The Bill James Handbook 2017

Baseball Info Solutions

www.baseballinfosolutions.com

Published by ACTA Sports

A Division of ACTA Publications

Cover Design by Tom A. Wright
Front Cover Photo by Winslow Townson, USA TODAY Sports
Back Cover Photo by Mark J. Rebilas, USA TODAY Sports

First Edition: November 2016

Published by:
ACTA Sports, a division of ACTA Publications
4848 North Clark Street
Chicago, IL 60640
(800) 397-2282
www.actasports.com www.actapublications.com

ISBN: 978-0-87946-567-4
ISSN: 1940-8668

Printed in the United States of America by McNaughton & Gunn

Dedication

This book is dedicated to my wife Lynn for her support and encouragement in pursuing a career in baseball and all of the sacrifices that entailed. You also gave me the greatest gift possible in our daughter Reagan. I hope she is as strong, caring, and creative as you are, while still being able to discuss in-depth future editions of this book with her dad.

I also need to send a special thank you to my parents for not only passing on their love of sports to my sister and me, but for all of the love and guidance they have provided throughout the years.

Finally, I'd be remiss if I did not acknowledge all of my co-workers at BIS whose many talents not only make this book possible, but also make a small town in Pennsylvania feel like a home away from home.

Kevin Morrissey

Table of Contents

Introduction

David Ortiz may be the iconic figure of 2000s baseball. He was a traditional middle-of-the-order hitter. He was not a fast runner. He was not a fielder at all. But he was patient, and he could hit for power. When he came to the plate, there was no mystery. He was going to work the count, and when he saw his pitch, he was going to swing hard. Opposing pitchers had to hope that he would swing and miss or that his invariably hard-hit balls would be hit at one of their fielders who could make a play on it.

Ortiz is interesting for many different reasons, but the thing I find so fascinating about his career is that it reached into this new era of baseball. Ortiz had one of the best seasons in MLB history as a 40-year-old, but the nostalgic image of him at bat did not perfectly match our memories of him from his prime because defensive shifts poached would-be hits from Ortiz every few games and because teams became much more aggressive in deploying left-handed relievers against him to try to gain an extra edge.

In part because of the *Handbook* and other new data-driven analytical work in recent seasons, teams have gotten more sophisticated. That sophistication has led to more nuanced strategies, like defensive shifts, that have chipped away at the strengths of opposing players. Ortiz had the talent to overcome those new challenges, but many one-dimensional players do not. As the number of stars in Ortiz's image has declined, a new generation of diversely talented stars has made the game more exciting than it's ever been.

If the cover is meant to represent Ortiz passing the torch to that next generation, then it's perfect that Jose Altuve is the player he is passing it to. Physically, Altuve will never measure up to Ortiz, but his play justifies his inclusion at Ortiz's side. Despite his height of 5'7", Altuve hit 24 home runs in 2016, the same number as 6'2" Bryce Harper and 6'4" Paul Goldschmidt. And don't think that Altuve padded his total with a bunch of cheap shots. As is fully explained in the new Long Outs and Home Run Distances section on page 23, 15 of Altuve's home runs flew at least 380 feet. Even more impressive, Altuve had another 19 flyball outs that traveled at least 380 feet in the air. That was four more than any other player. If anything, Altuve should have had even more home runs.

But really, Altuve's power numbers are beside the point. What makes Altuve such a great representation of the new generation of star players is his diverse skill set. Altuve stole 30 bases this season and averaged 3.54 seconds running from first to second on his stolen base attempts, tied for eighth fastest in baseball (from the Stolen Base Times section on page 369). Altuve was a major part of the Astros' league-leading 1,869 defensive shifts (from the Shifts section on page 61). Altuve hit safely 216 times and leads baseball with a three percent projected chance to set the all-time hit record of 4,257 hits (from The Favorite Toy section on page 581).

The Cubs were the best team in baseball this season and quite possibly the best team in more than a decade, and, like Altuve, their diversity led to their success. As you can find in the Team Statistics section on page 31, the Cubs were just 13th in baseball with 199 home runs, but they still had an elite offense because they led baseball with 656 walks, they manufactured runs with an MLB-best 96 hit-by-pitches, and, despite a modest 66 stolen bases, they were excellent on the basepaths. To that point, Kris Bryant and Ben Zobrist combined to steal just 14 bases, but they were both top 10 in baserunning gain, which captures extra bases taken and outs avoided on the basepaths (from the Baserunning section on page 357). Cubs starters led baseball with a 2.96 ERA and did so even though none of their starters struck out a batter per inning. Instead, they avoided walks and let their defense—that saved 107 runs, the most in baseball this season and the most by any team in the Defensive Runs Saved era (since 2003)—make plays behind them.

You'll find interesting statistics related to every star player you can think of. For example, Madison Bumgarner had the highest Game Score in a start in his complete-game one-hitter against the Diamondbacks on July 10. He won that start, but Bumgarner also had six tough losses, or losses with a Game Score over 50 (from the Leader Boards section on page 499). Altuve, Mike Trout, and Joey Votto finished in the top three in Win Shares even though none of their teams made the playoffs (from the Win Shares section on page 537).

But I think the real reason I love the *Handbook* is that you can also find interesting statistics on players you might not have realized were so interesting otherwise. Take Tyler Flowers, who started 2016 as the backup catcher on an Atlanta Braves team that was clearly in a rebuild—they finished in last place in the NL East with 93 losses. Despite his typical modest offensive performance, Flowers was a major contributor to the team thanks to his 14 Strike Zone Runs Saved, or runs saved due to his pitch-framing, which was tied for the most in baseball. That one elite skill made him an above-average defensive catcher overall even though he allowed 60 stolen bases and caught just 2 runners stealing all season (from the Fielding section on page 337).

All of that information and much more is at your fingertips in this *Handbook*. In the pages that follow, you'll find a variety of sections and statistics that aim to capture the amazing diversity of today's game and its players. We hope that you enjoy all of our hard work.

Scott Spratt
October 14, 2016

Starting Pitcher Rankings

Joe Rosales

It is interesting to think about the trajectory of a player's career. There is the natural rise and fall that comes with age that would exist for any projectile in motion, like a ball struck by a baseball bat. However, certain external factors—injuries, for instance—can cause some localized peaks and valleys resulting in a less smooth path. And then, of course, the player himself can sometimes affect his own path to some degree through a combination of desire, hard work, good choices, and intelligence—qualities that a baseball does not have. We can try to create projection systems to predict a player's trajectory—something that we even do later on in this book—but projections are often wrong. Not that that makes projection systems bad. Newton's laws of physics would also fail to accurately predict the ultimate landing spot of a batted ball if a bird happened to fly in front of it. But that's why it is fun to look back at how things actually played themselves out—because sometimes some feathers get ruffled.

Of the players that began the 2016 season ranked among the top 10 pitchers in baseball, eight of them finished the season that way. The two that fell out of the top 10 were Dallas Keuchel, who began the season ranked ninth, and Zack Greinke, who began the season ranked second. Of the two, Keuchel fell further. He dropped 17 spots down to 26th, whereas Greinke dropped 12 spots down to 14th. Still, it is difficult not to think of Greinke's decline as more consequential given the lofty heights that he started from and the earnest ambitions of the Diamondbacks going into the season.

Replacing those two in the top 10 were Johnny Cueto and Justin Verlander. Cueto began the season ranked at No. 13 and finished it at No. 10. The fact that he was outside the top 10 at all, though, is almost entirely due to his second half swoon in

2015. He was a top 10 pitcher for most of that year, and if he had continued to pitch the way he had up to that point in his career or if he had pitched the way that he pitched in 2016, he probably would not have dropped out. At the time of his struggles in late 2015, there was certainly some question as to whether this was the start of a larger decline, but ultimately his reinstatement in the top 10 is not a surprising one. Verlander, on the other hand, made some substantial strides. He finished the season ranked 6th, moving up 27 spots from his 33rd position at the start of the season.

Talking about who the No. 1 pitcher is on the list is boring. This is the third year that we have included this section in the *Handbook*, and Clayton Kershaw's name has never not been at the top, nor has there ever been any number other than 1 in any of the ranking columns next to his name. Except for very brief stints in 2014 and 2015 in which Kershaw relinquished his top spot to Max Scherzer, he has dominated the No. 1 ranking since first reaching it on May 16, 2013.

However, what makes the No. 1 ranking, and that date specifically, worth talking about now is the pitcher that Kershaw took the top spot away from...Justin Verlander. Since that day in May of 2013, after Verlander had reached his career peak and started his trip down, he fell as far as 98th place in the rankings, which happened on July 22, 2015. The last time he was ranked as high as sixth was May 26, 2014. But, amazingly, Verlander has pulled himself back up to a considerable height. And it has been a sustained effort. This past season, it actually took him until the very last day of the season, October 2, 2016, to reach sixth place again after a well-pitched but hard luck 1-0 loss to the Braves officially eliminated the Tigers from the playoffs. Now that is an interesting career trajectory!

The system that produces these Starting Pitcher Rankings is one devised by Bill James. The tables in this section of the book show a snapshot of the rankings on the first day of every month during the season, as well as the last day of the season. However, the rankings are recalculated every day, even during the offseason. For full details on how the system works, see Bill's article on www.billjamesonline.com from September 18, 2011 called *The World's #1 Starting Pitcher*. And if you are interested in exploring these rankings more thoroughly, you can also find those updated and stored daily at www.billjamesonline.com.

Starting Pitcher Rankings

Player	April 1 Score	Rank	May 1 Score	Rank	June 1 Score	Rank	July 1 Score	Rank	Aug 1 Score	Rank	Sept 1 Score	Rank	Oct 2 Score	Rank
Kershaw, Clayton	595.9	1	611.8	1	634.1	1	632.5	1	625.0	1	617.2	1	616.1	1
Scherzer, Max	540.0	3	541.8	3	553.7	4	573.4	2	587.2	2	600.0	2	593.7	2
Bumgarner, Madison	532.5	6	533.1	6	555.8	3	568.6	3	584.9	3	572.4	3	573.1	3
Kluber, Corey	503.5	8	510.9	9	516.7	10	539.7	8	550.7	6	564.3	4	569.2	4
Lester, Jon	500.4	10	519.7	8	528.2	8	547.5	7	528.6	12	544.1	9	564.4	5
Verlander, Justin	438.5	33	448.3	32	479.7	20	484.3	21	519.2	13	542.0	10	564.1	6
Sale, Chris	511.6	7	538.1	4	548.5	5	549.0	6	543.1	7	560.7	6	557.7	7
Price, David	532.5	5	527.8	7	532.7	7	535.1	9	541.6	9	550.3	7	552.4	8
Arrieta, Jake	538.9	4	562.3	2	572.8	2	568.4	4	558.5	4	562.1	5	552.4	9
Cueto, Johnny	481.1	13	497.9	13	524.6	9	532.6	11	533.6	11	527.7	12	543.2	10
Porcello, Rick	413.7	62	444.3	36	452.2	40	463.9	33	484.2	27	514.4	17	535.8	11
Hamels, Cole	498.7	11	503.6	11	511.3	11	535.0	10	534.9	10	544.6	8	532.4	12
Hendricks, Kyle	409.5	65	420.8	62	446.7	46	466.3	30	486.8	23	515.1	16	528.3	13
Greinke, Zack	554.1	2	537.7	5	540.0	6	558.7	5	551.7	5	534.4	11	526.6	14
Lackey, John	471.1	16	478.2	18	504.5	13	510.8	13	510.2	17	521.2	13	525.3	15
Quintana, Jose	461.1	23	482.0	16	500.4	15	496.1	17	513.3	15	520.5	14	517.2	16
Archer, Chris	461.2	22	462.9	23	465.5	30	472.9	25	493.0	22	508.5	18	515.2	17
Tanaka, Masahiro	423.3	48	447.4	35	470.7	25	477.1	24	485.1	25	503.0	23	511.1	18
Strasburg, Stephen	474.8	15	496.8	14	511.1	12	516.9	12	543.1	8	516.3	15	510.7	19
Happ, J.A.	420.6	53	438.8	43	460.3	33	464.3	32	494.0	21	503.6	22	510.2	20
Teheran, Julio	444.0	28	458.8	25	480.5	19	507.6	14	510.7	16	504.0	21	509.3	21
Estrada, Marco	424.7	45	440.4	40	477.9	21	499.9	16	499.1	18	496.6	25	505.8	22
Syndergaard, Noah	407.6	66	435.2	45	462.5	32	469.3	28	476.8	29	492.7	28	502.5	23
Kennedy, Ian	431.3	41	449.3	31	463.0	31	464.7	31	472.5	33	495.9	26	501.1	24
deGrom, Jacob	475.5	14	480.4	17	492.1	16	506.0	15	515.9	14	505.2	20	498.9	25
Keuchel, Dallas	502.0	9	500.9	12	487.5	17	488.9	20	494.9	19	506.3	19	498.8	26
Samardzija, Jeff	428.5	43	442.0	39	473.2	23	460.7	34	457.1	42	472.5	36	494.9	27
Carrasco, Carlos	441.6	29	457.1	26	449.3	43	478.1	23	494.4	20	495.6	27	494.4	28
Martinez, Carlos	392.5	73	421.2	60	426.2	57	453.5	41	462.8	38	479.2	32	492.3	29
Odorizzi, Jake	414.9	60	434.0	48	449.1	44	456.0	38	466.6	35	484.0	29	489.8	30
Hernandez, Felix	488.1	12	506.8	10	502.9	14	495.6	18	486.2	24	502.1	24	488.9	31
McHugh, Collin	438.7	32	429.6	49	449.6	42	457.1	36	455.1	44	458.4	45	481.1	32
Fernandez, Jose	321.5	139	354.5	113	408.3	72	442.8	52	453.5	46	466.9	39	480.4	33
Santana, Ervin	379.3	81	392.9	78	402.6	81	412.6	79	444.9	54	460.8	42	480.1	34
Liriano, Francisco	458.6	24	465.2	21	465.5	29	451.0	45	450.7	49	458.8	44	477.8	35
Roark, Tanner	328.8	135	366.2	102	396.1	85	418.7	72	435.5	64	458.2	46	477.4	36
Tillman, Chris	420.3	54	439.4	42	467.6	28	467.4	29	484.5	26	476.3	35	477.1	37
Dickey, R.A.	463.8	18	455.0	28	473.1	24	479.7	22	476.8	30	481.7	31	475.4	38
Iwakuma, Hisashi	437.0	35	442.2	38	453.2	39	459.1	35	466.5	36	476.4	34	473.8	39
Hammel, Jason	419.4	55	443.2	37	458.0	36	456.4	37	473.0	32	483.0	30	468.2	40
Colon, Bartolo	413.0	64	421.9	59	435.9	52	452.9	42	448.2	50	459.3	43	467.6	41
Gonzalez, Gio	440.7	31	459.2	24	454.4	38	450.3	47	461.4	39	478.4	33	466.9	42
Salazar, Danny	421.8	51	448.2	33	469.0	27	492.3	19	476.5	31	467.0	38	466.1	43
Ventura, Yordano	429.1	42	439.7	41	432.9	54	439.3	54	453.5	45	470.4	37	465.9	44
Sanchez, Aaron	300.0	162	339.7	135	377.0	105	404.0	89	440.1	58	447.5	58	465.2	45
Hellickson, Jeremy	361.8	106	382.7	88	411.4	70	423.6	66	443.8	56	448.5	57	463.0	46
Shoemaker, Matt	386.1	76	378.9	91	403.5	77	435.1	55	447.1	52	465.9	40	462.5	47
Gausman, Kevin	343.0	124	346.6	126	376.3	106	396.8	96	405.5	100	435.6	68	458.4	48
Pineda, Michael	373.8	88	382.9	86	383.7	99	423.0	69	436.6	63	443.6	61	457.8	49
Santiago, Hector	406.1	67	426.4	55	426.0	58	428.4	63	455.3	43	441.6	63	456.9	50
Eickhoff, Jerad	320.5	142	348.9	122	367.7	115	401.9	90	421.3	81	430.0	74	456.0	51
Duffy, Danny	379.4	80	350.9	118	358.2	127	391.5	101	433.2	65	452.5	48	455.7	52
Bauer, Trevor	395.7	72	381.3	89	407.7	74	445.3	50	441.1	57	453.8	47	454.7	53
Sabathia, CC	355.7	112	364.6	104	397.9	83	413.5	78	412.3	93	428.7	78	454.2	54
Cole, Gerrit	455.6	25	465.0	22	473.3	22	472.2	26	479.4	28	464.1	41	452.0	55
Fiers, Mike	414.8	61	421.2	61	427.7	56	439.9	53	439.6	60	453.3	55	451.0	56
Pomeranz, Drew	300.0	162	341.0	134	378.1	102	405.2	87	422.7	78	452.2	50	450.0	57
Straily, Dan	300.0	162	320.2	164	360.2	124	371.9	123	407.4	97	425.0	83	449.8	58
Jimenez, Ubaldo	422.8	49	427.0	53	414.9	67	418.3	73	410.2	94	415.2	98	448.9	59
Miley, Wade	424.2	46	430.0	48	438.9	49	428.8	62	444.2	55	439.4	65	448.2	60
Koehler, Tom	399.1	69	394.2	77	415.4	66	429.6	61	439.2	61	450.6	52	447.2	61
Bettis, Chad	351.1	117	383.4	83	384.1	98	386.5	106	415.5	87	423.6	86	446.9	62
Leake, Mike	434.1	38	429.5	50	454.6	37	452.7	43	451.1	48	452.2	49	446.7	63
Rodon, Carlos	363.9	101	382.9	84	395.2	86	410.0	82	399.8	106	430.3	73	446.5	64
Ray, Robbie	361.7	107	375.0	95	391.9	89	410.7	81	426.3	73	450.4	54	445.6	65
Kazmir, Scott	423.9	47	426.8	54	449.7	41	447.2	49	457.9	41	450.5	53	444.7	66
Gray, Jon	300.0	162	303.6	193	346.7	139	381.7	111	391.9	117	433.5	69	443.4	67
Chen, Wei-Yin	441.5	30	456.7	27	458.8	34	452.3	44	453.3	47	445.5	59	443.2	68
Gonzalez, Miguel	387.9	74	374.7	97	393.2	88	399.3	93	425.3	76	423.3	87	442.8	69
Maeda, Kenta			347.1	125	366.0	121	398.6	95	413.8	91	432.8	72	442.3	70
Anderson, Chase	376.1	85	375.1	94	397.8	84	400.3	91	408.2	96	424.3	85	442.0	71

Starting Pitcher Rankings

Player	April 1 Score	Rank	May 1 Score	Rank	June 1 Score	Rank	July 1 Score	Rank	Aug 1 Score	Rank	Sept 1 Score	Rank	Oct 2 Score	Rank
Fulmer, Michael			305.1	191	349.8	136	392.8	99	409.7	95	432.9	71	441.4	72
Moore, Matt	300.0	162	336.9	143	336.8	152	373.7	118	400.9	104	429.3	75	441.1	73
Shields, James	462.0	21	474.6	19	470.7	26	444.1	51	467.9	34	436.4	66	440.8	74
Stroman, Marcus	311.5	153	355.9	111	364.9	122	373.4	119	403.3	102	419.3	91	440.1	75
de la Rosa, Jorge	434.9	37	427.8	52	413.8	68	430.5	60	432.6	67	450.8	51	439.9	76
Nolasco, Ricky	319.4	144	349.7	119	356.2	130	367.5	126	387.8	115	408.4	105	439.9	77
Gray, Sonny	462.5	20	470.2	20	448.0	45	454.9	40	446.9	53	443.4	62	439.1	78
Zimmermann, Jordan	464.6	17	486.3	15	484.8	18	470.6	27	464.1	37	449.4	56	436.6	79
Weaver, Jered	421.3	52	424.9	57	419.0	63	419.7	71	425.9	74	420.4	90	435.9	80
Volquez, Edinson	444.5	27	452.3	29	458.6	35	450.2	48	458.5	40	445.3	60	434.8	81
Lewis, Colby	387.7	75	405.0	68	438.9	50	455.3	39	447.5	51	439.8	64	434.6	82
Gallardo, Yovani	427.9	44	423.9	58	416.1	65	419.9	70	422.3	80	426.5	82	434.4	83
Smyly, Drew	353.9	113	397.1	73	394.0	87	400.3	92	402.3	103	428.8	77	432.9	84
Finnegan, Brandon	300.0	162	327.9	151	351.5	133	372.2	122	380.5	120	422.2	88	432.6	85
Gibson, Kyle	416.8	57	413.3	66	405.6	76	414.2	76	432.3	68	422.1	89	430.8	86
Walker, Taijuan	371.3	94	395.6	75	403.1	78	423.5	67	415.8	85	411.8	101	428.9	87
Chatwood, Tyler	300.0	162	337.0	142	378.1	101	389.6	102	403.9	101	408.0	107	427.0	88
Peavy, Jake	422.7	50	409.5	67	424.2	60	433.5	58	440.0	59	433.2	70	425.5	89
Hill, Rich	300.0	162	345.2	127	384.3	96	377.5	113	392.7	111	393.6	116	424.6	90
Cashner, Andrew	396.3	71	404.1	70	408.0	73	409.1	83	427.1	70	427.8	80	422.8	91
Nelson, Jimmy	372.3	90	395.4	76	429.8	55	424.4	65	425.8	75	416.5	96	422.6	92
Garcia, Jaime	372.2	91	395.7	74	413.0	69	417.5	75	415.2	88	426.7	81	421.5	93
Harvey, Matt	436.7	36	437.5	44	403.5	53	450.5	46	436.9	62	429.1	76	421.4	94
Tomlin, Josh	334.2	133	348.7	124	374.4	108	408.7	84	420.6	82	399.2	115	420.9	95
Graveman, Kendall	310.1	155	328.4	149	340.3	151	356.1	134	386.8	116	413.4	99	420.4	96
Manaea, Sean			303.2	194	325.4	166	340.5	155	366.9	132	393.0	117	420.0	97
Davies, Zach	300.0	162	302.0	196	346.9	138	374.2	117	399.7	107	408.0	106	420.0	98
Miller, Shelby	437.5	34	429.0	51	425.3	59	423.3	68	415.7	86	412.0	100	419.2	99
Wacha, Michael	401.4	68	416.1	65	409.1	71	427.9	64	432.7	66	428.1	79	419.1	100
Wainwright, Adam	317.5	147	322.8	157	345.6	140	374.4	116	406.5	99	409.7	103	418.3	101
Wright, Steven	300.0	162	338.5	138	384.2	97	411.6	80	417.9	84	424.6	84	418.1	102
Perez, Martin	318.9	145	342.1	132	381.5	100	399.1	94	393.3	110	409.8	102	418.1	103
DeSclafani, Anthony	366.7	99	348.7	123	317.7	177	347.5	145	373.7	126	407.3	108	417.7	104
Guerra, Junior					344.3	142	378.5	112	414.0	90	406.3	110	415.4	105
Anderson, Tyler							333.2	164	363.3	134	405.5	111	415.1	106
Sanchez, Anibal	383.1	77	386.6	82	387.4	92	384.2	108	382.2	119	408.6	104	415.0	107
Nova, Ivan	318.6	146	302.9	195	331.8	158	339.5	157	364.6	133	392.6	119	413.4	108
Darvish, Yu	300.0	162	300.0	199	310.5	188	321.3	179	341.6	154	384.4	124	412.3	109
Peralta, Wily	366.8	98	362.5	106	367.1	118	363.7	129	355.9	139	385.4	123	411.7	110
Ross, Tyson	462.9	19	450.0	30	442.3	47	434.8	56	427.0	71	419.2	92	411.5	111
Richards, Garrett	431.4	40	448.0	34	441.8	48	434.3	57	426.5	72	418.8	93	411.0	112
Eovaldi, Nathan	376.3	84	388.2	79	420.5	62	405.6	86	415.1	89	418.8	94	411.0	113
McCullers, Lance	380.9	78	371.9	98	377.3	104	392.0	100	422.4	79	417.2	95	409.5	114
Fister, Doug	357.4	110	366.7	101	389.6	91	417.8	74	429.9	69	435.6	67	408.9	115
Buchholz, Clay	355.7	111	362.3	107	376.0	107	375.7	115	368.7	130	382.8	125	408.5	116
Wood, Alex	413.3	63	418.2	63	437.5	51	431.0	59	423.3	77	415.5	97	407.8	117
Rodriguez, Eduardo	358.8	109	339.3	136	317.6	179	318.9	183	346.4	148	368.3	138	405.5	118
Bradley, Archie	300.0	162	300.0	199	313.4	184	353.6	136	369.6	128	382.5	126	403.2	119
Conley, Adam	311.2	154	343.4	129	367.0	119	388.0	104	412.6	92	403.7	112	401.7	120
Velasquez, Vince	300.0	162	349.1	121	359.3	126	372.9	120	397.4	108	399.3	114	400.8	121
Matz, Steven	301.5	159	322.7	159	366.0	120	372.5	121	392.3	113	407.1	109	399.4	122
Paxton, James	300.0	162	300.0	199	298.1	395	326.0	173	361.2	135	373.2	132	398.8	123
Niese, Jon	396.4	70	404.3	69	420.5	61	413.6	77	406.6	98	401.7	113	394.0	124
Foltynewicz, Mike	300.0	162	300.0	199	336.0	154	332.9	165	355.1	142	386.1	122	393.2	125
Wisler, Matt	324.3	137	342.8	130	385.3	95	384.8	107	377.5	121	392.5	120	390.5	126
Friedrich, Christian	300.0	162	300.0	199	324.3	167	346.9	149	355.3	140	365.2	143	388.0	127
Hughes, Phil	415.4	59	425.2	56	417.5	64	408.3	85	400.6	105	392.8	118	385.1	128
de la Rosa, Rubby	369.2	96	387.3	81	403.1	79	395.6	97	387.8	114	380.1	128	383.0	129
Griffin, A.J.			322.6	160	330.0	161	340.2	156	355.1	141	373.9	131	380.9	130
Nola, Aaron	329.5	134	368.1	99	405.9	75	389.0	103	389.8	109	386.1	121	378.4	131
Snell, Blake			309.7	183	302.0	205	306.7	199	345.3	149	354.9	149	377.6	132
Boyd, Matt	300.0	162	300.0	199	305.6	193	310.2	194	338.9	160	369.4	136	377.2	133
Perdomo, Luis					300.7	209	312.5	190	330.3	167	359.4	146	374.8	134
Ross, Joe	308.9	156	336.3	146	367.5	116	382.3	110	374.6	124	366.8	140	374.3	135
Locke, Jeff	373.7	89	382.9	87	402.8	80	405.0	88	392.5	112	381.4	127	373.7	136
Vogelsong, Ryan	362.8	104	355.3	112	354.4	131	346.9	148	339.2	159	367.9	139	372.5	137
Bundy, Dylan							319.2	185	353.3	150	372.1	138
Duffey, Tyler	323.1	138	326.1	153	341.1	150	350.5	142	354.9	143	369.7	135	371.2	139
Karns, Nathan	349.3	118	363.3	105	391.2	90	393.9	98	386.2	117	378.4	129	370.7	140
Norris, Daniel	300.3	161	300.0	199	300.0	212	311.5	192	309.7	203	332.4	175	368.0	141
Garza, Matt	351.9	116	321.9	162	300.0	212	314.7	185	326.7	176	355.5	148	367.7	142
Urias, Julio					300.5	210	336.3	161	335.2	165	353.0	152	367.5	143
Andriese, Matt	300.0	162	300.0	199	341.2	149	348.3	144	340.5	156	348.2	155	366.5	144
Chacin, Jhoulys	300.0	162	328.2	150	350.8	134	342.1	153	335.8	163	334.1	172	366.2	145

Starting Pitcher Rankings

Player	April 1 Score	April 1 Rank	May 1 Score	May 1 Rank	June 1 Score	June 1 Rank	July 1 Score	July 1 Rank	Aug 1 Score	Aug 1 Rank	Sept 1 Score	Sept 1 Rank	Oct 2 Score	Oct 2 Rank
Corbin, Patrick	339.3	128	354.4	114	371.7	111	386.9	105	382.8	118	372.9	133	365.2	146
Miranda, Ariel											318.1	206	363.0	147
Pelfrey, Mike	345.2	122	342.6	131	357.8	128	359.4	132	377.3	122	370.8	134	362.6	148
Kuhl, Chad							304.9	202	319.7	184	347.9	156	362.2	149
Milone, Tommy	371.6	93	376.7	92	368.9	114	359.7	131	377.0	123	369.4	137	361.6	150
Holland, Derek	300.0	162	337.2	141	343.2	143	352.5	139	344.8	151	358.3	147	360.8	151
Latos, Mat	363.3	103	387.4	80	385.8	94	376.7	114	369.0	129	361.2	145	360.5	152
Rea, Colin	300.0	162	324.9	155	344.7	141	364.3	128	373.0	127	366.3	141	358.5	153
Young, Chris	374.5	86	382.9	85	378.0	103	383.4	109	373.8	125	366.1	142	358.3	154
Clemens, Paul							22.9	406	310.2	202	325.9	183	357.7	155
Norris, Bud	300.0	162	306.7	187	300.0	212	351.7	140	367.1	131	362.8	144	356.3	156
Adleman, Tim			308.7	185	321.4	172	313.9	187	306.2	215	318.7	205	353.4	157
Musgrove, Joe											324.5	189	353.0	158
Cessa, Luis											323.0	191	352.7	159
Lugo, Seth											322.5	192	351.5	160
Morgan, Adam	315.0	150	306.0	188	317.5	180	326.2	172	321.1	182	336.9	167	351.4	161
Skaggs, Tyler	300.0	162	300.0	199	300.0	212	300.0	214	323.6	178	335.3	170	349.8	162
Richard, Clayton	300.0	162	300.0	199	300.0	212	300.0	214	300.0	228	325.2	186	348.9	163
Shipley, Braden									308.6	205	333.5	174	348.4	164
Gsellman, Robert											304.0	232	348.4	165
Cosart, Jarred	341.7	126	338.4	139	330.6	159	323.1	176	332.4	171	346.3	158	348.2	166
Jackson, Edwin	300.0	162	300.0	199	300.0	212	300.0	214	311.6	199	321.5	197	347.9	167
Suarez, Albert					305.5	194	325.4	175	327.2	173	324.1	190	345.3	168
Feldman, Scott	377.7	83	374.9	96	367.2	117	367.8	125	360.8	136	353.0	151	345.3	169
McCarthy, Brandon	300.0	162	300.0	199	300.0	212	300.0	214	341.0	155	342.8	161	342.8	170
Tropeano, Nick	300.0	162	325.2	154	354.1	132	347.4	146	358.1	137	350.3	153	342.6	171
Ramirez, Erasmo	378.1	82	380.3	90	372.6	110	365.1	127	357.3	138	349.6	154	341.8	172
Cotton, Jharel													341.3	173
Urena, Jose	300.0	162	300.0	199	300.0	212	300.0	214	312.4	197	335.8	169	340.7	174
Danks, John	380.0	79	376.3	93	369.3	112	361.8	130	354.1	144	346.3	157	338.6	175
Hutchison, Drew	371.8	92	368.1	100	360.3	123	352.8	137	352.7	145	344.9	159	338.5	176
Stripling, Ross			322.8	158	330.1	160	322.6	178	314.8	192	337.0	166	338.2	177
Weaver, Luke											326.3	182	337.7	178
Cole, A.J.	300.0	162	300.0	199	300.0	212	300.0	214	300.0	228	314.1	211	337.7	179
Gee, Dillon	300.0	162	300.0	199	312.1	185	305.8	200	309.2	204	339.1	163	337.4	180
Thompson, Jake											311.5	214	337.3	181
Cain, Matt	300.0	162	312.7	172	341.6	147	336.4	160	343.0	152	344.7	160	337.0	182
Montgomery, Mike	300.0	162	300.0	199	300.0	212	300.0	214	311.0	201	322.1	193	336.4	183
Reyes, Alex											307.5	226	336.3	184
Mengden, Daniel							331.6	166	332.7	169	324.9	187	334.0	185
Phelps, David	300.0	162	300.0	199	300.0	212	300.0	214	300.0	228	341.4	162	333.7	186
Asher, Alec	300.0	162	300.0	199	300.0	212	300.0	214	300.0	228	300.0	239	333.5	187
Triggs, Andrew							303.8	208	300.0	228	333.6	173	332.3	188
Clevinger, Mike					302.0	204	300.0	214	300.0	228	309.4	218	331.5	189
Kelly, Joe	363.7	102	360.7	108	360.2	125	354.2	135	346.5	147	338.7	164	331.0	190
Peacock, Brad	300.0	162	300.0	199	300.0	212	300.0	214	300.0	228	300.0	239	330.5	191
Eflin, Zach							314.6	186	349.9	146	337.3	165	329.5	192
LeBlanc, Wade	300.0	162	300.0	199	300.0	212	319.8	182	321.6	181	336.2	168	328.4	193
Detwiler, Ross	300.0	162	300.0	199	300.0	212	300.0	214	300.0	228	324.8	188	328.1	194
Meyer, Alex					300.0	212	300.0	214	300.0	228	300.0	239	327.2	195
Morton, Charlie	347.2	119	365.3	103	357.6	129	350.1	143	342.3	153	334.6	171	326.8	196
Mitchell, Bryan	300.0	162	300.0	199	300.0	212	300.0	214	300.0	228	300.0	239	326.6	197
Collmenter, Josh	300.0	162	300.0	199	300.0	212	300.0	214	300.0	228	300.0	239	325.7	198
Nicasio, Juan	300.0	162	336.3	147	341.5	148	347.2	147	339.5	158	331.7	176	324.0	199
Vargas, Jason	319.6	143	300.0	199	300.0	212	300.0	214	300.0	228	300.0	239	323.5	200
Lamb, John	300.0	162	300.0	199	323.3	168	352.5	138	338.9	161	331.2	177	323.4	201
Berrios, Jose			300.6	197	304.1	196	300.0	214	307.7	208	307.5	225	322.7	202
Hoffman, Jeff											312.3	213	322.3	203
Green, Chad					300.0	212	300.0	214	306.7	213	328.6	179	322.2	204
Wilson, Tyler	300.0	162	310.1	182	336.3	153	351.4	141	337.3	162	329.5	178	321.8	205
Simon, Alfredo	347.0	121	338.8	137	342.2	146	343.5	150	335.8	164	328.0	180	320.3	206
Wright, Daniel			302.2	201	300.0	214	300.0	228	300.0	239	320.3	207
Stewart, Brock							301.7	211	300.0	228	310.6	217	319.9	208
Neal, Zach					300.0	212	300.0	214	300.0	228	317.0	207	319.5	209
Taillon, Jameson							327.7	169	344.9	150	376.6	130	319.4	210
Koch, Matt													318.7	211
De La Cruz, Joel							304.1	206	307.5	211	321.9	195	318.6	212
Blach, Ty													318.6	213
Iglesias, Raisel	334.3	132	356.6	110	348.9	137	341.4	154	333.6	168	325.9	184	318.1	214
Jungmann, Taylor	352.5	115	349.3	120	342.3	145	334.8	163	327.0	175	319.3	204	317.8	215
Harrell, Lucas	300.0	162							318.5	188	325.5	185	317.7	216
Brault, Steven									305.8	217	303.9	233	317.6	217
Perez, Williams	315.1	149	322.5	161	350.0	135	342.5	152	334.8	166	327.0	181	317.5	218
Stephenson, Robert			311.3	178	303.6	198	300.0	214	300.0	228	300.0	239	317.3	219

9

Starting Pitcher Rankings

Player	April 1 Score	Rank	May 1 Score	Rank	June 1 Score	Rank	July 1 Score	Rank	Aug 1 Score	Rank	Sept 1 Score	Rank	Oct 2 Score	Rank
Anderson, Cody	338.4	129	336.7	145	343.2	144	334.8	162	327.1	174	319.3	202	317.2	220
Marquez, German													315.6	221
Blair, Aaron			312.8	171	311.8	186	313.3	188	305.6	218	299.3	409	315.4	222
Severino, Luis	328.8	136	333.2	148	335.8	155	328.3	168	320.5	183	313.8	212	315.2	223
Lopez, Reynaldo									302.9	224	319.4	201	315.1	224
Wright, Mike	300.0	162	321.3	163	332.9	157	337.6	159	329.8	172	322.1	194	314.3	225
Ynoa, Gabriel													314.3	226
Whalen, Rob											321.9	196	314.1	227
Alcantara, Raul													314.1	228
Bailey, Homer	300.0	162	300.0	199	300.0	212	300.0	214	307.5	210	320.8	199	313.6	229
Jenkins, Tyrell									317.4	189	321.3	198	313.6	230
De Leon, Jose													312.4	231
Verrett, Logan	300.0	162	318.9	165	307.1	189	308.3	196	332.5	170	319.9	200	312.2	232
Nicolino, Justin	302.3	158	312.3	175	329.2	162	327.2	170	323.2	179	319.3	203	312.0	233
Gant, John							323.1	177	315.8	191	308.1	223	311.8	234
Smith, Josh	300.0	162	300.0	199	300.0	212	300.0	214	300.0	228	300.0	239	311.8	235
Glasnow, Tyler									305.9	216	300.0	239	310.4	236
Merritt, Ryan													309.5	237
Godley, Zack	300.0	162	300.0	199	300.0	212	304.6	204	314.5	193	316.2	208	308.7	238
Dean, Pat					319.7	175	319.8	181	312.1	198	300.9	236	308.7	239
Reed, Cody							305.3	201	313.5	194	316.0	209	308.2	240
Zastryzny, Rob													308.1	241
Cobb, Alex	300.0	162	300.0	199	300.0	212	300.0	214	300.0	228	300.0	239	307.9	242
McAllister, Zach	300.0	162	300.0	199	300.0	212	300.0	214	300.0	228	300.0	239	307.2	243
Rusin, Chris	320.9	141	318.7	166	317.7	178	329.8	167	322.1	180	314.3	210	306.6	244
Owens, Henry	313.4	151	313.6	170	311.0	187	303.5	209	300.0	228	300.0	239	306.4	245
Esch, Jake											302.2	235	306.1	246
Sampson, Keyvius	300.0	162	300.0	199	300.0	212	300.0	214	307.0	212	300.0	239	306.0	247
Klein, Phil	300.0	162	300.0	199	300.0	212	300.0	214	300.0	228	300.0	239	305.8	248
Cravy, Tyler	300.0	162	300.0	199	300.0	212	300.0	214	300.0	228	300.0	239	305.7	249
Whitley, Chase	300.0	162	300.0	199	300.0	212	300.0	214	300.0	228	300.0	239	305.5	250
Montero, Rafael	300.0	162	300.0	199	300.0	212	300.0	214	300.0	228	308.2	222	305.0	251
Butler, Eddie	300.0	162	300.0	199	328.3	163	325.9	174	318.9	186	311.1	215	303.4	252
Weber, Ryan	300.0	162	300.0	199	300.0	212	300.0	214	300.0	228	300.0	239	303.3	253
Farmer, Buck	300.0	162	300.0	199	300.0	212	300.0	214	300.0	228	300.0	239	303.2	254
Suter, Brent											300.0	239	303.2	255
Heaney, Andrew	343.7	123	341.6	133	333.8	156	326.3	171	318.6	187	310.8	216	303.1	256
Williams, Trevor													301.4	257
Anderson, Brett	362.3	105	353.3	115	322.3	170	300.0	214	300.0	228	300.0	239	300.9	258
Hahn, Jesse	300.0	162	311.5	177	322.5	169	310.4	193	316.2	190	308.5	220	300.7	259
Rodgers, Brady													300.4	260
Devenski, Chris			305.5	189	316.7	181	309.2	195	301.5	225	307.9	224	300.1	261
All Others													300	262

Run Impact of Events

Bill James

Not all singles are created equal. When a batter hits a single, that could be a bases-loaded, two-out single which plates two runs, or it could be a two-out, bases-empty single which will have no impact on the scoreboard 85% of the time. A leadoff single is much more likely to lead to runs being scored than is a single with one out. A single with a runner on third is virtually certain to lead to a run being scored; a single with a runner on first may or may not.

Every play in baseball has a "before" and an "after" state, and every base/out state has a value based on the number of runs the team can expect to score from that state. If a team has the bases loaded and nobody out, they have an expectation of scoring 2.09 (more) runs in that inning. If the batter strikes out, freezing the runners, the run expectation for the inning drops to 1.54 runs. The negative impact of the strikeout is .55 runs. If the next hitter grounds into an inning-ending double play, the expected runs in the inning drop to zero, so the double play has cost the team about 1.54 runs.

These run-impact (or run-expectation) charts have been around at least since the 1960s, and they have to be adjusted occasionally as the run scoring levels in the majors go up and down. What we are trying to do in this section is to use those charts to ask a few basic questions. Which hitters hit the most productive singles in the majors? The least productive singles? The most productive doubles?

This is a "clutch hitting" article—and then again it isn't. Certainly this issue is related to whether a player has hit well in the clutch, but it is important to note that that is not EXACTLY what we are figuring. We are trying to state facts, not judgments.

Suppose that a player hits a single with two out and a runner on second base. The runner scores; the batter goes to second on the throw home, so the run impact of the event is 1.000 runs. The base/out situation is exactly the same after the play as it was before, only there is one more run on the scoreboard.

Suppose, however, that the runner from second base is thrown out at home plate, ending the inning. Then the impact of the play is NEGATIVE, not positive.

You can point out—and correctly—that this is not the hitter's "fault", and that it may have nothing to do with the batter. Maybe the runner coming around from second didn't hustle; who knows? But saying that it is not the batter's fault is a JUDGMENT. Saying that the play hurt the team, rather than helped it, is a fact. We're not making judgments; we are recording facts.

There are a million other ways that this can be done, and I'm just trying to explain what we have done. You can treat that as two separate events—the "batting event" of the batter hitting the single, and the "base running event" of the runner from second scoring or being thrown out. That has problems, but you can do it that way—or you can say that there is a batting event, a base running event, and a fielding event, or you can say that there are two base running events or two fielding events.

Also, the concept of "clutch" hitting has several other meanings. This study looks at the RUN impact of each event, without considering the score of the game. But the impact on the game is different if the score of the game is 2-1 than it is if the score is 12-0. We didn't consider that. The impact of the event is different if it is in the heat of a pennant race than if both teams are out of the race. The eventual impact of the event is different if the team's pitcher goes out the next inning and allows five runs than it is if he retires the side one-two-three.

Those are all valid ways to study the issue, and maybe we'll study some of those things next year, but we didn't study any of those things this year. We just looked at the RUN impact of each event, based on the state of the inning before the event and the state of the inning after the event.

So...the player who produced the most runs with his singles, in 2016, was Dustin Pedroia of the Red Sox. Pedroia hit 149 singles, which led the major leagues. On average, his singles were about as valuable as anybody else's singles, but he led the majors in the runs added by his singles as well as the number of singles:

Players Producing the Most Runs with Singles

Player	Team	Singles	Runs on Singles
Pedroia, Dustin	Bos	149	63.1
Markakis, Nick	Atl	110	61.9
Prado, Martin	Mia	135	61.0
Hosmer, Eric	KC	111	59.0
Bogaerts, Xander	Bos	136	57.1

Pedroia's singles produced 63.1 runs for the Red Sox, the most for any major league player. We will also note this: that the number of runs Pedroia produced with his singles is greater than the number of runs that ANY hitter produced with doubles, triples, or walks, and more than anyone produced with home runs except for two players. The most interesting name on this list, however, is the #2 man, Nick Markakis. Markakis hit 110 singles, which would rank him 36th in the major leagues—but he hit singles that MATTERED. He hit singles that changed the inning. Although he hit 39 fewer singles than Pedroia, he almost matched Pedroia—and beat every other major leaguer—in the number of runs resulting from his singles. Markakis hit .240 with the bases empty—but .306 with men on base. That made his singles more valuable. A list of the players hitting the most valuable singles (one for one) contains a couple of the same names:

Players Hitting High-Impact Singles

Player	Team	Singles	Runs on Singles	Runs Per Single
Markakis, Nick	Atl	110	61.9	.563
Russell, Addison	ChC	76	41.3	.544
Rizzo, Anthony	ChC	91	49.3	.542
Ortiz, David	Bos	82	43.7	.533
Hosmer, Eric	KC	111	59.0	.532

David Ortiz is there...one more note from his remarkable Swan Song Season. The major league average was .436. Markakis created 14 more runs than he would have created had his singles been just ordinary, garden variety singles.

On the other end of that scale was a high-visibility player:

Players Hitting Low-Impact Singles

Player	Team	Singles	Runs on Singles	Runs Per Single
Altuve, Jose	Hou	145	48.9	.337
Hernandez, Cesar	Phi	130	46.9	.361
Cespedes, Yoenis	NYM	77	27.9	.363
Hamilton, Billy	Cin	82	29.8	.364
Eaton, Adam	CWS	124	45.6	.368

Jose Altuve was regarded for most of the season as a leading MVP candidate. Not trying to play into that discussion; Altuve is a great player, and he has a lot of good numbers. But he did hit the most meaningless singles of any major league player, among the 150 players who hit the most singles—and by far the most meaningless singles; nobody else is close to him in this regard. The other four guys on this list are in the .360s; Altuve is 24 points behind the world.

Moving on now to doubles; same concept. A bases-empty double is worth 1.14 runs when there is no one out, 0.32 runs when there are two men out. A bases-loaded, bases-clearing double is worth 2.05 runs with no one out, 2.62 runs when there are two men out.

The player who produced the most runs with his doubles was, again, the player who hit the most doubles:

Players Producing the Most Runs with Doubles

Player	Team	Doubles	Runs on Doubles
Ortiz, David	Bos	48	40.3
Gonzalez, Carlos	Col	42	36.3
Rizzo, Anthony	ChC	43	35.6
Yelich, Christian	Mia	38	35.3
Ramirez, Jose	Cle	46	34.6

But Ortiz isn't at the top of this list simply because he hit the most doubles. He also hit high-impact doubles, producing .84 runs per double as opposed to a major league average of .75. That's a good average, but nowhere near the highest in the majors:

Players Hitting High-Impact Doubles

Player	Team	Doubles	Runs on Doubles	Runs Per Double
Lucroy, Jonathan	Tex	24	23.2	.965
Suzuki, Kurt	Min	24	22.5	.937
Myers, Wil	SD	29	27.0	.930
Yelich, Christian	Mia	38	35.3	.929
Reynolds, Mark	Col	24	21.6	.900

Lucroy, traded to Texas in mid-season, hit only half as many doubles as the Big Papi, but did have a higher impact per double. A hitter was eligible for this list if he hit 22 or more doubles—this list, or the next one. 22 doubles because 150 major league players hit 22 or more doubles. These are the players who hit doubles at times when a double didn't change the game much:

Players Hitting Low-Impact Doubles

Player	Team	Doubles	Runs on Doubles	Runs Per Double
Escobar, Yunel	LAA	28	15.5	.553
Granderson, Curtis	NYM	24	13.5	.564
Gonzalez, Marwin	Hou	26	14.8	.571
Cabrera, Asdrubal	NYM	30	17.7	.590
Dickerson, Corey	TB	36	21.4	.594

A double by Escobar had less impact (on average) than a single by Markakis. Escobar hit .362 with runners in scoring position, but hit only eight doubles with men on base—as opposed to Lucroy, who hit fewer doubles than Escobar, but hit 15 doubles with men on base.

We can't really do triples, by this method, because there aren't enough players who hit enough triples to make interesting data. But continuing a theme, the player who produced the most runs by hitting home runs was simply the guy who hit the most homers:

Players Producing the Most Runs with Homers

Player	Team	Homers	Runs on Homers
Trumbo, Mark	Bal	47	67.1
Arenado, Nolan	Col	41	63.6
Encarnacion, Edwin	Tor	42	61.5
Carter, Chris	Mil	41	58.5
Davis, Khris	Oak	42	58.4

This doesn't HAVE to be true. A player who hit fewer homers COULD have produced more runs on homers than Trumbo; a player who hit fewer doubles than Ortiz COULD have produced more runs on doubles than Ortiz. It just didn't happen that way. Trumbo and Arenado, by the way, produced more runs with homers than any other player produced on any kind of hit. The player who hit the most meaningful home runs on average is now retired:

Players Hitting High-Impact Homers

Player	Team	Homers	Runs on Homers	Runs Per Homer
Teixeira, Mark	NYY	15	25.9	1.725
Shaw, Travis	Bos	16	27.1	1.693
Martin, Russell	Tor	20	33.7	1.687
Bour, Justin	Mia	15	25.1	1.671
Wieters, Matt	Bal	17	28.3	1.664

The average Home Run produced 1.40 Runs. Teixeira beat the average by about five runs, total. The player who hit the most low-impact home runs was Charlie Blackmon of Colorado:

Players Hitting Low-Impact Homers

Player	Team	Homers	Runs on Homers	Runs Per Homer
Blackmon, Charlie	Col	29	31.4	1.083
Nunez, Eduardo	SF	16	18.0	1.123
Kipnis, Jason	Cle	23	26.0	1.129
Alvarez, Pedro	Bal	22	25.1	1.139
McCann, Brian	NYY	20	22.9	1.143

Blackmon hit leadoff for the Rockies, and 26 of his 29 homers were hit with the bases empty. He may not stay as the leadoff man, but who knows; it's Colorado.

You might think that the "run value" of a home run is simply the number of homers plus the number of runners on base when the homers are hit, and that is sort of generally true but not absolutely true. If a runner is on third base with nobody out, there is a very high probability that he will score anyway. Hitting a home run in that situation increases the run expectation for the inning by one run, but not much more than one run.

We can do the same with walks, strikeouts...most anything. A bases-loaded walk produces 1.000 runs, regardless of how many are out in the inning. A leadoff walk produces .356 runs; a two-out, bases-empty walk has a value of .113 runs, so a bases-loaded walk has nine times the value of two-out, bases-empty walk. A walk with a runner on second, two out, increases the expected runs in the inning by only .103 runs. The average walk has a value of .284.

And...well, here we are again. The player who produced the most runs with walks was simply the player who drew the most walks, the big fish:

Players Producing the Most Runs with Walks

Player	Team	Walks	Runs on Walk
Trout, Mike	LAA	116	34.0
Santana, Carlos	Cle	99	31.4
Donaldson, Josh	Tor	109	31.0
Zobrist, Ben	ChC	96	30.1
Belt, Brandon	SF	104	29.8

But the player producing the most runs per walk was John Jaso:

Players Drawing Run-Productive Walks

Player	Team	Walks	Runs From Walks	Runs Per Walk
Jaso, John	Pit	45	16.2	.359
Pujols, Albert	LAA	49	16.9	.344
Semien, Marcus	Oak	51	17.3	.340
Nieuwenhuis, Kirk	Mil	56	18.9	.337
Kinsler, Ian	Det	45	15.1	.336

Jaso had a .436 on base percentage when there was already a runner on base, as opposed to .305 when the bases were empty, so he contributed to setting up some big innings. The player having the least luck drawing walks when a walk would really help was another catcher:

Players Drawing Walks That Had Little Impact

Player	Team	Walks	Runs From Walks	Runs Per Walk
Avila, Alex	CWS	38	8.8	.231
Bour, Justin	Mia	38	8.8	.232
Freese, David	Pit	45	10.7	.238
Goldschmidt, Paul	Ari	110	26.3	.239
Yelich, Christian	Mia	72	17.3	.240

Avila had an interesting year. He drew more walks (38) than he had hits (36); he and Matt Joyce were the only major league players with 200 plate appearances and more walks than hits, but the walks that he drew didn't tend to come at particularly helpful moments. At least, that's what the data shows; I don't know. I'm not a White Sox fan.

We've run out of positive things we can measure here, so we're going to switch to measuring negative outcomes. The player who cost his team the most runs with his strikeouts was, you will not be surprised to learn, also the player who struck out the most:

Players Costing their Team
the Most Runs with Strikeouts

Player	Team	Strikeouts	Runs Lost
Davis, Chris	Bal	219	60.0
Carter, Chris	Mil	206	59.6
Napoli, Mike	Cle	194	54.1
Upton, Justin	Det	179	46.5
Springer, George	Hou	178	46.4

Let me ask you a question: Which costs the team more, a strikeout with the bases loaded and no one out, a strikeout with the bases loaded and one out, or a strikeout with the bases loaded and two out?

The answer is, the most costly strikeout with the bases loaded is with one out. With the bases loaded and no one out, a team can expect to score 2.09 runs; with one out, 1.54 runs, with two out, .69 runs—so a strikeout with the bases loaded and no one out costs the team about .55 runs, with the bases loaded and two out, about .69 runs. But a strikeout with the bases loaded and one out costs the team .85 runs. A strikeout with the bases loaded and one out is (on average) the most costly strikeout you can have, followed closely by a strikeout with one out and runners on second and third, which has an average cost of .82 runs.

It makes sense when you think about it. It is the one-out strikeout which eliminates the possibility of scoring a run with an out. The great thing about having a runner on third/less than two out is that he can score on an out. The first out in the inning doesn't eliminate that possibility, because it still exists after the first out, and the third out in the inning doesn't eliminate that possibility, because it is already gone. The second out of the inning is the most costly one, if the runner doesn't score from third, because that out eliminates the possibility of scoring the run with an out.

Players with the Highest Cost Per Strikeout

Player	Team	Strikeouts	Runs Lost to Strikeouts	Runs Per Strikeout
Lucroy, Jonathan	Tex	100	33.4	.334
Encarnacion, Edwin	Tor	138	42.5	.308
Stanton, Giancarlo	Mia	140	42.4	.303
Pence, Hunter	SF	95	28.3	.298
Shaw, Travis	Bos	133	39.5	.297

There's never really a good time for a strikeout. The manager very rarely sends you up to the plate and says "This would be a good time for a strikeout, Chris." I've never known a manager who kept a photo of Adam Dunn on his desk. But the LEAST damaging strikeouts, for players who struck out 94 or more times, were by Ryan Shimpf.

Players with the Lowest Cost Per Strikeout

Player	Team	Strikeouts	Runs Lost to Strikeouts	Runs Per Strikeout
Schimpf, Ryan	SD	105	22.8	.217
Hernandez, Cesar	Phi	116	26.4	.228
Escobar, Alcides	KC	96	22.3	.232
Rupp, Cameron	Phi	114	26.8	.235
Longoria, Evan	TB	144	34.1	.237

If you can win a Bar Bet with that piece of information, I would recommend that you switch to a different bar. The player who cost his team the most runs by grounding into double plays was NOT, repeat NOT, simply the player who grounded into the most double plays. Miguel Cabrera grounded into the most double plays. But Albert Pujols cost his team more runs by grounding into double plays:

Players Costing their Team the Most Runs by Grounding into Double Plays

Player	Team	Double Plays	Runs Lost
Pujols, Albert	LAA	24	21.2
Cabrera, Miguel	Det	26	19.5
Pedroia, Dustin	Bos	24	18.7
Molina, Yadier	StL	22	18.6
Prado, Martin	Mia	24	18.4

In Pujols' defense, he also batted more times with a runner on first and less than two out than any other major league player, 176 times.

The variance on the cost of hitting a double play is not as high as for most other events because

1) There is always a runner on base when a batter grounds into a double play, and

2) There are never two out in the inning when a batter grounds into a double play.

Two of the "cost variables" which factor into all of the other events we have talked about are not in play in this case. It's like, there are some things that cost five times as much when you buy them at a convenience store as when you buy them at a discount store, and then there are other things that cost kind of the same no matter where you buy them, not EXACTLY the same but sort of the same. Double plays are like that; they are always costly. On average, the Double Play is the most high-impact event on our list here, other than the home run.

Also should be noted: Chase Utley in 2016 became the first regular player in the 21st century to make it through the season without grounding into a double play. The player who hit into the most expensive double plays, one for one, was Carlos Correa of Houston:

Players with the Highest Cost Per Double Play

Player	Team	GIDP	Runs Lost	Unit Cost
Correa, Carlos	Hou	12	13.0	1.086
Bradley Jr., Jackie	Bos	10	10.7	1.069
Desmond, Ian	Tex	12	12.0	1.001
Freese, David	Pit	16	15.8	.988
Joseph, Tommy	Phi	11	9.9	.904

While Maikel Franco hit into the LEAST costly double plays, on average.

Players with the Lowest Cost Per Double Play

Player	Team	GIDP	Runs Lost	Unit Cost
Franco, Maikel	Phi	13	7.4	.571
Gyorko, Jedd	StL	11	6.5	.593
Votto, Joey	Cin	16	9.8	.610
Granderson, Curtis	NYM	10	6.1	.611
Gonzalez, Adrian	LAD	16	9.8	.613

All 13 of Franco's double play balls occurred when there was a runner on first base ONLY, with no other runner on base, whereas 5 of Correa's 12 double plays were hit when there was a runner on third base.

Well, I have data like this on Fly Balls and Outs in Play, but I sense that this article has gone on long enough, so I think I'll put that in the closet, and close with this little essay. What we are looking for in the stats is improved understanding of the game. Baseball telecasts now are full of blatantly meaningless statistics. I saw one during the playoffs which gave the player's batting averages on pitches up and away (and down and away, and up and in, and down and in) when there were runners in scoring position. Who could possibly believe that there is an ability to hit pitches up and away with runners in scoring position? It's preposterous.

We're not always successful in avoiding that kind of thing ourselves. We publish a lot of meaningless stats ourselves. But we're trying. We are trying to find what the player does that is truly valuable, truly relevant to his team. We are trying to learn to measure all of the <u>real</u> skills that players actually have—an ability to go from first to third on a single, an ability to go to his left on a ground ball. Here we have looked at the value of what each player has done. I hope you got something out of it.

Long Flies and Big Flies

Bill James

In the 2016 regular season, Mark Trumbo hit 47 home runs and 58 long fly outs. Adeiny Hechavarria hit three home runs—but 67 long fly outs. It could be, perhaps, that one of these two needs to adjust his approach at the plate. It's a possibility, anyway.

I love this data, because it confirms an old prejudice of mine. I liked Freddie Patek when he first came to the Royals in 1971. He was a little bitty guy who just smacked the ball, kind of like he was playing ping pong; he slapped the ball over the infield like a ping pong player slapping the ball over the net. But after a year or two, he decided that he needed to hit the ball harder, which the pitchers were very happy to let him do. He would hit, it seemed to me, three long fly balls every game. I'm sure that wasn't the actual data; that was just the way it seemed. He would hit .225 or .228 or .234 or .212 every year with about three homers a year, but he would pay for the three homers with 150 long fly outs. It used to drive me crazy, as a 1970s Royals fan; why does he DO that?

So now we have actual data on Adeiny Hechavarria. Hechevarria hit .236 with 3 homers, which is a Freddie Patek season if I have ever seen one, and, sure enough, he hit more long fly outs than Mark Trumbo.

Well, I shouldn't beat up on Adeiny; that's not what I'm here for. Let me explain the data. The "320" under "Long Fly Outs" is the number of fly ball outs the player hit which went 320 to 339 feet. "340" means 340 to 359 feet, 360 means 360 to 379 feet, etc. Home Runs, same thing. Occasionally the Home Run total doesn't match the player's actual home run total because the player hit an inside-the-park home run, which we didn't include in these totals.

In the majors, 99.3% of balls hit 320 to 339 feet were outs; a little less than one percent were homers:

Flyball Distance	Out%	Home Run%
320 to 339 Feet	99.3%	0.7%
340 to 359 Feet	91%	9%
360 to 379 Feet	76%	24%
380 to 399 Feet	49%	51%
400 or more Feet	6%	94%

Overall, almost exactly one-fourth of Fly Balls hit 320 or more feet become homers; the other 75% become outs. Well...a few of them become doubles off the wall or something, but we're not talking about those. The batter hits a long fly ball; the home crowd cheers. The cheer gets louder as the outfielder retreats—but three times in four, it's an out.

Which explains something I will get to in a moment. Before Babe Ruth, it was universally believed by baseball men that hitting long fly balls was a sucker's game, that you would pay for the occasional fly ball that goes past the outfielders with so many long fly outs that you could never come out ahead on the deal. Babe Ruth established that this was not universally true, that if you were good enough at it, you could make it pay to hit long fly balls.

Now, we have reached the other extreme; now ALL the hitters like to hit fly balls. But here is what surprised me when I studied this data.

Suppose that you add together the number of long fly balls and home runs that a player hits; we'll call them Long Flies Total. Chris Carter and Adrian Beltre hit 118 Long Flies total; Carter hit 77 and 41, and Beltre hit 86 and 32. At 94 you have Todd Frazier (54 and 40) and Corey Seager (68 and 26). At 93 we have Wil Myers (65 and 28) and Brandon Belt (76 and 17). At 88 we have Justin Upton (57 and 31) and Buster Posey (74 and 14). At 73 you have Mitch Moreland (51 and 22) and Jacoby Ellsbury (64 and 9).

Do you see a pattern here? In many of these matches...you can make hundreds of matches like this out of the data. In many of these matches and I think most of them, it is the player who hit FEWER home runs who is actually the better hitter. The player who hits more home runs (given a certain number of long flies) usually strikes out more, hits fewer doubles and triples, and hits for a lower average.

I didn't expect that. I sorted the data that way looking for guys, like Adeiny Hechavarria, who maybe shouldn't be hitting long fly outs—but that's not what the data shows, really. The data suggests that it may be the big home run hitters who could benefit from adjusting their approach.

The only major league player (with significant playing time) who hit more home runs than long fly outs was Pedro Alvarez of Baltimore, who hit 22 home runs with only 18 long fly outs. Joc Pederson was almost even, 28 and 25.

Well...study the data; get out of it what you can. Thanks for reading.

Long Flies and Big Flies

Player	Long Out Distances						Home Run Distances					
	320	340	360	380	400+	Long	320	340	360	380	400+	HR
Trumbo, Mark	12	18	7	6	3	58	0	1	3	10	33	47
Cruz, Nelson	10	13	12	3	0	58	0	1	1	10	31	43
Encarnacion, Edwin	17	14	10	8	0	66	0	2	3	6	31	42
Davis, Khris	19	16	5	2	2	58	0	3	4	9	26	42
Dozier, Brian	17	16	14	7	0	69	1	2	5	11	22	42
Carter, Chris	24	12	8	15	0	77	0	0	5	7	29	41
Arenado, Nolan	19	20	16	7	4	85	1	0	7	9	24	41
Frazier, Todd	16	14	6	0	0	54	0	2	5	13	20	40
Bryant, Kris	14	17	15	8	4	80	0	0	7	6	26	39
Cano, Robinson	25	15	11	2	1	71	0	3	5	14	17	39
Davis, Chris	14	16	18	5	0	64	0	2	3	7	26	38
Ortiz, David	21	18	17	5	1	77	0	1	5	9	23	38
Cabrera, Miguel	18	18	12	7	4	81	0	2	5	9	22	38
Machado, Manny	18	18	12	2	2	76	0	2	4	6	25	37
Donaldson, Josh	17	14	8	10	0	65	0	2	2	8	24	37
Longoria, Evan	18	18	14	13	2	78	0	1	3	9	22	36
Kemp, Matt	15	24	9	11	2	82	0	0	5	7	23	35
Napoli, Mike	13	14	11	2	2	46	0	2	0	7	25	34
Santana, Carlos	20	15	8	8	0	67	0	0	7	7	20	34
Freeman, Freddie	24	19	15	5	0	80	0	1	5	9	19	34
Bruce, Jay	15	24	13	6	0	73	0	3	4	8	18	33
Odor, Rougned	17	15	14	9	1	66	0	6	4	7	16	33
Duvall, Adam	14	12	15	4	4	63	0	1	3	14	15	33
Beltre, Adrian	25	12	16	10	0	86	0	4	4	5	19	32
Gattis, Evan	10	7	5	5	1	38	1	3	4	8	16	32
Upton, Justin	16	14	3	5	3	57	0	3	2	5	21	31
Cespedes, Yoenis	14	23	10	4	1	66	0	1	5	4	21	31
Pujols, Albert	18	21	21	14	0	93	0	0	4	7	20	31
Tomas, Yasmany	16	7	5	5	4	51	0	0	5	10	16	31
Rizzo, Anthony	16	16	6	8	0	63	0	1	5	9	16	31
Betts, Mookie	15	29	15	5	2	79	0	5	6	13	7	31
Morales, Kendrys	15	13	16	13	1	72	0	2	4	4	20	30
Miller, Brad	10	13	7	4	0	46	0	4	4	2	20	30
Braun, Ryan	10	9	7	5	0	41	0	2	5	6	17	30
Gyorko, Jedd	15	11	5	3	1	50	0	1	6	7	16	30
Granderson, Curtis	16	16	10	7	0	64	1	6	3	6	14	30
Ramirez, Hanley	10	16	8	6	1	56	1	3	3	10	13	30
Seager, Kyle	18	21	11	9	0	77	1	4	4	9	12	30
Trout, Mike	25	16	13	3	1	69	0	1	0	5	23	29
Votto, Joey	14	19	15	3	0	66	0	1	2	9	17	29
Springer, George	14	14	10	4	1	60	0	1	2	10	15	29
Lamb, Jake	8	12	10	3	5	49	0	0	7	7	15	29
Jones, Adam	22	17	18	7	2	83	0	1	9	5	14	29
Blackmon, Charlie	13	15	15	9	3	75	0	2	5	11	11	29
Beltran, Carlos	18	12	8	4	0	57	0	3	9	9	8	29
Myers, Wil	18	12	10	6	0	65	0	2	4	5	17	28
Moss, Brandon	10	11	12	10	0	51	0	1	6	7	14	28
Kinsler, Ian	15	20	15	11	1	84	0	3	10	8	7	28
Stanton, Giancarlo	11	9	3	8	0	41	0	0	3	2	22	27
Grandal, Yasmani	13	9	6	5	0	41	0	1	1	4	21	27
Story, Trevor	14	11	7	5	0	44	0	0	1	6	20	27
Semien, Marcus	24	14	10	5	0	79	0	1	4	9	13	27
Turner, Justin	22	13	13	6	1	76	1	2	6	5	13	27
Martinez, Victor	34	9	12	12	2	79	0	3	5	7	12	27
Seager, Corey	13	15	13	12	2	68	0	2	2	1	21	26
Schoop, Jonathan	13	9	3	4	0	41	0	0	1	6	18	26
Bradley Jr., Jackie	11	15	5	4	0	48	0	3	3	3	17	26
Gonzalez, Carlos	8	13	14	10	2	57	0	0	1	4	20	25
Pederson, Joc	10	6	4	3	1	28	0	1	1	6	17	25
Sano, Miguel	9	11	6	3	0	41	0	1	4	3	17	25
Abreu, Jose	16	15	12	7	1	68	0	1	2	6	16	25
Howard, Ryan	9	13	9	6	2	44	0	1	3	7	14	25
Franco, Maikel	19	14	10	5	1	65	0	1	5	6	13	25
Hosmer, Eric	14	10	13	6	0	54	0	3	4	6	12	25
Murphy, Daniel	26	15	20	6	2	88	0	0	6	8	11	25
Goldschmidt, Paul	16	9	7	8	1	54	0	0	4	2	18	24
Grichuk, Randal	13	12	8	5	0	47	0	1	2	5	16	24
Tulowitzki, Troy	15	17	8	10	1	67	1	2	2	3	16	24
Harper, Bryce	17	13	8	3	1	58	0	0	4	6	14	24
Lucroy, Jonathan	8	19	11	7	0	60	0	0	2	9	13	24
Altuve, Jose	21	18	14	16	3	86	0	1	8	2	13	24
Dickerson, Corey	19	10	12	3	0	58	0	2	5	5	12	24
Espinosa, Danny	16	14	12	4	1	56	0	0	3	10	11	24

Long Flies and Big Flies

Player	Long Out Distances						Home Run Distances					
	320	340	360	380	400+	Long	320	340	360	380	400+	HR
McCutchen, Andrew	24	25	14	5	1	83	0	2	6	5	11	24
Saunders, Michael	11	12	6	6	1	52	0	2	4	8	10	24
Ozuna, Marcell	19	14	16	6	2	68	0	1	1	6	15	23
Kipnis, Jason	24	14	11	4	0	67	0	1	1	7	14	23
Walker, Neil	18	13	11	8	0	66	0	1	4	9	9	23
Cabrera, Asdrubal	17	22	13	6	0	68	0	2	5	10	6	23
Moreland, Mitch	12	15	10	4	0	51	0	1	1	3	17	22
Piscotty, Stephen	20	14	10	7	0	65	0	0	3	3	16	22
Desmond, Ian	16	10	7	2	0	44	0	1	5	2	14	22
Alvarez, Pedro	3	6	5	1	0	18	0	0	6	3	13	22
Ramos, Wilson	16	9	10	2	1	50	0	2	1	7	12	22
Polanco, Gregory	16	10	11	3	0	54	0	1	4	7	10	22
Martinez, J.D.	6	18	9	4	1	48	0	2	5	5	10	22
Perez, Salvador	16	14	4	3	0	50	0	0	6	7	9	22
Bautista, Jose	10	14	7	5	1	50	1	6	2	4	9	22
Joseph, Tommy	14	7	6	2	1	39	0	1	1	4	15	21
Castro, Starlin	15	16	11	3	0	55	1	0	2	4	14	21
Kang, Jung Ho	3	9	5	4	1	29	0	2	2	3	14	21
Carpenter, Matt	16	24	17	10	2	80	0	0	1	7	13	21
Yelich, Christian	18	10	4	2	2	46	0	1	5	3	12	21
Werth, Jayson	28	12	5	6	0	61	0	4	6	11	21
Bogaerts, Xander	15	8	9	6	1	56	0	1	3	6	11	21
Russell, Addison	21	5	6	6	1	52	0	0	5	8	8	21
Suarez, Eugenio	12	18	13	4	0	62	0	2	3	8	8	21
Mazara, Nomar	8	9	6	6	0	45	0	1	1	0	18	20
Upton Jr., Melvin	12	9	9	2	1	43	0	0	2	4	14	20
Schimpf, Ryan	4	9	9	3	0	28	1	0	2	5	12	20
Rendon, Anthony	24	22	8	7	1	80	0	0	3	6	11	20
Lind, Adam	14	13	9	5	0	51	0	2	4	3	11	20
Forsythe, Logan	16	13	11	4	0	58	0	1	6	2	11	20
Correa, Carlos	11	11	7	8	1	51	0	2	2	6	10	20
Holliday, Matt	12	8	10	4	0	42	0	2	3	6	9	20
Martin, Russell	6	15	6	5	0	45	0	2	2	8	8	20
McCann, Brian	19	11	12	1	0	53	1	3	5	3	8	20
Galvis, Freddy	10	7	8	4	0	51	0	2	5	6	7	20
Gregorius, Didi	23	16	1	2	0	59	1	3	8	8	0	20
Villar, Jonathan	17	9	9	3	0	46	0	1	4	3	11	19
Segura, Jean	22	9	9	6	5	64	0	1	2	9	7	19
Rodriguez, Sean	5	8	5	2	1	27	0	1	3	1	13	18
Castellanos, Nick	20	12	11	7	0	65	0	1	2	5	10	18
Gonzalez, Adrian	14	11	9	3	0	62	0	2	4	3	9	18
Calhoun, Kole	22	19	11	6	1	79	0	2	2	6	8	18
Zobrist, Ben	21	10	10	7	0	65	0	0	7	6	5	18
Gordon, Alex	15	16	10	2	0	56	0	1	0	3	13	17
Belt, Brandon	11	19	15	10	2	76	0	0	2	4	11	17
Valencia, Danny	8	8	9	5	0	38	0	0	2	5	10	17
Souza Jr., Steven	11	10	6	6	0	46	0	1	2	6	8	17
Diaz, Aledmys	16	9	9	2	0	53	0	0	2	8	7	17
Kepler, Max	16	8	8	3	0	44	0	1	4	5	7	17
Wieters, Matt	12	10	8	5	0	51	0	2	4	5	6	17
Adams, Matt	13	12	4	6	1	44	0	0	2	2	12	16
Cron, C.J.	22	10	1	4	0	47	0	1	1	2	12	16
Rupp, Cameron	14	9	4	2	0	35	0	1	2	1	12	16
Drury, Brandon	13	9	13	1	0	45	0	0	1	6	9	16
Smith, Seth	7	8	8	7	0	42	1	0	2	4	9	16
Shaw, Travis	10	12	12	2	1	52	0	0	2	6	8	16
Cozart, Zack	10	15	9	4	0	56	0	2	1	6	7	16
Flores, Wilmer	9	14	6	2	0	44	0	0	2	8	6	16
Rasmus, Colby	11	4	7	7	2	45	0	0	0	3	12	15
Bour, Justin	7	7	7	2	0	28	0	0	1	3	11	15
Marte, Jefry	11	8	3	1	0	30	0	1	1	3	10	15
Nunez, Eduardo	18	20	8	3	0	65	0	0	2	5	8	15
Herrera, Odubel	14	14	11	4	0	57	0	2	2	3	8	15
Solarte, Yangervis	13	7	10	4	0	46	0	2	1	5	7	15
Teixeira, Mark	6	12	6	2	0	33	1	4	2	2	6	15
Lindor, Francisco	17	17	13	3	0	71	0	1	4	5	5	15
Pedroia, Dustin	23	13	11	3	0	71	1	4	3	2	5	15
Martin, Leonys	7	10	7	4	0	41	0	4	4	4	3	15
Posey, Buster	17	28	9	5	1	74	0	0	1	3	10	14
Zimmerman, Ryan	22	10	6	5	1	55	0	0	0	5	9	14
Smoak, Justin	6	3	9	1	0	29	0	0	3	3	8	14
Morrison, Logan	12	6	5	4	0	36	0	0	3	3	8	14
Utley, Chase	18	8	11	8	0	54	0	0	3	4	7	14
Eaton, Adam	12	10	12	7	0	53	0	1	2	4	7	14
Reynolds, Mark	6	9	2	5	0	29	0	0	2	6	6	14
Cabrera, Melky	21	14	7	2	0	65	0	3	1	4	6	14

Long Flies and Big Flies

Player	Long Out Distances						Home Run Distances					
	320	340	360	380	400+	Long	320	340	360	380	400+	HR
Castillo, Welington	8	17	10	2	1	47	0	1	4	3	6	14
Norris, Derek	11	11	11	1	0	46	0	2	3	3	6	14
Garcia, Adonis	11	8	5	3	0	43	0	0	0	9	5	14
Gennett, Scooter	18	7	4	2	0	50	0	0	3	6	5	14
Vogt, Stephen	27	21	9	4	0	81	0	2	1	6	5	14
Baez, Javier	5	7	8	3	1	37	0	0	5	4	5	14
Headley, Chase	14	17	6	5	1	50	0	3	2	4	5	14
Lee, Dae-Ho	9	5	2	2	0	22	1	2	4	2	5	14
Gomez, Carlos	3	6	5	4	1	34	0	0	0	4	9	13
Turner, Trea	8	10	9	2	1	35	0	0	1	4	8	13
Freese, David	5	7	8	2	0	28	0	2	0	3	8	13
Nieuwenhuis, Kirk	5	8	4	2	0	24	0	0	3	2	8	13
Naquin, Tyler	4	6	6	1	0	19	0	1	0	5	7	13
Fowler, Dexter	13	10	8	7	0	50	0	1	2	3	7	13
Healy, Ryon	3	6	1	0	2	15	0	3	0	3	7	13
Valbuena, Luis	8	7	6	5	1	34	0	1	1	5	6	13
Pence, Hunter	6	6	4	4	0	26	0	1	3	3	6	13
Pearce, Steve	9	4	5	4	2	33	0	0	1	7	5	13
Gonzalez, Marwin	9	5	9	5	8	42	0	1	3	5	4	13
Crisp, Coco	18	10	5	1	0	57	0	1	4	4	4	13
Perez, Hernan	20	14	5	0	0	49	0	0	3	7	3	13
Markakis, Nick	27	16	12	6	0	86	0	0	5	5	3	13
McCann, James	9	3	9	5	1	37	0	0	0	1	11	12
Garcia, Avisail	8	6	3	3	0	30	0	1	2	0	9	12
Davis, Rajai	14	6	11	2	0	45	0	1	1	2	8	12
Conforto, Michael	10	13	8	4	0	43	0	1	3	2	6	12
Cuthbert, Cheslor	7	12	6	0	0	35	0	1	2	4	5	12
Saltalamacchia, Jarrod	8	9	5	4	1	36	0	2	2	3	5	12
Pagan, Angel	10	13	5	0	0	50	0	0	3	5	4	12
Plouffe, Trevor	8	6	6	3	0	40	0	0	3	5	4	12
Kiermaier, Kevin	8	11	8	1	0	35	1	3	3	1	4	12
Crawford, Brandon	17	16	15	5	1	70	0	1	4	6	1	12
LeMahieu, DJ	10	10	13	3	2	55	0	1	0	0	10	11
Realmuto, J.T.	17	11	6	5	0	47	0	0	1	2	8	11
Travis, Devon	12	8	6	2	0	40	0	1	0	4	6	11
Mercer, Jordy	20	10	5	2	0	62	0	0	2	3	6	11
Puig, Yasiel	12	6	4	3	0	31	1	1	0	3	6	11
Castro, Jason	7	4	2	0	1	27	0	2	1	2	6	11
Grossman, Robbie	5	5	6	1	0	22	0	1	1	4	5	11
Lawrie, Brett	12	6	5	1	0	31	0	0	2	3	5	11
Phillips, Brandon	13	13	7	6	0	69	0	0	4	2	5	11
Ramirez, Jose	21	15	11	3	0	67	0	0	3	4	4	11
Span, Denard	16	9	8	1	1	45	2	2	2	2	3	11
Mauer, Joe	14	12	3	5	0	54	0	4	2	4	1	11
Buxton, Byron	10	4	2	0	0	17	0	1	1	1	7	10
Hundley, Nick	14	9	2	1	0	32	0	0	1	3	6	10
Dickerson, Alex	5	5	8	2	0	30	1	1	1	1	6	10
Rosario, Eddie	6	9	1	3	0	30	0	1	3	1	5	10
Johnson, Kelly	6	4	5	3	1	28	0	1	3	1	5	10
Panik, Joe	14	11	10	6	0	55	0	0	1	5	4	10
Reddick, Josh	11	11	4	4	1	45	0	1	2	3	4	10
Hill, Aaron	13	14	10	4	0	55	0	0	3	5	2	10
Marte, Starling	14	10	8	2	1	43	0	0	0	2	7	9
Cain, Lorenzo	7	8	7	2	1	36	0	2	0	1	6	9
Guyer, Brandon	13	8	3	2	0	36	0	1	1	2	5	9
Anderson, Tim	5	5	2	9	0	25	0	0	2	3	4	9
Gomes, Yan	8	9	4	0	1	29	0	1	1	3	4	9
Ellsbury, Jacoby	14	9	13	3	0	64	0	1	3	1	4	9
Loney, James	11	10	7	4	0	45	0	2	3	1	3	9
Young, Chris	10	7	3	1	0	28	0	1	2	4	2	9
Hardy, J.J.	9	23	8	2	1	53	2	0	2	4	1	9
Flowers, Tyler	5	9	10	3	0	31	0	0	0	0	8	8
Fielder, Prince	6	8	5	5	0	37	0	0	1	0	7	8
Reyes, Jose	7	5	4	4	0	25	0	0	1	3	4	8
Prado, Martin	19	11	7	6	0	64	0	0	1	3	4	8
Andrus, Elvis	17	11	14	5	0	67	0	1	1	2	4	8
Descalso, Daniel	10	3	7	2	0	26	0	0	1	4	3	8
Bandy, Jett	6	11	1	2	0	31	0	1	0	4	3	8
Jaso, John	6	6	8	3	0	30	0	0	2	3	3	8
Chisenhall, Lonnie	13	7	8	3	0	37	0	1	1	3	3	8
White, Tyler	4	4	7	2	2	22	0	1	1	3	3	8
Kendrick, Howie	11	5	6	4	2	42	0	1	2	2	3	8
Bregman, Alex	7	5	2	2	0	26	0	2	1	2	3	8
Saladino, Tyler	3	3	4	1	0	25	0	0	4	1	3	8
Peralta, Jhonny	14	13	2	6	0	46	0	0	1	5	2	8
Hicks, Aaron	19	11	7	3	1	50	0	2	1	3	2	8

Long Flies and Big Flies

Player	Long Out Distances						Home Run Distances					
	320	340	360	380	400+	Long	320	340	360	380	400+	HR
Molina, Yadier	21	11	11	6	1	69	0	1	0	6	1	8
Suzuki, Kurt	13	9	5	1	0	42	0	0	4	3	1	8
Parra, Gerardo	11	7	6	5	0	38	0	0	0	1	6	7
Escobar, Alcides	16	11	12	1	0	62	0	0	1	0	6	7
Francoeur, Jeff	10	6	4	3	0	25	0	0	1	1	5	7
Dietrich, Derek	9	11	8	2	1	37	0	0	1	1	5	7
Uribe, Juan	6	9	6	4	0	29	0	0	1	2	4	7
Iannetta, Chris	4	6	6	4	0	27	0	0	3	0	4	7
Alonso, Yonder	19	15	12	2	0	69	0	3	0	0	4	7
Gardner, Brett	22	8	1	1	0	48	0	0	0	4	3	7
Pillar, Kevin	13	14	8	4	0	56	0	0	1	3	3	7
Holt, Brock	2	7	2	0	0	16	0	1	1	2	3	7
Peterson, Jace	10	6	7	5	0	36	0	0	0	5	2	7
Barnhart, Tucker	14	11	8	6	0	48	0	1	1	3	2	7
Leon, Sandy	10	3	2	3	0	23	0	2	0	3	2	7
Smolinski, Jake	10	7	6	3	0	35	0	1	1	4	1	7
Heyward, Jason	16	21	7	2	0	50	0	1	1	4	1	7
De Aza, Alejandro	6	15	5	2	0	34	1	0	1	2	2	6
Kim, Hyun Soo	11	4	6	4	0	37	0	0	3	1	2	6
Escobar, Eduardo	11	6	7	1	0	38	0	1	2	1	2	6
Hernandez, Cesar	7	9	6	2	0	41	0	2	1	1	2	6
Gillaspie, Conor	8	6	4	3	0	26	0	1	1	3	1	6
Ramirez, Alexei	12	14	5	1	0	43	0	0	3	2	1	6
Giavotella, Johnny	11	9	3	0	0	34	0	2	1	3	0	6
Navarro, Dioner	9	12	4	2	0	41	0	2	1	3	0	6
Bourn, Michael	12	8	6	2	0	33	0	0	0	1	4	5
Perez, Carlos	9	6	4	0	0	23	0	0	1	0	4	5
Butler, Billy	8	7	3	3	1	31	0	0	0	2	3	5
Orlando, Paulo	11	5	6	8	0	41	0	0	1	1	3	5
Escobar, Yunel	14	12	9	2	0	49	0	0	1	1	3	5
Profar, Jurickson	6	5	2	2	0	24	0	0	1	1	3	5
Duffy, Matt	15	7	4	2	0	35	0	0	1	2	2	5
Bourjos, Peter	4	9	7	0	0	30	0	0	1	2	2	5
Beckham, Gordon	11	11	8	2	0	34	0	0	1	2	2	5
Wong, Kolten	11	8	8	2	0	37	0	1	0	2	2	5
Rickard, Joey	8	8	2	4	0	33	0	0	2	1	2	5
Owings, Chris	15	10	5	2	0	46	0	0	0	4	1	5
Marisnick, Jake	5	4	5	3	1	24	0	0	2	2	1	5
Ahmed, Nick	10	14	3	3	0	38	0	1	0	1	2	4
Harrison, Josh	24	23	7	7	1	78	0	0	2	0	2	4
Polanco, Jorge	10	4	3	2	0	30	0	1	1	0	2	4
Iglesias, Jose	10	5	4	1	0	38	0	1	1	0	2	4
Simmons, Andrelton	7	12	11	2	0	42	0	0	0	3	1	4
Barney, Darwin	11	6	4	2	0	32	0	2	0	1	1	4
Maybin, Cameron	4	7	5	1	0	22	0	2	0	1	1	4
Aoki, Nori	13	9	1	2	0	36	0	0	1	3	0	4
Peraza, Jose	4	5	3	3	1	20	0	0	0	0	3	3
Inciarte, Ender	21	15	2	1	0	53	0	0	1	1	1	3
Hechavarria, Adeiny	21	15	7	3	2	67	0	1	0	1	1	3
Hamilton, Billy	13	7	1	1	0	30	0	0	2	0	1	3
Aybar, Erick	14	8	7	2	0	38	0	1	1	0	1	3
Merrifield, Whit	9	11	2	2	1	30	0	0	0	0	2	2
Jay, Jon	10	9	3	0	0	29	0	1	0	0	1	2
Revere, Ben	15	9	5	2	0	39	0	0	0	2	0	2
Pierzynski, A.J.	13	5	4	2	0	34	0	0	1	1	0	2
Lowrie, Jed	11	10	7	1	1	40	0	2	0	0	0	2
d'Arnaud, Chase	10	8	2	1	0	29	0	0	0	0	1	1
Dyson, Jarrod	3	4	4	0	0	16	0	0	0	1	0	1
Suzuki, Ichiro	10	4	6	4	0	34	0	0	0	1	0	1
Marte, Ketel	13	11	1	1	0	35	0	0	0	1	0	1
Blanco, Gregor	6	3	1	2	0	19	0	0	0	1	0	1
Gordon, Dee	4	9	1	0	0	25	0	0	1	0	0	1
Cervelli, Francisco	7	9	4	3	0	30	0	0	1	0	0	1
Burns, Billy	8	1	1	0	0	20	0	0	0	0	0	0

2016 Team Statistics

Scott Spratt

By the end of the season, every division winner won by at least four games over the second place team, but for much of the season, the AL East and the NL West told much different stories. In the former, the Baltimore Orioles held first place for 111 days and as late into the season as August 15. In the end, they finished four back of the Red Sox in one of the Wild Card spots. If that seems like a significant fall-off, then consider that the Orioles' length of stay in the top spot in the East fails to tell the full story of how hotly contested that division became. For the full week from September 8 through September 14, the East had four teams—the Red Sox, Blue Jays, Orioles, and Yankees—within four games of the division lead. In the previous decade, there was only one day where four teams in a division were within four games of the lead in September. That was on September 4, 2007, when the Diamondbacks, Padres, Dodgers, and Rockies were all within four games in the NL West.

Speaking of the NL West, this year's version appeared to be the Giants division to lose even before the Dodgers lost Clayton Kershaw for two months in the middle of the season. However, the Giants won just 30 games in the second half, tied for third fewest in baseball. One of their major issues shows up in the National League Pitching table. Despite finishing second in the league with 73 save opportunities, they successfully shut the door on only 43, just seventh most, and they cycled through a number of closers who continued to blow games. They lost hold of the division just five days after the Orioles did the same in the AL East.

That information just scratches the surface of what is available in the Team Statistics section. In addition to teams' traditional standings and won-lost records, there are league and team splits that show success by month, in one-run games, and much more. Beyond that, there are tables on each team's batting, pitching, and fielding statistics. Finally, there is a Team Pitching Staff Summary, a Team Defense table that shows Defensive Runs Saved split by team and position, and league positional splits for batting and fielding. There, you can discover interesting narratives such as that the Orioles had the worst outfield defense, costing the team 52 runs, but the third best infield defense including shifts, saving them 47 runs.

2016 American League Standings

Overall

EAST Team	W-L	Pct	GB	D1	LD1	LLd	CENTRAL Team	W-L	Pct	GB	D1	LD1	LLd	WEST Team	W-L	Pct	GB	D1	LD1	LLd
Boston Red Sox	93-69	.574	0.0	54	10/2	6.0	Cleveland Indians	94-67	.584	0.0	122	10/2	8.0	Texas Rangers	95-67	.586	0.0	148	10/2	10.5
Toronto Blue Jays	89-73	.549	4.0	29	9/6	2.0	Detroit Tigers	86-75	.534	8.0	4	4/9	1.0	Seattle Mariners	86-76	.531	9.0	31	6/2	2.5
Baltimore Orioles	89-73	.549	4.0	111	8/15	5.5	Kansas City Royals	81-81	.500	13.5	21	6/15	2.0	Houston Astros	84-78	.519	11.0	1	4/5	0.5
New York Yankees	84-78	.519	9.0	0	-	0.0	Chicago White Sox	78-84	.481	16.5	45	5/27	6.0	Los Angeles Angels	74-88	.457	21.0	3	4/15	0.5
Tampa Bay Rays	68-94	.420	25.0	0	-	0.0	Minnesota Twins	59-103	.364	35.5	0	-	0.0	Oakland Athletics	69-93	.426	26.0	6	4/24	1.0

Wild Card Clinch Dates: Baltimore 10/2, Toronto 10/2. Division Clinch Dates: Texas 9/23, Cleveland 9/26, Boston 9/28.
D1 = Number of days a team had at least a share of first place of their division; LD1 = Last date the team had at least a share of first place; LLd = The largest number of games that a team led their division by.

East Division

Tm	AT Home	Road	Versus East	Cent	West	NL	LHS	RHS	Day	Night	Grass	Turf	1-Rn	5+Rn	XInn	April	May	June	July	Aug	Sept	All-Star Pre	Post
Bos	47-34	46-35	43-33	15-18	21-12	14-6	20-17	73-52	27-23	66-46	82-61	11-8	20-24	30-11	7-4	14-10	18-10	10-16	15-10	17-13	19-10	49-38	44-31
Tor	46-35	43-38	40-36	18-15	18-15	13-7	24-20	65-53	35-26	54-47	38-33	51-40	21-25	29-15	4-9	11-14	17-12	15-12	16-8	17-11	13-16	51-40	38-33
Bal	50-31	39-42	40-36	23-9	12-22	14-6	23-23	66-50	27-18	62-55	80-63	9-10	21-16	24-21	6-2	14-9	14-13	19-9	12-14	13-16	17-12	51-36	38-37
NYY	48-33	36-45	35-41	21-12	20-13	8-12	25-26	59-52	26-27	58-51	78-65	6-13	24-12	17-22	4-3	8-14	16-13	15-12	13-13	17-11	15-15	44-44	40-34
TB	36-45	32-49	32-44	11-23	15-17	10-10	18-26	50-68	27-31	41-63	26-46	42-48	13-27	18-22	4-3	11-12	11-16	11-17	9-16	14-15	12-18	34-54	34-40

Central Division

Tm	AT Home	Road	Versus East	Cent	West	NL	LHS	RHS	Day	Night	Grass	Turf	1-Rn	5+Rn	XInn	April	May	June	July	Aug	Sept	All-Star Pre	Post
Cle	53-28	41-39	14-18	49-26	18-16	13-7	31-20	63-47	27-27	67-40	90-64	4-3	28-21	34-20	6-6	10-11	16-13	22-6	12-12	16-14	18-11	52-36	42-31
Det	45-35	41-40	19-15	38-37	16-16	13-7	25-22	61-53	33-27	53-48	81-72	5-3	26-17	23-20	5-4	13-10	11-17	17-11	16-10	15-13	14-14	46-43	40-32
KC	47-34	34-47	15-17	46-30	10-24	10-10	21-22	60-59	23-19	58-62	79-76	2-5	23-25	19-28	7-3	12-11	17-11	13-14	7-19	20-9	12-17	45-43	36-38
CWS	45-36	33-48	19-14	32-44	18-15	9-11	20-18	58-66	25-30	53-54	74-82	4-2	23-29	20-23	8-7	17-8	11-17	12-14	11-15	12-15	15-15	45-43	33-41
Min	30-51	29-52	10-24	24-52	17-15	8-12	21-25	38-78	20-38	39-65	57-99	2-4	15-29	14-33	6-10	7-17	8-19	10-17	15-11	9-20	10-19	32-56	27-47

West Division

Tm	AT Home	Road	Versus East	Cent	West	NL	LHS	RHS	Day	Night	Grass	Turf	1-Rn	5+Rn	XInn	April	May	June	July	Aug	Sept	All-Star Pre	Post
Tex	53-28	42-39	16-17	19-14	47-29	13-7	22-19	73-48	24-23	71-44	93-62	2-5	36-11	18-24	6-6	14-10	17-11	20-8	15-13	18-10	15-13	52-36	43-31
Sea	44-37	42-39	19-13	16-18	38-38	13-7	24-34	62-42	28-24	58-52	83-73	3-3	30-30	25-18	9-8	13-10	17-11	10-18	12-12	16-14	18-11	45-44	41-32
Hou	43-38	41-40	15-18	17-16	41-35	11-9	27-26	57-52	29-25	55-53	82-74	2-4	28-25	23-19	10-8	7-17	17-12	18-8	13-12	16-13	13-16	48-41	36-37
LAA	40-41	34-47	13-21	17-15	35-41	9-11	21-22	53-66	21-23	53-65	69-86	5-2	17-20	24-24	0-4	11-13	13-15	8-19	15-11	12-16	15-14	37-52	37-36
Oak	34-47	35-46	16-17	17-16	29-47	7-13	16-26	53-67	24-35	45-58	66-90	3-3	25-28	15-24	6-5	13-12	11-17	11-15	12-14	10-18	12-17	38-51	31-42

Team vs. Team Breakdown

	EAST Bos	Tor	Bal	NYY	TB	CENTRAL Cle	Det	KC	CWS	Min	WEST Tex	Sea	Hou	LAA	Oak
Boston Red Sox	-	9	11	11	12	4	2	2	3	4	3	4	5	4	5
Toronto Blue Jays	10	-	10	12	8	3	4	4	1	6	3	3	5	3	3
Baltimore Orioles	8	9	-	10	13	5	5	4	4	5	3	1	1	4	3
New York Yankees	8	7	9	-	11	5	3	5	3	5	3	3	4	6	4
Tampa Bay Rays	7	11	6	8	-	1	1	2	3	4	2	4	2	4	2
Cleveland Indians	2	4	1	2	5	-	14	14	11	10	2	3	3	6	4
Detroit Tigers	5	3	2	3	6	4	-	7	12	15	2	4	4	2	4
Kansas City Royals	4	2	2	2	5	5	12	-	14	15	1	3	4	1	1
Chicago White Sox	4	5	3	4	4	8	7	5	-	12	4	4	3	2	5
Minnesota Twins	3	1	1	2	3	9	4	4	7	-	5	4	2	4	2
Texas Rangers	3	3	4	4	2	5	4	6	2	2	-	12	15	10	10
Seattle Mariners	3	3	1	3	3	4	3	4	3	2	7	-	8	11	12
Houston Astros	2	2	6	2	3	4	2	3	3	5	4	11	-	13	13
Los Angeles Angels	3	4	2	1	3	1	4	5	5	2	9	8	6	-	12
Oakland Athletics	1	3	4	3	5	2	3	6	2	4	9	7	6	7	-

2016 National League Standings

Overall

EAST							CENTRAL							WEST						
Team	W-L	Pct	GB	D1	LD1	LLd	Team	W-L	Pct	GB	D1	LD1	LLd	Team	W-L	Pct	GB	D1	LD1	LLd
Washington Nationals	95-67	.586	0.0	176	10/2	10.5	Chicago Cubs	103-58	.640	0.0	180	10/2	19.0	Los Angeles Dodgers	91-71	.562	0.0	78	10/2	8.0
New York Mets	87-75	.537	8.0	9	5/28	0.5	St Louis Cardinals	86-76	.531	17.5	0	-	0.0	San Francisco Giants	87-75	.537	4.0	118	8/20	8.0
Miami Marlins	79-82	.491	15.5	0	-	0.0	Pittsburgh Pirates	78-83	.484	25.0	7	4/9	1.0	Colorado Rockies	75-87	.463	16.0	5	5/5	0.0
Philadelphia Phillies	71-91	.438	24.0	0	-	0.0	Milwaukee Brewers	73-89	.451	30.5	0	-	0.0	Arizona Diamondbacks	69-93	.426	22.0	0	-	0.0
Atlanta Braves	68-93	.422	26.5	0	-	0.0	Cincinnati Reds	68-94	.420	35.5	4	4/10	0.0	San Diego Padres	68-94	.420	23.0	0	-	0.0

Wild Card Clinch Dates: New York 10/1, San Francisco 10/2. Division Clinch Dates: Chicago 9/15, Washington 9/24, Los Angeles 9/25. D1 = Number of days a team had at least a share of first place of their division; LD1 = Last date the team had at least a share of first place; LLd = The largest number of games that a team led their division

East Division

Tm	AT		VERSUS						CONDITIONS				GAME			MONTHLY						ALL-STAR	
	Home	Road	East	Cent	West	AL	LHS	RHS	Day	Night	Grass	Turf	1-Rn	5+Rn	XInn	April	May	June	July	Aug	Sept	Pre	Post
Was	50-31	45-36	51-25	17-16	15-18	12-8	20-14	75-53	31-24	64-43	95-67	0-0	26-19	30-10	5-8	16-7	16-14	16-11	13-12	17-11	17-12	54-36	41-31
NYM	44-37	43-38	40-36	22-10	13-21	12-8	19-18	68-57	29-17	58-58	87-75	0-0	25-22	19-18	8-5	15-7	14-15	12-15	13-13	15-14	18-11	47-41	40-34
Mia	40-40	39-42	32-43	21-13	20-12	6-14	22-12	57-70	21-26	58-56	77-82	2-0	22-24	13-21	4-7	12-11	15-14	14-13	16-10	10-18	12-16	47-41	32-41
Phi	37-44	34-47	30-46	12-21	18-15	11-9	17-17	54-74	22-32	49-59	70-90	1-1	28-23	10-34	7-6	14-10	12-16	9-19	13-14	12-14	11-18	42-48	29-43
Atl	31-50	37-43	36-39	13-20	11-22	8-12	16-31	52-62	20-25	48-68	68-93	0-0	21-22	11-28	11-11	5-18	10-18	12-16	10-16	13-15	18-10	31-58	37-35

Central Division

Tm	AT		VERSUS						CONDITIONS				GAME			MONTHLY						ALL-STAR	
	Home	Road	East	Cent	West	AL	LHS	RHS	Day	Night	Grass	Turf	1-Rn	5+Rn	XInn	April	May	June	July	Aug	Sept	Pre	Post
ChC	57-24	46-34	19-14	50-25	19-14	15-5	28-17	75-41	45-28	58-30	103-58	0-0	22-23	42-13	9-4	17-5	18-10	16-12	12-14	22-6	18-11	53-35	50-23
StL	38-43	48-33	17-16	42-34	19-14	8-12	20-24	66-52	27-23	59-53	86-76	0-0	24-23	33-20	4-3	12-12	16-13	12-13	13-11	14-13	16-14	46-42	40-34
Pit	38-42	40-41	14-19	33-42	22-11	9-11	20-9	58-74	19-30	59-53	78-83	0-0	20-21	19-23	8-5	15-9	14-13	9-19	14-10	15-13	11-19	46-43	32-40
Mil	41-40	32-49	16-17	31-45	15-18	11-9	30-19	43-70	27-31	46-58	73-89	0-0	23-28	18-23	4-9	8-15	15-14	12-14	12-13	10-20	16-13	38-49	35-40
Cin	38-43	30-51	14-19	33-43	16-17	5-15	14-20	54-74	27-28	41-66	68-94	0-0	22-27	19-33	3-10	9-15	8-20	12-16	13-11	13-15	13-17	32-57	36-37

West Division

Tm	AT		VERSUS						CONDITIONS				GAME			MONTHLY						ALL-STAR	
	Home	Road	East	Cent	West	AL	LHS	RHS	Day	Night	Grass	Turf	1-Rn	5+Rn	XInn	April	May	June	July	Aug	Sept	Pre	Post
LAD	57-28	38-43	19-13	19-15	43-33	10-10	22-24	69-47	28-16	63-55	88-69	3-2	22-20	25-19	6-8	12-13	16-12	16-12	15-9	15-13	17-12	51-40	40-31
SF	45-36	42-39	17-16	17-16	45-31	8-12	30-22	57-53	33-22	54-53	84-75	0-0	28-27	24-10	11-7	12-13	21-8	17-10	11-13	11-16	15-15	57-33	30-42
Col	42-39	33-48	20-14	11-21	35-41	9-11	19-29	56-58	29-26	46-61	75-87	0-0	12-20	27-30	3-6	11-12	13-15	13-14	15-12	12-16	11-18	40-48	35-39
Ari	33-48	36-45	18-15	13-20	33-43	5-15	23-22	46-71	20-30	49-63	68-92	1-1	22-17	19-31	8-8	12-14	11-17	13-14	7-17	13-15	13-16	38-52	31-41
SD	39-42	29-52	14-19	14-19	34-42	6-14	21-22	47-72	15-35	53-59	67-89	1-5	19-31	14-19	6-6	9-15	11-18	13-13	12-14	10-17	13-17	38-51	30-43

Team vs. Team Breakdown

	EAST					CENTRAL					WEST				
	Was	NYM	Mia	Phi	Atl	ChC	StL	Pit	Mil	Cin	LAD	SF	Col	Ari	SD
Washington Nationals	-	12	10	14	15	2	5	4	2	4	1	4	2	5	3
New York Mets	7	-	12	12	9	5	3	3	5	6	3	4	1	1	4
Miami Marlins	9	7	-	9	7	3	4	6	4	4	6	2	5	4	3
Philadelphia Phillies	5	7	10	-	8	1	2	3	4	2	2	3	5	3	5
Atlanta Braves	4	10	11	11	-	3	2	3	2	3	1	3	1	2	4
Chicago Cubs	5	2	4	5	3	-	10	14	11	15	4	4	2	5	4
St Louis Cardinals	2	3	3	5	4	9	-	10	13	10	2	4	4	3	6
Pittsburgh Pirates	2	3	1	4	4	4	9	-	10	10	5	4	5	5	3
Milwaukee Brewers	4	2	2	3	5	8	6	9	-	8	2	1	5	4	3
Cincinnati Reds	3	0	3	4	4	4	9	9	11	-	2	3	5	3	3
Los Angeles Dodgers	5	4	1	4	5	3	4	2	5	5	-	8	12	12	11
San Francisco Giants	3	3	4	3	4	3	3	3	5	3	11	-	10	13	11
Colorado Rockies	4	6	2	2	6	4	2	2	1	2	7	9	-	9	10
Arizona Diamondbacks	2	5	2	4	5	2	4	1	3	3	7	6	10	-	10
San Diego Padres	4	3	3	2	2	2	1	3	4	4	8	8	9	9	-

American League Batting

Tm	G	AB	H	2B	3B	HR	(Hm	Rd)	TB	R	RBI	TBB	IBB	SO	HBP	SH	SF	ShO	SB	CS	SB%	GDP	LOB	Avg	OBP	Slg
Bos	162	5670	1598	343	25	208	(102	106)	2615	878	836	558	34	1160	43	8	40	6	83	24	.78	137	1771	.282	.348	.461
Cle	161	5484	1435	308	29	185	(99	86)	2356	777	733	531	16	1246	49	31	60	7	134	31	.81	137	1654	.262	.329	.430
Sea	162	5583	1446	251	17	223	(116	107)	2400	768	735	506	29	1288	72	24	41	6	56	28	.67	138	1661	.259	.326	.430
Tex	162	5525	1446	257	23	215	(103	112)	2394	765	746	436	23	1220	70	18	40	8	99	36	.73	114	1586	.262	.322	.433
Tor	162	5479	1358	276	18	221	(107	114)	2333	759	728	632	16	1362	55	26	40	8	54	24	.69	153	1666	.248	.330	.426
Det	161	5526	1476	252	30	211	(101	110)	2421	750	719	493	32	1303	53	17	38	12	58	29	.67	135	1635	.267	.331	.438
Bal	162	5524	1413	265	6	253	(131	122)	2449	744	710	468	19	1324	44	17	36	6	19	13	.59	119	1601	.256	.317	.443
Hou	162	5545	1367	291	29	198	(98	100)	2310	724	689	554	31	1452	47	27	31	8	102	44	.70	134	1599	.247	.319	.417
Min	162	5618	1409	288	35	200	(98	102)	2367	722	690	513	24	1426	44	27	43	8	91	32	.74	96	1660	.251	.316	.421
LAA	162	5431	1410	279	20	156	(81	75)	2197	717	686	471	21	991	51	36	49	7	73	34	.68	147	1644	.260	.322	.405
CWS	162	5550	1428	277	33	168	(83	85)	2275	686	655	455	16	1285	53	29	44	11	77	36	.68	122	1671	.257	.317	.410
NYY	162	5458	1378	245	20	183	(111	72)	2212	680	647	475	19	1188	42	21	49	13	72	22	.77	121	1664	.252	.315	.405
KC	162	5552	1450	264	33	147	(64	83)	2221	675	640	382	23	1224	45	38	34	10	121	35	.78	134	1620	.261	.312	.400
TB	162	5481	1333	288	32	216	(103	113)	2333	672	647	449	20	1482	69	18	28	10	60	37	.62	88	1543	.243	.307	.426
Oak	162	5500	1352	270	21	169	(67	102)	2171	653	634	442	19	1145	33	13	34	11	50	23	.68	142	1597	.246	.304	.395
AL	1214	82926	21299	4154	371	2953	(1464	1489)	35054	10970	10496	7365	342	19096	770	350	607	132	1149	448	.72	1917	24572	.257	.321	.423

American League Pitching

Tm	G	CG	Rel	IP	BFP	H	R	ER	HR	SH	SF	HB	TBB	IBB	SO	WP	Bk	W	L	Pct.	ShO	Sv-Op	Hld	OAvg	OOBP	OSlg	ERA
Tor	162	0	487	1459.1	6113	1340	666	613	183	13	33	59	461	10	1314	50	7	89	73	.549	10	43-65	72	.242	.305	.398	3.78
Cle	161	5	504	1445.0	6033	1330	676	617	186	27	31	34	461	34	1398	49	7	94	67	.584	11	37-48	54	.243	.304	.407	3.84
Bos	162	9	463	1439.2	6073	1342	694	640	176	24	35	65	490	16	1362	52	0	93	69	.574	5	43-61	81	.246	.314	.397	4.00
Hou	162	2	500	1468.0	6180	1441	701	663	181	18	31	39	453	19	1396	98	2	84	78	.519	8	44-64	102	.256	.314	.424	4.06
NYY	162	0	483	1428.1	6023	1358	702	660	214	21	22	57	444	15	1393	52	2	84	78	.519	10	48-64	80	.248	.310	.424	4.16
Sea	162	2	476	1457.0	6147	1410	707	647	213	23	36	55	460	30	1318	52	7	86	76	.531	8	49-74	97	.253	.314	.425	4.00
KC	162	3	472	1440.0	6182	1433	712	674	206	30	39	60	517	8	1287	55	7	81	81	.500	7	41-60	78	.259	.327	.423	4.21
TB	162	1	485	1426.1	6076	1395	713	665	210	33	47	32	491	25	1357	61	7	68	94	.420	8	42-60	75	.255	.318	.416	4.20
CWS	162	1	485	1446.2	6196	1422	715	659	185	29	49	68	521	30	1270	72	2	78	84	.481	10	43-71	86	.257	.326	.419	4.10
Bal	162	1	443	1432.0	6122	1408	715	671	183	17	38	51	545	23	1248	59	3	89	73	.549	9	54-68	58	.258	.328	.421	4.22
Det	161	3	476	1428.0	6048	1417	721	672	182	25	53	51	462	25	1232	44	4	86	75	.534	8	47-66	75	.260	.320	.421	4.24
LAA	162	4	527	1421.1	6120	1480	727	676	208	22	48	56	498	27	1136	47	10	74	88	.457	12	29-50	83	.269	.334	.440	4.28
Tex	162	7	481	1443.0	6186	1441	757	700	201	19	43	53	534	16	1154	45	5	95	67	.586	6	56-73	103	.260	.329	.424	4.37
Oak	162	2	492	1433.1	6144	1459	761	718	185	21	49	50	464	28	1188	70	3	69	93	.426	7	42-65	66	.263	.322	.422	4.51
Min	162	4	533	1443.0	6314	1617	889	814	221	26	46	41	479	26	1191	83	7	59	103	.364	3	26-46	46	.283	.340	.466	5.08
AL	1214	44	7301	21611.0	91957	21293	10856	10089	2934	348	600	771	7280	332	19244	889	73	1229	1199	.506	122	644-935	1156	.257	.320	.422	4.20

American League Fielding

Team	G	Inn	PO	Ast	OFAst	E	(Throw	Field)	TC	DP	GDP	SB	CS	SB%	CPkof	PPkof	PB	UER	UERA	FPct
Houston	162	1468.0	4404	1599	45	77	31	46	6080	135	113	67	31	.68	1	3	18	38	0.23	.987
Detroit	161	1428.0	4284	1537	17	75	29	46	5896	148	129	71	39	.65	3	5	5	49	0.31	.987
Boston	162	1439.2	4319	1427	35	75	36	39	5821	140	117	59	33	.64	3	1	37	54	0.34	.987
Baltimore	162	1432.0	4296	1579	30	80	37	43	5955	165	145	69	37	.65	3	0	4	44	0.28	.987
Toronto	162	1459.1	4378	1622	25	88	36	52	6088	144	127	84	20	.81	0	4	29	53	0.33	.986
New York	162	1428.1	4285	1536	26	86	38	48	5907	116	100	86	31	.74	3	3	14	42	0.26	.985
Seattle	162	1457.0	4371	1575	31	89	34	55	6035	158	135	81	32	.72	1	1	11	60	0.37	.985
Cleveland	161	1445.0	4335	1608	37	89	34	55	6032	126	103	51	32	.61	5	2	12	59	0.37	.985
Kansas City	162	1440.0	4320	1526	30	94	49	45	5940	134	117	55	42	.57	1	8	7	38	0.24	.984
Chicago	162	1446.2	4340	1536	43	95	39	56	5971	148	123	89	20	.82	5	1	8	56	0.35	.984
Texas	162	1443.0	4329	1655	27	97	39	58	6081	190	168	82	33	.71	0	2	11	57	0.36	.984
Oakland	162	1433.1	4300	1630	29	97	35	62	6027	152	125	75	22	.77	1	3	11	43	0.27	.984
Tampa Bay	162	1426.1	4279	1410	28	94	42	52	5783	129	109	91	31	.75	1	5	13	48	0.30	.984
Los Angeles	162	1421.1	4264	1483	34	97	56	41	5844	148	126	93	47	.66	3	11	7	51	0.32	.983
Minnesota	162	1443.0	4329	1610	31	126	54	72	6065	172	155	78	20	.80	0	8	9	75	0.47	.979
American League	1214	21611.0	64833	23333	468	1359	589	770	89525	2205	1892	1131	470	.71	30	57	196	767	0.32	.985

National League Batting

							BATTING														BASERUNNING					PERCENTAGES		
Tm	G	AB	H	2B	3B	HR	(Hm	Rd)	TB	R	RBI	TBB	IBB	SO	HBP	SH	SF	ShO		SB	CS	SB%	GDP	LOB	Avg	OBP	Slg
Col	162	5614	1544	318	47	204	(116	88)	2568	845	805	494	35	1330	40	54	34	5		66	39	.63	113	1626	.275	.336	.457
ChC	162	5503	1409	293	30	199	(90	109)	2359	808	767	656	45	1339	96	42	37	6		66	34	.66	107	1799	.256	.343	.429
StL	162	5548	1415	299	32	225	(104	121)	2453	779	745	526	28	1318	70	37	41	8		35	26	.57	117	1629	.255	.325	.442
Was	162	5490	1403	268	29	203	(102	101)	2338	763	735	536	49	1252	64	48	63	7		121	39	.76	102	1645	.256	.326	.426
Ari	162	5665	1479	285	56	190	(113	77)	2446	752	709	463	43	1427	50	43	38	6		137	31	.82	117	1642	.261	.320	.432
Pit	162	5542	1426	277	32	153	(70	83)	2226	729	696	561	39	1334	81	41	36	9		110	45	.71	133	1709	.257	.332	.402
LAD	162	5518	1376	272	21	189	(101	88)	2257	725	680	525	31	1321	58	30	32	12		45	26	.63	120	1658	.249	.319	.409
Cin	162	5487	1403	277	33	164	(88	76)	2238	716	678	452	37	1284	52	58	44	10		139	51	.73	129	.1579	.256	.316	.408
SF	162	5565	1437	280	54	130	(55	75)	2215	715	675	572	43	1107	42	42	46	13		79	36	.69	120	1794	.258	.329	.398
SD	162	5419	1275	257	26	177	(83	94)	2115	686	654	449	30	1500	58	36	36	15		125	45	.74	93	1448	.235	.299	.390
Mil	162	5330	1299	249	19	194	(102	92)	2168	671	641	599	34	1543	37	53	39	8		181	56	.76	131	1564	.244	.322	.407
NYM	162	5459	1342	240	19	218	(112	106)	2274	671	649	517	43	1302	62	35	41	10		42	18	.70	123	1670	.246	.316	.417
Mia	161	5547	1460	259	42	128	(58	70)	2187	655	626	447	40	1213	54	46	38	12		71	28	.72	140	1750	.263	.322	.394
Atl	161	5514	1404	295	27	122	(52	70)	2119	649	615	502	60	1240	59	64	52	12		75	34	.69	145	1755	.255	.321	.384
Phi	162	5434	1305	231	35	161	(78	83)	2089	610	574	424	33	1376	58	46	30	11		96	45	.68	112	1558	.240	.301	.384
NL	1214	82635	20977	4100	502	2657	(1324	1333)	34052	10774	10249	7723	590	19886	881	675	607	144		1388	553	.72	1802	24826	.254	.322	.412

National League Pitching

	HOW MUCH THEY PITCHED					WHAT THEY GAVE UP													THE RESULTS									
Tm	G	CG	Rel	IP	BFP	H	R	ER	HR	SH	SF	HB	TBB	IBB	SO	WP	Bk		W	L	Pct.	ShO	Sv-Op	Hld	OAvg	OOBP	OSlg	ERA
ChC	162	5	503	1459.2	5933	1125	556	511	163	31	35	63	495	24	1441	80	0		103	58	.640	15	38-53	74	.212	.285	.348	3.15
Was	162	1	508	1459.2	6036	1272	612	570	155	52	28	57	468	43	1476	47	4		95	67	.586	12	46-60	91	.234	.300	.376	3.51
NYM	162	1	538	1447.0	6067	1397	617	574	152	55	44	35	439	39	1396	50	7		87	75	.537	13	55-71	100	.254	.311	.395	3.57
SF	162	10	575	1460.1	6049	1334	631	593	158	41	34	46	439	30	1309	40	6		87	75	.537	11	43-73	125	.243	.303	.392	3.65
LAD	162	3	606	1453.0	6014	1266	638	598	165	35	30	53	464	51	1510	58	5		91	71	.562	15	47-69	100	.233	.298	.375	3.70
Mia	161	0	559	1435.0	6164	1358	682	646	152	48	50	61	595	62	1379	66	3		79	82	.491	12	55-84	97	.251	.329	.394	4.05
StL	162	2	481	1448.1	6164	1432	712	656	159	38	46	52	475	35	1290	50	1		86	76	.531	10	38-55	70	.258	.320	.402	4.08
Mil	162	0	513	1434.1	6188	1450	733	650	178	40	41	66	532	33	1175	48	2		73	89	.451	7	46-68	88	.263	.333	.426	4.08
Pit	162	5	525	1450.2	6292	1490	758	679	180	64	46	68	533	28	1232	71	7		78	83	.484	5	51-71	89	.267	.336	.436	4.21
SD	162	1	510	1440.0	6228	1425	770	708	183	27	42	53	569	44	1222	67	3		68	94	.420	9	35-53	74	.258	.330	.422	4.43
Atl	161	1	587	1447.2	6250	1414	779	725	177	52	50	70	547	55	1227	83	4		68	93	.422	9	39-58	64	.256	.328	.416	4.51
Phi	162	4	505	1437.0	6164	1468	796	739	213	49	55	51	466	30	1299	57	9		71	91	.438	12	43-63	80	.265	.325	.448	4.63
Cin	162	2	484	1442.0	6348	1457	854	786	258	54	35	78	636	31	1241	61	12		68	94	.420	8	28-53	57	.263	.345	.456	4.91
Col	162	2	533	1429.1	6289	1532	860	779	181	49	36	70	547	38	1223	72	5		75	87	.463	9	37-65	73	.274	.345	.446	4.91
Ari	162	2	575	1451.1	6437	1563	890	821	202	42	42	57	603	57	1318	69	7		69	93	.426	7	31-53	69	.275	.348	.454	5.09
NL	1214	39	8002	21695.1	92623	20983	10888	10035	2676	677	614	880	7808	600	19738	919	75		1198	1228	.494	154	632-949	1251	.254	.323	.413	4.16

National League Fielding

							Fielding													
Team	G	Inn	PO	Ast	OFAst	E	(Throw	Field)	TC	DP	GDP	SB	CS	SB%	CPkof	PPkof	PB	UER	UERA	FPct
San Francisco	162	1460.1	4381	1639	22	72	27	45	6092	136	120	71	35	.67	2	7	6	38	0.23	.988
Washington	162	1459.2	4379	1425	18	73	35	38	5877	142	124	54	29	.65	0	1	17	42	0.26	.988
Los Angeles	162	1453.0	4359	1448	26	80	35	45	5887	102	84	87	36	.71	1	8	13	40	0.25	.986
Miami	161	1435.0	4305	1507	28	86	37	49	5898	137	119	76	38	.67	0	4	9	36	0.23	.985
New York	162	1447.0	4341	1519	26	90	45	45	5950	138	117	135	45	.75	0	4	8	43	0.27	.985
Philadelphia	162	1437.0	4311	1503	29	97	36	61	5911	142	120	70	32	.69	1	5	10	57	0.36	.984
Arizona	162	1451.1	4354	1663	22	101	42	59	6118	143	125	63	35	.64	1	1	17	69	0.43	.983
Chicago	162	1459.2	4379	1634	20	101	60	41	6114	116	98	133	38	.78	10	8	12	45	0.28	.983
Atlanta	161	1447.2	4343	1565	34	101	39	62	6009	134	126	132	25	.84	0	10	14	54	0.34	.983
Cincinnati	162	1442.0	4326	1549	33	102	45	57	5977	142	118	108	45	.71	1	6	9	68	0.42	.983
St Louis	162	1448.1	4345	1747	23	107	49	58	6199	169	149	85	26	.77	0	5	10	56	0.35	.983
Pittsburgh	162	1450.2	4352	1745	35	111	44	67	6208	172	150	102	28	.78	1	4	17	79	0.49	.982
Colorado	162	1429.1	4288	1749	30	110	54	56	6147	148	128	100	31	.76	1	6	13	81	0.51	.982
San Diego	162	1440.0	4320	1623	23	109	45	64	6052	165	147	98	29	.77	0	3	13	62	0.39	.982
Milwaukee	162	1434.1	4303	1671	29	136	69	67	6110	145	122	92	59	.61	5	5	8	83	0.52	.978
National League	1214	21695.1	65086	23987	398	1476	662	814	90549	2131	1827	1406	531	.73	23	77	176	853	0.35	.984

Team Pitching Staff Summary

Team	Starters				Bullpen					
	IP	ERA	ERA Rank	W-L	IP	ERA	ERA Rank	W-L	Sv-Opp	Sv Pct
Arizona Diamondbacks	884.1	5.19	29	46-69	567.0	4.94	27	23-24	31-53	58%
Atlanta Braves	880.1	4.87	28	40-64	567.1	3.95	19	28-29	39-58	67%
Baltimore Orioles	886.0	4.72	24	57-58	546.0	3.40	3	32-15	54-68	79%
Boston Red Sox	969.1	4.22	8	68-42	470.1	3.56	8	25-27	43-61	70%
Chicago Cubs	989.0	2.96	1	81-39	470.2	3.56	8	22-19	38-53	72%
Chicago White Sox	977.0	4.33	13	54-62	469.2	3.68	17	24-22	43-71	61%
Cincinnati Reds	859.0	4.79	25	45-62	583.0	5.09	29	23-32	28-53	53%
Cleveland Indians	936.1	4.08	7	66-47	508.2	3.45	4	28-20	37-48	77%
Colorado Rockies	905.0	4.79	25	53-58	524.1	5.13	30	22-29	37-65	57%
Detroit Tigers	918.2	4.25	9	56-55	509.1	4.22	24	30-20	47-66	71%
Houston Astros	917.0	4.37	15	57-59	551.0	3.56	8	27-19	44-64	69%
Kansas City Royals	900.1	4.67	22	50-57	539.2	3.45	4	31-24	41-60	68%
Los Angeles Angels	877.1	4.60	20	50-66	544.0	3.77	18	24-22	29-50	58%
Los Angeles Dodgers	862.1	3.95	6	59-49	590.2	3.35	1	32-22	47-69	68%
Miami Marlins	875.1	4.32	12	47-53	559.2	3.63	14	32-29	55-84	65%
Milwaukee Brewers	883.1	4.40	17	50-64	551.0	3.61	12	23-25	46-68	68%
Minnesota Twins	875.1	5.39	30	37-71	567.2	4.63	26	22-32	26-46	57%
New York Mets	922.0	3.61	3	58-55	525.0	3.51	6	29-20	55-71	77%
New York Yankees	916.0	4.44	19	48-59	512.1	3.67	16	36-19	48-64	75%
Oakland Athletics	872.0	4.84	27	43-67	561.1	4.01	20	26-26	42-65	65%
Philadelphia Phillies	909.0	4.41	18	48-63	528.0	5.05	28	23-28	43-63	68%
Pittsburgh Pirates	865.2	4.67	22	50-61	585.0	3.57	11	28-22	51-71	72%
San Diego Padres	884.0	4.61	21	43-74	556.0	4.18	23	25-20	35-53	66%
San Francisco Giants	982.1	3.71	5	62-51	478.0	3.65	15	25-24	43-73	59%
Seattle Mariners	934.2	4.25	9	62-53	522.1	3.55	7	24-23	49-74	66%
St Louis Cardinals	934.1	4.33	13	58-55	514.0	3.62	13	28-21	38-55	69%
Tampa Bay Rays	920.0	4.26	11	48-61	506.1	4.09	21	20-33	42-60	70%
Texas Rangers	921.1	4.38	16	54-47	521.2	4.40	25	41-20	56-73	77%
Toronto Blue Jays	995.1	3.64	4	66-41	464.0	4.11	22	23-32	43-65	66%
Washington Nationals	960.0	3.60	2	72-44	499.2	3.37	2	23-23	46-60	77%

Team Defense
Defensive Runs Saved by Position and Team

Team	P	C	1B	2B	3B	SS	LF	CF	RF	Shifts	Total
Chicago Cubs	11	10	11	7	3	23	5	8	17	12	107
Houston Astros	10	9	5	-1	6	-3	18	7	8	22	81
San Francisco Giants	9	18	11	-1	19	19	3	-7	-13	12	70
Boston Red Sox	-3	0	0	11	8	-10	-2	12	32	6	54
Toronto Blue Jays	6	6	-5	8	3	13	-3	19	-6	12	53
Los Angeles Dodgers	5	13	3	-12	5	2	8	6	10	12	52
Cleveland Indians	2	4	-3	7	-1	17	-1	-21	11	22	37
Los Angeles Angels	3	8	1	4	-10	17	-5	6	6	4	34
Milwaukee Brewers	0	8	-4	-4	4	4	1	6	-9	23	29
Tampa Bay Rays	2	13	-3	-1	-7	-17	9	22	-5	9	22
Kansas City Royals	-8	-2	-6	7	-12	-4	15	20	10	1	21
Colorado Rockies	-8	-9	-5	2	21	3	-3	3	0	15	19
Miami Marlins	-5	-6	6	0	4	5	13	-11	8	2	16
New York Yankees	1	-3	-3	-10	7	-10	13	7	0	10	12
Texas Rangers	-4	-1	2	-7	16	4	3	-4	-10	10	9
St Louis Cardinals	13	0	0	4	-4	-6	-10	2	5	1	5
Washington Nationals	-7	1	-3	-5	7	5	-9	-2	-1	14	0
Arizona Diamondbacks	0	1	5	-2	-13	10	-18	12	-13	17	-1
Seattle Mariners	-9	-5	-6	14	12	-2	-13	-5	-9	22	-1
Chicago White Sox	2	-16	-4	0	-3	3	-5	-22	25	17	-3
Pittsburgh Pirates	4	-1	-5	9	3	-8	16	-32	-1	11	-4
San Diego Padres	-13	13	8	-6	-3	-34	10	0	-2	20	-7
New York Mets	-2	5	4	-4	-21	-13	9	3	5	5	-9
Atlanta Braves	-8	-11	9	-16	-9	-11	-7	11	13	18	-11
Baltimore Orioles	-7	-2	9	-1	15	7	-21	-11	-19	15	-15
Philadelphia Phillies	-2	-10	-15	-1	-11	4	-1	7	-2	8	-23
Cincinnati Reds	-14	-11	-15	-2	2	4	13	4	-18	8	-29
Minnesota Twins	6	-18	8	-1	-8	-16	-22	1	-9	9	-50
Detroit Tigers	-5	2	-10	14	-14	3	-1	-19	-30	10	-50
Oakland Athletics	-5	-15	-2	-12	-23	-6	-1	-17	-2	12	-71

Batting By Position

Pos	AB	H	2B	3B	HR	(Hm	Rd)	TB	R	RBI	TBB	IBB	SO	HBP	SH	SF	SB	CS	SB%	GDP	LOB	Avg	OBP	Slg
P	4677	619	91	8	24	(12	12)	798	243	265	169	0	2073	12	449	15	3	1	.75	77	1923	.132	.164	.171
C	17243	4187	855	42	550	(262	288)	6776	1888	2210	1569	94	4141	178	94	136	76	36	.68	446	5583	.243	.310	.393
1B	18204	4714	938	58	827	(403	424)	8249	2483	2695	2067	164	4499	189	12	155	147	74	.67	459	5562	.259	.338	.453
2B	18924	5236	986	139	585	(309	276)	8255	2646	2220	1511	84	3688	200	81	138	375	144	.72	385	5056	.277	.334	.436
3B	18647	4969	1001	90	718	(362	356)	8304	2535	2509	1674	102	3891	197	31	128	218	84	.72	429	5399	.266	.331	.445
SS	18494	4863	936	125	493	(244	249)	7528	2326	2146	1404	124	3770	163	101	153	356	130	.73	435	5370	.263	.318	.407
LF	18316	4651	968	118	595	(304	291)	7640	2482	2219	1699	73	4364	207	63	131	322	132	.71	411	5401	.254	.322	.417
CF	18677	4911	899	157	546	(297	249)	7762	2674	2042	1717	85	4347	189	103	105	632	208	.75	315	5040	.263	.329	.416
RF	18559	4808	925	96	709	(366	343)	8052	2540	2455	1817	111	4464	172	53	126	252	131	.66	399	5247	.259	.329	.434
DH	9073	2307	456	20	430	(208	222)	4093	1141	1373	930	60	2239	90	6	87	43	16	.73	255	2878	.254	.327	.451
PH	4746	1010	198	20	133	(55	78)	1647	541	610	529	35	1504	54	32	40	45	16	.74	108	1939	.213	.297	.347

Fielding By Position

Pos	Inn	PO	Ast	E	(Throw	Field)	TC	DP	GDP	FPct
P	43306.1	2242	4977	389	303	85	7608	365	264	.949
C	43306.1	39181	2645	283	199	69	42109	257	15	.993
1B	43306.1	40504	2853	269	53	198	43626	3979	231	.994
2B	43306.1	8569	13287	389	134	252	22245	3162	1045	.983
3B	43306.1	3202	9261	555	249	298	13018	916	709	.957
SS	43306.1	6660	13431	509	226	283	20600	2935	1348	.975
LF	43306.1	8512	309	155	38	114	8976	48	1	.983
CF	43306.1	11464	249	136	27	109	11849	50		.989
RF	43306.1	9585	308	150	22	126	10043	59		.985

Team Efficiency Summary

Joe Rosales

The 2016 American League division winners all finished the season with very similar records to each other. The Texas Rangers finished with the best record in the league at 95-67, the Cleveland Indians were just half a game behind at 94-67 (having had a late-season game rained out that did not need to be made up because it would not have affected the final standings), and the Boston Red Sox came in at 93-69. Over the course of a 162-game season, one might think that things even out enough that any differences between three teams that close in the standings would have to be subtle. Not so.

The Rangers, the team that earned the top seed heading into the playoffs, barely outscored their opponents in 2016, scoring 765 runs while allowing 757. On both sides of the ball, the Indians and Red Sox were ostensibly better than the Rangers. The Indians scored 777 runs while allowing 676. The Red Sox scored an MLB-best 878 runs while allowing 694. Based on those numbers, the Red Sox would have been expected to win 100 games and run away with the AL; the Indians would have been expected to do about as well as they actually did and win 92 games; and the Rangers would have been expected to win 82 games, which would only have been good enough for them to finish third in their division, never mind make the playoffs.

If we take these breakdowns further and focus on component stats (singles, doubles, home runs, walks, etc.) rather than aggregate run scoring, the differences are even more stark. The Rangers would still be expected to have won 82 games, the Indians would have inched up to 93 wins, but the Red Sox expected win total would jump to 104 games.

The Rangers were the most efficient team at finding ways to win ballgames in 2016. Without making any judgments on how they achieved it, they maximized the runs that they scored and allowed more so than any other team in baseball. By comparison, the Indians finished right where their underlying stats suggested they would, and the Red Sox tied for being the second least efficient team in baseball. These three teams basically ended up in the same place at the end of the season, but they got there in very different ways.

The tables on the following pages detail how efficient each team was in 2016 according to four different measures. Hitting Efficiency compares a team's actual runs scored to its expected runs scored as measured by Runs Created. Similarly, Pitching Efficiency compares a team's actual runs allowed to its expected runs allowed based on component statistics like walks and hits allowed. Run Efficiency is a measure of how a team's actual win total stacks up against its expected win total as determined using actual runs scored and allowed (i.e., the measure by which the Red Sox would have been expected to win 100 games). And finally, Overall Efficiency is a measure of how a team's actual win total compares to its expected win total as calculated from its expected runs scored and allowed (i.e., the measure by which the Red Sox would have been expected to win 104 games).

2016 American League Team Efficiency Summary

	RC	Runs	Hit Eff	Exp RA	RA	Pit Eff	Exp Wins	Wins	Runs Eff	Eff Wins	Wins	Overall Eff
Texas Rangers	753	765	102	747	757	99	82	95	116	82	95	116
Kansas City Royals	674	675	100	765	712	107	77	81	106	71	81	114
Los Angeles Angels	688	717	104	791	727	109	80	74	93	70	74	106
Baltimore Orioles	747	744	100	720	715	101	84	89	106	84	89	106
New York Yankees	687	680	99	702	702	100	78	84	107	79	84	106
Houston Astros	709	724	102	706	701	101	84	84	100	81	84	103
Chicago White Sox	704	686	97	738	715	103	78	78	100	77	78	101
Cleveland Indians	765	777	102	651	676	96	92	94	103	93	94	101
Oakland Athletics	631	653	103	734	761	96	69	69	100	69	69	100
Seattle Mariners	761	768	101	714	707	101	88	86	98	86	86	100
Toronto Blue Jays	747	759	102	656	666	98	92	89	97	91	89	97
Detroit Tigers	777	750	97	695	721	96	84	86	103	89	86	96
Boston Red Sox	891	878	99	666	694	96	100	93	93	104	93	89
Tampa Bay Rays	692	672	97	730	713	102	76	68	89	77	68	89
Minnesota Twins	739	722	98	879	889	99	64	59	92	67	59	88

2016 National League Team Efficiency Summary

	RC	Runs	Hit Eff	Exp RA	RA	Pit Eff	Exp Wins	Wins	Runs Eff	Eff Wins	Wins	Overall Eff
Philadelphia Phillies	610	610	100	767	796	96	60	71	118	63	71	113
Cincinnati Reds	688	716	104	882	854	103	67	68	102	61	68	111
San Diego Padres	621	686	110	750	770	97	72	68	95	66	68	103
Milwaukee Brewers	690	671	97	776	733	106	74	73	99	72	73	102
Pittsburgh Pirates	735	729	99	779	758	103	78	78	100	76	78	102
New York Mets	702	671	96	648	617	105	88	87	99	87	87	99
Miami Marlins	691	655	95	693	682	102	77	79	102	80	79	98
Los Angeles Dodgers	704	725	103	605	638	95	91	91	100	93	91	98
Arizona Diamondbacks	770	752	98	867	890	97	67	69	102	71	69	97
Atlanta Braves	665	649	98	742	779	95	66	68	103	72	68	95
St Louis Cardinals	773	779	101	689	712	97	88	86	97	90	86	95
Washington Nationals	762	763	100	584	612	95	99	95	96	102	95	93
Chicago Cubs	813	808	99	552	556	99	110	103	94	111	103	93
Colorado Rockies	835	845	101	825	860	96	80	75	94	82	75	92
San Francisco Giants	732	715	98	607	631	96	91	87	96	96	87	91

Anthony Rizzo
Dustin Pedroia
Nolan Arenado
Andrelton Simmons
Javier Baez

Starling Marte
Kevin Pillar
Mookie Betts
Buster Posey
Dallas Keuchel

THE FIELDING BIBLE
AWARDS 2016

The Fielding Bible Awards 2016

John Dewan

There are 12 experts who comprise the voting panel for the annual Fielding Bible Awards, now in its 11th year. Their intention is to stand up and say "This was the best fielder at this position in the major leagues last season." The panel awards ten winners each year, one at each position plus an additional award that goes to the best defensive multi-position player.

Some very, very close races added to the drama this year. In fact, the last ballot received broke two exact ties: at shortstop and at pitcher. The last ballot allowed Andrelton Simmons of the Los Angeles Angels to win his fourth consecutive award with a one-point victory (106 to 105 points) over the Giants' Brandon Crawford. It was the first of Simmons' four awards that was not a unanimous vote. Astro Dallas Keuchel won his third in a row going down to the wire with Zack Greinke of the Arizona Diamonbacks.

In addition to Simmons and Keuchel, four other players were repeat award winners this year, making six multiple winners among this year's group of ten.

Dustin Pedroia of the Red Sox won his fourth award (in six years) as baseball's best defensive second baseman. Three players are two-time winners. Nolan Arenado (Rockies) at third base, Starling Marte (Pirates) in left field, and Buster Posey (Giants) at catcher all repeated from last year.

There were four first-time winners: first baseman Anthony Rizzo (Chicago Cubs), center fielder Kevin Pillar (Toronto), right fielder Mookie Betts (Boston), and multi-position player Javier Baez (Chicago Cubs).

Here's a short refresher course on how the awards are determined: We asked our panel of 12 experts to rank 10 players at each position on a scale from one to ten. We then use the same voting technique as the Major League Baseball MVP voting. A first place vote gets 10 points, second place 9 points, third place 8 points, etc. Total up the points for each player and the player with the most points wins the award. A perfect score is 120.

Here are the Fielding Bible Awards for the 2016 season:

First Base – Anthony Rizzo, Chicago Cubs

Anthony Rizzo won his first Fielding Bible Award in 2016, but he won an even bigger battle eight years ago. Rizzo was diagnosed with cancer at age 18 in his first year of professional baseball in the Boston Red Sox organization. It was then-Red Sox pitcher Jon Lester who gave him hope that he could still be a major leaguer. Because Lester also had cancer at a young age, and beat it. It is not coincidental that they are now Chicago Cub teammates. Rizzo saved 11 runs for the Cubs defensively in 2016 leading all MLB first basemen. He received seven of 12 first place votes and out-pointed runner-up Brandon Belt 113 to 101.

Previous Winners:

2015	Paul Goldschmidt	2010	Daric Barton
2014	Adrian Gonzalez	2009	Albert Pujols
2013	Paul Goldschmidt	2008	Albert Pujols
2012	Mark Teixeira	2007	Albert Pujols
2011	Albert Pujols	2006	Albert Pujols

Second Base – Dustin Pedroia, Boston Red Sox

Dustin Pedroia now has four Fielding Bible Awards and four Gold Gloves. By the time you read this he might have five Gold Gloves, but he'll have to beat out Tiger Ian Kinsler, the 2015 FBA winner and the 2016 FBA runner-up at second base. The voting wasn't particularly close for the 2016 Fielding Bible Awards (114 to 104) but Kinsler had a great year defensively as well. Pedroia and Kinsler led all major league second basemen with 12 runs saved in 2016.

Previous Winners:

2015	Ian Kinsler	2010	Chase Utley
2014	Dustin Pedroia	2009	Aaron Hill
2013	Dustin Pedroia	2008	Brandon Phillips
2012	Darwin Barney	2007	Aaron Hill
2011	Dustin Pedroia	2006	Orlando Hudson

Third Base – Nolan Arenado, Colorado Rockies

It's back-to-back Fielding Bible Awards for Nolen Arenado. He received all but one of the first place votes at third base for a total of 119 points. He also finished well ahead in Defensive Runs Saved, saving 20 runs for the Rockies, a good margin ahead of the 15 runs saved by Adrian Beltre (Texas) and Kyle Seager (Seattle). Arenado also led all fielders (not just third basemen) recording 75 Good Fielding Plays where he made a play that was not likely to be an out or prevent an advancement with an average play.

Previous Winners:

2015	Nolan Arenado	2010	Evan Longoria
2014	Josh Donaldson	2009	Ryan Zimmerman
2013	Manny Machado	2008	Adrian Beltre
2012	Adrian Beltre	2007	Pedro Feliz
2011	Adrian Beltre	2006	Adrian Beltre

Shortstop – Andrelton Simmons, Los Angeles Angels

Four years in a row for Andrelton Simmons. No one is yet to win five in a row; Mark Buehrle, Yadier Molina and Albert Pujols have also won four in a row. But it was the slimmest of margins (106 to 105 points) over Brandon Crawford of the Giants. This, after Simmons and Crawford finished first and second on every ballot in the 2015 voting. No one is close to Simmons' five-year total of 131 Defensive Runs Saved. Crawford is second in the five years with 62, less than half of Simmons' total. However, Crawford did edge out Simmons in 2016 DRS, 20 to 18. Addison Russell of the Cubs was also in the top three with 19 runs saved.

Previous Winners:

2015	Andrelton Simmons	2010	Troy Tulowitzki
2014	Andrelton Simmons	2009	Jack Wilson
2013	Andrelton Simmons	2008	Jimmy Rollins
2012	Brendan Ryan	2007	Troy Tulowitzki
2011	Troy Tulowitzki	2006	Adam Everett

Left Field – Starling Marte, Pittsburgh Pirates

It's not the norm for your left fielder to have a wickedly strong throwing arm, but that is the case with Starling Marte. He led all outfielders in 2016 with 16 baserunner kills (direct throw to a base to nab the runner) with the next best left fielder at 9 (Ryan Braun). Throwing accounted for nine of Marte's MLB-leading 19 Defensive Runs Saved in left field. His ability to cover ground accounted for six more runs saved and making Good Plays while avoiding Misplays added another four runs saved, an all-around tremendous defensive performance for repeat-winner Marte. Marte's margin of victory over runner-up Yankee Brett Gardner was huge (119 to 90 points).

Previous Winners:

2015	Starling Marte	2010	Brett Gardner
2014	Alex Gordon	2009	Carl Crawford
2013	Alex Gordon	2008	Carl Crawford
2012	Alex Gordon	2007	Eric Byrnes
2011	Brett Gardner	2006	Carl Crawford

Center Field – Kevin Pillar, Toronto Blue Jays

Kevin Pillar upstaged Kevin Kiermaier. It was not easy as Kiermaier set a record for the highest single season total of Defensive Runs Saved in 2015 with 42. But in 2016 Pillar continued his reign as King of the Web Gem and added in 21 runs saved to boot. Kiermaier did have 25 DRS for the Tampa Bay Rays, but when it came to making catches, Pillar saved 47 bases compared to 34 for Kiermaier. The Fielding Bible Award voters rewarded Pillar with his first award in a close vote, 109 points to 106 points for Kiermaier.

Previous Winners:

2015	Kevin Kiermaier	2010	Michael Bourn
2014	Juan Lagares	2009	Franklin Gutierrez
2013	Carlos Gomez	2008	Carlos Beltran
2012	Mike Trout	2007	Andruw Jones
2011	Austin Jackson	2006	Carlos Beltran

Right Field – Mookie Betts, Boston Red Sox

Mookie's full name is Markus Lynn Betts, intentionally chosen by his parents so his initials are MLB. He is MLB and he is the best in MLB. Betts had the highest total of Defensive Runs Saved among any defender in baseball in 2016 with 32. He finished 10 runs ahead of runner-up Adam Eaton of the White Sox and 13 points ahead of him in the voting (116 to 103). See page 57 for a dramatic rundown of the battle for right field defensive supremacy during the 2016 season between Betts and Eaton.

Previous Winners:

2015	Jason Heyward	2010	Ichiro Suzuki
2014	Jason Heyward	2009	Ichiro Suzuki
2013	Gerardo Parra	2008	Franklin Gutierrez
2012	Jason Heyward	2007	Alex Rios
2011	Justin Upton	2006	Ichiro Suzuki

Catcher – Buster Posey, San Francisco Giants

Buster Posey excels at every aspect of catching. There are five categories of defense that are measured in Defensive Runs Saved (Pitcher Handling, Controlling the Running Game, Handling Bunts, Good Plays and Misplays, and Getting Extra Strikes). Posey's MLB-leading total of 23 Defensive Runs Saved breaks down with an above-average number in each one of these categories with 1, 2, 4, 5, and 11 runs saved by category, respectively. Fielding Bible voters acknowledged Posey with a first place vote on every ballot giving him his second straight Fielding Bible Award.

Previous Winners:

2015	Buster Posey	2010	Yadier Molina
2014	Jonathan Lucroy	2009	Yadier Molina
2013	Yadier Molina	2008	Yadier Molina
2012	Yadier Molina	2007	Yadier Molina
2011	Matt Wieters	2006	Ivan Rodriguez

Pitcher – Dallas Keuchel, Houston Astros

One day Zack Greinke (Diamondbacks) will win a Fielding Bible Award, but 2016 was not to be as the last ballot to come in gave a repeat award to Dallas Keuchel. Greinke had more first place votes than Keuchel, four vs. three, but an eighth place vote and a fifth place vote for Greinke did him in. The final point total was 103 to 100, Keuchel over Greinke. The voting panel recognized defensive excellence among pitchers throughout Major League Baseball, also giving first place votes to Bartolo Colon-Mets (3), Masahiro Tanaka-Yankees (1) and Jake Arrieta-Cubs (1).

Previous Winners:

2015	Dallas Keuchel	2010	Mark Buehrle
2014	Dallas Keuchel	2009	Mark Buehrle
2013	R.A. Dickey	2008	Kenny Rogers
2012	Mark Buehrle	2007	Johan Santana
2011	Mark Buehrle	2006	Greg Maddux

Multi-Position – Javier Baez, Chicago Cubs

Javy Baez was the epitome of defensive excellence at multiple positions. He saved 11 runs at second base, 4 runs at shortstop and one run at third base for the Cubs defensively in 2016. He also demonstrated his versatility by playing a few innings at first base and left field as well. Playing a lot of positions (five) and playing them well (16 DRS), that's what the Multi-Position Fielding Bible Award is all about. Royals outfielder Jarrod Dyson was runner up in the voting (90 points vs. 105 for Baez). Dyson played all three outfield positions and saved 19 runs in total. Cub manager Joe Maddon encouraged versatility and was also rewarded by Baez' teammate Kris Bryant who played six different positions and saved 10 runs. Bryant was third in the voting among multi-position players, and the Cubs led all of baseball with the highest total of Defensive Runs Saved as a team (107).

Previous Winners:

2015 Ender Inciarte   2014 Lorenzo Cain

Background of the Fielding Bible Awards

While *The Fielding Bible, The Fielding Bible—Volume II, The Fielding Bible—Volume III, and The Fielding Bible—Volume IV* put a lot of emphasis on the numbers, especially Defensive Runs Saved and the Range and Positioning System, we feel that visual observation and subjective judgment are still very important parts of determining the best defensive players. Also, we believe people have a right to know who is voting and all the players they are voting for. Therefore, in setting up the Fielding Bible Awards, we took the following steps:

1. *We appointed a panel of experts to vote.* We have a panel of 12 experts plus three "tie-breaker" ballots. (See below.)

2. *We rate everybody in one group.* The Gold Glove vote is divided into National League and American League. We make ours different by putting everybody together. Besides, is playing shortstop in the American League one thing and playing shortstop in the National League a different thing, or are they really very much the same thing? A few years back we had a great example of this decision. Without the Fielding Bible Award, Jack Wilson wins *nada*, because he switched leagues in mid-year. According to our panelists (and unlike the Gold Glove

voters), Jack was the best fielding shortstop in baseball in 2009. Period. He deserved to be recognized for that.

3. *We use a 10-man ballot and a 10-point scale.* We use a 10-man ballot. We give 10 points for first place, 9 points for second place, etc, down to 1 point for tenth place. We feel strongly that a 10-man ballot with weighted positions leads to more accurate outcomes.

4. *We defined the list of candidates.* Only players who actually were regulars at the position are candidates. This eliminates the possibility of a vote going to somebody who wasn't really playing the position.

5. *We are publishing the balloting.* We summarize the voting at each position, clearly identifying whom everybody voted for. Publishing the actual vote totals encourages the voters to take their votes more seriously. Also, we feel the public will have more respect for the voting if they have more insight into the process.

A perfect score is 120 points. If all 12 voters place one player first on their ballot, he scores 120. Only one player had a perfect score of 120 this year: Buster Posey.

Here are the tie-breaker rules (which came into play in our very first year, in 2010, and in 2013). They are applied one at a time until we have a winner:

1. Most first-place votes wins.
2. Count the tie-breaker ballots, highest point tally wins.
3. Award goes to player with the most Bases Saved.

Ballots were due four days after the end of the regular season. Here is this year's panel:

Since you have this book, you probably know **Bill James**, a baseball writer and analyst published for more than thirty years. Bill is the Senior Baseball Operations Advisor for the Boston Red Sox.

The **BIS Video Scouts** at Baseball Info Solutions (BIS) study every game of the season, multiple times, charting a huge list of valuable game details.

As an MLB Network on-air host of *MLB Now* and *MLB Tonight*, **Brian Kenny** brings an analytical perspective on the game of baseball to a national television audience. He also won a 2003 Sports Emmy Award as host of ESPN's *Baseball Tonight*.

Dave Cameron is the Managing Editor of FanGraphs. Until recently, he resided in Winston-Salem, North Carolina, where the local minor league team once forced him to watch Michael Morse play shortstop for an entire season. He has appreciated defensive value ever since.

Doug Glanville played nine seasons in Major League Baseball and was well known for his excellent outfield defense. Currently, he is a baseball analyst at ESPN on *Baseball Tonight*, *SportsCenter*, *Wednesday Night Baseball*, and ESPN.com, as well as a regular contributor to *The New York Times*, and he is the author of the book *The Game from Where I Stand*.

The man who created Strat-O-Matic Baseball, **Hal Richman**, continues to lead his company's annual in-depth analysis of each player's season. Hal cautions SOM players that his voting on this ballot may or may not reflect the eventual fielding ratings for players in his game. Ballots were due prior to the completion of his annual research effort to evaluate player defense.

Named the best sports columnist in America in 2012 by the National Sportswriters and Sportscasters Hall of Fame, **Joe Posnanski** is the National Columnist at NBC Sports.

For over twenty-five years, BIS owner and CEO **John Dewan** has collected, analyzed, and published in-depth baseball statistics and analysis. He has authored or co-authored four volumes of *The Fielding Bible*.

Mark Simon has been a researcher for ESPN Stats & Information since 2002 and currently helps oversee the Stats & Information blog and Twitter (@espnstatsinfo). He is a regular contributor on baseball (often writing on defense) for ESPNNY.com and ESPN.com, and is the author of *Numbers Don't Lie: The Biggest Numbers in Yankees History* (published by Triumph Books in June 2016).

Peter Gammons serves as on-air and online analyst for MLB Network, MLB.com and NESN (New England Sports Network). He is the 56th recipient of the J. G. Taylor Spink Award for outstanding baseball writing given by the BBWAA (Baseball Writers Association of America).

Rob Neyer has been a working writer for 25 years, and most recently has contributed to *The New York Times*, Vice Sports, and Complex. When he's not writing, he's thinking about not writing. Rob will live in Portland, Oregon for as long as they let him.

The **Tom Tango Fan Poll** represents the results of a poll taken at the website Tango on Baseball (www.tangotiger.net). Besides hosting the website, Tom is the Senior Data Architect—Stats at MLBAM and is the co-author of *The Book: Playing the Percentages in Baseball*.

Our three tie-breakers are **Ben Jedlovec**, President of Baseball Info Solutions and co-author of *The Fielding Bible—Volume III* and *The Fielding Bible—Volume IV*, **Dan Casey**, veteran Video Scout and Senior Operations Analyst at BIS, and **Sean Forman**, the founder of Baseball-Reference.com.

The Fielding Bible Awards

Below we show the final point tally for The Fielding Bible Awards in the 2016 season. We asked a panel of experts to complete a 10-man ballot ranking players from 1 to 10 based on their defensive abilities. We show the ranks in the tables below. We then awarded points in the same way as Major League Baseball's MVP voting: 10 points for a first place vote, 9 for second, etc., down to 1 point for 10th place. We cover all nine positions, looking at only their fielding work for the 2016 season. Position players are eligible if they played at least 600 innings while catchers require a minimum of 500 innings. Either can qualify with 10 Runs Saved, as well. Pitchers require a minimum of 120 innings pitched or 5 Runs Saved.

In 2014, we introduced a Multi-Position Award for fielders who are excellent defensive players but do not call any one position their home. For a player to qualify for the Multi-Position Award, he must have played at least 600 innings across all positions and played no more than 70 percent of those innings at any one position.

First Basemen

First Basemen	Bill	BIS Video Scouts	Brian	Dave	Doug	Hal	Joe	John	Mark	Peter	Rob	Tango Fan Poll	Total Points
Anthony Rizzo	2	1	2	1	1	3	1	1	1	1	2	3	113
Brandon Belt	1	6	3	4	2	2	3	2	2	2	3	1	101
Freddie Freeman	3	3	1	3	4	4	2	4	3	5	5		84
Paul Goldschmidt	4	4	4	6	7	1	5	5	8	4	1	2	81
Chris Davis	5	5	10	5	5	6	6	3	6	3	4	7	67
Wil Myers	10	2	5	2	3	8	8	8	7	8	6	9	56
Adrian Gonzalez		9	6	8	9	5	4	6	9	9	8	5	43
Mitch Moreland		7	9	7	6	7	9	9	4	7	7		38
Joe Mauer	6	8	8		8	9	7	7	5	10	9	10	34
Mark Teixeira	8		7	10		10		10	10			6	16
Others receiving points: Eric Hosmer 12, Yonder Alonso, 10, Hanley Ramirez 2, Mark Reynolds 2, Miguel Cabrera 1													

Second Basemen

Second Basemen	Bill	BIS Video Scouts	Brian	Dave	Doug	Hal	Joe	John	Mark	Peter	Rob	Tango Fan Poll	Total Points
Dustin Pedroia	2	1	2	1	1	2	2	2	1	1	1	2	114
Ian Kinsler	1	2	1	5	2	1	4	1	2	2	2	5	104
Robinson Cano	6	3	3	2	3	8		5	3	3	4	6	75
DJ LeMahieu	4	5	7	4	5	6		7	5	8	7	3	60
Javier Baez	3	6	4	8		3	1	6				1	56
Josh Harrison	7	4	5	9	6		7	3	4	4	6		55
Jason Kipnis	10	10	8	6	4		3		6	6	10		36
Cesar Hernandez		8	6	3			5			5	5		34
Joe Panik	9		9	7	7	9	9	9	9	10	8	4	31
Brian Dozier		7			9	7	8	10		7			18
Others receiving points: Kolten Wong 16, Jose Altuve 15, Dee Gordon 11, Darwin Barney 10, Brandon Phillips 10, Neil Walker 5, Devon Travis 3, Chase Utley 3, Logan Forsythe 2, Whit Merrifield 1, Jonathan Schoop 1													

Third Basemen

Third Basemen	Bill	BIS Video Scouts	Brian	Dave	Doug	Hal	Joe	John	Mark	Peter	Rob	Tango Fan Poll	Total Points
Nolan Arenado	1	1	1	2	1	1	1	1	1	1	1	1	119
Adrian Beltre	3	3	3	1	2	3	2	2	3	2	2	3	103
Manny Machado	4	2	4	3	3	2	3	3	2	3	3	2	98
Kyle Seager	2	4	2		4	7	4	4	4	5	7	8	70
Josh Donaldson	5	7	6	4	6	4	5	8	9	9	6	5	58
Anthony Rendon	7	5	8	9	8	5	7	6	7	4	4	7	55
Matt Duffy	6	8	5	6	5	6		5	5		8	4	52
Justin Turner		6	7	8			6	9		6	5	9	32
Travis Shaw	10		9		7			7	6	7	9		22
Chase Headley		9		7		8	9	10	10	8			16
Others receiving points: Kris Bryant 15, Evan Longoria 8, Martin Prado 8, Todd Frazier 2, David Freese 2													

Shortstops

Shortstops	Bill	BIS Video Scouts	Brian	Dave	Doug	Hal	Joe	John	Mark	Peter	Rob	Tango Fan Poll	Total Points
Andrelton Simmons	1	3	1	2	3	1	4	1	1	4	3	2	106
Brandon Crawford	3	2	2	1	4	2	2	2	4	2	2	1	105
Francisco Lindor	6	1	3	3	1	3	3	4	2	1	1	4	100
Addison Russell	2	4	4	4	2	6	1	3	3	3	4	3	93
Zack Cozart	4		7	6	7	8	6	8	6	7	6	8	48
Nick Ahmed	7	10	5	5	5	7	9	5	5		7	9	47
Adeiny Hechavarria	8	5	8		6	5	8	7	7	5	5	10	47
Troy Tulowitzki	10	6	6	10	9		5	6	8		8	5	37
Jose Iglesias	9	7		7		4				9	10	7	24
J.J. Hardy	5				8			9	10	6			17
Others receiving points: Danny Espinosa 14, Alcides Escobar 6, Freddy Galvis 6, Elvis Andrus 3, Carlos Correa 3, Corey Seager 2, Jonathan Villar 2													

Left Fielders

Left Fielders	Bill	BIS Video Scouts	Brian	Dave	Doug	Hal	Joe	John	Mark	Peter	Rob	Tango Fan Poll	Total Points
Starling Marte	1	1	1	1	1	1	2	1	1	1	1	1	119
Brett Gardner	2	4	2	6	3	4	6	2	3	3	4	3	90
Adam Duvall	3	3	3	7	2	7	1	3	2	2	7	9	83
Alex Gordon		2	4	3	8	2	3	6	8	7	3	2	73
Colby Rasmus	6	5	6	4	7	5	4	4	4	9	2	4	72
Christian Yelich	4	6	7	5	5	3	9	5	5	5	5		62
Melvin Upton Jr.		7	8	8	4	6	5	8	6	4	8	5	52
Ryan Braun	7	8	5		6		10	9	7	6	9	7	36
Yoenis Cespedes	5	10	10	2		8	7	7	10		6		34
Justin Upton	8				9			10	9	8			11
Others receiving points: Eddie Rosario 9, Angel Pagan 7, Brandon Guyer 4, Michael Conforto 2, Khris Davis 2, Brock Holt 2, Coco Crisp 1, Howie Kendrick 1													

Center Fielders

Center Fielders	Bill	BIS Video Scouts	Brian	Dave	Doug	Hal	Joe	John	Mark	Peter	Rob	Tango Fan Poll	Total Points
Kevin Pillar	1	1	2	2	1	2	1	2	2	1	1	7	109
Kevin Kiermaier	3	3	1	5	2	1	4	1	1	2	2	1	106
Billy Hamilton	4	2	3	1	3	4	2	3	3	4	3	3	97
Jackie Bradley Jr.	2	5	4	4	5	3	6	5	6	3	5	2	82
Ender Inciarte	5	4	5	3	4	5	5	4	4	5	4	4	80
Lorenzo Cain		9	7	6	8	7	3	6	5		6	10	43
Mike Trout	10	6	9	8	7	6	8	10	8	6	9	9	36
Jake Marisnick	6	8				8		8	10		8	5	24
Jacoby Ellsbury		7	8	7	6		9		9	8			23
Byron Buxton			6		10	10					7	6	16

Others receiving points: Jarrod Dyson 15, Odubel Herrera 11, Leonys Martin 5, Dexter Fowler 4, Michael Bourn 3, Joc Pederson 3, Randal Grichuk 2, Adam Jones 1

Right Fielders

Right Fielders	Bill	BIS Video Scouts	Brian	Dave	Doug	Hal	Joe	John	Mark	Peter	Rob	Tango Fan Poll	Total Points
Mookie Betts	1	1	1	2	2	2	1	1	1	1	1	2	116
Adam Eaton	3	2	3	1	3	3	2	2	2	2	2	4	103
Jason Heyward	4	3	2	3	1	1	3	3	3	3	3	1	102
George Springer	5	5	5	4	6	4	6	8		4	4	5	65
Nick Markakis	6	4	4		4	10	10	6	4	6	8		48
Josh Reddick	10	10		5	10	7		4		5		7	30
Carlos Gonzalez	8	9	7		5	8		10	7			6	28
Gregory Polanco		6	9	6		6	8	9			6		27
Kole Calhoun		8		9		5	5				5	9	25
Max Kepler	2	7	6		8								21

Others receiving points: Giancarlo Stanton 20, Yasiel Puig 17, Bryce Harper 15, Stephen Piscotty 14, Steven Souza Jr. 7, Paulo Orlando 6, Lonnie Chisenhall 5, Curtis Granderson 4, Hunter Pence 4, Aaron Hicks 3

Catchers

Catchers	Bill	BIS Video Scouts	Brian	Dave	Doug	Hal	Joe	John	Mark	Peter	Rob	Tango Fan Poll	Total Points
Buster Posey	1	1	1	1	1	1	1	1	1	1	1	1	120
Salvador Perez	3	5	2	6	3	2	2	9		4	7	2	76
Jonathan Lucroy	5	3	6	3	7	3	6	7		3	3	5	70
Russell Martin	2	9	8	2	5	7		2	5	6	2	6	67
Yasmani Grandal	8	2	4	9	2	9	7	4	2	2	8		64
Yadier Molina	4	7	5	5	10	4	5		4		4	3	59
Derek Norris	7	4	7		8		4	3	8	5	5		48
James McCann	10	6	3	4	9	8	3				9		36
Curt Casali		10	9		4	10	10	6	6				22
Carlos Perez					6	5	9	10	10				15

Others receiving points: Martin Maldonado 15, Francisco Cervelli 13, Brian McCann 11, David Ross 11, Jason Castro 6, Matt Wieters 5, Tucker Barnhart 4, Yan Gomes 4, Miguel Montero 4, Welington Castillo 3, Sandy Leon 3, Tyler Flowers 2, Wilson Ramos 2

Pitchers

Pitchers	Bill	BIS Video Scouts	Brian	Dave	Doug	Hal	Joe	John	Mark	Peter	Rob	Ben	Total Points
Dallas Keuchel	2	3	2	4	2	1	2	1	3	2	1	6	103
Zack Greinke	1	2	5	2	1	8	1	2	4	3	2	1	100
Bartolo Colon		1	3	1	3	4	4	4	1	7	6	4	83
Masahiro Tanaka	3	4	1		4	3	3	3	5	8	3	2	82
R.A. Dickey		7	4	3	8	5	5	5	8	10	4	5	57
Jake Arrieta	4	6	10		6	2		8	2	1	9		51
Mike Leake		8		5	9	7		6	7		5	8	33
Kenta Maeda		9	6		5	10				4	7	7	29
Justin Verlander		5	7				6		10	6		3	29
J.A. Happ	5	10		10	7		7	9		5		10	25

Others receiving points: Kyle Hendricks 13, Johnny Cueto 11, Madison Bumgarner 8, Michael Wacha 8, Corey Kluber 7, Clayton Kershaw 6, Jose Quintana 5, Danny Duffy 3, Carlos Carrasco 2, Tony Cingrani 2, Jeremy Hellickson 2, Chase Anderson 1

Multi-Position

Pitchers	Bill	BIS Video Scouts	Brian	Dave	Doug	Hal	Joe	John	Mark	Peter	Rob	Tango Fan Poll	Total Points
Javier Baez	7	1	2	7	1	1	1	1	3	1	1	1	105
Jarrod Dyson	1	3		3	2	2	2	2	1	2		2	90
Kris Bryant		2	1	1		8	5	4	2	6	3	3	75
Darwin Barney	2	6	8	10	3	3	3	3				4	57
Jedd Gyorko		5	3		5		4	7	4		5		44
Paulo Orlando	5	4		5	6		7	5	6	10			40
Marwin Gonzalez	6	8	4		10			6		7	4		32
Aaron Hicks		10		4	7	4				8		5	28
Sean Rodriguez					9	7		9	5		2	10	24
Jose Ramirez		7	6	6		10				4			22

Others receiving points: Yoenis Cespedes 18, Hernan Perez 17, Tyler Saladino 16, Wilmer Flores 14, Eddie Rosario 14, Matt Carpenter 12, Howie Kendrick 8, Gerardo Parra 7, Coco Crisp 7, David Freese 6, Rajai Davis 4, Eduardo Nunez 4, Brandon Guyer 3, Yasmany Tomas 3, Kelly Johnson 2, Chris Owings 2, Jake Smolinski 2

Shift Update

John Dewan

In 2014, MLB teams shifted 13,299 times and saved 196 runs.

In 2015, MLB teams shifted 17,744 times and saved 267 runs.

In 2016, MLB teams shifted 28,074 times and saved 359 runs.

As we have been saying for the last 10 years, the more you shift the more you save. By comparison, the 2011 season was the season before the shift trend started. Just five years ago. In 2011, MLB teams shifted 2,350 times and saved 40 runs.

The increase in shifts in 2016 was a whopping 58% over 2015. On one hand it's surprising because normally major league teams are slow to change. But on the other hand, the numbers show how effective shifting is and maybe we shouldn't be surprised that teams are buying into the strategy more and more.

Here is a complete team-by-team listing comparing 2016 to 2015:

American League

Team	2015	2016	Change
Astros	1,417	1,869	452
Rays	1,465	1,584	119
Mariners	352	1,482	1,130
Angels	436	1,478	1,042
Yankees	931	1,384	453
Blue Jays	884	872	-12
Athletics	610	840	230
Rangers	557	834	277
Twins	724	832	108
Indians	575	784	209
Orioles	902	787	-115
White Sox	389	781	392
Red Sox	527	692	165
Tigers	520	547	27
Royals	539	458	-81
Total	**10,828**	**15,224**	**4,396**
Average	**722**	**1,015**	**293**

National League

Team	2015	2016	Change
Brewers	382	1,486	1,104
Pirates	973	1,483	510
Rockies	1,010	1,354	344
Braves	211	1,025	814
Reds	426	876	450
Giants	552	858	306
Diamondbacks	587	822	235
Cardinals	311	813	502
Padres	569	813	244
Nationals	215	758	543
Dodgers	315	675	360
Mets	297	536	239
Phillies	384	502	118
Marlins	300	450	150
Cubs	384	399	15
Total	**6,916**	**12,850**	**5,934**
Average	**461**	**857**	**396**

*All totals reflect Shifts on Balls in Play

Every National League team increased their shifting in 2016. All but three AL teams increased. The Mariners had the biggest increase in number of shifts (from 352 to 1,482) and also increased their runs saved on shifts from just five in 2015 to 22 in 2016. At the other extreme, the Orioles shifted less in 2016 and it cost them. As a team, shifting saved them the most runs in baseball in 2015 with 29, but for some reason they shifted less in 2016 and they only had 15 Shift Runs Saved.

There is one last thing we want to point out. We did see a small drop-off in overall effectiveness in 2016.

Runs Saved per 100 Shifts

Season	Runs/100
2014	1.47
2015	1.50
2016	1.28

Is this drop-off indicative of diminishing returns on the shift as teams shift more often? It could be, but it could also simply be a statistical anomaly. It remains to be seen.

Hits Lost and Gained to the Shift

Joe Rosales

The proliferation of defensive shifts throughout baseball is one of those evolutions of the game that evokes our sense of nostalgia, the idea of bygone days when defensive alignments were not so elaborate. Not that everyone wishes there were fewer shifts being used, though there certainly are those people. For some of the more data-driven baseball enthusiasts out there, shifts represent a more informed way of approaching defensive positioning, so it has been gratifying to see things develop the way they have. But it is still difficult not to look at an infield with three fielders aligned to one side of second base, maybe with one of those infielders positioned more like an outfielder, and not think about how incongruous it looks compared to the traditional alignment that seems so much more natural. The word itself—shift—implies a departure from something standardized. No matter how commonplace shifts become, it is difficult not to consider "simpler" times whenever we see one. When a batter hits a groundball into a shift, whether it goes for a hit or an out, it is virtually impossible not to instinctively ask ourselves what would have happened if the defense had been positioned in a traditional alignment.

Given how intuitively this question occurs, we decided to add a section to the book this year that looks at how many hits a batter has lost or gained when hitting groundballs or short line drives into a shifted defense. What might not be as intuitive to everyone, though, is how we go about doing this, so I will explain after sharing some of the results.

In 2016, the player that suffered the most at the expense of the shift was Curtis Granderson. He had 34 hits taken away by the shift and 10 hits gained that he would not normally have been expected to get for a net of 24 hits lost to the shift. However, over the seven years that Baseball Info Solutions (BIS) has been tracking shift data, David Ortiz has been the player most victimized, having lost a net of 91 hits. There may not be any one player as singularly identified with the negative impact of defensive shifts than Ortiz, so this is not a surprise.

What is so interesting about this data, though, is that it shows so much more than just who the shifting casualties are. Some players are better at beating the shift than others, not every team shifts in the same way, not every team shifts against the same players, and, frankly, not every team shifts against the *correct* players. As a result, you get players like Carlos Gonzalez. He lost 31 hits in 2016. Only two players lost more: Granderson and Adrian Gonzalez. However, he also gained 32 hits, giving him a net of one hit gained. Despite all the shifting teams have done against him, it has basically been a net neutral. And at the other end of the spectrum, you get guys like Nomar Mazara and Hyun Soo Kim. Both were rookies this year, so opposing teams obviously had less data to go off of in preparing for these guys. But both ended up with a net of six hits gained on shifts despite being shifted over 100 times each on balls they put into play. Whatever teams thought they knew about these guys, they clearly did not know enough.

How do we come up with these hits lost and gained to the shift? To be clear, we are not counting in ones and zeros. By that, I mean that we are not reviewing every play and trying to make a subjective yes or no determination of whether a groundball that was hit into a shift would have gotten through with a traditional alignment. Instead we are taking a more objective approach that relies on BIS's Range and Positioning System.

From the data collected at BIS, we know the likelihood of an out being made, shift or not, on every ball in play based on where it was hit and how hard it was hit. With that information, we can objectively figure out how many hits were lost or gained depending on the outcome of a particular ball in play. For example, for a groundball that typically goes for a hit 60 percent of the time, if that particular ball makes it through the infield for a hit against the shifted defense, then that means that the hitter gained 0.4 hits on that play (1 actual hit - 0.6 expected hits). However, if the shifted defense is able to turn that groundball into an out, then the hitter has lost 0.6 hits (0 actual hits - 0.6 expected hits). We total up all these fractional gains and losses to arrive at the number of Hits Lost and Hits Gained a player ended up with. All final totals are then rounded to the nearest integer.

In the section that follows, you will find a table split into two halves. One half shows data for 2016 only and the other half shows aggregated data from 2010 (when BIS began collecting shift data) to the present. In both cases, you will find listed the number of shifts on balls in play that a player saw, how many hits he lost, how many hits he gained, and the net of his hits lost and gained.

Hits Lost and Gained to the Shift

Player	2016 Season				Career Since 2010			
	Shifts	Lost	Gained	Net	Shifts	Lost	Gained	Net
Granderson, Curtis	346	34	10	24	867	79	37	42
Morales, Kendrys	254	31	10	21	828	86	51	35
Ortiz, David	403	31	14	17	2269	209	118	91
Howard, Ryan	187	25	9	16	1682	172	89	83
Martinez, Victor	279	29	14	15	733	69	45	24
Pujols, Albert	255	31	16	15	884	100	62	38
Morrison, Logan	201	24	9	15	530	59	23	36
Gonzalez, Adrian	325	34	20	14	1217	110	68	42
McCann, Brian	274	25	12	13	1336	112	63	49
Fielder, Prince	207	21	9	12	1254	129	85	44
Rizzo, Anthony	375	30	18	12	1024	81	50	31
Davis, Chris	301	28	16	12	1133	98	69	29
Lind, Adam	234	23	11	12	630	61	43	18
Castro, Jason	140	18	7	11	291	33	18	15
Moreland, Mitch	293	29	18	11	737	63	49	14
Harper, Bryce	223	24	13	11	363	37	23	14
Calhoun, Kole	303	29	19	10	459	44	33	11
Grandal, Yasmani	147	17	7	10	259	26	14	12
Pierzynski, A.J.	134	16	6	10	340	33	19	14
Santana, Carlos	271	26	17	9	857	76	44	32
Duda, Lucas	107	13	4	9	698	60	28	32
Zobrist, Ben	131	16	7	9	271	28	18	10
Kemp, Matt	216	18	9	9	417	39	23	16
Shaw, Travis	224	18	9	9	295	23	16	7
Lamb, Jake	219	23	14	9	301	30	21	9
Conforto, Michael	164	15	6	9	190	17	8	9
Bour, Justin	156	16	8	8	293	32	19	13
Seager, Kyle	345	31	23	8	872	67	54	13
Donaldson, Josh	130	14	6	8	265	26	19	7
Encarnacion, Edwin	250	20	12	8	766	67	37	30
Alvarez, Pedro	195	21	13	8	776	86	57	29
Utley, Chase	229	20	12	8	489	41	31	10
Teixeira, Mark	206	15	8	7	1115	102	55	47
Moss, Brandon	223	18	11	7	876	67	43	24
Loney, James	137	14	7	7	342	37	24	13
Freeman, Freddie	328	28	21	7	748	67	47	20
Saunders, Michael	174	16	9	7	219	20	16	4
Belt, Brandon	313	21	14	7	602	40	31	9
Bruce, Jay	328	25	19	6	1017	84	61	23
Markakis, Nick	52	6	0	6	105	13	6	7
Smith, Seth	227	22	16	6	680	62	47	15
Avila, Alex	74	10	4	6	310	36	19	17
Carpenter, Matt	202	13	7	6	279	17	11	6
Stanton, Giancarlo	146	18	12	6	293	29	22	7
Wieters, Matt	211	16	10	6	403	34	22	12
Bautista, Jose	102	9	3	6	531	51	33	18
Rodriguez, Alex	43	8	3	5	165	24	10	14
Choo, Shin-Soo	85	10	5	5	283	30	22	8
Alonso, Yonder	254	22	17	5	370	35	25	10
Cabrera, Asdrubal	137	12	7	5	295	23	16	7
Wallace, Brett	113	15	10	5	157	19	12	7
Smoak, Justin	112	8	3	5	520	52	30	22
Davis, Khris	114	13	8	5	170	21	11	10
Jaso, John	181	21	16	5	341	37	25	12
Mesoraco, Devin	26	6	1	5	101	13	9	4
Gordon, Alex	183	14	9	5	478	39	30	9
McCutchen, Andrew	149	15	10	5	347	34	30	4
Duvall, Adam	139	11	6	5	141	11	7	4
Franco, Maikel	142	13	8	5	163	15	10	5
Polanco, Gregory	119	9	4	5	155	12	6	6
Springer, George	42	6	2	4	63	8	6	2
Muncy, Max	44	6	2	4	73	8	2	6
Bradley Jr., Jackie	203	22	18	4	250	26	20	6
Cespedes, Yoenis	127	12	8	4	389	33	34	-1
Story, Trevor	50	7	3	4	50	7	3	4
Odor, Rougned	224	16	12	4	256	19	14	5
Gyorko, Jedd	36	4	0	4	54	6	2	4
Nieuwenhuis, Kirk	81	7	3	4	99	9	4	5
Norris, Derek	43	4	0	4	81	8	4	4
Forsythe, Logan	87	9	5	4	128	14	10	4
Plouffe, Trevor	41	6	2	4	99	12	8	4
Valbuena, Luis	145	12	8	4	291	23	18	5
Vogt, Stephen	293	20	16	4	512	34	31	3

Hits Lost and Gained to the Shift

Player	2016 Season				Career Since 2010			
	Shifts	Lost	Gained	Net	Shifts	Lost	Gained	Net
Tulowitzki, Troy	120	12	8	4	201	20	13	7
Mauer, Joe	103	9	5	4	224	21	17	4
Rollins, Jimmy	61	6	3	3	170	18	10	8
Cabrera, Miguel	32	4	1	3	143	16	14	2
Gutierrez, Franklin	47	7	4	3	65	9	6	3
Napoli, Mike	91	8	5	3	238	21	16	5
Conger, Hank	68	6	3	3	257	21	14	7
Joyce, Matt	92	8	5	3	533	50	30	20
Martin, Russell	40	4	1	3	68	7	3	4
Coghlan, Chris	76	7	4	3	113	10	7	3
Nava, Daniel	46	6	3	3	107	14	6	8
Martin, Leonys	54	8	5	3	74	10	7	3
Vargas, Kennys	36	4	1	3	109	10	7	3
Suarez, Eugenio	85	9	6	3	102	10	7	3
Lindor, Francisco	44	4	1	3	51	4	1	3
Baez, Javier	93	8	5	3	136	12	9	3
Perez, Carlos	31	3	0	3	45	4	1	3
Arcia, Oswaldo	83	7	4	3	240	21	15	6
Abreu, Jose	51	5	2	3	124	11	9	2
Russell, Addison	46	4	1	3	47	4	1	3
Correa, Carlos	28	3	1	2	28	3	1	2
Seager, Corey	162	13	11	2	169	14	11	3
Tucker, Preston	62	7	5	2	145	13	12	1
Reed, A.J.	47	5	3	2	47	5	3	2
Bryant, Kris	234	19	17	2	292	24	23	1
Rasmus, Colby	200	13	11	2	592	44	24	20
Carter, Chris	156	10	8	2	424	29	21	8
Kipnis, Jason	75	7	5	2	120	13	8	5
Arenado, Nolan	153	13	11	2	166	14	13	1
Kiermaier, Kevin	77	7	5	2	132	11	11	0
Bell, Josh	30	4	2	2	30	4	2	2
Pederson, Joc	182	15	13	2	326	28	20	8
Cowart, Kaleb	29	4	2	2	29	4	2	2
Solarte, Yangervis	130	11	9	2	183	20	14	6
Upton, Justin	40	4	2	2	80	6	5	1
Jones, Adam	64	5	3	2	139	11	12	-1
Span, Denard	48	5	3	2	54	5	4	1
Ramirez, Hanley	36	4	2	2	69	9	7	2
Espinosa, Danny	74	6	4	2	115	10	6	4
Longoria, Evan	133	11	9	2	371	31	26	5
Headley, Chase	172	15	13	2	504	43	30	13
Votto, Joey	232	24	22	2	487	44	43	1
Young, Chris	53	3	1	2	229	17	12	5
Cabrera, Melky	42	3	1	2	61	4	3	1
Cruz, Nelson	130	12	10	2	275	25	23	2
Ross, David	26	2	0	2	34	3	0	3
Crisp, Coco	61	5	3	2	74	8	4	4
Frazier, Todd	102	7	5	2	160	11	10	1
Morneau, Justin	53	5	4	1	424	37	35	2
Peralta, David	69	7	6	1	217	21	21	0
Navarro, Dioner	87	7	6	1	243	27	15	12
Murphy, Daniel	127	12	11	1	163	16	13	3
De Aza, Alejandro	34	4	3	1	76	7	7	0
Upton Jr., Melvin	51	7	6	1	57	7	8	-1
Moustakas, Mike	64	5	4	1	617	47	35	12
Heyward, Jason	190	16	15	1	385	35	29	6
Adams, Matt	163	11	10	1	551	45	39	6
Gomes, Yan	36	2	1	1	95	9	5	4
Paulsen, Ben	29	4	3	1	72	9	4	5
Gillaspie, Conor	53	4	3	1	148	13	9	4
Chisenhall, Lonnie	53	3	2	1	96	4	4	0
Kinsler, Ian	46	4	3	1	135	11	11	0
Gregorius, Didi	57	5	4	1	64	6	6	0
Robinson, Clint	87	6	5	1	178	16	10	6
Wilson, Bobby	26	3	2	1	27	3	2	1
Grossman, Robbie	35	3	2	1	36	3	2	1
Paredes, Jimmy	27	3	2	1	89	5	8	-3
Panik, Joe	38	4	3	1	50	5	4	1
Kepler, Max	91	7	6	1	92	7	6	1
Rosario, Eddie	54	5	4	1	78	7	5	2
Schebler, Scott	117	12	11	1	125	13	11	2
Zunino, Mike	35	2	1	1	97	8	3	5
Cron, C.J.	32	2	1	1	62	3	3	0
Rupp, Cameron	41	6	5	1	46	6	5	1
Schoop, Jonathan	47	6	5	1	73	9	7	2
Sanchez, Gary	45	5	4	1	45	5	4	1

Hits Lost and Gained to the Shift

Player	2016 Season				Career Since 2010			
	Shifts	Lost	Gained	Net	Shifts	Lost	Gained	Net
Gattis, Evan	63	4	3	1	131	15	9	6
Cabrera, Ramon	29	2	1	1	30	2	2	0
Schimpf, Ryan	75	3	2	1	75	3	2	1
Myers, Wil	65	6	5	1	149	14	16	-2
Franklin, Nick	51	3	3	0	52	3	3	0
Barnhart, Tucker	62	4	4	0	73	5	4	1
Pearce, Steve	58	5	5	0	213	18	14	4
Dozier, Brian	209	17	17	0	313	28	22	6
Gennett, Scooter	55	4	4	0	66	6	4	2
Joseph, Tommy	27	3	3	0	27	3	3	0
Dietrich, Derek	81	6	6	0	112	8	8	0
Yelich, Christian	34	4	4	0	41	5	4	1
Dickerson, Alex	73	6	6	0	73	6	6	0
Bandy, Jett	36	1	1	0	36	1	1	0
Wong, Kolten	60	5	5	0	95	9	5	4
Asche, Cody	64	5	5	0	156	13	9	4
Drury, Brandon	28	3	3	0	29	3	3	0
Kang, Jung Ho	42	4	4	0	51	4	6	-2
Park, Byungho	38	3	3	0	38	3	3	0
Maxwell, Bruce	30	2	2	0	30	2	2	0
Puig, Yasiel	40	3	3	0	65	4	4	0
Smolinski, Jake	48	3	3	0	53	4	3	1
Turner, Justin	31	2	2	0	36	2	3	-1
Hill, Aaron	50	2	2	0	103	5	8	-3
Escobar, Eduardo	45	2	2	0	66	4	5	-1
Walker, Neil	131	11	11	0	246	20	18	2
Butler, Billy	46	5	5	0	92	10	7	3
Perez, Salvador	42	2	2	0	97	7	8	-1
Blackmon, Charlie	51	3	3	0	80	5	4	1
Iannetta, Chris	49	3	3	0	93	6	5	1
Posey, Buster	36	3	3	0	59	5	6	-1
Marte, Starling	27	2	2	0	43	3	6	-3
Escobar, Yunel	27	2	2	0	39	4	4	0
Van Slyke, Scott	31	3	3	0	49	5	4	1
Lowrie, Jed	104	10	10	0	170	15	13	2
Cozart, Zack	27	3	3	0	45	5	5	0
Cano, Robinson	253	21	21	0	490	48	41	7
Beltran, Carlos	275	23	23	0	702	63	51	12
Castillo, Welington	60	5	6	-1	101	7	10	-3
Guyer, Brandon	28	2	3	-1	32	3	3	0
Johnson, Kelly	105	10	11	-1	279	26	26	0
Fowler, Dexter	88	4	5	-1	123	8	7	1
Pennington, Cliff	36	2	3	-1	48	3	3	0
Braun, Ryan	37	3	4	-1	46	4	5	-1
Hosmer, Eric	233	21	22	-1	486	50	48	2
Descalso, Daniel	33	2	3	-1	57	4	5	-1
Suzuki, Kurt	34	2	3	-1	48	2	4	-2
Valencia, Danny	92	8	9	-1	189	20	18	2
Trumbo, Mark	69	4	5	-1	118	9	9	0
Gonzalez, Carlos	344	31	32	-1	697	66	63	3
Souza Jr., Steven	29	2	3	-1	39	4	4	0
Castellanos, Nick	41	2	3	-1	89	6	7	-1
Semien, Marcus	101	8	9	-1	140	12	9	3
Casali, Curt	27	2	3	-1	39	3	3	0
Miller, Brad	113	11	12	-1	144	14	15	-1
Machado, Manny	40	2	3	-1	58	6	5	1
Grichuk, Randal	84	6	7	-1	98	7	8	-1
Holt, Brock	32	2	3	-1	69	5	7	-2
Trout, Mike	94	6	8	-2	161	9	17	-8
Rua, Ryan	27	2	4	-2	30	3	4	-1
Sano, Miguel	76	5	7	-2	93	5	8	-3
Betts, Mookie	47	3	5	-2	55	3	6	-3
Healy, Ryon	34	2	4	-2	34	2	4	-2
Saltalamacchia, Jarrod	99	7	9	-2	469	38	21	17
Hicks, Aaron	33	3	5	-2	43	4	7	-3
Crawford, Brandon	106	8	10	-2	158	12	14	-2
Goldschmidt, Paul	47	3	5	-2	82	7	9	-2
Drew, Stephen	49	3	5	-2	303	23	17	6
Ellsbury, Jacoby	36	2	4	-2	58	4	7	-3
Beltre, Adrian	63	3	5	-2	132	8	11	-3
Montero, Miguel	86	5	8	-3	252	24	20	4
Reddick, Josh	212	17	20	-3	525	44	38	6
Herrmann, Chris	61	5	8	-3	68	6	8	-2
Altuve, Jose	38	2	5	-3	52	4	8	-4
Martinez, J.D.	74	5	8	-3	126	9	15	-6
Soler, Jorge	51	3	6	-3	74	5	7	-2

Hits Lost and Gained to the Shift

Player	2016 Season				Career Since 2010			
	Shifts	Lost	Gained	Net	Shifts	Lost	Gained	Net
Dickerson, Corey	164	6	9	-3	183	7	11	-4
Profar, Jurickson	33	2	5	-3	33	2	5	-3
Ozuna, Marcell	33	2	6	-4	46	2	7	-5
Leon, Sandy	75	4	8	-4	99	5	10	-5
Flaherty, Ryan	32	2	6	-4	143	17	10	7
Hardy, J.J.	44	3	7	-4	88	7	11	-4
Reynolds, Mark	102	8	13	-5	298	24	27	-3
Gonzalez, Marwin	73	4	9	-5	81	4	11	-7
Mazara, Nomar	186	16	22	-6	186	16	22	-6
Kim, Hyun Soo	105	8	14	-6	105	8	14	-6

Defensive Runs Saved Leaders

Ben Jedlovec

The Defensive Runs Saved (DRS) leader boards tell some interesting stories. Some observations jump out, like Joey Votto's uncharacteristically bad defensive season. Others help explain the successes and failures of different players and teams, like how the Cubs' incredible infield defense led the team to the lowest allowed team batting average on balls in play (BABIP) in history, relative to league average.

Perhaps the biggest DRS narrative this season was the race for the overall Defensive Runs Saved crown. Appropriate for a Summer Olympics year, the race played out like a long-distance run between two of baseball's best all-around players: Adam Eaton and Mookie Betts.

Eaton first took the DRS lead in right field on April 6th, his third game of the season. Eaton, of course, was a career center fielder, having spent 90 percent of his career MLB innings at the position prior to 2016. At times, he'd flashed his outstanding defensive abilities, including his 11 Runs Saved in 2014, his first season in Chicago. Unfortunately, he got off to a brutal start to 2015, making 17 Defensive Misplays in April and May alone, more than he logged in all of 2014. Mental errors, such as misreading the ball off the bat, and physical errors, frequently allowing balls to bounce out of his mitt, sunk his defensive contributions to a third-worst -14 Runs Saved by season's end. The White Sox dabbled in the offseason outfield free agent and trade market, eventually scooping up Austin Jackson, which allowed them to slide Eaton to the easier right field position.

Eaton took to right field like a duck takes to water. By April 16, he took the overall DRS lead with 5 Runs Saved (in nine games, seven of which he actually started in right field). He saved another run the next day and finished April a full 13 runs better than the average right fielder. No other fielder had more than 7 Runs Saved at that point in the month. Even the White Sox home broadcast crew of Jason Benetti and Steve Stone directly cited Eaton's DRS dominance on the air as the team was enjoying a not-coincidental run atop the AL Central in late April.

On May 29, Yasiel Puig had cut Eaton's DRS lead to two (15-13). Austin Jackson left that day's White Sox game with a turf toe injury, and Eaton and J.B. Shuck shared center-field duties during the week Jackson was out. But three games after he returned, on June 10, Jackson went down for the season with a meniscus tear in his right knee. The White Sox were stuck between a rock and a hard place: the choice between playing Eaton in center and the defensively challenged Avisail Garcia in right or playing offensively challenged J.B. Shuck in center and Eaton in right.

After a few games with the Eaton-Garcia option, the Sox reverted to the Shuck-Eaton option. Eaton held a 18-12 DRS lead over Brandon Crawford and Jason Heyward on July 1, and Crawford briefly caught Eaton right after the All-Star Break, but Eaton was sitting pretty at 21 Runs Saved on August 1.

Meanwhile, Mookie Betts started the year much more slowly. Betts was also acclimating to right field after spending most of 2015 in center. Jackie Bradley Jr's bat earned him a regular spot in the lineup, shifting Betts to right field. Mookie started out slowly, sitting at 1 Run Saved on May 1 and 2 Runs Saved on June 1, when Eaton already had 15. On July 1, Mookie had contributed 5 runs above average, half a win, but still trailed Eaton's 18. He reached 8 Runs Saved at the All-Star Break.

But then, two things happened. First, Betts took off. Settling into Fenway's unique right field, Betts jumped to 15 by August 1, seven runs in two weeks. Second, the White Sox stopped playing Shuck every day and shifted Eaton back to center for most of the rest of the season. Spending more time at the more difficult center field position, Eaton's DRS pace slowed dramatically.

On August 1, Eaton led 21-15, with Crawford and Nolan Arenado also in the mix. On August 23, it narrowed to a two-man race, with Eaton holding a narrow lead on Betts at 22-20. On September 5, Betts caught Eaton at 24, and five days later, Betts passed him for good.

Though Betts ran away with the DRS title (and the Fielding Bible Award), Eaton was technically better on a per inning basis.

In this section, you will find Defensive Runs Saved leaders and trailers for every defensive position, both for the 2016 season alone and for the last three years combined.

Defensive Runs Saved (or just Runs Saved for short) is a comprehensive accounting of how a player performs defensively. Depending on the position, Runs Saved is a combined measure of his range and positioning, his ability to field bunts, to turn double plays, to prevent baserunners from advancing either on balls in play or on stolen base attempts, to get extra strike calls, to limit earned runs, and to make extraordinary defensive plays while avoiding misplays. Positive numbers mean that a player saved his team runs, while negative numbers mean a player cost his team runs, with zero being average.

It is remarkable how consistent Defensive Runs Saved numbers can be from year to year. Five of nine positional DRS leaders from 2016 also led their position in 2015, with the exceptions being Betts (who wasn't playing right field last year), Anthony Rizzo (who finished second in 2015), Addison Russell (who split his time between second base and shortstop in 2015), and Bartolo Colon (last year's winner, Dallas Keuchel, is tied for second place one run behind Colon).

Infield Runs Saved Leaders

First Basemen 3-Year Leaders

Rizzo, Anthony	27
Gonzalez, Adrian	24
Goldschmidt, Paul	23
Davis, Chris	20
Belt, Brandon	20
Alonso, Yonder	15
Adams, Matt	14
Mauer, Joe	10
Duda, Lucas	9
Reynolds, Mark	9

Second Basemen 3-Year Leaders

Kinsler, Ian	51
Pedroia, Dustin	26
LeMahieu, DJ	22
Wong, Kolten	19
Barney, Darwin	14
Harrison, Josh	12
Forsythe, Logan	11
Gordon, Dee	9
Goins, Ryan	9
Baez, Javier	9

Third Basemen 3-Year Leaders

Arenado, Nolan	54
Beltre, Adrian	42
Donaldson, Josh	33
Machado, Manny	33
Seager, Kyle	26
Duffy, Matt	23
Prado, Martin	20
Rendon, Anthony	20
Uribe, Juan	19
Turner, Justin	18

Shortstops 3-Year Leaders

Simmons, Andrelton	71
Crawford, Brandon	48
Cozart, Zack	34
Ahmed, Nick	34
Russell, Addison	29
Lindor, Francisco	27
Tulowitzki, Troy	22
Hardy, J.J.	20
Hechavarria, Adeiny	15
Goins, Ryan	11

First Basemen 3-Year Trailers

Howard, Ryan	-28
Abreu, Jose	-14
Morrison, Logan	-11
Carter, Chris	-9
Fielder, Prince	-8
Santana, Carlos	-8

Second Basemen 3-Year Trailers

Odor, Rougned	-27
Murphy, Daniel	-25
Giavotella, Johnny	-13
Dietrich, Derek	-11
Carpenter, Matt	-9
Schimpf, Ryan	-9

Third Basemen 3-Year Trailers

Castellanos, Nick	-50
Valencia, Danny	-23
Escobar, Yunel	-22
Gillaspie, Conor	-18
Johnson, Chris	-16
Longoria, Evan	-15

Shortstops 3-Year Trailers

Ramirez, Alexei	-30
Reyes, Jose	-26
Cabrera, Asdrubal	-22
Miller, Brad	-21
Bogaerts, Xander	-20
Andrus, Elvis	-18

First Basemen 2016 Leaders

Rizzo, Anthony	11
Freeman, Freddie	9
Belt, Brandon	9
Davis, Chris	8
Myers, Wil	8
Moreland, Mitch	7
Mauer, Joe	6
Goldschmidt, Paul	4
Reynolds, Mark	4
Gonzalez, Adrian	3

Second Basemen 2016 Leaders

Kinsler, Ian	12
Pedroia, Dustin	12
Cano, Robinson	11
Baez, Javier	11
Harrison, Josh	8
Wong, Kolten	5
Merrifield, Whit	5
Hernandez, Cesar	4
Kipnis, Jason	4
Dozier, Brian	3

Third Basemen 2016 Leaders

Arenado, Nolan	20
Seager, Kyle	15
Beltre, Adrian	15
Machado, Manny	13
Duffy, Matt	11
Shaw, Travis	10
Rendon, Anthony	8
Headley, Chase	7
Turner, Justin	7
Freese, David	5

Shortstops 2016 Leaders

Crawford, Brandon	20
Russell, Addison	19
Simmons, Andrelton	18
Lindor, Francisco	17
Ahmed, Nick	13
Tulowitzki, Troy	10
Hechavarria, Adeiny	9
Espinosa, Danny	8
Cozart, Zack	8
Hardy, J.J.	6

First Basemen 2016 Trailers

Votto, Joey	-14
Howard, Ryan	-9
Joseph, Tommy	-6
Cabrera, Miguel	-6
Hosmer, Eric	-6
Smoak, Justin	-5

Second Basemen 2016 Trailers

Schimpf, Ryan	-9
Murphy, Daniel	-9
Odor, Rougned	-9
Lowrie, Jed	-8
Castro, Starlin	-8
Phillips, Brandon	-7

Third Basemen 2016 Trailers

Valencia, Danny	-18
Cuthbert, Cheslor	-12
Escobar, Yunel	-11
Castellanos, Nick	-11
Longoria, Evan	-9
Lamb, Jake	-8

Shortstops 2016 Trailers

Ramirez, Alexei	-20
Miller, Brad	-14
Bogaerts, Xander	-10
Mercer, Jordy	-9
Gregorius, Didi	-9
Polanco, Jorge	-8

Outfield Runs Saved Leaders

Left Fielders 3-Year Leaders		Center Fielders 3-Year Leaders		Right Fielders 3-Year Leaders	
Marte, Starling	50	Kiermaier, Kevin	68	Heyward, Jason	62
Gordon, Alex	37	Cain, Lorenzo	40	Betts, Mookie	36
Yelich, Christian	32	Hamilton, Billy	37	Eaton, Adam	22
Cespedes, Yoenis	30	Pillar, Kevin	37	Stanton, Giancarlo	19
Inciarte, Ender	21	Lagares, Juan	36	Reddick, Josh	17
Van Slyke, Scott	17	Inciarte, Ender	30	Chisenhall, Lonnie	14
Gardner, Brett	16	Martin, Leonys	29	Nava, Daniel	14
Duvall, Adam	15	Bradley Jr., Jackie	29	Polanco, Gregory	13
Lough, David	15	Dyson, Jarrod	28	Granderson, Curtis	12
Rasmus, Colby	13	Pollock, A.J.	25	Byrd, Marlon	11

Left Fielders 3-Year Trailers		Center Fielders 3-Year Trailers		Right Fielders 3-Year Trailers	
Kemp, Matt	-20	McCutchen, Andrew	-49	Beltran, Carlos	-25
Grossman, Robbie	-19	Fowler, Dexter	-31	Kemp, Matt	-24
Werth, Jayson	-18	Crisp, Coco	-29	Choo, Shin-Soo	-18
Kim, Hyun Soo	-13	Pagan, Angel	-27	Martinez, J.D.	-18
Asche, Cody	-13	Maybin, Cameron	-25	Arcia, Oswaldo	-17
Holliday, Matt	-13	Span, Denard	-19	Garcia, Avisail	-17

Left Fielders 2016 Leaders		Center Fielders 2016 Leaders		Right Fielders 2016 Leaders	
Marte, Starling	19	Kiermaier, Kevin	25	Betts, Mookie	32
Duvall, Adam	16	Pillar, Kevin	21	Eaton, Adam	22
Rasmus, Colby	14	Hamilton, Billy	15	Heyward, Jason	14
Gardner, Brett	12	Inciarte, Ender	13	Markakis, Nick	10
Upton Jr., Melvin	10	Bradley Jr., Jackie	11	Carrera, Ezequiel	8
Braun, Ryan	6	Marisnick, Jake	9	Reddick, Josh	6
Yelich, Christian	6	Broxton, Keon	9	Springer, George	5
Francoeur, Jeff	5	Ellsbury, Jacoby	8	Kepler, Max	5
Gordon, Alex	4	Cain, Lorenzo	8	Puig, Yasiel	5
Cespedes, Yoenis	4	Grichuk, Randal	7	Orlando, Paulo	5

Left Fielders 2016 Trailers		Center Fielders 2016 Trailers		Right Fielders 2016 Trailers	
Grossman, Robbie	-21	McCutchen, Andrew	-28	Martinez, J.D.	-22
Kim, Hyun Soo	-13	Naquin, Tyler	-17	Bruce, Jay	-11
Kemp, Matt	-12	Shuck, J.B.	-13	Trumbo, Mark	-9
Tomas, Yasmany	-8	Ozuna, Marcell	-12	Gutierrez, Franklin	-8
Holliday, Matt	-8	Maybin, Cameron	-11	Santana, Domingo	-8
Werth, Jayson	-8	Jones, Adam	-10	Tomas, Yasmany	-8

Pitcher/Catcher Runs Saved Leaders

Pitchers 3-Year Leaders		Catchers 3-Year Leaders	
Keuchel, Dallas	30	Posey, Buster	48
Greinke, Zack	21	Lucroy, Jonathan	31
Tanaka, Masahiro	16	Martin, Russell	30
Cueto, Johnny	14	Joseph, Caleb	28
Leake, Mike	13	Flowers, Tyler	27
Colon, Bartolo	13	Zunino, Mike	24
Dickey, R.A.	13	Maldonado, Martin	22
Kershaw, Clayton	12	Perez, Roberto	20
Cole, Gerrit	10	Plawecki, Kevin	20
2 tied with	10	Vazquez, Christian	19

Pitchers 3-Year Trailers		Catchers 3-Year Trailers	
Nelson, Jimmy	-18	Suzuki, Kurt	-38
Lackey, John	-15	Saltalamacchia,J	-33
Sabathia, CC	-12	Pierzynski, A.J.	-32
McAllister, Zach	-11	Hundley, Nick	-30
Syndergaard, Noah	-11	Navarro, Dioner	-30
Volquez, Edinson	-11		

Pitchers 2016 Leaders		Catchers 2016 Leaders	
Colon, Bartolo	8	Posey, Buster	23
Dickey, R.A.	7	Norris, Derek	15
Tanaka, Masahiro	7	Grandal, Yasmani	13
Keuchel, Dallas	7	Casali, Curt	11
Greinke, Zack	7	McCann, James	9
Arrieta, Jake	5	Perez, Carlos	8
Happ, J.A.	5	Maldonado, Martin	7
Verlander, Justin	5	Martin, Russell	7
Maeda, Kenta	5	Cervelli, Francisco	6
Anderson, Tyler	5	Wolters, Tony	5

Pitchers 2016 Trailers		Catchers 2016 Trailers	
Rodon, Carlos	-6	Hundley, Nick	-16
de la Rosa, Jorge	-6	Navarro, Dioner	-14
Nelson, Jimmy	-6	Realmuto, J.T.	-13
Syndergaard, Noah	-6	Suzuki, Kurt	-12
Nova, Ivan	-5		
Volquez, Edinson	-5		

2016 Career Register

Joe Rosales

The Career Register is the heart of this book. It is the largest section, by far, because it contains the complete career statistics of every active major league player up to date through the end of the 2016 regular season. While these statistics are certainly information that anyone can look up online these days, without them, the rest of this book would carry less weight, both literally and figuratively. The Career Register provides the baseline context from which the other sections in this book derive their substance. How meaningful would it be to scrutinize one player's information against another's from the Hitter Analysis section without being able to look up how each player actually performed? Or to see what a pitcher did, both this season and over the course of his career, to achieve his current ranking in the Starting Pitcher Rankings? Or to see the underlying stats that go into determining a player's Win Shares?

Of course, the Career Register is also interesting in its own right. Any curiosity that we have about a player is going to start with his baseline statistics, and the register allows you to look those up for whatever season you are interested in. Plus, the register isn't just limited to a player's major league stats. We fill it out with minor league statistics, biographical information, the number of games a player played at each defensive position in the most recent season, and a pronunciation guide for difficult names. We have tried to create as complete a player reference guide as possible for readers to use.

With respect to minor league statistics, we only include them for some players, and we do so according to the following criteria:

- We include the last five years of minor league statistics for players who have appeared in fewer than three major league seasons, whether or not those players spent any time in the minors in 2016.
- For players who exceed that three-year cutoff but who also spent time in the minors in 2016—likely because of a rehab assignment—we include only their 2016 minor league statistics, which is called out by an asterisk.
- For minor league data below Double-A:
  - If a player only played at one level in a given season, you will see that level explicitly specified.

- If a player played at multiple levels in a given season, his statistics will be grouped into a single row labeled Low.
- For all levels, in instances where a player either pitched in fewer than five games or hit in fewer than 10 games at a given level, we eliminate those statistics.
  - In the cases where we combine a player's statistics below Double-A into a single line called Low, those five and 10 game thresholds are applied to the aggregated stat line, not its stat lines from each of the individual levels.

If a player led either the American or National League in a particular category, that number will appear in **boldface**.

Age is seasonal as of June 30, 2017.

For pitchers, BFP is Batters Facing Pitcher; TBB is Total Bases on Balls (or Total Walks, intentional and unintentional); Op is Save Opportunities; Hld is Holds.

For the various levels of Class-A ball, we have used "A+" to indicate High-A and "A-" to indicate Low-A. To help readers decode our minor league abbreviations, there is a legend in the back of the book.

A pronunciation guide is provided underneath the name of select players.

In addition to a variety of traditional statistics, the Register also shows Runs Created (RC) for hitters and Component ERA (ERC) for pitchers. Runs Created is a comprehensive measurement of a player's offensive production distilled into a single number. It was originally developed by Bill James. Component ERA estimates what a pitcher's ERA should have been based only on his raw pitching statistics and acts as a good indicator of whether a pitcher deserved the ERA he ended the season with. The details of the current formulas for both RC and ERC are in the Baseball Glossary at the back of the *Handbook*.

A player's total career numbers in the postseason appear on one line above his total regular season career numbers. Since we work hard to bring you this publication by November 1, postseason data from 2016 is not included. In addition, the Japanese baseball season extends a bit beyond our deadline, so the Japanese statistics for posted players will not include a complete record of their most recent games. Those numbers will be updated in the following year's *Handbook*.

Fernando Abad

Pitches: L Bats: L Pos: RP-57   ah-BAHD   Ht: 6'1" Wt: 220 Born: 12/17/1985 Age: 31

Year	Team	Lg	G	GS	CG	GF	IP	BFP	H	R	ER	HR	SH	SF	HB	TBB	IBB	SO	WP	Bk	W	L	Pct	Sh	Sv-Op	Hld	ERC	ERA
2010	Hou	NL	22	0	0	6	19.0	76	14	6	6	3	0	1	0	5	0	12	0	0	0	1	.000	0	0-0	6	2.49	2.84
2011	Hou	NL	29	0	0	1	19.2	99	28	18	16	5	1	2	1	9	0	15	0	0	1	4	.200	0	0-2	7	8.06	7.32
2012	Hou	NL	37	6	0	8	46.0	208	57	27	26	6	2	1	3	19	1	38	4	0	0	6	.000	0	0-0	3	6.13	5.09
2013	Was	NL	39	0	0	17	37.2	166	42	14	14	3	0	0	1	10	0	32	0	0	0	3	.000	0	0-1	2	4.65	3.35
2014	Oak	AL	69	0	0	17	57.1	216	34	11	10	4	1	2	4	15	3	51	0	0	2	4	.333	0	0-2	9	1.64	1.57
2015	Oak	AL	62	0	0	17	47.2	205	45	23	22	11	3	3	1	19	3	45	4	0	2	2	.500	0	0-3	1	4.63	4.15
2016	2 Tms	AL	57	0	0	15	46.2	198	40	20	19	4	0	1	1	22	2	41	1	1	1	6	.143	0	1-5	8	3.50	3.66
16	Min	AL	39	0	0	8	34.0	138	27	11	10	2	0	1	0	14	2	29	0	1	1	4	.200	0	1-2	6	2.72	2.65
16	Bos	AL	18	0	0	7	12.2	60	13	9	9	2	0	0	1	8	0	12	1	0	0	2	.000	0	0-3	2	5.81	6.39
	Postseason		1	0	0	0	0.1	1	0	0	0	0	0	0	0	0	0	0	0	0	0	0	-	0	0-0	0	0.00	0.00
7 ML YEARS			315	6	0	81	274.0	1168	260	119	113	36	7	10	11	99	9	234	9	1	6	26	.188	0	1-13	36	3.97	3.71

Jose Abreu

Bats: R Throws: R Pos: 1B-152;DH-7   uh-BRAY-you   Ht: 6'3" Wt: 255 Born: 1/29/1987 Age: 30

Year	Team	Lg	G	AB	H	2B	3B	HR	(Hm	Rd)	TB	R	RBI	RC	TBB	IBB	SO	HBP	SH	SF	SB	CS	GDP	Avg	OBP	Slg	OPS
2014	CWS	AL	145	556	176	35	2	36	(15	21)	323	80	107	113	51	15	131	11	0	4	3	1	14	.317	.383	.581	.964
2015	CWS	AL	154	613	178	34	3	30	(16	14)	308	88	101	105	39	11	140	15	0	1	0	0	16	.290	.347	.502	.850
2016	CWS	AL	159	624	183	32	1	25	(15	10)	292	67	100	92	47	7	125	15	0	9	0	2	21	.293	.353	.468	.820
3 ML YEARS			458	1793	537	101	6	91	(46	45)	923	235	308	310	137	33	396	41	0	14	3	3	51	.299	.360	.515	.875

A.J. Achter

Pitches: R Bats: R Pos: RP-27   AHK-ter   Ht: 6'5" Wt: 215 Born: 8/27/1988 Age: 28

Year	Team	Lg	G	GS	CG	GF	IP	BFP	H	R	ER	HR	SH	SF	HB	TBB	IBB	SO	WP	Bk	W	L	Pct	Sh	Sv-Op	Hld	ERC	ERA
2016	Salt Lk*	AAA	29	1	0	11	46.1	183	31	19	18	9	2	0	1	14	0	33	2	0	2	2	.500	0	3- -	-	2.61	3.50
2014	Min	AL	7	0	0	1	11.0	49	14	7	4	2	0	0	0	3	0	5	0	0	1	0	1.000	0	0-0	5	5.74	3.27
2015	Min	AL	11	0	0	4	13.1	58	12	10	10	4	0	0	0	6	1	14	0	0	1	0	1.000	0	0-0	4	4.88	6.75
2016	LAA	AL	27	0	0	17	37.2	160	43	13	13	7	0	1	1	12	1	14	0	0	0	1	1.000	0	0-0	3	5.45	3.11
3 ML YEARS			45	0	0	22	62.0	267	69	30	27	13	0	1	1	21	2	33	0	0	2	1	.667	0	0-0	3	5.38	3.92

Dustin Ackley

Bats: L Throws: R Pos: 1B-13;RF-9;PH-6;DH-3;2B-1   Ht: 6'1" Wt: 205 Born: 2/26/1988 Age: 29

Year	Team	Lg	G	AB	H	2B	3B	HR	(Hm	Rd)	TB	R	RBI	RC	TBB	IBB	SO	HBP	SH	SF	SB	CS	GDP	Avg	OBP	Slg	OPS
2011	Sea	AL	90	333	91	16	7	6	(3	3)	139	39	36	53	40	1	79	0	0	3	6	0	3	.273	.348	.417	.766
2012	Sea	AL	153	607	137	22	2	12	(2	10)	199	84	50	62	59	7	124	0	1	1	13	3	3	.226	.294	.328	.622
2013	Sea	AL	113	384	97	18	2	4	(2	2)	131	40	31	45	37	1	72	1	4	1	2	3	6	.253	.319	.341	.660
2014	Sea	AL	143	502	123	27	4	14	(8	6)	200	64	65	54	32	1	90	3	3	2	8	4	10	.245	.293	.398	.692
2015	2 Tms	AL	108	238	55	11	3	10	(7	3)	102	28	30	23	18	0	45	1	3	4	2	2	3	.231	.284	.429	.712
2016	NYY	AL	28	61	9	0	0	0	(0	0)	9	6	4	2	8	0	9	0	0	0	0	0	0	.148	.243	.148	.390
15	Sea	AL	85	186	40	8	1	6	(4	2)	68	22	19	13	14	0	38	1	3	3	2	2	3	.215	.270	.366	.635
15	NYY	AL	23	52	15	3	2	4	(3	1)	34	6	11	10	4	0	7	0	0	1	0	0	0	.288	.333	.654	.987
6 ML YEARS			635	2125	512	94	18	46	(22	24)	780	261	216	239	194	10	419	5	11	12	31	12	25	.241	.304	.367	.671

Cristhian Adames

kris-tee-YAHN ah-DAHM-ess

Bats: B Throws: R Pos: PH-61;SS-47;2B-11;3B-11;PR-1   Ht: 6'0" Wt: 185 Born: 7/26/1991 Age: 25

Year	Team	Lg	G	AB	H	2B	3B	HR	(Hm	Rd)	TB	R	RBI	RC	TBB	IBB	SO	HBP	SH	SF	SB	CS	GDP	Avg	OBP	Slg	OPS
2014	Col	NL	7	15	1	0	0	0	(0	0)	1	1	0	0	0	0	5	0	0	0	0	0	1	.067	.067	.067	.133
2015	Col	NL	26	53	13	1	1	0	(0	0)	16	4	3	4	3	1	11	1	1	0	0	1	0	.245	.298	.302	.600
2016	Col	NL	121	225	49	7	3	2	(0	2)	68	25	17	17	24	0	47	4	3	0	2	3	5	.218	.304	.302	.607
3 ML YEARS			154	293	63	8	4	2	(0	2)	85	30	20	20	27	1	63	5	4	0	2	4	6	.215	.292	.290	.582

Austin Adams

Pitches: R Bats: R Pos: RP-19   Ht: 5'11" Wt: 200 Born: 8/19/1986 Age: 30

Year	Team	Lg	G	GS	CG	GF	IP	BFP	H	R	ER	HR	SH	SF	HB	TBB	IBB	SO	WP	Bk	W	L	Pct	Sh	Sv-Op	Hld	ERC	ERA
2016	Clmbs*	AAA	34	0	0	25	37.2	164	44	21	21	1	3	0	1	9	0	41	6	1	2	4	.333	0	8- -	-	3.94	4.54
2014	Cle	AL	6	0	0	1	7.0	30	9	7	7	1	0	0	0	1	0	4	0	0	0	0	-	0	0-0	0	5.04	9.00
2015	Cle	AL	28	0	0	9	33.1	149	37	15	14	2	2	0	0	13	0	23	1	0	2	0	1.000	0	1-1	0	4.29	3.78
2016	Cle	AL	19	0	0	11	18.1	88	27	22	20	5	0	0	0	7	1	17	0	0	0	0	-	0	0-0	0	8.11	9.82
3 ML YEARS			53	0	0	21	58.2	267	73	44	41	8	2	0	0	21	1	44	1	0	2	0	1.000	0	1-1	0	5.50	6.29

Matt Adams

Bats: L **Throws:** R **Pos:** 1B-86;PH-39   **Ht:** 6'3" **Wt:** 260 **Born:** 8/31/1988 **Age:** 28

Year	Team	Lg	G	AB	H	2B	3B	HR	(Hm	Rd)	TB	R	RBI	RC	TBB	IBB	SO	HBP	SH	SF	SB	CS	GDP	Avg	OBP	Slg	OPS
2012	StL	NL	27	86	21	6	0	2	(1	1)	33	8	13	9	5	0	24	0	0	0	0	0	3	.244	.286	.384	.669
2013	StL	NL	108	296	84	14	0	17	(10	7)	149	46	51	49	23	0	80	0	0	0	0	1	9	.284	.335	.503	.839
2014	StL	NL	142	527	152	34	5	15	(8	7)	241	55	68	65	26	5	114	3	0	7	3	2	9	.288	.321	.457	.779
2015	StL	NL	60	175	42	9	0	5	(1	4)	66	14	24	16	10	1	41	0	0	1	1	0	1	.240	.280	.377	.657
2016	StL	NL	118	297	74	18	0	16	(11	5)	140	37	54	46	25	1	81	2	0	3	0	1	5	.249	.309	.471	.780
	Postseason		26	93	21	3	0	4	(3	1)	36	10	11	12	8	2	24	1	0	0	0	0	2	.226	.294	.387	.681
	5 ML YEARS		455	1381	373	81	5	55	(31	24)	629	160	210	185	89	7	340	5	0	11	4	4	27	.270	.314	.455	.770

Tim Adleman

Pitches: R **Bats:** R **Pos:** SP-13   **Ht:** 6'5" **Wt:** 225 **Born:** 11/13/1987 **Age:** 29

Year	Team	Lg	G	GS	CG	GF	IP	BFP	H	R	ER	HR	SH	SF	HB	TBB	IBB	SO	WP	Bk	W	L	Pct	Sh	Sv-Op	Hld	ERC	ERA
2014	Bkrsfld	A+	8	0	0	2	8.0	49	18	13	11	3	0	0	1	7	0	8	0	0	1	.000	0	0- -	-	17.44	12.38
2014	Pnscla	AA	30	6	0	11	79.0	314	70	28	25	7	3	0	2	20	1	70	2	0	3	8	.273	0	0- -	-	3.01	2.85
2015	Pnscla	AA	27	26	0	0	150.0	611	134	52	44	7	6	0	2	49	2	113	6	0	9	10	.474	0	0- -	-	2.97	2.64
2016	Lsvlle	AAA	10	10	0	0	56.2	227	52	18	15	4	1	0	2	10	0	38	2	0	3	1	.750	0	0- -	-	2.78	2.38
2016	Cin	NL	13	13	0	0	69.2	287	64	32	31	13	6	1	5	20	1	47	0	0	4	4	.500	0	0-0	0	4.11	4.00

Ehire Adrianza

Bats: B **Throws:** R **Pos:** PH-21;SS-13;2B-7;3B-7   eh-EE-ray ah-dree-AHN-zah   **Ht:** 6'1" **Wt:** 170 **Born:** 8/21/1989 **Age:** 27

Year	Team	Lg	G	AB	H	2B	3B	HR	(Hm	Rd)	TB	R	RBI	RC	TBB	IBB	SO	HBP	SH	SF	SB	CS	GDP	Avg	OBP	Slg	OPS
2013	SF	NL	9	18	4	1	0	1	(0	1)	8	3	3	1	1	0	5	0	1	0	0	0	1	.222	.263	.444	.708
2014	SF	NL	53	97	23	6	0	0	(0	0)	29	10	5	6	5	1	22	1	2	1	1	1	2	.237	.279	.299	.578
2015	SF	NL	52	113	21	7	1	0	(0	0)	30	11	11	12	15	0	20	4	2	0	3	2	2	.186	.303	.265	.569
2016	SF	NL	40	63	16	2	0	2	(1	1)	24	3	7	6	2	0	13	2	4	0	0	1	0	.254	.299	.381	.679
	4 ML YEARS		154	291	64	16	1	3	(1	2)	91	27	26	25	23	1	60	7	9	1	4	4	5	.220	.292	.313	.605

Jesus Aguilar

Bats: R **Throws:** R **Pos:** 1B-7;PH-3   AGG-you-lahr   **Ht:** 6'3" **Wt:** 250 **Born:** 6/30/1990 **Age:** 27

Year	Team	Lg	G	AB	H	2B	3B	HR	(Hm	Rd)	TB	R	RBI	RC	TBB	IBB	SO	HBP	SH	SF	SB	CS	GDP	Avg	OBP	Slg	OPS
2016	Clmbs*	AAA	137	515	127	26	0	30	(-	-)	243	62	92	80	53	2	110	4	1	5	0	0	20	.247	.319	.472	.791
2014	Cle	AL	19	33	4	0	0	0	(0	0)	4	2	3	0	4	0	13	0	0	1	0	0	1	.121	.211	.121	.332
2015	Cle	AL	7	19	6	1	0	0	(0	0)	7	0	2	4	0	0	7	1	0	0	0	0	0	.316	.350	.368	.718
2016	Cle	AL	9	6	0	0	0	0	(0	0)	0	0	0	0	0	0	1	0	0	0	0	0	0	.000	.000	.000	.000
	3 ML YEARS		35	58	10	1	0	0	(0	0)	11	2	5	4	4	0	21	1	0	1	0	0	1	.172	.234	.190	.424

Nick Ahmed

Bats: R **Throws:** R **Pos:** SS-88;PH-3;PR-1   **Ht:** 6'2" **Wt:** 195 **Born:** 3/15/1990 **Age:** 27

Year	Team	Lg	G	AB	H	2B	3B	HR	(Hm	Rd)	TB	R	RBI	RC	TBB	IBB	SO	HBP	SH	SF	SB	CS	GDP	Avg	OBP	Slg	OPS
2014	Ari	NL	25	70	14	2	0	1	(1	0)	19	9	4	3	3	0	10	0	2	0	0	1	2	.200	.233	.271	.504
2015	Ari	NL	134	421	95	17	6	9	(4	5)	151	49	34	38	29	1	81	1	5	3	4	5	4	.226	.275	.359	.634
2016	Ari	NL	90	284	62	9	1	4	(1	3)	85	26	20	18	15	3	58	4	2	3	5	2	9	.218	.265	.299	.564
	3 ML YEARS		249	775	171	28	7	14	(6	8)	255	84	58	59	47	4	149	5	9	6	9	8	15	.221	.268	.329	.597

Andrew Albers

Pitches: L **Bats:** R **Pos:** RP-4; SP-2   **Ht:** 6'1" **Wt:** 200 **Born:** 10/6/1985 **Age:** 31

Year	Team	Lg	G	GS	CG	GF	IP	BFP	H	R	ER	HR	SH	SF	HB	TBB	IBB	SO	WP	Bk	W	L	Pct	Sh	Sv-Op	Hld	ERC	ERA
2016	Roch*	AAA	21	21	2	0	124.1	533	150	53	51	10	4	3	4	30	0	84	8	0	10	6	.625	0	0- -	-	4.71	3.69
2013	Min	AL	10	10	1	0	60.0	249	64	34	27	6	2	2	2	7	0	25	0	1	2	5	.286	1	0-0	0	3.45	4.05
2015	Tor	AL	1	0	0	0	2.2	11	1	1	1	1	0	0	0	2	0	1	0	0	0	0	-	0	0-0	0	3.75	3.38
2016	Min	AL	6	2	0	3	17.0	85	27	16	11	5	0	0	0	6	0	16	1	0	0	0	-	0	0-0	0	8.84	5.82
	3 ML YEARS		17	12	1	3	79.2	345	92	51	39	12	2	2	2	15	0	42	1	1	2	5	.286	1	0-0	0	4.49	4.41

Matt Albers

Pitches: R **Bats:** L **Pos:** RP-57; SP-1   **Ht:** 6'1" **Wt:** 225 **Born:** 1/20/1983 **Age:** 34

Year	Team	Lg	G	GS	CG	GF	IP	BFP	H	R	ER	HR	SH	SF	HB	TBB	IBB	SO	WP	Bk	W	L	Pct	Sh	Sv-Op	Hld	ERC	ERA
2006	Hou	NL	4	2	0	0	15.0	66	17	10	10	1	2	0	0	7	0	11	0	0	2	0	.000	0	0-0	0	4.97	6.00
2007	Hou	NL	31	18	0	2	110.2	508	127	77	72	18	6	8	7	50	6	71	7	0	4	11	.267	0	0-0	0	5.76	5.86
2008	Bal	AL	28	3	0	5	49.0	208	43	21	19	4	1	3	2	22	1	26	1	0	3	3	.500	0	0-2	6	3.62	3.49
2009	Bal	AL	56	0	0	13	67.0	309	80	43	41	3	5	2	2	36	3	49	3	0	3	6	.333	0	0-4	10	5.41	5.51
2010	Bal	AL	62	0	0	19	75.2	329	78	41	38	6	3	0	2	34	5	49	2	0	5	3	.625	0	0-2	7	4.35	4.52
2011	Bos	AL	56	0	0	10	64.2	289	62	35	34	7	4	2	5	31	1	68	2	0	4	4	.500	0	0-3	10	4.44	4.73
2012	2 Tms		63	0	0	12	60.1	241	46	21	16	9	1	2	2	22	3	44	1	0	3	1	.750	0	0-6	9	3.13	2.39
2013	Cle	AL	56	0	0	21	63.0	262	57	25	22	2	2	0	1	23	3	35	6	0	3	1	.750	0	0-0	1	2.99	3.14
2014	Hou	AL	8	0	0	1	10.0	42	10	1	1	0	0	1	0	3	0	8	0	0	0	0	-	0	0-1	3	3.46	0.90
2015	CWS	AL	30	0	0	5	37.1	149	31	6	5	0	0	3	1	9	2	28	0	0	2	0	1.000	0	0-0	6	2.52	1.21

Year	Team	Lg	G	GS	CG	GF	IP	BFP	H	R	ER	HR	SH	SF	HB	TBB	IBB	SO	WP	Bk	W	L	Pct	Sh	Sv-Op	Hld	ERC	ERA
2016	CWS	AL	58	1	0	11	51.1	237	67	44	36	10	3	2	3	19	1	30	4	0	2	6	.250	0	0-4	13	6.75	6.31
12	Bos	AL	40	0	0	8	39.1	157	30	14	10	6	0	2	1	15	3	25	0	0	2	0	1.000	0	0-4	7	3.16	2.29
12	Ari	NL	23	0	0	4	21.0	84	16	7	6	3	1	0	1	7	0	19	1	0	1	1	.500	0	0-2	2	3.07	2.57
11 ML YEARS			452	24	0	99	604.0	2640	618	324	294	63	27	22	26	256	25	419	26	0	29	37	.439	0	0-22	65	4.46	4.38

Hanser Alberto

HAHN-zer al-BAIR-tow

Bats: R **Throws:** R **Pos:** 3B-11;PR-10;SS-9;2B-6;DH-6;1B-4;PH-2 **Ht:** 5'11" **Wt:** 215 **Born:** 10/17/1992 **Age:** 24

								BATTING														RUNNING			AVERAGES			
Year	Team	Lg	G	AB	H	2B	3B	HR	(Hm	Rd)	TB	R	RBI	RC	TBB	IBB	SO	HBP	SH	SF	SB	CS	GDP	Avg	OBP	Slg	OPS
2012	2 Tms	Low	128	525	157	28	3	8	(-	-)	215	73	72	74	20	1	49	6	3	8	24	7	17	.299	.327	.410	.737
2013	Frisco	AA	100	356	76	6	4	4	(-	-)	102	37	40	26	16	1	41	5	1	6	13	5	10	.213	.253	.287	.540
2013	MrtlBh	A+	29	97	25	5	0	0	(-	-)	30	6	7	9	4	0	8	2	1	0	3	1	7	.258	.301	.309	.610
2014	MrtlBh	A+	70	262	71	15	3	5	(-	-)	107	37	43	34	10	0	25	3	6	4	10	4	8	.271	.301	.408	.709
2014	Frisco	AA	50	178	49	6	1	2	(-	-)	63	23	15	20	6	0	17	4	2	0	7	4	2	.275	.314	.354	.668
2015	RdRck	AAA	81	310	96	19	4	4	(-	-)	135	42	32	44	9	1	33	2	7	2	5	5	5	.310	.331	.435	.767
2016	RdRck	AAA	63	265	73	13	1	7	(-	-)	109	32	36	33	8	0	29	2	2	0	2	2	3	.275	.302	.411	.713
2015	Tex	AL	41	99	22	2	1	0	(0	0)	26	12	4	3	2	0	17	0	3	0	1	0	2	.222	.238	.263	.500
2016	Tex	AL	35	56	8	1	0	0	(0	0)	9	2	5	1	0	0	17	0	2	0	1	0	1	.143	.143	.161	.304
	Postseason		3	10	2	1	0	0	(0	0)	3	0	2	1	0	0	2	0	0	1	0	0	0	.200	.182	.300	.482
	2 ML YEARS		76	155	30	3	1	0	(0	0)	35	14	9	4	2	0	34	0	5	0	2	0	3	.194	.204	.226	.430

Al Alburquerque

AL-buh-kur-kee

Pitches: R **Bats:** R **Pos:** RP-2 **Ht:** 6'0" **Wt:** 195 **Born:** 6/10/1986 **Age:** 31

			HOW MUCH HE PITCHED						WHAT HE GAVE UP												THE RESULTS							
Year	Team	Lg	G	GS	CG	GF	IP	BFP	H	R	ER	HR	SH	SF	HB	TBB	IBB	SO	WP	Bk	W	L	Pct	Sh	Sv-Op	Hld	ERC	ERA
2016	Salt Lk*	AAA	24	0	0	19	23.2	107	24	12	10	0	0	2	0	13	0	27	3	0	1	0	1.000	0	8- -	-	3.92	3.80
2016	Tacom*	AAA	6	0	0	4	6.0	30	9	4	4	1	0	0	0	4	0	6	0	0	0	1	.000	0	0- -	-	9.02	6.00
2011	Det	AL	41	0	0	11	43.1	182	21	9	9	0	2	1	2	29	4	67	4	0	6	1	.857	0	0-0	6	1.73	1.87
2012	Det	AL	8	0	0	6	13.1	53	6	1	1	0	0	0	0	8	0	18	0	1	0	0	-	0	0-0	1	1.50	0.68
2013	Det	AL	53	0	0	12	49.0	220	39	25	25	5	0	0	0	34	5	70	9	1	4	3	.571	0	0-0	10	4.02	4.59
2014	Det	AL	72	0	0	15	57.1	236	46	16	16	7	0	2	3	21	1	63	2	2	3	1	.750	0	1-1	17	3.23	2.51
2015	Det	AL	67	0	0	12	62.0	271	63	29	29	4	1	2	1	33	3	58	5	4	4	1	.800	0	0-1	7	4.51	4.21
2016	LAA	AL	2	0	0	1	2.0	12	2	3	1	1	0	0	0	2	0	1	0	0	0	0	-	0	0-0	0	8.14	4.50
	Postseason		14	0	0	5	10.0	43	7	6	6	2	1	0	0	6	2	14	1	1	1	1	.500	0	0-0	3	3.51	5.40
	6 ML YEARS		243	0	0	51	227.0	974	177	83	81	17	3	6	8	127	13	277	20	8	17	6	.739	0	1-2	41	3.35	3.21

Arismendy Alcantara

ahr-ees-MEN-dee ahl-KAHN-tar-ah

Bats: B **Throws:** R **Pos:** PR-5;CF-4;2B-3;PH-3;SS-2;RF-1;DH-1 **Ht:** 5'10" **Wt:** 170 **Born:** 10/29/1991 **Age:** 25

								BATTING														RUNNING			AVERAGES			
Year	Team	Lg	G	AB	H	2B	3B	HR	(Hm	Rd)	TB	R	RBI	RC	TBB	IBB	SO	HBP	SH	SF	SB	CS	GDP	Avg	OBP	Slg	OPS
2016	Iowa*	AAA	54	198	52	9	5	5	(-	-)	86	32	21	31	15	0	61	0	0	1	21	0	2	.263	.313	.434	.747
2016	Nashv*	AAA	48	200	58	10	5	6	(-	-)	96	28	27	32	14	0	57	1	2	2	11	6	4	.290	.336	.480	.816
2014	ChC	NL	70	278	57	11	2	10	(5	5)	102	31	29	23	17	0	93	2	1	2	8	5	3	.205	.254	.367	.621
2015	ChC	NL	11	26	2	0	0	0	(0	0)	2	5	1	1	5	0	11	0	1	0	1	0	0	.077	.226	.077	.303
2016	Oak	AL	16	19	4	1	0	0	(0	0)	5	2	2	0	0	0	8	0	0	0	3	3	1	.211	.211	.263	.474
	3 ML YEARS		97	323	63	12	2	10	(5	5)	109	38	32	24	22	0	112	2	2	2	12	8	4	.195	.249	.337	.587

Raul Alcantara

ahl-KAHN-tar-ah

Pitches: R **Bats:** R **Pos:** SP-5 **Ht:** 6'4" **Wt:** 220 **Born:** 12/4/1992 **Age:** 24

			HOW MUCH HE PITCHED						WHAT HE GAVE UP												THE RESULTS							
Year	Team	Lg	G	GS	CG	GF	IP	BFP	H	R	ER	HR	SH	SF	HB	TBB	IBB	SO	WP	Bk	W	L	Pct	Sh	Sv-Op	Hld	ERC	ERA
2012	Burlgtn	A	27	17	0	2	102.2	441	119	64	58	12	3	2	7	38	0	57	2	4	6	11	.353	0	0- -	-	5.55	5.08
2013	2 Tms	Low	27	27	1	0	156.1	649	157	74	54	11	5	3	8	24	0	124	8	1	12	6	.667	1	0- -	-	3.13	3.11
2015	Stcktn	A+	15	15	0	0	48.2	202	54	21	21	3	1	2	2	8	0	29	1	1	0	2	.000	0	0- -	-	3.73	3.88
2016	Mdlnd	AA	17	17	0	0	90.0	390	100	52	48	11	5	3	3	27	1	73	6	0	5	6	.455	0	0- -	-	4.60	4.80
2016	Nashv	AAA	8	8	0	0	45.2	172	38	7	6	1	3	0	0	3	0	32	0	0	4	0	1.000	0	0- -	-	1.64	1.18
2016	Oak	AL	5	5	0	0	22.1	103	31	18	18	4	0	2	4	4	0	14	1	1	1	3	.250	0	0-0	0	8.76	7.25

Scott Alexander

ahr-ees-MEN-dee ahl-KAHN-tar-ah

Pitches: L **Bats:** L **Pos:** RP-17 **Ht:** 6'2" **Wt:** 190 **Born:** 7/10/1989 **Age:** 27

			HOW MUCH HE PITCHED						WHAT HE GAVE UP												THE RESULTS							
Year	Team	Lg	G	GS	CG	GF	IP	BFP	H	R	ER	HR	SH	SF	HB	TBB	IBB	SO	WP	Bk	W	L	Pct	Sh	Sv-Op	Hld	ERC	ERA
2012	2 Tms	Low	11	7	0	1	35.2	159	34	22	10	2	1	3	2	16	1	31	4	0	2	4	.333	0	0- -	-	3.76	2.52
2013	2 Tms	Low	17	0	0	8	42.0	162	25	8	6	0	0	1	2	14	0	37	2	0	3	1	.750	0	2- -	-	1.50	1.29
2013	NWArk	AA	24	0	0	5	33.0	150	38	20	19	0	2	0	3	18	1	40	3	0	2	0	1.000	0	1- -	-	5.19	5.18
2014	NWArk	AA	35	0	0	10	48.2	204	42	26	21	3	4	2	3	16	0	36	5	0	1	2	.333	0	3- -	-	3.03	3.88
2014	Omha	AAA	11	0	0	3	19.0	85	23	16	13	1	0	0	1	10	0	13	4	0	1	2	.333	0	0- -	-	6.99	6.16
2015	Omha	AAA	41	0	0	29	63.1	250	48	21	18	5	0	2	1	17	1	50	10	0	2	3	.400	0	14- -	-	2.27	2.56
2016	Omha	AAA	22	0	0	10	30.0	130	32	16	12	2	1	0	1	10	1	24	1	0	2	0	1.000	0	1- -	-	4.03	3.00

Year	Team	Lg	G	GS	CG	GF	IP	BFP	H	R	ER	HR	SH	SF	HB	TBB	IBB	SO	WP	Bk	W	L	Pct	Sh	Sv-Op	Hld	ERC	ERA
2016	Royals	R	5	2	0	0	7.1	34	8	4	4	0	0	1	2	2	0	12	2	0	0	0	-	0	0- -	-	4.28	4.91
2015	KC	AL	4	0	0	3	6.0	25	5	3	3	0	0	0	1	3	0	3	1	0	0	0	-	0	0-0	0	3.67	4.50
2016	KC	AL	17	0	0	4	19.0	84	24	7	7	1	0	1	0	7	0	16	0	0	0	0	-	0	0-1	0	5.24	3.32
2 ML YEARS			21	0	0	7	25.0	109	29	10	10	1	0	1	1	10	0	19	1	0	0	0	-	0	0-1	0	4.86	3.60

Jorge Alfaro

Bats: R Throws: R Pos: C-4;PH-2

Ht: 6'2" Wt: 225 Born: 6/11/1993 Age: 24

Year	Team	Lg	G	AB	H	2B	3B	HR	(Hm	Rd)	TB	R	RBI	RC	TBB	IBB	SO	HBP	SH	SF	SB	CS	GDP	Avg	OBP	Slg	OPS
2012	Hkry	A	74	272	71	21	5	5	(-	-)	117	40	34	39	16	0	84	9	0	3	7	3	8	.261	.320	.430	.750
2013	Hkry	Low	113	404	107	24	1	18	(-	-)	187	72	61	68	32	0	122	20	0	3	18	3	10	.265	.346	.463	.809
2014	MrtlBh	A+	100	398	104	22	5	13	(-	-)	175	63	73	56	23	0	100	12	0	4	6	5	6	.261	.318	.440	.758
2014	Frisco	AA	21	88	23	4	0	4	(-	-)	39	12	14	13	6	1	23	5	0	0	0	0	4	.261	.343	.443	.787
2015	Frisco	AA	49	190	48	15	2	5	(-	-)	82	22	21	26	9	0	61	8	0	0	2	1	3	.253	.314	.432	.746
2016	Rdng	AA	97	404	115	22	2	15	(-	-)	186	68	67	61	22	0	105	4	1	4	3	2	9	.285	.325	.460	.785
2016	Phi	NL	6	16	2	0	0	0	(0	0)	2	0	0	0	1	1	8	0	0	0	0	0	0	.125	.176	.125	.301

Cody Allen

Pitches: R Bats: R Pos: RP-67

Ht: 6'1" Wt: 210 Born: 11/20/1988 Age: 28

Year	Team	Lg	G	GS	CG	GF	IP	BFP	H	R	ER	HR	SH	SF	HB	TBB	IBB	SO	WP	Bk	W	L	Pct	Sh	Sv-Op	Hld	ERC	ERA
2012	Cle	AL	27	0	0	9	29.0	126	29	12	12	2	1	1	0	15	0	27	0	0	0	1	.000	0	0-1	1	4.39	3.72
2013	Cle	AL	77	0	0	12	70.1	301	62	22	19	7	4	4	1	26	2	88	9	0	6	1	.857	0	2-4	11	3.24	2.43
2014	Cle	AL	76	0	0	44	69.2	279	48	21	16	7	2	2	1	26	5	91	4	0	6	4	.600	0	24-28	9	2.32	2.07
2015	Cle	AL	70	0	0	58	69.1	286	56	26	23	2	1	2	2	25	2	99	9	0	2	5	.286	0	34-38	0	2.51	2.99
2016	Cle	AL	67	0	0	55	68.0	264	41	23	19	8	3	2	0	27	2	87	3	0	3	5	.375	0	32-35	0	2.14	2.51
	Postseason		1	0	0	0	0.1	2	1	1	0	0	0	0	0	0	0	1	0	0	0	0	-	0	0-0	0	14.52	0.00
5 ML YEARS			317	0	0	178	306.1	1256	236	104	89	26	11	11	4	119	11	392	25	0	17	16	.515	0	92-106	21	2.71	2.61

Abraham Almonte

Bats: B Throws: R Pos: RF-36;LF-34;PH-13;CF-2

Ht: 5'9" Wt: 210 Born: 6/27/1989 Age: 28

Year	Team	Lg	G	AB	H	2B	3B	HR	(Hm	Rd)	TB	R	RBI	RC	TBB	IBB	SO	HBP	SH	SF	SB	CS	GDP	Avg	OBP	Slg	OPS
2013	Sea	AL	25	72	19	4	0	2	(1	1)	29	10	9	9	6	0	21	0	2	2	1	0	2	.264	.313	.403	.715
2014	2 Tms		59	204	47	10	1	3	(2	1)	68	19	15	18	12	0	60	1	2	1	4	3	5	.230	.275	.333	.609
2015	2 Tms		82	232	58	12	5	5	(4	1)	95	36	24	28	21	0	52	0	3	2	7	1	5	.250	.310	.409	.719
2016	Cle	AL	67	182	48	20	1	1	(1	0)	73	24	22	20	8	1	42	1	0	3	8	0	5	.264	.294	.401	.695
14	Sea	AL	27	106	21	5	1	1	(0	1)	31	10	8	10	6	0	40	1	0	0	3	1	1	.198	.248	.292	.540
14	SD	NL	32	98	26	5	0	2	(2	0)	37	9	7	8	6	0	20	0	2	1	1	2	4	.265	.305	.378	.682
15	SD	NL	31	54	11	3	0	0	(0	0)	14	6	4	3	5	0	19	0	3	0	1	1	1	.204	.271	.259	.530
15	Cle	AL	51	178	47	9	5	5	(4	1)	81	30	20	25	16	0	33	0	0	2	6	0	4	.264	.321	.455	.776
4 ML YEARS			233	690	172	46	7	11	(8	3)	265	89	70	75	47	1	175	2	7	8	20	4	17	.249	.296	.384	.680

Albert Almora

Bats: R Throws: R Pos: CF-33;PH-10;LF-8;RF-2;PR-1

Ht: 6'2" Wt: 190 Born: 4/16/1994 Age: 23

Year	Team	Lg	G	AB	H	2B	3B	HR	(Hm	Rd)	TB	R	RBI	RC	TBB	IBB	SO	HBP	SH	SF	SB	CS	GDP	Avg	OBP	Slg	OPS
2012	2 Tms	Low	33	140	45	12	1	2	(-	-)	65	27	19	21	2	0	13	1	0	2	5	2	5	.321	.331	.464	.795
2013	Kane	A	61	249	82	17	4	3	(-	-)	116	39	23	43	17	1	30	3	1	2	4	4	7	.329	.376	.466	.842
2014	Dytona	A+	89	367	104	20	2	7	(-	-)	149	55	50	46	12	1	46	2	0	4	6	3	16	.283	.306	.406	.712
2014	Tenn	AA	36	142	33	7	2	2	(-	-)	50	20	10	11	2	0	22	1	0	0	1	6	6	.232	.248	.352	.600
2015	Tenn	AA	106	405	110	26	4	6	(-	-)	162	69	46	56	32	1	47	4	4	6	9	4	10	.272	.327	.400	.727
2016	Iowa	AAA	80	320	97	18	3	4	(-	-)	133	46	43	43	9	0	44	0	2	5	10	3	7	.303	.317	.416	.733
2016	ChC	NL	47	112	31	9	1	3	(1	2)	51	14	14	16	5	0	20	0	0	0	0	0	5	.277	.308	.455	.763

Yonder Alonso

YONN-dur ah-LONN-zo

Bats: L Throws: R Pos: 1B-145;PH-11;3B-7;DH-3;PR-2

Ht: 6'1" Wt: 230 Born: 4/8/1987 Age: 30

Year	Team	Lg	G	AB	H	2B	3B	HR	(Hm	Rd)	TB	R	RBI	RC	TBB	IBB	SO	HBP	SH	SF	SB	CS	GDP	Avg	OBP	Slg	OPS
2010	Cin	NL	22	29	6	2	0	0	(0	0)	8	2	3	0	0	0	10	0	0	0	0	0	1	.207	.207	.276	.483
2011	Cin	NL	47	88	29	4	0	5	(2	3)	48	9	15	16	10	0	21	0	0	0	0	0	2	.330	.398	.545	.943
2012	SD	NL	155	549	150	39	0	9	(3	6)	216	47	62	71	62	9	101	3	1	4	3	0	14	.273	.348	.393	.741
2013	SD	NL	97	334	94	11	0	6	(4	2)	123	34	45	46	32	5	47	2	0	7	6	0	9	.281	.341	.368	.710
2014	SD	NL	84	267	64	19	1	7	(3	4)	106	27	27	26	17	1	36	1	0	3	6	1	8	.240	.285	.397	.682
2015	SD	NL	103	354	100	18	1	5	(3	4)	135	50	31	40	42	3	48	3	0	3	2	5	13	.282	.361	.381	.742
2016	Oak	AL	156	482	122	34	0	7	(3	4)	177	52	56	58	45	1	74	1	0	4	3	1	15	.253	.316	.367	.683
7 ML YEARS			664	2103	565	127	2	39	(18	21)	813	221	239	257	208	19	337	10	1	21	20	7	62	.269	.334	.387	.721

Dan Altavilla

Pitches: R Bats: R Pos: RP-15   all-ta-VILL-ah   Ht: 5'11" Wt: 200 Born: 9/8/1992 Age: 24

			HOW MUCH HE PITCHED					WHAT HE GAVE UP										THE RESULTS						
Year	Team	Lg	G	GS	CG	GF	IP	BFP	H	R	ER	HR	SH	SF	HB	TBB	IBB	SO	WP	Bk	W	L	Pct	Sh	Sv-Op	Hld	ERC	ERA
2014	Everett	A-	14	14	0	0	66.0	293	74	36	32	7	0	0	4	32	0	66	4	0	5	3	.625	0	0--	-	5.58	4.36
2015	Bkrsfld	A+	28	28	1	0	148.1	628	138	82	67	11	1	7	7	53	0	134	13	2	6	12	.333	1	0--	-	3.55	4.07
2016	Jacksn	AA	43	0	0	35	56.2	235	40	15	12	3	5	1	3	22	1	65	2	0	7	3	.700	0	16--	-	2.32	1.91
2016	Sea	AL	15	0	0	7	12.1	48	11	1	1	0	0	1	1	1	0	10	1	0	0	0	-	0	0-1	1	2.09	0.73

Aaron Altherr

Bats: R Throws: R Pos: RF-42;LF-20;CF-10;PH-1   ALL-tair   Ht: 6'5" Wt: 215 Born: 1/14/1991 Age: 26

					BATTING														RUNNING			AVERAGES			
Year	Team	Lg	G	AB	H	2B	3B	HR	(Hm | Rd)	TB	R	RBI	RC	TBB	IBB	SO	HBP	SH	SF	SB	CS	GDP	Avg	OBP	Slg	OPS
2014	Phi	NL	2	5	0	0	0	0	(0 | 0)	0	0	0	0	0	0	2	0	0	0	0	0	0	.000	.000	.000	.000
2015	Phi	NL	39	137	33	11	4	5	(2 | 3)	67	25	22	23	16	0	41	5	1	2	6	2	3	.241	.338	.489	.827
2016	Phi	NL	57	198	39	6	0	4	(2 | 2)	57	23	22	20	23	2	69	6	0	0	7	2	4	.197	.300	.288	.587
	3 ML YEARS		98	340	72	17	4	9	(4 | 5)	124	48	44	43	39	2	112	11	1	2	13	4	7	.212	.311	.365	.676

Jose Altuve

Bats: R Throws: R Pos: 2B-148;DH-13;SS-1;PR-1   al-TOO-vay   Ht: 5'6" Wt: 165 Born: 5/6/1990 Age: 27

					BATTING														RUNNING			AVERAGES			
Year	Team	Lg	G	AB	H	2B	3B	HR	(Hm | Rd)	TB	R	RBI	RC	TBB	IBB	SO	HBP	SH	SF	SB	CS	GDP	Avg	OBP	Slg	OPS
2011	Hou	NL	57	221	61	10	1	2	(2 | 0)	79	26	12	18	5	0	29	2	5	1	7	3	5	.276	.297	.357	.654
2012	Hou	NL	147	576	167	34	4	7	(4 | 3)	230	80	37	76	40	0	74	6	4	4	33	11	8	.290	.340	.399	.740
2013	Hou	AL	152	626	177	31	2	5	(4 | 1)	227	64	52	67	32	5	85	2	4	8	35	13	24	.283	.316	.363	.678
2014	Hou	AL	158	660	225	47	3	7	(4 | 3)	299	85	59	106	36	7	53	5	1	5	56	9	20	.341	.377	.453	.830
2015	Hou	AL	154	638	200	40	4	15	(9 | 6)	293	86	66	98	33	8	67	9	3	6	38	13	17	.313	.353	.459	.812
2016	Hou	AL	161	640	216	42	5	24	(15 | 9)	340	108	96	132	60	11	70	7	3	7	30	10	15	.338	.396	.531	.928
	Postseason		6	26	4	0	0	0	(0 | 0)	4	2	2	1	1	0	3	0	0	0	1	1	1	.154	.185	.154	.339
	6 ML YEARS		829	3361	1046	204	19	60	(38 | 22)	1468	449	322	497	206	31	378	31	20	31	199	59	89	.311	.354	.437	.790

Dariel Alvarez

Bats: R Throws: R Pos: RF-1;PH-1   Ht: 6'2" Wt: 180 Born: 11/7/1988 Age: 28

					BATTING														RUNNING			AVERAGES			
Year	Team	Lg	G	AB	H	2B	3B	HR	(Hm | Rd)	TB	R	RBI	RC	TBB	IBB	SO	HBP	SH	SF	SB	CS	GDP	Avg	OBP	Slg	OPS
2013	2 Tms	Low	13	48	21	4	1	3	(- | -)	36	7	9	13	3	0	2	0	0	0	1	2	2	.438	.471	.750	1.221
2014	Bowie	AA	91	359	111	20	1	14	(- | -)	175	52	68	58	13	0	35	2	1	6	7	4	13	.309	.332	.487	.819
2014	Norfolk	AAA	44	173	52	17	2	1	(- | -)	76	23	19	25	8	0	27	0	0	2	1	1	6	.301	.328	.439	.767
2015	Norfolk	AAA	130	512	141	24	2	16	(- | -)	217	61	72	68	16	0	63	8	0	5	7	3	14	.275	.305	.424	.729
2016	Norfolk	AAA	130	524	151	38	0	4	(- | -)	201	53	49	68	28	3	80	2	2	4	7	2	11	.288	.324	.384	.708
2015	Bal	AL	12	29	7	1	0	1	(1 | 0)	11	3	1	3	2	0	8	0	0	0	0	0	0	.241	.290	.379	.670
2016	Bal	AL	2	3	1	1	0	0	(0 | 0)	2	0	0	1	1	0	0	0	0	0	0	0	0	.333	.500	.667	1.167
	2 ML YEARS		14	32	8	2	0	1	(1 | 0)	13	3	1	4	3	0	8	0	0	0	0	0	0	.250	.314	.406	.721

Dario Alvarez

Pitches: L Bats: L Pos: RP-26   Ht: 6'1" Wt: 170 Born: 1/17/1989 Age: 28

			HOW MUCH HE PITCHED					WHAT HE GAVE UP										THE RESULTS						
Year	Team	Lg	G	GS	CG	GF	IP	BFP	H	R	ER	HR	SH	SF	HB	TBB	IBB	SO	WP	Bk	W	L	Pct	Sh	Sv-Op	Hld	ERC	ERA
2016	LsVgs*	AAA	17	0	0	8	15.1	79	22	19	17	3	0	0	1	10	0	27	0	0	0	1	.000	0	0--	-	8.77	9.98
2016	Gwnntt*	AAA	8	0	0	1	8.0	33	4	1	1	0	0	0	1	4	1	14	1	0	0	0	-	0	0--	-	1.54	1.13
2016	RdRck*	AAA	6	0	0	2	8.0	33	8	3	2	1	0	1	0	3	0	10	1	0	2	0	1.000	0	1--	-	4.34	2.25
2014	NYM	NL	4	0	0	0	1.1	8	4	2	2	1	0	0	0	0	0	1	0	0	0	0	-	0	0-1	1	22.76	13.50
2015	NYM	NL	6	0	0	0	3.2	19	5	5	5	2	1	0	2	1	0	2	0	1	1	0	1.000	0	0-0	1	12.00	12.27
2016	2 Tms		26	0	0	9	26.2	113	28	16	15	6	0	1	3	7	2	41	5	0	3	1	.750	0	0-0	1	5.16	5.06
16	Atl	NL	16	0	0	4	15.0	61	11	5	5	3	0	0	1	5	2	28	4	0	3	1	.750	0	0-0	1	3.09	3.00
16	Tex	AL	10	0	0	5	11.2	52	17	11	10	3	0	1	2	2	0	13	1	0	0	0	-	0	0-0	0	8.34	7.71
	3 ML YEARS		36	0	0	9	31.2	140	37	23	22	9	1	1	5	8	2	44	5	1	4	1	.800	0	0-1	3	6.49	6.25

Henderson Alvarez

Pitches: R Bats: R Pos: P   Ht: 6'0" Wt: 205 Born: 4/18/1990 Age: 27

			HOW MUCH HE PITCHED					WHAT HE GAVE UP										THE RESULTS						
Year	Team	Lg	G	GS	CG	GF	IP	BFP	H	R	ER	HR	SH	SF	HB	TBB	IBB	SO	WP	Bk	W	L	Pct	Sh	Sv-Op	Hld	ERC	ERA
2016	Nashv*	AAA	5	5	0	0	18.2	78	17	9	8	3	0	0	1	6	0	17	0	0	1	0	1.000	0	0--	-	3.93	3.86
2011	Tor	AL	10	10	0	0	63.2	259	64	26	25	8	1	2	4	8	0	40	2	0	1	3	.250	0	0-0	0	3.49	3.53
2012	Tor	AL	31	31	1	0	187.1	807	216	110	101	29	2	4	3	54	2	79	3	1	9	14	.391	1	0-0	0	5.01	4.85
2013	Mia	NL	17	17	1	0	102.2	418	90	42	41	2	0	4	7	27	1	57	4	1	5	6	.455	1	0-0	0	2.66	3.59
2014	Mia	NL	30	30	3	0	187.0	772	198	65	55	14	7	4	8	33	3	111	4	0	12	7	.632	3	0-0	0	3.56	2.65
2015	Mia	NL	4	4	0	0	22.1	102	28	18	16	1	4	1	0	7	1	9	3	1	0	4	.000	0	0-0	0	4.57	6.45
	5 ML YEARS		92	92	5	0	563.0	2358	596	261	238	54	14	15	22	129	7	296	16	3	27	34	.443	5	0-0	0	3.89	3.80

Jose Alvarez

Pitches: L Bats: L Pos: RP-64   Ht: 5'11" Wt: 190 Born: 5/6/1989 Age: 28

Year	Team	Lg	G	GS	CG	GF	IP	BFP	H	R	ER	HR	SH	SF	HB	TBB	IBB	SO	WP	Bk	W	L	Pct	Sh	Sv-Op	Hld	ERC	ERA
2016	Salt Lk*	AAA	5	0	0	0	7.1	30	5	3	2	0	1	0	0	5	0	7	0	0	1	0	1.000	0	0- -	-	2.87	2.45
2013	Det	AL	14	6	0	0	38.2	172	42	26	25	7	2	2	2	16	1	31	0	1	1	5	.167	0	0-0	2	5.41	5.82
2014	LAA	AL	2	0	0	1	0.2	3	1	0	0	0	0	0	0	0	0	1	0	0	0	0	-	0	0-0	0	4.47	0.00
2015	LAA	AL	64	0	0	18	67.0	283	58	29	26	5	0	1	5	23	4	59	1	0	4	3	.571	0	0-1	7	3.13	3.49
2016	LAA	AL	64	0	0	12	57.1	256	71	29	22	4	1	1	1	15	4	51	2	0	1	3	.250	0	0-1	11	4.55	3.45
	Postseason		1	0	0	0	3.0	10	0	0	0	0	0	0	0	1	0	3	0	0	0	0	-	0	0-0	0	0.13	0.00
4 ML YEARS			144	6	0	31	163.2	714	172	84	73	16	3	4	8	54	9	142	3	1	6	11	.353	0	0-2	20	4.14	4.01

Pedro Alvarez

Bats: L Throws: R Pos: DH-85;PH-14;3B-12   Ht: 6'3" Wt: 250 Born: 2/6/1987 Age: 30

									BATTING												RUNNING			AVERAGES			
Year	Team	Lg	G	AB	H	2B	3B	HR	(Hm	Rd)	TB	R	RBI	RC	TBB	IBB	SO	HBP	SH	SF	SB	CS	GDP	Avg	OBP	Slg	OPS
2010	Pit	NL	95	347	89	21	1	16	(12	4)	160	42	64	50	37	1	119	0	0	2	0	0	8	.256	.326	.461	.788
2011	Pit	NL	74	235	45	9	1	4	(0	4)	68	18	19	14	24	1	80	2	1	0	1	0	11	.191	.272	.289	.561
2012	Pit	NL	149	525	128	25	1	30	(12	18)	245	64	85	77	57	6	180	1	0	3	1	0	10	.244	.317	.467	.784
2013	Pit	NL	152	558	130	22	2	36	(16	20)	264	70	100	66	48	7	186	4	0	4	2	0	16	.233	.296	.473	.770
2014	Pit	NL	122	398	92	13	1	18	(8	10)	161	46	56	42	45	6	113	2	0	0	8	3	12	.231	.312	.405	.717
2015	Pit	NL	150	437	106	18	0	27	(14	13)	205	60	77	52	48	9	131	2	0	4	2	0	6	.243	.318	.469	.787
2016	Bal	AL	109	337	84	20	0	22	(14	8)	170	43	49	46	37	1	97	0	0	2	1	0	6	.249	.322	.504	.826
	Postseason		7	23	6	1	0	3	(1	2)	16	4	7	5	2	1	10	0	0	1	0	0	0	.261	.308	.696	1.003
7 ML YEARS			851	2837	674	128	6	153	(76	77)	1273	343	450	347	296	31	906	11	1	15	15	3	69	.238	.311	.449	.759

Alexi Amarista

ah-mah-REE-stah

Bats: L Throws: R Pos: 2B-28;PH-17;SS-12;3B-5;LF-5;RF-5;PR-4   Ht: 5'6" Wt: 160 Born: 4/6/1989 Age: 28

									BATTING												RUNNING			AVERAGES			
Year	Team	Lg	G	AB	H	2B	3B	HR	(Hm	Rd)	TB	R	RBI	RC	TBB	IBB	SO	HBP	SH	SF	SB	CS	GDP	Avg	OBP	Slg	OPS
2016	ElPaso*	AAA	13	48	16	3	0	1	(-	-)	22	9	4	9	4	0	8	1	0	2	1	0	0	.333	.382	.458	.840
2011	LAA	AL	23	52	8	3	1	0	(0	0)	13	2	5	1	2	0	8	0	1	1	0	0	1	.154	.182	.250	.432
2012	2 Tms		106	275	66	15	5	5	(0	5)	106	36	32	31	17	1	42	0	6	2	8	4	2	.240	.282	.385	.668
2013	SD	NL	146	368	87	14	4	5	(1	4)	124	35	32	40	22	1	57	2	3	1	4	2	7	.236	.282	.337	.619
2014	SD	NL	148	423	101	13	2	5	(3	2)	133	39	40	43	29	5	69	1	8	5	12	1	6	.239	.286	.314	.600
2015	SD	NL	118	324	66	10	4	3	(1	2)	93	28	30	28	24	4	55	1	3	5	5	1	6	.204	.257	.287	.544
2016	SD	NL	65	140	36	2	0	0	(0	0)	38	9	11	14	8	2	26	0	1	1	9	2	5	.257	.295	.271	.567
12	LAA	AL	1	0	0	0	0	0	(0	0)	0	1	0	0	0	0	0	0	0	0	0	0	0	-	-	-	-
12	SD	NL	105	275	66	15	5	5	(0	5)	106	35	32	31	17	1	42	0	6	2	8	4	2	.240	.282	.385	.668
6 ML YEARS			606	1582	364	57	16	18	(5	13)	507	149	150	157	102	13	257	4	22	15	38	10	27	.230	.276	.320	.596

Brett Anderson

Pitches: L Bats: L Pos: SP-3; RP-1   Ht: 6'3" Wt: 230 Born: 2/1/1988 Age: 29

Year	Team	Lg	G	GS	CG	GF	IP	BFP	H	R	ER	HR	SH	SF	HB	TBB	IBB	SO	WP	Bk	W	L	Pct	Sh	Sv-Op	Hld	ERC	ERA
2009	Oak	AL	30	30	1	0	175.1	735	180	94	79	20	4	4	3	45	1	150	0	1	11	11	.500	1	0-0	0	3.84	4.06
2010	Oak	AL	19	19	0	0	112.1	470	112	41	35	6	3	2	7	22	2	75	4	2	7	6	.538	0	0-0	0	3.16	2.80
2011	Oak	AL	13	13	1	0	83.1	356	86	40	37	8	4	1	7	25	1	61	0	1	3	6	.333	0	0-0	0	4.20	4.00
2012	Oak	AL	6	6	0	0	35.0	137	29	11	10	1	0	0	1	7	1	25	1	0	4	2	.667	0	0-0	0	2.13	2.57
2013	Oak	AL	16	5	0	4	44.2	200	51	32	30	5	1	0	0	21	1	46	0	0	1	4	.200	0	3-3	1	5.27	6.04
2014	Col	NL	8	8	0	0	43.1	180	44	18	14	1	1	1	0	13	3	29	0	0	1	3	.250	0	0-0	0	3.20	2.91
2015	LAD	NL	31	31	1	0	180.1	750	194	82	74	18	3	2	2	46	2	116	4	2	10	9	.526	0	0-0	0	4.05	3.69
2016	LAD	NL	4	3	0	0	11.1	62	25	15	15	4	1	1	0	4	0	5	2	0	1	2	.333	0	0-0	0	14.27	11.91
	Postseason		3	2	0	1	9.1	40	10	7	7	1	0	0	0	3	0	10	1	0	1	1	.500	0	0-0	0	4.23	6.75
8 ML YEARS			127	115	3	4	685.2	2890	721	333	294	63	17	11	20	183	11	507	11	6	38	43	.469	1	3-3	1	3.92	3.86

Chase Anderson

Pitches: R Bats: R Pos: SP-30; RP-1   Ht: 6'1" Wt: 200 Born: 11/30/1987 Age: 29

Year	Team	Lg	G	GS	CG	GF	IP	BFP	H	R	ER	HR	SH	SF	HB	TBB	IBB	SO	WP	Bk	W	L	Pct	Sh	Sv-Op	Hld	ERC	ERA
2014	Ari	NL	21	21	0	0	114.1	486	117	56	51	16	4	4	2	40	2	105	4	0	9	7	.563	0	0-0	0	4.39	4.01
2015	Ari	NL	27	27	0	0	152.2	640	158	75	73	18	3	9	7	40	2	111	3	0	6	6	.500	0	0-0	0	4.08	4.30
2016	Mil	NL	31	30	0	1	151.2	647	155	83	74	28	4	3	4	53	0	120	4	0	9	11	.450	0	0-0	0	4.76	4.39
3 ML YEARS			79	78	0	1	418.2	1773	430	214	198	62	11	16	13	133	4	336	11	0	24	24	.500	0	0-0	0	4.41	4.26

Cody Anderson

Pitches: R Bats: R Pos: RP-10; SP-9   Ht: 6'4" Wt: 240 Born: 9/14/1990 Age: 26

Year	Team	Lg	G	GS	CG	GF	IP	BFP	H	R	ER	HR	SH	SF	HB	TBB	IBB	SO	WP	Bk	W	L	Pct	Sh	Sv-Op	Hld	ERC	ERA
2012	Lk Cty	A	24	23	0	1	98.1	403	92	40	35	8	1	2	1	29	0	72	5	2	4	7	.364	0	0- -	-	3.29	3.20
2013	Carlina	A+	23	23	0	0	123.1	488	105	34	32	6	4	3	5	31	0	112	7	1	9	4	.692	0	0- -	-	2.65	2.34
2014	Akron	AA	25	25	0	0	125.2	544	141	78	76	17	1	0	4	45	0	81	4	2	4	11	.267	0	0- -	-	5.10	5.44
2015	Akron	AA	10	10	0	0	52.0	202	44	12	10	2	2	1	1	9	0	36	2	0	3	2	.600	0	0- -	-	2.20	1.73

Year	Team	Lg	G	GS	CG	GF	IP	BFP	H	R	ER	HR	SH	SF	HB	TBB	IBB	SO	WP	Bk	W	L	Pct	Sh	Sv-Op	Hld	ERC	ERA
2016	Clmbs	AAA	13	6	0	4	32.1	141	32	15	13	4	0	0	2	10	0	40	2	-1	0	2	.000	0	1- -	-	3.98	3.62
2015	Cle	AL	15	15	1	0	91.1	365	77	32	31	9	3	3	1	24	1	44	0	1	7	3	.700	0	0-0	0	2.78	3.05
2016	Cle	AL	19	9	0	2	60.2	270	85	45	45	13	0	1	1	13	3	54	5	0	2	5	.286	0	0-0	0	6.67	6.68
	2 ML YEARS		34	24	1	2	152.0	635	162	77	76	22	3	4	2	37	4	98	5	1	9	8	.529	0	0-0	0	4.21	4.50

Tim Anderson

Bats: R **Throws:** R **Pos:** SS-98 **Ht:** 6'1" **Wt:** 185 **Born:** 6/23/1993 **Age:** 24

Year	Team	Lg	G	AB	H	2B	3B	HR	(Hm	Rd)	TB	R	RBI	RC	TBB	IBB	SO	HBP	SH	SF	SB	CS	GDP	Avg	OBP	Slg	OPS
2013	Knapol	A	68	267	74	10	5	1	(-	-)	97	45	21	39	23	0	78	7	2	2	24	4	5	.277	.348	.363	.711
2014	2 Tms	Low	74	303	89	18	7	8	(-	-)	145	50	33	46	9	0	73	5	0	2	10	4	4	.294	.323	.479	.801
2014	Brham	AA	10	44	16	3	0	1	(-	-)	22	7	7	7	0	0	9	0	1	0	0	1	0	.364	.364	.500	.864
2015	Brham	AA	125	513	160	21	12	5	(-	-)	220	79	46	82	24	0	114	7	4	2	49	13	6	.312	.350	.429	.779
2016	Charllt	AAA	55	247	75	10	2	4	(-	-)	101	39	20	33	8	0	58	0	1	0	11	4	5	.304	.325	.409	.734
2016	CWS	AL	99	410	116	22	6	9	(5	4)	177	57	30	45	13	0	117	1	6	1	10	2	15	.283	.306	.432	.738

Tyler Anderson

Pitches: L **Bats:** L **Pos:** SP-19 **Ht:** 6'4" **Wt:** 210 **Born:** 12/30/1989 **Age:** 27

Year	Team	Lg	G	GS	CG	GF	IP	BFP	H	R	ER	HR	SH	SF	HB	TBB	IBB	SO	WP	Bk	W	L	Pct	Sh	Sv-Op	Hld	ERC	ERA
2012	Ashvll	A	20	20	2	0	120.1	476	102	43	33	5	3	3	3	28	0	81	5	1	12	3	.800	1	0- -	-	2.44	2.47
2013	2 Tms	Low	16	16	0	0	89.2	367	71	40	28	10	3	3	2	27	0	76	5	0	4	3	.571	0	0- -	-	2.72	2.81
2014	Tulsa	AA	23	23	0	0	118.1	474	90	37	26	3	6	3	4	40	0	106	8	3	7	4	.636	0	0- -	-	2.29	1.98
2016	Col	NL	19	19	0	0	114.1	478	119	50	45	12	6	3	3	28	2	99	4	3	5	6	.455	0	0-0	0	3.85	3.54

Robert Andino

Bats: R **Throws:** R **Pos:** PH-7;2B-3;LF-2;3B-1;SS-1;PR-1 ann-DEE-no **Ht:** 5'11" **Wt:** 185 **Born:** 4/25/1984 **Age:** 33

Year	Team	Lg	G	AB	H	2B	3B	HR	(Hm	Rd)	TB	R	RBI	RC	TBB	IBB	SO	HBP	SH	SF	SB	CS	GDP	Avg	OBP	Slg	OPS
2016	NewOr*	AAA	108	419	112	24	2	13	(-	-)	179	52	46	59	30	0	111	2	1	1	8	1	12	.267	.319	.427	.746
2005	Fla	NL	17	44	7	4	0	0	(0	0)	11	4	1	1	5	1	8	0	1	0	1	0	2	.159	.245	.250	.495
2006	Fla	NL	11	24	4	1	0	0	(0	0)	5	0	2	0	1	0	6	0	1	2	1	0	0	.167	.185	.208	.394
2007	Fla	NL	7	13	5	1	0	0	(0	0)	6	0	0	1	0	0	2	0	0	0	0	0	0	.385	.385	.462	.846
2008	Fla	NL	44	63	13	2	0	2	(1	1)	21	7	9	7	4	0	23	0	1	0	0	0	1	.206	.254	.333	.587
2009	Bal	AL	78	198	44	7	0	2	(1	1)	57	31	10	11	15	1	47	0	0	2	3	3	6	.222	.274	.288	.562
2010	Bal	AL	16	61	18	4	0	2	(2	0)	28	6	6	4	3	0	13	1	0	1	1	1	3	.295	.333	.459	.792
2011	Bal	AL	139	457	120	22	0	5	(2	3)	157	63	36	52	41	0	83	3	9	1	13	3	14	.263	.327	.344	.670
2012	Bal	AL	127	384	81	13	1	7	(4	3)	117	41	28	31	37	0	100	2	7	1	5	5	13	.211	.283	.305	.588
2013	Sea	AL	29	76	14	4	0	0	(0	0)	18	5	4	3	7	0	27	0	2	0	0	0	3	.184	.253	.237	.490
2016	Mia	NL	13	24	7	0	0	0	(0	0)	7	2	1	3	0	0	4	0	0	0	0	0	0	.292	.292	.292	.583
	Postseason		6	12	5	1	0	0	(0	0)	6	3	0	4	0	0	2	0	1	0	0	0	0	.417	.417	.500	.917
	10 ML YEARS		481	1344	313	58	1	18	(10	8)	427	159	97	113	113	2	313	6	21	7	24	12	42	.233	.294	.318	.612

Matt Andriese

Pitches: R **Bats:** R **Pos:** SP-19; RP-10 ANN-dreese **Ht:** 6'3" **Wt:** 215 **Born:** 8/28/1989 **Age:** 27

Year	Team	Lg	G	GS	CG	GF	IP	BFP	H	R	ER	HR	SH	SF	HB	TBB	IBB	SO	WP	Bk	W	L	Pct	Sh	Sv-Op	Hld	ERC	ERA
2012	Lk Els	A+	27	26	0	0	146.0	603	140	72	58	9	2	3	4	38	0	131	10	1	10	8	.556	0	0- -	-	3.20	3.58
2013	SnAnt	AA	15	15	0	0	76.0	314	71	26	20	3	1	0	3	17	0	63	2	0	8	2	.800	0	0- -	-	2.80	2.37
2013	Tucsn	AAA	12	10	0	0	58.2	245	64	32	29	2	4	4	2	12	0	42	2	0	3	5	.375	0	0- -	-	3.55	4.45
2014	Drham	AAA	28	25	0	1	162.1	667	153	73	68	18	7	2	8	48	0	129	3	1	11	8	.579	0	0- -	-	3.72	3.77
2015	Drham	AAA	13	12	0	1	65.0	265	65	24	17	2	0	3	1	10	0	69	3	1	3	3	.500	0	0- -	-	2.76	2.35
2016	Drham	AAA	6	6	1	0	34.1	142	32	14	13	2	0	1	2	7	0	44	5	1	2	4	.333	0	0- -	-	2.90	3.41
2015	TB	AL	25	8	0	8	65.2	282	69	32	30	8	1	3	2	18	1	49	2	2	3	5	.375	0	2-2	0	4.08	4.11
2016	TB	AL	29	19	1	3	127.2	527	131	64	62	17	0	6	1	25	1	109	3	4	8	8	.500	1	1-1	4	3.68	4.37
	2 ML YEARS		54	27	1	11	193.1	809	200	96	92	25	1	9	3	43	2	158	5	6	11	13	.458	1	3-3	4	3.82	4.28

Elvis Andrus

Bats: R **Throws:** R **Pos:** SS-147 AHN-drews **Ht:** 6'0" **Wt:** 200 **Born:** 8/26/1988 **Age:** 28

Year	Team	Lg	G	AB	H	2B	3B	HR	(Hm	Rd)	TB	R	RBI	RC	TBB	IBB	SO	HBP	SH	SF	SB	CS	GDP	Avg	OBP	Slg	OPS
2009	Tex	AL	145	480	128	17	8	6	(3	3)	179	72	40	65	40	0	77	6	12	3	33	6	4	.267	.329	.373	.702
2010	Tex	AL	148	588	156	15	3	0	(0	0)	177	88	35	79	64	0	96	5	17	0	32	15	6	.265	.342	.301	.643
2011	Tex	AL	150	587	164	27	3	5	(2	3)	212	96	60	76	56	0	74	5	16	1	37	12	17	.279	.347	.361	.708
2012	Tex	AL	158	629	180	31	9	3	(1	2)	238	85	62	92	57	0	96	5	17	3	21	10	15	.286	.349	.378	.727
2013	Tex	AL	156	620	168	17	4	4	(0	4)	205	91	67	72	52	1	97	4	16	6	42	8	19	.271	.328	.331	.659
2014	Tex	AL	157	619	163	35	1	2	(1	1)	206	72	41	59	46	0	96	3	9	7	27	15	21	.263	.314	.333	.647
2015	Tex	AL	160	596	154	34	2	7	(4	3)	213	69	62	68	46	1	78	2	8	9	25	9	14	.258	.309	.357	.667
2016	Tex	AL	147	506	153	31	7	8	(3	5)	222	75	69	87	47	2	70	4	4	7	24	8	15	.302	.362	.439	.800
	Postseason		39	162	42	4	0	0	(0	0)	46	19	6	13	12	0	24	1	4	1	9	4	6	.259	.313	.284	.596
	8 ML YEARS		1221	4625	1266	207	37	35	(14	21)	1652	648	436	598	408	4	684	34	99	36	241	83	114	.274	.335	.357	.692

Dustin Antolin

Pitches: R Bats: R Pos: RP-1   Ht: 6'2" Wt: 230 Born: 8/9/1989 Age: 27

Year	Team	Lg	G	GS	CG	GF	IP	BFP	H	R	ER	HR	SH	SF	HB	TBB	IBB	SO	WP	Bk	W	L	Pct	Sh	Sv-Op	Hld	ERC	ERA
2012	Dnedin	A+	48	0	0	9	59.0	268	72	31	30	3	4	2	1	25	0	47	5	1	7	3	.700	0	1--	-	5.15	4.58
2013	Dnedin	A+	20	0	0	8	23.0	95	16	7	6	0	1	0	3	7	0	28	3	0	2	1	.667	0	2--	-	1.95	2.35
2013	Nham	AA	26	0	0	9	32.1	170	44	42	41	4	4	0	2	28	1	31	4	1	0	2	.000	0	2--	-	8.55	11.41
2014	Nham	AA	37	0	0	13	42.2	185	42	17	16	0	2	1	5	15	0	52	3	1	4	6	.400	0	0--	-	3.55	3.38
2015	Nham	AA	37	1	0	9	55.2	238	59	21	19	2	1	3	1	18	2	55	4	0	4	3	.571	0	2--	-	3.70	3.07
2016	Buffalo	AAA	46	1	0	30	53.0	225	41	15	12	3	2	0	3	28	0	61	1	0	2	3	.400	0	10--	-	3.27	2.04
2016	Tor	AL	1	0	0	0	2.0	11	4	3	3	1	0	0	0	1	0	1	0	0	0	0	-	0	0-0	0	14.72	13.50

Nori Aoki

Bats: L Throws: R Pos: LF-99;CF-15;PH-11;PR-1   AH-oh-kee   Ht: 5'9" Wt: 180 Born: 1/5/1982 Age: 35

Year	Team	Lg	G	AB	H	2B	3B	HR	(Hm	Rd)	TB	R	RBI	RC	TBB	IBB	SO	HBP	SH	SF	SB	CS	GDP	Avg	OBP	Slg	OPS
2016	Tacom*	AAA	24	96	31	5	0	1	(-	-)	39	17	7	16	8	0	13	1	1	2	4	0	1	.323	.374	.406	.780
2012	Mil	NL	151	520	150	37	4	10	(4	6)	225	81	50	80	43	1	55	13	7	5	30	8	6	.288	.355	.433	.787
2013	Mil	NL	155	597	171	20	3	8	(5	3)	221	80	37	80	55	1	40	11	8	3	20	12	9	.286	.356	.370	.726
2014	KC	AL	132	491	140	22	6	1	(0	1)	177	63	43	69	43	0	49	6	8	1	17	8	5	.285	.349	.360	.710
2015	SF	NL	93	355	102	12	3	5	(2	3)	135	42	26	49	30	0	25	6	1	0	14	5	8	.287	.353	.380	.733
2016	Sea	AL	118	417	118	24	4	4	(2	2)	162	63	28	51	34	0	45	9	5	1	7	9	9	.283	.349	.388	.738
	Postseason		14	41	8	0	0	0	(0	0)	8	7	3	5	5	0	3	1	0	1	1	0	2	.195	.292	.195	.487
	5 ML YEARS		649	2380	681	115	20	28	(13	15)	920	329	184	329	205	2	214	45	29	10	88	42	37	.286	.353	.387	.739

Jayson Aquino

Pitches: L Bats: L Pos: RP-3   a-KEE-no   Ht: 6'1" Wt: 225 Born: 11/22/1992 Age: 24

Year	Team	Lg	G	GS	CG	GF	IP	BFP	H	R	ER	HR	SH	SF	HB	TBB	IBB	SO	WP	Bk	W	L	Pct	Sh	Sv-Op	Hld	ERC	ERA
2012	GdJunc	R+	7	7	0	0	43.1	174	32	13	9	2	0	2	3	11	0	36	0	1	4	0	1.000	0	0--	-	2.10	1.87
2013	2 Tms	Low	15	14	0	0	87.0	365	87	48	42	5	4	4	5	26	0	73	2	1	0	10	.000	0	0--	-	3.68	4.34
2014	Mdest	A+	16	16	1	0	95.0	423	113	66	57	7	3	7	12	30	0	74	9	2	5	10	.333	0	0--	-	5.23	5.40
2015	3 Tms	Low	24	24	0	0	137.1	572	135	58	50	8	2	6	5	30	0	86	6	4	5	11	.313	0	0--	-	3.14	3.28
2016	Bowie	AA	20	19	1	1	115.1	501	130	55	50	7	5	4	5	33	0	77	6	2	5	10	.333	1	0--	-	4.24	3.90
2016	Norfolk	AAA	5	0	0	0	13.0	51	12	3	3	0	0	0	0	3	0	12	0	0	2	0	1.000	0	0--	-	2.51	2.08
2016	Bal	AL	3	0	0	2	2.1	8	1	0	0	0	0	0	0	0	0	3	0	0	0	0	-	0	0-0	0	0.40	0.00

Elvis Araujo

Pitches: L Bats: L Pos: RP-32   ah-ROW-hoe   Ht: 6'7" Wt: 275 Born: 7/15/1991 Age: 25

Year	Team	Lg	G	GS	CG	GF	IP	BFP	H	R	ER	HR	SH	SF	HB	TBB	IBB	SO	WP	Bk	W	L	Pct	Sh	Sv-Op	Hld	ERC	ERA
2012	Lk Cty	A	28	28	1	0	135.0	601	141	89	75	7	7	5	6	61	0	111	20	2	7	10	.412	0	0--	-	4.33	5.00
2014	Carlina	A+	25	0	0	15	29.0	126	23	16	13	1	2	5	0	13	1	29	6	0	1	1	.500	0	8--	-	2.53	4.03
2014	Akron	AA	18	0	0	6	21.0	90	20	7	6	2	0	1	0	15	2	21	2	0	1	0	1.000	0	3--	-	5.19	2.57
2015	Rdng	AA	7	0	0	3	9.2	44	9	8	8	1	0	1	0	6	0	11	0	0	1	2	.333	0	4--	-	5.00	7.45
2016	LV	AAA	18	0	0	8	20.2	84	15	7	5	2	0	0	1	6	0	19	1	0	1	0	1.000	0	1--	-	2.36	2.18
2015	Phi	NL	40	0	0	5	34.2	151	29	17	13	1	2	0	0	19	1	34	2	0	2	1	.667	0	0-0	2	3.15	3.38
2016	Phi	NL	32	0	0	9	27.1	134	35	22	17	4	2	1	2	17	2	29	0	1	2	1	.667	0	0-1	4	7.19	5.60
	2 ML YEARS		72	0	0	14	62.0	285	64	39	30	5	4	1	2	36	3	63	2	1	4	2	.667	0	0-1	6	4.81	4.35

Chris Archer

Pitches: R Bats: R Pos: SP-33   Ht: 6'3" Wt: 190 Born: 9/26/1988 Age: 28

Year	Team	Lg	G	GS	CG	GF	IP	BFP	H	R	ER	HR	SH	SF	HB	TBB	IBB	SO	WP	Bk	W	L	Pct	Sh	Sv-Op	Hld	ERC	ERA
2012	TB	AL	6	4	0	1	29.1	122	23	17	15	3	1	0	1	13	0	36	2	0	1	3	.250	0	0-0	0	3.24	4.60
2013	TB	AL	23	23	2	0	128.2	525	107	49	46	15	1	5	8	38	2	101	7	0	9	7	.563	2	0-0	0	3.13	3.22
2014	TB	AL	32	32	0	0	194.2	822	177	85	72	12	4	9	8	72	1	173	8	0	10	9	.526	0	0-0	0	3.36	3.33
2015	TB	AL	34	34	1	0	212.0	868	175	85	76	19	2	2	3	66	0	252	13	0	12	13	.480	1	0-0	0	2.79	3.23
2016	TB	AL	33	33	0	0	201.1	850	183	100	90	30	6	4	3	67	0	233	11	0	9	19	.321	0	0-0	0	3.66	4.02
	Postseason		2	0	0	0	1.2	6	1	0	0	0	0	0	0	0	0	2	0	0	0	0	-	0	0-0	0	0.75	0.00
	5 ML YEARS		128	126	3	1	766.0	3187	665	336	299	79	14	20	23	256	3	795	41	0	41	51	.446	3	0-0	0	3.23	3.51

Orlando Arcia

Bats: R Throws: R Pos: SS-53;PH-2   ARR-see-ya   Ht: 6'0" Wt: 165 Born: 8/4/1994 Age: 22

Year	Team	Lg	G	AB	H	2B	3B	HR	(Hm	Rd)	TB	R	RBI	RC	TBB	IBB	SO	HBP	SH	SF	SB	CS	GDP	Avg	OBP	Slg	OPS
2013	Wisc	A	120	442	111	14	5	4	(-	-)	147	67	39	49	35	2	40	6	2	1	20	9	15	.251	.314	.333	.647
2014	BrvdCt	A+	127	498	144	29	5	4	(-	-)	195	65	50	72	42	0	65	2	3	1	31	11	17	.289	.346	.392	.738
2015	Biloxi	AA	129	512	157	37	7	8	(-	-)	232	74	69	83	30	1	73	3	4	3	25	8	17	.307	.347	.453	.800
2016	ColSpr	AAA	100	404	108	19	6	8	(-	-)	163	59	53	53	29	2	77	3	2	2	15	8	18	.267	.320	.403	.723
2016	Mil	NL	55	201	44	10	3	4	(2	2)	72	21	17	20	15	0	47	0	0	0	8	0	6	.219	.273	.358	.631

Oswaldo Arcia

Bats: L **Throws:** R **Pos:** RF-39;LF-19;PH-13;DH-4;PR-1   ARR-see-ya   **Ht:** 6'0" **Wt:** 225 **Born:** 5/9/1991 **Age:** 26

								BATTING											RUNNING			AVERAGES			
Year	Team	Lg	G	AB	H	2B	3B	HR	(Hm | Rd)	TB	R	RBI	RC	TBB	IBB	SO	HBP	SH	SF	SB	CS	GDP	Avg	OBP	Slg	OPS
2013	Min	AL	97	351	88	17	2	14	(6 | 8)	151	34	43	37	23	0	117	4	0	0	1	2	4	.251	.304	.430	.734
2014	Min	AL	103	372	86	16	3	20	(12 | 8)	168	46	57	51	31	4	127	6	0	1	1	2	6	.231	.300	.452	.752
2015	Min	AL	19	58	16	0	0	2	(2 | 0)	22	6	8	8	4	4	15	2	0	1	0	0	2	.276	.338	.379	.718
2016	4 Tms		69	202	41	7	1	8	(3 | 5)	74	17	23	20	18	0	80	1	0	1	1	1	1	.203	.270	.366	.637
16	Min	AL	32	103	22	4	0	4	(2 | 2)	38	8	12	11	10	0	46	1	0	0	0	0	1	.214	.289	.369	.658
16	TB	AL	21	54	14	2	1	2	(1 | 1)	24	7	7	8	6	0	19	0	0	1	1	1	0	.259	.328	.444	.772
16	Mia	NL	2	2	0	0	0	0	(0 | 0)	0	0	0	0	0	0	1	0	0	0	0	0	0	.000	.000	.000	.000
16	SD	NL	14	43	5	1	0	2	(0 | 2)	12	2	4	1	2	0	14	0	0	0	0	0	0	.116	.156	.279	.435
4 ML YEARS			288	983	231	40	6	44	(23 | 21)	415	103	131	116	76	8	339	13	0	3	3	5	13	.235	.298	.422	.720

Nolan Arenado

Bats: R **Throws:** R **Pos:** 3B-160   ahr-eh-NOD-oh   **Ht:** 6'2" **Wt:** 205 **Born:** 4/16/1991 **Age:** 26

								BATTING											RUNNING			AVERAGES			
Year	Team	Lg	G	AB	H	2B	3B	HR	(Hm	Rd)	TB	R	RBI	RC	TBB	IBB	SO	HBP	SH	SF	SB	CS	GDP	Avg	OBP	Slg	OPS
2013	Col	NL	133	486	130	29	4	10	(5	5)	197	49	52	48	23	1	72	1	2	2	2	0	16	.267	.301	.405	.706
2014	Col	NL	111	432	124	34	2	18	(16	2)	216	58	61	60	25	1	58	4	1	5	2	1	13	.287	.328	.500	.828
2015	Col	NL	157	616	177	43	4	42	(20	22)	354	97	130	116	34	13	110	4	0	11	2	5	17	.287	.323	.575	.898
2016	Col	NL	160	618	182	35	6	41	(25	16)	352	116	133	128	68	10	103	2	0	8	2	3	17	.294	.362	.570	.932
4 ML YEARS			561	2152	613	141	16	111	(66	45)	1119	320	376	352	150	25	343	11	3	26	8	9	63	.285	.331	.520	.851

Shawn Armstrong

Pitches: R **Bats:** R **Pos:** RP-10   **Ht:** 6'2" **Wt:** 225 **Born:** 9/11/1990 **Age:** 26

			HOW MUCH HE PITCHED						WHAT HE GAVE UP											THE RESULTS						
Year	Team	Lg	G	GS	CG	GF	IP	BFP	H	R	ER	HR	SH	SF	HB	TBB	IBB	SO	WP	Bk	W	L	Pct	Sh	Sv-Op	Hld	ERC	ERA
2012	2 Tms	Low	28	0	0	13	47.1	196	32	10	10	0	2	1	6	25	1	56	3	1	1	3	.250	0	1- -	-	2.65	1.90
2012	Akron	AA	17	0	0	7	20.1	81	12	2	2	0	0	0	1	12	0	22	1	0	1	0	1.000	0	3- -	-	2.27	0.89
2013	Akron	AA	30	0	0	5	33.0	153	32	18	15	2	2	1	2	21	0	43	2	0	2	3	.400	0	0- -	-	4.69	4.09
2014	Akron	AA	44	0	0	34	51.0	207	39	12	12	3	2	0	1	19	1	68	2	0	6	2	.750	0	15- -	-	2.53	2.12
2014	Clmbs	AAA	5	0	0	1	5.0	22	4	3	3	1	0	2	0	3	0	4	2	0	0	0	-	0	0- -	-	4.36	5.40
2015	Clmbs	AAA	46	0	0	27	49.2	210	37	15	13	0	0	0	4	26	2	80	4	0	1	2	.333	0	16- -	-	2.57	2.36
2016	Clmbs	AAA	47	0	0	22	49.0	204	27	11	10	0	2	1	3	29	1	72	3	0	3	1	.750	0	9- -	-	1.96	1.84
2015	Cle	AL	8	0	0	5	8.0	30	5	2	2	1	0	0	0	2	0	11	0	0	0	0	-	0	0-0	0	1.84	2.25
2016	Cle	AL	10	0	0	2	10.2	44	9	3	3	1	1	0	0	5	2	7	1	0	0	0	-	0	0-0	0	3.25	2.53
2 ML YEARS			18	0	0	7	18.2	74	14	5	5	2	1	0	0	7	2	18	1	0	0	0	-	0	0-0	0	2.63	2.41

Jonathan Aro

Pitches: R **Bats:** R **Pos:** RP-1   ah-ROW   **Ht:** 6'0" **Wt:** 235 **Born:** 10/10/1990 **Age:** 26

			HOW MUCH HE PITCHED						WHAT HE GAVE UP											THE RESULTS						
Year	Team	Lg	G	GS	CG	GF	IP	BFP	H	R	ER	HR	SH	SF	HB	TBB	IBB	SO	WP	Bk	W	L	Pct	Sh	Sv-Op	Hld	ERC	ERA
2012	RedSx	R	11	4	0	3	38.2	163	45	21	20	4	1	0	0	9	0	34	5	0	3	4	.429	0	0- -	-	4.46	4.66
2013	Lowell	A-	15	1	0	9	54.2	219	44	17	13	2	4	3	2	12	2	49	1	0	5	3	.625	0	3- -	-	2.09	2.14
2014	2 Tms	Low	32	1	0	25	87.0	355	64	33	21	4	7	1	3	29	0	98	3	0	3	3	.500	0	8- -	-	2.21	2.17
2015	Portlnd	AA	8	0	0	3	22.1	94	15	12	7	0	1	1	1	8	0	19	0	0	3	2	.600	0	0- -	-	1.68	2.82
2015	Pwtckt	AAA	26	0	0	7	51.2	207	43	18	18	2	0	2	4	10	0	53	0	0	1	0	1.000	0	2- -	-	2.35	3.14
2016	Tacom	AAA	24	1	0	8	36.1	145	29	13	10	2	2	2	0	10	0	25	1	0	3	2	.600	0	1- -	-	2.30	2.48
2015	Bos	AL	6	0	0	2	10.1	49	15	8	8	2	0	1	0	4	0	8	0	0	0	1	.000	0	0-0	0	7.50	6.97
2016	Sea	AL	1	0	0	0	0.2	4	1	0	0	0	0	0	0	1	0	0	0	0	0	0	-	0	0-0	1	10.76	0.00
2 ML YEARS			7	0	0	2	11.0	53	16	8	8	2	0	1	0	5	0	8	0	0	0	1	.000	0	0-0	0	7.73	6.55

Jake Arrieta

Pitches: R **Bats:** R **Pos:** SP-31   air-ee-ETT-uh   **Ht:** 6'4" **Wt:** 225 **Born:** 3/6/1986 **Age:** 31

			HOW MUCH HE PITCHED						WHAT HE GAVE UP											THE RESULTS						
Year	Team	Lg	G	GS	CG	GF	IP	BFP	H	R	ER	HR	SH	SF	HB	TBB	IBB	SO	WP	Bk	W	L	Pct	Sh	Sv-Op	Hld	ERC	ERA
2010	Bal	AL	18	18	0	0	100.1	449	106	57	52	9	4	2	4	48	3	52	5	0	6	6	.500	0	0-0	0	4.74	4.66
2011	Bal	AL	22	22	0	0	119.1	523	115	70	67	21	3	2	4	59	2	93	0	0	10	8	.556	0	0-0	0	4.93	5.05
2012	Bal	AL	24	18	0	1	114.2	496	122	82	79	16	3	4	5	35	3	109	4	0	3	9	.250	0	0-0	1	4.47	6.20
2013	2 Tms		14	14	0	0	75.1	324	59	41	40	9	2	3	5	41	1	60	1	0	5	4	.556	0	0-0	0	3.82	4.78
2014	ChC	NL	25	25	1	0	156.2	614	114	46	44	5	5	3	4	41	2	167	8	0	10	5	.667	1	0-0	0	1.85	2.53
2015	ChC	NL	33	33	4	0	229.0	870	150	52	45	10	4	1	6	48	2	236	6	0	22	6	.786	3	0-0	0	1.53	1.77
2016	ChC	NL	31	31	1	0	197.1	795	138	72	68	16	2	1	6	76	1	190	16	0	18	8	.692	1	0-0	0	2.45	3.10
13	Bal	AL	5	5	0	0	23.2	111	25	19	19	2	0	3	2	17	1	23	1	0	1	2	.333	0	0-0	0	5.91	7.23
13	ChC	NL	9	9	0	0	51.2	213	34	22	21	7	2	0	3	24	0	37	0	0	4	2	.667	0	0-0	0	2.94	3.66
Postseason			3	3	1	0	19.2	78	14	8	8	2	0	0	3	4	1	28	0	0	2	1	.667	1	0-0	0	2.38	3.66
7 ML YEARS			167	161	6	1	992.2	4071	804	420	395	86	23	16	33	348	14	907	40	0	74	46	.617	5	0-0	1	2.91	3.58

Cody Asche

Bats: L **Throws:** R **Pos:** LF-57;PH-15   ASH-ee   **Ht:** 6'1" **Wt:** 205 **Born:** 6/30/1990 **Age:** 27

								BATTING											RUNNING			AVERAGES			
Year Team	Lg	G	AB	H	2B	3B	HR	(Hm | Rd)	TB	R	RBI	RC	TBB	IBB	SO	HBP	SH	SF	SB	CS	GDP	Avg	OBP	Slg	OPS
2016 LV*	AAA	29	111	31	8	0	6	(- | -)	57	20	15	20	11	0	26	1	0	1	0	1	1	.279	.350	.514	.863
2013 Phi	NL	50	162	38	8	1	5	(4 | 1)	63	18	22	18	15	3	43	1	0	1	1	0	1	.235	.302	.389	.691
2014 Phi	NL	121	397	100	25	0	10	(6 | 4)	155	43	46	44	33	4	102	0	3	1	0	1	7	.252	.309	.390	.699
2015 Phi	NL	129	425	104	22	3	12	(5 | 7)	168	41	39	47	26	3	111	4	0	1	1	2	4	.245	.294	.395	.689
2016 Phi	NL	71	197	42	15	0	4	(3 | 1)	69	22	18	17	18	0	54	2	0	1	3	1	1	.213	.284	.350	.635
4 ML YEARS		371	1181	284	70	4	31	(18 | 13)	455	124	125	126	92	10	310	7	3	4	5	4	13	.240	.298	.385	.684

Alec Asher

Pitches: R **Bats:** R **Pos:** SP-5   **Ht:** 6'4" **Wt:** 230 **Born:** 10/4/1991 **Age:** 25

			HOW MUCH HE PITCHED					WHAT HE GAVE UP												THE RESULTS						
Year Team	Lg	G	GS	CG	GF	IP	BFP	H	R	ER	HR	SH	SF	HB	TBB	IBB	SO	WP	Bk	W	L	Pct	Sh	Sv-Op	Hld	ERC	ERA
2012 Spkane	A-	20	0	0	13	35.0	145	29	12	12	4	1	1	1	11	0	50	1	1	2	3	.400	0	5- -	-	2.99	3.09
2013 MrtlBh	A+	26	25	0	0	133.1	562	120	60	43	10	3	3	6	40	1	139	6	2	9	7	.563	0	0- -	-	3.10	2.90
2014 Frisco	AA	28	28	0	0	154.0	631	139	74	65	18	6	6	3	32	1	122	6	0	11	11	.500	0	0- -	-	2.96	3.80
2015 Frisco	AA	8	8	0	0	43.0	183	39	20	19	3	1	0	2	18	0	43	5	0	1	4	.200	0	0- -	-	3.63	3.98
2015 RdRck	AAA	12	12	0	0	64.2	277	71	36	34	16	1	1	0	19	0	54	4	0	3	6	.333	0	0- -	-	5.27	4.73
2016 Rdng	AA	5	5	0	0	29.1	123	29	12	11	1	2	1	0	5	0	21	0	0	1	2	.333	0	0- -	-	2.63	3.38
2015 Phi	NL	7	7	0	0	29.0	138	42	30	30	8	2	1	1	10	0	16	2	2	0	6	.000	0	0-0	0	8.10	9.31
2016 Phi	NL	5	5	0	0	27.2	111	22	11	7	1	2	1	2	4	0	13	0	0	2	1	.667	0	0-0	0	1.93	2.28
2 ML YEARS		12	12	0	0	56.2	249	64	41	37	9	4	2	3	14	0	29	2	2	2	7	.222	0	0-0	0	4.76	5.88

Carlos Asuaje

Bats: L **Throws:** R **Pos:** 2B-6;PH-1   a-SWAH-hay   **Ht:** 5'9" **Wt:** 160 **Born:** 11/2/1991 **Age:** 25

								BATTING											RUNNING			AVERAGES			
Year Team	Lg	G	AB	H	2B	3B	HR	(Hm	Rd)	TB	R	RBI	RC	TBB	IBB	SO	HBP	SH	SF	SB	CS	GDP	Avg	OBP	Slg	OPS
2013 Lowell	A-	52	171	46	12	1	1	(-	-)	63	19	20	25	27	0	33	1	2	3	4	3	3	.269	.366	.368	.735
2014 2 Tms	Low	129	480	149	38	12	15	(-	-)	256	86	101	100	59	0	90	11	2	7	8	7	8	.310	.393	.533	.927
2015 Portlnd	AA	131	495	123	23	7	8	(-	-)	184	60	61	65	56	1	88	7	10	2	9	6	8	.248	.332	.372	.704
2016 ElPaso	AAA	134	535	172	32	11	9	(-	-)	253	98	69	97	49	0	82	3	5	5	10	5	10	.321	.378	.473	.851
2016 SD	NL	7	24	5	2	0	0	(0	0)	7	2	2	3	1	0	4	0	0	0	0	0	0	.208	.240	.292	.532

Tyler Austin

Bats: R **Throws:** R **Pos:** 1B-27;RF-3;PH-3;LF-2;DH-1   **Ht:** 6'2" **Wt:** 220 **Born:** 9/6/1991 **Age:** 25

								BATTING											RUNNING			AVERAGES			
Year Team	Lg	G	AB	H	2B	3B	HR	(Hm	Rd)	TB	R	RBI	RC	TBB	IBB	SO	HBP	SH	SF	SB	CS	GDP	Avg	OBP	Slg	OPS
2012 3 Tms	Low	108	406	131	35	6	17	(-	-)	229	90	79	92	50	3	97	5	0	3	23	2	10	.323	.401	.564	.965
2013 Trntn	AA	83	319	82	17	1	6	(-	-)	119	43	40	45	41	0	79	3	0	3	4	0	12	.257	.344	.373	.717
2014 Trntn	AA	105	396	109	20	5	9	(-	-)	166	56	47	58	36	0	80	2	0	3	3	2	7	.275	.336	.419	.756
2015 S-WB	AAA	73	264	62	8	0	4	(-	-)	82	33	27	28	26	0	81	4	1	4	8	1	15	.235	.309	.311	.619
2015 Trntn	AA	21	77	20	5	2	2	(-	-)	35	8	8	12	8	0	16	1	0	0	3	2	4	.260	.337	.455	.792
2016 Trntn	AA	50	177	46	10	1	4	(-	-)	70	22	29	28	30	0	46	1	0	2	1	1	5	.260	.367	.395	.762
2016 S-WB	AAA	57	201	65	24	0	13	(-	-)	128	39	49	51	32	0	59	0	0	1	5	0	9	.323	.415	.637	1.051
2016 NYY	AL	31	83	20	3	0	5	(5	0)	38	7	12	12	7	0	36	0	0	0	1	0	1	.241	.300	.458	.758

Alex Avila

Bats: L **Throws:** R **Pos:** C-54;DH-2;PH-1   ah-VEE-lah   **Ht:** 5'11" **Wt:** 210 **Born:** 1/29/1987 **Age:** 30

								BATTING											RUNNING			AVERAGES			
Year Team	Lg	G	AB	H	2B	3B	HR	(Hm	Rd)	TB	R	RBI	RC	TBB	IBB	SO	HBP	SH	SF	SB	CS	GDP	Avg	OBP	Slg	OPS
2009 Det	AL	29	61	17	4	0	5	(4	1)	36	9	14	12	10	0	18	0	0	1	0	0	0	.279	.375	.590	.965
2010 Det	AL	104	294	67	12	0	7	(4	3)	100	28	31	26	36	0	71	2	1	0	2	2	12	.228	.316	.340	.656
2011 Det	AL	141	464	137	33	4	19	(10	9)	235	63	82	86	73	9	131	3	3	8	3	1	8	.295	.389	.506	.895
2012 Det	AL	116	367	89	21	2	9	(7	2)	141	42	48	53	61	2	104	2	2	2	2	0	12	.243	.352	.384	.736
2013 Det	AL	102	330	75	14	1	11	(7	4)	124	39	47	37	44	0	112	1	1	3	0	0	10	.227	.317	.376	.693
2014 Det	AL	124	390	85	22	0	11	(3	8)	140	44	47	48	61	1	151	3	1	2	0	3	6	.218	.327	.359	.686
2015 Det	AL	67	178	34	5	0	4	(2	2)	51	21	13	20	40	0	66	0	1	0	0	1	4	.191	.339	.287	.626
2016 CWS	AL	57	169	36	6	0	7	(5	2)	63	19	11	17	38	0	78	1	0	1	0	0	3	.213	.359	.373	.732
Postseason		34	110	16	2	0	3	(2	1)	27	6	7	4	11	0	43	1	1	0	0	0	1	.145	.230	.245	.475
8 ML YEARS		740	2253	540	117	7	73	(42	31)	890	265	293	299	363	12	731	12	9	17	7	7	55	.240	.346	.395	.741

Luis Avilan

Pitches: L **Bats:** L **Pos:** RP-27   ah-VEE-lan   **Ht:** 6'2" **Wt:** 225 **Born:** 7/19/1989 **Age:** 27

				HOW MUCH HE PITCHED					WHAT HE GAVE UP											THE RESULTS						
Year Team	Lg	G	GS	CG	GF	IP	BFP	H	R	ER	HR	SH	SF	HB	TBB	IBB	SO	WP	Bk	W	L	Pct	Sh	Sv-Op	Hld	ERC	ERA
2016 OkCity*	AAA	33	0	0	10	34.0	154	35	19	16	3	1	2	3	16	3	37	1	0	0	3	.000	0	4- -	-	4.58	4.24
2012 Atl	NL	31	0	0	2	36.0	142	27	9	8	1	3	0	1	10	1	33	3	1	1	0	1.000	0	0-0	5	2.00	2.00
2013 Atl	NL	75	0	0	7	65.0	256	40	12	11	1	1	1	4	22	2	38	3	1	5	0	1.000	0	0-2	27	1.62	1.52
2014 Atl	NL	62	0	0	14	43.1	193	47	22	22	2	3	2	3	21	7	25	5	0	4	1	.800	0	0-2	8	4.55	4.57
2015 2 Tms	NL	73	0	0	9	53.1	220	48	24	24	6	1	2	1	15	2	49	2	1	2	5	.286	0	0-3	17	3.18	4.05
2016 LAD	NL	27	0	0	3	19.2	82	12	8	7	0	2	0	2	10	4	28	1	0	3	0	1.000	0	0-1	3	1.84	3.20

Year	Team	Lg	G	GS	CG	GF	IP	BFP	H	R	ER	HR	SH	SF	HB	TBB	IBB	SO	WP	Bk	W	L	Pct	Sh	Sv-Op	Hld	ERC	ERA
15	Atl	NL	50	0	0	7	37.2	154	35	15	15	4	0	1	0	10	2	31	1	1	2	4	.333	0	0-3	11	3.16	3.58
15	LAD	NL	23	0	0	2	15.2	66	13	9	9	2	1	1	0	5	0	18	1	0	0	1	.000	0	0-0	6	3.21	5.17
	Postseason		6	0	0	2	4.0	15	3	0	0	0	0	0	0	1	1	3	0	0	0	0	-	0	0-0	2	1.51	0.00
	5 ML YEARS		268	0	0	35	217.1	893	174	75	72	10	10	5	11	78	16	173	14	3	15	6	.714	0	0-8	60	2.61	2.98

Mike Aviles

uh-VEE-less

Bats: R **Throws:** R **Pos:** RF-32;2B-10;3B-9;PH-9;LF-8;SS-6;CF-1;DH-1;PR-1 **Ht:** 5'10" **Wt:** 205 **Born:** 3/13/1981 **Age:** 36

Year	Team	Lg	G	AB	H	2B	3B	HR	(Hm	Rd)	TB	R	RBI	RC	TBB	IBB	SO	HBP	SH	SF	SB	CS	GDP	Avg	OBP	Slg	OPS
2008	KC	AL	102	419	136	27	4	10	(4	6)	201	68	51	62	18	4	58	2	0	2	8	3	12	.325	.354	.480	.833
2009	KC	AL	36	120	22	3	1	1	(1	0)	30	10	8	4	4	0	26	0	2	1	1	0	3	.183	.208	.250	.458
2010	KC	AL	110	424	129	16	3	8	(4	4)	175	63	32	47	20	0	49	1	0	3	14	5	13	.304	.335	.413	.748
2011	2 Tms	AL	91	286	73	17	3	7	(4	3)	117	31	39	31	13	0	44	2	4	4	14	4	8	.255	.289	.409	.698
2012	Bos	AL	136	512	128	28	0	13	(7	6)	195	57	60	57	23	0	77	2	3	6	14	6	6	.250	.282	.381	.663
2013	Cle	AL	124	361	91	15	0	9	(3	6)	133	54	46	35	15	0	41	3	7	8	8	5	11	.252	.282	.368	.650
2014	Cle	AL	113	344	85	16	1	5	(2	3)	118	38	39	27	13	0	49	1	11	5	14	5	10	.247	.273	.343	.616
2015	Cle	AL	98	290	67	10	0	5	(1	4)	92	37	17	19	20	0	38	1	5	1	3	1	18	.231	.282	.317	.599
2016	Det	AL	68	167	35	5	1	1	(1	0)	45	17	6	9	9	0	27	2	3	0	2	2	5	.210	.258	.269	.528
11	KC	AL	53	185	41	11	3	5	(2	3)	73	14	31	18	9	0	27	2	3	3	10	2	5	.222	.261	.395	.656
11	Bos	AL	38	101	32	6	0	2	(2	0)	44	17	8	13	4	0	17	0	1	1	4	2	3	.317	.340	.436	.775
	9 ML YEARS		878	2923	766	137	13	59	(27	32)	1106	375	298	291	135	4	409	14	35	30	78	31	86	.262	.295	.378	.673

John Axford

Pitches: R **Bats:** R **Pos:** RP-68 **Ht:** 6'5" **Wt:** 220 **Born:** 4/1/1983 **Age:** 34

Year	Team	Lg	G	GS	CG	GF	IP	BFP	H	R	ER	HR	SH	SF	HB	TBB	IBB	SO	WP	Bk	W	L	Pct	Sh	Sv-Op	Hld	ERC	ERA
2009	Mil	NL	7	0	0	6	7.2	34	5	3	3	0	0	0	0	6	1	9	1	0	0	0	-	0	1-1	0	2.62	3.52
2010	Mil	NL	50	0	0	43	58.0	238	42	17	16	1	2	2	1	27	3	76	4	0	8	2	.800	0	24-27	0	2.33	2.48
2011	Mil	NL	74	0	0	63	73.2	305	59	19	16	4	1	1	0	25	1	86	8	0	2	2	.500	0	46-48	0	2.44	1.95
2012	Mil	NL	75	0	0	54	69.1	310	61	42	36	10	1	2	2	39	2	93	10	0	5	8	.385	0	35-44	3	4.33	4.67
2013	2 Tms	NL	75	0	0	16	65.0	289	73	32	29	10	4	1	2	26	3	65	5	0	7	7	.500	0	0-7	19	5.25	4.02
2014	2 Tms	NL	62	0	0	28	54.2	243	43	26	24	6	3	4	2	36	3	63	5	0	2	4	.333	0	10-13	2	3.96	3.95
2015	Col	NL	60	0	0	43	55.2	250	56	27	26	4	0	2	0	32	4	62	1	0	4	5	.444	0	25-31	2	4.45	4.20
2016	Oak	AL	68	0	0	13	65.2	289	65	30	29	6	2	2	3	30	1	60	4	0	6	4	.600	0	3-10	15	4.33	3.97
13	Mil	NL	62	0	0	13	54.2	245	62	29	27	10	3	1	1	23	3	54	5	0	6	7	.462	0	0-6	19	5.53	4.45
13	StL	NL	13	0	0	3	10.1	44	11	3	2	0	1	0	1	3	0	11	0	0	1	0	1.000	0	0-1	0	3.75	1.74
14	Cle	AL	49	0	0	24	43.2	196	34	21	19	6	3	3	1	30	3	51	4	0	2	3	.400	0	10-13	2	4.11	3.92
14	Pit	NL	13	0	0	4	11.0	47	9	5	5	0	0	1	1	6	0	12	1	0	0	1	.000	0	0-0	0	3.33	4.09
	Postseason		12	0	0	8	12.2	51	7	2	2	1	0	0	0	6	0	18	0	0	1	0	1.000	0	3-4	0	1.91	1.42
	8 ML YEARS		471	0	0	266	449.2	1958	404	196	179	41	13	14	10	221	18	514	38	0	34	32	.515	0	144-181	44	3.79	3.58

Erick Aybar

Bats: B **Throws:** R **Pos:** SS-104;3B-12;PH-10;2B-7;PR-3 EYE-barr **Ht:** 5'10" **Wt:** 195 **Born:** 1/14/1984 **Age:** 33

Year	Team	Lg	G	AB	H	2B	3B	HR	(Hm	Rd)	TB	R	RBI	RC	TBB	IBB	SO	HBP	SH	SF	SB	CS	GDP	Avg	OBP	Slg	OPS
2006	LAA	AL	34	40	10	1	1	0	(0	0)	13	5	2	4	0	0	8	0	0	0	1	0	1	.250	.250	.325	.575
2007	LAA	AL	79	194	46	5	1	1	(0	1)	56	18	19	16	10	0	32	2	3	2	4	4	8	.237	.279	.289	.568
2008	LAA	AL	98	346	96	18	5	3	(2	1)	133	53	39	49	14	0	45	5	9	1	7	2	2	.277	.314	.384	.699
2009	LAA	AL	137	504	157	23	9	5	(2	3)	213	70	58	73	30	1	54	5	12	5	14	7	9	.312	.353	.423	.776
2010	LAA	AL	138	534	135	18	4	5	(3	2)	176	69	29	51	35	1	81	7	11	2	22	8	7	.253	.306	.330	.636
2011	LAA	AL	143	556	155	33	8	10	(2	8)	234	71	59	72	31	1	68	6	9	3	30	6	13	.279	.322	.421	.743
2012	LAA	AL	141	517	150	31	5	8	(4	4)	215	67	45	63	22	1	61	5	7	2	20	4	11	.290	.324	.416	.740
2013	LAA	AL	138	550	149	33	5	6	(4	2)	210	68	54	61	23	1	59	3	8	5	12	7	14	.271	.301	.382	.683
2014	LAA	AL	156	589	164	30	4	7	(2	5)	223	77	68	74	36	4	62	3	5	8	16	9	10	.278	.321	.379	.700
2015	LAA	AL	156	597	161	30	1	3	(1	2)	202	74	44	60	25	1	73	4	7	5	15	6	12	.270	.301	.338	.639
2016	2 Tms		126	415	101	19	2	3	(0	3)	133	34	34	37	31	6	70	6	3	4	3	5	15	.243	.303	.320	.623
16	Atl	NL	97	335	81	14	2	2	(0	2)	105	27	26	26	20	5	59	6	3	4	3	5	14	.242	.293	.313	.607
16	Det	AL	29	80	20	5	0	1	(0	1)	28	7	8	11	11	1	11	0	0	0	0	0	1	.250	.341	.350	.691
	Postseason		17	61	16	3	1	0	(0	0)	21	4	4	7	1	0	5	0	4	0	4	0	2	.262	.274	.344	.618
	11 ML YEARS		1346	4842	1324	241	45	51	(20	31)	1808	606	451	560	257	16	613	48	72	37	144	58	102	.273	.314	.373	.688

Javier Baez

BYE-ezz

Bats: R **Throws:** R **Pos:** 3B-62;2B-59;SS-25;PH-18;1B-6;PR-3;LF-2 **Ht:** 6'0" **Wt:** 190 **Born:** 12/1/1992 **Age:** 24

Year	Team	Lg	G	AB	H	2B	3B	HR	(Hm	Rd)	TB	R	RBI	RC	TBB	IBB	SO	HBP	SH	SF	SB	CS	GDP	Avg	OBP	Slg	OPS
2014	ChC	NL	52	213	36	6	0	9	(3	6)	69	25	20	12	15	0	95	1	0	0	5	1	5	.169	.227	.324	.551
2015	ChC	NL	28	76	22	6	1	1	(1	0)	31	4	4	5	4	1	24	0	0	0	1	2	0	.289	.325	.408	.733
2016	ChC	NL	142	421	115	19	1	14	(8	6)	178	50	59	53	15	3	108	11	1	2	12	3	8	.273	.314	.423	.737
	Postseason		6	15	5	0	0	1	(1	0)	8	1	3	4	0	0	4	0	0	0	2	0	0	.333	.333	.533	.867
	3 ML YEARS		222	710	173	31	1	24	(12	12)	278	79	83	70	34	4	227	12	1	2	18	6	13	.244	.289	.392	.680

Pedro Baez

Pitches: R **Bats:** R **Pos:** RP-73   BYE-ezz   **Ht:** 6'0" **Wt:** 235 **Born:** 3/11/1988 **Age:** 29

Year Team	Lg	G	GS	CG	GF	IP	BFP	H	R	ER	HR	SH	SF	HB	TBB	IBB	SO	WP	Bk	W	L	Pct	Sh	Sv-Op	Hld	ERC	ERA
2014 LAD	NL	20	0	0	8	24.0	92	16	7	7	3	1	0	0	5	1	18	0	0	0	0	-	0	0-0	5	1.79	2.63
2015 LAD	NL	52	0	0	8	51.0	208	47	22	19	4	3	3	1	11	1	60	1	1	4	2	.667	0	0-3	11	2.87	3.35
2016 LAD	NL	73	0	0	10	74.0	295	52	27	25	11	1	2	2	22	0	83	3	2	3	2	.600	0	0-2	23	2.52	3.04
Postseason		4	0	0	0	2.2	15	3	5	5	1	0	0	1	3	0	3	0	0	0	0	-	0	0-0	0	12.09	16.88
3 ML YEARS		145	0	0	26	149.0	595	115	56	51	18	5	6	3	38	2	161	4	3	7	4	.636	0	0-5	39	2.52	3.08

Andrew Bailey

Pitches: R **Bats:** R **Pos:** RP-45   **Ht:** 6'3" **Wt:** 240 **Born:** 5/31/1984 **Age:** 33

Year Team	Lg	G	GS	CG	GF	IP	BFP	H	R	ER	HR	SH	SF	HB	TBB	IBB	SO	WP	Bk	W	L	Pct	Sh	Sv-Op	Hld	ERC	ERA
2016 LV*	AAA	5	0	0	3	6.0	24	4	1	1	0	0	0	0	2	0	12	1	0	1	0	1.000	0	1--	-	1.57	1.50
2016 Salt Lk*	AAA	8	0	0	1	9.0	37	7	3	2	0	1	0	0	3	0	11	0	0	2	1	.667	0	0--	-	2.01	2.00
2009 Oak	AL	68	0	0	54	83.1	323	49	17	17	5	3	2	0	24	3	91	6	0	6	3	.667	0	26-30	2	1.44	1.84
2010 Oak	AL	47	0	0	42	49.0	189	34	8	8	3	2	3	0	13	1	42	0	0	1	3	.250	0	25-28	1	1.82	1.47
2011 Oak	AL	42	0	0	37	41.2	170	34	18	15	3	1	1	0	12	2	41	0	0	0	4	.000	0	24-26	1	2.42	3.24
2012 Bos	AL	19	0	0	13	15.1	74	21	12	12	2	0	0	0	8	2	14	0	1	1	1	.500	0	6-9	1	6.73	7.04
2013 Bos	AL	30	0	0	17	28.2	116	23	12	12	7	1	0	0	12	0	39	0	0	3	1	.750	0	8-13	8	4.13	3.77
2015 NYY	AL	10	0	0	3	8.2	41	9	8	5	2	0	2	0	5	1	6	0	0	0	1	.000	0	0-0	0	6.39	5.19
2016 2 Tms	AL	45	0	0	14	43.2	190	41	26	26	7	3	3	2	17	0	41	3	1	3	1	.750	0	6-7	4	4.23	5.36
16 Phi	NL	33	0	0	4	32.1	144	32	23	23	6	3	2	1	15	0	33	2	1	3	1	.750	0	0-1	4	4.95	6.40
16 LAA	AL	12	0	0	10	11.1	46	9	3	3	1	0	1	1	2	0	8	1	0	0	0	-	0	6-6	0	2.38	2.38
7 ML YEARS		261	0	0	180	270.1	1103	211	101	95	29	10	11	2	91	9	274	9	2	14	14	.500	0	95-113	16	2.71	3.16

Homer Bailey

Pitches: R **Bats:** R **Pos:** SP-6   **Ht:** 6'4" **Wt:** 225 **Born:** 5/3/1986 **Age:** 31

Year Team	Lg	G	GS	CG	GF	IP	BFP	H	R	ER	HR	SH	SF	HB	TBB	IBB	SO	WP	Bk	W	L	Pct	Sh	Sv-Op	Hld	ERC	ERA
2016 Lsvlle*	AAA	7	7	0	0	24.0	113	31	17	15	7	0	1	1	9	0	19	1	1	1	2	.333	0	0--	-	7.24	5.63
2007 Cin	NL	9	9	0	0	45.1	205	43	32	29	3	1	6	3	28	1	28	1	1	4	2	.667	0	0-0	0	4.61	5.76
2008 Cin	NL	8	8	0	0	36.1	180	59	36	32	8	5	2	0	17	1	18	4	1	0	6	.000	0	0-0	0	9.31	7.93
2009 Cin	NL	20	20	0	0	113.1	496	115	61	57	12	4	4	3	52	1	86	6	0	8	5	.615	0	0-0	0	4.56	4.53
2010 Cin	NL	19	19	1	0	109.0	465	109	55	54	11	2	1	3	40	6	100	3	1	4	3	.571	1	0-0	0	4.01	4.46
2011 Cin	NL	22	22	0	0	132.0	561	136	68	65	18	4	4	5	33	2	106	4	0	9	7	.563	0	0-0	0	4.01	4.43
2012 Cin	NL	33	33	2	0	208.0	874	206	97	85	26	5	5	8	52	3	168	3	0	13	10	.565	1	0-0	0	3.73	3.68
2013 Cin	NL	32	32	2	0	209.0	849	181	85	81	20	8	4	10	54	2	199	5	2	11	12	.478	1	0-0	0	2.99	3.49
2014 Cin	NL	23	23	1	0	145.2	604	134	60	60	16	5	4	7	45	1	124	5	1	9	5	.643	1	0-0	0	3.57	3.71
2015 Cin	NL	2	2	0	0	11.1	51	16	7	7	3	0	0	0	4	2	3	0	0	1	1	1.000	0	0-0	0	7.64	5.56
2016 Cin	NL	6	6	0	0	23.0	111	35	19	17	2	0	2	2	7	0	27	1	0	2	3	.400	0	0-0	0	7.04	6.65
Postseason		2	1	0	0	9.0	32	3	1	1	0	1	1	1	1	0	12	0	0	0	0	-	0	0-0	0	0.52	1.00
10 ML YEARS		174	174	6	0	1033.0	4396	1034	520	487	119	34	32	41	332	19	859	32	6	60	54	.526	4	0-0	0	4.02	4.24

Jett Bandy

Bats: R **Throws:** R **Pos:** C-68;PH-3;DH-1;PR-1   **Ht:** 6'4" **Wt:** 235 **Born:** 3/26/1990 **Age:** 27

Year Team	Lg	G	AB	H	2B	3B	HR	(Hm	Rd)	TB	R	RBI	RC	TBB	IBB	SO	HBP	SH	SF	SB	CS	GDP	Avg	OBP	Slg	OPS
2012 InldEm	A+	94	324	80	22	1	7	(-	-)	125	42	46	42	20	1	51	15	3	3	1	1	5	.247	.318	.386	.703
2013 Ark	AA	78	245	59	17	2	4	(-	-)	92	26	28	29	14	0	39	9	1	3	0	1	5	.241	.303	.376	.678
2014 Ark	AA	93	312	78	12	0	13	(-	-)	129	38	40	47	33	2	63	15	1	2	2	4	7	.250	.348	.413	.762
2015 Salt Lk	AAA	87	309	90	21	0	11	(-	-)	144	47	60	51	16	0	63	13	1	5	0	0	8	.291	.347	.466	.813
2016 Salt Lk	AAA	24	95	26	7	0	2	(-	-)	39	13	21	13	2	0	19	5	0	3	2	1	5	.274	.314	.411	.725
2015 LAA	AL	2	2	1	0	0	1	(0	1)	4	1	1	1	0	0	0	0	0	0	0	0	0	.500	.500	2.000	2.500
2016 LAA	AL	70	209	49	9	0	8	(6	2)	82	23	25	20	11	0	38	4	3	4	1	0	5	.234	.281	.392	.673
2 ML YEARS		72	211	50	9	0	9	(6	3)	86	24	26	21	11	0	38	4	3	4	1	0	5	.237	.283	.408	.690

Manny Banuelos

Pitches: L **Bats:** R **Pos:** P   ban-yoo-WAY-lohss   **Ht:** 5'10" **Wt:** 215 **Born:** 3/13/1991 **Age:** 26

Year Team	Lg	G	GS	CG	GF	IP	BFP	H	R	ER	HR	SH	SF	HB	TBB	IBB	SO	WP	Bk	W	L	Pct	Sh	Sv-Op	Hld	ERC	ERA
2012 S-WB	AAA	6	6	0	0	24.0	110	29	13	12	2	0	2	1	10	0	22	1	1	0	2	.000	0	0--	-	5.36	4.50
2014 Tampa	A+	5	5	0	0	12.1	50	10	4	4	0	0	0	1	2	0	14	1	0	0	0	-	0	0--	-	1.88	2.92
2014 Trntn	AA	17	16	0	0	49.0	206	40	28	25	8	0	2	3	19	0	44	8	0	1	3	.250	0	0--	-	3.67	4.59
2015 Gwnntt	AAA	16	16	1	0	84.2	350	64	24	21	2	3	3	6	40	0	69	4	0	6	2	.750	1	0--	-	2.85	2.23
2016 Gwnntt	AAA	9	9	0	0	30.1	140	31	19	16	2	2	1	0	22	0	21	5	0	0	2	.000	0	0--	-	5.26	4.75
2015 Atl	NL	7	6	0	0	26.1	121	30	17	15	4	0	0	3	12	0	19	1	0	1	4	.200	0	0-0	0	6.01	5.13

Johnny Barbato

Pitches: R Bats: R Pos: RP-13   Ht: 6'1" Wt: 235 Born: 7/11/1992 Age: 24

			HOW MUCH HE PITCHED						WHAT HE GAVE UP										THE RESULTS						
Year	Team	Lg	G	GS	CG	GF	IP	BFP	H	R	ER	HR	SH	SF	HB	TBB	IBB	SO	WP	Bk	W	L	Pct	Sh	Sv-Op	Hld	ERC	ERA
2012	FtWyn	A	48	0	0	14	73.1	303	52	23	15	4	2	2	2	31	1	84	4	0	6	1	.857	0	3--		2.39	1.84
2013	Lk Els	A+	49	7	0	26	88.0	381	90	54	49	8	5	3	6	33	0	89	1	0	3	6	.333	0	14--		4.35	5.01
2014	SnAnt	AA	27	0	0	22	31.1	129	26	12	10	3	3	0	1	10	0	33	3	0	2	2	.500	0	16--		2.94	2.87
2015	Trntn	AA	26	0	0	2	42.1	180	42	19	19	4	1	3	3	14	1	44	1	0	2	2	.500	0	0--		4.01	4.04
2015	S-WB	AAA	14	0	0	5	25.0	95	13	1	1	1	2	0	0	11	1	26	1	0	4	0	1.000	0	3--		1.54	0.36
2016	S-WB	AAA	31	1	0	13	48.1	203	38	17	14	3	0	1	1	23	0	49	1	0	3	2	.600	0	3--		3.04	2.61
2016	NYY	AL	13	0	0	5	13.0	57	13	11	11	2	0	0	2	5	0	15	0	0	1	2	.333	0	0-0	0	5.11	7.62

Austin Barnes

Bats: R Throws: R Pos: C-9;PH-8;2B-7;3B-1;PR-1   Ht: 5'10" Wt: 195 Born: 12/28/1989 Age: 27

						BATTING																RUNNING			AVERAGES			
Year	Team	Lg	G	AB	H	2B	3B	HR	(Hm	Rd)	TB	R	RBI	RC	TBB	IBB	SO	HBP	SH	SF	SB	CS	GDP	Avg	OBP	Slg	OPS
2012	Grnsbr	A	123	478	152	36	3	12	(-	-)	230	76	65	96	59	0	61	9	17	3	9	2	14	.318	.401	.481	.882
2013	Jupiter	A+	98	350	91	15	1	4	(-	-)	120	42	38	51	52	0	59	10	0	5	5	2	15	.260	.367	.343	.710
2013	Jaxnvl	AA	19	62	21	2	2	1	(-	-)	30	10	7	13	12	0	10	0	0	0	0	0	0	.339	.446	.484	.930
2014	Jupiter	A+	44	180	57	11	2	1	(-	-)	75	24	14	29	19	1	25	1	0	3	3	3	7	.317	.385	.417	.802
2014	Jaxnvl	AA	78	284	84	20	2	12	(-	-)	144	56	43	63	50	0	36	6	3	5	8	0	7	.296	.406	.507	.913
2015	OkCity	AAA	81	292	92	17	2	9	(-	-)	140	40	42	58	35	1	36	3	1	4	12	2	7	.315	.389	.479	.869
2016	OkCity	AAA	85	336	99	22	5	6	(-	-)	149	59	39	61	43	0	53	4	1	1	18	3	6	.295	.380	.443	.824
2015	LAD	NL	20	29	6	2	0	0	(0	0)	8	4	1	3	6	0	6	1	1	0	1	0	2	.207	.361	.276	.637
2016	LAD	NL	21	32	5	1	0	0	(0	0)	6	3	2	3	5	0	9	0	0	0	0	0	0	.156	.270	.188	.458
	2 ML YEARS		41	61	11	3	0	0	(0	0)	14	7	3	6	11	0	15	1	1	0	1	0	2	.180	.315	.230	.545

Brandon Barnes

Bats: R Throws: R Pos: LF-29;CF-13;PH-11;RF-2;PR-1   Ht: 6'2" Wt: 210 Born: 5/15/1986 Age: 31

						BATTING																RUNNING			AVERAGES			
Year	Team	Lg	G	AB	H	2B	3B	HR	(Hm	Rd)	TB	R	RBI	RC	TBB	IBB	SO	HBP	SH	SF	SB	CS	GDP	Avg	OBP	Slg	OPS
2016	Albq*	AAA	64	238	67	13	2	5	(-	-)	99	30	32	32	15	1	58	0	1	1	11	5	4	.282	.323	.416	.739
2012	Hou	NL	43	98	20	3	0	1	(0	1)	26	8	7	4	5	0	29	1	1	0	1	1	1	.204	.250	.265	.515
2013	Hou	AL	136	408	98	17	4	8	(7	1)	141	46	41	47	21	0	127	8	6	2	11	11	5	.240	.289	.346	.635
2014	Col	NL	132	292	75	17	4	8	(7	1)	124	37	27	26	15	0	100	0	6	0	5	4	11	.257	.293	.425	.718
2015	Col	NL	106	255	64	13	2	2	(1	1)	87	30	17	24	21	3	67	3	1	1	4	2	6	.251	.314	.341	.655
2016	Col	NL	48	100	22	6	2	0	(0	0)	32	10	8	8	3	0	30	1	5	0	1	2	0	.220	.250	.320	.570
	5 ML YEARS		465	1153	279	56	9	19	(15	4)	410	131	100	109	65	3	353	13	19	3	22	20	23	.242	.289	.356	.645

Danny Barnes

Pitches: R Bats: L Pos: RP-12   Ht: 6'1" Wt: 195 Born: 10/21/1989 Age: 27

			HOW MUCH HE PITCHED						WHAT HE GAVE UP										THE RESULTS						
Year	Team	Lg	G	GS	CG	GF	IP	BFP	H	R	ER	HR	SH	SF	HB	TBB	IBB	SO	WP	Bk	W	L	Pct	Sh	Sv-Op	Hld	ERC	ERA
2012	Dnedin	A+	50	0	0	47	51.1	205	37	8	8	3	2	0	0	16	1	63	1	1	1	2	.333	0	34--		2.03	1.40
2014	Dnedin	A+	36	0	0	19	38.2	164	36	20	18	4	1	3	1	12	0	49	1	0	0	5	.000	0	7--		3.42	4.19
2015	Nham	AA	40	1	0	17	60.2	262	64	24	20	5	2	3	1	19	2	74	0	0	3	2	.600	0	4--		3.90	2.97
2016	Nham	AA	24	0	0	11	35.2	126	17	5	4	3	0	0	0	4	0	40	0	0	2	1	.667	0	1--		0.90	1.01
2016	Buffalo	AAA	17	0	0	9	25.2	88	6	1	1	0	0	0	2	2	0	37	0	0	1	0	1.000	0	5--		0.27	0.35
2016	Tor	AL	12	0	0	4	13.2	58	14	6	6	0	0	2	0	5	0	14	1	0	0	0	-	0	0-0	1	3.42	3.95

Jacob Barnes

Pitches: R Bats: R Pos: RP-27   Ht: 6'2" Wt: 220 Born: 4/14/1990 Age: 27

			HOW MUCH HE PITCHED						WHAT HE GAVE UP										THE RESULTS						
Year	Team	Lg	G	GS	CG	GF	IP	BFP	H	R	ER	HR	SH	SF	HB	TBB	IBB	SO	WP	Bk	W	L	Pct	Sh	Sv-Op	Hld	ERC	ERA
2012	Wisc	A	25	7	0	5	93.2	399	87	46	40	10	2	2	4	46	0	83	2	5	4	7	.364	0	3--		4.27	3.84
2013	BrvdCt	A+	21	14	1	2	105.1	442	98	43	36	6	6	5	3	36	0	66	3	1	9	6	.600	0	0--		3.31	3.08
2014	Hntsvl	AA	23	21	0	0	105.2	442	94	57	50	9	4	5	10	38	0	75	6	1	4	6	.250	0	0--		3.65	4.26
2015	Biloxi	AA	39	6	0	8	75.0	317	74	32	28	2	2	1	2	30	1	84	7	0	4	5	.444	0	0--		3.65	3.36
2016	ColSpr	AAA	17	0	0	8	22.1	84	14	3	3	1	1	0	0	7	0	23	3	0	2	1	.667	0	1--		1.66	1.21
2016	Mil	NL	27	0	0	7	26.2	106	24	9	8	1	1	0	6	1	26	2	0	0	1	.000	0	1-1	0	2.50	2.70

Matt Barnes

Pitches: R Bats: R Pos: RP-62   Ht: 6'4" Wt: 210 Born: 6/17/1990 Age: 27

			HOW MUCH HE PITCHED						WHAT HE GAVE UP										THE RESULTS						
Year	Team	Lg	G	GS	CG	GF	IP	BFP	H	R	ER	HR	SH	SF	HB	TBB	IBB	SO	WP	Bk	W	L	Pct	Sh	Sv-Op	Hld	ERC	ERA
2014	Bos	AL	5	0	0	3	9.0	39	11	4	4	1	0	1	0	2	0	8	0	0	0	0	-	0	0-0	0	4.72	4.00
2015	Bos	AL	32	2	0	7	43.0	199	56	28	26	9	2	0	2	15	0	39	4	0	3	4	.429	0	0-0	3	6.66	5.44
2016	Bos	AL	62	0	0	13	66.2	287	62	32	30	6	2	1	3	31	1	71	4	0	4	3	.571	0	1-2	16	4.06	4.05
	3 ML YEARS		99	2	0	23	118.2	525	129	64	60	16	4	2	5	48	1	118	8	0	7	7	.500	0	1-2	19	5.02	4.55

Tony Barnette

Pitches: R Bats: R Pos: RP-53   Ht: 6'1" Wt: 190 Born: 11/9/1983 Age: 33

			HOW MUCH HE PITCHED						WHAT HE GAVE UP										THE RESULTS						
Year	Team	Lg	G	GS	CG	GF	IP	BFP	H	R	ER	HR	SH	SF	HB	TBB	IBB	SO	WP	Bk	W	L	Pct	Sh	Sv-Op	Hld	ERC	ERA
2016	Tex	AL	53	0	0	9	60.1	246	54	16	14	4	1	2	4	16	1	49	6	0	7	3	.700	0	0-1	15	3.06	2.09

Darwin Barney

Bats: R **Throws:** R **Pos:** 2B-40;3B-32;SS-25;PH-8;PR-6;LF-5 | **Ht:** 5'10" **Wt:** 180 **Born:** 11/8/1985 **Age:** 31

							BATTING												RUNNING			AVERAGES			
Year	Team	Lg	G	AB	H	2B	3B	HR	(Hm | Rd)	TB	R	RBI	RC	TBB	IBB	SO	HBP	SH	SF	SB	CS	GDP	Avg	OBP	Slg	OPS
2010	ChC	NL	30	79	19	4	0	0	(0 | 0)	23	12	2	6	6	0	12	0	0	0	0	0	0	.241	.294	.291	.585
2011	ChC	NL	143	529	146	23	6	2	(2 | 0)	187	66	43	60	22	2	67	8	7	4	9	2	14	.276	.313	.353	.666
2012	ChC	NL	156	548	139	26	4	7	(7 | 0)	194	73	44	60	33	1	58	3	3	1	6	1	11	.254	.299	.354	.653
2013	ChC	NL	141	501	104	25	1	7	(4 | 3)	152	49	41	30	36	5	64	6	4	6	4	2	22	.208	.266	.303	.569
2014	2 Tms	NL	94	237	57	11	2	3	(2 | 1)	81	24	23	27	17	2	34	4	2	2	1	0	1	.241	.300	.342	.642
2015	2 Tms		17	27	7	1	0	2	(0 | 2)	14	4	4	4	1	0	2	0	2	0	0	0	0	.259	.286	.519	.804
2016	Tor	AL	104	279	75	13	2	4	(2 | 2)	104	35	19	27	22	1	48	1	2	2	2	2	8	.269	.322	.373	.695
14	ChC	NL	72	204	47	10	2	2	(2 | 0)	67	18	16	19	9	2	31	1	2	1	1	0	1	.230	.265	.328	.594
14	LAD	NL	22	33	10	1	0	1	(0 | 1)	14	6	7	8	8	0	3	3	0	1	0	0	0	.303	.467	.424	.891
15	LAD	NL	2	4	0	0	0	0	(0 | 0)	0	0	0	0	0	0	0	0	0	0	0	0	0	.000	.000	.000	.000
15	Tor	AL	15	23	7	1	0	2	(0 | 2)	14	4	4	4	1	0	2	0	2	0	0	0	0	.304	.333	.609	.942
	7 ML YEARS		685	2200	547	103	15	25	(17 | 8)	755	263	176	214	137	11	285	22	20	15	22	7	56	.249	.297	.343	.641

Tucker Barnhart

Bats: B **Throws:** R **Pos:** C-108;PH-9 | **Ht:** 5'11" **Wt:** 190 **Born:** 1/7/1991 **Age:** 26

							BATTING												RUNNING			AVERAGES			
Year	Team	Lg	G	AB	H	2B	3B	HR	(Hm | Rd)	TB	R	RBI	RC	TBB	IBB	SO	HBP	SH	SF	SB	CS	GDP	Avg	OBP	Slg	OPS
2014	Cin	NL	21	54	10	0	0	1	(1 | 0)	13	3	1	2	4	1	10	0	2	0	0	0	0	.185	.241	.241	.482
2015	Cin	NL	81	242	61	9	0	3	(2 | 1)	79	23	18	22	25	5	45	2	2	3	0	1	10	.252	.324	.326	.650
2016	Cin	NL	115	377	97	23	1	7	(6 | 1)	143	34	51	51	36	8	72	2	2	3	1	0	12	.257	.323	.379	.702
	3 ML YEARS		217	673	168	32	1	11	(9 | 2)	235	60	70	75	65	14	127	4	6	6	1	1	22	.250	.317	.349	.666

Kyle Barraclough

Pitches: R **Bats:** R **Pos:** RP-75 | BAIR-ah-claw | **Ht:** 6'3" **Wt:** 225 **Born:** 5/23/1990 **Age:** 27

			HOW MUCH HE PITCHED					WHAT HE GAVE UP									THE RESULTS						
Year	Team	Lg	G	GS	CG	GF	IP	BFP	H	R	ER	HR	SH	SF	HB	TBB	IBB	SO	WP	Bk	W	L	Pct	Sh	Sv-Op	Hld	ERC	ERA
2012	2 Tms	Low	15	3	0	5	35.1	148	26	15	12	2	3	3	2	13	1	33	5	0	0	3	.000	0	2--	-	2.39	3.06
2014	2 Tms	Low	48	0	0	18	58.1	256	49	22	16	0	2	1	1	34	0	78	8	0	2	2	.500	0	11--	-	3.20	2.47
2015	PlmBh	A+	11	0	0	7	15.0	63	9	4	1	0	0	0	0	9	0	23	3	0	1	0	1.000	0	4--	-	2.03	0.60
2015	Sprgfld	AA	23	0	0	16	24.2	113	19	9	9	0	0	1	2	20	0	28	5	0	1	0	1.000	0	8--	-	3.88	3.28
2015	Mia	NL	25	0	0	5	24.1	98	12	8	7	1	0	2	0	18	2	30	1	0	2	1	.667	0	0-1	6	2.25	2.59
2016	Mia	NL	75	0	0	6	72.2	306	45	24	23	1	2	2	2	44	1	113	8	0	6	3	.667	0	0-4	29	2.31	2.85
	2 ML YEARS		100	0	0	11	97.0	404	57	32	30	2	2	4	2	62	3	143	9	0	8	4	.667	0	0-5	35	2.29	2.78

Aaron Barrett

Pitches: R **Bats:** R **Pos:** P | **Ht:** 6'3" **Wt:** 230 **Born:** 1/2/1988 **Age:** 29

			HOW MUCH HE PITCHED					WHAT HE GAVE UP									THE RESULTS						
Year	Team	Lg	G	GS	CG	GF	IP	BFP	H	R	ER	HR	SH	SF	HB	TBB	IBB	SO	WP	Bk	W	L	Pct	Sh	Sv-Op	Hld	ERC	ERA
2012	2 Tms	Low	42	0	0	33	51.2	203	34	14	12	2	0	1	4	14	0	73	8	1	3	2	.600	0	17--	-	1.67	2.09
2013	Hrsbrg	AA	51	0	0	42	50.1	203	40	14	12	2	2	0	0	15	0	69	3	0	1	1	.500	0	26--	-	2.25	2.15
2014	Syrcse	AAA	10	0	0	5	10.1	37	5	0	0	0	0	0	0	1	0	8	0	0	1	0	1.000	0	2--	-	0.65	0.00
2014	Was	NL	50	0	0	12	40.2	174	33	17	12	1	1	2	1	20	2	49	6	1	3	0	1.000	0	0-0	8	2.87	2.66
2015	Was	NL	40	0	0	8	29.1	123	28	15	15	1	0	0	3	7	0	35	1	0	3	3	.500	0	0-3	10	3.17	4.60
	Postseason		2	0	0	0	0.1	3	1	0	0	0	0	0	0	2	1	0	1	0	0	0	-	0	0-0	0	44.72	0.00
	2 ML YEARS		90	0	0	20	70.0	297	61	32	27	2	1	2	4	27	2	84	7	1	6	3	.667	0	0-3	18	2.99	3.47

Jake Barrett

Pitches: R **Bats:** R **Pos:** RP-68 | **Ht:** 6'2" **Wt:** 240 **Born:** 7/22/1991 **Age:** 25

			HOW MUCH HE PITCHED					WHAT HE GAVE UP									THE RESULTS						
Year	Team	Lg	G	GS	CG	GF	IP	BFP	H	R	ER	HR	SH	SF	HB	TBB	IBB	SO	WP	Bk	W	L	Pct	Sh	Sv-Op	Hld	ERC	ERA
2012	Sbend	A	25	0	0	20	24.2	117	28	18	16	2	2	1	2	13	3	25	4	0	0	3	.000	0	6--	-	5.19	5.84
2013	Visalia	A+	28	0	0	27	27.1	118	21	7	6	2	0	0	3	9	0	37	4	0	2	1	.667	0	15--	-	2.67	1.98
2013	Mobile	AA	24	0	0	20	24.2	96	18	4	1	2	0	1	0	3	1	22	2	0	1	1	.500	0	14--	-	1.56	0.36
2014	Mobile	AA	25	0	0	17	26.1	110	25	7	7	0	1	1	0	12	3	24	2	0	1	2	.333	0	12--	-	3.23	2.39
2014	Reno	AAA	30	0	0	25	29.0	119	22	13	12	3	1	2	1	15	1	23	4	0	1	0	1.000	0	16--	-	3.43	3.72
2015	Reno	AAA	22	0	0	21	23.0	104	27	15	13	1	2	1	0	12	0	21	0	0	1	3	.250	0	11--	-	5.21	5.09
2015	Mobile	AA	25	0	0	10	30.0	131	34	14	14	2	1	3	0	11	0	30	2	0	3	0	1.000	0	4--	-	4.49	4.20
2016	Ari	NL	68	0	0	12	59.1	250	47	25	23	6	0	3	3	28	4	56	4	0	1	2	.333	0	4-9	8	3.33	3.49

Chris Bassitt

Pitches: R **Bats:** R **Pos:** SP-5 | **Ht:** 6'5" **Wt:** 220 **Born:** 2/22/1989 **Age:** 28

			HOW MUCH HE PITCHED					WHAT HE GAVE UP									THE RESULTS						
Year	Team	Lg	G	GS	CG	GF	IP	BFP	H	R	ER	HR	SH	SF	HB	TBB	IBB	SO	WP	Bk	W	L	Pct	Sh	Sv-Op	Hld	ERC	ERA
2014	CWS	AL	6	5	0	1	29.2	137	34	13	13	0	1	1	3	13	1	21	0	0	1	1	.500	0	0-0	0	4.57	3.94
2015	Oak	AL	18	13	0	3	86.0	361	78	36	34	5	1	1	9	30	0	64	5	0	1	8	.111	0	0-0	0	3.55	3.56
2016	Oak	AL	5	5	0	0	28.0	133	35	20	19	5	0	0	0	14	0	23	2	0	0	2	.000	0	0-0	0	6.44	6.11
	3 ML YEARS		29	23	0	4	143.2	631	147	69	66	10	2	2	12	57	1	108	7	0	2	11	.154	0	0-0	0	4.30	4.13

Antonio Bastardo

Pitches: L Bats: R Pos: RP-69   bah-STAHR-doh   Ht: 5'11" Wt: 205 Born: 9/21/1985 Age: 31

				HOW MUCH HE PITCHED					WHAT HE GAVE UP											THE RESULTS						
Year	Team	Lg	G	GS	CG	GF	IP	BFP	H	R	ER	HR	SH	SF	HB	TBB	IBB	SO	WP	Bk	W	L	Pct	Sh	Sv-Op	Hld	ERC	ERA
2009	Phi	NL	6	5	0	0	23.2	106	26	18	17	4	0	0	2	9	0	19	0	0	2	3	.400	0	0-0	0	5.41	6.46
2010	Phi	NL	25	0	0	2	18.2	86	19	9	9	1	0	0	2	9	0	26	0	0	2	0	1.000	0	0-1	2	4.46	4.34
2011	Phi	NL	64	0	0	15	58.0	225	28	17	17	6	2	2	0	26	0	70	4	0	6	1	.857	0	8-9	17	1.69	2.64
2012	Phi	NL	65	0	0	10	52.0	224	40	26	25	7	1	2	2	26	3	81	5	0	2	5	.286	0	1-5	26	3.42	4.33
2013	Phi	NL	48	0	0	15	42.2	179	33	12	11	2	4	1	1	21	1	47	4	0	3	2	.600	0	2-5	14	2.91	2.32
2014	Phi	NL	67	0	0	17	64.0	271	43	31	28	4	3	3	2	34	4	81	5	0	5	7	.417	0	0-2	12	2.54	3.94
2015	Pit	NL	66	0	0	18	57.1	239	39	19	19	4	2	0	3	26	2	64	8	0	4	1	.800	0	1-2	9	2.50	2.98
2016	2 Tms	NL	69	0	0	11	67.2	297	60	37	34	11	2	3	4	32	3	74	6	4	3	0	1.000	0	0-2	15	4.27	4.52
16	NYM	NL	41	0	0	11	43.2	195	41	24	23	8	2	1	3	21	2	46	1	2	0	0	-	0	0-1	7	4.78	4.74
16	Pit	NL	28	0	0	0	24.0	102	19	13	11	3	0	2	1	11	1	28	5	2	3	0	1.000	0	0-1	8	3.40	4.13
	Postseason		6	0	0	0	2.2	11	2	0	0	0	1	0	0	1	0	4	0	0	0	0	-	0	0-0	1	2.01	0.00
	8 ML YEARS		410	5	0	88	384.0	1627	288	169	160	39	14	11	16	183	13	462	32	4	27	19	.587	0	12-26	95	3.10	3.75

Trevor Bauer

Pitches: R Bats: R Pos: SP-28; RP-7   Ht: 6'1" Wt: 200 Born: 1/17/1991 Age: 26

				HOW MUCH HE PITCHED					WHAT HE GAVE UP											THE RESULTS						
Year	Team	Lg	G	GS	CG	GF	IP	BFP	H	R	ER	HR	SH	SF	HB	TBB	IBB	SO	WP	Bk	W	L	Pct	Sh	Sv-Op	Hld	ERC	ERA
2012	Ari	NL	4	4	0	0	16.1	77	14	13	11	2	1	1	1	13	0	17	2	0	1	2	.333	0	0-0	0	5.12	6.06
2013	Cle	AL	4	4	0	0	17.0	81	15	11	10	3	0	1	1	16	0	11	1	0	1	2	.333	0	0-0	0	6.47	5.29
2014	Cle	AL	26	26	0	0	153.0	663	151	76	71	16	1	8	11	60	4	143	6	0	5	8	.385	0	0-0	0	4.27	4.18
2015	Cle	AL	31	30	1	1	176.0	744	152	90	89	23	4	1	5	79	1	170	7	1	11	12	.478	0	0-0	0	3.86	4.55
2016	Cle	AL	35	28	1	3	190.0	811	179	96	90	20	4	7	9	70	1	168	3	0	12	8	.600	0	0-0	0	3.85	4.26
	5 ML YEARS		100	92	2	4	552.1	2376	511	286	271	64	10	18	27	238	6	509	19	1	30	32	.484	0	0-0	0	4.08	4.42

Buddy Baumann

Pitches: L Bats: L Pos: RP-11   Ht: 5'11" Wt: 195 Born: 12/9/1987 Age: 29

				HOW MUCH HE PITCHED					WHAT HE GAVE UP											THE RESULTS						
Year	Team	Lg	G	GS	CG	GF	IP	BFP	H	R	ER	HR	SH	SF	HB	TBB	IBB	SO	WP	Bk	W	L	Pct	Sh	Sv-Op	Hld	ERC	ERA
2012	NWArk	AA	32	0	0	10	59.0	258	47	31	27	7	4	4	3	33	3	58	4	0	3	2	.600	0	2--	-	3.76	4.12
2013	Omha	AAA	30	0	0	11	49.0	219	49	15	15	5	2	2	1	23	2	66	2	0	3	0	1.000	0	1--	-	4.29	2.76
2014	Omha	AAA	40	11	0	13	90.1	378	85	35	32	6	2	6	2	31	1	68	0	1	2	4	.333	0	2--	-	3.41	3.19
2015	Omha	AAA	34	6	0	9	77.0	328	65	29	26	5	3	2	8	25	2	84	5	0	3	4	.429	0	3--	-	3.01	3.04
2016	ElPaso	AAA	24	0	0	7	28.2	117	22	10	10	3	1	0	1	12	0	31	2	0	1	1	.500	0	2--	-	3.12	3.14
2016	SD	NL	11	0	0	2	9.2	40	7	4	4	0	0	0	1	4	0	10	0	0	1	0	1.000	0	0-0	2	2.41	3.72

Jose Bautista

Bats: R Throws: R Pos: RF-91;DH-26;1B-1   bah-TEE-stah   Ht: 6'0" Wt: 205 Born: 10/19/1980 Age: 36

								BATTING														RUNNING			AVERAGES			
Year	Team	Lg	G	AB	H	2B	3B	HR	(Hm	Rd)	TB	R	RBI	RC	TBB	IBB	SO	HBP	SH	SF	SB	CS	GDP	Avg	OBP	Slg	OPS
2004	4 Tms		64	88	18	3	0	0	(0	0)	21	6	2	2	7	0	40	0	1	0	0	1	1	.205	.263	.239	.502
2005	Pit	NL	11	28	4	1	0	0	(0	0)	5	3	1	0	3	0	7	0	0	0	1	0	2	.143	.226	.179	.404
2006	Pit	NL	117	400	94	20	3	16	(11	5)	168	58	51	55	46	2	110	16	3	4	2	4	12	.235	.335	.420	.755
2007	Pit	NL	142	532	135	36	2	15	(8	7)	220	75	63	71	68	1	101	4	4	6	6	3	16	.254	.339	.414	.753
2008	2 Tms		128	370	88	17	0	15	(5	10)	150	45	54	43	40	5	91	2	8	4	1	1	12	.238	.313	.405	.718
2009	Tor	AL	113	336	79	13	3	13	(5	8)	137	54	40	42	56	1	85	4	6	2	4	0	9	.235	.349	.408	.757
2010	Tor	AL	161	569	148	35	3	54	(33	21)	351	109	124	132	100	2	116	10	0	4	9	5	10	.260	.378	.617	.995
2011	Tor	AL	149	513	155	24	2	43	(20	23)	312	105	103	133	132	24	111	6	0	4	9	5	8	.302	.447	.608	1.056
2012	Tor	AL	92	332	80	14	0	27	(11	16)	175	64	65	58	59	2	63	4	0	4	5	2	11	.241	.358	.527	.886
2013	Tor	AL	118	452	117	24	0	28	(14	14)	225	82	73	81	69	2	84	3	0	4	7	2	13	.259	.358	.498	.856
2014	Tor	AL	155	553	158	27	0	35	(18	17)	290	101	103	102	104	11	96	9	1	6	6	2	18	.286	.403	.524	.928
2015	Tor	AL	153	543	136	29	3	40	(23	17)	291	108	114	113	110	2	106	5	0	8	8	2	19	.250	.377	.536	.913
2016	Tor	AL	116	423	99	24	1	22	(10	12)	191	68	69	75	87	1	103	3	0	4	2	2	21	.234	.366	.452	.817
04	Bal	AL	16	11	3	0	0	0	(0	0)	3	3	0	1	1	0	3	0	0	0	0	0	0	.273	.333	.273	.606
04	TB	AL	12	12	2	0	0	0	(0	0)	2	1	1	1	3	0	7	0	0	0	0	1	0	.167	.333	.167	.500
04	KC	AL	13	25	5	1	0	0	(0	0)	6	1	1	0	1	0	12	0	0	0	0	0	0	.200	.231	.240	.471
04	Pit	NL	23	40	8	2	0	0	(0	0)	10	1	0	1	2	0	18	0	1	0	0	0	1	.200	.238	.250	.488
08	Pit	NL	107	314	76	15	0	12	(3	9)	127	38	44	39	38	4	77	2	6	3	1	1	10	.242	.325	.404	.729
08	Tor	AL	21	56	12	2	0	3	(2	1)	23	7	10	4	2	1	14	0	2	1	0	0	2	.214	.237	.411	.648
	Postseason		11	41	12	3	0	4	(2	2)	27	7	11	12	8	0	7	0	0	0	0	0	0	.293	.408	.659	1.067
	13 ML YEARS		1519	5139	1311	267	17	308	(158	150)	2536	878	862	917	881	53	1113	66	23	50	60	26	152	.255	.368	.493	.861

Brandon Beachy

Pitches: R Bats: R Pos: P   BEE-chee   Ht: 6'2" Wt: 220 Born: 9/3/1986 Age: 30

				HOW MUCH HE PITCHED					WHAT HE GAVE UP											THE RESULTS						
Year	Team	Lg	G	GS	CG	GF	IP	BFP	H	R	ER	HR	SH	SF	HB	TBB	IBB	SO	WP	Bk	W	L	Pct	Sh	Sv-Op	Hld	ERC	ERA
2010	Atl	NL	3	3	0	0	15.0	67	16	9	5	4	0	0	0	7	3	15	1	0	0	2	.000	0	0-0	0	3.58	3.00
2011	Atl	NL	25	25	0	0	141.2	591	125	62	58	16	6	5	5	46	9	169	11	1	7	3	.700	0	0-0	0	3.27	3.68
2012	Atl	NL	13	13	1	0	81.0	319	49	24	18	6	1	2	1	29	1	68	4	0	5	5	.500	1	0-0	0	1.80	2.00
2013	Atl	NL	5	5	0	0	30.0	120	27	17	15	5	2	1	0	4	0	23	2	0	2	1	.667	0	0-0	0	2.90	4.50
2015	LAD	NL	2	2	0	0	8.0	39	10	7	7	1	1	0	0	6	2	5	0	0	0	1	.000	0	0-0	0	6.76	7.88
	5 ML YEARS		48	48	1	0	275.2	1136	227	119	103	28	10	8	6	92	15	280	18	1	14	12	.538	1	0-0	0	2.88	3.36

Chris Beck

Pitches: R Bats: R Pos: RP-25 Ht: 6'3" Wt: 225 Born: 9/4/1990 Age: 26

Year	Team	Lg	G	GS	CG	GF	IP	BFP	H	R	ER	HR	SH	SF	HB	TBB	IBB	SO	WP	Bk	W	L	Pct	Sh	Sv-Op	Hld	ERC	ERA
2012	Gr Falls	R+	15	6	0	0	40.1	175	51	27	21	3	0	3	0	12	0	36	3	1	4	3	.571	0	0- -	-	5.14	4.69
2013	WinSa	A+	21	21	1	0	118.2	500	117	51	41	11	4	4	4	42	0	57	3	0	11	8	.579	1	0- -	-	3.97	3.11
2013	Brham	AA	5	5	0	0	28.0	110	26	10	9	0	1	0	2	3	0	22	0	0	2	2	.500	0	0- -	-	2.32	2.89
2014	Brham	AA	20	20	1	0	116.2	492	116	50	44	7	4	3	5	31	1	57	4	0	5	8	.385	1	0- -	-	3.40	3.39
2014	Charllt	AAA	7	7	0	0	33.1	152	36	16	15	1	1	0	2	13	0	28	1	1	1	3	.250	0	0- -	-	4.07	4.05
2015	Charllt	AAA	10	10	0	0	54.1	226	50	20	19	3	0	1	2	14	0	40	3	0	3	2	.600	0	0- -	-	2.93	3.15
2016	Charllt	AAA	22	7	0	4	66.1	290	77	32	31	5	0	0	3	25	4	50	1	1	5	4	.556	0	0- -	-	4.93	4.21
2015	CWS	AL	1	1	0	0	6.0	31	10	5	4	0	1	0	0	4	0	3	0	0	0	1	.000	0	0-0	0	8.52	6.00
2016	CWS	AL	25	0	0	4	25.1	123	31	18	18	3	0	1	2	17	1	20	0	0	2	2	.500	0	0-1	5	6.95	6.39
	2 ML YEARS		26	1	0	4	31.1	154	41	23	22	3	1	1	2	21	1	23	0	0	2	3	.400	0	0-1	5	7.25	6.32

Gordon Beckham

Bats: R Throws: R Pos: 2B-51;PH-23;3B-18;SS-11 Ht: 6'0" Wt: 190 Born: 9/16/1986 Age: 30

| | | | | | | | | | BATTING | | | | | | | | | | RUNNING | | | AVERAGES | | | |
Year	Team	Lg	G	AB	H	2B	3B	HR	(Hm	Rd)	TB	R	RBI	RC	TBB	IBB	SO	HBP	SH	SF	SB	CS	GDP	Avg	OBP	Slg	OPS
2009	CWS	AL	103	378	102	28	1	14	(4	10)	174	58	63	61	41	0	65	6	1	4	7	4	10	.270	.347	.460	.808
2010	CWS	AL	131	444	112	25	2	9	(7	2)	168	58	49	52	37	0	92	7	6	4	4	6	9	.252	.317	.378	.695
2011	CWS	AL	150	499	115	23	0	10	(7	3)	168	60	44	48	35	0	111	13	7	3	5	3	6	.230	.296	.337	.633
2012	CWS	AL	151	525	123	24	0	16	(12	4)	195	62	60	58	40	0	89	7	8	2	5	4	10	.234	.296	.371	.668
2013	CWS	AL	103	371	99	22	1	5	(3	2)	138	46	24	36	28	2	56	4	1	4	5	1	10	.267	.322	.372	.694
2014	2 Tms	AL	127	446	101	27	0	9	(4	5)	155	53	44	32	22	2	81	7	3	5	3	0	17	.226	.271	.348	.618
2015	CWS	AL	100	211	44	8	0	6	(3	3)	70	24	20	17	19	1	43	2	1	4	0	1	6	.209	.275	.332	.607
2016	2 Tms	NL	88	245	52	16	1	5	(2	3)	85	25	31	22	26	1	52	4	0	1	1	0	12	.212	.294	.347	.641
14	CWS	AL	101	390	86	24	0	7	(3	4)	131	43	36	28	19	1	70	5	3	5	3	0	12	.221	.263	.336	.598
14	LAA	AL	26	56	15	3	0	2	(1	1)	24	10	8	4	3	1	11	2	0	0	0	0	5	.268	.328	.429	.756
16	Atl	NL	85	240	52	16	1	5	(2	3)	85	25	30	22	26	1	50	4	0	3	1	0	12	.217	.300	.354	.655
16	SF	NL	3	5	0	0	0	0	(0	0)	0	0	1	0	0	0	2	0	0	0	0	0	0	.000	.000	.000	.000
	Postseason		2	1	0	0	0	0	(0	0)	0	0	0	0	0	0	1	1	0	0	0	0	0	.000	.500	.000	.500
	8 ML YEARS		953	3119	748	173	5	74	(42	32)	1153	386	335	326	248	6	589	50	27	30	30	19	80	.240	.303	.370	.673

Tim Beckham

Bats: R Throws: R Pos: SS-25;2B-19;PH-9;3B-7;1B-6;DH-3;PR-1 Ht: 6'0" Wt: 195 Born: 1/27/1990 Age: 27

| | | | | | | | | | BATTING | | | | | | | | | | RUNNING | | | AVERAGES | | | |
Year	Team	Lg	G	AB	H	2B	3B	HR	(Hm	Rd)	TB	R	RBI	RC	TBB	IBB	SO	HBP	SH	SF	SB	CS	GDP	Avg	OBP	Slg	OPS
2013	TB	AL	5	7	3	0	0	0	(0	0)	3	1	1	1	0	0	0	0	0	1	0	0	0	.429	.375	.429	.804
2015	TB	AL	83	203	45	7	4	9	(3	6)	87	24	37	26	13	0	69	3	0	4	3	1	3	.222	.274	.429	.702
2016	TB	AL	64	198	49	12	5	5	(1	4)	86	25	16	23	14	0	67	1	2	0	2	1	3	.247	.300	.434	.735
	3 ML YEARS		152	408	97	19	9	14	(4	10)	176	50	54	50	27	0	136	4	2	5	5	2	6	.238	.288	.431	.720

Cam Bedrosian

Pitches: R Bats: R Pos: RP-45 beh-DROH-zhee-ann Ht: 6'0" Wt: 230 Born: 10/2/1991 Age: 25

Year	Team	Lg	G	GS	CG	GF	IP	BFP	H	R	ER	HR	SH	SF	HB	TBB	IBB	SO	WP	Bk	W	L	Pct	Sh	Sv-Op	Hld	ERC	ERA
2016	Salt Lk*	AAA	5	0	0	2	8.1	37	7	3	3	1	0	0	0	4	0	14	0	0	1	0	1.000	0	1- -	-	3.45	3.24
2014	LAA	AL	17	0	0	4	19.1	93	23	17	14	2	0	1	0	12	1	20	1	1	0	1	.000	0	0-1	1	5.88	6.52
2015	LAA	AL	34	0	0	10	33.1	156	40	21	20	3	1	2	2	19	2	34	2	0	0	1	.000	0	0-0	1	6.05	5.40
2016	LAA	AL	45	0	0	9	40.1	162	30	7	5	1	0	1	2	14	1	51	3	0	2	0	1.000	0	1-2	7	2.25	1.12
	3 ML YEARS		96	0	0	23	93.0	411	93	45	39	6	1	4	4	45	4	105	6	1	3	1	.750	0	1-3	9	4.25	3.77

Matt Belisle

Pitches: R Bats: R Pos: RP-40 bell-EYE-el Ht: 6'3" Wt: 230 Born: 6/6/1980 Age: 37

Year	Team	Lg	G	GS	CG	GF	IP	BFP	H	R	ER	HR	SH	SF	HB	TBB	IBB	SO	WP	Bk	W	L	Pct	Sh	Sv-Op	Hld	ERC	ERA
2003	Cin	NL	6	0	0	2	8.2	39	10	5	5	1	2	1	1	2	0	6	0	0	1	1	.500	0	0-1	0	4.73	5.19
2005	Cin	NL	60	5	0	17	85.2	382	101	49	42	11	4	2	6	26	6	59	3	0	4	8	.333	0	1-4	8	5.08	4.41
2006	Cin	NL	30	2	0	5	40.0	180	43	18	16	5	1	2	3	19	1	26	3	0	2	0	1.000	0	0-1	0	5.29	3.60
2007	Cin	NL	30	30	1	0	177.2	771	212	111	105	26	7	9	7	43	4	125	6	1	8	9	.471	0	0-0	0	5.05	5.32
2008	Cin	NL	6	6	0	0	29.2	142	47	27	24	4	1	2	0	6	0	14	2	0	1	4	.200	0	0-0	0	6.87	7.28
2009	Col	NL	24	0	0	6	31.0	133	35	21	19	6	0	2	1	5	1	22	1	0	3	1	.750	0	0-0	1	4.50	5.52
2010	Col	NL	76	0	0	11	92.0	365	84	34	30	7	4	2	2	16	5	91	3	1	7	5	.583	0	1-2	21	2.67	2.93
2011	Col	NL	74	0	0	10	72.0	301	77	33	26	5	4	0	4	14	3	58	2	0	10	4	.714	0	0-7	14	3.65	3.25
2012	Col	NL	80	0	0	14	80.0	348	91	36	33	5	4	0	3	18	6	69	1	1	3	8	.273	0	3-10	26	3.87	3.71
2013	Col	NL	72	0	0	16	73.0	301	76	37	33	6	2	1	0	15	2	62	3	0	5	7	.417	0	0-5	24	3.42	4.32
2014	Col	NL	66	1	0	13	64.2	282	74	35	35	5	4	5	1	19	2	43	3	0	4	7	.364	0	0-2	6	4.31	4.87
2015	StL	NL	34	0	0	10	33.2	149	34	10	10	1	2	1	3	15	2	25	0	0	1	1	.500	0	0-1	7	4.05	2.67
2016	Was	NL	40	0	0	6	46.0	186	43	13	9	2	1	1	1	7	3	32	2	0	0	0	-	0	0-0	4	2.43	1.76
	Postseason		2	0	0	0	2.0	7	0	0	0	0	0	0	1	0	2	0	0	0	0	-	0	0-0	1	0.27	0.00
	13 ML YEARS		598	44	1	110	834.0	3579	927	429	389	84	36	28	32	205	35	632	29	3	49	55	.471	0	5-33	111	4.19	4.20

Josh Bell

Bats: B **Throws:** R **Pos:** 1B-23;RF-16;PH-12 **Ht:** 6'2" **Wt:** 245 **Born:** 8/14/1992 **Age:** 24

Year	Team	Lg	G	AB	H	2B	3B	HR	(Hm	Rd)	TB	R	RBI	RC	TBB	IBB	SO	HBP	SH	SF	SB	CS	GDP	Avg	OBP	Slg	OPS
2012	WV	A	15	62	17	5	0	1	(-	-)	25	6	11	7	2	0	21	0	0	2	1	0	3	.274	.288	.403	.691
2013	WV	A	119	459	128	37	2	13	(-	-)	208	75	76	76	52	1	90	3	0	5	1	2	10	.279	.353	.453	.806
2014	Bradtn	A+	84	331	111	20	4	9	(-	-)	166	45	53	62	25	1	43	2	4	1	5	4	11	.335	.384	.502	.886
2014	Altna	AA	24	94	27	2	0	0	(-	-)	29	13	7	11	8	0	12	0	0	0	4	1	1	.287	.343	.309	.652
2015	Altna	AA	96	368	113	17	6	5	(-	-)	157	47	60	63	44	4	50	2	3	9	7	4	11	.307	.376	.427	.803
2015	Indy	AAA	35	121	42	7	3	2	(-	-)	61	20	18	28	21	2	15	1	0	2	2	0	4	.347	.441	.504	.946
2016	Indy	AAA	114	421	124	23	4	14	(-	-)	197	57	60	76	57	8	74	4	0	2	3	7	17	.295	.382	.468	.850
2016	Pit	NL	45	128	35	8	0	3	(2	1)	52	18	19	18	21	0	19	0	0	3	0	1	4	.273	.368	.406	.775

Brandon Belt

Bats: L **Throws:** L **Pos:** 1B-151;PH-5;LF-3 **Ht:** 6'5" **Wt:** 220 **Born:** 4/20/1988 **Age:** 29

Year	Team	Lg	G	AB	H	2B	3B	HR	(Hm	Rd)	TB	R	RBI	RC	TBB	IBB	SO	HBP	SH	SF	SB	CS	GDP	Avg	OBP	Slg	OPS
2011	SF	NL	63	187	42	6	1	9	(2	7)	77	21	18	20	20	1	57	2	0	0	3	2	3	.225	.306	.412	.718
2012	SF	NL	145	411	113	27	6	7	(5	2)	173	47	56	63	54	5	106	3	4	4	12	2	3	.275	.360	.421	.781
2013	SF	NL	150	509	147	39	4	17	(6	11)	245	76	67	82	52	4	125	6	1	3	5	2	4	.289	.360	.481	.841
2014	SF	NL	61	214	52	8	0	12	(2	10)	96	30	27	24	18	2	64	2	0	1	3	1	4	.243	.306	.449	.755
2015	SF	NL	137	492	138	33	5	18	(5	13)	235	73	68	78	56	2	147	4	0	4	9	3	3	.280	.356	.478	.834
2016	SF	NL	156	542	149	41	8	17	(6	11)	257	77	82	105	104	4	148	5	0	4	0	4	7	.275	.394	.474	.868
	Postseason		32	110	27	2	2	2	(1	1)	39	13	11	16	18	1	36	0	0	1	1	2	0	.245	.349	.355	.703
	6 ML YEARS		712	2355	641	154	24	80	(26	54)	1083	324	318	372	304	18	647	22	1	16	32	14	24	.272	.359	.460	.818

Carlos Beltran

Bats: B **Throws:** R **Pos:** DH-73;RF-69;PH-11 BELL-trahn **Ht:** 6'1" **Wt:** 215 **Born:** 4/24/1977 **Age:** 40

Year	Team	Lg	G	AB	H	2B	3B	HR	(Hm	Rd)	TB	R	RBI	RC	TBB	IBB	SO	HBP	SH	SF	SB	CS	GDP	Avg	OBP	Slg	OPS
1998	KC	AL	14	58	16	5	3	0	(0	0)	27	12	7	9	3	0	12	1	0	1	3	0	2	.276	.317	.466	.783
1999	KC	AL	156	663	194	27	7	22	(12	10)	301	112	108	100	46	2	123	4	0	10	27	8	17	.293	.337	.454	.791
2000	KC	AL	98	372	92	15	4	7	(4	3)	136	49	44	43	35	2	69	0	2	4	13	0	12	.247	.309	.366	.675
2001	KC	AL	155	617	189	32	12	24	(7	17)	317	106	101	118	52	2	120	5	1	5	31	1	7	.306	.362	.514	.876
2002	KC	AL	162	637	174	44	7	29	(19	10)	319	114	105	117	71	1	135	4	3	7	35	7	12	.273	.346	.501	.847
2003	KC	AL	141	521	160	14	10	26	(10	16)	272	102	100	117	72	4	81	2	0	7	41	4	8	.307	.389	.522	.911
2004	2 Tms		159	599	160	36	9	38	(15	23)	328	121	104	124	92	10	101	7	3	7	42	3	4	.267	.367	.548	.915
2005	NYM	NL	151	582	155	34	2	16	(6	10)	241	83	78	88	56	5	96	2	4	6	17	6	9	.266	.330	.414	.744
2006	NYM	NL	140	510	140	38	1	41	(15	26)	303	127	116	121	95	6	99	4	1	7	18	3	6	.275	.388	.594	.982
2007	NYM	NL	144	554	153	33	3	33	(11	22)	291	93	112	97	69	10	111	2	1	10	23	2	8	.276	.353	.525	.878
2008	NYM	NL	161	606	172	40	5	27	(14	13)	303	116	112	116	92	13	96	1	1	6	25	3	11	.284	.376	.500	.876
2009	NYM	NL	81	308	100	22	1	10	(3	7)	154	50	48	54	47	10	43	1	0	1	11	1	9	.325	.415	.500	.915
2010	NYM	NL	64	220	56	11	3	7	(3	4)	94	21	27	31	30	5	39	1	0	4	3	1	4	.255	.341	.427	.768
2011	2 Tms	NL	142	520	156	39	6	22	(14	8)	273	78	84	96	71	7	88	3	0	4	4	2	18	.300	.385	.525	.910
2012	StL	NL	151	547	147	26	1	32	(20	12)	271	83	97	87	65	15	124	2	1	4	13	6	9	.269	.346	.495	.842
2013	StL	NL	145	554	164	30	2	24	(12	12)	272	79	84	91	38	1	90	1	1	6	2	1	12	.296	.339	.491	.830
2014	NYY	AL	109	403	94	23	0	15	(11	4)	162	46	49	44	37	2	80	4	0	5	3	1	11	.233	.301	.402	.703
2015	NYY	AL	133	478	132	34	1	19	(10	9)	225	57	67	69	45	2	85	2	0	6	0	0	12	.276	.337	.471	.808
2016	2 Tms	AL	151	552	163	33	0	29	(19	10)	283	73	93	84	35	4	101	2	0	4	1	0	19	.295	.337	.513	.850
04	KC	AL	69	266	74	19	2	15	(8	7)	142	51	51	57	37	7	44	2	1	3	14	3	4	.278	.367	.534	.901
04	Hou	NL	90	333	86	17	7	23	(7	16)	186	70	53	67	55	3	57	5	2	4	28	0	4	.258	.368	.559	.926
11	NYM	NL	98	353	102	30	2	15	(9	6)	181	61	66	72	60	6	61	2	0	4	3	0	9	.289	.391	.513	.904
11	SF	NL	44	167	54	9	4	7	(5	2)	92	17	18	24	11	1	27	1	0	0	1	2	9	.323	.369	.551	.920
16	NYY	AL	99	359	109	21	0	22	(14	8)	196	50	64	55	22	3	70	2	0	4	0	0	13	.304	.344	.546	.890
16	Tex	AL	52	193	54	12	0	7	(5	2)	87	23	29	29	13	1	31	0	0	0	1	0	6	.280	.325	.451	.776
	Postseason		52	184	61	13	1	16	(7	9)	124	45	40	53	35	2	26	2	1	1	11	0	3	.332	.441	.674	1.115
	19 ML YEARS		2457	9301	2617	536	78	421	(205	216)	4572	1522	1536	1606	1051	101	1693	48	18	104	312	49	194	.281	.354	.492	.845

Adrian Beltre

Bats: R **Throws:** R **Pos:** 3B-141;DH-12 **Ht:** 5'11" **Wt:** 220 **Born:** 4/7/1979 **Age:** 38

Year	Team	Lg	G	AB	H	2B	3B	HR	(Hm	Rd)	TB	R	RBI	RC	TBB	IBB	SO	HBP	SH	SF	SB	CS	GDP	Avg	OBP	Slg	OPS
1998	LAD	NL	77	195	42	9	0	7	(5	2)	72	18	22	20	14	0	37	3	2	0	3	1	4	.215	.278	.369	.648
1999	LAD	NL	152	538	148	27	5	15	(6	9)	230	84	67	84	61	12	105	6	4	5	18	7	4	.275	.352	.428	.780
2000	LAD	NL	138	510	148	30	2	20	(7	13)	242	71	85	85	56	2	80	2	3	4	12	5	13	.290	.360	.475	.835
2001	LAD	NL	126	475	126	22	4	13	(4	9)	195	59	60	60	28	1	82	5	2	5	13	4	9	.265	.310	.411	.720
2002	LAD	NL	159	587	151	26	5	21	(7	14)	250	70	75	74	37	4	96	4	1	6	7	5	15	.257	.303	.426	.729
2003	LAD	NL	158	559	134	30	2	23	(13	10)	237	50	80	66	37	4	103	5	1	6	2	2	13	.240	.290	.424	.714
2004	LAD	NL	156	598	200	32	0	48	(23	25)	376	104	121	120	53	9	87	2	0	4	7	2	15	.334	.388	.629	1.017
2005	Sea	AL	156	603	154	36	1	19	(7	12)	249	69	87	75	38	6	108	5	0	4	3	1	15	.255	.303	.413	.716
2006	Sea	AL	156	620	166	39	4	25	(16	9)	288	88	89	85	47	4	118	10	1	3	11	5	15	.268	.328	.465	.792
2007	Sea	AL	149	595	164	41	2	26	(11	15)	287	87	99	79	38	2	104	2	0	4	14	2	18	.276	.319	.482	.802
2008	Sea	AL	143	556	148	29	1	25	(10	15)	254	74	77	71	50	10	90	2	0	4	8	2	11	.266	.327	.457	.784
2009	Sea	AL	111	449	119	27	0	8	(4	4)	170	54	44	47	19	1	74	7	0	2	13	2	19	.265	.304	.379	.683
2010	Bos	AL	154	589	189	49	2	28	(13	15)	326	84	102	103	40	10	82	5	0	7	2	1	25	.321	.365	.553	.919
2011	Tex	AL	124	487	144	33	0	32	(23	9)	273	82	105	80	25	0	53	5	0	8	1	1	13	.296	.331	.561	.892
2012	Tex	AL	156	604	194	33	2	36	(20	16)	339	95	102	109	36	8	82	5	0	9	1	0	8	.321	.359	.561	.921
2013	Tex	AL	161	631	199	32	0	30	(15	15)	321	88	92	97	50	12	78	7	0	2	1	0	17	.315	.371	.509	.880
2014	Tex	AL	148	549	178	33	1	19	(11	8)	270	79	77	99	57	13	74	5	0	5	1	1	15	.324	.388	.492	.879

91

Year	Team	Lg	G	AB	H	2B	3B	HR	(Hm	Rd)	TB	R	RBI	RC	TBB	IBB	SO	HBP	SH	SF	SB	CS	GDP	Avg	OBP	Slg	OPS
2015	Tex	AL	143	567	163	32	4	18	(13	5)	257	83	83	83	41	4	65	3	0	8	1	0	18	.287	.334	.453	.788
2016	Tex	AL	153	583	175	31	1	32	(14	18)	304	89	104	108	48	6	66	6	0	3	1	1	10	.300	.358	.521	.879
	Postseason		25	100	27	5	0	5	(1	4)	47	15	11	11	3	1	23	2	0	1	0	0	1	.270	.302	.470	.772
	19 ML YEARS		2720	10295	2942	591	36	445	(222	223)	4940	1428	1571	1545	775	108	1584	87	14	89	119	42	259	.286	.338	.480	.818

Andrew Benintendi

Bats: L Throws: L Pos: LF-29;CF-5;PH-3 **Ht: 5'10" Wt: 170 Born: 7/6/1994 Age: 22**

Year	Team	Lg	G	AB	H	2B	3B	HR	(Hm	Rd)	TB	R	RBI	RC	TBB	IBB	SO	HBP	SH	SF	SB	CS	GDP	Avg	OBP	Slg	OPS
2015	2 Tms	Low	54	198	62	7	4	11	(-	-)	110	36	31	46	35	2	24	2	1	3	10	3	4	.313	.416	.556	.972
2016	Salem	A+	34	135	46	13	7	1	(-	-)	76	30	32	31	15	2	9	3	0	2	8	2	3	.341	.413	.563	.976
2016	Portlnd	AA	63	237	70	18	5	8	(-	-)	122	40	44	43	24	2	30	0	0	2	8	7	2	.295	.357	.515	.872
2016	Bos	AL	34	105	31	11	1	2	(0	2)	50	16	14	20	10	0	25	1	1	1	1	0	0	.295	.359	.476	.835

Joaquin Benoit

Pitches: R Bats: R Pos: RP-51 ben-WAH **Ht: 6'4" Wt: 250 Born: 7/26/1977 Age: 39**

Year	Team	Lg	G	GS	CG	GF	IP	BFP	H	R	ER	HR	SH	SF	HB	TBB	IBB	SO	WP	Bk	W	L	Pct	Sh	Sv-Op	Hld	ERC	ERA
2001	Tex	AL	1	1	0	0	5.0	26	8	6	6	3	0	1	0	3	0	4	0	0	0	0	-	0	0-0	0	13.11	10.80
2002	Tex	AL	17	13	0	2	84.2	405	91	51	50	6	4	3	5	58	2	59	7	0	4	5	.444	0	1-1	0	5.52	5.31
2003	Tex	AL	25	17	0	1	105.0	462	99	67	64	23	1	4	3	51	0	87	3	1	8	5	.615	0	0-0	0	5.03	5.49
2004	Tex	AL	28	15	0	2	103.0	456	113	67	65	19	2	10	8	31	0	95	3	0	3	5	.375	0	0-0	0	5.10	5.68
2005	Tex	AL	32	9	0	6	87.0	369	69	39	36	9	2	1	2	38	0	78	1	0	4	4	.500	0	0-0	5	3.15	3.72
2006	Tex	AL	56	0	0	7	79.2	347	68	49	43	5	0	3	3	38	4	85	3	0	1	1	.500	0	0-2	7	3.30	4.86
2007	Tex	AL	70	0	0	22	82.0	337	68	28	26	6	3	2	2	28	2	87	3	0	7	4	.636	0	6-13	19	2.83	2.85
2008	Tex	AL	44	0	0	8	45.0	209	40	28	25	6	2	0	0	35	2	43	3	0	3	2	.600	0	1-4	13	5.02	5.00
2010	TB	AL	63	0	0	16	60.1	217	30	10	9	6	0	2	0	11	1	75	1	0	1	2	.333	0	1-4	25	1.14	1.34
2011	Det	AL	66	0	0	13	61.0	241	47	22	20	5	1	5	2	17	1	63	3	0	4	3	.571	0	2-7	29	2.46	2.95
2012	Det	AL	73	0	0	18	71.0	288	59	31	29	14	3	3	1	22	2	84	2	0	5	3	.625	0	2-6	30	3.48	3.68
2013	Det	AL	66	0	0	43	67.0	265	47	15	15	5	4	0	1	22	2	73	2	0	4	1	.800	0	24-26	9	2.15	2.01
2014	SD	NL	53	0	0	17	54.1	205	28	10	9	3	2	2	1	14	2	64	3	1	4	2	.667	0	11-12	16	1.20	1.49
2015	SD	NL	67	0	0	11	65.1	254	36	17	17	7	2	1	2	23	1	63	2	0	6	5	.545	0	2-6	28	1.78	2.34
2016	2 Tms		51	0	0	6	48.0	204	37	17	15	5	1	2	1	24	1	52	1	0	3	1	.750	0	1-4	18	3.26	2.81
16	Sea	AL	26	0	0	2	24.1	111	20	16	14	4	1	1	1	15	1	28	1	0	1	1	.500	0	0-2	8	4.30	5.18
16	Tor	AL	25	0	0	4	23.2	93	17	1	1	1	0	1	0	9	0	24	0	0	2	0	1.000	0	1-2	10	2.25	0.38
	Postseason		20	0	0	5	22.1	88	17	7	7	3	0	0	1	5	0	27	2	0	1	0	1.000	0	3-5	5	2.57	2.82
	15 ML YEARS		712	55	0	172	1018.1	4285	840	457	429	122	27	39	31	415	20	1012	37	2	57	43	.570	0	51-85	199	3.35	3.79

James Beresford

Bats: L Throws: R Pos: 1B-6;3B-3;PR-2;2B-1;PH-1 **Ht: 6'1" Wt: 170 Born: 1/19/1989 Age: 28**

Year	Team	Lg	G	AB	H	2B	3B	HR	(Hm	Rd)	TB	R	RBI	RC	TBB	IBB	SO	HBP	SH	SF	SB	CS	GDP	Avg	OBP	Slg	OPS
2012	NwBrit	AA	114	369	98	12	3	0	(-	-)	116	38	25	41	35	0	53	1	7	1	3	3	11	.266	.330	.314	.644
2013	NwBrit	AA	45	158	50	5	0	0	(-	-)	55	21	19	23	14	0	22	2	4	3	5	0	5	.316	.373	.348	.721
2013	Roch	AAA	58	198	59	7	1	0	(-	-)	68	34	21	26	16	0	29	2	5	1	5	2	3	.298	.355	.343	.698
2014	Roch	AAA	131	507	140	28	2	2	(-	-)	178	65	47	60	36	1	75	1	8	4	7	4	12	.276	.323	.351	.674
2015	Roch	AAA	129	498	153	21	1	1	(-	-)	179	58	50	64	29	0	57	0	3	6	2	2	11	.307	.341	.359	.701
2016	Roch	AAA	122	465	125	14	3	0	(-	-)	145	63	35	52	43	0	78	1	4	3	2	1	10	.269	.330	.312	.642
2016	Min	AL	10	22	5	1	0	0	(0	0)	6	0	0	0	0	0	6	0	1	0	0	0	0	.227	.261	.273	.534

Christian Bergman

Pitches: R Bats: R Pos: RP-14; SP-1 **Ht: 6'1" Wt: 195 Born: 5/4/1988 Age: 29**

Year	Team	Lg	G	GS	CG	GF	IP	BFP	H	R	ER	HR	SH	SF	HB	TBB	IBB	SO	WP	Bk	W	L	Pct	Sh	Sv-Op	Hld	ERC	ERA
2016	Albq*	AAA	10	10	0	0	51.2	215	52	24	21	8	3	3	2	12	0	33	1	0	3	3	.500	0	0--	-	4.01	3.66
2014	Col	NL	10	10	0	0	54.2	249	75	37	36	9	1	1	1	10	2	31	0	0	3	5	.375	0	0-0	0	5.74	5.93
2015	Col	NL	30	4	0	6	68.1	286	82	36	36	8	2	1	0	15	1	37	4	0	3	1	.750	0	0-0	0	4.75	4.74
2016	Col	NL	15	1	0	5	24.2	119	39	24	23	7	2	1	0	6	0	22	0	0	1	3	.250	0	0-1	0	8.27	8.39
	3 ML YEARS		55	15	0	11	147.2	654	196	97	95	24	5	3	1	31	3	90	4	0	7	9	.438	0	0-1	0	5.68	5.79

Jose Berrios

Pitches: R Bats: R Pos: SP-14 beh-REE-ohs **Ht: 6'0" Wt: 185 Born: 5/27/1994 Age: 23**

Year	Team	Lg	G	GS	CG	GF	IP	BFP	H	R	ER	HR	SH	SF	HB	TBB	IBB	SO	WP	Bk	W	L	Pct	Sh	Sv-Op	Hld	ERC	ERA
2012	2 Tms	Low	11	4	0	4	30.2	113	15	4	4	1	0	1	1	4	0	49	1	0	3	0	1.000	0	4--	-	0.86	1.17
2013	Crpds	A	19	19	0	0	103.2	455	105	58	46	6	2	3	9	40	0	100	13	1	7	7	.500	0	0--	-	4.12	3.99
2014	FtMyrs	A+	16	16	1	0	96.0	389	78	29	21	4	2	2	4	23	0	109	5	3	9	3	.750	1	0--	-	2.27	1.97
2014	NwBrit	AA	8	8	1	0	40.2	163	33	17	16	2	1	2	2	12	0	28	1	1	3	4	.429	1	0--	-	2.60	3.54
2015	Chatt	AA	15	15	1	0	90.2	367	77	32	31	6	3	3	5	20	0	92	0	0	8	3	.727	1	0--	-	2.79	3.08
2016	Roch	AAA	12	12	0	0	75.2	300	59	24	22	6	0	0	4	14	0	83	4	1	6	2	.750	0	0--	-	2.31	2.62
2016	Roch	AAA	17	17	1	0	111.1	432	74	39	31	8	3	3	3	36	0	125	3	0	10	5	.667	0	0--	-	2.06	2.51
2016	Min	AL	14	14	0	0	58.1	281	74	56	52	12	2	0	5	35	0	49	1	0	3	7	.300	0	0-0	0	7.85	8.02

Dellin Betances

Pitches: R Bats: R Pos: RP-73   DELL-inn buh-TAN-siss   Ht: 6'8" Wt: 265 Born: 3/23/1988 Age: 29

				HOW MUCH HE PITCHED				WHAT HE GAVE UP											THE RESULTS						
Year Team	Lg	G	GS	CG	GF	IP	BFP	H	R	ER	HR	SH	SF	HB	TBB	IBB	SO	WP	Bk	W	L	Pct	Sh	Sv-Op	Hld	ERC	ERA
2011 NYY	AL	2	1	0	0	2.2	16	1	2	2	0	0	1	1	6	0	2	0	0	0	0	-	0	0-0	0	7.94	6.75
2013 NYY	AL	6	0	0	3	5.0	26	9	6	6	1	0	0	0	2	0	10	0	0	0	0	-	0	0-0	0	9.81	10.80
2014 NYY	AL	70	0	0	8	90.0	341	46	15	14	4	2	3	4	24	1	135	2	1	5	0	1.000	0	1-5	22	1.24	1.40
2015 NYY	AL	74	0	0	17	84.0	332	45	17	14	6	1	1	3	40	2	131	9	0	6	4	.600	0	9-13	28	1.94	1.50
2016 NYY	AL	73	0	0	20	73.0	299	54	31	25	5	1	1	1	28	0	126	6	0	3	6	.333	0	12-17	28	2.48	3.08
Postseason		1	0	0	0	1.2	7	1	1	1	0	0	0	0	1	0	4	0	0	0	0	-	0	0-0	0	2.03	5.40
5 ML YEARS		225	1	0	48	254.2	1014	155	71	61	16	4	6	9	100	3	404	17	1	14	10	.583	0	22-35	78	1.94	2.16

Christian Bethancourt

BETH-an-court

Bats: R Throws: R Pos: C-41;PH-20;LF-8;RF-4;DH-2;2B-1;PR-1   Ht: 6'2" Wt: 210 Born: 9/2/1991 Age: 25

							BATTING											RUNNING			AVERAGES			
Year Team	Lg	G	AB	H	2B	3B	HR	(Hm | Rd)	TB	R	RBI	RC	TBB	IBB	SO	HBP	SH	SF	SB	CS	GDP	Avg	OBP	Slg	OPS
2013 Atl	NL	1	1	0	0	0	0	(0 | 0)	0	0	0	0	0	0	1	0	0	0	0	0	0	.000	.000	.000	.000
2014 Atl	NL	31	113	28	3	0	0	(0 | 0)	31	7	9	8	3	0	26	1	0	0	1	1	3	.248	.274	.274	.548
2015 Atl	NL	48	155	31	8	0	2	(1 | 1)	45	16	12	4	5	1	33	0	0	0	1	1	7	.200	.225	.290	.515
2016 SD	NL	73	193	44	9	0	6	(4 | 2)	71	20	25	15	10	0	56	0	0	1	1	2	9	.228	.265	.368	.633
4 ML YEARS		153	462	103	20	0	8	(5 | 3)	147	43	46	27	18	1	116	1	0	1	3	4	19	.223	.253	.318	.571

Chad Bettis

Pitches: R Bats: R Pos: SP-32   Ht: 6'1" Wt: 200 Born: 4/26/1989 Age: 28

				HOW MUCH HE PITCHED				WHAT HE GAVE UP											THE RESULTS						
Year Team	Lg	G	GS	CG	GF	IP	BFP	H	R	ER	HR	SH	SF	HB	TBB	IBB	SO	WP	Bk	W	L	Pct	Sh	Sv-Op	Hld	ERC	ERA
2013 Col	NL	16	8	0	0	44.2	208	55	34	28	6	3	1	2	20	2	30	2	1	1	3	.250	0	0-1	3	5.95	5.64
2014 Col	NL	21	0	0	9	24.2	127	42	26	25	4	5	0	1	10	2	13	5	0	0	2	.000	0	0-1	1	8.84	9.12
2015 Col	NL	20	20	0	0	115.0	502	120	56	54	11	7	2	3	42	2	98	6	0	8	6	.571	0	0-0	0	4.23	4.23
2016 Col	NL	32	32	1	0	186.0	814	204	107	99	22	10	3	7	59	5	138	4	0	14	8	.636	1	0-0	0	4.51	4.79
4 ML YEARS		89	60	1	9	370.1	1651	421	223	206	43	25	6	13	131	11	279	17	1	23	19	.548	1	0-2	4	4.84	5.01

Mookie Betts

Bats: R Throws: R Pos: RF-157;PH-1   Ht: 5'9" Wt: 180 Born: 10/7/1992 Age: 24

							BATTING											RUNNING			AVERAGES			
Year Team	Lg	G	AB	H	2B	3B	HR	(Hm | Rd)	TB	R	RBI	RC	TBB	IBB	SO	HBP	SH	SF	SB	CS	GDP	Avg	OBP	Slg	OPS
2014 Bos	AL	52	189	55	12	1	5	(1 | 4)	84	34	18	30	21	0	31	2	1	0	7	3	2	.291	.368	.444	.812
2015 Bos	AL	145	597	174	42	8	18	(9 | 9)	286	92	77	100	46	1	82	2	3	6	21	6	8	.291	.341	.479	.820
2016 Bos	AL	158	672	214	42	5	31	(17 | 14)	359	122	113	130	49	1	80	2	0	7	26	4	12	.318	.363	.534	.897
3 ML YEARS		355	1458	443	96	14	54	(27 | 27)	729	248	208	260	116	2	193	6	4	13	54	13	16	.304	.355	.500	.855

Joseph Biagini

Pitches: R Bats: R Pos: RP-60   bee-ah-gee-nee   Ht: 6'5" Wt: 240 Born: 5/29/1990 Age: 27

				HOW MUCH HE PITCHED				WHAT HE GAVE UP											THE RESULTS						
Year Team	Lg	G	GS	CG	GF	IP	BFP	H	R	ER	HR	SH	SF	HB	TBB	IBB	SO	WP	Bk	W	L	Pct	Sh	Sv-Op	Hld	ERC	ERA
2012 2 Tms	Low	23	21	0	0	93.0	408	90	65	56	9	0	5	3	47	0	99	13	0	2	8	.200	0	0- -	-	4.44	5.42
2013 Augsta	A	20	20	0	0	96.2	430	102	63	54	5	1	1	4	42	0	79	6	0	7	6	.538	0	0- -	-	4.31	5.03
2014 SnJos	A+	23	23	0	0	128.0	541	133	58	57	5	3	3	6	46	0	103	10	0	10	9	.526	0	0- -	-	4.01	4.01
2015 Rchmd	AA	23	22	0	0	130.1	533	112	45	35	5	4	0	4	34	0	84	7	0	10	7	.588	0	0- -	-	2.52	2.42
2016 Tor	AL	60	0	0	12	67.2	295	69	28	23	3	2	3	5	19	1	62	3	0	4	3	.571	0	1-3	8	3.52	3.06

Gregory Bird

Bats: L Throws: R Pos: 1B   Ht: 6'4" Wt: 220 Born: 11/9/1992 Age: 24

							BATTING											RUNNING			AVERAGES			
Year Team	Lg	G	AB	H	2B	3B	HR	(Hm | Rd)	TB	R	RBI	RC	TBB	IBB	SO	HBP	SH	SF	SB	CS	GDP	Avg	OBP	Slg	OPS
2012 2 Tms	Low	28	89	30	6	1	2	(- | -)	44	13	13	20	17	1	23	2	0	1	0	0	1	.337	.450	.494	.944
2013 CtnSC	A	130	458	132	36	3	20	(- | -)	234	84	84	105	107	4	132	6	0	2	1	1	9	.288	.428	.511	.938
2014 Tampa	A+	75	274	76	22	1	7	(- | -)	121	36	32	49	45	3	70	1	0	5	1	0	5	.277	.375	.442	.817
2014 Trntn	AA	27	95	24	8	0	7	(- | -)	53	16	11	20	18	0	27	2	0	1	0	0	0	.253	.373	.558	.937
2015 Trntn	AA	49	182	47	16	0	6	(- | -)	81	29	29	30	24	1	30	5	0	1	1	1	4	.258	.358	.445	.804
2015 S-WB	AAA	34	136	41	7	1	6	(- | -)	68	15	23	24	11	0	27	1	0	2	0	0	1	.301	.353	.500	.853
2015 NYY	AL	46	157	41	9	0	11	(5 | 6)	83	26	31	30	19	0	53	1	0	1	0	0	1	.261	.343	.529	.871
Postseason		1	3	1	0	0	0	(0 | 0)	1	0	0	0	0	0	1	0	0	0	0	0	0	.333	.333	.333	.667

Ty Blach

Pitches: L Bats: R Pos: SP-2; RP-2   block   Ht: 6'2" Wt: 200 Born: 10/20/1990 Age: 26

				HOW MUCH HE PITCHED				WHAT HE GAVE UP											THE RESULTS						
Year Team	Lg	G	GS	CG	GF	IP	BFP	H	R	ER	HR	SH	SF	HB	TBB	IBB	SO	WP	Bk	W	L	Pct	Sh	Sv-Op	Hld	ERC	ERA
2013 SnJos	A+	22	20	0	1	130.1	526	124	46	42	8	4	7	1	18	0	117	8	1	12	4	.750	0	0- -	-	2.64	2.90
2014 Rchmd	AA	25	25	1	0	141.0	596	142	53	49	8	7	3	3	39	2	91	5	0	8	8	.500	0	0- -	-	3.39	3.13
2015 Scrmto	AAA	27	27	2	0	165.1	699	189	92	82	16	9	5	2	31	0	93	6	0	11	12	.478	2	0- -	-	4.08	4.46
2016 Scrmto	AAA	26	26	3	0	162.2	655	147	65	62	9	5	7	2	38	0	113	6	1	14	7	.667	2	0- -	-	2.73	3.43
2016 SF	NL	4	2	0	2	17.0	62	8	2	2	1	1	0	0	5	0	10	0	1	1	0	1.000	0	0-0	0	1.18	1.06

Charlie Blackmon

Bats: L Throws: L Pos: CF-138;PH-5

Ht: 6'3" Wt: 210 Born: 7/1/1986 Age: 30

Year	Team	Lg	G	AB	H	2B	3B	HR	(Hm	Rd)	TB	R	RBI	RC	TBB	IBB	SO	HBP	SH	SF	SB	CS	GDP	Avg	OBP	Slg	OPS
2011	Col	NL	27	98	25	1	0	1	(1	0)	29	9	8	10	3	1	8	0	1	0	5	1	2	.255	.277	.296	.573
2012	Col	NL	42	113	32	8	0	2	(1	1)	46	15	9	11	4	0	17	3	1	0	1	2	4	.283	.325	.407	.732
2013	Col	NL	82	246	76	17	2	6	(3	3)	115	35	22	35	7	0	49	3	2	0	7	0	1	.309	.336	.467	.803
2014	Col	NL	154	593	171	27	3	19	(13	6)	261	82	72	87	31	5	96	13	6	5	28	10	3	.288	.335	.440	.775
2015	Col	NL	157	614	176	31	9	17	(7	10)	276	93	58	95	46	2	112	13	5	4	43	13	4	.287	.347	.450	.797
2016	Col	NL	143	578	187	35	5	29	(12	17)	319	111	82	110	43	4	102	13	3	4	17	9	2	.324	.381	.552	.933
	6 ML YEARS		605	2242	667	119	19	74	(37	37)	1046	345	251	348	134	12	384	45	18	13	101	35	16	.298	.348	.467	.814

Aaron Blair

Pitches: R Bats: R Pos: SP-15

Ht: 6'4" Wt: 250 Born: 5/26/1992 Age: 25

Year	Team	Lg	G	GS	CG	GF	IP	BFP	H	R	ER	HR	SH	SF	HB	TBB	IBB	SO	WP	Bk	W	L	Pct	Sh	Sv-Op	Hld	ERC	ERA
2013	2 Tms	Low	11	11	0	0	48.2	203	44	20	17	2	1	3	3	17	0	41	1	1	1	3	.250	0	0- -	-	3.24	3.14
2014	2 Tms	Low	19	19	1	0	107.2	463	95	56	51	8	1	4	11	35	0	125	9	0	5	4	.556	0	0- -	-	3.29	4.26
2014	Mobile	AA	8	8	0	0	46.1	182	30	11	10	4	2	0	2	16	0	46	3	0	4	1	.800	0	0- -	-	2.17	1.94
2015	Mobile	AA	13	13	1	0	83.1	332	70	28	25	8	2	1	3	23	0	64	8	0	6	3	.667	0	0- -	-	2.95	2.70
2015	Reno	AAA	13	12	0	0	77.0	316	67	31	27	5	2	2	1	27	1	56	2	0	7	2	.778	0	0- -	-	3.03	3.16
2016	Gwnntt	AAA	13	13	0	0	71.2	314	77	38	37	4	2	0	3	32	1	71	6	0	5	4	.556	0	0- -	-	4.58	4.65
2016	Atl	NL	15	15	0	0	70.0	324	82	61	59	14	3	7	6	34	4	46	0	0	2	7	.222	0	0-0	0	6.51	7.59

Andres Blanco

Bats: B Throws: R Pos: PH-33;3B-21;2B-20;1B-19;SS-10;LF-1

Ht: 5'10" Wt: 195 Born: 4/11/1984 Age: 33

Year	Team	Lg	G	AB	H	2B	3B	HR	(Hm	Rd)	TB	R	RBI	RC	TBB	IBB	SO	HBP	SH	SF	SB	CS	GDP	Avg	OBP	Slg	OPS
2004	KC	AL	19	60	19	2	2	0	(0	0)	25	9	5	12	5	0	6	1	1	0	1	2	0	.317	.379	.417	.795
2005	KC	AL	26	79	17	0	1	0	(0	0)	19	6	5	3	0	0	5	1	4	2	0	1	3	.215	.220	.241	.460
2006	KC	AL	33	87	21	4	1	0	(0	0)	27	9	9	9	5	0	14	1	3	0	0	1	0	.241	.290	.310	.601
2009	ChC	NL	53	123	31	8	0	1	(1	0)	42	15	12	9	8	3	14	1	6	0	0	2	4	.252	.303	.341	.644
2010	Tex	AL	68	166	46	10	1	0	(0	0)	58	17	13	19	11	1	24	3	3	2	0	2	0	.277	.330	.349	.679
2011	Tex	AL	36	76	17	3	0	2	(2	0)	26	9	3	4	4	0	14	0	2	0	0	1	1	.224	.263	.342	.605
2014	Phi	NL	25	47	13	5	0	1	(1	0)	21	4	3	6	2	1	6	0	4	0	0	0	4	.277	.306	.447	.753
2015	Phi	NL	106	233	68	22	3	7	(4	3)	117	32	25	34	21	0	44	4	3	0	1	1	11	.292	.360	.502	.863
2016	Phi	NL	90	190	48	15	1	4	(1	3)	77	26	21	26	11	0	41	7	0	1	2	3	7	.253	.316	.405	.721
	9 ML YEARS		456	1061	280	69	9	15	(9	6)	412	127	96	122	67	5	168	18	26	5	4	13	32	.264	.317	.388	.705

Gregor Blanco

Bats: L Throws: L Pos: PH-38;RF-34;LF-29;CF-18;PR-3

Ht: 5'11" Wt: 175 Born: 12/24/1983 Age: 33

Year	Team	Lg	G	AB	H	2B	3B	HR	(Hm	Rd)	TB	R	RBI	RC	TBB	IBB	SO	HBP	SH	SF	SB	CS	GDP	Avg	OBP	Slg	OPS
2008	Atl	NL	144	430	108	14	4	1	(0	1)	133	52	38	60	74	2	99	6	6	3	13	5	3	.251	.366	.309	.676
2009	Atl	NL	24	43	8	0	1	0	(0	0)	10	5	1	2	4	0	9	0	1	0	2	0	1	.186	.255	.233	.488
2010	2 Tms		85	237	67	9	4	1	(1	0)	87	31	14	30	29	1	50	0	2	1	11	4	5	.283	.360	.367	.727
2012	SF	NL	141	393	96	14	5	5	(2	3)	135	56	34	50	51	2	104	2	5	2	26	6	4	.244	.333	.344	.676
2013	SF	NL	141	452	120	17	6	3	(0	3)	158	50	41	54	52	4	95	1	3	3	14	9	10	.265	.341	.350	.690
2014	SF	NL	146	393	102	18	6	5	(2	3)	147	51	38	53	41	1	77	3	6	1	16	5	4	.260	.333	.374	.707
2015	SF	NL	115	327	95	19	3	5	(0	5)	135	59	26	41	40	7	59	2	0	3	13	5	3	.291	.368	.413	.781
2016	SF	NL	106	241	54	10	4	1	(1	0)	75	28	18	22	29	4	51	1	1	1	6	3	5	.224	.309	.311	.620
10	Atl	NL	36	58	18	1	1	0	(0	0)	21	9	3	8	8	1	15	0	0	0	1	2	2	.310	.394	.362	.756
10	KC	AL	49	179	49	8	3	1	(1	0)	66	22	11	22	21	0	35	0	2	1	10	2	3	.274	.348	.369	.717
	Postseason		33	123	23	3	2	2	(0	2)	36	20	10	14	17	0	22	1	2	0	2	0	0	.187	.291	.293	.583
	8 ML YEARS		902	2516	650	101	33	21	(6	15)	880	332	210	312	320	21	544	15	24	14	101	37	31	.258	.344	.350	.694

Joe Blanton

Pitches: R Bats: R Pos: RP-75

Ht: 6'3" Wt: 225 Born: 12/11/1980 Age: 36

Year	Team	Lg	G	GS	CG	GF	IP	BFP	H	R	ER	HR	SH	SF	HB	TBB	IBB	SO	WP	Bk	W	L	Pct	Sh	Sv-Op	Hld	ERC	ERA
2004	Oak	AL	3	0	0	1	8.0	30	6	5	5	1	0	0	0	2	0	6	0	0	0	0	-	0	0-0	0	2.52	5.63
2005	Oak	AL	33	33	2	0	201.1	835	178	86	79	23	2	7	5	67	3	116	4	2	12	12	.500	2	0-0	0	3.37	3.53
2006	Oak	AL	32	31	1	0	194.1	856	241	111	104	17	3	9	5	58	4	107	3	0	16	12	.571	1	0-0	0	5.09	4.82
2007	Oak	AL	34	34	3	0	230.0	950	240	106	101	16	5	8	4	40	4	140	3	1	14	10	.583	1	0-0	0	3.30	3.95
2008	2 Tms		33	33	0	0	197.2	855	211	110	103	22	2	4	4	66	3	111	2	0	9	12	.429	0	0-0	0	4.33	4.69
2009	Phi	NL	31	31	0	0	195.1	837	198	89	88	30	11	4	8	59	4	163	7	0	12	8	.600	0	0-0	0	4.25	4.05
2010	Phi	NL	29	28	0	0	175.2	765	206	104	94	27	5	7	3	43	6	134	2	0	9	6	.600	0	0-0	0	4.81	4.82
2011	Phi	NL	11	8	0	1	41.1	180	52	23	23	5	5	2	1	9	0	35	0	0	1	2	.333	0	0-0	0	5.13	5.01
2012	2 Tms		31	30	2	1	191.0	806	207	106	100	29	8	4	2	34	5	166	5	0	10	13	.435	1	0-0	0	4.00	4.71
2013	LAA	AL	28	20	0	7	132.2	611	180	96	89	29	1	5	4	34	4	108	9	0	2	14	.125	0	0-0	0	6.48	6.04
2015	2 Tms		36	4	0	13	76.0	309	69	26	24	7	1	3	1	16	5	79	2	0	7	2	.778	0	2-2	0	2.77	2.84
2016	LAD	NL	75	0	0	15	80.0	315	55	23	22	7	0	3	2	26	4	80	3	0	7	2	.778	0	0-1	28	2.17	2.48
08	Oak	AL	20	20	0	0	127.0	550	145	74	70	12	1	2	1	35	3	62	1	0	5	12	.294	0	0-0	0	4.33	4.96
08	Phi	NL	13	13	0	0	70.2	305	66	36	33	10	1	2	3	31	0	49	1	0	4	0	1.000	0	0-0	0	4.33	4.20
12	Phi	NL	21	20	2	1	133.1	560	141	74	68	22	6	3	1	18	2	115	4	0	8	9	.471	1	0-0	0	3.77	4.59
12	LAD	NL	10	10	0	0	57.2	246	66	32	32	7	2	1	0	16	3	51	1	0	2	4	.333	0	0-0	0	4.54	4.99

Year Team	Lg	G GS CG GF	IP	BFP	H	R	ER	HR SH SF HB	TBB IBB	SO	WP Bk	W	L	Pct	Sh	Sv-Op	Hld	ERC	ERA
15 KC	AL	15 4 0 6	41.2	172	43	19	18	6 1 2 0	7 1	40	0 0	2	2	.500	0	2-2	0	3.59	3.89
15 Pit	NL	21 0 0 7	34.1	137	26	7	6	1 0 1 1	9 4	39	2 0	5	0	1.000	0	0-0	0	1.84	1.57
Postseason		10 6 0 1	40.1	172	36	19	18	5 1 1 3	13 2	33	2 0	2	0	1.000	0	0-0	0	3.51	4.02
12 ML YEARS		376 252 8 38	1723.1	7349	1843	885	832	213 43 56 40	454 42	1245	40 3	99	93	.516	3	2-3	28	4.14	4.35

Jabari Blash

Bats: R **Throws:** R **Pos:** RF-18;PH-17;LF-4   **Ht:** 6'5" **Wt:** 235 **Born:** 7/4/1989 **Age:** 27

Year Team	Lg	G	AB	H	2B	3B	HR	(Hm Rd)	TB	R	RBI	RC	TBB IBB	SO	HBP SH SF	SB CS GDP	Avg	OBP	Slg	OPS
2012 Clinton	A	113	400	98	20	5	15	(- -)	173	71	50	65	60 0	134	9 0 2	13 7 8	.245	.355	.433	.787
2013 Hi Dsrt	A+	80	283	73	16	3	16	(- -)	143	42	53	52	40 0	85	6 0 3	14 8 9	.258	.358	.505	.864
2013 Jacksn	AA	29	97	30	3	0	9	(- -)	60	13	21	25	20 1	28	3 0 0	1 1 1	.309	.442	.619	1.060
2014 Jacksn	AA	37	127	30	7	1	6	(- -)	57	27	22	25	28 2	35	5 0 3	4 1 3	.236	.387	.449	.835
2014 Tacom	AAA	45	162	34	8	0	12	(- -)	78	23	37	25	17 0	57	8 0 2	2 2 2	.210	.312	.481	.794
2015 Tacom	AAA	56	197	52	8	0	22	(- -)	126	41	47	44	28 0	63	1 0 2	3 1 3	.264	.355	.640	.995
2015 Jacksn	AA	60	209	58	16	2	10	(- -)	108	38	34	43	31 0	60	6 0 2	5 0 7	.278	.383	.517	.900
2016 ElPaso	AAA	62	177	46	12	0	11	(- -)	91	30	30	40	41 1	66	8 0 3	1 2 3	.260	.415	.514	.929
2016 SD	NL	38	71	12	2	0	3	(1 2)	23	7	5	5	11 0	34	2 0 0	1 0 3	.169	.298	.324	.622

Michael Blazek

Pitches: R **Bats:** R **Pos:** RP-41   BLAY-zek   **Ht:** 6'0" **Wt:** 205 **Born:** 3/16/1989 **Age:** 28

Year Team	Lg	G GS CG GF	IP	BFP	H	R	ER	HR SH SF HB	TBB IBB	SO	WP Bk	W	L	Pct	Sh	Sv-Op	Hld	ERC	ERA
2016 ColSpr*	AAA	5 1 0 0	8.1	36	10	4	4	0 0 0 1	3 0	8	0 0	0	0	-	0	0--	-	5.07	4.32
2013 2 Tms	NL	18 0 0 7	17.1	84	16	12	11	3 1 1 1	13 0	14	0 0	0	1	.000	0	0-0	-	5.57	5.71
2015 Mil	NL	45 0 0 17	55.2	222	40	17	15	3 1 2 1	18 1	47	3 0	5	3	.625	0	0-0	4	2.11	2.43
2016 Mil	NL	41 0 0 7	41.1	201	52	31	26	7 1 4 2	27 3	36	2 0	3	1	.750	0	0-1	9	7.31	5.66
13 StL	NL	11 0 0 3	10.1	52	10	8	8	2 0 0 1	10 0	10	0 0	0	0	-	0	0-0	-	7.25	6.97
13 Mil	NL	7 0 0 4	7.0	32	6	4	3	1 1 1 0	3 0	4	0 0	0	1	.000	0	0-0	-	3.35	3.86
3 ML YEARS		104 0 0 31	114.1	507	108	60	52	13 3 7 4	58 4	97	5 0	8	5	.615	0	0-1	13	4.32	4.09

Richard Bleier

Pitches: L **Bats:** L **Pos:** RP-23   BLY-er   **Ht:** 6'3" **Wt:** 215 **Born:** 4/16/1987 **Age:** 30

Year Team	Lg	G GS CG GF	IP	BFP	H	R	ER	HR SH SF HB	TBB IBB	SO	WP Bk	W	L	Pct	Sh	Sv-Op	Hld	ERC	ERA
2012 Frisco	AA	22 0 0 10	32.0	132	34	15	14	3 1 0 0	7 2	17	0 0	0	2	.000	0	1--	-	3.64	3.94
2013 RdRck	AAA	8 2 0 0	19.0	83	23	9	8	1 2 1 0	7 1	8	0 0	1	1	.500	0	0--	-	4.83	3.79
2013 Frisco	AA	34 2 0 6	62.1	256	61	27	22	5 0 2 1	13 1	41	4 0	5	5	.500	0	4--	-	3.15	3.18
2014 Nham	AA	34 5 0 8	84.2	359	100	47	37	13 1 1 3	11 1	43	5 2	6	5	.545	0	1--	-	4.53	3.93
2015 Hrsbrg	AA	16 15 0 1	103.0	404	95	32	28	6 4 1 5	9 1	40	0 4	8	3	.727	0	0--	-	2.46	2.45
2015 Syrcse	AAA	12 11 1 0	68.2	278	75	24	21	0 1 1 2	7 0	25	2 0	6	2	.750	1	0--	-	2.96	2.75
2016 S-WB	AAA	12 10 0 2	58.0	240	66	25	24	2 2 0 1	11 0	25	2 1	2	3	.400	0	1--	-	3.74	3.72
2016 NYY	AL	23 0 0 8	23.0	92	20	6	5	0 0 1 1	4 0	13	0 0	0	0	-	0	0-0	2	2.11	1.96

Jerry Blevins

Pitches: L **Bats:** L **Pos:** RP-73   **Ht:** 6'6" **Wt:** 190 **Born:** 9/6/1983 **Age:** 33

Year Team	Lg	G GS CG GF	IP	BFP	H	R	ER	HR SH SF HB	TBB IBB	SO	WP Bk	W	L	Pct	Sh	Sv-Op	Hld	ERC	ERA
2007 Oak	AL	6 0 0 1	4.2	25	8	6	5	1 0 0 0	2 0	3	0 0	0	1	.000	0	0-0	-	9.08	9.64
2008 Oak	AL	36 0 0 8	37.2	156	32	14	13	2 0 1 3	13 2	35	0 0	1	3	.250	0	0-1	5	3.00	3.11
2009 Oak	AL	20 0 0 5	22.1	90	19	12	12	2 0 1 0	6 1	23	0 0	0	0	-	0	0-0	2	2.68	4.84
2010 Oak	AL	63 0 0 9	48.2	220	54	20	20	7 3 1 1	18 1	46	0 0	2	1	.667	0	1-2	11	4.81	3.70
2011 Oak	AL	26 0 0 11	28.1	122	24	14	9	2 2 3 1	14 1	26	0 0	0	0	-	0	0-0	0	3.45	2.86
2012 Oak	AL	63 0 0 17	65.1	261	45	20	18	7 5 2 5	25 5	54	2 0	5	1	.833	0	1-1	14	2.66	2.48
2013 Oak	AL	67 0 0 14	60.0	245	47	23	21	7 3 5 4	17 2	52	2 0	5	0	1.000	0	0-4	19	2.78	3.15
2014 Was	NL	64 0 0 25	57.1	240	48	31	31	3 3 3 1	23 6	66	2 0	2	3	.400	0	0-0	9	2.78	4.87
2015 NYM	NL	7 0 0 1	5.0	15	0	0	0	0 0 0 0	2 0	5	0 0	1	0	1.000	0	0-1	5	0.00	0.00
2016 NYM	NL	73 0 0 8	42.0	178	36	14	13	4 2 3 1	15 3	52	1 0	4	2	.667	0	2-3	16	3.02	2.79
Postseason		6 0 0 1	7.0	22	1	0	0	0 0 0 0	0 0	2	0 0	0	0	-	0	0-0	0	0.05	0.00
10 ML YEARS		425 0 0 99	371.1	1552	313	154	142	35 18 19 16	133 21	361	7 0	20	11	.645	0	4-12	64	3.10	3.44

Xander Bogaerts

Bats: R **Throws:** R **Pos:** SS-157   ZAN-derr BO-garts   **Ht:** 6'1" **Wt:** 210 **Born:** 10/1/1992 **Age:** 24

Year Team	Lg	G	AB	H	2B	3B	HR	(Hm Rd)	TB	R	RBI	RC	TBB IBB	SO	HBP SH SF	SB CS GDP	Avg	OBP	Slg	OPS
2013 Bos	AL	18	44	11	2	0	1	(0 1)	16	7	5	4	5 0	13	0 0 1	1 0 1	.250	.320	.364	.684
2014 Bos	AL	144	538	129	28	1	12	(7 5)	195	60	46	43	39 1	138	8 2 7	2 3 11	.240	.297	.362	.660
2015 Bos	AL	156	613	196	35	3	7	(5 2)	258	84	81	88	32 1	101	3 3 3	10 2 16	.320	.355	.421	.776
2016 Bos	AL	157	652	192	34	1	21	(11 10)	291	115	89	98	58 0	123	6 0 3	13 4 14	.294	.356	.446	.802
Postseason		12	27	8	3	1	0	(0 0)	13	9	2	5	6 0	9	0 0 0	1 0 1	.296	.412	.481	.893
4 ML YEARS		475	1847	528	99	5	41	(23 18)	760	266	221	233	134 2	375	17 5 14	26 9 42	.286	.337	.411	.749

Mike Bolsinger

Pitches: R Bats: R Pos: SP-6 BOWL-sing-er **Ht: 6'1" Wt: 215 Born: 1/29/1988 Age: 29**

Year Team	Lg	G	GS	CG	GF	IP	BFP	H	R	ER	HR	SH	SF	HB	TBB	IBB	SO	WP	Bk	W	L	Pct	Sh	Sv-Op	Hld	ERC	ERA
2016 OkCity*	AAA	13	2	0	3	29.0	124	32	12	11	2	0	3	0	10	0	34	2	0	2	1	.667	0	0- -	-	4.30	3.41
2016 Buffalo*	AAA	6	6	0	0	25.1	114	29	19	17	4	0	0	1	11	0	27	2	0	1	4	.200	0	0- -	-	5.69	6.04
2014 Ari	NL	10	9	0	0	52.1	238	66	36	32	7	3	4	0	17	1	48	0	1	1	6	.143	0	0-0	0	5.42	5.50
2015 LAD	NL	21	21	0	0	109.1	466	104	49	44	11	3	2	1	45	3	98	6	1	6	6	.500	0	0-0	0	3.87	3.62
2016 LAD	NL	6	6	0	0	27.2	122	33	21	21	7	2	0	2	9	1	25	0	0	1	4	.200	0	0-0	0	6.43	6.83
3 ML YEARS		37	36	0	0	189.1	826	203	106	97	25	8	6	3	71	5	171	6	2	8	16	.333	0	0-0	0	4.64	4.61

Emilio Bonifacio

Bats: B Throws: R Pos: PH-13;LF-12;CF-1 bone-ee-FAH-see-oh **Ht: 5'10" Wt: 210 Born: 4/23/1985 Age: 32**

Year Team	Lg	G	AB	H	2B	3B	HR	(Hm	Rd)	TB	R	RBI	RC	TBB	IBB	SO	HBP	SH	SF	SB	CS	GDP	Avg	OBP	Slg	OPS
2016 Gwnntt*	AAA	107	420	125	14	5	2	(-	-)	155	57	40	62	39	2	70	1	7	4	37	9	2	.298	.356	.369	.725
2007 Ari	NL	11	23	5	1	0	0	(0	0)	6	2	2	4	4	0	3	0	0	0	0	1	0	.217	.333	.261	.594
2008 2 Tms	NL	49	169	41	6	5	0	(0	0)	57	29	14	16	14	0	46	0	0	3	7	4	2	.243	.296	.337	.633
2009 Fla	NL	127	461	116	11	6	1	(1	0)	142	72	27	41	34	0	95	2	8	4	21	9	5	.252	.303	.308	.611
2010 Fla	NL	73	180	47	6	3	0	(0	0)	59	30	10	24	17	0	42	0	1	3	12	0	1	.261	.320	.328	.648
2011 Fla	NL	152	565	167	26	7	5	(1	4)	222	78	36	83	59	1	129	1	11	5	40	11	4	.296	.360	.393	.753
2012 Mia	NL	64	244	63	3	4	1	(1	0)	77	30	11	30	25	1	52	1	4	0	30	3	3	.258	.330	.316	.645
2013 2 Tms	AL	136	420	102	22	3	3	(1	2)	139	54	31	39	30	0	103	2	6	3	28	8	4	.243	.295	.331	.625
2014 2 Tms	AL	110	394	102	17	4	3	(2	1)	136	47	24	46	26	2	85	0	6	0	26	8	2	.259	.305	.345	.650
2015 CWS	AL	47	78	13	2	0	0	(0	0)	15	5	4	1	2	0	27	1	1	0	1	4	1	.167	.198	.192	.390
2016 Atl	NL	24	38	8	0	0	0	(0	0)	8	6	3	3	3	0	12	0	2	0	1	0	0	.211	.268	.211	.479
08 Ari	NL	8	12	2	1	0	0	(0	0)	3	3	2	1	0	0	5	0	0	0	1	0	0	.167	.167	.250	.417
08 Was	NL	41	157	39	5	5	0	(0	0)	54	26	12	15	14	0	41	0	0	3	6	4	2	.248	.305	.344	.649
13 Tor	AL	94	262	57	16	1	3	(1	2)	84	33	20	19	13	0	66	2	3	2	12	6	3	.218	.254	.321	.579
13 KC	AL	42	158	45	6	2	0	(0	0)	55	21	11	20	17	0	37	0	3	1	16	2	1	.285	.352	.348	.700
14 ChC	NL	69	276	77	14	3	2	(2	0)	103	35	18	37	16	2	49	0	6	0	14	6	1	.279	.318	.373	.692
14 Atl	NL	41	118	25	3	1	1	(0	1)	33	12	6	9	10	0	36	0	0	0	12	2	1	.212	.273	.280	.553
10 ML YEARS		793	2572	664	94	32	13	(6	7)	861	353	162	287	214	4	594	7	39	18	166	48	22	.258	.315	.335	.650

Julio Borbon

Bats: L Throws: L Pos: LF-3;CF-3 bore-BONE **Ht: 6'0" Wt: 195 Born: 2/20/1986 Age: 31**

Year Team	Lg	G	AB	H	2B	3B	HR	(Hm	Rd)	TB	R	RBI	RC	TBB	IBB	SO	HBP	SH	SF	SB	CS	GDP	Avg	OBP	Slg	OPS
2016 Bowie*	AA	111	424	117	11	4	6	(-	-)	154	61	27	56	36	1	59	2	7	1	30	10	16	.276	.335	.363	.698
2009 Tex	AL	46	157	49	4	0	4	(2	2)	65	30	20	27	15	0	28	1	6	0	19	4	3	.312	.376	.414	.790
2010 Tex	AL	137	438	121	11	4	3	(2	1)	149	60	42	48	19	0	59	2	8	1	15	7	5	.276	.309	.340	.649
2011 Tex	AL	32	89	24	1	3	0	(0	0)	31	10	11	14	3	0	9	2	3	1	6	2	2	.270	.305	.348	.654
2013 2 Tms		73	105	21	3	1	1	(0	1)	29	11	3	9	12	0	22	0	1	0	7	1	0	.200	.282	.276	.558
2016 Bal	AL	6	13	4	0	0	0	(0	0)	4	1	0	1	0	0	3	0	2	0	0	1	0	.308	.308	.308	.615
13 Tex	AL	1	1	0	0	0	0	(0	0)	0	0	0	0	0	0	0	0	0	0	0	0	0	.000	.000	.000	.000
13 ChC	NL	72	104	21	3	1	1	(0	1)	29	10	3	9	12	0	22	0	1	0	7	1	0	.202	.284	.279	.563
Postseason		8	9	1	0	0	0	(0	0)	1	4	0	1	0	0	3	0	0	0	0	0	0	.111	.111	.111	.222
5 ML YEARS		294	802	219	19	8	8	(4	4)	278	112	76	99	49	0	121	5	20	2	47	15	10	.273	.318	.347	.665

Wilfredo Boscan

Pitches: R Bats: R Pos: RP-5; SP-1 bohs-KAHN **Ht: 6'2" Wt: 175 Born: 10/26/1989 Age: 27**

Year Team	Lg	G	GS	CG	GF	IP	BFP	H	R	ER	HR	SH	SF	HB	TBB	IBB	SO	WP	Bk	W	L	Pct	Sh	Sv-Op	Hld	ERC	ERA
2012 Frisco	AA	34	9	0	5	98.1	405	92	45	41	10	2	1	3	28	2	89	6	0	7	5	.583	0	0- -	-	3.43	3.75
2013 SnAnt	AA	5	4	0	1	19.0	86	21	11	9	3	0	0	0	7	0	11	2	0	0	1	.000	0	0- -	-	4.79	4.26
2013 Tucsn	AAA	14	6	0	1	43.0	199	61	35	32	9	0	1	3	10	1	22	2	0	1	3	.250	0	1- -	-	6.98	6.70
2014 Portlnd	AA	20	5	0	4	62.2	272	75	38	27	6	1	4	1	15	0	44	4	0	1	7	.125	0	1- -	-	4.60	3.88
2015 Indy	AAA	25	23	0	1	126.0	547	130	53	43	3	6	8	7	45	3	86	9	2	10	3	.769	0	0- -	-	3.72	3.07
2016 Indy	AAA	17	16	1	1	84.0	351	97	39	35	5	7	1	4	14	0	51	1	0	6	7	.462	0	0- -	-	4.03	3.75
2016 Pit	NL	6	1	0	2	15.1	67	15	11	11	2	1	0	0	7	0	8	1	1	1	1	.500	0	0-0	0	4.37	6.46

Buddy Boshers

Pitches: L Bats: L Pos: RP-37 bo-SHEERS **Ht: 6'3" Wt: 205 Born: 5/9/1988 Age: 29**

Year Team	Lg	G	GS	CG	GF	IP	BFP	H	R	ER	HR	SH	SF	HB	TBB	IBB	SO	WP	Bk	W	L	Pct	Sh	Sv-Op	Hld	ERC	ERA
2012 InldEm	A+	26	0	0	11	39.1	167	30	15	11	4	1	1	0	16	1	48	1	0	4	2	.667	0	1- -	-	2.70	2.52
2012 Ark	AA	19	0	0	0	24.0	106	28	10	10	3	3	1	1	5	1	27	2	0	1	0	1.000	0	1- -	-	4.42	3.75
2013 Ark	AA	28	0	0	7	28.2	117	20	12	10	1	1	1	0	13	0	35	3	1	3	2	.600	0	1- -	-	2.28	3.14
2013 Salt Lk	AAA	16	0	0	2	19.2	88	18	11	8	1	3	0	0	12	1	26	3	1	1	0	1.000	0	1- -	-	3.92	3.66
2014 Salt Lk	AAA	11	0	0	0	13.0	57	10	9	9	1	0	0	0	13	0	12	0	0	1	0	1.000	0	0- -	-	5.28	6.23
2014 Ark	AA	29	8	0	3	61.0	255	47	21	18	1	2	2	1	27	0	70	10	0	2	3	.400	0	0- -	-	2.50	2.66
2016 Roch	AAA	22	0	0	8	26.0	105	18	8	3	1	1	0	0	11	0	29	2	0	1	1	.500	0	2- -	-	2.18	1.04
2013 LAA	AL	25	0	0	1	15.1	63	13	8	8	0	0	0	1	8	1	13	0	0	1	0	-	0	0-0	6	3.33	4.70
2016 Min	AL	37	0	0	9	36.0	152	35	21	17	3	0	3	1	7	1	37	1	0	1	0	1.000	0	0-0	2	3.00	4.25
2 ML YEARS		62	0	0	10	51.1	215	48	29	25	3	0	3	2	15	2	50	1	0	2	0	1.000	0	0-0	8	3.12	4.38

Justin Bour

Bats: L Throws: R Pos: 1B-82;PH-8;DH-1   BOOR   Ht: 6'3" Wt: 265 Born: 5/28/1988 Age: 29

							BATTING												RUNNING			AVERAGES			
Year	Team	Lg	G	AB	H	2B	3B	HR	(Hm | Rd)	TB	R	RBI	RC	TBB	IBB	SO	HBP	SH	SF	SB	CS	GDP	Avg	OBP	Slg	OPS
2014	Mia	NL	39	74	21	3	0	1	(1 | 0)	27	10	11	13	9	1	19	0	0	0	0	0	0	.284	.361	.365	.726
2015	Mia	NL	129	409	107	20	0	23	(10 | 13)	196	42	73	58	34	3	101	2	0	1	0	0	19	.262	.321	.479	.800
2016	Mia	NL	90	280	74	12	1	15	(9 | 6)	133	35	51	44	38	9	56	0	0	3	0	0	8	.264	.349	.475	.824
	3 ML YEARS		258	763	202	35	1	39	(20 | 19)	356	87	135	115	81	13	176	2	0	4	0	0	27	.265	.335	.467	.802

Peter Bourjos

Bats: R Throws: R Pos: RF-115;CF-10;PH-5;PR-1   BORE-juss   Ht: 6'1" Wt: 185 Born: 3/31/1987 Age: 30

							BATTING												RUNNING			AVERAGES			
Year	Team	Lg	G	AB	H	2B	3B	HR	(Hm | Rd)	TB	R	RBI	RC	TBB	IBB	SO	HBP	SH	SF	SB	CS	GDP	Avg	OBP	Slg	OPS
2010	LAA	AL	51	181	37	6	4	6	(1 | 5)	69	19	15	13	6	0	40	2	3	1	10	3	2	.204	.237	.381	.618
2011	LAA	AL	147	502	136	26	11	12	(7 | 5)	220	72	43	66	32	0	124	10	7	1	22	9	7	.271	.327	.438	.765
2012	LAA	AL	101	168	37	7	0	3	(1 | 2)	53	27	19	18	15	0	44	3	6	3	3	1	2	.220	.291	.315	.606
2013	LAA	AL	55	175	48	3	3	3	(1 | 2)	66	26	12	19	10	0	43	6	4	1	6	0	8	.274	.333	.377	.710
2014	StL	NL	119	264	61	9	5	4	(2 | 2)	92	32	24	27	20	1	78	4	5	1	9	3	5	.231	.294	.348	.643
2015	StL	NL	117	195	39	8	3	4	(2 | 2)	65	32	13	14	19	4	59	6	4	1	5	8	2	.200	.290	.333	.623
2016	Phi	NL	123	355	89	20	7	5	(1 | 4)	138	40	23	33	17	2	91	4	6	1	6	4	6	.251	.292	.389	.681
	Postseason		5	2	0	0	0	0	(0 | 0)	0	0	0	0	0	0	1	0	0	0	0	0	0	.000	.000	.000	.000
	7 ML YEARS		713	1840	447	79	33	37	(15 | 22)	703	248	149	190	119	7	479	35	35	9	61	28	32	.243	.300	.382	.682

Michael Bourn

Bats: L Throws: R Pos: CF-77;LF-21;RF-21;PH-8;PR-4   BORN   Ht: 5'11" Wt: 190 Born: 12/27/1982 Age: 34

							BATTING												RUNNING			AVERAGES			
Year	Team	Lg	G	AB	H	2B	3B	HR	(Hm | Rd)	TB	R	RBI	RC	TBB	IBB	SO	HBP	SH	SF	SB	CS	GDP	Avg	OBP	Slg	OPS
2006	Phi	NL	17	8	1	0	0	0	(0 | 0)	1	2	0	0	1	0	3	0	2	0	1	2	0	.125	.222	.125	.347
2007	Phi	NL	105	119	33	3	3	1	(1 | 0)	45	29	6	19	13	2	21	0	1	0	18	1	1	.277	.348	.378	.727
2008	Hou	NL	138	467	107	10	4	5	(3 | 2)	140	57	29	43	37	0	111	2	7	1	41	10	3	.229	.288	.300	.588
2009	Hou	NL	157	606	173	27	12	3	(2 | 1)	233	97	35	94	63	1	140	2	5	2	61	12	1	.285	.354	.384	.738
2010	Hou	NL	141	535	142	25	6	2	(0 | 2)	185	84	38	74	59	5	109	3	6	2	52	12	6	.265	.341	.346	.686
2011	2 Tms	NL	158	656	193	34	10	2	(2 | 0)	253	94	50	92	53	3	140	4	5	4	61	14	6	.294	.349	.386	.734
2012	Atl	NL	155	624	171	26	10	9	(2 | 7)	244	96	57	102	70	1	155	3	2	1	42	13	2	.274	.348	.391	.739
2013	Cle	AL	130	525	138	21	6	6	(2 | 4)	189	75	50	65	40	0	132	2	5	3	23	12	2	.263	.316	.360	.676
2014	Cle	AL	106	444	114	17	10	3	(3 | 0)	160	57	28	51	35	1	114	3	3	2	10	6	5	.257	.314	.360	.674
2015	2 Tms	NL	141	425	101	15	2	0	(0 | 0)	120	39	30	39	46	4	107	0	8	3	17	7	5	.238	.310	.282	.592
2016	2 Tms	NL	113	375	99	13	6	5	(1 | 4)	139	48	38	47	28	0	92	0	8	2	15	5	3	.264	.314	.371	.684
11	Hou	NL	105	429	130	26	7	1	(1 | 0)	173	64	32	66	38	2	90	3	2	1	39	7	5	.303	.363	.403	.766
11	Atl	NL	53	227	63	8	3	1	(1 | 0)	80	30	18	26	15	1	50	1	3	3	22	7	1	.278	.321	.352	.674
15	Cle	AL	95	289	71	12	1	0	(0 | 0)	85	29	19	27	29	0	76	0	7	1	13	5	2	.246	.313	.294	.608
15	Atl	NL	46	136	30	3	1	0	(0 | 0)	35	10	11	12	17	0	31	0	1	2	4	2	3	.221	.303	.257	.561
16	Ari	NL	89	329	86	12	6	3	(1 | 2)	119	43	30	38	22	0	83	0	6	1	13	5	3	.261	.307	.362	.669
16	Bal	AL	24	46	13	1	0	2	(0 | 2)	20	5	8	9	6	0	9	0	2	1	2	0	0	.283	.358	.435	.793
	Postseason		4	10	1	0	0	0	(0 | 0)	1	0	1	0	0	0	4	0	0	0	0	0	0	.100	.100	.100	.200
	11 ML YEARS		1361	4784	1272	191	69	36	(16 | 20)	1709	678	361	626	445	13	1124	19	52	23	341	94	34	.266	.329	.357	.687

Matt Bowman

Pitches: R Bats: R Pos: RP-59   Ht: 6'0" Wt: 175 Born: 5/31/1991 Age: 26

				HOW MUCH HE PITCHED				WHAT HE GAVE UP											THE RESULTS						
Year	Team	Lg	G	GS	CG	GF	IP	BFP	H	R	ER	HR	SH	SF	HB	TBB	IBB	SO	WP	Bk	W	L	Pct	Sh	Sv-Op	Hld	ERC	ERA
2012	Bklyn	A-	12	1	0	4	29.1	114	26	9	8	1	2	0	1	2	0	30	1	0	2	2	.500	0	3--	-	2.03	2.45
2013	2 Tms	Low	21	21	0	0	127.0	522	111	45	43	8	1	5	5	35	0	116	15	1	10	4	.714	0	0--	-	2.84	3.05
2014	Bnghtn	AA	17	17	0	0	98.1	417	102	45	34	7	3	0	4	27	1	92	3	0	7	6	.538	0	0--	-	3.76	3.11
2014	LsVgs	AAA	7	6	0	0	36.1	153	38	15	14	1	2	0	0	9	0	32	0	0	3	2	.600	0	0--	-	3.24	3.47
2015	LsVgs	AAA	28	26	2	1	140.0	643	184	97	86	15	8	5	2	51	1	77	8	1	7	16	.304	1	0--	-	5.87	5.53
2016	StL	NL	59	0	0	12	67.2	281	59	31	26	4	1	1	1	20	2	52	0	0	2	5	.286	0	0-1	13	2.71	3.46

Brad Boxberger

Pitches: R Bats: R Pos: RP-27   Ht: 6'2" Wt: 225 Born: 5/27/1988 Age: 29

				HOW MUCH HE PITCHED				WHAT HE GAVE UP											THE RESULTS						
Year	Team	Lg	G	GS	CG	GF	IP	BFP	H	R	ER	HR	SH	SF	HB	TBB	IBB	SO	WP	Bk	W	L	Pct	Sh	Sv-Op	Hld	ERC	ERA
2016	Charltt*	A+	7	5	0	1	6.1	29	7	2	2	1	0	0	0	4	0	7	0	0	0	0	-	0	0--	-	6.18	2.84
2012	SD	NL	24	0	0	4	27.2	120	22	12	8	3	0	1	2	18	1	33	0	0	0	0	-	0	0-0	1	4.28	2.60
2013	SD	NL	18	0	0	6	22.0	94	19	9	7	3	3	2	0	13	0	24	0	0	0	1	.000	0	1-1	0	4.43	2.86
2014	TB	AL	63	0	0	10	64.2	247	34	17	17	9	2	2	4	20	0	104	3	2	5	2	.714	0	2-5	18	1.84	2.37
2015	TB	AL	69	0	0	53	63.0	271	54	29	26	9	2	1	2	32	5	74	5	1	4	10	.286	0	41-47	2	4.01	3.71
2016	TB	AL	27	0	0	3	24.1	114	23	13	13	3	0	1	2	19	1	22	0	0	4	3	.571	0	0-3	7	5.75	4.81
	5 ML YEARS		201	0	0	76	201.2	846	152	80	71	27	7	7	10	102	7	257	8	3	13	16	.448	0	44-56	28	3.54	3.17

Matt Boyd

Pitches: L Bats: L Pos: SP-18; RP-2   Ht: 6'3" Wt: 215 Born: 2/2/1991 Age: 26

Year Team	Lg	G	GS	CG	GF	IP	BFP	H	R	ER	HR	SH	SF	HB	TBB	IBB	SO	WP	Bk	W	L	Pct	Sh	Sv-Op	Hld	ERC	ERA
2013 2 Tms	Low	8	5	0	0	24.0	88	14	7	7	2	0	0	0	4	0	23	1	0	0	3	.000	0	0- -	-	1.31	2.63
2014 Dnedin	A+	16	16	1	0	90.2	357	65	20	14	4	1	1	4	20	0	103	3	1	5	3	.625	0	0- -	-	1.81	1.39
2014 Nham	AA	10	10	0	0	42.2	197	55	33	33	5	0	2	3	13	0	44	3	0	1	4	.200	0	0- -	-	5.72	6.96
2015 Nham	AA	12	12	0	0	73.2	273	39	11	9	3	1	1	1	18	0	70	2	1	6	1	.857	0	0- -	-	1.20	1.10
2015 Buffalo	AAA	6	6	0	0	39.0	153	32	13	12	5	0	1	0	6	0	37	2	0	3	1	.750	0	0- -	-	2.49	2.77
2016 Toledo	AAA	11	11	0	0	64.0	259	53	20	16	5	1	1	2	18	1	57	0	0	2	5	.286	0	0- -	-	2.69	2.25
2015 2 Tms	AL	13	12	0	0	57.1	252	71	50	48	17	1	3	1	20	0	43	4	0	1	6	.143	0	0-0	0	7.04	7.53
2016 Det	AL	20	18	0	1	97.1	412	97	51	49	17	0	3	4	29	0	82	1	0	6	5	.545	0	0-0	0	4.35	4.53
15 Tor	AL	2	2	0	0	6.2	36	15	11	11	5	0	1	0	1	0	7	2	0	0	2	.000	0	0-0	0	17.16	14.85
15 Det	AL	11	10	0	0	50.2	216	56	39	37	12	1	2	1	19	0	36	2	0	1	4	.200	0	0-0	0	5.88	6.57
2 ML YEARS		33	30	0	1	154.2	664	168	101	97	34	1	6	5	49	0	125	5	0	7	11	.389	0	0-0	0	5.30	5.64

Blaine Boyer

Pitches: R Bats: R Pos: RP-61   Ht: 6'3" Wt: 225 Born: 7/11/1981 Age: 35

Year Team	Lg	G	GS	CG	GF	IP	BFP	H	R	ER	HR	SH	SF	HB	TBB	IBB	SO	WP	Bk	W	L	Pct	Sh	Sv-Op	Hld	ERC	ERA
2005 Atl	NL	43	0	0	5	37.2	158	32	13	13	1	1	1	2	17	0	33	2	0	4	2	.667	0	0-2	9	3.21	3.11
2006 Atl	NL	2	0	0	0	0.2	7	4	3	3	0	0	0	0	1	0	0	0	0	0	0	-	0	0-0	1	47.92	40.50
2007 Atl	NL	5	0	0	2	5.1	26	10	3	2	0	1	0	0	1	1	3	2	0	0	0	-	0	0-0	1	7.41	3.38
2008 Atl	NL	76	0	0	18	72.0	313	73	51	47	10	3	4	2	25	4	67	2	0	2	6	.250	0	1-5	14	4.19	5.88
2009 3 Tms	NL	48	0	0	21	54.2	241	56	36	25	1	4	1	5	20	0	29	2	0	0	2	.000	0	0-4	5	3.81	4.12
2010 Ari	NL	54	0	0	11	57.0	251	59	32	27	3	3	2	1	29	1	29	2	0	3	2	.600	0	0-4	5	4.45	4.26
2011 NYM	NL	5	0	0	3	6.2	33	13	8	8	2	1	0	1	1	0	1	0	0	0	2	.000	0	1-1	0	12.04	10.80
2014 SD	NL	32	0	0	11	40.1	160	34	16	16	2	2	1	0	8	0	29	1	0	0	1	.000	0	0-0	5	2.21	3.57
2015 Min	AL	68	0	0	12	65.0	268	62	24	18	5	3	2	0	19	4	33	5	0	3	6	.333	0	1-3	19	3.20	2.49
2016 Mil	NL	61	0	0	17	66.0	282	80	30	29	4	0	2	1	17	3	26	0	0	2	4	.333	0	1-3	5	4.54	3.95
09 Atl	NL	3	0	0	1	1.1	11	3	6	6	0	0	0	1	3	0	2	0	0	0	1	.000	0	0-0	0	23.46	40.50
09 StL	NL	15	0	0	4	16.1	70	14	10	8	1	3	0	1	5	0	9	0	0	0	0	-	0	0-0	2	2.82	4.41
09 Ari	NL	30	0	0	16	37.0	160	39	20	11	0	1	1	3	12	0	18	2	0	0	1	.000	0	0-0	2	3.71	2.68
10 ML YEARS		394	0	0	100	405.1	1739	423	216	188	28	18	13	12	138	13	250	16	0	14	25	.359	0	4-18	63	3.96	4.17

Brad Brach

Pitches: R Bats: R Pos: RP-71   BROCK   Ht: 6'6" Wt: 215 Born: 4/12/1986 Age: 31

Year Team	Lg	G	GS	CG	GF	IP	BFP	H	R	ER	HR	SH	SF	HB	TBB	IBB	SO	WP	Bk	W	L	Pct	Sh	Sv-Op	Hld	ERC	ERA
2011 SD	NL	9	0	0	4	7.0	38	9	5	4	0	0	0	1	7	4	11	1	0	0	2	.000	0	0-0	0	6.51	5.14
2012 SD	NL	67	0	0	13	66.2	280	50	28	28	11	1	3	2	33	7	75	4	0	2	4	.333	0	0-1	15	3.47	3.78
2013 SD	NL	33	0	0	6	31.0	141	36	15	11	3	0	3	0	19	0	31	4	0	1	0	1.000	0	0-0	2	6.03	3.19
2014 Bal	AL	46	0	0	8	62.1	254	48	24	22	6	2	4	1	25	1	54	2	0	7	1	.875	0	0-0	8	2.90	3.18
2015 Bal	AL	62	0	0	12	79.1	324	57	25	24	7	3	2	0	38	3	89	1	0	5	3	.625	0	1-2	14	2.78	2.72
2016 Bal	AL	71	0	0	16	79.0	311	57	23	18	7	0	3	0	25	1	92	4	1	10	4	.714	0	2-7	24	2.27	2.05
Postseason		2	0	0	0	2.1	10	1	0	0	0	0	0	0	2	0	1	0	0	1	0	1.000	0	0-0	0	2.03	0.00
6 ML YEARS		288	0	0	59	325.1	1348	257	120	107	34	6	15	4	147	16	352	16	1	25	14	.641	0	3-10	63	3.17	2.96

Silvino Bracho

Pitches: R Bats: R Pos: RP-26   BRAH-cho   Ht: 5'10" Wt: 190 Born: 7/17/1992 Age: 24

Year Team	Lg	G	GS	CG	GF	IP	BFP	H	R	ER	HR	SH	SF	HB	TBB	IBB	SO	WP	Bk	W	L	Pct	Sh	Sv-Op	Hld	ERC	ERA
2013 Msoula	R+	24	0	0	23	26.1	105	23	6	5	2	0	1	0	3	0	38	1	0	0	2	.000	0	11- -	-	2.17	1.71
2014 Sbend	A	45	0	0	38	43.1	163	25	10	10	3	2	1	2	8	1	70	3	0	3	2	.600	0	26- -	-	1.35	2.08
2015 Visalia	A+	6	0	0	6	6.0	20	1	0	0	0	0	0	0	1	0	14	0	0	0	0	-	0	3- -	-	0.19	0.00
2015 Mobile	AA	37	0	0	28	44.2	177	34	10	9	3	1	2	1	9	1	59	5	0	2	1	.667	0	16- -	-	1.96	1.81
2016 Reno	AAA	36	0	0	26	33.2	144	34	19	18	2	0	3	0	8	0	43	1	0	0	2	.000	0	15- -	-	3.13	4.81
2015 Ari	NL	13	0	0	3	12.1	50	9	2	2	2	0	0	1	4	1	17	1	0	0	0	-	0	1-1	0	2.95	1.46
2016 Ari	NL	26	0	0	11	24.2	119	31	22	20	7	0	1	3	10	1	17	3	0	0	2	.000	0	0-0	0	7.32	7.30
2 ML YEARS		39	0	0	14	37.0	169	40	24	22	9	0	1	4	14	2	34	4	0	0	2	.000	0	1-1	0	5.75	5.35

Archie Bradley

Pitches: R Bats: R Pos: SP-26   Ht: 6'4" Wt: 225 Born: 8/10/1992 Age: 24

Year Team	Lg	G	GS	CG	GF	IP	BFP	H	R	ER	HR	SH	SF	HB	TBB	IBB	SO	WP	Bk	W	L	Pct	Sh	Sv-Op	Hld	ERC	ERA
2012 Sbend	A	27	27	0	0	136.0	583	87	64	58	6	2	2	15	84	0	152	17	2	12	6	.667	0	0- -	-	2.97	3.84
2013 Visalia	A+	5	5	0	0	28.2	115	22	5	4	1	1	0	2	10	0	43	1	0	2	0	1.000	0	0- -	-	2.57	1.26
2013 Mobile	AA	21	21	2	0	123.1	506	93	35	27	5	5	4	4	59	2	119	1	0	12	5	.706	0	0- -	-	2.82	1.97
2014 Reno	AAA	5	5	0	0	24.1	113	26	14	14	0	1	2	4	12	0	23	2	1	1	4	.200	0	0- -	-	4.66	5.18
2014 Mobile	AA	12	12	1	0	54.2	240	45	27	25	2	2		5	36	1	46	3	0	2	3	.400	0	0- -	-	4.01	4.12
2016 Reno	AAA	7	7	0	0	40.2	157	26	9	9	0	1	0	2	18	0	47	3	0	5	1	.833	0	0- -	-	2.05	1.99
2015 Ari	NL	8	8	0	0	35.2	161	36	23	23	3	1	1	2	22	1	23	0	0	2	3	.400	0	0-0	0	5.12	5.80
2016 Ari	NL	26	26	0	0	141.2	638	154	84	79	16	2	7	4	67	8	143	7	2	8	9	.471	0	0-0	0	4.96	5.02
2 ML YEARS		34	34	0	0	177.1	799	190	107	102	19	3	8	6	89	9	166	7	2	10	12	.455	0	0-0	0	4.99	5.18

Jed Bradley

Pitches: L Bats: L Pos: RP-6   Ht: 6'3" Wt: 225 Born: 6/12/1990 Age: 27

					HOW MUCH HE PITCHED						WHAT HE GAVE UP									THE RESULTS						
Year Team	Lg	G	GS	CG	GF	IP	BFP	H	R	ER	HR	SH	SF	HB	TBB	IBB	SO	WP	Bk	W	L	Pct	Sh	Sv-Op	Hld	ERC	ERA
2012 BrvdCt	A+	20	20	1	0	107.1	495	136	76	66	9	3	5	6	43	0	60	6	1	5	10	.333	0	0- -	-	5.75	5.53
2013 BrvdCt	A+	16	16	1	0	78.1	347	81	42	36	6	4	2	2	39	0	58	5	0	4	4	.500	0	0- -	-	4.61	4.14
2014 BrvdCt	A+	10	10	0	0	60.1	237	54	21	20	4	1	0	1	10	0	53	1	0	5	2	.714	0	0- -	-	2.56	2.98
2014 Hntsvl	AA	17	17	0	0	87.0	393	106	52	44	8	3	4	5	36	1	71	4	0	5	8	.385	0	0- -	-	5.64	4.55
2015 ColSpr	AAA	20	1	0	4	26.0	128	45	27	26	1	0	2	0	10	0	15	4	0	2	4	.333	0	0- -	-	8.11	9.00
2015 Biloxi	AA	23	0	0	9	32.2	136	29	16	12	1	1	1	4	10	1	31	1	0	1	1	.500	0	0- -	-	3.11	3.31
2016 Biloxi	AA	17	0	0	3	24.2	118	33	18	17	2	2	1	4	6	2	19	2	0	3	2	.600	0	0- -	-	5.59	6.20
2016 Missi	AA	15	10	0	2	65.0	273	59	24	17	0	2	3	1	23	0	69	5	0	4	3	.571	0	0- -	-	2.78	2.35
2016 Atl	NL	6	0	0	1	7.0	33	7	4	4	0	0	1	0	6	2	4	1	0	1	1	.500	0	0-0	0	4.53	5.14

Jackie Bradley Jr.

Bats: L Throws: R Pos: CF-156;PR-1   Ht: 5'10" Wt: 200 Born: 4/19/1990 Age: 27

								BATTING												RUNNING			AVERAGES			
Year Team	Lg	G	AB	H	2B	3B	HR	(Hm	Rd)	TB	R	RBI	RC	TBB	IBB	SO	HBP	SH	SF	SB	CS	GDP	Avg	OBP	Slg	OPS
2013 Bos	AL	37	95	18	5	0	3	(2	1)	32	18	10	8	10	0	31	2	0	0	2	0	1	.189	.280	.337	.617
2014 Bos	AL	127	384	76	19	2	1	(1	0)	102	45	30	27	31	1	121	5	1	3	8	0	10	.198	.265	.266	.531
2015 Bos	AL	74	221	55	17	4	10	(5	5)	110	43	43	41	27	0	69	3	1	3	3	0	5	.249	.335	.498	.832
2016 Bos	AL	156	558	149	30	7	26	(12	14)	271	94	87	86	63	5	143	10	0	5	9	2	10	.267	.349	.486	.835
4 ML YEARS		394	1258	298	71	13	40	(20	20)	515	200	170	162	131	6	364	20	2	10	22	2	26	.237	.316	.409	.726

Michael Brantley

Bats: L Throws: L Pos: LF-11;PH-1   Ht: 6'2" Wt: 200 Born: 5/15/1987 Age: 30

								BATTING												RUNNING			AVERAGES			
Year Team	Lg	G	AB	H	2B	3B	HR	(Hm	Rd)	TB	R	RBI	RC	TBB	IBB	SO	HBP	SH	SF	SB	CS	GDP	Avg	OBP	Slg	OPS
2009 Cle	AL	28	112	35	4	0	0	(0	0)	39	10	11	16	8	0	19	0	1	0	4	4	3	.313	.358	.348	.707
2010 Cle	AL	72	297	73	9	3	3	(2	1)	97	38	22	32	22	0	38	0	4	2	10	2	6	.246	.296	.327	.623
2011 Cle	AL	114	451	120	24	4	7	(4	3)	173	63	46	56	34	2	76	3	3	5	13	5	11	.266	.318	.384	.702
2012 Cle	AL	149	552	159	37	4	6	(3	3)	222	63	60	76	53	12	56	0	0	4	12	9	7	.288	.348	.402	.750
2013 Cle	AL	151	556	158	26	3	10	(9	1)	220	66	73	86	40	1	67	4	3	8	17	4	11	.284	.332	.396	.728
2014 Cle	AL	156	611	200	45	2	20	(11	9)	309	94	97	114	52	4	56	8	0	5	23	1	16	.327	.385	.506	.890
2015 Cle	AL	137	529	164	45	0	15	(9	6)	254	68	84	94	60	8	51	2	0	5	15	1	14	.310	.379	.480	.859
2016 Cle	AL	11	39	9	2	0	0	(0	0)	11	5	7	5	3	1	6	0	0	1	1	0	1	.231	.279	.282	.561
Postseason		1	4	1	0	0	0	(0	0)	1	0	0	0	0	0	0	0	0	0	0	0	0	.250	.250	.250	.500
8 ML YEARS		818	3147	918	192	16	61	(38	23)	1325	407	400	479	272	28	369	17	11	30	95	26	69	.292	.348	.421	.769

Steven Brault

Pitches: L Bats: L Pos: SP-7; RP-1   Ht: 6'0" Wt: 190 Born: 4/29/1992 Age: 25

						HOW MUCH HE PITCHED						WHAT HE GAVE UP									THE RESULTS						
Year Team	Lg	G	GS	CG	GF	IP	BFP	H	R	ER	HR	SH	SF	HB	TBB	IBB	SO	WP	Bk	W	L	Pct	Sh	Sv-Op	Hld	ERC	ERA
2013 Abrdn	A-	12	12	0	0	43.0	169	35	14	10	1	0	1	2	12	0	38	1	0	1	2	.333	0	0- -	-	2.44	2.09
2014 2 Tms	Low	25	24	2	0	146.1	574	114	44	45	4	4	3	10	30	0	124	10	0	11	8	.579	0	0- -	-	2.07	2.77
2015 Bradtn	A+	13	13	0	0	65.2	273	62	28	22	3	4	0	2	21	0	45	3	0	4	1	.800	0	0- -	-	3.26	3.02
2015 Altna	AA	15	15	0	0	90.0	363	72	22	20	1	2	0	3	19	0	80	0	0	9	3	.750	0	0- -	-	1.90	2.00
2016 Indy	AAA	16	15	0	1	71.1	314	66	35	31	6	3	0	3	35	0	81	2	1	2	7	.222	0	0- -	-	4.02	3.91
2016 Pit	NL	8	7	0	0	33.1	166	45	26	18	5	3	0	2	17	1	29	1	0	0	3	.000	0	0-0	0	6.99	4.86

Ryan Braun

Bats: R Throws: R Pos: LF-127;PH-5;DH-3;RF-2   Ht: 6'2" Wt: 205 Born: 11/17/1983 Age: 33

								BATTING												RUNNING			AVERAGES			
Year Team	Lg	G	AB	H	2B	3B	HR	(Hm	Rd)	TB	R	RBI	RC	TBB	IBB	SO	HBP	SH	SF	SB	CS	GDP	Avg	OBP	Slg	OPS
2007 Mil	NL	113	451	146	26	6	34	(17	17)	286	91	97	94	29	1	112	7	0	5	15	5	13	.324	.370	.634	1.004
2008 Mil	NL	151	611	174	39	7	37	(23	14)	338	92	106	100	42	4	129	6	0	4	14	4	13	.285	.335	.553	.888
2009 Mil	NL	158	635	203	39	6	32	(15	17)	350	113	114	133	57	1	121	13	0	3	20	6	7	.320	.386	.551	.937
2010 Mil	NL	157	619	188	45	1	25	(13	12)	310	101	103	104	56	1	105	6	0	3	14	3	17	.304	.365	.501	.866
2011 Mil	NL	150	563	187	38	6	33	(16	17)	336	109	111	124	58	2	93	5	0	3	33	6	9	.332	.397	.597	.994
2012 Mil	NL	154	598	191	36	3	41	(24	17)	356	108	112	125	63	15	128	11	0	5	30	7	12	.319	.391	.595	.987
2013 Mil	NL	61	225	67	14	2	9	(5	4)	112	30	38	39	27	7	56	0	0	1	4	5	8	.298	.372	.498	.869
2014 Mil	NL	135	530	141	30	6	19	(8	11)	240	68	81	74	41	3	113	6	0	3	11	5	17	.266	.324	.453	.777
2015 Mil	NL	140	506	144	27	3	25	(8	17)	252	87	84	91	54	4	115	4	0	3	24	4	20	.285	.356	.498	.854
2016 Mil	NL	135	511	156	23	3	30	(15	15)	275	80	91	93	46	10	98	4	0	3	16	5	20	.305	.365	.538	.903
Postseason		15	58	22	9	0	2	(2	0)	37	7	12	13	4	0	13	1	0	1	1	0	0	.379	.422	.638	1.060
10 ML YEARS		1354	5249	1597	317	43	285	(144	141)	2855	879	937	977	473	48	1070	62	0	33	181	50	136	.304	.367	.544	.910

Alex Bregman

Bats: R Throws: R Pos: 3B-40;SS-6;2B-3;DH-3;LF-1;PH-1   Ht: 6'0" Wt: 180 Born: 3/30/1994 Age: 23

								BATTING												RUNNING			AVERAGES			
Year Team	Lg	G	AB	H	2B	3B	HR	(Hm	Rd)	TB	R	RBI	RC	TBB	IBB	SO	HBP	SH	SF	SB	CS	GDP	Avg	OBP	Slg	OPS
2015 2 Tms	Low	66	272	80	13	4	4	(-	-)	113	37	34	44	29	2	30	4	2	4	13	6	7	.294	.366	.415	.781
2016 CpChr	AA	62	236	70	16	2	14	(-	-)	132	54	46	55	42	3	26	6	1	0	5	3	5	.297	.415	.559	.975
2016 Fresno	AAA	18	78	26	6	0	6	(-	-)	50	17	15	17	5	0	12	0	0	0	2	1	2	.333	.373	.641	1.015
2016 Hou	AL	49	201	53	13	3	8	(3	5)	96	31	34	37	15	0	52	0	0	1	2	0	1	.264	.313	.478	.791

Bryce Brentz

Bats: R Throws: R Pos: LF-22;PH-5;PR-2;DH-1   Ht: 6'0" Wt: 210 Born: 12/30/1988 Age: 28

Year	Team	Lg	G	AB	H	2B	3B	HR	(Hm	Rd)	TB	R	RBI	RC	TBB	IBB	SO	HBP	SH	SF	SB	CS	GDP	Avg	OBP	Slg	OPS
2012	Portlnd	AA	122	456	135	30	1	17	(-	-)	218	62	76	78	40	3	130	4	0	4	7	5	9	.296	.355	.478	.833
2013	Pwtckt	AAA	82	326	86	16	1	17	(-	-)	155	36	56	49	20	1	86	3	0	0	1	0	11	.264	.312	.475	.788
2014	Pwtckt	AAA	63	230	56	11	2	12	(-	-)	107	42	53	38	32	0	58	3	0	2	1	1	9	.243	.341	.465	.806
2015	Pwtckt	AAA	59	220	51	9	0	8	(-	-)	84	28	26	27	24	0	74	2	0	4	0	0	6	.232	.308	.382	.690
2016	Pwtckt	AAA	54	204	51	17	1	4	(-	-)	82	16	21	23	8	0	52	0	0	0	2	0	7	.250	.278	.402	.680
2016	Portlnd	AAA	12	40	8	2	0	1	(-	-)	13	5	3	5	7	0	14	1	0	0	1	0	1	.200	.333	.325	.658
2014	Bos	AL	9	26	8	2	0	0	(0	0)	10	5	2	3	0	0	9	0	0	0	0	0	0	.308	.308	.385	.692
2016	Bos	AL	25	61	17	3	0	1	(0	1)	23	8	7	7	3	0	17	0	0	0	0	0	1	.279	.313	.377	.690
	2 ML YEARS		34	87	25	5	0	1	(0	1)	33	13	9	10	3	0	26	0	0	0	0	0	1	.287	.311	.379	.690

Craig Breslow

Pitches: L Bats: L Pos: RP-15   BREHZ-loh   Ht: 6'0" Wt: 190 Born: 8/8/1980 Age: 36

Year	Team	Lg	G	GS	CG	GF	IP	BFP	H	R	ER	HR	SH	SF	HB	TBB	IBB	SO	WP	Bk	W	L	Pct	Sh	Sv-Op	Hld	ERC	ERA
2016	NewOr*	AAA	14	0	0	5	23.2	115	34	18	17	3	0	1	0	11	0	29	0	0	1	3	.250	0	2- -	-	7.10	6.46
2005	SD	NL	14	0	0	3	16.1	78	15	6	4	1	0	1	1	13	0	14	1	0	0	0	-	0	0-0	1	4.98	2.20
2006	Bos	AL	13	0	0	3	12.0	55	12	5	5	0	0	2	1	6	1	12	2	1	0	2	.000	0	0-0	3	3.78	3.75
2008	2 Tms	AL	49	0	0	13	47.0	189	34	12	10	1	2	0	0	19	2	39	4	1	0	2	.000	0	1-2	5	2.12	1.91
2009	2 Tms	AL	77	0	0	9	69.2	281	48	31	26	8	4	1	3	29	0	55	3	1	8	7	.533	0	0-2	15	2.79	3.36
2010	Oak	AL	75	0	0	23	74.2	304	53	26	25	9	2	0	0	29	4	71	0	1	4	4	.500	0	5-7	16	2.53	3.01
2011	Oak	AL	67	0	0	10	59.1	261	69	29	25	4	3	2	2	21	1	44	3	0	0	2	.000	0	0-3	8	4.74	3.79
2012	2 Tms		63	0	0	16	63.1	261	52	22	19	5	3	3	2	22	2	61	2	0	3	0	1.000	0	0-1	9	2.86	2.70
2013	Bos	AL	61	0	0	13	59.2	237	49	16	12	3	0	2	2	18	0	33	2	0	5	2	.714	0	0-1	13	2.66	1.81
2014	Bos	AL	60	0	0	16	54.1	260	73	40	36	8	1	0	2	28	1	37	3	1	2	4	.333	0	1-2	2	7.14	5.96
2015	Bos	AL	45	2	0	18	65.0	280	69	33	30	12	3	5	2	23	5	46	2	0	0	4	.000	0	1-4	1	4.91	4.15
2016	Mia	NL	15	0	0	4	14.0	63	21	9	7	1	1	0	0	4	0	7	2	0	0	2	.000	0	0-1	1	6.62	4.50
08	Cle	AL	7	0	0	3	8.1	40	10	3	3	1	0	0	0	5	0	7	0	0	0	0	-	0	0-0	0	6.09	3.24
08	Min	AL	42	0	0	10	38.2	149	24	9	7	0	2	0	0	14	2	32	4	1	0	2	.000	0	1-2	5	1.49	1.63
09	Min	AL	17	0	0	5	14.1	64	11	11	10	3	2	0	1	11	0	11	3	0	1	2	.333	0	0-0	2	5.38	6.28
09	Oak	AL	60	0	0	4	55.1	217	37	20	16	5	2	1	2	18	0	44	0	1	7	5	.583	0	0-2	13	2.21	2.60
12	Ari	NL	40	0	0	12	43.1	180	38	15	13	5	2	1	0	13	0	42	1	0	2	0	1.000	0	0-0	4	3.19	2.70
12	Bos	AL	23	0	0	4	20.0	81	14	7	6	0	1	2	1	9	2	19	1	0	1	0	1.000	0	0-1	5	2.12	2.70
	Postseason		10	0	0	0	7.1	36	6	3	2	0	0	1	2	7	1	6	0	0	1	0	1.000	0	0-1	4	5.16	2.45
	11 ML YEARS		539	2	0	128	535.1	2269	495	229	199	52	19	16	15	212	16	419	24	5	22	29	.431	0	8-23	75	3.71	3.35

Austin Brice

Pitches: R Bats: R Pos: RP-15   Ht: 6'4" Wt: 235 Born: 6/19/1992 Age: 25

Year	Team	Lg	G	GS	CG	GF	IP	BFP	H	R	ER	HR	SH	SF	HB	TBB	IBB	SO	WP	Bk	W	L	Pct	Sh	Sv-Op	Hld	ERC	ERA
2012	Grnsbr	A	25	19	0	4	109.2	483	96	63	53	13	0	3	7	68	0	122	10	0	8	6	.571	0	3- -	-	4.70	4.35
2013	Grnsbr	A	26	23	0	1	113.0	541	118	84	72	11	2	2	14	82	0	111	7	0	8	11	.421	0	0- -	-	6.13	5.73
2014	Jupiter	A+	25	24	0	0	127.1	552	114	66	51	5	5	5	13	55	0	109	17	1	8	9	.471	0	0- -	-	3.58	3.60
2015	Jaxnvl	AA	25	25	0	0	125.1	556	114	74	65	11	3	5	12	69	0	127	10	0	6	9	.400	0	0- -	-	4.47	4.67
2016	Jaxnvl	AA	27	13	0	3	93.1	384	79	39	30	5	3	3	7	29	0	79	6	1	4	7	.364	0	2- -	-	2.92	2.89
2016	NewOr	AAA	5	0	0	3	8.2	28	3	1	1	1	0	0	0	1	0	10	0	0	0	0	-	0	2- -	-	0.71	1.04
2016	Mia	NL	15	0	0	2	14.0	59	9	12	11	2	0	0	2	5	1	14	0	0	0	1	.000	0	0-0	1	2.63	7.07

Parker Bridwell

Pitches: R Bats: R Pos: RP-2   Ht: 6'4" Wt: 185 Born: 8/2/1991 Age: 25

Year	Team	Lg	G	GS	CG	GF	IP	BFP	H	R	ER	HR	SH	SF	HB	TBB	IBB	SO	WP	Bk	W	L	Pct	Sh	Sv-Op	Hld	ERC	ERA
2012	Dlmrva	A	23	22	1	0	114.1	521	122	82	76	15	3	6	15	63	0	71	15	1	5	9	.357	0	0- -	-	5.98	5.98
2013	Dlmrva	A	26	26	0	0	142.2	631	141	86	75	9	3	6	9	59	0	144	8	0	8	9	.471	0	0- -	-	3.99	4.73
2014	Frdrck	A+	26	26	1	0	141.1	607	123	75	70	11	1	1	9	70	0	142	6	2	7	10	.412	0	0- -	-	3.86	4.46
2015	Bowie	AA	18	18	1	0	97.0	418	96	48	43	7	2	2	2	38	0	93	5	0	4	5	.444	0	0- -	-	3.87	3.99
2016	Bowie	AA	18	7	0	2	55.2	249	56	33	28	7	0	1	3	28	0	38	1	0	1	1	.500	0	1- -	-	4.92	4.53
2016	2 Tms	Low	5	0	0	0	11.0	41	5	3	3	1	0	0	1	3	0	11	0	0	3	1	.750	0	0- -	-	1.38	2.45
2016	Bal	AL	2	0	0	1	3.1	15	5	5	5	2	0	0	0	1	0	3	0	0	0	0	-	0	0-0	0	11.35	13.50

Reid Brignac

Bats: L Throws: R Pos: PH-7;3B-5;2B-4   BRINN-yak   Ht: 6'3" Wt: 210 Born: 1/16/1986 Age: 31

Year	Team	Lg	G	AB	H	2B	3B	HR	(Hm	Rd)	TB	R	RBI	RC	TBB	IBB	SO	HBP	SH	SF	SB	CS	GDP	Avg	OBP	Slg	OPS
2016	Gwnntt*	AAA	102	363	96	21	1	8	(-	-)	143	56	42	56	52	2	91	4	3	2	6	3	8	.264	.361	.394	.755
2008	TB	AL	4	10	0	0	0	0	(0	0)	0	1	0	0	1	0	5	0	0	0	0	0	0	.000	.091	.000	.091
2009	TB	AL	31	90	25	8	2	1	(0	1)	40	10	6	10	3	0	20	0	0	0	2	2	1	.278	.301	.444	.746
2010	TB	AL	113	301	77	13	1	8	(3	5)	116	39	45	38	20	3	77	3	0	2	3	3	6	.256	.307	.385	.692
2011	TB	AL	92	249	48	4	0	1	(0	1)	55	18	15	8	10	1	63	1	4	0	3	1	2	.193	.227	.221	.448
2012	TB	AL	16	21	2	0	0	0	(0	0)	2	1	1	0	1	0	5	0	0	0	0	0	0	.095	.136	.095	.232
2013	2 Tms		46	92	17	4	0	1	(0	1)	24	5	6	7	4	1	30	0	2	0	0	0	6	.185	.219	.261	.480
2014	Phi	NL	37	81	18	5	1	1	(1	0)	28	4	10	8	9	1	33	0	1	0	1	1	2	.222	.300	.346	.646
2015	Mia	NL	17	13	1	0	0	0	(0	0)	1	2	0	0	3	0	5	0	1	0	0	0	0	.077	.250	.077	.327
2016	Atl	NL	13	29	6	2	0	0	(0	0)	8	3	1	0	0	0	8	0	0	0	0	0	0	.207	.207	.276	.483

Year Team	Lg		BATTING																	RUNNING			AVERAGES			
		G	AB	H	2B	3B	HR	(Hm Rd)	TB	R	RBI	RC	TBB	IBB	SO	HBP	SH	SF	SB	CS	GDP	Avg	OBP	Slg	OPS
13 Col	NL	29	48	12	3	0	1	(0 1)	18	4	6	7	3	1	13	0	2	0	0	0	3	.250	.294	.375	.669
13 NYY	AL	17	44	5	1	0	0	(0 0)	6	1	0	0	1	0	17	0	0	0	0	0	3	.114	.133	.136	.270
Postseason		5	4	0	0	0	0	(0 0)	0	0	0	0	1	0	3	0	0	0	0	0	0	.000	.200	.000	.200
9 ML YEARS		369	886	194	36	4	12	(4 8)	274	83	84	71	51	6	246	4	8	2	9	7	17	.219	.264	.309	.573

Socrates Brito

Bats: L **Throws:** L **Pos:** CF-17;RF-16;LF-7;PH-2;PR-2   BREE-tow   **Ht:** 6'2" **Wt:** 205 **Born:** 9/6/1992 **Age:** 24

Year Team	Lg		BATTING																	RUNNING			AVERAGES			
		G	AB	H	2B	3B	HR	(Hm Rd)	TB	R	RBI	RC	TBB	IBB	SO	HBP	SH	SF	SB	CS	GDP	Avg	OBP	Slg	OPS
2012 Msoula	R+	69	279	87	15	5	4	(- -)	124	47	39	44	21	0	73	1	0	4	15	9	3	.312	.357	.444	.802
2013 Sbend	A	129	523	138	24	9	2	(- -)	186	61	49	62	37	1	124	2	1	3	27	9	3	.264	.313	.356	.669
2014 Visalia	A+	128	518	152	30	5	10	(- -)	222	82	62	80	36	1	109	2	0	5	38	10	6	.293	.339	.429	.767
2015 Mobile	AA	129	490	147	16	15	9	(- -)	220	70	57	76	29	1	84	1	0	2	20	6	7	.300	.339	.449	.788
2016 Reno	AAA	73	303	89	10	8	6	(- -)	133	46	39	42	13	1	60	0	0	1	7	6	4	.294	.322	.439	.761
2015 Ari	NL	18	33	10	3	1	0	(0 0)	15	5	1	5	1	0	7	0	0	0	1	0	0	.303	.324	.455	.778
2016 Ari	NL	40	95	17	3	1	4	(1 3)	34	10	12	6	2	0	23	0	0	0	2	0	3	.179	.196	.358	.554
2 ML YEARS		58	128	27	6	2	4	(1 3)	49	15	13	11	3	0	30	0	0	0	3	0	3	.211	.229	.383	.612

Zach Britton

Pitches: L **Bats:** L **Pos:** RP-69   **Ht:** 6'3" **Wt:** 195 **Born:** 12/22/1987 **Age:** 29

Year Team	Lg		HOW MUCH HE PITCHED					WHAT HE GAVE UP												THE RESULTS						
		G	GS	CG	GF	IP	BFP	H	R	ER	HR	SH	SF	HB	TBB	IBB	SO	WP	Bk	W	L	Pct	Sh	Sv-Op	Hld	ERC	ERA
2011 Bal	AL	28	28	0	0	154.1	666	162	93	79	12	8	7	1	62	3	97	7	0	11	11	.500	0	0-0	0	4.24	4.61
2012 Bal	AL	12	11	0	0	60.1	270	61	37	34	6	0	1	2	32	3	53	4	0	5	3	.625	0	0-0	0	4.70	5.07
2013 Bal	AL	8	7	0	0	40.0	182	52	23	22	4	1	1	1	17	1	18	1	0	2	3	.400	0	0-0	0	6.14	4.95
2014 Bal	AL	71	0	0	49	76.1	285	46	17	14	4	3	0	1	23	0	62	0	0	3	2	.600	0	37-41	7	1.62	1.65
2015 Bal	AL	64	0	0	58	65.2	253	51	16	14	3	0	0	1	14	1	79	5	0	4	1	.800	0	36-40	0	2.02	1.92
2016 Bal	AL	69	0	0	63	67.0	254	38	7	4	1	1	0	0	18	3	74	10	0	2	1	.667	0	**47-47**	0	1.18	0.54
Postseason		6	0	0	4	4.2	24	5	2	2	0	1	0	0	5	2	5	0	0	0	0	-	0	2-2	1	5.28	3.86
6 ML YEARS		252	46	0	170	463.2	1910	410	193	167	30	13	9	6	166	11	383	27	0	27	21	.563	0	120-128	7	3.12	3.24

Mike Broadway

Pitches: R **Bats:** R **Pos:** RP-4   **Ht:** 6'5" **Wt:** 215 **Born:** 3/30/1987 **Age:** 30

Year Team	Lg		HOW MUCH HE PITCHED					WHAT HE GAVE UP												THE RESULTS						
		G	GS	CG	GF	IP	BFP	H	R	ER	HR	SH	SF	HB	TBB	IBB	SO	WP	Bk	W	L	Pct	Sh	Sv-Op	Hld	ERC	ERA
2012 SnAnt	AA	33	0	0	10	39.2	184	51	32	28	4	0	1	1	13	0	45	4	0	0	2	.000	0	0- -	-	5.42	6.35
2013 Hrsbrg	AA	12	0	0	4	16.2	73	18	6	5	1	2	2	0	5	1	14	2	0	1	0	1.000	0	0- -	-	3.66	2.70
2013 Syrcse	AAA	18	0	0	13	23.2	93	16	6	6	2	0	1	0	7	0	26	1	0	1	1	.500	0	6- -	-	1.95	2.28
2014 Giants	R	5	0	0	1	6.0	25	8	1	1	0	0	0	0	1	0	6	0	0	0	0	-	0	0- -	-	5.89	1.50
2015 Scrmto	AAA	40	0	0	31	48.1	175	25	6	5	0	3	1	0	8	0	64	1	0	2	0	1.000	0	13- -	-	0.85	0.93
2016 Scrmto	AAA	26	0	0	18	29.2	133	32	14	13	4	0	2	4	11	1	30	2	0	0	3	.000	0	5- -	-	5.16	3.94
2015 SF	NL	21	0	0	5	17.1	77	20	10	10	1	1	0	1	7	1	13	0	1	0	2	.000	0	0-0	2	4.86	5.19
2016 SF	NL	4	0	0	2	5.1	25	9	7	7	2	0	0	0	1	0	4	0	0	0	0	-	0	0-0	0	9.90	11.81
2 ML YEARS		25	0	0	7	22.2	102	29	17	17	3	1	0	1	8	1	17	0	1	0	2	.000	0	0-0	2	5.98	6.75

Trevor Brown

Bats: R **Throws:** R **Pos:** C-60;PH-19;DH-2;3B-1   **Ht:** 6'2" **Wt:** 195 **Born:** 11/15/1991 **Age:** 25

Year Team	Lg		BATTING																	RUNNING			AVERAGES			
		G	AB	H	2B	3B	HR	(Hm Rd)	TB	R	RBI	RC	TBB	IBB	SO	HBP	SH	SF	SB	CS	GDP	Avg	OBP	Slg	OPS
2012 Slkzr	A-	33	122	27	8	0	0	(- -)	35	10	12	11	13	0	16	1	1	2	1	1	5	.221	.297	.287	.584
2013 2 Tms	Low	111	442	106	22	1	3	(- -)	139	53	44	41	31	0	62	5	2	5	10	9	8	.240	.294	.314	.608
2014 SnJos	A+	54	195	42	5	1	2	(- -)	55	19	22	14	12	1	33	1	0	4	0	0	5	.215	.259	.282	.541
2014 Fresno	AAA	23	72	23	4	0	0	(- -)	27	6	13	10	7	0	13	0	1	0	0	0	1	.319	.380	.375	.755
2015 Scrmto	AAA	83	283	74	17	0	2	(- -)	97	35	27	33	21	0	53	4	4	2	1	0	8	.261	.319	.343	.662
2015 SF	NL	13	39	9	3	0	0	(0 0)	12	1	5	3	3	0	8	0	0	1	1	1	0	.231	.279	.308	.587
2016 SF	NL	75	173	41	7	0	5	(1 4)	63	17	19	16	10	0	39	1	0	0	0	1	2	.237	.283	.364	.647
2 ML YEARS		88	212	50	10	0	5	(1 4)	75	18	24	19	13	0	47	1	0	1	1	2	2	.236	.282	.354	.636

Jonathan Broxton

Pitches: R **Bats:** R **Pos:** RP-66   **Ht:** 6'4" **Wt:** 285 **Born:** 6/16/1984 **Age:** 33

Year Team	Lg		HOW MUCH HE PITCHED					WHAT HE GAVE UP												THE RESULTS						
		G	GS	CG	GF	IP	BFP	H	R	ER	HR	SH	SF	HB	TBB	IBB	SO	WP	Bk	W	L	Pct	Sh	Sv-Op	Hld	ERC	ERA
2005 LAD	NL	14	0	0	5	13.2	68	13	11	9	0	0	2	1	12	2	22	2	0	1	0	1.000	0	0-1	1	4.65	5.93
2006 LAD	NL	68	0	0	20	76.1	320	61	25	22	7	3	1	1	33	6	97	7	0	4	1	.800	0	3-7	12	2.97	2.59
2007 LAD	NL	83	0	0	18	82.0	334	69	30	26	6	0	1	1	25	3	99	4	0	4	4	.500	0	2-8	32	2.71	2.85
2008 LAD	NL	70	0	0	32	69.0	285	54	29	24	2	3	3	3	27	5	88	3	0	3	5	.375	0	14-22	13	2.48	3.13
2009 LAD	NL	73	0	0	58	76.0	300	44	24	22	4	0	3	1	29	1	114	2	0	7	2	.778	0	36-42	5	1.65	2.61
2010 LAD	NL	64	0	0	46	62.1	271	64	30	28	4	3	1	2	28	5	73	1	0	5	6	.455	0	22-29	3	4.21	4.04
2011 LAD	NL	14	0	0	12	12.2	62	15	10	8	2	0	0	0	9	2	10	0	0	1	2	.333	0	7-8	0	6.47	5.68
2012 2 Tms		60	0	0	39	58.0	238	56	18	16	2	2	1	3	17	0	45	0	0	4	5	.444	0	27-33	10	3.34	2.48
2013 Cin	NL	34	0	0	8	30.2	133	27	17	14	4	1	2	4	12	2	25	0	0	2	2	.500	0	0-3	12	3.97	4.11
2014 2 Tms	NL	62	0	0	18	58.2	231	41	15	15	4	2	1	1	19	0	49	0	0	4	5	.571	0	7-15	23	2.14	2.30
2015 2 Tms	NL	66	0	0	15	60.1	257	61	32	31	7	5	1	0	22	1	63	0	0	4	5	.444	0	0-3	17	4.11	4.62
2016 StL	NL	66	0	0	14	60.2	259	52	32	29	8	7	2	3	24	5	57	1	0	4	2	.667	0	0-3	12	3.40	4.30
12 KC	AL	35	0	0	32	35.2	151	36	11	9	1	2	1	2	14	0	25	0	0	1	2	.333	0	23-27	0	3.93	2.27

	HOW MUCH HE PITCHED						WHAT HE GAVE UP												THE RESULTS							
Year Team	Lg	G	GS	CG	GF	IP	BFP	H	R	ER	HR	SH	SF	HB	TBB	IBB	SO	WP	Bk	W	L	Pct	Sh	Sv-Op	Hld	ERC	ERA
12 Cin	NL	25	0	0	7	22.1	87	20	7	7	1	0	0	1	3	0	20	0	0	3	3	.500	0	4-6	10	2.44	2.82
14 Cin	NL	51	0	0	16	48.1	189	32	10	10	3	2	1	1	17	0	37	0	0	4	2	.667	0	7-13	21	2.06	1.86
14 Mil	NL	11	0	0	2	10.1	42	9	5	5	1	0	0	0	2	0	12	0	0	0	1	.000	0	0-2	2	2.55	4.35
15 Mil	NL	40	0	0	10	36.2	156	41	24	24	5	2	1	0	10	1	37	0	0	1	2	.333	0	0-1	11	4.50	5.89
15 StL	NL	26	0	0	5	23.2	101	20	8	7	2	3	0	0	12	0	26	0	0	3	3	.500	0	0-2	6	3.53	2.66
Postseason		19	0	0	13	19.2	89	20	9	8	2	0	0	1	9	0	22	0	0	0	3	.000	0	3-5	1	4.50	3.66
12 ML YEARS		674	0	0	285	660.1	2758	557	273	244	49	21	19	20	257	32	742	20	0	43	37	.538	0	118-174	136	3.06	3.33

Keon Broxton

Bats: R **Throws:** R **Pos:** CF-68;PH-11;PR-1   **Ht:** 6'3" **Wt:** 195 **Born:** 5/7/1990 **Age:** 27

								BATTING												RUNNING			AVERAGES			
Year Team	Lg	G	AB	H	2B	3B	HR	(Hm	Rd)	TB	R	RBI	RC	TBB	IBB	SO	HBP	SH	SF	SB	CS	GDP	Avg	OBP	Slg	OPS
2012 Visalia	A+	130	490	131	24	1	19	(-	-)	214	84	62	72	40	0	136	4	0	2	21	8	5	.267	.326	.437	.763
2013 Mobile	AA	101	334	77	13	3	8	(-	-)	120	40	41	37	30	0	116	2	4	2	6	1	7	.231	.296	.359	.655
2014 Altna	AA	127	407	112	22	9	15	(-	-)	197	67	52	77	59	6	122	3	0	2	25	6	7	.275	.369	.484	.853
2015 Altna	AA	45	179	54	12	4	3	(-	-)	83	35	26	31	19	0	51	1	1	4	11	6	1	.302	.365	.464	.828
2015 Indy	AAA	88	312	80	15	8	7	(-	-)	132	51	42	52	47	0	105	2	1	5	28	9	3	.256	.352	.423	.776
2016 ColSpr	AAA	47	178	51	11	7	8	(-	-)	100	30	26	36	20	0	60	1	0	0	18	8	1	.287	.362	.562	.924
2015 Pit	NL	7	2	0	0	0	0	(0	0)	0	3	0	0	0	0	1	0	0	0	1	1	0	.000	.000	.000	.000
2016 Mil	NL	75	207	50	10	1	9	(2	7)	89	28	19	32	36	0	88	0	1	0	23	4	2	.242	.354	.430	.784
2 ML YEARS		82	209	50	10	1	9	(2	7)	89	31	19	32	36	0	89	0	1	0	24	5	2	.239	.351	.426	.777

Jay Bruce

Bats: L **Throws:** L **Pos:** RF-138;PH-7;DH-2;CF-1   **Ht:** 6'3" **Wt:** 225 **Born:** 4/3/1987 **Age:** 30

								BATTING												RUNNING			AVERAGES			
Year Team	Lg	G	AB	H	2B	3B	HR	(Hm	Rd)	TB	R	RBI	RC	TBB	IBB	SO	HBP	SH	SF	SB	CS	GDP	Avg	OBP	Slg	OPS
2008 Cin	NL	108	413	105	17	1	21	(13	8)	187	63	52	49	33	1	110	4	0	2	4	6	8	.254	.314	.453	.767
2009 Cin	NL	101	345	77	15	2	22	(13	9)	162	47	58	47	38	2	75	2	1	1	3	3	5	.223	.303	.470	.773
2010 Cin	NL	148	509	143	23	5	25	(19	6)	251	80	70	71	58	5	136	1	0	5	5	4	12	.281	.353	.493	.846
2011 Cin	NL	157	585	150	27	2	32	(16	16)	277	84	97	96	71	14	158	5	1	2	8	7	8	.256	.341	.474	.814
2012 Cin	NL	155	560	141	35	5	34	(21	13)	288	89	99	85	62	11	155	4	0	7	9	3	5	.252	.327	.514	.841
2013 Cin	NL	160	626	164	43	1	30	(16	14)	299	89	109	88	63	13	185	2	0	5	7	3	9	.262	.329	.478	.807
2014 Cin	NL	137	493	107	21	1	18	(10	8)	184	71	66	54	44	5	149	2	1	5	12	3	8	.217	.281	.373	.654
2015 Cin	NL	157	580	131	35	4	26	(13	13)	252	72	87	61	58	8	145	2	0	9	9	5	10	.226	.294	.434	.729
2016 2 Tms	NL	147	539	135	27	6	33	(17	16)	273	74	99	87	44	7	126	3	0	3	4	2	14	.250	.309	.506	.815
16 Cin	NL	97	370	98	22	6	25	(14	11)	207	60	80	67	27	3	83	2	0	3	4	2	11	.265	.316	.559	.875
16 NYM	NL	50	169	37	5	0	8	(3	5)	66	14	19	20	17	4	43	1	0	0	0	0	3	.219	.294	.391	.685
Postseason		9	31	8	2	0	2	(0	2)	16	3	6	4	4	0	4	1	0	0	0	1	0	.258	.361	.516	.877
9 ML YEARS		1270	4650	1153	243	27	241	(138	103)	2173	669	737	638	471	66	1239	25	3	39	61	36	79	.248	.318	.467	.785

Kris Bryant

Bats: R **Throws:** R **Pos:** 3B-107;LF-60;RF-14;1B-9;SS-1;CF-1;DH-1   **Ht:** 6'5" **Wt:** 230 **Born:** 1/4/1992 **Age:** 25

								BATTING												RUNNING			AVERAGES			
Year Team	Lg	G	AB	H	2B	3B	HR	(Hm	Rd)	TB	R	RBI	RC	TBB	IBB	SO	HBP	SH	SF	SB	CS	GDP	Avg	OBP	Slg	OPS
2013 3 Tms	Low	36	128	43	14	2	9	(-	-)	88	22	32	32	21	0	35	3	0	4	1	0	5	.336	.390	.688	1.078
2014 Tenn	AA	68	248	88	20	0	22	(-	-)	174	61	58	74	43	4	77	5	0	1	8	2	3	.355	.458	.702	1.160
2014 Iowa	AAA	70	244	72	14	1	21	(-	-)	151	57	52	62	43	4	85	9	0	1	7	2	1	.295	.418	.619	1.036
2015 ChC	NL	151	559	154	31	5	26	(12)	273	87	99	104	77	0	199	9	0	5	13	4	7	.275	.369	.488	.858
2016 ChC	NL	155	603	176	35	3	39	(17	22)	334	121	102	120	75	5	154	18	0	3	8	5	3	.292	.385	.554	.939
Postseason		9	34	6	1	1	2	(2	0)	15	2	5	4	3	0	12	0	0	0	0	0	3	.176	.243	.441	.684
2 ML YEARS		306	1162	330	66	8	65	(38	27)	607	208	201	224	152	5	353	27	0	8	21	9	10	.284	.377	.522	.900

Jake Buchanan

Pitches: R **Bats:** R **Pos:** SP-1; RP-1   **Ht:** 6'0" **Wt:** 235 **Born:** 9/24/1989 **Age:** 27

	HOW MUCH HE PITCHED						WHAT HE GAVE UP												THE RESULTS							
Year Team	Lg	G	GS	CG	GF	IP	BFP	H	R	ER	HR	SH	SF	HB	TBB	IBB	SO	WP	Bk	W	L	Pct	Sh	Sv-Op	Hld	ERC	ERA
2016 Iowa*	AAA	24	22	0	0	141.0	608	154	76	68	6	5	3	9	38	1	105	5	0	12	8	.600	0	0- -	-	3.92	4.34
2014 Hou	AL	17	2	0	0	35.1	154	41	19	18	4	3	0	1	12	1	20	2	0	1	3	.250	0	0-0	0	5.00	4.58
2015 Hou	AL	5	0	0	1	9.0	37	5	2	2	1	1	0	1	4	0	5	2	0	0	0	-	0	0-0	0	2.37	2.00
2016 ChC	NL	2	1	0	1	6.0	21	3	1	1	1	0	0	0	1	0	4	0	0	1	0	1.000	0	0-0	0	1.36	1.50
3 ML YEARS		24	3	0	11	50.1	212	49	22	21	6	4	0	2	17	1	29	4	0	2	3	.400	0	0-0	0	4.00	3.75

Clay Buchholz

Pitches: R **Bats:** L **Pos:** SP-21; RP-16   BUCK-holtz   **Ht:** 6'3" **Wt:** 190 **Born:** 8/14/1984 **Age:** 32

	HOW MUCH HE PITCHED						WHAT HE GAVE UP												THE RESULTS							
Year Team	Lg	G	GS	CG	GF	IP	BFP	H	R	ER	HR	SH	SF	HB	TBB	IBB	SO	WP	Bk	W	L	Pct	Sh	Sv-Op	Hld	ERC	ERA
2007 Bos	AL	4	3	1	0	22.2	88	14	6	4	0	0	1	0	10	0	22	0	0	3	1	.750	1	0-0	0	1.90	1.59
2008 Bos	AL	16	15	1	0	76.0	357	93	63	57	11	0	3	2	41	1	72	2	1	2	9	.182	0	0-0	0	6.40	6.75
2009 Bos	AL	16	16	0	0	92.0	399	91	44	43	13	2	3	2	36	1	68	1	0	7	4	.636	0	0-0	0	4.31	4.21
2010 Bos	AL	28	28	1	0	173.2	711	142	55	45	9	5	5	5	67	1	120	7	1	17	7	.708	1	0-0	0	2.88	2.33
2011 Bos	AL	14	14	0	0	82.2	353	76	34	32	10	1	4	2	31	1	60	3	0	6	3	.667	0	0-0	0	3.72	3.48
2012 Bos	AL	29	29	2	0	189.1	802	187	104	96	25	5	9	12	64	2	129	2	2	11	8	.579	1	0-0	0	4.29	4.56
2013 Bos	AL	16	16	1	0	108.1	416	75	23	21	4	1	2	1	36	0	96	1	0	12	1	.923	1	0-0	0	2.00	1.74
2014 Bos	AL	28	28	2	0	170.1	737	182	108	101	17	3	4	10	54	2	132	8	0	8	11	.421	2	0-0	0	4.37	5.34

Year Team	Lg	G	GS	CG	GF	IP	BFP	H	R	ER	HR	SH	SF	HB	TBB	IBB	SO	WP	Bk	W	L	Pct	Sh	Sv-Op	Hld	ERC	ERA
2015 Bos	AL	18	18	1	0	113.1	469	114	48	41	6	1	2	5	23	0	107	3	0	7	7	.500	0	0-0	0	3.23	3.26
2016 Bos	AL	37	21	0	7	139.1	588	130	80	74	21	2	6	5	55	1	93	1	0	8	10	.444	0	0-0	2	4.23	4.78
Postseason		5	5	0	0	25.2	114	28	13	12	4	0	0	2	9	1	20	2	1	0	0	-	0	0-0	0	5.04	4.21
10 ML YEARS		206	188	9	7	1167.2	4920	1104	565	514	116	20	39	45	417	9	899	28	4	81	61	.570	6	0-0	2	3.78	3.96

Ryan Buchter

Pitches: L Bats: L Pos: RP-67 BOOK-ter Ht: 6'4" Wt: 250 Born: 2/13/1987 Age: 30

Year Team	Lg	G	GS	CG	GF	IP	BFP	H	R	ER	HR	SH	SF	HB	TBB	IBB	SO	WP	Bk	W	L	Pct	Sh	Sv-Op	Hld	ERC	ERA
2012 Missi	AA	35	0	0	13	41.1	165	24	7	6	1	1	0	2	19	1	50	3	0	3	1	.750	0	4- -	-	1.84	1.31
2012 Gwnntt	AAA	9	0	0	4	8.0	53	10	13	9	1	2	1	0	17	0	5	2	0	0	2	.000	0	0- -	-	12.70	10.13
2013 Gwnntt	AAA	51	0	0	13	62.0	274	36	23	19	5	3	2	4	51	2	103	5	0	4	0	1.000	0	5- -	-	3.40	2.76
2014 Gwnntt	AAA	49	0	0	13	63.0	271	51	23	23	5	2	4	2	40	0	63	2	0	3	3	.500	0	1- -	-	3.98	3.29
2015 OkCity	AAA	27	0	0	9	32.2	140	27	6	6	0	4	0	1	16	1	39	2	0	0	0	-	0	3- -	-	2.83	1.65
2015 Iowa	AAA	16	0	0	3	18.0	72	9	4	4	0	1	0	1	9	1	23	1	0	2	0	1.000	0	0- -	-	1.49	2.00
2014 Atl	NL	1	0	0	0	1.0	3	0	0	0	0	0	0	0	1	0	1	0	0	1	0	1.000	0	0-0	0	1.26	0.00
2016 SD	NL	67	0	0	10	63.0	247	34	20	20	4	0	2	2	31	3	78	3	0	3	0	1.000	0	1-2	20	1.94	2.86
2 ML YEARS		68	0	0	10	64.0	250	34	20	20	4	0	2	2	32	3	79	3	0	4	0	1.000	0	1-2	20	1.93	2.81

Madison Bumgarner

Pitches: L Bats: R Pos: SP-34 Ht: 6'5" Wt: 250 Born: 8/1/1989 Age: 27

Year Team	Lg	G	GS	CG	GF	IP	BFP	H	R	ER	HR	SH	SF	HB	TBB	IBB	SO	WP	Bk	W	L	Pct	Sh	Sv-Op	Hld	ERC	ERA
2009 SF	NL	4	1	0	1	10.0	40	8	2	2	2	1	1	0	3	1	10	0	0	0	0	-	0	0-0	0	3.14	1.80
2010 SF	NL	18	18	0	0	111.0	472	119	40	37	11	0	4	5	26	2	86	1	1	7	6	.538	0	0-0	0	3.98	3.00
2011 SF	NL	33	33	0	0	204.2	844	202	82	73	12	12	4	5	46	5	191	0	1	13	13	.500	0	0-0	0	3.14	3.21
2012 SF	NL	32	32	2	0	208.1	849	183	87	78	23	7	4	7	49	6	191	3	2	16	11	.593	1	0-0	0	2.95	3.37
2013 SF	NL	31	31	0	0	201.1	803	146	68	62	15	10	4	6	62	6	199	6	0	13	9	.591	0	0-0	0	2.23	2.77
2014 SF	NL	33	33	4	0	217.1	873	194	81	72	21	9	5	6	43	3	219	4	1	18	10	.643	2	0-0	0	2.83	2.98
2015 SF	NL	32	32	4	0	218.1	869	181	73	71	21	5	4	7	39	2	234	1	0	18	9	.667	2	0-0	0	2.43	2.93
2016 SF	NL	34	34	4	0	226.2	912	179	79	69	26	3	6	8	54	0	251	4	1	15	9	.625	1	0-0	0	2.57	2.74
Postseason		14	12	2	1	88.1	342	63	22	21	7	6	1	4	15	1	77	0	0	7	3	.700	2	1-1	0	1.82	2.14
8 ML YEARS		217	214	14	1	1397.2	5662	1212	512	464	131	47	32	44	322	25	1381	19	6	100	67	.599	6	0-0	0	2.79	2.99

Dylan Bundy

Pitches: R Bats: B Pos: RP-22; SP-14 Ht: 6'1" Wt: 200 Born: 11/15/1992 Age: 24

Year Team	Lg	G	GS	CG	GF	IP	BFP	H	R	ER	HR	SH	SF	HB	TBB	IBB	SO	WP	Bk	W	L	Pct	Sh	Sv-Op	Hld	ERC	ERA
2012 2 Tms	Low	20	20	0	0	87.0	327	53	26	18	5	3	1	3	20	0	106	5	1	7	3	.700	0	0- -	-	1.52	1.86
2014 2 Tms	Low	9	9	0	0	41.1	173	38	15	15	0	2	2	1	16	0	37	2	0	1	3	.250	0	0- -	-	3.04	3.27
2015 Bowie	AA	8	8	0	0	22.0	90	21	10	9	0	1	0	1	5	0	25	2	0	0	3	.000	0	0- -	-	2.73	3.68
2012 Bal	AL	2	0	0	2	1.2	7	1	0	0	0	0	0	0	0	0	0	0	0	0	0	-	0	0-0	0	2.46	0.00
2016 Bal	AL	36	14	0	6	109.2	474	109	52	49	18	1	1	6	42	4	104	0	0	10	6	.625	0	0-0	3	4.61	4.02
2 ML YEARS		38	14	0	8	111.1	480	110	52	49	18	1	1	6	43	4	104	0	0	10	6	.625	0	0-0	3	4.58	3.96

Enrique Burgos

Pitches: R Bats: R Pos: RP-43 BURR-gose Ht: 6'4" Wt: 250 Born: 11/23/1990 Age: 26

Year Team	Lg	G	GS	CG	GF	IP	BFP	H	R	ER	HR	SH	SF	HB	TBB	IBB	SO	WP	Bk	W	L	Pct	Sh	Sv-Op	Hld	ERC	ERA
2012 Yakima	A-	25	0	0	16	38.1	163	28	11	10	1	2	1	2	19	0	40	3	0	2	3	.400	0	4- -	-	2.65	2.35
2013 Sbend	A	49	0	0	37	46.1	216	29	23	20	1	3	1	1	49	0	50	6	0	2	2	.500	0	17- -	-	3.90	3.88
2014 Visalia	A+	55	0	0	47	54.2	227	37	17	15	5	0	2	2	26	0	83	8	0	3	3	.500	0	29- -	-	2.70	2.47
2015 Mobile	AA	10	0	0	7	9.1	41	4	0	0	0	0	0	0	8	0	15	1	0	0	0	-	0	6- -	-	1.97	0.00
2015 Reno	AAA	15	0	0	11	15.0	78	19	10	10	3	1	0	2	12	2	23	1	0	0	1	.000	0	5- -	-	8.39	6.00
2016 Reno	AAA	24	0	0	6	27.2	121	23	7	6	1	0	1	1	17	0	29	1	0	3	0	1.000	0	1- -	-	3.65	1.95
2015 Ari	NL	30	0	0	8	27.0	121	27	15	14	2	0	1	0	15	0	39	6	0	2	2	.500	0	2-4	4	4.47	4.67
2016 Ari	NL	43	0	0	16	41.1	178	38	27	26	5	2	2	1	23	5	43	5	1	1	2	.333	0	1-4	7	4.39	5.66
2 ML YEARS		73	0	0	24	68.1	299	65	42	40	7	2	3	1	38	5	82	11	1	3	4	.429	0	3-8	9	4.42	5.27

Sean Burnett

Pitches: L Bats: L Pos: RP-10 Ht: 5'11" Wt: 185 Born: 9/17/1982 Age: 34

Year Team	Lg	G	GS	CG	GF	IP	BFP	H	R	ER	HR	SH	SF	HB	TBB	IBB	SO	WP	Bk	W	L	Pct	Sh	Sv-Op	Hld	ERC	ERA
2016 OkCity*	AAA	7	0	0	1	7.2	39	8	3	2	1	1	0	2	6	1	5	0	0	0	0	-	0	0- -	-	6.81	2.35
2016 Gwnntt*	AAA	6	0	0	1	5.1	20	3	0	0	0	0	0	0	1	0	5	1	0	0	0	-	0	0- -	-	0.99	0.00
2016 Roch*	AAA	29	0	0	14	29.1	113	20	9	7	1	2	1	0	7	1	18	4	0	0	3	.000	0	3- -	-	1.55	2.15
2016 Syrcse*	AAA	5	0	0	1	5.0	22	7	3	3	1	0	0	0	4	0	4	0	0	0	0	-	0	0- -	-	5.32	5.40
2004 Pit	NL	13	13	1	0	71.2	318	86	41	40	9	2	1	1	28	2	30	2	0	5	5	.500	1	0-0	0	5.49	5.02
2008 Pit	NL	58	0	0	16	56.2	253	57	31	30	7	4	3	2	34	3	42	4	0	1	1	.500	0	0-0	8	5.23	4.76
2009 2 Tms	NL	71	0	0	22	57.2	237	36	21	20	6	6	1	3	28	8	43	4	0	2	3	.400	0	1-3	11	2.43	3.12
2010 Was	NL	73	0	0	10	63.0	261	52	17	15	3	4	0	4	20	4	62	2	0	1	7	.125	0	3-4	20	2.43	2.14
2011 Was	NL	69	0	0	17	56.2	242	54	24	24	4	6	3	3	24	11	33	2	0	5	5	.500	0	4-11	15	3.85	3.81
2012 Was	NL	70	0	0	16	56.2	239	58	16	15	4	1	2	3	12	3	57	2	0	1	2	.333	0	2-5	31	3.38	2.38
2013 LAA	AL	13	0	0	1	9.2	40	9	1	1	1	2	0	0	4	0	7	1	0	0	0	-	0	0-0	5	3.90	0.93
2014 LAA	AL	3	0	0	0	0.2	3	1	1	1	0	1	0	0	0	0	0	0	0	0	0	-	0	0-0	1	4.47	13.50

Year Team	Lg	G	GS	CG	GF	IP	BFP	H	R	ER	HR	SH	SF	HB	TBB	IBB	SO	WP	Bk	W	L	Pct	Sh	Sv-Op	Hld	ERC	ERA
2016 Was	NL	10	0	0	2	5.2	22	5	2	2	1	0	0	0	1	0	3	0	0	0	0	-	0	0-0	-	3.16	3.18
09 Pit	NL	38	0	0	7	32.1	133	22	12	11	3	4	1	3	15	4	23	2	0	1	2	.333	0	1-2	6	2.77	3.06
09 Was	NL	33	0	0	1	25.1	104	14	9	9	3	2	0	0	13	4	20	2	0	1	1	.500	0	0-1	5	2.02	3.20
Postseason		2	0	0	0	1.0	7	3	4	3	1	0	0	0	1	0	1	0	0	0	0	-	0	0-0	1	32.12	27.00
9 ML YEARS		380	13	1	70	378.1	1615	358	154	148	37	22	9	13	148	24	277	17	0	15	23	.395	1	10-23	91	3.77	3.52

Andrew Burns

Bats: R **Throws:** R **Pos:** 3B-4;PH-4;PR-2;1B-1;LF-1 **Ht:** 6'2" **Wt:** 205 **Born:** 8/7/1990 **Age:** 26

Year Team	Lg	G	AB	H	2B	3B	HR	(Hm	Rd)	TB	R	RBI	RC	TBB	IBB	SO	HBP	SH	SF	SB	CS	GDP	Avg	OBP	Slg	OPS
2012 Lnsng	A	78	278	69	25	4	9	(-	-)	129	57	37	49	38	0	75	7	0	2	15	2	2	.248	.351	.464	.815
2013 Dnedin	A+	64	248	81	15	5	8	(-	-)	130	45	53	51	25	0	38	2	0	7	21	9	4	.327	.383	.524	.907
2013 Nham	AA	64	265	67	19	2	7	(-	-)	111	40	32	36	23	0	55	0	0	3	12	5	5	.253	.309	.419	.728
2014 Nham	AA	133	495	126	32	5	15	(-	-)	213	71	63	71	41	1	99	6	3	8	18	8	4	.255	.315	.430	.745
2015 Buffalo	AAA	126	478	140	26	4	4	(-	-)	178	60	45	63	38	0	69	5	5	1	6	9	17	.293	.351	.372	.723
2016 Buffalo	AAA	111	418	96	25	1	8	(-	-)	147	42	38	44	33	0	82	0	1	2	13	5	10	.230	.285	.352	.636
2016 Tor	AL	10	6	0	0	0	0	(0	0)	0	2	0	0	0	0	2	1	0	0	0	0	0	.000	.143	.000	.143

Billy Burns

Bats: B **Throws:** R **Pos:** CF-80;RF-7;PH-7;PR-7;LF-6;DH-4 **Ht:** 5'9" **Wt:** 170 **Born:** 8/30/1989 **Age:** 27

Year Team	Lg	G	AB	H	2B	3B	HR	(Hm	Rd)	TB	R	RBI	RC	TBB	IBB	SO	HBP	SH	SF	SB	CS	GDP	Avg	OBP	Slg	OPS
2016 Nashv*	AAA	10	41	12	1	0	0	(-	-)	13	7	4	5	2	0	12	0	1	0	4	0	0	.293	.326	.317	.643
2014 Oak	AL	13	6	1	0	0	0	(0	0)	1	4	0	0	0	0	0	0	0	0	3	1	0	.167	.167	.167	.333
2015 Oak	AL	125	520	153	18	9	5	(3	2)	204	70	42	72	26	1	81	6	1	2	26	8	5	.294	.334	.392	.726
2016 2 Tms	AL	97	311	73	11	4	0	(0	0)	92	39	13	23	10	2	37	6	3	2	17	5	3	.235	.271	.296	.566
16 Oak	AL	73	274	64	11	4	0	(0	0)	83	32	12	22	10	2	30	4	3	1	14	3	3	.234	.270	.303	.573
16 KC	AL	24	37	9	0	0	0	(0	0)	9	7	1	1	0	0	7	2	0	1	3	2	0	.243	.275	.243	.518
3 ML YEARS		235	837	227	29	13	5	(3	2)	297	113	55	95	36	3	118	12	4	4	46	14	8	.271	.309	.355	.664

Emmanuel Burriss

Bats: B **Throws:** R **Pos:** PH-24;PR-6;2B-5;SS-3;LF-3;1B-2;DH-1 **Ht:** 6'0" **Wt:** 190 **Born:** 1/17/1985 **Age:** 32

Year Team	Lg	G	AB	H	2B	3B	HR	(Hm	Rd)	TB	R	RBI	RC	TBB	IBB	SO	HBP	SH	SF	SB	CS	GDP	Avg	OBP	Slg	OPS
2016 LV*	AAA	50	175	46	6	1	0	(-	-)	54	21	13	17	9	2	25	0	1	2	6	1	5	.263	.296	.309	.604
2008 SF	NL	95	240	68	6	1	1	(0	1)	79	37	18	22	23	1	24	5	5	1	13	5	7	.283	.357	.329	.686
2009 SF	NL	61	202	48	6	0	0	(0	0)	54	18	13	15	14	1	34	2	1	1	11	4	3	.238	.292	.267	.560
2010 SF	NL	7	5	2	0	0	0	(0	0)	2	3	0	1	0	0	1	0	0	0	0	0	0	.400	.400	.400	.800
2011 SF	NL	59	137	28	1	0	0	(0	0)	29	14	4	6	6	0	17	3	6	0	11	3	2	.204	.253	.212	.465
2012 SF	NL	60	136	29	1	0	0	(0	0)	30	15	7	4	10	1	25	1	2	1	5	3	6	.213	.270	.221	.491
2015 Was	NL	5	3	2	0	0	0	(0	0)	2	2	0	2	2	0	0	0	0	0	0	0	0	.667	.800	.667	1.467
2016 Phi	NL	39	45	5	1	1	0	(0	0)	8	3	0	0	2	0	10	2	1	0	1	0	1	.111	.184	.178	.361
7 ML YEARS		326	768	182	15	2	1	(0	1)	204	92	42	50	57	3	111	13	15	3	41	15	19	.237	.300	.266	.565

Matt Buschmann

Pitches: R **Bats:** R **Pos:** RP-3 **Ht:** 6'3" **Wt:** 205 **Born:** 2/13/1984 **Age:** 33

Year Team	Lg	G	GS	CG	GF	IP	BFP	H	R	ER	HR	SH	SF	HB	TBB	IBB	SO	WP	Bk	W	L	Pct	Sh	Sv-Op	Hld	ERC	ERA
2012 Mont	AA	24	22	1	1	141.0	589	136	69	61	12	6	3	8	48	3	111	6	0	7	8	.467	0	0- -	-	3.83	3.89
2013 Mont	AA	11	11	0	0	63.2	267	59	24	19	6	1	1	3	23	1	63	4	0	6	3	.667	0	0- -	-	3.70	2.69
2013 Drham	AAA	18	17	0	1	97.0	407	80	37	32	4	2	1	6	44	0	104	4	0	8	2	.800	0	1- -	-	3.21	2.97
2014 Scrmto	AAA	23	22	1	0	133.1	577	142	76	67	15	2	3	6	49	1	123	8	0	9	7	.563	1	0- -	-	4.64	4.52
2015 Drham	AAA	13	13	0	0	78.2	326	68	35	34	9	0	1	4	29	0	63	5	0	6	5	.545	0	0- -	-	3.57	3.89
2015 Lsvlle	AAA	9	9	2	0	53.0	220	52	25	25	3	3	2	3	18	1	44	2	0	2	5	.286	1	0- -	-	3.76	4.25
2016 Reno	AAA	25	24	1	0	142.0	628	172	89	83	20	4	6	2	53	3	91	6	1	8	10	.444	1	0- -	-	5.63	5.26
2016 Ari	NL	3	0	0	2	4.1	15	2	1	1	1	0	0	0	1	1	3	0	0	0	0	-	0	0-0	0	1.46	2.08

Matt Bush

Pitches: R **Bats:** R **Pos:** RP-58 **Ht:** 5'9" **Wt:** 180 **Born:** 2/8/1986 **Age:** 31

Year Team	Lg	G	GS	CG	GF	IP	BFP	H	R	ER	HR	SH	SF	HB	TBB	IBB	SO	WP	Bk	W	L	Pct	Sh	Sv-Op	Hld	ERC	ERA
2016 Frisco	AA	12	0	0	9	17.0	63	9	5	5	2	0	1	1	4	0	18	2	0	0	2	.000	0	5- -	-	1.57	2.65
2016 Tex	AL	58	0	0	15	61.2	243	44	18	17	4	1	3	1	14	0	61	2	0	7	2	.778	0	1-4	22	1.83	2.48

Nick Buss

Bats: L **Throws:** R **Pos:** LF-24;RF-5;PH-5;PR-4;CF-3 **Ht:** 6'2" **Wt:** 190 **Born:** 12/15/1986 **Age:** 30

Year Team	Lg	G	AB	H	2B	3B	HR	(Hm	Rd)	TB	R	RBI	RC	TBB	IBB	SO	HBP	SH	SF	SB	CS	GDP	Avg	OBP	Slg	OPS
2012 Chatt	AA	132	492	134	24	10	8	(-	-)	202	70	57	68	38	1	71	5	19	4	19	13	4	.272	.328	.411	.739
2013 Albq	AAA	131	459	139	29	11	17	(-	-)	241	84	100	92	41	1	90	7	3	8	21	2	6	.303	.363	.525	.888
2014 Albq	AAA	26	92	24	3	3	1	(-	-)	36	12	16	12	8	0	12	2	1	1	0	2	0	.261	.330	.391	.721
2014 Scrmto	AAA	110	450	138	17	2	4	(-	-)	171	79	52	69	45	1	75	4	2	5	14	4	8	.307	.371	.380	.751
2015 Reno	AAA	92	284	84	14	3	4	(-	-)	116	43	33	44	24	1	35	4	2	6	10	4	7	.296	.352	.408	.761

Year	Team	Lg	G	AB	H	2B	3B	HR	(Hm	Rd)	TB	R	RBI	RC	TBB	IBB	SO	HBP	SH	SF	SB	CS	GDP	Avg	OBP	Slg	OPS
2016	Salt Lk	AAA	87	331	96	23	8	6	(-	-)	153	49	46	54	30	1	66	0	7	4	8	5	6	.290	.345	.462	.807
2013	LAD	NL	8	19	2	0	0	0	(0	0)	2	0	0	0	1	0	1	0	0	0	0	0	0	.105	.150	.105	.255
2016	LAA	AL	36	81	16	7	1	1	(0	1)	28	7	8	6	6	0	24	0	1	2	2	1	4	.198	.247	.346	.593
	2 ML YEARS		44	100	18	7	1	1	(0	1)	30	7	8	6	7	0	25	0	1	2	2	1	4	.180	.229	.300	.529

Drew Butera

Bats: R Throws: R Pos: C-51;1B-2;PH-2   bue-TARE-ah   Ht: 6'1" Wt: 200 Born: 8/9/1983 Age: 33

Year	Team	Lg	G	AB	H	2B	3B	HR	(Hm	Rd)	TB	R	RBI	RC	TBB	IBB	SO	HBP	SH	SF	SB	CS	GDP	Avg	OBP	Slg	OPS
2010	Min	AL	49	142	28	6	1	2	(0	2)	42	12	13	7	4	0	25	4	3	2	0	0	5	.197	.237	.296	.533
2011	Min	AL	93	234	39	9	1	2	(1	1)	56	19	23	11	11	0	42	2	6	1	0	0	7	.167	.210	.239	.449
2012	Min	AL	42	111	22	6	0	1	(1	0)	31	7	5	6	9	0	26	2	0	0	0	0	3	.198	.270	.279	.550
2013	2 Tms		6	10	1	0	0	0	(0	0)	1	0	0	0	0	0	5	0	0	0	0	0	0	.100	.100	.100	.200
2014	LAD	NL	61	170	32	6	1	3	(0	3)	49	16	14	10	17	1	41	2	1	2	0	0	1	.188	.267	.288	.555
2015	2 Tms		55	107	21	3	0	1	(0	1)	27	9	5	5	6	0	26	2	5	0	0	1	3	.196	.252	.252	.505
2016	KC	AL	56	123	35	10	1	4	(0	4)	59	18	16	15	8	0	36	0	2	0	0	0	2	.285	.328	.480	.808
13	Min	AL	2	3	0	0	0	0	(0	0)	0	0	0	0	0	0	1	0	0	0	0	0	0	.000	.000	.000	.000
13	LAD	NL	4	7	1	0	0	0	(0	0)	1	0	0	0	0	0	4	0	0	0	0	0	0	.143	.143	.143	.286
15	LAA	AL	10	21	4	0	0	0	(0	0)	4	3	0	0	0	0	2	0	0	0	0	1	0	.190	.190	.190	.381
15	KC	AL	45	86	17	3	0	1	(0	1)	23	6	5	6	6	0	24	2	5	0	0	0	3	.198	.266	.267	.533
	Postseason		3	1	0	0	0	0	(0	0)	0	0	0	0	1	0	0	0	0	0	0	0	0	.000	.500	.000	.500
	7 ML YEARS		362	897	178	40	4	13	(2	11)	265	81	76	55	55	1	201	12	17	5	0	1	18	.198	.253	.295	.548

Billy Butler

Bats: R Throws: R Pos: DH-53;PH-28;1B-25   Ht: 6'0" Wt: 260 Born: 4/18/1986 Age: 31

Year	Team	Lg	G	AB	H	2B	3B	HR	(Hm	Rd)	TB	R	RBI	RC	TBB	IBB	SO	HBP	SH	SF	SB	CS	GDP	Avg	OBP	Slg	OPS
2007	KC	AL	92	329	96	23	2	8	(5	3)	147	38	52	50	27	5	55	2	0	2	0	0	8	.292	.347	.447	.794
2008	KC	AL	124	443	122	22	0	11	(4	7)	177	44	55	57	33	0	57	0	0	2	0	1	23	.275	.324	.400	.724
2009	KC	AL	159	608	183	51	1	21	(16	5)	299	78	93	99	58	3	103	2	0	4	1	0	20	.301	.362	.492	.853
2010	KC	AL	158	595	189	45	0	15	(9	6)	279	77	78	91	69	8	78	5	0	9	0	0	32	.318	.388	.469	.857
2011	KC	AL	159	597	174	44	0	19	(9	10)	275	74	95	94	66	15	95	3	0	7	2	1	16	.291	.361	.461	.822
2012	KC	AL	161	614	192	32	1	29	(11	18)	313	72	107	102	54	9	111	7	0	4	2	1	20	.313	.373	.510	.882
2013	KC	AL	162	582	168	27	0	15	(6	9)	240	62	82	87	79	11	102	3	0	4	0	0	28	.289	.374	.412	.787
2014	KC	AL	151	549	149	32	0	9	(5	4)	208	57	66	65	41	3	96	5	0	8	0	0	21	.271	.323	.379	.702
2015	Oak	AL	151	538	135	28	1	15	(9	6)	210	63	65	64	52	4	101	7	0	4	0	0	26	.251	.323	.390	.713
2016	2 Tms	AL	97	250	71	18	0	5	(2	3)	104	27	35	33	21	1	42	0	0	3	0	0	13	.284	.336	.416	.752
16	Oak	AL	85	221	61	16	0	4	(2	2)	89	24	31	28	19	1	34	0	0	3	0	0	13	.276	.331	.403	.733
16	NYY	AL	12	29	10	2	0	1	(0	1)	15	3	4	5	2	0	8	0	0	0	0	0	0	.345	.375	.517	.892
	Postseason		13	42	11	3	0	0	(0	0)	14	3	8	7	5	0	5	0	0	2	1	0	3	.262	.327	.333	.660
	10 ML YEARS		1414	5105	1479	322	5	147	(76	71)	2252	592	728	742	500	59	840	34	0	47	5	3	207	.290	.354	.441	.795

Eddie Butler

Pitches: R Bats: R Pos: SP-9; RP-8   Ht: 6'2" Wt: 180 Born: 3/13/1991 Age: 26

			HOW MUCH HE PITCHED					WHAT HE GAVE UP										THE RESULTS							
Year	Team	Lg	G	GS	CG	GF	IP	BFP	H	R	ER	HR	SH	SF	HB	TBB	IBB	SO	WP	Bk	W	L	Pct	Sh	Sv-Op	Hld	ERC	ERA
2016	Albq*	AAA	15	15	1	0	89.0	380	93	47	44	9	1	5	0	26	0	35	4	0	8	3	.727	1	0--	-	3.89	4.45
2014	Col	NL	3	3	0	0	16.0	76	23	12	12	2	2	0	0	7	1	3	0	0	1	1	.500	0	0-0	0	6.98	6.75
2015	Col	NL	16	16	1	0	79.1	370	102	57	52	13	6	1	4	42	4	44	0	0	3	10	.231	0	0-0	0	7.12	5.90
2016	Col	NL	17	9	0	0	64.0	293	87	57	51	13	2	2	3	21	1	47	1	0	2	5	.286	0	0-0	0	7.00	7.17
	3 ML YEARS		36	28	1	0	159.1	739	212	126	115	28	10	3	7	70	6	94	1	0	6	16	.273	0	0-0	0	7.06	6.50

Byron Buxton

Bats: R Throws: R Pos: CF-92;PR-1   Ht: 6'2" Wt: 190 Born: 12/18/1993 Age: 23

Year	Team	Lg	G	AB	H	2B	3B	HR	(Hm	Rd)	TB	R	RBI	RC	TBB	IBB	SO	HBP	SH	SF	SB	CS	GDP	Avg	OBP	Slg	OPS
2012	2 Tms	Low	48	165	41	10	4	5	(-	-)	74	33	20	27	19	0	41	5	0	1	11	3	0	.248	.344	.448	.792
2013	2 Tms	Low	125	488	163	19	18	12	(-	-)	254	109	77	111	76	3	105	3	3	4	55	19	5	.334	.424	.520	.944
2014	FtMyrs	A+	30	121	29	4	2	4	(-	-)	49	19	16	16	10	0	33	3	0	0	6	2	0	.240	.313	.405	.718
2015	Chatt	AA	59	237	67	7	12	6	(-	-)	116	44	37	45	26	0	51	1	0	4	20	2	2	.283	.351	.489	.840
2015	Roch	AAA	13	55	22	3	1	1	(-	-)	30	11	8	12	4	0	12	0	0	0	2	1	0	.400	.441	.545	.986
2016	Roch	AAA	49	190	58	11	3	11	(-	-)	108	41	24	39	14	1	58	3	0	2	7	0	2	.305	.359	.568	.927
2015	Min	AL	46	129	27	7	1	2	(0	2)	42	16	6	10	6	0	44	1	2	0	2	1	1	.209	.250	.326	.576
2016	Min	AL	92	298	67	19	6	10	(6	4)	128	44	38	33	23	0	118	3	4	3	10	2	2	.225	.284	.430	.714
	2 ML YEARS		138	427	94	26	7	12	(6	6)	170	60	44	43	29	0	162	4	6	3	12	4	3	.220	.274	.398	.672

Marlon Byrd

Bats: R Throws: R Pos: RF-21;LF-14;PH-3;DH-1   Ht: 6'0" Wt: 245 Born: 8/30/1977 Age: 39

Year	Team	Lg	G	AB	H	2B	3B	HR	(Hm	Rd)	TB	R	RBI	RC	TBB	IBB	SO	HBP	SH	SF	SB	CS	GDP	Avg	OBP	Slg	OPS
2002	Phi	NL	10	35	8	2	0	1	(1	0)	13	2	1	0	1	0	8	0	0	0	0	2	0	.229	.250	.371	.621
2003	Phi	NL	135	495	150	28	4	7	(3	4)	207	86	45	72	44	3	94	7	4	3	11	1	8	.303	.366	.418	.784
2004	Phi	NL	106	346	79	13	2	5	(3	2)	111	48	33	33	22	1	68	7	2	1	2	2	10	.228	.287	.321	.608
2005	2 Tms	NL	79	229	61	15	2	2	(0	2)	86	20	26	30	19	1	50	2	5	4	5	1	5	.266	.323	.376	.698
2006	Was	NL	78	197	44	8	1	5	(1	4)	69	28	18	18	22	1	47	6	1	2	3	3	6	.223	.317	.350	.667

Year Team	Lg	G	AB	H	2B	3B	HR	(Hm	Rd)	TB	R	RBI	RC	TBB	IBB	SO	HBP	SH	SF	SB	CS	GDP	Avg	OBP	Slg	OPS
2007 Tex	AL	109	414	127	17	8	10	(4	6)	190	60	70	68	29	3	88	5	0	6	5	3	9	.307	.355	.459	.814
2008 Tex	AL	122	403	120	28	4	10	(7	3)	186	70	53	63	46	3	62	9	2	2	7	2	10	.298	.380	.462	.842
2009 Tex	AL	146	547	155	43	2	20	(14	6)	262	66	89	91	32	2	98	10	0	10	8	4	11	.283	.329	.479	.808
2010 ChC	NL	152	580	170	39	2	12	(6	6)	249	84	66	80	31	1	98	17	0	2	5	1	12	.293	.346	.429	.775
2011 ChC	NL	119	446	123	22	2	9	(4	5)	176	51	35	43	25	2	78	8	1	2	3	2	13	.276	.324	.395	.719
2012 2 Tms		48	143	30	2	0	1	(0	1)	35	10	9	8	5	1	31	2	1	2	0	3	3	.210	.243	.245	.488
2013 Phi	NL	147	532	155	35	5	24	(9	15)	272	75	88	85	31	2	144	8	1	7	2	4	11	.291	.336	.511	.847
2014 Phi	NL	154	591	156	28	2	25	(13	12)	261	71	85	74	35	7	185	8	0	3	3	2	6	.264	.324	.445	.757
2015 2 Tms	NL	135	506	125	25	5	23	(14	9)	229	58	73	61	29	2	145	4	0	5	2	1	10	.247	.290	.453	.743
2016 Cle	AL	34	115	31	6	0	5	(2	3)	52	11	19	18	11	1	38	0	0	3	0	0	1	.270	.326	.452	.778
05 Phi	NL	5	13	4	0	0	0	(0	0)	4	0	0	2	1	0	3	1	0	0	0	0	0	.308	.400	.308	.708
05 Was	NL	74	216	57	15	2	2	(0	2)	82	20	26	28	18	1	47	1	5	4	5	1	5	.264	.318	.380	.698
12 ChC	NL	13	43	3	0	0	0	(0	0)	3	1	2	0	3	1	10	1	0	0	0	1	2	.070	.149	.070	.219
12 Bos	AL	35	100	27	2	0	1	(0	1)	32	9	7	8	2	0	21	1	1	2	0	2	1	.270	.286	.320	.606
13 NYM	NL	117	425	121	26	5	21	(7	14)	220	61	71	68	25	2	124	7	1	6	2	4	6	.285	.330	.518	.848
13 Pit	NL	30	107	34	9	0	3	(2	1)	52	14	17	17	6	0	20	1	0	1	0	0	5	.318	.357	.486	.843
15 Cin	NL	96	359	85	13	3	19	(11	8)	161	46	42	37	23	1	101	3	0	3	2	1	6	.237	.286	.448	.735
15 SF	NL	39	147	40	12	2	4	(3	1)	68	12	31	24	6	1	44	1	0	2	0	0	4	.272	.301	.463	.764
Postseason		6	22	8	2	0	1	(1	0)	13	4	5	3	1	0	6	0	0	0	0	0	0	.364	.391	.591	.982
15 ML YEARS		1574	5579	1534	311	39	159	(81	78)	2400	740	710	746	382	30	1234	93	17	52	56	31	115	.275	.329	.430	.759

Asdrubal Cabrera

Bats: B Throws: R Pos: SS-135;PH-6   azz-DRUE-bull   **Ht: 6'0" Wt: 205 Born: 11/13/1985 Age: 31**

Year Team	Lg	G	AB	H	2B	3B	HR	(Hm	Rd)	TB	R	RBI	RC	TBB	IBB	SO	HBP	SH	SF	SB	CS	GDP	Avg	OBP	Slg	OPS
2007 Cle	AL	45	159	45	9	2	3	(1	2)	67	30	22	27	17	0	29	2	5	3	0	0	7	.283	.354	.421	.775
2008 Cle	AL	114	352	91	20	0	6	(5	1)	129	48	47	48	46	2	77	4	11	5	4	4	8	.259	.346	.366	.713
2009 Cle	AL	131	523	161	42	4	6	(4	2)	229	81	68	81	44	1	89	1	10	3	17	4	13	.308	.361	.438	.799
2010 Cle	AL	97	381	105	16	1	3	(2	1)	132	39	29	46	25	0	60	5	11	3	6	4	10	.276	.326	.346	.673
2011 Cle	AL	151	604	165	32	3	25	(13	12)	278	87	92	100	44	5	119	11	4	4	17	5	10	.273	.332	.460	.792
2012 Cle	AL	143	555	150	35	1	16	(10	6)	235	70	68	74	52	3	99	6	1	2	9	1	18	.270	.338	.423	.762
2013 Cle	AL	136	508	123	35	2	14	(8	6)	204	66	64	51	35	1	114	8	6	5	9	3	10	.242	.299	.402	.700
2014 2 Tms	AL	146	553	133	31	4	14	(6	8)	214	74	61	57	49	2	108	7	1	6	10	2	15	.241	.307	.387	.694
2015 TB	AL	143	505	134	28	5	15	(7	8)	217	66	58	53	36	4	107	3	1	6	6	3	14	.265	.315	.430	.744
2016 NYM	NL	141	521	146	30	1	23	(18	5)	247	65	62	76	38	3	103	7	0	2	5	1	14	.280	.336	.474	.810
14 Cle	AL	97	378	93	22	2	9	(5	4)	146	54	40	36	27	1	79	7	0	4	7	2	11	.246	.305	.386	.692
14 Was	NL	49	175	40	9	2	5	(1	4)	68	20	21	21	22	1	29	0	1	2	3	0	4	.229	.312	.389	.700
Postseason		16	65	13	1	0	2	(2	0)	20	7	8	6	2	0	18	0	3	1	0	0	3	.200	.221	.308	.528
10 ML YEARS		1247	4661	1253	278	23	125	(74	51)	1952	626	571	613	386	21	905	54	50	39	83	30	119	.269	.329	.419	.748

Mauricio Cabrera

Pitches: R Bats: R Pos: RP-41   **Ht: 6'3" Wt: 245 Born: 9/22/1993 Age: 23**

Year Team	Lg	G	GS	CG	GF	IP	BFP	H	R	ER	HR	SH	SF	HB	TBB	IBB	SO	WP	Bk	W	L	Pct	Sh	Sv-Op	Hld	ERC	ERA
2012 Danvle	R+	12	12	0	0	57.2	242	45	23	19	2	0	1	7	23	0	48	13	1	2	2	.500	0	0- -	-	2.92	2.97
2013 Rome	A	24	24	1	0	131.1	573	118	74	61	3	5	5	6	71	0	107	16	4	3	8	.273	0	0- -	-	3.69	4.18
2014 2 Tms	Low	22	5	0	4	33.0	147	27	25	21	1	2	0	4	21	0	31	7	2	1	1	.500	0	0- -	-	3.94	5.73
2015 Carlina	A+	23	0	0	9	31.0	140	30	22	19	1	1	2	0	17	0	28	8	1	2	2	.500	0	1- -	-	3.87	5.52
2015 Missi	AA	13	0	0	4	17.1	83	12	12	11	0	0	1	1	18	0	25	8	0	0	1	.000	0	0- -	-	4.58	5.71
2016 Missi	AA	25	0	0	9	33.2	146	20	15	12	0	0	0	3	22	2	35	2	0	3	3	.500	0	4- -	-	2.34	3.21
2016 Atl	NL	41	0	0	10	38.1	162	31	14	12	0	2	2	1	19	1	32	2	0	5	1	.833	0	6-7	8	2.79	2.82

Melky Cabrera

Bats: B Throws: L Pos: LF-147;DH-3;PH-1   **Ht: 5'10" Wt: 210 Born: 8/11/1984 Age: 32**

Year Team	Lg	G	AB	H	2B	3B	HR	(Hm	Rd)	TB	R	RBI	RC	TBB	IBB	SO	HBP	SH	SF	SB	CS	GDP	Avg	OBP	Slg	OPS
2005 NYY	AL	6	19	4	0	0	0	(0	0)	4	1	0	0	0	0	2	0	0	0	0	0	0	.211	.211	.211	.421
2006 NYY	AL	130	460	129	26	2	7	(3	4)	180	75	50	68	56	3	59	2	5	1	12	5	9	.280	.360	.391	.752
2007 NYY	AL	150	545	149	24	8	8	(4	4)	213	66	73	70	43	0	68	5	10	9	13	5	14	.273	.327	.391	.718
2008 NYY	AL	129	414	103	12	1	8	(4	4)	141	42	37	37	29	5	58	3	4	3	3	2	11	.249	.301	.341	.641
2009 NYY	AL	154	485	133	28	1	13	(9	4)	202	66	68	69	43	4	59	4	4	4	10	2	15	.274	.336	.416	.752
2010 Atl	NL	147	458	117	27	3	4	(1	3)	162	50	42	45	42	11	64	1	5	3	7	1	8	.255	.317	.354	.671
2011 KC	AL	155	658	201	44	5	18	(6	12)	309	102	87	92	35	1	94	1	7	5	20	10	13	.305	.339	.470	.809
2012 SF	NL	113	459	159	25	10	11	(2	9)	237	84	60	83	36	4	63	0	1	5	13	5	8	**.346**	.390	.516	.906
2013 Tor	AL	88	344	96	15	2	3	(3	0)	124	39	30	39	23	0	47	0	2	3	2	2	7	.279	.322	.360	.682
2014 Tor	AL	139	568	171	35	3	16	(7	9)	260	81	73	84	43	3	67	3	2	5	6	2	19	.301	.351	.458	.808
2015 CWS	AL	158	629	172	36	2	12	(6	6)	248	70	77	81	40	2	88	2	2	**10**	3	0	18	.273	.314	.394	.709
2016 CWS	AL	151	591	175	42	5	14	(6	8)	269	70	86	89	47	2	69	0	3	5	2	0	17	.296	.345	.455	.800
Postseason		22	75	16	2	0	1	(0	1)	21	8	7	5	3	0	16	0	2	0	0	0	0	.213	.244	.280	.524
12 ML YEARS		1520	5630	1609	314	42	114	(51	63)	2349	746	683	757	437	37	738	21	45	53	97	34	139	.286	.337	.417	.754

Miguel Cabrera

Bats: R Throws: R Pos: 1B-147;DH-8;PH-2;3B-1   Ht: 6'4" Wt: 240 Born: 4/18/1983 Age: 34

							BATTING													RUNNING			AVERAGES			
Year	Team	Lg	G	AB	H	2B	3B	HR	(Hm | Rd)	TB	R	RBI	RC	TBB	IBB	SO	HBP	SH	SF	SB	CS	GDP	Avg	OBP	Slg	OPS
2003	Fla	NL	87	314	84	21	3	12	(7 | 5)	147	39	62	51	25	3	84	2	4	1	0	2	12	.268	.325	.468	.793
2004	Fla	NL	160	603	177	31	1	33	(14 | 19)	309	101	112	92	68	5	148	6	0	8	5	2	20	.294	.366	.512	.879
2005	Fla	NL	158	613	198	43	2	33	(11 | 22)	344	106	116	108	64	12	125	2	0	6	1	0	20	.323	.385	.561	.947
2006	Fla	NL	158	576	195	50	2	26	(15 | 11)	327	112	114	132	86	27	108	10	0	4	9	6	18	.339	.430	.568	.998
2007	Fla	NL	157	588	188	38	2	34	(19 | 15)	332	91	119	122	79	23	127	5	1	7	2	1	17	.320	.401	.565	.965
2008	Det	AL	160	616	180	36	2	**37**	(19 | **18)**	**331**	85	127	109	56	6	126	3	0	9	1	0	16	.292	.349	.537	.887
2009	Det	AL	160	611	198	34	0	34	(19 | 15)	334	96	103	114	68	14	107	5	0	1	6	2	22	.324	.396	.547	.942
2010	Det	AL	150	548	180	45	1	38	(17 | 21)	341	111	**126**	122	89	**32**	95	3	0	3	3	3	17	.328	**.420**	.622	1.042
2011	Det	AL	**161**	572	197	**48**	0	30	(15 | 15)	335	111	105	**141**	108	22	89	3	0	5	2	1	24	**.344**	**.448**	.586	1.033
2012	Det	AL	161	622	205	40	0	**44**	(28 | 16)	**377**	109	**139**	123	66	17	98	3	0	6	4	1	28	.330	.393	**.606**	**.999**
2013	Det	AL	148	555	193	26	1	44	(17 | **27)**	353	103	137	146	90	19	94	5	0	2	3	0	19	**.348**	**.442**	**.636**	**1.078**
2014	Det	AL	159	611	191	**52**	1	25	(13 | 12)	320	101	109	110	60	10	117	3	0	**11**	1	1	21	.313	.371	.524	.895
2015	Det	AL	119	429	145	28	1	18	(7 | 11)	229	64	76	93	77	15	82	3	0	2	1	1	19	**.338**	**.440**	.534	.974
2016	Det	AL	158	595	188	31	1	38	(20 | 18)	335	92	108	106	75	**15**	116	4	0	5	0	0	**26**	.316	.393	.563	.956
	Postseason		55	205	57	10	0	13	(4 | 9)	106	29	38	34	27	7	48	2	1	0	3	0	7	.278	.368	.517	.885
	14 ML YEARS		2096	7853	2519	523	17	446	(221 | 225)	4414	1321	1553	1569	1011	220	1516	57	5	75	38	20	279	.321	.399	.562	.961

Ramon Cabrera

Bats: B Throws: R Pos: C-48;PH-15   Ht: 5'8" Wt: 195 Born: 11/5/1989 Age: 27

							BATTING													RUNNING			AVERAGES			
Year	Team	Lg	G	AB	H	2B	3B	HR	(Hm	Rd)	TB	R	RBI	RC	TBB	IBB	SO	HBP	SH	SF	SB	CS	GDP	Avg	OBP	Slg	OPS
2012	Altna	AA	112	384	106	22	2	3	(-	-)	141	47	50	50	39	1	44	0	4	1	0	3	11	.276	.342	.367	.709
2013	Erie	AA	84	312	95	22	2	0	(-	-)	121	44	54	53	44	0	34	3	0	3	4	0	6	.304	.392	.388	.780
2013	Toledo	AAA	39	149	36	9	1	1	(-	-)	50	13	15	16	14	0	21	1	1	0	0	1	8	.242	.311	.336	.647
2014	Erie	AA	107	394	109	17	0	5	(-	-)	141	42	47	49	33	0	37	0	0	4	1	0	9	.277	.329	.358	.687
2014	Altna	AA	12	46	11	5	0	1	(-	-)	19	5	5	5	3	0	6	0	0	0	1	0	1	.239	.286	.413	.699
2015	Lsvlle	AAA	86	317	92	14	0	2	(-	-)	112	29	35	41	27	0	44	0	4	3	1	1	10	.290	.343	.353	.696
2016	Lsvlle	AAA	15	54	14	1	0	0	(-	-)	15	3	2	4	1	0	6	0	0	1	0	0	4	.259	.268	.278	.546
2015	Cin	NL	13	30	11	1	0	1	(1	0)	15	4	3	4	0	0	5	0	0	0	0	0	1	.367	.367	.500	.867
2016	Cin	NL	61	171	42	10	0	3	(3	0)	61	11	23	16	8	1	30	1	2	3	1	1	5	.246	.279	.357	.635
	2 ML YEARS		74	201	53	11	0	4	(4	0)	76	15	26	20	8	1	35	1	2	3	1	1	6	.264	.291	.378	.669

Trevor Cahill

Pitches: R Bats: R Pos: RP-49; SP-1   KAY-hill   Ht: 6'4" Wt: 240 Born: 3/1/1988 Age: 29

			HOW MUCH HE PITCHED						WHAT HE GAVE UP											THE RESULTS						
Year	Team	Lg	G	GS	CG	GF	IP	BFP	H	R	ER	HR	SH	SF	HB	TBB	IBB	SO	WP	Bk	W	L	Pct	Sh	Sv-Op	Hld	ERC	ERA
2016	Iowa*	AAA	6	6	0	0	19.2	95	25	12	10	3	0	0	1	12	0	25	0	0	0	3	.000	0	0- -	-	7.23	4.58
2009	Oak	AL	32	32	0	0	178.2	773	185	99	92	27	4	7	4	72	1	90	5	0	10	13	.435	0	0-0	0	4.79	4.63
2010	Oak	AL	30	30	1	0	196.2	783	155	73	65	19	3	6	6	63	1	118	2	2	18	8	.692	1	0-0	0	2.81	2.97
2011	Oak	AL	34	**34**	0	0	207.2	901	214	102	96	19	8	6	8	82	1	147	15	0	12	14	.462	0	0-0	0	4.34	4.16
2012	Ari	NL	32	32	2	0	200.0	839	184	93	84	16	12	6	11	74	0	156	10	2	13	12	.520	1	0-0	0	3.66	3.78
2013	Ari	NL	26	25	0	1	146.2	636	143	70	65	13	9	9	6	65	2	102	**17**	0	8	10	.444	0	0-0	0	4.19	3.99
2014	Ari	NL	32	17	0	8	110.2	499	123	76	69	9	6	3	4	55	2	105	5	0	3	12	.200	0	1-2	6	5.11	5.61
2015	2 Tms	NL	26	3	0	6	43.1	187	44	27	26	4	3	1	2	16	1	36	2	0	1	3	.250	0	0-0	2	4.15	5.40
2016	ChC	NL	50	1	0	16	65.2	284	49	22	20	7	0	0	5	35	3	66	3	0	4	4	.500	0	0-1	5	3.42	2.74
15	Atl	NL	15	3	0	6	26.1	124	36	23	22	2	2	1	1	11	1	14	1	0	0	3	.000	0	0-0	0	6.22	7.52
15	ChC	NL	11	0	0	0	17.0	63	8	4	4	2	1	0	1	5	0	22	1	0	1	0	1.000	0	0-0	2	1.52	2.12
	Postseason		6	0	0	1	5.1	24	7	2	2	1	0	0	0	0	0	8	1	0	1	1	.500	0	0-1	2	3.29	3.38
	8 ML YEARS		262	174	3	31	1149.1	4902	1097	562	517	114	45	38	46	462	11	820	59	4	69	76	.476	2	1-3	6	4.01	4.05

Lorenzo Cain

Bats: R Throws: R Pos: CF-72;RF-29;PH-1;PR-1   Ht: 6'2" Wt: 205 Born: 4/13/1986 Age: 31

							BATTING													RUNNING			AVERAGES			
Year	Team	Lg	G	AB	H	2B	3B	HR	(Hm	Rd)	TB	R	RBI	RC	TBB	IBB	SO	HBP	SH	SF	SB	CS	GDP	Avg	OBP	Slg	OPS
2010	Mil	NL	43	147	45	11	1	1	(1	0)	61	17	13	23	9	0	28	1	0	1	7	1	1	.306	.348	.415	.763
2011	KC	AL	6	22	6	1	0	0	(0	0)	7	4	1	2	1	0	4	0	0	0	0	0	0	.273	.304	.318	.623
2012	KC	AL	61	222	59	9	2	7	(3	4)	93	27	31	32	15	0	56	3	0	4	10	0	4	.266	.316	.419	.734
2013	KC	AL	115	399	100	21	3	4	(3	1)	139	54	46	46	33	2	90	4	0	6	14	6	10	.251	.310	.348	.658
2014	KC	AL	133	471	142	29	4	5	(3	2)	194	55	53	67	24	2	108	4	0	3	28	5	9	.301	.339	.412	.751
2015	KC	AL	140	551	169	34	6	16	(9	7)	263	101	72	90	37	4	98	12	0	4	28	6	16	.307	.361	.477	.838
2016	KC	AL	103	397	114	19	1	9	(3	6)	162	56	56	53	31	3	84	2	0	4	14	5	15	.287	.339	.408	.747
	Postseason		31	122	36	7	0	1	(0	1)	46	24	19	26	16	3	23	1	1	2	8	1	1	.295	.376	.377	.753
	7 ML YEARS		601	2209	635	124	17	42	(22	20)	919	314	272	313	150	11	468	26	0	22	101	23	55	.287	.337	.416	.753

Matt Cain

Pitches: R Bats: R Pos: SP-17; RP-4   Ht: 6'3" Wt: 230 Born: 10/1/1984 Age: 32

			HOW MUCH HE PITCHED						WHAT HE GAVE UP											THE RESULTS						
Year	Team	Lg	G	GS	CG	GF	IP	BFP	H	R	ER	HR	SH	SF	HB	TBB	IBB	SO	WP	Bk	W	L	Pct	Sh	Sv-Op	Hld	ERC	ERA
2005	SF	NL	7	7	1	0	46.1	181	24	12	12	4	2	1	0	19	1	30	1	0	2	1	.667	0	0-0	0	1.61	2.33
2006	SF	NL	32	31	1	1	190.2	818	157	93	88	18	11	6	6	87	1	179	9	2	13	12	.520	1	0-0	0	3.35	4.15
2007	SF	NL	32	32	1	0	200.0	832	173	84	81	14	8	5	5	79	3	163	**12**	0	7	16	.304	0	0-0	0	3.23	3.65
2008	SF	NL	34	**34**	1	0	217.2	933	206	95	91	19	7	7	7	91	9	186	7	2	8	14	.364	1	0-0	0	3.84	3.76
2009	SF	NL	33	33	**4**	0	217.2	886	184	73	70	22	10	6	3	73	6	171	9	0	14	8	.636	0	0-0	0	3.06	2.89
2010	SF	NL	33	33	4	0	223.1	896	181	84	78	22	6	7	4	61	4	177	8	0	13	11	.542	2	0-0	0	2.65	3.14

107

Kole Calhoun

Bats: L **Throws:** L **Pos:** RF-154;DH-2;PH-1   **Ht:** 5'10" **Wt:** 205 **Born:** 10/14/1987 **Age:** 29

Year	Team	Lg	G	AB	H	2B	3B	HR	(Hm	Rd)	TB	R	RBI	RC	TBB	IBB	SO	HBP	SH	SF	SB	CS	GDP	Avg	OBP	Slg	OPS
									BATTING												RUNNING			AVERAGES			
2012	LAA	AL	21	23	4	1	0	0	(0	0)	5	2	1	0	2	1	6	0	0	0	1	1	0	.174	.240	.217	.457
2013	LAA	AL	58	195	55	7	2	8	(5	3)	90	29	32	33	21	0	41	1	0	5	2	2	5	.282	.347	.462	.808
2014	LAA	AL	127	493	134	31	3	17	(7	10)	222	90	58	75	38	0	104	2	2	2	5	3	5	.272	.325	.450	.776
2015	LAA	AL	159	630	161	23	2	26	(16	10)	266	78	83	85	45	1	164	5	2	4	4	1	6	.256	.308	.422	.731
2016	LAA	AL	157	594	161	35	5	18	(7	11)	260	91	75	93	67	0	118	6	0	5	2	3	10	.271	.348	.438	.786
	Postseason		3	15	5	0	0	0	(0	0)	5	1	0	1	0	0	1	0	0	0	0	0	0	.333	.333	.333	.667
	5 ML YEARS		522	1935	515	97	12	69	(35	34)	843	290	249	286	173	2	433	14	4	16	14	9	27	.266	.328	.436	.764

Arquimedes Caminero

Pitches: R **Bats:** R **Pos:** RP-57   ahr-keh-MEE-deez   **Ht:** 6'4" **Wt:** 245 **Born:** 6/16/1987 **Age:** 30

Year	Team	Lg	G	GS	CG	GF	IP	BFP	H	R	ER	HR	SH	SF	HB	TBB	IBB	SO	WP	Bk	W	L	Pct	Sh	Sv-Op	Hld	ERC	ERA
							HOW MUCH HE PITCHED				WHAT HE GAVE UP												THE RESULTS					
2013	Mia	NL	13	0	0	6	13.0	52	10	4	4	2	0	0	1	3	0	12	1	0	0	0	-	0	0-1	1	2.85	2.77
2014	Mia	NL	6	0	0	1	6.2	31	8	8	8	2	0	0	0	4	0	8	0	0	0	1	.000	0	0-0	0	7.83	10.80
2015	Pit	NL	73	0	0	19	74.2	318	63	31	30	7	1	1	6	29	2	73	6	1	5	1	.833	0	0-1	15	3.38	3.62
2016	2 Tms		57	0	0	11	60.2	280	67	31	24	7	2	1	5	33	1	50	2	0	2	3	.400	0	1-3	8	5.71	3.56
16	Pit	NL	39	0	0	9	41.0	187	46	17	16	4	1	1	4	22	0	32	1	0	1	2	.333	0	1-2	2	5.84	3.51
16	Sea	AL	18	0	0	2	19.2	93	21	14	8	3	1	0	1	11	1	18	1	0	1	1	.500	0	0-1	6	5.44	3.66
	4 ML YEARS		149	0	0	37	155.0	681	148	74	66	18	3	2	12	69	3	143	9	1	7	5	.583	0	1-5	24	4.38	3.83

Eric Campbell

Bats: R **Throws:** R **Pos:** 1B-21;PH-15;3B-7;LF-2;PR-2;2B-1   **Ht:** 6'3" **Wt:** 215 **Born:** 4/9/1987 **Age:** 30

Year	Team	Lg	G	AB	H	2B	3B	HR	(Hm	Rd)	TB	R	RBI	RC	TBB	IBB	SO	HBP	SH	SF	SB	CS	GDP	Avg	OBP	Slg	OPS
									BATTING												RUNNING			AVERAGES			
2016	LsVgs*	AAA	83	302	91	15	4	7	(-	-)	135	63	47	56	41	0	55	6	0	5	7	3	13	.301	.390	.447	.837
2014	NYM	NL	85	190	50	9	0	3	(2	1)	68	16	16	19	17	0	55	1	0	3	3	0	5	.263	.322	.358	.680
2015	NYM	NL	71	173	34	8	0	3	(0	3)	51	28	19	13	26	1	37	4	1	2	5	3	11	.197	.312	.295	.607
2016	NYM	NL	40	75	13	1	0	1	(0	1)	17	9	9	7	10	1	24	2	0	1	1	0	2	.173	.284	.227	.511
	3 ML YEARS		196	438	97	18	0	7	(2	5)	136	53	44	39	53	2	116	7	1	6	9	3	18	.221	.312	.311	.622

Leonel Campos

Pitches: R **Bats:** R **Pos:** RP-18   LEE-oh-nel KAM-pohs   **Ht:** 6'2" **Wt:** 215 **Born:** 7/17/1987 **Age:** 29

Year	Team	Lg	G	GS	CG	GF	IP	BFP	H	R	ER	HR	SH	SF	HB	TBB	IBB	SO	WP	Bk	W	L	Pct	Sh	Sv-Op	Hld	ERC	ERA
							HOW MUCH HE PITCHED				WHAT HE GAVE UP												THE RESULTS					
2016	ElPaso*	AAA	37	0	0	10	50.0	218	47	25	24	2	2	2	0	30	0	62	13	0	2	1	.667	0	1- -		4.16	4.32
2014	SD	NL	6	0	0	0	7.0	33	9	5	4	0	0	0	0	4	0	9	2	0	0	0	-	0	0-0	0	5.67	5.14
2015	SD	NL	1	0	0	0	1.0	5	1	1	1	0	0	0	0	1	0	1	0	0	0	0	-	0	0-0	0	5.48	9.00
2016	SD	NL	18	0	0	10	22.0	98	18	16	14	3	1	1	1	14	2	24	1	0	1	0	1.000	0	0-0	0	4.22	5.73
	3 ML YEARS		25	0	0	11	30.0	136	28	22	19	3	1	1	1	19	2	34	3	0	1	0	1.000	0	0-0	0	4.59	5.70

Vicente Campos

Pitches: R **Bats:** R **Pos:** RP-1   **Ht:** 6'3" **Wt:** 230 **Born:** 7/27/1992 **Age:** 24

Year	Team	Lg	G	GS	CG	GF	IP	BFP	H	R	ER	HR	SH	SF	HB	TBB	IBB	SO	WP	Bk	W	L	Pct	Sh	Sv-Op	Hld	ERC	ERA
							HOW MUCH HE PITCHED				WHAT HE GAVE UP												THE RESULTS					
2012	CtnSC	A	5	5	0	0	24.2	104	20	12	11	2	0	1	1	8	0	26	2	0	3	0	1.000	0	0- -	-	2.72	4.01
2013	CtnSC	A	26	19	0	5	87.0	357	82	37	33	5	6	3	3	16	0	77	4	1	4	2	.667	0	2- -	-	2.79	3.41
2015	3 Tms	Low	13	13	0	0	54.1	238	64	39	38	6	2	4	1	10	0	45	4	1	3	8	.273	0	0- -	-	4.26	6.29
2016	Tampa	A+	10	10	0	0	59.1	247	50	24	23	3	3	4	4	23	0	56	3	5	4	2	.667	0	0- -	-	3.14	3.49
2016	Trntn	AA	9	9	1	0	56.2	224	45	19	19	1	2	1	2	14	0	48	2	0	5	1	.833	1	0- -	-	2.11	3.02
2016	Ari	NL	1	0	0	0	5.2	24	4	3	2	2	0	0	0	2	0	4	0	0	0	0	-	0	0-0	0	3.60	3.18

Jeimer Candelario

Bats: B **Throws:** R **Pos:** 3B-3;PH-2   **Ht:** 6'1" **Wt:** 210 **Born:** 11/24/1993 **Age:** 23

Year	Team	Lg	G	AB	H	2B	3B	HR	(Hm	Rd)	TB	R	RBI	RC	TBB	IBB	SO	HBP	SH	SF	SB	CS	GDP	Avg	OBP	Slg	OPS
									BATTING												RUNNING			AVERAGES			
2012	Boise	A-	71	278	78	14	0	6	(-	-)	110	34	47	40	26	0	55	3	0	3	2	1	6	.281	.345	.396	.741
2013	Kane	A	130	500	128	35	1	11	(-	-)	198	71	57	74	68	1	88	2	0	2	1	0	18	.256	.346	.396	.742
2014	2 Tms	Low	125	462	103	29	5	11	(-	-)	175	56	63	47	41	1	89	2	0	2	0	4	9	.223	.288	.379	.667
2015	MrtlBh	A+	82	318	86	25	3	5	(-	-)	132	42	39	42	20	0	62	3	0	2	0	1	5	.270	.318	.415	.733

Year	Team	Lg		BATTING																				RUNNING			AVERAGES			
			G	AB	H	2B	3B	HR	(Hm	Rd)	TB	R	RBI	RC	TBB	IBB	SO	HBP	SH	SF	SB	CS	GDP	Avg	OBP	Slg	OPS
2015	Tenn	AA	46	158	46	10	1	5	(-	-)	73	21	25	29	22	1	21	1	0	1	0	0	7	.291	.379	.462	.841
2016	Tenn	AA	56	210	46	17	1	4	(-	-)	77	30	23	27	32	0	46	1	0	1	0	0	8	.219	.324	.367	.690
2016	Iowa	AAA	76	264	88	22	3	9	(-	-)	143	44	54	59	38	2	53	3	0	4	0	2	7	.333	.417	.542	.959
2016	ChC	NL	5	11	1	0	0	0	(0	0)	1	0	0	0	2	1	5	1	0	0	0	0	0	.091	.286	.091	.377

Mark Canha

Bats: R **Throws:** R **Pos:** PH-6;1B-5;3B-3;LF-3;RF-3;DH-1   CAN-uh   **Ht:** 6'2" **Wt:** 210 **Born:** 2/15/1989 **Age:** 28

Year	Team	Lg		BATTING																				RUNNING			AVERAGES			
			G	AB	H	2B	3B	HR	(Hm	Rd)	TB	R	RBI	RC	TBB	IBB	SO	HBP	SH	SF	SB	CS	GDP	Avg	OBP	Slg	OPS
2012	Jupiter	A+	114	406	119	24	3	6	(-	-)	167	65	68	68	54	2	75	9	1	8	1	3	6	.293	.382	.411	.793
2013	Jaxnvl	AA	128	425	116	32	2	13	(-	-)	191	63	58	76	54	0	102	15	5	5	6	1	9	.273	.371	.449	.820
2014	NewOr	AAA	127	465	141	28	3	20	(-	-)	235	83	82	92	57	0	112	8	0	7	3	1	9	.303	.384	.505	.889
2015	Oak	AL	124	441	112	22	3	16	(8	8)	188	61	70	62	33	0	96	8	0	3	7	2	9	.254	.315	.426	.742
2016	Oak	AL	16	41	5	0	0	3	(1	2)	14	4	6	0	0	0	20	1	1	1	0	1		.122	.140	.341	.481
	2 ML YEARS		140	482	117	22	3	19	(9	10)	202	65	76	62	33	0	116	9	1	4	7	3	10	.243	.301	.419	.720

Robinson Cano

Bats: L **Throws:** R **Pos:** 2B-157;DH-5   kuh-NOE   **Ht:** 6'0" **Wt:** 210 **Born:** 10/22/1982 **Age:** 34

Year	Team	Lg		BATTING																				RUNNING			AVERAGES			
			G	AB	H	2B	3B	HR	(Hm	Rd)	TB	R	RBI	RC	TBB	IBB	SO	HBP	SH	SF	SB	CS	GDP	Avg	OBP	Slg	OPS
2005	NYY	AL	132	522	155	34	4	14	(5	9)	239	78	62	59	16	1	68	3	7	3	1	3	16	.297	.320	.458	.778
2006	NYY	AL	122	482	165	41	1	15	(9	6)	253	62	78	74	18	3	54	2	1	5	5	2	19	.342	.365	.525	.890
2007	NYY	AL	160	617	189	41	7	19	(10	9)	301	93	97	94	39	5	85	8	1	4	4	5	19	.306	.353	.488	.841
2008	NYY	AL	159	597	162	35	3	14	(7	7)	245	70	72	64	26	3	65	5	1	5	2	4	18	.271	.305	.410	.715
2009	NYY	AL	**161**	637	204	48	2	25	(14	11)	331	103	85	79	30	2	63	3	0	4	5	7	22	.320	.352	.520	.871
2010	NYY	AL	160	626	200	41	3	29	(16	13)	334	103	109	118	57	14	77	8	0	5	3	2	19	.319	.381	.534	.914
2011	NYY	AL	159	623	188	46	7	28	(16	12)	332	104	118	111	38	11	96	12	0	8	8	2	18	.302	.349	.533	.882
2012	NYY	AL	161	627	196	48	1	33	(22	11)	345	105	94	110	61	10	96	7	0	2	3	2	22	.313	.379	.550	.929
2013	NYY	AL	160	605	190	41	0	27	(11	16)	312	81	107	120	65	16	85	6	0	5	7	1	18	.314	.383	.516	.899
2014	Sea	AL	157	595	187	37	2	14	(9	5)	270	77	82	106	61	20	68	6	0	3	10	3	19	.314	.382	.454	.836
2015	Sea	AL	156	624	179	34	1	21	(11	10)	278	82	79	84	43	5	107	3	0	4	2	6	26	.287	.334	.446	.779
2016	Sea	AL	161	655	195	33	2	39	(17	22)	349	107	103	100	47	8	100	8	0	5	0	1	18	.298	.350	.533	.882
	Postseason		51	203	45	10	3	8	(5	3)	85	22	33	23	11	3	28	2	0	1	0	2	7	.222	.267	.419	.686
	12 ML YEARS		1848	7210	2210	479	33	278	(147	131)	3589	1065	1086	1119	501	98	964	71	10	53	50	38	234	.307	.355	.498	.853

Carter Capps

Pitches: R **Bats:** R **Pos:** P   **Ht:** 6'5" **Wt:** 220 **Born:** 8/7/1990 **Age:** 26

Year	Team	Lg		HOW MUCH HE PITCHED						WHAT HE GAVE UP													THE RESULTS						
			G	GS	CG	GF	IP	BFP	H	R	ER	HR	SH	SF	HB	TBB	IBB	SO	WP	Bk	W	L	Pct	Sh	Sv-Op	Hld	ERC	ERA
2012	Sea	AL	18	0	0	2	25.0	109	25	11	11	0	1	1	0	11	0	28	1	0	0	0	-	0	0-0	2	3.49	3.96
2013	Sea	AL	53	0	0	11	59.0	270	73	37	36	12	2	1	2	23	4	66	5	0	3	3	.500	0	0-2	9	6.23	5.49
2014	Mia	NL	17	0	0	6	20.1	86	19	9	9	1	0	1	2	5	0	25	2	0	0	0	-	0	0-0	1	3.13	3.98
2015	Mia	NL	30	0	0	8	31.0	118	18	5	4	2	1	1	2	7	0	58	2	0	1	0	1.000	0	0-2	11	1.50	1.16
	4 ML YEARS		118	0	0	26	135.1	583	135	62	60	15	4	4	6	46	4	177	10	0	4	3	.571	0	0-4	23	4.01	3.99

Chris Capuano

Pitches: L **Bats:** L **Pos:** RP-16   capp-ue-AHH-noe   **Ht:** 6'2" **Wt:** 225 **Born:** 8/19/1978 **Age:** 38

Year	Team	Lg		HOW MUCH HE PITCHED						WHAT HE GAVE UP													THE RESULTS						
			G	GS	CG	GF	IP	BFP	H	R	ER	HR	SH	SF	HB	TBB	IBB	SO	WP	Bk	W	L	Pct	Sh	Sv-Op	Hld	ERC	ERA
2003	Ari	NL	9	5	0	2	33.0	139	27	19	17	3	4	1	6	11	1	23	3	0	2	4	.333	0	0-0	1	3.45	4.64
2004	Mil	NL	17	17	0	0	88.1	385	91	55	49	18	4	1	5	37	1	80	3	1	6	8	.429	0	0-0	0	5.37	4.99
2005	Mil	NL	35	**35**	0	0	219.0	949	212	105	97	31	14	5	12	91	6	176	3	**4**	18	12	.600	0	0-0	0	4.44	3.99
2006	Mil	NL	34	34	3	0	221.1	936	229	108	99	29	9	8	9	47	4	174	7	0	11	12	.478	2	0-0	0	3.84	4.03
2007	Mil	NL	29	25	0	0	150.0	669	170	93	85	20	10	3	8	54	2	132	10	0	5	12	.294	0	0-0	0	5.11	5.10
2010	Mil	NL	24	9	0	5	66.0	278	65	29	29	9	3	2	1	21	1	54	5	0	4	4	.500	0	0-0	1	3.98	3.95
2011	NYM	NL	33	31	1	0	186.0	802	198	99	94	27	9	1	5	53	5	168	4	0	11	12	.478	1	0-0	1	4.33	4.55
2012	LAD	NL	33	33	0	0	198.1	817	188	91	82	25	16	4	2	54	4	162	6	0	12	12	.500	0	0-0	0	3.51	3.72
2013	LAD	NL	24	20	0	0	105.2	457	125	57	50	11	6	3	0	24	5	81	5	0	4	7	.364	0	0-1	0	4.36	4.26
2014	2 Tms	AL	40	12	0	4	97.1	429	101	51	47	10	3	5	4	34	3	84	8	1	3	4	.429	0	0-1	4	4.14	4.35
2015	NYY	AL	22	4	0	7	40.2	196	52	38	36	6	2	1	3	22	1	38	0	0	0	4	.000	0	0-0	0	6.93	7.97
2016	Mil	NL	16	0	0	3	24.0	106	23	11	11	7	0	1	0	15	2	27	1	0	1	1	.500	0	0-1	0	6.43	4.13
14	Bos	AL	28	0	0	4	31.2	143	34	17	16	3	0	1	1	15	2	29	4	1	1	1	.500	0	0-1	4	4.72	4.55
14	NYY	AL	12	12	0	0	65.2	286	67	34	31	7	3	4	3	19	1	55	4	0	2	3	.400	0	0-0	0	3.86	4.25
	Postseason		1	0	0	0	3.0	11	0	0	0	0	1	0	0	3	0	3	0	0	1	0	1.000	0	0-0	0	1.03	0.00
	12 ML YEARS		316	225	4	21	1429.2	6163	1481	756	696	196	80	34	56	463	35	1199	55	6	77	92	.456	3	0-3	9	4.35	4.38

Matt Carasiti

Pitches: R **Bats:** R **Pos:** RP-19   **Ht:** 6'3" **Wt:** 205 **Born:** 7/23/1991 **Age:** 25

Year	Team	Lg		HOW MUCH HE PITCHED						WHAT HE GAVE UP													THE RESULTS						
			G	GS	CG	GF	IP	BFP	H	R	ER	HR	SH	SF	HB	TBB	IBB	SO	WP	Bk	W	L	Pct	Sh	Sv-Op	Hld	ERC	ERA
2012	GdJunc	R+	14	14	0	0	68.0	298	80	45	33	6	3	0	4	20	0	34	7	0	3	4	.429	0	0--	-	4.87	4.37
2013	Ashvll	A	20	20	0	0	88.1	455	136	93	82	9	4	3	6	43	0	60	11	9	2	10	.167	0	0--	-	7.36	7.94
2014	Ashvll	A	46	0	0	18	76.0	317	71	31	26	8	1	0	4	28	1	76	9	8	6	2	.750	0	2--	-	3.54	3.08

Year	Team	Lg	G	GS	CG	GF	IP	BFP	H	R	ER	HR	SH	SF	HB	TBB	IBB	SO	WP	Bk	W	L	Pct	Sh	Sv-Op	Hld	ERC	ERA
							HOW MUCH HE PITCHED					**WHAT HE GAVE UP**											**THE RESULTS**				
2015	Mdest	A+	49	0	0	42	56.2	246	54	28	19	3	4	3	2	22	1	57	3	1	3	7	.300	0	22--	-	3.50	3.02
2016	Hrtfrd	AA	38	0	0	33	39.0	150	28	13	10	5	0	2	1	7	1	43	1	0	0	2	.000	0	29--	-	2.07	2.31
2016	Albq	AAA	6	0	0	4	7.0	25	2	0	0	0	0	0	1	2	0	5	0	0	0	0	-	0	2--	-	0.75	0.00
2016	Col	NL	19	0	0	7	15.2	83	25	17	16	1	0	2	3	11	0	17	2	0	1	0	1.000	0	0-0	2	9.75	9.19

Stephen Cardullo

Bats: R **Throws:** R **Pos:** 1B-15;PH-12;RF-3;LF-2 **Ht:** 6'0" **Wt:** 215 **Born:** 8/31/1987 **Age:** 29

Year	Team	Lg	G	AB	H	2B	3B	HR	(Hm	Rd)	TB	R	RBI	RC	TBB	IBB	SO	HBP	SH	SF	SB	CS	GDP	Avg	OBP	Slg	OPS
								BATTING													**RUNNING**			**AVERAGES**			
2016	Albq	AAA	115	406	125	26	5	17	(-	-)	212	71	72	78	37	2	58	4	0	5	6	3	9	.308	.367	.522	.889
2016	Col	NL	27	56	12	3	1	2	(2	0)	23	5	6	5	3	0	12	0	0	0	0	0	2	.214	.254	.411	.665

Matt Carpenter

Bats: L **Throws:** R **Pos:** 3B-54;1B-45;2B-40;PH-3;DH-1 **Ht:** 6'3" **Wt:** 205 **Born:** 11/26/1985 **Age:** 31

Year	Team	Lg	G	AB	H	2B	3B	HR	(Hm	Rd)	TB	R	RBI	RC	TBB	IBB	SO	HBP	SH	SF	SB	CS	GDP	Avg	OBP	Slg	OPS
								BATTING													**RUNNING**			**AVERAGES**			
2011	StL	NL	7	15	1	0	0	0	(0	0)	2	0	0	0	4	0	4	0	0	0	0	0	0	.067	.263	.133	.396
2012	StL	NL	114	296	87	22	5	6	(3	3)	137	44	46	46	34	2	63	3	0	7	1	1	10	.294	.365	.463	.828
2013	StL	NL	157	626	**199**	55	7	11	(6	5)	301	**126**	78	119	72	1	98	9	3	7	3	3	4	.318	.392	.481	.873
2014	StL	NL	158	595	162	33	2	8	(4	4)	223	99	59	93	**95**	2	111	8	2	9	5	3	3	.272	.375	.375	.750
2015	StL	NL	154	574	156	**44**	3	28	(13	15)	290	101	84	108	81	5	151	6	0	4	4	3	5	.272	.365	.505	.871
2016	StL	NL	129	473	128	36	6	21	(9	12)	239	81	68	87	81	6	108	5	3	4	0	4	4	.271	.380	.505	.885
	Postseason		39	136	33	8	1	6	(4	2)	61	20	16	19	11	0	39	1	0	2	1	0	1	.243	.300	.449	.749
	6 ML YEARS		719	2579	733	191	23	74	(35	39)	1192	451	335	453	367	16	535	31	8	31	13	14	26	.284	.376	.462	.838

Carlos Carrasco

Pitches: R **Bats:** R **Pos:** SP-25 **Ht:** 6'4" **Wt:** 210 **Born:** 3/21/1987 **Age:** 30

Year	Team	Lg	G	GS	CG	GF	IP	BFP	H	R	ER	HR	SH	SF	HB	TBB	IBB	SO	WP	Bk	W	L	Pct	Sh	Sv-Op	Hld	ERC	ERA
							HOW MUCH HE PITCHED					**WHAT HE GAVE UP**												**THE RESULTS**				
2009	Cle	AL	5	5	0	0	22.1	112	40	23	22	6	0	1	1	11	1	11	0	1	0	4	.000	0	0-0	0	11.36	8.87
2010	Cle	AL	7	7	1	0	44.2	188	47	20	19	6	2	1	1	14	1	38	1	0	2	2	.500	0	0-0	0	4.42	3.83
2011	Cle	AL	21	21	1	0	124.2	536	130	68	64	15	3	7	4	40	3	85	3	0	8	9	.471	0	0-0	0	4.24	4.62
2013	Cle	AL	15	7	0	5	46.2	218	64	36	35	4	2	3	1	18	2	30	2	0	1	4	.200	0	0-0	0	6.11	6.75
2014	Cle	AL	40	14	1	12	134.0	529	103	40	38	7	2	3	3	29	1	140	4	0	8	7	.533	1	1-1	0	2.00	2.55
2015	Cle	AL	30	30	3	0	183.2	730	154	75	74	18	1	6	5	43	2	216	5	0	14	12	.538	1	0-0	0	2.72	3.63
2016	Cle	AL	25	25	1	0	146.1	599	134	64	54	21	1	3	3	34	2	150	4	1	11	8	.579	1	0-0	0	3.31	3.32
	7 ML YEARS		143	109	7	17	702.1	2912	672	326	306	77	11	24	17	189	12	670	19	2	44	46	.489	3	1-1	0	3.49	3.92

Ezequiel Carrera

ee-ZEEK-ee-ull

Bats: L **Throws:** L **Pos:** RF-65;LF-45;PR-11;PH-9;CF-5;DH-2 **Ht:** 5'11" **Wt:** 185 **Born:** 6/11/1987 **Age:** 30

Year	Team	Lg	G	AB	H	2B	3B	HR	(Hm	Rd)	TB	R	RBI	RC	TBB	IBB	SO	HBP	SH	SF	SB	CS	GDP	Avg	OBP	Slg	OPS
								BATTING													**RUNNING**			**AVERAGES**			
2011	Cle	AL	68	202	49	8	3	0	(0	0)	63	27	14	25	16	0	35	1	7	0	10	5	4	.243	.301	.312	.613
2012	Cle	AL	48	147	40	6	3	2	(0	2)	58	20	11	17	8	1	35	1	1	1	8	1	3	.272	.312	.395	.707
2013	2 Tms		15	17	3	0	0	0	(0	0)	3	3	1	1	1	0	5	2	1	0	0	0	1	.176	.300	.176	.476
2014	Det	AL	45	69	18	4	1	0	(0	0)	24	12	2	6	3	1	14	1	0	0	7	1	2	.261	.301	.348	.649
2015	Tor	AL	91	172	47	8	0	3	(1	2)	64	27	26	26	11	0	45	2	5	2	2	1	1	.273	.321	.372	.693
2016	Tor	AL	110	270	67	9	1	6	(5	1)	96	47	23	34	27	0	70	4	7	2	7	4	8	.248	.326	.356	.679
13	Phi	NL	13	13	1	0	0	0	(0	0)	1	2	0	0	1	0	4	2	0	0	0	0	0	.077	.250	.077	.327
13	Cle	AL	2	4	2	0	0	0	(0	0)	2	1	1	1	0	0	1	0	1	0	0	0	1	.500	.500	.500	1.000
	Postseason		5	3	0	0	0	0	(0	0)	0	0	0	0	1	0	0	0	0	0	1	0	0	.000	.250	.000	.250
	6 ML YEARS		377	877	224	35	8	11	(6	5)	308	136	77	109	66	2	204	11	21	5	34	12	19	.255	.314	.351	.665

Scott Carroll

Pitches: R **Bats:** R **Pos:** RP-3 **Ht:** 6'4" **Wt:** 215 **Born:** 9/24/1984 **Age:** 32

Year	Team	Lg	G	GS	CG	GF	IP	BFP	H	R	ER	HR	SH	SF	HB	TBB	IBB	SO	WP	Bk	W	L	Pct	Sh	Sv-Op	Hld	ERC	ERA
							HOW MUCH HE PITCHED					**WHAT HE GAVE UP**												**THE RESULTS**				
2016	Charllt*	AAA	16	12	0	0	60.0	280	78	48	37	8	0	3	3	25	0	31	2	0	2	8	.200	0	0--	-	6.39	5.55
2016	Frisco*	AA	7	7	0	0	37.0	147	27	12	12	2	0	1	3	7	0	24	1	0	2	1	.667	0	0--	-	1.93	2.92
2014	CWS	AL	26	19	0	5	129.1	573	147	81	69	13	3	4	12	45	1	64	5	1	5	10	.333	0	0-0	0	5.07	4.80
2015	CWS	AL	18	0	0	8	36.2	162	40	19	14	2	1	2	3	13	2	27	4	0	1	1	.500	0	0-0	0	4.31	3.44
2016	CWS	AL	3	0	0	2	2.1	10	2	3	3	0	0	0	1	1	0	2	0	0	0	0	-	0	0-0	0	4.61	11.57
	3 ML YEARS		47	19	0	15	168.1	745	189	103	86	15	4	6	16	59	3	93	9	1	6	11	.353	0	0-0	0	4.90	4.60

Chris Carter

Bats: R **Throws:** R **Pos:** 1B-155;PH-5;DH-2 **Ht:** 6'4" **Wt:** 245 **Born:** 12/18/1986 **Age:** 30

Year	Team	Lg	G	AB	H	2B	3B	HR	(Hm	Rd)	TB	R	RBI	RC	TBB	IBB	SO	HBP	SH	SF	SB	CS	GDP	Avg	OBP	Slg	OPS
								BATTING													**RUNNING**			**AVERAGES**			
2010	Oak	AL	24	70	13	1	0	3	(1	2)	23	8	7	5	7	0	21	0	0	1	1	0	3	.186	.256	.329	.585
2011	Oak	AL	15	44	6	0	0	0	(0	0)	6	2	0	2	2	0	20	0	0	0	0	0	1	.136	.174	.136	.310
2012	Oak	AL	67	218	52	12	0	16	(5	11)	112	38	39	36	39	1	83	0	0	3	0	0	4	.239	.350	.514	.864
2013	Hou	AL	148	506	113	24	2	29	(10	19)	228	64	82	74	70	1	**212**	4	0	5	2	0	8	.223	.320	.451	.770

Year	Team	Lg	G	AB	H	2B	3B	HR	(Hm	Rd)	TB	R	RBI	RC	TBB	IBB	SO	HBP	SH	SF	SB	CS	GDP	Avg	OBP	Slg	OPS
2014	Hou	AL	145	507	115	21	1	37	(21	16)	249	68	88	74	56	6	182	5	0	4	5	2	12	.227	.308	.491	.799
2015	Hou	AL	129	391	78	17	0	24	(17	7)	167	50	64	55	57	1	151	6	0	5	1	2	5	.199	.307	.427	.734
2016	Mil	NL	160	549	122	27	1	41	(24	17)	274	84	94	73	76	1	206	9	0	10	3	1	18	.222	.321	.499	.821
Postseason			6	17	5	1	0	1	(1	0)	9	3	1	3	3	0	7	0	0	0	0	0	0	.294	.400	.529	.929
7 ML YEARS			688	2285	499	102	4	150	(78	72)	1059	314	374	317	307	10	875	24	0	28	12	5	51	.218	.314	.463	.777

Curt Casali

Bats: R **Throws:** R **Pos:** C-76;DH-7;PH-4   cuh-SAL-ee   **Ht:** 6'2" **Wt:** 230 **Born:** 11/9/1988 **Age:** 28

Year	Team	Lg	G	AB	H	2B	3B	HR	(Hm	Rd)	TB	R	RBI	RC	TBB	IBB	SO	HBP	SH	SF	SB	CS	GDP	Avg	OBP	Slg	OPS
2016	Drham*	AAA	20	63	16	1	0	2	(-	-)	23	5	15	11	15	0	12	2	0	1	0	0	1	.254	.407	.365	.772
2014	TB	AL	30	72	12	3	0	0	(0	0)	15	10	3	3	8	0	23	2	2	0	0	0	2	.167	.268	.208	.477
2015	TB	AL	38	101	24	6	0	10	(7	3)	60	13	18	14	8	0	34	2	1	0	0	0	2	.238	.304	.594	.898
2016	TB	AL	84	226	42	10	0	8	(3	5)	76	23	25	18	25	1	82	2	3	0	0	0	2	.186	.273	.336	.609
3 ML YEARS			152	399	78	19	0	18	(10	8)	151	46	46	35	41	1	139	6	6	1	0	0	6	.195	.280	.378	.658

Andrew Cashner

Pitches: R **Bats:** R **Pos:** SP-27; RP-1   **Ht:** 6'6" **Wt:** 235 **Born:** 9/11/1986 **Age:** 30

Year	Team	Lg	G	GS	CG	GF	IP	BFP	H	R	ER	HR	SH	SF	HB	TBB	IBB	SO	WP	Bk	W	L	Pct	Sh	Sv-Op	Hld	ERC	ERA
2010	ChC	NL	53	0	0	9	54.1	248	55	31	29	8	6	2	4	30	5	50	4	1	2	6	.250	0	0-1	16	5.22	4.80
2011	ChC	NL	7	1	0	0	10.2	39	3	2	2	1	0	0	0	4	0	8	0	0	0	0	-	0	0-0	1	0.91	1.69
2012	SD	NL	33	5	0	5	46.1	196	42	23	22	5	3	1	1	19	1	52	2	0	3	4	.429	0	0-4	6	3.73	4.27
2013	SD	NL	31	26	1	2	175.0	707	151	68	60	12	6	3	4	47	3	128	5	0	10	9	.526	1	0-0	1	2.74	3.09
2014	SD	NL	19	19	2	0	123.1	506	110	42	35	7	3	4	1	29	3	93	2	0	5	7	.417	2	0-0	0	2.57	2.55
2015	SD	NL	31	31	0	0	184.2	804	200	111	89	19	8	6	6	66	2	165	3	0	6	16	.273	0	0-0	0	4.53	4.34
2016 2 Tms		NL	28	27	0	1	132.0	588	142	83	77	19	6	5	7	60	3	112	3	0	5	11	.313	0	0-0	0	5.28	5.25
16	SD	NL	16	16	0	0	79.1	347	80	47	42	13	4	3	6	30	0	67	1	0	4	7	.364	0	0-0	0	4.80	4.76
16	Mia	NL	12	11	0	1	52.2	241	62	36	35	6	2	2	1	30	3	45	2	0	1	4	.200	0	0-0	0	6.01	5.98
7 ML YEARS			202	109	3	17	726.1	3088	703	360	314	71	32	21	23	255	17	608	19	1	31	53	.369	3	0-5	24	3.79	3.89

Santiago Casilla

Pitches: R **Bats:** R **Pos:** RP-62   cuh-SEE-ya   **Ht:** 6'0" **Wt:** 210 **Born:** 7/25/1980 **Age:** 36

Year	Team	Lg	G	GS	CG	GF	IP	BFP	H	R	ER	HR	SH	SF	HB	TBB	IBB	SO	WP	Bk	W	L	Pct	Sh	Sv-Op	Hld	ERC	ERA
2004	Oak	AL	4	0	0	2	5.2	32	5	8	8	3	0	0	1	9	0	5	0	0	0	0	-	0	0-0	0	13.22	12.71
2005	Oak	AL	3	0	0	1	3.0	12	2	1	1	0	0	0	0	1	0	1	1	0	0	0	-	0	0-0	0	1.57	3.00
2006	Oak	AL	2	0	0	1	2.1	10	2	3	3	0	0	0	0	2	0	2	0	0	0	0	-	0	0-0	0	4.61	11.57
2007	Oak	AL	46	0	0	10	50.2	219	43	25	25	6	0	3	1	23	6	52	5	0	3	1	.750	0	2-5	12	3.39	4.44
2008	Oak	AL	51	0	0	9	50.1	229	60	22	22	5	3	2	3	20	2	43	6	0	2	1	.667	0	2-3	7	5.34	3.93
2009	Oak	AL	46	0	0	15	48.1	233	61	36	32	6	1	3	3	25	3	35	5	0	1	2	.333	0	0-0	5	6.32	5.96
2010	SF	NL	52	0	0	13	55.1	225	40	14	12	2	2	1	4	26	4	56	1	0	7	2	.778	0	2-3	11	2.68	1.95
2011	SF	NL	49	0	0	20	51.2	211	33	11	10	1	4	0	2	25	1	45	5	0	2	2	.500	0	6-7	6	2.11	1.74
2012	SF	NL	73	0	0	37	63.1	272	55	24	20	8	2	1	2	22	4	55	1	0	7	6	.538	0	25-31	12	3.24	2.84
2013	SF	NL	57	0	0	12	50.0	208	39	14	12	2	2	3	2	25	6	38	8	0	7	2	.778	0	2-3	22	2.88	2.16
2014	SF	NL	54	0	0	31	58.1	218	35	13	11	3	2	0	3	15	2	45	3	1	3	3	.500	0	19-23	10	1.56	1.70
2015	SF	NL	67	0	0	55	58.0	244	51	19	18	6	2	1	2	23	2	62	1	0	4	2	.667	0	38-44	0	3.52	2.79
2016	SF	NL	62	0	0	44	58.0	241	50	23	23	8	3	1	5	19	2	65	4	2	2	5	.286	0	31-40	3	3.43	3.57
Postseason			24	0	0	8	19.0	79	13	3	2	0	0	0	2	5	1	20	3	0	1	0	1.000	0	4-4	4	1.61	0.95
13 ML YEARS			566	0	0	252	555.0	2354	476	213	197	50	21	15	28	235	32	504	49	3	38	26	.594	0	127-159	88	3.43	3.19

Nick Castellanos

Bats: R **Throws:** R **Pos:** 3B-108;PH-2;DH-1   cahs-teh-YAHN-ohs   **Ht:** 6'4" **Wt:** 210 **Born:** 3/4/1992 **Age:** 25

Year	Team	Lg	G	AB	H	2B	3B	HR	(Hm	Rd)	TB	R	RBI	RC	TBB	IBB	SO	HBP	SH	SF	SB	CS	GDP	Avg	OBP	Slg	OPS
2013	Det	AL	11	18	5	0	0	0	(0	0)	5	1	0	1	0	0	1	0	0	0	0	0	0	.278	.278	.278	.556
2014	Det	AL	148	533	138	31	4	11	(6	5)	210	50	66	63	36	3	140	3	0	7	2	2	5	.259	.306	.394	.700
2015	Det	AL	154	549	140	33	6	15	(6	9)	230	42	73	66	39	1	152	1	0	6	0	3	21	.255	.303	.419	.721
2016	Det	AL	110	411	117	25	4	18	(5	13)	204	54	58	67	28	1	111	3	0	5	1	1	4	.285	.331	.496	.827
Postseason			3	10	1	0	0	1	(0	1)	4	1	1	0	2	1	1	0	0	0	0	0	0	.100	.250	.400	.650
4 ML YEARS			423	1511	400	89	14	44	(17	27)	649	147	197	197	103	5	404	7	0	18	3	6	32	.265	.311	.430	.741

Rusney Castillo

Bats: R **Throws:** R **Pos:** PR-5;LF-2;DH-2;CF-1;RF-1;PH-1   ROOZ-knee   **Ht:** 5'9" **Wt:** 195 **Born:** 7/9/1987 **Age:** 29

Year	Team	Lg	G	AB	H	2B	3B	HR	(Hm	Rd)	TB	R	RBI	RC	TBB	IBB	SO	HBP	SH	SF	SB	CS	GDP	Avg	OBP	Slg	OPS
2016	Pwtckt*	AAA	103	395	104	20	5	2	(-	-)	140	55	34	46	24	0	68	4	2	4	9	3	13	.263	.309	.354	.664
2014	Bos	AL	10	36	12	1	0	2	(2	0)	19	6	6	9	3	0	6	1	0	0	3	0	0	.333	.400	.528	.928
2015	Bos	AL	80	273	69	10	2	5	(4	1)	98	35	29	30	13	0	54	1	1	1	4	5	11	.253	.288	.359	.647
2016	Bos	AL	9	8	2	1	0	0	(0	0)	3	4	0	0	0	0	3	0	0	0	0	0	0	.250	.250	.375	.625
3 ML YEARS			99	317	83	12	2	7	(6	1)	120	45	35	39	16	0	63	2	1	1	7	5	11	.262	.301	.379	.679

Welington Castillo

Bats: R **Throws:** R **Pos:** C-107;PH-8;DH-1　　　WELL-ing-tunn　　　**Ht:** 5'10" **Wt:** 220 **Born:** 4/24/1987 **Age:** 30

Year Team	Lg	G	AB	H	2B	3B	HR	(Hm	Rd)	TB	R	RBI	RC	TBB	IBB	SO	HBP	SH	SF	SB	CS	GDP	Avg	OBP	Slg	OPS
2010 ChC	NL	7	20	6	4	0	1	(0	1)	13	3	5	3	1	0	7	0	0	0	0	0	0	.300	.333	.650	.983
2011 ChC	NL	4	13	2	0	0	0	(0	0)	2	0	0	0	0	0	4	0	0	0	0	0	1	.154	.154	.154	.308
2012 ChC	NL	52	170	45	11	0	5	(4	1)	71	16	22	22	17	2	51	2	0	1	0	0	4	.265	.337	.418	.754
2013 ChC	NL	113	380	104	23	0	8	(1	7)	151	41	32	44	34	3	97	11	1	2	2	0	13	.274	.349	.397	.746
2014 ChC	NL	110	380	90	19	0	13	(7	6)	148	28	46	44	26	0	102	7	2	2	0	0	7	.237	.296	.389	.686
2015 3 Tms		110	342	81	15	1	19	(7	12)	155	42	57	41	25	1	92	6	0	5	0	0	12	.237	.296	.453	.750
2016 Ari	NL	113	416	110	24	0	14	(6	8)	176	41	68	58	33	3	121	4	0	4	2	0	5	.264	.322	.423	.745
15 ChC	NL	24	43	7	2	0	2	(1	1)	15	5	5	2	3	1	12	1	0	0	0	0	0	.163	.234	.349	.583
15 Sea	AL	6	25	4	0	0	0	(0	0)	4	3	2	0	1	0	5	0	0	2	0	0	2	.160	.179	.160	.339
15 Ari	NL	80	274	70	13	1	17	(6	11)	136	34	50	39	21	0	75	5	0	3	0	0	10	.255	.317	.496	.813
7 ML YEARS		509	1721	438	96	1	60	(27	33)	716	171	230	212	136	9	474	30	3	14	4	0	42	.255	.318	.416	.734

Daniel Castro

Bats: R **Throws:** R **Pos:** SS-20;2B-16;3B-9;PH-8　　　**Ht:** 5'11" **Wt:** 190 **Born:** 11/14/1992 **Age:** 24

Year Team	Lg	G	AB	H	2B	3B	HR	(Hm	Rd)	TB	R	RBI	RC	TBB	IBB	SO	HBP	SH	SF	SB	CS	GDP	Avg	OBP	Slg	OPS
2013 Lynbrg	A+	26	88	25	1	1	0	(-	-)	28	10	7	10	7	0	6	0	1	0	3	1	1	.284	.337	.318	.655
2014 Lynbrg	A+	70	257	75	16	3	1	(-	-)	100	33	34	32	10	0	20	1	10	1	7	4	8	.292	.320	.389	.709
2014 Missi	AA	51	173	48	9	1	4	(-	-)	71	23	20	21	5	0	18	1	0	1	2	1	5	.277	.300	.410	.710
2015 Missi	AA	23	90	35	5	0	0	(-	-)	40	17	10	16	4	0	8	0	3	1	4	2	1	.389	.411	.444	.855
2015 Gwnntt	AAA	89	310	83	9	0	0	(-	-)	92	19	36	31	22	0	32	1	7	5	1	1	7	.268	.314	.297	.610
2016 Gwnntt	AAA	61	214	55	10	0	3	(-	-)	74	29	20	21	8	0	25	0	3	4	0	1	2	.257	.279	.346	.625
2015 Atl	NL	33	96	23	2	1	2	(2	0)	33	14	5	4	3	0	15	0	1	0	0	0	4	.240	.263	.344	.606
2016 Atl	NL	47	130	26	1	0	0	(0	0)	27	8	7	4	7	1	24	0	2	0	1	1	4	.200	.241	.208	.449
2 ML YEARS		80	226	49	3	1	2	(2	0)	60	22	12	8	10	1	39	0	3	0	1	1	8	.217	.250	.265	.515

Jason Castro

Bats: L **Throws:** R **Pos:** C-111;1B-3;PH-2　　　**Ht:** 6'3" **Wt:** 215 **Born:** 6/18/1987 **Age:** 30

Year Team	Lg	G	AB	H	2B	3B	HR	(Hm	Rd)	TB	R	RBI	RC	TBB	IBB	SO	HBP	SH	SF	SB	CS	GDP	Avg	OBP	Slg	OPS
2010 Hou	NL	67	195	40	8	1	2	(1	1)	56	26	8	12	22	2	41	0	0	0	0	0	4	.205	.286	.287	.573
2012 Hou	NL	87	257	66	15	2	6	(3	3)	103	29	29	33	31	2	61	1	2	4	0	0	8	.257	.334	.401	.735
2013 Hou	AL	120	435	120	35	1	18	(13	5)	211	63	56	76	50	3	130	2	0	4	2	1	11	.276	.350	.485	.835
2014 Hou	AL	126	465	103	21	2	14	(10	4)	170	43	56	45	34	1	151	9	1	3	1	0	11	.222	.286	.366	.651
2015 Hou	AL	104	337	71	19	0	11	(8	3)	123	38	31	29	33	1	115	2	0	3	0	0	5	.211	.283	.365	.648
2016 Hou	AL	113	329	69	16	3	11	(5	6)	124	41	32	34	45	0	123	1	1	0	2	1	9	.210	.307	.377	.684
Postseason		6	16	1	0	0	0	(0	0)	1	1	2	0	2	0	8	0	0	0	0	0	2	.063	.167	.063	.229
6 ML YEARS		617	2018	469	114	9	62	(40	22)	787	240	212	229	215	9	621	15	4	14	5	2	41	.232	.309	.390	.699

Miguel Castro

Pitches: R **Bats:** R **Pos:** RP-19　　　**Ht:** 6'5" **Wt:** 190 **Born:** 12/24/1994 **Age:** 22

		HOW MUCH HE PITCHED						WHAT HE GAVE UP											THE RESULTS							
Year Team	Lg	G	GS	CG	GF	IP	BFP	H	R	ER	HR	SH	SF	HB	TBB	IBB	SO	WP	Bk	W	L	Pct	Sh	Sv-Op	Hld	ERC	ERA
2014 3 Tms	Low	16	15	0	0	80.1	315	50	25	24	6	0	2	2	30	0	78	5	2	8	3	.727	0	0--	-	2.02	2.69
2015 Buffalo	AAA	13	5	0	2	19.2	99	26	15	10	4	1	1	2	12	0	21	2	0	1	3	.250	0	0--	-	8.07	4.58
2015 Albq	AAA	11	0	0	4	13.2	55	6	3	2	0	1	2	1	7	2	10	4	0	2	0	1.000	0	0--	-	1.26	1.32
2016 Albq	AAA	16	0	0	5	15.2	72	21	18	18	5	0	0	1	7	0	15	3	0	2	3	.400	0	0--	-	8.73	10.34
2015 2 Tms		18	0	0	12	17.2	83	21	13	12	4	0	2	0	10	2	18	2	1	0	3	.000	0	4-6	1	6.61	6.12
2016 Col	NL	19	0	0	4	14.2	67	18	10	10	3	1	0	1	5	0	12	0	0	0	0	-	0	0-1	7	6.21	6.14
15 Tor	AL	13	0	0	9	12.1	57	15	7	6	2	0	2	0	6	2	12	2	1	0	2	.000	0	4-6	1	5.86	4.38
15 Col	NL	5	0	0	3	5.1	26	6	6	6	2	0	0	0	4	0	6	0	0	1	1	.000	0	0-0	0	8.41	10.13
2 ML YEARS		37	0	0	16	32.1	150	39	23	22	7	1	2	1	15	2	30	2	1	0	3	.000	0	4-7	8	6.43	6.12

Starlin Castro

Bats: R **Throws:** R **Pos:** 2B-150;SS-3;PH-3;PR-1　　　STARR-linn　　　**Ht:** 6'2" **Wt:** 230 **Born:** 3/24/1990 **Age:** 27

Year Team	Lg	G	AB	H	2B	3B	HR	(Hm	Rd)	TB	R	RBI	RC	TBB	IBB	SO	HBP	SH	SF	SB	CS	GDP	Avg	OBP	Slg	OPS
2010 ChC	NL	125	463	139	31	5	3	(1	2)	189	53	41	56	29	7	71	6	4	4	10	8	14	.300	.347	.408	.755
2011 ChC	NL	158	674	207	36	9	10	(4	6)	291	91	66	93	35	2	96	2	0	4	22	9	20	.307	.341	.432	.773
2012 ChC	NL	162	646	183	29	12	14	(7	7)	278	78	78	91	36	5	100	4	0	5	25	13	15	.283	.323	.430	.753
2013 ChC	NL	161	666	163	34	2	10	(9	1)	231	59	44	55	30	0	129	7	1	1	9	6	21	.245	.284	.347	.631
2014 ChC	NL	134	528	134	33	1	14	(8	6)	211	58	65	72	35	4	100	4	0	2	4	4	18	.292	.339	.438	.777
2015 ChC	NL	151	547	145	23	2	11	(3	8)	205	52	69	54	21	6	91	5	1	4	5	5	18	.265	.296	.375	.671
2016 NYY	AL	151	577	156	29	1	21	(15	6)	250	63	70	69	24	1	118	3	1	5	4	0	15	.270	.300	.433	.734
Postseason		9	34	6	1	0	1	(1	0)	10	2	2	2	1	1	1	0	0	0	0	0	0	.176	.200	.294	.494
7 ML YEARS		1042	4101	1147	215	32	83	(42	41)	1675	454	433	490	210	25	705	31	7	25	79	45	121	.280	.318	.408	.726

Gavin Cecchini

Bats: R Throws: R Pos: PH-3;SS-2 | chick-KEE-nee | Ht: 6'2" Wt: 200 Born: 12/22/1993 Age: 23

Year	Team	Lg	G	AB	H	2B	3B	HR	(Hm	Rd)	TB	R	RBI	RC	TBB	IBB	SO	HBP	SH	SF	SB	CS	GDP	Avg	OBP	Slg	OPS
2012	2 Tms	Low	58	196	47	9	2	1	(-	-)	63	23	22	20	18	0	44	2	0	2	5	4	4	.240	.307	.321	.629
2013	Bklyn	A-	51	194	53	8	0	0	(-	-)	61	18	14	20	14	0	30	0	2	2	2	3	1	.273	.319	.314	.633
2014	2 Tms	Low	125	461	114	27	5	8	(-	-)	175	78	56	63	57	1	81	3	1	8	10	4	9	.247	.329	.380	.709
2015	Bnghtn	AA	109	439	139	26	4	7	(-	-)	194	64	51	74	42	0	55	2	0	2	3	4	8	.317	.377	.442	.819
2016	LsVgs	AAA	117	446	145	27	2	8	(-	-)	200	71	55	80	48	0	55	0	4	1	4	1	16	.325	.390	.448	.838
2016	NYM	NL	4	6	2	2	0	0	(0	0)	4	2	2	2	0	0	2	1	0	0	0	0	0	.333	.429	.667	1.095

Brett Cecil

Pitches: L Bats: R Pos: RP-54 | SEE-sill | Ht: 6'3" Wt: 235 Born: 7/2/1986 Age: 30

Year	Team	Lg	G	GS	CG	GF	IP	BFP	H	R	ER	HR	SH	SF	HB	TBB	IBB	SO	WP	Bk	W	L	Pct	Sh	Sv-Op	Hld	ERC	ERA
2009	Tor	AL	18	17	0	1	93.1	422	116	59	55	17	0	2	5	38	0	69	0	0	7	4	.636	0	0-0	0	6.53	5.30
2010	Tor	AL	28	28	0	0	172.2	726	175	87	81	18	1	6	1	54	2	105	7	1	15	7	.682	0	0-0	0	3.88	4.22
2011	Tor	AL	20	20	2	0	123.2	532	122	68	65	22	3	5	6	42	1	87	1	0	4	11	.267	1	0-0	0	4.47	4.73
2012	Tor	AL	21	9	0	2	61.1	270	70	40	39	11	3	3	3	23	0	51	0	0	2	4	.333	0	0-0	1	5.68	5.72
2013	Tor	AL	60	0	0	12	60.2	250	44	20	19	4	3	2	3	23	3	70	5	1	5	1	.833	0	1-3	11	2.42	2.82
2014	Tor	AL	66	0	0	17	53.1	234	46	16	16	2	0	3	1	27	4	76	1	0	2	3	.400	0	5-7	24	3.16	2.70
2015	Tor	AL	63	0	0	24	54.1	214	39	17	15	4	1	0	2	13	3	70	4	0	5	5	.500	0	5-8	9	1.95	2.48
2016	Tor	AL	54	0	0	8	36.2	157	39	17	16	6	1	1	2	8	0	45	0	0	1	7	.125	0	0-4	9	4.33	3.93
	Postseason		2	0	0	0	2.0	7	1	0	0	0	1	0	0	1	0	2	0	0	0	0	-	0	0-1	0	1.62	0.00
8 ML YEARS			330	74	2	64	656.0	2805	651	324	306	84	12	22	23	228	13	585	18	2	41	42	.494	1	11-22	54	4.14	4.20

Darrell Ceciliani

Bats: L Throws: L Pos: LF-8;RF-4;PR-1 | ses-see-lee-AH-nee | Ht: 6'1" Wt: 220 Born: 6/22/1990 Age: 27

Year	Team	Lg	G	AB	H	2B	3B	HR	(Hm	Rd)	TB	R	RBI	RC	TBB	IBB	SO	HBP	SH	SF	SB	CS	GDP	Avg	OBP	Slg	OPS
2012	Stluci	A+	23	85	28	6	1	1	(-	-)	39	19	10	16	10	0	13	1	0	1	2	0	0	.329	.402	.459	.861
2013	Bnghtn	AA	114	418	112	17	6	6	(-	-)	159	61	44	56	29	2	105	6	4	4	31	7	10	.268	.322	.380	.702
2014	Bnghtn	AA	107	395	114	17	4	7	(-	-)	160	59	54	55	22	1	89	6	1	6	16	7	6	.289	.331	.405	.736
2015	LsVgs	AAA	70	229	79	19	4	9	(-	-)	133	50	36	52	21	2	48	1	0	3	16	4	7	.345	.398	.581	.978
2016	Buffalo	AAA	82	304	81	17	3	10	(-	-)	134	40	40	45	26	1	52	1	0	3	11	5	7	.266	.323	.441	.764
2015	NYM	NL	39	68	14	2	0	1	(1	0)	19	5	3	6	4	0	25	2	0	0	5	1	0	.206	.270	.279	.550
2016	Tor	AL	13	27	3	2	0	0	(0	0)	5	2	1	0	1	0	14	1	0	0	0	0	0	.111	.172	.185	.358
2 ML YEARS			52	95	17	4	0	1	(1	0)	24	7	4	6	5	0	39	3	0	0	5	1	0	.179	.243	.253	.495

Xavier Cedeno

Pitches: L Bats: L Pos: RP-54 | seh-DAYN-yo | Ht: 6'0" Wt: 215 Born: 8/26/1986 Age: 30

Year	Team	Lg	G	GS	CG	GF	IP	BFP	H	R	ER	HR	SH	SF	HB	TBB	IBB	SO	WP	Bk	W	L	Pct	Sh	Sv-Op	Hld	ERC	ERA
2011	Hou	NL	3	0	0	0	1.2	11	7	5	5	2	0	0	0	0	0	0	0	0	0	0	-	0	0-0	0	43.10	27.00
2012	Hou	NL	44	0	0	12	31.0	138	30	15	13	2	3	2	1	14	1	36	3	0	0	1	.000	0	1-3	6	4.05	3.77
2013	2 Tms	NL	16	0	0	3	12.1	60	15	12	9	0	1	0	2	8	0	9	0	0	0	0	-	0	0-0	2	6.24	6.57
2014	Was	NL	9	0	0	4	7.0	30	10	4	3	1	0	0	0	0	0	5	0	0	0	0	-	0	0-0	0	5.27	3.86
2015	2 Tms	NL	66	0	0	10	46.0	189	40	13	12	4	0	0	2	14	2	47	6	0	4	1	.800	0	1-3	19	3.05	2.35
2016	TB	AL	54	0	0	7	41.1	174	36	17	17	2	1	2	0	13	1	43	3	0	3	4	.429	0	0-5	19	2.62	3.70
13	Hou	AL	5	0	0	0	6.1	37	10	11	8	0	1	0	2	7	0	3	0	0	0	0	-	0	0-0	0	11.27	11.37
13	Was	NL	11	0	0	3	6.0	23	5	1	1	0	0	0	0	1	0	6	0	0	0	0	-	0	0-0	2	1.84	1.50
15	Was	NL	5	0	0	1	3.0	15	3	2	2	1	0	0	1	2	0	4	2	0	0	0	-	0	0-2	0	8.41	6.00
15	TB	AL	61	0	0	9	43.0	174	37	11	10	3	0	0	1	12	2	43	4	0	4	1	.800	0	1-1	19	2.74	2.09
6 ML YEARS			192	0	0	36	139.1	602	138	66	59	12	4	5	6	49	4	140	12	0	7	6	.538	0	2-11	46	3.80	3.81

Juan Centeno

Bats: L Throws: R Pos: C-53;PH-2;DH-1 | sen-TAIN-no | Ht: 5'9" Wt: 195 Born: 11/16/1989 Age: 27

Year	Team	Lg	G	AB	H	2B	3B	HR	(Hm	Rd)	TB	R	RBI	RC	TBB	IBB	SO	HBP	SH	SF	SB	CS	GDP	Avg	OBP	Slg	OPS
2016	Roch*	AAA	15	49	12	1	0	1	(-	-)	16	5	5	5	4	0	4	1	1	0	1	0	2	.245	.315	.327	.641
2013	NYM	NL	4	10	3	0	0	0	(0	0)	3	0	1	1	0	0	1	0	0	0	0	0	0	.300	.300	.300	.600
2014	NYM	NL	10	30	6	0	0	0	(0	0)	6	1	2	2	3	0	5	0	0	0	0	0	2	.200	.273	.200	.473
2015	Mil	NL	10	21	1	0	0	0	(0	0)	1	0	0	0	2	0	7	0	0	0	0	0	0	.048	.130	.095	.226
2016	Min	AL	55	176	46	12	1	3	(1	2)	69	16	25	20	12	0	38	1	3	0	0	0	8	.261	.312	.392	.704
4 ML YEARS			79	237	56	13	1	3	(1	2)	80	17	28	23	17	0	51	1	3	0	0	0	10	.236	.290	.338	.628

Francisco Cervelli

Bats: R Throws: R Pos: C-95;PH-5;1B-2;DH-1 | sir-VEL-lee | Ht: 6'1" Wt: 205 Born: 3/6/1986 Age: 31

Year	Team	Lg	G	AB	H	2B	3B	HR	(Hm	Rd)	TB	R	RBI	RC	TBB	IBB	SO	HBP	SH	SF	SB	CS	GDP	Avg	OBP	Slg	OPS
2008	NYY	AL	3	5	0	0	0	0	(0	0)	0	0	0	0	0	0	3	0	0	0	0	0	1	.000	.000	.000	.000
2009	NYY	AL	42	94	28	4	0	1	(0	1)	35	13	11	11	2	0	11	0	4	1	0	3	1	.298	.315	.372	.682
2010	NYY	AL	93	266	72	11	3	0	(0	0)	89	27	38	40	33	1	42	6	8	4	1	1	7	.271	.359	.335	.694
2011	NYY	AL	43	124	33	4	0	4	(2	2)	49	17	22	17	9	0	29	2	1	1	4	1	4	.266	.324	.395	.719
2012	NYY	AL	3	1	0	0	0	0	(0	0)	0	1	0	0	0	0	0	0	0	0	0	0	0	.000	.500	.000	.500
2013	NYY	AL	17	52	14	3	0	3	(3	0)	26	12	11	13	8	0	9	1	0	0	0	0	0	.269	.377	.500	.877

113

Year Team	Lg	G	AB	H	2B	3B	HR	(Hm Rd)	TB	R	RBI	RC	TBB	IBB	SO	HBP	SH	SF	SB	CS	GDP	Avg	OBP	Slg	OPS
2014 NYY	AL	49	146	44	11	1	2	(1 1)	63	18	13	19	11	0	41	5	0	0	1	0	5	.301	.370	.432	.802
2015 Pit	NL	130	451	133	17	5	7	(6 1)	181	56	43	62	46	1	94	8	4	1	1	1	12	.295	.401	.401	.751
2016 Pit	NL	101	326	86	14	1	1	(0 1)	105	42	33	40	56	0	72	6	0	5	6	2	14	.264	.377	.322	.699
Postseason		4	6	1	0	0	0	(0 0)	1	0	0	0	0	0	2	1	0	0	0	0	0	.167	.286	.167	.452
9 ML YEARS		481	1465	410	64	10	18	(12 6)	548	186	168	198	166	3	301	28	17	12	13	8	45	.280	.361	.374	.736

Hunter Cervenka

Pitches: L Bats: L Pos: RP-68   sir-VEN-kuh   Ht: 6'1" Wt: 245 Born: 1/3/1990 Age: 27

Year Team	Lg	G	GS	CG	GF	IP	BFP	H	R	ER	HR	SH	SF	HB	TBB	IBB	SO	WP	Bk	W	L	Pct	Sh	Sv-Op	Hld	ERC	ERA
2012 3 Tms	Low	35	0	0	15	62.2	274	59	40	30	4	5	1	1	33	0	71	6	0	3	3	.500	0	1--	-	4.06	4.31
2013 Dytona	A+	11	0	0	7	21.2	94	13	8	7	0	1	0	2	15	0	21	3	0	1	0	1.000	0	5--	-	2.63	2.91
2013 Tenn	AA	30	0	0	11	38.1	163	29	14	13	1	5	0	1	20	1	33	3	1	5	1	.833	0	1--	-	2.76	3.05
2014 Tenn	AA	48	0	0	6	61.2	256	44	28	26	1	2	1	4	31	0	65	5	0	4	4	.500	0	1--	-	2.65	3.79
2015 Iowa	AAA	12	0	0	6	13.0	79	21	16	16	2	1	0	0	15	2	20	2	1	0	1	.000	0	0--	-	10.68	11.08
2015 Gwnntt	AAA	14	0	0	3	16.2	71	13	1	0	0	1	0	2	8	0	23	4	0	1	0	1.000	0	0--	-	2.96	0.00
2016 2 Tms	NL	68	0	0	11	43.1	182	31	19	17	3	1	0	1	28	5	42	6	0	1	0	1.000	0	0-0	11	3.23	3.53
16 Atl	NL	50	0	0	8	34.0	139	20	14	12	2	1	0	1	23	5	35	6	0	1	0	1.000	0	0-0	9	2.61	3.18
16 Mia	NL	18	0	0	3	9.1	43	11	5	5	1	0	0	0	5	0	7	0	0	0	0	-	0	0-0	2	5.73	4.82

Yoenis Cespedes

Bats: R Throws: R Pos: LF-80;CF-63;PH-6;DH-4   yo-EHN-ess SESS-peh-des   Ht: 5'10" Wt: 220 Born: 10/18/1985 Age: 31

Year Team	Lg	G	AB	H	2B	3B	HR	(Hm Rd)	TB	R	RBI	RC	TBB	IBB	SO	HBP	SH	SF	SB	CS	GDP	Avg	OBP	Slg	OPS
2012 Oak	AL	129	487	142	25	5	23	(11 12)	246	70	82	90	43	5	102	7	0	3	16	4	9	.292	.356	.505	.861
2013 Oak	AL	135	529	127	21	4	26	(14 12)	234	74	80	65	37	5	137	5	0	3	7	7	8	.240	.294	.442	.737
2014 2 Tms	AL	152	600	156	36	6	22	(13 9)	270	89	100	85	35	3	128	3	0	7	7	2	13	.260	.301	.450	.751
2015 2 Tms	AL	159	633	184	42	6	35	(10 25)	343	101	105	103	33	5	141	5	0	5	7	5	14	.291	.328	.542	.870
2016 NYM	NL	132	479	134	25	1	31	(14 17)	254	72	86	83	51	8	108	7	0	6	3	1	14	.280	.354	.530	.884
14 Oak	AL	101	399	102	26	3	17	(11 6)	185	62	67	55	28	3	80	1	0	4	3	2	8	.256	.303	.464	.767
14 Bos	AL	51	201	54	10	3	5	(2 3)	85	27	33	30	7	0	48	2	0	3	4	0	5	.269	.296	.423	.719
15 Det	AL	102	403	118	28	2	18	(5 13)	204	62	61	58	19	2	87	1	0	4	3	4	9	.293	.323	.506	.829
15 NYM	NL	57	230	66	14	4	17	(5 12)	139	39	44	45	14	3	54	4	0	1	4	1	5	.287	.337	.604	.942
Postseason		24	94	26	3	1	3	(2 1)	40	11	14	14	3	0	23	1	0	1	3	0	1	.277	.303	.426	.729
5 ML YEARS		707	2728	743	149	22	137	(62 75)	1347	406	453	426	199	26	616	27	0	24	40	19	58	.272	.325	.494	.819

Luis Cessa

Pitches: R Bats: R Pos: SP-9; RP-8   SESS-uh   Ht: 6'0" Wt: 205 Born: 4/25/1992 Age: 25

Year Team	Lg	G	GS	CG	GF	IP	BFP	H	R	ER	HR	SH	SF	HB	TBB	IBB	SO	WP	Bk	W	L	Pct	Sh	Sv-Op	Hld	ERC	ERA
2012 Bklyn	A-	13	13	0	0	72.1	285	64	21	20	4	4	0	2	13	0	44	0	0	5	4	.556	0	0--	-	2.53	2.49
2013 Savann	A	21	21	1	0	130.0	537	136	53	45	11	8	2	0	19	0	124	4	1	8	4	.667	0	0--	-	3.23	3.12
2014 Stluci	A+	20	20	1	0	114.2	472	110	54	51	7	3	5	3	27	0	83	6	0	7	8	.467	0	0--	-	3.09	4.00
2015 Bnghtn	AA	13	13	0	0	77.1	318	77	25	22	2	5	1	0	17	1	61	4	0	7	4	.636	0	0--	-	2.88	2.56
2015 LsVgs	AAA	5	5	0	0	24.1	119	40	25	23	3	1	0	1	4	0	24	0	0	0	3	.000	0	0--	-	7.11	8.51
2015 Toledo	AAA	7	7	0	0	37.2	170	46	27	25	2	0	3	2	15	0	34	1	1	1	3	.250	0	0--	-	5.27	5.97
2016 S-WB	AAA	15	14	1	0	77.1	309	66	33	26	8	2	3	0	23	0	69	3	0	6	3	.667	1	0--	-	3.00	3.03
2016 NYY	AL	17	9	0	5	70.1	285	64	36	34	16	1	1	3	14	0	46	2	0	4	4	.500	0	0-0	0	3.81	4.35

Jhoulys Chacin

Pitches: R Bats: R Pos: SP-22; RP-12   yoo-LEES cha-SEEN   Ht: 6'3" Wt: 215 Born: 1/7/1988 Age: 29

Year Team	Lg	G	GS	CG	GF	IP	BFP	H	R	ER	HR	SH	SF	HB	TBB	IBB	SO	WP	Bk	W	L	Pct	Sh	Sv-Op	Hld	ERC	ERA
2009 Col	NL	9	1	0	3	11.0	48	6	6	6	1	1	0	0	11	0	13	2	0	0	1	.000	0	0-0	0	3.87	4.91
2010 Col	NL	28	21	0	2	137.1	583	114	64	50	10	6	5	9	61	5	138	4	0	9	11	.450	0	0-0	0	3.33	3.28
2011 Col	NL	31	31	2	0	194.0	827	168	87	78	20	5	3	4	87	1	150	7	0	11	14	.440	1	0-0	0	3.61	3.62
2012 Col	NL	14	14	0	0	69.0	314	80	35	34	10	1	1	2	32	0	45	3	0	3	5	.375	0	0-0	0	5.73	4.43
2013 Col	NL	31	31	0	0	197.1	816	188	82	76	11	3	7	3	61	3	126	5	1	14	10	.583	0	0-0	0	3.26	3.47
2014 Col	NL	11	11	0	0	63.1	272	63	38	38	8	2	3	1	28	1	42	4	0	1	7	.125	0	0-0	0	4.52	5.40
2015 Ari	NL	5	4	0	0	26.2	111	24	11	10	4	1	0	0	10	0	21	0	0	2	1	.667	0	0-0	0	3.80	3.38
2016 2 Tms	NL	34	22	1	5	144.0	632	153	81	77	14	4	6	5	55	4	119	8	1	6	8	.429	0	0-0	0	4.42	4.81
16 Atl	NL	5	5	0	0	26.2	117	29	17	16	4	2	1	0	8	0	27	0	0	1	2	.333	0	0-0	0	4.42	5.40
16 LAA	AL	29	17	1	5	117.1	515	124	64	61	10	2	5	5	47	4	92	8	1	5	6	.455	0	0-0	0	4.42	4.68
8 ML YEARS		163	135	3	10	842.2	3603	796	404	369	78	23	25	24	345	14	654	33	2	46	57	.447	1	0-0	0	3.86	3.94

Andrew Chafin

Pitches: L Bats: R Pos: RP-32   Ht: 6'2" Wt: 225 Born: 6/17/1990 Age: 27

Year Team	Lg	G	GS	CG	GF	IP	BFP	H	R	ER	HR	SH	SF	HB	TBB	IBB	SO	WP	Bk	W	L	Pct	Sh	Sv-Op	Hld	ERC	ERA
2016 Reno*	AAA	7	1	0	0	9.1	36	6	3	2	0	2	0	0	2	0	8	0	0	1	1	.500	0	1--	-	1.17	1.93
2016 2 Tms*	Low	5	1	0	0	5.0	18	0	0	0	0	0	0	0	2	0	8	0	0	1	0	1.000	0	0--	-	0.17	0.00
2014 Ari	NL	3	3	0	0	14.0	60	13	6	6	0	2	0	1	8	1	10	2	0	0	1	.000	0	0-0	0	3.92	3.86
2015 Ari	NL	66	0	0	6	75.0	306	56	23	23	4	3	2	1	30	6	58	2	0	5	1	.833	0	2-2	16	2.30	2.76
2016 Ari	NL	32	0	0	1	22.2	98	22	18	17	1	1	0	1	11	1	28	2	0	0	1	.000	0	0-1	6	4.01	6.75
3 ML YEARS		101	3	0	7	111.2	464	91	47	46	4	6	2	3	49	8	96	6	0	5	3	.625	0	2-3	22	2.82	3.71

Joba Chamberlain

Pitches: R Bats: R Pos: RP-20 JOBB-ah CHAME-berr-linn **Ht: 6'3" Wt: 245 Born: 9/23/1985 Age: 31**

Year Team	Lg	G	GS	CG	GF	IP	BFP	H	R	ER	HR	SH	SF	HB	TBB	IBB	SO	WP	Bk	W	L	Pct	Sh	Sv-Op	Hld	ERC	ERA
2007 NYY	AL	19	0	0	3	24.0	91	12	2	1	1	1	0	1	6	0	34	1	0	2	0	1.000	0	1-1	8	1.16	0.38
2008 NYY	AL	42	12	0	5	100.1	417	87	32	29	5	2	1	2	39	3	118	4	2	4	3	.571	0	0-1	19	3.04	2.60
2009 NYY	AL	32	31	0	5	157.1	709	167	94	83	21	6	5	12	76	2	133	5	2	9	6	.600	0	0-0	0	5.32	4.75
2010 NYY	AL	73	0	0	18	71.2	305	71	37	35	6	0	1	1	22	2	77	5	1	3	4	.429	0	3-7	26	3.53	4.40
2011 NYY	AL	27	0	0	3	28.2	110	23	10	9	3	0	1	1	7	0	24	1	0	2	0	1.000	0	0-1	12	2.76	2.83
2012 NYY	AL	22	0	0	5	20.2	95	26	11	10	3	0	1	2	6	2	22	0	0	1	0	1.000	0	0-0	4	5.63	4.35
2013 NYY	AL	45	0	0	14	42.0	198	47	23	23	8	0	1	1	26	1	38	3	0	2	1	.667	0	1-1	5	6.38	4.93
2014 Det	AL	69	0	0	10	63.0	263	57	26	25	3	1	2	3	24	3	59	3	0	2	5	.286	0	2-6	29	3.29	3.57
2015 2 Tms	AL	36	0	0	15	27.2	128	38	20	15	6	1	0	1	9	0	23	2	0	0	2	.000	0	0-2	8	7.09	4.88
2016 Cle	AL	20	0	0	5	20.0	82	12	6	5	1	0	2	1	11	3	18	1	0	0	0	-	0	0-0	2	2.19	2.25
15 Det	AL	30	0	0	10	22.0	101	32	15	10	5	1	0	1	5	0	15	1	0	0	2	.000	0	0-2	8	7.34	4.09
15 KC	AL	6	0	0	5	5.2	27	6	5	5	1	0	0	0	4	0	8	1	0	0	0	-	0	0-0	0	6.14	7.94
Postseason		21	0	0	1	16.0	79	23	10	9	1	1	1	2	6	0	15	2	0	1	0	1.000	0	0-2	4	6.64	5.06
10 ML YEARS		385	43	0	78	555.1	2398	540	261	235	57	11	14	25	226	16	546	25	5	25	21	.543	0	7-19	111	4.11	3.81

Aroldis Chapman

Pitches: L Bats: L Pos: RP-59 ah-ROLL-diss **Ht: 6'4" Wt: 215 Born: 2/28/1988 Age: 29**

Year Team	Lg	G	GS	CG	GF	IP	BFP	H	R	ER	HR	SH	SF	HB	TBB	IBB	SO	WP	Bk	W	L	Pct	Sh	Sv-Op	Hld	ERC	ERA
2010 Cin	NL	15	0	0	3	13.1	51	9	4	3	0	0	0	0	5	0	19	2	0	2	2	.500	0	0-1	4	1.82	2.03
2011 Cin	NL	54	0	0	13	50.0	207	24	21	20	2	1	0	2	41	0	71	4	0	4	1	.800	0	1-3	13	2.69	3.60
2012 Cin	NL	68	0	0	52	71.2	276	35	13	12	4	0	1	4	23	0	122	4	0	5	5	.500	0	38-43	6	1.35	1.51
2013 Cin	NL	68	0	0	55	63.2	258	37	18	18	7	1	0	3	29	0	112	6	0	4	5	.444	0	38-43	0	2.33	2.54
2014 Cin	NL	54	0	0	44	54.0	202	21	12	12	1	1	1	2	24	0	106	4	0	0	3	.000	0	36-38	0	1.18	2.00
2015 Cin	NL	65	0	0	54	66.1	278	43	13	12	3	0	2	5	33	1	116	7	0	4	4	.500	0	33-36	0	2.45	1.63
2016 2 Tms	NL	59	0	0	52	58.0	222	32	12	10	2	0	1	0	18	0	90	8	1	4	1	.800	0	36-39	0	1.33	1.55
16 NYY	AL	31	0	0	29	31.1	120	20	8	7	2	0	0	0	8	0	44	2	1	3	0	1.000	0	20-21	0	1.59	2.01
16 ChC	NL	28	0	0	23	26.2	102	12	4	3	0	0	1	0	10	0	46	6	0	1	1	.500	0	16-18	0	1.04	1.01
Postseason		5	0	0	3	4.2	24	5	4	1	0	0	0	1	2	0	4	2	0	0	0	-	0	0-1	0	4.11	1.93
7 ML YEARS		383	0	0	273	377.0	1494	201	93	87	19	3	5	16	173	1	636	35	1	23	21	.523	0	182-203	23	1.78	2.08

Kevin Chapman

Pitches: L Bats: L Pos: RP-9 **Ht: 6'3" Wt: 230 Born: 2/19/1988 Age: 29**

Year Team	Lg	G	GS	CG	GF	IP	BFP	H	R	ER	HR	SH	SF	HB	TBB	IBB	SO	WP	Bk	W	L	Pct	Sh	Sv-Op	Hld	ERC	ERA
2016 Fresno*	AAA	51	0	0	14	61.0	288	68	36	33	5	4	0	7	27	1	76	3	0	3	4	.429	0	0--	-	5.01	4.87
2013 Hou	AL	25	0	0	2	20.1	87	13	6	4	1	2	0	1	13	2	15	3	0	1	1	.500	0	1-4	4	2.69	1.77
2014 Hou	AL	21	0	0	1	21.1	97	22	11	11	3	3	1	0	11	0	19	0	0	2	0	1.000	0	0-1	5	4.90	4.64
2015 Hou	AL	3	0	0	0	5.1	22	4	2	2	1	0	0	0	3	0	8	0	0	0	0	-	0	0-0	1	4.05	3.38
2016 Hou	AL	9	0	0	1	8.0	42	15	8	8	0	0	0	0	4	0	6	0	0	0	0	-	0	0-0	0	9.11	9.00
4 ML YEARS		58	0	0	4	55.0	248	54	27	25	5	5	1	1	31	2	48	3	0	3	1	.750	0	1-5	10	4.51	4.09

J.T. Chargois

Pitches: R Bats: B Pos: RP-25 SHAHG-wah **Ht: 6'3" Wt: 200 Born: 12/3/1990 Age: 26**

Year Team	Lg	G	GS	CG	GF	IP	BFP	H	R	ER	HR	SH	SF	HB	TBB	IBB	SO	WP	Bk	W	L	Pct	Sh	Sv-Op	Hld	ERC	ERA
2012 Elizab	R+	12	0	0	8	16.0	61	10	4	3	0	1	0	0	5	0	22	1	0	0	0	-	0	5--	-	1.45	1.69
2015 FtMyrs	A+	16	0	0	10	15.0	66	12	8	4	0	1	0	0	5	0	19	2	0	1	0	1.000	0	4--	-	1.94	2.40
2015 Chatt	AA	32	0	0	24	33.0	141	26	12	10	1	0	0	2	20	0	34	1	0	1	1	.500	0	11--	-	3.51	2.73
2016 Chatt	AA	11	0	0	11	11.2	48	8	3	2	1	1	0	0	5	0	14	0	0	0	0	-	0	7--	-	2.40	1.54
2016 Roch	AAA	28	0	0	16	35.0	141	27	7	5	1	2	1	0	8	0	41	6	0	2	1	.667	0	9--	-	1.81	1.29
2016 Min	AL	25	0	0	10	23.0	100	25	12	12	0	0	1	1	12	0	17	3	0	1	1	.500	0	0-0	2	4.67	4.70

Tyler Chatwood

Pitches: R Bats: R Pos: SP-27 **Ht: 6'0" Wt: 185 Born: 12/16/1989 Age: 27**

Year Team	Lg	G	GS	CG	GF	IP	BFP	H	R	ER	HR	SH	SF	HB	TBB	IBB	SO	WP	Bk	W	L	Pct	Sh	Sv-Op	Hld	ERC	ERA
2011 LAA	AL	27	25	0	0	142.0	633	166	81	75	14	6	3	6	71	4	74	3	1	6	11	.353	0	0-0	0	5.78	4.75
2012 Col	NL	19	12	0	3	64.2	294	74	43	39	9	4	2	0	33	2	41	4	0	5	6	.455	0	1-1	0	5.62	5.43
2013 Col	NL	20	20	1	0	111.1	476	118	44	39	5	2	4	4	41	5	66	1	0	8	5	.615	0	0-0	0	4.05	3.15
2014 Col	NL	4	4	0	0	24.0	101	21	13	12	4	0	2	2	8	0	20	2	0	1	1	1.000	0	0-0	0	3.91	4.50
2016 Col	NL	27	27	0	0	158.0	669	147	75	68	15	2	3	5	70	2	117	7	0	12	9	.571	0	0-0	0	4.01	3.87
5 ML YEARS		97	88	1	3	500.0	2173	526	256	233	47	14	14	17	223	13	318	26	1	32	31	.508	0	1-1	0	4.70	4.19

Jesse Chavez

Pitches: R Bats: R Pos: RP-62 CHAH-vezz **Ht: 6'2" Wt: 175 Born: 8/21/1983 Age: 33**

Year Team	Lg	G	GS	CG	GF	IP	BFP	H	R	ER	HR	SH	SF	HB	TBB	IBB	SO	WP	Bk	W	L	Pct	Sh	Sv-Op	Hld	ERC	ERA
2008 Pit	NL	15	0	0	6	15.0	74	20	11	11	2	3	1	0	9	2	16	2	0	0	0	1.000	0	0-2	6	6.76	6.60
2009 Pit	NL	73	0	0	24	67.1	286	69	33	30	11	1	1	1	22	3	47	5	0	1	4	.200	0	0-4	15	4.39	4.01
2010 2 Tms		51	0	0	26	62.2	280	69	44	41	11	5	3	1	23	7	45	2	0	5	5	.500	0	0-1	6	4.85	5.89
2011 KC	AL	4	0	0	3	7.2	39	12	9	9	3	0	0	0	5	0	8	0	0	0	0	-	0	0-0	0	11.48	10.57

Year	Team	Lg	G	GS	CG	GF	IP	BFP	H	R	ER	HR	SH	SF	HB	TBB	IBB	SO	WP	Bk	W	L	Pct	Sh	Sv-Op	Hld	ERC	ERA
2012	2 Tms	AL	13	2	0	3	24.2	123	34	29	27	7	0	1	3	11	1	30	1	0	1	1	.500	0	0-0	0	8.32	9.85
2013	Oak	AL	35	0	0	16	57.1	248	50	27	25	3	6	2	3	20	4	55	5	0	2	4	.333	0	1-2	1	2.85	3.92
2014	Oak	AL	32	21	0	5	146.0	621	142	64	56	17	1	4	5	49	3	136	1	0	8	8	.500	0	0-0	0	3.89	3.45
2015	Oak	AL	30	26	0	3	157.0	672	164	78	73	18	4	6	2	48	2	136	3	0	7	15	.318	0	1-1	0	4.08	4.18
2016	2 Tms	AL	62	0	0	9	67.0	282	71	36	33	12	0	1	2	18	3	63	1	0	2	2	.500	0	0-3	10	4.56	4.43
10	Atl	NL	28	0	0	16	36.2	162	40	24	24	6	3	2	1	12	3	29	0	0	3	2	.600	0	0-0	0	4.65	5.89
10	KC	AL	23	0	0	10	26.0	118	29	20	17	5	2	1	0	11	4	16	2	0	2	3	.400	0	0-1	6	5.13	5.88
12	Tor	AL	9	2	0	2	21.1	102	25	22	20	6	0	1	2	10	1	27	0	0	1	1	.500	0	0-0	0	6.90	8.44
12	Oak	AL	4	0	0	1	3.1	21	9	7	7	1	0	0	1	1	0	3	1	0	0	0	-	0	0-0	0	18.70	18.90
16	Tor	AL	39	0	0	6	41.1	173	43	22	21	9	0	1	2	10	0	42	1	0	1	2	.333	0	0-2	7	4.75	4.57
16	LAD	NL	23	0	0	3	25.2	109	28	14	12	3	0	0	0	8	3	21	0	0	1	0	1.000	0	0-1	3	4.24	4.21
9 ML YEARS			315	49	0	95	604.2	2625	631	331	305	84	20	19	17	205	25	536	26	0	26	40	.394	0	2-13	32	4.38	4.54

Wei-Yin Chen

Pitches: L **Bats:** R **Pos:** SP-22   way-yin   **Ht:** 6'0" **Wt:** 200 **Born:** 7/21/1985 **Age:** 31

Year	Team	Lg	G	GS	CG	GF	IP	BFP	H	R	ER	HR	SH	SF	HB	TBB	IBB	SO	WP	Bk	W	L	Pct	Sh	Sv-Op	Hld	ERC	ERA
2012	Bal	AL	32	32	0	0	192.2	818	186	97	86	29	5	8	5	57	0	154	2	1	12	11	.522	0	0-0	0	3.88	4.02
2013	Bal	AL	23	23	0	0	137.0	572	142	62	62	17	2	6	2	39	2	104	3	0	7	7	.500	0	0-0	0	4.11	4.07
2014	Bal	AL	31	31	0	0	185.2	772	193	77	73	23	5	4	3	35	2	136	2	0	16	6	.727	0	0-0	0	3.67	3.54
2015	Bal	AL	31	31	0	0	191.1	792	192	78	71	28	5	8	5	41	0	153	3	0	11	8	.579	0	0-0	0	3.80	3.34
2016	Mia	NL	22	22	0	0	123.1	520	134	69	68	22	3	4	3	24	0	100	1	0	5	5	.500	0	0-0	0	4.38	4.96
Postseason			3	3	0	0	15.1	69	22	9	8	2	0	0	0	2	0	10	0	0	1	1	.500	0	0-0	0	5.68	4.70
5 ML YEARS			139	139	0	0	830.0	3474	847	383	360	119	20	30	18	196	4	647	11	1	51	37	.580	0	0-0	0	3.93	3.90

Robinson Chirinos

Bats: R **Throws:** R **Pos:** C-54;DH-3;PR-3;PH-1   chee-REE-nos   **Ht:** 6'1" **Wt:** 210 **Born:** 6/5/1984 **Age:** 33

Year	Team	Lg	G	AB	H	2B	3B	HR	(Hm	Rd)	TB	R	RBI	RC	TBB	IBB	SO	HBP	SH	SF	SB	CS	GDP	Avg	OBP	Slg	OPS
2011	TB	AL	20	55	12	2	0	1	(1	0)	17	4	7	5	5	0	13	0	0	0	0	0	0	.218	.283	.309	.592
2013	Tex	AL	13	28	5	3	0	0	(0	0)	8	3	0	0	2	0	6	0	0	0	0	0	1	.179	.233	.286	.519
2014	Tex	AL	93	306	73	15	0	13	(6	7)	127	36	40	38	17	1	71	7	4	4	0	1	4	.239	.290	.415	.705
2015	Tex	AL	78	233	54	16	1	10	(4	6)	102	33	34	28	28	0	62	5	5	2	0	0	4	.232	.325	.438	.762
2016	Tex	AL	57	147	33	11	0	9	(1	8)	71	21	20	21	15	0	44	5	1	2	0	1	4	.224	.314	.483	.797
Postseason			3	11	3	0	0	1	(0	1)	6	1	3	3	0	0	2	0	0	0	0	0	0	.273	.273	.545	.818
5 ML YEARS			261	769	177	47	1	33	(12	21)	325	97	101	92	67	1	196	17	10	8	0	2	13	.230	.303	.423	.726

Lonnie Chisenhall

Bats: L **Throws:** R **Pos:** RF-118;PH-17;1B-3;CF-2;3B-1   CHIZ-en-hall   **Ht:** 6'2" **Wt:** 190 **Born:** 10/4/1988 **Age:** 28

Year	Team	Lg	G	AB	H	2B	3B	HR	(Hm	Rd)	TB	R	RBI	RC	TBB	IBB	SO	HBP	SH	SF	SB	CS	GDP	Avg	OBP	Slg	OPS
2011	Cle	AL	66	212	54	13	0	7	(2	5)	88	27	22	24	8	1	49	1	1	1	0	0	3	.255	.284	.415	.699
2012	Cle	AL	43	142	38	6	1	5	(4	1)	61	16	16	18	9	0	27	1	0	0	2	1	2	.268	.311	.430	.741
2013	Cle	AL	94	289	65	17	0	11	(4	7)	115	30	36	31	16	0	56	2	1	0	1	0	8	.225	.270	.398	.668
2014	Cle	AL	142	478	134	29	1	13	(6	7)	204	62	59	69	39	3	99	8	4	3	1	1	8	.280	.343	.427	.770
2015	Cle	AL	106	333	82	19	1	7	(3	4)	124	38	44	39	23	3	69	1	2	3	4	1	6	.246	.294	.372	.667
2016	Cle	AL	126	385	110	25	5	8	(4	4)	169	43	57	64	23	2	70	3	3	4	6	0	4	.286	.328	.439	.767
Postseason			1	4	3	0	0	0	(0	0)	3	0	0	0	0	0	1	0	0	0	0	0	0	.750	.750	.750	1.500
6 ML YEARS			577	1839	483	109	8	51	(23	28)	761	216	234	242	117	9	370	16	11	11	17	3	25	.263	.311	.414	.724

Ji-Man Choi

Bats: L **Throws:** R **Pos:** 1B-27;LF-20;PH-12;PR-5;DH-4   gee-man choy   **Ht:** 6'1" **Wt:** 230 **Born:** 5/19/1991 **Age:** 26

Year	Team	Lg	G	AB	H	2B	3B	HR	(Hm	Rd)	TB	R	RBI	RC	TBB	IBB	SO	HBP	SH	SF	SB	CS	GDP	Avg	OBP	Slg	OPS
2012	Clinton	A	66	242	72	14	1	8	(-	-)	112	43	43	49	39	5	55	12	1	0	0	2	7	.298	.420	.463	.883
2013	Hi Dsrt	A+	48	181	61	24	3	7	(-	-)	112	34	40	45	27	1	33	2	0	1	0	1	5	.337	.427	.619	1.045
2013	Jacksn	AA	61	198	53	10	3	9	(-	-)	96	21	39	38	32	2	28	4	0	2	2	2	5	.268	.377	.485	.862
2013	Tacom	AAA	13	45	11	2	0	2	(-	-)	19	9	6	6	4	0	7	2	1	0	0	0	2	.244	.333	.422	.756
2014	Tacom	AAA	70	237	67	7	2	5	(-	-)	93	41	30	42	36	0	42	3	3	2	2	2	10	.283	.381	.392	.774
2015	Tacom	AAA	18	57	17	4	0	1	(-	-)	24	8	16	10	10	1	14	0	0	0	0	1	2	.298	.403	.421	.824
2016	Salt Lk	AAA	53	188	65	18	1	5	(-	-)	100	31	31	44	31	1	34	2	1	5	4	3	4	.346	.434	.532	.966
2016	LAA	AL	54	112	19	4	0	5	(3	2)	38	9	12	8	16	1	27	0	0	1	2	4	2	.170	.271	.339	.611

Shin-Soo Choo

Bats: L **Throws:** L **Pos:** RF-43;DH-4;PH-2   SHIN-sue CHEW   **Ht:** 5'11" **Wt:** 210 **Born:** 7/13/1982 **Age:** 34

Year	Team	Lg	G	AB	H	2B	3B	HR	(Hm	Rd)	TB	R	RBI	RC	TBB	IBB	SO	HBP	SH	SF	SB	CS	GDP	Avg	OBP	Slg	OPS
2005	Sea	AL	10	18	1	0	0	0	(0	0)	1	1	1	0	3	0	4	0	0	0	0	0	0	.056	.190	.056	.246
2006	2 Tms	AL	49	157	44	12	3	3	(2	1)	71	23	22	24	18	2	50	2	1	5	3	3	3	.280	.360	.452	.812
2007	Cle	AL	6	17	5	0	0	0	(0	0)	5	5	5	3	2	1	5	0	0	1	0	0	0	.294	.350	.294	.644
2008	Cle	AL	94	317	98	28	3	14	(10	4)	174	68	66	72	44	4	78	5	0	4	4	3	5	.309	.397	.549	.946
2009	Cle	AL	156	583	175	38	6	20	(11	9)	285	87	86	111	78	5	151	17	0	7	21	2	9	.300	.394	.489	.883
2010	Cle	AL	144	550	165	31	2	22	(8	14)	266	81	90	106	83	11	118	11	0	2	22	7	11	.300	.401	.484	.885
2011	Cle	AL	85	313	81	11	3	8	(7	1)	122	37	36	38	36	3	78	6	0	2	12	5	7	.259	.344	.390	.733
2012	Cle	AL	155	598	169	43	2	16	(8	8)	264	88	67	96	73	0	150	14	0	1	21	7	11	.283	.373	.441	.815

Year	Team	Lg	G	AB	H	2B	3B	HR	(Hm	Rd)	TB	R	RBI	RC	TBB	IBB	SO	HBP	SH	SF	SB	CS	GDP	Avg	OBP	Slg	OPS
2013	Cin	NL	154	569	162	34	2	21	(10	11)	263	107	54	111	112	5	133	26	3	2	20	11	3	.285	.423	.462	.885
2014	Tex	AL	123	455	110	19	1	13	(5	8)	170	58	40	54	58	3	131	12	0	4	3	4	9	.242	.340	.374	.714
2015	Tex	AL	149	555	153	32	3	22	(12	10)	257	94	82	99	76	1	147	15	2	5	4	2	7	.276	.375	.463	.838
2016	Tex	AL	48	178	43	7	0	7	(2	5)	71	27	17	25	25	1	46	7	0	0	6	3	1	.242	.357	.399	.756
06	Sea	AL	4	11	1	1	0	0	(0	0)	2	0	0	0	0	0	4	1	0	0	0	0	1	.091	.167	.182	.348
06	Cle	AL	45	146	43	11	3	3	(2	1)	69	23	22	24	18	2	46	1	1	1	5	3	2	.295	.373	.473	.846
	Postseason		6	24	6	0	0	2	(0	2)	12	6	3	3	1	0	7	1	1	0	0	0	0	.250	.308	.500	.808
	12 ML YEARS		1173	4310	1206	255	25	146	(75	71)	1949	676	566	739	608	36	1091	115	6	30	118	48	66	.280	.381	.452	.833

Tony Cingrani

Pitches: L Bats: L Pos: RP-65   sin-GRAHN-ee   Ht: 6'4" Wt: 210 Born: 7/5/1989 Age: 27

			HOW MUCH HE PITCHED					WHAT HE GAVE UP										THE RESULTS						
Year	Team	Lg	G	GS	CG	GF	IP	BFP	H	R	ER	HR	SH	SF	HB	TBB	IBB	SO	WP	Bk	W	L	Pct	Sh	Sv-Op	Hld	ERC	ERA
2012	Cin	NL	3	0	0	1	5.0	22	4	1	1	1	0	0	0	2	0	9	0	0	0	0	-	0	0-0	0	3.38	1.80
2013	Cin	NL	23	18	0	0	104.2	420	72	37	34	14	4	4	2	43	1	120	4	0	7	4	.636	0	0-0	1	2.78	2.92
2014	Cin	NL	13	11	0	2	63.1	280	62	33	32	12	2	2	1	35	2	61	1	2	2	8	.200	0	0-0	0	5.29	4.55
2015	Cin	NL	35	1	0	7	33.1	155	31	21	21	3	1	2	3	25	3	39	2	1	0	3	.000	0	0-2	9	5.19	5.67
2016	Cin	NL	65	0	0	34	63.0	271	54	30	29	5	1	1	3	37	1	49	3	1	2	5	.286	0	17-23	8	4.12	4.14
	5 ML YEARS		139	30	0	44	269.1	1148	223	122	117	35	8	9	9	142	7	278	10	4	11	20	.355	0	17-25	18	3.96	3.91

Steve Cishek

Pitches: R Bats: R Pos: RP-62   SEE-sheck   Ht: 6'6" Wt: 215 Born: 6/18/1986 Age: 31

			HOW MUCH HE PITCHED					WHAT HE GAVE UP										THE RESULTS						
Year	Team	Lg	G	GS	CG	GF	IP	BFP	H	R	ER	HR	SH	SF	HB	TBB	IBB	SO	WP	Bk	W	L	Pct	Sh	Sv-Op	Hld	ERC	ERA
2010	Fla	NL	3	0	0	2	4.1	15	1	0	0	0	0	0	0	1	0	3	0	0	0	0	-	0	0-0	0	0.35	0.00
2011	Fla	NL	45	0	0	21	54.2	229	45	18	16	1	3	0	3	19	7	55	5	0	2	1	.667	0	3-3	2	2.38	2.63
2012	Mia	NL	68	0	0	36	63.2	275	54	26	19	3	3	2	6	29	6	68	1	1	5	2	.714	0	15-19	13	3.28	2.69
2013	Mia	NL	69	0	0	62	69.2	281	53	19	18	3	3	3	2	22	6	74	1	0	4	6	.400	0	34-36	1	2.15	2.33
2014	Mia	NL	67	0	0	55	65.1	275	58	26	23	3	5	3	1	21	2	84	1	0	4	5	.444	0	39-43	4	2.78	3.17
2015	2 Tms	NL	59	0	0	23	55.1	243	55	26	22	4	1	2	1	27	3	48	1	0	2	6	.250	0	4-9	6	4.17	3.58
2016	Sea	AL	62	0	0	40	64.0	258	44	21	20	8	1	0	4	21	2	76	4	0	4	6	.400	0	25-32	9	2.51	2.81
15	Mia	NL	32	0	0	15	32.0	144	37	19	16	2	1	2	0	14	3	28	0	0	2	6	.250	0	3-7	3	4.66	4.50
15	StL	NL	27	0	0	8	23.1	99	18	7	6	2	0	0	1	13	0	20	1	0	0	0	-	0	1-2	3	3.53	2.31
	7 ML YEARS		373	0	0	239	377.0	1576	310	136	118	22	16	10	17	140	26	408	13	1	21	26	.447	0	120-142	31	2.79	2.82

Alex Claudio

Pitches: L Bats: L Pos: RP-39   Ht: 6'3" Wt: 180 Born: 1/31/1992 Age: 25

			HOW MUCH HE PITCHED					WHAT HE GAVE UP										THE RESULTS						
Year	Team	Lg	G	GS	CG	GF	IP	BFP	H	R	ER	HR	SH	SF	HB	TBB	IBB	SO	WP	Bk	W	L	Pct	Sh	Sv-Op	Hld	ERC	ERA
2016	RdRck*	AAA	6	0	0	3	16.1	57	7	1	1	0	1	0	0	4	1	8	0	0	0	0	-	0	1--	-	0.76	0.55
2014	Tex	AL	15	0	0	5	12.1	54	14	4	4	0	0	0	0	4	0	14	0	1	0	0	-	0	0-0	0	3.79	2.92
2015	Tex	AL	18	0	0	6	15.2	66	12	6	5	4	0	2	1	6	2	13	1	0	1	1	.500	0	0-1	3	3.74	2.87
2016	Tex	AL	39	0	0	15	51.2	217	55	19	16	2	0	2	1	10	0	34	0	0	4	1	.800	0	0-0	2	3.28	2.79
	3 ML YEARS		72	0	0	26	79.2	337	81	29	25	6	0	4	2	20	2	61	1	1	5	2	.714	0	0-1	5	3.46	2.82

Paul Clemens

Pitches: R Bats: R Pos: SP-14; RP-4   Ht: 6'3" Wt: 215 Born: 2/14/1988 Age: 29

			HOW MUCH HE PITCHED					WHAT HE GAVE UP										THE RESULTS						
Year	Team	Lg	G	GS	CG	GF	IP	BFP	H	R	ER	HR	SH	SF	HB	TBB	IBB	SO	WP	Bk	W	L	Pct	Sh	Sv-Op	Hld	ERC	ERA
2016	NewOr*	AAA	14	14	2	0	75.1	316	66	38	36	6	4	2	3	25	0	66	2	0	6	4	.600	1	0--	-	3.14	4.30
2013	Hou	AL	35	5	0	8	73.1	323	82	48	44	16	0	5	2	26	1	49	2	0	4	7	.364	0	0-2	7	5.53	5.40
2014	Hou	AL	13	0	0	4	24.2	118	28	20	16	5	1	0	1	13	1	16	0	0	1	0	1.000	0	0-0	1	6.03	5.84
2016	2 Tms	NL	18	14	0	2	71.1	314	72	39	32	14	1	3	4	31	0	53	4	1	4	5	.444	0	0-1	0	5.21	4.04
16	Mia	NL	2	2	0	0	10.0	47	11	7	7	5	0	0	1	8	0	6	0	0	1	0	1.000	0	0-0	0	10.75	6.30
16	SD	NL	16	12	0	2	61.1	267	61	32	25	9	1	3	3	23	0	47	4	1	3	5	.375	0	0-1	0	4.45	3.67
	3 ML YEARS		66	19	0	14	169.1	755	182	107	92	35	2	8	7	70	2	118	6	1	8	13	.381	0	0-3	8	5.47	4.89

Steve Clevenger

Bats: L Throws: R Pos: C-20; PH-2; DH-1   CLEV-en-jer   Ht: 5'10" Wt: 210 Born: 4/5/1986 Age: 31

Year	Team	Lg	G	AB	H	2B	3B	HR	(Hm	Rd)	TB	R	RBI	RC	TBB	IBB	SO	HBP	SH	SF	SB	CS	GDP	Avg	OBP	Slg	OPS
2011	ChC	NL	2	4	1	1	0	0	(0	0)	2	1	0	0	0	0	0	1	0	0	0	0	0	.250	.400	.500	.900
2012	ChC	NL	69	199	40	12	0	1	(1	0)	55	16	16	12	16	0	39	0	0	0	0	1	10	.201	.260	.276	.537
2013	2 Tms		12	23	5	1	0	0	(0	0)	6	2	2	1	1	0	5	0	0	0	0	0	1	.217	.250	.261	.511
2014	Bal	AL	35	89	20	8	1	0	(0	0)	30	8	8	3	8	1	19	0	0	0	0	0	5	.225	.289	.337	.626
2015	Bal	AL	30	101	29	4	2	2	(2	0)	43	11	15	15	4	1	13	0	0	0	0	0	3	.287	.314	.426	.740
2016	Sea	AL	22	68	15	3	0	1	(0	1)	21	7	7	8	8	0	14	0	0	0	0	0	3	.221	.303	.309	.611
13	ChC	NL	8	8	1	0	0	0	(0	0)	1	1	0	0	1	0	3	0	0	0	0	0	0	.125	.222	.125	.347
13	Bal	AL	4	15	4	1	0	0	(0	0)	5	1	2	1	0	0	2	0	0	0	0	0	1	.267	.267	.333	.600
	6 ML YEARS		170	484	110	29	3	4	(3	1)	157	45	48	39	37	2	90	1	0	0	0	1	22	.227	.284	.324	.608

Mike Clevinger

Pitches: R Bats: R Pos: SP-10; RP-7   Ht: 6'4" Wt: 210 Born: 12/21/1990 Age: 26

Year Team	Lg	G	GS	CG	GF	IP	BFP	H	R	ER	HR	SH	SF	HB	TBB	IBB	SO	WP	Bk	W	L	Pct	Sh	Sv-Op	Hld	ERC	ERA
2012 Crpds	A	8	8	0	0	41.0	172	37	18	17	3	1	3	3	13	0	34	1	0	1	1	.500	0	0- -	-	3.34	3.73
2014 3 Tms	Low	23	22	0	1	99.2	428	94	58	49	11	3	2	7	43	0	100	8	1	4	4	.500	0	0- -	-	4.30	4.42
2015 Akron	AA	27	26	0	1	158.0	639	127	53	48	8	4	6	9	40	0	145	11	1	9	8	.529	0	0- -	-	2.40	2.73
2016 Clmbs	AAA	17	17	1	0	93.0	380	78	32	31	8	0	3	1	35	0	97	8	0	11	1	.917	0	0- -	-	3.12	3.00
2016 Cle	AL	17	10	0	3	53.0	233	50	31	31	8	0	1	0	29	0	50	2	0	3	3	.500	0	0-0	0	4.72	5.26

Tyler Clippard

Pitches: R Bats: R Pos: RP-69   Ht: 6'3" Wt: 200 Born: 2/14/1985 Age: 32

Year Team	Lg	G	GS	CG	GF	IP	BFP	H	R	ER	HR	SH	SF	HB	TBB	IBB	SO	WP	Bk	W	L	Pct	Sh	Sv-Op	Hld	ERC	ERA
2007 NYY	AL	6	6	0	0	27.0	124	29	19	19	6	0	0	0	17	1	18	2	1	3	1	.750	0	0-0	0	6.37	6.33
2008 Was	NL	2	2	0	0	10.1	48	12	5	5	2	0	0	0	7	1	8	1	0	1	1	.500	0	0-0	0	6.90	4.35
2009 Was	NL	41	0	0	8	60.1	246	36	20	18	9	3	1	1	32	1	67	1	1	4	2	.667	0	0-1	3	2.79	2.69
2010 Was	NL	78	0	0	18	91.0	378	69	33	31	8	3	7	2	41	4	112	1	1	11	8	.579	0	1-11	23	2.91	3.07
2011 Was	NL	72	0	0	8	88.1	329	48	18	18	11	4	3	0	26	2	104	1	0	3	0	1.000	0	0-7	38	1.61	1.83
2012 Was	NL	74	0	0	42	72.2	307	55	32	30	7	3	4	2	29	2	84	5	0	2	6	.250	0	32-37	13	2.73	3.72
2013 Was	NL	72	0	0	6	71.0	275	37	19	19	9	2	1	4	24	1	73	2	0	6	3	.667	0	0-3	33	1.79	2.41
2014 Was	NL	75	0	0	6	70.1	278	47	22	17	5	2	1	1	23	1	82	0	0	7	4	.636	0	1-7	40	1.98	2.18
2015 2 Tms		69	0	0	36	71.0	301	49	25	23	8	1	2	4	31	2	64	6	0	5	4	.556	0	19-25	8	2.72	2.92
2016 2 Tms		69	0	0	17	63.0	262	54	27	25	10	1	0	1	26	2	72	5	3	4	6	.400	0	3-6	25	3.80	3.57
15 Oak	AL	37	0	0	30	38.2	167	25	12	12	3	0	1	2	21	1	38	1	0	1	3	.250	0	17-21	0	2.62	2.79
15 NYM	NL	32	0	0	6	32.1	134	24	13	11	5	1	1	2	10	1	26	5	0	4	1	.800	0	2-4	8	2.82	3.06
16 Ari	NL	40	0	0	10	37.2	155	34	18	18	7	1	0	0	15	0	46	1	3	2	3	.400	0	1-3	13	4.23	4.30
16 NYY	AL	29	0	0	7	25.1	107	20	9	7	3	0	0	1	11	2	26	4	0	2	3	.400	0	2-3	12	3.19	2.49
Postseason		14	0	0	1	12.2	53	9	6	6	2	1	0	0	5	0	11	1	0	0	1	.000	0	0-0	8	2.77	4.26
10 ML YEARS		558	8	0	141	625.0	2548	436	220	205	75	19	20	15	256	17	684	24	6	46	35	.568	0	56-97	183	2.69	2.95

Jason Coats

Bats: R Throws: R Pos: RF-11;LF-7;PH-7;DH-5;PR-3   Ht: 6'2" Wt: 200 Born: 2/24/1990 Age: 27

Year Team	Lg	G	AB	H	2B	3B	HR	(Hm	Rd)	TB	R	RBI	RC	TBB	IBB	SO	HBP	SH	SF	SB	CS	GDP	Avg	OBP	Slg	OPS
2013 Knapol	A	133	516	140	38	3	12	(-	-)	220	63	84	74	31	0	85	8	4	4	12	3	18	.271	.320	.426	.747
2014 WinSa	A+	115	429	125	35	2	15	(-	-)	209	64	72	75	35	2	65	6	2	4	5	2	10	.291	.350	.487	.837
2014 Brham	AA	19	68	18	3	1	0	(-	-)	23	5	9	7	3	0	9	1	2	3	1	1	4	.265	.293	.338	.632
2015 Brham	AA	12	47	16	9	0	0	(-	-)	25	6	2	7	1	0	6	0	0	0	0	2	1	.340	.354	.532	.886
2015 Charllt	AAA	122	489	132	29	1	17	(-	-)	214	56	81	70	29	1	93	4	3	5	11	2	16	.270	.313	.438	.751
2016 Charllt	AAA	78	297	98	22	2	10	(-	-)	154	44	38	59	25	0	69	7	2	1	1	3	8	.330	.394	.519	.912
2016 CWS	AL	28	50	10	4	0	1	(0	1)	17	8	4	5	5	0	12	2	1	0	1	0	1	.200	.298	.340	.638

Alex Cobb

Pitches: R Bats: R Pos: SP-5   Ht: 6'3" Wt: 205 Born: 10/7/1987 Age: 29

Year Team	Lg	G	GS	CG	GF	IP	BFP	H	R	ER	HR	SH	SF	HB	TBB	IBB	SO	WP	Bk	W	L	Pct	Sh	Sv-Op	Hld	ERC	ERA
2011 TB	AL	9	9	0	0	52.2	224	49	21	20	3	0	1	1	21	1	37	2	0	3	2	.600	0	0-0	0	3.44	3.42
2012 TB	AL	23	23	2	0	136.1	569	130	67	61	11	3	6	9	40	2	106	8	1	11	9	.550	1	0-0	0	3.56	4.03
2013 TB	AL	22	22	1	0	143.1	578	120	46	44	13	1	2	3	45	4	134	5	1	11	3	.786	0	0-0	0	2.92	2.76
2014 TB	AL	27	27	0	0	166.1	681	142	56	53	11	4	4	10	47	1	149	8	0	10	9	.526	0	0-0	0	2.87	2.87
2016 TB	AL	5	5	0	0	22.0	104	32	22	21	5	1	1	0	7	0	16	0	0	1	2	.333	0	0-0	0	7.40	8.59
Postseason		2	2	0	0	11.2	51	13	3	2	0	0	0	1	3	0	10	1	0	1	0	1.000	0	0-0	0	3.75	1.54
5 ML YEARS		86	86	3	0	520.2	2156	473	212	199	43	9	14	23	160	8	442	23	2	36	25	.590	1	0-0	0	3.29	3.44

Chris Coghlan

KAHG-lin

Bats: L Throws: R Pos: LF-29;2B-20;PH-20;3B-18;RF-18;1B-6;DH-2   Ht: 6'0" Wt: 195 Born: 6/18/1985 Age: 32

Year Team	Lg	G	AB	H	2B	3B	HR	(Hm	Rd)	TB	R	RBI	RC	TBB	IBB	SO	HBP	SH	SF	SB	CS	GDP	Avg	OBP	Slg	OPS
2009 Fla	NL	128	504	162	31	6	9	(5	4)	232	84	47	91	53	2	77	4	3	1	8	5	3	.321	.390	.460	.850
2010 Fla	NL	91	358	96	20	3	5	(5	0)	137	60	28	43	33	1	84	4	3	2	10	3	3	.268	.335	.383	.718
2011 Fla	NL	65	269	62	20	1	5	(4	1)	99	33	22	23	22	3	49	4	1	2	7	6	3	.230	.296	.368	.664
2012 Mia	NL	39	93	13	1	0	1	(1	0)	17	10	10	2	9	1	12	0	1	2	0	2	4	.140	.212	.183	.394
2013 Mia	NL	70	195	50	10	3	1	(0	1)	69	10	10	20	17	1	43	1	0	1	2	0	2	.256	.318	.354	.672
2014 ChC	NL	125	385	109	28	5	9	(5	4)	174	50	41	59	39	2	81	3	3	2	7	4	5	.283	.352	.452	.804
2015 ChC	NL	148	440	110	25	6	16	(6	10)	195	64	41	63	58	6	94	3	1	1	11	2	8	.250	.341	.443	.784
2016 2 Tms		99	261	49	12	2	6	(1	5)	83	35	30	30	35	3	73	3	0	1	2	1	4	.188	.296	.318	.608
16 Oak	AL	51	158	23	5	0	5	(0	5)	43	14	14	10	13	1	47	1	0	0	1	1	2	.146	.215	.272	.487
16 ChC	NL	48	103	26	7	2	1	(1	0)	40	21	16	20	22	2	26	2	0	1	1	0	2	.252	.391	.388	.779
Postseason		6	12	1	0	0	0	(0	0)	1	1	0	0	0	0	4	0	0	0	0	0	0	.083	.083	.083	.167
8 ML YEARS		765	2505	651	147	26	52	(27	25)	1006	346	229	331	266	19	513	22	12	12	47	23	32	.260	.335	.402	.736

Phil Coke

Pitches: L Bats: L Pos: RP-6 Ht: 6'1" Wt: 210 Born: 7/19/1982 Age: 34

Year	Team	Lg	G	GS	CG	GF	IP	BFP	H	R	ER	HR	SH	SF	HB	TBB	IBB	SO	WP	Bk	W	L	Pct	Sh	Sv-Op	Hld	ERC	ERA
2016	S-WB*	AAA	20	11	0	3	70.0	298	68	29	23	3	1	4	2	21	2	61	3	0	5	3	.625	0	0- -	-	3.17	2.96
2008	NYY	AL	12	0	0	0	14.2	52	8	1	1	0	0	0	0	2	0	14	1	0	1	0	1.000	0	0-0	5	0.89	0.61
2009	NYY	AL	72	0	0	13	60.0	238	44	34	30	10	1	5	1	20	4	49	7	0	4	3	.571	0	2-7	21	2.84	4.50
2010	Det	AL	74	1	0	18	64.2	279	67	29	27	2	2	3	4	26	4	53	3	0	7	5	.583	0	2-4	17	4.00	3.76
2011	Det	AL	48	14	0	6	108.2	474	118	64	54	5	4	3	4	40	5	69	4	0	3	9	.250	0	1-2	8	4.13	4.47
2012	Det	AL	66	0	0	11	54.0	245	71	28	24	5	5	2	1	18	4	51	3	0	2	3	.400	0	1-3	5	5.56	4.00
2013	Det	AL	49	0	0	14	38.1	177	43	24	23	3	4	4	0	21	7	30	1	0	0	5	.000	0	1-3	20	4.81	5.40
2014	Det	AL	62	0	0	24	58.0	257	69	28	25	5	1	2	2	20	2	41	1	0	5	2	.714	0	1-2	5	4.96	3.88
2015	2 Tms		18	0	0	3	12.2	56	15	8	8	2	0	1	0	5	2	12	0	0	0	0	-	0	0-0	3	5.36	5.68
2016	2 Tms		6	0	0	3	10.0	45	10	5	4	1	0	0	1	7	1	4	0	0	0	0	-	0	0-0	0	5.75	3.60
15	ChC	NL	16	0	0	2	10.0	45	14	7	7	1	0	1	0	3	2	9	0	0	0	0	-	0	0-0	3	5.78	6.30
15	Tor	AL	2	0	0	1	2.2	11	1	1	1	1	0	0	0	2	0	3	0	0	0	0	-	0	0-0	0	3.75	3.38
16	NYY	AL	3	0	0	2	6.0	29	7	5	4	1	0	0	1	4	0	1	0	0	0	0	-	0	0-0	0	7.55	6.00
16	Pit		3	0	0	1	4.0	16	3	0	0	0	0	0	0	3	1	3	0	0	0	0	-	0	0-0	0	3.21	0.00
	Postseason		26	0	0	10	19.0	79	18	9	9	2	1	0	0	6	0	19	1	0	0	1	.000	0	3-3		3.52	4.26
	9 ML YEARS		407	15	0	92	421.0	1823	445	221	196	33	17	20	13	159	29	323	20	0	22	27	.449	0	8-21	83	4.20	4.19

Chris Colabello

Bats: R Throws: R Pos: 1B-8;PH-2;LF-1 cahl-uh-BELL-oh Ht: 6'4" Wt: 210 Born: 10/24/1983 Age: 33

Year	Team	Lg	G	AB	H	2B	3B	HR	(Hm	Rd)	TB	R	RBI	RC	TBB	IBB	SO	HBP	SH	SF	SB	CS	GDP	Avg	OBP	Slg	OPS
2016	Buffalo*	AAA	40	139	25	0	0	5	(-	-)	40	14	11	9	11	1	46	2	0	1	0	0	12	.180	.248	.288	.536
2013	Min	AL	55	160	31	3	0	7	(1	6)	55	14	17	13	20	0	58	1	0	0	0	1	5	.194	.287	.344	.631
2014	Min	AL	59	205	47	13	0	6	(2	4)	78	17	39	21	14	1	66	1	0	0	0	2	2	.229	.282	.380	.662
2015	Tor	AL	101	333	107	19	1	15	(7	8)	173	55	54	62	22	0	96	3	0	2	2	0	12	.321	.367	.520	.886
2016	Tor	AL	10	29	2	0	0	0	(0	0)	2	0	1	0	2	0	9	1	0	0	0	0	2	.069	.156	.069	.225
	Postseason		10	39	11	3	0	2	(1	1)	20	5	3	2	2	0	9	0	0	0	0	0	3	.282	.317	.513	.830
	4 ML YEARS		225	727	187	35	1	28	(10	18)	308	86	111	96	58	1	229	6	0	2	2	3	21	.257	.317	.424	.740

A.J. Cole

Pitches: R Bats: R Pos: SP-8 Ht: 6'5" Wt: 215 Born: 1/5/1992 Age: 25

Year	Team	Lg	G	GS	CG	GF	IP	BFP	H	R	ER	HR	SH	SF	HB	TBB	IBB	SO	WP	Bk	W	L	Pct	Sh	Sv-Op	Hld	ERC	ERA
2012	2 Tms	Low	27	27	0	0	133.2	558	138	72	55	14	4	2	7	29	0	133	5	2	6	10	.375	0	0- -	-	3.82	3.70
2013	Ptomc	A+	18	18	0	0	97.1	406	96	50	46	12	0	6	4	23	0	102	6	1	6	3	.667	0	0- -	-	3.69	4.25
2013	Hrsbrg	AA	7	7	0	0	45.1	175	31	13	11	3	0	0	0	10	1	49	1	0	4	2	.667	0	0- -	-	1.64	2.18
2014	Hrsbrg	AA	14	14	1	0	71.0	308	79	30	23	1	0	1	3	15	1	61	3	0	6	3	.667	1	0- -	-	3.44	2.92
2014	Syrcse	AAA	11	11	0	0	63.0	267	69	30	24	9	2	3	1	17	0	50	2	0	7	0	1.000	0	0- -	-	4.52	3.43
2015	Syrcse	AAA	21	19	0	0	105.2	443	91	40	37	9	1	3	4	34	1	76	2	0	5	6	.455	0	0- -	-	3.02	3.15
2016	Syrcse	AAA	22	22	2	0	124.2	532	131	64	59	16	2	1	1	35	1	109	9	0	8	8	.500	0	0- -	-	4.09	4.26
2015	Was	NL	3	1	0	1	9.1	44	14	11	6	1	1	1	0	1	1	9	1	0	0	0	-	0	1-1	0	5.38	5.79
2016	Was	NL	8	8	0	0	38.1	168	37	24	22	7	0	3	2	14	1	39	1	0	1	2	.333	0	0-0	0	4.39	5.17
	2 ML YEARS		11	9	0	1	47.2	212	51	35	28	8	1	4	2	15	2	48	2	0	1	2	.333	0	1-1	0	4.58	5.29

Gerrit Cole

Pitches: R Bats: R Pos: SP-21 Ht: 6'4" Wt: 230 Born: 9/8/1990 Age: 26

Year	Team	Lg	G	GS	CG	GF	IP	BFP	H	R	ER	HR	SH	SF	HB	TBB	IBB	SO	WP	Bk	W	L	Pct	Sh	Sv-Op	Hld	ERC	ERA
2013	Pit	NL	19	19	0	0	117.1	469	109	43	42	7	5	2	3	28	0	100	4	0	10	7	.588	0	0-0	0	3.02	3.22
2014	Pit	NL	22	22	0	0	138.0	571	127	58	56	11	10	0	9	40	1	138	9	1	11	5	.688	0	0-0	0	3.37	3.65
2015	Pit	NL	32	32	0	0	208.0	832	183	71	60	11	7	6	10	44	1	202	7	0	19	8	.704	0	0-0	0	2.66	2.60
2016	Pit	NL	21	21	1	0	116.0	506	131	57	50	7	4	6	6	36	3	98	5	1	7	10	.412	0	0-0	0	4.35	3.88
	Postseason		3	3	0	0	16.0	61	11	7	7	4	0	0	0	3	0	14	0	0	1	2	.333	0	0-0	0	2.50	3.94
	4 ML YEARS		94	94	1	0	579.1	2378	550	229	208	36	26	14	28	148	5	538	25	2	47	30	.610	0	0-0	0	3.22	3.23

Louis Coleman

Pitches: R Bats: R Pos: RP-61 Ht: 6'4" Wt: 205 Born: 4/4/1986 Age: 31

Year	Team	Lg	G	GS	CG	GF	IP	BFP	H	R	ER	HR	SH	SF	HB	TBB	IBB	SO	WP	Bk	W	L	Pct	Sh	Sv-Op	Hld	ERC	ERA
2011	KC	AL	48	0	0	11	59.2	244	44	20	19	6	1	1	3	26	6	64	4	0	1	4	.200	0	1-2	11	3.23	2.87
2012	KC	AL	42	0	0	18	51.0	217	41	23	21	10	3	0	1	26	3	65	1	0	0	0	-	0	0-0	2	4.07	3.71
2013	KC	AL	27	0	0	8	29.2	110	19	2	2	1	1	0	1	6	1	32	1	0	3	0	1.000	0	0-0	4	1.45	0.61
2014	KC	AL	31	0	0	10	34.0	154	39	21	21	6	0	1	1	18	1	24	3	0	1	0	1.000	0	1-1	1	6.25	5.56
2015	KC	AL	4	0	0	2	3.0	11	1	0	0	0	0	0	0	2	0	1	0	0	1	0	1.000	0	0-0	0	1.37	0.00
2016	LAD	NL	61	0	0	11	48.0	211	45	27	25	5	2	2	3	24	2	45	3	0	2	1	.667	0	0-2	10	4.33	4.69
	6 ML YEARS		213	0	0	60	225.1	947	189	93	88	31	7	4	9	102	13	231	12	0	8	5	.615	0	2-5	28	3.76	3.51

Tyler Collins

Bats: L **Throws:** L **Pos:** CF-29;LF-13;PH-12;RF-8;PR-2;DH-1 **Ht:** 5'11" **Wt:** 215 **Born:** 6/6/1990 **Age:** 27

Year	Team	Lg	G	AB	H	2B	3B	HR	(Hm	Rd)	TB	R	RBI	RC	TBB	IBB	SO	HBP	SH	SF	SB	CS	GDP	Avg	OBP	Slg	OPS
2016	Toledo*	AAA	68	257	55	7	0	7	(-	-)	83	29	30	23	20	0	69	2	0	2	4	1	10	.214	.274	.323	.597
2014	Det	AL	18	24	6	0	0	1	(0	1)	9	3	4	3	1	0	4	0	0	0	0	0	1	.250	.280	.375	.655
2015	Det	AL	60	192	51	11	3	4	(2	2)	80	18	25	27	13	0	43	1	1	0	2	1	2	.266	.316	.417	.732
2016	Det	AL	56	136	32	2	3	4	(2	2)	52	14	15	19	13	0	38	1	0	1	1	1	1	.235	.305	.382	.687
	3 ML YEARS		134	352	89	13	6	9	(4	5)	141	35	44	49	27	0	85	2	1	1	3	2	4	.253	.309	.401	.709

Josh Collmenter

Pitches: R **Bats:** R **Pos:** RP-15; SP-3   COLE-men-ter   **Ht:** 6'3" **Wt:** 240 **Born:** 2/7/1986 **Age:** 31

Year	Team	Lg	G	GS	CG	GF	IP	BFP	H	R	ER	HR	SH	SF	HB	TBB	IBB	SO	WP	Bk	W	L	Pct	Sh	Sv-Op	Hld	ERC	ERA
2011	Ari	NL	31	24	0	3	154.1	621	137	61	58	17	9	2	5	28	2	100	1	1	10	10	.500	0	0-0	0	2.82	3.38
2012	Ari	NL	28	11	0	7	90.1	375	92	39	37	13	5	0	0	22	2	80	1	0	5	3	.625	0	0-0	0	3.85	3.69
2013	Ari	NL	49	0	0	10	92.0	384	79	34	32	8	8	0	2	33	8	85	3	0	5	5	.500	0	0-1	5	3.01	3.13
2014	Ari	NL	33	28	1	2	179.1	719	163	75	69	18	8	5	4	39	2	115	2	0	11	9	.550	1	1-1	0	3.02	3.46
2015	Ari	NL	44	12	1	19	121.0	499	129	53	51	18	2	6	1	24	2	63	1	0	4	6	.400	1	1-1	1	4.05	3.79
2016	2 Tms	NL	18	3	0	10	41.1	173	36	17	17	7	3	0	3	16	1	33	0	0	3	0	1.000	0	0-0	0	4.11	3.70
16	Ari	NL	15	0	0	10	22.1	97	21	12	12	4	1	0	2	11	1	17	0	0	1	0	1.000	0	0-0	0	5.08	4.84
16	Atl	NL	3	3	0	0	19.0	76	15	5	5	3	2	0	1	5	0	16	0	0	2	0	1.000	0	0-0	0	3.03	2.37
	Postseason		1	1	0	0	7.0	26	2	1	1	1	0	0	1	2	0	6	0	0	1	0	1.000	0	0-0	0	1.18	1.29
	6 ML YEARS		203	78	2	51	678.1	2771	636	279	264	81	35	13	15	162	17	476	8	1	38	33	.535	2	2-3	6	3.32	3.50

Alex Colome

Pitches: R **Bats:** R **Pos:** RP-57   COHL-oh-may   **Ht:** 6'2" **Wt:** 220 **Born:** 12/31/1988 **Age:** 28

Year	Team	Lg	G	GS	CG	GF	IP	BFP	H	R	ER	HR	SH	SF	HB	TBB	IBB	SO	WP	Bk	W	L	Pct	Sh	Sv-Op	Hld	ERC	ERA
2013	TB	AL	3	3	0	0	16.0	71	14	8	4	2	0	0	1	9	0	12	1	0	1	1	.500	0	0-0	0	4.41	2.25
2014	TB	AL	5	3	0	1	23.2	97	19	7	7	1	0	1	0	10	0	13	3	0	2	0	1.000	0	0-0	0	2.77	2.66
2015	TB	AL	43	13	0	5	109.2	457	112	50	48	9	2	7	4	31	4	88	0	0	8	5	.615	0	0-5	8	3.78	3.94
2016	TB	AL	57	0	0	48	56.2	226	43	12	12	6	0	0	2	15	1	71	1	0	2	4	.333	0	37-40	1	2.46	1.91
	4 ML YEARS		108	19	0	54	206.0	851	188	77	71	18	2	8	7	65	5	184	13	0	13	10	.565	0	37-45	9	3.33	3.10

Bartolo Colon

Pitches: R **Bats:** R **Pos:** SP-33; RP-1   co-LONE   **Ht:** 5'11" **Wt:** 285 **Born:** 5/24/1973 **Age:** 44

Year	Team	Lg	G	GS	CG	GF	IP	BFP	H	R	ER	HR	SH	SF	HB	TBB	IBB	SO	WP	Bk	W	L	Pct	Sh	Sv-Op	Hld	ERC	ERA
1997	Cle	AL	19	17	1	0	94.0	427	107	66	59	12	4	1	3	45	1	66	5	0	4	7	.364	0	0-0	0	5.53	5.65
1998	Cle	AL	31	31	6	0	204.0	883	205	91	84	15	10	2	3	79	5	158	4	0	14	9	.609	2	0-0	0	3.87	3.71
1999	Cle	AL	32	32	1	0	205.0	858	185	97	90	24	5	4	7	76	5	161	4	0	18	5	.783	1	0-0	0	3.68	3.95
2000	Cle	AL	30	30	2	0	188.0	807	163	86	81	21	2	3	4	98	4	212	4	0	15	8	.652	1	0-0	0	3.97	3.88
2001	Cle	AL	34	34	1	0	222.1	947	220	106	101	26	8	4	2	90	2	201	4	1	14	12	.538	0	0-0	0	4.24	4.09
2002	2 Tms		33	33	8	0	233.1	966	219	85	76	20	19	6	2	70	5	149	4	0	20	8	.714	3	0-0	0	3.29	2.93
2003	CWS	AL	34	34	9	0	242.0	984	223	107	104	30	5	8	5	67	3	173	8	3	15	13	.536	0	0-0	0	3.47	3.87
2004	LAA	AL	34	34	0	0	208.1	897	215	122	116	38	5	8	3	71	1	158	1	0	18	12	.600	0	0-0	0	4.64	5.01
2005	LAA	AL	33	33	2	0	222.2	906	215	93	86	26	9	4	3	43	0	157	2	1	21	8	.724	0	0-0	0	3.28	3.48
2006	LAA	AL	10	10	1	0	56.1	251	71	39	32	11	4	1	3	11	0	31	1	0	1	5	.167	0	0-0	0	5.61	5.11
2007	LAA	AL	19	18	0	0	99.1	453	132	74	70	15	4	3	5	29	1	76	1	0	6	8	.429	0	0-0	1	6.17	6.34
2008	Bos	AL	7	7	0	0	39.0	173	44	23	17	5	3	2	2	10	0	27	0	0	4	2	.667	0	0-0	0	4.53	3.92
2009	CWS	AL	12	12	0	0	62.1	276	69	42	29	13	4	3	2	21	3	38	1	0	3	6	.333	0	0-0	0	5.22	4.19
2011	NYY	AL	29	26	1	0	164.1	694	172	85	73	21	2	6	3	40	3	135	0	0	8	10	.444	1	0-0	0	3.95	4.00
2012	Oak	AL	24	24	0	0	152.1	636	161	62	58	17	3	4	1	23	3	91	0	0	10	9	.526	0	0-0	0	3.45	3.43
2013	Oak	AL	30	30	3	0	190.1	769	193	60	56	14	3	6	0	29	0	117	1	0	18	6	.750	3	0-0	0	3.07	2.65
2014	NYM	NL	31	31	0	0	202.1	846	218	97	92	22	8	4	5	30	3	151	2	0	15	13	.536	0	0-0	0	3.63	4.09
2015	NYM	NL	33	31	1	1	194.2	815	217	94	90	25	9	7	4	24	5	136	0	0	14	13	.519	1	0-0	0	3.84	4.16
2016	NYM	NL	34	33	0	0	191.2	791	200	81	73	24	7	4	3	32	2	128	0	0	15	8	.652	0	0-0	0	3.63	3.43
02	Cle	AL	16	16	4	0	116.1	467	104	37	33	11	6	3	2	31	1	75	3	0	10	4	.714	2	0-0	0	3.09	2.55
02	Mon	NL	17	17	4	0	117.0	499	115	48	43	9	13	3	0	39	4	74	1	0	10	4	.714	1	0-0	0	3.48	3.31
	Postseason		17	10	1	2	67.0	278	66	27	26	6	2	2	2	26	4	52	0	0	3	5	.375	0	0-1	1	4.06	3.49
	19 ML YEARS		509	500	36	1	3172.1	13379	3229	1510	1387	379	114	80	60	888	46	2365	42	5	233	162	.590	13	0-0	1	3.90	3.93

Christian Colon

co-LONE

Bats: R **Throws:** R **Pos:** 2B-32;3B-15;PH-8;SS-4;DH-1;PR-1 **Ht:** 5'10" **Wt:** 185 **Born:** 5/14/1989 **Age:** 28

Year	Team	Lg	G	AB	H	2B	3B	HR	(Hm	Rd)	TB	R	RBI	RC	TBB	IBB	SO	HBP	SH	SF	SB	CS	GDP	Avg	OBP	Slg	OPS
2016	Omha*	AAA	19	77	21	5	0	1	(-	-)	29	9	5	10	6	0	11	1	1	0	2	0	5	.273	.333	.377	.710
2014	KC	AL	21	45	15	5	1	0	(0	0)	22	8	6	9	3	0	4	0	1	0	2	0	1	.333	.375	.489	.864
2015	KC	AL	43	107	31	5	0	0	(0	0)	36	8	6	12	11	0	17	0	1	0	3	2	2	.290	.356	.336	.692
2016	KC	AL	54	147	34	6	0	1	(1	0)	43	13	13	13	11	0	31	2	1	0	0	1	4	.231	.294	.293	.586
	Postseason		3	2	2	0	0	0	(0	0)	2	2	2	2	0	0	0	0	1	0	1	0	0	1.000	1.000	1.000	2.000
	3 ML YEARS		118	299	80	16	1	1	(1	0)	101	29	25	34	25	0	52	2	3	0	5	3	7	.268	.328	.338	.666

Joseph Colon

Pitches: R **Bats:** R **Pos:** RP-11   co-LONE   **Ht:** 6'0" **Wt:** 180 **Born:** 2/18/1990 **Age:** 27

			HOW MUCH HE PITCHED						WHAT HE GAVE UP												THE RESULTS							
Year	Team	Lg	G	GS	CG	GF	IP	BFP	H	R	ER	HR	SH	SF	HB	TBB	IBB	SO	WP	Bk	W	L	Pct	Sh	Sv-Op	Hld	ERC	ERA
2012	2 Tms	Low	22	22	0	0	126.0	520	121	61	48	9	5	4	4	39	0	83	5	0	9	10	.474	0	0--	-	3.52	3.43
2013	2 Tms	Low	17	17	0	0	92.0	379	83	41	33	2	0	0	5	27	0	76	3	2	5	4	.556	0	0--	-	2.87	3.23
2014	Akron	AA	25	25	1	0	138.0	579	132	56	52	8	2	1	6	55	0	96	5	2	8	7	.533	1	0--	-	3.81	3.39
2015	Akron	AA	21	1	0	5	31.1	132	28	11	11	1	1	0	0	11	0	23	1	0	2	0	1.000	0	0--	-	2.82	3.16
2015	Clmbs	AAA	12	0	0	2	17.1	73	19	6	6	2	1	0	0	3	0	24	4	0	1	0	1.000	0	0--	-	3.79	3.12
2016	Clmbs	AAA	20	0	0	5	22.0	85	8	4	2	0	0	2	1	12	0	21	1	0	0	1	.000	0	0--	-	1.23	0.82
2016	Cle	AL	11	0	0	5	10.0	50	12	9	8	2	0	0	0	7	1	10	1	1	1	3	.250	0	0-0	0	6.84	7.20

Gerardo Concepcion

Pitches: L **Bats:** L **Pos:** RP-3   heh-RAHR-doh kohn-sepp-SYOHN   **Ht:** 6'2" **Wt:** 200 **Born:** 2/29/1992 **Age:** 25

			HOW MUCH HE PITCHED						WHAT HE GAVE UP												THE RESULTS							
Year	Team	Lg	G	GS	CG	GF	IP	BFP	H	R	ER	HR	SH	SF	HB	TBB	IBB	SO	WP	Bk	W	L	Pct	Sh	Sv-Op	Hld	ERC	ERA
2012	Peoria	A	12	12	0	0	52.1	251	70	52	43	6	3	3	2	30	0	28	3	4	2	6	.250	0	0--	-	7.18	7.39
2014	3 Tms	Low	29	0	0	9	59.2	251	47	23	22	1	6	2	6	23	0	55	5	1	4	2	.667	0	1--	-	2.69	3.32
2015	MrtlBh	A+	7	0	0	3	12.2	55	9	6	5	0	2	1	0	8	0	14	1	0	0	2	.000	0	1--	-	2.63	3.55
2015	Tenn	AA	31	0	0	14	31.2	167	45	30	29	4	1	2	0	29	0	25	2	0	0	1	.000	0	0--	-	9.05	8.24
2016	Tenn	AA	10	0	0	1	17.2	62	5	0	0	0	0	2	4	1	1	17	1	0	1	0	1.000	0	0--	-	0.57	0.00
2016	Iowa	AAA	32	0	0	10	42.0	202	57	36	34	6	2	1	2	24	1	35	3	0	2	4	.333	0	1--	-	7.57	7.29
2016	ChC	NL	3	0	0	1	2.1	10	2	1	1	0	0	1	0	1	0	2	0	0	0	0	-	0	0-0	0	2.67	3.86

Michael Conforto

Bats: L **Throws:** R **Pos:** LF-73;PH-23;RF-9;CF-6;DH-4   **Ht:** 6'1" **Wt:** 215 **Born:** 3/1/1993 **Age:** 24

			BATTING																		RUNNING			AVERAGES			
Year	Team	Lg	G	AB	H	2B	3B	HR	(Hm	Rd)	TB	R	RBI	RC	TBB	IBB	SO	HBP	SH	SF	SB	CS	GDP	Avg	OBP	Slg	OPS
2014	Bklyn	A-	42	163	54	10	0	3	(-	-)	73	30	19	31	16	0	29	5	0	2	3	0	8	.331	.403	.448	.851
2015	Stluci	A+	46	184	52	12	0	7	(-	-)	85	25	28	30	17	6	26	3	0	2	0	1	8	.283	.350	.462	.811
2015	Bnghtn	AA	45	173	54	12	3	5	(-	-)	87	21	26	34	23	1	35	1	0	0	1	0	2	.312	.396	.503	.899
2016	LsVgs	AAA	33	128	54	8	2	9	(-	-)	93	30	28	39	13	0	18	2	0	0	2	2	3	.422	.483	.727	1.209
2015	NYM	NL	56	174	47	14	0	9	(4	5)	88	30	26	29	17	0	39	1	0	2	0	1	4	.270	.335	.506	.841
2016	NYM	NL	109	304	67	21	1	12	(7	5)	126	38	42	35	36	2	89	5	0	3	2	1	6	.220	.310	.414	.725
	Postseason		12	30	6	0	0	3	(2	1)	15	3	6	5	1	0	8	1	0	2	0	0	0	.200	.235	.500	.735
	2 ML YEARS		165	478	114	35	1	21	(11	10)	214	68	68	64	53	2	128	6	0	5	2	2	10	.238	.319	.448	.767

Hank Conger

Bats: B **Throws:** R **Pos:** C-47;PH-6   KONG-gerr   **Ht:** 6'2" **Wt:** 220 **Born:** 1/29/1988 **Age:** 29

			BATTING																		RUNNING			AVERAGES			
Year	Team	Lg	G	AB	H	2B	3B	HR	(Hm	Rd)	TB	R	RBI	RC	TBB	IBB	SO	HBP	SH	SF	SB	CS	GDP	Avg	OBP	Slg	OPS
2016	Drham*	AAA	30	109	18	4	1	3	(-	-)	33	7	11	6	4	0	24	1	1	1	0	0	3	.165	.200	.303	.503
2010	LAA	AL	13	29	5	1	1	0	(0	0)	8	2	5	3	5	0	9	0	0	0	0	0	1	.172	.294	.276	.570
2011	LAA	AL	59	177	37	8	0	6	(2	4)	63	14	19	18	17	2	37	1	2	0	0	0	2	.209	.282	.356	.638
2012	LAA	AL	7	18	3	0	0	0	(0	0)	3	0	1	1	1	0	0	1	1	1	0	0	1	.167	.238	.167	.405
2013	LAA	AL	92	233	58	13	1	7	(3	4)	94	23	21	24	17	2	61	4	0	1	0	0	6	.249	.310	.403	.713
2014	LAA	AL	80	231	51	12	0	4	(3	1)	75	24	25	25	22	0	57	2	4	1	0	2	6	.221	.293	.325	.618
2015	Hou	AL	73	201	46	11	0	11	(8	3)	90	25	33	26	23	0	63	2	1	2	0	1	6	.229	.311	.448	.759
2016	TB	AL	49	124	24	5	0	3	(1	2)	38	6	10	6	12	0	40	0	1	0	0	0	4	.194	.265	.306	.571
	Postseason		2	1	0	0	0	0	(0	0)	0	0	0	0	0	0	1	0	0	0	0	0	0	.000	.000	.000	.000
	7 ML YEARS		373	1013	224	50	2	31	(17	14)	371	94	114	103	97	4	267	10	9	5	0	4	26	.221	.294	.366	.660

Adam Conley

Pitches: L **Bats:** L **Pos:** SP-25   **Ht:** 6'3" **Wt:** 200 **Born:** 5/24/1990 **Age:** 27

			HOW MUCH HE PITCHED						WHAT HE GAVE UP												THE RESULTS							
Year	Team	Lg	G	GS	CG	GF	IP	BFP	H	R	ER	HR	SH	SF	HB	TBB	IBB	SO	WP	Bk	W	L	Pct	Sh	Sv-Op	Hld	ERC	ERA
2012	2 Tms	Low	26	26	0	0	127.0	534	117	59	49	4	1	6	3	43	0	135	8	1	11	5	.688	0	0--	-	3.04	3.47
2013	Jaxnvl	AA	26	25	3	0	138.2	581	125	61	50	7	4	2	7	37	0	129	1	0	11	7	.611	1	0--	-	2.86	3.25
2014	NewOr	AAA	12	11	0	1	60.0	266	65	41	40	3	3	1	3	26	0	48	1	0	3	5	.375	0	0--	-	4.54	6.00
2015	NewOr	AAA	19	18	1	0	107.0	436	85	34	30	4	2	1	5	40	1	81	1	0	9	3	.750	1	0--	-	2.68	2.52
2015	Mia	NL	15	11	0	0	67.0	281	65	28	28	7	1	4	3	21	1	59	0	0	4	1	.800	0	0-0	0	3.80	3.76
2016	Mia	NL	25	25	0	0	133.1	584	125	59	57	13	7	3	11	62	7	124	9	0	8	6	.571	0	0-0	0	4.21	3.85
	2 ML YEARS		40	36	0	1	200.1	865	190	87	85	20	8	7	14	83	8	183	9	0	12	7	.632	0	0-0	0	4.07	3.82

Willson Contreras

Bats: R **Throws:** R **Pos:** C-57;LF-24;PH-5;1B-3   **Ht:** 6'1" **Wt:** 210 **Born:** 5/13/1992 **Age:** 25

			BATTING																		RUNNING			AVERAGES			
Year	Team	Lg	G	AB	H	2B	3B	HR	(Hm	Rd)	TB	R	RBI	RC	TBB	IBB	SO	HBP	SH	SF	SB	CS	GDP	Avg	OBP	Slg	OPS
2012	Boise	A-	64	249	68	10	1	3	(-	-)	89	32	39	28	11	1	54	5	0	1	3	2	7	.273	.316	.357	.673
2013	Kane	A	86	310	77	11	5	11	(-	-)	131	46	46	44	26	0	66	7	1	1	8	3	11	.248	.320	.423	.742
2014	Dytona	A+	80	281	68	14	2	5	(-	-)	101	40	37	33	28	0	66	5	1	2	5	5	6	.242	.320	.359	.679
2015	Tenn	AA	126	454	151	34	4	8	(-	-)	217	71	75	91	57	0	62	7	0	3	4	4	22	.333	.413	.478	.891
2016	Iowa	AAA	55	204	72	16	3	9	(-	-)	121	40	43	51	28	1	32	6	0	2	4	4	6	.353	.442	.593	1.035
2016	ChC	NL	76	252	71	14	1	12	(8	4)	123	33	35	41	26	0	67	4	0	1	2	2	7	.282	.357	.488	.845

Patrick Corbin

Pitches: L Bats: L Pos: SP-24; RP-12   **Ht: 6'3" Wt: 210 Born: 7/19/1989 Age: 27**

			HOW MUCH HE PITCHED						WHAT HE GAVE UP											THE RESULTS						
Year	Team	Lg	G	GS	CG	GF	IP	BFP	H	R	ER	HR	SH	SF	HB	TBB	IBB	SO	WP	Bk	W	L	Pct	Sh	Sv-Op	Hld	ERC	ERA
2012	Ari	NL	22	17	0	3	107.0	454	117	56	54	14	2	5	4	25	2	86	1	0	6	8	.429	0	1-1	0	4.31	4.54
2013	Ari	NL	32	32	3	0	208.1	860	189	81	79	19	8	1	9	54	1	178	13	0	14	8	.636	0	0-0	0	3.14	3.41
2015	Ari	NL	16	16	0	0	85.0	357	91	34	34	9	2	1	2	17	0	78	4	0	6	5	.545	0	0-0	0	3.82	3.60
2016	Ari	NL	36	24	0	6	155.2	701	177	**109**	89	24	6	5	5	66	2	131	9	0	5	13	.278	0	1-1	2	5.47	5.15
	4 ML YEARS		106	89	3	9	556.0	2372	574	280	256	66	18	12	20	162	5	473	27	0	31	34	.477	0	2-2	2	4.09	4.14

Carlos Correa

Bats: R Throws: R Pos: SS-153;PH-1   coh-RAY-uh   **Ht: 6'4" Wt: 215 Born: 9/22/1994 Age: 22**

						BATTING													RUNNING			AVERAGES			
Year	Team	Lg	G	AB	H	2B	3B	HR	(Hm Rd)	TB	R	RBI	RC	TBB	IBB	SO	HBP	SH	SF	SB	CS	GDP	Avg	OBP	Slg	OPS
2012	2 Tms	Low	50	190	49	14	2	3	(- -)	76	28	12	24	12	1	44	1	1	0	6	1	1	.258	.305	.400	.705
2013	QuadC	A	117	450	144	33	3	9	(- -)	210	73	86	86	58	4	83	8	1	2	10	10	6	.320	.405	.467	.872
2014	Lancst	A+	62	249	81	16	6	6	(- -)	127	50	57	56	36	0	45	5	0	3	20	4	9	.325	.416	.510	.926
2015	CpChr	AA	29	117	45	15	2	7	(- -)	85	25	32	37	15	1	25	1	0	0	15	0	3	.385	.459	.726	1.185
2015	Fresno	AAA	24	98	27	6	1	3	(- -)	44	19	12	16	12	1	14	0	0	3	3	1	2	.276	.345	.449	.794
2015	Hou	AL	99	387	108	22	1	22	(12 10)	198	52	68	68	40	2	78	1	0	4	14	4	10	.279	.345	.512	.857
2016	Hou	AL	153	577	158	36	3	20	(8 12)	260	76	96	93	75	5	139	4	0	3	13	3	12	.274	.361	.451	.811
	Postseason		6	24	7	1	0	2	(2 0)	14	2	4	4	0	0	6	1	0	0	0	0	1	.292	.320	.583	.903
	2 ML YEARS		252	964	266	58	4	42	(20 22)	458	128	164	161	115	7	217	6	0	7	27	7	22	.276	.354	.475	.829

Jarred Cosart

Pitches: R Bats: R Pos: SP-13   KOH-zart   **Ht: 6'3" Wt: 205 Born: 5/25/1990 Age: 27**

					HOW MUCH HE PITCHED						WHAT HE GAVE UP									THE RESULTS						
Year	Team	Lg	G	GS	CG	GF	IP	BFP	H	R	ER	HR	SH	SF	HB	TBB	IBB	SO	WP	Bk	W	L	Pct	Sh	Sv-Op	Hld	ERC	ERA
2016	NewOr*	AAA	10	10	0	0	50.2	224	55	30	23	8	1	1	0	25	0	30	1	0	3	4	.429	0	0--	-	5.47	4.09
2013	Hou	AL	10	10	0	0	60.0	246	46	15	13	3	0	2	0	35	0	33	3	0	1	1	.500	0	0-0	0	3.31	1.95
2014	2 Tms		30	30	0	0	180.1	766	173	80	74	9	3	8	3	73	1	115	7	0	13	11	.542	0	0-0	0	3.61	3.69
2015	Mia	NL	14	13	0	0	69.2	296	63	35	35	10	2	1	1	33	1	47	7	0	2	5	.286	0	0-0	0	4.24	4.52
2016	2 Tms		13	13	0	0	57.0	268	61	41	38	4	1	1	2	39	2	38	3	0	0	4	.000	0	0-0	0	5.43	6.00
14	Hou	AL	20	20	0	0	116.1	507	119	61	57	7	2	6	3	51	1	75	7	0	9	7	.563	0	0-0	0	4.18	4.41
14	Mia	NL	10	10	0	0	64.0	259	54	19	17	2	1	2	0	22	0	40	0	0	4	4	.500	0	0-0	0	2.64	2.39
16	Mia	NL	4	4	0	0	19.2	92	19	14	13	0	1	1	0	16	2	11	2	0	0	1	.000	0	0-0	0	4.50	5.95
16	SD	NL	9	9	0	0	37.1	176	42	27	25	4	0	0	2	23	0	27	1	0	0	3	.000	0	0-0	0	5.93	6.03
	4 ML YEARS		67	66	0	0	367.0	1576	343	171	160	26	6	12	6	180	4	233	20	0	16	21	.432	0	0-0	0	3.96	3.92

Caleb Cotham

Pitches: R Bats: R Pos: RP-23   COTH-im   **Ht: 6'3" Wt: 215 Born: 11/6/1987 Age: 29**

					HOW MUCH HE PITCHED						WHAT HE GAVE UP									THE RESULTS						
Year	Team	Lg	G	GS	CG	GF	IP	BFP	H	R	ER	HR	SH	SF	HB	TBB	IBB	SO	WP	Bk	W	L	Pct	Sh	Sv-Op	Hld	ERC	ERA
2012	2 Tms	Low	23	19	0	0	101.1	422	103	44	41	5	0	2	3	29	2	76	2	0	5	7	.417	0	0--	-	3.53	3.64
2013	Trntn	AA	7	6	0	1	29.0	126	27	13	12	1	1	0	2	13	0	26	1	0	2	1	.667	0	0--	-	3.68	3.72
2013	S-WB	AAA	21	17	0	0	95.1	428	115	64	58	11	2	7	7	34	0	60	3	2	6	6	.500	0	0--	-	5.57	5.48
2014	S-WB	AAA	5	5	0	0	18.1	86	25	14	11	1	0	0	0	7	0	17	1	1	0	2	.000	0	0--	-	5.70	5.40
2014	Trntn	AA	5	5	0	0	25.1	106	25	17	17	3	0	0	0	13	0	16	1	0	0	2	.000	0	0--	-	4.86	6.04
2014	3 Tms	Low	8	1	0	2	10.0	38	7	0	0	0	0	0	1	0	0	11	1	0	0	0	-	0	0--	-	1.19	0.00
2015	Trntn	AA	15	0	0	5	26.0	105	20	8	8	1	0	0	1	8	0	31	1	0	4	2	.667	0	1--	-	2.29	2.77
2015	S-WB	AAA	20	0	0	12	31.0	124	25	7	6	1	0	1	2	5	0	30	2	0	2	2	.500	0	1--	-	2.01	1.74
2015	NYY	AL	12	0	0	4	9.2	45	14	7	7	4	1	0	0	1	0	11	0	0	1	0	1.000	0	0-0	0	7.50	6.52
2016	Cin	NL	23	0	0	3	24.1	117	32	21	20	3	1	2	3	12	2	21	1	0	0	3	.000	0	0-1	3	6.92	7.40
	2 ML YEARS		35	0	0	7	34.0	162	46	28	27	7	2	2	3	13	2	32	1	0	1	3	.250	0	0-1	3	7.17	7.15

Jharel Cotton

Pitches: R Bats: R Pos: SP-5   JUH-rel   **Ht: 5'11" Wt: 195 Born: 1/19/1992 Age: 25**

					HOW MUCH HE PITCHED						WHAT HE GAVE UP									THE RESULTS						
Year	Team	Lg	G	GS	CG	GF	IP	BFP	H	R	ER	HR	SH	SF	HB	TBB	IBB	SO	WP	Bk	W	L	Pct	Sh	Sv-Op	Hld	ERC	ERA
2012	Ogden	R+	5	1	0	0	15.0	55	9	2	2	0	1	1	0	3	0	20	1	0	1	0	1.000	0	0--	-	1.15	1.20
2013	Chatt	AA	8	0	0	3	10.0	48	15	12	9	0	0	1	0	3	0	11	1	0	0	2	.000	0	0--	-	5.66	8.10
2013	2 Tms	Low	13	11	1	1	64.0	254	46	24	24	4	2	0	1	20	1	61	4	0	2	5	.286	1	0--	-	2.12	3.38
2014	Rcuca	A+	25	20	1	4	126.2	519	113	70	57	18	5	6	1	34	0	138	5	0	6	10	.375	1	0--	-	3.29	4.05
2015	2 Tms	Low	5	3	0	0	25.2	100	18	6	6	1	0	0	0	8	0	34	2	0	1	0	1.000	0	0--	-	1.90	2.10
2015	Tulsa	AA	11	8	0	0	62.2	248	49	18	16	4	4	1	0	21	0	71	3	0	5	2	.714	0	0--	-	2.53	2.30
2015	OkCity	AAA	5	0	0	0	7.1	32	9	4	4	0	0	2	0	2	0	9	3	0	0	0	-	0	0--	-	4.15	4.91
2016	OkCity	AAA	22	16	1	2	97.1	403	80	59	53	17	4	2	0	32	0	119	10	0	8	5	.615	1	0--	-	3.26	4.90
2016	Nashv	AAA	6	6	1	0	38.1	147	28	12	12	3	1	0	0	7	1	36	2	0	3	1	.750	1	0--	-	1.79	2.82
2016	Oak	AL	5	5	0	0	29.1	112	20	10	7	4	0	0	0	4	0	23	1	0	2	0	1.000	0	0-0	0	1.70	2.15

Neal Cotts

Pitches: L **Bats:** L **Pos:** P **Ht:** 6'2" **Wt:** 200 **Born:** 3/25/1980 **Age:** 37

			HOW MUCH HE PITCHED						WHAT HE GAVE UP											THE RESULTS							
Year	Team	Lg	G	GS	CG	GF	IP	BFP	H	R	ER	HR	SH	SF	HB	TBB	IBB	SO	WP	Bk	W	L	Pct	Sh	Sv-Op	Hld	ERC	ERA
2016	Salt Lk*	AAA	14	0	0	2	13.2	55	12	5	5	1	1	0	0	3	0	13	1	0	0	0	-	0	1- -	-	2.59	3.29
2016	S-WB*	AAA	7	0	0	2	7.1	31	8	5	4	2	0	1	1	1	0	2	0	0	0	0	-	0	0- -	-	5.36	4.91
2016	RdRck*	AAA	20	0	0	7	23.2	100	23	10	10	2	2	1	0	10	2	23	0	0	2	2	.500	0	0- -	-	3.84	3.80
2003	CWS	AL	4	4	0	0	13.1	69	15	12	12	1	1	0	0	17	0	10	0	0	1	1	.500	0	0-0	0	8.43	8.10
2004	CWS	AL	56	1	0	12	65.1	281	61	45	41	13	0	1	3	30	2	58	8	0	4	4	.500	0	0-2	4	4.84	5.65
2005	CWS	AL	69	0	0	10	60.1	248	38	15	13	1	0	3	4	29	5	58	3	0	4	0	1.000	0	0-2	13	2.03	1.94
2006	CWS	AL	70	0	0	14	54.0	251	64	33	31	12	3	1	3	24	6	43	3	0	1	2	.333	0	1-4	14	6.24	5.17
2007	ChC	NL	16	0	0	4	16.2	76	15	9	9	1	1	2	3	9	0	14	0	0	0	1	.000	0	0-0	4	4.41	4.86
2008	ChC	NL	50	0	0	7	35.2	160	38	18	17	7	3	0	1	13	2	43	3	0	0	2	.000	0	0-2	9	4.87	4.29
2009	ChC	NL	19	0	0	3	11.0	55	14	9	9	3	0	0	1	9	0	9	0	0	0	2	.000	0	0-1	2	9.64	7.36
2013	Tex	AL	58	0	0	6	57.0	223	36	8	7	2	2	3	0	18	1	65	3	0	8	3	.727	0	1-4	11	1.57	1.11
2014	Tex	AL	73	0	0	18	66.2	286	66	33	32	6	2	1	3	23	3	63	4	2	2	9	.182	0	2-9	19	3.84	4.32
2015	2 Tms		68	0	0	10	63.1	269	58	26	24	12	3	2	4	22	2	58	2	0	1	0	1.000	0	0-0	5	4.21	3.41
15	Mil	NL	51	0	0	9	49.2	209	44	18	18	9	3	1	3	17	2	49	2	0	1	0	1.000	0	0-0	4	3.95	3.26
15	Min	AL	17	0	0	1	13.2	60	14	8	6	3	0	1	1	5	0	9	0	0	0	0	-	0	0-0	1	5.22	3.95
	Postseason		8	0	0	3	4.0	16	2	0	0	0	0	0	0	2	0	5	0	0	1	0	1.000	0	0-0	2	1.41	0.00
	10 ML YEARS		483	5	0	84	443.1	1918	405	208	195	58	15	13	22	194	21	421	26	2	21	24	.467	0	4-24	79	4.06	3.96

Daniel Coulombe

Pitches: L **Bats:** L **Pos:** RP-35 **KOO-lohm** **Ht:** 5'10" **Wt:** 190 **Born:** 10/26/1989 **Age:** 27

			HOW MUCH HE PITCHED						WHAT HE GAVE UP											THE RESULTS							
Year	Team	Lg	G	GS	CG	GF	IP	BFP	H	R	ER	HR	SH	SF	HB	TBB	IBB	SO	WP	Bk	W	L	Pct	Sh	Sv-Op	Hld	ERC	ERA
2016	Nashv*	AAA	20	0	0	1	25.0	96	18	4	3	0	0	0	0	6	1	35	3	0	0	0	-	0	0- -	-	1.55	1.08
2014	LAD	NL	5	0	0	0	4.1	22	5	3	2	1	0	0	0	2	0	4	2	0	0	0	-	0	0-0	0	5.49	4.15
2015	2 Tms		14	0	0	4	16.0	72	17	10	10	0	0	0	0	9	0	11	2	0	0	0	-	0	0-1	0	4.32	5.63
2016	Oak	AL	35	0	0	11	47.2	193	37	24	24	6	2	3	0	17	2	54	3	0	3	1	.750	0	0-1	2	2.84	4.53
15	LAD	NL	5	0	0	3	8.1	40	9	7	7	0	0	0	0	6	0	7	1	0	0	0	-	0	0-0	0	4.87	7.56
15	Oak	AL	9	0	0	1	7.2	32	8	3	3	0	0	0	0	3	0	4	1	0	0	0	-	0	0-1	0	3.72	3.52
	3 ML YEARS		54	0	0	15	68.0	287	59	37	36	7	2	3	0	28	2	69	7	0	3	1	.750	0	0-2	2	3.35	4.76

Kaleb Cowart

Bats: B **Throws:** R **Pos:** 3B-21;2B-16;PH-3;PR-2;1B-1 **Ht:** 6'3" **Wt:** 225 **Born:** 6/2/1992 **Age:** 25

			BATTING																				RUNNING			AVERAGES			
Year	Team	Lg	G	AB	H	2B	3B	HR	(Hm	Rd)	TB	R	RBI	RC	TBB	IBB	SO	HBP	SH	SF	SB	CS	GDP	Avg	OBP	Slg	OPS
2012	2 Tms	Low	135	526	145	31	7	16	(-	-)	238	90	103	89	67	0	111	4	1	7	14	7	11	.276	.358	.452	.810
2013	Ark	AA	132	498	110	20	1	6	(-	-)	150	48	42	43	38	0	124	3	4	3	14	5	11	.221	.279	.301	.580
2014	Ark	AA	126	435	97	18	4	6	(-	-)	141	48	54	46	43	2	99	3	2	4	26	7	12	.223	.295	.324	.619
2015	InldEm	A+	51	194	47	14	4	2	(-	-)	75	32	23	27	22	0	43	3	0	2	10	2	10	.242	.326	.387	.712
2015	Salt Lk	AAA	62	220	71	13	3	6	(-	-)	108	35	45	43	29	2	64	0	0	4	2	1	3	.323	.395	.491	.886
2016	Salt Lk	AAA	107	414	116	34	5	9	(-	-)	187	58	58	67	37	2	100	2	1	3	18	4	5	.280	.340	.452	.792
2015	LAA	AL	34	46	8	2	0	1	(1	0)	13	8	4	3	5	0	19	0	1	0	1	1	1	.174	.255	.283	.538
2016	LAA	AL	31	85	15	4	0	1	(0	1)	22	8	8	3	0	0	23	1	0	1	0	0	1	.176	.184	.259	.443
	2 ML YEARS		65	131	23	6	0	2	(1	1)	35	16	12	6	5	0	42	1	1	1	1	1	2	.176	.210	.267	.477

Collin Cowgill

Bats: R **Throws:** L **Pos:** RF-8;PR-4 **Ht:** 5'9" **Wt:** 190 **Born:** 5/22/1986 **Age:** 31

			BATTING																				RUNNING			AVERAGES			
Year	Team	Lg	G	AB	H	2B	3B	HR	(Hm	Rd)	TB	R	RBI	RC	TBB	IBB	SO	HBP	SH	SF	SB	CS	GDP	Avg	OBP	Slg	OPS
2016	Clmbs*	AAA	103	359	84	17	1	4	(-	-)	115	46	30	39	34	0	85	7	5	2	7	2	4	.234	.311	.320	.631
2011	Ari	NL	37	92	22	3	0	1	(1	0)	28	8	9	8	8	1	28	0	0	0	4	2	0	.239	.300	.304	.604
2012	Oak	AL	38	104	28	2	0	1	(1	0)	33	10	9	14	11	0	27	0	0	1	3	4	3	.269	.336	.317	.654
2013	2 Tms		73	152	32	5	2	4	(3	1)	53	18	16	12	7	0	42	0	3	0	1	0	1	.211	.245	.349	.594
2014	LAA	AL	106	260	65	10	1	5	(2	3)	92	35	21	31	26	0	74	5	2	0	4	0	4	.250	.300	.354	.684
2015	LAA	AL	55	69	13	2	1	1	(0	1)	20	10	2	3	4	0	19	0	1	0	2	1	1	.188	.233	.290	.523
2016	Cle	AL	9	12	1	0	0	0	(0	0)	1	0	0	0	2	0	7	0	0	0	0	0	1	.083	.214	.083	.298
13	NYM	NL	23	61	11	2	0	2	(2	0)	19	7	8	5	2	0	15	0	0	0	0	0	0	.180	.206	.311	.518
13	LAA	AL	50	91	21	3	2	2	(1	1)	34	11	8	7	5	0	27	0	3	0	1	0	1	.231	.271	.374	.644
	Postseason		3	1	1	0	0	0	(0	0)	1	0	2	1	0	0	0	0	0	0	0	0	0	1.000	1.000	1.000	2.000
	6 ML YEARS		318	689	161	22	4	12	(7	5)	227	83	57	68	58	1	197	5	6	1	14	7	10	.234	.297	.329	.627

Zack Cozart

Bats: R **Throws:** R **Pos:** SS-111;PH-9;DH-1;PR-1 **COE-zart** **Ht:** 6'0" **Wt:** 195 **Born:** 8/12/1985 **Age:** 31

			BATTING																				RUNNING			AVERAGES			
Year	Team	Lg	G	AB	H	2B	3B	HR	(Hm	Rd)	TB	R	RBI	RC	TBB	IBB	SO	HBP	SH	SF	SB	CS	GDP	Avg	OBP	Slg	OPS
2011	Cin	NL	11	37	12	0	0	2	(2	0)	18	6	3	3	0	0	6	1	0	0	0	0	2	.324	.324	.486	.811
2012	Cin	NL	138	561	138	33	4	15	(6	9)	224	72	35	51	31	0	113	3	2	3	4	0	11	.246	.288	.399	.687
2013	Cin	NL	151	567	144	30	3	12	(7	5)	216	74	63	56	26	2	102	2	13	10	0	0	18	.254	.284	.381	.665
2014	Cin	NL	147	506	112	18	5	4	(1	3)	152	48	38	36	25	3	79	7	5	0	7	0	13	.221	.268	.300	.568
2015	Cin	NL	53	194	50	10	1	9	(4	5)	89	28	28	23	14	1	29	2	1	3	3	3	4	.258	.310	.459	.769
2016	Cin	NL	121	464	117	28	2	16	(7	9)	197	67	50	53	37	3	84	2	1	4	4	1	9	.252	.308	.425	.732
	Postseason		6	24	5	0	0	0	(0	0)	5	2	0	1	3	0	5	1	0	0	0	0	0	.208	.321	.208	.530
	6 ML YEARS		621	2329	573	119	15	58	(27	31)	896	295	217	222	133	9	413	16	23	20	18	4	57	.246	.289	.385	.674

Tyler Cravy

Pitches: R **Bats**: R **Pos**: RP-18; SP-2   KRAY-vee   **Ht**: 6'2" **Wt**: 220 **Born**: 7/13/1989 **Age**: 27

			HOW MUCH HE PITCHED						WHAT HE GAVE UP												THE RESULTS						
Year	Team	Lg	G	GS	CG	GF	IP	BFP	H	R	ER	HR	SH	SF	HB	TBB	IBB	SO	WP	Bk	W	L	Pct	Sh	Sv-Op	Hld	ERC	ERA
2012	Wisc	A	24	0	0	20	50.2	218	45	24	19	5	1	0	7	15	2	53	10	0	2	5	.286	0	3- --	-	3.46	3.38
2013	BrvdCt	A+	25	9	0	6	79.1	316	61	22	18	1	0	1	6	24	0	59	5	0	4	2	.667	0	0- --	-	2.00	2.04
2014	Hntsvl	AA	14	12	0	0	73.1	281	47	17	14	7	4	1	6	15	0	64	1	1	8	1	.889	0	0- --	-	1.86	1.72
2015	ColSpr	AAA	17	17	0	0	95.1	400	92	44	42	6	4	4	4	31	0	75	6	2	7	7	.500	0	0- --	-	3.55	3.97
2016	ColSpr	AAA	21	9	0	1	56.1	250	56	40	37	5	2	2	1	28	0	65	4	1	3	3	.500	0	0- --	-	4.38	5.91
2015	Mil	NL	14	7	0	1	42.2	193	47	30	27	5	2	0	2	22	1	35	0	0	0	8	.000	0	0-1	0	5.46	5.70
2016	Mil	NL	20	2	0	4	28.1	116	21	9	9	3	1	1	1	12	1	22	0	0	0	1	.000	0	0-0	0	2.93	2.86
	2 ML YEARS		34	9	0	5	71.0	309	68	39	36	8	3	1	3	34	2	57	0	0	0	9	.000	0	0-1	0	4.40	4.56

Brandon Crawford

Bats: L **Throws**: R **Pos**: SS-155;PH-1   **Ht**: 6'2" **Wt**: 215 **Born**: 1/21/1987 **Age**: 30

						BATTING												RUNNING			AVERAGES			
Year	Team	Lg	G	AB	H	2B	3B	HR	(Hm | Rd)	TB	R	RBI	RC	TBB	IBB	SO	HBP	SH	SF	SB	CS	GDP	Avg	OBP	Slg	OPS
2011	SF	NL	66	196	40	5	2	3	(0 | 3)	58	22	21	20	23	1	31	0	1	4	1	3	4	.204	.288	.296	.584
2012	SF	NL	143	435	108	26	3	4	(1 | 3)	152	44	45	40	33	6	95	3	2	3	1	4	4	.248	.304	.349	.653
2013	SF	NL	149	499	124	24	3	9	(2 | 7)	181	52	43	42	42	6	96	5	1	3	1	2	10	.248	.311	.363	.674
2014	SF	NL	153	491	121	20	10	10	(4 | 6)	191	54	69	72	59	10	129	2	2	10	5	3	4	.246	.324	.389	.713
2015	SF	NL	143	507	130	33	4	21	(8 | 13)	234	65	84	69	39	9	119	11	0	4	6	4	18	.256	.321	.462	.782
2016	SF	NL	155	553	152	28	11	12	(4 | 8)	238	67	84	82	57	10	115	4	0	9	7	0	13	.275	.342	.430	.772
	Postseason		33	107	25	3	1	1	(0 | 1)	33	10	16	12	14	2	27	0	1	2	1	0	2	.234	.317	.308	.625
	6 ML YEARS		809	2681	675	136	33	59	(19 | 40)	1054	304	346	325	253	42	585	25	6	29	21	16	53	.252	.319	.393	.712

Carl Crawford

Bats: L **Throws**: L **Pos**: LF-21;PH-8;DH-4   **Ht**: 6'2" **Wt**: 230 **Born**: 8/5/1981 **Age**: 35

						BATTING												RUNNING			AVERAGES			
Year	Team	Lg	G	AB	H	2B	3B	HR	(Hm | Rd)	TB	R	RBI	RC	TBB	IBB	SO	HBP	SH	SF	SB	CS	GDP	Avg	OBP	Slg	OPS
2002	TB	AL	63	259	67	11	6	2	(1 | 1)	96	23	30	34	9	0	41	3	6	1	9	5	0	.259	.290	.371	.661
2003	TB	AL	151	630	177	18	9	5	(5 | 0)	228	80	54	80	26	4	102	1	1	3	55	10	5	.281	.309	.362	.671
2004	TB	AL	152	626	185	26	19	11	(6 | 5)	282	104	55	96	35	2	81	1	4	6	59	15	2	.296	.331	.450	.781
2005	TB	AL	156	644	194	33	15	15	(5 | 10)	302	101	81	102	27	1	84	5	5	6	46	8	11	.301	.331	.469	.800
2006	TB	AL	151	600	183	20	16	18	(7 | 11)	289	89	77	113	37	3	85	4	9	2	58	9	8	.305	.348	.482	.830
2007	TB	AL	143	584	184	37	9	11	(6 | 5)	272	93	80	97	32	5	112	5	1	2	50	10	11	.315	.355	.466	.820
2008	TB	AL	109	443	121	12	10	8	(3 | 5)	177	69	57	57	30	1	60	2	0	5	25	7	10	.273	.319	.400	.718
2009	TB	AL	156	606	185	28	8	15	(9 | 6)	274	96	68	91	51	1	99	8	2	5	60	16	7	.305	.364	.452	.816
2010	TB	AL	154	600	184	30	13	19	(11 | 8)	297	110	90	120	46	3	104	3	3	4	47	10	2	.307	.356	.495	.851
2011	Bos	AL	130	506	129	29	7	11	(4 | 7)	205	65	56	54	23	1	104	3	2	4	18	6	7	.255	.289	.405	.694
2012	Bos	AL	31	117	33	10	2	3	(2 | 1)	56	23	19	17	3	0	22	2	1	2	5	0	1	.282	.306	.479	.785
2013	LAD	NL	116	434	123	30	3	6	(5 | 1)	177	62	31	55	28	2	66	3	0	2	15	4	4	.283	.329	.407	.736
2014	LAD	NL	105	343	103	14	3	8	(5 | 3)	147	56	46	49	16	0	55	6	0	4	23	6	5	.300	.339	.429	.767
2015	LAD	NL	69	181	48	9	2	4	(1 | 3)	73	19	16	19	10	1	41	0	0	0	10	2	3	.265	.304	.403	.707
2016	LAD	NL	30	81	15	2	1	0	(0 | 0)	19	8	6	4	4	0	11	1	0	1	1	1	3	.185	.230	.235	.464
	Postseason		39	154	40	5	1	7	(5 | 2)	68	21	16	19	6	0	33	1	0	0	10	0	4	.260	.292	.442	.765
	15 ML YEARS		1716	6655	1931	309	123	136	(70 | 66)	2894	998	766	988	377	24	1067	47	34	48	480	109	79	.290	.330	.435	.765

Coco Crisp

Bats: B **Throws**: R **Pos**: LF-71;CF-36;DH-14;PH-10;PR-1   **Ht**: 5'10" **Wt**: 185 **Born**: 11/1/1979 **Age**: 37

						BATTING												RUNNING			AVERAGES			
Year	Team	Lg	G	AB	H	2B	3B	HR	(Hm | Rd)	TB	R	RBI	RC	TBB	IBB	SO	HBP	SH	SF	SB	CS	GDP	Avg	OBP	Slg	OPS
2002	Cle	AL	32	127	33	9	2	1	(1 | 0)	49	16	9	19	11	0	19	0	3	2	4	1	0	.260	.314	.386	.700
2003	Cle	AL	99	414	110	15	6	3	(3 | 0)	146	55	27	48	23	1	51	0	7	3	15	9	4	.266	.302	.353	.655
2004	Cle	AL	139	491	146	24	2	15	(8 | 7)	219	78	71	72	36	4	69	0	9	2	20	13	8	.297	.344	.446	.790
2005	Cle	AL	145	594	178	42	4	16	(4 | 12)	276	86	69	92	44	1	81	0	13	5	15	6	7	.300	.345	.465	.810
2006	Bos	AL	105	413	109	22	4	8	(4 | 4)	159	58	36	51	31	1	67	1	7	0	22	4	5	.264	.317	.385	.702
2007	Bos	AL	145	526	141	28	7	6	(1 | 5)	201	85	60	68	50	1	84	1	9	5	28	6	12	.268	.330	.382	.712
2008	Bos	AL	118	361	102	18	3	7	(1 | 6)	147	55	41	49	35	0	59	1	8	4	20	7	6	.283	.344	.407	.751
2009	KC	AL	49	180	41	8	5	3	(0 | 3)	68	30	14	25	29	1	23	1	4	1	13	2	4	.228	.336	.378	.714
2010	Oak	AL	75	290	81	14	4	8	(6 | 2)	127	51	38	49	30	0	49	0	3	5	32	3	6	.279	.342	.438	.779
2011	Oak	AL	136	531	140	27	5	8	(4 | 4)	201	69	54	69	41	2	65	1	4	6	49	9	11	.264	.314	.379	.693
2012	Oak	AL	120	455	118	25	7	11	(6 | 5)	190	68	46	71	45	0	64	0	6	2	39	4	9	.259	.325	.418	.742
2013	Oak	AL	131	513	134	22	3	22	(9 | 13)	228	93	66	78	61	3	65	0	2	8	21	5	7	.261	.335	.444	.779
2014	Oak	AL	126	463	114	21	3	9	(4 | 5)	168	68	47	67	66	2	66	0	1	6	19	5	3	.246	.336	.363	.699
2015	Oak	AL	44	126	22	6	0	0	(0 | 0)	28	11	6	13	13	0	25	0	0	2	0	0	2	.175	.252	.222	.474
2016	2 Tms	AL	122	446	103	27	4	13	(3 | 10)	177	54	55	67	46	2	78	0	4	2	10	5	7	.231	.302	.397	.698
16	Oak	AL	102	393	92	24	4	11	(3 | 8)	157	45	47	58	37	2	65	0	2	2	7	5	6	.234	.299	.399	.698
16	Cle	AL	20	53	11	3	0	2	(0 | 2)	20	9	8	9	9	0	13	0	2	0	3	0	1	.208	.323	.377	.700
	Postseason		31	103	29	5	1	1	(0 | 1)	39	15	8	12	9	0	19	0	0	1	4	0	3	.282	.336	.379	.715
	15 ML YEARS		1586	5930	1572	308	57	130	(54 | 76)	2384	877	639	831	561	18	865	5	80	51	309	79	91	.265	.327	.402	.729

Kyle Crockett

Pitches: L **Bats:** L **Pos:** RP-29 **Ht:** 6'2" **Wt:** 175 **Born:** 12/15/1991 **Age:** 25

			HOW MUCH HE PITCHED					WHAT HE GAVE UP												THE RESULTS							
Year	Team	Lg	G	GS	CG	GF	IP	BFP	H	R	ER	HR	SH	SF	HB	TBB	IBB	SO	WP	Bk	W	L	Pct	Sh	Sv-Op	Hld	ERC	ERA
2016	Clmbs*	AAA	29	0	0	3	30.0	130	29	13	13	2	1	0	1	11	2	26	0	0	1	1	.500	0	0--	-	3.50	3.90
2014	Cle	AL	43	0	0	7	30.0	122	26	6	6	2	2	0	3	8	2	28	0	1	4	1	.800	0	0-0	5	2.99	1.80
2015	Cle	AL	31	0	0	4	17.2	74	17	9	8	1	0	2	1	7	0	15	0	0	0	0	-	0	0-0	3	3.90	4.08
2016	Cle	AL	29	0	0	4	16.0	70	16	9	9	0	0	1	0	7	2	17	1	1	0	0	-	0	0-0	3	3.26	5.06
	3 ML YEARS		103	0	0	15	63.2	266	59	24	23	3	2	3	4	22	4	60	1	2	4	1	.800	0	0-0	11	3.30	3.25

C.J. Cron

CROHN

Bats: R **Throws:** R **Pos:** 1B-97;DH-10;PH-9 **Ht:** 6'4" **Wt:** 235 **Born:** 1/5/1990 **Age:** 27

							BATTING														RUNNING			AVERAGES			
Year	Team	Lg	G	AB	H	2B	3B	HR	(Hm	Rd)	TB	R	RBI	RC	TBB	IBB	SO	HBP	SH	SF	SB	CS	GDP	Avg	OBP	Slg	OPS
2014	LAA	AL	79	242	62	12	1	11	(5	6)	109	28	37	35	10	0	61	1	0	0	0	0	10	.256	.289	.450	.739
2015	LAA	AL	113	378	99	17	1	16	(11	5)	166	37	51	46	17	1	82	5	0	3	3	1	9	.262	.300	.439	.739
2016	LAA	AL	116	407	113	25	2	16	(7	9)	190	51	69	66	24	1	75	7	0	5	2	3	9	.278	.325	.467	.792
	Postseason		3	9	1	1	0	0	(0	0)	2	0	0	0	2	0	4	0	0	0	0	0	0	.111	.273	.222	.495
	3 ML YEARS		308	1027	274	54	4	43	(23	20)	465	116	157	147	51	2	218	13	0	8	5	4	28	.267	.308	.453	.760

Nelson Cruz

Bats: R **Throws:** R **Pos:** DH-107;RF-48 **Ht:** 6'2" **Wt:** 230 **Born:** 7/1/1980 **Age:** 36

							BATTING														RUNNING			AVERAGES			
Year	Team	Lg	G	AB	H	2B	3B	HR	(Hm	Rd)	TB	R	RBI	RC	TBB	IBB	SO	HBP	SH	SF	SB	CS	GDP	Avg	OBP	Slg	OPS
2005	Mil	NL	8	5	1	1	0	0	(0	0)	2	1	0	1	2	0	0	0	0	0	0	0	0	.200	.429	.400	.829
2006	Tex	AL	41	130	29	3	0	6	(3	3)	50	15	22	18	7	0	32	0	0	1	1	0	1	.223	.261	.385	.645
2007	Tex	AL	96	307	72	15	2	9	(4	5)	118	35	34	32	21	1	87	2	1	1	2	4	5	.235	.287	.384	.671
2008	Tex	AL	31	115	38	9	1	7	(4	3)	70	19	26	30	17	2	28	1	0	0	3	1	1	.330	.421	.609	1.030
2009	Tex	AL	128	462	120	21	1	33	(18	15)	242	75	76	72	49	6	118	2	0	2	20	4	9	.260	.332	.524	.856
2010	Tex	AL	108	399	127	31	3	22	(13	9)	230	60	78	77	38	5	81	1	1	6	17	4	12	.318	.374	.576	.950
2011	Tex	AL	124	475	125	28	1	29	(19	10)	242	64	87	79	33	1	116	2	0	3	9	5	8	.263	.312	.509	.821
2012	Tex	AL	159	585	152	45	0	24	(18	6)	269	86	90	80	48	2	140	5	0	4	8	4	7	.260	.319	.460	.779
2013	Tex	AL	109	413	110	18	0	27	(13	14)	209	49	76	69	35	2	109	4	0	4	5	1	14	.266	.327	.506	.833
2014	Bal	AL	159	613	166	32	2	40	(15	25)	322	87	108	93	55	8	140	5	0	5	4	5	17	.271	.333	.525	.859
2015	Sea	AL	152	590	178	22	1	44	(17	27)	334	90	93	108	59	9	164	5	1	0	3	2	6	.302	.369	.566	.936
2016	Sea	AL	155	589	169	27	1	43	(17	26)	327	96	105	101	62	5	159	9	0	7	2	0	15	.287	.360	.555	.915
	Postseason		41	154	45	10	0	16	(10	6)	103	31	34	35	12	2	36	1	0	0	1	1	4	.292	.347	.669	1.016
	12 ML YEARS		1270	4683	1287	252	12	284	(141	143)	2415	677	795	760	426	41	1174	36	2	34	74	30	95	.275	.338	.516	.853

Tony Cruz

Bats: R **Throws:** R **Pos:** C-4 **Ht:** 5'11" **Wt:** 215 **Born:** 8/18/1986 **Age:** 30

							BATTING														RUNNING			AVERAGES			
Year	Team	Lg	G	AB	H	2B	3B	HR	(Hm	Rd)	TB	R	RBI	RC	TBB	IBB	SO	HBP	SH	SF	SB	CS	GDP	Avg	OBP	Slg	OPS
2016	Omha*	AAA	92	318	84	18	0	7	(-	-)	123	32	55	46	41	3	74	1	0	3	2	1	9	.264	.347	.387	.734
2011	StL	NL	38	65	17	5	0	0	(0	0)	22	8	6	7	6	1	13	1	0	0	0	1	1	.262	.333	.338	.672
2012	StL	NL	51	126	32	9	1	1	(0	1)	46	11	11	9	3	0	19	0	0	2	0	1	4	.254	.267	.365	.632
2013	StL	NL	51	123	25	6	1	1	(0	1)	36	13	13	9	4	1	25	2	0	0	0	0	7	.203	.240	.293	.533
2014	StL	NL	50	135	27	5	0	1	(1	0)	35	11	17	9	13	1	28	0	2	0	0	3	6	.200	.270	.259	.530
2015	StL	NL	69	142	29	7	1	2	(0	2)	44	6	11	5	6	0	32	0	2	1	0	0	6	.204	.235	.310	.545
2016	KC	AL	4	4	0	0	0	0	(0	0)	0	0	1	0	0	0	3	0	0	1	0	0	0	.000	.000	.000	.000
	Postseason		8	11	2	1	0	1	(0	1)	6	2	2	2	2	0	6	0	0	0	0	0	0	.182	.308	.545	.853
	6 ML YEARS		263	595	130	32	3	5	(1	4)	183	49	59	39	32	3	120	3	4	4	0	5	24	.218	.260	.308	.568

Johnny Cueto

KWAY-toe

Pitches: R **Bats:** R **Pos:** SP-32 **Ht:** 5'11" **Wt:** 220 **Born:** 2/15/1986 **Age:** 31

					HOW MUCH HE PITCHED					WHAT HE GAVE UP										THE RESULTS							
Year	Team	Lg	G	GS	CG	GF	IP	BFP	H	R	ER	HR	SH	SF	HB	TBB	IBB	SO	WP	Bk	W	L	Pct	Sh	Sv-Op	Hld	ERC	ERA
2008	Cin	NL	31	31	0	0	174.0	769	178	101	93	29	9	5	14	68	1	158	6	1	9	14	.391	0	0-0	0	4.95	4.81
2009	Cin	NL	30	30	0	0	171.1	740	172	90	84	24	5	3	14	61	0	132	4	0	11	11	.500	0	0-0	0	4.57	4.41
2010	Cin	NL	31	31	1	0	185.2	780	181	79	75	19	9	3	6	56	5	138	5	2	12	7	.632	1	0-0	0	3.75	3.64
2011	Cin	NL	24	24	3	0	156.0	631	123	51	40	8	10	4	10	47	0	104	5	1	9	5	.643	1	0-0	0	2.55	2.31
2012	Cin	NL	33	33	2	0	217.0	888	205	73	67	15	6	6	12	49	5	170	1	3	19	9	.679	1	0-0	0	3.13	2.78
2013	Cin	NL	11	11	0	0	60.2	242	46	20	19	7	2	1	0	18	1	51	0	0	5	2	.714	0	0-0	0	2.57	2.82
2014	Cin	NL	34	34	4	0	243.2	961	169	69	61	22	7	1	15	65	2	242	1	1	20	9	.690	2	0-0	0	2.18	2.25
2015	2 Tms		32	32	2	0	212.0	866	194	87	81	21	5	4	8	46	1	176	0	4	11	13	.458	2	0-0	0	3.06	3.44
2016	SF	NL	32	32	5	0	219.2	881	195	71	66	15	7	3	8	45	1	198	3	1	18	5	.783	2	0-0	0	2.71	2.79
15	Cin	NL	19	19	1	0	130.2	516	93	42	38	11	4	3	6	29	1	120	0	4	7	6	.538	1	0-0	0	2.00	2.62
15	KC	AL	13	13	1	0	81.1	350	101	45	43	10	1	1	2	17	0	56	0	0	4	7	.364	1	0-0	0	5.05	4.76
	Postseason		7	7	1	0	33.2	143	30	21	20	6	1	1	1	12	0	22	0	0	2	3	.400	0	0-0	0	3.90	5.35
	9 ML YEARS		258	258	17	0	1640.0	6758	1463	641	588	160	60	30	91	455	16	1369	26	13	114	75	.603	8	0-0	0	3.23	3.23

William Cuevas

Pitches: R Bats: R Pos: RP-3   KWAY-vahs   **Ht:** 6'2" **Wt:** 215 **Born:** 10/14/1990 **Age:** 26

				HOW MUCH HE PITCHED			WHAT HE GAVE UP										THE RESULTS						
Year Team	Lg	G	GS	CG	GF	IP	BFP	H	R	ER	HR	SH	SF	HB	TBB	IBB	SO	WP	Bk	W	L	Pct	Sh	Sv-Op	Hld	ERC	ERA
2012 Lowell	A-	15	6	0	5	77.1	289	55	12	12	4	3	1	0	15	0	72	3	1	8	2	.800	0	0- -	-	1.68	1.40
2013 Salem	A+	26	26	1	0	135.1	573	139	82	76	13	5	5	4	40	0	109	12	1	8	9	.471	0	0- -	-	3.94	5.05
2014 Salem	A+	24	10	0	8	95.2	415	92	57	50	7	1	9	9	32	0	80	9	1	2	6	.250	0	1- -	-	3.75	4.70
2015 Portlnd	AA	19	19	0	0	95.1	410	84	43	36	4	1	4	3	41	0	91	9	0	8	5	.615	0	0- -	-	3.22	3.40
2015 Pwtckt	AAA	7	7	0	0	41.0	165	29	12	12	3	0	1	1	14	0	37	1	0	3	2	.600	0	0- -	-	2.26	2.63
2016 Pwtckt	AAA	25	18	1	2	131.0	567	134	71	61	18	6	4	5	45	0	85	4	0	6	8	.429	0	0- -	-	4.38	4.19
2016 Bos	AL	3	0	0	2	5.0	24	5	2	2	0	1	0	0	6	0	3	0	0	0	1	.000	0	0-0	0	6.82	3.60

Charlie Culberson

Bats: R Throws: R Pos: SS-11;PH-11;2B-10;3B-4;LF-2;PR-1   **Ht:** 6'0" **Wt:** 200 **Born:** 4/10/1989 **Age:** 28

								BATTING											RUNNING			AVERAGES			
Year Team	Lg	G	AB	H	2B	3B	HR	(Hm	Rd)	TB	R	RBI	RC	TBB	IBB	SO	HBP	SH	SF	SB	CS	GDP	Avg	OBP	Slg	OPS
2016 OkCity*	AAA	70	265	69	17	2	4	(-	-)	102	32	33	31	18	0	61	1	1	0	6	5	7	.260	.310	.385	.695
2012 SF	NL	6	22	3	0	0	0	(0	0)	3	0	1	0	0	0	7	0	1	0	0	0	0	.136	.136	.136	.273
2013 Col	NL	47	99	29	5	0	2	(0	2)	40	12	12	13	4	1	23	0	0	1	5	1	5	.293	.317	.404	.721
2014 Col	NL	95	210	41	7	2	3	(2	1)	61	17	24	14	12	2	62	5	4	2	2	2	6	.195	.253	.290	.544
2016 LAD	NL	34	67	20	3	0	1	(1	0)	26	6	7	9	1	0	13	0	0	0	1	0	2	.299	.309	.388	.697
4 ML YEARS		182	398	93	15	2	6	(3	3)	130	35	44	36	17	3	105	5	5	3	8	3	13	.234	.272	.327	.599

Brandon Cunniff

Pitches: R Bats: R Pos: RP-15   kin-IF   **Ht:** 6'0" **Wt:** 185 **Born:** 10/7/1988 **Age:** 28

				HOW MUCH HE PITCHED			WHAT HE GAVE UP										THE RESULTS						
Year Team	Lg	G	GS	CG	GF	IP	BFP	H	R	ER	HR	SH	SF	HB	TBB	IBB	SO	WP	Bk	W	L	Pct	Sh	Sv-Op	Hld	ERC	ERA
2013 Lynbrg	A+	20	0	0	11	31.2	133	20	8	7	2	1	2	1	21	2	39	2	1	1	0	1.000	0	0- -	-	2.89	1.99
2014 Lynbrg	A+	9	0	0	6	15.1	58	5	1	0	0	2	0	0	7	2	21	1	0	1	0	1.000	0	3- -	-	0.76	0.00
2014 Missi	AA	33	0	0	6	52.2	214	39	14	12	2	3	4	1	20	2	51	4	0	3	0	1.000	0	0- -	-	2.27	2.05
2015 Gwnntt	AAA	6	0	0	2	5.0	27	8	5	5	2	0	0	0	8	0	4	0	0	1	0	1.000	0	0- -	-	18.96	9.00
2016 Gwnntt	AAA	35	0	0	17	42.2	173	35	20	19	3	3	0	0	19	1	39	3	0	3	3	.500	0	2- -	-	3.16	4.01
2016 Missi	AA	8	0	0	4	12.2	49	6	1	1	0	1	0	1	5	1	10	1	0	0	1	.000	0	2- -	-	1.24	0.71
2015 Atl	NL	39	0	0	12	35.0	151	27	20	18	4	1	1	0	22	2	37	1	0	2	2	.500	0	0-2	5	3.71	4.63
2016 Atl	NL	15	0	0	3	17.0	74	14	9	8	2	2	1	2	9	1	16	1	0	2	0	1.000	0	0-0	0	4.11	4.24
2 ML YEARS		54	0	0	15	52.0	225	41	29	26	6	3	2	2	31	3	53	2	0	4	2	.667	0	0-2	5	3.84	4.50

Todd Cunningham

Bats: B Throws: R Pos: LF-17;PR-6;CF-1;RF-1;DH-1   **Ht:** 6'0" **Wt:** 205 **Born:** 3/20/1989 **Age:** 28

								BATTING											RUNNING			AVERAGES			
Year Team	Lg	G	AB	H	2B	3B	HR	(Hm	Rd)	TB	R	RBI	RC	TBB	IBB	SO	HBP	SH	SF	SB	CS	GDP	Avg	OBP	Slg	OPS
2016 Salt Lk*	AAA	99	349	97	16	2	6	(-	-)	135	66	43	59	51	0	56	7	7	3	23	5	10	.278	.378	.387	.765
2013 Atl	NL	8	8	2	0	0	0	(0	0)	2	2	0	1	0	0	3	0	0	0	0	0	0	.250	.250	.250	.500
2015 Atl	NL	39	86	19	4	0	0	(0	0)	23	13	4	3	5	1	17	2	0	0	2	1	1	.221	.280	.267	.547
2016 LAA	AL	20	27	4	3	0	0	(0	0)	7	5	1	0	1	0	6	0	1	0	0	1	1	.148	.179	.259	.438
3 ML YEARS		67	121	25	7	0	0	(0	0)	32	20	5	4	6	1	26	2	1	0	2	2	3	.207	.256	.264	.520

Zac Curtis

Pitches: L Bats: L Pos: RP-21   **Ht:** 5'9" **Wt:** 190 **Born:** 7/4/1992 **Age:** 24

				HOW MUCH HE PITCHED			WHAT HE GAVE UP										THE RESULTS						
Year Team	Lg	G	GS	CG	GF	IP	BFP	H	R	ER	HR	SH	SF	HB	TBB	IBB	SO	WP	Bk	W	L	Pct	Sh	Sv-Op	Hld	ERC	ERA
2014 Hlsbro	A-	24	0	0	22	27.0	109	18	5	3	0	1	0	0	12	0	42	1	0	2	1	.667	0	14- -	-	1.90	1.00
2015 Kane	A	53	0	0	45	54.0	206	33	9	8	2	4	1	1	12	0	75	5	0	4	4	.500	0	33- -	-	1.37	1.33
2016 Visalia	A+	8	0	0	3	10.1	49	12	8	6	0	0	0	1	5	0	22	3	0	1	0	1.000	0	2- -	-	4.80	5.23
2016 Mobile	AA	19	0	0	11	19.2	82	17	7	7	3	1	0	0	6	0	30	0	0	1	1	.500	0	4- -	-	3.25	3.20
2016 Ari	NL	21	0	0	2	13.1	67	13	10	10	2	0	0	3	13	1	10	0	0	0	1	.000	0	0-1	1	7.56	6.75

Cheslor Cuthbert

Bats: R Throws: R Pos: 3B-127;PH-2   CHESS-lohr   **Ht:** 6'1" **Wt:** 190 **Born:** 11/16/1992 **Age:** 24

								BATTING											RUNNING			AVERAGES			
Year Team	Lg	G	AB	H	2B	3B	HR	(Hm	Rd)	TB	R	RBI	RC	TBB	IBB	SO	HBP	SH	SF	SB	CS	GDP	Avg	OBP	Slg	OPS
2012 Wilmg	A+	124	475	114	18	0	7	(-	-)	153	47	59	47	37	0	80	2	0	3	6	3	8	.240	.296	.322	.618
2013 Wilmg	A+	60	225	63	21	2	2	(-	-)	94	32	31	34	27	0	37	0	0	2	1	2	8	.280	.354	.418	.772
2013 NWArk	AA	64	237	51	16	0	6	(-	-)	85	25	28	25	20	2	53	2	2	3	5	2	5	.215	.279	.359	.637
2014 NWArk	AA	96	355	98	19	1	10	(-	-)	149	35	48	54	36	2	67	1	0	3	9	3	12	.276	.342	.420	.761
2014 Omha	AAA	25	91	24	5	0	2	(-	-)	35	12	16	11	9	0	12	0	0	0	1	1	1	.264	.330	.385	.715
2015 Omha	AAA	104	397	110	22	1	11	(-	-)	167	55	51	59	37	1	60	1	1	2	5	2	14	.277	.339	.421	.759
2016 Omha	AAA	24	93	31	4	1	7	(-	-)	58	15	28	22	11	0	14	1	0	2	0	1	1	.333	.402	.624	1.026
2015 KC	AL	19	46	10	2	1	1	(1	0)	17	6	8	6	4	0	9	0	0	0	0	0	0	.217	.280	.370	.650
2016 KC	AL	128	475	130	28	1	12	(4	8)	196	49	46	57	32	0	96	0	1	2	2	0	14	.274	.318	.413	.731
2 ML YEARS		147	521	140	30	2	13	(5	8)	213	55	54	63	36	0	105	0	1	2	2	0	14	.269	.315	.409	.724

David Dahl

Bats: L **Throws:** R **Pos:** LF-54;CF-6;PH-6;RF-4   **Ht:** 6'2" **Wt:** 195 **Born:** 4/1/1994 **Age:** 23

								BATTING												RUNNING			AVERAGES			
Year	Team	Lg	G	AB	H	2B	3B	HR	(Hm | Rd)	TB	R	RBI	RC	TBB	IBB	SO	HBP	SH	SF	SB	CS	GDP	Avg	OBP	Slg	OPS
2012	GdJunc	R+	67	280	106	22	10	9	(- | -)	175	62	57	68	21	3	42	2	1	2	12	7	4	.379	.423	.625	1.048
2013	Ashvll	A	10	40	11	4	1	0	(- | -)	17	9	7	5	2	0	8	0	0	0	2	0	0	.275	.310	.425	.735
2014	2 Tms	Low	119	512	153	41	8	14	(- | -)	252	83	55	86	28	0	92	1	4	2	21	5	4	.299	.335	.492	.827
2015	NwBrit	AA	73	288	80	16	3	6	(- | -)	120	46	24	38	11	0	72	0	3	0	22	7	1	.278	.304	.417	.721
2016	Hrtfrd	AA	76	288	80	21	2	13	(- | -)	144	53	45	55	39	1	85	2	2	1	16	5	1	.278	.367	.500	.867
2016	Albq	AAA	16	62	30	6	2	5	(- | -)	55	17	16	22	6	1	11	0	0	0	1	2	1	.484	.529	.887	1.417
2016	Col	NL	63	222	70	12	4	7	(3 | 4)	111	42	24	35	15	0	59	0	0	0	5	0	3	.315	.359	.500	.859

Tyler Danish

Pitches: R **Bats:** R **Pos:** RP-3   **Ht:** 6'0" **Wt:** 200 **Born:** 9/12/1994 **Age:** 22

				HOW MUCH HE PITCHED					WHAT HE GAVE UP												THE RESULTS						
Year	Team	Lg	G	GS	CG	GF	IP	BFP	H	R	ER	HR	SH	SF	HB	TBB	IBB	SO	WP	Bk	W	L	Pct	Sh	Sv-Op	Hld	ERC	ERA
2013	2 Tms	Low	15	1	0	0	30.0	111	17	6	4	1	0	1	0	5	0	28	0	0	1	0	1.000	0	0--	-	1.08	1.20
2014	2 Tms	Low	25	25	0	0	129.2	524	115	43	30	7	1	1	4	33	0	103	3	1	8	3	.727	0	0--	-	2.79	2.08
2015	Brham	AA	26	26	2	0	142.0	635	175	82	71	13	2	5	5	60	0	90	3	0	8	12	.400	0	0--	-	5.76	4.50
2016	Brham	AA	12	12	1	0	75.1	308	71	38	37	3	2	1	0	16	0	47	2	0	3	7	.300	1	0--	-	2.67	4.42
2016	Charllt	AAA	7	5	0	0	29.1	134	39	21	19	0	0	1	1	10	0	21	2	0	1	3	.250	0	0--	-	5.13	5.83
2016	CWS	AL	3	0	0	2	1.2	12	6	2	2	0	0	0	0	3	1	0	0	0	0	0	-	0	0-0	0	31.12	10.80

John Danks

Pitches: L **Bats:** L **Pos:** SP-4   **Ht:** 6'1" **Wt:** 210 **Born:** 4/15/1985 **Age:** 32

				HOW MUCH HE PITCHED					WHAT HE GAVE UP												THE RESULTS						
Year	Team	Lg	G	GS	CG	GF	IP	BFP	H	R	ER	HR	SH	SF	HB	TBB	IBB	SO	WP	Bk	W	L	Pct	Sh	Sv-Op	Hld	ERC	ERA
2007	CWS	AL	26	26	0	0	139.0	622	160	92	85	28	7	4	4	54	4	109	3	0	6	13	.316	0	0-0	0	5.73	5.50
2008	CWS	AL	33	33	0	0	195.0	804	182	74	72	15	2	2	4	57	1	159	7	0	12	9	.571	0	0-0	0	3.26	3.32
2009	CWS	AL	32	32	1	0	200.1	839	184	89	84	28	5	6	5	73	1	149	1	0	13	11	.542	0	0-0	0	3.89	3.77
2010	CWS	AL	32	32	1	0	213.0	878	189	93	88	18	5	0	4	70	2	162	2	1	15	11	.577	1	0-0	0	3.18	3.72
2011	CWS	AL	27	27	2	0	170.1	728	182	89	82	19	4	6	7	46	5	135	6	0	8	12	.400	1	0-0	0	4.16	4.33
2012	CWS	AL	9	9	0	0	53.2	238	57	35	34	7	3	2	1	23	0	30	5	0	3	4	.429	0	0-0	0	4.82	5.70
2013	CWS	AL	22	22	0	0	138.1	583	151	81	73	28	1	5	4	27	0	89	3	0	4	14	.222	0	0-0	0	4.61	4.75
2014	CWS	AL	32	32	0	0	193.2	855	205	106	102	25	4	7	9	74	1	129	7	0	11	11	.500	0	0-0	0	4.70	4.74
2015	CWS	AL	30	30	2	0	177.2	768	195	104	93	24	8	6	3	56	1	124	8	1	7	15	.318	1	0-0	0	4.62	4.71
2016	CWS	AL	4	4	0	0	22.1	100	28	20	18	5	0	2	0	11	0	16	1	0	0	4	.000	0	0-0	0	7.24	7.25
	Postseason		1	1	0	0	6.2	30	7	3	3	1	0	0	0	3	0	7	0	0	1	0	1.000	0	0-0	0	4.81	4.05
	10 ML YEARS		247	247	6	0	1503.1	6415	1533	783	731	197	39	40	41	491	15	1102	43	2	79	104	.432	3	0-0	0	4.23	4.38

Chase d'Arnaud

dar-NO

Bats: R **Throws:** R **Pos:** PH-28;SS-21;3B-19;2B-10;LF-8;CF-4;PR-2;RF-1   **Ht:** 6'2" **Wt:** 205 **Born:** 1/21/1987 **Age:** 30

								BATTING												RUNNING			AVERAGES			
Year	Team	Lg	G	AB	H	2B	3B	HR	(Hm	Rd)	TB	R	RBI	RC	TBB	IBB	SO	HBP	SH	SF	SB	CS	GDP	Avg	OBP	Slg	OPS
2016	Gwnntt*	AAA	22	94	24	6	1	1	(-	-)	35	11	4	12	6	0	16	0	0	0	7	0	0	.255	.300	.372	.672
2011	Pit	NL	48	143	31	6	2	0	(0	0)	41	17	6	8	4	0	36	1	2	1	12	3	3	.217	.242	.287	.528
2012	Pit	NL	8	6	0	0	0	0	(0	0)	0	2	1	0	0	0	2	0	0	0	1	0	0	.000	.000	.000	.000
2014	Pit	NL	8	0	0	0	0	0	(0	0)	0	2	0	0	0	0	0	0	0	0	0	2	0	-	-	-	-
2015	Phi	NL	11	17	3	0	1	0	(0	0)	5	2	0	1	1	0	7	0	0	0	0	1	0	.176	.222	.294	.516
2016	Atl	NL	84	233	57	14	2	1	(1	0)	78	24	21	25	23	1	50	3	0	3	9	3	5	.245	.317	.335	.652
	5 ML YEARS		159	399	91	20	5	1	(1	0)	124	47	28	34	28	1	95	4	2	4	22	8	8	.228	.283	.311	.594

Travis d'Arnaud

dar-NO

Bats: R **Throws:** R **Pos:** C-73;PH-4   **Ht:** 6'2" **Wt:** 210 **Born:** 2/10/1989 **Age:** 28

								BATTING												RUNNING			AVERAGES			
Year	Team	Lg	G	AB	H	2B	3B	HR	(Hm	Rd)	TB	R	RBI	RC	TBB	IBB	SO	HBP	SH	SF	SB	CS	GDP	Avg	OBP	Slg	OPS
2013	NYM	NL	31	99	20	3	0	1	(1	0)	26	4	5	6	12	0	21	0	0	1	0	0	3	.202	.286	.263	.548
2014	NYM	NL	108	385	93	22	3	13	(5	8)	160	48	41	39	32	5	64	2	1	1	1	0	15	.242	.302	.416	.718
2015	NYM	NL	67	239	64	14	1	12	(6	6)	116	31	41	36	23	0	49	4	0	2	0	0	7	.268	.340	.485	.825
2016	NYM	NL	75	251	62	7	0	4	(4	0)	81	27	15	17	19	1	50	3	2	1	0	0	7	.247	.307	.323	.629
	Postseason		14	55	10	1	0	3	(2	1)	20	5	7	3	0	0	17	1	0	1	0	0	2	.182	.193	.364	.557
	4 ML YEARS		281	974	239	46	4	30	(16	14)	383	110	102	98	86	6	184	9	3	5	1	0	32	.245	.311	.393	.704

Yu Darvish

YOO DARR-vish

Pitches: R **Bats:** R **Pos:** SP-17   **Ht:** 6'5" **Wt:** 220 **Born:** 8/16/1986 **Age:** 30

				HOW MUCH HE PITCHED					WHAT HE GAVE UP												THE RESULTS						
Year	Team	Lg	G	GS	CG	GF	IP	BFP	H	R	ER	HR	SH	SF	HB	TBB	IBB	SO	WP	Bk	W	L	Pct	Sh	Sv-Op	Hld	ERC	ERA
2016	Frisco*	AA	5	5	0	0	20.0	79	14	7	5	1	0	1	0	7	0	24	1	0	1	1	.500	0	0--	-	2.07	2.25
2012	Tex	AL	29	29	0	0	191.1	816	156	89	83	14	2	7	10	89	1	221	8	0	16	9	.640	0	0-0	0	3.31	3.90
2013	Tex	AL	32	32	0	0	209.2	841	145	68	66	26	0	5	8	80	1	277	7	1	13	9	.591	0	0-0	0	2.70	2.83
2014	Tex	AL	22	22	2	0	144.1	605	133	54	49	13	1	2	2	49	0	182	14	1	10	7	.588	1	0-0	0	3.39	3.06
2016	Tex	AL	17	17	0	0	100.1	416	81	43	38	12	0	4	3	31	1	132	6	0	7	5	.583	0	0-0	0	2.87	3.41
	Postseason		1	1	0	0	6.2	27	5	3	2	0	1	1	1	0	0	7	0	0	1	0	1.000	0	0-0	0	1.38	2.70
	4 ML YEARS		100	100	2	0	645.2	2678	515	254	236	65	3	18	23	249	4	812	35	2	46	30	.605	1	0-0	0	3.06	3.29

Matt Davidson

Bats: R **Throws:** R **Pos:** DH-1   **Ht:** 6'3" **Wt:** 230 **Born:** 3/26/1991 **Age:** 26

								BATTING												RUNNING			AVERAGES			
Year Team	Lg	G	AB	H	2B	3B	HR	(Hm Rd)	TB	R	RBI	RC	TBB	IBB	SO	HBP	SH	SF	SB	CS	GDP	Avg	OBP	Slg	OPS
2012 Mobile	AA	135	486	127	28	2	23	(- -)	228	81	77	87	69	5	126	15	0	5	3	4	12	.261	.367	.469	.836
2013 Reno	AAA	115	443	124	32	3	17	(- -)	213	55	74	77	46	1	134	5	0	6	1	0	16	.280	.350	.481	.831
2014 Charllt	AAA	130	478	95	18	0	20	(- -)	173	59	55	51	49	1	164	8	1	3	0	0	5	.199	.283	.362	.644
2015 Charllt	AAA	141	528	107	22	0	23	(- -)	198	63	74	61	62	2	191	7	1	4	1	0	11	.203	.293	.375	.668
2016 Charllt	AAA	75	284	76	20	0	10	(- -)	126	35	46	46	32	2	86	5	2	3	0	0	7	.268	.349	.444	.792
2013 Ari	NL	31	76	18	6	0	3	(1 2)	33	8	12	12	10	1	24	1	0	0	0	1	1	.237	.333	.434	.768
2016 CWS	AL	1	2	1	0	0	0	(0 0)	1	1	1	0	0	0	1	0	0	0	0	0	0	.500	.500	.500	1.000
2 ML YEARS		32	78	19	6	0	3	(1 2)	34	9	13	12	10	1	25	1	0	0	0	1	1	.244	.337	.436	.773

Zach Davies

Pitches: R **Bats:** R **Pos:** SP-28   **Ht:** 6'0" **Wt:** 155 **Born:** 2/7/1993 **Age:** 24

		HOW MUCH HE PITCHED						WHAT HE GAVE UP												THE RESULTS						
Year Team	Lg	G	GS	CG	GF	IP	BFP	H	R	ER	HR	SH	SF	HB	TBB	IBB	SO	WP	Bk	W	L	Pct	Sh	Sv-Op	Hld	ERC	ERA
2012 Dlmrva	A	25	17	0	5	114.1	484	109	52	49	11	4	4	3	46	0	91	4	0	5	7	.417	0	1--	-	3.96	3.86
2013 Frdrck	A+	26	26	0	0	148.2	619	145	72	61	10	9	3	3	38	0	132	5	1	7	9	.438	0	0--	-	3.25	3.69
2014 Bowie	AA	21	20	0	0	110.0	465	106	50	41	8	3	1	4	32	1	109	3	0	10	7	.588	0	0--	-	3.38	3.35
2015 Norfolk	AAA	19	18	1	0	101.1	419	91	33	32	4	6	1	1	33	0	81	3	0	5	6	.455	0	0--	-	2.90	2.84
2015 ColSpr	AAA	5	5	0	0	27.0	128	38	17	15	2	1	0	1	12	0	21	1	0	1	2	.333	0	0--	-	6.69	5.00
2015 Mil	NL	6	6	0	0	34.0	139	36	14	14	2	1	0	0	15	0	24	0	0	3	2	.600	0	0-0	0	2.74	3.71
2016 Mil	NL	28	28	0	0	163.1	682	166	79	72	20	3	4	6	38	0	135	3	0	11	7	.611	0	0-0	0	3.83	3.97
2 ML YEARS		34	34	0	0	197.1	821	192	93	86	22	4	4	6	53	0	159	3	0	14	9	.609	0	0-0	0	3.64	3.92

Chris Davis

Bats: L **Throws:** R **Pos:** 1B-152;RF-3;DH-2   **Ht:** 6'3" **Wt:** 230 **Born:** 3/17/1986 **Age:** 31

								BATTING												RUNNING			AVERAGES			
Year Team	Lg	G	AB	H	2B	3B	HR	(Hm Rd)	TB	R	RBI	RC	TBB	IBB	SO	HBP	SH	SF	SB	CS	GDP	Avg	OBP	Slg	OPS
2008 Tex	AL	80	295	84	23	2	17	(8 9)	162	51	55	44	20	1	88	1	0	1	1	2	5	.285	.331	.549	.880
2009 Tex	AL	113	391	93	15	1	21	(11 10)	173	48	59	50	24	2	150	2	0	2	0	0	6	.238	.284	.442	.726
2010 Tex	AL	45	120	23	9	0	1	(0 1)	35	7	4	5	15	3	40	0	0	1	3	0	3	.192	.279	.292	.571
2011 2 Tms	AL	59	199	53	12	0	5	(2 3)	80	25	19	23	11	1	63	0	0	0	1	0	4	.266	.305	.402	.707
2012 Bal	AL	139	515	139	20	0	33	(22 11)	260	75	85	85	37	6	169	7	0	3	2	3	8	.270	.326	.501	.827
2013 Bal	AL	160	584	167	42	1	53	(28 25)	370	103	138	134	72	12	199	10	0	7	4	1	4	.286	.370	.634	1.004
2014 Bal	AL	127	450	88	16	0	26	(13 13)	182	65	72	58	60	9	173	9	1	5	2	1	2	.196	.300	.404	.704
2015 Bal	AL	160	573	150	31	0	47	(29 18)	322	100	117	117	84	6	208	8	0	5	2	3	6	.262	.361	.562	.923
2016 Bal	AL	157	566	125	21	0	38	(17 21)	260	99	84	82	88	3	219	8	0	3	1	0	6	.221	.332	.459	.792
11 Tex	AL	28	76	19	3	0	3	(1 2)	31	9	6	7	5	0	24	0	0	0	0	0	2	.250	.296	.408	.704
11 Bal	AL	31	123	34	9	0	2	(1 1)	49	16	13	16	6	1	39	0	0	0	1	0	2	.276	.310	.398	.708
Postseason		6	24	5	0	0	0	(0 0)	5	1	2	1	1	0	9	1	0	0	0	0	0	.208	.269	.208	.478
9 ML YEARS		1040	3693	922	189	4	241	(130 111)	1842	573	633	598	411	43	1309	45	1	27	16	10	44	.250	.330	.499	.829

Ike Davis

Bats: L **Throws:** L **Pos:** 1B-8;PH-1;PR-1   **Ht:** 6'4" **Wt:** 220 **Born:** 3/22/1987 **Age:** 30

								BATTING												RUNNING			AVERAGES			
Year Team	Lg	G	AB	H	2B	3B	HR	(Hm Rd)	TB	R	RBI	RC	TBB	IBB	SO	HBP	SH	SF	SB	CS	GDP	Avg	OBP	Slg	OPS
2016 RdRck*	AAA	39	142	38	12	0	4	(- -)	62	21	25	23	19	0	37	0	0	2	0	0	4	.268	.350	.437	.786
2016 S-WB*	AAA	26	92	20	1	0	5	(- -)	36	11	16	12	14	1	32	0	0	1	0	0	2	.217	.318	.391	.709
2010 NYM	NL	147	523	138	33	1	19	(8 11)	240	73	71	75	72	6	138	1	0	5	3	2	13	.264	.351	.440	.791
2011 NYM	NL	36	129	39	8	1	7	(5 2)	70	20	25	22	17	3	31	1	0	2	0	0	5	.302	.383	.543	.925
2012 NYM	NL	156	519	118	26	0	32	(11 21)	240	66	90	68	61	3	141	1	0	3	0	2	10	.227	.308	.462	.771
2013 NYM	NL	103	317	65	14	0	9	(5 4)	106	37	33	36	57	5	101	1	0	2	4	0	9	.205	.326	.334	.661
2014 2 Tms	NL	143	360	84	19	0	11	(9 2)	136	43	51	45	63	3	78	0	0	4	0	4	8	.233	.344	.378	.722
2015 Oak	AL	74	214	49	17	0	3	(1 2)	75	19	20	23	23	0	44	0	0	2	0	0	5	.229	.301	.350	.652
2016 NYY	AL	8	14	3	0	0	0	(0 0)	3	2	1	1	1	0	5	0	0	0	0	0	1	.214	.267	.214	.481
14 NYM	NL	12	24	5	1	0	1	(1 0)	9	4	5	4	6	0	4	0	0	0	0	0	0	.208	.367	.375	.742
14 Pit	NL	131	336	79	18	0	10	(8 2)	127	39	46	41	57	3	74	0	0	4	0	4	8	.235	.343	.378	.721
7 ML YEARS		667	2076	496	117	2	81	(39 42)	860	260	291	270	294	20	538	4	0	18	7	8	51	.239	.332	.414	.746

Khris Davis

Bats: R **Throws:** R **Pos:** LF-93;DH-53;PH-4   **Ht:** 5'10" **Wt:** 195 **Born:** 12/21/1987 **Age:** 29

								BATTING												RUNNING			AVERAGES			
Year Team	Lg	G	AB	H	2B	3B	HR	(Hm Rd)	TB	R	RBI	RC	TBB	IBB	SO	HBP	SH	SF	SB	CS	GDP	Avg	OBP	Slg	OPS
2013 Mil	NL	56	136	38	10	0	11	(5 6)	81	27	27	25	11	0	34	5	0	1	0	3	4	.279	.353	.596	.949
2014 Mil	NL	144	501	122	37	2	22	(12 10)	229	70	69	58	32	0	122	10	0	6	4	1	13	.244	.299	.457	.756
2015 Mil	NL	121	392	97	16	2	27	(16 11)	198	54	66	57	44	1	122	1	0	3	6	2	9	.247	.323	.505	.828
2016 Oak	AL	150	555	137	24	2	42	(19 23)	291	85	102	77	42	0	166	8	0	5	1	2	19	.247	.307	.524	.831
4 ML YEARS		471	1584	394	87	6	102	(52 50)	799	236	264	217	129	1	444	24	0	15	14	5	45	.249	.312	.504	.817

Rajai Davis

RAH-jay

Bats: R **Throws:** R **Pos:** CF-80;LF-66;PH-17;PR-6;RF-1;DH-1   **Ht:** 5'10" **Wt:** 195 **Born:** 10/19/1980 **Age:** 36

Year Team	Lg	G	AB	H	2B	3B	HR	(Hm	Rd)	TB	R	RBI	RC	TBB	IBB	SO	HBP	SH	SF	SB	CS	GDP	Avg	OBP	Slg	OPS
2006 Pit	NL	20	14	2	1	0	0	(0	0)	3	1	0	0	2	0	3	0	1	0	1	3	0	.143	.250	.214	.464
2007 2 Tms	NL	75	190	53	11	2	1	(0	1)	71	32	9	26	21	1	28	4	3	1	22	6	1	.279	.361	.374	.735
2008 2 Tms		113	214	52	5	4	3	(0	3)	74	30	19	24	8	0	40	1	2	1	29	6	1	.243	.272	.346	.618
2009 Oak	AL	125	390	119	27	5	3	(1	2)	165	65	48	63	29	0	70	7	2	4	41	12	12	.305	.360	.423	.784
2010 Oak	AL	143	525	149	28	3	5	(5	0)	198	66	52	62	26	0	78	4	1	5	50	11	10	.284	.320	.377	.697
2011 Tor	AL	95	320	76	21	6	1	(1	0)	112	44	29	32	15	0	63	1	1	1	34	11	4	.238	.273	.350	.623
2012 Tor	AL	142	447	115	24	3	8	(5	3)	169	64	43	59	29	3	102	6	1	4	46	**13**	8	.257	.309	.378	.687
2013 Tor	AL	108	331	86	16	2	6	(3	3)	124	49	24	36	21	0	67	5	1	2	45	6	8	.260	.312	.375	.687
2014 Det	AL	134	461	130	27	2	8	(4	4)	185	64	51	62	22	0	75	5	3	3	36	11	7	.282	.320	.401	.721
2015 Det	AL	112	341	88	16	11	8	(6	2)	150	55	30	37	22	0	76	3	1	3	18	8	5	.258	.306	.440	.746
2016 Cle	AL	134	454	113	23	2	12	(3	9)	176	74	48	62	33	0	106	5	1	2	**43**	6	9	.249	.306	.388	.693
07 Pit	NL	24	48	13	2	1	0	(0	0)	17	6	2	6	7	0	3	0	1	1	5	2	1	.271	.357	.354	.711
07 SF		51	142	40	9	1	1	(0	1)	54	26	7	20	14	1	25	4	2	0	17	4	0	.282	.363	.380	.743
08 SF	NL	12	18	1	0	0	0	(0	0)	1	2	0	0	1	0	6	0	0	0	4	0	0	.056	.105	.056	.161
08 Oak	AL	101	196	51	5	4	3	(0	3)	73	28	19	24	7	0	34	1	2	1	25	6	1	.260	.288	.372	.660
Postseason		3	6	2	0	0	0	(0	0)	2	0	0	1	0	0	0	0	0	0	0	0	0	.333	.333	.333	.667
11 ML YEARS		1201	3687	983	199	40	55	(28	27)	1427	544	353	463	228	4	708	41	17	26	365	93	65	.267	.314	.387	.701

Wade Davis

Pitches: R **Bats:** R **Pos:** RP-45   **Ht:** 6'5" **Wt:** 225 **Born:** 9/7/1985 **Age:** 31

Year Team	Lg	G	GS	CG	GF	IP	BFP	H	R	ER	HR	SH	SF	HB	TBB	IBB	SO	WP	Bk	W	L	Pct	Sh	Sv-Op	Hld	ERC	ERA
2009 TB	AL	6	6	1	0	36.1	150	33	19	15	2	0	0	0	13	1	36	1	0	2	2	.500	1	0-0	0	3.12	3.72
2010 TB	AL	29	29	0	0	168.0	722	165	77	76	24	3	6	5	62	2	113	4	0	12	10	.545	0	0-0	0	4.25	4.07
2011 TB	AL	29	29	1	0	184.0	795	190	96	91	23	5	7	8	63	1	105	6	0	11	10	.524	0	0-0	0	4.38	4.45
2012 TB	AL	54	0	0	15	70.1	284	48	20	19	5	0	1	0	29	2	87	2	0	3	0	1.000	0	0-1	6	2.25	2.43
2013 KC	AL	31	24	0	2	135.1	618	169	89	80	15	1	5	4	58	2	114	7	0	8	11	.421	0	0-0	0	5.88	5.32
2014 KC	AL	71	0	0	11	72.0	279	38	8	8	0	0	1	3	23	0	109	1	0	9	2	.818	0	3-6	**33**	1.23	1.00
2015 KC	AL	69	0	0	24	67.1	251	33	8	7	3	0	2	0	20	1	78	1	0	8	1	.889	0	17-18	18	1.16	0.94
2016 KC	AL	45	0	0	40	43.1	176	33	9	9	0	0	0	3	16	0	47	4	0	2	1	.667	0	27-30	0	2.35	1.87
Postseason		23	1	0	10	32.1	124	22	4	3	1	0	0	0	9	0	46	2	0	4	0	1.000	0	4-4	3	1.67	0.84
8 ML YEARS		334	88	2	92	776.2	3275	709	326	305	72	9	22	23	284	9	689	26	0	55	37	.598	1	47-55	57	3.52	3.53

Grant Dayton

Pitches: L **Bats:** L **Pos:** RP-25   **Ht:** 6'2" **Wt:** 195 **Born:** 11/25/1987 **Age:** 29

Year Team	Lg	G	GS	CG	GF	IP	BFP	H	R	ER	HR	SH	SF	HB	TBB	IBB	SO	WP	Bk	W	L	Pct	Sh	Sv-Op	Hld	ERC	ERA
2012 Jupiter	A+	31	6	0	5	60.0	245	48	19	14	1	0	1	2	18	0	71	3	0	2	5	.286	0	2--	-	2.24	2.10
2012 Jaxnvl	AA	7	0	0	0	13.0	55	12	6	6	2	2	0	0	4	1	19	0	0	2	1	.667	0	0--	-	3.46	4.15
2013 Jaxnvl	AA	30	0	0	11	38.0	160	33	10	10	4	1	0	1	12	0	56	2	0	4	4	.500	0	1--	-	3.11	2.37
2014 Jaxnvl	AA	11	0	0	4	16.1	71	17	2	2	0	2	0	0	4	0	18	0	0	0	1	.000	0	3--	-	2.90	1.10
2014 NewOr	AAA	39	0	0	11	55.2	238	53	24	23	10	1	1	1	22	3	61	1	0	2	2	.500	0	1--	-	4.34	3.72
2015 NewOr	AAA	25	0	0	8	35.0	131	25	11	11	1	2	2	1	5	1	35	4	0	2	1	.667	0	0--	-	1.51	2.83
2015 OkCity	AAA	9	0	0	3	11.2	53	16	12	12	1	0	0	1	3	0	13	2	0	1	1	.500	0	0--	-	6.01	9.26
2015 Tulsa	AA	8	0	0	2	10.2	47	9	3	3	1	0	0	0	7	2	17	2	0	0	2	.000	0	1--	-	3.13	2.53
2016 OkCity	AAA	26	0	0	11	36.1	140	22	12	10	2	1	0	1	8	1	63	0	0	2	2	.500	0	4--	-	1.40	2.48
2016 Tulsa	AA	12	0	0	5	15.2	58	8	6	4	0	0	0	0	3	0	28	0	0	3	0	1.000	0	1--	-	1.00	2.30
2016 LAD	NL	25	0	0	0	26.1	101	14	7	6	4	0	0	1	6	0	39	0	0	0	1	.000	0	0-2	6	1.56	2.05

Alejandro De Aza

Bats: L **Throws:** L **Pos:** PH-65;CF-46;LF-22;RF-14;PR-2   day-AH-zah   **Ht:** 6'0" **Wt:** 195 **Born:** 4/11/1984 **Age:** 33

Year Team	Lg	G	AB	H	2B	3B	HR	(Hm	Rd)	TB	R	RBI	RC	TBB	IBB	SO	HBP	SH	SF	SB	CS	GDP	Avg	OBP	Slg	OPS
2007 Fla	NL	45	144	33	8	2	0	(0	0)	45	14	8	11	6	1	37	1	5	2	2	0	2	.229	.261	.313	.574
2009 Fla	NL	22	20	5	1	0	0	(0	0)	6	6	3	4	5	0	5	0	1	1	0	0	0	.250	.385	.300	.685
2010 CWS	AL	19	30	9	3	0	0	(0	0)	12	7	2	4	1	0	4	0	1	0	2	1	0	.300	.323	.400	.723
2011 CWS	AL	54	152	50	11	3	4	(2	2)	79	29	23	34	17	1	34	1	1	2	12	5	2	.329	.400	.520	.920
2012 CWS	AL	131	524	147	29	6	9	(2	7)	215	81	50	79	47	3	109	9	4	1	26	12	1	.281	.349	.410	.760
2013 CWS	AL	153	607	160	27	4	17	(4	13)	246	84	62	82	50	1	147	6	6	6	20	8	8	.264	.323	.405	.728
2014 2 Tms	AL	142	477	120	24	8	8	(4	4)	184	56	41	58	39	2	119	6	3	3	17	10	7	.252	.314	.386	.700
2015 3 Tms		114	325	85	17	7	7	(3	4)	137	51	35	47	31	3	84	5	2	2	7	5	6	.262	.333	.422	.755
2016 NYM	NL	130	234	48	9	0	6	(2	4)	75	31	25	23	26	1	67	5	1	1	4	3	5	.205	.297	.321	.618
14 CWS	AL	122	395	96	19	5	5	(4	1)	140	45	31	45	33	2	100	6	2	3	15	7	6	.243	.309	.354	.663
14 Bal		20	82	24	5	3	3	(0	3)	44	11	10	13	6	0	19	0	1	0	2	3	1	.293	.341	.537	.877
15 Bal	AL	30	103	22	4	1	3	(1	2)	37	16	7	10	7	2	34	2	0	0	2	2	1	.214	.277	.359	.636
15 Bos	AL	60	161	47	9	5	4	(2	2)	78	23	25	30	12	1	36	2	2	1	3	1	2	.292	.347	.484	.831
15 SF	NL	24	61	16	4	1	0	(0	0)	22	12	3	7	12	0	14	1	0	1	2	2	3	.262	.387	.361	.747
Postseason		6	21	7	3	0	0	(0	0)	10	4	3	4	1	0	1	1	0	0	0	0	0	.333	.391	.476	.867
9 ML YEARS		810	2513	657	129	30	51	(17	34)	999	359	249	342	222	12	606	33	24	16	90	44	31	.261	.328	.398	.725

Ivan De Jesus Jr.

hay-SOOS

Bats: R **Throws:** R **Pos:** PH-33;SS-30;2B-22;3B-14;1B-12;LF-1;PR-1 **Ht:** 5'11" **Wt:** 200 **Born:** 5/1/1987 **Age:** 30

									BATTING											RUNNING			AVERAGES			
Year	Team	Lg	G	AB	H	2B	3B	HR	(Hm | Rd)	TB	R	RBI	RC	TBB	IBB	SO	HBP	SH	SF	SB	CS	GDP	Avg	OBP	Slg	OPS
2011	LAD	NL	17	32	6	0	0	0	(0 | 0)	6	2	1	1	2	0	11	0	1	0	0	0	1	.188	.235	.188	.423
2012	2 Tms		31	41	9	3	0	0	(0 | 0)	12	5	4	4	3	0	13	0	0	1	1	1	1	.220	.267	.293	.559
2015	Cin	NL	76	201	49	10	2	4	(4 | 0)	75	15	28	23	19	0	55	1	0	1	0	2	3	.244	.311	.373	.684
2016	Cin	NL	104	221	56	10	0	1	(0 | 1)	69	21	20	22	17	1	51	2	2	1	3	1	6	.253	.311	.312	.623
12	LAD	NL	23	33	9	3	0	0	(0 | 0)	12	5	4	4	3	0	7	0	0	1	1	1	1	.273	.324	.364	.688
12	Bos	AL	8	8	0	0	0	0	(0 | 0)	0	0	0	0	0	0	6	0	0	0	0	0	0	.000	.000	.000	.000
	4 ML YEARS		228	495	120	23	2	5	(4 | 1)	162	43	53	50	41	1	130	3	3	3	4	4	11	.242	.303	.327	.630

Joel De La Cruz

Pitches: R **Bats:** R **Pos:** RP-13; SP-9 **Ht:** 6'1" **Wt:** 240 **Born:** 6/9/1989 **Age:** 28

				HOW MUCH HE PITCHED					WHAT HE GAVE UP										THE RESULTS						
Year	Team	Lg	G	GS	CG	GF	IP	BFP	H	R	ER	HR	SH	SF	HB	TBB	IBB	SO	WP	Bk	W	L	Pct	Sh	Sv-Op	Hld	ERC	ERA
2012	2 Tms	Low	26	0	0	13	48.1	210	46	25	19	3	1	0	1	27	0	51	7	3	3	3	.500	0	3- -	-	4.32	3.54
2013	Tampa	A+	33	6	0	7	85.0	348	70	35	31	2	3	3	3	27	0	73	6	1	6	3	.667	0	1- -	-	2.48	3.28
2014	Trntn	AA	11	10	0	0	56.0	241	60	31	27	3	2	1	3	19	0	39	3	1	4	4	.500	0	0- -	-	4.18	4.34
2014	S-WB	AAA	17	12	0	2	65.2	289	74	43	33	6	2	4	2	18	0	38	5	1	3	5	.375	0	0- -	-	4.28	4.52
2015	Trntn	AA	8	2	0	3	23.1	101	24	12	9	2	0	1	2	5	0	13	2	0	1	2	.333	0	0- -	-	3.66	3.47
2015	S-WB	AAA	15	7	0	0	61.0	248	59	25	22	4	1	1	2	17	0	29	0	1	7	0	1.000	0	0- -	-	3.45	3.25
2016	Gwnntt	AAA	21	5	0	3	57.2	249	62	32	30	5	2	2	5	24	2	44	2	1	1	3	.250	0	0- -	-	4.95	4.68
2016	Atl	NL	22	9	0	2	62.2	276	65	40	34	10	3	2	2	22	0	37	0	0	0	7	.000	0	0-0	0	4.56	4.88

Jorge de la Rosa

Pitches: L **Bats:** L **Pos:** SP-24; RP-3 **Ht:** 6'1" **Wt:** 215 **Born:** 4/5/1981 **Age:** 36

				HOW MUCH HE PITCHED					WHAT HE GAVE UP										THE RESULTS						
Year	Team	Lg	G	GS	CG	GF	IP	BFP	H	R	ER	HR	SH	SF	HB	TBB	IBB	SO	WP	Bk	W	L	Pct	Sh	Sv-Op	Hld	ERC	ERA
2004	Mil	NL	5	5	0	0	22.2	113	29	20	16	1	1	1	1	14	0	5	3	0	0	3	.000	0	0-0	0	6.12	6.35
2005	Mil	NL	38	0	0	13	42.1	208	48	23	21	1	2	2	0	38	4	42	6	0	2	2	.500	0	0-2	5	6.04	4.46
2006	2 Tms		28	13	0	4	79.0	367	81	59	57	14	2	4	2	54	1	67	6	1	5	6	.455	0	0-0	1	6.05	6.49
2007	KC	AL	26	23	0	1	130.0	589	160	88	84	20	2	4	3	53	6	82	4	1	8	12	.400	0	0-0	0	5.93	5.82
2008	Col	NL	28	23	0	0	130.0	571	128	77	71	13	6	7	7	62	3	128	14	1	10	8	.556	0	0-0	0	4.50	4.92
2009	Col	NL	33	32	0	0	185.0	799	172	95	90	20	11	6	9	83	3	193	12	1	16	9	.640	0	0-0	0	4.11	4.38
2010	Col	NL	20	20	0	0	121.2	512	105	62	57	15	3	3	5	55	4	113	9	1	8	7	.533	0	0-0	0	3.86	4.22
2011	Col	NL	10	10	1	0	59.0	245	48	25	23	4	4	1	2	22	0	52	6	1	5	2	.714	0	0-0	0	2.88	3.51
2012	Col	NL	3	3	0	0	10.2	53	17	14	11	5	1	0	0	2	0	6	2	0	0	2	.000	0	0-0	0	9.22	9.28
2013	Col	NL	30	30	0	0	167.2	714	170	70	65	11	11	5	6	62	5	112	5	0	16	6	.727	0	0-0	0	3.92	3.49
2014	Col	NL	32	32	0	0	184.1	768	161	90	84	21	9	5	9	67	2	139	9	0	14	11	.560	0	0-0	0	3.55	4.10
2015	Col	NL	26	26	1	0	149.0	635	137	73	69	17	4	8	3	65	3	134	6	2	9	7	.563	0	0-0	0	3.94	4.17
2016	Col	NL	27	24	0	0	134.0	614	157	93	82	22	9	3	8	63	3	108	7	1	8	9	.471	0	0-0	0	6.16	5.51
06	Mil	NL	18	3	0	4	30.1	146	32	30	29	4	1	3	1	22	1	31	4	0	2	2	.500	0	0-0	1	5.90	8.60
06	KC	AL	10	10	0	0	48.2	221	49	29	28	10	1	1	1	32	0	36	2	1	3	4	.429	0	0-0	0	6.14	5.18
	13 ML YEARS		306	241	2	18	1415.1	6188	1413	789	730	165	60	51	54	640	34	1181	89	9	101	84	.546	0	0-2	6	4.53	4.64

Rubby de la Rosa

ROO-bee

Pitches: R **Bats:** R **Pos:** SP-10; RP-3 **Ht:** 6'0" **Wt:** 210 **Born:** 3/4/1989 **Age:** 28

				HOW MUCH HE PITCHED					WHAT HE GAVE UP										THE RESULTS						
Year	Team	Lg	G	GS	CG	GF	IP	BFP	H	R	ER	HR	SH	SF	HB	TBB	IBB	SO	WP	Bk	W	L	Pct	Sh	Sv-Op	Hld	ERC	ERA
2011	LAD	NL	13	10	0	2	60.2	254	54	26	25	6	2	0	0	31	3	60	3	0	4	5	.444	0	0-1	1	3.94	3.71
2012	LAD	NL	1	0	0	0	0.2	4	0	2	2	0	0	0	0	2	0	0	0	0	0	0	-	0	0-0	0	7.00	27.00
2013	Bos	AL	11	0	0	7	11.1	53	15	7	7	2	0	0	3	2	0	6	1	0	0	2	.000	0	0-0	0	6.76	5.56
2014	Bos	AL	19	18	0	1	101.2	441	116	51	50	12	3	5	2	35	0	74	3	1	4	8	.333	0	0-0	0	4.96	4.43
2015	Ari	NL	32	32	0	0	188.2	809	193	103	98	32	8	5	4	63	3	150	2	2	14	9	.609	0	0-0	0	4.49	4.67
2016	Ari	NL	13	10	0	1	50.2	222	43	26	24	8	1	1	4	20	1	54	2	1	4	5	.444	0	0-0	0	3.75	4.26
	6 ML YEARS		89	70	0	11	413.2	1783	421	215	206	60	14	11	13	153	7	344	11	4	26	29	.473	0	0-1	1	4.50	4.48

Jose De Leon

Pitches: R **Bats:** R **Pos:** SP-4 **Ht:** 6'2" **Wt:** 190 **Born:** 8/7/1992 **Age:** 24

				HOW MUCH HE PITCHED					WHAT HE GAVE UP										THE RESULTS						
Year	Team	Lg	G	GS	CG	GF	IP	BFP	H	R	ER	HR	SH	SF	HB	TBB	IBB	SO	WP	Bk	W	L	Pct	Sh	Sv-Op	Hld	ERC	ERA
2013	2 Tms	Low	14	13	0	0	53.0	250	67	48	41	6	0	2	9	21	0	53	9	0	3	5	.375	0	0- -	-	6.44	6.96
2014	2 Tms	Low	14	12	0	0	77.0	314	58	29	19	3	3	1	4	21	0	119	7	2	7	0	1.000	0	0- -	-	2.10	2.22
2015	Rcuca	A+	7	7	0	0	37.2	148	26	9	7	1	1	0	4	8	0	58	1	0	4	1	.800	0	0- -	-	1.78	1.67
2015	Tulsa	AA	16	16	1	0	76.2	317	61	35	31	11	2	1	2	29	1	105	2	0	2	6	.250	1	0- -	-	3.25	3.64
2016	OkCity	AAA	16	16	0	0	86.1	342	62	29	28	9	3	4	1	20	0	111	1	0	7	1	.875	0	0- -	-	2.05	2.92
2016	LAD	NL	4	4	0	0	17.0	80	19	17	12	5	3	1	3	7	1	15	0	0	2	0	1.000	0	0-0	0	6.82	6.35

Abel De Los Santos

Pitches: R **Bats:** R **Pos:** RP-5   ah-BELL   **Ht:** 6'2" **Wt:** 195 **Born:** 11/21/1992 **Age:** 24

Year	Team	Lg	G	GS	CG	GF	IP	BFP	H	R	ER	HR	SH	SF	HB	TBB	IBB	SO	WP	Bk	W	L	Pct	Sh	Sv-Op	Hld	ERC	ERA
2012	Spkane	A-	16	11	0	0	62.0	273	67	46	40	7	5	2	5	22	1	54	5	1	3	5	.375	0	0- -	-	4.76	5.81
2013	Spkane	A-	20	0	0	7	41.1	169	33	16	16	4	2	1	2	13	0	48	4	1	4	1	.800	0	1- -	-	2.84	3.48
2014	2 Tms	Low	41	0	0	33	56.0	230	36	15	12	2	2	2	5	18	3	65	3	2	5	3	.625	0	8- -	-	1.76	1.93
2015	Hrsbrg	AA	39	0	0	22	57.2	239	53	24	22	6	3	3	1	12	1	55	3	1	4	4	.500	0	8- -	-	2.91	3.43
2016	Hrsbrg	AA	14	0	0	9	14.0	62	9	6	6	2	0	0	1	10	0	13	2	0	0	0	-	0	5- -	-	3.82	3.86
2016	Syrcse	AAA	15	0	0	2	20.1	97	25	8	8	0	2	0	0	13	1	26	4	0	1	1	.500	0	0- -	-	5.45	3.54
2016	Pnscla	AA	17	0	0	4	23.1	90	11	5	4	1	0	1	0	7	1	25	0	1	1	2	.333	0	3- -	-	1.05	1.54
2015	Was	NL	2	0	0	2	1.2	8	2	1	1	1	0	0	0	1	0	3	0	0	0	0	-	0	0-0	0	10.04	5.40
2016	Cin	NL	5	0	0	1	5.2	28	7	7	7	1	0	1	1	4	0	2	1	0	0	0	-	0	0-0	0	8.33	11.12
	2 ML YEARS		7	0	0	3	7.1	36	9	8	8	2	0	1	1	5	0	5	1	0	0	0	-	0	0-0	0	8.80	9.82

Pat Dean

Pitches: L **Bats:** L **Pos:** RP-10; SP-9   **Ht:** 6'1" **Wt:** 195 **Born:** 5/25/1989 **Age:** 28

Year	Team	Lg	G	GS	CG	GF	IP	BFP	H	R	ER	HR	SH	SF	HB	TBB	IBB	SO	WP	Bk	W	L	Pct	Sh	Sv-Op	Hld	ERC	ERA
2012	FtMyrs	A+	28	28	0	0	153.1	655	177	74	68	11	2	3	5	33	0	81	0	1	10	8	.556	0	0- -	-	4.18	3.99
2013	NwBrit	AA	22	22	2	0	125.0	541	151	72	65	12	8	3	2	17	0	61	2	2	6	11	.353	1	0- -	-	4.16	4.68
2013	Roch	AAA	6	6	0	0	40.0	160	38	14	9	0	2	2	1	5	0	22	0	0	3	2	.600	0	0- -	-	2.27	2.03
2014	NwBrit	AA	26	26	1	0	144.0	647	192	91	77	20	4	4	8	31	0	83	3	0	8	9	.471	0	0- -	-	5.80	4.81
2015	Roch	AAA	27	27	5	0	179.0	715	170	60	56	10	4	4	3	36	0	98	2	0	12	11	.522	3	0- -	-	2.91	2.82
2016	Roch	AAA	16	16	1	0	87.1	390	113	58	54	10	0	3	2	19	0	49	2	0	5	7	.417	0	0- -	-	5.19	5.56
2016	Min	AL	19	9	0	4	67.1	300	88	47	47	13	1	2	0	23	1	50	1	0	1	6	.143	0	0-0	0	6.48	6.28

Jaff Decker

Bats: L **Throws:** L **Pos:** RF-13;PH-4;LF-3;CF-2;DH-1   JEFF   **Ht:** 5'9" **Wt:** 190 **Born:** 2/23/1990 **Age:** 27

										BATTING													RUNNING			AVERAGES			
Year	Team	Lg	G	AB	H	2B	3B	HR	(Hm	Rd)	TB	R	RBI	RC	TBB	IBB	SO	HBP	SH	SF	SB	CS	GDP	Avg	OBP	Slg	OPS
2016	Drham*	AAA	99	349	89	18	2	12	(-	-)	147	55	35	59	59	3	79	4	2	3	18	7	6	.255	.366	.421	.787
2013	SD	NL	13	26	4	0	0	1	(0	1)	7	3	2	0	3	0	4	0	1	1	0	1	0	.154	.233	.269	.503
2014	Pit	NL	5	5	0	0	0	0	(0	0)	0	0	0	0	0	0	3	0	0	0	0	0	0	.000	.000	.000	.000
2015	Pit	NL	23	28	6	1	1	0	(0	0)	9	8	1	4	7	0	9	0	1	0	0	0	0	.214	.371	.321	.693
2016	TB	AL	19	52	8	1	0	0	(0	0)	9	1	1	0	4	0	14	0	0	1	1	0	1	.154	.211	.173	.384
	4 ML YEARS		60	111	18	2	1	1	(0	1)	25	12	4	4	14	0	30	0	2	2	1	1	1	.162	.252	.225	.477

Jacob deGrom

Pitches: R **Bats:** L **Pos:** SP-24   duh-GRAHM   **Ht:** 6'4" **Wt:** 180 **Born:** 6/19/1988 **Age:** 29

Year	Team	Lg	G	GS	CG	GF	IP	BFP	H	R	ER	HR	SH	SF	HB	TBB	IBB	SO	WP	Bk	W	L	Pct	Sh	Sv-Op	Hld	ERC	ERA
2014	NYM	NL	22	22	0	0	140.1	565	117	44	42	7	5	3	1	43	2	144	1	0	9	6	.600	0	0-0	0	2.57	2.69
2015	NYM	NL	30	30	0	0	191.0	751	149	59	54	16	10	7	2	38	2	205	6	0	14	8	.636	0	0-0	0	2.13	2.54
2016	NYM	NL	24	24	1	0	148.0	604	142	53	50	15	5	3	3	36	0	143	4	0	7	8	.467	1	0-0	0	3.40	3.04
	Postseason		4	4	0	0	25.0	105	21	8	8	2	2	0	0	8	1	29	0	0	3	1	.750	0	0-0	0	2.65	2.88
	3 ML YEARS		76	76	1	0	479.1	1920	408	156	146	38	20	13	6	117	4	492	11	0	30	22	.577	1	0-0	0	2.63	2.74

Steve Delabar

Pitches: R **Bats:** R **Pos:** RP-7   DELL-uh-bar   **Ht:** 6'5" **Wt:** 215 **Born:** 7/17/1983 **Age:** 33

Year	Team	Lg	G	GS	CG	GF	IP	BFP	H	R	ER	HR	SH	SF	HB	TBB	IBB	SO	WP	Bk	W	L	Pct	Sh	Sv-Op	Hld	ERC	ERA
2016	Lsvlle*	AAA	17	0	0	8	24.0	108	22	8	7	2	0	1	0	16	0	25	3	0	1	0	1.000	0	4- -	-	4.51	2.63
2011	Sea	AL	6	0	0	4	7.0	28	5	2	2	1	0	0	1	4	1	7	0	0	1	1	.500	0	0-0	0	4.15	2.57
2012	2 Tms	AL	61	0	0	12	66.0	274	46	29	28	12	3	2	5	26	1	92	6	0	4	3	.571	0	0-2	12	3.18	3.82
2013	Tor	AL	55	0	0	14	58.2	253	50	25	21	4	3	3	2	29	5	82	4	1	5	5	.500	0	1-6	6	3.38	3.22
2014	Tor	AL	30	0	0	0	25.2	114	19	14	14	3	1	1	3	19	0	21	2	0	3	0	1.000	0	0-0	12	4.59	4.91
2015	Tor	AL	31	0	0	12	29.1	129	28	19	17	5	1	1	1	14	1	30	6	0	2	0	1.000	0	1-4	5	4.69	5.22
2016	Cin	NL	7	0	0	0	8.0	40	5	6	6	1	0	0	1	10	0	10	1	0	0	0	-	0	0-0	2	5.82	6.75
	12 Sea	AL	34	0	0	11	36.2	148	23	17	17	9	2	0	5	11	1	46	3	0	2	1	.667	0	0-2	3	3.07	4.17
	12 Tor	AL	27	0	0	1	29.1	126	23	12	11	3	1	2	0	15	0	46	3	0	2	2	.500	0	0-0	9	3.27	3.38
	6 ML YEARS		190	0	0	42	194.2	838	153	95	88	26	8	7	13	102	8	242	19	1	15	9	.625	0	2-12	37	3.79	4.07

Randall Delgado

Pitches: R **Bats:** R **Pos:** RP-79   **Ht:** 6'4" **Wt:** 220 **Born:** 2/9/1990 **Age:** 27

Year	Team	Lg	G	GS	CG	GF	IP	BFP	H	R	ER	HR	SH	SF	HB	TBB	IBB	SO	WP	Bk	W	L	Pct	Sh	Sv-Op	Hld	ERC	ERA
2011	Atl	NL	7	7	0	0	35.0	147	29	12	11	5	0	0	1	14	1	18	2	0	1	1	.500	0	0-0	0	3.48	2.83
2012	Atl	NL	18	17	0	0	92.2	401	89	48	45	8	5	3	4	42	4	76	5	1	4	9	.308	0	0-0	0	4.10	4.37
2013	Ari	NL	20	19	1	0	116.1	473	116	59	55	24	5	5	1	23	2	79	3	1	5	7	.417	1	0-0	0	4.03	4.26
2014	Ari	NL	47	4	0	6	77.2	339	71	44	42	6	2	2	3	35	2	86	5	0	4	4	.500	0	0-0	2	3.69	4.87
2015	Ari	NL	64	1	0	13	72.0	308	63	28	26	7	2	2	1	33	2	73	7	0	8	4	.667	0	1-3	12	3.59	3.25
2016	Ari	NL	79	0	0	14	75.0	337	77	39	37	8	3	5	2	36	3	68	7	0	5	2	.714	0	0-3	5	4.56	4.44
	6 ML YEARS		235	48	1	33	468.2	2005	445	230	216	58	17	17	12	183	14	400	29	2	27	27	.500	1	1-6	21	3.98	4.15

Matt den Dekker

Bats: L Throws: L Pos: PH-9;CF-6;RF-4;LF-3   Ht: 6'2" Wt: 210 Born: 8/10/1987 Age: 29

Year Team	Lg	G	AB	H	2B	3B	HR	(Hm	Rd)	TB	R	RBI	RC	TBB	IBB	SO	HBP	SH	SF	SB	CS	GDP	Avg	OBP	Slg	OPS
2016 Syrcse*	AAA	106	372	77	14	1	8	(-	-)	117	41	44	38	40	0	110	6	0	3	20	5	3	.207	.292	.315	.607
2013 NYM	NL	27	58	12	1	0	1	(0	1)	16	7	6	5	4	0	23	1	0	0	4	1	0	.207	.270	.276	.546
2014 NYM	NL	53	152	38	11	0	0	(0	0)	49	23	7	17	21	0	34	1	0	0	7	4	1	.250	.345	.322	.667
2015 Was	AA	55	99	25	6	1	5	(3	2)	48	12	12	12	9	0	20	0	2	0	1	1	0	.253	.315	.485	.800
2016 Was	NL	19	34	6	1	0	1	(1	0)	10	3	4	5	4	0	10	1	0	0	1	0	0	.176	.282	.294	.576
4 ML YEARS		154	343	81	19	1	7	(4	3)	123	45	29	39	38	0	87	3	2	0	12	6	1	.236	.318	.359	.676

Matt Dermody

Pitches: L Bats: R Pos: RP-5   Ht: 6'5" Wt: 190 Born: 7/4/1990 Age: 26

Year Team	Lg	G	GS	CG	GF	IP	BFP	H	R	ER	HR	SH	SF	HB	TBB	IBB	SO	WP	Bk	W	L	Pct	Sh	Sv-Op	Hld	ERC	ERA
2013 2 Tms	Low	16	3	0	1	43.1	178	46	12	8	0	2	0	1	4	0	51	1	0	5	1	.833	0	0--	-	2.66	1.66
2014 Lnsng	A	27	12	0	2	96.0	429	113	62	50	5	5	1	3	36	0	65	8	0	4	6	.400	0	0--	-	4.76	4.69
2015 Dnedin	A+	35	1	0	8	77.0	340	98	45	36	2	1	5	3	13	0	62	1	0	4	1	.800	0	1--	-	4.27	4.21
2016 Dnedin	A+	16	0	0	10	18.1	74	21	4	4	0	0	2	0	1	0	20	0	0	1	1	.500	0	3--	-	2.95	1.96
2016 Nham	AA	16	0	0	5	19.2	72	12	3	2	1	0	1	0	2	0	21	1	0	2	0	1.000	0	0--	-	1.13	0.92
2016 Buffalo	AAA	15	0	0	5	16.1	75	22	9	5	0	1	1	0	5	0	6	0	0	0	0	-	0	0--	-	4.87	2.76
2016 Tor	AL	5	0	0	1	3.0	16	6	4	4	1	0	0	1	0	0	5	1	0	0	0	-	0	0-0	0	12.18	12.00

Daniel Descalso

dess-CAL-so

Bats: L Throws: R Pos: SS-31;PH-30;1B-16;2B-14;LF-7;3B-4;DH-4;PR-1   Ht: 5'10" Wt: 190 Born: 10/19/1986 Age: 30

Year Team	Lg	G	AB	H	2B	3B	HR	(Hm	Rd)	TB	R	RBI	RC	TBB	IBB	SO	HBP	SH	SF	SB	CS	GDP	Avg	OBP	Slg	OPS
2010 StL	NL	11	34	9	2	0	0	(0	0)	11	6	4	5	2	0	6	1	0	0	1	0	0	.265	.324	.324	.648
2011 StL	NL	148	326	86	20	3	1	(1	0)	115	35	28	40	33	9	65	3	10	3	2	2	3	.264	.334	.353	.687
2012 StL	NL	143	374	85	10	7	4	(0	4)	121	41	26	29	37	3	83	5	7	3	6	3	5	.227	.303	.324	.627
2013 StL	NL	123	328	78	25	1	5	(1	4)	120	43	43	40	22	5	56	3	3	2	6	3	7	.238	.290	.366	.656
2014 StL	NL	104	161	39	11	0	0	(0	0)	50	20	10	15	20	0	33	2	1	0	1	3	2	.242	.333	.311	.644
2015 Col	NL	101	185	38	3	2	5	(1	4)	60	22	22	14	20	6	45	0	4	0	1	2	3	.205	.283	.324	.607
2016 Col	NL	99	250	66	12	2	8	(3	5)	106	38	38	45	34	3	56	1	0	4	3	0	2	.264	.349	.424	.773
Postseason		44	84	18	2	0	2	(1	1)	26	16	6	5	4	2	19	0	5	1	2	0	2	.214	.247	.310	.557
7 ML YEARS		729	1658	401	83	15	23	(6	17)	583	205	171	188	168	26	344	15	25	12	20	13	22	.242	.315	.352	.667

Anthony DeSclafani

DEE-skla-fa-nee

Pitches: R Bats: R Pos: SP-20   Ht: 6'1" Wt: 200 Born: 4/18/1990 Age: 27

Year Team	Lg	G	GS	CG	GF	IP	BFP	H	R	ER	HR	SH	SF	HB	TBB	IBB	SO	WP	Bk	W	L	Pct	Sh	Sv-Op	Hld	ERC	ERA
2014 Mia	NL	13	5	0	4	33.0	146	40	23	23	4	4	3	2	5	0	26	2	0	2	2	.500	0	0-0	0	4.56	6.27
2015 Cin	NL	31	31	0	0	184.2	785	194	93	83	17	10	5	5	55	5	151	6	0	9	13	.409	0	0-0	0	4.00	4.05
2016 Cin	NL	20	20	1	0	123.1	507	120	51	45	16	7	3	4	30	2	105	6	1	9	5	.643	1	0-0	0	3.67	3.28
3 ML YEARS		64	56	1	4	341.0	1438	354	167	151	37	21	11	11	90	7	282	14	1	20	20	.500	1	0-0	0	3.94	3.99

Delino DeShields

Bats: R Throws: R Pos: CF-33;LF-26;PR-16;DH-4;PH-3   Ht: 5'9" Wt: 200 Born: 8/16/1992 Age: 24

Year Team	Lg	G	AB	H	2B	3B	HR	(Hm	Rd)	TB	R	RBI	RC	TBB	IBB	SO	HBP	SH	SF	SB	CS	GDP	Avg	OBP	Slg	OPS
2012 2 Tms		135	537	154	24	8	12	(-	-)	230	113	61	108	83	5	131	9	5	3	101	19	5	.287	.389	.428	.818
2013 Lancst	A+	111	451	143	25	14	5	(-	-)	211	100	54	91	57	1	91	11	13	2	51	18	8	.317	.405	.468	.873
2014 CpChr	AA	114	411	97	14	2	11	(-	-)	148	75	57	63	61	0	112	11	18	6	53	14	3	.236	.346	.360	.706
2016 RdRck	AAA	54	207	54	10	0	3	(-	-)	73	37	17	31	35	0	60	1	4	2	21	7	1	.261	.367	.353	.720
2015 Tex	AL	121	425	111	22	10	2	(2	0)	159	83	37	66	53	1	101	3	7	4	25	8	1	.261	.344	.374	.718
2016 Tex	AL	74	182	38	7	0	4	(0	4)	57	36	13	16	15	0	54	2	3	1	8	3	1	.209	.275	.313	.588
Postseason		5	24	7	3	0	0	(0	0)	10	4	2	4	0	0	2	0	0	0	1	0	0	.292	.292	.417	.708
2 ML YEARS		195	607	149	29	10	6	(2	4)	216	119	50	82	68	1	155	5	10	5	33	11	2	.245	.324	.356	.680

Ian Desmond

Bats: R Throws: R Pos: CF-130;LF-29   Ht: 6'3" Wt: 215 Born: 9/20/1985 Age: 31

Year Team	Lg	G	AB	H	2B	3B	HR	(Hm	Rd)	TB	R	RBI	RC	TBB	IBB	SO	HBP	SH	SF	SB	CS	GDP	Avg	OBP	Slg	OPS
2009 Was	NL	21	82	23	7	2	4	(2	2)	46	9	12	10	5	0	14	0	1	1	1	0	2	.280	.318	.561	.879
2010 Was	NL	154	525	141	27	4	10	(8	2)	206	59	65	58	28	3	109	5	9	7	17	5	9	.269	.308	.392	.700
2011 Was	NL	154	584	148	27	5	8	(7	1)	209	65	49	65	35	2	139	4	11	5	25	10	9	.253	.298	.358	.656
2012 Was	NL	130	513	150	33	2	25	(16	9)	262	72	73	73	30	1	113	3	0	1	21	6	17	.292	.335	.511	.845
2013 Was	NL	158	600	168	38	3	20	(10	10)	272	77	80	81	43	3	145	2	0	5	21	6	16	.280	.331	.453	.784
2014 Was	NL	154	593	151	26	3	24	(12	12)	255	73	91	78	46	0	183	6	0	3	24	5	17	.255	.313	.430	.743
2015 Was	NL	156	583	136	27	2	19	(18	1)	224	69	62	59	45	0	187	3	6	4	13	5	9	.233	.290	.384	.674
2016 Tex	AL	156	625	178	29	3	22	(10	12)	279	107	86	92	44	2	160	5	0	3	21	6	11	.285	.335	.446	.782
Postseason		9	37	10	1	0	0	(0	0)	11	4	0	2	1	0	9	0	0	0	1	0	0	.270	.289	.297	.587
8 ML YEARS		1083	4105	1095	214	24	132	(76	56)	1753	531	518	516	276	11	1050	31	29	29	143	43	90	.267	.316	.427	.743

Odrisamer Despaigne

Pitches: R **Bats:** R **Pos:** RP-19   oh-DREE-sa-mehr des-PAHN-yay   **Ht:** 6'0" **Wt:** 200 **Born:** 4/4/1987 **Age:** 30

Year	Team	Lg	G	GS	CG	GF	IP	BFP	H	R	ER	HR	SH	SF	HB	TBB	IBB	SO	WP	Bk	W	L	Pct	Sh	Sv-Op	Hld	ERC	ERA
2016	Norfolk*	AAA	18	17	0	0	88.1	378	91	39	38	5	1	1	6	27	0	70	6	1	1	9	.100	0	0- -	-	3.86	3.87
2014	SD	NL	16	16	0	0	96.1	404	85	44	36	6	8	1	5	32	0	65	0	0	4	7	.364	0	0-0	0	3.12	3.36
2015	SD	NL	34	18	0	5	125.2	547	142	82	81	17	8	3	9	32	3	69	7	0	5	9	.357	0	0-0	0	4.75	5.80
2016	2 Tms		19	0	0	8	30.1	135	36	21	20	3	0	2	1	16	1	17	0	1	0	2	.000	0	0-2	1	6.02	5.93
16	Bal	AL	16	0	0	5	27.1	122	32	18	17	3	0	1	1	15	1	17	0	1	0	2	.000	0	0-2	1	6.11	5.60
16	Mia	NL	3	0	0	3	3.0	13	4	3	3	0	0	1	0	1	0	0	0	0	0	0	-	0	0-0	0	5.24	9.00
	3 ML YEARS		69	34	0	13	252.1	1086	263	147	137	26	16	6	15	80	4	151	7	1	9	18	.333	0	0-2	1	4.24	4.89

Ross Detwiler

Pitches: L **Bats:** R **Pos:** RP-9; SP-7   DETT-why-lerr   **Ht:** 6'3" **Wt:** 210 **Born:** 3/6/1986 **Age:** 31

Year	Team	Lg	G	GS	CG	GF	IP	BFP	H	R	ER	HR	SH	SF	HB	TBB	IBB	SO	WP	Bk	W	L	Pct	Sh	Sv-Op	Hld	ERC	ERA
2016	Clmbs*	AAA	12	12	0	0	62.2	266	64	33	32	6	2	1	3	21	0	41	3	0	2	4	.333	0	0- -	-	4.17	4.60
2007	Was	NL	1	0	0	1	1.0	4	0	0	0	0	0	0	0	0	0	1	0	0	0	0	-	0	0-0	0	0.00	0.00
2009	Was	NL	15	14	1	0	75.2	341	87	43	42	3	4	1	2	33	3	43	4	0	1	6	.143	0	0-0	0	4.65	5.00
2010	Was	NL	8	5	0	1	29.2	135	34	22	14	5	2	0	1	14	1	17	1	0	1	3	.250	0	0-0	0	5.83	4.25
2011	Was	NL	15	10	0	1	66.0	277	63	26	22	7	7	3	3	20	2	41	2	0	4	5	.444	0	0-0	1	3.64	3.00
2012	Was	NL	33	27	0	1	164.1	686	149	75	62	15	8	3	5	52	1	105	4	1	10	8	.556	0	0-0	1	3.30	3.40
2013	Was	NL	13	13	0	0	71.1	316	92	37	32	5	4	1	5	14	2	39	0	0	2	7	.222	0	0-0	0	4.96	4.04
2014	Was	NL	47	0	0	15	63.0	274	68	34	28	5	4	3	5	21	4	39	3	0	2	3	.400	0	1-2	3	4.36	4.00
2015	2 Tms		41	7	0	7	58.1	288	82	51	47	10	1	4	6	36	1	41	3	0	1	5	.167	0	0-2	2	8.67	7.25
2016	2 Tms	AL	16	7	0	0	48.2	220	59	34	33	5	0	1	1	19	0	26	3	0	2	4	.333	0	0-1	0	5.37	6.10
15	Tex	AL	17	7	0	4	43.0	208	62	37	34	9	1	3	3	20	0	28	3	0	0	5	.000	0	0-1	1	8.35	7.12
15	Atl	NL	24	0	0	3	15.1	80	20	14	13	1	0	1	3	16	1	13	0	0	1	0	1.000	0	0-1	1	9.42	7.63
16	Cle	AL	7	0	0	0	4.2	21	3	3	3	1	0	1	0	4	0	3	0	0	0	0	-	0	0-1	0	4.60	5.79
16	Oak	AL	9	7	0	0	44.0	199	56	31	30	4	0	0	1	15	0	23	3	0	2	4	.333	0	0-0	0	5.46	6.14
	Postseason		1	1	0	0	6.0	25	3	1	0	0	1	1	0	3	1	2	0	0	0	0	-	0	0-0	0	1.21	0.00
	9 ML YEARS		189	83	1	25	578.0	2541	634	322	280	55	30	16	28	209	13	352	20	1	23	41	.359	0	1-5	7	4.61	4.36

Chris Devenski

Pitches: R **Bats:** R **Pos:** RP-43; SP-5   **Ht:** 6'3" **Wt:** 210 **Born:** 11/13/1990 **Age:** 26

Year	Team	Lg	G	GS	CG	GF	IP	BFP	H	R	ER	HR	SH	SF	HB	TBB	IBB	SO	WP	Bk	W	L	Pct	Sh	Sv-Op	Hld	ERC	ERA
2012	2 Tms	Low	24	13	1	4	91.0	388	86	42	39	9	5	4	5	35	1	92	4	4	8	7	.533	1	2- -	-	3.93	3.86
2013	2 Tms	Low	29	18	0	3	118.2	551	166	91	87	16	6	4	8	40	0	97	5	1	8	5	.615	0	1- -	-	6.84	6.60
2014	Lancst	A+	17	11	0	2	76.2	319	70	42	35	8	2	1	3	12	0	77	1	0	5	5	.500	0	2- -	-	2.76	4.11
2014	CpChr	AA	10	5	0	1	41.1	174	33	21	18	7	0	1	0	18	0	37	2	0	5	3	.625	0	0- -	-	3.53	3.92
2015	CpChr	AA	24	17	0	5	119.2	501	117	43	40	12	1	3	2	33	0	104	4	0	7	4	.636	0	2- -	-	3.54	3.01
2016	Hou	AL	48	5	0	16	108.1	408	79	26	26	4	1	1	3	20	0	104	2	0	4	4	.500	0	1-1	5	1.74	2.16

Scott Diamond

Pitches: L **Bats:** L **Pos:** RP-1   **Ht:** 6'3" **Wt:** 205 **Born:** 7/30/1986 **Age:** 30

Year	Team	Lg	G	GS	CG	GF	IP	BFP	H	R	ER	HR	SH	SF	HB	TBB	IBB	SO	WP	Bk	W	L	Pct	Sh	Sv-Op	Hld	ERC	ERA
2016	Buffalo*	AAA	28	28	0	0	166.0	695	191	92	83	11	3	9	5	32	0	100	4	0	9	15	.375	0	0- -	-	4.08	4.50
2011	Min	AL	7	7	0	0	39.0	181	51	25	22	3	2	1	0	17	3	19	3	0	1	5	.167	0	0-0	0	5.69	5.08
2012	Min	AL	27	27	1	0	173.0	714	184	76	68	17	3	5	4	31	2	90	10	0	12	9	.571	1	0-0	0	3.68	3.54
2013	Min	AL	24	24	0	0	131.0	576	163	88	79	21	1	5	1	36	4	52	5	0	6	13	.316	0	0-0	0	5.45	5.43
2016	Tor	AL	1	0	0	1	1.0	7	2	3	3	0	0	0	0	2	0	0	0	0	0	0	-	0	0-0	0	16.69	27.00
	4 ML YEARS		59	58	1	1	344.0	1478	400	192	172	41	6	11	5	86	9	161	18	0	19	27	.413	1	0-0	0	4.59	4.50

Aledmys Diaz

Bats: R **Throws:** R **Pos:** SS-106;PH-6;2B-1   ah-LED-mees   **Ht:** 6'1" **Wt:** 195 **Born:** 8/1/1990 **Age:** 26

Year	Team	Lg	G	AB	H	2B	3B	HR	(Hm	Rd)	TB	R	RBI	RC	TBB	IBB	SO	HBP	SH	SF	SB	CS	GDP	Avg	OBP	Slg	OPS
2014	Sprgfld	AA	34	117	34	8	1	3	(-	-)	53	15	18	17	2	0	24	2	3	1	6	2	2	.291	.311	.453	.764
2014	PlmBh	A+	13	44	10	2	0	2	(-	-)	18	5	6	7	7	0	10	2	0	1	1	0	1	.227	.352	.409	.761
2015	Sprgfld	AA	102	375	99	26	2	10	(-	-)	159	47	46	52	29	0	62	4	1	0	6	5	10	.264	.324	.424	.748
2015	Memp	AAA	14	50	19	3	0	3	(-	-)	31	12	6	12	6	1	5	1	0	1	0	1	2	.380	.448	.620	1.068
2016	StL	NL	111	404	121	28	3	17	(7	10)	206	71	65	75	41	6	60	7	2	6	4	4	10	.300	.369	.510	.879

Dayan Diaz

Pitches: R **Bats:** R **Pos:** RP-6   DIE-yahn   **Ht:** 5'10" **Wt:** 195 **Born:** 2/10/1989 **Age:** 28

Year	Team	Lg	G	GS	CG	GF	IP	BFP	H	R	ER	HR	SH	SF	HB	TBB	IBB	SO	WP	Bk	W	L	Pct	Sh	Sv-Op	Hld	ERC	ERA
2012	Lxngtn	A	41	0	0	31	58.1	240	40	14	12	1	3	1	2	30	0	64	3	0	5	4	.556	0	19- -	-	2.45	1.85
2013	2 Tms	Low	8	1	0	4	14.0	61	11	3	3	2	0	0	1	6	0	19	3	0	0	1	.000	0	1- -	-	3.44	1.93
2013	Tenn	AA	1	0	0	1	7.0	31	5	4	4	1	1	0	1	3	0	10	2	0	0	0	-	0	0- -	-	3.27	5.14
2014	Salem	A+	24	0	0	22	33.2	135	21	8	5	1	0	3	1	14	0	40	4	2	0	1	.000	0	6- -	-	1.89	1.34
2014	Portlnd	AA	11	0	0	5	16.1	72	16	5	5	0	1	0	1	7	0	16	0	0	2	1	.667	0	1- -	-	3.55	2.76

Year	Team	Lg	G	GS	CG	GF	IP	BFP	H	R	ER	HR	SH	SF	HB	TBB	IBB	SO	WP	Bk	W	L	Pct	Sh	Sv-Op	Hld	ERC	ERA
2015	Portlnd	AA	9	0	0	6	15.2	56	7	2	2	0	0	0	0	2	0	17	1	1	0	0	-	0	2--	-	0.62	1.15
2015	Pwtckt	AAA	28	0	0	12	57.0	247	47	16	12	3	4	0	2	28	1	49	3	0	2	1	.667	0	4--	-	3.18	1.89
2016	Lsvlle	AAA	40	1	0	13	56.0	230	52	20	19	2	1	0	0	16	1	46	1	0	7	1	.875	0	1--	-	2.83	3.05
2016	Cin	NL	6	0	0	0	6.2	36	10	9	7	2	1	1	0	7	0	3	0	0	0	0	-	0	0-0	0	12.17	9.45

Edwin Diaz

Pitches: R Bats: R Pos: RP-49   **Ht: 6'3" Wt: 165 Born: 3/22/1994 Age: 23**

Year	Team	Lg	G	GS	CG	GF	IP	BFP	H	R	ER	HR	SH	SF	HB	TBB	IBB	SO	WP	Bk	W	L	Pct	Sh	Sv-Op	Hld	ERC	ERA
2012	Ms	R	9	1	0	0	19.0	90	12	13	11	2	0	0	5	17	0	20	0	0	2	1	.667	0	0--	-	4.92	5.21
2013	Pulski	R+	13	13	0	0	69.0	260	45	14	11	5	1	2	4	18	0	79	2	0	5	2	.714	0	0--	-	1.95	1.43
2014	Clinton	A	24	24	1	0	116.0	483	96	50	43	5	3	4	10	42	0	111	5	2	6	8	.429	1	0--	-	2.97	3.34
2015	Bkrsfld	A+	7	7	0	0	37.0	141	21	7	7	3	1	1	4	9	0	42	2	0	2	0	1.000	0	0--	-	1.67	1.70
2015	Jacksn	AA	20	20	0	0	104.1	443	102	56	53	5	2	3	7	37	0	103	2	1	5	10	.333	0	0--	-	3.73	4.57
2016	Jacksn	AA	16	6	0	4	40.2	162	32	13	10	3	1	1	2	7	0	54	2	1	3	3	.500	0	1--	-	2.13	2.21
2016	Sea	AL	49	0	0	23	51.2	217	45	16	16	5	0	0	3	15	2	88	6	1	0	4	.000	0	18-21	13	3.05	2.79

Elias Diaz

Bats: R Throws: R Pos: C-1   Eh-lee-ahs   **Ht: 6'0" Wt: 210 Born: 11/17/1990 Age: 26**

Year	Team	Lg	G	AB	H	2B	3B	HR	(Hm	Rd)	TB	R	RBI	RC	TBB	IBB	SO	HBP	SH	SF	SB	CS	GDP	Avg	OBP	Slg	OPS
2012	WV	A	92	313	65	14	1	3	(-	-)	90	32	26	24	22	0	51	3	3	6	2	2	15	.208	.262	.288	.549
2013	Bradtn	A+	57	183	51	12	2	2	(-	-)	73	30	15	30	31	0	33	1	3	2	4	4	3	.279	.382	.399	.781
2014	Altna	AA	91	326	107	20	0	6	(-	-)	145	41	54	57	30	0	51	1	2	8	3	2	11	.328	.378	.445	.823
2014	Indy	AAA	10	33	5	1	0	0	(-	-)	6	4	0	0	3	0	6	1	0	0	0	1	2	.152	.243	.182	.425
2015	Indy	AAA	93	325	88	16	4	4	(-	-)	124	33	47	42	29	0	47	0	2	5	1	4	9	.271	.330	.382	.711
2016	Indy	AAA	25	94	25	3	0	0	(-	-)	28	4	10	8	3	0	17	0	0	0	1	0	4	.266	.289	.298	.587
2015	Pit	NL	2	2	0	0	0	0	(0	0)	0	0	0	0	0	0	1	0	0	0	0	0	0	.000	.000	.000	.000
2016	Pit	NL	1	4	0	0	0	0	(0	0)	0	0	1	0	0	0	1	0	0	0	0	0	0	.000	.000	.000	.000
	2 ML YEARS		3	6	0	0	0	0	(0	0)	0	0	1	0	0	0	2	0	0	0	0	0	0	.000	.000	.000	.000

Jumbo Diaz

Pitches: R Bats: R Pos: RP-45   **Ht: 6'4" Wt: 280 Born: 2/27/1984 Age: 33**

Year	Team	Lg	G	GS	CG	GF	IP	BFP	H	R	ER	HR	SH	SF	HB	TBB	IBB	SO	WP	Bk	W	L	Pct	Sh	Sv-Op	Hld	ERC	ERA
2016	Lsvlle*	AAA	22	0	0	18	24.0	94	16	2	2	0	1	0	0	7	0	28	2	0	1	1	.500	0	11--	-	1.50	0.75
2014	Cin	NL	36	0	0	12	34.2	142	29	13	13	3	0	2	0	14	4	37	1	0	0	1	.000	0	0-1	8	3.00	3.38
2015	Cin	NL	61	0	0	16	60.1	255	58	29	28	9	3	2	3	18	3	70	5	1	2	1	.667	0	1-5	7	3.92	4.18
2016	Cin	NL	45	0	0	11	43.0	182	36	20	15	8	1	0	1	19	1	37	5	0	1	1	.500	0	0-1	4	3.97	3.14
	3 ML YEARS		142	0	0	39	138.0	579	123	62	56	20	4	4	4	51	8	144	11	1	3	3	.500	0	1-7	19	3.70	3.65

Alex Dickerson

Bats: L Throws: L Pos: LF-68;PH-16;DH-2   **Ht: 6'3" Wt: 235 Born: 5/26/1990 Age: 27**

Year	Team	Lg	G	AB	H	2B	3B	HR	(Hm	Rd)	TB	R	RBI	RC	TBB	IBB	SO	HBP	SH	SF	SB	CS	GDP	Avg	OBP	Slg	OPS
2012	Bradtn	A+	129	488	144	31	3	13	(-	-)	220	65	90	79	39	3	93	7	2	5	12	7	7	.295	.353	.451	.803
2013	Altna	AA	126	451	130	36	3	17	(-	-)	223	61	68	75	27	4	89	8	2	3	10	7	14	.288	.337	.494	.832
2014	SnAnt	AA	34	137	44	11	2	3	(-	-)	68	20	24	24	9	1	28	1	0	0	0	1	2	.321	.367	.496	.864
2015	ElPaso	AAA	125	459	141	36	9	12	(-	-)	231	82	71	88	45	2	96	8	0	7	4	0	10	.307	.374	.503	.877
2016	ElPaso	AAA	62	217	83	16	3	10	(-	-)	135	50	51	54	14	6	27	5	0	4	0	0	7	.382	.425	.622	1.047
2015	SD	NL	11	8	2	0	0	0	(0	0)	2	0	0	0	0	0	3	0	0	0	0	0	1	.250	.250	.250	.500
2016	SD	NL	84	253	65	16	2	10	(5	5)	115	39	37	40	26	2	44	4	0	2	5	1	5	.257	.333	.455	.788
	2 ML YEARS		95	261	67	16	2	10	(5	5)	117	39	37	40	26	2	47	4	0	2	5	1	6	.257	.331	.448	.779

Corey Dickerson

Bats: L Throws: R Pos: LF-76;DH-61;PH-15;RF-2   **Ht: 6'1" Wt: 205 Born: 5/22/1989 Age: 28**

Year	Team	Lg	G	AB	H	2B	3B	HR	(Hm	Rd)	TB	R	RBI	RC	TBB	IBB	SO	HBP	SH	SF	SB	CS	GDP	Avg	OBP	Slg	OPS
2013	Col	NL	69	194	51	13	5	5	(4	1)	89	32	17	23	16	0	41	0	1	2	2	2	1	.263	.316	.459	.775
2014	Col	NL	131	436	136	27	6	24	(15	9)	247	74	76	79	37	6	101	1	0	4	8	7	6	.312	.364	.567	.931
2015	Col	NL	65	224	68	18	2	10	(5	5)	120	30	31	39	10	0	56	0	0	0	3	1	3	.304	.333	.536	.869
2016	TB	AL	148	510	125	36	3	24	(7	17)	239	57	70	59	33	6	134	2	0	2	0	2	12	.245	.293	.469	.761
	4 ML YEARS		413	1364	380	94	16	63	(31	32)	695	193	194	200	96	12	332	3	1	8	10	12	22	.279	.326	.510	.835

R.A. Dickey

Pitches: R Bats: R Pos: SP-29; RP-1   **Ht: 6'3" Wt: 215 Born: 10/29/1974 Age: 42**

Year	Team	Lg	G	GS	CG	GF	IP	BFP	H	R	ER	HR	SH	SF	HB	TBB	IBB	SO	WP	Bk	W	L	Pct	Sh	Sv-Op	Hld	ERC	ERA
2001	Tex	AL	4	0	0	0	12.0	53	13	9	9	3	0	0	0	7	1	4	1	0	0	1	.000	0	0-0	0	6.57	6.75
2003	Tex	AL	38	13	1	6	116.2	513	135	68	66	16	4	3	5	38	5	94	5	2	9	8	.529	1	1-1	3	5.09	5.09
2004	Tex	AL	25	15	0	2	104.1	480	136	77	65	17	3	3	4	33	1	57	5	1	6	7	.462	0	1-1	0	6.08	5.61
2005	Tex	AL	9	4	0	2	29.2	134	29	23	22	4	0	1	2	17	0	15	2	0	1	2	.333	0	0-0	0	5.18	6.67
2006	Tex	AL	1	1	0	0	3.1	18	8	7	7	6	0	0	0	1	0	1	0	0	0	1	.000	0	0-0	0	32.05	18.90

Year	Team	Lg	G	GS	CG	GF	IP	BFP	H	R	ER	HR	SH	SF	HB	TBB	IBB	SO	WP	Bk	W	L	Pct	Sh	Sv-Op	Hld	ERC	ERA
2008	Sea	AL	32	14	0	9	112.1	500	124	65	65	15	4	6	2	51	4	58	11	1	5	8	.385	0	0-0	0	5.19	5.21
2009	Min	AL	35	1	0	13	64.1	293	74	34	33	8	2	2	4	30	1	42	4	0	1	1	.500	0	0-0	1	5.66	4.62
2010	NYM	NL	27	26	2	0	174.1	713	165	62	55	13	7	3	4	42	3	104	11	0	11	9	.550	1	0-0	1	3.11	2.84
2011	NYM	NL	33	32	1	0	208.2	876	202	85	76	18	16	7	9	54	2	134	9	1	8	13	.381	0	0-0	1	3.40	3.28
2012	NYM	NL	34	33	5	1	233.2	927	192	78	71	24	9	7	9	54	2	230	4	1	20	6	.769	3	0-0	1	2.70	2.73
2013	Tor	AL	34	34	3	0	224.2	943	207	113	105	35	2	6	10	71	0	177	7	1	14	13	.519	1	0-0	0	3.87	4.21
2014	Tor	AL	34	34	1	0	215.2	914	191	101	89	26	2	4	14	74	2	173	5	0	14	13	.519	0	0-0	0	3.58	3.71
2015	Tor	AL	33	33	2	0	214.1	884	195	97	93	25	3	11	11	61	1	126	9	2	11	11	.500	0	0-0	0	3.48	3.91
2016	Tor	AL	30	29	0	1	169.2	728	169	97	84	28	1	3	6	63	0	126	5	1	10	15	.400	0	0-0	0	4.57	4.46
Postseason			2	2	0	0	6.1	31	9	6	5	2	0	1	1	2	0	4	1	0	0	1	.000	0	0-0	0	8.58	7.11
14 ML YEARS			369	269	15	35	1883.2	7976	1840	916	840	238	53	56	80	596	22	1341	78	10	110	108	.505	6	2-2	6	3.97	4.01

Jake Diekman

Pitches: L **Bats:** L **Pos:** RP-66 DEEK-man **Ht:** 6'4" **Wt:** 200 **Born:** 1/21/1987 **Age:** 30

Year	Team	Lg	G	GS	CG	GF	IP	BFP	H	R	ER	HR	SH	SF	HB	TBB	IBB	SO	WP	Bk	W	L	Pct	Sh	Sv-Op	Hld	ERC	ERA
2012	Phi	NL	32	0	0	7	27.1	131	25	17	12	1	1	0	3	20	3	35	1	0	1	1	.500	0	0-1	4	4.45	3.95
2013	Phi	NL	45	0	0	11	38.1	164	34	15	11	1	2	1	0	16	2	41	2	1	1	4	.200	0	0-1	11	2.89	2.58
2014	Phi	NL	73	0	0	19	71.0	313	66	36	30	4	2	7	3	35	5	100	7	0	5	5	.500	0	0-4	18	3.73	3.80
2015	2 Tms		67	0	0	7	58.1	260	53	28	26	5	0	0	3	31	0	69	2	0	2	1	.667	0	0-3	16	4.11	4.01
2016	Tex	AL	66	0	0	14	53.0	221	36	22	20	4	0	2	3	26	1	59	3	0	4	2	.667	0	4-5	26	2.72	3.40
15	Phi	NL	41	0	0	6	36.2	175	40	23	21	3	0	0	2	24	0	49	1	0	2	1	.667	0	0-2	6	5.60	5.15
15	Tex	AL	26	0	0	1	21.2	85	13	5	5	2	0	0	1	7	0	20	1	0	0	0	-	0	0-1	10	1.89	2.08
Postseason			4	0	0	1	6.0	19	2	1	1	0	0	0	0	0	0	5	0	0	0	0	-	0	0-0	1	0.26	1.50
5 ML YEARS			283	0	0	58	248.0	1089	214	118	99	15	5	10	12	128	11	304	15	1	13	13	.500	0	4-14	75	3.54	3.59

Derek Dietrich

Bats: L **Throws:** R **Pos:** 2B-75;PH-27;1B-16;3B-13;LF-8 DEE-trick **Ht:** 6'0" **Wt:** 205 **Born:** 7/18/1989 **Age:** 27

Year	Team	Lg	G	AB	H	2B	3B	HR	(Hm	Rd)	TB	R	RBI	RC	TBB	IBB	SO	HBP	SH	SF	SB	CS	GDP	Avg	OBP	Slg	OPS
2013	Mia	NL	57	215	46	10	2	9	(3	6)	87	32	23	24	11	1	56	7	0	0	1	0	1	.214	.275	.405	.679
2014	Mia	NL	49	158	36	6	2	5	(1	4)	61	31	17	22	13	0	38	10	2	0	1	0	1	.228	.326	.386	.712
2015	Mia	NL	90	250	64	14	3	10	(3	7)	114	38	24	32	23	2	65	13	0	3	0	2	4	.256	.346	.456	.802
2016	Mia	NL	128	351	98	20	5	7	(3	4)	149	39	42	57	32	2	84	24	0	5	1	0	6	.279	.374	.425	.798
4 ML YEARS			324	974	244	50	12	31	(10	21)	411	140	106	135	79	5	243	54	2	8	3	2	12	.251	.338	.422	.760

Wilmer Difo

Bats: B **Throws:** R **Pos:** PH-14;2B-9;SS-5;3B-3;PR-3 DEE-fo **Ht:** 5'11" **Wt:** 200 **Born:** 4/2/1992 **Age:** 25

Year	Team	Lg	G	AB	H	2B	3B	HR	(Hm	Rd)	TB	R	RBI	RC	TBB	IBB	SO	HBP	SH	SF	SB	CS	GDP	Avg	OBP	Slg	OPS
2012	Nats	R	54	198	52	7	3	0	(-	-)	65	33	13	30	14	0	35	2	0	1	19	5	2	.263	.374	.328	.703
2013	4 Tms	Low	61	207	45	7	4	4	(-	-)	72	30	21	22	21	0	36	3	2	2	9	4	2	.217	.296	.348	.644
2014	Hgrstn	A	136	559	176	31	7	14	(-	-)	263	91	90	102	37	0	65	6	2	6	49	9	5	.315	.360	.470	.831
2015	Ptomc	A+	19	75	24	7	0	3	(-	-)	40	13	14	15	8	1	13	0	0	0	4	1	0	.320	.386	.533	.919
2015	Hrsbrg	AA	87	359	100	21	6	2	(-	-)	139	48	39	49	12	2	79	7	0	3	26	1	0	.279	.312	.387	.700
2016	Hrsbrg	AA	104	410	106	15	3	6	(-	-)	145	59	41	50	34	0	59	3	2	2	28	11	12	.259	.318	.354	.672
2015	Was	NL	15	11	2	0	0	0	(0	0)	2	1	0	0	0	0	2	0	0	0	3	0	0	.182	.182	.182	.364
2016	Was	NL	31	58	16	3	0	1	(1	0)	22	14	7	8	8	1	12	0	0	0	3	0	0	.276	.364	.379	.743
2 ML YEARS			46	69	18	3	0	1	(1	0)	24	15	7	9	8	1	14	0	0	0	3	0	0	.261	.338	.348	.685

Jose Dominguez

Pitches: R **Bats:** R **Pos:** RP-34 **Ht:** 6'0" **Wt:** 200 **Born:** 8/7/1990 **Age:** 26

Year	Team	Lg	G	GS	CG	GF	IP	BFP	H	R	ER	HR	SH	SF	HB	TBB	IBB	SO	WP	Bk	W	L	Pct	Sh	Sv-Op	Hld	ERC	ERA
2016	ElPaso*	AAA	27	0	0	17	35.2	159	28	17	15	1	0	1	4	25	2	36	5	1	3	3	.500	0	6--	-	3.86	3.79
2013	LAD	NL	9	0	0	2	8.1	39	11	3	2	0	0	0	1	3	0	4	1	0	0	0	-	0	0-0	1	5.47	2.16
2014	LAD	NL	5	0	0	2	6.1	30	7	8	8	2	0	0	1	3	0	8	0	0	0	0	-	0	0-0	0	7.23	11.37
2015	TB	AL	4	0	0	2	5.2	19	2	0	0	0	1	0	0	2	0	5	0	0	1	0	1.000	0	0-0	0	0.84	0.00
2016	SD	NL	34	0	0	6	35.2	155	34	23	20	5	1	1	4	17	1	20	2	0	1	0	1.000	0	0-1	4	4.94	5.05
4 ML YEARS			52	0	0	12	56.0	243	54	34	30	7	2	1	6	25	1	37	3	0	2	0	1.000	0	0-1	2	4.74	4.82

Matt Dominguez

Bats: R **Throws:** R **Pos:** 3B-3;1B-1;PH-1 **Ht:** 6'2" **Wt:** 220 **Born:** 8/28/1989 **Age:** 27

Year	Team	Lg	G	AB	H	2B	3B	HR	(Hm	Rd)	TB	R	RBI	RC	TBB	IBB	SO	HBP	SH	SF	SB	CS	GDP	Avg	OBP	Slg	OPS
2016	Buffalo*	AAA	127	475	128	18	0	18	(-	-)	200	47	67	65	29	0	70	5	0	5	0	1	15	.269	.315	.421	.736
2011	Fla	NL	17	45	11	4	0	0	(0	0)	15	2	2	3	2	0	8	1	0	0	0	0	2	.244	.292	.333	.625
2012	Hou	NL	31	109	31	2	2	5	(2	3)	52	14	16	13	4	1	17	0	0	0	0	0	4	.284	.310	.477	.787
2013	Hou	AL	152	543	131	25	0	21	(12	9)	219	56	77	59	30	1	96	7	2	7	0	1	17	.241	.286	.403	.690
2014	Hou	AL	157	564	121	17	0	16	(10	6)	186	51	57	42	29	2	125	5	2	7	0	1	23	.215	.256	.330	.586
2016	Tor	AL	5	11	0	0	0	0	(0	0)	0	0	0	0	1	0	3	0	0	0	0	0	0	.000	.083	.000	.083
5 ML YEARS			362	1272	294	48	2	42	(24	18)	472	123	152	117	66	4	249	13	4	14	0	2	46	.231	.273	.371	.644

Josh Donaldson

Bats: R **Throws:** R **Pos:** 3B-136;DH-19;PH-1   **Ht:** 6'1" **Wt:** 210 **Born:** 12/8/1985 **Age:** 31

Year Team	Lg	G	AB	H	2B	3B	HR	(Hm	Rd)	TB	R	RBI	RC	TBB	IBB	SO	HBP	SH	SF	SB	CS	GDP	Avg	OBP	Slg	OPS
2010 Oak	AL	14	32	5	1	0	1	(0	1)	9	1	4	3	2	0	12	0	0	0	0	0	0	.156	.206	.281	.487
2012 Oak	AL	75	274	66	16	0	9	(3	6)	109	34	33	33	14	0	61	5	0	1	4	1	6	.241	.289	.398	.687
2013 Oak	AL	158	579	174	37	3	24	(13	11)	289	89	93	112	76	2	110	6	1	6	5	2	15	.301	.384	.499	.883
2014 Oak	AL	158	608	155	31	2	29	(11	18)	277	93	98	105	76	5	130	7	0	4	8	0	16	.255	.342	.456	.798
2015 Tor	AL	158	620	184	41	2	41	(24	17)	352	122	123	131	73	0	133	6	2	10	6	0	16	.297	.371	.568	.939
2016 Tor	AL	155	577	164	32	5	37	(21	16)	317	122	99	121	109	6	119	9	2	3	7	1	16	.284	.404	.549	.953
Postseason		22	84	20	4	0	3	(2	1)	33	11	8	12	9	0	24	1	0	0	1	0	1	.238	.319	.393	.712
6 ML YEARS		718	2690	748	158	12	141	(72	69)	1353	461	450	505	350	13	565	33	5	24	30	4	69	.278	.365	.503	.868

Sean Doolittle

Pitches: L **Bats:** L **Pos:** RP-44   **Ht:** 6'2" **Wt:** 210 **Born:** 9/26/1986 **Age:** 30

Year Team	Lg	G	GS	CG	GF	IP	BFP	H	R	ER	HR	SH	SF	HB	TBB	IBB	SO	WP	Bk	W	L	Pct	Sh	Sv-Op	Hld	ERC	ERA
2016 Nashv*	AAA	6	0	0	0	6.0	23	4	1	1	1	0	0	0	1	0	10	0	0	0	0	-	0	0- -	-	1.88	1.50
2012 Oak	AL	44	0	0	7	47.1	191	40	18	16	3	2	2	0	11	1	60	0	0	2	1	.667	0	1-2	18	2.36	3.04
2013 Oak	AL	70	0	0	11	69.0	266	53	24	24	4	3	0	2	13	1	60	2	0	5	5	.500	0	2-7	26	2.00	3.13
2014 Oak	AL	61	0	0	40	62.2	236	38	19	19	5	2	1	0	8	1	89	0	0	2	4	.333	0	22-26	5	1.23	2.73
2015 Oak	AL	12	0	0	7	13.2	57	12	6	6	1	0	1	0	5	0	15	0	0	1	0	1.000	0	4-5	1	3.10	3.95
2016 Oak	AL	44	0	0	13	39.0	155	33	14	14	6	4	0	0	8	2	45	1	0	2	3	.400	0	4-6	10	2.79	3.23
Postseason		8	0	0	1	9.0	41	10	6	4	1	3	1	0	2	0	11	0	0	0	1	.000	0	0-3	2	3.75	4.00
5 ML YEARS		231	0	0	78	231.2	905	176	81	79	19	11	4	2	45	5	269	3	0	12	13	.480	0	33-46	60	1.99	3.07

Felix Doubront

Pitches: L **Bats:** L **Pos:** P   due-BRAWNDT   **Ht:** 6'2" **Wt:** 240 **Born:** 10/23/1987 **Age:** 29

Year Team	Lg	G	GS	CG	GF	IP	BFP	H	R	ER	HR	SH	SF	HB	TBB	IBB	SO	WP	Bk	W	L	Pct	Sh	Sv-Op	Hld	ERC	ERA
2010 Bos	AL	12	3	0	5	25.0	113	27	16	12	3	1	1	1	10	0	23	3	0	2	2	.500	0	2-3	1	4.72	4.32
2011 Bos	AL	11	0	0	1	10.1	47	12	7	7	1	0	1	0	8	0	6	0	0	0	0	-	0	1-1	0	6.97	6.10
2012 Bos	AL	29	29	0	0	161.0	709	162	95	87	24	1	6	5	71	0	167	5	0	11	10	.524	0	0-0	0	4.73	4.86
2013 Bos	AL	29	27	0	0	162.1	705	161	84	78	13	3	10	5	71	0	139	8	0	11	6	.647	0	0-0	0	4.18	4.32
2014 2 Tms		21	14	0	2	79.2	364	91	54	49	12	3	2	2	33	0	51	5	1	4	5	.444	0	0-0	0	5.33	5.54
2015 2 Tms		16	12	0	2	75.1	328	87	50	46	10	4	5	1	26	1	56	3	0	3	3	.500	0	1-1	0	5.09	5.50
14 Bos	AL	17	10	0	2	59.1	277	69	45	40	10	2	2	2	26	0	43	4	0	2	4	.333	0	0-0	0	5.66	6.07
14 ChC	NL	4	4	0	0	20.1	87	22	9	9	2	1	0	0	7	0	8	1	1	2	1	.667	0	0-0	0	4.36	3.98
15 Tor	AL	5	4	0	0	22.2	101	32	15	12	1	0	1	1	5	1	13	1	0	1	1	.500	0	0-0	0	5.56	4.76
15 Oak	AL	11	8	0	2	52.2	227	55	35	34	9	4	4	0	21	0	43	2	0	2	2	.500	0	1-1	0	4.89	5.81
Postseason		4	0	0	1	7.0	27	3	1	1	0	0	0	1	3	1	4	0	0	1	0	1.000	0	0-0	0	1.26	1.29
6 ML YEARS		118	85	0	10	513.2	2266	540	306	279	63	12	25	14	219	1	442	24	1	31	26	.544	0	4-5	1	4.74	4.89

Brian Dozier

Bats: R **Throws:** R **Pos:** 2B-151;DH-2;PH-2   DOE-zhur   **Ht:** 5'11" **Wt:** 200 **Born:** 5/15/1987 **Age:** 30

Year Team	Lg	G	AB	H	2B	3B	HR	(Hm	Rd)	TB	R	RBI	RC	TBB	IBB	SO	HBP	SH	SF	SB	CS	GDP	Avg	OBP	Slg	OPS
2012 Min	AL	84	316	74	11	1	6	(4	2)	105	33	33	24	16	0	58	1	4	3	9	2	10	.234	.271	.332	.603
2013 Min	AL	147	558	136	33	4	18	(8	10)	231	72	66	74	51	0	120	6	3	4	14	7	14	.244	.312	.414	.726
2014 Min	AL	156	598	145	33	1	23	(11	12)	249	112	71	87	89	1	129	9	3	8	21	7	8	.242	.345	.416	.762
2015 Min	AL	157	628	148	39	4	28	(13	15)	279	101	77	87	61	2	148	7	0	8	12	4	10	.236	.307	.444	.751
2016 Min	AL	155	615	165	35	5	42	(21	21)	336	104	99	102	61	6	138	8	2	5	18	2	12	.268	.340	.546	.886
5 ML YEARS		699	2715	668	151	15	117	(57	60)	1200	422	346	374	278	9	593	31	12	28	74	22	54	.246	.320	.442	.762

Hunter Dozier

Bats: R **Throws:** R **Pos:** RF-7;DH-1;PH-1   DOE-zhur   **Ht:** 6'4" **Wt:** 220 **Born:** 8/22/1991 **Age:** 25

Year Team	Lg	G	AB	H	2B	3B	HR	(Hm	Rd)	TB	R	RBI	RC	TBB	IBB	SO	HBP	SH	SF	SB	CS	GDP	Avg	OBP	Slg	OPS
2013 2 Tms	Low	69	273	84	30	0	7	(-	-)	135	49	52	55	38	0	37	4	0	2	3	1	3	.308	.397	.495	.892
2014 Wilmg	A+	66	224	66	18	0	4	(-	-)	96	36	39	41	35	2	56	5	0	3	7	3	6	.295	.397	.429	.826
2014 NWArk	AA	64	234	49	12	0	4	(-	-)	73	33	21	23	31	0	70	1	0	1	3	2	12	.209	.303	.312	.615
2015 NWArk	AA	128	475	100	27	1	12	(-	-)	165	65	53	48	45	1	151	1	0	2	6	2	7	.211	.279	.347	.627
2016 NWArk	AA	26	95	29	8	0	8	(-	-)	61	14	21	24	14	0	23	1	0	0	4	0	1	.305	.400	.642	1.042
2016 Omha	AAA	103	391	115	36	1	15	(-	-)	198	65	54	71	40	3	100	0	0	3	3	1	12	.294	.357	.506	.864
2016 KC	AL	8	19	4	1	0	0	(0	0)	5	4	1	1	2	0	8	0	0	0	0	0	0	.211	.286	.263	.549

Kyle Drabek

Pitches: R **Bats:** R **Pos:** RP-1   **Ht:** 6'2" **Wt:** 205 **Born:** 12/8/1987 **Age:** 29

Year Team	Lg	G	GS	CG	GF	IP	BFP	H	R	ER	HR	SH	SF	HB	TBB	IBB	SO	WP	Bk	W	L	Pct	Sh	Sv-Op	Hld	ERC	ERA
2016 Reno*	AAA	15	11	0	1	68.2	318	91	54	51	4	3	4	0	33	1	41	5	0	3	6	.333	0	0- -	-	6.05	6.68
2010 Tor	AL	3	3	0	0	17.0	69	18	9	9	2	1	2	0	5	0	12	2	0	0	3	.000	0	0-0	0	4.34	4.76
2011 Tor	AL	18	14	0	2	78.2	365	87	54	53	10	3	5	1	55	0	51	11	0	4	5	.444	0	0-0	0	6.30	6.06
2012 Tor	AL	13	13	0	0	71.1	317	67	41	37	10	0	1	1	47	0	47	7	0	4	7	.364	0	0-0	0	5.21	4.67
2013 Tor	AL	3	0	0	1	2.1	14	4	2	2	1	0	0	1	2	0	3	0	0	0	0	-	0	0-0	0	16.01	7.71

Year Team	Lg	HOW MUCH HE PITCHED						WHAT HE GAVE UP											THE RESULTS							
		G	GS	CG	GF	IP	BFP	H	R	ER	HR	SH	SF	HB	TBB	IBB	SO	WP	Bk	W	L	Pct	Sh	Sv-Op	Hld	ERC	ERA
2014 Tor	AL	2	0	0	1	3.0	13	2	0	0	0	0	0	0	2	0	5	0	0	0	0	-	0	0-0	0	2.54	0.00
2015 CWS	AL	3	0	0	3	5.1	26	9	3	3	1	0	0	0	2	0	3	0	0	0	0	-	0	0-0	0	9.16	5.06
2016 Ari	NL	1	0	0	0	2.0	11	1	1	1	0	0	0	0	4	0	2	0	0	0	0	-	0	0-0	0	6.31	4.50
7 ML YEARS		43	30	0	7	179.2	815	188	110	105	24	4	8	3	117	0	123	20	0	8	15	.348	0	0-0	0	5.80	5.26

Oliver Drake

Pitches: R Bats: R Pos: RP-14   Ht: 6'4" Wt: 215 Born: 1/13/1987 Age: 30

Year Team	Lg	HOW MUCH HE PITCHED						WHAT HE GAVE UP											THE RESULTS							
		G	GS	CG	GF	IP	BFP	H	R	ER	HR	SH	SF	HB	TBB	IBB	SO	WP	Bk	W	L	Pct	Sh	Sv-Op	Hld	ERC	ERA
2013 Bowie	AA	19	0	0	13	31.0	126	19	8	6	1	2	0	1	13	0	38	1	0	3	0	1.000	0	8- -	-	1.84	1.74
2014 Bowie	AA	50	0	0	47	52.2	210	41	19	18	2	1	0	0	17	0	71	4	0	2	4	.333	0	31- -	-	2.28	3.08
2015 Norfolk	AAA	42	0	0	34	44.0	169	23	4	4	1	0	1	0	16	0	66	2	0	1	2	.333	0	23- -	-	1.31	0.82
2016 Norfolk	AAA	47	1	0	22	56.1	231	44	20	17	5	0	0	1	25	0	79	2	0	1	4	.200	0	10- -	-	3.12	2.72
2015 Bal	AL	13	0	0	5	15.2	72	16	7	5	1	0	2	0	9	0	17	3	0	0	0	-	0	0-0	2	4.50	2.87
2016 Bal	AL	14	0	0	5	18.0	74	11	11	8	2	1	0	0	7	0	21	1	0	1	0	1.000	0	0-1	0	2.01	4.00
2 ML YEARS		27	0	0	10	33.2	146	27	18	13	3	1	2	0	16	0	38	4	0	1	0	1.000	0	0-1	2	3.10	3.48

Stephen Drew

Bats: L Throws: R Pos: PH-28;2B-21;3B-12;SS-12;DH-1   Ht: 6'0" Wt: 200 Born: 3/16/1983 Age: 34

Year Team	Lg	BATTING									RUNNING									AVERAGES			
		G	AB	H	2B	3B	HR	(Hm Rd)	TB	R	RBI	RC	TBB	IBB	SO	HBP	SH	SF	SB	CS	GDP	Avg	OBP	Slg	OPS
2006 Ari	NL	59	209	66	13	7	5	(3 2)	108	27	23	31	14	4	50	0	2	1	2	0	1	.316	.357	.517	.874
2007 Ari	NL	150	543	129	28	4	12	(6 6)	201	60	60	71	60	5	100	3	5	8	9	0	4	.238	.313	.370	.683
2008 Ari	NL	152	611	178	44	11	21	(9 12)	307	91	67	97	41	6	109	1	3	7	3	3	5	.291	.333	.502	.836
2009 Ari	NL	135	533	139	29	12	12	(4 8)	228	71	65	76	49	7	87	1	5	7	5	1	5	.261	.320	.428	.748
2010 Ari	NL	151	533	148	33	12	15	(5 10)	259	83	61	84	62	2	108	3	2	1	10	5	8	.278	.352	.458	.810
2011 Ari	NL	86	321	81	21	5	5	(3 2)	127	44	45	41	30	0	74	1	1	1	4	4	3	.252	.317	.396	.713
2012 2 Tms		79	287	64	13	1	7	(4 3)	100	38	28	30	37	2	76	0	0	3	1	2	2	.223	.309	.348	.657
2013 Bos	AL	124	442	112	29	8	13	(6 7)	196	57	67	63	54	3	124	1	0	4	6	0	9	.253	.333	.443	.777
2014 2 Tms	AL	85	271	44	14	1	7	(4 3)	81	18	26	19	27	3	75	0	1	1	1	1	1	.162	.237	.299	.536
2015 NYY	AL	131	383	77	16	1	17	(9 8)	146	43	44	40	37	1	71	1	4	3	0	2	7	.201	.271	.381	.652
2016 Was	NL	70	143	38	11	1	8	(6 2)	75	24	21	22	16	0	31	2	0	4	0	1	3	.266	.340	.524	.864
12 Ari	NL	40	135	26	8	1	2	(0 2)	42	17	12	12	19	1	35	0	0	1	0	1	1	.193	.290	.311	.601
12 Oak	AL	39	152	38	5	0	5	(4 1)	58	21	16	18	18	1	41	0	0	2	1	1	1	.250	.326	.382	.707
14 Bos	AL	39	131	23	6	1	4	(2 2)	43	11	11	12	14	2	39	0	0	0	1	1	1	.176	.255	.328	.583
14 NYY	AL	46	140	21	8	0	3	(2 1)	38	7	15	7	13	1	36	0	0	1	0	0	0	.150	.219	.271	.491
Postseason		28	104	22	3	2	3	(2 1)	38	10	9	8	5	0	33	0	0	1	1	0	1	.212	.245	.365	.611
11 ML YEARS		1222	4308	1085	251	63	122	(59 63)	1828	556	507	574	427	33	905	13	22	41	41	19	48	.252	.318	.424	.743

Brandon Drury

DROO-ree

Bats: R Throws: R Pos: LF-62;RF-32;3B-29;2B-16;PH-15;1B-1   Ht: 6'2" Wt: 210 Born: 8/21/1992 Age: 24

Year Team	Lg	BATTING									RUNNING									AVERAGES			
		G	AB	H	2B	3B	HR	(Hm Rd)	TB	R	RBI	RC	TBB	IBB	SO	HBP	SH	SF	SB	CS	GDP	Avg	OBP	Slg	OPS
2012 Rome	A	123	445	102	22	3	6	(- -)	148	47	51	40	20	0	73	7	3	5	3	4	14	.229	.270	.333	.603
2013 Sbend	A	134	526	159	51	4	15	(- -)	263	78	85	96	47	6	92	5	0	5	1	1	10	.302	.362	.500	.862
2014 Visalia	A+	107	430	129	35	1	19	(- -)	223	73	81	81	41	2	76	5	0	4	4	3	16	.300	.366	.519	.885
2014 Mobile	AA	29	105	31	7	0	4	(- -)	50	12	14	17	7	0	19	2	0	2	0	0	1	.295	.345	.476	.821
2015 Mobile	AA	67	273	76	14	1	3	(- -)	101	22	36	30	11	0	41	2	0	5	4	6	7	.278	.306	.370	.676
2015 Reno	AAA	63	251	83	26	0	2	(- -)	115	43	25	44	21	0	35	2	0	2	0	2	6	.331	.384	.458	.842
2015 Ari	NL	20	56	12	3	0	2	(0 2)	21	3	8	4	2	0	8	1	0	0	0	0	5	.214	.254	.375	.629
2016 Ari	NL	134	461	130	31	1	16	(12 4)	211	59	53	59	31	2	100	3	0	4	1	1	14	.282	.329	.458	.786
2 ML YEARS		154	517	142	34	1	18	(12 6)	232	62	61	63	33	2	108	4	0	4	1	1	19	.275	.321	.449	.770

Lucas Duda

DOO-duh

Bats: L Throws: R Pos: 1B-45;PH-5   Ht: 6'4" Wt: 255 Born: 2/3/1986 Age: 31

Year Team	Lg	BATTING									RUNNING									AVERAGES			
		G	AB	H	2B	3B	HR	(Hm Rd)	TB	R	RBI	RC	TBB	IBB	SO	HBP	SH	SF	SB	CS	GDP	Avg	OBP	Slg	OPS
2010 NYM	NL	29	84	17	6	0	4	(3 1)	35	11	13	5	6	0	22	1	0	1	0	0	2	.202	.261	.417	.678
2011 NYM	NL	100	301	88	21	3	10	(2 8)	145	38	50	44	33	3	57	7	1	5	1	0	5	.292	.370	.482	.852
2012 NYM	NL	121	401	96	15	0	15	(9 6)	156	43	57	58	51	0	120	4	0	3	1	0	5	.239	.329	.389	.718
2013 NYM	NL	100	318	71	16	0	15	(9 6)	132	42	33	38	55	4	102	9	0	2	0	3	1	.223	.352	.415	.767
2014 NYM	NL	153	514	130	27	0	30	(14 16)	247	74	92	91	69	8	135	9	0	4	3	2	9	.253	.349	.481	.830
2015 NYM	NL	135	471	115	33	0	27	(19 8)	229	67	73	69	66	7	138	14	0	3	0	2	12	.244	.352	.486	.838
2016 NYM	NL	47	153	35	7	0	7	(4 3)	63	20	23	18	15	2	36	2	0	2	0	0	1	.229	.302	.412	.714
Postseason		14	47	11	2	0	1	(0 1)	16	3	8	7	5	0	20	0	1	1	0	0	0	.234	.302	.340	.642
7 ML YEARS		685	2242	552	125	3	108	(60 48)	1007	295	341	323	295	24	610	46	1	20	5	7	35	.246	.343	.449	.792

Brian Duensing

Pitches: L Bats: L Pos: RP-14
DUNN-sing
Ht: 6'0" Wt: 200 Born: 2/22/1983 Age: 34

Year Team	Lg	G	GS	CG	GF	IP	BFP	H	R	ER	HR	SH	SF	HB	TBB	IBB	SO	WP	Bk	W	L	Pct	Sh	Sv-Op	Hld	ERC	ERA
2016 Omha*	AAA	12	0	0	5	20.1	82	16	7	7	0	2	0	0	5	0	19	1	0	1	0	1.000	0	2- -	-	1.78	3.10
2009 Min	AL	24	9	0	3	84.0	359	84	37	34	7	3	2	3	31	1	53	1	0	5	2	.714	0	0-0	1	4.00	3.64
2010 Min	AL	53	13	1	11	130.2	535	122	42	38	11	4	0	3	35	5	78	1	0	10	3	.769	1	0-0	9	3.18	2.62
2011 Min	AL	32	28	1	0	161.2	711	193	102	94	21	7	6	1	52	3	115	3	0	9	14	.391	1	0-0	0	5.12	5.23
2012 Min	AL	55	11	0	8	109.0	472	126	71	62	10	2	3	2	27	3	69	5	0	4	12	.250	0	0-1	7	4.31	5.12
2013 Min	AL	73	0	0	9	61.0	268	68	28	27	4	2	2	2	22	4	56	6	0	6	2	.750	0	1-4	15	4.35	3.98
2014 Min	AL	62	0	0	10	54.1	229	52	20	20	6	1	2	1	20	2	33	2	0	3	3	.500	0	0-4	7	3.84	3.31
2015 Min	AL	55	0	0	9	48.2	209	46	24	23	5	2	1	4	21	4	24	3	0	4	1	.800	0	1-2	6	4.17	4.25
2016 Bal	AL	14	0	0	4	13.1	55	13	6	6	2	0	0	0	3	1	10	1	0	1	0	1.000	0	0-0	0	3.47	4.05
Postseason		2	2	0	0	8.0	39	14	10	10	2	0	0	0	2	0	4	1	0	0	2	.000	0	0-0	0	9.43	11.25
8 ML YEARS		368	61	2	54	662.2	2838	704	330	304	66	21	16	16	211	23	438	22	0	42	37	.532	2	2-11	45	4.17	4.13

Tyler Duffey

Pitches: R Bats: R Pos: SP-26
Ht: 6'3" Wt: 220 Born: 12/27/1990 Age: 26

Year Team	Lg	G	GS	CG	GF	IP	BFP	H	R	ER	HR	SH	SF	HB	TBB	IBB	SO	WP	Bk	W	L	Pct	Sh	Sv-Op	Hld	ERC	ERA
2012 Elizab	R+	12	0	0	5	19.0	67	10	3	3	1	0	0	0	2	0	27	1	0	2	0	1.000	0	2- -	-	0.94	1.42
2013 2 Tms	Low	24	18	0	1	121.0	500	116	56	49	8	3	1	5	23	0	91	4	0	7	7	.500	0	0- -	-	2.97	3.64
2014 NwBrit	AA	18	18	0	0	111.1	452	104	52	47	14	2	6	5	19	0	84	4	0	8	3	.727	0	0- -	-	3.19	3.80
2015 Chatt	AA	8	8	0	0	52.2	210	46	19	15	0	1	1	1	12	0	54	1	0	2	2	.500	0	0- -	-	2.26	2.56
2015 Roch	AAA	14	14	1	0	85.1	349	73	32	24	1	1	3	1	18	0	68	3	0	5	6	.455	1	0- -	-	2.07	2.53
2016 Roch	AAA	5	5	1	0	30.2	125	24	10	10	4	0	0	0	12	0	25	0	0	1	1	.500	0	0- -	-	3.10	2.93
2015 Min	AL	10	10	0	0	58.0	242	56	20	20	4	3	0	0	20	0	53	1	0	5	1	.833	0	0-0	0	3.51	3.10
2016 Min	AL	26	26	0	0	133.0	596	167	103	95	25	2	2	6	32	3	114	9	1	9	12	.429	0	0-0	0	5.66	6.43
2 ML YEARS		36	36	0	0	191.0	838	223	123	115	29	5	2	6	52	3	167	10	1	14	13	.519	0	0-0	0	4.98	5.42

Danny Duffy

Pitches: L Bats: L Pos: SP-26; RP-16
Ht: 6'3" Wt: 205 Born: 12/21/1988 Age: 28

Year Team	Lg	G	GS	CG	GF	IP	BFP	H	R	ER	HR	SH	SF	HB	TBB	IBB	SO	WP	Bk	W	L	Pct	Sh	Sv-Op	Hld	ERC	ERA
2011 KC	AL	20	20	0	0	105.1	474	119	66	66	15	2	2	5	51	1	87	4	1	4	8	.333	0	0-0	0	5.76	5.64
2012 KC	AL	6	6	0	0	27.2	121	26	13	12	2	0	0	0	18	1	28	0	1	2	2	.500	0	0-0	0	4.58	3.90
2013 KC	AL	5	5	0	0	24.1	104	19	5	5	0	0	0	1	14	0	22	2	0	2	0	1.000	0	0-0	0	3.02	1.85
2014 KC	AL	31	25	0	1	149.1	606	113	52	42	12	3	4	5	53	2	113	5	0	9	12	.429	0	0-0	1	2.62	2.53
2015 KC	AL	30	24	0	1	136.2	588	137	64	62	15	3	5	9	53	0	102	11	0	7	8	.467	0	1-1	2	4.44	4.08
2016 KC	AL	42	26	1	5	179.2	731	163	71	70	27	4	2	7	42	0	188	4	0	12	3	.800	0	0-0	0	3.44	3.51
Postseason		9	0	0	1	10.2	44	10	6	6	2	1	1	0	4	0	14	0	0	2	0	1.000	0	0-0	0	4.35	5.06
6 ML YEARS		134	106	1	7	623.0	2624	577	271	257	71	12	13	27	231	4	540	26	2	36	33	.522	0	1-1	4	3.85	3.71

Matt Duffy

Bats: R Throws: R Pos: PH-2;3B-1
Ht: 6'3" Wt: 215 Born: 2/6/1989 Age: 28

Year Team	Lg	G	AB	H	2B	3B	HR	(Hm	Rd)	TB	R	RBI	RC	TBB	IBB	SO	HBP	SH	SF	SB	CS	GDP	Avg	OBP	Slg	OPS
2012 Lxngtn	A	134	492	138	32	1	16	(-	-)	220	73	70	91	48	0	106	41	0	6	6	3	11	.280	.387	.447	.834
2013 Lancst	A+	100	371	120	20	4	19	(-	-)	205	74	84	80	30	2	80	18	1	4	0	2	6	.323	.397	.553	.950
2013 CpChr	AA	24	89	22	4	0	5	(-	-)	41	11	10	12	3	0	22	3	0	0	1	1	3	.247	.295	.461	.755
2014 CpChr	AA	49	202	61	11	1	6	(-	-)	92	23	35	31	7	0	36	5	1	1	2	1	5	.302	.340	.455	.795
2014 OkCity	AAA	87	315	88	11	3	12	(-	-)	141	47	49	47	21	0	70	7	4	5	0	3	17	.279	.333	.448	.781
2015 Fresno	AAA	127	490	144	29	2	20	(-	-)	237	94	104	90	48	0	90	12	0	7	4	1	20	.294	.366	.484	.850
2016 Fresno	AAA	74	266	60	13	1	6	(-	-)	93	36	30	29	24	1	94	6	0	1	1	1	6	.226	.303	.350	.653
2016 RdRck	AAA	35	135	32	4	1	8	(-	-)	62	17	22	18	6	0	30	4	0	2	0	0	6	.237	.286	.459	.745
2015 Hou	AL	8	8	3	1	0	0	(0	0)	4	0	0	3	2	1	2	0	0	0	0	0	0	.375	.444	.500	.944
2016 Hou	AL	3	3	0	0	0	0	(0	0)	0	0	0	0	0	0	2	0	0	0	0	0	0	.000	.000	.000	.000
2 ML YEARS		11	11	3	1	0	0	(0	0)	4	0	0	3	2	1	4	0	0	0	0	0	0	.273	.333	.364	.697

Matt Duffy

Bats: R Throws: R Pos: 3B-70;SS-18;PH-3;DH-1
Ht: 6'2" Wt: 170 Born: 1/15/1991 Age: 26

Year Team	Lg	G	AB	H	2B	3B	HR	(Hm	Rd)	TB	R	RBI	RC	TBB	IBB	SO	HBP	SH	SF	SB	CS	GDP	Avg	OBP	Slg	OPS
2014 SF	NL	34	60	16	2	0	0	(0	0)	18	5	8	8	1	0	14	2	1	0	0	1	1	.267	.302	.300	.602
2015 SF	NL	149	573	169	28	6	12	(7	5)	245	77	77	84	30	0	96	5	2	2	12	0	22	.295	.334	.428	.762
2016 2 Tms		91	333	86	14	2	5	(1	4)	119	41	28	30	23	0	53	4	2	4	8	5	13	.258	.310	.357	.668
16 SF	NL	70	257	65	11	2	4	(1	3)	92	32	21	23	20	0	40	4	2	3	8	4	9	.253	.313	.358	.671
16 TB	AL	21	76	21	3	0	1	(0	1)	27	9	7	7	3	0	13	0	0	1	0	1	4	.276	.300	.355	.655
Postseason		8	6	1	0	0	0	(0	0)	1	2	0	0	0	0	2	1	0	0	0	0	0	.167	.167	.167	.333
3 ML YEARS		274	966	271	44	8	17	(8	9)	382	123	113	122	54	0	163	11	5	6	20	6	36	.281	.324	.395	.719

Zach Duke

Pitches: L Bats: L Pos: RP-81   Ht: 6'2" Wt: 210 Born: 4/19/1983 Age: 34

				HOW MUCH HE PITCHED				WHAT HE GAVE UP										THE RESULTS						
Year	Team	Lg	G	GS	CG	GF	IP	BFP	H	R	ER	HR	SH	SF	HB	TBB	IBB	SO	WP	Bk	W	L	Pct	Sh	Sv-Op	Hld	ERC	ERA
2005	Pit	NL	14	14	0	0	84.2	341	79	20	17	3	3	1	2	23	2	58	1	0	8	2	.800	0	0-0	0	2.96	1.81
2006	Pit	NL	34	34	2	0	215.1	935	255	116	107	17	13	4	7	68	6	117	8	1	10	15	.400	1	0-0	0	4.82	4.47
2007	Pit	NL	20	19	0	0	107.1	482	161	74	66	14	2	4	3	25	2	41	0	1	3	8	.273	0	0-0	0	6.96	5.53
2008	Pit	NL	31	31	1	0	185.0	829	230	111	99	19	14	4	7	47	1	87	2	2	5	14	.263	1	0-0	0	4.99	4.82
2009	Pit	NL	32	32	3	0	213.0	891	231	101	96	23	18	10	3	49	0	106	2	1	11	16	.407	1	0-0	0	4.05	4.06
2010	Pit	NL	29	29	0	0	159.0	730	212	115	101	25	9	6	4	51	2	96	4	3	8	15	.348	0	0-0	0	6.22	5.72
2011	Ari	NL	21	9	0	5	76.2	338	101	42	42	6	3	3	1	19	0	32	1	0	3	4	.429	0	1-1	0	5.27	4.93
2012	Was	NL	8	0	0	3	13.2	56	11	2	2	0	0	0	0	4	0	10	0	0	1	0	1.000	0	0-0	0	2.00	1.32
2013	2 Tms	NL	26	1	0	3	31.1	142	39	23	21	3	2	2	1	10	3	18	2	0	1	2	.333	0	0-0	1	5.04	6.03
2014	Mil	NL	74	0	0	13	58.2	238	49	19	16	3	0	0	0	17	1	74	3	0	5	1	.833	0	0-4	12	2.64	2.45
2015	CWS	AL	71	0	0	14	60.2	255	47	26	23	9	2	1	3	32	4	66	0	0	3	6	.333	0	1-3	26	3.82	3.41
2016	2 Tms		81	0	0	13	61.0	258	48	16	16	2	3	1	4	29	3	68	4	0	2	1	.667	0	2-5	26	2.93	2.36
13	Was	NL	12	1	0	1	20.2	101	31	22	20	2	2	2	1	8	3	11	1	0	1	1	.500	0	0-0	0	6.83	8.71
13	Cin	NL	14	0	0	2	10.2	41	8	1	1	1	0	0	0	2	0	7	1	0	0	1	.000	0	0-0	1	2.01	0.84
16	CWS	AL	53	0	0	9	37.2	159	31	11	11	2	2	1	2	16	3	42	2	0	2	0	1.000	0	1-4	20	2.97	2.63
16	StL	NL	28	0	0	4	23.1	99	17	5	5	0	1	0	2	13	0	26	2	0	0	1	.000	0	1-1	6	2.85	1.93
12 ML YEARS			441	169	6	51	1266.1	5495	1463	665	606	124	69	36	35	374	24	773	27	8	60	84	.417	3	4-13	65	4.65	4.31

Ryan Dull

Pitches: R Bats: R Pos: RP-70   Ht: 5'9" Wt: 175 Born: 10/2/1989 Age: 27

				HOW MUCH HE PITCHED				WHAT HE GAVE UP										THE RESULTS						
Year	Team	Lg	G	GS	CG	GF	IP	BFP	H	R	ER	HR	SH	SF	HB	TBB	IBB	SO	WP	Bk	W	L	Pct	Sh	Sv-Op	Hld	ERC	ERA
2012	2 Tms	Low	21	0	0	11	31.2	133	29	11	9	2	2	0	2	9	1	47	5	0	5	1	.833	0	5- -	-	3.11	2.56
2013	2 Tms	Low	35	0	0	30	48.1	182	29	10	10	1	3	2	1	6	1	66	3	0	2	4	.333	0	18- -	-	1.06	1.86
2013	Mdlnd	AA	10	0	0	8	11.2	54	15	9	6	2	0	0	0	3	0	12	2	0	0	1	.000	0	1- -	-	5.44	4.63
2014	Mdlnd	AA	40	0	0	24	56.1	239	52	24	18	6	3	1	3	15	4	61	5	1	5	5	.500	0	6- -	-	3.21	2.88
2015	Mdlnd	AA	35	0	0	27	45.0	173	29	3	3	1	0	1	0	13	1	52	0	0	3	1	.750	0	12- -	-	1.51	0.60
2015	Nashv	AAA	12	0	0	4	16.0	61	10	2	2	1	0	0	0	3	1	21	0	0	1	0	1.000	0	0- -	-	1.32	1.13
2015	Oak	AL	13	0	0	3	17.0	66	12	8	8	4	0	1	0	6	1	16	0	0	1	2	.333	0	1-2	3	3.19	4.24
2016	Oak	AL	70	0	0	9	74.1	290	50	23	20	10	0	5	1	15	4	73	6	0	5	5	.500	0	3-6	15	1.84	2.42
2 ML YEARS			83	0	0	12	91.1	356	62	31	28	14	0	6	1	21	5	89	6	0	6	7	.462	0	4-8	17	2.07	2.76

Mike Dunn

Pitches: L Bats: L Pos: RP-51   Ht: 6'0" Wt: 215 Born: 5/23/1985 Age: 32

				HOW MUCH HE PITCHED				WHAT HE GAVE UP										THE RESULTS						
Year	Team	Lg	G	GS	CG	GF	IP	BFP	H	R	ER	HR	SH	SF	HB	TBB	IBB	SO	WP	Bk	W	L	Pct	Sh	Sv-Op	Hld	ERC	ERA
2009	NYY	AL	4	0	0	3	4.0	20	3	3	3	1	0	0	0	5	0	5	1	0	0	0	-	0	0-0	0	7.17	6.75
2010	Atl	NL	25	0	0	5	19.0	88	15	4	4	1	0	0	0	17	2	27	2	0	2	0	1.000	0	0-0	1	4.19	1.89
2011	Fla	NL	72	0	0	11	63.0	267	51	28	24	9	4	2	2	31	2	68	3	0	5	6	.455	0	0-4	15	3.77	3.43
2012	Mia	NL	60	0	0	8	44.0	208	49	31	24	3	2	4	0	29	8	47	2	0	3	0	.000	0	1-6	18	5.10	4.91
2013	Mia	NL	75	0	0	15	67.2	282	53	21	20	5	1	3	0	28	4	72	2	0	3	4	.429	0	2-5	18	2.68	2.66
2014	Mia	NL	75	0	0	15	57.0	245	47	25	20	4	4	1	4	22	1	67	2	0	10	6	.625	0	1-4	22	3.03	3.16
2015	Mia	NL	72	0	0	9	54.0	235	46	27	27	6	0	1	2	29	1	65	2	0	2	5	.286	0	0-3	23	3.96	4.50
2016	Mia	NL	51	0	0	5	42.1	176	43	16	16	5	1	2	3	11	0	38	2	0	6	1	.857	0	0-4	8	4.13	3.40
Postseason			3	0	0	0	1.1	6	2	0	0	0	0	0	0	0	0	2	0	0	0	0	-	0	0-1	0	4.47	0.00
8 ML YEARS			434	0	0	71	351.0	1521	307	155	138	34	12	13	11	172	18	389	16	0	28	25	.528	0	4-26	105	3.72	3.54

Adam Duvall

Bats: R Throws: R Pos: LF-137;RF-6;1B-5;PH-4;3B-3   Ht: 6'1" Wt: 220 Born: 9/4/1988 Age: 28

				BATTING																		RUNNING			AVERAGES			
Year	Team	Lg	G	AB	H	2B	3B	HR	(Hm	Rd)	TB	R	RBI	RC	TBB	IBB	SO	HBP	SH	SF	SB	CS	GDP	Avg	OBP	Slg	OPS
2014	SF	NL	28	73	14	2	0	3	(2	1)	25	8	5	4	3	0	20	1	0	0	0	0	0	.192	.234	.342	.576
2015	Cin	NL	27	64	14	2	0	5	(3	2)	31	6	9	9	6	1	26	2	0	0	0	0	0	.219	.306	.484	.790
2016	Cin	NL	150	552	133	31	6	33	(16	17)	275	85	103	80	41	1	164	6	0	8	6	5	7	.241	.297	.498	.795
3 ML YEARS			205	689	161	35	6	41	(21	20)	331	99	117	93	50	2	210	9	0	8	6	5	7	.234	.291	.480	.771

Jarrod Dyson

juh-ROD

Bats: L Throws: R Pos: CF-57;RF-21;LF-19;PR-9;DH-6;PH-4   Ht: 5'10" Wt: 165 Born: 8/15/1984 Age: 32

				BATTING																		RUNNING			AVERAGES			
Year	Team	Lg	G	AB	H	2B	3B	HR	(Hm	Rd)	TB	R	RBI	RC	TBB	IBB	SO	HBP	SH	SF	SB	CS	GDP	Avg	OBP	Slg	OPS
2010	KC	AL	18	57	12	4	2	1	(1	0)	23	11	5	9	6	0	16	0	2	0	9	1	2	.211	.286	.404	.689
2011	KC	AL	26	44	9	1	0	0	(0	0)	10	3	3	7	7	0	14	0	1	1	11	1	0	.205	.308	.227	.535
2012	KC	AL	102	292	76	8	5	0	(0	0)	94	52	9	36	30	1	56	1	4	3	30	5	3	.260	.328	.322	.650
2013	KC	AL	87	213	55	9	4	2	(2	0)	78	30	17	28	21	1	45	1	3	1	34	6	4	.258	.326	.366	.692
2014	KC	AL	120	260	70	4	4	1	(1	0)	85	33	24	32	22	1	52	0	6	2	36	7	5	.269	.324	.327	.651
2015	KC	AL	90	200	50	8	6	2	(2	0)	76	31	18	25	14	0	37	4	6	1	26	3	3	.250	.311	.380	.691
2016	KC	AL	107	299	83	14	8	1	(1	0)	116	46	25	45	26	1	39	3	8	1	30	7	4	.278	.340	.388	.728
Postseason			19	20	2	0	0	0	(0	0)	2	3	0	0	2	0	6	0	1	0	4	2	1	.100	.182	.100	.282
7 ML YEARS			550	1365	355	48	29	7	(7	0)	482	211	101	182	126	4	259	9	30	9	176	30	23	.260	.325	.353	.678

Sam Dyson

Pitches: R Bats: R Pos: RP-73   Ht: 6'1" Wt: 205 Born: 5/7/1988 Age: 29

Year Team	Lg	G	GS	CG	GF	IP	BFP	H	R	ER	HR	SH	SF	HB	TBB	IBB	SO	WP	Bk	W	L	Pct	Sh	Sv-Op	Hld	ERC	ERA
2012 Tor	AL	2	0	0	0	0.2	8	4	3	3	0	0	0	0	2	0	1	0	0	0	0	-	0	0-0	0	56.02	40.50
2013 Mia	NL	5	1	0	1	11.0	54	16	12	11	2	1	1	1	5	1	5	0	0	0	2	.000	0	0-0	0	7.96	9.00
2014 Mia	NL	31	0	0	12	42.0	181	41	14	10	1	2	0	3	15	4	33	1	0	3	1	.750	0	0-1	0	3.36	2.14
2015 2 Tms		75	0	0	16	75.1	309	65	26	22	4	4	1	4	21	1	71	8	0	5	4	.556	0	2-4	21	2.77	2.63
2016 Tex	AL	73	0	0	53	70.1	285	63	19	19	5	1	0	3	23	0	55	3	0	3	2	.600	0	38-43	10	3.32	2.43
15 Mia	NL	44	0	0	10	44.0	190	41	21	18	3	3	1	3	17	1	41	6	0	3	3	.500	0	0-2	9	3.63	3.68
15 Tex	AL	31	0	0	6	31.1	119	24	5	4	1	1	0	1	4	0	30	2	0	2	1	.667	0	2-2	12	1.68	1.15
Postseason		4	0	0	1	3.2	18	6	1	1	1	0	0	0	1	1	2	0	0	0	0	-	0	1-2	0	8.17	2.45
5 ML YEARS		186	1	0	82	199.1	837	189	74	65	12	8	2	11	66	6	165	12	0	11	9	.550	0	40-48	31	3.46	2.93

Adam Eaton

Bats: L Throws: L Pos: RF-121;CF-48;LF-1;DH-1;PH-1   Ht: 5'8" Wt: 185 Born: 12/6/1988 Age: 28

Year Team	Lg	G	AB	H	2B	3B	HR	(Hm	Rd)	TB	R	RBI	RC	TBB	IBB	SO	HBP	SH	SF	SB	CS	GDP	Avg	OBP	Slg	OPS
2012 Ari	NL	22	85	22	3	2	2	(1	1)	35	19	5	13	14	0	15	3	1	0	2	3	0	.259	.382	.412	.794
2013 Ari	NL	66	250	63	10	4	3	(2	1)	90	40	22	27	17	0	44	6	3	1	5	2	4	.252	.314	.360	.674
2014 CWS	AL	123	486	146	26	10	1	(1	0)	195	76	35	77	43	0	83	5	2	2	15	9	4	.300	.362	.401	.763
2015 CWS	AL	153	610	175	28	9	14	(6	8)	263	98	56	96	58	2	131	14	5	2	18	8	5	.287	.361	.431	.792
2016 CWS	AL	157	619	176	29	9	14	(7	7)	265	91	59	92	63	2	115	14	7	3	14	5	6	.284	.362	.428	.790
5 ML YEARS		521	2050	582	96	34	34	(17	17)	848	324	177	305	195	4	388	42	18	8	54	27	19	.284	.357	.414	.771

Josh Edgin

Pitches: L Bats: R Pos: RP-16   EDGE-inn   Ht: 6'1" Wt: 245 Born: 12/17/1986 Age: 30

Year Team	Lg	G	GS	CG	GF	IP	BFP	H	R	ER	HR	SH	SF	HB	TBB	IBB	SO	WP	Bk	W	L	Pct	Sh	Sv-Op	Hld	ERC	ERA
2016 Stluci*	A+	6	3	0	1	4.1	17	2	1	1	0	0	1	0	1	0	7	0	0	0	0	-	0	0--	-	0.77	2.08
2016 LsVgs*	AAA	37	0	0	11	33.1	151	35	13	12	2	4	2	3	20	1	38	1	0	2	2	.500	0	2--	-	5.28	3.24
2012 NYM	NL	34	0	0	6	25.2	107	19	14	13	5	2	0	2	10	0	30	0	0	1	2	.333	0	0-2	5	3.52	4.56
2013 NYM	NL	34	0	0	5	28.2	122	26	12	12	2	1	0	2	12	3	20	0	0	1	1	.500	0	1-2	3	3.57	3.77
2014 NYM	NL	47	0	0	5	27.1	104	19	6	4	2	0	0	0	6	0	28	2	0	1	0	1.000	0	0-1	5	1.77	1.32
2016 NYM	NL	16	0	0	4	10.1	45	10	6	6	1	0	2	0	6	0	11	1	0	1	0	1.000	0	0-0	0	4.70	5.23
4 ML YEARS		131	0	0	20	92.0	378	74	38	35	10	3	3	4	34	3	89	3	0	4	3	.571	0	1-5	13	3.11	3.42

Carl Edwards Jr.

Pitches: R Bats: R Pos: RP-36   Ht: 6'3" Wt: 170 Born: 9/3/1991 Age: 25

Year Team	Lg	G	GS	CG	GF	IP	BFP	H	R	ER	HR	SH	SF	HB	TBB	IBB	SO	WP	Bk	W	L	Pct	Sh	Sv-Op	Hld	ERC	ERA
2012 2 Tms	Low	14	13	0	0	67.0	257	32	13	11	0	2	0	3	25	0	85	3	1	5	3	.625	0	0--	-	1.21	1.48
2013 2 Tms	Low	24	24	1	0	116.1	468	76	33	24	1	6	1	3	41	0	155	12	1	8	2	.800	0	0--	-	1.67	1.86
2014 Tenn	AA	10	10	0	0	48.0	193	30	14	13	1	2	2	1	21	0	46	3	0	1	2	.333	0	0--	-	1.88	2.44
2015 Tenn	AA	13	0	0	6	23.2	100	11	12	7	1	1	0	0	17	0	36	1	0	2	2	.500	0	4--	-	2.02	2.66
2015 Iowa	AAA	23	0	0	6	31.2	132	15	11	10	0	1	0	1	24	1	39	3	0	3	1	.750	0	2--	-	2.04	2.84
2016 Iowa	AAA	24	0	0	7	25.1	110	17	12	12	1	0	0	2	17	0	35	3	0	1	1	.500	0	1--	-	3.00	4.26
2015 ChC	NL	5	0	0	3	4.2	19	3	3	2	0	0	0	0	3	0	4	0	0	0	0	-	0	0-0	0	2.50	3.86
2016 ChC	NL	36	0	0	10	36.0	138	15	15	15	4	0	2	0	14	1	52	5	0	0	1	.000	0	2-3	6	1.33	3.75
2 ML YEARS		41	0	0	13	40.2	157	18	18	17	4	0	2	0	17	1	56	5	0	0	1	.000	0	2-3	6	1.44	3.76

Zach Eflin

Pitches: R Bats: R Pos: SP-11   Ht: 6'6" Wt: 215 Born: 4/8/1994 Age: 23

Year Team	Lg	G	GS	CG	GF	IP	BFP	H	R	ER	HR	SH	SF	HB	TBB	IBB	SO	WP	Bk	W	L	Pct	Sh	Sv-Op	Hld	ERC	ERA
2013 FtWyn	A	22	22	0	0	118.2	502	110	53	36	7	2	5	4	31	2	86	7	0	7	6	.538	0	0--	-	2.91	2.73
2014 Lk Els	A+	24	24	0	0	128.0	536	138	56	54	9	4	6	4	31	0	93	3	0	10	7	.588	0	0--	-	3.88	3.80
2015 Rdng	AA	23	23	0	0	131.2	541	136	63	54	12	6	1	4	23	2	68	3	0	8	6	.571	0	0--	-	3.46	3.69
2016 LV	AAA	11	11	0	0	68.1	263	49	24	22	2	0	3	3	11	0	55	4	0	5	2	.714	0	0--	-	1.60	2.90
2016 Phi	NL	11	11	2	0	63.1	272	67	42	39	7	4	1	1	17	1	31	1	0	3	5	.375	1	0-0	0	4.49	5.54

Cody Ege

Pitches: L Bats: L Pos: RP-18   ee-GHEE   Ht: 6'1" Wt: 190 Born: 5/8/1991 Age: 26

Year Team	Lg	G	GS	CG	GF	IP	BFP	H	R	ER	HR	SH	SF	HB	TBB	IBB	SO	WP	Bk	W	L	Pct	Sh	Sv-Op	Hld	ERC	ERA
2013 3 Tms	Low	17	0	0	6	30.0	113	19	8	3	0	0	2	0	5	0	39	2	0	4	0	1.000	0	2--	-	1.30	0.90
2014 MrtlBh	A+	37	0	0	17	62.2	262	62	28	27	4	2	1	4	17	2	76	6	0	4	1	.800	0	2--	-	3.52	3.88
2015 Hi Dsrt	A+	9	0	0	6	13.1	51	7	2	2	1	0	0	1	3	0	25	1	0	3	0	1.000	0	1--	-	1.37	1.35
2015 Frisco	AA	26	0	0	9	31.2	138	26	10	3	1	4	0	1	19	1	37	2	0	3	2	.600	0	1--	-	3.43	0.85
2015 Jaxnvl	AA	5	0	0	1	8.1	31	4	2	1	1	2	0	0	2	0	11	0	0	0	0	-	0	0--	-	1.26	1.08
2015 NewOr	AAA	8	0	0	3	12.0	43	6	2	1	0	0	0	0	2	0	13	0	0	0	0	-	0	0--	-	1.07	0.75
2016 NewOr	AAA	36	0	0	21	44.0	203	42	24	22	1	1	5	6	27	2	35	5	0	4	3	.571	0	5--	-	4.48	4.50
2016 Salt Lk	AAA	6	0	0	3	7.1	30	6	4	4	1	0	0	1	2	0	11	0	0	0	0	-	0	0--	-	3.43	4.91
2016 2 Tms		18	0	0	4	11.2	55	16	5	5	2	0	3	1	5	0	11	0	0	1	0	1.000	0	0-0	3	7.50	3.86
16 Mia	NL	5	0	0	1	3.0	19	8	4	4	1	0	2	1	2	0	2	0	0	0	0	-	0	0-0	0	22.12	12.00
16 LAA	AL	13	0	0	3	8.2	36	8	1	1	1	0	1	0	3	0	9	0	0	1	0	1.000	0	0-0	3	3.58	1.04

Brett Eibner

eye-b-nur

Bats: R **Throws:** R **Pos:** RF-28;CF-19;LF-13;PH-9;DH-4;PR-3   **Ht:** 6'4" **Wt:** 225 **Born:** 12/2/1988 **Age:** 28

Year	Team	Lg	G	AB	H	2B	3B	HR	(Hm	Rd)	TB	R	RBI	RC	TBB	IBB	SO	HBP	SH	SF	SB	CS	GDP	Avg	OBP	Slg	OPS
2012	Wilmg	A+	120	423	83	26	5	15	(-	-)	164	60	53	52	57	0	165	5	1	0	5	2	3	.196	.299	.388	.687
2013	NWArk	AA	114	441	107	17	9	19	(-	-)	199	74	41	69	53	0	149	6	1	3	7	3	6	.243	.330	.451	.781
2014	Omha	AAA	74	274	66	13	2	7	(-	-)	104	42	27	35	30	0	78	2	2	3	5	2	7	.241	.317	.380	.697
2014	Wilmg	A+	13	41	9	3	0	1	(-	-)	15	5	3	6	10	0	16	0	0	0	3	2	0	.220	.373	.366	.738
2015	Omha	AAA	103	389	118	23	1	19	(-	-)	200	65	81	74	38	3	79	0	2	2	10	0	9	.303	.364	.514	.878
2016	Omha	AAA	50	184	53	7	1	11	(-	-)	95	37	32	38	30	2	48	1	1	3	5	1	5	.288	.385	.516	.902
2016	2 Tms	AL	70	187	36	10	1	6	(4	2)	66	21	22	14	19	1	50	0	1	1	0	2	3	.193	.266	.353	.619
16	KC	AL	26	78	18	6	0	3	(2	1)	33	11	10	7	6	1	23	0	1	0	0	0	1	.231	.286	.423	.709
16	Oak	AL	44	109	18	4	1	3	(2	1)	33	10	12	7	13	0	27	0	0	1	0	2	2	.165	.252	.303	.555

Jerad Eickhoff

Pitches: R **Bats:** R **Pos:** SP-33   EYE-koff   **Ht:** 6'4" **Wt:** 245 **Born:** 7/2/1990 **Age:** 26

| | | | HOW MUCH HE PITCHED | | | | | | WHAT HE GAVE UP | | | | | | | | | | THE RESULTS | | | | | | |
Year	Team	Lg	G	GS	CG	GF	IP	BFP	H	R	ER	HR	SH	SF	HB	TBB	IBB	SO	WP	Bk	W	L	Pct	Sh	Sv-Op	Hld	ERC	ERA
2012	Hkry	A	26	25	0	0	126.2	545	132	75	66	22	3	5	5	38	0	90	8	2	13	7	.650	0	0- -	-	4.58	4.69
2013	MrtlBh	A+	21	21	0	0	116.0	476	110	52	44	9	3	4	7	26	2	80	11	0	7	3	.700	0	0- -	-	3.22	3.41
2013	Frisco	AA	6	6	0	0	29.0	128	34	24	24	6	1	0	1	14	0	13	1	0	1	1	.500	0	0- -	-	6.69	7.45
2014	Frisco	AA	27	26	0	0	154.1	636	129	76	70	17	4	2	7	52	0	144	12	0	10	9	.526	0	0- -	-	3.21	4.08
2015	RdRck	AAA	18	17	0	0	101.2	427	95	49	48	12	2	6	4	33	1	93	4	1	9	4	.692	0	0- -	-	3.70	4.25
2015	Phi	NL	8	8	0	0	51.0	203	40	16	15	5	0	1	0	13	0	49	1	0	3	3	.500	0	0-0	0	2.40	2.65
2016	Phi	NL	33	33	0	0	197.1	811	187	88	80	30	6	**10**	8	42	2	167	6	2	11	14	.440	0	0-0	0	3.56	3.65
	2 ML YEARS		41	41	0	0	248.1	1014	227	104	95	35	6	11	8	55	2	216	7	2	14	17	.452	0	0-0	0	3.31	3.44

Roenis Elias

Pitches: L **Bats:** L **Pos:** RP-2; SP-1   roh-EN-ees ehl-LEE-us   **Ht:** 6'1" **Wt:** 205 **Born:** 8/1/1988 **Age:** 28

| | | | HOW MUCH HE PITCHED | | | | | | WHAT HE GAVE UP | | | | | | | | | | THE RESULTS | | | | | | |
Year	Team	Lg	G	GS	CG	GF	IP	BFP	H	R	ER	HR	SH	SF	HB	TBB	IBB	SO	WP	Bk	W	L	Pct	Sh	Sv-Op	Hld	ERC	ERA
2016	Pwtckt*	AAA	21	19	1	0	125.0	533	115	56	50	10	3	7	6	57	0	113	2	1	10	5	.667	0	0- -	-	3.96	3.60
2014	Sea	AL	29	29	1	0	163.2	693	151	77	70	16	4	4	11	64	3	143	6	**4**	10	12	.455	1	0-0	0	3.89	3.85
2015	Sea	AL	22	20	0	0	115.1	490	106	57	53	15	1	4	9	44	1	97	1	1	5	8	.385	0	0-0	0	4.10	4.14
2016	Bos	AL	3	1	0	2	7.2	41	15	11	11	2	0	0	0	5	1	3	0	0	0	1	.000	0	0-0	0	13.11	12.91
	3 ML YEARS		54	50	1	2	286.2	1224	272	145	134	33	5	8	20	113	5	243	7	5	15	21	.417	1	0-0	1	4.18	4.21

Brian Ellington

Pitches: R **Bats:** R **Pos:** RP-32   **Ht:** 6'3" **Wt:** 215 **Born:** 8/4/1990 **Age:** 26

| | | | HOW MUCH HE PITCHED | | | | | | WHAT HE GAVE UP | | | | | | | | | | THE RESULTS | | | | | | |
Year	Team	Lg	G	GS	CG	GF	IP	BFP	H	R	ER	HR	SH	SF	HB	TBB	IBB	SO	WP	Bk	W	L	Pct	Sh	Sv-Op	Hld	ERC	ERA
2012	Jmstwn	A-	18	0	0	4	30.0	134	20	11	8	2	0	2	0	25	0	33	3	0	2	0	1.000	0	0- -	-	3.90	2.40
2013	3 Tms	Low	24	3	0	4	65.0	293	56	40	30	3	3	1	12	35	0	52	1	0	4	4	.500	0	0- -	-	4.12	4.15
2014	Jupiter	A+	35	0	0	15	47.1	217	51	28	25	2	1	1	3	24	0	56	2	1	2	2	.500	0	0- -	-	4.70	4.75
2015	Jaxnvl	AA	25	0	0	6	43.0	169	28	13	12	0	3	2	1	13	0	47	2	0	4	1	.800	0	0- -	-	1.53	2.51
2016	NewOr	AAA	32	0	0	11	34.2	147	17	12	12	2	1	1	2	26	0	54	4	0	1	0	1.000	0	2- -	-	2.58	3.12
2015	Mia	NL	23	0	0	9	25.0	105	17	10	8	1	0	2	2	13	2	18	1	0	2	1	.667	0	0-0	2	2.59	2.88
2016	Mia	NL	32	0	0	7	33.0	142	27	10	9	2	1	1	2	16	2	32	3	1	4	2	.667	0	0-0	3	3.24	2.45
	2 ML YEARS		55	0	0	16	58.0	247	44	20	17	3	1	3	4	29	4	50	4	1	6	3	.667	0	0-0	5	2.96	2.64

A.J. Ellis

Bats: R **Throws:** R **Pos:** C-57;PH-9   **Ht:** 6'2" **Wt:** 225 **Born:** 4/9/1981 **Age:** 36

Year	Team	Lg	G	AB	H	2B	3B	HR	(Hm	Rd)	TB	R	RBI	RC	TBB	IBB	SO	HBP	SH	SF	SB	CS	GDP	Avg	OBP	Slg	OPS
2008	LAD	NL	4	3	0	0	0	0	(0	0)	0	1	0	0	0	0	2	0	0	0	0	0	0	.000	.000	.000	.000
2009	LAD	NL	8	10	1	0	0	0	(0	0)	1	0	1	0	0	0	1	0	0	0	0	0	0	.100	.100	.100	.200
2010	LAD	NL	44	108	30	5	0	0	(0	0)	35	6	16	16	14	1	18	1	4	1	0	0	5	.278	.363	.324	.687
2011	LAD	NL	31	85	23	1	1	2	(0	2)	32	8	11	11	14	0	16	3	1	0	0	1	2	.271	.392	.376	.769
2012	LAD	NL	133	423	114	20	1	13	(6	7)	175	44	52	61	65	11	107	7	6	4	0	0	17	.270	.373	.414	.786
2013	LAD	NL	115	390	93	17	1	10	(2	8)	142	43	52	43	45	1	78	3	4	6	0	2	11	.238	.318	.364	.682
2014	LAD	NL	93	283	54	9	0	3	(0	3)	72	21	25	22	53	5	57	4	3	4	0	0	15	.191	.323	.254	.577
2015	LAD	NL	63	181	43	9	0	7	(3	4)	73	24	21	25	32	1	38	1	3	0	0	0	9	.238	.355	.403	.758
2016	2 Tms	NL	64	171	37	8	0	2	(1	1)	51	11	22	19	19	2	31	2	3	1	2	1	5	.216	.301	.298	.599
16	LAD	NL	53	139	27	5	0	1	(0	1)	35	8	13	10	16	2	24	2	3	1	1	1	5	.194	.285	.252	.537
16	Phi	NL	11	32	10	3	0	1	(1	0)	16	3	9	9	3	0	7	0	0	0	1	0	0	.313	.371	.500	.871
	Postseason		17	52	19	5	1	2	(2	0)	32	7	5	11	7	1	9	1	1	0	0	0	0	.365	.450	.615	1.065
	9 ML YEARS		555	1654	395	69	3	37	(12	25)	581	158	200	197	242	21	348	21	24	16	2	4	59	.239	.340	.351	.692

Jacoby Ellsbury

Bats: L Throws: L Pos: CF-148;PH-4;PR-2   Ht: 6'1" Wt: 195 Born: 9/11/1983 Age: 33

								BATTING												RUNNING			AVERAGES			
Year	Team	Lg	G	AB	H	2B	3B	HR	(Hm | Rd)	TB	R	RBI	RC	TBB	IBB	SO	HBP	SH	SF	SB	CS	GDP	Avg	OBP	Slg	OPS
2007	Bos	AL	33	116	41	7	1	3	(3 | 0)	59	20	18	26	8	0	15	1	0	2	9	0	2	.353	.394	.509	.902
2008	Bos	AL	145	554	155	22	7	9	(4 | 5)	218	98	47	71	41	2	80	7	4	3	50	11	10	.280	.336	.394	.729
2009	Bos	AL	153	624	188	27	10	8	(4 | 4)	259	94	60	97	49	3	74	6	6	6	70	12	13	.301	.355	.415	.770
2010	Bos	AL	18	78	15	4	0	0	(0 | 0)	19	10	5	4	4	0	9	1	0	0	7	1	0	.192	.241	.244	.485
2011	Bos	AL	158	660	212	46	5	32	(15 | 17)	364	119	105	134	52	1	98	9	3	5	39	15	8	.321	.376	.552	.928
2012	Bos	AL	74	303	82	18	0	4	(3 | 1)	112	43	26	37	19	0	43	0	0	1	14	3	5	.271	.313	.370	.682
2013	Bos	AL	134	577	172	31	8	9	(4 | 5)	246	92	53	90	47	3	92	5	1	2	52	4	12	.298	.355	.426	.781
2014	NYY	AL	149	575	156	27	5	16	(7 | 9)	241	71	70	84	49	5	93	3	0	7	39	5	9	.271	.328	.419	.747
2015	NYY	AL	111	452	116	15	2	7	(3 | 4)	156	66	33	51	35	1	86	7	1	3	21	9	6	.257	.318	.345	.663
2016	NYY	AL	148	551	145	24	5	9	(4 | 5)	206	71	56	77	54	1	84	2	4	3	20	8	11	.263	.330	.374	.703
	Postseason		39	134	40	11	2	0	(0 | 0)	55	26	17	25	13	2	24	0	0	1	11	2	4	.299	.358	.410	.769
	10 ML YEARS		1123	4490	1282	221	43	97	(47 | 50)	1880	684	473	671	358	16	674	41	19	32	321	68	76	.286	.342	.419	.760

Jake Elmore

Bats: R Throws: R Pos: PH-38;LF-14;3B-4;RF-4;2B-3;CF-2;PR-1   Ht: 5'10" Wt: 180 Born: 6/15/1987 Age: 30

								BATTING												RUNNING			AVERAGES			
Year	Team	Lg	G	AB	H	2B	3B	HR	(Hm	Rd)	TB	R	RBI	RC	TBB	IBB	SO	HBP	SH	SF	SB	CS	GDP	Avg	OBP	Slg	OPS
2016	ColSpr*	AAA	57	150	48	3	0	2	(-	-)	57	25	19	28	26	2	19	3	2	1	13	4	3	.320	.428	.380	.808
2012	Ari	NL	30	68	13	4	0	0	(0	0)	17	1	7	3	5	0	6	0	0	0	0	0	1	.191	.247	.250	.497
2013	Hou	AL	52	120	29	4	0	2	(1	1)	39	16	6	13	13	0	20	0	2	1	1	6	1	.242	.313	.325	.638
2014	Cin	NL	5	11	2	0	0	0	(0	0)	2	0	0	0	1	0	4	0	0	0	0	0	0	.182	.250	.182	.432
2015	TB	AL	51	141	29	5	0	2	(2	0)	40	10	16	10	12	1	25	0	2	3	1	1	6	.206	.263	.284	.547
2016	Mil	NL	59	78	17	2	0	0	(0	0)	19	7	4	7	17	1	17	2	2	0	2	3	1	.218	.371	.244	.615
	5 ML YEARS		197	418	90	15	0	4	(3	1)	117	34	33	33	48	2	72	2	6	4	4	10	9	.215	.297	.280	.577

Edwin Encarnacion

Bats: R Throws: R Pos: DH-86;1B-75   Ht: 6'1" Wt: 230 Born: 1/7/1983 Age: 34

								BATTING												RUNNING			AVERAGES			
Year	Team	Lg	G	AB	H	2B	3B	HR	(Hm	Rd)	TB	R	RBI	RC	TBB	IBB	SO	HBP	SH	SF	SB	CS	GDP	Avg	OBP	Slg	OPS
2005	Cin	NL	69	211	49	16	0	9	(3	6)	92	25	31	24	20	2	60	3	0	0	3	0	8	.232	.308	.436	.744
2006	Cin	NL	117	406	112	33	1	15	(7	8)	192	60	72	66	41	3	78	13	0	3	6	3	9	.276	.359	.473	.831
2007	Cin	NL	139	502	145	25	1	16	(10	6)	220	66	76	86	39	4	86	14	0	1	8	1	5	.289	.356	.438	.794
2008	Cin	NL	146	506	127	29	1	26	(15	11)	236	75	68	72	61	1	102	10	0	5	1	0	13	.251	.340	.466	.807
2009	2 Tms		85	293	66	11	2	13	(5	8)	120	35	39	37	37	0	67	5	0	3	2	1	5	.225	.320	.410	.729
2010	Tor	AL	96	332	81	16	0	21	(7	14)	160	47	51	41	29	1	60	2	0	4	1	0	9	.244	.305	.482	.787
2011	Tor	AL	134	481	131	36	0	17	(14	3)	218	70	55	67	43	2	77	3	0	3	8	2	17	.272	.334	.453	.787
2012	Tor	AL	151	542	152	24	0	42	(23	19)	302	93	110	124	84	12	94	11	0	7	13	3	6	.280	.384	.557	.941
2013	Tor	AL	142	530	144	29	1	36	(12	24)	283	90	104	102	82	7	62	4	0	5	7	1	20	.272	.370	.534	.904
2014	Tor	AL	128	477	128	27	2	34	(19	15)	261	75	98	86	62	6	82	2	0	1	2	0	18	.268	.354	.547	.901
2015	Tor	AL	146	528	146	31	0	39	(18	21)	294	94	111	110	77	5	98	9	0	10	3	2	14	.277	.372	.557	.929
2016	Tor	AL	160	601	158	34	0	42	(20	22)	318	99	127	104	87	3	138	5	0	8	2	0	22	.263	.357	.529	.886
09	Cin	NL	43	139	29	6	1	5	(3	2)	52	10	16	19	24	0	38	2	0	1	1	1	3	.209	.333	.374	.707
09	Tor	AL	42	154	37	5	1	8	(2	6)	68	25	23	18	13	0	29	3	0	3	1	0	2	.240	.306	.442	.748
	Postseason		11	40	11	2	0	1	(1	0)	16	5	5	6	7	3	8	0	0	0	0	0	1	.275	.383	.400	.783
	12 ML YEARS		1513	5409	1439	311	8	310	(153	157)	2696	829	942	919	662	46	1004	81	0	50	56	13	146	.266	.352	.498	.850

Nathan Eovaldi

Pitches: R Bats: R Pos: SP-21; RP-3   eh-VOLL-dee   Ht: 6'2" Wt: 225 Born: 2/13/1990 Age: 27

			HOW MUCH HE PITCHED						WHAT HE GAVE UP									THE RESULTS						
Year	Team	Lg	G	GS	CG	GF	IP	BFP	H	R	ER	HR	SH	SF	HB	TBB	IBB	SO	WP	Bk	W	L	Pct	Sh	Sv-Op	Hld	ERC	ERA
2011	LAD	NL	10	6	0	1	34.2	146	28	14	14	2	2	0	2	20	0	23	0	0	1	2	.333	0	0-0	0	3.75	3.63
2012	2 Tms	NL	22	22	0	0	119.1	526	133	59	57	10	1	6	3	47	3	78	1	0	4	13	.235	0	0-0	0	4.67	4.30
2013	Mia	NL	18	18	0	0	106.1	451	100	44	40	7	6	1	1	40	3	78	3	0	4	6	.400	0	0-0	0	3.41	3.39
2014	Mia	NL	33	33	0	0	199.2	854	223	107	97	14	9	5	7	43	5	142	6	0	6	14	.300	0	0-0	0	3.89	4.37
2015	NYY	AL	27	27	0	0	154.1	673	175	72	72	10	3	3	3	49	0	121	8	0	14	3	.824	0	0-0	0	4.34	4.20
2016	NYY	AL	24	21	0	2	124.2	525	123	66	66	23	1	1	1	40	2	97	5	0	9	8	.529	0	0-0	0	4.30	4.76
12	LAD	NL	10	10	0	0	56.1	241	63	27	26	5	0	3	0	20	2	34	1	0	1	6	.143	0	0-0	0	4.54	4.15
12	Mia	NL	12	12	0	0	63.0	285	70	32	31	5	1	3	3	27	1	44	0	0	3	7	.300	0	0-0	0	4.79	4.43
	6 ML YEARS		134	127	0	3	739.0	3175	782	362	346	66	22	16	17	239	13	539	23	0	38	46	.452	0	0-0	1	4.10	4.21

Robbie Erlin

Pitches: L Bats: R Pos: SP-2; RP-1   Ht: 6'0" Wt: 190 Born: 10/8/1990 Age: 26

			HOW MUCH HE PITCHED						WHAT HE GAVE UP									THE RESULTS						
Year	Team	Lg	G	GS	CG	GF	IP	BFP	H	R	ER	HR	SH	SF	HB	TBB	IBB	SO	WP	Bk	W	L	Pct	Sh	Sv-Op	Hld	ERC	ERA
2013	SD	NL	11	9	0	2	54.2	227	53	26	25	6	3	1	0	15	0	40	3	0	3	5	.500	0	0-0	0	3.50	4.12
2014	SD	NL	13	11	0	1	61.1	264	71	34	34	6	2	4	1	15	1	46	4	0	4	5	.444	0	0-0	0	4.39	4.99
2015	SD	NL	3	3	0	0	17.0	65	16	9	9	1	0	0	1	2	0	10	1	0	1	2	.333	0	0-0	0	2.84	4.76
2016	SD	NL	3	2	0	0	15.2	58	12	7	7	3	0	0	0	3	0	13	2	0	1	2	.333	0	0-0	0	2.77	4.02
	4 ML YEARS		30	25	0	3	148.2	614	152	76	75	16	5	5	2	35	1	109	10	0	9	12	.429	0	0-0	1	3.71	4.54

Jake Esch

Pitches: R **Bats:** R **Pos:** SP-3   esh   **Ht:** 6'3" **Wt:** 205 **Born:** 3/27/1990 **Age:** 27

			HOW MUCH HE PITCHED						WHAT HE GAVE UP										THE RESULTS							
Year	Team	Lg	G	GS	CG	GF	IP	BFP	H	R	ER	HR	SH	SF	HB	TBB	IBB	SO	WP	Bk	W	L	Pct	Sh	Sv-Op	Hld	ERC	ERA
2012	2 Tms	Low	16	6	0	3	68.2	279	58	30	24	4	2	2	1	24	1	53	4	3	4	3	.571	0	1--	-	2.87	3.15
2013	Jupiter	A+	23	19	0	0	94.0	418	99	57	49	5	1	6	7	38	0	57	3	0	2	10	.167	0	0--	-	4.32	4.69
2014	Jupiter	A+	25	24	1	0	135.1	580	147	73	61	7	4	4	5	34	0	105	5	0	6	6	.500	0	0--	-	3.77	4.06
2015	Jaxnvl	AA	15	15	0	0	85.1	351	69	34	33	5	3	4	2	33	1	68	1	0	6	5	.545	0	0--	-	2.83	3.48
2015	NewOr	AAA	6	6	0	0	30.0	137	41	20	18	3	1	1	2	9	1	20	0	0	1	3	.250	0	0--	-	6.13	5.40
2016	Jaxnvl	AA	22	22	0	0	118.1	500	117	53	53	8	8	6	5	37	0	82	2	1	10	9	.526	0	0--	-	3.64	4.03
2016	Mia	NL	3	3	0	0	13.0	59	17	8	8	4	0	0	1	6	1	10	0	0	0	1	.000	0	0-0	0	8.49	5.54

Alcides Escobar

Bats: R **Throws:** R **Pos:** SS-162   al-SEE-dess   **Ht:** 6'1" **Wt:** 185 **Born:** 12/16/1986 **Age:** 30

						BATTING													RUNNING			AVERAGES			
Year	Team	Lg	G	AB	H	2B	3B	HR	(Hm | Rd)	TB	R	RBI	RC	TBB	IBB	SO	HBP	SH	SF	SB	CS	GDP	Avg	OBP	Slg	OPS
2008	Mil	NL	9	4	2	0	0	0	(0 | 0)	2	2	0	0	0	0	1	0	0	0	0	0	0	.500	.500	.500	1.000
2009	Mil	NL	38	125	38	3	1	1	(0 | 1)	46	20	11	16	4	0	18	2	2	1	4	2	0	.304	.333	.368	.701
2010	Mil	NL	145	506	119	14	10	4	(3 | 1)	165	57	41	51	36	7	70	3	4	3	10	4	8	.235	.288	.326	.614
2011	KC	AL	158	548	139	21	8	4	(0 | 4)	188	69	46	46	25	1	73	4	18	3	26	9	10	.254	.290	.343	.633
2012	KC	AL	155	605	177	30	7	5	(5 | 0)	236	68	52	72	27	2	100	8	8	0	35	5	14	.293	.331	.390	.721
2013	KC	AL	158	607	142	20	4	4	(1 | 3)	182	57	52	51	19	1	84	3	9	4	22	0	12	.234	.259	.300	.559
2014	KC	AL	**162**	579	165	34	5	3	(2 | 1)	218	74	50	68	23	1	83	6	8	4	31	6	12	.285	.317	.377	.694
2015	KC	AL	148	612	157	20	5	3	(0 | 3)	196	76	47	60	26	1	75	8	11	5	17	5	10	.257	.293	.320	.614
2016	KC	AL	**162**	637	166	24	6	7	(5 | 2)	223	57	55	66	27	2	96	3	**10**	5	17	4	16	.261	.292	.350	.642
	Postseason		31	135	42	9	3	2	(1 | 1)	63	21	14	24	1	0	21	3	6	2	2	1	2	.311	.326	.467	.793
	9 ML YEARS		1135	4223	1105	166	46	31	(16 | 15)	1456	480	354	430	187	15	600	37	70	25	162	35	82	.262	.297	.345	.642

Eduardo Escobar

Bats: B **Throws:** R **Pos:** SS-71;3B-23;PH-11;2B-6;LF-2;DH-1;PR-1   **Ht:** 5'10" **Wt:** 185 **Born:** 1/5/1989 **Age:** 28

						BATTING													RUNNING			AVERAGES			
Year	Team	Lg	G	AB	H	2B	3B	HR	(Hm | Rd)	TB	R	RBI	RC	TBB	IBB	SO	HBP	SH	SF	SB	CS	GDP	Avg	OBP	Slg	OPS
2011	CWS	AL	9	7	2	0	0	0	(0 | 0)	2	0	0	1	0	0	1	0	0	0	0	0	0	.286	.286	.286	.571
2012	2 Tms	AL	50	131	28	4	1	0	(0 | 0)	34	18	9	12	11	0	31	1	2	1	3	0	0	.214	.278	.260	.537
2013	Min	AL	66	165	39	5	2	3	(2 | 1)	57	23	10	14	11	0	34	0	2	1	0	2	0	.236	.282	.345	.628
2014	Min	AL	133	433	119	35	2	6	(2 | 4)	176	52	37	53	24	1	93	2	4	2	1	1	6	.275	.315	.406	.721
2015	Min	AL	127	409	107	31	4	12	(2 | 10)	182	48	58	55	28	1	86	2	2	5	2	3	7	.262	.309	.445	.754
2016	Min	AL	105	352	83	14	2	6	(3 | 3)	119	32	37	38	21	1	72	1	2	1	1	3	7	.236	.280	.338	.618
	12 CWS	AL	36	87	18	4	1	0	(0 | 0)	24	14	3	7	9	0	23	0	1	0	2	0	0	.207	.281	.276	.557
	12 Min	AL	14	44	10	0	0	0	(0 | 0)	10	4	6	5	2	0	8	1	1	1	1	0	0	.227	.271	.227	.498
	6 ML YEARS		490	1497	378	89	11	27	(9 | 18)	570	173	151	173	95	3	317	6	12	10	7	9	20	.253	.298	.381	.679

Edwin Escobar

Pitches: L **Bats:** L **Pos:** RP-23; SP-2   **Ht:** 6'2" **Wt:** 225 **Born:** 4/22/1992 **Age:** 25

			HOW MUCH HE PITCHED						WHAT HE GAVE UP										THE RESULTS							
Year	Team	Lg	G	GS	CG	GF	IP	BFP	H	R	ER	HR	SH	SF	HB	TBB	IBB	SO	WP	Bk	W	L	Pct	Sh	Sv-Op	Hld	ERC	ERA
2012	Augsta	A	22	22	0	0	130.2	547	121	57	43	7	3	2	7	32	0	122	10	2	7	8	.467	0	0--	-	2.95	2.96
2013	SnJos	A+	16	14	0	0	74.2	314	68	33	24	3	2	4	1	17	0	92	0	1	3	4	.429	0	0--	-	2.52	2.89
2013	Rchmd	AA	10	10	0	0	54.0	218	44	18	16	2	2	0	2	13	0	53	1	0	5	4	.556	0	0--	-	2.26	2.67
2014	Fresno	AAA	20	20	0	0	111.0	499	128	69	63	16	5	5	6	37	2	96	4	2	3	8	.273	0	0--	-	5.14	5.11
2014	Pwtckt	AAA	5	5	0	0	27.1	120	33	15	13	3	0	1	0	8	0	20	0	0	0	2	.000	0	0--	-	4.92	4.28
2015	Pwtckt	AAA	19	6	0	5	49.2	221	52	29	28	8	1	3	2	25	0	24	0	0	3	3	.500	0	0--	-	5.45	5.07
2016	Reno	AAA	16	16	0	0	91.0	396	99	46	43	8	3	5	3	36	0	63	5	1	6	3	.667	0	0--	-	4.68	4.25
2014	Bos	AL	2	0	0	2	2.0	8	1	1	1	0	0	0	1	0	0	2	0	0	0	0	-	0	0-0	0	1.41	4.50
2016	Ari	NL	25	2	0	3	23.2	116	33	21	19	4	1	0	4	12	3	17	0	0	1	2	.333	0	0-1	4	8.10	7.23
	2 ML YEARS		27	2	0	5	25.2	124	34	22	20	4	1	0	5	12	3	19	0	0	1	2	.333	0	0-1	4	7.46	7.01

Yunel Escobar

Bats: R **Throws:** R **Pos:** 3B-129;PH-2   you-NELL   **Ht:** 6'2" **Wt:** 215 **Born:** 11/2/1982 **Age:** 34

						BATTING													RUNNING			AVERAGES			
Year	Team	Lg	G	AB	H	2B	3B	HR	(Hm | Rd)	TB	R	RBI	RC	TBB	IBB	SO	HBP	SH	SF	SB	CS	GDP	Avg	OBP	Slg	OPS
2007	Atl	NL	94	319	104	25	0	5	(3 | 2)	144	54	28	52	27	1	44	5	2	2	5	3	6	.326	.385	.451	.837
2008	Atl	NL	136	514	148	24	2	10	(5 | 5)	206	71	60	70	59	4	62	5	7	2	5	5	24	.288	.366	.401	.766
2009	Atl	NL	141	528	158	26	2	14	(7 | 7)	230	89	76	90	57	3	62	10	7	2	5	4	21	.299	.377	.436	.812
2010	2 Tms		135	497	127	19	0	4	(2 | 2)	158	60	35	53	56	1	57	5	9	0	6	2	18	.256	.337	.318	.655
2011	Tor	AL	145	513	149	24	3	11	(8 | 3)	212	77	48	84	61	1	70	6	5	5	3	3	14	.290	.369	.413	.782
2012	Tor	AL	145	558	141	22	1	9	(6 | 3)	192	58	51	51	35	1	70	4	7	4	5	1	21	.253	.300	.344	.644
2013	TB	AL	153	508	130	27	1	9	(5 | 4)	186	61	56	60	57	2	73	3	6	4	4	4	19	.256	.332	.366	.698
2014	TB	AL	137	476	123	18	0	7	(2 | 5)	162	33	39	49	43	3	60	4	4	2	1	1	15	.258	.324	.340	.664
2015	Was	NL	139	535	168	25	4	9	(5 | 4)	222	75	56	78	45	0	70	8	1	2	2	2	**24**	.314	.375	.415	.790
2016	LAA	AL	132	517	157	28	1	5	(4 | 1)	202	68	39	74	40	0	67	3	3	4	0	3	21	.304	.355	.391	.745
	10 Atl	NL	75	261	62	12	0	0	(0 | 0)	74	28	19	25	37	1	31	1	2	0	5	1	9	.238	.334	.284	.618
	10 Tor	AL	60	236	65	7	0	4	(2 | 2)	84	32	16	28	19	0	26	4	7	0	1	1	9	.275	.340	.356	.696
	Postseason		5	19	8	2	0	0	(0 | 0)	10	3	2	4	0	0	1	0	0	0	0	0	1	.421	.421	.526	.947
	10 ML YEARS		1345	4965	1405	238	11	83	(47 | 36)	1914	646	488	661	480	16	635	53	51	27	33	28	183	.283	.351	.385	.736

Danny Espinosa

Bats: B **Throws:** R **Pos:** SS-157;PH-1;PR-1   **Ht:** 6'0" **Wt:** 205 **Born:** 4/25/1987 **Age:** 30

									BATTING													RUNNING			AVERAGES			
Year Team	Lg	G	AB	H	2B	3B	HR	(Hm	Rd)	TB	R	RBI	RC	TBB	IBB	SO	HBP	SH	SF			SB	CS	GDP	Avg	OBP	Slg	OPS
2010 Was	NL	28	103	22	4	1	6	(4	2)	46	16	15	15	9	1	30	0	0	0			0	2	0	.214	.277	.447	.723
2011 Was	NL	158	573	135	29	5	21	(11	10)	237	72	66	83	57	4	166	19	5	4			17	6	6	.236	.323	.414	.737
2012 Was	NL	160	594	147	37	2	17	(7	10)	239	82	56	69	46	4	189	13	3	2			20	6	11	.247	.315	.402	.717
2013 Was	NL	44	158	25	9	0	3	(2	1)	43	11	12	8	4	0	47	3	1	1			0	1	0	.158	.193	.272	.465
2014 Was	NL	114	333	73	14	3	8	(5	3)	117	31	27	26	18	5	122	12	0	1			8	1	5	.219	.283	.351	.634
2015 Was	NL	118	367	88	21	1	13	(6	7)	150	59	37	40	33	5	106	6	3	3			5	2	6	.240	.311	.409	.719
2016 Was	NL	157	516	108	15	0	24	(12	12)	195	66	72	64	54	12	174	20	7	4			9	2	4	.209	.306	.378	.684
Postseason		7	19	1	0	0	0	(0	0)	1	0	0	0	2	0	8	0	2	0			0	0	0	.053	.143	.053	.195
7 ML YEARS		779	2644	598	129	12	92	(47	45)	1027	337	285	305	221	31	834	73	19	15			60	19	33	.226	.302	.388	.690

Carlos Estevez

Pitches: R **Bats:** R **Pos:** RP-63   **Ht:** 6'4" **Wt:** 210 **Born:** 12/28/1992 **Age:** 24

		HOW MUCH HE PITCHED						WHAT HE GAVE UP											THE RESULTS							
Year Team	Lg	G	GS	CG	GF	IP	BFP	H	R	ER	HR	SH	SF	HB	TBB	IBB	SO	WP	Bk	W	L	Pct	Sh	Sv-Op	Hld	ERC	ERA
2013 2 Tms	Low	24	0	0	4	39.1	163	34	19	16	4	3	1	1	15	0	36	5	0	6	1	.857	0	0- -	-	3.42	3.66
2014 Ashvll	A	33	0	0	5	53.1	226	62	34	28	4	1	2	1	11	0	50	7	0	1	3	.250	0	0- -	-	4.18	4.73
2015 Mdest	A+	14	0	0	10	19.2	72	12	3	3	0	0	0	0	5	0	25	0	0	5	0	1.000	0	5- -	-	1.31	1.37
2015 NwBrit	AA	34	0	0	26	36.0	157	39	19	18	2	2	3	1	9	0	43	2	0	0	3	.000	0	13- -	-	3.66	4.50
2016 Albq	AAA	5	0	0	2	5.2	26	6	2	2	0	0	0	0	3	0	4	0	0	1	0	1.000	0	0- -	-	4.05	3.18
2016 Col	NL	63	0	0	26	55.0	246	50	32	32	6	1	4	5	28	4	59	3	0	3	7	.300	0	11-18	11	4.23	5.24

Marco Estrada

Pitches: R **Bats:** R **Pos:** SP-29   **Ht:** 6'0" **Wt:** 200 **Born:** 7/5/1983 **Age:** 33

		HOW MUCH HE PITCHED						WHAT HE GAVE UP											THE RESULTS							
Year Team	Lg	G	GS	CG	GF	IP	BFP	H	R	ER	HR	SH	SF	HB	TBB	IBB	SO	WP	Bk	W	L	Pct	Sh	Sv-Op	Hld	ERC	ERA
2008 Was	NL	11	0	0	3	12.2	63	17	13	11	4	0	0	2	5	1	10	0	0	0	0	-	0	0-1	3	8.13	7.82
2009 Was	NL	4	1	0	1	7.1	33	6	6	5	1	1	0	0	4	0	9	1	0	0	1	.000	0	0-0	0	3.67	6.14
2010 Mil	NL	7	1	0	0	11.1	58	14	13	12	3	1	0	1	6	0	13	2	0	0	0	-	0	0-0	0	7.17	9.53
2011 Mil	NL	43	7	0	12	92.2	381	83	45	42	11	7	1	2	29	2	88	4	2	4	8	.333	0	0-3	4	3.39	4.08
2012 Mil	NL	29	23	0	0	138.1	562	129	62	56	18	7	3	0	29	0	143	4	1	5	7	.417	0	0-0	1	3.18	3.64
2013 Mil	NL	21	21	0	0	128.0	512	109	56	55	19	3	2	2	29	0	118	3	0	7	4	.636	0	0-0	0	3.01	3.87
2014 Mil	NL	39	18	0	3	150.2	624	137	77	73	29	4	4	3	44	0	127	2	1	7	6	.538	0	0-0	0	3.85	4.36
2015 Tor	AL	34	28	0	3	181.0	725	134	67	63	24	2	3	5	55	2	131	2	0	13	8	.619	0	0-0	0	2.64	3.13
2016 Tor	AL	29	29	0	0	176.0	721	132	73	68	23	0	3	4	65	1	165	5	0	9	9	.500	0	0-0	0	2.88	3.48
Postseason		7	3	0	2	25.1	100	21	9	9	2	0	0	0	3	0	24	1	0	2	1	.667	0	0-0	0	2.00	3.20
9 ML YEARS		217	128	0	22	898.0	3681	761	412	385	132	25	16	19	266	6	804	23	4	45	43	.511	0	0-4	8	3.22	3.86

Andre Ethier

Bats: L **Throws:** L **Pos:** PH-12;LF-4;DH-1   EE-thee-er   **Ht:** 6'2" **Wt:** 210 **Born:** 4/10/1982 **Age:** 35

									BATTING													RUNNING			AVERAGES			
Year Team	Lg	G	AB	H	2B	3B	HR	(Hm	Rd)	TB	R	RBI	RC	TBB	IBB	SO	HBP	SH	SF			SB	CS	GDP	Avg	OBP	Slg	OPS
2006 LAD	NL	126	396	122	20	7	11	(9	2)	189	50	55	62	34	2	77	5	0	6			5	5	11	.308	.365	.477	.842
2007 LAD	NL	153	447	127	32	2	13	(8	5)	202	50	64	65	46	12	68	4	0	8			0	4	10	.284	.350	.452	.802
2008 LAD	NL	141	525	160	38	5	20	(10	10)	268	90	77	99	59	0	88	4	1	7			6	3	6	.305	.375	.510	.885
2009 LAD	NL	160	596	162	42	3	31	(22	9)	303	92	106	94	72	10	116	13	0	4			6	4	19	.272	.361	.508	.869
2010 LAD	NL	139	517	151	33	1	23	(14	9)	255	71	82	89	59	11	102	3	0	6			2	1	11	.292	.364	.493	.857
2011 LAD	NL	135	487	142	30	0	11	(8	3)	205	67	62	73	58	9	103	3	0	3			0	1	8	.292	.368	.421	.789
2012 LAD	NL	149	556	158	36	1	20	(14	6)	256	79	89	89	50	6	124	9	0	3			2	2	13	.284	.351	.460	.812
2013 LAD	NL	142	482	131	33	2	12	(6	6)	204	54	52	62	61	11	95	7	0	3			4	3	9	.272	.360	.423	.783
2014 LAD	NL	130	341	85	17	6	4	(4	0)	126	29	42	42	31	3	74	6	1	1			2	2	5	.249	.322	.370	.691
2015 LAD	NL	142	395	116	20	7	14	(9	5)	192	54	53	59	43	2	75	4	0	3			2	3	11	.294	.366	.486	.852
2016 LAD	NL	16	24	5	1	0	1	(1	0)	9	2	2	1	2	1	6	0	0	0			0	0	1	.208	.269	.375	.644
Postseason		35	107	25	6	1	3	(1	2)	42	15	8	11	15	0	29	1	0	0			0	1	4	.234	.333	.393	.726
11 ML YEARS		1433	4766	1359	302	34	160	(105	55)	2209	638	684	735	515	67	928	58	2	44			29	28	104	.285	.359	.463	.822

Dana Eveland

Pitches: L **Bats:** L **Pos:** RP-33   EVE-land   **Ht:** 6'1" **Wt:** 235 **Born:** 10/29/1983 **Age:** 33

		HOW MUCH HE PITCHED						WHAT HE GAVE UP											THE RESULTS							
Year Team	Lg	G	GS	CG	GF	IP	BFP	H	R	ER	HR	SH	SF	HB	TBB	IBB	SO	WP	Bk	W	L	Pct	Sh	Sv-Op	Hld	ERC	ERA
2016 Drham*	AAA	20	1	0	4	29.2	111	16	2	1	1	1	0	4	6	0	21	0	0	1	0	1.000	0	0- -	-	1.38	0.30
2005 Mil	NL	27	0	0	3	31.2	146	40	21	21	2	0	1	1	18	3	23	1	0	1	1	.500	0	1-2	7	6.16	5.97
2006 Mil	NL	9	5	0	1	27.2	141	39	25	25	4	1	1	5	16	2	32	2	0	0	3	.000	0	0-1	0	8.30	8.13
2007 Ari	NL	5	1	0	0	5.0	28	8	8	8	0	0	1	0	5	0	3	1	0	1	0	1.000	0	0-0	0	9.25	14.40
2008 Oak	AL	29	29	1	0	168.0	737	172	82	81	10	2	5	12	77	2	118	6	1	9	9	.500	0	0-0	0	4.47	4.34
2009 Oak	AL	13	9	0	2	44.0	221	70	39	35	4	1	2	0	26	1	22	2	0	2	4	.333	0	0-0	0	8.50	7.16
2010 2 Tms		12	10	0	0	54.1	262	72	44	41	4	0	4	4	32	2	24	4	0	3	5	.375	0	0-0	0	6.90	6.79
2011 LAD	NL	5	5	0	0	29.2	118	28	10	10	1	1	0	2	6	0	16	0	0	3	2	.600	0	0-0	0	2.98	3.03
2012 Bal	AL	14	2	0	6	32.1	145	32	18	17	3	0	2	5	13	3	18	0	0	1	1	.500	0	0-0	1	4.38	4.73
2014 NYM	NL	30	0	0	10	27.1	115	24	8	8	2	0	0	4	6	1	27	0	0	1	1	.500	0	1-2	2	3.02	2.63
2015 Atl	NL	10	0	0	1	3.1	18	5	2	2	1	0	1	0	3	1	4	1	0	0	1	.000	0	0-0	1	10.42	5.40
2016 TB	AL	33	0	0	8	23.0	119	32	23	23	3	0	1	3	19	3	21	0	0	0	0	.000	0	0-0	3	8.98	9.00
10 Tor	AL	9	9	0	0	44.2	213	57	35	32	4	0	2	4	27	1	21	3	0	3	4	.429	0	0-0	0	6.69	6.45
10 Pit	NL	3	1	0	0	9.2	49	15	9	9	0	0	2	0	5	1	3	1	0	0	1	.000	0	0-0	0	7.85	8.38
11 ML YEARS		187	61	1	32	446.1	2050	522	280	271	34	5	18	36	221	18	308	17	1	20	28	.417	0	2-5	13	5.57	5.46

Jeurys Familia

Pitches: R Bats: R Pos: RP-78   jer-ISS fa-MEAL-ya   Ht: 6'3" Wt: 240 Born: 10/10/1989 Age: 27

		HOW MUCH HE PITCHED						WHAT HE GAVE UP												THE RESULTS						
Year	Team	Lg	G	GS	CG	GF	IP	BFP	H	R	ER	HR	SH	SF	HB	TBB	IBB	SO	WP	Bk	W	L	Pct	Sh	Sv-Op	Hld	ERC	ERA
2012	NYM	NL	8	1	0	4	12.1	52	10	8	8	0	0	0	0	9	0	10	0	0	0	0	-	0	0-0	0	3.76	5.84
2013	NYM	NL	9	0	0	3	10.2	52	12	5	5	2	2	0	0	9	1	8	3	0	0	0	-	0	1-1	0	7.20	4.22
2014	NYM	NL	76	0	0	16	77.1	322	59	26	19	3	4	2	2	32	5	73	9	0	2	5	.286	0	5-10	23	2.45	2.21
2015	NYM	NL	76	0	0	65	78.0	308	59	16	16	6	1	1	2	19	1	86	4	0	2	2	.500	0	43-48	1	2.19	1.85
2016	NYM	NL	78	0	0	67	77.2	321	63	25	22	1	2	1	1	31	6	84	3	0	3	4	.429	0	51-56	0	2.44	2.55
	Postseason		12	0	0	9	14.2	51	5	2	1	1	0	0	0	2	0	9	0	0	0	0	-	0	5-8	0	0.58	0.61
	5 ML YEARS		247	1	0	155	256.0	1055	203	80	70	12	9	4	5	100	13	261	19	0	7	11	.389	0	100-115	24	2.60	2.46

Buck Farmer

Pitches: R Bats: L Pos: RP-13; SP-1   Ht: 6'4" Wt: 225 Born: 2/20/1991 Age: 26

		HOW MUCH HE PITCHED						WHAT HE GAVE UP												THE RESULTS						
Year	Team	Lg	G	GS	CG	GF	IP	BFP	H	R	ER	HR	SH	SF	HB	TBB	IBB	SO	WP	Bk	W	L	Pct	Sh	Sv-Op	Hld	ERC	ERA
2016	Toledo*	AAA	20	20	0	0	100.0	426	105	48	43	11	2	2	3	28	0	93	3	0	5	6	.455	0	0--	-	4.08	3.87
2014	Det	AL	4	2	0	1	9.1	46	12	12	12	2	0	0	2	5	0	11	0	0	0	1	.000	0	0-0	0	8.29	11.57
2015	Det	AL	14	5	0	0	40.1	186	53	35	33	10	1	1	3	17	2	24	1	0	0	4	.000	0	0-0	0	7.65	7.36
2016	Det	AL	14	1	0	7	29.1	131	25	15	15	4	1	1	1	20	1	27	2	0	0	1	.000	0	0-0	0	4.71	4.60
	3 ML YEARS		32	8	0	8	79.0	363	90	62	60	16	2	2	6	42	3	62	3	0	0	6	.000	0	0-0	0	6.58	6.84

Danny Farquhar

Pitches: R Pos: RP-35   FAHR-kwahr   Ht: 5'9" Wt: 185 Born: 2/17/1987 Age: 30

		HOW MUCH HE PITCHED						WHAT HE GAVE UP												THE RESULTS						
Year	Team	Lg	G	GS	CG	GF	IP	BFP	H	R	ER	HR	SH	SF	HB	TBB	IBB	SO	WP	Bk	W	L	Pct	Sh	Sv-Op	Hld	ERC	ERA
2016	Drhm*	AAA	32	0	0	19	38.0	151	33	16	14	2	3	1	1	9	0	24	0	1	4	2	.667	0	2--	-	2.63	3.32
2011	Tor	AL	3	0	0	2	2.0	11	4	4	3	0	0	1	0	2	0	1	0	0	0	0	-	0	0-0	0	13.16	13.50
2013	Sea	AL	46	0	0	27	55.2	228	44	29	26	2	1	2	0	22	4	79	2	1	0	3	.000	0	16-20	2	2.44	4.20
2014	Sea	AL	66	0	0	22	71.0	290	58	23	21	5	1	1	4	22	1	81	6	2	3	1	.750	0	1-3	13	2.78	2.66
2015	Sea	AL	43	0	0	10	51.0	219	53	33	29	9	1	1	1	17	2	48	1	1	1	8	.111	0	1-3	8	4.60	5.12
2016	TB	AL	35	0	0	11	35.1	158	33	14	12	8	2	0	4	15	1	46	1	0	1	0	1.000	0	0-1	7	5.01	3.06
	5 ML YEARS		193	0	0	72	215.0	906	192	103	91	24	5	5	9	78	8	255	10	4	5	12	.294	0	18-27	30	3.53	3.81

Andrew Faulkner

Pitches: L Bats: R Pos: RP-9   Ht: 6'3" Wt: 205 Born: 9/12/1992 Age: 24

		HOW MUCH HE PITCHED						WHAT HE GAVE UP												THE RESULTS						
Year	Team	Lg	G	GS	CG	GF	IP	BFP	H	R	ER	HR	SH	SF	HB	TBB	IBB	SO	WP	Bk	W	L	Pct	Sh	Sv-Op	Hld	ERC	ERA
2012	Hkry	A	29	10	0	7	94.0	424	97	56	45	2	1	4	8	44	0	74	10	0	5	5	.500	0	0--	-	4.23	4.31
2013	Hkry	A	21	19	0	0	111.1	490	123	54	43	8	6	2	5	37	0	84	3	0	6	5	.545	0	0--	-	4.35	3.48
2014	MrtlBh	A+	21	18	0	1	104.0	420	86	26	24	1	3	5	3	31	0	100	3	0	10	1	.909	0	1--	-	2.35	2.08
2014	Frisco	AA	7	6	0	0	30.2	134	28	22	17	3	0	2	0	14	0	33	0	0	2	4	.333	0	0--	-	3.71	4.99
2015	Frisco	AA	28	15	0	3	92.1	405	84	50	43	9	4	3	6	47	0	90	1	0	7	4	.636	0	1--	-	4.24	4.19
2016	RdRck	AAA	6	0	0	3	8.0	26	2	0	0	0	0	0	0	1	0	13	0	0	0	0	-	0	0--	-	0.27	0.00
2016	RdRck	AAA	41	1	0	20	45.1	196	39	21	20	3	3	1	5	20	1	39	3	0	5	3	.625	0	4--	-	3.61	3.97
2015	Tex	AL	11	0	0	1	9.2	40	8	3	3	2	0	0	0	3	1	10	0	0	0	0	-	0	0-0	2	3.27	2.79
2016	Tex	AL	9	0	0	1	6.2	32	8	7	5	3	0	0	0	4	1	1	2	0	0	0	-	0	0-0	1	8.52	6.75
	2 ML YEARS		20	0	0	2	16.1	72	16	10	8	5	0	0	0	7	2	11	2	0	0	0	-	0	0-0	3	5.23	4.41

Taylor Featherston

Bats: R Throws: R Pos: PH-15;2B-4   Ht: 6'1" Wt: 185 Born: 10/8/1989 Age: 27

						BATTING																RUNNING			AVERAGES			
Year	Team	Lg	G	AB	H	2B	3B	HR	(Hm	Rd)	TB	R	RBI	RC	TBB	IBB	SO	HBP	SH	SF	SB	CS	GDP	Avg	OBP	Slg	OPS
2012	Ashvll	A	105	378	113	30	4	12	(-	-)	187	75	53	77	53	0	87	8	1	4	15	4	5	.299	.393	.495	.887
2013	Mdest	A+	116	469	137	31	10	13	(-	-)	227	87	81	80	30	0	110	9	2	6	17	4	14	.292	.342	.484	.826
2014	Tulsa	AA	127	497	129	33	4	16	(-	-)	218	69	57	73	38	3	114	9	3	3	14	6	3	.260	.322	.439	.760
2016	LV	AAA	99	402	102	23	4	13	(-	-)	172	56	37	55	25	1	98	9	1	2	6	3	4	.254	.311	.428	.738
2015	LAA	AL	101	154	25	5	1	2	(0	2)	38	23	9	7	7	0	46	3	4	1	4	2	3	.162	.212	.247	.459
2016	Phi	NL	19	26	3	1	0	0	(0	0)	4	2	1	0	2	0	11	0	0	0	2	0	0	.115	.179	.154	.332
	2 ML YEARS		120	180	28	6	1	2	(0	2)	42	25	10	7	9	0	57	3	4	1	6	2	3	.156	.207	.233	.441

Tim Federowicz

Bats: R Throws: R Pos: C-12;PH-9   fed-er-oh-vich   Ht: 5'10" Wt: 215 Born: 8/5/1987 Age: 29

						BATTING																RUNNING			AVERAGES			
Year	Team	Lg	G	AB	H	2B	3B	HR	(Hm	Rd)	TB	R	RBI	RC	TBB	IBB	SO	HBP	SH	SF	SB	CS	GDP	Avg	OBP	Slg	OPS
2016	Iowa*	AAA	65	229	67	12	0	8	(-	-)	103	25	39	37	18	1	51	4	0	2	3	0	9	.293	.352	.450	.802
2011	LAD	NL	7	13	2	0	0	0	(0	0)	2	0	1	1	2	0	4	1	0	0	0	0	0	.154	.313	.154	.466
2012	LAD	NL	3	3	1	0	0	0	(0	0)	1	0	0	1	1	0	2	0	0	0	0	0	0	.333	.500	.333	.833
2013	LAD	NL	56	160	37	8	0	4	(1	3)	57	12	16	9	10	5	56	0	2	1	0	0	3	.231	.275	.356	.631
2014	LAD	NL	23	71	8	3	0	1	(0	1)	14	2	5	0	3	0	18	1	2	1	0	0	3	.113	.158	.197	.355
2016	ChC	NL	17	31	6	2	0	0	(0	0)	8	3	3	2	1	0	12	0	0	1	0	0	1	.194	.212	.258	.470
	5 ML YEARS		106	278	54	13	0	5	(1	4)	82	17	25	13	17	5	92	2	4	3	0	0	9	.194	.243	.295	.538

Scott Feldman

Pitches: R **Bats:** L **Pos:** RP-35; SP-5 **Ht:** 6'7" **Wt:** 210 **Born:** 2/7/1983 **Age:** 34

Year	Team	Lg	G	GS	CG	GF	IP	BFP	H	R	ER	HR	SH	SF	HB	TBB	IBB	SO	WP	Bk	W	L	Pct	Sh	Sv-Op	Hld	ERC	ERA
2005	Tex	AL	8	0	0	3	9.1	37	9	1	1	0	0	0	0	2	1	4	0	0	0	1	.000	0	0-0	1	2.48	0.96
2006	Tex	AL	36	0	0	5	41.1	175	42	19	18	4	2	1	4	10	0	30	0	0	0	2	.000	0	0-1	7	3.94	3.92
2007	Tex	AL	29	0	0	10	39.0	192	44	26	25	3	0	2	3	32	5	19	2	2	1	2	.333	0	0-0	0	6.40	5.77
2008	Tex	AL	28	25	0	2	151.1	651	161	103	89	22	1	9	10	56	2	74	4	2	6	8	.429	0	0-0	0	5.03	5.29
2009	Tex	AL	34	31	0	0	189.2	791	178	87	86	18	1	3	9	65	0	113	5	2	17	8	.680	0	0-0	0	3.74	4.08
2010	Tex	AL	29	22	0	2	141.1	641	181	98	86	18	5	8	5	45	2	75	11	0	7	11	.389	0	0-0	0	5.71	5.48
2011	Tex	AL	11	2	0	5	32.0	129	25	14	14	3	0	1	2	10	0	22	2	0	2	1	.667	0	0-0	0	2.83	3.94
2012	Tex	AL	29	21	0	5	123.2	536	139	79	70	14	0	5	1	32	2	96	2	1	6	11	.353	0	0-0	0	4.27	5.09
2013	2 Tms		30	30	2	0	181.2	758	159	87	78	19	7	7	9	56	1	132	7	1	12	12	.500	1	0-0	0	3.24	3.86
2014	Hou	AL	29	29	2	0	180.1	765	185	86	75	16	2	7	11	50	5	107	6	1	8	12	.400	1	0-0	0	3.89	3.74
2015	Hou	AL	18	18	0	0	108.1	451	115	49	47	13	1	5	0	27	1	61	8	0	5	5	.500	0	0-0	0	4.01	3.90
2016	2 Tms	AL	40	5	0	13	77.0	338	87	42	34	10	5	3	3	19	3	56	0	0	7	4	.636	0	0-1	0	4.42	3.97
13	ChC	NL	15	15	1	0	91.0	376	79	42	35	10	6	4	3	25	0	67	4	0	7	6	.538	0	0-0	0	3.05	3.46
13	Bal		15	15	1	0	90.2	382	80	45	43	9	1	3	6	31	1	65	3	1	5	6	.455	1	0-0	0	3.44	4.27
16	Hou	AL	26	5	0	9	62.0	265	64	27	20	8	4	3	3	13	3	42	0	0	5	3	.625	0	0-1	0	3.75	2.90
16	Tor	AL	14	0	0	4	15.0	73	23	15	14	2	1	0	0	6	0	14	0	0	2	1	.667	0	0-0	0	7.53	8.40
	Postseason		9	0	0	1	13.2	56	8	5	5	0	2	0	2	6	2	11	0	0	1	0	1.000	0	0-1	0	1.75	3.29
12 ML YEARS			321	183	4	45	1275.0	5464	1325	691	623	140	24	51	57	404	22	789	47	9	71	77	.480	2	0-2	8	4.21	4.40

Michael Feliz

Pitches: R **Bats:** R **Pos:** RP-47 **Ht:** 6'4" **Wt:** 230 **Born:** 6/28/1993 **Age:** 24

Year	Team	Lg	G	GS	CG	GF	IP	BFP	H	R	ER	HR	SH	SF	HB	TBB	IBB	SO	WP	Bk	W	L	Pct	Sh	Sv-Op	Hld	ERC	ERA
2012	2 Tms	Low	13	9	0	1	64.2	265	53	24	22	3	0	2	1	23	0	63	2	1	6	1	.857	0	0- -	-	2.67	3.06
2013	TriCity	A-	14	10	0	2	69.0	273	53	19	15	2	2	1	3	13	1	78	4	0	4	2	.667	0	1- -	-	1.83	1.96
2014	QuadC	A	25	19	0	1	102.2	441	104	53	46	6	3	1	5	37	0	111	7	0	8	6	.571	0	0- -	-	3.92	4.03
2015	Lancst	A+	8	5	0	0	32.2	144	30	19	16	2	2	5	2	12	0	33	2	0	1	1	.500	0	0- -	-	3.33	4.41
2015	CpChr	AA	15	12	0	3	78.2	301	52	19	19	5	0	0	0	20	0	70	3	1	6	3	.667	0	1- -	-	1.67	2.17
2015	Hou	AL	5	0	0	5	8.0	38	9	7	7	2	0	0	1	4	0	7	0	0	0	0	-	0	0-0	0	6.79	7.88
2016	Hou	AL	47	0	0	17	65.0	270	55	33	32	10	0	2	0	22	0	95	6	0	8	1	.889	0	0-3	5	3.32	4.43
2 ML YEARS			52	0	0	22	73.0	308	64	40	39	12	0	2	1	26	0	102	6	1	8	1	.889	0	0-3	5	3.66	4.81

Neftali Feliz

Pitches: R **Bats:** R **Pos:** RP-62 neff-TAH-lee **Ht:** 6'3" **Wt:** 225 **Born:** 5/2/1988 **Age:** 29

Year	Team	Lg	G	GS	CG	GF	IP	BFP	H	R	ER	HR	SH	SF	HB	TBB	IBB	SO	WP	Bk	W	L	Pct	Sh	Sv-Op	Hld	ERC	ERA
2009	Tex	AL	20	0	0	3	31.0	117	13	6	6	2	1	0	3	8	0	39	0	0	1	0	1.000	0	2-3	9	1.14	1.74
2010	Tex	AL	70	0	0	59	69.0	269	43	21	21	5	1	0	5	18	1	71	5	0	4	3	.571	0	40-43	3	1.75	2.73
2011	Tex	AL	64	0	0	56	62.1	252	42	22	19	4	3	2	0	30	1	54	2	1	2	3	.400	0	32-38	0	2.45	2.74
2012	Tex	AL	8	7	1	0	42.2	175	28	15	15	5	0	0	2	23	0	37	0	0	3	1	.750	0	0-0	0	3.11	3.16
2013	Tex	AL	6	0	0	2	4.2	21	5	0	0	0	0	0	1	2	0	4	0	0	0	0	-	0	0-0	0	4.78	0.00
2014	Tex	AL	30	0	0	22	31.2	122	20	7	7	5	1	1	0	11	0	21	1	0	2	1	.667	0	13-14	2	2.38	1.99
2015	2 Tms	AL	48	0	0	24	48.0	212	57	34	34	5	1	1	1	18	6	39	4	0	3	4	.429	0	10-17	2	5.03	6.38
2016	Pit	NL	62	0	0	6	53.2	218	40	21	21	10	2	1	1	21	1	61	3	0	4	2	.667	0	2-4	29	3.30	3.52
15	Tex	AL	18	0	0	12	19.2	91	24	10	10	2	0	0	0	9	3	16	2	0	1	2	.333	0	6-9	0	5.26	4.58
15	Det	AL	30	0	0	12	28.1	121	33	24	24	3	1	1	1	9	3	23	2	0	2	2	.500	0	4-8	2	4.87	7.62
	Postseason		18	0	0	15	18.2	76	8	4	4	1	1	0	1	13	1	23	1	0	0	0	-	0	7-8	0	2.04	1.93
8 ML YEARS			308	7	1	172	343.1	1386	248	126	123	36	9	5	13	131	9	326	15	1	19	14	.576	0	99-119	43	2.71	3.22

Jose Fernandez

Pitches: R **Bats:** R **Pos:** SP-29 **Ht:** 6'3" **Wt:** 240 **Born:** 7/31/1992 **Age:** 24

Year	Team	Lg	G	GS	CG	GF	IP	BFP	H	R	ER	HR	SH	SF	HB	TBB	IBB	SO	WP	Bk	W	L	Pct	Sh	Sv-Op	Hld	ERC	ERA
2013	Mia	NL	28	28	0	0	172.2	681	111	47	42	10	3	4	5	58	5	187	3	1	12	6	.667	0	0-0	0	1.85	2.19
2014	Mia	NL	8	8	0	0	51.2	205	36	19	14	4	0	0	0	13	1	70	2	1	4	2	.667	0	0-0	0	1.80	2.44
2015	Mia	NL	11	11	0	0	64.2	265	61	21	21	4	0	4	2	14	0	79	2	0	6	1	.857	0	0-0	0	2.95	2.92
2016	Mia	NL	29	29	0	0	182.1	737	149	63	58	13	7	5	6	55	6	253	9	1	16	8	.667	0	0-0	0	2.66	2.86
4 ML YEARS			76	76	0	0	471.1	1888	357	150	135	31	10	13	13	140	12	589	16	3	38	17	.691	0	0-0	0	2.29	2.58

Prince Fielder

Bats: L **Throws:** R **Pos:** DH-80;1B-9;PH-1 **Ht:** 5'11" **Wt:** 275 **Born:** 5/9/1984 **Age:** 33

Year	Team	Lg	G	AB	H	2B	3B	HR	(Hm	Rd)	TB	R	RBI	RC	TBB	IBB	SO	HBP	SH	SF	SB	CS	GDP	Avg	OBP	Slg	OPS
2005	Mil	NL	39	59	17	4	0	2	(2	0)	27	2	10	10	2	0	17	0	0	1	0	0	0	.288	.306	.458	.764
2006	Mil	NL	157	569	154	35	1	28	(11	17)	275	82	81	84	59	5	125	12	0	8	7	2	17	.271	.347	.483	.831
2007	Mil	NL	158	573	165	35	2	50	(27	23)	354	109	119	125	90	21	121	14	0	4	2	2	9	.288	.395	.618	1.013
2008	Mil	NL	159	588	162	30	2	34	(18	16)	298	86	102	105	84	19	134	12	0	10	3	2	12	.276	.372	.507	.879
2009	Mil	NL	162	591	177	35	3	46	(23	23)	356	103	141	134	110	21	138	9	0	9	2	3	14	.299	.412	.602	1.014
2010	Mil	NL	161	578	151	25	0	32	(18	14)	272	94	83	94	114	17	138	21	0	1	1	0	12	.261	.401	.471	.871
2011	Mil	NL	162	569	170	36	1	38	(24	14)	322	95	120	120	107	32	106	10	0	6	1	1	17	.299	.415	.566	.981
2012	Det	AL	162	581	182	33	1	30	(18	12)	307	83	108	116	85	18	84	17	0	7	1	1	19	.313	.412	.528	.940
2013	Det	AL	162	624	174	36	0	25	(13	12)	285	82	106	94	75	5	117	9	0	4	1	1	20	.279	.362	.457	.819
2014	Tex	AL	42	150	37	8	0	3	(3	0)	54	19	16	18	25	11	24	2	0	1	0	0	5	.247	.360	.360	.720

Year	Team	Lg	G	AB	H	2B	3B	HR	(Hm	Rd)	TB	R	RBI	RC	TBB	IBB	SO	HBP	SH	SF	SB	CS	GDP	Avg	OBP	Slg	OPS
2015	Tex	AL	158	613	187	28	0	23	(11	12)	284	78	98	110	64	14	88	11	0	5	0	0	21	.305	.378	.463	.841
2016	Tex	AL	89	326	69	16	0	8	(6	2)	109	29	44	32	32	1	63	7	0	5	0	0	12	.212	.292	.334	.626
	Postseason		44	164	31	5	0	5	(4	1)	51	13	12	11	15	5	36	5	0	1	0	1	8	.189	.276	.311	.587
	12 ML YEARS		1611	5821	1645	321	10	319	(174	145)	2943	862	1028	1042	847	164	1155	124	0	61	18	11	158	.283	.382	.506	.887

Josh Fields

Pitches: R **Bats:** R **Pos:** RP-37   **Ht:** 6'0" **Wt:** 195 **Born:** 8/19/1985 **Age:** 31

			HOW MUCH HE PITCHED						WHAT HE GAVE UP										THE RESULTS							
Year	Team	Lg	G	GS	CG	GF	IP	BFP	H	R	ER	HR	SH	SF	HB	TBB	IBB	SO	WP	Bk	W	L	Pct	Sh	Sv-Op	Hld	ERC	ERA
2016	Fresno*	AAA	23	0	0	7	27.1	107	19	6	5	0	0	1	0	7	0	32	1	0	1	0	1.000	0	1--	-	1.51	1.65
2013	Hou	AL	41	0	0	16	38.0	160	31	21	21	8	1	0	0	18	4	40	0	0	1	3	.250	0	5-6	6	3.94	4.97
2014	Hou	AL	54	0	0	16	54.2	231	50	29	27	2	0	5	2	17	3	70	0	0	4	6	.400	0	4-8	5	2.87	4.45
2015	Hou	AL	54	0	0	19	50.2	209	39	20	20	2	2	1	1	19	3	67	1	0	4	1	.800	0	0-2	5	2.35	3.55
2016	2 Tms		37	0	0	12	35.0	158	43	22	18	4	0	1	1	11	2	42	0	0	1	0	1.000	0	0-0	2	5.12	4.63
16	Hou	AL	15	0	0	7	15.2	71	23	14	12	2	0	1	0	3	0	20	0	0	0	0	-	0	0-0	0	6.23	6.89
16	LAD	NL	22	0	0	5	19.1	87	20	8	6	2	0	0	1	8	2	22	0	0	1	0	1.000	0	0-0	2	4.27	2.79
	Postseason		2	0	0	1	1.2	8	1	2	2	1	0	0	0	2	0	4	0	0	0	0	-	0	0-1	0	8.92	10.80
	4 ML YEARS		186	0	0	63	178.1	758	163	92	86	16	3	7	4	65	12	219	1	0	10	10	.500	0	9-16	21	3.35	4.34

Casey Fien

Pitches: R **Bats:** R **Pos:** RP-39   FEEN   **Ht:** 6'2" **Wt:** 210 **Born:** 10/21/1983 **Age:** 33

			HOW MUCH HE PITCHED						WHAT HE GAVE UP										THE RESULTS							
Year	Team	Lg	G	GS	CG	GF	IP	BFP	H	R	ER	HR	SH	SF	HB	TBB	IBB	SO	WP	Bk	W	L	Pct	Sh	Sv-Op	Hld	ERC	ERA
2016	OkCity*	AAA	8	0	0	5	10.1	42	11	5	5	1	0	0	0	2	0	13	1	0	1	0	1.000	0	1--	-	3.71	4.35
2009	Det	AL	9	0	0	5	11.1	53	13	11	10	2	0	2	0	6	0	9	0	0	0	1	.000	0	0-0	0	5.92	7.94
2010	Det	AL	2	0	0	2	2.2	12	4	3	3	2	1	0	0	0	0	0	0	0	0	0	-	0	0-0	0	9.96	10.13
2012	Min	AL	35	0	0	7	35.0	141	25	9	8	3	1	2	1	9	4	32	0	0	2	1	.667	0	0-0	6	1.90	2.06
2013	Min	AL	73	0	0	20	62.0	244	51	28	27	9	3	2	0	12	3	73	2	0	5	2	.714	0	0-2	17	2.59	3.92
2014	Min	AL	73	0	0	15	63.1	260	64	29	28	7	2	4	0	10	0	51	2	0	5	6	.455	0	1-5	26	3.25	3.98
2015	Min	AL	62	0	0	6	63.1	257	61	26	25	6	2	3	0	8	0	41	0	0	4	6	.400	0	0-4	18	2.77	3.55
2016	2 Tms		39	0	0	7	39.1	169	45	24	24	13	1	0	0	10	3	35	1	0	1	1	.500	0	0-1	6	5.84	5.49
16	Min	AL	14	0	0	2	13.2	63	21	12	12	5	0	0	0	3	0	12	1	0	1	0	1.000	0	0-0	1	8.81	7.90
16	LAD	NL	25	0	0	5	25.2	106	24	12	12	8	1	0	0	7	3	23	0	0	0	1	.000	0	0-1	5	4.42	4.21
	7 ML YEARS		293	0	0	62	277.0	1136	263	130	125	42	10	13	1	55	10	241	5	0	17	17	.500	0	1-12	73	3.29	4.06

Mike Fiers

Pitches: R **Bats:** R **Pos:** SP-30; RP-1   FIRES   **Ht:** 6'2" **Wt:** 200 **Born:** 6/15/1985 **Age:** 32

			HOW MUCH HE PITCHED						WHAT HE GAVE UP										THE RESULTS							
Year	Team	Lg	G	GS	CG	GF	IP	BFP	H	R	ER	HR	SH	SF	HB	TBB	IBB	SO	WP	Bk	W	L	Pct	Sh	Sv-Op	Hld	ERC	ERA
2011	Mil	NL	2	0	0	2	2.0	10	2	0	0	0	0	0	0	3	0	2	0	0	0	0	-	0	0-0	0	8.25	0.00
2012	Mil	NL	23	22	0	1	127.2	539	125	56	53	12	4	4	2	36	0	135	4	0	9	10	.474	0	0-0	0	3.50	3.74
2013	Mil	NL	11	3	0	4	22.1	103	28	20	18	8	1	2	0	6	0	15	1	0	1	4	.200	0	0-0	0	6.65	7.25
2014	Mil	NL	14	10	0	1	71.2	274	46	19	17	7	2	1	0	17	1	76	1	0	6	5	.545	0	0-0	0	1.68	2.13
2015	2 Tms		31	30	1	0	180.1	761	162	83	74	24	3	8	6	64	5	180	8	0	7	10	.412	1	0-0	0	3.64	3.69
2016	Hou	AL	31	30	0	0	168.2	724	187	89	84	26	3	5	7	42	0	134	17	0	11	8	.579	0	0-0	0	4.66	4.48
15	Mil	NL	21	21	0	0	118.0	509	117	57	51	14	3	6	5	43	5	121	6	0	5	9	.357	0	0-0	0	4.11	3.89
15	Hou	AL	10	9	1	0	62.1	252	45	26	23	10	0	2	1	21	0	59	2	0	2	1	.667	1	0-0	0	2.78	3.32
	Postseason		1	0	0	0	1.0	4	1	1	1	0	1	0	0	0	0	0	0	0	0	0	-	0	0-0	0	1.95	9.00
	6 ML YEARS		112	95	1	8	572.2	2411	550	267	246	77	13	20	15	168	6	542	31	0	34	37	.479	1	0-0	0	3.75	3.87

Cole Figueroa

Bats: L **Throws:** R **Pos:** PH-14;2B-5;3B-2;SS-2;PR-1   figg-uh-ROE-ah   **Ht:** 5'10" **Wt:** 185 **Born:** 6/30/1987 **Age:** 30

			BATTING																		RUNNING			AVERAGES			
Year	Team	Lg	G	AB	H	2B	3B	HR	(Hm	Rd)	TB	R	RBI	RC	TBB	IBB	SO	HBP	SH	SF	SB	CS	GDP	Avg	OBP	Slg	OPS
2016	Indy*	AAA	20	75	23	3	1	2	(-	-)	34	12	11	11	3	0	9	0	0	0	2	1	2	.307	.333	.453	.787
2016	NewOr*	AAA	41	135	31	7	1	0	(-	-)	40	14	11	13	15	0	17	1	0	3	0	1	5	.230	.305	.296	.601
2014	TB	AL	23	43	10	2	1	0	(0	0)	14	6	6	4	4	0	4	0	0	2	0	0	0	.233	.286	.326	.611
2015	NYY	AL	2	8	2	1	0	0	(0	0)	4	2	0	0	0	0	0	0	0	0	0	0	0	.250	.250	.500	.750
2016	Pit	NL	23	26	4	0	0	0	(0	0)	4	0	3	1	1	0	2	0	0	0	1	0	0	.154	.185	.154	.339
	3 ML YEARS		48	77	16	4	1	0	(0	0)	22	8	9	5	5	0	6	0	0	2	1	0	0	.208	.250	.286	.536

Brandon Finnegan

Pitches: L **Bats:** L **Pos:** SP-31   **Ht:** 5'11" **Wt:** 200 **Born:** 4/14/1993 **Age:** 24

			HOW MUCH HE PITCHED						WHAT HE GAVE UP										THE RESULTS							
Year	Team	Lg	G	GS	CG	GF	IP	BFP	H	R	ER	HR	SH	SF	HB	TBB	IBB	SO	WP	Bk	W	L	Pct	Sh	Sv-Op	Hld	ERC	ERA
2014	KC	AL	7	0	0	4	7.0	28	6	1	1	0	0	0	0	1	0	10	0	0	0	1	.000	0	0-0	1	1.77	1.29
2015	2 Tms		20	4	0	3	48.0	197	37	19	19	8	3	1	1	21	0	45	0	0	5	2	.714	0	0-1	3	3.55	3.56
2016	Cin	NL	31	31	1	0	172.0	734	150	86	76	29	5	5	4	84	2	145	6	2	10	11	.476	0	0-0	0	4.30	3.98
15	KC	AL	14	0	0	3	24.1	99	16	8	8	3	1	1	1	13	0	21	0	0	3	0	1.000	0	0-1	3	3.14	2.96
15	Cin	NL	6	4	0	0	23.2	98	21	11	11	5	2	0	0	8	0	24	0	0	2	2	.500	0	0-0	0	3.96	4.18
	Postseason		7	0	0	0	6.0	31	9	7	7	0	3	0	0	5	1	4	0	0	1	1	.500	0	0-1	1	7.77	10.50
	3 ML YEARS		58	35	1	4	227.0	959	193	106	96	37	8	6	5	106	2	200	6	2	15	14	.517	0	0-1	1	4.05	3.81

Doug Fister

Pitches: R Bats: L Pos: SP-32 Ht: 6'8" Wt: 210 Born: 2/4/1984 Age: 33

			HOW MUCH HE PITCHED						WHAT HE GAVE UP										THE RESULTS							
Year	Team	Lg	G	GS	CG	GF	IP	BFP	H	R	ER	HR	SH	SF	HB	TBB	IBB	SO	WP	Bk	W	L	Pct	Sh	Sv-Op	Hld	ERC	ERA
2009	Sea	AL	11	10	0	1	61.0	256	63	29	28	11	0	0	2	15	0	36	1	0	3	4	.429	0	0-0	0	4.36	4.13
2010	Sea	AL	28	28	0	0	171.0	720	187	85	78	13	2	4	6	32	2	93	8	3	6	14	.300	0	0-0	0	3.73	4.11
2011	2 Tms	AL	32	31	3	0	216.1	875	193	76	68	11	4	9	12	37	2	146	3	1	11	13	.458	0	0-0	0	2.53	2.83
2012	Det	AL	26	26	2	0	161.2	673	156	73	62	15	3	0	7	37	1	137	1	0	10	10	.500	1	0-0	0	3.33	3.45
2013	Det	AL	33	32	1	0	208.2	881	229	91	85	14	2	5	16	44	2	159	7	0	14	9	.609	0	0-0	0	4.00	3.67
2014	Was	NL	25	25	1	0	164.0	662	153	52	44	18	6	2	7	24	0	98	5	0	16	6	.727	1	0-0	0	2.98	2.41
2015	Was	NL	25	15	0	2	103.0	449	120	56	48	14	7	5	6	24	3	63	1	0	5	7	.417	0	1-1	0	4.79	4.19
2016	Hou	AL	32	32	0	0	180.1	779	195	98	93	24	0	3	7	62	1	115	10	0	12	13	.480	0	0-0	0	4.76	4.64
11	Sea	AL	21	21	3	0	146.0	602	139	57	54	7	3	7	9	32	2	89	3	1	3	12	.200	0	0-0	0	3.02	3.33
11	Det	AL	11	10	0	0	70.1	273	54	19	14	4	1	2	3	5	0	57	0	0	8	1	.889	0	0-0	0	1.63	1.79
	Postseason		9	8	0	0	55.1	232	54	16	16	2	2	0	3	16	0	40	1	1	4	2	.667	0	0-0	0	3.32	2.60
8 ML YEARS			212	199	7	3	1266.0	5295	1296	560	506	120	24	28	63	275	11	847	36	4	77	76	.503	2	1-1	0	3.66	3.60

Ryan Flaherty

Bats: L Throws: R Pos: 3B-40;SS-13;1B-7;PH-7;RF-6;LF-3;PR-3;2B-1 Ht: 6'3" Wt: 220 Born: 7/27/1986 Age: 30

			BATTING																		RUNNING			AVERAGES			
Year	Team	Lg	G	AB	H	2B	3B	HR	(Hm	Rd)	TB	R	RBI	RC	TBB	IBB	SO	HBP	SH	SF	SB	CS	GDP	Avg	OBP	Slg	OPS
2012	Bal	AL	77	153	33	2	1	6	(3	3)	55	15	19	15	6	0	43	3	3	1	1	0	3	.216	.258	.359	.617
2013	Bal	AL	85	246	55	13	0	10	(6	4)	96	28	27	27	19	3	62	5	1	0	2	0	2	.224	.293	.390	.683
2014	Bal	AL	102	281	62	15	1	7	(7	0)	100	33	32	34	22	2	68	5	3	1	1	0	3	.221	.288	.356	.644
2015	Bal	AL	91	267	54	8	3	9	(2	7)	95	34	31	24	26	2	81	4	2	2	0	0	8	.202	.281	.356	.637
2016	Bal	AL	74	157	34	7	0	3	(3	0)	50	16	15	18	17	1	48	0	1	1	2	0	1	.217	.291	.318	.610
	Postseason		11	32	9	0	0	2	(0	2)	15	5	5	4	4	0	9	0	0	0	0	0	0	.281	.361	.469	.830
5 ML YEARS			429	1104	238	43	5	35	(21	14)	396	126	124	118	90	8	302	17	10	5	6	0	17	.216	.284	.359	.642

Yohan Flande

Pitches: L Bats: L Pos: RP-2 YO-hahn FLAHN-day Ht: 6'2" Wt: 180 Born: 1/27/1986 Age: 31

			HOW MUCH HE PITCHED						WHAT HE GAVE UP										THE RESULTS							
Year	Team	Lg	G	GS	CG	GF	IP	BFP	H	R	ER	HR	SH	SF	HB	TBB	IBB	SO	WP	Bk	W	L	Pct	Sh	Sv-Op	Hld	ERC	ERA
2016	Albq*	AAA	18	1	0	6	42.1	185	52	22	20	2	3	2	0	14	0	27	1	0	3	3	.500	0	0- -	-	4.81	4.25
2014	Col	NL	16	10	0	2	59.0	241	55	34	34	5	5	4	2	16	2	34	0	0	0	6	.000	0	0-0	1	3.26	5.19
2015	Col	NL	19	10	0	2	68.1	296	73	36	36	14	5	1	1	25	3	43	1	1	3	3	.500	0	0-0	0	5.11	4.74
2016	Col	NL	2	0	0	0	3.2	20	8	6	5	0	1	0	0	3	1	0	0	0	0	0	-	0	0-0	0	13.02	12.27
3 ML YEARS			37	20	0	4	131.0	557	136	76	75	19	11	5	3	44	6	77	1	1	3	9	.250	0	0-0	1	4.43	5.15

Kendry Flores

Pitches: R Bats: R Pos: SP-1 Ht: 6'2" Wt: 195 Born: 11/24/1991 Age: 25

			HOW MUCH HE PITCHED						WHAT HE GAVE UP										THE RESULTS							
Year	Team	Lg	G	GS	CG	GF	IP	BFP	H	R	ER	HR	SH	SF	HB	TBB	IBB	SO	WP	Bk	W	L	Pct	Sh	Sv-Op	Hld	ERC	ERA
2012	SlKzr	A-	10	8	0	0	42.1	184	44	26	21	4	1	1	0	11	0	34	3	0	1	3	.250	0	0- -	-	3.58	4.46
2013	Augsta	A	22	22	1	0	141.2	551	113	47	43	11	5	2	4	17	2	137	4	0	10	6	.625	0	0- -	-	1.97	2.73
2014	SnJos	A+	20	20	0	0	105.2	446	101	57	48	14	1	2	5	32	0	112	6	0	4	6	.400	0	0- -	-	3.86	4.09
2015	Jaxnvl	AA	9	9	0	0	56.2	211	33	14	13	3	1	1	2	15	0	42	2	1	3	3	.500	0	0- -	-	1.52	2.06
2015	NewOr	AAA	10	10	0	0	58.2	234	49	19	17	3	0	0	1	14	0	42	1	0	3	2	.600	0	0- -	-	2.40	2.61
2016	NewOr	AAA	18	16	0	0	91.1	409	103	51	46	8	4	3	6	39	1	74	4	1	3	6	.333	0	0- -	-	5.12	4.53
2015	Mia	NL	7	1	0	3	12.2	57	16	8	7	0	0	1	1	4	1	9	0	0	1	2	.333	0	0-0	0	4.70	4.97
2016	Mia	NL	1	1	0	0	3.0	13	1	0	0	0	0	0	0	3	0	1	0	0	0	0	-	0	0-0	0	2.02	0.00
2 ML YEARS			8	2	0	3	15.2	70	17	8	7	0	0	1	1	7	1	10	0	0	1	2	.333	0	0-0	0	4.14	4.02

Ramon Flores

Bats: L Throws: L Pos: RF-49;CF-29;PH-26;LF-13;1B-2 Ht: 5'10" Wt: 190 Born: 3/26/1992 Age: 25

			BATTING																		RUNNING			AVERAGES			
Year	Team	Lg	G	AB	H	2B	3B	HR	(Hm	Rd)	TB	R	RBI	RC	TBB	IBB	SO	HBP	SH	SF	SB	CS	GDP	Avg	OBP	Slg	OPS
2012	Tampa	A+	131	517	156	29	7	6	(-	-)	217	83	39	85	54	1	85	5	2	5	24	9	4	.302	.370	.420	.790
2013	Trntn	AA	136	534	139	25	6	6	(-	-)	194	79	55	75	77	0	98	2	3	4	7	6	11	.260	.353	.363	.717
2014	S-WB	AAA	63	235	58	17	4	7	(-	-)	104	30	23	37	33	0	45	1	0	2	3	2	5	.247	.339	.443	.782
2015	S-WB	AAA	73	276	79	11	2	7	(-	-)	115	43	34	46	39	1	43	3	0	3	3	2	5	.286	.377	.417	.794
2015	Tacom	AAA	14	52	22	6	0	2	(-	-)	34	11	7	16	11	1	6	0	0	0	0	0	2	.423	.524	.654	1.178
2015	NYY	AL	12	32	7	1	0	0	(0	0)	8	3	0	1	4	0	11	0	0	0	0	0	0	.219	.219	.250	.469
2016	Mil	NL	104	249	51	8	0	2	(1	1)	65	18	19	14	31	3	58	2	3	4	3	0	11	.205	.294	.261	.555
2 ML YEARS			116	281	58	9	0	2	(1	1)	73	21	19	15	31	3	62	2	4	4	3	0	11	.206	.286	.260	.546

Wilmer Flores

Bats: R Throws: R Pos: 3B-51;1B-27;2B-18;PH-15;SS-8;PR-1 Ht: 6'3" Wt: 205 Born: 8/6/1991 Age: 25

			BATTING																		RUNNING			AVERAGES			
Year	Team	Lg	G	AB	H	2B	3B	HR	(Hm	Rd)	TB	R	RBI	RC	TBB	IBB	SO	HBP	SH	SF	SB	CS	GDP	Avg	OBP	Slg	OPS
2013	NYM	NL	27	95	20	5	0	1	(0	1)	28	8	13	7	5	0	23	0	0	1	0	0	1	.211	.248	.295	.542
2014	NYM	NL	78	259	65	13	1	6	(4	2)	98	28	29	25	12	2	31	1	1	1	1	0	6	.251	.286	.378	.664
2015	NYM	NL	137	483	127	22	0	16	(8	8)	197	55	59	58	19	2	63	4	2	2	0	1	12	.263	.295	.408	.703
2016	NYM	NL	103	307	82	14	0	16	(12	4)	144	38	49	39	23	0	48	2	0	3	1	1	9	.267	.319	.469	.788
	Postseason		13	41	8	2	1	0	(0	0)	12	4	0	5	5	2	9	1	1	0	1	0	1	.195	.298	.293	.591
4 ML YEARS			345	1144	294	54	1	39	(24	15)	467	129	150	129	59	4	165	7	3	7	2	2	28	.257	.296	.408	.704

Pedro Florimon

Bats: B **Throws:** R **Pos:** 2B-8;PR-8;SS-6;PH-1   floh-ree-MOHN   **Ht:** 6'2" **Wt:** 185 **Born:** 12/10/1986 **Age:** 30

Year Team	Lg	G	AB	H	2B	3B	HR	(Hm	Rd)	TB	R	RBI	RC	TBB	IBB	SO	HBP	SH	SF	SB	CS	GDP	Avg	OBP	Slg	OPS
2016 Indy*	AAA	107	298	76	12	4	5	(-	-)	111	36	36	40	33	1	87	1	4	4	14	4	6	.255	.327	.372	.700
2011 Bal	AL	4	8	1	1	0	0	(0	0)	2	1	2	1	1	0	6	0	1	0	0	0	0	.125	.222	.250	.472
2012 Min	AL	43	137	30	5	2	1	(1	0)	42	16	10	8	10	0	30	0	3	0	3	1	3	.219	.272	.307	.579
2013 Min	AL	134	403	89	17	0	9	(3	6)	133	44	44	38	33	1	115	2	5	3	15	6	7	.221	.281	.330	.611
2014 Min	AL	33	76	7	1	1	0	(0	0)	10	7	1	0	8	0	22	0	2	0	6	0	2	.092	.179	.132	.310
2015 Pit	NL	24	23	2	0	1	0	(0	0)	4	5	1	0	2	0	12	0	0	0	1	0	0	.087	.160	.174	.334
2016 Pit	NL	18	24	5	1	1	0	(0	0)	8	4	4	1	1	0	12	0	0	0	0	1	0	.208	.240	.333	.573
6 ML YEARS		256	671	134	25	5	10	(4	6)	199	77	62	48	55	1	197	2	11	3	25	8	12	.200	.261	.297	.558

Dylan Floro

Pitches: R **Bats:** L **Pos:** RP-12   **Ht:** 6'2" **Wt:** 175 **Born:** 12/27/1990 **Age:** 26

Year Team	Lg	G	GS	CG	GF	IP	BFP	H	R	ER	HR	SH	SF	HB	TBB	IBB	SO	WP	Bk	W	L	Pct	Sh	Sv-Op	Hld	ERC	ERA
2012 HudVal	A-	18	0	0	11	30.0	122	26	11	8	0	4	0	0	4	3	21	2	0	4	1	.800	0	2- -	-	1.64	2.40
2013 2 Tms	Low	23	23	2	0	137.1	536	123	39	27	4	4	1	2	21	0	99	11	0	11	2	.846	1	0- -	-	2.30	1.77
2014 Mont	AA	28	28	3	0	178.2	746	209	80	69	4	3	3	3	24	0	112	11	2	11	13	.458	2	0- -	-	3.56	3.48
2015 Drham	AAA	25	22	1	1	132.2	571	160	78	74	10	5	6	0	21	0	81	3	1	9	12	.429	0	0- -	-	4.06	5.02
2016 Drham	AAA	32	0	0	13	50.0	207	53	21	16	6	0	0	1	9	0	40	1	0	1	2	.333	0	7- -	-	3.79	2.88
2016 TB	AL	12	0	0	4	15.0	72	23	8	7	0	0	1	0	5	1	14	2	0	0	1	.000	0	0-0	0	5.96	4.20

Tyler Flowers

Bats: R **Throws:** R **Pos:** C-81;PH-3   **Ht:** 6'4" **Wt:** 260 **Born:** 1/24/1986 **Age:** 31

Year Team	Lg	G	AB	H	2B	3B	HR	(Hm	Rd)	TB	R	RBI	RC	TBB	IBB	SO	HBP	SH	SF	SB	CS	GDP	Avg	OBP	Slg	OPS
2009 CWS	AL	10	16	3	1	0	0	(0	0)	4	3	0	2	3	0	8	1	0	0	0	0	1	.188	.350	.250	.600
2010 CWS	AL	8	11	1	0	0	0	(0	0)	1	2	0	1	4	0	5	0	0	0	0	0	0	.091	.333	.091	.424
2011 CWS	AL	38	110	23	5	1	5	(3	2)	45	13	16	13	14	0	38	3	0	2	0	1	2	.209	.310	.409	.719
2012 CWS	AL	52	136	29	6	0	7	(5	2)	56	19	13	13	12	0	56	4	1	0	2	1	2	.213	.296	.412	.708
2013 CWS	AL	84	256	50	11	0	10	(7	3)	91	24	24	14	14	1	94	4	0	1	0	1	9	.195	.247	.355	.603
2014 CWS	AL	127	407	98	16	1	15	(7	8)	161	42	50	43	25	0	159	8	1	1	0	1	10	.241	.297	.396	.693
2015 CWS	AL	112	331	79	12	0	9	(3	6)	118	21	39	36	21	0	104	6	2	1	0	1	8	.239	.295	.356	.652
2016 Atl	NL	83	281	76	18	0	8	(5	3)	118	27	41	46	29	1	91	11	0	3	0	0	3	.270	.357	.420	.777
8 ML YEARS		514	1548	359	69	2	54	(30	24)	594	151	183	168	122	2	555	37	4	9	2	5	35	.232	.302	.384	.686

Gavin Floyd

Pitches: R **Bats:** R **Pos:** RP-28   **Ht:** 6'4" **Wt:** 245 **Born:** 1/27/1983 **Age:** 34

Year Team	Lg	G	GS	CG	GF	IP	BFP	H	R	ER	HR	SH	SF	HB	TBB	IBB	SO	WP	Bk	W	L	Pct	Sh	Sv-Op	Hld	ERC	ERA
2004 Phi	NL	6	4	0	0	28.1	126	25	11	11	1	1	0	5	16	0	24	1	1	2	0	1.000	0	0-0	0	4.33	3.49
2005 Phi	NL	7	4	0	0	26.0	127	30	31	29	5	1	1	3	16	2	17	2	0	1	2	.333	0	0-0	0	6.82	10.04
2006 Phi	NL	11	11	1	0	54.1	264	70	48	44	14	2	5	3	32	3	34	2	0	4	3	.571	1	0-0	0	8.02	7.29
2007 CWS	AL	16	10	0	4	70.0	314	85	45	41	17	3	2	6	19	0	49	1	0	1	5	.167	0	0-0	0	6.22	5.27
2008 CWS	AL	33	33	1	0	206.1	878	190	107	88	30	7	5	9	70	6	145	9	0	17	8	.680	0	0-0	0	3.80	3.84
2009 CWS	AL	30	30	1	0	193.0	797	178	93	87	21	2	3	2	59	4	163	8	0	11	11	.500	0	0-0	0	3.38	4.06
2010 CWS	AL	31	31	1	0	187.1	798	199	92	85	14	3	4	6	58	4	151	9	1	10	13	.435	0	0-0	0	4.03	4.08
2011 CWS	AL	31	30	1	1	193.2	798	180	97	94	22	4	8	11	45	2	151	12	1	12	13	.480	0	0-0	0	3.36	4.37
2012 CWS	AL	29	29	0	0	168.0	724	166	84	80	22	3	3	14	63	2	144	8	0	12	11	.522	0	0-0	0	4.50	4.29
2013 CWS	AL	5	5	0	0	24.1	110	27	15	14	4	2	2	0	12	1	25	1	0	0	4	.000	0	0-0	0	5.48	5.18
2014 Atl	NL	9	9	0	0	54.1	229	55	23	16	6	4	2	3	13	0	45	6	0	2	2	.500	0	0-0	0	3.81	2.65
2015 Cle	AL	7	0	0	2	13.1	55	11	4	4	0	0	0	1	4	0	7	1	0	0	0	-	0	0-0	0	2.40	2.70
2016 Tor	AL	28	0	0	10	31.0	124	23	14	14	4	0	1	3	8	1	30	4	0	2	4	.333	0	0-1	6	2.71	4.06
Postseason		1	1	0	0	3.0	16	5	4	4	0	0	0	0	2	0	4	0	0	0	1	.000	0	0-0	0	14.65	12.00
13 ML YEARS		243	196	5	17	1250.0	5344	1239	664	607	160	32	36	66	415	25	985	64	3	74	76	.493	1	0-1	6	4.14	4.37

Brian Flynn

Pitches: L **Bats:** L **Pos:** RP-35; SP-1   **Ht:** 6'7" **Wt:** 250 **Born:** 4/19/1990 **Age:** 27

Year Team	Lg	G	GS	CG	GF	IP	BFP	H	R	ER	HR	SH	SF	HB	TBB	IBB	SO	WP	Bk	W	L	Pct	Sh	Sv-Op	Hld	ERC	ERA
2016 Omha*	AAA	9	4	0	0	23.2	101	22	8	8	1	0	0	0	12	0	28	2	0	2	1	.667	0	0- -	-	3.76	3.04
2013 Mia	NL	4	4	0	0	18.0	88	27	17	17	4	2	0	0	13	0	15	3	0	0	2	.000	0	0-0	0	10.17	8.50
2014 Mia	NL	2	1	0	0	7.0	35	12	7	7	0	0	0	0	3	0	6	1	0	0	1	.000	0	0-0	0	7.75	9.00
2016 KC	AL	36	1	0	11	55.1	221	38	19	16	5	4	1	1	23	0	44	8	0	1	2	.333	0	0-0	2	2.55	2.60
3 ML YEARS		42	6	0	11	80.1	344	77	43	40	9	6	1	1	39	0	65	12	0	1	5	.167	0	0-0	2	4.41	4.48

Mike Foltynewicz

Pitches: R **Bats:** R **Pos:** SP-22   fohl-tuh-NEH-vich   **Ht:** 6'4" **Wt:** 220 **Born:** 10/7/1991 **Age:** 25

Year Team	Lg	G	GS	CG	GF	IP	BFP	H	R	ER	HR	SH	SF	HB	TBB	IBB	SO	WP	Bk	W	L	Pct	Sh	Sv-Op	Hld	ERC	ERA
2016 Gwnntt*	AAA	5	5	0	0	27.0	104	13	7	5	0	1	0	2	14	0	25	1	0	1	2	.333	0	0- -	-	1.64	1.67

	HOW MUCH HE PITCHED							WHAT HE GAVE UP													THE RESULTS							
Year Team	Lg	G	GS	CG	GF	IP	BFP	H	R	ER	HR	SH	SF	HB	TBB	IBB	SO	WP	Bk	W	L	Pct	Sh	Sv-Op	Hld	ERC	ERA
2014 Hou	AL	16	0	0	9	18.2	84	23	11	11	3	0	0	0	7	0	14	3	0	0	1	.000	0	0-0	1	5.80	5.30
2015 Atl	NL	18	15	0	1	86.2	399	112	63	55	17	2	6	4	29	0	77	3	1	4	6	.400	0	0-0	1	6.43	5.71
2016 Atl	NL	22	22	0	0	123.1	525	125	61	59	18	5	4	6	35	2	111	13	1	9	5	.643	0	0-0	0	4.18	4.31
3 ML YEARS		56	37	0	10	228.2	1008	260	135	125	38	7	10	10	71	2	202	19	2	13	12	.520	0	0-0	2	5.13	4.92

Logan Forsythe

Bats: R **Throws:** R **Pos:** 2B-118;DH-7;PH-2   **Ht:** 6'1" **Wt:** 205 **Born:** 1/14/1987 **Age:** 30

		BATTING																				RUNNING			AVERAGES			
Year Team	Lg	G	AB	H	2B	3B	HR	(Hm	Rd)	TB	R	RBI	RC	TBB	IBB	SO	HBP	SH	SF	SB	CS	GDP	Avg	OBP	Slg	OPS
2011 SD	NL	62	150	32	9	1	0	(0	0)	43	12	12	15	12	3	33	3	2	2	3	1	3	.213	.281	.287	.568
2012 SD	NL	91	315	86	13	3	6	(5	1)	123	45	26	37	28	0	57	6	0	1	8	2	6	.273	.343	.390	.733
2013 SD	NL	75	220	47	6	1	6	(2	4)	73	22	19	16	19	2	54	2	1	1	6	1	5	.214	.281	.332	.613
2014 TB	AL	110	301	67	12	1	6	(2	4)	99	32	26	26	25	0	71	4	2	4	2	0	9	.223	.287	.329	.616
2015 TB	AL	153	540	152	33	2	17	(8	9)	240	69	68	73	55	2	111	14	0	6	9	4	12	.281	.359	.444	.804
2016 TB	AL	127	511	135	24	4	20	(12	8)	227	76	52	74	46	0	127	8	0	2	6	6	8	.264	.333	.444	.778
6 ML YEARS		618	2037	519	97	12	55	(29	26)	805	256	203	241	185	7	453	37	5	16	34	14	43	.255	.326	.395	.721

Dexter Fowler

Bats: B **Throws:** R **Pos:** CF-121;PH-4;DH-1   **Ht:** 6'5" **Wt:** 195 **Born:** 3/22/1986 **Age:** 31

		BATTING																				RUNNING			AVERAGES			
Year Team	Lg	G	AB	H	2B	3B	HR	(Hm	Rd)	TB	R	RBI	RC	TBB	IBB	SO	HBP	SH	SF	SB	CS	GDP	Avg	OBP	Slg	OPS
2008 Col	NL	13	26	4	0	0	0	(0	0)	4	3	0	0	0	0	5	1	0	0	0	1	0	.154	.185	.154	.339
2009 Col	NL	135	433	115	29	10	4	(2	2)	176	73	34	68	67	1	116	1	14	3	27	10	4	.266	.363	.406	.770
2010 Col	NL	132	439	114	20	14	6	(5	1)	180	73	36	68	57	0	104	2	7	0	13	8	5	.260	.347	.410	.757
2011 Col	NL	125	481	128	35	15	5	(3	2)	208	84	45	79	68	3	130	6	7	1	12	9	6	.266	.363	.432	.796
2012 Col	NL	143	454	136	18	11	13	(10	3)	215	72	53	81	68	1	128	0	6	2	12	5	5	.300	.389	.474	.863
2013 Col	NL	119	415	109	18	3	12	(7	5)	169	71	42	62	65	1	105	6	4	2	19	9	5	.263	.369	.407	.776
2014 Hou	AL	116	434	120	21	4	8	(5	3)	173	61	35	65	66	2	108	3	1	1	11	4	6	.276	.375	.399	.774
2015 ChC	NL	156	596	149	29	8	17	(11	6)	245	102	46	77	84	1	154	5	2	3	20	7	5	.250	.346	.411	.757
2016 ChC	NL	125	456	126	25	7	13	(4	9)	204	84	48	83	79	0	124	11	1	4	13	4	3	.276	.393	.447	.840
Postseason		13	50	13	2	0	2	(1	1)	21	7	5	5	3	0	9	0	2	2	1	0	1	.260	.291	.420	.711
9 ML YEARS		1064	3734	1001	195	72	78	(47	31)	1574	623	339	583	554	9	974	35	42	16	127	57	39	.268	.366	.422	.788

Maikel Franco

MY-kell

Bats: R **Throws:** R **Pos:** 3B-148;PH-4   **Ht:** 6'1" **Wt:** 215 **Born:** 8/26/1992 **Age:** 24

		BATTING																				RUNNING			AVERAGES			
Year Team	Lg	G	AB	H	2B	3B	HR	(Hm	Rd)	TB	R	RBI	RC	TBB	IBB	SO	HBP	SH	SF	SB	CS	GDP	Avg	OBP	Slg	OPS
2014 Phi	NL	16	56	10	2	0	0	(0	0)	12	5	5	1	1	0	13	0	0	1	0	0	1	.179	.190	.214	.404
2015 Phi	NL	80	304	85	22	1	14	(7	7)	151	45	50	48	26	2	52	4	0	1	1	0	8	.280	.343	.497	.840
2016 Phi	NL	152	581	148	23	1	25	(10	15)	248	67	88	74	40	7	106	5	0	4	1	1	13	.255	.306	.427	.733
3 ML YEARS		248	941	243	47	2	39	(17	22)	411	117	143	123	67	9	171	9	0	6	2	1	22	.258	.312	.437	.749

Jeff Francoeur

frann-COOR

Bats: R **Throws:** R **Pos:** LF-63;PH-49;RF-17;DH-3;3B-1;PR-1   **Ht:** 6'4" **Wt:** 225 **Born:** 1/8/1984 **Age:** 33

		BATTING																				RUNNING			AVERAGES			
Year Team	Lg	G	AB	H	2B	3B	HR	(Hm	Rd)	TB	R	RBI	RC	TBB	IBB	SO	HBP	SH	SF	SB	CS	GDP	Avg	OBP	Slg	OPS
2005 Atl	NL	70	257	77	20	1	14	(11	3)	141	41	45	50	11	3	58	4	0	2	3	2	4	.300	.336	.549	.884
2006 Atl	NL	162	651	169	24	6	29	(19	10)	292	83	103	91	23	6	132	9	0	3	1	6	15	.260	.293	.449	.742
2007 Atl	NL	162	642	188	40	0	19	(7	12)	285	84	105	97	42	5	129	5	0	7	5	2	14	.293	.338	.444	.782
2008 Atl	NL	155	599	143	33	3	11	(5	6)	215	70	71	49	39	5	111	10	0	4	0	1	18	.239	.294	.359	.653
2009 2 Tms	NL	157	593	166	32	4	15	(7	8)	251	72	76	59	23	5	92	6	1	9	6	4	13	.280	.309	.423	.732
2010 2 Tms		139	454	113	18	2	13	(5	8)	174	52	65	46	30	8	81	8	0	11	8	3	9	.249	.300	.383	.683
2011 KC	AL	153	601	171	47	4	20	(10	10)	286	77	87	83	37	3	123	8	0	10	22	10	17	.285	.329	.476	.805
2012 KC	AL	148	561	132	26	3	16	(7	9)	212	58	49	50	34	9	119	7	0	1	4	7	14	.235	.287	.378	.665
2013 2 Tms		81	245	50	10	2	3	(1	2)	73	20	17	11	9	2	61	2	0	0	3	0	7	.204	.238	.298	.536
2014 SD	NL	10	24	2	0	0	0	(0	0)	2	2	1	0	3	0	7	0	0	1	0	0	0	.083	.179	.083	.262
2015 Phi	NL	119	326	84	16	1	13	(9	4)	141	34	45	34	13	0	77	1	0	3	0	2	10	.258	.286	.433	.718
2016 2 Tms		125	307	78	15	1	7	(1	6)	116	33	34	30	20	2	90	0	1	3	2	2	5	.254	.297	.378	.675
09 Atl	NL	82	304	76	12	2	5	(3	2)	107	32	35	25	12	2	46	3	1	4	5	1	10	.250	.282	.352	.634
09 NYM	NL	75	289	90	20	2	10	(4	6)	144	40	41	34	11	3	46	3	0	5	1	3	3	.311	.338	.498	.836
10 NYM	NL	124	401	95	16	2	11	(5	6)	148	43	54	39	29	8	76	7	0	10	8	2	7	.237	.293	.369	.662
10 Tex	AL	15	53	18	2	0	2	(0	2)	26	9	11	7	1	0	5	1	0	1	0	1	2	.340	.357	.491	.848
13 KC	AL	59	183	38	8	2	3	(1	2)	59	19	13	10	8	2	49	2	0	0	2	0	5	.208	.249	.322	.571
13 SF		22	62	12	2	0	0	(0	0)	14	1	4	1	1	0	12	0	0	0	1	0	2	.194	.206	.226	.432
16 Atl	NL	99	257	64	13	0	7	(1	6)	98	29	33	27	16	2	75	0	0	3	2	0	4	.249	.290	.381	.671
16 Mia	NL	26	50	14	2	1	0	(0	0)	18	4	1	3	4	0	15	0	1	0	0	2	1	.280	.333	.360	.693
Postseason		13	41	7	2	1	0	(0	0)	11	3	2	3	3	1	7	1	1	0	0	2	1	.171	.244	.268	.513
12 ML YEARS		1481	5260	1373	281	27	160	(82	78)	2188	626	698	600	284	48	1080	60	2	54	54	39	126	.261	.303	.416	.719

Nick Franklin

Bats: B **Throws:** R **Pos:** LF-18;PH-13;1B-9;2B-8;RF-7;DH-6;SS-5;PR-1   **Ht:** 6'1" **Wt:** 190 **Born:** 3/2/1991 **Age:** 26

Year	Team	Lg	G	AB	H	2B	3B	HR	(Hm	Rd)	TB	R	RBI	RC	TBB	IBB	SO	HBP	SH	SF	SB	CS	GDP	Avg	OBP	Slg	OPS
2016	Drham*	AAA	64	240	61	16	1	5	(-	-)	94	26	28	33	26	1	56	0	0	4	10	1	5	.254	.322	.392	.714
2013	Sea	AL	102	369	83	20	1	12	(4	8)	141	38	45	48	42	1	113	0	0	1	6	1	2	.225	.303	.382	.686
2014	2 Tms	AL	28	81	13	2	1	1	(1	0)	20	7	6	6	6	0	32	1	0	2	2	0	2	.160	.222	.247	.469
2015	TB	AL	44	101	16	4	1	3	(2	1)	31	11	7	4	7	0	37	0	1	0	1	0	2	.158	.213	.307	.520
2016	TB	AL	60	174	47	10	1	6	(4	2)	77	18	26	25	12	1	42	3	2	0	6	1	1	.270	.328	.443	.771
14	Sea	AL	17	47	6	0	1	0	(0	0)	8	3	2	1	3	0	21	1	0	1	1	0	0	.128	.192	.170	.363
14	TB	AL	11	34	7	2	0	1	(1	0)	12	4	4	5	3	0	11	0	0	1	1	0	2	.206	.263	.353	.616
	4 ML YEARS		234	725	159	36	4	22	(11	11)	269	74	84	83	67	2	224	4	3	3	15	2	7	.219	.288	.371	.659

Jason Frasor

Pitches: R **Bats:** R **Pos:** P   FRAY-zer   **Ht:** 5'9" **Wt:** 180 **Born:** 8/9/1977 **Age:** 39

			HOW MUCH HE PITCHED					WHAT HE GAVE UP										THE RESULTS							
Year	Team	Lg	G	GS	CG	GF	IP	BFP	H	R	ER	HR	SH	SF	HB	TBB	IBB	SO	WP	Bk	W	L	Pct	Sh	Sv-Op	Hld	ERC	ERA
2004	Tor	AL	63	0	0	37	68.1	299	64	31	31	4	3	3	2	36	3	54	4	2	4	6	.400	0	17-19	8	3.97	4.08
2005	Tor	AL	67	0	0	12	74.2	305	67	31	27	8	2	1	3	28	2	62	1	0	3	5	.375	0	1-3	15	3.72	3.25
2006	Tor	AL	51	0	0	12	50.0	215	47	24	24	8	0	3	2	17	1	51	3	0	3	2	.600	0	0-1	12	3.98	4.32
2007	Tor	AL	51	0	0	18	57.0	242	47	29	29	3	1	2	2	23	1	59	2	1	1	5	.167	0	3-6	4	2.88	4.58
2008	Tor	AL	49	0	0	21	47.1	208	36	23	22	4	0	2	1	32	4	42	6	0	1	2	.333	0	0-1	4	3.62	4.18
2009	Tor	AL	61	0	0	36	57.2	227	43	17	16	4	1	2	2	16	3	56	2	0	7	3	.700	0	11-14	4	2.22	2.50
2010	Tor	AL	69	0	0	18	63.2	279	61	30	26	4	1	0	4	27	6	65	5	0	3	4	.429	0	4-8	14	3.72	3.68
2011	2 Tms	AL	64	0	0	10	60.0	261	58	25	24	7	2	4	3	26	3	57	3	0	3	3	.500	0	0-2	14	4.26	3.60
2012	Tor	AL	50	0	0	9	43.2	191	42	20	20	6	1	2	2	22	1	53	5	1	1	1	.500	0	0-3	12	4.74	4.12
2013	Tex	AL	61	0	0	11	49.0	200	36	15	14	4	1	2	0	20	3	48	2	0	4	3	.571	0	0-1	10	2.50	2.57
2014	2 Tms	AL	61	0	0	11	47.1	196	40	17	14	3	0	5	2	18	2	46	3	0	4	1	.800	0	0-2	15	3.05	2.66
2015	2 Tms	AL	32	0	0	10	28.0	124	27	5	4	1	1	1	0	18	3	22	2	0	1	0	1.000	0	0-1	4	4.22	1.29
11	Tor	AL	44	0	0	6	42.1	178	38	15	14	4	2	3	2	15	1	37	2	0	2	1	.667	0	0-2	10	3.46	2.98
11	CWS	AL	20	0	0	4	17.2	83	20	10	10	3	0	1	1	11	2	20	1	0	1	2	.333	0	0-0	4	6.37	5.09
14	Tex	AL	38	0	0	6	29.2	129	27	14	11	2	0	3	1	14	1	30	2	0	1	1	.500	0	0-2	10	3.68	3.34
14	KC	AL	23	0	0	5	17.2	67	13	3	3	1	0	2	1	4	1	16	1	0	3	0	1.000	0	0-0	5	2.07	1.53
15	KC	AL	26	0	0	10	23.1	104	24	5	4	1	1	1	0	15	2	18	2	0	1	0	1.000	0	0-1	2	4.72	1.54
15	Atl	NL	6	0	0	0	4.2	20	3	0	0	0	0	0	0	3	1	4	0	0	0	0	-	0	0-0	2	2.03	0.00
	Postseason		7	0	0	2	5.1	23	5	1	1	0	0	0	0	2	0	3	1	0	2	0	1.000	0	0-0	2	2.88	1.69
	12 ML YEARS		679	0	0	205	646.2	2747	568	267	251	56	13	27	23	283	32	615	38	4	35	35	.500	0	36-61	111	3.53	3.49

Adam Frazier

Bats: L **Throws:** R **Pos:** LF-20;2B-17;RF-16;PH-14;PR-7;3B-5;CF-1   **Ht:** 5'10" **Wt:** 175 **Born:** 12/14/1991 **Age:** 25

Year	Team	Lg	G	AB	H	2B	3B	HR	(Hm	Rd)	TB	R	RBI	RC	TBB	IBB	SO	HBP	SH	SF	SB	CS	GDP	Avg	OBP	Slg	OPS
2013	Jmstwn	A-	58	224	72	7	1	0	(-	-)	81	34	27	34	25	1	31	6	0	3	5	8	2	.321	.399	.362	.761
2014	Bradtn	A+	121	492	124	21	2	1	(-	-)	152	62	42	49	37	0	61	3	6	2	14	8	5	.252	.307	.309	.616
2015	Altna	AA	103	377	122	21	4	2	(-	-)	157	59	30	62	34	0	42	3	9	0	11	7	2	.324	.384	.416	.801
2016	Indy	AAA	68	261	87	16	4	0	(-	-)	111	34	22	44	29	0	27	2	5	2	17	15	2	.333	.401	.425	.827
2016	Pit	NL	66	146	44	8	1	2	(2	0)	60	21	11	23	12	0	26	1	0	1	4	1	0	.301	.356	.411	.767

Todd Frazier

Bats: R **Throws:** R **Pos:** 3B-149;1B-7;DH-2   **Ht:** 6'3" **Wt:** 220 **Born:** 2/12/1986 **Age:** 31

Year	Team	Lg	G	AB	H	2B	3B	HR	(Hm	Rd)	TB	R	RBI	RC	TBB	IBB	SO	HBP	SH	SF	SB	CS	GDP	Avg	OBP	Slg	OPS
2011	Cin	NL	41	112	26	5	0	6	(2	4)	49	17	15	13	7	0	27	2	0	0	1	0	2	.232	.289	.438	.727
2012	Cin	NL	128	422	115	26	6	19	(10	9)	210	55	67	59	36	1	103	3	0	4	3	2	9	.273	.331	.498	.829
2013	Cin	NL	150	531	124	29	4	19	(12	7)	216	63	73	67	50	1	125	14	2	3	6	5	14	.234	.314	.407	.721
2014	Cin	NL	157	597	163	22	1	29	(20	9)	274	88	80	84	52	2	139	7	0	4	20	8	9	.273	.336	.459	.795
2015	Cin	NL	157	619	158	43	1	35	(19	16)	308	82	89	73	44	3	137	7	1	7	13	8	10	.255	.309	.498	.806
2016	CWS	AL	158	590	133	21	4	40	(16	24)	274	89	98	71	64	1	163	4	1	7	15	5	11	.225	.302	.464	.767
	Postseason		5	10	2	1	0	0	(0	0)	3	0	1	0	1	0	3	0	0	0	0	0	0	.200	.273	.300	.573
	6 ML YEARS		791	2871	719	146	11	148	(79	69)	1331	394	422	367	253	8	694	37	4	25	58	28	64	.250	.317	.464	.780

Freddie Freeman

Bats: L **Throws:** R **Pos:** 1B-158   **Ht:** 6'5" **Wt:** 220 **Born:** 9/12/1989 **Age:** 27

Year	Team	Lg	G	AB	H	2B	3B	HR	(Hm	Rd)	TB	R	RBI	RC	TBB	IBB	SO	HBP	SH	SF	SB	CS	GDP	Avg	OBP	Slg	OPS
2010	Atl	NL	20	24	4	1	0	1	(0	1)	8	3	1	0	0	0	8	0	0	0	0	0	1	.167	.167	.333	.500
2011	Atl	NL	157	571	161	32	6	21	(9	12)	256	67	76	79	53	3	142	6	0	5	4	4	15	.282	.346	.448	.795
2012	Atl	NL	147	540	140	33	2	23	(12	11)	246	91	94	82	64	4	129	7	0	9	2	0	10	.259	.340	.456	.796
2013	Atl	NL	147	551	176	27	2	23	(16	7)	276	89	109	124	66	10	121	7	0	5	1	0	13	.319	.396	.501	.897
2014	Atl	NL	162	607	175	43	4	18	(7	11)	280	93	78	101	90	4	145	8	0	3	3	4	18	.288	.386	.461	.847
2015	Atl	NL	118	416	115	27	0	18	(5	13)	196	62	66	77	56	4	98	7	0	2	3	1	6	.276	.370	.471	.841
2016	Atl	NL	158	589	178	43	6	34	(15	19)	335	102	91	119	89	18	171	10	0	5	6	1	12	.302	.400	.569	.968
	Postseason		5	20	8	2	0	0	(0	0)	10	4	0	2	2	0	5	0	0	0	0	0	0	.400	.455	.500	.955
	7 ML YEARS		909	3298	949	206	14	138	(64	74)	1597	507	515	582	418	43	814	45	0	29	19	10	73	.288	.373	.484	.857

Mike Freeman

Bats: L Throws: R Pos: PH-10;2B-5;PR-4;SS-2;DH-2;LF-1;RF-1   Ht: 6'0" Wt: 190 Born: 8/4/1987 Age: 29

Year	Team	Lg	G	AB	H	2B	3B	HR	(Hm	Rd)	TB	R	RBI	RC	TBB	IBB	SO	HBP	SH	SF	SB	CS	GDP	Avg	OBP	Slg	OPS
2012	Visalia	A+	135	537	166	24	5	3	(-	-)	209	91	59	89	60	1	88	2	6	5	30	4	3	.309	.377	.389	.767
2013	Mobile	AA	131	454	112	20	4	1	(-	-)	135	60	40	56	65	1	84	6	6	5	29	10	8	.247	.345	.297	.643
2014	Mobile	AA	52	196	42	7	3	5	(-	-)	70	27	16	22	20	0	41	2	2	1	7	1	2	.214	.292	.357	.649
2014	Reno	AAA	71	218	67	11	7	1	(-	-)	95	37	25	37	21	0	25	0	0	2	6	0	6	.307	.365	.436	.801
2015	Reno	AAA	113	398	126	23	5	3	(-	-)	168	79	41	66	34	2	51	1	1	1	10	0	6	.317	.371	.422	.793
2016	Reno	AAA	88	341	108	17	6	1	(-	-)	140	56	24	58	38	1	75	2	2	1	11	1	1	.317	.387	.411	.798
2016	Tacom	AAA	26	105	32	6	0	3	(-	-)	47	15	15	18	13	1	19	0	0	1	1	0	2	.305	.378	.448	.826
2016	2 Tms		21	22	5	1	0	0	(0	0)	6	1	1	1	2	0	7	0	0	0	0	0	2	.227	.292	.273	.564
16	Ari	NL	8	9	0	0	0	0	(0	0)	0	0	0	0	2	0	5	0	0	0	0	0	1	.000	.182	.000	.182
16	Sea	AL	13	13	5	1	0	0	(0	0)	6	1	1	1	0	0	2	0	0	0	0	0	1	.385	.385	.462	.846

Sam Freeman

Pitches: L Bats: R Pos: RP-7   Ht: 5'11" Wt: 180 Born: 6/24/1987 Age: 30

Year	Team	Lg	G	GS	CG	GF	IP	BFP	H	R	ER	HR	SH	SF	HB	TBB	IBB	SO	WP	Bk	W	L	Pct	Sh	Sv-Op	Hld	ERC	ERA
2016	ColSpr*	AAA	30	3	0	4	55.1	249	63	34	32	4	2	1	3	28	0	46	3	0	2	1	.667	0	2- -	-	5.43	5.20
2012	StL	NL	24	0	0	7	20.0	86	17	13	12	2	1	0	1	10	0	18	0	0	0	2	.000	0	0-0	2	3.84	5.40
2013	StL	NL	13	0	0	2	12.1	50	8	3	3	0	1	0	0	5	0	8	2	0	1	0	1.000	0	0-0	1	1.67	2.19
2014	StL	NL	44	0	0	9	38.0	169	34	13	11	2	1	1	4	19	0	35	3	0	2	0	1.000	0	0-0	11	3.89	2.61
2015	Tex	AL	54	0	0	10	38.1	171	31	13	13	4	0	1	3	25	0	40	0	0	0	0	-	0	0-0	12	4.31	3.05
2016	Mil	NL	7	0	0	4	7.2	44	13	11	11	2	0	2	0	9	0	8	1	0	0	0	-	0	0-0	0	13.79	12.91
	Postseason		1	0	0	0	0.0	2	0	0	0	0	0	0	0	2	0	0	0	0	0	0	-	0	0-0	0	-	-
	5 ML YEARS		142	0	0	32	116.1	520	103	53	50	10	3	4	8	68	0	109	6	0	3	2	.600	0	0-0	26	4.29	3.87

David Freese

Bats: R Throws: R Pos: 3B-78;1B-58;PH-24;2B-2   FREEZE   Ht: 6'2" Wt: 225 Born: 4/28/1983 Age: 34

Year	Team	Lg	G	AB	H	2B	3B	HR	(Hm	Rd)	TB	R	RBI	RC	TBB	IBB	SO	HBP	SH	SF	SB	CS	GDP	Avg	OBP	Slg	OPS
2009	StL	NL	17	31	10	2	0	1	(0	1)	15	3	7	4	2	0	7	0	0	1	0	0	1	.323	.353	.484	.837
2010	StL	NL	70	240	71	12	1	4	(3	1)	97	28	36	36	21	0	59	4	4	1	1	1	7	.296	.361	.404	.765
2011	StL	NL	97	333	99	16	1	10	(6	4)	147	41	55	50	24	0	75	4	0	2	1	0	18	.297	.350	.441	.791
2012	StL	NL	144	501	147	25	1	20	(8	12)	234	70	79	79	57	2	122	7	0	2	3	3	19	.293	.372	.467	.839
2013	StL	NL	138	462	121	26	1	9	(4	5)	176	53	60	48	47	1	106	9	0	3	1	2	26	.262	.340	.381	.721
2014	LAA	AL	134	462	120	25	1	10	(6	4)	177	53	55	55	38	0	124	6	0	5	1	3	10	.260	.321	.383	.704
2015	LAA	AL	121	424	109	27	0	14	(9	5)	178	53	56	60	31	0	107	12	0	3	1	1	12	.257	.323	.420	.743
2016	Pit	NL	141	437	118	23	0	13	(5	8)	180	63	55	61	45	2	142	10	0	0	1	0	15	.270	.352	.412	.764
	Postseason		51	174	49	15	1	8	(4	4)	90	21	30	31	19	2	47	2	0	1	0	1	8	.282	.357	.517	.874
	8 ML YEARS		862	2890	795	156	5	81	(41	40)	1204	364	403	393	265	5	742	52	4	17	8	10	108	.275	.345	.417	.762

Carlos Frias

Pitches: R Bats: R Pos: RP-1   FREE-us   Ht: 6'4" Wt: 195 Born: 11/13/1989 Age: 27

Year	Team	Lg	G	GS	CG	GF	IP	BFP	H	R	ER	HR	SH	SF	HB	TBB	IBB	SO	WP	Bk	W	L	Pct	Sh	Sv-Op	Hld	ERC	ERA
2016	OkCity*	AAA	8	4	0	2	36.1	151	37	19	18	2	2	3	0	11	0	27	0	0	3	3	.500	0	0- -	1	3.56	4.46
2014	LAD	NL	15	2	0	7	32.1	137	33	22	22	4	0	0	0	7	1	29	2	0	1	1	.500	0	0-0	1	3.50	6.12
2015	LAD	NL	17	13	0	1	77.2	333	88	38	35	7	4	4	3	26	1	43	3	0	5	5	.500	0	0-0	0	4.78	4.06
2016	LAD	NL	1	0	0	1	4.0	15	2	0	0	0	0	0	0	1	0	3	0	0	0	0	-	0	0-0	0	0.94	0.00
	3 ML YEARS		33	15	0	9	114.0	485	123	60	57	11	4	4	3	34	2	75	5	0	6	6	.500	0	0-0	1	4.23	4.50

Christian Friedrich

Pitches: L Bats: R Pos: SP-23; RP-1   FREE-drick   Ht: 6'4" Wt: 215 Born: 7/8/1987 Age: 29

Year	Team	Lg	G	GS	CG	GF	IP	BFP	H	R	ER	HR	SH	SF	HB	TBB	IBB	SO	WP	Bk	W	L	Pct	Sh	Sv-Op	Hld	ERC	ERA
2012	Col	NL	16	16	0	0	84.2	377	102	61	58	14	6	2	2	30	0	74	8	0	5	8	.385	0	0-0	0	5.71	6.17
2014	Col	NL	16	3	0	3	24.1	110	25	21	16	3	1	2	2	10	1	27	5	0	0	4	.000	0	0-0	3	4.59	5.92
2015	Col	NL	68	0	0	13	58.1	270	75	37	34	5	4	6	1	25	2	45	3	0	0	4	.000	0	0-0	9	5.76	5.25
2016	SD	NL	24	23	0	0	129.1	567	131	74	69	13	3	5	2	52	2	100	7	0	5	12	.294	0	0-0	0	4.14	4.80
	4 ML YEARS		124	42	0	16	296.2	1324	333	193	177	35	14	15	7	117	5	246	23	0	10	28	.263	0	0-0	12	4.93	5.37

Eric Fryer

Bats: R Throws: R Pos: C-54;PH-8;PR-6   Ht: 6'2" Wt: 215 Born: 8/26/1985 Age: 31

Year	Team	Lg	G	AB	H	2B	3B	HR	(Hm	Rd)	TB	R	RBI	RC	TBB	IBB	SO	HBP	SH	SF	SB	CS	GDP	Avg	OBP	Slg	OPS
2011	Pit	NL	10	26	7	0	0	0	(0	0)	7	5	0	2	3	1	7	0	0	0	1	1	0	.269	.345	.269	.614
2012	Pit	NL	6	4	1	0	0	0	(0	0)	1	0	0	1	1	0	1	0	0	0	0	0	0	.250	.400	.250	.650
2013	Min	AL	6	13	5	1	0	1	(1	0)	9	2	4	5	3	0	1	0	0	0	0	0	1	.385	.500	.692	1.192
2014	Min	AL	28	75	16	4	0	1	(0	1)	23	11	5	6	5	0	15	1	0	0	1	0	0	.213	.272	.307	.578
2015	Min	AL	15	22	5	2	0	0	(0	0)	7	2	2	3	5	0	11	0	0	0	0	0	0	.227	.370	.318	.689
2016	2 Tms	NL	60	116	31	4	1	0	(0	0)	37	19	13	13	13	0	25	1	0	2	0	3	1	.267	.336	.319	.655
16	StL	NL	24	38	14	2	0	0	(0	0)	16	7	5	5	3	0	7	0	0	1	0	1	0	.368	.415	.421	.836
16	Pit	NL	36	78	17	2	1	0	(0	0)	21	12	8	8	10	0	18	1	0	1	0	2	1	.218	.300	.269	.569
	6 ML YEARS		125	256	65	11	1	2	(1	1)	84	39	24	30	30	1	62	1	2	2	2	4	2	.254	.332	.328	.660

Rey Fuentes

Bats: L **Throws:** L **Pos:** RF-9;LF-3;DH-1;PR-1
foo-WHEN-tayz
Ht: 6'0" **Wt:** 160 **Born:** 2/12/1991 **Age:** 26

Year	Team	Lg	G	AB	H	2B	3B	HR	(Hm	Rd)	TB	R	RBI	RC	TBB	IBB	SO	HBP	SH	SF	SB	CS	GDP	Avg	OBP	Slg	OPS
2012	SnAnt	AA	136	473	103	20	4	4	(-	-)	143	53	34	50	52	1	133	6	7	3	35	9	2	.218	.301	.302	.604
2013	SnAnt	AA	93	345	109	21	2	6	(-	-)	152	56	35	65	41	2	71	6	9	2	29	10	2	.316	.396	.441	.837
2013	Tucsn	AAA	14	55	23	4	0	0	(-	-)	27	17	8	15	10	0	10	1	1	0	6	1	1	.418	.515	.491	1.006
2014	ElPaso	AAA	46	157	41	9	3	1	(-	-)	59	29	16	22	17	0	27	1	3	0	13	2	1	.261	.337	.376	.713
2014	SnAnt	AA	42	170	55	6	2	4	(-	-)	77	25	17	32	16	1	37	2	5	1	12	1	1	.324	.386	.453	.839
2015	Omha	AAA	107	396	122	10	4	9	(-	-)	167	70	46	65	30	1	72	3	14	2	29	6	7	.308	.360	.422	.781
2016	Omha	AAA	65	240	61	9	3	0	(-	-)	76	32	14	28	23	2	62	4	1	4	17	5	2	.254	.325	.317	.641
2013	SD	NL	23	33	5	0	0	0	(0	0)	5	4	1	1	3	0	16	0	0	0	3	0	0	.152	.222	.152	.374
2016	KC	AL	13	41	13	1	0	0	(0	0)	14	2	5	5	3	0	8	0	0	0	0	2	0	.317	.364	.341	.705
	2 ML YEARS		36	74	18	1	0	0	(0	0)	19	6	6	6	6	0	24	0	0	0	3	2	0	.243	.300	.257	.557

Carson Fulmer

Pitches: R **Bats:** R **Pos:** RP-8
Ht: 6'0" **Wt:** 195 **Born:** 12/13/1993 **Age:** 23

			HOW MUCH HE PITCHED						WHAT HE GAVE UP										THE RESULTS						
Year	Team	Lg	G	GS	CG	GF	IP	BFP	H	R	ER	HR	SH	SF	HB	TBB	IBB	SO	WP	Bk	W	L	Pct	Sh	Sv-Op	Hld	ERC	ERA
2015	2 Tms	Low	9	9	0	0	23.0	93	17	5	5	2	1	0	2	9	0	26	3	0	0	0	-	0	0- -	-	2.98	1.96
2016	Brham	AA	17	17	0	0	87.0	393	82	51	46	7	4	4	3	51	0	90	7	1	4	9	.308	0	0- -	-	4.41	4.76
2016	CWS	AL	8	0	0	4	11.2	53	12	11	11	2	0	0	2	7	0	10	2	0	0	2	.000	0	0-1	0	6.57	8.49

Michael Fulmer

Pitches: R **Bats:** R **Pos:** SP-26
Ht: 6'3" **Wt:** 210 **Born:** 3/15/1993 **Age:** 24

			HOW MUCH HE PITCHED						WHAT HE GAVE UP										THE RESULTS						
Year	Team	Lg	G	GS	CG	GF	IP	BFP	H	R	ER	HR	SH	SF	HB	TBB	IBB	SO	WP	Bk	W	L	Pct	Sh	Sv-Op	Hld	ERC	ERA
2012	Savann	A	21	21	1	0	108.1	454	92	37	33	6	4	1	6	38	0	101	8	0	7	6	.538	0	0- -	-	2.98	2.74
2013	2 Tms	Low	9	9	0	0	46.0	193	33	17	17	1	1	3	5	19	0	42	1	0	3	3	.500	0	0- -	-	2.49	3.33
2014	Stluci	A+	19	19	0	0	95.0	435	112	52	42	7	3	1	8	31	0	86	6	0	6	10	.375	0	0- -	-	4.83	3.98
2015	Bnghtn	AA	15	15	0	0	86.0	349	73	25	18	3	4	0	1	23	0	83	3	1	6	2	.750	0	0- -	-	2.42	1.88
2015	Erie	AA	6	6	0	0	31.2	124	27	10	10	4	0	0	0	7	0	33	2	0	4	1	.800	0	0- -	-	2.86	2.84
2016	Det	AL	26	26	1	0	159.0	647	136	57	54	19	4	4	9	42	1	132	1	1	11	7	.611	0	0-0	-	3.02	3.06

Yovani Gallardo

Pitches: R **Bats:** R **Pos:** SP-23
guy-YARR-doe
Ht: 6'2" **Wt:** 205 **Born:** 2/27/1986 **Age:** 31

			HOW MUCH HE PITCHED						WHAT HE GAVE UP										THE RESULTS						
Year	Team	Lg	G	GS	CG	GF	IP	BFP	H	R	ER	HR	SH	SF	HB	TBB	IBB	SO	WP	Bk	W	L	Pct	Sh	Sv-Op	Hld	ERC	ERA
2007	Mil	NL	20	17	0	1	110.1	466	103	48	45	8	4	3	2	37	2	101	3	0	9	5	.643	0	0-0	0	3.30	3.67
2008	Mil	NL	4	4	0	0	24.0	97	22	5	5	3	2	1	0	8	0	20	0	0	0	0	-	0	0-0	0	3.66	1.88
2009	Mil	NL	30	30	1	0	185.2	793	150	78	77	21	5	3	5	94	5	204	9	0	13	12	.520	0	0-0	0	3.57	3.73
2010	Mil	NL	31	31	2	0	185.0	803	178	89	79	12	11	4	3	75	5	200	7	1	14	7	.667	2	0-0	0	3.61	3.84
2011	Mil	NL	33	33	1	0	207.1	865	193	92	81	27	10	7	1	59	1	207	12	0	17	10	.630	1	0-0	0	3.43	3.52
2012	Mil	NL	33	33	0	0	204.0	860	185	86	83	26	11	6	0	81	3	204	5	0	16	9	.640	0	0-0	0	3.72	3.66
2013	Mil	NL	31	31	0	0	180.2	773	180	92	84	18	8	7	3	66	1	144	5	0	12	10	.545	0	0-0	0	3.98	4.18
2014	Mil	NL	32	32	0	0	192.1	817	195	86	75	21	8	3	4	54	2	146	8	0	8	11	.421	0	0-0	0	3.79	3.51
2015	Tex	AL	33	33	0	0	184.1	793	193	76	70	15	1	3	1	68	0	121	10	0	13	11	.542	0	0-0	0	4.13	3.42
2016	Bal	AL	23	23	0	0	118.0	526	126	74	71	16	1	6	1	61	2	85	6	0	6	8	.429	0	0-0	0	5.26	5.42
	Postseason		6	5	0	0	31.0	129	26	11	8	2	1	0	0	14	3	21	4	0	2	2	.500	0	0-0	0	3.05	2.32
	10 ML YEARS		270	267	4	1	1591.2	6793	1525	726	670	167	61	43	20	603	21	1432	65	1	108	83	.565	3	0-0	0	3.82	3.79

Joey Gallo

Bats: L **Throws:** R **Pos:** 3B-5;DH-5;PH-5;PR-3;1B-1
Ht: 6'5" **Wt:** 235 **Born:** 11/19/1993 **Age:** 23

Year	Team	Lg	G	AB	H	2B	3B	HR	(Hm	Rd)	TB	R	RBI	RC	TBB	IBB	SO	HBP	SH	SF	SB	CS	GDP	Avg	OBP	Slg	OPS
2012	2 Tms	Low	59	206	56	12	1	22	(-	-)	136	53	52	56	48	3	78	3	0	3	6	0	0	.272	.412	.660	1.072
2013	2 Tms	Low	111	411	103	23	5	40	(-	-)	256	86	88	88	50	1	172	5	0	1	15	1	2	.251	.338	.623	.961
2014	MrtlBh	A+	58	189	61	9	3	21	(-	-)	139	53	50	61	51	3	64	2	0	4	5	3	3	.323	.463	.735	1.199
2014	Frisco	AA	68	250	58	10	0	21	(-	-)	131	44	56	45	36	4	115	3	1	1	2	0	1	.232	.334	.524	.858
2015	Frisco	AA	34	121	38	10	1	9	(-	-)	77	21	31	31	24	0	49	0	0	1	1	0	1	.314	.425	.636	1.061
2015	RdRck	AAA	53	200	39	9	0	14	(-	-)	90	20	32	27	27	2	90	0	1	0	1	0	1	.195	.289	.450	.739
2016	RdRck	AAA	102	359	86	17	6	25	(-	-)	190	71	66	72	68	4	150	5	0	1	2	0	2	.240	.367	.529	.896
2015	Tex	AL	36	108	22	3	1	6	(4	2)	45	16	14	13	15	3	57	0	0	0	3	0	0	.204	.301	.417	.717
2016	Tex	AL	17	25	1	0	0	1	(1	0)	4	2	1	0	5	0	19	0	0	0	1	0	0	.040	.200	.160	.360
	2 ML YEARS		53	133	23	3	1	7	(5	2)	49	18	15	13	20	3	76	0	0	0	4	0	0	.173	.281	.368	.649

Freddy Galvis

Bats: B **Throws:** R **Pos:** SS-156;PH-2;PR-1
GAL-viss
Ht: 5'10" **Wt:** 185 **Born:** 11/14/1989 **Age:** 27

Year	Team	Lg	G	AB	H	2B	3B	HR	(Hm	Rd)	TB	R	RBI	RC	TBB	IBB	SO	HBP	SH	SF	SB	CS	GDP	Avg	OBP	Slg	OPS
2012	Phi	NL	58	190	43	15	1	3	(3	0)	69	14	24	14	7	0	29	0	3	0	0	0	6	.226	.254	.363	.617
2013	Phi	NL	70	205	48	5	4	6	(4	2)	79	13	19	20	13	2	45	1	3	0	1	0	5	.234	.283	.385	.668
2014	Phi	NL	43	119	21	3	1	4	(2	2)	38	14	12	9	8	0	30	0	0	1	1	0	1	.176	.227	.319	.546
2015	Phi	NL	151	559	147	14	5	7	(6	1)	192	63	50	64	30	1	103	3	7	4	10	1	11	.263	.302	.343	.645
2016	Phi	NL	158	584	141	26	3	20	(11	9)	233	61	67	59	25	6	136	3	8	4	17	6	16	.241	.274	.399	.673
	5 ML YEARS		480	1657	400	63	14	40	(26	14)	611	165	172	166	83	9	343	7	21	9	29	7	38	.241	.279	.369	.648

Eddie Gamboa

Pitches: R **Bats:** R **Pos:** RP-7   **Ht:** 6'1" **Wt:** 215 **Born:** 12/21/1984 **Age:** 32

				HOW MUCH HE PITCHED					WHAT HE GAVE UP										THE RESULTS							
Year	Team	Lg	G	GS	CG	GF	IP	BFP	H	R	ER	HR	SH	SF	HB	TBB	IBB	SO	WP	Bk	W	L	Pct	Sh	Sv-Op	Hld	ERC	ERA
2012	Bowie	AA	23	13	0	2	92.0	375	103	41	34	4	3	6	0	17	1	71	3	0	8	4	.667	0	1--	-	3.63	3.33
2013	Bowie	AA	16	16	2	0	99.0	405	82	49	40	6	3	1	7	31	0	79	15	2	4	6	.400	1	0--	-	2.88	3.64
2013	Norfolk	AAA	9	9	1	0	43.1	205	41	35	30	2	1	0	8	28	0	35	6	0	2	5	.286	0	0--	-	4.97	6.23
2014	Norfolk	AAA	14	12	0	0	77.2	332	70	41	35	7	2	7	5	28	1	74	8	0	4	5	.444	0	0--	-	3.51	4.06
2014	Bowie	AA	5	5	0	0	31.0	132	19	14	11	1	0	2	1	18	1	30	11	1	1	2	.333	0	0--	-	2.26	3.19
2015	Norfolk	AAA	26	19	0	2	113.1	507	94	61	58	6	2	3	9	84	1	79	16	4	8	11	.421	0	0--	-	4.45	4.61
2016	Drham	AAA	27	12	0	3	94.0	378	65	36	28	0	0	4	4	39	0	89	11	0	6	4	.600	0	0--	-	2.08	2.68
2016	TB	AL	7	0	0	3	13.1	54	9	3	2	1	0	0	0	8	0	11	0	0	0	2	.000	0	0-0	1	3.05	1.35

Ben Gamel

Bats: L **Throws:** L **Pos:** RF-29;PR-5;PH-4;LF-2;CF-1   **Ht:** 5'11" **Wt:** 185 **Born:** 5/17/1992 **Age:** 25

									BATTING												RUNNING			AVERAGES			
Year	Team	Lg	G	AB	H	2B	3B	HR	(Hm	Rd)	TB	R	RBI	RC	TBB	IBB	SO	HBP	SH	SF	SB	CS	GDP	Avg	OBP	Slg	OPS
2012	CtnSC	A	110	444	136	23	5	2	(-	-)	175	56	61	61	23	0	71	4	0	5	19	10	10	.306	.342	.394	.737
2013	Tampa	A+	96	364	99	28	4	3	(-	-)	144	50	49	57	48	2	77	1	3	7	21	5	7	.272	.352	.396	.748
2013	Trntn	AA	16	67	16	4	0	1	(-	-)	23	5	5	6	4	0	18	0	1	0	1	0	0	.239	.282	.343	.625
2014	Trntn	AA	131	544	142	31	3	2	(-	-)	185	58	51	60	36	0	88	2	1	3	13	5	10	.261	.308	.340	.648
2015	S-WB	AAA	129	500	150	28	14	10	(-	-)	236	77	64	86	46	5	108	1	1	3	13	5	9	.300	.358	.472	.830
2016	S-WB	AAA	116	483	149	26	5	6	(-	-)	203	80	51	77	43	3	94	2	1	4	19	8	7	.308	.365	.420	.785
2016	2 Tms	AL	33	48	9	2	0	1	(0	1)	14	9	5	4	6	0	16	0	3	0	0	0	1	.188	.278	.292	.569
16	NYY	AL	6	8	1	0	0	0	(0	0)	1	1	0	0	1	0	1	0	1	0	0	0	1	.125	.222	.125	.347
16	Sea	AL	27	40	8	2	0	1	(0	1)	13	8	5	4	5	0	15	0	2	0	0	0	0	.200	.289	.325	.614

John Gant

Pitches: R **Bats:** R **Pos:** RP-13; SP-7   **Ht:** 6'3" **Wt:** 200 **Born:** 8/6/1992 **Age:** 24

									WHAT HE GAVE UP										THE RESULTS								
Year	Team	Lg	G	GS	CG	GF	IP	BFP	H	R	ER	HR	SH	SF	HB	TBB	IBB	SO	WP	Bk	W	L	Pct	Sh	Sv-Op	Hld	ERC	ERA
2012	2 Tms	Low	12	12	0	0	59.2	273	72	36	33	7	0	2	1	19	0	52	10	2	3	4	.429	0	0--	-	4.97	4.98
2013	Bklyn	A-	13	13	1	0	71.2	293	53	30	23	1	1	2	5	28	0	81	3	2	6	4	.600	1	0--	-	2.39	2.89
2014	Savann	A	21	21	2	0	123.0	510	107	47	35	5	1	2	3	40	0	114	7	1	11	5	.688	2	0--	-	2.79	2.56
2015	Bnghtn	AA	11	11	0	0	59.1	265	67	38	29	2	3	3	1	26	0	43	2	1	4	5	.444	0	0--	-	4.54	4.40
2015	Stluci	A+	6	6	0	0	40.1	162	27	9	8	4	0	1	1	10	0	48	0	0	2	0	1.000	0	0--	-	1.85	1.79
2015	Missi	AA	7	7	0	0	40.2	157	28	11	9	1	3	1	0	14	0	43	2	1	4	0	1.000	0	0--	-	1.90	1.99
2016	Gwnntt	AAA	12	10	0	1	56.0	245	58	29	26	5	1	1	0	22	0	57	7	0	3	3	.500	0	0--	-	4.13	4.18
2016	Atl	NL	20	7	0	6	50.0	222	54	32	27	7	3	2	2	21	3	49	4	0	1	4	.200	0	0-0	0	4.97	4.86

Adonis Garcia

Bats: R **Throws:** R **Pos:** 3B-123;PH-5;LF-4;DH-2   ah-DOH-niss   **Ht:** 5'9" **Wt:** 205 **Born:** 4/12/1985 **Age:** 32

									BATTING												RUNNING			AVERAGES			
Year	Team	Lg	G	AB	H	2B	3B	HR	(Hm	Rd)	TB	R	RBI	RC	TBB	IBB	SO	HBP	SH	SF	SB	CS	GDP	Avg	OBP	Slg	OPS
2012	Tampa	A+	29	106	25	7	1	1	(-	-)	37	11	15	10	9	0	18	0	0	0	0	2	3	.236	.296	.349	.645
2012	Trntn	AA	28	118	34	12	0	4	(-	-)	58	17	14	19	5	0	18	2	0	1	2	1	1	.288	.325	.492	.817
2013	S-WB	AAA	50	199	51	9	1	3	(-	-)	71	17	10	22	11	0	21	5	1	0	4	4	8	.256	.312	.357	.668
2014	S-WB	AAA	86	342	109	20	3	9	(-	-)	162	58	45	58	17	0	51	4	0	5	11	3	12	.319	.353	.474	.827
2015	Gwnntt	AAA	87	331	94	17	1	3	(-	-)	122	43	47	40	15	2	41	1	0	3	5	1	9	.284	.314	.369	.683
2016	Gwnntt	AAA	19	73	26	7	0	4	(-	-)	45	14	18	17	3	0	12	4	0	0	2	1	0	.356	.413	.616	1.029
2015	Atl	NL	58	191	53	12	0	10	(8	2)	95	20	26	16	5	0	35	0	0	2	0	0	9	.277	.293	.497	.790
2016	Atl	NL	134	532	145	29	0	14	(5	9)	216	65	65	60	24	4	93	6	0	0	3	2	18	.273	.311	.406	.717
	2 ML YEARS		192	723	198	41	0	24	(13	11)	311	85	91	76	29	4	128	6	0	2	3	2	27	.274	.307	.430	.737

Avisail Garcia

Bats: R **Throws:** R **Pos:** DH-63;RF-46;LF-11;PH-5   ah-vee-sigh-EEL   **Ht:** 6'4" **Wt:** 240 **Born:** 6/12/1991 **Age:** 26

									BATTING												RUNNING			AVERAGES			
Year	Team	Lg	G	AB	H	2B	3B	HR	(Hm	Rd)	TB	R	RBI	RC	TBB	IBB	SO	HBP	SH	SF	SB	CS	GDP	Avg	OBP	Slg	OPS
2012	Det	AL	23	47	15	0	0	0	(0	0)	15	7	3	5	3	1	10	1	0	0	0	2	1	.319	.373	.319	.692
2013	2 Tms	AL	72	244	69	7	3	7	(3	4)	103	31	31	30	9	0	59	1	0	2	3	3	8	.283	.309	.422	.731
2014	CWS	AL	46	172	42	8	0	7	(2	5)	71	19	29	20	14	1	44	2	0	2	4	1	5	.244	.305	.413	.718
2015	CWS	AL	148	553	142	17	2	13	(8	5)	202	66	59	58	36	3	141	8	0	4	7	7	13	.257	.309	.365	.675
2016	CWS	AL	120	413	101	18	2	12	(5	7)	159	59	51	56	34	0	115	4	0	2	4	4	9	.245	.307	.385	.692
13	Det	AL	30	83	20	3	1	2	(1	1)	31	12	10	7	4	0	21	0	0	1	0	1	3	.241	.273	.373	.646
13	CWS	AL	42	161	49	4	2	5	(2	3)	72	19	21	23	5	0	38	1	0	1	3	2	5	.304	.327	.447	.775
	Postseason		12	23	6	1	0	0	(0	0)	7	0	4	4	2	0	5	0	0	0	1	0	0	.261	.320	.304	.624
	5 ML YEARS		409	1429	369	50	7	39	(18	21)	550	182	173	169	96	5	369	16	0	10	18	17	36	.258	.310	.385	.695

Greg Garcia

Bats: L **Throws:** R **Pos:** 3B-31;SS-30;PH-28;2B-26;PR-4   **Ht:** 6'0" **Wt:** 190 **Born:** 8/8/1989 **Age:** 27

									BATTING												RUNNING			AVERAGES			
Year	Team	Lg	G	AB	H	2B	3B	HR	(Hm	Rd)	TB	R	RBI	RC	TBB	IBB	SO	HBP	SH	SF	SB	CS	GDP	Avg	OBP	Slg	OPS
2016	Memp*	AAA	30	104	28	4	1	0	(-	-)	34	13	8	12	11	1	20	2	3	0	2	2	3	.269	.350	.327	.677
2014	StL	NL	14	14	2	1	0	0	(0	0)	3	2	1	1	1	0	6	3	0	0	0	0	0	.143	.333	.214	.548

Year	Team	Lg	G	AB	H	2B	3B	HR	(Hm	Rd)	TB	R	RBI	RC	TBB	IBB	SO	HBP	SH	SF	SB	CS	GDP	Avg	OBP	Slg	OPS
2015	StL	NL	49	75	18	5	0	2	(1	1)	29	7	4	7	10	1	12	1	1	0	0	0	0	.240	.337	.387	.724
2016	StL	NL	99	214	59	11	0	3	(0	3)	79	33	17	31	38	4	50	4	0	1	1	1	3	.276	.393	.369	.762
	Postseason		3	3	0	0	0	0	(0	0)	0	0	0	0	0	0	1	0	0	0	0	0	0	.000	.000	.000	.000
	3 ML YEARS		162	303	79	17	0	5	(1	4)	111	42	22	39	49	5	68	8	1	1	1	1	5	.261	.377	.366	.743

Jaime Garcia

Pitches: L **Bats:** L **Pos:** SP-30; RP-2   HY-may   **Ht:** 6'2" **Wt:** 215 **Born:** 7/8/1986 **Age:** 30

			HOW MUCH HE PITCHED						WHAT HE GAVE UP										THE RESULTS						
Year	Team	Lg	G	GS	CG	GF	IP	BFP	H	R	ER	HR	SH	SF	HB	TBB	IBB	SO	WP	Bk	W	L	Pct	Sh	Sv-Op	Hld	ERC	ERA
2008	StL	NL	10	1	0	4	16.0	69	14	10	10	4	0	0	1	8	0	8	3	0	1	1	.500	0	0-0	3	5.15	5.63
2010	StL	NL	28	28	1	0	163.1	695	151	64	49	9	3	3	3	64	4	132	4	1	13	8	.619	1	0-0	0	3.34	2.70
2011	StL	NL	32	32	2	0	194.2	826	207	100	77	15	10	5	2	50	2	156	12	1	13	7	.650	2	0-0	0	3.73	3.56
2012	StL	NL	20	20	0	0	121.2	515	136	58	53	7	8	7	0	30	1	98	12	1	7	7	.500	0	0-0	0	3.86	3.92
2013	StL	NL	9	9	0	0	55.1	234	57	26	22	6	2	0	0	15	0	43	3	0	5	2	.714	0	0-0	0	3.78	3.58
2014	StL	NL	7	7	0	0	43.2	177	39	20	20	6	0	0	3	7	0	39	1	0	3	1	.750	0	0-0	0	3.08	4.12
2015	StL	NL	20	20	0	0	129.2	510	106	37	35	6	3	3	3	30	0	97	1	0	10	6	.625	0	0-0	0	2.31	2.43
2016	StL	NL	32	30	1	0	171.2	741	179	94	89	26	7	2	7	57	3	150	8	0	10	13	.435	1	0-0	0	4.56	4.67
	Postseason		7	7	0	0	29.2	132	33	18	13	4	3	0	1	12	2	26	1	0	0	3	.000	0	0-0	0	5.02	3.94
	8 ML YEARS		158	147	4	4	896.0	3767	889	409	355	79	33	20	19	261	10	723	47	3	62	45	.579	4	0-0	3	3.61	3.57

Leury Garcia

Bats: B **Throws:** R **Pos:** CF-16;PR-2   lay-OOH-ree   **Ht:** 5'8" **Wt:** 170 **Born:** 3/18/1991 **Age:** 26

									BATTING											RUNNING			AVERAGES			
Year	Team	Lg	G	AB	H	2B	3B	HR	(Hm | Rd)	TB	R	RBI	RC	TBB	IBB	SO	HBP	SH	SF	SB	CS	GDP	Avg	OBP	Slg	OPS
2016	Charlit*	AAA	84	310	97	9	4	6	(- | -)	132	45	35	50	24	3	64	3	4	1	18	8	6	.313	.367	.426	.793
2013	2 Tms	AL	45	101	20	1	1	0	(0 | 0)	23	10	2	4	7	0	34	0	2	1	7	2	0	.198	.248	.228	.475
2014	CWS	AL	74	145	24	3	0	1	(0 | 1)	30	13	6	0	5	1	48	0	4	1	11	1	6	.166	.192	.207	.399
2015	CWS	AL	18	14	3	0	0	0	(0 | 0)	3	0	1	2	1	0	7	0	0	0	1	0	0	.214	.267	.214	.481
2016	CWS	AL	18	48	11	1	1	1	(1 | 0)	17	6	5	5	1	0	13	1	0	0	2	1	0	.229	.240	.354	.614
13	Tex	AL	25	52	10	0	1	0	(0 | 0)	12	8	1	2	3	0	16	0	2	0	1	0	0	.192	.236	.231	.467
13	CWS	AL	20	49	10	1	0	0	(0 | 0)	11	2	1	2	4	0	18	0	0	1	6	2	0	.204	.259	.224	.484
	4 ML YEARS		155	308	58	5	2	2	(1 | 1)	73	29	14	11	14	1	102	1	6	2	21	4	6	.188	.225	.237	.462

Luis Garcia

Pitches: R **Bats:** R **Pos:** RP-17   **Ht:** 6'3" **Wt:** 230 **Born:** 1/30/1987 **Age:** 30

			HOW MUCH HE PITCHED						WHAT HE GAVE UP										THE RESULTS						
Year	Team	Lg	G	GS	CG	GF	IP	BFP	H	R	ER	HR	SH	SF	HB	TBB	IBB	SO	WP	Bk	W	L	Pct	Sh	Sv-Op	Hld	ERC	ERA
2016	LV*	AAA	48	0	0	26	54.2	219	38	13	13	3	2	1	5	24	0	53	8	1	6	3	.667	0	13- -	-	2.76	2.14
2013	Phi	NL	24	0	0	6	31.1	138	27	15	13	3	0	0	1	23	0	23	3	0	1	1	.500	0	0-0	1	4.85	3.73
2014	Phi	NL	13	0	0	5	14.0	69	14	12	10	2	1	0	0	13	0	12	4	0	1	0	1.000	0	0-0	0	6.43	6.43
2015	Phi	NL	72	0	0	14	66.2	304	72	28	26	4	3	2	0	37	8	63	6	1	4	6	.400	0	2-4	16	4.59	3.51
2016	Phi	NL	17	0	0	7	15.1	76	21	11	11	2	0	1	1	8	1	14	2	0	1	1	.500	0	0-1	1	7.04	6.46
	4 ML YEARS		126	0	0	32	127.1	587	134	66	60	11	4	3	2	81	9	112	15	1	7	8	.467	0	2-5	18	5.14	4.24

Yimi Garcia

Pitches: R **Bats:** R **Pos:** RP-9   YIM-ee   **Ht:** 6'1" **Wt:** 220 **Born:** 8/18/1990 **Age:** 26

			HOW MUCH HE PITCHED						WHAT HE GAVE UP										THE RESULTS						
Year	Team	Lg	G	GS	CG	GF	IP	BFP	H	R	ER	HR	SH	SF	HB	TBB	IBB	SO	WP	Bk	W	L	Pct	Sh	Sv-Op	Hld	ERC	ERA
2014	LAD	NL	8	0	0	5	10.0	36	6	2	2	2	0	0	0	1	0	9	0	0	0	0	-	0	0-0	1	1.59	1.80
2015	LAD	NL	59	1	0	15	56.2	225	44	23	21	8	0	2	2	10	1	68	1	0	3	5	.375	0	1-6	11	2.40	3.34
2016	LAD	NL	9	0	0	1	8.1	35	9	3	3	0	2	2	1	1	0	4	0	0	0	0	-	0	0-2	1	3.23	3.24
	Postseason		1	0	0	0	1.0	4	0	0	0	0	0	0	0	1	0	3	0	0	0	0	-	0	0-0	0	0.95	0.00
	3 ML YEARS		76	1	0	21	75.0	296	59	28	26	10	2	4	3	12	1	81	1	0	3	5	.375	0	1-8	13	2.39	3.12

Brett Gardner

Bats: L **Throws:** L **Pos:** LF-147;PH-5;CF-3;PR-1   **Ht:** 5'11" **Wt:** 195 **Born:** 8/24/1983 **Age:** 33

									BATTING											RUNNING			AVERAGES			
Year	Team	Lg	G	AB	H	2B	3B	HR	(Hm | Rd)	TB	R	RBI	RC	TBB	IBB	SO	HBP	SH	SF	SB	CS	GDP	Avg	OBP	Slg	OPS
2008	NYY	AL	42	127	29	5	2	0	(0 | 0)	38	18	16	17	8	0	30	2	1	3	13	1	0	.228	.283	.299	.582
2009	NYY	AL	108	248	67	6	6	3	(1 | 2)	94	48	23	38	26	0	40	3	6	1	26	5	3	.270	.345	.379	.724
2010	NYY	AL	150	477	132	20	7	5	(5 | 0)	181	97	47	77	79	1	101	5	5	3	47	9	6	.277	.383	.379	.762
2011	NYY	AL	159	510	132	19	8	7	(4 | 3)	188	87	36	77	60	1	93	8	8	2	49	13	5	.259	.345	.369	.713
2012	NYY	AL	16	31	10	2	0	0	(0 | 0)	12	7	3	7	5	0	7	0	1	0	2	2	0	.323	.417	.387	.804
2013	NYY	AL	145	539	147	33	10	8	(6 | 2)	224	81	52	88	52	1	127	8	7	3	24	8	8	.273	.344	.416	.759
2014	NYY	AL	148	555	142	25	8	17	(8 | 9)	234	87	58	81	56	0	134	6	13	6	21	5	3	.256	.327	.422	.749
2015	NYY	AL	151	571	148	26	3	16	(12 | 4)	228	94	66	90	68	1	135	6	3	8	20	5	8	.259	.343	.399	.742
2016	NYY	AL	148	547	143	22	6	7	(5 | 2)	198	80	41	77	70	0	106	8	4	5	16	4	6	.261	.351	.362	.713
	Postseason		34	69	14	1	0	0	(0 | 0)	15	8	7	5	4	0	20	0	2	1	5	2	0	.203	.243	.217	.461
	9 ML YEARS		1067	3605	950	158	50	63	(41 | 22)	1397	599	342	552	424	4	773	46	55	24	218	52	39	.264	.346	.388	.734

Dustin Garneau

Bats: R **Throws:** R **Pos:** C-23;PH-3 | GARR-noh | **Ht:** 6'0" **Wt:** 200 **Born:** 8/13/1987 **Age:** 29

Year	Team	Lg	G	AB	H	2B	3B	HR	(Hm	Rd)	TB	R	RBI	RC	TBB	IBB	SO	HBP	SH	SF	SB	CS	GDP	Avg	OBP	Slg	OPS
2012	Mdest	A+	86	300	73	18	3	6	(-	-)	115	35	29	41	40	0	41	2	2	4	2	3	6	.243	.332	.383	.716
2013	Tulsa	AA	96	326	77	17	1	13	(-	-)	135	36	47	45	25	0	57	13	4	4	4	2	2	.236	.313	.414	.727
2014	Tulsa	AA	34	115	31	7	0	2	(-	-)	44	14	20	17	14	0	19	4	0	2	2	3	2	.270	.363	.383	.746
2014	ColSpr	AAA	44	148	32	9	2	5	(-	-)	60	17	22	18	14	0	21	3	1	0	2	1	4	.216	.297	.405	.702
2015	Albq	AAA	81	303	83	16	0	15	(-	-)	144	44	61	50	28	2	44	2	3	4	2	1	6	.274	.335	.475	.811
2016	Albq	AAA	52	185	54	11	0	15	(-	-)	110	31	35	40	15	0	43	8	1	2	2	0	3	.292	.367	.595	.961
2015	Col	NL	22	70	11	3	0	2	(0	2)	20	6	8	5	6	2	14	0	0	0	0	0	2	.157	.224	.286	.509
2016	Col	NL	24	68	16	6	0	1	(0	1)	25	7	6	6	6	0	22	0	0	1	0	0	1	.235	.293	.368	.661
	2 ML YEARS		46	138	27	9	0	3	(0	3)	45	13	14	11	12	2	36	0	0	1	0	0	3	.196	.258	.326	.584

Perci Garner

Pitches: R **Bats:** R **Pos:** RP-8 | **Ht:** 6'3" **Wt:** 225 **Born:** 12/13/1988 **Age:** 28

			HOW MUCH HE PITCHED					WHAT HE GAVE UP									THE RESULTS						
Year	Team	Lg	G	GS	CG	GF	IP	BFP	H	R	ER	HR	SH	SF	HB	TBB	IBB	SO	WP	Bk	W	L	Pct	Sh	Sv-Op	Hld	ERC	ERA
2012	Clrwtr	A+	26	26	0	0	134.0	597	135	82	72	9	6	7	6	63	0	91	10	1	7	9	.438	0	0- -	-	4.29	4.84
2013	Clrwtr	A+	22	22	0	0	121.1	542	130	75	58	6	3	2	8	62	0	95	10	1	6	6	.500	0	0- -	-	4.89	4.30
2014	Rdng	AA	19	16	0	1	81.2	378	79	53	44	3	2	6	4	62	1	62	6	0	4	5	.444	0	0- -	-	5.02	4.85
2014	Clrwtr	A+	7	0	0	5	12.0	58	9	5	4	0	0	0	0	15	0	13	2	0	0	0	-	0	0- -	-	5.17	3.00
2015	Lynbg	A+	18	1	0	3	30.2	128	27	12	10	0	0	2	1	12	0	33	6	0	3	1	.750	0	1- -	-	2.87	2.93
2016	Akron	AA	23	0	0	9	51.0	198	37	13	11	1	1	1	2	11	0	47	4	0	5	1	.833	0	2- -	-	1.71	1.94
2016	Clmbs	AAA	18	0	0	9	27.2	108	15	5	5	1	1	0	0	11	1	23	1	0	2	0	1.000	0	5- -	-	1.46	1.63
2016	Cle	AL	8	0	0	0	9.1	46	12	6	5	0	0	2	5	1	12	1	0	0	0	-	0	0-0	0	6.12	4.82

Ryan Garton

Pitches: R **Bats:** R **Pos:** RP-37 | **Ht:** 5'11" **Wt:** 185 **Born:** 12/5/1989 **Age:** 27

			HOW MUCH HE PITCHED					WHAT HE GAVE UP									THE RESULTS						
Year	Team	Lg	G	GS	CG	GF	IP	BFP	H	R	ER	HR	SH	SF	HB	TBB	IBB	SO	WP	Bk	W	L	Pct	Sh	Sv-Op	Hld	ERC	ERA
2012	HudVal	A-	21	0	0	13	27.0	108	19	9	6	0	0	0	0	8	0	31	1	1	4	0	1.000	0	7- -	-	1.61	2.00
2013	BG	A	40	0	0	30	70.0	300	54	19	19	3	5	1	5	34	6	62	4	0	4	3	.571	0	8- -	-	2.87	2.44
2014	Charltt	A+	40	0	0	25	67.0	281	61	29	23	3	1	1	1	28	0	44	5	0	6	2	.750	0	4- -	-	3.39	3.09
2015	Mont	AA	41	0	0	8	61.0	259	44	22	20	2	1	1	2	32	1	70	3	0	6	1	.857	0	0- -	-	2.66	2.95
2016	Drham	AAA	22	0	0	5	32.0	138	31	14	11	1	2	2	1	10	0	39	2	0	4	0	1.000	0	2- -	-	3.14	3.09
2016	TB	AL	37	0	0	14	39.1	171	44	20	19	5	1	0	0	11	2	33	2	0	1	2	.333	0	1-1	2	4.33	4.35

Matt Garza

Pitches: R **Bats:** R **Pos:** SP-19 | **Ht:** 6'4" **Wt:** 220 **Born:** 11/26/1983 **Age:** 33

			HOW MUCH HE PITCHED					WHAT HE GAVE UP									THE RESULTS						
Year	Team	Lg	G	GS	CG	GF	IP	BFP	H	R	ER	HR	SH	SF	HB	TBB	IBB	SO	WP	Bk	W	L	Pct	Sh	Sv-Op	Hld	ERC	ERA
2006	Min	AL	10	9	0	0	50.0	232	62	33	32	6	0	3	0	23	0	38	1	0	3	6	.333	0	0-0	0	5.82	5.76
2007	Min	AL	16	15	0	1	83.0	367	96	44	34	8	1	4	4	32	4	67	4	0	5	7	.417	0	0-0	0	5.08	3.69
2008	TB	AL	30	30	3	0	184.2	772	170	83	76	19	3	9	6	59	2	128	3	2	11	9	.550	2	0-0	0	3.47	3.70
2009	TB	AL	32	32	0	0	203.0	861	177	93	89	25	2	8	11	79	0	189	3	0	8	12	.400	0	0-0	0	3.69	3.95
2010	TB	AL	32	32	1	0	204.2	855	193	94	89	28	1	6	7	63	2	150	12	2	15	10	.600	1	1-1	0	3.80	3.91
2011	ChC	NL	31	31	2	0	198.0	839	186	90	73	14	11	2	3	63	5	197	6	0	10	10	.500	0	0-0	0	3.21	3.32
2012	ChC	NL	18	18	0	0	103.2	424	90	48	45	15	5	1	4	32	0	96	1	0	5	7	.417	0	0-0	0	3.50	3.91
2013	2 Tms		24	24	1	0	155.1	652	150	73	66	20	8	3	5	42	3	136	6	0	10	6	.625	0	0-0	0	3.66	3.82
2014	Mil	NL	27	27	1	0	163.1	680	143	77	66	12	9	4	4	50	2	126	3	1	8	8	.500	1	0-0	0	2.92	3.64
2015	Mil	NL	26	25	0	1	148.2	666	176	102	93	23	7	2	2	57	3	104	7	0	6	14	.300	0	0-0	0	5.51	5.63
2016	Mil	NL	19	19	0	0	101.2	461	117	67	51	11	4	4	3	36	2	70	3	0	6	8	.429	0	0-0	0	4.78	4.51
13	ChC	NL	11	11	0	0	71.0	293	61	26	25	8	2	1	4	20	2	62	2	0	6	1	.857	0	0-0	0	3.12	3.17
13	Tex	AL	13	13	1	0	84.1	359	89	47	41	12	6	2	1	22	1	74	4	0	4	5	.444	0	0-0	0	4.14	4.38
	Postseason		5	5	0	0	31.0	131	26	13	12	5	0	1	4	14	0	29	2	0	2	1	.667	0	0-0	0	3.95	3.48
	11 ML YEARS		266	262	10	3	1596.0	6809	1560	804	714	181	51	46	49	536	23	1301	49	5	87	97	.473	4	1-1	0	3.88	4.03

Evan Gattis

Bats: R **Throws:** R **Pos:** DH-71;C-55;PH-11 | GAT-iss | **Ht:** 6'4" **Wt:** 270 **Born:** 8/18/1986 **Age:** 30

Year	Team	Lg	G	AB	H	2B	3B	HR	(Hm	Rd)	TB	R	RBI	RC	TBB	IBB	SO	HBP	SH	SF	SB	CS	GDP	Avg	OBP	Slg	OPS
2016	CpChr*	AA	11	40	15	2	0	5	(-	-)	32	8	10	11	1	0	4	1	0	0	0	0	0	.375	.405	.800	1.205
2013	Atl	NL	105	354	86	21	0	21	(8	13)	170	44	65	43	21	4	81	4	0	3	0	0	10	.243	.291	.480	.771
2014	Atl	NL	108	369	97	17	1	22	(12	10)	182	41	52	45	22	3	97	8	0	2	0	0	9	.263	.317	.493	.810
2015	Hou	AL	153	566	139	20	11	27	(15	12)	262	66	88	73	30	3	119	3	0	5	0	1	13	.246	.285	.463	.748
2016	Hou	AL	128	447	112	19	0	32	(19	13)	227	58	72	64	43	6	127	4	0	5	2	1	12	.251	.319	.508	.826
	Postseason		10	37	9	0	0	0	(0	0)	9	4	2	3	2	0	9	0	0	0	0	0	1	.243	.282	.243	.525
	4 ML YEARS		494	1736	434	77	12	102	(54	48)	841	209	277	225	116	16	424	19	0	15	2	2	44	.250	.302	.484	.786

Kevin Gausman

Pitches: R **Bats:** L **Pos:** SP-30 GAHZ-man **Ht:** 6'3" **Wt:** 190 **Born:** 1/6/1991 **Age:** 26

			HOW MUCH HE PITCHED					WHAT HE GAVE UP											THE RESULTS						
Year	Team	Lg	G	GS	CG	GF	IP	BFP	H	R	ER	HR	SH	SF	HB	TBB	IBB	SO	WP	Bk	W	L	Pct	Sh	Sv-Op	Hld	ERC	ERA
2013	Bal	AL	20	5	0	3	47.2	201	51	30	30	8	2	1	0	13	2	49	4	0	3	5	.375	0	0-2	2	4.41	5.66
2014	Bal	AL	20	20	1	0	113.1	476	111	48	45	7	3	7	1	38	0	88	9	0	7	7	.500	0	0-0	0	3.52	3.57
2015	Bal	AL	25	17	0	1	112.1	470	109	56	53	17	2	3	2	29	1	103	7	0	4	7	.364	0	0-0	1	3.74	4.25
2016	Bal	AL	30	30	0	0	179.2	757	183	76	72	28	4	3	5	47	1	174	8	0	9	12	.429	0	0-0	0	4.13	3.61
	Postseason		3	0	0	1	8.0	27	4	1	1	0	0	1	0	2	0	7	0	0	0	0	-	0	0-0	0	1.05	1.13
	4 ML YEARS		95	72	1	4	453.0	1904	454	210	200	60	11	14	8	127	4	414	28	0	23	31	.426	0	0-2	3	3.91	3.97

Cory Gearrin

Pitches: R **Bats:** R **Pos:** RP-56 GARE-inn **Ht:** 6'3" **Wt:** 200 **Born:** 4/14/1986 **Age:** 31

			HOW MUCH HE PITCHED					WHAT HE GAVE UP											THE RESULTS						
Year	Team	Lg	G	GS	CG	GF	IP	BFP	H	R	ER	HR	SH	SF	HB	TBB	IBB	SO	WP	Bk	W	L	Pct	Sh	Sv-Op	Hld	ERC	ERA
2016	Scrmto*	AAA	8	0	0	1	8.0	29	5	1	1	0	0	0	0	2	0	9	1	0	0	0	-	0	0- -	-	1.37	1.13
2011	Atl	NL	18	0	0	4	18.1	85	17	16	16	0	0	1	2	12	4	25	1	0	1	1	.500	0	0-1	3	3.84	7.85
2012	Atl	NL	22	0	0	7	20.0	80	17	4	4	1	0	0	2	5	0	20	2	0	0	1	.000	0	0-1	4	2.86	1.80
2013	Atl	NL	37	0	0	12	31.0	133	30	13	13	2	1	0	4	16	2	23	3	0	2	1	.667	0	1-3	1	4.73	3.77
2015	SF	NL	7	0	0	0	3.2	13	1	2	2	0	0	0	0	1	0	5	0	0	0	0	-	0	0-0	3	0.47	4.91
2016	SF	NL	56	0	0	10	48.1	197	42	24	23	4	0	2	1	14	2	45	1	0	3	2	.600	0	3-7	15	2.89	4.28
	5 ML YEARS		140	0	0	33	121.1	508	107	59	58	7	1	3	9	48	8	118	7	0	6	5	.545	0	4-12	26	3.37	4.30

Dillon Gee

Pitches: R **Bats:** R **Pos:** RP-19; SP-14 JEE **Ht:** 6'1" **Wt:** 205 **Born:** 4/28/1986 **Age:** 31

			HOW MUCH HE PITCHED					WHAT HE GAVE UP											THE RESULTS						
Year	Team	Lg	G	GS	CG	GF	IP	BFP	H	R	ER	HR	SH	SF	HB	TBB	IBB	SO	WP	Bk	W	L	Pct	Sh	Sv-Op	Hld	ERC	ERA
2010	NYM	NL	5	5	0	0	33.0	136	25	10	8	2	3	0	0	15	2	17	0	0	2	2	.500	0	0-0	0	2.66	2.18
2011	NYM	NL	30	27	1	1	160.2	706	150	85	79	18	10	5	14	71	4	114	6	1	13	6	.684	0	0-0	0	4.23	4.43
2012	NYM	NL	17	17	0	0	109.2	463	108	56	50	12	2	3	6	29	0	97	0	1	6	7	.462	0	0-0	0	3.74	4.10
2013	NYM	NL	32	32	2	0	199.0	841	208	84	80	24	9	3	7	47	0	142	4	0	12	11	.522	0	0-0	0	3.97	3.62
2014	NYM	NL	22	22	0	0	137.1	570	128	61	61	18	7	3	5	43	0	94	3	1	7	8	.467	0	0-0	0	3.77	4.00
2015	NYM	NL	8	7	0	0	39.2	183	55	29	26	5	2	2	1	11	3	25	0	0	0	3	.000	0	0-0	0	5.98	5.90
2016	KC	AL	33	14	0	3	125.0	551	146	67	65	24	3	3	6	37	3	89	1	1	8	9	.471	0	0-0	0	5.47	4.68
	7 ML YEARS		147	124	3	4	804.1	3450	820	392	369	103	36	19	39	253	12	578	14	4	48	46	.511	0	0-0	0	4.22	4.13

Steve Geltz

Pitches: R **Bats:** R **Pos:** RP-27 **Ht:** 5'10" **Wt:** 210 **Born:** 11/1/1987 **Age:** 29

			HOW MUCH HE PITCHED					WHAT HE GAVE UP											THE RESULTS						
Year	Team	Lg	G	GS	CG	GF	IP	BFP	H	R	ER	HR	SH	SF	HB	TBB	IBB	SO	WP	Bk	W	L	Pct	Sh	Sv-Op	Hld	ERC	ERA
2016	Drham*	AAA	31	0	0	16	35.2	152	30	13	12	3	2	0	1	17	0	40	5	0	0	2	.000	0	3- -	-	3.50	3.03
2012	LAA	AL	2	0	0	2	2.0	11	2	1	1	0	0	1	0	3	0	1	0	0	0	0	-	0	0-0	0	7.45	4.50
2014	TB	AL	11	0	0	1	8.1	37	6	3	3	0	0	2	5	0	14	0	0	0	1	.000	0	0-1	0	6.25	3.24
2015	TB	AL	70	2	0	12	67.1	269	45	31	28	8	2	0	2	26	3	61	4	0	2	6	.250	0	2-5	20	2.48	3.74
2016	TB	AL	27	0	0	11	26.2	112	24	17	17	11	0	1	1	9	0	23	3	0	0	2	.000	0	0-1	1	5.51	5.74
	4 ML YEARS		110	2	0	26	104.1	429	77	52	49	22	2	2	5	43	3	99	7	0	2	9	.182	0	2-7	21	3.59	4.23

Scooter Gennett

Bats: L **Throws:** R **Pos:** 2B-127;PH-13;DH-1 jen-ETT **Ht:** 5'10" **Wt:** 185 **Born:** 5/1/1990 **Age:** 27

			BATTING																		RUNNING			AVERAGES			
Year	Team	Lg	G	AB	H	2B	3B	HR	(Hm	Rd)	TB	R	RBI	RC	TBB	IBB	SO	HBP	SH	SF	SB	CS	GDP	Avg	OBP	Slg	OPS
2013	Mil	NL	69	213	69	11	2	6	(0	6)	102	29	21	35	10	0	42	1	5	1	2	1	0	.324	.356	.479	.834
2014	Mil	NL	137	440	127	31	3	9	(6	3)	191	55	54	59	22	5	67	0	8	4	6	3	11	.289	.320	.434	.754
2015	Mil	NL	114	375	99	18	4	6	(5	1)	143	42	29	36	12	5	68	4	0	0	1	3	11	.264	.294	.381	.675
2016	Mil	NL	136	498	131	30	1	14	(8	6)	205	58	56	61	38	1	114	2	1	2	8	1	11	.263	.317	.412	.728
	4 ML YEARS		456	1526	426	90	10	35	(19	16)	641	184	160	191	82	11	291	7	14	7	17	8	33	.279	.318	.420	.738

Craig Gentry

Bats: R **Throws:** R **Pos:** LF-12;PR-3;CF-1;PH-1 JEN-tree **Ht:** 6'2" **Wt:** 190 **Born:** 11/29/1983 **Age:** 33

			BATTING																		RUNNING			AVERAGES			
Year	Team	Lg	G	AB	H	2B	3B	HR	(Hm	Rd)	TB	R	RBI	RC	TBB	IBB	SO	HBP	SH	SF	SB	CS	GDP	Avg	OBP	Slg	OPS
2009	Tex	AL	11	17	2	1	0	0	(0	0)	3	4	1	1	2	0	5	0	0	0	0	0	0	.118	.211	.176	.387
2010	Tex	AL	20	33	7	0	0	0	(0	0)	7	4	3	1	1	0	11	0	0	1	1	0	1	.212	.229	.212	.441
2011	Tex	AL	64	133	36	5	1	1	(1	0)	46	26	13	21	10	1	27	6	3	1	18	0	2	.271	.347	.346	.693
2012	Tex	AL	122	240	73	12	3	1	(0	1)	94	31	26	33	14	1	41	10	5	0	13	7	4	.304	.367	.392	.759
2013	Tex	AL	106	246	69	12	4	2	(2	0)	95	39	22	42	29	2	46	8	3	1	24	3	5	.280	.373	.386	.759
2014	Oak	AL	94	232	59	6	1	0	(0	0)	67	38	12	27	17	2	44	5	2	0	20	2	2	.254	.319	.289	.608
2015	Oak	AL	26	50	6	0	2	0	(0	0)	10	6	3	2	4	0	15	1	0	1	1	1	0	.120	.196	.200	.396
2016	LAA	AL	14	34	5	1	0	0	(0	0)	6	2	2	1	3	0	6	1	1	0	0	0	2	.147	.237	.176	.413
	Postseason		14	17	5	0	0	0	(0	0)	5	2	1	3	1	0	4	1	1	0	2	1	0	.294	.368	.294	.663
	8 ML YEARS		457	985	257	37	11	4	(3	1)	328	150	82	128	80	6	195	31	14	4	77	13	16	.261	.335	.333	.668

Gonzalez Germen

Pitches: R Bats: R Pos: RP-40 | hare-MEN | Ht: 6'1" Wt: 200 Born: 9/23/1987 Age: 29

		HOW MUCH HE PITCHED						WHAT HE GAVE UP									THE RESULTS						
Year Team	Lg	G	GS	CG	GF	IP	BFP	H	R	ER	HR	SH	SF	HB	TBB	IBB	SO	WP	Bk	W	L	Pct	Sh	Sv-Op	Hld	ERC	ERA
2016 Albq*	AAA	11	0	0	5	13.2	58	11	4	1	0	1	0	1	5	1	16	1	0	1	0	1.000	0	3- -	-	2.08	0.66
2013 NYM	NL	29	0	0	8	34.1	149	32	15	15	1	0	0	0	16	1	33	2	0	1	2	.333	0	1-3	1	3.37	3.93
2014 NYM	NL	25	0	0	9	30.1	133	30	16	16	7	1	0	1	14	1	31	1	0	0	0	-	0	0-1	0	5.31	4.75
2015 2 Tms	NL	35	1	0	9	38.2	176	41	19	19	4	1	0	0	26	3	33	3	0	0	0	-	0	1-3	2	5.50	4.42
2016 Col	NL	40	0	0	8	40.2	182	41	25	24	5	1	1	1	25	3	32	5	0	2	1	.667	0	1-2	0	5.22	5.31
15 ChC	NL	6	0	0	2	6.0	29	8	5	5	0	1	0	0	5	2	8	0	0	0	0	-	0	0-0	0	6.58	7.50
15 Col	NL	29	1	0	3	32.2	147	33	14	14	4	0	0	0	21	1	25	3	0	0	0	-	0	1-3	2	5.29	3.86
4 ML YEARS		129	1	0	30	144.0	640	144	75	74	17	3	1	2	81	8	129	11	0	3	3	.500	0	3-9	3	4.86	4.63

Johnny Giavotella

Bats: R Throws: R Pos: 2B-97;PH-2;PR-2 | gee-uh-vo-TELL-uh | Ht: 5'8" Wt: 185 Born: 7/10/1987 Age: 29

							BATTING													RUNNING			AVERAGES			
Year Team	Lg	G	AB	H	2B	3B	HR	(Hm	Rd)	TB	R	RBI	RC	TBB	IBB	SO	HBP	SH	SF	SB	CS	GDP	Avg	OBP	Slg	OPS
2011 KC	AL	46	178	44	9	4	2	(2	0)	67	20	21	15	6	0	32	1	0	2	5	2	4	.247	.273	.376	.649
2012 KC	AL	53	181	43	7	1	1	(1	0)	55	21	15	14	8	0	35	0	0	0	3	0	4	.238	.270	.304	.574
2013 KC	AL	14	41	9	3	0	0	(0	0)	12	4	4	5	5	0	4	2	0	0	0	0	0	.220	.333	.293	.626
2014 KC	AL	12	37	8	1	0	1	(0	1)	12	8	5	2	1	0	5	2	0	1	0	1	1	.216	.268	.324	.593
2015 LAA	AL	129	453	123	25	5	4	(3	1)	170	51	49	63	32	0	59	2	9	6	2	1	7	.272	.318	.375	.694
2016 LAA	AL	99	346	90	20	1	6	(3	3)	130	44	31	31	13	0	39	1	4	3	4	3	11	.260	.287	.376	.662
6 ML YEARS		353	1236	317	65	11	14	(9	5)	446	148	125	130	65	0	174	8	13	12	14	7	27	.256	.295	.361	.656

Kyle Gibson

Pitches: R Bats: R Pos: SP-25 | | Ht: 6'6" Wt: 215 Born: 10/23/1987 Age: 29

		HOW MUCH HE PITCHED						WHAT HE GAVE UP									THE RESULTS						
Year Team	Lg	G	GS	CG	GF	IP	BFP	H	R	ER	HR	SH	SF	HB	TBB	IBB	SO	WP	Bk	W	L	Pct	Sh	Sv-Op	Hld	ERC	ERA
2013 Min	AL	10	10	0	0	51.0	238	69	38	37	7	0	2	5	20	0	29	4	0	2	4	.333	0	0-0	0	6.98	6.53
2014 Min	AL	31	31	0	0	179.1	757	178	91	89	12	4	3	2	57	0	107	11	0	13	12	.520	0	0-0	0	3.54	4.47
2015 Min	AL	32	32	1	0	194.2	821	186	88	83	16	6	3	6	65	6	145	7	0	11	11	.500	0	0-0	0	3.63	3.84
2016 Min	AL	25	25	1	0	147.1	653	175	89	83	20	3	4	4	55	3	104	9	0	6	11	.353	0	0-0	0	5.47	5.07
4 ML YEARS		98	98	2	0	572.1	2469	608	306	292	57	13	15	18	197	9	385	31	0	32	38	.457	0	0-0	0	4.33	4.59

Ken Giles

Pitches: R Bats: R Pos: RP-69 | | Ht: 6'2" Wt: 205 Born: 9/20/1990 Age: 26

		HOW MUCH HE PITCHED						WHAT HE GAVE UP									THE RESULTS						
Year Team	Lg	G	GS	CG	GF	IP	BFP	H	R	ER	HR	SH	SF	HB	TBB	IBB	SO	WP	Bk	W	L	Pct	Sh	Sv-Op	Hld	ERC	ERA
2014 Phi	NL	44	0	0	11	45.2	166	25	7	6	1	2	1	0	11	1	64	1	0	3	1	.750	0	1-1	13	1.15	1.18
2015 Phi	NL	69	0	0	28	70.0	298	59	23	14	2	1	2	1	25	2	87	1	0	6	3	.667	0	15-20	12	2.53	1.80
2016 Hou	AL	69	0	0	24	65.2	286	60	32	30	8	2	1	2	25	1	102	14	0	2	5	.286	0	15-20	18	3.66	4.11
3 ML YEARS		182	0	0	63	181.1	750	144	62	50	11	5	4	3	61	4	253	16	0	11	9	.550	0	31-41	43	2.49	2.48

Conor Gillaspie

Bats: L Throws: R Pos: PH-57;3B-45;1B-7;PR-1 | guh-LESS-pee | Ht: 6'1" Wt: 195 Born: 7/18/1987 Age: 29

							BATTING													RUNNING			AVERAGES			
Year Team	Lg	G	AB	H	2B	3B	HR	(Hm	Rd)	TB	R	RBI	RC	TBB	IBB	SO	HBP	SH	SF	SB	CS	GDP	Avg	OBP	Slg	OPS
2016 Scrmto*	AAA	12	51	16	3	0	1	(-	-)	22	6	4	7	1	0	6	0	0	0	1	0	1	.314	.327	.431	.758
2008 SF	NL	8	5	1	0	0	0	(0	0)	1	1	0	1	2	0	0	0	0	0	0	0	0	.200	.429	.200	.629
2011 SF	NL	15	19	5	0	0	1	(1	0)	8	2	2	4	2	0	1	0	0	0	0	0	0	.263	.333	.421	.754
2012 SF	NL	6	20	3	1	0	0	(0	0)	4	2	2	0	0	0	2	0	0	0	0	0	0	.150	.150	.200	.350
2013 CWS	AL	134	408	100	14	3	13	(8	5)	159	46	40	46	37	4	79	1	0	6	0	1	7	.245	.305	.390	.695
2014 CWS	AL	130	464	131	31	5	7	(3	4)	193	50	57	68	36	4	78	3	0	3	0	4	5	.282	.336	.416	.752
2015 2 Tms	AL	75	237	54	15	2	4	(3	1)	85	14	24	20	13	2	47	1	0	2	0	1	4	.228	.269	.359	.627
2016 SF	NL	101	191	50	8	4	6	(3	3)	84	24	25	23	12	3	28	1	0	1	1	2	3	.262	.307	.440	.747
15 CWS	AL	58	173	41	11	1	3	(2	1)	63	10	15	14	9	1	34	1	0	2	0	1	2	.237	.276	.364	.640
15 LAA	AL	17	64	13	4	1	1	(1	0)	22	4	9	6	4	1	13	0	0	0	0	0	2	.203	.250	.344	.594
7 ML YEARS		469	1344	344	69	14	31	(18	13)	534	139	150	162	102	13	235	6	0	12	1	8	17	.256	.309	.397	.706

Cole Gillespie

Bats: R Throws: R Pos: PH-32;LF-4;RF-3;1B-1;CF-1 | gil-EH-spee | Ht: 6'2" Wt: 215 Born: 6/20/1984 Age: 33

							BATTING													RUNNING			AVERAGES			
Year Team	Lg	G	AB	H	2B	3B	HR	(Hm	Rd)	TB	R	RBI	RC	TBB	IBB	SO	HBP	SH	SF	SB	CS	GDP	Avg	OBP	Slg	OPS
2016 NewOr*	AAA	37	121	23	5	0	1	(-	-)	31	7	11	9	14	0	23	1	0	0	1	0	3	.190	.279	.256	.536
2010 Ari	NL	45	104	24	8	0	2	(2	0)	38	11	12	10	7	1	29	1	0	1	1	1	2	.231	.283	.365	.649
2011 Ari	NL	5	6	2	0	1	0	(1	0)	5	2	4	3	1	0	1	0	0	0	0	0	0	.333	.429	.833	1.262
2013 2 Tms	NL	28	59	12	2	0	0	(0	0)	14	6	4	5	7	1	13	1	1	0	0	0	2	.203	.294	.237	.531
2014 2 Tms	AL	35	74	18	2	0	1	(0	1)	23	9	5	7	6	0	13	0	0	0	2	2	3	.243	.300	.311	.611
2015 Mia	NL	67	145	42	10	2	2	(1	1)	62	17	16	21	10	0	27	0	1	1	4	1	5	.290	.333	.428	.761
2016 Mia	NL	41	51	12	3	2	0	(0	0)	19	7	5	5	3	0	14	0	0	1	0	0	1	.235	.273	.373	.645
13 SF	NL	3	9	0	0	0	0	(0	0)	0	0	0	0	1	1	0	0	0	0	0	0	0	.000	.100	.000	.100
13 ChC	NL	25	50	12	2	0	0	(0	0)	14	6	4	5	6	0	13	1	1	0	0	0	2	.240	.328	.280	.608
14 Sea	AL	34	71	18	2	0	1	(0	1)	23	9	5	7	6	0	13	0	0	0	2	2	3	.254	.312	.324	.636
14 Tor	AL	1	3	0	0	0	0	(0	0)	0	0	0	0	0	0	0	0	0	0	0	0	0	.000	.000	.000	.000
6 ML YEARS		221	439	110	25	4	6	(4	2)	161	52	46	51	34	2	97	2	3	4	7	4	13	.251	.305	.367	.672

Sean Gilmartin

Pitches: L **Bats:** L **Pos:** RP-13; SP-1   **Ht:** 6'2" **Wt:** 200 **Born:** 5/8/1990 **Age:** 27

		HOW MUCH HE PITCHED						WHAT HE GAVE UP											THE RESULTS							
Year Team	Lg	G	GS	CG	GF	IP	BFP	H	R	ER	HR	SH	SF	HB	TBB	IBB	SO	WP	Bk	W	L	Pct	Sh	Sv-Op	Hld	ERC	ERA
2012 Missi	AA	20	20	3	0	119.1	483	111	49	47	9	3	2	4	26	0	86	2	1	5	8	.385	0	0- -	-	3.02	3.54
2012 Gwnntt	AAA	7	7	0	0	37.2	167	41	22	20	6	3	1	0	13	1	25	0	0	1	2	.333	0	0- -	-	4.63	4.78
2013 Gwnntt	AAA	17	17	0	0	91.0	412	112	61	58	12	3	6	1	33	1	65	4	0	3	8	.273	0	0- -	-	5.50	5.74
2014 NwBrit	AA	12	12	0	0	72.0	302	76	30	25	2	3	4	3	16	0	74	3	1	7	3	.700	0	0- -	-	3.39	3.13
2014 Roch	AAA	14	14	0	0	73.2	308	69	39	35	7	2	1	1	28	1	59	3	0	2	4	.333	0	0- -	-	3.71	4.28
2016 LsVgs	AAA	19	18	1	1	107.1	469	122	63	58	12	4	3	0	31	0	94	6	0	9	7	.563	0	0- -	-	4.44	4.86
2015 NYM	NL	50	1	0	13	57.1	235	50	17	17	2	2	1	2	18	5	54	1	0	3	2	.600	0	0-1	2	2.67	2.67
2016 NYM	NL	14	1	0	3	17.2	79	21	14	14	4	1	0	1	7	1	11	0	0	0	1	.000	0	0-0	1	6.39	7.13
Postseason		1	0	0	1	0.2	2	0	0	0	0	0	0	0	0	0	0	0	0	0	0	-	0	0-0	0	0.00	0.00
2 ML YEARS		64	2	0	16	75.0	314	71	31	31	6	3	1	3	25	6	65	1	0	3	3	.500	0	0-1	3	3.46	3.72

Chris Gimenez

Bats: R **Throws:** R **Pos:** C-59;1B-4;3B-3;DH-1;PH-1   JIMM-inn-ezz   **Ht:** 6'2" **Wt:** 230 **Born:** 12/27/1982 **Age:** 34

		BATTING																	RUNNING			AVERAGES			
Year Team	Lg	G	AB	H	2B	3B	HR	(Hm | Rd)	TB	R	RBI	RC	TBB	IBB	SO	HBP	SH	SF	SB	CS	GDP	Avg	OBP	Slg	OPS
2009 Cle	AL	45	111	16	2	0	3	(0 | 3)	27	12	7	3	17	0	36	0	1	1	1	1	3	.144	.256	.243	.499
2010 Cle	AL	28	58	11	5	0	1	(1 | 0)	19	6	8	5	8	0	22	0	1	0	0	0	1	.190	.288	.328	.615
2011 Sea	AL	24	59	12	1	0	1	(0 | 1)	16	6	6	5	10	0	13	0	0	1	0	1	1	.203	.314	.271	.585
2012 TB	AL	42	100	26	4	0	1	(0 | 1)	33	10	9	10	8	0	24	0	1	0	0	0	4	.260	.315	.330	.645
2013 TB	AL	4	3	1	1	0	0	(0 | 0)	2	0	0	0	1	0	1	0	0	0	0	0	0	.333	.500	.667	1.167
2014 2 Tms	AL	42	116	28	10	0	0	(0 | 0)	38	13	11	12	12	1	29	0	0	0	0	1	3	.241	.313	.328	.640
2015 Tex	AL	36	98	25	6	1	5	(3 | 2)	48	19	14	15	10	0	19	1	4	0	2	0	2	.255	.330	.490	.820
2016 Cle	AL	68	139	30	4	0	4	(1 | 3)	46	17	11	8	10	0	41	1	4	1	0	0	8	.216	.272	.331	.602
14 Tex	AL	34	107	28	10	0	0	(0 | 0)	38	13	11	12	11	1	26	0	0	0	0	1	3	.262	.331	.355	.686
14 Cle	AL	8	9	0	0	0	0	(0 | 0)	0	0	0	0	1	0	3	0	0	0	0	0	0	.000	.100	.000	.100
Postseason		2	8	2	0	0	0	(0 | 0)	2	1	0	0	0	0	1	0	1	0	0	0	0	.250	.250	.250	.500
8 ML YEARS		289	684	149	33	1	15	(5 | 10)	229	83	66	58	76	1	185	2	11	3	3	3	23	.218	.297	.335	.632

Lucas Giolito

Pitches: R **Bats:** R **Pos:** SP-4; RP-2   jee-oh-LEE-toh   **Ht:** 6'6" **Wt:** 255 **Born:** 7/14/1994 **Age:** 22

		HOW MUCH HE PITCHED						WHAT HE GAVE UP											THE RESULTS							
Year Team	Lg	G	GS	CG	GF	IP	BFP	H	R	ER	HR	SH	SF	HB	TBB	IBB	SO	WP	Bk	W	L	Pct	Sh	Sv-Op	Hld	ERC	ERA
2013 2 Tms	Low	11	11	0	0	36.2	147	28	9	8	1	0	2	2	14	0	39	5	0	2	1	.667	0	0- -	-	2.58	1.96
2014 Hgrstn	A	20	20	0	0	98.0	386	70	28	24	7	0	1	1	28	0	110	1	0	10	2	.833	0	0- -	-	2.07	2.20
2015 Ptomc	A+	13	11	0	0	69.2	292	65	24	21	1	2	1	3	20	0	86	7	1	3	5	.375	0	0- -	-	2.86	2.71
2015 Hrsbrg	AA	8	8	0	0	47.1	202	48	21	20	2	1	0	3	17	0	45	2	0	4	2	.667	0	0- -	-	3.90	3.80
2016 Hrsbrg	AA	14	14	0	0	71.0	313	67	37	25	2	3	1	4	34	0	72	3	0	5	3	.625	0	0- -	-	3.73	3.17
2016 Syrcse	AAA	7	7	0	0	37.1	149	31	11	9	3	0	0	1	10	0	40	1	0	1	2	.333	0	0- -	-	2.71	2.17
2016 Was	NL	6	4	0	1	21.1	101	26	18	16	7	0	0	0	12	0	11	1	1	0	1	.000	0	0-0	0	8.14	6.75

Chad Girodo

Pitches: L **Bats:** L **Pos:** RP-14   jih-ROD-oh   **Ht:** 6'1" **Wt:** 190 **Born:** 2/6/1991 **Age:** 26

		HOW MUCH HE PITCHED						WHAT HE GAVE UP											THE RESULTS							
Year Team	Lg	G	GS	CG	GF	IP	BFP	H	R	ER	HR	SH	SF	HB	TBB	IBB	SO	WP	Bk	W	L	Pct	Sh	Sv-Op	Hld	ERC	ERA
2013 Lnsng	A	14	0	0	4	23.2	96	21	11	11	0	2	0	0	5	0	24	1	0	1	1	.500	0	0- -	-	2.14	4.18
2014 Dnedin	A+	47	1	0	19	76.2	316	70	25	21	2	1	2	3	20	1	81	2	0	7	3	.700	0	3- -	-	2.74	2.47
2015 Dnedin	A+	20	0	0	10	27.1	106	17	4	4	1	0	0	2	7	0	32	0	1	2	2	.500	0	0- -	-	1.60	1.32
2015 Nham	AA	21	0	0	13	29.0	110	26	3	2	0	0	0	0	2	0	23	0	0	2	0	1.000	0	2- -	-	1.82	0.62
2016 Buffalo	AAA	29	0	0	7	35.2	155	45	16	15	5	1	1	0	13	0	24	0	0	2	1	.667	0	1- -	-	6.03	3.79
2016 Tor	AL	14	0	0	2	10.1	44	11	5	5	3	0	0	1	2	0	5	1	0	0	0	-	0	0-0	0	5.34	4.35

Mychal Givens

Pitches: R **Bats:** R **Pos:** RP-66   michael   **Ht:** 6'0" **Wt:** 210 **Born:** 5/13/1990 **Age:** 27

		HOW MUCH HE PITCHED						WHAT HE GAVE UP											THE RESULTS							
Year Team	Lg	G	GS	CG	GF	IP	BFP	H	R	ER	HR	SH	SF	HB	TBB	IBB	SO	WP	Bk	W	L	Pct	Sh	Sv-Op	Hld	ERC	ERA
2013 Dlmrva	A	28	0	0	12	42.2	179	34	20	20	1	1	3	4	19	0	36	11	1	2	3	.400	0	3- -	-	2.92	4.22
2014 Frdrck	A+	18	0	0	6	33.1	141	21	20	12	2	1	1	2	16	0	27	4	3	1	2	.333	0	3- -	-	2.31	3.24
2014 Bowie	AA	18	0	0	8	25.1	122	19	12	11	0	2	0	6	23	0	28	9	0	0	0	-	0	0- -	-	4.68	3.91
2015 Bowie	AA	35	0	0	20	57.1	227	38	14	11	1	1	2	3	16	0	79	9	0	4	2	.667	0	15- -	-	1.64	1.73
2015 Bal	AL	22	0	0	5	30.0	117	20	7	6	1	1	1	1	6	0	38	0	0	2	0	1.000	0	0-0	4	1.49	1.80
2016 Bal	AL	66	0	0	8	74.2	313	59	28	26	6	2	1	6	36	2	96	3	0	8	2	.800	0	0-1	13	3.44	3.13
2 ML YEARS		88	0	0	13	104.2	430	79	35	32	7	3	2	7	42	2	134	3	0	10	2	.833	0	0-1	17	2.81	2.75

Tyler Glasnow

Pitches: R **Bats:** L **Pos:** SP-4; RP-3   **Ht:** 6'8" **Wt:** 225 **Born:** 8/23/1993 **Age:** 23

		HOW MUCH HE PITCHED						WHAT HE GAVE UP											THE RESULTS							
Year Team	Lg	G	GS	CG	GF	IP	BFP	H	R	ER	HR	SH	SF	HB	TBB	IBB	SO	WP	Bk	W	L	Pct	Sh	Sv-Op	Hld	ERC	ERA
2012 2 Tms	Low	12	11	0	0	38.1	157	23	17	8	3	0	1	2	17	0	44	5	0	0	3	.000	0	0- -	-	2.18	1.88
2013 WV	A	24	24	0	0	111.1	452	54	35	27	9	2	1	9	61	0	164	11	1	9	3	.750	0	0- -	-	2.13	2.18
2014 Bradtn	A+	23	23	0	0	124.1	493	74	29	24	3	3	5	3	57	0	157	5	2	12	5	.706	0	0- -	-	1.87	1.74

Year	Team	Lg	G	GS	CG	GF	IP	BFP	H	R	ER	HR	SH	SF	HB	TBB	IBB	SO	WP	Bk	W	L	Pct	Sh	Sv-Op	Hld	ERC	ERA
2015	Altna	AA	12	12	0	0	63.0	248	41	22	17	2	1	3	0	19	0	82	4	0	5	3	.625	0	0- -	-	1.59	2.43
2015	Indy	AAA	8	8	0	0	41.0	174	33	16	10	1	1	0	1	22	0	48	2	0	2	1	.667	0	0- -	-	3.13	2.20
2016	Indy	AAA	20	20	0	0	110.2	438	65	23	23	4	2	2	0	62	0	133	6	0	8	3	.727	0	0- -	-	2.20	1.87
2016	Pit	NL	7	4	0	0	23.1	105	22	13	11	2	1	0	3	13	0	24	2	1	0	2	.000	0	0-0	0	4.80	4.24

Koda Glover

Pitches: R Bats: R Pos: RP-19   Ht: 6'5" Wt: 225 Born: 4/13/1993 Age: 24

Year	Team	Lg	G	GS	CG	GF	IP	BFP	H	R	ER	HR	SH	SF	HB	TBB	IBB	SO	WP	Bk	W	L	Pct	Sh	Sv-Op	Hld	ERC	ERA
2015	2 Tms	Low	19	0	0	15	30.0	117	22	8	6	2	2	1	2	0	38	0	0	1	1	.500	0	5- -	-	1.50	1.80
2016	Ptomc	A+	7	0	0	5	9.2	36	3	0	0	0	0	0	0	4	0	15	0	0	0	0	-	0	2- -	-	0.76	0.00
2016	Hrsbrg	AA	17	0	0	12	22.1	93	20	9	8	1	2	0	0	7	0	29	0	0	2	0	1.000	0	4- -	-	2.80	3.22
2016	Syrcse	AAA	16	0	0	8	24.0	88	16	6	6	2	2	0	1	3	0	22	0	0	1	1	.500	0	2- -	-	1.60	2.25
2016	Was	NL	19	0	0	4	19.2	83	15	12	11	3	0	0	1	7	1	16	1	0	2	0	1.000	0	0-2	2	2.99	5.03

Zack Godley

Pitches: R Bats: R Pos: RP-18; SP-9   Ht: 6'3" Wt: 240 Born: 4/21/1990 Age: 27

Year	Team	Lg	G	GS	CG	GF	IP	BFP	H	R	ER	HR	SH	SF	HB	TBB	IBB	SO	WP	Bk	W	L	Pct	Sh	Sv-Op	Hld	ERC	ERA
2013	2 Tms	Low	14	0	0	0	26.2	104	22	7	6	0	1	1	0	5	0	28	6	0	2	0	1.000	0	0- -	-	1.84	2.03
2014	2 Tms	Low	40	0	0	30	55.1	241	49	24	19	3	3	1	2	24	1	77	7	0	4	3	.571	0	15- -	-	3.29	3.09
2015	Visalia	A+	14	12	0	0	75.1	306	64	26	19	3	3	0	3	19	0	78	2	0	8	3	.727	0	0- -	-	2.50	2.27
2015	Mobile	AA	7	5	0	1	24.1	100	21	12	11	2	1	0	3	10	0	12	0	0	2	1	.667	0	0- -	-	3.92	4.07
2016	Mobile	AA	8	8	1	0	49.1	201	48	27	21	4	1	3	4	11	0	31	6	0	2	5	.286	0	0- -	-	3.54	3.83
2016	Reno	AAA	7	6	0	0	32.2	146	37	16	12	3	1	0	1	15	1	38	1	0	2	1	.667	0	0- -	-	5.15	3.31
2015	Ari	NL	9	6	0	1	36.2	150	29	13	13	4	1	3	1	17	1	34	2	0	5	1	.833	0	0-0	0	3.67	3.19
2016	Ari	NL	27	9	0	1	74.2	335	86	54	53	13	7	1	4	25	4	60	5	0	5	4	.556	0	0-1	0	5.31	6.39
	2 ML YEARS		36	15	0	2	111.1	485	115	67	66	17	8	2	7	42	5	94	7	0	10	5	.667	0	0-1	0	4.76	5.34

Erik Goeddel

guh-DELL

Pitches: R Bats: R Pos: RP-36   Ht: 6'3" Wt: 190 Born: 12/20/1988 Age: 28

Year	Team	Lg	G	GS	CG	GF	IP	BFP	H	R	ER	HR	SH	SF	HB	TBB	IBB	SO	WP	Bk	W	L	Pct	Sh	Sv-Op	Hld	ERC	ERA
2016	LsVgs*	AAA	24	1	0	4	28.2	130	28	15	13	2	5	2	1	15	1	34	1	0	1	1	.500	0	1- -	-	4.18	4.08
2014	NYM	NL	6	0	0	5	6.2	26	3	2	2	0	0	0	0	4	1	6	1	0	0	0	-	0	0-0	0	1.37	2.70
2015	NYM	NL	35	0	0	9	33.1	132	24	9	9	1	0	3	2	9	2	34	2	0	1	1	.500	0	0-0	2	1.89	2.43
2016	NYM	NL	36	0	0	10	35.2	157	33	20	18	5	0	1	1	14	1	36	5	0	2	2	.500	0	0-1	2	3.83	4.54
	Postseason		1	0	0	0	0.0	4	4	3	3	1	0	0	0	0	0	0	0	0	0	0	-	0	0-0	0	-	-
	3 ML YEARS		77	0	0	24	75.2	315	60	31	29	6	0	4	3	27	4	76	8	0	3	3	.500	0	0-1	4	2.71	3.45

Tyler Goeddel

guh-DELL

Bats: R Throws: R Pos: LF-69;PH-23;RF-12;PR-3   Ht: 6'4" Wt: 180 Born: 10/20/1992 Age: 24

Year	Team	Lg	G	AB	H	2B	3B	HR	(Hm	Rd)	TB	R	RBI	RC	TBB	IBB	SO	HBP	SH	SF	SB	CS	GDP	Avg	OBP	Slg	OPS
2012	BG	A	103	329	81	19	2	6	(-	-)	122	52	46	48	38	0	94	7	3	2	30	5	8	.246	.335	.371	.706
2013	BG	A	112	450	112	18	12	7	(-	-)	175	63	65	61	40	1	98	3	1	3	30	5	7	.249	.313	.389	.701
2014	Charltt	A+	113	424	114	25	8	6	(-	-)	173	41	61	64	46	1	98	7	0	2	20	9	9	.269	.349	.408	.757
2015	Mont	AA	123	473	132	17	10	12	(-	-)	205	68	72	77	48	1	98	6	1	5	28	9	7	.279	.350	.433	.783
2016	Phi	NL	92	213	41	3	3	4	(3	1)	62	17	16	15	17	0	52	2	1	1	3	0	4	.192	.258	.291	.549

David Goforth

Pitches: R Bats: R Pos: RP-10   Ht: 5'10" Wt: 205 Born: 10/11/1988 Age: 28

Year	Team	Lg	G	GS	CG	GF	IP	BFP	H	R	ER	HR	SH	SF	HB	TBB	IBB	SO	WP	Bk	W	L	Pct	Sh	Sv-Op	Hld	ERC	ERA
2012	Wisc	A	28	28	0	0	150.2	651	154	91	78	16	3	3	9	63	0	93	11	8	10	8	.556	0	0- -	-	4.65	4.66
2013	BrvdCt	A+	14	14	0	0	78.1	328	67	33	27	4	3	2	5	28	0	58	4	0	7	5	.583	0	0- -	-	3.05	3.10
2013	Hntsvl	AA	20	4	1	9	46.2	189	32	19	17	1	2	1	1	18	0	36	5	0	4	3	.571	1	5- -	-	1.98	3.28
2014	Hntsvl	AA	54	0	0	44	64.2	282	60	28	27	2	3	0	2	29	2	46	4	0	5	4	.556	0	27- -	-	3.40	3.76
2015	ColSpr	AAA	38	0	0	19	47.0	198	36	15	14	2	4	1	0	27	4	34	10	0	0	4	.000	0	4- -	-	2.97	2.68
2016	ColSpr	AAA	42	0	0	22	51.1	238	56	30	28	3	1	3	2	35	2	38	8	1	3	4	.429	0	2- -	-	5.57	4.91
2015	Mil	NL	20	0	0	9	24.2	111	32	13	11	4	2	2	0	8	2	24	2	0	1	0	1.000	0	0-0	0	5.87	4.01
2016	Mil	NL	10	0	0	7	10.2	55	18	14	13	3	0	0	0	4	1	9	1	0	0	0	-	0	0-0	0	9.27	10.97
	2 ML YEARS		30	0	0	16	35.1	166	50	27	24	7	2	2	0	12	3	33	3	0	1	0	1.000	0	0-0	0	6.86	6.11

Ryan Goins

GO-inns

Bats: L Throws: R Pos: 2B-37;SS-28;3B-6;PH-6;PR-3;1B-2;LF-2;RF-1   Ht: 5'10" Wt: 180 Born: 2/13/1988 Age: 29

Year	Team	Lg	G	AB	H	2B	3B	HR	(Hm	Rd)	TB	R	RBI	RC	TBB	IBB	SO	HBP	SH	SF	SB	CS	GDP	Avg	OBP	Slg	OPS
2016	Buffalo*	AAA	28	98	26	6	0	2	(-	-)	38	9	10	12	8	0	23	0	3	1	0	1	4	.265	.318	.388	.706
2013	Tor	AL	34	119	30	5	0	2	(2	0)	41	11	8	11	2	0	28	0	0	0	0	1	1	.252	.264	.345	.609
2014	Tor	AL	67	181	34	6	3	1	(1	0)	49	14	15	7	5	0	42	1	0	1	0	1	4	.188	.209	.271	.479

Year	Team	Lg	G	AB	H	2B	3B	HR	(Hm	Rd)	TB	R	RBI	RC	TBB	IBB	SO	HBP	SH	SF	SB	CS	GDP	Avg	OBP	Slg	OPS
2015	Tor	AL	128	376	94	16	4	5	(4	1)	133	52	45	48	39	0	83	1	7	5	2	1	12	.250	.318	.354	.672
2016	Tor	AL	77	183	34	9	2	3	(1	2)	56	13	12	9	9	0	48	1	3	0	1	1	6	.186	.228	.306	.534
	Postseason		11	36	5	1	0	1	(1	0)	9	4	4	3	1	0	12	0	3	0	0	0	1	.139	.162	.250	.412
4 ML YEARS			306	859	192	36	9	11	(8	3)	279	90	80	75	55	0	201	2	16	6	3	3	23	.224	.270	.325	.595

Paul Goldschmidt

Bats: R **Throws:** R **Pos:** 1B-157;DH-1   **Ht:** 6'3" **Wt:** 225 **Born:** 9/10/1987 **Age:** 29

Year	Team	Lg	G	AB	H	2B	3B	HR	(Hm	Rd)	TB	R	RBI	RC	TBB	IBB	SO	HBP	SH	SF	SB	CS	GDP	Avg	OBP	Slg	OPS
2011	Ari	NL	48	156	39	9	1	8	(2	6)	74	28	26	26	20	0	53	0	0	1	4	0	4	.250	.333	.474	.808
2012	Ari	NL	145	514	147	43	1	20	(10	10)	252	82	82	86	60	4	130	4	0	9	18	3	9	.286	.359	.490	.850
2013	Ari	NL	160	602	182	36	3	36	(17	19)	332	103	125	131	99	19	145	3	0	5	15	7	25	.302	.401	.551	.952
2014	Ari	NL	109	406	122	39	1	19	(10	9)	220	75	69	83	64	10	110	2	0	3	9	3	10	.300	.396	.542	.938
2015	Ari	NL	159	567	182	38	2	33	(13	20)	323	103	110	135	118	29	151	2	0	7	21	5	16	.321	.435	.570	1.005
2016	Ari	NL	158	579	172	33	3	24	(15	9)	283	106	95	113	110	15	150	7	0	8	32	5	14	.297	.411	.489	.899
	Postseason		4	16	7	0	0	2	(1	1)	13	4	6	5	2	0	5	1	0	0	1	0	0	.438	.526	.813	1.339
6 ML YEARS			779	2824	844	198	11	140	(67	73)	1484	497	507	574	471	77	739	18	0	33	99	23	78	.299	.398	.525	.924

Yan Gomes

Bats: R **Throws:** R **Pos:** C-73;PH-2;DH-1   YAHN GOHMS   **Ht:** 6'2" **Wt:** 215 **Born:** 7/19/1987 **Age:** 29

Year	Team	Lg	G	AB	H	2B	3B	HR	(Hm	Rd)	TB	R	RBI	RC	TBB	IBB	SO	HBP	SH	SF	SB	CS	GDP	Avg	OBP	Slg	OPS
2012	Tor	AL	43	98	20	4	0	4	(3	1)	36	9	13	11	6	0	32	3	1	3	0	0	3	.204	.264	.367	.631
2013	Cle	AL	88	293	86	18	2	11	(6	5)	141	45	38	42	18	0	67	7	0	4	2	0	12	.294	.345	.481	.826
2014	Cle	AL	135	485	135	25	3	21	(9	12)	229	61	74	65	24	3	120	3	0	6	0	0	13	.278	.313	.472	.785
2015	Cle	AL	95	363	84	22	0	12	(5	7)	142	38	45	25	13	1	104	7	0	6	0	0	11	.231	.267	.391	.659
2016	Cle	AL	74	251	42	11	1	9	(4	5)	82	22	34	18	9	0	69	2	0	2	0	0	7	.167	.201	.327	.527
	Postseason		1	4	2	1	0	0	(0	0)	3	0	0	0	0	0	0	0	0	0	0	0	0	.500	.500	.750	1.250
5 ML YEARS			435	1490	367	80	6	57	(27	30)	630	175	204	161	70	4	392	22	1	21	2	0	46	.246	.286	.423	.709

Carlos Gomez

Bats: R **Throws:** R **Pos:** CF-85;LF-28;RF-6;DH-5;PR-4;PH-1   **Ht:** 6'3" **Wt:** 220 **Born:** 12/4/1985 **Age:** 31

Year	Team	Lg	G	AB	H	2B	3B	HR	(Hm	Rd)	TB	R	RBI	RC	TBB	IBB	SO	HBP	SH	SF	SB	CS	GDP	Avg	OBP	Slg	OPS
2007	NYM	NL	58	125	29	3	0	2	(1	1)	38	14	12	11	8	2	27	3	0	3	12	3	0	.232	.288	.304	.592
2008	Min	AL	153	577	149	24	7	7	(3	4)	208	79	59	66	25	0	142	7	3	2	33	11	7	.258	.296	.360	.657
2009	Min	AL	137	315	72	15	5	3	(1	2)	106	51	28	33	22	0	72	4	7	1	14	7	1	.229	.287	.337	.623
2010	Mil	NL	97	291	72	11	3	5	(3	2)	104	38	24	28	17	1	72	4	6	0	18	3	10	.247	.298	.357	.655
2011	Mil	NL	94	231	52	11	3	8	(4	4)	93	37	24	25	15	0	64	2	8	2	16	2	2	.225	.276	.403	.679
2012	Mil	NL	137	415	108	19	4	19	(11	8)	192	72	51	59	20	1	98	8	3	2	37	6	6	.260	.305	.463	.768
2013	Mil	NL	147	536	152	27	10	24	(15	9)	271	80	73	81	37	2	146	10	1	6	40	7	11	.284	.338	.506	.843
2014	Mil	NL	148	574	163	34	4	23	(13	10)	274	95	73	98	47	0	141	19	1	3	34	12	11	.284	.356	.477	.833
2015	2 Tms		115	435	111	29	1	12	(6	6)	178	61	56	63	31	1	101	7	3	1	17	9	5	.255	.314	.409	.724
2016	2 Tms	AL	118	411	95	22	1	13	(8	5)	158	45	53	54	34	2	136	5	3	0	18	5	11	.231	.298	.384	.682
15	Mil	NL	74	286	75	20	1	8	(6	2)	121	42	43	45	23	0	70	5	0	0	7	6	4	.262	.328	.423	.751
15	Hou	AL	41	149	36	9	0	4	(0	4)	57	19	13	18	8	1	31	2	3	1	10	3	1	.242	.288	.383	.670
16	Hou	AL	85	295	62	16	1	5	(2	3)	95	27	29	29	21	2	100	4	3	0	13	2	11	.210	.272	.322	.594
16	Tex	AL	33	116	33	6	0	8	(6	2)	63	18	24	25	13	0	36	1	0	0	5	3	0	.284	.362	.543	.905
	Postseason		15	33	9	0	0	3	(1	2)	18	6	5	5	1	0	8	2	2	0	2	1	0	.273	.333	.545	.879
10 ML YEARS			1204	3910	1003	195	38	116	(65	51)	1622	572	453	518	256	9	999	69	38	21	239	65	64	.257	.312	.415	.727

Jeanmar Gomez

Pitches: R **Bats:** R **Pos:** RP-70   JENN-marr   **Ht:** 6'3" **Wt:** 215 **Born:** 2/10/1988 **Age:** 29

			HOW MUCH HE PITCHED					WHAT HE GAVE UP								THE RESULTS						
Year	Team	Lg	G	GS	CG	GF	IP	BFP	H	R	ER	HR	SH	SF	HB	TBB	IBB	SO	WP	Bk	W	L	Pct	Sh	Sv-Op	Hld	ERC	ERA
2010	Cle	AL	11	11	0	0	57.2	265	73	36	30	7	0	3	2	22	3	34	1	0	4	5	.444	0	0-0	0	5.75	4.68
2011	Cle	AL	11	10	0	0	58.1	259	73	31	29	6	0	2	1	15	1	31	2	0	5	3	.625	0	0-0	0	4.99	4.47
2012	Cle	AL	20	17	0	1	90.2	395	95	66	60	15	2	7	4	34	5	47	2	0	5	8	.385	0	0-0	0	4.83	5.96
2013	Pit	NL	34	8	0	6	80.2	333	65	35	30	6	4	6	3	28	3	53	6	0	3	0	1.000	0	0-0	3	2.75	3.35
2014	Pit	NL	44	0	0	20	62.0	270	70	24	22	6	3	2	2	23	7	38	2	0	2	2	.500	0	1-1	5	4.70	3.19
2015	Phi	NL	65	0	0	21	74.2	319	82	28	25	4	1	4	2	17	4	50	3	0	2	3	.400	0	0-3	7	3.63	3.01
2016	Phi	NL	70	0	0	59	68.2	297	78	38	37	6	0	3	2	22	2	47	3	0	3	5	.375	0	37-43	0	4.58	4.85
	Postseason		1	0	0	0	4.0	17	3	2	0	0	1	0	0	2	0	0	0	0	0	0	-	0	0-0	0	2.40	0.00
7 ML YEARS			255	46	0	107	492.2	2138	536	258	233	50	10	27	16	161	25	300	19	0	24	26	.480	0	38-47	13	4.35	4.26

Marco Gonzales

Pitches: L **Bats:** L **Pos:** P   **Ht:** 6'1" **Wt:** 195 **Born:** 2/16/1992 **Age:** 25

			HOW MUCH HE PITCHED					WHAT HE GAVE UP								THE RESULTS						
Year	Team	Lg	G	GS	CG	GF	IP	BFP	H	R	ER	HR	SH	SF	HB	TBB	IBB	SO	WP	Bk	W	L	Pct	Sh	Sv-Op	Hld	ERC	ERA
2013	2 Tms	Low	8	6	0	0	23.1	93	18	8	7	1	0	0	0	8	0	23	2	0	0	0	-	0	0--	-	2.35	2.70
2014	PlmBh	A+	6	6	0	0	37.2	150	34	8	6	1	0	0	0	8	0	32	0	0	2	2	.500	0	0--	-	2.44	1.43
2014	Sprgfld	AA	7	7	0	0	38.2	160	33	14	10	2	0	0	0	10	1	46	2	0	3	2	.600	0	0--	-	2.37	2.33
2014	Memp	AAA	8	8	0	0	45.2	188	43	18	17	7	4	1	3	9	0	39	2	0	4	1	.800	0	0--	-	3.58	3.35
2015	Memp	AAA	14	14	0	0	69.1	312	91	43	42	10	4	1	1	24	1	51	1	0	1	5	.167	0	0--	-	6.17	5.45

Year Team	Lg	G	GS	CG	GF	IP	BFP	H	R	ER	HR	SH	SF	HB	TBB	IBB	SO	WP	Bk	W	L	Pct	Sh	Sv-Op	Hld	ERC	ERA
						HOW MUCH HE PITCHED					WHAT HE GAVE UP											THE RESULTS					
2014 StL	NL	10	5	0	0	34.2	156	32	16	16	4	0	1	1	21	1	31	0	0	4	2	.667	0	0-0	1	4.59	4.15
2015 StL	NL	1	1	0	0	2.2	16	7	4	4	1	0	1	0	1	0	1	0	0	0	0	-	0	0-0	0	17.70	13.50
Postseason		6	0	0	0	6.0	24	4	3	3	0	1	0	0	2	0	4	0	0	2	1	.667	0	0-1	0	1.57	4.50
2 ML YEARS		11	6	0	0	37.1	172	39	20	20	5	0	2	1	22	1	32	0	0	4	2	.667	0	0-0	1	5.36	4.82

Adrian Gonzalez

Bats: L Throws: L Pos: 1B-151;PH-6;DH-2   Ht: 6'2" Wt: 215 Born: 5/8/1982 Age: 35

Year Team	Lg	G	AB	H	2B	3B	HR	(Hm	Rd)	TB	R	RBI	RC	TBB	IBB	SO	HBP	SH	SF	SB	CS	GDP	Avg	OBP	Slg	OPS
						BATTING														RUNNING			AVERAGES			
2004 Tex	AL	16	42	10	3	0	1	(1	0)	16	7	7	7	2	0	6	0	0	0	0	0	0	.238	.273	.381	.654
2005 Tex	AL	43	150	34	7	1	6	(3	3)	61	17	17	13	10	2	37	0	0	2	0	0	3	.227	.272	.407	.678
2006 SD	NL	156	570	173	38	1	24	(10	14)	285	83	82	82	52	9	113	3	1	5	0	1	24	.304	.362	.500	.862
2007 SD	NL	161	646	182	46	3	30	(10	20)	324	101	100	108	65	9	140	3	0	6	0	0	6	.282	.347	.502	.849
2008 SD	NL	162	616	172	32	1	36	(14	22)	314	103	119	107	74	18	142	7	0	3	0	0	24	.279	.361	.510	.871
2009 SD	NL	160	552	153	27	2	40	(12	28)	304	90	99	109	119	22	109	5	1	4	1	1	23	.277	.407	.551	.958
2010 SD	NL	160	591	176	33	0	31	(11	20)	302	87	101	122	93	35	114	2	2	4	0	0	15	.298	.393	.511	.904
2011 Bos	AL	159	630	213	45	3	27	(10	17)	345	108	117	121	74	20	119	6	0	5	1	0	28	.338	.410	.548	.957
2012 2 Tms		159	629	188	47	1	18	(9	9)	291	75	108	113	42	5	110	5	0	8	2	0	10	.299	.344	.463	.806
2013 LAD	NL	157	583	171	32	0	22	(11	11)	269	69	100	89	47	6	98	1	0	10	1	0	12	.293	.342	.461	.803
2014 LAD	NL	159	591	163	41	0	27	(13	14)	285	83	116	95	56	9	112	2	0	11	1	1	13	.276	.335	.482	.817
2015 LAD	NL	156	571	157	33	0	28	(17	11)	274	76	90	84	62	10	107	6	0	3	0	1	21	.275	.350	.480	.830
2016 LAD	NL	156	568	162	31	0	18	(6	12)	247	69	90	85	55	9	117	4	0	6	0	2	16	.285	.349	.435	.784
12 Bos	AL	123	484	145	37	0	15	(8	7)	227	63	86	89	31	4	81	5	0	7	0	0	9	.300	.343	.469	.812
12 LAD	NL	36	145	43	10	1	3	(1	2)	64	12	22	24	11	1	29	0	0	1	2	0	1	.297	.344	.441	.785
Postseason		23	87	26	3	0	5	(3	2)	44	14	15	11	9	1	21	0	0	0	0	0	1	.299	.365	.506	.870
13 ML YEARS		1804	6739	1954	415	12	308	(127	181)	3317	968	1146	1135	751	154	1324	44	4	67	6	6	195	.290	.362	.492	.854

Carlos Gonzalez

Bats: L Throws: L Pos: RF-148;PH-3   Ht: 6'1" Wt: 220 Born: 10/17/1985 Age: 31

Year Team	Lg	G	AB	H	2B	3B	HR	(Hm	Rd)	TB	R	RBI	RC	TBB	IBB	SO	HBP	SH	SF	SB	CS	GDP	Avg	OBP	Slg	OPS
						BATTING														RUNNING			AVERAGES			
2008 Oak	AL	85	302	73	22	4	4	(3	1)	109	31	26	30	13	1	81	0	1	4	1	7		.242	.273	.361	.634
2009 Col	NL	89	278	79	14	7	13	(7	6)	146	53	29	42	28	3	70	3	5	3	16	4	3	.284	.353	.525	.878
2010 Col	NL	145	587	197	34	9	34	(26	8)	351	111	117	118	40	8	135	2	0	7	26	8	9	.336	.376	.598	.974
2011 Col	NL	127	481	142	27	3	26	(16	10)	253	92	92	95	48	8	105	7	0	6	20	5	11	.295	.363	.526	.889
2012 Col	NL	135	518	157	31	5	22	(13	9)	264	89	85	88	56	11	115	2	0	3	20	5	11	.303	.371	.510	.881
2013 Col	NL	110	391	118	23	6	26	(12	14)	231	72	70	69	41	2	118	1	0	3	21	3	7	.302	.367	.591	.958
2014 Col	NL	70	260	62	15	1	11	(5	6)	112	35	38	32	19	2	70	1	0	1	3	0	7	.238	.292	.431	.723
2015 Col	NL	153	554	150	25	2	40	(24	16)	299	87	97	94	46	6	133	1	1	6	2	0	11	.271	.325	.540	.864
2016 Col	NL	150	584	174	42	2	25	(18	7)	295	87	100	99	46	6	129	1	0	1	2	2	10	.298	.350	.505	.855
Postseason		4	17	10	2	0	1	(1	0)	15	5	1	5	2	0	1	0	0	0	2	1	0	.588	.632	.882	1.514
9 ML YEARS		1064	3955	1152	233	36	201	(124	77)	2060	657	654	667	337	47	956	18	7	30	114	28	76	.291	.347	.521	.868

Chi Chi Gonzalez

Pitches: R Bats: R Pos: SP-3   Ht: 6'3" Wt: 215 Born: 1/15/1992 Age: 25

Year Team	Lg	G	GS	CG	GF	IP	BFP	H	R	ER	HR	SH	SF	HB	TBB	IBB	SO	WP	Bk	W	L	Pct	Sh	Sv-Op	Hld	ERC	ERA
						HOW MUCH HE PITCHED					WHAT HE GAVE UP											THE RESULTS					
2013 2 Tms	Low	14	14	0	0	42.2	183	45	24	18	2	2	0	1	16	0	35	1	1	0	4	.000	0	0--	-	4.06	3.80
2014 MrtlBh	A+	11	11	0	0	65.0	276	56	22	19	3	1	1	6	16	0	49	5	0	5	2	.714	0	0--	-	2.66	2.63
2014 Frisco	AA	15	14	0	1	73.0	309	67	30	22	3	4	3	4	25	0	64	3	0	7	4	.636	0	0--	-	3.21	2.71
2015 RdRck	AAA	16	16	0	0	88.1	377	95	40	35	3	1	2	4	31	0	56	1	1	8	7	.533	0	0--	-	4.11	3.57
2016 RdRck	AAA	25	24	0	0	138.0	591	154	73	72	8	6	5	4	44	0	91	5	0	8	10	.444	0	0--	-	4.31	4.70
2015 Tex	AL	14	10	1	1	67.0	280	49	33	29	6	1	2	3	32	1	30	2	1	4	6	.400	1	0-0	0	3.90	3.90
2016 Tex	AL	3	3	0	0	10.1	62	21	13	10	1	0	1	0	9	0	7	0	0	0	2	.000	0	0-0	0	12.48	8.71
Postseason		1	0	0	0	1.2	8	2	1	1	1	0	0	0	2	0	0	0	0	0	0	-	0	0-0	0	15.09	5.40
2 ML YEARS		17	13	1	1	77.1	342	70	46	39	7	1	3	3	41	1	37	2	1	4	8	.333	1	0-0	0	4.07	4.54

Erik Gonzalez

Bats: R Throws: R Pos: SS-8;PH-6;2B-5;3B-2;RF-2   Ht: 6'3" Wt: 195 Born: 8/31/1991 Age: 25

Year Team	Lg	G	AB	H	2B	3B	HR	(Hm	Rd)	TB	R	RBI	RC	TBB	IBB	SO	HBP	SH	SF	SB	CS	GDP	Avg	OBP	Slg	OPS
						BATTING														RUNNING			AVERAGES			
2012 MhVlly	A-	60	214	47	9	1	2	(-	-)	64	30	18	18	11	1	50	2	3	0	9	1	4	.220	.264	.299	.563
2013 2 Tms	Low	132	508	129	32	12	9	(-	-)	212	75	76	63	29	0	109	1	3	5	11	6	13	.254	.293	.417	.710
2014 Carlina	A+	74	308	89	14	7	3	(-	-)	126	44	46	44	23	1	65	0	3	2	15	6	12	.289	.336	.409	.745
2014 Akron	AA	31	129	46	6	3	1	(-	-)	61	21	16	24	7	0	23	0	0	0	6	1	2	.357	.390	.473	.863
2015 Akron	AA	72	311	88	18	4	6	(-	-)	132	38	46	41	11	0	56	1	1	3	10	5	12	.283	.307	.424	.731
2015 Clmbs	AAA	65	238	53	6	3	3	(-	-)	74	32	23	21	15	0	47	3	5	0	8	2	7	.223	.277	.311	.588
2016 Clmbs	AAA	104	429	127	31	1	11	(-	-)	193	62	53	62	19	2	88	3	7	2	12	10	8	.296	.329	.450	.779
2016 Cle	AL	21	16	5	0	0	0	(0	0)	5	2	0	1	1	0	8	0	0	0	0	1	0	.313	.353	.313	.665

Gio Gonzalez

Pitches: L Bats: R Pos: SP-32
JEE-oh
Ht: 6'0" Wt: 205 Born: 9/19/1985 Age: 31

				HOW MUCH HE PITCHED						WHAT HE GAVE UP											THE RESULTS						
Year	Team	Lg	G	GS	CG	GF	IP	BFP	H	R	ER	HR	SH	SF	HB	TBB	IBB	SO	WP	Bk	W	L	Pct	Sh	Sv-Op	Hld	ERC	ERA
2008	Oak	AL	10	7	0	3	34.0	163	32	34	29	9	2	1	3	25	1	34	1	0	1	4	.200	0	0-0	0	6.54	7.68
2009	Oak	AL	20	17	0	0	98.2	455	113	68	63	14	2	3	1	56	2	109	2	0	6	7	.462	0	0-0	0	5.96	5.75
2010	Oak	AL	33	33	1	0	200.2	851	171	75	72	15	5	2	4	92	1	171	4	1	15	9	.625	0	0-0	0	3.39	3.23
2011	Oak	AL	32	32	0	0	202.0	864	175	81	70	17	3	2	8	91	1	197	6	1	16	12	.571	0	0-0	0	3.56	3.12
2012	Was	NL	32	32	2	0	199.1	822	149	69	64	9	9	7	5	76	3	207	10	1	21	8	.724	1	0-0	0	2.37	2.89
2013	Was	NL	32	32	1	0	195.2	819	169	79	73	17	7	1	2	76	1	192	4	1	11	8	.579	1	0-0	0	3.23	3.36
2014	Was	NL	27	27	0	0	158.2	653	134	66	63	10	7	4	3	56	0	162	2	0	10	10	.500	0	0-0	0	2.91	3.57
2015	Was	NL	31	31	0	0	175.2	758	181	79	74	8	3	9	4	69	3	169	4	0	11	8	.579	0	0-0	0	3.92	3.79
2016	Was	NL	32	32	0	0	177.1	765	179	98	90	19	8	5	9	59	2	171	7	0	11	11	.500	0	0-0	0	4.08	4.57
	Postseason		3	3	0	0	14.0	63	10	7	5	0	0	1	0	12	0	11	2	0	0	0	-	0	0-0	0	3.46	3.21
9 ML YEARS			249	243	4	3	1442.0	6150	1303	649	598	118	46	34	39	600	14	1412	40	4	102	77	.570	2	0-0	0	3.57	3.73

Marwin Gonzalez

MARR-win
Bats: B Throws: R Pos: 1B-92;3B-22;LF-18;2B-14;PH-13;SS-11;PR-4;DH-3;CF-1
Ht: 6'1" Wt: 205 Born: 3/14/1989 Age: 28

								BATTING													RUNNING			AVERAGES			
Year	Team	Lg	G	AB	H	2B	3B	HR	(Hm	Rd)	TB	R	RBI	RC	TBB	IBB	SO	HBP	SH	SF	SB	CS	GDP	Avg	OBP	Slg	OPS
2012	Hou	NL	80	205	48	13	0	2	(1	1)	67	21	12	12	13	0	29	0	1	0	3	3	9	.234	.280	.327	.607
2013	Hou	AL	72	204	45	8	0	4	(2	2)	65	22	14	10	9	0	37	0	8	1	6	2	5	.221	.252	.319	.571
2014	Hou	AL	103	285	79	15	1	6	(3	3)	114	33	23	26	17	0	58	4	4	0	2	4	6	.277	.327	.400	.727
2015	Hou	AL	120	344	96	18	1	12	(6	6)	152	44	34	39	16	0	74	3	7	0	4	5	9	.279	.317	.442	.759
2016	Hou	AL	141	484	123	26	3	13	(8	5)	194	55	51	47	22	1	118	5	6	1	12	6	16	.254	.293	.401	.694
	Postseason		4	3	0	0	0	0	(0	0)	0	0	0	0	0	0	2	0	0	0	0	0	0	.000	.000	.000	.000
5 ML YEARS			516	1522	391	80	5	37	(20	17)	592	175	134	134	77	1	316	12	26	2	27	20	45	.257	.298	.389	.687

Miguel Gonzalez

Pitches: R Bats: R Pos: SP-23; RP-1
Ht: 6'1" Wt: 170 Born: 5/27/1984 Age: 33

				HOW MUCH HE PITCHED						WHAT HE GAVE UP											THE RESULTS						
Year	Team	Lg	G	GS	CG	GF	IP	BFP	H	R	ER	HR	SH	SF	HB	TBB	IBB	SO	WP	Bk	W	L	Pct	Sh	Sv-Op	Hld	ERC	ERA
2016	Charltt*	AAA	5	5	0	0	21.1	92	27	12	11	5	1	2	1	4	0	25	1	0	1	1	.500	0	0- -		6.07	4.64
2012	Bal	AL	18	15	0	0	105.1	434	92	38	38	13	1	2	5	35	2	77	3	2	9	4	.692	0	0-0	0	3.49	3.25
2013	Bal	AL	30	28	0	1	171.1	712	157	81	72	24	3	6	3	53	3	120	4	0	11	8	.579	0	0-0	0	3.58	3.78
2014	Bal	AL	27	26	1	0	159.0	671	155	61	57	25	0	3	8	51	1	111	4	1	10	9	.526	1	0-0	0	4.25	3.23
2015	Bal	AL	26	26	0	0	144.2	622	151	81	79	24	2	2	8	51	2	109	4	0	9	12	.429	1	0-0	0	4.88	4.91
2016	CWS	AL	24	23	0	0	135.0	566	132	61	56	11	1	5	6	35	1	95	3	0	5	8	.385	0	0-0	0	3.45	3.73
	Postseason		2	2	0	0	12.2	52	9	3	2	0	1	0	2	4	1	12	1	0	1	0	1.000	0	0-0	0	2.07	1.42
5 ML YEARS			125	118	1	1	715.1	3005	687	322	302	97	7	18	30	225	9	512	18	3	44	41	.518	1	0-0	0	3.94	3.80

Severino Gonzalez

Pitches: R Bats: R Pos: RP-27
Ht: 6'2" Wt: 155 Born: 9/28/1992 Age: 24

				HOW MUCH HE PITCHED						WHAT HE GAVE UP											THE RESULTS						
Year	Team	Lg	G	GS	CG	GF	IP	BFP	H	R	ER	HR	SH	SF	HB	TBB	IBB	SO	WP	Bk	W	L	Pct	Sh	Sv-Op	Hld	ERC	ERA
2013	2 Tms	Low	24	13	0	1	97.0	380	76	27	21	5	2	4	3	22	1	113	2	1	6	5	.545	0	0- -	-	2.17	1.95
2014	Rdng	AA	27	27	0	0	158.2	675	169	89	81	23	2	3	9	34	0	115	3	1	9	13	.409	0	0- -	-	4.23	4.59
2015	LV	AAA	16	16	0	0	88.0	381	106	54	50	8	1	1	5	18	0	45	3	0	2	7	.222	0	0- -	-	4.66	5.11
2016	Rdng	AA	6	0	0	2	10.2	44	9	2	2	0	1	0	0	2	0	9	0	0	2	0	1.000	0	0- -	-	1.80	1.69
2016	LV	AAA	15	1	0	1	35.1	150	37	14	13	3	0	1	2	6	0	26	3	0	0	1	.000	0	0- -	-	3.50	3.31
2015	Phi	NL	7	7	0	0	30.2	143	44	27	27	5	1	4	4	7	0	28	0	1	3	3	.500	0	0-0	0	7.06	7.92
2016	Phi	NL	27	0	0	12	35.1	151	40	22	22	4	0	3	1	7	1	34	0	1	1	2	.333	0	0-0	1	4.17	5.60
2 ML YEARS			34	7	0	12	66.0	294	84	49	49	9	1	7	5	14	1	62	0	2	4	5	.444	0	0-0	1	5.45	6.68

Brian Goodwin

Bats: L Throws: R Pos: PH-9;RF-8;LF-5;CF-1
Ht: 6'0" Wt: 205 Born: 11/2/1990 Age: 26

								BATTING													RUNNING			AVERAGES			
Year	Team	Lg	G	AB	H	2B	3B	HR	(Hm	Rd)	TB	R	RBI	RC	TBB	IBB	SO	HBP	SH	SF	SB	CS	GDP	Avg	OBP	Slg	OPS
2012	Hrsbrg	AA	42	166	37	8	1	5	(-	-)	62	17	14	19	18	0	50	2	0	0	3	3	1	.223	.306	.373	.680
2012	Hgrstn	A	58	216	70	18	1	9	(-	-)	117	47	38	54	43	0	39	3	1	3	15	4	1	.324	.438	.542	.979
2013	Hrsbrg	AA	122	457	115	19	11	10	(-	-)	186	82	40	70	66	0	121	8	1	1	19	11	4	.252	.355	.407	.762
2014	Syrcse	AAA	81	275	60	10	4	4	(-	-)	90	31	32	34	50	0	95	1	3	0	6	4	6	.218	.340	.327	.668
2015	Hrsbrg	AA	114	429	97	17	4	8	(-	-)	146	58	46	44	38	2	93	2	0	3	15	7	7	.226	.290	.340	.631
2016	Syrcse	AAA	119	436	121	25	1	14	(-	-)	190	51	67	70	46	1	106	3	2	5	15	3	7	.278	.347	.436	.783
2016	Was	NL	22	42	12	4	1	0	(0	0)	18	1	5	6	2	0	14	0	0	0	0	0	1	.286	.318	.429	.747

Nick Goody

Pitches: R Bats: R Pos: RP-27
Ht: 5'11" Wt: 195 Born: 7/6/1991 Age: 25

				HOW MUCH HE PITCHED						WHAT HE GAVE UP											THE RESULTS						
Year	Team	Lg	G	GS	CG	GF	IP	BFP	H	R	ER	HR	SH	SF	HB	TBB	IBB	SO	WP	Bk	W	L	Pct	Sh	Sv-Op	Hld	ERC	ERA
2012	3 Tms	Low	23	0	0	18	32.0	123	20	4	4	0	0	0	1	9	0	52	1	0	1	2	.333	0	7- -	-	1.44	1.13
2014	Tampa	A+	12	4	0	0	15.1	62	10	4	4	1	0	0	0	5	0	27	1	0	2	0	1.000	0	0- -	-	2.01	2.35
2014	Trntn	AA	15	0	0	5	16.0	78	20	12	12	3	3	1	0	10	2	19	1	0	0	3	.000	0	0- -	-	6.83	6.75
2015	Trntn	AA	29	0	0	20	41.2	171	29	8	8	2	1	1	2	14	0	59	2	0	1	1	.500	0	4- -	-	2.07	1.73
2015	S-WB	AAA	14	0	0	8	20.2	82	14	3	3	0	2	0	0	7	0	25	3	0	1	1	.500	0	4- -	-	1.64	1.31

Year	Team	Lg	G	GS	CG	GF	IP	BFP	H	R	ER	HR	SH	SF	HB	TBB	IBB	SO	WP	Bk	W	L	Pct	Sh	Sv-Op	Hld	ERC	ERA
	HOW MUCH HE PITCHED								**WHAT HE GAVE UP**												**THE RESULTS**							
2016	S-WB	AAA	18	0	0	11	23.1	87	12	5	5	4	1	0	0	4	1	35	2	0	0	1	.000	0	5- -	-	1.32	1.93
2015	NYY	AL	7	0	0	5	5.2	26	6	3	3	0	0	0	1	3	0	3	0	0	0	0	-	0	0-0	0	4.90	4.76
2016	NYY	AL	27	0	0	10	29.0	128	30	15	15	7	1	1	1	12	1	34	0	0	0	0	-	0	0-0	0	5.42	4.66
	2 ML YEARS		34	0	0	15	34.2	154	36	18	18	7	1	1	2	15	1	37	0	0	0	0	-	0	0-0	0	5.36	4.67

Alex Gordon

Bats: L **Throws:** R **Pos:** LF-126;PH-3

Ht: 6'1" **Wt:** 220 **Born:** 2/10/1984 **Age:** 33

Year	Team	Lg	G	AB	H	2B	3B	HR	(Hm	Rd)	TB	R	RBI	RC	TBB	IBB	SO	HBP	SH	SF	SB	CS	GDP	Avg	OBP	Slg	OPS
									BATTING												**RUNNING**			**AVERAGES**			
2007	KC	AL	151	543	134	36	4	15	(8	7)	223	60	60	69	41	4	137	13	1	2	14	4	12	.247	.314	.411	.725
2008	KC	AL	134	493	128	35	1	16	(9	7)	213	72	59	71	66	5	120	6	1	5	9	2	8	.260	.351	.432	.783
2009	KC	AL	49	164	38	6	0	6	(2	4)	62	28	22	16	21	0	43	2	1	1	5	0	5	.232	.324	.378	.703
2010	KC	AL	74	242	52	10	0	8	(5	3)	86	34	20	23	34	1	62	2	2	1	1	5	9	.215	.315	.355	.671
2011	KC	AL	151	611	185	45	4	23	(12	11)	307	101	87	103	67	2	139	7	0	3	17	8	9	.303	.376	.502	.879
2012	KC	AL	161	642	189	**51**	5	14	(6	8)	292	93	72	94	73	3	140	3	0	3	10	5	14	.294	.368	.455	.822
2013	KC	AL	156	633	168	27	6	20	(10	10)	267	90	81	90	52	7	141	9	0	6	11	3	4	.265	.327	.422	.749
2014	KC	AL	156	563	150	34	1	19	(11	8)	243	87	74	95	65	5	126	11	0	4	12	3	11	.266	.351	.432	.783
2015	KC	AL	104	354	96	18	0	13	(4	9)	153	40	48	60	49	7	92	14	0	5	2	5	2	.271	.377	.432	.809
2016	KC	AL	128	445	98	16	2	17	(8	9)	169	62	40	48	52	3	148	8	0	1	8	1	9	.220	.312	.380	.692
	Postseason		31	108	24	10	0	3	(1	2)	43	17	17	13	14	2	30	4	0	0	4	0	3	.222	.333	.398	.731
	10 ML YEARS		1264	4690	1238	278	23	151	(75	76)	2015	667	563	669	520	37	1148	75	5	31	89	36	83	.264	.345	.430	.774

Dee Gordon

Bats: L **Throws:** R **Pos:** 2B-78;PR-3;PH-2

Ht: 5'11" **Wt:** 170 **Born:** 4/22/1988 **Age:** 29

Year	Team	Lg	G	AB	H	2B	3B	HR	(Hm	Rd)	TB	R	RBI	RC	TBB	IBB	SO	HBP	SH	SF	SB	CS	GDP	Avg	OBP	Slg	OPS
									BATTING												**RUNNING**			**AVERAGES**			
2011	LAD	NL	56	224	68	9	2	0	(0	0)	81	34	11	25	7	0	27	0	2	0	24	7	1	.304	.325	.362	.686
2012	LAD	NL	87	303	69	9	2	1	(0	1)	85	38	17	22	20	0	62	3	2	2	32	10	5	.228	.280	.281	.561
2013	LAD	NL	38	94	22	1	1	1	(1	0)	28	9	6	9	10	2	21	1	1	0	10	2	0	.234	.314	.298	.612
2014	LAD	NL	148	609	176	24	**12**	2	(2	0)	230	92	34	76	31	0	107	4	3	3	**64**	19	6	.289	.326	.378	.704
2015	Mia	NL	145	615	**205**	24	8	4	(2	2)	257	88	46	94	25	2	91	2	6	5	58	**20**	6	**.333**	.359	.418	.776
2016	Mia	NL	79	325	87	7	6	1	(1	0)	109	47	14	33	18	1	55	0	1	1	30	7	4	.268	.305	.335	.641
	Postseason		6	17	3	0	0	0	(0	0)	3	0	2	0	2	0	6	0	0	0	1	1	0	.176	.263	.176	.440
	6 ML YEARS		553	2170	627	74	31	9	(6	3)	790	308	128	259	111	5	363	10	15	11	218	65	19	.289	.325	.364	.689

Terrance Gore

Bats: R **Throws:** R **Pos:** PR-15;LF-2;DH-2

Ht: 5'7" **Wt:** 165 **Born:** 6/8/1991 **Age:** 26

Year	Team	Lg	G	AB	H	2B	3B	HR	(Hm	Rd)	TB	R	RBI	RC	TBB	IBB	SO	HBP	SH	SF	SB	CS	GDP	Avg	OBP	Slg	OPS
									BATTING												**RUNNING**			**AVERAGES**			
2016	NWArk*	AA	88	253	59	2	1	0	(-	-)	63	31	11	29	26	1	58	4	19	0	44	5	2	.233	.314	.249	.563
2014	KC	AL	11	1	0	0	0	0	(0	0)	0	5	0	1	0	0	0	1	0	0	5	0	0	.000	.500	.000	.500
2015	KC	AL	9	3	0	0	0	0	(0	0)	0	1	0	0	0	0	1	1	0	0	3	0	0	.000	.250	.000	.250
2016	KC	AL	17	3	0	0	0	0	(0	0)	0	6	0	0	0	0	1	0	0	0	11	2	0	.000	.000	.000	.000
	Postseason		8	0	0	0	0	0	(0	0)	0	2	0	0	0	0	0	0	0	0	4	1	0	-	-	-	-
	3 ML YEARS		37	7	0	0	0	0	(0	0)	0	12	0	1	0	0	2	2	0	0	19	2	0	.000	.222	.000	.222

Tom Gorzelanny

Pitches: L **Bats:** R **Pos:** RP-7

gore-zah-LAWN-ee

Ht: 6'2" **Wt:** 210 **Born:** 7/12/1982 **Age:** 34

Year	Team	Lg	G	GS	CG	GF	IP	BFP	H	R	ER	HR	SH	SF	HB	TBB	IBB	SO	WP	Bk	W	L	Pct	Sh	Sv-Op	Hld	ERC	ERA
	HOW MUCH HE PITCHED								**WHAT HE GAVE UP**												**THE RESULTS**							
2016	Clmbs*	AAA	19	0	0	3	18.2	79	13	8	7	0	0	1	1	11	1	19	1	0	1	1	.500	0	1- -	-	2.60	3.38
2016	Norfolk*	AAA	7	0	0	2	6.0	36	11	7	3	0	0	0	0	5	0	5	1	0	0	0	-	0	0- -	-	9.50	4.50
2005	Pit	NL	3	1	0	0	6.0	32	10	8	8	1	1	0	0	3	0	3	0	0	1	0	1.000	0	0-0	0	8.76	12.00
2006	Pit	NL	11	11	0	0	61.2	267	50	29	26	3	7	4	4	31	2	40	3	0	2	5	.286	0	0-0	0	3.23	3.79
2007	Pit	NL	32	32	1	0	201.2	874	214	90	87	18	3	9	11	68	3	135	5	1	14	10	.583	1	0-0	0	4.31	3.88
2008	Pit	NL	21	21	0	0	105.1	490	120	79	78	20	3	6	1	70	0	67	5	1	6	9	.400	0	0-0	0	6.86	6.66
2009	2 Tms	NL	22	7	0	2	47.0	204	45	30	29	6	3	3	1	17	0	47	1	0	7	3	.700	0	0-1	2	3.88	5.55
2010	ChC	NL	29	23	0	3	136.1	604	136	70	62	11	4	6	2	68	4	119	0	0	7	9	.438	0	1-1	1	4.30	4.09
2011	Was	NL	30	15	0	1	105.0	447	102	50	47	15	8	4	6	33	5	95	5	1	4	6	.400	0	0-1	4	4.03	4.03
2012	Was	NL	45	1	0	11	72.0	306	65	27	23	7	3	2	2	30	1	62	4	0	4	2	.667	0	1-1	9	3.68	2.88
2013	Mil	NL	43	10	0	4	85.1	356	77	41	37	11	1	2	2	31	1	83	2	0	3	6	.333	0	0-1	6	3.70	3.90
2014	Mil	NL	23	0	0	7	21.0	95	22	3	2	1	0	0	2	8	0	23	0	0	0	0	-	0	0-0	0	4.15	0.86
2015	Det	AL	48	0	0	14	39.1	181	45	28	26	4	2	0	2	23	2	36	1	0	2	2	.500	0	0-0	5	5.89	5.95
2016	Cle	AL	7	0	0	1	3.0	18	4	7	7	1	0	0	0	5	1	4	0	0	1	0	1.000	0	0-0	1	13.17	21.00
09	Pit	NL	9	0	0	2	8.2	36	6	5	5	0	1	0	0	4	0	7	0	0	3	1	.750	0	0-1	1	2.02	5.19
09	ChC	NL	13	7	0	0	38.1	168	39	25	24	6	2	3	1	13	0	40	1	0	4	2	.667	0	0-0	1	4.33	5.63
	Postseason		1	0	0	1	0.1	2	1	0	0	0	0	0	0	0	0	0	0	0	0	0	-	0	0-0	0	14.52	0.00
	12 ML YEARS		314	121	1	43	883.2	3874	890	462	432	98	35	36	33	387	19	714	26	3	50	53	.485	1	2-5	25	4.46	4.40

Anthony Gose

Bats: L **Throws:** L **Pos:** CF-30

GOASE

Ht: 6'1" **Wt:** 190 **Born:** 8/10/1990 **Age:** 26

Year	Team	Lg	G	AB	H	2B	3B	HR	(Hm	Rd)	TB	R	RBI	RC	TBB	IBB	SO	HBP	SH	SF	SB	CS	GDP	Avg	OBP	Slg	OPS
2016	Toledo*	AAA	50	184	34	8	2	1	(-	-)	49	22	13	13	15	0	75	3	2	2	6	1	3	.185	.255	.266	.521
2016	Erie*	AA	40	156	35	4	0	6	(-	-)	57	16	27	18	17	0	54	0	0	0	11	4	4	.224	.301	.365	.666
2012	Tor	AL	56	166	37	7	3	1	(0	1)	53	25	11	21	17	0	59	2	4	0	15	3	1	.223	.303	.319	.622
2013	Tor	AL	52	147	38	6	5	2	(2	0)	60	15	12	13	5	0	37	0	1	0	4	3	5	.259	.283	.408	.691
2014	Tor	AL	94	239	54	8	1	2	(2	0)	70	31	13	19	25	0	74	5	4	1	15	5	9	.226	.311	.293	.604
2015	Det	AL	140	485	123	24	8	5	(1	4)	178	73	26	45	45	0	145	3	2	0	23	11	11	.254	.321	.367	.688
2016	Det	AL	30	91	19	2	2	2	(1	1)	31	11	7	6	9	0	38	1	0	0	0	1	1	.209	.287	.341	.628
	5 ML YEARS		372	1128	271	47	19	12	(6	6)	392	155	69	104	101	0	353	11	11	1	57	23	27	.240	.309	.348	.656

Tuffy Gosewisch

Bats: R **Throws:** R **Pos:** C-31;PH-3

GOES-uh-wish

Ht: 5'11" **Wt:** 200 **Born:** 8/17/1983 **Age:** 33

Year	Team	Lg	G	AB	H	2B	3B	HR	(Hm	Rd)	TB	R	RBI	RC	TBB	IBB	SO	HBP	SH	SF	SB	CS	GDP	Avg	OBP	Slg	OPS
2016	Reno*	AAA	58	199	68	13	1	9	(-	-)	110	33	26	42	15	1	30	4	1	0	0	0	6	.342	.399	.553	.952
2013	Ari	NL	14	45	8	2	0	0	(0	0)	10	1	3	0	0	0	8	0	1	1	0	0	3	.178	.174	.222	.396
2014	Ari	NL	41	129	29	8	0	1	(0	1)	40	6	7	5	3	0	24	0	0	0	0	0	6	.225	.242	.310	.553
2015	Ari	NL	38	128	27	6	0	1	(1	0)	36	9	13	8	8	0	23	1	0	1	2	1	2	.211	.261	.281	.542
2016	Ari	NL	33	90	14	1	1	3	(1	2)	26	8	7	6	7	0	22	1	1	0	0	0	1	.156	.224	.289	.513
	4 ML YEARS		126	392	78	17	1	5	(2	3)	112	24	30	19	18	0	77	2	2	2	2	1	12	.199	.237	.286	.522

Phil Gosselin

GAHSS-eh-lin

Bats: R **Throws:** R **Pos:** PH-83;2B-35;3B-10;1B-6;LF-2;RF-1;DH-1

Ht: 6'1" **Wt:** 200 **Born:** 10/3/1988 **Age:** 28

Year	Team	Lg	G	AB	H	2B	3B	HR	(Hm	Rd)	TB	R	RBI	RC	TBB	IBB	SO	HBP	SH	SF	SB	CS	GDP	Avg	OBP	Slg	OPS
2013	Atl	NL	4	6	2	0	0	0	(0	0)	2	2	0	1	1	1	2	0	0	0	0	0	0	.333	.429	.333	.762
2014	Atl	NL	46	128	34	4	0	1	(1	0)	41	17	3	10	5	0	27	2	1	0	2	2	1	.266	.304	.320	.624
2015	2 Tms	NL	44	106	33	9	1	3	(2	1)	53	19	15	22	9	0	16	2	0	1	2	1	2	.311	.373	.500	.873
2016	Ari	NL	122	220	61	12	1	2	(1	1)	81	26	13	24	15	0	46	1	2	2	3	0	0	.277	.324	.368	.692
15	Atl	NL	20	40	13	4	0	0	(0	0)	17	2	2	6	2	0	5	0	0	0	2	0	0	.325	.357	.425	.782
15	Ari	NL	24	66	20	5	1	3	(2	1)	36	17	13	16	7	0	11	2	0	1	0	1	2	.303	.382	.545	.927
	4 ML YEARS		216	460	130	25	2	6	(4	2)	177	64	31	57	30	1	91	5	3	3	7	3	3	.283	.331	.385	.716

Trevor Gott

Pitches: R **Bats:** R **Pos:** RP-9

Ht: 6'0" **Wt:** 185 **Born:** 8/26/1992 **Age:** 24

			HOW MUCH HE PITCHED					WHAT HE GAVE UP										THE RESULTS							
Year	Team	Lg	G	GS	CG	GF	IP	BFP	H	R	ER	HR	SH	SF	HB	TBB	IBB	SO	WP	Bk	W	L	Pct	Sh	Sv-Op	Hld	ERC	ERA
2013	2 Tms	Low	31	0	0	11	36.0	147	27	13	10	1	0	2	2	15	0	41	1	0	2	2	.500	0	4- -	-	2.59	2.50
2014	Lk Els	A+	29	0	0	25	31.1	133	28	13	11	3	4	2	1	9	2	31	1	0	2	4	.333	0	16- -	-	2.98	3.16
2014	SnAnt	AA	10	0	0	0	11.2	55	11	8	6	0	3	0	0	9	0	11	0	0	0	0	-	0	0- -	-	4.30	4.63
2014	Ark	AA	13	0	0	8	17.2	68	11	3	3	0	1	1	0	7	0	18	1	0	2	1	.667	0	2- -	-	1.64	1.53
2015	Ark	AA	18	0	0	16	19.2	81	19	9	7	0	1	1	1	7	0	20	1	0	1	0	1.000	0	8- -	-	3.36	3.20
2015	Salt Lk	AAA	7	0	0	4	8.1	37	7	0	0	0	2	0	1	5	0	10	0	0	0	0	-	0	0- -	-	3.68	0.00
2016	Syrcse	AAA	33	0	0	8	39.1	174	44	20	19	2	3	2	3	13	1	31	1	0	3	3	.500	0	1- -	-	4.37	4.35
2015	LAA	AL	48	0	0	7	47.2	202	43	18	16	2	2	3	3	16	3	27	1	0	4	2	.667	0	0-4	14	3.03	3.02
2016	Was	NL	9	0	0	1	6.0	28	6	1	1	0	0	1	1	3	1	6	0	0	0	0	-	0	0-0	1	3.93	1.50
	2 ML YEARS		57	0	0	8	53.2	230	49	19	17	2	2	4	4	19	4	33	1	0	4	2	.667	0	0-4	15	3.13	2.85

Matt Grace

Pitches: L **Bats:** L **Pos:** RP-5

Ht: 6'4" **Wt:** 215 **Born:** 12/14/1988 **Age:** 28

			HOW MUCH HE PITCHED					WHAT HE GAVE UP										THE RESULTS							
Year	Team	Lg	G	GS	CG	GF	IP	BFP	H	R	ER	HR	SH	SF	HB	TBB	IBB	SO	WP	Bk	W	L	Pct	Sh	Sv-Op	Hld	ERC	ERA
2012	Ptomc	A+	26	24	2	1	141.1	632	178	95	76	10	5	2	3	48	0	83	13	0	9	12	.429	1	0- -	-	5.25	4.84
2013	Ptomc	A+	14	0	0	2	28.1	120	26	11	10	0	3	1	3	7	0	24	2	0	3	0	1.000	0	1- -	-	2.74	3.18
2013	Hrsbrg	AA	28	0	0	4	38.0	158	42	17	16	2	1	1	1	7	1	31	3	0	6	3	.667	0	1- -	-	3.62	3.79
2014	Hrsbrg	AA	22	0	0	8	35.1	154	32	10	4	0	1	1	1	12	1	32	1	0	3	1	.750	0	3- -	-	2.49	1.02
2014	Syrcse	AAA	28	0	0	4	41.2	160	28	6	6	1	1	0	0	12	1	30	0	0	2	0	1.000	0	0- -	-	1.85	1.30
2015	Syrcse	AAA	38	0	0	10	48.2	198	43	16	13	1	7	2	0	16	0	31	0	0	0	2	.000	0	1- -	-	2.72	2.40
2016	Syrcse	AAA	35	0	0	10	47.1	199	54	17	15	1	1	1	0	9	2	32	4	0	1	3	.250	0	1- -	-	3.45	2.85
2015	Was	NL	26	0	0	5	17.0	84	26	11	8	0	0	2	1	8	2	14	1	0	2	1	.667	0	0-2	4	6.71	4.24
2016	Was	NL	5	0	0	1	3.0	10	1	0	0	0	0	0	0	0	0	4	0	0	0	0	-	0	0-0	0	0.25	0.00
	2 ML YEARS		31	0	0	6	20.0	94	27	11	8	0	0	2	1	8	2	18	1	0	2	1	.667	0	0-2	4	5.31	3.60

J.R. Graham

Pitches: R **Bats:** R **Pos:** RP-1

Ht: 5'11" **Wt:** 195 **Born:** 1/14/1990 **Age:** 27

			HOW MUCH HE PITCHED					WHAT HE GAVE UP										THE RESULTS							
Year	Team	Lg	G	GS	CG	GF	IP	BFP	H	R	ER	HR	SH	SF	HB	TBB	IBB	SO	WP	Bk	W	L	Pct	Sh	Sv-Op	Hld	ERC	ERA
2012	Lynbrg	A+	17	17	1	0	102.2	398	88	34	30	6	4	2	2	17	0	68	2	0	9	1	.900	0	0- -	-	2.35	2.63
2012	Missi	AA	9	9	0	0	45.1	187	35	17	16	2	0	1	2	17	0	42	2	0	3	1	.750	0	0- -	-	2.57	3.18
2013	Missi	AA	8	8	0	0	35.2	150	39	16	16	0	1	1	0	10	1	28	1	0	1	3	.250	0	0- -	-	3.45	4.04
2014	Missi	AA	27	19	0	1	71.1	319	79	47	44	2	10	4	6	26	1	50	1	0	1	5	.167	0	0- -	-	4.29	5.55
2016	Roch	AAA	8	0	0	7	8.1	42	11	10	10	1	1	0	0	7	0	7	2	1	0	2	.000	0	3- -	-	8.07	10.80

			HOW MUCH HE PITCHED						WHAT HE GAVE UP										THE RESULTS							
Year	Team	Lg	G	GS	CG	GF	IP	BFP	H	R	ER	HR	SH	SF	HB	TBB	IBB	SO	WP	Bk	W	L	Pct	Sh	Sv-Op	Hld	ERC	ERA
2016	Trntn	AA	17	0	0	6	29.2	122	26	7	6	1	0	1	1	9	0	33	2	2	2	1	.667	0	5- -	-	2.76	1.82
2015	Min	AL	39	1	0	19	63.2	283	73	41	35	10	2	2	4	21	0	53	5	1	1	1	.500	0	0-1	0	5.31	4.95
2016	Min	AL	1	0	0	0	1.2	9	3	2	2	0	0	0	0	1	0	2	0	0	0	0	-	0	0-0	0	8.83	10.80
	2 ML YEARS		40	1	0	19	65.1	292	76	43	37	10	2	2	4	22	0	55	5	1	1	1	.500	0	0-1	0	5.40	5.10

Yasmani Grandal

Bats: B **Throws:** R **Pos:** C-115;PH-16;1B-4   yahz-MAH-nee gran-DAHL   **Ht:** 6'1" **Wt:** 235 **Born:** 11/8/1988 **Age:** 28

							BATTING															RUNNING			AVERAGES			
Year	Team	Lg	G	AB	H	2B	3B	HR	(Hm	Rd)	TB	R	RBI	RC	TBB	IBB	SO	HBP	SH	SF	SB	CS	GDP	Avg	OBP	Slg	OPS
2012	SD	NL	60	192	57	7	1	8	(3	5)	90	28	36	37	31	1	39	1	0	2	0	0	8	.297	.394	.469	.863
2013	SD	NL	28	88	19	8	0	1	(1	0)	30	13	9	12	18	2	18	1	0	1	0	0	1	.216	.352	.341	.693
2014	SD	NL	128	377	85	19	1	15	(7	8)	151	47	49	45	58	1	115	1	0	6	3	0	7	.225	.327	.401	.728
2015	LAD	NL	115	355	83	12	0	16	(8	8)	143	43	47	47	65	1	92	2	1	3	0	1	16	.234	.353	.403	.756
2016	LAD	NL	126	390	89	14	1	27	(20	7)	186	49	72	63	64	1	116	2	0	1	1	3	11	.228	.339	.477	.816
	Postseason		3	10	1	0	0	0	(0	0)	1	0	2	0	1	0	6	0	0	0	0	0	0	.100	.182	.100	.282
	5 ML YEARS		457	1402	333	60	3	67	(39	28)	600	180	213	204	236	6	380	8	1	13	4	4	43	.238	.348	.428	.776

Curtis Granderson

Bats: L **Throws:** R **Pos:** RF-110;CF-36;PH-10;LF-7;DH-1;PR-1   **Ht:** 6'1" **Wt:** 200 **Born:** 3/16/1981 **Age:** 36

							BATTING															RUNNING			AVERAGES			
Year	Team	Lg	G	AB	H	2B	3B	HR	(Hm	Rd)	TB	R	RBI	RC	TBB	IBB	SO	HBP	SH	SF	SB	CS	GDP	Avg	OBP	Slg	OPS
2004	Det	AL	9	25	6	1	1	0	(0	0)	9	2	0	2	3	0	8	0	0	0	0	0	1	.240	.321	.360	.681
2005	Det	AL	47	162	44	6	3	8	(5	3)	80	18	20	26	10	0	43	0	2	0	1	1	2	.272	.314	.494	.808
2006	Det	AL	159	596	155	31	9	19	(7	12)	261	90	68	89	66	0	174	4	7	6	8	5	4	.260	.335	.438	.773
2007	Det	AL	158	612	185	38	23	23	(10	13)	338	122	74	106	52	3	141	5	5	2	26	1	3	.302	.361	.552	.913
2008	Det	AL	141	553	155	26	13	22	(11	11)	273	112	66	100	71	1	111	3	1	1	12	4	7	.280	.365	.494	.858
2009	Det	AL	160	631	157	23	8	30	(10	20)	286	91	71	92	72	4	141	2	3	2	20	6	1	.249	.327	.453	.780
2010	NYY	AL	136	466	115	17	7	24	(14	10)	218	76	67	71	53	3	116	2	4	3	12	2	3	.247	.324	.468	.792
2011	NYY	AL	156	583	153	26	10	41	(21	20)	322	136	119	113	85	0	169	12	4	7	25	10	12	.262	.364	.552	.916
2012	NYY	AL	160	596	138	18	4	43	(26	17)	293	102	106	92	75	4	195	5	1	7	10	3	5	.232	.319	.492	.811
2013	NYY	AL	61	214	49	13	2	7	(2	5)	87	31	15	23	27	1	69	1	2	1	8	2	1	.229	.317	.407	.723
2014	NYM	NL	155	564	128	27	2	20	(7	13)	219	73	66	70	79	1	141	6	0	5	8	2	1	.227	.326	.388	.714
2015	NYM	NL	157	580	150	33	2	26	(12	14)	265	98	70	104	91	3	151	7	0	4	11	6	3	.259	.364	.457	.821
2016	NYM	NL	150	545	129	24	5	30	(13	17)	253	88	59	66	74	7	130	9	0	5	4	2	10	.237	.335	.464	.799
	Postseason		50	184	45	8	3	9	(6	3)	86	26	29	35	29	1	45	1	1	3	9	3	2	.245	.346	.467	.813
	13 ML YEARS		1649	6127	1564	283	89	293	(138	155)	2904	1039	801	957	758	27	1589	56	29	43	145	44	53	.255	.340	.474	.814

Juan Graterol

Bats: R **Throws:** R **Pos:** C-9   **Ht:** 6'1" **Wt:** 205 **Born:** 2/14/1989 **Age:** 28

							BATTING															RUNNING			AVERAGES			
Year	Team	Lg	G	AB	H	2B	3B	HR	(Hm	Rd)	TB	R	RBI	RC	TBB	IBB	SO	HBP	SH	SF	SB	CS	GDP	Avg	OBP	Slg	OPS
2012	Wilmg	A+	61	196	59	12	0	2	(-	-)	77	26	18	26	7	0	24	4	4	0	0	2	12	.301	.338	.393	.731
2013	NWArk	AA	56	182	52	6	0	3	(-	-)	67	17	17	22	6	0	22	2	4	1	3	0	7	.286	.314	.368	.682
2014	NWArk	AA	70	246	69	17	0	4	(-	-)	98	17	28	31	9	0	29	3	5	1	0	0	11	.280	.314	.398	.711
2015	S-WB	AAA	20	70	14	1	0	1	(-	-)	18	8	9	3	1	0	10	0	0	1	0	0	6	.200	.208	.257	.465
2016	Salt Lk	AAA	68	227	68	10	0	2	(-	-)	84	24	23	30	10	0	27	5	2	2	2	1	13	.300	.340	.370	.710
2016	LAA	AL	9	14	4	2	0	0	(0	0)	6	2	3	1	0	0	3	0	1	0	0	0	0	.286	.286	.429	.714

Kendall Graveman

Pitches: R **Bats:** R **Pos:** SP-31   **Ht:** 6'2" **Wt:** 200 **Born:** 12/21/1990 **Age:** 26

						HOW MUCH HE PITCHED				WHAT HE GAVE UP												THE RESULTS					
Year	Team	Lg	G	GS	CG	GF	IP	BFP	H	R	ER	HR	SH	SF	HB	TBB	IBB	SO	WP	Bk	W	L	Pct	Sh	Sv-Op	Hld	ERC	ERA
2014	Tor	AL	5	0	0	1	4.2	18	4	2	2	0	0	0	0	0	0	4	1	0	0	0	-	0	0-0	0	1.44	3.86
2015	Oak	AL	21	21	1	0	115.2	502	126	57	52	15	1	2	5	38	0	77	4	0	6	9	.400	0	0-0	0	4.72	4.05
2016	Oak	AL	31	31	2	0	186.0	786	196	87	85	22	2	6	7	47	2	108	2	0	10	11	.476	1	0-0	0	4.08	4.11
	3 ML YEARS		57	52	3	1	306.1	1306	326	146	139	37	3	8	12	85	2	189	7	0	16	20	.444	1	0-0	0	4.27	4.08

Jon Gray

Pitches: R **Bats:** R **Pos:** SP-29   **Ht:** 6'4" **Wt:** 235 **Born:** 11/5/1991 **Age:** 25

						HOW MUCH HE PITCHED				WHAT HE GAVE UP												THE RESULTS					
Year	Team	Lg	G	GS	CG	GF	IP	BFP	H	R	ER	HR	SH	SF	HB	TBB	IBB	SO	WP	Bk	W	L	Pct	Sh	Sv-Op	Hld	ERC	ERA
2013	2 Tms	Low	9	9	0	0	37.1	144	25	11	8	0	1	1	1	8	0	51	1	1	4	0	1.000	0	0- -	-	1.41	1.93
2014	Tulsa	AA	24	24	0	0	124.1	508	107	58	54	10	6	5	4	41	0	113	5	0	10	5	.667	0	0- -	-	3.10	3.91
2015	Albq	AAA	21	20	1	0	114.1	507	129	61	55	9	2	1	4	41	2	110	9	1	6	6	.500	0	0- -	-	4.58	4.33
2015	Col	NL	9	9	0	0	40.2	185	52	26	25	4	2	4	2	14	2	40	3	0	0	2	.000	0	0-0	0	5.60	5.53
2016	Col	NL	29	29	1	0	168.0	712	153	92	86	18	5	5	12	59	2	185	7	0	10	10	.500	1	0-0	0	3.71	4.61
	2 ML YEARS		38	38	1	0	208.2	897	205	118	111	22	7	9	14	73	4	225	10	0	10	12	.455	1	0-0	0	4.06	4.79

Sonny Gray

Pitches: R Bats: R Pos: SP-22　　　　　　　　Ht: 5'10" Wt: 190 Born: 11/7/1989 Age: 27

			HOW MUCH HE PITCHED						WHAT HE GAVE UP										THE RESULTS						
Year	Team	Lg	G	GS	CG	GF	IP	BFP	H	R	ER	HR	SH	SF	HB	TBB	IBB	SO	WP	Bk	W	L	Pct	Sh	Sv-Op	Hld	ERC	ERA
2013	Oak	AL	12	10	0	0	64.0	261	51	22	19	4	0	3	0	20	0	67	2	1	5	3	.625	0	0-0	0	2.42	2.67
2014	Oak	AL	33	33	2	0	219.0	899	187	84	75	15	8	5	7	74	2	183	15	0	14	10	.583	2	0-0	0	2.99	3.08
2015	Oak	AL	31	31	3	0	208.0	831	166	71	63	17	1	4	2	59	0	169	13	0	14	7	.667	2	0-0	0	2.53	2.73
2016	Oak	AL	22	22	0	0	117.0	517	133	80	74	18	0	7	2	42	0	94	15	0	5	11	.313	0	0-0	0	5.16	5.69
	Postseason		2	2	0	0	13.0	53	10	3	3	1	1	0	0	6	1	12	0	0	0	1	.000	0	0-0	0	2.87	2.08
	4 ML YEARS		98	96	5	0	608.0	2508	537	257	231	54	9	19	11	195	2	513	45	1	38	31	.551	4	0-0	0	3.15	3.42

Chad Green

Pitches: R Bats: L Pos: SP-8; RP-4　　　　　　　　Ht: 6'3" Wt: 210 Born: 5/24/1991 Age: 26

			HOW MUCH HE PITCHED						WHAT HE GAVE UP										THE RESULTS						
Year	Team	Lg	G	GS	CG	GF	IP	BFP	H	R	ER	HR	SH	SF	HB	TBB	IBB	SO	WP	Bk	W	L	Pct	Sh	Sv-Op	Hld	ERC	ERA
2013	2 Tms	Low	12	2	0	2	20.1	84	19	8	8	1	0	0	0	6	0	16	0	0	4	0	1.000	0	1- -	-	3.00	3.54
2014	Wmich	A	23	23	0	0	130.1	523	121	51	45	8	3	6	3	28	0	125	5	0	6	4	.600	0	0- -	-	2.89	3.11
2015	Erie	AA	27	27	1	0	148.2	655	170	84	65	9	7	5	7	43	2	137	5	0	5	14	.263	0	0- -	-	4.29	3.93
2016	S-WB	AAA	16	16	0	0	94.2	365	68	21	16	3	1	2	1	21	0	100	2	0	7	6	.538	0	0- -	-	1.68	1.52
2016	NYY	AL	12	8	0	4	45.2	198	49	26	24	12	1	1	1	15	0	52	1	0	2	4	.333	0	1-1	0	5.46	4.73

Grant Green

Bats: R Throws: R Pos: 2B-15;PH-7　　　　　　　　Ht: 6'3" Wt: 180 Born: 9/27/1987 Age: 29

			BATTING																RUNNING			AVERAGES			
Year	Team	Lg	G	AB	H	2B	3B	HR	(Hm | Rd)	TB	R	RBI	RC	TBB	IBB	SO	HBP	SH	SF	SB	CS	GDP	Avg	OBP	Slg	OPS
2016	Scrmto*	AAA	94	348	111	18	4	7	(- | -)	158	46	52	53	11	0	58	0	1	4	2	1	9	.319	.336	.454	.790
2013	2 Tms	AL	45	140	35	8	1	1	(1 | 0)	48	16	17	16	10	0	44	1	0	2	0	0	3	.250	.301	.343	.644
2014	LAA	AL	43	99	27	5	0	1	(1 | 0)	35	7	11	8	2	0	20	0	0	2	1	4	3	.273	.282	.354	.635
2015	LAA	AL	21	42	8	0	0	1	(0 | 1)	11	6	3	1	2	1	14	0	0	0	0	1	2	.190	.227	.262	.489
2016	SF	AL	18	46	12	2	0	1	(1 | 0)	17	7	7	1	3	0	8	0	0	1	0	0	3	.261	.300	.370	.670
13	Oak	AL	5	15	0	0	0	0	(1 | 0)	0	0	1	0	0	0	6	0	0	1	0	0	0	.000	.000	.000	.000
13	LAA	AL	40	125	35	8	1	1	(1 | 0)	48	16	16	16	10	0	38	1	0	1	0	0	3	.280	.336	.384	.720
	4 ML YEARS		127	327	82	15	1	4	(3 | 1)	111	36	38	26	17	1	86	1	0	5	1	5	11	.251	.286	.339	.625

Shane Greene

Pitches: R Bats: R Pos: RP-47; SP-3　　　　　　　　Ht: 6'4" Wt: 210 Born: 11/17/1988 Age: 28

			HOW MUCH HE PITCHED						WHAT HE GAVE UP										THE RESULTS						
Year	Team	Lg	G	GS	CG	GF	IP	BFP	H	R	ER	HR	SH	SF	HB	TBB	IBB	SO	WP	Bk	W	L	Pct	Sh	Sv-Op	Hld	ERC	ERA
2014	NYY	AL	15	14	0	0	78.2	345	81	38	33	8	0	1	6	29	0	81	1	0	5	4	.556	0	0-0	0	4.43	3.78
2015	Det	AL	18	16	0	0	83.2	373	103	67	64	13	2	4	6	27	4	50	1	0	4	8	.333	0	0-0	0	5.83	6.88
2016	Det	AL	50	3	0	4	60.1	256	58	39	39	3	2	2	4	22	1	59	0	0	5	4	.556	0	2-3	16	3.65	5.82
	3 ML YEARS		83	33	0	5	222.2	974	242	144	136	24	4	7	16	78	5	190	2	0	14	16	.467	0	2-3	16	4.72	5.50

Luke Gregerson

Pitches: R Bats: L Pos: RP-59　　　　　　　　Ht: 6'3" Wt: 205 Born: 5/14/1984 Age: 33

			HOW MUCH HE PITCHED						WHAT HE GAVE UP										THE RESULTS						
Year	Team	Lg	G	GS	CG	GF	IP	BFP	H	R	ER	HR	SH	SF	HB	TBB	IBB	SO	WP	Bk	W	L	Pct	Sh	Sv-Op	Hld	ERC	ERA
2009	SD	NL	72	0	0	7	75.0	318	62	29	27	3	3	1	3	31	9	93	4	0	2	4	.333	0	1-7	27	2.72	3.24
2010	SD	NL	80	0	0	9	78.1	297	47	30	28	8	1	1	1	18	2	89	0	0	4	7	.364	0	2-7	40	1.56	3.22
2011	SD	NL	61	0	0	11	55.2	241	57	23	17	2	5	1	2	19	3	34	2	0	3	3	.500	0	0-4	16	3.55	2.75
2012	SD	NL	77	0	0	15	72.0	294	57	19	19	7	5	0	3	21	3	72	3	0	2	0	1.000	0	9-13	24	2.64	2.39
2013	SD	NL	73	0	0	17	66.1	268	49	24	20	3	4	1	4	18	2	64	1	0	6	8	.429	0	4-9	25	2.07	2.71
2014	Oak	AL	72	0	0	17	72.1	284	58	20	17	6	3	1	4	15	3	59	6	0	5	5	.500	0	3-11	22	2.25	2.12
2015	Hou	AL	64	0	0	53	61.0	239	48	24	21	5	2	0	2	10	2	59	1	0	7	3	.700	0	31-36	23	2.09	3.10
2016	Hou	AL	59	0	0	25	57.2	230	38	23	21	5	0	2	2	18	2	67	6	0	4	3	.571	0	15-21	15	1.99	3.28
	Postseason		5	0	0	3	4.2	21	3	1	1	1	0	0	1	3	0	8	1	0	0	0	-	0	3-3	1	4.60	1.93
	8 ML YEARS		558	0	0	154	538.0	2171	416	192	170	39	23	7	18	150	26	537	23	0	33	33	.500	0	65-108	169	2.32	2.84

Didi Gregorius

Bats: L Throws: R Pos: SS-153;PH-2　　dee-dee greh-GORE-ee-us　　　　Ht: 6'3" Wt: 205 Born: 2/18/1990 Age: 27

			BATTING																RUNNING			AVERAGES			
Year	Team	Lg	G	AB	H	2B	3B	HR	(Hm | Rd)	TB	R	RBI	RC	TBB	IBB	SO	HBP	SH	SF	SB	CS	GDP	Avg	OBP	Slg	OPS
2012	Cin	NL	8	20	6	0	0	0	(0 | 0)	6	1	2	2	0	0	6	0	1	0	0	0	0	.300	.300	.300	.600
2013	Ari	NL	103	357	90	16	3	7	(3 | 4)	133	47	28	42	37	5	65	6	2	1	0	2	4	.252	.332	.373	.704
2014	Ari	NL	80	270	61	9	5	6	(3 | 3)	98	35	27	37	22	3	52	3	2	2	3	0	1	.226	.290	.363	.653
2015	NYY	AL	155	525	139	24	2	9	(6 | 3)	194	57	56	64	33	0	85	11	3	5	5	3	4	.265	.318	.370	.688
2016	NYY	AL	153	562	155	32	2	20	(11 | 9)	251	68	70	71	19	2	82	6	5	5	7	1	9	.276	.304	.447	.751
	Postseason		1	3	1	0	0	0	(0 | 0)	1	0	0	0	0	0	0	0	0	0	0	0	0	.333	.333	.333	.667
	5 ML YEARS		499	1734	451	81	12	42	(23 | 19)	682	208	183	216	111	10	289	26	13	14	15	6	18	.260	.312	.393	.705

Zack Greinke

Pitches: R Bats: R Pos: SP-26   GRAIN-key   Ht: 6'2" Wt: 200 Born: 10/21/1983 Age: 33

Year Team	Lg	G	GS	CG	GF	IP	BFP	H	R	ER	HR	SH	SF	HB	TBB	IBB	SO	WP	Bk	W	L	Pct	Sh	Sv-Op	Hld	ERC	ERA
2004 KC	AL	24	24	0	0	145.0	599	143	64	64	26	3	2	8	26	3	100	1	1	8	11	.421	0	0-0	0	3.85	3.97
2005 KC	AL	33	33	2	0	183.0	829	233	125	118	23	4	4	13	53	0	114	4	2	5	17	.227	0	0-0	0	5.71	5.80
2006 KC	AL	3	0	0	1	6.1	28	7	3	3	1	0	0	0	3	2	5	0	0	1	0	1.000	0	0-0	0	4.93	4.26
2007 KC	AL	52	14	0	7	122.0	507	122	52	50	12	3	4	3	36	5	106	3	1	7	7	.500	0	1-1	12	3.77	3.69
2008 KC	AL	32	32	1	0	202.1	851	202	87	78	21	2	4	4	56	1	183	8	1	13	10	.565	0	0-0	0	3.68	3.47
2009 KC	AL	33	33	6	0	229.1	915	195	64	55	11	8	3	4	51	0	242	5	0	16	8	.667	3	0-0	0	2.39	2.16
2010 KC	AL	33	33	3	0	220.0	919	219	114	102	18	6	7	7	55	1	181	4	0	10	14	.417	0	0-0	0	3.48	4.17
2011 Mil	NL	28	28	0	0	171.2	715	161	82	73	19	6	1	4	45	0	201	10	0	16	6	.727	0	0-0	0	3.35	3.83
2012 2 Tms		34	34	0	0	212.1	868	200	84	82	18	7	2	2	54	0	200	8	0	15	5	.750	0	0-0	0	3.17	3.48
2013 LAD	NL	28	28	1	0	177.2	717	152	54	52	13	13	1	7	46	1	148	5	0	15	4	.789	1	0-0	0	2.78	2.63
2014 LAD	NL	32	32	0	0	202.1	821	190	69	61	19	2	4	2	43	3	207	12	0	17	8	.680	0	0-0	0	3.03	2.71
2015 LAD	NL	32	32	1	0	222.2	843	148	43	41	14	6	2	5	40	1	200	7	0	19	3	.864	0	0-0	0	1.56	1.66
2016 Ari	NL	26	26	1	0	158.2	667	161	80	77	23	7	4	0	41	3	134	1	0	13	7	.650	1	0-0	0	3.86	4.37
12 Mil	NL	21	21	0	0	123.0	504	120	49	47	7	3	0	0	28	0	122	4	0	9	3	.750	0	0-0	0	3.02	3.44
12 LAA	AL	13	13	0	0	89.1	364	80	35	35	11	4	2	2	26	0	78	4	0	6	2	.750	0	0-0	0	3.38	3.53
Postseason		9	9	0	0	58.1	232	50	26	23	7	1	1	2	9	0	54	1	0	3	3	.500	0	0-0	0	2.65	3.55
13 ML YEARS		390	349	15	8	2253.1	9279	2133	921	856	218	67	38	59	549	20	2021	68	5	155	100	.608	5	1-1	12	3.27	3.42

Randal Grichuk

Bats: R Throws: R Pos: CF-115;PH-17;LF-4;RF-3;PR-1   GRICH-ick   Ht: 6'1" Wt: 205 Born: 8/13/1991 Age: 25

Year Team	Lg	G	AB	H	2B	3B	HR	(Hm	Rd)	TB	R	RBI	RC	TBB	IBB	SO	HBP	SH	SF	SB	CS	GDP	Avg	OBP	Slg	OPS
2016 Memp*	AAA	23	81	22	4	1	6	(-	-)	46	12	18	14	2	0	14	2	0	1	0	0	2	.272	.302	.568	.870
2014 StL	NL	47	110	27	6	1	3	(2	1)	44	11	8	7	5	0	31	4	0	1	0	2	4	.245	.278	.400	.678
2015 StL	NL	103	323	89	23	7	17	(10	7)	177	49	47	47	22	2	110	4	0	1	4	2	6	.276	.329	.548	.877
2016 StL	NL	132	446	107	29	3	24	(12	12)	214	66	68	62	28	0	141	3	0	1	5	4	9	.240	.289	.480	.769
Postseason		13	43	8	0	0	3	(1	2)	17	5	4	2	1	0	17	0	0	0	0	0	0	.186	.205	.395	.600
3 ML YEARS		282	879	223	58	11	44	(24	20)	435	126	123	116	55	2	282	7	1	2	9	8	19	.254	.302	.495	.797

A.J. Griffin

Pitches: R Bats: R Pos: SP-23   Ht: 6'5" Wt: 230 Born: 1/28/1988 Age: 29

Year Team	Lg	G	GS	CG	GF	IP	BFP	H	R	ER	HR	SH	SF	HB	TBB	IBB	SO	WP	Bk	W	L	Pct	Sh	Sv-Op	Hld	ERC	ERA
2012 Oak	AL	15	15	0	0	82.1	336	74	29	28	10	0	2	1	19	0	64	0	0	7	1	.875	0	0-0	0	3.06	3.06
2013 Oak	AL	32	32	1	0	200.0	823	171	91	85	36	4	4	4	54	2	171	7	0	14	10	.583	1	0-0	0	3.33	3.83
2016 Tex	AL	23	23	0	0	119.0	509	116	68	67	28	0	3	7	46	1	107	0	1	7	4	.636	0	0-0	0	5.14	5.07
Postseason		1	1	0	0	5.0	21	7	2	2	1	1	0	0	0	0	1	0	0	0	0	-	0	0-0	0	5.60	3.60
3 ML YEARS		70	70	1	0	401.1	1668	361	188	180	74	4	9	12	119	3	342	7	1	28	15	.651	1	0-0	0	3.78	4.04

Jason Grilli

Pitches: R Bats: R Pos: RP-67   GRILL-ee   Ht: 6'5" Wt: 235 Born: 11/11/1976 Age: 40

Year Team	Lg	G	GS	CG	GF	IP	BFP	H	R	ER	HR	SH	SF	HB	TBB	IBB	SO	WP	Bk	W	L	Pct	Sh	Sv-Op	Hld	ERC	ERA
2000 Fla	NL	1	1	0	0	6.2	35	11	4	4	0	2	0	2	2	0	3	0	0	1	0	1.000	0	0-0	0	7.84	5.40
2001 Fla	NL	6	5	0	1	26.2	115	30	18	18	6	1	0	2	11	0	17	0	0	2	2	.500	0	0-0	0	6.44	6.08
2004 CWS	AL	8	8	1	0	45.0	203	52	38	37	11	2	1	3	20	0	26	2	0	2	3	.400	0	0-0	0	6.67	7.40
2005 Det	AL	3	2	0	0	16.0	63	14	6	6	1	1	1	0	6	0	5	0	0	1	1	.500	0	0-0	0	3.27	3.38
2006 Det	AL	51	0	0	18	62.0	270	61	31	29	6	2	4	5	25	3	31	5	0	2	3	.400	0	0-0	9	4.23	4.21
2007 Det	AL	57	0	0	13	79.2	352	81	46	42	5	1	5	5	32	1	62	5	0	5	3	.625	0	0-2	11	4.09	4.74
2008 2 Tms		60	0	0	16	75.0	323	67	27	25	2	1	3	2	38	7	69	4	0	3	3	.500	0	1-2	4	3.34	3.00
2009 2 Tms		52	0	0	11	45.2	212	50	27	27	4	2	1	1	27	0	49	2	0	2	3	.400	0	1-1	7	5.25	5.32
2011 Pit	NL	28	0	0	4	32.2	140	24	10	9	2	1	0	4	15	5	37	3	0	2	1	.667	0	1-1	9	2.79	2.48
2012 Pit	NL	64	0	0	11	58.2	244	45	20	19	7	2	1	2	22	4	90	0	0	1	6	.143	0	2-5	32	2.85	2.91
2013 Pit	NL	54	0	0	41	50.0	202	40	15	15	4	1	0	1	13	0	74	1	0	0	2	.000	0	33-35	2	2.44	2.70
2014 2 Tms		62	0	0	22	54.0	235	51	26	24	4	5	3	4	21	2	57	1	0	1	5	.167	0	12-17	12	3.73	4.00
2015 Atl	NL	36	0	0	29	33.2	140	28	13	11	2	0	1	0	10	1	45	2	0	3	4	.429	0	24-26	0	2.43	2.94
2016 2 Tms		67	0	0	14	59.0	251	44	28	27	10	0	3	2	32	1	81	2	0	7	6	.538	0	4-8	23	3.80	4.12
08 Det	AL	9	0	0	4	13.2	59	12	5	5	1	0	0	1	7	1	10	1	0	0	1	.000	0	0-1	0	3.85	3.29
08 Col	NL	51	0	0	12	61.1	264	55	22	20	1	1	3	1	31	6	59	3	0	3	2	.600	0	1-1	4	3.23	2.93
09 Col	NL	22	0	0	6	19.1	99	29	13	13	2	1	1	0	13	2	22	2	0	1	1	1.000	0	1-1	3	8.02	6.05
09 Tex	AL	30	0	0	5	26.1	113	21	14	14	2	1	0	1	14	0	27	0	0	2	2	.500	0	0-0	4	3.44	4.78
14 Pit	NL	22	0	0	16	20.1	93	22	11	11	4	1	0	1	11	1	21	0	0	0	2	.000	0	11-15	1	5.99	4.87
14 LAA	AL	40	0	0	6	33.2	142	29	15	13	0	4	3	3	10	1	36	1	0	1	3	.250	0	1-2	11	2.53	3.48
16 Atl	NL	21	0	0	8	17.0	81	16	11	10	2	0	1	1	13	1	23	1	0	1	2	.333	0	2-4	2	5.33	5.29
16 Tor	AL	46	0	0	6	42.0	170	28	17	17	8	0	2	1	19	0	58	1	0	6	4	.600	0	2-4	21	3.19	3.64
Postseason		11	0	0	4	8.1	33	4	0	0	0	0	0	0	4	1	7	0	0	1	1	.500	0	1-1	1	1.21	0.00
14 ML YEARS		549	16	1	180	644.2	2785	598	309	293	64	21	23	33	274	26	646	27	0	32	42	.432	0	78-97	109	3.89	4.09

Justin Grimm

Pitches: R Bats: R Pos: RP-68   Ht: 6'3" Wt: 210 Born: 8/16/1988 Age: 28

			HOW MUCH HE PITCHED						WHAT HE GAVE UP											THE RESULTS					
Year	Team	Lg	G	GS	CG	GF	IP	BFP	H	R	ER	HR	SH	SF	HB	TBB	IBB	SO	WP	Bk	W	L	Pct	Sh	Sv-Op	Hld	ERC	ERA
2012	Tex	AL	5	2	0	3	14.0	65	22	14	14	1	0	2	0	3	0	13	3	0	1	1	.500	0	0-0	0	6.54	9.00
2013	2 Tms		27	17	0	3	98.0	442	120	70	65	15	4	2	2	34	1	76	4	0	7	9	.438	0	0-0	3	5.61	5.97
2014	ChC	NL	73	0	0	19	69.0	292	59	32	29	4	1	3	4	27	2	70	8	0	5	2	.714	0	0-1	11	3.14	3.78
2015	ChC	NL	62	0	0	11	49.2	204	31	18	11	4	0	3	1	26	1	67	8	0	3	5	.375	0	3-6	15	2.48	1.99
2016	ChC	NL	68	0	0	11	52.2	225	47	24	24	5	0	0	1	23	2	65	7	0	2	1	.667	0	0-0	10	3.59	4.10
13	Tex		17	17	0	0	89.0	406	116	67	63	15	2	2	1	31	1	68	4	0	7	7	.500	0	0-0	0	6.21	6.37
13	ChC	NL	10	0	0	3	9.0	36	4	3	2	0	2	0	1	3	0	8	0	0	0	2	.000	0	0-0	3	1.12	2.00
	Postseason		3	0	0	0	2.0	8	1	0	0	0	0	0	0	0	0	4	0	0	0	0	-	0	0-0	0	0.47	0.00
	5 ML YEARS		235	19	0	47	283.1	1228	279	158	143	29	5	10	8	113	6	291	30	0	18	18	.500	0	3-7	39	4.06	4.54

Robbie Grossman

Bats: B Throws: L Pos: LF-75;DH-18;PH-7;PR-2;CF-1   Ht: 6'0" Wt: 215 Born: 9/16/1989 Age: 27

			BATTING																	RUNNING			AVERAGES			
Year	Team	Lg	G	AB	H	2B	3B	HR	(Hm	Rd)	TB	R	RBI	RC	TBB	IBB	SO	HBP	SH	SF	SB	CS	GDP	Avg	OBP	Slg	OPS
2016	Clmbs*	AAA	34	117	30	5	0	6	(-	-)	53	14	13	21	21	2	25	0	1	2	3	1	2	.256	.370	.453	.823
2013	Hou	AL	63	257	69	14	0	4	(3	1)	95	29	21	37	23	0	70	2	5	1	6	7	2	.268	.332	.370	.702
2014	Hou	AL	103	360	84	14	2	6	(2	4)	120	42	37	48	55	1	105	2	3	2	9	3	7	.233	.337	.333	.670
2015	Hou	AL	24	49	7	2	0	1	(1	0)	12	7	5	4	5	0	17	0	0	0	0	0	0	.143	.222	.245	.467
2016	Min	AL	99	332	93	19	1	11	(8	3)	147	49	37	52	55	0	96	2	0	0	2	3	3	.280	.386	.443	.828
	4 ML YEARS		289	998	253	49	3	22	(14	8)	374	127	100	141	138	1	288	6	8	3	17	13	12	.254	.347	.375	.721

Robert Gsellman

Pitches: R Bats: R Pos: SP-7; RP-1   guh-ZELL-man   Ht: 6'4" Wt: 205 Born: 7/18/1993 Age: 23

			HOW MUCH HE PITCHED						WHAT HE GAVE UP											THE RESULTS					
Year	Team	Lg	G	GS	CG	GF	IP	BFP	H	R	ER	HR	SH	SF	HB	TBB	IBB	SO	WP	Bk	W	L	Pct	Sh	Sv-Op	Hld	ERC	ERA
2012	Kngspt	R+	11	5	0	5	43.2	194	42	27	19	3	1	2	5	18	0	33	2	0	1	3	.250	0	0--	-	4.08	3.92
2013	3 Tms	Low	19	19	0	0	108.0	448	99	43	31	5	3	1	7	23	0	83	3	0	6	6	.500	0	0--	-	2.79	2.58
2014	Savann	A	20	20	4	0	116.0	500	122	42	33	2	6	7	9	34	0	92	6	0	10	6	.625	1	0--	-	3.67	2.56
2015	Stluci	A+	8	8	0	0	51.0	196	37	10	10	1	0	1	3	11	0	37	2	1	6	0	1.000	0	0--	-	1.81	1.76
2015	Bnghtn	AA	16	16	0	0	92.1	387	89	47	36	4	5	4	1	26	1	49	6	0	7	7	.500	0	0--	-	3.06	3.51
2016	Bnghtn	AA	11	11	0	0	66.1	266	57	23	20	2	0	0	6	15	0	48	3	0	3	4	.429	0	0--	-	2.64	2.71
2016	LsVgs	AAA	9	9	0	0	48.2	215	56	35	31	8	3	0	0	16	0	40	1	0	1	5	.167	0	0--	-	5.08	5.73
2016	NYM	NL	8	7	0	0	44.2	185	42	12	12	1	4	2	1	15	2	42	1	0	4	2	.667	0	0-0	0	3.05	2.42

Mayckol Guaipe

Pitches: R Bats: R Pos: RP-5   michael GOO-why-pay   Ht: 6'4" Wt: 235 Born: 8/11/1990 Age: 26

			HOW MUCH HE PITCHED						WHAT HE GAVE UP											THE RESULTS					
Year	Team	Lg	G	GS	CG	GF	IP	BFP	H	R	ER	HR	SH	SF	HB	TBB	IBB	SO	WP	Bk	W	L	Pct	Sh	Sv-Op	Hld	ERC	ERA
2012	2 Tms	Low	13	13	0	0	70.1	299	73	37	28	5	3	4	8	17	0	40	4	0	5	0	1.000	0	0--	-	3.96	3.58
2013	Hi Dsrt	A+	35	3	0	18	59.0	261	59	39	37	5	1	2	8	29	0	57	3	0	3	4	.429	0	5--	-	4.99	5.64
2014	Jacksn	AA	40	0	0	32	56.0	226	45	20	18	4	3	2	3	9	0	56	1	0	1	3	.250	0	12--	-	2.15	2.89
2015	Tacom	AAA	38	0	0	19	47.0	194	49	17	15	3	1	0	1	10	0	36	2	0	0	4	.000	0	5--	-	3.48	2.87
2016	Tacom	AAA	12	0	0	7	14.1	57	10	5	5	1	1	0	1	4	1	13	1	0	0	1	.000	0	4--	-	2.06	3.14
2015	Sea	AL	21	0	0	2	26.2	121	34	19	16	5	1	1	3	13	1	22	1	0	0	3	.000	0	0-3	2	7.61	5.40
2016	Sea	AL	5	0	0	0	7.1	34	8	6	4	0	0	1	0	4	0	5	0	0	0	0	-	0	0-0	0	4.28	4.91
	2 ML YEARS		26	0	0	2	34.0	155	42	25	20	5	1	2	3	17	1	27	1	0	0	3	.000	0	0-3	2	6.83	5.29

Deolis Guerra

Pitches: R Bats: R Pos: RP-44   day-OH-lis GAIR-uh   Ht: 6'5" Wt: 245 Born: 4/17/1989 Age: 28

			HOW MUCH HE PITCHED						WHAT HE GAVE UP											THE RESULTS					
Year	Team	Lg	G	GS	CG	GF	IP	BFP	H	R	ER	HR	SH	SF	HB	TBB	IBB	SO	WP	Bk	W	L	Pct	Sh	Sv-Op	Hld	ERC	ERA
2012	NwBrit	AA	7	0	0	2	12.2	44	5	1	1	0	0	0	1	1	0	15	2	0	2	0	1.000	0	1--	-	0.57	0.71
2012	Roch	AAA	29	0	0	7	57.1	245	59	33	31	7	2	0	1	21	1	56	5	0	2	3	.400	0	0--	-	4.45	4.87
2014	Roch	AAA	36	1	0	11	52.0	223	51	28	25	5	0	1	0	18	0	54	3	0	2	2	.500	0	0--	-	3.68	4.33
2015	Indy	AAA	25	0	0	9	36.2	137	21	6	5	1	0	2	0	8	1	37	3	0	2	1	.667	0	4--	-	1.16	1.23
2015	Pit	NL	10	0	0	4	16.2	74	26	12	12	5	0	0	0	3	0	17	2	0	2	0	1.000	0	0-0	0	8.96	6.48
2016	LAA	AL	44	0	0	11	53.1	220	52	23	19	6	1	1	2	7	0	36	2	1	3	0	1.000	0	0-4	5	3.08	3.21
	2 ML YEARS		54	0	0	15	70.0	294	78	35	31	11	1	1	3	10	0	53	4	1	5	0	1.000	0	0-4	5	4.27	3.99

Javy Guerra

Pitches: R Bats: R Pos: RP-7   GEHR-uh   Ht: 6'1" Wt: 225 Born: 10/31/1985 Age: 31

			HOW MUCH HE PITCHED						WHAT HE GAVE UP											THE RESULTS					
Year	Team	Lg	G	GS	CG	GF	IP	BFP	H	R	ER	HR	SH	SF	HB	TBB	IBB	SO	WP	Bk	W	L	Pct	Sh	Sv-Op	Hld	ERC	ERA
2016	Salt Lk*	AAA	43	1	0	30	51.2	235	48	30	25	5	0	3	0	31	0	57	5	0	3	2	.600	0	12--	-	4.31	4.35
2011	LAD	NL	47	0	0	38	46.2	195	37	12	12	2	3	1	3	18	1	38	2	0	2	2	.500	0	21-23	0	2.73	2.31
2012	LAD	NL	45	0	0	17	45.0	196	44	13	13	1	4	2	1	23	5	37	1	0	2	3	.400	0	8-13	4	3.76	2.60
2013	LAD	NL	9	0	0	5	10.2	50	15	9	8	1	0	1	1	6	0	12	0	0	0	0	-	0	0-0	0	7.24	6.75
2014	CWS	AL	42	0	0	10	46.1	198	41	15	15	4	3	2	4	20	5	38	2	0	2	4	.333	0	1-6	7	3.60	2.91
2015	CWS	AL	3	0	0	0	1.2	7	2	0	0	0	0	0	0	1	0	0	0	0	0	0	-	0	0-0	1	5.91	0.00
2016	LAA	AL	7	0	0	1	6.1	30	5	4	4	1	0	0	1	7	1	4	1	0	0	0	-	0	0-0	0	6.80	5.68
	6 ML YEARS		153	0	0	71	156.2	681	144	53	52	8	9	8	11	75	12	129	6	0	6	9	.400	0	30-42	12	3.74	2.99

Junior Guerra

Pitches: R Bats: R Pos: SP-20   GAIR-uh   Ht: 6'0" Wt: 205 Born: 1/16/1985 Age: 32

		HOW MUCH HE PITCHED					WHAT HE GAVE UP										THE RESULTS					
Year	Team	Lg	G	GS	CG	GF	IP	BFP	H	R	ER	HR	SH	SF	HB	TBB	IBB	SO	WP	Bk	W	L	Pct	Sh	Sv-Op	Hld	ERC	ERA
2015	Brham	AA	5	3	0	2	19.2	74	15	5	5	2	0	0	2	4	0	26	2	0	2	3	.400	0	0- -	-	2.69	2.29
2015	Charllt	AAA	26	8	0	13	63.2	264	44	24	24	5	4	2	1	29	0	79	6	1	2	4	.333	0	7- -	-	2.54	3.39
2016	ColSpr	AAA	5	5	0	0	26.2	106	18	12	12	2	1	1	0	11	0	25	1	0	0	2	.000	0	0- -	-	2.32	4.05
2015	CWS	AL	3	0	0	3	4.0	18	7	3	3	1	0	0	0	1	1	3	1	0	0	0	-	0	0-0	0	9.70	6.75
2016	Mil	NL	20	20	0	0	121.2	492	94	40	38	10	3	2	3	43	2	100	7	1	9	3	.750	0	0-0	0	2.68	2.81
	2 ML YEARS		23	20	0	3	125.2	510	101	43	41	11	3	2	3	44	3	103	8	1	9	3	.750	0	0-0	0	2.86	2.94

Tayron Guerrero

Pitches: R Bats: R Pos: RP-1   ty-ROHN guh-RAIR-oh   Ht: 6'8" Wt: 210 Born: 1/9/1991 Age: 26

		HOW MUCH HE PITCHED					WHAT HE GAVE UP										THE RESULTS					
Year	Team	Lg	G	GS	CG	GF	IP	BFP	H	R	ER	HR	SH	SF	HB	TBB	IBB	SO	WP	Bk	W	L	Pct	Sh	Sv-Op	Hld	ERC	ERA
2012	2 Tms	Low	9	7	0	0	25.1	100	17	8	7	0	0	1	1	14	0	17	6	0	1	1	.500	0	0- -	-	2.55	2.49
2013	3 Tms	Low	22	4	0	2	40.1	193	37	33	22	1	2	1	6	33	0	44	11	0	2	5	.286	0	0- -	-	5.21	4.91
2014	2 Tms	Low	39	0	0	17	49.1	201	32	11	8	3	0	0	1	20	0	56	3	1	6	1	.857	0	4- -	-	2.08	1.46
2015	SnAnt	AA	37	0	0	27	42.1	184	33	22	13	1	3	2	0	20	0	46	4	0	1	5	.167	0	13- -	-	2.93	2.76
2015	ElPaso	AAA	11	0	0	2	13.2	57	8	6	6	0	0	0	1	11	0	15	4	0	0	0	-	0	1- -	-	3.06	3.95
2016	ElPaso	AAA	13	0	0	3	12.0	57	12	9	8	2	0	0	0	9	0	11	2	0	0	0	-	0	0- -	-	5.89	6.00
2016	SnAnt	AA	19	0	0	7	23.2	97	20	14	13	2	1	1	0	10	0	25	0	0	0	3	.000	0	0- -	-	3.30	4.94
2016	Jaxnvl	AA	12	0	0	10	14.0	57	11	3	3	0	0	0	2	3	0	15	1	0	1	1	.500	0	4- -	-	2.16	1.93
2016	SD	NL	1	0	0	1	2.0	9	3	1	1	0	0	0	0	1	0	0	0	0	0	0	-	0	0-0	0	7.26	4.50

Jason Gurka

Pitches: L Bats: L Pos: RP-6   gurr-KAH   Ht: 6'0" Wt: 170 Born: 1/10/1988 Age: 29

		HOW MUCH HE PITCHED					WHAT HE GAVE UP										THE RESULTS					
Year	Team	Lg	G	GS	CG	GF	IP	BFP	H	R	ER	HR	SH	SF	HB	TBB	IBB	SO	WP	Bk	W	L	Pct	Sh	Sv-Op	Hld	ERC	ERA
2012	Frdrck	A+	20	1	0	6	45.1	179	30	12	11	1	2	1	7	12	2	43	0	0	1	2	.333	0	1- -	-	1.91	2.18
2012	Bowie	AA	12	0	0	5	20.0	94	19	8	8	3	1	1	4	12	0	22	0	0	2	3	.400	0	1- -	-	5.73	3.60
2013	Bowie	AA	20	0	0	9	39.2	170	35	13	13	2	2	0	6	18	1	46	1	0	2	2	.500	0	4- -	-	3.92	2.95
2014	Bowie	AA	30	3	0	5	64.0	260	50	21	17	4	3	1	2	18	0	60	2	0	3	1	.750	0	0- -	-	2.35	2.39
2015	NwBrit	AA	14	0	0	6	23.1	91	17	6	6	0	1	0	1	6	0	20	2	1	3	0	1.000	0	0- -	-	1.77	2.31
2015	Albq	AAA	21	1	0	6	39.2	167	42	14	14	3	1	1	3	12	1	33	1	0	2	1	.667	0	0- -	-	4.25	3.18
2016	Albq	AAA	18	0	0	8	21.1	95	25	6	4	3	1	0	1	6	2	31	0	0	0	1	.000	0	4- -	-	4.85	1.69
2015	Col	NL	9	0	0	4	7.2	39	16	8	8	1	0	0	0	2	0	7	0	0	0	0	-	0	0-0	0	11.05	9.39
2016	Col	NL	6	0	0	5	9.2	45	16	10	10	1	0	1	0	2	0	7	0	0	0	0	-	0	0-0	0	7.42	9.31
	2 ML YEARS		15	0	0	9	17.1	84	32	18	18	2	0	1	0	4	0	14	0	0	0	0	-	0	0-0	0	8.98	9.35

Yulieski Gurriel

yoo-lee-ES-kee goo-REE-el

Bats: R Throws: R Pos: 3B-21;DH-7;1B-5;PH-3;LF-1   Ht: 6'0" Wt: 190 Born: 6/9/1984 Age: 33

					BATTING															RUNNING			AVERAGES			
Year	Team	Lg	G	AB	H	2B	3B	HR	(Hm	Rd)	TB	R	RBI	RC	TBB	IBB	SO	HBP	SH	SF	SB	CS	GDP	Avg	OBP	Slg	OPS
2016	Hou	AL	36	130	34	7	0	3	(1	2)	50	13	15	13	5	0	12	1	0	1	1	1	7	.262	.292	.385	.677

Jandel Gustave

Pitches: R Bats: R Pos: RP-14   hahn-DELL goo-STAH-vay   Ht: 6'2" Wt: 210 Born: 10/12/1992 Age: 24

		HOW MUCH HE PITCHED					WHAT HE GAVE UP										THE RESULTS					
Year	Team	Lg	G	GS	CG	GF	IP	BFP	H	R	ER	HR	SH	SF	HB	TBB	IBB	SO	WP	Bk	W	L	Pct	Sh	Sv-Op	Hld	ERC	ERA
2012	Astros	R	10	4	0	0	28.0	137	24	23	18	0	0	3	5	27	0	22	7	2	2	1	.667	0	0- -	-	4.96	5.79
2013	Grnvlle	R+	10	10	0	0	43.2	193	38	23	13	2	1	3	4	23	0	49	2	0	2	3	.400	0	0- -	-	3.77	2.68
2014	QuadC	A	23	14	0	5	79.0	371	94	57	44	3	1	2	13	29	0	82	14	1	5	5	.500	0	2- -	-	5.11	5.01
2015	CpChr	AA	46	0	0	38	58.2	248	51	18	14	2	2	2	2	21	5	49	3	1	5	2	.714	0	20- -	-	3.13	2.15
2016	Fresno	AAA	47	0	0	20	57.0	247	46	27	24	1	1	5	8	23	1	55	4	2	3	3	.500	0	3- -	-	2.92	3.79
2016	Hou	AL	14	0	0	4	15.1	60	13	6	6	2	0	0	0	4	0	16	2	0	1	0	1.000	0	0-0	0	3.04	3.52

Franklin Gutierrez

Bats: R Throws: R Pos: RF-64;PH-35;DH-15;LF-9;PR-1   Ht: 6'2" Wt: 200 Born: 2/21/1983 Age: 34

					BATTING															RUNNING			AVERAGES			
Year	Team	Lg	G	AB	H	2B	3B	HR	(Hm	Rd)	TB	R	RBI	RC	TBB	IBB	SO	HBP	SH	SF	SB	CS	GDP	Avg	OBP	Slg	OPS
2005	Cle	AL	7	1	0	0	0	0	(0	0)	0	2	0	0	1	0	0	0	0	0	0	0	0	.000	.500	.000	.500
2006	Cle	AL	43	136	37	9	0	1	(1	0)	49	21	8	12	3	0	28	0	2	0	0	0	4	.272	.288	.360	.648
2007	Cle	AL	100	271	72	13	2	13	(10	3)	128	41	36	36	21	1	77	1	5	3	8	3	7	.266	.318	.472	.790
2008	Cle	AL	134	399	99	26	2	8	(6	2)	153	54	41	37	27	1	87	8	4	2	9	3	10	.248	.307	.383	.691
2009	Sea	AL	153	565	160	24	1	18	(7	11)	240	85	70	80	46	3	122	13	6	5	16	5	14	.283	.339	.425	.764
2010	Sea	AL	152	568	139	25	3	12	(6	6)	206	61	64	61	50	5	137	1	2	8	25	3	10	.245	.303	.363	.666
2011	Sea	AL	92	322	72	13	0	1	(0	1)	88	26	19	25	16	1	56	1	3	2	13	2	6	.224	.261	.273	.534
2012	Sea	AL	40	150	39	10	1	4	(2	2)	63	18	17	19	9	0	31	2	1	1	3	1	5	.260	.309	.420	.729
2013	Sea	AL	41	145	36	7	0	10	(4	6)	73	18	24	16	5	0	43	0	1	0	3	1	2	.248	.273	.503	.777
2015	Sea	AL	59	171	50	11	0	15	(6	9)	106	27	35	36	14	1	54	3	0	1	0	0	5	.292	.354	.620	.974
2016	Sea	AL	98	248	61	9	0	14	(8	6)	112	33	39	36	29	0	85	3	0	3	1	0	6	.246	.329	.452	.780
	Postseason		10	29	6	0	0	1	(0	1)	9	5	4	3	5	0	11	0	0	0	0	0	1	.207	.324	.310	.634
	11 ML YEARS		919	2976	765	147	9	96	(52	44)	1218	386	353	352	221	12	720	22	31	22	78	18	69	.257	.311	.409	.720

Brandon Guyer

Bats: R **Throws:** R **Pos:** LF-51;RF-19;CF-18;PH-18;DH-10 GUY-er **Ht:** 6'2" **Wt:** 200 **Born:** 1/28/1986 **Age:** 31

Year	Team	Lg	G	AB	H	2B	3B	HR	(Hm	Rd)	TB	R	RBI	RC	TBB	IBB	SO	HBP	SH	SF	SB	CS	GDP	Avg	OBP	Slg	OPS
2011	TB	AL	15	41	8	1	0	2	(1	1)	15	7	3	2	1	0	9	0	1	0	0	0	1	.195	.214	.366	.580
2012	TB	AL	3	7	1	0	0	1	(0	1)	4	2	1	0	0	0	1	0	0	0	0	0	0	.143	.143	.571	.714
2014	TB	AL	97	259	69	15	1	3	(1	2)	95	37	26	37	16	0	52	11	7	1	6	1	3	.266	.334	.367	.701
2015	TB	AL	128	332	88	21	2	8	(5	3)	137	51	28	51	25	0	61	24	3	1	10	4	5	.265	.359	.413	.771
2016	2 Tms	AL	101	293	78	17	1	9	(7	2)	124	39	32	46	19	1	55	31	1	1	3	2	6	.266	.372	.423	.795
16	TB	AL	63	212	51	12	1	7	(6	1)	86	27	18	29	12	1	42	23	1	1	2	1	3	.241	.347	.406	.752
16	Cle	AL	38	81	27	5	0	2	(1	1)	38	12	14	17	7	0	13	8	0	0	1	1	3	.333	.438	.469	.907
5 ML YEARS			344	932	244	54	4	23	(14	9)	375	136	90	136	61	1	178	66	12	3	19	7	15	.262	.349	.402	.752

Jedd Gyorko

Bats: R **Throws:** R **Pos:** 2B-46;3B-39;SS-26;PH-22;1B-11 JERK-oh **Ht:** 5'10" **Wt:** 215 **Born:** 9/23/1988 **Age:** 28

Year	Team	Lg	G	AB	H	2B	3B	HR	(Hm	Rd)	TB	R	RBI	RC	TBB	IBB	SO	HBP	SH	SF	SB	CS	GDP	Avg	OBP	Slg	OPS
2013	SD	NL	125	486	121	26	0	23	(13	10)	216	62	63	48	33	1	123	4	0	2	1	1	14	.249	.301	.444	.745
2014	SD	NL	111	400	84	17	1	10	(7	3)	133	37	51	42	36	1	100	4	0	3	3	2	8	.210	.280	.333	.612
2015	SD	NL	128	421	104	15	0	16	(9	7)	167	34	57	46	27	1	107	5	0	5	0	1	13	.247	.297	.397	.694
2016	StL	NL	128	400	97	9	1	30	(12	18)	198	58	59	54	37	1	96	0	0	1	0	0	11	.243	.306	.495	.801
4 ML YEARS			492	1707	406	67	2	79	(41	38)	714	191	230	190	133	4	426	13	0	11	4	4	46	.238	.296	.418	.714

Jesse Hahn

Pitches: R **Bats:** R **Pos:** SP-9 **Ht:** 6'4" **Wt:** 215 **Born:** 7/30/1989 **Age:** 27

Year	Team	Lg	G	GS	CG	GF	IP	BFP	H	R	ER	HR	SH	SF	HB	TBB	IBB	SO	WP	Bk	W	L	Pct	Sh	Sv-Op	Hld	ERC	ERA
2016	Nashv*	AAA	15	15	0	0	66.2	301	72	36	32	4	0	3	3	34	0	46	3	0	1	7	.125	0	0 - -	-	4.86	4.32
2014	SD	NL	14	12	0	2	73.1	306	57	26	25	4	3	1	4	32	1	70	4	0	7	4	.636	0	0-0	0	2.91	3.07
2015	Oak	AL	16	16	1	0	96.2	406	88	46	36	5	1	2	8	25	1	64	7	0	6	6	.500	1	0-0	0	3.00	3.35
2016	Oak	AL	9	9	0	0	46.1	203	57	32	31	8	1	1	0	19	1	23	2	0	2	4	.333	0	0-0	0	6.22	6.02
3 ML YEARS			39	37	1	2	216.1	915	202	104	92	17	5	4	12	76	3	157	13	0	15	14	.517	1	0-0	0	3.59	3.83

David Hale

Pitches: R **Bats:** R **Pos:** RP-2 **Ht:** 6'2" **Wt:** 210 **Born:** 9/27/1987 **Age:** 29

Year	Team	Lg	G	GS	CG	GF	IP	BFP	H	R	ER	HR	SH	SF	HB	TBB	IBB	SO	WP	Bk	W	L	Pct	Sh	Sv-Op	Hld	ERC	ERA
2016	Norfolk*	AAA	20	20	0	0	94.0	431	133	65	61	10	1	3	2	23	0	56	2	0	4	7	.364	0	0 - -	-	6.00	5.84
2013	Atl	NL	2	2	0	0	11.0	46	11	1	1	0	0	0	0	1	0	14	0	0	1	0	1.000	0	0-0	0	2.18	0.82
2014	Atl	NL	45	6	0	13	87.1	383	89	38	32	5	1	3	3	39	8	44	5	0	4	5	.444	0	0-0	4	4.05	3.30
2015	Col	NL	17	12	0	0	78.1	346	95	56	53	14	3	2	2	20	2	61	11	0	5	5	.500	0	0-0	0	5.33	6.09
2016	Col	NL	2	0	0	0	2.0	12	4	3	3	1	0	0	0	2	0	1	0	0	0	0	-	0	0-0	0	17.51	13.50
Postseason			1	0	0	1	0.1	1	0	0	0	0	0	0	0	0	0	0	0	0	0	0	-	0	0-0	0	0.00	0.00
4 ML YEARS			66	20	0	13	178.2	787	199	98	89	20	4	5	5	62	10	120	16	0	10	10	.500	0	0-0	4	4.60	4.48

Cody Hall

Pitches: R **Bats:** R **Pos:** RP-2 **Ht:** 6'4" **Wt:** 235 **Born:** 1/6/1988 **Age:** 29

Year	Team	Lg	G	GS	CG	GF	IP	BFP	H	R	ER	HR	SH	SF	HB	TBB	IBB	SO	WP	Bk	W	L	Pct	Sh	Sv-Op	Hld	ERC	ERA
2012	2 Tms	Low	45	0	0	35	47.2	205	48	13	10	0	2	0	5	16	2	64	1	0	4	1	.800	0	21- -	-	3.52	1.89
2013	SnJos	A+	26	0	0	5	33.2	125	15	8	5	2	2	0	1	7	0	48	2	0	2	0	1.000	0	2- -	-	0.96	1.34
2013	Rchmd	AA	20	0	0	15	26.1	105	17	8	7	4	1	0	2	8	0	27	1	0	2	2	.500	0	8- -	-	2.46	2.39
2014	Rchmd	AA	47	0	0	28	51.2	204	42	18	18	3	3	0	0	14	1	57	1	1	1	4	.200	0	11- -	-	2.38	3.14
2015	Scrmto	AAA	43	0	0	8	67.2	293	67	30	26	3	2	4	0	26	0	55	2	0	1	3	.250	0	3- -	-	3.52	3.46
2016	Reno	AAA	12	0	0	5	14.2	76	23	13	13	2	2	0	1	7	1	10	0	0	0	0	-	0	0- -	-	8.07	7.98
2015	SF	NL	7	0	0	1	8.1	41	10	6	6	1	0	0	1	4	0	7	0	0	0	0	-	0	0-0	0	5.92	6.48
2016	Mia	NL	2	0	0	2	3.0	16	4	4	4	1	0	0	0	3	1	3	0	0	0	0	-	0	0-0	0	9.98	12.00
2 ML YEARS			9	0	0	3	11.1	57	14	10	10	2	0	0	1	7	1	10	0	0	0	0	-	0	0-0	0	6.93	7.94

Cole Hamels

Pitches: L **Bats:** L **Pos:** SP-32 **Ht:** 6'4" **Wt:** 205 **Born:** 12/27/1983 **Age:** 33

Year	Team	Lg	G	GS	CG	GF	IP	BFP	H	R	ER	HR	SH	SF	HB	TBB	IBB	SO	WP	Bk	W	L	Pct	Sh	Sv-Op	Hld	ERC	ERA
2006	Phi	NL	23	23	0	0	132.1	558	117	66	60	19	6	8	3	48	4	145	5	0	9	8	.529	0	0-0	0	3.61	4.08
2007	Phi	NL	28	28	2	0	183.1	743	163	72	69	25	5	5	3	43	4	177	5	0	15	5	.750	0	0-0	0	3.12	3.39
2008	Phi	NL	33	33	2	0	227.1	914	193	80	78	28	6	2	1	53	7	196	0	0	14	10	.583	2	0-0	0	2.76	3.09
2009	Phi	NL	32	32	2	0	193.2	814	206	95	93	24	7	5	4	43	4	168	1	0	10	11	.476	2	0-0	0	3.98	4.32
2010	Phi	NL	33	33	1	0	208.2	856	185	74	71	26	7	0	6	61	5	211	3	0	12	11	.522	0	0-0	0	3.36	3.06
2011	Phi	NL	32	31	3	0	216.0	880	169	68	67	19	9	3	5	44	2	194	3	3	14	9	.609	0	0-0	0	2.23	2.79
2012	Phi	NL	31	31	2	0	215.1	867	190	80	73	24	6	4	3	52	3	216	3	2	17	6	.739	2	0-0	0	2.98	3.05
2013	Phi	NL	33	33	1	0	220.0	905	205	94	88	21	11	3	9	50	5	202	4	0	8	14	.364	0	0-0	0	3.15	3.60
2014	Phi	NL	30	30	0	0	204.2	829	176	60	56	14	7	7	8	59	3	198	6	1	9	9	.500	0	0-0	0	2.88	2.46
2015	2 Tms		32	32	2	0	212.1	880	190	88	86	22	6	2	10	62	3	215	9	4	13	8	.619	1	0-0	0	3.28	3.65
2016	Tex	AL	32	32	0	0	200.2	848	185	83	74	24	1	2	8	77	1	200	4	1	15	5	.750	0	0-0	0	3.90	3.32

Year	Team	Lg	G	GS	CG	GF	IP	BFP	H	R	ER	HR	SH	SF	HB	TBB	IBB	SO	WP	Bk	W	L	Pct	Sh	Sv-Op	Hld	ERC	ERA
15 Phi		NL	20	20	1	0	128.2	537	113	53	52	12	5	1	6	39	3	137	7	2	6	7	.462	1	0-0	0	3.13	3.64
15 Tex		AL	12	12	1	0	83.2	343	77	35	34	10	1	1	4	23	0	78	2	2	7	1	.875	0	0-0	0	3.54	3.66
Postseason			15	15	1	0	95.0	381	75	38	32	11	4	2	2	23	2	91	0	0	7	5	.583	1	0-0	0	2.51	3.03
11 ML YEARS			339	338	15	0	2214.1	9064	1979	869	815	246	71	41	63	592	41	2122	43	11	136	96	.586	7	0-0	0	3.17	3.31

Billy Hamilton

Bats: B **Throws:** R **Pos:** CF-115;PH-5;PR-2

Ht: 6'0" **Wt:** 160 **Born:** 9/9/1990 **Age:** 26

						BATTING														RUNNING			AVERAGES			
Year	Team	Lg	G	AB	H	2B	3B	HR	(Hm | Rd)	TB	R	RBI	RC	TBB	IBB	SO	HBP	SH	SF	SB	CS	GDP	Avg	OBP	Slg	OPS
2013 Cin	NL	13	19	7	2	0	0	(0	0)	9	9	1	5	2	0	4	0	1	0	13	1	0	.368	.429	.474	.902
2014 Cin	NL	152	563	141	25	8	6	(3	3)	200	72	48	64	34	0	117	1	9	4	56	23	1	.250	.292	.355	.648
2015 Cin	NL	114	412	93	8	3	4	(2	2)	119	56	28	32	28	0	75	1	9	5	57	8	5	.226	.274	.289	.563
2016 Cin	NL	119	411	107	19	3	3	(2	1)	141	69	17	46	36	0	93	1	11	1	58	8	5	.260	.321	.343	.664
4 ML YEARS		398	1405	348	54	14	13	(7	6)	469	206	94	147	100	0	289	3	30	9	184	40	11	.248	.297	.334	.631

Josh Hamilton

Bats: L **Throws:** L **Pos:** OF

Ht: 6'4" **Wt:** 240 **Born:** 5/21/1981 **Age:** 36

						BATTING														RUNNING			AVERAGES			
Year	Team	Lg	G	AB	H	2B	3B	HR	(Hm | Rd)	TB	R	RBI	RC	TBB	IBB	SO	HBP	SH	SF	SB	CS	GDP	Avg	OBP	Slg	OPS
2007 Cin	NL	90	298	87	17	2	19	(11	8)	165	52	47	58	33	4	65	4	0	2	3	3	6	.292	.368	.554	.922
2008 Tex	AL	156	624	190	35	5	32	(19	13)	331	98	130	119	64	9	126	7	0	9	9	1	6	.304	.371	.530	.901
2009 Tex	AL	89	336	90	19	2	10	(6	4)	143	43	54	51	24	2	79	1	0	4	8	3	5	.268	.315	.426	.741
2010 Tex	AL	133	518	186	40	3	32	(22	10)	328	95	100	121	43	5	95	5	1	4	8	1	11	.359	.411	.633	1.044
2011 Tex	AL	121	487	145	31	5	25	(14	11)	261	80	94	78	39	13	93	2	0	10	8	1	9	.298	.346	.536	.882
2012 Tex	AL	148	562	160	31	2	43	(22	21)	324	103	128	108	60	13	162	5	0	9	7	4	9	.285	.354	.577	.930
2013 LAA	AL	151	576	144	32	5	21	(9	12)	249	73	79	67	47	4	158	4	0	9	4	0	16	.250	.307	.432	.739
2014 LAA	AL	89	338	89	21	0	10	(0	10)	140	43	44	49	32	5	108	5	0	6	3	3	2	.263	.331	.414	.745
2015 Tex	AL	50	170	43	8	0	8	(7	1)	75	22	25	19	10	0	52	0	0	2	0	0	1	.253	.291	.441	.732
Postseason		42	163	33	9	0	6	(2	4)	60	18	23	17	15	7	30	0	0	3	4	1	5	.202	.265	.368	.633
9 ML YEARS		1027	3909	1134	234	24	200	(110	90)	2016	609	701	670	352	55	938	33	1	55	50	16	66	.290	.349	.516	.865

Jason Hammel

Pitches: R **Bats:** R **Pos:** SP-30

Ht: 6'6" **Wt:** 225 **Born:** 9/2/1982 **Age:** 34

				HOW MUCH HE PITCHED						WHAT HE GAVE UP											THE RESULTS							
Year	Team	Lg	G	GS	CG	GF	IP	BFP	H	R	ER	HR	SH	SF	HB	TBB	IBB	SO	WP	Bk	W	L	Pct	Sh	Sv-Op	Hld	ERC	ERA
2006 TB	AL	9	9	0	0	44.0	208	61	38	38	7	0	3	1	21	0	32	3	2	0	6	.000	0	0-0	0	7.40	7.77
2007 TB	AL	24	14	0	2	85.0	384	100	58	58	12	2	0	2	40	1	64	3	0	3	5	.375	0	0-0	0	5.86	6.14
2008 TB	AL	40	5	0	21	78.1	346	83	45	40	11	2	2	2	35	4	44	7	0	4	4	.500	0	2-2	1	4.94	4.60
2009 Col	NL	34	30	1	0	176.2	771	203	94	85	17	10	9	9	42	6	133	4	0	10	8	.556	0	0-0	0	4.37	4.33
2010 Col	NL	30	30	0	0	177.2	770	201	97	95	18	11	6	6	47	1	141	13	2	10	9	.526	0	0-0	0	4.41	4.81
2011 Col	NL	32	27	0	2	170.1	739	175	100	90	21	11	6	6	68	3	94	8	1	7	13	.350	0	1-1	0	4.54	4.76
2012 Bal	AL	20	20	1	0	118.0	493	104	48	45	9	3	1	2	42	2	113	3	0	8	6	.571	1	0-0	0	3.14	3.43
2013 Bal	AL	26	23	0	1	139.1	611	155	81	77	22	2	8	8	48	1	96	1	0	7	8	.467	0	1-1	1	5.19	4.97
2014 2 Tms		30	29	0	1	176.1	715	154	70	68	23	3	4	8	44	2	158	6	0	10	11	.476	0	0-0	0	3.21	3.47
2015 ChC	NL	31	31	0	0	170.2	710	158	79	71	23	4	6	6	40	4	172	10	0	10	7	.588	0	0-0	0	3.32	3.74
2016 ChC	NL	30	30	0	0	166.2	692	148	77	71	25	7	3	9	53	0	144	9	0	15	10	.600	0	0-0	0	3.72	3.83
14 ChC	NL	17	17	0	0	108.2	429	88	36	36	10	2	3	5	23	2	104	4	0	8	5	.615	0	0-0	0	2.51	2.98
14 Oak	AL	13	12	0	1	67.2	286	66	34	32	13	1	1	3	21	0	54	2	0	2	6	.250	0	0-0	0	4.42	4.26
Postseason		6	5	0	1	19.1	88	20	15	15	4	0	0	1	14	2	19	0	0	0	2	.000	0	0-0	0	6.73	6.98
11 ML YEARS		306	248	2	27	1503.0	6439	1542	787	738	188	55	48	59	480	24	1191	67	5	84	87	.491	1	4-4	2	4.22	4.42

Brad Hand

Pitches: L **Bats:** L **Pos:** RP-82

Ht: 6'3" **Wt:** 220 **Born:** 3/20/1990 **Age:** 27

				HOW MUCH HE PITCHED						WHAT HE GAVE UP											THE RESULTS							
Year	Team	Lg	G	GS	CG	GF	IP	BFP	H	R	ER	HR	SH	SF	HB	TBB	IBB	SO	WP	Bk	W	L	Pct	Sh	Sv-Op	Hld	ERC	ERA
2011 Fla	NL	12	12	0	0	60.0	263	53	32	28	10	4	3	1	35	1	38	0	1	1	8	.111	0	0-0	0	4.68	4.20
2012 Mia	NL	1	1	0	0	3.2	23	6	7	7	1	0	0	0	6	1	3	0	0	1	0	.000	0	0-0	0	14.74	17.18
2013 Mia	NL	7	2	0	2	20.2	82	13	7	7	2	0	0	0	8	0	15	1	0	1	1	.500	0	0-0	0	2.10	3.05
2014 Mia	NL	32	16	0	5	111.0	474	112	56	54	10	6	2	2	39	3	67	5	0	3	8	.273	0	1-1	0	3.91	4.38
2015 Mia	NL	38	12	0	4	93.1	408	107	55	55	9	5	2	3	32	1	67	2	0	4	7	.364	0	0-0	2	4.83	5.30
2016 SD	NL	82	0	0	16	89.1	364	63	32	29	8	2	2	1	36	4	111	7	0	4	4	.500	0	1-7	21	2.44	2.92
6 ML YEARS		172	43	0	30	378.0	1614	354	189	180	40	17	9	7	156	10	301	15	1	13	29	.310	0	2-8	23	3.85	4.29

Ryan Hanigan

Bats: R **Throws:** R **Pos:** C-34;DH-1;PH-1

HANN-eh-gann

Ht: 6'0" **Wt:** 220 **Born:** 8/16/1980 **Age:** 36

						BATTING														RUNNING			AVERAGES			
Year	Team	Lg	G	AB	H	2B	3B	HR	(Hm | Rd)	TB	R	RBI	RC	TBB	IBB	SO	HBP	SH	SF	SB	CS	GDP	Avg	OBP	Slg	OPS
2007 Cin	NL	5	10	3	1	0	0	(0	0)	4	3	2	1	1	1	2	0	0	0	0	0	0	.300	.364	.400	.764
2008 Cin	NL	31	85	23	2	0	2	(1	1)	31	9	9	12	10	1	9	3	0	0	0	0	2	.271	.367	.365	.732
2009 Cin	NL	90	251	66	6	1	3	(3	0)	83	22	11	25	37	7	31	2	2	1	0	0	6	.263	.361	.331	.692
2010 Cin	NL	70	203	61	11	0	5	(2	3)	87	25	40	41	33	4	21	4	1	2	0	0	6	.300	.405	.429	.834
2011 Cin	NL	91	266	71	6	0	6	(4	2)	95	27	31	38	35	3	32	2	1	0	0	0	3	.267	.356	.357	.714
2012 Cin	NL	112	317	87	14	0	2	(0	2)	107	25	24	40	44	13	37	3	4	3	0	0	6	.274	.365	.338	.703
2013 Cin	NL	75	222	44	8	0	2	(1	1)	58	17	21	18	29	9	27	6	2	1	0	1	7	.198	.306	.261	.567
2014 TB	AL	84	225	49	9	0	5	(4	1)	73	18	34	24	31	0	39	3	2	2	1	0	6	.218	.318	.324	.642

Year Team	Lg	G	AB	H	2B	3B	HR	(Hm	Rd)	TB	R	RBI	RC	TBB	IBB	SO	HBP	SH	SF	SB	CS	GDP	Avg	OBP	Slg	OPS
								BATTING												**RUNNING**			**AVERAGES**			
2015 Bos	AL	54	174	43	8	0	2	(2	0)	57	28	16	18	20	0	39	4	1	1	0	0	6	.247	.337	.328	.664
2016 Bos	AL	35	105	18	4	0	1	(0	1)	25	9	14	4	7	0	27	1	0	0	0	0	5	.171	.230	.238	.468
Postseason		7	22	3	0	0	0	(0	0)	3	3	3	1	0	0	3	1	0	0	0	0	1	.136	.174	.136	.310
10 ML YEARS		647	1858	465	69	1	28	(17	11)	620	183	202	225	247	38	264	28	13	10	1	1	50	.250	.345	.334	.679

Mitch Haniger

Bats: R **Throws:** R **Pos:** CF-22;LF-9;RF-4;PH-4   **Ht:** 6'2" **Wt:** 215 **Born:** 12/23/1990 **Age:** 26

Year Team	Lg	G	AB	H	2B	3B	HR	(Hm	Rd)	TB	R	RBI	RC	TBB	IBB	SO	HBP	SH	SF	SB	CS	GDP	Avg	OBP	Slg	OPS
2012 Wisc	A	14	49	14	4	0	1	(-	-)	21	9	8	8	7	0	13	1	0	1	1	0	0	.286	.379	.429	.808
2013 2 Tms	Low	129	473	125	36	5	11	(-	-)	204	76	68	75	57	1	92	7	0	6	9	2	6	.264	.348	.431	.779
2014 Hntsvl	AA	67	243	62	7	1	10	(-	-)	101	41	34	34	19	1	41	4	2	3	4	0	5	.255	.316	.416	.732
2015 Mobile	AA	55	153	43	10	1	1	(-	-)	58	23	19	21	16	1	32	2	0	3	4	4	2	.281	.351	.379	.730
2015 Visalia	A+	49	202	67	16	3	12	(-	-)	125	40	36	47	17	0	39	2	0	5	8	2	2	.332	.381	.619	.999
2016 Mobile	AA	55	197	57	14	2	5	(-	-)	90	21	30	38	30	0	37	8	0	1	4	3	2	.289	.403	.457	.859
2016 Reno	AAA	74	261	89	20	3	20	(-	-)	175	58	64	73	39	0	62	5	1	6	8	1	6	.341	.428	.670	1.098
2016 Ari	NL	34	109	25	2	1	5	(4	1)	44	9	17	16	12	2	27	1	0	1	0	0	3	.229	.309	.404	.713

Alen Hanson

Bats: B **Throws:** R **Pos:** PH-11;2B-8;PR-8   **Ht:** 5'11" **Wt:** 180 **Born:** 10/22/1992 **Age:** 24

Year Team	Lg	G	AB	H	2B	3B	HR	(Hm	Rd)	TB	R	RBI	RC	TBB	IBB	SO	HBP	SH	SF	SB	CS	GDP	Avg	OBP	Slg	OPS
2012 WV	A	124	489	151	33	13	16	(-	-)	258	99	62	98	55	1	105	4	7	3	35	19	2	.309	.381	.528	.909
2013 Bradtn	A+	92	367	103	23	8	7	(-	-)	163	51	48	56	33	1	70	2	2	5	24	14	2	.281	.339	.444	.783
2013 Altna	AA	35	137	35	4	5	1	(-	-)	52	13	10	16	8	0	26	1	3	1	6	2	2	.255	.299	.380	.679
2014 Altna	AA	118	482	135	21	12	11	(-	-)	213	64	58	71	31	0	88	3	8	3	25	11	2	.280	.326	.442	.768
2015 Indy	AAA	117	475	125	17	12	6	(-	-)	184	66	43	62	37	1	91	0	12	5	35	12	9	.263	.313	.387	.701
2016 Indy	AAA	110	432	115	15	7	8	(-	-)	168	58	32	57	32	1	78	2	10	2	36	15	7	.266	.318	.389	.707
2016 Pit	NL	27	31	7	1	0	0	(0	0)	8	5	1	1	2	1	5	0	0	0	2	1	0	.226	.273	.258	.531

J.A. Happ

Pitches: L **Bats:** L **Pos:** SP-32   JAY   **Ht:** 6'5" **Wt:** 205 **Born:** 10/19/1982 **Age:** 34

Year Team	Lg	G	GS	CG	GF	IP	BFP	H	R	ER	HR	SH	SF	HB	TBB	IBB	SO	WP	Bk	W	L	Pct	Sh	Sv-Op	Hld	ERC	ERA
						HOW MUCH HE PITCHED					**WHAT HE GAVE UP**												**THE RESULTS**				
2007 Phi	NL	1	1	0	0	4.0	21	7	5	5	3	0	0	0	2	0	5	0	0	0	1	.000	0	0-0	0	15.13	11.25
2008 Phi	NL	8	4	0	1	31.2	138	28	13	13	3	2	1	1	14	1	26	1	0	1	0	1.000	0	0-0	1	3.55	3.69
2009 Phi	NL	35	23	3	4	166.0	685	149	55	54	20	7	6	5	56	2	119	2	0	12	4	.750	2	0-0	0	3.57	2.93
2010 2 Tms	NL	16	16	1	0	87.1	374	73	37	33	8	5	4	1	47	1	70	4	0	6	4	.600	1	0-0	0	3.69	3.40
2011 Hou	NL	28	28	0	0	156.1	698	157	103	93	21	12	8	2	83	5	134	3	2	6	15	.286	0	0-0	0	4.86	5.35
2012 2 Tms	NL	28	24	0	3	144.2	627	147	79	79	19	9	4	2	56	1	144	7	0	10	11	.476	0	0-0	1	4.37	4.79
2013 Tor	AL	18	18	0	0	92.2	415	91	53	47	10	1	3	2	45	0	77	5	0	5	7	.417	0	0-0	0	4.36	4.56
2014 Tor	AL	30	26	0	2	158.0	673	160	79	74	22	1	5	2	51	0	133	1	0	11	11	.500	0	0-0	0	4.17	4.22
2015 2 Tms	AL	32	31	0	0	172.0	717	173	71	69	16	2	0	2	45	4	151	6	0	11	8	.579	0	0-0	0	3.56	3.61
2016 Tor	AL	32	32	0	0	195.0	796	168	72	69	22	2	2	6	60	0	163	3	2	20	4	.833	0	0-0	0	3.22	3.18
10 Phi	NL	3	3	0	0	15.1	70	13	4	3	1	1	1	0	12	0	9	1	0	1	0	1.000	0	0-0	0	4.40	1.76
10 Hou	NL	13	13	1	0	72.0	304	60	33	30	7	4	3	1	35	1	61	3	0	5	4	.556	1	0-0	0	3.53	3.75
12 Hou	NL	18	18	0	0	104.1	457	112	58	56	17	7	2	1	39	0	98	5	0	7	9	.438	0	0-0	0	4.86	4.83
12 Tor	NL	10	6	0	3	40.1	170	35	21	21	2	2	2	1	17	1	46	2	0	3	2	.600	0	0-0	1	3.16	4.69
15 Sea	AL	21	20	0	0	108.2	468	121	58	56	13	1	0	2	32	3	82	4	0	4	6	.400	0	0-0	0	4.49	4.64
15 Pit	NL	11	11	0	0	63.1	249	52	13	13	3	1	0	0	13	1	69	2	0	7	2	.778	0	0-0	0	2.12	1.85
Postseason		8	1	0	0	9.1	46	12	5	5	1	0	0	0	8	0	10	0	0	0	0	-	0	0-0	1	7.96	4.82
10 ML YEARS		228	203	4	10	1207.2	5144	1153	567	534	144	41	33	23	459	14	1022	32	4	82	65	.558	3	0-0	2	3.94	3.98

Blaine Hardy

Pitches: L **Bats:** L **Pos:** RP-21   **Ht:** 6'2" **Wt:** 215 **Born:** 3/14/1987 **Age:** 30

Year Team	Lg	G	GS	CG	GF	IP	BFP	H	R	ER	HR	SH	SF	HB	TBB	IBB	SO	WP	Bk	W	L	Pct	Sh	Sv-Op	Hld	ERC	ERA
						HOW MUCH HE PITCHED					**WHAT HE GAVE UP**												**THE RESULTS**				
2016 Toledo*	AAA	32	0	0	5	31.1	115	20	6	6	1	2	0	1	5	2	19	1	0	1	0	1.000	0	1--	1	1.32	1.72
2014 Det	AL	38	0	0	7	39.0	167	34	12	11	1	1	2	1	20	3	31	1	0	2	1	.667	0	0-1	4	3.28	2.54
2015 Det	AL	70	0	0	11	61.1	265	61	23	21	2	3	4	1	22	2	55	5	0	5	3	.625	0	0-3	13	3.38	3.08
2016 Det	AL	21	0	0	10	25.2	112	25	11	10	2	1	0	0	12	1	20	1	0	1	0	1.000	0	0-0	0	3.95	3.51
3 ML YEARS		129	0	0	28	126.0	544	120	46	42	5	5	6	2	54	6	106	7	0	8	4	.667	0	0-4	17	3.47	3.00

J.J. Hardy

Bats: R **Throws:** R **Pos:** SS-115   **Ht:** 6'1" **Wt:** 200 **Born:** 8/19/1982 **Age:** 34

Year Team	Lg	G	AB	H	2B	3B	HR	(Hm	Rd)	TB	R	RBI	RC	TBB	IBB	SO	HBP	SH	SF	SB	CS	GDP	Avg	OBP	Slg	OPS
2005 Mil	NL	124	372	92	22	1	9	(6	3)	143	46	50	49	44	7	48	1	8	2	0	0	10	.247	.327	.384	.711
2006 Mil	NL	35	128	31	5	0	5	(4	1)	51	13	14	13	10	0	23	0	0	1	1	1	4	.242	.293	.398	.693
2007 Mil	NL	151	592	164	30	1	26	(15	11)	274	89	80	84	40	1	73	1	4	1	2	3	13	.277	.323	.463	.786
2008 Mil	NL	146	569	161	31	4	24	(14	10)	272	78	74	78	52	3	98	1	5	2	2	1	18	.283	.343	.478	.821
2009 Mil	NL	115	414	95	16	2	11	(6	5)	148	53	47	32	43	0	85	2	1	5	0	1	14	.229	.302	.357	.659
2010 Min	NL	101	340	91	19	3	6	(1	5)	134	44	38	41	28	1	54	0	3	4	1	1	8	.268	.320	.394	.714
2011 Bal	AL	129	527	142	27	0	30	(15	15)	259	76	80	78	31	3	92	2	2	5	0	0	10	.269	.310	.491	.801
2012 Bal	AL	158	663	158	30	2	22	(15	7)	258	85	68	71	38	4	106	3	7	2	0	0	21	.238	.282	.389	.671

Year	Team	Lg	G	AB	H	2B	3B	HR	(Hm	Rd)	TB	R	RBI	RC	TBB	IBB	SO	HBP	SH	SF	SB	CS	GDP	Avg	OBP	Slg	OPS
												BATTING											**RUNNING**		**AVERAGES**		
2013	Bal	AL	159	601	158	27	0	25	(11	14)	260	66	76	71	38	3	73	0	3	2	2	1	14	.263	.306	.433	.738
2014	Bal	AL	141	529	142	28	0	9	(5	4)	197	56	52	60	29	1	104	4	3	4	0	0	12	.268	.309	.372	.682
2015	Bal	AL	114	411	90	14	0	8	(4	4)	128	45	37	32	20	0	88	0	2	4	0	0	11	.219	.253	.311	.564
2016	Bal	AL	115	405	109	29	0	9	(4	5)	165	43	48	50	26	1	68	0	1	6	0	0	14	.269	.309	.407	.716
	Postseason		20	76	18	5	0	1	(1	0)	26	6	7	8	6	1	12	0	0	0	0	0	1	.237	.293	.342	.635
	12 ML YEARS		1488	5551	1433	278	13	184	(100	84)	2289	694	664	659	399	24	912	14	39	38	8	8	149	.258	.308	.412	.720

Bryce Harper

Bats: L **Throws:** R **Pos:** RF-143;PH-4   **Ht:** 6'3" **Wt:** 215 **Born:** 10/16/1992 **Age:** 24

Year	Team	Lg	G	AB	H	2B	3B	HR	(Hm	Rd)	TB	R	RBI	RC	TBB	IBB	SO	HBP	SH	SF	SB	CS	GDP	Avg	OBP	Slg	OPS
												BATTING											**RUNNING**		**AVERAGES**		
2012	Was	NL	139	533	144	26	9	22	(10	12)	254	98	59	82	56	0	120	2	3	3	18	6	8	.270	.340	.477	.817
2013	Was	NL	118	424	116	24	3	20	(13	7)	206	71	58	73	61	4	94	5	3	4	11	4	4	.274	.368	.486	.854
2014	Was	NL	100	352	96	10	2	13	(5	8)	149	41	32	43	38	4	104	1	3	1	2	2	6	.273	.344	.423	.768
2015	Was	NL	153	521	172	38	1	**42**	(23	19)	338	**118**	99	**138**	124	15	131	5	0	4	6	4	15	.330	**.460**	**.649**	**1.109**
2016	Was	NL	147	506	123	24	2	24	(12	12)	223	84	86	90	108	**20**	117	3	0	10	21	10	11	.243	.373	.441	.814
	Postseason		9	40	8	2	1	4	(2	2)	24	6	6	4	2	0	11	0	0	0	0	0	0	.200	.238	.600	.838
	5 ML YEARS		657	2336	651	122	17	121	(63	58)	1170	412	334	426	387	43	566	16	9	22	58	26	44	.279	.382	.501	.883

Lucas Harrell

Pitches: R **Bats:** B **Pos:** SP-9   HAH-rell   **Ht:** 6'2" **Wt:** 205 **Born:** 6/3/1985 **Age:** 32

Year	Team	Lg	G	GS	CG	GF	IP	BFP	H	R	ER	HR	SH	SF	HB	TBB	IBB	SO	WP	Bk	W	L	Pct	Sh	Sv-Op	Hld	ERC	ERA
					HOW MUCH HE PITCHED						**WHAT HE GAVE UP**											**THE RESULTS**						
2016	Erie*	AA	5	5	0	0	24.2	110	24	11	9	1	0	0	1	14	0	16	2	0	2	1	.667	0	0- -	-	4.31	3.28
2016	Gwnntt*	AAA	9	5	0	1	32.0	147	35	13	10	1	2	0	1	19	0	27	1	0	2	1	.667	0	0- -	-	4.99	2.81
2010	CWS	AL	8	3	0	3	24.0	119	34	18	13	2	1	0	0	17	1	15	1	0	1	0	1.000	0	0-0	0	7.77	4.88
2011	2 Tms		9	2	0	2	18.0	86	23	12	9	0	1	1	1	8	0	15	1	0	0	2	.000	0	0-0	0	5.16	4.50
2012	Hou	NL	32	32	1	0	193.2	827	185	90	81	13	8	10	1	78	5	140	10	3	11	11	.500	1	0-0	0	3.59	3.76
2013	Hou	AL	36	22	0	8	153.2	707	174	111	100	20	6	5	6	**88**	5	89	8	0	6	**17**	.261	0	0-1	0	5.95	5.86
2014	Hou	AL	3	3	0	0	12.1	66	19	14	13	2	0	2	0	9	1	9	1	0	0	3	.000	0	0-0	0	8.91	9.49
2016	2 Tms		9	9	0	0	47.0	208	46	24	22	4	2	2	4	25	0	36	5	0	3	2	.600	0	0-0	0	4.78	4.21
11	CWS	AL	3	0	0	2	5.0	26	11	4	4	0	0	0	0	1	0	5	0	0	0	0	-	0	0-0	0	10.11	7.20
11	Hou	NL	6	2	0	0	13.0	60	12	8	5	0	1	1	1	7	0	10	1	1	0	2	.000	0	0-0	0	3.57	3.46
16	Atl	NL	5	5	0	0	29.1	124	25	13	11	1	1	1	3	12	0	21	3	0	2	2	.500	0	0-0	0	3.28	3.38
16	Tex	AL	4	4	0	0	17.2	84	21	11	11	3	1	1	1	13	0	15	2	0	1	0	1.000	0	0-0	0	7.64	5.60
	6 ML YEARS		97	71	1	13	448.2	2013	481	269	238	41	18	20	12	225	12	304	26	4	21	35	.375	1	0-1	0	4.90	4.77

Will Harris

Pitches: R **Bats:** R **Pos:** RP-66   **Ht:** 6'4" **Wt:** 250 **Born:** 8/28/1984 **Age:** 32

Year	Team	Lg	G	GS	CG	GF	IP	BFP	H	R	ER	HR	SH	SF	HB	TBB	IBB	SO	WP	Bk	W	L	Pct	Sh	Sv-Op	Hld	ERC	ERA
					HOW MUCH HE PITCHED						**WHAT HE GAVE UP**											**THE RESULTS**						
2012	Col	NL	20	0	0	10	17.2	89	27	18	16	3	2	1	1	6	1	19	4	0	1	1	.500	0	0-0	3	7.39	8.15
2013	Ari	NL	61	0	0	11	52.2	217	50	17	17	3	0	4	2	15	1	53	4	0	4	1	.800	0	0-1	4	3.25	2.91
2014	Ari	NL	29	0	0	8	29.0	120	27	14	14	3	1	1	2	9	2	35	1	0	0	3	.000	0	0-1	3	3.62	4.34
2015	Hou	AL	68	0	0	18	71.0	276	42	18	15	8	2	1	1	22	1	68	2	0	5	5	.500	0	2-6	13	1.79	1.90
2016	Hou	AL	66	0	0	19	64.0	255	52	17	16	3	1	2	1	15	1	69	4	0	1	2	.333	0	12-15	**28**	2.21	2.25
	Postseason		4	0	0	0	3.0	16	8	5	4	0	0	0	0	0	0	2	0	0	0	1	.000	0	0-0	3	12.84	12.00
	5 ML YEARS		244	0	0	66	234.1	957	198	84	78	20	6	9	7	67	6	244	15	0	11	12	.478	0	14-23	51	2.80	3.00

Josh Harrison

Bats: R **Throws:** R **Pos:** 2B-128;PH-5;RF-1;PR-1   **Ht:** 5'8" **Wt:** 195 **Born:** 7/8/1987 **Age:** 29

Year	Team	Lg	G	AB	H	2B	3B	HR	(Hm	Rd)	TB	R	RBI	RC	TBB	IBB	SO	HBP	SH	SF	SB	CS	GDP	Avg	OBP	Slg	OPS
												BATTING											**RUNNING**		**AVERAGES**		
2011	Pit	NL	65	195	53	13	2	1	(1	0)	73	21	16	19	3	0	24	0	5	1	4	1	6	.272	.281	.374	.656
2012	Pit	NL	104	249	58	9	5	3	(1	2)	86	34	16	22	10	0	37	7	7	3	7	3	3	.233	.279	.345	.624
2013	Pit	NL	60	88	22	1	2	3	(1	2)	36	10	14	11	2	0	10	3	2	0	2	0	4	.250	.290	.409	.699
2014	Pit	NL	143	520	164	38	7	13	(4	9)	255	77	52	84	22	1	81	4	2	2	18	7	6	.315	.347	.490	.837
2015	Pit	NL	114	418	120	29	4	4	(2	2)	163	57	28	48	19	1	71	7	3	2	10	8	4	.287	.327	.390	.699
2016	Pit	NL	131	487	138	25	7	4	(2	2)	189	57	59	61	18	0	76	5	4	8	19	4	10	.283	.311	.388	.699
	Postseason		4	7	2	0	0	0	(0	0)	2	1	0	0	0	0	2	1	0	0	0	1	0	.286	.375	.286	.661
	6 ML YEARS		617	1957	555	115	24	28	(11	17)	802	256	185	245	74	2	299	26	23	16	60	23	33	.284	.316	.410	.726

Matt Harrison

Pitches: L **Bats:** L **Pos:** P   **Ht:** 6'4" **Wt:** 240 **Born:** 9/16/1985 **Age:** 31

Year	Team	Lg	G	GS	CG	GF	IP	BFP	H	R	ER	HR	SH	SF	HB	TBB	IBB	SO	WP	Bk	W	L	Pct	Sh	Sv-Op	Hld	ERC	ERA
					HOW MUCH HE PITCHED						**WHAT HE GAVE UP**											**THE RESULTS**						
2008	Tex	AL	15	15	1	0	83.2	372	100	57	51	12	1	5	2	31	2	42	2	2	9	3	.750	1	0-0	0	5.53	5.49
2009	Tex	AL	11	11	2	0	63.1	283	81	43	43	9	1	1	2	23	0	34	0	0	4	5	.444	0	0-0	0	6.17	6.11
2010	Tex	AL	37	6	0	9	78.1	356	80	45	41	10	2	8	2	39	3	46	4	0	3	2	.600	0	2-3	3	4.71	4.71
2011	Tex	AL	31	30	0	0	185.2	772	180	79	70	13	8	5	1	57	1	126	6	1	14	9	.609	0	0-0	0	3.40	3.39
2012	Tex	AL	32	32	4	0	213.1	876	210	82	78	22	1	2	1	59	0	133	2	0	18	11	.621	2	0-0	0	3.63	3.40
2013	Tex	AL	2	2	0	0	10.2	51	14	11	10	2	0	1	0	7	2	12	0	0	0	2	.000	0	0-0	0	7.54	8.44

Year	Team	Lg	G	GS	CG	GF	IP	BFP	H	R	ER	HR	SH	SF	HB	TBB	IBB	SO	WP	Bk	W	L	Pct	Sh	Sv-Op	Hld	ERC	ERA
2014	Tex	AL	4	4	0	0	17.1	84	20	8	8	1	1	0	1	12	0	10	1	0	1	1	.500	0	0-0	-	5.98	4.15
2015	Tex	AL	3	3	0	0	16.0	69	19	12	12	3	0	1	0	6	0	5	0	1	1	2	.333	0	0-0	-	5.94	6.75
	Postseason		5	4	0	0	18.1	83	20	13	11	2	0	0	0	9	1	16	1	0	1	2	.333	0	0-0	-	4.88	5.40
	8 ML YEARS		135	103	7	9	668.1	2863	704	337	313	72	14	23	9	234	8	408	15	4	50	35	.588	4	2-3	3	4.31	4.21

Donnie Hart

Pitches: L **Bats:** L **Pos:** RP-22   **Ht:** 5'11" **Wt:** 180 **Born:** 9/6/1990 **Age:** 26

Year	Team	Lg	G	GS	CG	GF	IP	BFP	H	R	ER	HR	SH	SF	HB	TBB	IBB	SO	WP	Bk	W	L	Pct	Sh	Sv-Op	Hld	ERC	ERA
2013	Abrdn	A-	19	0	0	13	24.0	103	24	10	6	0	0	2	3	7	2	26	0	0	3	1	.750	0	5--	-	3.31	2.25
2014	Dlmrva	A	24	0	0	16	29.1	123	25	13	12	2	1	0	1	11	1	31	3	0	1	3	.250	0	4--	-	3.04	3.68
2015	2 Tms	Low	46	0	0	31	52.0	211	40	10	8	0	4	0	3	14	2	46	4	0	6	2	.750	0	13--	-	1.92	1.38
2016	Bowie	AA	40	0	0	11	46.1	185	41	17	14	1	0	0	4	7	1	50	0	0	3	1	.750	0	4--	-	2.38	2.72
2016	Bal	AL	22	0	0	3	18.1	71	12	1	1	1	2	1	0	6	1	12	0	0	0	0	-	0	0-0	4	1.76	0.49

Matt Harvey

Pitches: R **Bats:** R **Pos:** SP-17   **Ht:** 6'4" **Wt:** 215 **Born:** 3/27/1989 **Age:** 28

Year	Team	Lg	G	GS	CG	GF	IP	BFP	H	R	ER	HR	SH	SF	HB	TBB	IBB	SO	WP	Bk	W	L	Pct	Sh	Sv-Op	Hld	ERC	ERA
2012	NYM	NL	10	10	0	0	59.1	245	42	19	18	5	3	3	3	26	0	70	3	0	3	5	.375	0	0-0	-	2.75	2.73
2013	NYM	NL	26	26	1	0	178.1	690	135	46	45	7	5	4	4	31	1	191	2	0	9	5	.643	1	0-0	-	1.76	2.27
2015	NYM	NL	29	29	0	0	189.1	755	156	62	57	18	7	2	5	37	2	188	4	0	13	8	.619	0	0-0	-	2.44	2.71
2016	NYM	NL	17	17	0	0	92.2	402	111	55	50	8	5	4	1	25	1	76	4	0	4	10	.286	0	0-0	-	4.65	4.86
	Postseason		4	4	0	0	26.2	109	21	10	9	2	0	1	1	8	1	27	0	0	2	0	1.000	0	0-0	-	2.49	3.04
	4 ML YEARS		82	82	1	0	519.2	2092	444	182	170	38	20	13	13	119	4	525	13	0	29	28	.509	1	0-0	0	2.59	2.94

Chris Hatcher

Pitches: R **Bats:** R **Pos:** RP-37   **Ht:** 6'1" **Wt:** 200 **Born:** 1/12/1985 **Age:** 32

Year	Team	Lg	G	GS	CG	GF	IP	BFP	H	R	ER	HR	SH	SF	HB	TBB	IBB	SO	WP	Bk	W	L	Pct	Sh	Sv-Op	Hld	ERC	ERA
2011	Fla	NL	11	0	0	4	10.1	48	14	8	8	2	0	3	0	4	1	8	2	0	0	0	-	0	0-0	0	6.69	6.97
2012	Mia	NL	11	0	0	7	14.2	66	17	9	7	3	0	0	1	6	0	10	1	0	0	0	-	0	0-0	0	6.19	4.30
2013	Mia	NL	7	0	0	2	8.2	44	13	13	12	1	0	0	0	4	1	7	0	0	0	1	.000	0	0-0	0	6.92	12.46
2014	Mia	NL	52	0	0	15	56.0	232	55	22	21	4	1	1	0	12	1	60	1	2	0	3	.000	0	0-2	6	3.03	3.38
2015	LAD	NL	49	0	0	12	39.0	166	35	19	16	4	2	1	3	13	2	45	3	0	3	5	.375	0	4-6	13	3.46	3.69
2016	LAD	NL	37	0	0	10	40.2	181	40	26	25	8	1	0	1	21	4	43	4	0	5	4	.556	0	0-1	4	5.07	5.53
	Postseason		4	0	0	1	3.2	12	0	0	0	0	0	0	0	1	0	5	0	0	0	0	-	0	0-0	2	0.09	0.00
	6 ML YEARS		167	0	0	50	169.1	737	174	97	89	22	4	5	5	60	9	173	11	2	8	13	.381	0	4-9	23	4.26	4.73

Steve Hathaway

Pitches: L **Bats:** L **Pos:** RP-24   **Ht:** 6'1" **Wt:** 185 **Born:** 9/13/1990 **Age:** 26

Year	Team	Lg	G	GS	CG	GF	IP	BFP	H	R	ER	HR	SH	SF	HB	TBB	IBB	SO	WP	Bk	W	L	Pct	Sh	Sv-Op	Hld	ERC	ERA
2014	Sbend	A	8	0	0	1	14.1	64	12	9	6	0	0	0	0	6	0	18	0	0	0	0	-	0	1--	-	2.40	3.77
2015	2 Tms	Low	45	0	0	7	43.2	188	35	19	14	0	3	0	2	15	1	48	4	0	5	3	.625	0	2--	-	2.18	2.89
2016	Mobile	AA	13	0	0	2	15.1	60	14	3	2	0	0	1	0	3	0	10	0	0	1	1	.500	0	0--	-	2.32	1.17
2016	Reno	AAA	28	0	0	6	29.2	124	21	11	11	2	3	1	1	19	3	29	1	0	1	2	.333	0	1--	-	3.24	3.34
2016	Ari	NL	24	0	0	0	14.2	65	18	8	8	1	0	0	0	6	0	15	0	0	0	0	-	0	0-0	2	5.31	4.91

Drew Hayes

Pitches: R **Bats:** R **Pos:** RP-6   **Ht:** 6'1" **Wt:** 205 **Born:** 9/3/1987 **Age:** 29

Year	Team	Lg	G	GS	CG	GF	IP	BFP	H	R	ER	HR	SH	SF	HB	TBB	IBB	SO	WP	Bk	W	L	Pct	Sh	Sv-Op	Hld	ERC	ERA
2012	Pnscla	AA	56	1	0	8	63.1	275	53	24	24	3	5	4	2	38	2	64	6	0	2	3	.400	0	1--	-	3.66	3.41
2013	Pnscla	AA	51	0	0	17	63.0	292	73	42	38	7	6	0	6	33	4	61	9	0	4	3	.571	0	2--	-	5.92	5.43
2014	Pnscla	AA	52	1	0	16	71.1	311	63	33	32	4	3	2	6	39	0	76	4	0	5	3	.625	0	4--	-	4.06	4.04
2015	Lsvlle	AAA	43	0	0	17	58.0	253	58	22	19	2	4	4	1	30	3	56	3	0	4	4	.500	0	3--	-	4.10	2.95
2016	Lsvlle	AAA	38	2	0	14	59.0	261	61	37	27	3	4	2	2	27	2	41	2	0	4	5	.444	0	1--	-	4.20	4.12
2016	Cin	NL	6	0	0	1	9.2	48	15	10	9	3	0	0	0	6	1	8	0	0	0	0	-	0	0-1	0	10.39	8.38

Jeremy Hazelbaker

Bats: L **Throws:** R **Pos:** LF-52;PH-46;CF-21;PR-12;RF-6   **Ht:** 6'3" **Wt:** 190 **Born:** 8/14/1987 **Age:** 29

Year	Team	Lg	G	AB	H	2B	3B	HR	(Hm	Rd)	TB	R	RBI	RC	TBB	IBB	SO	HBP	SH	SF	SB	CS	GDP	Avg	OBP	Slg	OPS
2012	Portlnd	AA	114	436	119	21	6	19	(-	-)	209	77	64	74	35	2	114	9	6	2	33	11	2	.273	.338	.479	.818
2013	Pwtckt	AAA	121	428	110	13	2	11	(-	-)	160	62	54	57	36	3	131	1	10	5	37	7	4	.257	.313	.374	.687
2014	Chatt	AA	87	271	68	9	8	4	(-	-)	105	31	33	36	30	2	70	0	2	0	15	7	5	.251	.326	.387	.713
2014	Albq	AAA	22	90	20	3	2	4	(-	-)	39	12	11	9	2	0	27	0	0	0	6	2	0	.222	.239	.433	.672
2015	Tulsa	AA	14	53	13	2	2	0	(-	-)	19	5	2	6	3	0	11	0	2	0	6	0	0	.245	.286	.358	.644
2015	Sprgfld	AA	40	143	44	13	3	3	(-	-)	72	30	20	30	18	1	33	3	3	1	10	6	3	.308	.394	.503	.897
2015	Memp	AAA	58	207	70	10	7	10	(-	-)	124	38	46	49	23	0	60	2	0	1	8	2	3	.338	.408	.599	1.007
2016	Memp	AAA	13	40	13	3	0	1	(-	-)	19	8	11	8	6	0	12	2	2	0	2	1	0	.325	.438	.475	.913
2016	StL	NL	114	200	47	7	3	12	(3	9)	96	35	34	29	18	2	64	0	4	2	5	2	1	.235	.295	.480	.775

Chase Headley

Bats: B Throws: R Pos: 3B-140;PH-5;DH-1   HEDD-lee   Ht: 6'2" Wt: 215 Born: 5/9/1984 Age: 33

Year	Team	Lg	G	AB	H	2B	3B	HR	(Hm	Rd)	TB	R	RBI	RC	TBB	IBB	SO	HBP	SH	SF	SB	CS	GDP	Avg	OBP	Slg	OPS
2007	SD	NL	8	18	4	1	0	0	(0	0)	5	1	0	1	2	0	4	1	0	0	0	0	2	.222	.333	.278	.611
2008	SD	NL	91	331	89	19	2	9	(4	5)	139	34	38	42	30	1	104	5	0	2	4	1	5	.269	.337	.420	.757
2009	SD	NL	156	543	142	31	2	12	(7	5)	213	62	64	68	62	3	133	5	0	2	10	2	19	.262	.342	.392	.734
2010	SD	NL	161	610	161	29	3	11	(3	8)	229	77	58	70	56	3	139	3	1	4	17	5	11	.264	.327	.375	.702
2011	SD	NL	113	381	110	28	1	4	(1	3)	152	43	44	61	52	8	92	2	1	3	13	2	6	.289	.374	.399	.773
2012	SD	NL	161	604	173	31	2	31	(13	18)	301	95	115	112	86	2	157	4	0	5	17	6	7	.286	.376	.498	.875
2013	SD	NL	141	520	130	35	2	13	(5	8)	208	59	50	64	67	7	142	11	0	2	8	4	9	.250	.347	.400	.747
2014	2 Tms		135	470	114	20	1	13	(7	6)	175	55	49	54	51	1	122	9	0	1	7	3	17	.243	.328	.372	.700
2015	NYY	AL	156	580	150	29	1	11	(6	5)	214	74	62	71	51	0	135	7	0	4	0	2	17	.259	.324	.369	.693
2016	NYY	AL	140	467	118	18	1	14	(11	3)	180	58	51	64	51	3	118	6	0	5	8	2	7	.253	.331	.385	.716
14	SD	NL	77	279	64	12	1	7	(2	5)	99	27	32	29	22	0	73	5	0	1	4	1	12	.229	.296	.355	.651
14	NYY	AL	58	191	50	8	0	6	(5	1)	76	28	17	25	29	1	49	4	0	0	3	2	5	.262	.371	.398	.768
	Postseason		1	2	0	0	0	0	(0	0)	0	0	0	0	1	0	1	0	0	0	0	0	0	.000	.333	.000	.333
10 ML YEARS			1262	4524	1191	241	15	118	(57	61)	1816	558	531	607	508	28	1146	53	2	28	84	27	100	.263	.343	.401	.744

Ryon Healy

Bats: R Throws: R Pos: 3B-72   Ht: 6'5" Wt: 225 Born: 1/10/1992 Age: 25

Year	Team	Lg	G	AB	H	2B	3B	HR	(Hm	Rd)	TB	R	RBI	RC	TBB	IBB	SO	HBP	SH	SF	SB	CS	GDP	Avg	OBP	Slg	OPS
2013	2 Tms	Low	47	174	40	10	1	6	(-	-)	70	16	29	18	5	1	28	2	0	3	2	1	6	.230	.255	.402	.658
2014	Stcktn	A+	136	561	160	28	2	16	(-	-)	240	73	83	78	28	1	79	3	0	8	0	0	20	.285	.318	.428	.746
2015	Mdlnd	AA	124	507	153	31	1	10	(-	-)	216	63	62	74	30	0	82	1	1	4	0	1	21	.302	.339	.426	.766
2016	Mdlnd	AA	36	145	49	12	3	8	(-	-)	91	27	34	35	18	0	35	0	0	1	1	0	0	.338	.409	.628	1.036
2016	Nashv	AAA	49	192	61	16	1	6	(-	-)	97	33	30	34	13	1	40	2	0	3	0	1	4	.318	.362	.505	.867
2016	Oak	AL	72	269	82	20	0	13	(8	5)	141	36	37	43	12	1	60	1	1	0	0	0	7	.305	.337	.524	.861

Andrew Heaney

Pitches: L Bats: L Pos: SP-1   HEE-nee   Ht: 6'2" Wt: 195 Born: 6/5/1991 Age: 26

| | | | HOW MUCH HE PITCHED | | | | | WHAT HE GAVE UP | | | | | | | | | | THE RESULTS | | | | | | |
Year	Team	Lg	G	GS	CG	GF	IP	BFP	H	R	ER	HR	SH	SF	HB	TBB	IBB	SO	WP	Bk	W	L	Pct	Sh	Sv-Op	Hld	ERC	ERA
2014	Mia	NL	7	5	0	2	29.1	126	32	19	19	6	2	0	3	7	0	20	2	0	0	3	.000	0	0-0	0	5.17	5.83
2015	LAA	AL	18	18	0	0	105.2	438	99	41	41	9	1	3	6	28	1	78	4	0	6	4	.600	0	0-0	0	3.35	3.49
2016	LAA	AL	1	1	0	0	6.0	25	7	4	4	2	0	0	0	0	0	7	0	0	0	1	.000	0	0-0	0	4.78	6.00
3 ML YEARS			26	24	0	2	141.0	589	138	64	64	17	3	3	9	35	1	105	6	0	6	8	.429	0	0-0	0	3.77	4.09

Adeiny Hechavarria

Bats: R Throws: R Pos: SS-153;PH-8;PR-1   a-DAY-nee hetch-a-VA-ree-a   Ht: 6'0" Wt: 195 Born: 4/15/1989 Age: 28

Year	Team	Lg	G	AB	H	2B	3B	HR	(Hm	Rd)	TB	R	RBI	RC	TBB	IBB	SO	HBP	SH	SF	SB	CS	GDP	Avg	OBP	Slg	OPS
2012	Tor	AL	41	126	32	8	0	1	(1	1)	46	10	15	15	4	0	32	1	5	1	0	0	2	.254	.280	.365	.645
2013	Mia	NL	148	543	123	14	8	3	(1	2)	162	30	42	37	30	1	96	0	4	1	11	10	19	.227	.267	.298	.565
2014	Mia	NL	146	536	148	20	10	1	(0	1)	191	53	34	49	26	5	86	1	4	6	7	5	21	.276	.308	.356	.664
2015	Mia	NL	130	470	132	17	6	5	(3	2)	176	54	48	49	23	4	78	2	0	4	7	2	18	.281	.315	.374	.689
2016	Mia	NL	155	508	120	17	6	3	(1	2)	158	52	38	40	33	7	73	1	2	3	1	0	10	.236	.283	.311	.594
5 ML YEARS			620	2183	555	76	30	14	(6	8)	733	199	177	190	116	17	365	5	15	15	26	17	70	.254	.292	.336	.627

Austin Hedges

Bats: R Throws: R Pos: C-7;PH-1   Ht: 6'1" Wt: 210 Born: 8/18/1992 Age: 24

Year	Team	Lg	G	AB	H	2B	3B	HR	(Hm	Rd)	TB	R	RBI	RC	TBB	IBB	SO	HBP	SH	SF	SB	CS	GDP	Avg	OBP	Slg	OPS
2012	FtWyn	A	96	337	94	28	0	10	(-	-)	152	44	56	51	23	1	62	7	2	4	14	9	8	.279	.334	.451	.785
2013	Lk Els	A+	66	233	63	22	1	4	(-	-)	99	34	30	35	22	0	45	6	1	4	5	4	7	.270	.343	.425	.768
2013	SnAnt	AA	20	67	15	3	0	0	(-	-)	18	4	8	5	6	1	9	1	1	0	3	1	1	.224	.297	.269	.566
2014	SnAnt	AA	113	427	96	19	2	6	(-	-)	137	31	44	36	23	1	89	3	2	2	1	3	19	.225	.268	.321	.589
2015	ElPaso	AAA	21	71	23	8	0	2	(-	-)	37	12	15	14	8	0	0	0	0	1	1	0	1	.324	.392	.521	.914
2016	ElPaso	AAA	82	313	102	20	1	21	(-	-)	187	55	82	64	13	2	51	3	0	5	1	1	8	.326	.353	.597	.951
2015	SD	NL	56	137	23	2	0	3	(2	1)	34	13	11	7	8	1	38	1	3	3	0	0	1	.168	.215	.248	.463
2016	SD	NL	8	24	3	1	0	0	(0	0)	4	2	1	0	0	0	7	1	0	1	0	1	0	.125	.154	.167	.321
2 ML YEARS			64	161	26	3	0	3	(2	1)	38	15	12	7	8	1	45	2	3	4	0	1	1	.161	.206	.236	.442

Chris Heisey

HY-zee

Bats: R Throws: R Pos: PH-44;LF-25;RF-16;CF-3;DH-1;PR-1   Ht: 6'1" Wt: 220 Born: 12/14/1984 Age: 32

Year	Team	Lg	G	AB	H	2B	3B	HR	(Hm	Rd)	TB	R	RBI	RC	TBB	IBB	SO	HBP	SH	SF	SB	CS	GDP	Avg	OBP	Slg	OPS
2010	Cin	NL	97	201	51	10	1	8	(2	6)	87	33	21	22	16	1	57	6	1	2	1	2	3	.254	.324	.433	.757
2011	Cin	NL	120	279	71	9	1	18	(11	7)	136	44	50	40	19	3	78	5	1	4	6	1	5	.254	.309	.487	.797
2012	Cin	NL	120	347	92	16	5	7	(4	3)	139	44	31	43	18	0	81	7	3	0	6	3	8	.265	.315	.401	.715
2013	Cin	NL	87	224	53	11	1	9	(6	3)	93	29	23	26	9	0	51	5	4	2	3	0	4	.237	.279	.415	.694
2014	Cin	NL	119	275	61	15	2	8	(4	4)	104	34	22	22	15	0	64	2	5	2	9	2	3	.222	.265	.378	.643

| | | | | | | | | | BATTING | | | | | | | | | | | | RUNNING | | | AVERAGES | | | |
Year	Team	Lg	G	AB	H	2B	3B	HR	(Hm Rd)	TB	R	RBI	RC	TBB	IBB	SO	HBP	SH	SF	SB	CS	GDP	Avg	OBP	Slg	OPS
2015	LAD	NL	33	55	10	2	0	2	(2 0)	18	8	9	10	15	2	17	0	0	2	0	1	1	.182	.347	.327	.674
2016	Was	NL	83	139	30	3	1	9	(4 5)	62	18	17	14	13	0	44	2	0	1	0	1	0	.216	.290	.446	.736
	Postseason		6	6	0	0	0	0	(0 0)	0	1	0	0	0	0	2	0	0	0	0	0	1	.000	.000	.000	.000
	7 ML YEARS		659	1520	368	66	11	61	(33 28)	639	210	173	176	105	6	392	27	14	13	25	10	20	.242	.300	.420	.721

Ben Heller

Pitches: R **Bats:** R **Pos:** RP-10 **Ht:** 6'3" **Wt:** 205 **Born:** 8/5/1991 **Age:** 25

| | | | HOW MUCH HE PITCHED | | | | | | WHAT HE GAVE UP | | | | | | | | | | THE RESULTS | | | | | | | |
Year	Team	Lg	G	GS	CG	GF	IP	BFP	H	R	ER	HR	SH	SF	HB	TBB	IBB	SO	WP	Bk	W	L	Pct	Sh	Sv-Op	Hld	ERC	ERA
2013	MhVlly	A-	21	1	0	8	37.1	163	37	16	13	0	0	0	2	14	1	39	4	0	1	3	.250	0	2- -	-	3.34	3.13
2014	2 Tms	Low	45	0	0	22	53.0	218	27	16	14	4	1	0	5	29	0	81	6	1	5	1	.833	0	5- -	-	2.24	2.38
2015	Lynbrg	A+	36	0	0	31	34.1	148	30	18	17	0	1	1	2	13	0	43	6	0	0	2	.000	0	12- -	-	2.78	4.46
2015	Akron	AA	5	0	0	0	6.0	26	5	1	1	0	0	0	0	1	0	15	5	0	0	0	-	0	0- -	-	1.60	1.50
2016	Akron	AA	15	0	0	14	16.1	60	3	1	1	1	0	0	2	5	0	23	0	0	1	0	1.000	0	7- -	-	0.67	0.55
2016	Clmbs	AAA	28	0	0	13	25.1	104	20	7	7	1	1	0	4	7	2	25	2	1	2	2	.500	0	5- -	-	2.60	2.49
2016	S-WB	AAA	6	0	0	6	6.1	25	3	1	1	0	1	0	0	2	0	7	0	0	0	1	.000	0	1- -	-	0.95	1.42
2016	NYY	AL	10	0	0	4	7.0	40	11	5	5	3	0	0	2	4	1	6	0	0	1	0	1.000	0	0-1	1	11.69	6.43

Jeremy Hellickson

Pitches: R **Bats:** R **Pos:** SP-32 **Ht:** 6'1" **Wt:** 190 **Born:** 4/8/1987 **Age:** 30

| | | | HOW MUCH HE PITCHED | | | | | | WHAT HE GAVE UP | | | | | | | | | | THE RESULTS | | | | | | | |
Year	Team	Lg	G	GS	CG	GF	IP	BFP	H	R	ER	HR	SH	SF	HB	TBB	IBB	SO	WP	Bk	W	L	Pct	Sh	Sv-Op	Hld	ERC	ERA
2010	TB	AL	10	4	0	0	36.1	149	32	14	14	5	0	1	2	8	2	33	2	0	4	0	1.000	0	0-1	0	3.10	3.47
2011	TB	AL	29	29	2	0	189.0	774	146	64	62	21	1	2	4	72	8	117	8	1	13	10	.565	1	0-0	0	2.89	2.95
2012	TB	AL	31	31	0	0	177.0	741	163	68	61	25	4	3	4	59	3	124	5	0	10	11	.476	0	0-0	0	3.73	3.10
2013	TB	AL	32	31	0	1	174.0	737	185	103	100	24	2	5	4	50	0	135	7	2	12	10	.545	0	0-0	0	4.40	5.17
2014	TB	AL	13	13	0	0	63.2	281	71	35	32	8	0	1	2	21	1	54	0	0	1	5	.167	0	0-0	0	4.70	4.52
2015	Ari	NL	27	27	0	0	146.0	636	151	79	75	22	8	6	6	43	3	121	5	0	9	12	.429	0	0-0	0	4.25	4.62
2016	Phi	NL	32	32	1	0	189.0	772	173	86	78	24	4	6	6	45	0	154	6	1	12	10	.545	1	0-0	0	3.31	3.71
	Postseason		2	2	0	0	5.0	22	5	3	3	3	0	0	0	3	0	1	0	0	0	1	.000	0	0-0	0	8.99	5.40
	7 ML YEARS		174	167	3	1	975.0	4090	921	449	422	129	19	24	28	298	17	738	41	4	61	58	.513	2	0-1	0	3.71	3.90

Heath Hembree

Pitches: R **Bats:** R **Pos:** RP-38 HEHM-bree **Ht:** 6'4" **Wt:** 210 **Born:** 1/13/1989 **Age:** 28

| | | | HOW MUCH HE PITCHED | | | | | | WHAT HE GAVE UP | | | | | | | | | | THE RESULTS | | | | | | | |
Year	Team	Lg	G	GS	CG	GF	IP	BFP	H	R	ER	HR	SH	SF	HB	TBB	IBB	SO	WP	Bk	W	L	Pct	Sh	Sv-Op	Hld	ERC	ERA
2016	Pwtckt*	AAA	13	0	0	13	13.1	49	6	1	1	0	0	0	0	3	0	22	0	0	0	0	-	0	8- -	-	0.78	0.68
2013	SF	NL	9	0	0	2	7.2	29	4	0	0	0	0	0	0	2	0	12	0	0	0	0	.000	0	0-0	0	1.02	0.00
2014	Bos	AL	6	0	0	3	10.0	43	11	5	5	1	0	0	0	5	2	6	1	0	0	0	.000	0	0-0	0	4.94	4.50
2015	Bos	AL	22	0	0	9	25.1	106	25	10	10	5	0	0	0	9	2	15	1	0	2	0	1.000	0	0-0	1	4.46	3.55
2016	Bos	AL	38	0	0	8	51.0	223	51	23	15	6	0	1	0	17	1	47	0	0	4	1	.800	0	0-2	5	3.78	2.65
	4 ML YEARS		75	0	0	22	94.0	401	91	38	30	12	0	1	0	33	5	80	2	0	6	1	.857	0	0-2	6	3.78	2.87

Jim Henderson

Pitches: R **Bats:** L **Pos:** RP-44 **Ht:** 6'5" **Wt:** 220 **Born:** 10/21/1982 **Age:** 34

| | | | HOW MUCH HE PITCHED | | | | | | WHAT HE GAVE UP | | | | | | | | | | THE RESULTS | | | | | | | |
Year	Team	Lg	G	GS	CG	GF	IP	BFP	H	R	ER	HR	SH	SF	HB	TBB	IBB	SO	WP	Bk	W	L	Pct	Sh	Sv-Op	Hld	ERC	ERA
2016	Bnghtn*	AA	5	3	0	0	4.2	25	8	8	8	0	1	0	0	5	0	4	1	0	0	0	.000	0	0- -	-	11.21	15.43
2016	LsVgs*	AAA	8	0	0	6	8.0	34	8	4	4	1	1	1	0	4	0	10	0	1	0	2	.000	0	2- -	-	4.85	4.50
2012	Mil	NL	36	0	0	6	30.2	131	26	12	12	1	1	3	1	13	0	45	1	0	1	3	.250	0	3-7	14	2.96	3.52
2013	Mil	NL	61	0	0	45	60.0	247	44	18	18	8	1	0	2	24	2	75	0	0	5	5	.500	0	28-32	5	2.93	2.70
2014	Mil	NL	14	0	0	3	11.1	50	14	10	9	3	1	0	0	4	1	17	0	0	2	1	.667	0	0-0	2	6.49	7.15
2016	NYM	NL	44	0	0	8	35.0	155	34	17	16	7	1	1	2	14	0	40	0	1	2	2	.500	0	0-2	11	4.75	4.11
	4 ML YEARS		155	0	0	62	137.0	583	118	57	55	19	4	4	5	55	3	177	1	1	10	11	.476	0	31-41	32	3.65	3.61

Kyle Hendricks

Pitches: R **Bats:** R **Pos:** SP-30; RP-1 **Ht:** 6'3" **Wt:** 190 **Born:** 12/7/1989 **Age:** 27

| | | | HOW MUCH HE PITCHED | | | | | | WHAT HE GAVE UP | | | | | | | | | | THE RESULTS | | | | | | | |
Year	Team	Lg	G	GS	CG	GF	IP	BFP	H	R	ER	HR	SH	SF	HB	TBB	IBB	SO	WP	Bk	W	L	Pct	Sh	Sv-Op	Hld	ERC	ERA
2014	ChC	NL	13	13	0	0	80.1	321	72	24	22	4	4	1	4	15	2	47	0	0	7	2	.778	0	0-0	0	2.61	2.46
2015	ChC	NL	32	32	1	0	180.0	739	166	82	79	17	6	0	8	43	1	167	3	1	8	7	.533	1	0-0	0	3.18	3.95
2016	ChC	NL	31	30	2	0	190.0	745	142	53	45	15	4	3	8	44	3	170	5	0	16	8	.667	1	0-0	0	**2.19**	**2.13**
	Postseason		2	2	0	0	8.2	35	9	5	5	4	0	0	0	1	0	11	0	0	0	0	-	0	0-0	0	5.49	5.19
	3 ML YEARS		76	75	3	0	450.1	1805	380	159	146	36	14	4	20	102	6	384	8	1	31	17	.646	2	0-0	0	2.65	2.92

Liam Hendriks

Pitches: R **Bats:** R **Pos:** RP-53 **Ht:** 6'0" **Wt:** 200 **Born:** 2/10/1989 **Age:** 28

| | | | HOW MUCH HE PITCHED | | | | | | WHAT HE GAVE UP | | | | | | | | | | THE RESULTS | | | | | | | |
Year	Team	Lg	G	GS	CG	GF	IP	BFP	H	R	ER	HR	SH	SF	HB	TBB	IBB	SO	WP	Bk	W	L	Pct	Sh	Sv-Op	Hld	ERC	ERA
2011	Min	AL	4	4	0	0	23.1	100	29	16	16	3	0	0	0	6	0	16	1	0	0	2	.000	0	0-0	0	5.26	6.17
2012	Min	AL	16	16	1	0	85.1	381	106	61	53	17	3	1	4	26	3	50	4	0	1	8	.111	0	0-0	0	6.03	5.59
2013	Min	AL	10	8	0	1	47.1	224	67	39	36	10	0	2	3	14	1	34	1	0	1	3	.250	0	0-0	0	7.16	6.85
2014	2 Tms	AL	9	6	0	0	32.2	143	38	21	19	3	0	2	3	7	0	23	1	0	1	2	.333	0	0-0	1	4.56	5.23

Year Team	Lg	G	GS	CG	GF	IP	BFP	H	R	ER	HR	SH	SF	HB	TBB	IBB	SO	WP	Bk	W	L	Pct	Sh	Sv-Op	Hld	ERC	ERA
2015 Tor	AL	58	0	0	14	64.2	261	59	23	21	3	0	2	2	11	1	71	4	0	5	0	1.000	0	0-2	5	2.51	2.92
2016 Oak	AL	53	0	0	10	64.2	275	69	31	27	6	0	4	1	14	3	71	3	0	0	4	.000	0	0-1	10	3.63	3.76
14 Tor	AL	3	3	0	0	13.1	57	12	9	9	3	0	0	2	4	0	8	0	0	1	0	1.000	0	0-0	0	4.58	6.08
14 KC	AL	6	3	0	0	19.1	86	26	12	10	0	0	2	1	3	0	15	1	0	0	2	.000	0	0-0	1	4.52	4.66
Postseason		3	0	0		5.0	18	5	3	3	0	0	1	0	0	0	2	0	0	0	0	-	0	0-0	0	2.23	5.40
6 ML YEARS		150	34	1	25	318.0	1384	368	191	172	42	3	12	13	78	8	265	14	0	8	19	.296	0	0-3	16	4.70	4.87

Guillermo Heredia

Bats: R **Throws:** L **Pos:** LF-35;RF-14;PH-5;PR-3;CF-1   ghee-YAIR-moh   **Ht:** 5'10" **Wt:** 180 **Born:** 1/31/1991 **Age:** 26

Year Team	Lg	G	AB	H	2B	3B	HR	(Hm	Rd)	TB	R	RBI	RC	TBB	IBB	SO	HBP	SH	SF	SB	CS	GDP	Avg	OBP	Slg	OPS
2016 Jacksn	AA	58	205	60	7	2	2	(-	-)	77	39	34	36	36	0	32	9	1	9	2	5	11	.293	.405	.376	.781
2016 Tacom	AAA	35	138	43	6	1	2	(-	-)	57	27	13	23	12	0	15	4	1	2	3	0	6	.312	.378	.413	.791
2016 Sea	AL	45	92	23	3	0	1	(1	0)	29	12	12	12	12	0	15	2	1	0	1	1	1	.250	.349	.315	.664

Cesar Hernandez

Bats: B **Throws:** R **Pos:** 2B-149;PH-5;SS-4   **Ht:** 5'10" **Wt:** 160 **Born:** 5/23/1990 **Age:** 27

Year Team	Lg	G	AB	H	2B	3B	HR	(Hm	Rd)	TB	R	RBI	RC	TBB	IBB	SO	HBP	SH	SF	SB	CS	GDP	Avg	OBP	Slg	OPS
2013 Phi	NL	34	121	35	5	0	0	(0	0)	40	17	10	13	9	0	26	1	0	0	0	3	2	.289	.344	.331	.674
2014 Phi	NL	66	114	27	2	0	1	(1	0)	32	13	4	7	9	1	33	0	1	1	1	1	1	.237	.290	.281	.571
2015 Phi	NL	127	405	110	20	4	1	(1	0)	141	57	35	52	40	1	86	2	4	1	19	5	6	.272	.339	.348	.687
2016 Phi	NL	155	547	161	14	11	6	(4	2)	215	67	39	82	66	4	116	2	5	2	17	13	6	.294	.371	.393	.764
4 ML YEARS		382	1187	333	41	15	8	(6	2)	428	154	88	154	124	6	261	5	10	4	37	22	15	.281	.350	.361	.711

David Hernandez

Pitches: R **Bats:** R **Pos:** RP-70   **Ht:** 6'3" **Wt:** 245 **Born:** 5/13/1985 **Age:** 32

Year Team	Lg	G	GS	CG	GF	IP	BFP	H	R	ER	HR	SH	SF	HB	TBB	IBB	SO	WP	Bk	W	L	Pct	Sh	Sv-Op	Hld	ERC	ERA
2009 Bal	AL	20	19	0	0	101.1	462	118	62	61	27	2	3	1	46	0	68	3	0	4	10	.286	0	0-0	0	6.55	5.42
2010 Bal	AL	41	8	0	16	79.1	348	72	40	38	9	1	3	4	42	4	72	9	0	8	8	.500	0	2-6	2	4.28	4.31
2011 Ari	NL	74	0	0	28	69.1	291	49	27	26	4	3	2	2	30	1	77	7	1	5	3	.625	0	11-14	23	2.40	3.38
2012 Ari	NL	72	0	0	21	68.1	278	48	21	19	4	0	1	3	22	1	98	4	1	2	3	.400	0	4-10	25	2.10	2.50
2013 Ari	NL	62	0	0	12	62.1	263	50	33	31	10	2	0	4	24	4	66	6	0	5	6	.455	0	2-8	15	3.45	4.48
2015 Ari	NL	40	0	0	7	33.2	144	33	18	16	6	1	0	3	11	0	33	1	0	1	5	.167	0	0-0	7	4.62	4.28
2016 Phi	NL	70	0	0	16	72.2	322	77	31	31	11	1	1	2	32	5	80	6	0	3	4	.429	0	1-3	15	4.95	3.84
Postseason		4	0	0	1	5.0	17	2	2	2	1	0	0	0	0	0	5	0	0	0	0	-	0	0-0	0	0.74	3.60
7 ML YEARS		379	27	0	100	487.0	2108	447	232	222	71	10	10	19	207	15	494	36	2	28	39	.418	0	20-41	87	4.11	4.10

Felix Hernandez

Pitches: R **Bats:** R **Pos:** SP-25   **Ht:** 6'3" **Wt:** 225 **Born:** 4/8/1986 **Age:** 31

Year Team	Lg	G	GS	CG	GF	IP	BFP	H	R	ER	HR	SH	SF	HB	TBB	IBB	SO	WP	Bk	W	L	Pct	Sh	Sv-Op	Hld	ERC	ERA
2005 Sea	AL	12	12	0	0	84.1	328	61	26	25	5	1	2	2	23	0	77	3	0	4	4	.500	0	0-0	0	2.08	2.67
2006 Sea	AL	31	31	2	0	191.0	816	195	105	96	23	2	3	6	60	2	176	11	0	12	14	.462	1	0-0	0	4.11	4.52
2007 Sea	AL	30	30	1	0	190.1	808	209	88	83	20	6	1	3	53	4	165	7	1	14	7	.667	1	0-0	0	4.27	3.92
2008 Sea	AL	31	31	2	0	200.2	857	198	85	77	17	4	6	8	80	7	175	8	1	9	11	.450	0	0-0	0	4.05	3.45
2009 Sea	AL	34	34	2	0	238.2	977	200	81	66	15	6	11	8	71	0	217	17	1	19	5	.792	1	0-0	0	2.72	2.49
2010 Sea	AL	34	34	6	0	249.2	1001	194	80	63	17	6	3	8	70	1	232	14	1	13	12	.520	1	0-0	0	2.39	2.27
2011 Sea	AL	33	33	5	0	233.2	964	218	99	90	19	3	7	7	67	0	222	12	1	14	14	.500	0	0-0	0	3.31	3.47
2012 Sea	AL	33	33	5	0	232.0	939	209	84	79	14	2	2	12	56	0	223	13	2	13	9	.591	5	0-0	0	2.94	3.06
2013 Sea	AL	31	31	0	0	204.1	823	185	74	69	15	4	6	3	46	1	216	13	0	12	10	.545	0	0-0	0	2.82	3.04
2014 Sea	AL	34	34	0	0	236.0	912	170	68	56	16	4	5	5	46	1	248	18	0	15	6	.714	0	0-0	0	1.81	2.14
2015 Sea	AL	31	31	2	0	201.2	826	180	80	79	23	4	4	9	58	0	191	10	0	18	9	.667	2	0-0	0	3.37	3.53
2016 Sea	AL	25	25	0	0	153.1	655	138	76	65	19	3	0	10	65	0	122	6	0	11	8	.579	0	0-0	0	4.07	3.82
12 ML YEARS		359	359	25	0	2415.2	9906	2157	946	848	203	45	50	81	695	16	2264	132	7	154	109	.586	11	0-0	0	3.11	3.16

Gorkys Hernandez

Bats: R **Throws:** R **Pos:** CF-14;RF-6;PH-6;LF-2   GORE-keez   **Ht:** 6'1" **Wt:** 190 **Born:** 9/7/1987 **Age:** 29

Year Team	Lg	G	AB	H	2B	3B	HR	(Hm	Rd)	TB	R	RBI	RC	TBB	IBB	SO	HBP	SH	SF	SB	CS	GDP	Avg	OBP	Slg	OPS
2016 Scrmto*	AAA	116	437	132	22	3	8	(-	-)	184	74	51	73	52	2	77	6	5	3	20	13	11	.302	.382	.421	.803
2012 2 Tms	NL	70	156	30	2	3	3	(2	1)	47	18	13	15	13	0	42	3	1	0	7	2	2	.192	.267	.301	.569
2015 Pit	NL	8	5	0	0	0	0	(0	0)	0	0	0	0	0	0	0	0	0	0	1	0	0	.000	.000	.000	.000
2016 SF	NL	26	54	14	5	0	2	(1	1)	25	7	4	5	3	0	11	0	0	0	0	1	0	.259	.298	.463	.761
12 Pit	NL	25	24	2	0	0	0	(0	0)	2	2	2	0	1	0	5	1	0	0	2	0	1	.083	.154	.083	.237
12 Mia	NL	45	132	28	2	3	3	(2	1)	45	16	11	15	12	0	37	2	1	0	5	2	1	.212	.288	.341	.629
3 ML YEARS		104	215	44	7	3	5	(3	2)	72	25	17	20	16	0	53	3	1	0	8	3	2	.205	.269	.335	.604

Kiké Hernandez

kee-KAY

Bats: R **Throws:** R **Pos:** PH-51;LF-41;CF-22;2B-11;RF-7;3B-5;SS-2;DH-1 **Ht:** 5'11" **Wt:** 200 **Born:** 8/24/1991 **Age:** 25

						BATTING														RUNNING			AVERAGES			
Year	Team	Lg	G	AB	H	2B	3B	HR	(Hm | Rd)	TB	R	RBI	RC	TBB	IBB	SO	HBP	SH	SF	SB	CS	GDP	Avg	OBP	Slg	OPS
2014	2 Tms		42	121	30	6	3	3	(1 | 2)	51	13	14	18	12	0	21	1	0	0	0	0	1	.248	.321	.421	.742
2015	LAD	NL	76	202	62	12	2	7	(2 | 5)	99	24	22	32	11	0	46	2	1	2	0	2	3	.307	.346	.490	.836
2016	LAD	NL	109	216	41	8	0	7	(5 | 2)	70	25	18	16	28	1	64	0	0	0	2	0	3	.190	.283	.324	.607
14	Hou	AL	24	81	23	4	2	1	(1 | 0)	34	10	8	14	8	0	11	0	0	0	0	0	0	.284	.348	.420	.768
14	Mia	NL	18	40	7	2	1	2	(0 | 2)	17	3	6	4	4	0	10	1	0	0	0	0	1	.175	.267	.425	.692
	Postseason		4	13	4	0	0	0	(0 | 0)	4	3	0	1	2	1	4	0	0	0	1	0	1	.308	.400	.308	.708
	3 ML YEARS		227	539	133	26	5	17	(8 | 9)	220	62	54	66	51	1	131	3	1	2	2	2	7	.247	.314	.408	.722

Marco Hernandez

Bats: L **Throws:** R **Pos:** 2B-14;PH-12;3B-10;PR-5;SS-2;DH-1 **Ht:** 6'0" **Wt:** 200 **Born:** 9/6/1992 **Age:** 24

						BATTING														RUNNING			AVERAGES			
Year	Team	Lg	G	AB	H	2B	3B	HR	(Hm | Rd)	TB	R	RBI	RC	TBB	IBB	SO	HBP	SH	SF	SB	CS	GDP	Avg	OBP	Slg	OPS
2012	2 Tms	Low	110	426	110	14	7	7	(- | -)	159	57	50	46	19	0	76	0	4	5	10	4	7	.258	.287	.373	.660
2013	Kane	A	111	417	106	17	3	4	(- | -)	141	45	34	42	16	1	72	4	4	2	21	7	8	.254	.287	.338	.625
2014	Dytona	A+	122	441	119	13	7	3	(- | -)	155	61	55	52	30	2	90	2	7	6	22	8	7	.270	.315	.351	.667
2015	Portlnd	AA	68	282	92	21	4	5	(- | -)	136	30	31	46	9	0	49	1	2	0	4	2	5	.326	.349	.482	.832
2015	Pwtckt	AAA	46	181	49	9	2	4	(- | -)	74	27	22	22	8	2	39	0	0	1	1	0	1	.271	.300	.409	.709
2016	Pwtckt	AAA	57	223	69	7	4	5	(- | -)	99	26	29	34	12	0	51	0	1	1	4	2	4	.309	.343	.444	.787
2016	Bos	AL	40	51	15	1	0	1	(0 | 1)	19	11	5	6	5	0	10	0	0	0	1	0	0	.294	.357	.373	.730

Oscar Hernandez

Bats: R **Throws:** R **Pos:** C-4 **Ht:** 6'1" **Wt:** 230 **Born:** 7/9/1993 **Age:** 23

						BATTING														RUNNING			AVERAGES			
Year	Team	Lg	G	AB	H	2B	3B	HR	(Hm | Rd)	TB	R	RBI	RC	TBB	IBB	SO	HBP	SH	SF	SB	CS	GDP	Avg	OBP	Slg	OPS
2012	Prnctn	R+	49	160	37	9	1	5	(- | -)	63	25	24	24	23	0	31	8	0	4	0	1	8	.231	.349	.394	.742
2013	2 Tms	Low	46	176	40	6	0	6	(- | -)	64	23	34	19	13	2	25	2	0	1	9	1	3	.227	.286	.364	.650
2014	BG	A	94	362	90	18	5	9	(- | -)	145	43	63	44	25	1	78	4	1	5	3	6	6	.249	.301	.401	.701
2016	Visalia	A+	34	112	33	10	0	3	(- | -)	52	15	15	22	18	0	26	2	1	0	1	0	3	.295	.402	.464	.866
2016	Mobile	AA	42	144	28	6	0	7	(- | -)	55	12	18	13	5	0	27	1	0	0	3	0	3	.194	.227	.382	.609
2015	Ari	NL	18	31	5	1	0	0	(0 | 0)	6	4	1	2	3	0	15	1	1	0	0	0	0	.161	.257	.194	.451
2016	Ari	NL	4	11	2	0	0	1	(0 | 1)	5	1	1	0	0	0	0	0	0	0	0	0	1	.182	.182	.455	.636
	2 ML YEARS		22	42	7	1	0	1	(0 | 1)	11	5	2	2	3	0	15	1	1	0	0	0	1	.167	.239	.262	.501

Roberto Hernandez

Pitches: R **Bats:** R **Pos:** SP-2 **Ht:** 6'4" **Wt:** 270 **Born:** 8/30/1980 **Age:** 36

				HOW MUCH HE PITCHED					WHAT HE GAVE UP									THE RESULTS							
Year	Team	Lg	G	GS	CG	GF	IP	BFP	H	R	ER	HR	SH	SF	HB	TBB	IBB	SO	WP	Bk	W	L	Pct	Sh	Sv-Op	Hld	ERC	ERA
2016	Buffalo*	AAA	13	13	0	0	71.1	309	74	37	35	10	1	2	6	23	0	48	2	0	4	4	.500	0	0--	-	4.63	4.42
2006	Cle	AL	38	7	0	12	74.2	340	88	46	45	9	2	4	7	31	3	58	3	1	1	10	.091	0	0-3	10	5.69	5.42
2007	Cle	AL	32	32	2	0	215.0	879	199	78	73	16	2	4	11	61	2	137	5	1	19	8	.704	1	0-0	0	3.32	3.06
2008	Cle	AL	22	22	1	0	120.2	549	126	80	73	7	1	4	9	70	0	58	8	1	8	7	.533	1	0-0	0	5.07	5.44
2009	Cle	AL	24	24	0	0	125.1	596	151	97	88	16	4	2	8	70	0	79	5	1	5	12	.294	0	0-0	0	6.38	6.32
2010	Cle	AL	33	33	4	0	210.1	880	203	98	88	17	2	10	9	72	0	124	3	0	13	14	.481	1	0-0	0	3.77	3.77
2011	Cle	AL	32	32	0	0	188.2	833	205	125	110	22	9	7	14	60	3	109	3	1	7	15	.318	0	0-0	0	4.59	5.25
2012	Cle	AL	3	3	0	0	14.1	62	17	15	12	4	0	2	1	3	0	2	1	0	0	3	.000	0	0-0	0	6.03	7.53
2013	TB	AL	32	24	1	3	151.0	643	164	87	82	24	3	5	13	38	8	113	3	0	6	13	.316	0	1-1	0	4.74	4.89
2014	2 Tms	NL	32	29	0	1	164.2	722	156	84	75	19	10	5	9	73	7	105	5	0	8	11	.421	0	0-1	0	4.17	4.10
2015	Hou	AL	20	11	0	6	84.2	357	90	48	41	9	0	3	1	26	2	42	1	0	3	5	.375	0	0-0	0	4.20	4.36
2016	Atl	NL	2	2	0	0	9.0	39	13	8	8	4	0	1	0	1	0	6	0	0	1	1	.500	0	0-0	0	8.36	8.00
14	Phi	NL	23	20	0	1	121.0	527	108	57	52	11	7	3	7	55	7	75	4	0	6	8	.429	0	0-1	0	3.72	3.87
14	LAD	NL	9	9	0	0	43.2	195	48	27	23	8	3	2	2	18	0	30	1	0	2	3	.400	0	0-0	0	5.50	4.74
	Postseason		3	3	0	0	15.0	66	13	12	12	2	0	0	0	11	0	12	0	0	0	1	.000	0	0-0	0	5.02	7.20
	11 ML YEARS		270	219	8	22	1358.1	5900	1412	766	695	147	33	47	82	505	25	833	37	5	71	99	.418	3	1-5	10	4.49	4.60

Teoscar Hernandez

Bats: R **Throws:** R **Pos:** LF-22;CF-15;RF-6;PH-6;PR-2 tay-OH-skar **Ht:** 6'2" **Wt:** 180 **Born:** 10/15/1992 **Age:** 24

						BATTING														RUNNING			AVERAGES			
Year	Team	Lg	G	AB	H	2B	3B	HR	(Hm | Rd)	TB	R	RBI	RC	TBB	IBB	SO	HBP	SH	SF	SB	CS	GDP	Avg	OBP	Slg	OPS
2012	2 Tms	Low	59	202	49	13	2	5	(- | -)	81	27	23	28	22	0	66	3	1	2	11	1	3	.243	.323	.401	.724
2013	QuadC	A	123	499	135	25	9	13	(- | -)	217	97	55	74	41	0	135	4	17	4	24	11	6	.271	.328	.435	.763
2014	Lancst	A+	96	391	115	33	8	17	(- | -)	215	72	75	85	49	0	117	5	5	5	31	6	7	.294	.376	.550	.925
2014	CpChr	AA	23	95	27	4	1	4	(- | -)	45	12	10	12	2	0	36	0	1	2	2	3	1	.284	.299	.474	.773
2015	CpChr	AA	121	470	103	12	2	17	(- | -)	170	92	48	51	33	1	126	4	5	2	33	7	11	.219	.275	.362	.637
2016	CpChr	AA	69	279	85	19	0	6	(- | -)	122	53	30	50	32	0	55	5	3	2	29	11	2	.305	.384	.437	.821
2016	Fresno	AAA	38	144	45	9	3	4	(- | -)	72	20	23	26	13	0	25	0	1	2	5	4	3	.313	.365	.500	.865
2016	Hou	AL	41	100	23	7	0	4	(1 | 3)	42	15	11	11	11	1	28	0	0	1	0	2	5	.230	.304	.420	.724

Dilson Herrera

Bats: R **Throws:** R **Pos:** 2B · DILL-sun · **Ht:** 5'10" **Wt:** 205 **Born:** 3/3/1994 **Age:** 23

Year Team	Lg	G	AB	H	2B	3B	HR	(Hm	Rd)	TB	R	RBI	RC	TBB	IBB	SO	HBP	SH	SF	SB	CS	GDP	Avg	OBP	Slg	OPS
2012 2 Tms	Low	60	227	65	12	5	8	(-	-)	111	48	29	39	19	0	47	0	10	0	12	4	3	.286	.341	.489	.830
2013 2 Tms	Low	116	442	118	27	3	11	(-	-)	184	75	60	64	40	1	116	8	6	7	14	6	6	.267	.334	.416	.750
2014 Stluci	A+	67	283	87	16	2	3	(-	-)	116	48	23	44	18	0	44	4	2	2	14	3	4	.307	.355	.410	.765
2014 Bnghtn	AA	61	241	82	17	3	10	(-	-)	135	50	48	54	29	0	52	2	0	6	9	4	5	.340	.406	.560	.967
2015 LsVgs	AAA	81	327	107	23	2	11	(-	-)	167	68	50	62	28	0	59	3	3	3	13	9	2	.327	.382	.511	.893
2016 LsVgs	AAA	86	359	99	24	2	13	(-	-)	166	61	55	53	27	0	72	1	1	1	6	7	5	.276	.327	.462	.790
2016 Lsvlle	AAA	24	64	17	0	2	2	(-	-)	27	10	9	10	11	0	15	1	2	2	1	2	1	.266	.372	.422	.794
2014 NYM	NL	18	59	13	0	1	3	(0	3)	24	6	11	7	7	0	17	0	0	0	0	0	3	.220	.303	.407	.710
2015 NYM	NL	31	90	19	3	1	3	(2	1)	33	7	6	11	11	1	23	2	0	0	2	0	2	.211	.311	.367	.677
2 ML YEARS		49	149	32	3	2	6	(2	4)	57	13	17	18	18	1	40	2	0	0	2	0	5	.215	.308	.383	.690

Kelvin Herrera

Pitches: R **Bats:** R **Pos:** RP-72 · **Ht:** 5'10" **Wt:** 200 **Born:** 12/31/1989 **Age:** 27

Year Team	Lg	G	GS	CG	GF	IP	BFP	H	R	ER	HR	SH	SF	HB	TBB	IBB	SO	WP	Bk	W	L	Pct	Sh	Sv-Op	Hld	ERC	ERA
2011 KC	AL	2	0	0	0	2.0	9	2	3	3	1	1	0	1	0	0	0	0	1	0	1	.000	0	0-0	1	7.30	13.50
2012 KC	AL	76	0	0	10	84.1	344	79	24	22	4	5	0	2	21	6	77	3	1	4	3	.571	0	3-4	19	2.84	2.35
2013 KC	AL	59	0	0	16	58.1	245	48	27	25	9	0	3	2	21	2	74	5	0	5	7	.417	0	2-4	20	3.35	3.86
2014 KC	AL	70	0	0	12	70.0	285	54	12	11	0	4	0	3	26	0	59	1	0	4	3	.571	0	0-1	20	2.31	1.41
2015 KC	AL	72	0	0	8	69.2	286	52	23	21	5	1	5	2	26	1	64	4	0	4	3	.571	0	0-7	21	2.53	2.71
2016 KC	AL	72	0	0	23	72.0	283	57	23	22	6	1	1	3	12	0	86	3	0	2	6	.250	0	12-15	26	2.20	2.75
Postseason		22	0	0	0	28.2	115	21	5	4	0	0	1	0	10	0	38	0	0	2	0	1.000	0	0-0	6	1.90	1.26
6 ML YEARS		351	0	0	69	356.1	1452	292	112	104	25	12	9	13	106	9	360	16	1	19	23	.452	0	17-31	107	2.65	2.63

Odubel Herrera

Bats: L **Throws:** R **Pos:** CF-155;PH-7;PR-1 · oh-DOO-bull · **Ht:** 5'11" **Wt:** 205 **Born:** 12/29/1991 **Age:** 25

Year Team	Lg	G	AB	H	2B	3B	HR	(Hm	Rd)	TB	R	RBI	RC	TBB	IBB	SO	HBP	SH	SF	SB	CS	GDP	Avg	OBP	Slg	OPS
2012 MrtlBh	A+	126	500	142	22	6	5	(-	-)	191	72	46	69	33	3	99	7	7	4	27	5	9	.284	.335	.382	.717
2013 Frisco	AA	101	389	100	12	7	2	(-	-)	132	37	30	39	17	0	67	1	3	2	15	5	11	.257	.289	.339	.628
2013 MrtlBh	A+	29	95	28	2	1	1	(-	-)	35	13	5	16	16	0	19	1	2	1	2	2	1	.295	.398	.368	.767
2014 MrtlBh	A+	29	111	33	3	1	0	(-	-)	38	26	11	19	23	0	21	0	1	2	9	3	1	.297	.412	.342	.754
2014 Frisco	AA	96	368	118	16	4	2	(-	-)	148	47	47	57	29	1	70	3	6	2	12	7	4	.321	.373	.402	.775
2015 Phi	NL	147	495	147	30	3	8	(4	4)	207	64	41	66	28	0	129	8	5	1	16	8	6	.297	.344	.418	.762
2016 Phi	NL	159	583	167	21	6	15	(7	8)	245	87	49	93	63	7	134	6	2	2	25	7	6	.286	.361	.420	.781
2 ML YEARS		306	1078	314	51	9	23	(11	12)	452	151	90	159	91	7	263	14	7	3	41	15	12	.291	.353	.419	.773

Chris Herrmann

HERR-men

Bats: L **Throws:** R **Pos:** C-31;PH-16;RF-4;LF-3;1B-2;CF-2;PR-1 · **Ht:** 6'0" **Wt:** 200 **Born:** 11/24/1987 **Age:** 29

Year Team	Lg	G	AB	H	2B	3B	HR	(Hm	Rd)	TB	R	RBI	RC	TBB	IBB	SO	HBP	SH	SF	SB	CS	GDP	Avg	OBP	Slg	OPS
2012 Min	AL	7	18	1	0	0	0	(0	0)	1	0	1	0	1	0	5	0	0	0	0	0	0	.056	.105	.056	.161
2013 Min	AL	57	157	32	7	0	4	(1	3)	51	16	18	15	18	0	49	0	3	0	0	1	3	.204	.286	.325	.611
2014 Min	AL	33	75	16	3	0	0	(0	0)	19	8	4	5	4	0	17	0	0	0	0	0	2	.213	.253	.253	.506
2015 Min	AL	45	103	15	5	1	2	(2	0)	28	13	10	8	7	0	37	2	1	0	0	0	1	.146	.214	.272	.486
2016 Ari	NL	56	148	42	5	4	6	(3	3)	73	21	28	31	16	1	44	0	1	1	4	0	2	.284	.352	.493	.845
5 ML YEARS		198	501	106	20	5	12	(6	6)	172	58	61	59	46	1	152	2	5	1	5	1	8	.212	.280	.343	.623

Frank Herrmann

Pitches: R **Bats:** L **Pos:** RP-14 · **Ht:** 6'4" **Wt:** 220 **Born:** 5/30/1984 **Age:** 33

Year Team	Lg	G	GS	CG	GF	IP	BFP	H	R	ER	HR	SH	SF	HB	TBB	IBB	SO	WP	Bk	W	L	Pct	Sh	Sv-Op	Hld	ERC	ERA
2016 LV*	AAA	27	0	0	10	31.1	123	24	6	6	2	0	0	0	6	2	31	1	0	6	1	.857	0	0--	-	1.82	1.72
2010 Cle	AL	40	0	0	8	44.2	189	48	22	20	6	1	2	2	9	0	24	2	0	1	0	1.000	0	1-2	7	4.12	4.03
2011 Cle	AL	40	0	0	17	56.1	253	71	35	32	7	2	0	0	16	1	34	1	0	4	0	1.000	0	0-0	0	5.20	5.11
2012 Cle	AL	15	0	0	7	19.1	71	12	5	5	1	0	0	0	4	0	14	0	0	0	0	-	0	0-0	0	1.42	2.33
2016 Phi	NL	14	0	0	4	15.0	69	20	16	14	7	1	0	1	5	0	14	3	0	1	2	.333	0	0-0	0	9.12	8.40
4 ML YEARS		109	0	0	36	135.1	582	151	78	71	21	4	2	3	34	1	86	6	0	5	3	.625	0	1-2	7	4.60	4.72

Keith Hessler

Pitches: L **Bats:** L **Pos:** RP-17 · **Ht:** 6'4" **Wt:** 240 **Born:** 3/15/1989 **Age:** 28

Year Team	Lg	G	GS	CG	GF	IP	BFP	H	R	ER	HR	SH	SF	HB	TBB	IBB	SO	WP	Bk	W	L	Pct	Sh	Sv-Op	Hld	ERC	ERA
2012 Sbend	A	39	7	0	5	90.0	387	86	40	32	3	3	5	5	44	0	75	9	1	2	5	.286	0	1--	-	4.00	3.20
2013 Visalia	A+	26	26	0	0	137.0	623	161	97	89	24	10	8	10	64	1	126	7	0	8	7	.533	0	0--	-	6.36	5.85
2014 Visalia	A+	44	0	0	12	59.1	275	79	31	29	3	2	2	5	18	0	78	4	0	4	2	.667	0	1--	-	5.54	4.40
2015 Visalia	A+	10	0	0	2	14.2	55	11	0	0	0	0	0	0	2	0	20	1	0	1	0	1.000	0	0--	-	1.46	0.00
2015 Mobile	AA	24	0	0	7	25.1	95	17	2	2	1	2	0	0	5	3	32	1	0	3	1	.750	0	1--	-	1.39	0.71
2015 Reno	AAA	17	0	0	2	19.0	75	14	12	12	3	1	0	0	8	0	13	1	0	1	1	.500	0	0--	-	3.25	5.68
2016 Mobile	AA	7	0	0	2	5.1	26	7	3	3	0	0	0	1	3	0	5	2	0	0	0	-	0	1--	-	6.62	5.06
2016 ElPaso	AAA	28	0	0	5	36.2	150	32	13	12	1	0	1	1	12	0	42	2	0	1	1	.500	0	2--	-	2.79	2.95

Year Team	Lg	G	GS	CG	GF	IP	BFP	H	R	ER	HR	SH	SF	HB	TBB	IBB	SO	WP	Bk	W	L	Pct	Sh	Sv-Op	Hld	ERC	ERA
						HOW MUCH HE PITCHED			WHAT HE GAVE UP														THE RESULTS				
2015 Ari	NL	18	0	0	1	12.1	57	16	11	11	4	0	0	0	4	1	12	1	0	0	1	.000	0	0-2	1	6.95	8.03
2016 2 Tms	NL	17	0	0	5	21.2	103	24	10	10	2	1	0	1	13	2	11	0	0	1	0	1.000	0	0-0	1	5.33	4.15
16 Ari	NL	2	0	0	1	3.0	17	5	3	3	0	0	0	1	2	0	2	0	0	0	0	-	0	0-0	0	9.70	9.00
16 SD	NL	15	0	0	4	18.2	86	19	7	7	2	1	0	0	11	2	9	0	0	1	0	1.000	0	0-0	1	4.68	3.38
2 ML YEARS		35	0	0	6	34.0	160	40	21	21	6	1	0	1	17	3	23	1	0	1	1	.500	0	0-2	2	5.94	5.56

Chris Heston

Pitches: R Bats: R Pos: RP-4 **Ht: 6'3" Wt: 195 Born: 4/10/1988 Age: 29**

Year Team	Lg	G	GS	CG	GF	IP	BFP	H	R	ER	HR	SH	SF	HB	TBB	IBB	SO	WP	Bk	W	L	Pct	Sh	Sv-Op	Hld	ERC	ERA
						HOW MUCH HE PITCHED			WHAT HE GAVE UP														THE RESULTS				
2016 Scrmto*	AAA	15	14	0	1	81.1	354	82	42	41	8	6	5	4	32	2	53	4	0	2	9	.182	0	1--	-	4.24	4.54
2014 SF	NL	3	1	0	2	5.1	24	6	3	3	0	0	1	0	3	0	4	1	0	0	0	-	0	0-0	0	4.74	5.06
2015 SF	NL	31	31	2	0	177.2	746	169	82	78	16	2	0	13	64	3	141	5	1	12	11	.522	1	0-0	0	3.94	3.95
2016 SF	NL	4	0	0	0	5.0	29	9	6	6	0	1	0	0	6	2	3	3	0	1	1	.500	0	0-0	0	10.88	10.80
3 ML YEARS		38	32	2	2	188.0	799	184	91	87	16	3	1	13	73	5	148	9	1	13	12	.520	1	0-0	0	4.13	4.16

Jason Heyward

Bats: L Throws: L Pos: RF-131;CF-24;PH-2 **Ht: 6'5" Wt: 240 Born: 8/9/1989 Age: 27**

Year Team	Lg	G	AB	H	2B	3B	HR	(Hm	Rd)	TB	R	RBI	RC	TBB	IBB	SO	HBP	SH	SF	SB	CS	GDP	Avg	OBP	Slg	OPS
								BATTING												RUNNING			AVERAGES			
2010 Atl	NL	142	520	144	29	5	18	(9	9)	237	83	72	96	91	2	128	10	0	2	11	6	13	.277	.393	.456	.849
2011 Atl	NL	128	396	90	18	2	14	(5	9)	154	50	42	49	51	4	93	4	0	3	9	2	7	.227	.319	.389	.708
2012 Atl	NL	158	587	158	30	6	27	(9	18)	281	93	82	87	58	1	152	2	0	3	21	8	5	.269	.335	.479	.814
2013 Atl	NL	104	382	97	22	1	14	(10	4)	163	67	38	55	48	1	73	8	1	0	2	4	7	.254	.349	.427	.776
2014 Atl	NL	149	573	155	26	3	11	(5	6)	220	74	58	84	67	3	98	6	0	3	20	4	2	.271	.351	.384	.735
2015 StL	NL	154	547	160	33	4	13	(5	8)	240	79	60	78	56	4	90	2	0	3	23	3	13	.293	.359	.439	.797
2016 ChC	NL	142	530	122	27	1	7	(3	4)	172	61	49	53	54	0	93	5	1	2	11	4	12	.230	.306	.325	.631
Postseason		13	53	11	2	0	2	(0	2)	19	3	6	5	3	0	18	0	0	0	0	0	1	.208	.250	.358	.608
7 ML YEARS		977	3535	926	185	22	104	(46	58)	1467	507	401	502	425	15	727	37	2	16	97	31	59	.262	.346	.415	.761

Aaron Hicks

Bats: B Throws: R Pos: RF-86;LF-25;CF-24;PH-6;PR-6;DH-2 **Ht: 6'1" Wt: 205 Born: 10/2/1989 Age: 27**

Year Team	Lg	G	AB	H	2B	3B	HR	(Hm	Rd)	TB	R	RBI	RC	TBB	IBB	SO	HBP	SH	SF	SB	CS	GDP	Avg	OBP	Slg	OPS
								BATTING												RUNNING			AVERAGES			
2013 Min	AL	81	281	54	11	3	8	(3	5)	95	37	27	25	24	0	84	2	4	2	9	3	0	.192	.259	.338	.597
2014 Min	AL	69	186	40	8	0	1	(0	1)	51	22	18	22	36	0	56	0	2	1	4	3	2	.215	.341	.274	.615
2015 Min	AL	97	352	90	11	3	11	(6	5)	140	48	33	45	34	2	66	2	0	2	13	5	6	.256	.323	.398	.721
2016 NYY	AL	123	327	71	13	1	8	(7	1)	110	32	31	28	30	1	68	0	1	3	3	4	7	.217	.281	.336	.617
4 ML YEARS		370	1146	255	43	7	28	(16	12)	396	139	109	120	124	3	274	4	7	8	29	13	15	.223	.299	.346	.644

John Hicks

Bats: R Throws: R Pos: 1B-1 **Ht: 6'2" Wt: 230 Born: 8/31/1989 Age: 27**

Year Team	Lg	G	AB	H	2B	3B	HR	(Hm	Rd)	TB	R	RBI	RC	TBB	IBB	SO	HBP	SH	SF	SB	CS	GDP	Avg	OBP	Slg	OPS
								BATTING												RUNNING			AVERAGES			
2012 Hi Dsrt	A+	121	506	158	32	2	15	(-	-)	239	87	79	85	28	2	73	3	0	1	22	8	11	.312	.342	.472	.824
2013 Jacksn	AA	80	296	70	14	1	4	(-	-)	98	40	29	32	22	0	62	6	1	2	13	4	8	.236	.301	.331	.632
2014 Jacksn	AA	53	189	56	10	2	3	(-	-)	79	29	27	29	20	0	42	0	1	1	6	3	6	.296	.362	.418	.780
2014 Tacom	AAA	28	101	28	2	1	2	(-	-)	38	13	20	13	7	0	24	2	0	2	1	0	3	.277	.330	.376	.707
2015 Tacom	AAA	83	298	73	15	1	6	(-	-)	108	39	35	32	17	0	71	0	1	4	9	2	6	.245	.282	.362	.645
2016 Erie	AA	14	49	19	1	1	1	(-	-)	25	7	4	10	4	0	9	0	0	1	1	0	2	.388	.426	.510	.936
2016 Toledo	AAA	70	241	73	20	0	8	(-	-)	117	38	42	41	17	0	59	3	3	0	3	1	3	.303	.356	.485	.842
2015 Sea	AL	17	32	2	1	0	0	(0	0)	3	1	1	0	1	0	18	0	1	0	1	1	0	.063	.091	.094	.185
2016 Det	AL	1	2	1	1	0	0	(0	0)	2	1	0	0	0	0	0	0	0	0	0	0	0	.500	.500	1.000	1.500
2 ML YEARS		18	34	3	2	0	0	(0	0)	5	2	1	0	1	0	18	0	1	0	1	1	0	.088	.114	.147	.261

Aaron Hill

Bats: R Throws: R Pos: 3B-103;2B-24;PH-18;DH-1 **Ht: 5'11" Wt: 200 Born: 3/21/1982 Age: 35**

Year Team	Lg	G	AB	H	2B	3B	HR	(Hm	Rd)	TB	R	RBI	RC	TBB	IBB	SO	HBP	SH	SF	SB	CS	GDP	Avg	OBP	Slg	OPS
								BATTING												RUNNING			AVERAGES			
2005 Tor	AL	105	361	99	25	3	3	(3	0)	139	49	40	50	34	0	41	5	3	4	2	1	5	.274	.342	.385	.727
2006 Tor	AL	155	546	159	28	3	6	(4	2)	211	70	50	68	42	5	66	9	4	5	5	2	15	.291	.349	.386	.735
2007 Tor	AL	160	608	177	47	2	17	(8	9)	279	87	78	88	41	1	102	0	3	5	4	3	21	.291	.333	.459	.792
2008 Tor	AL	55	205	54	14	0	2	(1	1)	74	19	20	24	16	0	31	3	4	1	4	2	4	.263	.324	.361	.685
2009 Tor	AL	158	682	195	37	0	36	(21	15)	340	103	108	110	42	1	98	5	1	4	6	2	17	.286	.330	.499	.829
2010 Tor	AL	138	528	108	22	0	26	(15	11)	208	70	68	57	41	2	85	8	1	2	2	2	8	.205	.271	.394	.665
2011 2 Tms		137	520	128	27	3	8	(4	4)	185	61	61	65	35	1	72	7	2	7	21	7	10	.246	.299	.356	.655
2012 Ari	NL	156	609	184	44	6	26	(14	12)	318	93	85	101	52	7	86	4	1	4	14	5	15	.302	.360	.522	.882
2013 Ari	NL	87	327	95	21	1	11	(7	4)	151	45	41	45	29	2	48	5	0	1	1	4	6	.291	.356	.462	.818
2014 Ari	NL	133	501	122	26	3	10	(6	4)	184	52	60	48	28	0	92	5	0	7	4	3	16	.244	.287	.367	.654
2015 Ari	NL	116	313	72	18	0	6	(3	3)	108	32	39	30	31	0	54	1	0	8	7	2	9	.230	.295	.345	.640
2016 2 Tms		125	378	99	14	0	10	(3	7)	143	48	38	47	41	2	59	3	0	4	4	2	6	.262	.336	.378	.714
11 Tor	AL	104	396	89	15	1	6	(3	3)	124	38	45	38	23	1	53	4	0	6	16	3	8	.225	.270	.313	.584
11 Ari	NL	33	124	39	12	2	2	(1	1)	61	23	16	23	12	0	19	3	2	1	5	4	2	.315	.386	.492	.878

					BATTING															RUNNING			AVERAGES			
Year	Team	Lg	G	AB	H	2B	3B	HR	(Hm Rd)	TB	R	RBI	RC	TBB	IBB	SO	HBP	SH	SF	SB	CS	GDP	Avg	OBP	Slg	OPS
16	Mil	NL	78	254	72	11	0	8	(3 5)	107	34	29	36	30	0	43	2	0	4	4	2	5	.283	.359	.421	.780
16	Bos	AL	47	124	27	3	0	2	(0 2)	36	14	9	11	11	2	16	1	0	0	0	0	1	.218	.287	.290	.577
	Postseason		5	18	5	0	0	1	(1 0)	8	3	1	2	5	0	3	0	0	0	0	0	1	.278	.435	.444	.879
	12 ML YEARS		1525	5578	1492	323	21	161	(89 72)	2340	729	688	729	432	21	834	55	19	50	74	35	132	.267	.324	.420	.743

Rich Hill

Pitches: L Bats: L Pos: SP-20 **Ht: 6'5" Wt: 220 Born: 3/11/1980 Age: 37**

			HOW MUCH HE PITCHED						WHAT HE GAVE UP										THE RESULTS							
Year	Team	Lg	G	GS	CG	GF	IP	BFP	H	R	ER	HR	SH	SF	HB	TBB	IBB	SO	WP	Bk	W	L	Pct	Sh	Sv-Op	Hld	ERC	ERA
2005	ChC	NL	10	4	0	1	23.2	115	25	24	24	3	1	0	1	17	1	21	0	0	0	2	.000	0	0-0	0	5.81	9.13
2006	ChC	NL	17	16	2	1	99.1	417	83	51	46	16	8	3	2	39	1	90	3	0	6	7	.462	1	0-0	0	3.59	4.17
2007	ChC	NL	32	32	0	0	195.0	812	170	89	85	27	9	4	12	63	3	183	1	1	11	8	.579	0	0-0	0	3.56	3.92
2008	ChC	NL	5	5	0	0	19.2	89	13	9	9	2	0	2	1	18	0	15	1	0	1	0	1.000	0	0-0	0	4.38	4.12
2009	Bal	AL	14	13	0	0	57.2	275	68	53	50	7	2	2	1	40	2	46	1	1	3	3	.500	0	0-0	0	6.55	7.80
2010	Bos	AL	6	0	0	0	4.0	18	5	0	0	0	0	0	0	1	0	3	0	0	1	0	1.000	0	0-0	0	4.05	0.00
2011	Bos	AL	9	0	0	3	8.0	30	3	0	0	0	0	0	1	3	0	12	1	0	0	0	-	0	0-0	3	1.10	0.00
2012	Bos	AL	25	0	0	3	19.2	83	17	4	4	0	0	0	0	11	1	21	0	0	1	0	1.000	0	0-0	6	3.24	1.83
2013	Cle	AL	63	0	0	3	38.2	182	38	30	27	3	1	2	2	29	6	51	6	1	1	2	.333	0	0-2	13	5.07	6.28
2014	2 Tms	AL	16	0	0	2	5.1	29	7	2	2	0	0	0	1	6	1	9	1	0	0	0	-	0	0-0	1	8.55	3.38
2015	Bos	AL	4	4	1	0	29.0	106	14	5	5	2	0	0	2	5	0	36	0	0	2	1	.667	1	0-0	0	1.13	1.55
2016	2 Tms	AL	20	20	0	0	110.1	439	77	29	26	4	1	2	8	33	0	129	0	0	12	5	.706	0	0-0	0	2.04	2.12
14	LAA	AL	2	0	0	0	0.0	4	1	1	1	0	0	0	0	3	0	0	0	0	0	0	-	0	0-0	0	-	-
14	NYY	AL	14	0	0	2	5.1	25	6	1	1	0	0	0	1	3	1	9	0	0	0	0	-	0	0-0	1	5.10	1.69
16	Oak	AL	14	14	0	0	76.0	311	55	22	19	2	0	1	8	28	0	90	0	0	9	3	.750	0	0-0	0	2.44	2.25
16	LAD	NL	6	6	0	0	34.1	128	22	7	7	2	1	1	0	5	0	39	0	0	3	2	.600	0	0-0	0	1.34	1.83
	Postseason		1	1	0	0	3.0	18	6	3	3	1	0	0	1	2	0	3	0	0	0	1	.000	0	0-0	0	15.68	9.00
	12 ML YEARS		221	94	3	13	610.1	2595	520	296	278	64	22	15	31	265	15	616	14	3	38	28	.576	2	0-2	24	3.59	4.10

Dalier Hinojosa

Pitches: R Bats: R Pos: RP-10 DAH-lee-air ee-no-HOE-sah **Ht: 6'1" Wt: 230 Born: 2/10/1986 Age: 31**

			HOW MUCH HE PITCHED						WHAT HE GAVE UP										THE RESULTS							
Year	Team	Lg	G	GS	CG	GF	IP	BFP	H	R	ER	HR	SH	SF	HB	TBB	IBB	SO	WP	Bk	W	L	Pct	Sh	Sv-Op	Hld	ERC	ERA
2014	Pwtckt	AAA	41	0	0	12	61.2	254	39	27	26	5	3	4	1	33	2	65	6	2	3	5	.375	0	3--	-	2.53	3.79
2015	Pwtckt	AAA	19	0	0	3	42.0	178	39	21	15	2	0	3	1	17	0	39	2	0	3	1	.750	0	0--	-	3.46	3.21
2015	LV	AAA	10	0	0	5	13.0	57	14	8	8	1	0	1	0	5	0	13	2	0	0	1	.000	0	0--	-	4.26	5.54
2016	LV	AAA	22	0	0	11	24.1	108	25	9	8	2	3	2	0	14	1	23	0	0	1	3	.250	0	1--	-	4.79	2.96
2015	2 Tms		19	0	0	5	24.2	102	15	3	2	1	0	0	1	11	1	23	1	0	2	0	1.000	0	0-1	3	1.89	0.73
2016	Phi	NL	10	0	0	4	11.0	44	10	4	4	1	0	1	0	3	0	8	0	0	0	1	.000	0	0-1	1	3.14	3.27
15	Bos	AL	1	0	0	1	1.2	9	0	0	0	0	0	0	0	3	0	2	0	0	0	0	-	0	0-0	0	4.82	0.00
15	Phi	NL	18	0	0	4	23.0	93	15	3	2	1	0	0	1	8	1	21	1	0	2	0	1.000	0	0-1	3	1.68	0.78
	2 ML YEARS		29	0	0	9	35.2	146	25	7	6	2	0	1	1	14	1	31	1	0	2	1	.667	0	0-2	4	2.25	1.51

Luke Hochevar

Pitches: R Bats: R Pos: RP-40 HOE-chay-vur **Ht: 6'5" Wt: 225 Born: 9/15/1983 Age: 33**

			HOW MUCH HE PITCHED						WHAT HE GAVE UP										THE RESULTS							
Year	Team	Lg	G	GS	CG	GF	IP	BFP	H	R	ER	HR	SH	SF	HB	TBB	IBB	SO	WP	Bk	W	L	Pct	Sh	Sv-Op	Hld	ERC	ERA
2007	KC	AL	4	1	0	1	12.2	54	11	4	3	1	1	0	3	4	0	5	1	0	0	1	.000	0	0-0	0	3.86	2.13
2008	KC	AL	22	22	0	0	129.0	566	143	84	79	12	1	2	5	47	1	72	7	0	6	12	.333	0	0-0	0	4.67	5.51
2009	KC	AL	25	25	2	0	143.0	631	167	109	104	23	2	0	8	46	0	106	9	0	7	13	.350	1	0-0	0	5.46	6.55
2010	KC	AL	18	17	1	0	103.0	450	110	61	55	9	2	2	4	37	1	76	2	1	6	6	.500	0	0-0	0	4.34	4.81
2011	KC	AL	31	31	0	0	198.0	835	192	110	103	23	2	2	7	62	4	128	7	2	11	11	.500	0	0-0	0	3.80	4.68
2012	KC	AL	32	32	2	0	185.1	800	202	127	118	27	4	3	13	61	3	144	8	0	8	16	.333	1	0-0	0	4.99	5.73
2013	KC	AL	58	0	0	22	70.1	262	41	15	15	8	2	0	1	17	1	82	2	0	5	2	.714	0	2-5	9	1.62	1.92
2015	KC	AL	49	0	0	16	50.2	214	49	23	21	7	0	1	3	16	0	49	3	0	1	1	.500	0	1-2	6	3.90	3.73
2016	KC	AL	40	0	0	1	37.1	151	31	17	16	6	1	1	3	9	0	40	2	0	2	3	.400	0	0-4	14	3.28	3.86
	Postseason		9	0	0	3	10.2	38	6	0	0	0	0	0	0	1	0	4	0	0	2	0	1.000	0	0-0	0	0.85	0.00
	9 ML YEARS		279	128	5	40	929.1	3963	946	550	514	116	15	11	45	299	10	702	41	3	46	65	.414	2	3-11	29	4.25	4.98

Jeff Hoffman

Pitches: R Bats: R Pos: SP-6; RP-2 **Ht: 6'5" Wt: 225 Born: 1/8/1993 Age: 24**

			HOW MUCH HE PITCHED						WHAT HE GAVE UP										THE RESULTS							
Year	Team	Lg	G	GS	CG	GF	IP	BFP	H	R	ER	HR	SH	SF	HB	TBB	IBB	SO	WP	Bk	W	L	Pct	Sh	Sv-Op	Hld	ERC	ERA
2015	Dnedin	A+	11	11	0	0	56.0	227	59	26	20	4	1	1	2	15	0	38	6	0	3	3	.500	0	0--	-	4.11	3.21
2015	NwBrit	AA	7	7	0	0	36.1	143	27	14	13	3	1	1	2	10	1	29	1	0	2	3	.500	0	0--	-	2.39	3.22
2016	Albq	AAA	22	22	0	0	118.2	512	117	60	53	11	3	9	7	44	0	124	5	0	6	9	.400	0	0--	-	4.07	4.02
2016	Col	NL	8	6	0	0	31.1	147	37	29	17	7	1	0	0	17	1	22	4	0	0	4	.000	0	0-0	0	6.55	4.88

Bryan Holaday

Bats: R Throws: R Pos: C-40;PR-2;3B-1;LF-1;DH-1 HAHL-ih-daye **Ht: 6'0" Wt: 205 Born: 11/19/1987 Age: 29**

					BATTING															RUNNING			AVERAGES			
Year	Team	Lg	G	AB	H	2B	3B	HR	(Hm Rd)	TB	R	RBI	RC	TBB	IBB	SO	HBP	SH	SF	SB	CS	GDP	Avg	OBP	Slg	OPS
2012	Det	AL	6	12	3	1	0	0	(0 0)	4	3	0	1	0	0	2	0	1	0	0	0	0	.250	.250	.333	.583
2013	Det	AL	16	27	8	1	0	1	(1 0)	12	8	2	3	2	0	3	1	3	0	0	0	0	.296	.367	.444	.811
2014	Det	AL	62	156	36	5	1	0	(0 0)	43	14	15	11	8	0	37	1	2	4	1	1	4	.231	.266	.276	.542
2015	Det	AL	24	64	18	5	0	2	(1 1)	29	3	13	9	1	0	13	0	0	0	0	0	0	.281	.292	.453	.745

Year	Team	Lg	G	AB	H	2B	3B	HR	(Hm	Rd)	TB	R	RBI	RC	TBB	IBB	SO	HBP	SH	SF	SB	CS	GDP	Avg	OBP	Slg	OPS
2016	2 Tms	AL	44	117	27	7	1	2	(1	1)	42	17	14	14	7	0	28	2	1	2	0	1	1	.231	.281	.359	.640
16	Tex	AL	30	84	20	6	1	2	(1	1)	34	14	13	12	5	0	16	2	1	2	0	1	0	.238	.290	.405	.695
16	Bos	AL	14	33	7	1	0	0	(0	0)	8	3	1	2	2	0	12	0	0	0	0	0	1	.212	.257	.242	.500
	Postseason		1	2	0	0	0	0	(0	0)	0	0	0	0	0	0	1	0	0	0	0	0	0	.000	.000	.000	.000
	5 ML YEARS		152	376	92	19	2	5	(3	2)	130	45	44	38	18	0	83	4	7	6	1	2	5	.245	.282	.346	.628

Jonathan Holder

Pitches: R **Bats:** R **Pos:** RP-8   **Ht:** 6'2" **Wt:** 235 **Born:** 6/9/1993 **Age:** 24

			HOW MUCH HE PITCHED						WHAT HE GAVE UP											THE RESULTS							
Year	Team	Lg	G	GS	CG	GF	IP	BFP	H	R	ER	HR	SH	SF	HB	TBB	IBB	SO	WP	Bk	W	L	Pct	Sh	Sv-Op	Hld	ERC	ERA
2014	2 Tms	Low	12	8	0	0	36.1	154	42	21	16	1	1	0	4	13	0	34	3	0	2	3	.400	0	0- -	-	4.45	3.96
2015	2 Tms	Low	22	21	1	1	112.1	457	97	34	29	3	2	2	5	21	0	86	2	0	7	5	.583	0	0- -	-	2.25	2.32
2016	Trntn	AA	28	0	0	21	41.0	155	27	10	10	2	0	1	3	7	0	59	0	0	3	1	.750	0	10- -	-	1.60	2.20
2016	S-WB	AAA	12	0	0	11	20.1	68	7	2	2	1	0	0	0	0	0	35	0	0	2	0	1.000	0	6- -	-	0.35	0.89
2016	NYY	AL	8	0	0	1	8.1	36	8	5	5	1	0	1	0	4	0	5	0	0	0	0	-	0	0-0	0	4.34	5.40

Derek Holland

Pitches: L **Bats:** B **Pos:** SP-20; RP-2   **Ht:** 6'2" **Wt:** 215 **Born:** 10/9/1986 **Age:** 30

			HOW MUCH HE PITCHED						WHAT HE GAVE UP											THE RESULTS							
Year	Team	Lg	G	GS	CG	GF	IP	BFP	H	R	ER	HR	SH	SF	HB	TBB	IBB	SO	WP	Bk	W	L	Pct	Sh	Sv-Op	Hld	ERC	ERA
2009	Tex	AL	33	21	1	0	138.1	611	160	98	94	26	2	3	4	47	0	107	3	3	8	13	.381	1	0-1	2	5.52	6.12
2010	Tex	AL	14	10	0	2	57.1	253	55	30	26	6	0	2	4	24	0	54	0	1	3	4	.429	0	0-0	1	4.17	4.08
2011	Tex	AL	32	32	4	0	198.0	843	201	97	87	22	1	3	6	67	1	162	2	1	16	5	.762	4	0-0	0	4.15	3.95
2012	Tex	AL	29	27	0	1	175.1	730	162	100	91	32	5	4	3	52	0	145	1	0	12	7	.632	0	0-0	0	3.86	4.67
2013	Tex	AL	33	33	2	0	213.0	894	210	90	81	20	8	9	3	64	0	189	9	1	10	9	.526	2	0-0	0	3.64	3.42
2014	Tex	AL	6	5	0	0	37.0	145	34	8	6	0	2	1	0	5	1	25	1	0	2	0	1.000	0	0-0	0	2.07	1.46
2015	Tex	AL	10	10	1	0	58.2	245	59	32	32	11	3	1	5	17	2	41	1	0	4	3	.571	1	0-0	0	4.71	4.91
2016	Tex	AL	22	20	0	0	107.1	461	116	62	59	15	1	2	2	35	2	67	2	0	7	9	.438	0	0-0	0	4.61	4.95
	Postseason		14	5	0	2	37.2	161	37	23	21	10	0	0	1	16	0	24	2	0	3	1	.750	0	0-0	2	5.47	5.02
	8 ML YEARS		179	158	8	3	985.0	4182	997	517	476	132	22	25	27	311	6	790	19	6	62	50	.554	8	0-1	3	4.17	4.35

Greg Holland

Pitches: R **Bats:** R **Pos:** P   **Ht:** 5'10" **Wt:** 205 **Born:** 11/20/1985 **Age:** 31

			HOW MUCH HE PITCHED						WHAT HE GAVE UP											THE RESULTS							
Year	Team	Lg	G	GS	CG	GF	IP	BFP	H	R	ER	HR	SH	SF	HB	TBB	IBB	SO	WP	Bk	W	L	Pct	Sh	Sv-Op	Hld	ERC	ERA
2010	KC	AL	15	0	0	10	18.2	87	23	15	14	3	1	0	0	8	0	23	2	0	0	1	.000	0	0-0	0	5.88	6.75
2011	KC	AL	46	0	0	15	60.0	233	37	13	12	3	1	1	1	19	3	74	7	0	5	1	.833	0	4-6	18	1.60	1.80
2012	KC	AL	67	0	0	36	67.0	289	58	22	22	2	4	3	0	34	7	91	3	1	7	4	.636	0	16-20	9	3.07	2.96
2013	KC	AL	68	0	0	61	67.0	255	40	11	9	3	1	1	0	18	1	103	2	0	2	1	.667	0	47-50	1	1.41	1.21
2014	KC	AL	65	0	0	60	62.1	240	37	13	10	3	1	1	0	20	0	90	9	0	1	3	.250	0	46-48	0	1.54	1.44
2015	KC	AL	48	0	0	40	44.2	193	39	20	19	2	3	1	0	26	1	49	7	0	3	2	.600	0	32-37	0	3.68	3.83
	Postseason		11	0	0	10	11.0	43	4	1	1	0	0	0	0	5	1	15	0	0	0	0	-	0	7-7	0	0.86	0.82
	6 ML YEARS		309	0	0	222	319.2	1297	234	94	86	16	11	7	1	125	12	430	30	1	18	12	.600	0	145-161	28	2.29	2.42

Matt Holliday

Bats: R **Throws:** R **Pos:** LF-85;1B-10;PH-10;DH-8   **Ht:** 6'4" **Wt:** 240 **Born:** 1/15/1980 **Age:** 37

									BATTING												RUNNING			AVERAGES			
Year	Team	Lg	G	AB	H	2B	3B	HR	(Hm	Rd)	TB	R	RBI	RC	TBB	IBB	SO	HBP	SH	SF	SB	CS	GDP	Avg	OBP	Slg	OPS
2004	Col	NL	121	400	116	31	3	14	(10	4)	195	65	57	61	31	0	86	6	1	1	3	3	9	.290	.349	.488	.837
2005	Col	NL	125	479	147	24	7	19	(12	7)	242	68	87	88	36	1	79	7	0	4	14	3	11	.307	.361	.505	.866
2006	Col	NL	155	602	196	45	5	34	(22	12)	353	119	114	112	47	3	110	15	0	5	10	5	22	.326	.387	.586	.973
2007	Col	NL	158	636	216	50	6	36	(25	11)	386	120	137	134	63	7	126	10	0	4	11	4	23	.340	.405	.607	1.012
2008	Col	NL	139	539	173	38	2	25	(15	10)	290	107	88	104	74	6	104	8	0	2	28	2	9	.321	.409	.538	.947
2009	2 Tms		156	581	182	39	3	24	(16	8)	299	94	109	112	72	8	101	10	0	7	14	7	14	.313	.394	.515	.909
2010	StL	NL	158	596	186	45	1	28	(13	15)	317	95	103	107	69	10	93	8	0	2	9	5	13	.312	.390	.532	.922
2011	StL	NL	124	446	132	36	0	22	(12	10)	234	83	75	81	60	4	93	8	0	2	2	1	21	.296	.388	.525	.912
2012	StL	NL	157	599	177	36	2	27	(13	14)	298	95	102	99	75	3	132	9	0	5	4	4	15	.295	.379	.497	.877
2013	StL	NL	141	520	156	31	1	22	(14	8)	255	103	94	99	69	5	86	9	0	4	6	1	31	.300	.389	.490	.879
2014	StL	NL	156	574	156	37	0	20	(13	7)	253	83	90	97	74	4	100	17	0	2	4	1	20	.272	.370	.441	.811
2015	StL	NL	73	229	64	16	1	4	(0	4)	94	24	35	44	39	5	49	6	0	3	2	1	9	.279	.394	.410	.804
2016	StL	NL	110	382	94	20	1	20	(9	11)	176	48	62	51	35	1	71	8	0	1	0	0	9	.246	.322	.461	.782
09	Oak	AL	93	346	99	23	1	11	(7	4)	157	52	54	62	46	3	58	6	0	2	12	3	8	.286	.378	.454	.831
09	StL	NL	63	235	83	16	2	13	(9	4)	142	42	55	50	26	5	43	4	0	5	2	4	5	.353	.419	.604	1.023
	Postseason		72	279	69	9	1	13	(5	8)	119	42	37	31	17	0	58	6	0	0	1	1	5	.247	.305	.427	.731
	13 ML YEARS		1773	6583	1995	448	32	295	(174	121)	3392	1104	1153	1189	744	57	1230	121	1	40	107	37	206	.303	.382	.515	.897

Brock Holt

Bats: L **Throws:** R **Pos:** LF-64;3B-17;PH-10;2B-8;SS-7;RF-5;PR-2;DH-1   **Ht:** 5'10" **Wt:** 180 **Born:** 6/11/1988 **Age:** 29

									BATTING												RUNNING			AVERAGES			
Year	Team	Lg	G	AB	H	2B	3B	HR	(Hm	Rd)	TB	R	RBI	RC	TBB	IBB	SO	HBP	SH	SF	SB	CS	GDP	Avg	OBP	Slg	OPS
2012	Pit	NL	24	65	19	2	1	0	(0	0)	23	6	3	10	4	0	14	0	2	1	0	0	1	.292	.329	.354	.682
2013	Bos	AL	26	59	12	2	0	0	(0	0)	14	9	11	7	7	0	4	0	3	3	1	0	0	.203	.275	.237	.513

Year Team	Lg	G	AB	H	2B	3B	HR	(Hm	Rd)	TB	R	RBI	RC	TBB	IBB	SO	HBP	SH	SF	SB	CS	GDP	Avg	OBP	Slg	OPS
2014 Bos	AL	106	449	126	23	5	4	(1	3)	171	68	29	56	33	0	98	2	5	3	12	2	7	.281	.331	.381	.711
2015 Bos	AL	129	454	127	27	6	2	(1	1)	172	56	45	65	46	0	97	3	4	2	8	1	7	.280	.349	.379	.727
2016 Bos	AL	94	290	74	16	0	7	(4	3)	111	45	34	36	27	0	58	3	1	3	4	3	5	.255	.322	.383	.705
5 ML YEARS		379	1317	358	70	12	13	(6	7)	491	184	122	174	117	0	271	8	15	12	25	6	20	.272	.332	.373	.705

Tyler Holt

Bats: R **Throws:** R **Pos:** PH-41;CF-32;RF-23;LF-19;PR-8   **Ht:** 5'10" **Wt:** 200 **Born:** 3/10/1989 **Age:** 28

Year Team	Lg	G	AB	H	2B	3B	HR	(Hm	Rd)	TB	R	RBI	RC	TBB	IBB	SO	HBP	SH	SF	SB	CS	GDP	Avg	OBP	Slg	OPS
2014 Cle	AL	36	71	19	2	0	0	(0	0)	21	4	2	6	3	0	25	1	1	0	2	2	1	.268	.307	.296	.602
2015 2 Tms		14	31	3	0	0	0	(0	0)	3	4	0	0	3	0	11	0	0	0	1	0	0	.097	.176	.097	.273
2016 Cin	NL	106	179	42	5	3	0	(0	0)	53	21	13	19	23	0	48	2	3	1	4	3	6	.235	.327	.296	.623
15 Cle	AL	9	20	2	0	0	0	(0	0)	2	2	0	0	1	0	9	0	0	0	0	0	0	.100	.143	.100	.243
15 Cin	NL	5	11	1	0	0	0	(0	0)	1	2	0	0	2	0	2	0	0	0	1	0	0	.091	.231	.091	.322
3 ML YEARS		156	281	64	7	3	0	(0	0)	77	29	15	25	29	0	84	3	4	1	7	5	7	.228	.306	.274	.580

Destin Hood

Bats: R **Throws:** R **Pos:** LF-5;PH-5;RF-2;PR-1   **Ht:** 6'2" **Wt:** 205 **Born:** 4/3/1990 **Age:** 27

Year Team	Lg	G	AB	H	2B	3B	HR	(Hm	Rd)	TB	R	RBI	RC	TBB	IBB	SO	HBP	SH	SF	SB	CS	GDP	Avg	OBP	Slg	OPS
2012 Hrsbrg	AA	94	355	87	20	3	3	(-	-)	122	45	45	39	24	2	89	6	0	4	6	1	8	.245	.301	.344	.644
2013 Hrsbrg	AA	112	392	88	18	5	4	(-	-)	128	44	40	35	27	0	116	4	1	5	5	7	8	.224	.278	.327	.605
2014 Hrsbrg	AA	19	73	24	1	0	1	(-	-)	28	9	5	11	2	0	18	1	0	0	6	0	0	.329	.355	.384	.739
2014 Syrcse	AAA	84	309	91	24	2	10	(-	-)	149	43	36	51	22	1	65	2	0	1	4	3	9	.294	.344	.482	.827
2015 Clmbs	AAA	17	59	10	2	2	0	(-	-)	16	3	2	3	4	0	21	0	0	0	1	0	0	.169	.222	.271	.493
2015 Akron	AA	40	140	41	11	3	3	(-	-)	67	20	19	23	10	0	36	2	0	2	4	1	3	.293	.344	.479	.823
2015 Rdng	AA	42	167	48	13	1	7	(-	-)	84	19	37	26	7	0	42	0	1	1	1	1	7	.287	.314	.503	.817
2016 NewOr	AAA	126	476	127	29	3	15	(-	-)	207	61	80	67	37	0	113	1	0	8	11	6	12	.267	.316	.435	.751
2016 Mia	NL	13	25	6	1	0	1	(0	1)	10	3	2	1	0	0	11	0	0	0	0	1	0	.240	.240	.400	.640

J.J. Hoover

Pitches: R **Bats:** R **Pos:** RP-18   **Ht:** 6'3" **Wt:** 240 **Born:** 8/13/1987 **Age:** 29

		HOW MUCH HE PITCHED						WHAT HE GAVE UP										THE RESULTS						
Year Team	Lg	G	GS	CG	GF	IP	BFP	H	R	ER	HR	SH	SF	HB	TBB	IBB	SO	WP	Bk	W	L	Pct	Sh	Sv-Op	Hld	ERC	ERA
2016 Lsvlle*	AAA	32	0	0	14	38.1	164	39	15	15	2	0	1	1	11	0	50	1	0	4	2	.667	0	4- -	-	3.47	3.52
2012 Cin	NL	28	0	0	6	30.2	123	17	7	7	2	2	2	0	13	1	31	0	0	1	0	1.000	0	1-2	1	1.64	2.05
2013 Cin	NL	69	0	0	23	66.0	269	47	21	21	6	3	3	2	26	6	67	1	0	5	5	.500	0	3-5	13	2.46	2.86
2014 Cin	NL	54	0	0	22	62.2	275	56	36	34	13	1	5	1	31	3	75	0	0	1	10	.091	0	0-4	1	4.52	4.88
2015 Cin	NL	67	0	0	12	64.1	264	44	24	21	7	5	2	2	31	1	52	3	0	8	2	.800	0	1-7	18	2.87	2.94
2016 Cin	NL	18	0	0	8	18.2	97	29	29	28	9	0	0	1	12	1	15	0	0	1	2	.333	0	1-2	1	12.20	13.50
Postseason		3	0	0	0	3.1	10	0	0	0	0	0	0	0	2	0	2	0	0	0	0	-	0	0-0	0	0.45	0.00
5 ML YEARS		236	0	0	71	242.1	1028	193	117	111	37	11	12	6	113	12	240	4	0	16	19	.457	0	6-20	34	3.56	4.12

Eric Hosmer

Bats: L **Throws:** L **Pos:** 1B-154;DH-4   HOZZ-mer   **Ht:** 6'4" **Wt:** 225 **Born:** 10/24/1989 **Age:** 27

Year Team	Lg	G	AB	H	2B	3B	HR	(Hm	Rd)	TB	R	RBI	RC	TBB	IBB	SO	HBP	SH	SF	SB	CS	GDP	Avg	OBP	Slg	OPS
2011 KC	AL	128	523	153	27	3	19	(3	16)	243	66	78	71	34	7	82	1	0	5	11	5	13	.293	.334	.465	.799
2012 KC	AL	152	535	124	22	2	14	(8	6)	192	65	60	61	56	4	95	2	0	5	16	1	10	.232	.304	.359	.663
2013 KC	AL	159	623	188	34	3	17	(10	7)	279	86	79	88	51	4	100	1	1	4	11	4	15	.302	.353	.448	.801
2014 KC	AL	131	503	136	35	1	9	(5	4)	200	54	58	62	35	4	93	3	0	6	4	2	12	.270	.318	.398	.716
2015 KC	AL	158	599	178	33	5	18	(10	8)	275	98	93	94	61	6	108	3	1	3	7	3	16	.297	.363	.459	.822
2016 KC	AL	158	605	161	24	5	25	(8	17)	262	80	104	87	57	5	132	1	0	4	5	3	18	.266	.328	.433	.761
Postseason		31	123	34	5	1	3	(1	2)	50	18	29	21	12	2	33	0	0	3	1	1	1	.276	.333	.407	.740
6 ML YEARS		886	3388	940	175	15	102	(44	58)	1451	449	472	463	294	30	610	11	2	27	54	18	84	.277	.335	.428	.763

T.J. House

Pitches: L **Bats:** R **Pos:** RP-4   **Ht:** 6'1" **Wt:** 205 **Born:** 9/29/1989 **Age:** 27

		HOW MUCH HE PITCHED						WHAT HE GAVE UP										THE RESULTS						
Year Team	Lg	G	GS	CG	GF	IP	BFP	H	R	ER	HR	SH	SF	HB	TBB	IBB	SO	WP	Bk	W	L	Pct	Sh	Sv-Op	Hld	ERC	ERA
2016 Clmbs*	AAA	33	12	0	3	72.1	342	89	44	32	6	2	2	2	43	0	50	5	0	5	3	.625	0	1- -	-	6.23	3.98
2014 Cle	AL	19	18	0	1	102.0	429	113	41	38	10	1	1	7	22	1	80	1	0	5	3	.625	0	0-0	0	4.30	3.35
2015 Cle	AL	4	4	0	0	13.0	73	21	19	19	1	0	1	2	12	1	7	0	0	0	4	.000	0	0-0	0	10.45	13.15
2016 Cle	AL	4	0	0	0	2.2	14	6	1	1	0	0	1	1	0	0	2	0	0	0	0	-	0	0-0	0	11.69	3.38
3 ML YEARS		27	22	0	1	117.2	516	140	61	58	11	1	3	10	34	2	89	1	0	5	7	.417	0	0-0	0	5.08	4.44

Ryan Howard

Bats: L **Throws:** L **Pos:** 1B-83;PH-21;DH-9   **Ht:** 6'4" **Wt:** 250 **Born:** 11/19/1979 **Age:** 37

								BATTING													RUNNING			AVERAGES			
Year	Team	Lg	G	AB	H	2B	3B	HR	(Hm	Rd)	TB	R	RBI	RC	TBB	IBB	SO	HBP	SH	SF	SB	CS	GDP	Avg	OBP	Slg	OPS
2004	Phi	NL	19	39	11	5	0	2	(1	1)	22	5	5	7	2	0	13	1	0	0	0	0	2	.282	.333	.564	.897
2005	Phi	NL	88	312	90	17	2	22	(11	11)	177	52	63	50	33	8	100	1	0	2	0	1	6	.288	.356	.567	.924
2006	Phi	NL	159	581	182	25	1	58	(29	29)	383	104	149	138	108	37	181	9	0	6	0	0	7	.313	.425	.659	1.084
2007	Phi	NL	144	529	142	26	0	47	(23	24)	309	94	136	119	107	35	199	5	0	7	1	0	13	.268	.392	.584	.976
2008	Phi	NL	162	610	153	26	4	48	(26	22)	331	105	146	117	81	17	199	3	0	6	1	1	11	.251	.339	.543	.881
2009	Phi	NL	160	616	172	37	4	45	(18	27)	352	105	141	117	75	8	186	6	0	6	8	1	11	.279	.360	.571	.931
2010	Phi	NL	143	550	152	23	5	31	(16	15)	278	87	108	94	59	11	157	8	0	3	1	1	14	.276	.353	.505	.859
2011	Phi	NL	152	557	141	30	1	33	(17	16)	272	81	116	91	75	16	172	7	0	5	1	0	10	.253	.346	.488	.835
2012	Phi	NL	71	260	57	11	0	14	(10	4)	110	28	56	35	25	7	99	4	0	3	0	0	8	.219	.295	.423	.718
2013	Phi	NL	80	286	76	20	2	11	(9	2)	133	34	43	36	23	4	95	2	0	6	0	0	6	.266	.319	.465	.784
2014	Phi	NL	153	569	127	18	1	23	(12	11)	216	65	95	71	67	7	190	7	0	5	0	0	10	.223	.310	.380	.690
2015	Phi	NL	129	467	107	29	1	23	(13	10)	207	53	77	57	27	2	138	5	0	3	0	0	11	.229	.277	.443	.720
2016	Phi	NL	112	331	65	10	0	25	(13	12)	150	35	59	35	27	2	114	1	0	3	0	1	7	.196	.257	.453	.710
	Postseason		46	170	44	13	1	8	(6	2)	83	22	33	28	26	7	67	1	0	2	1	1	1	.259	.357	.488	.845
	13 ML YEARS		1572	5707	1475	277	21	382	(198	184)	2940	848	1194	967	709	154	1843	59	0	55	12	5	116	.258	.343	.515	.859

J.P. Howell

Pitches: L **Bats:** L **Pos:** RP-64   **Ht:** 6'0" **Wt:** 180 **Born:** 4/25/1983 **Age:** 34

			HOW MUCH HE PITCHED						WHAT HE GAVE UP										THE RESULTS							
Year	Team	Lg	G	GS	CG	GF	IP	BFP	H	R	ER	HR	SH	SF	HB	TBB	IBB	SO	WP	Bk	W	L	Pct	Sh	Sv-Op	Hld	ERC	ERA
2005	KC	AL	15	15	0	0	72.2	328	73	55	50	9	3	3	6	39	0	54	7	0	3	5	.375	0	0-0	0	5.18	6.19
2006	TB	AL	8	8	0	0	42.1	187	52	25	24	4	0	2	3	14	0	33	1	0	1	3	.250	0	0-0	0	5.51	5.10
2007	TB	AL	10	10	0	0	51.0	244	69	45	43	8	2	1	3	21	0	49	3	0	1	6	.143	0	0-0	0	6.84	7.59
2008	TB	AL	64	0	0	9	89.1	370	62	29	22	6	6	1	4	39	1	92	5	0	6	1	.857	0	3-5	14	2.51	2.22
2009	TB	AL	69	0	0	41	66.2	278	47	22	21	7	2	1	3	33	3	79	3	1	7	5	.583	0	17-25	4	2.99	2.84
2011	TB	AL	46	0	0	5	30.2	138	30	24	21	5	1	1	2	18	1	26	2	2	2	3	.400	0	1-2	10	5.43	6.16
2012	TB	AL	55	0	0	10	50.1	203	39	17	17	7	2	0	4	22	2	42	1	0	1	0	1.000	0	0-0	3	3.68	3.04
2013	LAD	NL	67	0	0	6	62.0	246	42	15	15	2	1	3	1	23	3	54	3	0	4	1	.800	0	0-0	11	1.92	2.18
2014	LAD	NL	68	0	0	8	49.0	199	31	14	13	2	4	0	1	25	1	48	3	0	3	3	.500	0	0-0	27	2.26	2.39
2015	LAD	NL	65	0	0	18	44.0	190	47	9	7	3	0	1	2	14	1	39	3	1	6	1	.857	0	1-4	9	4.07	1.43
2016	LAD	NL	64	0	0	11	50.2	220	56	23	23	4	1	2	3	15	2	44	3	0	1	1	.500	0	0-1	4	4.30	4.09
	Postseason		24	0	0	3	20.1	89	21	7	7	2	1	3	2	7	1	23	2	0	0	3	.000	0	0-1	4	4.34	3.10
	11 ML YEARS		531	33	0	108	608.2	2603	548	278	256	57	22	15	32	263	14	560	34	4	35	29	.547	0	22-36	80	3.79	3.79

Jared Hoying

Bats: L **Throws:** R **Pos:** RF-17;LF-13;PH-10;PR-9;DH-3;CF-1   **Ht:** 6'3" **Wt:** 205 **Born:** 5/18/1989 **Age:** 28

								BATTING													RUNNING			AVERAGES			
Year	Team	Lg	G	AB	H	2B	3B	HR	(Hm	Rd)	TB	R	RBI	RC	TBB	IBB	SO	HBP	SH	SF	SB	CS	GDP	Avg	OBP	Slg	OPS
2012	MrtlBh	A+	58	218	60	12	2	4	(-	-)	88	37	17	32	21	4	52	5	4	0	8	4	0	.275	.352	.404	.756
2012	Frisco	AA	64	247	68	7	3	4	(-	-)	93	39	25	32	18	0	50	3	3	2	9	5	2	.275	.330	.377	.706
2013	Frisco	AA	40	153	37	9	3	5	(-	-)	67	17	24	21	13	0	45	1	0	1	3	1	1	.242	.304	.438	.741
2013	RdRck	AAA	53	188	50	5	5	8	(-	-)	89	31	24	26	6	0	60	1	0	1	4	2	2	.266	.291	.473	.764
2014	RdRck	AAA	135	509	138	33	7	26	(-	-)	263	86	78	87	41	1	140	2	1	3	20	7	5	.271	.325	.517	.842
2015	RdRck	AAA	129	485	104	25	6	23	(-	-)	210	66	60	58	29	3	110	3	1	1	20	6	4	.214	.263	.433	.696
2016	RdRck	AAA	100	390	105	20	6	16	(-	-)	185	62	66	66	37	1	78	4	0	4	18	4	4	.269	.336	.474	.810
2016	Tex	AL	39	46	10	2	0	0	(0	0)	12	8	5	3	3	0	8	0	0	0	1	0	1	.217	.265	.261	.526

James Hoyt

Pitches: R **Bats:** R **Pos:** RP-22   **Ht:** 6'6" **Wt:** 230 **Born:** 9/30/1986 **Age:** 30

			HOW MUCH HE PITCHED						WHAT HE GAVE UP										THE RESULTS							
Year	Team	Lg	G	GS	CG	GF	IP	BFP	H	R	ER	HR	SH	SF	HB	TBB	IBB	SO	WP	Bk	W	L	Pct	Sh	Sv-Op	Hld	ERC	ERA
2013	Lynbrg	A+	17	3	0	1	49.2	213	39	27	27	3	0	4	1	25	0	72	10	0	3	2	.600	0	0- -	-	3.06	4.89
2013	Missi	AA	22	0	0	4	32.2	130	17	9	9	1	0	1	0	13	0	33	5	0	0	1	.000	0	1- -	-	1.44	2.48
2014	Missi	AA	28	0	0	12	31.2	126	19	5	4	1	3	1	0	10	0	43	2	0	2	2	.500	0	6- -	-	1.44	1.14
2014	Gwnntt	AAA	24	0	0	12	28.0	140	38	18	17	4	1	2	2	14	2	34	6	0	1	1	.500	0	1- -	-	6.89	5.46
2015	Fresno	AAA	47	0	0	30	49.0	211	48	23	19	1	0	2	3	11	2	66	5	0	0	1	.000	0	9- -	-	2.83	3.49
2016	Fresno	AAA	49	0	0	44	55.0	212	29	14	10	2	4	1	0	19	2	93	4	0	4	3	.571	0	29- -	-	1.30	1.64
2016	Hou	AL	22	0	0	7	22.0	91	16	12	11	5	1	1	1	9	1	28	3	0	1	1	.500	0	0-1	1	3.55	4.50

Daniel Hudson

Pitches: R **Bats:** R **Pos:** RP-70   **Ht:** 6'3" **Wt:** 230 **Born:** 3/9/1987 **Age:** 30

			HOW MUCH HE PITCHED						WHAT HE GAVE UP										THE RESULTS							
Year	Team	Lg	G	GS	CG	GF	IP	BFP	H	R	ER	HR	SH	SF	HB	TBB	IBB	SO	WP	Bk	W	L	Pct	Sh	Sv-Op	Hld	ERC	ERA
2009	CWS	AL	6	2	0	1	18.2	82	16	9	7	3	0	1	1	9	0	14	1	0	1	1	.500	0	0-0	0	4.15	3.38
2010	2 Tms		14	14	0	0	95.1	372	68	26	26	8	2	2	4	27	1	84	5	0	8	2	.800	0	0-0	0	2.26	2.45
2011	Ari	NL	33	33	3	0	222.0	921	217	98	86	17	6	6	8	50	1	169	4	1	16	12	.571	0	0-0	0	3.26	3.49
2012	Ari	NL	9	9	0	0	45.1	202	62	37	37	9	2	1	0	12	0	37	2	0	3	2	.600	0	0-0	0	6.56	7.35
2014	Ari	NL	3	0	0	0	2.2	13	4	4	4	0	0	0	0	2	0	0	0	0	1	1	.000	0	0-0	0	4.08	13.50
2015	Ari	NL	64	1	0	13	67.2	290	64	34	29	7	1	3	0	25	2	71	5	0	4	3	.571	0	4-6	20	3.58	3.86
2016	Ari	NL	70	0	0	17	60.1	268	65	40	35	4	2	1	0	23	3	58	5	0	3	2	.600	0	5-7	17	4.51	5.22
	10 CWS	AL	3	3	0	0	15.2	71	17	11	11	1	1	1	0	11	0	14	2	0	1	1	.500	0	0-0	0	5.69	6.32
	10 Ari	NL	11	11	0	0	79.2	301	51	15	15	7	1	1	4	16	1	70	3	0	7	1	.875	0	0-0	0	1.70	1.69
	Postseason		1	1	0	0	5.1	24	9	5	5	1	0	0	0	0	0	6	0	0	0	1	.000	0	0-0	0	7.35	8.44
	7 ML YEARS		199	59	3	31	512.0	2148	496	248	224	50	11	13	17	145	7	435	22	1	35	23	.603	0	9-13	37	3.55	3.94

David Huff

Pitches: L **Bats:** B **Pos:** SP-2   **Ht:** 6'1" **Wt:** 210 **Born:** 8/22/1984 **Age:** 32

			HOW MUCH HE PITCHED							WHAT HE GAVE UP										THE RESULTS							
Year	Team	Lg	G	GS	CG	GF	IP	BFP	H	R	ER	HR	SH	SF	HB	TBB	IBB	SO	WP	Bk	W	L	Pct	Sh	Sv-Op	Hld	ERC	ERA
2016	Omha*	AAA	12	0	0	5	23.2	99	29	11	11	3	0	1	0	2	0	29	0	1	1	1	.500	0	1--	-	4.30	4.18
2016	Salt Lk*	AAA	6	6	0	0	28.2	136	42	23	22	5	0	1	0	9	0	23	0	0	1	2	.333	0	0--	-	6.99	6.91
2009	Cle	AL	23	23	0	0	128.1	574	159	82	80	16	2	2	1	41	1	65	1	0	11	8	.579	0	0-0	0	5.33	5.61
2010	Cle	AL	15	15	1	0	79.2	369	101	61	55	14	3	3	3	34	1	37	2	0	2	11	.154	0	0-0	0	6.50	6.21
2011	Cle	AL	11	10	0	1	50.2	227	55	35	23	6	0	3	0	17	1	36	4	0	2	6	.250	0	0-0	0	4.23	4.09
2012	Cle	AL	6	4	0	0	26.2	114	30	14	10	5	0	1	1	5	0	19	0	0	3	1	.750	0	0-0	0	4.67	3.38
2013	2 Tms		14	2	0	4	37.2	151	33	23	23	7	1	1	1	9	1	31	1	0	3	1	.750	0	0-0	0	3.45	5.50
2014	2 Tms		46	0	0	16	59.0	258	61	25	22	5	2	0	1	23	2	39	1	0	4	1	.800	0	0-0	4	4.10	3.36
2015	LAD	NL	3	1	0	1	6.0	30	11	6	6	2	1	0	1	1	0	4	0	0	0	0	-	0	0-0	0	11.33	9.00
2016	LAA	AL	2	2	0	0	5.1	32	13	10	7	4	1	1	0	2	0	3	0	0	0	2	.000	0	0-0	0	19.54	11.81
13	Cle	AL	3	0	0	1	3.0	15	7	5	5	0	0	0	0	1	0	5	0	0	0	0	-	0	0-0	0	12.85	15.00
13	NYY	AL	11	2	0	3	34.2	136	26	18	18	7	1	1	1	8	1	26	1	0	3	1	.750	0	0-0	0	2.82	4.67
14	SF	NL	16	0	0	3	20.0	92	27	15	14	2	0	0	1	6	0	11	0	0	1	0	1.000	0	0-0	1	5.92	6.30
14	NYY	AL	30	0	0	13	39.0	166	34	10	8	3	2	0	0	17	2	28	1	0	3	1	.750	0	0-0	3	3.25	1.85
	8 ML YEARS		120	57	1	22	393.1	1755	463	256	226	59	10	11	8	132	6	234	9	0	25	30	.455	0	0-0	4	5.23	5.17

Jared Hughes

Pitches: R **Bats:** R **Pos:** RP-67   **Ht:** 6'7" **Wt:** 245 **Born:** 7/4/1985 **Age:** 31

			HOW MUCH HE PITCHED							WHAT HE GAVE UP										THE RESULTS							
Year	Team	Lg	G	GS	CG	GF	IP	BFP	H	R	ER	HR	SH	SF	HB	TBB	IBB	SO	WP	Bk	W	L	Pct	Sh	Sv-Op	Hld	ERC	ERA
2011	Pit	NL	12	0	0	1	11.0	46	9	5	5	1	1	0	0	4	0	10	0	0	0	1	.000	0	0-0	2	2.85	4.09
2012	Pit	NL	66	0	0	20	75.2	316	65	30	24	7	1	0	5	22	4	50	5	0	2	2	.500	0	2-4	11	2.99	2.85
2013	Pit	NL	29	0	0	8	32.0	148	37	17	17	2	2	1	2	16	1	23	2	0	2	3	.400	0	0-0	3	5.27	4.78
2014	Pit	NL	63	0	0	16	64.1	256	51	21	14	4	6	2	6	19	5	36	2	0	7	5	.583	0	0-2	13	2.68	1.96
2015	Pit	NL	76	0	0	11	67.0	284	70	21	17	3	6	4	7	19	2	36	3	0	3	1	.750	0	0-3	21	3.93	2.28
2016	Pit	NL	67	0	0	18	59.1	257	62	24	20	6	4	2	5	22	3	34	5	0	1	1	.500	0	1-3	4	4.55	3.03
	Postseason		1	0	0	0	1.0	7	3	2	2	0	0	0	0	1	0	1	0	0	0	0	-	0	0-0	0	19.55	18.00
	6 ML YEARS		313	0	0	74	309.1	1307	294	118	97	23	20	9	25	102	15	189	17	0	15	13	.536	0	3-12	54	3.63	2.82

Phil Hughes

Pitches: R **Bats:** R **Pos:** SP-11; RP-1   **Ht:** 6'5" **Wt:** 240 **Born:** 6/24/1986 **Age:** 31

			HOW MUCH HE PITCHED							WHAT HE GAVE UP										THE RESULTS							
Year	Team	Lg	G	GS	CG	GF	IP	BFP	H	R	ER	HR	SH	SF	HB	TBB	IBB	SO	WP	Bk	W	L	Pct	Sh	Sv-Op	Hld	ERC	ERA
2007	NYY	AL	13	13	0	0	72.2	306	64	39	36	8	2	1	2	29	0	58	4	0	5	3	.625	0	0-0	0	3.61	4.46
2008	NYY	AL	8	8	0	0	34.0	157	43	26	25	3	1	1	0	15	0	23	2	0	0	4	.000	0	0-0	0	5.84	6.62
2009	NYY	AL	51	7	0	6	86.0	351	68	31	29	8	0	4	5	28	1	96	4	2	8	3	.727	0	3-6	18	2.86	3.03
2010	NYY	AL	31	29	0	0	176.1	730	162	83	82	25	2	5	0	58	1	146	9	1	18	8	.692	0	0-0	0	3.65	4.19
2011	NYY	AL	17	14	1	1	74.2	334	84	48	48	9	3	3	4	27	2	47	3	0	5	5	.500	1	0-0	0	4.92	5.79
2012	NYY	AL	32	32	1	0	191.1	815	196	101	89	35	1	4	6	46	0	165	3	0	16	13	.552	0	0-0	0	4.21	4.19
2013	NYY	AL	30	29	0	0	145.2	642	170	91	84	24	3	11	4	42	4	121	6	0	4	14	.222	0	0-0	0	5.13	5.19
2014	Min	AL	32	32	1	0	209.2	855	221	88	82	16	3	7	5	16	1	186	1	0	16	10	.615	0	0-0	0	3.05	3.52
2015	Min	AL	27	25	1	1	155.1	651	184	76	76	29	1	3	2	16	0	94	1	0	11	9	.550	0	0-0	0	4.59	4.40
2016	Min	AL	12	11	1	0	59.0	259	76	40	39	11	1	2	0	13	0	34	0	0	1	7	.125	0	0-0	0	5.68	5.95
	Postseason		18	5	0	2	39.2	176	41	20	20	5	1	0	0	18	3	38	3	0	2	4	.333	0	0-1	0	4.49	4.54
	10 ML YEARS		253	200	5	8	1204.2	5100	1268	623	590	168	17	43	30	290	9	970	33	3	84	76	.525	1	3-6	18	4.09	4.41

Nick Hundley

Bats: R **Throws:** R **Pos:** C-79; PH-4   **Ht:** 6'1" **Wt:** 205 **Born:** 9/8/1983 **Age:** 33

							BATTING														RUNNING			AVERAGES			
Year	Team	Lg	G	AB	H	2B	3B	HR	(Hm	Rd)	TB	R	RBI	RC	TBB	IBB	SO	HBP	SH	SF	SB	CS	GDP	Avg	OBP	Slg	OPS
2008	SD	NL	60	198	47	7	1	5	(4	1)	71	21	24	17	11	0	52	2	0	5	0	0	1	.237	.278	.359	.636
2009	SD	NL	78	256	61	15	2	8	(4	4)	104	23	30	33	28	1	76	1	1	3	5	1	2	.238	.313	.406	.719
2010	SD	NL	85	273	68	18	2	8	(7	1)	114	33	43	37	25	0	66	1	2	6	0	5	8	.249	.308	.418	.726
2011	SD	NL	82	281	81	16	5	9	(6	3)	134	34	29	40	22	3	74	4	0	1	1	1	3	.288	.347	.477	.824
2012	SD	NL	58	204	32	7	1	3	(1	2)	50	14	22	6	15	2	56	2	1	3	0	3	4	.157	.219	.245	.464
2013	SD	NL	114	373	87	19	0	13	(6	7)	145	35	44	36	26	5	98	5	1	3	1	0	7	.233	.290	.389	.679
2014	2 Tms		83	218	53	7	0	6	(4	2)	78	18	22	21	10	0	63	0	2	3	1	0	3	.243	.273	.358	.631
2015	Col	NL	103	366	110	21	5	10	(7	3)	171	45	43	44	21	0	76	1	0	1	5	6	8	.301	.339	.467	.807
2016	Col	NL	83	289	75	20	1	10	(4	6)	127	30	48	41	25	3	65	1	1	1	0	0	12	.260	.320	.439	.759
14	SD	NL	33	59	16	3	0	1	(1	0)	22	1	3	5	0	0	13	0	0	0	0	0	1	.271	.271	.373	.644
14	Bal	AL	50	159	37	4	0	5	(3	2)	56	17	19	16	10	0	50	0	2	3	1	0	2	.233	.273	.352	.625
	Postseason		5	15	1	0	0	0	(0	0)	1	0	1	0	0	0	5	0	0	0	0	0	0	.067	.067	.067	.133
	9 ML YEARS		746	2458	614	130	17	72	(43	29)	994	253	305	275	183	14	626	17	8	26	13	16	48	.250	.303	.404	.708

Cedric Hunter

Bats: L **Throws:** L **Pos:** LF-10; PH-4; RF-2   **Ht:** 5'11" **Wt:** 200 **Born:** 3/10/1988 **Age:** 29

							BATTING														RUNNING			AVERAGES			
Year	Team	Lg	G	AB	H	2B	3B	HR	(Hm	Rd)	TB	R	RBI	RC	TBB	IBB	SO	HBP	SH	SF	SB	CS	GDP	Avg	OBP	Slg	OPS
2012	Memp	AAA	129	355	95	19	2	5	(-	-)	133	40	44	51	44	2	43	6	3	4	7	4	7	.268	.355	.375	.684
2013	Clmbs	AAA	32	96	24	5	0	2	(-	-)	35	14	11	10	8	1	14	0	1	1	2	2	3	.250	.305	.365	.669
2013	Akron	AA	61	234	69	20	4	12	(-	-)	133	32	39	45	17	0	35	2	0	3	2	3	4	.295	.344	.568	.912
2014	Missi	AA	120	399	118	30	4	14	(-	-)	198	60	72	81	57	4	52	7	1	6	14	5	11	.296	.388	.496	.884
2015	Gwnntt	AAA	138	474	134	21	4	12	(-	-)	199	52	77	68	34	2	67	2	1	4	11	6	14	.283	.331	.420	.751

Year Team	Lg	G	AB	H	2B	3B	HR	(Hm	Rd)	TB	R	RBI	RC	TBB	IBB	SO	HBP	SH	SF	SB	CS	GDP	Avg	OBP	Slg	OPS
								BATTING												**RUNNING**			**AVERAGES**			
2016 LV	AAA	98	330	97	16	0	10	(-	-)	143	33	53	46	15	0	56	0	4	1	6	3	4	.294	.324	.433	.757
2011 SD	NL	6	4	1	0	0	0	(0	0)	1	1	0	0	1	0	0	0	0	0	0	1	0	.250	.400	.250	.650
2016 Phi	NL	13	34	3	0	0	1	(0	1)	6	3	1	0	2	0	6	0	0	0	0	0	1	.088	.139	.176	.315
2 ML YEARS		19	38	4	0	0	1	(0	1)	7	4	1	0	3	0	6	0	0	0	0	1	1	.105	.171	.184	.355

Tommy Hunter

Pitches: R Bats: R Pos: RP-33 **Ht: 6'3" Wt: 250 Born: 7/3/1986 Age: 30**

Year Team	Lg	G	GS	CG	GF	IP	BFP	H	R	ER	HR	SH	SF	HB	TBB	IBB	SO	WP	Bk	W	L	Pct	Sh	Sv-Op	Hld	ERC	ERA
				HOW MUCH HE PITCHED							**WHAT HE GAVE UP**											**THE RESULTS**					
2016 Clmbs*	AAA	14	2	0	2	15.0	60	14	5	5	2	0	0	0	2	0	10	0	0	2	1	.667	0	1--	-	2.90	3.00
2008 Tex	AL	3	3	0	0	11.0	63	23	20	20	4	0	0	1	3	0	9	0	0	0	2	.000	0	0-0	0	12.66	16.36
2009 Tex	AL	19	19	1	0	112.0	475	113	55	51	13	2	1	2	33	2	64	6	1	9	6	.600	0	0-0	0	3.86	4.10
2010 Tex	AL	23	22	1	0	128.0	536	126	55	53	21	3	2	3	33	0	68	1	0	13	4	**.765**	0	0-0	0	3.95	3.73
2011 2 Tms	AL	20	11	0	2	84.2	367	100	50	44	12	2	2	4	15	1	45	0	0	4	4	.500	0	0-1	1	4.65	4.68
2012 Bal	AL	33	20	0	5	133.2	573	161	85	81	32	3	6	4	27	2	77	0	1	7	8	.467	0	0-1	1	5.63	5.45
2013 Bal	AL	68	0	0	20	86.1	336	71	28	27	11	1	0	2	14	1	68	0	0	6	5	.545	0	4-6	21	2.53	2.81
2014 Bal	AL	60	0	0	24	60.2	241	55	22	20	4	1	2	1	12	3	45	2	0	3	2	.600	0	11-17	12	2.65	2.97
2015 2 Tms	AL	58	0	0	17	60.1	249	61	29	28	7	1	3	1	14	2	47	2	0	4	2	.667	0	1-2	7	3.65	4.18
2016 2 Tms	AL	33	0	0	8	34.0	139	35	13	12	1	1	0	2	8	1	23	0	0	2	2	.500	0	0-1	1	3.43	3.18
11 Tex	AL	8	0	0	2	15.1	62	12	6	5	1	1	1	0	5	0	10	0	0	1	1	.500	0	0-1	0	2.44	2.93
11 Bal	AL	12	11	0	0	69.1	305	88	44	39	11	1	1	4	10	1	35	0	0	3	3	.500	0	0-0	1	5.19	5.06
15 Bal	AL	39	0	0	12	44.2	180	41	19	18	3	1	3	1	11	2	32	2	0	2	2	.500	0	0-1	6	2.92	3.63
15 ChC	NL	19	0	0	5	15.2	69	20	10	10	4	0	0	0	3	0	15	0	0	2	0	1.000	0	1-1	1	5.91	5.74
16 Cle	AL	21	0	0	5	21.2	90	21	10	9	1	1	0	2	5	1	17	0	0	2	2	.500	0	0-1	0	3.22	3.74
16 Bal	AL	12	0	0	3	12.1	49	14	3	3	0	0	0	0	3	0	6	0	0	0	0	-	0	0-0	1	3.82	2.19
Postseason		7	3	0	2	14.1	65	19	8	7	2	0	2	1	2	0	15	0	1	0	2	.000	0	0-0	0	5.35	4.40
9 ML YEARS		317	75	2	76	710.2	2979	745	357	336	105	14	16	20	159	12	446	11	2	48	35	.578	0	16-28	42	4.08	4.26

Jason Hursh

Pitches: R Bats: R Pos: RP-2 **Ht: 6'3" Wt: 200 Born: 10/2/1991 Age: 25**

Year Team	Lg	G	GS	CG	GF	IP	BFP	H	R	ER	HR	SH	SF	HB	TBB	IBB	SO	WP	Bk	W	L	Pct	Sh	Sv-Op	Hld	ERC	ERA
				HOW MUCH HE PITCHED							**WHAT HE GAVE UP**											**THE RESULTS**					
2013 Rome	A	9	9	0	0	27.0	108	20	9	2	1	0	0	1	10	0	15	4	0	1	1	.500	0	0--	-	2.40	0.67
2014 Missi	AA	27	26	1	0	148.1	615	151	70	59	5	8	2	7	43	0	83	6	0	11	7	.611	1	0--	-	3.58	3.58
2015 Missi	AA	24	15	0	5	82.1	379	111	52	47	3	2	1	0	32	0	60	2	0	3	6	.333	0	2--	-	5.59	5.14
2015 Gwnntt	AAA	10	0	0	2	15.0	64	16	9	9	2	0	1	1	5	0	5	0	0	1	0	1.000	0	0--	-	4.83	5.40
2016 Missi	AA	35	0	0	14	57.0	236	42	16	13	0	4	1	3	23	0	42	6	1	3	2	.600	0	3--	-	2.24	2.05
2016 Gwnntt	AAA	8	0	0	2	16.0	66	15	3	3	0	0	1	2	8	0	8	0	0	0	0	-	0	0--	-	4.20	1.69
2016 Atl	NL	2	0	0	0	1.1	11	4	5	5	0	0	0	0	3	0	1	1	0	0	0	-	0	0-0	0	25.85	33.75

Drew Hutchison

Pitches: R Bats: L Pos: RP-6; SP-3 **Ht: 6'3" Wt: 205 Born: 8/22/1990 Age: 26**

Year Team	Lg	G	GS	CG	GF	IP	BFP	H	R	ER	HR	SH	SF	HB	TBB	IBB	SO	WP	Bk	W	L	Pct	Sh	Sv-Op	Hld	ERC	ERA
				HOW MUCH HE PITCHED							**WHAT HE GAVE UP**											**THE RESULTS**					
2016 Buffalo*	AAA	18	18	0	0	102.0	417	78	40	37	11	0	3	7	35	0	110	1	1	6	5	.545	0	0--	-	2.93	3.26
2016 Indy*	AAA	7	6	0	0	36.0	160	37	23	18	5	0	3	1	15	0	28	2	0	1	1	.500	0	0--	-	4.62	4.50
2012 Tor	AL	11	11	0	0	58.2	257	59	31	30	8	1	1	5	20	0	49	1	0	5	3	.625	0	0-0	0	4.43	4.60
2014 Tor	AL	32	32	1	0	184.2	786	173	92	92	23	4	**10**	7	60	1	184	4	2	11	13	.458	1	0-0	0	3.70	4.48
2015 Tor	AL	30	28	1	0	150.1	664	179	103	93	22	0	6	11	44	0	129	7	0	13	5	.722	1	0-0	0	5.44	5.57
2016 2 Tms		9	3	0	3	24.0	104	28	14	14	6	1	2	2	7	0	22	0	0	1	0	1.000	0	0-1	0	6.24	5.25
16 Tor	AL	3	2	0	0	12.2	53	13	7	7	4	0	0	1	4	0	12	0	0	1	0	1.000	0	0-1	0	5.98	4.97
16 Pit	NL	6	1	0	3	11.1	51	15	7	7	2	1	2	1	3	0	10	0	0	0	0	-	0	0-0	0	6.50	5.56
4 ML YEARS		82	74	2	3	417.2	1811	439	240	229	59	6	19	25	131	1	384	12	2	30	21	.588	2	0-1	0	4.55	4.93

Chris Iannetta

Bats: R Throws: R Pos: C-93;DH-1 eye-ah-NETT-ah **Ht: 6'0" Wt: 230 Born: 4/8/1983 Age: 34**

Year Team	Lg	G	AB	H	2B	3B	HR	(Hm	Rd)	TB	R	RBI	RC	TBB	IBB	SO	HBP	SH	SF	SB	CS	GDP	Avg	OBP	Slg	OPS
								BATTING												**RUNNING**			**AVERAGES**			
2006 Col	NL	21	77	20	4	0	2	(0	2)	30	12	10	9	13	2	17	1	1	1	0	1	1	.260	.370	.390	.759
2007 Col	NL	67	197	43	8	3	4	(1	3)	69	22	27	27	29	3	58	5	1	2	0	0	3	.218	.330	.350	.681
2008 Col	NL	104	333	88	22	2	18	(11	7)	168	50	65	65	56	0	92	14	2	2	0	0	6	.264	.390	.505	.895
2009 Col	NL	93	289	66	15	2	16	(8	8)	133	41	52	47	43	3	75	11	1	6	0	1	4	.228	.344	.460	.804
2010 Col	NL	61	188	37	6	1	9	(7	2)	72	20	27	21	30	2	48	4	0	1	1	0	4	.197	.318	.383	.701
2011 Col	NL	112	345	82	17	1	14	(10	4)	143	51	55	62	70	5	89	5	2	4	6	3	10	.238	.370	.414	.785
2012 LAA	AL	79	221	53	6	1	9	(3	6)	88	27	26	27	29	0	60	2	0	1	1	3	4	.240	.332	.398	.730
2013 LAA	AL	115	325	73	15	0	11	(1	10)	121	40	39	44	68	2	100	2	0	4	0	1	8	.225	.358	.372	.731
2014 LAA	AL	108	306	77	22	0	7	(6	1)	120	41	43	56	54	3	91	8	0	5	3	0	9	.252	.373	.392	.765
2015 LAA	AL	92	272	51	10	0	10	(3	7)	91	28	24	27	41	1	83	1	0	3	0	0	11	.188	.293	.335	.628
2016 Sea	AL	94	295	62	14	0	7	(5	2)	97	23	24	27	38	0	83	2	1	2	0	0	4	.210	.303	.329	.631
Postseason		3	10	1	0	0	1	(1	0)	4	1	1	0	1	0	2	0	0	0	0	0	0	.100	.182	.400	.582
11 ML YEARS		946	2848	652	139	10	107	(55	52)	1132	355	402	412	471	21	796	55	8	31	11	10	58	.229	.346	.397	.743

Jose Iglesias

ee-GLAY-see-us

Bats: R Throws: R Pos: SS-136;PH-2;PR-1

Ht: 5'11" Wt: 185 Born: 1/5/1990 Age: 27

Year	Team	Lg	G	AB	H	2B	3B	HR	(Hm	Rd)	TB	R	RBI	RC	TBB	IBB	SO	HBP	SH	SF	SB	CS	GDP	Avg	OBP	Slg	OPS
2011	Bos	AL	10	6	2	0	0	0	(0	0)	2	3	0	0	0	0	2	0	0	0	0	0	0	.333	.333	.333	.667
2012	Bos	AL	25	68	8	2	0	0	(0	1)	13	5	2	0	4	0	16	3	2	0	1	0	2	.118	.200	.191	.391
2013	2 Tms	AL	109	350	106	16	2	3	(1	2)	135	39	29	45	15	0	60	11	4	2	5	2	7	.303	.349	.386	.735
2015	Det	AL	120	416	125	17	3	2	(1	1)	154	44	23	47	25	2	44	6	4	3	11	8	10	.300	.347	.370	.717
2016	Det	AL	137	467	119	26	0	4	(1	3)	157	57	32	47	28	1	50	8	7	3	7	4	12	.255	.306	.336	.643
13	Bos	AL	63	215	71	10	2	1	(0	1)	88	27	19	34	11	0	30	6	0	2	3	1	4	.330	.376	.409	.785
13	Det	AL	46	135	35	6	0	2	(1	1)	47	12	10	11	4	0	30	5	4	0	2	1	3	.259	.306	.348	.654
	Postseason		11	26	6	0	0	0	(0	0)	6	2	1	0	1	0	5	1	3	0	0	1	1	.231	.286	.231	.516
	5 ML YEARS		401	1307	360	61	5	10	(3	7)	461	148	86	139	72	3	172	28	17	8	24	14	31	.275	.325	.353	.678

Raisel Iglesias

rye-SELL

Pitches: R Bats: R Pos: RP-32; SP-5

Ht: 6'2" Wt: 185 Born: 1/4/1990 Age: 27

Year	Team	Lg	G	GS	CG	GF	IP	BFP	H	R	ER	HR	SH	SF	HB	TBB	IBB	SO	WP	Bk	W	L	Pct	Sh	Sv-Op	Hld	ERC	ERA
2015	Lsvlle	AAA	6	6	0	0	29.0	121	26	12	11	4	3	0	0	8	0	21	1	0	1	3	.250	0	0--	-	3.22	3.41
2015	Cin	NL	18	16	0	1	95.1	395	81	45	44	11	4	0	7	28	0	104	2	2	3	7	.300	0	0-0	0	3.24	4.15
2016	Cin	NL	37	5	0	15	78.1	325	63	22	22	7	1	2	5	26	1	83	3	1	3	2	.600	0	6-8	7	2.90	2.53
	2 ML YEARS		55	21	0	16	173.2	720	144	67	66	18	5	2	12	54	1	187	5	3	6	9	.400	0	6-8	7	3.09	3.42

Ender Inciarte

END-er in-see-ARR-tay

Bats: L Throws: L Pos: CF-120;LF-10;PH-4;PR-1

Ht: 5'11" Wt: 190 Born: 10/29/1990 Age: 26

Year	Team	Lg	G	AB	H	2B	3B	HR	(Hm	Rd)	TB	R	RBI	RC	TBB	IBB	SO	HBP	SH	SF	SB	CS	GDP	Avg	OBP	Slg	OPS
2014	Ari	NL	118	418	116	18	2	4	(1	3)	150	54	27	49	25	0	53	0	4	0	19	3	3	.278	.318	.359	.677
2015	Ari	NL	132	524	159	27	5	6	(1	5)	214	73	45	69	26	0	58	4	2	5	21	10	8	.303	.338	.408	.747
2016	Atl	NL	131	522	152	24	7	3	(1	2)	199	85	29	58	45	5	68	4	5	2	16	7	8	.291	.351	.381	.732
	3 ML YEARS		381	1464	427	69	14	13	(3	10)	563	212	101	176	96	5	179	8	11	7	56	20	19	.292	.337	.385	.722

Omar Infante

in-FAHN-tay

Bats: R Throws: R Pos: 2B-39

Ht: 5'11" Wt: 195 Born: 12/26/1981 Age: 35

Year	Team	Lg	G	AB	H	2B	3B	HR	(Hm	Rd)	TB	R	RBI	RC	TBB	IBB	SO	HBP	SH	SF	SB	CS	GDP	Avg	OBP	Slg	OPS
2016	Gwnntt*	AAA	27	110	23	5	1	1	(-	-)	33	8	9	6	3	0	16	0	1	2	0	1	1	.209	.226	.300	.526
2002	Det	AL	18	72	24	3	0	1	(0	1)	30	4	6	12	3	0	10	0	0	0	0	1	0	.333	.360	.417	.777
2003	Det	AL	69	221	49	6	1	0	(0	0)	57	24	8	16	18	0	37	0	3	2	6	3	1	.222	.278	.258	.536
2004	Det	AL	142	503	133	27	9	16	(7	9)	226	69	55	69	40	3	112	1	7	5	13	7	4	.264	.317	.449	.766
2005	Det	AL	121	406	90	28	2	9	(3	6)	149	36	43	38	16	0	73	2	8	2	8	0	5	.222	.254	.367	.621
2006	Det	AL	78	224	62	11	4	4	(0	4)	93	35	25	26	14	0	45	3	2	5	3	2	5	.277	.325	.415	.740
2007	Det	AL	66	166	45	6	1	2	(0	2)	59	24	17	23	9	0	29	0	2	1	4	1	4	.271	.307	.355	.662
2008	Atl	NL	96	317	93	24	3	3	(1	2)	132	45	40	45	22	2	44	2	2	5	0	1	4	.293	.338	.416	.755
2009	Atl	NL	70	203	62	9	1	2	(1	1)	79	24	27	29	19	0	28	1	2	4	2	0	5	.305	.361	.389	.750
2010	Atl	NL	134	471	151	15	3	8	(1	7)	196	65	47	70	29	1	62	0	4	2	7	6	14	.321	.359	.416	.775
2011	Fla	NL	148	579	160	24	8	7	(2	5)	221	55	49	66	34	1	67	2	17	8	4	2	12	.276	.315	.382	.696
2012	2 Tms	NL	149	554	152	30	7	12	(5	7)	232	69	53	58	21	0	55	1	8	4	17	3	9	.274	.300	.419	.719
2013	Det	AL	118	453	144	24	3	10	(7	3)	204	54	51	64	20	1	44	0	0	3	5	2	11	.318	.345	.450	.795
2014	KC	AL	135	528	133	21	3	6	(2	4)	178	50	66	55	33	3	68	2	5	7	9	3	7	.252	.295	.337	.632
2015	KC	AL	124	440	97	23	7	2	(0	2)	140	39	44	31	9	0	69	0	2	4	2	2	8	.220	.234	.318	.552
2016	KC	AL	39	134	32	9	1	0	(0	0)	43	16	11	12	9	0	23	0	2	4	0	0	0	.239	.279	.321	.600
12	Mia	NL	85	328	94	23	2	8	(2	6)	145	42	33	36	12	0	42	1	4	2	10	1	7	.287	.312	.442	.754
12	Det	AL	64	226	58	7	5	4	(3	1)	87	27	20	22	9	0	23	0	4	2	7	2	2	.257	.283	.385	.668
	Postseason		45	161	41	7	0	1	(1	0)	51	16	9	16	12	2	40	1	1	2	3	1	4	.255	.307	.317	.624
	15 ML YEARS		1507	5271	1427	260	53	82	(29	53)	2039	609	542	614	296	11	776	14	64	53	80	33	89	.271	.308	.387	.695

Hernan Iribarren

air-NAHN ee-ree-BAR-en

Bats: L Throws: R Pos: PH-12;CF-6;2B-5;1B-2;RF-2;PR-1

Ht: 6'1" Wt: 195 Born: 6/29/1984 Age: 33

Year	Team	Lg	G	AB	H	2B	3B	HR	(Hm	Rd)	TB	R	RBI	RC	TBB	IBB	SO	HBP	SH	SF	SB	CS	GDP	Avg	OBP	Slg	OPS
2016	Lsvlle*	AAA	101	373	122	20	1	3	(-	-)	153	46	35	59	33	6	60	0	2	2	3	5	11	.327	.380	.410	.790
2008	Mil	NL	12	14	2	1	0	0	(0	0)	3	1	1	1	1	0	3	0	0	0	0	0	0	.143	.200	.214	.414
2009	Mil	NL	12	13	3	2	0	0	(0	0)	5	1	1	2	1	0	5	0	0	0	0	0	0	.231	.286	.385	.670
2016	Cin	NL	24	45	14	0	3	0	(0	0)	20	6	2	6	0	0	11	0	0	0	1	0	2	.311	.311	.444	.756
	3 ML YEARS		48	72	19	3	3	0	(0	0)	28	8	4	9	2	0	19	0	0	0	1	0	2	.264	.284	.389	.673

Hisashi Iwakuma

he-SAH-shee ee-wuh-KOO-muh

Pitches: R Bats: R Pos: SP-33

Ht: 6'3" Wt: 210 Born: 4/12/1981 Age: 36

Year	Team	Lg	G	GS	CG	GF	IP	BFP	H	R	ER	HR	SH	SF	HB	TBB	IBB	SO	WP	Bk	W	L	Pct	Sh	Sv-Op	Hld	ERC	ERA
2012	Sea	AL	30	16	0	6	125.1	519	117	49	44	17	1	1	3	43	3	101	5	0	9	5	.643	0	2-2	0	3.87	3.16
2013	Sea	AL	33	33	0	0	219.2	866	179	69	65	25	3	6	2	42	4	185	10	0	14	6	.700	0	0-0	0	2.43	2.66

Year	Team	Lg	G	GS	CG	GF	IP	BFP	H	R	ER	HR	SH	SF	HB	TBB	IBB	SO	WP	Bk	W	L	Pct	Sh	Sv-Op	Hld	ERC	ERA
2014	Sea	AL	28	28	0	0	179.0	709	167	70	70	20	0	1	2	21	2	154	2	0	15	9	.625	0	0-0	0	2.77	3.52
2015	Sea	AL	20	20	1	0	129.2	516	117	53	51	18	4	3	1	21	1	111	1	0	9	5	.643	1	0-0	0	2.93	3.54
2016	Sea	AL	33	33	0	0	199.0	836	218	95	91	28	6	7	5	46	3	147	4	0	16	12	.571	0	0-0	0	4.37	4.12
5 ML YEARS			144	130	1	6	852.2	3446	798	336	321	108	14	18	13	173	13	698	22	0	63	37	.630	1	2-2	0	3.21	3.39

Austin Jackson

Bats: R **Throws:** R **Pos:** CF-54;PR-1   **Ht:** 6'1" **Wt:** 205 **Born:** 2/1/1987 **Age:** 30

Year	Team	Lg	G	AB	H	2B	3B	HR	(Hm	Rd)	TB	R	RBI	RC	TBB	IBB	SO	HBP	SH	SF	SB	CS	GDP	Avg	OBP	Slg	OPS
2010	Det	AL	151	618	181	34	10	4	(0	4)	247	103	41	84	47	4	170	4	3	3	27	6	5	.293	.345	.400	.745
2011	Det	AL	153	591	147	22	11	10	(5	5)	221	90	45	67	56	3	181	4	14	3	22	5	11	.249	.317	.374	.690
2012	Det	AL	137	543	163	29	10	16	(6	10)	260	103	66	90	67	0	134	2	2	3	12	9	9	.300	.377	.479	.856
2013	Det	AL	129	552	150	30	7	12	(3	9)	230	99	49	73	52	0	129	4	3	3	8	4	12	.272	.337	.417	.754
2014	2 Tms	AL	154	597	153	30	6	4	(2	2)	207	71	47	58	47	0	144	2	1	9	20	6	15	.256	.308	.347	.655
2015	2 Tms		136	491	131	25	3	9	(5	4)	189	56	48	63	29	0	126	3	3	1	17	10	5	.267	.311	.385	.696
2016	CWS	AL	54	181	46	12	2	0	(0	0)	62	24	18	24	17	0	39	1	2	2	2	1	3	.254	.318	.343	.661
14	Det	AL	100	374	102	25	5	4	(2	2)	149	52	33	42	35	0	85	2	1	8	9	4	9	.273	.332	.398	.730
14	Sea	AL	54	223	51	5	1	0	(0	0)	58	19	14	16	12	0	59	0	0	1	11	2	6	.229	.267	.260	.527
15	Sea	AL	107	419	114	18	3	8	(5	3)	162	46	38	52	24	0	107	1	3	1	15	9	4	.272	.312	.387	.699
15	ChC	NL	29	72	17	7	0	1	(0	1)	27	10	10	11	5	0	19	2	0	0	2	1	1	.236	.304	.375	.679
	Postseason		40	141	31	7	1	2	(1	1)	46	19	11	15	20	0	58	1	2	0	3	2	2	.220	.321	.326	.647
7 ML YEARS			914	3573	971	182	49	55	(21	34)	1416	546	314	459	315	7	923	20	28	24	108	41	60	.272	.332	.396	.728

Edwin Jackson

Pitches: R **Bats:** R **Pos:** SP-13; RP-8   **Ht:** 6'2" **Wt:** 215 **Born:** 9/9/1983 **Age:** 33

Year	Team	Lg	G	GS	CG	GF	IP	BFP	H	R	ER	HR	SH	SF	HB	TBB	IBB	SO	WP	Bk	W	L	Pct	Sh	Sv-Op	Hld	ERC	ERA
2003	LAD	NL	4	3	0	0	22.0	91	17	6	6	2	1	1	1	11	1	19	3	0	2	1	.667	0	0-0	0	3.36	2.45
2004	LAD	NL	8	5	0	1	24.2	113	31	20	20	7	1	0	0	11	1	16	0	0	2	1	.667	0	0-0	0	7.21	7.30
2005	LAD	NL	7	6	0	0	28.2	134	31	22	20	2	0	2	1	17	0	13	2	1	2	2	.500	0	0-0	0	5.13	6.28
2006	TB	AL	23	1	0	7	36.1	174	42	27	22	2	2	2	1	25	0	27	3	1	0	0	-	0	0-0	0	5.86	5.45
2007	TB	AL	32	31	1	0	161.0	755	195	116	103	19	5	6	4	88	3	128	7	1	5	15	.250	1	0-0	0	6.11	5.76
2008	TB	AL	32	31	0	0	183.1	792	199	91	90	23	3	3	2	77	1	108	7	1	14	11	.560	0	0-1	0	4.99	4.42
2009	Det	AL	33	33	1	0	214.0	890	200	93	86	27	4	2	5	70	3	161	6	0	13	9	.591	0	0-0	0	3.72	3.62
2010	2 Tms		32	32	1	0	209.1	902	214	111	104	21	6	4	6	78	4	181	20	0	10	12	.455	1	0-0	0	4.20	4.47
2011	2 Tms		32	31	1	0	199.2	861	225	92	84	16	15	6	2	62	4	148	9	2	12	9	.571	1	0-0	0	4.34	3.79
2012	Was	NL	31	31	1	0	189.2	790	173	90	85	23	9	8	2	58	5	168	3	0	10	11	.476	0	0-0	0	3.36	4.03
2013	ChC	NL	31	31	0	0	175.1	777	197	110	97	16	8	3	5	59	7	135	14	0	8	18	.308	0	0-0	0	4.46	4.98
2014	ChC	NL	28	27	0	0	140.2	633	168	105	99	18	6	4	3	63	3	123	9	0	6	15	.286	0	0-0	0	5.75	6.33
2015	2 Tms		47	0	0	18	55.2	228	44	25	19	4	1	3	1	21	1	40	5	1	4	3	.571	0	1-2	5	2.75	3.07
2016	2 Tms		21	13	0	3	84.0	373	92	56	55	14	2	4	1	41	3	61	6	0	5	7	.417	0	0-0	0	5.55	5.89
10	Ari	NL	21	21	1	0	134.1	587	141	80	77	13	6	2	5	60	2	104	13	0	6	10	.375	1	0-0	0	4.72	5.16
10	CWS	AL	11	11	0	0	75.0	315	73	31	27	8	0	2	1	18	2	77	7	0	4	2	.667	0	0-0	0	3.32	3.24
11	CWS	AL	19	19	1	0	121.2	522	134	55	53	8	6	4	0	39	2	97	7	1	7	7	.500	1	0-0	0	4.10	3.92
11	StL	NL	13	12	0	1	78.0	339	91	37	31	8	9	2	2	23	2	51	2	1	5	2	.714	0	0-0	0	4.73	3.58
15	ChC	NL	23	0	0	11	31.0	134	30	14	11	0	1	2	1	12	1	23	3	1	2	1	.667	0	0-1	0	3.19	3.19
15	Atl	NL	24	0	0	7	24.2	94	14	11	8	4	0	1	0	9	0	17	2	0	2	2	.500	0	1-1	5	2.16	2.92
16	Mia	NL	8	0	0	3	10.2	47	13	7	7	2	0	0	0	6	1	7	1	0	0	1	.000	0	0-0	0	7.01	5.91
16	SD	NL	13	13	0	0	73.1	326	79	49	48	12	2	4	1	35	2	54	5	0	5	6	.455	0	0-0	0	5.35	5.89
	Postseason		9	5	0	2	28.0	124	30	17	17	6	2	0	0	15	1	23	0	0	1	2	.333	0	0-0	1	5.97	5.46
14 ML YEARS			361	275	5	30	1724.1	7513	1828	964	890	194	63	48	34	681	36	1328	94	7	93	114	.449	3	1-3	5	4.56	4.65

Luke Jackson

Pitches: R **Bats:** R **Pos:** RP-8   **Ht:** 6'2" **Wt:** 210 **Born:** 8/24/1991 **Age:** 25

Year	Team	Lg	G	GS	CG	GF	IP	BFP	H	R	ER	HR	SH	SF	HB	TBB	IBB	SO	WP	Bk	W	L	Pct	Sh	Sv-Op	Hld	ERC	ERA
2012	2 Tms	Low	26	26	1	0	129.2	569	130	72	67	6	2	5	9	65	0	146	9	1	10	7	.588	0	0--	-	4.45	4.65
2013	MrtlBh	A+	19	19	0	0	101.0	417	79	30	27	6	1	1	3	47	0	104	6	0	9	4	.692	0	0--	-	3.05	2.41
2013	Frisco	AA	6	4	0	0	27.0	103	13	2	2	0	0	1	0	12	0	30	3	0	2	0	1.000	0	0--	-	1.29	0.67
2014	Frisco	AA	15	14	0	1	83.1	335	58	28	28	5	1	3	4	24	0	83	8	1	8	2	.800	0	1--	-	2.01	3.02
2014	RdRck	AAA	11	10	0	0	40.0	201	56	49	46	9	0	3	2	28	0	43	2	0	1	3	.250	0	0--	-	9.20	10.35
2015	RdRck	AAA	39	5	0	9	66.1	294	62	37	32	3	1	4	1	35	0	79	11	0	2	3	.400	0	0--	-	3.82	4.34
2016	RdRck	AAA	16	0	0	2	22.0	90	13	7	6	2	1	0	1	15	0	27	1	0	1	0	1.000	0	2--	-	3.18	2.45
2016	Frisco	AA	20	0	0	5	24.1	118	27	18	13	4	1	0	2	17	1	32	5	0	0	1	.000	0	1--	-	6.65	4.81
2015	Tex	AL	7	0	0	4	6.1	27	5	3	3	1	0	0	0	2	0	6	1	0	0	0	-	0	0-0	0	2.81	4.26
2016	Tex	AL	8	0	0	2	11.2	62	22	14	14	4	1	0	1	8	0	3	0	0	0	0	-	0	0-0	0	13.93	10.80
2 ML YEARS			15	0	0	6	18.0	89	27	17	17	5	1	0	1	10	0	9	1	0	0	0	-	0	0-0	0	9.41	8.50

Paul Janish

Bats: R **Throws:** R **Pos:** 3B-9;SS-6;PR-1   YONN-ish   **Ht:** 6'2" **Wt:** 200 **Born:** 10/12/1982 **Age:** 34

Year	Team	Lg	G	AB	H	2B	3B	HR	(Hm	Rd)	TB	R	RBI	RC	TBB	IBB	SO	HBP	SH	SF	SB	CS	GDP	Avg	OBP	Slg	OPS
2016	Norfolk*	AAA	76	246	61	8	0	0	(-	-)	69	26	18	25	28	0	33	4	4	1	3	8	.248	.333	.280	.614
2008	Cin	NL	38	80	15	2	0	1	(1	0)	20	5	6	5	7	0	18	2	0	0	0	0	2	.188	.270	.250	.520
2009	Cin	NL	90	256	54	21	0	1	(1	0)	78	36	16	18	26	1	40	5	5	0	2	0	8	.211	.296	.305	.601
2010	Cin	NL	82	200	52	10	0	5	(0	5)	77	23	25	31	22	2	30	2	3	1	1	3	4	.260	.338	.385	.723
2011	Cin	NL	114	336	72	14	1	0	(0	0)	88	27	23	21	18	1	46	4	3	5	3	2	7	.214	.259	.262	.521

189

Year	Team	Lg	G	AB	H	2B	3B	HR	(Hm	Rd)	TB	R	RBI	RC	TBB	IBB	SO	HBP	SH	SF	SB	CS	GDP	Avg	OBP	Slg	OPS
2012	Atl	NL	55	167	31	6	1	0	(0	0)	39	18	9	13	17	0	30	2	0	0	1	0	1	.186	.269	.234	.502
2013	Atl	NL	52	41	7	2	0	0	(0	0)	9	7	2	1	3	0	11	0	0	1	0	0	3	.171	.222	.220	.442
2015	Bal	AL	14	35	10	3	0	0	(0	0)	13	4	3	3	0	0	3	0	0	1	0	0	0	.286	.278	.371	.649
2016	Bal	AL	14	31	6	1	0	0	(0	0)	7	3	0	3	3	0	3	1	0	0	0	0	0	.194	.286	.226	.512
	Postseason		2	1	0	0	0	0	(0	0)	0	0	0	0	0	0	0	0	0	1	0	0	0	.000	.000	.000	.000
	8 ML YEARS		459	1146	247	59	2	7	(2	5)	331	123	84	95	96	4	181	16	11	8	7	5	25	.216	.284	.289	.572

Travis Jankowski

Bats: L Throws: R Pos: CF-87;RF-22;PH-15;PR-12;LF-9   Ht: 6'2" Wt: 185 Born: 6/15/1991 Age: 26

Year	Team	Lg	G	AB	H	2B	3B	HR	(Hm	Rd)	TB	R	RBI	RC	TBB	IBB	SO	HBP	SH	SF	SB	CS	GDP	Avg	OBP	Slg	OPS
2012	2 Tms	Low	61	246	69	10	4	1	(-	-)	90	33	27	29	13	0	45	1	1	4	17	7	4	.280	.314	.366	.680
2013	Lk Els	A+	122	493	141	19	6	1	(-	-)	175	89	38	76	54	0	96	2	3	4	71	14	3	.286	.356	.355	.711
2014	SnAnt	AA	29	100	24	4	1	0	(-	-)	30	14	10	10	8	0	14	1	1	2	10	2	2	.240	.297	.300	.597
2014	3 Tms	Low	17	65	15	2	0	0	(-	-)	17	13	5	7	10	1	9	1	1	0	7	1	3	.231	.342	.262	.604
2015	SnAnt	AA	73	282	89	11	5	1	(-	-)	113	50	13	49	36	1	40	1	2	0	23	8	5	.316	.395	.401	.796
2015	ElPaso	AAA	24	97	38	6	2	0	(-	-)	48	19	12	23	13	0	10	1	1	1	9	3	0	.392	.464	.495	.959
2015	SD	NL	34	90	19	2	2	2	(0	2)	31	9	12	10	4	0	24	0	2	0	2	1	1	.211	.245	.344	.589
2016	SD	NL	131	335	82	13	2	2	(1	1)	105	53	12	34	42	0	100	2	3	0	30	12	5	.245	.332	.313	.646
	2 ML YEARS		165	425	101	15	4	4	(1	3)	136	62	24	44	46	0	124	2	5	0	32	13	6	.238	.315	.320	.635

Kenley Jansen

Pitches: R Bats: B Pos: RP-71   KEN-lee JANN-sen   Ht: 6'5" Wt: 270 Born: 9/30/1987 Age: 29

			HOW MUCH HE PITCHED						WHAT HE GAVE UP									THE RESULTS							
Year	Team	Lg	G	GS	CG	GF	IP	BFP	H	R	ER	HR	SH	SF	HB	TBB	IBB	SO	WP	Bk	W	L	Pct	Sh	Sv-Op	Hld	ERC	ERA
2010	LAD	NL	25	0	0	8	27.0	109	12	2	2	0	1	0	1	15	1	41	1	0	1	0	1.000	0	4-4	4	1.40	0.67
2011	LAD	NL	51	0	0	13	53.2	218	30	17	17	3	0	1	2	26	0	96	0	2	2	1	.667	0	5-6	9	1.96	2.85
2012	LAD	NL	65	0	0	40	65.0	252	33	18	17	6	0	1	3	22	1	99	3	0	5	3	.625	0	25-32	8	1.55	2.35
2013	LAD	NL	75	0	0	45	76.2	292	48	16	16	6	0	0	3	18	1	111	2	0	4	3	.571	0	28-32	16	1.65	1.88
2014	LAD	NL	68	0	0	57	65.1	268	55	20	20	5	1	2	0	19	2	101	2	0	2	3	.400	0	44-49	0	2.60	2.76
2015	LAD	NL	54	0	0	50	52.1	200	33	14	14	6	0	2	2	8	0	80	0	0	2	1	.667	0	36-38	1	1.58	2.41
2016	LAD	NL	71	0	0	63	68.2	251	35	14	14	4	3	1	2	11	2	104	1	0	3	2	.600	0	47-53	1	1.03	1.83
	Postseason		10	0	0	10	8.2	37	7	2	2	0	0	0	1	4	1	16	0	0	0	0	-	0	5-5	0	2.37	2.08
	7 ML YEARS		409	0	0	276	408.2	1590	246	101	100	30	5	7	13	119	7	632	9	2	19	13	.594	0	189-214	38	1.64	2.20

John Jaso

Bats: L Throws: R Pos: 1B-108;PH-29;RF-1   JAY-soe   Ht: 6'2" Wt: 205 Born: 9/19/1983 Age: 33

Year	Team	Lg	G	AB	H	2B	3B	HR	(Hm	Rd)	TB	R	RBI	RC	TBB	IBB	SO	HBP	SH	SF	SB	CS	GDP	Avg	OBP	Slg	OPS
2008	TB	AL	5	10	2	0	0	0	(0	0)	2	2	0	0	0	0	2	0	0	0	0	0	1	.200	.200	.200	.400
2010	TB	AL	109	339	89	18	3	5	(1	4)	128	57	44	57	59	1	39	2	1	3	4	0	8	.263	.372	.378	.750
2011	TB	AL	89	246	55	15	1	5	(3	2)	87	26	27	20	25	0	36	1	1	0	1	2	9	.224	.298	.354	.651
2012	Sea	AL	108	294	81	19	2	10	(6	4)	134	41	50	68	56	1	51	5	1	5	5	0	6	.276	.394	.456	.850
2013	Oak	AL	70	207	56	12	0	3	(0	3)	77	31	21	36	38	0	45	2	1	1	2	1	5	.271	.387	.372	.759
2014	Oak	AL	99	307	81	18	3	9	(5	4)	132	42	40	44	28	1	60	7	0	2	2	0	5	.264	.337	.430	.767
2015	TB	AL	70	185	53	17	0	5	(3	2)	85	23	22	32	28	1	39	1	0	2	1	2	5	.286	.380	.459	.839
2016	Pit	NL	132	380	102	25	3	8	(4	4)	157	45	42	55	45	0	74	5	1	1	0	4	8	.268	.353	.413	.766
	Postseason		5	14	3	0	0	0	(0	0)	3	0	1	1	1	0	3	0	0	0	0	0	0	.214	.267	.214	.481
	8 ML YEARS		682	1968	519	124	12	45	(22	23)	802	267	246	312	279	4	346	23	5	14	15	9	47	.264	.359	.408	.767

Jon Jay

Bats: L Throws: L Pos: CF-72;RF-9;LF-8;PH-7;PR-1   Ht: 5'11" Wt: 195 Born: 3/15/1985 Age: 32

Year	Team	Lg	G	AB	H	2B	3B	HR	(Hm	Rd)	TB	R	RBI	RC	TBB	IBB	SO	HBP	SH	SF	SB	CS	GDP	Avg	OBP	Slg	OPS
2010	StL	NL	105	287	86	19	2	4	(2	2)	121	47	27	40	24	0	50	3	8	1	2	4	5	.300	.359	.422	.780
2011	StL	NL	159	455	135	24	2	10	(5	5)	193	56	37	56	28	1	81	7	9	4	6	7	11	.297	.344	.424	.768
2012	StL	NL	117	443	135	22	4	4	(3	1)	177	70	40	65	34	3	71	15	9	1	19	7	9	.305	.373	.400	.773
2013	StL	NL	157	548	151	27	2	7	(2	5)	203	75	67	74	52	7	103	14	9	5	10	5	13	.276	.351	.370	.721
2014	StL	NL	140	413	125	16	3	3	(0	3)	156	52	46	57	28	3	78	20	3	4	6	3	17	.303	.372	.378	.750
2015	StL	NL	79	210	44	5	1	1	(0	1)	54	25	10	11	19	5	36	11	3	2	0	2	7	.210	.306	.257	.563
2016	SD	NL	90	347	101	26	1	2	(1	1)	135	49	26	55	19	0	78	6	1	0	2	0	5	.291	.339	.389	.728
	Postseason		58	190	44	4	1	0	(0	0)	50	24	15	20	19	1	30	4	4	2	5	2	4	.232	.312	.263	.575
	7 ML YEARS		847	2703	777	139	15	31	(13	18)	1039	374	253	358	204	19	497	76	42	17	45	28	67	.287	.352	.384	.737

Jeremy Jeffress

Pitches: R Bats: R Pos: RP-59   JEFF-ress   Ht: 6'0" Wt: 205 Born: 9/21/1987 Age: 29

			HOW MUCH HE PITCHED						WHAT HE GAVE UP									THE RESULTS							
Year	Team	Lg	G	GS	CG	GF	IP	BFP	H	R	ER	HR	SH	SF	HB	TBB	IBB	SO	WP	Bk	W	L	Pct	Sh	Sv-Op	Hld	ERC	ERA
2010	Mil	NL	10	0	0	5	10.0	42	8	4	3	0	0	1	0	6	1	8	1	0	1	0	1.000	0	0-0	0	2.96	2.70
2011	KC	AL	14	0	0	6	15.1	67	12	8	8	1	2	0	0	11	0	13	1	0	1	1	.500	0	1-2	0	3.87	4.70
2012	KC	AL	13	0	0	6	13.1	73	19	14	10	0	1	0	0	13	0	13	1	0	0	0	-	0	0-0	0	7.87	6.75
2013	Tor	AL	10	0	0	3	10.1	43	8	1	1	1	0	0	0	5	0	12	0	0	1	0	1.000	0	0-0	0	3.17	0.87
2014	2 Tms		32	0	0	12	32.0	135	35	10	10	1	3	1	2	10	2	29	1	0	1	1	.500	0	0-1	6	4.06	2.81
2015	Mil	NL	72	0	0	18	68.0	285	64	22	20	5	3	0	3	22	5	67	4	2	5	0	1.000	0	0-5	23	3.36	2.65
2016	2 Tms		59	0	0	41	58.0	241	55	17	15	2	2	1	4	18	3	42	3	0	3	2	.600	0	27-28	6	3.26	2.33

Year Team	Lg	HOW MUCH HE PITCHED						WHAT HE GAVE UP												THE RESULTS							
		G	GS	CG	GF	IP	BFP	H	R	ER	HR	SH	SF	HB	TBB	IBB	SO	WP	Bk	W	L	Pct	Sh	Sv-Op	Hld	ERC	ERA
14 Tor	AL	3	0	0	3	3.1	21	8	4	4	0	0	1	2	3	0	4	0	0	0	0	-	0	0-0	0	19.06	10.80
14 Mil	NL	29	0	0	9	28.2	114	27	6	6	1	3	0	0	7	2	25	1	0	1	1	.500	0	0-1	6	2.75	1.88
16 Mil	NL	47	0	0	40	44.2	190	45	13	11	2	2	1	4	11	3	35	0	0	2	2	.500	0	27-28	5	3.38	2.22
16 Tex	AL	12	0	0	1	13.1	51	10	4	4	0	0	0	0	7	0	7	3	0	1	0	1.000	0	0-0	6	2.84	2.70
7 ML YEARS		210	0	0	81	207.0	886	201	76	67	10	10	3	9	85	11	184	11	2	12	4	.750	0	28-36	35	3.72	2.91

Tyrell Jenkins

Pitches: R Bats: R Pos: SP-8; RP-6 **Ht: 6'4" Wt: 210 Born: 7/20/1992 Age: 24**

Year Team	Lg	HOW MUCH HE PITCHED						WHAT HE GAVE UP												THE RESULTS							
		G	GS	CG	GF	IP	BFP	H	R	ER	HR	SH	SF	HB	TBB	IBB	SO	WP	Bk	W	L	Pct	Sh	Sv-Op	Hld	ERC	ERA
2012 QuadC	A	19	19	0	0	82.1	359	84	53	47	5	3	2	3	36	0	80	11	0	4	4	.500	0	0- -	-	4.23	5.14
2013 2 Tms	Low	13	13	2	0	59.1	261	64	34	31	4	1	1	1	25	0	40	6	0	4	4	.500	1	0- -	-	4.45	4.70
2014 PlmBh	A+	13	13	0	0	74.0	309	74	32	27	6	1	4	1	23	0	41	8	3	6	5	.545	0	0- -	-	3.71	3.28
2015 Missi	AA	16	16	3	0	93.0	396	84	41	31	3	2	2	2	41	0	59	1	0	5	5	.500	0	0- -	-	3.33	3.00
2015 Gwnntt	AAA	9	9	0	0	45.1	196	43	20	18	4	3	3	2	20	0	29	2	0	3	4	.429	0	0- -	-	4.06	3.57
2016 Gwnntt	AAA	17	12	0	0	83.2	357	86	30	23	3	0	5	1	35	0	55	2	1	9	3	.750	0	0- -	-	3.98	2.47
2016 Atl	NL	14	8	0	2	52.0	237	55	35	34	11	3	3	1	33	1	26	1	0	2	4	.333	0	0-0	0	6.38	5.88

Dan Jennings

Pitches: L Bats: L Pos: RP-64 **Ht: 6'3" Wt: 210 Born: 4/17/1987 Age: 30**

Year Team	Lg	HOW MUCH HE PITCHED						WHAT HE GAVE UP												THE RESULTS							
		G	GS	CG	GF	IP	BFP	H	R	ER	HR	SH	SF	HB	TBB	IBB	SO	WP	Bk	W	L	Pct	Sh	Sv-Op	Hld	ERC	ERA
2012 Mia	NL	22	0	0	4	19.0	86	18	5	4	2	0	0	2	11	1	8	0	0	1	0	1.000	0	0-0	2	4.85	1.89
2013 Mia	NL	47	0	0	6	40.2	171	39	17	17	1	0	2	0	16	2	38	3	0	2	4	.333	0	0-2	5	3.27	3.76
2014 Mia	NL	47	0	0	12	40.1	182	45	11	6	3	2	3	0	17	1	38	2	0	0	2	.000	0	0-2	3	4.50	1.34
2015 CWS	AL	53	0	0	17	56.1	244	55	28	25	3	4	1	0	24	6	46	4	0	2	3	.400	0	0-0	4	3.52	3.99
2016 CWS	AL	64	0	0	15	60.2	259	57	18	14	1	2	6	3	28	0	46	4	0	4	3	.571	0	1-3	10	3.65	2.08
5 ML YEARS		233	0	0	54	217.0	942	214	79	66	10	8	12	5	96	10	176	13	0	9	12	.429	0	1-7	20	3.80	2.74

Desmond Jennings

Bats: R Throws: R Pos: LF-33;CF-30;DH-2;PH-2;PR-1 **Ht: 6'2" Wt: 210 Born: 10/30/1986 Age: 30**

Year Team	Lg	BATTING														RUNNING			AVERAGES			
		G	AB	H	2B	3B	HR	(Hm Rd)	TB	R	RBI	RC	TBB	IBB	SO	HBP	SH	SF	SB	CS	GDP	Avg	OBP	Slg	OPS
2010 TB	AL	17	21	4	1	1	0	(0 0)	7	5	2	2	2	0	4	1	0	0	2	2	0	.190	.292	.333	.625
2011 TB	AL	63	247	64	9	4	10	(3 7)	111	44	25	45	31	1	59	6	3	0	20	6	1	.259	.356	.449	.805
2012 TB	AL	132	505	124	19	7	13	(9 4)	196	85	47	62	46	1	120	5	4	7	31	2	7	.246	.314	.388	.702
2013 TB	AL	139	527	133	31	6	14	(8 6)	218	82	54	74	64	0	115	3	3	5	20	8	6	.252	.334	.414	.748
2014 TB	AL	123	479	117	30	2	10	(2 8)	181	64	36	55	47	0	108	6	9	1	15	6	10	.244	.319	.378	.697
2015 TB	AL	28	97	26	2	1	1	(0 1)	33	9	7	10	8	0	17	1	0	2	5	3	2	.268	.324	.340	.664
2016 TB	AL	65	200	40	7	1	7	(2 5)	70	22	20	15	21	0	58	2	1	1	2	0	4	.200	.281	.350	.631
Postseason		11	33	10	2	0	2	(2 0)	18	5	4	6	5	0	5	0	0	0	1	0	0	.303	.395	.545	.940
7 ML YEARS		567	2076	508	99	22	55	(22 33)	816	311	191	263	219	2	481	24	22	10	95	27	30	.245	.322	.393	.716

Kyle Jensen

Bats: R Throws: L Pos: PH-9;1B-4;LF-4;RF-1;DH-1;PR-1 **Ht: 6'3" Wt: 240 Born: 5/20/1988 Age: 29**

Year Team	Lg	BATTING														RUNNING			AVERAGES			
		G	AB	H	2B	3B	HR	(Hm Rd)	TB	R	RBI	RC	TBB	IBB	SO	HBP	SH	SF	SB	CS	GDP	Avg	OBP	Slg	OPS
2012 Jaxnvl	AA	132	445	104	21	2	24	(- -)	201	70	84	71	69	0	162	3	0	4	1	1	11	.234	.338	.452	.789
2013 Jaxnvl	AA	70	245	58	16	0	16	(- -)	122	43	42	45	33	0	73	12	0	1	5	3	6	.237	.354	.498	.852
2013 NewOr	AAA	60	202	47	15	0	12	(- -)	98	31	36	30	17	0	71	2	1	4	1	0	0	.233	.293	.485	.778
2014 NewOr	AAA	133	497	129	29	0	27	(- -)	239	70	92	81	48	1	147	7	0	4	1	0	7	.260	.331	.481	.812
2015 OkCity	AAA	128	417	108	28	3	20	(- -)	202	59	71	65	31	2	110	4	0	4	0	0	9	.259	.314	.484	.798
2016 Reno	AAA	133	498	144	34	2	30	(- -)	272	77	120	95	44	1	169	6	0	7	1	1	11	.289	.350	.546	.896
2016 Ari	NL	17	31	6	0	1	2	(2 0)	14	5	7	5	2	0	13	1	0	0	0	0	1	.194	.265	.452	.716

Kevin Jepsen

Pitches: R Bats: R Pos: RP-58 **Ht: 6'3" Wt: 235 Born: 7/26/1984 Age: 32**

Year Team	Lg	HOW MUCH HE PITCHED						WHAT HE GAVE UP												THE RESULTS							
		G	GS	CG	GF	IP	BFP	H	R	ER	HR	SH	SF	HB	TBB	IBB	SO	WP	Bk	W	L	Pct	Sh	Sv-Op	Hld	ERC	ERA
2008 LAA	AL	9	0	0	0	8.1	36	8	5	4	0	0	0	0	4	0	7	1	0	0	1	.000	0	0-0	3	3.46	4.32
2009 LAA	AL	54	0	0	13	54.2	237	63	33	30	2	0	2	0	19	2	48	6	0	6	4	.600	0	1-2	17	4.27	4.94
2010 LAA	AL	68	0	0	4	59.0	253	54	26	26	2	4	2	2	29	5	61	8	0	2	4	.333	0	0-4	27	3.53	3.97
2011 LAA	AL	16	0	0	5	13.0	68	21	11	11	2	1	1	1	9	4	6	5	0	1	2	.333	0	0-1	2	9.45	7.62
2012 LAA	AL	49	0	0	11	44.2	178	39	17	15	3	3	1	2	12	1	38	1	0	3	2	.600	0	2-4	18	2.93	3.02
2013 LAA	AL	45	0	0	7	36.0	164	41	21	18	3	3	1	1	14	4	36	2	0	1	3	.250	0	0-2	8	4.50	4.50
2014 LAA	AL	74	0	0	10	65.0	260	45	19	19	4	0	1	2	23	2	75	5	0	2	4	.333	0	2-4	22	2.16	2.63
2015 2 Tms	AL	75	0	0	23	69.2	285	52	20	18	5	1	5	0	27	1	59	5	0	3	6	.333	0	15-20	24	2.48	2.33
2016 2 Tms	AL	58	0	0	24	49.2	224	62	35	33	12	0	6	0	21	2	35	4	0	2	6	.250	0	7-11	5	6.77	5.98
15 LAA	AL	46	0	0	6	41.2	176	34	15	13	4	1	5	0	20	1	34	2	0	2	5	.286	0	5-9	22	3.31	2.81
15 Min	AL	29	0	0	17	28.0	109	18	5	5	1	0	0	0	7	0	25	3	0	1	1	.500	0	10-11	2	1.46	1.61
16 Min	AL	33	0	0	19	30.2	141	42	22	21	7	0	3	0	12	1	22	2	0	2	5	.286	0	7-11	2	7.33	6.16
16 Tex	AL	25	0	0	5	19.0	83	20	13	12	5	0	3	0	9	1	13	2	0	0	1	.000	0	0-0	3	5.90	5.68
Postseason		8	0	0	0	7.0	38	12	6	5	2	0	0	0	6	1	4	0	0	1	1	.500	0	0-0	1	12.28	6.43
9 ML YEARS		448	0	0	97	400.0	1705	385	187	174	33	12	19	8	158	21	365	37	0	18	30	.375	0	27-48	126	3.74	3.92

Ubaldo Jimenez

Pitches: R Bats: R Pos: SP-25; RP-4   ooh-BALL-doh   Ht: 6'5" Wt: 210 Born: 1/22/1984 Age: 33

Year	Team	Lg	G	GS	CG	GF	IP	BFP	H	R	ER	HR	SH	SF	HB	TBB	IBB	SO	WP	Bk	W	L	Pct	Sh	Sv-Op	Hld	ERC	ERA
2006	Col	NL	2	1	0	0	7.2	30	5	4	3	1	0	0	0	3	0	3	0	0	0	0	-	0	0-0	0	2.48	3.52
2007	Col	NL	15	15	0	0	82.0	354	70	46	39	10	3	1	6	37	4	68	3	0	4	4	.500	0	0-0	0	3.80	4.28
2008	Col	NL	34	34	1	0	198.2	868	182	97	88	11	7	4	10	103	4	172	16	0	12	12	.500	0	0-0	0	3.92	3.99
2009	Col	NL	33	33	1	0	218.0	914	183	87	84	13	15	6	10	85	6	198	8	3	15	12	.556	0	0-0	0	3.03	3.47
2010	Col	NL	33	33	4	0	221.2	894	164	73	71	10	7	1	9	92	7	214	16	1	19	8	.704	2	0-0	0	2.57	2.88
2011	2 Tms		32	32	2	0	188.1	822	186	111	98	17	2	2	9	78	5	180	8	0	10	13	.435	1	0-0	0	4.13	4.68
2012	Cle	AL	31	31	0	0	176.2	805	190	116	106	25	2	3	8	95	3	143	16	1	9	17	.346	0	0-0	0	5.55	5.40
2013	Cle	AL	32	32	0	0	182.2	777	163	75	67	16	1	11	3	80	0	194	8	0	13	9	.591	0	0-0	0	3.61	3.30
2014	Bal	AL	25	22	0	0	125.1	553	113	68	67	14	3	1	4	77	0	116	4	0	6	9	.400	0	0-0	1	4.62	4.81
2015	Bal	AL	32	32	0	0	184.0	791	182	89	84	20	1	4	11	68	1	168	6	0	12	10	.545	0	0-0	0	4.21	4.11
2016	Bal	AL	29	25	1	2	142.1	638	150	93	86	16	1	1	3	72	1	125	5	1	8	12	.400	0	1-1	0	4.97	5.44
11	Col	NL	21	21	2	0	123.0	532	118	68	61	10	2	2	7	51	5	118	6	0	6	9	.400	0	1-0	0	3.94	4.46
11	Cle	AL	11	11	0	0	65.1	290	68	43	37	7	0	0	2	27	0	62	2	0	4	4	.500	0	0-0	0	4.48	5.10
	Postseason		5	5	0	0	28.0	123	26	11	11	3	0	1	1	16	2	24	1	0	0	2	.000	0	0-0	0	4.47	3.54
11 ML YEARS			298	290	9	2	1727.1	7446	1588	859	793	153	42	34	73	790	31	1581	90	6	108	106	.505	3	1-1	1	3.92	4.13

Chris Johnson

Bats: R Throws: R Pos: 1B-81;PH-40;3B-11;LF-2   Ht: 6'3" Wt: 225 Born: 10/1/1984 Age: 32

Year	Team	Lg	G	AB	H	2B	3B	HR	(Hm	Rd)	TB	R	RBI	RC	TBB	IBB	SO	HBP	SH	SF	SB	CS	GDP	Avg	OBP	Slg	OPS
2009	Hou	NL	11	22	2	0	0	0	(0	0)	2	1	1	0	1	0	6	0	0	0	0	0	0	.091	.130	.091	.221
2010	Hou	NL	94	341	105	22	2	11	(6	5)	164	40	52	55	15	2	91	2	0	4	3	0	8	.308	.337	.481	.818
2011	Hou	NL	107	378	95	21	3	7	(2	5)	143	32	42	42	16	3	97	7	0	4	2	2	2	.251	.291	.378	.670
2012	2 Tms	NL	136	488	137	28	5	15	(8	7)	220	48	76	75	31	2	132	4	1	4	5	1	18	.281	.326	.451	.777
2013	Atl	NL	142	514	165	34	0	12	(4	8)	235	54	68	77	29	5	116	2	0	2	0	0	20	.321	.358	.457	.816
2014	Atl	NL	153	582	153	27	0	10	(5	5)	210	43	58	59	23	2	159	2	2	2	6	0	23	.263	.292	.361	.653
2015	2 Tms	NL	83	243	62	11	0	3	(3	0)	82	18	18	22	10	0	74	1	0	1	2	1	5	.255	.286	.337	.624
2016	Mia	NL	113	243	54	11	0	5	(1	4)	80	20	24	17	19	2	78	1	1	0	0	0	13	.222	.281	.329	.611
12	Hou	NL	92	341	95	21	3	8	(8	0)	146	36	41	47	23	1	92	3	0	1	4	1	12	.279	.329	.428	.757
12	Ari	NL	44	147	42	7	2	7	(0	7)	74	12	35	28	8	1	40	1	1	3	1	0	6	.286	.321	.503	.824
15	Atl	NL	56	153	36	7	0	2	(2	0)	49	12	11	11	7	0	49	1	0	1	2	1	3	.235	.272	.320	.592
15	Cle	AL	27	90	26	4	0	1	(1	0)	33	6	7	11	3	0	25	0	0	0	0	0	2	.289	.312	.367	.678
	Postseason		4	16	7	0	0	0	(0	0)	7	1	5	4	0	0	5	0	0	0	0	0	0	.438	.438	.438	.875
8 ML YEARS			839	2811	773	154	10	63	(29	34)	1136	256	339	347	144	16	753	19	4	17	18	4	89	.275	.313	.404	.717

Erik Johnson

Pitches: R Bats: R Pos: SP-6   Ht: 6'3" Wt: 230 Born: 12/30/1989 Age: 27

Year	Team	Lg	G	GS	CG	GF	IP	BFP	H	R	ER	HR	SH	SF	HB	TBB	IBB	SO	WP	Bk	W	L	Pct	Sh	Sv-Op	Hld	ERC	ERA
2016	Charllt*	AAA	8	8	1	0	49.0	204	44	18	16	7	1	2	0	17	0	35	5	0	2	1	.667	0	0- -	-	3.60	2.94
2013	CWS	AL	5	5	0	0	27.2	128	32	16	10	5	0	2	1	11	0	18	2	0	3	2	.600	0	0-0	0	5.55	3.25
2014	CWS	AL	5	5	0	0	23.2	109	27	18	17	1	0	1	2	15	1	18	3	0	1	1	.500	0	0-0	0	5.82	6.46
2015	CWS	AL	6	6	0	0	35.0	151	32	14	13	8	1	3	1	17	0	30	3	0	3	1	.750	0	0-0	0	5.01	3.34
2016	2 Tms		6	6	0	0	31.1	146	46	29	29	14	0	3	0	11	0	21	2	0	0	6	.000	0	0-0	0	9.73	8.33
16	CWS	AL	2	2	0	0	11.2	53	14	9	9	5	0	1	0	6	0	11	0	0	0	2	.000	0	0-0	0	8.53	6.94
16	SD	NL	4	4	0	0	19.2	93	32	20	20	9	0	2	0	5	0	10	2	0	0	4	.000	0	0-0	0	10.46	9.15
4 ML YEARS			22	22	0	0	117.2	534	137	77	69	28	1	9	4	54	1	87	10	0	7	10	.412	0	0-0	0	6.52	5.28

Jim Johnson

Pitches: R Bats: R Pos: RP-65   Ht: 6'6" Wt: 250 Born: 6/27/1983 Age: 34

Year	Team	Lg	G	GS	CG	GF	IP	BFP	H	R	ER	HR	SH	SF	HB	TBB	IBB	SO	WP	Bk	W	L	Pct	Sh	Sv-Op	Hld	ERC	ERA
2006	Bal	AL	1	1	0	0	3.0	21	9	8	8	1	0	1	1	3	0	0	0	0	0	1	.000	0	0-0	0	26.81	24.00
2007	Bal	AL	1	0	0	1	2.0	11	3	2	2	1	0	1	0	2	0	1	0	0	0	0	-	0	0-0	0	8.58	9.00
2008	Bal	AL	54	0	0	18	68.2	281	54	18	17	0	2	1	3	28	3	38	1	1	2	4	.333	0	1-1	19	2.45	2.23
2009	Bal	AL	64	0	0	29	70.0	300	73	32	32	8	2	2	3	23	3	49	2	1	4	6	.400	0	10-16	14	4.28	4.11
2010	Bal	AL	26	0	0	6	26.1	117	32	11	10	2	3	0	1	5	1	22	4	0	1	1	.500	0	1-6	11	4.26	3.42
2011	Bal	AL	69	0	0	20	91.0	366	80	30	27	5	4	2	2	21	3	58	2	1	6	5	.545	0	9-14	18	2.58	2.67
2012	Bal	AL	71	0	0	63	68.2	269	55	21	19	3	1	0	3	15	1	41	1	0	2	1	.667	0	51-54	0	2.22	2.49
2013	Bal	AL	74	0	0	63	70.1	291	72	26	23	5	2	0	7	18	4	56	2	0	3	8	.273	0	50-59	0	3.89	2.94
2014	2 Tms	AL	54	0	0	21	53.1	263	69	46	42	5	3	2	6	35	6	42	4	0	5	2	.714	0	2-3	2	7.13	7.09
2015	2 Tms	AL	72	0	0	15	66.2	291	77	36	33	5	3	3	5	20	2	50	3	0	2	6	.250	0	10-17	25	4.70	4.46
2016	Atl	NL	65	0	0	36	64.2	266	57	23	22	3	0	1	3	20	0	68	6	0	2	6	.250	0	20-23	1	2.95	3.06
14	Oak	AL	38	0	0	18	40.1	200	60	33	32	5	2	2	3	23	3	28	4	0	4	2	.667	0	2-3	2	8.28	7.14
14	Det	AL	16	0	0	3	13.0	63	9	13	10	0	1	0	3	12	3	14	0	0	1	0	1.000	0	0-0	0	3.86	6.92
15	Atl	NL	49	0	0	13	48.0	196	45	14	12	2	3	2	1	14	2	33	2	0	2	3	.400	0	9-13	20	3.02	2.25
15	LAD	NL	23	0	0	2	18.2	95	32	22	21	3	0	1	2	6	0	17	1	0	0	3	.000	0	1-4	5	9.81	10.13
	Postseason		5	0	0	3	5.1	25	8	6	5	2	0	0	0	1	0	4	0	0	0	1	.000	0	2-3	0	8.18	8.44
11 ML YEARS			551	1	0	272	584.2	2476	581	253	235	37	20	13	34	190	23	425	25	3	27	40	.403	0	154-193	97	3.70	3.62

Kelly Johnson

Bats: L **Throws:** R **Pos:** PH-53;2B-52;3B-21;LF-15;1B-3;SS-1 **Ht:** 6'1" **Wt:** 200 **Born:** 2/22/1982 **Age:** 35

									BATTING										RUNNING			AVERAGES			
Year	Team	Lg	G	AB	H	2B	3B	HR	(Hm | Rd)	TB	R	RBI	RC	TBB	IBB	SO	HBP	SH	SF	SB	CS	GDP	Avg	OBP	Slg	OPS
2005	Atl	NL	87	290	70	12	3	9	(2 | 7)	115	46	40	41	40	1	75	1	2	1	2	1	11	.241	.334	.397	.731
2007	Atl	NL	147	521	144	26	10	16	(5 | 11)	238	91	68	87	79	3	117	4	2	2	9	5	8	.276	.375	.457	.831
2008	Atl	NL	150	547	157	39	6	12	(5 | 7)	244	86	69	87	52	2	113	2	9	4	11	6	3	.287	.349	.446	.795
2009	Atl	NL	106	303	68	20	3	8	(4 | 4)	118	47	29	31	32	1	54	3	6	2	7	2	4	.224	.303	.389	.692
2010	Ari	NL	154	585	166	36	5	26	(16 | 10)	290	93	71	92	79	1	148	2	3	2	13	7	12	.284	.370	.496	.865
2011	2 Tms		147	545	121	27	7	21	(10 | 11)	225	75	58	70	60	2	163	4	4	0	16	6	3	.222	.304	.413	.717
2012	Tor	AL	142	507	114	19	2	16	(10 | 6)	185	61	55	63	62	4	159	5	2	4	14	2	8	.225	.313	.365	.678
2013	TB	AL	118	366	86	12	2	16	(6 | 10)	150	41	52	49	35	1	99	3	0	3	7	4	5	.235	.305	.410	.715
2014	3 Tms	AL	106	265	57	14	2	7	(5 | 2)	96	29	27	30	29	0	71	2	0	1	2	2	3	.215	.296	.362	.659
2015	2 Tms	NL	111	310	82	11	0	14	(7 | 7)	135	38	47	41	23	2	81	0	0	1	2	1	8	.265	.314	.435	.750
2016	2 Tms	NL	131	304	75	14	0	10	(4 | 6)	119	25	34	37	25	2	65	2	0	2	4	0	6	.247	.306	.391	.698
11	Ari	NL	114	430	90	23	5	18	(10 | 8)	177	59	49	53	44	2	132	3	4	0	13	3	3	.209	.287	.412	.699
11	Tor	AL	33	115	31	4	2	3	(0 | 3)	48	16	9	17	16	0	31	1	0	0	3	3	0	.270	.364	.417	.781
14	NYY	AL	77	201	44	9	2	6	(5 | 1)	75	21	22	25	23	0	50	2	0	1	2	1	2	.219	.304	.373	.677
14	Bos	AL	10	25	4	1	0	0	(0 | 0)	5	1	1	0	0	0	10	0	0	0	0	0	1	.160	.160	.200	.360
14	Bal	AL	19	39	9	4	0	1	(0 | 1)	16	7	4	5	6	0	11	0	0	0	0	1	0	.231	.333	.410	.744
15	Atl	NL	62	182	50	5	0	9	(5 | 4)	82	20	34	27	13	1	43	0	0	1	1	1	4	.275	.321	.451	.772
15	NYM	NL	49	128	32	6	0	5	(2 | 3)	53	18	13	14	10	1	38	0	0	0	1	0	4	.250	.304	.414	.718
16	Atl	NL	49	121	26	6	0	1	(0 | 1)	35	8	10	9	10	1	25	0	0	1	1	0	4	.215	.273	.289	.562
16	NYM	NL	82	183	49	8	0	9	(4 | 5)	84	17	24	28	15	1	40	2	0	1	3	0	2	.268	.328	.459	.787
	Postseason		17	16	2	0	1	0	(0 | 0)	4	0	0	1	1	0	6	1	0	0	0	0	0	.125	.222	.250	.472
	11 ML YEARS		1399	4543	1140	230	40	155	(74 | 81)	1915	632	550	628	516	19	1145	28	28	22	87	36	70	.251	.330	.422	.751

Micah Johnson

Bats: L **Throws:** R **Pos:** PH-5;2B-3;LF-1;PR-1 **Ht:** 6'0" **Wt:** 210 **Born:** 12/18/1990 **Age:** 26

									BATTING										RUNNING			AVERAGES			
Year	Team	Lg	G	AB	H	2B	3B	HR	(Hm | Rd)	TB	R	RBI	RC	TBB	IBB	SO	HBP	SH	SF	SB	CS	GDP	Avg	OBP	Slg	OPS
2012	Gr Falls	R+	69	271	74	10	5	4	(- | -)	106	49	25	44	43	1	74	1	2	0	19	6	9	.273	.375	.391	.766
2013	2 Tms	Low	126	515	162	24	15	7	(- | -)	237	104	57	96	50	2	94	4	8	2	83	26	3	.315	.378	.460	.838
2014	Brham	AA	37	146	48	9	1	3	(- | -)	68	18	16	28	21	0	27	1	1	1	10	7	1	.329	.414	.466	.880
2014	Charltt	AAA	65	273	75	10	5	2	(- | -)	101	30	28	33	16	0	42	1	9	3	12	6	4	.275	.314	.370	.684
2015	Charltt	AAA	78	311	98	17	3	8	(- | -)	145	54	36	58	32	0	63	0	4	8	28	7	4	.315	.375	.466	.841
2016	OkCity	AAA	120	464	121	23	3	5	(- | -)	165	72	37	56	41	0	105	1	8	1	26	11	8	.261	.321	.356	.677
2015	CWS	AL	36	100	23	4	0	0	(0 | 0)	27	10	4	8	9	0	30	2	2	0	3	2	0	.230	.306	.270	.576
2016	LAD	NL	7	6	1	0	0	0	(0 | 0)	1	1	0	0	0	0	1	0	0	0	0	0	0	.167	.167	.167	.333
	2 ML YEARS		43	106	24	4	0	0	(0 | 0)	28	11	4	8	9	0	31	2	2	0	3	2	0	.226	.299	.264	.563

Steve Johnson

Pitches: R **Bats:** R **Pos:** RP-16 **Ht:** 6'1" **Wt:** 220 **Born:** 8/31/1987 **Age:** 29

			HOW MUCH HE PITCHED						WHAT HE GAVE UP										THE RESULTS							
Year	Team	Lg	G	GS	CG	GF	IP	BFP	H	R	ER	HR	SH	SF	HB	TBB	IBB	SO	WP	Bk	W	L	Pct	Sh	Sv-Op	Hld	ERC	ERA
2016	Tacom*	AAA	11	0	0	1	22.0	84	14	5	5	1	0	0	2	6	0	26	2	0	3	0	1.000	0	0- -	-	1.86	2.05
2012	Bal	AL	12	4	0	3	38.1	151	23	9	9	4	1	0	0	18	1	46	1	0	4	0	1.000	0	0-0	0	2.31	2.11
2013	Bal	AL	9	1	0	2	15.2	73	14	13	13	2	0	0	0	13	1	20	1	0	1	1	.500	0	0-0	1	5.23	7.47
2015	Bal	AL	6	0	0	2	5.1	29	8	6	6	2	0	0	0	5	0	3	1	0	0	0	-	0	0-0	0	12.01	10.13
2016	Sea	AL	16	0	0	12	16.2	75	13	8	8	3	0	1	0	11	0	17	1	0	1	0	1.000	0	0-0	1	4.28	4.32
	4 ML YEARS		43	5	0	19	76.0	328	58	36	36	11	1	1	0	47	2	86	4	0	6	1	.857	0	0-0	2	3.87	4.26

Adam Jones

Bats: R **Throws:** R **Pos:** CF-152 **Ht:** 6'2" **Wt:** 215 **Born:** 8/1/1985 **Age:** 31

									BATTING										RUNNING			AVERAGES			
Year	Team	Lg	G	AB	H	2B	3B	HR	(Hm	Rd)	TB	R	RBI	RC	TBB	IBB	SO	HBP	SH	SF	SB	CS	GDP	Avg	OBP	Slg	OPS
2006	Sea	AL	32	74	16	4	0	1	(0	1)	23	6	8	4	2	0	22	0	0	0	3	1	3	.216	.237	.311	.548
2007	Sea	AL	41	65	16	2	1	2	(1	1)	26	16	4	5	4	0	21	1	1	0	2	1	0	.246	.300	.400	.700
2008	Bal	AL	132	477	129	21	7	9	(4	5)	191	61	57	56	23	0	108	7	2	5	10	3	12	.270	.311	.400	.711
2009	Bal	AL	119	473	131	22	3	19	(11	8)	216	83	70	71	36	3	93	7	0	3	10	4	13	.277	.335	.457	.792
2010	Bal	AL	149	581	165	25	5	19	(9	10)	257	76	69	72	23	1	119	13	2	2	7	7	17	.284	.325	.442	.767
2011	Bal	AL	151	567	159	26	2	25	(19	6)	264	68	83	77	29	2	113	9	1	12	12	4	16	.280	.319	.466	.785
2012	Bal	AL	162	648	186	39	3	32	(15	17)	327	103	82	101	34	0	126	13	0	2	16	7	15	.287	.334	.505	.839
2013	Bal	AL	160	653	186	35	1	33	(17	16)	322	100	108	101	25	4	136	8	0	3	14	5	15	.285	.318	.493	.811
2014	Bal	AL	159	644	181	30	2	29	(14	15)	302	88	96	92	19	1	133	12	0	7	7	1	11	.281	.311	.469	.780
2015	Bal	AL	137	546	147	25	3	27	(17	10)	259	74	82	73	24	3	102	8	0	3	3	1	21	.269	.308	.474	.782
2016	Bal	AL	152	619	164	19	0	29	(14	15)	270	86	83	82	39	2	115	5	1	8	2	0	13	.265	.310	.436	.746
	Postseason		13	53	8	0	0	1	(1	0)	11	6	4	3	3	0	15	1	0	1	1	0	1	.151	.207	.208	.414
	11 ML YEARS		1394	5347	1480	248	27	225	(121	104)	2457	761	742	734	258	16	1088	83	7	45	86	32	136	.277	.318	.460	.777

JaCoby Jones

Bats: R **Throws:** R **Pos:** 3B-6;CF-5;DH-2;PH-2;PR-2 **Ht:** 6'2" **Wt:** 205 **Born:** 5/10/1992 **Age:** 25

									BATTING										RUNNING			AVERAGES			
Year	Team	Lg	G	AB	H	2B	3B	HR	(Hm	Rd)	TB	R	RBI	RC	TBB	IBB	SO	HBP	SH	SF	SB	CS	GDP	Avg	OBP	Slg	OPS
2013	Jmstwn	A-	15	61	19	2	2	1	(-	-)	28	14	10	10	3	0	14	2	0	1	3	2	1	.311	.358	.459	.817
2014	WV	A	117	445	128	21	3	23	(-	-)	224	72	70	79	33	0	132	12	3	8	17	9	8	.288	.347	.503	.851
2015	Bradtn	A+	93	379	96	18	3	10	(-	-)	150	48	58	50	31	0	113	4	4	5	14	4	7	.253	.313	.396	.708

Year Team	Lg	G	AB	H	2B	3B	HR	(Hm	Rd)	TB	R	RBI	RC	TBB	IBB	SO	HBP	SH	SF	SB	CS	GDP	Avg	OBP	Slg	OPS
2015 Erie	AA	37	136	34	7	2	6	(-	-)	63	26	20	23	17	0	52	2	0	5	10	3	4	.250	.331	.463	.794
2016 Erie	AA	20	77	24	6	2	4	(-	-)	46	11	20	17	10	0	23	1	0	1	2	1	0	.312	.393	.597	.991
2016 Toledo	AAA	79	292	71	14	5	3	(-	-)	104	33	23	34	25	1	97	4	0	3	11	4	7	.243	.309	.356	.665
2016 Det	AL	13	28	6	3	0	0	(0	0)	9	3	2	2	0	0	12	0	0	0	0	0	1	.214	.214	.321	.536

Nate Jones

Pitches: R Bats: R Pos: RP-71　　　　**Ht: 6'5" Wt: 220 Born: 1/28/1986 Age: 31**

Year Team	Lg	G	GS	CG	GF	IP	BFP	H	R	ER	HR	SH	SF	HB	TBB	IBB	SO	WP	Bk	W	L	Pct	Sh	Sv-Op	Hld	ERC	ERA
2012 CWS	AL	65	0	0	11	71.2	301	67	19	19	4	2	4	1	32	3	65	5	0	8	0	1.000	0	0-3	7	3.67	2.39
2013 CWS	AL	70	0	0	17	78.0	315	69	40	36	5	3	6	1	26	1	89	8	1	4	5	.444	0	0-4	16	3.09	4.15
2014 CWS	AL	2	0	0	0	0.0	5	2	4	4	0	0	0	0	3	0	0	0	0	0	0	-	0	0-1	0	-	-
2015 CWS	AL	19	0	0	3	19.0	72	12	7	7	5	2	0	0	6	0	27	0	0	2	2	.500	0	0-1	6	2.87	3.32
2016 CWS	AL	71	0	0	11	70.2	274	48	20	18	7	2	2	3	15	3	80	7	0	5	3	.625	0	3-12	28	1.87	2.29
5 ML YEARS		227	0	0	42	239.1	967	198	90	84	21	9	12	5	82	7	261	20	1	19	10	.655	0	3-21	57	2.96	3.16

Caleb Joseph

Bats: R Throws: R Pos: C-48;1B-2　　　　**Ht: 6'3" Wt: 180 Born: 6/18/1986 Age: 31**

Year Team	Lg	G	AB	H	2B	3B	HR	(Hm	Rd)	TB	R	RBI	RC	TBB	IBB	SO	HBP	SH	SF	SB	CS	GDP	Avg	OBP	Slg	OPS
2014 Bal	AL	82	246	51	16	3	9	(4	5)	87	22	28	22	17	0	69	3	6	3	0	1	6	.207	.264	.354	.618
2015 Bal	AL	100	320	75	16	1	11	(5	6)	126	38	49	44	27	2	72	3	3	1	0	0	7	.234	.299	.394	.693
2016 Bal	AL	49	132	23	3	0	0	(0	0)	26	7	0	0	7	0	28	0	2	0	0	0	6	.174	.216	.197	.413
Postseason		3	9	2	0	0	0	(0	0)	2	0	1	1	0	0	4	0	0	1	0	0	0	.222	.200	.222	.422
3 ML YEARS		231	698	149	28	1	20	(9	11)	239	67	77	66	51	2	169	6	11	4	0	1	19	.213	.271	.342	.614

Tommy Joseph

Bats: R Throws: R Pos: 1B-97;PH-25　　　　**Ht: 6'1" Wt: 255 Born: 7/16/1991 Age: 25**

Year Team	Lg	G	AB	H	2B	3B	HR	(Hm	Rd)	TB	R	RBI	RC	TBB	IBB	SO	HBP	SH	SF	SB	CS	GDP	Avg	OBP	Slg	OPS
2012 Rchmd	AA	80	304	79	16	0	8	(-	-)	119	32	38	38	25	0	64	1	0	5	0	3	9	.260	.313	.391	.705
2012 Rdng	AA	28	100	25	8	0	3	(-	-)	42	12	10	14	9	0	32	3	1	1	0	1	4	.250	.327	.420	.747
2013 LV	AAA	21	67	14	1	0	3	(-	-)	24	6	14	6	4	0	15	1	0	0	0	1	2	.209	.264	.358	.622
2013 2 Tms	Low	12	45	5	2	0	0	(-	-)	7	0	1	0	2	0	14	0	0	0	0	0	1	.111	.149	.156	.304
2014 Rdng	AA	21	78	22	4	1	5	(-	-)	43	8	19	15	5	0	13	3	0	1	0	0	2	.282	.345	.551	.896
2015 LV	AAA	45	166	32	9	0	3	(-	-)	50	9	18	10	3	0	33	3	2	1	0	0	6	.193	.220	.301	.521
2015 Phillies	R	13	33	16	3	0	3	(-	-)	28	6	10	13	7	0	1	0	0	0	0	0	1	.485	.585	.848	1.434
2016 LV	AAA	27	95	33	7	0	6	(-	-)	58	11	17	20	4	0	12	0	0	1	0	1	5	.347	.370	.611	.981
2016 Phi	NL	107	315	81	15	0	21	(10	11)	159	47	47	37	22	0	75	4	0	6	1	1	11	.257	.308	.505	.813

Matt Joyce

Bats: L Throws: R Pos: PH-81;RF-43;LF-26;DH-4　　　　**Ht: 6'2" Wt: 200 Born: 8/3/1984 Age: 32**

Year Team	Lg	G	AB	H	2B	3B	HR	(Hm	Rd)	TB	R	RBI	RC	TBB	IBB	SO	HBP	SH	SF	SB	CS	GDP	Avg	OBP	Slg	OPS
2008 Det	AL	92	242	61	16	3	12	(6	6)	119	40	33	36	31	0	65	2	0	2	0	2	3	.252	.339	.492	.831
2009 TB	AL	11	32	6	1	0	3	(2	1)	16	3	7	5	3	0	7	1	0	1	1	0	0	.188	.270	.500	.770
2010 TB	AL	77	216	52	15	3	10	(4	6)	103	30	40	41	40	2	55	2	0	3	2	2	2	.241	.360	.477	.837
2011 TB	AL	141	462	128	32	2	19	(11	8)	221	69	75	77	49	9	106	4	0	7	13	1	7	.277	.347	.478	.825
2012 TB	AL	124	399	96	18	3	17	(4	13)	171	55	59	59	55	4	102	6	1	1	4	3	10	.241	.341	.429	.769
2013 TB	AL	140	413	97	22	0	18	(8	10)	173	61	47	51	59	0	87	2	0	7	7	3	8	.235	.328	.419	.747
2014 TB	AL	140	418	106	23	2	9	(2	7)	160	51	52	52	62	4	111	4	0	9	2	5	11	.254	.349	.383	.732
2015 LAA	AL	93	247	43	12	1	5	(4	1)	72	17	21	15	30	1	67	4	1	2	0	3	5	.174	.272	.291	.564
2016 Pit	NL	140	231	56	10	1	13	(10	3)	107	45	42	47	59	4	67	3	0	0	1	1	9	.242	.403	.463	.866
Postseason		12	32	5	1	0	1	(0	1)	9	1	4	3	1	0	13	0	0	0	1	0	0	.156	.182	.281	.463
9 ML YEARS		958	2660	645	149	15	106	(51	55)	1142	371	376	383	388	24	667	28	2	32	30	20	55	.242	.341	.429	.771

Aaron Judge

Bats: R Throws: R Pos: RF-27;PH-1　　　　**Ht: 6'7" Wt: 275 Born: 4/26/1992 Age: 25**

Year Team	Lg	G	AB	H	2B	3B	HR	(Hm	Rd)	TB	R	RBI	RC	TBB	IBB	SO	HBP	SH	SF	SB	CS	GDP	Avg	OBP	Slg	OPS
2014 2 Tms	Low	131	467	144	24	4	17	(-	-)	227	80	78	99	89	2	131	3	0	4	1	0	10	.308	.419	.486	.905
2015 Trntn	AA	63	250	71	16	3	12	(-	-)	129	36	44	46	24	1	70	3	0	3	1	0	9	.284	.350	.516	.866
2015 S-WB	AAA	61	228	51	10	0	8	(-	-)	85	27	28	28	29	0	74	0	0	3	6	2	6	.224	.308	.373	.680
2016 S-WB	AAA	93	352	95	18	1	19	(-	-)	172	62	65	66	47	0	98	8	0	3	5	0	7	.270	.366	.489	.854
2016 NYY	AL	27	84	15	2	0	4	(3	1)	29	10	10	6	9	0	42	1	0	1	0	1	2	.179	.263	.345	.608

Taylor Jungmann

Pitches: R **Bats:** R **Pos:** SP-6; RP-2 YOUNG-men **Ht:** 6'6" **Wt:** 210 **Born:** 12/18/1989 **Age:** 27

Year	Team	Lg	G	GS	CG	GF	IP	BFP	H	R	ER	HR	SH	SF	HB	TBB	IBB	SO	WP	Bk	W	L	Pct	Sh	Sv-Op	Hld	ERC	ERA
2012	BrvdCt	A+	26	26	1	0	153.0	656	159	70	60	7	3	0	11	46	0	99	10	2	11	6	.647	0	0- -	-	3.83	3.53
2013	Hntsvl	AA	26	26	0	0	139.1	595	117	75	67	11	5	2	10	73	1	82	9	1	10	10	.500	0	0- -	-	3.86	4.33
2014	Hntsvl	AA	9	9	0	0	52.0	220	52	21	16	4	5	0	3	15	0	46	6	0	4	4	.500	0	0- -	-	3.73	2.77
2014	Nashv	AAA	19	18	0	0	101.2	435	88	48	45	7	2	1	12	46	0	101	10	1	8	6	.571	0	0- -	-	3.83	3.98
2015	ColSpr	AAA	11	9	0	0	59.1	258	61	44	42	2	0	1	4	29	0	54	10	0	2	3	.400	0	0- -	-	4.50	6.37
2016	ColSpr	AAA	8	8	0	0	31.0	171	39	37	34	6	2	1	8	35	0	24	4	0	1	3	.250	0	0- -	-	10.90	9.87
2016	Biloxi	AA	13	13	0	0	75.1	307	53	24	21	2	1	2	2	35	0	81	7	0	3	4	.429	0	0- -	-	2.41	2.51
2015	Mil	NL	21	21	1	0	119.1	501	106	55	50	11	2	5	8	47	1	107	8	0	9	8	.529	0	0-0	-	3.69	3.77
2016	Mil	NL	8	6	0	2	26.2	126	30	24	23	4	1	2	3	17	1	18	0	0	0	5	.000	0	0-0	-	6.66	7.76
	2 ML YEARS		29	27	1	2	146.0	627	136	79	73	15	3	7	11	64	2	125	8	0	9	13	.409	0	0-0	0	4.20	4.50

Tommy Kahnle

Pitches: R **Bats:** R **Pos:** RP-29 KAIN-lee **Ht:** 6'1" **Wt:** 235 **Born:** 8/7/1989 **Age:** 27

Year	Team	Lg	G	GS	CG	GF	IP	BFP	H	R	ER	HR	SH	SF	HB	TBB	IBB	SO	WP	Bk	W	L	Pct	Sh	Sv-Op	Hld	ERC	ERA
2016	Charllt*	AAA	23	0	0	8	27.0	109	17	9	9	0	0	0	1	12	2	36	2	0	1	1	.500	0	7- -	-	1.75	3.00
2014	Col	NL	54	0	0	7	68.2	285	51	39	32	7	2	3	1	31	2	63	7	0	2	1	.667	0	0-2	8	2.91	4.19
2015	Col	NL	36	0	0	8	33.1	155	31	22	18	3	1	2	0	28	1	39	3	0	0	1	.000	0	2-3	10	5.31	4.86
2016	CWS	AL	29	0	0	12	27.1	119	21	8	8	2	0	0	0	20	3	25	3	0	0	1	.000	0	1-2	4	3.74	2.63
	3 ML YEARS		119	0	0	27	129.1	559	103	69	58	12	3	5	1	79	6	127	13	0	2	3	.400	0	3-7	22	3.67	4.04

Ryan Kalish

Bats: L **Throws:** L **Pos:** PH-6;LF-2;RF-1 KAY-lish **Ht:** 6'0" **Wt:** 215 **Born:** 3/28/1988 **Age:** 29

Year	Team	Lg	G	AB	H	2B	3B	HR	(Hm	Rd)	TB	R	RBI	RC	TBB	IBB	SO	HBP	SH	SF	SB	CS	GDP	Avg	OBP	Slg	OPS
2016	Iowa*	AAA	21	57	21	4	2	0	(-	-)	29	15	4	14	10	0	9	2	0	1	3	1	0	.368	.471	.509	.980
2010	Bos	AL	53	163	41	11	1	4	(2	2)	66	26	24	23	12	0	38	1	2	1	10	1	5	.252	.305	.405	.710
2012	Bos	AL	36	96	22	3	0	0	(0	0)	25	12	5	3	6	0	26	0	0	1	3	2	4	.229	.272	.260	.532
2014	ChC	NL	57	121	30	4	4	0	(0	0)	42	13	5	9	8	1	28	0	1	0	3	2	3	.248	.295	.347	.642
2016	ChC	NL	7	7	2	0	0	0	(0	0)	2	1	2	2	1	0	1	1	0	0	0	0	0	.286	.444	.286	.730
	4 ML YEARS		153	387	95	18	5	4	(2	2)	135	52	36	37	27	1	92	2	4	2	16	5	12	.245	.297	.349	.645

Jung Ho Kang

Bats: R **Throws:** R **Pos:** 3B-92;PH-13;DH-1 GAHNG **Ht:** 6'0" **Wt:** 220 **Born:** 4/5/1987 **Age:** 30

Year	Team	Lg	G	AB	H	2B	3B	HR	(Hm	Rd)	TB	R	RBI	RC	TBB	IBB	SO	HBP	SH	SF	SB	CS	GDP	Avg	OBP	Slg	OPS
2016	Indy	AAA	16	48	7	0	0	2	(-	-)	13	5	7	3	7	0	11	0	0	2	0	1	0	.146	.246	.271	.516
2015	Pit	NL	126	421	121	24	2	15	(5	10)	194	60	58	60	28	0	99	17	0	1	5	4	10	.287	.355	.461	.816
2016	Pit	NL	103	318	81	19	0	21	(10	11)	163	45	62	47	36	1	79	14	0	2	3	1	11	.255	.354	.513	.867
	2 ML YEARS		229	739	202	43	2	36	(15	21)	357	105	120	107	64	1	178	31	0	3	8	5	21	.273	.355	.483	.838

Nathan Karns

Pitches: R **Bats:** R **Pos:** SP-15; RP-7 **Ht:** 6'3" **Wt:** 225 **Born:** 11/25/1987 **Age:** 29

Year	Team	Lg	G	GS	CG	GF	IP	BFP	H	R	ER	HR	SH	SF	HB	TBB	IBB	SO	WP	Bk	W	L	Pct	Sh	Sv-Op	Hld	ERC	ERA
2013	Was	NL	3	3	0	0	12.0	61	17	11	10	5	1	0	1	6	0	11	0	0	0	1	.000	0	0-0	0	9.80	7.50
2014	TB	AL	2	2	0	0	12.0	49	7	6	6	3	0	0	2	4	0	13	0	0	1	1	.500	0	0-0	0	3.12	4.50
2015	TB	AL	27	26	0	0	147.0	621	132	62	60	19	3	4	5	56	1	145	15	0	7	5	.583	0	0-0	0	3.77	3.67
2016	Sea	AL	22	15	0	2	94.1	417	95	55	54	11	0	2	3	45	1	101	5	1	6	2	.750	0	1-1	0	4.65	5.15
	4 ML YEARS		54	46	0	2	265.1	1148	251	134	130	38	4	6	11	111	2	270	20	1	14	9	.609	0	1-1	0	4.29	4.41

Munenori Kawasaki

Bats: L **Throws:** R **Pos:** 2B-10;PH-5;3B-1;PR-1 moo-neh-NO-ree kah-wah-SAH-kee **Ht:** 5'11" **Wt:** 175 **Born:** 6/3/1981 **Age:** 36

Year	Team	Lg	G	AB	H	2B	3B	HR	(Hm	Rd)	TB	R	RBI	RC	TBB	IBB	SO	HBP	SH	SF	SB	CS	GDP	Avg	OBP	Slg	OPS
2016	Iowa*	AAA	102	314	80	11	2	1	(-	-)	98	42	39	41	49	4	61	1	9	5	20	8	10	.255	.352	.312	.664
2012	Sea	AL	61	104	20	1	0	0	(0	0)	21	13	7	7	8	0	18	1	2	0	2	2	2	.192	.257	.202	.459
2013	Tor	AL	96	240	55	6	5	1	(1	0)	74	27	24	28	32	0	41	4	10	3	7	1	5	.229	.326	.308	.634
2014	Tor	AL	82	240	62	7	1	0	(0	0)	71	31	17	27	22	0	49	3	8	1	1	0	3	.258	.327	.296	.623
2015	Tor	AL	23	28	6	2	0	0	(0	0)	8	6	2	4	4	0	6	0	2	0	0	1	1	.214	.313	.286	.598
2016	ChC	NL	14	21	7	2	0	0	(0	0)	9	3	1	4	4	0	5	1	0	0	2	0	1	.333	.462	.429	.890
	5 ML YEARS		276	633	150	18	6	1	(1	0)	183	80	51	68	70	0	119	9	22	4	12	4	12	.237	.320	.289	.609

Scott Kazmir

Pitches: L **Bats:** L **Pos:** SP-26 KAZ-meer **Ht:** 6'0" **Wt:** 195 **Born:** 1/24/1984 **Age:** 33

Year	Team	Lg	G	GS	CG	GF	IP	BFP	H	R	ER	HR	SH	SF	HB	TBB	IBB	SO	WP	Bk	W	L	Pct	Sh	Sv-Op	Hld	ERC	ERA
2004	TB	AL	8	8	0	0	33.1	152	33	22	21	4	0	0	2	21	0	41	3	0	2	3	.400	0	0-0	0	5.36	5.67
2005	TB	AL	32	32	0	0	186.0	818	172	90	78	12	6	9	10	100	3	174	7	1	10	9	.526	0	0-0	0	4.13	3.77
2006	TB	AL	24	24	1	0	144.2	610	132	59	52	15	0	5	2	52	3	163	6	0	10	8	.556	1	0-0	0	3.47	3.24
2007	TB	AL	34	34	0	0	206.2	887	196	91	80	18	6	3	7	89	1	239	10	0	13	9	.591	0	0-0	0	3.97	3.48

Year	Team	Lg	G	GS	CG	GF	IP	BFP	H	R	ER	HR	SH	SF	HB	TBB	IBB	SO	WP	Bk	W	L	Pct	Sh	Sv-Op	Hld	ERC	ERA
2008	TB	AL	27	27	0	0	152.1	641	123	61	59	23	4	5	4	70	2	166	5	0	12	8	.600	0	0-0	0	3.69	3.49
2009	2 Tms	AL	26	26	0	0	147.1	647	149	85	80	16	1	4	6	60	0	117	13	0	10	9	.526	0	0-0	0	4.36	4.89
2010	LAA	AL	28	28	0	0	150.0	682	158	103	99	25	3	6	12	79	2	93	6	0	9	15	.375	0	0-0	0	5.74	5.94
2011	LAA	AL	1	1	0	0	1.2	14	5	5	5	1	0	0	2	2	0	0	0	1	0	0	-	0	0-0	0	35.08	27.00
2013	Cle	AL	29	29	0	0	158.0	672	162	76	71	19	2	1	3	47	1	162	5	1	10	9	.526	0	0-0	0	4.02	4.04
2014	Oak	AL	32	32	2	0	190.1	777	171	81	75	16	5	1	4	50	1	164	9	1	15	9	.625	0	0-0	0	3.00	3.55
2015	2 Tms	AL	31	31	0	0	183.0	763	162	77	63	20	5	6	6	59	0	155	5	2	7	11	.389	0	0-0	0	3.41	3.10
2016	LAD	NL	26	26	0	0	136.1	590	133	71	69	21	2	3	7	52	3	134	5	0	10	6	.625	0	0-0	0	4.41	4.56
09	TB	AL	20	20	0	0	111.0	504	121	77	73	15	1	4	5	50	0	91	10	0	8	7	.533	0	0-0	0	5.18	5.92
09	LAA	AL	6	6	0	0	36.1	143	28	8	7	1	0	0	1	10	0	26	3	0	2	2	.500	0	0-0	0	2.13	1.73
15	Oak	AL	18	18	0	0	109.2	440	84	35	29	7	3	4	3	35	0	101	2	2	5	5	.500	0	0-0	0	2.45	2.38
15	Hou	AL	13	13	0	0	73.1	323	78	42	34	13	2	2	6	24	0	54	3	0	2	6	.250	0	0-0	0	5.01	4.17
	Postseason		9	8	0	0	41.2	197	42	25	24	6	3	2	3	27	0	30	2	0	1	2	.333	0	0-0	0	5.63	5.18
	12 ML YEARS		298	297	3	0	1689.2	7253	1596	821	752	190	34	43	68	681	16	1608	74	6	108	96	.529	1	0-0	0	4.02	4.01

Keone Kela

Pitches: R **Bats:** R **Pos:** RP-35 KEY-oh-nee KELL-uh **Ht:** 6'1" **Wt:** 215 **Born:** 4/16/1993 **Age:** 24

Year	Team	Lg	G	GS	CG	GF	IP	BFP	H	R	ER	HR	SH	SF	HB	TBB	IBB	SO	WP	Bk	W	L	Pct	Sh	Sv-Op	Hld	ERC	ERA
2012	Rngrs	R	9	0	0	1	11.1	43	4	4	2	0	0	0	1	4	0	15	0	0	0	1	.000	0	0--	-	0.91	1.59
2013	3 Tms	Low	27	0	0	9	39.0	182	43	17	15	1	1	1	6	15	0	52	7	4	5	4	.556	0	3--	-	4.49	3.46
2014	MrtlBh	A+	8	0	0	8	10.1	44	9	3	3	0	0	0	0	4	0	13	3	0	0	1	.000	0	5--	-	2.60	2.61
2014	Frisco	AA	36	0	0	23	38.2	166	22	14	8	1	0	1	2	27	0	55	4	0	2	1	.667	0	5--	-	2.53	1.86
2015	Tex	AL	68	0	0	11	60.1	243	52	18	16	4	1	0	0	18	0	68	6	1	7	5	.583	0	1-4	22	2.79	2.39
2016	Tex	AL	35	0	0	2	34.0	150	30	23	23	6	2	1	3	17	0	45	2	1	5	1	.833	0	0-1	15	4.68	6.09
	Postseason		3	0	0	1	3.0	11	1	1	1	1	0	0	0	2	0	2	0	0	1	0	1.000	0	0-0	1	3.27	3.00
	2 ML YEARS		103	0	0	13	94.1	393	82	41	39	10	3	1	3	35	0	113	8	2	12	6	.667	0	1-5	37	3.44	3.72

Shawn Kelley

Pitches: R **Bats:** R **Pos:** RP-67 **Ht:** 6'2" **Wt:** 230 **Born:** 4/26/1984 **Age:** 33

Year	Team	Lg	G	GS	CG	GF	IP	BFP	H	R	ER	HR	SH	SF	HB	TBB	IBB	SO	WP	Bk	W	L	Pct	Sh	Sv-Op	Hld	ERC	ERA
2009	Sea	AL	41	0	0	12	46.0	191	45	23	23	9	2	2	3	9	1	41	2	1	5	4	.556	0	0-4	9	4.02	4.50
2010	Sea	AL	22	0	0	7	25.0	112	26	11	11	5	0	0	1	12	2	26	0	0	3	1	.750	0	0-0	3	5.38	3.96
2011	Sea	AL	10	0	0	2	12.2	47	7	0	0	0	0	0	0	3	1	10	0	0	0	0	-	0	0-0	1	1.01	0.00
2012	Sea	AL	47	0	0	10	44.1	190	43	20	16	5	4	3	0	15	6	45	2	1	2	4	.333	0	0-2	6	3.49	3.25
2013	NYY	AL	57	0	0	13	53.1	227	47	28	26	8	0	2	0	23	2	71	8	0	4	2	.667	0	0-1	11	3.80	4.39
2014	NYY	AL	59	0	0	15	51.2	220	45	26	26	5	3	1	1	20	4	67	3	0	3	6	.333	0	4-7	12	3.20	4.53
2015	SD	NL	53	0	0	14	51.1	205	41	18	14	4	0	4	0	15	4	63	0	0	2	2	.500	0	0-0	7	2.40	2.45
2016	Was	NL	67	0	0	26	58.0	224	41	19	17	9	0	2	0	11	2	80	2	0	3	2	.600	0	7-9	13	2.06	2.64
	8 ML YEARS		356	0	0	99	342.1	1416	295	145	133	45	9	14	5	108	22	403	17	2	22	21	.512	0	11-23	62	3.15	3.50

Carson Kelly

Bats: R **Throws:** R **Pos:** C-10 **Ht:** 6'2" **Wt:** 220 **Born:** 7/14/1994 **Age:** 22

Year	Team	Lg	G	AB	H	2B	3B	HR	(Hm	Rd)	TB	R	RBI	RC	TBB	IBB	SO	HBP	SH	SF	SB	CS	GDP	Avg	OBP	Slg	OPS
2012	Jhscty	R+	56	213	48	10	0	9	(-	-)	85	24	25	22	10	0	33	1	1	0	0	0	5	.225	.263	.399	.662
2013	2 Tms	Low	113	417	107	22	1	6	(-	-)	149	53	45	50	33	1	56	8	7	2	1	0	18	.257	.322	.357	.679
2014	Peoria	A	98	363	90	17	4	6	(-	-)	133	41	49	47	37	1	54	7	4	4	1	0	14	.248	.326	.366	.692
2015	PlmBh	A+	108	389	85	18	1	8	(-	-)	129	30	51	34	22	0	64	3	0	5	0	0	17	.219	.263	.332	.594
2016	Sprgfld	AA	64	216	62	7	0	6	(-	-)	87	29	18	30	14	0	46	3	2	1	0	1	5	.287	.338	.403	.740
2016	Memp	AAA	32	113	33	10	0	0	(-	-)	43	14	14	16	11	0	17	0	1	1	0	0	6	.292	.352	.381	.733
2016	StL	NL	10	13	2	1	0	0	(0	0)	3	1	1	0	0	0	2	1	0	0	0	0	0	.154	.214	.231	.445

Casey Kelly

Pitches: R **Bats:** R **Pos:** RP-9; SP-1 **Ht:** 6'3" **Wt:** 215 **Born:** 10/4/1989 **Age:** 27

Year	Team	Lg	G	GS	CG	GF	IP	BFP	H	R	ER	HR	SH	SF	HB	TBB	IBB	SO	WP	Bk	W	L	Pct	Sh	Sv-Op	Hld	ERC	ERA
2016	Gwnntt*	AAA	15	12	0	0	74.0	302	64	33	29	6	1	0	3	28	0	47	5	0	3	6	.333	0	0--	-	3.40	3.53
2012	SD	NL	6	6	0	0	29.0	136	39	23	20	5	3	0	2	10	1	26	0	0	2	3	.400	0	0-0	0	6.65	6.21
2015	SD	NL	3	2	0	0	11.1	56	19	13	10	1	0	0	1	3	0	7	0	0	0	2	.000	0	0-0	0	7.89	7.94
2016	Atl	NL	10	1	0	3	21.2	102	30	14	14	1	0	1	2	7	3	7	1	0	0	3	.000	0	0-1	0	5.68	5.82
	3 ML YEARS		19	9	0	4	62.0	294	88	50	44	7	3	1	5	20	4	40	1	0	2	8	.200	0	0-1	0	6.53	6.39

Don Kelly

Bats: L **Throws:** R **Pos:** 1B-12;PR-1 **Ht:** 6'4" **Wt:** 215 **Born:** 2/15/1980 **Age:** 37

Year	Team	Lg	G	AB	H	2B	3B	HR	(Hm	Rd)	TB	R	RBI	RC	TBB	IBB	SO	HBP	SH	SF	SB	CS	GDP	Avg	OBP	Slg	OPS
2016	NewOr*	AAA	72	202	40	2	1	1	(-	-)	47	19	19	14	24	1	40	1	1	2	1	1	5	.198	.284	.233	.517
2007	Pit	NL	25	27	4	0	0	0	(0	0)	4	2	0	1	3	0	3	2	0	0	1	0	1	.148	.281	.148	.429
2009	Det	AL	31	56	14	3	1	0	(0	0)	19	8	3	7	4	0	10	1	1	0	1	0	0	.250	.311	.339	.651
2010	Det	AL	119	238	58	4	0	7	(4	5)	89	30	27	26	8	0	42	2	1	2	3	0	1	.244	.272	.374	.646
2011	Det	AL	113	257	63	8	3	7	(1	6)	98	35	28	27	14	0	32	3	6	1	2	1	8	.245	.291	.381	.672
2012	Det	AL	75	113	21	2	1	1	(1	0)	28	14	7	6	14	0	22	0	0	0	2	0	2	.186	.276	.248	.523
2013	Det	AL	112	216	48	6	1	6	(4	2)	74	33	23	27	27	1	28	2	2	4	2	0	4	.222	.309	.343	.652

Year	Team	Lg				BATTING															RUNNING			AVERAGES			
			G	AB	H	2B	3B	HR	(Hm Rd)	TB	R	RBI	RC	TBB	IBB	SO	HBP	SH	SF	SB	CS	GDP	Avg	OBP	Slg	OPS
2014	Det	AL	95	163	40	5	1	0	(0 0)	47	24	7	14	20	1	29	1	1	0	6	1	6	.245	.332	.288	.620
2015	Mia	NL	2	1	0	0	0	0	(0 0)	0	0	0	0	0	0	0	0	0	0	0	0	0	.000	.000	.000	.000
2016	Mia	NL	13	27	4	0	2	0	(0 0)	8	2	3	1	2	0	5	0	0	1	0	0	2	.148	.200	.296	.496
	Postseason		24	34	9	1	0	1	(0 1)	13	5	3	3	3	0	9	0	0	1	1	0	0	.265	.316	.382	.698
	9 ML YEARS		585	1098	252	28	9	23	(10 13)	367	148	98	109	92	2	171	11	11	8	16	2	24	.230	.294	.334	.628

Joe Kelly

Pitches: R **Bats:** R **Pos:** RP-14; SP-6 **Ht:** 6'1" **Wt:** 190 **Born:** 6/9/1988 **Age:** 29

Year	Team	Lg			HOW MUCH HE PITCHED						WHAT HE GAVE UP											THE RESULTS						
			G	GS	CG	GF	IP	BFP	H	R	ER	HR	SH	SF	HB	TBB	IBB	SO	WP	Bk	W	L	Pct	Sh	Sv-Op	Hld	ERC	ERA
2016	Pwtckt*	AAA	17	4	0	11	35.0	136	29	6	6	1	0	3	1	6	0	46	2	0	1	1	.500	0	2--	-	2.08	1.54
2012	StL	NL	24	16	0	4	107.0	457	112	50	42	10	4	1	3	36	2	75	4	0	5	7	.417	0	0-0	0	4.17	3.53
2013	StL	NL	37	15	0	8	124.0	532	124	42	37	10	2	2	5	44	4	79	3	0	10	5	.667	0	0-1	2	3.88	2.69
2014	2 Tms		17	17	0	0	96.1	415	88	48	45	8	2	4	7	42	0	66	3	0	6	4	.600	0	0-0	0	3.92	4.20
2015	Bos	AL	25	25	0	0	134.1	587	145	76	72	15	0	5	6	49	0	110	9	0	10	6	.625	0	0-0	0	4.68	4.82
2016	Bos	AL	20	6	0	6	40.0	188	44	23	23	5	0	4	2	24	0	48	0	0	4	0	1.000	0	0-1	2	5.80	5.18
14	StL	NL	7	7	0	0	35.0	156	41	19	17	3	1	1	3	10	0	25	3	0	2	2	.500	0	0-0	0	4.82	4.37
14	Bos	AL	10	10	0	0	61.1	259	47	29	28	5	1	3	4	32	0	41	0	0	4	2	.667	0	0-0	0	3.43	4.11
	Postseason		11	4	0	1	29.1	127	26	13	12	2	1	0	1	13	1	24	1	0	0	1	.000	0	0-0	0	3.42	3.68
	5 ML YEARS		123	79	0	18	501.2	2179	513	239	219	48	8	16	23	195	6	378	19	0	35	22	.614	0	0-2	4	4.31	3.93

Ty Kelly

Bats: B **Throws:** R **Pos:** PH-18; 3B-10; LF-8; PR-3; 2B-2; 1B-1; CF-1; RF-1 **Ht:** 6'0" **Wt:** 180 **Born:** 7/20/1988 **Age:** 28

Year	Team	Lg				BATTING															RUNNING			AVERAGES			
			G	AB	H	2B	3B	HR	(Hm Rd)	TB	R	RBI	RC	TBB	IBB	SO	HBP	SH	SF	SB	CS	GDP	Avg	OBP	Slg	OPS
2012	Frdrck	A+	76	263	91	17	0	9	(- -)	135	47	41	63	54	0	41	3	2	2	2	3	12	.346	.460	.513	.973
2012	Norfolk	AAA	11	36	10	1	0	1	(- -)	14	3	2	5	4	0	3	0	0	0	1	0	0	.278	.350	.389	.739
2012	Bowie	AA	46	172	53	11	2	1	(- -)	71	24	27	29	21	0	28	2	1	3	1	0	8	.308	.384	.413	.797
2013	Bowie	AA	72	283	80	21	2	1	(- -)	108	51	47	48	51	0	49	2	1	6	4	2	5	.283	.389	.382	.771
2013	Tacom	AAA	54	197	63	6	1	3	(- -)	80	34	17	40	51	2	41	0	2	3	3	7	4	.320	.456	.406	.862
2014	Tacom	AAA	134	456	120	19	2	15	(- -)	188	81	80	79	85	0	96	3	3	2	11	3	7	.263	.381	.412	.793
2015	Memp	AAA	79	227	46	5	4	2	(- -)	65	23	21	23	38	0	43	1	1	2	3	3	4	.203	.317	.286	.604
2015	Buffalo	AAA	38	144	38	4	0	1	(- -)	45	16	12	15	14	1	10	1	0	1	0	2	2	.264	.331	.313	.644
2016	LsVgs	AAA	81	271	89	21	1	2	(- -)	118	45	35	49	38	0	42	1	3	3	5	6	3	.328	.409	.435	.844
2016	NYM	NL	39	58	14	1	1	1	(0 1)	20	9	7	8	11	0	9	0	0	2	0	0	2	.241	.352	.345	.697

Matt Kemp

Bats: R **Throws:** R **Pos:** RF-97; LF-54; PH-3; DH-2 **Ht:** 6'4" **Wt:** 210 **Born:** 9/23/1984 **Age:** 32

Year	Team	Lg				BATTING															RUNNING			AVERAGES			
			G	AB	H	2B	3B	HR	(Hm Rd)	TB	R	RBI	RC	TBB	IBB	SO	HBP	SH	SF	SB	CS	GDP	Avg	OBP	Slg	OPS
2006	LAD	NL	52	154	39	7	1	7	(4 3)	69	30	23	20	9	1	53	0	0	3	6	0	1	.253	.289	.448	.737
2007	LAD	NL	98	292	100	12	5	10	(9 1)	152	47	42	49	16	0	66	0	0	3	10	5	6	.342	.373	.521	.894
2008	LAD	NL	155	606	176	38	5	18	(14 4)	278	93	76	86	46	6	153	1	1	3	35	11	11	.290	.340	.459	.799
2009	LAD	NL	159	606	180	25	7	26	(13 13)	297	97	101	100	52	6	139	3	0	6	34	8	14	.297	.352	.490	.842
2010	LAD	NL	162	602	150	25	6	28	(15 13)	271	82	89	89	53	4	170	4	0	9	19	15	14	.249	.310	.450	.760
2011	LAD	NL	161	602	195	33	4	39	(19 20)	353	115	126	129	74	24	159	6	0	7	40	11	16	.324	.399	.586	.986
2012	LAD	NL	106	403	122	22	2	23	(11 12)	217	74	69	75	40	8	103	3	0	3	9	4	10	.303	.367	.538	.906
2013	LAD	NL	73	263	71	15	0	6	(0 6)	104	35	33	27	22	3	76	2	0	3	9	0	11	.270	.328	.395	.723
2014	LAD	NL	150	541	155	38	3	25	(17 8)	274	77	89	79	52	3	145	0	0	6	8	5	21	.287	.346	.506	.852
2015	SD	NL	154	596	158	31	3	23	(10 13)	264	80	100	81	39	0	147	5	0	8	12	2	17	.265	.312	.443	.755
2016	2 Tms	NL	156	623	167	39	0	35	(14 21)	311	89	108	85	36	6	156	1	0	12	1	0	17	.268	.304	.499	.803
16	SD	NL	100	409	107	24	0	23	(8 15)	200	54	69	58	16	3	100	0	0	6	0	0	8	.262	.285	.489	.774
16	Atl	NL	56	214	60	15	0	12	(6 6)	111	35	39	27	20	3	56	1	0	6	1	0	9	.280	.336	.519	.855
	Postseason		20	79	20	3	0	3	(2 1)	32	6	7	2	5	0	28	0	0	0	0	2	3	.253	.298	.405	.703
	11 ML YEARS		1426	5288	1513	285	36	240	(131 109)	2590	819	856	805	439	61	1367	25	1	63	183	61	138	.286	.340	.490	.830

Tony Kemp

Bats: L **Throws:** R **Pos:** LF-37; PH-19; DH-8; PR-8; 2B-5; CF-1; RF-1 **Ht:** 5'6" **Wt:** 165 **Born:** 10/31/1991 **Age:** 25

Year	Team	Lg				BATTING															RUNNING			AVERAGES			
			G	AB	H	2B	3B	HR	(Hm Rd)	TB	R	RBI	RC	TBB	IBB	SO	HBP	SH	SF	SB	CS	GDP	Avg	OBP	Slg	OPS
2013	2 Tms	Low	75	275	75	8	3	2	(- -)	95	46	22	39	40	0	47	3	2	4	21	11	6	.273	.366	.345	.712
2014	Lancst	A+	72	295	99	19	4	4	(- -)	138	79	37	66	45	2	35	6	5	3	28	7	6	.336	.433	.468	.901
2014	CpChr	AA	59	233	68	11	4	4	(- -)	99	42	21	40	28	0	32	7	5	2	13	6	5	.292	.381	.425	.806
2015	CpChr	AA	50	193	69	10	1	0	(- -)	81	36	19	40	35	0	28	1	0	1	15	8	3	.358	.457	.420	.876
2015	Fresno	AAA	71	271	74	9	3	3	(- -)	98	42	29	37	21	0	37	5	12	2	20	6	6	.273	.334	.362	.696
2016	Fresno	AAA	69	255	78	9	4	2	(- -)	101	36	24	41	34	0	34	2	8	3	10	8	3	.306	.389	.396	.785
2016	Hou	AL	59	120	26	4	3	1	(1 0)	39	15	7	11	14	0	27	0	1	1	2	1	5	.217	.296	.325	.621

Howie Kendrick

Bats: R **Throws:** R **Pos:** LF-94;2B-32;PH-19;3B-17;1B-11;DH-1 **Ht:** 5'11" **Wt:** 220 **Born:** 7/12/1983 **Age:** 33

Year	Team	Lg	G	AB	H	2B	3B	HR	(Hm	Rd)	TB	R	RBI	RC	TBB	IBB	SO	HBP	SH	SF	SB	CS	GDP	Avg	OBP	Slg	OPS
2006	LAA	AL	72	267	76	21	1	4	(2	2)	111	25	30	32	9	2	44	4	0	3	6	0	5	.285	.314	.416	.730
2007	LAA	AL	88	338	109	24	2	5	(3	2)	152	55	39	41	9	2	61	4	1	1	5	4	15	.322	.347	.450	.796
2008	LAA	AL	92	340	104	26	2	3	(1	2)	143	43	37	50	12	3	58	4	1	4	11	4	8	.306	.333	.421	.754
2009	LAA	AL	105	374	109	21	3	10	(5	5)	166	61	61	58	20	1	71	4	2	0	11	4	8	.291	.334	.444	.778
2010	LAA	AL	158	616	172	41	4	10	(4	6)	251	67	75	81	28	2	94	5	4	5	14	4	16	.279	.313	.407	.721
2011	LAA	AL	140	537	153	30	6	18	(5	13)	249	86	63	69	33	3	119	10	3	0	14	6	18	.285	.338	.464	.802
2012	LAA	AL	147	550	158	32	3	8	(4	4)	220	57	67	65	29	1	115	4	6	5	14	6	26	.287	.325	.400	.725
2013	LAA	AL	122	478	142	21	4	13	(9	4)	210	55	54	57	23	5	89	6	3	3	6	3	16	.297	.335	.439	.775
2014	LAA	AL	157	617	181	33	5	7	(0	7)	245	85	75	94	48	8	110	4	3	2	14	5	15	.293	.347	.397	.744
2015	LAD	NL	117	464	137	22	2	9	(6	3)	190	64	54	62	27	1	82	2	1	1	6	2	17	.295	.336	.409	.746
2016	LAD	NL	146	487	124	26	2	8	(3	5)	178	65	40	55	50	2	96	3	0	3	10	2	20	.255	.326	.366	.691
	Postseason		21	81	17	2	1	2	(1	1)	27	9	6	5	1	0	18	0	2	1	3	0	2	.210	.217	.333	.550
	11 ML YEARS		1344	5068	1465	297	34	95	(42	53)	2115	663	595	664	288	30	939	50	24	27	111	40	164	.289	.332	.417	.749

Ian Kennedy

Pitches: R **Bats:** R **Pos:** SP-33 **Ht:** 6'0" **Wt:** 200 **Born:** 12/19/1984 **Age:** 32

Year	Team	Lg	G	GS	CG	GF	IP	BFP	H	R	ER	HR	SH	SF	HB	TBB	IBB	SO	WP	Bk	W	L	Pct	Sh	Sv-Op	Hld	ERC	ERA
2007	NYY	AL	3	3	0	0	19.0	77	13	6	4	1	0	0	0	9	0	15	0	0	1	0	1.000	0	0-0	0	2.42	1.89
2008	NYY	AL	10	9	0	1	39.2	194	50	37	36	5	1	4	1	26	0	27	3	0	0	4	.000	0	0-0	0	6.93	8.17
2009	NYY	AL	1	0	0	0	1.0	6	0	0	0	0	0	0	1	2	0	1	0	0	0	0	-	0	0-0	1	7.00	0.00
2010	Ari	NL	32	32	0	0	194.0	810	163	87	82	26	11	5	10	70	2	168	16	0	9	10	.474	0	0-0	0	3.47	3.80
2011	Ari	NL	33	33	1	0	222.0	900	186	73	71	19	9	9	9	55	0	198	11	1	21	4	.840	1	0-0	0	2.71	2.88
2012	Ari	NL	33	33	1	0	208.1	899	216	101	93	28	13	5	14	55	4	187	5	4	15	12	.556	0	0-0	0	4.18	4.02
2013	2 Tms	NL	31	31	0	0	181.1	794	180	108	99	27	8	5	12	73	1	163	10	1	7	10	.412	0	0-0	0	4.64	4.91
2014	SD	NL	33	33	0	0	201.0	846	189	85	81	16	9	8	4	70	4	207	11	0	13	13	.500	0	0-0	0	3.47	3.63
2015	SD	NL	30	30	0	0	168.1	713	166	95	80	31	8	2	7	52	4	174	5	1	9	15	.375	0	0-0	0	4.37	4.28
2016	KC	NL	33	33	0	0	195.2	818	173	81	80	33	1	5	13	66	1	184	4	0	11	11	.500	0	0-0	0	3.94	3.68
13	Ari	NL	21	21	0	0	124.0	549	128	79	72	18	8	5	10	48	1	108	9	0	3	8	.273	0	0-0	0	4.82	5.23
13	SD	NL	10	10	0	0	57.1	245	52	29	27	9	0	0	2	25	0	55	1	1	4	2	.667	0	0-0	0	4.26	4.24
	Postseason		2	2	0	0	12.2	57	13	6	6	1	0	2	3	3	0	8	1	0	0	1	.000	0	0-0	0	4.25	4.26
	10 ML YEARS		239	237	2	1	1430.1	6057	1336	673	626	186	60	43	71	478	16	1324	65	7	86	79	.521	1	0-0	1	3.84	3.94

Logan Kensing

Pitches: R **Bats:** R **Pos:** RP-3 **Ht:** 6'1" **Wt:** 190 **Born:** 7/3/1982 **Age:** 34

Year	Team	Lg	G	GS	CG	GF	IP	BFP	H	R	ER	HR	SH	SF	HB	TBB	IBB	SO	WP	Bk	W	L	Pct	Sh	Sv-Op	Hld	ERC	ERA
2016	Toledo*	AAA	52	0	0	15	49.2	210	46	19	19	1	1	1	1	18	2	48	4	0	1	1	.500	0	0--	-	2.99	3.44
2004	Fla	NL	5	3	0	2	13.2	66	19	15	15	5	0	1	1	9	0	7	2	0	0	3	.000	0	0-0	0	10.74	9.88
2005	Fla	NL	3	0	0	0	5.2	31	11	7	7	2	0	1	0	3	0	4	0	0	0	0	-	0	0-0	1	12.96	11.12
2006	Fla	NL	37	0	0	10	37.2	161	30	19	19	6	3	0	3	19	2	45	0	0	1	3	.250	0	1-7	14	4.02	4.54
2007	Fla	NL	9	0	0	0	13.1	59	11	2	2	0	1	0	2	7	2	13	0	0	3	0	1.000	0	0-0	0	3.15	1.35
2008	Fla	NL	48	0	0	7	55.1	254	50	26	26	7	1	2	4	33	5	55	7	0	3	1	.750	0	0-3	5	4.50	4.23
2009	2 Tms	NL	32	0	0	12	35.1	172	54	35	35	8	3	1	0	17	1	19	4	1	1	2	.333	0	1-3	1	8.78	8.92
2013	Col	NL	1	0	0	1	0.2	2	0	0	0	0	0	0	0	1	0	1	0	0	0	0	-	0	0-0	0	3.22	0.00
2015	Sea	NL	19	0	0	4	15.1	64	12	10	10	2	0	1	0	7	0	13	2	0	2	1	.667	0	0-0	9	3.31	5.87
2016	Det	AL	3	0	0	0	4.2	21	8	1	1	0	0	0	0	2	0	1	0	0	0	0	-	0	0-0	0	8.67	1.93
09	Fla	NL	6	0	0	2	7.1	40	14	8	8	1	1	0	0	5	0	7	2	1	0	1	.000	0	0-0	0	11.61	9.82
09	Was	NL	26	0	0	10	28.0	132	40	27	27	7	2	1	0	12	1	12	2	0	1	1	.500	0	1-3	1	8.04	8.68
	9 ML YEARS		157	3	0	36	181.2	830	195	115	115	30	8	6	10	98	10	158	15	1	10	10	.500	0	2-13	30	5.70	5.70

Max Kepler

Bats: L **Throws:** L **Pos:** RF-108;CF-4;1B-2;PR-2;PH-1 **Ht:** 6'4" **Wt:** 205 **Born:** 2/10/1993 **Age:** 24

Year	Team	Lg	G	AB	H	2B	3B	HR	(Hm	Rd)	TB	R	RBI	RC	TBB	IBB	SO	HBP	SH	SF	SB	CS	GDP	Avg	OBP	Slg	OPS
2012	Elizab	R+	59	232	69	16	5	10	(-	-)	125	40	49	50	27	0	33	8	0	2	7	0	5	.297	.387	.539	.925
2013	Crpds	A	61	236	56	11	3	9	(-	-)	100	35	40	33	24	1	43	2	0	1	2	0	2	.237	.312	.424	.736
2014	FtMyrs	A+	102	364	96	20	6	5	(-	-)	143	53	59	50	34	0	62	5	2	2	6	2	4	.264	.333	.393	.726
2015	Chatt	AA	112	407	131	32	13	9	(-	-)	216	76	71	93	67	4	63	2	1	5	18	4	3	.322	.416	.531	.947
2016	Roch	AAA	30	110	31	4	6	1	(-	-)	50	16	19	19	16	1	14	0	0	2	1	1	4	.282	.367	.455	.822
2015	Min	AL	3	7	1	0	0	0	(0	0)	1	0	0	0	0	0	3	0	0	0	0	0	0	.143	.143	.143	.286
2016	Min	AL	113	396	93	20	2	17	(8	9)	168	52	63	52	42	3	93	3	1	5	6	2	2	.235	.309	.424	.734
	2 ML YEARS		116	403	94	20	2	17	(8	9)	169	52	63	52	42	3	96	3	1	5	6	2	2	.233	.307	.419	.726

Clayton Kershaw

Pitches: L **Bats:** L **Pos:** SP-21 **Ht:** 6'4" **Wt:** 225 **Born:** 3/19/1988 **Age:** 29

Year	Team	Lg	G	GS	CG	GF	IP	BFP	H	R	ER	HR	SH	SF	HB	TBB	IBB	SO	WP	Bk	W	L	Pct	Sh	Sv-Op	Hld	ERC	ERA
2008	LAD	NL	22	21	0	0	107.2	470	109	51	51	11	3	3	1	52	3	100	7	0	5	5	.500	0	0-0	1	4.53	4.26
2009	LAD	NL	31	30	0	1	171.0	701	119	55	53	7	11	2	1	91	4	185	11	2	8	8	.500	0	0-0	0	2.60	2.79
2010	LAD	NL	32	32	1	0	204.1	848	160	73	66	13	8	4	7	81	9	212	5	2	13	10	.565	1	0-0	0	2.72	2.91
2011	LAD	NL	33	33	5	0	233.1	912	174	66	59	15	11	2	3	54	2	248	5	1	21	5	.808	2	0-0	0	2.00	2.28
2012	LAD	NL	33	33	2	0	227.2	901	170	70	64	16	18	4	5	63	5	229	6	2	14	9	.609	2	0-0	0	2.20	2.53
2013	LAD	NL	33	33	3	0	236.0	908	164	55	48	11	8	3	3	52	2	232	12	2	16	9	.640	2	0-0	0	1.65	1.83

Year	Team	Lg	G	GS	CG	GF	IP	BFP	H	R	ER	HR	SH	SF	HB	TBB	IBB	SO	WP	Bk	W	L	Pct	Sh	Sv-Op	Hld	ERC	ERA
			HOW MUCH HE PITCHED						WHAT HE GAVE UP												THE RESULTS							
2014	LAD	NL	27	27	6	0	198.1	749	139	42	39	9	6	1	2	31	0	239	7	2	21	3	.875	2	0-0	0	1.53	1.77
2015	LAD	NL	33	33	4	0	232.2	890	163	64	55	15	4	0	5	42	1	301	9	3	16	7	.696	3	0-0	0	1.67	2.13
2016	LAD	NL	21	21	3	0	149.0	544	97	31	28	8	4	1	2	11	1	172	5	3	12	4	.750	3	0-0	0	1.23	1.69
	Postseason		13	10	0	0	64.2	266	52	36	33	8	4	1	1	23	2	77	9	0	2	6	.250	0	0-0	1	3.02	4.59
	9 ML YEARS		265	263	24	1	1760.0	6923	1295	505	463	105	73	20	29	477	27	1918	67	17	126	60	.677	15	0-0	1	2.06	2.37

Dallas Keuchel

Pitches: L Bats: L Pos: SP-26   KY-kull   Ht: 6'3" Wt: 205 Born: 1/1/1988 Age: 29

Year	Team	Lg	G	GS	CG	GF	IP	BFP	H	R	ER	HR	SH	SF	HB	TBB	IBB	SO	WP	Bk	W	L	Pct	Sh	Sv-Op	Hld	ERC	ERA
			HOW MUCH HE PITCHED						WHAT HE GAVE UP												THE RESULTS							
2012	Hou	NL	16	16	1	0	85.1	377	93	56	50	14	9	3	1	39	1	38	2	0	3	8	.273	0	0-0	0	5.39	5.27
2013	Hou	AL	31	22	0	2	153.2	682	184	96	88	20	2	3	5	52	3	123	7	0	6	10	.375	0	0-0	0	5.33	5.15
2014	Hou	AL	29	29	5	0	200.0	808	187	71	65	11	4	5	7	48	2	146	7	0	12	9	.571	1	0-0	0	3.02	2.93
2015	Hou	AL	33	33	3	0	232.0	911	185	68	64	17	1	3	2	51	0	216	9	0	20	8	.714	2	0-0	0	2.26	2.48
2016	Hou	AL	26	26	1	0	168.0	701	168	88	85	20	2	1	2	48	1	144	9	0	9	12	.429	1	0-0	0	3.84	4.55
	Postseason		3	2	0	1	14.0	58	10	4	4	2	1	0	0	5	2	14	1	0	2	0	1.000	0	0-0	0	2.39	2.57
	5 ML YEARS		135	126	10	2	839.0	3479	817	379	352	82	18	15	17	238	7	667	34	0	50	47	.515	4	0-0	2	3.58	3.78

Spencer Kieboom

Bats: R Throws: R Pos: PH-1   KEE-boom   Ht: 6'0" Wt: 210 Born: 3/16/1991 Age: 26

Year	Team	Lg	G	AB	H	2B	3B	HR	(Hm	Rd)	TB	R	RBI	RC	TBB	IBB	SO	HBP	SH	SF	SB	CS	GDP	Avg	OBP	Slg	OPS
			BATTING																		RUNNING			AVERAGES			
2012	Auburn	A-	41	128	36	6	0	0	(-	-)	39	13	20	16	19	0	24	2	6	0	0	0	4	.258	.362	.305	.667
2014	Hgrstn	A	87	330	102	28	4	9	(-	-)	165	50	61	58	21	0	67	4	0	6	2	2	7	.309	.352	.500	.852
2015	Ptomc	A+	71	246	61	16	1	2	(-	-)	85	30	26	32	36	1	30	1	0	2	1	1	10	.248	.344	.346	.689
2016	Hrsbrg	AA	94	309	71	11	0	5	(-	-)	97	27	31	35	43	0	60	2	1	4	0	0	10	.230	.324	.314	.638
2016	Was	NL	1	0	0	0	0	0	(0	0)	0	1	0	0	1	0	0	0	0	0	0	0	0	-	1.000	-	-

Dean Kiekhefer

Pitches: L Bats: L Pos: RP-26   KEEK-heff-er   Ht: 6'0" Wt: 175 Born: 6/7/1989 Age: 28

Year	Team	Lg	G	GS	CG	GF	IP	BFP	H	R	ER	HR	SH	SF	HB	TBB	IBB	SO	WP	Bk	W	L	Pct	Sh	Sv-Op	Hld	ERC	ERA
			HOW MUCH HE PITCHED						WHAT HE GAVE UP												THE RESULTS							
2012	PlmBh	A+	46	0	0	35	60.1	248	61	23	15	3	5	3	1	4	1	41	1	0	2	2	.500	0	14--	0	2.52	2.24
2013	Sprgfld	AA	11	0	0	5	16.1	69	20	9	7	1	0	0	0	1	0	10	0	0	0	2	.000	0	0--	0	3.69	3.86
2013	PlmBh	A+	25	0	0	16	44.0	188	48	18	16	1	6	0	1	8	2	28	0	0	4	3	.571	0	7--	0	3.16	3.27
2014	Sprgfld	AA	15	0	0	11	14.2	61	18	10	7	2	0	0	1	0	0	10	0	1	0	2	.000	0	7--	0	4.32	4.30
2014	Memp	AAA	40	0	0	6	56.2	222	48	17	16	7	1	1	3	5	1	52	5	0	3	3	.500	0	1--	0	2.43	2.54
2015	Memp	AAA	50	1	0	17	59.2	248	68	21	16	5	1	1	0	7	1	37	0	0	2	1	.667	0	2--	0	3.62	2.41
2016	Memp	AAA	29	0	0	14	34.2	137	32	8	8	2	1	1	0	8	2	20	0	0	6	1	.857	0	2--	0	2.77	2.08
2016	StL	NL	26	0	0	10	22.0	98	24	13	13	2	0	1	2	7	4	14	0	0	0	0	-	0	0-0	2	4.19	5.32

Kevin Kiermaier

Bats: L Throws: R Pos: CF-104;PH-2   KEER-my-urr   Ht: 6'1" Wt: 215 Born: 4/22/1990 Age: 27

Year	Team	Lg	G	AB	H	2B	3B	HR	(Hm	Rd)	TB	R	RBI	RC	TBB	IBB	SO	HBP	SH	SF	SB	CS	GDP	Avg	OBP	Slg	OPS
			BATTING																		RUNNING			AVERAGES			
2013	TB	AL	1	0	0	0	0	0	(0	0)	0	0	0	0	0	0	0	0	0	0	0	0	0	-	-	-	-
2014	TB	AL	108	331	87	16	8	10	(4	6)	149	35	35	37	23	2	71	3	5	2	5	4	3	.263	.315	.450	.765
2015	TB	AL	151	505	133	25	12	10	(5	5)	212	62	40	66	24	0	95	2	2	2	18	5	7	.263	.298	.420	.718
2016	TB	AL	105	366	90	20	2	12	(5	7)	150	55	37	54	40	1	74	7	0	1	21	3	5	.246	.331	.410	.741
	Postseason		1	0	0	0	0	0	(0	0)	0	0	0	0	0	0	0	0	0	0	0	0	0	-	-	-	-
	4 ML YEARS		365	1202	310	61	22	32	(14	18)	511	152	112	157	87	3	240	12	7	5	44	12	15	.258	.313	.425	.738

Hyun Soo Kim

Bats: L Throws: R Pos: LF-91;PH-11   hee-YUHN   Ht: 6'2" Wt: 210 Born: 1/12/1988 Age: 29

Year	Team	Lg	G	AB	H	2B	3B	HR	(Hm	Rd)	TB	R	RBI	RC	TBB	IBB	SO	HBP	SH	SF	SB	CS	GDP	Avg	OBP	Slg	OPS
			BATTING																		RUNNING			AVERAGES			
2016	Bal	AL	95	305	92	16	1	6	(2	4)	128	36	22	50	36	0	51	4	0	1	1	3	5	.302	.382	.420	.801

Craig Kimbrel

Pitches: R Bats: R Pos: RP-57   KIM-brull   Ht: 6'0" Wt: 210 Born: 5/28/1988 Age: 29

Year	Team	Lg	G	GS	CG	GF	IP	BFP	H	R	ER	HR	SH	SF	HB	TBB	IBB	SO	WP	Bk	W	L	Pct	Sh	Sv-Op	Hld	ERC	ERA
			HOW MUCH HE PITCHED						WHAT HE GAVE UP												THE RESULTS							
2010	Atl	NL	21	0	0	7	20.2	88	9	2	1	0	0	0	0	16	1	40	4	0	4	0	1.000	0	1-1	2	1.72	0.44
2011	Atl	NL	79	0	0	64	77.0	306	48	19	18	3	1	2	1	32	1	127	4	0	4	3	.571	0	46-54	1	1.88	2.10
2012	Atl	NL	63	0	0	56	62.2	231	27	7	7	3	0	0	2	14	0	116	5	0	3	1	.750	0	42-45	0	0.93	1.01
2013	Atl	NL	68	0	0	60	67.0	258	39	10	9	4	0	0	3	20	2	98	3	0	4	3	.571	0	50-54	0	1.58	1.21
2014	Atl	NL	63	0	0	54	61.2	244	30	13	11	2	3	0	2	26	0	95	6	0	0	3	.000	0	47-51	0	1.41	1.61
2015	SD	NL	61	0	0	53	59.1	239	40	19	17	6	0	0	1	22	1	87	4	0	4	2	.667	0	39-43	1	2.31	2.58
2016	Bos	AL	57	0	0	47	53.0	220	28	22	20	4	1	1	4	30	0	83	6	0	2	6	.250	0	31-33	3	2.32	3.40
	Postseason		9	0	0	6	6.2	21	1	2	1	0	0	0	0	3	0	10	0	0	1	0	1.000	0	1-1	1	0.54	1.35
	7 ML YEARS		412	0	0	341	401.1	1586	221	92	83	22	5	3	13	160	5	646	32	0	21	18	.538	0	256-281	3	1.65	1.86

Ian Kinsler

Bats: R **Throws:** R **Pos:** 2B-151;PH-3;DH-1;PR-1   **Ht:** 6'0" **Wt:** 200 **Born:** 6/22/1982 **Age:** 35

								BATTING													RUNNING			AVERAGES			
Year Team	Lg	G	AB	H	2B	3B	HR	(Hm Rd)	TB	R	RBI	RC	TBB	IBB	SO	HBP	SH	SF	SB	CS	GDP	Avg	OBP	Slg	OPS
2006 Tex	AL	120	423	121	27	1	14	(10 4)	192	65	55	65	40	1	64	3	1	7	11	4	12	.286	.347	.454	.801
2007 Tex	AL	130	483	127	22	2	20	(12 8)	213	96	61	79	62	2	83	9	8	4	23	2	14	.263	.355	.441	.796
2008 Tex	AL	121	518	165	41	4	18	(4 14)	268	102	71	106	45	1	67	6	7	7	26	2	12	.319	.375	.517	.892
2009 Tex	AL	144	566	143	32	4	31	(20 11)	277	101	86	99	59	0	77	6	3	6	31	5	9	.253	.327	.488	.814
2010 Tex	AL	103	391	112	20	1	9	(4 5)	161	73	45	59	56	2	57	7	2	4	15	5	11	.286	.382	.412	.794
2011 Tex	AL	155	620	158	34	4	32	(16 16)	296	121	77	100	89	2	71	8	4	2	30	4	17	.255	.355	.477	.832
2012 Tex	AL	157	655	168	42	5	19	(14 5)	277	105	72	83	60	0	90	10	1	5	21	9	14	.256	.326	.423	.749
2013 Tex	AL	136	545	151	31	2	13	(5 8)	225	85	72	84	51	0	59	8	3	7	15	11	5	.277	.344	.413	.757
2014 Det	AL	161	**684**	188	40	4	17	(9 8)	287	100	92	89	29	1	79	5	3	5	15	4	20	.275	.307	.420	.727
2015 Det	AL	154	624	185	35	7	11	(6 5)	267	94	73	81	43	0	80	3	0	5	10	6	13	.296	.342	.428	.770
2016 Det	AL	153	618	178	29	4	28	(13 15)	299	117	83	105	45	0	115	13	0	3	14	6	5	.288	.348	.484	.831
Postseason		37	134	39	7	1	4	(1 3)	60	18	20	24	24	1	19	1	1	1	6	5	3	.291	.400	.448	.848
11 ML YEARS		1534	6127	1696	353	38	212	(113 99)	2761	1059	787	950	579	9	842	78	32	55	211	58	132	.277	.344	.451	.795

Brandon Kintzler

Pitches: R **Bats:** R **Pos:** RP-54   **Ht:** 6'0" **Wt:** 190 **Born:** 8/1/1984 **Age:** 32

		HOW MUCH HE PITCHED						WHAT HE GAVE UP												THE RESULTS							
Year Team	Lg	G	GS	CG	GF	IP	BFP	H	R	ER	HR	SH	SF	HB	TBB	IBB	SO	WP	Bk	W	L	Pct	Sh	Sv-Op	Hld	ERC	ERA
2016 Roch*	AAA	10	0	0	3	15.1	61	15	6	6	0	1	1	1	3	0	11	5	0	4	1	.800	0	0- -	-	2.91	3.52
2010 Mil	NL	7	0	0	2	7.1	33	10	6	6	2	1	0	0	4	1	9	1	0	0	1	.000	0	0-0	0	8.67	7.36
2011 Mil	NL	9	0	0	3	14.2	61	14	9	6	3	0	2	0	3	0	15	0	1	1	1	.500	0	0-0	0	3.65	3.68
2012 Mil	NL	14	0	0	1	16.2	72	18	7	7	1	0	0	0	7	1	14	1	0	3	0	1.000	0	0-0	2	4.30	3.78
2013 Mil	NL	71	0	0	11	77.0	305	66	26	23	2	4	2	1	16	2	58	1	0	3	3	.500	0	0-4	26	2.21	2.69
2014 Mil	NL	64	0	0	13	58.1	239	62	22	21	8	4	1	0	16	3	31	1	0	3	3	.500	0	0-3	8	4.28	3.24
2015 Mil	NL	7	0	0	4	7.0	36	12	6	5	1	0	0	0	5	0	7	1	0	0	1	.000	0	0-0	0	10.76	6.43
2016 Min	AL	54	0	0	36	54.1	224	59	22	19	5	0	0	2	8	1	35	0	0	0	2	.000	0	17-20	1	3.68	3.15
7 ML YEARS		226	0	0	70	235.1	970	241	98	87	22	9	5	3	59	8	169	5	1	10	11	.476	0	17-27	37	3.66	3.33

Jason Kipnis

Bats: L **Throws:** R **Pos:** 2B-151;DH-4;PH-1   KIP-niss   **Ht:** 5'11" **Wt:** 195 **Born:** 4/3/1987 **Age:** 30

								BATTING													RUNNING			AVERAGES			
Year Team	Lg	G	AB	H	2B	3B	HR	(Hm Rd)	TB	R	RBI	RC	TBB	IBB	SO	HBP	SH	SF	SB	CS	GDP	Avg	OBP	Slg	OPS
2011 Cle	AL	36	136	37	9	1	7	(3 4)	69	24	19	22	11	0	34	2	0	1	5	0	0	.272	.333	.507	.841
2012 Cle	AL	152	591	152	22	4	14	(5 9)	224	86	76	88	67	2	109	5	3	6	31	7	12	.257	.335	.379	.714
2013 Cle	AL	149	564	160	36	4	17	(7 10)	255	86	84	99	76	3	143	3	5	10	30	7	10	.284	.366	.452	.818
2014 Cle	AL	129	500	120	25	1	6	(3 3)	165	61	41	44	50	2	100	2	1	2	22	3	15	.240	.310	.330	.640
2015 Cle	AL	141	565	171	43	7	9	(6 3)	255	86	52	92	57	6	107	9	4	6	12	8	5	.303	.372	.451	.823
2016 Cle	AL	156	610	168	41	4	23	(13 10)	286	91	82	90	60	0	146	6	5	7	15	3	21	.275	.343	.469	.811
Postseason		1	4	0	0	0	0	(0 0)	0	0	0	0	0	0	0	0	0	0	0	0	0	.000	.000	.000	.000
6 ML YEARS		763	2966	808	176	21	76	(37 39)	1254	434	354	435	321	13	639	27	18	32	115	28	63	.272	.345	.423	.768

Michael Kirkman

Pitches: L **Bats:** L **Pos:** RP-2   **Ht:** 6'4" **Wt:** 215 **Born:** 9/18/1986 **Age:** 30

		HOW MUCH HE PITCHED						WHAT HE GAVE UP												THE RESULTS							
Year Team	Lg	G	GS	CG	GF	IP	BFP	H	R	ER	HR	SH	SF	HB	TBB	IBB	SO	WP	Bk	W	L	Pct	Sh	Sv-Op	Hld	ERC	ERA
2016 ElPaso*	AAA	5	0	0	1	6.0	22	3	3	3	0	0	0	1	0	0	6	1	0	0	0	-	0	1- -	-	0.80	4.50
2016 ColSpr*	AAA	42	0	0	5	32.0	153	40	12	10	2	2	2	1	17	0	34	3	0	1	0	1.000	0	0- -	-	5.80	2.81
2010 Tex	AL	14	0	0	2	16.1	68	9	3	3	0	0	2	0	10	1	16	0	0	0	0	-	0	0-1	2	1.76	1.65
2011 Tex	AL	15	0	0	7	27.1	122	26	22	20	5	1	2	3	12	2	21	2	0	1	1	.500	0	0-0	1	4.81	6.59
2012 Tex	AL	28	0	0	9	35.1	151	24	16	15	5	0	1	1	17	1	38	2	0	1	2	.333	0	0-2	1	2.88	3.82
2013 Tex	AL	25	0	0	1	22.0	115	36	20	20	2	0	1	0	15	4	25	2	0	0	2	.000	0	1-2	0	8.74	8.18
2014 Tex	AL	12	0	0	1	5.2	22	5	1	1	0	0	0	2	1	0	3	0	0	0	1	.000	0	0-0	2	3.64	1.59
2016 2 Tms	NL	2	0	0	0	2.1	15	7	5	5	0	0	0	0	1	0	1	0	0	0	0	-	0	0-0	0	16.68	19.29
16 SD	NL	1	0	0	0	1.1	10	6	4	4	0	0	0	0	0	0	0	0	0	0	0	-	0	0-0	-	26.58	27.00
16 Mil	NL	1	0	0	0	1.0	5	1	1	1	0	0	0	0	1	0	1	0	0	0	0	-	0	0-0	-	5.48	9.00
Postseason		3	0	0	2	2.2	13	4	1	1	0	1	0	0	2	0	2	0	0	0	0	-	0	0-0	-	8.14	3.38
6 ML YEARS		96	0	0	26	109.0	493	107	67	64	12	1	6	6	56	8	104	6	0	2	6	.250	0	1-5	6	4.51	5.28

Patrick Kivlehan

Bats: R **Throws:** R **Pos:** RF-6;PH-2;LF-1   KIV-leh-hann   **Ht:** 6'2" **Wt:** 215 **Born:** 12/22/1989 **Age:** 27

								BATTING													RUNNING			AVERAGES			
Year Team	Lg	G	AB	H	2B	3B	HR	(Hm Rd)	TB	R	RBI	RC	TBB	IBB	SO	HBP	SH	SF	SB	CS	GDP	Avg	OBP	Slg	OPS
2012 Everett	A-	72	282	85	17	3	12	(- -)	144	46	52	55	19	0	93	13	2	0	14	1	2	.301	.373	.511	.883
2013 2 Tms	Low	128	489	148	25	3	16	(- -)	227	74	90	86	43	1	107	10	0	7	15	6	9	.303	.366	.464	.830
2014 Hi Dsrt	A+	34	142	40	9	2	9	(- -)	80	24	35	27	12	0	32	0	0	8	2	2	8	.282	.331	.563	.895
2014 Jacksn	AA	104	377	113	23	7	11	(- -)	183	60	68	70	44	1	78	4	0	5	9	4	7	.300	.374	.485	.860
2015 Tacom	AAA	123	472	121	25	1	22	(- -)	214	58	73	70	36	1	113	5	0	5	14	3	10	.256	.313	.453	.766
2016 RdRck	AAA	37	141	26	8	1	0	(- -)	37	17	16	8	11	0	36	2	0	1	2	2	5	.184	.252	.262	.514
2016 Tacom	AAA	43	157	46	8	2	8	(- -)	82	21	25	26	8	0	49	0	0	0	2	2	3	.293	.327	.522	.850
2016 ElPaso	AAA	20	72	22	2	1	3	(- -)	35	8	8	12	5	0	23	0	0	0	1	0	1	.306	.351	.486	.837
2016 2 Tms	NL	8	21	4	0	0	1	(1 0)	7	5	2	3	2	0	11	1	0	0	0	0	0	.190	.292	.333	.625
16 SD	NL	5	16	4	0	0	1	(1 0)	7	5	2	3	2	0	9	1	0	0	0	0	0	.250	.368	.438	.806
16 Cin	NL	3	5	0	0	0	0	(0 0)	0	0	0	0	0	0	2	0	0	0	0	0	0	.000	.000	.000	.000

Phil Klein

Pitches: R Bats: R Pos: RP-10; SP-2   Ht: 6'7" Wt: 255 Born: 4/30/1989 Age: 28

Year Team	Lg	G	GS	CG	GF	IP	BFP	H	R	ER	HR	SH	SF	HB	TBB	IBB	SO	WP	Bk	W	L	Pct	Sh	Sv-Op	Hld	ERC	ERA
2016 RdRck*	AAA	8	1	0	1	12.2	57	14	7	6	2	0	1	0	5	0	12	1	0	0	0	-	0	0- -	-	4.96	4.26
2016 LV*	AAA	14	10	0	0	65.1	251	44	13	11	4	1	0	5	13	1	76	4	0	5	1	.833	0	0- -	-	1.77	1.52
2014 Tex	AL	17	0	0	3	19.0	79	11	6	6	3	0	0	2	10	5	23	1	1	1	2	.333	0	0-0	0	2.69	2.84
2015 Tex	AL	11	2	0	3	17.1	86	23	15	13	4	0	0	0	10	0	12	1	0	0	1	1.000	0	0-0	2	7.62	6.75
2016 2 Tms		12	2	0	5	19.1	86	23	15	15	2	2	1	1	9	1	19	1	0	0	1	.000	0	0-0	0	5.80	6.98
16 Tex		8	0	0	5	8.2	35	8	5	5	2	0	0	0	2	0	12	1	0	0	1	.000	0	0-0	0	3.87	5.19
16 Phi	NL	4	2	0	0	10.2	51	15	10	10	0	2	1	1	7	1	7	0	0	0	0	-	0	0-0	0	7.31	8.44
3 ML YEARS		40	4	0	11	55.2	251	57	36	34	9	2	1	3	29	6	54	3	1	2	3	.400	0	0-0	2	5.19	5.50

Corey Kluber

Pitches: R Bats: R Pos: SP-32   CLUE-burr   Ht: 6'4" Wt: 215 Born: 4/10/1986 Age: 31

Year Team	Lg	G	GS	CG	GF	IP	BFP	H	R	ER	HR	SH	SF	HB	TBB	IBB	SO	WP	Bk	W	L	Pct	Sh	Sv-Op	Hld	ERC	ERA
2011 Cle	AL	3	0	0	2	4.1	25	6	4	4	0	0	0	2	3	0	5	1	0	0	0	-	0	0-0	0	8.12	8.31
2012 Cle	AL	12	12	0	0	63.0	281	76	44	36	9	1	0	4	18	0	54	2	0	2	5	.286	0	0-0	0	5.38	5.14
2013 Cle	AL	26	24	0	1	147.1	608	153	67	63	15	4	2	5	33	0	136	1	0	11	5	.688	0	0-0	0	3.83	3.85
2014 Cle	AL	34	34	3	1	235.2	951	207	72	64	14	5	2	6	51	3	269	3	0	18	9	.667	1	0-0	0	2.57	2.44
2015 Cle	AL	32	32	4	0	222.0	886	189	92	86	22	7	4	11	45	3	245	6	1	9	16	.360	0	0-0	0	2.74	3.49
2016 Cle	AL	32	32	3	0	215.0	860	170	82	75	22	6	2	7	57	1	227	5	1	18	9	.667	2	0-0	0	2.62	3.14
6 ML YEARS		139	134	10	3	887.1	3611	801	361	328	82	23	10	35	207	7	936	18	2	58	44	.569	3	0-0	0	3.03	3.33

Corey Knebel

Pitches: R Bats: R Pos: RP-35   kuh-NAY-bull   Ht: 6'4" Wt: 220 Born: 11/26/1991 Age: 25

Year Team	Lg	G	GS	CG	GF	IP	BFP	H	R	ER	HR	SH	SF	HB	TBB	IBB	SO	WP	Bk	W	L	Pct	Sh	Sv-Op	Hld	ERC	ERA
2016 ColSpr*	AAA	11	2	0	3	13.2	46	5	2	2	0	0	2	0	3	0	14	0	0	1	0	1.000	0	2- -	-	0.62	1.32
2014 Det	AL	8	0	0	4	8.2	39	11	7	6	0	0	0	0	3	0	11	1	0	0	0	-	0	0-0	0	4.65	6.23
2015 Mil	NL	48	0	0	15	50.1	209	44	18	18	8	0	0	2	17	1	58	1	0	0	0	-	0	0-1	3	3.69	3.22
2016 Mil	NL	35	0	0	7	32.2	145	32	20	17	3	0	1	1	16	3	38	1	0	1	4	.200	0	2-4	13	4.18	4.68
3 ML YEARS		91	0	0	26	91.2	393	87	45	41	11	0	1	3	36	4	107	3	0	1	4	.200	0	2-5	16	3.96	4.03

Matt Koch

Pitches: R Bats: L Pos: RP-5; SP-2   cook   Ht: 6'3" Wt: 215 Born: 11/2/1990 Age: 26

Year Team	Lg	G	GS	CG	GF	IP	BFP	H	R	ER	HR	SH	SF	HB	TBB	IBB	SO	WP	Bk	W	L	Pct	Sh	Sv-Op	Hld	ERC	ERA
2012 Bklyn	A-	13	2	0	2	23.1	104	25	13	13	1	1	3	3	7	0	19	2	0	0	2	.000	0	0- -	-	4.11	5.01
2013 Savann	A	18	15	1	1	82.1	350	100	52	43	7	1	4	2	4	0	68	3	0	6	4	.600	0	0- -	-	3.82	4.70
2014 Stluci	A+	22	22	0	0	120.1	529	141	67	62	7	2	2	13	32	0	63	8	3	10	4	.714	0	0- -	-	4.69	4.64
2015 Bnghtn	AA	35	8	0	3	88.1	367	95	37	34	5	5	3	4	15	1	55	5	0	4	8	.333	0	0- -	-	3.50	3.46
2016 Mobile	AA	14	14	0	0	74.2	319	87	41	39	7	3	5	3	13	0	49	0	0	2	4	.333	0	0- -	-	4.24	4.70
2016 Reno	AAA	7	7	0	0	46.2	194	55	18	16	3	1	0	0	6	1	25	1	0	4	2	.667	0	0- -	-	3.78	3.09
2016 Ari	NL	7	2	0	4	18.0	69	9	4	4	1	1	0	2	4	0	10	0	0	1	1	.500	0	1-1	0	1.29	2.00

Tom Koehler

Pitches: R Bats: R Pos: SP-33   COLE-err   Ht: 6'3" Wt: 235 Born: 6/29/1986 Age: 31

Year Team	Lg	G	GS	CG	GF	IP	BFP	H	R	ER	HR	SH	SF	HB	TBB	IBB	SO	WP	Bk	W	L	Pct	Sh	Sv-Op	Hld	ERC	ERA
2012 Mia	NL	8	1	0	0	13.1	56	15	8	8	4	0	0	0	2	1	13	0	0	0	1	.000	0	0-0	0	4.99	5.40
2013 Mia	NL	29	23	0	2	143.0	601	140	72	70	14	3	2	5	54	2	92	7	0	5	10	.333	0	0-0	0	4.08	4.41
2014 Mia	NL	32	32	0	0	191.1	803	177	84	81	16	6	5	7	71	0	153	4	0	10	10	.500	0	0-0	0	3.63	3.81
2015 Mia	NL	32	31	0	0	187.1	800	180	96	85	22	6	5	5	77	3	137	2	0	11	14	.440	0	0-0	0	4.17	4.08
2016 Mia	NL	33	33	0	0	176.2	774	176	93	85	22	6	5	5	83	7	147	9	0	9	13	.409	0	0-0	0	4.58	4.33
5 ML YEARS		134	120	0	2	711.2	3034	688	353	329	78	21	17	23	287	13	542	22	0	35	48	.422	0	0-0	0	4.12	4.16

George Kontos

Pitches: R Bats: R Pos: RP-57   KAHN-tose   Ht: 6'3" Wt: 215 Born: 6/12/1985 Age: 32

Year Team	Lg	G	GS	CG	GF	IP	BFP	H	R	ER	HR	SH	SF	HB	TBB	IBB	SO	WP	Bk	W	L	Pct	Sh	Sv-Op	Hld	ERC	ERA
2011 NYY	AL	7	0	0	4	6.0	24	4	2	2	1	0	0	0	3	0	6	0	0	0	0	-	0	0-0	0	3.20	3.00
2012 SF	NL	44	0	0	9	43.2	177	34	15	12	3	0	2	0	12	0	44	1	0	2	1	.667	0	0-1	5	2.23	2.47
2013 SF	NL	52	0	0	9	55.1	238	60	30	27	7	1	4	2	18	2	47	1	0	2	2	.500	0	0-1	5	4.59	4.39
2014 SF	NL	24	0	0	7	32.1	125	24	10	10	1	0	0	0	11	3	27	1	0	4	0	1.000	0	0-0	1	2.07	2.78
2015 SF	NL	73	0	0	12	73.1	284	57	20	19	9	1	3	0	12	3	44	3	0	4	4	.500	0	0-2	14	2.14	2.33
2016 SF	NL	57	0	0	17	53.1	216	42	19	15	3	1	1	2	20	3	35	1	0	3	2	.600	0	0-2	9	2.68	2.53
Postseason		8	0	0	1	5.1	22	6	4	4	1	1	0	0	1	0	2	0	0	0	0	-	0	0-0	1	4.65	6.75
6 ML YEARS		257	0	0	58	264.0	1064	221	96	85	24	3	10	4	76	11	203	7	0	15	9	.625	0	0-6	34	2.76	2.90

Erik Kratz

Bats: R Throws: R Pos: C-30;1B-1;DH-1;PH-1   Ht: 6'4" Wt: 245 Born: 6/15/1980 Age: 37

Year Team	Lg	G	AB	H	2B	3B	HR	(Hm	Rd)	TB	R	RBI	RC	TBB	IBB	SO	HBP	SH	SF	SB	CS	GDP	Avg	OBP	Slg	OPS
2016 Salt Lk*	AAA	12	39	9	3	0	0	(-	-)	12	6	7	3	1	0	12	1	0	0	0	0	1	.231	.268	.308	.576
2016 Buffalo*	AAA	19	58	9	1	0	0	(-	-)	10	6	1	2	7	0	11	2	1	0	0	0	3	.155	.269	.172	.441
2010 Pit	NL	9	34	4	0	0	0	(0	0)	4	2	1	0	2	0	9	0	0	0	0	0	0	.118	.167	.118	.284
2011 Phi	NL	2	6	2	1	0	0	(0	0)	3	0	0	1	0	0	1	0	0	0	0	0	0	.333	.333	.500	.833
2012 Phi	NL	50	141	35	9	0	9	(6	3)	71	14	26	20	11	2	34	2	0	3	0	0	2	.248	.306	.504	.809
2013 Phi	NL	68	197	42	7	0	9	(5	4)	76	21	26	15	18	4	45	1	0	2	0	0	11	.213	.280	.386	.666
2014 2 Tms	AL	47	110	24	4	0	5	(1	4)	43	12	13	7	4	1	22	0	0	1	0	0	4	.218	.243	.391	.634
2015 2 Tms		16	26	5	2	0	0	(0	0)	7	3	3	1	1	0	5	0	0	1	0	0	0	.192	.214	.269	.484
2016 2 Tms		33	85	8	2	0	1	(1	0)	13	3	4	0	1	0	32	0	1	0	0	0	3	.094	.105	.153	.258
14 Tor	AL	34	81	16	3	0	3	(1	2)	28	8	10	5	3	0	12	0	0	0	0	0	3	.198	.226	.346	.572
14 KC	AL	13	29	8	1	0	2	(0	2)	15	4	3	2	1	1	10	0	0	1	0	0	1	.276	.290	.517	.808
15 KC	AL	4	4	0	0	0	0	(0	0)	0	0	1	0	0	0	2	0	0	0	0	0	0	.000	.000	.000	.000
15 Phi	NL	12	22	5	2	0	0	(0	0)	7	3	2	1	1	0	3	0	0	0	0	0	0	.227	.261	.318	.579
16 Hou	AL	15	29	2	1	0	0	(0	0)	3	0	0	0	1	0	14	0	0	0	0	0	1	.069	.100	.103	.203
16 Pit	NL	18	56	6	1	0	1	(1	0)	10	3	4	0	0	0	18	0	1	0	0	0	2	.107	.107	.179	.286
7 ML YEARS		225	599	120	25	0	24	(13	11)	217	55	73	44	37	7	148	3	1	7	0	0	20	.200	.248	.362	.610

Ian Krol

Pitches: L Bats: L Pos: RP-63   KROHL   Ht: 6'1" Wt: 210 Born: 5/9/1991 Age: 26

Year Team	Lg	G	GS	CG	GF	IP	BFP	H	R	ER	HR	SH	SF	HB	TBB	IBB	SO	WP	Bk	W	L	Pct	Sh	Sv-Op	Hld	ERC	ERA
2016 Gwnntt*	AAA	12	0	0	3	12.1	53	10	6	6	1	0	0	0	6	0	14	1	0	1	2	.333	0	1--	-	3.18	4.38
2013 Was	NL	32	0	0	10	27.1	117	28	12	12	5	2	1	0	8	1	22	2	0	2	1	.667	0	0-1	2	4.24	3.95
2014 Det	AL	45	0	0	5	32.2	154	42	23	18	6	0	1	2	13	4	28	1	1	0	0	-	0	1-4	10	6.35	4.96
2015 Det	AL	33	0	0	6	28.0	129	31	19	18	4	2	0	2	17	1	26	0	0	2	3	.400	0	0-1	1	6.23	5.79
2016 Atl	NL	63	0	0	7	51.0	217	54	19	18	4	1	1	3	13	3	56	5	0	2	0	1.000	0	0-2	10	3.84	3.18
4 ML YEARS		173	0	0	28	139.0	617	155	73	66	19	5	3	7	51	9	132	8	1	6	4	.600	0	1-8	23	4.96	4.27

Chad Kuhl

Pitches: R Bats: R Pos: SP-14   cool   Ht: 6'3" Wt: 215 Born: 9/10/1992 Age: 24

Year Team	Lg	G	GS	CG	GF	IP	BFP	H	R	ER	HR	SH	SF	HB	TBB	IBB	SO	WP	Bk	W	L	Pct	Sh	Sv-Op	Hld	ERC	ERA
2013 Jmstwn	A-	13	13	0	0	55.1	222	53	22	13	0	1	2	5	6	0	33	1	0	3	4	.429	0	0--	-	2.50	2.11
2014 Bradtn	A+	28	28	0	0	153.1	626	141	67	59	9	1	7	15	42	0	100	3	0	13	5	.722	0	0--	-	3.36	3.46
2015 Altna	AA	26	26	1	0	152.2	620	134	53	42	10	8	3	4	41	0	101	6	0	11	5	.688	0	0--	-	2.83	2.48
2016 Indy	AAA	16	16	0	0	83.2	339	81	27	22	9	2	2	4	16	0	66	2	0	6	3	.667	0	0--	-	3.40	2.37
2016 Pit	NL	14	14	0	0	70.2	301	73	34	33	7	2	2	4	20	0	53	2	0	5	4	.556	0	0-0	0	4.04	4.20

Tommy La Stella

Bats: L Throws: R Pos: PH-37;3B-33;2B-9   Ht: 5'11" Wt: 180 Born: 1/31/1989 Age: 28

Year Team	Lg	G	AB	H	2B	3B	HR	(Hm	Rd)	TB	R	RBI	RC	TBB	IBB	SO	HBP	SH	SF	SB	CS	GDP	Avg	OBP	Slg	OPS
2016 Iowa*	AAA	12	44	12	2	0	1	(-	-)	17	6	3	5	2	0	9	0	0	0	0	0	2	.273	.304	.386	.691
2014 Atl	NL	93	319	80	16	1	1	(1	0)	101	22	31	36	36	2	40	1	3	1	2	1	8	.251	.328	.317	.644
2015 ChC	NL	33	67	18	6	0	1	(1	0)	27	4	11	10	5	0	7	1	0	1	2	0	1	.269	.324	.403	.727
2016 ChC	NL	74	148	40	12	1	2	(1	1)	60	17	11	20	18	1	27	2	0	0	0	1	1	.270	.357	.405	.763
Postseason		6	10	0	0	0	0	(0	0)	0	0	0	0	0	0	3	0	0	0	0	0	0	.000	.000	.000	.000
3 ML YEARS		200	534	138	34	2	4	(3	1)	188	43	53	66	59	3	74	4	3	2	4	2	11	.258	.336	.352	.688

John Lackey

Pitches: R Bats: R Pos: SP-29   Ht: 6'6" Wt: 235 Born: 10/23/1978 Age: 38

Year Team	Lg	G	GS	CG	GF	IP	BFP	H	R	ER	HR	SH	SF	HB	TBB	IBB	SO	WP	Bk	W	L	Pct	Sh	Sv-Op	Hld	ERC	ERA
2002 LAA	AL	18	18	1	0	108.1	465	113	52	44	10	0	4	4	33	0	69	7	2	9	4	.692	0	0-0	0	4.03	3.66
2003 LAA	AL	33	33	2	0	204.0	885	223	117	105	31	2	6	10	66	4	151	11	1	10	16	.385	2	0-0	0	4.88	4.63
2004 LAA	AL	33	32	1	0	198.1	855	215	108	103	22	9	4	6	60	4	144	11	1	14	13	.519	1	0-0	0	4.39	4.67
2005 LAA	AL	33	33	1	0	209.0	892	208	85	80	13	1	2	11	71	3	199	18	0	14	5	.737	0	0-0	0	3.76	3.44
2006 LAA	AL	33	33	3	0	217.2	922	203	98	86	14	8	6	9	72	4	190	16	0	13	11	.542	2	0-0	0	3.31	3.56
2007 LAA	AL	33	33	2	0	224.0	929	219	87	75	18	1	1	12	52	2	179	9	1	19	9	.679	2	0-0	0	3.40	3.01
2008 LAA	AL	24	24	3	0	163.1	675	161	71	68	26	5	1	10	40	1	130	5	0	12	5	.706	0	0-0	0	4.10	3.75
2009 LAA	AL	27	27	1	0	176.1	748	177	84	75	17	9	10	9	47	1	139	6	0	11	8	.579	1	0-0	0	3.73	3.83
2010 Bos	AL	33	33	0	0	215.0	930	233	114	110	18	4	5	9	72	2	156	3	0	14	11	.560	0	0-0	0	4.37	4.40
2011 Bos	AL	28	28	0	0	160.0	743	203	119	114	20	2	6	19	56	1	108	11	0	12	12	.500	0	0-0	0	6.11	6.41
2013 Bos	AL	29	29	2	0	189.1	778	179	80	74	26	3	3	6	40	0	161	4	0	10	13	.435	0	0-0	0	3.42	3.52
2014 2 Tms		31	31	1	0	198.0	833	206	94	84	24	6	3	4	47	1	164	4	2	14	10	.583	0	0-0	0	3.81	3.82
2015 StL	NL	33	33	1	0	218.0	896	211	71	67	21	11	4	4	53	5	175	5	3	13	10	.565	0	0-0	0	3.34	2.77
2016 ChC	NL	29	29	0	0	188.1	748	146	74	70	23	8	8	9	53	1	180	4	0	11	8	.579	0	0-0	0	2.81	3.35
14 Bos	AL	21	21	1	0	137.1	572	137	60	55	15	2	3	0	32	0	116	3	1	11	7	.611	0	0-0	0	3.46	3.60
14 StL	NL	10	10	0	0	60.2	261	69	34	29	9	4	0	1	15	1	48	1	1	3	3	.500	0	0-0	0	4.63	4.30
Postseason		23	20	0	0	127.1	526	116	46	44	5	3	4	3	39	5	99	7	0	8	5	.615	0	0-0	1	2.89	3.11
14 ML YEARS		417	416	18	0	2669.2	11299	2697	1254	1150	283	69	63	121	762	29	2145	114	10	176	135	.566	8	0-0	0	3.91	3.88

Tyler Ladendorf

Bats: R Throws: R Pos: 2B-30;PR-12;3B-3;PH-2;CF-1;RF-1   Ht: 5'11" Wt: 195 Born: 3/7/1988 Age: 29

Year	Team	Lg	G	AB	H	2B	3B	HR	(Hm	Rd)	TB	R	RBI	RC	TBB	IBB	SO	HBP	SH	SF	SB	CS	GDP	Avg	OBP	Slg	OPS
2012	Mdlnd	AA	104	416	100	20	1	9	(-	-)	149	59	54	52	42	0	89	11	4	3	7	4	14	.240	.324	.358	.682
2013	Mdlnd	AA	83	266	70	16	1	6	(-	-)	106	34	40	38	27	2	45	5	2	2	2	0	8	.263	.340	.398	.738
2014	Scrmto	AAA	78	273	81	18	3	2	(-	-)	111	44	43	45	35	0	56	2	0	4	3	1	4	.297	.376	.407	.782
2015	Nashv	AAA	20	83	22	2	1	1	(-	-)	29	3	8	9	5	0	23	1	0	1	0	1	1	.265	.311	.349	.661
2016	Nashv	AAA	35	128	30	5	0	1	(-	-)	38	17	6	10	7	0	26	0	2	0	0	0	0	.234	.274	.297	.571
2015	Oak	AL	9	17	4	0	1	0	(0	0)	6	3	2	0	1	0	2	0	0	0	0	0	0	.235	.278	.353	.631
2016	Oak	AL	45	48	4	0	0	0	(0	0)	4	6	1	0	1	0	13	0	1	0	2	0	3	.083	.102	.083	.185
	2 ML YEARS		54	65	8	0	1	0	(0	0)	10	9	3	0	2	0	15	0	1	0	2	0	3	.123	.149	.154	.303

Juan Lagares

Bats: R Throws: R Pos: CF-68;PH-20;PR-5;RF-2;LF-1   luh-GAR-ess   Ht: 6'1" Wt: 215 Born: 3/17/1989 Age: 28

Year	Team	Lg	G	AB	H	2B	3B	HR	(Hm	Rd)	TB	R	RBI	RC	TBB	IBB	SO	HBP	SH	SF	SB	CS	GDP	Avg	OBP	Slg	OPS
2013	NYM	NL	121	392	95	21	5	4	(1	3)	138	35	34	36	20	4	96	2	5	2	6	3	6	.242	.281	.352	.633
2014	NYM	NL	116	416	117	24	3	4	(2	2)	159	46	47	53	20	1	87	7	3	6	13	4	6	.281	.321	.382	.703
2015	NYM	NL	143	441	114	16	5	6	(4	2)	158	47	41	51	16	2	87	4	1	3	7	3	6	.259	.289	.358	.647
2016	NYM	NL	79	142	34	7	2	3	(2	1)	54	15	9	12	11	1	27	2	4	1	4	2	4	.239	.301	.380	.682
	Postseason		13	23	8	2	0	0	(0	0)	10	7	0	3	1	0	3	0	1	0	2	0	0	.348	.375	.435	.810
	4 ML YEARS		459	1391	360	68	15	17	(7	10)	509	143	131	152	67	8	297	15	13	12	30	12	22	.259	.298	.366	.664

Junior Lake

Bats: R Throws: R Pos: RF-19;PR-5;1B-1;PH-1   Ht: 6'2" Wt: 230 Born: 3/27/1990 Age: 27

Year	Team	Lg	G	AB	H	2B	3B	HR	(Hm	Rd)	TB	R	RBI	RC	TBB	IBB	SO	HBP	SH	SF	SB	CS	GDP	Avg	OBP	Slg	OPS
2016	Buffalo*	AAA	82	281	65	12	2	6	(-	-)	99	33	31	33	33	1	77	2	0	2	10	4	4	.231	.314	.352	.667
2013	ChC	NL	64	236	67	16	0	6	(4	2)	101	26	16	26	13	0	68	4	1	0	4	4	2	.284	.332	.428	.760
2014	ChC	NL	108	308	65	10	3	9	(5	4)	108	30	25	18	14	0	110	1	1	2	7	3	3	.211	.246	.351	.597
2015	2 Tms		29	80	16	7	0	1	(0	1)	26	4	5	6	4	0	29	0	0	0	4	0	1	.200	.238	.325	.563
2016	Tor	AL	22	35	7	3	0	1	(0	1)	13	5	2	4	4	0	11	0	0	0	1	0	0	.200	.282	.371	.653
15	ChC	NL	21	58	13	4	0	1	(0	1)	20	2	5	6	4	0	20	0	0	0	4	0	1	.224	.274	.345	.619
15	Bal	AL	8	22	3	3	0	0	(0	0)	6	2	0	0	0	0	9	0	0	0	0	0	0	.136	.136	.273	.409
	4 ML YEARS		223	659	155	36	3	17	(9	8)	248	65	48	54	35	0	218	5	2	2	16	7	6	.235	.278	.376	.655

Blake Lalli

Bats: L Throws: R Pos: PH-8;1B-4   LAHL-ee   Ht: 6'1" Wt: 210 Born: 5/12/1983 Age: 34

Year	Team	Lg	G	AB	H	2B	3B	HR	(Hm	Rd)	TB	R	RBI	RC	TBB	IBB	SO	HBP	SH	SF	SB	CS	GDP	Avg	OBP	Slg	OPS
2016	Gwnntt*	AAA	110	348	89	22	0	1	(-	-)	114	28	36	36	22	2	60	2	4	4	1	1	17	.256	.301	.328	.628
2012	ChC	NL	6	15	2	0	0	0	(0	0)	2	1	2	1	1	0	3	0	0	0	0	0	0	.133	.188	.133	.321
2013	Mil	NL	16	24	3	0	0	0	(0	0)	3	1	2	0	0	0	7	0	0	0	0	0	0	.125	.125	.125	.250
2016	Atl	NL	10	13	2	1	0	0	(0	0)	3	0	1	0	0	0	3	0	0	0	0	0	1	.154	.154	.231	.385
	3 ML YEARS		32	52	7	1	0	0	(0	0)	8	2	5	1	1	0	13	0	0	0	0	0	1	.135	.151	.154	.305

Ryan LaMarre

Bats: R Throws: L Pos: LF-2;PR-2;RF-1;PH-1   la-MARR   Ht: 6'1" Wt: 210 Born: 11/21/1988 Age: 28

Year	Team	Lg	G	AB	H	2B	3B	HR	(Hm	Rd)	TB	R	RBI	RC	TBB	IBB	SO	HBP	SH	SF	SB	CS	GDP	Avg	OBP	Slg	OPS
2012	Pnscla	AA	133	482	127	22	3	5	(-	-)	170	68	32	68	60	0	119	10	4	2	30	10	5	.263	.356	.353	.708
2013	Pnscla	AA	126	451	111	19	4	10	(-	-)	168	55	39	58	44	1	93	11	6	3	23	13	8	.246	.326	.373	.699
2014	Lsvlle	AAA	17	50	10	2	0	1	(-	-)	15	6	6	5	8	0	17	0	1	0	1	1	0	.200	.310	.300	.610
2015	Lsvlle	AAA	91	300	77	17	1	8	(-	-)	120	33	18	38	18	0	88	5	3	3	11	4	7	.257	.307	.400	.707
2016	Pwtckt	AAA	86	317	96	15	0	10	(-	-)	141	44	41	55	28	1	80	8	0	5	17	6	6	.303	.369	.445	.814
2015	Cin	NL	21	25	2	0	0	0	(0	0)	2	2	0	0	0	0	9	0	1	0	0	0	1	.080	.080	.080	.160
2016	Bos	AL	6	5	0	0	0	0	(0	0)	0	1	0	0	1	0	2	0	0	0	0	0	1	.000	.167	.000	.167
	2 ML YEARS		27	30	2	0	0	0	(0	0)	2	3	0	0	1	0	11	0	1	0	0	0	2	.067	.097	.067	.163

Jake Lamb

Bats: L Throws: R Pos: 3B-142;PH-17   Ht: 6'3" Wt: 215 Born: 10/9/1990 Age: 26

Year	Team	Lg	G	AB	H	2B	3B	HR	(Hm	Rd)	TB	R	RBI	RC	TBB	IBB	SO	HBP	SH	SF	SB	CS	GDP	Avg	OBP	Slg	OPS
2014	Ari	NL	37	126	29	4	1	4	(2	2)	47	15	11	7	6	0	37	0	0	1	1	1	4	.230	.263	.373	.636
2015	Ari	NL	107	350	92	15	5	6	(1	5)	135	38	34	39	36	3	97	1	0	3	2	2	5	.263	.331	.386	.716
2016	Ari	NL	151	523	130	31	9	29	(19	10)	266	81	91	84	64	5	154	3	0	4	6	1	13	.249	.332	.509	.840
	3 ML YEARS		295	999	251	50	15	39	(22	17)	448	134	136	130	106	8	288	4	0	8	10	4	22	.251	.323	.448	.772

John Lamb

Pitches: L Bats: L Pos: SP-14 **Ht:** 6'4" **Wt:** 205 **Born:** 7/10/1990 **Age:** 26

		HOW MUCH HE PITCHED					WHAT HE GAVE UP											THE RESULTS						
Year Team	Lg	G	GS	CG	GF	IP	BFP	H	R	ER	HR	SH	SF	HB	TBB	IBB	SO	WP	Bk	W	L	Pct	Sh	Sv-Op	Hld	ERC	ERA
2012 2 Tms	Low	6	6	0	0	13.0	58	15	10	10	2	0	0	4	0	14	1	0	0	1	.000	0	0- -	-	4.86	6.92
2013 Wilmg	A+	19	19	0	0	92.2	399	109	61	58	13	2	3	4	19	0	76	1	0	4	12	.250	0	0- -	-	4.79	5.63
2014 Omha	AAA	27	26	0	0	138.1	616	137	78	61	19	7	2	9	68	0	131	8	0	8	10	.444	0	0- -	-	4.92	3.97
2015 Omha	AAA	17	17	0	0	94.1	382	80	35	28	7	2	3	4	29	0	96	1	2	9	1	.900	0	0- -	-	2.97	2.67
2016 Lsvlle	AAA	6	6	0	0	29.1	130	35	18	17	1	1	1	2	9	0	26	0	0	2	2	.500	0	0- -	-	4.62	5.22
2015 Cin	NL	10	10	0	0	49.2	220	58	32	32	8	2	1	2	19	0	58	0	0	1	5	.167	0	0-0	0	5.69	5.80
2016 Cin	NL	14	14	0	0	70.0	318	84	54	50	14	8	1	1	31	0	58	1	1	1	7	.125	0	0-0	0	6.28	6.43
2 ML YEARS		24	24	0	0	119.2	538	142	86	82	22	10	2	3	50	0	116	1	1	2	12	.143	0	0-0	0	6.04	6.17

Andrew Lambo

Bats: L Throws: L Pos: PH-1 **Ht:** 6'3" **Wt:** 220 **Born:** 8/11/1988 **Age:** 28

		BATTING																	RUNNING			AVERAGES			
Year Team	Lg	G	AB	H	2B	3B	HR	(Hm Rd)	TB	R	RBI	RC	TBB	IBB	SO	HBP	SH	SF	SB	CS	GDP	Avg	OBP	Slg	OPS
2016 Nashv*	AAA	56	216	55	10	3	4	(- -)	83	29	30	28	21	0	43	1	0	2	1	0	9	.255	.321	.384	.705
2013 Pit	NL	18	30	7	2	0	1	(0 1)	12	4	2	1	3	0	11	0	0	0	0	1		.233	.303	.400	.703
2014 Pit	NL	21	39	10	4	0	0	(0 0)	14	3	1	1	0	0	8	0	0	0	0	0	2	.256	.256	.359	.615
2015 Pit	NL	20	25	1	1	0	0	(0 0)	2	1	0	0	2	0	8	0	0	0	0	0		.040	.111	.080	.191
2016 Oak	AL	1	1	0	0	0	0	(0 0)	0	0	0	0	0	0	0	0	0	0	0	0		.000	.000	.000	.000
4 ML YEARS		60	95	18	7	0	1	(0 1)	28	8	3	2	5	0	27	0	0	0	0	1	2	.189	.230	.295	.525

Mat Latos

Pitches: R Bats: R Pos: SP-12; RP-5 LAY-tos **Ht:** 6'6" **Wt:** 245 **Born:** 12/9/1987 **Age:** 29

		HOW MUCH HE PITCHED						WHAT HE GAVE UP												THE RESULTS						
Year Team	Lg	G	GS	CG	GF	IP	BFP	H	R	ER	HR	SH	SF	HB	TBB	IBB	SO	WP	Bk	W	L	Pct	Sh	Sv-Op	Hld	ERC	ERA
2009 SD	NL	10	10	0	0	50.2	212	43	29	26	7	3	1	0	23	1	39	0	2	4	5	.444	0	0-0	0	3.72	4.62
2010 SD	NL	31	31	1	0	184.2	748	150	63	60	16	4	1	2	50	3	189	5	1	14	10	.583	1	0-0	0	2.52	2.92
2011 SD	NL	31	31	0	0	194.1	799	168	82	75	16	8	7	1	62	3	185	5	0	9	14	.391	0	0-0	0	2.93	3.47
2012 Cin	NL	33	33	0	0	209.1	858	179	87	81	25	9	3	4	64	9	185	3	1	14	4	.778	0	0-0	0	3.08	3.48
2013 Cin	NL	32	32	1	0	210.2	881	197	82	74	14	12	3	10	58	5	187	8	0	14	7	.667	0	0-0	0	3.16	3.16
2014 Cin	NL	16	16	0	0	102.1	420	92	42	37	9	8	1	2	26	2	74	1	0	5	5	.500	0	0-0	0	2.94	3.25
2015 3 Tms		24	21	0	2	116.1	494	120	67	64	13	6	5	1	32	1	100	10	1	4	10	.286	0	0-0	0	3.84	4.95
2016 2 Tms		17	12	0	0	70.0	309	74	40	38	11	2	5	1	30	1	42	1	0	7	3	.700	0	0-0	0	4.96	4.89
15 Mia	NL	16	16	0	0	88.1	372	85	46	44	8	4	3	1	25	0	79	9	0	4	7	.364	0	0-0	0	3.36	4.48
15 LAD	NL	6	5	0	0	24.1	106	31	19	18	3	2	2	0	6	1	18	1	1	0	3	.000	0	0-0	0	5.22	6.66
15 LAA	AL	2	0	0	1	3.2	16	4	2	2	2	0	0	0	1	0	3	0	0	0	0	-	-	0-0	0	7.04	4.91
16 CWS	AL	11	11	0	0	60.1	265	63	33	31	10	2	4	1	25	1	32	1	0	6	2	.750	0	0-0	0	4.89	4.62
16 Was	NL	6	1	0	0	9.2	44	11	7	7	1	0	1	0	5	0	10	0	0	1	1	.500	0	0-0	0	5.37	6.52
Postseason		2	1	0	0	8.1	39	11	7	6	2	0	0	0	2	0	5	0	0	0	1	.000	0	0-0	0	6.03	6.48
8 ML YEARS		194	186	4	3	1138.1	4721	1023	492	455	111	52	26	21	345	25	1001	33	5	71	58	.550	1	0-0	0	3.17	3.60

Derek Law

Pitches: R Bats: R Pos: RP-61 **Ht:** 6'2" **Wt:** 210 **Born:** 9/14/1990 **Age:** 26

		HOW MUCH HE PITCHED						WHAT HE GAVE UP												THE RESULTS						
Year Team	Lg	G	GS	CG	GF	IP	BFP	H	R	ER	HR	SH	SF	HB	TBB	IBB	SO	WP	Bk	W	L	Pct	Sh	Sv-Op	Hld	ERC	ERA
2012 Augsta	A	32	0	0	8	55.2	235	45	20	18	6	2	0	2	23	0	67	8	0	5	2	.714	0	2- -	-	3.24	2.91
2013 3 Tms	Low	46	0	0	27	66.1	263	51	21	17	2	1	1	2	12	3	102	11	0	5	3	.625	0	14- -	-	1.72	2.31
2014 Rchmd	AA	27	0	0	24	28.0	113	19	8	8	1	0	2	1	14	0	29	1	0	2	0	1.000	0	13- -	-	2.54	2.57
2015 Rchmd	AA	28	0	0	21	25.2	116	31	16	13	1	1	1	0	8	0	33	6	0	1	0	1.000	0	13- -	-	4.34	4.56
2016 SF	NL	61	0	0	12	55.0	214	44	13	13	3	0	0	0	9	0	50	1	0	4	2	.667	0	1-2	14	1.93	2.13

Brett Lawrie

Bats: R Throws: R Pos: 2B-92; DH-2 LORI **Ht:** 6'0" **Wt:** 210 **Born:** 1/18/1990 **Age:** 27

		BATTING																	RUNNING			AVERAGES			
Year Team	Lg	G	AB	H	2B	3B	HR	(Hm Rd)	TB	R	RBI	RC	TBB	IBB	SO	HBP	SH	SF	SB	CS	GDP	Avg	OBP	Slg	OPS
2011 Tor	AL	43	150	44	8	4	9	(5 4)	87	26	25	33	16	1	31	3	2	0	7	1	0	.293	.373	.580	.953
2012 Tor	AL	125	494	135	26	3	11	(7 4)	200	73	48	65	33	0	86	5	2	8	13	8	9	.273	.324	.405	.729
2013 Tor	AL	107	401	102	18	3	11	(4 7)	159	41	46	45	30	1	68	7	1	3	9	5	8	.254	.315	.397	.712
2014 Tor	AL	70	259	64	9	0	12	(7 5)	109	27	38	39	16	0	49	5	0	2	0	0	0	.247	.301	.421	.722
2015 Oak	AL	149	562	146	29	3	16	(6 10)	229	64	60	65	28	1	144	5	3	4	5	2	8	.260	.299	.407	.706
2016 CWS	AL	94	351	87	22	0	12	(5 7)	145	35	36	43	30	2	109	2	0	1	7	3	3	.248	.310	.413	.723
6 ML YEARS		588	2217	578	112	13	71	(34 37)	929	266	253	290	153	5	487	27	8	12	41	19	28	.261	.315	.419	.734

Tommy Layne

Pitches: L Bats: L Pos: RP-63 **Ht:** 6'2" **Wt:** 195 **Born:** 11/2/1984 **Age:** 32

		HOW MUCH HE PITCHED						WHAT HE GAVE UP												THE RESULTS						
Year Team	Lg	G	GS	CG	GF	IP	BFP	H	R	ER	HR	SH	SF	HB	TBB	IBB	SO	WP	Bk	W	L	Pct	Sh	Sv-Op	Hld	ERC	ERA
2012 SD	NL	26	0	0	5	16.2	68	9	6	6	0	1	0	3	3	0	25	0	0	2	0	1.000	0	2-3	7	1.20	3.24
2013 SD	NL	14	0	0	2	8.2	39	10	4	2	1	1	0	2	5	0	6	1	0	0	2	.000	0	0-0	0	7.38	2.08
2014 Bos	AL	30	0	0	3	19.0	76	14	4	2	0	0	1	1	8	1	14	2	0	2	1	.667	0	0-1	9	2.32	0.95
2015 Bos	AL	64	0	0	9	47.2	207	41	22	21	3	2	1	2	27	2	45	1	0	2	1	.667	0	1-2	9	3.80	3.97

Year	Team	Lg	G	GS	CG	GF	IP	BFP	H	R	ER	HR	SH	SF	HB	TBB	IBB	SO	WP	Bk	W	L	Pct	Sh	Sv-Op	Hld	ERC	ERA
2016	2 Tms	AL	63	0	0	16	44.2	187	37	18	18	3	2	0	3	21	3	38	2	0	2	1	.667	0	1-3	12	3.41	3.63
16	Bos	AL	34	0	0	12	28.2	120	27	12	12	1	1	0	1	14	2	25	1	0	0	1	.000	0	0-1	2	3.82	3.77
16	NYY	AL	29	0	0	4	16.0	67	10	6	6	2	1	0	2	7	1	13	1	0	2	0	1.000	0	1-2	10	2.72	3.38
	5 ML YEARS		197	0	0	35	136.2	577	111	54	49	7	6	2	11	64	6	128	6	0	8	5	.615	0	4-9	37	3.26	3.23

Mike Leake

Pitches: R **Bats:** R **Pos:** SP-30
LEEK
Ht: 5'10" **Wt:** 170 **Born:** 11/12/1987 **Age:** 29

Year	Team	Lg	G	GS	CG	GF	IP	BFP	H	R	ER	HR	SH	SF	HB	TBB	IBB	SO	WP	Bk	W	L	Pct	Sh	Sv-Op	Hld	ERC	ERA
2010	Cin	NL	24	22	0	0	138.1	604	158	77	65	19	7	3	3	49	2	91	2	0	8	4	.667	0	0-0	0	5.12	4.23
2011	Cin	NL	29	26	0	2	167.2	693	159	74	72	23	3	6	8	38	3	118	2	1	12	9	.571	0	0-0	0	3.53	3.86
2012	Cin	NL	30	30	2	0	179.0	757	201	97	91	26	6	7	3	41	3	116	3	0	8	9	.471	0	0-0	0	4.50	4.58
2013	Cin	NL	31	31	0	0	192.1	801	193	78	72	21	8	5	6	48	4	122	2	0	14	7	.667	0	0-0	0	3.69	3.37
2014	Cin	NL	33	33	0	0	214.1	902	217	93	88	23	7	7	13	50	3	164	4	0	11	13	.458	0	0-0	0	3.77	3.70
2015	2 Tms	NL	30	30	2	0	192.0	778	174	80	79	22	6	3	3	49	5	119	6	2	11	10	.524	1	0-0	0	3.18	3.70
2016	StL	NL	30	30	0	0	176.2	757	203	101	92	20	5	10	7	30	1	125	7	0	9	12	.429	0	0-0	0	4.22	4.69
15	Cin	NL	21	21	1	0	136.2	556	123	55	54	14	6	2	2	34	4	90	3	1	9	5	.643	0	0-0	0	3.01	3.56
15	SF	NL	9	9	1	0	55.1	222	51	25	25	8	0	1	1	15	1	29	3	1	2	5	.286	1	0-0	0	3.61	4.07
	Postseason		1	1	0	0	4.1	20	6	5	5	2	1	0	0	2	0	1	0	0	0	1	.000	0	0-0	0	10.00	10.38
	7 ML YEARS		207	202	4	2	1260.1	5292	1305	600	559	154	42	41	43	305	21	855	26	3	73	64	.533	1	0-0	0	3.94	3.99

Wade LeBlanc

Pitches: L **Bats:** L **Pos:** RP-11; SP-8
lah-BLAHNK
Ht: 6'3" **Wt:** 210 **Born:** 8/7/1984 **Age:** 32

Year	Team	Lg	G	GS	CG	GF	IP	BFP	H	R	ER	HR	SH	SF	HB	TBB	IBB	SO	WP	Bk	W	L	Pct	Sh	Sv-Op	Hld	ERC	ERA
2016	Buffalo*	AAA	14	14	0	0	89.2	369	84	20	17	3	2	1	3	21	0	85	2	1	7	2	.778	0	0- -	-	2.81	1.71
2008	SD	NL	5	4	0	0	21.1	104	29	19	19	7	1	0	0	15	2	14	0	0	1	3	.250	0	0-0	0	9.57	8.02
2009	SD	NL	9	9	0	0	46.1	194	35	19	19	6	3	1	4	19	1	30	0	0	3	1	.750	0	0-0	0	3.28	3.69
2010	SD	NL	26	25	0	0	146.0	625	157	69	69	24	7	2	2	51	5	110	2	0	8	12	.400	0	0-0	0	4.84	4.25
2011	SD	NL	14	14	0	0	79.2	339	84	42	41	7	3	3	1	28	1	51	1	1	5	6	.455	0	0-0	0	4.21	4.63
2012	Mia	NL	25	9	0	1	68.2	284	71	30	28	7	5	1	1	19	1	43	1	0	2	5	.286	0	0-0	1	3.94	3.67
2013	2 Tms		17	7	0	1	55.0	259	72	40	33	7	2	1	3	20	3	33	0	0	1	5	.167	0	0-0	0	5.97	5.40
2014	2 Tms	AL	11	3	0	3	29.2	121	27	13	13	2	0	2	2	7	2	21	1	0	1	1	.500	0	0-0	0	2.96	3.94
2016	2 Tms		19	8	0	7	62.0	252	59	30	26	14	0	2	0	11	0	51	0	0	4	0	1.000	0	2-2	1	3.72	3.77
13	Mia	NL	13	7	0	0	48.2	222	63	30	28	6	2	1	2	15	2	31	0	0	1	5	.167	0	0-0	0	5.67	5.18
13	Hou	AL	4	0	0	1	6.1	37	9	10	5	1	0	0	1	5	1	2	0	0	0	0	-	0	0-0	0	8.25	7.11
14	LAA	AL	10	3	0	2	28.2	114	25	11	11	2	0	1	1	6	1	21	1	0	1	1	.500	0	0-0	0	2.63	3.45
14	NYY	AL	1	0	0	1	1.0	7	2	2	2	0	0	1	1	1	1	0	0	0	0	0	-	0	0-0	0	13.81	18.00
16	Sea	AL	11	8	0	3	50.0	208	52	27	25	14	0	0	0	9	0	41	0	0	3	0	1.000	0	1-1	0	4.58	4.50
16	Pit	NL	8	0	0	4	12.0	44	7	3	1	0	0	2	0	2	0	10	0	0	1	0	1.000	0	1-1	1	1.03	0.75
	8 ML YEARS		126	79	0	12	508.2	2178	534	262	248	74	21	12	13	170	15	353	5	1	25	33	.431	0	2-2	2	4.52	4.39

Jose Leclerc

Pitches: R **Bats:** R **Pos:** RP-12
leh-KLURK
Ht: 6'0" **Wt:** 190 **Born:** 12/19/1993 **Age:** 23

Year	Team	Lg	G	GS	CG	GF	IP	BFP	H	R	ER	HR	SH	SF	HB	TBB	IBB	SO	WP	Bk	W	L	Pct	Sh	Sv-Op	Hld	ERC	ERA
2013	Hkry	A	39	0	0	20	59.0	254	53	26	22	2	4	2	6	21	0	77	3	0	3	4	.429	0	5- -	-	3.25	3.36
2014	MrtlBh	A+	42	0	0	37	57.1	243	39	23	21	8	1	1	2	37	1	79	5	1	4	1	.800	0	14- -	-	3.69	3.30
2015	Frisco	AA	26	22	0	0	103.0	472	97	66	66	8	1	1	2	73	0	98	13	2	6	8	.429	0	0- -	-	5.05	5.77
2016	Frisco	AA	10	2	0	2	23.0	95	17	11	9	1	1	2	1	10	0	28	2	0	0	5	.000	0	1- -	-	2.62	3.52
2016	RdRck	AAA	29	0	0	4	43.0	176	23	13	13	3	2	2	0	28	0	50	3	1	2	2	.500	0	1- -	-	2.39	2.72
2016	Tex	AL	12	0	0	5	15.0	66	11	4	3	0	0	1	0	13	2	15	1	0	0	0	-	0	0-0	0	3.46	1.80

Sam LeCure

Pitches: R **Bats:** R **Pos:** P
leh-CURE
Ht: 6'0" **Wt:** 210 **Born:** 5/4/1984 **Age:** 33

Year	Team	Lg	G	GS	CG	GF	IP	BFP	H	R	ER	HR	SH	SF	HB	TBB	IBB	SO	WP	Bk	W	L	Pct	Sh	Sv-Op	Hld	ERC	ERA
2016	OkCity*	AAA	31	12	0	8	91.0	387	97	48	46	10	3	4	2	25	1	73	2	1	5	5	.500	0	2- -	-	4.11	4.55
2010	Cin	NL	15	6	0	4	48.0	217	50	24	24	6	1	2	5	25	3	37	1	0	2	5	.286	0	0-0	0	5.36	4.50
2011	Cin	NL	43	4	0	7	77.2	307	57	33	32	10	0	4	0	21	3	73	0	0	2	1	.667	0	0-0	5	2.55	3.71
2012	Cin	NL	48	0	0	12	57.1	237	46	22	20	3	4	1	1	23	2	61	2	0	3	3	.500	0	0-1	7	2.73	3.14
2013	Cin	NL	63	0	0	15	61.0	251	50	18	18	4	1	0	1	24	0	66	0	0	2	1	.667	0	1-3	17	2.95	2.66
2014	Cin	NL	62	0	0	16	56.2	251	62	27	24	6	2	3	3	24	1	48	5	0	1	4	.200	0	0-1	17	4.99	3.81
2015	Cin	NL	19	0	0	1	20.0	83	16	9	7	2	1	0	0	7	0	15	0	0	0	2	.000	0	0-1	3	2.77	3.15
	Postseason		4	0	0	1	5.0	19	3	0	0	0	0	1	0	2	1	5	0	0	1	0	1.000	0	0-0	0	1.39	0.00
	6 ML YEARS		250	10	0	55	320.2	1346	281	133	125	31	13	7	14	124	9	300	8	0	10	16	.385	0	1-6	49	3.48	3.51

Dae-Ho Lee

Bats: R **Throws:** R **Pos:** 1B-84; PH-25; DH-7
day-ho
Ht: 6'4" **Wt:** 250 **Born:** 6/21/1982 **Age:** 35

Year	Team	Lg	G	AB	H	2B	3B	HR	(Hm	Rd)	TB	R	RBI	RC	TBB	IBB	SO	HBP	SH	SF	SB	CS	GDP	Avg	OBP	Slg	OPS
2016	Sea	AL	104	292	74	9	0	14	(8	6)	125	33	49	40	20	2	74	5	0	0	0	0	8	.253	.312	.428	.740

DJ LeMahieu

Bats: R **Throws:** R **Pos:** 2B-146;PH-1   la-MAY-hugh   **Ht:** 6'4" **Wt:** 215 **Born:** 7/13/1988 **Age:** 28

									BATTING											RUNNING			AVERAGES			
Year	Team	Lg	G	AB	H	2B	3B	HR	(Hm	Rd)	TB	R	RBI	RC	TBB	IBB	SO	HBP	SH	SF	SB	CS	GDP	Avg	OBP	Slg	OPS
2011	ChC	NL	37	60	15	2	0	0	(0	0)	17	3	4	3	1	0	12	0	1	0	0	0	2	.250	.262	.283	.546
2012	Col	NL	81	229	68	12	4	2	(1	1)	94	26	22	28	13	4	42	0	3	2	1	2	8	.297	.332	.410	.742
2013	Col	NL	109	404	113	21	3	2	(1	1)	146	39	28	42	19	2	67	1	7	3	18	7	13	.280	.311	.361	.673
2014	Col	NL	149	494	132	15	5	5	(2	3)	172	59	42	47	33	7	97	2	7	2	10	10	13	.267	.315	.348	.663
2015	Col	NL	150	564	170	21	5	6	(3	3)	219	85	61	75	50	4	107	1	3	2	23	3	20	.301	.358	.388	.746
2016	Col	NL	146	552	192	32	8	11	(7	4)	273	104	66	104	66	2	80	3	8	6	11	7	19	**.348**	.416	.495	.911
6 ML YEARS			672	2303	690	103	25	26	(14	12)	921	316	223	299	182	19	405	7	29	15	63	29	75	.300	.351	.400	.751

Arnold Leon

Pitches: R **Bats:** R **Pos:** RP-2   lay-OHN   **Ht:** 6'1" **Wt:** 210 **Born:** 9/6/1988 **Age:** 28

				HOW MUCH HE PITCHED				WHAT HE GAVE UP											THE RESULTS							
Year	Team	Lg	G	GS	CG	GF	IP	BFP	H	R	ER	HR	SH	SF	HB	TBB	IBB	SO	WP	Bk	W	L	Pct	Sh	Sv-Op	Hld	ERC	ERA
2012	Stcktn	A+	12	0	0	4	15.1	77	26	13	9	1	0	0	1	5	0	25	3	0	0	1	.000	0	0- -	-	7.94	5.28
2012	Mdlnd	AA	10	0	0	3	15.2	64	17	5	4	0	1	1	0	3	0	18	1	0	1	0	1.000	0	1- -	-	3.15	2.30
2012	Scrmto	AAA	22	0	0	5	35.2	144	26	9	7	4	2	0	2	15	0	31	5	0	3	0	1.000	0	0- -	-	3.08	1.77
2013	Mdlnd	AA	13	13	0	0	72.2	313	87	40	31	9	2	1	4	11	0	48	2	0	4	5	.444	0	0- -	-	4.59	3.84
2013	Scrmto	AAA	12	11	0	0	71.1	300	81	36	35	4	0	2	3	13	0	49	3	0	5	3	.625	0	0- -	-	3.89	4.42
2014	Scrmto	AAA	27	27	0	0	145.0	640	170	84	80	12	0	7	6	51	0	128	14	2	10	7	.588	0	0- -	-	4.97	4.97
2015	Nashv	AAA	20	6	0	3	58.0	243	52	21	19	7	0	2	2	19	0	55	3	2	2	5	.286	0	1- -	-	3.49	2.95
2015	Oak	AL	19	0	0	9	26.2	115	30	14	13	3	1	2	0	9	3	19	0	0	0	2	.000	0	0-0	0	4.50	4.39
2016	Tor	AL	2	0	0	0	2.1	11	3	2	2	1	0	0	0	1	0	2	0	0	0	0	-	0	0-1	0	8.35	7.71
2 ML YEARS			21	0	0	9	29.0	126	33	16	15	4	1	2	0	10	3	21	0	0	0	2	.000	0	0-1	0	4.79	4.66

Sandy Leon

Bats: B **Throws:** R **Pos:** C-74;PH-8;DH-2   lay-OHN   **Ht:** 5'10" **Wt:** 225 **Born:** 3/13/1989 **Age:** 28

									BATTING											RUNNING			AVERAGES			
Year	Team	Lg	G	AB	H	2B	3B	HR	(Hm	Rd)	TB	R	RBI	RC	TBB	IBB	SO	HBP	SH	SF	SB	CS	GDP	Avg	OBP	Slg	OPS
2016	Pwtckt*	AAA	36	115	28	3	1	2	(-	-)	39	12	13	13	11	1	24	2	0	2	0	0	5	.243	.315	.339	.655
2012	Was	NL	12	30	8	2	0	0	(0	0)	10	2	2	2	4	0	11	2	0	0	0	0	1	.267	.389	.333	.722
2013	Was	NL	2	1	0	0	0	0	(0	0)	0	0	0	0	0	0	1	0	0	0	0	0	0	.000	.000	.000	.000
2014	Was	NL	20	64	10	1	0	1	(0	1)	14	7	3	2	6	0	20	0	0	0	0	0	1	.156	.229	.219	.447
2015	Bos	AL	41	114	21	2	0	0	(0	0)	23	8	3	7	7	1	28	1	6	0	0	1	4	.184	.238	.202	.439
2016	Bos	AL	78	252	78	17	2	7	(2	5)	120	36	35	44	23	1	66	2	4	2	0	0	4	.310	.369	.476	.845
5 ML YEARS			153	461	117	22	2	8	(2	6)	167	53	43	49	40	2	126	5	10	2	0	1	10	.254	.319	.362	.681

Dominic Leone

Pitches: R **Bats:** R **Pos:** RP-25   LEE-own   **Ht:** 5'11" **Wt:** 210 **Born:** 10/26/1991 **Age:** 25

				HOW MUCH HE PITCHED				WHAT HE GAVE UP											THE RESULTS							
Year	Team	Lg	G	GS	CG	GF	IP	BFP	H	R	ER	HR	SH	SF	HB	TBB	IBB	SO	WP	Bk	W	L	Pct	Sh	Sv-Op	Hld	ERC	ERA
2016	Reno*	AAA	33	0	0	4	35.0	137	25	14	13	4	1	0	1	11	3	36	6	0	5	2	.714	0	1- -	-	2.41	3.34
2014	Sea	AL	57	0	0	3	66.1	272	52	18	16	4	1	3	3	25	3	70	4	0	8	2	.800	0	0-2	7	2.71	2.17
2015	2 Tms		13	0	0	6	15.0	74	19	15	14	2	0	1	1	9	2	9	2	0	0	5	.000	0	0-1	1	6.63	8.40
2016	Ari	NL	25	0	0	8	27.0	131	45	21	19	7	0	3	1	12	1	23	4	0	0	1	.000	0	0-1	0	10.37	6.33
15	Sea	AL	10	0	0	5	11.1	54	11	9	8	1	0	0	0	9	2	7	2	0	0	4	.000	0	0-0	1	4.93	6.35
15	Ari	NL	3	0	0	1	3.2	20	8	6	6	1	0	1	1	0	0	2	0	0	0	1	.000	0	0-1	0	12.63	14.73
3 ML YEARS			95	0	0	17	108.1	477	116	54	49	13	1	7	5	46	6	102	10	0	8	8	.500	0	0-4	8	4.87	4.07

Jon Lester

Pitches: L **Bats:** L **Pos:** SP-32   **Ht:** 6'4" **Wt:** 240 **Born:** 1/7/1984 **Age:** 33

				HOW MUCH HE PITCHED				WHAT HE GAVE UP											THE RESULTS							
Year	Team	Lg	G	GS	CG	GF	IP	BFP	H	R	ER	HR	SH	SF	HB	TBB	IBB	SO	WP	Bk	W	L	Pct	Sh	Sv-Op	Hld	ERC	ERA
2006	Bos	AL	15	15	0	0	81.1	367	91	43	43	7	2	8	5	43	1	60	5	0	7	2	.778	0	0-0	0	5.52	4.76
2007	Bos	AL	12	11	0	0	63.0	275	61	33	32	10	1	5	1	31	0	50	1	0	4	0	1.000	0	0-0	0	4.78	4.57
2008	Bos	AL	33	33	2	0	210.1	874	202	78	75	14	6	3	10	66	1	152	3	1	16	6	.727	2	0-0	0	3.55	3.21
2009	Bos	AL	32	32	2	0	203.1	843	186	80	77	20	2	6	3	64	0	225	6	0	15	8	.652	0	0-0	0	3.35	3.41
2010	Bos	AL	32	32	2	0	208.0	861	167	81	75	14	4	6	10	83	0	225	6	0	19	9	.679	0	0-0	0	3.00	3.25
2011	Bos	AL	31	31	0	0	191.2	799	166	77	74	20	2	2	11	75	0	182	4	0	15	9	.625	0	0-0	0	3.62	3.47
2012	Bos	AL	33	33	3	0	205.1	876	216	117	110	25	5	7	4	68	2	166	6	0	9	14	.391	0	0-0	0	4.36	4.82
2013	Bos	AL	33	33	1	0	213.1	903	209	94	89	19	1	1	7	67	0	177	5	0	15	8	.652	1	0-0	0	3.69	3.75
2014	2 Tms	AL	32	32	1	0	219.2	885	194	76	60	16	6	5	5	48	0	220	3	0	16	11	.593	1	0-0	0	2.70	2.46
2015	ChC	NL	32	32	1	0	205.0	828	183	83	76	16	5	4	7	47	0	207	8	0	11	12	.478	0	0-0	0	2.88	3.34
2016	ChC	NL	32	32	2	0	202.2	796	154	57	55	21	4	4	6	52	0	197	4	0	19	5	.792	0	0-0	0	2.47	2.44
14	Bos	AL	21	21	0	0	143.0	580	128	52	40	9	5	2	4	32	0	149	2	0	10	7	.588	0	0-0	0	2.73	2.73
14	Oak	AL	11	11	1	0	76.2	305	66	24	20	7	1	3	1	16	0	71	1	0	6	4	.600	1	0-0	0	2.65	2.35
Postseason			16	14	0	2	98.0	396	80	33	31	11	6	1	2	25	0	87	2	0	6	6	.500	0	0-0	0	2.70	2.85
11 ML YEARS			317	316	14	0	2003.2	8307	1829	819	766	182	38	51	69	644	4	1861	51	1	146	84	.635	4	0-0	0	3.40	3.44

Colby Lewis

Pitches: R Bats: R Pos: SP-19 **Ht: 6'4" Wt: 240 Born: 8/2/1979 Age: 37**

Year	Team	Lg	G	GS	CG	GF	IP	BFP	H	R	ER	HR	SH	SF	HB	TBB	IBB	SO	WP	Bk	W	L	Pct	Sh	Sv-Op	Hld	ERC	ERA
2002	Tex	AL	15	4	0	4	34.1	168	42	26	24	4	2	0	2	26	2	28	3	1	1	3	.250	0	0-2	1	7.22	6.29
2003	Tex	AL	26	26	0	0	127.0	594	163	104	103	23	2	2	5	70	1	88	5	0	10	9	.526	0	0-0	0	7.38	7.30
2004	Tex	AL	3	3	0	0	15.1	71	13	7	7	1	0	0	1	13	0	11	0	0	1	1	.500	0	0-0	0	4.98	4.11
2006	Det	AL	2	0	0	1	3.0	18	8	1	1	1	0	0	0	1	0	5	0	0	0	0	-	0	0-0	0	17.35	3.00
2007	Oak	AL	26	1	0	8	37.2	170	44	28	27	7	1	2	3	14	3	23	1	1	0	2	.000	0	0-1	5	5.79	6.45
2010	Tex	AL	32	32	1	0	201.0	844	174	90	83	21	4	4	6	65	0	196	9	0	12	13	.480	0	0-0	0	3.15	3.72
2011	Tex	AL	32	32	2	0	200.1	839	187	103	98	35	4	5	6	56	1	169	4	0	14	10	.583	1	0-0	0	3.82	4.40
2012	Tex	AL	16	16	2	0	105.0	427	99	48	40	16	1	2	6	14	0	93	2	0	6	6	.500	0	0-0	0	3.28	3.43
2014	Tex	AL	29	29	2	0	170.1	762	211	107	98	25	3	9	8	48	5	133	3	1	10	14	.417	1	0-0	0	5.46	5.18
2015	Tex	AL	33	33	2	0	204.2	861	211	114	106	26	2	11	11	42	2	142	5	0	17	9	.654	1	0-0	0	3.86	4.66
2016	Tex	AL	19	19	1	0	116.1	472	103	53	48	19	1	3	3	28	0	73	1	0	6	5	.545	0	0-0	0	3.37	3.71
	Postseason		9	8	0	0	53.0	220	35	16	14	7	0	0	3	25	0	45	3	0	4	1	.800	0	0-0	0	2.94	2.38
11 ML YEARS			233	195	10	13	1215.0	5226	1255	681	635	178	20	38	51	377	14	961	33	3	77	72	.517	3	0-3	4	4.37	4.70

Adam Liberatore

Pitches: L Bats: L Pos: RP-58 LEE-ber-ah-toor **Ht: 6'3" Wt: 240 Born: 5/12/1987 Age: 30**

Year	Team	Lg	G	GS	CG	GF	IP	BFP	H	R	ER	HR	SH	SF	HB	TBB	IBB	SO	WP	Bk	W	L	Pct	Sh	Sv-Op	Hld	ERC	ERA
2012	Mont	AA	33	0	0	24	52.0	223	53	18	17	4	3	1	6	20	1	27	1	0	3	4	.429	0	8--	-	4.53	2.94
2012	Drham	AAA	16	0	0	6	21.0	89	18	3	3	0	0	1	0	8	0	21	4	0	1	1	.500	0	1--	-	2.52	1.29
2013	Drham	AAA	43	0	0	12	60.1	255	50	27	24	1	7	3	1	25	0	69	4	0	5	3	.625	0	0--	-	2.68	3.58
2014	Drham	AAA	54	0	0	20	65.0	247	43	14	12	1	1	0	1	15	0	86	3	0	6	1	.857	0	4--	-	1.47	1.66
2015	OkCity	AAA	19	0	0	7	21.2	91	18	9	9	2	3	1	1	10	0	18	1	0	0	1	.000	0	3--	-	3.56	3.74
2015	LAD	NL	39	0	0	5	29.2	122	26	14	14	3	0	1	0	9	4	29	1	0	2	2	.500	0	0-1	10	2.85	4.25
2016	LAD	NL	58	0	0	9	42.2	176	34	16	16	2	0	2	2	17	4	47	1	0	2	2	.500	0	0-2	13	2.70	3.38
2 ML YEARS			97	0	0	14	72.1	298	60	30	30	5	0	3	2	26	8	76	2	0	4	4	.500	0	0-3	23	2.76	3.73

Pat Light

Pitches: R Bats: R Pos: RP-17 **Ht: 6'5" Wt: 220 Born: 3/29/1991 Age: 26**

Year	Team	Lg	G	GS	CG	GF	IP	BFP	H	R	ER	HR	SH	SF	HB	TBB	IBB	SO	WP	Bk	W	L	Pct	Sh	Sv-Op	Hld	ERC	ERA
2012	Lowell	A-	12	12	0	0	30.1	117	27	9	8	1	0	0	1	5	0	30	2	0	2	0	.000	0	0--	-	2.45	2.37
2013	2 Tms	Low	13	12	0	0	34.1	166	48	33	28	4	0	1	1	16	0	31	5	0	1	4	.200	0	0--	-	6.92	7.34
2014	2 Tms	Low	25	25	1	0	132.1	578	150	76	71	11	4	9	6	37	0	76	5	0	8	6	.571	0	0--	-	4.40	4.83
2015	Portlnd	AA	21	0	0	16	29.2	118	18	11	8	3	0	0	0	11	0	32	2	0	1	1	.500	0	3--	-	1.94	2.43
2015	Pwtckt	AAA	26	0	0	18	33.0	154	31	19	19	2	1	1	1	26	0	35	1	0	2	4	.333	0	2--	-	5.05	5.18
2016	Pwtckt	AAA	25	0	0	18	31.0	131	21	8	8	1	0	2	0	17	1	36	5	0	1	1	.500	0	7--	-	2.38	2.32
2016	Roch	AAA	6	0	0	5	7.0	29	5	2	2	0	1	0	1	2	0	6	1	0	1	0	1.000	0	2--	-	2.02	2.57
2016	2 Tms	AL	17	0	0	1	16.2	91	22	22	21	4	0	0	1	16	2	16	5	0	0	1	.000	0	0-1	0	9.33	11.34
16	Bos	AL	2	0	0	1	2.2	18	7	8	7	2	0	0	1	1	0	2	0	0	0	0	-	0	0-0	0	22.77	23.63
16	Min	AL	15	0	0	0	14.0	73	15	14	14	2	0	0	0	15	2	14	5	0	0	1	.000	0	0-1	0	7.08	9.00

Tim Lincecum

Pitches: R Bats: L Pos: SP-9 LIN-suh-come **Ht: 5'11" Wt: 170 Born: 6/15/1984 Age: 33**

Year	Team	Lg	G	GS	CG	GF	IP	BFP	H	R	ER	HR	SH	SF	HB	TBB	IBB	SO	WP	Bk	W	L	Pct	Sh	Sv-Op	Hld	ERC	ERA
2016	Salt Lk*	AAA	7	7	0	0	38.1	161	30	21	16	2	2	1	3	14	0	37	2	1	0	3	.000	0	0--	-	2.72	3.76
2007	SF	NL	24	24	0	0	146.1	618	122	70	65	12	5	7	2	65	5	150	10	0	7	5	.583	0	0-0	0	3.21	4.00
2008	SF	NL	34	33	2	0	227.0	928	182	72	66	11	11	3	6	84	1	265	17	2	18	5	.783	1	0-0	0	2.69	2.62
2009	SF	NL	32	32	4	0	225.1	905	168	69	62	10	12	5	6	68	2	261	11	0	15	7	.682	2	0-0	0	2.14	2.48
2010	SF	NL	33	33	1	0	212.1	897	194	84	81	18	9	5	5	76	7	231	9	0	16	10	.615	1	0-0	0	3.37	3.43
2011	SF	NL	33	33	1	0	217.0	900	176	74	66	15	13	1	6	86	5	220	9	0	13	14	.481	1	0-0	0	2.92	2.74
2012	SF	NL	33	33	0	0	186.0	825	190	111	107	23	11	6	4	90	3	190	17	2	10	15	.400	0	0-0	0	4.50	5.18
2013	SF	NL	32	32	1	0	197.2	841	184	102	96	21	10	4	7	76	3	193	11	2	10	14	.417	1	0-0	0	3.76	4.37
2014	SF	NL	33	26	1	3	155.2	673	154	86	82	19	4	4	5	63	0	134	15	1	12	9	.571	1	1-1	0	4.33	4.74
2015	SF	NL	15	15	0	0	76.1	333	75	37	35	7	3	2	1	38	2	60	5	0	7	4	.636	0	0-0	0	4.35	4.13
2016	LAA	AL	9	9	0	0	38.1	200	68	41	39	11	1	2	2	23	0	32	3	0	2	6	.250	0	0-0	0	12.19	9.16
	Postseason		13	6	1	0	56.1	217	34	16	15	3	1	3	1	14	0	65	0	0	5	2	.714	1	0-0	2	1.45	2.40
10 ML YEARS			278	270	10	3	1682.0	7120	1506	746	699	147	79	39	44	669	33	1736	107	7	110	89	.553	7	1-1	0	3.48	3.74

Adam Lind

Bats: L Throws: L Pos: 1B-101;PH-23;DH-16 **Ht: 6'2" Wt: 195 Born: 7/17/1983 Age: 33**

Year	Team	Lg	G	AB	H	2B	3B	HR	(Hm	Rd)	TB	R	RBI	RC	TBB	IBB	SO	HBP	SH	SF	SB	CS	GDP	Avg	OBP	Slg	OPS
2006	Tor	AL	18	60	22	8	0	2	(0	2)	36	8	8	13	5	0	12	0	0	0	0	0	0	.367	.415	.600	1.015
2007	Tor	AL	89	290	69	14	0	11	(10	1)	116	34	46	38	16	0	65	1	2	2	1	2	7	.238	.278	.400	.678
2008	Tor	AL	88	326	92	16	4	9	(2	7)	143	48	40	39	16	3	59	2	1	4	2	0	8	.282	.316	.439	.755
2009	Tor	AL	151	587	179	46	0	35	(14	21)	330	93	114	114	58	7	110	5	0	4	1	1	15	.305	.370	.562	.932
2010	Tor	AL	150	569	135	32	3	23	(15	8)	242	57	72	65	38	3	144	3	0	3	0	0	10	.237	.287	.425	.712
2011	Tor	AL	125	499	125	16	0	26	(12	14)	219	56	87	67	32	4	107	3	0	8	1	1	12	.251	.295	.439	.734
2012	Tor	AL	93	321	82	14	2	11	(6	5)	133	28	45	47	29	1	61	0	0	3	0	0	10	.255	.314	.414	.729
2013	Tor	AL	143	465	134	26	1	23	(9	14)	231	67	67	76	51	5	103	1	0	4	1	0	20	.288	.357	.497	.854

			BATTING																	RUNNING			AVERAGES			
Year	Team	Lg	G	AB	H	2B	3B	HR	(Hm	Rd)	TB	R	RBI	RC	TBB	IBB	SO	HBP	SH	SF	SB	CS	GDP	Avg	OBP	Slg	OPS
2014	Tor	AL	96	290	93	24	2	6	(5	1)	139	38	40	54	28	3	48	0	0	0	0	0	8	.321	.381	.479	.860
2015	Mil	NL	149	502	139	32	6	20	(10	10)	231	72	87	91	66	11	100	1	0	3	0	0	7	.277	.360	.460	.820
2016	Sea	AL	126	401	96	17	0	20	(15	5)	173	48	58	47	26	3	89	1	0	2	0	1	14	.239	.286	.431	.717
11 ML YEARS			1228	4310	1166	245	12	186	(98	88)	1993	549	664	651	365	40	898	17	3	33	6	5	111	.271	.328	.462	.790

Francisco Lindor

Bats: B **Throws:** R **Pos:** SS-155;PH-3;DH-1   lin-DOHR   **Ht:** 5'11" **Wt:** 190 **Born:** 11/14/1993 **Age:** 23

			BATTING																	RUNNING			AVERAGES			
Year	Team	Lg	G	AB	H	2B	3B	HR	(Hm	Rd)	TB	R	RBI	RC	TBB	IBB	SO	HBP	SH	SF	SB	CS	GDP	Avg	OBP	Slg	OPS
2012	Lk Cty	A	122	490	126	24	3	6	(-	-)	174	83	42	68	61	8	78	11	4	1	27	12	19	.257	.352	.355	.707
2013	Carlina	A+	83	327	100	19	6	1	(-	-)	134	51	27	55	35	0	39	2	6	3	20	5	7	.306	.373	.410	.783
2013	Akron	AA	21	76	22	3	1	1	(-	-)	30	14	7	13	14	0	7	1	0	0	5	2	1	.289	.407	.395	.801
2014	Akron	AA	88	342	95	13	4	6	(-	-)	134	51	48	51	40	0	61	1	1	3	25	9	11	.278	.352	.392	.744
2014	Clmbs	AAA	38	165	45	4	0	5	(-	-)	64	24	14	18	9	1	36	0	4	2	3	7	3	.273	.307	.388	.695
2015	Clmbs	AAA	59	229	65	11	5	2	(-	-)	92	26	22	33	25	0	38	0	5	3	9	7	1	.284	.350	.402	.752
2015	Cle	AL	99	390	122	22	4	12	(8	4)	188	50	51	64	27	0	69	1	13	7	12	2	12	.313	.353	.482	.835
2016	Cle	AL	158	604	182	30	3	15	(6	9)	263	99	78	87	57	3	88	5	3	15	19	5	18	.301	.358	.435	.794
2 ML YEARS			257	994	304	52	7	27	(14	13)	451	149	129	151	84	3	157	6	16	22	31	7	30	.306	.356	.454	.810

Francisco Liriano

Pitches: L **Bats:** L **Pos:** SP-29; RP-2   **Ht:** 6'2" **Wt:** 225 **Born:** 10/26/1983 **Age:** 33

			HOW MUCH HE PITCHED					WHAT HE GAVE UP											THE RESULTS						
Year	Team	Lg	G	GS	CG	GF	IP	BFP	H	R	ER	HR	SH	SF	HB	TBB	IBB	SO	WP	Bk	W	L	Pct	Sh	Sv-Op	Hld	ERC	ERA
2005	Min	AL	6	4	0	2	23.2	93	19	15	15	4	0	0	0	7	0	33	0	0	1	2	.333	0	0-0	0	3.15	5.70
2006	Min	AL	28	16	0	2	121.0	473	89	31	29	9	4	2	1	32	0	144	9	1	12	3	.800	0	1-1	1	2.12	2.16
2008	Min	AL	14	14	0	0	76.0	329	74	40	33	7	2	3	1	32	1	67	3	0	6	4	.600	0	0-0	0	3.97	3.91
2009	Min	AL	29	24	0	0	136.2	609	147	93	88	21	5	6	6	65	0	122	5	1	5	13	.278	0	0-0	0	5.46	5.80
2010	Min	AL	31	31	0	0	191.2	806	184	77	77	9	6	2	10	58	0	201	10	1	14	10	.583	0	0-0	0	3.34	3.62
2011	Min	AL	26	24	1	0	134.1	591	125	81	76	14	0	6	7	75	1	112	9	0	9	10	.474	1	0-0	0	4.58	5.09
2012	2 Tms	AL	34	28	0	2	156.2	693	143	97	93	19	4	8	7	87	5	167	11	1	6	12	.333	0	0-0	1	4.47	5.34
2013	Pit	NL	26	26	2	0	161.0	666	134	54	54	9	3	1	0	63	0	163	7	2	16	8	.667	0	0-0	0	2.86	3.02
2014	Pit	NL	29	29	0	0	162.1	691	130	68	61	13	6	5	4	81	3	175	12	0	7	10	.412	0	0-0	0	3.28	3.38
2015	Pit	NL	31	31	0	0	186.2	773	155	75	70	15	2	1	5	70	1	205	10	1	12	7	.632	0	0-0	0	3.04	3.38
2016	2 Tms		31	29	0	0	163.0	731	157	98	85	26	7	6	9	85	1	168	9	0	8	13	.381	0	0-0	0	4.96	4.69
12 Min		AL	22	17	0	2	100.0	440	89	63	59	12	2	7	4	55	4	109	6	1	3	10	.231	0	0-0	1	4.27	5.31
12 CWS			12	11	0	0	56.2	253	54	34	34	7	2	1	3	32	1	58	5	0	3	2	.600	0	0-0	0	4.83	5.40
16 Pit		NL	21	21	0	0	113.2	523	115	76	69	19	7	5	7	69	1	116	8	0	6	11	.353	0	0-0	0	5.71	5.46
16 Tor			10	8	0	0	49.1	208	42	22	16	7	0	1	2	16	0	52	1	0	2	2	.500	0	0-0	0	3.34	2.92
Postseason			4	3	0	0	20.2	84	14	9	8	1	0	0	2	7	0	18	2	0	1	0	1.000	0		0	2.20	3.48
11 ML YEARS			285	256	3	8	1513.0	6455	1357	729	681	146	39	40	50	655	12	1557	85	7	96	92	.511	1	1-1	2	3.74	4.05

Jose Lobaton

Bats: B **Throws:** R **Pos:** C-38;PH-1   LOE-bah-tone   **Ht:** 6'1" **Wt:** 205 **Born:** 10/21/1984 **Age:** 32

			BATTING																	RUNNING			AVERAGES			
Year	Team	Lg	G	AB	H	2B	3B	HR	(Hm	Rd)	TB	R	RBI	RC	TBB	IBB	SO	HBP	SH	SF	SB	CS	GDP	Avg	OBP	Slg	OPS
2009	SD	NL	7	17	3	0	0	0	(0	0)	3	0	0	0	0	0	5	0	0	0	0	0	1	.176	.176	.176	.353
2011	TB	AL	15	34	4	1	0	0	(0	0)	5	2	0	0	4	0	8	1	0	0	0	0	2	.118	.231	.147	.378
2012	TB	AL	69	167	37	10	0	2	(1	1)	53	16	20	19	24	1	46	2	2	2	0	1	6	.222	.323	.317	.640
2013	TB	AL	100	277	69	15	2	7	(5	2)	109	38	32	32	30	0	65	0	2	2	0	1	5	.249	.320	.394	.714
2014	Was	NL	66	214	50	9	0	2	(2	0)	65	15	12	13	15	1	61	1	0	0	0	0	5	.234	.287	.304	.591
2015	Was	NL	44	136	27	4	0	3	(1	2)	40	11	20	14	15	1	40	1	1	2	0	0	5	.199	.279	.294	.573
2016	Was	NL	39	99	23	3	1	3	(2	1)	37	10	8	9	12	1	18	1	1	1	0	0	4	.232	.319	.374	.692
Postseason			4	7	2	0	0	1	(1	0)	5	1	1	1	0	0	2	0	0	0	0	0	0	.286	.286	.714	1.000
7 ML YEARS			340	944	213	42	3	17	(11	6)	312	95	92	87	100	4	243	6	6	7	0	2	28	.226	.302	.331	.632

Kyle Lobstein

Pitches: L **Bats:** L **Pos:** RP-14   LOB-steen   **Ht:** 6'3" **Wt:** 220 **Born:** 8/12/1989 **Age:** 27

			HOW MUCH HE PITCHED					WHAT HE GAVE UP											THE RESULTS						
Year	Team	Lg	G	GS	CG	GF	IP	BFP	H	R	ER	HR	SH	SF	HB	TBB	IBB	SO	WP	Bk	W	L	Pct	Sh	Sv-Op	Hld	ERC	ERA
2016	Indy*	AAA	19	6	0	4	50.1	214	55	26	23	3	1	1	1	17	2	42	1	0	1	3	.250	0	1--	-	4.18	4.11
2014	Det	AL	7	6	0	1	39.1	164	35	20	19	3	1	1	0	14	2	27	0	0	1	2	.333	0	0-0	0	3.07	4.35
2015	Det	AL	13	11	0	2	63.2	280	78	43	42	7	0	1	0	23	1	32	2	1	3	8	.273	0	0-0	0	5.38	5.94
2016	Pit	NL	14	0	0	3	25.0	110	25	11	11	2	1	0	2	12	1	15	2	0	2	0	1.000	0	0-0	0	4.56	3.96
3 ML YEARS			34	17	0	6	128.0	554	138	74	72	12	2	2	2	49	4	74	4	1	6	10	.375	0	0-0	0	4.47	5.06

Jeff Locke

Pitches: L **Bats:** L **Pos:** SP-19; RP-11   LOCK   **Ht:** 6'0" **Wt:** 195 **Born:** 11/20/1987 **Age:** 29

			HOW MUCH HE PITCHED					WHAT HE GAVE UP											THE RESULTS						
Year	Team	Lg	G	GS	CG	GF	IP	BFP	H	R	ER	HR	SH	SF	HB	TBB	IBB	SO	WP	Bk	W	L	Pct	Sh	Sv-Op	Hld	ERC	ERA
2011	Pit	NL	4	4	0	0	16.2	78	21	12	12	3	1	1	1	10	0	5	0	0	0	3	.000	0	0-0	0	7.62	6.48
2012	Pit	NL	8	6	0	1	34.1	148	36	21	21	6	1	0	1	11	0	34	0	0	1	3	.250	0	0-0	0	4.68	5.50
2013	Pit	NL	30	30	0	0	166.1	711	146	69	65	11	8	10	6	84	4	125	8	2	10	7	.588	0	0-0	0	3.72	3.52

Year	Team	Lg	G	GS	CG	GF	IP	BFP	H	R	ER	HR	SH	SF	HB	TBB	IBB	SO	WP	Bk	W	L	Pct	Sh	Sv-Op	Hld	ERC	ERA
2014	Pit	NL	21	21	0	0	131.1	548	127	63	57	16	6	3	4	40	2	89	1	0	7	6	.538	0	0-0	0	3.81	3.91
2015	Pit	NL	30	30	0	0	168.1	736	179	95	84	15	7	8	7	60	4	129	5	0	8	11	.421	0	0-0	0	4.30	4.49
2016	Pit	NL	30	19	1	4	127.1	564	151	81	77	17	8	2	3	44	4	73	7	0	9	8	.529	1	0-0	0	5.25	5.44
6 ML YEARS			123	110	1	5	644.1	2785	660	341	316	68	31	24	22	249	14	455	21	2	35	38	.479	1	0-0	0	4.33	4.41

Adam Loewen

Pitches: L Bats: L Pos: RP-8   Ht: 6'6" Wt: 245 Born: 4/9/1984 Age: 33

Year	Team	Lg	G	GS	CG	GF	IP	BFP	H	R	ER	HR	SH	SF	HB	TBB	IBB	SO	WP	Bk	W	L	Pct	Sh	Sv-Op	Hld	ERC	ERA
2016	Reno*	AAA	40	1	0	2	46.0	207	42	21	20	0	4	1	2	31	3	54	1	1	5	3	.625	0	0- --	-	3.96	3.91
2006	Bal	AL	22	19	0	1	112.1	504	111	72	67	8	1	4	8	62	0	98	3	1	6	6	.500	0	0-0	1	4.70	5.37
2007	Bal	AL	6	6	0	0	30.1	143	27	14	12	1	1	0	3	26	0	22	1	1	2	0	1.000	0	0-0	0	5.11	3.56
2008	Bal	AL	7	4	0	0	21.1	102	25	19	19	5	0	2	0	18	0	14	2	0	0	2	.000	0	0-0	1	8.37	8.02
2015	Phi	NL	20	0	0	7	19.1	93	20	15	15	3	1	1	3	17	1	22	5	0	1	0	1.000	0	0-0	1	7.51	6.98
2016	Ari	NL	8	0	0	3	6.0	31	7	10	10	1	0	2	1	6	0	3	1	0	1	0	1.000	0	0-0	1	9.05	15.00
5 ML YEARS			63	29	0	11	189.1	873	190	130	123	18	3	9	15	129	1	159	12	2	10	8	.556	0	0-0	3	5.56	5.85

Boone Logan

Pitches: L Bats: R Pos: RP-66   Ht: 6'5" Wt: 215 Born: 8/13/1984 Age: 32

Year	Team	Lg	G	GS	CG	GF	IP	BFP	H	R	ER	HR	SH	SF	HB	TBB	IBB	SO	WP	Bk	W	L	Pct	Sh	Sv-Op	Hld	ERC	ERA
2006	CWS	AL	21	0	0	4	17.1	93	21	18	16	2	1	1	3	15	2	15	1	0	0	0	-	0	1-2	2	7.56	8.31
2007	CWS	AL	68	0	0	13	50.2	226	59	30	28	7	2	6	0	20	3	35	2	0	2	1	.667	0	0-2	11	5.18	4.97
2008	CWS	AL	55	0	0	12	42.1	197	57	31	28	7	2	4	0	14	3	42	1	0	2	3	.400	0	0-1	3	6.24	5.95
2009	Atl	NL	20	0	0	7	17.1	82	21	12	10	1	0	0	1	9	3	10	0	0	1	1	.500	0	0-0	1	5.29	5.19
2010	NYY	AL	51	0	0	8	40.0	169	34	13	13	3	0	1	1	20	3	38	1	0	2	0	1.000	0	0-0	13	3.50	2.93
2011	NYY	AL	64	0	0	6	41.2	185	43	20	16	4	2	1	4	13	1	46	1	0	5	3	.625	0	0-2	10	4.04	3.46
2012	NYY	AL	80	0	0	8	55.1	239	48	23	23	6	1	3	2	28	6	68	3	0	7	2	.778	0	1-4	23	3.78	3.74
2013	NYY	AL	61	0	0	9	39.0	159	33	15	14	7	3	3	0	13	4	50	3	0	5	2	.714	0	0-2	11	3.38	3.23
2014	Col	NL	35	0	0	8	25.0	116	31	20	19	6	2	2	1	11	1	32	3	0	2	3	.400	0	0-4	5	6.84	6.84
2015	Col	NL	60	0	0	12	35.1	168	40	17	17	3	1	2	5	17	1	44	3	0	0	3	.000	0	0-4	23	5.43	4.33
2016	Col	NL	66	0	0	4	46.1	187	27	23	19	4	2	0	2	20	5	57	4	0	2	5	.286	0	1-4	27	1.96	3.69
Postseason			13	0	0	1	7.2	30	7	2	2	1	0	0	0	1	0	9	0	0	0	0	-	0	0-0	2	2.83	2.35
11 ML YEARS			581	0	0	96	410.1	1821	414	222	203	50	16	19	20	180	34	437	22	0	28	23	.549	0	3-25	131	4.45	4.45

Kyle Lohse

Pitches: R Bats: R Pos: SP-2   LOESH   Ht: 6'2" Wt: 215 Born: 10/4/1978 Age: 38

Year	Team	Lg	G	GS	CG	GF	IP	BFP	H	R	ER	HR	SH	SF	HB	TBB	IBB	SO	WP	Bk	W	L	Pct	Sh	Sv-Op	Hld	ERC	ERA
2016	RdRck*	AAA	10	10	0	0	58.2	244	60	37	33	8	0	4	4	14	0	41	3	0	3	5	.375	0	0- --	-	4.18	5.06
2001	Min	AL	19	16	0	2	90.1	402	102	60	57	16	1	5	8	29	0	64	5	0	4	7	.364	0	0-0	0	5.43	5.68
2002	Min	AL	32	31	1	0	180.2	783	181	92	85	26	3	3	9	70	2	124	8	0	13	8	.619	1	0-1	0	4.55	4.23
2003	Min	AL	33	33	2	0	201.0	850	211	107	103	28	8	5	5	45	1	130	10	1	14	11	.560	1	0-0	0	4.00	4.61
2004	Min	AL	35	34	1	1	194.0	883	240	128	115	28	5	7	7	76	5	111	6	0	9	13	.409	1	0-0	0	5.89	5.34
2005	Min	AL	31	30	0	1	178.2	769	211	85	83	22	3	7	9	44	5	86	4	1	9	13	.409	0	0-0	0	4.91	4.18
2006	2 Tms		34	19	0	6	126.2	566	150	83	82	15	8	9	6	44	4	97	3	1	5	10	.333	0	0-0	0	5.21	5.83
2007	2 Tms	NL	34	32	2	0	192.2	829	207	109	99	22	14	4	12	57	3	122	3	0	9	12	.429	1	0-0	0	4.45	4.62
2008	StL	NL	33	33	0	0	200.0	839	211	88	84	18	6	4	3	49	3	119	5	0	15	6	.714	0	0-0	0	3.77	3.78
2009	StL	NL	23	22	1	0	117.2	512	125	69	62	16	3	4	3	36	2	77	3	1	6	10	.375	1	0-0	0	4.33	4.74
2010	StL	NL	18	18	0	0	92.0	431	129	75	67	9	5	4	3	35	2	54	1	0	4	8	.333	0	0-0	0	6.50	6.55
2011	StL	NL	30	30	1	0	188.1	775	178	80	71	16	8	6	3	42	1	111	1	0	14	8	.636	1	0-0	0	3.05	3.39
2012	StL	NL	33	33	0	0	211.0	864	192	74	67	19	11	7	4	38	1	143	1	0	16	3	.842	0	0-0	0	2.72	2.86
2013	Mil	NL	32	32	2	0	198.2	806	196	78	74	26	8	2	3	36	1	125	1	0	11	10	.524	1	0-0	0	3.45	3.35
2014	Mil	NL	31	31	2	0	198.1	817	183	87	78	22	9	9	8	45	0	141	1	0	13	9	.591	2	0-0	0	3.21	3.54
2015	Mil	NL	37	22	0	5	152.1	665	180	99	99	29	7	4	4	43	3	108	5	0	5	13	.278	0	2-2	2	5.42	5.85
2016	Tex	NL	2	2	0	0	9.1	48	15	13	13	4	0	1	0	5	1	3	0	0	0	2	.000	0	0-0	0	11.00	12.54
06	Min	AL	22	8	0	5	63.2	295	80	50	50	8	1	3	6	25	2	46	1	1	2	5	.286	0	0-0	0	6.10	7.07
06	Cin	NL	12	11	0	1	63.0	271	70	33	32	7	7	2	0	19	2	51	2	0	3	5	.375	0	0-0	0	4.36	4.57
07	Cin	NL	21	21	2	0	131.2	561	143	76	67	16	8	4	6	33	1	80	3	0	6	12	.333	1	0-0	0	4.32	4.58
07	Phi	NL	13	11	0	0	61.0	268	64	33	32	6	6	0	6	24	2	42	0	0	3	0	1.000	0	0-0	0	4.71	4.72
Postseason			13	8	0	3	46.1	199	49	26	25	8	1	0	1	13	1	39	1	0	2	5	.286	0	0-0	0	4.46	4.86
16 ML YEARS			457	418	12	15	2531.2	10839	2711	1327	1239	316	99	78	87	694	34	1615	57	4	147	143	.507	9	2-3	2	4.27	4.40

James Loney

Bats: L Throws: L Pos: 1B-97;PH-8   Ht: 6'3" Wt: 235 Born: 5/7/1984 Age: 33

Year	Team	Lg	G	AB	H	2B	3B	HR	(Hm	Rd)	TB	R	RBI	RC	TBB	IBB	SO	HBP	SH	SF	SB	CS	GDP	Avg	OBP	Slg	OPS
2016	ElPaso*	AAA	44	158	54	7	0	2	(-	-)	67	22	28	25	9	0	12	0	0	2	0	0	9	.342	.373	.424	.797
2006	LAD	NL	48	102	29	6	5	4	(1	3)	57	20	18	17	8	1	10	1	0	0	1	0	8	.284	.342	.559	.901
2007	LAD	NL	96	344	114	18	4	15	(5	10)	185	41	67	71	28	5	48	1	0	2	0	1	6	.331	.381	.538	.919
2008	LAD	NL	161	595	172	35	6	13	(5	8)	258	66	90	79	45	6	85	3	1	7	7	4	25	.289	.338	.434	.772
2009	LAD	NL	158	576	162	25	2	13	(1	12)	230	73	90	84	70	10	68	0	1	4	7	3	16	.281	.357	.399	.756
2010	LAD	NL	161	588	157	41	2	10	(6	4)	232	67	88	81	52	9	95	4	0	4	10	5	14	.267	.329	.395	.723
2011	LAD	NL	158	531	153	30	1	12	(7	5)	221	56	65	71	42	7	67	1	3	5	4	0	8	.288	.339	.416	.755
2012	2 Tms		144	434	108	20	0	6	(0	6)	146	37	41	34	28	7	51	0	1	2	0	3	21	.249	.293	.336	.630
2013	TB	AL	158	549	164	33	4	13	(7	6)	236	54	75	75	44	6	77	0	1	4	3	1	16	.299	.348	.430	.778
2014	TB	AL	155	600	174	27	0	9	(4	5)	228	59	69	68	41	2	80	4	0	6	4	0	21	.290	.336	.380	.716

		BATTING																RUNNING			AVERAGES			
Year Team	Lg	G	AB	H	2B	3B	HR	(Hm Rd)	TB	R	RBI	RC	TBB	IBB	SO	HBP	SH	SF	SB	CS	GDP	Avg	OBP	Slg	OPS
2015 TB	AL	104	361	101	16	0	4	(3 1)	129	25	32	40	23	5	34	1	0	3	2	4	10	.280	.322	.357	.680
2016 NYM	NL	100	343	91	16	1	9	(2 7)	136	30	34	35	16	3	37	5	1	1	0	0	11	.265	.307	.397	.703
12 LAD	NL	114	334	85	18	0	4	(0 4)	115	32	33	28	23	7	39	0	1	1	0	3	16	.254	.302	.344	.646
12 Bos	AL	30	100	23	2	0	2	(0 2)	31	5	8	6	5	0	12	0	0	1	0	0	5	.230	.264	.310	.574
Postseason		22	79	28	5	0	3	(1 2)	42	6	16	16	9	1	13	1	0	0	0	0	4	.354	.427	.532	.959
11 ML YEARS		1443	5023	1425	267	21	108	(41 67)	2058	528	669	655	397	61	652	20	8	38	38	21	156	.284	.336	.410	.746

Evan Longoria

Bats: R **Throws:** R **Pos:** 3B-152;DH-8   **Ht:** 6'2" **Wt:** 210 **Born:** 10/7/1985 **Age:** 31

		BATTING																RUNNING			AVERAGES			
Year Team	Lg	G	AB	H	2B	3B	HR	(Hm Rd)	TB	R	RBI	RC	TBB	IBB	SO	HBP	SH	SF	SB	CS	GDP	Avg	OBP	Slg	OPS
2008 TB	AL	122	448	122	31	2	27	(18 9)	238	67	85	72	46	4	122	6	0	8	7	0	8	.272	.343	.531	.874
2009 TB	AL	157	584	164	44	0	33	(16 17)	307	100	113	102	72	11	140	8	0	7	9	0	27	.281	.364	.526	.889
2010 TB	AL	151	574	169	46	5	22	(10 12)	291	96	104	99	72	12	124	5	0	10	15	5	15	.294	.372	.507	.879
2011 TB	AL	133	483	118	26	1	31	(14 17)	239	78	99	91	80	6	93	6	0	5	3	2	11	.244	.355	.495	.850
2012 TB	AL	74	273	79	14	0	17	(8 9)	144	39	55	55	33	6	61	3	0	3	2	3	14	.289	.369	.527	.896
2013 TB	AL	160	614	165	39	3	32	(15 17)	306	91	88	90	70	10	162	3	0	6	1	0	16	.269	.343	.498	.842
2014 TB	AL	**162**	624	158	26	1	22	(12 10)	252	83	91	83	57	11	133	9	1	9	5	0	15	.253	.320	.404	.724
2015 TB	AL	160	604	163	35	1	21	(10 11)	263	74	73	77	51	8	132	6	0	9	3	1	11	.270	.328	.435	.764
2016 TB	AL	160	633	173	41	4	36	(17 19)	330	81	98	95	42	6	144	3	0	7	0	3	13	.273	.318	.521	.840
Postseason		30	115	22	5	0	4	(4 5)	54	16	21	13	11	0	38	0	0	0	1	0	4	.191	.262	.470	.731
9 ML YEARS		1279	4837	1311	302	17	241	(120 121)	2370	709	806	764	523	74	1111	49	1	64	45	14	130	.271	.344	.490	.834

Javier Lopez

Pitches: L **Bats:** L **Pos:** RP-68   **Ht:** 6'4" **Wt:** 220 **Born:** 7/11/1977 **Age:** 39

		HOW MUCH HE PITCHED					WHAT HE GAVE UP											THE RESULTS						
Year Team	Lg	G	GS	CG	GF	IP	BFP	H	R	ER	HR	SH	SF	HB	TBB	IBB	SO	WP	Bk	W	L	Pct	Sh	Sv-Op	Hld	ERC	ERA
2003 Col	NL	75	0	0	11	58.1	242	58	25	24	5	1	0	4	12	2	40	1	3	4	1	.800	0	1-2	15	3.44	3.70
2004 Col	NL	64	0	0	10	40.2	187	45	34	34	1	1	0	3	26	4	20	3	0	1	2	.333	0	0-1	12	5.28	7.52
2005 2 Tms		32	0	0	6	16.1	87	26	20	20	2	1	0	1	11	3	12	0	0	1	1	.500	0	2-4	6	8.82	11.02
2006 Bos	AL	27	0	0	8	16.2	69	13	10	5	1	0	1	2	10	1	11	0	0	1	0	1.000	0	1-1	6	3.96	2.70
2007 Bos	AL	61	0	0	11	40.2	174	36	16	14	2	1	1	4	18	2	26	1	0	2	1	.667	0	0-2	13	3.59	3.10
2008 Bos	AL	70	0	0	10	59.1	247	53	18	16	4	1	1	2	27	0	38	1	0	2	0	1.000	0	0-1	10	3.73	2.43
2009 Bos	AL	14	0	0	5	11.2	64	20	13	12	1	1	1	2	9	0	5	1	0	2	0	.000	0	0-0	11	11.00	9.26
2010 2 Tms	NL	77	0	0	18	57.2	235	50	17	15	2	1	2	2	20	3	38	3	0	4	2	.667	0	0-0	11	2.85	2.34
2011 SF	NL	70	0	0	17	53.0	222	42	16	16	0	3	0	3	26	6	40	1	0	5	2	.714	0	1-3	20	2.69	2.72
2012 SF	NL	70	0	0	19	36.0	153	37	13	10	1	1	1	0	14	3	28	2	0	3	0	1.000	0	7-9	18	3.60	2.50
2013 SF	NL	69	0	0	14	39.1	161	30	10	8	1	4	1	0	12	5	37	1	0	4	2	.667	0	1-1	15	1.82	1.83
2014 SF	NL	65	0	0	14	37.2	167	31	14	13	2	3	2	2	19	6	22	1	0	1	1	.500	0	0-2	12	3.00	3.11
2015 SF	NL	77	0	0	14	39.1	147	19	8	7	1	0	0	0	16	3	26	1	0	1	0	1.000	0	0-0	20	1.26	1.60
2016 SF	NL	68	0	0	6	26.2	118	24	13	12	3	1	0	2	15	0	15	0	0	1	3	.250	0	1-4	20	4.56	4.05
05 Col	NL	3	0	0	1	2.0	13	7	5	5	0	0	0	0	0	0	1	0	0	0	0	-	0	0-1	0	18.39	22.50
05 Ari	NL	29	0	0	5	14.1	74	19	15	15	2	1	0	1	11	3	11	0	0	1	1	.500	0	2-3	6	7.63	9.42
10 Pit	NL	50	0	0	14	38.2	166	39	14	12	2	1	2	2	18	3	22	3	0	2	2	.500	0	0-0	6	4.24	2.79
10 SF	NL	27	0	0	4	19.0	69	11	3	3	0	0	0	0	2	0	16	0	0	2	0	1.000	0	0-0	5	0.90	1.42
Postseason		31	0	0	2	17.1	72	16	6	6	0	1	1	0	6	1	15	1	0	1	1	.500	0	0-0	9	2.72	3.12
14 ML YEARS		839	0	0	163	533.1	2273	484	227	206	26	19	10	27	235	38	358	16	3	30	17	.638	0	14-30	178	3.48	3.48

Raffy Lopez

Bats: L **Throws:** R **Pos:** PH-5;C-4;1B-1   **Ht:** 5'9" **Wt:** 200 **Born:** 10/2/1987 **Age:** 29

		BATTING																RUNNING			AVERAGES			
Year Team	Lg	G	AB	H	2B	3B	HR	(Hm Rd)	TB	R	RBI	RC	TBB	IBB	SO	HBP	SH	SF	SB	CS	GDP	Avg	OBP	Slg	OPS
2012 3 Tms	Low	70	251	70	19	2	2	(- -)	99	37	28	37	31	0	31	1	1	4	2	0	7	.279	.355	.394	.750
2013 Tenn	AA	95	316	78	22	0	8	(- -)	124	44	43	46	49	4	67	1	1	0	0	1	9	.247	.350	.392	.742
2014 Tenn	AA	45	148	44	13	0	4	(- -)	69	21	24	29	29	5	26	0	0	0	1	1	2	.297	.412	.466	.879
2014 Iowa	AAA	61	207	59	4	1	1	(- -)	68	17	27	29	28	1	52	3	1	0	0	0	9	.285	.378	.329	.707
2015 Iowa	AAA	46	156	43	8	1	0	(- -)	53	14	17	19	14	0	37	0	0	1	3	1	2	.276	.333	.340	.673
2015 Salt Lk	AAA	21	62	15	2	0	1	(- -)	20	10	7	8	11	0	13	0	1	1	0	0	0	.242	.351	.323	.674
2016 Lsvlle	AAA	47	155	33	10	0	1	(- -)	46	12	17	12	9	0	39	2	1	2	1	0	2	.213	.262	.297	.559
2014 ChC	NL	7	11	2	0	0	0	(0 0)	2	0	1	1	2	0	4	0	0	0	0	0	0	.182	.286	.182	.468
2016 Cin	NL	8	7	0	0	0	0	(0 0)	0	0	0	0	0	0	3	0	0	1	0	0	0	.000	.000	.000	.000
2 ML YEARS		15	18	2	0	0	0	(0 0)	2	0	1	1	2	0	7	0	0	1	0	0	0	.111	.190	.111	.302

Reynaldo Lopez

Pitches: R **Bats:** R **Pos:** SP-6; RP-5   ray-NAHL-doh   **Ht:** 6'0" **Wt:** 185 **Born:** 1/4/1994 **Age:** 23

		HOW MUCH HE PITCHED					WHAT HE GAVE UP											THE RESULTS						
Year Team	Lg	G	GS	CG	GF	IP	BFP	H	R	ER	HR	SH	SF	HB	TBB	IBB	SO	WP	Bk	W	L	Pct	Sh	Sv-Op	Hld	ERC	ERA
2014 2 Tms	Low	16	16	0	0	83.1	312	42	12	10	1	2	0	2	26	0	70	3	1	7	3	.700	0	0- -	-	1.18	1.08
2015 Ptomc	A+	19	19	1	0	99.0	404	93	47	45	4	4	3	6	28	0	94	9	0	6	7	.462	0	0- -	-	3.16	4.09
2016 Hrsbrg	AA	14	14	0	0	76.1	329	69	35	27	7	3	5	3	25	0	100	5	1	3	5	.375	0	0- -	-	3.26	3.18
2016 Syrcse	AAA	5	5	1	0	33.0	129	21	12	12	6	0	1	1	10	1	26	0	0	2	2	.500	1	0- -	-	2.40	3.27
2016 Was	NL	11	6	0	1	44.0	201	47	27	24	4	3	2	0	22	2	42	5	0	5	3	.625	0	0-0	1	4.60	4.91

Michael Lorenzen

Pitches: R Bats: R Pos: RP-35   Ht: 6'3" Wt: 215 Born: 1/4/1992 Age: 25

			HOW MUCH HE PITCHED					WHAT HE GAVE UP											THE RESULTS						
Year	Team	Lg	G	GS	CG	GF	IP	BFP	H	R	ER	HR	SH	SF	HB	TBB	IBB	SO	WP	Bk	W	L	Pct	Sh	Sv-Op	Hld	ERC	ERA
2013	3 Tms	Low	15	1	0	6	15.0	67	14	5	4	1	0	0	3	7	1	14	0	0	1	1	.500	0	4--	-	4.41	2.40
2013	Pnscla	AA	7	0	0	0	6.0	28	6	3	3	1	1	0	0	6	0	5	0	0	0	0	-	0	0--	-	7.48	4.50
2014	Pnscla	AA	24	24	0	0	120.2	504	112	50	42	9	6	5	6	44	0	84	7	0	4	6	.400	0	0--	-	3.64	3.13
2015	Lsvlle	AAA	6	6	1	0	43.0	165	34	9	9	3	1	0	0	8	0	19	2	0	4	2	.667	1	0--	-	2.09	1.88
2015	Cin	NL	27	21	0	1	113.1	515	131	70	68	18	2	1	6	57	6	83	4	0	4	9	.308	0	0-0	1	6.09	5.40
2016	Cin	NL	35	0	0	4	50.0	202	41	16	16	5	0	0	6	13	0	48	2	2	2	1	.667	0	0-2	10	3.11	2.88
	2 ML YEARS		62	21	0	5	163.1	717	172	86	84	23	2	1	12	70	6	131	6	2	6	10	.375	0	0-2	11	5.12	4.63

David Lough

Bats: L Throws: L Pos: LF-15;RF-11;PH-8;PR-1   LOW   Ht: 5'10" Wt: 175 Born: 1/20/1986 Age: 31

			BATTING																	RUNNING			AVERAGES			
Year	Team	Lg	G	AB	H	2B	3B	HR	(Hm	Rd)	TB	R	RBI	RC	TBB	IBB	SO	HBP	SH	SF	SB	CS	GDP	Avg	OBP	Slg	OPS
2016	LV*	AAA	45	126	34	7	1	1	(-	-)	46	17	9	16	11	1	17	1	0	1	2	0	3	.270	.331	.365	.696
2012	KC	AL	20	59	14	2	1	0	(0	0)	18	9	2	5	4	0	9	1	0	1	1	0	2	.237	.292	.305	.597
2013	KC	AL	96	315	90	17	4	5	(1	4)	130	35	33	38	10	0	52	3	4	3	5	2	3	.286	.311	.413	.724
2014	Bal	AL	112	174	43	6	3	4	(3	1)	67	31	16	19	15	0	33	1	6	1	8	5	3	.247	.309	.385	.694
2015	Bal	AL	84	134	27	1	1	4	(3	1)	42	14	12	13	5	0	36	2	3	0	2	4	0	.201	.241	.313	.555
2016	Phi	NL	30	67	16	3	1	0	(0	0)	21	6	4	7	9	1	8	2	0	1	1	2	0	.239	.342	.313	.655
	Postseason		2	1	0	0	0	0	(0	0)	0	0	0	0	0	0	0	0	0	0	0	0	0	.000	.000	.000	.000
	5 ML YEARS		342	749	190	29	10	13	(7	6)	278	95	67	82	43	1	138	9	13	6	17	13	8	.254	.300	.371	.671

Aaron Loup

Pitches: L Bats: L Pos: RP-21   LOOP   Ht: 5'11" Wt: 210 Born: 12/19/1987 Age: 29

			HOW MUCH HE PITCHED					WHAT HE GAVE UP											THE RESULTS						
Year	Team	Lg	G	GS	CG	GF	IP	BFP	H	R	ER	HR	SH	SF	HB	TBB	IBB	SO	WP	Bk	W	L	Pct	Sh	Sv-Op	Hld	ERC	ERA
2016	Buffalo*	AAA	20	0	0	1	19.2	81	21	4	4	0	0	0	0	3	0	26	0	0	3	0	1.000	0	1--	-	2.85	1.83
2012	Tor	AL	33	0	0	3	30.2	117	26	10	9	0	2	1	0	2	0	21	1	1	0	2	.000	0	0-1	6	1.59	2.64
2013	Tor	AL	64	0	0	12	69.1	282	66	23	19	5	2	4	7	13	4	53	2	0	4	6	.400	0	2-3	8	3.20	2.47
2014	Tor	AL	71	0	0	15	68.2	283	50	25	24	4	3	3	6	30	5	56	5	0	4	4	.500	0	4-8	13	2.75	3.15
2015	Tor	AL	60	0	0	6	42.1	186	47	24	21	6	2	0	6	7	0	46	0	0	2	5	.286	0	0-4	9	4.54	4.46
2016	Tor	AL	21	0	0	2	14.1	62	15	8	8	2	0	3	3	4	0	15	3	0	0	0	-	0	0-1	1	5.13	5.02
	Postseason		4	0	0	0	2.0	7	1	1	1	0	0	0	0	2	0	0	0	0	0	0	-	0	0-0	0	3.75	4.50
	5 ML YEARS		249	0	0	38	225.1	930	204	90	81	17	9	11	22	56	9	191	11	1	10	17	.370	0	6-17	37	3.17	3.24

Mark Lowe

Pitches: R Bats: L Pos: RP-54   Ht: 6'3" Wt: 210 Born: 6/7/1983 Age: 34

			HOW MUCH HE PITCHED					WHAT HE GAVE UP											THE RESULTS						
Year	Team	Lg	G	GS	CG	GF	IP	BFP	H	R	ER	HR	SH	SF	HB	TBB	IBB	SO	WP	Bk	W	L	Pct	Sh	Sv-Op	Hld	ERC	ERA
2006	Sea	AL	15	0	0	3	18.2	75	12	4	4	1	1	0	2	9	1	20	1	0	1	0	1.000	0	0-0	6	2.61	1.93
2007	Sea	AL	4	0	0	1	2.2	13	2	2	2	1	0	0	0	3	0	3	0	0	0	0	-	0	0-0	2	7.69	6.75
2008	Sea	AL	57	0	0	19	63.2	303	78	44	38	6	3	3	4	34	0	55	2	0	1	5	.167	0	1-5	1	6.10	5.37
2009	Sea	AL	75	0	0	18	80.0	339	71	39	29	7	0	4	0	29	1	69	4	0	2	7	.222	0	3-13	26	3.16	3.26
2010	2 Tms	AL	14	0	0	5	13.1	61	18	9	8	2	0	1	0	6	1	12	1	0	1	3	.250	0	0-0	4	6.82	5.40
2011	Tex	AL	52	0	0	10	45.0	196	46	26	19	6	1	1	0	19	4	42	3	0	2	3	.400	0	1-3	11	4.38	3.80
2012	Tex	AL	36	0	0	12	39.1	162	35	15	15	5	0	3	0	13	0	28	4	2	0	2	.000	0	0-0	1	3.41	3.43
2013	LAA	AL	11	0	0	2	11.2	56	11	12	12	1	2	0	0	11	1	7	2	0	1	0	1.000	0	0-0	1	5.60	9.26
2014	Cle	AL	7	0	0	1	7.0	39	10	7	3	2	0	1	0	6	4	6	1	0	1	0	1.000	0	0-0	0	8.50	3.86
2015	2 Tms	AL	57	0	0	13	55.0	215	46	15	12	4	0	2	1	12	1	61	2	0	1	3	.250	0	1-5	17	2.49	1.96
2016	Det	AL	54	0	0	26	49.1	224	57	41	39	12	0	6	1	21	2	49	2	0	1	3	.250	0	0-1	8	6.14	7.11
10	Sea	AL	11	0	0	4	10.1	45	11	5	4	1	0	1	0	5	1	7	1	0	1	3	.250	0	0-0	4	4.70	3.48
10	Tex	AL	3	0	0	1	3.0	16	7	4	4	1	0	0	0	1	0	5	0	0	0	0	-	0	0-0	0	15.67	12.00
15	Sea	AL	34	0	0	8	36.0	144	31	6	4	1	0	1	0	11	1	47	1	0	0	1	.000	0	0-2	12	2.67	1.00
15	Tor	AL	23	0	0	5	19.0	71	15	9	8	3	0	2	1	1	0	14	0	0	1	2	.333	0	1-3	5	2.07	3.79
	Postseason		10	0	0	2	6.0	30	8	9	9	1	0	0	1	3	0	7	0	0	0	1	.000	0	0-0	0	7.61	13.50
	11 ML YEARS		382	0	0	110	385.2	1683	386	214	181	47	7	21	8	163	15	352	22	2	10	27	.270	0	6-27	77	4.33	4.22

Jed Lowrie

Bats: B Throws: R Pos: 2B-82;DH-5;PH-3;SS-2   LAU-ree   Ht: 6'0" Wt: 180 Born: 4/17/1984 Age: 33

			BATTING																	RUNNING			AVERAGES			
Year	Team	Lg	G	AB	H	2B	3B	HR	(Hm	Rd)	TB	R	RBI	RC	TBB	IBB	SO	HBP	SH	SF	SB	CS	GDP	Avg	OBP	Slg	OPS
2008	Bos	AL	81	260	67	25	3	2	(0	2)	104	34	46	35	35	0	68	1	2	8	1	0	8	.258	.339	.400	.739
2009	Bos	AL	32	68	10	2	0	2	(1	1)	18	5	11	5	6	0	20	0	0	2	0	0	0	.147	.211	.265	.475
2010	Bos	AL	55	171	49	14	0	9	(3	6)	90	31	24	32	25	0	25	1	0	0	1	1	2	.287	.381	.526	.907
2011	Bos	AL	88	309	78	14	4	6	(3	3)	118	40	36	33	23	2	60	2	1	6	1	1	6	.252	.303	.382	.685
2012	Hou	NL	97	340	83	18	0	16	(9	7)	149	43	42	45	43	0	65	2	0	2	2	0	3	.244	.331	.438	.769
2013	Oak	AL	154	603	175	45	2	15	(7	8)	269	80	75	88	50	3	91	2	3	4	1	0	17	.290	.344	.446	.791
2014	Oak	AL	136	502	125	29	3	6	(4	2)	178	59	50	52	51	5	79	5	2	6	0	0	14	.249	.321	.355	.676
2015	Hou	AL	69	230	51	14	0	9	(5	4)	92	35	30	29	28	5	43	3	0	2	1	0	3	.222	.312	.400	.712
2016	Oak	AL	87	338	89	12	1	2	(1	1)	109	30	27	36	26	0	65	1	0	4	0	0	10	.263	.314	.322	.637
	Postseason		22	60	9	2	0	1	(0	1)	14	6	5	4	7	0	16	1	1	1	0	0	1	.150	.246	.233	.480
	9 ML YEARS		799	2821	727	173	13	67	(33	34)	1127	357	341	355	287	15	516	17	8	34	7	2	63	.258	.326	.400	.726

Jonathan Lucroy

Bats: R **Throws:** R **Pos:** C-126;PH-11;1B-6;DH-3   LOO-croy   **Ht:** 6'0" **Wt:** 200 **Born:** 6/13/1986 **Age:** 31

Year	Team	Lg	G	AB	H	2B	3B	HR	(Hm	Rd)	TB	R	RBI	RC	TBB	IBB	SO	HBP	SH	SF	SB	CS	GDP	Avg	OBP	Slg	OPS
2010	Mil	NL	75	277	70	9	0	4	(4	0)	91	24	26	23	18	1	44	1	0	1	4	2	9	.253	.300	.329	.628
2011	Mil	NL	136	430	114	16	1	12	(8	4)	168	45	59	50	29	0	99	2	4	3	2	1	7	.265	.313	.391	.703
2012	Mil	NL	96	316	101	17	4	12	(7	5)	162	46	58	61	22	1	44	4	1	3	4	1	12	.320	.368	.513	.881
2013	Mil	NL	147	521	146	26	6	18	(9	9)	237	59	82	78	46	2	69	5	0	8	9	1	16	.280	.340	.455	.795
2014	Mil	NL	153	585	176	53	2	13	(6	7)	272	73	69	90	66	3	71	2	0	2	4	4	13	.301	.373	.465	.837
2015	Mil	NL	103	371	98	20	3	7	(3	4)	145	51	43	46	36	0	64	1	1	6	1	0	18	.264	.326	.391	.717
2016	2 Tms		142	490	143	24	3	24	(15	9)	245	67	81	74	47	5	100	3	0	4	5	0	16	.292	.355	.500	.855
16	Mil	NL	95	338	101	17	3	13	(9	4)	163	48	50	46	33	3	70	1	0	4	5	0	12	.299	.359	.482	.841
16	Tex	AL	47	152	42	7	0	11	(6	5)	82	19	31	28	14	2	30	2	0	0	0	0	4	.276	.345	.539	.885
	Postseason		10	32	8	1	0	1	(1	0)	12	3	5	4	0	0	8	0	0	0	0	0	0	.250	.250	.375	.625
	7 ML YEARS		852	2990	848	164	19	90	(52	38)	1320	365	418	422	264	12	491	18	6	27	29	9	91	.284	.343	.441	.784

Cory Luebke

Pitches: L **Bats:** R **Pos:** RP-9   LOOB-kee   **Ht:** 6'4" **Wt:** 210 **Born:** 3/4/1985 **Age:** 32

			HOW MUCH HE PITCHED					WHAT HE GAVE UP										THE RESULTS							
Year	Team	Lg	G	GS	CG	GF	IP	BFP	H	R	ER	HR	SH	SF	HB	TBB	IBB	SO	WP	Bk	W	L	Pct	Sh	Sv-Op	Hld	ERC	ERA
2016	Indy*	AAA	11	0	0	4	18.1	78	17	5	5	2	0	0	2	3	0	29	1	0	1	0	1.000	0	1- -	-	3.13	2.45
2010	SD	NL	4	3	0	1	17.2	76	17	8	8	3	0	0	1	6	0	18	0	0	1	1	.500	0	0-0	0	4.30	4.08
2011	SD	NL	46	17	0	3	139.2	555	105	54	51	12	3	4	2	44	3	154	5	2	6	10	.375	0	0-0	3	2.43	3.29
2012	SD	NL	5	5	0	0	31.0	130	28	10	9	1	2	0	0	8	0	23	0	0	3	1	.750	0	0-0	0	2.51	2.61
2016	Pit	NL	9	0	0	5	8.2	53	15	9	9	2	1	1	1	11	2	9	0	0	0	1	.000	0	0-0	0	13.85	9.35
	4 ML YEARS		64	25	0	9	197.0	814	165	81	77	18	6	5	4	69	5	204	5	2	10	13	.435	0	0-0	3	3.00	3.52

Seth Lugo

Pitches: R **Bats:** R **Pos:** RP-9; SP-8   LOO-go   **Ht:** 6'4" **Wt:** 225 **Born:** 11/17/1989 **Age:** 27

			HOW MUCH HE PITCHED					WHAT HE GAVE UP										THE RESULTS							
Year	Team	Lg	G	GS	CG	GF	IP	BFP	H	R	ER	HR	SH	SF	HB	TBB	IBB	SO	WP	Bk	W	L	Pct	Sh	Sv-Op	Hld	ERC	ERA
2013	2 Tms	Low	12	12	0	0	66.1	267	56	25	25	5	2	1	2	19	0	66	3	0	4	6	.400	0	0- -	-	2.83	3.39
2014	Stluci	A+	27	4	0	10	105.0	455	100	55	48	12	2	1	4	38	0	114	7	0	8	3	.727	0	3- -	-	3.84	4.11
2015	Bnghtn	AA	19	19	0	0	109.0	466	108	54	46	8	3	3	5	30	1	97	6	0	6	5	.545	0	0- -	-	3.47	3.80
2015	LsVgs	AAA	5	5	0	0	27.0	114	27	13	12	3	0	0	2	5	0	30	2	0	2	2	.500	0	0- -	-	3.56	4.00
2016	LsVgs	AAA	21	14	0	1	73.1	341	103	63	53	10	6	1	1	20	0	62	4	0	3	4	.429	0	0- -	-	6.19	6.50
2016	NYM	NL	17	8	0	2	64.0	260	49	19	19	7	8	4	4	21	3	45	1	1	5	2	.714	0	0-0	0	2.81	2.67

Jordan Lyles

Pitches: R **Bats:** R **Pos:** RP-35; SP-5   **Ht:** 6'4" **Wt:** 230 **Born:** 10/19/1990 **Age:** 26

			HOW MUCH HE PITCHED					WHAT HE GAVE UP										THE RESULTS							
Year	Team	Lg	G	GS	CG	GF	IP	BFP	H	R	ER	HR	SH	SF	HB	TBB	IBB	SO	WP	Bk	W	L	Pct	Sh	Sv-Op	Hld	ERC	ERA
2016	Albq*	AAA	8	8	0	0	44.2	199	57	33	27	5	0	1	3	18	0	29	2	0	4	2	.667	0	0- -	-	6.36	5.44
2011	Hou	NL	20	15	0	2	94.0	415	107	61	56	14	7	1	5	26	1	67	0	0	2	8	.200	0	0-0	0	4.87	5.36
2012	Hou	NL	25	25	1	0	141.1	628	159	97	80	20	6	4	5	42	4	99	2	0	5	12	.294	1	0-0	0	4.67	5.09
2013	Hou	AL	27	25	0	1	141.2	642	165	98	88	17	0	3	11	49	1	93	5	2	7	9	.438	0	1-1	1	5.20	5.59
2014	Col	NL	22	22	0	0	126.2	546	127	64	61	12	4	3	4	46	1	90	6	0	7	4	.636	0	0-0	0	4.17	4.33
2015	Col	NL	10	10	0	0	49.0	212	54	32	28	2	3	1	3	19	1	30	2	0	2	5	.286	0	0-0	0	4.51	5.14
2016	Col	NL	40	5	0	7	58.2	273	69	46	38	4	1	2	4	28	2	32	5	0	4	5	.444	0	1-4	3	5.32	5.83
	6 ML YEARS		144	102	1	10	611.1	2716	681	398	351	69	21	14	36	210	10	411	20	2	27	43	.386	1	2-5	4	4.77	5.17

Lance Lynn

Pitches: R **Bats:** R **Pos:** P   **Ht:** 6'5" **Wt:** 280 **Born:** 5/12/1987 **Age:** 30

			HOW MUCH HE PITCHED					WHAT HE GAVE UP										THE RESULTS							
Year	Team	Lg	G	GS	CG	GF	IP	BFP	H	R	ER	HR	SH	SF	HB	TBB	IBB	SO	WP	Bk	W	L	Pct	Sh	Sv-Op	Hld	ERC	ERA
2011	StL	NL	18	2	0	2	34.2	136	25	12	12	3	1	0	1	11	1	40	1	0	1	1	.500	0	1-2	3	2.37	3.12
2012	StL	NL	35	29	0	2	176.0	744	168	76	74	16	4	3	10	64	3	180	3	0	18	7	.720	0	0-0	1	3.87	3.78
2013	StL	NL	33	33	0	0	201.2	856	189	92	89	14	11	8	11	76	0	198	6	0	15	10	.600	0	0-0	0	3.67	3.97
2014	StL	NL	33	33	2	0	203.2	866	185	72	62	13	6	4	7	72	1	181	7	0	15	10	.600	1	0-0	0	3.24	2.74
2015	StL	NL	31	31	0	0	175.1	751	172	66	59	13	9	2	5	68	5	167	2	0	12	11	.522	0	0-0	0	3.83	3.03
	Postseason		24	7	0	3	52.0	232	56	30	26	6	2	3	1	26	5	50	0	0	5	4	.556	0	0-0	3	4.98	4.50
	5 ML YEARS		150	128	2	4	791.1	3353	739	318	296	59	31	17	34	291	10	766	19	0	61	39	.610	1	1-2	4	3.58	3.37

Tyler Lyons

Pitches: L **Bats:** L **Pos:** RP-30   **Ht:** 6'4" **Wt:** 210 **Born:** 2/21/1988 **Age:** 29

			HOW MUCH HE PITCHED					WHAT HE GAVE UP										THE RESULTS							
Year	Team	Lg	G	GS	CG	GF	IP	BFP	H	R	ER	HR	SH	SF	HB	TBB	IBB	SO	WP	Bk	W	L	Pct	Sh	Sv-Op	Hld	ERC	ERA
2013	StL	NL	12	8	0	1	53.0	223	49	29	28	5	1	0	3	16	0	43	0	0	2	4	.333	0	0-0	0	3.46	4.75
2014	StL	NL	11	4	0	1	36.2	155	33	23	18	4	1	1	2	11	2	36	0	0	0	4	.000	0	0-0	0	3.29	4.42
2015	StL	NL	17	8	0	0	60.0	255	59	29	25	12	3	2	1	15	0	60	4	0	3	1	.750	0	0-0	0	4.04	3.75
2016	StL	NL	30	0	0	10	48.0	187	35	18	18	9	1	1	0	14	0	46	2	0	2	0	1.000	0	0-0	4	2.83	3.38
	4 ML YEARS		70	20	0	13	197.2	820	176	99	89	30	6	4	6	56	2	185	6	0	7	9	.438	0	0-0	4	3.45	4.05

Dixon Machado

Bats: R **Throws:** R **Pos:** SS-6;2B-2;PH-2;PR-1   **Ht:** 6'1" **Wt:** 170 **Born:** 2/22/1992 **Age:** 25

									BATTING												RUNNING			AVERAGES			
Year	Team	Lg	G	AB	H	2B	3B	HR	(Hm	Rd)	TB	R	RBI	RC	TBB	IBB	SO	HBP	SH	SF	SB	CS	GDP	Avg	OBP	Slg	OPS
2012	Lkland	A+	119	421	82	16	1	2	(-	-)	106	59	37	35	51	0	61	1	16	1	23	5	14	.195	.283	.252	.534
2013	2 Tms	Low	44	177	41	7	2	1	(-	-)	55	22	14	15	11	1	24	0	5	0	1	0	6	.232	.277	.311	.587
2014	Lkland	A+	41	159	40	8	1	1	(-	-)	53	30	8	20	23	0	34	1	3	1	2	1	5	.252	.348	.333	.681
2014	Erie	AA	90	292	89	23	1	5	(-	-)	129	45	32	53	40	0	36	3	4	3	8	5	10	.305	.391	.442	.832
2015	Toledo	AAA	127	509	133	22	1	4	(-	-)	169	61	48	58	36	0	85	4	15	3	15	3	16	.261	.313	.332	.645
2016	Toledo	AAA	131	492	131	28	2	4	(-	-)	175	59	48	68	58	0	75	6	10	3	17	5	14	.266	.349	.356	.705
2015	Det	AL	24	68	16	3	0	0	(0	0)	19	6	5	5	7	0	14	0	3	0	1	0	3	.235	.307	.279	.586
2016	Det	AL	8	10	1	0	0	0	(0	0)	1	1	0	0	3	0	4	0	0	0	0	0	0	.100	.308	.100	.408
	2 ML YEARS		32	78	17	3	0	0	(0	0)	20	7	5	5	10	0	18	0	3	0	1	0	3	.218	.307	.256	.563

Manny Machado

Bats: R **Throws:** R **Pos:** 3B-114;SS-45   muh-CHAH-doe   **Ht:** 6'3" **Wt:** 185 **Born:** 7/6/1992 **Age:** 24

									BATTING												RUNNING			AVERAGES			
Year	Team	Lg	G	AB	H	2B	3B	HR	(Hm	Rd)	TB	R	RBI	RC	TBB	IBB	SO	HBP	SH	SF	SB	CS	GDP	Avg	OBP	Slg	OPS
2012	Bal	AL	51	191	50	8	3	7	(7	0)	85	24	26	29	9	0	38	0	1	1	2	0	6	.262	.294	.445	.739
2013	Bal	AL	156	667	189	51	3	14	(5	9)	288	88	71	87	29	0	113	2	9	3	6	7	15	.283	.314	.432	.746
2014	Bal	AL	82	327	91	14	0	12	(9	3)	141	38	32	44	20	2	68	3	2	2	2	0	13	.278	.324	.431	.755
2015	Bal	AL	162	633	181	30	1	35	(21	14)	318	102	86	107	70	2	111	4	2	4	20	8	17	.286	.359	.502	.861
2016	Bal	AL	157	640	188	40	1	37	(18	19)	341	105	96	103	48	9	120	3	0	5	0	3	14	.294	.343	.533	.876
	Postseason		6	19	3	1	0	1	(0	1)	7	2	2	1	2	0	6	0	2	0	0	0	1	.158	.238	.368	.607
	5 ML YEARS		608	2458	699	143	8	105	(60	45)	1173	357	311	370	176	13	450	12	14	15	30	18	65	.284	.333	.477	.811

Jean Machi

Pitches: R **Bats:** R **Pos:** P   GENE ma-CHEE   **Ht:** 6'0" **Wt:** 255 **Born:** 2/1/1982 **Age:** 35

			HOW MUCH HE PITCHED						WHAT HE GAVE UP										THE RESULTS						
Year	Team	Lg	G	GS	CG	GF	IP	BFP	H	R	ER	HR	SH	SF	HB	TBB	IBB	SO	WP	Bk	W	L	Pct	Sh	Sv-Op	Hld	ERC	ERA
2016	Iowa*	AAA	20	0	0	5	29.1	120	29	13	12	5	2	1	1	9	1	26	1	0	2	1	.667	0	1- -	-	4.39	3.68
2016	Scrmto*	AAA	28	0	0	21	32.1	135	30	17	13	4	0	2	3	8	0	27	0	1	2	2	.500	0	12- -	-	3.62	3.62
2012	SF	NL	8	0	0	5	6.2	28	7	5	5	2	0	0	0	1	0	4	0	0	0	0	-	0	0-0	-	4.56	6.75
2013	SF	NL	51	0	0	9	53.0	211	46	15	14	2	1	1	0	12	3	51	2	0	3	1	.750	0	0-2	11	2.30	2.38
2014	SF	NL	71	0	0	13	66.1	249	45	19	19	5	5	1	1	18	3	51	5	1	7	1	.875	0	2-5	17	1.93	2.58
2015	2 Tms		59	0	0	17	58.0	257	59	35	33	8	2	3	1	22	0	42	3	0	2	0	1.000	0	4-4	4	4.31	5.12
15	SF	NL	33	0	0	8	35.0	159	38	21	20	3	2	2	1	14	0	22	1	0	1	0	1.000	0	0-0	2	4.43	5.14
15	Bos	AL	26	0	0	9	23.0	98	21	14	13	5	0	1	0	8	0	20	2	0	1	0	1.000	0	4-4	2	4.09	5.09
	Postseason		7	0	0	0	5.2	28	9	5	5	2	0	0	0	2	0	4	0	0	0	0	-	0	0-1	-	9.46	7.94
	4 ML YEARS		189	0	0	44	184.0	745	157	74	71	17	8	5	2	53	6	148	10	1	12	2	.857	0	6-11	32	2.84	3.47

Ryan Madson

Pitches: R **Bats:** L **Pos:** RP-63   **Ht:** 6'6" **Wt:** 225 **Born:** 8/28/1980 **Age:** 36

			HOW MUCH HE PITCHED						WHAT HE GAVE UP										THE RESULTS						
Year	Team	Lg	G	GS	CG	GF	IP	BFP	H	R	ER	HR	SH	SF	HB	TBB	IBB	SO	WP	Bk	W	L	Pct	Sh	Sv-Op	Hld	ERC	ERA
2003	Phi	NL	1	0	0	0	2.0	6	0	0	0	0	0	0	0	0	0	0	0	0	0	0	-	0	0-0	-	0.00	0.00
2004	Phi	NL	52	1	0	14	77.0	312	68	23	20	6	1	1	5	19	4	55	7	0	9	3	.750	0	1-2	7	2.95	2.34
2005	Phi	NL	78	0	0	10	87.0	365	84	44	40	11	5	5	6	25	6	79	6	1	6	5	.545	0	0-7	32	3.83	4.14
2006	Phi	NL	50	17	0	8	134.1	620	176	92	85	20	9	3	10	50	4	99	12	0	11	9	.550	0	2-4	6	6.50	5.69
2007	Phi	NL	38	0	0	9	56.0	237	48	19	19	5	2	2	2	23	4	43	2	2	2	2	.500	0	1-2	7	3.28	3.05
2008	Phi	NL	76	0	0	14	82.2	340	79	29	28	6	3	2	1	23	4	67	2	1	4	2	.667	0	1-3	17	3.20	3.05
2009	Phi	NL	79	0	0	28	77.1	320	73	29	28	7	3	1	3	22	3	78	1	0	5	5	.500	0	10-16	26	3.39	3.26
2010	Phi	NL	55	0	0	21	53.0	217	42	16	15	4	2	0	4	13	3	64	2	0	6	2	.750	0	5-10	15	2.42	2.55
2011	Phi	NL	62	0	0	46	60.2	246	54	16	16	2	6	1	1	16	8	62	0	0	4	2	.667	0	32-34	3	2.45	2.37
2015	KC	AL	68	0	0	12	63.1	248	47	17	15	5	0	3	2	14	1	58	1	0	1	2	.333	0	3-5	20	2.08	2.13
2016	Oak	AL	63	0	0	53	64.2	270	63	27	26	7	2	1	2	20	3	49	4	1	6	7	.462	0	30-37	3	3.74	3.62
	Postseason		42	0	0	11	43.1	185	45	14	14	6	3	2	1	13	2	58	2	0	4	1	.800	0	2-7	9	4.19	2.91
	11 ML YEARS		622	18	0	215	758.0	3181	734	312	292	73	33	19	36	225	40	654	37	5	54	39	.581	0	85-120	136	3.61	3.47

Kenta Maeda

Pitches: R **Bats:** R **Pos:** SP-32   mah-AY-duh   **Ht:** 6'1" **Wt:** 175 **Born:** 4/11/1988 **Age:** 29

			HOW MUCH HE PITCHED						WHAT HE GAVE UP										THE RESULTS						
Year	Team	Lg	G	GS	CG	GF	IP	BFP	H	R	ER	HR	SH	SF	HB	TBB	IBB	SO	WP	Bk	W	L	Pct	Sh	Sv-Op	Hld	ERC	ERA
2012	HiroCrp	IND	29	29	5	0	206.1	820	161	46	35	6	-	-	9	44	1	171	2	0	14	7	.667	1	0- -	-	1.99	1.53
2013	HiroCrp	IND	26	26	3	0	175.2	690	129	46	41	13	-	-	2	40	1	158	1	0	15	7	.682	1	0- -	-	1.96	2.10
2014	HiroCrp	IND	27	27	1	0	187.0	746	164	61	54	12	-	-	2	41	1	161	4	1	11	9	.550	1	0- -	-	2.59	2.60
2015	HiroCrp	IND	28	28	5	0	199.1	791	162	49	48	5	-	-	6	38	0	170	3	0	15	8	.652	0	0- -	-	2.00	2.17
2016	LAD	NL	32	32	0	0	175.2	716	150	72	68	20	0	3	8	50	6	179	6	0	16	11	.593	0	0-0	0	3.09	3.48

Matt Magill

Pitches: R Bats: R Pos: RP-5   Ht: 6'3" Wt: 210 Born: 11/10/1989 Age: 27

			HOW MUCH HE PITCHED						WHAT HE GAVE UP												THE RESULTS							
Year	Team	Lg	G	GS	CG	GF	IP	BFP	H	R	ER	HR	SH	SF	HB	TBB	IBB	SO	WP	Bk	W	L	Pct	Sh	Sv-Op	Hld	ERC	ERA
2012	Chatt	AA	26	26	0	0	146.1	623	127	71	61	8	7	4	3	61	1	168	10	0	11	8	.579	0	0- -	-	3.15	3.75
2013	Albq	AAA	18	16	0	1	85.2	362	72	34	33	7	5	4	1	50	0	101	5	2	6	2	.750	0	0- -	-	3.94	3.47
2014	Albq	AAA	36	12	0	5	84.2	385	80	53	49	8	2	3	6	59	1	70	13	0	7	6	.538	0	0- -	-	5.23	5.21
2016	Lsvlle	AAA	29	0	0	2	42.1	181	54	24	21	6	0	0	0	21	0	43	4	0	4	1	.800	0	0- -	-	4.53	4.46
2016	Pnscla	AA	9	0	0	1	9.2	46	12	7	7	0	1	0	0	6	0	16	3	0	0	0	-	0	1- -	-	5.55	6.52
2013	LAD	NL	6	6	0	0	27.2	137	27	25	20	6	1	2	1	28	1	26	1	0	0	2	.000	0	0-0	0	7.48	6.51
2016	Cin	NL	5	0	0	2	4.1	20	5	3	3	1	1	0	0	5	0	1	0	0	0	0	-	0	0-0	0	10.68	6.23
	2 ML YEARS		11	6	0	2	32.0	157	32	28	23	7	2	2	1	33	1	27	1	0	0	2	.000	0	0-0	0	7.87	6.47

Damien Magnifico

Pitches: R Bats: R Pos: RP-3   Ht: 6'1" Wt: 195 Born: 5/24/1991 Age: 26

			HOW MUCH HE PITCHED						WHAT HE GAVE UP												THE RESULTS							
Year	Team	Lg	G	GS	CG	GF	IP	BFP	H	R	ER	HR	SH	SF	HB	TBB	IBB	SO	WP	Bk	W	L	Pct	Sh	Sv-Op	Hld	ERC	ERA
2012	Helena	R+	9	1	0	3	21.2	100	21	17	14	2	1	0	0	15	0	25	6	3	0	3	.000	0	0- -	-	4.93	5.82
2013	2 Tms	Low	21	18	0	2	80.2	357	83	46	41	6	0	3	6	41	2	63	9	0	5	3	.625	0	0- -	-	4.83	4.57
2014	BrvdCt	A+	22	22	2	0	120.1	503	110	61	50	11	3	2	4	43	0	76	12	0	8	6	.571	2	0- -	-	3.55	3.74
2015	Biloxi	AA	42	0	0	33	53.2	221	41	10	7	3	1	2	1	22	0	38	2	0	4	1	.800	0	20- -	-	2.65	1.17
2016	ColSpr	AAA	52	0	0	43	62.0	272	57	32	28	2	4	2	1	33	0	61	16	0	6	7	.462	0	18- -	-	3.69	4.06
2016	Mil	NL	3	0	0	3	3.0	15	2	2	2	0	0	1	1	3	0	0	2	0	0	0	-	0	0-0	0	4.81	6.00

Greg Mahle

mah-lee

Pitches: L Bats: L Pos: RP-24   Ht: 6'2" Wt: 230 Born: 4/17/1993 Age: 24

			HOW MUCH HE PITCHED						WHAT HE GAVE UP												THE RESULTS							
Year	Team	Lg	G	GS	CG	GF	IP	BFP	H	R	ER	HR	SH	SF	HB	TBB	IBB	SO	WP	Bk	W	L	Pct	Sh	Sv-Op	Hld	ERC	ERA
2014	2 Tms	Low	23	0	0	10	37.1	155	25	17	11	1	2	1	3	15	0	49	8	0	1	2	.333	0	2- -	-	2.14	2.65
2015	InldEm	A+	21	0	0	18	22.2	93	26	10	9	1	1	0	2	3	0	31	2	0	0	1	.000	0	9- -	-	3.98	3.57
2015	Ark	AA	31	0	0	26	35.1	147	34	16	12	1	1	3	0	11	0	36	3	0	3	3	.500	0	16- -	-	3.07	3.06
2016	Salt Lk	AAA	30	0	0	11	32.2	153	48	29	28	7	2	1	2	12	0	24	1	1	1	1	.500	0	2- -	-	8.21	7.71
2016	LAA	AL	24	0	0	1	18.1	86	23	13	11	4	1	0	2	10	2	14	1	0	1	0	1.000	0	0-0	6	7.64	5.40

Mikie Mahtook

MIKE-ee MAH-took

Bats: R Throws: R Pos: LF-26;CF-23;RF-18;PR-4;PH-3   Ht: 6'1" Wt: 200 Born: 11/30/1989 Age: 27

			BATTING																		RUNNING			AVERAGES			
Year	Team	Lg	G	AB	H	2B	3B	HR	(Hm	Rd)	TB	R	RBI	RC	TBB	IBB	SO	HBP	SH	SF	SB	CS	GDP	Avg	OBP	Slg	OPS
2012	Charltt	A+	92	341	99	15	7	5	(-	-)	143	44	37	55	29	2	71	10	0	6	19	6	7	.290	.358	.419	.777
2012	Mont	AA	39	153	38	10	1	4	(-	-)	62	17	25	19	11	0	31	3	0	2	4	3	3	.248	.308	.405	.713
2013	Mont	AA	132	511	130	30	8	7	(-	-)	197	71	68	68	43	0	102	10	0	4	25	8	18	.254	.322	.386	.708
2014	Drham	AAA	132	489	143	33	6	12	(-	-)	224	56	68	85	46	4	137	10	0	5	18	5	9	.292	.362	.458	.820
2015	Drham	AAA	98	385	96	27	3	4	(-	-)	141	35	45	46	22	0	98	9	0	2	10	1	3	.249	.304	.366	.670
2016	Drham	AAA	27	105	32	5	3	1	(-	-)	46	16	7	19	12	0	24	2	0	1	5	1	1	.305	.383	.438	.821
2015	TB	AL	41	105	31	5	1	9	(3	6)	65	22	19	22	6	0	31	3	1	0	4	3	0	.295	.351	.619	.970
2016	TB	AL	65	185	36	9	0	3	(1	2)	54	16	11	5	7	0	68	2	1	1	0	1	2	.195	.275	.292	.523
	2 ML YEARS		106	290	67	14	1	12	(4	8)	119	38	30	27	13	0	99	5	2	1	4	4	2	.231	.275	.410	.685

Luke Maile

MAY-lee

Bats: R Throws: R Pos: C-37;1B-4;DH-1;PH-1   Ht: 6'3" Wt: 225 Born: 2/6/1991 Age: 26

			BATTING																		RUNNING			AVERAGES			
Year	Team	Lg	G	AB	H	2B	3B	HR	(Hm	Rd)	TB	R	RBI	RC	TBB	IBB	SO	HBP	SH	SF	SB	CS	GDP	Avg	OBP	Slg	OPS
2012	HudVal	A-	61	216	60	10	3	3	(-	-)	85	30	41	35	31	0	36	4	0	1	3	1	4	.278	.377	.394	.771
2013	BG	A	95	361	102	25	3	4	(-	-)	145	45	49	55	41	0	54	0	0	5	8	2	10	.283	.351	.402	.753
2014	Mont	AA	97	351	94	19	3	5	(-	-)	134	43	37	48	35	0	76	5	0	2	2	1	13	.268	.341	.382	.723
2015	Drham	AAA	89	294	61	9	1	5	(-	-)	87	38	29	28	35	0	50	4	1	3	1	1	11	.207	.298	.296	.594
2016	Drham	AAA	58	194	47	13	0	2	(-	-)	66	13	12	21	16	0	36	3	1	0	0	1	5	.242	.310	.340	.650
2015	TB	AL	15	35	6	3	0	0	(0	0)	9	2	2	0	0	0	8	0	0	0	0	0	3	.171	.171	.257	.429
2016	TB	AL	42	119	27	7	0	3	(2	1)	43	10	15	11	4	1	36	0	0	3	0	0	2	.227	.252	.361	.613
	2 ML YEARS		57	154	33	10	0	3	(2	1)	52	12	17	11	4	1	44	0	0	3	0	0	5	.214	.234	.338	.572

Martin Maldonado

mar-TEEN

Bats: R Throws: R Pos: C-69;PH-8   Ht: 6'0" Wt: 230 Born: 8/16/1986 Age: 30

			BATTING																		RUNNING			AVERAGES			
Year	Team	Lg	G	AB	H	2B	3B	HR	(Hm	Rd)	TB	R	RBI	RC	TBB	IBB	SO	HBP	SH	SF	SB	CS	GDP	Avg	OBP	Slg	OPS
2011	Mil	NL	3	1	0	0	0	0	(0	0)	0	0	0	0	0	0	1	0	0	0	0	0	0	.000	.000	.000	.000
2012	Mil	NL	78	233	62	9	0	8	(6	2)	95	22	30	28	17	0	56	2	4	0	1	1	5	.266	.321	.408	.729
2013	Mil	NL	67	183	31	7	1	4	(1	3)	52	13	22	14	13	1	53	3	3	0	0	0	5	.169	.236	.284	.520
2014	Mil	NL	52	111	26	5	0	4	(2	2)	43	14	16	14	11	1	32	3	1	0	0	0	4	.234	.320	.387	.707
2015	Mil	NL	79	229	48	7	0	4	(4	0)	67	19	22	20	23	3	65	1	1	2	0	1	6	.210	.282	.293	.575
2016	Mil	NL	76	208	42	7	0	8	(6	2)	73	21	21	23	35	9	56	6	3	1	1	0	6	.202	.332	.351	.683
	6 ML YEARS		355	965	209	35	1	28	(19	9)	330	89	111	99	99	14	263	15	12	3	2	2	23	.217	.299	.342	.640

Sean Manaea

Pitches: L Bats: R Pos: SP-24; RP-1   muh-NIE-uh   Ht: 6'5" Wt: 245 Born: 2/1/1992 Age: 25

				HOW MUCH HE PITCHED						WHAT HE GAVE UP											THE RESULTS						
Year	Team	Lg	G	GS	CG	GF	IP	BFP	H	R	ER	HR	SH	SF	HB	TBB	IBB	SO	WP	Bk	W	L	Pct	Sh	Sv-Op	Hld	ERC	ERA
2014	Wilmg	A+	25	25	1	0	121.2	514	102	54	42	5	3	4	5	54	0	146	4	0	7	8	.467	1	0--	-	3.13	3.11
2015	2 Tms	Low	5	5	0	0	24.2	100	24	13	9	1	1	1	2	5	0	28	1	0	1	0	1.000	0	0--	-	3.19	3.28
2015	Mdlnd	AA	7	7	0	0	42.2	173	34	11	9	3	1	0	1	15	0	51	1	0	6	0	1.000	0	0--	-	2.75	1.90
2016	Oak	AL	25	24	0	0	144.2	594	135	65	62	20	4	4	4	37	1	124	3	0	7	9	.438	0	0-0	0	3.53	3.86

Trey Mancini

Bats: R Throws: R Pos: DH-4;PH-1   Ht: 6'4" Wt: 215 Born: 3/18/1992 Age: 25

									BATTING												RUNNING			AVERAGES			
Year	Team	Lg	G	AB	H	2B	3B	HR	(Hm	Rd)	TB	R	RBI	RC	TBB	IBB	SO	HBP	SH	SF	SB	CS	GDP	Avg	OBP	Slg	OPS
2013	Abrdn	A-	68	256	84	18	2	3	(-	-)	115	43	35	45	20	2	43	5	0	4	3	1	6	.328	.382	.449	.832
2014	2 Tms	Low	137	543	154	32	3	10	(-	-)	222	67	83	73	28	0	95	9	0	6	1	2	22	.284	.326	.409	.735
2015	Frdrck	A+	52	207	65	14	3	8	(-	-)	109	28	32	36	9	1	35	0	0	1	4	2	7	.314	.341	.527	.868
2015	Bowie	AA	84	326	117	29	3	13	(-	-)	191	60	57	72	22	1	58	1	0	5	2	1	11	.359	.395	.586	.981
2016	Bowie	AA	17	63	19	4	0	7	(-	-)	44	18	14	17	10	0	17	2	0	0	0	0	4	.302	.413	.698	1.112
2016	Norfolk	AAA	125	483	135	22	5	13	(-	-)	206	60	54	74	48	1	123	4	0	1	2	2	13	.280	.349	.427	.775
2016	Bal	AL	5	14	5	1	0	3	(3	0)	15	3	5	5	0	0	4	1	0	0	0	0	0	.357	.400	1.071	1.471

Seth Maness

Pitches: R Bats: R Pos: RP-29   MAY-ness   Ht: 6'0" Wt: 190 Born: 10/14/1988 Age: 28

				HOW MUCH HE PITCHED						WHAT HE GAVE UP											THE RESULTS						
Year	Team	Lg	G	GS	CG	GF	IP	BFP	H	R	ER	HR	SH	SF	HB	TBB	IBB	SO	WP	Bk	W	L	Pct	Sh	Sv-Op	Hld	ERC	ERA
2013	StL	NL	66	0	0	4	62.0	249	65	17	16	4	4	0	1	13	7	35	2	0	5	2	.714	0	1-3	15	3.41	2.32
2014	StL	NL	73	0	0	17	80.1	317	77	29	26	7	5	4	2	11	3	55	2	1	6	4	.600	0	3-3	11	2.90	2.91
2015	StL	NL	76	0	0	13	63.1	270	77	35	30	7	4	1	0	13	4	46	2	0	4	2	.667	0	3-6	20	4.65	4.26
2016	StL	NL	29	0	0	13	31.2	134	34	14	12	2	1	1	0	8	2	16	2	0	2	2	.500	0	0-0	1	3.56	3.41
	Postseason		17	0	0	2	12.1	49	13	3	2	1	1	1	0	1	0	6	0	0	1	0	1.000	0	0-1	1	3.09	1.46
	4 ML YEARS		244	0	0	47	237.1	970	253	95	84	20	14	6	4	45	16	152	8	1	17	10	.630	0	7-12	47	3.57	3.19

Jeff Manship

Pitches: R Bats: R Pos: RP-53   Ht: 6'2" Wt: 205 Born: 1/16/1985 Age: 32

				HOW MUCH HE PITCHED						WHAT HE GAVE UP											THE RESULTS						
Year	Team	Lg	G	GS	CG	GF	IP	BFP	H	R	ER	HR	SH	SF	HB	TBB	IBB	SO	WP	Bk	W	L	Pct	Sh	Sv-Op	Hld	ERC	ERA
2009	Min	AL	11	5	0	1	31.2	146	39	21	20	4	1	3	1	15	0	21	2	0	1	1	.500	0	0-0	0	6.11	5.68
2010	Min	AL	13	1	0	1	29.0	124	34	20	17	3	1	1	0	6	0	21	0	0	2	1	.667	0	0-0	0	4.31	5.28
2011	Min	AL	5	0	0	1	3.1	19	5	3	3	0	0	2	0	4	1	2	0	0	0	0	-	0	0-0	0	8.73	8.10
2012	Min	AL	12	0	0	2	21.2	98	29	19	19	4	1	0	1	7	1	12	0	0	0	0	-	0	0-0	1	6.67	7.89
2013	Col	NL	11	4	0	3	30.2	139	37	25	24	6	0	3	0	12	1	18	0	0	0	5	.000	0	0-0	0	5.87	7.04
2014	Phi	NL	20	0	0	7	23.0	105	24	17	17	1	3	0	0	14	5	16	0	0	1	2	.333	0	0-0	1	4.30	6.65
2015	Cle	AL	32	0	0	7	39.1	144	20	4	4	1	0	4	1	10	0	33	0	0	1	0	1.000	0	0-0	3	1.14	0.92
2016	Cle	AL	53	0	0	8	43.1	189	40	20	15	7	0	1	0	22	2	36	0	0	2	1	.667	0	0-1	6	4.41	3.12
	8 ML YEARS		157	10	0	30	222.0	964	228	129	119	26	6	14	3	90	10	159	2	0	7	10	.412	0	0-1	10	4.36	4.82

Joe Mantiply

Pitches: L Bats: R Pos: RP-5   Ht: 6'4" Wt: 215 Born: 3/1/1991 Age: 26

				HOW MUCH HE PITCHED						WHAT HE GAVE UP											THE RESULTS						
Year	Team	Lg	G	GS	CG	GF	IP	BFP	H	R	ER	HR	SH	SF	HB	TBB	IBB	SO	WP	Bk	W	L	Pct	Sh	Sv-Op	Hld	ERC	ERA
2013	Conn	A-	13	12	0	0	35.1	147	31	12	8	2	0	3	2	10	0	30	1	0	0	1	.000	0	0--	-	2.88	2.04
2014	Wmich	A	38	0	0	17	71.0	282	57	19	19	2	1	1	3	19	0	76	2	0	6	3	.667	0	8--	-	2.31	2.41
2014	Erie	AA	8	0	0	1	10.2	46	12	5	4	1	0	2	0	3	0	10	1	0	0	0	-	0	1--	-	4.26	3.38
2015	Erie	AA	32	0	0	13	53.1	221	49	18	15	4	3	2	1	12	1	44	1	0	2	2	.500	0	2--	-	2.81	2.53
2015	Toledo	AAA	7	0	0	5	10.0	35	6	1	1	0	1	0	0	1	0	7	0	0	2	0	1.000	0	1--	-	0.98	0.90
2016	Erie	AA	49	0	0	11	51.0	205	40	17	14	1	1	4	2	11	0	62	4	0	3	1	.750	0	1--	-	1.92	2.47
2016	Toledo	AAA	7	1	0	2	8.1	36	11	4	4	1	0	1	0	1	0	7	1	0	1	1	.500	0	0--	-	4.94	4.32
2016	Det	AL	5	0	0	3	2.2	16	7	5	5	1	1	0	0	2	1	2	0	0	0	0	-	0	0-0	0	19.98	16.88

Manuel Margot

Bats: R Throws: R Pos: CF-9;RF-1;PH-1;PR-1   mar-GOH   Ht: 5'11" Wt: 180 Born: 9/28/1994 Age: 22

									BATTING												RUNNING			AVERAGES			
Year	Team	Lg	G	AB	H	2B	3B	HR	(Hm	Rd)	TB	R	RBI	RC	TBB	IBB	SO	HBP	SH	SF	SB	CS	GDP	Avg	OBP	Slg	OPS
2013	Lowell	A-	49	185	50	8	2	1	(-	-)	65	29	21	26	22	1	40	1	5	3	18	8	0	.270	.346	.351	.697
2014	2 Tms	Low	115	420	123	25	5	12	(-	-)	194	65	59	73	39	0	54	3	5	2	42	15	8	.293	.356	.462	.818
2015	Salem	A+	46	181	51	6	5	3	(-	-)	76	35	17	27	11	0	15	1	2	3	20	5	4	.282	.321	.420	.741
2015	Portlnd	AA	64	258	70	21	4	3	(-	-)	108	38	33	37	21	1	36	1	0	2	19	8	4	.271	.326	.419	.745
2016	ElPaso	AAA	124	517	157	21	12	6	(-	-)	220	98	55	81	36	0	64	4	5	4	30	11	2	.304	.351	.426	.777
2016	SD	NL	10	37	9	4	1	0	(0	0)	15	4	3	5	0	0	7	0	0	0	2	0	0	.243	.243	.405	.649

Jhan Marinez

Pitches: R Bats: R Pos: RP-46   Ht: 6'1" Wt: 200 Born: 8/12/1988 Age: 28

			HOW MUCH HE PITCHED						WHAT HE GAVE UP											THE RESULTS						
Year	Team	Lg	G	GS	CG	GF	IP	BFP	H	R	ER	HR	SH	SF	HB	TBB	IBB	SO	WP	Bk	W	L	Pct	Sh	Sv-Op	Hld	ERC	ERA
2016	Drhm*	AAA	6	0	0	5	8.0	35	10	2	2	0	0	0	0	3	0	9	1	0	2	1	.667	0	1--	-	4.81	2.25
2010	Fla	NL	4	0	0	2	2.2	14	3	3	2	1	0	0	0	3	0	3	0	0	1	1	.500	0	0-2	0	10.25	6.75
2012	CWS	AL	2	0	0	1	2.2	11	2	0	0	0	1	0	0	2	1	1	0	0	0	0	-	0	0-0	0	2.87	0.00
2016	2 Tms		46	0	0	12	62.1	269	62	25	22	4	2	1	6	21	3	50	4	0	0	1	.000	0	0-0	5	3.86	3.18
16	TB	AL	3	0	0	2	3.2	13	2	1	1	1	0	0	0	0	0	3	0	0	0	0	-	0	0-0	0	1.32	2.45
16	Mil	NL	43	0	0	10	58.2	256	60	24	21	3	2	1	6	21	3	47	4	0	0	1	.000	0	0-0	5	4.02	3.22
3 ML YEARS			52	0	0	15	67.2	294	67	28	24	5	3	1	6	26	4	54	4	0	1	2	.333	0	0-2	5	4.04	3.19

Michael Mariot

Pitches: R Bats: R Pos: RP-25   MAIR-ee-aht   Ht: 6'0" Wt: 190 Born: 10/20/1988 Age: 28

			HOW MUCH HE PITCHED						WHAT HE GAVE UP											THE RESULTS						
Year	Team	Lg	G	GS	CG	GF	IP	BFP	H	R	ER	HR	SH	SF	HB	TBB	IBB	SO	WP	Bk	W	L	Pct	Sh	Sv-Op	Hld	ERC	ERA
2016	LV*	AAA	26	0	0	9	32.1	122	16	8	8	3	1	0	1	13	0	24	1	0	1	2	.333	0	1--	-	1.70	2.23
2014	KC	AL	17	0	0	8	25.0	118	31	21	18	2	0	2	0	12	1	21	5	1	1	0	1.000	0	0-0	0	5.43	6.48
2015	KC	AL	2	0	0	1	3.0	12	2	1	1	1	0	0	0	2	0	1	0	0	0	0	-	0	0-0	0	5.24	3.00
2016	Phi	NL	25	0	0	4	21.2	95	18	14	14	5	0	0	0	14	1	23	2	0	1	0	1.000	0	2-3	4	4.98	5.82
3 ML YEARS			44	0	0	13	49.2	225	51	36	33	8	0	2	0	28	2	45	7	1	2	0	1.000	0	2-3	4	5.23	5.98

Jake Marisnick

mah-RIZ-nick

Bats: R Throws: R Pos: CF-74;LF-26;PR-12;RF-5;DH-5;PH-4   Ht: 6'4" Wt: 220 Born: 3/30/1991 Age: 26

			BATTING																		RUNNING			AVERAGES			
Year	Team	Lg	G	AB	H	2B	3B	HR	(Hm	Rd)	TB	R	RBI	RC	TBB	IBB	SO	HBP	SH	SF	SB	CS	GDP	Avg	OBP	Slg	OPS
2013	Mia	NL	40	109	20	2	1	1	(1	0)	27	6	5	7	6	0	27	1	1	1	3	1	1	.183	.231	.248	.478
2014	2 Tms		65	221	55	8	0	3	(3	0)	72	21	19	19	8	3	67	3	2	3	11	3	2	.249	.281	.326	.607
2015	Hou	AL	133	339	80	15	4	9	(4	5)	130	46	36	40	18	0	105	5	6	4	24	9	2	.236	.281	.383	.665
2016	Hou	AL	118	287	60	18	1	5	(1	4)	95	40	21	23	16	0	83	3	4	1	10	5	4	.209	.257	.331	.588
14	Mia	NL	14	48	8	0	0	0	(0	0)	8	3	0	1	3	1	19	0	0	0	5	0	0	.167	.216	.167	.382
14	Hou	AL	51	173	47	8	0	3	(3	0)	64	18	19	18	5	2	48	3	2	3	6	3	2	.272	.299	.370	.669
Postseason			4	7	3	1	0	0	(0	0)	4	1	0	2	0	0	2	0	0	0	0	0	0	.429	.429	.571	1.000
4 ML YEARS			356	956	215	43	6	18	(9	9)	324	113	81	89	48	3	282	12	13	9	48	18	9	.225	.268	.339	.607

Nick Markakis

mar-KAY-kiss

Bats: L Throws: L Pos: RF-150;DH-5;PH-2;1B-1   Ht: 6'1" Wt: 215 Born: 11/17/1983 Age: 33

			BATTING																		RUNNING			AVERAGES			
Year	Team	Lg	G	AB	H	2B	3B	HR	(Hm	Rd)	TB	R	RBI	RC	TBB	IBB	SO	HBP	SH	SF	SB	CS	GDP	Avg	OBP	Slg	OPS
2006	Bal	AL	147	491	143	25	2	16	(9	7)	220	72	62	67	43	3	72	3	3	2	0	15	.291	.351	.448	.799
2007	Bal	AL	161	637	191	43	3	23	(15	8)	309	97	112	103	61	5	112	5	1	6	18	6	22	.300	.362	.485	.848
2008	Bal	AL	157	595	182	48	1	20	(11	9)	292	106	87	113	99	7	113	2	0	1	10	7	10	.306	.406	.491	.897
2009	Bal	AL	161	642	188	45	2	18	(8	10)	291	94	101	97	56	0	98	3	0	10	6	2	12	.293	.347	.453	.801
2010	Bal	AL	160	629	187	45	3	12	(8	4)	274	79	60	99	73	9	93	2	0	5	7	2	18	.297	.370	.436	.805
2011	Bal	AL	160	641	182	31	1	15	(8	7)	260	72	73	90	62	6	75	7	0	6	12	3	16	.284	.351	.406	.756
2012	Bal	AL	104	420	125	28	3	13	(9	4)	198	59	54	69	42	3	51	4	0	5	1	1	11	.298	.363	.471	.834
2013	Bal	AL	160	634	172	24	0	10	(6	4)	226	89	59	66	55	3	76	3	0	8	1	2	17	.271	.329	.356	.685
2014	Bal	AL	155	642	177	27	1	14	(8	6)	248	81	50	82	62	4	84	4	0	2	4	2	10	.276	.342	.386	.729
2015	Atl	NL	156	612	181	38	1	3	(1	2)	230	73	53	81	70	11	83	3	0	1	2	1	17	.296	.370	.376	.746
2016	Atl	NL	158	599	161	38	0	13	(7	6)	238	67	89	82	71	9	101	5	0	9	2	2	16	.269	.346	.397	.744
Postseason			7	31	8	1	0	1	(1	0)	12	4	3	4	1	0	3	0	0	0	1	0	0	.258	.281	.387	.668
11 ML YEARS			1679	6542	1889	392	17	157	(90	67)	2786	889	800	949	694	60	958	41	4	55	63	28	164	.289	.358	.426	.784

Justin Marks

Pitches: L Bats: L Pos: RP-4   Ht: 6'3" Wt: 205 Born: 1/12/1988 Age: 29

			HOW MUCH HE PITCHED						WHAT HE GAVE UP											THE RESULTS						
Year	Team	Lg	G	GS	CG	GF	IP	BFP	H	R	ER	HR	SH	SF	HB	TBB	IBB	SO	WP	Bk	W	L	Pct	Sh	Sv-Op	Hld	ERC	ERA
2012	NWArk	AA	17	17	0	0	85.1	362	79	39	36	8	0	6	2	38	0	73	4	2	3	5	.375	0	0--	-	3.95	3.80
2013	Omha	AAA	24	20	0	3	129.2	576	138	68	66	7	2	3	4	61	0	117	4	0	6	13	.316	0	0--	-	4.52	4.58
2014	Omha	AAA	13	2	0	0	30.1	147	38	25	19	4	2	0	4	11	0	27	1	0	3	2	.600	0	0--	-	5.92	5.64
2014	RdRck	AAA	5	0	0	2	5.1	26	6	3	3	0	0	0	0	4	1	8	1	0	1	0	1.000	0	0--	-	4.88	5.06
2015	Reno	AAA	28	19	0	2	108.2	481	121	72	68	12	5	4	3	50	2	84	7	3	5	9	.357	0	0--	-	5.22	5.63
2016	Drhm	AAA	25	23	1	1	140.0	585	125	70	60	14	0	4	4	53	1	127	5	0	7	11	.389	1	0--	-	3.54	3.86
2014	KC	AL	1	0	0	0	2.0	13	4	3	3	0	0	0	0	3	0	2	0	0	0	0	-	0	0-0	0	14.34	13.50
2016	TB	AL	4	0	0	0	9.0	42	7	1	1	1	0	0	0	9	0	6	0	0	0	0	-	0	0-0	0	5.27	1.00
2 ML YEARS			5	0	0	0	11.0	55	11	4	4	1	0	0	0	12	0	8	0	0	0	0	-	0	0-0	0	6.78	3.27

Matt Marksberry

Pitches: L Bats: L Pos: RP-4   Ht: 6'1" Wt: 180 Born: 8/25/1990 Age: 26

			HOW MUCH HE PITCHED						WHAT HE GAVE UP											THE RESULTS						
Year	Team	Lg	G	GS	CG	GF	IP	BFP	H	R	ER	HR	SH	SF	HB	TBB	IBB	SO	WP	Bk	W	L	Pct	Sh	Sv-Op	Hld	ERC	ERA
2013	Danvle	R+	12	6	0	0	33.2	149	32	22	19	1	1	2	4	16	0	40	5	0	1	3	.250	0	0--	-	4.05	5.08
2014	2 Tms	Low	24	22	0	0	115.0	493	104	58	48	10	3	3	3	53	0	100	13	0	6	10	.375	0	0--	-	3.81	3.76
2015	Carlina	A+	22	0	0	9	35.2	143	22	11	11	2	1	1	2	13	1	35	1	0	3	1	.750	0	2--	-	1.88	2.78
2015	Gwnntt	AAA	11	0	0	1	10.1	41	10	3	3	0	1	0	1	9	0	8	0	0	0	0	-	0	1--	-	2.18	2.61

Year Team	Lg	G	GS	CG	GF	IP	BFP	H	R	ER	HR	SH	SF	HB	TBB	IBB	SO	WP	Bk	W	L	Pct	Sh	Sv-Op	Hld	ERC	ERA
2016 Missi	AA	6	0	0	4	8.2	29	3	1	1	0	0	1	0	2	0	7	0	0	0	0	-	0	2--	-	0.60	1.04
2016 Gwnntt	AAA	28	0	0	3	34.0	147	34	10	10	2	1	0	0	15	1	32	1	1	4	2	.667	0	0--	-	3.91	2.65
2015 Atl	NL	31	0	0	4	23.1	108	22	16	13	2	0	2	1	16	2	21	3	0	0	3	.000	0	0-3	5	4.71	5.01
2016 Atl	NL	4	0	0	1	3.1	17	5	2	2	1	0	0	1	1	0	2	0	0	0	0	-	0	0-0	0	9.61	5.40
2 ML YEARS		35	0	0	5	26.2	125	27	18	15	3	0	2	2	17	2	23	3	0	0	3	.000	0	0-3	5	5.28	5.06

German Marquez

hair-MAHN

Pitches: R Bats: R Pos: SP-3; RP-3   **Ht: 6'1" Wt: 185 Born: 2/22/1995 Age: 22**

Year Team	Lg	G	GS	CG	GF	IP	BFP	H	R	ER	HR	SH	SF	HB	TBB	IBB	SO	WP	Bk	W	L	Pct	Sh	Sv-Op	Hld	ERC	ERA
2013 Prnctn	R+	12	12	0	0	53.1	225	46	27	24	2	2	3	2	20	0	38	2	0	2	5	.286	0	0--	-	2.94	4.05
2014 BG	A	22	18	0	0	98.0	398	83	43	35	5	1	0	4	29	0	95	5	0	5	7	.417	0	0--	-	2.74	3.21
2015 Charltt	A+	26	23	0	1	139.0	596	147	68	55	6	4	7	13	29	0	104	7	2	7	13	.350	0	0--	-	3.60	3.56
2016 Hrtfrd	AA	21	21	0	0	135.2	553	124	53	43	9	5	2	7	33	1	126	5	1	9	6	.600	0	0--	-	3.03	2.85
2016 Albq	AAA	5	5	0	0	31.0	124	30	15	15	5	0	0	0	6	0	29	0	0	2	0	1.000	0	0--	-	3.58	4.35
2016 Col	NL	6	3	0	0	20.2	98	28	12	12	2	2	1	3	6	0	15	0	0	1	1	.500	0	0-0	0	6.21	5.23

Deven Marrero

Bats: R Throws: R Pos: 2B-6;3B-4;SS-4;PH-2;DH-1;PR-1   **Ht: 6'1" Wt: 195 Born: 8/25/1990 Age: 26**

Year Team	Lg	G	AB	H	2B	3B	HR	(Hm	Rd)	TB	R	RBI	RC	TBB	IBB	SO	HBP	SH	SF	SB	CS	GDP	Avg	OBP	Slg	OPS
2012 Lowell	A-	64	246	66	14	3	2	(-	-)	92	45	24	38	34	0	48	1	2	1	24	6	6	.268	.358	.374	.732
2013 Salem	A+	85	332	85	20	0	2	(-	-)	111	50	21	44	42	0	60	1	1	0	21	2	7	.256	.341	.334	.676
2013 Portlnd	AA	19	72	17	0	0	0	(-	-)	17	7	5	7	10	0	16	0	1	2	6	0	2	.236	.321	.236	.558
2014 Portlnd	AA	68	268	78	19	2	5	(-	-)	116	42	39	45	34	0	57	2	0	3	12	7	8	.291	.371	.433	.804
2014 Pwtckt	AAA	50	186	39	11	0	1	(-	-)	53	23	20	14	12	0	37	1	2	1	4	1	6	.210	.260	.285	.545
2015 Pwtckt	AAA	102	375	96	13	1	6	(-	-)	129	49	29	44	33	0	87	2	5	4	12	5	10	.256	.316	.344	.660
2016 Pwtckt	AAA	96	363	72	11	1	1	(-	-)	88	30	27	20	22	0	90	1	0	2	10	3	15	.198	.245	.242	.487
2015 Bos	AL	25	53	12	0	0	1	(0	1)	15	8	3	4	3	0	19	0	0	0	2	1	0	.226	.268	.283	.551
2016 Bos	AL	13	12	1	0	0	0	(0	0)	1	0	0	0	2	0	5	0	0	0	0	0	0	.083	.214	.083	.298
2 ML YEARS		38	65	13	0	0	1	(0	1)	16	8	3	4	5	0	24	0	0	0	2	1	0	.200	.257	.246	.503

Evan Marshall

Pitches: R Bats: R Pos: RP-15   **Ht: 6'2" Wt: 225 Born: 4/18/1990 Age: 27**

Year Team	Lg	G	GS	CG	GF	IP	BFP	H	R	ER	HR	SH	SF	HB	TBB	IBB	SO	WP	Bk	W	L	Pct	Sh	Sv-Op	Hld	ERC	ERA
2016 Reno*	AAA	33	0	0	5	33.1	151	36	17	17	1	2	2	3	16	2	28	1	0	1	1	.500	0	0--	-	4.57	4.59
2014 Ari	NL	57	0	0	11	49.1	210	50	17	15	3	2	1	2	17	3	54	3	0	4	4	.500	0	0-1	19	3.76	2.74
2015 Ari	NL	13	0	0	4	13.1	61	20	9	9	3	0	0	0	5	1	7	1	0	0	2	.000	0	0-2	8	8.27	6.08
2016 Ari	NL	15	0	0	8	15.1	79	28	18	15	2	0	0	1	8	2	9	1	0	0	1	.000	0	0-0	1	10.46	8.80
3 ML YEARS		85	0	0	23	78.0	350	98	44	39	8	2	1	3	30	6	70	5	0	4	7	.364	0	0-3	22	5.66	4.50

Jefry Marte

marr-TAY

Bats: R Throws: R Pos: 1B-29;LF-27;3B-22;PH-12;DH-4;PR-4   **Ht: 6'1" Wt: 220 Born: 6/21/1991 Age: 26**

Year Team	Lg	G	AB	H	2B	3B	HR	(Hm	Rd)	TB	R	RBI	RC	TBB	IBB	SO	HBP	SH	SF	SB	CS	GDP	Avg	OBP	Slg	OPS
2012 Bnghtn	AA	129	462	116	20	3	9	(-	-)	169	61	58	57	43	1	76	6	0	2	9	5	20	.251	.322	.366	.687
2013 Mdlnd	AA	66	245	68	17	1	2	(-	-)	93	33	28	36	25	1	49	4	0	4	8	1	4	.278	.349	.380	.729
2014 Mdlnd	AA	107	405	104	17	0	10	(-	-)	151	50	53	54	45	0	69	3	1	6	9	3	11	.257	.331	.373	.704
2015 Toledo	AAA	95	357	98	25	3	15	(-	-)	174	49	66	60	31	0	64	7	0	4	8	5	6	.275	.341	.487	.828
2016 Salt Lk	AAA	44	162	43	12	1	3	(-	-)	66	22	24	24	22	0	35	2	0	3	3	3	3	.265	.354	.407	.762
2015 Det	AL	33	80	17	4	0	4	(1	3)	33	9	11	6	8	0	22	0	2	0	0	0	2	.213	.284	.413	.697
2016 LAA	AL	88	258	65	14	0	15	(10	5)	124	38	44	31	18	0	59	5	0	3	2	2	8	.252	.310	.481	.790
2 ML YEARS		121	338	82	18	0	19	(11	8)	157	47	55	37	26	0	81	5	2	3	2	2	10	.243	.304	.464	.768

Kelvin Marte

marr-TAY

Pitches: L Bats: R Pos: RP-2   **Ht: 5'9" Wt: 170 Born: 11/24/1987 Age: 29**

Year Team	Lg	G	GS	CG	GF	IP	BFP	H	R	ER	HR	SH	SF	HB	TBB	IBB	SO	WP	Bk	W	L	Pct	Sh	Sv-Op	Hld	ERC	ERA
2012 2 Tms	Low	17	10	0	1	48.1	212	57	32	24	3	3	1	4	11	0	37	2	1	2	3	.400	0	0--	-	4.46	4.47
2013 SnJos	A+	25	15	0	2	105.1	424	102	46	43	14	5	0	4	19	0	80	2	1	6	4	.600	0	0--	-	3.50	3.67
2014 Rchmd	AA	18	15	1	0	87.0	363	89	37	37	8	2	1	1	23	0	55	0	0	8	3	.727	1	0--	-	3.70	3.83
2014 Fresno	AAA	6	6	0	0	36.1	154	42	24	22	6	3	2	0	8	0	21	5	1	1	2	.333	0	0--	-	4.75	5.45
2015 Rchmd	AA	26	19	1	2	130.0	534	118	41	38	5	2	4	8	40	2	77	2	1	10	6	.625	1	0--	-	3.09	2.63
2016 Indy	AAA	34	4	0	6	73.2	302	65	31	30	4	2	2	2	21	1	57	2	1	4	3	.571	0	2--	-	2.81	3.67
2016 Pit	NL	2	0	0	1	3.1	17	5	5	0	2	0	0	0	2	0	1	0	0	0	0	-	0	0-0	0	12.33	0.00

Ketel Marte

Bats: B **Throws:** R **Pos:** SS-119;PH-1;PR-1 kuh-TELL marr-TAY **Ht:** 6'1" **Wt:** 165 **Born:** 10/12/1993 **Age:** 23

Year	Team	Lg	G	AB	H	2B	3B	HR	(Hm	Rd)	TB	R	RBI	RC	TBB	IBB	SO	HBP	SH	SF	SB	CS	GDP	Avg	OBP	Slg	OPS
2012	2 Tms	Low	69	265	66	4	2	0	(-	-)	74	39	24	22	14	0	38	0	7	0	15	4	5	.249	.287	.279	.566
2013	2 Tms	Low	117	464	137	15	7	1	(-	-)	169	79	37	56	19	0	50	1	11	3	20	11	9	.295	.322	.364	.687
2014	Jacksn	AA	109	443	134	27	6	2	(-	-)	179	63	46	61	19	1	65	1	4	5	23	10	6	.302	.329	.404	.733
2014	Tacom	AAA	19	80	25	5	0	2	(-	-)	36	16	9	14	8	0	13	0	0	2	6	0	1	.313	.367	.450	.817
2015	Tacom	AAA	65	261	82	12	2	3	(-	-)	107	41	29	42	20	0	32	0	3	3	20	3	4	.314	.359	.410	.769
2015	Sea	AL	57	219	62	14	3	2	(1	1)	88	25	17	33	24	0	43	0	2	2	8	4	1	.283	.351	.402	.753
2016	Sea	AL	119	437	113	21	2	1	(1	0)	141	55	33	41	18	0	84	2	3	6	11	5	10	.259	.287	.323	.610
	2 ML YEARS		176	656	175	35	5	3	(2	1)	229	80	50	74	42	0	127	2	5	8	19	9	11	.267	.309	.349	.658

Starling Marte

Bats: R **Throws:** R **Pos:** LF-114;CF-16;PH-6;PR-1 marr-TAY **Ht:** 6'1" **Wt:** 185 **Born:** 10/9/1988 **Age:** 28

Year	Team	Lg	G	AB	H	2B	3B	HR	(Hm	Rd)	TB	R	RBI	RC	TBB	IBB	SO	HBP	SH	SF	SB	CS	GDP	Avg	OBP	Slg	OPS
2012	Pit	NL	47	167	43	3	6	5	(3	2)	73	18	17	21	8	0	50	3	2	2	12	5	5	.257	.300	.437	.737
2013	Pit	NL	135	510	143	26	10	12	(5	7)	225	83	35	74	25	2	138	24	6	1	41	15	6	.280	.343	.441	.784
2014	Pit	NL	135	495	144	29	6	13	(5	8)	224	73	56	70	33	0	131	17	0	0	30	11	5	.291	.356	.453	.808
2015	Pit	NL	153	579	166	30	2	19	(10	9)	257	84	81	81	27	3	123	19	3	5	30	10	14	.287	.337	.444	.780
2016	Pit	NL	129	489	152	34	5	9	(2	7)	223	71	46	77	23	5	104	16	1	0	47	12	8	.311	.362	.456	.818
	Postseason		8	32	4	1	0	1	(0	1)	8	2	1	1	1	0	7	1	0	0	1	0	2	.125	.176	.250	.426
	5 ML YEARS		599	2240	648	122	29	58	(25	33)	1002	329	235	323	116	10	546	79	12	8	160	53	38	.289	.345	.447	.792

Cody Martin

Pitches: R **Bats:** R **Pos:** RP-7; SP-2 **Ht:** 6'3" **Wt:** 230 **Born:** 9/4/1989 **Age:** 27

			HOW MUCH HE PITCHED					WHAT HE GAVE UP											THE RESULTS							
Year	Team	Lg	G	GS	CG	GF	IP	BFP	H	R	ER	HR	SH	SF	HB	TBB	IBB	SO	WP	Bk	W	L	Pct	Sh	Sv-Op	Hld	ERC	ERA
2012	2 Tms	Low	22	19	1	0	107.1	445	93	49	35	7	3	6	7	34	2	123	1	0	12	7	.632	1	0- -	-	3.05	2.93
2013	Missi	AA	16	11	0	2	67.0	281	63	23	21	3	1	1	0	27	0	71	2	1	3	3	.500	0	0- -	-	3.43	2.82
2013	Gwnntt	AAA	13	11	1	1	69.2	292	59	30	27	6	3	2	2	31	0	66	0	0	3	4	.429	0	1- -	-	3.47	3.49
2014	Gwnntt	AAA	27	26	1	1	156.0	667	151	66	61	17	6	2	7	56	0	142	0	0	7	8	.467	0	1- -	-	3.98	3.52
2015	Gwnntt	AAA	7	6	0	1	34.1	135	24	11	8	2	3	1	1	9	0	33	1	0	1	3	.250	0	1- -	-	1.90	2.10
2015	Nashv	AAA	11	11	0	0	60.0	270	59	36	34	6	3	3	3	31	2	58	5	0	4	4	.500	0	0- -	-	4.53	5.10
2016	Tacom	AAA	25	20	0	1	114.1	469	106	48	46	6	1	4	5	33	0	114	4	0	10	7	.588	0	0- -	-	3.17	3.62
2015	2 Tms		25	2	0	4	30.2	141	40	27	27	8	2	2	2	12	0	27	2	0	2	5	.286	0	0-3	7	7.54	7.92
2016	Sea	AL	9	2	0	3	25.2	107	28	11	11	5	2	1	1	9	0	15	0	0	1	2	.333	0	0-0	-	5.55	3.86
15	Atl	NL	21	0	0	2	21.2	92	24	13	13	4	2	1	1	7	0	24	1	0	2	3	.400	0	0-3	7	5.37	5.40
15	Oak	AL	4	2	0	2	9.0	49	16	14	14	4	0	1	1	5	0	3	1	0	0	2	.000	0	0-0	0	13.36	14.00
	2 ML YEARS		34	4	0	7	56.1	248	68	38	38	13	4	3	3	21	0	42	2	0	3	7	.300	0	0-3	7	6.62	6.07

Leonys Martin

Bats: L **Throws:** R **Pos:** CF-143 lay-OH-nees mar-TEEN **Ht:** 6'2" **Wt:** 200 **Born:** 3/6/1988 **Age:** 29

Year	Team	Lg	G	AB	H	2B	3B	HR	(Hm	Rd)	TB	R	RBI	RC	TBB	IBB	SO	HBP	SH	SF	SB	CS	GDP	Avg	OBP	Slg	OPS
2011	Tex	AL	8	8	3	1	0	0	(0	0)	4	2	0	1	0	0	1	0	0	0	0	0	0	.375	.375	.500	.875
2012	Tex	AL	24	46	8	5	2	0	(0	0)	17	6	6	4	4	0	12	0	1	1	3	0	2	.174	.235	.370	.605
2013	Tex	AL	147	457	119	21	6	8	(3	5)	176	66	49	58	28	0	104	8	12	3	36	9	6	.260	.313	.385	.698
2014	Tex	AL	155	533	146	13	7	7	(4	3)	194	68	40	64	39	3	114	2	7	2	31	12	4	.274	.325	.364	.689
2015	Tex	AL	95	288	63	12	0	5	(1	4)	90	26	25	22	16	1	69	2	3	1	14	5	5	.219	.264	.313	.576
2016	Sea	AL	143	518	128	17	3	15	(7	8)	196	72	47	64	44	0	149	3	4	7	24	6	10	.247	.306	.378	.684
	6 ML YEARS		572	1850	467	69	18	35	(15	20)	677	240	167	213	131	4	449	15	27	14	108	32	27	.252	.305	.366	.671

Rafael Martin

Pitches: R **Bats:** R **Pos:** RP-8 mar-TEEN **Ht:** 6'3" **Wt:** 225 **Born:** 5/16/1984 **Age:** 33

			HOW MUCH HE PITCHED					WHAT HE GAVE UP											THE RESULTS							
Year	Team	Lg	G	GS	CG	GF	IP	BFP	H	R	ER	HR	SH	SF	HB	TBB	IBB	SO	WP	Bk	W	L	Pct	Sh	Sv-Op	Hld	ERC	ERA
2012	Syrcse	AAA	13	0	0	2	17.2	85	16	14	14	2	1	1	3	11	0	15	3	1	0	0	-	0	0- -	-	4.94	7.13
2012	Hrsbrg	AA	15	0	0	4	17.0	83	21	15	14	4	1	3	0	12	0	14	2	0	0	0	-	0	0- -	-	7.85	7.41
2013	Lynbrg	Low	21	0	0	4	31.0	123	15	5	3	1	1	1	1	14	0	39	2	0	0	0	-	0	2- -	-	1.47	0.87
2014	Hrsbrg	AA	11	0	0	3	20.0	80	15	7	6	1	1	0	1	5	0	20	0	0	2	1	.667	0	1- -	-	2.10	2.70
2014	Syrcse	AAA	25	0	0	16	33.2	126	20	4	3	0	0	0	0	7	0	42	0	0	1	1	.500	0	10- -	-	1.13	0.80
2015	Syrcse	AAA	46	0	0	31	56.0	222	41	21	20	4	3	2	1	16	2	68	2	0	5	5	.500	0	12- -	-	2.13	3.21
2016	Syrcse	AAA	50	0	0	44	49.1	215	43	26	25	7	1	1	1	25	3	50	3	0	2	4	.333	0	22- -	-	4.01	4.56
2015	Was	NL	13	0	0	5	12.1	56	12	9	7	4	0	1	1	5	0	25	0	0	2	0	1.000	0	0-0	0	5.66	5.11
2016	Was	NL	8	0	0	2	3.2	12	0	1	1	0	0	0	0	1	0	5	0	0	0	0	-	0	0-0	0	0.09	2.45
	2 ML YEARS		21	0	0	7	16.0	68	12	10	8	4	0	1	1	6	0	30	0	0	2	0	1.000	0	0-0	0	3.70	4.50

Russell Martin

Bats: R **Throws:** R **Pos:** C-127;PH-10;DH-5;2B-1;3B-1   **Ht:** 5'10" **Wt:** 205 **Born:** 2/15/1983 **Age:** 34

Year	Team	Lg	G	AB	H	2B	3B	HR	(Hm	Rd)	TB	R	RBI	RC	TBB	IBB	SO	HBP	SH	SF	SB	CS	GDP	Avg	OBP	Slg	OPS
2006	LAD	NL	121	415	117	26	4	10	(8	2)	181	65	65	58	45	8	57	4	1	3	10	5	17	.282	.355	.436	.792
2007	LAD	NL	151	540	158	32	3	19	(8	11)	253	87	87	84	67	1	89	7	0	6	21	9	16	.293	.374	.469	.843
2008	LAD	NL	155	553	155	25	0	13	(6	7)	219	87	69	89	90	8	83	5	0	2	18	6	16	.280	.385	.396	.781
2009	LAD	NL	143	505	126	19	0	7	(3	4)	166	63	53	62	69	9	80	11	2	1	11	6	18	.250	.352	.329	.680
2010	LAD	NL	97	331	82	13	0	5	(2	3)	110	45	26	40	48	7	61	4	1	3	6	2	7	.248	.347	.332	.679
2011	NYY	AL	125	417	99	17	0	18	(8	10)	170	57	65	56	50	1	81	5	1	3	8	2	19	.237	.324	.408	.732
2012	NYY	AL	133	422	89	18	0	21	(13	8)	170	50	53	50	53	0	95	8	2	0	6	1	13	.211	.311	.403	.713
2013	Pit	NL	127	438	99	21	0	15	(6	9)	165	51	55	47	58	2	108	8	1	1	9	5	13	.226	.327	.377	.703
2014	Pit	NL	111	379	110	20	0	11	(3	8)	163	45	67	66	59	5	78	15	2	5	4	4	16	.290	.402	.430	.832
2015	Tor	AL	129	441	106	23	2	23	(13	10)	202	76	77	66	53	1	106	8	0	5	4	5	22	.240	.329	.458	.787
2016	Tor	AL	137	455	105	16	0	20	(8	12)	181	62	74	69	64	1	148	10	1	5	2	1	12	.231	.335	.398	.733
	Postseason		48	162	33	8	0	4	(2	2)	53	20	17	15	21	0	38	9	0	2	1	0	4	.204	.325	.327	.652
	11 ML YEARS		1429	4896	1246	230	9	162	(78	84)	1980	688	691	687	656	43	986	85	11	34	99	46	169	.254	.350	.404	.755

Carlos Martinez

Pitches: R **Bats:** R **Pos:** SP-31   **Ht:** 6'0" **Wt:** 190 **Born:** 9/21/1991 **Age:** 25

			HOW MUCH HE PITCHED						WHAT HE GAVE UP												THE RESULTS						
Year	Team	Lg	G	GS	CG	GF	IP	BFP	H	R	ER	HR	SH	SF	HB	TBB	IBB	SO	WP	Bk	W	L	Pct	Sh	Sv-Op	Hld	ERC	ERA
2013	StL	NL	21	1	0	5	28.1	124	31	16	16	1	1	1	3	9	1	24	0	0	2	1	.667	0	1-1	3	4.20	5.08
2014	StL	NL	57	7	0	13	89.1	386	90	41	40	4	7	1	4	36	8	84	8	1	2	4	.333	0	1-6	17	3.79	4.03
2015	StL	NL	31	29	0	1	179.2	755	168	65	60	13	9	4	8	63	5	184	8	1	14	7	.667	0	0-0	1	3.51	3.01
2016	StL	NL	31	31	0	0	195.1	809	169	68	66	15	2	2	11	70	1	174	8	0	16	9	.640	0	0-0	3	3.29	3.04
	Postseason		16	0	0	1	16.2	65	10	6	6	0	1	1	1	7	1	13	1	0	0	1	.000	0	0-0	5	1.70	3.24
	4 ML YEARS		140	68	0	19	492.2	2074	458	190	182	33	19	8	26	178	15	466	24	2	34	21	.618	0	2-7	21	3.51	3.32

J.D. Martinez

Bats: R **Throws:** R **Pos:** RF-118;DH-1;PH-1   **Ht:** 6'3" **Wt:** 220 **Born:** 8/21/1987 **Age:** 29

Year	Team	Lg	G	AB	H	2B	3B	HR	(Hm	Rd)	TB	R	RBI	RC	TBB	IBB	SO	HBP	SH	SF	SB	CS	GDP	Avg	OBP	Slg	OPS
2011	Hou	NL	53	208	57	13	0	6	(3	3)	88	29	35	30	13	1	48	2	0	3	0	1	4	.274	.319	.423	.742
2012	Hou	NL	113	395	95	14	3	11	(5	6)	148	34	55	45	40	0	96	1	0	2	0	2	18	.241	.311	.375	.685
2013	Hou	AL	86	296	74	17	0	7	(4	3)	112	24	36	29	10	0	82	0	0	3	2	0	8	.250	.272	.378	.650
2014	Det	AL	123	441	139	30	3	23	(13	10)	244	57	76	75	30	5	126	3	0	6	6	3	8	.315	.358	.553	.912
2015	Det	AL	158	596	168	33	2	38	(20	18)	319	93	102	100	53	7	178	5	0	3	3	2	11	.282	.344	.535	.879
2016	Det	AL	120	460	141	35	2	22	(13	9)	246	69	68	77	49	2	128	3	0	5	1	2	13	.307	.373	.535	.908
	Postseason		3	12	3	1	0	2	(0	2)	10	2	5	3	0	0	4	0	0	0	0	0	0	.250	.250	.833	1.083
	6 ML YEARS		653	2396	674	142	10	107	(58	49)	1157	306	372	356	195	15	658	14	0	22	12	10	62	.281	.336	.483	.819

Jose Martinez

Bats: R **Throws:** R **Pos:** PH-6;LF-4;1B-1;PR-1   **Ht:** 6'6" **Wt:** 215 **Born:** 7/25/1988 **Age:** 28

Year	Team	Lg	G	AB	H	2B	3B	HR	(Hm	Rd)	TB	R	RBI	RC	TBB	IBB	SO	HBP	SH	SF	SB	CS	GDP	Avg	OBP	Slg	OPS
2012	Brham	AA	114	436	108	15	1	5	(-	-)	140	54	42	47	41	0	87	2	2	1	6	3	9	.248	.315	.321	.636
2013	Missi	AA	124	431	123	19	0	6	(-	-)	160	46	39	55	37	1	63	1	4	2	6	9	12	.285	.342	.371	.713
2014	Lynbrg	A+	66	257	82	14	3	4	(-	-)	114	32	34	45	26	0	37	0	0	5	5	1	4	.319	.375	.444	.819
2015	Omha	AAA	98	341	131	25	3	10	(-	-)	192	57	60	86	48	1	55	3	1	3	8	2	8	.384	.461	.563	1.024
2016	Omha	AAA	37	141	42	10	0	3	(-	-)	61	18	18	23	14	0	24	1	0	4	2	0	5	.298	.356	.433	.789
2016	Memp	AAA	87	301	81	18	1	8	(-	-)	125	34	42	43	25	3	50	1	1	1	9	1	14	.269	.326	.415	.742
2016	StL	NL	12	16	7	1	0	0	(0	0)	8	4	1	4	2	0	1	0	0	0	0	0	0	.438	.500	.500	1.000

Michael Martinez

Bats: B **Throws:** R **Pos:** 2B-21;CF-11;RF-11;PR-11;LF-9;PH-7;SS-6;3B-2   **Ht:** 5'9" **Wt:** 180 **Born:** 9/16/1982 **Age:** 34

Year	Team	Lg	G	AB	H	2B	3B	HR	(Hm	Rd)	TB	R	RBI	RC	TBB	IBB	SO	HBP	SH	SF	SB	CS	GDP	Avg	OBP	Slg	OPS
2016	Clmbs*	AAA	27	104	30	8	1	2	(-	-)	46	12	12	16	9	1	21	1	0	0	2	2	1	.288	.351	.442	.793
2011	Phi	NL	88	209	41	5	2	3	(1	2)	59	25	24	20	18	0	35	0	5	2	3	0	2	.196	.258	.282	.540
2012	Phi	NL	45	115	20	3	0	2	(1	1)	29	10	7	5	5	2	21	0	2	0	0	0	4	.174	.208	.252	.461
2013	Phi	NL	29	40	7	0	0	0	(0	0)	7	5	3	3	0	0	12	0	0	1	1	0	1	.175	.175	.175	.350
2014	Pit	NL	26	39	5	1	0	0	(0	0)	6	2	2	1	4	1	13	0	1	0	0	0	0	.128	.209	.154	.363
2015	Cle	AL	16	30	8	2	0	0	(0	0)	10	7	2	3	1	0	12	0	1	0	0	1	0	.267	.290	.333	.624
2016	2 Tms	AL	63	101	24	4	0	1	(0	1)	31	16	4	4	4	0	23	0	1	0	0	2	1	.238	.267	.307	.574
16	Cle	AL	59	95	23	4	0	1	(0	1)	30	15	4	4	3	0	21	0	1	0	0	2	1	.242	.265	.316	.581
16	Bos	AL	4	6	1	0	0	0	(0	0)	1	1	0	0	1	0	2	0	0	0	0	0	0	.167	.286	.167	.452
	Postseason		2	0	0	0	0	0	(0	0)	0	1	0	0	0	0	0	0	0	0	0	0	0	-	-	-	-
	6 ML YEARS		267	534	105	15	2	6	(2	4)	142	65	42	36	32	3	116	0	10	2	4	3	9	.197	.241	.266	.507

Nick Martinez

Pitches: R **Bats:** L **Pos:** RP-7; SP-5   **Ht:** 6'1" **Wt:** 200 **Born:** 8/5/1990 **Age:** 26

			HOW MUCH HE PITCHED						WHAT HE GAVE UP												THE RESULTS							
Year	Team	Lg	G	GS	CG	GF	IP	BFP	H	R	ER	HR	SH	SF	HB	TBB	IBB	SO	WP	Bk	W	L	Pct	Sh	Sv-Op	Hld	ERC	ERA
2016	RdRck*	AAA	18	16	0	0	99.0	415	109	47	43	7	4	5	6	17	0	67	2	0	7	6	.538	0	0- -	-	3.83	3.91
2014	Tex	AL	29	24	0	3	140.1	610	150	79	71	18	1	6	3	55	1	77	7	0	5	12	.294	0	0-0	2	4.76	4.55
2015	Tex	AL	24	21	0	1	125.0	558	135	66	55	16	1	5	13	46	2	77	4	0	7	7	.500	0	0-0	0	4.99	3.96
2016	Tex	AL	12	5	0	2	38.2	179	45	24	24	8	0	0	5	19	1	16	0	0	2	3	.400	0	0-0	0	6.86	5.59
3 ML YEARS			65	50	0	6	304.0	1347	330	169	150	42	2	11	21	120	4	170	11	0	14	22	.389	0	0-0	2	5.11	4.44

Victor Martinez

Bats: B **Throws:** R **Pos:** DH-138;PH-11;1B-5   **Ht:** 6'2" **Wt:** 210 **Born:** 12/23/1978 **Age:** 38

			BATTING																	RUNNING			AVERAGES			
Year	Team	Lg	G	AB	H	2B	3B	HR	(Hm	Rd)	TB	R	RBI	RC	TBB	IBB	SO	HBP	SH	SF	SB	CS	GDP	Avg	OBP	Slg	OPS
2002	Cle	AL	12	32	9	1	0	1	(1	0)	13	2	5	5	3	0	2	0	0	1	0	0	1	.281	.333	.406	.740
2003	Cle	AL	49	159	46	4	0	1	(0	1)	53	15	16	17	13	0	21	1	0	1	1	1	8	.289	.345	.333	.678
2004	Cle	AL	141	520	147	38	1	23	(8	15)	256	77	108	90	60	11	69	5	0	6	0	1	16	.283	.359	.492	.851
2005	Cle	AL	147	547	167	33	0	20	(10	10)	260	73	80	90	63	9	78	5	0	7	0	1	16	.305	.378	.475	.853
2006	Cle	AL	153	572	181	37	0	16	(4	12)	266	82	93	96	71	8	78	3	0	6	0	0	27	.316	.391	.465	.856
2007	Cle	AL	147	562	169	40	0	25	(12	13)	284	78	114	108	62	12	76	10	0	11	0	0	19	.301	.374	.505	.879
2008	Cle	AL	73	266	74	17	0	2	(2	0)	97	30	35	36	24	4	32	1	0	3	0	0	12	.278	.337	.365	.701
2009	2 Tms	AL	155	588	178	33	1	23	(7	16)	282	88	108	101	75	3	74	3	0	6	1	0	17	.303	.381	.480	.861
2010	Bos	AL	127	493	149	32	1	20	(10	10)	243	64	79	74	40	5	52	0	0	5	1	0	17	.302	.351	.493	.844
2011	Det	AL	145	540	178	40	0	12	(5	7)	254	76	103	103	46	6	51	2	0	7	1	0	20	.330	.380	.470	.850
2013	Det	AL	159	605	182	36	0	14	(7	7)	260	68	83	75	54	10	62	1	0	8	0	2	23	.301	.355	.430	.785
2014	Det	AL	151	561	188	33	0	32	(15	17)	317	87	103	115	70	28	42	4	0	6	3	2	17	.335	.409	.565	.974
2015	Det	AL	120	440	108	20	0	11	(6	5)	161	39	64	41	31	8	52	7	0	7	0	0	18	.245	.301	.366	.667
2016	Det	AL	154	553	160	22	0	27	(12	15)	263	65	86	82	50	8	90	4	0	3	0	0	19	.289	.351	.476	.826
	09 Cle	AL	99	377	107	21	1	15	(6	9)	175	56	67	64	51	3	51	2	0	5	0	0	11	.284	.368	.464	.832
	09 Bos	AL	56	211	71	12	0	8	(1	7)	107	32	41	37	24	0	23	1	0	1	1	0	6	.336	.405	.507	.912
	Postseason		39	149	47	8	1	6	(4	2)	75	22	22	25	11	3	23	3	0	0	0	0	3	.315	.374	.503	.878
14 ML YEARS			1733	6438	1936	386	3	227	(99	128)	3009	844	1077	1033	662	112	779	46	0	77	7	7	230	.301	.366	.467	.833

Darin Mastroianni

Bats: R **Throws:** R **Pos:** RF-4;PR-2;LF-1;CF-1   mass-tree-AH-nee   **Ht:** 5'11" **Wt:** 190 **Born:** 8/26/1985 **Age:** 31

			BATTING																	RUNNING			AVERAGES			
Year	Team	Lg	G	AB	H	2B	3B	HR	(Hm	Rd)	TB	R	RBI	RC	TBB	IBB	SO	HBP	SH	SF	SB	CS	GDP	Avg	OBP	Slg	OPS
2016	Roch*	AAA	51	180	46	6	1	0	(-	-)	54	20	15	20	18	0	39	2	1	2	8	3	1	.256	.327	.300	.627
2016	Frisco*	AA	23	95	22	6	0	1	(-	-)	31	14	6	9	5	0	15	2	0	0	5	2	2	.232	.284	.326	.611
2011	Tor	AL	1	2	0	0	0	0	(0	0)	0	0	0	0	0	0	1	0	1	0	0	0	0	.000	.000	.000	.000
2012	Min	AL	77	163	41	3	2	3	(2	1)	57	22	17	24	18	0	45	1	3	1	21	3	4	.252	.328	.350	.678
2013	Min	AL	30	65	12	2	0	0	(0	0)	14	5	5	1	3	0	23	1	3	1	2	1	2	.185	.229	.215	.444
2014	2 Tms	AL	21	43	5	0	0	1	(1	0)	8	7	2	0	1	0	10	0	0	0	1	0	4	.116	.136	.186	.322
2016	Min	AL	7	9	0	0	0	0	(0	0)	0	1	0	0	2	0	4	0	0	0	1	0	0	.000	.182	.000	.182
	14 Min	AL	7	11	0	0	0	0	(0	0)	0	3	0	0	1	0	5	0	0	0	1	0	0	.000	.083	.000	.083
	14 Tor	AL	14	32	5	0	0	1	(1	0)	8	4	2	0	0	0	5	0	0	0	0	0	4	.156	.156	.250	.406
5 ML YEARS			136	282	58	5	2	4	(3	1)	79	35	24	25	24	0	83	2	7	2	25	4	10	.206	.271	.280	.551

Jeff Mathis

Bats: R **Throws:** R **Pos:** C-38;PH-3   **Ht:** 6'0" **Wt:** 205 **Born:** 3/31/1983 **Age:** 34

			BATTING																	RUNNING			AVERAGES			
Year	Team	Lg	G	AB	H	2B	3B	HR	(Hm	Rd)	TB	R	RBI	RC	TBB	IBB	SO	HBP	SH	SF	SB	CS	GDP	Avg	OBP	Slg	OPS
2005	LAA	AL	5	3	1	0	0	0	(0	0)	1	1	0	0	0	0	1	0	0	0	0	0	0	.333	.333	.333	.667
2006	LAA	AL	23	55	8	2	0	2	(1	1)	16	9	6	4	7	1	14	0	0	0	0	0	0	.145	.238	.291	.529
2007	LAA	AL	59	171	36	12	0	4	(3	1)	60	24	23	13	15	0	49	2	3	4	0	1	3	.211	.276	.351	.627
2008	LAA	AL	94	283	55	8	0	9	(4	5)	90	35	42	33	30	4	90	3	8	4	2	2	1	.194	.275	.318	.593
2009	LAA	AL	84	237	50	8	0	5	(3	2)	73	26	28	24	22	0	73	4	8	1	2	3	2	.211	.288	.308	.596
2010	LAA	AL	68	205	40	6	1	3	(2	1)	57	19	18	10	6	0	59	1	3	3	3	0	3	.195	.219	.278	.497
2011	LAA	AL	93	247	43	12	0	3	(1	2)	64	18	22	12	15	2	75	2	14	3	1	2	3	.174	.225	.259	.484
2012	Tor	AL	71	211	46	13	0	8	(5	3)	83	25	27	18	9	0	68	0	6	1	1	0	2	.218	.249	.393	.642
2013	Mia	NL	73	232	42	7	1	5	(3	2)	66	14	29	15	21	4	76	1	1	1	0	0	5	.181	.251	.284	.535
2014	Mia	NL	64	175	35	7	0	2	(1	1)	48	12	12	11	15	2	64	0	5	0	0	0	2	.200	.263	.274	.537
2015	Mia	NL	32	93	15	4	1	2	(1	1)	27	9	12	3	7	1	24	0	0	3	0	0	1	.161	.214	.290	.504
2016	Mia	NL	41	126	30	4	1	2	(0	2)	42	12	15	10	4	0	36	1	1	0	0	0	1	.238	.267	.333	.601
	Postseason		10	20	9	5	0	0	(0	0)	14	2	2	3	0	0	5	0	1	0	0	0	0	.450	.450	.700	1.150
12 ML YEARS			707	2038	401	83	4	45	(24	21)	627	204	234	153	151	14	629	14	49	21	9	8	24	.197	.254	.308	.562

Brian Matusz

Pitches: L **Bats:** L **Pos:** RP-7; SP-1   MATT-uss   **Ht:** 6'5" **Wt:** 190 **Born:** 2/11/1987 **Age:** 30

			HOW MUCH HE PITCHED						WHAT HE GAVE UP												THE RESULTS							
Year	Team	Lg	G	GS	CG	GF	IP	BFP	H	R	ER	HR	SH	SF	HB	TBB	IBB	SO	WP	Bk	W	L	Pct	Sh	Sv-Op	Hld	ERC	ERA
2016 2 Tms*	Low	6	4	0	1	20.0	70	9	2	2	1	0	0	0	1	0	25	0	0	0	0	-	0	0- -	-	0.63	0.90
2009	Bal	AL	8	8	0	0	44.2	196	52	24	23	6	2	2	0	14	0	38	0	0	5	2	.714	0	0-0	0	4.91	4.63
2010	Bal	AL	32	32	0	0	175.2	760	173	88	84	19	6	6	7	63	3	143	1	0	10	12	.455	0	0-0	0	3.98	4.30
2011	Bal	AL	12	12	0	0	49.2	245	67	60	59	18	1	2	0	24	1	38	0	0	1	9	.100	0	0-0	0	10.88	10.69
2012	Bal	AL	34	16	0	2	98.0	441	112	61	53	15	2	3	0	41	4	81	0	0	6	10	.375	0	0-0	4	5.25	4.87
2013	Bal	AL	65	0	0	9	51.0	208	43	21	20	3	1	2	2	16	2	50	0	0	2	1	.667	0	0-4	18	2.77	3.53
2014	Bal	AL	63	0	0	11	51.2	226	51	23	20	7	0	2	3	17	4	53	3	0	2	3	.400	0	0-3	14	3.98	3.48

Year Team	Lg	G	GS	CG	GF	IP	BFP	H	R	ER	HR	SH	SF	HB	TBB	IBB	SO	WP	Bk	W	L	Pct	Sh	Sv-Op	Hld	ERC	ERA
2015 Bal	AL	58	0	0	16	49.0	206	38	18	16	5	2	1	3	20	3	56	2	0	1	4	.200	0	0-2	2	3.02	2.94
2016 2 Tms		8	1	0	2	9.0	53	17	14	14	6	1	1	0	9	0	3	1	0	0	0	-	0	0-0	1	19.43	14.00
16 Bal	AL	7	1	0	2	6.0	35	11	8	8	3	0	1	0	7	0	1	0	0	0	0	-	0	0-0	1	17.60	12.00
16 ChC	NL	1	1	0	0	3.0	18	6	6	6	3	1	0	1	2	0	2	1	0	0	0	-	0	0-0	0	23.01	18.00
Postseason		7	0	0	3	5.1	20	3	2	2	2	0	0	0	2	1	7	1	0	0	1	.000	0	0-0	2	3.15	3.38
8 ML YEARS		280	69	0	40	528.2	2335	567	309	289	79	15	19	16	204	17	462	7	0	27	41	.397	0	0-9	39	4.83	4.92

Steven Matz

Pitches: L Bats: R Pos: SP-22 **Ht: 6'2" Wt: 200 Born: 5/29/1991 Age: 26**

Year Team	Lg	G	GS	CG	GF	IP	BFP	H	R	ER	HR	SH	SF	HB	TBB	IBB	SO	WP	Bk	W	L	Pct	Sh	Sv-Op	Hld	ERC	ERA
2012 Kngspt	R+	6	6	0	0	29.0	119	16	10	5	1	0	0	1	17	0	34	0	0	2	1	.667	0	0- -	-	2.14	1.55
2013 Savann	A	21	21	1	0	106.1	428	86	36	31	4	1	2	5	38	0	121	1	0	5	6	.455	1	0- -	-	2.75	2.62
2014 Stluci	A+	12	12	0	0	69.0	289	66	21	17	0	3	1	5	21	0	62	2	0	4	4	.500	0	0- -	-	3.11	2.22
2014 Bnghtn	AA	12	12	1	0	71.1	287	66	23	18	3	3	2	2	14	0	69	0	0	6	5	.545	0	0- -	-	2.68	2.27
2015 LsVgs	AAA	15	14	0	0	90.1	359	69	25	22	6	2	1	1	31	0	94	0	0	7	4	.636	0	0- -	-	2.51	2.19
2015 NYM	NL	6	6	0	0	35.2	149	34	9	9	4	1	1	1	10	0	34	0	0	4	0	1.000	0	0-0	0	3.55	2.27
2016 NYM	NL	22	22	0	0	132.1	547	129	53	50	14	8	1	5	31	2	129	3	1	9	8	.529	0	0-0	0	3.49	3.40
Postseason		3	3	0	0	14.2	64	17	6	6	0	0	0	0	4	1	13	0	0	0	1	.000	0	0-0	0	3.60	3.68
2 ML YEARS		28	28	0	0	168.0	696	163	62	59	18	9	2	6	41	2	163	3	1	13	8	.619	0	0-0	0	3.50	3.16

Joe Mauer

Bats: L Throws: R Pos: 1B-95;DH-33;PH-7 **Ht: 6'5" Wt: 225 Born: 4/19/1983 Age: 34**

Year Team	Lg	G	AB	H	2B	3B	HR	(Hm	Rd)	TB	R	RBI	RC	TBB	IBB	SO	HBP	SH	SF	SB	CS	GDP	Avg	OBP	Slg	OPS
2004 Min	AL	35	107	33	8	1	6	(4	2)	61	18	17	21	11	0	14	1	0	3	1	0	1	.308	.369	.570	.939
2005 Min	AL	131	489	144	26	2	9	(4	5)	201	61	55	78	61	12	64	1	0	3	13	1	9	.294	.372	.411	.783
2006 Min	AL	140	521	181	36	4	13	(3	10)	264	86	84	103	79	21	54	1	0	7	8	3	24	**.347**	.429	.507	.936
2007 Min	AL	109	406	119	27	3	7	(2	5)	173	62	60	69	57	10	51	3	2	3	7	1	11	.293	.382	.426	.808
2008 Min	AL	146	536	176	31	4	9	(7	2)	242	98	85	103	84	8	50	1	1	11	1	1	21	**.328**	.413	.451	.864
2009 Min	AL	138	523	191	30	1	28	(16	12)	307	94	96	123	76	14	63	2	0	5	4	1	13	**.365**	.444	**.587**	1.031
2010 Min	AL	137	510	167	43	1	9	(1	8)	239	88	75	91	65	14	53	3	0	6	1	4	19	.327	.402	.469	.871
2011 Min	AL	82	296	85	15	0	3	(0	3)	109	38	30	39	32	7	38	3	0	2	0	0	9	.287	.360	.368	.729
2012 Min	AL	147	545	174	31	4	10	(4	6)	243	81	85	108	90	10	88	2	1	3	8	4	23	.319	**.416**	.446	.861
2013 Min	AL	113	445	144	35	0	11	(5	6)	212	62	47	74	61	7	89	0	0	2	0	1	7	.324	.404	.476	.880
2014 Min	AL	120	455	126	27	2	4	(3	1)	169	60	55	66	60	12	96	1	0	3	2	0	12	.277	.361	.371	.732
2015 Min	AL	158	592	157	34	2	10	(6	4)	225	69	66	85	67	12	112	1	1	5	2	1	22	.265	.338	.380	.718
2016 Min	AL	134	494	129	22	4	11	(3	8)	192	68	49	75	79	10	93	1	0	2	2	0	11	.261	.363	.389	.752
Postseason		9	35	10	1	0	0	(0	0)	11	1	1	2	4	0	7	0	0	0	0	0	0	.286	.359	.314	.673
13 ML YEARS		1590	5919	1826	365	28	130	(58	72)	2637	885	804	1035	822	137	865	20	5	54	50	17	182	.308	.391	.446	.837

Brandon Maurer

Pitches: R Bats: R Pos: RP-71 MAUW-er **Ht: 6'5" Wt: 230 Born: 7/3/1990 Age: 26**

Year Team	Lg	G	GS	CG	GF	IP	BFP	H	R	ER	HR	SH	SF	HB	TBB	IBB	SO	WP	Bk	W	L	Pct	Sh	Sv-Op	Hld	ERC	ERA
2013 Sea	AL	22	14	0	3	90.0	402	114	66	63	16	1	2	6	27	0	70	9	0	5	8	.385	0	0-0	0	6.20	6.30
2014 Sea	AL	38	7	0	4	69.2	301	74	39	36	6	2	3	0	19	2	55	3	0	1	4	.200	0	0-1	5	3.70	4.65
2015 SD	NL	53	0	0	10	51.0	206	39	19	17	3	1	2	1	15	1	59	1	0	7	4	.636	0	0-1	12	2.23	3.00
2016 SD	NL	71	0	0	36	69.2	300	65	37	35	7	0	1	2	23	5	72	3	0	0	5	.000	0	13-19	13	3.35	4.52
4 ML YEARS		184	21	0	53	280.1	1209	292	161	151	32	4	8	9	84	8	236	16	0	13	21	.382	0	13-21	30	4.06	4.85

Bruce Maxwell

Bats: L Throws: R Pos: C-29;PH-4;DH-3 **Ht: 6'1" Wt: 250 Born: 12/20/1990 Age: 26**

Year Team	Lg	G	AB	H	2B	3B	HR	(Hm	Rd)	TB	R	RBI	RC	TBB	IBB	SO	HBP	SH	SF	SB	CS	GDP	Avg	OBP	Slg	OPS
2012 2 Tms	Low	67	249	69	18	0	0	(-	-)	87	30	26	34	31	1	38	0	1	1	1	0	9	.277	.356	.349	.705
2013 2 Tms	Low	104	374	103	22	0	7	(-	-)	146	44	49	54	43	1	63	1	3	4	0	0	9	.275	.348	.390	.739
2014 Stcktn	A+	79	289	79	11	1	6	(-	-)	110	33	35	43	41	1	58	2	0	2	0	1	3	.273	.365	.381	.746
2014 Mdlnd	AA	25	85	12	3	0	0	(-	-)	15	8	2	1	9	0	32	0	0	0	0	1	6	.141	.223	.176	.400
2015 Mdlnd	AA	96	338	82	16	0	2	(-	-)	104	32	48	36	39	1	54	1	1	2	0	1	14	.243	.321	.308	.629
2016 Nashv	AAA	60	193	62	12	0	10	(-	-)	104	27	41	40	24	0	38	0	0	0	1	0	5	.321	.393	.539	.932
2016 Oak	AL	33	92	26	6	1	1	(1	0)	37	8	14	13	8	0	24	0	0	1	0	0	2	.283	.337	.402	.739

Trevor May

Pitches: R Bats: R Pos: RP-44 **Ht: 6'5" Wt: 240 Born: 9/23/1989 Age: 27**

Year Team	Lg	G	GS	CG	GF	IP	BFP	H	R	ER	HR	SH	SF	HB	TBB	IBB	SO	WP	Bk	W	L	Pct	Sh	Sv-Op	Hld	ERC	ERA
2014 Min	AL	10	9	0	0	45.2	213	59	41	40	7	0	1	2	22	1	44	3	0	3	6	.333	0	0-0	0	6.80	7.88
2015 Min	AL	48	16	0	9	114.2	492	127	53	51	11	3	4	4	26	2	110	4	0	8	9	.471	0	0-2	5	4.06	4.00
2016 Min	AL	44	0	0	10	42.2	187	39	26	25	7	0	0	2	17	1	60	10	0	2	2	.500	0	0-2	6	4.07	5.27
3 ML YEARS		102	25	0	19	203.0	892	225	120	116	25	3	5	8	65	4	214	17	0	13	17	.433	0	0-4	13	4.64	5.14

Cameron Maybin

Bats: R Throws: R Pos: CF-91;PR-3;DH-1;PH-1   Ht: 6'3" Wt: 215 Born: 4/4/1987 Age: 30

Year	Team	Lg	G	AB	H	2B	3B	HR	(Hm	Rd)	TB	R	RBI	RC	TBB	IBB	SO	HBP	SH	SF	SB	CS	GDP	Avg	OBP	Slg	OPS
2016	Toledo*	AAA	23	85	16	9	0	2	(-	-)	31	14	11	10	14	0	17	1	0	0	4	1	2	.188	.310	.365	.675
2007	Det	AL	24	49	7	3	0	1	(0	1)	13	8	2	2	3	0	21	1	0	0	5	0	0	.143	.208	.265	.473
2008	Fla	NL	8	32	16	2	0	0	(0	0)	18	9	2	8	3	0	8	0	1	0	4	0	0	.500	.543	.563	1.105
2009	Fla	NL	54	176	44	12	2	4	(1	3)	72	30	13	15	17	1	51	1	4	1	1	3	2	.250	.318	.409	.727
2010	Fla	NL	82	291	68	7	3	8	(5	3)	105	46	28	37	24	1	92	5	1	1	9	2	4	.234	.302	.361	.663
2011	SD	NL	137	516	136	24	8	9	(2	7)	203	82	40	69	44	2	125	2	4	2	40	8	6	.264	.323	.393	.716
2012	SD	NL	147	507	123	20	5	8	(3	5)	177	67	45	52	44	4	110	4	3	3	26	7	12	.243	.306	.349	.656
2013	SD	NL	14	51	8	1	0	1	(0	1)	12	7	5	0	4	1	9	1	1	0	4	1	3	.157	.232	.235	.467
2014	SD	NL	95	251	59	13	4	1	(0	1)	83	24	15	22	19	2	56	1	0	1	4	3	8	.235	.290	.331	.621
2015	Atl	NL	141	505	135	18	2	10	(5	5)	187	65	59	64	45	1	102	1	1	3	23	6	16	.267	.327	.370	.697
2016	Det	AL	94	349	110	14	5	4	(3	1)	146	65	43	60	36	0	69	3	2	1	15	6	8	.315	.383	.418	.801
	10 ML YEARS		796	2727	706	114	29	46	(19	27)	1016	403	252	329	239	9	643	19	17	12	131	36	59	.259	.322	.373	.694

Mike Mayers

Pitches: R Bats: R Pos: RP-3; SP-1   MY-erz   Ht: 6'3" Wt: 200 Born: 12/6/1991 Age: 25

Year	Team	Lg	G	GS	CG	GF	IP	BFP	H	R	ER	HR	SH	SF	HB	TBB	IBB	SO	WP	Bk	W	L	Pct	Sh	Sv-Op	Hld	ERC	ERA
2013	2 Tms	Low	10	8	0	0	36.1	149	35	14	12	3	0	0	1	11	1	27	3	1	1	3	.250	0	0- -	-	3.55	2.97
2014	PlmBh	A+	12	12	1	0	72.2	306	84	35	30	5	2	3	2	13	0	61	1	0	2	7	.222	0	0- -	-	4.03	3.72
2014	Sprgfld	AA	13	13	0	0	76.1	325	81	29	24	2	1	4	4	23	0	52	2	1	6	5	.545	0	0- -	-	3.77	2.83
2015	Sprgfld	AA	10	10	1	0	46.2	211	53	39	34	8	1	2	5	21	0	36	7	1	1	4	.200	1	0- -	-	6.18	6.56
2016	Sprgfld	AA	9	9	0	0	54.2	224	47	17	14	4	0	1	1	17	0	43	3	1	5	2	.714	0	0- -	-	2.90	2.30
2016	Memp	AAA	16	16	1	0	89.1	379	87	44	37	8	1	2	5	31	2	84	2	0	4	8	.333	0	0- -	-	3.88	3.73
2016	StL	NL	4	1	0	0	5.1	35	16	16	16	3	0	1	1	3	0	2	0	0	1	1	.500	0	0-0	0	25.90	27.00

Nomar Mazara

Bats: L Throws: L Pos: RF-112;LF-38;PH-11;DH-1;PR-1   Ht: 6'4" Wt: 215 Born: 4/26/1995 Age: 22

Year	Team	Lg	G	AB	H	2B	3B	HR	(Hm	Rd)	TB	R	RBI	RC	TBB	IBB	SO	HBP	SH	SF	SB	CS	GDP	Avg	OBP	Slg	OPS
2012	Rngrs	R	54	201	53	13	3	6	(-	-)	90	40	39	37	37	0	70	3	0	2	5	2	5	.264	.383	.448	.830
2013	Hkry	A	126	453	107	23	2	13	(-	-)	173	48	62	56	44	0	131	6	0	3	1	2	6	.236	.310	.382	.692
2014	Hkry	A	106	398	105	21	2	19	(-	-)	187	68	73	69	57	2	99	3	0	3	4	3	9	.264	.358	.470	.828
2014	Frisco	AA	24	85	26	7	1	3	(-	-)	44	10	16	16	9	0	22	2	0	1	0	0	3	.306	.381	.518	.899
2015	Frisco	AA	111	409	116	22	2	13	(-	-)	181	57	56	69	47	0	92	5	0	9	2	0	10	.284	.357	.443	.800
2015	RdRck	AAA	20	81	29	4	0	1	(-	-)	36	11	13	14	5	1	10	2	0	0	0	0	1	.358	.409	.444	.854
2016	Tex	AL	145	516	137	13	3	20	(7	13)	216	59	64	67	39	1	112	6	0	7	0	2	12	.266	.320	.419	.739

Vin Mazzaro

Pitches: R Bats: R Pos: RP-2   muh-ZA-roh   Ht: 6'2" Wt: 220 Born: 9/27/1986 Age: 30

Year	Team	Lg	G	GS	CG	GF	IP	BFP	H	R	ER	HR	SH	SF	HB	TBB	IBB	SO	WP	Bk	W	L	Pct	Sh	Sv-Op	Hld	ERC	ERA
2016	Scrmto*	AAA	38	4	0	3	67.0	278	61	27	24	4	1	1	4	26	0	43	4	0	2	2	.500	0	1- -	-	3.60	3.22
2009	Oak	AL	17	17	0	0	91.1	423	120	61	54	12	1	3	4	39	3	59	5	0	4	9	.308	0	0-0	0	6.49	5.32
2010	Oak	AL	24	18	0	4	122.1	537	127	70	58	19	4	4	4	50	0	79	5	0	6	8	.429	0	0-0	0	4.86	4.27
2011	KC	AL	7	4	0	2	28.1	131	39	26	26	4	3	3	1	15	1	10	2	0	1	1	.500	0	0-0	0	7.67	8.26
2012	KC	AL	18	6	0	4	44.0	198	55	29	28	3	1	2	3	19	2	26	1	0	4	3	.571	0	0-0	0	5.80	5.73
2013	Pit	NL	57	0	0	17	73.2	304	68	23	23	3	3	1	3	21	3	46	5	1	8	2	.800	0	1-3	6	2.95	2.81
2014	Pit	NL	5	0	0	1	10.1	46	8	4	4	2	1	0	1	5	0	7	0	0	0	0	-	0	0-0	0	3.99	3.48
2015	Mia	NL	10	0	0	5	12.0	55	15	6	5	0	0	2	0	6	1	6	0	0	0	0	-	0	0-0	0	5.04	3.75
2016	SF	NL	2	0	0	0	1.0	13	7	9	6	0	0	0	1	1	0	9	0	0	1	0	1.000	0	0-0	0	55.13	54.00
	Postseason		3	0	0	0	1.2	5	0	0	0	0	0	0	0	0	0	2	0	0	0	0	-	0	0-0	0	0.00	0.00
	8 ML YEARS		140	45	0	33	383.0	1707	439	228	204	43	13	15	17	156	10	233	18	1	24	23	.511	0	1-3	6	5.23	4.79

Zach McAllister

Pitches: R Bats: R Pos: RP-51; SP-2   Ht: 6'6" Wt: 240 Born: 12/8/1987 Age: 29

Year	Team	Lg	G	GS	CG	GF	IP	BFP	H	R	ER	HR	SH	SF	HB	TBB	IBB	SO	WP	Bk	W	L	Pct	Sh	Sv-Op	Hld	ERC	ERA
2011	Cle	AL	4	4	0	0	17.2	84	26	16	12	1	0	0	0	7	1	14	0	0	0	1	.000	0	0-0	0	6.41	6.11
2012	Cle	AL	22	22	0	0	125.1	543	133	78	59	19	2	5	1	38	0	110	0	2	6	8	.429	0	0-0	0	4.37	4.24
2013	Cle	AL	24	24	0	0	134.1	579	134	65	56	13	0	3	6	49	2	101	7	1	9	9	.500	0	0-0	0	4.06	3.75
2014	Cle	AL	22	15	0	2	86.0	377	96	54	50	7	1	5	0	28	1	74	3	0	4	7	.364	0	0-0	1	4.24	5.23
2015	Cle	AL	61	1	0	9	69.0	299	70	28	23	7	1	1	3	23	4	84	3	0	4	4	.500	0	1-2	12	3.95	3.00
2016	Cle	AL	53	2	0	11	52.1	233	53	21	20	6	1	0	2	23	2	54	3	0	3	2	.600	0	0-1	7	4.43	3.44
	6 ML YEARS		186	68	0	22	484.2	2115	512	262	220	53	5	14	12	168	10	437	16	3	26	31	.456	0	1-3	20	4.28	4.09

Matt McBride

Bats: R Throws: R Pos: C-16;PH-3;1B-1;RF-1;DH-1   Ht: 6'2" Wt: 215 Born: 5/23/1985 Age: 32

Year Team	Lg	G	AB	H	2B	3B	HR	(Hm	Rd)	TB	R	RBI	RC	TBB	IBB	SO	HBP	SH	SF	SB	CS	GDP	Avg	OBP	Slg	OPS
2016 Nashv*	AAA	70	247	66	20	1	7	(-	-)	109	33	30	37	26	0	49	1	0	0	0	1	4	.267	.339	.441	.781
2012 Col	NL	31	78	16	2	0	2	(1	1)	24	8	11	7	1	0	17	1	0	1	0	0	4	.205	.222	.308	.530
2014 Col	NL	21	31	7	2	0	2	(1	1)	15	6	6	4	2	0	12	1	0	0	0	0	0	.226	.294	.484	.778
2015 Col	NL	20	42	7	0	0	0	(0	0)	7	5	0	0	0	0	4	1	0	0	0	0	0	.167	.186	.167	.353
2016 Oak	AL	20	43	9	3	0	0	(0	0)	12	4	2	2	1	0	10	0	0	0	0	0	0	.209	.227	.279	.506
4 ML YEARS		92	194	39	7	0	4	(2	2)	58	23	19	13	4	0	43	3	0	1	0	0	4	.201	.228	.299	.527

Brian McCann

Bats: L Throws: R Pos: C-92;DH-31;PH-15;1B-3   Ht: 6'3" Wt: 225 Born: 2/20/1984 Age: 33

Year Team	Lg	G	AB	H	2B	3B	HR	(Hm	Rd)	TB	R	RBI	RC	TBB	IBB	SO	HBP	SH	SF	SB	CS	GDP	Avg	OBP	Slg	OPS
2005 Atl	NL	59	180	50	7	0	5	(2	3)	72	20	23	25	18	5	26	1	4	1	1	1	5	.278	.345	.400	.745
2006 Atl	NL	130	442	147	34	0	24	(10	14)	253	61	93	94	41	8	54	3	0	6	2	0	12	.333	.388	.572	.961
2007 Atl	NL	139	504	136	38	0	18	(6	12)	228	51	92	68	35	7	74	5	2	6	0	1	19	.270	.320	.452	.772
2008 Atl	NL	145	509	153	42	1	23	(10	13)	266	68	87	84	57	4	64	4	0	3	5	0	17	.301	.373	.523	.896
2009 Atl	NL	138	488	137	35	1	21	(12	9)	237	63	94	83	49	3	83	5	3	6	4	1	17	.281	.349	.486	.834
2010 Atl	NL	143	479	129	25	0	21	(13	8)	217	63	77	76	74	10	98	9	0	4	5	2	12	.269	.375	.453	.828
2011 Atl	NL	128	466	126	19	0	24	(15	9)	217	51	71	76	57	14	89	2	0	2	3	2	10	.270	.351	.466	.817
2012 Atl	NL	121	439	101	14	0	20	(11	9)	175	44	67	45	44	7	76	1	0	3	3	0	15	.230	.300	.399	.698
2013 Atl	NL	102	356	91	13	0	20	(12	8)	164	43	57	51	39	3	66	5	0	2	0	1	9	.256	.336	.461	.796
2014 NYY	AL	140	495	115	15	1	23	(19	4)	201	57	75	58	32	1	77	7	0	4	0	0	16	.232	.286	.406	.692
2015 NYY	AL	135	465	108	15	1	26	(16	10)	203	68	94	77	52	3	97	11	0	7	0	0	7	.232	.320	.437	.756
2016 NYY	AL	130	429	104	13	0	20	(11	9)	177	56	58	51	54	2	99	7	0	2	1	0	15	.242	.335	.413	.748
Postseason		13	47	9	1	0	3	(2	1)	19	4	9	5	5	0	16	0	0	1	0	0	0	.191	.264	.404	.668
12 ML YEARS		1510	5252	1397	270	4	245	(137	108)	2410	645	888	788	552	67	903	60	9	46	24	8	154	.266	.340	.459	.799

James McCann

Bats: R Throws: R Pos: C-99;PH-6;DH-5   Ht: 6'2" Wt: 210 Born: 6/13/1990 Age: 27

Year Team	Lg	G	AB	H	2B	3B	HR	(Hm	Rd)	TB	R	RBI	RC	TBB	IBB	SO	HBP	SH	SF	SB	CS	GDP	Avg	OBP	Slg	OPS
2014 Det	AL	9	12	3	1	0	0	(0	0)	4	2	0	1	0	0	2	0	0	0	1	0	0	.250	.250	.333	.583
2015 Det	AL	114	401	106	18	5	7	(5	2)	155	32	41	34	16	0	90	3	4	1	0	1	17	.264	.297	.387	.683
2016 Det	AL	105	344	76	9	1	12	(7	5)	123	31	48	30	23	0	109	2	1	3	0	1	12	.221	.272	.358	.629
3 ML YEARS		228	757	185	28	6	19	(12	7)	282	65	89	65	39	0	201	5	5	4	1	2	29	.244	.284	.373	.657

Brandon McCarthy

Pitches: R Bats: R Pos: SP-9; RP-1   Ht: 6'7" Wt: 235 Born: 7/7/1983 Age: 33

| | | HOW MUCH HE PITCHED | | | | | WHAT HE GAVE UP | | | | | | | | | | THE RESULTS | | | | | | |
Year Team	Lg	G	GS	CG	GF	IP	BFP	H	R	ER	HR	SH	SF	HB	TBB	IBB	SO	WP	Bk	W	L	Pct	Sh	Sv-Op	Hld	ERC	ERA
2005 CWS	AL	12	10	0	0	67.0	277	62	30	30	13	1	1	2	17	0	48	1	1	3	2	.600	0	0-0	0	3.83	4.03
2006 CWS	AL	53	2	0	13	84.2	354	77	44	44	17	3	1	0	33	9	69	5	0	4	7	.364	0	0-1	11	4.10	4.68
2007 Tex	AL	23	22	0	0	101.2	459	111	62	55	9	3	5	3	48	0	59	4	1	5	10	.333	0	0-0	0	4.89	4.87
2008 Tex	AL	5	5	0	0	22.0	93	20	11	10	3	0	2	1	8	0	10	0	0	1	1	.500	0	0-0	0	3.87	4.09
2009 Tex	AL	17	17	1	0	97.1	420	96	55	50	13	0	5	3	36	0	65	0	0	7	4	.636	1	0-0	0	4.22	4.62
2011 Oak	AL	25	25	5	0	170.2	690	168	73	63	11	4	9	0	25	1	123	3	0	9	9	.500	1	0-0	0	2.80	3.32
2012 Oak	AL	18	18	0	0	111.0	469	115	44	40	10	5	4	6	24	2	73	3	0	8	6	.571	0	0-0	0	3.67	3.24
2013 Ari	NL	22	22	2	0	135.0	577	161	71	68	13	6	5	1	21	3	76	1	1	5	11	.313	1	0-0	0	4.29	4.53
2014 2 Tms		32	32	1	0	200.0	836	222	100	90	25	3	4	3	33	4	175	4	0	10	15	.400	1	0-0	0	3.98	4.05
2015 LAD	NL	4	4	0	0	23.0	94	24	15	15	9	0	0	0	4	0	29	0	0	3	0	1.000	0	0-0	0	5.39	5.87
2016 LAD	NL	10	9	0	0	40.0	171	29	24	22	2	1	2	2	26	1	44	2	0	2	3	.400	0	0-1	0	3.37	4.95
14 Ari	NL	18	18	0	0	109.2	466	131	65	61	15	2	3	2	20	4	93	3	0	3	10	.231	0	0-0	0	4.64	5.01
14 NYY	AL	14	14	1	0	90.1	370	91	35	29	10	1	1	1	13	0	82	1	0	7	5	.583	1	0-0	0	3.23	2.89
11 ML YEARS		221	166	9	13	1052.1	4440	1085	529	487	125	26	34	25	275	20	771	20	3	57	68	.456	4	0-2	11	3.91	4.17

Kevin McCarthy

Pitches: R Bats: R Pos: RP-10   Ht: 6'3" Wt: 200 Born: 2/22/1992 Age: 25

| | | HOW MUCH HE PITCHED | | | | | WHAT HE GAVE UP | | | | | | | | | | THE RESULTS | | | | | | |
Year Team	Lg	G	GS	CG	GF	IP	BFP	H	R	ER	HR	SH	SF	HB	TBB	IBB	SO	WP	Bk	W	L	Pct	Sh	Sv-Op	Hld	ERC	ERA
2013 Burlgtn	R+	10	5	0	1	42.1	172	49	18	16	2	0	0	0	5	0	32	2	0	4	2	.667	0	0- -	-	3.61	3.40
2015 2 Tms	Low	22	0	0	14	45.0	172	34	10	8	2	2	2	0	6	1	31	3	1	4	4	.500	0	6- -	-	1.59	1.60
2015 NWArk	AA	11	0	0	3	17.1	84	24	11	11	1	1	2	0	8	1	9	3	1	1	0	1.000	0	0- -	-	6.00	5.71
2016 NWArk	AA	22	0	0	16	34.2	135	26	12	12	3	1	0	1	8	1	29	0	0	3	2	.600	0	11- -	-	2.19	3.12
2016 Omha	AAA	25	0	0	15	33.1	140	28	15	10	4	1	0	1	16	2	30	1	0	2	4	.333	0	5- -	-	3.73	2.70
2016 KC	AL	10	0	0	1	8.1	41	11	8	6	1	1	0	0	5	0	7	0	0	1	0	1.000	0	0-1	0	6.83	6.48

Lance McCullers

Pitches: R **Bats:** L **Pos:** SP-14   **Ht:** 6'1" **Wt:** 205 **Born:** 10/2/1993 **Age:** 23

			HOW MUCH HE PITCHED				WHAT HE GAVE UP								THE RESULTS							
Year Team	Lg	G GS CG GF	IP	BFP	H	R	ER	HR SH SF HB	TBB IBB	SO WP Bk	W	L	Pct	Sh	Sv-Op	Hld	ERC	ERA
2012 2 Tms	Low	8 8 0 0	26.0	113	20	13	10	2 0 1 1	12 0	29 3 0	0	4	.000	0	0--	-	2.93	3.46
2013 QuadC	A	25 19 0 3	104.2	447	92	49	37	3 6 1 6	49 1	117 4 2	6	5	.545	0	0--	-	3.41	3.18
2014 Lancst	A+	25 18 0 6	97.0	436	95	63	59	18 0 0 7	56 0	115 11 1	3	6	.333	0	4--	-	5.67	5.47
2015 CpChr	AA	7 5 0 2	32.0	129	16	4	2	1 0 0 2	14 0	48 4 0	3	1	.750	0	1--	-	1.53	0.56
2015 Hou	AL	22 22 1 0	125.2	520	106	49	45	10 0 3 5	43 2	129 8 1	6	7	.462	0	0-0	0	3.02	3.22
2016 Hou	AL	14 14 0 0	81.0	352	80	29	29	5 0 0 0	45 1	106 9 2	6	5	.545	0	0-0	0	4.42	3.22
Postseason		1 1 0 0	6.1	25	2	2	2	1 0 0 2	2 0	7 0 0	0	0	-	0	0-0	0	1.80	2.84
2 ML YEARS		36 36 1 0	206.2	872	186	78	74	15 0 3 5	88 3	235 17 3	12	12	.500	0	0-0	0	3.55	3.22

Andrew McCutchen

Bats: R **Throws:** R **Pos:** CF-151;PH-2   **Ht:** 5'10" **Wt:** 190 **Born:** 10/10/1986 **Age:** 30

		BATTING																		RUNNING			AVERAGES			
Year Team	Lg	G	AB	H	2B	3B	HR	(Hm Rd)	TB	R	RBI	RC	TBB	IBB	SO	HBP	SH	SF	SB	CS	GDP	Avg	OBP	Slg	OPS
2009 Pit	NL	108	433	124	26	9	12	(8 4)	204	74	54	78	54	2	83	2	0	4	22	5	3	.286	.365	.471	.836
2010 Pit	NL	154	570	163	35	5	16	(8 8)	256	94	56	86	70	1	89	5	1	7	33	10	6	.286	.365	.449	.814
2011 Pit	NL	158	572	148	34	5	23	(10 13)	261	87	89	102	89	3	126	9	2	6	23	10	7	.259	.364	.456	.820
2012 Pit	NL	157	593	**194**	29	6	31	(15 16)	328	107	96	**125**	70	13	132	5	0	5	20	12	9	.327	.400	.553	.953
2013 Pit	NL	157	583	185	38	5	21	(9 12)	296	97	84	105	78	12	101	9	0	4	27	10	13	.317	.404	.508	.911
2014 Pit	NL	146	548	172	38	6	25	(10 15)	297	89	83	**109**	84	8	115	10	0	6	18	3	9	.314	**.410**	**.542**	**.952**
2015 Pit	NL	157	566	165	36	3	23	(13 10)	276	91	96	120	98	12	133	12	0	9	11	5	9	.292	.401	.488	.889
2016 Pit	NL	153	598	153	26	3	24	(10 14)	257	81	79	83	69	7	143	5	0	3	6	7	15	.256	.336	.430	.766
Postseason		8	28	9	1	0	0	(0 0)	10	3	0	3	6	1	4	0	0	0	0	0	0	.321	.441	.357	.798
8 ML YEARS		1190	4463	1304	262	42	175	(83 92)	2175	720	637	808	612	58	922	57	3	44	160	62	71	.292	.381	.487	.869

T.J. McFarland

Pitches: L **Bats:** L **Pos:** RP-16   **Ht:** 6'3" **Wt:** 220 **Born:** 6/8/1989 **Age:** 28

			HOW MUCH HE PITCHED				WHAT HE GAVE UP								THE RESULTS							
Year Team	Lg	G GS CG GF	IP	BFP	H	R	ER	HR SH SF HB	TBB IBB	SO WP Bk	W	L	Pct	Sh	Sv-Op	Hld	ERC	ERA
2016 Norfolk*	AAA	8 4 0 1	26.1	114	33	13	13	3 0 0 2	7 0	11 3 0	1	1	.500	0	0--	-	5.64	4.44
2013 Bal	AL	38 1 0 8	74.2	331	83	37	35	7 2 1 0	28 5	58 2 0	4	1	.800	0	0-0	0	4.40	4.22
2014 Bal	AL	37 1 0 14	58.2	255	70	22	18	2 5 0 4	13 2	34 0 0	4	2	.667	0	0-0	5	4.23	2.76
2015 Bal	AL	30 0 0 7	40.1	188	52	26	22	4 0 0 0	18 5	26 3 0	2	2	.500	0	0-0	3	5.68	4.91
2016 Bal	AL	16 0 0 2	24.2	112	33	19	19	3 0 3 2	10 2	7 1 0	2	2	.500	0	0-3	0	6.74	6.93
4 ML YEARS		121 2 0 31	198.1	886	238	104	94	16 7 4 6	69 14	125 6 0	12	7	.632	0	0-3	8	4.88	4.27

Jake McGee

Pitches: L **Bats:** L **Pos:** RP-57   **Ht:** 6'3" **Wt:** 230 **Born:** 8/6/1986 **Age:** 30

			HOW MUCH HE PITCHED				WHAT HE GAVE UP								THE RESULTS							
Year Team	Lg	G GS CG GF	IP	BFP	H	R	ER	HR SH SF HB	TBB IBB	SO WP Bk	W	L	Pct	Sh	Sv-Op	Hld	ERC	ERA
2010 TB	AL	8 0 0 3	5.0	20	2	1	1	0 0 0 0	3 0	6 0 0	0	0	-	0	0-0	0	1.32	1.80
2011 TB	AL	37 0 0 9	28.0	124	30	14	14	5 1 0 0	12 1	27 0 0	5	2	.714	0	0-0	4	5.09	4.50
2012 TB	AL	69 0 0 13	55.1	212	33	13	12	3 0 2 1	11 4	73 3 0	5	2	.714	0	0-2	19	1.26	1.95
2013 TB	AL	71 0 0 6	62.2	260	52	28	28	8 1 3 1	22 5	75 4 0	5	3	.625	0	1-5	27	3.07	4.02
2014 TB	AL	73 0 0 31	71.1	274	48	15	15	2 1 1 2	16 1	90 1 0	5	2	.714	0	19-23	14	1.55	1.89
2015 TB	AL	39 0 0 6	37.1	147	27	11	10	3 0 1 1	8 1	48 1 0	1	2	.333	0	6-10	19	1.92	2.41
2016 Col	NL	57 0 0 25	45.2	205	56	25	24	9 0 0 3	16 1	38 4 0	2	3	.400	0	15-19	4	6.26	4.73
Postseason		5 0 0 1	3.1	17	3	2	2	0 1 0 1	3 1	3 0 0	0	1	.000	0	0-0	2	5.03	5.40
7 ML YEARS		354 0 0 93	305.1	1242	248	107	104	30 3 7 8	88 13	357 13 0	23	14	.622	0	41-59	87	2.68	3.07

Casey McGehee

Bats: R **Throws:** R **Pos:** 3B-27;PH-3;1B-1   McGEE   **Ht:** 6'1" **Wt:** 220 **Born:** 10/12/1982 **Age:** 34

		BATTING																		RUNNING			AVERAGES			
Year Team	Lg	G	AB	H	2B	3B	HR	(Hm Rd)	TB	R	RBI	RC	TBB	IBB	SO	HBP	SH	SF	SB	CS	GDP	Avg	OBP	Slg	OPS
2016 Toledo*	AAA	116	438	139	37	0	6	(- -)	194	56	50	74	38	3	73	2	0	2	6	3	13	.317	.373	.443	.816
2008 ChC	NL	9	24	4	1	0	0	(0 0)	5	1	5	0	0	0	8	0	0	1	0	0	1	.167	.160	.208	.368
2009 Mil	NL	116	355	107	20	1	16	(6 10)	177	58	66	65	34	2	67	1	0	4	0	2	13	.301	.360	.499	.859
2010 Mil	NL	157	610	174	38	1	23	(13 10)	283	70	104	93	50	5	102	2	0	8	1	1	18	.285	.337	.464	.801
2011 Mil	NL	155	546	122	24	2	13	(8 5)	189	46	67	50	45	4	104	1	0	8	0	3	19	.223	.280	.346	.626
2012 2 Tms	NL	114	318	69	16	1	9	(1 8)	114	36	41	30	29	0	70	2	0	3	1	1	10	.217	.284	.358	.643
2014 Mia	NL	160	616	177	29	1	4	(1 3)	220	56	76	78	67	3	102	1	0	7	4	2	**31**	.287	.355	.357	.712
2015 2 Tms	NL	109	237	47	12	0	2	(1 1)	65	14	20	8	21	0	50	0	0	0	1	1	18	.198	.264	.274	.538
2016 Det	AL	30	92	21	1	0	0	(0 0)	22	4	1	2	3	0	14	1	0	0	0	0	5	.228	.260	.239	.500
12 Pit	NL	92	265	61	13	1	8	(1 7)	100	27	35	26	24	0	60	2	0	2	1	1	7	.230	.297	.377	.674
12 NYY	AL	22	53	8	3	0	1	(0 1)	14	9	6	4	5	0	10	0	0	1	0	0	3	.151	.220	.264	.484
15 SF	NL	49	127	27	5	0	2	(1 1)	38	7	11	4	11	0	28	0	0	0	1	1	15	.213	.274	.299	.575
15 Mia	NL	60	110	20	7	0	0	(0 0)	27	7	9	4	10	0	22	0	0	0	1	0	3	.182	.250	.245	.495
Postseason		6	5	1	0	0	0	(0 0)	1	0	0	1	1	0	2	0	0	0	0	0	0	.200	.333	.200	.533
8 ML YEARS		850	2798	721	141	6	67	(30 37)	1075	285	380	326	249	14	517	8	0	31	7	10	115	.258	.317	.384	.701

Dustin McGowan

Pitches: R Bats: R Pos: RP-55   Ht: 6'3" Wt: 235 Born: 3/24/1982 Age: 35

					HOW MUCH HE PITCHED					WHAT HE GAVE UP										THE RESULTS						
Year	Team	Lg	G	GS	CG	GF	IP	BFP	H	R	ER	HR	SH	SF	HB	TBB	IBB	SO	WP	Bk	W	L	Pct	Sh	Sv-Op	Hld	ERC	ERA
2005	Tor	AL	13	7	0	2	45.1	205	49	34	32	7	0	4	7	17	0	34	7	0	1	3	.250	0	0-0	1	5.47	6.35
2006	Tor	AL	16	3	0	3	27.1	143	35	27	22	2	0	1	2	25	2	22	3	1	1	2	.333	0	0-1	1	7.72	7.24
2007	Tor	AL	27	27	2	0	169.2	705	146	80	77	14	0	6	2	61	3	144	13	0	12	10	.545	1	0-0	0	3.07	4.08
2008	Tor	AL	19	19	1	0	111.1	474	115	60	54	9	2	8	5	38	1	85	5	0	6	7	.462	0	0-0	0	4.13	4.37
2011	Tor	AL	5	4	0	1	21.0	96	20	15	15	4	0	1	1	13	0	20	3	0	0	2	.000	0	0-0	0	5.50	6.43
2013	Tor	AL	25	0	0	8	25.2	114	19	11	7	2	0	0	2	12	1	26	3	0	0	0	-	0	0-1	6	2.83	2.45
2014	Tor	AL	53	8	0	9	82.0	354	80	41	38	13	0	2	3	33	1	61	2	0	5	3	.625	0	1-5	10	4.50	4.17
2015	Phi	NL	14	1	0	3	23.1	118	29	21	18	7	0	0	0	20	1	21	1	0	1	2	.333	0	0-0	0	9.07	6.94
2016	Mia	NL	55	0	0	24	67.0	279	49	26	21	7	0	2	2	33	7	63	4	0	1	3	.250	0	1-2	3	2.98	2.82
	9 ML YEARS		227	69	3	49	572.2	2488	542	315	284	65	2	24	24	252	16	476	41	1	27	32	.458	1	2-9	21	4.14	4.46

Collin McHugh

Pitches: R Bats: R Pos: SP-33   mick-HYOO   Ht: 6'2" Wt: 190 Born: 6/19/1987 Age: 30

					HOW MUCH HE PITCHED					WHAT HE GAVE UP										THE RESULTS						
Year	Team	Lg	G	GS	CG	GF	IP	BFP	H	R	ER	HR	SH	SF	HB	TBB	IBB	SO	WP	Bk	W	L	Pct	Sh	Sv-Op	Hld	ERC	ERA
2012	NYM	NL	8	4	0	1	21.1	99	27	21	18	5	2	1	2	8	2	17	0	0	0	4	.000	0	0-0	0	6.83	7.59
2013	2 Tms	NL	7	5	0	2	26.0	125	45	29	29	6	2	2	0	5	0	11	0	0	0	4	.000	0	0-0	0	8.82	10.04
2014	Hou	AL	25	25	0	0	154.2	619	117	53	47	13	6	4	6	41	1	157	6	0	11	9	.550	0	0-0	0	2.34	2.73
2015	Hou	AL	32	32	0	0	203.2	859	207	89	88	19	5	4	9	53	2	171	5	0	19	7	.731	0	0-0	0	3.75	3.89
2016	Hou	AL	33	33	1	0	184.2	796	206	92	89	25	1	5	5	54	1	177	9	0	13	10	.565	0	0-0	0	4.69	4.34
13	NYM	NL	3	1	0	2	7.0	34	12	8	8	2	0	1	0	3	0	3	0	0	0	1	.000	0	0-0	0	10.77	10.29
13	Col	NL	4	4	0	0	19.0	91	33	21	21	4	2	1	0	2	0	8	0	0	0	3	.000	0	0-0	0	8.14	9.95
	Postseason		2	2	0	0	10.0	40	9	5	5	2	0	0	1	2	0	2	0	0	1	1	.500	0	0-0	0	3.93	4.50
	5 ML YEARS		105	99	1	3	590.1	2498	602	284	271	68	16	16	22	161	6	533	20	0	43	34	.558	0	0-0	0	3.93	4.13

Michael McKenry

Bats: R Throws: R Pos: PH-3   Ht: 5'10" Wt: 205 Born: 3/4/1985 Age: 32

									BATTING												RUNNING			AVERAGES			
Year	Team	Lg	G	AB	H	2B	3B	HR	(Hm	Rd)	TB	R	RBI	RC	TBB	IBB	SO	HBP	SH	SF	SB	CS	GDP	Avg	OBP	Slg	OPS
2016	RdRck*	AAA	13	41	9	5	0	0	(-	-)	14	9	9	6	11	0	13	1	0	1	0	0	1	.220	.389	.341	.730
2016	Memp*	AAA	24	82	28	5	4	5	(-	-)	56	20	20	22	14	0	19	1	0	0	2	2	1	.341	.443	.683	1.126
2016	Gwnntt*	AAA	14	45	12	2	0	1	(-	-)	17	6	3	6	7	0	16	0	0	0	0	0	0	.267	.365	.378	.743
2016	ColSpr*	AAA	14	32	8	2	0	1	(-	-)	13	6	6	8	15	0	8	1	0	0	0	0	2	.250	.500	.406	.906
2010	Col	NL	6	8	0	0	0	0	(0	0)	0	0	0	0	1	0	5	0	0	0	0	0	0	.000	.111	.000	.111
2011	Pit	NL	58	180	40	12	0	2	(1	1)	58	17	11	12	14	2	49	0	5	2	0	1	3	.222	.276	.322	.598
2012	Pit	NL	88	240	56	14	0	12	(3	9)	106	25	39	32	29	1	73	3	0	3	0	0	7	.233	.320	.442	.762
2013	Pit	NL	41	115	25	6	0	3	(2	1)	40	9	14	11	5	0	24	2	0	0	0	0	2	.217	.262	.348	.610
2014	Col	NL	57	168	53	9	0	8	(4	4)	86	23	22	28	22	1	42	1	1	0	0	3	6	.315	.398	.512	.910
2015	Col	NL	58	127	26	7	3	4	(3	1)	51	20	17	15	22	0	41	2	0	1	2	2	2	.205	.329	.402	.731
2016	StL	NL	3	1	0	0	0	0	(0	0)	0	0	0	0	0	0	1	0	1	0	0	0	0	.000	.000	.000	.000
	7 ML YEARS		311	839	200	48	3	29	(13	16)	341	94	103	98	93	4	235	8	7	6	2	6	20	.238	.318	.406	.725

Kris Medlen

Pitches: R Bats: B Pos: SP-6   MEDD-linn   Ht: 5'10" Wt: 190 Born: 10/7/1985 Age: 31

					HOW MUCH HE PITCHED					WHAT HE GAVE UP										THE RESULTS						
Year	Team	Lg	G	GS	CG	GF	IP	BFP	H	R	ER	HR	SH	SF	HB	TBB	IBB	SO	WP	Bk	W	L	Pct	Sh	Sv-Op	Hld	ERC	ERA
2016	Omha*	AAA	8	5	0	1	19.2	92	25	20	19	9	0	0	1	7	0	18	0	0	0	3	.000	0	0--	1	8.37	8.69
2009	Atl	NL	37	4	0	10	67.2	294	65	34	32	5	6	2	2	30	2	72	3	1	3	5	.375	0	0-2	1	3.90	4.26
2010	Atl	NL	31	14	0	5	107.2	438	108	48	44	13	7	3	3	21	1	83	1	1	6	2	.750	0	0-0	1	3.60	3.68
2011	Atl	NL	2	0	0	1	2.1	8	1	0	0	0	0	0	0	0	0	2	0	0	0	0	.000	0	0-0	0	0.40	0.00
2012	Atl	NL	50	12	2	7	138.0	520	103	26	24	6	1	0	0	23	0	120	3	0	10	1	.909	1	1-2	7	1.69	1.57
2013	Atl	NL	32	31	0	1	197.0	820	194	77	68	18	9	2	8	47	1	157	2	0	15	12	.556	0	0-0	0	3.48	3.11
2015	KC	AL	15	8	0	2	58.1	243	56	30	26	6	0	1	2	18	0	40	3	0	6	2	.750	0	0-0	0	3.71	4.01
2016	KC	AL	6	6	0	0	24.1	119	30	25	21	2	0	2	0	20	0	18	1	0	1	3	.250	0	0-0	0	7.15	7.77
	Postseason		4	2	0	1	16.1	69	15	12	9	4	1	2	2	2	0	16	0	0	0	2	.000	0	0-0	0	3.80	4.96
	7 ML YEARS		173	75	2	26	595.1	2442	557	240	215	50	23	10	15	159	4	492	13	2	41	25	.621	1	1-4	9	3.24	3.25

Adalberto Mejia

Pitches: L Bats: R Pos: RP-1   ah-dahl-BAIR-toe meh-HEE-yah   Ht: 6'3" Wt: 195 Born: 6/20/1993 Age: 24

					HOW MUCH HE PITCHED					WHAT HE GAVE UP										THE RESULTS						
Year	Team	Lg	G	GS	CG	GF	IP	BFP	H	R	ER	HR	SH	SF	HB	TBB	IBB	SO	WP	Bk	W	L	Pct	Sh	Sv-Op	Hld	ERC	ERA
2012	Augsta	A	30	14	1	2	106.2	463	122	57	47	4	3	5	4	21	1	79	6	2	10	7	.588	0	0--	-	3.71	3.97
2013	SnJos	A+	16	16	0	0	87.0	355	75	34	32	11	2	0	1	23	0	89	5	0	7	4	.636	0	0--	-	3.02	3.31
2014	Rchmd	AA	22	21	0	0	108.0	459	119	62	56	9	1	6	0	31	0	82	2	0	7	9	.438	0	0--	-	4.13	4.67
2015	Rchmd	AA	12	9	0	0	51.1	210	38	14	14	2	5	0	1	18	0	38	2	0	5	2	.714	0	0--	-	2.20	2.45
2016	Rchmd	AA	11	11	0	0	65.0	254	48	16	14	4	1	0	1	16	0	58	3	1	3	2	.600	0	0--	-	2.02	1.94
2016	Scrmto	AAA	7	7	0	0	40.2	172	42	19	19	5	1	0	0	11	0	43	0	1	4	1	.800	0	0--	-	3.89	4.20
2016	Min	AL	1	0	0	0	2.1	13	5	2	2	0	0	1	0	1	0	0	0	0	0	0	-	0	0-0	0	10.38	7.71

Mark Melancon

Pitches: R **Bats:** R **Pos:** RP-75 muh-LANN-sun **Ht:** 6'2" **Wt:** 210 **Born:** 3/28/1985 **Age:** 32

Year	Team	Lg	G	GS	CG	GF	IP	BFP	H	R	ER	HR	SH	SF	HB	TBB	IBB	SO	WP	Bk	W	L	Pct	Sh	Sv-Op	Hld	ERC	ERA
2009	NYY	AL	13	0	0	4	16.1	74	13	8	7	0	0	0	4	10	0	10	3	0	0	1	.000	0	0-1	0	3.94	3.86
2010	2 Tms		22	0	0	4	21.1	90	19	13	10	2	0	1	1	8	0	22	2	0	2	0	1.000	0	0-1	8	3.53	4.22
2011	Hou	NL	71	0	0	47	74.1	309	65	28	23	5	2	0	2	26	6	66	1	0	8	4	.667	0	20-25	3	2.98	2.78
2012	Bos	AL	41	0	0	17	45.0	194	45	31	31	8	1	2	3	12	1	41	2	0	0	2	.000	0	1-2	2	4.24	6.20
2013	Pit	NL	72	0	0	24	71.0	279	60	15	11	1	0	1	1	8	0	70	6	0	3	2	.600	0	16-21	26	1.78	1.39
2014	Pit	NL	72	0	0	48	71.0	277	51	15	15	2	1	1	3	11	1	71	3	0	3	5	.375	0	33-37	14	1.54	1.90
2015	Pit	NL	78	0	0	63	76.2	293	57	20	19	4	1	1	2	14	2	62	3	0	3	2	.600	0	51-53	1	1.82	2.23
2016	2 Tms	NL	75	0	0	67	71.1	270	52	16	13	3	0	2	1	12	0	65	4	0	2	2	.500	0	47-51	1	1.66	1.64
10	NYY	AL	2	0	0	2	4.0	19	7	5	4	1	0	1	0	0	0	3	0	0	0	0	-	0	0-0	0	7.95	9.00
10	Hou	AL	20	0	0	2	17.1	71	12	8	6	1	0	0	1	8	0	19	2	0	2	0	1.000	0	0-1	8	2.65	3.12
16	Pit	NL	45	0	0	39	41.2	163	31	10	7	2	0	2	1	9	0	38	1	0	1	1	.500	0	30-33	0	1.89	1.51
16	Was	NL	30	0	0	28	29.2	107	21	6	6	1	0	0	0	3	0	27	3	0	1	1	.500	0	17-18	0	1.41	1.82
	Postseason		6	0	0	3	5.2	22	6	4	4	2	0	0	0	1	0	3	0	0	1	0	1.000	0	0-1	0	5.58	6.35
	8 ML YEARS		444	0	0	274	447.0	1786	362	148	129	25	5	8	17	101	10	407	24	0	21	18	.538	0	168-191	54	2.29	2.60

Tim Melville

Pitches: R **Bats:** R **Pos:** SP-2; RP-1 **Ht:** 6'4" **Wt:** 225 **Born:** 10/9/1989 **Age:** 27

Year	Team	Lg	G	GS	CG	GF	IP	BFP	H	R	ER	HR	SH	SF	HB	TBB	IBB	SO	WP	Bk	W	L	Pct	Sh	Sv-Op	Hld	ERC	ERA
2012	NWArk	AA	6	5	0	0	23.1	112	27	22	20	4	0	2	3	15	1	19	3	0	2	1	.667	0	0--	-	7.10	7.71
2014	NWArk	AA	26	26	0	0	129.1	593	144	92	79	14	8	5	2	68	0	105	7	0	2	11	.154	0	0--	-	5.32	5.50
2015	Toledo	AAA	27	27	1	0	151.2	655	141	89	78	14	7	8	7	68	1	102	4	1	7	10	.412	0	0--	-	4.00	4.63
2016	Lsvlle	AAA	6	6	0	0	8.1	41	10	7	4	1	0	0	1	5	0	7	1	0	1	1	.500	0	0--	-	5.92	4.32
2016	Cin	NL	3	2	0	0	9.0	54	16	12	11	5	2	0	1	9	0	8	1	0	0	1	.000	0	0-0	0	16.62	11.00

Yohander Mendez

Pitches: L **Bats:** L **Pos:** RP-2 yo-HAHN-dair **Ht:** 6'5" **Wt:** 200 **Born:** 1/17/1995 **Age:** 22

Year	Team	Lg	G	GS	CG	GF	IP	BFP	H	R	ER	HR	SH	SF	HB	TBB	IBB	SO	WP	Bk	W	L	Pct	Sh	Sv-Op	Hld	ERC	ERA
2013	Spkane	A-	8	8	0	0	33.1	151	31	18	14	4	0	2	3	17	0	23	1	0	1	2	.333	0	0--	-	4.51	3.78
2014	2 Tms	Low	10	9	0	0	36.2	143	34	13	11	4	0	2	0	4	0	35	5	2	3	1	.750	0	0--	-	2.70	2.70
2015	Hickry	A	21	8	0	6	66.1	269	57	20	18	2	3	1	2	15	0	74	6	1	3	3	.500	0	3--	-	2.35	2.44
2016	Hi Dsrt	A+	7	7	0	0	33.0	130	21	9	9	2	0	0	0	11	0	45	1	0	4	1	.800	0	0--	-	1.76	2.45
2016	Frisco	AA	10	10	0	0	46.2	191	39	18	16	2	1	1	4	14	0	46	5	0	4	1	.800	0	0--	-	2.81	3.09
2016	RdRck	AAA	7	4	0	1	31.1	119	12	2	2	0	1	0	1	16	0	22	2	0	4	1	.800	0	0--	-	1.20	0.57
2016	Tex	AL	2	0	0	0	3.0	17	5	6	6	0	0	0	0	2	0	0	0	0	0	0	-	0	0-0	0	7.72	18.00

Daniel Mengden

Pitches: R **Bats:** R **Pos:** SP-14 MENG-den **Ht:** 6'2" **Wt:** 190 **Born:** 2/19/1993 **Age:** 24

Year	Team	Lg	G	GS	CG	GF	IP	BFP	H	R	ER	HR	SH	SF	HB	TBB	IBB	SO	WP	Bk	W	L	Pct	Sh	Sv-Op	Hld	ERC	ERA
2014	2 Tms	Low	6	1	0	2	11.0	44	9	4	4	0	0	0	1	1	0	17	1	0	0	0	-	0	0--	-	1.73	3.27
2015	3 Tms	Low	26	22	0	3	130.2	554	128	60	54	11	5	3	6	36	0	125	12	2	10	4	.714	0	1--	-	3.53	3.72
2016	Nashv	AAA	13	13	0	0	75.1	294	54	15	14	4	2	2	3	17	1	67	1	0	8	2	.800	0	0--	-	1.87	1.67
2016	Oak	AL	14	14	0	0	72.0	332	83	54	52	9	2	1	4	33	0	71	5	0	2	9	.182	0	0-0	0	5.56	6.50

Jordy Mercer

Bats: R **Throws:** R **Pos:** SS-146;PH-3 **Ht:** 6'3" **Wt:** 205 **Born:** 8/27/1986 **Age:** 30

Year	Team	Lg	G	AB	H	2B	3B	HR	(Hm	Rd)	TB	R	RBI	RC	TBB	IBB	SO	HBP	SH	SF	SB	CS	GDP	Avg	OBP	Slg	OPS
2012	Pit	NL	42	62	13	5	1	1	(1	1)	23	7	5	6	4	0	14	1	0	1	0	1	0	.210	.265	.371	.636
2013	Pit	NL	103	333	95	22	2	8	(1	7)	145	33	27	46	22	6	62	4	5	1	3	2	7	.285	.336	.435	.772
2014	Pit	NL	149	506	129	27	2	12	(3	9)	196	56	55	45	35	12	89	4	5	5	4	1	14	.255	.305	.387	.693
2015	Pit	NL	116	394	96	21	0	3	(0	3)	126	34	34	34	27	7	73	2	4	3	3	2	7	.244	.293	.320	.613
2016	Pit	NL	149	519	133	22	3	11	(4	7)	194	66	59	58	51	8	83	5	7	2	1	1	11	.256	.328	.374	.701
	Postseason		7	14	2	0	0	0	(0	0)	2	0	0	0	1	1	5	0	0	0	0	0	0	.143	.200	.143	.343
	5 ML YEARS		559	1814	466	97	8	35	(9	26)	684	196	180	189	139	33	321	16	21	12	11	7	39	.257	.313	.377	.691

Whit Merrifield

Bats: R **Throws:** R **Pos:** 2B-65;LF-13;3B-5;RF-4;PH-4;1B-1;PR-1 **Ht:** 6'0" **Wt:** 195 **Born:** 1/24/1989 **Age:** 28

Year	Team	Lg	G	AB	H	2B	3B	HR	(Hm	Rd)	TB	R	RBI	RC	TBB	IBB	SO	HBP	SH	SF	SB	CS	GDP	Avg	OBP	Slg	OPS
2012	Wilmg	A+	101	380	98	20	3	8	(-	-)	148	59	36	56	41	0	69	4	10	5	11	5	11	.258	.333	.389	.722
2012	NWArk	AA	24	96	25	2	1	1	(-	-)	32	12	8	10	8	0	19	0	1	1	3	2	5	.260	.314	.333	.648
2013	NWArk	AA	94	322	87	20	5	3	(-	-)	126	31	43	42	22	0	57	2	5	2	17	7	14	.270	.319	.391	.710
2014	NWArk	AA	44	162	45	13	1	5	(-	-)	75	22	20	28	22	0	21	1	4	1	5	4	3	.278	.366	.463	.829
2014	Omha	AAA	76	321	109	28	3	3	(-	-)	152	57	29	56	17	1	52	2	2	3	11	7	6	.340	.373	.474	.847
2015	Omha	AAA	135	544	144	29	5	5	(-	-)	198	83	38	68	39	1	66	4	4	3	32	9	13	.265	.317	.364	.681
2016	Omha	AAA	69	274	73	19	0	8	(-	-)	116	46	29	42	22	1	55	2	2	4	20	2	4	.266	.321	.423	.745
2016	KC	AL	81	311	88	22	3	2	(2	0)	122	44	29	38	19	1	72	0	1	1	8	3	1	.283	.323	.392	.716

Ryan Merritt

Pitches: L Bats: L Pos: RP-3; SP-1   Ht: 6'0" Wt: 180 Born: 2/21/1992 Age: 25

		HOW MUCH HE PITCHED						WHAT HE GAVE UP										THE RESULTS						
Year	Team	Lg	G	GS	CG	GF	IP	BFP	H	R	ER	HR	SH	SF	HB	TBB	IBB	SO	WP	Bk	W	L	Pct	Sh	Sv-Op	Hld	ERC	ERA
2012	MhVlly	A-	14	14	0	0	66.0	299	82	42	30	3	4	6	1	17	1	40	2	1	3	4	.429	0	0- -	-	4.39	4.09
2013	2 Tms	Low	26	25	0	0	135.1	560	149	67	53	11	2	4	6	19	0	97	8	6	6	9	.400	0	0- -	-	3.72	3.52
2014	Carlina	A+	25	25	2	0	160.1	631	128	56	46	12	3	5	5	25	0	127	0	3	13	3	.813	0	0- -	-	2.10	2.58
2015	Akron	AA	22	22	2	0	141.0	572	145	63	55	8	7	2	8	16	1	89	3	1	10	7	.588	2	0- -	-	3.11	3.51
2015	Clmbs	AAA	5	5	0	0	30.0	132	38	14	14	1	2	0	1	6	0	16	0	1	2	0	1.000	0	0- -	-	4.43	4.20
2016	Clmbs	AAA	24	24	2	0	143.1	596	156	67	59	15	5	3	6	23	0	92	2	0	11	8	.579	1	0- -	-	3.87	3.70
2016	Cle	AL	4	1	0	1	11.0	37	6	2	2	0	1	0	0	0	0	6	0	0	1	0	1.000	0	0-0	0	0.67	1.64

Devin Mesoraco

Bats: R Throws: R Pos: C-13;PH-3   mezz-er-OCK-oh   Ht: 6'1" Wt: 220 Born: 6/19/1988 Age: 29

							BATTING													RUNNING			AVERAGES			
Year	Team	Lg	G	AB	H	2B	3B	HR	(Hm	Rd)	TB	R	RBI	RC	TBB	IBB	SO	HBP	SH	SF	SB	CS	GDP	Avg	OBP	Slg	OPS
2011	Cin	NL	18	50	9	3	0	2	(2	0)	18	5	6	5	3	1	10	0	0	0	0	0	1	.180	.226	.360	.586
2012	Cin	NL	54	165	35	8	0	5	(4	1)	58	17	14	10	17	4	33	1	0	1	1	1	2	.212	.288	.352	.640
2013	Cin	NL	103	323	77	13	0	9	(5	4)	117	31	42	30	24	4	61	0	0	5	0	2	9	.238	.287	.362	.649
2014	Cin	NL	114	384	105	25	0	25	(14	11)	205	54	80	76	41	4	103	12	0	3	1	3	5	.273	.359	.534	.893
2015	Cin	NL	23	45	8	1	1	0	(0	0)	11	2	2	3	5	0	9	1	0	0	1	0	0	.178	.275	.244	.519
2016	Cin	NL	16	50	7	1	0	0	(0	0)	8	2	1	0	5	0	10	0	0	0	0	1	3	.140	.218	.160	.378
	Postseason		1	1	0	0	0	0	(0	0)	0	0	0	0	0	0	0	0	0	0	0	0	0	.000	.000	.000	.000
	6 ML YEARS		328	1017	241	51	1	41	(25	16)	417	111	145	124	95	13	226	14	0	9	3	7	20	.237	.308	.410	.718

Alex Meyer

Pitches: R Bats: R Pos: SP-6; RP-1   MY-er   Ht: 6'9" Wt: 225 Born: 1/3/1990 Age: 27

				HOW MUCH HE PITCHED						WHAT HE GAVE UP										THE RESULTS						
Year	Team	Lg	G	GS	CG	GF	IP	BFP	H	R	ER	HR	SH	SF	HB	TBB	IBB	SO	WP	Bk	W	L	Pct	Sh	Sv-Op	Hld	ERC	ERA
2012	2 Tms	Low	25	25	1	0	129.0	521	97	44	41	6	6	5	45	0	139	9	0	10	6	.625	1	0- -	-	2.41	2.86
2013	NwBrit	AA	13	13	0	0	70.0	299	60	29	25	3	0	2	3	29	0	84	5	1	4	3	.571	0	0- -	-	3.09	3.21
2014	Roch	AAA	27	27	0	0	130.1	565	116	58	51	10	7	5	8	64	0	153	5	0	7	7	.500	0	0- -	-	3.90	3.52
2015	Roch	AAA	38	8	0	6	92.0	418	101	54	49	4	3	3	5	48	1	100	6	0	4	5	.444	0	0- -	-	4.91	4.79
2015	Min	AL	2	0	0	0	2.2	15	4	5	5	2	1	0	0	3	0	3	0	0	0	0	-	0	0-0	0	16.82	16.88
2016	2 Tms	AL	7	6	0	0	25.1	117	25	16	16	3	0	2	2	17	0	29	3	0	1	3	.250	0	0-0	0	5.15	5.68
16	Min	AL	2	1	0	0	3.2	23	8	5	5	1	0	0	4	0	5	2	0	0	1	.000	0	0-0	0	16.88	12.27
16	LAA	AL	5	5	0	0	21.2	94	17	11	11	2	0	2	0	13	0	24	1	0	1	2	.333	0	0-0	0	3.57	4.57
	2 ML YEARS		9	6	0	0	28.0	132	29	21	21	5	1	0	2	20	0	32	3	0	1	3	.250	0	0-0	0	6.10	6.75

Will Middlebrooks

Bats: R Throws: R Pos: 3B-8;PH-2   Ht: 6'3" Wt: 220 Born: 9/9/1988 Age: 28

							BATTING													RUNNING			AVERAGES			
Year	Team	Lg	G	AB	H	2B	3B	HR	(Hm	Rd)	TB	R	RBI	RC	TBB	IBB	SO	HBP	SH	SF	SB	CS	GDP	Avg	OBP	Slg	OPS
2016	ColSpr*	AAA	68	248	70	22	2	10	(-	-)	126	38	47	39	9	2	59	2	1	4	1	1	6	.282	.308	.508	.816
2012	Bos	AL	75	267	77	14	0	15	(9	6)	136	34	54	46	13	0	70	3	0	3	4	1	8	.288	.325	.509	.835
2013	Bos	AL	94	348	79	18	0	17	(4	13)	148	41	49	29	20	3	98	2	1	3	3	1	13	.227	.271	.425	.696
2014	Bos	AL	63	215	41	10	0	2	(1	1)	57	14	19	15	15	1	70	4	0	0	1	1	7	.191	.256	.265	.522
2015	SD	NL	83	255	54	7	2	9	(1	8)	92	23	29	20	11	0	60	0	0	4	2	1	4	.212	.241	.361	.602
2016	Mil	NL	10	27	3	0	0	0	(0	0)	3	2	1	1	4	0	13	0	0	0	0	0	4	.111	.226	.111	.337
	Postseason		10	25	4	2	0	0	(0	0)	6	2	1	2	3	1	10	0	0	0	0	0	0	.160	.250	.240	.490
	5 ML YEARS		325	1112	254	49	2	43	(15	28)	436	114	152	111	63	4	311	9	1	10	10	4	32	.228	.273	.392	.665

Wade Miley

Pitches: L Bats: L Pos: SP-30   MY-lee   Ht: 6'0" Wt: 220 Born: 11/13/1986 Age: 30

				HOW MUCH HE PITCHED						WHAT HE GAVE UP										THE RESULTS						
Year	Team	Lg	G	GS	CG	GF	IP	BFP	H	R	ER	HR	SH	SF	HB	TBB	IBB	SO	WP	Bk	W	L	Pct	Sh	Sv-Op	Hld	ERC	ERA
2011	Ari	NL	8	7	0	0	40.0	180	48	20	20	6	3	1	0	18	0	25	1	0	4	2	.667	0	0-0	0	5.90	4.50
2012	Ari	NL	32	29	0	0	194.2	807	193	79	72	14	8	3	2	37	0	144	6	1	16	11	.593	0	0-0	0	3.05	3.33
2013	Ari	NL	33	33	0	0	202.2	847	201	88	80	21	6	2	4	66	4	147	13	0	10	10	.500	0	0-0	0	3.88	3.55
2014	Ari	NL	33	33	0	0	201.1	866	207	103	97	23	8	9	4	75	3	183	9	0	8	12	.400	0	0-0	0	4.31	4.34
2015	Bos	AL	32	32	1	0	193.2	831	201	98	96	17	3	4	4	64	0	147	10	1	11	11	.500	0	0-0	0	4.01	4.46
2016	2 Tms	AL	30	30	1	0	166.0	711	187	100	99	25	2	5	6	49	1	137	8	2	9	13	.409	1	0-0	0	4.98	5.37
16	Sea	AL	19	19	1	0	112.0	469	117	62	62	18	2	3	3	34	1	82	5	2	7	8	.467	1	0-0	0	4.58	4.98
16	Bal	AL	11	11	0	0	54.0	242	70	38	37	7	0	2	3	15	0	55	3	0	2	5	.286	0	0-0	0	5.83	6.17
	6 ML YEARS		168	164	2	0	998.1	4242	1037	488	464	106	30	22	20	309	8	783	47	4	58	59	.496	1	0-0	0	4.08	4.18

Andrew Miller

Pitches: L Bats: L Pos: RP-70   Ht: 6'7" Wt: 205 Born: 5/21/1985 Age: 32

				HOW MUCH HE PITCHED						WHAT HE GAVE UP										THE RESULTS						
Year	Team	Lg	G	GS	CG	GF	IP	BFP	H	R	ER	HR	SH	SF	HB	TBB	IBB	SO	WP	Bk	W	L	Pct	Sh	Sv-Op	Hld	ERC	ERA
2006	Det	AL	8	0	0	3	10.1	51	8	9	7	0	0	0	2	10	0	6	1	0	0	1	.000	0	0-0	1	4.79	6.10
2007	Det	AL	13	13	0	0	64.0	309	73	44	40	8	3	1	7	39	0	56	4	1	5	5	.500	0	0-0	0	6.31	5.63
2008	Fla	NL	29	20	0	1	107.1	492	120	78	70	7	10	7	4	56	4	89	4	0	6	10	.375	0	0-0	0	5.04	5.87
2009	Fla	NL	20	14	0	1	80.0	366	85	52	43	7	6	4	2	43	1	59	10	0	3	5	.375	0	0-0	1	4.90	4.84
2010	Fla	NL	9	7	0	1	32.2	171	51	34	31	6	5	2	1	26	2	28	5	0	1	5	.167	0	0-0	0	10.20	8.54
2011	Bos	AL	17	12	0	2	65.0	310	77	43	40	4	6	5	3	41	0	50	2	1	6	3	.667	0	0-0	0	6.48	5.54

Year	Team	Lg	G	GS	CG	GF	IP	BFP	H	R	ER	HR	SH	SF	HB	TBB	IBB	SO	WP	Bk	W	L	Pct	Sh	Sv-Op	Hld	ERC	ERA
2012	Bos	AL	53	0	0	4	40.1	169	28	15	15	3	0	3	2	20	1	51	1	0	3	2	.600	0	0-0	13	2.76	3.35
2013	Bos	AL	37	0	0	11	30.2	135	25	12	9	3	1	0	2	17	0	48	2	0	1	2	.333	0	0-1	6	3.83	2.64
2014	2 Tms	AL	73	0	0	15	62.1	242	33	16	14	3	2	2	5	17	2	103	3	0	5	5	.500	0	1-2	22	1.36	2.02
2015	NYY	AL	60	0	0	53	61.2	246	33	16	14	5	1	2	5	20	1	100	2	0	3	2	.600	0	36-38	0	1.61	2.04
2016	2 Tms	AL	70	0	0	23	74.1	275	42	13	12	8	1	1	2	9	0	123	1	0	10	1	.909	0	12-14	25	1.27	1.45
14	Bos	AL	50	0	0	12	42.1	170	25	13	11	2	2	2	4	13	2	69	2	0	3	5	.375	0	0-0	13	1.62	2.34
14	Bal	AL	23	0	0	3	20.0	72	8	3	3	1	0	0	1	4	0	34	1	0	2	0	1.000	0	1-2	9	0.86	1.35
16	NYY	AL	44	0	0	16	45.1	172	28	8	7	5	1	1	2	7	0	77	0	0	6	1	.857	0	9-11	16	1.55	1.39
16	Cle	AL	26	0	0	7	29.0	103	14	5	5	3	0	0	0	2	0	46	1	0	4	0	1.000	0	3-3	9	0.87	1.55
	Postseason		6	0	0	1	8.1	27	1	0	0	0	0	0	1	1	0	10	0	0	0	0	-	0	0-0	2	0.20	0.00
	11 ML YEARS		389	66	0	114	628.2	2766	575	331	295	58	35	27	35	298	11	713	35	2	43	41	.512	0	49-55	70	3.97	4.22

Brad Miller

Bats: L **Throws:** R **Pos:** SS-105;1B-39;PH-8;DH-7;LF-1

Ht: 6'2" **Wt:** 200 **Born:** 10/18/1989 **Age:** 27

									BATTING										RUNNING			AVERAGES			
Year	Team	Lg	G	AB	H	2B	3B	HR	(Hm | Rd)	TB	R	RBI	RC	TBB	IBB	SO	HBP	SH	SF	SB	CS	GDP	Avg	OBP	Slg	OPS
2013	Sea	AL	76	306	81	11	6	8	(3 | 5)	128	41	36	41	24	0	52	1	2	2	5	3	2	.265	.318	.418	.737
2014	Sea	AL	123	367	81	15	4	10	(4 | 6)	134	47	36	41	34	2	95	2	3	3	4	2	2	.221	.288	.365	.653
2015	Sea	AL	144	438	113	22	4	11	(6 | 5)	176	44	46	58	47	0	101	2	4	6	13	4	7	.258	.329	.402	.730
2016	TB	AL	152	548	133	29	6	30	(22 | 8)	264	73	81	74	47	0	149	3	0	3	6	4	5	.243	.304	.482	.786
	4 ML YEARS		495	1659	408	77	20	59	(35 | 24)	702	205	199	214	152	2	397	8	9	14	28	13	16	.246	.310	.423	.733

Justin Miller

Pitches: R **Bats:** R **Pos:** RP-40

Ht: 6'3" **Wt:** 215 **Born:** 6/13/1987 **Age:** 30

				HOW MUCH HE PITCHED						WHAT HE GAVE UP										THE RESULTS						
Year	Team	Lg	G	GS	CG	GF	IP	BFP	H	R	ER	HR	SH	SF	HB	TBB	IBB	SO	WP	Bk	W	L	Pct	Sh	Sv-Op	Hld	ERC	ERA
2016	Albq*	AAA	12	0	0	2	12.0	56	15	10	9	1	0	0	0	4	0	8	0	0	0	0	-	0	0--	-	4.27	6.75
2014	Det	AL	8	0	0	4	12.1	53	14	9	7	2	1	2	0	2	0	5	0	0	1	0	1.000	0	0-0	0	4.21	5.11
2015	Col	NL	34	0	0	9	13.1	129	21	15	15	2	0	0	0	11	0	38	2	0	3	3	.500	0	1-2	7	1.75	4.05
2016	Col	NL	40	0	0	13	42.2	194	50	27	27	6	0	3	2	20	0	45	3	1	1	1	.500	0	0-0	1	5.92	5.70
	3 ML YEARS		82	0	0	26	88.1	376	85	51	49	10	1	5	2	33	0	88	5	1	5	4	.556	0	1-2	8	3.96	4.99

Mike Miller

Bats: R **Throws:** R **Pos:** 2B-1

Ht: 5'9" **Wt:** 170 **Born:** 9/27/1989 **Age:** 27

									BATTING										RUNNING			AVERAGES			
Year	Team	Lg	G	AB	H	2B	3B	HR	(Hm | Rd)	TB	R	RBI	RC	TBB	IBB	SO	HBP	SH	SF	SB	CS	GDP	Avg	OBP	Slg	OPS
2012	Lowell	A-	66	264	69	14	1	1	(- | -)	88	39	15	35	29	0	35	1	1	0	21	3	7	.261	.337	.333	.670
2013	Grnvlle	A	15	45	16	6	0	0	(- | -)	22	8	2	10	5	0	5	2	1	0	3	1	1	.356	.442	.489	.931
2014	Salem	A+	49	192	59	8	0	0	(- | -)	67	24	18	26	15	0	25	3	6	0	7	4	6	.307	.367	.349	.716
2014	Portlnd	AA	23	93	28	4	0	3	(- | -)	41	15	12	15	6	0	14	2	0	0	3	1	2	.301	.356	.441	.797
2015	Portlnd	AA	40	165	45	9	2	1	(- | -)	61	26	12	21	11	0	21	2	2	3	6	2	3	.273	.320	.370	.690
2015	Pwtckt	AAA	74	247	54	10	1	3	(- | -)	75	17	19	19	14	0	34	0	4	3	6	3	3	.219	.258	.304	.561
2016	Pwtckt	AAA	90	312	71	13	1	1	(- | -)	89	38	20	28	27	0	40	3	5	2	12	4	13	.228	.294	.285	.579
2016	Bos	AL	1	1	0	0	0	0	(0 | 0)	0	0	0	0	0	0	0	0	0	0	0	0	0	.000	.000	.000	.000

Shelby Miller

Pitches: R **Bats:** R **Pos:** SP-20

Ht: 6'3" **Wt:** 225 **Born:** 10/10/1990 **Age:** 26

				HOW MUCH HE PITCHED						WHAT HE GAVE UP										THE RESULTS						
Year	Team	Lg	G	GS	CG	GF	IP	BFP	H	R	ER	HR	SH	SF	HB	TBB	IBB	SO	WP	Bk	W	L	Pct	Sh	Sv-Op	Hld	ERC	ERA
2016	Reno*	AAA	8	8	1	0	50.2	209	55	24	22	4	2	0	1	10	0	55	1	0	5	1	.833	1	0--	-	3.78	3.91
2012	StL	NL	6	1	0	1	13.2	54	9	2	2	0	0	0	1	4	0	16	0	0	1	0	1.000	0	0-0	1	1.65	1.32
2013	StL	NL	31	31	1	0	173.1	722	152	65	59	20	7	3	5	57	0	169	2	0	15	9	.625	1	0-0	0	3.34	3.06
2014	StL	NL	32	31	1	0	183.0	764	160	78	76	22	7	4	2	73	4	127	4	0	10	9	.526	1	0-0	0	3.56	3.74
2015	Atl	NL	33	33	2	0	205.1	860	183	82	69	13	8	4	6	73	8	171	5	2	6	17	.261	2	0-0	0	3.12	3.02
2016	Ari	NL	20	20	1	0	101.0	460	127	72	69	14	3	3	2	42	3	70	3	0	3	12	.200	1	0-0	0	6.03	6.15
	Postseason		5	2	0	0	13.2	61	16	8	8	1	1	1	1	6	0	12	0	0	0	0	-	0	0-0	1	5.46	5.27
	5 ML YEARS		122	116	5	1	676.1	2860	631	299	275	69	25	14	16	249	15	553	14	2	35	47	.427	5	0-0	1	3.66	3.66

Alec Mills

Pitches: R **Bats:** R **Pos:** RP-3

Ht: 6'4" **Wt:** 190 **Born:** 11/30/1991 **Age:** 25

				HOW MUCH HE PITCHED						WHAT HE GAVE UP										THE RESULTS						
Year	Team	Lg	G	GS	CG	GF	IP	BFP	H	R	ER	HR	SH	SF	HB	TBB	IBB	SO	WP	Bk	W	L	Pct	Sh	Sv-Op	Hld	ERC	ERA
2012	Idaho	R+	17	7	0	4	50.2	233	58	33	26	7	1	1	5	17	1	50	9	0	1	4	.200	0	3--	-	5.15	4.62
2013	Lxngtn	A	18	3	0	13	45.1	175	28	11	8	1	1	0	2	9	0	47	5	0	2	3	.400	0	6--	-	1.32	1.59
2014	2 Tms	Low	14	13	0	0	57.1	221	45	18	15	0	2	3	3	14	0	47	4	0	4	3	.571	0	0--	-	2.07	2.35
2015	Wilmg	A+	21	21	1	0	113.1	472	122	42	38	3	1	3	3	14	0	111	6	2	7	7	.500	0	0--	-	3.02	3.02
2016	NWArk	AA	12	12	0	0	67.2	258	57	19	18	2	1	0	1	12	0	68	4	0	2	4	.333	0	0--	-	2.18	2.39
2016	Omha	AAA	12	11	0	0	58.0	250	62	29	27	8	0	1	2	19	1	54	3	1	4	3	.571	0	0--	-	4.59	4.19
2016	KC	AL	3	0	0	2	3.1	19	3	5	5	0	0	1	0	5	0	4	0	0	0	0	-	0	0-0	0	8.02	13.50

Tommy Milone

Pitches: L Bats: L Pos: SP-12; RP-7 — mah-LONE — Ht: 6'0" Wt: 220 Born: 2/16/1987 Age: 30

Year	Team	Lg	G	GS	CG	GF	IP	BFP	H	R	ER	HR	SH	SF	HB	TBB	IBB	SO	WP	Bk	W	L	Pct	Sh	Sv-Op	Hld	ERC	ERA
2016	Roch*	AAA	7	7	0	0	48.2	188	41	11	9	4	1	0	1	4	0	41	1	0	4	0	1.000	0	0--	-	2.08	1.66
2011	Was	NL	5	5	0	0	26.0	110	28	11	11	2	3	2	2	4	2	15	0	0	1	0	1.000	0	0-0	0	3.55	3.81
2012	Oak	AL	31	31	1	0	190.0	791	207	90	79	24	3	3	4	36	2	137	2	0	13	10	.565	0	0-0	0	4.04	3.74
2013	Oak	AL	28	26	1	0	156.1	667	160	83	72	25	0	6	2	39	2	126	1	0	12	9	.571	0	0-0	0	3.98	4.14
2014	2 Tms	AL	22	21	0	1	118.0	519	128	63	55	16	1	2	5	37	2	75	0	0	6	4	.600	0	0-0	0	4.55	4.19
2015	Min	AL	24	23	0	1	128.2	543	128	64	56	17	6	7	1	36	1	91	3	0	9	5	.643	0	1-1	0	3.79	3.92
2016	Min	AL	19	12	0	3	69.1	311	84	53	44	15	4	3	1	22	3	49	3	1	3	5	.375	0	0-0	1	5.77	5.71
14	Oak	AL	16	16	0	0	96.1	405	91	42	38	12	1	2	4	26	2	61	0	0	6	3	.667	0	0-0	0	3.53	3.55
14	Min	AL	6	5	0	1	21.2	114	37	21	17	4	0	0	1	11	0	14	0	0	0	1	.000	0	0-0	0	9.76	7.06
	Postseason		1	1	0	0	6.0	25	5	1	1	0	0	0	1	1	0	6	1	0	0	0	-	0	0-0	0	2.26	1.50
	6 ML YEARS		129	118	2	5	688.1	2941	735	364	317	99	17	23	15	174	12	493	9	1	44	33	.571	0	1-1	1	4.21	4.14

Juan Minaya

Pitches: R Bats: R Pos: RP-11 — Ht: 6'4" Wt: 210 Born: 9/18/1990 Age: 26

Year	Team	Lg	G	GS	CG	GF	IP	BFP	H	R	ER	HR	SH	SF	HB	TBB	IBB	SO	WP	Bk	W	L	Pct	Sh	Sv-Op	Hld	ERC	ERA
2012	TriCity	A-	17	2	0	5	36.2	165	34	21	19	0	0	1	4	17	0	31	3	0	2	2	.500	0	0--	-	3.51	4.66
2013	QuadC	A	24	5	0	15	54.2	255	63	34	29	5	3	4	4	23	1	57	3	0	3	6	.333	0	8--	-	5.08	4.77
2014	Lancst	A+	29	1	0	10	45.0	198	43	25	22	6	1	1	0	22	1	53	5	1	2	3	.400	0	1--	-	4.33	4.40
2014	CpChr	AA	6	0	0	0	8.2	38	9	3	3	1	0	0	0	4	0	11	1	0	0	0	-	0	0--	-	4.68	3.12
2015	CpChr	AA	29	0	0	10	44.1	190	43	16	16	2	1	2	5	16	1	48	9	0	1	0	1.000	0	1--	-	3.82	3.25
2015	Fresno	AAA	6	0	0	0	10.1	39	6	1	1	0	1	0	1	5	0	11	1	0	0	0	-	0	0--	-	2.14	0.87
2016	Fresno	AAA	17	0	0	5	25.1	109	25	15	11	1	2	2	1	10	1	19	0	0	1	3	.250	0	0--	-	3.66	3.91
2016	Charllt	AAA	17	0	0	5	26.2	114	23	11	10	2	1	0	1	10	2	28	0	0	4	3	.571	0	1--	-	3.03	3.38
2016	CWS	AL	11	0	0	3	10.1	47	10	6	5	0	0	0	0	5	0	6	0	0	1	0	1.000	0	0-0	0	4.19	4.35

Ariel Miranda

Pitches: L Bats: L Pos: SP-10; RP-2 — Ht: 6'2" Wt: 190 Born: 1/10/1989 Age: 28

Year	Team	Lg	G	GS	CG	GF	IP	BFP	H	R	ER	HR	SH	SF	HB	TBB	IBB	SO	WP	Bk	W	L	Pct	Sh	Sv-Op	Hld	ERC	ERA
2015	2 Tms	Low	6	6	0	0	25.0	100	17	10	10	2	1	0	1	8	0	30	0	1	1	1	.500	0	0--	-	2.15	3.60
2015	Bowie	AA	8	8	0	0	45.0	193	40	23	18	1	2	5	2	18	0	41	3	0	5	2	.714	0	0--	-	3.07	3.60
2016	Norfolk	AAA	19	19	0	0	100.2	420	95	47	44	11	3	3	2	31	0	87	1	0	4	7	.364	0	0--	-	3.57	3.93
2016	2 Tms	AL	12	10	0	1	58.0	232	47	28	25	12	0	2	0	18	0	44	2	0	5	2	.714	0	0-0	0	3.44	3.88
16	Bal	AL	1	0	0	0	2.0	11	4	3	3	0	0	0	0	0	0	4	0	0	0	0	-	0	0-0	0	6.75	13.50
16	Sea	AL	11	10	0	1	56.0	221	43	25	22	12	0	2	0	18	0	40	2	0	5	2	.714	0	0-0	0	3.32	3.54

Bryan Mitchell

Pitches: R Bats: L Pos: SP-5 — Ht: 6'3" Wt: 210 Born: 4/19/1991 Age: 26

Year	Team	Lg	G	GS	CG	GF	IP	BFP	H	R	ER	HR	SH	SF	HB	TBB	IBB	SO	WP	Bk	W	L	Pct	Sh	Sv-Op	Hld	ERC	ERA
2014	NYY	AL	3	1	0	1	11.0	44	10	3	3	0	0	0	2	3	0	7	0	0	0	1	.000	0	0-0	0	3.34	2.45
2015	NYY	AL	20	2	0	8	29.2	143	37	24	21	4	0	0	2	16	1	29	6	0	0	2	.000	0	1-1	1	6.51	6.37
2016	NYY	AL	5	5	0	0	25.0	107	26	13	9	1	1	0	0	12	0	11	0	0	1	2	.333	0	0-0	0	4.32	3.24
	3 ML YEARS		28	8	0	9	65.2	294	73	40	33	5	1	0	4	31	1	47	6	0	1	5	.167	0	1-1	1	5.12	4.52

Yadier Molina

Bats: R Throws: R Pos: C-146;1B-2;PH-2 — YAH-dee-air — Ht: 5'11" Wt: 205 Born: 7/13/1982 Age: 34

Year	Team	Lg	G	AB	H	2B	3B	HR	(Hm	Rd)	TB	R	RBI	RC	TBB	IBB	SO	HBP	SH	SF	SB	CS	GDP	Avg	OBP	Slg	OPS
2004	StL	NL	51	135	36	6	0	2	(1	1)	48	12	15	15	13	3	20	0	2	1	0	1	4	.267	.329	.356	.684
2005	StL	NL	114	385	97	15	1	8	(6	2)	138	36	49	46	23	3	30	2	8	3	2	3	10	.252	.295	.358	.654
2006	StL	NL	129	417	90	26	0	6	(2	4)	134	29	49	35	26	2	41	8	8	2	1	2	15	.216	.274	.321	.595
2007	StL	NL	111	353	97	15	0	6	(4	2)	130	30	40	38	34	5	43	3	2	4	1	1	18	.275	.340	.368	.708
2008	StL	NL	124	444	135	18	0	7	(2	5)	174	37	56	57	32	4	29	1	3	5	0	2	21	.304	.349	.392	.740
2009	StL	NL	140	481	141	23	1	6	(5	1)	184	45	54	64	50	2	39	6	1	9	9	3	27	.293	.366	.383	.749
2010	StL	NL	136	465	122	19	0	6	(1	5)	159	34	62	55	42	6	51	7	2	5	8	4	19	.262	.329	.342	.671
2011	StL	NL	139	475	145	32	1	14	(5	9)	221	55	65	64	33	4	44	1	5	4	4	5	21	.305	.349	.465	.814
2012	StL	NL	138	505	159	28	0	22	(9	13)	253	65	76	91	45	4	55	5	3	5	12	3	10	.315	.373	.501	.874
2013	StL	NL	136	505	161	44	0	12	(5	7)	241	68	80	84	30	4	55	3	0	3	3	2	14	.319	.359	.477	.836
2014	StL	NL	110	404	114	21	0	7	(3	4)	156	40	38	47	28	4	55	6	1	6	1	1	14	.282	.333	.386	.719
2015	StL	NL	136	488	132	23	2	4	(1	3)	171	34	61	48	32	3	59	0	1	9	3	1	16	.270	.310	.350	.660
2016	StL	NL	147	534	164	38	1	8	(4	4)	228	56	58	74	39	1	63	6	0	2	3	2	22	.307	.360	.427	.787
	Postseason		89	315	90	17	0	3	(2	1)	116	25	31	32	25	5	38	1	1	1	1	1	11	.286	.339	.368	.707
	13 ML YEARS		1611	5591	1593	308	6	108	(50	58)	2237	541	703	718	427	45	584	48	41	50	47	30	211	.285	.338	.400	.738

Dustin Molleken

Pitches: R Bats: L Pos: RP-4   Ht: 6'4" Wt: 230 Born: 8/21/1984 Age: 32

			HOW MUCH HE PITCHED							WHAT HE GAVE UP										THE RESULTS						
Year	Team	Lg	G	GS	CG	GF	IP	BFP	H	R	ER	HR	SH	SF	HB	TBB	IBB	SO	WP	Bk	W	L	Pct	Sh	Sv-Op	Hld	ERC	ERA
2012	ColSpr	AAA	40	0	0	18	48.2	222	58	33	28	5	3	2	5	18	2	36	4	1	3	0	1.000	0	1--	-	5.43	5.18
2013	Nashv	AAA	10	0	0	6	14.1	56	9	5	5	0	0	0	1	4	0	13	0	0	0	0	-	0	1--	-	1.51	3.14
2014	Nashv	AAA	54	0	0	15	74.1	328	71	44	40	7	4	2	5	35	2	89	6	0	5	2	.714	0	4--	-	4.26	4.84
2015	Clmbs	AAA	40	3	0	17	52.2	224	45	21	19	4	2	2	2	27	2	52	1	0	5	3	.625	0	1--	-	3.68	3.25
2016	Toledo	AAA	42	5	0	10	60.1	252	49	26	24	4	1	3	2	30	1	56	5	0	2	4	.333	0	1--	-	3.37	3.58
2016	Det	AL	4	0	0	1	8.1	42	12	4	4	0	0	1	0	5	0	8	2	0	0	0	-	0	0-0	0	6.52	4.32

Yoan Moncada

Bats: B Throws: R Pos: 3B-5;DH-3;PR-2;PH-1   yo-AHN   Ht: 6'2" Wt: 205 Born: 5/27/1995 Age: 22

						BATTING																RUNNING			AVERAGES			
Year	Team	Lg	G	AB	H	2B	3B	HR	(Hm	Rd)	TB	R	RBI	RC	TBB	IBB	SO	HBP	SH	SF	SB	CS	GDP	Avg	OBP	Slg	OPS
2015	Grnvlle	A	81	306	85	19	3	8	(-	-)	134	61	38	62	42	1	83	10	2	3	49	3	3	.278	.380	.438	.817
2016	Salem	A+	61	228	70	25	3	4	(-	-)	113	57	34	55	45	3	60	5	3	3	36	8	4	.307	.427	.496	.923
2016	Portlnd	AA	45	177	49	6	3	11	(-	-)	94	37	28	36	27	1	64	2	1	0	9	4	2	.277	.379	.531	.910
2016	Bos	AL	8	19	4	1	0	0	(0	0)	5	3	1	0	1	0	12	0	0	0	0	0	0	.211	.250	.263	.513

Raul Mondesi

Bats: B Throws: R Pos: 2B-42;SS-7;PH-1;PR-1   Ht: 6'1" Wt: 185 Born: 7/27/1995 Age: 21

						BATTING																RUNNING			AVERAGES			
Year	Team	Lg	G	AB	H	2B	3B	HR	(Hm	Rd)	TB	R	RBI	RC	TBB	IBB	SO	HBP	SH	SF	SB	CS	GDP	Avg	OBP	Slg	OPS
2012	Idaho	R+	50	207	60	7	2	3	(-	-)	80	35	30	30	19	1	65	1	1	4	11	2	5	.290	.346	.386	.733
2013	Lxngtn	A	125	482	126	13	7	7	(-	-)	174	61	47	57	34	1	118	2	15	3	24	10	5	.261	.311	.361	.672
2014	Wilmg	A+	110	435	92	14	12	8	(-	-)	154	54	33	41	24	0	122	3	8	2	17	4	7	.211	.256	.354	.610
2015	NWArk	AA	81	304	74	11	5	6	(-	-)	113	36	33	34	17	0	88	0	12	5	19	6	5	.243	.279	.372	.651
2016	NWArk	AA	29	116	31	5	1	5	(-	-)	53	20	17	21	13	1	30	0	1	1	17	1	0	.267	.338	.457	.795
2016	Omha	AAA	14	56	17	2	4	1	(-	-)	30	9	9	10	2	0	19	0	3	0	5	0	0	.304	.328	.536	.863
2016	KC	AL	47	135	25	1	3	2	(0	2)	38	16	13	9	6	0	48	2	6	0	9	1	1	.185	.231	.281	.512
	Postseason		1	1	0	0	0	0	(0	0)	0	0	0	0	0	0	1	0	0	0	0	0	0	.000	.000	.000	.000

Miguel Montero

Bats: L Throws: R Pos: C-71;PH-19;DH-1   Ht: 5'11" Wt: 210 Born: 7/9/1983 Age: 33

						BATTING																RUNNING			AVERAGES			
Year	Team	Lg	G	AB	H	2B	3B	HR	(Hm	Rd)	TB	R	RBI	RC	TBB	IBB	SO	HBP	SH	SF	SB	CS	GDP	Avg	OBP	Slg	OPS
2006	Ari	NL	6	16	4	1	0	0	(0	0)	5	0	3	2	1	0	3	0	0	0	0	0	0	.250	.294	.313	.607
2007	Ari	NL	84	214	48	7	0	10	(7	3)	85	30	37	19	20	2	35	3	1	6	0	0	7	.224	.292	.397	.689
2008	Ari	NL	70	184	47	16	1	5	(1	4)	80	24	18	21	19	3	49	2	1	1	0	0	1	.255	.330	.435	.765
2009	Ari	NL	128	425	125	30	0	16	(5	11)	203	61	59	65	38	5	78	3	2	2	1	2	6	.294	.355	.478	.832
2010	Ari	NL	85	297	79	20	2	9	(0	9)	130	36	43	38	29	3	71	2	0	3	0	1	10	.266	.332	.438	.770
2011	Ari	NL	140	493	139	36	1	18	(8	10)	231	65	86	84	47	10	97	8	1	4	1	1	14	.282	.351	.469	.820
2012	Ari	NL	141	486	139	25	2	15	(4	11)	213	65	88	92	73	6	130	12	0	2	0	0	15	.286	.391	.438	.829
2013	Ari	NL	116	413	95	14	0	11	(8	3)	142	44	42	42	51	4	110	5	0	6	0	0	18	.230	.318	.344	.662
2014	Ari	NL	136	489	119	23	0	13	(5	8)	181	40	72	63	56	11	97	9	0	4	0	4	12	.243	.329	.370	.699
2015	ChC	NL	113	347	86	11	0	15	(8	7)	142	36	53	52	49	5	103	4	0	3	1	1	9	.248	.345	.409	.754
2016	ChC	NL	86	241	52	8	1	8	(2	6)	86	33	33	31	38	5	58	3	0	2	1	0	8	.216	.327	.357	.684
	Postseason		17	48	10	2	0	0	(0	0)	12	5	3	3	7	2	16	0	0	0	0	0	0	.208	.309	.250	.559
	11 ML YEARS		1105	3605	933	191	7	120	(48	72)	1498	434	534	509	421	54	831	51	5	35	4	9	100	.259	.342	.416	.757

Rafael Montero

Pitches: R Bats: R Pos: RP-6; SP-3   Ht: 6'0" Wt: 185 Born: 10/17/1990 Age: 26

						HOW MUCH HE PITCHED							WHAT HE GAVE UP										THE RESULTS						
Year	Team	Lg	G	GS	CG	GF	IP	BFP	H	R	ER	HR	SH	SF	HB	TBB	IBB	SO	WP	Bk	W	L	Pct	Sh	Sv-Op	Hld	ERC	ERA
2016	LsVgs*	AAA	16	16	0	0	80.0	385	111	70	64	12	2	5	0	40	3	68	3	1	4	6	.400	0	0--	-	7.12	7.20
2016	Bnghtn*	AA	9	9	1	0	49.0	200	35	17	12	4	1	1	4	19	0	40	1	1	4	3	.571	0	0--	-	2.73	2.20
2014	NYM	NL	10	8	0	1	44.1	194	44	21	20	8	0	0	0	23	0	42	0	0	1	3	.250	0	0-0	0	5.16	4.06
2015	NYM	NL	5	1	0	1	10.0	46	9	6	5	0	1	0	0	5	3	13	0	0	1	0	1.000	0	0-0	1	2.50	4.50
2016	NYM	NL	9	3	0	1	19.0	93	23	17	17	4	0	0	0	16	1	20	2	0	0	1	.000	0	0-0	0	8.15	8.05
	3 ML YEARS		24	12	0	3	73.1	333	76	44	42	12	1	0	0	44	4	75	2	0	1	5	.167	0	0-0	1	5.48	5.15

Mike Montgomery

Pitches: L Bats: L Pos: RP-42; SP-7   Ht: 6'5" Wt: 215 Born: 7/1/1989 Age: 27

						HOW MUCH HE PITCHED							WHAT HE GAVE UP										THE RESULTS						
Year	Team	Lg	G	GS	CG	GF	IP	BFP	H	R	ER	HR	SH	SF	HB	TBB	IBB	SO	WP	Bk	W	L	Pct	Sh	Sv-Op	Hld	ERC	ERA
2012	Omha	AAA	17	17	1	0	91.2	428	110	74	58	12	7	6	3	43	0	67	4	1	3	6	.333	0	0--	-	5.81	5.69
2012	NWArk	AA	10	10	0	0	58.0	259	69	44	43	12	2	2	3	21	0	44	5	0	2	6	.250	0	0--	-	6.12	6.67
2013	Drham	AAA	20	19	1	0	108.2	474	111	65	57	9	4	2	6	48	0	77	15	0	7	8	.467	0	0--	-	4.52	4.72
2014	Drham	AAA	25	25	0	0	126.0	539	117	68	60	9	2	6	5	48	0	98	11	1	10	5	.667	0	0--	-	3.55	4.29
2015	Tacom	AAA	11	11	0	0	65.1	270	59	32	30	3	2	2	3	19	0	58	7	0	4	3	.571	0	0--	-	2.98	4.13
2015	Sea	AL	16	16	2	0	90.0	395	92	49	46	11	0	4	9	37	1	64	10	0	4	6	.400	2	0-0	0	4.56	4.60
2016	2 Tms		49	7	0	18	100.0	414	79	33	28	8	3	2	10	38	2	92	10	0	4	5	.444	0	0-0	5	3.13	2.52
16	Sea	AL	32	2	0	13	61.2	250	49	18	16	3	2	1	6	18	2	54	5	0	3	4	.429	0	0-0	3	2.61	2.34
16	ChC	NL	17	5	0	5	38.1	164	30	15	12	5	1	1	4	20	0	38	5	0	1	1	.500	0	0-0	2	4.01	2.82
	2 ML YEARS		65	23	2	18	190.0	809	171	82	74	19	3	6	19	75	3	156	20	0	8	11	.421	2	0-0	5	3.79	3.51

Adam Moore

Bats: R Throws: R Pos: C-9   Ht: 6'3" Wt: 220 Born: 5/8/1984 Age: 33

								BATTING													RUNNING			AVERAGES			
Year	Team	Lg	G	AB	H	2B	3B	HR	(Hm	Rd)	TB	R	RBI	RC	TBB	IBB	SO	HBP	SH	SF	SB	CS	GDP	Avg	OBP	Slg	OPS
2016	Clmbs*	AAA	86	299	74	14	0	7	(-	-)	109	35	31	36	26	1	63	4	0	0	0	0	16	.247	.316	.365	.681
2009	Sea	AL	6	23	5	1	0	1	(1	0)	9	4	2	2	0	0	7	1	0	0	1	0	1	.217	.250	.391	.641
2010	Sea	AL	60	205	40	6	0	4	(1	3)	58	12	15	9	8	1	63	2	1	2	0	1	3	.195	.230	.283	.513
2011	Sea	AL	2	6	1	1	0	0	(0	0)	2	0	0	0	0	0	2	0	0	0	0	0	0	.167	.167	.333	.500
2012	KC	AL	4	11	2	1	0	1	(1	0)	6	1	2	2	1	0	3	0	0	0	0	0	0	.182	.250	.545	.795
2013	KC	AL	5	10	3	1	0	0	(0	0)	4	1	0	1	1	0	2	0	0	0	1	0	0	.300	.364	.400	.764
2014	SD	NL	9	10	2	1	0	0	(0	0)	3	1	1	2	2	1	5	0	0	0	0	0	0	.200	.333	.300	.633
2015	Cle	AL	1	4	1	0	0	0	(0	0)	1	0	1	0	0	0	2	0	0	0	0	0	0	.250	.250	.250	.500
2016	Cle	AL	9	5	0	0	0	0	(0	0)	0	0	0	0	0	0	4	0	0	0	0	0	0	.000	.000	.000	.000
	8 ML YEARS		96	274	54	11	0	6	(3	3)	83	19	21	16	12	2	88	3	1	2	2	1	4	.197	.237	.303	.540

Matt Moore

Pitches: L Bats: L Pos: SP-33   Ht: 6'3" Wt: 210 Born: 6/18/1989 Age: 28

			HOW MUCH HE PITCHED						WHAT HE GAVE UP											THE RESULTS					
Year	Team	Lg	G	GS	CG	GF	IP	BFP	H	R	ER	HR	SH	SF	HB	TBB	IBB	SO	WP	Bk	W	L	Pct	Sh	Sv-Op	Hld	ERC	ERA
2011	TB	AL	3	1	0	0	9.1	40	9	3	3	1	0	0	0	3	0	15	2	0	1	0	1.000	0	0-0	1	3.54	2.89
2012	TB	AL	31	31	0	0	177.1	759	158	85	75	18	3	4	7	81	5	175	8	1	11	11	.500	0	0-0	0	3.83	3.81
2013	TB	AL	27	27	1	0	150.1	642	119	58	55	14	5	6	4	76	1	143	17	1	17	4	.810	1	0-0	0	3.36	3.29
2014	TB	AL	2	2	0	0	10.0	44	10	3	3	1	0	0	0	5	0	6	0	0	0	2	.000	0	0-0	0	4.48	2.70
2015	TB	AL	12	12	0	0	63.0	278	74	40	38	9	0	3	4	23	1	46	6	0	3	4	.429	0	0-0	0	5.63	5.43
2016	2 Tms		33	33	0	0	198.1	838	184	93	90	25	4	4	6	72	1	178	6	1	13	12	.520	0	0-0	0	3.83	4.08
16	TB	AL	21	21	0	0	130.0	549	125	62	59	20	3	2	5	40	0	109	3	1	7	7	.500	0	0-0	0	4.02	4.08
16	SF	NL	12	12	0	0	68.1	289	59	31	31	5	1	2	1	32	1	69	3	0	6	5	.545	0	0-0	0	3.47	4.08
	Postseason		4	2	0	0	16.1	69	12	9	8	1	0	0	2	6	1	15	2	0	1	1	.500	0	0-0	0	2.60	4.41
	6 ML YEARS		108	106	1	0	608.1	2601	554	282	264	68	12	17	21	260	8	563	39	3	45	33	.577	1	0-0	1	3.89	3.91

Franklin Morales

Pitches: L Bats: L Pos: RP-5   Ht: 6'1" Wt: 210 Born: 1/24/1986 Age: 31

			HOW MUCH HE PITCHED						WHAT HE GAVE UP											THE RESULTS					
Year	Team	Lg	G	GS	CG	GF	IP	BFP	H	R	ER	HR	SH	SF	HB	TBB	IBB	SO	WP	Bk	W	L	Pct	Sh	Sv-Op	Hld	ERC	ERA
2016	Buffalo*	AAA	9	0	0	0	9.0	34	6	2	2	1	0	0	0	4	0	6	2	0	1	0	1.000	0	0- -	-	2.79	2.00
2007	Col	NL	8	8	0	0	39.1	163	34	15	15	2	4	2	2	14	1	26	0	0	3	2	.600	0	0-0	0	3.04	3.43
2008	Col	NL	5	5	0	0	25.1	120	28	18	18	2	2	2	1	17	2	9	1	3	1	2	.333	0	0-0	0	5.58	6.39
2009	Col	NL	40	2	0	14	40.0	179	38	22	20	4	3	0	1	23	4	41	2	0	3	2	.600	0	7-8	7	4.38	4.50
2010	Col	NL	35	0	0	15	28.2	140	28	22	20	5	1	3	2	24	2	27	3	2	0	4	.000	0	3-6	1	6.53	6.28
2011	2 Tms		50	0	0	13	46.1	193	40	21	19	6	2	1	2	19	1	42	2	1	1	2	.333	0	0-0	10	3.77	3.69
2012	Bos	AL	37	9	0	5	76.1	325	64	38	32	11	0	3	6	30	3	76	3	5	3	4	.429	0	1-1	8	3.68	3.77
2013	Bos	AL	20	1	0	3	25.1	112	24	13	13	2	0	0	3	15	2	21	3	0	2	2	.500	0	0-1	4	4.86	4.62
2014	Col	NL	38	22	0	4	142.1	646	166	90	85	24	7	7	6	65	4	100	5	4	6	9	.400	0	0-0	0	5.97	5.37
2015	KC	AL	67	0	0	12	62.1	258	58	24	22	4	2	2	4	14	0	41	6	2	4	2	.667	0	0-1	8	3.04	3.18
2016	Tor	AL	5	0	0	2	4.0	16	3	4	4	1	0	0	0	2	0	2	0	1	0	0	—	0	0-0	0	4.30	9.00
11	Col	NL	14	0	0	4	14.0	59	10	6	6	2	1	1	0	8	1	11	1	0	0	1	.000	0	0-0	2	3.36	3.86
11	Bos	AL	36	0	0	9	32.1	134	30	15	13	4	1	0	2	11	0	31	1	1	1	1	.500	0	0-0	8	3.96	3.62
	Postseason		14	2	0	2	16.1	83	23	17	17	1	0	0	3	10	1	9	0	1	0	0	—	0	0-1	1	7.77	9.37
	10 ML YEARS		305	47	0	68	490.0	2152	483	267	248	61	21	19	28	223	19	385	25	18	23	30	.434	0	11-17	38	4.57	4.56

Kendrys Morales

Bats: B Throws: R Pos: DH-138;1B-7;RF-5;PH-5   KEN-dreez   Ht: 6'1" Wt: 225 Born: 6/20/1983 Age: 34

								BATTING													RUNNING			AVERAGES			
Year	Team	Lg	G	AB	H	2B	3B	HR	(Hm	Rd)	TB	R	RBI	RC	TBB	IBB	SO	HBP	SH	SF	SB	CS	GDP	Avg	OBP	Slg	OPS
2006	LAA	AL	57	197	46	10	1	5	(1	4)	73	21	22	19	17	1	28	0	0	1	1	1	11	.234	.293	.371	.664
2007	LAA	AL	43	119	35	10	0	4	(2	2)	57	12	15	15	6	2	21	1	0	0	0	1	5	.294	.333	.479	.812
2008	LAA	AL	27	61	13	2	0	3	(0	3)	24	7	8	3	4	0	7	1	0	0	0	1	3	.213	.273	.393	.666
2009	LAA	AL	152	566	173	43	2	34	(21	13)	322	86	108	105	46	10	117	2	0	8	3	7	15	.306	.355	.569	.924
2010	LAA	AL	51	193	56	5	0	11	(7	4)	94	29	39	34	12	3	31	5	0	1	0	1	5	.290	.346	.487	.833
2012	LAA	AL	134	484	132	26	1	22	(10	12)	226	61	73	68	31	1	116	4	0	3	0	1	17	.273	.320	.467	.787
2013	Sea	AL	156	602	167	34	0	23	(12	11)	270	64	80	85	49	6	114	5	0	1	0	0	21	.277	.336	.449	.785
2014	2 Tms		98	367	80	20	0	8	(4	4)	124	28	42	29	27	3	68	3	0	4	0	0	12	.218	.274	.338	.612
2015	KC	AL	158	569	165	41	2	22	(10	12)	276	81	106	98	58	4	103	8	0	4	0	0	24	.290	.362	.485	.847
2016	KC	AL	154	558	147	24	0	30	(12	18)	261	65	93	86	48	2	120	7	0	5	0	0	20	.263	.327	.468	.795
14	Min	AL	39	154	36	11	0	1	(0	1)	50	12	18	11	6	1	27	0	0	2	0	0	4	.234	.259	.325	.584
14	Sea	AL	59	213	44	9	0	7	(4	3)	74	16	24	18	21	2	41	3	0	2	0	0	8	.207	.285	.347	.632
	Postseason		32	98	22	1	0	6	(4	2)	41	8	17	12	6	0	20	1	0	2	0	0	1	.224	.271	.418	.689
	10 ML YEARS		1030	3716	1014	215	6	162	(79	83)	1727	454	586	542	298	32	725	36	0	27	4	12	127	.273	.331	.465	.795

Colin Moran

Bats: L Throws: R Pos: 3B-8;PH-1   Ht: 6'4" Wt: 204 Born: 10/1/1992 Age: 24

								BATTING													RUNNING			AVERAGES			
Year	Team	Lg	G	AB	H	2B	3B	HR	(Hm	Rd)	TB	R	RBI	RC	TBB	IBB	SO	HBP	SH	SF	SB	CS	GDP	Avg	OBP	Slg	OPS
2013	Grnsbr	A	42	154	46	8	1	4	(-	-)	68	19	23	25	15	0	25	1	0	5	1	0	2	.299	.354	.442	.796
2014	Jupiter	A+	89	361	106	21	0	5	(-	-)	142	34	33	50	28	1	53	0	0	3	1	2	10	.294	.342	.393	.735

Year Team	Lg	G	AB	H	2B	3B	HR	(Hm	Rd)	TB	R	RBI	RC	TBB	IBB	SO	HBP	SH	SF	SB	CS	GDP	Avg	OBP	Slg	OPS
2014 CpChr	AA	28	112	34	6	0	2	(-	-)	46	12	22	16	9	2	23	0	0	2	0	1	2	.304	.350	.411	.760
2015 CpChr	AA	96	366	112	25	2	9	(-	-)	168	47	67	66	43	1	79	4	0	4	1	0	11	.306	.381	.459	.840
2016 Fresno	AAA	117	459	119	18	1	10	(-	-)	169	50	69	58	47	1	124	2	0	3	3	2	10	.259	.329	.368	.697
2016 Hou	AL	9	23	3	1	0	0	(0	0)	4	1	2	0	1	0	8	1	0	0	0	0	4	.130	.200	.174	.374

Mitch Moreland

Bats: L **Throws:** L **Pos:** 1B-139;PH-14;DH-5   **Ht:** 6'2" **Wt:** 230 **Born:** 9/6/1985 **Age:** 31

Year Team	Lg	G	AB	H	2B	3B	HR	(Hm	Rd)	TB	R	RBI	RC	TBB	IBB	SO	HBP	SH	SF	SB	CS	GDP	Avg	OBP	Slg	OPS
2010 Tex	AL	47	145	37	4	0	9	(3	6)	68	20	25	27	25	5	36	1	0	2	3	1	3	.255	.364	.469	.833
2011 Tex	AL	134	464	120	22	1	16	(7	9)	192	60	51	56	39	6	92	4	2	3	2	2	9	.259	.320	.414	.733
2012 Tex	AL	114	327	90	18	0	15	(10	5)	153	41	50	46	23	5	71	1	2	4	1	1	8	.275	.321	.468	.789
2013 Tex	AL	147	462	107	24	1	23	(10	13)	202	60	60	55	45	1	117	3	0	8	0	0	11	.232	.299	.437	.736
2014 Tex	AL	52	167	41	9	1	2	(1	1)	58	18	23	20	12	0	43	1	2	2	0	0	7	.246	.297	.347	.644
2015 Tex	AL	132	471	131	27	4	23	(9	14)	227	51	85	74	32	2	112	7	0	5	1	0	9	.278	.330	.482	.812
2016 Tex	AL	147	460	107	21	0	22	(13	9)	194	49	60	56	35	5	118	8	0	0	1	0	8	.233	.298	.422	.720
Postseason		30	89	19	4	0	3	(3	0)	32	7	11	12	8	1	21	1	1	0	0	0	3	.213	.286	.360	.645
7 ML YEARS		773	2496	633	125	3	110	(53	57)	1094	299	354	334	211	24	589	25	6	24	8	4	55	.254	.315	.438	.754

Adam Morgan

Pitches: L **Bats:** L **Pos:** SP-21; RP-2   **Ht:** 6'1" **Wt:** 200 **Born:** 2/27/1990 **Age:** 27

	HOW MUCH HE PITCHED						WHAT HE GAVE UP											THE RESULTS							
Year Team	Lg	G	GS	CG	GF	IP	BFP	H	R	ER	HR	SH	SF	HB	TBB	IBB	SO	WP	Bk	W	L	Pct	Sh	Sv-Op	Hld	ERC	ERA
2012 Clrwtr	A+	21	20	1	0	123.0	490	103	46	45	7	3	4	2	28	1	140	3	1	4	10	.286	0	0- -	-	2.39	3.29
2012 Rdng	AA	6	6	0	0	35.2	143	34	14	14	7	1	0	0	11	0	29	3	0	4	1	.800	0	0- -	-	3.33	3.53
2013 LV	AAA	16	16	0	0	71.1	321	84	41	32	10	4	2	5	26	1	49	3	2	2	7	.222	0	0- -	-	5.54	4.04
2015 LV	AAA	13	13	0	0	68.1	309	81	45	36	7	4	5	1	27	0	33	1	0	6	0	.000	0	0- -	-	5.17	4.74
2016 LV	AAA	8	7	0	1	50.1	201	43	19	17	4	2	2	2	10	0	51	1	0	6	1	.857	0	0- -	-	2.60	3.04
2015 Phi	NL	15	15	0	0	84.1	352	88	45	42	14	1	3	4	17	0	49	2	1	5	7	.417	0	0-0	0	4.21	4.48
2016 Phi	NL	23	21	0	0	113.1	507	141	81	76	23	3	4	4	29	3	95	2	0	2	11	.154	0	0-0	0	5.72	6.04
2 ML YEARS		38	36	0	1	197.2	859	229	126	118	37	4	7	8	46	3	144	4	1	7	18	.280	0	0-0	0	5.06	5.37

Shawn Morimando

Pitches: L **Bats:** L **Pos:** RP-2   **Ht:** 6'0" **Wt:** 200 **Born:** 11/20/1992 **Age:** 24

	HOW MUCH HE PITCHED						WHAT HE GAVE UP											THE RESULTS							
Year Team	Lg	G	GS	CG	GF	IP	BFP	H	R	ER	HR	SH	SF	HB	TBB	IBB	SO	WP	Bk	W	L	Pct	Sh	Sv-Op	Hld	ERC	ERA
2012 Lk Cty	A	22	22	1	0	110.1	467	96	51	44	11	2	7	5	52	0	69	15	5	7	6	.538	0	0- -	-	3.88	3.59
2013 Carlina	A+	27	27	1	0	135.0	583	115	68	56	8	1	5	3	76	0	102	6	3	8	13	.381	0	0- -	-	3.70	3.73
2014 Carlina	A+	18	18	0	0	96.0	396	72	42	32	7	2	2	3	35	0	70	4	2	8	3	.727	0	0- -	-	2.53	3.00
2014 Akron	AA	10	10	0	0	56.1	246	63	31	24	2	0	5	0	17	0	38	4	0	2	6	.250	0	0- -	-	3.84	3.83
2015 Akron	AA	28	28	0	0	158.2	655	139	62	56	9	4	7	1	65	0	128	7	0	10	12	.455	0	0- -	-	3.24	3.18
2016 Akron	AA	16	16	0	0	93.1	384	77	34	32	5	2	1	3	36	0	73	3	0	10	3	.769	0	0- -	-	2.94	3.09
2016 Clmbs	AAA	11	11	0	0	59.0	253	64	26	23	5	0	2	2	21	0	46	1	0	5	2	.714	0	0- -	-	4.51	3.51
2016 Cle	AL	2	0	0	0	4.2	27	9	6	6	2	0	0	0	5	0	5	0	0	0	0	-	0	0-0	0	17.18	11.57

Mike Morin

Pitches: R **Bats:** R **Pos:** RP-60   MORE-in   **Ht:** 6'4" **Wt:** 220 **Born:** 5/3/1991 **Age:** 26

	HOW MUCH HE PITCHED						WHAT HE GAVE UP											THE RESULTS							
Year Team	Lg	G	GS	CG	GF	IP	BFP	H	R	ER	HR	SH	SF	HB	TBB	IBB	SO	WP	Bk	W	L	Pct	Sh	Sv-Op	Hld	ERC	ERA
2016 Salt Lk*	AAA	11	0	0	4	10.0	38	8	4	4	2	0	0	1	1	0	11	0	0	0	1	.000	0	2- -	-	2.98	3.60
2014 LAA	AL	60	0	0	10	59.0	246	51	22	19	3	2	4	3	19	6	54	3	0	4	4	.500	0	0-2	9	2.76	2.90
2015 LAA	AL	47	0	0	10	35.1	151	36	28	25	3	2	2	2	9	2	41	0	0	4	2	.667	0	1-1	5	3.61	6.37
2016 LAA	AL	60	0	0	8	55.2	227	52	31	27	6	2	1	1	15	1	49	1	1	2	2	.500	0	0-1	12	3.37	4.37
Postseason		1	0	0	0	1.0	6	3	2	2	1	0	1	0	0	0	1	1	0	0	0	-	0	0-0	0	25.51	18.00
3 ML YEARS		167	0	0	28	150.0	624	139	81	71	12	6	7	6	43	9	144	4	1	10	8	.556	0	1-4	26	3.18	4.26

Justin Morneau

Bats: L **Throws:** R **Pos:** DH-53;PH-7   MOR-noh   **Ht:** 6'4" **Wt:** 220 **Born:** 5/15/1981 **Age:** 36

Year Team	Lg	G	AB	H	2B	3B	HR	(Hm	Rd)	TB	R	RBI	RC	TBB	IBB	SO	HBP	SH	SF	SB	CS	GDP	Avg	OBP	Slg	OPS
2003 Min	AL	40	106	24	4	0	4	(1	3)	40	14	16	11	9	1	30	0	0	0	0	0	4	.226	.287	.377	.664
2004 Min	AL	74	280	76	17	0	19	(9	10)	150	39	58	48	28	8	54	2	0	2	0	0	4	.271	.340	.536	.875
2005 Min	AL	141	490	117	23	4	22	(9	13)	214	62	79	58	44	0	94	4	0	5	0	2	12	.239	.304	.437	.741
2006 Min	AL	157	592	190	37	1	34	(17	17)	331	97	130	118	53	9	93	5	3	3	3	3	10	.321	.375	.559	.934
2007 Min	AL	157	590	160	31	3	31	(15	16)	290	84	111	95	64	11	91	5	0	9	1	1	17	.271	.343	.492	.834
2008 Min	AL	163	623	187	47	4	23	(11	12)	311	97	129	122	76	16	85	3	0	10	0	1	20	.300	.374	.499	.873
2009 Min	AL	135	508	139	31	1	30	(14	16)	262	85	100	91	72	12	86	3	0	7	0	0	12	.274	.363	.516	.878
2010 Min	AL	81	296	102	25	1	18	(4	14)	183	53	56	65	50	7	62	0	0	2	0	0	9	.345	.437	.618	1.055
2011 Min	AL	69	264	60	16	0	4	(0	4)	88	19	30	28	19	1	44	3	0	2	0	0	6	.227	.285	.333	.618
2012 Min	AL	134	505	135	26	2	19	(7	12)	222	63	77	63	49	8	102	6	0	10	1	0	19	.267	.333	.440	.773
2013 2 Tms		152	572	148	36	0	17	(9	8)	235	62	77	71	50	4	110	2	0	6	0	0	13	.259	.323	.411	.734
2014 Col	NL	135	502	160	32	3	17	(6	11)	249	62	82	88	34	4	60	6	0	3	0	3	7	.319	.364	.496	.860
2015 Col	NL	49	168	52	10	3	3	(2	1)	77	19	15	26	13	2	25	1	0	0	0	0	6	.310	.363	.458	.821
2016 CWS	AL	58	203	53	14	1	6	(3	3)	87	16	25	21	12	1	52	1	0	2	0	0	5	.261	.303	.429	.731

Year	Team	Lg	G	AB	H	2B	3B	HR	(Hm	Rd)	TB	R	RBI	RC	TBB	IBB	SO	HBP	SH	SF	SB	CS	GDP	Avg	OBP	Slg	OPS
13	Min	AL	127	495	128	32	0	17	(9	8)	211	56	74	64	37	3	98	6	0	5	0	0	10	.259	.315	.426	.741
13	Pit	NL	25	77	20	4	0	0	(0	0)	24	6	3	7	13	1	12	1	0	1	0	0	0	.260	.370	.312	.681
	Postseason		13	53	16	4	0	2	(1	1)	26	8	4	4	1	0	5	0	0	0	0	0	2	.302	.315	.491	.805
	14 ML YEARS		1545	5699	1603	349	23	247	(113	134)	2739	772	985	905	573	92	988	46	0	74	5	10	139	.281	.348	.481	.828

Max Moroff

Bats: B Throws: R Pos: PH-2 **Ht: 5'10" Wt: 185 Born: 5/13/1993 Age: 24**

Year	Team	Lg	G	AB	H	2B	3B	HR	(Hm	Rd)	TB	R	RBI	RC	TBB	IBB	SO	HBP	SH	SF	SB	CS	GDP	Avg	OBP	Slg	OPS
2012	Pirates	R	23	67	23	3	0	1	(-	-)	29	17	7	16	17	0	11	1	2	2	7	3	2	.343	.471	.433	.904
2013	WV	A	115	429	100	18	3	8	(-	-)	148	75	48	53	65	0	102	2	7	3	8	8	7	.233	.335	.345	.680
2014	Bradtn	A+	130	467	114	30	6	1	(-	-)	159	57	50	54	54	0	129	3	7	3	21	15	4	.244	.324	.340	.665
2015	Altna	AA	136	523	153	28	6	7	(-	-)	214	79	51	84	70	3	111	1	13	5	17	13	8	.293	.374	.409	.783
2016	Indy	AAA	133	421	97	18	4	8	(-	-)	147	61	45	61	90	1	129	2	5	2	9	7	6	.230	.367	.349	.716
2016	Pit	NL	2	2	0	0	0	0	(0	0)	0	0	0	0	0	0	2	0	0	0	0	0	0	.000	.000	.000	.000

A.J. Morris

Pitches: R Bats: R Pos: RP-7 **Ht: 6'2" Wt: 195 Born: 12/1/1986 Age: 30**

				HOW MUCH HE PITCHED						WHAT HE GAVE UP										THE RESULTS							
Year	Team	Lg	G	GS	CG	GF	IP	BFP	H	R	ER	HR	SH	SF	HB	TBB	IBB	SO	WP	Bk	W	L	Pct	Sh	Sv-Op	Hld	ERC	ERA
2012	Dytona	A+	39	0	0	20	52.1	209	36	17	13	1	1	1	2	15	1	42	6	0	5	2	.714	0	7- -	-	1.69	2.24
2013	Tenn	AA	31	10	0	3	72.0	318	74	50	38	4	2	1	2	35	0	53	6	0	4	2	.667	0	0- -	-	4.38	4.75
2014	Altna	AA	14	9	0	1	59.0	238	48	17	13	4	2	0	4	18	1	40	1	0	5	1	.833	0	0- -	-	2.81	1.98
2014	2 Tms	Low	5	0	0	1	8.0	30	4	2	2	1	1	0	0	1	0	8	0	0	-	0	-	0	0- -	-	1.05	2.25
2014	Indy	AAA	7	7	1	0	37.2	161	46	20	19	2	0	0	1	11	0	28	5	0	2	4	.333	1	0- -	-	4.86	4.54
2015	Indy	AAA	44	3	0	9	84.2	349	76	31	23	3	1	2	7	22	0	72	5	0	5	3	.625	0	3- -	-	2.91	2.44
2016	Lsvlle	AAA	18	6	0	1	38.2	167	46	24	17	5	0	0	1	11	0	32	4	0	2	2	.000	0	0- -	-	5.12	3.96
2016	Cin	NL	7	0	0	3	10.0	47	9	7	7	2	0	1	0	8	0	9	0	0	0	0	-	0	0-0	0	5.76	6.30

Bryan Morris

Pitches: R Bats: L Pos: RP-24 **Ht: 6'3" Wt: 220 Born: 3/28/1987 Age: 30**

				HOW MUCH HE PITCHED						WHAT HE GAVE UP										THE RESULTS							
Year	Team	Lg	G	GS	CG	GF	IP	BFP	H	R	ER	HR	SH	SF	HB	TBB	IBB	SO	WP	Bk	W	L	Pct	Sh	Sv-Op	Hld	ERC	ERA
2012	Pit	NL	5	0	0	2	5.0	20	2	2	1	0	0	1	1	2	0	6	1	0	0	0	-	0	0-0	0	1.32	1.80
2013	Pit	NL	55	0	0	21	65.0	270	57	25	25	8	0	5	2	28	5	37	6	0	5	7	.417	0	0-0	7	3.78	3.46
2014	2 Tms		60	0	0	10	64.1	272	58	17	13	6	7	3	4	24	6	50	8	1	8	1	.889	0	0-7	17	3.50	1.82
2015	Mia	NL	67	0	0	18	63.0	277	67	26	22	3	4	0	3	26	0	47	2	0	5	4	.556	0	0-2	18	4.31	3.14
2016	Mia	NL	24	0	0	4	17.2	74	15	7	6	4	0	0	0	10	1	13	0	0	0	0	-	0	1-3	6	5.19	3.06
14	Pit	NL	21	0	0	7	23.2	103	25	11	10	4	2	2	2	12	3	14	3	1	4	0	1.000	0	0-3	4	5.75	3.80
14	Mia	NL	39	0	0	3	40.2	169	33	6	3	2	5	1	2	12	3	36	5	0	4	1	.800	0	0-4	13	2.39	0.66
	Postseason		1	0	0	1	1.0	4	1	0	0	0	0	0	0	0	0	1	0	0	0	0	-	0	0-0	0	1.95	0.00
	5 ML YEARS		211	0	0	55	215.0	913	199	77	67	21	11	9	11	90	12	153	17	1	18	12	.600	0	1-12	48	3.89	2.80

Logan Morrison

Bats: L Throws: L Pos: 1B-83;DH-17;PH-9 **Ht: 6'2" Wt: 240 Born: 8/25/1987 Age: 29**

								BATTING													RUNNING			AVERAGES			
Year	Team	Lg	G	AB	H	2B	3B	HR	(Hm	Rd)	TB	R	RBI	RC	TBB	IBB	SO	HBP	SH	SF	SB	CS	GDP	Avg	OBP	Slg	OPS
2010	Fla	NL	62	244	69	20	7	2	(1	1)	109	43	18	41	41	0	51	2	0	0	1	1	4	.283	.390	.447	.837
2011	Fla	NL	123	462	114	25	4	23	(12	11)	216	54	72	55	54	3	99	5	0	4	2	1	9	.247	.330	.468	.797
2012	Mia	NL	93	296	68	15	1	11	(4	7)	118	30	36	27	31	2	58	4	0	3	1	0	9	.230	.308	.399	.707
2013	Mia	NL	85	293	71	13	4	6	(1	5)	110	32	36	37	38	5	56	2	0	0	0	0	10	.242	.333	.375	.709
2014	Sea	AL	99	336	88	20	0	11	(7	4)	141	41	38	46	24	1	59	3	0	2	5	2	9	.262	.315	.420	.735
2015	Sea	AL	146	457	103	15	3	17	(7	10)	175	47	54	53	47	5	81	4	1	2	8	4	7	.225	.302	.383	.685
2016	TB	AL	107	353	84	18	1	14	(6	8)	146	45	43	50	37	1	89	6	0	2	4	2	4	.238	.319	.414	.733
	7 ML YEARS		715	2441	597	126	20	84	(38	46)	1015	292	297	309	272	17	493	26	1	13	20	10	52	.245	.325	.416	.741

Brandon Morrow

Pitches: R Bats: R Pos: RP-18 **Ht: 6'3" Wt: 205 Born: 7/26/1984 Age: 32**

				HOW MUCH HE PITCHED						WHAT HE GAVE UP										THE RESULTS							
Year	Team	Lg	G	GS	CG	GF	IP	BFP	H	R	ER	HR	SH	SF	HB	TBB	IBB	SO	WP	Bk	W	L	Pct	Sh	Sv-Op	Hld	ERC	ERA
2016	2 Tms*	Low	6	4	0	0	16.2	73	23	12	10	1	0	1	0	3	0	14	0	0	1	1	.500	0	0- -	-	5.17	5.40
2016	ElPaso*	AAA	12	2	0	6	21.0	99	29	15	15	2	0	0	0	9	0	21	2	0	0	0	-	0	2- -	-	6.40	6.43
2007	Sea	AL	60	0	0	18	63.1	289	56	29	29	3	4	4	1	50	5	66	4	0	3	4	.429	0	0-2	18	4.47	4.12
2008	Sea	AL	45	5	0	14	64.2	265	40	26	24	10	1	0	0	34	1	75	5	0	3	4	.429	0	10-12	3	2.84	3.34
2009	Sea	AL	26	10	0	9	69.2	313	66	38	34	10	1	2	0	44	1	63	3	0	2	4	.333	0	6-8	1	4.99	4.39
2010	Tor	AL	26	26	1	0	146.1	629	136	76	73	11	2	4	9	66	0	178	8	0	10	7	.588	1	0-0	0	3.99	4.49
2011	Tor	AL	30	30	3	0	179.1	777	162	103	94	21	4	9	12	69	1	203	12	1	11	11	.500	0	0-0	0	3.79	4.72
2012	Tor	AL	21	21	3	0	124.2	504	98	45	41	12	1	3	2	41	0	108	3	0	10	7	.588	3	0-0	0	2.73	2.96
2013	Tor	AL	10	10	0	0	54.1	242	63	39	34	12	0	3	1	18	1	42	1	0	2	3	.400	0	0-0	0	5.60	5.63
2014	Tor	AL	13	6	0	2	33.1	148	37	21	21	2	1	0	0	18	0	30	1	1	1	3	.250	0	0-0	0	5.09	5.67
2015	SD	NL	5	5	0	0	33.0	126	29	10	10	3	1	1	0	7	0	23	0	0	2	0	1.000	0	0-0	0	2.84	2.73
2016	SD	NL	18	0	0	2	16.0	68	19	4	3	2	2	1	0	3	0	8	0	0	1	0	1.000	0	0-1	2	4.40	1.69
	10 ML YEARS		254	113	4	55	784.2	3361	706	391	363	86	17	27	25	350	10	796	37	2	45	43	.511	4	16-23	25	3.88	4.16

Michael Morse

Bats: R **Throws:** R **Pos:** PH-5;1B-1;DH-1 **Ht:** 6'5" **Wt:** 245 **Born:** 3/22/1982 **Age:** 35

Year	Team	Lg	G	AB	H	2B	3B	HR	(Hm	Rd)	TB	R	RBI	RC	TBB	IBB	SO	HBP	SH	SF	SB	CS	GDP	Avg	OBP	Slg	OPS
2005	Sea	AL	72	230	64	10	1	3	(3	0)	85	27	23	28	18	0	50	8	0	2	3	1	9	.278	.349	.370	.718
2006	Sea	AL	21	43	16	5	0	1	(0	0)	21	5	11	9	3	0	7	0	0	2	1	0	2	.372	.396	.488	.884
2007	Sea	AL	9	18	8	2	0	0	(0	0)	10	1	3	6	1	0	4	1	0	0	0	0	0	.444	.500	.556	1.056
2008	Sea	AL	5	9	2	1	0	0	(0	0)	3	0	0	1	1	0	4	1	0	0	0	0	0	.222	.364	.333	.697
2009	Was	NL	32	52	13	3	0	3	(3	0)	25	4	10	8	3	0	16	0	0	0	0	0	1	.250	.291	.481	.772
2010	Was	NL	98	266	77	12	2	15	(6	9)	138	36	41	42	22	1	64	4	0	1	0	1	6	.289	.352	.519	.870
2011	Was	NL	146	522	158	36	0	31	(11	20)	287	73	95	96	36	5	126	13	0	4	2	3	9	.303	.360	.550	.910
2012	Was	NL	102	406	118	17	1	18	(7	11)	191	53	62	57	16	0	97	4	0	4	0	1	14	.291	.321	.470	.791
2013	2 Tms	AL	88	312	67	13	0	13	(5	8)	119	34	27	24	21	1	87	3	0	1	0	0	12	.215	.270	.381	.651
2014	SF	NL	131	438	122	32	3	16	(6	10)	208	48	61	55	31	0	121	9	0	4	0	0	19	.279	.336	.475	.811
2015	2 Tms	NL	98	229	53	7	1	5	(1	4)	77	14	19	20	23	0	76	4	0	0	0	0	10	.231	.313	.336	.649
2016	Pit	NL	6	8	0	0	0	0	(0	0)	0	0	0	0	0	0	2	0	0	0	0	0	0	.000	.000	.000	.000
13	Sea	AL	76	283	64	13	0	13	(5	8)	116	31	27	24	20	1	80	3	0	1	0	0	10	.226	.283	.410	.693
13	Bal	AL	12	29	3	0	0	0	(0	0)	3	3	0	0	1	0	7	0	0	0	0	0	2	.103	.133	.103	.237
15	Mia	NL	53	160	34	4	0	4	(0	4)	50	8	12	9	12	0	55	2	0	0	0	0	6	.213	.276	.313	.588
15	Pit	NL	45	69	19	3	1	1	(1	0)	27	6	7	11	11	0	21	2	0	0	0	0	4	.275	.390	.391	.782
	Postseason		16	40	12	1	0	2	(2	0)	19	5	7	5	1	0	9	0	0	1	0	0	1	.300	.310	.475	.785
	12 ML YEARS		808	2533	698	138	8	104	(42	62)	1164	295	352	346	175	7	654	47	0	18	6	6	82	.276	.332	.460	.791

Charlie Morton

Pitches: R **Bats:** R **Pos:** SP-4 **Ht:** 6'5" **Wt:** 235 **Born:** 11/12/1983 **Age:** 33

Year	Team	Lg	G	GS	CG	GF	IP	BFP	H	R	ER	HR	SH	SF	HB	TBB	IBB	SO	WP	Bk	W	L	Pct	Sh	Sv-Op	Hld	ERC	ERA
2008	Atl	NL	16	15	0	0	74.2	345	80	56	51	9	5	4	2	41	2	48	2	0	4	8	.333	0	0-0	0	5.21	6.15
2009	Pit	NL	18	18	1	0	97.0	416	102	49	49	7	1	1	5	40	0	62	4	0	5	9	.357	1	0-0	0	4.56	4.55
2010	Pit	NL	17	17	0	0	79.2	382	112	79	67	15	6	6	7	26	3	59	5	1	2	12	.143	0	0-0	0	7.10	7.57
2011	Pit	NL	29	29	2	0	171.2	769	186	82	73	6	12	6	13	77	5	110	9	1	10	10	.500	1	0-0	0	4.52	3.83
2012	Pit	NL	9	9	0	0	50.1	223	62	30	26	5	5	2	2	11	1	25	4	0	2	6	.250	0	0-0	0	4.74	4.65
2013	Pit	NL	20	20	0	0	116.0	493	113	51	42	6	6	2	16	36	1	85	5	0	7	4	.636	0	0-0	0	3.84	3.26
2014	Pit	NL	26	26	0	0	157.1	666	143	76	65	9	7	5	19	57	2	126	8	0	6	12	.333	0	0-0	0	3.64	3.72
2015	Pit	NL	23	23	0	0	129.0	563	137	77	69	13	4	0	12	41	6	96	2	1	9	9	.500	0	0-0	0	4.41	4.81
2016	Phi	NL	4	4	0	0	17.1	71	15	8	8	1	1	0	0	8	0	19	1	1	1	1	.500	0	0-0	0	3.42	4.15
	Postseason		1	1	0	0	5.2	24	3	2	2	1	1	0	0	4	0	4	0	0	0	1	.000	0	0-0	0	3.16	3.18
	9 ML YEARS		162	161	3	0	893.0	3928	950	508	450	71	47	26	76	337	20	630	40	4	46	71	.393	2	0-0	0	4.53	4.54

Jon Moscot

Pitches: R **Bats:** R **Pos:** SP-5 **Ht:** 6'4" **Wt:** 210 **Born:** 8/15/1991 **Age:** 25

Year	Team	Lg	G	GS	CG	GF	IP	BFP	H	R	ER	HR	SH	SF	HB	TBB	IBB	SO	WP	Bk	W	L	Pct	Sh	Sv-Op	Hld	ERC	ERA
2012	2 Tms	Low	12	11	0	0	27.1	115	22	12	8	2	1		2	11	0	27	4	0	0	2	.000	0	0--	-	3.12	2.63
2013	Bkrsfld	A+	22	22	0	0	115.2	491	109	66	59	17	5	3	6	36	2	112	8	1	2	14	.125	0	0--	-	3.88	4.59
2013	Pnscla	AA	6	6	0	0	31.0	138	34	12	11	3	2	0	3	12	1	28	3	0	2	1	.667	0	0--	-	4.92	3.19
2014	Pnscla	AA	25	25	2	0	149.1	634	145	60	52	11	8	7	8	43	2	111	5	0	7	10	.412	0	0--	-	3.47	3.13
2015	Lsvlle	AAA	9	9	0	0	54.1	225	50	20	19	5	3	3	0	19	0	34	7	0	7	1	.875	0	0--	-	3.44	3.15
2016	Lsvlle	AAA	9	9	0	0	49.2	220	58	29	29	9	3	1	4	16	0	31	0	0	4	4	.500	0	0--	-	5.73	5.26
2015	Cin	NL	3	3	0	0	11.2	50	11	6	6	2	0	1	0	5	0	6	1	0	1	1	.500	0	0-0	0	4.37	4.63
2016	Cin	NL	5	5	0	0	21.1	105	26	22	19	10	3	1	1	10	1	10	0	0	0	3	.000	0	0-0	0	8.22	8.02
	2 ML YEARS		8	8	0	0	33.0	155	37	28	25	12	3	2	1	15	1	16	1	0	1	4	.200	0	0-0	0	6.81	6.82

Brandon Moss

Bats: L **Throws:** R **Pos:** 1B-64;LF-58;PH-24;RF-21 **Ht:** 6'1" **Wt:** 210 **Born:** 9/16/1983 **Age:** 33

Year	Team	Lg	G	AB	H	2B	3B	HR	(Hm	Rd)	TB	R	RBI	RC	TBB	IBB	SO	HBP	SH	SF	SB	CS	GDP	Avg	OBP	Slg	OPS
2007	Bos	AL	15	25	7	2	1	0	(0	0)	11	6	1	3	4	0	6	0	0	0	0	0	1	.280	.379	.440	.819
2008	2 Tms		79	236	58	15	3	8	(4	4)	103	19	34	30	21	1	70	1	0	5	1	2	2	.246	.304	.436	.741
2009	Pit	NL	133	385	91	20	4	7	(4	3)	140	47	41	37	34	3	84	4	0	1	1	5	7	.236	.304	.364	.668
2010	Pit	NL	17	26	4	1	0	0	(0	0)	5	2	2	2	1	0	6	0	0	0	0	0	1	.154	.185	.192	.377
2011	Phi	NL	5	6	0	0	0	0	(0	0)	0	0	0	0	0	0	2	0	0	0	0	0	1	.000	.000	.000	.000
2012	Oak	AL	84	265	76	18	0	21	(9	12)	158	48	52	50	26	2	90	3	0	2	1	1	5	.291	.358	.596	.954
2013	Oak	AL	145	446	114	23	3	30	(10	20)	233	73	87	79	50	3	140	6	0	3	4	2	4	.256	.337	.522	.859
2014	Oak	AL	147	500	117	23	2	25	(12	13)	219	70	81	78	67	7	153	10	0	3	1	0	6	.234	.334	.438	.772
2015	2 Tms		145	469	106	24	2	19	(4	15)	191	47	58	43	49	4	148	5	0	3	0	1	12	.226	.304	.407	.711
2016	StL	NL	128	413	93	19	2	28	(13	15)	200	66	67	57	39	3	141	7	0	5	1	0	8	.225	.300	.484	.784
08	Bos	AL	34	78	23	5	1	2	(1	1)	36	7	11	11	6	0	25	0	0	2	1	1	1	.295	.337	.462	.799
08	Pit	AL	45	158	35	10	2	6	(3	3)	67	12	23	19	15	1	45	1	0	3	0	1	2	.222	.288	.424	.712
15	Cle	AL	94	337	73	17	1	15	(2	13)	137	36	50	32	32	2	106	3	0	3	0	0	9	.217	.288	.407	.695
15	StL	NL	51	132	33	7	1	4	(2	2)	54	11	8	11	17	2	42	2	0	0	0	1	3	.250	.344	.409	.753
	Postseason		14	41	7	0	0	3	(0	3)	16	4	7	5	6	1	24	2	0	0	0	0	0	.171	.306	.390	.696
	10 ML YEARS		898	2771	667	145	17	138	(56	82)	1260	378	423	379	291	23	840	36	0	22	9	11	47	.241	.319	.455	.773

Jason Motte

Pitches: R **Bats:** R **Pos:** RP-30   **Ht:** 6'0" **Wt:** 205 **Born:** 6/22/1982 **Age:** 35

Year	Team	Lg	G	GS	CG	GF	IP	BFP	H	R	ER	HR	SH	SF	HB	TBB	IBB	SO	WP	Bk	W	L	Pct	Sh	Sv-Op	Hld	ERC	ERA
2016 Albq*	AAA		6	0	0	1	5.2	21	3	2	2	1	0	0	0	3	0	5	0	0	0	0	-	0	0- -	-	2.83	3.18
2008 StL	NL		12	0	0	4	11.0	40	5	2	1	0	1	0	0	3	0	16	0	0	0	0	-	0	1-1	4	0.89	0.82
2009 StL	NL		69	0	0	14	56.2	244	57	32	30	10	0	3	2	23	1	54	2	1	4	4	.500	0	0-3	15	4.86	4.76
2010 StL	NL		56	0	0	13	52.1	208	41	13	13	5	1	3	0	18	3	54	1	0	4	2	.667	0	2-3	12	2.68	2.24
2011 StL	NL		78	0	0	27	68.0	268	49	22	17	2	1	3	5	16	2	63	1	0	5	2	.714	0	9-13	18	1.87	2.25
2012 StL	NL		67	0	0	58	72.0	279	49	23	22	9	2	1	2	17	1	86	0	0	4	5	.444	0	**42-49**	0	2.08	2.75
2014 StL	NL		29	0	0	10	25.0	112	29	14	13	7	0	2	0	9	0	17	1	0	1	0	1.000	0	0-0	1	6.22	4.68
2015 ChC	NL		57	0	0	18	48.1	206	48	21	21	4	3	2	2	11	5	34	2	0	8	1	.889	0	6-7	9	3.18	3.91
2016 Col	NL		30	0	0	8	23.2	109	28	15	13	6	0	1	2	8	1	24	0	0	0	1	.000	0	0-0	6	6.20	4.94
Postseason			19	0	0	16	21.2	79	12	6	5	2	0	0	0	2	0	10	0	0	1	1	.500	0	8-8	0	1.07	2.08
8 ML YEARS			398	0	0	152	357.0	1464	306	142	130	43	8	15	13	105	13	348	7	1	26	15	.634	0	60-76	65	3.13	3.28

Taylor Motter

Bats: R **Throws:** R **Pos:** SS-9;LF-7;2B-6;RF-6;3B-4;PH-4;PR-3;1B-1   **Ht:** 6'1" **Wt:** 195 **Born:** 9/18/1989 **Age:** 27

Year	Team	Lg	G	AB	H	2B	3B	HR	(Hm	Rd)	TB	R	RBI	RC	TBB	IBB	SO	HBP	SH	SF	SB	CS	GDP	Avg	OBP	Slg	OPS
2012 BG	A	99	303	74	17	2	5	(-	-)	110	41	37	44	50	2	60	3	4	5	24	12	10	.244	.357	.363	.720
2013 2 Tms	Low	71	221	65	16	2	3	(-	-)	94	27	21	36	24	0	30	1	5	1	20	8	5	.294	.364	.425	.790
2014 Mont	AA	119	452	125	19	3	16	(-	-)	198	60	61	68	34	1	71	5	6	9	15	7	20	.277	.328	.438	.766
2015 Drhm	AAA	127	486	142	43	1	14	(-	-)	229	74	72	89	57	1	95	5	1	9	26	8	11	.292	.366	.471	.837
2016 Drhm	AAA	88	350	80	17	0	13	(-	-)	136	44	46	44	33	1	65	2	0	2	20	4	9	.229	.297	.389	.686
2016 TB	AL	34	80	15	3	0	2	(0	2)	24	11	9	7	11	0	19	1	0	1	0	1	1	.188	.290	.300	.590

Mike Moustakas

Bats: L **Throws:** R **Pos:** 3B-26;PH-1   moo-STOCK-us   **Ht:** 6'0" **Wt:** 215 **Born:** 9/11/1988 **Age:** 28

Year	Team	Lg	G	AB	H	2B	3B	HR	(Hm	Rd)	TB	R	RBI	RC	TBB	IBB	SO	HBP	SH	SF	SB	CS	GDP	Avg	OBP	Slg	OPS
2011 KC	AL	89	338	89	18	1	5	(3	2)	124	26	30	31	22	0	51	1	2	2	2	0	5	.263	.309	.367	.675
2012 KC	AL	149	563	136	34	1	20	(10	10)	232	69	73	64	39	4	124	7	0	5	5	2	4	.242	.296	.412	.708
2013 KC	AL	136	472	110	26	0	12	(5	7)	172	42	42	35	32	1	83	5	1	4	2	4	13	.233	.287	.364	.651
2014 KC	AL	140	457	97	21	1	15	(5	10)	165	45	54	44	35	1	74	3	1	4	1	0	12	.212	.271	.361	.632
2015 KC	AL	147	549	156	34	1	22	(9	13)	258	73	82	85	43	1	76	13	4	5	1	2	14	.284	.348	.470	.817
2016 KC	AL	27	104	25	6	0	7	(4	3)	52	12	13	10	9	0	13	0	0	0	1	5	.240	.301	.500	.801
Postseason		31	117	26	3	0	6	(3	3)	47	14	15	12	5	0	17	1	1	1	0	0	2	.222	.258	.402	.660
6 ML YEARS		688	2483	613	139	4	81	(36	45)	1003	267	294	269	180	7	421	29	8	20	11	9	53	.247	.303	.404	.707

Steven Moya

Bats: L **Throws:** R **Pos:** RF-18;LF-8;PH-4;DH-3   MOY-uh   **Ht:** 6'7" **Wt:** 260 **Born:** 8/9/1991 **Age:** 25

Year	Team	Lg	G	AB	H	2B	3B	HR	(Hm	Rd)	TB	R	RBI	RC	TBB	IBB	SO	HBP	SH	SF	SB	CS	GDP	Avg	OBP	Slg	OPS
2016 Toledo*	AAA	97	409	116	23	3	20	(-	-)	205	60	66	64	15	2	96	1	0	1	3	0	10	.284	.310	.501	.811
2014 Det	AL	11	8	3	0	0	0	(0	0)	3	2	0	1	0	0	2	0	0	0	0	0	0	.375	.375	.375	.750
2015 Det	AL	9	22	4	0	1	0	(0	0)	6	1	0	1	3	0	10	0	0	0	0	0	0	.182	.280	.273	.553
2016 Det	AL	31	94	24	4	2	5	(3	2)	47	9	11	8	5	0	38	0	0	1	0	1	0	.255	.290	.500	.790
3 ML YEARS		51	124	31	4	3	5	(3	2)	56	12	11	10	8	0	50	0	0	1	0	1	0	.250	.293	.452	.745

Peter Moylan

Pitches: R **Bats:** R **Pos:** RP-50   **Ht:** 6'2" **Wt:** 225 **Born:** 12/2/1978 **Age:** 38

Year	Team	Lg	G	GS	CG	GF	IP	BFP	H	R	ER	HR	SH	SF	HB	TBB	IBB	SO	WP	Bk	W	L	Pct	Sh	Sv-Op	Hld	ERC	ERA
2016 Omha*	AAA		12	0	0	11	12.2	51	8	2	1	0	0	0	2	5	2	10	1	0	1	1	.500	0	5- -	-	1.89	0.71
2006 Atl	NL		15	0	0	5	15.0	68	18	8	8	1	1	0	0	5	1	14	0	0	0	0	-	0	0-0	0	4.47	4.80
2007 Atl	NL		80	0	0	16	90.0	359	65	27	18	6	4	4	7	31	**12**	63	2	0	5	3	.625	0	1-2	8	2.36	1.80
2008 Atl	NL		7	0	0	2	5.2	25	5	1	1	0	0	0	1	1	0	5	0	0	1	0	1.000	0	1-2	4	3.51	1.59
2009 Atl	NL		87	0	0	6	73.0	309	65	29	23	0	4	3	2	35	8	61	1	0	6	2	.750	0	0-5	25	3.06	2.84
2010 Atl	NL		85	0	0	7	63.2	271	53	24	21	5	5	2	2	37	6	52	3	0	6	2	.750	0	1-4	21	3.75	2.97
2011 Atl	NL		13	0	0	2	8.1	38	12	3	3	0	0	0	0	3	0	10	0	0	2	1	.667	0	0-0	2	5.87	3.24
2012 Atl	NL		8	0	0	3	5.0	21	3	3	1	1	0	0	2	2	0	2	1	0	1	0	1.000	0	1-1	2	2.40	1.80
2013 LAD	NL		14	0	0	7	15.1	70	23	11	11	3	0	0	0	7	1	6	0	0	1	0	1.000	0	0-0	1	8.59	6.46
2015 Atl	NL		22	0	0	2	10.1	44	12	5	4	1	0	0	0	0	0	8	0	1	1	0	1.000	0	0-1	3	3.20	3.48
2016 KC	AL		50	0	0	11	44.2	191	42	19	17	4	1	5	2	16	0	34	3	0	2	0	1.000	0	0-0	7	3.67	3.43
Postseason			4	0	0	0	1.0	6	1	0	0	0	0	0	0	0	0	1	0	0	0	0	-	0	0-1	0	1.26	0.00
10 ML YEARS			381	0	0	61	331.0	1396	298	130	107	22	16	14	14	137	28	255	10	1	24	9	.727	0	4-15	72	3.42	2.91

Edward Mujica

Pitches: R **Bats:** R **Pos:** P   moo-HEE-kah   **Ht:** 6'3" **Wt:** 220 **Born:** 5/10/1984 **Age:** 33

Year	Team	Lg	G	GS	CG	GF	IP	BFP	H	R	ER	HR	SH	SF	HB	TBB	IBB	SO	WP	Bk	W	L	Pct	Sh	Sv-Op	Hld	ERC	ERA
2016 LV*	AAA		36	0	0	29	39.0	165	42	19	16	3	3	1	0	4	0	27	0	0	3	0	.000	0	23- -	-	3.07	3.69
2016 Omha*	AAA		9	0	0	7	12.0	55	17	11	11	2	1	0	1	2	0	14	0	0	1	0	1.000	0	2- -	-	6.26	8.25
2016 Roch*	AAA		6	0	0	4	6.2	27	6	1	1	0	0	0	0	2	0	8	0	0	0	0	-	0	3- -	-	2.57	1.35
2006 Cle	AL		10	0	0	2	18.1	78	25	6	6	1	0	2	1	0	0	12	0	0	0	1	.000	0	0-0	0	4.50	2.95

			HOW MUCH HE PITCHED							WHAT HE GAVE UP													THE RESULTS							
Year	Team	Lg	G	GS	CG	GF	IP	BFP	H	R	ER	HR	SH	SF	HB	TBB	IBB	SO	WP	Bk	W	L	Pct	Sh	Sv-Op	Hld	ERC	ERA
2007	Cle	AL	10	0	0	5	13.0	60	19	12	12	3	0	1	0	2	0	7	0	0	0	0	-	0	0-0	0	6.63	8.31
2008	Cle	AL	33	0	0	13	38.2	168	46	29	29	5	0	4	1	10	3	27	1	0	3	2	.600	0	0-2	1	4.82	6.75
2009	SD	NL	67	4	0	15	93.2	393	101	47	41	14	1	3	0	19	4	76	3	1	3	5	.375	0	2-3	11	4.00	3.94
2010	SD	NL	59	0	0	24	69.2	268	59	29	28	14	1	0	0	6	0	72	1	0	2	1	.667	0	0-1	4	2.68	3.62
2011	Fla	NL	67	0	0	11	76.0	297	64	27	25	7	5	1	2	14	5	63	1	0	9	6	.600	0	0-3	17	2.46	2.96
2012	2 Tms	NL	70	0	0	16	65.1	258	56	24	22	7	1	1	1	12	3	47	1	0	0	3	.000	0	2-8	30	2.58	3.03
2013	StL	NL	65	0	0	49	64.2	255	60	20	20	9	3	1	1	5	1	46	0	1	2	1	.667	0	37-41	5	2.75	2.78
2014	Bos	NL	64	0	0	31	60.0	253	69	28	26	6	2	2	0	14	2	43	1	0	2	4	.333	0	8-9	3	4.28	3.90
2015	2 Tms	NL	49	0	0	13	47.1	194	52	28	25	10	2	1	1	7	2	30	1	3	3	5	.375	0	1-5	4	4.49	4.75
12	Mia	NL	41	0	0	14	39.0	161	36	21	19	6	0	1	1	9	2	26	0	0	0	3	.000	0	2-6	12	3.35	4.38
12	StL	NL	29	0	0	2	26.1	97	20	3	3	1	1	0	0	3	1	21	1	0	0	0	-	0	0-2	18	1.57	1.03
15	Bos	AL	11	0	0	4	13.2	56	15	7	7	3	1	0	1	3	0	8	0	2	1	1	.500	0	0-1	0	5.32	4.61
15	Oak	AL	38	0	0	9	33.2	138	37	21	18	7	1	1	0	4	2	22	1	1	2	4	.333	0	1-4	4	4.17	4.81
	Postseason		11	0	0	3	9.2	39	10	3	3	1	0	1	0	1	0	4	0	0	1	0	1.000	0	0-0	2	3.16	2.79
	10 ML YEARS		494	4	0	179	546.2	2224	551	250	234	76	15	16	7	89	20	423	9	5	24	28	.462	0	50-72	75	3.48	3.85

Conor Mullee

Pitches: R Bats: R Pos: RP-3   Ht: 6'4" Wt: 195 Born: 2/25/1988 Age: 29

			HOW MUCH HE PITCHED							WHAT HE GAVE UP													THE RESULTS							
Year	Team	Lg	G	GS	CG	GF	IP	BFP	H	R	ER	HR	SH	SF	HB	TBB	IBB	SO	WP	Bk	W	L	Pct	Sh	Sv-Op	Hld	ERC	ERA
2012	StnIsld	A-	6	0	0	0	5.0	19	3	2	2	1	0	0	0	1	0	4	0	1	0	0	-	0	0--	-	1.85	3.60
2014	2 Tms	Low	21	0	0	7	38.2	151	23	12	6	1	0	2	2	13	0	37	6	1	3	1	.750	0	2--	-	1.60	1.40
2015	Tampa	A+	10	0	0	8	12.2	51	10	5	3	0	1	0	0	2	0	11	1	0	1	1	.500	0	4--	-	1.54	2.13
2015	Trntn	AA	24	0	0	9	42.1	180	40	18	16	3	2	1	3	14	1	40	4	0	3	3	.500	0	1--	-	3.54	3.40
2016	S-WB	AAA	25	0	0	15	36.1	137	21	5	4	1	1	1	0	11	0	45	0	0	4	0	1.000	0	6--	-	1.39	0.99
2016	NYY	AL	3	0	0	1	3.0	14	0	1	1	0	0	0	1	4	0	4	0	0	0	0	-	0	0-0	0	2.44	3.00

Max Muncy

Bats: L Throws: R Pos: 2B-21;RF-17;PH-9;LF-4;DH-3;PR-2;3B-1   Ht: 6'0" Wt: 210 Born: 8/25/1990 Age: 26

			BATTING																	RUNNING			AVERAGES			
Year	Team	Lg	G	AB	H	2B	3B	HR	(Hm	Rd)	TB	R	RBI	RC	TBB	IBB	SO	HBP	SH	SF	SB	CS	GDP	Avg	OBP	Slg	OPS
2012	Burlgtn	A	64	229	63	20	2	4	(-	-)	99	34	23	41	41	2	37	1	0	3	3	•1	2	.275	.383	.432	.816
2013	Stcktn	A+	93	351	100	13	1	21	(-	-)	178	67	76	74	64	9	68	7	0	6	1	1	2	.285	.400	.507	.907
2013	Mdlnd	AA	47	172	43	12	2	4	(-	-)	71	22	24	25	24	1	34	0	0	1	0	1	3	.250	.340	.413	.753
2014	Mdlnd	AA	122	435	115	23	3	7	(-	-)	165	59	63	73	87	5	92	2	0	6	7	2	1	.264	.385	.379	.764
2015	Nashv	AAA	60	212	58	14	1	4	(-	-)	86	24	35	31	26	1	58	1	0	4	0	1	5	.274	.350	.406	.755
2016	Nashv	AAA	64	223	56	7	2	8	(-	-)	91	34	26	37	35	0	54	5	1	4	5	0	1	.251	.360	.408	.768
2015	Oak	AL	45	102	21	8	1	3	(1	2)	40	14	9	9	9	0	31	0	0	1	0	0	0	.206	.268	.392	.660
2016	Oak	AL	51	113	21	2	0	2	(1	1)	29	13	8	10	20	1	24	0	0	0	0	0	2	.186	.308	.257	.565
	2 ML YEARS		96	215	42	10	1	5	(2	3)	69	27	17	19	29	1	55	0	0	1	0	0	2	.195	.290	.321	.611

Daniel Murphy

Bats: L Throws: R Pos: 2B-117;1B-21;PH-7;3B-1;DH-1   Ht: 6'1" Wt: 220 Born: 4/1/1985 Age: 32

			BATTING																	RUNNING			AVERAGES			
Year	Team	Lg	G	AB	H	2B	3B	HR	(Hm	Rd)	TB	R	RBI	RC	TBB	IBB	SO	HBP	SH	SF	SB	CS	GDP	Avg	OBP	Slg	OPS
2008	NYM	NL	49	131	41	9	3	2	(1	1)	62	24	17	26	18	1	28	1	0	1	0	2	4	.313	.397	.473	.871
2009	NYM	NL	155	508	135	38	4	12	(7	5)	217	60	63	60	38	4	69	0	4	6	4	2	13	.266	.313	.427	.741
2011	NYM	NL	109	391	125	28	2	6	(2	4)	175	49	49	57	24	2	42	3	3	2	5	5	14	.320	.362	.448	.809
2012	NYM	NL	156	571	166	40	3	6	(1	5)	230	62	65	78	36	5	82	1	0	4	10	2	12	.291	.332	.403	.735
2013	NYM	NL	161	658	188	38	4	13	(6	7)	273	92	78	86	32	2	95	2	0	5	23	3	13	.286	.319	.415	.733
2014	NYM	NL	143	596	172	37	2	9	(4	5)	240	79	57	78	39	3	86	2	0	5	13	5	15	.289	.332	.403	.734
2015	NYM	NL	130	499	140	38	2	14	(7	7)	224	56	73	71	31	10	38	2	0	2	2	2	15	.281	.322	.449	.770
2016	Was	NL	142	531	184	**47**	5	25	(10	15)	316	88	104	115	35	10	57	8	0	8	5	3	4	.347	.390	**.595**	**.985**
	Postseason		14	58	19	2	0	7	(3	4)	42	13	11	14	6	1	13	0	0	0	1	1	1	.328	.391	.724	1.115
	8 ML YEARS		1045	3885	1151	275	25	87	(38	49)	1737	510	506	571	253	37	497	19	7	37	62	24	90	.296	.339	.447	.786

John Ryan Murphy

Bats: R Throws: R Pos: C-25;PH-1   Ht: 5'11" Wt: 205 Born: 5/13/1991 Age: 26

			BATTING																	RUNNING			AVERAGES			
Year	Team	Lg	G	AB	H	2B	3B	HR	(Hm	Rd)	TB	R	RBI	RC	TBB	IBB	SO	HBP	SH	SF	SB	CS	GDP	Avg	OBP	Slg	OPS
2016	Roch*	AAA	83	263	62	14	0	3	(-	-)	85	24	39	25	21	0	51	0	0	6	0	0	3	.236	.286	.323	.609
2013	NYY	AL	16	26	4	1	0	0	(0	0)	5	3	1	0	1	0	9	0	0	0	0	0	0	.154	.185	.192	.377
2014	NYY	AL	32	81	23	4	0	1	(1	0)	30	7	9	10	4	0	22	0	0	0	0	0	0	.284	.318	.370	.688
2015	NYY	AL	67	155	43	9	1	3	(1	2)	63	21	14	17	12	0	43	1	1	3	0	0	4	.277	.327	.406	.734
2016	Min	AL	26	82	12	3	0	1	(1	0)	18	4	3	0	5	0	19	0	2	1	0	0	3	.146	.193	.220	.413
	4 ML YEARS		141	344	82	17	1	5	(3	2)	116	35	27	27	22	0	93	1	3	4	0	0	7	.238	.283	.337	.620

Tom Murphy

Bats: R Throws: R Pos: C-12;PH-11   Ht: 6'1" Wt: 220 Born: 4/3/1991 Age: 26

			BATTING																	RUNNING			AVERAGES			
Year	Team	Lg	G	AB	H	2B	3B	HR	(Hm	Rd)	TB	R	RBI	RC	TBB	IBB	SO	HBP	SH	SF	SB	CS	GDP	Avg	OBP	Slg	OPS
2012	TriCity	A-	55	212	61	13	3	6	(-	-)	98	26	38	34	14	1	52	7	1	2	1	1	3	.288	.349	.462	.811
2013	Ashvll	A	80	288	83	26	2	19	(-	-)	170	55	74	64	37	0	87	10	3	3	4	5	2	.288	.385	.590	.975
2013	Tulsa	AA	20	69	20	5	0	3	(-	-)	34	9	9	11	4	0	16	1	0	0	0	0	1	.290	.338	.493	.831
2014	Tulsa	AA	27	94	20	4	0	5	(-	-)	39	16	15	13	14	0	27	1	0	0	0	0	4	.213	.321	.415	.736

Year Team	Lg	G	AB	H	2B	3B	HR	(Hm	Rd)	TB	R	RBI	RC	TBB	IBB	SO	HBP	SH	SF	SB	CS	GDP	Avg	OBP	Slg	OPS
2015 NwBrit	AA	72	265	66	17	1	13	(-	-)	124	36	44	41	23	1	80	5	0	1	5	2	3	.249	.320	.468	.788
2015 Albq	AAA	33	129	35	9	2	7	(-	-)	69	19	19	20	5	1	43	1	0	1	0	1	3	.271	.301	.535	.836
2016 Albq	AAA	80	303	99	26	7	19	(-	-)	196	53	59	67	16	0	78	1	0	1	1	1	5	.327	.361	.647	1.008
2015 Col	NL	11	35	9	1	0	3	(3	0)	19	5	9	9	4	1	10	0	0	0	0	0	0	.257	.333	.543	.876
2016 Col	NL	21	44	12	2	0	5	(5	0)	29	8	13	10	4	0	19	1	0	0	1	0	2	.273	.347	.659	1.006
2 ML YEARS		32	79	21	3	0	8	(8	0)	48	13	22	19	8	1	29	1	0	0	1	0	2	.266	.341	.608	.949

Colton Murray

Pitches: R Bats: R Pos: RP-24 **Ht: 6'0" Wt: 195 Born: 4/22/1990 Age: 27**

Year Team	Lg	G	GS	CG	GF	IP	BFP	H	R	ER	HR	SH	SF	HB	TBB	IBB	SO	WP	Bk	W	L	Pct	Sh	Sv-Op	Hld	ERC	ERA
2012 2 Tms	Low	44	0	0	24	60.1	262	60	34	25	4	1	3	5	21	1	62	7	1	1	4	.200	0	8--	-	3.89	3.73
2013 Clrwtr	A+	47	0	0	33	66.1	291	66	38	37	6	2	2	2	27	2	75	7	0	5	7	.417	0	11--	-	4.02	5.02
2014 Clrwtr	A+	11	0	0	8	17.1	75	16	4	4	0	1	0	8	1	17	3	0	2	2	.500	0	2--	-	3.06	2.08
2014 Rdng	AA	36	2	0	14	59.0	235	39	22	15	5	2	1	2	22	0	60	4	0	1	5	.167	0	6--	-	2.27	2.29
2015 LV	AAA	31	0	0	15	42.0	171	24	16	13	2	0	2	1	21	0	41	2	0	2	2	.500	0	2--	-	1.98	2.79
2015 Rdng	AA	21	0	0	10	35.2	147	31	10	10	1	0	2	0	10	0	36	0	0	6	1	.857	0	1--	-	2.44	2.52
2016 LV	AAA	27	0	0	6	36.2	153	31	14	12	2	0	1	2	15	0	36	2	0	2	2	.500	0	0--	-	3.22	2.95
2015 Phi	NL	8	0	0	6	7.2	37	11	5	5	2	0	0	0	2	0	9	1	0	0	1	.000	0	0-0	0	6.98	5.87
2016 Phi	NL	24	0	0	4	31.2	142	34	22	22	6	2	1	2	13	1	31	5	0	1	1	.500	0	0-0	1	5.37	6.25
2 ML YEARS		32	0	0	10	39.1	179	45	27	27	8	2	1	2	15	1	40	6	0	1	2	.333	0	0-0	1	5.68	6.18

Joe Musgrove

Pitches: R Bats: R Pos: SP-10; RP-1 **Ht: 6'5" Wt: 265 Born: 12/4/1992 Age: 24**

Year Team	Lg	G	GS	CG	GF	IP	BFP	H	R	ER	HR	SH	SF	HB	TBB	IBB	SO	WP	Bk	W	L	Pct	Sh	Sv-Op	Hld	ERC	ERA
2012 2 Tms	Low	6	1	0	0	17.0	72	19	8	8	0	0	0	1	4	0	19	1	0	0	1	.000	0	0--	-	3.68	4.24
2013 Astros	R	11	3	0	4	32.2	149	43	22	16	1	0	1	2	4	0	30	3	0	1	3	.250	0	0--	-	4.32	4.41
2014 TriCity	A-	15	13	0	0	77.0	301	64	25	24	4	3	0	2	10	1	67	0	0	7	1	.875	0	0--	-	2.02	2.81
2015 2 Tms	Low	11	7	0	3	55.2	218	50	13	10	2	2	1	3	2	0	66	2	0	8	1	.889	0	0--	-	2.03	1.62
2015 CpChr	AA	8	7	0	1	45.0	174	35	13	11	7	1	0	0	6	0	33	2	0	4	0	1.000	0	1--	-	2.25	2.20
2016 CpChr	AA	6	4	0	1	26.1	102	19	2	1	1	0	0	0	3	0	30	1	0	2	1	.667	0	0--	-	1.40	0.34
2016 Fresno	AAA	10	10	0	0	59.0	237	60	26	25	8	0	0	1	7	0	57	1	0	5	3	.625	0	0--	-	3.42	3.81
2016 Hou	AL	11	10	0	1	62.0	256	59	28	28	9	0	1	3	16	0	55	0	0	4	4	.500	0	0-0	0	3.80	4.06

Wil Myers

Bats: R Throws: R Pos: 1B-149;RF-7;LF-3;PH-3;3B-1 **Ht: 6'3" Wt: 205 Born: 12/10/1990 Age: 26**

Year Team	Lg	G	AB	H	2B	3B	HR	(Hm	Rd)	TB	R	RBI	RC	TBB	IBB	SO	HBP	SH	SF	SB	CS	GDP	Avg	OBP	Slg	OPS
2013 TB	AL	88	335	98	23	0	13	(5	8)	160	50	53	52	33	6	91	1	0	4	5	2	10	.293	.354	.478	.831
2014 TB	AL	87	325	72	14	0	6	(2	4)	104	37	35	32	34	3	90	0	0	2	6	1	10	.222	.294	.320	.614
2015 SD	NL	60	225	57	13	1	8	(3	5)	96	40	29	35	27	0	55	1	0	0	5	2	2	.253	.336	.427	.763
2016 SD	NL	157	599	155	29	4	28	(18	10)	276	99	94	97	68	1	160	4	0	5	28	6	12	.259	.336	.461	.797
Postseason		5	20	2	0	0	0	(0	0)	2	0	0	0	1	0	7	0	0	0	0	0	0	.100	.143	.100	.243
4 ML YEARS		392	1484	382	79	5	55	(28	27)	636	226	211	216	162	10	396	6	0	11	44	11	34	.257	.331	.429	.759

Mike Napoli

Bats: R Throws: R Pos: 1B-98;DH-51;PH-1 NAPP-uh-lee **Ht: 6'1" Wt: 225 Born: 10/31/1981 Age: 35**

Year Team	Lg	G	AB	H	2B	3B	HR	(Hm	Rd)	TB	R	RBI	RC	TBB	IBB	SO	HBP	SH	SF	SB	CS	GDP	Avg	OBP	Slg	OPS
2006 LAA	AL	99	268	61	13	0	16	(10	6)	122	47	42	40	51	0	90	5	0	1	2	3	2	.228	.360	.455	.815
2007 LAA	AL	75	219	54	11	1	10	(5	5)	97	40	34	35	33	2	63	5	1	5	5	2	5	.247	.351	.443	.794
2008 LAA	AL	78	227	62	9	1	20	(10	10)	133	39	49	46	35	5	70	5	1	6	7	3	3	.273	.374	.586	.960
2009 LAA	AL	114	382	104	22	1	20	(10	10)	188	60	56	53	40	1	103	7	0	3	3	3	3	.272	.350	.492	.842
2010 LAA	AL	140	453	108	24	1	26	(13	13)	212	60	68	60	42	2	137	11	0	4	4	2	15	.238	.316	.468	.784
2011 Tex	AL	113	369	118	25	0	30	(13	17)	233	72	75	90	58	2	85	3	0	2	4	2	10	.320	.414	.631	1.046
2012 Tex	AL	108	352	80	9	2	24	(11	13)	165	53	56	54	56	5	125	7	0	2	1	0	9	.227	.343	.469	.812
2013 Bos	AL	139	498	129	38	2	23	(11	12)	240	79	92	79	73	3	187	6	0	1	1	1	15	.259	.360	.482	.842
2014 Bos	AL	119	415	103	20	0	17	(6	11)	174	49	55	54	78	3	133	4	0	3	3	2	12	.248	.370	.419	.789
2015 2 Tms	AL	133	407	91	20	1	18	(13	5)	167	46	50	50	57	3	118	4	0	1	3	3	11	.224	.324	.410	.734
2016 Cle	AL	150	557	133	22	1	34	(22	12)	259	92	101	88	78	2	194	5	0	5	5	1	15	.239	.335	.465	.800
15 Bos	AL	98	329	68	18	1	13	(9	4)	127	37	40	36	45	2	99	3	0	1	3	1	10	.207	.307	.386	.693
15 Tex	AL	35	78	23	2	0	5	(4	1)	40	9	10	14	12	1	19	1	0	0	0	2	1	.295	.396	.513	.908
Postseason		51	145	36	6	0	7	(1	6)	63	20	27	25	21	2	49	3	0	2	1	1	3	.248	.351	.434	.785
11 ML YEARS		1268	4147	1043	213	10	238	(124	114)	1990	637	678	649	601	28	1305	62	2	33	38	22	103	.252	.352	.480	.832

Tyler Naquin

Bats: L Throws: R Pos: CF-105;PH-11;RF-4;PR-4 NAY-kwin **Ht: 6'2" Wt: 195 Born: 4/24/1991 Age: 26**

Year Team	Lg	G	AB	H	2B	3B	HR	(Hm	Rd)	TB	R	RBI	RC	TBB	IBB	SO	HBP	SH	SF	SB	CS	GDP	Avg	OBP	Slg	OPS
2012 MhVlly	A-	36	137	37	11	2	0	(-	-)	52	22	13	21	17	0	26	7	0	0	4	3	5	.270	.379	.380	.758
2013 Carlna	A+	108	448	124	27	6	9	(-	-)	190	69	42	67	41	0	112	6	2	1	14	7	8	.277	.345	.424	.769
2013 Akron	AA	18	80	18	3	0	1	(-	-)	24	9	6	5	5	0	22	0	0	0	1	3	0	.225	.271	.300	.571
2014 Akron	AA	76	304	95	12	5	4	(-	-)	129	54	30	51	29	0	71	2	1	5	14	3	4	.313	.371	.424	.795

Year	Team	Lg	G	AB	H	2B	3B	HR	(Hm	Rd)	TB	R	RBI	RC	TBB	IBB	SO	HBP	SH	SF	SB	CS	GDP	Avg	OBP	Slg	OPS
2015	Akron	AA	34	141	49	12	1	1	(-	-)	66	16	10	29	15	1	24	3	0	1	7	1	3	.348	.419	.468	.887
2015	Clmbs	AAA	50	186	49	13	0	6	(-	-)	80	34	17	30	25	2	49	2	3	2	6	2	3	.263	.353	.430	.784
2016	Clmbs	AAA	17	70	20	3	1	1	(-	-)	28	6	8	10	8	0	15	0	0	1	1	2	1	.286	.354	.400	.754
2016	Cle	AL	116	321	95	18	5	14	(9	5)	165	52	43	53	36	4	112	4	2	2	6	3	4	.296	.372	.514	.886

Omar Narvaez

Bats: L **Throws:** R **Pos:** C-34;PH-1 nar-VAH-es **Ht:** 5'11" **Wt:** 215 **Born:** 2/10/1992 **Age:** 25

Year	Team	Lg	G	AB	H	2B	3B	HR	(Hm	Rd)	TB	R	RBI	RC	TBB	IBB	SO	HBP	SH	SF	SB	CS	GDP	Avg	OBP	Slg	OPS
2012	Prnctn	R+	43	151	46	7	1	1	(-	-)	58	24	16	23	17	1	19	2	2	1	4	2	4	.305	.380	.384	.764
2013	HudVal	A-	39	150	40	6	2	0	(-	-)	50	13	13	15	8	0	21	2	1	1	0	2	6	.267	.311	.333	.644
2014	2 Tms	Low	85	267	76	11	0	2	(-	-)	93	25	36	38	36	0	32	3	1	9	3	2	12	.285	.365	.348	.713
2015	WinSa	A+	98	339	93	10	0	1	(-	-)	106	38	27	42	40	1	31	2	1	3	1	0	12	.274	.352	.313	.664
2016	Brham	AA	13	45	10	2	0	0	(-	-)	12	4	5	3	4	0	8	0	0	0	0	0	1	.222	.286	.267	.552
2016	Charllt	AAA	41	143	35	6	0	2	(-	-)	47	14	11	14	9	0	17	1	2	1	0	0	7	.245	.292	.329	.621
2016	CWS	AL	34	101	27	4	0	1	(1	0)	34	13	10	15	14	1	14	0	0	2	0	0	0	.267	.350	.337	.687

Chris Narveson

Pitches: L **Bats:** L **Pos:** RP-6 NARR-vih-son **Ht:** 6'3" **Wt:** 205 **Born:** 12/20/1981 **Age:** 35

			HOW MUCH HE PITCHED						WHAT HE GAVE UP									THE RESULTS							
Year	Team	Lg	G	GS	CG	GF	IP	BFP	H	R	ER	HR	SH	SF	HB	TBB	IBB	SO	WP	Bk	W	L	Pct	Sh	Sv-Op	Hld	ERC	ERA
2016	NewOr*	AAA	20	15	0	1	89.2	369	76	36	34	10	4	1	1	30	0	68	5	0	4	6	.400	0	0- -	-	3.13	3.41
2006	StL	NL	5	1	0	1	9.1	40	6	5	5	1	0	0	1	5	0	12	1	1	0	0	-	0	0-0	0	3.06	4.82
2009	Mil	NL	21	4	0	5	47.0	205	45	22	20	7	2	3	2	16	1	46	4	0	2	0	1.000	0	0-0	0	3.96	3.83
2010	Mil	NL	37	28	0	2	167.2	724	172	96	93	21	8	5	5	59	3	137	6	0	12	9	.571	0	0-1	3	4.30	4.99
2011	Mil	NL	30	28	0	0	161.2	699	160	82	80	17	6	4	1	65	1	126	4	1	11	8	.579	0	0-0	0	4.06	4.45
2012	Mil	NL	2	2	0	0	9.0	41	10	8	7	2	1	2	0	4	0	5	0	0	1	1	.500	0	0-0	0	5.69	7.00
2013	Mil	NL	2	0	0	1	2.0	8	1	0	0	0	0	0	0	1	0	1	0	0	0	0	-	0	0-0	0	1.41	0.00
2015	Mia	NL	15	2	0	3	30.1	121	24	15	15	7	0	0	0	9	0	32	0	0	3	1	.750	0	0-0	0	3.40	4.45
2016	Mia	NL	6	0	0	2	8.1	38	10	8	8	3	0	0	1	2	1	6	1	0	1	0	1.000	0	0-1	0	6.69	8.64
	Postseason		6	0	0	2	7.1	33	7	9	9	5	0	1	0	2	1	13	0	0	0	0	-	0	0-0	0	6.33	11.05
	8 ML YEARS		118	65	0	14	435.1	1876	428	236	228	58	17	14	10	161	6	364	17	2	30	19	.612	0	0-2	3	4.14	4.71

Joe Nathan

Pitches: R **Bats:** R **Pos:** RP-10 NARR-vih-son **Ht:** 6'4" **Wt:** 230 **Born:** 11/22/1974 **Age:** 42

			HOW MUCH HE PITCHED						WHAT HE GAVE UP									THE RESULTS							
Year	Team	Lg	G	GS	CG	GF	IP	BFP	H	R	ER	HR	SH	SF	HB	TBB	IBB	SO	WP	Bk	W	L	Pct	Sh	Sv-Op	Hld	ERC	ERA
2016	Tenn*	AA	7	0	0	0	6.2	23	3	2	2	2	0	0	0	0	0	6	0	0	0	1	.000	0	0- -	-	1.09	2.70
2016	Rchmd*	AA	6	0	0	6	6.0	22	3	0	0	0	0	0	0	1	0	7	0	0	1	0	1.000	0	2- -	0	0.80	0.00
1999	SF	NL	19	14	0	2	90.1	395	84	45	42	17	2	0	1	46	0	54	2	0	7	4	.636	0	1-1	0	4.78	4.18
2000	SF	NL	20	15	0	0	93.1	426	89	63	54	12	5	5	4	63	4	61	5	0	5	2	.714	0	0-1	0	5.23	5.21
2002	SF	NL	4	0	0	3	3.2	12	1	0	0	0	0	0	0	0	0	2	0	0	0	0	-	0	0-0	0	0.17	0.00
2003	SF	NL	78	0	0	9	79.0	316	51	26	26	7	2	4	3	33	3	83	4	1	12	4	.750	0	0-3	20	2.34	2.96
2004	Min	AL	73	0	0	63	72.1	284	48	14	13	3	2	0	2	23	3	89	5	0	1	2	.333	0	44-47	0	1.78	1.62
2005	Min	AL	69	0	0	58	70.0	276	46	22	21	5	1	2	0	22	1	94	2	0	7	4	.636	0	43-48	0	1.83	2.70
2006	Min	AL	64	0	0	61	68.1	262	38	12	12	3	3	2	1	16	4	95	3	0	7	0	1.000	0	36-38	0	1.18	1.58
2007	Min	AL	68	0	0	60	71.2	282	54	15	15	4	2	2	1	19	2	77	3	0	4	2	.667	0	37-41	0	2.08	1.88
2008	Min	AL	68	0	0	57	67.2	261	43	13	10	5	1	0	2	18	4	74	2	0	1	2	.333	0	39-45	0	1.67	1.33
2009	Min	AL	70	0	0	62	68.2	271	42	16	16	7	1	0	2	22	1	89	4	0	2	2	.500	0	47-52	0	1.89	2.10
2011	Min	AL	48	0	0	33	44.2	191	38	26	24	7	1	2	3	14	2	43	3	0	2	1	.667	0	14-17	8	3.38	4.84
2012	Tex	AL	66	0	0	62	64.1	257	55	23	20	7	1	3	2	13	1	78	5	0	3	5	.375	0	37-40	0	2.73	2.80
2013	Tex	AL	67	0	0	61	64.2	250	36	10	10	2	3	2	1	22	3	73	4	0	6	2	.750	0	43-46	0	1.39	1.39
2014	Det	AL	62	0	0	54	58.0	259	60	32	31	5	2	1	4	29	3	54	4	1	5	4	.556	0	35-42	0	4.53	4.81
2015	Det	AL	1	0	0	1	0.1	1	0	0	0	0	0	0	0	0	0	0	0	0	0	0	-	0	1-1	0	0.00	0.00
2016	2 Tms	NL	10	0	0	1	6.1	28	5	0	0	0	0	0	0	4	0	9	1	0	2	0	1.000	0	0-1	0	3.01	0.00
16	ChC	NL	3	0	0	0	2.0	10	2	0	0	0	0	0	0	2	0	4	0	0	1	0	1.000	0	0-0	0	5.48	0.00
16	SF	NL	7	0	0	1	4.1	18	3	0	0	0	0	0	0	2	0	5	1	0	1	0	1.000	0	0-1	0	2.02	0.00
	Postseason		10	0	0	5	10.0	52	14	9	9	2	0	1	0	8	3	12	1	0	0	2	.000	0	1-3	0	8.32	8.10
	16 ML YEARS		787	29	0	587	923.1	3771	690	317	294	84	25	24	23	344	31	976	47	2	64	34	.653	0	377-423	28	2.62	2.87

Daniel Nava

Bats: B **Throws:** L **Pos:** LF-37;PH-13;1B-6;RF-2;DH-1 NAH-vah **Ht:** 5'11" **Wt:** 200 **Born:** 2/22/1983 **Age:** 34

Year	Team	Lg	G	AB	H	2B	3B	HR	(Hm	Rd)	TB	R	RBI	RC	TBB	IBB	SO	HBP	SH	SF	SB	CS	GDP	Avg	OBP	Slg	OPS
2016	Salt Lk*	AAA	22	85	31	6	0	1	(-	-)	40	5	13	16	6	0	10	1	0	0	1	1	2	.365	.413	.471	.884
2010	Bos	AL	60	161	39	14	1	1	(1	0)	58	23	26	26	19	1	46	8	0	0	1	1	5	.242	.351	.360	.711
2012	Bos	AL	88	267	65	21	4	6	(1	5)	104	38	33	33	37	1	63	9	2	2	3	0	5	.243	.352	.390	.742
2013	Bos	AL	134	458	139	29	0	12	(5	7)	204	77	66	79	51	2	93	15	4	8	0	2	10	.303	.385	.445	.831
2014	Bos	AL	113	363	98	21	0	4	(0	4)	131	41	37	49	33	1	81	10	0	2	4	2	5	.270	.346	.361	.706
2015	2 Tms	AL	60	139	27	4	0	1	(1	0)	34	13	10	15	20	0	36	5	1	1	1	0	4	.194	.315	.245	.560
2016	2 Tms	AL	54	130	29	6	0	1	(1	0)	38	11	13	11	10	0	30	5	0	3	0	0	2	.223	.297	.292	.590
15	Bos	AL	29	66	10	2	0	0	(0	0)	12	6	7	5	8	0	17	2	1	1	0	0	3	.152	.260	.182	.442
15	TB	AL	31	73	17	2	0	1	(1	0)	22	7	3	10	12	0	19	3	0	0	1	0	1	.233	.364	.301	.665
16	LAA	AL	45	119	28	5	0	1	(1	0)	36	10	13	11	9	0	26	5	0	3	0	0	2	.235	.309	.303	.611
16	KC	AL	9	11	1	1	0	0	(0	0)	2	1	0	0	1	0	4	0	0	0	0	0	0	.091	.167	.182	.348
	Postseason		9	25	5	1	0	0	(0	0)	6	1	2	2	3	0	9	0	0	1	0	1	1	.200	.286	.240	.526
	6 ML YEARS		509	1518	397	95	1	25	(9	16)	569	203	185	213	170	5	349	52	7	16	9	5	31	.262	.353	.375	.727

Dioner Navarro

Bats: B **Throws:** R **Pos:** C-90;PH-11;DH-3   dee-AHN-err   **Ht:** 5'9" **Wt:** 215 **Born:** 2/9/1984 **Age:** 33

Year	Team	Lg	G	AB	H	2B	3B	HR	(Hm	Rd)	TB	R	RBI	RC	TBB	IBB	SO	HBP	SH	SF	SB	CS	GDP	Avg	OBP	Slg	OPS
2004	NYY	AL	5	7	3	0	0	0	(0	0)	3	2	1	1	0	0	0	0	0	0	0	0	1	.429	.429	.429	.857
2005	LAD	NL	50	176	48	9	0	3	(3	0)	66	21	14	18	20	1	21	2	1	0	0	0	3	.273	.354	.375	.729
2006	2 Tms		81	268	68	9	0	6	(4	2)	95	28	28	27	31	6	51	1	1	1	2	1	7	.254	.332	.354	.687
2007	TB	AL	119	388	88	19	2	9	(5	4)	138	44	44	35	33	3	67	1	7	5	3	1	11	.227	.286	.356	.641
2008	TB	AL	120	427	126	27	0	7	(4	3)	174	43	54	59	34	1	49	3	3	3	0	4	16	.295	.349	.407	.757
2009	TB	AL	115	376	82	15	0	8	(4	4)	121	38	32	22	18	1	51	5	8	3	5	2	14	.218	.261	.322	.583
2010	TB	AL	48	124	24	5	0	1	(1	0)	32	11	7	4	12	0	20	1	5	0	0	1	3	.194	.270	.258	.528
2011	LAD	NL	64	176	34	6	1	5	(3	2)	57	13	17	14	20	4	35	1	3	2	0	0	3	.193	.276	.324	.600
2012	Cin	NL	24	69	20	3	1	2	(0	2)	31	6	12	10	2	1	12	0	1	1	0	0	1	.290	.306	.449	.755
2013	ChC	NL	89	240	72	7	0	13	(9	4)	118	31	34	43	23	1	36	2	0	1	0	1	4	.300	.365	.492	.856
2014	Tor	AL	139	481	132	22	0	12	(9	3)	190	40	69	68	32	1	76	1	0	6	3	0	12	.274	.317	.395	.712
2015	Tor	AL	54	171	42	7	0	5	(3	2)	64	17	20	21	17	1	29	0	0	4	0	0	0	.246	.307	.374	.682
2016	2 Tms	AL	101	304	63	13	2	6	(5	1)	98	26	35	27	23	0	71	2	2	3	1	2	5	.207	.265	.322	.587
06	LAD	NL	25	75	21	2	0	2	(1	1)	29	5	8	8	11	4	18	0	0	1	0	1	0	.280	.372	.387	.759
06	TB	AL	56	193	47	7	0	4	(3	1)	66	23	20	19	20	2	33	1	1	1	1	1	6	.244	.316	.342	.658
16	CWS	AL	85	271	57	13	2	6	(5	1)	92	25	32	25	20	0	63	2	2	3	1	2	5	.210	.267	.339	.606
16	Tor	AL	16	33	6	0	0	0	(0	0)	6	1	3	2	3	0	8	0	0	0	0	0	0	.182	.250	.182	.432
	Postseason		23	75	19	5	0	0	(0	0)	24	5	5	6	6	0	18	0	0	0	0	1	3	.253	.309	.320	.629
	13 ML YEARS		1009	3207	802	142	6	77	(50	27)	1187	322	367	349	265	20	518	19	31	29	14	12	80	.250	.309	.370	.679

Zach Neal

Pitches: R **Bats:** R **Pos:** RP-18; SP-6   **Ht:** 6'3" **Wt:** 220 **Born:** 11/9/1988 **Age:** 28

Year	Team	Lg	G	GS	CG	GF	IP	BFP	H	R	ER	HR	SH	SF	HB	TBB	IBB	SO	WP	Bk	W	L	Pct	Sh	Sv-Op	Hld	ERC	ERA
2012	Jupiter	A+	9	8	0	0	44.2	180	41	7	6	2	0	1	0	10	1	33	0	0	4	1	.800	0	0- -	-	2.62	1.21
2012	Jaxnvl	AA	21	10	0	4	68.2	290	77	36	29	4	4	4	3	12	0	45	1	0	4	6	.400	0	0- -	-	3.77	3.80
2013	Mdlnd	AA	28	28	1	0	165.2	696	172	95	80	18	3	5	6	36	1	96	2	2	8	12	.400	1	0- -	-	3.77	4.35
2014	Mdlnd	AA	5	5	0	0	31.0	125	25	5	2	0	0	0	3	4	0	25	1	0	3	0	1.000	0	0- -	-	1.81	0.58
2014	Scrmto	AAA	20	19	0	0	119.1	500	137	70	54	15	3	2	4	16	0	80	2	0	7	7	.500	0	0- -	-	4.20	4.07
2015	Mdlnd	AA	7	7	0	0	36.1	160	43	26	26	7	1	1	1	15	0	22	0	0	3	3	.500	0	0- -	-	6.21	6.44
2015	Nashv	AAA	21	20	2	0	131.1	553	151	71	61	10	4	5	5	20	0	78	2	0	7	10	.412	0	0- -	-	3.96	4.18
2016	Nashv	AAA	11	11	0	0	61.2	254	62	27	22	5	3	3	1	8	0	32	1	0	2	2	.778	0	0- -	-	2.97	3.21
2016	Oak	AL	24	6	0	7	70.0	281	72	35	33	9	0	2	1	6	0	27	2	1	2	4	.333	0	2-3	0	3.28	4.24

Jimmy Nelson

Pitches: R **Bats:** R **Pos:** SP-32   **Ht:** 6'6" **Wt:** 250 **Born:** 6/5/1989 **Age:** 28

Year	Team	Lg	G	GS	CG	GF	IP	BFP	H	R	ER	HR	SH	SF	HB	TBB	IBB	SO	WP	Bk	W	L	Pct	Sh	Sv-Op	Hld	ERC	ERA
2013	Mil	NL	4	1	0	0	10.0	37	2	1	1	0	0	1	0	5	0	8	1	0	0	0	-	0	0-0	0	0.64	0.90
2014	Mil	NL	14	12	0	1	69.1	311	82	42	38	6	1	2	8	19	0	57	4	0	2	9	.182	0	0-0	0	4.96	4.93
2015	Mil	NL	30	30	0	0	177.1	752	163	89	81	18	4	7	13	65	4	148	11	1	11	13	.458	0	0-0	0	3.79	4.11
2016	Mil	NL	32	32	0	0	179.1	807	186	108	92	25	7	4	17	86	2	140	8	0	8	16	.333	0	0-0	0	5.29	4.62
	4 ML YEARS		80	75	0	1	436.0	1907	433	240	212	49	12	14	38	175	6	353	24	1	21	38	.356	0	0-0	0	4.47	4.38

Hector Neris

Pitches: R **Bats:** R **Pos:** RP-79   NAIR-ess   **Ht:** 6'2" **Wt:** 215 **Born:** 6/14/1989 **Age:** 28

Year	Team	Lg	G	GS	CG	GF	IP	BFP	H	R	ER	HR	SH	SF	HB	TBB	IBB	SO	WP	Bk	W	L	Pct	Sh	Sv-Op	Hld	ERC	ERA
2014	Phi	NL	1	0	0	1	1.0	3	0	0	0	0	0	0	0	0	0	1	0	0	1	0	1.000	0	0-0	0	0.00	0.00
2015	Phi	NL	32	0	0	1	40.1	170	38	19	17	8	1	0	4	10	0	41	3	0	2	2	.500	0	0-0	2	4.21	3.79
2016	Phi	NL	79	0	0	13	80.1	328	59	26	23	9	1	2	3	30	3	102	4	1	4	4	.500	0	2-6	28	2.73	2.58
	3 ML YEARS		112	0	0	22	121.2	501	97	45	40	17	2	2	7	40	3	144	7	1	7	6	.538	0	2-6	30	3.15	2.96

Pat Neshek

Pitches: R **Bats:** B **Pos:** RP-60   NEE-sheck   **Ht:** 6'3" **Wt:** 220 **Born:** 9/4/1980 **Age:** 36

Year	Team	Lg	G	GS	CG	GF	IP	BFP	H	R	ER	HR	SH	SF	HB	TBB	IBB	SO	WP	Bk	W	L	Pct	Sh	Sv-Op	Hld	ERC	ERA
2006	Min	AL	32	0	0	3	37.0	138	23	9	9	6	0	1	0	6	0	53	0	0	4	2	.667	0	0-2	10	1.68	2.19
2007	Min	AL	74	0	0	20	70.1	278	44	25	23	7	4	5	2	27	5	74	2	0	7	2	.778	0	0-3	15	2.12	2.94
2008	Min	AL	15	0	0	3	13.1	56	12	7	7	2	1	1	0	4	1	15	0	0	1	0	1.000	0	0-2	6	3.29	4.73
2010	Min	AL	11	0	0	3	9.0	43	7	5	5	1	0	0	1	8	0	9	0	0	0	1	.000	0	0-1	1	5.13	5.00
2011	SD	NL	25	0	0	13	24.2	112	19	12	11	4	1	0	1	22	1	20	1	0	1	1	.500	0	0-0	0	5.37	4.01
2012	Oak	AL	24	0	0	5	19.2	77	10	3	3	3	0	2	1	6	1	16	1	0	2	1	.667	0	0-2	4	1.66	1.37
2013	Oak	AL	45	0	0	17	40.1	177	40	17	15	6	0	3	0	15	2	29	1	0	2	1	.667	0	0-0	1	4.06	3.35
2014	StL	NL	71	0	0	17	67.1	255	44	14	14	4	2	2	2	9	2	68	1	0	7	2	.778	0	6-10	25	1.38	1.87
2015	Hou	AL	66	0	0	8	54.2	223	49	25	22	8	4	1	2	12	1	51	1	0	3	6	.333	0	1-4	38	3.23	3.62
2016	Hou	AL	60	0	0	9	47.0	185	33	17	16	6	3	1	0	11	7	43	1	0	2	2	.500	0	0-0	18	1.89	3.06
	Postseason		13	0	0	4	10.1	38	6	3	3	2	0	0	0	0	0	10	0	0	0	2	.000	0	0-1	3	1.20	2.61
	10 ML YEARS		423	0	0	98	383.1	1544	281	134	125	47	15	16	9	120	20	378	8	0	28	19	.596	0	7-24	108	2.49	2.93

Juan Nicasio

Pitches: R **Bats:** R **Pos:** RP-40; SP-12   nih-KAH-see-oh   **Ht:** 6'4" **Wt:** 250 **Born:** 8/31/1986 **Age:** 30

			HOW MUCH HE PITCHED						WHAT HE GAVE UP										THE RESULTS						
Year	Team	Lg	G	GS	CG	GF	IP	BFP	H	R	ER	HR	SH	SF	HB	TBB	IBB	SO	WP	Bk	W	L	Pct	Sh	Sv-Op	Hld	ERC	ERA
2011	Col	NL	13	13	0	0	71.2	299	73	35	33	8	1	0	1	18	3	58	1	0	4	4	.500	0	0-0	0	3.69	4.14
2012	Col	NL	11	11	0	0	58.0	257	72	37	34	7	3	1	1	22	1	54	4	0	2	3	.400	0	0-0	0	5.74	5.28
2013	Col	NL	31	31	0	0	157.2	703	168	97	90	17	6	1	5	64	7	119	6	2	9	9	.500	0	0-0	0	4.52	5.14
2014	Col	NL	33	14	0	7	93.2	409	107	59	56	19	5	2	1	63	3	63	3	1	6	6	.500	0	0-0	1	5.43	5.38
2015	LAD	NL	53	1	0	12	58.1	260	59	25	25	1	3	0	1	32	6	65	2	0	1	3	.250	0	1-3	14	4.00	3.86
2016	Pit	NL	52	12	0	9	118.0	513	117	64	59	15	5	7	7	45	3	138	3	0	10	7	.588	0	0-2	6	4.33	4.50
	6 ML YEARS		193	82	0	28	557.1	2441	596	317	297	67	23	11	16	212	21	497	19	3	32	32	.500	0	1-5	21	4.59	4.80

Brett Nicholas

Bats: L **Throws:** R **Pos:** C-15   **Ht:** 6'2" **Wt:** 220 **Born:** 7/18/1988 **Age:** 28

									BATTING											RUNNING			AVERAGES			
Year	Team	Lg	G	AB	H	2B	3B	HR	(Hm	Rd)	TB	R	RBI	RC	TBB	IBB	SO	HBP	SH	SF	SB	CS	GDP	Avg	OBP	Slg	OPS
2012	MrtlBh	A+	122	446	127	33	0	8	(-	-)	184	49	63	69	44	3	58	6	0	8	5	1	8	.285	.351	.413	.764
2013	Frisco	AA	136	506	146	25	3	21	(-	-)	240	71	91	89	46	7	123	13	0	10	2	1	8	.289	.357	.474	.831
2014	RdRck	AAA	127	452	124	20	1	10	(-	-)	176	40	58	59	27	2	112	7	1	4	4	1	11	.274	.322	.389	.712
2015	RdRck	AAA	109	403	108	22	0	12	(-	-)	166	49	63	53	27	1	79	2	1	5	2	2	12	.268	.314	.412	.725
2016	RdRck	AAA	101	400	115	27	1	13	(-	-)	183	57	58	65	38	1	88	3	3	3	2	2	15	.288	.351	.458	.809
2016	Tex	AL	15	40	11	5	0	2	(1	1)	22	5	4	7	4	0	9	1	0	0	0	0	2	.275	.356	.550	.906

Justin Nicolino

Pitches: L **Bats:** L **Pos:** SP-13; RP-5   **Ht:** 6'3" **Wt:** 195 **Born:** 11/22/1991 **Age:** 25

					HOW MUCH HE PITCHED					WHAT HE GAVE UP										THE RESULTS						
Year	Team	Lg	G	GS	CG	GF	IP	BFP	H	R	ER	HR	SH	SF	HB	TBB	IBB	SO	WP	Bk	W	L	Pct	Sh	Sv-Op	Hld	ERC	ERA
2012	Lnsng	A	28	22	0	0	124.1	495	112	41	34	6	3	2	5	21	1	119	4	1	10	4	.714	0	0- -	-	2.54	2.46
2013	Jupiter	A+	18	18	1	0	96.2	385	89	27	24	4	2	3	2	18	0	64	1	1	5	2	.714	0	0- -	-	2.61	2.23
2013	Jaxnvl	AA	9	9	1	0	45.1	205	63	29	25	2	4	2	2	12	0	31	1	0	3	2	.600	0	0- -	-	5.64	4.96
2014	Jaxnvl	AA	28	28	2	0	170.1	686	163	68	55	10	7	4	5	20	1	81	2	0	14	4	.778	2	0- -	-	2.62	2.91
2015	NewOr	AAA	20	20	0	0	115.0	487	134	51	45	11	5	2	4	29	2	63	0	0	7	7	.500	0	0- -	-	4.64	3.52
2016	NewOr	AAA	14	14	0	0	85.0	345	87	43	39	10	3	7	0	13	0	49	4	0	7	6	.538	0	0- -	-	3.40	4.13
2015	Mia	NL	12	12	0	0	74.0	301	72	33	33	8	5	3	3	20	2	23	2	0	5	4	.556	0	0-0	0	3.73	4.01
2016	Mia	NL	18	13	0	0	79.1	346	96	45	44	8	4	6	3	20	1	37	1	0	3	6	.333	0	0-0	0	4.87	4.99
	2 ML YEARS		30	25	0	0	153.1	647	168	78	77	16	9	9	6	40	3	60	3	0	8	10	.444	0	0-0	0	4.31	4.52

Jon Niese

Pitches: L **Bats:** L **Pos:** SP-20; RP-9   NIECE   **Ht:** 6'3" **Wt:** 215 **Born:** 10/27/1986 **Age:** 30

					HOW MUCH HE PITCHED					WHAT HE GAVE UP										THE RESULTS						
Year	Team	Lg	G	GS	CG	GF	IP	BFP	H	R	ER	HR	SH	SF	HB	TBB	IBB	SO	WP	Bk	W	L	Pct	Sh	Sv-Op	Hld	ERC	ERA
2008	NYM	NL	3	3	0	0	14.0	69	20	11	11	2	1	0	0	8	0	11	0	0	1	1	.500	0	0-0	0	7.71	7.07
2009	NYM	NL	5	5	0	0	25.2	110	27	12	12	1	2	1	0	9	0	18	1	0	1	1	.500	0	0-0	0	3.76	4.21
2010	NYM	NL	30	30	2	0	173.2	770	192	97	81	20	9	4	9	62	3	148	5	0	9	10	.474	1	0-0	0	4.77	4.20
2011	NYM	NL	27	26	0	0	157.1	694	178	88	77	14	16	2	5	44	4	138	3	0	11	11	.500	0	0-0	0	4.27	4.40
2012	NYM	NL	30	30	0	0	190.1	788	174	77	72	22	8	4	4	49	2	155	6	0	13	9	.591	0	0-0	0	3.21	3.40
2013	NYM	NL	24	24	1	0	143.0	621	158	68	59	10	6	0	4	48	1	105	5	0	8	8	.500	1	0-0	0	4.32	3.71
2014	NYM	NL	30	30	0	0	187.2	786	193	80	71	17	10	5	7	45	0	138	3	0	9	11	.450	0	0-0	0	3.72	3.40
2015	NYM	NL	33	29	0	1	176.2	770	192	93	81	20	16	4	9	55	2	113	2	0	9	10	.474	0	0-0	0	4.49	4.13
2016	2 Tms	NL	29	20	0	3	121.0	546	145	77	74	25	5	2	3	47	3	88	11	0	8	7	.533	0	0-0	0	6.06	5.50
16	Pit	NL	23	18	0	2	110.0	491	132	63	60	21	5	1	3	38	2	76	9	0	8	6	.571	0	0-0	0	5.80	4.91
16	NYM	NL	6	2	0	1	11.0	55	13	14	14	4	0	1	0	9	1	12	2	0	0	1	.000	0	0-0	0	8.86	11.45
	Postseason		6	0	0	0	5.1	22	5	3	3	0	0	0	0	1	0	6	0	0	0	0	-	0	0-0	2	2.27	5.06
	9 ML YEARS		211	197	3	4	1189.1	5154	1279	603	538	131	73	22	41	367	15	914	36	0	69	68	.504	2	0-0	0	4.32	4.07

Kirk Nieuwenhuis

Bats: L **Throws:** R **Pos:** CF-83;RF-28;PH-22;LF-5   NEW-enn-hice   **Ht:** 6'3" **Wt:** 225 **Born:** 8/7/1987 **Age:** 29

									BATTING											RUNNING			AVERAGES			
Year	Team	Lg	G	AB	H	2B	3B	HR	(Hm	Rd)	TB	R	RBI	RC	TBB	IBB	SO	HBP	SH	SF	SB	CS	GDP	Avg	OBP	Slg	OPS
2012	NYM	NL	91	282	71	12	1	7	(5	2)	106	40	28	28	25	0	98	2	3	2	4	4	2	.252	.315	.376	.691
2013	NYM	NL	47	95	18	3	1	3	(2	1)	32	10	14	8	12	1	32	0	0	1	2	0	1	.189	.278	.337	.615
2014	NYM	NL	61	112	29	14	1	3	(1	2)	54	16	16	16	16	3	39	0	0	2	4	0	1	.259	.346	.482	.828
2015	2 Tms		74	128	25	11	0	4	(3	1)	48	21	14	10	10	0	49	3	0	0	2	2	2	.195	.270	.375	.645
2016	Mil	NL	125	335	70	18	1	13	(11	2)	129	38	44	40	56	1	133	1	0	0	8	9	5	.209	.324	.385	.709
15	NYM	NL	64	106	22	9	0	4	(3	1)	43	17	13	10	8	0	40	3	0	0	2	1	2	.208	.282	.406	.688
15	LAA	AL	10	22	3	2	0	0	(0	0)	5	4	1	0	2	0	9	0	0	0	0	1	0	.136	.208	.227	.436
	Postseason		4	4	0	0	0	0	(0	0)	0	0	0	0	0	0	2	0	0	0	0	0	0	.000	.000	.000	.000
	5 ML YEARS		398	952	213	58	4	30	(22	8)	369	125	116	102	119	5	351	6	3	5	20	15	11	.224	.312	.388	.700

Brandon Nimmo

Bats: L **Throws:** R **Pos:** PH-14;LF-13;RF-7;CF-4   NIH-moe   **Ht:** 6'3" **Wt:** 205 **Born:** 3/27/1993 **Age:** 24

							BATTING													RUNNING			AVERAGES			
Year	Team	Lg	G	AB	H	2B	3B	HR	(Hm | Rd)	TB	R	RBI	RC	TBB	IBB	SO	HBP	SH	SF	SB	CS	GDP	Avg	OBP	Slg	OPS
2012	Bklyn	A-	69	266	66	20	2	6	(- | -)	108	41	40	42	46	1	78	7	1	1	1	5	3	.248	.372	.406	.778
2013	Savann	A	110	395	108	16	6	2	(- | -)	142	62	40	64	71	1	131	11	1	2	10	7	7	.273	.397	.359	.756
2014	Stluci	A+	62	227	73	9	5	4	(- | -)	104	59	25	50	50	1	51	2	0	0	9	3	3	.322	.448	.458	.906
2014	Bnghtn	AA	65	240	57	12	4	6	(- | -)	95	38	26	35	36	0	54	1	2	0	5	1	4	.238	.339	.396	.735
2015	Bnghtn	AA	68	269	75	12	3	2	(- | -)	99	26	16	37	26	2	55	6	0	1	0	2	4	.279	.354	.368	.722
2015	LsVgs	AAA	32	91	24	3	1	3	(- | -)	38	19	8	16	18	1	20	2	0	1	5	4	0	.264	.393	.418	.810
2016	LsVgs	AAA	97	392	138	25	8	11	(- | -)	212	72	61	86	46	1	73	3	2	1	7	8	10	.352	.423	.541	.964
2016	NYM	NL	32	73	20	1	0	1	(1 | 0)	24	12	6	9	6	0	20	1	0	0	0	0	0	.274	.338	.329	.666

Aaron Nola

Pitches: R **Bats:** R **Pos:** SP-20   NO-luh   **Ht:** 6'2" **Wt:** 195 **Born:** 6/4/1993 **Age:** 24

					HOW MUCH HE PITCHED				WHAT HE GAVE UP											THE RESULTS						
Year	Team	Lg	G	GS	CG	GF	IP	BFP	H	R	ER	HR	SH	SF	HB	TBB	IBB	SO	WP	Bk	W	L	Pct	Sh	Sv-Op	Hld	ERC	ERA
2014	Clrwtr	A+	7	6	0	0	31.1	121	24	12	11	4	2	1	0	5	0	30	1	0	2	3	.400	0	0--	-	2.15	3.16
2014	Rdng	AA	5	5	0	0	24.0	98	25	7	7	4	1	0	0	5	0	15	0	0	2	0	1.000	0	0--	-	4.09	2.63
2015	Rdng	AA	12	12	0	0	76.2	288	59	17	16	4	3	2	3	9	0	59	0	0	7	3	.700	0	0--	-	1.82	1.88
2015	LV	AAA	6	6	0	0	32.2	141	38	14	13	3	0	0	0	9	0	33	0	0	3	1	.750	0	0--	-	4.47	3.58
2015	Phi	NL	13	13	0	0	77.2	318	74	31	31	11	1	1	2	19	1	68	0	0	6	2	.750	0	0-0	0	3.62	3.59
2016	Phi	NL	20	20	0	0	111.0	483	116	68	59	10	5	4	6	29	3	121	2	0	6	9	.400	0	0-0	0	3.80	4.78
	2 ML YEARS		33	33	0	0	188.2	801	190	99	90	21	6	5	8	48	4	189	2	0	12	11	.522	0	0-0	0	3.73	4.29

Ricky Nolasco

Pitches: R **Bats:** R **Pos:** SP-32   **Ht:** 6'2" **Wt:** 235 **Born:** 12/13/1982 **Age:** 34

					HOW MUCH HE PITCHED				WHAT HE GAVE UP											THE RESULTS						
Year	Team	Lg	G	GS	CG	GF	IP	BFP	H	R	ER	HR	SH	SF	HB	TBB	IBB	SO	WP	Bk	W	L	Pct	Sh	Sv-Op	Hld	ERC	ERA
2006	Fla	NL	35	22	0	0	140.0	613	157	86	75	20	8	6	10	41	5	99	7	0	11	11	.500	0	0-0	2	4.89	4.82
2007	Fla	NL	5	4	0	0	21.1	99	26	16	13	3	3	5	1	9	2	11	1	0	1	2	.333	0	0-0	0	5.71	5.48
2008	Fla	NL	34	32	0	0	212.1	868	192	88	83	28	6	9	6	42	6	186	1	3	15	8	.652	1	0-0	0	3.03	3.52
2009	Fla	NL	31	31	2	0	185.0	785	188	111	104	23	8	5	2	44	7	195	2	0	13	9	.591	0	0-0	0	3.62	5.06
2010	Fla	NL	26	26	1	0	157.2	665	169	82	79	24	5	5	2	33	1	147	5	0	14	9	.609	0	0-0	0	4.11	4.51
2011	Fla	NL	33	33	2	0	206.0	891	244	117	107	20	11	5	3	44	8	148	6	0	10	12	.455	1	0-0	0	4.34	4.67
2012	Mia	NL	31	31	3	0	191.0	832	214	100	95	18	19	6	8	47	9	125	8	1	12	13	.480	2	0-0	0	4.14	4.48
2013	2 Tms	NL	34	33	0	0	199.1	834	195	90	82	17	10	3	10	46	1	165	5	0	13	11	.542	0	0-0	0	3.38	3.70
2014	Min	AL	27	27	1	0	159.0	695	203	96	95	22	4	5	5	38	1	115	5	0	6	12	.333	0	0-0	0	5.53	5.38
2015	Min	AL	9	8	0	1	37.1	173	50	31	28	3	0	2	1	14	2	35	1	1	5	2	.714	0	0-0	0	5.82	6.75
2016	2 Tms	AL	32	32	1	0	197.2	817	202	104	97	26	3	9	5	44	0	144	7	0	8	14	.364	1	0-0	0	3.87	4.42
	13	Mia	18	18	0	0	112.1	468	112	50	48	11	7	3	4	25	1	90	4	0	5	8	.385	0	0-0	0	3.49	3.85
	13	LAD	16	15	0	0	87.0	366	83	40	34	6	3	0	6	21	0	75	1	0	8	3	.727	0	0-0	0	3.25	3.52
	16	Min	21	21	0	0	124.2	527	139	77	71	18	2	9	3	29	0	93	4	0	4	8	.333	0	0-0	0	4.53	5.13
	16	LAA	11	11	1	0	73.0	290	63	27	26	8	1	0	2	15	0	51	3	0	4	6	.400	1	0-0	0	2.82	3.21
	Postseason		1	1	0	0	4.0	16	3	3	3	1	1	0	0	1	0	4	0	0	0	1	.000	0	0-0	0	3.01	6.75
	11 ML YEARS		297	279	11	1	1706.2	7272	1840	921	858	204	77	60	53	402	42	1370	48	5	108	103	.512	5	0-0	2	4.07	4.52

Nick Noonan

Bats: L **Throws:** R **Pos:** SS-5;2B-2   **Ht:** 6'1" **Wt:** 185 **Born:** 5/4/1989 **Age:** 28

								BATTING													RUNNING			AVERAGES			
Year	Team	Lg	G	AB	H	2B	3B	HR	(Hm	Rd)	TB	R	RBI	RC	TBB	IBB	SO	HBP	SH	SF	SB	CS	GDP	Avg	OBP	Slg	OPS
2016	ElPaso*	AAA	99	342	103	28	0	5	(-	-)	146	49	43	50	21	0	70	0	7	4	0	1	10	.301	.338	.427	.765
2013	SF	NL	62	105	23	2	0	0	(0	0)	25	12	5	5	6	3	24	0	0	0	0	0	1	.219	.261	.238	.499
2015	SF	NL	14	22	2	1	0	1	(1	0)	6	2	3	0	2	0	8	0	0	0	0	0	1	.091	.167	.273	.439
2016	SD	NL	7	18	3	0	0	0	(0	0)	3	0	1	0	1	0	5	0	0	1	0	1	0	.167	.200	.167	.367
	3 ML YEARS		83	145	28	3	0	1	(1	0)	34	14	9	5	9	3	37	0	0	1	0	1	2	.193	.239	.234	.473

Bud Norris

Pitches: R **Bats:** R **Pos:** SP-19; RP-16   **Ht:** 6'0" **Wt:** 215 **Born:** 3/2/1985 **Age:** 32

					HOW MUCH HE PITCHED				WHAT HE GAVE UP											THE RESULTS						
Year	Team	Lg	G	GS	CG	GF	IP	BFP	H	R	ER	HR	SH	SF	HB	TBB	IBB	SO	WP	Bk	W	L	Pct	Sh	Sv-Op	Hld	ERC	ERA
2009	Hou	NL	11	10	0	0	55.2	249	59	29	28	9	1	3	3	25	1	54	3	0	6	3	.667	0	0-0	0	5.26	4.53
2010	Hou	NL	27	27	0	0	153.2	683	151	94	84	18	6	4	6	77	3	158	5	2	9	10	.474	0	0-0	0	4.61	4.92
2011	Hou	NL	31	31	0	0	186.0	795	177	93	78	24	9	4	5	70	7	176	3	2	6	11	.353	0	0-0	0	3.96	3.77
2012	Hou	NL	29	29	0	0	168.1	733	165	90	87	23	7	2	8	66	2	165	8	0	7	13	.350	0	0-0	0	4.34	4.65
2013	2 Tms	AL	32	30	0	2	176.2	773	196	89	82	17	6	3	5	67	0	147	4	0	10	12	.455	0	0-0	0	4.75	4.18
2014	Bal	AL	28	28	0	0	165.1	687	149	68	67	20	1	4	14	52	2	139	3	0	15	8	.652	0	0-0	0	3.72	3.65
2015	2 Tms	AL	38	11	0	7	83.0	377	100	68	62	18	6	3	2	31	0	71	2	0	3	11	.214	0	0-2	2	5.96	6.72
2016	2 Tms	NL	35	19	0	8	113.0	495	116	67	64	14	9	3	5	49	4	102	7	0	6	10	.375	0	0-0	1	4.59	5.10
	13	Hou	21	21	0	0	126.0	541	135	62	55	11	4	3	4	43	0	90	3	0	6	9	.400	0	0-0	0	4.34	3.93
	13	Bal	11	9	0	2	50.2	232	61	27	27	6	2	0	1	24	0	57	1	0	4	3	.571	0	0-0	0	5.81	4.80
	15	Bal	18	11	0	2	66.1	305	84	57	52	14	3	2	3	25	0	50	0	0	2	9	.182	0	0-1	0	6.60	7.06
	15	SD	20	0	0	5	16.2	72	16	11	10	1	0	0	1	6	0	21	2	0	1	2	.333	0	0-1	2	3.62	5.40
	16	Atl	22	10	0	0	70.1	301	68	34	33	6	3	3	2	28	1	60	3	0	3	7	.300	0	0-0	1	3.89	4.22
	16	LAD	13	9	0	0	42.2	194	48	33	31	8	0	0	1	21	3	42	4	0	3	3	.500	0	0-0	0	5.82	6.54
	Postseason		2	2	0	0	10.2	46	11	4	4	1	0	0	0	2	0	9	1	0	1	0	1.000	0	0-0	0	3.22	3.38
	8 ML YEARS		231	185	0	10	1101.2	4792	1113	598	552	140	36	25	48	437	19	1012	35	4	62	78	.443	0	0-2	3	4.47	4.51

Daniel Norris

Pitches: L **Bats:** L **Pos:** SP-13; RP-1   **Ht:** 6'2" **Wt:** 195 **Born:** 4/25/1993 **Age:** 24

			HOW MUCH HE PITCHED						WHAT HE GAVE UP										THE RESULTS						
Year Team	Lg	G	GS	CG	GF	IP	BFP	H	R	ER	HR	SH	SF	HB	TBB	IBB	SO	WP	Bk	W	L	Pct	Sh	Sv-Op	Hld	ERC	ERA
2016 Toledo*	AAA	14	14	0	0	73.1	320	78	40	37	2	2	2	1	28	1	77	6	0	5	7	.417	0	0- -	-	3.86	4.54
2014 Tor	AL	5	1	0	2	6.2	30	5	4	4	1	0	1	0	5	0	4	0	0	0	0	-	0	0-0	1	4.31	5.40
2015 2 Tms	AL	13	13	0	0	60.0	251	53	31	25	9	1	4	2	19	0	45	3	0	3	2	.600	0	0-0	0	3.55	3.75
2016 Det	AL	14	13	0	1	69.1	302	75	30	26	10	0	3	0	22	0	71	1	0	4	2	.667	0	0-0	0	4.46	3.38
15 Tor	AL	5	5	0	0	23.1	103	23	11	10	3	1	2	2	12	0	18	2	0	1	1	.500	0	0-0	0	5.10	3.86
15 Det	AL	8	8	0	0	36.2	148	30	20	15	6	0	2	0	7	0	27	1	0	2	1	.667	0	0-0	0	2.64	3.68
3 ML YEARS		32	27	0	3	136.0	583	133	65	55	20	1	8	2	46	0	120	4	0	7	4	.636	0	0-0	1	4.05	3.64

Derek Norris

Bats: R **Throws:** R **Pos:** C-116;PH-8;1B-3   **Ht:** 6'0" **Wt:** 230 **Born:** 2/14/1989 **Age:** 28

								BATTING														RUNNING			AVERAGES			
Year Team	Lg	G	AB	H	2B	3B	HR	(Hm	Rd)	TB	R	RBI	RC	TBB	IBB	SO	HBP	SH	SF	SB	CS	GDP	Avg	OBP	Slg	OPS
2012 Oak	AL	60	209	42	8	1	7	(3	4)	73	19	34	27	21	1	66	1	0	1	5	1	6	.201	.276	.349	.625
2013 Oak	AL	98	264	65	16	0	9	(6	3)	108	41	30	40	37	1	71	4	1	2	5	0	5	.246	.345	.409	.754
2014 Oak	AL	127	385	104	19	1	10	(7	3)	155	46	55	66	54	2	86	1	1	1	2	2	12	.270	.361	.403	.763
2015 SD	NL	147	515	129	33	2	14	(9	5)	208	65	62	66	35	1	131	6	0	1	4	1	5	.250	.305	.404	.709
2016 SD	NL	125	415	77	17	0	14	(8	6)	136	50	42	28	36	5	139	4	0	3	9	2	9	.186	.255	.328	.583
Postseason		7	18	2	0	0	0	(0	0)	2	1	1	1	0	0	9	0	0	0	0	1	0	.111	.111	.111	.222
5 ML YEARS		557	1788	417	93	4	54	(33	21)	680	221	223	227	183	10	493	16	2	8	25	6	37	.233	.309	.380	.689

Ivan Nova

Pitches: R **Bats:** R **Pos:** SP-26; RP-6   ee-VAHN   **Ht:** 6'5" **Wt:** 235 **Born:** 1/12/1987 **Age:** 30

				HOW MUCH HE PITCHED						WHAT HE GAVE UP										THE RESULTS						
Year Team	Lg	G	GS	CG	GF	IP	BFP	H	R	ER	HR	SH	SF	HB	TBB	IBB	SO	WP	Bk	W	L	Pct	Sh	Sv-Op	Hld	ERC	ERA
2010 NYY	AL	10	7	0	3	42.0	185	44	22	21	4	1	1	1	17	2	26	2	0	1	2	.333	0	0-1	0	4.31	4.50
2011 NYY	AL	28	27	0	1	165.1	704	163	74	68	13	2	6	6	57	3	98	11	0	16	4	.800	0	0-0	0	3.76	3.70
2012 NYY	AL	28	28	0	0	170.1	748	194	100	95	28	3	6	10	56	3	153	6	2	12	8	.600	0	0-0	0	5.32	5.02
2013 NYY	AL	23	20	3	2	139.1	586	135	49	48	9	2	3	14	44	3	116	3	0	9	6	.600	2	0-0	0	3.77	3.10
2014 NYY	AL	4	4	0	0	20.2	96	32	19	19	6	0	2	2	6	0	12	1	0	2	2	.500	0	0-0	0	9.40	8.27
2015 NYY	AL	17	17	0	0	94.0	413	99	54	53	13	3	2	7	33	0	63	5	0	6	11	.353	0	0-0	0	4.75	5.07
2016 2 Tms	AL	32	26	3	3	162.0	684	175	81	75	23	5	6	9	28	1	127	10	0	12	8	.600	0	1-1	0	4.12	4.17
16 NYY	AL	21	15	0	3	97.1	421	107	54	53	19	1	2	6	25	1	75	7	0	7	6	.538	0	1-1	0	4.98	4.90
16 Pit	NL	11	11	3	0	64.2	263	68	27	22	4	4	4	3	3	0	52	3	0	5	2	.714	0	0-0	0	2.93	3.06
Postseason		2	1	0	0	8.1	34	7	4	4	2	0	0	0	4	0	8	0	0	1	1	.500	0	0-0	0	4.66	4.32
7 ML YEARS		142	129	6	9	793.2	3416	842	399	379	96	16	26	49	241	12	595	38	2	58	41	.586	2	1-2	0	4.44	4.30

Eduardo Nunez

Bats: R **Throws:** R **Pos:** 3B-81;SS-55;2B-6;DH-5;PH-5;PR-2   **Ht:** 6'0" **Wt:** 195 **Born:** 6/15/1987 **Age:** 30

								BATTING														RUNNING			AVERAGES			
Year Team	Lg	G	AB	H	2B	3B	HR	(Hm	Rd)	TB	R	RBI	RC	TBB	IBB	SO	HBP	SH	SF	SB	CS	GDP	Avg	OBP	Slg	OPS
2010 NYY	AL	30	50	14	1	0	1	(0	1)	18	12	7	8	3	0	2	0	0	0	5	0	4	.280	.321	.360	.681
2011 NYY	AL	112	309	82	18	2	5	(2	3)	119	38	30	42	22	2	37	1	0	6	22	6	6	.265	.313	.385	.698
2012 NYY	AL	38	89	26	4	1	1	(1	0)	35	14	11	15	6	0	12	1	0	4	11	2	1	.292	.330	.393	.723
2013 NYY	AL	90	304	79	17	4	3	(2	1)	113	38	28	31	20	1	51	3	4	5	10	3	3	.260	.307	.372	.679
2014 Min	AL	72	204	51	7	4	4	(4	0)	78	26	24	21	5	0	31	1	3	0	9	3	7	.250	.271	.382	.654
2015 Min	AL	72	188	53	14	1	4	(3	1)	81	23	20	25	12	0	29	1	2	1	8	4	1	.282	.327	.431	.758
2016 2 Tms	AL	141	553	159	24	4	16	(8	8)	239	73	67	74	29	3	88	5	2	6	40	10	8	.288	.325	.432	.758
16 Min	AL	91	371	110	15	1	12	(6	6)	163	49	47	54	15	0	58	3	2	5	27	6	6	.296	.325	.439	.764
16 SF	NL	50	182	49	9	3	4	(2	2)	76	24	20	20	14	3	30	2	0	1	13	4	2	.269	.327	.418	.744
Postseason		6	11	3	1	1	1	(0	1)	9	4	1	1	0	0	0	0	0	0	2	0	0	.273	.273	.818	1.091
7 ML YEARS		555	1697	464	85	16	34	(20	14)	683	224	187	216	97	6	250	11	17	17	105	28	30	.273	.314	.402	.716

Renato Nunez

Bats: R **Throws:** R **Pos:** DH-6;PH-5   **Ht:** 6'1" **Wt:** 220 **Born:** 4/4/1994 **Age:** 23

								BATTING														RUNNING			AVERAGES			
Year Team	Lg	G	AB	H	2B	3B	HR	(Hm	Rd)	TB	R	RBI	RC	TBB	IBB	SO	HBP	SH	SF	SB	CS	GDP	Avg	OBP	Slg	OPS
2012 As	R	42	160	52	18	3	4	(-	-)	88	31	42	36	17	0	32	6	0	3	4	0	7	.325	.403	.550	.953
2013 Beloit	A	128	508	131	27	0	19	(-	-)	215	69	85	66	28	0	136	5	1	3	2	2	18	.258	.301	.423	.725
2014 Stcktn	A+	124	509	142	28	3	29	(-	-)	263	75	96	90	34	0	113	13	0	6	2	0	12	.279	.336	.517	.853
2015 Mdlnd	AA	93	381	106	23	0	18	(-	-)	183	62	61	62	28	1	66	4	0	3	1	0	4	.278	.332	.480	.812
2016 Nashv	AAA	128	505	115	20	2	23	(-	-)	208	61	74	60	31	1	119	7	0	7	2	0	7	.228	.278	.412	.690
2016 Oak	AL	9	15	2	0	0	0	(0	0)	2	0	1	0	0	0	3	0	0	0	0	0	0	.133	.133	.133	.267

Vidal Nuno

Pitches: L **Bats:** L **Pos:** RP-54; SP-1   vee-DAHL NOON-yoh   **Ht:** 5'11" **Wt:** 210 **Born:** 7/26/1987 **Age:** 29

				HOW MUCH HE PITCHED						WHAT HE GAVE UP										THE RESULTS						
Year Team	Lg	G	GS	CG	GF	IP	BFP	H	R	ER	HR	SH	SF	HB	TBB	IBB	SO	WP	Bk	W	L	Pct	Sh	Sv-Op	Hld	ERC	ERA
2013 NYY	AL	5	3	0	2	20.0	82	16	5	5	2	0	0	1	6	0	9	0	0	1	2	.333	0	0-0	0	2.81	2.25
2014 2 Tms	AL	31	28	0	1	161.2	679	157	89	82	25	3	7	6	46	1	129	5	0	2	12	.143	0	0-0	0	3.98	4.56
2015 2 Tms	AL	35	10	0	8	89.0	376	90	38	37	15	1	7	5	22	2	81	3	2	1	5	.167	0	0-0	4	4.20	3.74
2016 Sea	AL	55	1	0	14	58.2	247	67	23	23	11	0	2	2	11	2	51	0	2	1	1	.500	0	0-2	12	4.80	3.53
14 NYY	AL	17	14	0	1	78.0	339	86	52	47	15	0	6	2	26	1	60	4	0	2	5	.286	0	0-0	0	5.18	5.42

242

Year Team	Lg	G	GS	CG	GF	IP	BFP	H	R	ER	HR	SH	SF	HB	TBB	IBB	SO	WP	Bk	W	L	Pct	Sh	Sv-Op	Hld	ERC	ERA
14 Ari	NL	14	14	0	0	83.2	340	71	37	35	10	3	1	4	20	0	69	1	0	0	7	.000	0	0-0	0	2.96	3.76
15 Ari	NL	3	0	0	1	14.1	58	10	3	3	1	0	0	0	5	1	19	0	1	0	1	.000	0	0-0	0	2.01	1.88
15 Sea	AL	32	10	0	7	74.2	318	80	35	34	14	1	7	5	17	1	62	3	1	1	4	.200	0	0-0	4	4.67	4.10
4 ML YEARS		126	42	0	25	329.1	1384	330	155	147	53	4	16	14	85	5	270	8	4	5	20	.200	0	0-2	16	4.11	4.02

Scott Oberg

Pitches: R **Bats:** R **Pos:** RP-24   **Ht:** 6'2" **Wt:** 205 **Born:** 3/13/1990 **Age:** 27

Year Team	Lg	G	GS	CG	GF	IP	BFP	H	R	ER	HR	SH	SF	HB	TBB	IBB	SO	WP	Bk	W	L	Pct	Sh	Sv-Op	Hld	ERC	ERA
2012 GdJunc	R+	25	0	0	22	27.0	111	20	9	7	2	3	0	0	6	0	29	0	0	0	2	.000	0	13- --	-	1.83	2.33
2013 Mdest	A+	56	0	0	49	53.1	221	34	14	11	4	3	0	0	27	1	61	3	0	1	6	.143	0	33- --	-	2.34	1.86
2014 Tulsa	AA	27	0	0	24	27.1	109	22	8	8	1	0	1	1	6	0	21	1	0	0	1	.000	0	15- --	-	2.15	2.63
2015 Albq	AAA	7	0	0	4	8.0	39	14	1	1	0	0	0	1	2	0	11	0	0	1	0	1.000	0	2- --	-	7.17	1.13
2016 Albq	AAA	27	0	0	22	29.2	113	16	8	8	1	1	0	1	11	0	36	1	0	1	0	1.000	0	9- --	-	1.52	2.43
2015 Col	NL	64	0	0	11	58.1	259	58	35	33	10	3	1	6	31	2	44	6	1	3	4	.429	0	1-3	15	5.60	5.09
2016 Col	NL	24	0	0	9	26.0	113	26	15	15	3	0	0	1	11	2	20	3	0	1	1	.500	0	1-2	1	4.33	5.19
2 ML YEARS		88	0	0	20	84.1	372	84	50	48	13	3	1	7	42	4	64	9	1	4	5	.444	0	2-5	16	5.19	5.12

Brett Oberholtzer

Pitches: L **Bats:** L **Pos:** RP-35; SP-2   OH-ber-holt-zer   **Ht:** 6'1" **Wt:** 225 **Born:** 7/1/1989 **Age:** 27

Year Team	Lg	G	GS	CG	GF	IP	BFP	H	R	ER	HR	SH	SF	HB	TBB	IBB	SO	WP	Bk	W	L	Pct	Sh	Sv-Op	Hld	ERC	ERA
2013 Hou	AL	13	10	2	1	71.2	293	66	26	22	7	0	1	1	13	0	45	0	0	4	5	.444	1	0-0	0	2.82	2.76
2014 Hou	AL	24	24	0	0	143.2	623	170	73	70	12	5	10	3	28	0	94	2	3	5	13	.278	0	0-0	0	4.22	4.39
2015 Hou	AL	8	8	0	0	38.1	171	44	21	19	4	1	2	1	17	0	27	2	0	2	2	.500	0	0-0	0	5.31	4.46
2016 2 Tms		37	2	0	14	70.1	321	85	47	46	18	1	1	1	29	1	54	1	0	3	3	.500	0	1-1	0	6.55	5.89
16 Phi	NL	26	0	0	10	50.1	226	58	28	27	11	1	1	0	20	0	38	1	0	2	2	.500	0	1-1	0	5.79	4.83
16 LAA	AL	11	2	0	4	20.0	95	27	19	19	7	0	0	1	9	1	16	0	0	1	1	.500	0	0-0	0	8.61	8.55
4 ML YEARS		82	44	2	15	324.0	1408	365	167	157	41	7	14	6	87	1	220	5	3	14	23	.378	1	1-1	0	4.49	4.36

Peter O'Brien

Bats: R **Throws:** R **Pos:** LF-16;PH-12;1B-1   **Ht:** 6'4" **Wt:** 235 **Born:** 7/15/1990 **Age:** 26

Year Team	Lg	G	AB	H	2B	3B	HR	(Hm	Rd)	TB	R	RBI	RC	TBB	IBB	SO	HBP	SH	SF	SB	CS	GDP	Avg	OBP	Slg	OPS
2012 2 Tms	Low	52	212	45	10	0	10	(-	-)	85	29	34	21	10	1	62	3	0	2	0	1	10	.212	.256	.401	.656
2013 2 Tms	Low	119	447	130	39	4	22	(-	-)	243	78	96	85	41	2	134	6	0	12	0	1	13	.291	.350	.544	.893
2014 Tampa	A+	30	112	36	1	1	10	(-	-)	77	19	19	25	4	1	29	2	0	1	0	0	1	.321	.353	.688	1.040
2014 Trntn	AA	72	274	67	14	1	23	(-	-)	152	47	51	45	16	0	77	4	0	0	0	0	8	.245	.296	.555	.851
2015 Reno	AAA	131	490	139	35	9	26	(-	-)	270	77	107	89	31	0	124	7	1	5	1	3	11	.284	.332	.551	.883
2016 Reno	AAA	105	406	103	20	5	24	(-	-)	205	64	75	61	23	0	147	2	0	3	2	0	5	.254	.295	.505	.800
2015 Ari	NL	8	10	4	1	0	1	(1	0)	8	1	3	3	2	0	5	0	0	0	0	0	0	.400	.500	.800	1.300
2016 Ari	NL	28	64	9	1	0	5	(2	3)	25	6	9	3	3	2	27	0	0	0	0	0	2	.141	.179	.391	.570
2 ML YEARS		36	74	13	2	0	6	(3	3)	33	7	12	6	5	2	32	0	0	0	0	0	2	.176	.228	.446	.674

Darren O'Day

Pitches: R **Bats:** R **Pos:** RP-34   **Ht:** 6'4" **Wt:** 220 **Born:** 10/22/1982 **Age:** 34

Year Team	Lg	G	GS	CG	GF	IP	BFP	H	R	ER	HR	SH	SF	HB	TBB	IBB	SO	WP	Bk	W	L	Pct	Sh	Sv-Op	Hld	ERC	ERA
2008 LAA	AL	30	0	0	17	43.1	194	49	24	22	2	2	1	4	14	6	29	1	0	0	1	.000	0	0-0	1	4.20	4.57
2009 2 Tms		68	0	0	15	58.2	233	41	14	12	3	1	3	5	18	1	56	1	0	2	1	.667	0	2-2	20	2.20	1.84
2010 Tex	AL	72	0	0	14	62.0	240	43	15	14	5	1	3	5	12	2	45	0	0	6	2	.750	0	0-2	22	1.93	2.03
2011 Tex	AL	16	0	0	7	16.2	74	17	10	10	7	1	1	2	5	0	18	0	0	1	0	1.000	0	0-0	3	6.45	5.40
2012 Bal	AL	69	0	0	10	67.0	263	49	17	17	6	3	1	3	14	2	69	0	0	7	1	.875	0	0-2	15	2.06	2.28
2013 Bal	AL	68	0	0	18	62.0	247	47	16	15	7	1	1	5	15	1	59	1	0	5	3	.625	0	2-6	20	2.60	2.18
2014 Bal	AL	68	0	0	18	68.2	271	42	14	13	6	1	2	8	19	4	73	0	0	5	2	.714	0	4-8	25	1.92	1.70
2015 Bal	AL	68	0	0	19	65.1	257	47	13	11	5	0	1	5	14	1	82	0	0	6	2	.750	0	6-11	18	2.09	1.52
2016 Bal	AL	34	0	0	6	31.0	131	25	13	13	6	0	0	1	13	2	38	0	0	3	1	.750	0	3-5	10	3.70	3.77
09 NYM	NL	4	0	0	1	3.0	17	5	2	0	0	0	1	1	1	0	2	0	0	0	0	-	0	0-0	0	7.72	0.00
09 Tex	AL	64	0	0	14	55.2	216	36	12	12	3	1	2	4	17	1	54	1	0	2	1	.667	0	2-2	20	1.95	1.94
Postseason		20	0	0	1	14.1	57	11	8	8	4	1	0	1	3	0	15	0	0	0	3	.000	0	0-0	5	3.46	5.02
9 ML YEARS		493	0	0	124	474.2	1910	360	136	127	47	10	13	38	124	19	469	3	0	34	14	.708	0	17-36	134	2.53	2.41

Rougned Odor

Bats: L **Throws:** R **Pos:** 2B-146;DH-3;PH-2   ROOG-ned oh-DORE   **Ht:** 5'11" **Wt:** 195 **Born:** 2/3/1994 **Age:** 23

Year Team	Lg	G	AB	H	2B	3B	HR	(Hm	Rd)	TB	R	RBI	RC	TBB	IBB	SO	HBP	SH	SF	SB	CS	GDP	Avg	OBP	Slg	OPS
2014 Tex	AL	114	386	100	14	7	9	(4	5)	155	39	48	46	17	1	71	5	6	3	4	7	5	.259	.297	.402	.698
2015 Tex	AL	120	426	111	21	9	16	(7	9)	198	54	61	62	23	2	79	14	2	5	6	7	3	.261	.316	.465	.781
2016 Tex	AL	150	605	164	33	4	33	(17	16)	304	89	88	77	19	0	135	4	0	4	14	7	6	.271	.296	.502	.798
Postseason		5	18	5	1	0	1	(0	1)	9	7	2	3	1	0	4	2	0	0	0	0	0	.278	.381	.500	.881
3 ML YEARS		384	1417	375	68	20	58	(28	30)	657	182	197	185	59	3	285	23	8	12	24	21	16	.265	.302	.464	.766

Jake Odorizzi

Pitches: R Bats: R Pos: SP-33   oh-duh-RIZZ-ee   Ht: 6'2" Wt: 190 Born: 3/27/1990 Age: 27

				HOW MUCH HE PITCHED				WHAT HE GAVE UP												THE RESULTS						
Year	Team	Lg	G	GS	CG	GF	IP	BFP	H	R	ER	HR	SH	SF	HB	TBB	IBB	SO	WP	Bk	W	L	Pct	Sh	Sv-Op	Hld	ERC	ERA
2012	KC	AL	2	2	0	0	7.1	34	8	4	4	1	0	0	0	4	0	4	0	0	0	1	.000	0	0-0	0	5.34	4.91
2013	TB	AL	7	4	0	2	29.2	122	28	13	13	3	0	1	2	8	0	22	1	0	0	1	.000	0	1-1	0	3.62	3.94
2014	TB	AL	31	31	0	0	168.0	719	156	79	77	20	3	8	5	59	0	174	3	0	11	13	.458	0	0-0	0	3.68	4.13
2015	TB	AL	28	28	0	0	169.1	700	149	65	63	18	4	3	3	46	0	150	5	1	9	9	.500	0	0-0	0	3.02	3.35
2016	TB	AL	33	33	0	0	187.2	773	170	80	77	29	3	6	4	54	3	166	3	1	10	6	.625	0	0-0	0	3.56	3.69
	5 ML YEARS		101	98	0	2	562.0	2348	511	241	234	71	10	18	14	171	3	516	12	2	30	30	.500	0	1-1	0	3.46	3.75

Eric O'Flaherty

Pitches: L Bats: L Pos: RP-39   Ht: 6'2" Wt: 210 Born: 2/5/1985 Age: 32

				HOW MUCH HE PITCHED				WHAT HE GAVE UP												THE RESULTS						
Year	Team	Lg	G	GS	CG	GF	IP	BFP	H	R	ER	HR	SH	SF	HB	TBB	IBB	SO	WP	Bk	W	L	Pct	Sh	Sv-Op	Hld	ERC	ERA
2016 2 Tms*		Low	5	2	0	0	5.0	23	8	3	1	1	1	0	0	0	0	7	0	0	0	1	.000	0	0- -	-	6.56	1.80
2006	Sea	AL	15	0	0	5	11.0	57	18	9	5	2	1	0	0	6	3	6	2	0	0	0	-	0	0-0	1	8.63	4.09
2007	Sea	AL	56	0	0	9	52.1	221	45	26	26	1	0	2	5	20	1	36	4	1	7	1	.875	0	0-1	4	3.04	4.47
2008	Sea	AL	7	0	0	1	6.2	42	16	15	15	2	0	1	2	4	2	4	0	0	0	1	.000	0	0-0	2	17.12	20.25
2009	Atl	NL	78	0	0	8	56.1	236	52	23	19	2	1	1	6	18	4	39	2	0	2	1	.667	0	0-2	15	3.26	3.04
2010	Atl	NL	56	0	0	7	44.0	181	37	14	12	2	1	1	0	18	2	36	3	0	3	2	.600	0	0-1	9	2.97	2.45
2011	Atl	NL	78	0	0	7	73.2	301	59	9	8	2	7	2	3	21	8	67	1	0	2	4	.333	0	0-4	32	2.13	0.98
2012	Atl	NL	64	0	0	7	57.1	230	47	14	11	3	3	1	2	19	2	46	1	0	3	0	1.000	0	0-3	28	2.71	1.73
2013	Atl	NL	19	0	0	2	18.0	70	12	5	5	2	0	1	0	5	1	11	0	0	3	0	1.000	0	0-1	12	1.93	2.50
2014	Oak	AL	21	0	0	6	20.0	80	15	5	5	3	1	0	2	4	0	15	3	0	1	0	1.000	0	1-2	3	2.68	2.25
2015	2 Tms		41	0	0	8	30.0	159	47	30	27	2	2	0	2	18	2	21	1	0	1	2	.333	0	0-1	4	7.97	8.10
2016	Atl	NL	39	0	0	8	28.2	136	39	25	22	3	1	0	2	11	2	22	3	0	1	4	.200	0	0-1	3	6.29	6.91
15	Oak	AL	25	0	0	5	21.1	108	29	17	14	1	2	0	0	13	1	15	0	0	1	2	.333	0	0-1	3	6.26	5.91
15	NYM	NL	16	0	0	3	8.2	51	18	13	13	1	0	0	2	5	1	6	1	0	0	0	-	0	0-0	1	12.63	13.50
	Postseason		1	0	0	0	1.0	4	2	0	0	0	0	0	0	0	0	0	0	0	0	0	-	0	0-0	0	9.49	0.00
	11 ML YEARS		474	0	0	66	398.0	1713	387	175	155	24	17	8	25	144	27	303	20	1	23	15	.605	0	1-16	113	3.63	3.51

Alexi Ogando

Pitches: R Bats: R Pos: RP-36   oh-GONE-doh   Ht: 6'4" Wt: 200 Born: 10/5/1983 Age: 33

				HOW MUCH HE PITCHED				WHAT HE GAVE UP												THE RESULTS						
Year	Team	Lg	G	GS	CG	GF	IP	BFP	H	R	ER	HR	SH	SF	HB	TBB	IBB	SO	WP	Bk	W	L	Pct	Sh	Sv-Op	Hld	ERC	ERA
2016	Reno*	AAA	6	0	0	0	5.1	32	10	8	8	0	0	0	0	7	1	2	1	0	1	0	1.000	0	0- -	-	12.47	13.50
2010	Tex	AL	44	0	0	12	41.2	171	31	6	6	2	3	2	1	16	2	39	3	0	4	1	.800	0	0-2	7	2.34	1.30
2011	Tex	AL	31	29	1	2	169.0	693	149	73	66	16	2	3	7	43	0	126	5	0	13	8	.619	1	0-0	0	3.01	3.51
2012	Tex	AL	58	1	0	11	66.0	263	49	26	24	9	0	3	2	17	1	66	5	0	2	0	1.000	0	3-6	12	2.50	3.27
2013	Tex	AL	23	18	0	0	104.1	428	87	38	36	11	2	3	5	41	1	72	6	1	7	4	.636	0	0-0	0	3.44	3.11
2014	Tex	AL	27	0	0	10	25.0	122	33	19	19	1	1	0	1	15	1	22	4	0	2	3	.400	0	1-2	7	6.34	6.84
2015	Bos	AL	64	0	0	16	65.1	277	59	29	29	12	0	2	3	28	2	53	1	2	3	1	.750	0	0-4	12	4.43	3.99
2016	Atl	NL	36	0	0	11	32.0	148	32	18	14	2	3	4	1	23	5	29	3	0	2	1	.667	0	0-0	3	4.90	3.94
	Postseason		18	0	0	2	19.0	81	16	6	5	3	0	0	0	10	2	23	1	0	2	0	1.000	0	0-3	4	3.95	2.37
	7 ML YEARS		283	48	1	62	503.1	2102	440	209	194	53	11	17	20	183	12	407	27	3	33	18	.647	1	4-14	41	3.42	3.47

Nefi Ogando

Pitches: R Bats: R Pos: RP-14   Ht: 6'0" Wt: 230 Born: 6/3/1989 Age: 28

				HOW MUCH HE PITCHED				WHAT HE GAVE UP												THE RESULTS						
Year	Team	Lg	G	GS	CG	GF	IP	BFP	H	R	ER	HR	SH	SF	HB	TBB	IBB	SO	WP	Bk	W	L	Pct	Sh	Sv-Op	Hld	ERC	ERA
2012	Grnvlle	A	38	0	0	12	75.1	331	72	34	31	3	1	1	5	34	1	54	7	1	4	4	.500	0	2- -	-	3.81	3.70
2013	Salem	A+	33	0	0	15	55.0	240	49	34	25	5	1	4	2	27	0	44	8	0	2	3	.400	0	3- -	-	3.86	4.09
2014	Rdng	AA	48	0	0	27	56.0	262	64	41	39	6	4	4	6	28	0	57	3	1	5	1	.833	0	7- -	-	5.76	6.27
2015	Rdng	AA	24	0	0	11	34.2	144	25	11	11	2	0	1	1	19	1	33	4	0	2	3	.400	0	2- -	-	2.97	2.86
2015	LV	AAA	21	0	0	6	28.1	127	27	11	9	1	0	0	4	12	1	22	1	0	2	2	.500	0	1- -	-	3.85	2.86
2016	NewOr	AAA	22	0	0	11	24.1	103	18	9	9	2	0	0	3	11	0	19	1	0	0	0	-	0	2- -	-	3.21	3.33
2015	Phi	NL	4	0	0	1	4.0	21	7	5	4	0	0	0	0	2	0	2	0	0	0	0	-	0	0-0	0	8.06	9.00
2016	Mia	NL	14	0	0	5	15.2	65	10	5	4	0	0	1	0	8	0	8	1	0	0	0	-	0	0-0	1	1.93	2.30
	2 ML YEARS		18	0	0	6	19.2	86	17	10	8	0	0	1	0	10	0	10	1	0	0	0	-	0	0-0	1	2.97	3.66

Seung Hwan Oh

Pitches: R Bats: R Pos: RP-76   sing whan   Ht: 5'10" Wt: 205 Born: 7/15/1982 Age: 34

				HOW MUCH HE PITCHED				WHAT HE GAVE UP												THE RESULTS						
Year	Team	Lg	G	GS	CG	GF	IP	BFP	H	R	ER	HR	SH	SF	HB	TBB	IBB	SO	WP	Bk	W	L	Pct	Sh	Sv-Op	Hld	ERC	ERA
2016	StL	NL	76	0	0	35	79.2	313	55	20	17	5	2	1	2	18	3	103	3	0	6	3	.667	0	19-23	14	1.69	1.92

Ross Ohlendorf

Pitches: R Bats: R Pos: RP-64   OH-lenn-dorf   Ht: 6'4" Wt: 240 Born: 8/8/1982 Age: 34

				HOW MUCH HE PITCHED				WHAT HE GAVE UP												THE RESULTS						
Year	Team	Lg	G	GS	CG	GF	IP	BFP	H	R	ER	HR	SH	SF	HB	TBB	IBB	SO	WP	Bk	W	L	Pct	Sh	Sv-Op	Hld	ERC	ERA
2007	NYY	AL	6	0	0	3	6.1	26	5	2	2	1	0	0	0	2	0	9	0	0	0	0	-	0	0-0	1	2.94	2.84
2008	2 Tms		30	5	0	3	62.2	300	86	49	45	10	1	1	1	31	3	46	10	1	1	4	.200	0	0-0	4	7.16	6.46
2009	Pit	NL	29	29	0	0	176.2	725	165	80	77	25	11	8	7	53	1	109	2	1	11	10	.524	0	0-0	0	3.84	3.92
2010	Pit	NL	21	21	0	0	108.1	475	106	54	49	12	9	8	6	44	2	79	5	0	1	11	.083	0	0-0	0	4.20	4.07
2011	Pit	NL	9	9	0	0	38.2	194	60	38	35	9	5	3	6	15	2	27	2	0	1	3	.250	0	0-0	0	9.12	8.15

Year	Team	Lg	G	GS	CG	GF	IP	BFP	H	R	ER	HR	SH	SF	HB	TBB	IBB	SO	WP	Bk	W	L	Pct	Sh	Sv-Op	Hld	ERC	ERA
										HOW MUCH HE PITCHED					WHAT HE GAVE UP					THE RESULTS							

HOW MUCH HE PITCHED / WHAT HE GAVE UP / THE RESULTS

Year	Team	Lg	G	GS	CG	GF	IP	BFP	H	R	ER	HR	SH	SF	HB	TBB	IBB	SO	WP	Bk	W	L	Pct	Sh	Sv-Op	Hld	ERC	ERA
2012	SD	NL	13	9	0	2	48.2	233	62	44	42	7	4	0	1	24	0	39	2	1	4	4	.500	0	0-0	0	6.37	7.77
2013	Was	NL	16	7	0	1	60.1	247	56	22	22	8	3	0	1	14	1	45	1	0	4	1	.800	0	0-1	1	3.30	3.28
2015	Tex	AL	21	0	0	6	19.1	85	21	8	8	4	0	1	0	7	2	19	0	0	3	1	.750	0	1-2	7	4.96	3.72
2016	Cin	NL	64	0	0	34	65.2	290	59	35	34	14	3	0	6	32	1	68	4	0	5	7	.417	0	2-5	3	4.98	4.66
08	NYY	AL	25	0	0	3	40.0	187	50	31	29	7	0	0	1	19	3	36	6	0	1	1	.500	0	0-0	4	6.39	6.53
08	Pit	NL	5	5	0	0	22.2	113	36	18	16	3	1	1	0	12	0	13	4	1	0	3	.000	0	0-0	0	8.59	6.35
	Postseason		4	0	0	1	4.1	22	6	3	3	1	0	0	2	1	0	5	0	0	0	0	-	0	1-1	0	8.64	6.23
9 ML YEARS			209	80	0	49	586.2	2575	620	332	314	90	36	21	28	222	12	444	26	3	30	41	.423	0	3-8	16	4.86	4.82

Steven Okert

Pitches: L Bats: L Pos: RP-16   Ht: 6'3" Wt: 210 Born: 7/9/1991 Age: 25

HOW MUCH HE PITCHED / WHAT HE GAVE UP / THE RESULTS

Year	Team	Lg	G	GS	CG	GF	IP	BFP	H	R	ER	HR	SH	SF	HB	TBB	IBB	SO	WP	Bk	W	L	Pct	Sh	Sv-Op	Hld	ERC	ERA
2012	2 Tms	Low	17	0	0	2	28.2	131	28	9	7	0	4	1	4	12	0	28	1	0	2	0	1.000	0	0- -	-	3.68	2.20
2013	Augsta	A	44	0	0	15	60.2	259	55	27	20	3	7	2	1	24	1	59	2	0	2	2	.500	0	2- -	-	3.21	2.97
2014	SnJos	A+	33	0	0	29	35.1	152	33	6	6	2	2	0	2	11	1	54	0	0	1	2	.333	0	19- -	-	3.18	1.53
2014	Rchmd	AA	24	0	0	11	33.0	131	24	11	10	3	3	1	0	11	1	38	0	1	1	0	1.000	0	5- -	-	2.34	2.73
2015	Scrmto	AAA	52	0	0	11	61.1	270	62	32	26	7	3	2	2	29	1	69	1	0	4	3	.571	0	3- -	-	4.65	3.82
2016	Scrmto	AAA	41	0	0	12	47.1	211	52	27	20	2	2	2	0	11	1	60	2	0	4	3	.571	0	3- -	-	3.33	3.80
2016	SF	NL	16	0	0	3	14.0	58	14	5	5	2	0	0	0	4	1	14	0	0	0	0	-	0	0-1	2	3.87	3.21

Hector Olivera

Bats: R Throws: R Pos: LF-5;PH-1   oh-li-VAIR-ah   Ht: 6'2" Wt: 230 Born: 4/5/1985 Age: 32

BATTING / RUNNING / AVERAGES

Year	Team	Lg	G	AB	H	2B	3B	HR	(Hm	Rd)	TB	R	RBI	RC	TBB	IBB	SO	HBP	SH	SF	SB	CS	GDP	Avg	OBP	Slg	OPS
2015	Gwnntt	AAA	10	39	9	3	0	0	(-	-)	12	5	3	3	2	0	4	1	0	0	0	0	1	.231	.286	.308	.593
2015	3 Tms	Low	12	33	6	1	0	0	(-	-)	7	5	0	2	4	0	3	0	0	0	0	0	3	.182	.270	.212	.482
2015	Atl	NL	24	79	20	4	1	2	(0	2)	32	4	11	11	5	0	12	2	0	1	0	0	2	.253	.310	.405	.715
2016	Atl	NL	6	19	4	1	0	0	(0	0)	5	2	2	1	1	0	5	0	0	1	0	0	1	.211	.238	.263	.501
2 ML YEARS			30	98	24	5	1	2	(0	2)	37	6	13	12	6	0	17	2	0	2	0	0	3	.245	.296	.378	.674

Matt Olson

Bats: L Throws: R Pos: RF-5;1B-4;PH-4   Ht: 6'5" Wt: 230 Born: 3/29/1994 Age: 23

BATTING / RUNNING / AVERAGES

Year	Team	Lg	G	AB	H	2B	3B	HR	(Hm	Rd)	TB	R	RBI	RC	TBB	IBB	SO	HBP	SH	SF	SB	CS	GDP	Avg	OBP	Slg	OPS
2012	2 Tms	Low	50	188	53	16	1	9	(-	-)	98	32	45	35	19	1	50	3	0	3	0	0	5	.282	.352	.521	.873
2013	Beloit	A	134	481	108	32	0	23	(-	-)	209	69	93	72	72	1	148	2	0	3	4	3	5	.225	.326	.435	.761
2014	Stcktn	A+	138	512	134	31	1	37	(-	-)	278	111	97	116	117	4	137	5	0	0	2	0	6	.262	.404	.543	.947
2015	Mdlnd	AA	133	466	116	37	0	17	(-	-)	204	82	75	89	105	6	139	6	0	8	5	1	7	.249	.388	.438	.826
2016	Nashv	AAA	131	464	109	34	1	17	(-	-)	196	69	60	70	71	2	132	0	2	3	1	0	9	.235	.335	.422	.757
2016	Oak	AL	11	21	2	1	0	0	(0	0)	3	3	0	1	7	0	4	0	0	0	0	0	1	.095	.321	.143	.464

Tyler Olson

Pitches: L Bats: R Pos: RP-1   Ht: 6'3" Wt: 195 Born: 10/2/1989 Age: 27

HOW MUCH HE PITCHED / WHAT HE GAVE UP / THE RESULTS

Year	Team	Lg	G	GS	CG	GF	IP	BFP	H	R	ER	HR	SH	SF	HB	TBB	IBB	SO	WP	Bk	W	L	Pct	Sh	Sv-Op	Hld	ERC	ERA
2013	Everett	A-	18	8	1	3	54.0	243	61	33	26	1	1	3	3	20	0	48	6	0	2	4	.333	1	1- -	-	4.25	4.33
2014	Hi Dsrt	A+	5	5	0	0	23.0	100	21	8	8	0	0	4	1	10	0	27	2	0	2	1	.667	0	0- -	-	3.15	3.13
2014	Jacksn	AA	22	22	1	0	125.1	528	126	55	49	8	7	4	7	25	0	100	2	0	10	7	.588	0	0- -	-	3.27	3.52
2015	Tacom	AAA	25	6	0	3	54.1	243	61	40	27	7	1	2	2	17	0	53	0	2	3	5	.375	0	1- -	-	4.67	4.47
2016	S-WB	AAA	11	3	0	1	27.1	117	31	17	16	2	1	0	1	8	1	21	1	0	1	2	.333	0	0- -	-	4.39	5.27
2016	Omha	AAA	5	0	0	1	6.1	31	10	3	2	1	1	0	0	2	0	2	0	0	0	0	-	0	0- -	-	7.54	2.84
2016	Clmbs	AAA	9	0	0	3	10.2	51	12	9	7	1	0	0	1	6	1	10	1	0	1	0	1.000	0	0- -	-	5.48	5.91
2015	Sea	AL	11	0	0	4	13.1	65	18	8	8	2	2	0	1	10	7	8	0	1	1	1	.500	0	0-0	1	7.64	5.40
2016	NYY	AL	1	0	0	1	2.2	13	3	2	2	0	0	1	0	2	0	0	0	0	0	0	-	0	0-0	0	5.24	6.75
2 ML YEARS			12	0	0	5	16.0	78	21	10	10	2	2	1	1	12	7	8	0	1	1	1	.500	0	0-0	1	7.21	5.63

Shawn O'Malley

Bats: B Throws: R Pos: SS-36;RF-19;LF-15;2B-12;PR-10;PH-9;3B-7;CF-5   Ht: 5'11" Wt: 175 Born: 12/28/1987 Age: 29

BATTING / RUNNING / AVERAGES

Year	Team	Lg	G	AB	H	2B	3B	HR	(Hm	Rd)	TB	R	RBI	RC	TBB	IBB	SO	HBP	SH	SF	SB	CS	GDP	Avg	OBP	Slg	OPS
2016	Tacom*	AAA	25	82	26	5	1	1	(-	-)	36	15	13	16	13	0	18	1	3	1	5	1	1	.317	.412	.439	.851
2014	LAA	AL	11	16	3	0	0	0	(0	0)	3	3	1	1	0	0	8	0	0	0	2	0	0	.188	.188	.188	.375
2015	Sea	AL	24	42	11	1	0	1	(0	1)	15	10	7	11	12	0	14	0	2	1	3	0	0	.262	.418	.357	.775
2016	Sea	AL	89	210	48	9	2	2	(2	0)	67	24	17	23	18	0	59	3	1	0	6	2	4	.229	.299	.319	.618
3 ML YEARS			124	268	62	10	2	3	(2	1)	85	37	25	35	30	0	81	3	3	1	11	2	4	.231	.315	.317	.632

Logan Ondrusek

Pitches: R Bats: R Pos: RP-7   ahn-DREW-seck   Ht: 6'8" Wt: 230 Born: 2/13/1985 Age: 32

		HOW MUCH HE PITCHED				WHAT HE GAVE UP											THE RESULTS							
Year Team	Lg	G	GS	CG	GF	IP	BFP	H	R	ER	HR	SH	SF	HB	TBB	IBB	SO	WP	Bk	W	L	Pct	Sh	Sv-Op	Hld	ERC	ERA
2016 Bowie*	AA	5	0	0	2	7.0	32	10	6	5	2	1	0	0	1	0	9	0	0	0	1	.000	0	0- -	-	6.78	6.43
2010 Cin	NL	60	0	0	11	58.2	240	49	25	24	7	1	1	0	20	1	39	2	0	5	0	1.000	0	0-2	6	3.08	3.68
2011 Cin	NL	66	0	0	14	61.1	268	55	25	22	6	3	4	2	28	7	41	6	0	5	5	.500	0	0-3	14	3.58	3.23
2012 Cin	NL	63	0	0	20	54.2	243	51	23	21	8	1	1	3	31	4	39	5	0	5	2	.714	0	2-4	13	4.81	3.46
2013 Cin	NL	52	0	0	18	55.0	233	53	26	25	8	4	0	1	16	1	53	5	1	3	1	.750	0	0-1	5	3.75	4.09
2014 Cin	NL	40	0	0	10	41.0	189	50	26	25	5	2	1	1	16	1	42	3	0	3	3	.500	0	0-3	4	5.43	5.49
2016 Bal	AL	7	0	0	1	6.1	29	9	7	7	1	0	0	0	3	0	4	0	0	0	0	-	0	0-0	1	7.78	9.95
Postseason		3	0	0	1	3.0	13	1	1	1	1	0	0	0	1	0	1	0	0	0	0	-	0	0-0	-	2.68	3.00
6 ML YEARS		288	0	0	74	277.0	1202	267	132	124	35	11	7	7	114	14	218	21	1	21	11	.656	0	2-13	43	4.09	4.03

Paulo Orlando

Bats: R Throws: R Pos: RF-89;CF-37;PH-5;DH-1;PR-1   Ht: 6'2" Wt: 210 Born: 11/1/1985 Age: 31

		BATTING																		RUNNING			AVERAGES			
Year Team	Lg	G	AB	H	2B	3B	HR	(Hm	Rd)	TB	R	RBI	RC	TBB	IBB	SO	HBP	SH	SF	SB	CS	GDP	Avg	OBP	Slg	OPS
2012 NWArk	AA	116	420	117	18	2	6	(-	-)	157	54	40	56	30	2	57	4	3	5	21	6	11	.279	.329	.374	.703
2013 Omha	AAA	92	293	81	9	3	5	(-	-)	111	41	46	38	22	0	56	1	7	3	8	3	3	.276	.326	.379	.705
2014 Omha	AAA	136	501	151	21	9	6	(-	-)	208	61	63	80	39	1	86	5	5	4	34	9	9	.301	.355	.415	.770
2015 Omha	AAA	41	170	47	11	0	3	(-	-)	67	20	17	23	8	1	32	1	1	2	9	0	1	.276	.309	.394	.704
2015 KC	AL	86	241	60	14	6	7	(4	3)	107	31	27	30	5	0	53	2	2	1	3	3	0	.249	.269	.444	.713
2016 KC	AL	128	457	138	24	4	5	(3	2)	185	52	43	59	13	1	105	7	3	3	14	3	12	.302	.329	.405	.734
Postseason		12	11	3	0	0	0	(0	0)	3	3	1	1	0	0	2	0	0	1	0	0	0	.273	.250	.273	.523
2 ML YEARS		214	698	198	38	10	12	(7	5)	292	83	70	89	18	1	158	9	5	4	17	6	12	.284	.309	.418	.727

Ryan O'Rourke

Pitches: L Bats: R Pos: RP-26   Ht: 6'3" Wt: 230 Born: 4/30/1988 Age: 29

		HOW MUCH HE PITCHED						WHAT HE GAVE UP												THE RESULTS							
Year Team	Lg	G	GS	CG	GF	IP	BFP	H	R	ER	HR	SH	SF	HB	TBB	IBB	SO	WP	Bk	W	L	Pct	Sh	Sv-Op	Hld	ERC	ERA
2012 2 Tms	Low	38	2	0	12	74.1	324	83	51	46	8	2	3	1	20	2	72	9	0	2	6	.250	0	2- -	-	4.22	5.57
2013 FtMyrs	A+	17	0	0	7	28.1	110	19	7	7	3	1	1	0	8	0	21	2	0	5	1	.833	0	3- -	-	2.02	2.22
2013 NwBrit	AA	17	0	0	5	17.1	72	15	10	9	1	1	1	0	7	2	19	3	0	2	2	.000	0	2- -	-	2.54	4.67
2014 NwBrit	AA	50	0	0	17	40.2	174	36	24	19	5	1	2	0	16	1	52	1	0	2	4	.333	0	4- -	-	3.46	4.20
2015 Roch	AAA	20	0	0	8	13.2	61	13	9	9	1	0	2	0	7	0	22	1	0	0	0	-	0	0- -	-	3.95	5.93
2016 Roch	AAA	33	0	0	12	28.0	111	26	9	6	1	2	0	1	6	2	29	0	1	1	1	.500	0	1- -	-	2.72	1.93
2015 Min	AL	28	0	0	7	22.0	97	16	15	15	3	1	1	0	15	2	24	2	0	0	0	-	0	0-0	0	3.69	6.14
2016 Min	AL	26	0	0	6	25.0	101	18	13	11	3	2	1	1	10	0	24	2	1	0	1	.000	0	0-0	0	2.91	3.96
2 ML YEARS		54	0	0	13	47.0	198	34	28	26	6	3	2	1	25	2	48	4	1	0	1	.000	0	0-0	0	3.27	4.98

Rafael Ortega

Bats: L Throws: R Pos: LF-46;PH-11;CF-10;RF-9;PR-2;DH-1   Ht: 5'11" Wt: 160 Born: 5/15/1991 Age: 26

		BATTING																		RUNNING			AVERAGES			
Year Team	Lg	G	AB	H	2B	3B	HR	(Hm	Rd)	TB	R	RBI	RC	TBB	IBB	SO	HBP	SH	SF	SB	CS	GDP	Avg	OBP	Slg	OPS
2012 Mdest	A+	114	495	140	23	8	8	(-	-)	203	81	60	73	46	1	93	4	4	7	36	18	8	.283	.344	.410	.754
2013 Tulsa	AA	42	158	36	4	2	1	(-	-)	47	22	10	16	19	0	26	1	0	0	9	4	3	.228	.315	.297	.612
2014 Sprgfld	AA	101	358	89	8	3	7	(-	-)	124	56	31	44	45	1	57	1	6	4	16	10	4	.249	.331	.346	.677
2015 Memp	AAA	131	437	126	22	6	2	(-	-)	166	66	42	67	55	1	71	2	6	2	17	6	4	.288	.369	.380	.749
2016 Salt Lk	AAA	78	322	102	18	7	4	(-	-)	146	47	31	50	15	0	39	1	2	1	14	8	1	.317	.348	.453	.801
2012 Col	NL	2	4	2	0	0	0	(0	0)	2	0	0	2	1	0	2	1	0	0	1	0	0	.500	.667	.500	1.167
2016 LAA	AL	66	185	43	8	0	1	(0	1)	54	24	16	19	13	0	23	0	3	0	8	3	5	.232	.283	.292	.575
2 ML YEARS		68	189	45	8	0	1	(0	1)	56	24	16	21	14	0	25	1	3	0	9	3	5	.238	.294	.296	.590

David Ortiz

Bats: L Throws: L Pos: DH-140;PH-11;1B-1   Ht: 6'3" Wt: 230 Born: 11/18/1975 Age: 41

		BATTING																		RUNNING			AVERAGES			
Year Team	Lg	G	AB	H	2B	3B	HR	(Hm	Rd)	TB	R	RBI	RC	TBB	IBB	SO	HBP	SH	SF	SB	CS	GDP	Avg	OBP	Slg	OPS
1997 Min	AL	15	49	16	3	0	1	(0	1)	22	10	6	7	2	0	19	0	0	0	0	0	1	.327	.353	.449	.802
1998 Min	AL	86	278	77	20	0	9	(2	7)	124	47	46	46	39	3	72	5	0	4	1	0	8	.277	.371	.446	.817
1999 Min	AL	10	20	0	0	0	0	(0	0)	0	1	0	0	5	0	12	0	0	0	0	0	2	.000	.200	.000	.200
2000 Min	AL	130	415	117	36	1	10	(7	3)	185	59	63	66	57	2	81	0	0	6	1	0	13	.282	.364	.446	.810
2001 Min	AL	89	303	71	17	1	18	(6	12)	144	46	48	46	40	8	68	1	1	2	1	0	6	.234	.324	.475	.799
2002 Min	AL	125	412	112	32	1	20	(5	15)	206	52	75	62	43	0	87	3	0	8	1	2	5	.272	.339	.500	.839
2003 Bos	AL	128	448	129	39	2	31	(17	14)	265	79	101	80	58	8	83	1	0	2	0	0	9	.288	.369	.592	.961
2004 Bos	AL	150	582	175	47	3	41	(17	24)	351	94	139	127	75	8	133	4	0	8	0	0	12	.301	.380	.603	.983
2005 Bos	AL	159	601	180	40	1	47	(20	27)	363	119	148	127	102	9	124	1	0	9	1	0	13	.300	.397	.604	1.001
2006 Bos	AL	151	558	160	29	2	54	(22	32)	355	115	137	129	119	23	117	4	0	5	1	0	12	.287	.413	.636	1.049
2007 Bos	AL	149	549	182	52	1	35	(16	19)	341	116	117	138	111	12	103	4	0	3	3	1	16	.332	.445	.621	1.066
2008 Bos	AL	109	416	110	30	1	23	(12	11)	214	74	89	82	70	12	74	1	1	3	1	0	11	.264	.369	.507	.877
2009 Bos	AL	150	541	129	35	1	28	(18	10)	250	77	99	79	74	5	134	5	0	7	0	2	9	.238	.332	.462	.794
2010 Bos	AL	145	518	140	36	1	32	(15	17)	274	86	102	94	82	14	145	2	0	4	0	1	12	.270	.370	.529	.899
2011 Bos	AL	146	525	162	40	1	29	(13	16)	291	84	96	97	78	12	83	1	0	1	1	1	24	.309	.398	.554	.953
2012 Bos	AL	90	324	103	26	0	23	(13	10)	198	65	60	75	56	13	51	0	0	3	0	1	6	.318	.415	.611	1.026
2013 Bos	AL	137	518	160	38	2	30	(12	18)	292	84	103	102	76	27	88	1	0	5	4	0	21	.309	.395	.564	.959
2014 Bos	AL	142	518	136	27	0	35	(11	24)	268	59	104	91	75	22	95	3	0	6	0	0	18	.263	.355	.517	.873

Year	Team	Lg	G	AB	H	2B	3B	HR	(Hm	Rd)	TB	R	RBI	RC	TBB	IBB	SO	HBP	SH	SF	SB	CS	GDP	Avg	OBP	Slg	OPS
									BATTING												RUNNING			AVERAGES			
2015	Bos	AL	146	528	144	37	0	37	(15	22)	292	73	108	87	77	16	95	0	0	9	0	1	16	.273	.360	.553	.913
2016	Bos	AL	151	537	169	48	1	38	(20	18)	333	79	127	123	80	15	86	0	0	7	2	0	22	.315	.401	.620	1.021
	Postseason		82	295	87	21	2	17	(12	5)	163	51	60	69	57	11	71	2	0	3	0	1	4	.295	.409	.553	.962
	20 ML YEARS		2408	8640	2472	632	19	541	(241	300)	4765	1419	1768	1668	1319	209	1750	38	2	92	17	9	236	.286	.380	.552	.931

Josh Osich

Pitches: L **Bats:** L **Pos:** RP-59 OH-sitch **Ht:** 6'2" **Wt:** 230 **Born:** 9/3/1988 **Age:** 28

Year	Team	Lg	G	GS	CG	GF	IP	BFP	H	R	ER	HR	SH	SF	HB	TBB	IBB	SO	WP	Bk	W	L	Pct	Sh	Sv-Op	Hld	ERC	ERA
						HOW MUCH HE PITCHED				WHAT HE GAVE UP												THE RESULTS					
2012	SnJos	A+	27	2	0	6	32.1	138	34	14	13	1	1	1	0	11	0	34	3	0	0	2	.000	0	1--	-	3.67	3.62
2013	SnJos	A+	34	0	0	20	40.1	162	32	13	11	1	1	0	0	10	1	48	4	1	3	1	.750	0	12--	-	1.94	2.45
2013	Rchmd	AA	22	0	0	9	29.2	122	26	16	16	2	2	0	0	12	0	28	4	0	2	3	.400	0	3--	-	3.28	4.85
2014	Rchmd	AA	28	0	0	3	33.1	143	28	18	14	4	2	0	1	20	0	27	4	0	1	0	1.000	0	0--	-	4.33	3.78
2015	Rchmd	AA	31	0	0	28	34.0	137	23	6	6	1	2	0	1	10	1	34	4	0	0	1	.000	0	19--	-	1.66	1.59
2015	Scrmto	AAA	6	0	0	5	7.0	27	3	1	0	0	0	0	0	2	0	11	1	0	1	0	1.000	0	1--	-	0.80	0.00
2016	Scrmto	AAA	7	0	0	1	7.0	29	6	1	1	0	0	0	0	2	0	8	2	0	0	0	-	0	0--	-	2.21	1.29
2015	SF	NL	35	0	0	6	28.2	120	24	12	7	4	1	1	0	8	0	27	2	0	2	0	1.000	0	0-2	11	2.88	2.20
2016	SF	NL	59	0	0	9	36.1	160	31	20	19	7	1	0	3	19	1	25	2	0	1	3	.250	0	0-3	18	4.65	4.71
	2 ML YEARS		94	0	0	15	65.0	280	55	32	26	11	2	1	3	27	1	52	4	0	3	3	.500	0	0-5	29	3.83	3.60

Sean O'Sullivan

Pitches: R **Bats:** R **Pos:** SP-4; RP-1 **Ht:** 6'1" **Wt:** 245 **Born:** 9/1/1987 **Age:** 29

Year	Team	Lg	G	GS	CG	GF	IP	BFP	H	R	ER	HR	SH	SF	HB	TBB	IBB	SO	WP	Bk	W	L	Pct	Sh	Sv-Op	Hld	ERC	ERA
						HOW MUCH HE PITCHED				WHAT HE GAVE UP												THE RESULTS					
2016	Pwtckt*	AAA	19	19	1	0	105.1	441	112	49	47	7	3	3	8	27	0	85	1	0	9	6	.600	0	0--	-	4.05	4.02
2009	LAA	AL	12	10	0	1	51.2	227	60	34	34	12	2	4	1	16	1	29	1	0	4	2	.667	0	0-0	0	5.66	5.92
2010	2 Tms	AL	19	14	0	3	83.2	368	90	53	51	15	0	3	1	31	2	43	4	2	4	6	.400	0	0-0	0	4.93	5.49
2011	KC	AL	12	10	0	1	58.1	273	78	52	47	10	3	4	2	26	1	19	3	0	2	6	.250	0	0-1	0	7.03	7.25
2013	SD	NL	7	3	0	2	25.0	118	31	12	11	0	1	2	1	14	1	12	0	0	0	2	.000	0	0-0	0	5.40	3.96
2014	Phi	NL	3	2	0	1	12.2	52	15	9	9	3	1	0	0	2	0	7	0	0	0	1	.000	0	0-0	0	5.29	6.39
2015	Phi	NL	13	13	0	0	71.0	328	94	49	48	16	4	5	6	20	5	35	3	0	1	6	.143	0	0-0	0	6.67	6.08
2016	Bos	AL	5	4	0	1	21.1	98	30	17	16	3	0	1	2	6	0	13	2	0	2	0	1.000	0	0-0	0	6.85	6.75
10	LAA	AL	5	1	0	2	13.0	49	7	3	3	1	0	0	0	4	2	6	0	0	1	0	1.000	0	0-0	0	1.33	2.08
10	KC	AL	14	13	0	1	70.2	319	83	50	48	14	0	3	1	27	0	37	4	2	3	6	.333	0	0-0	0	5.76	6.11
	7 ML YEARS		71	56	0	9	323.2	1464	398	226	216	59	11	19	13	115	10	158	13	2	13	23	.361	0	0-1	0	5.98	6.01

Roberto Osuna

Pitches: R **Bats:** R **Pos:** RP-72 **Ht:** 6'2" **Wt:** 215 **Born:** 2/7/1995 **Age:** 22

Year	Team	Lg	G	GS	CG	GF	IP	BFP	H	R	ER	HR	SH	SF	HB	TBB	IBB	SO	WP	Bk	W	L	Pct	Sh	Sv-Op	Hld	ERC	ERA
						HOW MUCH HE PITCHED				WHAT HE GAVE UP												THE RESULTS					
2012	2 Tms	Low	12	9	0	0	43.2	180	32	14	11	2	1	2	3	15	0	49	3	1	2	0	1.000	0	0--	-	2.34	2.27
2013	Lnsng	A	10	10	0	0	42.1	176	39	26	26	6	2	0	2	11	0	51	8	0	3	5	.375	0	0--	-	3.55	5.53
2014	2 Tms	Low	8	8	0	0	23.0	104	28	16	16	3	1	0	3	9	0	32	0	0	0	2	.000	0	0--	-	6.26	6.26
2015	Tor	AL	68	0	0	39	69.2	271	48	21	20	7	1	2	1	16	2	75	5	0	1	6	.143	0	20-23	7	1.89	2.58
2016	Tor	AL	72	0	0	61	74.0	288	55	23	22	9	1	3	3	14	4	82	4	1	4	3	.571	0	36-42	0	2.20	2.68
	Postseason		7	0	0	6	8.1	28	3	2	2	1	0	0	0	1	0	6	0	0	0	1	.000	0	1-1	0	0.74	2.16
	2 ML YEARS		140	0	0	100	143.2	559	103	44	42	16	2	5	4	30	6	157	9	1	5	9	.357	0	56-65	7	2.05	2.63

Dan Otero

Pitches: R **Bats:** R **Pos:** RP-62 oh-TEHR-oh **Ht:** 6'3" **Wt:** 205 **Born:** 2/19/1985 **Age:** 32

Year	Team	Lg	G	GS	CG	GF	IP	BFP	H	R	ER	HR	SH	SF	HB	TBB	IBB	SO	WP	Bk	W	L	Pct	Sh	Sv-Op	Hld	ERC	ERA
						HOW MUCH HE PITCHED				WHAT HE GAVE UP												THE RESULTS					
2012	SF	NL	12	0	0	4	12.1	57	19	11	8	0	0	0	2	2	1	8	1	0	0	0	-	0	0-0	0	6.18	5.84
2013	Oak	AL	33	0	0	8	39.0	159	42	7	6	1	0	0	0	6	1	27	0	0	2	0	1.000	0	0-1	8	2.90	1.38
2014	Oak	AL	72	0	0	14	86.2	349	80	24	22	4	4	3	2	15	7	45	1	0	8	2	.800	0	1-4	12	2.46	2.28
2015	Oak	AL	41	0	0	6	46.2	204	64	35	35	7	1	3	2	6	2	28	1	0	2	4	.333	0	0-1	2	5.70	6.75
2016	Cle	AL	62	0	0	20	70.2	269	54	14	12	2	3	0	0	10	1	57	2	0	5	1	.833	0	1-2	3	1.60	1.53
	Postseason		5	0	0	0	7.0	28	7	2	2	0	1	0	0	1	0	3	0	0	0	1	.000	0	0-0	1	2.52	2.57
	5 ML YEARS		220	0	0	52	255.1	1038	259	91	83	13	9	6	6	39	12	165	5	0	17	7	.708	0	2-8	25	2.95	2.93

Adam Ottavino

Pitches: R **Bats:** B **Pos:** RP-34 ott-tah-VEE-no **Ht:** 6'5" **Wt:** 220 **Born:** 11/22/1985 **Age:** 31

Year	Team	Lg	G	GS	CG	GF	IP	BFP	H	R	ER	HR	SH	SF	HB	TBB	IBB	SO	WP	Bk	W	L	Pct	Sh	Sv-Op	Hld	ERC	ERA
						HOW MUCH HE PITCHED				WHAT HE GAVE UP												THE RESULTS					
2016	Albq*	AAA	6	0	0	0	5.2	21	2	3	3	1	0	0	0	3	0	6	0	0	0	1	.000	0	0--	-	1.84	4.76
2010	StL	NL	5	3	0	0	22.1	110	37	21	21	5	1	0	0	9	1	12	1	0	0	2	.000	0	0-0	0	9.22	8.46
2012	Col	NL	53	0	0	6	79.0	339	76	42	40	9	3	1	0	34	7	81	8	0	5	1	.833	0	0-2	6	4.01	4.56
2013	Col	NL	51	0	0	5	78.1	335	73	27	23	5	6	4	2	31	5	78	9	1	1	3	.250	0	0-0	8	3.42	2.64
2014	Col	NL	75	0	0	16	65.0	272	67	26	26	6	2	3	4	16	1	70	4	0	1	4	.200	0	1-6	21	3.87	3.60
2015	Col	NL	10	0	0	5	10.1	35	3	0	0	0	0	0	1	2	0	13	0	0	1	0	1.000	0	3-3	3	0.56	0.00
2016	Col	NL	34	0	0	19	27.0	107	18	9	8	3	0	0	2	7	0	35	4	0	1	3	.250	0	7-12	4	2.17	2.67
	6 ML YEARS		228	3	0	51	282.0	1198	274	125	118	28	12	8	10	99	14	289	26	1	9	13	.409	0	11-23	42	3.80	3.77

Dillon Overton

Pitches: L Bats: L Pos: SP-5; RP-2 Ht: 6'2" Wt: 175 Born: 8/17/1991 Age: 25

		HOW MUCH HE PITCHED				WHAT HE GAVE UP													THE RESULTS							
Year Team	Lg	G	GS	CG	GF	IP	BFP	H	R	ER	HR	SH	SF	HB	TBB	IBB	SO	WP	Bk	W	L	Pct	Sh	Sv-Op	Hld	ERC	ERA
2014 2 Tms	Low	12	12	0	0	37.0	146	30	12	8	0	2	0	3	4	0	53	0	0	0	3	.000	0	0- -	-	1.75	1.95
2015 Stcktn	A+	14	12	0	2	61.1	247	62	29	26	7	0	2	3	12	0	59	1	0	2	4	.333	0	0- -	-	3.77	3.82
2015 Mdlnd	AA	13	13	0	0	64.2	266	65	22	22	4	1	0	0	15	0	47	1	0	5	2	.714	0	0- -	-	3.24	3.06
2016 Nashv	AAA	21	20	1	0	125.2	530	132	50	46	6	2	2	2	31	0	105	1	1	13	5	.722	0	0- -	-	3.47	3.29
2016 Oak	AL	7	5	0	2	24.1	128	48	31	31	12	0	2	1	7	0	17	1	0	1	3	.250	0	0-0	0	13.58	11.47

Henry Owens

Pitches: L Bats: L Pos: SP-5 Ht: 6'6" Wt: 220 Born: 7/21/1992 Age: 24

		HOW MUCH HE PITCHED				WHAT HE GAVE UP													THE RESULTS							
Year Team	Lg	G	GS	CG	GF	IP	BFP	H	R	ER	HR	SH	SF	HB	TBB	IBB	SO	WP	Bk	W	L	Pct	Sh	Sv-Op	Hld	ERC	ERA
2012 Grnvlle	A	23	22	0	0	101.2	450	100	58	55	10	4	2	6	47	0	130	5	0	12	5	.706	0	0- -	-	4.43	4.87
2013 Salem	A+	20	20	0	0	104.2	431	66	39	34	6	3	1	7	53	0	123	8	0	8	5	.615	0	0- -	-	2.51	2.92
2013 Portlnd	AA	6	6	0	0	30.1	125	18	8	6	3	0	0	2	15	0	46	3	0	3	1	.750	0	0- -	-	2.51	1.78
2014 Portlnd	AA	20	20	3	0	121.0	493	89	36	35	6	0	1	3	47	0	126	6	0	14	4	.778	2	0- -	-	2.42	2.60
2014 Pwtckt	AAA	6	6	0	0	38.0	156	32	17	17	4	1	1	3	12	0	44	0	0	3	1	.750	0	0- -	-	3.29	4.03
2015 Pwtckt	AAA	21	21	0	0	122.1	499	84	47	43	7	0	5	3	56	0	103	4	1	3	8	.273	0	0- -	-	2.48	3.16
2016 Pwtckt	AAA	24	24	1	0	137.2	595	107	60	54	13	5	3	13	81	0	135	3	0	10	7	.588	1	0- -	-	3.94	3.53
2015 Bos	AL	11	11	0	0	63.0	272	62	35	32	7	0	2	3	24	0	50	4	1	4	4	.500	0	0-0	0	4.18	4.57
2016 Bos	AL	5	5	0	0	22.0	103	23	17	17	5	0	1	1	20	1	21	3	0	0	2	.000	0	0-0	0	8.02	6.95
2 ML YEARS		16	16	0	0	85.0	375	85	52	49	12	0	3	4	44	1	71	7	1	4	6	.400	0	0-0	0	5.09	5.19

Chris Owings

Bats: R Throws: R Pos: SS-70;CF-49;PH-4;2B-1;PR-1 Ht: 5'10" Wt: 185 Born: 8/12/1991 Age: 25

		BATTING																		RUNNING			AVERAGES			
Year Team	Lg	G	AB	H	2B	3B	HR	(Hm	Rd)	TB	R	RBI	RC	TBB	IBB	SO	HBP	SH	SF	SB	CS	GDP	Avg	OBP	Slg	OPS
2013 Ari	NL	20	55	16	5	0	0	(0	0)	21	5	5	7	6	1	10	0	0	0	2	0	0	.291	.361	.382	.742
2014 Ari	NL	91	310	81	15	6	6	(1	5)	126	34	26	38	16	0	67	2	2	2	8	1	4	.261	.300	.406	.706
2015 Ari	NL	147	515	117	27	5	4	(3	1)	166	59	43	41	26	3	144	1	7	3	16	4	9	.227	.264	.322	.587
2016 Ari	NL	119	437	121	24	11	5	(5	0)	182	52	49	60	20	4	87	5	2	2	21	2	8	.277	.315	.416	.731
4 ML YEARS		377	1317	335	71	22	15	(9	6)	495	150	123	146	68	8	308	8	11	7	47	7	21	.254	.294	.376	.669

Marcell Ozuna

Bats: R Throws: R Pos: CF-123;LF-11;RF-9;PH-6 oh-ZUNE-uh Ht: 6'1" Wt: 225 Born: 11/12/1990 Age: 26

		BATTING																		RUNNING			AVERAGES			
Year Team	Lg	G	AB	H	2B	3B	HR	(Hm	Rd)	TB	R	RBI	RC	TBB	IBB	SO	HBP	SH	SF	SB	CS	GDP	Avg	OBP	Slg	OPS
2013 Mia	NL	70	275	73	17	4	3	(0	3)	107	31	32	35	13	0	57	2	1	0	5	1	6	.265	.303	.389	.693
2014 Mia	NL	153	565	152	26	5	23	(12	11)	257	72	85	74	41	1	164	1	0	5	3	1	12	.269	.317	.455	.772
2015 Mia	NL	123	459	119	27	0	10	(2	8)	176	47	44	48	30	1	110	3	0	2	2	3	10	.259	.308	.383	.691
2016 Mia	NL	148	557	148	23	6	23	(12	11)	252	75	76	69	43	2	115	4	0	4	3	3	11	.266	.321	.452	.773
4 ML YEARS		494	1856	492	93	15	59	(26	33)	792	225	237	226	127	4	446	10	1	11	10	8	39	.265	.314	.427	.741

Jordan Pacheco

Bats: R Throws: R Pos: PH-20;3B-4;1B-3;2B-3;DH-1 puh-CHECK-oh Ht: 6'1" Wt: 200 Born: 1/30/1986 Age: 31

		BATTING																		RUNNING			AVERAGES			
Year Team	Lg	G	AB	H	2B	3B	HR	(Hm	Rd)	TB	R	RBI	RC	TBB	IBB	SO	HBP	SH	SF	SB	CS	GDP	Avg	OBP	Slg	OPS
2011 Col	NL	21	84	24	1	0	2	(2	0)	31	5	14	12	3	0	9	1	0	0	0	0	2	.286	.318	.369	.687
2012 Col	NL	132	475	147	32	3	5	(4	1)	200	51	54	64	22	2	61	3	1	4	7	2	13	.309	.341	.421	.762
2013 Col	NL	95	247	59	15	0	1	(1	0)	77	23	22	21	10	0	38	3	1	1	0	0	4	.239	.276	.312	.588
2014 2 Tms	NL	69	153	39	10	1	0	(0	0)	51	10	16	17	9	0	27	1	1	1	0	0	6	.255	.299	.333	.632
2015 Ari	NL	29	66	16	0	0	2	(2	0)	22	8	8	8	9	0	14	1	0	2	1	0	6	.242	.333	.333	.667
2016 Cin	NL	31	51	8	4	0	0	(0	0)	12	1	0	0	0	0	14	0	0	0	0	0	1	.157	.157	.235	.392
14 Col	NL	22	72	17	6	1	0	(0	0)	25	4	8	8	6	0	15	1	0	1	0	0	3	.236	.300	.347	.647
14 Ari	NL	47	81	22	4	0	0	(0	0)	26	6	8	9	3	0	12	0	1	0	0	0	3	.272	.298	.321	.619
6 ML YEARS		377	1076	293	62	4	10	(9	1)	393	98	114	120	53	2	163	9	3	8	8	2	32	.272	.310	.365	.675

Angel Pagan

Bats: B Throws: R Pos: LF-123;CF-4;PH-4 AIN-jell pah-GAHN Ht: 6'2" Wt: 200 Born: 7/2/1981 Age: 35

		BATTING																		RUNNING			AVERAGES			
Year Team	Lg	G	AB	H	2B	3B	HR	(Hm	Rd)	TB	R	RBI	RC	TBB	IBB	SO	HBP	SH	SF	SB	CS	GDP	Avg	OBP	Slg	OPS
2006 ChC	NL	77	170	42	6	2	5	(4	1)	67	28	18	21	15	0	28	0	1	1	4	2	3	.247	.306	.394	.701
2007 ChC	NL	71	148	39	10	2	4	(3	1)	65	21	21	23	10	0	32	0	1	2	4	1	0	.264	.306	.439	.745
2008 NYM	NL	31	91	25	7	1	0	(0	0)	34	12	13	15	11	0	18	0	1	2	4	0	0	.275	.346	.374	.720
2009 NYM	NL	88	343	105	22	11	6	(5	1)	167	54	32	53	25	2	56	0	5	3	14	7	3	.306	.350	.487	.837
2010 NYM	NL	151	579	168	31	7	11	(6	5)	246	80	69	90	44	5	97	1	6	3	37	9	9	.290	.340	.425	.765
2011 NYM	NL	123	478	125	24	4	7	(4	3)	178	68	56	64	44	4	62	1	4	5	32	7	4	.262	.322	.372	.694
2012 SF	NL	154	605	174	38	15	8	(1	7)	266	95	56	91	48	5	97	0	2	4	29	7	6	.288	.338	.440	.778
2013 SF	NL	71	280	79	16	3	5	(3	2)	116	44	30	41	23	0	36	0	0	2	9	4	1	.282	.334	.414	.749
2014 SF	NL	96	383	115	21	2	3	(1	2)	149	56	27	50	25	1	53	1	1	3	16	6	5	.300	.342	.389	.731
2015 SF	NL	133	512	134	21	3	3	(1	2)	170	55	37	48	32	0	93	1	0	6	12	4	12	.262	.303	.332	.635
2016 SF	NL	129	495	137	24	5	12	(6	6)	207	71	55	70	42	1	66	0	0	3	15	4	11	.277	.331	.418	.750
Postseason		16	69	13	3	1	2	(1	1)	24	10	6	3	4	0	12	0	0	1	1	1	0	.188	.230	.348	.578
11 ML YEARS		1124	4084	1143	220	55	64	(34	30)	1665	584	414	566	319	18	638	4	21	34	176	51	54	.280	.330	.408	.738

Joe Panik

Bats: L **Throws:** R **Pos:** 2B-126;PH-4   PAN-ick   **Ht:** 6'1" **Wt:** 190 **Born:** 10/30/1990 **Age:** 26

									BATTING											RUNNING			AVERAGES			
Year	Team	Lg	G	AB	H	2B	3B	HR	(Hm | Rd)	TB	R	RBI	RC	TBB	IBB	SO	HBP	SH	SF	SB	CS	GDP	Avg	OBP	Slg	OPS
2014	SF	NL	73	269	82	10	2	1	(0 | 1)	99	31	18	33	16	0	33	0	1	1	0	0	4	.305	.343	.368	.711
2015	SF	NL	100	382	119	27	2	8	(4 | 4)	174	59	37	60	38	0	42	5	3	4	3	2	7	.312	.378	.455	.833
2016	SF	NL	127	464	111	21	7	10	(3 | 7)	176	67	62	56	50	5	47	4	3	5	5	0	14	.239	.315	.379	.695
	Postseason		17	73	17	2	2	1	(1 | 0)	26	7	8	7	4	0	6	0	1	0	0	0	1	.233	.273	.356	.629
	3 ML YEARS		300	1115	312	58	11	19	(7 | 12)	449	157	117	149	104	5	122	9	7	10	8	2	25	.280	.343	.403	.746

Jonathan Papelbon

Pitches: R **Bats:** R **Pos:** RP-37   PAHP-ill-bonn   **Ht:** 6'5" **Wt:** 230 **Born:** 11/23/1980 **Age:** 36

				HOW MUCH HE PITCHED					WHAT HE GAVE UP										THE RESULTS							
Year	Team	Lg	G	GS	CG	GF	IP	BFP	H	R	ER	HR	SH	SF	HB	TBB	IBB	SO	WP	Bk	W	L	Pct	Sh	Sv-Op	Hld	ERC	ERA
2005	Bos	AL	17	3	0	4	34.0	148	33	11	10	4	1	0	3	17	2	34	1	0	3	1	.750	0	0-1	4	4.82	2.65
2006	Bos	AL	59	0	0	49	68.1	257	40	8	7	3	1	2	1	13	2	75	2	0	4	2	.667	0	35-41	5	1.22	0.92
2007	Bos	AL	59	0	0	53	58.1	224	30	12	12	5	0	0	4	15	0	84	0	0	1	3	.250	0	37-40	2	1.43	1.85
2008	Bos	AL	67	0	0	62	69.1	273	58	24	18	4	4	1	0	8	0	77	2	0	5	4	.556	0	41-46	0	1.92	2.34
2009	Bos	AL	66	0	0	59	68.0	285	54	15	14	5	1	2	4	24	1	76	0	0	1	1	.500	0	38-41	0	2.78	1.85
2010	Bos	AL	65	0	0	53	67.0	287	57	34	29	7	5	0	2	28	4	76	4	0	5	7	.417	0	37-45	0	3.32	3.90
2011	Bos	AL	63	0	0	54	64.1	255	50	22	21	3	0	1	3	10	1	87	1	0	4	1	.800	0	31-34	0	1.86	2.94
2012	Phi	NL	70	0	0	64	70.0	284	56	22	19	8	3	0	4	18	1	92	0	0	5	6	.455	0	38-42	0	2.75	2.44
2013	Phi	NL	61	0	0	54	61.2	254	59	23	20	6	0	3	1	11	1	57	2	0	5	1	.833	0	29-36	0	2.98	2.92
2014	Phi	NL	66	0	0	52	66.1	259	45	15	15	2	3	0	5	15	1	63	1	0	2	3	.400	0	39-43	0	1.68	2.04
2015	2 Tms	NL	59	0	0	51	63.1	260	53	22	15	7	2	2	7	12	2	56	0	1	4	3	.571	0	24-26	1	2.82	2.13
2016	Was	NL	37	0	0	30	35.0	152	37	18	17	3	1	0	0	14	3	31	1	0	2	4	.333	0	19-22	1	4.17	4.37
15	Phi	NL	37	0	0	34	39.2	161	31	9	7	3	1	0	4	8	1	40	0	0	2	1	.667	0	17-17	0	2.36	1.59
15	Was	NL	22	0	0	17	23.2	99	22	13	8	4	1	2	3	4	1	16	0	1	2	2	.500	0	7-9	1	3.64	3.04
	Postseason		18	0	0	12	27.0	100	14	3	3	0	0	1	0	8	3	23	0	0	2	1	.667	0	7-9	0	1.01	1.00
	12 ML YEARS		689	3	0	585	725.2	2938	572	226	197	57	21	11	34	185	18	808	14	1	41	36	.532	0	368-417	8	2.41	2.44

Jimmy Paredes

pah-REY-dez

Bats: B **Throws:** R **Pos:** PH-44;LF-23;RF-20;2B-2;3B-2;DH-1;PR-1   **Ht:** 6'3" **Wt:** 200 **Born:** 11/25/1988 **Age:** 28

									BATTING											RUNNING			AVERAGES			
Year	Team	Lg	G	AB	H	2B	3B	HR	(Hm	Rd)	TB	R	RBI	RC	TBB	IBB	SO	HBP	SH	SF	SB	CS	GDP	Avg	OBP	Slg	OPS
2016	Bowie*	AA	10	37	9	2	0	1	(-	-)	14	4	5	4	4	1	12	0	0	0	1	0	0	.243	.317	.378	.695
2011	Hou	NL	46	168	48	8	2	2	(0	2)	66	16	18	23	9	0	47	0	1	1	5	4	3	.286	.320	.393	.713
2012	Hou	NL	24	74	14	1	1	0	(0	0)	17	7	3	3	6	0	21	0	0	2	2	1	0	.189	.244	.230	.474
2013	Hou	AL	48	125	24	4	0	1	(1	0)	31	8	10	8	6	0	44	1	1	2	4	4	1	.192	.231	.248	.479
2014	2 Tms	AL	27	63	18	4	0	2	(2	0)	28	12	8	6	2	0	16	0	0	0	4	0	1	.286	.308	.444	.752
2015	Bal	AL	104	363	100	17	2	10	(6	4)	151	46	42	47	19	0	111	0	0	2	4	4	8	.275	.310	.416	.726
2016	2 Tms	AL	83	158	35	8	0	5	(3	2)	58	15	19	17	7	0	48	0	1	1	0	1	0	.222	.253	.367	.620
14	KC	AL	9	10	2	0	0	0	(0	0)	2	3	0	0	0	0	3	0	0	0	2	0	0	.200	.200	.200	.400
14	Bal	AL	18	53	16	4	0	2	(2	0)	26	9	8	6	2	0	13	0	0	0	2	0	1	.302	.327	.491	.818
16	Tor	AL	7	15	4	1	0	1	(1	0)	8	2	2	2	2	0	4	0	0	0	0	0	0	.267	.353	.533	.886
16	Phi	NL	76	143	31	7	0	4	(2	2)	50	13	17	15	5	0	44	0	1	1	0	1	0	.217	.242	.350	.591
	Postseason		1	0	0	0	0	0	(0	0)	0	0	0	0	1	0	0	0	0	0	0	0	0	-	1.000	-	-
	6 ML YEARS		332	951	239	42	5	20	(12	8)	351	104	100	104	49	0	287	1	3	8	19	14	13	.251	.286	.369	.656

Byungho Park

Bats: R **Throws:** R **Pos:** DH-36;1B-24;PH-1   bee-YUNG   **Ht:** 6'1" **Wt:** 220 **Born:** 7/10/1986 **Age:** 30

									BATTING											RUNNING			AVERAGES			
Year	Team	Lg	G	AB	H	2B	3B	HR	(Hm	Rd)	TB	R	RBI	RC	TBB	IBB	SO	HBP	SH	SF	SB	CS	GDP	Avg	OBP	Slg	OPS
2012	Nexen	IND	133	469	136	34	0	31	(-	-)	263	76	105	105	73	3	111	11	0	7	20	9	6	.290	.393	.561	.954
2013	Nexen	IND	128	450	143	17	0	37	(-	-)	271	91	117	119	92	4	96	8	0	6	10	2	7	.318	.437	.602	1.039
2014	Nexen	IND	128	459	139	16	2	52	(-	-)	315	126	124	132	96	3	142	12	0	4	8	3	13	.303	.433	.686	1.119
2015	Nexen	IND	140	528	181	35	1	53	(-	-)	377	129	146	153	78	6	161	12	0	4	10	3	10	.343	.436	.714	1.150
2016	Roch	AAA	31	116	26	5	0	10	(-	-)	61	18	19	18	6	0	32	6	0	0	0	0	4	.224	.297	.526	.823
2016	Min	AL	62	215	41	9	1	12	(8	4)	88	28	24	17	21	0	80	5	0	3	1	0	3	.191	.275	.409	.684

Blake Parker

Pitches: R **Bats:** R **Pos:** RP-17   **Ht:** 6'3" **Wt:** 225 **Born:** 6/19/1985 **Age:** 32

				HOW MUCH HE PITCHED					WHAT HE GAVE UP										THE RESULTS							
Year	Team	Lg	G	GS	CG	GF	IP	BFP	H	R	ER	HR	SH	SF	HB	TBB	IBB	SO	WP	Bk	W	L	Pct	Sh	Sv-Op	Hld	ERC	ERA
2016	Tacom*	AAA	38	0	0	32	39.2	150	24	13	12	4	0	1	1	11	0	56	2	0	1	2	.333	0	19- -	-	1.80	2.72
2012	ChC	NL	7	0	0	0	6.0	32	10	7	4	3	0	0	0	5	1	6	0	0	0	0	-	0	0-0	0	14.02	6.00
2013	ChC	NL	49	0	0	18	46.1	195	39	17	14	6	4	0	2	15	1	55	2	0	1	2	.333	0	1-1	7	2.91	2.72
2014	ChC	NL	18	0	0	10	21.0	91	24	13	12	3	0	1	0	4	0	24	1	0	1	1	.500	0	0-0	0	4.24	5.14
2016	2 Tms	AL	17	0	0	5	17.1	79	17	9	9	1	0	0	2	9	1	15	0	0	1	0	1.000	0	1-1	1	4.41	4.67
16	Sea	AL	1	0	0	0	1.0	5	1	0	0	0	0	0	0	1	0	0	0	0	0	0	-	0	0-0	0	5.48	0.00
16	NYY	AL	16	0	0	5	16.1	74	16	9	9	1	0	0	2	8	1	15	0	0	1	0	1.000	0	1-1	1	4.35	4.96
	4 ML YEARS		91	0	0	33	90.2	397	90	46	39	11	0	2	4	33	3	100	3	0	3	3	.500	0	2-2	8	4.09	3.87

Jarrett Parker

Bats: L Throws: L Pos: PH-25;RF-21;LF-17;DH-4;CF-1   Ht: 6'4" Wt: 210 Born: 1/1/1989 Age: 28

Year	Team	Lg	G	AB	H	2B	3B	HR	(Hm	Rd)	TB	R	RBI	RC	TBB	IBB	SO	HBP	SH	SF	SB	CS	GDP	Avg	OBP	Slg	OPS
2012	SnJos	A+	122	409	101	21	7	15	(-	-)	181	71	67	73	70	3	175	8	2	2	28	6	2	.247	.366	.443	.809
2013	Rchmd	AA	131	444	109	18	5	18	(-	-)	191	72	57	70	60	0	161	15	5	0	13	11	7	.245	.355	.430	.785
2014	Rchmd	AA	100	363	100	20	6	12	(-	-)	168	52	58	65	45	2	103	10	0	1	11	4	8	.275	.370	.463	.833
2014	Fresno	AAA	24	79	22	5	0	3	(-	-)	36	13	10	12	9	0	23	1	0	0	1	2	1	.278	.360	.456	.815
2015	Scrmto	AAA	124	434	123	25	3	23	(-	-)	223	74	74	86	62	3	164	4	0	4	19	7	3	.283	.375	.514	.889
2016	Scrmto	AAA	53	194	53	8	2	16	(-	-)	113	44	35	40	26	0	66	2	0	0	1	1	0	.273	.365	.582	.947
2015	SF	NL	21	49	17	2	0	6	(1	5)	37	11	14	12	5	0	21	0	0	0	1	1	1	.347	.407	.755	1.163
2016	SF	NL	63	127	30	3	1	5	(3	2)	50	22	14	17	19	1	44	5	0	0	0	1	3	.236	.358	.394	.751
	2 ML YEARS		84	176	47	5	1	11	(4	7)	87	33	28	29	24	1	65	5	0	0	1	2	4	.267	.371	.494	.865

Jarrod Parker

Pitches: R Bats: R Pos: P   Ht: 6'1" Wt: 195 Born: 11/24/1988 Age: 28

			HOW MUCH HE PITCHED						WHAT HE GAVE UP										THE RESULTS						
Year	Team	Lg	G	GS	CG	GF	IP	BFP	H	R	ER	HR	SH	SF	HB	TBB	IBB	SO	WP	Bk	W	L	Pct	Sh	Sv-Op	Hld	ERC	ERA
2011	Ari	NL	1	1	0	0	5.2	22	4	0	0	2	0	0	1	0	1	0	0	0	0	0	-	0	0-0	0	1.36	0.00
2012	Oak	AL	29	29	0	0	181.1	751	166	71	70	11	7	8	3	63	3	140	10	0	13	8	.619	0	0-0	0	3.24	3.47
2013	Oak	AL	32	32	1	0	197.0	818	178	92	87	25	8	4	7	63	2	134	7	0	12	8	.600	0	0-0	0	3.57	3.97
	Postseason		4	3	0	0	18.0	77	21	11	10	1	2	0	1	4	0	12	2	0	1	2	.333	0	0-0	0	4.29	5.00
	3 ML YEARS		62	62	1	0	384.0	1591	348	163	157	36	17	12	10	127	5	275	17	0	25	16	.610	0	0-0	0	3.37	3.68

Chris Parmelee

Bats: L Throws: L Pos: 1B-6   PAR-muh-lee   Ht: 6'1" Wt: 220 Born: 2/24/1988 Age: 29

Year	Team	Lg	G	AB	H	2B	3B	HR	(Hm	Rd)	TB	R	RBI	RC	TBB	IBB	SO	HBP	SH	SF	SB	CS	GDP	Avg	OBP	Slg	OPS
2016	S-WB*	AAA	64	214	53	10	0	11	(-	-)	96	29	29	34	29	2	42	0	0	2	0	0	3	.248	.335	.449	.783
2011	Min	AL	21	76	27	6	0	4	(2	2)	45	8	14	19	12	0	13	0	0	0	0	0	3	.355	.443	.592	1.035
2012	Min	AL	64	192	44	10	2	5	(1	4)	73	18	19	18	13	1	52	4	0	1	0	0	4	.229	.290	.380	.671
2013	Min	AL	101	294	67	13	0	8	(2	6)	104	21	24	27	33	0	81	3	0	3	1	1	6	.228	.309	.354	.663
2014	Min	AL	87	250	64	11	0	7	(3	4)	96	27	28	19	17	0	64	2	0	1	0	3	7	.256	.307	.384	.691
2015	Bal	AL	32	97	21	7	1	4	(3	1)	42	11	9	9	4	0	26	1	0	0	0	1	1	.216	.255	.433	.688
2016	NYY	AL	6	8	4	1	0	2	(2	0)	11	4	4	3	0	0	3	0	0	0	0	0	0	.500	.500	1.375	1.875
	6 ML YEARS		311	917	227	48	3	30	(13	17)	371	89	98	95	79	1	239	10	0	5	1	5	21	.248	.313	.405	.717

Bobby Parnell

Pitches: R Bats: R Pos: RP-6   Ht: 6'3" Wt: 205 Born: 9/8/1984 Age: 32

			HOW MUCH HE PITCHED						WHAT HE GAVE UP										THE RESULTS						
Year	Team	Lg	G	GS	CG	GF	IP	BFP	H	R	ER	HR	SH	SF	HB	TBB	IBB	SO	WP	Bk	W	L	Pct	Sh	Sv-Op	Hld	ERC	ERA
2016	Toledo*	AAA	44	0	0	21	43.1	187	43	23	19	2	1	4	0	18	1	30	2	0	2	1	.667	0	12- -	-	3.67	3.95
2008	NYM	NL	6	0	0	3	5.0	19	3	3	3	0	0	0	0	2	0	3	1	0	0	0	-	0	0-0	0	1.59	5.40
2009	NYM	NL	68	8	0	14	88.1	413	101	56	52	8	3	1	4	46	2	74	6	1	4	8	.333	0	1-5	16	5.37	5.30
2010	NYM	NL	41	0	0	10	35.0	149	41	13	11	1	2	0	0	8	2	33	0	0	0	1	.000	0	0-2	9	3.80	2.83
2011	NYM	NL	60	0	0	23	59.1	268	60	29	24	4	6	0	2	27	4	64	8	1	4	6	.400	0	6-12	11	4.01	3.64
2012	NYM	NL	74	0	0	23	68.2	288	65	24	19	4	4	2	1	20	2	61	1	0	5	4	.556	0	7-12	18	3.08	2.49
2013	NYM	NL	49	0	0	41	50.0	198	38	17	12	1	2	3	1	12	3	44	1	0	5	5	.500	0	22-26	0	1.78	2.16
2014	NYM	NL	1	0	0	0	1.0	6	2	1	1	0	0	0	0	1	0	1	0	0	0	0	-	0	0-1	0	12.01	9.00
2015	NYM	NL	30	0	0	8	24.0	112	30	20	17	0	1	1	0	17	1	13	4	0	2	4	.333	0	1-3	5	6.12	6.38
2016	Det	AL	6	0	0	2	5.1	27	7	4	4	1	0	0	0	5	1	4	2	0	0	0	-	0	0-0	0	8.82	6.75
	9 ML YEARS		335	8	0	124	336.2	1480	347	167	143	19	18	7	8	138	15	297	23	2	20	28	.417	0	37-61	59	3.96	3.82

Gerardo Parra

heh-RAHR-doh PAR-uh

Bats: L Throws: L Pos: LF-60;1B-19;RF-16;CF-11;PH-6;PR-2   Ht: 5'11" Wt: 210 Born: 5/6/1987 Age: 30

Year	Team	Lg	G	AB	H	2B	3B	HR	(Hm	Rd)	TB	R	RBI	RC	TBB	IBB	SO	HBP	SH	SF	SB	CS	GDP	Avg	OBP	Slg	OPS
2009	Ari	NL	120	455	132	21	8	5	(4	1)	184	59	60	58	25	1	89	1	4	6	5	7	18	.290	.324	.404	.729
2010	Ari	NL	133	364	95	19	6	3	(1	2)	135	31	30	38	23	10	76	2	3	1	1	0	8	.261	.308	.371	.679
2011	Ari	NL	141	445	130	20	8	8	(3	5)	190	55	46	71	43	16	82	3	0	2	15	1	8	.292	.357	.427	.784
2012	Ari	NL	133	385	105	21	2	7	(5	2)	151	58	36	50	33	4	77	4	6	2	15	9	4	.273	.335	.392	.727
2013	Ari	NL	156	601	161	43	4	10	(6	4)	242	79	48	69	48	3	100	3	7	4	10	10	12	.268	.323	.403	.726
2014	2 Tms	NL	150	529	138	22	4	9	(3	6)	195	64	40	46	32	5	100	5	6	2	9	7	10	.261	.308	.369	.677
2015	2 Tms	NL	155	547	159	36	5	14	(8	6)	247	83	51	71	28	3	92	5	4	5	14	4	8	.291	.328	.452	.780
2016	Col	NL	102	368	93	27	3	7	(5	2)	147	45	39	29	9	1	73	1	1	2	6	4	16	.253	.271	.399	.670
14	Ari	NL	104	406	105	18	3	6	(2	4)	147	51	30	37	24	3	72	4	4	2	5	5	6	.259	.305	.362	.667
14	Mil	NL	46	123	33	4	1	3	(1	2)	48	13	10	9	8	2	28	1	2	0	4	2	4	.268	.318	.390	.708
15	Mil	NL	100	323	106	24	5	9	(4	5)	167	53	31	47	20	2	57	3	1	4	9	3	7	.328	.369	.517	.886
15	Bal	AL	55	224	53	12	0	5	(4	1)	80	30	20	24	8	1	35	2	3	1	5	1	1	.237	.268	.357	.625
	Postseason		5	18	1	1	0	0	(0	0)	2	1	0	0	1	0	7	0	0	0	0	0	0	.056	.105	.111	.216
	8 ML YEARS		1090	3694	1013	209	40	63	(35	28)	1491	474	350	432	241	43	689	24	31	24	75	42	84	.274	.321	.404	.724

Curtis Partch

Pitches: R Bats: R Pos: RP-2   PARCH   **Ht:** 6'5" **Wt:** 240 **Born:** 2/13/1987 **Age:** 30

			HOW MUCH HE PITCHED						WHAT HE GAVE UP										THE RESULTS							
Year	Team	Lg	G	GS	CG	GF	IP	BFP	H	R	ER	HR	SH	SF	HB	TBB	IBB	SO	WP	Bk	W	L	Pct	Sh	Sv-Op	Hld	ERC	ERA
2016	Indy*	AAA	42	0	0	12	60.1	243	41	17	15	1	3	0	1	30	1	60	5	0	2	2	.500	0	4- -	-	2.31	2.24
2013	Cin	NL	14	0	0	4	23.1	106	17	16	16	8	3	1	4	17	1	16	0	0	0	1	.000	0	0-0	0	6.32	6.17
2014	Cin	NL	6	0	0	4	7.0	30	2	0	0	0	0	0	0	7	0	6	0	0	1	0	1.000	0	0-0	0	1.81	0.00
2016	Pit	NL	2	0	0	0	0.2	6	2	3	3	0	0	0	0	2	0	0	1	0	0	0	-	0	0-0	0	29.63	40.50
	3 ML YEARS		22	0	0	8	31.0	142	21	19	19	8	3	1	4	26	1	22	1	0	1	1	.500	0	0-0	0	5.62	5.52

Jordan Patterson

Bats: L Throws: L Pos: RF-5;PH-3;1B-2;LF-2   **Ht:** 6'4" **Wt:** 215 **Born:** 2/12/1992 **Age:** 25

			BATTING																		RUNNING			AVERAGES			
Year	Team	Lg	G	AB	H	2B	3B	HR	(Hm	Rd)	TB	R	RBI	RC	TBB	IBB	SO	HBP	SH	SF	SB	CS	GDP	Avg	OBP	Slg	OPS
2013	GdJunc	R+	60	206	60	12	0	10	(-	-)	102	44	37	41	19	0	37	16	5	3	10	6	3	.291	.389	.495	.884
2014	Ashvll	A	125	453	126	27	0	14	(-	-)	195	69	66	77	46	2	118	17	6	10	25	8	3	.278	.359	.430	.790
2015	Mdest	A+	77	303	92	26	12	10	(-	-)	172	62	43	63	19	0	88	17	0	0	9	6	4	.304	.378	.568	.945
2015	NwBrit	AA	48	185	53	19	0	7	(-	-)	93	26	32	32	11	0	42	5	0	1	9	4	4	.286	.342	.503	.844
2016	Albq	AAA	119	427	125	24	7	14	(-	-)	205	75	62	81	47	2	118	13	3	5	10	0	9	.293	.376	.480	.856
2016	Col	NL	10	18	8	1	0	0	(0	0)	9	1	2	2	1	0	1	0	0	0	0	1	0	.444	.474	.500	.974

Spencer Patton

Pitches: R Bats: R Pos: RP-16   **Ht:** 6'1" **Wt:** 200 **Born:** 2/20/1988 **Age:** 29

			HOW MUCH HE PITCHED						WHAT HE GAVE UP										THE RESULTS							
Year	Team	Lg	G	GS	CG	GF	IP	BFP	H	R	ER	HR	SH	SF	HB	TBB	IBB	SO	WP	Bk	W	L	Pct	Sh	Sv-Op	Hld	ERC	ERA
2016	Iowa*	AAA	35	0	0	28	36.0	143	21	4	3	0	1	1	2	15	0	59	0	0	1	0	1.000	0	11- -	-	1.64	0.75
2014	Tex	AL	9	0	0	2	9.1	35	6	1	1	0	0	0	0	2	0	8	0	0	1	0	1.000	0	0-0	2	1.29	0.96
2015	Tex	AL	27	0	0	6	24.0	109	24	24	24	5	1	0	4	12	0	28	1	0	1	1	.500	0	0-0	3	6.04	9.00
2016	ChC	NL	16	0	0	7	21.1	101	20	16	13	3	0	0	1	14	0	22	0	0	1	1	.500	0	0-0	1	5.01	5.48
	3 ML YEARS		52	0	0	15	54.2	245	50	41	38	7	1	0	5	28	0	58	1	0	3	2	.600	0	0-0	6	4.68	6.26

David Paulino

Pitches: R Bats: R Pos: RP-2; SP-1   **Ht:** 6'7" **Wt:** 215 **Born:** 2/6/1994 **Age:** 23

			HOW MUCH HE PITCHED						WHAT HE GAVE UP										THE RESULTS							
Year	Team	Lg	G	GS	CG	GF	IP	BFP	H	R	ER	HR	SH	SF	HB	TBB	IBB	SO	WP	Bk	W	L	Pct	Sh	Sv-Op	Hld	ERC	ERA
2015	3 Tms	Low	13	12	0	1	67.1	267	49	23	21	1	0	0	3	19	0	72	4	3	5	3	.625	0	1- -	-	1.91	2.81
2016	CpChr	AA	14	9	0	2	64.0	246	47	16	13	3	1	1	3	11	0	72	0	0	5	2	.714	0	1- -	-	1.80	1.83
2016	Hou	AL	3	1	0	1	7.0	29	6	4	4	0	0	0	1	3	0	2	2	0	0	1	.000	0	0-0	0	3.40	5.14

Ben Paulsen

Bats: L Throws: R Pos: 1B-23;PH-10;LF-7   **Ht:** 6'4" **Wt:** 210 **Born:** 10/27/1987 **Age:** 29

			BATTING																		RUNNING			AVERAGES			
Year	Team	Lg	G	AB	H	2B	3B	HR	(Hm	Rd)	TB	R	RBI	RC	TBB	IBB	SO	HBP	SH	SF	SB	CS	GDP	Avg	OBP	Slg	OPS
2016	Albq*	AAA	78	288	80	17	5	6	(-	-)	125	44	40	42	24	0	64	0	0	2	1	0	4	.278	.331	.434	.765
2014	Col	NL	31	63	20	4	0	4	(1	3)	36	8	10	11	2	1	19	1	0	0	0	0	1	.317	.348	.571	.920
2015	Col	NL	116	325	90	19	4	11	(6	5)	150	42	49	42	23	0	92	2	1	3	1	2	5	.277	.326	.462	.787
2016	Col	NL	39	92	20	5	0	1	(0	1)	28	8	11	10	5	1	27	0	0	0	0	0	2	.217	.258	.304	.562
	3 ML YEARS		186	480	130	28	4	16	(7	9)	214	58	70	63	30	2	138	3	1	3	1	2	8	.271	.316	.446	.762

James Paxton

Pitches: L Bats: L Pos: SP-20   **Ht:** 6'4" **Wt:** 235 **Born:** 11/6/1988 **Age:** 28

			HOW MUCH HE PITCHED						WHAT HE GAVE UP										THE RESULTS							
Year	Team	Lg	G	GS	CG	GF	IP	BFP	H	R	ER	HR	SH	SF	HB	TBB	IBB	SO	WP	Bk	W	L	Pct	Sh	Sv-Op	Hld	ERC	ERA
2016	Tacom*	AAA	11	11	0	0	50.2	204	43	24	21	6	0	0	0	15	0	53	4	0	4	3	.571	0	0- -	-	3.03	3.73
2013	Sea	AL	4	4	0	0	24.0	94	15	5	4	2	0	0	0	7	2	21	0	0	3	0	1.000	0	0-0	0	1.61	1.50
2014	Sea	AL	13	13	0	0	74.0	303	60	29	25	3	3	1	1	29	2	59	7	0	6	4	.600	0	0-0	0	2.69	3.04
2015	Sea	AL	13	13	0	0	67.0	297	67	34	29	8	0	3	0	29	1	56	5	0	3	4	.429	0	0-0	0	4.22	3.90
2016	Sea	AL	20	20	0	0	121.0	511	134	62	51	9	0	6	1	24	3	117	5	0	6	7	.462	0	0-0	0	3.70	3.79
	4 ML YEARS		50	50	0	0	286.0	1205	276	130	109	22	3	10	2	89	8	253	17	0	18	15	.545	0	0-0	0	3.36	3.43

James Pazos

Pitches: L Bats: R Pos: RP-7   pah-ZOHSS   **Ht:** 6'2" **Wt:** 235 **Born:** 5/5/1991 **Age:** 26

			HOW MUCH HE PITCHED						WHAT HE GAVE UP										THE RESULTS							
Year	Team	Lg	G	GS	CG	GF	IP	BFP	H	R	ER	HR	SH	SF	HB	TBB	IBB	SO	WP	Bk	W	L	Pct	Sh	Sv-Op	Hld	ERC	ERA
2012	Stnlld	A-	28	0	0	9	40.1	168	29	9	8	0	0	1	0	19	0	39	3	0	2	2	.500	0	3- -	-	2.18	1.79
2013	2 Tms	Low	25	0	0	13	34.1	142	28	15	15	3	1	2	3	9	0	33	2	0	3	1	.750	0	1- -	-	2.79	3.93
2014	Tampa	A+	18	1	0	16	25.0	106	23	13	11	0	0	1	2	6	0	33	1	0	0	2	.000	0	4- -	-	2.62	3.96
2014	Trntn	AA	28	0	0	15	42.0	168	28	7	7	0	0	1	1	19	0	42	4	0	0	1	.000	0	6- -	-	2.04	1.50
2015	Trntn	AA	6	0	0	4	9.2	32	4	2	2	1	0	1	0	0	0	12	1	0	0	0	-	0	1- -	-	0.60	1.86
2015	S-WB	AAA	21	0	0	6	33.0	138	25	6	4	0	0	1	2	15	0	37	2	0	3	1	.750	0	2- -	-	2.55	1.09
2016	S-WB	AAA	23	0	0	8	27.1	118	19	8	8	1	1	0	0	19	0	41	0	0	2	2	.500	0	1- -	-	3.08	2.63
2015	NYY	AL	11	0	0	1	5.0	21	3	0	0	0	1	0	0	3	0	3	1	0	0	0	-	0	0-0	0	2.03	0.00
2016	NYY	AL	7	0	0	1	3.1	17	7	5	5	2	0	0	0	1	0	3	0	0	1	0	1.000	0	0-0	0	16.29	13.50
	2 ML YEARS		18	0	0	2	8.1	38	10	5	5	2	1	0	0	4	0	6	1	0	1	0	1.000	0	0-0	0	6.72	5.40

Brad Peacock

Pitches: R Bats: R Pos: SP-5; RP-5   Ht: 6'1" Wt: 210 Born: 2/2/1988 Age: 29

Year	Team	Lg	G	GS	CG	GF	IP	BFP	H	R	ER	HR	SH	SF	HB	TBB	IBB	SO	WP	Bk	W	L	Pct	Sh	Sv-Op	Hld	ERC	ERA
2016	Fresno*	AAA	22	21	1	1	117.0	507	122	64	56	11	5	4	6	40	1	119	9	0	5	6	.455	1	0- -	-	4.24	4.31
2011	Was	NL	3	2	0	0	12.0	48	7	1	1	0	0	0	0	6	0	4	1	0	2	0	1.000	0	0-1	0	1.71	0.75
2013	Hou	AL	18	14	0	1	83.1	365	78	51	48	15	1	1	3	37	0	77	4	0	5	6	.455	0	0-0	0	4.54	5.18
2014	Hou	AL	28	24	0	3	131.2	589	136	80	69	20	0	6	4	70	4	119	6	0	4	9	.308	0	0-0	1	5.29	4.72
2015	Hou	AL	1	1	0	0	5.0	22	5	3	3	0	0	1	1	2	0	3	0	0	0	1	.000	0	0-0	0	4.20	5.40
2016	Hou	AL	10	5	0	3	31.2	127	21	15	13	6	0	0	0	14	0	28	2	0	0	1	.000	0	0-0	0	3.04	3.69
	5 ML YEARS		60	46	0	7	263.2	1151	247	150	134	41	1	8	8	129	4	231	13	0	11	17	.393	0	0-1	3	4.57	4.57

Steve Pearce

Bats: R Throws: R Pos: 1B-40;2B-15;DH-13;PH-9;LF-7;RF-6;3B-2   Ht: 5'11" Wt: 200 Born: 4/13/1983 Age: 34

Year	Team	Lg	G	AB	H	2B	3B	HR	(Hm	Rd)	TB	R	RBI	RC	TBB	IBB	SO	HBP	SH	SF	SB	CS	GDP	Avg	OBP	Slg	OPS
2007	Pit	NL	23	68	20	5	1	0	(0	0)	27	13	6	9	5	0	12	0	0	0	2	1	2	.294	.342	.397	.740
2008	Pit	NL	37	109	27	7	0	4	(0	4)	46	6	15	13	5	0	22	3	0	2	2	0	1	.248	.294	.422	.716
2009	Pit	NL	60	165	34	13	1	4	(3	1)	61	19	16	17	21	0	43	0	0	0	1	0	2	.206	.296	.370	.665
2010	Pit	NL	15	29	8	2	1	0	(0	0)	12	4	5	5	7	0	6	0	0	2	0	0	0	.276	.395	.414	.809
2011	Pit	NL	50	94	19	2	0	1	(1	0)	24	8	10	5	7	0	21	1	1	2	0	0	6	.202	.260	.255	.515
2012	3 Tms		61	159	38	8	1	4	(2	2)	60	16	26	24	20	1	41	3	2	4	1	2	4	.239	.328	.377	.705
2013	Bal	AL	44	119	31	7	0	4	(3	1)	50	14	13	20	15	2	25	4	0	1	1	0	0	.261	.362	.420	.782
2014	Bal	AL	102	338	99	26	0	21	(12	9)	188	51	49	66	40	1	76	4	0	1	5	0	4	.293	.373	.556	.930
2015	Bal	AL	92	294	64	13	1	15	(7	8)	124	42	40	33	23	1	69	7	0	1	1	1	11	.218	.289	.422	.711
2016	2 Tms	AL	85	264	76	13	1	13	(6	7)	130	35	35	43	34	2	54	3	0	1	0	3	5	.288	.374	.492	.867
12	Bal	AL	28	71	18	4	0	3	(2	1)	31	8	14	12	8	0	17	0	2	2	0	1	1	.254	.321	.437	.758
12	Hou	NL	21	63	16	4	1	0	(0	0)	22	2	8	9	7	1	16	3	0	2	1	1	3	.254	.347	.349	.696
12	NYY	AL	12	25	4	0	0	1	(0	1)	7	6	4	3	5	0	8	0	0	0	0	0	0	.160	.300	.280	.580
16	TB	AL	60	204	63	11	1	10	(4	6)	106	26	29	37	26	2	40	1	0	1	0	3	4	.309	.388	.520	.908
16	Bal	AL	25	60	13	2	0	3	(2	1)	24	9	6	6	8	0	14	2	0	0	0	0	1	.217	.329	.400	.729
	Postseason		7	27	4	1	0	0	(0	0)	5	4	1	2	2	0	3	1	0	0	0	0	0	.148	.233	.185	.419
	10 ML YEARS		569	1639	416	96	6	66	(34	32)	722	208	215	235	177	7	369	25	3	13	13	7	35	.254	.333	.441	.774

Jake Peavy

Pitches: R Bats: R Pos: SP-21; RP-10   Ht: 6'1" Wt: 195 Born: 5/31/1981 Age: 36

Year	Team	Lg	G	GS	CG	GF	IP	BFP	H	R	ER	HR	SH	SF	HB	TBB	IBB	SO	WP	Bk	W	L	Pct	Sh	Sv-Op	Hld	ERC	ERA
2002	SD	NL	17	17	0	0	97.2	430	106	54	49	11	5	2	3	33	4	90	4	1	6	7	.462	0	0-0	0	4.41	4.52
2003	SD	NL	32	32	0	0	194.2	827	173	94	89	33	7	5	6	82	3	156	2	0	12	11	.522	0	0-0	0	4.13	4.11
2004	SD	NL	27	27	0	0	166.1	694	146	49	42	13	5	6	11	53	4	173	1	1	15	6	.714	0	0-0	0	3.18	2.27
2005	SD	NL	30	30	3	0	203.0	812	162	70	65	18	4	5	7	50	3	216	3	1	13	7	.650	3	0-0	0	2.49	2.88
2006	SD	NL	32	32	2	0	202.1	846	187	93	92	23	5	1	6	62	11	215	4	0	11	14	.440	0	0-0	0	3.42	4.09
2007	SD	NL	34	34	0	0	223.1	898	169	67	63	13	5	7	6	68	5	240	4	0	19	6	.760	0	0-0	0	2.27	2.54
2008	SD	NL	27	27	1	0	173.2	709	146	57	55	17	7	1	5	59	1	166	6	0	10	11	.476	0	0-0	0	3.12	2.85
2009	2 Tms		16	16	1	0	101.2	410	80	41	39	8	3	2	1	34	0	110	2	2	9	6	.600	0	0-0	0	2.63	3.45
2010	CWS	AL	17	17	1	0	107.0	450	98	55	55	13	1	5	5	34	2	93	2	1	7	6	.538	1	0-0	0	3.59	4.63
2011	CWS	AL	19	18	1	0	111.2	470	117	61	61	10	1	5	3	24	4	95	4	0	7	7	.500	1	0-0	0	3.59	4.92
2012	CWS	AL	32	32	4	0	219.0	882	191	88	82	27	1	6	10	49	1	194	3	2	11	12	.478	1	0-0	0	3.07	3.37
2013	2 Tms	AL	23	23	2	0	144.2	590	130	70	67	20	2	3	2	36	0	121	0	2	12	5	.706	0	0-0	0	3.25	4.17
2014	2 Tms	AL	32	32	0	0	202.2	852	196	91	84	23	8	11	9	63	2	158	5	2	7	13	.350	0	0-0	0	3.83	3.73
2015	SF	NL	19	19	0	0	110.2	448	99	45	44	12	5	1	2	25	1	78	2	1	8	6	.571	0	0-0	0	2.97	3.58
2016	SF	NL	31	21	0	3	118.2	520	134	76	73	18	4	2	2	36	1	102	4	1	5	9	.357	0	0-0	0	4.82	5.54
09	SD	NL	13	13	1	0	81.2	335	69	38	36	7	2	2	1	28	0	92	2	1	6	6	.500	0	0-0	0	3.00	3.97
09	CWS	AL	3	3	0	0	20.0	75	11	3	3	1	1	0	0	6	0	18	0	1	3	0	1.000	0	0-0	0	1.38	1.35
13	CWS	AL	13	13	1	0	80.0	324	74	41	38	14	1	2	1	17	0	76	0	1	8	4	.667	0	0-0	0	3.49	4.28
13	Bos	AL	10	10	1	0	64.2	266	56	29	29	6	1	1	1	19	0	45	0	1	4	1	.800	0	0-0	0	2.96	4.04
14	Bos	AL	20	20	0	0	124.0	538	131	67	65	20	4	5	3	46	1	100	2	1	1	9	.100	0	0-0	0	4.83	4.72
14	SF	NL	12	12	0	0	78.2	314	65	24	19	3	4	6	6	17	1	58	3	1	6	4	.600	0	0-0	0	2.40	2.17
	Postseason		9	9	0	0	38.1	178	53	34	34	4	3	1	0	17	4	21	1	0	1	5	.167	0	0-0	0	6.48	7.98
	15 ML YEARS		388	377	15	3	2377.0	9838	2134	1011	960	259	63	62	78	708	42	2207	46	14	152	126	.547	6	0-0	0	3.30	3.63

Joc Pederson

Bats: L Throws: L Pos: CF-132;PH-17;PR-1   JOCK   Ht: 6'1" Wt: 220 Born: 4/21/1992 Age: 25

Year	Team	Lg	G	AB	H	2B	3B	HR	(Hm	Rd)	TB	R	RBI	RC	TBB	IBB	SO	HBP	SH	SF	SB	CS	GDP	Avg	OBP	Slg	OPS
2014	LAD	NL	18	28	4	0	0	0	(0	0)	4	1	0	1	9	0	11	0	1	0	0	0	1	.143	.351	.143	.494
2015	LAD	NL	151	480	101	19	1	26	(13	13)	200	67	54	62	92	6	170	9	2	2	4	7	5	.210	.346	.417	.763
2016	LAD	NL	137	406	100	26	0	25	(13	12)	201	64	68	71	63	4	130	4	1	2	6	2	5	.246	.352	.495	.847
	Postseason		5	4	0	0	0	0	(0	0)	0	0	0	1	4	1	1	0	0	0	0	0	0	.000	.500	.000	.500
	3 ML YEARS		306	914	205	45	1	51	(26	25)	405	132	122	134	164	10	311	13	4	4	10	9	11	.224	.349	.443	.792

Dustin Pedroia

Bats: R **Throws:** R **Pos:** 2B-152;PH-2;PR-1   peh-DROY-uh   **Ht:** 5'9" **Wt:** 175 **Born:** 8/17/1983 **Age:** 33

Year	Team	Lg	G	AB	H	2B	3B	HR	(Hm	Rd)	TB	R	RBI	RC	TBB	IBB	SO	HBP	SH	SF	SB	CS	GDP	Avg	OBP	Slg	OPS
2006	Bos	AL	31	89	17	4	0	2	(1	1)	27	5	7	3	7	0	7	1	1	0	0	1	1	.191	.258	.303	.561
2007	Bos	AL	139	520	165	39	1	8	(5	3)	230	86	50	79	47	1	42	7	5	2	7	1	8	.317	.380	.442	.823
2008	Bos	AL	157	653	**213**	54	2	17	(7	10)	322	118	83	107	50	1	52	7	7	9	20	1	17	.326	.376	.493	.869
2009	Bos	AL	154	626	185	48	1	15	(10	5)	280	**115**	72	104	74	3	45	5	3	6	20	8	19	.296	.371	.447	.819
2010	Bos	AL	75	302	87	24	1	12	(4	8)	149	53	41	52	37	1	38	4	2	6	9	1	7	.288	.367	.493	.860
2011	Bos	AL	159	635	195	37	3	21	(13	8)	301	102	91	114	86	6	85	1	2	7	26	8	12	.307	.387	.474	.861
2012	Bos	AL	141	563	163	39	3	15	(9	6)	253	81	65	84	48	3	60	5	1	6	20	6	9	.290	.347	.449	.797
2013	Bos	AL	160	641	193	42	2	9	(7	2)	266	91	84	99	73	4	75	3	0	7	17	5	24	.301	.372	.415	.787
2014	Bos	AL	135	551	153	33	0	7	(2	5)	207	72	53	65	51	1	75	1	0	6	6	6	14	.278	.337	.376	.712
2015	Bos	AL	93	381	111	19	1	12	(4	8)	168	46	42	55	38	1	51	2	1	3	2	2	6	.291	.356	.441	.797
2016	Bos	AL	154	633	201	36	1	15	(7	8)	284	105	74	100	61	0	73	0	1	3	7	4	24	.318	.376	.449	.825
	Postseason		44	178	44	13	0	5	(2	3)	72	30	25	22	19	0	25	2	1	2	3	1	4	.247	.323	.404	.728
	11 ML YEARS		1398	5594	1683	375	15	133	(69	64)	2487	874	662	862	572	21	603	36	23	55	134	43	141	.301	.366	.445	.811

Mike Pelfrey

Pitches: R **Bats:** R **Pos:** SP-22; RP-2   PELL-free   **Ht:** 6'7" **Wt:** 240 **Born:** 1/14/1984 **Age:** 33

Year	Team	Lg	G	GS	CG	GF	IP	BFP	H	R	ER	HR	SH	SF	HB	TBB	IBB	SO	WP	Bk	W	L	Pct	Sh	Sv-Op	Hld	ERC	ERA
2006	NYM	NL	4	4	0	0	21.1	99	25	14	13	1	1	1	3	12	0	13	2	0	2	1	.667	0	0-0	0	6.05	5.48
2007	NYM	NL	15	13	0	0	72.2	342	85	47	45	6	6	3	9	39	1	45	3	0	3	8	.273	0	0-0	0	5.99	5.57
2008	NYM	NL	32	32	2	0	200.2	851	209	86	83	12	11	5	13	64	1	110	2	0	13	11	.542	0	0-0	0	4.04	3.72
2009	NYM	NL	31	31	0	0	184.1	824	213	112	103	18	8	5	7	66	8	107	1	**6**	10	12	.455	0	0-0	0	4.83	5.03
2010	NYM	NL	34	33	0	1	204.0	870	213	88	83	12	17	4	6	68	5	113	1	1	15	9	.625	0	1-1	0	3.89	3.66
2011	NYM	NL	34	33	2	0	193.2	860	220	111	102	21	10	8	7	65	7	105	2	2	7	13	.350	0	0-0	0	4.70	4.74
2012	NYM	NL	3	3	0	0	19.2	85	24	5	5	0	1	0	0	4	0	13	1	0	0	0	-	0	0-0	0	3.82	2.29
2013	Min	AL	29	29	0	0	152.2	680	184	92	88	13	1	7	6	53	0	101	1	0	5	13	.278	0	0-0	0	5.13	5.19
2014	Min	AL	5	5	0	0	23.2	119	29	23	21	5	2	2	2	18	0	10	1	0	0	3	.000	0	0-0	0	8.18	7.99
2015	Min	AL	30	30	0	0	164.2	714	198	86	78	11	3	3	12	45	1	86	5	0	6	11	.353	0	0-0	0	4.89	4.26
2016	Det	AL	24	22	0	0	119.0	541	160	76	67	15	2	5	6	46	0	56	3	0	4	10	.286	0	0-0	0	6.69	5.07
	11 ML YEARS		241	235	4	1	1356.1	5985	1560	740	688	114	62	43	71	480	23	759	22	9	65	91	.417	0	1-1	0	4.86	4.57

Ariel Pena

Pitches: R **Bats:** R **Pos:** RP-1   arr-ee-EL   **Ht:** 6'3" **Wt:** 245 **Born:** 5/20/1989 **Age:** 28

Year	Team	Lg	G	GS	CG	GF	IP	BFP	H	R	ER	HR	SH	SF	HB	TBB	IBB	SO	WP	Bk	W	L	Pct	Sh	Sv-Op	Hld	ERC	ERA
2012	Ark	AA	19	19	0	0	114.1	475	94	43	38	14	2	2	1	42	0	111	7	0	6	6	.500	0	0--	-	3.15	2.99
2012	Hntsvl	AA	7	7	0	0	32.1	153	40	26	26	5	4	2	5	23	0	29	3	0	0	2	.000	0	0--	-	8.42	7.24
2013	Hntsvl	AA	27	27	0	0	142.1	604	115	63	59	17	4	5	2	79	1	131	10	0	8	9	.471	0	0--	-	3.85	3.73
2014	Nashv	AAA	25	24	0	0	128.1	548	96	69	65	12	4	2	5	75	0	140	12	0	9	8	.529	0	0--	-	3.52	4.56
2015	ColSpr	AAA	43	7	0	5	82.2	349	77	41	38	7	2	3	3	32	1	83	6	0	2	2	.500	0	0--	-	3.71	4.14
2016	ColSpr	AAA	16	5	0	2	37.2	190	51	36	35	7	2	2	1	32	0	35	2	0	2	2	.500	0	0--	-	9.22	8.36
2015	Mil	NL	6	5	0	0	27.1	120	24	14	13	2	2	1	2	14	2	27	2	0	2	1	.667	0	0-0	0	3.78	4.28
2016	Mil	NL	1	0	0	0	1.2	11	5	5	5	3	0	0	0	2	0	0	0	0	0	0	-	0	0-0	0	47.67	27.00
	2 ML YEARS		7	5	0	0	29.0	131	29	19	18	5	2	1	2	16	2	27	2	0	2	1	.667	0	0-0	0	5.40	5.59

Brayan Pena

Bats: B **Throws:** R **Pos:** PH-5;C-3;1B-1   BRIAN   **Ht:** 5'9" **Wt:** 240 **Born:** 1/7/1982 **Age:** 35

Year	Team	Lg	G	AB	H	2B	3B	HR	(Hm	Rd)	TB	R	RBI	RC	TBB	IBB	SO	HBP	SH	SF	SB	CS	GDP	Avg	OBP	Slg	OPS
2005	Atl	NL	18	39	7	2	0	0	(0	0)	9	2	4	0	1	1	7	0	0	0	0	0	1	.179	.200	.231	.431
2006	Atl	NL	23	41	11	2	0	1	(0	1)	16	9	5	4	2	0	5	0	0	0	0	0	2	.268	.302	.390	.693
2007	Atl	NL	16	33	7	0	0	1	(1	0)	10	2	3	0	0	0	3	0	0	0	0	1	2	.212	.212	.303	.515
2008	Atl	NL	14	14	4	1	0	0	(0	0)	5	3	0	0	1	0	2	0	0	0	0	0	0	.286	.333	.357	.690
2009	KC	AL	64	165	45	10	0	6	(3	3)	73	17	18	18	12	2	18	0	4	2	0	0	5	.273	.318	.442	.761
2010	KC	AL	60	158	40	10	0	1	(0	1)	53	11	19	16	12	0	27	1	1	2	2	0	8	.253	.306	.335	.642
2011	KC	AL	72	222	55	11	0	3	(0	3)	75	17	24	23	12	0	24	2	0	4	0	0	6	.248	.288	.338	.625
2012	KC	AL	68	212	50	10	1	2	(1	1)	68	16	25	19	9	0	24	0	1	4	0	1	7	.236	.262	.321	.583
2013	Det	AL	71	229	68	11	0	4	(1	3)	91	19	22	19	6	0	26	2	2	4	0	2	7	.297	.315	.397	.713
2014	Cin	NL	115	348	88	18	1	5	(3	2)	123	23	26	31	20	2	42	0	1	3	2	3	8	.253	.291	.353	.645
2015	Cin	NL	108	333	91	17	0	0	(0	0)	108	17	18	34	29	1	34	2	2	1	2	0	10	.273	.334	.324	.659
2016	StL	NL	9	13	2	1	0	0	(0	0)	3	0	0	0	1	0	2	0	0	0	0	0	0	.154	.214	.231	.445
	Postseason		1	3	1	0	0	0	(0	0)	1	0	1	0	0	0	0	0	0	0	0	0	1	.333	.333	.333	.667
	12 ML YEARS		638	1807	468	93	2	23	(9	14)	634	136	164	164	105	6	214	7	11	20	6	7	56	.259	.299	.351	.650

Felix Pena

Pitches: R **Bats:** R **Pos:** RP-11   **Ht:** 6'2" **Wt:** 185 **Born:** 2/25/1990 **Age:** 27

Year	Team	Lg	G	GS	CG	GF	IP	BFP	H	R	ER	HR	SH	SF	HB	TBB	IBB	SO	WP	Bk	W	L	Pct	Sh	Sv-Op	Hld	ERC	ERA
2012	2 Tms	Low	21	6	0	2	73.0	319	69	38	29	6	5	2	7	27	0	52	5	0	4	2	.667	0	0--	-	3.53	3.58
2013	Kane	A	21	17	1	1	103.1	440	102	57	45	5	1	3	7	32	0	77	8	0	4	7	.364	0	0--	-	3.57	3.92
2014	Dytona	A+	19	19	1	0	96.0	408	88	43	34	6	2	1	4	34	0	76	6	0	4	6	.400	0	0--	-	3.33	3.19

	HOW MUCH HE PITCHED					WHAT HE GAVE UP													THE RESULTS							
Year Team	Lg	G	GS	CG	GF	IP	BFP	H	R	ER	HR	SH	SF	HB	TBB	IBB	SO	WP	Bk	W	L	Pct	Sh	Sv-Op	Hld	ERC	ERA
2014 Tenn	AA	6	6	0	0	27.2	126	30	23	23	5	5	0	2	17	0	26	1	0	2	4	.333	0	0- -	-	6.57	7.48
2015 Tenn	AA	25	23	1	1	129.2	539	111	60	54	10	2	3	5	49	1	140	12	5	7	8	.467	0	0- -	-	3.22	3.75
2016 Iowa	AAA	36	0	0	10	63.1	256	46	24	24	4	1	3	2	23	3	81	1	0	3	4	.429	0	3- -	-	2.34	3.41
2016 ChC	NL	11	0	0	2	9.0	35	5	4	4	1	0	0	0	3	1	13	1	0	0	0	-	0	1-1	2	1.57	4.00

Francisco Pena

Bats: R **Throws:** R **Pos:** C-14;PH-2;PR-1   **Ht:** 6'2" **Wt:** 230 **Born:** 10/12/1989 **Age:** 27

							BATTING												RUNNING			AVERAGES			
Year Team	Lg	G	AB	H	2B	3B	HR	(Hm | Rd)	TB	R	RBI	RC	TBB	IBB	SO	HBP	SH	SF	SB	CS	GDP	Avg	OBP	Slg	OPS
2016 Norfolk*	AAA	54	191	47	11	1	4	(- | -)	72	17	23	22	15	0	25	0	0	2	0	1	9	.246	.298	.377	.675
2014 KC	AL	1	0	0	0	0	0	(0 | 0)	0	0	0	0	0	0	0	0	0	0	0	0	0	-	-	-	-
2015 KC	AL	8	7	1	0	0	0	(0 | 0)	1	0	0	0	0	0	3	0	0	0	0	0	1	.143	.143	.143	.286
2016 Bal	AL	14	40	8	0	0	1	(1 | 0)	11	5	3	4	2	0	14	0	1	0	0	0	1	.200	.238	.275	.513
3 ML YEARS		23	47	9	0	0	1	(1 | 0)	12	5	3	4	2	0	17	0	1	0	0	0	3	.191	.224	.255	.480

Ramiro Pena

Bats: B **Throws:** R **Pos:** 2B-17;3B-12;PH-8;SS-4;PR-1   **Ht:** 5'11" **Wt:** 200 **Born:** 7/18/1985 **Age:** 31

							BATTING												RUNNING			AVERAGES			
Year Team	Lg	G	AB	H	2B	3B	HR	(Hm | Rd)	TB	R	RBI	RC	TBB	IBB	SO	HBP	SH	SF	SB	CS	GDP	Avg	OBP	Slg	OPS
2016 Scrmto*	AAA	57	216	64	12	1	5	(- | -)	93	24	24	33	21	2	35	2	4	2	5	6	6	.296	.361	.431	.792
2009 NYY	AL	69	115	33	6	1	1	(1 | 0)	44	17	10	15	5	0	20	0	1	0	4	1	2	.287	.317	.383	.699
2010 NYY	AL	85	154	35	1	1	0	(0 | 0)	38	18	18	10	6	0	27	1	4	2	7	1	4	.227	.258	.247	.504
2011 NYY	AL	23	40	4	0	0	1	(1 | 0)	7	5	4	0	2	0	11	1	2	1	0	0	1	.100	.159	.175	.334
2012 NYY	AL	3	4	1	0	0	0	(0 | 0)	1	0	0	0	0	0	0	0	0	0	0	0	0	.250	.250	.250	.500
2013 Atl	NL	50	97	27	5	1	3	(2 | 1)	43	14	12	12	8	0	18	0	1	1	0	2	1	.278	.330	.443	.773
2014 Atl	NL	81	147	36	6	0	3	(2 | 1)	51	9	9	14	13	3	38	0	4	1	1	0	0	.245	.304	.347	.651
2016 SF	NL	30	87	26	6	1	1	(0 | 1)	37	9	10	10	2	1	16	2	0	0	0	0	0	.299	.330	.425	.755
7 ML YEARS		341	644	162	24	4	9	(6 | 3)	221	72	63	61	36	4	130	4	12	5	12	4	8	.252	.293	.343	.636

Hunter Pence

Bats: R **Throws:** R **Pos:** RF-102;PH-4   **Ht:** 6'4" **Wt:** 220 **Born:** 4/13/1983 **Age:** 34

							BATTING												RUNNING			AVERAGES			
Year Team	Lg	G	AB	H	2B	3B	HR	(Hm | Rd)	TB	R	RBI	RC	TBB	IBB	SO	HBP	SH	SF	SB	CS	GDP	Avg	OBP	Slg	OPS
2007 Hou	NL	108	456	147	30	9	17	(7 | 10)	246	57	69	77	26	0	95	1	0	1	11	5	10	.322	.360	.539	.899
2008 Hou	NL	157	595	160	34	4	25	(14 | 11)	277	78	83	82	40	2	124	4	0	3	11	10	14	.269	.318	.466	.783
2009 Hou	NL	159	585	165	26	5	25	(14 | 11)	276	76	72	80	58	1	109	1	0	3	14	11	25	.282	.346	.472	.818
2010 Hou	NL	156	614	173	29	3	25	(14 | 11)	283	93	91	89	41	2	105	0	0	3	18	9	11	.282	.325	.461	.786
2011 2 Tms	NL	154	606	190	38	5	22	(5 | 17)	304	84	97	102	56	3	124	1	0	5	8	2	15	.314	.370	.502	.871
2012 2 Tms	NL	160	617	156	26	4	24	(9 | 15)	262	87	104	81	56	2	145	7	1	7	5	2	15	.253	.319	.425	.743
2013 SF	NL	162	629	178	35	5	27	(10 | 17)	304	91	99	91	52	3	115	3	0	3	22	3	17	.283	.339	.483	.822
2014 SF	NL	162	650	180	29	10	20	(5 | 15)	289	106	74	96	52	3	130	3	0	3	13	6	13	.277	.332	.445	.777
2015 SF	NL	52	207	57	13	1	9	(3 | 6)	99	30	40	28	16	0	48	0	0	0	4	1	8	.275	.327	.478	.806
2016 SF	NL	106	395	114	23	1	13	(6 | 7)	178	58	57	65	43	1	95	1	0	3	1	1	10	.289	.357	.451	.808
11 Hou	NL	100	399	123	26	3	11	(4 | 7)	188	49	62	63	30	1	86	1	0	2	7	1	7	.308	.356	.471	.828
11 Phi	NL	54	207	67	12	2	11	(1 | 10)	116	35	35	39	26	2	38	0	0	3	1	1	8	.324	.394	.560	.954
12 Phi	NL	101	398	108	15	2	17	(7 | 10)	178	59	59	50	37	1	85	3	0	2	4	2	14	.271	.336	.447	.784
12 SF	NL	59	219	48	11	2	7	(2 | 5)	84	28	45	31	19	1	60	4	1	5	1	0	1	.219	.287	.384	.671
Postseason		38	147	39	8	0	2	(0 | 2)	53	22	16	14	12	1	28	0	0	1	4	3	3	.265	.319	.361	.679
10 ML YEARS		1376	5354	1520	283	47	207	(87 | 120)	2518	760	786	791	440	17	1090	21	1	31	107	50	138	.284	.339	.470	.809

Cliff Pennington

Bats: B **Throws:** R **Pos:** 2B-58;SS-17;PH-9;1B-3;PR-3;3B-1;DH-1   **Ht:** 5'11" **Wt:** 195 **Born:** 6/15/1984 **Age:** 33

							BATTING												RUNNING			AVERAGES			
Year Team	Lg	G	AB	H	2B	3B	HR	(Hm | Rd)	TB	R	RBI	RC	TBB	IBB	SO	HBP	SH	SF	SB	CS	GDP	Avg	OBP	Slg	OPS
2008 Oak	AL	36	99	24	5	0	0	(0 | 0)	29	14	9	12	13	0	18	2	2	1	4	1	1	.242	.339	.293	.632
2009 Oak	AL	60	208	58	11	3	4	(3 | 1)	87	27	21	29	19	0	46	1	1	0	7	5	5	.279	.342	.418	.760
2010 Oak	AL	156	508	127	26	8	6	(2 | 4)	187	64	46	66	50	0	96	3	12	3	29	5	7	.250	.319	.368	.687
2011 Oak	AL	148	515	136	26	2	8	(3 | 5)	190	57	58	73	42	1	104	1	8	4	14	9	5	.264	.325	.369	.687
2012 Oak	AL	125	418	90	18	2	6	(0 | 6)	130	50	28	37	35	0	90	2	5	2	15	6	1	.215	.278	.311	.589
2013 Ari	NL	96	269	65	13	1	1	(1 | 0)	83	25	18	23	26	5	54	1	2	1	2	0	7	.242	.310	.309	.618
2014 Ari	NL	68	177	45	5	3	2	(1 | 1)	62	21	10	19	20	0	36	3	1	0	6	1	1	.254	.340	.350	.690
2015 2 Tms		105	210	44	6	0	3	(1 | 2)	59	24	21	18	27	2	49	1	7	4	3	0	6	.210	.298	.281	.578
2016 LAA	AL	74	172	36	4	2	3	(2 | 1)	53	18	10	11	13	0	55	0	3	0	1	0	4	.209	.265	.308	.573
15 Ari	NL	72	135	32	3	0	1	(1 | 0)	38	15	10	10	16	2	29	0	4	2	3	0	4	.237	.314	.281	.595
15 Tor	AL	33	75	12	3	0	2	(0 | 2)	21	9	11	8	11	0	20	1	3	2	0	0	2	.160	.270	.280	.550
Postseason		9	15	4	0	0	0	(0 | 0)	4	1	1	2	4	0	4	0	0	0	0	0	0	.267	.421	.267	.688
9 ML YEARS		868	2576	625	114	21	33	(13 | 20)	880	300	221	288	245	8	548	14	41	15	81	27	37	.243	.310	.342	.652

David Peralta

Bats: L Throws: L Pos: RF-44;CF-8;PH-3 pah-RALL-tah **Ht: 6'1" Wt: 210 Born: 8/14/1987 Age: 29**

													BATTING										RUNNING			AVERAGES			
Year	Team	Lg	G	AB	H	2B	3B	HR	(Hm	Rd)	TB	R	RBI	RC	TBB	IBB	SO	HBP	SH	SF	SB	CS	GDP	Avg	OBP	Slg	OPS
2014	Ari	NL	88	329	94	12	9	8	(5	3)	148	40	36	38	16	0	60	1	1	1	6	3	9	.286	.320	.450	.770
2015	Ari	NL	149	462	144	26	10	17	(8	9)	241	61	78	83	44	2	107	4	0	7	9	4	7	.312	.371	.522	.893
2016	Ari	NL	48	171	43	9	5	4	(3	1)	74	23	15	15	8	1	42	3	0	1	2	0	3	.251	.295	.433	.728
	3 ML YEARS		285	962	281	47	24	29	(16	13)	463	124	129	136	68	3	209	8	1	9	17	7	19	.292	.341	.481	.822

Jhonny Peralta

Bats: R Throws: R Pos: 3B-67;SS-7;PH-7;DH-1 pah-RALL-tah **Ht: 6'2" Wt: 225 Born: 5/28/1982 Age: 35**

													BATTING										RUNNING			AVERAGES			
Year	Team	Lg	G	AB	H	2B	3B	HR	(Hm	Rd)	TB	R	RBI	RC	TBB	IBB	SO	HBP	SH	SF	SB	CS	GDP	Avg	OBP	Slg	OPS
2003	Cle	AL	77	242	55	10	1	4	(3	1)	79	24	21	24	20	0	65	4	2	2	1	3	5	.227	.295	.326	.621
2004	Cle	AL	8	25	6	1	0	0	(0	0)	7	2	2	2	3	0	6	0	0	0	0	1	0	.240	.321	.280	.601
2005	Cle	AL	141	504	147	35	4	24	(14	10)	262	82	78	87	58	3	128	3	1	4	0	2	12	.292	.366	.520	.885
2006	Cle	AL	149	569	146	28	3	13	(7	6)	219	84	68	66	56	0	152	1	3	3	0	1	19	.257	.323	.385	.708
2007	Cle	AL	152	574	155	27	1	21	(16	5)	247	87	72	85	61	2	146	4	1	7	4	4	12	.270	.341	.430	.771
2008	Cle	AL	154	605	167	42	4	23	(11	12)	286	104	89	84	48	2	126	4	2	5	3	1	26	.276	.331	.473	.804
2009	Cle	AL	151	582	148	35	1	11	(2	9)	218	57	83	63	51	0	134	4	2	6	0	2	20	.254	.316	.375	.690
2010	2 Tms	AL	148	551	137	30	2	15	(4	11)	216	60	81	71	53	2	103	1	0	10	1	0	11	.249	.311	.392	.703
2011	Det	AL	146	525	157	25	3	21	(13	8)	251	68	86	77	40	2	95	2	0	9	0	2	17	.299	.345	.478	.824
2012	Det	AL	150	531	127	32	3	13	(6	7)	204	58	63	53	49	3	105	2	1	2	1	2	20	.239	.305	.384	.689
2013	Det	AL	107	409	124	30	1	11	(7	4)	187	50	55	62	32	2	98	1	1	3	3	3	9	.303	.358	.457	.815
2014	StL	NL	157	560	147	38	0	21	(8	13)	248	61	75	74	58	2	112	6	0	4	3	2	19	.263	.336	.443	.779
2015	StL	NL	155	579	159	26	1	17	(9	8)	238	64	71	65	50	6	111	5	0	6	1	4	23	.275	.334	.411	.745
2016	StL	NL	82	289	75	17	1	8	(4	4)	118	37	29	31	20	0	56	1	0	3	0	0	5	.260	.307	.408	.715
10	Cle	AL	91	334	82	23	2	7	(3	4)	130	37	43	41	32	1	69	1	0	6	1	0	7	.246	.308	.389	.698
10	Det	AL	57	217	55	7	0	8	(1	7)	86	23	38	30	21	1	34	0	0	4	0	0	4	.253	.314	.396	.710
	Postseason		58	211	54	15	0	8	(5	3)	93	18	26	25	15	0	45	1	1	1	2	0	9	.256	.307	.441	.748
	14 ML YEARS		1777	6545	1750	376	24	202	(104	98)	2780	838	873	844	602	24	1437	38	13	63	17	27	198	.267	.330	.425	.754

Joel Peralta

Pitches: R Bats: R Pos: RP-31 joe-ELL pah-RALL-tah **Ht: 5'10" Wt: 210 Born: 3/23/1976 Age: 41**

				HOW MUCH HE PITCHED					WHAT HE GAVE UP										THE RESULTS						
Year	Team	Lg	G	GS	CG	GF	IP	BFP	H	R	ER	HR	SH	SF	HB	TBB	IBB	SO	WP	Bk	W	L	Pct	Sh	Sv-Op	Hld	ERC	ERA
2016	Iowa*	AAA	5	0	0	2	4.0	17	3	5	2	0	0	0	0	0	0	4	1	0	0	0	-	0	2- -	-	1.00	4.50
2005	LAA	AL	28	0	0	10	34.2	145	28	15	15	6	2	1	0	14	2	30	2	0	1	0	1.000	0	0-0	0	3.40	3.89
2006	KC	AL	64	0	0	21	73.2	304	74	37	36	10	1	3	2	17	2	57	5	0	1	3	.250	0	1-3	17	3.80	4.40
2007	KC	AL	62	0	0	18	87.2	366	93	39	37	9	2	4	2	19	5	66	2	0	1	3	.250	0	1-5	7	3.75	3.80
2008	KC	AL	40	0	0	12	52.2	224	56	37	35	15	1	3	2	14	0	38	1	0	1	2	.333	0	0-1	1	5.38	5.98
2009	Col	NL	27	0	0	6	24.2	113	27	17	17	3	0	1	3	12	2	22	0	0	3	0	.000	0	0-1	6	5.51	6.20
2010	Was	NL	39	0	0	10	49.0	189	30	12	11	5	2	1	1	9	4	49	0	0	1	0	1.000	0	0-2	9	1.43	2.02
2011	TB	AL	71	0	0	18	67.2	256	44	23	22	7	2	2	0	18	3	61	3	0	3	4	.429	0	6-8	19	1.84	2.93
2012	TB	AL	77	0	0	9	67.0	264	49	28	27	9	0	1	1	17	2	84	5	0	2	6	.250	0	2-5	37	2.36	3.63
2013	TB	AL	80	0	0	12	71.1	291	47	31	27	7	2	0	0	34	1	74	1	0	3	8	.273	0	1-4	41	2.53	3.41
2014	TB	AL	69	0	0	12	63.1	265	60	31	31	9	2	1	1	15	1	74	2	0	3	4	.429	0	1-7	18	3.41	4.41
2015	LAD	NL	33	0	0	7	29.0	121	28	14	14	6	0	0	0	8	1	24	1	0	3	1	.750	0	3-3	3	4.04	4.34
2016	2 Tms		31	0	0	5	27.1	119	30	19	18	9	0	1	1	8	0	33	0	0	1	1	.500	0	0-2	11	5.97	5.93
16	Sea	AL	26	0	0	5	23.1	100	24	14	14	7	0	1	0	7	0	28	0	0	1	0	1.000	0	0-2	11	5.16	5.40
16	ChC	NL	5	0	0	0	4.0	19	6	5	4	2	0	0	1	1	0	5	0	0	0	1	.000	0	0-0	0	11.48	9.00
	Postseason		7	0	0	2	6.2	26	4	0	0	0	0	0	0	3	0	5	1	0	0	0	-	0	0-1	1	1.68	0.00
	12 ML YEARS		621	0	0	140	648.0	2657	566	303	290	95	14	18	13	185	23	612	22	0	20	35	.364	0	15-41	169	3.28	4.03

Wandy Peralta

Pitches: L Bats: L Pos: RP-10 **Ht: 6'0" Wt: 210 Born: 7/27/1991 Age: 25**

				HOW MUCH HE PITCHED					WHAT HE GAVE UP										THE RESULTS						
Year	Team	Lg	G	GS	CG	GF	IP	BFP	H	R	ER	HR	SH	SF	HB	TBB	IBB	SO	WP	Bk	W	L	Pct	Sh	Sv-Op	Hld	ERC	ERA
2012	Reds	R	14	4	0	4	45.1	227	62	47	33	3	1	0	2	22	0	40	7	0	3	6	.333	0	0- -	-	6.21	6.55
2013	Dayton	A	44	4	0	12	85.1	383	91	45	36	9	5	3	2	41	1	79	14	4	2	7	.222	0	1- -	-	4.87	3.80
2014	Bkrsfld	A+	28	28	0	0	142.0	631	164	92	76	19	4	4	3	55	0	93	13	2	7	12	.368	0	0- -	-	5.28	4.82
2015	Pnscla	AA	29	20	0	2	116.2	524	129	74	66	7	5	4	7	60	0	80	8	1	7	7	.500	0	0- -	-	5.17	5.09
2016	Pnscla	AA	13	0	0	3	17.2	73	17	6	6	1	0	2	0	3	0	20	2	0	1	0	1.000	0	0- -	-	2.67	3.06
2016	Lsvlle	AAA	37	2	0	15	58.0	234	44	18	15	2	4	1	2	23	0	38	2	0	4	1	.800	0	3- -	-	2.55	2.33
2016	Cin	NL	10	0	0	3	7.1	39	11	7	7	1	0	0	1	7	0	5	0	0	0	0	-	0	0-0	2	10.93	8.59

Wily Peralta

Pitches: R Bats: R Pos: SP-23 pah-RALL-tah **Ht: 6'1" Wt: 255 Born: 5/8/1989 Age: 28**

				HOW MUCH HE PITCHED					WHAT HE GAVE UP										THE RESULTS						
Year	Team	Lg	G	GS	CG	GF	IP	BFP	H	R	ER	HR	SH	SF	HB	TBB	IBB	SO	WP	Bk	W	L	Pct	Sh	Sv-Op	Hld	ERC	ERA
2016	ColSpr*	AAA	10	10	0	0	41.1	189	55	31	29	5	2	0	0	17	1	39	5	1	1	3	.250	0	0- -	-	6.29	6.31
2012	Mil	NL	6	5	0	1	29.0	113	24	8	8	0	3	0	0	11	0	23	1	0	2	1	.667	0	0-0	0	2.61	2.48
2013	Mil	NL	32	32	2	0	183.1	802	187	107	89	19	11	3	7	73	3	129	12	0	11	15	.423	1	0-0	0	4.32	4.37
2014	Mil	NL	32	32	0	0	198.2	838	198	88	78	23	9	3	7	61	0	154	7	0	17	11	.607	0	0-0	0	3.98	3.53
2015	Mil	NL	20	20	0	0	108.2	478	130	60	57	14	4	3	4	37	2	60	5	1	5	10	.333	0	0-0	0	5.40	4.72
2016	Mil	NL	23	23	0	0	127.2	554	152	73	69	19	6	4	3	43	1	93	0	0	7	11	.389	0	0-0	0	5.52	4.86
	5 ML YEARS		113	112	2	1	647.1	2785	691	336	301	75	33	13	21	225	6	459	25	1	42	48	.467	1	0-0	0	4.54	4.18

Jose Peraza

per-AH-zuh

Bats: R Throws: R Pos: SS-31;CF-13;2B-12;LF-8;PH-8;PR-2;DH-1   **Ht: 6'0" Wt: 180 Born: 4/30/1994 Age: 23**

								BATTING												RUNNING			AVERAGES			
Year	Team	Lg	G	AB	H	2B	3B	HR	(Hm Rd)	TB	R	RBI	RC	TBB	IBB	SO	HBP	SH	SF	SB	CS	GDP	Avg	OBP	Slg	OPS
2012	2 Tms	Low	53	206	61	7	3	1	(- -)	77	38	28	30	13	0	24	4	5	0	25	5	2	.296	.350	.374	.724
2013	Rome	A	114	448	129	18	8	1	(- -)	166	72	47	67	34	1	64	6	9	7	64	15	8	.288	.341	.371	.712
2014	Lynbrg	A+	66	284	97	13	8	1	(- -)	129	44	27	51	10	1	32	3	3	4	35	7	5	.342	.365	.454	.820
2014	Missi	AA	44	185	62	7	3	1	(- -)	78	35	17	30	7	0	15	1	2	0	25	8	5	.335	.363	.422	.784
2015	Gwnntt	AAA	96	391	115	10	7	3	(- -)	148	52	37	51	15	3	35	2	12	7	26	7	7	.294	.318	.379	.697
2015	OkCity	AAA	22	90	26	3	1	1	(- -)	34	11	5	11	2	0	10	0	2	0	7	0	1	.289	.304	.378	.682
2016	Lsvlle	AAA	71	288	81	15	3	2	(- -)	108	40	21	37	21	0	43	2	10	1	10	7	4	.281	.333	.375	.708
2015	LAD	NL	7	22	4	1	1	0	(0 0)	7	3	1	2	2	1	2	0	1	0	3	0	0	.182	.250	.318	.568
2016	Cin	NL	72	241	78	8	2	3	(1 2)	99	25	25	32	7	0	33	5	0	3	21	10	3	.324	.352	.411	.762
	2 ML YEARS		79	263	82	9	3	3	(1 2)	106	28	26	34	9	1	35	5	1	3	24	10	3	.312	.343	.403	.746

Luis Perdomo

Pitches: R Bats: R Pos: SP-20; RP-15   **Ht: 6'2" Wt: 185 Born: 5/9/1993 Age: 24**

				HOW MUCH HE PITCHED					WHAT HE GAVE UP												THE RESULTS					
Year	Team	Lg	G	GS	CG	GF	IP	BFP	H	R	ER	HR	SH	SF	HB	TBB	IBB	SO	WP	Bk	W	L	Pct	Sh	Sv-Op	Hld	ERC	ERA
2013	Jhscty	R+	12	10	0	0	41.2	207	59	44	25	4	0	2	4	14	0	29	6	0	1	6	.143	0	0- -	-	6.33	5.40
2014	2 Tms	Low	14	13	0	1	72.0	317	77	47	34	5	3	2	4	22	0	57	5	1	4	6	.400	0	0- -	-	4.02	4.25
2015	2 Tms	Low	23	22	1	0	126.2	542	134	68	56	8	6	3	5	37	0	118	10	1	6	12	.333	0	0- -	-	3.89	3.98
2016	SD	NL	35	20	1	8	146.2	662	187	99	93	23	0	4	7	46	7	105	10	0	9	10	.474	0	0-0	0	5.91	5.71

Carlos Perez

Bats: R Throws: R Pos: C-82;PH-3;PR-2;1B-1;DH-1   **Ht: 6'0" Wt: 210 Born: 10/27/1990 Age: 26**

								BATTING												RUNNING			AVERAGES			
Year	Team	Lg	G	AB	H	2B	3B	HR	(Hm Rd)	TB	R	RBI	RC	TBB	IBB	SO	HBP	SH	SF	SB	CS	GDP	Avg	OBP	Slg	OPS
2012	2 Tms	Low	97	361	103	28	6	5	(- -)	158	59	50	59	41	1	55	4	5	5	3	3	12	.285	.360	.438	.798
2013	CpChr	AA	16	53	15	4	0	1	(- -)	22	6	5	8	4	0	11	2	1	0	0	0	1	.283	.356	.415	.771
2013	OkCity	AAA	75	264	71	14	0	2	(- -)	91	29	32	32	25	0	39	0	3	4	1	1	5	.269	.328	.345	.672
2014	OkCity	AAA	88	301	78	16	2	6	(- -)	116	33	34	40	29	0	54	1	6	3	3	0	10	.259	.323	.385	.709
2015	Salt Lk	AAA	17	72	26	8	0	2	(- -)	40	11	12	16	7	0	7	0	0	0	1	0	2	.361	.418	.556	.973
2016	Salt Lk	AAA	10	39	14	4	0	3	(- -)	27	9	10	8	1	0	7	0	0	0	0	2	1	.359	.375	.692	1.067
2015	LAA	AL	86	260	65	13	0	4	(4 0)	90	20	21	26	19	0	49	0	2	2	2	0	7	.250	.299	.346	.645
2016	LAA	AL	87	268	56	16	0	5	(2 3)	87	25	31	22	12	0	49	1	8	2	1	0	6	.209	.244	.325	.568
	2 ML YEARS		173	528	121	29	0	9	(6 3)	177	45	52	48	31	0	98	1	10	4	3	0	13	.229	.271	.335	.607

Hernan Perez

air-NAHN

Bats: R Throws: R Pos: 3B-60;RF-36;PH-20;2B-11;CF-8;1B-6;SS-3;LF-2   **Ht: 6'1" Wt: 215 Born: 3/26/1991 Age: 26**

								BATTING												RUNNING			AVERAGES			
Year	Team	Lg	G	AB	H	2B	3B	HR	(Hm Rd)	TB	R	RBI	RC	TBB	IBB	SO	HBP	SH	SF	SB	CS	GDP	Avg	OBP	Slg	OPS
2016	ColSpr*	AAA	16	62	21	4	1	1	(- -)	30	10	11	11	3	0	10	0	1	1	2	0	1	.339	.364	.484	.848
2012	Det	AL	2	2	1	0	0	0	(0 0)	1	1	0	0	0	0	0	0	0	0	0	0	0	.500	.500	.500	1.000
2013	Det	AL	34	66	13	0	1	0	(0 0)	15	13	5	4	2	0	15	0	2	1	1	0	2	.197	.217	.227	.445
2014	Det	AL	8	5	1	0	0	0	(0 0)	1	1	0	0	1	0	1	0	0	0	0	0	0	.200	.333	.200	.533
2015	2 Tms		112	263	64	15	2	1	(0 1)	86	14	21	23	5	1	59	0	3	1	5	1	6	.243	.257	.327	.584
2016	Mil	NL	123	404	110	18	3	13	(7 6)	173	50	56	56	18	0	94	1	3	4	34	7	6	.272	.302	.428	.730
15	Det	AL	22	33	2	0	0	0	(0 0)	2	1	0	0	1	0	11	0	0	0	1	0	2	.061	.088	.061	.149
15	Mil	NL	90	230	62	15	2	1	(0 1)	84	13	21	23	4	1	48	0	3	1	4	1	4	.270	.281	.365	.646
	Postseason		4	2	0	0	0	0	(0 0)	0	1	0	0	0	0	0	0	0	0	0	0	1	.000	.000	.000	.000
	5 ML YEARS		279	740	189	33	6	14	(7 7)	276	79	82	83	26	1	169	1	8	6	40	8	14	.255	.279	.373	.652

Martin Perez

mar-TEEN

Pitches: L Bats: L Pos: SP-33   **Ht: 6'0" Wt: 200 Born: 4/4/1991 Age: 26**

				HOW MUCH HE PITCHED					WHAT HE GAVE UP												THE RESULTS					
Year	Team	Lg	G	GS	CG	GF	IP	BFP	H	R	ER	HR	SH	SF	HB	TBB	IBB	SO	WP	Bk	W	L	Pct	Sh	Sv-Op	Hld	ERC	ERA
2012	Tex	AL	12	6	0	2	38.0	177	47	26	23	3	1	1	2	15	1	25	5	2	1	4	.200	0	0-0	0	5.33	5.45
2013	Tex	AL	20	20	1	0	124.1	529	129	55	50	15	2	3	3	37	0	84	9	2	10	6	.625	0	0-0	0	4.14	3.62
2014	Tex	AL	8	8	2	0	51.1	207	50	25	25	3	1	0	1	19	1	35	1	0	4	3	.571	2	0-0	0	3.82	4.38
2015	Tex	AL	14	14	0	0	78.2	339	88	45	39	3	0	3	2	24	1	48	1	0	3	6	.333	0	0-0	0	4.04	4.46
2016	Tex	AL	33	33	0	0	198.2	855	205	110	97	18	9	8	4	76	0	103	3	2	10	11	.476	0	0-0	0	4.24	4.39
	Postseason		1	1	0	0	5.0	21	6	4	4	0	1	0	0	3	1	2	0	0	0	1	.000	0	0-0	0	5.47	7.20
	5 ML YEARS		87	81	3	2	491.0	2107	519	261	234	42	13	15	12	171	3	295	19	6	28	30	.483	2	0-0	0	4.22	4.29

Oliver Perez

Pitches: L Bats: L Pos: RP-64   **Ht: 6'3" Wt: 225 Born: 8/15/1981 Age: 35**

				HOW MUCH HE PITCHED					WHAT HE GAVE UP												THE RESULTS					
Year	Team	Lg	G	GS	CG	GF	IP	BFP	H	R	ER	HR	SH	SF	HB	TBB	IBB	SO	WP	Bk	W	L	Pct	Sh	Sv-Op	Hld	ERC	ERA
2002	SD	NL	16	15	0	0	90.0	387	71	37	35	13	5	3	5	48	1	94	3	0	4	5	.444	0	0-0	0	3.93	3.50
2003	2 Tms	NL	24	24	0	0	126.2	579	129	80	77	22	5	2	4	77	3	141	7	1	4	10	.286	0	0-0	0	5.66	5.47
2004	Pit	NL	30	30	2	0	196.0	805	145	71	65	22	9	5	9	81	2	239	2	1	12	10	.545	1	0-0	0	2.99	2.98
2005	Pit	NL	20	20	0	0	103.0	471	102	68	67	23	5	4	6	70	1	97	3	0	7	5	.583	0	0-0	0	6.44	5.85

HOW MUCH HE PITCHED						WHAT HE GAVE UP													THE RESULTS							
Year Team	Lg	G	GS	CG	GF	IP	BFP	H	R	ER	HR	SH	SF	HB	TBB	IBB	SO	WP	Bk	W	L	Pct	Sh	Sv-Op	Hld	ERC	ERA
2006 2 Tms	NL	22	22	1	0	112.2	529	129	90	82	20	5	10	6	68	0	102	5	1	3	13	.188	1	0-0	0	6.62	6.55
2007 NYM	NL	29	29	0	0	177.0	765	153	90	70	22	4	7	7	79	1	174	6	0	15	10	.600	0	0-0	0	3.76	3.56
2008 NYM	NL	34	**34**	0	0	194.0	847	167	100	91	24	9	7	11	**105**	4	180	9	1	10	7	.588	0	0-0	0	4.21	4.22
2009 NYM	NL	14	14	0	0	66.0	324	69	51	50	12	5	4	4	58	2	62	2	0	3	4	.429	0	0-0	0	7.16	6.82
2010 NYM	NL	17	7	0	4	46.1	234	54	37	35	9	1	3	4	42	3	37	4	0	0	5	.000	0	0-0	0	8.27	6.80
2012 Sea	AL	33	0	0	6	29.2	123	27	7	7	1	1	1	0	10	2	24	2	0	1	3	.250	0	0-2	5	2.82	2.12
2013 Sea	AL	61	0	0	22	53.0	229	50	23	22	6	1	0	1	26	3	74	1	0	3	3	.500	0	2-3	8	4.23	3.74
2014 Ari	NL	68	0	0	11	58.2	256	50	25	19	5	4	0	7	24	2	76	3	3	3	4	.429	0	0-1	15	3.53	2.91
2015 2 Tms		70	0	0	15	41.0	183	39	24	19	4	1	0	4	15	2	51	3	0	2	4	.333	0	0-3	10	3.81	4.17
2016 Was	NL	64	0	0	7	40.0	182	38	22	22	4	1	1	7	20	3	46	5	0	2	3	.400	0	0-1	15	4.72	4.95
03 SD	NL	19	19	0	0	103.2	473	103	65	62	20	4	2	3	65	2	117	6	1	4	7	.364	0	0-0	0	5.74	5.38
03 Pit	NL	5	5	0	0	23.0	106	26	15	15	2	1	0	1	12	1	24	1	0	0	3	.000	0	0-0	0	5.29	5.87
06 Pit	NL	15	15	0	0	76.0	364	88	64	56	13	5	8	3	51	0	61	4	1	2	10	.167	0	0-0	0	6.85	6.63
06 NYM	NL	7	7	1	0	36.2	165	41	26	26	7	0	2	3	17	0	41	1	0	1	3	.250	1	0-0	0	6.16	6.38
15 Ari	NL	48	0	0	11	29.0	128	25	12	10	2	1	0	4	11	1	37	2	0	2	1	.667	0	0-3	7	3.38	3.10
15 Hou	AL	22	0	0	4	12.0	55	14	12	9	2	0	0	0	4	1	14	1	0	0	3	.000	0	0-0	3	4.89	6.75
Postseason		4	2	0	0	12.0	54	15	7	7	3	2	0	1	4	1	7	0	0	1	0	1.000	0	0-0	1	6.75	5.25
14 ML YEARS		502	195	3	65	1334.0	5914	1223	725	661	187	56	47	75	723	29	1397	55	7	69	86	.445	2	2-10	53	4.64	4.46

Roberto Perez

Bats: R Throws: R Pos: C-61   Ht: 5'11" Wt: 220 Born: 12/23/1988 Age: 28

			BATTING																		RUNNING			AVERAGES			
Year Team	Lg	G	AB	H	2B	3B	HR	(Hm	Rd)	TB	R	RBI	RC	TBB	IBB	SO	HBP	SH	SF		SB	CS	GDP	Avg	OBP	Slg	OPS
2014 Cle	AL	29	85	23	5	0	1	(1	0)	31	10	4	8	5	0	26	0	5	0		0	0	2	.271	.311	.365	.676
2015 Cle	AL	70	184	42	9	1	7	(4	3)	74	30	21	24	33	1	64	2	5	2		0	0	9	.228	.348	.402	.751
2016 Cle	AL	61	153	28	6	1	3	(1	2)	45	14	17	17	23	0	44	0	5	3		0	0	4	.183	.285	.294	.579
3 ML YEARS		160	422	93	20	2	11	(6	5)	150	54	42	49	61	1	134	2	15	5		0	0	15	.220	.318	.355	.674

Salvador Perez

Bats: R Throws: R Pos: C-128;DH-7;PH-3;1B-1   Ht: 6'3" Wt: 240 Born: 5/10/1990 Age: 27

			BATTING																		RUNNING			AVERAGES			
Year Team	Lg	G	AB	H	2B	3B	HR	(Hm	Rd)	TB	R	RBI	RC	TBB	IBB	SO	HBP	SH	SF		SB	CS	GDP	Avg	OBP	Slg	OPS
2011 KC	AL	39	148	49	8	2	3	(1	2)	70	20	21	26	7	0	20	1	0	2		0	0	5	.331	.361	.473	.834
2012 KC	AL	76	289	87	16	0	11	(3	8)	136	38	39	36	12	3	27	1	0	3		0	0	14	.301	.328	.471	.798
2013 KC	AL	138	496	145	25	3	13	(6	7)	215	48	79	77	21	2	63	4	0	5		0	0	13	.292	.323	.433	.757
2014 KC	AL	150	578	150	28	2	17	(8	9)	233	57	70	55	22	2	85	3	0	3		1	0	22	.260	.289	.403	.692
2015 KC	AL	142	531	138	25	0	21	(9	12)	226	52	70	60	13	4	82	4	0	5		1	0	23	.260	.280	.426	.706
2016 KC	AL	139	514	127	28	2	22	(11	11)	225	57	64	61	22	3	119	8	0	2		0	0	12	.247	.288	.438	.725
Postseason		31	116	27	4	0	5	(3	2)	46	14	14	10	5	0	19	3	0	0		0	0	3	.233	.282	.397	.679
6 ML YEARS		684	2556	696	130	9	87	(38	49)	1105	272	343	315	97	14	396	21	0	20		2	0	89	.272	.302	.432	.734

Williams Perez

Pitches: R Bats: R Pos: SP-11   Ht: 6'0" Wt: 240 Born: 5/21/1991 Age: 26

HOW MUCH HE PITCHED								WHAT HE GAVE UP												THE RESULTS							
Year Team	Lg	G	GS	CG	GF	IP	BFP	H	R	ER	HR	SH	SF	HB	TBB	IBB	SO	WP	Bk	W	L	Pct	Sh	Sv-Op	Hld	ERC	ERA
2012 Danvle	R+	13	9	0	1	56.1	234	54	31	26	5	0	1	4	9	0	54	1	0	4	3	.571	0	1--	-	3.09	4.15
2013 2 Tms	Low	23	22	1	0	125.0	524	123	55	49	9	4	4	5	36	0	106	6	0	11	6	.647	0	0--	-	3.55	3.53
2014 Missi	AA	26	25	0	0	133.0	555	119	49	43	4	7	4	11	39	0	94	9	2	7	6	.538	0	0--	-	2.96	2.91
2015 Gwnntt	AAA	8	8	0	0	38.2	154	32	8	5	1	1	1	1	10	0	36	0	0	3	1	.750	0	0--	-	2.32	1.16
2015 Atl	NL	23	20	1	1	116.2	514	130	66	62	13	3	5	9	51	2	73	4	1	7	6	.538	0	1-1	0	5.41	4.78
2016 Atl	NL	11	11	0	0	53.2	233	57	37	36	7	4	2	2	15	3	27	4	0	2	3	.400	0	0-0	0	4.16	6.04
2 ML YEARS		34	31	1	1	170.1	747	187	103	98	20	7	7	11	66	5	100	8	1	9	9	.500	0	1-1	0	5.01	5.18

Yefri Perez

Bats: B Throws: R Pos: PR-9;SS-2;2B-1;PH-1   Ht: 5'11" Wt: 170 Born: 2/24/1991 Age: 26

			BATTING																		RUNNING			AVERAGES			
Year Team	Lg	G	AB	H	2B	3B	HR	(Hm	Rd)	TB	R	RBI	RC	TBB	IBB	SO	HBP	SH	SF		SB	CS	GDP	Avg	OBP	Slg	OPS
2012 Jmstwn	A-	45	143	40	8	0	1	(-	-)	51	18	16	16	8	0	12	2	1	1		4	5	5	.280	.325	.357	.681
2013 3 Tms	Low	48	188	43	8	2	3	(-	-)	64	26	18	20	9	0	24	1	2	0		20	2	1	.229	.268	.340	.608
2014 Grnsbr	A	118	421	121	17	0	1	(-	-)	141	65	29	52	26	1	54	5	8	2		30	9	7	.287	.335	.335	.670
2015 Jupiter	A+	135	517	124	10	1	1	(-	-)	139	74	22	46	31	0	95	4	8	3		71	21	10	.240	.286	.269	.555
2016 Jaxnvl	AA	84	328	85	7	3	1	(-	-)	101	49	28	41	39	0	66	1	3	6		39	11	0	.259	.334	.308	.642
2016 Mia	NL	12	3	2	1	0	0	(0	0)	3	5	0	1	0	0	1	0	0	0		4	2	0	.667	.667	1.000	1.667

Glen Perkins

Pitches: L Bats: L Pos: RP-2   Ht: 6'0" Wt: 205 Born: 3/2/1983 Age: 34

HOW MUCH HE PITCHED								WHAT HE GAVE UP												THE RESULTS							
Year Team	Lg	G	GS	CG	GF	IP	BFP	H	R	ER	HR	SH	SF	HB	TBB	IBB	SO	WP	Bk	W	L	Pct	Sh	Sv-Op	Hld	ERC	ERA
2006 Min	AL	4	0	0	1	5.2	20	3	1	1	0	0	0	0	0	0	6	0	0	0	0	-	0	0-0	1	0.60	1.59
2007 Min	AL	19	0	0	3	28.2	115	23	10	10	2	1	1	2	12	0	20	2	0	0	0	-	0	0-0	3	3.32	3.14
2008 Min	AL	26	26	0	0	151.0	661	183	81	74	25	7	4	3	39	2	74	2	1	12	4	.750	0	0-0	0	5.30	4.41
2009 Min	AL	18	17	0	1	96.1	423	120	64	63	13	1	3	1	23	0	45	2	1	6	7	.462	0	0-0	0	5.14	5.89
2010 Min	AL	13	1	0	5	21.2	98	29	16	14	3	1	2	4	5	1	14	0	0	1	1	.500	0	0-0	0	6.56	5.82
2011 Min	AL	65	0	0	17	61.2	253	55	19	17	2	5	1	1	21	5	65	3	0	4	4	.500	0	2-5	17	2.81	2.48
2012 Min	AL	70	0	0	43	70.1	281	57	25	20	8	3	2	3	16	3	78	3	0	3	1	.750	0	16-20	11	2.63	2.56

Year Team	Lg	G	GS	CG	GF	IP	BFP	H	R	ER	HR	SH	SF	HB	TBB	IBB	SO	WP	Bk	W	L	Pct	Sh	Sv-Op	Hld	ERC	ERA
		HOW MUCH HE PITCHED						**WHAT HE GAVE UP**												**THE RESULTS**							
2013 Min	AL	61	0	0	53	62.2	240	43	16	16	5	2	1	3	15	0	77	0	0	2	0	1.000	0	36-40	0	2.01	2.30
2014 Min	AL	63	0	0	56	61.2	260	62	29	25	7	2	5	2	11	2	66	3	0	4	3	.571	0	34-41	0	3.33	3.65
2015 Min	AL	60	0	0	45	57.0	238	58	21	21	9	1	0	0	10	2	54	4	0	3	5	.375	0	32-35	3	3.56	3.32
2016 Min	AL	2	0	0	1	2.0	12	5	2	2	0	0	1	0	1	0	3	2	0	0	0	-	0	0-1	0	13.27	9.00
Postseason		1	0	0	0	0.1	3	2	0	0	0	0	0	0	0	0	0	0	0	0	0	-	0	0-0	0	39.65	0.00
11 ML YEARS		401	44	0	225	618.2	2601	638	284	263	74	23	20	19	153	13	502	21	2	35	25	.583	0	120-142	35	3.89	3.83

Jace Peterson

Bats: L **Throws:** R **Pos:** 2B-87;PH-19;LF-15;3B-1;CF-1;PR-1   JAYCE   **Ht:** 6'0" **Wt:** 215 **Born:** 5/9/1990 **Age:** 27

Year Team	Lg	G	AB	H	2B	3B	HR	(Hm	Rd)	TB	R	RBI	RC	TBB	IBB	SO	HBP	SH	SF	SB	CS	GDP	Avg	OBP	Slg	OPS
		BATTING																		**RUNNING**			**AVERAGES**			
2016 Gwnntt*	AAA	26	97	18	3	2	0	(-	-)	25	8	6	6	11	1	15	1	1	0	2	2	3	.186	.275	.258	.533
2014 SD	NL	27	53	6	0	0	0	(0	0)	6	3	0	0	2	1	18	1	2	0	2	0	1	.113	.161	.113	.274
2015 Atl	NL	152	528	126	23	5	6	(1	5)	177	55	52	56	56	4	120	3	7	3	12	10	5	.239	.314	.335	.649
2016 Atl	NL	115	350	89	16	1	7	(3	4)	128	45	29	42	52	2	69	1	2	3	5	5	9	.254	.350	.366	.715
3 ML YEARS		294	931	221	39	6	13	(4	9)	311	103	81	98	110	7	207	5	11	6	19	15	15	.237	.319	.334	.653

Gregorio Petit

peh-TEET

Bats: R **Throws:** R **Pos:** 2B-50;SS-32;3B-10;LF-6;PR-6;PH-5;DH-2;RF-1   **Ht:** 5'10" **Wt:** 200 **Born:** 12/10/1984 **Age:** 32

Year Team	Lg	G	AB	H	2B	3B	HR	(Hm	Rd)	TB	R	RBI	RC	TBB	IBB	SO	HBP	SH	SF	SB	CS	GDP	Avg	OBP	Slg	OPS
		BATTING																		**RUNNING**			**AVERAGES**			
2016 Salt Lk*	AAA	17	55	18	3	0	0	(-	-)	21	7	3	8	5	1	13	0	1	1	2	0	1	.327	.377	.382	.759
2008 Oak	AL	14	23	8	2	0	0	(0	0)	10	4	0	2	2	0	9	0	0	0	0	0	0	.348	.400	.435	.835
2009 Oak	AL	11	31	7	1	0	0	(0	0)	8	2	1	1	0	0	6	0	0	0	0	0	2	.226	.226	.258	.484
2014 Hou	AL	37	97	27	8	0	2	(1	1)	41	14	9	10	1	0	25	2	0	0	0	1	1	.278	.300	.423	.723
2015 NYY	AL	20	42	7	3	0	0	(0	0)	10	7	5	2	3	1	16	0	1	1	0	0	0	.167	.217	.238	.455
2016 LAA	AL	89	204	50	13	1	2	(0	2)	71	21	17	21	15	1	51	1	2	1	1	1	7	.245	.299	.348	.647
5 ML YEARS		171	397	99	27	1	4	(1	3)	140	48	32	36	21	2	107	3	3	2	1	2	10	.249	.291	.353	.643

Yusmeiro Petit

Pitches: R **Bats:** R **Pos:** RP-35; SP-1   yooz-MAIR-oh peh-TEET   **Ht:** 6'1" **Wt:** 255 **Born:** 11/22/1984 **Age:** 32

Year Team	Lg	G	GS	CG	GF	IP	BFP	H	R	ER	HR	SH	SF	HB	TBB	IBB	SO	WP	Bk	W	L	Pct	Sh	Sv-Op	Hld	ERC	ERA
		HOW MUCH HE PITCHED						**WHAT HE GAVE UP**												**THE RESULTS**							
2006 Fla	NL	15	1	0	5	26.1	129	46	28	28	7	1	1	0	9	1	20	0	0	1	1	.500	0	0-0	0	10.07	9.57
2007 Ari	NL	14	10	0	2	57.0	243	58	30	29	12	1	1	0	18	1	40	0	1	3	4	.429	0	0-0	0	4.56	4.58
2008 Ari	NL	19	8	0	6	56.1	229	45	29	27	12	4	2	1	14	2	42	3	1	3	5	.375	0	0-0	0	3.08	4.31
2009 Ari	NL	23	17	0	3	89.2	407	102	62	58	19	3	0	0	34	1	74	3	0	3	10	.231	0	0-0	0	5.44	5.82
2012 SF	NL	1	1	0	0	4.2	22	7	2	2	0	1	0	0	4	0	1	1	0	0	0	-	0	0-0	0	9.14	3.86
2013 SF	NL	8	7	1	0	48.0	196	46	19	19	4	2	0	0	11	1	47	0	0	4	1	.800	1	0-0	0	3.08	3.56
2014 SF	NL	39	12	1	14	117.0	461	97	51	48	12	0	3	1	22	5	133	0	0	5	5	.500	0	0-0	0	2.40	3.69
2015 SF	NL	42	1	0	15	76.0	316	75	32	31	11	1	6	1	15	2	59	3	0	1	1	.500	0	1-1	0	3.48	3.67
2016 Was	NL	36	1	0	16	62.0	265	67	33	31	12	3	1	0	15	3	49	3	1	3	5	.375	0	1-2	0	4.42	4.50
Postseason		4	0	0	0	12.2	47	7	2	2	0	0	0	0	4	1	13	1	0	3	0	1.000	0	0-0	0	1.18	1.42
9 ML YEARS		197	58	2	60	537.0	2268	543	286	273	89	16	14	3	142	16	465	13	3	23	32	.418	1	2-3	1	4.00	4.58

Jake Petricka

Pitches: R **Bats:** R **Pos:** RP-9   puh-TRICH-kuh   **Ht:** 6'5" **Wt:** 220 **Born:** 6/5/1988 **Age:** 29

Year Team	Lg	G	GS	CG	GF	IP	BFP	H	R	ER	HR	SH	SF	HB	TBB	IBB	SO	WP	Bk	W	L	Pct	Sh	Sv-Op	Hld	ERC	ERA
		HOW MUCH HE PITCHED						**WHAT HE GAVE UP**												**THE RESULTS**							
2013 CWS	AL	16	0	0	3	19.1	85	20	7	7	0	1	1	1	10	1	10	4	0	1	1	.500	0	0-1	0	4.18	3.26
2014 CWS	AL	67	0	0	33	73.0	307	67	24	24	3	3	4	2	33	4	55	2	0	1	6	.143	0	14-18	10	3.52	2.96
2015 CWS	AL	62	0	0	18	52.0	220	56	21	21	2	3	1	1	18	4	33	2	0	4	3	.571	0	2-3	12	3.91	3.63
2016 CWS	AL	9	0	0	1	8.0	39	8	5	4	1	1	0	0	8	0	7	3	0	0	0	-	0	0-0	1	6.76	4.50
4 ML YEARS		154	0	0	55	152.1	651	151	57	56	6	8	6	4	69	9	105	11	0	6	10	.375	0	16-22	23	3.90	3.31

Tommy Pham

Bats: R **Throws:** R **Pos:** CF-34;LF-30;PH-16;PR-6;RF-5   FAM   **Ht:** 6'1" **Wt:** 210 **Born:** 3/8/1988 **Age:** 29

Year Team	Lg	G	AB	H	2B	3B	HR	(Hm	Rd)	TB	R	RBI	RC	TBB	IBB	SO	HBP	SH	SF	SB	CS	GDP	Avg	OBP	Slg	OPS
		BATTING																		**RUNNING**			**AVERAGES**			
2016 Memp*	AAA	33	110	26	5	1	3	(-	-)	42	15	17	16	18	0	29	0	0	0	8	2	2	.236	.344	.382	.726
2014 StL	NL	6	2	0	0	0	0	(0	0)	0	0	0	0	0	0	2	0	0	0	0	0	0	.000	.000	.000	.000
2015 StL	NL	52	153	41	7	5	5	(1	4)	73	28	18	26	19	1	41	0	0	1	2	0	1	.268	.347	.477	.824
2016 StL	NL	78	159	36	7	0	9	(3	6)	70	26	17	21	20	1	71	3	1	0	2	2	3	.226	.324	.440	.764
Postseason		3	5	1	0	0	1	(1	0)	4	1	2	0	0	0	2	0	0	0	0	0	0	.200	.200	.800	1.000
3 ML YEARS		136	314	77	14	5	14	(4	10)	143	54	35	47	39	2	114	3	1	1	4	2	4	.245	.333	.455	.789

Josh Phegley

Bats: R Throws: R Pos: C-25;PH-1   FEG-lee   Ht: 5'10" Wt: 230 Born: 2/12/1988 Age: 29

Year Team	Lg	G	AB	H	2B	3B	HR	(Hm	Rd)	TB	R	RBI	RC	TBB	IBB	SO	HBP	SH	SF	SB	CS	GDP	Avg	OBP	Slg	OPS
2013 CWS	AL	65	204	42	7	0	4	(2	2)	61	14	22	12	5	0	41	0	2	2	2	0	6	.206	.223	.299	.522
2014 CWS	AL	11	37	8	2	0	3	(3	0)	19	4	7	2	0	0	11	0	0	1	0	0	0	.216	.211	.514	.724
2015 Oak	AL	73	225	56	16	1	9	(6	3)	101	27	34	32	14	0	51	3	0	1	0	0	5	.249	.300	.449	.749
2016 Oak	AL	26	78	20	6	0	1	(1	0)	29	11	10	8	5	0	13	2	0	1	0	0	4	.256	.314	.372	.686
4 ML YEARS		175	544	126	31	1	17	(12	5)	210	56	73	54	24	0	116	5	2	5	2	0	15	.232	.268	.386	.654

David Phelps

Pitches: R Bats: R Pos: RP-59; SP-5   Ht: 6'2" Wt: 200 Born: 10/9/1986 Age: 30

Year Team	Lg	G	GS	CG	GF	IP	BFP	H	R	ER	HR	SH	SF	HB	TBB	IBB	SO	WP	Bk	W	L	Pct	Sh	Sv-Op	Hld	ERC	ERA
2012 NYY	AL	33	11	0	5	99.2	414	81	38	37	14	4	3	6	38	2	96	2	2	4	4	.500	0	0-0	2	3.48	3.34
2013 NYY	AL	22	12	0	3	86.2	376	88	50	48	8	1	2	5	35	1	79	2	0	6	5	.545	0	0-1	1	4.38	4.98
2014 NYY	AL	32	17	1	5	113.0	497	115	62	55	13	4	3	7	46	2	92	2	1	5	5	.500	0	1-1	5	4.52	4.38
2015 Mia	NL	23	19	0	1	112.0	482	119	59	56	11	2	5	4	33	0	77	2	0	4	8	.333	0	0-0	4	4.13	4.50
2016 Mia	NL	64	5	0	6	86.2	352	61	23	22	6	1	2	2	38	6	114	0	1	7	6	.538	0	4-10	25	2.47	2.28
Postseason		3	0	0	1	3.1	19	7	4	3	0	0	0	0	1	0	2	0	0	0	2	.000	0	0-0	0	8.97	8.10
5 ML YEARS		174	64	1	20	498.0	2121	464	232	218	52	12	15	24	190	11	458	8	4	26	28	.481	0	5-12	33	3.82	3.94

Brandon Phillips

Bats: R Throws: R Pos: 2B-138;DH-3   Ht: 6'0" Wt: 210 Born: 6/28/1981 Age: 36

Year Team	Lg	G	AB	H	2B	3B	HR	(Hm	Rd)	TB	R	RBI	RC	TBB	IBB	SO	HBP	SH	SF	SB	CS	GDP	Avg	OBP	Slg	OPS
2002 Cle	AL	11	31	8	3	1	0	(0	0)	13	5	4	5	3	0	6	1	1	0	0	0	0	.258	.343	.419	.762
2003 Cle	AL	112	370	77	18	1	6	(3	3)	115	36	33	22	14	0	77	3	5	1	4	5	12	.208	.242	.311	.553
2004 Cle	AL	6	22	4	2	0	0	(0	0)	6	1	1	0	2	0	5	0	0	0	0	2	1	.182	.250	.273	.523
2005 Cle	AL	6	9	0	0	0	0	(0	0)	0	1	0	0	0	0	4	0	0	0	0	0	0	.000	.000	.000	.000
2006 Cin	NL	149	536	148	28	1	17	(9	8)	229	65	75	74	35	3	88	6	4	6	25	2	19	.276	.324	.427	.751
2007 Cin	NL	158	650	187	26	6	30	(17	13)	315	107	94	88	33	4	109	12	2	5	32	8	26	.288	.331	.485	.816
2008 Cin	NL	141	559	146	24	7	21	(13	8)	247	80	78	74	39	6	93	5	0	6	23	10	13	.261	.312	.442	.754
2009 Cin	NL	153	584	161	30	5	20	(10	10)	261	78	98	80	44	3	75	6	2	8	25	9	21	.276	.329	.447	.776
2010 Cin	NL	155	626	172	33	5	18	(10	8)	269	100	59	77	46	1	83	6	1	6	16	12	14	.275	.332	.430	.762
2011 Cin	NL	150	610	183	38	2	18	(14	4)	279	94	82	92	44	3	85	9	5	6	14	9	15	.300	.353	.457	.810
2012 Cin	NL	147	580	163	30	1	18	(15	3)	249	86	77	78	28	2	79	8	3	4	15	2	19	.281	.321	.429	.750
2013 Cin	NL	151	606	158	24	2	18	(7	11)	240	80	103	82	39	6	98	8	4	9	5	3	19	.261	.310	.396	.706
2014 Cin	NL	121	462	123	25	0	8	(3	5)	172	44	51	53	23	1	74	6	2	6	2	3	13	.266	.306	.372	.678
2015 Cin	NL	148	588	173	19	2	12	(9	3)	232	69	70	78	27	1	68	4	1	3	23	3	13	.294	.328	.395	.723
2016 Cin	NL	141	550	160	34	1	11	(6	5)	229	74	64	65	18	3	68	8	2	6	14	8	17	.291	.320	.416	.736
Postseason		9	40	13	4	0	2	(0	2)	23	3	8	10	0	0	5	0	0	1	1	0	0	.325	.317	.575	.892
15 ML YEARS		1749	6783	1863	334	34	197	(116	81)	2856	920	889	868	395	33	1012	84	37	61	198	76	202	.275	.320	.421	.741

Zach Phillips

Pitches: L Bats: L Pos: RP-8   Ht: 6'1" Wt: 200 Born: 9/21/1986 Age: 30

Year Team	Lg	G	GS	CG	GF	IP	BFP	H	R	ER	HR	SH	SF	HB	TBB	IBB	SO	WP	Bk	W	L	Pct	Sh	Sv-Op	Hld	ERC	ERA
2016 Norfolk*	AAA	49	0	0	15	60.2	266	60	32	30	3	2	2	2	30	2	84	1	0	9	3	.750	0	1--	-	4.12	4.45
2011 Bal	AL	10	0	0	2	8.0	33	6	1	1	1	0	0	0	2	0	8	0	0	0	0	-	0	0-0	0	2.24	1.13
2012 Bal	AL	6	0	0	3	6.0	28	7	4	4	2	0	0	0	3	1	5	0	0	0	0	-	0	0-0	0	6.85	6.00
2013 Mia	NL	3	0	0	0	1.2	11	3	1	1	0	1	0	0	3	0	1	0	0	0	1	.000	0	0-0	0	14.26	5.40
2016 Pit	NL	8	0	0	0	6.2	28	8	2	2	1	0	0	0	1	0	6	1	0	0	0	-	0	0-0	1	4.62	2.70
4 ML YEARS		27	0	0	5	22.1	100	24	8	8	4	1	0	0	9	1	20	1	0	0	1	.000	0	0-0	1	4.90	3.22

A.J. Pierzynski

Bats: L Throws: R Pos: C-64;PH-18   perr-ZINN-ski   Ht: 6'3" Wt: 250 Born: 12/30/1976 Age: 40

Year Team	Lg	G	AB	H	2B	3B	HR	(Hm	Rd)	TB	R	RBI	RC	TBB	IBB	SO	HBP	SH	SF	SB	CS	GDP	Avg	OBP	Slg	OPS
1998 Min	AL	7	10	3	0	0	0	(0	0)	3	1	1	2	1	0	2	1	0	1	0	0	0	.300	.385	.300	.685
1999 Min	AL	9	22	6	2	0	0	(0	0)	8	3	3	3	1	0	4	1	0	0	0	0	0	.273	.333	.364	.697
2000 Min	AL	33	88	27	5	1	2	(1	1)	40	12	11	14	5	0	14	2	0	1	1	0	1	.307	.354	.455	.809
2001 Min	AL	114	381	110	33	2	7	(3	4)	168	51	55	50	16	4	57	4	1	3	1	7	7	.289	.322	.441	.763
2002 Min	AL	130	440	132	31	6	6	(2	4)	193	54	49	60	13	1	61	11	2	3	1	2	14	.300	.334	.439	.773
2003 Min	AL	137	487	152	35	3	11	(6	5)	226	63	74	80	24	12	55	15	2	5	3	1	13	.312	.360	.464	.824
2004 SF	NL	131	471	128	28	2	11	(3	8)	193	45	77	58	19	4	27	15	2	3	0	1	27	.272	.319	.410	.729
2005 CWS	AL	128	460	118	21	0	18	(12	6)	193	61	56	55	23	5	68	12	1	1	0	2	13	.257	.308	.420	.728
2006 CWS	AL	140	509	150	24	0	16	(9	7)	222	65	64	68	22	6	72	8	3	7	1	0	10	.295	.333	.436	.769
2007 CWS	AL	136	472	124	24	0	14	(8	6)	190	54	50	49	25	5	66	8	1	3	1	1	21	.263	.309	.403	.712
2008 CWS	AL	134	534	150	31	1	13	(7	6)	222	66	60	64	19	5	71	8	3	6	0	1	14	.281	.312	.416	.728
2009 CWS	AL	138	504	151	22	1	13	(8	5)	214	57	49	59	24	6	52	1	3	3	1	1	13	.300	.331	.425	.755
2010 CWS	AL	128	474	128	29	0	9	(7	2)	184	43	56	51	15	2	39	6	6	2	3	4	17	.270	.300	.388	.688
2011 CWS	AL	129	464	133	29	1	8	(5	3)	188	38	48	53	23	6	33	5	2	6	1	0	19	.287	.323	.405	.728
2012 CWS	AL	135	479	133	18	4	27	(18	9)	240	68	77	79	28	5	78	8	1	4	0	0	8	.278	.326	.501	.827
2013 Tex	AL	134	503	137	24	1	17	(10	7)	214	48	70	61	11	2	76	9	0	6	1	1	14	.272	.297	.425	.722
2014 2 Tms		102	338	85	12	1	5	(1	4)	114	25	37	31	14	2	54	5	1	4	0	1	13	.251	.288	.337	.625
2015 Atl	NL	113	407	122	24	1	9	(5	4)	175	38	49	51	19	2	37	7	0	3	0	2	19	.300	.339	.430	.769
2016 Atl	NL	81	247	54	15	0	2	(1	1)	75	15	23	16	6	1	29	3	0	3	1	0	13	.219	.243	.304	.547

Year	Team	Lg	G	AB	H	2B	3B	HR	(Hm	Rd)	TB	R	RBI	RC	TBB	IBB	SO	HBP	SH	SF	SB	CS	GDP	Avg	OBP	Slg	OPS
14	Bos	AL	72	256	65	10	1	4	(1	3)	89	19	31	23	9	2	40	4	1	4	0	0	11	.254	.286	.348	.633
14	StL	NL	30	82	20	2	0	1	(0	1)	25	6	6	8	5	0	14	1	0	0	0	1	2	.244	.295	.305	.600
	Postseason		32	106	31	5	1	5	(3	2)	53	16	18	20	11	1	14	2	1	1	2	3	2	.292	.367	.500	.867
	19 ML YEARS		2059	7290	2043	407	24	188	(106	82)	3062	807	909	904	308	68	895	129	28	58	15	23	241	.280	.319	.420	.739

Kevin Pillar

Bats: R **Throws:** R **Pos:** CF-146　　pih-LAHR　　**Ht:** 6'0" **Wt:** 205 **Born:** 1/4/1989 **Age:** 28

Year	Team	Lg	G	AB	H	2B	3B	HR	(Hm	Rd)	TB	R	RBI	RC	TBB	IBB	SO	HBP	SH	SF	SB	CS	GDP	Avg	OBP	Slg	OPS
2013	Tor	AL	36	102	21	4	0	3	(1	2)	34	11	13	9	4	0	29	2	2	0	0	1	0	.206	.250	.333	.583
2014	Tor	AL	53	116	31	9	0	2	(2	0)	46	19	7	8	4	0	28	1	0	1	1	2	3	.267	.295	.397	.692
2015	Tor	AL	159	586	163	31	2	12	(6	6)	234	76	56	73	28	1	85	5	4	5	25	4	9	.278	.314	.399	.713
2016	Tor	AL	146	548	146	35	2	7	(3	4)	206	59	53	66	24	0	90	6	3	3	14	6	12	.266	.303	.376	.679
	Postseason		11	42	12	5	0	1	(0	1)	20	6	6	7	3	0	8	0	0	0	2	1	1	.286	.333	.476	.810
	4 ML YEARS		394	1352	361	79	4	24	(12	12)	520	165	129	156	60	1	232	14	9	9	40	13	24	.267	.303	.385	.688

Manny Pina

Bats: R **Throws:** R **Pos:** C-17;PH-15;DH-1　　**Ht:** 6'0" **Wt:** 215 **Born:** 6/5/1987 **Age:** 30

Year	Team	Lg	G	AB	H	2B	3B	HR	(Hm	Rd)	TB	R	RBI	RC	TBB	IBB	SO	HBP	SH	SF	SB	CS	GDP	Avg	OBP	Slg	OPS
2016	ColSpr*	AAA	63	237	78	21	3	5	(-	-)	120	35	43	44	17	3	39	1	3	4	1	1	4	.329	.371	.506	.877
2011	KC	AL	4	14	3	2	0	0	(0	0)	5	2	0	1	1	0	2	0	0	0	0	0	1	.214	.267	.357	.624
2012	KC	AL	1	2	0	0	0	0	(0	0)	0	0	0	0	0	0	0	0	0	0	0	0	0	.000	.000	.000	.000
2016	Mil	NL	33	71	18	4	0	2	(1	1)	28	4	12	8	10	0	15	0	0	0	0	1	2	.254	.346	.394	.740
	3 ML YEARS		38	87	21	6	0	2	(1	1)	33	6	12	9	11	0	17	0	0	0	0	1	3	.241	.327	.379	.706

Branden Pinder

Pitches: R **Bats:** R **Pos:** RP-1　　**Ht:** 6'4" **Wt:** 215 **Born:** 1/26/1989 **Age:** 28

				HOW MUCH HE PITCHED					WHAT HE GAVE UP										THE RESULTS						
Year	Team	Lg	G	GS	CG	GF	IP	BFP	H	R	ER	HR	SH	SF	HB	TBB	IBB	SO	WP	Bk	W	L	Pct	Sh	Sv-Op	Hld	ERC	ERA
2012	Tampa	A+	41	0	0	28	67.2	307	70	27	21	1	5	1	5	29	7	67	8	0	2	6	.250	0	9- -	-	3.75	2.79
2013	Trntn	AA	19	0	0	13	24.1	117	28	19	17	2	2	2	2	16	1	22	1	1	1	1	.500	0	5- -	-	6.08	6.29
2013	Tampa	A+	21	5	0	6	49.0	192	39	20	19	4	0	4	4	11	0	50	4	0	1	2	.333	0	1- -	-	2.63	3.49
2014	Trntn	AA	12	0	0	9	16.0	57	7	1	1	0	1	0	0	2	0	18	1	0	2	0	1.000	0	4- -	-	0.60	0.56
2014	S-WB	AAA	13	0	0	6	16.2	69	17	7	7	2	0	1	0	5	0	12	1	0	1	0	1.000	0	1- -	-	4.03	3.78
2015	S-WB	AAA	23	0	0	12	35.1	147	31	15	11	3	0	2	0	10	0	36	4	1	1	3	.250	0	1- -	-	2.82	2.80
2015	NYY	AL	25	0	0	10	27.2	122	28	9	9	4	0	1	0	14	1	25	0	1	0	2	.000	0	0-0	0	4.85	2.93
2016	NYY	AL	1	0	0	0	1.0	6	3	2	2	0	0	0	0	1	0	1	0	0	0	0	-	0	0-0	0	22.91	18.00
	2 ML YEARS		26	0	0	10	28.2	128	31	11	11	4	0	1	0	15	1	26	0	1	0	2	.000	0	0-0	0	5.33	3.45

Chad Pinder

Bats: R **Throws:** R **Pos:** 2B-13;SS-7;PH-7;DH-2;PR-1　　**Ht:** 6'2" **Wt:** 195 **Born:** 3/29/1992 **Age:** 25

Year	Team	Lg	G	AB	H	2B	3B	HR	(Hm	Rd)	TB	R	RBI	RC	TBB	IBB	SO	HBP	SH	SF	SB	CS	GDP	Avg	OBP	Slg	OPS
2013	Vrmnt	A-	42	140	28	4	0	3	(-	-)	41	14	8	13	12	0	41	6	0	3	1	0	5	.200	.286	.293	.579
2014	Stcktn	A+	94	403	116	32	5	13	(-	-)	197	61	55	65	22	0	99	8	1	2	12	9	16	.288	.336	.489	.824
2015	Mdlnd	AA	117	477	151	32	2	15	(-	-)	232	71	86	83	28	1	103	8	4	5	7	5	15	.317	.361	.486	.847
2016	Nashv	AAA	107	426	110	23	3	14	(-	-)	181	72	51	58	25	0	108	9	1	4	5	1	8	.258	.310	.425	.735
2016	Oak	AL	22	51	12	4	0	1	(0	1)	19	4	4	4	3	0	14	0	0	1	0	0	1	.235	.273	.373	.645

Michael Pineda

Pitches: R **Bats:** R **Pos:** SP-32　　pah-NAY-dah　　**Ht:** 6'7" **Wt:** 260 **Born:** 1/18/1989 **Age:** 28

				HOW MUCH HE PITCHED					WHAT HE GAVE UP										THE RESULTS						
Year	Team	Lg	G	GS	CG	GF	IP	BFP	H	R	ER	HR	SH	SF	HB	TBB	IBB	SO	WP	Bk	W	L	Pct	Sh	Sv-Op	Hld	ERC	ERA
2011	Sea	AL	28	28	0	0	171.0	696	133	76	71	18	4	3	5	55	1	173	9	0	9	10	.474	0	0-0	0	2.73	3.74
2014	NYY	AL	13	13	0	0	76.1	290	56	18	16	5	2	1	0	7	0	59	3	1	5	5	.500	0	0-0	0	1.51	1.89
2015	NYY	AL	27	27	1	0	160.2	668	176	83	78	21	4	6	3	21	0	156	4	0	12	10	.545	0	0-0	0	3.82	4.37
2016	NYY	AL	32	32	0	0	175.2	756	184	98	94	27	0	3	6	53	1	207	7	0	6	12	.333	0	0-0	0	4.45	4.82
	4 ML YEARS		100	100	1	0	583.2	2410	549	275	259	71	10	13	14	136	2	595	23	1	32	37	.464	0	0-0	0	3.33	3.99

Josmil Pinto

Bats: R **Throws:** R **Pos:** PH-6　　HOSE-meel PEEN-toe　　**Ht:** 5'11" **Wt:** 225 **Born:** 3/31/1989 **Age:** 28

Year	Team	Lg	G	AB	H	2B	3B	HR	(Hm	Rd)	TB	R	RBI	RC	TBB	IBB	SO	HBP	SH	SF	SB	CS	GDP	Avg	OBP	Slg	OPS
2016	ColSpr*	AAA	86	286	88	21	3	11	(-	-)	148	46	51	53	26	0	67	0	0	3	0	0	5	.308	.362	.517	.879
2013	Min	AL	21	76	26	5	0	4	(3	1)	43	10	12	15	6	0	22	1	0	0	0	0	3	.342	.398	.566	.963
2014	Min	AL	57	169	37	8	0	7	(4	3)	66	25	18	13	24	0	50	1	0	3	0	1	7	.219	.315	.391	.705
2016	Mil	NL	6	5	0	0	0	0	(0	0)	0	1	0	0	1	0	4	0	0	0	0	0	0	.000	.167	.000	.167
	3 ML YEARS		84	250	63	13	0	11	(7	4)	109	36	30	28	31	0	76	2	0	3	0	1	10	.252	.336	.436	.772

Jose Pirela

Bats: R Throws: R Pos: 2B-12;PH-4;RF-1   Ht: 6'0" Wt: 220 Born: 11/21/1989 Age: 27

Year	Team	Lg	G	AB	H	2B	3B	HR	(Hm	Rd)	TB	R	RBI	RC	TBB	IBB	SO	HBP	SH	SF	SB	CS	GDP	Avg	OBP	Slg	OPS
2016	ElPaso*	AAA	35	137	35	7	3	2	(-	-)	54	19	16	16	9	1	21	0	0	0	1	1	6	.255	.301	.394	.696
2014	NYY	AL	7	24	8	1	2	0	(0	0)	13	6	3	4	1	0	4	0	0	0	0	0	1	.333	.360	.542	.902
2015	NYY	AL	37	74	17	3	0	1	(1	0)	23	7	5	3	2	0	16	0	1	1	1	0	4	.230	.247	.311	.558
2016	SD	NL	15	39	6	2	0	0	(0	0)	8	2	0	0	1	0	9	0	1	0	0	1	0	.154	.175	.205	.380
	3 ML YEARS		59	137	31	6	2	1	(1	0)	44	15	8	7	4	0	29	0	2	1	1	1	5	.226	.246	.321	.568

Stephen Piscotty

Bats: R Throws: R Pos: RF-146;CF-10;PH-6;1B-1   Ht: 6'3" Wt: 210 Born: 1/14/1991 Age: 26

Year	Team	Lg	G	AB	H	2B	3B	HR	(Hm	Rd)	TB	R	RBI	RC	TBB	IBB	SO	HBP	SH	SF	SB	CS	GDP	Avg	OBP	Slg	OPS
2012	QuadC	A	55	210	62	18	1	4	(-	-)	94	29	27	37	18	1	25	9	0	0	3	0	9	.295	.376	.448	.823
2013	PlmBh	A+	63	243	71	14	2	9	(-	-)	116	30	35	39	18	2	27	3	0	0	4	5	4	.292	.348	.477	.826
2013	Sprgfld	AA	49	184	55	9	0	6	(-	-)	82	17	24	31	19	1	19	1	1	2	7	3	12	.299	.364	.446	.810
2014	Memp	AAA	136	500	144	32	0	9	(-	-)	203	70	69	76	43	2	61	10	1	2	11	5	18	.288	.355	.406	.761
2015	Memp	AAA	87	320	87	28	2	11	(-	-)	152	54	41	56	46	0	62	3	0	3	5	6	13	.272	.366	.475	.841
2015	StL	NL	63	233	71	15	4	7	(4	3)	115	29	39	41	20	2	56	1	0	2	2	1	7	.305	.359	.494	.853
2016	StL	NL	153	582	159	35	3	22	(13	9)	266	86	85	97	51	0	133	12	1	2	7	5	14	.273	.343	.457	.800
	Postseason		4	16	6	1	0	3	(1	2)	16	5	6	8	2	0	8	0	0	0	0	0	0	.375	.444	1.000	1.444
	2 ML YEARS		216	815	230	50	7	29	(17	12)	381	115	124	138	71	2	189	13	1	4	9	6	21	.282	.348	.467	.815

Kevin Plawecki

Bats: R Throws: R Pos: C-45;PH-3   plah-WEH-kee   Ht: 6'2" Wt: 210 Born: 2/26/1991 Age: 26

Year	Team	Lg	G	AB	H	2B	3B	HR	(Hm	Rd)	TB	R	RBI	RC	TBB	IBB	SO	HBP	SH	SF	SB	CS	GDP	Avg	OBP	Slg	OPS
2012	Bklyn	A-	61	216	54	8	0	7	(-	-)	83	26	27	31	25	0	24	8	0	3	0	0	7	.250	.345	.384	.729
2013	2 Tms	Low	125	449	137	38	1	8	(-	-)	201	60	80	82	42	2	53	24	1	5	1	0	15	.305	.390	.448	.838
2014	Bnghtn	AA	58	224	73	18	0	6	(-	-)	109	33	43	41	16	0	27	5	0	4	0	0	12	.326	.378	.487	.864
2014	LsVgs	AAA	43	152	43	6	0	5	(-	-)	64	25	21	23	14	1	21	1	2	1	0	0	4	.283	.345	.421	.766
2015	LsVgs	AAA	22	85	19	5	1	1	(-	-)	29	7	9	7	3	0	12	2	0	0	0	0	3	.224	.267	.341	.608
2016	LsVgs	AAA	55	190	57	11	0	8	(-	-)	92	27	40	32	13	0	19	2	0	2	0	1	9	.300	.348	.484	.832
2015	NYM	NL	73	233	51	9	0	3	(1	2)	69	18	21	22	17	4	60	4	1	3	0	0	4	.219	.280	.296	.576
2016	NYM	NL	48	132	26	6	0	1	(0	1)	35	6	11	11	17	2	33	2	0	0	0	0	1	.197	.296	.265	.563
	2 ML YEARS		121	365	77	15	0	4	(1	3)	104	24	32	33	34	6	93	6	1	3	0	0	5	.211	.287	.285	.572

Trevor Plouffe

Bats: R Throws: R Pos: 3B-63;1B-13;DH-7;PH-1;PR-1   PLOOF   Ht: 6'2" Wt: 215 Born: 6/15/1986 Age: 31

Year	Team	Lg	G	AB	H	2B	3B	HR	(Hm	Rd)	TB	R	RBI	RC	TBB	IBB	SO	HBP	SH	SF	SB	CS	GDP	Avg	OBP	Slg	OPS
2010	Min	AL	22	41	6	1	0	2	(1	1)	13	7	6	2	0	0	14	0	2	1	0	0	0	.146	.143	.317	.460
2011	Min	AL	81	286	68	18	1	8	(3	5)	112	47	31	31	25	0	71	4	2	3	3	3	6	.238	.305	.392	.697
2012	Min	AL	119	422	99	19	1	24	(15	9)	192	56	55	48	37	0	92	4	0	2	1	3	9	.235	.301	.455	.756
2013	Min	AL	129	477	121	22	1	14	(8	6)	187	44	52	49	34	1	112	6	1	4	2	1	11	.254	.309	.392	.701
2014	Min	AL	136	520	134	40	2	14	(8	6)	220	69	80	74	53	2	109	4	0	5	2	1	12	.258	.328	.423	.751
2015	Min	AL	152	573	140	35	4	22	(13	9)	249	74	86	79	50	0	124	4	1	4	2	1	28	.244	.307	.435	.742
2016	Min	AL	84	319	83	13	1	12	(7	5)	134	35	47	38	19	0	60	2	1	3	1	0	11	.260	.303	.420	.723
	7 ML YEARS		723	2638	651	148	10	96	(55	41)	1107	332	357	321	218	3	582	24	7	22	11	9	77	.247	.308	.420	.727

Adam Plutko

Pitches: R Bats: R Pos: RP-2   Ht: 6'3" Wt: 200 Born: 10/3/1991 Age: 25

| | | | HOW MUCH HE PITCHED | | | | | WHAT HE GAVE UP | | | | | | | | | | | THE RESULTS | | | | | | |
Year	Team	Lg	G	GS	CG	GF	IP	BFP	H	R	ER	HR	SH	SF	HB	TBB	IBB	SO	WP	Bk	W	L	Pct	Sh	Sv-Op	Hld	ERC	ERA
2014	2 Tms	Low	28	28	0	0	149.2	615	148	73	67	12	3	2	3	30	0	144	6	0	7	10	.412	0	0- -	-	3.21	4.03
2015	Lynbrg	A+	8	8	1	0	49.2	182	30	7	7	3	1	2	1	5	0	47	1	0	4	2	.667	0	0- -	-	1.19	1.27
2015	Akron	AA	19	19	1	0	116.1	464	96	39	37	9	3	3	2	23	0	90	4	0	9	5	.643	0	0- -	-	2.33	2.86
2016	Akron	AA	13	13	0	0	71.2	284	64	27	26	5	1	2	0	12	0	63	1	0	3	3	.500	0	0- -	-	2.48	3.27
2016	Clmbs	AAA	15	15	0	0	90.0	379	87	42	41	8	3	2	0	34	1	67	1	1	6	5	.545	0	0- -	-	3.76	4.10
2016	Cle	AL	2	0	0	1	3.2	18	5	3	3	1	0	0	0	2	0	3	1	0	0	0	-	0	0-0	0	8.17	7.36

Gregory Polanco

puh-LAHN-ko

Bats: L Throws: L Pos: RF-111;LF-29;PH-8;CF-5;DH-4;PR-1   Ht: 6'5" Wt: 230 Born: 9/14/1991 Age: 25

Year	Team	Lg	G	AB	H	2B	3B	HR	(Hm	Rd)	TB	R	RBI	RC	TBB	IBB	SO	HBP	SH	SF	SB	CS	GDP	Avg	OBP	Slg	OPS
2014	Pit	NL	89	277	65	9	0	7	(5	2)	95	50	33	32	30	1	59	0	2	2	14	5	1	.235	.307	.343	.650
2015	Pit	NL	153	593	152	35	6	9	(6	3)	226	83	52	73	55	6	121	1	1	2	27	10	5	.256	.320	.381	.701
2016	Pit	NL	144	527	136	34	4	22	(9	13)	244	79	86	73	53	6	119	0	1	6	17	6	13	.258	.323	.463	.786
	Postseason		1	4	0	0	0	0	(0	0)	0	0	0	0	0	0	2	0	0	0	0	0	0	.000	.000	.000	.000
	3 ML YEARS		386	1397	353	78	10	38	(20	18)	565	212	171	178	138	13	299	1	4	10	58	21	19	.253	.318	.404	.723

Jorge Polanco

Bats: B **Throws:** R **Pos:** SS-47;3B-9;PH-8;2B-5;DH-1   puh-LAHN-ko   **Ht:** 5'11" **Wt:** 200 **Born:** 7/5/1993 **Age:** 23

							BATTING													RUNNING			AVERAGES			
Year Team	Lg	G	AB	H	2B	3B	HR	(Hm	Rd)	TB	R	RBI	RC	TBB	IBB	SO	HBP	SH	SF	SB	CS	GDP	Avg	OBP	Slg	OPS
2016 Roch*	AAA	75	293	81	14	6	9	(-	-)	134	32	39	46	27	1	51	1	0	4	5	4	6	.276	.335	.457	.793
2014 Min	AL	5	6	2	1	1	0	(0	0)	5	2	3	4	2	0	2	0	0	0	0	0	0	.333	.500	.833	1.333
2015 Min	AL	4	10	3	0	0	0	(0	0)	3	1	1	3	2	0	1	0	0	0	1	0	0	.300	.417	.300	.717
2016 Min	AL	69	245	69	15	4	4	(1	3)	104	24	27	36	17	0	46	3	2	3	4	3	3	.282	.332	.424	.757
3 ML YEARS		78	261	74	16	5	4	(1	3)	112	27	31	43	21	0	49	3	2	3	5	3	3	.284	.340	.429	.769

A.J. Pollock

Bats: R **Throws:** R **Pos:** CF-12   **Ht:** 6'1" **Wt:** 195 **Born:** 12/5/1987 **Age:** 29

							BATTING													RUNNING			AVERAGES			
Year Team	Lg	G	AB	H	2B	3B	HR	(Hm	Rd)	TB	R	RBI	RC	TBB	IBB	SO	HBP	SH	SF	SB	CS	GDP	Avg	OBP	Slg	OPS
2012 Ari	NL	31	81	20	4	1	2	(2	0)	32	8	8	9	9	1	11	0	1	2	2	2	2	.247	.315	.395	.710
2013 Ari	NL	137	443	119	28	5	8	(3	5)	181	64	38	58	33	1	82	2	3	1	12	3	5	.269	.322	.409	.730
2014 Ari	NL	75	265	80	19	6	7	(7	0)	132	41	24	43	19	0	46	2	1	0	14	3	4	.302	.353	.498	.851
2015 Ari	NL	157	609	192	39	6	20	(9	11)	303	111	76	106	53	0	89	2	0	9	39	7	19	.315	.367	.498	.865
2016 Ari	NL	12	41	10	0	0	2	(0	2)	16	9	4	5	5	0	8	0	0	0	4	0	1	.244	.326	.390	.716
5 ML YEARS		412	1439	421	90	18	39	(21	18)	664	233	150	221	119	2	236	6	5	12	70	15	31	.293	.346	.461	.808

Drew Pomeranz

Pitches: L **Bats:** R **Pos:** SP-30; RP-1   POMM-er-anze   **Ht:** 6'6" **Wt:** 240 **Born:** 11/22/1988 **Age:** 28

			HOW MUCH HE PITCHED					WHAT HE GAVE UP											THE RESULTS							
Year Team	Lg	G	GS	CG	GF	IP	BFP	H	R	ER	HR	SH	SF	HB	TBB	IBB	SO	WP	Bk	W	L	Pct	Sh	Sv-Op	Hld	ERC	ERA
2011 Col	NL	4	4	0	0	18.1	77	19	11	11	0	1	0	1	5	0	13	1	0	2	1	.667	0	0-0	0	3.36	5.40
2012 Col	NL	22	22	0	0	96.2	434	97	57	53	14	8	4	4	46	2	83	8	1	2	9	.182	0	0-0	0	4.78	4.93
2013 Col	NL	8	0	0	0	21.2	105	25	15	15	4	1	1	1	19	1	19	0	0	0	4	.000	0	0-0	0	8.04	6.23
2014 Oak	AL	20	10	0	4	69.0	278	51	22	18	7	1	0	1	26	0	64	0	0	5	4	.556	0	0-0	0	2.70	2.35
2015 Oak	AL	53	9	0	9	86.0	357	71	44	35	8	4	5	3	31	1	82	2	0	5	6	.455	0	3-6	12	3.05	3.66
2016 2 Tms		31	30	0	1	170.2	703	137	65	63	22	3	3	1	65	3	186	10	0	11	12	.478	0	0-0	0	3.13	3.32
16 SD	NL	17	17	0	0	102.0	411	67	30	28	8	2	3	1	41	2	115	7	0	8	7	.533	0	0-0	0	2.17	2.47
16 Bos	AL	14	13	0	1	68.2	292	70	35	35	14	1	0	0	24	1	71	3	0	3	5	.375	0	0-0	0	4.73	4.59
6 ML YEARS		138	79	0	14	462.1	1954	400	214	195	55	18	13	11	192	7	447	21	1	25	36	.410	0	3-6	12	3.59	3.80

Dalton Pompey

Bats: B **Throws:** R **Pos:** PR-7;LF-2;DH-2   pom-PAY   **Ht:** 6'2" **Wt:** 195 **Born:** 12/11/1992 **Age:** 24

							BATTING													RUNNING			AVERAGES			
Year Team	Lg	G	AB	H	2B	3B	HR	(Hm	Rd)	TB	R	RBI	RC	TBB	IBB	SO	HBP	SH	SF	SB	CS	GDP	Avg	OBP	Slg	OPS
2016 Buffalo*	AAA	93	337	91	14	1	4	(-	-)	119	48	28	46	40	0	72	2	1	2	18	7	7	.270	.349	.353	.702
2014 Tor	AL	17	39	9	1	2	1	(1	0)	17	5	4	3	4	0	12	0	0	0	1	0	0	.231	.302	.436	.738
2015 Tor	AL	34	94	21	8	0	2	(1	1)	35	17	6	9	7	0	23	2	0	0	5	1	1	.223	.291	.372	.664
2016 Tor	AL	8	2	0	0	0	0	(0	0)	0	3	0	0	0	0	1	0	0	0	2	1	0	.000	.000	.000	.000
Postseason		5	1	1	0	0	0	(0	0)	1	0	1	0	0	0	0	0	0	0	4	0	0	1.000	1.000	1.000	2.000
3 ML YEARS		59	135	30	9	2	3	(2	1)	52	25	10	12	11	0	36	2	0	0	8	2	1	.222	.291	.385	.676

Rick Porcello

Pitches: R **Bats:** R **Pos:** SP-33   pore-SELL-oh   **Ht:** 6'5" **Wt:** 205 **Born:** 12/27/1988 **Age:** 28

			HOW MUCH HE PITCHED					WHAT HE GAVE UP											THE RESULTS							
Year Team	Lg	G	GS	CG	GF	IP	BFP	H	R	ER	HR	SH	SF	HB	TBB	IBB	SO	WP	Bk	W	L	Pct	Sh	Sv-Op	Hld	ERC	ERA
2009 Det	AL	31	31	0	0	170.2	720	176	81	75	23	4	2	3	52	0	89	6	1	14	9	.609	0	0-0	0	4.24	3.96
2010 Det	AL	27	27	0	0	162.2	700	188	96	89	18	1	2	7	38	2	84	11	3	10	12	.455	0	0-0	0	4.56	4.92
2011 Det	AL	31	31	0	0	182.0	784	210	103	96	18	5	5	8	46	1	104	12	0	14	9	.609	0	0-0	0	4.57	4.75
2012 Det	AL	31	31	0	0	176.1	783	226	101	90	16	2	3	6	44	3	107	6	0	10	12	.455	0	0-0	0	5.16	4.59
2013 Det	AL	32	29	1	1	177.0	736	185	87	85	18	4	3	4	42	4	142	6	1	13	8	.619	0	0-0	0	3.79	4.32
2014 Det	AL	32	31	3	1	204.2	840	211	89	78	18	3	4	4	41	4	129	0	0	15	13	.536	3	0-0	0	3.50	3.43
2015 Bos	AL	28	28	0	0	172.0	737	196	103	94	25	2	5	10	38	0	149	12	1	9	15	.375	0	0-0	0	4.76	4.92
2016 Bos	AL	33	33	3	0	223.0	890	193	85	78	23	2	3	13	32	0	189	3	0	22	4	.846	0	0-0	0	2.64	3.15
Postseason		8	2	0	4	16.1	71	18	10	8	0	0	1	2	2	2	13	1	0	0	2	.000	0	0-0	0	3.06	4.41
8 ML YEARS		245	241	7	2	1468.1	6190	1585	745	685	159	23	27	54	333	14	993	56	6	107	82	.566	3	0-0	0	4.06	4.20

Buster Posey

Bats: R **Throws:** R **Pos:** C-123;1B-15;PH-7;DH-5   **Ht:** 6'1" **Wt:** 215 **Born:** 3/27/1987 **Age:** 30

							BATTING													RUNNING			AVERAGES			
Year Team	Lg	G	AB	H	2B	3B	HR	(Hm	Rd)	TB	R	RBI	RC	TBB	IBB	SO	HBP	SH	SF	SB	CS	GDP	Avg	OBP	Slg	OPS
2009 SF	NL	7	17	2	0	0	0	(0	0)	2	1	0	0	0	0	4	0	0	0	0	0	0	.118	.118	.118	.235
2010 SF	NL	108	406	124	23	2	18	(6	12)	205	58	67	70	30	5	55	4	0	3	0	2	12	.305	.357	.505	.862
2011 SF	NL	45	162	46	5	0	4	(1	3)	63	17	21	26	18	3	30	4	0	1	3	0	4	.284	.368	.389	.756
2012 SF	NL	148	530	178	39	1	24	(7	17)	291	78	103	111	69	7	96	2	0	9	1	1	19	.336	.408	.549	.957
2013 SF	NL	148	520	153	34	1	15	(8	7)	234	61	72	77	60	8	70	8	0	7	2	1	15	.294	.371	.450	.821
2014 SF	NL	147	547	170	28	2	22	(11	11)	268	72	89	94	47	5	69	3	0	8	0	1	16	.311	.364	.490	.854
2015 SF	NL	150	557	177	28	0	19	(6	13)	262	74	95	96	56	10	52	3	0	7	2	0	17	.318	.379	.470	.849
2016 SF	NL	146	539	155	33	2	14	(7	7)	234	82	80	82	64	7	68	3	0	8	6	1	18	.288	.362	.434	.796
Postseason		48	188	46	3	0	4	(1	3)	61	16	21	18	20	4	40	1	0	1	1	1	4	.245	.319	.324	.644
8 ML YEARS		899	3278	1005	190	8	116	(46	70)	1559	443	527	556	344	45	444	27	0	43	14	6	101	.307	.373	.476	.848

Brooks Pounders

Pitches: R Bats: R Pos: RP-13   **Ht:** 6'5" **Wt:** 265 **Born:** 9/26/1990 **Age:** 26

			HOW MUCH HE PITCHED							WHAT HE GAVE UP									THE RESULTS						
Year	Team	Lg	G	GS	CG	GF	IP	BFP	H	R	ER	HR	SH	SF	HB	TBB	IBB	SO	WP	Bk	W	L	Pct	Sh	Sv-Op	Hld	ERC	ERA
2012	2 Tms	Low	28	23	0	2	134.0	590	139	73	59	7	4	3	10	44	1	132	12	1	9	6	.600	0	0- -	-	3.88	3.96
2013	NWArk	AA	27	19	1	1	116.0	493	107	63	58	12	1	6	11	42	0	100	3	0	5	7	.417	1	1- -	-	3.93	4.50
2014	2 Tms	Low	9	8	0	0	30.1	130	29	18	15	0	2	0	1	12	0	37	2	0	0	2	.000	0	0- -	-	3.24	4.45
2015	3 Tms	Low	7	7	0	0	19.0	79	18	10	7	1	1	0	3	4	0	19	0	0	1	0	1.000	0	0- -	-	3.41	3.32
2015	NWArk	AA	8	8	0	0	49.1	198	39	16	12	3	1	0	3	19	0	32	1	1	3	4	.429	0	0- -	-	2.99	2.19
2016	Omha	AAA	31	7	0	7	80.1	342	67	29	28	5	2	1	5	37	3	90	4	1	5	3	.625	0	0- -	-	3.33	3.14
2016	KC	AL	13	0	0	6	12.2	58	19	13	13	6	0	1	0	3	0	13	0	1	2	1	.667	0	0-0	1	9.56	9.24

Martin Prado

Bats: R Throws: R Pos: 3B-150;PH-4;DH-1   mar-TEEN PRAH-doe   **Ht:** 6'0" **Wt:** 215 **Born:** 10/27/1983 **Age:** 33

			BATTING																			RUNNING			AVERAGES			
Year	Team	Lg	G	AB	H	2B	3B	HR	(Hm	Rd)	TB	R	RBI	RC	TBB	IBB	SO	HBP	SH	SF	SB	CS	GDP	Avg	OBP	Slg	OPS
2006	Atl	NL	24	42	11	1	1	1	(1	0)	17	3	9	9	5	0	7	0	2	0	0	0	2	.262	.340	.405	.745
2007	Atl	NL	28	59	17	3	0	0	(0	0)	20	5	2	6	3	0	6	0	0	0	0	0	0	.288	.323	.339	.662
2008	Atl	NL	78	228	73	18	4	2	(1	1)	105	36	33	39	21	0	29	1	2	2	3	1	3	.320	.377	.461	.838
2009	Atl	NL	128	450	138	38	0	11	(4	7)	209	64	49	57	36	1	59	2	11	4	1	3	17	.307	.358	.464	.822
2010	Atl	NL	140	599	184	40	3	15	(4	11)	275	100	66	86	40	2	86	3	3	6	5	3	13	.307	.350	.459	.809
2011	Atl	NL	129	551	143	26	2	13	(9	4)	212	66	57	57	34	1	52	1	1	3	4	8	16	.260	.302	.385	.687
2012	Atl	NL	156	617	186	42	6	10	(6	4)	270	81	70	96	58	2	69	2	4	9	17	4	19	.301	.359	.438	.796
2013	Ari	NL	155	609	172	36	2	14	(7	7)	254	70	82	72	47	2	53	2	0	6	3	5	29	.282	.333	.417	.750
2014	2 Tms		143	536	151	26	4	12	(7	5)	221	62	58	66	26	0	80	7	0	4	3	1	20	.282	.321	.412	.733
2015	Mia	NL	129	500	144	22	2	9	(5	4)	197	52	63	70	37	4	68	5	1	8	1	0	9	.288	.338	.394	.732
2016	Mia	NL	153	600	183	37	3	8	(6	2)	250	70	75	89	49	4	69	4	0	5	2	2	24	.305	.359	.417	.775
14	Ari	NL	106	403	109	17	4	5	(3	2)	149	44	43	43	23	0	57	6	0	4	2	1	17	.270	.317	.370	.686
14	NYY	AL	37	133	42	9	0	7	(4	3)	72	18	16	23	3	0	23	1	0	0	1	0	3	.316	.336	.541	.877
	Postseason		1	5	1	0	0	0	(0	0)	1	0	0	0	0	0	1	0	0	0	0	0	0	.200	.200	.200	.400
	11 ML YEARS		1263	4791	1402	289	27	95	(50	45)	2030	609	564	647	356	16	578	27	24	47	39	27	152	.293	.342	.424	.766

Alex Presley

Bats: L Throws: L Pos: PH-22;LF-13;RF-13;CF-7;PR-1   **Ht:** 5'10" **Wt:** 195 **Born:** 7/25/1985 **Age:** 31

			BATTING																			RUNNING			AVERAGES			
Year	Team	Lg	G	AB	H	2B	3B	HR	(Hm	Rd)	TB	R	RBI	RC	TBB	IBB	SO	HBP	SH	SF	SB	CS	GDP	Avg	OBP	Slg	OPS
2016	Toledo*	AAA	41	169	50	10	3	3	(-	-)	75	23	14	27	18	0	27	2	1	3	4	6	2	.296	.365	.444	.808
2010	Pit	NL	19	23	6	1	0	0	(0	0)	7	2	0	1	1	0	8	0	1	0	1	1	0	.261	.292	.304	.596
2011	Pit	NL	52	215	64	12	6	4	(1	3)	100	27	20	35	13	1	40	1	1	1	9	3	1	.298	.339	.465	.804
2012	Pit	NL	104	346	82	14	7	10	(2	8)	140	46	25	31	18	0	72	2	4	0	9	7	5	.237	.279	.405	.683
2013	2 Tms		57	185	51	5	2	3	(2	1)	69	17	15	17	9	0	39	1	0	0	1	4	3	.276	.313	.373	.686
2014	Hou	AL	89	254	62	6	1	6	(4	2)	88	22	19	29	13	0	44	1	1	2	5	1	3	.244	.281	.346	.628
2015	Hou	AL	8	12	3	0	0	0	(0	0)	3	1	1	2	1	0	5	0	0	0	0	0	0	.250	.308	.250	.558
2016	2 Tms		50	121	24	2	0	3	(1	2)	35	12	11	12	11	1	25	1	0	1	0	2	2	.198	.269	.289	.558
13	Pit	NL	29	72	19	1	1	2	(2	0)	28	8	4	5	1	0	18	0	0	0	0	1	1	.264	.274	.389	.663
13	Min	AL	28	113	32	4	1	1	(0	1)	41	9	11	12	8	0	21	1	0	0	1	3	2	.283	.336	.363	.699
16	Mil	NL	47	116	23	2	0	3	(1	2)	34	12	11	12	11	1	25	1	0	1	0	2	2	.198	.274	.293	.564
16	Det	AL	3	5	1	0	0	0	(0	0)	1	0	0	0	0	0	0	0	0	0	0	0	0	.200	.200	.200	.400
	7 ML YEARS		379	1156	292	40	16	26	(10	16)	442	127	91	127	66	2	233	6	7	4	25	18	14	.253	.295	.382	.678

Ryan Pressly

Pitches: R Bats: R Pos: RP-72   **Ht:** 6'3" **Wt:** 210 **Born:** 12/15/1988 **Age:** 28

			HOW MUCH HE PITCHED							WHAT HE GAVE UP									THE RESULTS						
Year	Team	Lg	G	GS	CG	GF	IP	BFP	H	R	ER	HR	SH	SF	HB	TBB	IBB	SO	WP	Bk	W	L	Pct	Sh	Sv-Op	Hld	ERC	ERA
2013	Min	AL	49	0	0	18	76.2	315	71	37	33	5	2	3	0	27	1	49	7	0	3	3	.500	0	0-0	1	3.31	3.87
2014	Min	AL	25	0	0	5	28.1	122	30	10	9	3	2	1	0	8	2	14	1	0	2	0	1.000	0	0-1	2	3.98	2.86
2015	Min	AL	27	0	0	6	27.2	119	27	9	9	0	1	1	0	12	1	22	2	0	3	2	.600	0	0-0	4	3.31	2.93
2016	Min	AL	72	0	0	10	75.1	328	79	34	31	8	4	2	2	23	2	67	7	0	6	7	.462	0	1-6	13	4.01	3.70
	4 ML YEARS		173	0	0	39	208.0	884	207	90	82	16	9	9	3	70	6	152	17	0	14	12	.538	0	1-7	20	3.66	3.55

David Price

Pitches: L Bats: L Pos: SP-35   **Ht:** 6'5" **Wt:** 215 **Born:** 8/26/1985 **Age:** 31

			HOW MUCH HE PITCHED							WHAT HE GAVE UP									THE RESULTS						
Year	Team	Lg	G	GS	CG	GF	IP	BFP	H	R	ER	HR	SH	SF	HB	TBB	IBB	SO	WP	Bk	W	L	Pct	Sh	Sv-Op	Hld	ERC	ERA
2008	TB	AL	5	1	0	0	14.0	57	9	4	3	1	0	1	4	4	0	12	0	0	0	0	-	0	0-0	1	1.86	1.93
2009	TB	AL	23	23	0	0	128.1	557	119	72	63	17	3	2	4	54	0	102	2	0	10	7	.588	0	0-0	0	4.05	4.42
2010	TB	AL	32	31	2	0	208.2	861	170	71	63	15	4	3	5	79	1	188	5	3	19	6	.760	1	0-0	0	2.91	2.72
2011	TB	AL	34	34	0	0	224.1	918	192	93	87	22	4	9	9	63	5	218	2	0	12	13	.480	2	0-0	0	2.97	3.49
2012	TB	AL	31	31	2	0	211.0	836	173	63	60	16	2	3	5	59	2	205	8	1	20	5	.800	1	0-0	0	2.67	2.56
2013	TB	AL	27	27	4	0	186.2	740	178	78	69	16	1	2	3	27	0	151	6	0	10	8	.556	0	0-0	0	2.89	3.33
2014	2 Tms	AL	34	34	3	0	248.1	1009	230	100	90	25	4	3	5	38	1	271	2	0	15	12	.556	0	0-0	0	2.79	3.26
2015	2 Tms	AL	32	32	3	0	220.1	888	190	70	60	17	4	8	3	47	2	225	4	0	18	5	.783	1	0-0	0	2.54	2.45
2016	Bos	AL	35	35	2	0	230.0	951	227	106	102	30	8	7	7	50	1	228	4	0	17	9	.654	0	0-0	0	3.63	3.99
14	TB	AL	23	23	2	0	170.2	689	156	68	59	20	3	3	5	23	1	189	2	0	11	8	.579	0	0-0	0	2.79	3.11
14	Det	AL	11	11	1	0	77.2	320	74	32	31	5	1	0	0	15	0	82	0	0	4	4	.500	0	0-0	0	2.77	3.59

			HOW MUCH HE PITCHED						WHAT HE GAVE UP												THE RESULTS							
Year	Team	Lg	G	GS	CG	GF	IP	BFP	H	R	ER	HR	SH	SF	HB	TBB	IBB	SO	WP	Bk	W	L	Pct	Sh	Sv-Op	Hld	ERC	ERA
15	Det	AL	21	21	3	0	146.0	592	133	50	41	13	4	5	3	29	2	138	3	0	9	4	.692	1	0-0	0	2.83	2.53
15	Tor	AL	11	11	0	0	74.1	296	57	20	19	4	0	3	0	18	0	87	1	0	9	1	.900	0	0-0	0	2.00	2.30
	Postseason		14	8	0	5	63.1	263	62	38	36	11	0	1	3	12	0	59	1	0	2	7	.222	0	1-1	0	3.79	5.12
9 ML YEARS			253	248	16	0	1671.2	6817	1488	657	597	159	30	36	42	421	12	1600	33	4	121	65	.651	3	0-0	1	2.99	3.21

Jurickson Profar

JURR-ick-sun PRO-farr

Bats: B **Throws:** R **Pos:** 3B-25;2B-19;1B-17;LF-14;PH-14;SS-11;DH-6;PR-2   **Ht:** 6'0" **Wt:** 190 **Born:** 2/20/1993 **Age:** 24

			BATTING																			RUNNING			AVERAGES			
Year	Team	Lg	G	AB	H	2B	3B	HR	(Hm	Rd)	TB	R	RBI	RC	TBB	IBB	SO	HBP	SH	SF	SB	CS	GDP	Avg	OBP	Slg	OPS
2016	RdRck*	AAA	42	169	48	9	0	5	(-	-)	72	28	26	26	16	0	26	3	1	0	4	3	5	.284	.356	.426	.782
2012	Tex	AL	9	17	3	2	0	1	(0	1)	8	2	2	1	0	0	4	0	0	0	0	0	1	.176	.176	.471	.647
2013	Tex	AL	85	286	67	11	0	6	(3	3)	96	30	26	30	26	0	63	5	6	1	2	4	1	.234	.308	.336	.644
2016	Tex	AL	90	272	65	6	3	5	(4	1)	92	35	20	30	30	0	61	3	2	0	2	1	7	.239	.321	.338	.660
	Postseason		1	1	1	0	0	0	(0	0)	1	0	0	0	0	0	0	0	0	0	0	0	0	1.000	1.000	1.000	2.000
3 ML YEARS			184	575	135	19	3	12	(7	5)	196	67	48	61	56	0	128	8	8	1	4	5	9	.235	.311	.341	.652

Yasiel Puig

yah-SEE-el PWEEG

Bats: R **Throws:** R **Pos:** RF-90;PH-17;LF-5;CF-4   **Ht:** 6'2" **Wt:** 240 **Born:** 12/7/1990 **Age:** 26

			BATTING																			RUNNING			AVERAGES			
Year	Team	Lg	G	AB	H	2B	3B	HR	(Hm	Rd)	TB	R	RBI	RC	TBB	IBB	SO	HBP	SH	SF	SB	CS	GDP	Avg	OBP	Slg	OPS
2016	OkCity*	AAA	19	69	24	3	1	4	(-	-)	41	12	12	15	6	0	8	0	0	0	1	2		.348	.400	.594	.994
2013	LAD	NL	104	382	122	21	2	19	(9	10)	204	66	42	62	36	6	97	11	0	3	11	8	6	.319	.391	.534	.925
2014	LAD	NL	148	558	165	37	9	16	(8	8)	268	92	69	95	67	3	124	12	2	1	11	7	7	.296	.382	.480	.863
2015	LAD	NL	79	282	72	12	3	11	(6	5)	123	30	38	35	26	1	66	2	0	1	3	3	1	.255	.322	.436	.758
2016	LAD	NL	104	334	88	14	2	11	(6	5)	139	45	45	46	24	0	74	7	0	3	5	2	10	.263	.323	.416	.740
	Postseason		17	57	16	1	2	0	(0	0)	21	10	5	6	2	0	25	2	0	0	0	1	2	.281	.328	.368	.696
4 ML YEARS			435	1556	447	84	16	57	(29	28)	734	233	194	238	153	10	361	32	2	8	30	20	24	.287	.361	.472	.833

Albert Pujols

POO-holes

Bats: R **Throws:** R **Pos:** DH-123;1B-28;PH-1   **Ht:** 6'3" **Wt:** 240 **Born:** 1/16/1980 **Age:** 37

			BATTING																			RUNNING			AVERAGES			
Year	Team	Lg	G	AB	H	2B	3B	HR	(Hm	Rd)	TB	R	RBI	RC	TBB	IBB	SO	HBP	SH	SF	SB	CS	GDP	Avg	OBP	Slg	OPS
2001	StL	NL	161	590	194	47	4	37	(18	19)	360	112	130	132	69	6	93	9	1	7	1	3	21	.329	.403	.610	1.013
2002	StL	NL	157	590	185	40	2	34	(14	20)	331	118	127	121	72	13	69	9	0	4	2	4	20	.314	.394	.561	.955
2003	StL	NL	157	591	**212**	**51**	1	43	(21	**22)**	**394**	**137**	124	**160**	79	12	65	10	0	5	5	1	13	**.359**	.439	.667	1.106
2004	StL	NL	154	592	196	51	2	46	(18	**28)**	**389**	**133**	123	143	84	12	52	7	0	9	5	5	21	.331	.415	.657	1.072
2005	StL	NL	161	591	195	38	2	41	(23	18)	360	**129**	117	**139**	97	**27**	65	9	0	3	16	2	19	.330	.430	.609	1.039
2006	StL	NL	143	535	177	33	1	49	(24	25)	359	119	137	**146**	92	28	50	4	0	3	7	2	20	.331	.431	**.671**	**1.102**
2007	StL	NL	158	565	185	38	1	32	(12	20)	321	99	103	118	99	22	58	7	0	8	2	6	**27**	.327	.429	.568	.997
2008	StL	NL	148	524	187	44	0	37	(19	18)	**342**	100	116	**130**	104	**34**	54	5	0	8	7	3	16	.357	.462	**.653**	**1.114**
2009	StL	NL	160	568	186	45	1	**47**	(22	25)	**374**	**124**	135	**145**	115	**44**	64	9	0	8	16	4	23	.327	**.443**	.658	**1.101**
2010	StL	NL	159	587	183	39	1	**42**	(17	25)	350	**115**	118	131	103	**38**	76	4	0	6	14	4	23	.312	.414	.596	1.011
2011	StL	NL	147	579	173	29	0	37	(16	21)	313	105	99	100	61	15	58	4	0	7	9	1	**29**	.299	.366	.541	.906
2012	LAA	AL	154	607	173	50	0	30	(14	16)	313	85	105	100	52	16	76	5	0	6	8	1	19	.285	.343	.516	.859
2013	LAA	AL	99	391	101	19	0	17	(8	9)	171	49	64	54	40	8	55	5	0	7	1	1	18	.258	.330	.437	.767
2014	LAA	AL	159	633	172	37	1	28	(13	15)	295	89	105	86	48	11	71	5	0	9	5	1	**28**	.272	.324	.466	.790
2015	LAA	AL	157	602	147	22	0	40	(20	20)	289	85	95	82	50	10	72	6	0	3	5	3	15	.244	.307	.480	.787
2016	LAA	AL	152	593	159	19	0	31	(18	13)	271	71	119	91	49	6	75	2	0	6	4	0	24	.268	.323	.457	.780
	Postseason		77	279	90	18	1	19	(7	12)	167	55	54	68	49	20	40	5	0	1	1	2	6	.323	.431	.599	1.030
16 ML YEARS			2426	9138	2825	602	16	591	(277	314)	5232	1670	1817	1878	1214	302	1053	100	1	99	107	41	336	.309	.392	.573	.965

Matt Purke

Pitches: L **Bats:** L **Pos:** RP-12   **Ht:** 6'4" **Wt:** 215 **Born:** 7/17/1990 **Age:** 26

			HOW MUCH HE PITCHED							WHAT HE GAVE UP									THE RESULTS							
Year	Team	Lg	G	GS	CG	GF	IP	BFP	H	R	ER	HR	SH	SF	HB	TBB	IBB	SO	WP	Bk	W	L	Pct	Sh	Sv-Op	Hld	ERC	ERA
2013	2 Tms	Low	18	18	0	0	90.0	381	92	45	38	6	2	4	5	25	0	82	10	1	6	4	.600	0	0- -	-	3.74	3.80
2014	Hrsbrg	AA	8	8	0	0	31.1	150	42	32	28	5	2	2	1	18	0	22	2	1	1	6	.143	0	0- -	-	7.59	8.04
2015	2 Tms	Low	10	10	0	0	39.2	163	39	19	14	2	1	1	4	10	0	24	1	1	2	3	.400	0	0- -	-	3.24	3.18
2015	Hrsbrg	AA	10	5	0	0	24.1	110	33	21	17	2	2	0	1	7	0	19	1	0	1	3	.250	0	0- -	-	5.81	6.29
2016	Charllt	AAA	26	1	0	14	38.1	169	30	20	15	4	0	2	1	23	0	38	10	0	0	0	-	0	2- -	-	3.70	3.52
2016	CWS	AL	12	0	0	7	18.0	84	20	12	11	0	4	0	1	12	1	15	2	0	0	1	.000	0	0-0	-	4.87	5.50

Zach Putnam

Pitches: R **Bats:** R **Pos:** RP-25   **Ht:** 6'2" **Wt:** 220 **Born:** 7/3/1987 **Age:** 29

			HOW MUCH HE PITCHED							WHAT HE GAVE UP									THE RESULTS							
Year	Team	Lg	G	GS	CG	GF	IP	BFP	H	R	ER	HR	SH	SF	HB	TBB	IBB	SO	WP	Bk	W	L	Pct	Sh	Sv-Op	Hld	ERC	ERA
2011	Cle	AL	8	0	0	3	7.1	34	10	5	5	1	0	0	2	0	0	9	1	0	1	1	.500	0	0-1	0	5.82	6.14
2012	Col	NL	2	0	0	1	2.0	9	3	0	0	0	1	0	0	1	0	0	0	0	0	0	-	0	0-0	0	7.26	0.00
2013	ChC	NL	5	0	0	1	3.1	19	9	7	7	1	0	1	0	4	0	0	0	0	0	0	-	0	0-0	0	15.42	18.90
2014	CWS	AL	49	0	0	13	54.2	213	39	14	12	2	1	1	1	20	1	46	5	0	5	3	.625	0	6-7	16	2.21	1.98
2015	CWS	AL	49	0	0	16	48.2	212	42	24	22	7	4	4	4	24	5	64	5	0	3	3	.500	0	0-3	6	4.14	4.07
2016	CWS	AL	25	0	0	6	27.1	114	25	7	7	2	0	2	0	11	1	30	2	0	1	0	1.000	0	0-0	2	3.43	2.30
6 ML YEARS			138	0	0	39	143.1	601	128	57	53	13	6	7	7	56	7	153	13	0	10	7	.588	0	6-11	24	3.55	3.33

Kevin Quackenbush

Pitches: R Bats: R Pos: RP-60   Ht: 6'4" Wt: 235 Born: 11/28/1988 Age: 28

		HOW MUCH HE PITCHED						WHAT HE GAVE UP										THE RESULTS						
Year Team	Lg	G	GS	CG	GF	IP	BFP	H	R	ER	HR	SH	SF	HB	TBB	IBB	SO	WP	Bk	W	L	Pct	Sh	Sv-Op	Hld	ERC	ERA
2016 ElPaso*	AAA	9	0	0	7	13.0	53	12	3	3	0	0	1	0	2	0	16	1	0	1	0	1.000	0	2- -	-	2.10	2.08
2014 SD	NL	56	0	0	18	54.1	222	42	15	15	2	1	3	2	18	4	56	1	1	3	3	.500	0	6-7	10	2.25	2.48
2015 SD	NL	57	0	0	19	58.1	243	52	28	26	6	1	4	1	20	3	58	0	1	3	2	.600	0	0-1	2	3.28	4.01
2016 SD	NL	60	0	0	17	59.2	253	55	27	26	8	2	2	0	22	2	42	2	0	7	7	.500	0	2-3	9	3.67	3.92
3 ML YEARS		173	0	0	54	172.1	718	149	70	67	16	4	9	3	60	9	156	3	2	13	12	.520	0	8-11	21	3.08	3.50

Chad Qualls

Pitches: R Bats: R Pos: RP-44   Ht: 6'4" Wt: 235 Born: 8/17/1978 Age: 38

		HOW MUCH HE PITCHED						WHAT HE GAVE UP										THE RESULTS						
Year Team	Lg	G	GS	CG	GF	IP	BFP	H	R	ER	HR	SH	SF	HB	TBB	IBB	SO	WP	Bk	W	L	Pct	Sh	Sv-Op	Hld	ERC	ERA
2004 Hou	NL	25	0	0	4	33.0	141	34	13	13	3	0	1	4	8	1	24	0	0	4	0	1.000	0	1-2	9	4.02	3.55
2005 Hou	NL	77	0	0	19	79.2	329	73	33	29	7	4	3	6	23	2	60	1	0	6	4	.600	0	0-0	22	3.42	3.28
2006 Hou	NL	81	0	0	13	88.2	356	76	38	37	10	4	4	6	28	6	56	0	0	7	3	.700	0	0-6	23	3.36	3.76
2007 Hou	NL	79	0	0	16	82.2	345	84	29	28	10	6	2	3	25	5	78	2	0	6	5	.545	0	5-10	21	4.07	3.05
2008 Ari	NL	77	0	0	21	73.2	300	61	29	23	4	4	3	3	18	2	71	6	0	4	8	.333	0	9-17	22	2.40	2.81
2009 Ari	NL	51	0	0	44	52.0	217	53	23	21	5	1	0	2	7	2	45	2	0	2	2	.500	0	24-29	0	3.17	3.63
2010 2 Tms		70	0	0	29	59.0	281	85	56	48	7	4	4	2	21	4	49	4	0	3	4	.429	0	12-19	11	6.63	7.32
2011 SD	NL	77	0	0	20	74.1	306	73	30	29	7	7	1	0	20	5	43	4	0	6	8	.429	0	0-5	22	3.38	3.51
2012 3 Tms		60	0	0	15	52.1	231	63	34	31	7	2	2	0	14	4	27	3	0	2	1	.667	0	0-5	14	4.78	5.33
2013 Mia	NL	66	0	0	12	62.0	252	57	18	18	4	4	0	2	19	7	49	1	0	5	2	.714	0	0-2	15	3.09	2.61
2014 Hou	AL	58	0	0	41	51.1	213	54	22	19	5	2	0	2	5	2	43	1	0	1	5	.167	0	19-25	2	3.22	3.33
2015 Hou	AL	60	0	0	17	49.1	202	46	24	24	6	1	4	2	9	1	46	3	0	3	5	.375	0	4-6	10	3.13	4.38
2016 Col	NL	44	0	0	14	32.2	152	43	22	19	5	1	1	0	9	1	22	1	0	2	0	1.000	0	0-1	4	5.54	5.23
10 Ari	NL	43	0	0	28	38.0	190	61	41	35	5	4	2	1	15	4	34	3	0	1	4	.200	0	12-16	3	7.80	8.29
10 TB		27	0	0	1	21.0	91	24	15	13	2	0	2	1	6	0	15	1	0	2	0	1.000	0	0-3	8	4.64	5.57
12 Phi	NL	35	0	0	6	31.1	140	39	18	16	7	1	0	0	9	3	19	2	0	1	1	.500	0	0-5	12	5.74	4.60
12 NYY	AL	8	0	0	4	7.1	33	10	5	5	0	0	1	0	3	1	2	1	0	1	0	1.000	0	0-0	0	5.38	6.14
12 Pit	NL	17	0	0	5	13.2	58	14	11	10	0	1	1	0	2	0	6	0	0	-	0	-	0	0-0	2	2.48	6.59
Postseason		17	0	0	0	22.2	94	24	13	13	3	1	0	0	7	3	17	0	0	1	1	.500	0	0-2	2	4.20	5.16
13 ML YEARS		825	0	0	265	790.2	3325	802	371	339	80	40	25	32	206	42	613	28	0	51	47	.520	0	74-127	175	3.72	3.86

Juniel Querecuto

Bats: B Throws: R Pos: 2B-2;3B-1;SS-1   hoo-nee-EL keh-reh-KOO-toh   Ht: 5'9" Wt: 155 Born: 9/19/1992 Age: 24

							BATTING													RUNNING			AVERAGES			
Year Team	Lg	G	AB	H	2B	3B	HR	(Hm	Rd)	TB	R	RBI	RC	TBB	IBB	SO	HBP	SH	SF	SB	CS	GDP	Avg	OBP	Slg	OPS
2012 BG	A	106	386	96	17	2	0	(-	-)	117	53	32	40	38	0	79	1	9	2	13	6	10	.249	.316	.303	.619
2014 2 Tms	Low	115	447	121	13	3	2	(-	-)	146	54	45	46	27	0	63	1	6	1	5	6	7	.271	.313	.327	.640
2015 Charltt	A+	41	150	44	7	1	1	(-	-)	56	23	23	21	14	0	26	1	3	1	1	1	3	.293	.355	.373	.729
2015 Mont	AA	44	129	27	5	1	1	(-	-)	37	22	10	10	14	0	18	1	3	1	0	3	6	.209	.290	.287	.576
2016 Mont	AA	60	220	53	11	3	3	(-	-)	79	26	27	25	21	0	43	0	2	3	0	0	6	.241	.303	.359	.662
2016 Drham	AAA	36	120	29	8	0	0	(-	-)	37	11	11	11	6	1	31	2	1	0	3	1	4	.242	.289	.308	.597
2016 TB	AL	4	11	1	0	1	0	(0	0)	3	1	2	1	0	0	6	0	0	0	0	0	0	.091	.091	.273	.364

Roman Quinn

Bats: B Throws: R Pos: LF-12;RF-4;CF-3   Ht: 5'10" Wt: 170 Born: 5/14/1993 Age: 24

							BATTING													RUNNING			AVERAGES			
Year Team	Lg	G	AB	H	2B	3B	HR	(Hm	Rd)	TB	R	RBI	RC	TBB	IBB	SO	HBP	SH	SF	SB	CS	GDP	Avg	OBP	Slg	OPS
2012 Wmspt	A-	66	267	75	9	11	1	(-	-)	109	56	23	46	28	0	61	11	1	2	30	6	1	.281	.370	.408	.778
2013 Lakwd	A	67	260	62	7	3	5	(-	-)	90	37	21	34	27	0	64	6	4	1	32	9	3	.238	.323	.346	.669
2014 Clrwtr	A+	88	327	84	10	3	7	(-	-)	121	51	36	47	36	0	80	9	6	4	32	12	3	.257	.343	.370	.713
2015 Rdng	AA	58	232	71	6	6	4	(-	-)	101	44	15	38	18	0	42	0	7	0	29	10	1	.306	.356	.435	.791
2016 Rdng	AA	71	286	82	14	6	6	(-	-)	126	58	25	50	30	0	68	4	1	1	31	8	3	.287	.361	.441	.802
2016 Phi	NL	15	57	15	4	0	0	(0	0)	19	10	6	9	8	0	19	2	2	0	5	1	0	.263	.373	.333	.706

Jose Quintana

Pitches: L Bats: R Pos: SP-32   KIN-tahn-ah   Ht: 6'1" Wt: 220 Born: 1/24/1989 Age: 28

		HOW MUCH HE PITCHED						WHAT HE GAVE UP										THE RESULTS						
Year Team	Lg	G	GS	CG	GF	IP	BFP	H	R	ER	HR	SH	SF	HB	TBB	IBB	SO	WP	Bk	W	L	Pct	Sh	Sv-Op	Hld	ERC	ERA
2012 CWS	AL	25	22	0	2	136.1	568	142	62	57	14	5	1	3	42	4	81	10	2	6	6	.500	0	0-0	0	4.13	3.76
2013 CWS	AL	33	33	0	0	200.0	832	188	83	78	23	3	6	5	56	2	164	2	1	9	7	.563	0	0-0	0	3.47	3.51
2014 CWS	AL	32	32	0	0	200.1	830	197	87	74	10	4	6	2	52	3	178	7	0	9	11	.450	0	0-0	0	3.15	3.32
2015 CWS	AL	32	32	1	0	206.1	862	218	81	77	16	4	4	8	44	4	177	5	0	9	10	.474	1	0-0	0	3.67	3.36
2016 CWS	AL	32	32	0	0	208.0	837	192	76	74	22	2	2	4	50	1	181	10	1	13	12	.520	0	0-0	0	3.23	3.20
5 ML YEARS		154	151	1	2	951.0	3929	937	389	360	85	18	19	22	244	14	781	34	4	46	46	.500	1	0-0	0	3.48	3.41

Ryan Raburn

Bats: R **Throws:** R **Pos:** PH-56;LF-47;DH-6;1B-5;RF-2 RAY-burn **Ht:** 6'0" **Wt:** 185 **Born:** 4/17/1981 **Age:** 36

Year	Team	Lg	G	AB	H	2B	3B	HR	(Hm	Rd)	TB	R	RBI	RC	TBB	IBB	SO	HBP	SH	SF	SB	CS	GDP	Avg	OBP	Slg	OPS
2004	Det	AL	12	29	4	1	0	0	(0	0)	5	4	1	1	2	0	15	0	0	0	1	0	0	.138	.194	.172	.366
2007	Det	AL	49	138	42	12	2	4	(2	2)	70	28	27	21	8	1	33	0	1	1	3	0	7	.304	.340	.507	.847
2008	Det	AL	92	182	43	10	1	4	(2	2)	67	26	20	20	16	1	49	0	1	0	3	1	2	.236	.298	.368	.666
2009	Det	AL	113	261	76	11	2	16	(9	7)	139	44	45	42	26	2	60	2	1	1	5	4	6	.291	.359	.533	.891
2010	Det	AL	113	371	104	25	1	15	(5	10)	176	54	62	54	27	0	92	8	1	3	2	2	8	.280	.340	.474	.814
2011	Det	AL	121	387	99	22	2	14	(7	7)	167	53	49	48	21	2	114	3	4	3	1	1	4	.256	.297	.432	.729
2012	Det	AL	66	205	35	14	0	1	(0	1)	52	14	12	8	13	0	53	2	1	1	1	1	7	.171	.226	.254	.480
2013	Cle	AL	87	243	66	18	0	16	(8	8)	132	40	55	47	29	0	67	4	0	1	0	0	8	.272	.357	.543	.901
2014	Cle	AL	74	195	39	7	0	4	(0	4)	58	18	22	11	13	1	51	1	0	3	0	0	8	.200	.250	.297	.547
2015	Cle	AL	82	173	52	16	1	8	(2	6)	94	22	29	30	23	3	44	4	0	1	0	0	5	.301	.393	.543	.936
2016	Col	NL	113	223	49	10	2	9	(5	4)	90	30	30	24	28	0	80	2	0	3	0	0	6	.220	.309	.404	.712
	Postseason		10	31	9	2	0	2	(1	1)	17	4	5	4	5	0	9	0	0	0	0	0	3	.290	.389	.548	.937
	11 ML YEARS		922	2407	609	146	11	91	(40	51)	1050	333	352	306	206	10	658	26	9	17	16	9	57	.253	.317	.436	.753

Alexei Ramirez

Bats: R **Throws:** R **Pos:** SS-127;PH-14;RF-3;2B-1;DH-1 ah-lexx-AY **Ht:** 6'2" **Wt:** 180 **Born:** 9/22/1981 **Age:** 35

Year	Team	Lg	G	AB	H	2B	3B	HR	(Hm	Rd)	TB	R	RBI	RC	TBB	IBB	SO	HBP	SH	SF	SB	CS	GDP	Avg	OBP	Slg	OPS
2008	CWS	AL	136	480	139	22	2	21	(13	8)	228	65	77	78	18	3	61	3	4	4	13	9	14	.290	.317	.475	.792
2009	CWS	AL	148	542	150	14	1	15	(9	6)	211	71	68	74	49	3	66	1	6	8	14	5	15	.277	.333	.389	.723
2010	CWS	AL	156	585	165	29	2	18	(11	7)	252	83	70	72	27	2	82	2	7	5	13	8	12	.282	.313	.431	.744
2011	CWS	AL	158	614	165	31	2	15	(7	8)	245	81	70	74	51	1	84	6	8	5	7	5	19	.269	.328	.399	.727
2012	CWS	AL	158	593	157	24	4	9	(6	3)	216	59	73	70	16	2	77	4	4	4	20	7	15	.265	.287	.364	.651
2013	CWS	AL	158	637	181	39	2	6	(5	1)	242	68	48	67	26	2	68	3	4	4	30	9	17	.284	.313	.380	.693
2014	CWS	AL	158	622	170	35	2	15	(8	7)	254	82	74	79	24	0	81	6	1	4	21	4	21	.273	.305	.408	.713
2015	CWS	AL	154	583	145	33	0	10	(7	3)	208	54	62	50	31	2	68	1	1	6	17	7	18	.249	.285	.357	.642
2016	2 Tms		145	478	115	22	2	6	(3	3)	159	38	48	48	21	3	63	4	1	2	8	9	7	.241	.277	.333	.610
16	SD	NL	128	421	101	19	2	5	(3	2)	139	33	41	40	17	3	56	4	0	2	6	9	7	.240	.275	.330	.605
16	TB	AL	17	57	14	3	0	1	(0	1)	20	5	7	8	4	0	7	0	1	0	2	0	1	.246	.295	.351	.646
	Postseason		4	12	3	0	0	0	(0	0)	3	1	2	1	1	0	1	0	0	2	0	0	0	.250	.267	.250	.517
	9 ML YEARS		1371	5134	1387	249	17	115	(69	46)	2015	601	590	612	263	18	650	30	36	42	143	63	139	.270	.307	.392	.700

Erasmo Ramirez

Pitches: R **Bats:** R **Pos:** RP-63; SP-1 eh-RASS-moh **Ht:** 5'11" **Wt:** 200 **Born:** 5/2/1990 **Age:** 27

Year	Team	Lg	G	GS	CG	GF	IP	BFP	H	R	ER	HR	SH	SF	HB	TBB	IBB	SO	WP	Bk	W	L	Pct	Sh	Sv-Op	Hld	ERC	ERA
2012	Sea	AL	16	8	0	2	59.0	238	47	26	22	6	1	5	3	12	1	48	0	0	1	3	.250	0	0-0	0	2.42	3.36
2013	Sea	AL	14	13	0	0	72.1	321	79	44	40	12	0	3	3	26	0	57	0	0	5	3	.625	0	0-0	0	5.04	4.98
2014	Sea	AL	17	14	0	0	75.1	338	82	44	44	13	1	1	6	34	2	60	3	0	1	6	.143	0	0-0	0	5.68	5.26
2015	TB	AL	34	27	0	5	163.1	666	145	73	68	16	1	9	4	40	0	126	3	0	11	6	.647	0	0-0	0	3.11	3.75
2016	TB	AL	64	1	0	13	90.2	378	90	39	38	14	7	2	4	26	5	63	7	0	7	11	.389	0	2-6	15	4.13	3.77
	5 ML YEARS		145	63	0	20	460.2	1941	443	226	212	61	10	12	35	138	8	354	13	0	25	29	.463	0	2-6	15	3.90	4.14

Hanley Ramirez

Bats: R **Throws:** R **Pos:** 1B-133;DH-11;PH-3 **Ht:** 6'2" **Wt:** 235 **Born:** 12/23/1983 **Age:** 33

Year	Team	Lg	G	AB	H	2B	3B	HR	(Hm	Rd)	TB	R	RBI	RC	TBB	IBB	SO	HBP	SH	SF	SB	CS	GDP	Avg	OBP	Slg	OPS
2005	Bos	AL	2	2	0	0	0	0	(0	0)	0	0	0	0	0	0	2	0	0	0	0	0	0	.000	.000	.000	.000
2006	Fla	NL	158	633	185	46	11	17	(9	8)	304	119	59	101	56	0	128	4	5	2	51	15	7	.292	.353	.480	.833
2007	Fla	NL	154	639	212	48	6	29	(15	14)	359	125	81	115	52	3	95	7	4	4	51	14	10	.332	.386	.562	.948
2008	Fla	NL	153	589	177	34	4	33	(17	16)	318	**125**	67	116	92	9	122	8	0	4	35	12	5	.301	.400	.540	.940
2009	Fla	NL	151	576	197	42	1	24	(17	7)	313	101	106	122	61	14	101	9	1	5	27	8	9	**.342**	.410	.543	.954
2010	Fla	NL	142	543	163	28	2	21	(9	12)	258	92	76	90	64	12	93	7	0	5	32	10	14	.300	.378	.475	.853
2011	Fla	NL	92	338	82	16	0	10	(5	5)	128	55	45	46	44	3	66	2	1	0	20	10	6	.243	.333	.379	.712
2012	2 Tms	NL	157	604	155	29	4	24	(11	13)	264	79	92	81	54	4	132	6	0	3	21	7	17	.257	.322	.437	.759
2013	LAD	NL	86	304	105	25	2	20	(8	12)	194	62	57	69	27	3	52	3	0	2	10	2	5	.345	.402	.638	1.040
2014	LAD	NL	128	449	127	35	0	13	(8	5)	201	64	71	69	56	2	84	6	0	1	14	5	10	.283	.369	.448	.817
2015	Bos	AL	105	401	100	12	1	19	(8	11)	171	59	53	47	21	2	71	4	0	4	6	3	11	.249	.291	.426	.717
2016	Bos	AL	147	549	157	28	1	30	(19	11)	277	81	111	94	60	5	120	7	0	4	9	3	17	.286	.361	.505	.866
12	Mia	NL	93	353	87	18	2	14	(7	7)	151	49	48	42	37	1	72	3	0	2	14	4	11	.246	.322	.428	.749
12	LAD	NL	64	251	68	11	2	10	(4	6)	113	30	44	39	17	3	60	3	0	1	7	3	6	.271	.324	.450	.774
	Postseason		13	45	16	5	1	1	(0	1)	26	7	9	9	6	3	7	2	0	0	2	0	2	.356	.453	.578	1.031
	12 ML YEARS		1475	5627	1660	343	32	240	(129	111)	2787	962	818	950	587	57	1066	63	11	34	276	89	111	.295	.366	.495	.861

JC Ramirez

Pitches: R **Bats:** R **Pos:** RP-70 **Ht:** 6'4" **Wt:** 250 **Born:** 8/16/1988 **Age:** 28

Year	Team	Lg	G	GS	CG	GF	IP	BFP	H	R	ER	HR	SH	SF	HB	TBB	IBB	SO	WP	Bk	W	L	Pct	Sh	Sv-Op	Hld	ERC	ERA
2016	Lsvlle*	AAA	5	0	0	3	6.0	24	4	0	0	0	0	2	0	3	0	10	0	0	0	0			0--		2.13	0.00
2013	Phi	NL	18	0	0	2	24.0	116	30	22	20	6	1	4	0	15	1	16	0	0	0	1	.000	0	0-0	3	7.59	7.50
2015	2 Tms		20	0	0	6	23.2	106	25	14	14	3	0	1	1	11	3	16	1	0	1	2	.333	0	0-3	2	4.79	5.32
2016	2 Tms		70	0	0	16	78.2	335	77	41	38	12	2	7	4	22	2	59	7	0	3	4	.429	0	2-6	13	3.97	4.35
15	Ari	NL	12	0	0	4	15.1	63	15	7	7	1	0	0	0	4	2	11	1	0	1	1	.500	0	0-2	2	3.04	4.11

Year	Team	Lg	G	GS	CG	GF	IP	BFP	H	R	ER	HR	SH	SF	HB	TBB	IBB	SO	WP	Bk	W	L	Pct	Sh	Sv-Op	Hld	ERC	ERA
15	Sea	AL	8	0	0	2	8.1	43	10	7	7	2	0	0	1	7	1	5	0	0	0	1	.000	0	0-1	0	8.47	7.56
16	Cin	NL	27	0	0	7	32.1	139	35	24	23	7	1	3	0	9	2	28	3	0	1	3	.250	0	1-4	1	4.74	6.40
16	LAA	AL	43	0	0	9	46.1	196	42	17	15	5	1	4	4	13	0	31	4	0	2	1	.667	0	1-2	12	3.45	2.91
	3 ML YEARS		108	0	0	24	126.1	557	132	77	72	21	3	11	5	48	6	91	8	0	4	7	.364	0	2-9	18	4.77	5.13

Jose Ramirez

Pitches: R Bats: R Pos: RP-33   Ht: 6'1" Wt: 215 Born: 1/21/1990 Age: 27

Year	Team	Lg	G	GS	CG	GF	IP	BFP	H	R	ER	HR	SH	SF	HB	TBB	IBB	SO	WP	Bk	W	L	Pct	Sh	Sv-Op	Hld	ERC	ERA
2016	Gwnntt*	AAA	36	0	0	22	41.1	173	34	10	10	3	3	2	1	18	0	45	3	0	3	2	.600	0	6- -	-	3.17	2.18
2014	NYY	AL	8	0	0	5	10.0	49	11	6	6	2	0	0	2	7	0	10	0	0	0	2	.000	0	0-0	0	7.60	5.40
2015	2 Tms	AL	8	0	0	2	7.2	52	15	14	11	0	0	0	3	10	1	5	3	0	1	0	1.000	0	0-0	0	14.28	12.91
2016	Atl	NL	33	0	0	5	32.2	143	26	16	13	2	0	3	4	18	4	33	3	0	2	2	.500	0	0-0	3	3.51	3.58
15	NYY	AL	3	0	0	1	3.0	20	6	5	5	0	0	0	1	4	0	2	3	0	0	0	-	0	0-0	0	15.12	15.00
15	Sea	AL	5	0	0	1	4.2	32	9	9	6	0	0	0	2	6	1	3	0	0	1	0	1.000	0	0-0	0	13.76	11.57
	3 ML YEARS		49	0	0	12	50.1	244	52	36	30	4	0	3	9	35	5	48	6	0	3	4	.429	0	0-0	3	5.75	5.36

Jose Ramirez

Bats: B Throws: R Pos: 3B-117;LF-48;2B-9;SS-5;PR-3;PH-2   Ht: 5'9" Wt: 180 Born: 9/17/1992 Age: 24

Year	Team	Lg	G	AB	H	2B	3B	HR	(Hm	Rd)	TB	R	RBI	RC	TBB	IBB	SO	HBP	SH	SF	SB	CS	GDP	Avg	OBP	Slg	OPS
2013	Cle	AL	15	12	4	0	1	0	(0	0)	6	5	0	2	2	0	2	0	0	0	0	1	0	.333	.429	.500	.929
2014	Cle	AL	68	237	62	10	2	2	(1	1)	82	27	17	25	13	0	35	1	13	2	10	1	3	.262	.300	.346	.646
2015	Cle	AL	97	315	69	14	3	6	(1	5)	107	50	27	28	32	0	39	1	5	2	10	4	5	.219	.291	.340	.631
2016	Cle	AL	152	565	176	46	3	11	(8	3)	261	84	76	101	44	1	62	4	1	4	22	7	10	.312	.363	.462	.825
	4 ML YEARS		332	1129	311	70	9	19	(10	9)	456	166	120	156	91	1	138	6	19	8	42	13	18	.275	.331	.404	.735

Neil Ramirez

Pitches: R Bats: R Pos: RP-18   Ht: 6'4" Wt: 215 Born: 5/25/1989 Age: 28

Year	Team	Lg	G	GS	CG	GF	IP	BFP	H	R	ER	HR	SH	SF	HB	TBB	IBB	SO	WP	Bk	W	L	Pct	Sh	Sv-Op	Hld	ERC	ERA
2016	Roch*	AAA	16	0	0	6	20.1	82	14	7	7	2	1	2	1	7	0	27	0	0	0	0	-	0	0- -	-	2.41	3.10
2014	ChC	NL	50	0	0	10	43.2	177	29	11	7	2	0	0	2	17	0	53	3	1	3	3	.500	0	3-5	16	2.12	1.44
2015	ChC	NL	19	0	0	4	14.0	60	12	5	5	1	0	2	0	6	0	15	2	0	1	0	1.000	0	0-0	2	3.14	3.21
2016	3 Tms	NL	18	0	0	7	24.0	107	22	16	16	8	0	3	0	18	2	24	5	0	0	0	-	0	0-0	1	6.88	6.00
16	ChC	NL	8	0	0	4	7.2	35	5	4	4	1	0	2	0	8	2	10	3	0	0	0	-	0	0-0	1	4.41	4.70
16	Mil	NL	2	0	0	0	1.2	7	2	2	2	2	0	0	0	0	0	3	0	0	0	0	-	0	0-0	0	10.43	10.80
16	Min	AL	8	0	0	3	14.2	65	15	10	10	5	0	1	0	10	0	11	2	0	0	0	-	0	0-0	0	7.60	6.14
	3 ML YEARS		87	0	0	21	81.2	344	63	32	28	11	0	5	2	41	2	92	10	1	4	3	.571	0	3-5	19	3.52	3.09

Noe Ramirez

Pitches: R Bats: R Pos: RP-14   no-AY   Ht: 6'3" Wt: 205 Born: 12/22/1989 Age: 27

Year	Team	Lg	G	GS	CG	GF	IP	BFP	H	R	ER	HR	SH	SF	HB	TBB	IBB	SO	WP	Bk	W	L	Pct	Sh	Sv-Op	Hld	ERC	ERA
2012	Grnvlle	A	16	16	0	0	84.2	350	89	43	39	12	2	5	3	19	0	82	2	1	2	7	.222	0	0- -	-	4.19	4.15
2013	Salem	A+	21	0	0	5	47.0	182	41	13	11	0	2	1	4	9	0	44	3	0	2	1	.667	0	1- -	-	2.46	2.11
2013	Portlnd	AA	15	0	0	9	28.2	113	22	9	9	4	1	1	2	8	0	31	0	0	1	1	.500	0	5- -	-	2.99	2.83
2014	Portlnd	AA	42	0	0	31	67.1	268	56	17	16	0	4	1	3	16	1	56	6	1	2	1	.667	0	18- -	-	2.16	2.14
2015	Pwtckt	AAA	30	1	0	20	42.2	176	33	13	11	1	2	3	1	18	0	38	1	0	4	1	.800	0	3- -	-	2.55	2.32
2016	Pwtckt	AAA	30	0	0	21	43.2	177	39	11	9	3	1	0	1	11	0	54	4	0	2	3	.400	0	7- -	-	2.86	1.85
2015	Bos	AL	17	0	0	3	13.0	61	13	12	6	3	0	0	2	7	0	13	1	0	0	0	-	0	0-0	4	6.15	4.15
2016	Bos	AL	14	0	0	7	13.0	61	16	9	9	4	0	2	2	8	1	15	0	0	0	0	-	0	0-0	4	9.08	6.23
	2 ML YEARS		31	0	0	10	26.0	122	29	21	15	7	0	2	4	15	1	28	1	0	0	1	.000	0	0-0	4	7.55	5.19

A.J. Ramos

Pitches: R Bats: R Pos: RP-67   Ht: 5'10" Wt: 200 Born: 9/20/1986 Age: 30

Year	Team	Lg	G	GS	CG	GF	IP	BFP	H	R	ER	HR	SH	SF	HB	TBB	IBB	SO	WP	Bk	W	L	Pct	Sh	Sv-Op	Hld	ERC	ERA
2012	Mia	NL	11	0	0	4	9.1	40	8	4	4	2	0	0	1	4	0	13	0	0	0	0	-	0	0-1	1	4.65	3.86
2013	Mia	NL	68	0	0	18	80.0	338	58	32	28	4	1	3	2	43	3	86	1	0	3	4	.429	0	0-4	11	2.80	3.15
2014	Mia	NL	68	0	0	12	64.0	270	36	16	15	1	3	1	3	43	7	73	7	0	7	0	1.000	0	0-3	20	2.19	2.11
2015	Mia	NL	71	0	0	51	70.1	277	45	18	18	6	1	2	3	26	0	87	2	0	2	4	.333	0	32-38	4	2.21	2.30
2016	Mia	NL	67	0	0	52	64.0	278	52	21	20	1	2	4	4	35	3	73	6	0	1	4	.200	0	40-43	2	3.15	2.81
	5 ML YEARS		285	0	0	137	287.2	1203	199	91	85	14	7	10	13	151	13	332	16	0	13	12	.520	0	72-89	38	2.66	2.66

Cesar Ramos

Pitches: L Bats: L Pos: RP-12; SP-4   Ht: 6'2" Wt: 200 Born: 6/22/1984 Age: 33

Year	Team	Lg	G	GS	CG	GF	IP	BFP	H	R	ER	HR	SH	SF	HB	TBB	IBB	SO	WP	Bk	W	L	Pct	Sh	Sv-Op	Hld	ERC	ERA
2016	Toledo*	AAA	8	3	0	0	21.0	96	29	14	14	2	0	1	2	6	0	19	4	0	2	3	.400	0	0- -	-	6.34	6.00
2009	SD	NL	5	2	0	0	14.2	62	19	5	5	0	0	0	0	4	0	12	0	0	0	1	.000	0	0-0	0	4.78	3.07
2010	SD	NL	14	0	0	4	8.1	47	18	11	11	1	0	0	0	4	0	9	1	1	0	1	.000	0	0-0	2	11.97	11.88
2011	TB	AL	59	0	0	9	43.2	192	36	22	19	4	1	2	3	25	8	31	1	0	0	1	.000	0	0-2	3	3.64	3.92

Year	Team	Lg	G	GS	CG	GF	IP	BFP	H	R	ER	HR	SH	SF	HB	TBB	IBB	SO	WP	Bk	W	L	Pct	Sh	Sv-Op	Hld	ERC	ERA
								HOW MUCH HE PITCHED				**WHAT HE GAVE UP**										**THE RESULTS**						
2012	TB	AL	17	1	0	9	30.0	120	19	7	7	2	0	0	2	10	0	29	0	0	1	0	1.000	0	0-0	0	1.98	2.10
2013	TB	AL	48	0	0	25	67.1	288	66	31	31	6	2	4	2	22	6	53	3	0	2	2	.500	0	1-1	1	3.55	4.14
2014	TB	AL	43	7	0	14	82.2	360	73	39	34	8	3	3	1	39	7	66	4	0	2	6	.250	0	0-0	2	3.53	3.70
2015	LAA	AL	65	0	0	21	52.1	221	55	17	16	2	3	3	3	15	0	43	5	0	2	1	.667	0	0-2	5	3.78	2.75
2016	Tex	AL	16	4	0	2	47.2	212	60	34	32	12	0	3	1	20	1	27	0	0	3	3	.500	0	1-1	0	7.20	6.04
8 ML YEARS			267	14	0	84	346.2	1502	346	166	155	35	9	15	12	139	22	268	14	1	10	15	.400	0	2-6	13	4.12	4.02

Edubray Ramos

Pitches: R Bats: R Pos: RP-42　　　eh-DOO-bray　　　**Ht:** 6'0" **Wt:** 160 **Born:** 12/19/1992 **Age:** 24

Year	Team	Lg	G	GS	CG	GF	IP	BFP	H	R	ER	HR	SH	SF	HB	TBB	IBB	SO	WP	Bk	W	L	Pct	Sh	Sv-Op	Hld	ERC	ERA
								HOW MUCH HE PITCHED				**WHAT HE GAVE UP**										**THE RESULTS**						
2014	2 Tms	Low	19	1	0	12	32.0	124	19	3	3	0	1	0	2	7	1	37	3	0	1	0	1.000	0	6--	-	1.22	0.84
2015	Clrwtr	A+	29	0	0	16	49.1	181	31	9	8	2	0	2	1	6	0	47	4	2	3	4	.429	0	8--	-	1.25	1.46
2015	Rdng	AA	18	0	0	7	20.1	89	17	9	8	0	2	2	2	10	2	18	0	1	1	2	.333	0	0--	-	2.99	3.54
2016	Rdng	AA	11	0	0	10	15.0	56	9	5	4	1	0	1	1	1	0	15	1	0	1	1	.500	0	7--	-	1.20	2.40
2016	LV	AAA	15	0	0	8	23.2	90	15	1	1	0	0	0	1	3	0	26	1	0	1	0	1.000	0	3--	-	1.14	0.38
2016	Phi	NL	42	0	0	6	40.0	160	36	18	17	5	1	0	0	11	1	40	1	1	1	3	.250	0	0-2	15	3.28	3.83

Wilson Ramos

Bats: R Throws: R Pos: C-128;PH-7　　　　**Ht:** 6'1" **Wt:** 255 **Born:** 8/10/1987 **Age:** 29

Year	Team	Lg	G	AB	H	2B	3B	HR	(Hm	Rd)	TB	R	RBI	RC	TBB	IBB	SO	HBP	SH	SF	SB	CS	GDP	Avg	OBP	Slg	OPS
								BATTING													**RUNNING**			**AVERAGES**			
2010	2 Tms		22	79	22	7	0	1	(1	0)	32	5	5	10	2	0	12	1	0	0	0	0	2	.278	.305	.405	.710
2011	Was	NL	113	389	104	22	1	15	(8	7)	173	48	52	43	38	8	76	2	4	2	0	2	19	.267	.334	.445	.779
2012	Was	NL	25	83	22	2	0	3	(1	2)	33	11	10	12	12	2	19	0	0	1	0	0	1	.265	.354	.398	.752
2013	Was	NL	78	287	78	9	0	16	(6	10)	135	29	59	40	15	1	42	0	0	1	0	1	12	.272	.307	.470	.777
2014	Was	NL	88	341	91	12	0	11	(3	8)	136	32	47	35	17	2	57	0	0	3	0	0	17	.267	.299	.399	.698
2015	Was	NL	128	475	109	16	0	15	(10	5)	170	41	68	39	21	2	101	0	0	8	0	0	16	.229	.258	.358	.616
2016	Was	NL	131	482	148	25	0	22	(12	10)	239	58	80	78	35	2	79	2	0	4	0	0	17	.307	.354	.496	.850
10	Min	AL	7	27	8	3	0	0	(0	0)	11	2	1	3	0	0	3	1	0	0	0	0	1	.296	.321	.407	.729
10	Was	NL	15	52	14	4	0	1	(1	0)	21	3	4	7	2	0	9	0	0	0	0	0	1	.269	.296	.404	.700
Postseason			4	17	2	0	0	0	(0	0)	2	1	0	0	1	0	6	0	1	0	0	0	1	.118	.167	.118	.284
7 ML YEARS			585	2136	574	93	1	83	(41	42)	918	224	321	257	140	17	386	5	4	19	0	3	84	.269	.313	.430	.742

Anthony Ranaudo

Pitches: R Bats: R Pos: SP-5; RP-4　　　ran-AW-doh　　　**Ht:** 6'7" **Wt:** 240 **Born:** 9/9/1989 **Age:** 27

Year	Team	Lg	G	GS	CG	GF	IP	BFP	H	R	ER	HR	SH	SF	HB	TBB	IBB	SO	WP	Bk	W	L	Pct	Sh	Sv-Op	Hld	ERC	ERA
								HOW MUCH HE PITCHED				**WHAT HE GAVE UP**										**THE RESULTS**						
2016	Charltt*	AAA	16	16	2	0	96.2	384	92	38	36	15	3	1	3	11	0	65	2	0	6	5	.545	0	0--	-	3.22	3.35
2014	Bos	AL	7	7	0	0	39.1	170	39	21	21	10	0	4	0	16	0	15	2	0	4	3	.571	0	0-0	0	5.14	4.81
2015	Tex	AL	4	2	0	0	15.1	73	18	13	13	2	2	1	1	8	0	11	0	0	0	1	.000	0	0-0	0	5.96	7.63
2016	2 Tms	AL	9	5	0	2	31.1	151	36	33	33	10	1	2	0	20	0	18	1	0	1	1	.500	0	0-0	0	7.52	9.48
16	Tex	AL	2	0	0	0	3.2	21	2	7	7	1	1	0	0	8	0	2	0	0	1	0	1.000	0	0-0	0	10.14	17.18
16	CWS	AL	7	5	0	2	27.2	130	34	26	26	9	0	2	0	12	0	16	1	0	0	1	.000	0	0-0	0	7.12	8.46
3 ML YEARS			20	14	0	2	86.0	394	93	67	67	22	3	7	1	44	0	44	3	0	5	5	.500	0	0-0	0	6.14	7.01

Colby Rasmus

Bats: L Throws: L Pos: LF-87;CF-21;RF-11;PH-9;DH-2　　　**Ht:** 6'2" **Wt:** 195 **Born:** 8/11/1986 **Age:** 30

Year	Team	Lg	G	AB	H	2B	3B	HR	(Hm	Rd)	TB	R	RBI	RC	TBB	IBB	SO	HBP	SH	SF	SB	CS	GDP	Avg	OBP	Slg	OPS
								BATTING													**RUNNING**			**AVERAGES**			
2009	StL	NL	147	474	119	22	2	16	(7	9)	193	72	52	60	36	3	95	3	5	2	3	1	5	.251	.307	.407	.714
2010	StL	NL	144	464	128	28	3	23	(11	12)	231	85	66	76	63	9	148	1	2	4	12	8	5	.276	.361	.498	.859
2011	2 Tms		129	471	106	24	6	14	(4	10)	184	75	53	50	50	2	116	0	2	3	5	2	10	.225	.298	.391	.688
2012	Tor	AL	151	565	126	21	5	23	(8	15)	226	75	75	74	47	5	149	7	2	4	4	3	7	.223	.289	.400	.689
2013	Tor	AL	118	417	115	26	1	22	(14	8)	209	57	66	76	37	0	135	3	0	1	0	1	4	.276	.338	.501	.840
2014	Tor	AL	104	346	78	21	1	18	(7	11)	155	45	40	38	29	2	124	1	0	0	4	0	1	.225	.287	.448	.735
2015	Hou	AL	137	432	103	23	2	25	(12	13)	205	67	61	67	47	0	154	2	1	3	2	1	6	.238	.314	.475	.789
2016	Hou	AL	107	369	76	10	0	15	(6	9)	131	38	54	46	43	0	121	0	1	4	4	1	5	.206	.286	.355	.641
11	StL	NL	94	338	83	14	6	11	(4	7)	142	61	40	43	45	2	77	0	1	2	5	2	8	.246	.332	.420	.753
11	Tor	AL	35	133	23	10	0	3	(0	3)	42	14	13	7	5	0	39	0	1	1	0	0	2	.173	.201	.316	.517
Postseason			9	26	11	4	0	4	(1	3)	27	5	7	8	9	2	8	0	0	0	1	0	1	.423	.571	1.038	1.610
8 ML YEARS			1037	3538	851	175	20	156	(69	87)	1534	514	467	487	352	21	1042	17	13	21	34	17	43	.241	.311	.434	.744

Cory Rasmus

Pitches: R Bats: R Pos: RP-18; SP-1　　　　**Ht:** 6'0" **Wt:** 200 **Born:** 11/6/1987 **Age:** 29

Year	Team	Lg	G	GS	CG	GF	IP	BFP	H	R	ER	HR	SH	SF	HB	TBB	IBB	SO	WP	Bk	W	L	Pct	Sh	Sv-Op	Hld	ERC	ERA
								HOW MUCH HE PITCHED				**WHAT HE GAVE UP**										**THE RESULTS**						
2013	2 Tms		19	0	0	6	21.2	103	24	15	13	6	0	1	0	13	2	20	0	1	1	1	.500	0	0-1	2	6.55	5.40
2014	LAA	AL	30	6	0	7	56.0	225	42	17	16	5	0	2	0	17	1	57	0	0	3	2	.600	0	0-0	0	2.31	2.57
2015	LAA	AL	16	1	0	5	20.2	88	15	12	12	3	1	0	1	11	2	27	0	0	0	0	-	0	0-1	1	3.41	5.84
2016	LAA	AL	19	1	0	4	24.2	114	25	16	16	4	0	1	1	16	1	17	2	2	0	2	.000	0	0-1	0	5.71	5.84
13	Atl	NL	3	0	0	2	6.2	31	8	6	6	4	0	0	0	3	0	6	0	0	0	0	-	0	0-0	0	9.21	8.10
13	LAA	AL	16	0	0	4	15.0	72	16	9	7	2	0	1	0	10	2	14	0	1	1	1	.500	0	0-1	2	5.34	4.20
Postseason			1	0	0	1	2.2	9	0	0	0	0	0	0	0	1	0	2	0	0	0	0	-	0	0-0	0	0.16	0.00
4 ML YEARS			84	8	0	22	123.0	530	106	60	57	18	1	4	2	57	6	121	2	3	4	5	.444	0	0-3	3	3.81	4.17

Josh Ravin

Pitches: R **Bats:** R **Pos:** RP-10   **Ht:** 6'4" **Wt:** 215 **Born:** 1/21/1988 **Age:** 29

Year	Team	Lg	G	GS	CG	GF	IP	BFP	H	R	ER	HR	SH	SF	HB	TBB	IBB	SO	WP	Bk	W	L	Pct	Sh	Sv-Op	Hld	ERC	ERA
2012	Pnscla	AA	20	0	0	3	24.0	113	23	16	13	3	1	1	1	20	0	22	5	0	1	3	.250	0	0- -	-	5.98	4.88
2013	Pnscla	AA	38	0	0	10	40.1	187	44	26	25	4	3	0	3	27	1	39	10	0	1	3	.250	0	0- -	-	6.08	5.58
2013	Lsvlle	AAA	10	0	0	2	10.2	53	12	9	8	1	0	0	0	11	0	9	1	0	0	0	-	0	0- -	-	7.50	6.75
2014	Chatt	AA	12	0	0	9	14.2	63	12	7	5	1	0	1	0	7	0	17	0	0	1	1	.500	0	4- -	-	3.10	3.07
2014	Albq	AAA	11	0	0	6	10.2	50	12	6	5	1	0	0	0	7	0	8	0	0	1	0	1.000	0	2- -	-	5.78	4.22
2015	OkCity	AAA	22	0	0	10	28.0	124	23	12	12	2	1	2	1	16	0	38	4	0	3	1	.750	0	3- -	-	3.60	3.86
2016	2 Tms	Low	5	3	0	0	6.0	23	3	3	2	1	0	0	0	0	0	12	1	0	0	0	-	0	0- -	-	0.85	3.00
2015	LAD	NL	9	0	0	4	9.1	47	13	7	7	3	0	0	1	4	0	12	1	0	2	1	.667	0	0-0	0	8.54	6.75
2016	LAD	NL	10	0	0	4	9.2	35	2	1	1	1	0	0	0	4	0	13	2	0	0	0	-	0	0-0	0	0.83	0.93
	2 ML YEARS		19	0	0	8	19.0	82	15	8	8	4	0	0	1	8	0	25	3	0	2	1	.667	0	0-0	0	3.82	3.79

Robbie Ray

Pitches: L **Bats:** L **Pos:** SP-32   **Ht:** 6'2" **Wt:** 195 **Born:** 10/1/1991 **Age:** 25

Year	Team	Lg	G	GS	CG	GF	IP	BFP	H	R	ER	HR	SH	SF	HB	TBB	IBB	SO	WP	Bk	W	L	Pct	Sh	Sv-Op	Hld	ERC	ERA
2014	Det	AL	9	6	0	1	28.2	136	43	26	26	5	1	1	0	11	0	19	2	1	1	4	.200	0	0-0	1	7.72	8.16
2015	Ari	NL	23	23	0	0	127.2	545	121	56	50	9	7	6	8	49	3	119	2	0	5	12	.294	0	0-0	0	3.75	3.52
2016	Ari	NL	32	32	0	0	174.1	776	185	105	95	24	3	2	6	71	4	218	8	0	8	15	.348	0	0-0	0	4.78	4.90
	3 ML YEARS		64	61	0	1	330.2	1457	349	187	171	38	11	9	14	131	7	356	12	1	14	31	.311	0	0-0	1	4.61	4.65

Colin Rea

Pitches: R **Bats:** R **Pos:** SP-19; RP-1   ray   **Ht:** 6'5" **Wt:** 225 **Born:** 7/1/1990 **Age:** 26

Year	Team	Lg	G	GS	CG	GF	IP	BFP	H	R	ER	HR	SH	SF	HB	TBB	IBB	SO	WP	Bk	W	L	Pct	Sh	Sv-Op	Hld	ERC	ERA
2012	FtWyn	A	31	19	0	4	103.0	460	106	61	47	9	6	3	8	47	0	80	8	0	5	10	.333	0	0- -	-	4.68	4.11
2013	2 Tms	Low	31	12	0	5	86.0	389	77	45	39	4	3	6	5	61	3	83	10	2	2	6	.250	0	0- -	-	4.48	4.08
2014	Lk Els	A+	28	28	0	0	139.0	597	151	65	60	11	2	0	7	37	0	118	4	2	11	9	.550	0	0- -	-	4.10	3.88
2015	SnAnt	AA	12	12	0	0	75.0	283	50	15	9	1	1	0	1	11	0	60	1	0	3	2	.600	0	0- -	-	1.28	1.08
2015	ElPaso	AAA	6	6	0	0	26.2	120	29	14	12	2	0	0	2	12	1	20	0	0	2	2	.500	0	0- -	-	4.83	4.05
2015	SD	NL	6	6	0	0	31.2	133	29	16	15	2	1	2	1	11	0	26	0	0	2	2	.500	0	0-0	0	3.29	4.26
2016	2 Tms	NL	20	19	0	0	102.2	454	102	63	55	12	4	2	8	44	4	80	0	1	5	5	.500	0	0-0	0	4.50	4.82
16	SD	NL	19	18	0	0	99.1	443	101	63	55	12	3	2	8	44	4	76	0	1	5	5	.500	0	0-0	0	4.73	4.98
16	Mia	NL	1	1	0	0	3.1	11	1	0	0	0	1	0	0	0	0	4	0	0	0	0	-	0	0-0	0	0.21	0.00
	2 ML YEARS		26	25	0	0	134.1	587	131	79	70	14	5	4	9	55	4	106	0	1	7	7	.500	0	0-0	0	4.21	4.69

J.T. Realmuto

Bats: R **Throws:** R **Pos:** C-129;PH-10;DH-2;PR-1   ray-al-MOO-toh   **Ht:** 6'1" **Wt:** 210 **Born:** 3/18/1991 **Age:** 26

Year	Team	Lg	G	AB	H	2B	3B	HR	(Hm	Rd)	TB	R	RBI	RC	TBB	IBB	SO	HBP	SH	SF	SB	CS	GDP	Avg	OBP	Slg	OPS
2014	Mia	NL	11	29	7	1	1	0	(0	0)	10	4	9	4	1	0	8	0	0	0	0	0	2	.241	.267	.345	.611
2015	Mia	NL	126	441	114	21	7	10	(6	4)	179	49	47	44	19	2	70	2	1	4	8	4	11	.259	.290	.406	.696
2016	Mia	NL	137	509	154	31	0	11	(3	8)	218	60	48	63	28	1	100	5	0	3	12	4	12	.303	.343	.428	.771
	3 ML YEARS		274	979	275	53	8	21	(9	12)	407	113	104	111	48	3	178	7	1	7	20	8	25	.281	.317	.416	.733

Anthony Recker

Bats: R **Throws:** R **Pos:** C-28;PH-6   **Ht:** 6'2" **Wt:** 240 **Born:** 8/29/1983 **Age:** 33

Year	Team	Lg	G	AB	H	2B	3B	HR	(Hm	Rd)	TB	R	RBI	RC	TBB	IBB	SO	HBP	SH	SF	SB	CS	GDP	Avg	OBP	Slg	OPS
2016	Clmbs*	AAA	19	61	15	5	0	2	(-	-)	26	10	10	11	14	0	17	1	0	0	1	0	1	.246	.395	.426	.821
2016	Gwnntt*	AAA	40	136	33	6	0	6	(-	-)	57	20	18	19	16	0	45	1	0	1	0	0	4	.243	.325	.419	.744
2011	Oak	AL	5	17	3	1	0	0	(0	0)	4	3	0	0	4	0	7	0	0	0	0	0	0	.176	.333	.235	.569
2012	2 Tms		22	49	7	2	0	1	(0	1)	12	4	4	0	6	0	15	2	1	0	0	0	1	.143	.263	.245	.508
2013	NYM	NL	50	135	29	7	0	6	(4	2)	54	17	19	13	13	1	49	0	1	2	0	1	1	.215	.280	.400	.680
2014	NYM	NL	58	174	35	9	0	7	(3	4)	65	18	27	17	10	0	64	1	2	1	1	1	2	.201	.246	.374	.620
2015	NYM	NL	32	80	10	1	0	2	(0	2)	17	6	5	3	11	2	35	1	0	1	0	1	1	.125	.239	.213	.452
2016	Atl	NL	33	90	25	8	0	2	(0	2)	39	6	15	19	16	1	22	2	3	1	1	0	0	.278	.394	.433	.828
12	Oak	AL	13	31	4	1	0	0	(0	0)	5	3	0	0	4	0	13	1	1	0	0	0	0	.129	.250	.161	.411
12	ChC	NL	9	18	3	1	0	1	(0	1)	7	1	4	0	2	0	2	1	0	0	0	0	1	.167	.286	.389	.675
	6 ML YEARS		200	545	109	28	0	18	(7	11)	191	54	70	52	60	4	192	6	7	5	3	2	5	.200	.284	.350	.635

Josh Reddick

Bats: L **Throws:** R **Pos:** RF-110;PH-9;DH-2   **Ht:** 6'2" **Wt:** 195 **Born:** 2/19/1987 **Age:** 30

Year	Team	Lg	G	AB	H	2B	3B	HR	(Hm	Rd)	TB	R	RBI	RC	TBB	IBB	SO	HBP	SH	SF	SB	CS	GDP	Avg	OBP	Slg	OPS
2009	Bos	AL	27	59	10	4	0	2	(0	2)	20	5	4	4	2	0	17	1	0	0	0	0	0	.169	.210	.339	.549
2010	Bos	AL	29	62	12	3	1	0	(1	0)	20	5	5	1	1	0	15	0	0	0	1	0	1	.194	.206	.323	.529
2011	Bos	AL	87	254	71	18	3	7	(2	5)	116	41	28	33	19	1	50	1	0	4	1	2	1	.280	.327	.457	.784
2012	Oak	AL	156	611	148	29	5	32	(18	14)	283	85	85	73	55	8	151	2	1	4	11	1	15	.242	.305	.463	.768
2013	Oak	AL	114	385	87	19	2	12	(2	10)	146	54	56	53	46	1	86	2	1	7	9	2	4	.226	.307	.379	.686
2014	Oak	AL	109	363	96	16	7	12	(5	7)	162	53	54	54	28	0	63	1	0	3	1	1	3	.264	.316	.446	.763
2015	Oak	AL	149	526	143	25	4	20	(7	13)	236	67	77	83	49	1	65	0	1	2	10	2	7	.272	.333	.449	.781
2016	2 Tms		115	398	112	17	1	10	(5	5)	161	53	37	54	39	5	56	0	0	1	8	3	8	.281	.345	.405	.749

Year Team	Lg	G	AB	H	2B	3B	HR	(Hm Rd)	TB	R	RBI	RC	TBB	IBB	SO	HBP	SH	SF	SB	CS	GDP	Avg	OBP	Slg	OPS
16 Oak	AL	68	243	72	11	1	8	(3 5)	109	33	28	42	28	5	34	0	0	1	5	0	7	.296	.368	.449	.816
16 LAD	NL	47	155	40	6	0	2	(2 0)	52	20	9	12	11	0	22	0	0	0	3	3	1	.258	.307	.335	.643
Postseason		11	38	8	1	0	2	(0 2)	15	5	2	2	5	1	15	0	0	0	0	0	1	.211	.302	.395	.697
8 ML YEARS		786	2658	679	131	23	96	(40 56)	1144	363	346	355	239	16	503	7	3	21	41	11	39	.255	.316	.430	.747

A.J. Reed

Bats: L Throws: L Pos: 1B-35;DH-9;PH-8   **Ht: 6'4" Wt: 275 Born: 5/10/1993 Age: 24**

Year Team	Lg	G	AB	H	2B	3B	HR	(Hm Rd)	TB	R	RBI	RC	TBB	IBB	SO	HBP	SH	SF	SB	CS	GDP	Avg	OBP	Slg	OPS
2014 2 Tms	Low	68	249	72	20	1	12	(- -)	130	43	54	49	30	1	54	5	0	1	2	0	4	.289	.375	.522	.898
2015 Lancst	A+	82	318	110	16	4	23	(- -)	203	75	81	88	59	1	73	4	0	4	0	0	9	.346	.449	.638	1.088
2015 CpChr	AA	53	205	68	14	1	11	(- -)	117	38	46	47	27	2	49	1	0	4	0	0	5	.332	.405	.571	.976
2016 Fresno	AAA	70	261	76	22	1	15	(- -)	145	42	50	53	32	1	67	1	0	2	0	0	8	.291	.368	.556	.924
2016 Hou	AL	45	122	20	3	0	3	(2 1)	32	11	8	7	18	0	48	0	0	1	0	0	1	.164	.270	.262	.532

Addison Reed

Pitches: R Bats: L Pos: RP-80   **Ht: 6'4" Wt: 230 Born: 12/27/1988 Age: 28**

Year Team	Lg	G	GS	CG	GF	IP	BFP	H	R	ER	HR	SH	SF	HB	TBB	IBB	SO	WP	Bk	W	L	Pct	Sh	Sv-Op	Hld	ERC	ERA
2011 CWS	AL	6	0	0	2	7.1	33	10	3	3	1	0	0	0	1	0	12	0	0	0	0	-	0	0-0	0	5.24	3.68
2012 CWS	AL	62	0	0	44	55.0	238	57	30	29	6	0	4	2	18	3	54	0	1	3	2	.600	0	29-33	4	4.09	4.75
2013 CWS	AL	68	0	0	59	71.1	295	56	31	30	6	3	6	2	23	2	72	2	0	5	4	.556	0	40-48	0	2.56	3.79
2014 Ari	NL	62	0	0	55	59.1	252	57	31	28	11	1	1	1	15	2	69	3	0	1	7	.125	0	32-38	0	3.76	4.25
2015 2 Tms	NL	55	0	0	14	56.0	241	58	21	21	3	1	0	0	19	6	51	2	0	3	3	.500	0	4-8	14	3.52	3.38
2016 NYM	NL	80	0	0	13	77.2	304	60	18	17	4	3	2	0	13	4	91	4	0	4	2	.667	0	1-5	40	1.72	1.97
15 Ari	NL	38	0	0	11	40.2	181	47	19	19	2	1	0	0	14	5	34	2	0	2	2	.500	0	3-5	8	4.10	4.20
15 NYM	NL	17	0	0	3	15.1	60	11	2	2	1	0	0	0	5	1	17	0	0	1	1	.500	0	1-3	6	2.10	1.17
Postseason		9	0	0	0	7.0	29	6	6	5	0	0	1	0	1	1	3	0	0	0	1	.000	0	0-0	2	1.56	6.43
6 ML YEARS		333	0	0	187	326.2	1363	298	134	128	31	8	13	5	89	17	349	11	1	16	18	.471	0	106-132	58	3.02	3.53

Cody Reed

Pitches: L Bats: L Pos: SP-10   **Ht: 6'5" Wt: 225 Born: 4/15/1993 Age: 24**

Year Team	Lg	G	GS	CG	GF	IP	BFP	H	R	ER	HR	SH	SF	HB	TBB	IBB	SO	WP	Bk	W	L	Pct	Sh	Sv-Op	Hld	ERC	ERA
2013 Idaho	R+	15	6	0	1	29.2	145	31	24	20	0	2	1	4	23	0	25	4	0	0	1	.000	0	0- -	-	5.48	6.07
2014 Lxngtn	A	19	19	0	0	84.0	387	105	66	51	5	8	3	3	36	0	58	11	1	3	9	.250	0	0- -	-	5.47	5.46
2015 Wilmg	A+	13	10	1	2	67.1	278	62	19	16	3	1	3	1	18	0	65	3	0	5	5	.500	0	1- -	-	2.84	2.14
2015 NWArk	AA	5	5	0	0	28.2	120	26	16	11	3	0	2	1	8	0	19	1	0	2	2	.500	0	0- -	-	3.23	3.45
2015 Pnscla	AA	8	8	0	0	49.2	201	39	14	12	1	5	1	2	16	0	60	1	1	6	2	.750	0	0- -	-	2.32	2.17
2016 Lsvlle	AAA	13	13	0	0	73.0	301	71	28	25	6	3	1	3	20	0	65	1	0	6	4	.600	0	0- -	-	3.55	3.08
2016 Cin	NL	10	10	0	0	47.2	230	67	47	39	12	1	1	4	19	2	43	2	2	0	7	.000	0	0-0	0	8.00	7.36

Michael Reed

Bats: R Throws: R Pos: CF-5;LF-2;PH-1   **Ht: 6'0" Wt: 215 Born: 11/18/1992 Age: 24**

Year Team	Lg	G	AB	H	2B	3B	HR	(Hm Rd)	TB	R	RBI	RC	TBB	IBB	SO	HBP	SH	SF	SB	CS	GDP	Avg	OBP	Slg	OPS
2012 2 Tms	Low	59	211	53	5	1	1	(- -)	63	34	25	27	32	0	66	1	4	1	14	1	1	.251	.351	.299	.650
2013 Wisc	A	118	455	130	23	13	1	(- -)	182	68	40	77	71	3	108	4	7	2	26	10	15	.286	.385	.400	.785
2014 BrvdCt	A+	110	365	93	20	5	5	(- -)	138	50	47	65	78	0	79	9	2	3	33	13	8	.255	.396	.378	.774
2015 Biloxi	AA	93	313	87	20	5	5	(- -)	132	43	49	57	53	1	80	3	0	8	25	7	6	.278	.379	.422	.801
2015 ColSpr	AAA	38	126	31	13	2	0	(- -)	48	19	21	18	20	0	31	1	0	1	1	0	3	.246	.351	.381	.732
2016 ColSpr	AAA	121	411	102	20	2	8	(- -)	150	68	45	62	74	1	124	4	0	3	20	8	12	.248	.366	.365	.731
2015 Mil	NL	7	6	2	1	0	0	(0 0)	3	2	0	1	0	0	3	0	0	0	0	0	0	.333	.333	.500	.833
2016 Mil	NL	8	22	4	0	0	0	(0 0)	4	3	0	1	2	0	7	0	0	0	1	0	1	.182	.250	.182	.432
2 ML YEARS		15	28	6	1	0	0	(0 0)	7	5	0	2	2	0	10	0	0	0	1	0	1	.214	.267	.250	.517

Rob Refsnyder

REF-snide-er

Bats: R Throws: R Pos: 1B-25;RF-23;2B-8;LF-5;PR-4;PH-2;3B-1   **Ht: 6'0" Wt: 200 Born: 3/26/1991 Age: 26**

Year Team	Lg	G	AB	H	2B	3B	HR	(Hm Rd)	TB	R	RBI	RC	TBB	IBB	SO	HBP	SH	SF	SB	CS	GDP	Avg	OBP	Slg	OPS
2012 CtnSC	A	46	162	39	8	0	4	(- -)	59	22	22	21	16	0	25	3	0	1	11	1	7	.241	.319	.364	.683
2013 2 Tms	Low	130	467	137	32	3	6	(- -)	193	75	57	90	84	0	82	13	2	3	23	6	13	.293	.413	.413	.826
2014 Trntn	AA	60	228	78	19	5	6	(- -)	125	35	30	45	14	0	38	2	0	0	5	5	4	.342	.385	.548	.933
2014 S-WB	AAA	77	287	85	19	1	8	(- -)	130	47	33	51	41	0	67	2	1	2	4	4	8	.296	.386	.453	.839
2015 S-WB	AAA	117	450	122	28	2	9	(- -)	181	66	56	72	56	1	73	9	1	6	12	2	12	.271	.359	.402	.761
2016 S-WB	AAA	54	209	66	10	1	2	(- -)	84	25	20	33	17	1	30	1	0	3	6	0	4	.316	.365	.402	.767
2015 NYY	AL	16	43	13	3	0	2	(1 1)	22	3	5	6	3	1	7	0	0	0	0	0	3	.302	.348	.512	.859
2016 NYY	AL	58	152	38	9	0	0	(1 1)	47	25	12	14	18	2	30	1	0	3	4	1	5	.250	.328	.309	.637
Postseason		1	3	0	0	0	0	(0 0)	0	0	0	0	0	0	0	0	0	0	0	0	0	.000	.000	.000	.000
2 ML YEARS		74	195	51	12	0	2	(1 1)	69	28	17	20	21	3	37	1	0	3	4	1	8	.262	.332	.354	.686

Nolan Reimold

RYE-mold

Bats: R **Throws:** R **Pos:** LF-62;RF-32;PH-13;PR-10;CF-8;DH-2   **Ht:** 6'4" **Wt:** 205 **Born:** 10/12/1983 **Age:** 33

Year	Team	Lg	G	AB	H	2B	3B	HR	(Hm	Rd)	TB	R	RBI	RC	TBB	IBB	SO	HBP	SH	SF	SB	CS	GDP	Avg	OBP	Slg	OPS
2009	Bal	AL	104	358	100	18	2	15	(8	7)	167	49	45	57	47	1	77	3	0	3	8	2	8	.279	.365	.466	.831
2010	Bal	AL	39	116	24	5	0	3	(0	3)	38	9	14	6	12	0	26	1	0	2	0	0	6	.207	.282	.328	.610
2011	Bal	AL	87	267	66	10	3	13	(8	5)	121	40	45	48	28	1	57	6	0	4	7	2	4	.247	.328	.453	.781
2012	Bal	AL	16	67	21	6	0	5	(0	5)	42	10	10	15	2	0	14	0	0	0	1	0	3	.313	.333	.627	.960
2013	Bal	AL	40	128	25	3	0	5	(3	2)	43	17	12	7	10	2	41	0	0	2	0	1	4	.195	.250	.336	.586
2014	2 Tms		29	69	16	5	0	3	(1	2)	30	5	13	9	6	0	32	0	0	3	1	0	0	.232	.282	.435	.717
2015	Bal	AL	61	170	42	5	1	6	(5	1)	67	24	20	27	23	2	47	2	0	0	0	0	2	.247	.344	.394	.738
2016	Bal	AL	104	203	45	9	1	6	(3	3)	74	25	15	20	22	0	62	1	0	1	1	2	8	.222	.300	.365	.664
14	Tor	AL	22	52	11	4	0	2	(0	2)	21	3	9	6	6	0	22	0	0	2	1	0	0	.212	.283	.404	.687
14	Ari	NL	7	17	5	1	0	1	(1	0)	9	2	4	3	0	0	10	0	0	1	0	0	0	.294	.278	.529	.807
	8 ML YEARS		480	1378	339	61	7	56	(28	28)	582	179	174	189	150	6	356	13	0	15	18	7	35	.246	.323	.422	.745

Tony Renda

Bats: R **Throws:** R **Pos:** PH-15;2B-9;LF-4;RF-4;3B-1   **Ht:** 5'8" **Wt:** 175 **Born:** 1/24/1991 **Age:** 26

Year	Team	Lg	G	AB	H	2B	3B	HR	(Hm	Rd)	TB	R	RBI	RC	TBB	IBB	SO	HBP	SH	SF	SB	CS	GDP	Avg	OBP	Slg	OPS
2012	Auburn	A-	71	295	78	9	0	0	(-	-)	87	47	32	35	31	0	33	5	0	3	15	3	8	.264	.341	.295	.636
2013	Hgrstn	A	135	521	153	43	3	3	(-	-)	211	99	51	90	68	1	65	8	4	5	30	6	8	.294	.380	.405	.785
2014	Ptomc	A+	107	414	127	21	4	0	(-	-)	156	75	47	66	43	0	59	10	0	5	19	5	6	.307	.381	.377	.758
2015	Hrsbrg	AA	54	206	55	10	1	1	(-	-)	70	31	23	26	19	1	15	2	0	1	14	3	6	.267	.333	.340	.673
2015	Trntn	AA	73	274	74	20	1	2	(-	-)	102	42	21	36	24	0	24	1	2	3	10	3	12	.270	.328	.372	.700
2016	Pnscla	AA	68	261	85	25	3	2	(-	-)	122	36	28	47	14	0	20	5	0	2	15	1	5	.326	.369	.467	.836
2016	Lsvlle	AAA	30	105	29	3	1	1	(-	-)	37	13	9	13	10	0	16	2	4	0	2	3	4	.276	.350	.352	.703
2016	Cin	NL	32	60	11	2	0	0	(0	0)	13	4	3	1	5	0	11	0	2	0	0	0	4	.183	.246	.217	.463

Anthony Rendon

Bats: R **Throws:** R **Pos:** 3B-155;PH-4;PR-1   ren-DOAN   **Ht:** 6'1" **Wt:** 210 **Born:** 6/6/1990 **Age:** 27

Year	Team	Lg	G	AB	H	2B	3B	HR	(Hm	Rd)	TB	R	RBI	RC	TBB	IBB	SO	HBP	SH	SF	SB	CS	GDP	Avg	OBP	Slg	OPS
2013	Was	NL	98	351	93	23	1	7	(3	4)	139	40	35	43	31	3	69	5	2	5	1	1	7	.265	.329	.396	.725
2014	Was	NL	153	613	176	39	6	21	(10	11)	290	111	83	97	58	2	104	5	2	5	17	3	11	.287	.351	.473	.824
2015	Was	NL	80	311	82	16	0	5	(3	2)	113	43	25	39	36	0	70	4	0	4	1	2	8	.264	.344	.363	.707
2016	Was	NL	156	567	153	38	2	20	(11	9)	255	91	85	95	65	2	117	7	0	8	12	6	5	.270	.348	.450	.797
	Postseason		4	19	7	0	0	0	(0	0)	7	0	1	3	1	0	2	0	0	0	1	0	0	.368	.400	.368	.768
	4 ML YEARS		487	1842	504	116	9	53	(27	26)	797	285	228	274	190	7	360	21	4	22	31	12	31	.274	.345	.433	.777

Hunter Renfroe

Bats: R **Throws:** R **Pos:** RF-9;PH-3   **Ht:** 6'1" **Wt:** 220 **Born:** 1/28/1992 **Age:** 25

Year	Team	Lg	G	AB	H	2B	3B	HR	(Hm	Rd)	TB	R	RBI	RC	TBB	IBB	SO	HBP	SH	SF	SB	CS	GDP	Avg	OBP	Slg	OPS
2013	2 Tms	Low	43	170	46	14	0	6	(-	-)	78	26	25	24	9	1	49	1	1	2	2	0	3	.271	.308	.459	.767
2014	Lk Els	A+	69	278	82	21	3	16	(-	-)	157	46	52	58	28	3	81	7	0	3	9	3	5	.295	.370	.565	.935
2014	SnAnt	AA	60	224	52	12	0	5	(-	-)	79	17	23	25	25	0	53	0	0	2	2	1	6	.232	.307	.353	.659
2015	SnAnt	AA	112	421	109	22	3	14	(-	-)	179	50	54	58	33	1	112	3	0	6	4	1	8	.259	.313	.425	.738
2015	ElPaso	AAA	21	90	30	5	2	6	(-	-)	57	15	24	19	4	0	20	0	0	1	1	0	3	.333	.358	.633	.991
2016	ElPaso	AAA	133	533	162	34	5	30	(-	-)	296	95	104	97	22	3	115	4	0	4	5	2	11	.304	.334	.555	.889
2016	SD	NL	11	35	13	3	0	4	(4	0)	28	8	14	10	1	1	5	0	0	0	0	0	1	.371	.389	.800	1.189

Ben Revere

Bats: L **Throws:** R **Pos:** CF-74;LF-25;PH-15;PR-2   **Ht:** 5'9" **Wt:** 175 **Born:** 5/3/1988 **Age:** 29

Year	Team	Lg	G	AB	H	2B	3B	HR	(Hm	Rd)	TB	R	RBI	RC	TBB	IBB	SO	HBP	SH	SF	SB	CS	GDP	Avg	OBP	Slg	OPS
2010	Min	AL	13	28	5	0	0	0	(0	0)	5	1	2	0	2	0	5	0	0	0	0	1	1	.179	.233	.179	.412
2011	Min	AL	117	450	120	9	5	0	(0	0)	139	56	30	51	26	1	41	2	3	0	34	9	7	.267	.310	.309	.619
2012	Min	AL	124	511	150	13	6	0	(0	0)	175	70	32	62	29	0	54	3	6	4	40	9	8	.294	.333	.342	.675
2013	Phi	NL	88	315	96	9	3	0	(0	0)	111	37	17	39	16	1	36	0	5	0	22	8	10	.305	.338	.352	.691
2014	Phi	NL	151	601	184	13	7	2	(1	1)	217	71	28	71	13	1	49	4	7	1	49	8	11	.306	.325	.361	.686
2015	2 Tms		152	592	181	22	7	2	(1	1)	223	84	45	78	32	0	64	2	5	3	31	7	5	.306	.342	.377	.719
2016	Was	NL	103	350	76	9	7	2	(2	0)	105	44	24	29	18	0	34	3	2	2	14	5	12	.217	.260	.300	.560
15	Phi	NL	96	366	109	13	4	1	(1	0)	137	49	26	45	19	0	36	1	2	0	24	5	4	.298	.334	.374	.709
15	Tor	AL	56	226	72	9	1	1	(0	1)	86	35	19	33	13	0	28	1	3	3	7	2	1	.319	.354	.381	.734
	Postseason		11	47	12	1	0	0	(0	0)	13	7	1	4	4	0	7	0	0	0	2	0	0	.255	.314	.277	.590
	7 ML YEARS		748	2847	812	75	35	6	(4	2)	975	363	178	330	136	3	283	14	28	10	190	47	54	.285	.320	.342	.662

Alex Reyes

Pitches: R Bats: R Pos: RP-7; SP-5   Ht: 6'3" Wt: 175 Born: 8/29/1994 Age: 22

			HOW MUCH HE PITCHED					WHAT HE GAVE UP										THE RESULTS						
Year	Team	Lg	G	GS	CG	GF	IP	BFP	H	R	ER	HR	SH	SF	HB	TBB	IBB	SO	WP	Bk	W	L	Pct	Sh	Sv-Op	Hld	ERC	ERA
2013	Jhscty	R+	12	12	0	0	58.1	253	54	26	22	1	2	2	4	28	0	68	8	1	6	4	.600	0	0- -	-	3.67	3.39
2014	Peoria	A	21	21	1	0	109.0	465	82	54	44	6	2	2	3	61	0	137	10	3	7	7	.500	0	0- -	-	3.12	3.63
2015	2 Tms	Low	14	14	0	0	66.2	271	49	20	16	0	1	0	4	31	0	99	4	2	2	5	.286	0	0- -	-	2.55	2.16
2015	Sprgfld	AA	8	8	0	0	34.2	143	21	14	12	1	1	1	1	18	0	52	5	1	3	2	.600	0	0- -	-	2.09	3.12
2016	Memp	AAA	14	14	0	0	65.1	291	63	38	36	6	4	1	4	32	0	93	7	1	2	3	.400	0	0- -	-	4.37	4.96
2016	StL	NL	12	5	0	3	46.0	189	33	8	8	1	1	1	0	23	1	52	3	1	4	1	.800	0	1-1	1	2.43	1.57

Jo-Jo Reyes

Pitches: L Bats: L Pos: RP-1   Ht: 6'2" Wt: 230 Born: 11/20/1984 Age: 32

			HOW MUCH HE PITCHED					WHAT HE GAVE UP										THE RESULTS						
Year	Team	Lg	G	GS	CG	GF	IP	BFP	H	R	ER	HR	SH	SF	HB	TBB	IBB	SO	WP	Bk	W	L	Pct	Sh	Sv-Op	Hld	ERC	ERA
2016	NewOr*	AAA	38	0	0	8	60.1	253	60	23	23	2	2	0	2	17	0	51	7	0	3	2	.600	0	4- -	-	3.28	3.43
2007	Atl	NL	11	10	0	0	50.2	230	55	39	35	9	5	2	1	30	2	27	1	0	2	2	.500	0	0-0	0	6.06	6.22
2008	Atl	NL	23	22	0	0	113.0	512	134	77	73	18	9	3	3	52	4	78	2	0	3	11	.214	0	0-0	0	5.97	5.81
2009	Atl	NL	6	5	0	0	27.0	119	27	25	21	4	1	1	1	13	3	21	0	0	0	2	.000	0	0-0	0	4.73	7.00
2010	Atl	NL	1	0	0	0	3.1	20	10	9	9	2	0	0	0	3	0	2	0	0	0	0	-	0	0-0	0	26.51	24.30
2011	2 Tms	AL	29	25	1	1	140.2	641	176	99	87	21	3	3	7	48	0	87	7	0	7	11	.389	0	0-0	0	5.87	5.57
2015	LAA	AL	1	0	0	0	0.1	1	0	0	0	0	0	0	0	0	0	0	0	0	1	0	1.000	0	0-0	0	0.00	0.00
2016	Mia	NL	1	0	0	1	2.0	10	3	2	2	0	0	0	0	1	0	0	0	0	0	0	-	0	0-0	0	6.48	9.00
11	Tor	AL	20	20	1	0	110.0	504	140	78	66	14	3	3	6	35	0	64	6	0	5	8	.385	0	0-0	0	5.71	5.40
11	Bal	AL	9	5	0	1	30.2	137	36	21	21	7	0	0	1	13	0	23	1	0	2	3	.400	0	0-0	0	6.42	6.16
7 ML YEARS			72	62	1	2	337.0	1536	405	251	227	54	18	9	12	147	9	215	10	0	13	26	.333	0	0-0	0	5.99	6.06

Jose Reyes

Bats: B Throws: R Pos: 3B-50;SS-13   Ht: 6'0" Wt: 195 Born: 6/11/1983 Age: 34

			BATTING																			RUNNING			AVERAGES			
Year	Team	Lg	G	AB	H	2B	3B	HR	(Hm	Rd)	TB	R	RBI	RC	TBB	IBB	SO	HBP	SH	SF	SB	CS	GDP	Avg	OBP	Slg	OPS
2003	NYM	NL	69	274	84	12	4	5	(1	4)	119	47	32	46	13	0	36	0	2	3	13	3	1	.307	.334	.434	.769
2004	NYM	NL	53	220	56	16	2	2	(1	1)	82	33	14	25	5	0	31	0	4	0	19	2	1	.255	.271	.373	.644
2005	NYM	NL	161	696	190	24	17	7	(2	5)	269	99	58	84	27	0	78	2	4	4	60	15	7	.273	.300	.386	.687
2006	NYM	NL	153	647	194	30	17	19	(9	10)	315	122	81	121	53	6	81	1	2	0	64	17	6	.300	.354	.487	.841
2007	NYM	NL	160	681	191	36	12	12	(7	5)	287	119	57	99	77	13	78	1	5	1	78	21	6	.280	.354	.421	.775
2008	NYM	NL	159	688	204	37	19	16	(9	7)	327	113	68	117	66	8	82	1	5	3	56	15	9	.297	.358	.475	.833
2009	NYM	NL	36	147	41	7	2	2	(1	1)	58	18	15	20	18	1	19	0	0	1	11	2	2	.279	.355	.395	.750
2010	NYM	NL	133	563	159	29	10	11	(8	3)	241	83	54	76	31	4	63	2	4	3	30	10	8	.282	.321	.428	.749
2011	NYM	NL	126	537	181	31	16	7	(4	3)	265	101	44	90	43	9	41	0	2	4	39	7	5	.337	.384	.493	.877
2012	Mia	NL	160	642	184	37	12	11	(4	7)	278	86	57	92	63	9	56	0	5	6	40	11	10	.287	.347	.433	.780
2013	Tor	AL	93	382	113	20	0	10	(7	3)	163	58	37	61	34	2	47	1	0	2	15	6	6	.296	.353	.427	.780
2014	Tor	AL	143	610	175	33	4	9	(5	4)	243	94	51	77	38	1	73	1	2	4	30	2	4	.287	.328	.398	.726
2015	2 Tms		116	481	132	25	2	7	(5	2)	182	57	53	63	26	0	62	0	9	3	24	6	6	.274	.310	.378	.688
2016	NYM	NL	60	255	68	13	4	8	(6	2)	113	45	24	35	23	1	49	0	0	1	9	2	3	.267	.326	.443	.769
15	Tor	AL	69	288	82	17	0	4	(3	1)	111	36	34	42	17	0	38	0	4	2	16	2	3	.285	.322	.385	.708
15	Col	NL	47	193	50	8	2	3	(2	1)	71	21	19	21	9	0	24	0	5	1	8	4	3	.259	.291	.368	.659
Postseason			10	44	11	1	1	1	(1	0)	17	7	5	6	3	1	5	0	0	0	3	1	0	.250	.298	.386	.684
14 ML YEARS			1622	6823	1972	350	121	126	(69	57)	2942	1075	645	1006	517	54	796	9	44	35	488	119	74	.289	.338	.431	.769

Mark Reynolds

Bats: R Throws: R Pos: 1B-115;PH-7;2B-1   Ht: 6'2" Wt: 220 Born: 8/3/1983 Age: 33

			BATTING																			RUNNING			AVERAGES			
Year	Team	Lg	G	AB	H	2B	3B	HR	(Hm	Rd)	TB	R	RBI	RC	TBB	IBB	SO	HBP	SH	SF	SB	CS	GDP	Avg	OBP	Slg	OPS
2007	Ari	NL	111	366	102	20	4	17	(7	10)	181	62	62	62	37	4	129	5	1	5	0	1	5	.279	.349	.495	.843
2008	Ari	NL	152	539	129	28	3	28	(13	15)	247	87	97	82	64	0	204	3	1	6	11	2	10	.239	.320	.458	.779
2009	Ari	NL	155	578	150	30	1	44	(19	25)	314	98	102	94	76	3	223	5	0	3	24	9	8	.260	.349	.543	.892
2010	Ari	NL	145	499	99	17	2	32	(21	11)	216	79	85	77	83	7	211	9	0	5	7	4	8	.198	.320	.433	.753
2011	Bal	AL	155	534	118	27	1	37	(17	20)	258	84	86	77	75	2	196	7	0	4	6	4	11	.221	.323	.483	.806
2012	Bal	AL	135	457	101	26	0	23	(11	12)	196	65	69	68	73	2	159	6	0	2	1	3	19	.221	.335	.429	.763
2013	2 Tms	AL	135	445	98	14	0	21	(9	12)	175	55	67	55	51	1	154	5	0	3	3	1	9	.220	.306	.393	.699
2014	Mil	NL	130	378	74	9	0	22	(9	13)	149	47	45	41	47	3	122	3	1	4	5	1	8	.196	.287	.394	.681
2015	StL	NL	140	382	88	21	2	13	(4	9)	152	35	48	38	44	2	121	4	0	2	3	2	10	.230	.315	.398	.713
2016	Col	NL	118	393	111	24	0	14	(8	6)	177	61	53	60	42	1	112	4	0	2	1	2	6	.282	.356	.450	.806
13	Cle	AL	99	335	72	8	0	15	(8	7)	125	40	48	39	43	1	123	3	0	3	3	0	7	.215	.307	.373	.680
13	NYY	AL	36	110	26	6	0	6	(1	5)	50	15	19	16	8	0	31	2	0	0	0	1	2	.236	.300	.455	.755
Postseason			16	52	7	0	0	2	(1	1)	13	3	3	2	3	0	20	3	0	0	1	0	1	.135	.224	.250	.474
10 ML YEARS			1376	4571	1070	216	13	251	(118	133)	2065	673	714	654	592	25	1631	51	3	36	60	30	94	.234	.326	.452	.778

Matt Reynolds

Pitches: L Bats: L Pos: RP-8   Ht: 6'5" Wt: 240 Born: 10/2/1984 Age: 32

			HOW MUCH HE PITCHED					WHAT HE GAVE UP										THE RESULTS						
Year	Team	Lg	G	GS	CG	GF	IP	BFP	H	R	ER	HR	SH	SF	HB	TBB	IBB	SO	WP	Bk	W	L	Pct	Sh	Sv-Op	Hld	ERC	ERA
2016	Rchmd*	AA	8	0	0	2	5.0	17	2	0	0	0	0	0	0	1	0	7	0	0	0	0	-	0	0- -	-	0.67	0.00
2016	Scrmto*	AAA	12	0	0	1	13.2	48	5	0	0	0	0	0	1	2	0	12	1	0	1	0	1.000	0	0- -	-	0.60	0.00
2010	Col	NL	21	0	0	2	18.0	70	10	4	4	2	1	1	2	5	0	17	1	0	1	0	1.000	0	0-0	2	1.87	2.00
2011	Col	NL	73	0	0	9	50.2	211	48	24	23	10	1	4	0	18	5	50	5	2	1	2	.333	0	0-2	18	4.18	4.09
2012	Col	NL	71	0	0	16	57.1	249	65	31	28	11	6	3	0	17	4	51	5	1	3	1	.750	0	0-0	2	4.96	4.40

Year	Team	Lg	G	GS	CG	GF	IP	BFP	H	R	ER	HR	SH	SF	HB	TBB	IBB	SO	WP	Bk	W	L	Pct	Sh	Sv-Op	Hld	ERC	ERA
			HOW MUCH HE PITCHED						**WHAT HE GAVE UP**												**THE RESULTS**							
2013	Ari	NL	30	0	0	9	27.1	111	25	7	6	2	0	1	1	5	1	23	0	0	0	2	.000	0	2-3	5	2.71	1.98
2015	Ari	NL	18	0	0	3	13.2	62	14	7	7	6	0	0	1	7	2	18	0	0	0	0	-	0	0-1	3	7.30	4.61
2016	SF	NL	8	0	0	4	6.0	30	7	5	5	0	0	1	0	5	2	3	1	0	0	1	.000	0	0-0	0	5.14	7.50
6 ML YEARS			221	0	0	43	173.0	733	169	78	73	31	8	10	4	57	14	162	12	3	5	6	.455	0	2-6	30	4.19	3.80

Matt Reynolds

Bats: R Throws: R Pos: SS-21;PH-17;3B-7;2B-4;LF-1;PR-1   Ht: 6'1" Wt: 200 Born: 12/3/1990 Age: 26

Year	Team	Lg	G	AB	H	2B	3B	HR	(Hm	Rd)	TB	R	RBI	RC	TBB	IBB	SO	HBP	SH	SF	SB	CS	GDP	Avg	OBP	Slg	OPS
								BATTING														**RUNNING**		**AVERAGES**			
2012	Savann	A	42	158	41	8	0	3	(-	-)	58	18	13	21	12	0	26	7	0	2	5	1	7	.259	.335	.367	.702
2013	Stluci	A+	117	433	98	21	6	5	(-	-)	146	59	49	48	36	1	80	13	1	5	9	2	15	.226	.302	.337	.639
2014	Bnghtn	AA	58	211	75	5	3	1	(-	-)	89	33	21	40	29	0	41	0	0	2	6	3	1	.355	.430	.422	.852
2014	LsVgs	AAA	68	267	89	16	4	5	(-	-)	128	54	40	51	21	1	60	5	2	6	14	4	4	.333	.385	.479	.864
2015	LsVgs	AAA	115	445	119	32	5	6	(-	-)	179	70	65	61	32	0	92	5	1	7	13	4	14	.267	.319	.402	.721
2016	LsVgs	AAA	71	269	71	15	2	2	(-	-)	96	43	24	35	26	0	64	3	1	0	9	2	12	.264	.336	.357	.692
2016	NYM	NL	47	89	20	8	0	3	(2	1)	37	11	13	10	4	0	34	1	2	0	0	1	3	.225	.266	.416	.682

Clayton Richard

Pitches: L Bats: L Pos: RP-27; SP-9   Ht: 6'5" Wt: 240 Born: 9/12/1983 Age: 33

Year	Team	Lg	G	GS	CG	GF	IP	BFP	H	R	ER	HR	SH	SF	HB	TBB	IBB	SO	WP	Bk	W	L	Pct	Sh	Sv-Op	Hld	ERC	ERA
			HOW MUCH HE PITCHED						**WHAT HE GAVE UP**													**THE RESULTS**						
2008	CWS	AL	13	8	0	3	47.2	215	61	37	32	5	0	1	0	13	2	29	1	1	2	5	.286	0	0-0	0	5.06	6.04
2009	2 Tms		38	26	1	3	153.0	663	154	81	75	17	8	5	3	71	0	114	7	3	9	5	.643	0	0-0	0	4.60	4.41
2010	SD	NL	33	33	1	0	201.2	861	206	89	84	16	6	2	4	78	6	153	4	2	14	9	.609	1	0-0	0	4.09	3.75
2011	SD	NL	18	18	0	0	99.2	427	104	52	43	8	4	1	2	38	2	53	3	1	5	9	.357	0	0-0	0	4.22	3.88
2012	SD	NL	33	33	1	0	218.2	910	228	110	97	31	3	6	6	42	4	107	4	2	14	14	.500	1	0-0	0	3.87	3.99
2013	SD	NL	12	11	0	1	52.2	239	65	44	41	13	6	1	0	21	1	24	0	0	2	5	.286	0	0-0	0	6.55	7.01
2015	ChC	NL	23	3	0	0	42.1	181	47	18	18	3	0	0	1	7	1	22	4	0	4	2	.667	0	0-0	2	3.56	3.83
2016	2 Tms		36	9	0	9	67.2	306	81	35	25	4	0	3	2	31	3	41	3	0	3	4	.429	0	1-1	5	5.24	3.33
09	CWS	AL	26	14	1	3	89.0	387	94	50	46	10	3	4	3	37	0	66	5	2	4	3	.571	0	0-0	0	4.76	4.65
09	SD	NL	12	12	0	0	64.0	276	60	31	29	7	5	1	0	34	0	48	2	1	5	2	.714	0	0-0	0	4.38	4.08
16	ChC	NL	25	0	0	9	14.0	72	23	14	10	0	0	2	2	7	3	7	1	0	0	1	.000	0	1-1	4	7.74	6.43
16	SD	NL	11	9	0	0	53.2	234	58	21	15	4	0	1	0	24	0	34	2	0	3	3	.500	0	0-0	1	4.61	2.52
Postseason			8	0	0	0	11.0	42	8	1	1	0	0	0	0	4	0	9	0	0	0	0	-	0	0-0	2	2.05	0.82
8 ML YEARS			206	141	3	16	883.1	3802	946	466	415	97	27	19	18	301	19	543	26	9	53	53	.500	2	1-1	3	4.39	4.23

Garrett Richards

Pitches: R Bats: R Pos: SP-6   Ht: 6'3" Wt: 210 Born: 5/27/1988 Age: 29

Year	Team	Lg	G	GS	CG	GF	IP	BFP	H	R	ER	HR	SH	SF	HB	TBB	IBB	SO	WP	Bk	W	L	Pct	Sh	Sv-Op	Hld	ERC	ERA
			HOW MUCH HE PITCHED						**WHAT HE GAVE UP**													**THE RESULTS**						
2011	LAA	AL	7	3	0	2	14.0	62	16	11	9	4	0	0	0	7	0	9	2	0	0	2	.000	0	0-0	0	6.97	5.79
2012	LAA	AL	30	9	0	4	71.0	318	77	46	37	7	2	4	3	34	1	47	2	0	4	3	.571	0	1-3	5	5.04	4.69
2013	LAA	AL	47	17	1	6	145.0	620	151	73	67	12	9	3	1	44	4	101	11	0	7	8	.467	0	1-2	5	3.78	4.16
2014	LAA	AL	26	26	1	0	168.2	678	124	51	49	5	0	3	7	51	1	164	22	1	13	4	.765	1	0-0	0	2.06	2.61
2015	LAA	AL	32	32	1	0	207.1	865	181	94	84	20	6	10	5	76	2	176	17	0	15	12	.556	1	0-0	0	3.32	3.65
2016	LAA	AL	6	6	0	0	34.2	148	31	16	9	2	2	0	1	15	1	34	3	0	1	3	.250	0	0-0	0	3.39	2.34
6 ML YEARS			148	93	3	12	640.2	2691	580	291	255	50	19	20	17	227	9	531	57	1	40	32	.556	2	2-5	10	3.32	3.58

Joey Rickard

Bats: R Throws: L Pos: RF-51;LF-31;CF-13;PR-8;PH-3   Ht: 6'1" Wt: 185 Born: 5/21/1991 Age: 26

Year	Team	Lg	G	AB	H	2B	3B	HR	(Hm	Rd)	TB	R	RBI	RC	TBB	IBB	SO	HBP	SH	SF	SB	CS	GDP	Avg	OBP	Slg	OPS
								BATTING														**RUNNING**		**AVERAGES**			
2012	HudVal	A-	47	183	51	11	0	2	(-	-)	68	35	14	29	16	2	32	12	0	2	11	3	3	.279	.371	.372	.742
2013	BG	A	127	452	122	29	5	8	(-	-)	185	79	63	83	78	0	98	16	5	8	30	10	8	.270	.390	.409	.799
2014	Mont	AA	68	206	50	8	0	1	(-	-)	61	33	17	24	28	0	39	4	4	5	9	4	4	.243	.337	.296	.634
2015	Charltt	A+	23	71	19	3	0	0	(-	-)	22	8	12	12	20	0	13	2	0	1	3	2	2	.268	.436	.310	.746
2015	Mont	AA	65	236	76	19	6	2	(-	-)	113	38	32	52	39	0	42	3	1	3	19	4	2	.322	.420	.479	.899
2015	Drham	AAA	29	89	32	6	2	0	(-	-)	42	16	11	19	10	0	20	3	1	1	1	0	0	.360	.437	.472	.909
2016	Bal	AL	85	257	69	13	0	5	(2	3)	97	32	19	32	18	0	54	2	3	2	4	1	3	.268	.319	.377	.696

Rene Rivera

Bats: R Throws: R Pos: C-59;PH-4;1B-1;DH-1   ruh-NAY   Ht: 5'10" Wt: 215 Born: 7/31/1983 Age: 33

Year	Team	Lg	G	AB	H	2B	3B	HR	(Hm	Rd)	TB	R	RBI	RC	TBB	IBB	SO	HBP	SH	SF	SB	CS	GDP	Avg	OBP	Slg	OPS
								BATTING														**RUNNING**		**AVERAGES**			
2004	Sea	AL	2	3	0	0	0	0	(0	0)	0	0	0	0	0	0	1	0	0	0	0	0	0	.000	.000	.000	.000
2005	Sea	AL	16	48	19	3	0	1	(0	1)	25	3	6	8	1	0	11	0	1	0	0	0	0	.396	.408	.521	.929
2006	Sea	AL	35	99	15	4	0	2	(1	1)	25	8	4	4	3	0	29	1	3	0	1	0	2	.152	.184	.253	.437
2011	Min	AL	45	104	15	3	0	1	(0	1)	21	9	5	3	8	0	32	1	0	1	0	0	2	.144	.211	.202	.412
2013	SD	NL	23	67	17	3	1	0	(0	0)	22	4	7	6	2	1	16	0	0	2	0	0	0	.254	.268	.328	.596
2014	SD	NL	103	294	74	18	1	11	(1	10)	127	27	44	41	27	3	76	3	3	2	0	0	6	.252	.319	.432	.751
2015	TB	AL	110	298	53	14	0	5	(4	1)	82	16	26	16	11	0	86	3	5	2	0	0	4	.178	.213	.275	.489
2016	NYM	NL	65	185	41	4	0	6	(4	2)	63	12	26	19	16	3	54	1	1	2	0	0	4	.222	.291	.341	.632
8 ML YEARS			399	1098	234	49	2	26	(10	16)	365	79	118	97	68	7	305	11	13	9	1	0	19	.213	.264	.332	.596

T.J. Rivera

Bats: R Throws: R Pos: 2B-26;3B-9;PH-6;1B-1   Ht: 6'1" Wt: 205 Born: 10/27/1988 Age: 28

					BATTING															RUNNING			AVERAGES			
Year	Team	Lg	G	AB	H	2B	3B	HR	(Hm	Rd)	TB	R	RBI	RC	TBB	IBB	SO	HBP	SH	SF	SB	CS	GDP	Avg	OBP	Slg	OPS
2012	2 Tms	Low	128	516	165	29	4	9	(-	-)	229	73	66	86	40	2	71	5	7	4	11	5	16	.320	.372	.444	.815
2013	Stluci	A+	125	502	145	23	1	2	(-	-)	176	76	51	66	34	1	73	13	7	3	6	2	19	.289	.348	.351	.698
2014	Stluci	A+	61	252	86	16	0	4	(-	-)	114	42	47	44	14	1	37	5	0	3	2	1	11	.341	.383	.452	.836
2014	Bnghtn	AA	54	201	72	13	0	1	(-	-)	88	28	28	36	11	1	27	4	0	5	1	0	6	.358	.394	.438	.831
2015	Bnghtn	AA	56	220	75	10	0	5	(-	-)	100	37	27	37	12	0	22	2	0	0	1	1	11	.341	.380	.455	.835
2015	LsVgs	AAA	54	183	56	17	1	2	(-	-)	81	26	21	28	7	0	25	4	2	0	0	0	6	.306	.345	.443	.788
2016	LsVgs	AAA	105	405	143	31	1	11	(-	-)	209	67	85	80	23	2	54	7	2	5	3	3	6	.353	.393	.516	.909
2016	NYM	NL	33	105	35	4	1	3	(2	1)	50	10	16	16	3	0	17	1	0	4	0	0	2	.333	.345	.476	.821

Yadiel Rivera

Bats: R Throws: R Pos: 3B-15;2B-13;PH-6;SS-5;PR-1   YA-dee-el   Ht: 6'3" Wt: 185 Born: 5/2/1992 Age: 25

					BATTING															RUNNING			AVERAGES			
Year	Team	Lg	G	AB	H	2B	3B	HR	(Hm	Rd)	TB	R	RBI	RC	TBB	IBB	SO	HBP	SH	SF	SB	CS	GDP	Avg	OBP	Slg	OPS
2012	Wisc	A	127	465	115	26	5	12	(-	-)	187	60	49	56	26	0	119	4	6	5	7	3	12	.247	.290	.402	.692
2013	BrvdCt	A+	129	478	115	16	2	5	(-	-)	150	51	37	47	32	0	80	9	4	1	13	8	8	.241	.300	.314	.614
2014	BrvdCt	A+	66	231	59	8	2	3	(-	-)	80	35	17	26	16	0	50	4	1	2	5	3	6	.255	.312	.346	.659
2014	Hntsvl	AA	58	183	48	9	6	2	(-	-)	75	31	13	23	10	1	36	1	2	0	5	2	4	.262	.304	.410	.714
2015	Biloxi	AA	52	184	51	9	3	1	(-	-)	69	23	16	24	17	0	30	2	5	0	8	7	4	.277	.345	.375	.720
2015	ColSpr	AAA	81	289	68	8	4	1	(-	-)	87	32	28	22	10	0	53	2	3	2	4	3	12	.235	.264	.301	.565
2016	ColSpr	AAA	83	304	69	7	8	2	(-	-)	98	38	41	25	10	0	78	6	2	4	4	3	13	.227	.262	.322	.585
2015	Mil	NL	7	14	1	0	0	0	(0	0)	1	0	0	0	0	0	4	0	1	0	0	0	0	.071	.071	.071	.143
2016	Mil	NL	35	66	14	4	0	0	(0	0)	18	12	3	3	2	0	20	0	3	0	0	0	4	.212	.235	.273	.508
	2 ML YEARS		42	80	15	4	0	0	(0	0)	19	12	3	3	2	0	24	0	4	0	0	0	4	.188	.207	.238	.445

Felipe Rivero

Pitches: L Bats: L Pos: RP-75   Ht: 6'2" Wt: 210 Born: 7/5/1991 Age: 25

			HOW MUCH HE PITCHED					WHAT HE GAVE UP										THE RESULTS						
Year	Team	Lg	G	GS	CG	GF	IP	BFP	H	R	ER	HR	SH	SF	HB	TBB	IBB	SO	WP	Bk	W	L	Pct	Sh	Sv-Op	Hld	ERC	ERA
2012	BG	A	27	21	0	0	113.1	476	115	56	43	5	3	6	6	29	1	98	7	2	8	8	.500	0	0--	-	3.44	3.41
2013	Charltt	A+	25	23	2	2	127.0	542	122	63	48	7	5	3	7	52	1	91	8	0	9	7	.563	0	0--	-	3.84	3.40
2014	Hrsbrg	AA	10	10	0	0	43.2	197	45	30	20	4	3	1	2	18	0	38	2	0	2	7	.222	0	0--	-	4.28	4.12
2015	Syrcse	AAA	8	0	0	2	6.2	32	8	5	5	0	0	0	0	5	0	5	0	0	0	2	.000	0	0--	-	5.88	6.75
2015	Was	NL	49	0	0	17	48.1	189	35	15	15	2	0	1	1	11	2	43	2	1	2	1	.667	0	2-3	6	1.74	2.79
2016	2 Tms	NL	75	0	0	11	77.0	327	66	39	35	7	0	2	6	33	3	92	3	0	1	6	.143	0	1-4	26	3.61	4.53
16	Was		47	0	0	8	49.2	203	43	26	25	4	0	1	5	15	2	53	1	0	0	3	.000	0	1-2	16	3.26	4.53
16	Pit		28	0	0	3	27.1	124	23	13	10	3	0	1	1	18	1	39	2	0	1	3	.250	0	0-2	10	4.25	3.29
	2 ML YEARS		124	0	0	28	125.1	516	101	54	50	9	0	3	7	44	5	135	5	1	3	7	.300	0	3-7	32	2.84	3.59

Anthony Rizzo

Bats: L Throws: L Pos: 1B-154;PH-2;2B-1   Ht: 6'3" Wt: 240 Born: 8/8/1989 Age: 27

					BATTING															RUNNING			AVERAGES			
Year	Team	Lg	G	AB	H	2B	3B	HR	(Hm	Rd)	TB	R	RBI	RC	TBB	IBB	SO	HBP	SH	SF	SB	CS	GDP	Avg	OBP	Slg	OPS
2011	SD	NL	49	128	18	8	1	1	(1	0)	31	9	9	7	21	1	46	4	0	0	2	1	2	.141	.281	.242	.523
2012	ChC	NL	87	337	96	15	0	15	(7	8)	156	44	48	57	27	1	62	3	0	1	3	2	7	.285	.342	.463	.805
2013	ChC	NL	160	606	141	40	2	23	(13	10)	254	71	80	74	76	7	127	6	0	2	6	5	12	.233	.323	.419	.742
2014	ChC	NL	140	524	150	28	1	32	(14	18)	276	89	78	99	73	7	116	15	0	4	5	4	8	.286	.386	.527	.913
2015	ChC	NL	160	586	163	38	3	31	(11	20)	300	94	101	115	78	9	105	30	0	7	17	6	9	.278	.387	.512	.899
2016	ChC	NL	155	583	170	43	4	32	(12	20)	317	94	109	119	74	8	108	16	0	3	3	5	13	.292	.385	.544	.928
	Postseason		9	32	6	0	0	2	(2	0)	12	4	2	1	2	0	8	1	0	0	0	0	1	.188	.257	.375	.632
	6 ML YEARS		751	2764	738	172	11	134	(58	76)	1334	401	425	471	349	33	564	74	0	17	36	23	51	.267	.362	.483	.845

Donn Roach

Pitches: R Bats: R Pos: RP-4   Ht: 6'0" Wt: 195 Born: 12/14/1989 Age: 27

			HOW MUCH HE PITCHED					WHAT HE GAVE UP										THE RESULTS						
Year	Team	Lg	G	GS	CG	GF	IP	BFP	H	R	ER	HR	SH	SF	HB	TBB	IBB	SO	WP	Bk	W	L	Pct	Sh	Sv-Op	Hld	ERC	ERA
2016	Tacom*	AAA	22	17	0	1	108.0	456	116	57	49	7	2	4	4	19	1	62	4	0	6	6	.500	0	1--	-	3.53	4.08
2016	Toledo*	AAA	5	5	0	0	29.2	120	29	11	10	1	0	1	1	5	0	21	4	0	3	1	.750	0	0--	-	2.82	3.03
2014	SD	NL	16	1	0	5	30.1	140	36	17	16	2	3	1	4	15	1	17	4	0	1	0	1.000	0	0-0	0	5.87	4.75
2015	ChC	NL	1	1	0	0	3.1	18	8	4	4	0	0	0	0	1	0	1	0	0	0	1	.000	0	0-0	0	12.26	10.80
2016	Sea	AL	4	0	0	1	5.1	28	7	5	5	1	0	1	1	2	0	2	1	0	2	0	1.000	0	0-0	0	6.64	8.44
	3 ML YEARS		21	2	0	6	39.0	186	51	26	25	3	3	2	5	18	1	20	5	0	3	1	.750	0	0-0	0	6.47	5.77

Tanner Roark

Pitches: R Bats: R Pos: SP-33; RP-1   ROW-ark   Ht: 6'2" Wt: 235 Born: 10/5/1986 Age: 30

			HOW MUCH HE PITCHED					WHAT HE GAVE UP										THE RESULTS						
Year	Team	Lg	G	GS	CG	GF	IP	BFP	H	R	ER	HR	SH	SF	HB	TBB	IBB	SO	WP	Bk	W	L	Pct	Sh	Sv-Op	Hld	ERC	ERA
2013	Was	NL	14	5	0	1	53.2	204	38	11	9	1	3	2	0	11	0	40	0	0	7	1	.875	0	0-0	1	1.54	1.51
2014	Was	NL	31	31	1	0	198.2	798	178	64	63	16	5	2	8	39	1	138	0	0	15	10	.600	1	0-0	0	2.76	2.85
2015	Was	NL	40	12	0	8	111.0	467	119	55	54	17	4	4	5	26	3	70	0	0	4	7	.364	0	1-2	4	4.39	4.38
2016	Was	NL	34	33	0	0	210.0	855	173	72	66	17	10	1	13	73	4	172	6	1	16	10	.615	0	0-0	1	3.08	2.83
	Postseason		2	0	0	1	2.2	12	3	1	1	1	0	0	0	0	0	3	0	0	0	1	.000	0	0-0	0	4.33	3.38
	4 ML YEARS		119	81	1	9	573.1	2324	508	202	192	51	22	9	24	149	8	420	6	1	42	28	.600	1	1-2	6	3.05	3.01

Daniel Robertson

Bats: R **Throws:** R **Pos:** LF-6;RF-3;CF-1;PH-1;PR-1 **Ht:** 5'8" **Wt:** 205 **Born:** 9/30/1985 **Age:** 31

																			RUNNING			AVERAGES			
Year	Team	Lg	G	AB	H	2B	3B	HR	(Hm | Rd)	TB	R	RBI	RC	TBB	IBB	SO	HBP	SH	SF	SB	CS	GDP	Avg	OBP	Slg	OPS
2016	Tacom*	AAA	114	408	117	19	7	6	(- | -)	168	50	46	65	42	0	41	4	3	3	13	2	14	.287	.357	.412	.768
2014	Tex	AL	70	177	48	9	1	0	(0 | 0)	59	23	21	23	17	0	28	0	2	1	6	4	3	.271	.333	.333	.667
2015	LAA	AL	37	75	21	2	0	0	(0 | 0)	23	10	7	8	2	1	7	0	3	0	0	0	1	.280	.299	.307	.605
2016	Sea	AL	9	19	5	1	0	0	(0 | 0)	6	1	1	1	1	0	3	0	1	0	0	1	2	.263	.300	.316	.616
	3 ML YEARS		116	271	74	12	1	0	(0 | 0)	88	34	29	32	20	1	38	0	6	1	6	5	6	.273	.322	.325	.647

David Robertson

Pitches: R **Bats:** R **Pos:** RP-62 **Ht:** 5'11" **Wt:** 195 **Born:** 4/9/1985 **Age:** 32

			HOW MUCH HE PITCHED					WHAT HE GAVE UP									THE RESULTS							
Year	Team	Lg	G	GS	CG	GF	IP	BFP	H	R	ER	HR	SH	SF	HB	TBB	IBB	SO	WP	Bk	W	L	Pct	Sh	Sv-Op	Hld	ERC	ERA
2008	NYY	AL	25	0	0	8	30.1	131	29	18	18	3	0	3	0	15	2	36	6	0	4	0	1.000	0	0-0	0	4.12	5.34
2009	NYY	AL	45	0	0	20	43.2	191	36	19	16	4	0	0	1	23	1	63	6	0	2	1	.667	0	1-1	5	3.51	3.30
2010	NYY	AL	64	0	0	10	61.1	273	59	26	26	5	5	3	3	33	6	71	7	2	4	5	.444	0	1-3	14	4.29	3.82
2011	NYY	AL	70	0	0	8	66.2	272	40	9	8	1	1	0	1	35	6	100	6	1	4	0	1.000	0	1-4	34	1.85	1.08
2012	NYY	AL	65	0	0	17	60.2	248	52	19	18	5	0	1	1	19	0	81	1	1	2	7	.222	0	2-5	30	2.95	2.67
2013	NYY	AL	70	0	0	9	66.1	262	51	15	15	5	3	0	2	18	1	77	1	0	5	1	.833	0	3-5	33	2.37	2.04
2014	NYY	AL	63	0	0	55	64.1	259	45	23	22	7	1	0	1	23	2	96	0	0	4	5	.444	0	39-44	0	2.41	3.08
2015	CWS	AL	60	0	0	53	63.1	250	46	27	24	7	0	0	1	13	2	86	4	0	6	5	.545	0	34-41	0	2.00	3.41
2016	CWS	AL	62	0	0	48	62.1	267	53	24	24	6	3	2	1	32	4	75	1	0	5	3	.625	0	37-44	0	3.63	3.47
	Postseason		19	0	0	7	17.0	73	15	7	7	2	1	0	1	5	3	17	1	0	3	0	1.000	0	0-0	2	2.99	3.71
	9 ML YEARS		524	0	0	228	519.0	2153	411	180	171	43	13	9	11	211	24	685	32	4	36	27	.571	0	118-147	116	2.88	2.97

Clint Robinson

Bats: L **Throws:** L **Pos:** PH-57;1B-46;LF-3;DH-1 **Ht:** 6'5" **Wt:** 240 **Born:** 2/16/1985 **Age:** 32

																					RUNNING		AVERAGES			
Year	Team	Lg	G	AB	H	2B	3B	HR	(Hm	Rd)	TB	R	RBI	RC	TBB	IBB	SO	HBP	SH	SF	SB	CS	GDP	Avg	OBP	Slg	OPS
2012	KC	AL	4	4	0	0	0	0	(0	0)	0	0	0	0	0	0	2	0	0	0	0	0	0	.000	.000	.000	.000
2014	LAD	NL	9	9	3	0	0	0	(0	0)	3	3	2	2	1	0	1	0	0	0	0	0	0	.333	.400	.333	.733
2015	Was	NL	126	309	84	15	1	10	(5	5)	131	44	34	47	37	4	52	5	0	1	0	0	6	.272	.358	.424	.782
2016	Was	NL	104	196	46	4	0	5	(1	4)	65	16	26	22	20	0	38	2	1	5	0	0	4	.235	.305	.332	.637
	4 ML YEARS		243	518	133	19	1	15	(6	9)	199	63	62	71	58	4	93	7	1	6	0	0	10	.257	.336	.384	.720

Shane Robinson

Bats: R **Throws:** R **Pos:** LF-34;CF-19;PR-12;PH-7;RF-5;DH-1 **Ht:** 5'9" **Wt:** 170 **Born:** 10/30/1984 **Age:** 32

																					RUNNING		AVERAGES			
Year	Team	Lg	G	AB	H	2B	3B	HR	(Hm	Rd)	TB	R	RBI	RC	TBB	IBB	SO	HBP	SH	SF	SB	CS	GDP	Avg	OBP	Slg	OPS
2016	Salt Lk*	AAA	19	73	23	4	0	0	(-	-)	27	14	4	10	3	0	8	1	2	1	4	0	1	.315	.346	.370	.716
2009	StL	NL	11	25	6	1	0	0	(0	0)	7	1	1	1	0	0	2	0	0	1	1	0	1	.240	.231	.280	.511
2011	StL	NL	9	7	0	0	0	0	(0	0)	0	0	0	0	1	0	2	0	0	0	0	0	1	.000	.125	.000	.125
2012	StL	NL	102	166	42	8	0	3	(1	2)	59	20	16	15	14	2	32	0	0	1	1	0	5	.253	.309	.355	.665
2013	StL	NL	99	144	36	2	1	2	(1	1)	46	22	16	18	23	0	17	0	0	4	5	1	2	.250	.345	.319	.664
2014	StL	NL	47	60	9	1	1	0	(0	0)	12	3	4	0	6	0	10	0	0	0	0	1	3	.150	.227	.200	.427
2015	Min	AL	83	180	45	7	3	0	(0	0)	58	28	16	21	12	0	29	1	3	1	6	1	4	.250	.299	.322	.621
2016	LAA	AL	65	98	17	3	0	1	(0	1)	23	16	10	6	10	0	17	1	2	0	3	2	3	.173	.257	.235	.492
	Postseason		18	24	5	1	0	1	(0	1)	9	4	4	0	1	0	4	0	0	0	0	0	1	.208	.240	.375	.615
	7 ML YEARS		416	680	155	22	5	6	(2	4)	205	90	63	61	66	2	109	2	5	7	16	5	19	.228	.295	.301	.597

Hansel Robles

Pitches: R **Bats:** R **Pos:** RP-68 **ROH-blace** **Ht:** 5'11" **Wt:** 185 **Born:** 8/13/1990 **Age:** 26

			HOW MUCH HE PITCHED					WHAT HE GAVE UP									THE RESULTS							
Year	Team	Lg	G	GS	CG	GF	IP	BFP	H	R	ER	HR	SH	SF	HB	TBB	IBB	SO	WP	Bk	W	L	Pct	Sh	Sv-Op	Hld	ERC	ERA
2012	Bklyn	A-	12	12	0	0	72.2	272	47	14	9	0	1	1	4	10	0	66	2	1	6	1	.857	0	0--	-	1.26	1.11
2013	2 Trms	Low	18	17	0	0	95.1	409	95	44	40	8	5	4	8	31	0	71	4	1	5	5	.500	0	0--	-	4.00	3.78
2014	Bnghtn	AA	30	18	1	3	110.2	477	107	57	53	10	3	5	7	43	0	106	4	1	7	6	.538	1	0--	-	4.04	4.31
2015	LsVgs	AAA	5	0	0	0	7.2	30	6	0	0	0	0	0	0	1	0	10	0	0	1	0	1.000	0	0--	-	1.49	0.00
2015	NYM	NL	57	0	0	7	54.0	217	37	24	22	8	1	1	2	18	1	61	2	1	4	3	.571	0	0-4	12	2.57	3.67
2016	NYM	NL	68	0	0	15	77.2	331	69	32	30	7	1	5	1	36	4	85	3	0	6	4	.600	0	1-3	13	3.62	3.48
	Postseason		3	0	0	2	3.0	9	0	0	0	0	0	0	0	0	0	4	0	0	0	0	-	0	0-0	0	0.00	0.00
	2 ML YEARS		125	0	0	22	131.2	548	106	59	52	15	2	6	3	54	5	146	5	1	10	7	.588	0	1-7	25	3.18	3.55

Brady Rodgers

Pitches: R **Bats:** R **Pos:** RP-4; SP-1 **Ht:** 6'2" **Wt:** 210 **Born:** 9/17/1990 **Age:** 26

			HOW MUCH HE PITCHED					WHAT HE GAVE UP									THE RESULTS							
Year	Team	Lg	G	GS	CG	GF	IP	BFP	H	R	ER	HR	SH	SF	HB	TBB	IBB	SO	WP	Bk	W	L	Pct	Sh	Sv-Op	Hld	ERC	ERA
2012	TriCity	A-	12	12	0	0	62.1	258	60	26	20	5	1	3	3	11	0	49	2	0	7	2	.778	0	0--	-	3.05	2.89
2013	Lancst	A+	27	18	0	6	112.0	486	135	71	67	14	1	4	8	23	0	104	4	1	10	8	.556	0	1--	-	4.99	5.38
2014	CpChr	AA	26	17	0	3	120.2	503	135	73	64	15	6	2	5	19	2	87	2	0	5	12	.294	0	2--	-	4.15	4.77
2015	Fresno	AAA	21	21	0	0	115.2	504	136	61	58	13	4	3	1	25	0	89	3	0	9	7	.563	0	0--	-	4.40	4.51
2016	Fresno	AAA	22	22	3	0	132.0	530	129	46	42	7	3	2	1	23	1	116	0	0	12	4	.750	1	0--	-	2.87	2.86
2016	Hou	AL	5	1	0	2	8.1	48	15	14	14	0	0	1	1	7	0	3	0	0	0	1	.000	0	0-0	0	10.43	15.12

Fernando Rodney

Pitches: R Bats: R Pos: RP-67 Ht: 5'11" Wt: 230 Born: 3/18/1977 Age: 40

Year	Team	Lg	G	GS	CG	GF	IP	BFP	H	R	ER	HR	SH	SF	HB	TBB	IBB	SO	WP	Bk	W	L	Pct	Sh	Sv-Op	Hld	ERC	ERA
2002	Det	AL	20	0	0	10	18.0	89	25	15	12	2	2	1	0	10	2	10	0	1	1	3	.250	0	0-4	0	6.77	6.00
2003	Det	AL	27	0	0	11	29.2	143	35	20	20	2	3	3	1	17	1	33	0	0	1	3	.250	0	3-6	3	5.46	6.07
2005	Det	AL	39	0	0	26	44.0	185	39	14	14	5	2	0	2	17	3	42	2	0	2	3	.400	0	9-15	3	3.59	2.86
2006	Det	AL	63	0	0	30	71.2	304	51	36	28	6	2	0	8	34	4	65	3	0	7	4	.636	0	7-11	18	3.01	3.52
2007	Det	AL	48	0	0	12	50.2	223	46	27	24	5	4	2	3	21	0	54	4	0	2	6	.250	0	1-3	12	3.74	4.26
2008	Det	AL	38	0	0	25	40.1	188	34	22	22	3	1	2	3	30	5	49	3	0	0	6	.000	0	13-19	5	4.29	4.91
2009	Det	AL	73	0	0	65	75.2	330	70	38	37	8	4	2	2	41	4	61	5	0	2	5	.286	0	37-38	0	4.31	4.40
2010	LAA	AL	72	0	0	30	68.0	308	70	33	32	4	1	0	5	35	1	53	4	0	4	3	.571	0	14-21	21	4.63	4.24
2011	LAA	AL	39	0	0	15	32.0	150	26	18	16	1	3	0	3	28	0	26	2	0	3	5	.375	0	3-7	10	4.66	4.50
2012	TB	AL	76	0	0	65	74.2	282	43	9	5	2	4	3	2	15	1	76	4	0	2	2	.500	0	48-50	0	1.22	0.60
2013	TB	AL	68	0	0	55	66.2	290	53	27	25	3	1	1	1	36	3	82	4	1	5	4	.556	0	37-45	0	3.02	3.38
2014	Sea	AL	69	0	0	64	66.1	286	61	24	21	3	4	1	3	28	3	76	4	0	1	6	.143	0	**48-51**	0	3.42	2.85
2015	2 Tms		68	0	0	32	62.2	277	59	36	33	9	1	1	8	29	3	58	6	0	7	5	.583	0	16-23	9	4.76	4.74
2016	2 Tms	NL	67	0	0	41	65.1	283	54	27	25	5	3	1	5	37	3	74	5	1	2	4	.333	0	25-28	8	3.85	3.44
15	Sea	AL	54	0	0	28	50.2	227	51	32	32	8	1	1	5	25	3	43	5	0	5	5	.500	0	16-22	7	5.25	5.68
15	ChC	NL	14	0	0	4	12.0	50	8	4	1	1	0	0	3	4	0	15	1	0	2	0	1.000	0	0-1	2	2.88	0.75
16	SD	NL	28	0	0	24	28.2	109	13	2	1	0	0	0	2	12	0	33	1	1	0	1	.000	0	17-17	0	1.30	0.31
16	Mia	NL	39	0	0	17	36.2	174	41	25	24	5	3	1	3	25	3	41	4	0	2	3	.400	0	8-11	8	6.45	5.89
Postseason			12	0	0	2	11.2	53	8	8	6	1	3	0	1	10	1	16	1	0	1	0	1.000	0	0-2	3	4.14	4.63
14 ML YEARS			767	0	0	481	765.2	3338	666	346	314	58	35	16	47	378	33	759	46	3	39	59	.398	0	261-321	89	3.69	3.69

Carlos Rodon

Pitches: L Bats: L Pos: SP-28 roh-DON Ht: 6'3" Wt: 235 Born: 12/10/1992 Age: 24

Year	Team	Lg	G	GS	CG	GF	IP	BFP	H	R	ER	HR	SH	SF	HB	TBB	IBB	SO	WP	Bk	W	L	Pct	Sh	Sv-Op	Hld	ERC	ERA
2014	2 Tms	Low	6	3	0	0	12.1	55	11	5	4	0	0	0	0	5	0	20	1	0	0	0	-	0	0- -	-	2.64	2.92
2015	CWS	AL	26	23	1	1	139.1	607	130	63	58	11	6	5	8	71	0	139	7	0	9	6	.600	0	0-0	0	4.25	3.75
2016	CWS	AL	28	28	0	0	165.0	715	176	82	74	23	4	6	6	54	3	168	11	1	9	10	.474	0	0-0	0	4.57	4.04
2 ML YEARS			54	51	1	1	304.1	1322	306	145	132	34	10	11	14	125	3	307	18	1	18	16	.529	0	0-0	0	4.43	3.90

Alex Rodriguez

Bats: R Throws: R Pos: DH-57;PH-8;3B-1 Ht: 6'3" Wt: 230 Born: 7/27/1975 Age: 41

Year	Team	Lg	G	AB	H	2B	3B	HR	(Hm	Rd)	TB	R	RBI	RC	TBB	IBB	SO	HBP	SH	SF	SB	CS	GDP	Avg	OBP	Slg	OPS
1994	Sea	AL	17	54	11	0	0	0	(0	0)	11	4	2	3	3	0	20	0	1	1	3	0	0	.204	.241	.204	.445
1995	Sea	AL	48	142	33	6	2	5	(1	4)	58	15	19	15	6	0	42	0	1	0	4	2	0	.232	.264	.408	.672
1996	Sea	AL	146	601	215	**54**	1	36	(18	18)	**379**	**141**	123	144	59	1	104	4	6	7	15	4	15	**.358**	.414	.631	1.045
1997	Sea	AL	141	587	176	40	3	23	(16	7)	291	100	84	100	41	1	99	5	4	1	29	6	14	.300	.350	.496	.846
1998	Sea	AL	161	**686**	213	35	5	42	(18	24)	384	123	124	135	45	0	121	10	3	4	46	13	12	.310	.360	.560	.919
1999	Sea	AL	129	502	143	25	0	42	(20	22)	294	110	111	102	56	2	109	5	1	8	21	7	12	.285	.357	.586	.943
2000	Sea	AL	148	554	175	34	2	41	(13	28)	336	134	132	138	100	5	121	7	0	11	15	4	10	.316	.420	.606	1.026
2001	Tex	AL	162	632	201	34	1	**52**	(26	26)	393	133	135	148	75	6	131	16	0	9	18	3	17	.318	.399	.622	1.021
2002	Tex	AL	162	624	187	27	2	**57**	(34	23)	389	125	**142**	152	87	12	122	10	0	4	9	4	14	.300	.392	.623	1.015
2003	Tex	AL	161	607	181	30	6	47	(26	21)	364	**124**	118	131	87	10	126	15	0	6	17	3	16	.298	.396	**.600**	.995
2004	NYY	AL	155	601	172	24	2	36	(17	19)	308	112	106	112	80	6	131	10	0	7	28	4	18	.286	.375	.512	.888
2005	NYY	AL	162	605	194	29	1	48	(26	22)	369	**124**	130	137	91	8	139	16	0	3	21	6	8	.321	.421	**.610**	**1.031**
2006	NYY	AL	154	572	166	26	1	35	(20	15)	299	113	121	112	90	8	139	8	0	4	15	4	22	.290	.392	.523	.914
2007	NYY	AL	158	583	183	31	0	**54**	(26	28)	376	**143**	156	159	95	11	120	21	0	9	24	4	15	.314	.422	**.645**	**1.067**
2008	NYY	AL	138	510	154	33	0	35	(21	14)	292	104	103	97	65	9	117	14	0	5	18	3	16	.302	.392	**.573**	.965
2009	NYY	AL	124	444	127	17	1	30	(18	12)	236	78	100	89	80	7	97	8	0	3	14	2	13	.286	.402	.532	.933
2010	NYY	AL	137	522	141	29	2	30	(15	15)	264	74	125	93	59	1	98	3	0	11	4	3	7	.270	.341	.506	.847
2011	NYY	AL	99	373	103	21	0	16	(9	7)	172	67	62	61	47	1	80	5	0	3	4	1	13	.276	.362	.461	.823
2012	NYY	AL	122	463	126	17	1	18	(8	10)	199	74	57	66	51	3	116	10	0	5	13	1	13	.272	.353	.430	.783
2013	NYY	AL	44	156	38	7	0	7	(2	5)	66	21	19	19	23	1	43	2	0	0	4	2	5	.244	.348	.423	.771
2015	NYY	AL	151	523	131	22	1	33	(18	15)	254	83	86	83	84	5	145	6	0	7	4	0	17	.250	.356	.486	.842
2016	NYY	AL	65	225	45	7	0	9	(2	7)	79	19	31	19	14	0	67	1	0	3	0	3	4	.200	.247	.351	.598
Postseason			76	278	72	16	0	13	(5	8)	127	43	41	43	39	4	77	9	1	3	8	3	6	.259	.365	.457	.822
22 ML YEARS			2784	10566	3115	548	31	696	(354	342)	5813	2021	2086	2115	1338	97	2287	176	16	111	329	76	261	.295	.380	.550	.930

Eduardo Rodriguez

Pitches: L Bats: L Pos: SP-20 Ht: 6'2" Wt: 220 Born: 4/7/1993 Age: 24

Year	Team	Lg	G	GS	CG	GF	IP	BFP	H	R	ER	HR	SH	SF	HB	TBB	IBB	SO	WP	Bk	W	L	Pct	Sh	Sv-Op	Hld	ERC	ERA
2012	Dlmrva	A	22	22	1	0	107.0	454	103	56	44	4	3	6	5	30	0	73	2	2	5	7	.417	0	0- -	-	3.13	3.70
2013	Frdrck	A+	14	14	0	0	85.1	351	78	36	27	4	4	2	2	25	0	66	2	0	6	4	.600	0	0- -	-	2.97	2.85
2013	Bowie	AA	11	11	0	0	59.2	252	53	28	28	5	0	2	2	24	1	59	1	1	4	3	.571	0	0- -	-	3.48	4.22
2014	Bowie	AA	16	16	1	0	82.2	362	90	50	44	5	1	3	0	29	1	69	4	5	3	7	.300	0	0- -	-	4.04	4.79
2014	Portlnd	AA	6	6	0	0	37.1	147	30	4	4	1	1	1	2	8	0	39	2	0	3	1	.750	0	0- -	-	2.17	0.96
2015	Pwtckt	AAA	8	8	1	0	48.1	190	46	22	16	2	1	2	0	7	0	44	1	0	4	3	.571	0	0- -	-	2.57	2.98
2016	Pwtckt	AAA	7	7	0	0	38.0	154	33	15	13	6	2	1	1	7	0	24	0	0	0	4	.000	0	0- -	-	2.97	3.08
2015	Bos	AL	21	21	0	0	121.2	522	120	55	52	13	5	4	4	37	1	98	4	1	10	6	.625	0	0-0	0	3.73	3.85
2016	Bos	AL	20	20	0	0	107.0	458	99	58	56	16	1	4	3	40	1	100	0	0	3	7	.300	0	0-0	0	3.96	4.71
2 ML YEARS			41	41	0	0	228.2	980	219	113	108	29	6	8	7	77	2	198	4	1	13	13	.500	0	0-0	0	3.84	4.25

Fernando Rodriguez

Pitches: R Bats: R Pos: RP-34 　　　　　Ht: 6'3" Wt: 235 Born: 6/18/1984 Age: 33

Year	Team	Lg	G	GS	CG	GF	IP	BFP	H	R	ER	HR	SH	SF	HB	TBB	IBB	SO	WP	Bk	W	L	Pct	Sh	Sv-Op	Hld	ERC	ERA
2009	LAA	AL	1	0	0	0	0.2	6	1	3	2	1	0	0	0	2	0	1	1	0	0	0	-	0	0-0	0	31.03	27.00
2011	Hou	NL	47	0	0	11	52.1	231	51	24	23	6	5	0	3	30	5	57	2	0	2	3	.400	0	0-0	6	4.90	3.96
2012	Hou	NL	71	0	0	9	70.1	309	68	45	42	10	2	2	1	34	7	78	10	0	2	10	.167	0	0-4	13	4.39	5.37
2014	Oak	AL	7	0	0	3	9.0	33	4	1	1	0	0	0	0	2	0	4	0	0	0	1	1.000	0	0-0	1	0.76	1.00
2015	Oak	AL	56	0	0	12	58.2	242	43	27	25	4	1	1	1	24	1	65	4	0	4	2	.667	0	0-2	6	2.51	3.84
2016	Oak	AL	34	0	0	4	40.2	163	30	19	19	3	1	1	1	17	0	37	2	0	2	0	1.000	0	0-0	5	2.76	4.20
6 ML YEARS			216	0	0	39	231.2	984	197	119	112	24	9	4	6	109	13	242	19	0	11	15	.423	0	0-6	31	3.58	4.35

Francisco Rodriguez

Pitches: R Bats: R Pos: RP-61 　　　　　Ht: 6'0" Wt: 195 Born: 1/7/1982 Age: 35

Year	Team	Lg	G	GS	CG	GF	IP	BFP	H	R	ER	HR	SH	SF	HB	TBB	IBB	SO	WP	Bk	W	L	Pct	Sh	Sv-Op	Hld	ERC	ERA
2002	LAA	AL	5	0	0	4	5.2	21	3	0	0	0	0	0	1	2	1	13	0	0	0	0	-	0	0-0	0	1.52	0.00
2003	LAA	AL	59	0	0	23	86.0	334	50	30	29	12	2	4	2	35	5	95	7	0	8	3	.727	0	2-6	7	2.25	3.03
2004	LAA	AL	69	0	0	29	84.0	335	51	21	17	2	2	1	1	33	1	123	5	0	4	1	.800	0	12-19	27	1.64	1.82
2005	LAA	AL	66	0	0	58	67.1	279	45	20	20	7	1	1	0	32	3	91	8	0	2	5	.286	0	**45-50**	0	2.52	2.67
2006	LAA	AL	69	0	0	58	73.0	296	52	16	14	6	3	0	1	28	5	98	10	0	2	3	.400	0	**47-51**	0	2.35	1.73
2007	LAA	AL	64	0	0	56	67.1	285	50	22	21	3	1	4	1	34	4	90	7	1	5	2	.714	0	40-46	0	2.74	2.81
2008	LAA	AL	76	0	0	69	68.1	288	54	21	17	4	1	1	2	34	4	77	6	0	2	3	.400	0	**62-69**	0	3.06	2.24
2009	NYM	NL	70	0	0	66	68.0	295	51	34	28	7	4	1	1	38	6	73	1	0	3	6	.333	0	35-42	0	3.18	3.71
2010	NYM	NL	53	0	0	46	57.1	236	45	14	14	3	1	1	2	21	4	67	3	1	4	2	.667	0	25-30	0	2.53	2.20
2011	2 Tms		73	0	0	36	71.2	307	67	22	21	4	2	1	2	26	4	79	4	0	6	2	.750	0	23-29	17	3.25	2.64
2012	Mil	NL	78	0	0	13	72.0	305	65	37	35	8	1	3	0	31	1	72	6	0	2	7	.222	0	3-10	32	3.73	4.38
2013	2 Tms		48	0	0	23	46.2	193	42	14	14	7	3	0	1	14	4	54	2	0	3	2	.600	0	10-10	5	3.44	2.70
2014	Mil	NL	69	0	0	66	68.0	268	49	23	23	14	2	0	1	18	1	73	0	0	5	5	.500	0	44-49	0	2.77	3.04
2015	Mil	NL	60	0	0	55	57.0	216	38	15	14	6	1	2	0	11	1	62	3	0	1	3	.250	0	38-40	0	1.69	2.21
2016	Det	AL	61	0	0	55	58.1	235	45	24	21	6	0	3	1	21	1	52	4	0	3	4	.429	0	44-**49**	0	2.81	3.24
11	NYM	NL	42	0	0	34	42.2	187	44	15	15	3	2	1	2	16	4	46	2	0	2	2	.500	0	23-26	0	3.94	3.16
11	Mil	NL	31	0	0	2	29.0	120	23	7	6	1	0	0	0	10	0	33	2	0	4	0	1.000	0	0-3	17	2.32	1.86
13	Mil	NL	25	0	0	18	24.2	97	17	3	3	2	2	0	0	9	3	26	0	0	1	1	.500	0	10-10	1	2.10	1.09
13	Bal	AL	23	0	0	5	22.0	96	25	11	11	5	1	0	1	5	1	28	2	0	2	1	.667	0	0-0	4	5.11	4.50
Postseason			26	0	0	8	36.2	158	32	15	12	5	1	3	1	18	2	49	5	0	5	4	.556	0	3-5	6	3.99	2.95
15 ML YEARS			920	0	0	657	950.2	3893	707	313	288	89	24	22	16	378	41	1119	66	2	50	48	.510	0	430-500	88	2.67	2.73

Joely Rodriguez

Pitches: L Bats: L Pos: RP-12 　　joe-EL-ee　　Ht: 6'1" Wt: 200 Born: 11/14/1991 Age: 25

Year	Team	Lg	G	GS	CG	GF	IP	BFP	H	R	ER	HR	SH	SF	HB	TBB	IBB	SO	WP	Bk	W	L	Pct	Sh	Sv-Op	Hld	ERC	ERA
2012	StCol	A-	14	14	0	0	64.0	269	74	37	32	2	2	3	1	15	0	32	6	0	3	4	.429	0	0- -	-	3.98	4.50
2013	2 Tms	Low	26	26	0	0	140.0	579	142	60	42	8	2	1	4	39	0	101	10	0	9	8	.529	0	0- -	-	3.59	2.70
2014	Altna	AA	30	21	2	4	134.0	574	151	80	72	10	5	2	1	43	1	73	6	1	6	11	.353	0	1- -	-	4.40	4.84
2015	LV	AAA	13	13	1	0	68.1	318	89	48	48	3	2	1	1	37	2	33	4	1	2	6	.250	0	0- -	-	6.11	6.32
2015	Rdng	AA	19	8	0	3	61.0	266	73	41	40	8	3	1	0	20	0	41	7	1	5	4	.556	0	0- -	-	5.23	5.90
2016	Rdng	AA	33	0	0	14	49.0	198	46	18	14	3	4	1	0	16	1	41	5	0	7	0	1.000	0	2- -	-	3.30	2.57
2016	Clrwtr	A+	7	0	0	0	8.1	29	3	0	0	0	0	0	0	1	0	10	0	0	0	0	-	0	3- -	-	0.44	0.00
2016	LV	AAA	13	0	0	1	19.1	77	16	6	6	0	1	1	0	6	0	18	0	0	0	0	-	0	0- -	-	2.26	2.79
2016	Phi	NL	12	0	0	1	9.2	39	8	3	3	0	0	0	1	4	1	7	0	0	0	0	-	0	0- -	3	2.91	2.79

Sean Rodriguez

Bats: R Throws: R Pos: 1B-57;2B-29;SS-27;PH-25;RF-17;3B-11;LF-10;PR-9;CF-5 　　Ht: 6'0" Wt: 200 Born: 4/26/1985 Age: 32

Year	Team	Lg	G	AB	H	2B	3B	HR	(Hm	Rd)	TB	R	RBI	RC	TBB	IBB	SO	HBP	SH	SF	SB	CS	GDP	Avg	OBP	Slg	OPS
2008	LAA	AL	59	167	34	8	1	3	(2	1)	53	18	10	12	14	0	55	3	2	1	3	1	3	.204	.276	.317	.593
2009	LAA	AL	12	25	5	0	0	2	(0	2)	11	4	4	2	3	0	7	0	0	1	0	0	0	.200	.276	.440	.716
2010	TB	AL	118	343	86	19	2	9	(5	4)	136	53	40	38	21	1	97	8	5	1	13	3	10	.251	.308	.397	.705
2011	TB	AL	131	373	83	20	3	8	(4	4)	133	45	36	41	38	2	87	18	5	2	11	7	8	.223	.323	.357	.679
2012	TB	AL	112	301	64	14	1	6	(3	3)	98	36	32	32	27	1	75	3	8	3	5	0	7	.213	.281	.326	.607
2013	TB	AL	96	195	48	10	1	5	(3	2)	75	21	23	21	17	0	59	5	3	2	1	3	3	.246	.320	.385	.704
2014	TB	AL	96	237	50	13	3	12	(7	5)	105	30	41	29	10	0	66	6	3	3	2	1	3	.211	.258	.443	.701
2015	Pit	NL	139	224	55	12	1	4	(2	2)	81	25	17	17	5	0	63	6	5	0	2	2	9	.246	.281	.362	.642
2016	Pit	NL	140	300	81	16	1	18	(7	11)	153	49	56	53	33	2	102	5	1	3	2	1	6	.270	.349	.510	.859
Postseason			13	28	5	1	0	1	(0	1)	9	6	2	1	2	0	5	0	0	0	0	0	0	.179	.233	.321	.555
9 ML YEARS			903	2165	506	112	13	67	(33	34)	845	281	259	245	168	6	611	54	32	16	39	18	51	.234	.303	.390	.693

Chaz Roe

Pitches: R Bats: R Pos: RP-30 　　ROW　　Ht: 6'5" Wt: 190 Born: 10/9/1986 Age: 30

Year	Team	Lg	G	GS	CG	GF	IP	BFP	H	R	ER	HR	SH	SF	HB	TBB	IBB	SO	WP	Bk	W	L	Pct	Sh	Sv-Op	Hld	ERC	ERA
2016	Norfolk*	AAA	33	0	0	12	37.2	146	27	10	10	1	2	1	1	10	1	45	2	0	1	2	.333	0	4- -	-	1.82	2.39
2013	Ari	NL	21	0	0	4	22.1	95	18	10	10	3	2	1	0	13	3	24	1	0	1	0	1.000	0	0-2	1	3.78	4.03
2014	NYY	AL	3	0	0	2	2.0	13	3	3	2	0	0	1	0	3	0	4	1	0	0	0	-	0	0-0	0	9.89	9.00
2015	Bal	AL	36	0	0	6	41.1	177	44	19	19	4	1	1	1	17	2	38	0	0	4	2	.667	0	0-1	4	4.62	4.14

Year	Team	Lg	HOW MUCH HE PITCHED						WHAT HE GAVE UP											THE RESULTS							
			G	GS	CG	GF	IP	BFP	H	R	ER	HR	SH	SF	HB	TBB	IBB	SO	WP	Bk	W	L	Pct	Sh	Sv-Op	Hld	ERC	ERA
2016	2 Tms		30	0	0	11	29.2	124	22	12	12	2	0	2	1	14	1	37	1	0	2	0	1.000	0	0-1	3	2.82	3.64
16	Bal	AL	9	0	0	6	9.2	44	8	4	4	2	0	0	0	7	0	11	1	0	1	0	1.000	0	0-0	0	5.07	4.22
16	Atl	NL	21	0	0	5	20.0	80	14	8	8	0	0	2	1	7	1	26	0	0	1	0	1.000	0	0-1	3	1.86	3.60
4 ML YEARS			90	0	0	23	95.1	409	87	44	43	9	3	5	2	47	6	103	3	0	7	2	.778	0	0-4	8	3.94	4.06

Jason Rogers

Bats: R **Throws:** R **Pos:** PH-17;1B-5;3B-4 **Ht:** 6'1" **Wt:** 250 **Born:** 3/13/1988 **Age:** 29

Year	Team	Lg	BATTING																	RUNNING			AVERAGES			
			G	AB	H	2B	3B	HR	(Hm | Rd)	TB	R	RBI	RC	TBB	IBB	SO	HBP	SH	SF	SB	CS	GDP	Avg	OBP	Slg	OPS
2016	Indy*	AAA	105	372	98	18	2	6	(- | -)	138	38	40	50	43	1	78	1	0	4	1	0	15	.263	.338	.371	.709
2014	Mil	NL	8	9	1	1	0	0	(0 | 0)	2	0	0	0	1	0	1	0	0	0	0	0	0	.111	.200	.222	.422
2015	Mil	NL	86	152	45	6	2	4	(2 | 2)	67	22	16	22	15	0	34	2	0	0	0	0	2	.296	.367	.441	.808
2016	Pit	NL	23	25	2	0	1	0	(0 | 0)	4	2	2	3	7	0	9	1	0	0	0	0	1	.080	.303	.160	.463
3 ML YEARS			117	186	48	7	3	4	(2 | 2)	73	24	18	25	23	0	44	3	0	0	0	0	3	.258	.349	.392	.742

Taylor Rogers

Pitches: L **Bats:** L **Pos:** RP-57 **Ht:** 6'3" **Wt:** 170 **Born:** 12/17/1990 **Age:** 26

Year	Team	Lg	HOW MUCH HE PITCHED						WHAT HE GAVE UP											THE RESULTS							
			G	GS	CG	GF	IP	BFP	H	R	ER	HR	SH	SF	HB	TBB	IBB	SO	WP	Bk	W	L	Pct	Sh	Sv-Op	Hld	ERC	ERA
2012	2 Tms	Low	15	10	0	0	63.1	264	53	25	16	7	1	1	5	17	0	74	5	0	4	3	.571	0	0- -	-	3.02	2.27
2013	2 Tms	Low	25	24	3	0	140.2	578	133	58	45	6	5	3	9	36	0	93	9	0	11	7	.611	2	0- -	-	3.15	2.88
2014	NwBrit	AA	24	24	1	0	145.0	606	150	63	53	4	1	2	6	37	0	113	4	0	11	6	.647	0	0- -	-	3.42	3.29
2015	Roch	AAA	28	27	2	1	174.0	732	190	83	77	9	7	6	4	44	2	126	4	2	11	12	.478	0	0- -	-	3.81	3.98
2016	Roch	AAA	7	2	0	1	18.0	85	24	15	9	1	1	2	0	6	0	15	0	0	1	1	.500	0	0- -	-	5.19	4.50
2016	Min	AL	57	0	0	8	61.1	264	63	29	27	7	0	1	5	16	3	64	1	0	3	1	.750	0	0-0	9	3.99	3.96

Miguel Rojas

Bats: R **Throws:** R **Pos:** 2B-45;1B-41;SS-33;PH-18;3B-16;PR-10 **Ht:** 5'11" **Wt:** 195 **Born:** 2/24/1989 **Age:** 28

Year	Team	Lg	BATTING																	RUNNING			AVERAGES			
			G	AB	H	2B	3B	HR	(Hm	Rd)	TB	R	RBI	RC	TBB	IBB	SO	HBP	SH	SF	SB	CS	GDP	Avg	OBP	Slg	OPS
2014	LAD	NL	85	149	27	3	0	1	(0	1)	33	16	9	6	10	1	28	2	1	0	0	0	5	.181	.242	.221	.464
2015	Mia	NL	60	142	40	7	1	1	(1	0)	52	13	17	15	11	1	16	0	2	2	0	1	4	.282	.329	.366	.695
2016	Mia	NL	123	194	48	12	0	1	(0	1)	63	27	14	14	11	2	27	1	6	2	2	1	10	.247	.288	.325	.613
Postseason			1	1	0	0	0	0	(0	0)	0	0	0	0	0	0	0	0	0	0	0	0	0	.000	.000	.000	.000
3 ML YEARS			268	485	115	22	1	3	(1	2)	148	56	40	35	32	4	71	3	9	4	2	2	19	.237	.286	.305	.591

David Rollins

Pitches: L **Bats:** L **Pos:** RP-11 **Ht:** 6'1" **Wt:** 210 **Born:** 12/21/1989 **Age:** 27

Year	Team	Lg	HOW MUCH HE PITCHED						WHAT HE GAVE UP											THE RESULTS							
			G	GS	CG	GF	IP	BFP	H	R	ER	HR	SH	SF	HB	TBB	IBB	SO	WP	Bk	W	L	Pct	Sh	Sv-Op	Hld	ERC	ERA
2012	2 Tms	Low	24	24	0	0	108.2	448	91	43	36	7	4	1	4	45	0	100	5	0	7	4	.636	0	0- -	-	3.22	2.98
2013	Lancst	A+	23	14	0	7	97.1	405	81	50	43	9	1	3	4	32	0	96	3	1	8	5	.615	0	3- -	-	2.98	3.98
2013	CpChr	AA	6	4	0	0	33.0	142	38	18	16	4	1	1	1	10	0	32	1	1	3	0	.000	0	0- -	-	4.93	4.36
2014	CpChr	AA	27	12	0	9	78.0	331	74	38	33	7	0	3	2	22	1	77	0	2	3	4	.429	0	1- -	-	3.29	3.81
2015	Tacom	AAA	7	0	0	0	9.1	34	7	0	0	0	0	0	0	1	0	8	1	0	0	0	-	0	0- -	-	1.43	0.00
2016	Tacom	AAA	37	0	0	14	45.1	174	39	20	19	4	2	1	0	6	2	32	2	0	5	0	1.000	0	2- -	-	2.29	3.77
2015	Sea	AL	20	0	0	7	25.0	118	37	21	21	3	1	0	2	8	1	21	0	0	0	2	.000	0	0-0	1	7.14	7.56
2016	Sea	AL	11	0	0	6	9.1	47	12	8	8	2	0	0	0	7	1	6	1	0	1	0	1.000	0	0-0	0	7.88	7.71
2 ML YEARS			31	0	0	13	34.1	165	49	29	29	5	1	0	2	15	2	27	1	0	1	2	.333	0	0-0	1	7.34	7.60

Jimmy Rollins

Bats: B **Throws:** R **Pos:** SS-35;DH-4;PH-3 **Ht:** 5'7" **Wt:** 175 **Born:** 11/27/1978 **Age:** 38

Year	Team	Lg	BATTING																	RUNNING			AVERAGES			
			G	AB	H	2B	3B	HR	(Hm	Rd)	TB	R	RBI	RC	TBB	IBB	SO	HBP	SH	SF	SB	CS	GDP	Avg	OBP	Slg	OPS
2000	Phi	NL	14	53	17	1	1	0	(0	0)	20	5	5	8	2	0	7	0	0	0	3	0	0	.321	.345	.377	.723
2001	Phi	NL	158	656	180	29	12	14	(8	6)	275	97	54	96	48	2	108	2	9	5	46	8	5	.274	.323	.419	.743
2002	Phi	NL	154	637	156	33	10	11	(3	8)	242	82	60	72	54	3	103	4	6	4	31	13	14	.245	.306	.380	.686
2003	Phi	NL	156	628	165	42	6	8	(5	3)	243	85	62	76	54	4	113	0	5	2	20	12	9	.263	.320	.387	.707
2004	Phi	NL	154	657	190	43	12	14	(8	6)	299	119	73	108	57	3	73	3	6	2	30	9	4	.289	.348	.455	.803
2005	Phi	NL	158	677	196	38	11	12	(5	7)	292	115	54	100	47	8	71	4	2	2	41	6	9	.290	.338	.431	.770
2006	Phi	NL	158	689	191	45	9	25	(15	10)	329	127	83	114	57	2	80	5	0	7	36	4	12	.277	.334	.478	.811
2007	Phi	NL	162	716	212	38	20	30	(18	12)	380	139	94	124	49	5	85	7	0	6	41	6	11	.296	.344	.531	.875
2008	Phi	NL	137	556	154	38	9	11	(5	6)	243	76	59	95	58	7	55	5	3	3	47	3	11	.277	.349	.437	.786
2009	Phi	NL	155	672	168	43	5	21	(10	11)	284	100	77	88	44	1	70	2	2	5	31	8	7	.250	.296	.423	.719
2010	Phi	NL	88	350	85	16	3	8	(4	4)	131	48	41	54	40	2	32	1	0	3	17	1	4	.243	.320	.374	.694
2011	Phi	NL	142	567	150	22	2	16	(7	9)	226	87	63	82	58	5	59	3	0	3	30	8	9	.268	.338	.399	.736
2012	Phi	NL	156	632	158	33	5	23	(11	12)	270	102	68	88	62	2	96	0	2	3	30	5	9	.250	.316	.427	.743
2013	Phi	NL	160	600	151	36	2	6	(4	2)	209	65	39	70	59	6	93	1	3	3	22	6	12	.252	.318	.348	.667
2014	Phi	NL	138	538	131	22	4	17	(7	10)	212	78	55	69	64	2	100	1	3	3	28	6	6	.243	.323	.394	.717
2015	LAD	NL	144	517	116	24	3	13	(6	7)	185	71	41	38	44	0	86	0	1	1	12	8	12	.224	.285	.358	.643
2016	CWS	AL	41	149	33	8	1	2	(0	2)	49	25	8	12	16	0	33	0	0	1	5	2	2	.221	.295	.329	.624
Postseason			50	195	48	12	1	3	(1	2)	71	27	15	16	16	0	36	2	1	1	11	4	6	.246	.308	.364	.673
17 ML YEARS			2275	9294	2455	511	115	231	(116	115)	3889	1421	936	1294	813	52	1264	38	42	53	470	105	136	.264	.324	.418	.743

Enny Romero

Pitches: L Bats: L Pos: RP-52
ENN-nee
Ht: 6'3" Wt: 215 Born: 1/24/1991 Age: 26

			HOW MUCH HE PITCHED						WHAT HE GAVE UP														THE RESULTS						
Year	Team	Lg	G	GS	CG	GF	IP	BFP	H	R	ER	HR	SH	SF	HB	TBB	IBB	SO	WP	Bk	W	L	Pct	Sh	Sv-Op	Hld	ERC	ERA
2013	TB	AL	1	1	0	0	4.2	18	1	0	0	0	0	0	0	4	0	0	0	0	0	0	-	0	0-0	0	1.35	0.00
2015	TB	AL	23	0	0	7	30.0	140	39	18	17	1	1	1	0	13	0	31	2	0	0	2	.000	0	0-2	3	5.38	5.10
2016	TB	AL	52	0	0	15	45.2	204	42	31	30	7	0	4	0	28	1	50	1	0	2	0	1.000	0	1-2	6	4.79	5.91
	3 ML YEARS		76	1	0	22	80.1	362	82	49	47	8	1	5	0	45	1	81	3	0	2	2	.500	0	1-4	9	4.78	5.27

Stefen Romero

Bats: R Throws: R Pos: LF-6;PH-4;RF-2;1B-1
STEFF-ehn
Ht: 6'2" Wt: 220 Born: 10/17/1988 Age: 28

						BATTING																	RUNNING			AVERAGES			
Year	Team	Lg	G	AB	H	2B	3B	HR	(Hm	Rd)	TB	R	RBI	RC	TBB	IBB	SO	HBP	SH	SF	SB	CS	GDP	Avg	OBP	Slg	OPS
2016	Tacom*	AAA	106	418	127	24	6	21	(-	-)	226	70	85	81	36	4	67	4	0	4	1	1	9	.304	.361	.541	.902
2014	Sea	AL	72	177	34	6	2	3	(1	2)	53	19	11	7	4	0	48	6	2	1	0	4	5	.192	.234	.299	.533
2015	Sea	AL	13	21	4	1	0	1	(0	1)	8	6	3	3	3	0	6	0	0	0	0	0	0	.190	.292	.381	.673
2016	Sea	AL	9	17	4	1	0	0	(0	0)	5	1	3	3	1	0	4	0	0	1	0	0	0	.235	.263	.294	.557
	3 ML YEARS		94	215	42	8	2	4	(1	3)	66	26	17	13	8	0	58	6	2	2	0	4	5	.195	.242	.307	.549

Andrew Romine

Bats: B Throws: R Pos: 3B-44;CF-22;1B-20;PR-17;SS-14;2B-12;DH-4;PH-4;RF-2;LF-1
ROW-mine
Ht: 6'1" Wt: 200 Born: 12/24/1985 Age: 31

						BATTING																	RUNNING			AVERAGES			
Year	Team	Lg	G	AB	H	2B	3B	HR	(Hm	Rd)	TB	R	RBI	RC	TBB	IBB	SO	HBP	SH	SF	SB	CS	GDP	Avg	OBP	Slg	OPS
2010	LAA	AL	5	11	1	0	0	0	(0	0)	1	0	0	0	0	0	4	0	1	0	0	0	0	.091	.091	.091	.182
2011	LAA	AL	10	16	2	0	0	0	(0	0)	2	2	0	0	1	0	6	0	1	0	1	0	0	.125	.176	.125	.301
2012	LAA	AL	12	17	7	0	0	0	(0	0)	7	2	1	5	3	0	3	0	1	0	1	0	0	.412	.500	.412	.912
2013	LAA	AL	47	108	28	3	0	0	(0	0)	31	9	10	12	7	0	24	1	6	1	1	0	2	.259	.308	.287	.595
2014	Det	AL	94	251	57	6	0	2	(1	1)	69	30	12	17	18	0	60	0	4	0	12	2	5	.227	.279	.275	.554
2015	Det	AL	109	184	47	5	0	2	(0	2)	58	25	15	13	11	1	46	3	4	1	10	5	4	.255	.307	.315	.622
2016	Det	AL	109	174	41	5	2	2	(1	1)	56	21	16	15	13	0	38	4	3	0	8	0	5	.236	.304	.322	.626
	Postseason		3	11	2	0	0	0	(0	0)	2	0	0	0	0	0	4	0	0	0	0	0	0	.182	.182	.182	.364
	7 ML YEARS		386	761	183	19	2	6	(2	4)	224	89	54	62	53	1	181	8	20	2	33	7	16	.240	.296	.294	.590

Austin Romine

Bats: R Throws: R Pos: C-50;1B-6;PH-5;DH-4;PR-1
ROW-mine
Ht: 6'1" Wt: 220 Born: 11/22/1988 Age: 28

						BATTING																	RUNNING			AVERAGES			
Year	Team	Lg	G	AB	H	2B	3B	HR	(Hm	Rd)	TB	R	RBI	RC	TBB	IBB	SO	HBP	SH	SF	SB	CS	GDP	Avg	OBP	Slg	OPS
2011	NYY	AL	9	19	3	0	0	0	(0	0)	3	2	0	0	1	0	5	0	0	0	0	0	0	.158	.200	.158	.358
2013	NYY	AL	60	135	28	9	0	1	(0	1)	40	15	10	8	8	0	37	1	3	1	1	0	7	.207	.255	.296	.551
2014	NYY	AL	7	13	3	1	0	0	(0	0)	4	2	1	2	0	0	4	0	0	0	0	0	0	.231	.308	.308	.538
2015	NYY	AL	1	2	0	0	0	0	(0	0)	0	0	0	0	0	0	0	0	0	0	0	0	0	.000	.000	.000	.000
2016	NYY	AL	62	165	40	11	0	4	(1	3)	63	17	26	19	7	1	31	0	1	3	1	0	7	.242	.269	.382	.650
	5 ML YEARS		139	334	74	21	0	5	(1	4)	110	36	37	29	16	1	77	1	4	4	2	0	14	.222	.256	.329	.586

Sergio Romo

Pitches: R Bats: R Pos: RP-40
Ht: 5'11" Wt: 185 Born: 3/4/1983 Age: 34

			HOW MUCH HE PITCHED						WHAT HE GAVE UP														THE RESULTS						
Year	Team	Lg	G	GS	CG	GF	IP	BFP	H	R	ER	HR	SH	SF	HB	TBB	IBB	SO	WP	Bk	W	L	Pct	Sh	Sv-Op	Hld	ERC	ERA
2016	Scrmto*	AAA	7	0	0	0	6.1	27	8	4	4	1	0	0	0	0	0	11	0	0	1	1	.500	0	0- -	0	4.23	5.68
2008	SF	NL	29	0	0	8	34.0	130	16	13	8	3	2	1	3	8	1	33	0	0	3	1	.750	0	0-0	5	1.27	2.12
2009	SF	NL	45	0	0	9	34.0	143	30	15	15	1	2	0	1	11	0	41	2	0	5	2	.714	0	2-2	10	2.76	3.97
2010	SF	NL	68	0	0	13	62.0	247	46	16	15	6	4	2	4	14	2	70	0	0	5	3	.625	0	0-4	21	2.26	2.18
2011	SF	NL	65	0	0	16	48.0	175	29	8	8	2	2	0	0	5	1	70	0	0	3	1	.750	0	1-2	23	1.08	1.50
2012	SF	NL	69	0	0	27	55.1	215	37	11	11	5	2	0	3	10	1	63	2	0	4	2	.667	0	14-15	23	1.72	1.79
2013	SF	NL	65	0	0	52	60.1	250	53	20	17	5	1	1	1	12	3	58	1	0	5	8	.385	0	38-43	0	2.47	2.54
2014	SF	NL	64	0	0	35	58.0	230	43	24	24	9	2	0	4	12	2	59	2	0	6	4	.600	0	23-28	11	2.54	3.72
2015	SF	NL	70	0	0	14	57.1	230	51	20	19	3	2	0	1	10	2	71	4	0	0	5	.000	0	2-4	34	2.37	2.98
2016	SF	NL	40	0	0	13	30.2	117	26	9	9	2	0	0	0	7	1	33	1	0	1	0	1.000	0	4-4	11	3.13	2.64
	Postseason		25	0	0	13	21.1	81	16	5	5	2	0	0	0	2	0	20	1	0	3	1	.750	0	4-6	4	1.68	2.11
	9 ML YEARS		515	0	0	187	439.2	1737	331	136	126	39	15	4	17	89	13	498	12	0	32	26	.552	0	84-102	141	2.10	2.58

Bruce Rondon

Pitches: R Bats: R Pos: RP-37
rohn-DOHN
Ht: 6'3" Wt: 275 Born: 12/9/1990 Age: 26

			HOW MUCH HE PITCHED						WHAT HE GAVE UP														THE RESULTS						
Year	Team	Lg	G	GS	CG	GF	IP	BFP	H	R	ER	HR	SH	SF	HB	TBB	IBB	SO	WP	Bk	W	L	Pct	Sh	Sv-Op	Hld	ERC	ERA
2016	Toledo*	AAA	22	0	0	18	21.2	102	23	9	9	1	4	0	1	16	3	30	1	0	2	2	.500	0	9- -	-	5.30	3.74
2013	Det	AL	30	0	0	12	28.2	122	28	11	11	2	1	2	0	11	0	30	7	1	1	2	.333	0	1-3	5	3.69	3.45
2015	Det	AL	35	0	0	15	31.0	145	31	22	20	3	3	2	2	19	1	36	2	0	1	0	1.000	0	5-9	3	4.97	5.81
2016	Det	AL	37	0	0	7	36.1	144	23	12	12	5	2	0	3	12	1	45	1	1	5	2	.714	0	0-2	6	2.43	2.97
	3 ML YEARS		102	0	0	34	96.0	411	82	45	43	10	6	4	5	42	2	111	10	2	7	4	.636	0	6-14	14	3.60	4.03

Hector Rondon

Pitches: R **Bats:** R **Pos:** RP-54   rohn-DOHN   **Ht:** 6'3" **Wt:** 230 **Born:** 2/26/1988 **Age:** 29

Year Team	Lg	G	GS	CG	GF	IP	BFP	H	R	ER	HR	SH	SF	HB	TBB	IBB	SO	WP	Bk	W	L	Pct	Sh	Sv-Op	Hld	ERC	ERA
2013 ChC	NL	45	0	0	14	54.2	242	52	29	29	6	4	3	3	25	5	44	4	0	2	1	.667	0	0-1	2	4.10	4.77
2014 ChC	NL	64	0	0	44	63.1	255	52	21	17	2	0	1	0	15	0	63	0	0	4	4	.500	0	29-33	1	2.10	2.42
2015 ChC	NL	72	0	0	47	70.0	281	55	19	13	4	3	1	3	15	2	69	5	1	6	4	.600	0	30-34	8	2.12	1.67
2016 ChC	NL	54	0	0	35	51.0	200	42	20	20	8	1	2	2	8	0	58	3	0	2	3	.400	0	18-23	7	2.75	3.53
Postseason		5	0	0	5	5.0	21	5	2	2	1	0	0	0	1	0	4	0	0	0	0	-	0	2-2	0	3.86	3.60
4 ML YEARS		235	0	0	140	239.0	978	201	89	79	20	8	7	8	63	7	234	12	1	14	12	.538	0	77-91	18	2.68	2.97

Jorge Rondon

Pitches: R **Bats:** R **Pos:** RP-2   rohn-DOHN   **Ht:** 6'1" **Wt:** 215 **Born:** 2/16/1988 **Age:** 29

Year Team	Lg	G	GS	CG	GF	IP	BFP	H	R	ER	HR	SH	SF	HB	TBB	IBB	SO	WP	Bk	W	L	Pct	Sh	Sv-Op	Hld	ERC	ERA
2016 Indy*	AAA	43	0	0	31	57.1	237	45	19	17	2	2	1	2	24	3	37	2	0	6	4	.600	0	12- -	-	2.64	2.67
2014 StL	NL	1	0	0	0	1.0	4	0	0	0	0	0	0	0	1	0	0	0	0	0	0	-	0	0-0	0	0.95	0.00
2015 2 Tms		10	0	0	3	14.1	81	28	26	21	3	0	0	0	9	0	9	1	0	0	1	.000	0	0-0	0	11.96	13.19
2016 Pit	NL	2	0	0	1	3.2	20	9	7	7	1	0	0	0	1	0	4	1	0	0	0	-	0	0-0	0	15.46	17.18
15 Col	NL	2	0	0	1	1.0	15	8	11	10	0	0	0	0	3	0	1	0	0	0	0	-	0	0-0	0	69.50	90.00
15 Bal	AL	8	0	0	2	13.1	66	20	15	11	3	0	0	0	6	0	8	1	0	0	1	.000	0	0-0	0	8.22	7.43
3 ML YEARS		13	0	0	4	19.0	105	37	33	28	4	0	0	0	11	0	13	2	0	0	1	.000	0	0-0	0	11.84	13.26

Jose Rondon

Bats: R **Throws:** R **Pos:** SS-7;PH-1   rohn-DOHN   **Ht:** 6'1" **Wt:** 195 **Born:** 3/3/1994 **Age:** 23

Year Team	Lg	G	AB	H	2B	3B	HR	(Hm	Rd)	TB	R	RBI	RC	TBB	IBB	SO	HBP	SH	SF	SB	CS	GDP	Avg	OBP	Slg	OPS
2012 2 Tms	Low	54	212	56	14	3	1	(-	-)	79	30	21	25	16	0	27	2	4	3	6	5	4	.264	.318	.373	.690
2013 Orem	R+	68	276	81	22	2	1	(-	-)	110	45	50	42	30	0	31	2	1	7	13	8	7	.293	.359	.399	.757
2014 3 Tms	Low	111	441	139	26	5	1	(-	-)	178	61	36	66	31	0	73	3	12	1	13	8	9	.315	.363	.404	.767
2015 Lk Els	A+	57	237	71	12	3	3	(-	-)	98	50	22	37	21	1	38	2	3	1	17	6	4	.300	.360	.414	.774
2015 SnAnt	AA	28	100	19	2	1	0	(-	-)	23	6	9	3	4	0	15	0	2	1	1	3	3	.190	.219	.230	.449
2016 SnAnt	AA	96	376	105	21	2	5	(-	-)	145	45	44	47	15	1	66	3	12	3	13	4	5	.279	.310	.386	.695
2016 ElPaso	AAA	24	80	24	4	0	1	(-	-)	31	8	9	9	1	0	12	0	0	1	0	1	0	.300	.305	.388	.692
2016 SD	NL	8	25	3	0	0	0	(0	0)	3	1	1	1	1	0	4	0	0	0	0	0	1	.120	.154	.120	.274

Adam Rosales

Bats: R **Throws:** R **Pos:** 3B-41;2B-36;PH-22;SS-15;PR-8;LF-2;1B-1;RF-1;DH-1   **Ht:** 6'2" **Wt:** 200 **Born:** 5/20/1983 **Age:** 34

Year Team	Lg	G	AB	H	2B	3B	HR	(Hm	Rd)	TB	R	RBI	RC	TBB	IBB	SO	HBP	SH	SF	SB	CS	GDP	Avg	OBP	Slg	OPS
2008 Cin	NL	18	29	6	1	0	0	(0	0)	7	0	2	2	1	0	4	0	0	0	1	0	0	.207	.233	.241	.475
2009 Cin	NL	87	230	49	10	1	4	(2	2)	73	23	19	22	26	0	46	5	2	3	1	2	2	.213	.303	.317	.620
2010 Oak	AL	80	255	69	8	2	7	(1	6)	102	31	31	31	19	0	65	1	2	2	2	2	1	.271	.321	.400	.721
2011 Oak	AL	24	61	6	0	0	2	(0	2)	12	5	8	0	4	0	13	1	0	2	0	0	4	.098	.162	.197	.358
2012 Oak	AL	42	99	22	5	0	2	(1	1)	33	12	8	6	11	1	24	0	0	1	0	0	0	.222	.297	.333	.631
2013 2 Tms	AL	68	147	28	5	0	5	(2	3)	48	15	12	6	10	1	34	4	4	1	0	0	4	.190	.259	.327	.586
2014 Tex	AL	56	164	43	7	0	4	(2	2)	62	20	19	23	13	0	42	3	0	0	4	2	5	.262	.328	.378	.706
2015 Tex	AL	55	114	26	4	0	3	(1	2)	39	14	7	9	10	0	30	1	0	0	4	4	4	.228	.296	.342	.638
2016 SD	AL	105	214	49	12	3	13	(9	4)	106	37	35	34	29	2	88	1	0	4	4	0	2	.229	.319	.495	.814
13 Oak	AL	51	136	26	5	0	4	(2	2)	43	11	8	5	10	1	31	4	4	0	0	0	4	.191	.267	.316	.583
13 Tex	AL	17	11	2	0	0	1	(0	1)	5	4	4	1	0	0	3	0	0	1	0	0	0	.182	.167	.455	.621
9 ML YEARS		535	1313	298	52	6	40	(18	22)	482	157	141	133	123	4	346	16	8	13	16	10	26	.227	.298	.367	.665

Alberto Rosario

Bats: R **Throws:** R **Pos:** C-17;PH-5;3B-1   **Ht:** 5'10" **Wt:** 190 **Born:** 1/10/1987 **Age:** 30

Year Team	Lg	G	AB	H	2B	3B	HR	(Hm	Rd)	TB	R	RBI	RC	TBB	IBB	SO	HBP	SH	SF	SB	CS	GDP	Avg	OBP	Slg	OPS
2012 Ark	AA	50	163	36	7	0	1	(-	-)	46	14	17	10	6	0	32	3	1	1	3	3	.221	.260	.282	.542
2012 Salt Lk	AAA	21	77	17	3	0	1	(-	-)	23	6	8	6	4	0	17	1	1	0	4	1	1	.221	.268	.299	.567
2013 Portlnd	AA	11	36	6	0	0	0	(-	-)	6	3	4	1	3	0	4	1	0	1	0	0	1	.167	.244	.167	.411
2013 Pwtckt	AAA	30	90	21	3	0	2	(-	-)	30	13	6	9	7	0	22	2	3	0	0	0	3	.233	.303	.333	.636
2014 Chatt	AA	25	47	13	1	0	1	(-	-)	17	3	7	5	3	0	15	0	0	0	0	0	1	.277	.320	.362	.682
2015 Sprgfld	AA	44	149	27	8	0	1	(-	-)	38	9	5	8	9	2	20	3	4	0	0	0	2	.181	.242	.255	.497
2016 Memp	AAA	39	114	32	5	0	0	(-	-)	37	8	13	12	6	0	20	2	0	2	0	0	6	.281	.323	.325	.647
2016 StL	NL	20	38	7	2	0	0	(0	0)	9	3	2	1	2	0	5	0	1	0	0	0	2	.184	.225	.237	.462

Eddie Rosario

Bats: L **Throws:** R **Pos:** LF-57;CF-37;PH-4;RF-1   **Ht:** 6'1" **Wt:** 180 **Born:** 9/28/1991 **Age:** 25

Year Team	Lg	G	AB	H	2B	3B	HR	(Hm	Rd)	TB	R	RBI	RC	TBB	IBB	SO	HBP	SH	SF	SB	CS	GDP	Avg	OBP	Slg	OPS
2012 2 Tms	Low	100	411	123	35	4	13	(-	-)	205	62	74	69	32	1	71	1	0	5	11	11	10	.299	.347	.499	.846
2013 FtMyrs	A+	52	207	68	13	5	6	(-	-)	109	40	35	39	17	1	29	2	0	5	3	6	5	.329	.377	.527	.903
2013 NwBrit	AA	70	289	82	19	3	4	(-	-)	119	40	38	40	21	1	67	0	1	2	7	4	3	.284	.330	.412	.742
2014 NwBrit	AA	79	316	75	20	3	8	(-	-)	125	40	34	35	17	0	68	1	0	2	8	4	5	.237	.277	.396	.672
2015 Roch	AAA	23	95	23	2	1	3	(-	-)	36	11	12	10	5	0	17	0	0	0	1	1	2	.242	.280	.379	.659

BATTING / RUNNING / AVERAGES

Year	Team	Lg	G	AB	H	2B	3B	HR	(Hm	Rd)	TB	R	RBI	RC	TBB	IBB	SO	HBP	SH	SF	SB	CS	GDP	Avg	OBP	Slg	OPS
2016	Roch	AAA	41	160	51	14	0	7	(-	-)	86	26	25	28	7	1	25	0	0	2	5	3	4	.319	.343	.538	.881
2015	Min	AL	122	453	121	18	**15**	13	(10	3)	208	60	50	58	15	3	118	0	3	3	11	6	5	.267	.289	.459	.748
2016	Min	AL	92	335	90	17	2	10	(4	6)	141	52	32	35	12	2	91	2	2	3	5	2	4	.269	.295	.421	.716
	2 ML YEARS		214	788	211	35	17	23	(14	9)	349	112	82	93	27	5	209	2	5	6	16	8	9	.268	.292	.443	.735

Trevor Rosenthal

Pitches: R Bats: R Pos: RP-45   Ht: 6'2" Wt: 230 Born: 5/29/1990 Age: 27

Year	Team	Lg	G	GS	CG	GF	IP	BFP	H	R	ER	HR	SH	SF	HB	TBB	IBB	SO	WP	Bk	W	L	Pct	Sh	Sv-Op	Hld	ERC	ERA
2012	StL	NL	19	0	0	7	22.2	89	14	7	7	2	1	0	1	7	0	25	1	0	0	2	.000	0	0-0	3	1.89	2.78
2013	StL	NL	74	0	0	15	75.1	311	63	25	22	4	3	0	6	20	0	108	3	0	2	4	.333	0	3-8	29	2.68	2.63
2014	StL	NL	72	0	0	59	70.1	308	57	25	25	2	2	4	4	42	5	87	1	1	2	6	.250	0	45-51	2	3.36	3.20
2015	StL	NL	68	0	0	57	68.2	287	62	16	16	3	1	0	1	25	3	83	7	0	2	4	.333	0	48-51	0	3.04	2.10
2016	StL	NL	45	0	0	27	40.1	197	48	22	20	3	1	0	3	29	0	56	0	0	2	4	.333	0	14-18	0	6.59	4.46
	Postseason		23	0	0	15	26.0	102	15	2	2	0	0	0	0	11	3	42	1	1	1	0	1.000	0	7-9	2	1.41	0.69
	5 ML YEARS		278	0	0	165	277.1	1192	244	95	90	14	8	4	15	123	8	359	12	1	8	20	.286	0	110-128	34	3.39	2.92

David Ross

Bats: R Throws: R Pos: C-58;PH-10   Ht: 6'2" Wt: 230 Born: 3/19/1977 Age: 40

Year	Team	Lg	G	AB	H	2B	3B	HR	(Hm	Rd)	TB	R	RBI	RC	TBB	IBB	SO	HBP	SH	SF	SB	CS	GDP	Avg	OBP	Slg	OPS
2002	LAD	NL	8	10	2	1	0	1	(0	1)	6	2	2	2	2	0	4	1	0	0	0	0	0	.200	.385	.600	.985
2003	LAD	NL	40	124	32	7	0	10	(5	5)	69	19	18	18	13	0	42	2	0	1	0	0	4	.258	.336	.556	.892
2004	LAD	NL	70	165	28	3	1	5	(2	3)	48	13	15	11	15	1	62	5	0	5	0	0	3	.170	.253	.291	.544
2005	2 Tms	NL	51	125	30	8	1	3	(2	1)	49	11	15	13	6	0	28	2	2	3	0	0	3	.240	.279	.392	.671
2006	Cin	NL	90	247	63	15	1	21	(13	8)	143	37	52	43	37	7	75	3	4	5	0	0	4	.255	.353	.579	.932
2007	Cin	NL	112	311	63	10	0	17	(12	5)	124	32	39	27	30	4	92	0	5	2	0	0	9	.203	.271	.399	.670
2008	2 Tms		60	142	32	9	0	3	(1	2)	50	18	13	19	32	4	39	1	6	1	0	1	3	.225	.369	.352	.721
2009	Atl	NL	54	128	35	9	0	7	(2	5)	65	18	20	20	21	0	39	1	1	0	0	0	1	.273	.380	.508	.888
2010	Atl	NL	59	121	35	13	2	2	(2	0)	58	15	28	22	20	0	28	1	2	1	0	1	5	.289	.392	.479	.871
2011	Atl	NL	52	152	40	7	0	6	(2	4)	65	14	23	22	16	0	51	0	2	0	0	1	1	.263	.333	.428	.761
2012	Atl	NL	62	176	45	7	0	9	(4	5)	79	18	23	21	18	0	60	0	0	2	1	0	5	.256	.321	.449	.770
2013	Bos	AL	36	102	22	5	0	4	(3	1)	39	11	10	7	11	0	42	1	2	0	1	0	3	.216	.298	.382	.681
2014	Bos	AL	50	152	28	7	0	7	(4	3)	56	16	15	13	16	1	58	0	2	1	0	1	3	.184	.260	.368	.629
2015	ChC	NL	72	159	28	9	0	1	(1	0)	40	6	9	8	20	7	61	0	2	1	1	0	1	.176	.267	.252	.518
2016	ChC	NL	67	166	38	6	0	10	(7	3)	74	24	32	25	30	6	54	0	4	5	0	1	3	.229	.338	.446	.784
05	Pit	NL	40	108	24	8	0	3	(2	1)	41	9	15	9	6	0	24	1	1	3	0	0	3	.222	.263	.380	.642
05	SD	NL	11	17	6	0	1	0	(0	0)	8	2	0	4	0	0	4	1	1	0	0	0	0	.353	.389	.471	.859
08	Cin	NL	52	134	31	9	0	3	(1	2)	49	17	13	19	32	4	36	1	5	1	0	1	3	.231	.381	.366	.747
08	Bos	AL	8	8	1	0	0	0	(0	0)	1	1	0	0	0	0	3	0	1	0	0	0	0	.125	.125	.125	.250
	Postseason		17	36	9	3	0	1	(1	0)	15	3	4	4	4	1	13	0	1	0	0	0	0	.250	.325	.417	.742
	15 ML YEARS		883	2280	521	116	5	106	(60	46)	965	254	314	271	287	30	735	17	32	27	3	5	49	.229	.316	.423	.739

Joe Ross

Pitches: R Bats: R Pos: SP-19   Ht: 6'4" Wt: 225 Born: 5/21/1993 Age: 24

Year	Team	Lg	G	GS	CG	GF	IP	BFP	H	R	ER	HR	SH	SF	HB	TBB	IBB	SO	WP	Bk	W	L	Pct	Sh	Sv-Op	Hld	ERC	ERA
2012	3 Tms	Low	15	15	0	0	54.2	233	51	28	26	4	1	4	1	22	0	56	3	0	0	4	.000	0	0- -	-	3.48	4.28
2013	FtWyn	A	23	23	0	0	122.1	524	124	55	51	7	8	6	5	40	1	79	4	0	5	8	.385	0	0- -	-	3.72	3.75
2014	Lk Els	A+	19	19	0	0	101.2	436	101	52	45	6	4	3	7	28	2	87	3	0	8	6	.571	0	0- -	-	3.47	3.98
2015	Hrsbrg	AA	9	9	0	0	51.1	206	46	18	16	3	3	0	3	12	0	54	1	0	2	2	.500	0	0- -	-	2.92	2.81
2015	Syrcse	AAA	5	5	0	0	24.2	93	15	6	6	2	0	0	0	7	0	15	2	0	3	1	.750	0	0- -	-	1.65	2.19
2015	Was	NL	16	13	0	1	76.2	314	64	33	31	7	3	1	2	21	0	69	1	0	5	5	.500	0	0-0	0	2.74	3.64
2016	Was	NL	19	19	0	0	105.0	447	108	43	40	9	7	3	6	29	3	93	2	0	7	5	.583	0	0-0	0	3.84	3.43
	2 ML YEARS		35	32	0	1	181.2	761	172	76	71	16	10	4	8	50	3	162	3	0	12	10	.545	0	0-0	0	3.36	3.52

Tyson Ross

Pitches: R Bats: R Pos: SP-1   Ht: 6'6" Wt: 245 Born: 4/22/1987 Age: 30

Year	Team	Lg	G	GS	CG	GF	IP	BFP	H	R	ER	HR	SH	SF	HB	TBB	IBB	SO	WP	Bk	W	L	Pct	Sh	Sv-Op	Hld	ERC	ERA
2010	Oak	AL	26	2	0	9	39.1	169	39	24	24	4	1	4	0	20	0	32	5	0	1	4	.200	0	1-2	2	4.60	5.49
2011	Oak	AL	9	6	0	1	36.0	145	33	12	11	1	1	0	0	13	1	24	2	0	3	3	.500	0	0-0	0	3.09	2.75
2012	Oak	AL	18	13	0	3	73.1	342	96	56	53	7	3	3	5	37	3	46	2	1	2	11	.154	0	0-0	0	6.68	6.50
2013	SD	NL	35	16	0	8	125.0	504	100	51	44	8	3	5	7	44	4	119	7	0	3	8	.273	0	0-0	0	2.84	3.17
2014	SD	NL	31	31	2	0	195.2	811	165	75	61	13	10	4	9	72	2	195	12	0	13	14	.481	1	0-0	0	3.07	2.81
2015	SD	NL	33	**33**	1	0	196.0	823	172	78	71	9	3	3	8	**84**	3	212	**14**	0	10	12	.455	0	0-0	0	3.33	3.26
2016	SD	NL	1	1	0	0	5.1	27	9	8	7	0	0	0	2	1	0	5	1	0	0	1	.000	0	0-0	0	8.24	11.81
	7 ML YEARS		153	102	3	21	670.2	2821	614	304	271	42	21	19	31	271	13	633	43	1	32	53	.376	1	1-2	2	3.58	3.64

Robbie Ross Jr.

Pitches: L **Bats**: L **Pos**: RP-54   **Ht**: 5'11" **Wt**: 215 **Born**: 6/24/1989 **Age**: 28

			HOW MUCH HE PITCHED					WHAT HE GAVE UP											THE RESULTS							
Year	Team	Lg	G	GS	CG	GF	IP	BFP	H	R	ER	HR	SH	SF	HB	TBB	IBB	SO	WP	Bk	W	L	Pct	Sh	Sv-Op	Hld	ERC	ERA
2012	Tex	AL	58	0	0	9	65.0	265	55	21	16	3	1	2	2	23	3	47	1	1	6	0	1.000	0	0-0	9	2.83	2.22
2013	Tex	AL	65	0	0	16	62.1	267	63	21	21	4	0	0	5	19	2	58	2	0	4	2	.667	0	0-1	15	3.79	3.03
2014	Tex	AL	27	12	0	4	78.1	365	103	65	54	9	2	2	7	30	2	51	6	0	3	6	.333	0	0-0	2	6.34	6.20
2015	Bos	AL	54	0	0	18	60.2	259	59	28	26	7	2	2	3	20	2	53	1	0	0	2	.000	0	6-8	12	3.89	3.86
2016	Bos	AL	54	0	0	8	55.1	238	47	21	20	2	0	1	8	23	0	56	7	0	3	2	.600	0	0-0	8	3.42	3.25
	5 ML YEARS		258	12	0	55	321.2	1394	327	156	137	25	5	7	25	115	9	265	17	1	16	12	.571	0	6-9	46	4.12	3.83

Michael Roth

Pitches: L **Bats**: L **Pos**: RP-1   **Ht**: 6'1" **Wt**: 210 **Born**: 2/15/1990 **Age**: 27

			HOW MUCH HE PITCHED					WHAT HE GAVE UP											THE RESULTS							
Year	Team	Lg	G	GS	CG	GF	IP	BFP	H	R	ER	HR	SH	SF	HB	TBB	IBB	SO	WP	Bk	W	L	Pct	Sh	Sv-Op	Hld	ERC	ERA
2016	RdRck*	AAA	28	23	1	0	145.1	591	136	50	48	9	3	2	5	42	0	94	1	0	11	5	.688	1	0- -	-	3.28	2.97
2013	LAA	AL	15	1	0	5	20.0	89	24	16	16	0	1	0	1	6	0	17	2	0	1	1	.500	0	0-0	0	4.26	7.20
2014	LAA	AL	7	0	0	2	12.1	60	16	12	12	2	0	1	3	9	2	9	0	0	1	0	1.000	0	0-0	0	9.10	8.76
2016	Tex	AL	1	0	0	1	3.2	22	10	6	6	3	0	0	0	1	0	3	0	0	0	0	-	0	0-0	0	22.83	14.73
	3 ML YEARS		23	1	0	8	36.0	171	50	34	34	5	1	1	4	16	2	29	2	0	2	1	.667	0	0-0	0	7.44	8.50

Ben Rowen

Pitches: R **Bats**: R **Pos**: RP-4   **Ht**: 6'4" **Wt**: 200 **Born**: 11/15/1988 **Age**: 28

			HOW MUCH HE PITCHED					WHAT HE GAVE UP											THE RESULTS							
Year	Team	Lg	G	GS	CG	GF	IP	BFP	H	R	ER	HR	SH	SF	HB	TBB	IBB	SO	WP	Bk	W	L	Pct	Sh	Sv-Op	Hld	ERC	ERA
2012	MrtlBh	A+	38	0	0	31	57.1	213	41	10	10	2	0	2	4	3	0	52	1	1	5	0	1.000	0	19- -	-	1.45	1.57
2013	Frisco	AA	31	0	0	24	33.2	127	23	3	2	1	0	0	0	11	0	28	0	0	3	0	1.000	0	10- -	-	1.89	0.53
2013	RdRck	AAA	20	0	0	12	32.0	121	18	5	3	0	0	0	0	6	1	30	0	0	3	1	.750	0	3- -	-	0.96	0.84
2014	RdRck	AAA	34	0	0	21	47.0	203	47	22	18	2	1	1	6	9	0	31	0	0	3	0	1.000	0	5- -	-	3.29	3.45
2015	Bowie	AA	20	0	0	13	27.2	104	24	7	7	1	0	1	1	3	1	18	0	0	2	0	1.000	0	1- -	-	2.15	2.28
2015	Norfolk	AAA	6	0	0	1	9.2	39	8	3	3	0	2	1	0	3	1	6	0	0	0	0	-	0	0- -	-	2.08	2.79
2015	Iowa	AAA	8	0	0	1	9.1	32	6	0	0	0	1	0	0	1	1	7	0	0	2	0	1.000	0	0- -	-	1.06	0.00
2015	Buffalo	AAA	14	0	0	6	18.0	68	12	4	4	0	0	0	2	2	1	11	0	0	0	1	.000	0	1- -	-	1.33	2.00
2016	Buffalo	AAA	37	0	0	12	47.1	192	46	13	13	1	1	0	0	11	3	33	1	0	0	4	.000	0	1- -	-	2.73	2.47
2016	ColSpr	AAA	8	0	0	2	10.2	44	11	2	2	0	1	0	0	3	0	12	0	0	0	0	-	0	0- -	-	3.19	1.69
2014	Tex	AL	8	0	0	4	8.2	39	10	4	4	0	1	2	0	4	3	7	0	0	0	0	-	0	0-0	0	3.81	4.15
2016	Mil	NL	4	0	0	1	3.0	19	10	6	5	0	0	0	0	0	0	2	0	0	0	0	-	0	0-0	0	17.08	15.00
	2 ML YEARS		12	0	0	5	11.2	58	20	10	9	0	1	2	0	4	3	9	0	0	0	0	-	0	0-0	0	6.75	6.94

Ryan Rua

ROO-ah

Bats: R **Throws**: R **Pos**: LF-60;1B-31;PH-12;PR-6;CF-4;DH-4;RF-3;3B-2   **Ht**: 6'2" **Wt**: 205 **Born**: 3/11/1990 **Age**: 27

			BATTING																		RUNNING			AVERAGES			
Year	Team	Lg	G	AB	H	2B	3B	HR	(Hm	Rd)	TB	R	RBI	RC	TBB	IBB	SO	HBP	SH	SF	SB	CS	GDP	Avg	OBP	Slg	OPS
2014	Tex	AL	28	105	31	7	0	2	(1	1)	44	11	14	13	2	0	18	2	0	0	1	0	6	.295	.321	.419	.740
2015	Tex	AL	28	83	16	5	0	4	(2	2)	33	10	7	5	3	0	32	0	0	0	0	0	2	.193	.221	.398	.619
2016	Tex	AL	99	240	62	8	1	8	(3	5)	96	40	22	25	21	2	76	6	0	2	9	0	8	.258	.331	.400	.731
	3 ML YEARS		155	428	109	20	1	14	(6	8)	173	61	43	43	26	2	126	8	0	2	10	0	16	.255	.308	.404	.712

Darin Ruf

ROUGH

Bats: R **Throws**: R **Pos**: PH-24;1B-14;LF-13   **Ht**: 6'3" **Wt**: 250 **Born**: 7/28/1986 **Age**: 30

			BATTING																		RUNNING			AVERAGES			
Year	Team	Lg	G	AB	H	2B	3B	HR	(Hm	Rd)	TB	R	RBI	RC	TBB	IBB	SO	HBP	SH	SF	SB	CS	GDP	Avg	OBP	Slg	OPS
2016	LV*	AAA	95	350	103	18	2	20	(-	-)	185	56	65	66	29	1	78	7	0	4	0	0	7	.294	.356	.529	.885
2012	Phi	NL	12	33	11	2	1	3	(1	2)	24	4	10	5	2	1	12	0	0	2	0	0	1	.333	.351	.727	1.079
2013	Phi	NL	73	251	62	11	0	14	(11	3)	115	36	30	33	33	1	91	7	0	2	0	0	4	.247	.348	.458	.806
2014	Phi	NL	52	102	24	8	0	3	(3	0)	41	13	8	9	8	0	32	4	1	2	0	0	2	.235	.310	.402	.712
2015	Phi	NL	106	268	63	12	0	12	(6	6)	111	30	39	34	21	0	69	5	0	3	1	0	7	.235	.300	.414	.714
2016	Phi	NL	43	83	17	2	0	3	(1	2)	28	8	9	4	4	0	25	0	0	2	0	1	5	.205	.236	.337	.573
	5 ML YEARS		286	737	177	35	1	35	(22	13)	319	91	96	85	68	2	229	16	1	11	1	1	19	.240	.314	.433	.747

Justin Ruggiano

roo-jee-AH-no

Bats: R **Throws**: R **Pos**: CF-6;PH-2;LF-1;RF-1   **Ht**: 6'1" **Wt**: 210 **Born**: 4/12/1982 **Age**: 35

			BATTING																		RUNNING			AVERAGES			
Year	Team	Lg	G	AB	H	2B	3B	HR	(Hm	Rd)	TB	R	RBI	RC	TBB	IBB	SO	HBP	SH	SF	SB	CS	GDP	Avg	OBP	Slg	OPS
2016	RdRck*	AAA	44	164	37	10	1	7	(-	-)	70	26	23	24	23	0	53	1	0	2	3	1	3	.226	.321	.427	.748
2007	TB	AL	7	14	3	0	0	0	(0	0)	3	2	3	1	1	0	5	0	0	0	0	0	0	.214	.267	.214	.481
2008	TB	AL	45	76	15	4	0	2	(2	0)	25	9	7	4	4	0	27	1	0	0	2	2	2	.197	.247	.329	.576
2011	TB	AL	46	105	26	4	0	4	(3	1)	42	11	13	16	4	0	26	0	1	1	1	1	2	.248	.273	.400	.673
2012	Mia	NL	91	288	90	23	1	13	(4	9)	154	38	36	46	29	0	84	0	1	1	14	6	6	.313	.374	.535	.909
2013	Mia	NL	128	424	94	18	1	18	(3	15)	168	49	50	42	41	1	114	5	1	0	15	8	9	.222	.298	.396	.694
2014	ChC	NL	81	224	63	13	1	6	(2	4)	96	29	24	32	18	0	70	3	1	4	2	4	2	.281	.337	.429	.766
2015	2 Tms		57	125	31	8	1	6	(1	5)	59	20	15	20	14	0	41	2	0	0	5	2	1	.248	.333	.472	.805
2016	2 Tms		9	24	8	1	0	2	(0	2)	15	4	7	4	2	0	10	0	0	0	0	0	0	.333	.385	.625	1.010
	15	Sea	AL	36	70	15	4	0	2	(1	1)	25	8	3	9	11	0	27	1	0	0	3	2	0	.214	.321	.357	.678
	15	LAD	NL	21	55	16	4	1	4	(0	4)	34	12	12	11	3	0	14	1	0	0	2	0	1	.291	.350	.618	.968

Year	Team	Lg	G	AB	H	2B	3B	HR	(Hm	Rd)	TB	R	RBI	RC	TBB	IBB	SO	HBP	SH	SF	SB	CS	GDP	Avg	OBP	Slg	OPS
16	Tex	AL	1	4	1	1	0	0	(0	0)	2	0	1	1	0	0	1	0	0	0	0	0	0	.250	.250	.500	.750
16	NYM	NL	8	20	7	0	0	2	(0	2)	13	4	6	4	2	0	9	0	0	0	0	1	1	.350	.409	.650	1.059
	Postseason		3	4	0	0	0	0	(0	0)	0	0	0	0	0	0	3	0	0	0	0	0	0	.000	.000	.000	.000
	8 ML YEARS		464	1280	330	71	4	51	(15	36)	562	162	159	166	113	1	377	11	4	6	39	24	23	.258	.322	.439	.761

Carlos Ruiz

Bats: R **Throws:** R **Pos:** C-56;PH-5;DH-1;PR-1 **Ht:** 5'10" **Wt:** 215 **Born:** 1/22/1979 **Age:** 38

Year	Team	Lg	G	AB	H	2B	3B	HR	(Hm	Rd)	TB	R	RBI	RC	TBB	IBB	SO	HBP	SH	SF	SB	CS	GDP	Avg	OBP	Slg	OPS
2006	Phi	NL	27	69	18	1	1	3	(2	1)	30	5	10	10	5	2	8	1	2	1	0	0	3	.261	.316	.435	.751
2007	Phi	NL	115	374	97	29	2	6	(4	2)	148	42	54	49	42	10	49	5	5	3	6	1	17	.259	.340	.396	.735
2008	Phi	NL	117	320	70	14	0	4	(2	2)	96	47	31	28	44	6	38	4	4	1	1	2	14	.219	.320	.300	.620
2009	Phi	NL	107	322	82	26	1	9	(5	4)	137	32	43	49	47	8	39	4	4	2	3	2	8	.255	.355	.425	.780
2010	Phi	NL	121	371	112	28	1	8	(3	5)	166	43	53	62	55	13	54	6	0	1	0	1	8	.302	.400	.447	.847
2011	Phi	NL	132	410	116	23	0	6	(1	5)	157	49	40	59	48	10	48	10	3	1	1	0	7	.283	.371	.383	.754
2012	Phi	NL	114	372	121	32	0	16	(8	8)	201	56	68	75	29	6	50	16	0	4	4	0	6	.325	.394	.540	.935
2013	Phi	NL	92	310	83	16	0	5	(4	1)	114	30	37	34	18	3	39	7	4	2	1	0	11	.268	.320	.368	.688
2014	Phi	NL	110	381	96	25	1	6	(2	4)	141	43	31	50	46	1	60	12	1	5	4	2	11	.252	.347	.370	.717
2015	Phi	NL	86	284	60	13	1	2	(1	1)	81	23	22	19	28	2	43	4	3	1	1	1	13	.211	.290	.285	.575
2016	2 Tms	NL	62	201	53	8	0	3	(1	2)	70	21	15	25	27	1	33	5	0	0	3	1	4	.264	.365	.348	.713
16	Phi	NL	48	165	43	6	0	3	(1	2)	58	18	12	21	24	1	28	4	0	0	3	1	3	.261	.368	.352	.719
16	LAD	NL	14	36	10	2	0	0	(0	0)	12	3	3	4	3	0	5	1	0	0	0	0	1	.278	.350	.333	.683
	Postseason		46	142	36	8	1	4	(3	1)	58	19	15	24	24	3	16	5	1	0	3	0	2	.254	.380	.408	.789
	11 ML YEARS		1083	3414	908	215	7	68	(33	35)	1341	391	404	460	389	62	461	74	26	21	24	10	102	.266	.352	.393	.745

Rio Ruiz

Bats: L **Throws:** R **Pos:** PH-3;3B-2 **Ht:** 6'1" **Wt:** 230 **Born:** 5/22/1994 **Age:** 23

Year	Team	Lg	G	AB	H	2B	3B	HR	(Hm	Rd)	TB	R	RBI	RC	TBB	IBB	SO	HBP	SH	SF	SB	CS	GDP	Avg	OBP	Slg	OPS
2012	2 Tms	Low	38	135	34	11	3	1	(-	-)	54	21	18	18	16	1	32	1	0	0	2	0	1	.252	.336	.400	.736
2013	QuadC	A	114	416	108	33	1	12	(-	-)	179	46	63	64	50	0	92	0	1	5	12	3	9	.260	.335	.430	.766
2014	Lancst	A+	131	516	151	37	2	11	(-	-)	225	76	77	92	82	2	91	0	0	4	4	4	14	.293	.387	.436	.823
2015	Missi	AA	127	420	98	21	1	5	(-	-)	136	48	46	50	63	1	94	1	3	2	2	2	16	.233	.333	.324	.657
2016	Gwnntt	AAA	133	465	126	24	3	10	(-	-)	186	52	62	69	61	3	116	2	0	5	1	4	10	.271	.355	.400	.755
2016	Atl	NL	5	7	2	0	1	0	(0	0)	4	1	2	2	0	0	2	0	0	0	1	0	0	.286	.286	.571	.857

Cameron Rupp

Bats: R **Throws:** R **Pos:** C-104;PH-1 **Ht:** 6'2" **Wt:** 260 **Born:** 9/28/1988 **Age:** 28

Year	Team	Lg	G	AB	H	2B	3B	HR	(Hm	Rd)	TB	R	RBI	RC	TBB	IBB	SO	HBP	SH	SF	SB	CS	GDP	Avg	OBP	Slg	OPS
2013	Phi	NL	4	13	4	1	0	0	(0	0)	5	1	2	2	1	0	4	0	0	0	0	0	0	.308	.357	.385	.742
2014	Phi	NL	18	60	11	4	0	0	(0	0)	15	4	6	3	4	0	20	0	0	0	0	0	5	.183	.234	.250	.484
2015	Phi	NL	81	270	63	9	1	9	(4	5)	101	24	28	29	24	5	71	3	0	2	0	1	8	.233	.301	.374	.675
2016	Phi	NL	105	389	98	26	1	16	(8	8)	174	36	54	53	24	0	114	5	0	1	1	0	11	.252	.303	.447	.750
	4 ML YEARS		208	732	176	40	2	25	(12	13)	295	65	90	87	53	5	209	8	0	3	1	1	24	.240	.298	.403	.701

Chris Rusin

Pitches: L **Bats:** L **Pos:** RP-22; SP-7 RUSS-inn **Ht:** 6'2" **Wt:** 195 **Born:** 10/22/1986 **Age:** 30

			HOW MUCH HE PITCHED						WHAT HE GAVE UP											THE RESULTS							
Year	Team	Lg	G	GS	CG	GF	IP	BFP	H	R	ER	HR	SH	SF	HB	TBB	IBB	SO	WP	Bk	W	L	Pct	Sh	Sv-Op	Hld	ERC	ERA
2012	ChC	NL	7	7	0	0	29.2	135	38	22	21	4	0	0	3	11	0	21	0	0	2	3	.400	0	0-0	0	6.46	6.37
2013	ChC	NL	13	13	0	0	66.1	282	66	30	29	8	1	1	3	24	3	36	1	0	2	6	.250	0	0-0	0	4.21	3.93
2014	ChC	NL	4	0	0	2	12.2	58	16	10	10	1	1	0	0	5	1	8	1	0	0	0	-	0	0-0	0	5.24	7.11
2015	Col	NL	24	22	0	0	131.2	594	170	88	78	19	2	0	3	41	5	86	2	2	6	10	.375	1	0-0	0	5.80	5.33
2016	Col	NL	29	7	0	1	84.1	350	82	36	35	5	7	0	3	23	2	69	4	0	3	5	.375	0	0-1	3	3.30	3.74
	5 ML YEARS		77	49	2	3	324.2	1419	372	186	173	37	11	1	12	104	11	220	8	2	13	24	.351	1	0-1	3	4.82	4.80

Addison Russell

Bats: R **Throws:** R **Pos:** SS-148;PH-6 **Ht:** 6'0" **Wt:** 200 **Born:** 1/23/1994 **Age:** 23

Year	Team	Lg	G	AB	H	2B	3B	HR	(Hm	Rd)	TB	R	RBI	RC	TBB	IBB	SO	HBP	SH	SF	SB	CS	GDP	Avg	OBP	Slg	OPS
2012	3 Tms	Low	55	217	80	10	9	7	(-	-)	129	46	45	54	23	0	48	2	1	1	16	2	3	.369	.432	.594	1.027
2013	Stcktn	A+	107	429	118	29	10	17	(-	-)	218	85	60	87	61	0	116	11	0	3	21	3	8	.275	.377	.508	.885
2014	Mdlnd	AA	13	48	16	3	1	1	(-	-)	24	7	8	10	8	0	8	1	0	0	3	2	3	.333	.439	.500	.939
2014	Tenn	AA	50	193	57	11	0	12	(-	-)	104	32	36	33	9	0	36	2	0	0	2	2	7	.295	.333	.539	.872
2015	Iowa	AAA	11	44	14	4	0	1	(-	-)	21	7	9	7	1	0	7	0	0	1	1	0	0	.318	.326	.477	.803
2015	ChC	NL	142	475	115	29	1	13	(8	5)	185	60	54	53	42	2	149	3	1	2	4	3	8	.242	.307	.389	.696
2016	ChC	NL	151	525	125	25	3	21	(11	10)	219	67	95	73	55	6	135	12	0	6	5	1	11	.238	.321	.417	.738
	Postseason		4	12	3	0	1	0	(0	0)	5	0	1	1	0	0	3	0	1	0	1	0	0	.250	.250	.417	.667
	2 ML YEARS		293	1000	240	54	4	34	(19	15)	404	127	149	126	97	8	284	15	1	8	9	4	19	.240	.314	.404	.718

James Russell

Pitches: L Bats: L Pos: RP-7   Ht: 6'4" Wt: 205 Born: 1/8/1986 Age: 31

			HOW MUCH HE PITCHED						WHAT HE GAVE UP											THE RESULTS						
Year Team	Lg	G	GS	CG	GF	IP	BFP	H	R	ER	HR	SH	SF	HB	TBB	IBB	SO	WP	Bk	W	L	Pct	Sh	Sv-Op	Hld	ERC	ERA
2016 LV*	AAA	29	13	0	4	79.2	348	88	43	38	11	2	2	2	19	0	49	1	0	3	5	.375	0	0- -	-	4.29	4.29
2010 ChC	NL	57	0	0	11	49.0	219	55	37	27	11	3	4	4	11	0	42	2	0	1	1	.500	0	0-2	6	5.12	4.96
2011 ChC	NL	64	5	0	10	67.2	292	76	37	31	12	4	6	2	14	4	43	1	0	1	6	.143	0	0-2	6	4.51	4.12
2012 ChC	NL	77	0	0	19	69.1	292	67	28	25	5	2	3	1	23	7	55	1	1	7	1	.875	0	2-5	13	3.35	3.25
2013 ChC	NL	74	0	0	7	52.2	214	46	21	21	7	1	1	1	18	6	37	1	0	1	6	.143	0	0-8	19	3.37	3.59
2014 2 Tms	NL	66	1	0	15	57.2	238	45	20	19	3	7	1	1	20	3	42	1	0	0	2	.000	0	1-3	6	2.37	2.97
2015 ChC	NL	49	0	0	8	34.0	148	42	24	20	3	1	1	0	9	2	20	0	0	0	2	.000	0	1-3	8	4.75	5.29
2016 Phi	NL	7	0	0	1	4.1	27	9	9	9	2	0	1	0	5	0	4	0	0	0	0	-	0	0-1	1	18.54	18.69
14 ChC	NL	44	0	0	7	33.1	142	24	14	13	3	5	1	1	16	2	26	1	0	0	2	.000	0	1-3	5	2.76	3.51
14 Atl	NL	22	1	0	8	24.1	96	21	6	6	0	2	0	0	4	1	16	0	0	0	0	-	0	0-0	1	1.86	2.22
7 ML YEARS		394	6	0	71	334.2	1430	340	176	152	43	18	17	9	100	22	243	6	1	10	18	.357	0	4-24	59	3.95	4.09

Josh Rutledge

Bats: R Throws: R Pos: 3B-17;PH-7;2B-5;SS-1;PR-1   Ht: 6'1" Wt: 190 Born: 4/21/1989 Age: 28

								BATTING											RUNNING			AVERAGES			
Year Team	Lg	G	AB	H	2B	3B	HR	(Hm Rd)	TB	R	RBI	RC	TBB	IBB	SO	HBP	SH	SF	SB	CS	GDP	Avg	OBP	Slg	OPS
2012 Col	NL	73	277	76	20	5	8	(5 3)	130	37	37	37	9	0	54	4	0	1	7	0	8	.274	.306	.469	.775
2013 Col	NL	88	285	67	6	1	7	(5 2)	96	45	19	28	22	1	62	2	4	1	12	0	2	.235	.294	.337	.630
2014 Col	NL	105	309	83	16	7	4	(1 3)	125	44	33	42	20	0	83	6	5	2	2	3	6	.269	.323	.405	.728
2015 Bos	AL	39	74	21	1	0	1	(1 0)	25	11	10	11	5	1	26	2	1	3	0	0	3	.284	.333	.338	.671
2016 Bos	AL	28	49	13	6	0	0	(0 0)	19	9	3	5	6	0	19	0	1	0	2	0	3	.265	.345	.388	.733
5 ML YEARS		333	994	260	49	13	20	(12 8)	395	146	102	123	62	2	244	14	11	7	23	3	19	.262	.312	.397	.709

Brendan Ryan

Bats: R Throws: R Pos: SS-16;LF-1;PR-1   Ht: 6'1" Wt: 190 Born: 3/26/1982 Age: 35

								BATTING											RUNNING			AVERAGES			
Year Team	Lg	G	AB	H	2B	3B	HR	(Hm Rd)	TB	R	RBI	RC	TBB	IBB	SO	HBP	SH	SF	SB	CS	GDP	Avg	OBP	Slg	OPS
2016 Syrcse*	AAA	21	76	20	4	1	1	(- -)	29	7	8	9	4	0	17	1	1	1	1	0	2	.263	.305	.382	.686
2016 Salt Lk*	AAA	59	190	44	6	1	0	(- -)	52	16	15	16	18	0	48	0	2	2	6	3	6	.232	.295	.274	.569
2007 StL	NL	67	180	52	9	0	4	(2 2)	73	30	12	21	15	0	19	1	3	0	7	0	3	.289	.347	.406	.752
2008 StL	NL	80	197	48	9	0	0	(0 0)	57	30	10	12	16	0	31	2	3	0	7	2	4	.244	.307	.289	.596
2009 StL	NL	129	390	114	19	7	3	(1 2)	156	55	37	48	24	3	56	6	6	3	14	7	9	.292	.340	.400	.740
2010 StL	NL	139	439	98	19	3	2	(0 2)	129	50	36	37	33	5	60	2	9	3	11	4	6	.223	.279	.294	.573
2011 Sea	AL	123	436	108	19	3	3	(0 3)	142	51	39	46	34	0	87	10	9	5	13	3	7	.248	.313	.326	.639
2012 Sea	AL	141	407	79	19	3	3	(2 1)	113	42	31	35	44	0	98	5	8	6	11	5	4	.194	.277	.278	.555
2013 2 Tms	AL	104	319	63	12	0	4	(1 3)	87	30	22	17	23	1	73	2	4	1	4	2	11	.197	.255	.273	.528
2014 NYY	AL	49	114	19	4	0	0	(0 0)	23	5	8	2	4	0	30	3	1	2	0	2	2	.167	.211	.202	.413
2015 NYY	AL	47	96	22	6	2	0	(0 0)	32	10	8	9	5	0	29	1	1	0	0	0	1	.229	.275	.333	.608
2016 LAA	AL	17	13	1	0	0	0	(0 0)	1	1	0	0	0	0	7	0	1	0	0	0	0	.077	.077	.077	.154
13 Sea	AL	87	260	50	10	0	3	(1 2)	69	23	21	14	21	1	60	1	4	1	4	2	11	.192	.254	.265	.520
13 NYY	AL	17	59	13	2	0	1	(0 1)	18	7	1	3	2	0	13	1	0	0	0	0	0	.220	.258	.305	.563
Postseason		3	12	1	1	0	0	(0 0)	2	1	0	0	0	0	2	0	0	0	0	0	0	.083	.083	.167	.250
10 ML YEARS		896	2591	604	116	18	19	(6 13)	813	304	203	227	198	9	490	32	45	20	67	25	47	.233	.294	.314	.607

Kyle Ryan

Pitches: L Bats: L Pos: RP-56   Ht: 6'5" Wt: 215 Born: 9/25/1991 Age: 25

			HOW MUCH HE PITCHED						WHAT HE GAVE UP											THE RESULTS						
Year Team	Lg	G	GS	CG	GF	IP	BFP	H	R	ER	HR	SH	SF	HB	TBB	IBB	SO	WP	Bk	W	L	Pct	Sh	Sv-Op	Hld	ERC	ERA
2016 Toledo*	AAA	8	0	0	2	7.0	29	3	0	0	0	0	0	0	6	0	5	0	0	0	0	-	0	0- -	-	2.12	0.00
2014 Det	AL	6	1	0	1	10.1	41	10	3	3	0	0	0	0	2	0	4	0	1	2	0	1.000	0	0-0	0	2.57	2.61
2015 Det	AL	16	6	0	3	56.1	237	60	29	28	9	2	1	1	20	0	30	1	0	2	4	.333	0	0-0	0	4.94	4.47
2016 Det	AL	56	0	0	14	55.2	226	48	21	19	2	2	1	3	15	5	35	1	0	4	2	.667	0	0-1	4	2.55	3.07
3 ML YEARS		78	7	0	18	122.1	504	118	53	50	11	4	2	4	37	5	69	2	1	8	6	.571	0	0-1	4	3.59	3.68

Hyun-Jin Ryu

Pitches: L Bats: R Pos: SP-1   he-YUN-jin ree-YOO   Ht: 6'3" Wt: 250 Born: 3/25/1987 Age: 30

			HOW MUCH HE PITCHED						WHAT HE GAVE UP											THE RESULTS						
Year Team	Lg	G	GS	CG	GF	IP	BFP	H	R	ER	HR	SH	SF	HB	TBB	IBB	SO	WP	Bk	W	L	Pct	Sh	Sv-Op	Hld	ERC	ERA
2016 Rcuca*	A+	5	5	0	0	18.0	71	15	7	4	2	0	0	0	1	0	14	0	0	1	1	.500	0	0- -	-	1.94	2.00
2013 LAD	NL	30	30	2	0	192.0	783	182	67	64	15	7	3	1	49	4	154	5	0	14	8	.636	1	0-0	0	3.13	3.00
2014 LAD	NL	26	26	0	0	152.0	631	152	60	57	8	6	2	3	29	2	139	2	0	14	7	.667	0	0-0	0	3.00	3.38
2016 LAD	NL	1	1	0	0	4.2	24	8	6	6	1	0	0	0	2	1	4	0	0	0	1	.000	0	0-0	0	9.03	11.57
Postseason		3	3	0	0	16.0	63	14	5	5	1	0	0	0	3	0	9	0	0	1	0	1.000	0	0-0	0	2.44	2.81
3 ML YEARS		57	57	2	0	348.2	1438	342	133	127	24	13	5	4	80	7	297	7	0	28	16	.636	1	0-0	0	3.14	3.28

Marc Rzepczynski

Pitches: L **Bats:** L **Pos:** RP-70   zepp-CHINN-ski   **Ht:** 6'2" **Wt:** 220 **Born:** 8/29/1985 **Age:** 31

Year	Team	Lg	G	GS	CG	GF	IP	BFP	H	R	ER	HR	SH	SF	HB	TBB	IBB	SO	WP	Bk	W	L	Pct	Sh	Sv-Op	Hld	ERC	ERA
2009	Tor	AL	11	11	0	0	61.1	261	51	27	25	7	2	1	1	30	0	60	4	1	2	4	.333	0	0-0	0	3.65	3.67
2010	Tor	AL	14	12	0	0	63.2	287	72	37	35	8	1	2	5	30	1	57	4	1	4	4	.500	0	0-0	2	5.71	4.95
2011	2 Tms		71	0	0	7	62.0	256	50	27	23	3	2	0	4	26	1	61	6	0	2	6	.250	0	0-4	18	3.04	3.34
2012	StL	NL	70	0	0	14	46.2	196	46	22	22	7	0	0	0	17	2	33	3	0	1	3	.250	0	0-5	18	4.21	4.24
2013	2 Tms		38	0	0	10	30.2	129	27	13	11	2	1	1	4	10	3	29	0	0	0	0	-	0	0-0	6	3.28	3.23
2014	Cle	AL	73	0	0	8	46.0	196	42	19	14	1	1	2	3	19	3	46	2	0	0	3	.000	0	1-2	13	3.27	2.74
2015	2 Tms		72	0	0	7	35.0	158	40	29	22	3	2	2	3	14	4	41	2	0	2	4	.333	0	0-4	16	4.94	5.66
2016	2 Tms		70	0	0	15	47.2	215	46	17	14	1	1	1	4	29	8	46	5	0	1	0	1.000	0	0-1	11	4.15	2.64
11	Tor	AL	43	0	0	6	39.1	158	28	16	13	2	1	0	3	15	0	33	5	0	2	3	.400	0	0-3	10	2.52	2.97
11	StL	NL	28	0	0	1	22.2	98	22	11	10	1	1	0	1	11	1	28	1	0	0	3	.000	0	0-1	8	4.01	3.97
13	StL	NL	11	0	0	4	10.1	50	16	9	9	1	0	1	1	4	1	9	0	0	0	0	-	0	0-0	0	7.69	7.84
13	Cle	AL	27	0	0	6	20.1	79	11	4	2	1	1	0	3	6	2	20	0	0	0	0	-	0	0-0	6	1.57	0.89
15	Cle	AL	45	0	0	6	20.1	94	23	15	10	1	1	0	1	10	3	24	1	0	2	3	.400	0	0-2	12	4.66	4.43
15	SD	NL	27	0	0	1	14.2	64	17	14	12	2	1	2	2	4	1	17	1	0	0	1	.000	0	0-2	4	5.32	7.36
16	Oak	AL	56	0	0	15	36.0	169	38	14	12	1	0	0	2	24	6	37	5	0	1	0	1.000	0	0-1	6	4.75	3.00
16	Was	NL	14	0	0	0	11.2	46	8	3	2	0	1	1	2	5	2	9	0	0	0	0	-	0	0-0	5	2.39	1.54
	Postseason		18	0	0	1	10.2	44	10	5	5	0	0	0	1	2	0	13	1	0	1	0	1.000	0	0-1	7	2.64	4.22
8 ML YEARS			419	23	0	61	393.0	1698	374	191	166	32	10	9	24	175	22	373	26	2	12	24	.333	0	1-16	84	4.04	3.80

CC Sabathia

Pitches: L **Bats:** L **Pos:** SP-30   **Ht:** 6'6" **Wt:** 300 **Born:** 7/21/1980 **Age:** 36

Year	Team	Lg	G	GS	CG	GF	IP	BFP	H	R	ER	HR	SH	SF	HB	TBB	IBB	SO	WP	Bk	W	L	Pct	Sh	Sv-Op	Hld	ERC	ERA
2001	Cle	AL	33	33	0	0	180.1	763	149	93	88	19	3	5	7	95	1	171	7	3	17	5	.773	0	0-0	0	3.86	4.39
2002	Cle	AL	33	33	2	0	210.0	891	198	109	102	17	5	10	1	88	2	149	6	3	13	11	.542	0	0-0	0	3.74	4.37
2003	Cle	AL	30	30	2	0	197.2	832	190	85	79	19	10	4	6	66	3	141	4	2	13	9	.591	1	0-0	0	3.70	3.60
2004	Cle	AL	30	30	1	0	188.0	787	176	90	86	20	3	6	7	72	3	139	1	1	11	10	.524	1	0-0	0	3.91	4.12
2005	Cle	AL	31	31	1	0	196.2	823	185	92	88	19	6	3	7	62	1	161	7	0	15	10	.600	0	0-0	0	3.55	4.03
2006	Cle	AL	28	28	6	0	192.2	802	182	83	69	17	8	5	7	44	3	172	3	0	12	11	.522	2	0-0	0	3.13	3.22
2007	Cle	AL	34	34	4	0	241.0	975	238	94	86	20	6	6	8	37	1	209	1	0	19	7	.731	1	0-0	0	3.12	3.21
2008	2 Tms		35	35	10	0	253.0	1023	223	85	76	19	9	6	7	59	1	251	2	2	17	10	.630	5	0-0	0	2.78	2.70
2009	NYY	AL	34	34	2	0	230.0	938	197	96	86	18	4	9	9	67	7	197	5	0	19	8	.704	1	0-0	0	2.89	3.37
2010	NYY	AL	34	34	2	0	237.2	970	209	92	84	20	5	8	7	74	6	197	8	1	21	7	.750	1	0-0	0	3.11	3.18
2011	NYY	AL	33	33	3	0	237.1	985	230	87	79	17	8	7	7	61	4	230	2	1	19	8	.704	1	0-0	0	3.27	3.00
2012	NYY	AL	28	28	2	0	200.0	833	184	89	75	22	4	3	8	44	2	197	4	1	15	6	.714	0	0-0	0	3.10	3.38
2013	NYY	AL	32	32	2	0	211.0	908	224	122	112	28	8	8	4	65	5	175	7	1	14	13	.519	0	0-0	0	4.32	4.78
2014	NYY	AL	8	8	0	0	46.0	209	58	31	27	10	1	1	4	10	0	48	2	0	3	4	.429	0	0-0	0	5.98	5.28
2015	NYY	AL	29	29	1	0	167.1	726	188	92	88	28	5	6	6	50	3	137	5	1	6	10	.375	0	0-0	0	5.01	4.73
2016	NYY	AL	30	30	0	0	179.2	768	172	83	78	22	5	2	9	65	1	152	2	1	9	12	.429	0	0-0	0	4.04	3.91
08	Cle	AL	18	18	3	0	122.1	507	117	54	52	13	3	3	3	34	1	123	1	2	6	8	.429	2	0-0	0	3.52	3.83
08	Mil	NL	17	17	7	0	130.2	516	106	31	24	6	6	3	4	25	0	128	1	0	11	2	.846	3	0-0	0	2.13	1.65
	Postseason		19	18	1	0	107.1	478	116	57	54	14	5	0	5	51	8	101	4	1	9	5	.643	0	0-0	0	5.19	4.53
16 ML YEARS			482	482	38	0	3168.1	13233	3003	1423	1303	315	90	89	104	959	43	2726	66	17	223	141	.613	12	0-0	0	3.54	3.70

Tyler Saladino

Bats: R **Throws:** R **Pos:** 2B-41;SS-32;3B-10;PR-6;PH-3;1B-2;DH-2;LF-1;CF-1;RF-1   **Ht:** 6'0" **Wt:** 200 **Born:** 7/20/1989 **Age:** 27

Year	Team	Lg	G	AB	H	2B	3B	HR	(Hm	Rd)	TB	R	RBI	RC	TBB	IBB	SO	HBP	SH	SF	SB	CS	GDP	Avg	OBP	Slg	OPS
2012	Brham	AA	112	418	99	15	4	4	(-	-)	134	71	39	61	75	0	91	8	2	6	38	8	5	.237	.359	.321	.680
2012	Charllt	AAA	15	49	11	2	0	0	(-	-)	13	9	6	4	4	0	16	1	1	0	1	0	1	.224	.296	.265	.562
2013	Brham	AA	118	424	97	17	2	5	(-	-)	133	49	55	49	51	0	86	6	6	6	28	6	15	.229	.316	.314	.630
2014	Charllt	AAA	82	294	91	16	4	9	(-	-)	142	41	43	53	27	0	50	1	1	2	7	1	4	.310	.367	.483	.850
2015	Charllt	AAA	52	196	50	7	2	4	(-	-)	73	28	29	31	22	0	33	4	2	7	25	2	6	.255	.332	.372	.704
2015	CWS	AL	68	236	53	6	4	4	(4	0)	79	33	20	19	12	0	51	2	3	1	8	2	9	.225	.267	.335	.602
2016	CWS	AL	93	298	84	14	0	8	(5	3)	122	33	38	38	13	0	62	3	2	3	11	5	11	.282	.315	.409	.725
2 ML YEARS			161	534	137	20	4	12	(9	3)	201	66	58	57	25	0	113	5	5	4	19	7	20	.257	.294	.376	.670

Fernando Salas

Pitches: R **Bats:** R **Pos:** RP-75   SAH-lahss   **Ht:** 6'2" **Wt:** 200 **Born:** 5/30/1985 **Age:** 32

Year	Team	Lg	G	GS	CG	GF	IP	BFP	H	R	ER	HR	SH	SF	HB	TBB	IBB	SO	WP	Bk	W	L	Pct	Sh	Sv-Op	Hld	ERC	ERA
2010	StL	NL	27	0	0	11	30.2	133	28	13	12	4	1	1	0	15	2	29	2	0	0	0	-	0	0-1	1	4.03	3.52
2011	StL	NL	68	0	0	46	75.0	295	50	20	19	7	3	0	2	23	3	75	2	0	5	6	.455	0	24-30	6	1.94	2.28
2012	StL	NL	65	0	0	23	58.2	256	56	28	28	5	5	0	1	27	5	60	4	0	1	4	.200	0	0-3	7	3.85	4.30
2013	StL	NL	27	0	0	14	28.0	118	27	15	14	3	1	4	1	6	1	22	1	0	0	3	.000	0	0-2	2	3.22	4.50
2014	LAA	AL	57	0	0	11	58.2	239	50	22	22	5	4	1	1	14	4	61	1	1	5	0	1.000	0	0-1	8	2.54	3.38
2015	LAA	AL	72	0	0	13	63.2	269	61	34	30	8	5	2	3	12	5	74	3	0	5	2	.714	0	0-2	17	3.17	4.24
2016	2 Tms		75	0	0	24	73.2	293	63	32	32	12	0	2	0	19	1	64	1	0	3	7	.300	0	6-11	20	3.19	3.91
16	LAA	AL	58	0	0	22	56.1	231	52	28	28	9	0	2	0	19	1	45	0	0	3	6	.333	0	6-11	13	3.87	4.47
16	NYM	NL	17	0	0	2	17.1	62	11	4	4	3	0	0	0	0	0	19	1	0	0	1	.000	0	0-0	7	1.36	2.08
	Postseason		18	0	0	3	20.1	83	16	10	8	2	0	0	1	4	1	18	1	1	1	0	1.000	0	0-0	4	2.05	3.54
7 ML YEARS			391	0	0	142	388.1	1603	335	164	157	44	19	12	8	114	21	385	15	1	19	22	.463	0	30-50	61	3.00	3.64

Danny Salazar

Pitches: R Bats: R Pos: SP-25 SAL-uh-zarr Ht: 6'0" Wt: 195 Born: 1/11/1990 Age: 27

Year Team	Lg	G	GS	CG	GF	IP	BFP	H	R	ER	HR	SH	SF	HB	TBB	IBB	SO	WP	Bk	W	L	Pct	Sh	Sv-Op	Hld	ERC	ERA
2013 Cle	AL	10	10	0	0	52.0	211	44	18	18	7	1	0	0	15	0	65	3	0	2	3	.400	0	0-0	0	3.05	3.12
2014 Cle	AL	20	20	1	0	110.0	474	117	57	52	13	1	5	3	35	4	120	3	0	6	8	.429	1	0-0	0	4.30	4.25
2015 Cle	AL	30	30	0	0	185.0	757	156	79	71	23	3	4	7	53	1	195	3	2	14	10	.583	0	0-0	0	3.10	3.45
2016 Cle	AL	25	25	0	0	137.1	584	121	61	59	16	0	4	2	63	3	161	9	3	11	6	.647	0	0-0	0	3.80	3.87
Postseason		1	1	0	0	4.0	18	4	3	3	1	0	0	0	2	1	4	0	0	0	1	.000	0	0-0	0	5.04	6.75
4 ML YEARS		85	85	1	0	484.1	2026	438	215	200	59	5	13	12	166	8	541	18	5	33	27	.550	1	0-0	0	3.56	3.72

Chris Sale

Pitches: L Bats: L Pos: SP-32 SAIL Ht: 6'6" Wt: 180 Born: 3/30/1989 Age: 28

Year Team	Lg	G	GS	CG	GF	IP	BFP	H	R	ER	HR	SH	SF	HB	TBB	IBB	SO	WP	Bk	W	L	Pct	Sh	Sv-Op	Hld	ERC	ERA
2010 CWS	AL	21	0	0	8	23.1	92	15	5	5	2	1	0	0	10	0	32	1	0	2	1	.667	0	4-4	2	2.30	1.93
2011 CWS	AL	58	0	0	17	71.0	288	52	22	22	6	3	0	2	27	3	79	2	0	2	2	.500	0	8-10	16	2.55	2.79
2012 CWS	AL	30	29	1	0	192.0	772	167	66	65	19	1	3	6	51	5	192	6	0	17	8	.680	0	0-1	0	3.00	3.05
2013 CWS	AL	30	30	4	0	214.1	866	184	81	73	23	2	4	14	46	2	226	8	1	11	14	.440	1	0-0	0	2.92	3.07
2014 CWS	AL	26	26	2	0	174.0	685	129	48	42	13	2	3	11	39	2	208	3	0	12	4	.750	0	0-0	0	2.18	2.17
2015 CWS	AL	31	31	1	0	208.2	854	185	88	79	23	2	3	13	42	0	274	7	0	13	11	.542	0	0-0	0	3.00	3.41
2016 CWS	AL	32	32	6	0	226.2	907	190	88	84	27	5	3	17	45	2	233	2	0	17	10	.630	1	0-0	0	2.88	3.34
7 ML YEARS		228	148	14	25	1110.0	4464	922	398	370	113	16	16	63	260	14	1244	29	1	74	50	.597	2	12-15	18	2.78	3.00

Jarrod Saltalamacchia

Bats: B Throws: R Pos: C-68;PH-18;1B-11;DH-1 salt-ah-luh-MOCK-ee-ah Ht: 6'4" Wt: 235 Born: 5/2/1985 Age: 32

Year Team	Lg	G	AB	H	2B	3B	HR	(Hm	Rd)	TB	R	RBI	RC	TBB	IBB	SO	HBP	SH	SF	SB	CS	GDP	Avg	OBP	Slg	OPS
2007 2 Tms		93	308	82	13	1	11	(6	5)	130	39	33	32	19	1	75	1	0	1	0	0	8	.266	.310	.422	.732
2008 Tex	AL	61	198	50	13	0	3	(2	1)	72	27	26	29	31	1	74	0	0	1	0	2	1	.253	.352	.364	.716
2009 Tex	AL	84	283	66	12	0	9	(6	3)	105	34	34	30	22	1	97	1	3	1	0	2	3	.233	.290	.371	.661
2010 2 Tms	AL	12	24	4	3	0	0	(0	0)	7	2	2	3	6	0	5	0	0	0	0	0	0	.167	.333	.292	.625
2011 Bos	AL	103	358	84	23	3	16	(6	10)	161	52	56	43	24	1	119	3	0	1	1	0	7	.235	.288	.450	.737
2012 Bos	AL	121	405	90	17	1	25	(12	13)	184	55	59	49	38	0	139	1	0	4	0	1	5	.222	.288	.454	.742
2013 Bos	AL	121	425	116	40	0	14	(9	5)	198	68	65	60	43	3	139	0	0	2	4	1	7	.273	.338	.466	.804
2014 Mia	NL	114	373	82	20	0	11	(5	6)	135	43	44	34	55	4	143	2	0	5	0	1	11	.220	.320	.362	.681
2015 2 Tms	AL	79	200	45	15	0	9	(7	2)	87	26	24	21	23	0	69	2	1	1	0	0	5	.225	.310	.435	.745
2016 Det	AL	92	246	42	5	1	12	(5	7)	85	30	38	26	41	1	104	0	0	5	0	0	1	.171	.284	.346	.630
07 Atl	NL	47	141	40	6	0	4	(4	0)	58	11	12	13	10	1	28	1	0	1	0	0	4	.284	.333	.411	.745
07 Tex	AL	46	167	42	7	1	7	(2	5)	72	28	21	19	9	0	47	0	0	0	0	0	4	.251	.290	.431	.721
10 Tex	AL	2	5	1	0	0	0	(0	0)	1	0	1	1	0	0	1	0	0	0	0	0	0	.200	.200	.200	.400
10 Bos	AL	10	19	3	3	0	0	(0	0)	6	2	1	2	6	0	4	0	0	0	0	0	0	.158	.360	.316	.676
15 Mia	NL	9	29	2	1	0	1	(1	0)	6	3	1	0	4	0	12	0	0	0	0	0	2	.069	.182	.207	.389
15 Ari	NL	70	171	43	14	0	8	(6	2)	81	23	23	21	19	0	57	2	1	1	0	0	3	.251	.332	.474	.805
Postseason		10	32	6	1	0	0	(0	0)	7	1	5	2	3	0	19	0	0	0	0	0	0	.188	.257	.219	.476
10 ML YEARS		880	2820	661	161	6	110	(58	52)	1164	376	381	327	302	12	964	10	4	21	5	7	48	.234	.309	.413	.721

Jeff Samardzija

Pitches: R Bats: R Pos: SP-32 suh-MAHR-jah Ht: 6'5" Wt: 225 Born: 1/23/1985 Age: 32

Year Team	Lg	G	GS	CG	GF	IP	BFP	H	R	ER	HR	SH	SF	HB	TBB	IBB	SO	WP	Bk	W	L	Pct	Sh	Sv-Op	Hld	ERC	ERA
2008 ChC	NL	26	0	0	6	27.2	124	24	12	7	0	1	1	1	15	2	25	2	0	1	0	1.000	0	1-4	3	3.08	2.28
2009 ChC	NL	20	2	0	7	34.2	161	46	29	29	7	4	1	1	15	1	21	2	0	1	3	.250	0	0-0	0	7.13	7.53
2010 ChC	NL	7	3	0	0	19.1	100	21	22	18	4	0	0	2	20	1	9	1	0	2	2	.500	0	0-0	0	8.45	8.38
2011 ChC	NL	75	0	0	18	88.0	380	64	35	29	5	3	2	5	50	3	87	8	0	8	4	.667	0	0-2	13	3.05	2.97
2012 ChC	NL	28	28	1	0	174.2	723	157	79	74	20	5	4	4	56	2	180	10	0	9	13	.409	0	0-0	0	3.41	3.81
2013 ChC	NL	33	33	2	0	213.2	914	210	109	103	25	4	2	8	78	3	214	11	0	8	13	.381	1	0-0	0	4.11	4.34
2014 2 Tms		33	33	2	0	219.2	879	191	86	73	20	3	7	10	43	3	202	10	0	7	13	.350	0	0-0	0	2.74	2.99
2015 CWS	AL	32	32	2	0	214.0	910	228	122	118	29	4	9	12	49	0	163	5	0	11	13	.458	2	0-0	0	4.24	4.96
2016 SF	NL	32	32	1	0	203.1	829	190	88	86	24	6	4	1	54	4	167	2	0	12	11	.522	0	0-0	0	3.36	3.81
14 ChC	NL	17	17	0	0	108.0	449	99	44	34	7	3	4	6	31	3	103	6	0	2	7	.222	0	0-0	0	3.14	2.83
14 Oak	AL	16	16	2	0	111.2	430	92	42	39	13	0	3	4	12	0	99	4	0	5	6	.455	0	0-0	0	2.34	3.14
Postseason		1	0	0	0	1.0	4	2	1	1	0	0	0	0	0	0	0	0	0	0	0	-	0	0-0	0	9.49	9.00
9 ML YEARS		286	163	8	31	1195.0	5020	1131	582	537	134	30	30	44	380	19	1068	51	0	59	72	.450	3	1-6	16	3.68	4.04

Adrian Sampson

Pitches: R Bats: R Pos: SP-1 Ht: 6'2" Wt: 210 Born: 10/7/1991 Age: 25

Year Team	Lg	G	GS	CG	GF	IP	BFP	H	R	ER	HR	SH	SF	HB	TBB	IBB	SO	WP	Bk	W	L	Pct	Sh	Sv-Op	Hld	ERC	ERA
2012 StCol	A-	11	9	0	0	42.2	184	38	19	14	2	2	2	2	17	0	44	3	0	0	1	.000	0	0--	-	3.23	2.95
2013 Bradtn	A+	25	24	1	0	140.0	611	177	87	80	18	4	7	7	22	0	85	6	3	5	8	.385	0	0--	-	5.03	5.14
2014 Altna	AA	24	24	2	0	148.0	594	125	45	42	10	6	6	6	30	1	99	3	0	10	5	.667	1	0--	-	2.47	2.55
2015 Indy	AAA	21	21	0	0	124.1	533	137	59	55	8	2	4	4	29	2	95	9	0	8	8	.500	0	0--	-	3.82	3.98
2015 Tacom	AAA	7	7	0	0	38.1	182	60	38	31	5	1	3	0	8	0	28	1	0	2	4	.333	0	0--	-	6.78	7.28
2016 Tacom	AAA	13	13	0	0	80.1	324	81	30	29	5	2	4	1	12	0	61	1	0	7	4	.636	0	0--	-	3.01	3.25
2016 Sea	AL	1	1	0	0	4.2	21	8	4	4	2	0	0	0	1	0	2	0	0	0	1	.000	0	0-0	0	11.33	7.71

Keyvius Sampson

Pitches: R **Bats:** R **Pos:** RP-16; SP-2　　　　KEY-vuss　　　　**Ht:** 6'2" **Wt:** 225 **Born:** 1/6/1991 **Age:** 26

			HOW MUCH HE PITCHED						WHAT HE GAVE UP									THE RESULTS						
Year	Team	Lg	G	GS	CG	GF	IP	BFP	H	R	ER	HR	SH	SF	HB	TBB	IBB	SO	WP	Bk	W	L	Pct	Sh	Sv-Op	Hld	ERC	ERA
2012	SnAnt	AA	26	25	0	0	122.1	532	108	70	68	11	4	3	4	57	1	122	8	2	8	11	.421	0	0- -	-	3.67	5.00
2013	Tucsn	AAA	9	9	0	0	38.0	182	44	32	30	5	6	2	1	29	0	25	2	1	2	3	.400	0	0- -	-	6.97	7.11
2013	SnAnt	AA	19	18	0	0	103.1	411	74	31	26	9	3	1	3	33	2	110	6	0	10	4	.714	0	0- -	-	2.32	2.26
2014	ElPaso	AAA	38	14	0	5	91.2	425	91	73	68	19	3	3	3	68	0	94	8	0	2	5	.286	0	0- -	-	6.47	6.68
2015	Lsvlle	AAA	8	7	0	1	39.0	178	40	22	22	1	2	2	2	22	0	33	2	0	2	4	.333	0	0- -	-	4.46	5.08
2015	Pnscla	AA	8	8	0	0	43.2	189	35	11	9	2	1	0	2	24	0	41	3	0	1	2	.333	0	0- -	-	3.33	1.85
2016	Lsvlle	AA	18	9	0	1	62.1	242	38	14	13	3	1	1	1	21	0	62	2	0	3	3	.500	0	0- -	-	1.67	1.88
2015	Cin	NL	13	12	0	0	52.1	251	67	43	38	7	2	2	0	26	0	42	4	0	2	6	.250	0	0-0	0	6.23	6.54
2016	Cin	NL	18	2	0	2	39.1	188	40	24	19	9	2	0	2	27	2	42	3	0	0	1	.000	0	0-0	0	6.31	4.35
	2 ML YEARS		31	14	0	2	91.2	439	107	67	57	16	4	2	2	53	2	84	7	0	2	7	.222	0	0-0	0	6.26	5.60

Aaron Sanchez

Pitches: R **Bats:** R **Pos:** SP-30　　　　　　　　**Ht:** 6'4" **Wt:** 220 **Born:** 7/1/1992 **Age:** 24

			HOW MUCH HE PITCHED						WHAT HE GAVE UP									THE RESULTS						
Year	Team	Lg	G	GS	CG	GF	IP	BFP	H	R	ER	HR	SH	SF	HB	TBB	IBB	SO	WP	Bk	W	L	Pct	Sh	Sv-Op	Hld	ERC	ERA
2014	Tor	AL	24	0	0	6	33.0	121	14	5	4	1	2	0	1	9	0	27	1	0	2	2	.500	0	3-3	7	0.96	1.09
2015	Tor	AL	41	11	0	4	92.1	380	74	35	33	9	2	1	3	44	2	61	8	0	7	6	.538	0	0-1	10	3.47	3.22
2016	Tor	AL	30	30	0	0	192.0	790	161	69	64	15	1	2	5	63	0	161	5	0	15	2	.882	0	0-0	0	2.90	3.00
	Postseason		9	0	0	1	7.1	31	7	1	0	0	1	0	0	2	0	6	0	0	1	0	1.000	0	0-0	0	2.62	0.00
	3 ML YEARS		95	41	0	10	317.1	1291	249	109	101	25	5	3	9	116	2	249	14	0	24	10	.706	0	3-4	17	2.79	2.86

Anibal Sanchez

Pitches: R **Bats:** R **Pos:** SP-26; RP-9　　　　ah-NEE-bahl　　　　**Ht:** 6'0" **Wt:** 205 **Born:** 2/27/1984 **Age:** 33

			HOW MUCH HE PITCHED						WHAT HE GAVE UP									THE RESULTS						
Year	Team	Lg	G	GS	CG	GF	IP	BFP	H	R	ER	HR	SH	SF	HB	TBB	IBB	SO	WP	Bk	W	L	Pct	Sh	Sv-Op	Hld	ERC	ERA
2006	Fla	NL	18	17	2	0	114.1	469	90	39	36	9	3	1	4	46	1	72	4	1	10	3	.769	0	0-0	0	2.96	2.83
2007	Fla	NL	6	6	0	0	30.0	151	43	17	16	3	2	2	2	19	1	14	3	0	2	1	.667	0	0-0	0	7.90	4.80
2008	Fla	NL	10	10	0	0	51.2	241	54	35	32	7	4	2	6	27	2	50	1	0	2	5	.286	0	0-0	0	5.40	5.57
2009	Fla	NL	16	16	0	0	86.0	383	84	39	37	10	2	2	1	46	5	71	0	1	4	8	.333	0	0-0	0	4.51	3.87
2010	Fla	NL	32	32	1	0	195.0	841	192	89	77	10	13	3	7	70	5	157	7	0	13	12	.520	1	0-0	0	3.56	3.55
2011	Fla	NL	32	32	3	0	196.1	830	187	85	80	20	12	1	5	64	8	202	4	5	8	9	.471	2	0-0	0	3.57	3.67
2012	2 Tms		31	31	1	0	195.2	820	200	95	84	20	5	7	5	48	3	167	7	1	9	13	.409	1	0-0	0	3.70	3.86
2013	Det	AL	29	29	1	0	182.0	746	156	56	52	9	4	4	2	54	1	202	7	0	14	8	.636	1	0-0	0	2.63	2.57
2014	Det	AL	22	21	0	0	126.0	514	108	55	48	4	3	4	3	30	1	102	5	0	8	5	.615	0	0-0	0	2.35	3.43
2015	Det	AL	25	25	1	0	157.0	660	152	89	87	29	5	2	1	49	1	138	5	3	10	10	.500	1	0-0	0	4.14	4.99
2016	Det	AL	35	26	0	3	153.1	668	171	108	100	30	4	6	5	53	1	135	7	2	7	13	.350	0	0-0	0	5.40	5.87
	12 Mia	NL	19	19	0	0	121.0	504	119	59	53	12	4	5	2	33	2	110	4	1	5	7	.417	0	0-0	0	3.55	3.94
	12 Det	AL	12	12	1	0	74.2	316	81	36	31	8	1	2	3	15	1	57	3	0	4	6	.400	1	0-0	0	3.95	3.74
	Postseason		7	6	0	0	38.2	161	31	14	12	5	0	1	0	14	1	43	4	0	2	4	.333	0	0-0	1	2.96	2.79
	11 ML YEARS		256	245	9	3	1487.1	6323	1437	707	649	151	57	34	41	506	29	1310	50	13	87	87	.500	7	0-0	0	3.74	3.93

Carlos Sanchez

Bats: B **Throws:** R **Pos:** 2B-33;3B-6;PH-6;PR-6;SS-4;DH-3　　　　**Ht:** 5'11" **Wt:** 195 **Born:** 6/29/1992 **Age:** 25

			BATTING																		RUNNING			AVERAGES			
Year	Team	Lg	G	AB	H	2B	3B	HR	(Hm	Rd)	TB	R	RBI	RC	TBB	IBB	SO	HBP	SH	SF	SB	CS	GDP	Avg	OBP	Slg	OPS
2016	Charllt*	AAA	61	235	60	11	2	8	(-	-)	99	31	29	32	17	0	55	2	4	2	10	4	6	.255	.309	.421	.730
2014	CWS	AL	28	100	25	5	0	0	(0	0)	30	6	5	5	3	0	25	0	0	1	1	1	1	.250	.269	.300	.569
2015	CWS	AL	120	389	87	23	1	5	(2	3)	127	40	31	30	19	0	81	5	6	1	2	2	9	.224	.268	.326	.595
2016	CWS	AL	53	154	32	9	1	4	(2	2)	55	15	21	14	5	0	42	1	2	1	0	1	1	.208	.236	.357	.593
	3 ML YEARS		201	643	144	37	2	9	(4	5)	212	61	57	49	27	0	148	6	8	3	3	4	11	.224	.261	.330	.590

Gary Sanchez

Bats: R **Throws:** R **Pos:** C-36;DH-17　　　　**Ht:** 6'2" **Wt:** 230 **Born:** 12/2/1992 **Age:** 24

			BATTING																		RUNNING			AVERAGES			
Year	Team	Lg	G	AB	H	2B	3B	HR	(Hm	Rd)	TB	R	RBI	RC	TBB	IBB	SO	HBP	SH	SF	SB	CS	GDP	Avg	OBP	Slg	OPS
2012	2 Tms	Low	116	435	126	29	1	18	(-	-)	211	65	85	73	32	0	106	5	0	2	15	4	13	.290	.344	.485	.829
2013	Tampa	A+	94	362	92	21	0	13	(-	-)	152	38	61	50	28	1	71	5	0	4	3	1	8	.254	.313	.420	.733
2013	Trntn	AA	23	92	23	6	0	2	(-	-)	35	12	10	14	13	0	16	4	0	1	0	0	3	.250	.364	.380	.744
2014	Trntn	AA	110	429	116	19	0	13	(-	-)	174	48	65	61	43	0	91	2	0	3	1	1	15	.270	.338	.406	.743
2015	Trntn	AA	58	233	61	14	0	12	(-	-)	111	33	36	37	18	1	50	2	0	1	6	0	2	.262	.319	.476	.795
2015	S-WB	AAA	35	132	39	9	0	6	(-	-)	66	17	26	22	11	0	28	1	0	2	1	2	7	.295	.349	.500	.849
2016	S-WB	AAA	71	284	80	21	1	10	(-	-)	133	39	50	47	21	0	45	5	0	3	7	1	4	.282	.339	.468	.807
2015	NYY	AL	2	2	0	0	0	0	(0	0)	0	0	0	0	0	0	1	0	0	0	0	0	0	.000	.000	.000	.000
2016	NYY	AL	53	201	60	12	0	20	(10	10)	132	34	42	40	24	2	57	2	0	2	1	0	5	.299	.376	.657	1.032
	2 ML YEARS		55	203	60	12	0	20	(10	10)	132	34	42	40	24	2	58	2	0	2	1	0	5	.296	.372	.650	1.023

Hector Sanchez

Bats: B Throws: R Pos: C-14;PH-14   Ht: 6'0" Wt: 235 Born: 11/17/1989 Age: 27

Year	Team	Lg	G	AB	H	2B	3B	HR	(Hm	Rd)	TB	R	RBI	RC	TBB	IBB	SO	HBP	SH	SF	SB	CS	GDP	Avg	OBP	Slg	OPS
2016	ElPaso*	AAA	55	176	57	16	0	13	(-	-)	112	25	40	42	20	0	40	1	0	2	0	0	3	.324	.392	.636	1.028
2011	SF	NL	13	31	8	2	0	0	(0	0)	10	0	1	2	3	0	6	0	0	0	0	0	1	.258	.324	.323	.646
2012	SF	NL	74	218	61	15	0	3	(1	2)	85	22	34	22	5	0	52	1	0	3	0	0	8	.280	.295	.390	.685
2013	SF	NL	63	129	32	4	0	3	(0	3)	45	8	19	14	7	0	29	3	0	1	0	0	1	.248	.300	.349	.649
2014	SF	NL	66	163	32	8	0	3	(1	2)	49	8	28	12	8	1	55	2	0	4	0	1	2	.196	.237	.301	.538
2015	SF	NL	28	56	10	4	0	1	(0	1)	17	5	5	3	2	0	14	0	1	0	0	0	1	.179	.207	.304	.510
2016	2 Tms		28	49	13	1	0	3	(0	3)	23	3	8	6	4	0	10	1	0	0	0	0	0	.265	.333	.469	.803
16	CWS	AL	2	7	1	0	0	0	(0	0)	1	0	1	0	1	0	2	0	0	0	0	0	0	.143	.250	.143	.393
16	SD	NL	26	42	12	1	0	3	(0	3)	22	3	7	6	3	0	8	1	0	0	0	0	0	.286	.348	.524	.872
	Postseason		4	11	1	0	0	0	(0	0)	1	1	0	1	2	0	7	0	0	0	0	0	0	.091	.231	.091	.322
	6 ML YEARS		272	646	156	34	0	13	(2	11)	229	46	95	59	29	1	166	7	1	8	0	1	13	.241	.278	.354	.633

Pablo Sandoval

Bats: B Throws: R Pos: 3B-2;PH-2   Ht: 5'11" Wt: 255 Born: 8/11/1986 Age: 30

Year	Team	Lg	G	AB	H	2B	3B	HR	(Hm	Rd)	TB	R	RBI	RC	TBB	IBB	SO	HBP	SH	SF	SB	CS	GDP	Avg	OBP	Slg	OPS
2008	SF	NL	41	145	50	10	1	3	(1	2)	71	24	24	24	4	1	14	1	0	4	0	0	6	.345	.357	.490	.847
2009	SF	NL	153	572	189	44	5	25	(13	12)	318	79	90	113	52	13	83	4	0	5	5	5	10	.330	.387	.556	.943
2010	SF	NL	152	563	151	34	3	13	(9	4)	230	61	63	55	47	12	81	1	0	5	3	2	26	.268	.323	.409	.732
2011	SF	NL	117	426	134	26	3	23	(7	16)	235	55	70	72	32	9	63	0	1	7	2	4	12	.315	.357	.552	.909
2012	SF	NL	108	396	112	25	2	12	(7	5)	177	59	63	60	38	4	59	1	0	7	1	1	13	.283	.342	.447	.789
2013	SF	NL	141	525	146	27	2	14	(6	8)	219	52	79	78	47	5	79	6	0	6	0	0	19	.278	.341	.417	.758
2014	SF	NL	157	588	164	26	3	16	(9	7)	244	68	73	78	39	6	85	4	0	7	0	0	16	.279	.324	.415	.739
2015	Bos	AL	126	470	115	25	1	10	(4	6)	172	43	47	46	25	1	73	7	1	2	0	0	14	.245	.292	.366	.658
2016	Bos	AL	3	6	0	0	0	0	(0	0)	0	0	0	0	1	0	4	0	0	0	0	0	0	.000	.143	.000	.143
	Postseason		39	154	53	13	0	6	(3	3)	84	21	20	27	10	3	22	2	0	1	0	0	7	.344	.389	.545	.935
	9 ML YEARS		998	3691	1061	217	20	116	(56	60)	1666	441	509	526	285	51	541	24	2	43	11	12	116	.287	.339	.451	.790

Jerry Sands

Bats: R Throws: R Pos: DH-10;PH-7;1B-4;LF-3;RF-1   Ht: 6'4" Wt: 225 Born: 9/28/1987 Age: 29

Year	Team	Lg	G	AB	H	2B	3B	HR	(Hm	Rd)	TB	R	RBI	RC	TBB	IBB	SO	HBP	SH	SF	SB	CS	GDP	Avg	OBP	Slg	OPS
2016	Charltt*	AAA	73	270	68	12	1	8	(-	-)	106	32	37	35	26	1	62	1	2	2	0	1	8	.252	.318	.393	.710
2011	LAD	NL	61	198	50	15	0	4	(2	2)	77	20	26	25	25	0	51	1	2	1	3	3	5	.253	.338	.389	.727
2012	LAD	NL	9	23	4	2	0	0	(0	0)	6	2	1	1	1	0	9	0	0	0	0	0	0	.174	.208	.261	.469
2014	TB	AL	12	21	4	0	0	1	(1	0)	7	1	4	1	0	0	6	1	0	0	0	0	2	.190	.227	.333	.561
2015	Cle	AL	50	123	29	5	1	4	(2	2)	48	11	19	15	9	0	36	0	0	1	0	0	0	.236	.286	.390	.676
2016	CWS	AL	24	55	13	0	0	1	(0	1)	16	2	7	6	3	0	24	0	0	0	0	0	3	.236	.276	.291	.567
	5 ML YEARS		156	420	100	22	1	10	(5	5)	154	36	57	48	38	0	126	2	2	2	3	3	10	.238	.303	.367	.670

Miguel Sano

Bats: R Throws: R Pos: 3B-42;RF-38;DH-35;PH-2   sah-NO   Ht: 6'4" Wt: 260 Born: 5/11/1993 Age: 24

Year	Team	Lg	G	AB	H	2B	3B	HR	(Hm	Rd)	TB	R	RBI	RC	TBB	IBB	SO	HBP	SH	SF	SB	CS	GDP	Avg	OBP	Slg	OPS
2012	Beloit	A	129	457	118	28	4	28	(-	-)	238	75	100	93	80	4	144	8	0	8	8	3	10	.258	.373	.521	.893
2013	FtMyrs	A+	56	206	68	15	2	16	(-	-)	135	51	48	55	29	2	61	6	0	2	9	2	2	.330	.424	.655	1.079
2013	NwBrit	AA	67	233	55	15	3	19	(-	-)	133	35	55	47	36	2	81	4	0	3	2	1	6	.236	.344	.571	.915
2015	Chatt	AA	66	241	66	18	1	15	(-	-)	131	55	48	51	38	2	68	3	0	4	5	1	5	.274	.374	.544	.918
2015	Min	AL	80	279	75	17	1	18	(10	8)	148	46	52	62	53	1	119	1	0	2	1	1	4	.269	.385	.530	.916
2016	Min	AL	116	437	103	22	1	25	(11	14)	202	57	66	62	54	1	178	1	0	3	1	0	8	.236	.319	.462	.781
	2 ML YEARS		196	716	178	39	2	43	(21	22)	350	103	118	124	107	2	297	2	0	5	2	1	12	.249	.346	.489	.835

Carlos Santana

Bats: B Throws: R Pos: DH-92;1B-64;PH-4   Ht: 5'11" Wt: 210 Born: 4/8/1986 Age: 31

Year	Team	Lg	G	AB	H	2B	3B	HR	(Hm	Rd)	TB	R	RBI	RC	TBB	IBB	SO	HBP	SH	SF	SB	CS	GDP	Avg	OBP	Slg	OPS
2010	Cle	AL	46	150	39	13	0	6	(2	4)	70	23	22	25	37	2	29	1	0	4	3	0	3	.260	.401	.467	.868
2011	Cle	AL	155	552	132	35	2	27	(14	13)	252	84	79	81	97	7	133	2	0	7	5	3	15	.239	.351	.457	.808
2012	Cle	AL	143	507	128	27	2	18	(7	11)	213	72	76	77	91	4	101	3	0	8	3	5	21	.252	.365	.420	.785
2013	Cle	AL	154	541	145	39	1	20	(12	8)	246	75	74	93	93	6	110	4	0	4	3	1	7	.268	.377	.455	.832
2014	Cle	AL	152	541	125	25	0	27	(13	14)	231	68	85	88	113	5	124	3	0	3	5	2	13	.231	.365	.427	.792
2015	Cle	AL	154	550	127	29	2	19	(6	13)	217	72	85	80	108	8	122	3	0	5	11	3	20	.231	.357	.395	.752
2016	Cle	AL	158	582	151	31	3	34	(20	14)	290	89	87	104	99	0	99	2	0	5	5	2	18	.259	.366	.498	.865
	Postseason		1	4	2	1	0	0	(0	0)	3	0	0	0	0	0	1	0	0	0	0	0	0	.500	.500	.750	1.250
	7 ML YEARS		962	3423	847	199	10	151	(74	77)	1519	483	508	548	638	32	718	18	0	36	35	16	97	.247	.365	.444	.809

Danny Santana

Bats: B Throws: R Pos: CF-40;LF-17;PR-8;RF-6;2B-3;SS-3;DH-3;PH-3;3B-1   Ht: 5'11" Wt: 185 Born: 11/7/1990 Age: 26

Year	Team	Lg	G	AB	H	2B	3B	HR	(Hm	Rd)	TB	R	RBI	RC	TBB	IBB	SO	HBP	SH	SF	SB	CS	GDP	Avg	OBP	Slg	OPS
2014	Min	AL	101	405	129	27	7	7	(3	4)	191	70	40	72	19	0	98	3	2	1	20	4	3	.319	.353	.472	.824
2015	Min	AL	91	261	56	10	5	0	(0	0)	76	30	21	16	6	1	68	3	7	0	8	4	7	.215	.241	.291	.532
2016	Min	AL	75	233	56	10	2	2	(0	2)	76	29	14	18	12	0	55	1	1	1	12	9	1	.240	.279	.326	.606
3 ML YEARS			267	899	241	47	14	9	(3	6)	343	129	75	106	37	1	221	7	10	2	40	17	11	.268	.302	.382	.683

Domingo Santana

Bats: R Throws: R Pos: RF-62;PH-14;LF-4;CF-3   Ht: 6'5" Wt: 220 Born: 8/5/1992 Age: 24

Year	Team	Lg	G	AB	H	2B	3B	HR	(Hm	Rd)	TB	R	RBI	RC	TBB	IBB	SO	HBP	SH	SF	SB	CS	GDP	Avg	OBP	Slg	OPS
2014	Hou	AL	6	17	0	0	0	0	(0	0)	0	1	0	0	1	0	14	0	0	0	0	0	0	.000	.056	.000	.056
2015	2 Tms		52	160	38	7	0	8	(3	5)	69	20	26	28	20	0	63	5	0	2	4	1	2	.238	.337	.431	.768
2016	Mil	NL	77	246	63	14	0	11	(3	8)	110	34	32	36	32	0	91	2	0	1	2	3	7	.256	.345	.447	.792
15	Hou	AL	14	39	10	2	0	2	(0	2)	18	6	8	8	2	0	17	1	0	0	2	1	1	.256	.310	.462	.771
15	Mil	NL	38	121	28	5	0	6	(3	3)	51	14	18	20	18	0	46	4	0	2	2	0	1	.231	.345	.421	.766
3 ML YEARS			135	423	101	21	0	19	(6	13)	179	55	58	64	53	0	168	7	0	3	6	4	9	.239	.331	.423	.754

Ervin Santana

Pitches: R Bats: R Pos: SP-30   Ht: 6'2" Wt: 175 Born: 12/12/1982 Age: 34

Year	Team	Lg	G	GS	CG	GF	IP	BFP	H	R	ER	HR	SH	SF	HB	TBB	IBB	SO	WP	Bk	W	L	Pct	Sh	Sv-Op	Hld	ERC	ERA
2005	LAA	AL	23	23	1	0	133.2	583	139	73	69	17	1	4	8	47	2	99	4	0	12	8	.600	1	0-0	0	4.51	4.65
2006	LAA	AL	33	33	0	0	204.0	846	181	106	97	21	4	10	11	70	2	141	10	2	16	8	.667	0	0-0	0	3.51	4.28
2007	LAA	AL	28	26	0	1	150.0	675	174	103	96	26	3	2	8	58	3	126	7	0	7	14	.333	0	0-0	0	5.69	5.76
2008	LAA	AL	32	32	2	0	219.0	897	198	89	85	23	3	5	8	47	2	214	5	1	16	7	.696	1	0-0	0	3.00	3.49
2009	LAA	AL	24	23	2	0	139.2	614	159	83	78	24	2	1	10	47	4	107	4	0	8	8	.500	2	0-0	1	5.47	5.03
2010	LAA	AL	33	33	4	0	222.2	954	221	104	97	27	8	8	12	73	2	169	11	1	17	10	.630	1	0-0	0	4.10	3.92
2011	LAA	AL	33	33	4	0	228.2	949	207	95	86	26	4	7	8	72	4	178	10	1	11	12	.478	1	0-0	0	3.45	3.38
2012	LAA	AL	30	30	1	0	178.0	764	165	109	102	**39**	2	2	9	61	2	133	4	0	9	13	.409	1	0-0	0	4.38	5.16
2013	KC	AL	32	32	0	0	211.0	859	190	85	76	26	2	3	6	51	3	161	6	0	9	10	.474	0	0-0	0	3.19	3.24
2014	Atl	NL	31	31	0	0	196.0	817	193	90	86	16	12	**12**	4	63	4	179	9	0	14	10	.583	0	0-0	0	3.68	3.95
2015	Min	AL	17	17	0	0	108.0	457	104	50	48	12	4	2	4	36	2	82	3	0	7	5	.583	0	0-0	0	3.82	4.00
2016	Min	AL	30	30	2	0	181.1	748	168	78	68	19	1	5	4	53	2	149	11	3	7	11	.389	1	0-0	0	3.39	3.38
Postseason			8	2	0	3	22.2	101	21	17	14	4	1	1	3	9	1	14	0	0	2	2	.500	0	0-0	0	4.55	5.56
12 ML YEARS			346	343	16	1	2172.0	9163	2099	1065	988	276	46	61	92	678	32	1738	84	8	133	116	.534	8	0-0	1	3.89	4.09

Hector Santiago

Pitches: L Bats: R Pos: SP-33   Ht: 6'0" Wt: 215 Born: 12/16/1987 Age: 29

Year	Team	Lg	G	GS	CG	GF	IP	BFP	H	R	ER	HR	SH	SF	HB	TBB	IBB	SO	WP	Bk	W	L	Pct	Sh	Sv-Op	Hld	ERC	ERA
2011	CWS	AL	2	0	0	1	5.1	18	1	0	0	0	0	0	0	1	1	2	1	0	0	0	-	0	0-0	0	0.16	0.00
2012	CWS	AL	42	4	0	19	70.1	306	54	26	26	10	2	1	7	40	1	79	5	2	4	1	.800	0	4-6	4	4.11	3.33
2013	CWS	AL	34	23	0	4	149.0	656	137	69	59	17	3	3	15	72	2	137	2	0	4	9	.308	0	0-0	0	4.43	3.56
2014	LAA	AL	30	24	0	2	127.1	544	120	63	53	15	1	3	3	53	3	108	5	1	6	9	.400	0	0-0	1	4.02	3.75
2015	LAA	AL	33	32	0	0	180.2	776	150	80	72	**29**	4	4	10	71	5	162	1	3	9	9	.500	0	0-0	0	3.82	3.59
2016	2 Tms		33	33	0	0	182.0	785	169	100	95	33	5	6	5	**79**	1	144	3	1	13	10	.565	0	0-0	0	4.48	4.70
16	LAA	AL	22	22	0	0	120.2	515	104	61	57	20	3	4	4	57	0	107	2	1	10	4	.714	0	0-0	0	4.20	4.25
16	Min	AL	11	11	0	0	61.1	270	65	39	38	13	2	2	1	22	0	37	1	0	3	6	.333	0	0-0	0	5.05	5.58
Postseason			1	0	0	0	1.1	7	1	2	2	1	0	0	0	2	0	0	0	0	0	0	-	0	0-0	0	12.98	13.50
6 ML YEARS			174	116	0	26	714.2	3085	637	338	305	104	15	17	40	316	12	632	17	7	36	38	.486	0	4-6	5	4.13	3.84

Sergio Santos

Pitches: R Bats: R Pos: P   Ht: 6'4" Wt: 215 Born: 7/4/1983 Age: 33

Year	Team	Lg	G	GS	CG	GF	IP	BFP	H	R	ER	HR	SH	SF	HB	TBB	IBB	SO	WP	Bk	W	L	Pct	Sh	Sv-Op	Hld	ERC	ERA
2010	CWS	AL	56	0	0	13	51.2	235	53	18	17	2	2	1	3	26	3	56	8	0	2	2	.500	0	1-3	14	4.22	2.96
2011	CWS	AL	63	0	0	50	63.1	260	41	25	25	6	1	1	3	29	5	92	5	0	4	5	.444	0	30-36	2	2.46	3.55
2012	Tor	AL	6	0	0	4	5.0	24	6	5	5	1	0	1	0	4	0	4	1	0	0	1	.000	0	2-4	0	7.98	9.00
2013	Tor	AL	29	0	0	6	25.2	90	11	5	5	1	0	2	0	4	2	28	1	0	1	1	.500	0	1-3	8	0.69	1.75
2014	Tor	AL	26	0	0	14	21.0	106	28	22	20	5	0	2	0	18	2	29	4	0	0	3	.000	0	5-8	0	9.19	8.57
2015	2 Tms		14	0	0	8	16.1	73	16	9	9	3	0	1	0	7	1	18	4	0	0	0	-	0	0-0	0	4.40	4.96
15	LAD	NL	12	0	0	6	13.1	61	13	7	7	2	0	1	0	7	1	15	4	0	0	0	-	0	0-0	0	4.48	4.73
15	NYY	AL	2	0	0	2	3.0	12	3	2	2	1	0	0	0	0	0	3	0	0	0	0	-	0	0-0	0	3.79	6.00
6 ML YEARS			194	0	0	95	183.0	788	155	84	81	18	3	8	6	88	13	227	23	0	7	12	.368	0	39-54	24	3.52	3.98

Luis Sardinas

sar-DEEN-yas

Bats: B **Throws:** R **Pos:** SS-50;PR-6;PH-5;2B-4;1B-3;3B-3;LF-1   **Ht:** 6'1" **Wt:** 180 **Born:** 5/16/1993 **Age:** 24

Year	Team	Lg	G	AB	H	2B	3B	HR	(Hm	Rd)	TB	R	RBI	RC	TBB	IBB	SO	HBP	SH	SF	SB	CS	GDP	Avg	OBP	Slg	OPS
2016	Tacom*	AAA	44	163	41	4	0	0	(-	-)	45	17	17	13	9	1	20	2	1	2	7	4	4	.252	.295	.276	.572
2014	Tex	AL	43	115	30	6	0	0	(0	0)	36	12	8	9	5	0	21	2	3	0	5	1	5	.261	.303	.313	.616
2015	Mil	NL	36	97	19	0	1	0	(0	0)	21	8	4	5	6	1	25	0	1	1	0	0	3	.196	.240	.216	.457
2016	2 Tms		66	180	44	6	1	4	(1	3)	64	25	18	22	12	3	48	1	4	0	4	2	3	.244	.295	.356	.651
16	Sea	AL	32	72	13	0	0	2	(1	1)	19	12	5	1	1	0	25	1	3	0	1	1	3	.181	.203	.264	.467
16	SD	NL	34	108	31	6	1	2	(0	2)	45	13	13	21	11	3	23	0	1	0	3	1	0	.287	.353	.417	.770
	3 ML YEARS		145	392	93	12	2	4	(1	3)	121	45	30	36	23	4	94	3	8	1	9	3	11	.237	.284	.309	.593

Michael Saunders

Bats: L **Throws:** R **Pos:** LF-106;RF-22;DH-9;PH-9;CF-1   **Ht:** 6'4" **Wt:** 225 **Born:** 11/19/1986 **Age:** 30

Year	Team	Lg	G	AB	H	2B	3B	HR	(Hm	Rd)	TB	R	RBI	RC	TBB	IBB	SO	HBP	SH	SF	SB	CS	GDP	Avg	OBP	Slg	OPS
2009	Sea	AL	46	122	27	1	3	0	(0	0)	34	13	4	8	6	0	40	0	1	0	4	1	1	.221	.258	.279	.537
2010	Sea	AL	100	289	61	11	2	10	(5	5)	106	29	33	31	35	0	84	0	2	1	6	3	1	.211	.295	.367	.662
2011	Sea	AL	58	161	24	5	0	2	(1	1)	35	16	8	2	12	1	56	0	5	1	6	2	1	.149	.207	.217	.424
2012	Sea	AL	139	507	125	31	3	19	(8	11)	219	71	57	67	43	0	132	1	1	1	21	4	6	.247	.306	.432	.738
2013	Sea	AL	132	406	96	23	3	12	(5	7)	161	59	46	49	54	4	118	1	1	6	13	5	6	.236	.323	.397	.720
2014	Sea	AL	78	231	63	11	3	8	(4	4)	104	38	34	37	26	1	59	0	2	4	4	5	2	.273	.341	.450	.791
2015	Tor	AL	9	31	6	0	0	0	(0	0)	6	2	3	3	5	0	10	0	0	0	0	0	1	.194	.306	.194	.499
2016	Tor	AL	140	490	124	32	3	24	(10	14)	234	70	57	66	59	2	157	5	1	3	1	2	14	.253	.338	.478	.815
	8 ML YEARS		702	2237	526	114	17	75	(33	42)	899	298	242	263	240	8	656	7	13	16	55	22	32	.235	.309	.402	.711

Warwick Saupold

Pitches: R **Bats:** R **Pos:** RP-6   SOW-pold   **Ht:** 6'1" **Wt:** 195 **Born:** 1/16/1990 **Age:** 27

			HOW MUCH HE PITCHED						WHAT HE GAVE UP										THE RESULTS						
Year	Team	Lg	G	GS	CG	GF	IP	BFP	H	R	ER	HR	SH	SF	HB	TBB	IBB	SO	WP	Bk	W	L	Pct	Sh	Sv-Op	Hld	ERC	ERA
2012	2 Tms	Low	35	6	0	9	89.0	376	90	40	31	5	4	1	6	21	1	82	4	1	4	3	.571	0	2--	-	3.45	3.13
2013	Erie	AA	22	22	1	0	129.0	547	124	54	47	12	4	2	8	51	0	82	6	0	7	6	.538	0	0--	-	4.13	3.28
2014	Erie	AA	27	27	2	0	140.0	608	141	92	78	16	3	2	7	65	0	125	16	1	8	11	.421	0	0--	-	4.78	5.01
2015	Erie	AA	23	15	0	6	103.1	436	102	49	46	5	3	6	3	36	0	71	11	0	5	6	.455	0	1--	-	3.61	4.01
2015	Toledo	AAA	6	3	0	1	20.1	77	14	10	10	1	0	1	1	6	0	23	0	0	1	2	.333	0	0--	-	2.10	4.43
2016	Toledo	AAA	18	11	1	1	74.1	297	64	20	19	3	1	0	2	22	1	50	3	0	7	2	.778	0	0--	-	2.73	2.30
2016	Det	AL	6	0	0	2	9.2	49	17	8	8	0	0	2	1	3	0	10	0	0	1	1	.500	0	0-0	0	7.91	7.45

Rob Scahill

Pitches: R **Bats:** L **Pos:** RP-31   SKAY-hill   **Ht:** 6'2" **Wt:** 220 **Born:** 2/15/1987 **Age:** 30

			HOW MUCH HE PITCHED						WHAT HE GAVE UP										THE RESULTS						
Year	Team	Lg	G	GS	CG	GF	IP	BFP	H	R	ER	HR	SH	SF	HB	TBB	IBB	SO	WP	Bk	W	L	Pct	Sh	Sv-Op	Hld	ERC	ERA
2016	Indy*	AAA	13	0	0	7	18.0	88	23	13	13	0	0	2	0	8	0	18	2	0	0	2	.000	0	3--	-	4.75	4.00
2016	ColSpr*	AAA	8	0	0	3	9.1	42	11	5	5	1	1	0	1	5	0	4	1	0	0	0	-	0	0-0	0	6.50	4.82
2012	Col	NL	6	0	0	3	8.2	33	7	1	1	0	0	0	0	3	0	4	0	0	0	0	-	0	0-0	0	2.43	1.04
2013	Col	NL	23	0	0	6	33.1	149	40	19	19	5	3	0	4	9	1	20	1	0	1	0	1.000	0	0-0	1	5.55	5.13
2014	Col	NL	12	0	0	3	15.0	72	17	8	8	3	0	2	1	9	2	11	0	0	1	0	1.000	0	0-1	0	6.37	4.80
2015	Pit	NL	28	0	0	13	30.2	142	33	15	9	3	1	1	1	16	5	24	1	0	2	4	.333	0	0-0	1	4.70	2.64
2016	2 Tms	NL	31	0	0	12	34.2	147	34	14	13	2	0	1	4	9	0	27	1	0	0	0	-	0	0-0	2	3.60	3.38
16	Pit	NL	15	0	0	5	16.1	71	18	9	8	1	0	1	2	6	0	13	1	0	0	0	-	0	0-0	1	4.89	4.41
16	Mil	NL	16	0	0	7	18.1	76	16	5	5	1	0	0	2	3	0	14	0	0	0	0	-	0	0-0	1	2.58	2.45
	5 ML YEARS		100	0	0	37	122.1	543	131	57	50	13	4	4	10	46	8	86	3	0	4	4	.500	0	0-1	4	4.63	3.68

Logan Schafer

Bats: L **Throws:** L **Pos:** LF-12;RF-8;CF-3;PH-3;PR-3;DH-1   **Ht:** 6'1" **Wt:** 200 **Born:** 9/8/1986 **Age:** 30

Year	Team	Lg	G	AB	H	2B	3B	HR	(Hm	Rd)	TB	R	RBI	RC	TBB	IBB	SO	HBP	SH	SF	SB	CS	GDP	Avg	OBP	Slg	OPS
2016	Roch*	AAA	63	216	57	7	1	4	(-	-)	78	29	19	28	22	1	35	3	3	0	5	2	2	.264	.340	.361	.701
2011	Mil	NL	8	3	1	0	0	0	(0	0)	1	1	0	0	1	0	1	0	0	0	0	0	0	.333	.500	.333	.833
2012	Mil	NL	16	23	7	1	2	0	(0	0)	12	3	5	4	1	0	3	0	0	1	0	1	0	.304	.320	.522	.842
2013	Mil	NL	134	298	63	15	3	4	(2	2)	96	29	33	31	25	1	60	3	11	0	7	1	5	.211	.279	.322	.601
2014	Mil	NL	65	116	21	9	1	0	(0	0)	32	13	8	11	15	3	27	1	3	1	2	1	0	.181	.278	.276	.554
2015	Mil	NL	69	122	27	6	1	1	(1	0)	38	17	6	8	12	0	29	2	6	1	1	0	3	.221	.299	.311	.611
2016	Min	AL	26	63	15	3	1	0	(0	0)	20	8	1	7	8	0	16	2	1	0	0	0	0	.238	.342	.317	.660
	6 ML YEARS		318	625	134	34	8	5	(3	2)	199	71	53	61	62	4	136	8	22	3	10	3	8	.214	.292	.318	.611

Scott Schebler

Bats: L **Throws:** R **Pos:** RF-41;CF-18;PH-16;LF-13   SHEB-ler   **Ht:** 6'0" **Wt:** 225 **Born:** 10/6/1990 **Age:** 26

Year	Team	Lg	G	AB	H	2B	3B	HR	(Hm	Rd)	TB	R	RBI	RC	TBB	IBB	SO	HBP	SH	SF	SB	CS	GDP	Avg	OBP	Slg	OPS
2012	Gt Lks	A	137	515	134	32	8	6	(-	-)	200	67	67	64	30	3	99	10	2	3	17	11	8	.260	.312	.388	.700
2013	Rcuca	A+	125	477	141	29	13	27	(-	-)	277	95	91	99	35	0	140	15	4	3	16	5	5	.296	.360	.581	.941
2014	Chatt	AA	135	489	137	23	14	28	(-	-)	272	82	73	100	45	4	110	22	1	3	10	4	8	.280	.365	.556	.921
2015	OkCity	AAA	121	432	104	16	9	13	(-	-)	177	57	50	62	40	8	93	12	0	1	15	2	6	.241	.322	.410	.731

290

Year	Team	Lg	G	AB	H	2B	3B	HR	(Hm	Rd)	TB	R	RBI	RC	TBB	IBB	SO	HBP	SH	SF	SB	CS	GDP	Avg	OBP	Slg	OPS
2016	Lsvlle	AAA	75	289	90	18	8	13	(-	-)	163	40	43	59	19	3	59	9	0	2	2	0	5	.311	.370	.564	.934
2015	LAD	NL	19	36	9	0	0	3	(1	2)	18	6	4	4	3	1	13	1	0	0	2	1	0	.250	.325	.500	.825
2016	Cin	NL	82	257	68	12	2	9	(5	4)	111	36	40	36	19	2	59	6	0	0	2	4	5	.265	.330	.432	.762
	2 ML YEARS		101	293	77	12	2	12	(6	6)	129	42	44	40	22	3	72	7	0	0	4	5	5	.263	.329	.440	.769

Tanner Scheppers

Pitches: R Bats: R Pos: RP-10
Ht: 6'4" Wt: 200 Born: 1/17/1987 Age: 30

Year	Team	Lg	G	GS	CG	GF	IP	BFP	H	R	ER	HR	SH	SF	HB	TBB	IBB	SO	WP	Bk	W	L	Pct	Sh	Sv-Op	Hld	ERC	ERA
2016	RdRck*	AAA	6	1	0	0	6.0	26	4	0	0	0	0	0	1	2	0	6	1	0	0	0	-	0	0- -	-	1.92	0.00
2012	Tex	AL	39	0	0	13	32.1	152	47	18	16	6	3	1	2	9	3	30	4	0	1	1	.500	0	1-1	5	7.05	4.45
2013	Tex	AL	76	0	0	11	76.2	302	58	21	16	6	0	0	7	24	4	59	4	0	6	2	.750	0	1-3	27	2.71	1.88
2014	Tex	AL	8	4	0	0	23.0	111	31	24	23	6	0	1	3	10	0	17	2	0	0	1	.000	0	0-0	1	8.21	9.00
2015	Tex	AL	42	0	0	7	38.1	176	37	25	24	6	0	3	2	23	3	32	1	0	4	1	.800	0	0-3	12	5.09	5.63
2016	Tex	AL	10	0	0	5	8.2	35	6	4	4	0	0	0	0	3	1	5	2	0	1	1	.500	0	1-1	1	1.57	4.15
	5 ML YEARS		175	4	0	36	179.0	776	179	92	83	24	3	5	14	69	11	143	13	0	12	6	.667	0	3-8	46	4.51	4.17

Max Scherzer

SHERR-zer

Pitches: R Bats: R Pos: SP-34
Ht: 6'3" Wt: 210 Born: 7/27/1984 Age: 32

Year	Team	Lg	G	GS	CG	GF	IP	BFP	H	R	ER	HR	SH	SF	HB	TBB	IBB	SO	WP	Bk	W	L	Pct	Sh	Sv-Op	Hld	ERC	ERA
2008	Ari	NL	16	7	0	2	56.0	237	48	24	19	5	4	2	5	21	1	66	2	0	0	4	.000	0	0-0	0	3.45	3.05
2009	Ari	NL	30	30	0	0	170.1	741	166	94	78	20	5	6	10	63	1	174	5	1	9	11	.450	0	0-0	0	4.12	4.12
2010	Det	AL	31	31	0	0	195.2	800	174	84	76	20	5	5	7	70	1	184	8	0	12	11	.522	0	0-0	0	3.56	3.50
2011	Det	AL	33	33	0	0	195.0	833	207	101	96	29	3	7	7	56	1	174	12	0	15	9	.625	0	0-0	0	4.48	4.43
2012	Det	AL	32	32	0	0	187.2	787	179	82	78	23	5	1	5	60	2	231	2	1	16	7	.696	0	0-0	0	3.77	3.74
2013	Det	AL	32	32	0	0	214.1	836	152	73	69	18	2	8	4	56	0	240	6	1	21	3	.875	0	0-0	0	2.07	2.90
2014	Det	AL	33	33	1	0	220.1	904	196	80	77	18	4	8	6	63	1	252	10	1	18	5	.783	1	0-0	0	3.04	3.15
2015	Was	NL	33	33	4	0	228.2	899	176	74	71	27	11	2	5	34	2	276	10	1	14	12	.538	3	0-0	0	2.11	2.79
2016	Was	NL	34	34	1	0	228.1	902	165	77	75	31	7	3	6	56	2	284	2	1	20	7	.741	0	0-0	0	2.35	2.96
	Postseason		12	10	0	0	62.2	258	46	27	26	5	1	0	4	25	1	80	3	0	4	3	.571	0	0-0	1	2.75	3.73
	9 ML YEARS		274	265	6	2	1696.1	6939	1463	689	639	191	46	42	55	479	11	1881	57	6	125	69	.644	4	0-0	0	3.09	3.39

Ryan Schimpf

Bats: L Throws: R Pos: 2B-68;3B-14;PH-9;LF-1
Ht: 5'9" Wt: 180 Born: 4/11/1988 Age: 29

Year	Team	Lg	G	AB	H	2B	3B	HR	(Hm	Rd)	TB	R	RBI	RC	TBB	IBB	SO	HBP	SH	SF	SB	CS	GDP	Avg	OBP	Slg	OPS
2012	Dnedin	A+	96	361	96	29	3	14	(-	-)	173	59	61	64	48	2	89	4	0	6	4	2	1	.266	.353	.479	.832
2012	Nham	AA	33	111	31	8	0	8	(-	-)	63	21	15	26	23	2	32	2	1	0	3	1	1	.279	.412	.568	.979
2013	Nham	AA	126	442	93	21	3	23	(-	-)	189	67	65	68	79	1	138	7	0	1	3	3	6	.210	.338	.428	.766
2014	Nham	AA	50	185	50	16	1	15	(-	-)	113	35	37	42	28	4	56	3	0	3	3	0	1	.270	.374	.611	.981
2014	Buffalo	AAA	67	212	40	7	1	9	(-	-)	76	29	21	23	24	1	59	7	1	2	0	1	2	.189	.290	.358	.648
2015	Nham	AA	76	258	70	20	0	20	(-	-)	150	43	56	57	42	1	54	4	0	3	2	1	2	.271	.378	.581	.959
2015	Buffalo	AAA	31	110	22	6	0	3	(-	-)	37	12	7	9	11	1	23	0	0	1	0	2	1	.200	.270	.336	.607
2016	ElPaso	AAA	51	166	59	17	0	15	(-	-)	121	36	48	47	20	1	33	3	0	1	0	1	1	.355	.432	.729	1.160
2016	SD	NL	89	276	60	17	5	20	(7	13)	147	48	51	61	42	3	105	9	0	3	1	1	3	.217	.336	.533	.869

Jonathan Schoop

SCOPE

Bats: R Throws: R Pos: 2B-162
Ht: 6'1" Wt: 225 Born: 10/16/1991 Age: 25

Year	Team	Lg	G	AB	H	2B	3B	HR	(Hm	Rd)	TB	R	RBI	RC	TBB	IBB	SO	HBP	SH	SF	SB	CS	GDP	Avg	OBP	Slg	OPS
2013	Bal	AL	5	14	4	0	0	1	(1	0)	7	5	1	1	1	0	2	0	0	0	0	0	2	.286	.333	.500	.833
2014	Bal	AL	137	455	95	18	0	16	(5	11)	161	48	45	32	13	0	122	8	5	0	2	0	12	.209	.244	.354	.598
2015	Bal	AL	86	305	85	17	0	15	(9	6)	147	34	39	40	9	0	79	4	1	2	2	0	9	.279	.306	.482	.788
2016	Bal	AL	162	615	164	38	1	25	(13	12)	279	82	82	72	21	0	137	8	0	3	1	2	16	.267	.298	.454	.752
	Postseason		7	21	4	1	0	0	(0	0)	5	3	2	2	3	0	4	0	0	0	2	0	0	.190	.292	.238	.530
	4 ML YEARS		390	1389	348	73	1	57	(28	29)	594	169	167	145	44	0	340	20	6	5	5	2	39	.251	.283	.428	.710

A.J. Schugel

SHOO-gul

Pitches: R Bats: R Pos: RP-36
Ht: 6'0" Wt: 205 Born: 6/27/1989 Age: 28

Year	Team	Lg	G	GS	CG	GF	IP	BFP	H	R	ER	HR	SH	SF	HB	TBB	IBB	SO	WP	Bk	W	L	Pct	Sh	Sv-Op	Hld	ERC	ERA
2012	Ark	AA	27	27	0	0	140.1	575	117	64	45	9	6	4	6	55	1	109	5	0	8	8	.429	0	0- -	-	3.14	2.89
2013	Salt Lk	AAA	19	19	0	0	89.1	415	121	74	70	12	0	4	4	33	0	76	7	0	4	6	.400	0	0- -	-	6.54	7.05
2014	Mobile	AA	26	26	0	0	147.2	613	142	60	57	3	4	6	6	50	2	117	5	0	6	4	.600	0	0- -	-	3.30	3.47
2015	Reno	AAA	9	9	1	0	38.0	193	65	45	43	4	1	4	2	17	0	27	6	0	2	7	.222	0	0- -	-	9.03	10.18
2015	Mobile	AA	12	12	0	0	77.1	308	74	21	19	5	2	0	2	15	0	52	7	0	7	2	.778	0	0- -	-	3.03	2.21
2016	Indy	AAA	13	0	0	4	18.0	68	13	8	8	0	0	1	1	3	0	18	1	0	1	2	.333	0	0- -	-	1.57	4.00
2015	Ari	NL	5	0	0	2	9.0	51	17	13	5	2	0	0	0	5	2	5	0	0	0	0	-	0	0-0	0	10.46	5.00
2016	Pit	NL	36	0	0	11	52.0	204	41	22	21	4	0	0	1	13	0	46	2	0	2	2	.500	0	1-2	3	2.40	3.63
	2 ML YEARS		41	0	0	13	61.0	255	58	35	26	6	0	0	1	18	2	51	2	0	2	2	.500	0	1-2	3	3.40	3.84

Bo Schultz

Pitches: R **Bats:** R **Pos:** RP-16   **Ht:** 6'3" **Wt:** 230 **Born:** 9/25/1985 **Age:** 31

			HOW MUCH HE PITCHED						WHAT HE GAVE UP									THE RESULTS						
Year	Team	Lg	G	GS	CG	GF	IP	BFP	H	R	ER	HR	SH	SF	HB	TBB	IBB	SO	WP	Bk	W	L	Pct	Sh	Sv-Op	Hld	ERC	ERA
2016	Buffalo*	AAA	26	0	0	9	33.2	130	30	15	14	2	1	0	1	7	0	21	1	0	3	2	.600	0	2--	-	2.79	3.74
2014	Ari	NL	4	0	0	3	8.0	36	13	7	7	1	0	1	0	1	1	5	0	0	0	1	.000	0	0-0	0	6.86	7.88
2015	Tor	AL	31	0	0	10	43.0	173	32	19	17	7	0	2	1	14	0	31	2	0	0	1	.000	0	1-3	4	2.92	3.56
2016	Tor	AL	16	0	0	8	16.1	68	17	10	10	3	0	1	0	3	0	10	0	0	0	1	.000	0	0-0	0	3.98	5.51
	3 ML YEARS		51	0	0	21	67.1	277	62	36	34	11	0	4	1	18	1	46	2	0	0	3	.000	0	1-3	4	3.59	4.54

Patrick Schuster

Pitches: L **Bats:** R **Pos:** RP-11   **Ht:** 6'2" **Wt:** 190 **Born:** 10/30/1990 **Age:** 26

			HOW MUCH HE PITCHED						WHAT HE GAVE UP									THE RESULTS						
Year	Team	Lg	G	GS	CG	GF	IP	BFP	H	R	ER	HR	SH	SF	HB	TBB	IBB	SO	WP	Bk	W	L	Pct	Sh	Sv-Op	Hld	ERC	ERA
2012	Visalia	A+	47	2	0	10	64.1	280	56	37	35	5	0	4	10	32	2	67	6	0	4	5	.444	0	1--	-	4.20	4.90
2013	Visalia	A+	55	0	0	10	44.1	175	30	14	9	3	0	0	0	18	1	45	2	0	0	1	.000	0	0--	-	2.24	1.83
2014	Mobile	AA	36	0	0	7	26.2	103	12	7	6	2	0	2	1	15	0	19	3	0	3	2	.600	0	0--	-	1.94	2.03
2014	Reno	AAA	21	0	0	4	18.0	82	21	10	9	2	0	1	1	10	1	20	3	0	0	0	-	0	0--	-	6.06	4.50
2015	Mobile	AA	22	0	0	5	25.0	107	23	11	9	2	0	2	2	12	0	20	4	0	0	1	.000	0	0--	-	3.61	3.24
2015	Pnscla	AA	30	0	0	6	29.0	125	27	11	11	1	2	1	2	14	1	25	1	0	2	1	.667	0	0--	-	3.82	3.41
2016	Nashv	AAA	32	0	0	16	38.2	156	27	5	5	0	1	2	2	12	0	39	4	1	1	0	1.000	0	7--	-	1.76	1.16
2016	LV	AAA	6	0	0	2	6.0	29	4	1	1	0	0	0	1	6	0	7	0	0	0	0	-	0	0--	-	4.21	1.50
2016	2 Tms		11	0	0	3	8.2	54	15	19	18	1	1	1	2	10	0	8	2	0	0	1	.000	0	0-0	0	12.90	18.69
16	Oak	AL	5	0	0	3	6.2	35	9	8	8	0	0	1	0	6	0	6	0	0	0	0	-	0	0-0	0	7.20	10.80
16	Phi	NL	6	0	0	0	2.0	19	6	11	10	1	1	0	2	4	0	2	2	0	0	1	.000	0	0-0	0	34.98	45.00

Kyle Schwarber

Bats: L **Throws:** R **Pos:** LF-2   SHWAR-burr   **Ht:** 6'0" **Wt:** 235 **Born:** 3/5/1993 **Age:** 24

			BATTING																		RUNNING			AVERAGES			
Year	Team	Lg	G	AB	H	2B	3B	HR	(Hm	Rd)	TB	R	RBI	RC	TBB	IBB	SO	HBP	SH	SF	SB	CS	GDP	Avg	OBP	Slg	OPS
2014	3 Tms	Low	72	262	90	18	2	18	(-	-)	166	55	53	67	39	2	57	4	0	6	5	2	6	.344	.428	.634	1.061
2015	Tenn	AA	58	197	63	10	1	13	(-	-)	114	39	39	50	42	1	49	1	1	2	1	0	5	.320	.438	.579	1.017
2015	Iowa	AAA	17	60	20	7	1	3	(-	-)	38	7	10	14	7	0	23	0	0	0	0	0	3	.333	.403	.633	1.036
2015	ChC	NL	69	232	57	6	1	16	(7	9)	113	52	43	39	36	1	77	4	0	1	3	3	4	.246	.355	.487	.842
2016	ChC	NL	2	4	0	0	0	0	(0	0)	0	0	0	0	1	0	2	0	0	0	0	0	0	.000	.200	.000	.200
	Postseason		9	27	9	0	0	5	(3	2)	24	6	8	7	4	0	8	0	0	0	0	0	0	.333	.419	.889	1.308
	2 ML YEARS		71	236	57	6	1	16	(7	9)	113	52	43	39	37	1	79	4	0	1	3	3	4	.242	.353	.479	.831

Robby Scott

Pitches: L **Bats:** B **Pos:** RP-7   **Ht:** 6'3" **Wt:** 220 **Born:** 8/29/1989 **Age:** 27

			HOW MUCH HE PITCHED						WHAT HE GAVE UP									THE RESULTS						
Year	Team	Lg	G	GS	CG	GF	IP	BFP	H	R	ER	HR	SH	SF	HB	TBB	IBB	SO	WP	Bk	W	L	Pct	Sh	Sv-Op	Hld	ERC	ERA
2012	RedSx	R	14	0	0	11	20.1	76	13	2	1	0	1	0	1	5	0	23	1	0	0	0	-	0	1--	-	1.48	0.44
2013	Salem	A+	31	0	0	15	67.2	278	51	27	21	6	3	5	2	30	2	44	5	0	4	4	.500	0	2--	-	2.95	2.79
2014	Portlnd	AA	35	1	0	16	59.2	242	55	17	13	3	3	3	0	15	0	51	5	1	8	2	.800	0	3--	-	2.81	1.96
2015	Portlnd	AA	25	2	0	10	43.2	179	32	14	10	3	0	3	1	13	0	41	3	1	1	1	.500	0	0--	-	2.14	2.06
2015	Pwtckt	AAA	13	1	0	1	31.2	150	47	31	27	5	1	2	0	9	0	27	0	0	1	1	.500	0	1--	-	6.84	7.67
2016	Pwtckt	AAA	32	6	0	7	78.0	300	57	22	22	9	0	0	4	14	0	73	3	0	4	3	.571	0	0--	-	2.20	2.54
2016	Bos	AL	7	0	0	1	6.0	25	6	0	0	1	0	0	0	2	0	5	1	0	1	0	1.000	0	0-0	1	3.19	0.00

Evan Scribner

Pitches: R **Bats:** R **Pos:** RP-12   SKRIBB-nurr   **Ht:** 6'3" **Wt:** 190 **Born:** 7/19/1985 **Age:** 31

			HOW MUCH HE PITCHED						WHAT HE GAVE UP									THE RESULTS						
Year	Team	Lg	G	GS	CG	GF	IP	BFP	H	R	ER	HR	SH	SF	HB	TBB	IBB	SO	WP	Bk	W	L	Pct	Sh	Sv-Op	Hld	ERC	ERA
2011	SD	NL	10	0	0	5	14.0	64	18	11	11	1	0	0	0	4	0	10	0	0	0	0	-	0	0-0	0	4.92	7.07
2012	Oak	AL	30	0	0	13	35.1	148	30	11	10	2	0	0	0	12	0	30	1	0	2	0	1.000	0	1-1	1	2.70	2.55
2013	Oak	AL	18	0	0	12	26.2	114	26	13	13	3	0	0	0	7	0	19	2	0	0	0	-	0	0-0	0	3.38	4.39
2014	Oak	AL	13	0	0	6	11.2	47	11	6	6	4	0	0	1	0	0	11	0	0	1	0	1.000	0	0-0	0	3.89	4.63
2015	Oak	AL	54	0	0	14	60.0	238	58	31	29	14	0	1	2	4	0	64	2	0	2	2	.500	0	0-4	8	3.57	4.35
2016	Sea	AL	12	0	0	0	14.0	49	5	0	0	1	0	1	1	2	1	15	0	0	0	0	-	0	0-0	3	0.53	0.00
	Postseason		1	0	0	1	2.0	6	0	0	0	0	0	0	0	0	0	3	0	0	0	0	-	0	0-0	0	0.00	0.00
	6 ML YEARS		137	0	0	50	161.2	660	148	72	69	24	1	1	4	29	1	149	5	0	5	2	.714	0	1-5	12	3.13	3.84

Xavier Scruggs

Bats: R **Throws:** R **Pos:** 1B-19;PH-3;LF-2   ex-ZAY-vee-er   **Ht:** 6'0" **Wt:** 215 **Born:** 9/23/1987 **Age:** 29

			BATTING																		RUNNING			AVERAGES			
Year	Team	Lg	G	AB	H	2B	3B	HR	(Hm	Rd)	TB	R	RBI	RC	TBB	IBB	SO	HBP	SH	SF	SB	CS	GDP	Avg	OBP	Slg	OPS
2016	NewOr*	AAA	93	317	92	24	0	21	(-	-)	179	69	50	73	58	4	90	6	0	1	4	2	10	.290	.408	.565	.973
2014	StL	NL	9	15	3	1	0	0	(0	0)	4	0	2	2	2	0	7	1	0	0	0	0	0	.200	.333	.267	.600
2015	StL	NL	17	42	11	2	0	0	(0	0)	13	5	7	5	0	0	10	1	0	0	1	0	2	.262	.279	.310	.589
2016	Mia	NL	24	62	13	3	0	1	(0	1)	19	1	5	6	5	0	20	2	0	1	0	0	1	.210	.290	.306	.596
	3 ML YEARS		50	119	27	6	0	1	(0	1)	36	6	14	13	7	0	37	4	0	1	1	0	3	.227	.292	.303	.595

Corey Seager

Bats: L Throws: R Pos: SS-155;PH-7   SEE-gurr   Ht: 6'4" Wt: 215 Born: 4/27/1994 Age: 23

Year	Team	Lg	G	AB	H	2B	3B	HR	(Hm	Rd)	TB	R	RBI	RC	TBB	IBB	SO	HBP	SH	SF	SB	CS	GDP	Avg	OBP	Slg	OPS
2012	Ogden	R+	46	175	54	9	2	8	(-	-)	91	34	33	36	21	1	33	2	1	3	8	2	4	.309	.383	.520	.903
2013	2 Tms	Low	101	372	100	20	4	16	(-	-)	176	55	72	64	46	4	89	3	1	4	10	4	10	.269	.351	.473	.824
2014	Rcuca	A+	80	327	115	34	2	18	(-	-)	207	61	70	81	30	2	76	5	0	3	5	1	6	.352	.411	.633	1.044
2014	Chatt	AA	38	148	51	16	3	2	(-	-)	79	28	27	29	10	0	39	0	1	2	1	1	6	.345	.381	.534	.915
2015	Tulsa	AA	20	80	30	7	1	5	(-	-)	54	17	15	20	5	1	11	0	0	1	1	1	2	.375	.407	.675	1.082
2015	OkCity	AAA	105	421	117	30	2	13	(-	-)	190	64	61	66	32	2	65	5	0	6	3	0	9	.278	.332	.451	.783
2015	LAD	NL	27	98	33	8	1	4	(3	1)	55	17	17	19	14	1	19	1	0	0	2	0	2	.337	.425	.561	.986
2016	LAD	NL	157	627	193	40	5	26	(18	8)	321	105	72	110	54	5	133	4	0	2	3	3	12	.308	.365	.512	.877
	Postseason		5	16	3	1	0	0	(0	0)	4	2	0	0	1	0	8	0	0	0	0	0	0	.188	.235	.250	.485
	2 ML YEARS		184	725	226	48	6	30	(21	9)	376	122	89	129	68	6	152	5	0	2	5	3	14	.312	.374	.519	.892

Kyle Seager

Bats: L Throws: R Pos: 3B-156;DH-2   SEE-gurr   Ht: 6'0" Wt: 210 Born: 11/3/1987 Age: 29

Year	Team	Lg	G	AB	H	2B	3B	HR	(Hm	Rd)	TB	R	RBI	RC	TBB	IBB	SO	HBP	SH	SF	SB	CS	GDP	Avg	OBP	Slg	OPS
2011	Sea	AL	53	182	47	13	0	3	(0	3)	69	22	13	16	13	0	36	2	2	2	3	1	4	.258	.312	.379	.691
2012	Sea	AL	155	594	154	35	1	20	(5	15)	251	62	86	88	46	1	110	5	2	4	13	5	9	.259	.316	.423	.738
2013	Sea	AL	160	615	160	32	2	22	(8	14)	262	79	69	90	68	1	122	7	0	5	9	3	8	.260	.338	.426	.764
2014	Sea	AL	159	590	158	27	4	25	(16	9)	268	71	96	96	52	3	118	8	1	3	7	5	12	.268	.334	.454	.788
2015	Sea	AL	161	623	166	37	0	26	(7	19)	281	85	74	75	54	6	98	5	0	4	6	6	17	.266	.328	.451	.779
2016	Sea	AL	158	597	166	36	3	30	(11	19)	298	89	99	110	69	10	108	8	0	2	3	1	18	.278	.359	.499	.859
	6 ML YEARS		846	3201	851	180	10	126	(47	79)	1429	408	437	475	302	21	592	35	5	20	41	21	68	.266	.334	.446	.780

Rob Segedin

Bats: R Throws: R Pos: PH-18;1B-9;LF-7;RF-7;3B-6   Ht: 6'2" Wt: 220 Born: 11/10/1988 Age: 28

Year	Team	Lg	G	AB	H	2B	3B	HR	(Hm	Rd)	TB	R	RBI	RC	TBB	IBB	SO	HBP	SH	SF	SB	CS	GDP	Avg	OBP	Slg	OPS
2012	Tampa	A+	73	290	86	21	1	7	(-	-)	130	44	41	49	29	2	53	3	0	4	9	4	2	.297	.362	.448	.810
2012	Trntn	AA	48	165	31	6	0	3	(-	-)	46	16	13	11	13	0	33	2	0	2	0	0	3	.188	.253	.279	.532
2013	Trntn	AA	18	71	24	10	0	3	(-	-)	43	16	17	16	6	0	18	2	0	3	0	1	1	.338	.390	.606	.996
2014	Trntn	AA	92	325	92	21	1	8	(-	-)	139	46	49	61	52	1	60	13	0	4	1	0	12	.283	.398	.428	.826
2014	S-WB	AAA	21	77	11	2	0	1	(-	-)	16	7	11	2	4	0	14	1	0	0	0	0	6	.143	.188	.208	.396
2015	S-WB	AAA	46	162	45	8	1	4	(-	-)	67	24	15	24	15	0	34	3	1	0	2	0	5	.278	.350	.414	.764
2015	Trntn	AA	25	89	27	4	0	3	(-	-)	40	8	19	15	11	0	17	1	0	2	1	1	1	.303	.379	.449	.828
2016	OkCity	AAA	103	373	119	23	9	21	(-	-)	223	71	69	84	40	0	81	7	0	4	3	4	13	.319	.392	.598	.989
2016	LAD	NL	40	73	17	2	1	2	(1	1)	27	9	12	8	6	0	22	2	0	2	0	0	1	.233	.301	.370	.671

Jean Segura

Bats: R Throws: R Pos: 2B-142;SS-23;PH-2   GENE seg-ER-uh   Ht: 5'10" Wt: 205 Born: 3/17/1990 Age: 27

Year	Team	Lg	G	AB	H	2B	3B	HR	(Hm	Rd)	TB	R	RBI	RC	TBB	IBB	SO	HBP	SH	SF	SB	CS	GDP	Avg	OBP	Slg	OPS
2012	2 Tms		45	151	39	4	3	0	(0	0)	49	19	14	16	13	3	23	0	1	1	7	1	1	.258	.315	.325	.640
2013	Mil	NL	146	588	173	20	10	12	(7	5)	249	74	49	72	25	1	84	6	2	2	44	13	17	.294	.329	.423	.752
2014	Mil	NL	146	513	126	14	5	6	(3	2)	167	61	31	45	28	5	70	4	10	2	20	9	13	.246	.289	.326	.614
2015	Mil	NL	142	560	144	16	5	6	(4	2)	188	57	50	57	13	2	93	6	3	2	25	6	14	.257	.281	.336	.616
2016	Ari	NL	153	637	203	41	7	20	(12	8)	318	102	64	107	39	1	101	12	4	2	33	10	6	.319	.368	.499	.867
12	LAA	AL	1	3	0	0	0	0	(0	0)	0	0	0	0	0	0	2	0	0	0	0	0	0	.000	.000	.000	.000
12	Mil	NL	44	148	39	4	3	0	(0	0)	49	19	14	16	13	3	21	0	1	1	7	1	1	.264	.321	.331	.652
	5 ML YEARS		632	2449	685	95	31	43	(26	17)	971	313	208	297	118	12	371	28	20	9	129	39	51	.280	.319	.396	.716

Steve Selsky

Bats: R Throws: R Pos: RF-11;PH-9;LF-3;CF-2;PR-1   Ht: 6'0" Wt: 205 Born: 7/20/1989 Age: 27

Year	Team	Lg	G	AB	H	2B	3B	HR	(Hm	Rd)	TB	R	RBI	RC	TBB	IBB	SO	HBP	SH	SF	SB	CS	GDP	Avg	OBP	Slg	OPS
2012	2 Tms	Low	128	495	157	32	6	18	(-	-)	255	79	74	98	38	2	111	13	1	6	18	3	5	.317	.377	.515	.892
2013	Pnscla	AA	32	83	15	2	0	0	(-	-)	17	7	12	5	10	1	20	2	3	1	0	0	4	.181	.287	.205	.486
2013	Bkrsfld	A+	91	340	101	19	5	13	(-	-)	169	54	68	67	37	0	79	15	0	2	9	4	7	.297	.388	.497	.885
2014	Pnscla	AA	64	166	50	8	0	1	(-	-)	61	23	21	28	29	2	42	5	0	5	2	4	6	.301	.410	.367	.777
2014	Lsvlle	AAA	55	121	29	7	1	1	(-	-)	41	15	11	16	21	0	47	2	0	1	0	0	1	.240	.359	.339	.697
2015	Lsvlle	AAA	51	180	57	10	2	2	(-	-)	77	23	29	31	19	1	44	2	0	1	3	1	5	.317	.386	.428	.814
2016	Lsvlle	AAA	85	296	83	24	1	9	(-	-)	136	40	37	51	29	0	74	11	0	3	2	1	9	.280	.363	.459	.822
2016	Cin	NL	24	51	16	2	0	2	(1	1)	24	9	7	8	2	0	22	0	1	0	1	0	1	.314	.340	.471	.810

Marcus Semien

Bats: R Throws: R Pos: SS-159   SIM-ee-inn   Ht: 6'0" Wt: 195 Born: 9/17/1990 Age: 26

Year	Team	Lg	G	AB	H	2B	3B	HR	(Hm	Rd)	TB	R	RBI	RC	TBB	IBB	SO	HBP	SH	SF	SB	CS	GDP	Avg	OBP	Slg	OPS
2013	CWS	AL	21	69	18	4	0	2	(2	0)	28	7	7	7	1	0	22	0	0	1	2	2	1	.261	.268	.406	.673
2014	CWS	AL	64	231	54	10	2	6	(4	2)	86	30	28	31	21	0	70	1	2	0	3	0	6	.234	.300	.372	.673
2015	Oak	AL	155	556	143	23	7	15	(5	10)	225	65	45	57	42	1	132	1	1	1	11	5	16	.257	.310	.405	.715
2016	Oak	AL	159	568	135	27	2	27	(10	17)	247	72	75	77	51	1	139	0	1	1	10	2	12	.238	.300	.435	.735
	4 ML YEARS		399	1424	350	64	11	50	(21	29)	586	174	155	172	115	2	363	2	4	3	26	9	35	.246	.302	.412	.714

Luis Severino

Pitches: R Bats: R Pos: SP-11; RP-11

Ht: 6'2" Wt: 215 Born: 2/20/1994 Age: 23

Year	Team	Lg	G	GS	CG	GF	IP	BFP	H	R	ER	HR	SH	SF	HB	TBB	IBB	SO	WP	Bk	W	L	Pct	Sh	Sv-Op	Hld	ERC	ERA
2013	2 Tms	Low	10	8	0	0	44.0	179	37	14	12	1	0	2	2	10	0	53	3	0	4	2	.667	0	0- -	-	2.27	2.45
2014	2 Tms	Low	18	18	0	0	88.0	357	73	28	24	2	4	0	3	21	1	98	4	0	4	3	.571	0	0- -	-	2.20	2.45
2014	Trntn	AA	6	6	0	0	25.0	100	20	8	7	1	0	0	0	6	0	29	0	1	2	2	.500	0	0- -	-	2.07	2.52
2015	Trntn	AA	8	8	0	0	38.0	157	32	17	14	2	2	1	2	10	0	48	1	1	2	2	.500	0	0- -	-	2.58	3.32
2015	S-WB	AAA	11	11	0	0	61.1	239	40	18	13	0	1	1	3	17	0	50	3	0	7	0	1.000	0	0- -	-	1.54	1.91
2016	S-WB	AAA	13	12	0	0	77.1	323	75	31	30	4	1	1	2	18	0	78	5	0	8	1	.889	0	0- -	-	3.03	3.49
2015	NYY	AL	11	11	0	0	62.1	255	53	21	20	9	0	0	2	22	0	56	2	1	5	3	.625	0	0-0	0	3.57	2.89
2016	NYY	AL	22	11	0	3	71.0	312	78	48	46	11	0	0	3	25	1	66	3	0	3	8	.273	0	0-0	1	5.00	5.83
	2 ML YEARS		33	22	0	3	133.1	567	131	69	66	20	0	0	5	47	1	122	5	1	8	11	.421	0	0-0	1	4.31	4.46

Pedro Severino

Bats: R Throws: R Pos: C-15;PR-3;PH-2

Ht: 6'0" Wt: 215 Born: 7/20/1993 Age: 23

Year	Team	Lg	G	AB	H	2B	3B	HR	(Hm	Rd)	TB	R	RBI	RC	TBB	IBB	SO	HBP	SH	SF	SB	CS	GDP	Avg	OBP	Slg	OPS
2012	Nats	R	38	109	24	3	1	0	(-	-)	29	9	8	9	9	0	9	4	2	1	0	0	3	.220	.301	.266	.567
2013	Hgrstn	A	84	282	68	19	2	1	(-	-)	94	28	45	26	13	0	54	1	3	3	1	0	7	.241	.274	.333	.608
2014	Ptomc	A+	94	291	72	15	1	9	(-	-)	116	41	36	37	21	0	57	5	6	3	2	0	5	.247	.306	.399	.705
2015	Hrsbrg	AA	91	329	81	13	0	5	(-	-)	109	33	34	32	19	1	51	1	6	2	1	2	12	.246	.288	.331	.619
2016	Syrcse	AAA	82	291	79	13	0	2	(-	-)	98	25	21	32	19	0	44	2	1	4	3	4	9	.271	.316	.337	.653
2015	Was	NL	2	4	1	1	0	0	(0	0)	2	1	0	0	0	0	1	0	0	0	0	0	0	.250	.250	.500	.750
2016	Was	NL	16	28	9	2	0	2	(1	1)	17	6	4	5	5	0	3	1	0	0	0	0	0	.321	.441	.607	1.048
	2 ML YEARS		18	32	10	3	0	2	(1	1)	19	7	4	5	5	0	4	1	0	0	0	0	0	.313	.421	.594	1.015

Richie Shaffer

Bats: R Throws: R Pos: 1B-11;DH-5;3B-4;RF-2;PH-1;PR-1   SHAY-fer

Ht: 6'3" Wt: 220 Born: 3/15/1991 Age: 26

Year	Team	Lg	G	AB	H	2B	3B	HR	(Hm	Rd)	TB	R	RBI	RC	TBB	IBB	SO	HBP	SH	SF	SB	CS	GDP	Avg	OBP	Slg	OPS
2012	HudVal	A-	33	117	36	5	2	4	(-	-)	57	25	26	23	16	1	31	4	0	1	0	0	1	.308	.406	.487	.893
2013	Charltt	A+	122	469	119	33	1	11	(-	-)	187	55	73	62	35	2	106	6	0	9	6	0	4	.254	.308	.399	.707
2014	Mont	AA	119	427	95	28	4	19	(-	-)	188	58	64	64	56	1	119	5	1	2	4	0	10	.222	.318	.440	.759
2015	Mont	AA	39	149	39	10	0	7	(-	-)	70	22	27	27	23	0	49	1	1	1	3	0	3	.262	.362	.470	.832
2015	Drham	AAA	69	244	66	17	1	19	(-	-)	142	42	45	50	31	3	74	3	0	4	1	1	3	.270	.355	.582	.937
2016	Drham	AAA	119	428	97	27	0	11	(-	-)	157	49	48	56	65	1	135	1	0	2	4	1	8	.227	.329	.367	.695
2015	TB	AL	31	74	14	3	0	4	(2	2)	29	11	6	4	10	0	32	3	0	1	0	1	2	.189	.307	.392	.699
2016	TB	AL	20	48	12	6	0	1	(0	1)	21	5	4	6	5	0	18	0	0	1	0	1	0	.250	.315	.438	.752
	2 ML YEARS		51	122	26	9	0	5	(2	3)	50	16	10	10	15	0	50	3	0	2	0	2	2	.213	.310	.410	.720

Bryan Shaw

Pitches: R Bats: B Pos: RP-75

Ht: 6'1" Wt: 220 Born: 11/8/1987 Age: 29

Year	Team	Lg	G	GS	CG	GF	IP	BFP	H	R	ER	HR	SH	SF	HB	TBB	IBB	SO	WP	Bk	W	L	Pct	Sh	Sv-Op	Hld	ERC	ERA
2011	Ari	NL	33	0	0	8	28.1	122	30	9	8	2	0	0	4	8	1	24	1	0	1	0	1.000	0	0-0	9	4.31	2.54
2012	Ari	NL	64	0	0	19	59.1	252	60	29	23	4	4	2	2	24	3	41	4	1	1	6	.143	0	2-4	10	4.08	3.49
2013	Cle	AL	70	0	0	11	75.0	316	60	31	27	4	4	2	4	28	2	73	5	0	7	3	.700	0	1-5	12	2.71	3.24
2014	Cle	AL	80	0	0	16	76.1	313	61	26	22	6	5	2	2	22	4	64	4	1	5	5	.500	0	2-9	24	2.45	2.59
2015	Cle	AL	74	0	0	19	64.0	265	59	24	21	8	1	0	1	19	1	54	3	0	3	3	.500	0	2-6	23	3.47	2.95
2016	Cle	AL	75	0	0	9	66.2	275	56	26	24	8	2	1	1	28	3	69	2	0	2	5	.286	0	1-4	25	3.47	3.24
	Postseason		5	0	0	1	5.2	18	1	0	0	0	0	1	0	1	0	5	0	0	0	0	-	0	0-0	1	0.22	0.00
	6 ML YEARS		396	0	0	82	369.2	1543	326	145	125	32	16	7	14	129	14	325	19	2	19	22	.463	0	8-28	103	3.25	3.04

Travis Shaw

Bats: L Throws: R Pos: 3B-105;1B-50;PH-8;DH-2;PR-2;LF-1

Ht: 6'4" Wt: 230 Born: 4/16/1990 Age: 27

Year	Team	Lg	G	AB	H	2B	3B	HR	(Hm	Rd)	TB	R	RBI	RC	TBB	IBB	SO	HBP	SH	SF	SB	CS	GDP	Avg	OBP	Slg	OPS
2012	Salem	A+	99	354	108	31	3	16	(-	-)	193	69	73	81	59	3	81	7	0	3	11	2	8	.305	.411	.545	.957
2012	Portlnd	AA	31	110	25	13	0	3	(-	-)	47	13	12	18	21	0	34	1	0	1	1	1	1	.227	.353	.427	.781
2013	Portlnd	AA	127	444	98	21	4	16	(-	-)	175	57	50	66	78	2	117	5	0	2	7	3	3	.221	.342	.394	.736
2014	Portlnd	AA	47	177	54	8	1	11	(-	-)	97	35	37	39	29	1	23	1	1	0	5	3	8	.305	.406	.548	.954
2014	Pwtckt	AAA	81	313	82	21	1	10	(-	-)	135	43	41	45	28	2	76	1	0	4	2	0	8	.262	.324	.431	.754
2015	Pwtckt	AAA	77	289	72	12	2	5	(-	-)	103	29	30	34	26	1	54	4	1	2	0	1	7	.249	.318	.356	.674
2015	Bos	AL	65	226	61	10	0	13	(8	5)	110	31	36	35	18	1	57	2	0	2	0	1	4	.270	.327	.487	.814
2016	Bos	AL	145	480	116	34	2	16	(7	9)	202	63	71	64	43	4	133	3	0	4	5	1	10	.242	.306	.421	.726
	2 ML YEARS		210	706	177	44	2	29	(15	14)	312	94	107	99	61	5	190	5	0	6	5	2	11	.251	.312	.442	.754

James Shields

Pitches: R Bats: R Pos: SP-33

Ht: 6'3" Wt: 215 Born: 12/20/1981 Age: 35

Year	Team	Lg	G	GS	CG	GF	IP	BFP	H	R	ER	HR	SH	SF	HB	TBB	IBB	SO	WP	Bk	W	L	Pct	Sh	Sv-Op	Hld	ERC	ERA
2006	TB	AL	21	21	1	0	124.2	540	141	69	67	18	4	3	5	38	5	104	9	0	6	8	.429	0	0-0	0	4.92	4.84
2007	TB	AL	31	31	1	0	215.0	874	202	98	92	28	4	5	10	36	0	184	9	0	12	8	.600	0	0-0	0	3.24	3.85
2008	TB	AL	33	33	3	0	215.0	877	208	94	85	24	6	0	12	40	0	160	6	0	14	8	.636	2	0-0	0	3.41	3.56
2009	TB	AL	33	33	0	0	219.2	930	239	113	101	29	6	3	1	52	1	167	3	1	11	12	.478	0	0-0	0	4.16	4.14

Year Team	Lg	G	GS	CG	GF	IP	BFP	H	R	ER	HR	SH	SF	HB	TBB	IBB	SO	WP	Bk	W	L	Pct	Sh	Sv-Op	Hld	ERC	ERA
2010 TB	AL	34	33	0	0	203.1	899	246	128	117	34	5	2	5	51	2	187	13	2	13	15	.464	1	0-0	0	5.21	5.18
2011 TB	AL	33	33	11	0	249.1	975	195	83	78	26	5	3	5	65	1	225	4	0	16	12	.571	4	0-0	0	2.58	2.82
2012 TB	AL	33	33	3	0	227.2	944	208	103	89	25	3	2	11	58	2	223	7	1	15	10	.600	2	0-0	0	3.28	3.52
2013 KC	AL	34	34	2	0	228.2	946	215	82	80	20	6	7	8	68	0	196	11	2	13	9	.591	0	0-0	0	3.45	3.15
2014 KC	AL	34	34	1	0	227.0	939	224	95	81	23	3	7	11	44	0	180	12	2	14	8	.636	1	0-0	0	3.41	3.21
2015 SD	NL	33	33	0	0	202.1	860	189	93	88	33	6	1	9	81	5	216	7	1	13	7	.650	0	0-0	0	4.34	3.91
2016 2 Tms		33	33	1	0	181.2	822	208	122	118	40	2	5	8	82	3	135	10	0	6	19	.240	0	0-0	0	6.24	5.85
16 SD	NL	11	11	0	0	67.1	284	69	33	32	9	1	1	1	27	2	57	3	0	2	7	.222	0	0-0	0	4.63	4.28
16 CWS	AL	22	22	1	0	114.1	538	139	89	86	31	1	4	7	55	1	78	7	0	4	12	.250	0	0-0	0	7.24	6.77
Postseason		11	11	0	0	59.1	269	76	37	36	8	1	1	6	15	0	45	6	0	3	6	.333	0	0-0	0	5.80	5.46
11 ML YEARS		352	351	23	0	2294.1	9606	2275	1080	996	300	50	38	85	615	19	1977	91	9	133	116	.534	9	0-0	0	3.88	3.91

Braden Shipley

Pitches: R **Bats:** R **Pos:** SP-11; RP-2   **Ht:** 6'1" **Wt:** 190 **Born:** 2/22/1992 **Age:** 25

Year Team	Lg	G	GS	CG	GF	IP	BFP	H	R	ER	HR	SH	SF	HB	TBB	IBB	SO	WP	Bk	W	L	Pct	Sh	Sv-Op	Hld	ERC	ERA
2013 2 Tms	Low	12	12	0	0	39.2	175	44	24	22	3	1	2	2	14	0	40	3	1	0	3	.000	0	0--	-	4.53	4.99
2014 2 Tms	Low	18	18	0	0	106.0	441	103	54	46	8	3	1	9	32	0	109	9	0	6	6	.500	0	0--	-	3.81	3.91
2015 Mobile	AA	28	27	1	0	156.2	663	146	68	61	7	6	5	5	56	0	118	5	0	9	11	.450	0	0--	-	3.28	3.50
2016 Reno	AAA	19	19	1	0	119.1	498	131	53	49	7	4	3	0	22	0	77	1	0	8	5	.615	0	0--	-	3.51	3.70
2016 Ari	NL	13	11	0	0	70.0	306	80	43	41	14	2	2	1	28	1	43	1	0	4	5	.444	0	0-0	0	5.82	5.27

Matt Shoemaker

Pitches: R **Bats:** R **Pos:** SP-27   SHOO-may-kerr   **Ht:** 6'2" **Wt:** 225 **Born:** 9/27/1986 **Age:** 30

Year Team	Lg	G	GS	CG	GF	IP	BFP	H	R	ER	HR	SH	SF	HB	TBB	IBB	SO	WP	Bk	W	L	Pct	Sh	Sv-Op	Hld	ERC	ERA
2013 LAA	AL	1	1	0	0	5.0	19	2	0	0	0	0	0	0	2	0	5	1	0	0	0	-	0	0-0	0	0.95	0.00
2014 LAA	AL	27	20	0	5	136.0	543	122	49	46	14	3	5	4	24	0	124	5	0	16	4	.800	0	0-0	0	2.84	3.04
2015 LAA	AL	25	24	0	1	135.1	569	135	74	67	24	4	4	4	35	2	116	3	0	7	10	.412	0	0-0	0	4.12	4.46
2016 LAA	AL	27	27	1	0	160.0	668	166	71	69	18	2	5	7	30	1	143	2	0	9	13	.409	1	0-0	0	3.71	3.88
Postseason		1	1	0	0	6.0	23	5	1	1	0	1	0	0	0	0	6	0	0	0	0	-	0	0-0	0	1.37	1.50
4 ML YEARS		80	72	1	6	436.1	1799	425	190	182	56	9	14	15	91	3	388	11	0	32	27	.542	1	0-0	0	3.51	3.75

Chasen Shreve

Pitches: L **Bats:** L **Pos:** RP-37   CHAY-sen shreev   **Ht:** 6'4" **Wt:** 195 **Born:** 7/12/1990 **Age:** 26

Year Team	Lg	G	GS	CG	GF	IP	BFP	H	R	ER	HR	SH	SF	HB	TBB	IBB	SO	WP	Bk	W	L	Pct	Sh	Sv-Op	Hld	ERC	ERA
2016 S-WB*	AAA	13	1	0	0	16.2	60	4	3	3	1	0	0	0	7	0	20	0	0	0	0	-	0	0--	-	0.80	1.62
2014 Atl	NL	15	0	0	4	12.1	50	10	1	1	0	1	0	0	3	0	15	1	0	0	0	-	0	0-0	2	1.88	0.73
2015 NYY	AL	59	0	0	13	58.1	251	49	21	20	10	2	0	1	33	2	64	4	0	6	2	.750	0	0-1	10	4.39	3.09
2016 NYY	AL	37	0	0	11	33.0	142	29	19	19	8	1	0	3	13	0	33	0	0	2	1	.667	0	1-1	1	4.70	5.18
3 ML YEARS		111	0	0	28	103.2	443	88	41	40	18	4	0	4	49	2	112	5	0	8	3	.727	0	1-2	13	4.16	3.47

J.B. Shuck

Bats: L **Throws:** L **Pos:** CF-60;DH-10;PR-9;PH-8;LF-3;RF-2   **Ht:** 5'11" **Wt:** 195 **Born:** 6/18/1987 **Age:** 30

Year Team	Lg	G	AB	H	2B	3B	HR	(Hm	Rd)	TB	R	RBI	RC	TBB	IBB	SO	HBP	SH	SF	SB	CS	GDP	Avg	OBP	Slg	OPS
2016 Charlt*	AAA	37	154	46	9	2	2	(-	-)	65	20	17	23	11	2	13	0	2	3	4	2		.299	.339	.422	.761
2011 Hou	NL	37	81	22	2	1	0	(0	0)	26	9	3	9	11	1	7	0	0	0	2	0	3	.272	.359	.321	.680
2013 LAA	AL	129	437	128	20	3	2	(1	1)	160	60	39	54	27	0	54	1	6	7	8	4	10	.293	.331	.366	.697
2014 2 Tms	AL	38	110	16	1	0	2	(1	1)	23	12	9	3	3	1	12	0	1	0	2	0	1	.145	.168	.209	.377
2015 CWS	AL	79	143	38	8	2	0	(0	0)	50	15	15	20	16	0	16	1	3	2	7	5	2	.266	.340	.350	.689
2016 CWS	AL	81	224	46	5	2	4	(2	2)	67	27	14	12	12	0	21	1	3	1	3	3	5	.205	.248	.299	.547
14 LAA	AL	22	84	14	1	0	2	(1	1)	21	10	9	3	3	1	11	0	1	0	2	0	0	.167	.195	.250	.445
14 Cle	AL	16	26	2	0	0	0	(0	0)	2	2	0	0	0	0	1	0	0	0	0	0	1	.077	.077	.077	.154
5 ML YEARS		364	995	250	36	8	8	(4	4)	326	123	80	98	69	2	110	3	13	10	22	12	21	.251	.299	.328	.627

Kevin Siegrist

Pitches: L **Bats:** L **Pos:** RP-67   SEE-grist   **Ht:** 6'5" **Wt:** 230 **Born:** 7/20/1989 **Age:** 27

Year Team	Lg	G	GS	CG	GF	IP	BFP	H	R	ER	HR	SH	SF	HB	TBB	IBB	SO	WP	Bk	W	L	Pct	Sh	Sv-Op	Hld	ERC	ERA
2013 StL	NL	45	0	0	15	39.2	152	17	2	2	1	0	0	1	18	1	50	0	0	3	1	.750	0	0-0	11	1.27	0.45
2014 StL	NL	37	0	0	5	30.1	140	32	23	23	5	1	1	2	16	0	37	1	0	1	4	.200	0	0-0	16	5.59	6.82
2015 StL	NL	81	0	0	13	74.2	312	53	20	18	4	3	4	3	34	2	90	0	0	7	1	.875	0	6-10	28	2.52	2.17
2016 StL	NL	67	0	0	11	61.2	248	42	20	19	10	0	3	1	26	2	66	5	0	6	3	.667	0	3-8	17	2.91	2.77
Postseason		12	0	0	0	9.0	39	10	6	5	4	0	1	0	1	0	8	2	0	0	1	.000	0	0-0	2	5.50	5.00
4 ML YEARS		230	0	0	44	206.1	852	144	65	62	20	4	8	7	94	5	243	6	0	17	9	.654	0	9-20	72	2.74	2.70

Andrelton Simmons

Bats: R **Throws:** R **Pos:** SS-124 ANN-drel-ton **Ht:** 6'2" **Wt:** 200 **Born:** 9/4/1989 **Age:** 27

Year Team	Lg	G	AB	H	2B	3B	HR	(Hm	Rd)	TB	R	RBI	RC	TBB	IBB	SO	HBP	SH	SF	SB	CS	GDP	Avg	OBP	Slg	OPS
2012 Atl	NL	49	166	48	8	2	3	(3	0)	69	17	19	23	12	1	21	1	0	3	1	0	5	.289	.335	.416	.751
2013 Atl	NL	157	606	150	27	6	17	(5	12)	240	76	59	60	40	1	55	3	5	4	6	5	16	.248	.296	.396	.692
2014 Atl	NL	146	540	132	18	4	7	(3	4)	179	44	46	41	32	4	60	0	2	2	4	5	25	.244	.286	.331	.617
2015 Atl	NL	147	535	142	23	2	4	(2	2)	181	60	44	48	36	6	48	6	1	2	5	3	19	.265	.321	.338	.660
2016 LAA	AL	124	448	126	22	2	4	(4	0)	164	48	44	52	28	0	38	2	1	4	10	1	16	.281	.324	.366	.690
Postseason		5	16	4	1	0	0	(0	0)	5	0	2	1	2	0	3	0	1	0	0	0	1	.250	.333	.313	.646
5 ML YEARS		623	2295	598	98	16	35	(17	18)	833	245	212	224	151	12	222	12	9	15	26	14	81	.261	.308	.363	.671

Shae Simmons

Pitches: R **Bats:** R **Pos:** RP-7 SHAY **Ht:** 5'11" **Wt:** 190 **Born:** 9/3/1990 **Age:** 26

Year Team	Lg	G	GS	CG	GF	IP	BFP	H	R	ER	HR	SH	SF	HB	TBB	IBB	SO	WP	Bk	W	L	Pct	Sh	Sv-Op	Hld	ERC	ERA
2012 2 Tms	Low	16	1	0	7	24.2	105	16	8	4	0	0	0	0	16	1	36	5	0	2	2	.500	0	2--	-	2.36	1.46
2013 Missi	AA	11	0	0	2	11.0	44	5	3	3	0	1	0	0	7	0	16	1	0	0	0	-	0	0--	-	1.59	2.45
2013 Rome	A	39	0	0	34	42.1	176	26	12	7	0	1	1	4	15	0	66	5	0	1	1	.500	0	24--	-	1.62	1.49
2014 Missi	AA	20	0	0	19	23.0	89	15	2	2	0	0	0	1	6	0	30	0	0	0	0	-	0	14--	-	1.50	0.78
2016 Gwnntt	AAA	12	4	0	8	12.0	53	7	2	2	0	0	0	2	9	0	14	1	1	0	0	-	0	1--	-	3.00	1.50
2016 2 Tms	Low	7	6	0	0	6.1	29	4	5	2	0	0	1	1	3	0	9	3	0	0	0	-	0	0--	-	2.07	2.84
2014 Atl	NL	26	0	0	6	21.2	89	15	8	7	1	1	1	0	11	1	23	1	0	1	2	.333	0	1-1	9	2.45	2.91
2016 Atl	NL	7	0	0	2	6.2	25	6	1	1	0	0	0	0	3	0	3	0	0	0	0	-	0	0-0	0	1.63	1.35
2 ML YEARS		33	0	0	8	28.1	114	21	9	8	1	1	1	0	11	1	26	1	0	1	2	.333	0	1-1	9	2.25	2.54

Alfredo Simon

Pitches: R **Bats:** R **Pos:** SP-11; RP-4 si-MOHN **Ht:** 6'6" **Wt:** 265 **Born:** 5/8/1981 **Age:** 36

Year Team	Lg	G	GS	CG	GF	IP	BFP	H	R	ER	HR	SH	SF	HB	TBB	IBB	SO	WP	Bk	W	L	Pct	Sh	Sv-Op	Hld	ERC	ERA
2016 Lsvlle*	AAA	5	5	0	0	15.0	68	17	8	8	1	1	2	0	6	0	7	0	0	0	2	.000	0	0--	-	4.47	4.80
2008 Bal	AL	4	1	0	0	13.0	59	16	10	9	4	0	1	2	2	0	8	2	0	0	0	-	0	0-0	0	6.45	6.23
2009 Bal	AL	2	2	0	0	6.1	28	8	7	7	5	0	0	0	2	0	3	0	0	0	1	.000	0	0-0	0	10.74	9.95
2010 Bal	AL	49	0	0	35	49.1	222	54	30	27	10	1	2	2	22	2	37	1	0	4	2	.667	0	17-21	1	5.66	4.93
2011 Bal	AL	23	16	0	1	115.2	499	128	69	63	15	1	4	4	40	6	83	2	2	4	9	.308	0	0-0	0	4.83	4.90
2012 Cin	NL	36	0	0	13	61.0	269	65	22	18	2	2	3	6	22	1	52	9	0	3	2	.600	0	1-1	1	4.16	2.66
2013 Cin	NL	63	0	0	20	87.2	359	68	31	28	8	5	2	8	26	2	63	4	0	6	4	.600	0	1-3	6	2.75	2.87
2014 Cin	NL	32	32	0	0	196.1	818	181	80	75	22	7	4	12	56	7	127	3	0	15	10	.600	0	0-0	0	3.49	3.44
2015 Det	AL	31	31	2	0	187.0	820	201	112	105	24	9	6	8	68	1	117	14	0	13	12	.520	1	0-0	0	4.73	5.05
2016 Cin	NL	15	11	0	1	58.2	298	89	64	61	15	1	3	8	31	2	39	0	0	2	7	.222	0	0-0	0	9.77	9.36
Postseason		2	0	0	1	2.1	11	3	0	0	0	1	0	0	1	0	1	0	0	0	0	-	0	0-0	0	4.93	0.00
9 ML YEARS		255	93	2	70	775.0	3372	810	425	393	105	26	25	50	269	21	529	38	2	47	47	.500	1	19-25	8	4.60	4.56

Tony Sipp

Pitches: L **Bats:** L **Pos:** RP-60 **Ht:** 6'0" **Wt:** 190 **Born:** 7/12/1983 **Age:** 33

Year Team	Lg	G	GS	CG	GF	IP	BFP	H	R	ER	HR	SH	SF	HB	TBB	IBB	SO	WP	Bk	W	L	Pct	Sh	Sv-Op	Hld	ERC	ERA
2009 Cle	AL	46	0	0	8	40.0	168	27	16	13	5	3	1	0	25	2	48	3	0	2	0	1.000	0	0-0	9	3.29	2.93
2010 Cle	AL	70	0	0	16	63.0	266	48	30	29	12	3	2	2	39	3	69	4	0	2	2	.500	0	1-3	15	4.42	4.14
2011 Cle	AL	69	0	0	17	62.1	251	45	22	21	10	1	2	0	24	3	57	2	1	6	3	.667	0	0-1	24	2.87	3.03
2012 Cle	AL	63	0	0	7	55.0	233	47	29	27	9	2	1	1	23	1	51	3	0	1	2	.333	0	1-2	12	3.80	4.42
2013 Ari	NL	56	0	0	11	37.2	175	35	22	20	6	3	1	3	22	2	42	3	1	3	2	.600	0	0-2	3	4.90	4.78
2014 Hou	AL	56	0	0	13	50.2	198	28	19	19	5	2	0	0	17	2	63	3	0	4	3	.571	0	4-6	11	1.57	3.38
2015 Hou	AL	60	0	0	12	54.1	216	41	13	12	5	2	1	1	15	1	62	4	0	3	4	.429	0	0-3	13	2.34	1.99
2016 Hou	AL	60	0	0	13	43.2	195	52	26	24	12	0	1	1	18	0	40	0	0	1	2	.333	0	1-2	12	6.80	4.95
Postseason		6	0	0	0	5.1	20	1	1	0	0	0	0	0	2	0	5	0	0	0	1	.000	0	0-1	3	0.42	0.00
8 ML YEARS		480	0	0	97	406.2	1702	323	177	165	64	16	9	8	183	14	432	22	2	22	18	.550	0	7-19	99	3.56	3.65

Tyler Skaggs

Pitches: L **Bats:** L **Pos:** SP-10 **Ht:** 6'4" **Wt:** 215 **Born:** 7/13/1991 **Age:** 25

Year Team	Lg	G	GS	CG	GF	IP	BFP	H	R	ER	HR	SH	SF	HB	TBB	IBB	SO	WP	Bk	W	L	Pct	Sh	Sv-Op	Hld	ERC	ERA
2016 Salt Lk*	AAA	7	7	0	0	32.1	124	19	9	6	2	3	2	0	8	0	45	1	0	3	2	.600	0	0--	-	1.39	1.67
2012 Ari	NL	6	6	0	0	29.1	133	30	20	19	6	1	0	2	13	0	21	1	0	1	3	.250	0	0-0	0	5.31	5.83
2013 Ari	NL	7	7	0	0	38.2	170	38	23	22	7	0	2	2	15	2	36	2	0	2	3	.400	0	0-0	0	4.56	5.12
2014 LAA	AL	18	18	0	0	113.0	464	107	59	54	9	2	4	4	30	1	86	7	0	5	5	.500	0	0-0	0	3.31	4.30
2016 LAA	AL	10	10	0	0	49.2	219	51	23	23	5	0	3	2	23	0	50	0	0	3	4	.429	0	0-0	0	4.67	4.17
4 ML YEARS		41	41	0	0	230.2	986	226	125	118	27	3	10	10	81	3	193	10	0	11	15	.423	0	0-0	0	4.05	4.60

Blake Smith

Pitches: R Bats: L Pos: RP-5   Ht: 6'2" Wt: 220 Born: 12/9/1987 Age: 29

| | | HOW MUCH HE PITCHED | | | | | WHAT HE GAVE UP | | | | | | | | | | THE RESULTS | | | | | |
Year Team	Lg	G	GS	CG	GF	IP	BFP	H	R	ER	HR	SH	SF	HB	TBB	IBB	SO	WP	Bk	W	L	Pct	Sh	Sv-Op	Hld	ERC	ERA
2013 Rcuca	A+	21	0	0	11	19.2	103	20	20	17	2	1	0	4	19	0	12	4	1	1	1	.500	0	0--	-	7.10	7.78
2014 Rcuca	A+	22	0	0	16	28.0	120	23	13	11	2	1	0	2	13	0	28	3	0	1	3	.250	0	9--	-	3.41	3.54
2014 Chatt	AA	26	0	0	7	33.1	153	35	19	15	2	0	1	3	16	1	33	5	0	1	4	.200	0	2--	-	4.59	4.05
2015 Tulsa	AA	16	0	0	8	16.2	71	8	4	3	1	5	2	2	9	2	16	3	0	0	3	.000	0	3--	-	1.81	1.62
2015 Charllt	AAA	24	0	0	12	30.0	134	29	11	11	1	0	0	0	15	2	42	5	0	1	2	.333	0	0--	-	3.59	3.30
2016 Charllt	AAA	39	0	0	8	71.1	294	64	28	28	6	1	3	0	24	0	75	8	0	3	1	.750	0	1--	-	3.20	3.53
2016 CWS	AL	5	0	0	1	4.1	21	7	3	3	1	0	0	1	0	0	1	0	0	0	0	-	0	0-0	0	8.00	6.23

Carson Smith

Pitches: R Bats: R Pos: RP-3   Ht: 6'6" Wt: 215 Born: 10/19/1989 Age: 27

| | | HOW MUCH HE PITCHED | | | | | WHAT HE GAVE UP | | | | | | | | | | THE RESULTS | | | | | |
Year Team	Lg	G	GS	CG	GF	IP	BFP	H	R	ER	HR	SH	SF	HB	TBB	IBB	SO	WP	Bk	W	L	Pct	Sh	Sv-Op	Hld	ERC	ERA
2014 Sea	AL	9	0	0	1	8.1	29	2	0	0	0	0	0	0	3	0	10	0	0	1	0	1.000	0	0-0	3	0.55	0.00
2015 Sea	AL	70	0	0	24	70.0	284	49	19	18	2	3	0	7	22	4	92	6	0	2	5	.286	0	13-18	22	2.04	2.31
2016 Bos	AL	3	0	0	0	2.2	11	2	1	0	0	0	0	0	1	0	2	0	0	0	0	-	0	0-0	0	2.01	0.00
3 ML YEARS		82	0	0	25	81.0	324	53	20	18	2	3	0	7	26	4	104	6	0	3	5	.375	0	13-18	25	1.81	2.00

Chris Smith

Pitches: R Bats: R Pos: RP-13   Ht: 6'0" Wt: 190 Born: 4/9/1981 Age: 36

| | | HOW MUCH HE PITCHED | | | | | WHAT HE GAVE UP | | | | | | | | | | THE RESULTS | | | | | |
Year Team	Lg	G	GS	CG	GF	IP	BFP	H	R	ER	HR	SH	SF	HB	TBB	IBB	SO	WP	Bk	W	L	Pct	Sh	Sv-Op	Hld	ERC	ERA
2016 Nashv*	AAA	22	22	0	0	130.2	552	120	64	57	11	1	2	2	45	2	121	9	0	6	8	.429	0	0--	-	3.32	3.93
2008 Bos	AL	12	0	0	3	18.1	78	18	16	16	6	1	1	0	7	0	13	0	0	1	0	1.000	0	0-0	0	5.53	7.85
2009 Mil	NL	35	0	0	12	46.0	200	41	21	21	11	1	0	3	19	0	35	1	0	0	0	-	0	0-1	0	4.68	4.11
2010 Mil	NL	3	0	0	1	3.1	14	4	2	2	0	0	0	0	1	0	4	0	0	0	0	-	0	0-0	0	4.29	5.40
2016 Oak	AL	13	0	0	8	24.2	100	14	9	8	2	0	2	0	13	0	29	0	0	0	0	-	0	0-0	0	2.18	2.92
4 ML YEARS		63	0	0	24	92.1	392	77	48	47	19	2	3	3	40	0	81	1	0	1	0	1.000	0	0-1	0	4.11	4.58

Jake Smith

Pitches: R Bats: R Pos: RP-4   Ht: 6'4" Wt: 190 Born: 6/2/1990 Age: 27

| | | HOW MUCH HE PITCHED | | | | | WHAT HE GAVE UP | | | | | | | | | | THE RESULTS | | | | | |
Year Team	Lg	G	GS	CG	GF	IP	BFP	H	R	ER	HR	SH	SF	HB	TBB	IBB	SO	WP	Bk	W	L	Pct	Sh	Sv-Op	Hld	ERC	ERA
2012 Giants	R	6	0	0	2	8.2	35	5	2	0	0	0	1	0	2	0	13	0	0	0	0	-	0	0--	-	1.04	0.00
2013 SlkzR	A-	19	4	0	1	42.1	186	37	19	17	2	0	0	4	21	0	54	11	0	2	2	.500	0	0--	-	3.71	3.61
2014 2 Tms	Low	51	1	0	24	64.2	284	55	32	26	3	5	4	1	34	3	85	9	1	3	6	.333	0	0--	-	3.26	3.62
2015 SnJos	A+	56	0	0	30	84.1	323	50	28	22	7	4	5	2	21	0	118	5	1	4	4	.500	0	16--	-	1.55	2.35
2016 Rchmd	AA	22	0	0	8	20.1	104	17	19	16	1	1	1	3	23	1	26	3	0	2	1	.667	0	1--	-	5.92	7.08
2016 SnAnt	AA	6	0	0	4	5.2	22	3	1	1	0	0	0	0	2	0	4	1	0	0	0	-	0	1--	-	1.21	1.59
2016 SD	NL	4	0	0	1	4.0	17	5	2	2	1	0	0	1	1	0	3	0	0	1	0	1.000	0	0-0	0	7.92	4.50

Joe Smith

Pitches: R Bats: R Pos: RP-54   Ht: 6'2" Wt: 205 Born: 3/22/1984 Age: 33

| | | HOW MUCH HE PITCHED | | | | | WHAT HE GAVE UP | | | | | | | | | | THE RESULTS | | | | | |
Year Team	Lg	G	GS	CG	GF	IP	BFP	H	R	ER	HR	SH	SF	HB	TBB	IBB	SO	WP	Bk	W	L	Pct	Sh	Sv-Op	Hld	ERC	ERA
2007 NYM	NL	54	0	0	14	44.1	205	48	18	17	3	2	0	7	21	4	45	2	0	3	2	.600	0	0-0	10	5.04	3.45
2008 NYM	NL	82	0	0	12	63.1	271	51	28	25	4	4	0	4	31	4	52	1	0	6	3	.667	0	0-3	18	3.23	3.55
2009 Cle	AL	37	0	0	5	34.0	142	30	16	13	4	1	1	0	13	0	30	2	0	0	0	-	0	0-1	10	3.49	3.44
2010 Cle	AL	53	0	0	7	40.0	170	30	18	17	4	1	0	1	24	2	32	0	1	2	2	.500	0	0-1	17	3.53	3.83
2011 Cle	AL	71	0	0	13	67.0	267	52	16	15	1	2	2	2	21	1	45	2	0	3	3	.500	0	0-3	16	2.19	2.01
2012 Cle	AL	72	0	0	12	67.0	278	53	27	22	4	1	1	2	25	4	53	1	1	7	4	.636	0	0-3	21	2.60	2.96
2013 Cle	AL	70	0	0	20	63.0	259	54	17	16	5	3	0	3	23	2	54	3	0	6	2	.750	0	3-8	25	3.23	2.29
2014 LAA	AL	76	0	0	26	74.2	285	45	16	15	4	3	0	6	15	3	68	4	0	7	2	.778	0	15-19	18	1.47	1.81
2015 LAA	AL	70	0	0	13	65.1	271	64	26	26	4	2	1	2	19	4	57	1	0	5	5	.500	0	5-9	32	3.36	3.58
2016 2 Tms		54	0	0	19	52.0	217	47	20	20	8	1	1	6	18	3	40	0	1	2	5	.286	0	6-9	17	4.19	3.46
16 LAA	AL	38	0	0	16	37.2	160	36	16	16	4	1	1	5	13	3	25	0	1	1	4	.200	0	6-9	6	4.15	3.82
16 ChC		16	0	0	3	14.1	57	11	4	4	4	0	0	1	5	0	15	0	0	1	1	.500	0	0-0	1	4.20	2.51
Postseason		3	0	0	1	2.2	10	1	0	0	0	0	0	0	0	0	3	0	0	0	0	-	0	0-0	0	0.28	0.00
10 ML YEARS		639	0	0	141	570.2	2365	474	202	186	41	20	6	33	210	27	476	16	3	41	28	.594	0	29-56	174	3.03	2.93

Josh Smith

Pitches: R Bats: R Pos: RP-30; SP-2   Ht: 6'2" Wt: 220 Born: 8/7/1987 Age: 29

| | | HOW MUCH HE PITCHED | | | | | WHAT HE GAVE UP | | | | | | | | | | THE RESULTS | | | | | |
Year Team	Lg	G	GS	CG	GF	IP	BFP	H	R	ER	HR	SH	SF	HB	TBB	IBB	SO	WP	Bk	W	L	Pct	Sh	Sv-Op	Hld	ERC	ERA
2012 Bkrsfld	A+	27	27	1	0	147.0	626	143	71	62	15	2	5	9	46	0	140	8	0	9	8	.529	0	0--	-	3.84	3.80
2013 Pnscla	AA	28	28	0	0	160.0	674	148	65	58	16	9	5	7	50	2	139	5	0	11	9	.550	0	0--	-	3.46	3.26
2014 Lsvlle	AAA	28	24	1	1	159.0	719	174	90	83	8	5	8	7	66	1	123	2	1	10	7	.588	0	0--	-	4.38	4.70
2015 Lsvlle	AAA	15	12	0	1	86.1	365	84	37	36	2	1	4	6	24	1	69	1	0	3	5	.375	0	0--	-	3.18	3.75
2015 Pnscla	AA	9	9	1	0	56.0	226	51	23	19	5	1	4	2	9	0	53	0	0	5	4	.556	0	0--	-	2.76	3.05
2016 Lsvlle	AAA	9	8	0	0	45.0	184	44	20	19	5	0	2	1	13	0	38	2	0	4	4	.500	0	0--	-	3.80	3.80
2015 Cin	NL	9	7	0	0	32.2	161	42	27	25	5	0	2	5	21	3	30	0	0	0	4	.000	0	0-0	0	7.82	6.89
2016 Cin	NL	32	2	0	8	59.2	260	57	32	31	11	1	1	1	26	1	48	1	0	3	3	.500	0	0-0	1	4.56	4.68
2 ML YEARS		41	9	0	8	92.1	421	99	59	56	16	1	3	6	47	4	78	1	0	3	7	.300	0	0-0	1	5.67	5.46

Kevan Smith

Bats: R **Throws:** R **Pos:** C-6;DH-1   **Ht:** 6'4" **Wt:** 230 **Born:** 6/28/1988 **Age:** 29

Year	Team	Lg	G	AB	H	2B	3B	HR	(Hm	Rd)	TB	R	RBI	RC	TBB	IBB	SO	HBP	SH	SF	SB	CS	GDP	Avg	OBP	Slg	OPS
2012	2 Tms	Low	108	417	117	30	2	10	(-	-)	181	56	83	63	30	1	79	10	1	7	0	1	13	.281	.338	.434	.772
2013	WinSa	A+	101	384	110	26	3	12	(-	-)	178	66	73	69	38	0	66	15	2	3	4	1	13	.286	.370	.464	.834
2014	Brham	AA	106	389	113	21	3	10	(-	-)	170	45	49	67	46	5	68	9	2	3	1	1	13	.290	.376	.437	.813
2015	Charllt	AAA	97	319	83	13	2	6	(-	-)	118	41	36	41	29	0	66	5	5	2	0	1	13	.260	.330	.370	.699
2016	Charllt	AAA	49	183	40	9	0	8	(-	-)	73	18	24	22	16	0	36	3	2	1	0	0	12	.219	.291	.399	.690
2016	CWS	AL	7	16	2	0	0	0	(0	0)	2	2	0	0	0	0	6	0	0	0	0	0	1	.125	.125	.125	.250

Mallex Smith

Bats: L **Throws:** R **Pos:** CF-35;LF-22;PH-16;PR-3;RF-1   **Ht:** 5'9" **Wt:** 180 **Born:** 5/6/1993 **Age:** 24

Year	Team	Lg	G	AB	H	2B	3B	HR	(Hm	Rd)	TB	R	RBI	RC	TBB	IBB	SO	HBP	SH	SF	SB	CS	GDP	Avg	OBP	Slg	OPS
2012	2 Tms	Low	35	128	39	2	1	2	(-	-)	49	29	15	20	11	0	27	2	4	1	17	4	2	.305	.366	.383	.749
2013	FtWyn	A	110	424	111	17	2	4	(-	-)	144	81	29	65	59	0	84	12	11	1	64	16	4	.262	.367	.340	.707
2014	2 Tms	Low	120	477	148	29	7	5	(-	-)	206	99	31	94	69	0	103	6	10	2	88	26	2	.310	.403	.432	.834
2015	Missi	AA	57	206	70	5	2	2	(-	-)	85	35	22	40	27	2	41	2	3	2	23	6	2	.340	.418	.413	.830
2015	Gwnntt	AAA	69	278	78	12	6	0	(-	-)	102	49	13	40	24	0	44	1	3	1	34	7	1	.281	.339	.367	.706
2016	Atl	NL	72	189	45	7	4	3	(0	3)	69	28	22	26	20	0	48	2	3	1	16	8	3	.238	.316	.365	.681

Seth Smith

Bats: L **Throws:** L **Pos:** RF-74;LF-35;PH-33;DH-12   **Ht:** 6'3" **Wt:** 210 **Born:** 9/30/1982 **Age:** 34

Year	Team	Lg	G	AB	H	2B	3B	HR	(Hm	Rd)	TB	R	RBI	RC	TBB	IBB	SO	HBP	SH	SF	SB	CS	GDP	Avg	OBP	Slg	OPS
2007	Col	NL	7	8	5	0	1	0	(0	0)	7	4	0	3	0	0	1	0	0	0	0	0	0	.625	.625	.875	1.500
2008	Col	NL	67	108	28	7	0	4	(2	2)	47	13	15	18	15	0	23	0	0	0	1	0	0	.259	.350	.435	.785
2009	Col	NL	133	335	98	20	4	15	(8	7)	171	61	55	63	46	3	67	2	1	3	4	1	5	.293	.378	.510	.889
2010	Col	NL	133	358	88	19	5	17	(12	5)	168	55	52	51	35	1	67	2	0	3	2	1	5	.246	.314	.469	.783
2011	Col	NL	147	476	135	32	9	15	(9	6)	230	67	59	73	46	7	93	4	0	7	10	2	9	.284	.347	.483	.830
2012	Oak	AL	125	383	92	23	2	14	(6	8)	161	55	52	52	50	7	98	5	0	3	2	2	4	.240	.333	.420	.754
2013	Oak	AL	117	368	93	27	0	8	(3	5)	144	49	40	46	39	4	94	3	0	0	0	0	10	.253	.329	.391	.721
2014	SD	NL	136	443	118	31	5	12	(8	4)	195	55	48	68	69	3	87	4	0	4	1	1	9	.266	.367	.440	.807
2015	Sea	AL	136	395	98	31	5	12	(7	5)	175	54	42	54	47	4	99	4	1	5	0	0	15	.248	.330	.443	.773
2016	Sea	AL	137	378	94	15	0	16	(12	4)	157	62	63	62	48	1	89	8	0	4	0	0	11	.249	.342	.415	.758
	Postseason		18	42	11	2	0	2	(1	1)	19	6	7	7	5	2	13	1	0	0	0	0	0	.262	.354	.452	.807
	10 ML YEARS		1138	3252	849	205	31	113	(67	46)	1455	475	426	490	395	30	718	32	2	29	20	7	68	.261	.344	.447	.792

Will Smith

Pitches: L **Bats:** R **Pos:** RP-53   **Ht:** 6'5" **Wt:** 265 **Born:** 7/10/1989 **Age:** 27

			HOW MUCH HE PITCHED						WHAT HE GAVE UP										THE RESULTS						
Year	Team	Lg	G	GS	CG	GF	IP	BFP	H	R	ER	HR	SH	SF	HB	TBB	IBB	SO	WP	Bk	W	L	Pct	Sh	Sv-Op	Hld	ERC	ERA
2012	KC	AL	16	16	0	0	89.2	396	111	54	53	12	2	5	1	33	1	59	4	0	6	9	.400	0	0-0	0	5.75	5.32
2013	KC	AL	19	1	0	4	33.1	131	24	16	12	6	0	4	1	7	0	43	0	0	2	1	.667	0	0-3	6	2.47	3.24
2014	Mil	NL	78	0	0	6	65.2	286	62	31	27	6	1	1	3	31	6	86	7	0	1	3	.250	0	1-6	30	4.02	3.70
2015	Mil	NL	76	0	0	11	63.1	264	52	23	19	5	1	2	1	24	1	91	5	0	7	2	.778	0	0-4	20	2.91	2.70
2016	2 Tms	NL	53	0	0	4	40.1	167	31	19	15	3	1	1	1	18	1	48	3	0	2	4	.333	0	0-5	23	2.92	3.35
16	Mil	NL	27	0	0	3	22.0	92	18	13	9	3	1	1	1	9	1	22	3	0	1	3	.250	0	0-4	12	3.48	3.68
16	SF	NL	26	0	0	1	18.1	75	13	6	6	0	0	0	0	9	0	26	0	0	1	1	.500	0	0-1	11	2.26	2.95
	5 ML YEARS		242	17	0	25	292.1	1244	280	143	126	32	5	13	7	113	9	327	19	0	18	19	.486	0	1-18	79	3.93	3.88

Justin Smoak

Bats: B **Throws:** L **Pos:** 1B-111;PH-16   SMOKE   **Ht:** 6'4" **Wt:** 220 **Born:** 12/5/1986 **Age:** 30

Year	Team	Lg	G	AB	H	2B	3B	HR	(Hm	Rd)	TB	R	RBI	RC	TBB	IBB	SO	HBP	SH	SF	SB	CS	GDP	Avg	OBP	Slg	OPS
2010	2 Tms	AL	100	348	76	14	0	13	(4	9)	129	40	48	42	46	4	91	0	0	3	1	0	9	.218	.307	.371	.678
2011	Sea	AL	123	427	100	24	0	15	(10	5)	169	38	55	55	55	4	105	3	0	4	1	0	10	.234	.323	.396	.719
2012	Sea	AL	132	483	105	14	0	19	(4	15)	176	49	51	50	49	2	111	1	0	2	1	0	12	.217	.290	.364	.654
2013	Sea	AL	131	454	108	19	0	20	(9	11)	187	53	50	60	64	1	119	2	0	1	0	0	11	.238	.334	.412	.746
2014	Sea	AL	80	248	50	13	0	7	(4	3)	84	28	30	23	24	0	66	2	0	2	0	1	8	.202	.275	.339	.614
2015	Tor	AL	132	296	67	16	1	18	(8	10)	139	44	59	49	29	0	86	2	0	1	0	0	10	.226	.299	.470	.768
2016	Tor	AL	126	299	65	10	0	14	(10	4)	117	33	34	33	40	1	112	2	0	0	1	0	7	.217	.314	.391	.705
10	Tex	AL	70	235	49	10	0	8	(4	4)	83	29	34	30	38	4	57	0	0	2	1	0	6	.209	.316	.353	.670
10	Sea	AL	30	113	27	4	0	5	(0	5)	46	11	14	12	8	0	34	0	0	1	0	0	3	.239	.287	.407	.694
	Postseason		8	8	0	0	0	0	(0	0)	0	0	0	0	0	0	3	0	0	0	0	0	0	.000	.000	.000	.000
	7 ML YEARS		824	2555	571	110	1	106	(49	57)	1001	285	327	312	307	12	690	12	0	13	3	1	67	.223	.308	.392	.700

Josh Smoker

Pitches: L **Bats:** L **Pos:** RP-20   **Ht:** 6'2" **Wt:** 250 **Born:** 11/26/1988 **Age:** 28

			HOW MUCH HE PITCHED						WHAT HE GAVE UP										THE RESULTS						
Year	Team	Lg	G	GS	CG	GF	IP	BFP	H	R	ER	HR	SH	SF	HB	TBB	IBB	SO	WP	Bk	W	L	Pct	Sh	Sv-Op	Hld	ERC	ERA
2012	3 Tms	Low	6	0	0	4	9.2	43	8	8	8	1	1	0	3	6	0	6	2	0	1	1	.500	0	1--	-	5.48	7.45

Year	Team	Lg	G	GS	CG	GF	IP	BFP	H	R	ER	HR	SH	SF	HB	TBB	IBB	SO	WP	Bk	W	L	Pct	Sh	Sv-Op	Hld	ERC	ERA
2015	2 Tms	Low	20	0	0	12	28.0	117	23	11	10	1	1	0	0	8	1	34	2	0	2	0	1.000	0	6--	-	2.17	3.21
2015	Bnghtn	AA	21	0	0	7	21.0	89	16	8	7	0	2	1	0	11	0	26	1	1	1	0	1.000	0	0--	-	2.56	3.00
2016	LsVgs	AAA	52	0	0	11	57.0	253	66	32	26	5	2	3	0	18	1	81	7	0	3	2	.600	0	3--	-	4.44	4.11
2016	NYM	NL	20	0	0	4	15.1	65	16	10	8	4	0	0	1	4	1	25	0	0	3	0	1.000	0	0-0	2	5.11	4.70

Jake Smolinski

smoh-LYNN-skee

Bats: R **Throws:** R **Pos:** CF-49;RF-29;LF-18;PH-11;PR-2;DH-1   **Ht:** 5'11" **Wt:** 205 **Born:** 2/9/1989 **Age:** 28

Year	Team	Lg	G	AB	H	2B	3B	HR	(Hm	Rd)	TB	R	RBI	RC	TBB	IBB	SO	HBP	SH	SF	SB	CS	GDP	Avg	OBP	Slg	OPS
2016	Nashv*	AAA	39	145	36	14	0	3	(-	-)	59	20	15	19	11	0	23	2	1	0	6	1	3	.248	.310	.407	.717
2014	Tex	AL	24	86	30	5	0	3	(1	2)	44	12	12	15	3	0	24	3	0	0	0	0	1	.349	.391	.512	.903
2015	2 Tms	AL	76	166	32	7	2	6	(2	4)	61	24	26	17	19	0	39	3	0	4	1	1	3	.193	.281	.367	.649
2016	Oak	AL	99	290	69	6	2	7	(4	3)	100	28	27	28	19	0	44	7	1	2	1	2	11	.238	.299	.345	.644
15	Tex	AL	35	60	8	1	0	1	(0	1)	12	12	6	4	11	0	20	1	0	2	1	0	1	.133	.270	.200	.470
15	Oak	AL	41	106	24	6	2	5	(2	3)	49	12	20	13	8	0	19	2	0	2	0	1	2	.226	.288	.462	.750
3 ML YEARS			199	542	131	18	4	16	(7	9)	205	64	65	60	41	0	107	13	1	6	2	3	15	.242	.307	.378	.686

Drew Smyly

Pitches: L **Bats:** L **Pos:** SP-30   SMY-lee   **Ht:** 6'3" **Wt:** 190 **Born:** 6/13/1989 **Age:** 28

Year	Team	Lg	G	GS	CG	GF	IP	BFP	H	R	ER	HR	SH	SF	HB	TBB	IBB	SO	WP	Bk	W	L	Pct	Sh	Sv-Op	Hld	ERC	ERA
2012	Det	AL	23	18	0	0	99.1	416	93	49	44	12	2	3	2	33	1	94	3	0	4	3	.571	0	0-0	1	3.68	3.99
2013	Det	AL	63	0	0	9	76.0	303	62	20	20	4	0	1	1	17	1	81	5	0	6	0	1.000	0	2-6	21	2.21	2.37
2014	2 Tms	AL	28	25	1	0	153.0	618	136	57	55	18	1	3	1	42	2	133	8	0	9	10	.474	1	0-0	1	3.17	3.24
2015	TB	AL	12	12	0	0	66.2	275	58	24	23	11	1	1	1	20	0	77	2	0	5	2	.714	0	0-0	0	3.45	3.11
2016	TB	AL	30	30	0	0	175.1	738	174	103	95	32	5	11	2	49	2	167	10	0	7	12	.368	0	0-0	0	4.13	4.88
14	Det	AL	21	18	0	0	105.1	445	111	48	46	14	0	3	1	31	1	89	4	0	6	9	.400	0	0-0	1	4.26	3.93
14	TB	AL	7	7	1	0	47.2	173	25	9	9	4	1	0	0	11	1	44	4	0	3	1	.750	1	0-0	0	1.28	1.70
Postseason			10	0	0	1	7.0	30	3	3	2	0	0	0	0	6	1	7	0	0	1	0	1.000	0	0-0	2	1.81	2.57
5 ML YEARS			156	85	1	9	570.1	2350	523	253	237	77	9	19	7	161	6	552	28	0	31	27	.534	1	2-6	23	3.44	3.74

Blake Snell

Pitches: L **Bats:** L **Pos:** SP-19   **Ht:** 6'4" **Wt:** 180 **Born:** 12/4/1992 **Age:** 24

Year	Team	Lg	G	GS	CG	GF	IP	BFP	H	R	ER	HR	SH	SF	HB	TBB	IBB	SO	WP	Bk	W	L	Pct	Sh	Sv-Op	Hld	ERC	ERA
2012	Prnctn	R+	11	11	1	0	47.1	189	34	12	11	4	0	0	4	17	0	53	2	0	5	1	.833	1	0--	-	2.73	2.09
2013	BG	A	23	23	0	0	99.0	447	90	55	47	8	5	0	2	73	0	106	13	1	4	9	.308	0	0--	-	4.88	4.27
2014	2 Tms	Low	24	24	1	0	115.1	491	95	50	41	2	3	3	5	56	0	119	13	1	8	8	.500	1	0--	-	3.04	3.20
2015	Mont	A	12	12	0	0	68.2	268	45	13	12	5	1	1	1	29	0	79	5	0	6	2	.750	0	0--	-	2.35	1.57
2015	Drham	AAA	9	9	0	0	44.1	171	29	11	9	2	2	0	1	13	0	57	5	0	6	2	.750	0	0--	-	1.74	1.83
2016	Drham	AAA	12	12	0	0	63.0	270	56	23	21	4	0	1	2	28	0	90	6	0	3	5	.375	0	0--	-	3.50	3.00
2016	TB	AL	19	19	0	0	89.0	401	93	44	35	5	2	2	0	51	0	98	6	1	6	8	.429	0	0-0	0	4.69	3.54

Brandon Snyder

Bats: R **Throws:** R **Pos:** PH-33;3B-2;1B-1;LF-1   **Ht:** 6'2" **Wt:** 225 **Born:** 11/23/1986 **Age:** 30

Year	Team	Lg	G	AB	H	2B	3B	HR	(Hm	Rd)	TB	R	RBI	RC	TBB	IBB	SO	HBP	SH	SF	SB	CS	GDP	Avg	OBP	Slg	OPS
2016	Gwnntt*	AAA	43	147	48	8	0	3	(-	-)	65	19	26	24	8	0	35	1	1	3	6	0	5	.327	.358	.442	.801
2010	Bal	AL	10	20	6	2	0	0	(0	0)	8	1	3	3	0	0	3	0	0	0	0	1	0	.300	.300	.400	.700
2011	Bal	AL	6	13	3	1	0	0	(0	0)	4	2	1	1	3	0	4	1	0	0	0	0	0	.231	.412	.308	.719
2012	Tex	AL	40	65	18	2	0	3	(1	2)	29	11	9	7	3	0	26	0	1	0	0	0	1	.277	.309	.446	.755
2013	Bos	AL	27	50	9	3	0	2	(2	0)	18	5	7	1	0	0	16	2	0	0	0	0	0	.180	.212	.360	.572
2016	Atl	NL	37	46	11	5	1	4	(3	1)	30	8	9	5	1	0	16	0	0	0	0	0	1	.239	.255	.652	.907
5 ML YEARS			120	194	47	13	1	9	(6	3)	89	27	29	17	7	0	65	3	1	0	0	1	2	.242	.279	.459	.738

Miguel Socolovich

Pitches: R **Bats:** R **Pos:** RP-15   **Ht:** 6'1" **Wt:** 205 **Born:** 7/24/1986 **Age:** 30

Year	Team	Lg	G	GS	CG	GF	IP	BFP	H	R	ER	HR	SH	SF	HB	TBB	IBB	SO	WP	Bk	W	L	Pct	Sh	Sv-Op	Hld	ERC	ERA
2016	Memp*	AAA	45	0	0	18	51.2	214	42	24	18	2	3	2	1	16	3	59	0	0	2	6	.250	0	5--	-	2.30	3.14
2012	2 Tms		12	0	0	2	16.1	72	15	11	11	3	0	0	0	9	0	12	1	0	0	0	-	0	0-1	1	4.79	6.06
2015	StL	NL	28	0	0	11	29.2	125	25	7	6	1	2	0	0	10	1	27	1	0	4	1	.800	0	0-0	1	2.45	1.82
2016	StL	NL	15	0	0	6	18.0	64	5	4	4	2	0	1	0	5	0	16	0	0	1	0	1.000	0	0-0	0	0.78	2.00
12	Bal	AL	6	0	0	1	10.1	47	11	8	8	2	0	0	0	6	0	6	0	1	0	0	-	0	0-1	1	5.91	6.97
12	ChC	NL	6	0	0	1	6.0	25	4	3	3	1	0	0	0	3	0	6	1	0	0	0	-	0	0-0	1	3.05	4.50
3 ML YEARS			55	0	0	19	64.0	261	45	22	21	6	2	1	0	24	1	55	1	1	5	1	.833	0	0-1	2	2.33	2.95

Donovan Solano

Bats: R **Throws:** R **Pos:** 2B-6;3B-2;DH-1;PR-1   sol-ON-oh   **Ht:** 5'10" **Wt:** 205 **Born:** 12/17/1987 **Age:** 29

						BATTING														RUNNING			AVERAGES			
Year	Team	Lg	G	AB	H	2B	3B	HR	(Hm | Rd)	TB	R	RBI	RC	TBB	IBB	SO	HBP	SH	SF	SB	CS	GDP	Avg	OBP	Slg	OPS
2016	S-WB*	AAA	131	511	163	33	3	7	(- | -)	223	64	67	79	25	1	79	2	1	7	2	1	14	.319	.349	.436	.785
2012	Mia	NL	93	285	84	11	3	2	(0 | 2)	107	29	28	35	21	1	58	2	3	5	7	0	5	.295	.342	.375	.717
2013	Mia	NL	102	361	90	13	1	3	(0 | 3)	114	33	34	38	23	3	57	7	2	2	3	1	11	.249	.305	.316	.621
2014	Mia	NL	111	310	78	11	1	3	(1 | 2)	100	26	28	35	19	0	61	3	7	1	1	2	5	.252	.300	.323	.623
2015	Mia	NL	55	90	17	3	1	0	(0 | 0)	22	6	7	3	1	0	18	2	1	0	0	0	4	.189	.215	.244	.459
2016	NYY	AL	9	22	5	2	0	1	(0 | 1)	10	5	2	3	1	0	3	0	0	0	0	0	0	.227	.261	.455	.715
	5 ML YEARS		370	1068	274	40	6	9	(1 | 8)	353	99	99	114	65	4	197	14	13	8	11	3	25	.257	.306	.331	.636

Yangervis Solarte

yawn-HAIR-vees soh-LAHR-tay

Bats: B **Throws:** R **Pos:** 3B-95;2B-15;PH-5;1B-2   **Ht:** 5'11" **Wt:** 205 **Born:** 7/7/1987 **Age:** 29

						BATTING														RUNNING			AVERAGES			
Year	Team	Lg	G	AB	H	2B	3B	HR	(Hm	Rd)	TB	R	RBI	RC	TBB	IBB	SO	HBP	SH	SF	SB	CS	GDP	Avg	OBP	Slg	OPS
2014	2 Tms		131	469	122	19	1	10	(5	5)	173	56	48	59	53	1	58	4	3	6	0	1	13	.260	.336	.369	.705
2015	SD	NL	152	526	142	33	4	14	(5	9)	225	63	63	74	34	0	56	6	2	3	1	0	15	.270	.320	.428	.748
2016	SD	NL	109	405	116	26	1	15	(4	11)	189	55	71	68	30	1	63	5	0	3	1	1	7	.286	.341	.467	.808
14	NYY	AL	75	252	64	14	0	6	(3	3)	96	26	31	33	30	0	34	3	1	3	0	0	8	.254	.337	.381	.718
14	SD	NL	56	217	58	5	1	4	(2	2)	77	30	17	26	23	1	24	1	2	3	0	1	5	.267	.336	.355	.691
	3 ML YEARS		392	1400	380	78	6	39	(14	25)	587	174	182	201	117	2	177	15	5	12	2	2	35	.271	.332	.419	.751

Jorge Soler

HOR-hay so-LAIR

Bats: R **Throws:** R **Pos:** LF-53;PH-21;RF-7;DH-7   **Ht:** 6'4" **Wt:** 215 **Born:** 2/25/1992 **Age:** 25

						BATTING														RUNNING			AVERAGES			
Year	Team	Lg	G	AB	H	2B	3B	HR	(Hm	Rd)	TB	R	RBI	RC	TBB	IBB	SO	HBP	SH	SF	SB	CS	GDP	Avg	OBP	Slg	OPS
2014	ChC	NL	24	89	26	8	1	5	(1	4)	51	11	20	15	6	0	24	0	0	2	1	0	3	.292	.330	.573	.903
2015	ChC	NL	101	366	96	18	1	10	(7	3)	146	39	47	43	32	5	121	3	0	3	3	1	9	.262	.324	.399	.723
2016	ChC	NL	86	227	54	9	0	12	(6	6)	99	37	31	31	31	0	66	3	0	3	0	0	5	.238	.333	.436	.769
	Postseason		7	19	9	3	0	3	(2	1)	21	6	5	8	6	0	5	0	0	0	0	0	0	.474	.600	1.105	1.705
	3 ML YEARS		211	682	176	35	2	27	(14	13)	296	87	98	89	69	5	211	6	0	8	4	1	17	.258	.328	.434	.762

Sammy Solis

SOH-lees

Pitches: L **Bats:** R **Pos:** RP-37   **Ht:** 6'5" **Wt:** 250 **Born:** 8/10/1988 **Age:** 28

			HOW MUCH HE PITCHED						WHAT HE GAVE UP										THE RESULTS						
Year	Team	Lg	G	GS	CG	GF	IP	BFP	H	R	ER	HR	SH	SF	HB	TBB	IBB	SO	WP	Bk	W	L	Pct	Sh	Sv-Op	Hld	ERC	ERA
2013	2 Tms	Low	14	13	0	0	59.2	243	59	23	22	3	1	2	0	19	0	43	3	0	2	1	.667	0	0- -	-	3.50	3.32
2015	Hrsbrg	AA	11	1	0	4	13.1	64	19	10	10	0	1	1	2	5	0	11	3	0	0	3	.000	0	2- -	-	6.33	6.75
2015	Syrcse	AAA	9	0	0	3	13.1	53	8	3	3	0	1	1	1	5	0	11	1	0	0	0	-	0	2- -	-	1.64	2.03
2016	Syrcse	AAA	6	0	0	0	9.0	34	5	1	1	0	1	0	0	3	0	14	0	0	0	0	-	0	0- -	-	1.28	1.00
2015	Was	NL	18	0	0	6	21.1	94	25	11	8	2	1	2	1	4	2	17	0	0	1	1	.500	0	0-0	1	4.08	3.38
2016	Was	NL	37	0	0	10	41.0	172	31	12	11	1	3	0	1	21	2	47	2	0	2	4	.333	0	0-1	9	2.70	2.41
	2 ML YEARS		55	0	0	16	62.1	266	56	23	19	3	4	2	2	25	4	64	2	0	3	5	.375	0	0-1	10	3.17	2.74

Layne Somsen

Pitches: R **Bats:** R **Pos:** RP-2   **Ht:** 6'0" **Wt:** 190 **Born:** 6/5/1989 **Age:** 28

			HOW MUCH HE PITCHED						WHAT HE GAVE UP										THE RESULTS						
Year	Team	Lg	G	GS	CG	GF	IP	BFP	H	R	ER	HR	SH	SF	HB	TBB	IBB	SO	WP	Bk	W	L	Pct	Sh	Sv-Op	Hld	ERC	ERA
2013	Billings	R+	17	0	0	1	43.1	176	37	13	8	1	1	2	1	15	0	40	3	0	4	1	.800	0	1- -	-	2.74	1.66
2014	2 Tms	Low	32	3	0	14	59.0	234	44	24	20	5	0	1	1	20	1	64	4	0	3	3	.500	0	3- -	-	2.51	3.05
2015	Pnscla	AA	12	1	0	2	32.1	133	23	11	10	1	2	1	1	16	0	31	2	0	2	0	1.000	0	0- -	-	2.56	2.76
2015	Lsvlle	AAA	15	3	0	0	29.2	126	24	10	9	2	2	1	0	14	0	29	0	0	1	0	1.000	0	0- -	-	3.06	2.73
2016	Lsvlle	AAA	10	0	0	2	19.0	72	10	4	4	2	0	0	0	7	0	19	2	0	0	0	-	0	0- -	-	1.68	1.89
2016	OkCity	AAA	6	0	0	1	5.2	42	14	13	9	1	1	0	0	9	0	4	1	0	0	2	.000	0	0- -	-	19.55	14.29
2016	Cin	NL	2	0	0	1	2.1	16	6	5	5	2	0	0	0	3	0	2	0	0	0	0	-	0	0-0	0	28.23	19.29

Joakim Soria

wah-KEEM SORE-ee-uh

Pitches: R **Bats:** R **Pos:** RP-70   **Ht:** 6'3" **Wt:** 200 **Born:** 5/18/1984 **Age:** 33

			HOW MUCH HE PITCHED						WHAT HE GAVE UP										THE RESULTS						
Year	Team	Lg	G	GS	CG	GF	IP	BFP	H	R	ER	HR	SH	SF	HB	TBB	IBB	SO	WP	Bk	W	L	Pct	Sh	Sv-Op	Hld	ERC	ERA
2007	KC	AL	62	0	0	38	69.0	270	46	20	19	3	1	3	1	19	3	75	2	0	2	3	.400	0	17-21	9	1.63	2.48
2008	KC	AL	63	0	0	57	67.1	260	39	13	12	5	2	6	6	19	1	66	1	1	2	3	.400	0	42-45	0	1.72	1.60
2009	KC	AL	47	0	0	41	53.0	222	44	14	13	5	1	1	6	16	1	69	3	0	3	2	.600	0	30-33	0	2.80	2.21
2010	KC	AL	66	0	0	56	65.2	270	53	13	13	4	3	4	2	16	1	71	3	1	1	2	.333	0	43-46	0	2.27	1.78
2011	KC	AL	60	0	0	47	60.1	256	60	29	27	7	3	2	1	17	0	60	1	0	5	5	.500	0	28-35	0	3.80	4.03
2013	Tex	AL	26	0	0	9	23.2	101	18	10	10	2	1	0	1	14	2	28	2	0	1	0	1.000	0	0-0	6	3.45	3.80
2014	2 Tms	AL	48	0	0	37	44.1	182	38	19	16	2	1	2	2	6	2	48	1	0	2	4	.333	0	18-20	1	2.04	3.25
2015	2 Tms	AL	72	0	0	40	67.2	272	55	20	19	8	1	1	4	19	1	64	5	0	3	1	.750	0	24-30	11	2.87	2.53
2016	KC	AL	70	0	0	18	66.0	293	70	31	30	10	4	2	2	27	0	68	2	3	5	8	.385	0	1-8	20	4.86	4.05
14	Tex	AL	35	0	0	32	33.1	133	25	12	10	1	1	1	1	4	1	42	0	0	1	3	.250	0	17-19	1	1.38	2.70
14	Det	AL	13	0	0	5	11.0	49	13	7	6	2	0	1	1	2	1	6	1	0	1	1	.500	0	1-1	0	4.92	4.91

Year	Team	Lg	G	GS	CG	GF	IP	BFP	H	R	ER	HR	SH	SF	HB	TBB	IBB	SO	WP	Bk	W	L	Pct	Sh	Sv-Op	Hld	ERC	ERA
							HOW MUCH HE PITCHED						WHAT HE GAVE UP										THE RESULTS					
15	Det	AL	43	0	0	35	41.0	165	32	13	13	8	1	0	2	11	1	36	0	0	3	1	.750	0	23-26	0	3.15	2.85
15	Pit	NL	29	0	0	5	26.2	107	23	7	6	0	0	1	0	8	0	28	5	0	0	0	-	0	1-4	11	2.39	2.03
	Postseason		3	0	0	1	2.0	13	4	5	5	0	0	0	0	3	1	3	0	0	0	1	.000	0	0-1	0	12.98	22.50
	9 ML YEARS		514	0	0	343	517.2	2126	423	169	159	46	17	18	20	153	11	549	20	5	24	28	.462	0	203-238	47	2.73	2.76

Geovany Soto

Bats: R **Throws:** R **Pos:** C-23;1B-1;3B-1;PH-1   **Ht:** 6'1" **Wt:** 225 **Born:** 1/20/1983 **Age:** 34

Year	Team	Lg	G	AB	H	2B	3B	HR	(Hm	Rd)	TB	R	RBI	RC	TBB	IBB	SO	HBP	SH	SF	SB	CS	GDP	Avg	OBP	Slg	OPS
2016	Salt Lk*	AAA	10	36	7	4	0	1	(-	-)	14	2	8	3	1	0	7	0	1	0	0	0	0	.194	.216	.389	.605
2005	ChC	NL	1	1	0	0	0	0	(0	0)	0	0	0	0	0	0	0	0	0	0	0	0	0	.000	.000	.000	.000
2006	ChC	NL	11	25	5	1	0	0	(0	0)	6	1	2	0	0	0	5	1	0	0	0	0	0	.200	.231	.240	.471
2007	ChC	NL	18	54	21	6	0	3	(2	1)	36	12	8	13	5	0	14	0	0	1	0	0	1	.389	.433	.667	1.100
2008	ChC	NL	141	494	141	35	2	23	(11	12)	249	66	86	81	62	6	121	2	0	5	0	1	11	.285	.364	.504	.868
2009	ChC	NL	102	331	72	19	1	11	(6	5)	126	27	47	34	50	3	77	3	0	5	1	0	19	.218	.321	.381	.702
2010	ChC	NL	105	322	90	19	0	17	(12	5)	160	47	53	59	62	4	83	0	0	3	0	1	5	.280	.393	.497	.890
2011	ChC	NL	125	421	96	26	0	17	(7	10)	173	46	54	43	45	3	124	6	0	2	0	0	12	.228	.310	.411	.721
2012	2 Tms		99	324	64	12	1	11	(3	8)	111	45	39	30	30	1	76	3	2	1	1	0	14	.198	.270	.343	.613
2013	Tex	AL	54	163	40	9	0	9	(7	2)	76	20	22	23	20	0	60	0	1	0	1	2	2	.245	.328	.466	.794
2014	2 Tms		24	80	20	6	0	1	(1	0)	29	8	11	6	6	0	19	0	1	0	0	0	6	.250	.302	.363	.665
2015	CWS	AL	78	187	41	8	0	9	(6	3)	76	20	21	19	21	0	63	1	1	0	0	1	3	.219	.301	.406	.708
2016	LAA	AL	26	78	21	5	0	4	(0	4)	38	11	9	12	6	0	21	0	2	0	0	0	1	.269	.321	.487	.809
12	ChC	NL	52	176	35	6	1	6	(2	4)	61	26	14	15	19	1	35	2	0	0	0	0	6	.199	.284	.347	.631
12	Tex		47	148	29	6	0	5	(1	4)	50	19	25	15	11	0	41	1	2	1	1	0	6	.196	.253	.338	.591
14	Tex	AL	10	38	9	2	0	1	(1	0)	14	5	3	1	0	0	11	0	0	0	0	0	3	.237	.237	.368	.605
14	Oak	AL	14	42	11	4	0	0	(0	0)	15	3	8	5	6	0	8	0	1	0	0	0	3	.262	.354	.357	.711
	Postseason		7	20	3	1	0	1	(0	1)	7	1	2	1	3	0	6	0	0	0	0	0	0	.150	.261	.350	.611
	12 ML YEARS		784	2480	611	146	4	105	(55	50)	1080	303	352	320	307	17	663	16	7	18	3	5	71	.246	.331	.435	.767

Steven Souza Jr.

Bats: R **Throws:** R **Pos:** RF-111;DH-6;CF-3;PH-3   SOO-zuh   **Ht:** 6'4" **Wt:** 225 **Born:** 4/24/1989 **Age:** 28

Year	Team	Lg	G	AB	H	2B	3B	HR	(Hm	Rd)	TB	R	RBI	RC	TBB	IBB	SO	HBP	SH	SF	SB	CS	GDP	Avg	OBP	Slg	OPS
2014	Was	NL	21	23	3	0	0	2	(1	1)	9	2	2	1	3	0	7	0	0	0	0	0	1	.130	.231	.391	.622
2015	TB	AL	110	373	84	15	1	16	(6	10)	149	59	40	40	46	0	144	5	1	1	12	6	7	.225	.318	.399	.717
2016	TB	AL	120	430	106	17	1	17	(7	10)	176	58	49	53	31	0	159	5	0	2	7	6	5	.247	.303	.409	.713
	3 ML YEARS		251	826	193	32	2	35	(14	21)	334	119	91	94	80	0	310	10	1	3	19	12	13	.234	.308	.404	.712

Denard Span

Bats: L **Throws:** L **Pos:** CF-137;PH-9   **Ht:** 6'0" **Wt:** 210 **Born:** 2/27/1984 **Age:** 33

Year	Team	Lg	G	AB	H	2B	3B	HR	(Hm	Rd)	TB	R	RBI	RC	TBB	IBB	SO	HBP	SH	SF	SB	CS	GDP	Avg	OBP	Slg	OPS
2008	Min	AL	93	347	102	16	7	6	(2	4)	150	70	47	68	50	3	60	4	8	2	18	7	3	.294	.387	.432	.819
2009	Min	AL	145	578	180	16	10	8	(5	3)	240	97	68	100	70	3	89	10	12	6	23	10	7	.311	.392	.415	.807
2010	Min	AL	153	629	166	24	10	3	(0	3)	219	85	58	85	60	0	74	4	10	2	26	4	12	.264	.331	.348	.679
2011	Min	AL	70	284	75	11	5	2	(1	1)	102	37	16	32	27	0	36	0	6	1	6	1	3	.264	.328	.359	.687
2012	Min	AL	128	516	146	38	4	4	(2	2)	204	71	41	69	47	0	62	0	4	1	17	6	10	.283	.342	.395	.738
2013	Was	NL	153	610	170	28	11	4	(2	2)	232	75	47	74	42	0	70	2	7	1	20	6	11	.279	.327	.380	.707
2014	Was	NL	147	610	184	39	8	5	(1	4)	254	94	37	94	50	1	65	3	3	3	31	7	6	.302	.355	.416	.771
2015	Was	NL	61	246	74	17	0	5	(0	5)	106	38	22	45	25	0	26	1	1	2	11	0	5	.301	.365	.431	.796
2016	SF	NL	143	572	152	23	5	11	(5	6)	218	70	53	70	53	2	79	4	6	2	12	7	8	.266	.331	.381	.712
	Postseason		10	47	12	1	0	0	(0	0)	13	1	1	2	1	0	5	0	0	0	1	0	2	.255	.271	.277	.547
	9 ML YEARS		1093	4392	1249	212	60	48	(18	30)	1725	637	389	637	424	9	568	27	51	19	164	48	65	.284	.350	.393	.742

Cory Spangenberg

Bats: L **Throws:** R **Pos:** 2B-13;PH-1   SPAN-jen-burg   **Ht:** 6'0" **Wt:** 195 **Born:** 3/16/1991 **Age:** 26

Year	Team	Lg	G	AB	H	2B	3B	HR	(Hm	Rd)	TB	R	RBI	RC	TBB	IBB	SO	HBP	SH	SF	SB	CS	GDP	Avg	OBP	Slg	OPS
2014	SD	NL	20	62	18	2	1	2	(1	1)	28	7	9	9	2	0	14	0	1	0	4	2	1	.290	.313	.452	.764
2015	SD	NL	108	303	82	11	5	4	(3	1)	121	38	21	40	28	1	75	2	8	3	9	4	4	.271	.338	.399	.733
2016	SD	NL	14	48	11	1	1	1	(0	1)	17	6	8	7	4	0	13	1	0	0	1	0	0	.229	.302	.354	.656
	3 ML YEARS		142	413	111	20	7	7	(4	3)	166	51	38	56	34	1	102	3	9	3	14	6	5	.269	.327	.402	.729

George Springer

Bats: R **Throws:** R **Pos:** RF-147;DH-12;CF-1;PR-1   **Ht:** 6'3" **Wt:** 215 **Born:** 9/19/1989 **Age:** 27

Year	Team	Lg	G	AB	H	2B	3B	HR	(Hm	Rd)	TB	R	RBI	RC	TBB	IBB	SO	HBP	SH	SF	SB	CS	GDP	Avg	OBP	Slg	OPS
2014	Hou	AL	78	295	68	8	1	20	(5	15)	138	45	51	45	39	4	114	9	0	2	5	2	4	.231	.336	.468	.804
2015	Hou	AL	102	388	107	19	2	16	(9	7)	178	59	41	60	50	0	109	8	2	3	16	4	4	.276	.367	.459	.826
2016	Hou	AL	162	644	168	29	5	29	(13	16)	294	116	82	100	88	2	178	11	0	1	9	10	12	.261	.359	.457	.815
	Postseason		6	23	5	2	0	1	(0	1)	10	5	3	3	3	0	11	0	0	0	0	0	0	.217	.308	.435	.742
	3 ML YEARS		342	1327	343	56	8	65	(27	38)	610	220	174	205	177	6	401	28	2	6	30	16	20	.258	.356	.460	.816

Jacob Stallings

Bats: R Throws: R Pos: C-4;PH-2   Ht: 6'5" Wt: 225 Born: 12/22/1989 Age: 27

								BATTING												RUNNING			AVERAGES			
Year	Team	Lg	G	AB	H	2B	3B	HR	(Hm	Rd)	TB	R	RBI	RC	TBB	IBB	SO	HBP	SH	SF	SB	CS	GDP	Avg	OBP	Slg	OPS
2012	StCol	A-	66	226	52	16	2	1	(-	-)	75	26	30	27	32	1	73	1	3	3	2	0	3	.230	.324	.332	.656
2013	Bradtn	A+	78	251	55	16	2	6	(-	-)	93	36	23	37	45	0	62	7	2	1	1	1	12	.219	.352	.371	.722
2014	Bradtn	A+	68	212	51	11	0	4	(-	-)	74	22	30	26	28	0	52	2	5	2	1	2	1	.241	.332	.349	.681
2015	Altna	AA	75	265	73	14	1	3	(-	-)	98	25	32	33	15	0	65	3	1	8	4	1	7	.275	.313	.370	.683
2016	Indy	AAA	80	257	55	17	0	6	(-	-)	90	23	28	22	11	1	66	2	5	0	0	1	2	.214	.252	.350	.602
2016	Pit	NL	5	15	6	1	0	0	(0	0)	7	0	2	3	0	0	4	0	0	0	1	0	0	.400	.400	.467	.867

Craig Stammen

Pitches: R Bats: R Pos: P   STAMM-enn   Ht: 6'4" Wt: 230 Born: 3/9/1984 Age: 33

			HOW MUCH HE PITCHED						WHAT HE GAVE UP										THE RESULTS						
Year	Team	Lg	G	GS	CG	GF	IP	BFP	H	R	ER	HR	SH	SF	HB	TBB	IBB	SO	WP	Bk	W	L	Pct	Sh	Sv-Op	Hld	ERC	ERA
2016	Clmbs*	AAA	10	0	0	5	13.0	57	16	8	8	2	1	1	0	2	0	11	0	0	0	3	.000	0	0- -	-	4.66	5.54
2016	Akron*	AA	10	0	0	1	11.1	47	9	2	1	1	2	0	0	3	0	9	0	0	0	1	.000	0	0- -	-	2.31	0.79
2009	Was	NL	19	19	1	0	105.2	448	112	67	60	14	4	3	3	24	1	48	7	0	4	7	.364	0	0-0	-	4.03	5.11
2010	Was	NL	35	19	0	3	128.0	562	151	78	73	13	5	6	1	41	4	85	3	0	4	4	.500	0	0-0	1	4.79	5.13
2011	Was	NL	7	0	0	2	10.1	38	3	1	1	0	0	0	0	4	0	12	1	0	1	1	.500	0	0-0	1	0.67	0.87
2012	Was	NL	59	0	0	15	88.1	370	70	27	23	7	5	1	2	36	4	87	3	0	6	1	.857	0	1-2	10	2.84	2.34
2013	Was	NL	55	0	0	14	81.2	339	78	30	25	4	8	4	2	27	3	79	2	1	7	6	.538	0	0-1	7	3.32	2.76
2014	Was	NL	49	0	0	15	72.2	304	78	34	31	5	3	1	3	14	2	56	1	1	4	5	.444	0	0-0	7	3.61	3.84
2015	Was	NL	5	0	0	0	4.0	17	2	0	0	0	0	1	0	3	1	3	0	0	0	0	-	0	0-0	1	1.66	0.00
	Postseason		6	0	0	0	7.0	34	8	4	4	1	1	1	3	2	0	5	0	0	0	0	-	0	0-0	1	6.41	5.14
	7 ML YEARS		229	38	1	49	490.2	2078	494	237	213	43	25	16	11	149	15	370	17	2	26	24	.520	0	1-3	28	3.70	3.91

Giancarlo Stanton

Bats: R Throws: R Pos: RF-106;PH-11;DH-2   john-CAHR-loh   Ht: 6'6" Wt: 245 Born: 11/8/1989 Age: 27

								BATTING												RUNNING			AVERAGES			
Year	Team	Lg	G	AB	H	2B	3B	HR	(Hm	Rd)	TB	R	RBI	RC	TBB	IBB	SO	HBP	SH	SF	SB	CS	GDP	Avg	OBP	Slg	OPS
2010	Fla	NL	100	359	93	21	1	22	(7	15)	182	45	59	56	34	6	123	2	0	1	5	2	7	.259	.326	.507	.833
2011	Fla	NL	150	516	135	30	5	34	(16	18)	277	79	87	81	70	6	166	9	0	6	5	5	11	.262	.356	.537	.893
2012	Mia	NL	123	449	130	30	1	37	(16	21)	273	75	86	79	46	9	143	5	0	1	6	2	5	.290	.361	.608	.969
2013	Mia	NL	116	425	106	26	0	24	(15	9)	204	62	62	66	74	5	140	4	0	1	1	0	10	.249	.365	.480	.845
2014	Mia	NL	145	539	155	31	1	37	(24	13)	299	89	105	109	94	24	170	3	0	2	13	1	16	.288	.395	.555	.950
2015	Mia	NL	74	279	74	12	1	27	(13	14)	169	47	67	54	34	6	95	2	0	3	4	2	5	.265	.346	.606	.952
2016	Mia	NL	119	413	99	20	1	27	(13	14)	202	56	74	56	50	5	140	4	0	2	0	0	6	.240	.326	.489	.815
	7 ML YEARS		827	2980	792	170	10	208	(104	104)	1606	453	540	501	402	61	977	29	0	16	34	12	60	.266	.357	.539	.896

Max Stassi

Bats: R Throws: R Pos: C-8;PH-2;PR-1   STASS-ee   Ht: 5'10" Wt: 200 Born: 3/15/1991 Age: 26

								BATTING												RUNNING			AVERAGES			
Year	Team	Lg	G	AB	H	2B	3B	HR	(Hm	Rd)	TB	R	RBI	RC	TBB	IBB	SO	HBP	SH	SF	SB	CS	GDP	Avg	OBP	Slg	OPS
2016	Fresno*	AAA	69	243	56	12	1	7	(-	-)	91	21	32	27	20	0	65	2	1	0	1	0	7	.230	.294	.374	.669
2013	Hou	AL	3	7	2	0	0	0	(0	0)	2	0	1	0	0	0	2	1	0	0	0	0	1	.286	.375	.286	.661
2014	Hou	AL	7	20	7	2	0	0	(0	0)	9	2	4	4	0	0	6	0	0	0	0	0	0	.350	.350	.450	.800
2015	Hou	AL	11	15	6	0	0	1	(1	0)	9	4	2	3	1	0	5	0	1	0	0	0	0	.400	.438	.600	1.038
2016	Hou	AL	9	13	1	0	0	0	(0	0)	1	1	0	0	0	0	5	0	0	0	0	0	0	.077	.077	.077	.154
	4 ML YEARS		30	55	16	2	0	1	(1	0)	21	7	7	7	1	0	18	1	1	0	0	0	2	.291	.316	.382	.698

Robert Stephenson

Pitches: R Bats: R Pos: SP-8   Ht: 6'2" Wt: 200 Born: 2/24/1993 Age: 24

			HOW MUCH HE PITCHED						WHAT HE GAVE UP										THE RESULTS						
Year	Team	Lg	G	GS	CG	GF	IP	BFP	H	R	ER	HR	SH	SF	HB	TBB	IBB	SO	WP	Bk	W	L	Pct	Sh	Sv-Op	Hld	ERC	ERA
2012	2 Tms	Low	15	15	0	0	65.0	273	54	34	23	6	2	1	4	23	0	72	12	2	3	4	.429	0	0- -	-	3.14	3.18
2013	2 Tms	Low	18	18	0	0	97.2	390	75	39	29	8	3	1	3	22	0	118	11	2	7	5	.583	0	0- -	-	2.21	2.67
2014	Pnscla	AA	27	26	0	0	136.2	601	114	81	72	18	3	9	5	74	0	140	9	0	7	10	.412	0	0- -	-	4.00	4.74
2015	Pnscla	AA	14	14	1	0	78.1	325	53	36	32	8	5	4	4	43	0	89	5	0	4	7	.364	0	0- -	-	3.15	3.68
2015	Lsvlle	AAA	11	11	0	0	55.2	242	51	25	25	2	3	2	2	27	0	51	5	0	4	4	.500	0	0- -	-	3.61	4.04
2016	Lsvlle	AAA	24	24	1	0	136.2	591	115	72	67	17	6	5	3	71	0	120	5	0	8	9	.471	0	0- -	-	3.89	4.41
2016	Cin	NL	8	8	0	0	37.0	170	41	26	25	9	0	0	4	19	1	31	2	1	2	3	.400	0	0-0	0	6.78	6.08

Brock Stewart

Pitches: R Bats: L Pos: SP-5; RP-2   Ht: 6'3" Wt: 210 Born: 10/3/1991 Age: 25

			HOW MUCH HE PITCHED						WHAT HE GAVE UP										THE RESULTS						
Year	Team	Lg	G	GS	CG	GF	IP	BFP	H	R	ER	HR	SH	SF	HB	TBB	IBB	SO	WP	Bk	W	L	Pct	Sh	Sv-Op	Hld	ERC	ERA
2014	Ogden	R+	17	1	0	7	34.1	159	36	20	13	1	1	0	2	17	0	45	10	0	3	2	.600	0	3- -	-	4.27	3.41
2015	2 Tms	Low	25	19	0	0	101.0	437	113	52	50	10	2	2	5	24	0	103	7	1	4	6	.400	0	0- -	-	4.27	4.46
2016	Tulsa	AA	10	10	1	0	59.1	227	41	12	9	0	2	3	2	11	0	65	1	0	3	4	.429	0	0- -	-	1.44	1.37
2016	OkCity	AAA	9	9	0	0	50.2	197	41	14	14	4	1	1	0	6	0	54	0	0	4	0	1.000	0	0- -	-	1.94	2.49
2016	LAD	NL	7	5	0	0	28.0	126	33	18	18	7	1	0	0	12	1	25	0	0	2	2	.500	0	0-0	0	6.34	5.79

Chris Stewart

Bats: R **Throws:** R **Pos:** C-31;PH-6;1B-1 **Ht:** 6'4" **Wt:** 210 **Born:** 2/19/1982 **Age:** 35

Year	Team	Lg	G	AB	H	2B	3B	HR	(Hm Rd)	TB	R	RBI	RC	TBB	IBB	SO	HBP	SH	SF	SB	CS	GDP	Avg	OBP	Slg	OPS
2016	Altna*	AA	10	25	5	0	0	0	(- -)	5	6	3	3	8	0	1	1	0	1	0	0	1	.200	.400	.200	.600
2006	CWS	AL	6	8	0	0	0	0	(0 0)	0	0	0	0	0	0	2	0	0	0	0	0	0	.000	.000	.000	.000
2007	Tex	AL	17	37	9	2	0	0	(0 0)	11	4	3	3	3	0	6	0	3	0	0	0	2	.243	.300	.297	.597
2008	NYY	AL	1	3	0	0	0	0	(0 0)	0	0	0	0	0	0	1	0	0	0	0	0	0	.000	.000	.000	.000
2010	SD	NL	2	0	0	0	0	0	(0 0)	0	0	0	0	0	0	0	0	0	0	0	0	0	-	-	-	-
2011	SF	NL	67	162	33	8	0	3	(1 2)	50	20	10	10	16	4	18	2	3	0	0	0	2	.204	.283	.309	.592
2012	NYY	AL	55	141	34	8	0	1	(1 0)	45	15	13	10	10	0	21	1	3	2	2	0	1	.241	.292	.319	.611
2013	NYY	AL	109	294	62	6	0	4	(3 1)	80	28	25	24	30	0	49	6	6	4	4	0	2	.211	.293	.272	.566
2014	Pit	NL	49	136	40	5	0	0	(0 0)	45	9	10	15	12	2	27	3	2	1	0	1	2	.294	.362	.331	.693
2015	Pit	NL	58	159	46	8	0	0	(0 0)	54	9	15	17	6	0	29	2	3	2	0	0	3	.289	.320	.340	.659
2016	Pit	NL	34	98	21	4	0	1	(0 1)	28	10	7	7	12	2	15	3	0	0	0	0	2	.214	.319	.286	.604
	Postseason		1	0	0	0	0	0	(0 0)	0	0	0	0	0	0	0	0	0	0	0	0	0	-	-	-	-
	10 ML YEARS		398	1038	245	41	0	9	(5 4)	313	95	83	86	89	8	168	17	20	9	6	1	20	.236	.304	.302	.606

Drew Storen

Pitches: R **Bats:** B **Pos:** RP-57 STORE-inn **Ht:** 6'1" **Wt:** 195 **Born:** 8/11/1987 **Age:** 29

Year	Team	Lg	G	GS	CG	GF	IP	BFP	H	R	ER	HR	SH	SF	HB	TBB	IBB	SO	WP	Bk	W	L	Pct	Sh	Sv-Op	Hld	ERC	ERA
2010	Was	NL	54	0	0	22	55.1	232	48	24	22	4	3	2	3	22	3	52	3	0	4	4	.500	0	5-7	10	3.19	3.58
2011	Was	NL	73	0	0	52	75.1	303	57	24	23	8	1	1	2	20	4	74	2	0	6	3	.667	0	43-48	3	2.35	2.75
2012	Was	NL	37	0	0	17	30.1	116	22	8	8	0	0	2	1	8	0	24	1	0	3	1	.750	0	4-5	10	1.79	2.37
2013	Was	NL	68	0	0	20	61.2	267	65	34	31	7	3	1	1	19	2	58	2	0	4	2	.667	0	3-8	24	4.08	4.52
2014	Was	NL	65	0	0	18	56.1	224	44	8	7	2	3	2	3	11	3	46	4	0	2	1	.667	0	11-14	20	1.93	1.12
2015	Was	NL	58	0	0	35	55.0	228	45	23	21	3	4	1	5	16	2	67	2	0	2	2	.500	0	29-34	5	2.79	3.44
2016	2 Tms	AL	57	0	0	14	51.2	228	56	30	30	7	1	0	7	13	1	48	0	1	3	3	.571	0	3-4	10	4.68	5.23
16	Tor	AL	38	0	0	13	33.1	156	43	23	23	6	1	0	6	10	1	32	0	1	1	3	.250	0	3-4	8	6.70	6.21
16	Sea	AL	19	0	0	1	18.1	72	13	7	7	1	0	0	1	3	0	16	0	0	3	0	1.000	0	0-0	2	1.67	3.44
	Postseason		6	0	0	5	5.1	25	7	5	5	0	0	1	0	3	0	7	0	0	1	1	.500	0	1-3	0	5.85	8.44
	7 ML YEARS		412	0	0	178	385.2	1598	337	151	142	31	15	9	22	109	15	369	14	1	25	16	.610	0	98-120	82	2.97	3.31

Trevor Story

Bats: R **Throws:** R **Pos:** SS-96;PH-2 **Ht:** 6'1" **Wt:** 180 **Born:** 11/15/1992 **Age:** 24

Year	Team	Lg	G	AB	H	2B	3B	HR	(Hm Rd)	TB	R	RBI	RC	TBB	IBB	SO	HBP	SH	SF	SB	CS	GDP	Avg	OBP	Slg	OPS
2012	Ashvll	A	122	477	132	43	6	18	(- -)	241	96	63	92	60	0	121	9	0	3	15	3	3	.277	.367	.505	.872
2013	Mdest	A+	130	497	116	34	5	12	(- -)	196	71	65	66	45	0	183	7	4	1	23	1	2	.233	.305	.394	.700
2014	2 Tms	Low	52	191	63	18	7	5	(- -)	110	40	28	48	32	1	62	3	0	0	20	4	3	.330	.434	.576	1.010
2014	Tulsa	AA	56	205	41	8	1	9	(- -)	78	29	20	25	28	0	82	2	2	1	3	1	1	.200	.302	.380	.683
2015	NwBrit	AA	69	256	72	20	6	10	(- -)	134	46	40	53	35	2	73	5	0	4	15	2	0	.281	.373	.523	.897
2015	Albq	AAA	61	256	71	20	4	10	(- -)	129	37	40	42	16	1	68	2	0	1	7	1	1	.277	.324	.504	.828
2016	Col	NL	97	372	101	21	4	27	(16 11)	211	67	72	67	35	2	130	5	2	1	8	5	5	.272	.341	.567	.909

Matt Strahm

Pitches: L **Bats:** R **Pos:** RP-21 **Ht:** 6'3" **Wt:** 185 **Born:** 11/12/1991 **Age:** 25

Year	Team	Lg	G	GS	CG	GF	IP	BFP	H	R	ER	HR	SH	SF	HB	TBB	IBB	SO	WP	Bk	W	L	Pct	Sh	Sv-Op	Hld	ERC	ERA
2012	Idaho	R+	19	0	0	6	30.1	151	34	29	19	1	0	3	4	17	0	42	5	1	1	3	.250	0	0--	-	5.08	5.64
2014	Idaho	R+	10	1	0	3	19.1	79	10	6	5	1	1	0	1	10	0	27	1	0	1	0	1.000	0	1--	-	1.89	2.33
2015	2 Tms	Low	29	11	0	9	94.0	375	60	32	27	8	3	1	7	31	0	121	5	0	3	7	.300	0	5--	-	2.14	2.59
2016	NWArk	AA	22	18	0	0	102.1	425	102	47	39	14	1	2	6	23	0	107	1	1	3	8	.273	0	0--	-	3.90	3.43
2016	KC	AL	21	0	0	1	22.0	88	13	4	3	0	1	0	1	11	1	30	1	0	2	2	.500	0	0-0	6	1.84	1.23

Dan Straily

Pitches: R **Bats:** R **Pos:** SP-31; RP-3 STRAY-lee **Ht:** 6'2" **Wt:** 220 **Born:** 12/1/1988 **Age:** 28

Year	Team	Lg	G	GS	CG	GF	IP	BFP	H	R	ER	HR	SH	SF	HB	TBB	IBB	SO	WP	Bk	W	L	Pct	Sh	Sv-Op	Hld	ERC	ERA
2012	Oak	AL	7	7	0	0	39.1	172	36	19	17	11	1	1	2	16	1	32	0	0	2	1	.667	0	0-0	0	4.94	3.89
2013	Oak	AL	27	27	0	0	152.1	640	132	74	67	16	4	5	7	57	0	124	7	0	10	8	.556	0	0-0	0	3.46	3.96
2014	2 Tms		14	8	0	0	52.0	231	53	44	39	10	0	1	2	24	1	47	2	0	1	3	.250	0	0-0	0	5.22	6.75
2015	Hou	AL	4	3	0	0	16.2	76	16	11	10	2	0	1	2	8	0	14	1	0	0	1	.000	0	0-0	0	4.38	5.40
2016	Cin	NL	34	31	0	0	191.1	792	154	80	80	31	6	3	11	73	4	162	3	1	14	8	.636	0	0-0	0	3.58	3.76
14	Oak	AL	7	7	0	0	38.1	159	33	24	21	9	0	1	1	15	1	34	2	0	1	2	.333	0	0-0	0	4.31	4.93
14	ChC	NL	7	1	0	0	13.2	72	20	20	18	1	0	0	1	9	0	13	0	0	0	1	.000	0	0-0	0	7.78	11.85
	Postseason		1	1	0	0	6.0	22	4	3	3	1	0	0	1	0	0	8	0	0	0	0	-	0	0-0	0	1.99	4.50
	5 ML YEARS		86	76	0	0	451.2	1911	391	225	213	70	11	10	23	178	6	379	13	1	27	21	.563	0	0-0	0	3.87	4.24

Stephen Strasburg

Pitches: R Bats: R Pos: SP-24   STRAHS-berg   Ht: 6'4" Wt: 235 Born: 7/20/1988 Age: 28

Year Team	Lg	G	GS	CG	GF	IP	BFP	H	R	ER	HR	SH	SF	HB	TBB	IBB	SO	WP	Bk	W	L	Pct	Sh	Sv-Op	Hld	ERC	ERA
2010 Was	NL	12	12	0	0	68.0	274	56	25	22	5	2	2	0	17	0	92	2	0	5	3	.625	0	0-0	0	2.41	2.91
2011 Was	NL	5	5	0	0	24.0	88	15	5	4	0	1	1	0	2	0	24	0	0	1	1	.500	0	0-0	0	0.97	1.50
2012 Was	NL	28	28	0	0	159.1	653	136	62	56	15	6	4	4	48	1	197	5	0	15	6	.714	0	0-0	0	2.97	3.16
2013 Was	NL	30	30	1	0	183.0	731	136	71	61	16	5	1	12	56	1	191	7	3	8	9	.471	1	0-0	0	2.58	3.00
2014 Was	NL	34	34	0	0	215.0	868	198	86	75	23	9	4	5	43	4	242	7	0	14	11	.560	0	0-0	0	3.02	3.14
2015 Was	NL	23	23	0	0	127.1	523	115	56	49	14	5	1	3	26	0	155	4	0	11	7	.611	0	0-0	0	2.92	3.46
2016 Was	NL	24	24	0	0	147.2	598	119	59	59	15	5	1	2	44	1	183	2	0	15	4	.789	0	0-0	0	2.72	3.60
Postseason		1	1	0	0	5.0	25	8	2	1	0	1	0	1	1	0	2	0	0	0	1	.000	0	0-0	0	6.68	1.80
7 ML YEARS		156	156	1	0	924.1	3735	775	364	326	88	33	14	26	236	7	1084	27	3	69	41	.627	1	0-0	0	2.75	3.17

Chris Stratton

Pitches: R Bats: R Pos: RP-7   Ht: 6'3" Wt: 190 Born: 8/22/1990 Age: 26

Year Team	Lg	G	GS	CG	GF	IP	BFP	H	R	ER	HR	SH	SF	HB	TBB	IBB	SO	WP	Bk	W	L	Pct	Sh	Sv-Op	Hld	ERC	ERA
2012 SlKzr	A-	8	5	0	0	16.1	72	14	6	5	1	1	0	2	10	0	16	1	0	0	1	.000	0	0--	-	4.37	2.76
2013 Augsta	A	22	22	1	0	132.0	554	128	48	48	5	4	4	3	47	1	123	6	0	9	3	.750	0	0--	-	3.44	3.27
2014 SnJos	A+	19	18	0	0	99.0	427	103	61	56	13	4	3	2	36	0	102	5	0	7	8	.467	0	0--	-	4.49	5.09
2014 Rchmd	AA	5	5	0	0	23.0	107	29	10	9	2	1	2	0	12	0	18	2	0	1	1	.500	0	0--	-	6.04	3.52
2015 Rchmd	AA	9	9	0	0	50.0	212	40	26	23	3	2	1	1	22	1	39	2	0	1	5	.167	0	0--	-	2.88	4.14
2015 Scrmto	AAA	17	17	1	0	98.0	415	88	46	42	6	4	3	5	40	0	72	4	0	4	5	.444	0	0--	-	3.51	3.86
2016 Scrmto	AAA	21	20	1	0	125.2	526	120	57	54	6	7	3	4	39	1	103	6	0	12	6	.667	0	0--	-	3.26	3.87
2016 SF	NL	7	0	0	7	10.0	43	11	4	4	1	0	0	0	5	0	6	0	0	1	0	1.000	0	0-0	0	5.31	3.60

Huston Street

Pitches: R Bats: R Pos: RP-26   Ht: 6'0" Wt: 205 Born: 8/2/1983 Age: 33

Year Team	Lg	G	GS	CG	GF	IP	BFP	H	R	ER	HR	SH	SF	HB	TBB	IBB	SO	WP	Bk	W	L	Pct	Sh	Sv-Op	Hld	ERC	ERA
2005 Oak	AL	67	0	0	47	78.1	306	53	17	15	3	3	2	2	26	4	72	1	0	5	1	.833	0	23-27	0	1.87	1.72
2006 Oak	AL	69	0	0	55	70.2	290	64	28	26	4	3	3	2	13	3	67	4	0	4	4	.500	0	37-48	1	2.49	3.31
2007 Oak	AL	48	0	0	35	50.0	199	35	20	16	5	2	1	0	12	3	63	0	0	5	2	.714	0	16-21	5	1.84	2.88
2008 Oak	AL	63	0	0	37	70.0	287	58	29	29	6	3	3	1	27	6	69	2	0	7	5	.583	0	18-25	6	2.98	3.73
2009 Col	NL	64	0	0	52	61.2	240	43	22	21	7	3	2	0	13	4	70	0	0	4	1	.800	0	35-37	2	1.83	3.06
2010 Col	NL	44	0	0	39	47.1	187	39	21	19	5	0	1	2	11	4	45	2	1	4	4	.500	0	20-25	0	2.66	3.61
2011 Col	NL	62	0	0	47	58.1	239	62	28	25	10	3	1	1	9	1	55	0	0	1	4	.200	0	29-33	4	4.03	3.86
2012 SD	NL	40	0	0	36	39.0	144	17	8	8	2	1	1	0	11	1	47	1	0	2	1	.667	0	23-24	0	0.99	1.85
2013 SD	NL	58	0	0	52	56.2	222	44	17	17	12	0	1	0	14	1	46	4	0	2	5	.286	0	33-35	0	3.00	2.70
2014 2 Tms		61	0	0	51	59.1	229	42	9	9	4	1	0	0	14	3	57	0	0	2	2	.500	0	41-44	0	1.77	1.37
2015 LAA	AL	62	0	0	51	62.1	255	52	22	22	7	2	3	0	20	5	57	6	0	3	3	.500	0	40-45	0	2.85	3.18
2016 LAA	AL	26	0	0	21	22.1	105	31	16	16	5	0	1	0	12	2	14	0	0	3	2	.600	0	9-12	0	8.09	6.45
14 SD	NL	33	0	0	28	33.0	121	18	4	4	3	0	0	0	7	0	34	0	0	1	0	1.000	0	24-25	0	1.33	1.09
14 LAA	AL	28	0	0	23	26.1	108	24	5	5	1	1	0	0	7	3	23	0	0	1	2	.333	0	17-19	0	2.53	1.71
Postseason		10	0	0	7	12.0	54	14	9	9	2	1	1	0	6	1	8	0	0	0	3	.000	0	3-4	0	5.92	6.75
12 ML YEARS		664	0	0	523	676.0	2703	540	237	223	70	21	19	8	182	37	662	20	1	42	34	.553	0	324-376	18	2.53	2.97

Hunter Strickland

Pitches: R Bats: R Pos: RP-72   Ht: 6'4" Wt: 220 Born: 9/24/1988 Age: 28

Year Team	Lg	G	GS	CG	GF	IP	BFP	H	R	ER	HR	SH	SF	HB	TBB	IBB	SO	WP	Bk	W	L	Pct	Sh	Sv-Op	Hld	ERC	ERA
2014 SF	NL	9	0	0	5	7.0	25	5	0	0	0	0	0	0	0	0	9	0	0	1	0	1.000	0	1-1	1	1.08	0.00
2015 SF	NL	55	0	0	11	51.1	191	34	14	14	4	0	0	2	10	1	50	1	0	3	3	.500	0	0-2	20	1.72	2.45
2016 SF	NL	72	0	0	14	61.0	250	50	21	21	4	0	3	2	19	3	57	3	0	3	3	.500	0	3-8	18	2.61	3.10
Postseason		8	0	0	3	8.1	34	9	7	7	6	0	0	0	2	0	8	1	0	1	0	1.000	0	1-2	1	8.47	7.56
3 ML YEARS		136	0	0	30	119.1	466	89	35	35	8	0	3	4	29	4	116	4	0	7	6	.538	0	4-11	39	2.11	2.64

Ross Stripling

Pitches: R Bats: R Pos: SP-14; RP-8   Ht: 6'3" Wt: 210 Born: 11/23/1989 Age: 27

Year Team	Lg	G	GS	CG	GF	IP	BFP	H	R	ER	HR	SH	SF	HB	TBB	IBB	SO	WP	Bk	W	L	Pct	Sh	Sv-Op	Hld	ERC	ERA
2012 Ogden	R+	14	12	0	0	36.1	138	26	7	5	0	0	0	0	6	0	37	4	0	1	0	1.000	0	0--	-	1.40	1.24
2013 Rcuca	A+	6	6	0	0	33.2	134	24	11	11	1	1	1	0	11	0	34	2	0	2	0	1.000	0	0--	-	1.91	2.94
2013 Chatt	AA	21	16	0	1	94.0	387	91	33	29	4	4	2	0	19	1	83	4	0	6	4	.600	0	1--	-	2.75	2.78
2015 Tulsa	AA	13	13	1	0	67.1	273	61	29	29	7	1	1	0	19	0	55	4	0	3	6	.333	0	0--	-	3.20	3.88
2016 OkCity	AAA	5	4	0	0	16.2	71	20	7	7	2	1	1	0	2	0	17	1	0	0	2	.000	0	0--	-	4.18	3.78
2016 LAD	NL	22	14	0	4	100.0	419	96	46	44	10	3	1	1	30	3	74	6	0	5	9	.357	0	0-0	0	3.46	3.96

Marcus Stroman

Pitches: R Bats: R Pos: SP-32 **Ht: 5'8" Wt: 180 Born: 5/1/1991 Age: 26**

Year	Team	Lg	G	GS	CG	GF	IP	BFP	H	R	ER	HR	SH	SF	HB	TBB	IBB	SO	WP	Bk	W	L	Pct	Sh	Sv-Op	Hld	ERC	ERA
2014	Tor	AL	26	20	1	1	130.2	534	125	56	53	7	0	2	3	28	1	111	9	1	11	6	.647	1	1-1	0	2.93	3.65
2015	Tor	AL	4	4	0	0	27.0	103	20	5	5	2	0	0	1	6	0	18	2	1	4	0	1.000	0	0-0	0	2.16	1.67
2016	Tor	AL	32	32	0	0	204.0	855	209	104	99	21	2	2	4	54	0	166	9	1	9	10	.474	0	0-0	0	3.81	4.37
	Postseason		3	3	0	0	19.1	84	22	10	9	1	0	1	0	4	0	10	1	0	1	0	1.000	0	0-0	0	3.66	4.19
3 ML YEARS			62	56	1	1	361.2	1492	354	165	157	30	2	4	8	88	1	295	20	3	24	16	.600	1	1-1	0	3.36	3.91

Pedro Strop

Pitches: R Bats: R Pos: RP-54 STROPE **Ht: 6'1" Wt: 220 Born: 6/13/1985 Age: 32**

Year	Team	Lg	G	GS	CG	GF	IP	BFP	H	R	ER	HR	SH	SF	HB	TBB	IBB	SO	WP	Bk	W	L	Pct	Sh	Sv-Op	Hld	ERC	ERA
2009	Tex	AL	7	0	0	3	7.0	30	6	6	6	0	0	0	0	4	0	9	0	0	0	0	-	0	0-0	0	3.27	7.71
2010	Tex	AL	15	0	0	5	10.2	60	17	12	12	2	1	0	1	11	0	11	5	1	0	0	-	0	0-0	1	11.92	10.13
2011	2 Tms	AL	23	0	0	6	22.0	90	15	5	5	0	2	1	1	10	0	21	2	2	2	1	.667	0	0-2	4	2.15	2.05
2012	Bal	AL	70	0	0	17	66.1	283	52	18	18	2	1	1	4	37	2	58	5	0	5	2	.714	0	3-10	24	3.22	2.44
2013	2 Tms		66	0	0	22	57.1	254	45	30	29	5	7	0	6	26	2	66	8	1	2	5	.286	0	1-4	17	3.21	4.55
2014	ChC	NL	65	0	0	13	61.0	244	40	19	15	2	0	1	4	25	3	71	6	1	2	4	.333	0	2-6	21	2.12	2.21
2015	ChC	NL	76	0	0	12	68.0	270	39	24	22	5	1	3	4	29	6	81	6	0	2	6	.250	0	3-5	28	1.94	2.91
2016	ChC	NL	54	0	0	8	47.1	187	27	16	15	4	0	2	4	15	1	60	7	0	2	2	.500	0	0-4	21	1.78	2.85
11	Tex	AL	11	0	0	4	9.2	44	7	4	4	0	1	1	1	7	0	9	2	2	0	1	.000	0	0-1	0	3.34	3.72
11	Bal	AL	12	0	0	2	12.1	46	8	1	1	0	1	0	0	3	0	12	0	0	2	0	1.000	0	0-1	4	1.39	0.73
13	Bal	AL	29	0	0	15	22.1	111	23	19	18	4	4	0	2	15	2	24	5	1	0	3	.000	0	0-3	3	5.81	7.25
13	Bal	AL	37	0	0	7	35.0	143	22	11	11	1	3	0	4	11	0	42	3	0	2	2	.500	0	1-1	14	1.80	2.83
	Postseason		8	0	0	2	7.1	28	3	1	1	1	1	0	1	2	0	8	0	0	1	0	1.000	0	0-0	2	1.47	1.23
8 ML YEARS			376	0	0	86	339.2	1418	241	130	122	20	12	8	24	157	14	377	39	5	15	20	.429	0	9-31	116	2.69	3.23

Drew Stubbs

Bats: R Throws: R Pos: LF-19;RF-19;PR-16;CF-15;PH-9;DH-2 **Ht: 6'4" Wt: 205 Born: 10/4/1984 Age: 32**

Year	Team	Lg	G	AB	H	2B	3B	HR	(Hm	Rd)	TB	R	RBI	RC	TBB	IBB	SO	HBP	SH	SF	SB	CS	GDP	Avg	OBP	Slg	OPS
2016	RdRck*	AAA	12	39	9	4	0	2	(-	-)	19	10	10	8	10	0	8	0	0	2	2	1	2	.231	.373	.487	.860
2009	Cin	NL	42	180	48	5	1	8	(7	1)	79	27	17	22	15	0	49	0	1	0	10	4	1	.267	.323	.439	.762
2010	Cin	NL	150	514	131	19	6	22	(13	9)	228	91	77	74	55	2	168	5	3	6	30	6	6	.255	.329	.444	.773
2011	Cin	NL	158	604	147	22	3	15	(9	6)	220	92	44	66	63	1	205	7	6	1	40	10	2	.243	.321	.364	.686
2012	Cin	NL	136	493	105	13	2	14	(6	8)	164	75	40	45	42	0	166	2	6	1	30	7	2	.213	.277	.333	.610
2013	Cle		146	430	100	21	2	10	(4	6)	155	59	45	50	44	1	141	2	2	3	17	2	3	.233	.305	.360	.665
2014	Col	NL	132	388	112	22	4	15	(12	3)	187	67	43	58	30	1	136	1	2	3	20	3	4	.289	.339	.482	.821
2015	2 Tms		78	123	24	4	2	5	(4	1)	47	20	10	13	14	1	60	1	2	1	5	1	1	.195	.283	.382	.665
2016	3 Tms		59	80	18	0	0	3	(2	1)	27	13	7	10	12	0	38	1	0	1	9	1	1	.225	.330	.338	.667
15	Col	NL	51	102	22	3	2	5	(4	1)	44	14	10	12	9	1	50	1	2	0	2	1	1	.216	.286	.431	.717
15	Tex	AL	27	21	2	1	0	0	(0	0)	3	6	0	1	5	0	10	0	0	1	3	0	0	.095	.269	.143	.412
16	Atl	NL	20	38	9	0	0	1	(1	0)	12	6	3	4	4	0	20	0	0	0	4	0	1	.237	.310	.316	.625
16	Tex	AL	19	20	6	0	0	2	(1	1)	12	6	3	3	4	0	7	0	0	1	4	0	0	.300	.400	.600	1.000
16	Bal	AL	20	22	3	0	0	0	(0	0)	3	1	1	3	4	0	11	1	0	0	1	1	0	.136	.296	.136	.433
	Postseason		12	29	5	1	1	0	(0	0)	8	4	1	1	2	0	8	0	0	0	0	0	0	.172	.226	.276	.502
8 ML YEARS			901	2812	685	106	20	92	(57	35)	1107	444	283	338	275	6	963	19	22	15	161	34	20	.244	.314	.394	.707

Daniel Stumpf

Pitches: L Bats: L Pos: RP-7 **Ht: 6'2" Wt: 200 Born: 1/4/1991 Age: 26**

Year	Team	Lg	G	GS	CG	GF	IP	BFP	H	R	ER	HR	SH	SF	HB	TBB	IBB	SO	WP	Bk	W	L	Pct	Sh	Sv-Op	Hld	ERC	ERA
2012	Burlgtn	R+	19	0	0	10	29.0	115	20	6	5	1	1	1	0	8	0	34	3	0	2	1	.667	0	5--	-	1.66	1.55
2013	Lxngtn	A	25	25	4	0	137.2	554	103	58	47	10	1	4	7	50	0	117	6	0	10	10	.500	1	0--	-	2.68	3.07
2014	Wilmg	A+	32	8	0	16	74.0	316	82	34	31	1	1	2	1	19	0	79	5	0	3	8	.273	0	2--	-	3.57	3.77
2015	NWArk	AA	42	1	0	15	70.2	296	55	31	28	6	2	2	2	31	0	76	6	0	5	4	.556	0	3--	-	3.02	3.57
2016	NWArk	AA	14	0	0	6	21.1	85	14	5	5	0	4	0	2	4	0	26	1	0	2	0	1.000	0	1--	-	1.41	2.11
2016	Phi	NL	7	0	0	3	5.0	25	9	6	6	1	0	0	0	2	0	2	1	0	0	0	-	0	0-0	1	10.22	10.80

Tyler Sturdevant

Pitches: R Bats: R Pos: RP-16 **Ht: 6'0" Wt: 185 Born: 12/20/1985 Age: 31**

Year	Team	Lg	G	GS	CG	GF	IP	BFP	H	R	ER	HR	SH	SF	HB	TBB	IBB	SO	WP	Bk	W	L	Pct	Sh	Sv-Op	Hld	ERC	ERA
2012	Carlina	A+	5	0	0	2	7.0	23	2	0	0	0	0	0	0	2	0	3	0	0	1	0	1.000	0	0--	-	0.56	0.00
2012	Akron	AA	6	0	0	1	9.2	42	10	5	4	1	0	1	2	3	0	10	0	0	0	0	-	0	0--	-	4.90	3.72
2012	Clmbs	AAA	18	0	0	12	20.0	94	29	14	14	5	2	0	0	9	1	15	0	0	0	3	.000	0	0--	-	8.37	6.30
2014	Akron	AA	24	0	0	13	31.0	117	19	5	5	1	4	0	2	9	1	30	2	0	1	1	.500	0	7--	-	1.47	1.45
2014	Clmbs	AAA	22	0	0	7	26.2	111	26	13	12	3	1	1	0	8	0	24	0	0	1	1	.500	0	1--	-	3.66	4.05
2015	Clmbs	AAA	26	0	0	11	31.1	124	24	11	11	5	0	0	2	10	0	30	1	0	1	1	.500	0	3--	-	3.25	3.16
2016	Drham	AAA	34	0	0	20	39.1	165	39	16	16	6	3	2	2	12	2	49	2	0	3	2	.600	0	4--	-	4.21	3.66
2016	TB	AL	16	0	0	6	18.1	75	18	8	8	1	2	0	1	6	1	14	0	0	0	1	.000	0	0-0	3	3.68	3.93

Albert Suarez

Pitches: R Bats: R Pos: SP-12; RP-10   SWAH-rez   Ht: 6'3" Wt: 235 Born: 10/8/1989 Age: 27

			HOW MUCH HE PITCHED						WHAT HE GAVE UP											THE RESULTS						
Year	Team	Lg	G	GS	CG	GF	IP	BFP	H	R	ER	HR	SH	SF	HB	TBB	IBB	SO	WP	Bk	W	L	Pct	Sh	Sv-Op	Hld	ERC	ERA
2012	Charltt	A+	25	25	1	0	125.2	540	132	74	57	11	1	6	12	30	1	62	3	0	5	9	.357	1	0- -	-	3.99	4.08
2014	Mont	AA	11	11	0	0	56.0	249	67	34	27	4	3	3	2	19	2	32	1	0	3	6	.333	0	0- -	-	4.85	4.34
2015	Ark	AA	27	27	1	0	163.0	652	142	64	54	14	2	1	1	40	0	121	4	0	11	9	.550	0	0- -	-	2.78	2.98
2016	Scrmto	AAA	9	7	0	0	45.2	195	46	26	22	3	5	4	2	14	0	39	1	0	4	3	.571	0	0- -	-	3.68	4.34
2016	SF	NL	22	12	0	2	84.0	355	84	42	40	11	4	3	4	26	5	54	1	0	3	5	.375	0	0-0	1	4.07	4.29

Eugenio Suarez

ay-yoo-HAY-nee-oh SWAH-rez

Bats: R Throws: R Pos: 3B-151;PH-6;SS-2;DH-1   Ht: 5'11" Wt: 205 Born: 7/18/1991 Age: 25

						BATTING															RUNNING			AVERAGES			
Year	Team	Lg	G	AB	H	2B	3B	HR	(Hm	Rd)	TB	R	RBI	RC	TBB	IBB	SO	HBP	SH	SF	SB	CS	GDP	Avg	OBP	Slg	OPS
2014	Det	AL	85	244	59	9	1	4	(2	2)	82	33	23	30	22	1	67	5	5	1	3	2	3	.242	.316	.336	.652
2015	Cin	NL	97	372	104	19	2	13	(4	9)	166	42	48	49	17	0	94	3	4	2	4	1	7	.280	.315	.446	.761
2016	Cin	NL	159	565	140	25	2	21	(10	11)	232	78	70	77	51	0	155	8	0	3	11	5	10	.248	.317	.411	.728
	Postseason		1	1	0	0	0	0	(0	0)	0	0	0	0	0	0	0	0	0	0	0	0	0	.000	.000	.000	.000
	3 ML YEARS		341	1181	303	53	5	38	(16	22)	480	153	141	156	90	1	316	16	9	6	18	8	20	.257	.316	.406	.723

Jesus Sucre

SUE-cray

Bats: R Throws: R Pos: C-9   Ht: 6'0" Wt: 225 Born: 4/30/1988 Age: 29

						BATTING															RUNNING			AVERAGES			
Year	Team	Lg	G	AB	H	2B	3B	HR	(Hm	Rd)	TB	R	RBI	RC	TBB	IBB	SO	HBP	SH	SF	SB	CS	GDP	Avg	OBP	Slg	OPS
2016	Tacom*	AAA	29	99	27	4	1	0	(-	-)	33	7	11	9	3	0	15	1	1	0	0	1	2	.273	.301	.333	.634
2013	Sea	AL	8	26	5	0	0	0	(0	0)	5	1	3	1	2	0	1	0	0	1	0	0	2	.192	.241	.192	.434
2014	Sea	AL	21	61	13	2	0	0	(0	0)	15	4	5	6	0	0	17	0	3	0	0	0	0	.213	.213	.246	.459
2015	Sea	AL	52	127	20	6	0	1	(1	0)	29	9	7	1	6	0	21	0	9	0	0	0	6	.157	.195	.228	.424
2016	Sea	AL	9	25	12	2	0	1	(0	1)	17	4	5	9	2	0	5	2	0	0	0	0	1	.480	.552	.680	1.232
	4 ML YEARS		90	239	50	10	0	2	(1	1)	66	18	20	17	10	0	44	2	12	1	0	0	9	.209	.246	.276	.522

Eric Surkamp

Pitches: L Bats: L Pos: SP-9   SIR-camp   Ht: 6'5" Wt: 220 Born: 7/16/1987 Age: 29

					HOW MUCH HE PITCHED							WHAT HE GAVE UP										THE RESULTS						
Year	Team	Lg	G	GS	CG	GF	IP	BFP	H	R	ER	HR	SH	SF	HB	TBB	IBB	SO	WP	Bk	W	L	Pct	Sh	Sv-Op	Hld	ERC	ERA
2016	Nashv*	AAA	5	5	0	0	29.1	120	22	12	10	3	0	1	2	10	0	34	1	0	3	1	.750	0	0- -	-	2.80	3.07
2011	SF	NL	6	6	0	0	26.2	126	32	18	17	1	2	2	2	17	1	13	0	0	2	2	.500	0	0-0	0	6.03	5.74
2013	SF	NL	1	1	0	0	2.2	18	9	7	7	2	0	0	0	0	0	0	0	0	0	1	.000	0	0-0	0	32.56	23.63
2014	CWS	AL	35	0	0	2	24.1	107	22	14	13	3	3	0	1	13	3	20	0	0	2	0	1.000	0	0-0	7	4.18	4.81
2015	LAD	NL	1	0	0	0	3.1	16	4	4	4	2	0	0	2	1	0	4	0	0	0	0	-	0	0-0	0	12.47	10.80
2016	Oak	AL	9	9	0	0	38.2	197	55	32	30	8	0	3	5	21	2	22	1	0	0	5	.000	0	0-0	0	8.48	6.98
	5 ML YEARS		52	16	0	2	95.2	464	122	75	71	16	5	5	12	52	6	59	1	0	4	8	.333	0	0-0	7	7.28	6.68

Andrew Susac

Bats: R Throws: R Pos: C-6;PH-3   SOO-sack   Ht: 6'1" Wt: 215 Born: 3/22/1990 Age: 27

						BATTING															RUNNING			AVERAGES			
Year	Team	Lg	G	AB	H	2B	3B	HR	(Hm	Rd)	TB	R	RBI	RC	TBB	IBB	SO	HBP	SH	SF	SB	CS	GDP	Avg	OBP	Slg	OPS
2016	Scrmto*	AAA	58	209	57	12	1	8	(-	-)	95	28	36	34	24	0	45	1	0	5	0	0	7	.273	.343	.455	.798
2016	ColSpr*	AAA	11	40	5	1	0	0	(-	-)	6	2	3	0	2	1	16	0	0	1	0	0	1	.125	.163	.150	.313
2014	SF	NL	35	88	24	8	0	3	(1	2)	41	13	19	16	7	0	28	0	0	0	0	0	0	.273	.326	.466	.792
2015	SF	NL	52	133	29	7	2	3	(2	1)	49	14	14	13	14	0	43	1	0	0	0	0	2	.218	.297	.368	.666
2016	Mil	NL	9	17	4	1	0	1	(0	1)	8	3	2	2	2	0	5	0	0	0	0	0	0	.235	.316	.471	.786
	Postseason		4	4	1	0	0	0	(0	0)	1	0	0	1	0	0	1	0	0	0	0	0	0	.250	.250	.250	.500
	3 ML YEARS		96	238	57	16	2	7	(3	4)	98	30	35	31	23	0	76	1	0	0	0	0	2	.239	.309	.412	.721

Brent Suter

Pitches: L Bats: L Pos: RP-12; SP-2   SOO-ter   Ht: 6'5" Wt: 195 Born: 8/29/1989 Age: 27

					HOW MUCH HE PITCHED							WHAT HE GAVE UP										THE RESULTS						
Year	Team	Lg	G	GS	CG	GF	IP	BFP	H	R	ER	HR	SH	SF	HB	TBB	IBB	SO	WP	Bk	W	L	Pct	Sh	Sv-Op	Hld	ERC	ERA
2012	2 Tms	Low	14	2	0	4	52.1	221	60	26	21	4	2	3	0	11	1	50	3	0	4	2	.667	0	2- -	-	3.99	3.61
2013	2 Tms	Low	24	23	1	1	139.0	584	139	61	53	11	4	2	3	41	0	113	1	1	7	10	.412	0	0- -	-	3.64	3.43
2014	Hntsvl	AA	28	27	1	0	152.1	630	144	72	67	14	5	0	7	53	1	118	6	0	10	10	.500	0	0- -	-	3.80	3.96
2015	Biloxi	AA	20	11	0	0	83.0	337	71	20	18	2	6	2	5	33	1	64	0	0	5	3	.625	0	0- -	-	3.12	1.95
2015	ColSpr	AAA	6	6	0	0	35.1	141	35	15	13	4	2	3	0	6	0	19	1	0	3	1	.750	0	0- -	-	3.31	3.31
2016	ColSpr	AAA	26	15	0	2	110.2	453	129	45	43	5	5	3	3	14	0	75	0	0	6	6	.500	0	2- -	-	3.79	3.50
2016	Mil	NL	14	2	0	4	21.2	91	25	8	8	3	1	0	1	5	0	15	1	0	2	2	.500	0	0-0	2	4.90	3.32

Ichiro Suzuki

EE-chee-row soo-ZOO-kee

Bats: L **Throws:** R **Pos:** PH-70;RF-54;LF-14;CF-14;DH-3

Ht: 5'11" **Wt:** 175 **Born:** 10/22/1973 **Age:** 43

Year Team	Lg	G	AB	H	2B	3B	HR	(Hm	Rd)	TB	R	RBI	RC	TBB	IBB	SO	HBP	SH	SF	SB	CS	GDP	Avg	OBP	Slg	OPS
2001 Sea	AL	157	**692**	242	34	8	8	(5	3)	316	127	69	124	30	10	53	8	4	4	**56**	14	3	**.350**	.381	.457	.838
2002 Sea	AL	157	647	208	27	8	8	(4	4)	275	111	51	110	68	**27**	62	5	3	5	31	**15**	8	.321	.388	.425	.813
2003 Sea	AL	159	679	212	29	8	13	(8	5)	296	111	62	107	36	7	69	6	3	1	34	8	3	.312	.352	.436	.788
2004 Sea	AL	161	**704**	262	24	5	8	(4	4)	320	101	60	125	49	**19**	63	4	2	3	36	11	6	**.372**	.414	.455	.869
2005 Sea	AL	**162**	679	206	21	12	15	(8	7)	296	111	68	109	48	23	66	4	2	6	33	8	5	.303	.350	.436	.786
2006 Sea	AL	161	**695**	224	20	9	9	(6	3)	289	110	49	107	49	16	71	5	1	2	45	2	2	.322	.370	.416	.786
2007 Sea	AL	161	678	238	22	7	6	(3	3)	292	111	68	128	49	13	77	3	4	2	37	8	7	.351	.396	.431	.827
2008 Sea	AL	162	686	213	20	7	6	(3	3)	265	103	42	100	51	12	65	5	3	4	43	4	8	.310	.361	.386	.747
2009 Sea	AL	146	639	**225**	31	4	11	(6	5)	297	88	46	111	32	**15**	71	4	2	1	26	9	1	.352	.386	.465	.851
2010 Sea	AL	**162**	680	214	30	3	6	(1	5)	268	74	43	96	45	13	86	3	3	1	42	9	3	.315	.359	.394	.754
2011 Sea	AL	161	**677**	184	22	3	5	(4	1)	227	80	47	80	39	13	69	0	1	4	40	7	11	.272	.310	.335	.645
2012 2 Tms	AL	**162**	629	178	28	6	9	(6	3)	245	77	55	63	22	5	61	2	5	5	29	7	12	.283	.307	.390	.696
2013 NYY	AL	150	520	136	15	3	7	(5	2)	178	57	35	56	26	4	63	1	6	2	20	6	4	.262	.297	.342	.639
2014 NYY	AL	143	359	102	13	2	1	(1	0)	122	42	22	39	21	1	68	1	2	2	15	3	3	.284	.324	.340	.664
2015 Mia	NL	153	398	91	5	6	1	(1	0)	111	45	21	30	31	1	51	0	5	4	11	5	8	.229	.282	.279	.561
2016 Mia	NL	143	327	95	15	5	1	(1	0)	123	48	22	44	30	1	42	3	3	2	10	2	4	.291	.354	.376	.730
12 Sea	AL	95	402	105	15	5	4	(1	3)	142	49	28	33	17	4	40	0	0	4	15	2	10	.261	.288	.353	.642
12 NYY	AL	67	227	73	13	1	5	(5	0)	103	28	27	30	5	1	21	2	5	1	14	5	2	.322	.340	.454	.794
Postseason		19	78	27	4	0	1	(1	0)	34	10	8	11	7	2	9	0	1	0	4	3	0	.346	.400	.436	.836
16 ML YEARS		2500	9689	3030	356	96	114	(66	48)	3920	1396	760	1429	626	180	1037	54	49	48	508	116	90	.313	.356	.405	.761

Kurt Suzuki

Bats: R **Throws:** R **Pos:** C-99;PH-7;DH-4

Ht: 5'11" **Wt:** 205 **Born:** 10/4/1983 **Age:** 33

Year Team	Lg	G	AB	H	2B	3B	HR	(Hm	Rd)	TB	R	RBI	RC	TBB	IBB	SO	HBP	SH	SF	SB	CS	GDP	Avg	OBP	Slg	OPS
2007 Oak	AL	68	213	53	13	0	7	(4	3)	87	27	39	33	24	0	39	3	3	5	0	0	4	.249	.327	.408	.735
2008 Oak	AL	148	530	148	25	1	7	(5	2)	196	54	42	66	44	2	69	11	2	1	2	3	20	.279	.346	.370	.716
2009 Oak	AL	147	570	156	37	1	15	(8	7)	240	74	88	77	28	0	59	8	1	7	8	2	14	.274	.313	.421	.734
2010 Oak	AL	131	495	120	18	2	13	(8	5)	181	55	71	54	33	3	49	12	0	4	3	2	22	.242	.303	.366	.669
2011 Oak	AL	134	460	109	26	0	14	(8	6)	177	54	44	42	38	1	64	7	3	7	2	2	14	.237	.301	.385	.686
2012 2 Tms		118	408	96	20	0	6	(3	3)	134	36	43	39	20	3	73	5	4	5	2	0	5	.235	.276	.328	.605
2013		94	285	66	13	1	5	(2	3)	96	25	32	34	22	6	35	3	2	4	2	0	2	.232	.290	.337	.627
2014 Min	AL	131	452	130	34	0	3	(1	2)	173	37	61	65	34	0	46	9	1	7	0	1	9	.288	.345	.383	.727
2015 Min	AL	131	433	104	17	0	5	(3	2)	136	36	50	46	29	4	59	7	6	4	0	0	14	.240	.296	.314	.610
2016 Min	AL	106	345	89	24	1	8	(4	4)	139	34	49	45	18	0	48	5	1	4	0	0	9	.258	.301	.403	.704
12 Oak	AL	75	262	57	15	0	1	(1	0)	75	19	18	16	9	0	53	3	2	2	1	0	3	.218	.250	.286	.536
12 Was	NL	43	146	39	5	0	5	(2	3)	59	17	25	23	11	3	20	2	2	3	1	0	2	.267	.321	.404	.725
13 Was	NL	79	252	56	11	1	3	(0	3)	78	19	25	26	20	6	32	3	2	4	2	0	2	.222	.283	.310	.593
13 Oak	AL	15	33	10	2	0	2	(2	0)	18	6	7	8	2	0	3	0	0	0	0	0	0	.303	.343	.545	.888
Postseason		5	17	4	0	0	0	(0	0)	4	0	2	2	2	0	4	0	0	0	0	0	0	.235	.316	.235	.551
10 ML YEARS		1208	4191	1071	227	6	83	(46	37)	1559	432	519	501	290	19	541	70	23	48	19	10	113	.256	.311	.372	.683

Dansby Swanson

Bats: R **Throws:** R **Pos:** SS-37;PH-1

Ht: 6'1" **Wt:** 190 **Born:** 2/11/1994 **Age:** 23

Year Team	Lg	G	AB	H	2B	3B	HR	(Hm	Rd)	TB	R	RBI	RC	TBB	IBB	SO	HBP	SH	SF	SB	CS	GDP	Avg	OBP	Slg	OPS
2015 Hlsbro	A-	22	83	24	7	3	1	(-	-)	40	19	11	16	14	2	14	1	0	1	0	0	0	.289	.394	.482	.876
2016 Carlina	A+	21	78	26	12	0	1	(-	-)	41	14	10	19	15	2	13	0	0	0	7	1	1	.333	.441	.526	.967
2016 Missi	AA	84	333	87	13	5	8	(-	-)	134	54	45	49	35	2	71	7	0	2	7	2	6	.261	.342	.402	.745
2016 Atl	NL	38	129	39	7	1	3	(1	2)	57	20	17	17	13	5	34	0	1	2	3	0	2	.302	.361	.442	.803

Anthony Swarzak

Pitches: R **Bats:** R **Pos:** RP-26

SWORE-zack

Ht: 6'4" **Wt:** 215 **Born:** 9/10/1985 **Age:** 31

Year Team	Lg	G	GS	CG	GF	IP	BFP	H	R	ER	HR	SH	SF	HB	TBB	IBB	SO	WP	Bk	W	L	Pct	Sh	Sv-Op	Hld	ERC	ERA
2016 S-WB*	AAA	15	6	1	9	46.2	188	47	20	20	4	0	1	0	8	0	43	1	0	1	4	.200	0	7- -	-	3.21	3.86
2009 Min	AL	12	12	0	0	59.0	268	76	43	41	12	1	1	2	20	0	34	0	0	3	7	.300	0	0-0	0	6.50	6.25
2011 Min	AL	27	11	0	2	102.0	441	111	53	49	9	2	3	6	26	1	55	3	1	4	7	.364	0	0-0	0	4.11	4.32
2012 Min	AL	44	5	0	9	96.2	413	106	57	54	15	3	6	0	31	8	62	3	0	3	6	.333	0	0-1	1	4.63	5.03
2013 Min	AL	48	0	0	8	96.0	387	89	33	31	7	2	5	1	22	1	69	1	0	3	2	.600	0	0-2	3	2.94	2.91
2014 Min	AL	50	4	0	11	86.0	378	100	48	44	5	1	2	0	28	5	47	0	2	3	2	.600	0	0-1	3	4.29	4.60
2015 Cle	AL	10	0	0	3	13.1	61	18	9	5	1	0	0	0	4	1	13	0	0	0	0	-	0	0-0	0	5.34	3.38
2016 NYY	AL	26	0	0	6	31.0	124	28	19	19	10	0	1	1	7	0	31	1	0	1	2	.333	0	0-1	1	4.51	5.52
7 ML YEARS		217	32	0	39	484.0	2072	528	262	243	59	9	18	10	138	16	311	8	3	17	26	.395	0	0-5	8	4.34	4.52

Blake Swihart

Bats: B **Throws:** R **Pos:** LF-13;C-6   SWY-hart   **Ht:** 6'1" **Wt:** 200 **Born:** 4/3/1992 **Age:** 25

Year	Team	Lg	G	AB	H	2B	3B	HR	(Hm	Rd)	TB	R	RBI	RC	TBB	IBB	SO	HBP	SH	SF	SB	CS	GDP	Avg	OBP	Slg	OPS
2012	Grnvlle	A	92	344	90	17	4	7	(-	-)	136	44	53	44	26	0	68	0	0	8	6	2	5	.262	.307	.395	.702
2013	Salem	A+	103	376	112	29	7	2	(-	-)	161	45	42	60	41	2	63	1	1	3	7	8	9	.298	.366	.428	.794
2014	Portlnd	AA	92	347	104	23	3	12	(-	-)	169	47	55	61	29	1	65	1	0	3	7	1	8	.300	.353	.487	.840
2014	Pwtckt	AAA	18	69	18	3	1	1	(-	-)	26	6	9	7	2	0	15	0	0	0	1	0	1	.261	.282	.377	.659
2015	Pwtckt	AAA	20	74	23	3	0	0	(-	-)	26	7	11	9	6	0	14	0	0	0	1	1	2	.311	.363	.351	.714
2016	Pwtckt	AAA	29	103	25	4	0	1	(-	-)	32	13	8	12	17	1	17	0	0	2	2	1	5	.243	.344	.311	.655
2015	Bos	AL	84	288	79	17	1	5	(2	3)	113	47	31	34	18	0	77	1	2	0	4	2	8	.274	.319	.392	.712
2016	Bos	AL	19	62	16	0	3	0	(0	0)	22	9	5	8	11	0	17	0	0	1	0	1	0	.258	.365	.355	.720
	2 ML YEARS		103	350	95	17	4	5	(2	3)	135	56	36	42	29	0	94	1	2	1	4	3	8	.271	.328	.386	.714

Noah Syndergaard

Pitches: R **Bats:** L **Pos:** SP-30; RP-1   sin-DER-gard   **Ht:** 6'6" **Wt:** 240 **Born:** 8/29/1992 **Age:** 24

			HOW MUCH HE PITCHED					WHAT HE GAVE UP									THE RESULTS						
Year	Team	Lg	G	GS	CG	GF	IP	BFP	H	R	ER	HR	SH	SF	HB	TBB	IBB	SO	WP	Bk	W	L	Pct	Sh	Sv-Op	Hld	ERC	ERA
2012	Lnsng	A	27	19	0	0	103.2	420	81	41	30	3	0	4	3	31	0	122	1	0	8	5	.615	0	1- -	-	2.22	2.60
2013	Stlcui	A+	12	12	0	0	63.2	258	61	25	22	3	1	1	1	16	0	64	4	1	3	3	.500	0	0- -	-	3.07	3.11
2013	Bnghtn	AA	11	11	0	0	54.0	214	46	23	18	8	0	0	0	12	0	69	2	0	6	1	.857	0	0- -	-	2.95	3.00
2014	LsVgs	AAA	26	26	0	0	133.0	583	154	77	68	11	4	4	6	43	1	145	6	0	9	7	.563	0	0- -	-	4.76	4.60
2015	LsVgs	AAA	5	5	1	0	29.2	113	20	7	6	2	1	0	0	8	0	34	1	0	3	0	1.000	1	0- -	-	1.82	1.82
2015	NYM	NL	24	24	0	0	150.0	603	126	60	54	19	5	3	3	31	2	166	6	0	9	7	.563	0	0-0	0	2.70	3.24
2016	NYM	NL	31	30	0	0	183.2	744	168	61	53	11	3	4	2	43	2	218	10	1	14	9	.609	0	0-0	1	2.79	2.60
	Postseason		4	3	0	0	19.0	78	15	7	7	0	1	0	0	8	1	26	1	0	2	1	.667	0	0-0	1	2.33	3.32
	2 ML YEARS		55	54	0	0	333.2	1347	294	121	107	30	8	7	5	74	4	384	16	1	23	16	.590	0	0-0	1	2.75	2.89

Matt Szczur

Bats: R **Throws:** R **Pos:** LF-50;PH-49;CF-15;RF-15;PR-9   SEE-zur   **Ht:** 6'0" **Wt:** 200 **Born:** 7/20/1989 **Age:** 27

			BATTING																	RUNNING			AVERAGES			
Year	Team	Lg	G	AB	H	2B	3B	HR	(Hm	Rd)	TB	R	RBI	RC	TBB	IBB	SO	HBP	SH	SF	SB	CS	GDP	Avg	OBP	Slg	OPS
2014	ChC	NL	33	62	14	2	0	2	(1	1)	22	6	5	7	4	0	11	0	0	0	0	0	1	.226	.273	.355	.628
2015	ChC	NL	47	72	16	5	0	1	(1	0)	24	5	8	6	6	0	15	0	1	1	2	0	1	.222	.278	.333	.612
2016	ChC	NL	107	185	48	9	1	5	(4	1)	74	30	24	20	13	2	39	1	1	0	2	4	2	.259	.312	.400	.712
	3 ML YEARS		187	319	78	16	1	8	(6	2)	120	41	37	33	23	2	65	1	2	1	4	4	4	.245	.297	.376	.673

Jameson Taillon

Pitches: R **Bats:** R **Pos:** SP-18   TIE-yohn   **Ht:** 6'5" **Wt:** 240 **Born:** 11/18/1991 **Age:** 25

			HOW MUCH HE PITCHED					WHAT HE GAVE UP									THE RESULTS						
Year	Team	Lg	G	GS	CG	GF	IP	BFP	H	R	ER	HR	SH	SF	HB	TBB	IBB	SO	WP	Bk	W	L	Pct	Sh	Sv-Op	Hld	ERC	ERA
2012	Bradtn	A+	23	23	2	0	125.0	522	109	57	53	10	4	1	6	37	0	98	14	0	6	8	.429	0	0- -	-	3.01	3.82
2013	Altna	AA	20	19	0	0	110.1	478	112	54	45	8	0	2	5	36	0	106	6	0	4	7	.364	0	0- -	-	3.82	3.67
2013	Indy	AAA	6	6	0	0	37.0	162	31	16	16	1	2	1	4	16	3	37	3	0	1	3	.250	0	0- -	-	3.01	3.89
2016	Indy	AAA	10	10	0	0	61.2	236	44	14	14	2	2	3	1	6	0	61	1	0	4	2	.667	0	0- -	-	1.37	2.04
2016	Pit	NL	18	18	0	0	104.0	418	99	40	39	13	4	1	3	17	1	85	1	2	5	4	.556	0	0-0	0	3.21	3.38

Masahiro Tanaka

Pitches: R **Bats:** R **Pos:** SP-31   mah-sah-HEE-roh tuh-NAH-kah   **Ht:** 6'3" **Wt:** 215 **Born:** 11/1/1988 **Age:** 28

			HOW MUCH HE PITCHED					WHAT HE GAVE UP									THE RESULTS						
Year	Team	Lg	G	GS	CG	GF	IP	BFP	H	R	ER	HR	SH	SF	HB	TBB	IBB	SO	WP	Bk	W	L	Pct	Sh	Sv-Op	Hld	ERC	ERA
2014	NYY	AL	20	20	3	0	136.1	542	123	47	42	15	2	3	4	21	0	141	4	0	13	5	.722	1	0-0	0	2.83	2.77
2015	NYY	AL	24	24	1	0	154.0	609	126	66	60	25	1	8	1	27	0	139	4	0	12	7	.632	0	0-0	0	2.65	3.51
2016	NYY	AL	31	31	0	0	199.2	805	179	75	68	22	4	3	3	36	0	165	7	0	14	4	.778	0	0-0	0	2.80	3.07
	Postseason		1	1	0	0	5.0	21	4	2	2	2	0	0	0	3	0	3	0	0	0	1	.000	0	0-0	0	6.06	3.60
	3 ML YEARS		75	75	4	0	490.0	1956	428	188	170	62	7	14	8	84	0	445	15	0	39	16	.709	1	0-0	0	2.77	3.12

Raimel Tapia

Bats: L **Throws:** L **Pos:** PH-11;CF-9;LF-2;RF-1   rye-MELL   **Ht:** 6'2" **Wt:** 160 **Born:** 2/4/1994 **Age:** 23

			BATTING																	RUNNING			AVERAGES			
Year	Team	Lg	G	AB	H	2B	3B	HR	(Hm	Rd)	TB	R	RBI	RC	TBB	IBB	SO	HBP	SH	SF	SB	CS	GDP	Avg	OBP	Slg	OPS
2013	GdJunc	R+	66	258	92	20	6	7	(-	-)	145	53	47	54	15	2	31	5	5	3	10	9	4	.357	.399	.562	.961
2014	Ashvll	A	122	481	157	32	1	9	(-	-)	218	93	72	85	35	2	90	11	8	4	33	16	5	.326	.382	.453	.836
2015	Mdest	A+	131	544	166	34	9	12	(-	-)	254	74	71	87	24	3	105	5	7	13	26	10	6	.305	.333	.467	.800
2016	Hrtfrd	AA	104	424	137	20	5	8	(-	-)	191	79	34	68	25	2	49	3	2	3	17	14	7	.323	.363	.450	.813
2016	Albq	AAA	24	104	36	5	5	0	(-	-)	51	14	14	18	2	0	12	1	0	3	6	3	2	.346	.355	.490	.845
2016	Col	NL	22	38	10	0	0	0	(0	0)	10	4	3	5	2	0	11	0	0	1	3	0	0	.263	.293	.263	.556

Chris Taylor

Bats: R **Throws:** R **Pos:** PH-15;3B-10;2B-7;SS-6;DH-1;PR-1   **Ht:** 6'1" **Wt:** 195 **Born:** 8/29/1990 **Age:** 26

Year	Team	Lg	G	AB	H	2B	3B	HR	(Hm	Rd)	TB	R	RBI	RC	TBB	IBB	SO	HBP	SH	SF	SB	CS	GDP	Avg	OBP	Slg	OPS
2016	Tacom*	AAA	63	247	77	19	4	3	(-	-)	113	41	29	45	29	0	49	2	1	1	12	5	7	.312	.387	.457	.845
2016	OkCity*	AAA	15	57	21	6	2	0	(-	-)	31	7	8	14	6	0	16	1	0	0	5	0	2	.368	.438	.544	.981
2014	Sea	AL	47	136	39	8	0	0	(0	0)	47	16	9	18	11	0	39	2	1	1	5	2	3	.287	.347	.346	.692
2015	Sea	AL	37	94	16	3	1	0	(0	0)	21	9	1	1	6	0	31	0	2	0	3	2	0	.170	.220	.223	.443
2016	2 Tms		36	61	13	2	2	1	(0	1)	22	8	7	5	4	1	15	0	0	0	0	0	3	.213	.262	.361	.622
16	Sea	AL	2	3	1	0	0	0	(0	0)	1	0	0	0	0	0	2	0	0	0	0	0	0	.333	.333	.333	.667
16	LAD	NL	34	58	12	2	2	1	(0	1)	21	8	7	5	4	1	13	0	0	0	0	0	3	.207	.258	.362	.620
	3 ML YEARS		120	291	68	13	3	1	(0	1)	90	33	17	24	21	1	85	2	3	1	8	4	6	.234	.289	.309	.598

Michael Taylor

Bats: R **Throws:** R **Pos:** CF-64;PH-10;PR-6;RF-5;LF-1   **Ht:** 6'3" **Wt:** 210 **Born:** 3/26/1991 **Age:** 26

Year	Team	Lg	G	AB	H	2B	3B	HR	(Hm	Rd)	TB	R	RBI	RC	TBB	IBB	SO	HBP	SH	SF	SB	CS	GDP	Avg	OBP	Slg	OPS
2016	Syrcse*	AAA	31	117	24	5	1	1	(-	-)	34	17	9	11	12	0	33	1	0	0	7	1	3	.205	.285	.291	.575
2014	Was	NL	17	39	8	3	0	1	(0	1)	14	5	5	3	3	0	17	1	0	0	0	2	1	.205	.279	.359	.638
2015	Was	NL	138	472	108	15	2	14	(6	8)	169	49	63	60	35	9	158	1	1	2	16	3	5	.229	.282	.358	.640
2016	Was	NL	76	221	51	11	0	7	(1	6)	83	28	16	20	14	0	77	1	0	1	14	3	2	.231	.278	.376	.654
	3 ML YEARS		231	732	167	29	2	22	(7	15)	266	82	84	83	52	9	252	3	1	3	30	8	8	.228	.281	.363	.644

Junichi Tazawa

Pitches: R **Bats:** R **Pos:** RP-53   joo-NEE-chee tah-ZAH-wah   **Ht:** 5'11" **Wt:** 200 **Born:** 6/6/1986 **Age:** 31

Year	Team	Lg	G	GS	CG	GF	IP	BFP	H	R	ER	HR	SH	SF	HB	TBB	IBB	SO	WP	Bk	W	L	Pct	Sh	Sv-Op	Hld	ERC	ERA
2009	Bos	AL	6	4	0	1	25.1	130	43	23	21	4	0	3	3	9	0	13	0	0	2	3	.400	0	0-0	0	9.14	7.46
2011	Bos	AL	3	0	0	2	3.0	13	3	2	2	1	0	0	0	1	0	4	0	0	0	0	-	0	0-0	0	5.31	6.00
2012	Bos	AL	37	0	0	13	44.0	172	37	7	7	1	1	1	2	5	0	45	0	0	1	1	.500	0	1-1	5	1.94	1.43
2013	Bos	AL	71	0	0	10	68.1	284	70	25	24	9	2	5	1	12	1	72	3	1	5	4	.556	0	0-8	25	3.55	3.16
2014	Bos	AL	71	0	0	12	63.0	261	58	23	20	5	1	1	0	17	1	64	5	0	4	3	.571	0	0-5	16	2.97	2.86
2015	Bos	AL	61	0	0	13	58.2	247	65	28	27	5	0	1	1	13	1	56	9	1	2	7	.222	0	3-10	16	3.96	4.14
2016	Bos	AL	53	0	0	5	49.2	208	47	23	23	9	0	1	1	14	1	54	4	0	3	2	.600	0	0-2	16	3.89	4.17
	Postseason		13	0	0	0	7.1	26	6	1	1	0	0	0	0	1	0	6	1	0	1	0	1.000	0	0-0	6	1.84	1.23
	7 ML YEARS		302	4	0	56	312.0	1315	323	131	124	34	4	12	8	71	4	308	21	2	17	20	.459	0	4-26	78	3.72	3.58

Julio Teheran

Pitches: R **Bats:** R **Pos:** SP-30   tay-RAHN   **Ht:** 6'2" **Wt:** 205 **Born:** 1/27/1991 **Age:** 26

Year	Team	Lg	G	GS	CG	GF	IP	BFP	H	R	ER	HR	SH	SF	HB	TBB	IBB	SO	WP	Bk	W	L	Pct	Sh	Sv-Op	Hld	ERC	ERA
2011	Atl	NL	5	3	0	0	19.2	87	21	11	11	4	2	1	0	8	0	10	1	0	1	1	.500	0	0-0	0	5.19	5.03
2012	Atl	NL	2	1	0	0	6.1	24	5	4	4	0	0	0	0	1	0	5	0	0	0	0	-	0	0-0	0	1.64	5.68
2013	Atl	NL	30	30	0	0	185.2	774	173	69	66	22	8	5	13	45	4	170	2	0	14	8	.636	0	0-0	0	3.45	3.20
2014	Atl	NL	33	33	4	0	221.0	884	188	82	71	22	13	4	4	51	4	186	1	1	14	13	.519	2	0-0	0	2.71	2.89
2015	Atl	NL	33	33	0	0	200.2	843	189	99	90	27	10	3	9	73	3	171	2	0	11	8	.579	0	0-0	0	4.07	4.04
2016	Atl	NL	30	30	1	0	188.0	758	157	70	67	22	4	1	9	41	2	167	7	1	7	10	.412	1	0-0	0	2.79	3.21
	Postseason		1	1	0	0	2.2	17	8	6	6	1	0	1	0	1	0	5	1	0	0	1	.000	0	0-0	0	20.77	20.25
	6 ML YEARS		133	130	5	0	821.1	3370	733	335	309	97	37	14	35	219	13	709	13	2	47	40	.540	3	0-0	0	3.26	3.39

Mark Teixeira

Bats: B **Throws:** R **Pos:** 1B-110;DH-4;PH-4   tuh-SHARE-uh   **Ht:** 6'3" **Wt:** 225 **Born:** 4/11/1980 **Age:** 37

Year	Team	Lg	G	AB	H	2B	3B	HR	(Hm	Rd)	TB	R	RBI	RC	TBB	IBB	SO	HBP	SH	SF	SB	CS	GDP	Avg	OBP	Slg	OPS
2003	Tex	AL	146	529	137	29	5	26	(19	7)	254	66	84	78	44	5	120	14	0	2	1	2	14	.259	.331	.480	.811
2004	Tex	AL	145	545	153	34	2	38	(18	20)	305	101	112	120	68	12	117	10	0	2	4	1	6	.281	.370	.560	.929
2005	Tex	AL	162	644	194	41	3	43	(30	13)	370	112	144	148	72	5	124	11	0	3	4	0	18	.301	.379	.575	.954
2006	Tex	AL	162	628	177	45	1	33	(12	21)	323	99	110	114	89	12	128	4	0	6	2	0	17	.282	.371	.514	.886
2007	2 Tms		132	494	151	33	2	30	(14	16)	278	86	105	116	72	13	112	7	0	7	2	0	7	.306	.400	.563	.963
2008	2 Tms		157	574	177	41	0	33	(19	14)	317	102	121	119	97	13	93	7	0	7	2	0	17	.308	.410	.552	.962
2009	NYY	AL	156	609	178	43	3	39	(24	15)	344	103	122	112	81	9	114	12	0	5	2	0	13	.292	.383	.565	.948
2010	NYY	AL	158	601	154	36	0	33	(19	14)	289	113	108	110	93	6	122	13	0	5	0	1	15	.256	.365	.481	.846
2011	NYY	AL	156	589	146	26	1	39	(22	17)	291	90	111	106	76	3	110	11	0	8	4	1	12	.248	.341	.494	.835
2012	NYY	AL	123	451	113	27	1	24	(12	12)	214	66	84	69	54	1	83	7	0	12	2	1	11	.251	.332	.475	.807
2013	NYY	AL	15	53	8	1	0	3	(2	1)	18	5	12	6	8	2	19	1	0	1	0	0	1	.151	.270	.340	.609
2014	NYY	AL	123	440	95	14	0	22	(10	12)	175	56	62	51	58	3	109	6	0	4	1	1	13	.216	.313	.398	.711
2015	NYY	AL	111	392	100	22	0	31	(14	17)	215	57	79	71	59	6	95	6	0	5	2	0	7	.255	.357	.548	.906
2016	NYY	AL	116	387	79	16	0	15	(10	5)	140	43	44	41	47	1	105	2	0	2	2	0	7	.204	.292	.362	.654
07	Tex	AL	78	286	85	24	1	13	(5	8)	150	48	49	58	45	10	66	3	0	1	0	0	5	.297	.397	.524	.921
07	Atl	NL	54	208	66	9	1	17	(9	8)	128	38	56	58	27	3	46	4	0	1	2	0	2	.317	.404	.615	1.020
08	Atl	NL	103	381	108	27	0	20	(11	9)	195	63	78	69	65	9	70	3	0	2	0	0	13	.283	.390	.512	.902
08	LAA	AL	54	193	69	14	0	13	(8	5)	122	39	43	50	32	4	23	4	0	5	2	0	4	.358	.449	.632	1.081
	Postseason		40	153	34	6	0	3	(2	1)	49	21	14	15	24	2	34	4	0	2	1	0	3	.222	.339	.320	.659
	14 ML YEARS		1862	6936	1862	408	18	409	(225	184)	3533	1099	1298	1261	918	91	1441	111	0	64	26	7	158	.268	.360	.509	.869

Ruben Tejada

Bats: R Throws: R Pos: 3B-23;PH-8;SS-7;2B-4;PR-1 Ht: 5'11" Wt: 200 Born: 10/27/1989 Age: 27

Year	Team	Lg	G	AB	H	2B	3B	HR	(Hm	Rd)	TB	R	RBI	RC	TBB	IBB	SO	HBP	SH	SF	SB	CS	GDP	Avg	OBP	Slg	OPS
2016	Scrmto*	AAA	40	144	44	11	1	1	(-	-)	60	18	21	20	7	0	21	2	1	2	0	1	6	.306	.342	.417	.759
2010	NYM	NL	78	216	46	12	0	1	(0	1)	61	28	15	16	22	3	38	8	6	3	2	2	2	.213	.305	.282	.588
2011	NYM	NL	96	328	93	15	1	0	(0	0)	110	31	36	41	35	3	50	6	4	3	5	1	6	.284	.360	.335	.696
2012	NYM	NL	114	464	134	26	0	1	(0	1)	163	53	25	49	27	0	73	5	3	2	4	4	9	.289	.333	.351	.685
2013	NYM	NL	57	208	42	12	0	0	(0	0)	54	20	10	15	15	0	24	1	3	0	2	1	3	.202	.259	.260	.519
2014	NYM	NL	119	355	84	11	0	5	(1	4)	110	30	34	42	50	11	73	8	4	2	1	2	8	.237	.342	.310	.652
2015	NYM	NL	116	360	94	23	0	3	(2	1)	126	36	28	42	38	5	70	5	2	2	2	1	6	.261	.338	.350	.688
2016	2 Tms	NL	36	66	11	5	0	0	(0	0)	16	9	5	2	7	0	13	1	1	0	0	0	1	.167	.247	.242	.489
16	StL	NL	23	34	6	2	0	0	(0	0)	8	6	3	0	2	0	8	1	0	0	0	0	1	.176	.225	.235	.460
16	SF	NL	13	32	5	3	0	0	(0	0)	8	3	2	2	5	0	5	0	1	0	0	0	0	.156	.270	.250	.520
	Postseason		2	5	0	0	0	0	(0	0)	0	0	1	0	1	0	5	0	0	0	0	0	0	.000	.167	.000	.167
	7 ML YEARS		616	1997	504	104	1	10	(3	7)	640	207	153	207	194	22	341	34	23	15	16	11	35	.252	.327	.320	.647

Tomas Telis

Bats: B Throws: R Pos: PH-7;C-3 TOH-mahs tay-LEES Ht: 5'8" Wt: 220 Born: 6/18/1991 Age: 26

Year	Team	Lg	G	AB	H	2B	3B	HR	(Hm	Rd)	TB	R	RBI	RC	TBB	IBB	SO	HBP	SH	SF	SB	CS	GDP	Avg	OBP	Slg	OPS
2016	NewOr*	AAA	91	336	104	16	3	6	(-	-)	144	46	45	53	27	1	42	2	1	2	4	2	15	.310	.362	.429	.791
2014	Tex	AL	18	68	17	2	0	0	(0	0)	19	7	8	7	1	0	10	1	1	0	0	0	2	.250	.271	.279	.551
2015	2 Tms		23	38	6	0	0	0	(0	0)	6	2	2	1	1	1	4	2	0	0	0	0	2	.158	.220	.158	.377
2016	Mia	NL	10	13	4	0	0	1	(0	1)	7	1	4	3	0	0	2	0	0	0	0	0	0	.308	.308	.538	.846
15	Tex	AL	6	11	2	0	0	0	(0	0)	2	1	2	1	0	0	1	1	0	0	0	0	0	.182	.250	.182	.432
15	Mia	NL	17	27	4	0	0	0	(0	0)	4	1	0	0	1	1	3	1	0	0	0	0	2	.148	.207	.148	.355
	3 ML YEARS		51	119	27	2	0	1	(0	1)	32	10	14	11	2	1	16	3	1	0	0	0	4	.227	.258	.269	.527

Ryan Tepera

Pitches: R Bats: R Pos: RP-20 tuh-PAIR-uh Ht: 6'2" Wt: 195 Born: 11/3/1987 Age: 29

			HOW MUCH HE PITCHED					WHAT HE GAVE UP										THE RESULTS						
Year	Team	Lg	G	GS	CG	GF	IP	BFP	H	R	ER	HR	SH	SF	HB	TBB	IBB	SO	WP	Bk	W	L	Pct	Sh	Sv-Op	Hld	ERC	ERA
2012	Nham	AA	16	15	0	0	74.1	345	82	44	40	4	3	5	7	37	0	57	6	0	7	3	.700	0	0- -	-	5.01	4.84
2012	Dnedin	A+	5	5	1	0	21.0	101	27	19	18	3	0	0	2	12	0	14	1	1	1	3	.250	0	0- -	-	7.33	7.71
2013	Nham	AA	33	20	0	8	116.0	517	109	65	58	11	4	5	12	56	0	105	6	0	10	8	.556	0	1- -	-	4.40	4.50
2014	Buffalo	AAA	51	0	0	23	64.0	278	66	29	26	4	2	1	1	24	4	67	5	0	7	3	.700	0	2- -	-	3.82	3.66
2015	Buffalo	AAA	21	0	0	6	34.0	130	16	5	4	1	0	1	0	13	1	37	3	0	3	1	.750	0	3- -	-	1.20	1.06
2016	Buffalo	AAA	37	0	0	29	45.1	181	33	13	13	3	2	1	1	16	0	48	3	0	1	2	.333	0	18- -	-	2.39	2.58
2015	Tor	AL	32	0	0	12	33.0	128	23	14	12	8	0	0	3	6	0	22	2	0	0	2	.000	0	1-1	0	2.87	3.27
2016	Tor	AL	20	0	0	13	18.1	85	17	8	6	1	1	0	3	8	1	18	3	0	0	1	.000	0	0-0	0	3.81	2.95
	Postseason		1	0	0	0	1.2	12	5	4	4	0	0	3	0	2	0	0	1	0	0	0	-	0	0-0	0	20.56	21.60
	2 ML YEARS		52	0	0	25	51.1	213	40	22	18	9	1	0	6	14	1	40	5	0	0	3	.000	0	1-1	0	3.26	3.16

Nick Tepesch

Pitches: R Bats: R Pos: SP-1 TEPP-esh Ht: 6'4" Wt: 240 Born: 10/12/1988 Age: 28

			HOW MUCH HE PITCHED					WHAT HE GAVE UP										THE RESULTS						
Year	Team	Lg	G	GS	CG	GF	IP	BFP	H	R	ER	HR	SH	SF	HB	TBB	IBB	SO	WP	Bk	W	L	Pct	Sh	Sv-Op	Hld	ERC	ERA
2016	RdRck*	AAA	11	11	0	0	65.2	279	75	33	30	5	0	2	4	11	0	31	0	0	4	2	.667	0	0- -	-	4.06	4.11
2016	Omha*	AAA	5	2	0	2	16.0	63	11	7	7	0	0	2	0	7	0	8	2	0	0	1	.000	0	0- -	-	2.04	3.94
2013	Tex	AL	19	17	0	1	93.0	407	100	53	50	12	1	4	7	27	3	76	0	0	4	6	.400	0	0-0	0	4.49	4.84
2014	Tex	AL	23	22	0	1	126.0	537	128	66	61	15	3	4	7	44	2	56	1	0	5	11	.313	0	0-0	0	4.37	4.36
2016	LAD	NL	1	1	0	0	4.0	19	7	5	5	1	0	0	0	0	0	3	0	0	0	1	.000	0	0-0	0	7.95	11.25
	3 ML YEARS		43	40	0	2	223.0	963	235	124	116	28	4	8	14	71	5	135	1	0	9	18	.333	0	0-0	0	4.48	4.68

Joe Thatcher

Pitches: L Bats: L Pos: P Ht: 6'2" Wt: 230 Born: 10/4/1981 Age: 35

			HOW MUCH HE PITCHED					WHAT HE GAVE UP										THE RESULTS						
Year	Team	Lg	G	GS	CG	GF	IP	BFP	H	R	ER	HR	SH	SF	HB	TBB	IBB	SO	WP	Bk	W	L	Pct	Sh	Sv-Op	Hld	ERC	ERA
2016	OkCity*	AAA	17	0	0	0	15.0	63	14	6	6	0	1	0	0	5	0	21	0	1	0	0	-	0	0- -	-	2.78	3.60
2016	Iowa*	AAA	10	1	0	2	7.1	35	10	5	5	0	1	1	0	3	1	11	0	1	0	0	-	0	0- -	-	5.04	6.14
2007	SD	NL	22	0	0	5	21.0	85	13	6	3	1	0	0	1	6	2	16	0	0	2	2	.500	0	0-0	2	1.49	1.29
2008	SD	NL	25	0	0	7	25.2	128	42	25	24	4	2	3	0	13	2	17	0	0	0	4	.000	0	0-3	5	8.91	8.42
2009	SD	NL	52	0	0	7	45.0	188	37	14	14	2	1	2	4	18	7	55	2	1	1	0	1.000	0	0-1	9	2.87	2.80
2010	SD	NL	65	0	0	12	35.0	137	23	5	5	1	3	2	4	7	2	45	0	0	1	0	1.000	0	0-0	11	1.37	1.29
2011	SD	NL	18	0	0	5	10.0	44	8	5	5	1	0	0	0	7	1	9	0	0	0	0	-	0	0-0	2	3.96	4.50
2012	SD	NL	55	0	0	13	31.2	141	30	13	12	2	2	2	3	14	3	39	0	1	1	4	.200	0	1-1	14	3.82	3.41
2013	2 Tms	NL	72	0	0	16	39.1	164	40	14	14	4	1	2	1	10	0	36	3	0	3	2	.600	0	0-4	15	3.75	3.20
2014	2 Tms		53	0	0	9	30.1	135	36	16	13	3	1	2	4	4	1	27	1	0	2	1	.667	0	0-1	6	4.42	3.86
2015	Hou	AL	43	0	0	3	22.2	100	23	8	8	1	2	2	0	12	0	26	0	0	1	3	.250	0	0-0	6	4.28	3.18
13	SD	NL	50	0	0	13	30.0	121	28	7	7	3	0	1	1	4	0	29	2	0	3	1	.750	0	0-2	11	2.83	2.10
13	Ari	NL	22	0	0	3	9.1	43	12	7	7	1	1	1	0	6	0	7	1	0	0	1	.000	0	0-2	4	7.19	6.75
14	Ari	NL	37	0	0	7	24.0	100	23	10	7	3	1	1	2	3	1	25	1	0	1	0	1.000	0	0-1	4	3.14	2.63
14	LAA	AL	16	0	0	2	6.1	35	13	6	6	0	0	1	2	1	0	2	0	0	1	1	.500	0	0-0	2	9.96	8.53
	9 ML YEARS		405	0	0	77	260.2	1122	252	106	98	19	12	15	14	91	18	270	6	2	11	16	.407	0	1-10	70	3.58	3.38

Josh Thole

Bats: L Throws: R Pos: C-50;PH-1   tol-ee   Ht: 6'1" Wt: 205 Born: 10/28/1986 Age: 30

Year Team	Lg	G	AB	H	2B	3B	HR	(Hm	Rd)	TB	R	RBI	RC	TBB	IBB	SO	HBP	SH	SF	SB	CS	GDP	Avg	OBP	Slg	OPS
2009 NYM	NL	17	53	17	2	1	0	(0	0)	21	2	9	9	4	0	5	0	0	2	1	0	1	.321	.356	.396	.752
2010 NYM	NL	73	202	56	7	1	3	(2	1)	74	17	17	28	24	1	25	1	0	8	1	0	8	.277	.357	.366	.723
2011 NYM	NL	114	340	91	17	0	3	(1	2)	117	22	40	39	38	6	47	4	1	3	0	2	8	.268	.345	.344	.690
2012 NYM	NL	104	340	75	15	0	1	(0	1)	93	24	21	24	27	6	50	1	4	1	0	0	12	.234	.294	.290	.584
2013 Tor	AL	45	120	21	3	1	1	(0	1)	29	11	8	7	12	0	25	1	2	0	0	0	3	.175	.256	.242	.497
2014 Tor	AL	57	133	33	4	0	0	(0	0)	37	11	7	11	14	0	25	0	3	0	0	3	4	.248	.320	.278	.598
2015 Tor	AL	18	49	10	2	0	0	(0	0)	12	5	2	2	3	0	9	0	0	0	0	0	2	.204	.250	.245	.495
2016 Tor	AL	50	118	20	3	0	1	(0	1)	26	7	7	4	13	0	28	1	2	0	0	0	4	.169	.254	.220	.474
8 ML YEARS		478	1336	323	53	3	9	(3	6)	409	99	111	124	135	13	214	8	12	8	2	5	42	.242	.313	.306	.620

Jake Thompson

Pitches: R Bats: R Pos: SP-10   Ht: 6'4" Wt: 235 Born: 1/31/1994 Age: 23

Year Team	Lg	G	GS	CG	GF	IP	BFP	H	R	ER	HR	SH	SF	HB	TBB	IBB	SO	WP	Bk	W	L	Pct	Sh	Sv-Op	Hld	ERC	ERA
2012 Tigers	R	7	7	0	0	28.1	106	14	6	6	1	1	0	1	10	0	31	3	1	1	2	.333	0	0- -	-	1.36	1.91
2013 Wmich	A	17	16	0	0	83.1	370	79	38	29	4	2	0	11	32	0	91	4	0	3	3	.500	0	0- -	-	3.79	3.13
2014 Lkland	A+	16	16	0	0	83.0	342	75	31	29	3	1	1	7	25	0	79	4	1	6	4	.600	0	0- -	-	3.14	3.14
2014 Frisco	AA	7	6	0	0	35.2	148	28	13	13	3	0	1	1	18	0	44	1	0	3	1	.750	0	0- -	-	3.39	3.28
2015 Frisco	AA	17	17	1	0	87.2	386	94	51	46	7	3	0	7	30	0	78	5	0	6	6	.500	0	0- -	-	4.42	4.72
2015 Rdng	AA	7	7	0	0	45.0	166	33	9	9	3	1	1	0	12	0	34	2	0	5	1	.833	0	0- -	-	2.20	1.80
2016 LV	AAA	21	21	0	0	129.2	517	105	44	36	10	4	3	6	37	1	87	5	0	11	5	.688	0	0- -	-	2.72	2.50
2016 Phi	NL	10	10	0	0	53.2	237	53	34	34	10	2	3	4	28	1	32	4	0	3	6	.333	0	0-0	0	5.51	5.70

Trayce Thompson

Bats: R Throws: R Pos: CF-32;RF-28;LF-24;PH-13   Ht: 6'3" Wt: 225 Born: 3/15/1991 Age: 26

Year Team	Lg	G	AB	H	2B	3B	HR	(Hm	Rd)	TB	R	RBI	RC	TBB	IBB	SO	HBP	SH	SF	SB	CS	GDP	Avg	OBP	Slg	OPS
2012 WinSa	A+	116	449	114	28	5	22	(-	-)	218	77	90	76	45	1	144	6	2	8	18	3	2	.254	.325	.486	.810
2012 Brham	AA	14	50	14	1	1	3	(-	-)	26	10	6	10	8	0	16	0	0	1	2	0	1	.280	.379	.520	.899
2013 Brham	AA	135	507	116	24	5	15	(-	-)	195	78	73	70	60	0	139	13	2	8	25	8	5	.229	.321	.385	.706
2014 Brham	AA	133	518	123	34	6	16	(-	-)	217	86	59	76	65	0	151	4	3	5	20	5	5	.237	.324	.419	.743
2015 Charllt	AAA	104	388	101	23	4	13	(-	-)	171	53	39	53	23	0	79	2	2	2	11	5	8	.260	.304	.441	.744
2015 CWS	AL	44	122	36	8	3	5	(3	2)	65	17	16	20	13	0	26	0	0	0	1	0	3	.295	.363	.533	.896
2016 LAD	NL	80	236	53	11	0	13	(9	4)	103	31	32	26	26	0	66	0	0	0	5	1	3	.225	.302	.436	.738
2 ML YEARS		124	358	89	19	3	18	(12	6)	168	48	48	46	39	0	92	0	0	0	6	1	6	.249	.322	.469	.792

Tyler Thornburg

Pitches: R Bats: R Pos: RP-67   Ht: 5'11" Wt: 190 Born: 9/29/1988 Age: 28

Year Team	Lg	G	GS	CG	GF	IP	BFP	H	R	ER	HR	SH	SF	HB	TBB	IBB	SO	WP	Bk	W	L	Pct	Sh	Sv-Op	Hld	ERC	ERA
2012 Mil	NL	8	3	0	0	22.0	95	24	11	11	8	1	0	1	7	0	20	1	0	0	0	-	0	0-0	0	6.44	4.50
2013 Mil	NL	18	7	0	4	66.2	270	53	17	15	1	4	1	3	26	2	48	2	1	3	1	.750	0	0-0	0	2.59	2.03
2014 Mil	NL	27	0	0	4	29.2	131	24	14	14	1	1	1	0	21	0	28	4	0	3	1	.750	0	0-0	5	3.71	4.25
2015 Mil	NL	24	0	0	9	34.1	151	31	22	14	7	0	2	3	12	1	34	3	1	0	2	.000	0	0-0	1	4.20	3.67
2016 Mil	NL	67	0	0	23	67.0	263	38	19	16	6	0	1	2	25	1	90	4	0	8	5	.615	0	13-21	20	1.82	2.15
5 ML YEARS		144	10	0	43	219.2	910	170	83	70	23	6	5	9	91	4	220	14	2	14	9	.609	0	13-21	26	3.08	2.87

Matt Thornton

Pitches: L Bats: L Pos: RP-18   Ht: 6'6" Wt: 235 Born: 9/15/1976 Age: 40

Year Team	Lg	G	GS	CG	GF	IP	BFP	H	R	ER	HR	SH	SF	HB	TBB	IBB	SO	WP	Bk	W	L	Pct	Sh	Sv-Op	Hld	ERC	ERA
2004 Sea	AL	19	1	0	8	32.2	148	30	15	15	2	2	1	0	25	1	30	2	0	1	2	.333	0	0-0	0	4.75	4.13
2005 Sea	AL	55	0	0	15	57.0	262	54	33	33	13	1	1	0	42	2	57	7	0	0	4	.000	0	0-1	5	6.06	5.21
2006 CWS	AL	63	0	0	20	54.0	227	46	20	20	5	1	3	1	21	4	49	1	0	5	3	.625	0	2-5	18	3.12	3.33
2007 CWS	AL	68	0	0	13	56.1	249	59	31	30	4	0	2	2	26	6	55	3	0	4	4	.500	0	2-7	17	4.35	4.79
2008 CWS	AL	74	0	0	12	67.1	268	48	20	20	5	1	1	2	19	2	77	3	0	5	3	.625	0	1-6	20	2.07	2.67
2009 CWS	AL	70	0	0	17	72.1	291	58	22	22	5	2	1	1	20	2	87	4	0	6	3	.667	0	4-9	24	2.40	2.74
2010 CWS	AL	61	0	0	13	60.2	239	41	18	18	3	0	2	2	20	5	81	1	0	5	4	.556	0	8-10	21	1.89	2.67
2011 CWS	AL	62	0	0	20	59.2	262	60	34	22	3	3	3	0	21	5	63	2	0	2	5	.286	0	3-7	20	3.32	3.32
2012 CWS	AL	74	0	0	18	65.0	266	63	27	25	4	1	0	3	17	4	53	2	0	4	10	.286	0	3-7	20	3.29	3.46
2013 2 Tms	AL	60	0	0	6	43.1	187	47	20	18	4	4	1	2	15	1	30	2	0	0	4	.000	0	0-1	19	4.50	3.74
2014 2 Tms	AL	64	0	0	8	36.0	152	33	9	7	0	2	2	5	8	2	28	0	0	1	3	.250	0	0-4	18	2.69	1.75
2015 Was	NL	60	0	0	12	41.1	171	33	12	10	2	2	1	1	11	3	23	1	0	2	1	.667	0	0-1	18	2.12	2.18
2016 SD	NL	18	0	0	8	17.0	77	22	12	11	2	0	0	1	6	0	9	0	0	1	0	1.000	0	0-0	6	6.10	5.82
13 CWS	AL	40	0	0	3	28.0	116	25	14	12	4	2	0	2	10	1	21	1	0	0	3	.000	0	0-1	18	3.94	3.86
13 Bos	AL	20	0	0	3	15.1	71	22	6	6	0	2	1	0	5	0	9	1	0	0	1	.000	0	0-0	1	5.55	3.52
14 NYY	AL	46	0	0	6	24.2	107	23	9	7	0	2	2	4	6	2	20	0	0	0	3	.000	0	0-4	12	2.83	2.55
14 Was	AL	18	0	0	2	11.1	45	10	0	0	0	0	0	1	2	0	8	0	0	1	0	1.000	0	0-0	6	2.39	0.00
Postseason		6	0	0	1	5.2	26	5	1	1	0	1	0	0	4	2	3	0	0	1	0	1.000	0	0-0	1	3.13	1.59
13 ML YEARS		748	1	0	170	662.2	2799	594	273	251	52	19	18	20	251	37	642	28	0	36	46	.439	0	23-58	206	3.31	3.41

Chris Tillman

Pitches: R **Bats:** R **Pos:** SP-30   **Ht:** 6'5" **Wt:** 200 **Born:** 4/15/1988 **Age:** 29

			HOW MUCH HE PITCHED					WHAT HE GAVE UP												THE RESULTS						
Year	Team	Lg	G	GS	CG	GF	IP	BFP	H	R	ER	HR	SH	SF	HB	TBB	IBB	SO	WP	Bk	W	L	Pct	Sh	Sv-Op	Hld	ERC	ERA
2009	Bal	AL	12	12	0	0	65.0	285	77	40	39	15	0	0	2	24	1	39	4	0	2	5	.286	0	0-0	0	6.28	5.40
2010	Bal	AL	11	11	0	0	53.2	236	51	37	35	9	1	3	1	31	1	31	2	0	2	5	.286	0	0-0	0	5.12	5.87
2011	Bal	AL	13	13	0	0	62.0	287	77	41	38	5	1	1	4	25	0	46	1	1	3	5	.375	0	0-0	0	5.58	5.52
2012	Bal	AL	15	15	0	0	86.0	347	66	38	28	12	1	2	1	24	0	66	5	0	9	3	.750	0	0-0	0	2.65	2.93
2013	Bal	AL	33	33	1	0	206.1	845	184	87	85	33	4	6	3	68	2	179	6	1	16	7	.696	0	0-0	0	3.72	3.71
2014	Bal	AL	34	**34**	1	0	207.1	871	189	83	77	21	1	5	4	66	1	150	8	0	13	6	.684	1	0-0	0	3.33	3.34
2015	Bal	AL	31	31	0	0	173.0	741	176	97	96	20	3	8	5	64	1	120	4	0	11	11	.500	0	0-0	0	4.32	4.99
2016	Bal	AL	30	30	0	0	172.0	715	155	73	72	19	2	4	7	66	1	140	9	0	16	6	.727	0	0-0	0	3.78	3.77
Postseason			2	2	0	0	9.1	42	11	7	7	3	0	0	0	3	0	9	0	0	1	0	1.000	0	0-0	0	6.29	6.75
8 ML YEARS			179	179	2	0	1025.1	4327	975	496	470	134	13	29	27	368	7	771	39	2	72	48	.600	1	0-0	0	3.98	4.13

Charlie Tilson

Bats: L **Throws:** L **Pos:** CF-1   **Ht:** 5'11" **Wt:** 195 **Born:** 12/2/1992 **Age:** 24

					BATTING															RUNNING			AVERAGES			
Year	Team	Lg	G	AB	H	2B	3B	HR	(Hm	Rd)	TB	R	RBI	RC	TBB	IBB	SO	HBP	SH	SF	SB	CS	GDP	Avg	OBP	Slg	OPS
2013	2 Tms	Low	109	410	124	9	7	4	(-	-)	159	50	30	58	30	1	64	2	7	1	15	6	5	.302	.352	.388	.740
2014	PlmBh	A+	89	370	114	8	8	5	(-	-)	153	54	36	55	24	1	76	4	4	0	10	7	6	.308	.357	.414	.770
2014	Sprgfld	AA	31	139	33	4	1	2	(-	-)	45	19	17	11	6	0	28	0	0	0	2	3	1	.237	.269	.324	.593
2015	Sprgfld	AA	134	539	159	20	9	4	(-	-)	209	85	32	78	46	2	72	2	4	3	46	19	2	.295	.351	.388	.739
2016	Memp	AAA	100	351	99	16	8	4	(-	-)	143	53	34	54	33	0	51	3	4	4	15	3	6	.282	.345	.407	.753
2016	CWS	AL	1	2	1	0	0	0	(0	0)	1	0	0	0	0	0	0	0	0	0	0	0	0	.500	.500	.500	1.000

Andrew Toles

Bats: L **Throws:** R **Pos:** PH-23;LF-18;CF-9;RF-8;PR-1   **Ht:** 5'10" **Wt:** 185 **Born:** 5/24/1992 **Age:** 25

					BATTING															RUNNING			AVERAGES			
Year	Team	Lg	G	AB	H	2B	3B	HR	(Hm	Rd)	TB	R	RBI	RC	TBB	IBB	SO	HBP	SH	SF	SB	CS	GDP	Avg	OBP	Slg	OPS
2012	Prnctn	R+	51	199	56	13	3	7	(-	-)	96	31	33	32	12	3	36	2	0	1	14	5	5	.281	.327	.482	.810
2013	BG	A	121	519	169	35	16	2	(-	-)	242	79	57	91	22	1	105	7	1	3	62	17	6	.326	.359	.466	.826
2014	2 Tms	Low	52	223	59	10	2	1	(-	-)	76	32	15	25	12	0	37	2	3	3	24	10	7	.265	.304	.341	.645
2016	Rcuca	A+	22	92	34	8	2	0	(-	-)	46	22	9	19	6	0	13	1	1	0	9	3	1	.370	.414	.500	.914
2016	Tulsa	AA	43	175	55	14	3	5	(-	-)	90	27	22	33	12	0	30	2	0	1	13	3	2	.314	.363	.514	.877
2016	OkCity	AAA	17	56	18	5	0	2	(-	-)	29	6	7	8	2	0	8	0	0	1	1	5	1	.321	.339	.518	.857
2016	LAD	NL	48	105	33	9	1	3	(1	2)	53	19	16	21	8	2	25	1	0	1	1	1	1	.314	.365	.505	.870

Shawn Tolleson

Pitches: R **Bats:** R **Pos:** RP-37   TAHL-eh-son   **Ht:** 6'2" **Wt:** 225 **Born:** 1/19/1988 **Age:** 29

			HOW MUCH HE PITCHED					WHAT HE GAVE UP												THE RESULTS						
Year	Team	Lg	G	GS	CG	GF	IP	BFP	H	R	ER	HR	SH	SF	HB	TBB	IBB	SO	WP	Bk	W	L	Pct	Sh	Sv-Op	Hld	ERC	ERA
2012	LAD	NL	40	0	0	12	37.2	160	30	19	18	4	2	1	1	20	1	39	0	0	3	1	.750	0	0-0	2	3.59	4.30
2013	LAD	NL	1	0	0	0	0.0	2	0	0	0	0	0	0	0	2	0	0	0	0	0	0	-	0	0-0	0	-	-
2014	Tex	AL	64	0	0	10	71.2	296	56	23	22	10	2	3	1	28	5	69	4	0	3	1	.750	0	0-0	7	3.06	2.76
2015	Tex	AL	73	0	0	53	72.1	298	66	25	24	9	2	1	2	17	5	76	0	0	6	4	.600	0	35-37	6	3.11	2.99
2016	Tex	AL	37	0	0	19	36.1	168	53	32	31	8	0	1	0	10	2	29	1	0	2	2	.500	0	11-15	1	7.17	7.68
Postseason			2	0	0	1	3.0	10	1	0	0	0	0	0	0	0	0	3	0	0	0	0	-	0	0-0	0	0.25	0.00
5 ML YEARS			215	0	0	94	218.0	924	205	99	95	31	6	6	4	77	13	213	5	0	14	8	.636	0	46-52	16	3.82	3.92

Ashur Tolliver

Pitches: L **Bats:** L **Pos:** RP-5   **Ht:** 6'0" **Wt:** 170 **Born:** 1/24/1988 **Age:** 29

			HOW MUCH HE PITCHED					WHAT HE GAVE UP												THE RESULTS						
Year	Team	Lg	G	GS	CG	GF	IP	BFP	H	R	ER	HR	SH	SF	HB	TBB	IBB	SO	WP	Bk	W	L	Pct	Sh	Sv-Op	Hld	ERC	ERA
2013	2 Tms	Low	19	1	0	7	48.1	196	42	16	16	4	1	1	1	14	0	42	4	0	1	0	1.000	0	1- -	-	2.96	2.98
2014	Bowie	AA	18	1	0	7	22.2	97	27	9	8	1	0	0	0	5	0	25	0	0	3	1	.750	0	0- -	-	4.08	3.18
2014	Frdrck	A+	9	0	0	6	14.1	61	14	4	4	1	0	1	0	2	0	15	0	0	0	1	.000	0	2- -	-	2.60	2.51
2015	Bowie	AA	39	2	0	9	58.2	249	51	19	19	2	1	2	0	29	0	61	4	1	1	2	.333	0	1- -	-	3.29	2.91
2016	Bowie	AA	18	0	0	6	26.0	103	22	9	7	4	2	0	0	8	0	25	0	0	1	1	.500	0	2- -	-	3.35	2.42
2016	Norfolk	AAA	11	0	0	3	12.2	54	11	2	2	0	0	0	1	6	0	16	0	0	0	0	-	0	0- -	-	3.28	1.42
2016	Bal	AL	5	0	0	2	4.2	22	5	4	3	1	0	0	0	3	0	5	0	0	1	0	1.000	0	0-0	0	6.25	5.79

Yasmany Tomas

Bats: R **Throws:** R **Pos:** RF-91;LF-60;PH-4;1B-1   yahz-MAH-nee toh-MAHS   **Ht:** 6'2" **Wt:** 250 **Born:** 11/14/1990 **Age:** 26

					BATTING															RUNNING			AVERAGES			
Year	Team	Lg	G	AB	H	2B	3B	HR	(Hm	Rd)	TB	R	RBI	RC	TBB	IBB	SO	HBP	SH	SF	SB	CS	GDP	Avg	OBP	Slg	OPS
2015	Ari	NL	118	406	111	19	3	9	(4	5)	163	40	48	32	17	0	110	2	0	1	5	2	16	.273	.305	.401	.707
2016	Ari	NL	140	530	144	30	1	31	(16	15)	269	72	83	71	31	4	136	1	0	1	2	4	18	.272	.313	.508	.820
2 ML YEARS			258	936	255	49	4	40	(20	20)	432	112	131	103	48	4	246	3	0	2	7	6	34	.272	.309	.462	.771

Josh Tomlin

Pitches: R Bats: R Pos: SP-29; RP-1 Ht: 6'1" Wt: 190 Born: 10/19/1984 Age: 32

Year	Team	Lg	G	GS	CG	GF	IP	BFP	H	R	ER	HR	SH	SF	HB	TBB	IBB	SO	WP	Bk	W	L	Pct	Sh	Sv-Op	Hld	ERC	ERA
2010	Cle	AL	12	12	1	0	73.0	301	72	38	37	10	3	3	3	19	3	43	1	0	6	4	.600	0	0-0	0	3.89	4.56
2011	Cle	AL	26	26	0	0	165.1	662	157	80	78	24	1	3	3	21	2	89	3	0	12	7	.632	0	0-0	0	3.11	4.25
2012	Cle	AL	21	16	0	0	103.1	452	126	74	73	18	2	3	3	25	3	56	4	0	5	8	.385	0	0-0	0	5.34	6.36
2013	Cle	AL	1	0	0	0	2.0	9	2	0	0	0	0	0	0	0	0	0	0	0	0	0	-	0	0-0	0	1.68	0.00
2014	Cle	AL	25	16	1	6	104.0	446	120	66	55	18	1	3	1	14	3	94	6	0	6	9	.400	1	0-0	0	4.28	4.76
2015	Cle	AL	10	10	2	0	65.2	251	47	22	22	13	0	0	2	8	0	57	1	0	7	2	.778	0	0-0	0	2.24	3.02
2016	Cle	AL	30	29	0	1	174.0	725	187	97	85	36	4	4	3	20	2	118	4	0	13	9	.591	0	0-0	0	4.06	4.40
7 ML YEARS			125	109	4	7	687.1	2846	711	377	350	119	11	16	15	107	13	457	19	0	49	39	.557	1	0-0	0	3.83	4.58

Kelby Tomlinson

Bats: R Throws: R Pos: PH-24;2B-19;SS-7;3B-3;LF-3 Ht: 6'3" Wt: 180 Born: 6/16/1990 Age: 27

Year	Team	Lg	G	AB	H	2B	3B	HR	(Hm	Rd)	TB	R	RBI	RC	TBB	IBB	SO	HBP	SH	SF	SB	CS	GDP	Avg	OBP	Slg	OPS
2012	Augsta	A	123	450	101	9	4	1	(-	-)	121	57	36	45	53	0	105	5	6	6	36	11	5	.224	.309	.269	.578
2013	2 Tms	Low	39	162	45	8	1	1	(-	-)	58	22	18	20	15	0	39	1	0	1	6	2	6	.278	.341	.358	.699
2013	Rchmd	AA	33	96	19	5	0	0	(-	-)	24	13	4	8	16	0	27	0	4	0	3	1	1	.198	.313	.250	.563
2014	Rchmd	AA	126	433	116	9	6	1	(-	-)	140	63	32	57	44	1	82	5	8	4	49	12	7	.268	.340	.323	.663
2015	Rchmd	AA	64	253	82	18	3	1	(-	-)	109	43	28	45	25	0	37	3	5	3	16	6	3	.324	.387	.431	.818
2015	Scrmto	AAA	33	136	43	1	1	2	(-	-)	52	21	15	19	7	0	22	2	2	2	5	3	2	.316	.354	.382	.736
2016	Scrmto	AAA	31	185	53	8	1	0	(-	-)	63	28	20	27	22	0	26	3	1	1	12	3	4	.286	.370	.341	.710
2015	SF	NL	54	178	54	6	3	2	(2	0)	72	23	20	22	14	0	40	1	0	0	5	4	3	.303	.358	.404	.762
2016	SF	NL	52	106	31	4	0	0	(0	0)	35	13	6	18	12	1	18	1	1	0	5	1	1	.292	.370	.330	.700
2 ML YEARS			106	284	85	10	3	2	(2	0)	107	36	26	40	26	1	58	2	1	0	10	5	4	.299	.362	.377	.739

Michael Tonkin

Pitches: R Bats: R Pos: RP-65
TAHN-kin Ht: 6'7" Wt: 220 Born: 11/19/1989 Age: 27

Year	Team	Lg	G	GS	CG	GF	IP	BFP	H	R	ER	HR	SH	SF	HB	TBB	IBB	SO	WP	Bk	W	L	Pct	Sh	Sv-Op	Hld	ERC	ERA
2013	Min	AL	9	0	0	6	11.1	47	9	6	1	0	0	0	0	3	0	10	1	0	0	0	-	0	0-0	0	1.82	0.79
2014	Min	AL	25	0	0	8	19.0	87	23	13	10	2	2	1	2	6	0	16	1	0	0	0	-	0	0-0	0	5.36	4.74
2015	Min	AL	26	0	0	10	23.1	99	21	9	9	4	0	1	1	9	2	19	1	0	0	0	-	0	0-0	5	3.99	3.47
2016	Min	AL	65	0	0	23	71.2	315	80	46	40	13	2	0	3	24	0	80	5	0	3	2	.600	0	0-2	2	5.25	5.02
4 ML YEARS			125	0	0	47	125.1	548	133	74	60	19	4	2	6	42	2	125	8	0	3	2	.600	0	0-2	11	4.68	4.31

Carlos Torres

Pitches: R Bats: R Pos: RP-72 Ht: 6'1" Wt: 180 Born: 10/22/1982 Age: 34

Year	Team	Lg	G	GS	CG	GF	IP	BFP	H	R	ER	HR	SH	SF	HB	TBB	IBB	SO	WP	Bk	W	L	Pct	Sh	Sv-Op	Hld	ERC	ERA
2009	CWS	AL	8	5	0	2	28.1	130	30	20	19	5	3	3	2	17	2	22	0	0	1	2	.333	0	0-0	0	6.05	6.04
2010	CWS	AL	5	1	0	1	13.2	71	23	13	13	2	0	1	0	9	1	13	0	0	0	1	.000	0	0-0	0	9.84	8.56
2012	Col	NL	31	0	0	9	53.0	231	49	31	31	2	6	4	4	26	1	42	6	0	5	3	.625	0	0-0	1	3.85	5.26
2013	NYM	NL	33	9	0	6	86.1	352	79	34	33	15	4	1	4	17	1	75	4	1	4	6	.400	0	0-0	3	3.47	3.44
2014	NYM	NL	73	1	0	20	97.0	405	89	35	33	11	2	1	2	38	4	96	6	0	8	6	.571	0	2-5	12	3.77	3.06
2015	NYM	NL	59	0	0	19	57.2	243	61	32	30	5	1	3	0	18	6	48	5	0	5	6	.455	0	0-1	11	3.86	4.68
2016	Mil	NL	72	0	0	12	82.1	339	65	26	25	8	3	2	4	30	3	78	1	1	3	3	.500	0	2-5	20	2.94	2.73
7 ML YEARS			281	16	0	69	418.1	1771	396	191	184	48	19	15	16	155	18	374	22	2	26	27	.491	0	4-11	47	3.88	3.96

Jose Torres

Pitches: L Bats: L Pos: RP-4 Ht: 6'2" Wt: 175 Born: 9/24/1993 Age: 23

Year	Team	Lg	G	GS	CG	GF	IP	BFP	H	R	ER	HR	SH	SF	HB	TBB	IBB	SO	WP	Bk	W	L	Pct	Sh	Sv-Op	Hld	ERC	ERA
2012	As	R	12	12	0	0	52.0	232	52	29	25	2	2	2	2	29	1	41	3	2	3	1	.750	0	0--	-	4.38	4.33
2013	Vrmnt	A-	9	5	0	2	30.2	136	28	15	9	2	0	0	1	12	0	21	4	0	3	2	.600	0	0--	-	3.28	2.64
2014	Vrmnt	A-	14	9	0	4	61.2	264	62	37	30	4	1	6	3	22	0	47	6	0	6	6	.000	0	2--	-	3.91	4.38
2015	2 Tms	Low	47	0	0	24	77.1	313	55	24	22	4	10	4	4	24	2	84	3	0	4	5	.444	0	8--	-	2.09	2.56
2016	SnAnt	AA	25	0	0	9	36.1	136	20	5	5	1	2	1	0	12	1	36	1	1	1	2	.333	0	2--	-	1.35	1.24
2016	Lk Els	A+	20	0	0	7	25.1	105	21	11	10	2	0	1	0	10	0	25	2	0	0	2	.000	0	1--	-	3.00	3.55
2016	SD	NL	4	0	0	1	3.0	14	3	0	0	0	0	0	0	2	0	3	1	0	0	0	-	0	0-0	1	4.23	0.00

Ronald Torreyes

tore-RAY-ess
Bats: R Throws: R Pos: 3B-34;SS-15;2B-14;PR-9;DH-3;PH-3;RF-2 Ht: 5'10" Wt: 150 Born: 9/2/1992 Age: 24

Year	Team	Lg	G	AB	H	2B	3B	HR	(Hm	Rd)	TB	R	RBI	RC	TBB	IBB	SO	HBP	SH	SF	SB	CS	GDP	Avg	OBP	Slg	OPS
2012	Dytona	A+	115	421	111	23	5	6	(-	-)	162	62	47	57	32	1	29	10	5	6	13	4	2	.264	.326	.385	.711
2013	Tenn	AA	65	224	59	14	4	2	(-	-)	87	32	25	33	22	0	15	6	9	4	4	0	8	.263	.340	.388	.728
2013	CpChr	AA	38	151	42	6	2	0	(-	-)	52	19	12	16	6	0	14	1	4	0	1	1	3	.278	.310	.344	.654
2014	OkCity	AAA	126	460	137	20	5	2	(-	-)	173	65	46	62	25	0	26	10	21	3	12	9	10	.298	.345	.376	.721
2015	Fresno	AAA	19	70	14	1	0	0	(-	-)	15	7	5	1	1	0	9	0	1	0	1	1	3	.200	.211	.214	.426
2015	Nham	AA	16	50	7	2	0	0	(-	-)	9	4	9	1	4	0	2	0	0	0	2	0	4	.140	.204	.180	.384
2015	Tulsa	AA	62	249	73	13	2	4	(-	-)	102	39	19	36	20	0	23	2	1	2	3	3	3	.293	.348	.410	.758

Year Team	Lg	G	AB	H	2B	3B	HR	(Hm	Rd)	TB	R	RBI	RC	TBB	IBB	SO	HBP	SH	SF	SB	CS	GDP	Avg	OBP	Slg	OPS
2015 OkCity	AAA	13	49	15	2	1	0	(-	-)	19	10	3	6	2	0	4	1	0	1	0	0	2	.306	.340	.388	.727
2015 LAD	NL	8	6	2	1	0	0	(0	0)	3	1	1	2	1	0	1	0	1	0	0	0	0	.333	.429	.500	.929
2016 NYY	AL	72	155	40	7	4	1	(0	1)	58	20	12	19	10	0	20	1	1	1	2	1	4	.258	.305	.374	.680
2 ML YEARS		80	161	42	8	4	1	(0	1)	61	21	13	21	11	0	21	1	2	1	2	1	4	.261	.310	.379	.689

Devon Travis

Bats: R Throws: R Pos: 2B-99;DH-3;PH-2   DEV-in   Ht: 5'9" Wt: 190 Born: 2/21/1991 Age: 26

Year Team	Lg	G	AB	H	2B	3B	HR	(Hm	Rd)	TB	R	RBI	RC	TBB	IBB	SO	HBP	SH	SF	SB	CS	GDP	Avg	OBP	Slg	OPS
2012 Conn	A-	25	93	26	2	2	3	(-	-)	41	17	11	15	8	0	10	3	2	1	3	1	3	.280	.352	.441	.793
2013 2 Tms	Low	132	504	177	28	4	16	(-	-)	261	93	76	112	53	2	64	10	2	7	22	4	8	.351	.418	.518	.936
2014 Erie	AA	100	396	118	20	7	10	(-	-)	182	68	52	68	37	1	60	2	2	4	16	5	16	.298	.358	.460	.817
2015 Tor	AL	62	217	66	18	0	8	(4	4)	108	38	35	40	18	0	43	2	0	1	3	1	4	.304	.361	.498	.859
2016 Tor	AL	101	410	123	28	1	11	(2	9)	186	54	50	61	20	0	87	0	1	1	4	1	6	.300	.332	.454	.785
2 ML YEARS		163	627	189	46	1	19	(6	13)	294	92	85	101	38	0	130	2	1	2	7	2	10	.301	.342	.469	.811

Blake Treinen

Pitches: R Bats: R Pos: RP-73   TRY-nen   Ht: 6'5" Wt: 225 Born: 6/30/1988 Age: 29

Year Team	Lg	G	GS	CG	GF	IP	BFP	H	R	ER	HR	SH	SF	HB	TBB	IBB	SO	WP	Bk	W	L	Pct	Sh	Sv-Op	Hld	ERC	ERA
2014 Was	NL	15	7	0	6	50.2	214	57	17	14	1	0	0	2	13	1	30	1	0	2	3	.400	0	0-0	0	3.86	2.49
2015 Was	NL	60	0	0	17	67.2	280	62	32	29	4	1	1	2	32	6	65	4	0	2	5	.286	0	0-3	10	3.76	3.86
2016 Was	NL	73	0	0	17	67.0	263	51	19	17	5	2	2	0	31	6	63	1	0	4	1	.800	0	1-3	22	2.92	2.28
3 ML YEARS		148	7	0	40	185.1	757	170	68	60	10	3	3	4	76	13	158	6	0	8	9	.471	0	1-6	32	3.48	2.91

Andrew Triggs

Pitches: R Bats: R Pos: RP-18; SP-6   Ht: 6'4" Wt: 220 Born: 3/16/1989 Age: 28

Year Team	Lg	G	GS	CG	GF	IP	BFP	H	R	ER	HR	SH	SF	HB	TBB	IBB	SO	WP	Bk	W	L	Pct	Sh	Sv-Op	Hld	ERC	ERA
2012 2 Tms	Low	22	0	0	11	46.0	189	35	15	9	2	1	1	1	10	0	51	0	0	1	1	.500	0	4--	-	1.83	1.76
2013 Wilmg	A+	39	0	0	37	60.1	259	58	29	17	1	3	4	7	12	1	63	6	2	5	3	.625	0	9--	-	2.87	2.54
2014 NWArk	AA	43	1	0	32	61.1	260	55	28	20	4	2	3	5	16	1	38	2	0	4	3	.571	0	19--	-	2.97	2.93
2015 Bowie	AA	43	0	0	30	61.0	235	42	9	7	0	2	1	7	11	1	70	6	0	0	2	.000	0	17--	-	1.59	1.03
2016 Nashv	AAA	16	0	0	9	18.1	81	16	7	6	0	0	1	4	5	1	21	0	0	2	1	.667	0	2--	-	2.83	2.95
2016 Oak	AL	24	6	0	7	56.1	238	56	30	27	5	1	1	3	13	1	55	2	0	1	1	.500	0	0-0	0	3.46	4.31

Nick Tropeano

Pitches: R Bats: R Pos: SP-13   TROH-pee-ah-no   Ht: 6'4" Wt: 200 Born: 8/27/1990 Age: 26

Year Team	Lg	G	GS	CG	GF	IP	BFP	H	R	ER	HR	SH	SF	HB	TBB	IBB	SO	WP	Bk	W	L	Pct	Sh	Sv-Op	Hld	ERC	ERA
2014 Hou	AL	4	4	0	0	21.2	91	19	12	11	0	1	1	1	9	1	13	1	0	1	3	.250	0	0-0	0	2.92	4.57
2015 LAA	AL	8	7	0	0	37.2	161	40	18	16	2	2	1	0	10	0	38	0	0	3	2	.600	0	0-0	0	3.53	3.82
2016 LAA	AL	13	13	0	0	68.1	296	70	27	27	14	1	3	2	31	1	68	4	0	3	2	.600	0	0-0	0	5.41	3.56
3 ML YEARS		25	24	0	0	127.2	548	129	57	54	16	4	5	3	50	2	119	5	0	7	7	.500	0	0-0	0	4.40	3.81

Mike Trout

Bats: R Throws: R Pos: CF-148;DH-11;PH-1;PR-1   Ht: 6'2" Wt: 235 Born: 8/7/1991 Age: 25

Year Team	Lg	G	AB	H	2B	3B	HR	(Hm	Rd)	TB	R	RBI	RC	TBB	IBB	SO	HBP	SH	SF	SB	CS	GDP	Avg	OBP	Slg	OPS
2011 LAA	AL	40	123	27	6	0	5	(1	4)	48	20	16	14	9	0	30	2	0	1	4	0	2	.220	.281	.390	.672
2012 LAA	AL	139	559	182	27	8	30	(16	14)	315	129	83	127	67	4	139	6	0	7	49	5	7	.326	.399	.564	.963
2013 LAA	AL	157	589	190	39	9	27	(13	14)	328	109	97	141	110	10	136	9	0	8	33	7	8	.323	.432	.557	.988
2014 LAA	AL	157	602	173	39	9	36	(19	17)	338	115	111	131	83	6	184	10	0	10	16	2	6	.287	.377	.561	.939
2015 LAA	AL	159	575	172	32	6	41	(20	21)	339	104	90	131	92	14	158	10	0	5	11	7	11	.299	.402	.590	.991
2016 LAA	AL	159	549	173	32	5	29	(14	15)	302	123	100	137	116	12	137	11	0	5	30	7	5	.315	.441	.550	.991
Postseason		3	12	1	0	0	1	(0 | 1)	4	1	1	1	0		3	0	2	0	0	1	0	1	.083	.267	.333	.600
6 ML YEARS		811	2997	917	175	37	168	(83	85)	1670	600	497	681	477	46	784	48	0	36	143	28	39	.306	.405	.557	.963

Mark Trumbo

Bats: R Throws: R Pos: RF-95;DH-59;1B-6;LF-1   Ht: 6'4" Wt: 225 Born: 1/16/1986 Age: 31

Year Team	Lg	G	AB	H	2B	3B	HR	(Hm	Rd)	TB	R	RBI	RC	TBB	IBB	SO	HBP	SH	SF	SB	CS	GDP	Avg	OBP	Slg	OPS
2010 LAA	AL	8	15	1	0	0	0	(0	0)	1	2	2	0	1	0	8	0	0	0	0	0	0	.067	.125	.067	.192
2011 LAA	AL	149	539	137	31	1	29	(14	15)	257	65	87	69	25	6	120	5	0	4	9	4	17	.254	.291	.477	.768
2012 LAA	AL	144	544	146	19	3	32	(12	20)	267	66	95	80	36	3	153	4	0	2	4	5	12	.268	.317	.491	.808
2013 LAA	AL	159	620	145	30	2	34	(19	15)	281	85	100	74	54	6	184	0	0	4	5	2	18	.234	.294	.453	.747
2014 Ari	NL	88	328	77	15	1	14	(7	7)	136	37	61	44	28	3	89	1	0	5	2	3	8	.235	.293	.415	.707
2015 2 Tms	AL	142	508	133	23	3	22	(12	10)	228	62	64	58	36	1	132	0	0	1	0	0	12	.262	.310	.449	.759
2016 Bal	AL	159	613	157	27	1	47	(25	22)	327	94	108	102	51	1	170	3	0	0	2	0	14	.256	.316	.533	.850
15 Ari	NL	46	174	45	10	3	9	(4	5)	88	23	23	21	10	0	39	0	0	0	0	0	4	.259	.299	.506	.805
15 Sea	AL	96	334	88	13	0	13	(8	5)	140	39	41	37	26	1	93	0	0	1	0	0	8	.263	.316	.419	.735
7 ML YEARS		849	3167	796	145	11	178	(89	89)	1497	411	517	427	231	20	856	13	0	16	22	14	81	.251	.303	.473	.776

Chin-hui Tsao

Pitches: R **Bats:** R **Pos:** RP-2 | chin-wee sow | **Ht:** 6'1" **Wt:** 210 **Born:** 6/2/1981 **Age:** 36

			HOW MUCH HE PITCHED						WHAT HE GAVE UP											THE RESULTS					
Year	Team	Lg	G	GS	CG	GF	IP	BFP	H	R	ER	HR	SH	SF	HB	TBB	IBB	SO	WP	Bk	W	L	Pct	Sh	Sv-Op	Hld	ERC	ERA
2016	OkCity*	AAA	17	0	0	14	16.1	71	17	7	6	0	2	0	0	5	1	14	0	0	1	1	.500	0	6- -	-	3.06	3.31
2003	Col	NL	9	8	0	1	43.1	196	48	30	29	11	3	0	4	20	1	29	0	0	3	3	.500	0	0-0	0	6.56	6.02
2004	Col	NL	10	0	0	5	9.1	37	7	4	4	2	1	0	0	1	0	11	0	0	0	0	-	0	1-2	1	2.21	3.86
2005	Col	NL	10	0	0	9	11.0	56	16	8	8	3	1	1	1	5	1	4	1	0	1	0	1.000	0	3-4	0	8.44	6.55
2007	LAD	NL	21	0	0	6	24.2	97	18	12	12	3	0	0	1	8	0	16	0	0	1	0	.000	0	0-1	3	2.74	4.38
2015	LAD	NL	5	0	0	0	7.0	37	15	9	8	3	0	0	0	3	1	7	0	0	1	1	.500	0	0-0	0	15.20	10.29
2016	LAD	NL	2	0	0	2	1.2	9	1	1	1	0	0	0	0	3	0	0	0	0	0	1	.000	0	0-0	0	6.15	5.40
	6 ML YEARS		57	8	0	23	97.0	432	105	64	62	22	5	1	6	40	3	67	1	0	5	6	.455	0	4-7	4	5.77	5.75

Preston Tucker

Bats: L **Throws:** L **Pos:** DH-22;LF-19;PH-12;RF-3;PR-1 | **Ht:** 6'0" **Wt:** 215 **Born:** 7/6/1990 **Age:** 26

			BATTING																	RUNNING			AVERAGES			
Year	Team	Lg	G	AB	H	2B	3B	HR	(Hm	Rd)	TB	R	RBI	RC	TBB	IBB	SO	HBP	SH	SF	SB	CS	GDP	Avg	OBP	Slg	OPS
2012	TriCity	A-	42	165	53	7	0	8	(-	-)	84	32	38	32	18	0	16	2	0	2	1	2	4	.321	.390	.509	.899
2013	Lancst	A+	75	298	97	18	1	15	(-	-)	162	61	74	62	29	1	45	2	0	4	3	0	4	.326	.384	.544	.928
2013	CpChr	AA	60	237	62	14	1	10	(-	-)	108	36	29	38	27	1	46	4	0	0	1	6		.262	.347	.456	.803
2014	CpChr	AA	65	261	72	17	0	17	(-	-)	140	41	43	48	26	5	46	3	0	0	3	3	5	.276	.348	.536	.885
2014	OkCity	AAA	73	275	79	18	0	7	(-	-)	118	38	51	44	31	3	74	0	0	3	2	0	4	.287	.356	.429	.785
2015	Fresno	AAA	33	129	38	4	0	11	(-	-)	75	20	35	26	12	1	25	1	0	1	1	0	6	.295	.357	.581	.938
2016	Fresno	AAA	53	209	63	14	3	8	(-	-)	107	35	29	37	15	1	49	2	0	3	1	1	2	.301	.349	.512	.861
2015	Hou	AL	98	300	73	19	0	13	(5	8)	131	35	33	34	20	0	68	3	0	0	0	2	3	.243	.297	.437	.734
2016	Hou	AL	48	134	22	8	1	4	(2	2)	44	11	8	4	8	0	40	2	0	0	0	0	2	.164	.222	.328	.551
	Postseason		3	2	0	0	0	0	(0	0)	0	0	0	0	1	0	2	0	0	0	0	0	0	.000	.333	.000	.333
	2 ML YEARS		146	434	95	27	1	17	(7	10)	175	46	41	38	28	0	108	5	0	0	0	2	5	.219	.274	.403	.677

Matt Tuiasosopo

Bats: R **Throws:** R **Pos:** PH-3 | too-ee-ah-suh-SOH-poe | **Ht:** 6'2" **Wt:** 235 **Born:** 5/10/1986 **Age:** 31

			BATTING																	RUNNING			AVERAGES			
Year	Team	Lg	G	AB	H	2B	3B	HR	(Hm	Rd)	TB	R	RBI	RC	TBB	IBB	SO	HBP	SH	SF	SB	CS	GDP	Avg	OBP	Slg	OPS
2016	Gwnntt*	AAA	64	211	52	17	0	11	(-	-)	102	33	28	37	31	0	71	4	0	2	0	0	5	.246	.351	.483	.834
2008	Sea	AL	14	44	7	2	1	0	(0	0)	11	1	2	1	2	0	16	1	0	0	0	0	0	.159	.213	.250	.463
2009	Sea	AL	7	22	5	1	0	1	(0	1)	9	2	2	2	2	0	5	0	0	1	0	0	0	.227	.280	.409	.689
2010	Sea	AL	50	127	22	5	0	4	(0	4)	39	12	11	8	9	0	49	1	1	0	0	0	3	.173	.234	.307	.541
2013	Det	AL	81	164	40	7	0	7	(5	2)	68	26	30	26	25	0	57	2	0	0	0	0	3	.244	.351	.415	.765
2016	Atl	NL	3	3	0	0	0	0	(0	0)	0	0	0	0	0	0	1	0	0	0	0	0	0	.000	.000	.000	.000
	5 ML YEARS		155	360	74	15	1	12	(5	7)	127	41	45	37	38	0	128	4	1	1	0	0	6	.206	.288	.353	.641

Samuel Tuivailala

Pitches: R **Bats:** R **Pos:** RP-12 | TOO-ee-vah-la-la | **Ht:** 6'3" **Wt:** 225 **Born:** 10/19/1992 **Age:** 24

			HOW MUCH HE PITCHED						WHAT HE GAVE UP											THE RESULTS					
Year	Team	Lg	G	GS	CG	GF	IP	BFP	H	R	ER	HR	SH	SF	HB	TBB	IBB	SO	WP	Bk	W	L	Pct	Sh	Sv-Op	Hld	ERC	ERA
2016	Memp*	AAA	42	0	0	33	46.2	210	47	27	27	3	1	1	1	22	3	72	3	0	3	2	.600	0	17- -	-	4.01	5.21
2014	StL	NL	2	0	0	0	1.0	10	5	4	4	2	0	0	0	2	0	1	0	0	0	0	-	0	0-0	0	72.46	36.00
2015	StL	NL	14	0	0	5	14.2	65	13	5	5	2	0	0	0	8	1	20	3	0	0	1	.000	0	0-0	2	4.06	3.07
2016	StL	NL	12	0	0	4	9.0	47	12	6	6	0	0	0	2	6	0	7	1	0	0	0	-	0	0-0	0	7.05	6.00
	3 ML YEARS		28	0	0	9	24.2	122	30	15	15	4	0	0	2	16	1	28	4	0	0	1	.000	0	0-0	2	7.02	5.47

Troy Tulowitzki

Bats: R **Throws:** R **Pos:** SS-128;DH-3 | too-luh-WIT-skee | **Ht:** 6'3" **Wt:** 205 **Born:** 10/10/1984 **Age:** 32

			BATTING																	RUNNING			AVERAGES			
Year	Team	Lg	G	AB	H	2B	3B	HR	(Hm	Rd)	TB	R	RBI	RC	TBB	IBB	SO	HBP	SH	SF	SB	CS	GDP	Avg	OBP	Slg	OPS
2006	Col	NL	25	96	23	2	0	1	(0	1)	28	15	6	10	10	3	25	1	1	0	3	0	1	.240	.318	.292	.609
2007	Col	NL	155	609	177	33	5	24	(15	9)	292	104	99	95	57	3	130	9	5	2	7	6	14	.291	.359	.479	.838
2008	Col	NL	101	377	99	24	2	8	(4	4)	151	48	46	42	38	5	56	2	2	2	1	6	16	.263	.332	.401	.732
2009	Col	NL	151	543	161	25	9	32	(17	15)	300	101	92	96	73	4	112	3	0	9	20	11	20	.297	.377	.552	.930
2010	Col	NL	122	470	148	32	3	27	(15	12)	267	89	95	88	48	4	78	5	1	5	11	2	17	.315	.381	.568	.949
2011	Col	NL	143	537	162	36	2	30	(17	13)	292	81	105	101	59	12	79	4	1	5	9	3	16	.302	.372	.544	.916
2012	Col	NL	47	181	52	8	2	8	(3	5)	88	33	27	27	19	1	19	2	0	1	2	2	7	.287	.360	.486	.846
2013	Col	NL	126	446	139	27	0	25	(14	11)	241	72	82	80	57	5	85	4	0	5	1	0	9	.312	.391	.540	.931
2014	Col	NL	91	315	107	18	1	21	(14	7)	190	71	52	70	50	4	57	5	0	5	1	1	4	.340	.432	.603	1.035
2015	2 Tms		128	486	136	27	0	17	(11	6)	214	77	70	69	38	5	114	6	0	4	1	0	17	.280	.337	.440	.777
2016	Tor	AL	131	492	125	21	0	24	(13	11)	218	54	79	71	43	1	101	5	0	4	1	0	14	.254	.318	.443	.761
15	Col	NL	87	323	97	19	0	12	(7	5)	152	46	53	53	24	4	72	1	0	3	0	0	13	.300	.348	.471	.818
15	Tor	AL	41	163	39	8	0	5	(4	1)	62	31	17	16	14	1	42	5	0	1	1	0	4	.239	.317	.380	.697
	Postseason		26	101	21	7	0	3	(1	2)	37	8	17	10	6	0	31	1	0	1	0	0	3	.208	.257	.366	.623
	11 ML YEARS		1220	4552	1329	253	24	217	(123	94)	2281	745	753	749	492	47	856	46	10	42	57	31	135	.292	.364	.501	.865

Jacob Turner

Pitches: R Bats: R Pos: RP-16; SP-2   Ht: 6'5" Wt: 215 Born: 5/21/1991 Age: 26

				HOW MUCH HE PITCHED						WHAT HE GAVE UP										THE RESULTS							
Year	Team	Lg	G	GS	CG	GF	IP	BFP	H	R	ER	HR	SH	SF	HB	TBB	IBB	SO	WP	Bk	W	L	Pct	Sh	Sv-Op	Hld	ERC	ERA
2016	Charllt*	AAA	18	18	1	0	107.0	463	125	60	56	10	2	8	3	29	0	85	10	0	4	7	.364	1	0--	-	4.63	4.71
2011	Det	AL	3	3	0	0	12.2	60	17	13	12	3	0	1	1	4	0	8	0	0	0	1	.000	0	0-0	0	7.03	8.53
2012	2 Tms		10	10	0	0	55.0	231	50	32	27	9	1	2	0	16	3	36	5	0	2	5	.286	0	0-0	0	3.42	4.42
2013	Mia	NL	20	20	1	0	118.0	514	116	55	49	11	8	5	4	54	5	77	11	0	3	8	.273	0	0-0	0	4.25	3.74
2014	2 Tms	NL	28	18	0	4	113.0	501	148	81	77	12	6	4	1	33	2	71	6	1	6	11	.353	0	0-0	1	5.59	6.13
2016	CWS	AL	18	2	0	8	24.2	122	33	27	18	5	0	2	2	16	1	18	2	0	1	2	.333	0	0-0	2	8.38	6.57
12	Det	AL	3	3	0	0	12.1	61	17	11	11	4	0	1	0	7	1	7	1	0	1	1	.500	0	0-0	0	8.66	8.03
12	Mia	NL	7	7	0	0	42.2	170	33	21	16	5	1	1	0	9	2	29	4	0	1	4	.200	0	0-0	0	2.20	3.38
14	Mia	NL	20	12	0	4	78.1	352	106	54	52	8	2	3	1	23	1	54	3	1	4	7	.364	0	0-0	0	5.84	5.97
14	ChC	NL	8	6	0	0	34.2	149	42	27	25	4	4	1	0	10	1	17	3	0	2	4	.333	0	0-0	1	5.03	6.49
	5 ML YEARS		79	53	1	12	323.1	1428	364	208	183	40	15	14	8	123	11	210	24	1	12	27	.308	0	0-0	3	4.95	5.09

Justin Turner

Bats: R Throws: R Pos: 3B-144;PH-10;DH-2;1B-1   Ht: 5'11" Wt: 205 Born: 11/23/1984 Age: 32

						BATTING														RUNNING			AVERAGES			
Year	Team	Lg	G	AB	H	2B	3B	HR	(Hm	Rd)	TB	R	RBI	RC	TBB	IBB	SO	HBP	SH	SF	SB	CS	GDP	Avg	OBP	Slg	OPS
2009	Bal	AL	12	18	3	0	0	0	(0	0)	3	2	3	1	4	0	3	0	0	0	0	0	1	.167	.318	.167	.485
2010	2 Tms		9	17	1	1	0	0	(0	0)	2	1	0	0	1	0	3	0	0	0	0	0	0	.059	.111	.118	.229
2011	NYM	NL	117	435	113	30	0	4	(3	1)	155	49	51	59	39	2	59	10	2	1	7	2	9	.260	.334	.356	.690
2012	NYM	NL	94	171	46	13	1	2	(2	0)	67	20	19	19	9	0	24	4	0	1	1	1	6	.269	.319	.392	.711
2013	NYM	NL	86	200	56	13	1	2	(0	2)	77	12	16	17	11	1	34	1	1	1	0	1	6	.280	.319	.385	.704
2014	LAD	NL	109	288	98	21	1	7	(5	2)	142	46	43	55	28	1	58	4	0	2	6	1	6	.340	.404	.493	.897
2015	LAD	NL	126	385	113	26	1	16	(8	8)	189	55	60	65	36	1	71	13	1	4	5	2	10	.294	.370	.491	.861
2016	LAD	NL	151	556	153	34	3	27	(11	16)	274	79	90	96	48	1	107	10	0	8	4	1	16	.275	.339	.493	.832
10	Bal	AL	5	9	0	0	0	0	(0	0)	0	0	0	0	0	0	3	0	0	0	0	0	0	.000	.000	.000	.000
10	NYM	NL	4	8	1	1	0	0	(0	0)	2	1	0	0	1	0	0	0	0	0	0	0	0	.125	.222	.250	.472
	Postseason		7	21	10	6	0	0	(0	0)	16	2	4	7	1	1	4	0	0	0	1	0	0	.476	.500	.762	1.262
	8 ML YEARS		704	2070	583	138	7	58	(29	29)	909	264	282	312	176	6	359	42	4	17	23	8	57	.282	.348	.439	.787

Trea Turner

Bats: R Throws: R Pos: CF-45;2B-30;SS-2;PR-1   TRAY   Ht: 6'1" Wt: 185 Born: 6/30/1993 Age: 24

						BATTING														RUNNING			AVERAGES			
Year	Team	Lg	G	AB	H	2B	3B	HR	(Hm	Rd)	TB	R	RBI	RC	TBB	IBB	SO	HBP	SH	SF	SB	CS	GDP	Avg	OBP	Slg	OPS
2014	2 Tms	Low	69	279	90	16	2	5	(-	-)	125	45	24	55	35	1	67	5	1	1	23	4	4	.323	.406	.448	.854
2015	SnAnt	AA	58	227	73	13	3	5	(-	-)	107	31	35	42	24	0	48	0	2	1	11	4	5	.322	.385	.471	.856
2015	Hrsbrg	AA	10	39	14	4	1	0	(-	-)	20	6	4	7	1	0	8	0	0	1	4	0	2	.359	.366	.513	.879
2015	Syrcse	AAA	48	188	59	7	3	3	(-	-)	81	31	15	31	13	0	41	0	1	3	14	2	2	.314	.353	.431	.784
2016	Syrcse	AAA	83	331	100	22	8	6	(-	-)	156	61	33	63	37	1	72	0	1	2	25	2	3	.302	.370	.471	.842
2015	Was	NL	27	40	9	1	0	1	(0	1)	13	5	1	2	4	0	12	0	0	0	2	2	0	.225	.295	.325	.620
2016	Was	NL	73	307	105	14	8	13	(7	6)	174	53	40	62	14	0	59	1	0	2	33	6	1	.342	.370	.567	.937
	2 ML YEARS		100	347	114	15	8	14	(7	7)	187	58	41	64	18	0	71	1	0	2	35	8	1	.329	.361	.539	.900

Koji Uehara

Pitches: R Bats: R Pos: RP-50   KOH-jee ooh-ih-HAR-uh   Ht: 6'2" Wt: 195 Born: 4/3/1975 Age: 42

						HOW MUCH HE PITCHED					WHAT HE GAVE UP										THE RESULTS							
Year	Team	Lg	G	GS	CG	GF	IP	BFP	H	R	ER	HR	SH	SF	HB	TBB	IBB	SO	WP	Bk	W	L	Pct	Sh	Sv-Op	Hld	ERC	ERA
2009	Bal	AL	12	12	0	0	66.2	279	71	34	30	7	1	3	0	12	1	48	0	0	2	4	.333	0	0-0	0	3.56	4.05
2010	Bal	AL	43	0	0	22	44.0	174	37	15	14	5	1	0	0	5	0	55	1	0	1	2	.333	0	13-15	6	2.22	2.86
2011	2 Tms	AL	65	0	0	22	65.0	243	38	17	17	11	1	1	0	9	1	85	0	0	2	3	.400	0	0-1	22	1.48	2.35
2012	Tex	AL	37	0	0	13	36.0	130	20	7	7	4	1	1	0	3	0	43	1	0	0	0	--	0	1-1	7	1.12	1.75
2013	Bos	AL	73	0	0	40	74.1	265	33	10	9	5	1	1	1	9	2	101	1	0	4	1	.800	0	21-24	13	0.79	1.09
2014	Bos	AL	64	0	0	50	64.1	249	51	18	18	10	3	1	0	8	0	80	1	0	6	5	.545	0	26-31	1	2.35	2.52
2015	Bos	AL	43	0	0	38	40.1	160	28	14	10	3	1	1	0	9	1	47	4	0	2	4	.333	0	25-27	0	1.67	2.23
2016	Bos	AL	50	0	0	12	47.0	184	34	18	18	8	1	0	2	11	1	63	1	0	2	3	.400	0	7-9	18	2.58	3.45
11	Bal	AL	43	0	0	19	47.0	174	25	9	9	6	1	1	0	8	1	62	0	0	1	1	.500	0	0-1	13	1.27	1.72
11	Tex	AL	22	0	0	3	18.0	69	13	8	8	5	0	0	0	1	0	23	0	0	1	2	.333	0	0-0	9	2.21	4.00
	Postseason		17	0	0	13	16.0	60	12	6	6	4	0	0	0	2	0	20	0	0	1	1	.500	0	7-7	0	2.63	3.38
	8 ML YEARS		387	12	0	197	437.2	1684	312	132	123	53	10	8	4	66	6	522	9	0	19	22	.463	0	93-108	67	1.84	2.53

Justin Upton

Bats: R Throws: R Pos: LF-146;CF-6;DH-2;PH-2;PR-1   Ht: 6'2" Wt: 205 Born: 8/25/1987 Age: 29

						BATTING														RUNNING			AVERAGES			
Year	Team	Lg	G	AB	H	2B	3B	HR	(Hm	Rd)	TB	R	RBI	RC	TBB	IBB	SO	HBP	SH	SF	SB	CS	GDP	Avg	OBP	Slg	OPS
2007	Ari	NL	43	140	31	8	3	2	(2	0)	51	17	11	13	11	4	37	1	0	0	2	0	3	.221	.283	.364	.647
2008	Ari	NL	108	356	89	19	6	15	(12	3)	165	52	42	47	54	6	121	4	0	3	1	4	3	.250	.353	.463	.816
2009	Ari	NL	138	526	158	30	7	26	(14	12)	280	84	86	94	55	3	137	2	1	4	20	5	10	.300	.366	.532	.899
2010	Ari	NL	133	495	135	27	3	17	(8	9)	219	73	69	73	64	5	152	4	1	7	18	8	20	.273	.356	.442	.799
2011	Ari	NL	159	592	171	39	5	31	(20	11)	313	105	88	103	59	9	126	19	0	4	21	9	8	.289	.369	.529	.898
2012	Ari	NL	150	554	155	24	4	17	(11	6)	238	107	67	82	63	5	121	5	0	6	18	8	7	.280	.355	.430	.785
2013	Atl	NL	149	558	147	27	2	27	(13	14)	259	94	70	84	75	4	161	5	1	4	8	1	12	.263	.354	.464	.818
2014	Atl	NL	154	566	153	34	2	29	(18	11)	278	77	102	84	60	1	171	6	0	8	8	4	10	.270	.342	.491	.833

(continued)

Year Team	Lg	G	AB	H	2B	3B	HR	(Hm	Rd)	TB	R	RBI	RC	TBB	IBB	SO	HBP	SH	SF	SB	CS	GDP	Avg	OBP	Slg	OPS
2015 SD	NL	150	542	136	26	3	26	(15	11)	246	85	81	85	68	5	159	4	0	5	19	5	10	.251	.336	.454	.790
2016 Det	AL	153	570	140	28	2	31	(14	17)	265	81	87	77	50	3	179	4	0	2	9	4	15	.246	.310	.465	.775
Postseason		15	48	11	2	1	2	(0	2)	21	7	4	7	10	1	13	2	0	0	1	0	0	.229	.383	.438	.821
10 ML YEARS		1337	4899	1315	262	37	221	(127	94)	2314	775	703	742	559	45	1364	54	3	43	124	48	98	.268	.347	.472	.819

Melvin Upton Jr.

Bats: R **Throws:** R **Pos:** LF-121;CF-27;PH-12;RF-3;DH-1;PR-1   **Ht:** 6'3" **Wt:** 185 **Born:** 8/21/1984 **Age:** 32

Year Team	Lg	G	AB	H	2B	3B	HR	(Hm	Rd)	TB	R	RBI	RC	TBB	IBB	SO	HBP	SH	SF	SB	CS	GDP	Avg	OBP	Slg	OPS
2004 TB	AL	45	159	41	8	2	4	(2	2)	65	19	12	22	15	0	46	1	1	1	4	1	1	.258	.324	.409	.733
2006 TB	AL	50	175	43	5	0	1	(1	0)	51	20	10	17	13	0	40	1	0	0	11	3	1	.246	.302	.291	.593
2007 TB	AL	129	474	142	25	1	24	(13	11)	241	86	82	93	65	4	154	4	1	4	22	8	14	.300	.386	.508	.894
2008 TB	AL	145	531	145	37	2	9	(4	5)	213	85	67	87	97	4	134	2	3	7	44	16	13	.273	.383	.401	.784
2009 TB	AL	144	560	135	33	4	11	(7	4)	209	79	55	68	57	0	152	3	3	3	42	14	7	.241	.313	.373	.686
2010 TB	AL	154	536	127	38	4	18	(7	11)	227	89	62	74	67	1	164	2	1	4	42	9	13	.237	.322	.424	.745
2011 TB	AL	153	560	136	27	4	23	(9	14)	240	82	81	79	71	4	161	4	2	3	36	12	16	.243	.331	.429	.759
2012 TB	AL	146	573	141	29	3	28	(17	11)	260	79	78	71	45	0	169	1	4	8	31	6	13	.246	.298	.454	.752
2013 Atl	NL	126	391	72	14	0	9	(7	2)	113	30	26	21	44	2	151	3	1	6	12	5	7	.184	.268	.289	.557
2014 Atl	NL	141	519	108	19	5	12	(6	6)	173	67	35	47	57	5	173	1	3	2	20	7	6	.208	.287	.333	.620
2015 SD	NL	87	205	53	12	4	5	(2	3)	88	23	17	33	21	2	62	0	2	0	9	3	1	.259	.327	.429	.757
2016 2 Tms		149	492	117	15	3	20	(7	13)	198	64	61	62	37	1	155	2	1	6	27	8	6	.238	.291	.402	.693
16 SD	NL	92	344	88	11	2	16	(6	10)	151	46	45	51	23	1	106	2	1	3	20	5	5	.256	.304	.439	.743
16 Tor	AL	57	148	29	4	1	4	(1	3)	47	18	16	11	14	0	49	0	0	3	7	3	1	.196	.261	.318	.578
Postseason		28	104	27	6	1	7	(2	5)	56	20	18	17	9	1	32	0	0	1	9	2	4	.260	.316	.538	.854
12 ML YEARS		1469	5175	1260	262	32	164	(82	82)	2078	723	586	674	589	23	1561	24	22	44	300	92	98	.243	.321	.402	.723

Jose Urena

Pitches: R **Bats:** R **Pos:** RP-16; SP-12   oo-RAY-nuh   **Ht:** 6'2" **Wt:** 200 **Born:** 9/12/1991 **Age:** 25

		HOW MUCH HE PITCHED						WHAT HE GAVE UP										THE RESULTS							
Year Team	Lg	G	GS	CG	GF	IP	BFP	H	R	ER	HR	SH	SF	HB	TBB	IBB	SO	WP	Bk	W	L	Pct	Sh	Sv-Op	Hld	ERC	ERA
2012 Grnsbr	A	27	22	1	4	138.1	572	143	67	52	13	3	2	1	29	0	101	7	2	9	6	.600	0	2- -	-	3.54	3.38
2013 Jupiter	A+	27	26	0	0	149.2	618	148	69	62	8	3	5	6	29	0	107	3	0	10	7	.588	0	0- -	-	3.08	3.73
2014 Jaxnvl	AA	25	25	0	0	162.0	652	155	65	60	14	7	6	2	29	1	121	4	0	13	8	.619	0	0- -	-	2.99	3.33
2015 NewOr	AAA	11	11	1	0	67.2	276	65	23	20	4	2	1	3	19	0	41	3	0	6	1	.857	0	0- -	-	3.41	2.66
2016 NewOr	AAA	12	12	0	0	48.1	204	41	18	17	4	1	2	5	21	0	41	1	2	3	3	.500	0	0- -	-	3.73	3.17
2015 Mia	NL	20	9	0	4	61.2	274	73	37	36	5	3	5	3	25	2	28	2	1	1	5	.167	0	0-1	1	4.70	5.25
2016 Mia	NL	28	12	0	4	83.2	373	91	59	57	11	3	4	6	29	6	58	0	0	4	9	.308	0	1-3	1	4.70	6.13
2 ML YEARS		48	21	0	8	145.1	647	164	96	93	16	6	9	9	54	8	86	2	1	5	14	.263	0	1-4	1	4.94	5.76

Julio Urias

Pitches: L **Bats:** L **Pos:** SP-15; RP-3   oo-ree-AHS   **Ht:** 6'0" **Wt:** 215 **Born:** 8/12/1996 **Age:** 20

		HOW MUCH HE PITCHED						WHAT HE GAVE UP										THE RESULTS							
Year Team	Lg	G	GS	CG	GF	IP	BFP	H	R	ER	HR	SH	SF	HB	TBB	IBB	SO	WP	Bk	W	L	Pct	Sh	Sv-Op	Hld	ERC	ERA
2013 Gt Lks	A	18	18	0	0	54.1	211	44	15	15	5	0	0	1	16	0	67	2	0	2	0	1.000	0	0- -	-	2.83	2.48
2014 Rcuca	A+	25	20	0	1	87.2	356	60	25	23	4	0	2	7	37	0	109	5	1	2	2	.500	0	0- -	-	2.48	2.36
2015 Tulsa	AA	13	13	0	0	68.1	268	54	24	21	4	3	0	1	15	0	74	1	1	3	4	.429	0	0- -	-	2.16	2.77
2016 OkCity	AAA	11	7	0	1	45.0	168	31	7	7	2	3	1	1	8	0	49	0	1	5	1	.833	0	0- -	-	1.59	1.40
2016 LAD	NL	18	15	0	1	77.0	336	81	32	29	5	4	1	4	31	0	84	3	0	5	2	.714	0	0-0	0	4.37	3.39

Juan Uribe

Bats: R **Throws:** R **Pos:** 3B-68;PH-5;DH-1   oo-REE-bay   **Ht:** 6'0" **Wt:** 245 **Born:** 3/22/1979 **Age:** 38

Year Team	Lg	G	AB	H	2B	3B	HR	(Hm	Rd)	TB	R	RBI	RC	TBB	IBB	SO	HBP	SH	SF	SB	CS	GDP	Avg	OBP	Slg	OPS
2001 Col	NL	72	273	82	15	11	8	(3	5)	143	32	53	44	8	1	55	2	0	0	3	0	6	.300	.325	.524	.849
2002 Col	NL	155	566	136	25	7	6	(4	2)	193	69	49	53	34	1	120	5	7	6	9	2	17	.240	.286	.341	.627
2003 Col	NL	87	316	80	19	3	10	(6	4)	135	45	33	45	17	0	60	3	6	1	7	2	3	.253	.297	.427	.724
2004 CWS	AL	134	502	142	31	6	23	(16	7)	254	82	74	81	32	1	96	3	11	5	9	11	10	.283	.327	.506	.833
2005 CWS	AL	146	481	121	23	3	16	(10	6)	198	58	71	59	34	0	77	4	11	10	4	6	7	.252	.301	.412	.712
2006 CWS	AL	132	463	109	28	2	21	(13	8)	204	53	71	52	13	1	82	3	9	7	1	1	10	.235	.257	.441	.698
2007 CWS	AL	150	513	120	18	2	20	(15	5)	202	55	68	52	34	2	112	4	7	5	1	9	6	.234	.284	.394	.678
2008 CWS	AL	110	324	80	22	1	7	(5	2)	125	38	40	43	22	0	64	1	5	1	1	3	5	.247	.296	.386	.682
2009 SF	NL	122	398	115	26	4	16	(9	7)	197	50	55	55	25	2	82	1	3	5	3	1	7	.289	.329	.495	.824
2010 SF	NL	148	521	129	24	2	24	(13	11)	229	64	85	68	45	6	92	4	0	5	1	2	20	.248	.310	.440	.749
2011 LAD	NL	77	270	55	12	0	4	(3	1)	79	21	28	13	17	2	60	6	0	2	2	0	12	.204	.264	.293	.557
2012 LAD	NL	66	162	31	9	0	2	(1	1)	46	15	17	13	13	0	37	2	1	1	0	1	6	.191	.258	.284	.542
2013 LAD	NL	132	388	108	22	2	12	(6	6)	170	47	50	51	30	3	81	2	3	3	5	0	12	.278	.331	.438	.769
2014 LAD	NL	103	386	120	23	0	9	(5	4)	170	36	54	48	15	2	77	1	0	2	1	0	15	.311	.337	.440	.777
2015 3 Tms	NL	119	360	91	17	0	14	(6	8)	150	40	43	41	34	3	80	2	0	1	2	0	12	.253	.320	.417	.737
2016 Cle	NL	73	238	49	9	0	7	(4	3)	79	19	25	15	15	1	49	3	0	3	0	0	6	.206	.259	.332	.591
15 LAD	NL	29	81	20	2	0	1	(0	1)	25	6	6	6	5	0	9	0	0	1	1	0	5	.247	.287	.309	.596
15 Atl	NL	46	151	43	6	0	7	(3	4)	70	17	17	20	15	2	37	1	0	0	1	0	5	.285	.353	.464	.817
15 NYM	NL	44	128	28	9	0	6	(3	3)	55	17	20	15	14	1	34	1	0	0	0	0	2	.219	.301	.430	.730
Postseason		45	158	33	6	0	5	(4	1)	54	16	25	16	7	0	44	1	3	1	2	0	5	.209	.246	.342	.587
16 ML YEARS		1826	6161	1568	323	43	199	(119	80)	2574	724	816	733	388	25	1224	46	63	57	48	39	154	.255	.301	.418	.719

Chase Utley

Bats: L **Throws:** R **Pos:** 2B-134;PH-15;3B-1   UTT-lee   **Ht:** 6'1" **Wt:** 195 **Born:** 12/17/1978 **Age:** 38

								BATTING													RUNNING			AVERAGES			
Year	Team	Lg	G	AB	H	2B	3B	HR	(Hm	Rd)	TB	R	RBI	RC	TBB	IBB	SO	HBP	SH	SF	SB	CS	GDP	Avg	OBP	Slg	OPS
2003	Phi	NL	43	134	32	10	1	2	(1	1)	50	13	21	19	11	0	22	6	0	1	2	0	3	.239	.322	.373	.696
2004	Phi	NL	94	267	71	11	2	13	(8	5)	125	36	57	37	15	1	40	2	1	2	4	1	6	.266	.308	.468	.776
2005	Phi	NL	147	543	158	39	6	28	(12	16)	293	93	105	102	69	5	109	9	0	7	16	3	10	.291	.376	.540	.915
2006	Phi	NL	160	658	203	40	4	32	(16	16)	347	131	102	122	63	1	132	14	0	4	15	4	9	.309	.379	.527	.906
2007	Phi	NL	132	530	176	48	5	22	(14	8)	300	104	103	111	50	1	99	25	1	7	9	1	7	.332	.410	.566	.976
2008	Phi	NL	159	607	177	41	4	33	(20	13)	325	113	104	113	64	14	104	27	1	8	14	2	9	.292	.380	.535	.915
2009	Phi	NL	156	571	161	28	4	31	(16	15)	290	112	93	115	88	3	110	24	0	4	23	0	5	.282	.397	.508	.905
2010	Phi	NL	115	425	117	20	2	16	(10	6)	189	75	65	83	63	3	63	18	0	5	13	2	4	.275	.387	.445	.832
2011	Phi	NL	103	398	103	21	6	11	(8	3)	169	54	44	57	39	4	47	14	1	2	14	0	3	.259	.344	.425	.769
2012	Phi	NL	83	301	77	15	2	11	(8	3)	129	48	45	49	43	7	43	12	0	6	11	1	4	.256	.365	.429	.793
2013	Phi	NL	131	476	135	25	6	18	(8	10)	226	73	69	78	45	4	79	5	0	5	8	3	12	.284	.348	.475	.823
2014	Phi	NL	155	589	159	36	6	11	(6	5)	240	74	78	86	53	12	85	13	0	9	10	1	8	.270	.339	.407	.746
2015	2 Tms	NL	107	373	79	21	2	8	(3	5)	128	37	39	30	32	4	64	10	0	8	4	0	7	.212	.286	.343	.629
2016	LAD	NL	138	512	129	26	3	14	(4	10)	203	79	52	72	40	1	115	11	1	1	2	2	0	.252	.319	.396	.716
15	Phi	NL	73	249	54	12	1	5	(1	4)	83	23	30	19	22	4	35	4	0	7	3	0	6	.217	.284	.333	.617
15	LAD	NL	34	124	25	9	1	3	(2	1)	45	14	9	11	10	0	29	6	0	1	1	0	1	.202	.291	.363	.654
	Postseason		49	167	44	7	1	10	(5	5)	83	39	25	35	34	3	39	5	0	1	10	2	3	.263	.401	.497	.898
	14 ML YEARS		1723	6384	1777	381	53	250	(134	116)	3014	1042	977	1074	675	60	1102	190	5	69	145	20	87	.278	.361	.472	.833

Pat Valaika

Bats: R **Throws:** R **Pos:** 3B-6;2B-5;SS-2;PH-2;PR-2   vuh-LAKE-uh   **Ht:** 5'11" **Wt:** 200 **Born:** 9/9/1992 **Age:** 24

								BATTING													RUNNING			AVERAGES			
Year	Team	Lg	G	AB	H	2B	3B	HR	(Hm	Rd)	TB	R	RBI	RC	TBB	IBB	SO	HBP	SH	SF	SB	CS	GDP	Avg	OBP	Slg	OPS
2013	TriCity	A-	42	146	35	15	2	1	(-	-)	57	27	18	21	23	0	33	2	4	3	5	3	4	.240	.345	.390	.735
2014	2 Tms	Low	120	458	137	26	6	12	(-	-)	211	71	70	74	33	2	127	2	8	5	19	8	5	.299	.345	.461	.806
2015	NwBrit	AA	124	468	110	25	5	8	(-	-)	169	57	57	49	30	1	117	2	6	6	19	8	5	.235	.281	.361	.642
2016	Hrtfrd	AA	108	431	116	33	3	13	(-	-)	194	66	67	60	28	0	95	2	9	4	8	9	8	.269	.314	.450	.764
2016	Albq	AAA	28	110	23	8	1	1	(-	-)	36	8	13	8	2	0	28	1	0	2	2	0	0	.209	.226	.327	.553
2016	Col	NL	13	19	5	1	0	1	(0	1)	9	3	2	1	0	0	8	0	0	0	0	0	0	.263	.263	.474	.737

Luis Valbuena

Bats: L **Throws:** R **Pos:** 3B-81;1B-8;PH-4;2B-1   val-BWAY-nah   **Ht:** 5'10" **Wt:** 215 **Born:** 11/30/1985 **Age:** 31

								BATTING													RUNNING			AVERAGES			
Year	Team	Lg	G	AB	H	2B	3B	HR	(Hm	Rd)	TB	R	RBI	RC	TBB	IBB	SO	HBP	SH	SF	SB	CS	GDP	Avg	OBP	Slg	OPS
2008	Sea	AL	14	49	12	5	0	0	(0	0)	17	6	1	5	4	0	11	1	0	0	0	0	0	.245	.315	.347	.662
2009	Cle	AL	103	368	92	25	3	10	(2	8)	153	52	31	35	26	0	83	0	2	2	2	3	8	.250	.298	.416	.714
2010	Cle	AL	91	275	53	12	0	2	(1	1)	71	22	24	21	28	1	61	3	2	2	1	2	5	.193	.273	.258	.531
2011	Cle	AL	17	43	9	0	0	1	(0	1)	12	4	1	2	1	0	9	0	0	0	1	0	0	.209	.227	.279	.506
2012	ChC	NL	90	265	58	20	0	4	(2	2)	90	26	28	27	36	1	55	0	0	2	0	2	6	.219	.310	.340	.650
2013	ChC	NL	108	331	72	15	1	12	(4	8)	125	34	37	43	53	4	63	4	1	2	1	4	4	.218	.331	.378	.708
2014	ChC	NL	149	478	119	33	4	16	(7	9)	208	68	51	65	65	4	113	2	1	1	1	2	8	.249	.341	.435	.776
2015	Hou	AL	132	434	97	18	0	25	(15	10)	190	62	56	51	50	1	106	6	0	3	1	0	13	.224	.310	.438	.748
2016	Hou	AL	90	292	76	17	1	13	(9	4)	134	38	40	47	44	2	81	1	3	2	1	1	5	.260	.357	.459	.816
	Postseason		6	17	3	0	0	1	(0	1)	6	2	2	2	4	0	8	0	0	0	0	0	0	.176	.333	.353	.686
	9 ML YEARS		798	2535	588	145	9	83	(40	43)	1000	312	269	296	307	13	582	17	9	14	8	14	49	.232	.317	.394	.712

Jose Valdez

Pitches: R **Bats:** R **Pos:** RP-25   **Ht:** 6'1" **Wt:** 200 **Born:** 3/1/1990 **Age:** 27

			HOW MUCH HE PITCHED						WHAT HE GAVE UP										THE RESULTS						
Year	Team	Lg	G	GS	CG	GF	IP	BFP	H	R	ER	HR	SH	SF	HB	TBB	IBB	SO	WP	Bk	W	L	Pct	Sh	Sv-Op	Hld	ERC	ERA
2012	Tigers	R	23	0	0	23	22.0	90	15	3	2	0	0	0	0	10	0	28	5	1	0	1	.000	0	15- -	-	1.98	0.82
2013	2 Tms	Low	50	0	0	46	49.1	207	32	16	15	1	0	0	1	34	1	67	6	2	2	2	.500	0	33- -	-	2.82	2.74
2014	Erie	AA	47	0	0	41	57.0	246	56	27	26	6	0	1	1	26	1	66	3	1	2	3	.400	0	18- -	-	4.33	4.11
2015	Toledo	AAA	43	0	0	24	57.0	247	49	23	21	3	3	1	0	38	2	43	5	1	4	5	.444	0	5- -	-	4.01	3.32
2016	Toledo	AAA	8	0	0	5	10.1	42	7	4	4	2	1	0	1	5	1	8	1	0	0	0	-	0	0- -	-	3.62	3.48
2016	Erie	AA	8	0	0	5	9.2	46	13	7	6	1	0	1	0	7	0	8	2	0	2	1	.667	0	0- -	-	7.89	5.59
2016	Salt Lk	AAA	22	0	0	14	25.2	100	13	3	2	1	0	0	0	11	0	28	4	1	0	1	.000	0	5- -	-	1.46	0.70
2015	Det	AL	7	0	0	3	9.0	39	10	4	4	2	0	0	0	4	0	4	2	0	0	1	.000	0	0-1	0	6.01	4.00
2016	LAA	AL	25	0	0	4	23.1	100	17	11	11	4	0	0	0	16	0	22	2	1	2	3	.400	0	0-1	5	4.24	4.24
	2 ML YEARS		32	0	0	7	32.1	139	27	15	15	6	0	0	0	20	0	26	4	1	2	4	.333	0	0-2	5	4.71	4.18

Danny Valencia

vuh-LENN-see-yah

Bats: R **Throws:** R **Pos:** 3B-68;RF-37;1B-18;DH-6;PH-5;LF-1   **Ht:** 6'2" **Wt:** 210 **Born:** 9/19/1984 **Age:** 32

								BATTING													RUNNING			AVERAGES			
Year	Team	Lg	G	AB	H	2B	3B	HR	(Hm	Rd)	TB	R	RBI	RC	TBB	IBB	SO	HBP	SH	SF	SB	CS	GDP	Avg	OBP	Slg	OPS
2010	Min	AL	85	299	93	18	1	7	(4	3)	134	30	40	50	20	0	46	0	0	3	2	0	11	.311	.351	.448	.799
2011	Min	AL	154	564	139	28	2	15	(9	6)	216	63	72	57	40	2	102	0	0	4	2	6	15	.246	.294	.383	.677
2012	2 Tms	AL	44	154	29	6	1	3	(3	0)	46	14	21	7	3	0	38	0	0	4	0	1	6	.188	.199	.299	.497
2013	Bal	AL	52	161	49	14	1	8	(4	4)	89	20	23	25	8	0	33	0	0	1	0	2	5	.304	.335	.553	.888
2014	2 Tms	AL	86	264	68	16	1	4	(1	3)	98	20	30	25	14	0	62	2	0	4	1	1	8	.258	.296	.371	.667
2015	2 Tms	AL	105	345	100	23	1	18	(7	11)	179	59	66	57	29	3	80	1	1	2	2	2	13	.290	.345	.519	.864
2016	Oak	AL	130	471	135	22	1	17	(4	13)	210	72	51	69	41	1	115	3	0	2	1	1	11	.287	.346	.446	.792

Year	Team	Lg	G	AB	H	2B	3B	HR	(Hm	Rd)	TB	R	RBI	RC	TBB	IBB	SO	HBP	SH	SF	SB	CS	GDP	Avg	OBP	Slg	OPS
12	Min	AL	34	126	25	6	1	2	(2	0)	39	13	17	7	3	0	32	0	0	3	0	1	5	.198	.212	.310	.522
12	Bos	AL	10	28	4	0	0	1	(1	0)	7	1	4	0	0	0	6	0	0	1	0	0	1	.143	.138	.250	.388
14	KC	AL	36	110	31	5	0	2	(0	2)	42	8	11	8	7	0	27	1	0	1	0	0	4	.282	.328	.382	.710
14	Tor	AL	50	154	37	11	1	2	(1	1)	56	12	19	17	7	0	35	1	0	3	1	1	4	.240	.273	.364	.636
15	Tor	AL	58	162	48	13	0	7	(4	3)	82	26	29	26	9	0	40	0	1	1	2	1	4	.296	.331	.506	.838
15	Oak	AL	47	183	52	10	1	11	(3	8)	97	33	37	31	20	3	40	1	0	1	0	1	9	.284	.356	.530	.886
	Postseason		3	9	2	1	0	0	(0	0)	3	1	2	1	1	0	3	0	0	1	0	0	0	.222	.273	.333	.606
	7 ML YEARS		656	2258	613	127	8	72	(32	40)	972	278	303	290	155	6	476	6	1	20	8	13	69	.271	.317	.430	.748

Scott Van Slyke

Bats: R Throws: R Pos: LF-19;PH-19;RF-10;1B-7;PR-2;CF-1 Ht: 6'4" Wt: 215 Born: 7/24/1986 Age: 30

Year	Team	Lg	G	AB	H	2B	3B	HR	(Hm	Rd)	TB	R	RBI	RC	TBB	IBB	SO	HBP	SH	SF	SB	CS	GDP	Avg	OBP	Slg	OPS
2012	LAD	NL	27	54	9	2	0	2	(1	1)	17	4	7	4	2	0	14	0	1	0	1	0	2	.167	.196	.315	.511
2013	LAD	NL	53	129	31	8	0	7	(4	3)	60	13	19	15	20	0	37	1	0	2	1	1	7	.240	.342	.465	.807
2014	LAD	NL	98	212	63	13	1	11	(2	9)	111	32	29	34	28	0	71	4	0	2	4	2	3	.297	.386	.524	.910
2015	LAD	NL	96	222	53	14	0	6	(4	2)	85	19	30	26	23	2	62	4	1	3	3	1	5	.239	.317	.383	.700
2016	LAD	NL	52	102	23	6	0	1	(0	1)	32	10	7	5	5	1	24	5	0	1	1	2	3	.225	.292	.314	.606
	Postseason		3	1	0	0	0	0	(0	0)	0	0	0	0	0	0	0	0	0	0	0	0	0	.000	.000	.000	.000
	5 ML YEARS		326	719	179	43	1	27	(11	16)	305	78	92	84	78	3	208	14	2	8	10	6	20	.249	.331	.424	.755

Cesar Vargas

Pitches: R Bats: R Pos: SP-7 Ht: 6'2" Wt: 220 Born: 12/30/1991 Age: 25

					HOW MUCH HE PITCHED						WHAT HE GAVE UP											THE RESULTS							
Year	Team	Lg	G	GS	CG	GF	IP	BFP	H	R	ER	HR	SH	SF	HB	TBB	IBB	SO	WP	Bk	W	L	Pct	Sh	Sv-Op	Hld	ERC	ERA
2012	2 Tms	Low	13	4	0	4	46.0	192	46	20	16	2	2	0	1	12	0	38	7	0	3	2	.600	0	2- -	-	3.26	3.13
2013	2 Tms	Low	25	25	1	0	120.2	506	109	67	55	7	3	4	5	43	0	92	8	0	4	8	.333	0	0- -	-	3.28	4.10
2014	2 Tms	Low	44	0	0	30	69.2	275	53	26	20	4	5	2	0	14	0	76	7	0	4	2	.667	0	14- -	-	1.86	2.58
2015	Trntn	AA	43	0	0	16	67.2	291	65	25	21	1	3	2	3	22	1	65	7	0	6	0	1.000	0	4- -	-	3.08	2.79
2016	SD	NL	7	7	0	0	34.0	154	41	19	19	1	0	2	1	15	1	28	0	0	0	3	.000	0	0-0	0	5.95	5.03

Jason Vargas

Pitches: L Bats: L Pos: SP-3 Ht: 6'0" Wt: 215 Born: 2/2/1983 Age: 34

					HOW MUCH HE PITCHED						WHAT HE GAVE UP											THE RESULTS							
Year	Team	Lg	G	GS	CG	GF	IP	BFP	H	R	ER	HR	SH	SF	HB	TBB	IBB	SO	WP	Bk	W	L	Pct	Sh	Sv-Op	Hld	ERC	ERA
2005	Fla	NL	17	13	1	0	73.2	325	71	34	33	4	4	1	4	31	4	59	0	0	5	5	.500	0	0-0	0	3.68	4.03
2006	Fla	NL	12	5	0	3	43.0	213	50	39	35	9	4	4	4	30	3	25	2	0	1	2	.333	0	0-0	0	7.30	7.33
2007	NYM	NL	2	2	0	0	10.1	51	17	14	14	4	0	0	0	2	1	4	1	1	0	1	.000	0	0-0	0	8.95	12.19
2009	Sea	AL	23	14	0	4	91.2	385	98	53	50	16	3	6	3	24	1	54	1	0	3	6	.333	0	0-0	0	4.64	4.91
2010	Sea	AL	31	31	0	0	192.2	811	187	86	81	18	4	7	1	54	3	116	1	4	9	12	.429	0	0-0	0	3.37	3.78
2011	Sea	AL	32	32	4	0	201.0	857	205	105	95	22	3	4	4	59	4	131	3	1	10	13	.435	3	0-0	0	3.86	4.25
2012	Sea	AL	33	33	2	0	217.1	887	201	94	93	35	3	6	3	55	1	141	5	0	14	11	.560	0	0-0	0	3.57	3.85
2013	LAA	AL	24	24	3	0	150.0	644	162	68	67	17	3	3	5	46	2	109	0	1	9	8	.529	2	0-0	0	4.40	4.02
2014	KC	AL	30	30	1	0	187.0	790	197	82	77	19	3	1	6	41	4	128	1	1	11	10	.524	0	0-0	0	3.76	3.71
2015	KC	AL	9	9	0	0	43.0	183	46	20	19	5	0	0	1	12	0	27	0	0	5	2	.714	0	0-0	0	4.22	3.98
2016	KC	AL	3	3	0	0	12.0	47	8	3	3	1	0	0	0	3	0	11	0	0	0	0	-	0	0-0	0	1.73	2.25
	Postseason		3	3	0	0	15.1	61	11	6	6	3	0	0	0	6	0	11	1	0	1	0	1.000	0	0-0	0	3.20	3.52
	11 ML YEARS		216	196	11	7	1221.2	5193	1242	598	567	150	27	32	31	357	23	805	14	8	67	70	.489	6	0-0	0	3.97	4.18

Kennys Vargas

Bats: B Throws: R Pos: 1B-32;DH-13;PH-4 KEN-ee Ht: 6'5" Wt: 290 Born: 8/1/1990 Age: 26

Year	Team	Lg	G	AB	H	2B	3B	HR	(Hm	Rd)	TB	R	RBI	RC	TBB	IBB	SO	HBP	SH	SF	SB	CS	GDP	Avg	OBP	Slg	OPS
2016	Roch*	AAA	96	330	77	16	1	15	(-	-)	140	41	58	56	66	2	89	2	0	4	1	0	7	.233	.424	.785	
2014	Min	AL	53	215	59	10	1	9	(8	1)	98	26	38	27	12	2	63	3	0	4	0	0	5	.274	.316	.456	.772
2015	Min	AL	58	175	42	4	0	5	(5	0)	61	18	17	13	9	0	54	0	0	0	0	0	7	.240	.277	.349	.626
2016	Min	AL	47	152	35	11	0	10	(4	6)	76	27	20	21	24	1	57	0	0	1	0	0	2	.230	.333	.500	.833
	3 ML YEARS		158	542	136	25	1	24	(17	7)	235	71	75	61	45	3	174	3	0	5	0	0	14	.251	.309	.434	.743

Christian Vazquez

Bats: R Throws: R Pos: C-56;PH-3 VAZ-kehz Ht: 5'9" Wt: 195 Born: 8/21/1990 Age: 26

Year	Team	Lg	G	AB	H	2B	3B	HR	(Hm	Rd)	TB	R	RBI	RC	TBB	IBB	SO	HBP	SH	SF	SB	CS	GDP	Avg	OBP	Slg	OPS
2012	Salem	A+	81	293	78	17	0	7	(-	-)	116	43	41	44	40	0	70	4	3	2	2	2	7	.266	.360	.396	.756
2012	Portlnd	AA	20	73	15	4	0	0	(-	-)	19	11	5	5	8	0	9	0	0	1	0	0	1	.205	.280	.260	.541
2013	Portlnd	AA	96	342	99	19	1	5	(-	-)	135	48	48	55	47	0	44	3	3	4	7	5	9	.289	.376	.395	.771
2014	Pwtckt	AAA	66	244	68	17	0	3	(-	-)	94	35	20	32	21	2	52	1	2	2	0	1	14	.279	.336	.385	.721
2016	Pwtckt	AAA	42	152	41	9	0	2	(-	-)	56	19	16	21	15	1	31	3	0	1	2	0	6	.270	.345	.368	.713
2014	Bos	AL	55	175	42	9	0	1	(1	0)	54	15	20	19	19	1	33	0	3	4	0	0	4	.240	.308	.309	.617
2016	Bos	AL	57	172	39	9	1	1	(1	0)	53	21	12	11	10	1	39	2	0	0	0	0	3	.227	.277	.308	.585
	2 ML YEARS		112	347	81	18	1	2	(2	0)	107	36	32	30	29	2	72	2	3	4	0	0	7	.233	.293	.308	.602

Vince Velasquez

Pitches: R **Bats:** R **Pos:** SP-24   **Ht:** 6'3" **Wt:** 205 **Born:** 6/7/1992 **Age:** 25

		HOW MUCH HE PITCHED						WHAT HE GAVE UP												THE RESULTS							
Year	Team	Lg	G	GS	CG	GF	IP	BFP	H	R	ER	HR	SH	SF	HB	TBB	IBB	SO	WP	Bk	W	L	Pct	Sh	Sv-Op	Hld	ERC	ERA
2012	TriCity	A-	9	9	0	0	45.2	190	37	19	17	2	0	4	3	17	0	51	4	2	4	1	.800	0	0--	-	2.83	3.35
2013	2 Tms	Low	28	19	0	4	124.2	518	104	53	49	9	2	5	8	41	0	142	6	1	9	6	.600	0	3--	-	2.97	3.54
2014	2 Tms	Low	18	13	0	2	63.2	264	50	26	25	6	1	0	6	25	1	91	2	0	7	5	.583	0	0--	-	3.23	3.53
2015	CpChr	AA	9	5	0	1	33.0	130	20	9	7	2	2	0	1	13	0	45	1	0	4	0	1.000	0	0--	-	1.94	1.91
2015	Hou	AL	19	7	0	5	55.2	231	50	28	27	5	0	0	2	21	0	58	3	0	1	1	.500	0	0-0	0	3.58	4.37
2016	Phi	NL	24	24	1	0	131.0	551	129	64	60	21	9	5	1	45	1	152	3	0	8	6	.571	1	0-0	0	4.25	4.12
	2 ML YEARS		43	31	1	5	186.2	782	179	92	87	26	9	5	3	66	1	210	6	0	9	7	.563	1	0-0	0	4.05	4.19

Will Venable

Bats: L **Throws:** L **Pos:** PH-9;RF-4;LF-1   VENN-uh-bull   **Ht:** 6'3" **Wt:** 205 **Born:** 10/29/1982 **Age:** 34

			BATTING																			RUNNING			AVERAGES			
Year	Team	Lg	G	AB	H	2B	3B	HR	(Hm	Rd)	TB	R	RBI	RC	TBB	IBB	SO	HBP	SH	SF	SB	CS	GDP	Avg	OBP	Slg	OPS
2016	LV*	AAA	41	127	26	7	0	2	(-	-)	39	12	19	13	17	2	28	2	1	2	2	2	2	.205	.304	.307	.611
2016	OkCity*	AAA	46	156	43	6	1	4	(-	-)	63	23	25	22	15	1	32	1	0	0	3	2	2	.276	.343	.404	.747
2008	SD	NL	28	110	29	4	2	2	(0	2)	43	16	10	15	13	1	21	0	0	1	1	1	1	.264	.339	.391	.730
2009	SD	NL	95	293	75	14	2	12	(5	7)	129	38	38	34	25	2	89	4	2	0	6	1	6	.256	.323	.440	.763
2010	SD	NL	131	392	96	11	7	13	(6	7)	160	60	51	57	45	8	128	3	0	5	29	7	3	.245	.324	.408	.732
2011	SD	NL	121	370	91	14	7	9	(6	3)	146	49	44	52	31	4	92	5	1	4	26	3	2	.246	.310	.395	.704
2012	SD	NL	148	417	110	26	8	9	(2	7)	179	62	45	66	41	2	94	5	5	2	24	6	2	.264	.335	.429	.765
2013	SD	NL	151	481	129	22	8	22	(15	7)	233	64	53	56	29	4	118	2	2	1	22	6	6	.268	.312	.484	.796
2014	SD	NL	146	406	91	13	2	8	(5	3)	132	47	33	41	33	2	107	4	3	2	11	6	6	.224	.288	.325	.613
2015	2 Tms		135	349	85	13	3	6	(1	5)	122	40	33	46	37	3	94	2	2	0	16	1	8	.244	.320	.350	.669
2016	LAD	NL	12	18	1	1	0	0	(0	0)	2	2	0	0	0	0	5	1	0	0	0	0	0	.056	.105	.111	.216
15	SD	NL	98	283	73	10	3	6	(1	5)	107	34	30	39	25	1	73	0	0	0	11	1	8	.258	.318	.378	.696
15	Tex	AL	37	66	12	3	0	0	(0	0)	15	6	3	7	12	2	21	2	2	0	5	0	0	.182	.325	.227	.552
	Postseason		4	2	1	0	0	0	(0	0)	1	0	0	1	0	0	1	0	0	0	0	0	0	.500	.500	.500	1.000
	9 ML YEARS		967	2836	707	118	39	81	(40	41)	1146	378	307	367	254	26	748	26	15	15	135	31	34	.249	.315	.404	.719

Pat Venditte

Pitches: B **Bats:** L **Pos:** RP-15   ven-DET-ee   **Ht:** 6'1" **Wt:** 185 **Born:** 6/30/1985 **Age:** 32

			HOW MUCH HE PITCHED						WHAT HE GAVE UP												THE RESULTS							
Year	Team	Lg	G	GS	CG	GF	IP	BFP	H	R	ER	HR	SH	SF	HB	TBB	IBB	SO	WP	Bk	W	L	Pct	Sh	Sv-Op	Hld	ERC	ERA
2012	S-WB	AAA	7	0	0	0	13.0	56	11	4	4	1	1	1	1	6	1	12	0	0	1	1	.500	0	0--	-	3.47	2.77
2013	3 Tms	Low	13	6	0	0	17.1	71	14	8	6	0	1	1	1	5	0	17	2	0	0	2	.000	0	0--	-	2.22	3.12
2013	Trntn	AA	8	0	0	1	11.1	49	13	5	5	1	0	0	0	3	1	13	1	1	1	2	.333	0	0--	-	4.13	3.97
2014	Trntn	AA	15	0	0	6	22.0	83	11	3	2	2	0	0	0	5	0	30	0	0	0	1	.000	0	1--	-	1.18	0.82
2014	S-WB	AAA	26	2	0	7	56.1	239	54	21	21	4	3	2	1	17	0	53	3	2	2	5	.286	0	0--	-	3.30	3.36
2015	Nashv	AAA	23	1	0	2	40.2	166	27	8	7	2	3	1	2	15	0	40	1	2	1	0	1.000	0	0--	-	2.05	1.55
2016	Buffalo	AAA	25	2	0	4	35.0	161	39	17	17	3	0	1	3	13	0	52	0	0	2	1	.667	0	0--	-	4.70	4.37
2016	Tacom	AAA	5	0	0	0	8.1	33	7	1	1	0	0	0	0	3	0	11	0	0	1	0	1.000	0	0--	-	2.55	1.08
2015	Oak	AL	26	0	0	7	28.2	119	22	14	14	3	1	1	0	12	0	23	0	0	2	2	.500	0	0-0	2	2.90	4.40
2016	2 Tms	AL	15	0	0	7	22.0	102	24	18	14	5	0	3	2	11	1	19	0	0	0	0	-	0	0-0	1	6.23	5.73
16	Tor	AL	8	0	0	3	8.2	44	11	8	5	1	0	2	1	4	0	7	0	0	0	0	-	0	0-0	1	6.06	5.19
16	Sea	AL	7	0	0	4	13.1	58	13	10	9	4	0	1	1	7	1	12	0	0	0	0	-	0	0-0	0	6.34	6.08
	2 ML YEARS		41	0	0	14	50.2	221	46	32	28	8	1	4	2	23	1	42	0	0	2	2	.500	0	0-0	3	4.25	4.97

Yordano Ventura

Pitches: R **Bats:** R **Pos:** SP-32   your-DON-oh ven-TOUR-uh   **Ht:** 6'0" **Wt:** 195 **Born:** 6/3/1991 **Age:** 26

			HOW MUCH HE PITCHED						WHAT HE GAVE UP												THE RESULTS							
Year	Team	Lg	G	GS	CG	GF	IP	BFP	H	R	ER	HR	SH	SF	HB	TBB	IBB	SO	WP	Bk	W	L	Pct	Sh	Sv-Op	Hld	ERC	ERA
2013	KC	AL	3	3	0	0	15.1	64	13	6	6	3	0	0	0	6	0	11	1	0	0	1	.000	0	0-0	0	3.83	3.52
2014	KC	AL	31	30	0	0	183.0	782	168	70	65	14	3	4	5	69	1	159	11	1	14	10	.583	0	0-0	0	3.44	3.20
2015	KC	AL	28	28	0	0	163.1	693	154	75	74	14	1	4	9	58	1	156	10	0	13	8	.619	0	0-0	0	3.71	4.08
2016	KC	AL	32	32	2	0	186.0	816	190	96	92	23	3	4	8	78	1	144	13	1	11	12	.478	0	0-0	0	4.61	4.45
	Postseason		10	9	0	0	46.1	202	50	24	24	8	0	1	1	17	1	36	1	0	1	2	.333	0	0-1	0	4.99	4.66
	4 ML YEARS		94	93	2	0	547.2	2355	525	247	237	54	7	12	22	211	3	470	35	2	38	31	.551	0	0-0	0	3.92	3.89

Drew VerHagen

Pitches: R **Bats:** R **Pos:** RP-19   verr-HAY-gen   **Ht:** 6'6" **Wt:** 230 **Born:** 10/22/1990 **Age:** 26

			HOW MUCH HE PITCHED						WHAT HE GAVE UP												THE RESULTS							
Year	Team	Lg	G	GS	CG	GF	IP	BFP	H	R	ER	HR	SH	SF	HB	TBB	IBB	SO	WP	Bk	W	L	Pct	Sh	Sv-Op	Hld	ERC	ERA
2014	Det	AL	1	1	0	0	5.0	20	5	3	3	0	0	0	0	3	0	4	0	0	0	1	.000	0	0-0	0	4.67	5.40
2015	Det	AL	20	0	0	2	26.1	106	18	6	6	1	1	0	1	14	2	13	1	0	2	0	1.000	0	0-1	3	2.61	2.44
2016	Det	AL	19	0	0	4	19.0	90	28	15	15	3	0	1	1	7	1	10	1	0	1	0	1.000	0	0-0	2	7.50	7.11
	3 ML YEARS		40	1	0	6	50.1	216	51	24	24	4	1	1	2	24	3	27	2	0	3	1	.750	0	0-1	5	4.51	4.29

Justin Verlander

Pitches: R **Bats:** R **Pos:** SP-34   **Ht:** 6'5" **Wt:** 225 **Born:** 2/20/1983 **Age:** 34

Year	Team	Lg	G	GS	CG	GF	IP	BFP	H	R	ER	HR	SH	SF	HB	TBB	IBB	SO	WP	Bk	W	L	Pct	Sh	Sv-Op	Hld	ERC	ERA
2005	Det	AL	2	2	0	0	11.1	54	15	9	9	1	0	0	1	5	0	7	1	0	0	2	.000	0	0-0	0	6.41	7.15
2006	Det	AL	30	30	1	0	186.0	776	187	78	75	21	2	4	6	60	1	124	5	1	17	9	.654	1	0-0	0	4.12	3.63
2007	Det	AL	32	32	1	0	201.2	866	181	88	82	20	3	1	19	67	3	183	17	2	18	6	.750	1	0-0	0	3.53	3.66
2008	Det	AL	33	33	1	0	201.0	880	195	119	108	18	4	6	14	87	8	163	6	3	11	17	.393	0	0-0	0	4.17	4.84
2009	Det	AL	35	35	3	0	240.0	982	219	99	92	20	6	4	6	63	5	269	8	4	19	9	.679	1	0-0	0	3.06	3.45
2010	Det	AL	33	33	4	0	224.1	925	190	89	84	14	6	8	6	71	0	219	11	2	18	9	.667	0	0-0	0	2.79	3.37
2011	Det	AL	34	34	4	0	251.0	969	174	73	67	24	2	3	3	57	0	250	7	2	24	5	.828	2	0-0	0	1.92	2.40
2012	Det	AL	33	33	6	0	238.1	956	192	81	70	19	4	3	5	60	2	239	2	1	17	8	.680	1	0-0	0	2.45	2.64
2013	Det	AL	34	34	0	0	218.1	925	212	94	84	19	2	6	4	75	1	217	3	1	13	12	.520	0	0-0	0	3.68	3.46
2014	Det	AL	32	32	0	0	206.0	893	223	114	104	18	6	5	5	65	1	159	5	1	15	12	.556	0	0-0	0	4.19	4.54
2015	Det	AL	20	20	1	0	133.1	535	113	56	50	13	1	6	3	32	1	113	2	0	5	8	.385	1	0-0	0	2.75	3.38
2016	Det	AL	34	34	2	0	227.2	903	171	81	77	30	4	7	8	57	1	254	6	0	16	9	.640	0	0-0	0	2.54	3.04
	Postseason		16	16	1	0	98.1	401	77	40	37	13	1	1	1	30	0	112	6	1	7	5	.583	1	0-0	0	2.77	3.39
	12 ML YEARS		352	352	23	0	2339.0	9664	2072	981	902	217	40	53	80	699	23	2197	73	17	173	106	.620	7	0-0	0	3.15	3.47

Logan Verrett

Pitches: R **Bats:** R **Pos:** RP-23; SP-12   vuh-RETT   **Ht:** 6'2" **Wt:** 190 **Born:** 6/19/1990 **Age:** 27

Year	Team	Lg	G	GS	CG	GF	IP	BFP	H	R	ER	HR	SH	SF	HB	TBB	IBB	SO	WP	Bk	W	L	Pct	Sh	Sv-Op	Hld	ERC	ERA
2012	2 Tms	Low	17	17	2	0	103.1	415	87	43	31	11	0	3	3	13	0	93	5	0	5	2	.714	1	0--	-	2.32	2.70
2013	Bnghtn	AA	24	24	0	0	146.0	586	136	72	69	21	3	3	3	31	0	132	4	1	12	6	.667	0	0--	-	3.41	4.25
2014	LsVgs	AAA	28	28	1	0	162.0	699	188	94	78	17	3	9	7	34	0	119	9	1	11	5	.688	0	0--	-	4.44	4.33
2015	LsVgs	AAA	18	11	0	0	64.2	273	69	35	33	6	2	3	1	19	0	53	4	0	5	3	.625	0	0--	-	4.11	4.59
2015	2 Tms		18	4	0	4	47.2	190	34	20	19	6	2	3	2	15	4	39	1	0	1	2	.333	0	1-2	2	2.48	3.59
2016	NYM	NL	35	12	0	10	91.2	406	100	55	53	16	3	3	4	43	3	66	4	1	3	8	.273	0	0-0	5	5.68	5.20
15	Tex	AL	4	0	0	1	9.0	42	11	7	6	1	0	2	0	4	1	3	1	0	0	1	.000	0	0-0	0	5.30	6.00
15	NYM	NL	14	4	0	3	38.2	148	23	13	13	5	2	1	2	11	3	36	0	0	1	1	.500	0	1-2	2	1.90	3.03
	2 ML YEARS		53	16	0	14	139.1	596	134	75	72	22	5	6	6	58	7	105	5	1	4	10	.286	0	1-2	0	4.49	4.65

Carlos Villanueva

Pitches: R **Bats:** R **Pos:** RP-51   vee-yah-noo-WAY-vah   **Ht:** 6'2" **Wt:** 220 **Born:** 11/28/1983 **Age:** 33

Year	Team	Lg	G	GS	CG	GF	IP	BFP	H	R	ER	HR	SH	SF	HB	TBB	IBB	SO	WP	Bk	W	L	Pct	Sh	Sv-Op	Hld	ERC	ERA
2006	Mil	NL	10	6	0	2	53.2	215	43	22	22	8	1	0	4	11	1	39	0	0	2	2	.500	0	0-0	0	2.85	3.69
2007	Mil	NL	59	6	0	8	114.1	489	101	52	50	16	4	1	3	53	3	99	3	0	8	5	.615	0	1-3	16	4.03	3.94
2008	Mil	NL	47	9	0	9	108.1	464	112	53	49	18	9	1	3	30	1	93	4	0	4	7	.364	0	1-1	11	4.29	4.07
2009	Mil	NL	64	6	0	23	96.0	422	102	58	57	13	4	0	6	35	8	83	4	0	4	10	.286	0	3-8	9	4.44	5.34
2010	Mil	NL	50	0	0	5	52.2	231	48	27	27	7	0	3	4	22	1	67	5	0	2	0	1.000	0	1-4	14	4.08	4.61
2011	Tor	AL	33	13	0	3	107.0	454	103	49	48	11	1	6	4	32	3	68	4	0	6	4	.600	0	0-1	5	3.57	4.04
2012	Tor	AL	38	16	0	9	125.1	521	113	59	58	23	2	4	3	46	4	122	6	1	7	7	.500	0	0-0	2	4.08	4.16
2013	ChC	NL	47	15	0	5	128.2	524	117	58	58	14	7	3	3	40	4	103	0	0	7	8	.467	0	0-1	2	3.43	4.06
2014	ChC	NL	42	5	0	15	77.2	343	89	42	40	6	3	2	3	19	4	72	3	0	5	7	.417	0	2-2	5	4.10	4.64
2015	StL	NL	35	0	0	20	61.0	250	50	21	20	6	1	2	2	21	2	55	1	0	4	3	.571	0	2-2	0	2.98	2.95
2016	SD	NL	51	0	0	11	74.0	321	89	50	49	17	2	2	3	14	4	61	2	0	2	2	.500	0	1-2	4	5.39	5.96
	Postseason		3	0	0	0	5.2	18	0	0	0	0	0	0	0	1	0	3	0	0	0	0	-	0	0-0	1	0.04	0.00
	11 ML YEARS		476	76	0	110	998.2	4234	967	491	478	139	34	24	34	323	35	862	32	1	51	55	.481	0	11-24	61	3.95	4.31

Jonathan Villar

Bats: B **Throws:** R **Pos:** SS-108;3B-42;2B-11;PH-4   vee-YARR   **Ht:** 6'1" **Wt:** 215 **Born:** 5/2/1991 **Age:** 26

Year	Team	Lg	G	AB	H	2B	3B	HR	(Hm	Rd)	TB	R	RBI	RC	TBB	IBB	SO	HBP	SH	SF	SB	CS	GDP	Avg	OBP	Slg	OPS
2013	Hou	AL	58	210	51	9	2	1	(0	1)	67	26	8	22	24	1	71	0	7	0	18	8	5	.243	.321	.319	.640
2014	Hou	AL	87	263	55	13	2	7	(3	4)	93	31	27	24	19	1	80	2	4	1	17	4	4	.209	.267	.354	.620
2015	Hou	AL	53	116	33	7	1	2	(0	2)	48	18	11	15	10	0	29	0	1	1	7	2	3	.284	.339	.414	.752
2016	Mil	NL	156	589	168	38	3	19	(6	13)	269	92	63	102	79	4	174	2	5	4	62	18	7	.285	.369	.457	.826
	Postseason		1	0	0	0	0	0	(0	0)	0	1	0	0	0	0	0	0	0	0	1	0	0	-	-	-	-
	4 ML YEARS		354	1178	307	67	8	29	(9	20)	477	167	109	163	132	6	354	4	17	6	104	32	19	.261	.336	.405	.741

Nick Vincent

Pitches: R **Bats:** R **Pos:** RP-60   **Ht:** 6'0" **Wt:** 185 **Born:** 7/12/1986 **Age:** 30

Year	Team	Lg	G	GS	CG	GF	IP	BFP	H	R	ER	HR	SH	SF	HB	TBB	IBB	SO	WP	Bk	W	L	Pct	Sh	Sv-Op	Hld	ERC	ERA
2012	SD	NL	27	0	0	3	26.1	105	19	5	5	2	1	0	1	7	0	28	1	0	2	0	1.000	0	0-1	5	2.13	1.71
2013	SD	NL	45	0	0	7	46.1	180	33	11	11	1	4	0	2	11	3	49	0	0	6	3	.667	0	1-1	10	1.67	2.14
2014	SD	NL	63	0	0	7	55.0	215	44	22	22	5	3	0	2	11	1	62	1	0	1	2	.333	0	0-2	20	2.39	3.60
2015	SD	NL	26	0	0	8	23.0	100	25	8	6	0	1	0	0	10	1	22	0	0	1	0	1.000	0	0-2	6	3.95	2.35
2016	Sea	AL	60	0	0	15	60.1	247	53	26	25	11	1	1	1	15	5	65	0	0	4	4	.500	0	3-9	17	3.28	3.73
	5 ML YEARS		221	0	0	40	211.0	847	174	72	69	19	9	2	6	54	10	226	2	0	13	10	.565	0	4-15	52	2.61	2.94

Arodys Vizcaino

Pitches: R **Bats:** R **Pos:** RP-43 ah-ROH-dis vees-kai-EE-no **Ht:** 6'0" **Wt:** 230 **Born:** 11/13/1990 **Age:** 26

			HOW MUCH HE PITCHED					WHAT HE GAVE UP									THE RESULTS							
Year Team	Lg	G	GS	CG	GF	IP	BFP	H	R	ER	HR	SH	SF	HB	TBB	IBB	SO	WP	Bk	W	L	Pct	Sh	Sv-Op	Hld	ERC	ERA
2011 Atl	NL	17	0	0	2	17.1	77	16	9	9	1	0	0	1	9	1	17	5	0	1	1	.500	0	0-2	5	3.89	4.67
2014 ChC	NL	5	0	0	5	5.0	22	5	3	3	1	0	0	0	3	0	4	0	0	0	0	-	0	0-0	0	5.79	5.40
2015 Atl	NL	36	0	0	25	33.2	139	27	7	6	1	2	0	0	13	2	37	7	0	3	1	.750	0	9-10	3	2.42	1.60
2016 Atl	NL	43	0	0	24	38.2	182	37	25	19	3	1	0	1	26	3	50	3	1	1	4	.200	0	10-14	0	4.52	4.42
4 ML YEARS		101	0	0	56	94.2	420	85	44	37	6	3	0	2	51	6	108	15	1	5	6	.455	0	19-26	8	3.69	3.52

Dan Vogelbach

Bats: L **Throws:** R **Pos:** 1B-4;PH-4;DH-1 voh-GULL-bock **Ht:** 6'0" **Wt:** 250 **Born:** 12/17/1992 **Age:** 24

						BATTING														RUNNING			AVERAGES			
Year Team	Lg	G	AB	H	2B	3B	HR	(Hm	Rd)	TB	R	RBI	RC	TBB	IBB	SO	HBP	SH	SF	SB	CS	GDP	Avg	OBP	Slg	OPS
2012 2 Tms	Low	61	245	79	21	3	17	(-	-)	157	39	62	61	35	1	48	2	0	1			3	.322	.410	.641	1.051
2013 2 Tms	Low	131	483	137	23	3	19	(-	-)	217	68	76	85	73	3	89	2	0	8	5	4	11	.284	.375	.449	.824
2014 Dytona	A+	132	482	129	28	1	16	(-	-)	207	71	76	78	66	1	91	5	0	7	4	4	15	.268	.357	.429	.787
2015 Tenn	AA	76	254	69	16	1	7	(-	-)	108	41	39	48	57	1	61	0	0	2	1	1	12	.272	.403	.425	.828
2016 Iowa	AAA	89	305	97	18	2	16	(-	-)	167	53	64	71	55	5	67	3	0	2	0	0	9	.318	.425	.548	.972
2016 Tacom	AAA	44	154	37	7	0	7	(-	-)	65	26	32	30	42	2	34	1	0	1	0	0	7	.240	.404	.422	.826
2016 Sea	AL	8	12	1	0	0	0	(0	0)	1	0	0	0	1	0	6	0	0	0	0	0	0	.083	.154	.083	.237

Ryan Vogelsong

Pitches: R **Bats:** R **Pos:** SP-14; RP-10 VOH-gull-song **Ht:** 6'4" **Wt:** 215 **Born:** 7/22/1977 **Age:** 39

				HOW MUCH HE PITCHED				WHAT HE GAVE UP											THE RESULTS							
Year Team	Lg	G	GS	CG	GF	IP	BFP	H	R	ER	HR	SH	SF	HB	TBB	IBB	SO	WP	Bk	W	L	Pct	Sh	Sv-Op	Hld	ERC	ERA
2000 SF	NL	4	0	0	3	6.0	24	4	0	0	0	0	0	0	2	0	6	0	0	0	0	-	0	0-0	0	1.57	0.00
2001 2 Tms	NL	15	2	0	8	34.2	164	39	31	26	6	0	1	2	20	1	24	2	0	0	5	.000	0	0-0	1	6.20	6.75
2003 Pit	NL	6	5	0	0	22.0	108	30	19	16	1	3	1	2	9	3	15	1	0	2	2	.500	0	0-0	0	5.72	6.55
2004 Pit	NL	31	26	0	4	133.0	610	148	97	96	22	8	6	10	67	7	92	3	0	6	13	.316	0	0-0	0	5.89	6.50
2005 Pit	NL	44	0	0	19	81.1	369	82	43	40	5	1	4	8	40	1	52	7	0	2	2	.500	0	0-1	4	4.51	4.43
2006 Pit	NL	20	0	0	7	38.0	178	44	27	27	2	5	4	7	16	2	27	4	1	0	0	-	0	0-0	0	5.31	6.39
2011 SF	NL	30	28	1	1	179.2	752	164	62	54	15	10	3	5	61	6	139	1	1	13	7	.650	1	0-0	0	3.32	2.71
2012 SF	NL	31	31	0	0	189.2	788	171	76	71	17	7	4	8	62	7	158	3	0	14	9	.609	0	0-0	0	3.33	3.37
2013 SF	NL	19	19	0	0	103.2	467	124	73	66	11	4	4	6	38	2	67	3	0	4	6	.400	0	0-0	0	5.64	5.73
2014 SF	NL	32	32	1	0	184.2	780	178	86	82	18	10	3	9	58	2	151	2	0	8	13	.381	0	0-0	0	3.71	4.00
2015 SF	NL	33	22	0	6	135.0	598	140	76	70	17	3	6	3	58	2	108	1	0	9	11	.450	0	0-1	0	4.62	4.67
2016 Pit	NL	24	14	0	2	82.1	366	80	51	44	11	6	0	4	40	2	61	0	1	3	7	.300	0	0-0	1	4.62	4.81
01 SF	NL	13	0	0	8	28.2	130	29	21	18	5	0	1	2	14	0	17	2	0	0	3	.000	0	0-0	1	5.26	5.65
01 Pit	NL	2	2	0	0	6.0	34	10	10	8	1	0	0	0	6	1	7	0	0	0	2	.000	0	0-0	0	11.03	12.00
Postseason		8	7	0	1	37.0	155	32	12	12	1	0	0	1	16	0	29	0	0	3	0	1.000	0	0-0	0	3.11	2.92
12 ML YEARS		289	179	2	50	1190.0	5204	1204	641	592	129	57	36	64	471	35	900	31	2	61	75	.449	1	0-2	3	4.34	4.48

Stephen Vogt

Bats: L **Throws:** R **Pos:** C-113;DH-23;PH-11;1B-1 VOTE **Ht:** 6'0" **Wt:** 225 **Born:** 11/1/1984 **Age:** 32

						BATTING														RUNNING			AVERAGES			
Year Team	Lg	G	AB	H	2B	3B	HR	(Hm	Rd)	TB	R	RBI	RC	TBB	IBB	SO	HBP	SH	SF	SB	CS	GDP	Avg	OBP	Slg	OPS
2012 TB	AL	18	25	0	0	0	0	(0	0)	0	0	0	0	2	0	2	0	0	0	0	0	0	.000	.074	.000	.074
2013 Oak	AL	47	135	34	6	1	4	(3	1)	54	18	16	15	9	1	28	0	2	2	0	1	2	.252	.295	.400	.695
2014 Oak	AL	84	269	75	10	2	9	(4	5)	116	26	35	38	16	2	39	1	0	1	1	0	2	.279	.321	.431	.752
2015 Oak	AL	136	445	116	21	3	18	(5	13)	197	58	71	75	56	6	97	2	0	8	0	2	9	.261	.341	.443	.783
2016 Oak	AL	137	490	123	30	2	14	(4	10)	199	54	56	51	35	3	83	4	0	3	0	0	6	.251	.305	.406	.711
Postseason		6	19	3	0	1	0	(0	0)	5	2	1	1	2	0	8	0	0	0	0	0	0	.158	.238	.263	.501
5 ML YEARS		422	1364	348	67	8	45	(16	29)	566	156	178	179	118	12	249	7	2	14	1	3	19	.255	.315	.415	.730

Edinson Volquez

Pitches: R **Bats:** R **Pos:** SP-34 VOHL-kezz **Ht:** 6'0" **Wt:** 220 **Born:** 7/3/1983 **Age:** 33

				HOW MUCH HE PITCHED				WHAT HE GAVE UP											THE RESULTS							
Year Team	Lg	G	GS	CG	GF	IP	BFP	H	R	ER	HR	SH	SF	HB	TBB	IBB	SO	WP	Bk	W	L	Pct	Sh	Sv-Op	Hld	ERC	ERA
2005 Tex	AL	6	3	0	0	12.2	75	25	22	20	3	0	1	2	10	0	11	0	0	0	4	.000	0	0-0	0	14.15	14.21
2006 Tex	AL	8	8	0	0	33.1	164	52	28	27	7	0	1	1	17	0	15	0	0	1	6	.143	0	0-0	0	9.27	7.29
2007 Tex	AL	6	6	0	0	34.0	149	34	18	17	4	0	2	2	15	0	29	0	0	2	1	.667	0	0-0	0	4.63	4.50
2008 Cin	NL	33	32	0	1	196.0	838	167	82	70	14	6	5	14	93	5	206	10	1	17	6	.739	0	0-0	0	3.61	3.21
2009 Cin	NL	9	9	0	0	49.2	218	34	25	24	6	2	1	5	32	0	47	2	1	4	2	.667	0	0-0	0	3.77	4.35
2010 Cin	NL	12	12	0	0	62.2	275	59	30	30	6	3	1	3	35	0	67	5	0	4	3	.571	0	0-0	0	4.60	4.31
2011 Cin	NL	20	20	0	0	108.2	489	106	72	69	19	5	6	4	45	3	104	5	2	5	7	.417	0	0-0	0	5.42	5.71
2012 SD	NL	32	32	1	0	182.2	802	160	88	84	14	5	4	9	105	6	174	9	1	11	11	.500	1	0-0	0	4.04	4.14
2013 2 Tms	NL	33	32	0	0	170.1	777	193	114	108	19	9	4	3	77	2	142	16	0	9	12	.429	0	0-0	0	5.11	5.71
2014 Pit	NL	32	31	1	0	192.2	809	166	75	65	17	13	6	14	71	6	140	15	0	13	7	.650	0	0-0	0	3.37	3.04
2015 KC	AL	34	33	1	0	200.1	850	190	89	79	16	5	7	8	72	1	155	3	0	13	9	.591	0	0-0	0	3.66	3.55
2016 KC	AL	34	34	0	0	189.1	853	217	124	113	23	6	6	7	76	1	139	5	1	10	11	.476	0	0-0	0	5.20	5.37
13 SD	NL	27	27	0	0	142.1	659	168	100	95	14	7	3	3	69	2	116	11	0	9	10	.474	0	0-0	0	5.45	6.01
13 LAD	NL	6	5	0	0	28.0	118	25	14	13	5	2	1	0	8	0	26	5	0	0	2	.000	0	0-0	0	3.45	4.18
Postseason		7	7	0	0	35.1	154	27	22	21	4	1	3	2	23	2	26	0	0	1	4	.200	0	0-0	0	3.98	5.35
12 ML YEARS		259	252	3	1	1432.1	6299	1403	767	706	148	54	44	72	668	24	1229	70	6	89	79	.530	1	0-0	0	4.42	4.44

Joey Votto

Bats: L Throws: R Pos: 1B-154;PH-3;DH-1 VAH-toe **Ht: 6'2" Wt: 220 Born: 9/10/1983 Age: 33**

Year	Team	Lg	G	AB	H	2B	3B	HR	(Hm	Rd)	TB	R	RBI	RC	TBB	IBB	SO	HBP	SH	SF	SB	CS	GDP	Avg	OBP	Slg	OPS
2007	Cin	NL	24	84	27	7	0	4	(4	0)	46	11	17	17	5	1	15	0	0	0	1	0	0	.321	.360	.548	.907
2008	Cin	NL	151	526	156	32	3	24	(14	10)	266	69	84	91	59	9	102	2	0	2	7	5	7	.297	.368	.506	.874
2009	Cin	NL	131	469	151	38	1	25	(14	11)	266	82	84	99	70	10	106	4	0	1	4	1	8	.322	.414	.567	.981
2010	Cin	NL	150	547	177	36	2	37	(18	19)	328	106	113	132	91	8	125	7	0	3	16	5	11	.324	.424	.600	1.024
2011	Cin	NL	161	599	185	40	3	29	(13	16)	318	101	103	131	110	15	129	4	0	6	8	6	20	.309	.416	.531	.947
2012	Cin	NL	111	374	126	44	0	14	(10	4)	212	59	56	97	94	18	85	5	0	2	5	3	8	.337	.474	.567	1.041
2013	Cin	NL	162	581	177	30	3	24	(11	13)	285	101	73	121	135	19	138	4	0	6	6	3	15	.305	.435	.491	.926
2014	Cin	NL	62	220	56	16	0	6	(6	0)	90	32	23	36	47	2	49	3	0	2	1	1	5	.255	.390	.409	.799
2015	Cin	NL	158	545	171	33	2	29	(14	15)	295	95	80	135	143	15	135	5	0	2	11	3	11	.314	.459	.541	1.000
2016	Cin	NL	158	556	181	34	2	29	(16	13)	306	101	97	130	108	15	120	5	0	2	8	1	16	.326	.434	.550	.985
Postseason			9	32	8	0	0	0	(0	0)	8	3	1	3	4	0	9	0	0	1	0	0	1	.250	.324	.250	.574
10 ML YEARS			1268	4501	1407	310	16	221	(120	101)	2412	757	730	989	862	112	1004	39	0	32	67	28	101	.313	.425	.536	.961

Michael Wacha

Pitches: R Bats: R Pos: SP-24; RP-3 WOCK-uh **Ht: 6'6" Wt: 215 Born: 7/1/1991 Age: 25**

Year	Team	Lg	G	GS	CG	GF	IP	BFP	H	R	ER	HR	SH	SF	HB	TBB	IBB	SO	WP	Bk	W	L	Pct	Sh	Sv-Op	Hld	ERC	ERA
2013	StL	NL	15	9	0	2	64.2	260	52	20	20	5	1	3	0	19	0	65	3	0	4	1	.800	0	0-1	0	2.52	2.78
2014	StL	NL	19	19	0	0	107.0	447	95	41	38	6	1	2	5	33	0	94	2	0	5	6	.455	0	0-0	0	3.00	3.20
2015	StL	NL	30	30	0	0	181.1	762	162	74	68	19	8	3	6	58	4	153	4	1	17	7	.708	0	0-0	0	3.28	3.38
2016	StL	NL	27	24	0	1	138.0	606	159	86	78	15	4	5	1	45	6	114	6	0	7	7	.500	0	0-0	0	4.66	5.09
Postseason			7	6	0	1	35.1	144	24	16	16	7	0	0	1	16	4	38	0	0	4	3	.571	0	0-0	0	3.15	4.08
4 ML YEARS			91	82	0	3	491.0	2075	468	221	204	45	14	13	12	155	10	426	15	1	33	21	.611	0	0-1	0	3.48	3.74

Tyler Wagner

Pitches: R Bats: R Pos: RP-3 **Ht: 6'3" Wt: 205 Born: 1/24/1991 Age: 26**

Year	Team	Lg	G	GS	CG	GF	IP	BFP	H	R	ER	HR	SH	SF	HB	TBB	IBB	SO	WP	Bk	W	L	Pct	Sh	Sv-Op	Hld	ERC	ERA
2012	Helena	R+	14	13	0	0	48.2	233	63	51	42	6	0	1	3	22	0	47	4	0	1	4	.200	0	0--	-	6.36	7.77
2013	Wisc	A	27	25	1	2	148.2	613	129	59	53	10	3	4	3	56	0	116	12	0	10	8	.556	1	0--	-	3.18	3.21
2014	BrvdCt	A+	25	25	1	0	150.0	595	118	41	31	10	4	6	1	48	0	118	6	1	13	6	.684	0	0--	-	2.53	1.86
2015	Biloxi	AA	25	25	2	0	152.1	609	130	45	38	7	4	4	3	45	0	120	4	1	11	5	.688	1	0--	-	2.71	2.25
2016	Reno	AAA	5	5	0	0	26.2	114	29	15	9	1	1	0	0	11	0	15	3	0	1	4	.200	0	0--	-	4.29	3.04
2015	Mil	NL	3	3	0	0	13.2	67	22	11	11	1	2	1	0	7	0	5	1	0	0	2	.000	0	0-0	0	8.26	7.24
2016	Ari	NL	3	0	0	0	10.0	40	9	3	2	0	0	0	0	2	0	7	0	0	0	1	1.000	0	0-0	0	2.21	1.80
2 ML YEARS			6	3	0	0	23.2	107	31	14	13	1	2	1	0	9	0	12	1	0	1	2	.333	0	0-0	0	5.43	4.94

Adam Wainwright

Pitches: R Bats: R Pos: SP-33 **Ht: 6'7" Wt: 235 Born: 8/30/1981 Age: 35**

Year	Team	Lg	G	GS	CG	GF	IP	BFP	H	R	ER	HR	SH	SF	HB	TBB	IBB	SO	WP	Bk	W	L	Pct	Sh	Sv-Op	Hld	ERC	ERA
2005	StL	NL	2	0	0	1	2.0	9	2	3	3	1	0	0	0	1	0	0	0	0	0	0	-	0	0-0	0	7.30	13.50
2006	StL	NL	61	0	0	10	75.0	309	64	26	26	6	4	1	4	22	2	72	3	0	2	1	.667	0	3-5	17	2.92	3.12
2007	StL	NL	32	32	1	0	202.0	882	212	93	83	13	9	5	9	70	4	136	6	0	14	12	.538	0	0-0	0	4.01	3.70
2008	StL	NL	20	20	1	0	132.0	544	122	51	47	12	6	4	3	34	1	91	3	0	11	3	.786	0	0-0	0	3.14	3.20
2009	StL	NL	34	34	1	0	233.0	970	216	75	68	17	10	5	3	66	1	212	7	0	19	8	.704	0	0-0	0	3.08	2.63
2010	StL	NL	33	33	5	0	230.1	910	186	68	62	15	13	4	6	56	2	213	2	0	20	11	.645	2	0-0	0	2.36	2.42
2012	StL	NL	32	32	3	0	198.2	831	196	96	87	15	9	6	6	52	3	184	5	2	14	13	.519	2	0-0	0	3.41	3.94
2013	StL	NL	34	34	5	0	241.2	956	223	83	79	15	13	2	6	35	2	219	5	0	19	9	.679	2	0-0	0	2.60	2.94
2014	StL	NL	32	32	5	0	227.0	898	184	60	60	10	8	3	7	50	5	179	4	1	20	9	.690	3	0-0	0	2.20	2.38
2015	StL	NL	7	4	0	2	28.0	111	25	7	5	0	2	0	0	4	0	20	0	0	2	1	.667	0	0-0	0	1.97	1.61
2016	StL	NL	33	33	1	0	198.2	847	220	108	102	22	8	9	5	59	4	161	1	0	13	9	.591	1	0-0	0	4.50	4.62
Postseason			24	12	1	9	89.0	361	82	33	30	9	2	2	2	15	0	96	3	0	4	4	.500	0	4-5	0	2.85	3.03
11 ML YEARS			320	254	22	13	1768.1	7267	1650	674	622	126	82	41	47	449	24	1487	36	3	134	76	.638	10	3-5	17	3.07	3.17

Jordan Walden

Pitches: R Bats: R Pos: P **Ht: 6'5" Wt: 250 Born: 11/16/1987 Age: 29**

Year	Team	Lg	G	GS	CG	GF	IP	BFP	H	R	ER	HR	SH	SF	HB	TBB	IBB	SO	WP	Bk	W	L	Pct	Sh	Sv-Op	Hld	ERC	ERA
2010	LAA	AL	16	0	0	5	15.1	65	13	4	4	1	0	0	0	7	0	23	1	1	0	1	.000	0	1-1	6	3.21	2.35
2011	LAA	AL	62	0	0	42	60.1	253	49	22	20	3	4	2	1	26	3	67	6	0	5	5	.500	0	32-42	2	2.82	2.98
2012	LAA	AL	45	0	0	20	39.0	172	35	15	15	3	0	1	0	18	1	48	7	0	3	2	.600	0	1-2	8	3.42	3.46
2013	Atl	NL	50	0	0	9	47.0	193	39	19	18	4	1	0	1	14	4	54	6	0	4	3	.571	0	1-3	14	2.63	3.45
2014	Atl	NL	58	0	0	8	50.0	205	33	17	16	2	0	1	1	27	1	62	9	0	0	2	.000	0	3-5	20	2.41	2.88
2015	StL	NL	12	0	0	2	10.1	42	7	1	1	0	0	1	0	4	1	12	2	0	0	1	.000	0	1-1	8	1.63	0.87
Postseason			2	0	0	0	2.2	13	3	4	4	0	0	0	0	1	0	3	0	0	0	0	-	0	0-0	0	5.24	13.50
6 ML YEARS			243	0	0	86	222.0	930	176	78	74	13	5	5	2	96	10	266	31	1	12	14	.462	0	39-54	58	2.76	3.00

Kyle Waldrop

Bats: L Throws: L Pos: PH-10;LF-2;RF-2;DH-1   Ht: 6'2" Wt: 215 Born: 11/26/1991 Age: 25

Year	Team	Lg	G	AB	H	2B	3B	HR	(Hm	Rd)	TB	R	RBI	RC	TBB	IBB	SO	HBP	SH	SF	SB	CS	GDP	Avg	OBP	Slg	OPS
2012	Dayton	A	117	416	118	21	6	8	(-	-)	175	59	50	63	38	5	77	4	7	4	10	6	14	.284	.346	.421	.767
2013	Bkrsfld	A+	129	504	130	32	4	21	(-	-)	233	66	54	72	32	0	121	2	0	2	20	8	5	.258	.304	.462	.766
2014	Bkrsfld	A+	65	256	92	20	1	6	(-	-)	132	54	32	55	22	0	56	3	2	5	11	2	6	.359	.409	.516	.925
2014	Pnscla	AA	66	232	73	17	3	8	(-	-)	120	27	35	41	17	1	44	0	1	2	3	4	8	.315	.359	.517	.876
2015	Pnscla	AA	67	242	67	13	3	6	(-	-)	104	21	31	32	12	1	61	2	0	3	2	2	2	.277	.313	.430	.742
2015	Lsvlle	AAA	55	205	38	6	0	1	(-	-)	47	8	13	7	7	1	54	0	0	1	0	1	4	.185	.211	.229	.441
2016	Lsvlle	AAA	96	325	82	21	0	5	(-	-)	118	37	27	37	20	4	58	4	0	4	4	2	9	.252	.300	.363	.663
2015	Cin	NL	1	1	0	0	0	0	(0	0)	0	0	0	0	0	0	1	0	0	0	0	0	0	.000	.000	.000	.000
2016	Cin	NL	15	22	5	1	0	0	(0	0)	6	1	1	1	1	0	5	0	0	0	0	1	0	.227	.261	.273	.534
	2 ML YEARS		16	23	5	1	0	0	(0	0)	6	1	1	1	1	0	6	0	0	0	0	1	0	.217	.250	.261	.511

Neil Walker

Bats: B Throws: R Pos: 2B-111;PH-2   Ht: 6'3" Wt: 210 Born: 9/10/1985 Age: 31

Year	Team	Lg	G	AB	H	2B	3B	HR	(Hm	Rd)	TB	R	RBI	RC	TBB	IBB	SO	HBP	SH	SF	SB	CS	GDP	Avg	OBP	Slg	OPS
2009	Pit	NL	17	36	7	1	0	0	(0	0)	8	5	0	2	4	0	11	0	0	0	1	0	1	.194	.275	.222	.497
2010	Pit	NL	110	426	126	29	3	12	(5	7)	197	57	66	66	34	1	83	3	2	4	2	3	4	.296	.349	.462	.811
2011	Pit	NL	159	596	163	36	4	12	(4	8)	243	76	83	77	54	5	112	4	0	8	9	6	15	.273	.334	.408	.742
2012	Pit	NL	129	472	132	27	0	14	(7	7)	201	62	69	72	47	1	104	2	1	8	7	5	11	.280	.342	.426	.768
2013	Pit	NL	133	478	120	24	4	16	(8	8)	200	62	53	62	50	4	85	15	5	3	1	2	14	.251	.339	.418	.757
2014	Pit	NL	137	512	139	25	3	23	(10	13)	239	74	76	72	45	2	88	11	1	2	2	2	12	.271	.342	.467	.809
2015	Pit	NL	151	543	146	32	3	16	(8	8)	232	69	71	73	44	5	110	8	0	8	4	1	9	.269	.328	.427	.756
2016	NYM	NL	113	412	116	9	1	23	(10	13)	196	57	55	66	42	3	84	1	0	3	3	1	11	.282	.347	.476	.823
	Postseason		8	31	2	1	0	0			3	1	1	1	2	0	9	0	0	0	0	0	0	.065	.121	.097	.218
	8 ML YEARS		949	3475	949	183	18	116	(52	64)	1516	462	473	490	320	21	677	44	9	36	29	20	77	.273	.339	.436	.775

Taijuan Walker

Pitches: R Bats: R Pos: SP-25   TIE-wahn   Ht: 6'4" Wt: 235 Born: 8/13/1992 Age: 24

			HOW MUCH HE PITCHED						WHAT HE GAVE UP										THE RESULTS							
Year	Team	Lg	G	GS	CG	GF	IP	BFP	H	R	ER	HR	SH	SF	HB	TBB	IBB	SO	WP	Bk	W	L	Pct	Sh	Sv-Op	Hld	ERC	ERA
2013	Sea	AL	3	3	0	0	15.0	60	11	7	6	0	0	2	0	4	0	12	0	0	1	0	1.000	0	0-0	0	1.63	3.60
2014	Sea	AL	8	5	1	2	38.0	160	31	12	11	2	0	0	3	18	1	34	2	1	2	3	.400	0	0-0	0	3.34	2.61
2015	Sea	AL	29	29	1	0	169.2	706	163	92	86	25	4	5	9	40	1	157	4	1	11	8	.579	0	0-0	0	3.74	4.56
2016	Sea	AL	25	25	1	0	134.1	573	129	75	63	27	3	3	8	37	2	119	4	1	8	11	.421	1	0-0	0	4.20	4.22
	4 ML YEARS		65	62	3	2	357.0	1499	334	186	166	54	7	10	20	99	4	322	10	3	22	22	.500	1	0-0	0	3.78	4.18

Brett Wallace

Bats: L Throws: R Pos: PH-58;3B-42;1B-20;DH-3   Ht: 6'2" Wt: 250 Born: 8/26/1986 Age: 30

Year	Team	Lg	G	AB	H	2B	3B	HR	(Hm	Rd)	TB	R	RBI	RC	TBB	IBB	SO	HBP	SH	SF	SB	CS	GDP	Avg	OBP	Slg	OPS
2010	Hou	NL	51	144	32	6	1	2	(1	1)	46	14	13	10	8	3	50	7	0	0	0	0	3	.222	.296	.319	.615
2011	Hou	NL	115	336	87	22	0	5	(2	3)	124	37	29	31	36	4	91	3	1	2	1	1	12	.259	.334	.369	.703
2012	Hou	NL	66	229	58	10	1	9	(1	8)	97	24	24	27	18	1	73	6	0	1	0	0	2	.253	.323	.424	.746
2013	Hou	AL	79	262	58	14	1	13	(7	6)	113	35	36	34	18	0	104	5	0	0	1	1	5	.221	.284	.431	.716
2015	SD	NL	64	96	29	6	0	5	(4	1)	50	14	16	18	10	1	31	1	0	0	0	0	1	.302	.374	.521	.895
2016	SD	NL	119	217	41	10	0	6	(3	3)	69	19	20	24	29	3	83	9	0	1	0	0	2	.189	.309	.318	.627
	6 ML YEARS		494	1284	305	68	3	40	(18	22)	499	143	138	144	119	12	432	31	1	4	2	2	25	.238	.316	.389	.705

Colin Walsh

Bats: B Throws: R Pos: PH-27;3B-11;LF-2;2B-1   Ht: 6'1" Wt: 200 Born: 9/26/1989 Age: 27

Year	Team	Lg	G	AB	H	2B	3B	HR	(Hm	Rd)	TB	R	RBI	RC	TBB	IBB	SO	HBP	SH	SF	SB	CS	GDP	Avg	OBP	Slg	OPS
2012	2 Tms	Low	99	361	112	18	5	16	(-	-)	188	70	69	80	60	4	66	7	0	5	4	3	8	.310	.413	.521	.934
2013	PlmBh	A+	94	351	92	20	6	4	(-	-)	136	59	34	56	58	1	68	2	1	0	11	1	9	.262	.370	.387	.757
2013	Sprgfld	AA	32	118	26	5	0	2	(-	-)	37	15	6	13	16	0	24	0	0	0	3	0	1	.220	.313	.314	.627
2014	Mdlnd	AA	25	101	29	5	0	1	(-	-)	37	13	10	14	11	0	26	1	0	3	1	1	14	.287	.353	.366	.720
2014	Scrmto	AAA	48	148	40	4	0	2	(-	-)	50	16	18	20	19	3	38	1	2	1	1	0	5	.270	.360	.338	.698
2015	Mdlnd	AA	134	487	147	39	2	13	(-	-)	229	97	49	112	124	4	131	5	2	1	17	7	12	.302	.447	.470	.918
2016	Nashv	AAA	59	201	52	12	1	4	(-	-)	78	31	26	33	41	0	63	1	0	2	0	0	5	.259	.384	.388	.772
2016	Mil	NL	38	47	4	1	0	0	(0	0)	5	4	2	3	15	0	22	1	0	0	0	0	1	.085	.317	.106	.424

Zach Walters

Bats: B Throws: R Pos: PH-2;1B-1;LF-1;RF-1   Ht: 6'2" Wt: 210 Born: 9/5/1989 Age: 27

Year	Team	Lg	G	AB	H	2B	3B	HR	(Hm	Rd)	TB	R	RBI	RC	TBB	IBB	SO	HBP	SH	SF	SB	CS	GDP	Avg	OBP	Slg	OPS
2016	OkCity*	AAA	94	333	92	18	4	10	(-	-)	148	45	53	50	25	1	63	2	1	5	3	1	6	.276	.326	.444	.770
2013	Was	NL	8	8	3	0	1	0	(0	0)	5	2	1	2	1	0	0	0	0	0	0	0	1	.375	.444	.625	1.069
2014	2 Tms		62	127	23	3	0	10	(4	6)	56	16	17	10	9	0	48	1	0	0	0	0	0	.181	.241	.441	.682
2015	Cle	AL	12	30	4	0	0	0	(0	0)	4	0	3	0	0	0	15	0	0	0	0	0	0	.133	.133	.133	.267

Year	Team	Lg	G	AB	H	2B	3B	HR	(Hm	Rd)	TB	R	RBI	RC	TBB	IBB	SO	HBP	SH	SF	SB	CS	GDP	Avg	OBP	Slg	OPS
														BATTING							**RUNNING**			**AVERAGES**			
2016	LAD	NL	3	5	0	0	0	0	(0	0)	0	0	0	0	0	0	2	0	0	0	0	0	0	.000	.000	.000	.000
14	Was	NL	32	39	8	1	0	3	(0	3)	18	7	5	4	4	0	16	0	0	0	0	0	0	.205	.279	.462	.741
14	Cle	AL	30	88	15	2	0	7	(4	3)	38	9	12	6	5	0	32	1	0	0	0	0	0	.170	.223	.432	.655
4 ML YEARS			85	170	30	3	1	10	(4	6)	65	18	21	12	10	0	65	1	0	0	0	0	1	.176	.227	.382	.609

Chien-Ming Wang

Pitches: R Bats: R Pos: RP-38

CHENN-MING WONG

Ht: 6'4" Wt: 225 Born: 3/31/1980 Age: 37

Year	Team	Lg	G	GS	CG	GF	IP	BFP	H	R	ER	HR	SH	SF	HB	TBB	IBB	SO	WP	Bk	W	L	Pct	Sh	Sv-Op	Hld	ERC	ERA
							HOW MUCH HE PITCHED					**WHAT HE GAVE UP**											**THE RESULTS**					
2005	NYY	AL	18	17	0	0	116.1	486	113	58	52	9	3	4	6	32	3	47	3	0	8	5	.615	0	0-0	0	3.47	4.02
2006	NYY	AL	34	33	2	1	218.0	900	233	92	88	12	3	2	2	52	4	76	6	1	19	6	.760	1	1-1	0	3.62	3.63
2007	NYY	AL	30	30	1	0	199.1	823	199	84	82	9	2	3	8	59	1	104	9	1	19	7	.731	0	0-0	0	3.54	3.70
2008	NYY	AL	15	15	1	0	95.0	402	90	44	43	4	0	3	3	35	1	54	0	0	8	2	.800	0	0-0	0	3.39	4.07
2009	NYY	AL	12	9	0	2	42.0	206	66	46	45	7	3	1	2	19	1	29	3	0	1	6	.143	0	0-0	0	8.67	9.64
2011	Was	NL	11	11	0	0	62.1	264	67	35	28	8	2	2	1	13	0	25	2	0	4	3	.571	0	0-0	0	3.97	4.04
2012	Was	NL	10	5	0	0	32.1	158	50	24	24	5	4	3	3	15	0	15	5	0	2	3	.400	0	0-0	0	8.80	6.68
2013	Tor	AL	6	6	0	0	27.0	123	40	24	23	5	0	0	0	9	0	14	2	0	1	2	.333	0	0-0	0	7.66	7.67
2016	KC	AL	38	0	0	24	53.1	231	60	27	25	6	1	0	2	18	0	30	1	0	6	0	1.000	0	0-0	0	4.87	4.22
Postseason			4	4	0	0	19.0	90	28	19	16	5	2	0	3	5	0	7	0	0	1	3	.250	0	0-0	0	8.53	7.58
9 ML YEARS			174	126	4	27	845.2	3593	918	434	410	65	18	18	27	252	10	394	31	2	68	34	.667	1	1-1	0	4.17	4.36

Adam Warren

Pitches: R Bats: R Pos: RP-57; SP-1

Ht: 6'1" Wt: 225 Born: 8/25/1987 Age: 29

Year	Team	Lg	G	GS	CG	GF	IP	BFP	H	R	ER	HR	SH	SF	HB	TBB	IBB	SO	WP	Bk	W	L	Pct	Sh	Sv-Op	Hld	ERC	ERA
							HOW MUCH HE PITCHED					**WHAT HE GAVE UP**											**THE RESULTS**					
2012	NYY	AL	1	1	0	0	2.1	17	8	6	6	2	0	0	0	2	0	1	0	0	0	0	-	0	0-0	0	33.34	23.14
2013	NYY	AL	34	2	0	17	77.0	331	80	29	29	10	0	0	2	30	2	64	3	0	3	2	.600	0	1-1	6	4.60	3.39
2014	NYY	AL	69	0	0	11	78.2	324	63	27	26	4	5	4	3	24	1	76	4	0	3	6	.333	0	3-6	23	2.45	2.97
2015	NYY	AL	43	17	0	5	131.1	534	114	51	48	10	2	2	7	39	1	104	7	0	7	7	.500	0	1-1	3	3.07	3.29
2016	2 Tms		58	1	0	7	65.1	277	59	37	34	11	3	2	1	29	6	52	3	0	7	4	.636	0	0-3	12	4.14	4.68
16	ChC	NL	29	1	0	4	35.0	152	31	24	23	7	2	1	0	19	4	27	0	0	3	2	.600	0	0-1	6	4.53	5.91
16	NYY	AL	29	0	0	3	30.1	125	28	13	11	4	1	1	1	10	2	25	3	0	4	2	.667	0	0-2	6	3.71	3.26
5 ML YEARS			205	21	0	40	354.2	1483	324	150	143	37	10	8	13	124	10	297	17	0	20	19	.513	0	5-11	39	3.57	3.63

Tony Watson

Pitches: L Bats: L Pos: RP-70

Ht: 6'4" Wt: 225 Born: 5/30/1985 Age: 32

Year	Team	Lg	G	GS	CG	GF	IP	BFP	H	R	ER	HR	SH	SF	HB	TBB	IBB	SO	WP	Bk	W	L	Pct	Sh	Sv-Op	Hld	ERC	ERA
							HOW MUCH HE PITCHED					**WHAT HE GAVE UP**											**THE RESULTS**					
2011	Pit	NL	43	0	0	6	41.0	174	34	18	18	6	2	1	1	20	4	37	0	0	2	2	.500	0	0-1	10	3.75	3.95
2012	Pit	NL	68	0	0	10	53.1	215	37	21	20	5	2	1	1	23	1	53	1	0	5	2	.714	0	0-2	16	2.62	3.38
2013	Pit	NL	67	0	0	14	71.2	280	51	19	19	5	3	1	6	12	1	54	2	0	3	1	.750	0	2-4	22	1.88	2.39
2014	Pit	NL	78	0	0	3	77.1	305	64	16	14	5	5	3	6	15	0	81	0	0	10	2	.833	0	2-9	34	2.54	1.63
2015	Pit	NL	77	0	0	4	75.1	293	55	17	16	3	1	3	4	17	1	62	1	0	4	1	.800	0	1-3	41	1.92	1.91
2016	Pit	NL	70	0	0	27	67.2	272	52	26	23	10	4	3	3	20	1	58	0	0	2	5	.286	0	15-20	23	2.92	3.06
Postseason			5	0	0	0	5.0	21	4	1	1	1	0	0	1	1	0	2	0	0	0	0	-	0	0-0	1	3.57	1.80
6 ML YEARS			403	0	0	64	386.1	1539	293	117	110	34	17	13	21	107	8	345	4	0	26	13	.667	0	20-39	146	2.48	2.56

Jered Weaver

Pitches: R Bats: R Pos: SP-31

Ht: 6'7" Wt: 210 Born: 10/4/1982 Age: 34

Year	Team	Lg	G	GS	CG	GF	IP	BFP	H	R	ER	HR	SH	SF	HB	TBB	IBB	SO	WP	Bk	W	L	Pct	Sh	Sv-Op	Hld	ERC	ERA
							HOW MUCH HE PITCHED					**WHAT HE GAVE UP**											**THE RESULTS**					
2006	LAA	AL	19	19	0	0	123.0	490	94	36	35	15	2	3	2	33	1	105	2	0	11	2	.846	0	0-0	0	2.57	2.56
2007	LAA	AL	28	28	0	0	161.0	695	178	77	70	17	5	5	2	45	3	115	4	0	13	7	.650	0	0-0	0	4.24	3.91
2008	LAA	AL	30	30	0	0	176.2	745	173	88	85	20	1	4	6	54	4	152	3	0	11	10	.524	0	0-0	0	3.80	4.33
2009	LAA	AL	33	33	4	0	211.0	882	196	91	88	26	6	8	4	66	3	174	3	0	16	8	.667	2	0-0	0	3.56	3.75
2010	LAA	AL	34	**34**	0	0	224.1	905	187	83	75	23	2	5	0	54	0	**233**	7	1	13	12	.520	0	0-0	0	2.59	3.01
2011	LAA	AL	33	33	4	0	235.2	926	182	65	63	20	5	5	3	56	0	198	8	0	18	8	.692	2	0-0	0	2.27	2.41
2012	LAA	AL	30	30	3	0	188.2	739	147	63	59	20	0	4	4	45	0	142	2	0	**20**	5	.800	2	0-0	0	2.48	2.81
2013	LAA	AL	24	24	0	0	154.1	634	139	58	56	17	1	3	7	37	0	117	2	0	11	8	.579	0	0-0	0	3.17	3.27
2014	LAA	AL	34	**34**	1	0	213.1	888	193	87	85	27	5	4	6	65	1	169	3	0	**18**	9	.667	0	0-0	0	3.46	3.59
2015	LAA	AL	26	26	1	0	159.0	669	163	84	82	24	5	2	12	33	3	90	2	0	7	12	.368	1	0-0	0	4.09	4.64
2016	LAA	AL	31	31	1	0	178.0	767	209	106	100	**37**	1	6	4	51	2	103	1	2	12	12	.500	1	0-0	0	5.59	5.06
Postseason			7	4	0	2	27.2	107	15	8	8	5	0	1	0	12	0	28	0	0	2	1	.667	0	0-0	1	2.37	2.60
11 ML YEARS			322	322	14	0	2025.0	8340	1861	838	798	246	33	48	51	539	17	1598	37	3	150	93	.617	8	0-0	0	3.36	3.55

Luke Weaver

Pitches: R Bats: R Pos: SP-8; RP-1

Ht: 6'2" Wt: 170 Born: 8/21/1993 Age: 23

Year	Team	Lg	G	GS	CG	GF	IP	BFP	H	R	ER	HR	SH	SF	HB	TBB	IBB	SO	WP	Bk	W	L	Pct	Sh	Sv-Op	Hld	ERC	ERA
							HOW MUCH HE PITCHED					**WHAT HE GAVE UP**											**THE RESULTS**					
2014	2 Tms	Low	6	6	0	0	9.1	46	15	8	8	1	0	0	1	4	0	12	0	1	0	1	.000	0	0--	-	8.66	7.71
2015	PlmBh	A+	19	19	0	0	105.1	426	98	34	19	2	5	6	0	19	0	88	8	1	8	5	.615	0	0--	-	2.37	1.62
2016	Sprgfld	AA	12	12	0	0	77.0	308	62	23	12	4	0	1	2	10	0	88	5	0	6	3	.667	0	0--	-	1.85	1.40
2016	StL	NL	9	8	0	0	36.1	167	46	29	23	7	2	3	2	12	0	45	1	0	1	4	.200	0	0-0	-	6.23	5.70

Daniel Webb

Pitches: R Bats: R Pos: RP-1 **Ht: 6'3" Wt: 215 Born: 8/18/1989 Age: 27**

Year	Team	Lg	G	GS	CG	GF	IP	BFP	H	R	ER	HR	SH	SF	HB	TBB	IBB	SO	WP	Bk	W	L	Pct	Sh	Sv-Op	Hld	ERC	ERA
2016	Charllt*	AAA	7	0	0	6	10.2	44	12	5	4	1	1	0	0	0	0	5	1	0	2	1	.667	0	2- -	-	3.09	3.38
2013	CWS	AL	9	0	0	4	11.1	46	9	4	4	0	0	1	0	4	0	10	1	0	0	0	-	0	0-0	1	2.20	3.18
2014	CWS	AL	57	0	0	26	67.2	296	59	31	30	6	1	3	2	42	5	58	13	0	6	5	.545	0	0-2	4	4.18	3.99
2015	CWS	AL	27	0	0	6	30.0	150	41	26	21	3	0	1	1	22	1	22	2	0	1	0	1.000	0	0-1	0	7.82	6.30
2016	CWS	AL	1	0	0	1	1.0	6	2	0	0	0	0	0	0	1	0	3	0	0	0	0	-	0	0-0	0	12.01	0.00
	4 ML YEARS		94	0	0	37	110.0	498	111	61	55	9	1	5	3	69	6	93	16	0	7	5	.583	0	0-3	5	4.94	4.50

Ryan Webb

Pitches: R Bats: R Pos: RP-18 **Ht: 6'6" Wt: 245 Born: 2/5/1986 Age: 31**

Year	Team	Lg	G	GS	CG	GF	IP	BFP	H	R	ER	HR	SH	SF	HB	TBB	IBB	SO	WP	Bk	W	L	Pct	Sh	Sv-Op	Hld	ERC	ERA
2009	SD	NL	28	0	0	9	25.2	117	27	14	11	3	2	1	1	11	1	19	4	0	2	1	.667	0	0-0	6	4.54	3.86
2010	SD	NL	54	0	0	15	59.0	253	64	21	19	1	1	1	1	19	5	44	2	1	3	1	.750	0	0-2	9	3.61	2.90
2011	Fla	NL	53	0	0	10	50.2	214	48	20	18	2	3	1	2	20	5	31	1	1	2	4	.333	0	0-4	8	3.39	3.20
2012	Mia	NL	65	0	0	21	60.1	270	72	30	27	2	0	2	4	20	8	44	0	0	4	3	.571	0	0-0	10	4.44	4.03
2013	Mia	NL	66	0	0	19	80.1	332	70	30	26	5	11	5	2	27	5	54	4	0	2	6	.250	0	0-3	4	2.91	2.91
2014	Bal	AL	51	0	0	13	49.1	207	50	21	21	2	1	0	1	12	2	37	1	1	3	3	.500	0	0-0	11	3.15	3.83
2015	Cle	AL	40	0	0	11	50.2	204	46	21	18	4	1	1	2	12	1	31	1	0	1	0	1.000	0	0-0	2	2.99	3.20
2016	TB	AL	18	0	0	7	17.1	76	27	11	10	2	0	0	0	3	1	11	3	0	0	0	-	0	0-0	0	6.85	5.19
	8 ML YEARS		375	0	0	105	393.1	1673	404	168	150	21	19	11	13	124	29	271	16	3	17	18	.486	0	0-9	48	3.61	3.43

Ryan Weber

Pitches: R Bats: R Pos: RP-14; SP-2 **Ht: 6'1" Wt: 180 Born: 8/12/1990 Age: 26**

Year	Team	Lg	G	GS	CG	GF	IP	BFP	H	R	ER	HR	SH	SF	HB	TBB	IBB	SO	WP	Bk	W	L	Pct	Sh	Sv-Op	Hld	ERC	ERA
2012	2 Tms	Low	35	16	0	9	117.1	514	136	72	64	5	5	5	7	23	2	94	1	0	7	9	.438	0	2- -	-	3.89	4.91
2013	2 Tms	Low	24	16	1	1	96.2	403	95	54	44	7	4	1	11	15	2	83	1	0	6	6	.500	0	0- -	-	3.26	4.10
2014	Missi	AA	32	13	0	2	101.1	436	129	59	51	7	7	5	1	16	0	62	1	2	5	6	.455	0	0- -	-	4.52	4.53
2015	Missi	AA	11	3	0	1	26.1	101	23	8	8	1	0	1	0	1	0	24	0	0	0	2	.000	0	1- -	-	1.77	2.73
2015	Gwnntt	AAA	27	6	0	4	73.1	281	60	18	18	7	3	1	3	9	0	35	2	0	6	3	.667	0	3- -	-	2.30	2.21
2016	Gwnntt	AAA	26	5	0	9	62.0	268	65	21	19	1	3	2	4	14	2	41	4	0	2	3	.400	0	1- -	-	3.22	2.76
2015	Atl	NL	5	5	0	0	28.1	109	25	15	15	3	0	0	2	6	0	19	0	0	0	3	.000	0	0-0	0	3.26	4.76
2016	Atl	NL	16	2	0	6	36.1	157	46	22	22	7	1	0	2	5	2	23	1	0	1	1	.500	0	0-1	0	5.40	5.45
	2 ML YEARS		21	7	0	6	64.2	266	71	37	37	10	1	0	4	11	2	42	1	0	1	4	.200	0	0-1	0	4.44	5.15

Jemile Weeks

Bats: B Throws: R Pos: 2B-17;3B-1 jah-MYLE **Ht: 5'9" Wt: 170 Born: 1/26/1987 Age: 30**

Year	Team	Lg	G	AB	H	2B	3B	HR	(Hm	Rd)	TB	R	RBI	RC	TBB	IBB	SO	HBP	SH	SF	SB	CS	GDP	Avg	OBP	Slg	OPS
2016	ElPaso*	AAA	10	36	11	1	3	0	(-	-)	18	7	1	7	6	0	3	0	0	0	2	0	2	.306	.405	.500	.905
2011	Oak	AL	97	406	123	26	8	2	(1	1)	171	50	36	64	21	1	62	4	2	4	22	11	3	.303	.340	.421	.761
2012	Oak	AL	118	444	98	15	8	2	(1	1)	135	54	20	42	50	0	70	5	9	3	16	5	5	.221	.305	.304	.609
2013	Oak	AL	8	9	1	0	0	0	(0	0)	1	3	0	0	0	0	5	0	0	0	0	0	0	.111	.111	.111	.222
2014	2 Tms	AL	17	37	11	3	1	0	(0	0)	16	8	3	6	4	0	2	1	2	1	2	0	1	.297	.372	.432	.805
2015	Bos	AL	3	9	3	0	0	0	(0	0)	3	1	1	1	0	0	2	0	0	0	0	0	0	.333	.333	.333	.667
2016	SD	NL	17	50	7	1	1	0	(0	0)	10	5	2	1	3	0	14	1	3	0	1	0	1	.140	.204	.200	.404
	14 Bal	AL	3	11	3	0	1	0	(0	0)	5	2	0	1	0	0	0	0	2	0	0	0	1	.273	.273	.455	.727
	14 Bos	AL	14	26	8	3	0	0	(0	0)	11	6	3	5	4	0	2	1	0	1	2	0	0	.308	.406	.423	.829
	6 ML YEARS		260	955	243	45	18	4	(2	2)	336	121	62	114	78	1	155	11	16	8	41	16	10	.254	.316	.352	.667

Rickie Weeks Jr.

Bats: R Throws: R Pos: PH-68;LF-36;DH-6;RF-2 **Ht: 5'10" Wt: 220 Born: 9/13/1982 Age: 34**

Year	Team	Lg	G	AB	H	2B	3B	HR	(Hm	Rd)	TB	R	RBI	RC	TBB	IBB	SO	HBP	SH	SF	SB	CS	GDP	Avg	OBP	Slg	OPS
2003	Mil	NL	7	12	2	1	0	0	(0	0)	3	1	0	0	1	0	6	1	0	0	0	0	0	.167	.286	.250	.536
2005	Mil	NL	96	360	86	13	2	13	(8	5)	142	56	42	49	40	2	96	11	2	1	15	2	11	.239	.333	.394	.727
2006	Mil	NL	95	359	100	15	3	8	(6	2)	145	73	34	53	30	1	92	19	2	3	19	5	6	.279	.363	.404	.766
2007	Mil	NL	118	409	96	21	6	16	(5	11)	177	87	36	65	78	5	116	14	3	2	25	2	3	.235	.374	.433	.807
2008	Mil	NL	129	475	111	22	7	14	(3	11)	189	89	46	67	66	0	115	14	1	4	19	5	5	.234	.342	.398	.740
2009	Mil	NL	37	147	40	5	2	9	(7	2)	76	28	24	27	12	0	39	3	0	0	2	2	1	.272	.340	.517	.857
2010	Mil	NL	160	651	175	32	4	29	(16	13)	302	112	83	110	76	0	184	25	0	2	11	4	5	.269	.366	.464	.830
2011	Mil	NL	118	453	122	26	2	20	(10	10)	212	77	49	68	50	3	107	8	1	3	9	2	6	.269	.350	.468	.818
2012	Mil	NL	157	588	135	29	4	21	(10	11)	235	85	63	77	74	2	169	13	0	2	16	3	9	.230	.328	.400	.728
2013	Mil	NL	104	350	73	20	1	10	(6	4)	125	40	24	28	40	0	105	9	0	0	7	3	13	.209	.306	.357	.663
2014	Mil	NL	121	252	69	19	1	8	(4	4)	114	36	29	38	25	0	73	8	0	1	3	4	7	.274	.357	.452	.809
2015	Sea	AL	37	84	14	1	0	2	(0	2)	21	7	9	7	9	0	25	2	0	0	0	0	3	.167	.263	.250	.513
2016	Ari	NL	108	180	43	9	1	9	(6	3)	81	29	27	26	20	0	54	4	0	1	5	0	8	.239	.327	.450	.777
	Postseason		14	45	6	1	1	2	(2	0)	15	5	4	2	2	0	8	2	0	0	0	0	3	.133	.204	.333	.537
	13 ML YEARS		1287	4320	1066	213	33	159	(81	78)	1822	720	466	615	521	13	1181	131	9	19	131	32	77	.247	.344	.422	.766

J.B. Wendelken

Pitches: R Bats: R Pos: RP-8 Ht: 6'0" Wt: 220 Born: 3/24/1993 Age: 24

			HOW MUCH HE PITCHED						WHAT HE GAVE UP											THE RESULTS						
Year	Team	Lg	G	GS	CG	GF	IP	BFP	H	R	ER	HR	SH	SF	HB	TBB	IBB	SO	WP	Bk	W	L	Pct	Sh	Sv-Op	Hld	ERC	ERA
2012	RedSx	R	13	0	0	3	21.1	79	11	3	3	0	1	0	0	3	0	28	0	1	2	0	1.000	0	2- -	-	0.78	1.27
2013	3 Tms	Low	36	0	0	23	79.0	343	79	31	30	5	4	1	3	28	0	78	10	2	2	2	.500	0	12- -	-	3.74	3.42
2014	WinSa	A+	27	27	1	0	145.1	650	181	105	85	15	6	8	5	33	0	129	4	0	7	10	.412	0	0- -	-	4.87	5.26
2015	Brham	AA	27	0	0	17	43.0	176	36	14	13	4	0	1	0	11	0	56	0	0	6	2	.750	0	5- -	-	2.58	2.72
2015	Charllt	AAA	12	0	0	6	16.0	68	14	11	8	2	0	1	0	5	0	13	0	0	0	0	-	0	0- -	-	3.11	4.50
2016	Nashv	AAA	39	0	0	16	46.0	217	48	25	21	5	2	0	4	26	2	65	5	0	1	4	.200	0	5- -	-	5.17	4.11
2016	Oak	AL	8	0	0	3	12.2	64	18	15	14	3	0	0	0	9	0	12	2	0	0	0	-	0	0-0	0	9.17	9.95

Joey Wendle

Bats: L Throws: R Pos: 2B-28;PH-2;PR-1 Ht: 6'1" Wt: 190 Born: 4/26/1990 Age: 27

						BATTING														RUNNING			AVERAGES			
Year	Team	Lg	G	AB	H	2B	3B	HR	(Hm	Rd)	TB	R	RBI	RC	TBB	IBB	SO	HBP	SH	SF	SB	CS	GDP	Avg	OBP	Slg	OPS
2012	MhVlly	A-	61	245	80	15	4	4	(-	-)	115	32	37	44	15	1	25	5	0	2	4	1	3	.327	.375	.469	.844
2013	Carlina	A+	107	413	122	32	5	16	(-	-)	212	73	64	82	44	1	79	10	1	6	10	2	10	.295	.372	.513	.885
2014	Akron	AA	87	336	85	20	5	8	(-	-)	139	46	50	45	26	1	56	4	0	4	4	2	4	.253	.311	.414	.725
2015	Nashv	AAA	137	577	167	42	8	10	(-	-)	255	80	57	85	22	1	114	9	5	5	12	2	9	.289	.323	.442	.765
2016	Nashv	AAA	125	491	137	31	9	12	(-	-)	222	81	61	74	26	2	112	7	1	1	14	4	10	.279	.324	.452	.776
2016	Oak	AL	28	96	25	1	0	1	(0	1)	29	11	11	10	6	0	16	0	0	2	2	0	3	.260	.298	.302	.600

Jayson Werth

Bats: R Throws: R Pos: LF-131;DH-6;PH-4;RF-2 Ht: 6'5" Wt: 235 Born: 5/20/1979 Age: 38

						BATTING														RUNNING			AVERAGES			
Year	Team	Lg	G	AB	H	2B	3B	HR	(Hm	Rd)	TB	R	RBI	RC	TBB	IBB	SO	HBP	SH	SF	SB	CS	GDP	Avg	OBP	Slg	OPS
2002	Tor	AL	15	46	12	2	1	0	(0	0)	16	4	6	5	6	0	11	0	0	1	1	0	4	.261	.340	.348	.687
2003	Tor	AL	26	48	10	4	0	2	(0	2)	20	7	10	6	3	0	22	0	0	0	1	0	0	.208	.255	.417	.672
2004	LAD	NL	89	290	76	11	3	16	(11	5)	141	56	47	47	30	0	85	4	1	1	4	1	1	.262	.338	.486	.825
2005	LAD	NL	102	337	79	22	2	7	(1	6)	126	46	43	44	48	2	114	6	1	3	11	2	10	.234	.338	.374	.711
2007	Phi	NL	94	255	76	11	3	8	(1	7)	117	43	49	57	44	1	73	2	2	1	7	1	0	.298	.404	.459	.863
2008	Phi	NL	134	418	114	16	3	24	(11	13)	208	73	67	74	57	1	119	4	0	3	20	1	2	.273	.363	.498	.861
2009	Phi	NL	159	571	153	26	1	36	(21	15)	289	98	99	107	91	8	156	8	0	6	20	3	11	.268	.373	.506	.879
2010	Phi	NL	156	554	164	46	2	27	(18	9)	295	106	85	91	82	6	147	7	0	9	13	3	11	.296	.388	.532	.921
2011	Was	NL	150	561	130	26	1	20	(10	10)	218	69	58	74	74	5	160	10	0	4	19	3	10	.232	.330	.389	.718
2012	Was	NL	81	300	90	21	3	5	(4	1)	132	42	31	48	42	2	57	1	0	1	8	2	3	.300	.387	.440	.827
2013	Was	NL	129	462	147	24	0	25	(13	12)	246	84	82	94	60	3	101	5	0	5	10	1	9	.318	.398	.532	.931
2014	Was	NL	147	534	156	37	1	16	(5	11)	243	85	82	104	83	3	113	9	0	3	9	1	9	.292	.394	.455	.849
2015	Was	NL	88	331	73	16	1	12	(6	6)	127	51	42	38	38	0	84	3	0	6	1	0	8	.221	.302	.384	.685
2016	Was	NL	143	525	128	28	0	21	(9	12)	219	84	69	68	71	0	139	6	0	1	5	1	17	.244	.335	.417	.752
	Postseason		53	191	47	10	2	14	(10	4)	103	33	27	30	33	4	63	1	0	1	5	0	3	.246	.358	.539	.898
	14 ML YEARS		1513	5232	1408	290	21	219	(110	109)	2397	848	770	857	729	31	1381	63	4	49	128	20	95	.269	.362	.458	.820

Rob Whalen

Pitches: R Bats: R Pos: SP-5 Ht: 6'2" Wt: 220 Born: 1/31/1994 Age: 23

			HOW MUCH HE PITCHED						WHAT HE GAVE UP											THE RESULTS						
Year	Team	Lg	G	GS	CG	GF	IP	BFP	H	R	ER	HR	SH	SF	HB	TBB	IBB	SO	WP	Bk	W	L	Pct	Sh	Sv-Op	Hld	ERC	ERA
2013	Kngspt	R+	12	12	0	0	72.1	296	50	26	15	1	2	2	7	17	0	76	4	0	3	2	.600	0	0- -	-	1.67	1.87
2014	2 Tms	Low	14	12	0	1	69.2	282	48	19	15	2	1	1	5	21	1	63	8	0	9	2	.818	0	0- -	-	1.90	1.94
2015	2 Tms	Low	18	17	0	1	96.2	409	83	45	36	6	0	2	8	38	0	68	11	0	5	7	.417	0	0- -	-	3.35	3.35
2016	Missi	AA	18	18	0	0	101.1	423	87	35	28	4	6	1	4	37	0	94	2	0	7	5	.583	0	0- -	-	2.93	2.49
2016	Atl	NL	5	5	0	0	24.2	110	20	20	18	4	2	1	3	12	0	25	1	0	1	2	.333	0	0-0	0	4.14	6.57

Zack Wheeler

Pitches: R Bats: L Pos: P Ht: 6'4" Wt: 195 Born: 5/30/1990 Age: 27

			HOW MUCH HE PITCHED						WHAT HE GAVE UP											THE RESULTS						
Year	Team	Lg	G	GS	CG	GF	IP	BFP	H	R	ER	HR	SH	SF	HB	TBB	IBB	SO	WP	Bk	W	L	Pct	Sh	Sv-Op	Hld	ERC	ERA
2012	Bnghtn	AA	19	19	1	0	116.0	474	92	46	42	2	2	8	11	43	0	117	6	1	10	6	.625	1	0- -	-	2.74	3.26
2012	Buffalo	AAA	6	6	1	0	33.0	134	23	13	12	2	3	2	1	16	0	31	2	0	2	2	.500	1	0- -	-	2.70	3.27
2013	LsVgs	AAA	13	13	0	0	68.2	291	61	35	30	9	1	2	2	27	0	73	1	0	4	2	.667	0	0- -	-	3.75	3.93
2013	NYM	NL	17	17	0	0	100.0	431	90	42	38	10	3	7	4	46	2	84	6	0	7	5	.583	0	0-0	0	3.88	3.42
2014	NYM	NL	32	32	1	0	185.1	794	167	84	73	14	5	3	11	79	3	187	9	0	11	11	.500	1	0-0	0	3.68	3.54
	2 ML YEARS		49	49	1	0	285.1	1225	257	126	111	24	8	10	15	125	5	271	15	0	18	16	.529	1	0-0	0	3.75	3.50

Tyler White

Bats: R Throws: R Pos: 1B-58;DH-14;PH-14;3B-3;2B-2;PR-1 Ht: 5'11" Wt: 225 Born: 10/29/1990 Age: 26

						BATTING														RUNNING			AVERAGES			
Year	Team	Lg	G	AB	H	2B	3B	HR	(Hm	Rd)	TB	R	RBI	RC	TBB	IBB	SO	HBP	SH	SF	SB	CS	GDP	Avg	OBP	Slg	OPS
2013	3 Tms	Low	64	239	77	14	0	6	(-	-)	109	40	52	46	27	1	24	9	0	3	3	2	5	.322	.406	.456	.863
2014	2 Tms	Low	114	389	113	33	2	15	(-	-)	195	69	64	83	63	1	67	19	0	5	0	1	8	.290	.410	.501	.911
2015	CpChr	AA	59	190	54	6	0	7	(-	-)	81	33	40	37	42	1	35	2	0	2	1	0	7	.284	.415	.426	.842
2015	Fresno	AAA	57	213	77	19	1	7	(-	-)	119	37	59	55	42	1	38	2	0	2	0	1	6	.362	.467	.559	1.026
2016	Fresno	AAA	44	174	42	4	1	13	(-	-)	87	28	29	27	16	0	30	0	0	0	1	1	6	.241	.305	.500	.805
2016	Hou	AL	86	249	54	16	0	8	(2	6)	94	24	28	25	23	1	65	2	0	2	1	0	6	.217	.286	.378	.664

Chase Whitley

Pitches: R Bats: R Pos: RP-4; SP-1   Ht: 6'3" Wt: 215 Born: 6/14/1989 Age: 28

Year	Team	Lg	G	GS	CG	GF	IP	BFP	H	R	ER	HR	SH	SF	HB	TBB	IBB	SO	WP	Bk	W	L	Pct	Sh	Sv-Op	Hld	ERC	ERA
2016	Mont*	AA	6	6	0	0	27.2	107	17	12	9	3	0	1	2	8	0	22	1	0	2	1	.667	0	0- -	-	2.06	2.93
2014	NYY	AL	24	12	0	3	75.2	330	94	44	44	10	1	2	4	18	0	60	2	0	4	3	.571	0	0-0	0	5.37	5.23
2015	NYY	AL	4	4	0	0	19.1	84	20	9	9	3	0	0	2	5	0	16	2	0	1	2	.333	0	0-0	0	4.47	4.19
2016	TB	AL	5	1	0	0	14.1	61	13	7	4	2	0	0	0	3	0	15	0	0	0	0	-	0	0-0	3	2.91	2.51
3 ML YEARS			33	17	0	3	109.1	475	127	60	57	15	1	2	6	26	0	91	4	0	5	5	.500	0	0-0	3	4.85	4.69

Joe Wieland

Pitches: R Bats: R Pos: SP-1   WEE-land   Ht: 6'2" Wt: 205 Born: 1/21/1990 Age: 27

Year	Team	Lg	G	GS	CG	GF	IP	BFP	H	R	ER	HR	SH	SF	HB	TBB	IBB	SO	WP	Bk	W	L	Pct	Sh	Sv-Op	Hld	ERC	ERA
2016	Tacom*	AAA	26	24	0	1	124.1	559	154	82	75	15	1	4	5	39	0	118	10	0	14	6	.700	0	0- -	-	5.42	5.43
2012	SD	NL	5	5	0	0	27.2	119	26	16	14	5	1	2	1	9	2	24	1	0	0	4	.000	0	0-0	0	3.94	4.55
2014	SD	NL	4	2	0	0	11.1	54	16	9	9	3	0	1	0	5	0	8	0	1	1	0	1.000	0	0-0	0	8.09	7.15
2015	LAD	NL	2	2	0	0	8.2	40	10	8	8	2	0	1	0	5	1	4	0	0	0	1	.000	0	0-0	0	6.56	8.31
2016	Sea	AL	1	1	0	0	5.0	23	9	6	6	1	0	0	0	0	0	3	0	0	0	1	.000	0	0-0	0	8.24	10.80
4 ML YEARS			12	10	0	0	52.2	236	61	39	37	11	1	4	1	19	3	39	1	1	1	6	.143	0	0-0	0	5.57	6.32

Matt Wieters

Bats: B Throws: R Pos: C-117;PH-9;DH-2   WEE-ters   Ht: 6'5" Wt: 230 Born: 5/21/1986 Age: 31

							BATTING													RUNNING			AVERAGES			
Year	Team	Lg	G	AB	H	2B	3B	HR	(Hm | Rd)	TB	R	RBI	RC	TBB	IBB	SO	HBP	SH	SF	SB	CS	GDP	Avg	OBP	Slg	OPS
2009	Bal	AL	96	354	102	15	1	9	(5 | 4)	146	35	43	43	28	2	86	1	0	2	0	0	11	.288	.340	.412	.753
2010	Bal	AL	130	446	111	22	1	11	(3 | 8)	168	37	55	47	47	7	94	2	0	7	0	1	13	.249	.319	.377	.695
2011	Bal	AL	139	500	131	28	0	22	(13 | 9)	225	72	68	76	48	3	84	2	0	1	1	0	16	.262	.328	.450	.778
2012	Bal	AL	144	526	131	27	1	23	(11 | 12)	229	67	83	73	60	4	112	4	0	3	3	0	17	.249	.329	.435	.764
2013	Bal	AL	148	523	123	29	0	22	(13 | 9)	218	59	79	65	43	5	104	0	1	12	2	0	7	.235	.287	.417	.704
2014	Bal	AL	26	104	32	5	0	5	(2 | 3)	52	13	18	17	6	0	19	0	0	2	0	1	1	.308	.339	.500	.839
2015	Bal	AL	75	258	69	14	1	8	(3 | 5)	109	24	25	33	21	0	67	0	0	3	0	0	4	.267	.319	.422	.742
2016	Bal	AL	124	423	103	17	1	17	(10 | 7)	173	48	66	56	32	1	85	5	1	3	1	0	10	.243	.302	.409	.711
Postseason			6	24	3	1	0	0	(0 | 0)	4	2	0	0	2	0	4	0	0	0	0	0	0	.125	.192	.167	.359
8 ML YEARS			882	3134	802	157	5	117	(60 | 57)	1320	355	437	410	285	22	651	14	2	33	7	2	79	.256	.318	.421	.739

Tom Wilhelmsen

Pitches: R Bats: R Pos: RP-50   will-HELM-senn   Ht: 6'6" Wt: 220 Born: 12/16/1983 Age: 33

Year	Team	Lg	G	GS	CG	GF	IP	BFP	H	R	ER	HR	SH	SF	HB	TBB	IBB	SO	WP	Bk	W	L	Pct	Sh	Sv-Op	Hld	ERC	ERA
2016	RdRck*	AAA	5	0	0	2	8.0	30	5	1	1	1	0	0	0	1	0	5	0	0	0	1	.000	0	0- -	-	1.45	1.13
2011	Sea	AL	25	0	0	10	32.2	136	25	13	12	2	0	2	2	13	0	30	6	1	2	0	1.000	0	0-0	3	2.78	3.31
2012	Sea	AL	73	0	0	48	79.1	326	59	24	22	5	1	2	2	29	3	87	3	0	4	3	.571	0	29-34	7	2.38	2.50
2013	Sea	AL	59	0	0	40	59.0	251	45	28	27	2	3	3	1	33	5	45	6	0	0	3	.000	0	24-29	2	2.87	4.12
2014	Sea	AL	57	2	0	18	79.1	317	47	22	20	6	1	3	2	36	6	72	4	0	3	2	.600	0	1-3	8	2.03	2.27
2015	Sea	AL	53	0	0	20	62.0	267	56	24	22	3	4	3	2	29	3	60	2	0	2	2	.500	0	13-15	7	3.49	3.19
2016	2 Tms	AL	50	0	0	5	46.1	209	60	35	35	11	0	1	2	19	0	28	0	0	2	4	.333	0	1-4	12	7.39	6.80
16	Tex	AL	21	0	0	3	21.1	109	38	25	25	7	0	1	2	9	0	11	0	0	2	3	.400	0	0-2	3	11.90	10.55
16	Sea	AL	29	0	0	2	25.0	100	22	10	10	4	0	0	0	10	0	17	0	0	0	1	.000	0	1-2	9	4.04	3.60
6 ML YEARS			317	2	0	141	358.2	1506	292	146	138	29	9	14	11	159	17	322	21	1	13	14	.481	0	68-85	39	3.16	3.46

Andy Wilkins

Bats: L Throws: R Pos: PH-22;1B-3;RF-1   Ht: 6'1" Wt: 225 Born: 9/13/1988 Age: 28

							BATTING													RUNNING			AVERAGES			
Year	Team	Lg	G	AB	H	2B	3B	HR	(Hm	Rd)	TB	R	RBI	RC	TBB	IBB	SO	HBP	SH	SF	SB	CS	GDP	Avg	OBP	Slg	OPS
2012	Brham	AA	116	435	104	28	1	17	(-	-)	185	68	69	65	63	2	94	1	0	3	6	4	5	.239	.335	.425	.760
2013	Brham	AA	67	243	70	16	0	10	(-	-)	116	37	49	47	38	2	58	2	0	2	3	0	5	.288	.386	.477	.863
2013	Charllt	AAA	58	215	57	13	0	7	(-	-)	91	25	30	29	14	1	52	2	0	3	2	1	1	.265	.312	.423	.735
2014	Charllt	AAA	127	491	144	38	1	30	(-	-)	274	79	85	91	34	5	91	1	0	3	0	1	8	.293	.338	.558	.896
2015	Buffalo	AAA	21	72	19	4	0	0	(-	-)	23	9	9	9	11	0	13	0	0	2	0	0	2	.264	.353	.319	.672
2015	OkCity	AAA	105	362	90	25	1	18	(-	-)	171	53	70	56	36	4	81	0	1	13	0	0	3	.249	.307	.472	.779
2016	ColSpr	AAA	91	327	77	20	2	12	(-	-)	137	44	56	47	41	4	91	2	0	4	3	0	5	.235	.321	.419	.740
2014	CWS	AL	17	43	6	2	0	0	(0	0)	8	2	2	0	2	0	22	0	0	0	0	0	0	.140	.178	.186	.364
2016	Mil	NL	26	24	3	1	0	1	(1	0)	7	3	3	1	3	0	10	0	0	0	1	0	1	.125	.222	.292	.514
2 ML YEARS			43	67	9	3	0	1	(1	0)	15	5	5	1	5	0	32	0	0	0	1	0	2	.134	.194	.224	.418

Jerome Williams

Pitches: R Bats: R Pos: RP-11   Ht: 6'3" Wt: 260 Born: 12/4/1981 Age: 35

Year	Team	Lg	G	GS	CG	GF	IP	BFP	H	R	ER	HR	SH	SF	HB	TBB	IBB	SO	WP	Bk	W	L	Pct	Sh	Sv-Op	Hld	ERC	ERA
2016	Memp*	AAA	9	9	2	0	57.0	243	64	31	31	11	2	1	2	15	1	34	4	1	5	3	.625	1	0- -	-	5.09	4.89
2003	SF	NL	21	21	2	0	131.0	545	116	54	48	10	6	3	7	49	3	88	2	1	7	5	.583	1	0-0	0	3.42	3.30
2004	SF	NL	22	22	0	0	129.1	559	123	69	61	14	4	9	17	44	1	80	2	1	10	7	.588	0	0-0	0	4.14	4.24
2005	2 Tms	NL	22	20	0	0	122.2	532	119	62	58	14	11	8	10	49	1	70	2	0	6	10	.375	0	0-0	1	4.34	4.26
2006	ChC	NL	5	2	0	1	12.1	61	15	12	10	2	0	3	1	11	1	5	0	0	0	2	.000	0	0-0	0	8.42	7.30
2007	Was	NL	6	6	0	0	30.0	140	34	26	24	6	1	1	0	18	0	15	2	1	0	5	.000	0	0-0	0	6.43	7.20

Year	Team	Lg	G	GS	CG	GF	IP	BFP	H	R	ER	HR	SH	SF	HB	TBB	IBB	SO	WP	Bk	W	L	Pct	Sh	Sv-Op	Hld	ERC	ERA
2011	LAA	AL	10	6	0	1	44.0	184	45	20	18	6	0	1	1	15	0	28	0	0	4	0	1.000	0	0-0	0	4.45	3.68
2012	LAA	AL	32	15	1	7	137.2	572	139	73	70	17	0	4	5	35	1	98	1	0	6	8	.429	1	1-1	0	3.91	4.58
2013	LAA	AL	37	25	0	8	169.1	728	181	93	86	23	1	3	4	55	2	107	5	0	9	10	.474	0	0-0	0	4.53	4.57
2014	3 Tms		37	11	0	14	115.0	497	125	64	61	12	3	2	6	36	2	82	2	0	6	7	.462	0	0-3	2	4.47	4.77
2015	Phi	NL	33	21	0	3	121.0	553	161	83	78	22	2	4	5	34	3	74	4	0	4	12	.250	0	1-2	4	6.27	5.80
2016	StL	NL	11	0	0	9	17.1	81	22	15	11	4	0	1	2	6	1	8	0	0	0	0	-	0	0-0	0	6.80	5.71
05	SF	NL	4	3	0	0	16.2	73	21	12	12	2	1	0	1	4	1	11	0	0	0	2	.000	0	0-0	0	5.32	6.48
05	ChC	NL	18	17	0	0	106.0	459	98	50	46	12	10	8	9	45	0	59	2	0	6	8	.429	0	0-0	1	4.19	3.91
14	Hou	AL	26	0	0	14	47.2	219	59	33	32	7	3	1	3	16	1	38	2	0	1	4	.200	0	0-3	2	5.70	6.04
14	Tex	AL	2	2	0	0	10.0	48	18	11	11	0	0	0	0	3	0	6	0	0	1	1	.500	0	0-0	0	8.02	9.90
14	Phi	NL	9	9	0	0	57.1	230	48	20	18	5	0	1	3	17	1	38	0	0	4	2	.667	0	0-0	0	2.83	2.83
	Postseason		1	1	0	0	2.0	13	5	3	3	0	1	0	0	1	0	1	0	0	0	0	-	0	0-0	0	12.20	13.50
	11 ML YEARS		236	149	3	43	1029.2	4452	1080	571	525	130	28	39	58	352	15	655	20	3	52	66	.441	2	2-6	7	4.55	4.59

Mason Williams

Bats: L **Throws:** R **Pos:** RF-7;LF-2;CF-2;PR-2;DH-1   **Ht:** 6'1" **Wt:** 185 **Born:** 8/21/1991 **Age:** 25

							BATTING														RUNNING			AVERAGES			
Year	Team	Lg	G	AB	H	2B	3B	HR	(Hm	Rd)	TB	R	RBI	RC	TBB	IBB	SO	HBP	SH	SF	SB	CS	GDP	Avg	OBP	Slg	OPS
2012	2 Tms	Low	91	359	107	22	4	11	(-	-)	170	68	35	59	24	1	47	4	7	3	20	13	3	.298	.346	.474	.820
2013	Tampa	A+	100	406	106	21	3	3	(-	-)	142	56	24	49	39	0	61	2	11	3	15	9	7	.261	.327	.350	.676
2013	Trntn	AA	17	72	11	3	1	1	(-	-)	19	7	4	2	1	0	18	0	3	0	0	0	2	.153	.164	.264	.428
2014	Trntn	AA	128	507	113	18	4	5	(-	-)	154	67	40	48	47	1	68	1	7	1	21	8	21	.223	.290	.304	.593
2015	Trntn	AA	34	120	38	7	0	0	(-	-)	45	14	11	20	19	1	17	0	4	1	11	6	0	.317	.407	.375	.782
2015	S-WB	AAA	20	81	26	7	1	0	(-	-)	35	12	11	13	8	1	6	0	2	0	2	1	3	.321	.382	.432	.814
2016	2 Tms	Low	12	46	14	2	1	0	(-	-)	18	2	1	6	1	0	5	0	0	0	0	0	1	.304	.319	.391	.710
2016	S-WB	AAA	31	125	37	8	1	0	(-	-)	47	19	23	15	5	0	21	0	4	4	1	1	0	.296	.313	.376	.689
2015	NYY	AL	8	21	6	3	0	1	(0	1)	12	3	3	4	1	0	3	0	0	0	0	0	0	.286	.318	.571	.890
2016	NYY	AL	12	27	8	1	0	0	(0	0)	9	4	2	3	1	0	12	0	1	0	0	0	0	.296	.321	.333	.655
	2 ML YEARS		20	48	14	4	0	1	(0	1)	21	7	5	7	2	0	15	0	1	0	0	0	0	.292	.320	.438	.758

Trevor Williams

Pitches: R **Bats:** R **Pos:** RP-6; SP-1   **Ht:** 6'3" **Wt:** 230 **Born:** 4/25/1992 **Age:** 25

			HOW MUCH HE PITCHED						WHAT HE GAVE UP												THE RESULTS						
Year	Team	Lg	G	GS	CG	GF	IP	BFP	H	R	ER	HR	SH	SF	HB	TBB	IBB	SO	WP	Bk	W	L	Pct	Sh	Sv-Op	Hld	ERC	ERA
2013	3 Tms	Low	12	12	0	0	34.0	145	31	15	9	0	0	1	1	8	0	24	0	0	0	2	.000	0	0- -		2.34	2.38
2014	Jupiter	A+	23	23	0	0	129.0	537	138	49	40	5	4	6	0	29	0	90	4	0	8	6	.571	0	0- -		3.40	2.79
2015	Jaxnvl	AA	22	21	0	0	117.0	500	126	53	52	9	3	1	1	36	0	88	3	0	7	8	.467	0	0- -		4.04	4.00
2016	Indy	AAA	20	19	0	0	110.1	459	103	43	31	5	7	4	4	30	2	74	2	1	9	6	.600	0	0- -		2.97	2.53
2016	Pit	NL	7	1	0	1	12.2	61	19	13	11	4	0	0	0	5	0	11	0	0	1	1	.500	0	0-1	0	8.89	7.82

Mac Williamson

Bats: R **Throws:** R **Pos:** RF-23;PH-21;LF-13;DH-1   **Ht:** 6'4" **Wt:** 240 **Born:** 7/15/1990 **Age:** 26

							BATTING														RUNNING			AVERAGES			
Year	Team	Lg	G	AB	H	2B	3B	HR	(Hm	Rd)	TB	R	RBI	RC	TBB	IBB	SO	HBP	SH	SF	SB	CS	GDP	Avg	OBP	Slg	OPS
2012	2 Tms		33	131	42	8	0	9	(-	-)	77	26	32	27	8	0	24	4	0	1	0	0	7	.321	.375	.588	.963
2013	SnJos	A+	136	520	152	31	2	25	(-	-)	262	94	89	102	51	3	132	21	0	5	10	1	13	.292	.375	.504	.879
2014	SnJos	A+	23	85	27	7	0	3	(-	-)	43	16	11	19	13	0	14	2	0	0	6	1	3	.318	.420	.506	.926
2015	Rchmd	AA	69	259	76	16	2	5	(-	-)	111	41	42	42	25	4	53	5	0	1	3	1	8	.293	.366	.429	.794
2015	Scrmto	AAA	54	189	47	12	0	8	(-	-)	83	35	31	33	26	1	55	11	0	1	1	0	3	.249	.370	.439	.809
2016	Scrmto	AAA	54	208	56	14	0	11	(-	-)	103	35	42	33	12	3	53	3	0	3	2	1	7	.269	.314	.495	.809
2015	SF	NL	10	32	7	0	1	0	(0	0)	9	2	1	1	0	0	8	1	0	1	0	0	1	.219	.235	.281	.517
2016	SF	NL	54	112	25	3	0	6	(1	5)	46	14	15	11	13	0	35	2	0	0	0	1	4	.223	.315	.411	.726
	2 ML YEARS		64	144	32	3	1	6	(1	5)	55	16	16	12	13	0	43	3	0	1	0	1	5	.222	.298	.382	.680

Alex Wilson

Pitches: R **Bats:** R **Pos:** RP-62   **Ht:** 6'0" **Wt:** 215 **Born:** 11/3/1986 **Age:** 30

			HOW MUCH HE PITCHED						WHAT HE GAVE UP												THE RESULTS						
Year	Team	Lg	G	GS	CG	GF	IP	BFP	H	R	ER	HR	SH	SF	HB	TBB	IBB	SO	WP	Bk	W	L	Pct	Sh	Sv-Op	Hld	ERC	ERA
2013	Bos	AL	26	0	0	9	27.2	127	34	16	15	0	0	1	1	14	1	22	1	0	1	1	.500	0	0-0	1	5.19	4.88
2014	Bos	AL	18	0	0	3	28.1	109	20	8	6	3	0	1	2	5	0	19	1	0	1	0	1.000	0	0-1	0	2.81	1.91
2015	Det	AL	59	1	0	16	70.0	273	61	19	17	5	2	2	2	11	1	38	2	0	3	3	.500	0	2-4	7	2.47	2.19
2016	Det	AL	62	0	0	6	73.0	297	68	26	24	5	0	5	1	21	5	49	2	0	4	0	1.000	0	0-4	14	3.09	2.96
	4 ML YEARS		165	1	0	34	199.0	806	183	69	62	13	2	9	6	51	7	128	6	0	9	4	.692	0	2-9	22	3.00	2.80

Bobby Wilson

Bats: R **Throws:** R **Pos:** C-75   **Ht:** 6'0" **Wt:** 230 **Born:** 4/8/1983 **Age:** 34

							BATTING														RUNNING			AVERAGES			
Year	Team	Lg	G	AB	H	2B	3B	HR	(Hm	Rd)	TB	R	RBI	RC	TBB	IBB	SO	HBP	SH	SF	SB	CS	GDP	Avg	OBP	Slg	OPS
2008	LAA	AL	7	6	1	0	0	0	(0	0)	1	0	1	0	1	0	3	0	0	0	0	0	0	.167	.286	.167	.452
2009	LAA	AL	12	5	1	1	0	0	(0	0)	2	0	0	0	0	0	1	0	1	0	0	0	0	.200	.200	.400	.600
2010	LAA	AL	40	96	22	6	0	4	(3	1)	40	12	15	12	8	0	23	0	2	0	0	0	3	.229	.288	.417	.705
2011	LAA	AL	57	111	21	8	0	1	(0	1)	32	5	8	7	10	1	16	0	4	2	0	2	2	.189	.252	.288	.540
2012	LAA	AL	75	171	36	5	0	3	(2	1)	50	19	13	13	15	0	33	1	13	1	0	0	7	.211	.277	.292	.569
2014	Ari	NL	2	4	1	0	0	0	(0	0)	1	0	0	0	0	0	0	0	0	0	0	0	0	.250	.250	.250	.500
2015	2 Tms	AL	56	132	25	5	0	1	(1	0)	33	8	14	12	11	0	39	1	2	1	0	1	1	.189	.255	.250	.505

Batting (continued)

Year Team	Lg	G	AB	H	2B	3B	HR	(Hm Rd)	TB	R	RBI	RC	TBB	IBB	SO	HBP	SH	SF	SB	CS	GDP	Avg	OBP	Slg	OPS
2016 3 Tms	AL	75	228	54	6	0	7	(4 3)	81	25	33	25	11	0	64	1	7	4	0	0	6	.237	.270	.355	.626
15 TB	AL	25	55	8	0	0	0	(0 0)	8	3	4	2	4	0	20	0	0	0	0	0	1	.145	.203	.145	.349
15 Tex	AL	31	77	17	5	0	1	(1 0)	25	5	10	10	7	0	19	1	2	1	0	1	0	.221	.291	.325	.615
16 Det	AL	5	13	2	0	0	0	(0 0)	2	0	2	1	1	0	3	0	0	1	0	0	1	.154	.200	.154	.354
16 Tex	AL	42	128	32	4	0	3	(2 1)	45	11	22	18	5	0	33	1	4	3	0	0	2	.250	.277	.352	.629
16 TB	AL	28	87	20	2	0	4	(2 2)	34	14	9	6	5	0	28	0	3	0	0	0	3	.230	.272	.391	.663
8 ML YEARS		324	753	161	31	0	16	(10 6)	240	69	84	69	56	1	179	3	29	8	0	3	20	.214	.268	.319	.587

C.J. Wilson

Pitches: L **Bats:** L **Pos:** P **Ht:** 6'1" **Wt:** 210 **Born:** 11/18/1980 **Age:** 36

Year Team	Lg	G	GS	CG	GF	IP	BFP	H	R	ER	HR	SH	SF	HB	TBB	IBB	SO	WP	Bk	W	L	Pct	Sh	Sv-Op	Hld	ERC	ERA
2005 Tex	AL	24	6	0	5	48.0	220	63	39	37	5	1	2	2	18	1	30	4	1	1	7	.125	0	1-1	4	6.03	6.94
2006 Tex	AL	44	0	0	12	44.1	191	39	23	20	7	1	0	5	18	1	43	0	0	2	4	.333	0	1-2	7	4.25	4.06
2007 Tex	AL	66	0	0	22	68.1	285	50	25	23	4	2	4	6	33	1	63	5	0	2	1	.667	0	12-14	15	3.01	3.03
2008 Tex	AL	50	0	0	41	46.1	214	49	35	31	8	1	1	2	27	2	41	3	0	2	2	.500	0	24-28	1	5.77	6.02
2009 Tex	AL	74	0	0	30	73.2	323	66	29	23	3	3	0	6	32	3	84	3	0	5	6	.455	0	14-18	19	3.40	2.81
2010 Tex	AL	33	33	3	0	204.0	850	161	83	76	10	1	3	10	93	1	170	7	1	15	8	.652	0	0-0	0	3.03	3.35
2011 Tex	AL	34	34	3	0	223.1	915	191	89	73	16	3	5	10	74	0	206	6	0	16	7	.696	1	0-0	0	3.07	2.94
2012 LAA	AL	34	34	0	0	202.1	865	181	102	86	19	4	6	6	91	2	173	4	1	13	10	.565	0	0-0	0	3.75	3.83
2013 LAA	AL	33	33	0	0	212.1	913	200	93	80	15	4	2	8	85	3	188	14	2	17	7	.708	0	0-0	0	3.66	3.39
2014 LAA	AL	31	31	1	0	175.2	761	169	95	88	17	3	7	11	85	5	151	9	0	13	10	.565	1	0-0	0	4.46	4.51
2015 LAA	AL	21	21	0	0	132.0	553	118	59	57	13	2	4	10	46	2	110	11	1	8	8	.500	0	0-0	0	3.60	3.89
Postseason		11	10	0	0	53.0	237	49	35	31	10	3	1	4	30	0	44	3	0	1	6	.143	0	0-0	0	5.08	5.26
11 ML YEARS		444	192	7	110	1430.1	6090	1287	672	594	117	25	34	76	602	20	1259	66	6	94	70	.573	2	52-63	46	3.69	3.74

Justin Wilson

Pitches: L **Bats:** L **Pos:** RP-66 **Ht:** 6'2" **Wt:** 205 **Born:** 8/18/1987 **Age:** 29

Year Team	Lg	G	GS	CG	GF	IP	BFP	H	R	ER	HR	SH	SF	HB	TBB	IBB	SO	WP	Bk	W	L	Pct	Sh	Sv-Op	Hld	ERC	ERA
2012 Pit	NL	8	0	0	3	4.2	26	10	1	1	0	1	0	0	3	0	7	1	0	0	0	-	0	0-0	0	11.83	1.93
2013 Pit	NL	58	0	0	8	73.2	295	50	17	17	4	3	1	3	28	1	59	5	0	6	1	.857	0	0-3	14	2.20	2.08
2014 Pit	NL	70	0	0	15	60.0	256	49	30	28	4	0	0	3	30	5	61	4	0	3	4	.429	0	0-3	16	3.29	4.20
2015 NYY	AL	74	0	0	3	61.0	244	49	21	21	3	2	0	2	20	0	66	4	0	5	0	1.000	0	0-2	29	2.63	3.10
2016 Det	AL	66	0	0	10	58.2	251	61	29	27	6	1	0	1	17	2	65	4	0	4	5	.444	0	1-6	25	3.87	4.14
Postseason		4	0	0	0	4.1	18	3	1	1	0	0	0	0	3	0	4	1	0	0	0	-	0	0-0	0	2.92	2.08
5 ML YEARS		276	0	0	39	258.0	1072	219	98	94	17	7	1	9	98	8	258	18	0	18	10	.643	0	1-14	84	3.06	3.28

Tyler Wilson

Pitches: R **Bats:** R **Pos:** SP-13; RP-11 **Ht:** 6'2" **Wt:** 185 **Born:** 9/25/1989 **Age:** 27

Year Team	Lg	G	GS	CG	GF	IP	BFP	H	R	ER	HR	SH	SF	HB	TBB	IBB	SO	WP	Bk	W	L	Pct	Sh	Sv-Op	Hld	ERC	ERA
2012 2 Tms	Low	25	25	0	0	143.0	575	125	68	61	16	0	2	7	30	0	143	5	2	10	10	.500	0	0--	-	2.98	3.84
2013 Frdrck	A+	11	11	0	0	62.1	264	57	34	31	4	1	1	2	25	0	48	1	0	1	1	.500	0	0--	-	3.43	4.48
2013 Bowie	AA	16	16	1	0	89.1	374	85	40	38	13	1	4	2	22	0	70	5	0	7	5	.583	0	0--	-	3.55	3.83
2014 Bowie	AA	16	16	0	0	96.2	408	101	47	40	10	2	4	1	22	0	91	8	0	10	5	.667	0	0--	-	3.69	3.72
2014 Norfolk	AAA	12	12	0	0	70.0	285	61	30	28	8	6	2	1	21	0	66	7	1	4	3	.571	0	0--	-	3.18	3.60
2015 Norfolk	AAA	17	17	0	0	94.1	385	94	35	34	8	2	1	4	18	0	63	0	0	5	5	.500	0	0--	-	3.37	3.24
2016 Norfolk	AAA	6	6	0	0	23.2	94	26	12	12	1	1	0	0	3	0	20	3	0	2	0	1.000	0	0--	-	3.33	4.56
2015 Bal	AL	9	5	0	2	36.0	149	39	14	14	1	0	2	1	11	1	13	0	0	2	2	.500	0	0-0	0	3.90	3.50
2016 Bal	AL	24	13	0	5	94.0	414	110	57	55	15	1	3	4	24	1	55	2	0	4	6	.400	0	0-0	0	5.01	5.27
2 ML YEARS		33	18	0	7	130.0	563	149	71	69	16	1	5	5	35	2	68	2	0	6	8	.429	0	0-0	0	4.71	4.78

Alex Wimmers

Pitches: R **Bats:** L **Pos:** RP-16 **Ht:** 6'2" **Wt:** 215 **Born:** 11/1/1988 **Age:** 28

Year Team	Lg	G	GS	CG	GF	IP	BFP	H	R	ER	HR	SH	SF	HB	TBB	IBB	SO	WP	Bk	W	L	Pct	Sh	Sv-Op	Hld	ERC	ERA
2013 Twins	R	6	6	0	0	15.0	78	25	15	12	1	0	1	2	5	0	18	2	0	0	1	.000	0	0--	-	7.88	7.20
2014 FtMyrs	A+	18	7	0	2	62.1	282	71	44	28	2	1	3	3	25	0	70	3	2	3	3	.500	0	0--	-	4.50	4.04
2014 NwBrit	AA	13	1	0	2	21.2	89	19	9	9	3	0	0	0	6	0	27	1	0	1	0	1.000	0	1--	-	3.16	3.74
2015 Chatt	AA	30	18	0	6	115.1	489	117	58	58	7	4	8	1	43	0	100	5	0	8	4	.667	0	0--	-	3.87	4.53
2016 Chatt	AA	6	5	0	0	7.0	30	10	5	5	0	0	0	0	1	0	6	0	0	1	0	1.000	0	0--	-	4.97	6.43
2016 Roch	AAA	39	0	0	20	49.2	214	42	22	20	2	1	1	2	24	1	50	6	0	2	1	.667	0	11--	-	3.23	3.62
2016 Min	AL	16	0	0	2	17.1	72	14	8	8	2	0	2	0	11	1	14	0	0	1	3	.250	0	0-1	1	4.15	4.15

Daniel Winkler

Pitches: R **Bats:** R **Pos:** RP-3 **Ht:** 6'3" **Wt:** 205 **Born:** 2/2/1990 **Age:** 27

Year Team	Lg	G	GS	CG	GF	IP	BFP	H	R	ER	HR	SH	SF	HB	TBB	IBB	SO	WP	Bk	W	L	Pct	Sh	Sv-Op	Hld	ERC	ERA
2012 Ashvll	A	25	25	0	0	145.1	644	152	80	72	16	2	7	22	47	0	136	4	1	11	10	.524	0	0--	-	4.70	4.46
2013 Mdest	A+	22	22	0	0	130.1	510	84	48	43	15	1	6	9	37	0	152	4	1	12	5	.706	0	0--	-	2.19	2.97
2013 Tulsa	AA	5	5	0	0	26.2	108	23	11	9	3	0	1	1	10	0	23	2	0	1	2	.333	0	0--	-	3.60	3.04

Year Team	Lg	G	GS	CG	GF	IP	BFP	H	R	ER	HR	SH	SF	HB	TBB	IBB	SO	WP	Bk	W	L	Pct	Sh	Sv-Op	Hld	ERC	ERA
2014 Tulsa	AA	12	12	1	0	70.0	262	33	11	11	5	1	0	6	17	0	71	1	0	5	2	.714	1	0--	-	1.28	1.41
2015 Atl	NL	2	0	0	0	1.2	8	2	2	2	2	0	0	0	1	0	2	0	0	0	0	-	0	0-0	0	14.99	10.80
2016 Atl	NL	3	0	0	0	2.1	8	0	0	0	0	0	0	0	1	0	4	0	0	0	0	-	0	0-0	0	0.20	0.00
2 ML YEARS		5	0	0	0	4.0	16	2	2	2	2	0	0	0	2	0	6	0	0	0	0	-	0	0-0	0	4.08	4.50

Matt Wisler

Pitches: R **Bats:** R **Pos:** SP-26; RP-1 — WISS-lurr — **Ht:** 6'3" **Wt:** 205 **Born:** 9/12/1992 **Age:** 24

Year Team	Lg	G	GS	CG	GF	IP	BFP	H	R	ER	HR	SH	SF	HB	TBB	IBB	SO	WP	Bk	W	L	Pct	Sh	Sv-Op	Hld	ERC	ERA
2012 FtWyn	A	24	23	1	0	114.0	461	95	39	32	1	5	5	5	28	0	113	5	2	5	4	.556	1	0--	-	2.22	2.53
2013 Lk Els	A+	6	6	0	0	31.0	119	22	7	7	1	0	0	1	6	0	28	0	1	2	1	.667	0	0--	-	1.64	2.03
2013 SnAnt	AA	20	20	0	0	105.0	417	85	36	35	7	1	5	2	27	0	103	3	0	8	5	.615	0	0--	-	2.45	3.00
2014 SnAnt	AA	6	6	0	0	30.0	120	26	7	7	2	3	0	0	6	0	35	2	0	1	0	1.000	0	0--	-	2.42	2.10
2014 ElPaso	AAA	22	22	0	0	116.2	514	131	68	65	19	1	3	5	36	0	101	6	1	9	5	.643	0	0--	-	5.01	5.01
2015 Gwnntt	AAA	12	12	0	0	65.0	273	68	34	31	5	3	0	1	13	0	49	1	1	3	4	.429	0	0--	-	3.43	4.29
2015 Atl	NL	20	19	0	0	109.0	478	119	59	57	16	4	5	4	40	4	72	2	3	8	8	.500	0	0-0	0	4.91	4.71
2016 Atl	NL	27	26	0	1	156.2	671	159	90	87	26	2	3	4	49	3	115	5	1	7	13	.350	0	1-1	0	4.32	5.00
2 ML YEARS		47	45	0	1	265.2	1149	278	149	144	42	6	8	8	89	7	187	7	4	15	21	.417	0	1-1	0	4.56	4.88

Chris Withrow

Pitches: R **Bats:** R **Pos:** RP-46 — with-ROE — **Ht:** 6'3" **Wt:** 240 **Born:** 4/1/1989 **Age:** 28

Year Team	Lg	G	GS	CG	GF	IP	BFP	H	R	ER	HR	SH	SF	HB	TBB	IBB	SO	WP	Bk	W	L	Pct	Sh	Sv-Op	Hld	ERC	ERA
2016 Gwnntt*	AAA	11	0	0	6	10.0	43	7	6	5	1	0	1	0	6	0	12	0	0	0	1	.000	0	5--	-	3.15	4.50
2013 LAD	NL	26	0	0	4	34.2	134	20	10	10	5	0	0	0	13	0	43	2	0	3	0	1.000	0	1-2	6	2.11	2.60
2014 LAD	NL	20	0	0	0	21.1	90	10	8	7	1	0	1	0	18	0	28	4	0	0	0	-	0	0-1	6	2.74	2.95
2016 Atl	NL	46	0	0	6	37.2	158	29	16	15	5	2	1	2	17	1	28	1	0	3	0	1.000	0	0-3	12	3.41	3.58
Postseason		4	0	0	0	5.0	23	3	3	3	0	1	0	0	6	0	3	1	1	0	1	.000	0	0-0	0	4.17	5.40
3 ML YEARS		92	0	0	10	93.2	382	59	34	32	11	2	2	3	48	1	99	7	0	6	0	1.000	0	1-6	22	2.78	3.07

Nick Wittgren

Pitches: R **Bats:** R **Pos:** RP-48 — **Ht:** 6'2" **Wt:** 210 **Born:** 5/29/1991 **Age:** 26

Year Team	Lg	G	GS	CG	GF	IP	BFP	H	R	ER	HR	SH	SF	HB	TBB	IBB	SO	WP	Bk	W	L	Pct	Sh	Sv-Op	Hld	ERC	ERA
2012 2 Tms	Low	23	0	0	21	30.2	122	25	4	4	0	0	1	1	5	0	47	1	0	0	2	.000	0	13--	-	1.77	1.17
2013 Jupiter	A+	48	0	0	38	54.1	214	42	7	5	1	3	0	2	10	1	59	0	0	2	1	.667	0	25--	-	1.76	0.83
2014 Jaxnvl	AA	52	0	0	42	66.0	280	73	31	26	6	2	2	2	14	4	56	2	1	5	5	.500	0	20--	-	3.90	3.55
2015 NewOr	AAA	51	0	0	39	62.1	251	58	22	21	6	5	0	1	8	0	64	1	0	1	6	.143	0	19--	-	2.70	3.03
2016 NewOr	AAA	10	0	0	8	12.2	46	6	2	2	1	0	0	0	4	0	11	1	0	1	0	1.000	0	2--	-	1.32	1.42
2016 Mia	NL	48	0	0	9	51.2	213	50	18	18	6	3	2	1	10	2	42	1	0	4	3	.571	0	0-2	6	3.21	3.14

Tony Wolters

Bats: L **Throws:** R **Pos:** C-59;PH-8;2B-7;SS-3 — WAHL-ters — **Ht:** 5'10" **Wt:** 200 **Born:** 6/9/1992 **Age:** 25

Year Team	Lg	G	AB	H	2B	3B	HR	(Hm	Rd)	TB	R	RBI	RC	TBB	IBB	SO	HBP	SH	SF	SB	CS	GDP	Avg	OBP	Slg	OPS
2012 Carlina	A+	125	485	126	30	8	8	(-	-)	196	66	58	63	36	0	104	8	5	9	5	9	16	.260	.320	.404	.724
2013 Carlina	A+	80	289	80	13	6	3	(-	-)	102	36	33	41	41	0	58	3	4	3	3	6	4	.277	.369	.353	.722
2014 Akron	AA	94	341	85	15	2	1	(-	-)	107	36	34	37	35	1	74	3	2	6	3	2	10	.249	.319	.314	.633
2015 Akron	AA	65	239	50	7	2	2	(-	-)	67	23	17	20	21	0	63	7	2	2	3	2	5	.209	.290	.280	.570
2016 Col	NL	71	205	53	15	2	3	(2	1)	81	27	30	30	21	2	53	0	4	0	4	1	1	.259	.327	.395	.723

Kolten Wong

Bats: L **Throws:** R **Pos:** 2B-88;PH-28;CF-8;LF-6;RF-4;PR-4 — COLT-enn — **Ht:** 5'9" **Wt:** 185 **Born:** 10/10/1990 **Age:** 26

Year Team	Lg	G	AB	H	2B	3B	HR	(Hm	Rd)	TB	R	RBI	RC	TBB	IBB	SO	HBP	SH	SF	SB	CS	GDP	Avg	OBP	Slg	OPS
2013 StL	NL	32	59	9	1	0	0	(0	0)	10	6	0	0	3	0	12	0	0	0	3	0	0	.153	.194	.169	.363
2014 StL	NL	113	402	100	14	3	12	(10	2)	156	52	42	41	21	3	71	4	5	1	20	4	12	.249	.292	.388	.680
2015 StL	NL	150	557	146	28	4	11	(5	6)	215	71	61	67	36	2	95	15	0	5	15	8	10	.262	.321	.386	.707
2016 StL	NL	121	313	75	7	7	5	(3	2)	111	39	23	36	34	2	52	9	0	5	7	0	3	.240	.327	.355	.682
Postseason		19	49	10	4	1	4	(3	1)	28	5	7	5	1	1	11	0	0	0	2	0	2	.204	.220	.571	.791
4 ML YEARS		416	1331	330	50	14	28	(18	10)	492	168	126	144	94	7	230	28	5	11	45	12	27	.248	.309	.370	.678

Alex Wood

Pitches: L **Bats:** R **Pos:** SP-10; RP-4 — **Ht:** 6'4" **Wt:** 215 **Born:** 1/12/1991 **Age:** 26

Year Team	Lg	G	GS	CG	GF	IP	BFP	H	R	ER	HR	SH	SF	HB	TBB	IBB	SO	WP	Bk	W	L	Pct	Sh	Sv-Op	Hld	ERC	ERA
2013 Atl	NL	31	11	0	9	77.2	327	76	29	27	3	6	4	1	27	1	77	4	2	3	3	.500	0	0-0	1	3.40	3.13
2014 Atl	NL	35	24	1	2	171.2	694	151	58	53	16	7	3	6	45	1	170	5	0	11	11	.500	0	0-0	0	3.04	2.78
2015 2 Tms	NL	32	32	0	0	189.2	801	198	86	81	15	15	3	4	59	4	139	6	1	12	12	.500	0	0-0	0	3.94	3.84
2016 LAD	NL	14	10	0	0	60.1	255	56	30	25	5	0	2	3	20	0	66	4	0	1	4	.200	0	0-0	0	3.49	3.73

HOW MUCH HE PITCHED						WHAT HE GAVE UP												THE RESULTS							
Year Team	Lg	G	GS	CG	GF	IP	BFP	H	R	ER	HR	SH	SF	HB	TBB	IBB	SO	WP	Bk	W	L	Pct	Sh	Sv-Op	Hld	ERC	ERA
15 Atl	NL	20	20	0	0	119.1	509	132	50	47	8	11	1	2	36	2	90	5	0	7	6	.538	0	0-0	0	4.15	3.54
15 LAD	NL	12	12	0	0	70.1	292	66	36	34	7	4	2	2	23	2	49	1	1	5	6	.455	0	0-0	0	3.58	4.35
Postseason		3	0	0	0	5.1	26	7	8	4	2	0	0	0	2	1	5	1	0	0	0	-	0	0-0	0	7.19	6.75
4 ML YEARS		112	77	1	11	499.1	2077	481	203	186	39	28	12	14	151	6	452	19	3	27	30	.474	0	0-0	3	3.49	3.35

Blake Wood

Pitches: R Bats: R Pos: RP-70 **Ht: 6'5" Wt: 240 Born: 8/8/1985 Age: 31**

HOW MUCH HE PITCHED						WHAT HE GAVE UP												THE RESULTS							
Year Team	Lg	G	GS	CG	GF	IP	BFP	H	R	ER	HR	SH	SF	HB	TBB	IBB	SO	WP	Bk	W	L	Pct	Sh	Sv-Op	Hld	ERC	ERA
2010 KC	AL	51	0	0	13	49.2	220	54	29	28	6	2	6	1	22	5	31	3	0	1	3	.250	0	0-4	15	4.83	5.07
2011 KC	AL	55	0	0	20	69.2	303	66	30	29	5	5	3	3	32	7	62	2	0	5	3	.625	0	1-3	5	3.82	3.75
2013 Cle	AL	2	0	0	1	1.1	8	1	0	0	0	0	0	0	3	0	1	0	0	0	0	-	0	0-0	0	8.88	0.00
2014 Cle	AL	7	0	0	3	6.1	30	4	5	5	0	0	0	1	7	2	7	0	0	0	1	.000	0	0-0	0	3.89	7.11
2016 Cin	NL	70	0	0	21	76.2	330	72	38	34	9	1	2	2	38	3	81	8	0	6	5	.545	0	1-6	15	4.35	3.99
5 ML YEARS		185	0	0	58	203.2	891	197	102	96	20	8	11	7	102	17	182	13	0	12	12	.500	0	2-13	35	4.30	4.24

Travis Wood

Pitches: L Bats: R Pos: RP-77 **Ht: 5'11" Wt: 175 Born: 2/6/1987 Age: 30**

HOW MUCH HE PITCHED						WHAT HE GAVE UP												THE RESULTS							
Year Team	Lg	G	GS	CG	GF	IP	BFP	H	R	ER	HR	SH	SF	HB	TBB	IBB	SO	WP	Bk	W	L	Pct	Sh	Sv-Op	Hld	ERC	ERA
2010 Cin	NL	17	17	0	0	102.2	419	85	45	40	9	3	3	4	26	1	86	0	1	5	4	.556	0	0-0	0	2.64	3.51
2011 Cin	NL	22	18	0	0	106.0	463	118	57	57	10	9	7	4	40	5	76	2	0	6	6	.500	0	0-0	0	4.73	4.84
2012 ChC	NL	26	26	0	0	156.0	649	133	80	74	25	9	4	8	54	3	119	2	1	6	13	.316	0	0-0	0	3.65	4.27
2013 ChC	NL	32	32	0	0	200.0	822	163	73	69	18	7	4	8	66	2	144	6	0	9	12	.429	0	0-0	0	2.90	3.11
2014 ChC	NL	31	31	0	0	173.2	781	190	110	97	20	8	4	7	76	1	146	2	0	8	13	.381	0	0-0	0	5.00	5.03
2015 ChC	NL	54	9	0	12	100.2	419	86	48	43	11	1	2	1	39	5	118	2	0	5	4	.556	0	4-4	3	3.27	3.84
2016 ChC	NL	77	0	0	16	61.0	252	45	24	20	8	1	0	1	24	2	47	0	0	4	0	1.000	0	0-1	12	2.83	2.95
Postseason		7	0	0	0	11.0	41	7	4	4	0	0	0	1	2	1	15	0	0	1	0	1.000	0	0-0	0	1.13	3.27
7 ML YEARS		259	133	0	30	900.0	3804	820	437	400	101	38	24	33	325	19	736	14	2	43	52	.453	0	4-5	15	3.63	4.00

Vance Worley

Pitches: R Bats: R Pos: RP-31; SP-4 **Ht: 6'2" Wt: 250 Born: 9/25/1987 Age: 29**

HOW MUCH HE PITCHED						WHAT HE GAVE UP												THE RESULTS							
Year Team	Lg	G	GS	CG	GF	IP	BFP	H	R	ER	HR	SH	SF	HB	TBB	IBB	SO	WP	Bk	W	L	Pct	Sh	Sv-Op	Hld	ERC	ERA
2010 Phi	NL	5	2	0	2	13.0	51	8	2	2	1	2	0	0	4	0	12	1	0	1	1	.500	0	0-0	0	1.66	1.38
2011 Phi	NL	25	21	1	0	131.2	553	116	47	44	10	9	5	3	46	2	119	2	1	11	3	.786	0	0-0	2	3.12	3.01
2012 Phi	NL	23	23	0	0	133.0	590	154	69	62	12	11	3	6	47	4	107	1	0	6	9	.400	0	0-0	0	4.87	4.20
2013 Min	AL	10	10	0	0	48.2	234	82	43	39	9	0	1	3	15	1	25	1	0	1	5	.167	0	0-0	0	9.17	7.21
2014 Pit	NL	18	17	1	0	110.2	458	112	43	35	9	6	4	3	22	1	79	4	0	8	4	.667	1	0-0	0	3.35	2.85
2015 Pit	NL	23	8	0	6	71.2	310	81	36	32	6	3	2	2	21	3	49	3	0	4	6	.400	0	0-1	0	4.34	4.02
2016 Bal	AL	35	4	0	13	86.2	365	84	37	34	11	0	3	3	35	0	56	3	0	2	2	.500	0	1-1	0	4.37	3.53
Postseason		2	0	0	0	1.1	8	3	1	1	0	0	0	0	1	0	0	0	0	0	0	-	0	0-0	1	12.64	6.75
7 ML YEARS		139	85	2	21	595.1	2561	637	277	248	58	31	18	20	190	11	447	15	1	33	30	.524	1	1-2	2	4.26	3.75

Danny Worth

Bats: R Throws: R Pos: 2B-6;3B-5;PH-4;SS-2;DH-2;PR-1 **Ht: 6'1" Wt: 195 Born: 9/30/1985 Age: 31**

BATTING																			RUNNING			AVERAGES			
Year Team	Lg	G	AB	H	2B	3B	HR	(Hm	Rd)	TB	R	RBI	RC	TBB	IBB	SO	HBP	SH	SF	SB	CS	GDP	Avg	OBP	Slg	OPS
2016 Fresno*	AAA	84	303	100	22	2	11	(-	-)	159	62	48	71	54	1	72	4	1	6	5	1	5	.330	.431	.525	.955
2010 Det	AL	39	106	27	5	0	2	(2	0)	38	10	8	11	6	0	13	0	3	0	1	2	0	.255	.295	.358	.653
2011 Det	AL	30	37	10	2	0	0	(0	0)	12	6	3	3	2	0	9	0	0	0	0	0	0	.270	.308	.324	.632
2012 Det	AL	43	74	16	3	0	0	(0	0)	19	9	3	7	13	0	23	0	2	1	0	0	0	.216	.330	.257	.586
2013 Det	AL	3	2	0	0	0	0	(0	0)	0	0	0	0	0	0	1	0	0	1	0	0	1	.000	.000	.000	.000
2014 Det	AL	20	42	7	1	0	0	(0	0)	8	5	5	2	2	0	12	1	0	1	0	1	0	.167	.217	.190	.408
2016 Hou	AL	16	39	7	2	0	0	(0	0)	9	4	1	0	1	0	6	0	0	0	0	0	0	.179	.204	.231	.431
Postseason		4	1	0	0	0	0	(0	0)	0	0	0	0	0	0	1	0	0	0	0	0	0	.000	.000	.000	.000
6 ML YEARS		151	300	67	13	0	2	(2	0)	86	34	20	23	24	0	64	1	5	2	1	3	4	.223	.281	.287	.568

Daniel Wright

Pitches: R Bats: R Pos: SP-7; RP-2 **Ht: 6'2" Wt: 205 Born: 4/3/1991 Age: 26**

HOW MUCH HE PITCHED						WHAT HE GAVE UP												THE RESULTS							
Year Team	Lg	G	GS	CG	GF	IP	BFP	H	R	ER	HR	SH	SF	HB	TBB	IBB	SO	WP	Bk	W	L	Pct	Sh	Sv-Op	Hld	ERC	ERA
2013 Billings	R+	14	0	0	0	42.2	192	57	30	28	4	0	3	2	5	0	43	7	1	3	3	.500	0	0--	-	4.88	5.91
2014 2 Tms	Low	28	25	0	0	152.1	619	141	67	60	20	3	4	11	22	0	141	11	1	14	7	.667	0	0--	-	3.17	3.54
2015 Pnscla	AA	27	27	0	0	155.0	649	154	83	78	6	7	4	7	47	0	130	3	0	10	11	.476	0	0--	-	3.48	4.53
2016 Pnscla	AA	8	2	0	0	20.0	73	10	1	1	0	0	0	0	4	0	22	0	1	2	0	1.000	0	0--	-	0.87	0.45
2016 Lsvlle	AAA	17	12	2	2	63.2	387	109	66	50	10	4	7	4	25	1	65	2	0	6	5	.545	0	0--	-	5.65	6.13
2016 2 Tms		9	7	0	0	39.2	179	57	32	27	7	2	2	5	8	0	21	2	0	1	5	.167	0	0-0	0	7.25	6.13
16 Cin	NL	4	2	0	0	13.0	64	25	16	11	2	1	1	0	2	0	6	1	0	0	2	.000	0	0-0	0	9.35	7.62
16 LAA	AL	5	5	0	0	26.2	115	32	16	16	5	1	5	5	6	0	15	1	0	1	3	.250	0	0-0	0	6.27	5.40

David Wright

Bats: R Throws: R Pos: 3B-36;PH-1   Ht: 6'0" Wt: 205 Born: 12/20/1982 Age: 34

Year	Team	Lg	G	AB	H	2B	3B	HR	(Hm	Rd)	TB	R	RBI	RC	TBB	IBB	SO	HBP	SH	SF	SB	CS	GDP	Avg	OBP	Slg	OPS
2004	NYM	NL	69	263	77	17	1	14	(8	6)	138	41	40	42	14	0	40	3	0	3	6	0	7	.293	.332	.525	.857
2005	NYM	NL	160	575	176	42	1	27	(12	15)	301	99	102	105	72	2	113	7	0	3	17	7	16	.306	.388	.523	.912
2006	NYM	NL	154	582	181	40	5	26	(13	13)	309	96	116	119	66	13	113	5	0	8	20	5	15	.311	.381	.531	.912
2007	NYM	NL	160	604	196	42	1	30	(16	14)	330	113	107	127	94	6	115	6	0	7	34	5	14	.325	.416	.546	.963
2008	NYM	NL	160	626	189	42	2	33	(21	12)	334	115	124	116	94	5	118	4	0	11	15	5	15	.302	.390	.534	.924
2009	NYM	NL	144	535	164	39	3	10	(5	5)	239	88	72	86	74	8	140	3	0	6	27	9	16	.307	.390	.447	.837
2010	NYM	NL	157	587	166	36	3	29	(12	17)	295	87	103	97	69	9	161	2	0	12	19	11	12	.283	.354	.503	.856
2011	NYM	NL	102	389	99	23	1	14	(5	9)	166	60	61	58	52	4	97	3	0	3	13	2	5	.254	.345	.427	.771
2012	NYM	NL	156	581	178	41	2	21	(12	9)	286	91	93	105	81	16	112	3	0	5	15	10	15	.306	.391	.492	.883
2013	NYM	NL	112	430	132	23	6	18	(6	12)	221	63	58	78	55	5	79	5	0	2	17	3	11	.307	.390	.514	.904
2014	NYM	NL	134	535	144	30	1	8	(6	2)	200	54	63	60	42	5	113	4	0	5	8	5	22	.269	.324	.374	.698
2015	NYM	NL	38	152	44	7	0	5	(1	4)	66	24	17	25	22	0	36	0	0	0	2	1	4	.289	.379	.434	.814
2016	NYM	NL	37	137	31	8	0	7	(2	5)	60	18	14	19	26	0	55	0	0	0	3	2	0	.226	.350	.438	.788
	Postseason		24	91	18	5	0	2	(1	1)	29	10	13	11	15	2	28	0	0	0	1	1	2	.198	.311	.319	.630
	13 ML YEARS		1583	5996	1777	390	26	242	(119	123)	2945	949	970	1037	761	73	1292	45	0	65	196	65	152	.296	.376	.491	.867

Mike Wright

Pitches: R Bats: R Pos: SP-12; RP-6   Ht: 6'6" Wt: 215 Born: 1/3/1990 Age: 27

Year	Team	Lg	G	GS	CG	GF	IP	BFP	H	R	ER	HR	SH	SF	HB	TBB	IBB	SO	WP	Bk	W	L	Pct	Sh	Sv-Op	Hld	ERC	ERA
2012	Frdrck	A+	8	8	0	0	46.1	186	47	16	15	3	2	1	1	5	0	35	0	0	5	2	.714	0	0- -	-	2.94	2.91
2012	Bowie	AA	12	12	0	0	62.1	267	71	38	34	7	1	0	3	17	0	45	6	0	5	3	.625	0	0- -	-	4.74	4.91
2013	Bowie	AA	26	26	0	0	143.2	625	152	65	52	9	3	4	10	39	1	136	9	1	11	3	.786	0	0- -	-	3.84	3.26
2014	Norfolk	AAA	26	26	0	0	142.2	622	159	87	73	10	6	5	5	41	2	103	3	0	5	11	.313	0	0- -	-	4.15	4.61
2015	Norfolk	AAA	15	14	0	0	81.0	315	59	21	20	4	0	2	3	25	0	63	4	0	9	1	.900	0	0- -	-	2.24	2.22
2016	Norfolk	AAA	13	13	0	0	76.1	306	72	30	26	8	1	2	1	14	0	48	2	0	4	4	.500	0	0- -	-	3.07	3.07
2015	Bal	AL	12	9	0	0	44.2	204	52	30	30	9	0	2	5	18	3	26	2	0	3	5	.375	0	0-0	0	6.20	6.04
2016	Bal	AL	18	12	0	5	74.2	328	81	53	48	12	1	5	9	26	0	50	2	0	3	4	.429	0	0-0	0	5.38	5.79
	2 ML YEARS		30	21	0	5	119.1	532	133	83	78	21	1	7	14	44	3	76	4	0	6	9	.400	0	0-0	0	5.69	5.88

Steven Wright

Pitches: R Bats: R Pos: SP-24   Ht: 6'2" Wt: 215 Born: 8/30/1984 Age: 32

Year	Team	Lg	G	GS	CG	GF	IP	BFP	H	R	ER	HR	SH	SF	HB	TBB	IBB	SO	WP	Bk	W	L	Pct	Sh	Sv-Op	Hld	ERC	ERA
2013	Bos	AL	4	1	0	2	13.1	59	12	8	8	0	0	0	1	9	0	10	2	0	2	0	1.000	0	0-0	0	4.22	5.40
2014	Bos	AL	6	1	0	3	21.0	86	21	8	6	2	0	0	4	0	22	1	0	0	1	.000	0	0-0	0	3.25	2.57
2015	Bos	AL	16	9	0	3	72.2	310	67	38	33	12	1	1	1	27	0	52	2	0	5	4	.556	0	0-0	0	3.99	4.09
2016	Bos	AL	24	24	4	0	156.2	656	138	74	58	12	2	2	8	57	1	127	10	0	13	6	.684	1	0-0	0	3.34	3.33
	4 ML YEARS		50	35	4	8	263.2	1111	238	128	105	26	3	3	10	97	1	211	15	0	20	11	.645	1	0-0	0	3.56	3.58

Kirby Yates

Pitches: R Bats: L Pos: RP-41   Ht: 5'10" Wt: 210 Born: 3/25/1987 Age: 30

Year	Team	Lg	G	GS	CG	GF	IP	BFP	H	R	ER	HR	SH	SF	HB	TBB	IBB	SO	WP	Bk	W	L	Pct	Sh	Sv-Op	Hld	ERC	ERA
2016	S-WB*	AAA	14	0	0	10	16.2	69	12	3	3	0	1	0	1	6	0	19	2	1	0	1	.000	0	4- -	-	2.02	1.62
2014	TB	AL	37	0	0	12	36.0	156	33	16	15	4	0	1	3	15	3	42	2	0	0	2	.000	0	1-2	0	3.94	3.75
2015	TB	AL	20	0	0	10	20.1	92	23	18	18	10	0	0	1	7	0	21	0	0	1	0	1.000	0	0-0	0	7.58	7.97
2016	NYY	AL	41	0	0	11	41.1	184	41	24	24	5	1	1	4	19	1	50	1	0	2	1	.667	0	0-2	2	4.77	5.23
	3 ML YEARS		98	0	0	33	97.2	432	97	58	57	19	1	2	8	41	4	113	3	0	3	3	.500	0	1-4	2	5.04	5.25

Christian Yelich

Bats: L Throws: R Pos: LF-120;CF-31;PH-5;DH-1   YELL-itch   Ht: 6'3" Wt: 195 Born: 12/5/1991 Age: 25

Year	Team	Lg	G	AB	H	2B	3B	HR	(Hm	Rd)	TB	R	RBI	RC	TBB	IBB	SO	HBP	SH	SF	SB	CS	GDP	Avg	OBP	Slg	OPS
2013	Mia	NL	62	240	69	12	1	4	(0	4)	95	34	16	35	31	1	66	1	0	1	10	0	4	.288	.370	.396	.766
2014	Mia	NL	144	582	165	30	6	9	(2	7)	234	94	54	87	70	3	137	3	3	2	21	7	9	.284	.362	.402	.764
2015	Mia	NL	126	476	143	30	2	7	(1	6)	198	63	44	64	47	2	101	2	0	0	16	5	13	.300	.366	.416	.782
2016	Mia	NL	155	578	172	38	3	21	(8	13)	279	78	98	89	72	4	138	4	0	5	9	4	20	.298	.376	.483	.859
	4 ML YEARS		487	1876	549	110	12	41	(11	30)	806	269	212	275	220	10	442	10	3	8	56	16	46	.293	.368	.430	.798

Gabriel Ynoa

Pitches: R Bats: R Pos: RP-7; SP-3   ee-NOH-uh   Ht: 6'2" Wt: 205 Born: 5/26/1993 Age: 24

Year	Team	Lg	G	GS	CG	GF	IP	BFP	H	R	ER	HR	SH	SF	HB	TBB	IBB	SO	WP	Bk	W	L	Pct	Sh	Sv-Op	Hld	ERC	ERA
2012	Bklyn	A-	13	13	0	0	76.2	302	61	25	19	2	1	3	0	10	0	64	4	0	5	2	.714	0	0- -	-	1.68	2.23
2013	Savann	A	22	22	1	0	135.2	542	123	45	41	9	3	6	1	16	0	106	2	0	15	4	.789	0	0- -	-	2.33	2.72
2014	Stluci	A+	14	14	0	0	82.0	352	95	40	36	7	4	4	1	13	0	64	0	0	8	2	.800	0	0- -	-	3.89	3.95
2014	Bnghtn	AA	11	11	2	0	66.1	280	74	32	31	9	1	1	3	12	1	42	2	0	3	2	.600	0	0- -	-	4.29	4.21
2015	Bnghtn	AA	25	24	2	0	152.1	638	157	70	66	14	6	2	6	31	1	82	3	1	9	9	.500	1	0- -	-	3.57	3.90
2016	LsVgs	AAA	25	25	0	0	154.1	656	170	77	68	15	8	6	6	40	2	78	2	1	12	5	.706	0	0- -	-	4.28	3.97
2016	NYM	NL	10	3	0	2	18.1	88	26	13	13	0	0	2	1	7	0	17	0	0	1	0	1.000	0	0-0	0	5.80	6.38

Michael Ynoa

Pitches: R Bats: R Pos: RP-23 · ee-NOH-uh · Ht: 6'7" Wt: 210 Born: 9/24/1991 Age: 25

Year	Team	Lg	G	GS	CG	GF	IP	BFP	H	R	ER	HR	SH	SF	HB	TBB	IBB	SO	WP	Bk	W	L	Pct	Sh	Sv-Op	Hld	ERC	ERA
2012	2 Tms	Low	14	12	0	0	30.2	150	31	25	22	3	1	0	4	25	0	25	11	1	1	4	.200	0	0- -	-	6.27	6.46
2013	2 Tms	Low	22	21	0	1	75.2	333	68	39	31	5	0	1	9	35	0	68	7	1	3	3	.500	0	1- -	-	3.95	3.69
2014	Stcktn	A+	31	0	0	6	45.2	201	42	28	28	5	2	3	5	21	2	64	7	0	4	2	.667	0	0- -	-	4.28	5.52
2015	WinSa	A+	28	0	0	16	38.0	169	37	14	11	2	0	1	7	16	0	40	4	0	0	2	.000	0	6- -	-	4.41	2.61
2016	Charllt	AAA	18	0	0	6	23.2	108	25	12	12	2	2	1	3	12	2	20	3	0	1	3	.250	0	4- -	-	5.09	4.56
2016	CWS	AL	23	0	0	7	30.0	135	20	11	10	0	1	2	5	17	2	30	4	0	1	0	1.000	0	0-0	1	2.57	3.00

Table header spanning: HOW MUCH HE PITCHED / WHAT HE GAVE UP / THE RESULTS

Rafael Ynoa

Bats: B Throws: R Pos: LF-2;PH-2 · ee-NO-uh · Ht: 6'0" Wt: 190 Born: 8/7/1987 Age: 29

Year	Team	Lg	G	AB	H	2B	3B	HR	(Hm	Rd)	TB	R	RBI	RC	TBB	IBB	SO	HBP	SH	SF	SB	CS	GDP	Avg	OBP	Slg	OPS
2016	Albq*	AAA	122	482	126	30	3	3	(-	-)	171	65	33	59	45	2	87	2	2	2	7	4	11	.261	.326	.355	.681
2014	Col	NL	19	67	23	6	1	0	(0	0)	31	5	13	13	4	0	9	0	0	0	0	0	1	.343	.380	.463	.843
2015	Col	NL	72	127	33	8	1	0	(0	0)	43	14	9	13	3	0	28	0	1	0	1	0	2	.260	.277	.339	.616
2016	Col	NL	3	5	0	0	0	0	(0	0)	0	0	0	0	0	0	2	0	0	0	0	0	0	.000	.000	.000	.000
	3 ML YEARS		94	199	56	14	2	0	(0	0)	74	19	22	26	7	0	39	0	1	0	1	0	3	.281	.306	.372	.678

Chris Young

Pitches: R Bats: R Pos: RP-21; SP-13 · Ht: 6'10" Wt: 255 Born: 5/25/1979 Age: 38

Year	Team	Lg	G	GS	CG	GF	IP	BFP	H	R	ER	HR	SH	SF	HB	TBB	IBB	SO	WP	Bk	W	L	Pct	Sh	Sv-Op	Hld	ERC	ERA
2004	Tex	AL	7	7	0	0	36.1	158	36	21	19	7	1	0	2	10	0	27	1	0	3	2	.600	0	0-0	0	4.26	4.71
2005	Tex	AL	31	31	0	0	164.2	700	162	84	78	19	2	4	7	45	2	137	3	0	12	7	.632	0	0-0	0	3.71	4.26
2006	SD	NL	31	31	0	0	179.1	735	134	72	69	28	8	3	6	69	4	164	6	1	11	5	.688	0	0-0	0	3.12	3.46
2007	SD	NL	30	30	0	0	173.0	705	118	66	60	10	3	6	7	72	0	167	7	4	9	8	.529	0	0-0	0	2.35	3.12
2008	SD	NL	18	18	1	0	102.1	434	84	46	45	13	4	1	1	48	4	93	3	1	7	6	.538	0	0-0	0	3.50	3.96
2009	SD	NL	14	14	0	0	76.0	336	70	47	44	12	4	5	2	40	3	50	1	0	4	6	.400	0	0-0	0	4.55	5.21
2010	SD	NL	4	4	0	0	20.0	82	10	2	2	1	1	0	0	11	0	15	1	0	2	0	1.000	0	0-0	0	1.72	0.90
2011	NYM	NL	4	4	0	0	24.0	95	12	5	5	3	1	0	1	11	0	22	0	0	1	0	1.000	0	0-0	0	2.04	1.88
2012	NYM	NL	20	20	0	0	115.0	493	119	58	53	16	9	4	2	36	5	80	3	0	4	9	.308	0	0-0	0	4.19	4.15
2014	Sea	AL	30	29	0	0	165.0	688	143	70	67	26	4	9	3	60	3	108	5	1	12	9	.571	0	0-0	0	3.63	3.65
2015	KC	AL	34	18	0	3	123.1	500	91	44	42	16	4	2	0	43	0	83	5	0	11	6	.647	0	0-1	2	2.66	3.06
2016	KC	AL	34	13	0	7	88.2	406	104	63	61	28	0	4	1	43	1	94	3	0	3	9	.250	0	1-1	1	7.16	6.19
	Postseason		5	3	0	1	22.1	84	12	5	5	2	1	1	0	8	1	27	1	0	2	0	1.000	0	0-0	0	1.60	2.01
	12 ML YEARS		257	219	1	10	1267.2	5332	1083	578	545	179	41	38	32	488	22	1040	38	7	79	67	.541	0	1-2	3	3.55	3.87

Chris Young

Bats: R Throws: R Pos: LF-63;PH-16;CF-3;RF-3;DH-2;PR-1 · Ht: 6'2" Wt: 200 Born: 9/5/1983 Age: 33

Year	Team	Lg	G	AB	H	2B	3B	HR	(Hm	Rd)	TB	R	RBI	RC	TBB	IBB	SO	HBP	SH	SF	SB	CS	GDP	Avg	OBP	Slg	OPS
2006	Ari	NL	30	70	17	4	0	2	(1	1)	27	10	10	11	6	0	12	1	0	1	2	1	0	.243	.308	.386	.693
2007	Ari	NL	148	569	135	29	3	32	(14	18)	266	85	68	68	43	1	141	6	1	5	27	6	5	.237	.295	.467	.763
2008	Ari	NL	160	625	155	42	7	22	(9	13)	277	85	85	84	62	2	165	1	6	5	14	5	10	.248	.315	.443	.758
2009	Ari	NL	134	433	92	28	4	15	(7	8)	173	54	42	47	59	2	133	4	3	2	11	4	3	.212	.311	.400	.711
2010	Ari	NL	156	584	150	33	0	27	(20	7)	264	94	91	86	74	0	145	2	1	3	28	7	10	.257	.341	.452	.793
2011	Ari	NL	156	567	134	38	3	20	(14	6)	238	89	71	84	80	4	139	4	1	7	22	9	3	.236	.331	.420	.751
2012	Ari	NL	101	325	75	24	0	14	(5	9)	141	36	41	46	36	0	79	2	0	8	3	4	3	.231	.311	.434	.745
2013	Oak	AL	107	335	67	18	3	12	(4	8)	127	46	40	32	36	3	93	2	0	2	10	3	7	.200	.280	.379	.659
2014	2 Tms		111	325	72	20	0	11	(8	3)	125	40	38	37	32	2	70	5	1	3	8	3	3	.222	.299	.385	.683
2015	NYY	AL	140	318	80	20	1	14	(6	8)	144	53	42	46	30	2	73	3	3	2	3	1	6	.252	.320	.453	.773
2016	Bos	AL	76	203	56	18	0	9	(2	7)	101	29	24	28	21	0	50	3	0	4	2	4	4	.276	.352	.498	.850
	14 NYM	NL	88	254	52	12	0	8	(6	2)	88	31	28	25	25	2	54	4	1	3	7	3	3	.205	.283	.346	.630
	14 NYY	AL	23	71	20	8	0	3	(2	1)	37	9	10	12	7	0	16	1	0	0	1	0	0	.282	.354	.521	.876
	Postseason		13	45	14	2	0	5	(3	2)	31	9	9	12	10	0	19	1	0	0	3	2	0	.311	.446	.689	1.135
	11 ML YEARS		1319	4354	1033	274	21	178	(90	88)	1883	621	552	569	479	16	1100	33	16	30	137	44	55	.237	.316	.432	.748

Eric Young

Bats: B Throws: R Pos: PR-4;CF-2;DH-2 · Ht: 5'10" Wt: 195 Born: 5/25/1985 Age: 32

Year	Team	Lg	G	AB	H	2B	3B	HR	(Hm	Rd)	TB	R	RBI	RC	TBB	IBB	SO	HBP	SH	SF	SB	CS	GDP	Avg	OBP	Slg	OPS
2016	ColSpr*	AAA	116	289	77	9	2	3	(-	-)	99	48	30	39	31	2	51	3	4	2	23	6	3	.266	.342	.343	.684
2009	Col	NL	30	57	14	1	0	1	(1	0)	18	7	1	2	4	0	12	0	0	0	4	4	1	.246	.295	.316	.611
2010	Col	NL	51	172	42	5	1	0	(0	0)	49	26	8	16	17	0	32	0	0	0	17	6	2	.244	.312	.285	.597
2011	Col	NL	77	198	49	4	3	0	(0	0)	59	34	10	27	26	0	38	3	1	1	27	4	1	.247	.342	.298	.640
2012	Col	NL	98	174	55	7	2	4	(2	2)	78	36	15	29	13	0	31	4	5	0	14	2	1	.316	.377	.448	.825
2013	2 Tms	NL	148	539	134	27	7	2	(1	1)	181	70	32	58	46	1	100	2	10	1	46	11	6	.249	.310	.336	.645
2014	NYM	NL	100	280	64	10	5	1	(0	1)	87	48	17	30	24	1	60	5	5	2	30	6	2	.229	.299	.311	.610
2015	2 Tms	NL	53	85	13	4	2	0	(0	0)	21	16	5	6	6	1	18	1	2	0	6	2	1	.153	.217	.247	.464
2016	NYY	AL	6	1	0	0	0	0	(0	0)	0	2	0	0	0	0	0	0	0	0	1	0	0	.000	.000	.000	.000
	13 Col	NL	57	165	40	9	3	1	(0	1)	58	22	6	14	11	0	33	0	4	0	8	4	1	.242	.290	.352	.641
	13 NYM	NL	91	374	94	18	4	1	(1	0)	123	48	26	44	35	1	67	2	6	1	38	7	5	.251	.318	.329	.647

						BATTING																RUNNING			AVERAGES			
Year	Team	Lg	G	AB	H	2B	3B	HR	(Hm	Rd)	TB	R	RBI	RC	TBB	IBB	SO	HBP	SH	SF		SB	CS	GDP	Avg	OBP	Slg	OPS
15	Atl	NL	35	77	13	4	2	0	(0	0)	21	7	5	6	6	1	17	0	2	0		3	0	1	.169	.229	.273	.502
15	NYM	NL	18	8	0	0	0	0	(0	0)	0	9	0	0	0	0	1	1	0	0		3	2	0	.000	.111	.000	.111
	Postseason		2	1	0	0	0	0	(0	0)	0	0	0	0	0	0	0	0	0	0		0	0	0	.000	.000	.000	.000
8 ML YEARS			563	1506	371	58	20	8	(4	4)	493	239	88	168	136	3	291	15	23	4		145	35	14	.246	.314	.327	.642

Madison Younginer

Pitches: R Bats: R Pos: RP-8

Ht: 6'4" Wt: 205 Born: 11/3/1990 Age: 26

			HOW MUCH HE PITCHED					WHAT HE GAVE UP											THE RESULTS							
Year	Team	Lg	G	GS	CG	GF	IP	BFP	H	R	ER	HR	SH	SF	HB	TBB	IBB	SO	WP	Bk	W	L	Pct	Sh	Sv-Op	Hld	ERC	ERA
2012	3 Tms	Low	17	16	0	0	67.1	314	81	58	50	9	1	2	5	37	0	51	8	1	1	8	.111	0	0--	-	6.56	6.68
2013	3 Tms	Low	28	0	0	13	45.1	204	44	22	22	2	1	0	3	25	0	57	5	0	6	0	1.000	0	1--	-	4.32	4.37
2014	Salem	A+	35	0	0	17	57.1	253	61	31	26	0	3	2	1	25	0	55	5	2	3	3	.500	0	2--	-	3.90	4.08
2015	Portlnd	AA	39	0	0	22	73.2	312	62	30	25	4	3	3	5	25	0	55	8	0	8	4	.667	0	2--	-	2.89	3.05
2016	Gwnntt	AAA	11	0	0	3	13.2	73	18	16	11	1	0	1	2	11	1	13	1	0	0	0	-	0	1--	-	7.62	7.24
2016	Missi	AA	35	0	0	24	42.1	170	33	14	14	1	3	1	3	12	0	47	2	0	0	3	.000	0	14--	-	2.30	2.98
2016	Atl	NL	8	0	0	1	7.0	37	12	5	5	0	1	1	1	4	0	4	0	0	0	0	-	0	0-0	1	9.01	6.43

Rob Zastryzny

Pitches: L Bats: R Pos: RP-7; SP-1

za-STRIZ-nee

Ht: 6'3" Wt: 205 Born: 3/26/1992 Age: 25

			HOW MUCH HE PITCHED					WHAT HE GAVE UP											THE RESULTS							
Year	Team	Lg	G	GS	CG	GF	IP	BFP	H	R	ER	HR	SH	SF	HB	TBB	IBB	SO	WP	Bk	W	L	Pct	Sh	Sv-Op	Hld	ERC	ERA
2013	2 Tms	Low	11	7	0	0	24.0	101	24	6	6	0	0	0	2	8	0	22	1	0	1	0	1.000	0	0--	-	3.53	2.25
2014	Dytona	A+	23	23	0	0	110.0	479	121	58	57	10	5	0	7	33	0	110	8	0	4	6	.400	0	0--	-	4.44	4.66
2015	Tenn	AA	14	14	0	0	60.2	282	77	47	42	9	3	3	0	28	0	48	1	0	2	5	.286	0	0--	-	6.27	6.23
2016	Tenn	AA	9	9	0	0	54.2	225	50	29	26	6	0	0	1	20	0	42	3	1	3	2	.600	0	0--	-	3.71	4.28
2016	Iowa	AAA	15	14	0	1	81.0	339	67	42	39	7	10	3	2	31	1	77	6	0	7	3	.700	0	0--	-	3.04	4.33
2016	ChC	NL	8	1	0	1	16.0	66	12	3	2	0	0	2	1	5	0	17	0	0	1	0	1.000	0	0-0	0	2.01	1.13

Brad Ziegler

Pitches: R Bats: R Pos: RP-69

ZIGG-lerr

Ht: 6'4" Wt: 220 Born: 10/10/1979 Age: 37

			HOW MUCH HE PITCHED					WHAT HE GAVE UP											THE RESULTS							
Year	Team	Lg	G	GS	CG	GF	IP	BFP	H	R	ER	HR	SH	SF	HB	TBB	IBB	SO	WP	Bk	W	L	Pct	Sh	Sv-Op	Hld	ERC	ERA
2008	Oak	AL	47	0	0	21	59.2	229	47	8	7	2	4	3	1	22	3	30	0	0	3	0	1.000	0	11-13	9	2.60	1.06
2009	Oak	AL	69	0	0	23	73.1	313	82	27	25	2	1	3	1	28	4	54	0	0	2	4	.333	0	7-10	14	4.25	3.07
2010	Oak	AL	64	0	0	12	60.2	257	54	24	22	4	1	1	3	28	9	41	0	1	3	7	.300	0	0-4	18	3.48	3.26
2011	2 Tms		66	0	0	16	58.1	239	53	21	14	0	1	2	1	19	3	44	1	0	3	2	.600	0	1-2	10	2.68	2.16
2012	Ari	NL	77	0	0	15	68.2	263	54	21	19	2	2	2	1	21	2	42	1	0	6	1	.857	0	0-2	17	2.33	2.49
2013	Ari	NL	78	0	0	33	73.0	297	61	20	18	3	2	2	3	22	6	44	0	0	8	1	.889	0	13-15	11	2.51	2.22
2014	Ari	NL	68	0	0	11	67.0	281	60	29	26	3	2	2	3	24	6	54	0	0	5	3	.625	0	1-9	29	3.22	3.49
2015	Ari	NL	66	0	0	46	68.0	263	48	17	14	3	1	0	1	17	3	36	2	0	0	3	.000	0	30-32	6	1.74	1.85
2016	2 Tms		69	0	0	42	68.0	289	67	21	17	2	2	1	3	26	7	58	1	0	4	7	.364	0	22-28	8	3.49	2.25
11	Oak	AL	43	0	0	12	37.2	160	38	14	10	0	1	1	1	13	3	29	1	0	3	2	.600	0	1-2	6	3.21	2.39
11	Ari	NL	23	0	0	4	20.2	79	15	7	4	0	0	1	0	6	0	15	0	0	0	0	-	0	0-0	4	1.77	1.74
16	Ari	NL	36	0	0	30	38.1	165	41	13	12	1	1	1	2	15	5	27	0	0	2	3	.400	0	18-20	0	3.98	2.82
16	Bos	AL	33	0	0	12	29.2	124	26	8	5	1	1	0	1	11	2	31	1	0	2	4	.333	0	4-8	8	2.89	1.52
	Postseason		2	0	0	0	0.1	7	4	4	4	0	0	0	0	2	1	0	0	0	0	0	-	0	0-0	0	115.8	108.0
9 ML YEARS			604	0	0	219	596.2	2431	526	188	162	23	16	18	17	207	43	403	5	1	34	28	.548	0	85-115	120	2.91	2.44

Ryan Zimmerman

Bats: R Throws: R Pos: 1B-114;DH-1

Ht: 6'3" Wt: 225 Born: 9/28/1984 Age: 32

						BATTING																RUNNING			AVERAGES			
Year	Team	Lg	G	AB	H	2B	3B	HR	(Hm	Rd)	TB	R	RBI	RC	TBB	IBB	SO	HBP	SH	SF		SB	CS	GDP	Avg	OBP	Slg	OPS
2005	Was	NL	20	58	23	10	0	0	(0	0)	33	6	6	9	3	0	12	0	0	1		0	0	1	.397	.419	.569	.988
2006	Was	NL	157	614	176	47	3	20	(10	10)	289	84	110	101	61	7	120	2	1	4		11	8	15	.287	.351	.471	.822
2007	Was	NL	162	653	174	43	5	24	(11	13)	299	99	91	86	61	3	125	3	0	5		4	1	26	.266	.330	.458	.788
2008	Was	NL	106	428	121	24	1	14	(7	7)	189	51	51	48	31	1	71	3	0	5		4	1	12	.283	.333	.442	.774
2009	Was	NL	157	610	178	37	3	33	(17	16)	320	110	106	96	72	9	119	2	0	9		2	0	22	.292	.364	.525	.888
2010	Was	NL	142	525	161	32	0	25	(9	16)	268	85	85	97	69	6	98	4	0	5		4	1	16	.307	.388	.510	.899
2011	Was	NL	101	395	114	21	2	12	(7	5)	175	52	49	58	41	4	73	1	0	3		3	1	14	.289	.355	.443	.798
2012	Was	NL	145	578	163	36	1	25	(16	9)	276	93	95	84	57	8	116	2	0	4		5	2	20	.282	.346	.478	.824
2013	Was	NL	147	568	156	26	2	26	(7	19)	264	84	79	83	60	2	133	2	0	3		6	0	16	.275	.344	.465	.809
2014	Was	NL	61	214	60	19	1	5	(1	4)	96	26	38	32	22	0	37	0	0	4		0	0	6	.280	.342	.449	.790
2015	Was	NL	95	346	86	25	1	16	(9	7)	161	43	73	49	33	0	79	1	0	10		1	0	13	.249	.308	.465	.773
2016	Was	NL	115	427	93	18	1	15	(9	6)	158	60	46	36	29	1	104	5	0	6		4	1	12	.218	.272	.370	.642
	Postseason		9	25	9	1	0	2	(1	1)	16	3	4	5	0	0	6	0	0	1		0	0	0	.360	.346	.640	.986
12 ML YEARS			1408	5416	1505	338	20	215	(103	112)	2528	793	829	776	539	41	1087	25	1	58		41	15	173	.278	.343	.467	.809

Jordan Zimmermann

Pitches: R Bats: R Pos: SP-18; RP-1

Ht: 6'2" Wt: 225 Born: 5/23/1986 Age: 31

			HOW MUCH HE PITCHED					WHAT HE GAVE UP											THE RESULTS							
Year	Team	Lg	G	GS	CG	GF	IP	BFP	H	R	ER	HR	SH	SF	HB	TBB	IBB	SO	WP	Bk	W	L	Pct	Sh	Sv-Op	Hld	ERC	ERA
2016	Toledo*	AAA	5	5	0	0	20.1	81	19	10	3	2	1	1	1	4	0	11	1	0	0	1	.000	0	0--	-	3.23	1.33
2009	Was	NL	16	16	0	0	91.1	391	95	51	47	10	5	3	4	29	0	92	0	0	3	5	.375	0	0-0	0	4.25	4.63
2010	Was	NL	7	7	0	0	31.0	135	31	20	17	8	1	1	2	10	1	27	0	0	1	2	.333	0	0-0	0	5.02	4.94
2011	Was	NL	26	26	1	0	161.1	662	154	62	57	12	8	2	7	31	2	124	3	1	8	11	.421	0	0-0	0	3.02	3.18

			HOW MUCH HE PITCHED						WHAT HE GAVE UP												THE RESULTS							
Year	Team	Lg	G	GS	CG	GF	IP	BFP	H	R	ER	HR	SH	SF	HB	TBB	IBB	SO	WP	Bk	W	L	Pct	Sh	Sv-Op	Hld	ERC	ERA
2012	Was	NL	32	32	0	0	195.2	805	186	69	64	18	8	4	8	43	2	153	3	0	12	8	.600	0	0-0	0	3.22	2.94
2013	Was	NL	32	32	4	0	213.1	865	192	81	77	19	9	4	7	40	0	161	3	0	19	9	.679	2	0-0	0	2.79	3.25
2014	Was	NL	32	32	3	0	199.2	800	185	67	59	13	5	3	6	29	0	182	4	0	14	5	.737	2	0-0	0	2.64	2.66
2015	Was	NL	33	33	0	0	201.2	831	204	89	82	24	8	2	8	39	3	164	2	1	13	10	.565	0	0-0	0	3.63	3.66
2016	Det	AL	19	18	0	1	105.1	450	118	63	57	14	1	5	2	26	0	66	3	0	9	7	.563	0	0-0	0	4.48	4.87
Postseason			3	2	0	0	12.2	47	10	6	6	1	1	0	0	1	0	11	0	0	0	1	.000	0			1.80	4.26
8 ML YEARS			197	196	8	1	1199.1	4939	1165	502	460	118	45	24	44	247	8	969	18	2	79	57	.581	4	0-0	0	3.31	3.45

Ben Zobrist

ZOH-brist

Bats: B **Throws:** R **Pos:** 2B-119;LF-27;RF-24;PH-4;1B-1;SS-1　　　　**Ht:** 6'3" **Wt:** 210 **Born:** 5/26/1981 **Age:** 36

					BATTING																	RUNNING			AVERAGES			
Year	Team	Lg	G	AB	H	2B	3B	HR	(Hm	Rd)	TB	R	RBI	RC	TBB	IBB	SO	HBP	SH	SF	SB	CS	GDP	Avg	OBP	Slg	OPS
2006	TB	AL	52	183	41	6	2	2	(2	0)	57	10	18	13	10	1	26	0	2	3	2	3	2	.224	.260	.311	.572
2007	TB	AL	31	97	15	2	0	1	(0	1)	20	8	9	0	3	0	21	1	2	2	2	0	1	.155	.184	.206	.391
2008	TB	AL	62	198	50	10	2	12	(4	8)	100	32	30	31	25	1	37	2	0	2	3	0	4	.253	.339	.505	.844
2009	TB	AL	152	501	149	28	7	27	(18	9)	272	91	91	109	91	4	104	2	1	4	17	6	7	.297	.405	.543	.948
2010	TB	AL	151	541	129	28	2	10	(3	7)	191	77	75	84	92	1	107	3	7	12	24	3	10	.238	.346	.353	.699
2011	TB	AL	156	588	158	46	6	20	(9	11)	276	99	91	100	77	1	128	2	2	5	19	6	9	.269	.353	.469	.822
2012	TB	AL	157	560	151	39	7	20	(8	12)	264	88	74	102	97	7	103	3	2	6	14	9	13	.270	.377	.471	.848
2013	TB	AL	157	612	168	36	3	12	(7	5)	246	77	71	85	72	4	91	7	1	6	11	3	18	.275	.354	.402	.756
2014	TB	AL	146	570	155	34	3	10	(4	6)	225	83	52	75	75	4	84	1	2	6	10	5	8	.272	.354	.395	.749
2015	2 Tms	AL	126	467	129	36	4	13	(5	8)	210	76	56	72	62	3	56	1	0	5	3	4	8	.276	.359	.450	.809
2016	ChC	NL	147	523	142	31	3	18	(5	13)	233	94	76	81	96	6	82	4	4	4	6	4	17	.272	.386	.446	.831
15	Oak	AL	67	235	63	20	2	6	(2	4)	105	39	33	38	33	2	26	0	0	3	1	1	5	.268	.354	.447	.801
15	KC	AL	59	232	66	16	1	7	(3	4)	105	37	23	34	29	1	30	1	0	2	2	3	3	.284	.364	.453	.816
Postseason			37	132	34	10	0	4	(2	2)	56	22	9	12	13	2	20	1	1	1	1	0	3	.258	.327	.424	.751
11 ML YEARS			1337	4840	1287	296	38	145	(65	80)	2094	735	643	752	700	32	839	26	23	55	111	43	97	.266	.358	.433	.791

Mike Zunino

zoo-NEE-no

Bats: R **Throws:** R **Pos:** C-52;PH-3;DH-2　　　　**Ht:** 6'2" **Wt:** 220 **Born:** 3/25/1991 **Age:** 26

					BATTING																	RUNNING			AVERAGES			
Year	Team	Lg	G	AB	H	2B	3B	HR	(Hm	Rd)	TB	R	RBI	RC	TBB	IBB	SO	HBP	SH	SF	SB	CS	GDP	Avg	OBP	Slg	OPS
2016	Tacom*	AAA	79	280	80	15	0	17	(-	-)	146	47	57	56	35	0	69	8	0	4	0	1	3	.286	.376	.521	.898
2013	Sea	AL	52	173	37	5	0	5	(3	2)	57	22	14	13	16	0	49	3	0	1	1	0	5	.214	.290	.329	.620
2014	Sea	AL	131	438	87	20	2	22	(10	12)	177	51	60	39	17	1	158	17	0	4	0	3	13	.199	.254	.404	.658
2015	Sea	AL	112	350	61	11	0	11	(6	5)	105	28	28	14	21	0	132	5	8	2	0	1	6	.174	.230	.300	.530
2016	Sea	AL	55	164	34	7	0	12	(9	3)	77	16	31	28	21	0	65	6	0	1	0	0	0	.207	.318	.470	.787
4 ML YEARS			350	1125	219	43	2	50	(28	22)	416	117	133	94	75	1	404	31	8	8	1	4	24	.195	.262	.370	.632

Tony Zych

zick

Pitches: R **Bats:** R **Pos:** RP-12　　　　**Ht:** 6'3" **Wt:** 190 **Born:** 8/7/1990 **Age:** 26

					HOW MUCH HE PITCHED									WHAT HE GAVE UP										THE RESULTS							
Year	Team	Lg	G	GS	CG	GF	IP	BFP	H	R	ER	HR	SH	SF	HB	TBB	IBB	SO	WP	Bk	W	L	Pct	Sh	Sv-Op	Hld	ERC	ERA
2012	Dytona	A+	27	0	0	24	36.2	145	32	16	13	0	1	1	2	7	1	36	2	0	3	3	.500	0	6- -	-	2.23	3.19
2012	Tenn	AA	20	0	0	5	24.2	112	26	12	12	1	0	0	3	12	0	28	1	0	2	1	.667	0	0- -	-	4.77	4.38
2013	Tenn	AA	47	0	0	16	56.0	243	51	30	19	2	4	2	1	21	1	40	2	0	5	5	.500	0	3- -	-	2.99	3.05
2014	Tenn	AA	45	0	0	16	58.1	254	75	36	33	3	2	3	3	18	0	35	3	0	4	5	.444	0	2- -	-	5.44	5.09
2015	Jacksn	AA	15	0	0	14	16.2	62	11	4	4	0	0	0	3	0	0	18	0	1	0	0	-	0	5- -	-	1.28	2.16
2015	Tacom	AAA	25	0	0	14	31.2	135	34	12	12	2	1	0	2	9	0	37	4	0	1	2	.333	0	4- -	-	4.08	3.41
2015	Sea	AL	13	1	0	4	18.1	76	17	6	5	1	0	0	2	3	0	24	1	0	0	0	-	0	0-0	1	2.88	2.45
2016	Sea	AL	12	0	0	3	13.2	60	10	6	5	0	0	1	1	10	2	21	0	0	1	0	1.000	0	0-0	1	3.18	3.29
2 ML YEARS			25	1	0	7	32.0	136	27	12	10	1	0	1	3	13	2	45	1	0	1	0	1.000	0	0-0	2	3.04	2.81

2016 Fielding Statistics

Lindsay Zeck

Mookie Betts, right fielder for the Boston Red Sox, saved his team 32 runs during the 2016 baseball season. This led all defensive players. In second place, despite only playing in 105 games in 2016, was center fielder Kevin Kiermaier of the Tampa Bay Rays with 25. The majority of both Betts' and Kiermaier's Runs Saved were due to their range and positioning, with 23 and 15, respectively. Adam Eaton of the Chicago White Sox dropped to tied for 5th overall in DRS with 20 (when combining his Runs Saved for right field and center field) after leading for much of the season. He led all right fielders in Runs Saved on throws (9) and in outfield kills (14)—throwing a baserunner out without the use of a relay man.

In 2016, the Pirates had the best defensive left fielder in the league—Starling Marte with 19 Runs Saved—and the worst defensive center fielder in the league— Andrew McCutchen with -28 Runs Saved. In fact, no player cost his team more total runs (28) or range and positioning runs (23) than McCutchen cost the Pirates this season.

The following tables display defensive information for both regulars and backups at all of the eight non-pitcher positions. They include traditional statistics such as putouts, assists, errors, and fielding percentage, as well as Runs Saved information. They also include the total number of Bases Saved. The columns in the section on the far right of each table give the number of Runs Saved due to different components of overall Runs Saved. The column on the far right displays the total number of runs that Baseball Info Solutions estimates each fielder saved or cost his team defensively in 2016.

For all fielders, two of the Runs Saved components are Range and Positioning (R/P) and Good Fielding Plays/Defensive Misplays + Errors (GFP/DME). All infielders have a GDP component to Runs Saved, but for first and third basemen, that component also includes Bunt Runs Saved. For outfielders, the third component is Outfield Arm Runs Saved (Throws), and for catchers the third component is Strike Zone Runs Saved. Catchers also have a column titled "Other" which includes the combined total of Bunt Runs Saved and Adjusted Earned Runs Saved.

First Basemen - Regulars

Player	Tm	G	GS	Inn	PO	A	E	DP	Pct.	Bases Saved	R/P	GFP/DME	Bunts/GDP	Total
Rizzo, Anthony	ChC	154	151	1337.0	1268	125	6	98	.996	+13	9	0	2	11
Belt, Brandon	SF	151	148	1330.1	1284	94	8	110	.994	+14	10	-1	0	9
Freeman, Freddie	Atl	158	158	1411.2	1305	107	5	116	.996	+9	6	2	1	9
Myers, Wil	SD	149	147	1294.0	1246	76	3	139	.998	+9	6	1	1	8
Davis, Chris	Bal	152	152	1327.0	1325	62	10	138	.993	+5	4	4	0	8
Moreland, Mitch	Tex	139	118	1080.2	1036	65	2	138	.998	+7	5	3	-1	7
Mauer, Joe	Min	95	93	831.2	811	53	2	91	.998	+4	3	3	0	6
Reynolds, Mark	Col	115	102	907.0	939	79	7	91	.993	+3	2	0	2	4
Goldschmidt, Paul	Ari	157	157	1389.1	1378	116	4	127	.997	+2	1	1	2	4
Gonzalez, Adrian	LAD	151	146	1295.1	1105	85	2	77	.998	0	1	2	0	3
Cron, C.J.	LAA	97	93	818.2	761	48	6	78	.993	+1	0	2	1	3
Teixeira, Mark	NYY	110	100	872.2	867	39	3	65	.997	-1	-1	3	0	2
Loney, James	NYM	97	88	784.0	664	62	8	72	.989	-2	-2	3	1	2
Zimmerman, Ryan	Was	114	108	969.0	852	44	4	88	.996	-1	-1	1	-2	-2
Lind, Adam	Sea	101	88	797.0	731	50	5	75	.994	-6	-4	1	1	-2
Alonso, Yonder	Oak	145	128	1136.1	1155	70	4	118	.997	-5	-4	1	0	-3
Napoli, Mike	Cle	98	98	859.1	831	52	13	64	.985	-3	-2	-1	-1	-4
Carter, Chris	Mil	155	151	1338.0	1316	73	11	122	.992	-1	-1	-3	-1	-5
Ramirez, Hanley	Bos	133	133	1145.0	1000	39	4	100	.996	-4	-3	-2	0	-5
Abreu, Jose	CWS	152	152	1355.2	1243	84	10	131	.993	-10	-7	1	1	-5
Cabrera, Miguel	Det	147	147	1262.0	1186	95	7	124	.995	-10	-7	1	0	-6
Hosmer, Eric	KC	154	154	1351.0	1240	74	6	118	.995	-15	-11	4	1	-6
Votto, Joey	Cin	154	154	1342.0	1168	107	8	124	.994	-15	-11	-2	-1	-14

Second Basemen - Regulars

Player	Tm	G	GS	Inn	PO	A	E	DP	Pct.	Range	Bases Saved	R/P	GFP/DME	GDP	Total
Kinsler, Ian	Det	151	149	1299.0	303	432	9	109	.988	5.09	+10	8	1	3	12
Pedroia, Dustin	Bos	152	151	1292.2	245	362	6	98	.990	4.23	+11	8	3	1	12
Cano, Robinson	Sea	157	156	1376.1	311	429	3	123	.996	4.84	+9	7	1	3	11
Harrison, Josh	Pit	128	122	1077.2	262	365	7	97	.989	5.24	+8	6	2	0	8
Kipnis, Jason	Cle	151	151	1309.1	198	421	12	70	.981	4.25	+9	6	0	-2	4
Hernandez, Cesar	Phi	149	143	1247.1	241	390	12	102	.981	4.55	0	0	1	3	4
LeMahieu, DJ	Col	146	144	1242.2	276	422	6	91	.991	5.06	+3	2	3	-2	3
Panik, Joe	SF	126	118	1081.0	233	363	5	82	.992	4.96	+2	2	1	0	3
Dozier, Brian	Min	151	151	1331.0	286	419	8	118	.989	4.77	+2	1	3	-1	3
Travis, Devon	Tor	99	96	859.1	150	276	11	59	.975	4.46	+8	6	-4	0	2
Forsythe, Logan	TB	118	118	1028.1	206	264	9	69	.981	4.11	+2	1	0	0	1
Walker, Neil	NYM	111	110	961.2	181	297	7	65	.986	4.47	+2	2	-1	-1	0
Segura, Jean	Ari	142	133	1172.0	218	382	9	80	.985	4.61	-1	-1	0	1	0
Giavotella, Johnny	LAA	97	90	768.2	165	186	5	54	.986	4.11	-2	-1	1	-1	-1
Schoop, Jonathan	Bal	162	162	1429.0	278	447	8	123	.989	4.57	-5	-4	-1	4	-1
Altuve, Jose	Hou	148	147	1307.0	206	361	7	73	.988	3.90	-4	-3	0	1	-2
Zobrist, Ben	ChC	119	113	976.1	177	250	7	52	.984	3.94	+1	1	-2	-2	-3
Utley, Chase	LAD	134	118	1064.1	195	266	5	49	.989	3.90	0	0	0	-3	-3
Gennett, Scooter	Mil	127	121	1062.0	206	344	14	73	.975	4.66	0	0	-2	-2	-4
Lawrie, Brett	CWS	92	92	817.2	157	242	9	59	.978	4.39	-9	-6	2	0	-4
Phillips, Brandon	Cin	138	138	1177.0	249	345	14	89	.977	4.54	-9	-7	0	0	-7
Castro, Starlin	NYY	150	143	1266.0	221	377	12	70	.980	4.25	-3	-2	-2	-4	-8
Murphy, Daniel	Was	117	115	1016.1	194	265	9	76	.981	4.06	-13	-10	0	1	-9
Odor, Rougned	Tex	146	144	1271.0	283	428	22	129	.970	5.03	-17	-13	1	3	-9

Third Basemen - Regulars

Player	Tm	G	GS	Inn	PO	A	E	DP	Pct.	Range	Bases Saved	R/P	GFP/DME	Bunts/GDP	Total
Arenado, Nolan	Col	160	159	1377.1	99	378	13	39	.973	3.12	+24	18	4	-2	20
Beltre, Adrian	Tex	141	141	1219.0	104	301	10	43	.976	2.99	+17	13	-1	3	15
Seager, Kyle	Sea	156	156	1399.2	110	373	22	46	.956	3.11	+13	10	1	4	15
Machado, Manny	Bal	114	114	998.0	86	236	7	26	.979	2.90	+12	10	2	1	13
Shaw, Travis	Bos	105	99	851.1	76	197	16	20	.945	2.89	+8	6	2	2	10
Rendon, Anthony	Was	155	150	1345.0	134	239	9	25	.976	2.50	+9	7	0	1	8
Turner, Justin	LAD	144	138	1224.2	67	240	9	15	.972	2.26	+10	8	-1	0	7
Headley, Chase	NYY	140	134	1169.0	90	278	10	25	.974	2.83	+9	7	1	-1	7

Player	Tm	G	GS	Inn	PO	A	E	DP	Pct.	Range	Bases Saved	R/P	GFP/ DME	Bunts/ GDP	Total
Bryant, Kris	ChC	107	100	857.0	58	187	12	18	.953	2.57	+6	5	1	-2	4
Prado, Martin	Mia	150	146	1264.2	73	240	9	30	.972	2.23	+4	3	1	-1	3
Donaldson, Josh	Tor	136	134	1188.0	110	237	14	27	.961	2.63	+14	10	-4	-4	2
Suarez, Eugenio	Cin	151	149	1308.2	103	271	23	27	.942	2.57	-1	-1	0	2	1
Ramirez, Jose	Cle	117	91	865.2	55	174	5	16	.979	2.38	-4	-3	1	1	-1
Frazier, Todd	CWS	149	149	1320.1	91	293	11	33	.972	2.62	-1	-1	-1	0	-2
Solarte, Yangervis	SD	95	89	773.0	59	190	9	19	.965	2.90	-2	-2	0	0	-2
Franco, Maikel	Phi	148	147	1291.1	93	223	13	16	.960	2.20	-5	-4	-2	0	-6
Garcia, Adonis	Atl	123	123	1084.1	79	199	18	17	.939	2.31	-8	-6	1	-2	-7
Lamb, Jake	Ari	142	132	1186.1	91	251	20	13	.945	2.59	-8	-6	-1	-1	-8
Longoria, Evan	TB	152	152	1316.0	103	254	9	30	.975	2.44	-14	-11	0	2	-9
Escobar, Yunel	LAA	129	129	1086.2	95	188	19	22	.937	2.34	-13	-10	1	-2	-11
Castellanos, Nick	Det	108	107	898.0	66	184	9	12	.965	2.51	-15	-11	0	0	-11
Cuthbert, Cheslor	KC	127	123	1096.1	77	216	16	15	.948	2.41	-16	-12	1	-1	-12

Shortstops - Regulars

Player	Tm	G	GS	Inn	PO	A	E	DP	Pct.	Range	Bases Saved	R/P	GFP/ DME	GDP	Total
Crawford, Brandon	SF	155	148	1309.0	209	413	11	90	.983	4.28	+21	16	3	1	20
Russell, Addison	ChC	148	141	1262.2	152	388	14	60	.975	3.85	+26	20	0	-1	19
Simmons, Andrelton	LAA	124	123	1045.0	198	337	10	82	.982	4.61	+22	16	0	2	18
Lindor, Francisco	Cle	155	153	1364.2	214	448	12	83	.982	4.37	+28	21	-2	-2	17
Tulowitzki, Troy	Tor	128	128	1128.2	158	366	9	72	.983	4.18	+12	9	1	0	10
Hechavarria, Adeiny	Mia	153	135	1222.0	203	359	13	72	.977	4.14	+12	9	1	-1	9
Cozart, Zack	Cin	111	110	966.2	192	300	10	69	.980	4.58	+13	10	0	-2	8
Espinosa, Danny	Was	157	152	1358.0	181	404	18	96	.970	3.88	+5	4	3	1	8
Anderson, Tim	CWS	98	97	859.2	142	244	14	50	.965	4.04	+9	7	-1	0	6
Hardy, J.J.	Bal	115	115	990.0	140	326	6	80	.987	4.24	+4	3	0	3	6
Villar, Jonathan	Mil	108	104	915.2	152	321	17	67	.965	4.65	+8	6	0	-1	5
Galvis, Freddy	Phi	156	153	1350.0	210	407	8	93	.987	4.11	+5	3	2	0	5
Story, Trevor	Col	96	94	823.0	139	293	10	64	.977	4.72	+10	7	-3	0	4
Iglesias, Jose	Det	136	131	1163.0	180	389	5	92	.991	4.40	-2	-1	2	2	3
Seager, Corey	LAD	155	149	1345.0	195	356	18	67	.968	3.69	+7	5	-2	-3	0
Marte, Ketel	Sea	119	116	1032.2	140	315	21	69	.956	3.97	-1	-1	-1	0	-2
Andrus, Elvis	Tex	147	146	1294.0	229	413	17	105	.974	4.47	-3	-2	-1	0	-3
Correa, Carlos	Hou	153	152	1355.2	202	426	14	81	.978	4.17	-6	-4	-2	3	-3
Diaz, Aledmys	StL	106	102	910.0	122	275	16	68	.961	3.93	-6	-5	0	1	-4
Aybar, Erick	TOT	104	98	882.0	126	265	13	51	.968	3.99	-8	-5	0	0	-5
Escobar, Alcides	KC	162	162	1412.0	221	426	14	95	.979	4.12	-7	-5	0	-1	-6
Semien, Marcus	Oak	159	158	1385.1	235	477	21	109	.971	4.63	-9	-7	0	1	-6
Cabrera, Asdrubal	NYM	135	134	1154.0	175	329	7	77	.986	3.93	-13	-10	3	0	-7
Gregorius, Didi	NYY	153	148	1309.1	180	380	15	68	.974	3.85	-7	-5	-2	-2	-9
Mercer, Jordy	Pit	146	142	1245.1	187	411	9	95	.985	4.32	-14	-11	1	1	-9
Bogaerts, Xander	Bos	157	157	1378.2	195	355	12	73	.979	3.59	-15	-11	2	-1	-10
Miller, Brad	TB	105	95	854.0	132	215	14	45	.961	3.66	-16	-12	-1	-1	-14
Ramirez, Alexei	TOT	127	119	1059.2	162	317	14	84	.972	4.07	-29	-22	1	1	-20

Left Fielders - Regulars

Player	Tm	G	GS	Inn	PO	A	E	DP	Pct.	Range	Bases Saved	R/P	GFP/ DME	Throws	Total
Marte, Starling	Pit	114	111	966.2	168	17	4	2	.979	1.72	+12	6	4	9	19
Duvall, Adam	Cin	137	136	1173.1	270	8	8	0	.972	2.13	+25	15	0	1	16
Gardner, Brett	NYY	147	137	1219.0	249	9	3	2	.989	1.90	+22	10	3	-1	12
Upton Jr., Melvin	TOT	121	101	912.2	177	8	3	1	.984	1.82	+9	4	4	2	10
Yelich, Christian	Mia	120	120	1061.0	192	5	3	1	.985	1.67	+15	6	-1	1	6
Braun, Ryan	Mil	127	127	1101.2	208	12	3	3	.987	1.80	+5	2	0	4	6
Gordon, Alex	KC	126	125	1100.1	222	6	2	1	.991	1.86	+5	2	1	1	4
Upton, Justin	Det	146	142	1258.0	253	4	4	0	.985	1.84	+8	2	3	-4	1
Davis, Khris	Oak	93	93	796.1	159	4	5	3	.970	1.84	+9	6	-3	-4	-1
Pagan, Angel	SF	123	121	1047.0	218	5	6	2	.974	1.92	-5	-1	-2	-1	-4
Aoki, Nori	Sea	99	88	768.2	160	4	0	2	1.000	1.92	-3	-1	-1	-2	-4
Cabrera, Melky	CWS	147	147	1293.0	232	12	3	0	.988	1.70	-24	-13	4	4	-5
Saunders, Michael	Tor	106	100	884.2	153	5	2	0	.988	1.61	-14	-7	1	0	-6
Werth, Jayson	Was	131	131	1140.0	197	5	1	1	.995	1.59	-20	-10	1	0	-8

Center Fielders - Regulars

Player	Tm	G	GS	Inn	PO	A	E	DP	Pct.	Range	Bases Saved	Runs Saved R/P	Runs Saved GFP/DME	Runs Saved Throws	Runs Saved Total
Kiermaier, Kevin	TB	104	102	872.1	264	7	2	1	.993	2.80	+34	15	6	4	25
Pillar, Kevin	Tor	146	143	1293.0	337	6	6	2	.983	2.39	+47	24	-2	-1	21
Hamilton, Billy	Cin	115	108	942.1	276	9	3	4	.990	2.72	+11	8	4	3	15
Inciarte, Ender	Atl	120	117	1044.0	332	12	3	4	.991	2.97	+10	8	1	4	13
Bradley Jr., Jackie	Bos	156	155	1375.2	365	13	3	3	.992	2.47	+4	2	2	7	11
Ellsbury, Jacoby	NYY	148	138	1217.1	272	5	3	1	.989	2.05	+19	8	1	-1	8
Grichuk, Randal	StL	115	106	949.1	221	8	0	1	1.000	2.17	-4	1	3	3	7
Trout, Mike	LAA	148	146	1260.1	360	7	4	1	.989	2.62	+13	4	2	0	6
Herrera, Odubel	Phi	155	147	1301.1	372	11	9	4	.977	2.65	+1	3	-2	5	6
Buxton, Byron	Min	92	88	773.2	243	2	4	0	.984	2.85	+5	4	1	-2	3
Pederson, Joc	LAD	132	114	1032.0	258	3	2	0	.992	2.28	+10	4	-1	-2	1
Fowler, Dexter	ChC	121	117	1027.1	219	6	4	1	.983	1.97	+2	1	0	0	1
Blackmon, Charlie	Col	138	135	1183.0	293	4	3	0	.990	2.26	+3	3	0	-5	-2
Martin, Leonys	Sea	143	142	1275.0	353	11	3	3	.992	2.57	-19	-9	1	6	-2
Desmond, Ian	Tex	130	128	1109.0	293	6	9	2	.971	2.43	-1	-5	-2	1	-6
Span, Denard	SF	137	132	1191.1	286	3	1	1	.997	2.18	-15	-4	0	-3	-7
Jones, Adam	Bal	152	150	1300.0	349	4	2	1	.994	2.44	-26	-10	0	0	-10
Maybin, Cameron	Det	91	89	775.1	223	0	4	0	.982	2.59	-2	-3	-3	-5	-11
Ozuna, Marcell	Mia	123	122	1069.0	276	5	5	0	.983	2.37	-19	-11	-2	1	-12
Naquin, Tyler	Cle	105	90	799.2	183	6	1	0	.995	2.13	-36	-18	1	0	-17
McCutchen, Andrew	Pit	151	151	1318.0	317	6	3	0	.991	2.21	-49	-23	-2	-3	-28

Right Fielders - Regulars

Player	Tm	G	GS	Inn	PO	A	E	DP	Pct.	Range	Bases Saved	Runs Saved R/P	Runs Saved GFP/DME	Runs Saved Throws	Runs Saved Total
Betts, Mookie	Bos	157	157	1381.2	346	14	1	4	.997	2.34	+45	23	5	4	32
Eaton, Adam	CWS	121	110	980.1	296	15	3	3	.990	2.86	+14	9	4	9	22
Heyward, Jason	ChC	131	112	1029.2	218	4	2	2	.991	1.94	+29	15	1	-2	14
Markakis, Nick	Atl	150	149	1339.0	311	5	4	2	.988	2.12	+16	7	2	1	10
Reddick, Josh	TOT	110	100	897.1	205	8	6	1	.973	2.14	+9	4	2	0	6
Kepler, Max	Min	108	100	907.1	219	8	7	4	.970	2.25	+5	3	-1	3	5
Springer, George	Hou	147	147	1308.0	304	12	2	2	.994	2.17	-10	-3	5	3	5
Piscotty, Stephen	StL	146	136	1220.1	256	6	4	1	.985	1.93	+27	12	-3	-5	4
Stanton, Giancarlo	Mia	106	106	919.1	215	5	4	0	.982	2.15	+13	7	-4	1	4
Polanco, Gregory	Pit	111	103	906.2	203	9	5	4	.977	2.10	+10	4	-3	3	4
Gonzalez, Carlos	Col	148	145	1261.0	251	8	3	0	.989	1.85	+4	2	0	2	4
Souza Jr., Steven	TB	111	108	947.2	226	8	3	1	.987	2.22	+11	6	-1	-2	3
Chisenhall, Lonnie	Cle	118	99	887.0	186	7	3	1	.985	1.96	+2	3	-1	1	3
Granderson, Curtis	NYM	110	100	905.0	206	7	0	0	1.000	2.12	+9	4	1	-3	2
Calhoun, Kole	LAA	154	153	1316.1	306	9	5	1	.984	2.15	-5	-5	3	4	2
Bourjos, Peter	Phi	115	92	827.0	185	2	1	0	.995	2.04	+4	3	0	-3	0
Pence, Hunter	SF	102	102	908.1	193	7	0	0	1.000	1.98	-3	-2	-1	0	-3
Harper, Bryce	Was	143	142	1245.2	256	5	2	1	.992	1.89	-11	-4	-1	2	-3
Mazara, Nomar	Tex	112	97	885.1	236	6	2	2	.992	2.46	-8	-6	1	2	-3
Kemp, Matt	TOT	97	97	827.1	165	8	2	2	.989	1.88	-9	-4	-1	-1	-6
Bautista, Jose	Tor	91	90	787.0	149	5	2	0	.987	1.76	-14	-6	0	-2	-8
Trumbo, Mark	Bal	95	95	783.0	163	10	5	1	.972	1.99	-17	-10	2	-1	-9
Bruce, Jay	TOT	138	138	1189.2	265	10	6	3	.979	2.08	-8	-5	1	-7	-11
Martinez, J.D.	Det	118	118	1027.1	201	3	6	0	.971	1.79	-36	-18	0	-4	-22

Catchers - Regulars

Player	Tm	G	GS	Inn	PO	A	E	DP	PB	Pct.	SBA	CS	PCS	CS%	CERA	Runs Saved GFP/DME	Runs Saved SB	Runs Saved SZ	Runs Saved Other	Runs Saved Total
Posey, Buster	SF	123	122	1069.2	1003	65	3	8	2	.997	70	23	5	.33	3.51	5	2	11	5	23
Norris, Derek	SD	116	113	983.0	875	58	9	5	8	.990	89	13	7	.15	4.43	2	-3	8	8	15
Grandal, Yasmani	LAD	115	106	954.1	1022	55	5	4	10	.995	75	16	8	.21	3.72	-2	-1	14	2	13
McCann, James	Det	99	96	843.2	756	44	4	9	4	.995	58	25	6	.43	4.18	1	7	0	1	9
Perez, Carlos	LAA	82	76	670.1	571	43	3	7	4	.995	50	15	6	.30	4.24	2	2	1	3	8
Martin, Russell	Tor	127	119	1069.1	989	55	4	3	9	.996	70	9	2	.13	3.60	1	-6	11	1	7
Cervelli, Francisco	Pit	95	94	808.0	693	71	7	7	8	.991	82	15	1	.18	3.85	-2	-2	5	5	6
Lucroy, Jonathan	TOT	126	121	1063.1	918	75	6	9	8	.994	109	40	4	.37	4.33	4	5	4	-9	4
Castro, Jason	Hou	111	102	908.2	865	53	4	8	12	.996	58	13	1	.22	4.26	1	-1	6	-2	4

Player	Tm	G	GS	Inn	PO	A	E	DP	PB	Pct.	SBA	CS	PCS	CS%	CERA	Runs Saved GFP/DME	SB	SZ	Other	Total
Perez, Salvador	KC	128	128	1105.2	989	77	4	4	5	.996	70	30	7	.43	4.15	3	6	-8	2	3
Molina, Yadier	StL	146	142	1218.1	1113	60	2	5	8	.998	84	17	1	.20	3.88	2	-6	3	3	2
Castillo, Welington	Ari	107	103	925.0	799	72	7	7	10	.992	61	21	3	.34	5.04	5	2	-5	0	2
Flowers, Tyler	Atl	81	76	686.0	607	29	3	1	7	.995	62	2	1	.03	4.58	-3	-7	14	-2	2
Ramos, Wilson	Was	128	122	1096.1	1094	61	3	6	10	.997	48	16	3	.33	3.47	0	-1	1	-1	-1
Leon, Sandy	Bos	74	67	600.1	561	35	1	6	7	.998	33	13	1	.39	3.90	0	3	-4	0	-1
Wieters, Matt	Bal	117	111	980.1	871	50	11	6	1	.988	63	20	3	.32	3.98	0	0	-6	3	-3
Wilson, Bobby	TOT	75	71	620.0	554	20	4	5	5	.993	47	7	1	.15	4.37	2	-3	1	-3	-3
Barnhart, Tucker	Cin	108	106	931.2	817	74	7	6	5	.992	92	24	10	.26	5.04	4	3	-2	-8	-3
d'Arnaud, Travis	NYM	73	70	615.2	608	36	1	4	4	.998	73	12	5	.16	4.27	1	-4	3	-4	-4
McCann, Brian	NYY	92	86	757.0	773	36	4	4	6	.995	59	12	2	.20	4.18	-2	-5	2	0	-5
Vogt, Stephen	Oak	113	103	921.1	766	45	7	5	5	.991	64	13	7	.20	4.23	-2	-2	-9	3	-10
Rupp, Cameron	Phi	104	104	911.1	825	44	5	5	7	.994	58	13	4	.22	4.78	0	-2	-5	-3	-10
Iannetta, Chris	Sea	93	86	776.1	722	42	5	2	6	.993	61	16	4	.26	4.29	-3	1	-4	-4	-10
Suzuki, Kurt	Min	99	92	797.0	679	28	5	2	1	.993	59	7	5	.12	5.52	3	-3	-5	-7	-12
Realmuto, J.T.	Mia	129	124	1113.0	1068	81	10	8	8	.991	73	22	6	.30	4.23	3	1	-5	-12	-13
Navarro, Dioner	TOT	90	80	726.2	633	40	9	2	6	.987	54	10	3	.19	4.22	-2	-1	-9	-2	-14
Hundley, Nick	Col	79	77	678.1	554	38	7	3	8	.988	64	7	2	.11	4.99	-1	-4	-10	-1	-16

All Other Fielders

Player	Tm	Pos	G	GS	Inn	PO	A	E	DP	Pct.	Rng	BSv	RS
Ackley, D	NYY	1B	13	10	85	80	7	0	7	1.000	-	+2	1
	NYY	2B	1	0	1	0	0	0	0	-	.00	0	0
	NYY	RF	9	6	54	9	1	0	1	1.000	1.66	+1	2
Adames, C	Col	2B	11	5	54	15	14	1	3	.967	4.86	-3	-2
	Col	3B	11	1	22	1	3	0	1	1.000	1.64	+1	1
	Col	SS	47	37	339	52	121	5	20	.972	4.59	+3	2
Adams, M	StL	1B	86	69	602	617	71	7	62	.990	-	+4	1
Adrianza, E	SF	2B	7	3	24	3	8	0	2	1.000	4.13	0	0
	SF	3B	7	1	19	0	1	0	0	1.000	.47	0	0
	SF	SS	13	6	68	8	24	2	2	.941	4.21	+1	0
Aguilar, J	Cle	1B	7	1	16	18	0	0	2	1.000	-	0	0
Ahmed, N	Ari	SS	88	80	721	112	273	10	61	.975	4.80	+12	13
Alberto, H	Tex	1B	4	1	13	13	1	0	2	1.000	-	0	0
	Tex	2B	6	3	33	8	9	1	2	.944	4.64	+1	1
	Tex	3B	11	4	45	1	14	0	1	1.000	3.00	+1	1
	Tex	SS	9	6	59	13	33	0	10	1.000	6.98	+7	6
Alcantara, A	Oak	2B	3	3	27	6	5	0	1	1.000	3.71	0	-1
	Oak	SS	2	1	10	1	4	0	0	1.000	4.50	0	0
	Oak	CF	4	0	8	4	0	0	0	1.000	4.50	0	0
	Oak	RF	1	0	2	1	0	0	0	1.000	4.50	0	0
Almonte, A	Cle	LF	34	19	184	31	1	1	0	.970	1.56	+1	0
	Cle	CF	2	1	10	3	0	0	0	1.000	2.70	0	0
	Cle	RF	36	25	226	41	5	1	1	.979	1.83	+1	6
Almora, A	ChC	LF	8	2	26	9	1	0	2	1.000	3.46	+2	2
	ChC	CF	33	18	193	60	0	0	0	1.000	2.80	+5	0
	ChC	RF	2	2	18	5	0	0	0	1.000	2.50	+2	1
Alonso, Y	Oak	3B	7	4	38	2	9	1	0	.917	2.61	-2	-2
Altherr, A	Phi	LF	20	12	119	31	1	0	1	1.000	2.41	+1	2
	Phi	CF	10	7	60	16	0	0	0	1.000	2.40	-3	-1
	Phi	RF	42	35	303	62	2	1	0	.985	1.90	+2	2
Altuve, J	Hou	SS	1	0	4	0	2	0	0	1.000	4.50	0	0
Alvarez, D	Bal	RF	1	1	10	1	0	0	0	1.000	.90	0	0
Alvarez, P	Bal	3B	12	6	53	0	5	4	0	.556	.85	-4	-4
Amarista, A	SD	2B	28	15	167	33	50	1	11	.988	4.48	-3	-3
	SD	3B	5	4	37	6	5	0	2	1.000	2.68	-1	0
	SD	SS	12	7	70	12	17	1	6	.967	3.75	-1	-1
	SD	LF	5	3	30	5	0	0	0	1.000	1.48	0	0
	SD	RF	5	2	24	5	0	0	0	1.000	1.85	+2	1
Andino, R	Mia	2B	3	3	21	4	5	0	1	1.000	3.86	0	0
	Mia	3B	1	0	1	0	0	0	0	-	.00	-1	0
	Mia	SS	1	0	2	0	0	0	0	-	.00	0	0
	Mia	LF	2	1	11	5	1	0	0	1.000	4.91	+2	2
Aoki, N	Sea	CF	15	14	123	28	1	1	0	.967	2.12	0	0
Arcia, O	Mil	SS	53	53	465	98	160	5	31	.981	5.00	-2	-1
Arcia, O	TOT	LF	19	17	144	22	2	1	0	.960	1.50	0	1
	TOT	RF	39	33	289	83	1	1	0	.988	2.62	-9	-7
Asche, C	Phi	LF	57	54	441	104	3	1	0	.991	2.19	-4	-5
Asuaje, C	SD	2B	6	6	53	14	19	1	3	.971	5.60	-1	-1
Austin, T	NYY	1B	27	20	187	166	15	0	17	1.000	-	-2	-2
	NYY	LF	2	0	3	0	0	0	0	-	.00	0	0
	NYY	RF	3	2	12	4	0	0	0	1.000	3.00	-1	-1
Aviles, M	Det	2B	10	5	51	7	21	0	3	1.000	4.94	+3	2
	Det	3B	9	5	51	3	9	3	1	.800	2.12	-3	-3
	Det	SS	6	5	41	4	7	2	4	.846	2.41	0	0
	Det	LF	8	5	39	4	1	0	0	1.000	1.15	-1	-1
	Det	CF	1	1	6	1	0	0	0	1.000	1.50	0	0
	Det	RF	32	22	215	35	1	1	0	.973	1.50	-3	-4
Aybar, E	TOT	2B	7	1	20	2	8	0	2	1.000	4.50	+1	1
	TOT	3B	12	11	90	4	9	0	1	1.000	1.30	-3	-2
Baez, J	ChC	1B	6	2	21	18	4	0	1	1.000	-	-1	0
	ChC	2B	59	38	383	88	127	6	23	.973	5.05	+11	11
	ChC	3B	62	36	371	27	91	7	4	.944	2.87	+3	1
	ChC	SS	25	21	194	40	61	2	13	.981	4.69	+2	4
	ChC	CF	1	0	2	0	0	0	0	-	.00	0	0
Barnes, A	LAD	2B	7	2	22	4	9	0	3	1.000	5.32	0	0
	LAD	3B	1	0	1	0	0	0	0	-	.00	0	0
Barnes, B	Col	LF	29	13	152	30	3	1	1	.971	1.96	+3	5
	Col	CF	13	6	66	16	0	0	0	1.000	2.19	+4	2
	Col	RF	2	1	10	1	0	0	0	1.000	.90	+1	0
Barney, D	Tor	2B	40	32	297	55	105	4	35	.976	4.85	+4	5
	Tor	3B	32	23	210	14	48	4	4	.939	2.65	+1	1
	Tor	SS	25	18	180	23	57	0	6	1.000	4.00	+4	2

Player	Tm	Pos	G	GS	Inn	PO	A	E	DP	Pct.	Rng	BSv	RS
	Tor	LF	5	4	37	4	0	0	0	1.000	.97	+1	1
Bautista, J	Tor	1B	1	0	3	3	0	0	0	1.000	-	0	0
Beckham, G	TOT	2B	51	38	342	61	118	2	17	.989	4.71	-5	-5
	TOT	3B	18	12	110	9	16	1	3	.962	2.04	-4	-4
	TOT	SS	11	7	71	11	23	1	7	.971	4.29	-3	-2
Beckham, T	TB	1B	6	5	42	38	1	0	4	1.000	-	+1	1
	TB	2B	19	16	159	30	44	0	12	1.000	4.19	0	-1
	TB	3B	7	4	42	0	7	0	1	1.000	1.50	+2	1
	TB	SS	25	23	195	27	64	4	14	.958	4.19	+2	1
Bell, J	Pit	1B	23	19	150	157	14	3	11	.983	-	-1	-3
	Pit	RF	16	14	108	17	0	1	0	.944	1.41	-9	-5
Belt, B	SF	LF	3	1	12	1	0	0	0	1.000	.75	+1	1
Beltran, C	TOT	RF	69	67	512	97	4	1	1	.990	1.78	-11	-6
Benintendi, A	Bos	LF	29	27	232	48	0	1	0	.980	1.86	-2	-1
	Bos	CF	5	3	30	7	0	0	0	1.000	2.10	0	0
Beresford, J	Min	1B	6	4	37	28	5	1	6	.971	-	+1	1
	Min	2B	1	0	1	0	1	0	0	1.000	9.00	0	0
	Min	3B	3	2	21	1	5	0	2	1.000	2.57	-1	-1
Bethancourt, C	SD	2B	1	0	0	0	0	0	0	-	.00	0	0
	SD	LF	8	3	43	9	0	1	0	.900	1.90	-3	-2
	SD	RF	4	4	31	6	0	0	0	1.000	1.74	-1	0
Blanco, A	Phi	1B	1	1	44	35	4	0	5	1.000	-	0	0
	Phi	2B	20	13	128	28	38	2	7	.971	4.63	-3	-3
	Phi	3B	21	15	146	10	31	4	3	.911	2.53	-6	-5
	Phi	SS	10	7	62	8	15	0	4	1.000	3.32	-1	-1
	Phi	LF	1	0	1	1	0	0	0	1.000	9.00	+1	1
Blanco, G	SF	LF	29	18	185	36	1	0	0	1.000	1.80	+1	0
	SF	CF	18	14	127	26	0	0	0	1.000	1.85	0	0
	SF	RF	34	24	230	49	1	1	0	.980	1.96	-13	-7
Blash, J	SD	LF	4	2	18	2	0	0	0	1.000	1.02	+1	0
	SD	RF	18	14	129	41	1	0	0	1.000	2.92	+6	2
Bonifacio, E	Atl	LF	12	6	68	16	0	0	0	1.000	2.11	+2	0
	Atl	CF	1	1	8	1	0	0	0	1.000	1.13	-3	-1
Borbon, J	Bal	LF	3	2	19	8	0	0	0	1.000	3.79	-1	-1
	Bal	CF	3	2	18	3	0	0	0	1.000	1.50	-1	-1
Bour, J	Mia	1B	82	80	611	545	34	3	50	.995	-	0	0
Bourjos, P	Phi	CF	10	5	53	17	0	0	0	1.000	2.91	+3	1
Bourn, M	TOT	LF	21	6	83	14	3	1	0	.944	1.84	-2	0
	TOT	CF	77	65	610	169	2	5	0	.972	2.52	+19	4
	TOT	RF	21	15	131	26	1	1	0	.964	1.85	-6	-3
Brantley, M	Cle	LF	11	10	89	18	1	0	0	1.000	1.91	0	1
Braun, R	Mil	RF	2	0	1	1	0	0	0	1.000	9.00	0	0
Bregman, A	Hou	2B	3	1	12	2	5	0	0	1.000	5.00	0	0
	Hou	3B	40	40	347	28	80	8	8	.931	2.80	+4	5
	Hou	SS	6	4	39	6	9	1	4	.938	3.46	-1	-1
	Hou	LF	1	0	1	0	0	0	1	.000	.00	0	0
Brentz, B	Bos	LF	22	17	143	25	1	1	0	.963	1.64	-1	-2
Brignac, R	Atl	2B	4	2	19	4	5	0	1	1.000	4.34	0	0
	Atl	3B	5	3	32	4	13	1	1	.944	4.83	0	1
Brito, S	Ari	LF	7	3	30	7	1	1	0	.889	2.37	+1	1
	Ari	CF	14	14	124	24	0	1	0	.960	1.89	+1	0
	Ari	RF	16	6	70	15	0	1	0	.938	1.94	+3	1
Brown, T	SF	3B	1	0	1	0	0	0	0	-	.00	0	0
Broxton, K	Mil	CF	68	58	511	143	0	4	0	.973	2.52	+24	9
Bruce, J	TOT	CF	1	0	0	0	0	0	0	-	.00	0	0
Bryant, K	ChC	1B	9	6	55	35	3	0	3	1.000	-	+2	1
	ChC	SS	1	0	1	0	0	0	0	-	.00	0	0
	ChC	LF	60	36	353	69	3	1	0	.986	1.83	+5	3
	ChC	CF	1	0	1	1	0	0	0	1.000	9.00	+1	1
	ChC	RF	14	12	99	13	0	0	0	1.000	1.18	+2	1
Burns, A	Tor	1B	1	0	1	0	0	0	0	-	-	0	0
	Tor	3B	4	0	9	0	6	0	1	1.000	6.00	+1	1
	Tor	LF	1	1	0	1	0	0	0	-	.00	0	0
Burns, B	TOT	LF	6	2	25	7	0	0	0	1.000	2.52	+1	0
	TOT	CF	80	67	613	153	4	2	1	.987	2.31	-9	-4
	TOT	RF	7	6	45	11	0	0	0	1.000	2.20	0	-1
Burriss, E	Phi	1B	2	0	4	6	1	0	0	1.000	-	+1	2
	Phi	2B	5	3	33	5	3	0	1	1.000	2.20	-3	-3
	Phi	SS	3	0	5	0	1	0	0	1.000	1.80	0	0
	Phi	LF	3	2	17	2	0	0	0	1.000	1.06	0	0
Buss, N	LAA	LF	24	20	174	31	1	0	0	1.000	1.66	+3	3
	LAA	CF	3	2	18	4	0	0	0	1.000	2.00	-3	-2

All Other Fielders

Player	Tm	Pos	G	GS	Inn	PO	A	E	DP	Pct.	Rng	BSv	RS
	LAA	RF	5	1	18	4	0	0	0	1.000	2.00	+1	1
Butera, D	KC	1B	2	0	2	2	0	0	0	1.000	-	0	0
Butler, B	TOT	1B	25	17	130	113	9	3	10	.976	-	-4	-2
Byrd, M	Cle	LF	14	11	100	18	0	0	0	1.000	1.62	+1	0
	Cle	RF	21	19	155	24	3	0	1	1.000	1.57	-2	1
Cabrera, M	Det	3B	1	1	8	2	0	0	0	1.000	2.25	0	0
Cain, L	KC	CF	72	72	615	196	2	3	0	.985	2.90	+17	8
	KC	RF	29	29	260	61	1	0	0	1.000	2.15	+4	3
Campbell, E	NYM	1B	21	15	134	114	12	1	11	.992	-	0	0
	NYM	2B	1	0	1	1	0	0	0	1.000	13.50	0	0
	NYM	3B	7	5	47	2	6	0	0	1.000	1.53	0	0
	NYM	LF	2	0	3	2	0	0	0	1.000	6.00	+1	0
Candelario, J	ChC	3B	3	2	22	1	3	1	0	.800	1.61	0	0
Canha, M	Oak	1B	5	3	30	31	7	1	3	.974	-	-1	0
	Oak	3B	3	1	13	3	1	0	1	1.000	2.77	+1	0
	Oak	LF	3	2	18	3	0	0	0	1.000	1.50	0	0
	Oak	RF	3	2	16	3	0	0	0	1.000	1.69	-1	0
Cardullo, S	Col	1B	15	10	92	104	8	2	7	.982	-	+1	0
	Col	LF	2	1	11	5	1	0	0	1.000	4.91	+1	0
	Col	RF	3	0	3	1	0	0	0	1.000	3.00	0	0
Carpenter, M	StL	1B	45	35	312	304	16	1	38	.997	-	0	1
	StL	2B	40	37	318	60	103	4	22	.976	4.61	-9	-8
	StL	3B	54	52	431	20	95	8	12	.935	2.40	0	2
Carrera, E	Tor	LF	45	27	239	41	2	1	1	.977	1.62	+3	2
	Tor	CF	5	4	34	4	0	0	0	1.000	1.06	-7	-3
	Tor	RF	65	37	370	87	6	0	2	1.000	2.26	+5	8
Castillo, R	Bos	LF	2	1	10	3	0	0	0	1.000	2.70	+1	0
	Bos	CF	1	1	9	3	0	0	0	1.000	3.00	+1	1
	Bos	RF	1	0	1	0	0	0	0	-	.00	0	0
Castro, D	Atl	2B	16	10	101	24	29	0	7	1.000	4.74	+1	0
	Atl	3B	9	5	54	4	9	0	1	1.000	2.15	+1	0
	Atl	SS	20	14	127	15	48	0	10	1.000	4.46	-4	-2
Castro, J	Hou	1B	3	0	11	7	1	0	0	1.000	-	0	0
Castro, S	NYY	SS	3	3	20	6	6	0	2	1.000	5.40	0	0
Cecchini, G	NYM	SS	2	0	6	0	1	0	0	1.000	1.50	-1	-1
Ceciliani, D	Tor	LF	8	7	61	9	0	0	0	1.000	1.33	-2	-1
	Tor	RF	4	1	13	3	0	1	0	.750	2.08	+1	0
Cervelli, F	Pit	1B	2	1	9	7	0	0	2	1.000		-1	0
Cespedes, Y	NYM	LF	80	61	551	135	4	4	0	.972	2.27	-1	4
	NYM	CF	63	61	495	115	5	1	0	.992	2.18	-10	-7
Chisenhall, L	Cle	1B	3	0	7	8	0	0	0	1.000	-	0	0
	Cle	3B	1	0	2	1	0	0	0	1.000	4.50	0	0
	Cle	CF	2	1	8	4	0	0	0	1.000	4.50	+1	0
Choi, J	LAA	1B	27	15	152	127	11	1	15	.993	-	+2	2
	LAA	LF	20	14	113	26	0	0	0	1.000	2.07	-5	-2
Choo, S	Tex	RF	43	42	358	85	4	3	0	.967	2.24	-4	-4
Coats, J	CWS	LF	7	3	34	4	0	0	0	1.000	1.07	+3	1
	CWS	RF	11	8	68	13	0	0	0	1.000	1.71	0	0
Coghlan, C	TOT	1B	6	1	27	19	0	0	2	1.000	-	0	0
	TOT	2B	20	16	130	19	51	1	12	.986	4.85	-2	-2
	TOT	3B	18	15	136	11	28	1	5	.975	2.58	-3	-3
	TOT	LF	29	26	190	35	2	0	0	1.000	1.75	+5	3
	TOT	RF	18	15	114	25	0	0	0	1.000	1.97	+2	0
Colabello, C	Tor	1B	8	8	62	74	3	0	6	1.000	-	+1	1
	Tor	LF	1	0	1	0	0	0	0	-	.00	0	0
Collins, T	Det	LF	13	5	60	16	0	0	0	1.000	2.40	+1	1
	Det	CF	29	22	207	58	2	1	1	.984	2.61	-7	-4
	Det	RF	8	5	50	5	0	0	0	1.000	.91	0	-1
Colon, C	KC	2B	32	29	247	45	94	0	18	1.000	5.06	+10	7
	KC	3B	15	10	93	8	21	1	0	.967	2.82	0	0
	KC	SS	4	0	9	1	2	0	0	1.000	3.00	+1	1
Conforto, M	NYM	LF	73	66	562	116	3	3	1	.975	1.91	0	-1
	NYM	CF	6	5	39	9	0	0	0	1.000	2.08	+2	1
	NYM	RF	9	5	42	9	1	0	0	1.000	2.13	+1	1
Contreras, W	ChC	1B	3	2	19	22	1	0	1	1.000	-	-1	-1
	ChC	LF	24	21	181	26	1	0	0	1.000	1.35	-2	-1
Cowart, K	LAA	1B	1	1	2	3	0	0	1	1.000	-	0	0
	LAA	2B	16	12	92	21	29	2	8	.962	4.89	+1	1
	LAA	3B	21	10	122	8	30	1	3	.974	2.80	0	0
Cowgill, C	Cle	RF	8	4	43	10	0	0	0	1.000	2.09	0	0
Crawford, C	LAD	LF	21	18	151	28	0	0	0	1.000	1.67	-1	-4
Crisp, C	TOT	LF	71	64	562	106	3	3	0	.973	1.74	+6	1

Player	Tm	Pos	G	GS	Inn	PO	A	E	DP	Pct.	Rng	BSv	RS
	TOT	CF	36	34	291	73	1	0	1	1.000	2.29	-16	-11
Cruz, N	Sea	RF	48	48	401	76	2	1	1	.987	1.75	-7	-3
Culberson, C	LAD	2B	10	9	64	10	15	1	2	.962	3.52	-3	-2
	LAD	3B	4	2	15	2	3	1	0	.833	3.00	+1	1
	LAD	SS	11	8	60	8	16	0	3	1.000	3.60	+2	2
	LAD	LF	2	0	5	2	0	0	0	1.000	3.60	+1	1
Cunningham, T	LAA	LF	17	6	77	19	2	1	1	.955	2.45	0	2
	LAA	CF	1	0	3	0	0	0	0	-	.00	0	0
	LAA	RF	1	0	1	0	0	0	0	-	.00	0	0
Dahl, D	Col	LF	54	46	423	65	3	2	0	.971	1.45	-2	-3
	Col	CF	6	5	45	10	1	0	0	1.000	2.20	0	1
	Col	RF	4	1	13	4	0	0	0	1.000	2.70	+1	1
dArnaud,C'	Atl	2B	10	10	89	12	27	1	1	.976	4.06	-1	-1
	Atl	3B	19	16	145	12	24	0	1	1.000	2.23	0	0
	Atl	SS	21	16	147	20	38	1	7	.983	3.54	-1	-2
	Atl	LF	8	5	46	15	1	0	0	1.000	3.13	0	2
	Atl	CF	4	3	34	10	0	0	0	1.000	2.65	-6	-3
	Atl	RF	1	1	8	2	0	0	0	1.000	2.25	+2	1
Davis, C	Bal	RF	3	3	24	5	0	0	0	1.000	1.88	-4	-2
Davis, I	NYY	1B	8	4	39	39	3	0	2	1.000		0	0
Davis, R	Cle	LF	66	40	387	83	4	2	0	.978	2.02	-8	-3
	Cle	CF	80	66	595	151	5	3	2	.981	2.36	-10	-5
	Cle	RF	1	1	6	1	0	0	0	1.000	1.50	0	0
De Aza, A	NYM	LF	22	8	91	15	0	1	0	.938	1.48	+2	2
	NYM	CF	46	29	285	71	0	1	0	.986	2.24	+5	1
	NYM	RF	14	8	83	20	0	0	0	1.000	2.16	-2	-2
De Jesus, I	Cin	1B	12	4	52	44	0	1	5	.978	-	-1	-2
	Cin	2B	22	9	111	21	35	0	10	1.000	4.55	+3	2
	Cin	3B	14	7	81	5	16	1	1	.955	2.33	-1	0
	Cin	SS	30	22	215	41	73	1	16	.991	4.76	-1	0
	Cin	LF	1	0	1	0	0	0	0	-	.00	0	0
Decker, J	TB	LF	3	3	24	7	1	0	1	1.000	3.00	-1	1
	TB	CF	2	1	10	3	1	0	0	1.000	3.60	-1	-1
	TB	RF	3	3	86	18	1	0	1	1.000	1.99	-1	-2
den Dekker, M	Was	LF	3	2	21	4	0	0	0	1.000	1.71	+2	1
	Was	CF	6	3	34	12	0	0	0	1.000	3.15	+1	1
	Was	RF	4	1	18	8	0	0	0	1.000	4.00	+1	1
Descalso, D	Col	1B	16	11	101	106	3	3	14	.973	-	0	0
	Col	2B	14	11	103	17	33	1	8	.980	4.38	0	0
	Col	3B	4	2	18	3	0	0	0	1.000	1.50	0	0
	Col	SS	31	31	254	41	65	3	16	.972	3.75	-1	-2
	Col	LF	7	7	42	9	0	0	0	1.000	1.93	+2	1
DeShields, D	Tex	LF	26	19	143	21	0	1	0	.955	1.32	+4	1
	Tex	CF	33	30	281	81	1	2	0	.976	2.63	+1	-1
Desmond, I	Tex	LF	29	27	251	37	2	3	0	.929	1.40	0	2
Diaz, A	StL	2B	1	0	2	1	2	0	1	1.000	13.50	0	0
Dickerson, A	SD	1B	68	65	544	104	0	3	0	.972	1.72	+9	1
Dickerson, C	TB	LF	76	69	599	132	2	2	0	.985	2.01	+1	2
	TB	RF	2	1	14	2	0	0	0	1.000	1.32	0	0
Dietrich, D	Mia	1B	16	12	90	79	4	0	12	1.000	-	0	0
	Mia	2B	75	71	585	120	165	4	33	.986	4.38	-4	-3
	Mia	3B	13	7	66	5	14	0	2	1.000	2.58	+1	2
	Mia	LF	8	6	42	10	0	0	0	1.000	2.14	+1	1
Difo, W	Was	2B	9	7	65	6	19	1	1	.962	3.46	0	0
	Was	3B	3	3	19	1	3	0	0	1.000	1.86	0	0
	Was	SS	5	3	28	5	9	1	1	.933	4.50	+2	0
Dominguez, M	Tor	1B	1	1	9	9	0	0	1	1.000	-	0	0
	Tor	3B	3	2	20	7	4	0	0	1.000	4.95	+1	1
Dozier, H	KC	RF	7	5	44	13	0	0	0	1.000	2.66	+1	1
Drew, S	Was	2B	21	15	144	33	44	3	9	.963	4.80	+3	2
	Was	3B	12	8	86	5	19	0	1	1.000	2.50	+3	1
	Was	SS	12	7	68	11	13	0	4	1.000	3.19	-4	-3
Drury, B	Ari	1B	1	0	1	1	0	0	0	1.000	-	0	0
	Ari	2B	16	8	82	15	25	1	6	.976	4.39	0	0
	Ari	3B	29	25	224	17	42	3	4	.952	2.37	-5	-4
	Ari	LF	62	52	469	90	0	1	0	.989	1.73	+1	-7
	Ari	RF	32	27	235	50	0	1	0	.980	1.91	+2	-2
Duda, L	NYM	1B	45	40	354	313	23	3	26	.991		+1	0
Duffy, M	Hou	3B	1	0	2	0	0	0	0	1.000	4.50	0	0
Duffy, M	TOT	3B	70	66	593	44	142	5	5	.974	2.82	+15	11
	TOT	SS	18	18	153	15	40	0	8	1.000	3.24	-1	0
Duvall, A	Cin	1B	5	3	32	33	6	0	1	1.000	-	+2	1

All Other Fielders

Player	Tm	Pos	G	GS	Inn	PO	A	E	DP	Pct.	Rng	BSv	RS
	Cin	3B	3	1	13	1	2	0	0	1.000	2.03	+1	1
	Cin	RF	6	5	44	5	0	0	0	1.000	1.03	-3	-2
Dyson, J	KC	LF	19	12	120	27	2	0	0	1.000	2.18	+7	5
	KC	CF	57	50	462	132	4	1	0	.993	2.65	+13	9
	KC	RF	21	21	177	37	5	1	0	.977	2.14	0	5
Eaton, A	CWS	LF	1	1	8	1	0	0	0	1.000	1.13	0	0
	CWS	CF	48	43	374	120	3	2	1	.984	2.96	-6	-2
Eibner, B	TOT	LF	13	11	94	22	0	0	0	1.000	2.11	+5	2
	TOT	CF	19	17	149	42	1	0	1	1.000	2.60	-2	-2
	TOT	RF	28	21	190	47	1	1	0	.980	2.27	+6	1
Elmore, J	Mil	2B	3	1	11	4	5	0	2	1.000	7.15	0	0
	Mil	3B	4	1	24	1	8	2	1	.818	3.38	0	0
	Mil	LF	14	8	77	10	0	0	0	1.000	1.17	-2	-2
	Mil	CF	2	2	11	1	0	0	0	1.000	.82	-1	-1
	Mil	RF	4	2	18	3	0	0	0	1.000	1.53	0	0
Encarnacion, E	Tor	1B	75	74	636	602	27	2	57	.997	-	-1	0
Escobar, E	Min	2B	6	2	27	5	8	0	3	1.000	4.33	-1	0
	Min	3B	23	20	180	13	35	1	4	.980	2.40	+2	1
	Min	SS	71	66	579	87	200	9	62	.970	4.46	-8	-7
	Min	LF	2	0	4	0	0	0	0	-	.00	0	0
Ethier, A	LAD	LF	4	2	24	5	0	0	0	1.000	1.90	0	-1
Featherston, T	Phi	2B	3	2	26	9	6	0	3	1.000	5.26	+1	1
Fielder, P	Tex	1B	9	9	70	60	4	2	9	.970	-	-1	-1
Figueroa, C	Pit	2B	5	2	23	2	5	0	1	1.000	2.74	0	0
	Pit	3B	2	0	6	0	3	0	1	1.000	4.50	+1	1
	Pit	SS	2	0	7	0	2	0	0	1.000	2.57	0	0
Flaherty, R	Bal	1B	7	2	22	18	3	0	3	1.000	-	+1	1
	Bal	2B	1	0	1	0	1	0	0	1.000	9.00	0	0
	Bal	3B	40	33	308	17	78	3	9	.969	2.78	+5	6
	Bal	SS	13	3	45	12	17	0	4	1.000	5.80	-3	-2
	Bal	LF	3	2	17	2	0	0	0	1.000	1.06	-2	-1
	Bal	RF	6	2	26	4	0	0	0	1.000	1.38	+1	0
Flores, R	Mil	1B	2	1	6	3	0	0	0	1.000	-	0	0
	Mil	LF	13	9	79	18	2	0	0	1.000	2.28	+1	1
	Mil	CF	29	19	175	40	0	0	0	1.000	2.05	-1	-3
	Mil	RF	49	37	339	76	2	1	0	.987	2.07	+1	0
Flores, W	NYM	1B	27	18	163	135	15	1	14	.993	-	+3	2
	NYM	2B	18	13	119	24	42	2	8	.971	5.01	-4	-3
	NYM	3B	51	45	385	36	55	6	8	.938	2.13	-11	-9
	NYM	SS	8	2	35	9	8	1	1	.944	4.41	-3	-2
Florimon, P	Pit	2B	8	2	33	7	6	0	1	1.000	3.58	0	0
	Pit	SS	6	1	21	2	8	0	3	1.000	4.35	+1	1
Francoeur, J	TOT	3B	1	0	1	0	0	0	0	-	.00	-1	-1
	TOT	LF	63	48	436	71	5	1	0	.987	1.57	+3	5
	TOT	RF	17	15	142	29	4	2	1	.943	2.10	-3	2
Franklin, N	TB	1B	9	6	63	58	4	0	7	1.000	-	-1	-1
	TB	2B	8	7	57	6	14	4	3	.833	3.16	0	0
	TB	SS	5	5	36	3	9	1	1	.923	3.03	-1	-1
	TB	LF	18	16	132	35	0	1	0	.972	2.39	-6	-4
	TB	RF	7	5	49	10	0	0	0	1.000	1.84	0	0
Frazier, A	Pit	2B	17	13	100	15	30	3	7	.938	4.05	+1	0
	Pit	3B	5	2	18	1	8	1	2	.900	4.50	-2	-1
	Pit	LF	20	10	107	17	0	1	0	.944	1.43	+2	0
	Pit	CF	1	0	3	1	0	0	0	1.000	3.00	-2	-1
	Pit	RF	16	2	65	11	1	1	0	.923	1.67	-1	-1
Frazier, T	CWS	1B	7	7	61	59	3	1	4	.984	-	0	0
Freeman, M	TOT	2B	5	2	23	8	7	0	3	1.000	5.87	0	0
	TOT	SS	2	1	12	2	2	0	0	1.000	3.00	0	0
	TOT	LF	1	0	1	0	0	0	0	-	.00	0	0
	TOT	RF	1	1	9	1	0	0	0	1.000	1.00	-1	0
Freese, D	Pit	1B	58	34	341	344	31	3	42	.992	-	+2	0
	Pit	2B	2	0	5	0	0	0	0	-	.00	0	0
	Pit	3B	78	71	626	40	157	8	17	.961	2.83	+5	5
Fuentes, R	KC	LF	3	3	24	5	0	0	0	1.000	1.88	0	0
	KC	RF	9	9	74	18	1	1	0	.950	2.31	-4	-3
Gallo, J	Tex	1B	1	1	9	11	0	1	3	.917	-	-1	-1
	Tex	3B	5	1	18	3	6	0	0	1.000	4.50	+1	1
Gamel, B	TOT	LF	2	2	15	4	0	0	0	1.000	2.40	-1	0
	TOT	CF	1	1	9	6	0	0	0	1.000	6.00	-1	0
	TOT	RF	29	5	108	19	0	0	0	1.000	1.58	-1	-2
Garcia, A	Atl	LF	4	4	29	6	0	0	0	1.000	1.86	-4	-2
Garcia, A	CWS	LF	11	9	81	15	2	0	0	1.000	1.89	-1	-1

Player	Tm	Pos	G	GS	Inn	PO	A	E	DP	Pct.	Rng	BSv	RS
	CWS	RF	46	42	380	103	3	2	1	.981	2.51	+3	2
Garcia, G	StL	2B	26	15	151	31	43	2	7	.974	4.42	+1	1
	StL	3B	31	11	127	6	22	1	4	.966	1.98	+1	1
	StL	SS	30	24	226	19	78	5	17	.951	3.86	+1	1
Garcia, L	CWS	CF	16	14	119	30	0	0	0	1.000	2.28	-3	-2
Gardner, B	NYY	CF	3	2	11	1	0	0	0	1.000	.82	0	0
Gearrin, C	SF	LF	1	0	0	0	0	0	0	-	-	0	0
Gentry, C	LAA	LF	12	10	90	26	1	1	0	.964	2.70	+3	1
	LAA	CF	1	0	3	2	0	0	0	1.000	6.00	0	0
Gillaspie, C	SF	1B	7	3	32	29	2	0	3	1.000	-	+2	1
	SF	3B	45	34	305	11	62	2	6	.973	2.16	+6	4
Gillespie, C	Mia	1B	1	0	2	3	0	0	0	1.000	-	0	0
	Mia	LF	4	3	27	5	1	0	0	1.000	1.98	-3	0
	Mia	CF	1	0	3	1	0	0	0	1.000	3.00	0	0
	Mia	RF	3	2	19	7	0	1	0	.875	3.32	-4	-3
Gimenez, C	Cle	1B	4	0	6	3	0	0	1	1.000	-	0	0
	Cle	3B	1	1	10	1	2	0	1	1.000	2.79	-1	-1
Goeddel, T	Phi	LF	69	49	427	75	4	3	3	.963	1.66	-6	-6
	Phi	RF	12	7	69	13	1	0	0	1.000	1.82	-3	-3
Goins, R	Tor	1B	2	0	5	4	1	0	0	1.000	-	0	0
	Tor	2B	37	33	291	64	95	3	20	.981	4.92	-1	2
	Tor	3B	6	2	21	2	4	1	0	.857	2.57	-1	-1
	Tor	SS	28	16	151	31	65	1	16	.990	5.73	+1	1
	Tor	LF	2	0	9	2	0	0	0	1.000	2.00	0	0
	Tor	RF	1	0	3	1	0	0	0	1.000	3.00	0	0
Gomez, C	TOT	LF	28	24	213	53	0	0	0	1.000	2.24	+1	-1
	TOT	CF	85	80	705	165	7	1	1	.994	2.20	-18	-4
	TOT	RF	6	5	34	7	0	1	0	.875	1.85	0	-1
Gonzalez, E	Cle	2B	5	0	11	1	2	0	0	1.000	2.45	+1	1
	Cle	3B	2	0	2	0	0	0	0	-	.00	0	0
	Cle	SS	8	1	18	5	6	0	2	1.000	5.40	-1	-1
	Cle	RF	2	1	10	1	0	0	0	1.000	.90	0	0
Gonzalez, M	Hou	1B	92	74	677	640	69	6	57	.992	-	0	1
	Hou	2B	18	8	79	14	20	1	6	.971	3.87	0	1
	Hou	3B	22	16	158	12	42	1	2	.982	3.07	+1	1
	Hou	SS	11	6	66	9	18	0	3	1.000	3.66	+2	1
	Hou	LF	18	14	110	26	1	0	0	1.000	2.22	+1	1
	Hou	CF	1	0	1	0	0	0	0	-	.00	0	0
Goodwin, B	Was	LF	5	2	17	3	0	0	0	1.000	1.62	+1	0
	Was	CF	1	1	4	1	0	0	0	1.000	2.25	+1	0
	Was	RF	8	7	58	10	0	0	0	1.000	1.54	-2	-1
Gordon, D	Mia	2B	78	73	655	150	186	7	51	.980	4.61	+2	1
Gore, T	KC	LF	2	0	5	3	0	0	0	1.000	5.40	+1	1
Gose, A	Det	CF	30	27	238	59	1	0	0	1.000	2.27	-2	-3
Gosselin, P	Ari	1B	6	4	41	44	7	0	3	1.000	-	+2	1
	Ari	2B	35	21	195	36	50	0	12	1.000	3.96	-2	-2
	Ari	3B	10	5	41	3	7	0	0	1.000	2.21	-1	-1
	Ari	LF	2	2	18	6	0	0	0	1.000	3.00	+2	1
	Ari	RF	1	0	0	0	0	0	0	-	.00	0	0
Grandal, Y	LAD	1B	4	2	19	24	1	0	1	1.000	-	+1	1
Granderson, C	NYM	LF	7	6	54	13	0	0	0	1.000	2.18	-3	0
	NYM	CF	36	32	251	54	1	0	0	1.000	1.97	+1	1
Green, G	SF	2B	15	11	99	17	24	2	6	.953	3.73	-3	-3
Grichuk, R	StL	LF	4	3	27	7	0	0	0	1.000	2.33	+3	1
	StL	RF	3	2	18	4	0	1	0	.800	2.00	0	0
Grossman, R	Min	LF	75	72	635	123	4	8	1	.941	1.80	-27	-21
	Min	CF	1	0	2	0	0	0	0	-	.00	0	0
Gurriel, Y	Hou	1B	5	4	36	35	4	0	9	1.000	-	0	0
	Hou	3B	21	20	176	13	30	1	1	.977	2.20	-1	0
	Hou		1	1	8	0	0	0	0	-	.00	-1	0
Gutierrez, F	Sea	LF	9	8	63	10	1	0	0	1.000	1.57	0	0
	Sea	RF	64	47	413	95	0	0	0	1.000	2.07	-7	-8
Guyer, B	TOT	LF	51	42	368	80	2	3	0	.965	2.00	+4	2
	TOT	CF	18	14	136	40	0	1	0	.976	2.65	-4	-3
	TOT	RF	19	15	122	30	1	0	0	1.000	2.29	+1	-1
Gyorko, J	StL	1B	11	8	64	61	5	0	6	1.000	-	0	0
	StL	2B	46	39	338	63	136	1	32	.995	5.30	+5	6
	StL	3B	39	28	272	21	54	3	7	.962	2.48	+2	2
	StL	SS	26	25	218	38	74	6	18	.949	4.62	-6	-3
Haniger, M	Ari	LF	9	6	52	8	1	0	0	1.000	1.56	+2	2
	Ari	CF	22	20	182	51	1	0	0	1.000	2.58	+7	2
	Ari	RF	4	3	24	3	0	1	0	.750	1.13	-2	-3

All Other Fielders

Player	Tm	Pos	G	GS	Inn	PO	A	E	DP	Pct.	Rng	BSv	RS
Hanson, A	Pit	2B	8	5	47	13	11	2	6	.923	4.63	-2	-2
Harrison, J	Pit	RF	1	0	1	0	0	0	0	-	.00	0	0
Hazelbaker, J	StL	LF	52	19	241	42	0	1	0	.977	1.57	-2	-2
	StL	CF	21	15	127	33	0	3	0	.917	2.34	+2	-1
	StL	RF	6	4	34	4	0	0	0	1.000	1.06	0	0
Healy, R	Oak	3B	72	72	638	42	144	9	9	.954	2.63	-2	-2
Heisey, C	Was	LF	25	10	124	34	0	0	0	1.000	2.46	-3	-2
	Was	CF	3	2	16	2	0	0	0	1.000	1.13	0	0
	Was	RF	16	9	105	23	0	0	0	1.000	1.98	+1	1
Heredia, G	Sea	LF	35	17	198	55	3	1	1	.983	2.63	+1	2
	Sea	CF	1	1	9	1	0	0	0	1.000	1.00	-1	0
	Sea	RF	14	0	27	10	0	0	0	1.000	3.29	+3	1
Hernandez, C	Phi	SS	4	2	20	6	6	0	3	1.000	5.49	0	0
Hernandez, G	SF	LF	2	0	5	4	0	0	0	1.000	7.20	0	0
	SF	CF	14	11	95	21	1	0	0	1.000	2.08	0	1
	SF	RF	6	2	26	3	1	0	0	1.000	1.38	-2	0
Hernandez, K	LAD	2B	11	5	49	7	11	0	0	1.000	3.31	-2	-2
	LAD	3B	5	1	15	1	5	2	0	.750	3.68	-1	-1
	LAD	SS	2	1	11	0	1	0	0	1.000	.82	0	0
	LAD	LF	41	22	207	40	3	0	1	1.000	1.87	+5	4
	LAD	CF	22	16	126	34	0	0	0	1.000	2.44	+2	1
	LAD	RF	7	1	18	4	1	0	0	1.000	2.50	0	1
Hernandez, M	Bos	2B	14	3	45	9	12	1	4	.955	4.20	-3	-2
	Bos	3B	10	6	59	5	10	1	4	.938	2.29	-3	-3
	Bos	SS	2	1	10	0	2	0	0	1.000	1.80	-1	-1
Hernandez, T	Hou	LF	22	13	125	19	0	0	0	1.000	1.36	+2	1
	Hou	CF	15	10	86	17	1	1	0	.947	1.89	0	0
	Hou	RF	6	5	45	10	0	1	0	.909	2.00	0	0
Herrmann, C	Ari	1B	2	0	5	2	0	0	2	1.000	-	0	0
	Ari	LF	3	3	24	4	0	0	0	1.000	1.50	0	0
	Ari	CF	2	1	10	0	0	0	0	-	.00	0	0
	Ari	RF	4	2	22	5	1	1	0	.857	2.49	0	-1
Heyward, J	ChC	CF	24	21	171	51	1	0	0	1.000	2.74	+4	4
Hicks, A	NYY	LF	25	20	170	36	2	0	1	1.000	2.01	-2	1
	NYY	CF	24	20	178	54	0	0	0	1.000	2.73	+3	0
	NYY	RF	86	52	497	96	1	1	0	.990	1.76	+5	3
Hicks, J	Det	1B	1	0	3	3	1	0	0	1.000	-	0	0
Hill, A	TOT	2B	24	16	166	33	54	0	9	1.000	4.72	-1	0
	TOT	3B	103	85	745	57	150	5	17	.976	2.50	+7	3
Holaday, B	TOT	3B	1	0	1	0	1	0	1	1.000	9.00	0	0
	TOT	LF	1	0	3	1	0	0	0	1.000	3.00	0	0
Holliday, M	StL	1B	10	9	62	65	10	0	5	1.000	-	+2	1
	StL	LF	85	82	644	111	2	0	0	1.000	1.58	-4	-8
Holt, B	Bos	2B	8	4	44	10	11	0	1	1.000	4.30	+2	1
	Bos	3B	17	11	93	10	29	2	3	.951	3.77	+1	1
	Bos	SS	7	4	41	6	12	0	1	1.000	3.95	+1	1
	Bos	LF	64	55	479	103	6	2	2	.982	2.05	-3	3
	Bos	RF	5	2	23	4	0	0	0	1.000	1.57	-2	-1
Holt, T	Cin	LF	19	4	63	12	0	0	0	1.000	1.72	0	0
	Cin	CF	32	20	218	68	1	0	0	1.000	2.85	-8	-3
	Cin	RF	23	9	99	14	0	1	0	.933	1.27	-4	-4
Hood, D	Mia	LF	5	4	34	8	0	0	0	1.000	2.12	-3	-1
	Mia	RF	2	1	9	3	0	0	0	1.000	3.00	+1	1
Howard, R	Phi	1B	83	81	644	557	45	11	47	.982	-	-7	-9
Hoying, J	Tex	LF	13	7	71	10	1	1	0	.917	1.39	-1	-1
	Tex	CF	1	0	2	0	0	0	0	-	.00	0	0
	Tex	RF	17	1	36	7	0	0	0	1.000	1.75	-1	-1
Hunter, C	Phi	LF	10	7	66	12	1	0	0	1.000	1.76	-2	0
	Phi	RF	2	2	15	5	0	0	0	1.000	3.00	-2	-2
Inciarte, E	Atl	LF	10	9	84	19	2	1	0	.955	2.26	-2	2
Infante, O	KC	2B	39	38	336	66	102	4	17	.977	4.50	-3	-3
Iribarren, H	Cin	1B	2	0	3	2	0	0	1	1.000	-	0	0
	Cin	2B	5	1	55	5	2	0	2	1.000	4.20	0	0
	Cin	CF	6	4	41	11	0	0	0	1.000	2.43	+1	1
	Cin	RF	2	2	16	2	0	0	0	1.000	1.13	-1	-1
Jackson, A	CWS	CF	54	52	465	118	3	2	2	.984	2.34	-11	-5
Janish, P	Bal	3B	9	9	73	11	12	0	0	1.000	2.84	+1	0
	Bal	SS	6	1	17	2	6	0	2	1.000	4.24	0	0
Jankowski, T	SD	LF	9	3	37	10	0	1	0	.909	2.45	+4	2
	SD	CF	87	77	697	193	0	0	0	1.000	2.49	+16	3
	SD	RF	22	2	55	18	0	0	0	1.000	2.93	+7	3
Jaso, J	Pit	1B	108	99	748	749	46	5	81	.994	-	0	-3
	Pit	RF	1	0	1	0	0	0	0	-	.00	0	0
Jay, J	SD	LF	8	5	46	15	0	0	0	1.000	2.93	-3	-1
	SD	CF	72	68	599	155	4	1	1	.994	2.39	-6	-5
	SD	RF	9	9	76	20	0	0	0	1.000	2.38	+2	1
Jennings, D	TB	LF	33	28	257	55	2	0	1	1.000	2.00	+13	7
	TB	CF	30	26	229	57	1	2	0	.967	2.28	+7	0
Jensen, K	Ari	1B	4	1	12	10	0	0	1	1.000	-	0	0
	Ari	LF	4	3	31	9	0	0	0	1.000	2.61	+1	1
	Ari	RF	1	0	2	0	0	0	0	-	.00	0	0
Johnson, C	Mia	1B	81	43	433	360	23	3	37	.992	-	+3	2
	Mia	3B	11	7	59	5	12	0	1	1.000	2.59	-1	-1
	Mia	LF	2	0	4	0	0	0	0	-	.00	0	0
Johnson, K	TOT	1B	3	2	14	12	1	0	1	1.000	-	0	0
	TOT	2B	52	42	368	69	95	6	17	.965	4.01	-6	-5
	TOT	3B	21	15	147	10	27	2	6	.949	2.26	+2	2
	TOT	SS	1	0	3	1	0	0	0	1.000	3.00	0	0
	TOT	LF	15	8	79	17	0	0	0	1.000	1.94	+1	1
Johnson, M	LAD	2B	3	0	4	2	0	0	0	1.000	4.50	0	0
	LAD	LF	1	0	1	0	0	0	0	-	.00	0	0
Jones, J	Det	3B	6	4	34	1	6	0	0	1.000	1.85	+1	1
	Det	CF	5	3	28	8	0	0	0	1.000	2.57	+2	0
Joseph, C	Bal	1B	2	0	2	1	0	0	0	1.000	-	0	0
Joseph, T	Phi	1B	97	74	681	612	36	7	69	.989	-	-3	-6
Joyce, M	Pit	LF	26	14	136	26	1	0	0	1.000	1.79	-8	-2
	Pit	RF	43	30	267	55	0	0	0	1.000	1.86	-1	0
Judge, A	NYY	RF	27	24	216	35	2	1	0	.974	1.54	-5	-1
Kalish, R	ChC	LF	2	1	11	0	0	0	0	-	.00	0	0
	ChC	RF	1	0	2	3	0	0	0	1.000	13.50	0	0
Kang, J	Pit	3B	92	83	728	49	191	17	20	.934	2.97	+1	-1
Kawasaki, M	ChC	2B	4	0	50	10	14	1	6	.960	4.32	-1	-1
	ChC	3B	1	0	1	0	0	0	0	-	.00	0	0
Kelly, D	Mia	1B	12	6	68	63	9	0	5	1.000	-	+1	0
Kelly, T	NYM	1B	1	0	2	3	0	0	0	1.000	-	0	0
	NYM	2B	2	0	4	0	0	0	0	-	.00	0	0
	NYM	3B	10	5	58	4	11	0	0	1.000	2.34	+1	1
	NYM	LF	8	5	50	7	3	0	1	1.000	1.81	+1	3
	NYM	CF	1	0	1	0	0	0	0	-	.00	0	0
	NYM	RF	1	0	3	2	0	0	0	1.000	6.00	0	0
Kemp, M	TOT	LF	54	54	466	110	1	1	1	.991	2.15	-14	-12
Kemp, T	Hou	2B	5	1	18	2	5	1	1	.875	3.50	0	0
	Hou	LF	37	24	227	33	2	1	0	.972	1.39	-4	-3
	Hou	CF	1	0	2	1	0	0	0	1.000	4.50	0	0
	Hou	RF	1	0	3	0	0	0	0	-	.00	0	0
Kendrick, H	LAD	1B	11	7	70	56	3	1	6	.983	-	0	0
	LAD	2B	32	23	210	32	57	3	11	.967	3.81	-4	-4
	LAD	3B	17	14	126	5	26	1	2	.969	2.21	-2	-1
	LAD	LF	94	79	675	131	5	0	0	1.000	1.81	+8	0
Kepler, M	Min	1B	2	0	4	5	0	0	0	1.000	-	0	0
	Min	CF	4	1	21	5	1	0	0	1.000	2.57	+2	1
Kim, H	Bal	LF	91	78	665	110	4	0	0	1.000	1.54	-12	-13
Kivlehan, P	TOT	LF	1	1	9	1	0	1	0	.500	1.00	+1	0
	TOT	RF	6	5	40	13	0	1	0	.929	2.95	-2	-1
Kratz, E	TOT	1B	1	0	0	1	0	0	0	1.000	-	0	0
La Stella, T	ChC	2B	9	7	50	11	9	1	2	.952	3.60	0	0
	ChC	3B	33	24	208	12	32	4	4	.917	1.91	-3	-2
Ladendorf, T	Oak	2B	30	11	119	32	44	1	8	.987	5.76	+3	0
	Oak	3B	3	2	18	2	7	0	0	1.000	4.50	+1	0
	Oak	CF	1	0	0	0	0	0	0	-	.00	0	0
	Oak	RF	1	0	1	0	0	0	0	-	.00	0	0
Lagares, J	NYM	LF	1	0	1	0	0	0	0	-	.00	0	0
	NYM	CF	68	29	326	98	1	1	0	.990	2.74	+14	8
	NYM	RF	2	2	18	2	0	0	0	1.000	1.02	-1	0
Lake, J	Tor	1B	1	0	5	3	0	0	2	1.000	-	-1	-1
	Tor	RF	19	10	93	16	0	1	0	.941	1.55	-1	-1
Lalli, B	Atl	1B	4	1	14	10	0	0	5	1.000	-	0	0
LaMarre, R	Bos	LF	2	1	13	3	0	0	0	1.000	2.08	0	0
	Bos	RF	1	0	1	0	0	0	0	-	.00	0	0
Lee, D	Sea	1B	84	70	622	554	28	2	68	.997	-	-4	-3
Lopez, R	Cin	1B	1	0	1	1	0	0	0	1.000	-	0	0
Lough, D	Phi	LF	15	9	96	17	1	0	0	1.000	1.69	+1	1
	Phi	RF	11	8	70	21	0	0	0	1.000	2.70	-1	-1
Lowrie, J	Oak	2B	82	80	708	141	235	6	60	.984	4.78	-11	-8

All Other Fielders

Player	Tm	Pos	G	GS	Inn	PO	A	E	DP	Pct.	Rng	BSv	RS
	Oak	SS	2	0	3	0	1	0	0	1.000	3.00	0	0
Lucroy, J	TOT	1B	6	5	41	40	0	0	2	1.000	-	-1	-1
Machado, D	Det	2B	2	0	2	0	0	0	0	-	.00	0	0
	Det	SS	6	3	30	5	12	0	1	1.000	5.10	+2	2
Machado, M	Bal	SS	45	43	380	75	125	6	33	.971	4.74	+4	3
Mahtook, M	TB	LF	26	16	151	28	1	0	0	1.000	1.73	+1	1
	TB	CF	23	17	164	51	1	0	0	1.000	2.85	+5	2
	TB	RF	18	17	130	27	1	0	1	1.000	1.94	-5	-2
Maile, L	TB	1B	4	0	14	12	1	0	1	1.000		+1	1
Margot, M	SD	CF	9	7	64	26	0	0	0	1.000	3.68	+9	3
	SD	RF	1	1	8	5	0	0	0	1.000	5.63	+2	1
Marisnick, J	Hou	LF	26	22	194	38	1	0	0	1.000	1.81	+8	8
	Hou	CF	74	60	570	160	8	1	1	.994	2.65	+6	9
	Hou	RF	5	3	26	5	0	0	0	1.000	1.73	+1	1
Markakis, N	Atl	1B	1	1	10	10	0	0	0	1.000	-	-1	0
Marrero, D	Bos	2B	6	2	18	2	5	1	1	.875	3.50	0	0
	Bos	3B	4	1	17	0	5	0	0	1.000	2.65	+1	1
	Bos	SS	4	0	7	1	0	0	0	1.000	1.29	0	0
Marte, J	LAA	1B	29	25	205	169	14	2	18	.989	-	0	0
	LAA	3B	22	19	160	10	34	2	2	.957	2.48	+3	1
	LAA	LF	27	22	172	39	2	1	0	.976	2.15	-3	-2
Marte, S	Pit	CF	16	9	96	28	0	0	0	1.000	2.62	-6	-2
Martin, R	Tor	2B	1	0	2	0	1	0	0	1.000	4.50	-1	-1
	Tor	3B	1	0	1	0	1	0	0	1.000	9.00	0	0
Martinez, J	StL	1B	2	0	2	4	0	0	0	1.000	-	0	0
	StL	LF	4	2	22	2	0	0	0	1.000	.82	-2	-1
Martinez, M	TOT	2B	21	7	87	19	18	1	4	.974	3.83	-1	0
	TOT	3B	2	1	14	0	3	2	1	.600	1.93	0	0
	TOT	SS	6	4	36	6	11	1	3	.944	4.25	0	1
	TOT	LF	9	1	29	2	0	0	0	1.000	.62	+1	1
	TOT	CF	11	3	32	5	1	0	1	1.000	1.69	0	0
	TOT	RF	11	6	68	17	1	0	1	1.000	2.38	+2	2
Martinez, V	Det	1B	5	5	44	36	0	0	4	1.000	-	-1	-1
Mastroianni, D	Min	LF	1	0	2	0	0	0	0	-	.00	0	0
	Min	CF	1	1	8	1	0	0	0	1.000	1.13	-1	0
	Min	RF	4	2	19	3	0	0	0	1.000	1.42	+1	0
Mazara, N	Tex	LF	38	33	284	64	1	0	0	1.000	2.06	+2	-2
McBride, M	Oak	1B	1	0	1	2	0	0	0	1.000	-	0	0
	Oak	RF	1	0	1	0	0	0	0	-	.00	0	0
McCann, B	NYY	1B	3	0	5	5	0	0	0	1.000	-	0	0
McGehee, C	Det	1B	1	0	1	3	0	0	0	1.000	-	0	0
	Det	3B	27	23	211	14	35	0	2	1.000	2.09	-2	0
Merrifield, W	KC	1B	1	1	9	9	0	0	1	1.000	-	0	0
	KC	2B	65	55	503	92	156	4	39	.984	4.44	+5	5
	KC	3B	5	3	30	1	8	1	2	.900	2.70	-2	-1
	KC	SS	13	11	91	20	2	0	1	1.000	2.18	+2	3
	KC	RF	4	3	27	8	1	0	1	1.000	3.00	-1	-1
Middlebrooks, W	Mil	3B	8	8	63	6	19	0	3	1.000	3.59	+2	2
Miller, B	TB	1B	39	37	303	277	12	4	17	.986	-	-2	-2
	TB	LF	1	1	6	0	0	1	0	.000	.00	-1	-1
Miller, M	Bos	2B	1	0	1	0	0	0	0	-	.00	0	0
Miller, S	Ari	LF	1	0	1	0	0	0	0	-	.00	0	0
Molina, Y	StL	1B	2	1	7	5	1	0	0	1.000	-	0	0
Moncada, Y	Bos	3B	5	4	35	2	12	1	0	.933	3.60	-1	0
Mondesi, R	KC	2B	42	40	355	75	96	3	23	.983	4.34	+1	-2
	KC	SS	7	0	19	3	5	1	1	.889	3.79	+1	1
Morales, K	KC	1B	7	6	53	46	3	0	4	1.000	-	-1	0
	KC	RF	5	5	37	8	0	0	0	1.000	1.95	-2	-1
Moran, C	Hou	3B	8	6	58	5	13	1	1	.947	2.79	+1	1
Morrison, L	TB	1B	83	78	685	566	42	4	63	.993	-	-2	-4
Morse, M	Pit	1B	1	1	8	5	0	0	1	1.000	-	0	0
Moss, B	StL	1B	64	40	397	401	26	4	49	.991	-	-1	-3
	StL	LF	58	42	355	65	3	0	2	1.000	1.72	0	2
	StL	RF	21	19	152	30	1	0	0	1.000	1.84	+6	1
Motter, T	TB	1B	1	1	8	4	1	0	0	1.000	-	0	0
	TB	2B	6	4	39	6	18	1	4	.960	5.54	-1	-1
	TB	3B	4	3	28	2	11	0	4	1.000	4.18	0	0
	TB	SS	9	7	57	3	15	1	4	.947	2.83	-1	-1
	TB	LF	7	4	38	7	1	0	0	1.000	1.91	0	3
	TB	RF	6	2	30	8	0	0	0	1.000	2.40	+1	0
Moustakas, M	KC	3B	26	26	221	29	40	2	4	.972	2.81	+2	1
Moya, S	Det	LF	8	8	62	11	1	1	0	.923	1.74	+1	-2

Player	Tm	Pos	G	GS	Inn	PO	A	E	DP	Pct.	Rng	BSv	RS
	Det	RF	18	16	131	27	3	2	2	.938	2.06	-7	-4
Muncy, M	Oak	2B	21	19	159	24	51	0	9	1.000	4.25	0	0
	Oak	3B	1	1	9	0	3	1	1	.750	3.00	0	0
	Oak	LF	4	0	9	2	0	0	0	1.000	2.00	-2	-1
	Oak	RF	17	13	108	27	1	0	0	1.000	2.33	+1	1
Murphy, D	Was	1B	21	17	152	134	16	1	14	.993	-	0	0
	Was	3B	1	1	9	1	1	1	0	.667	2.00	-2	-2
Myers, W	SD	3B	1	0	1	0	0	0	0	-	.00	0	0
	SD	LF	3	1	8	3	0	0	0	1.000	3.38	0	0
	SD	RF	7	5	47	12	0	0	0	1.000	2.30	-2	-1
Naquin, T	Cle	RF	4	2	21	0	0	1	0	.000	.00	-1	-1
Nava, D	TOT	1B	6	1	22	17	2	0	2	1.000		0	0
	TOT	LF	37	32	239	58	3	0	0	1.000	2.30	-11	-8
	TOT	RF	2	0	5	4	0	0	0	1.000	7.20	+2	1
Nieuwenhuis, K	Mil	LF	5	2	24	4	0	0	0	1.000	1.50	0	0
	Mil	CF	83	68	590	157	5	0	0	1.000	2.47	0	2
	Mil	RF	28	22	199	29	3	3	1	.914	1.44	-2	-1
Nimmo, B	NYM	LF	13	11	87	21	0	1	0	.955	2.18	0	0
	NYM	CF	4	0	9	1	0	0	0	1.000	1.00	-1	0
	NYM	RF	7	4	43	7	0	0	0	1.000	1.47	+2	1
Noonan, N	SD	2B	2	1	10	1	4	0	0	1.000	4.50	0	0
	SD	SS	5	5	41	10	17	1	4	.964	5.88	-6	-4
Norris, D	SD	1B	3	0	6	7	0	0	0	1.000	-	0	0
Nunez, E	TOT	2B	6	4	33	8	9	2	3	.895	4.64	-3	-3
	TOT	3B	81	72	647	48	134	5	19	.973	2.53	+1	-2
	TOT	SS	55	51	454	58	138	6	33	.970	3.89	-1	-3
OBrien, P'	Ari	1B	1	0	1	0	1	0	0	1.000	-	0	0
	Ari	LF	16	13	106	17	0	1	0	.944	1.44	0	-1
Olivera, H	Atl	LF	5	5	43	7	0	0	0	1.000	1.47	-2	-1
Olson, M	Oak	1B	4	2	20	24	0	0	2	1.000	-	0	0
	Oak	RF	5	4	37	7	0	0	0	1.000	1.70	+1	0
O'Malley, S	Sea	2B	12	3	48	8	13	1	2	.955	3.97	+3	3
	Sea	3B	7	3	31	5	6	0	0	1.000	3.16	-2	-2
	Sea	SS	36	29	274	45	85	2	19	.985	4.26	-1	0
	Sea	LF	15	9	80	14	0	0	0	1.000	1.58	+1	1
	Sea	CF	5	3	34	9	0	0	0	1.000	2.38	-5	-3
	Sea	RF	19	2	44	10	1	0	0	1.000	2.25	+1	2
Orlando, P	KC	LF	37	36	317	77	2	1	1	.988	2.25	+10	5
	KC	RF	89	79	728	158	4	3	1	.982	2.00	+14	5
Ortega, R	LAA	LF	46	37	339	77	6	3	1	.965	2.21	-5	-2
	LAA	CF	10	6	54	12	0	0	0	1.000	2.00	+2	1
	LAA	RF	9	4	46	14	1	0	0	1.000	2.93	+3	1
Ortiz, D	Bos	1B	1	1	5	5	0	0	0	1.000	-	+1	1
Owings, C	Ari	2B	1	0	2	0	1	0	0	1.000	4.50	0	0
	Ari	SS	70	65	586	93	175	8	43	.971	4.12	-7	-3
	Ari	CF	49	47	403	93	4	0	1	1.000	2.17	+5	2
Ozuna, M	Mia	LF	11	11	95	17	0	0	0	1.000	1.60	+3	1
	Mia	RF	9	9	71	17	3	0	0	1.000	2.55	+5	6
Pacheco, J	Cin	1B	3	1	12	7	0	0	0	1.000	-	0	0
	Cin	2B	3	2	17	2	7	0	1	1.000	4.67	+1	0
	Cin	3B	4	4	31	2	4	0	0	1.000	.87	0	0
Pagan, A	SF	CF	4	4	36	12	0	0	0	1.000	3.00	-3	-2
Paredes, J	TOT	2B	2	1	13	1	2	1	0	.750	2.08	0	0
	TOT	3B	2	1	10	3	4	1	0	.875	6.30	-1	-1
	TOT	LF	23	10	103	27	0	0	0	1.000	2.36	-2	0
	TOT	RF	20	15	134	28	2	1	1	.968	2.01	0	2
Park, B	Min	1B	24	24	207	189	17	1	25	.995	-	+5	2
Parker, J	SF	LF	17	11	114	21	1	0	0	1.000	1.74	-1	-1
	SF	CF	1	1	3	1	0	0	0	1.000	2.45	+1	0
	SF	RF	21	15	132	29	0	0	0	1.000	1.98	-5	-4
Parmelee, C	NYY	1B	6	2	22	21	4	0	0	1.000	-	+1	0
Parra, G	Col	1B	19	16	135	120	7	0	11	1.000	-	-5	-3
	Col	LF	60	46	435	78	7	3	0	.966	1.76	-5	-4
	Col	CF	11	11	84	17	0	0	0	1.000	1.83	+1	1
	Col	RF	16	14	122	21	2	2	0	.920	1.70	-4	-5
Patterson, J	Col	1B	2	2	20	22	1	0	0	1.000	-	+1	0
	Col	LF	2	1	7	3	0	0	0	1.000	3.86	+1	0
	Col	RF	5	0	9	1	0	0	0	1.000	1.00	0	0
Patton, S	ChC	LF	1	0	0	0	0	0	0	-	.00	0	0
Paulsen, B	Col	1B	23	18	152	145	5	1	10	.993	-	-4	-4
	Col	LF	7	3	31	8	0	0	0	1.000	2.35	-2	0
Pearce, S	TOT	1B	40	31	278	244	22	3	26	.989	-	+4	2

All Other Fielders

Player	Tm	Pos	G	GS	Inn	PO	A	E	DP	Pct.	Rng	BSv	RS
	TOT	2B	15	14	121	23	40	1	10	.984	4.69	+1	0
	TOT	3B	2	1	13	1	1	0	0	1.000	1.42	0	0
	TOT	LF	7	7	49	10	0	0	0	1.000	1.84	-2	-1
	TOT	RF	6	5	35	2	1	0	0	1.000	.77	-1	-1
Pena, B	StL	1B	1	0	1	2	0	0	0	1.000	-	0	0
Pena, R	SF	2B	17	13	110	16	35	3	8	.944	4.17	-2	-2
	SF	3B	12	5	49	5	11	2	2	.889	2.92	+1	1
	SF	SS	4	2	23	4	7	0	2	1.000	4.30	+1	1
Pennington, C	LAA	1B	3	0	4	2	1	0	1	1.000	-	0	0
	LAA	2B	58	34	335	66	98	1	27	.994	4.41	+4	3
	LAA	3B	1	0	1	1	0	0	0	1.000	9.00	0	0
	LAA	SS	17	10	108	25	34	1	8	.983	4.90	+1	1
Peralta, D	Ari	CF	8	4	52	15	0	0	0	1.000	2.61	+2	1
	Ari	RF	44	36	333	84	0	1	0	1.000	2.27	+8	2
Peralta, J	StL	3B	67	67	570	39	125	4	15	.976	2.59	-8	-7
	StL	SS	7	7	57	11	18	0	6	1.000	4.61	-2	-1
Peraza, J	Cin	2B	12	7	72	15	22	1	6	.974	4.63	-1	1
	Cin	SS	31	29	250	41	66	2	8	.982	3.85	-1	-4
	Cin	LF	8	8	71	13	0	0	0	1.000	1.65	0	-1
	Cin	CF	13	11	97	24	0	0	0	1.000	2.23	-8	-4
Perez, C	LAA	1B	1	0	3	2	0	0	1	1.000	-	0	0
Perez, H	Mil	1B	6	4	39	35	9	0	5	1.000	-	+2	3
	Mil	2B	11	8	71	18	24	2	8	.955	5.32	-1	0
	Mil	3B	60	45	411	29	96	9	9	.933	2.74	+5	1
	Mil	SS	3	1	18	1	5	0	0	1.000	3.00	0	0
	Mil	LF	2	0	3	0	0	0	0	-	.00	0	0
	Mil	CF	8	7	67	14	0	1	0	.933	1.88	-1	-2
	Mil	RF	36	31	261	80	1	1	0	.988	2.79	+7	1
Perez, S	KC	1B	1	0	3	3	0	0	0	1.000	-	0	0
Perez, Y	Mia	2B	1	0	3	2	1	0	0	1.000	9.00	0	0
	Mia	SS	2	0	2	1	1	0	0	1.000	7.71	0	0
Peterson, J	Atl	2B	87	77	694	150	235	11	54	.972	4.99	-10	-6
	Atl	3B	1	1	10	0	0	0	0	-	.00	0	0
	Atl	LF	15	11	98	25	0	2	0	.926	2.30	+1	-2
	Atl	CF	1	1	8	2	0	0	0	1.000	2.25	0	0
Petit, G	LAA	2B	50	26	226	49	66	4	18	.966	4.59	0	1
	LAA	3B	10	4	51	4	13	1	0	.944	3.02	-1	0
	LAA	SS	32	26	224	31	78	3	13	.973	4.39	0	-3
	LAA	LF	6	5	47	19	0	0	0	1.000	3.64	-1	-1
	LAA	RF	1	0	3	0	0	0	0	-	.00	0	0
Pham, T	StL	LF	30	11	124	18	0	0	0	1.000	1.31	+1	-1
	StL	CF	34	25	239	50	2	0	1	1.000	1.96	-7	-3
	StL	RF	5	1	15	3	0	0	0	1.000	1.80	-1	0
Pinder, C	Oak	2B	13	9	80	9	23	3	1	.914	3.60	-3	-2
	Oak	SS	7	3	35	6	10	0	3	1.000	4.11	0	0
Pirela, J	SD	2B	12	9	78	10	16	1	4	.963	3.01	-1	-1
	SD	RF	1	1	6	0	0	0	0	-	.00	0	0
Piscotty, S	StL	1B	1	0	2	1	0	0	0	1.000	-	0	0
	StL	CF	10	9	71	16	1	0	0	1.000	2.15	-2	-1
Plouffe, T	Min	1B	13	13	113	106	10	1	10	.991	-	+2	0
	Min	3B	63	60	519	31	114	6	13	.960	2.51	-7	-4
Polanco, G	Pit	LF	29	24	202	38	1	1	0	.975	1.73	-3	-1
	Pit	CF	5	2	21	5	0	0	0	1.000	2.11	-2	-1
Polanco, J	Min	2B	5	5	43	9	14	1	3	.958	4.81	+1	0
	Min	3B	9	9	77	2	17	3	2	.864	2.22	0	0
	Min	SS	47	45	406	49	128	11	26	.941	3.92	-8	-8
Pollock, A	Ari	CF	12	11	86	31	1	0	0	1.000	3.35	+6	3
Pompey, D	Tor	LF	2	0	2	1	0	0	0	1.000	4.50	0	0
Posey, B	SF	1B	15	11	98	95	8	1	11	.990	-	+1	1
Presley, A	TOT	LF	13	12	111	23	0	1	0	.958	1.86	-2	-1
	TOT	CF	7	1	21	5	0	0	0	1.000	2.14	+1	0
	TOT	RF	13	13	100	32	1	0	0	1.000	2.96	-2	-1
Profar, J	Tex	1B	17	13	101	111	10	0	12	1.000	-	+1	-1
	Tex	2B	19	15	139	35	55	2	14	.978	5.83	+2	1
	Tex	3B	25	16	156	9	33	4	1	.913	2.42	-2	-1
	Tex	SS	11	10	90	11	26	1	9	.974	3.71	+1	1
	Tex	LF	14	8	75	11	1	0	0	1.000	1.44	+2	2
Puig, Y	LAD	LF	5	2	27	6	0	1	0	.857	2.00	+2	1
	LAD	CF	4	2	22	6	0	0	0	1.000	2.49	+3	1
	LAD	RF	90	77	696	160	6	3	0	.982	2.15	+6	5
Pujols, A	LAA	1B	28	28	234	200	16	2	20	.991	-	-5	-4
Querecuto, J	TB	2B	2	2	16	2	2	0	0	1.000	2.25	0	0

Player	Tm	Pos	G	GS	Inn	PO	A	E	DP	Pct.	Rng	BSv	RS
	TB	3B	1	1	9	1	1	0	0	1.000	2.00	0	0
	TB	SS	1	0	2	0	0	0	0	-	.00	0	0
Quinn, R	Phi	LF	12	8	80	18	0	0	0	1.000	2.02	+1	0
	Phi	CF	3	3	23	8	1	0	0	1.000	3.52	0	1
	Phi	RF	4	3	22	7	0	1	0	.875	2.91	0	0
Raburn, R	Col	1B	5	3	23	14	5	1	2	.950	-	-1	-2
	Col	LF	47	44	311	51	1	2	1	.963	1.51	+3	0
	Col	RF	2	1	10	1	0	0	0	1.000	.90	+1	0
Ramirez, A	TOT	2B	1	1	8	1	1	0	0	1.000	2.25	+1	0
	TOT	RF	3	3	22	3	0	0	0	1.000	1.23	0	-1
Ramirez, J	Cle	2B	9	3	38	5	10	1	1	.938	3.58	+2	0
	Cle	SS	5	3	28	5	6	0	2	1.000	3.54	+1	0
	Cle	LF	48	47	375	72	1	1	0	.986	1.75	-1	-2
Rasmus, C	Hou	LF	87	75	672	122	11	0	1	1.000	1.78	+4	14
	Hou	CF	21	14	125	33	0	0	0	1.000	2.45	+1	3
	Hou	RF	11	6	72	18	1	0	1	1.000	2.38	+4	3
Reed, A	Hou	1B	35	27	232	214	13	2	20	.991	-	0	0
Reed, M	Mil	LF	2	2	17	6	0	0	0	1.000	3.18	0	0
	Mil	CF	5	5	40	12	1	1	0	.929	2.93	+4	0
Refsnyder, R	NYY	1B	25	21	175	166	5	3	11	.983	-	-2	0
	NYY	2B	8	5	41	5	9	2	2	.875	3.07	-3	-2
	NYY	3B	1	0	1	0	0	0	0	-	.00	0	0
	NYY	LF	5	4	26	6	0	0	0	1.000	2.08	+1	0
	NYY	RF	23	14	133	22	3	0	0	1.000	1.70	+1	4
Reimold, N	Bal	LF	62	41	371	76	3	0	1	1.000	1.92	-2	0
	Bal	CF	8	4	48	9	0	1	0	.900	1.69	0	0
	Bal	RF	32	12	133	32	0	0	0	1.000	2.17	+2	0
Renda, T	Cin	2B	9	5	50	8	19	1	4	.964	4.86	+1	2
	Cin	3B	1	1	8	0	3	0	0	1.000	3.38	0	0
	Cin	LF	4	3	23	7	0	0	0	1.000	2.70	-2	-1
	Cin	RF	4	4	29	8	0	0	0	1.000	2.51	0	0
Renfroe, H	SD	RF	9	8	74	14	1	2	0	.882	1.83	-2	-1
Revere, B	Was	LF	25	14	134	29	0	1	0	.967	1.95	+2	0
	Was	CF	74	66	580	141	2	1	1	.993	2.22	+2	3
Reyes, J	NYM	3B	50	50	427	26	83	6	6	.948	2.30	-4	-6
	NYM	SS	13	10	100	9	26	0	5	1.000	3.15	-2	-1
Reynolds, M	Col	2B	1	0	1	0	0	0	0	-	.00	0	0
Reynolds, M	NYM	2B	4	2	18	1	3	0	0	1.000	2.00	0	0
	NYM	3B	7	1	17	2	5	0	0	1.000	3.78	0	0
	NYM	SS	21	16	149	23	47	2	13	.972	4.22	-1	-1
	NYM	LF	1	1	6	2	0	0	0	1.000	3.00	-1	0
Rickard, J	Bal	LF	31	27	240	56	4	0	0	1.000	2.25	-4	-3
	Bal	CF	13	6	60	10	0	0	0	1.000	1.50	0	0
	Bal	RF	51	31	293	61	2	0	0	1.000	1.94	-8	-5
Rivera, R	NYM	1B	1	0	1	1	1	0	0	1.000	-	0	0
Rivera, T	NYM	1B	1	0	3	2	1	0	0	1.000	-	0	0
	NYM	2B	26	18	171	30	48	0	12	1.000	4.11	-3	-1
	NYM	3B	9	5	49	4	7	3	1	.786	2.02	-1	-1
Rivera, Y	Mil	2B	13	8	70	21	29	2	7	.962	6.43	+2	1
	Mil	3B	15	4	56	5	10	3	2	.833	2.41	0	0
	Mil	SS	5	4	36	7	11	0	2	1.000	4.50	0	1
Rizzo, A	ChC	2B	1	0	0	0	1	0	0	1.000	27.00	0	0
Robertson, D	Sea	LF	6	4	36	7	0	1	0	.875	1.73	-2	-1
	Sea	CF	1	1	7	1	0	0	0	1.000	1.29	+1	0
	Sea	RF	3	1	10	3	0	0	0	1.000	2.70	0	0
Robinson, C	Was	1B	46	37	339	279	12	2	30	.993	-	-2	-1
	Was	LF	3	2	18	6	0	0	0	1.000	3.00	0	0
Robinson, S	LAA	LF	34	16	170	56	2	1	0	.983	3.08	+6	4
	LAA	CF	19	8	83	18	0	0	0	1.000	1.95	-1	1
	LAA	RF	5	4	32	13	0	0	0	1.000	3.66	+3	1
Rodriguez, A	NYY	3B	1	0	0	0	0	0	0	-	.00	0	0
Rodriguez, S	Pit	1B	57	5	174	176	14	1	17	.995	-	0	0
	Pit	2B	29	18	166	45	60	0	17	1.000	5.70	+2	3
	Pit	3B	11	6	61	3	13	1	1	.941	2.35	-2	-2
	Pit	SS	27	19	178	23	46	4	11	.945	3.50	-1	0
	Pit	LF	10	3	38	5	0	0	0	1.000	1.17	0	0
	Pit	CF	5	0	12	1	0	0	0	1.000	.75	0	0
	Pit	RF	17	13	102	24	0	1	0	.960	2.12	+1	1
Rogers, J	Pit	1B	5	3	18	20	0	0	3	1.000	-	0	0
	Pit	3B	4	0	11	1	1	0	0	1.000	1.59	0	0
Rojas, M	Mia	1B	41	3	104	85	12	0	9	1.000	-	+1	0
	Mia	2B	45	14	171	25	44	0	5	1.000	3.64	+1	2

Player	Tm	Pos	G	GS	Inn	PO	A	E	DP	Pct.	Rng	BSv	RS
	Mia	3B	16	1	43	1	10	0	1	1.000	2.30	+2	1
	Mia	SS	33	26	209	46	76	4	18	.968	5.26	-4	-4
Rollins, J	CWS	SS	35	34	299	47	86	2	18	.985	4.00	-3	-3
Romero, S	Sea	1B	1	1	6	3	0	0	0	1.000	-	0	0
	Sea	LF	6	3	29	6	1	1	0	.875	2.17	-1	-2
	Sea	RF	2	0	6	2	0	0	0	1.000	3.00	0	0
Romine, A	Det	1B	20	3	54	60	1	0	5	1.000	-	-1	-1
	Det	2B	12	7	64	16	16	0	6	1.000	4.50	+1	0
	Det	3B	44	10	136	7	35	1	1	.977	2.78	+1	1
	Det	SS	14	12	101	12	32	1	4	.978	3.92	-1	-2
	Det	LF	1	0	1	0	0	0	0	-	.00	0	0
	Det	CF	22	13	131	34	0	0	0	1.000	2.34	0	0
	Det	RF	2	0	4	1	1	0	1	1.000	4.15	0	1
Romine, A	NYY	1B	6	2	26	18	1	0	1	1.000	-	0	0
Rondon, J	SD	SS	7	7	63	9	24	2	6	.943	4.71	-6	-6
Rosales, A	SD	1B	1	0	1	0	0	0	0	-	-	0	0
	SD	2B	36	22	199	36	53	4	16	.957	4.02	+2	2
	SD	3B	41	24	253	12	62	4	7	.949	2.63	0	1
	SD	SS	15	6	71	6	31	0	4	1.000	4.69	0	-1
	SD	LF	2	1	9	2	0	0	0	1.000	2.00	+1	1
	SD	RF	1	0	1	0	0	0	0	-	.00	0	0
Rosario, A	StL	3B	1	0	1	0	1	0	0	1.000	9.00	0	0
Rosario, E	Min	LF	57	51	461	96	4	1	0	.990	1.95	-1	0
	Min	CF	37	30	292	79	6	3	0	.966	2.62	-2	2
	Min	RF	1	0	2	1	0	0	0	1.000	4.50	0	0
Rua, R	Tex	1B	31	20	169	152	4	1	12	.994	-	-1	-2
	Tex	3B	2	0	5	0	2	0	0	1.000	3.60	0	0
	Tex	LF	60	42	373	74	4	1	2	.987	1.88	+7	2
	Tex	CF	4	1	14	4	0	0	0	1.000	2.57	+2	1
	Tex	RF	3	3	24	7	0	0	0	1.000	2.63	0	0
Ruf, D	Phi	1B	14	6	63	62	4	0	8	1.000	-	-3	-2
	Phi	LF	13	11	86	16	0	1	0	.941	1.67	0	0
Ruggiano, J	TOT	LF	1	1	9	4	0	0	0	1.000	4.00	+1	1
	TOT	CF	6	6	42	15	0	1	0	.938	3.21	-2	-1
	TOT	RF	1	0	1	0	0	0	0	-	.00	0	0
Ruiz, R	Atl	3B	2	1	12	0	5	0	0	1.000	3.75	0	0
Rutledge, J	Bos	2B	5	2	23	6	7	0	3	1.000	5.09	0	0
	Bos	3B	17	10	97	2	20	2	2	.917	2.04	+1	1
	Bos	SS	1	0	1	0	0	0	0	-	.00	0	0
Ryan, B	LAA	SS	16	3	44	9	13	0	2	1.000	4.47	+1	1
	LAA	LF	1	0	1	1	0	0	0	1.000	9.00	0	0
Saladino, T	CWS	1B	2	0	2	3	0	0	0	1.000	-	0	0
	CWS	2B	41	39	345	60	111	1	28	.994	4.47	+1	1
	CWS	3B	10	10	88	4	22	3	4	.897	2.65	-1	-1
	CWS	SS	32	28	259	39	89	4	19	.970	4.45	-1	2
	CWS	LF	1	0	3	3	0	0	0	1.000	9.00	0	0
	CWS	CF	1	0	0	0	0	0	0	-	.00	0	0
	CWS	RF	1	0	1	0	1	0	0	1.000	13.50	0	1
Saltalamacchia, J	Det	1B	11	6	64	53	3	2	4	.966	-	0	-2
Sanchez, C	CWS	2B	33	31	284	50	75	3	14	.977	3.96	+6	3
	CWS	3B	6	3	38	2	6	0	1	1.000	1.89	0	0
	CWS	SS	4	3	29	4	9	0	4	1.000	4.03	-2	-2
Sandoval, P	Bos	3B	2	1	11	1	3	1	0	.800	3.27	-1	-1
Sands, J	CWS	1B	4	3	28	27	4	0	2	1.000	-	+1	1
	CWS	CF	3	0	9	0	0	0	0	-	.00	-1	0
	CWS	RF	1	0	1	0	0	0	0	-	.00	0	0
Sano, M	Min	3B	42	42	376	35	94	15	10	.896	3.09	-2	-2
	Min	RF	38	37	313	75	0	3	0	.962	2.16	-13	-8
Santana, C	Cle	1B	64	62	557	513	53	5	48	.991	-	+3	1
Santana, D	Min	2B	3	0	9	0	0	0	0	-	.00	-1	-1
	Min	3B	1	1	10	1	4	1	0	.833	4.50	+1	1
	Min	SS	3	2	24	6	8	0	1	1.000	5.25	+1	1
	Min	LF	17	15	127	24	1	2	0	.926	1.77	-2	-1
	Min	CF	40	39	324	105	1	1	1	.991	2.94	-12	-7
	Min	RF	6	5	42	7	0	0	0	1.000	1.50	-1	-1
Santana, D	Mil	LF	4	3	27	1	0	0	0	1.000	.33	-1	-1
	Mil	CF	3	2	21	1	0	0	0	1.000	.43	-2	-1
	Mil	RF	62	57	514	104	2	2	0	.981	1.86	-15	-8
Sardinas, L	TOT	1B	3	0	7	5	1	0	2	1.000	-	0	0
	TOT	2B	4	2	19	7	7	0	2	1.000	6.63	0	0
	TOT	3B	3	3	26	0	7	0	0	1.000	2.42	-1	-1
	TOT	SS	50	47	393	58	125	7	32	.963	4.19	-4	-5
Saunders, M	TOT	LF	1	1	9	0	0	0	0	-	.00	-1	0
	Tor	CF	1	0	1	0	0	0	0	-	.00	0	0
	Tor	RF	22	22	172	35	0	0	0	1.000	1.83	-7	-5
Schafer, L	Min	LF	12	10	93	17	0	0	0	1.000	1.64	-1	0
	Min	CF	3	3	22	8	1	0	0	1.000	3.68	+3	2
	Min	RF	8	6	52	13	1	0	0	1.000	2.42	-2	-2
Schebler, S	Cin	LF	13	9	86	17	0	1	0	.944	1.79	-6	-2
	Cin	CF	18	17	133	30	1	1	0	.969	2.10	-4	-4
	Cin	RF	41	39	336	89	4	1	0	.989	2.49	-3	-4
Schimpf, R	SD	2B	68	66	581	106	193	6	50	.980	4.63	-7	-9
	SD	3B	14	12	109	6	28	0	2	1.000	2.82	+4	3
	SD	LF	1	1	8	2	0	0	0	1.000	2.25	0	0
Schwarber, K	ChC	LF	2	2	8	1	0	0	0	1.000	1.17	-1	0
Scruggs, X	Mia	1B	19	17	128	129	8	0	13	1.000	-	+3	2
	Mia	LF	2	1	11	2	0	0	0	1.000	1.64	-2	-1
Segedin, R	LAD	1B	9	3	31	27	1	1	3	.966	-	-3	-2
	LAD	3B	6	5	42	4	8	0	0	1.000	2.59	-1	-1
	LAD	LF	7	3	23	8	0	0	0	1.000	3.09	+3	1
	LAD	RF	7	6	44	11	0	0	0	1.000	2.25	-1	1
Segura, J	Ari	SS	23	17	144	22	46	1	12	.986	4.24	0	0
Selsky, S	Cin	LF	3	1	16	8	0	0	0	1.000	4.60	+1	1
	Cin	CF	2	2	11	4	0	0	0	1.000	3.27	-1	0
	Cin	RF	11	6	66	17	1	0	0	1.000	2.44	-2	-1
Shaffer, R	TB	1B	11	8	77	64	7	1	6	.986	-	0	0
	TB	3B	4	1	15	4	0	0	0	1.000	2.45	+1	1
	TB	RF	2	1	7	1	0	0	0	1.000	1.29	0	0
Shaw, T	Bos	1B	50	28	290	251	19	0	27	1.000	-	+6	4
	Bos	LF	1	0	3	1	0	0	0	1.000	3.00	0	0
Shuck, J	CWS	LF	3	2	19	6	1	0	0	1.000	3.32	+1	1
	CWS	CF	60	52	485	122	3	2	0	.984	2.32	-19	-13
	CWS	RF	2	2	17	1	0	0	0	1.000	.53	0	0
Smith, M	Atl	LF	22	17	162	27	2	0	0	1.000	1.61	+1	2
	Atl	CF	35	32	280	95	3	1	0	.990	3.15	+10	5
	Atl	RF	1	1	9	0	0	0	0	-	.00	0	0
Smith, S	Sea	LF	35	30	258	49	3	1	0	.981	1.82	-10	-8
	Sea	RF	74	61	472	106	4	0	1	1.000	2.10	-1	1
Smoak, J	Tor	1B	111	79	738	753	38	3	69	.996	-	-4	-5
Smolinski, J	Oak	LF	18	11	111	24	0	0	0	1.000	1.94	+2	1
	Oak	CF	49	48	420	117	3	1	1	.992	2.57	-1	-2
	Oak	RF	29	18	183	40	0	0	0	1.000	1.97	+1	-2
Snyder, B	Atl	1B	1	0	4	1	2	0	0	1.000	-	+1	0
	Atl	3B	2	2	16	5	2	1	0	.875	3.94	0	0
	Atl	LF	1	1	4	0	0	0	0	-	.00	0	0
Solano, D	NYY	2B	6	5	41	12	13	0	3	1.000	5.49	+1	1
	NYY	3B	2	1	13	0	0	1	0	.000	.00	-1	-1
Solarte, Y	SD	1B	2	1	18	23	1	0	5	1.000	-	0	0
	SD	2B	15	12	97	20	34	2	8	.964	5.01	0	0
Soler, J	ChC	LF	53	51	371	65	1	0	0	1.000	1.60	0	-5
	ChC	RF	7	5	41	4	0	1	0	.800	.88	0	0
Soto, G	LAA	1B	1	0	3	2	1	1	0	.750	-	0	0
	LAA	3B	1	0	1	0	1	0	0	1.000	9.00	0	0
Souza Jr., S	TB	CF	3	2	15	6	0	1	0	.857	3.60	-2	-1
Spangenberg, C	SD	2B	13	13	108	22	35	5	12	.919	4.75	+1	2
Springer, G	Hou	CF	1	1	8	4	0	0	0	1.000	4.50	+3	1
Stewart, C	Pit	1B	1	0	1	0	1	0	0	1.000	-	0	0
Strop, P	ChC	LF	1	0	1	0	0	0	0	-	.00	0	0
Stubbs, D	TOT	LF	19	4	64	9	0	0	0	1.000	1.27	-1	-2
	TOT	CF	15	7	84	20	0	0	0	1.000	2.14	-4	-3
	TOT	RF	19	9	86	16	0	1	0	.941	1.67	-3	-2
Suarez, E	Cin	SS	2	1	10	3	3	0	1	1.000	5.40	0	0
Suzuki, I	Mia	LF	14	11	103	20	4	0	1	1.000	2.09	+2	5
	Mia	CF	14	10	105	24	2	0	0	1.000	2.23	+2	0
	Mia	RF	54	38	367	81	0	1	0	.988	1.99	+6	0
Swanson, D	Atl	SS	37	36	313	44	79	6	17	.953	3.54	-1	0
Swihart, B	Bos	LF	13	13	114	30	1	0	0	1.000	2.45	+2	1
Szczur, M	ChC	LF	50	14	201	33	0	0	0	1.000	1.48	+5	2
	ChC	CF	15	6	67	29	0	0	0	1.000	3.88	+5	1
	ChC	RF	15	9	85	21	0	0	0	1.000	2.21	+1	0
Tapia, R	Col	LF	2	1	10	0	0	0	0	-	.00	-1	0
	Col	CF	9	5	52	14	0	0	0	1.000	2.42	+3	1
	Col	RF	1	0	1	0	0	0	0	-	.00	0	0
Taylor, C	TOT	2B	7	5	39	9	12	1	3	.955	4.81	-1	-1

All Other Fielders

Player	Tm	Pos	G	GS	Inn	PO	A	E	DP	Pct.	Rng	BSv	RS
	TOT	3B	10	2	28	2	5	0	0	1.000	2.25	0	0
	TOT	SS	6	5	46	9	10	2	0	.905	3.72	0	0
Taylor, M	Was	LF	1	1	6	1	0	0	0	1.000	1.50	+1	1
	Was	CF	64	46	438	121	5	1	0	.992	2.59	-10	-4
	Was	RF	5	1	15	3	0	0	0	1.000	1.80	+1	1
Tejada, R	TOT	2B	4	0	9	2	2	0	2	1.000	4.15	0	0
	TOT	3B	23	13	128	7	33	4	4	.909	2.81	+1	1
	TOT	SS	7	4	37	1	14	2	2	.882	3.62	-1	0
Thompson, T	LAD	LF	24	13	110	16	0	0	0	1.000	1.07	-7	-4
	LAD	CF	32	26	229	54	0	0	0	1.000	2.12	+8	2
	LAD	RF	28	22	193	26	2	2	0	.933	1.31	+4	3
Tilson, C	CWS	CF	1	1	4	1	0	0	0	1.000	2.08	0	0
Toles, A	LAD	LF	18	13	110	26	3	1	0	.967	2.37	+10	8
	LAD	CF	9	3	36	8	0	0	0	1.000	2.02	+2	0
	LAD	RF	8	7	59	21	0	1	0	.955	3.22	-6	-3
Tomas, Y	Ari	1B	1	0	2	2	0	0	0	1.000	-	0	0
	Ari	LF	60	51	467	67	3	3	0	.959	1.35	-6	-8
	Ari	RF	91	80	697	125	4	4	2	.970	1.67	-4	-8
Tomlinson, K	SF	2B	19	17	141	21	43	1	9	.985	4.08	+1	1
	SF	3B	3	1	13	1	3	0	0	1.000	2.77	0	0
	SF	SS	7	4	40	2	9	2	2	.846	2.48	-2	-1
	SF	LF	3	2	20	5	1	0	0	1.000	2.70	+2	2
Torreyes, R	NYY	2B	14	9	79	14	15	0	9	1.000	3.29	-3	-1
	NYY	3B	34	27	245	12	76	2	9	.978	3.23	+2	1
	NYY	SS	15	11	99	12	22	1	1	.971	3.09	0	-1
	NYY	RF	2	0	4	1	0	0	0	1.000	2.25	0	0
Trumbo, M	Bal	1B	6	4	37	30	2	0	4	1.000	-	0	0
	Bal	LF	1	1	8	3	0	1	0	.750	3.38	-3	-2
Tucker, P	Hou	LF	19	13	130	19	0	1	0	.950	1.32	-3	-3
	Hou	RF	3	1	14	4	0	0	0	1.000	2.57	-1	-1
Turner, J	LAD	1B	1	0	1	1	0	0	0	1.000	-	0	0
Turner, T	Was	2B	30	25	234	52	71	1	19	.992	4.73	+4	2
	Was	SS	2	0	6	3	5	0	2	1.000	12.00	0	0
	Was	CF	45	44	388	99	1	2	0	.980	2.32	-6	-2
Upton, J	Det	CF	6	6	41	14	0	0	0	1.000	3.07	-3	-1
Upton Jr., M	TOT	CF	27	25	211	57	1	0	1	1.000	2.47	+1	0
	TOT	RF	3	3	26	6	0	0	0	1.000	2.08	+1	0
Uribe, J	Cle	3B	68	68	552	43	128	7	12	.961	2.79	+2	1
Utley, C	LAD	3B	1	0	2	0	0	0	0	-	.00	0	0
Valaika, P	Col	2B	5	2	20	3	5	0	0	1.000	3.60	0	0
	Col	3B	6	0	12	1	1	1	0	.667	1.50	-2	0
	Col	SS	2	0	7	1	1	0	0	1.000	2.70	0	0
Valbuena, L	Hou	1B	8	7	60	61	6	0	4	1.000	-	+2	2
	Hou	2B	1	0	2	0	0	0	0	-	.00	0	0
	Hou	3B	81	77	683	54	143	6	17	.970	2.60	-2	-1
Valencia, D	Oak	1B	18	15	131	134	9	1	8	.993	-	+1	1
	Oak	3B	68	67	583	41	122	13	9	.926	2.52	-23	-18
	Oak	LF	1	1	8	2	0	0	0	1.000	2.25	-2	-1
	Oak	RF	37	36	298	65	6	0	1	1.000	2.14	-5	0
Van Slyke, S	LAD	1B	7	4	36	40	4	1	2	.978	-	+1	1
	LAD	LF	19	9	88	18	0	1	0	.947	1.84	+6	2
	LAD	CF	1	1	9	3	0	0	0	1.000	3.00	+1	1
	LAD	RF	10	8	74	15	0	0	0	1.000	1.82	-1	-1
Vargas, K	Min	1B	32	28	251	240	14	1	27	.996	-	-2	-1
Venable, W	LAD	LF	1	1	6	1	0	0	0	1.000	1.50	0	0
	LAD	RF	4	2	22	5	0	0	0	1.000	2.05	0	0
Villar, J	Mil	2B	11	8	69	16	22	0	5	1.000	4.96	-1	-1
	Mil	3B	42	40	347	30	59	12	3	.881	2.31	-4	-4
Vogelbach, D	Sea	1B	4	3	25	20	1	0	3	1.000	-	0	-1
Vogt, S	Oak	1B	1	0	2	1	0	0	0	1.000	-	0	0
Waldrop, K	Cin	LF	2	1	9	2	0	0	0	1.000	1.93	0	0
	Cin	RF	2	1	8	2	0	0	0	1.000	2.25	0	0
Wallace, B	SD	1B	20	13	121	127	7	1	11	.993	-	0	0
	SD	3B	42	33	266	18	36	5	4	.915	1.82	-6	-5
Walsh, C	Mil	2B	1	0	1	1	0	0	0	1.000	9.00	0	0
	Mil	3B	11	9	64	6	17	1	2	.958	3.22	0	0
	Mil	LF	2	0	2	0	0	0	0	-	.00	-1	-1
Walters, Z	LAD	1B	1	0	1	1	0	0	0	1.000	-	0	0
	LAD	LF	1	0	1	0	0	0	0	-	.00	0	0
	LAD	RF	1	1	7	1	0	0	0	1.000	1.29	0	0
Weeks, J	SD	2B	17	17	138	36	48	1	10	.988	5.47	+4	4
	SD	3B	1	0	1	0	0	0	0	-	.00	0	0

Player	Tm	Pos	G	GS	Inn	PO	A	E	DP	Pct.	Rng	BSv	RS
Weeks Jr., R	Ari	LF	36	25	206	36	2	3	0	.927	1.66	-7	-7
	Ari	RF	2	1	9	0	0	0	0	-	.00	-1	0
Wendle, J	Oak	2B	28	24	211	45	71	2	20	.983	4.96	+2	1
Werth, J	Was	RF	2	2	18	4	0	0	0	1.000	2.00	0	0
White, T	Hou	1B	58	50	452	410	25	4	32	.991	-	+3	2
	Hou	2B	2	1	11	1	1	0	0	1.000	1.64	0	-1
	Hou	3B	3	0	5	0	0	0	0	-	.00	0	0
Wilkins, A	Mil	1B	3	1	10	11	0	1	1	.917	-	-1	-1
	Mil	RF	1	0	2	0	0	0	0	-	.00	0	0
Williams, M	NYY	LF	2	1	10	5	0	0	0	1.000	4.50	0	0
	NYY	CF	2	2	17	3	0	0	0	1.000	1.59	-1	-1
	NYY	RF	7	4	43	10	0	0	0	1.000	2.09	+1	0
Williamson, M	SF	LF	3	1	19	22	1	1	0	.958	2.67	+4	3
	SF	RF	23	19	164	40	0	1	0	.976	2.20	+4	1
Wolters, T	Col	2B	7	0	9	0	8	0	0	1.000	7.71	+1	1
	Col	SS	3	0	6	0	2	1	1	.667	3.00	0	-1
Wong, K	StL	2B	88	71	635	132	256	8	67	.980	5.50	+8	5
	StL	LF	6	3	35	7	0	0	0	1.000	1.80	-3	-1
	StL	CF	8	7	62	16	0	0	0	1.000	2.32	+2	0
	StL	RF	4	0	9	3	0	0	0	1.000	3.00	0	0
Wood, T	ChC	LF	3	0	5	1	0	0	0	1.000	1.80	+1	0
Worth, D	Hou	2B	6	4	39	5	13	0	4	1.000	4.15	+1	1
	Hou	3B	5	3	39	4	7	1	0	.917	2.54	0	0
	Hou	SS	2	0	3	0	3	0	1	1.000	9.00	+1	0
Wright, D	NYM	3B	36	36	317	23	58	4	5	.953	2.30	-12	-8
Yelich, C	Mia	CF	31	29	258	68	1	3	0	.958	2.41	-1	0
Ynoa, R	Col	LF	2	0	8	1	0	1	0	.500	1.13	-1	-1
Young, C	Bos	LF	63	48	446	87	0	0	0	1.000	1.76	-7	-3
	Bos	CF	3	3	25	12	0	0	0	1.000	4.32	-1	0
	Bos	RF	3	2	20	4	0	0	0	1.000	1.80	+2	1
Young, E	NYY	CF	2	0	5	3	0	0	0	1.000	5.40	0	0
Zobrist, B	ChC	1B	1	0	0	1	0	0	0	1.000	-	0	0
	ChC	SS	1	0	2	0	0	0	0	-	.00	0	0
	ChC	LF	27	11	128	16	0	0	0	1.000	1.13	0	0
	ChC	RF	24	18	159	27	1	0	0	1.000	1.59	0	0

All Other Catchers

Player	Tm	G	GS	Inn	PO	A	E	DP	PB	Pct.	SBA	CS	PCS	CS%	CERA	GFP/DME	SB	SZ	Other	Total
Alfaro, Jorge	Phi	4	4	31.0	27	0	0	0	1	1.000	0	0	1	-	7.55	-1	0	0	0	-1
Avila, Alex	CWS	54	52	453.0	414	21	2	3	4	.995	32	7	0	.22	4.15	0	1	0	-2	-1
Bandy, Jett	LAA	68	60	520.0	412	39	3	4	2	.993	46	17	2	.37	4.53	1	3	-1	-1	2
Barnes, Austin	LAD	9	5	50.0	47	1	0	0	0	1.000	2	0	0	.00	6.30	0	0	0	0	0
Bethancourt, Christian	SD	41	35	322.2	248	32	2	3	5	.993	22	6	0	.27	4.55	-2	1	1	2	2
Brown, Trevor	SF	60	40	390.2	316	26	2	0	4	.994	31	7	0	.23	4.19	-2	0	-3	0	-5
Butera, Drew	KC	51	34	325.1	288	16	6	1	1	.981	19	4	1	.21	4.37	-2	-2	-1	0	-5
Cabrera, Ramon	Cin	48	42	387.1	333	17	4	2	2	.989	34	3	5	.09	4.69	0	-1	-8	1	-8
Casali, Curt	TB	76	62	560.1	538	37	4	4	4	.993	36	11	3	.31	4.10	3	1	5	2	11
Centeno, Juan	Min	53	47	438.2	321	34	6	3	5	.983	21	3	0	.14	4.74	0	-1	-5	1	-5
Chirinos, Robinson	Tex	54	46	399.0	287	23	1	2	3	.997	28	6	2	.21	4.89	4	-1	-3	-1	-1
Clevenger, Steve	Sea	20	20	169.0	152	11	2	0	1	.988	15	4	1	.27	4.37	1	-2	-1	0	-2
Conger, Hank	TB	47	38	325.0	300	16	3	1	2	.991	40	5	3	.13	4.98	0	-2	2	-2	-2
Contreras, Willson	ChC	57	41	389.2	389	31	6	0	6	.986	34	12	1	.35	4.02	0	4	0	-3	1
Cruz, Tony	KC	4	0	9.0	9	0	0	0	1	1.000	0	0	0	-	7.00	0	0	0	0	0
Diaz, Elias	Pit	1	1	9.0	7	4	0	0	0	1.000	0	0	1	-	3.00	0	0	0	0	0
Ellis, A.J.	TOT	57	50	450.1	447	33	1	3	3	.998	37	7	4	.19	3.38	0	-1	-3	1	-3
Federowicz, Tim	ChC	12	7	63.0	42	7	1	1	0	.980	3	0	0	.00	2.86	-1	-1	0	-1	-3
Fryer, Eric	TOT	54	31	306.1	274	19	3	1	3	.990	28	7	0	.25	4.44	0	2	-3	0	-1
Garneau, Dustin	Col	23	18	168.0	134	11	1	0	0	.993	15	5	1	.33	4.98	0	1	0	0	1
Gattis, Evan	Hou	55	49	445.1	448	34	2	4	5	.996	27	12	1	.44	3.44	-5	3	2	4	4
Gimenez, Chris	Cle	59	42	389.2	355	26	3	2	5	.992	21	4	2	.19	3.88	-1	-2	-2	1	-4
Gomes, Yan	Cle	73	65	582.1	539	32	3	3	4	.995	29	10	1	.34	3.63	-1	2	-3	2	0
Gosewisch, Tuffy	Ari	31	27	234.0	241	20	1	1	3	.996	16	4	0	.25	6.35	-1	0	0	-1	-2
Graterol, Juan	LAA	9	4	42.0	31	3	0	0	0	1.000	5	1	0	.20	1.71	1	0	0	0	1
Hanigan, Ryan	Bos	34	30	264.0	258	26	0	3	18	1.000	25	7	0	.28	3.55	-2	0	-2	1	-3
Hedges, Austin	SD	7	7	61.2	47	2	1	1	0	.980	4	2	0	.50	2.92	0	0	0	-1	-1
Hernandez, Oscar	Ari	4	3	29.0	25	0	0	0	1	1.000	0	0	0	-	3.41	0	0	0	0	0
Herrmann, Chris	Ari	31	29	263.1	226	19	1	0	3	.996	17	6	1	.35	4.34	1	1	-1	0	1
Holaday, Bryan	TOT	40	35	314.2	219	19	1	5	1	.996	19	6	2	.32	4.12	2	1	0	-1	2
Joseph, Caleb	Bal	48	40	355.1	322	24	2	4	2	.994	32	10	0	.31	4.28	0	0	2	0	2
Kelly, Carson	StL	10	2	36.0	30	2	0	0	0	1.000	0	0	0	-	5.25	0	0	0	0	0
Kratz, Erik	TOT	30	24	222.0	173	15	2	1	2	.989	16	7	1	.44	4.18	0	2	0	0	2
Lobaton, Jose	Was	38	32	277.2	293	16	1	1	6	.997	25	7	0	.28	3.57	1	0	1	0	2
Lopez, Raffy	Cin	4	1	10.0	8	1	0	0	0	1.000	1	0	0	.00	4.50	0	0	0	0	0
Maile, Luke	TB	37	34	301.0	278	27	3	1	4	.990	25	7	0	.28	3.14	0	1	2	2	5
Maldonado, Martin	Mil	69	63	559.0	486	39	7	3	3	.987	46	16	4	.35	3.94	2	3	2	0	7
Mathis, Jeff	Mia	38	36	310.0	304	32	3	3	1	.991	32	9	1	.28	3.28	1	0	5	2	8
Maxwell, Bruce	Oak	29	25	215.0	178	9	1	1	0	.995	8	0	0	.00	4.27	0	-1	-1	1	-1
McBride, Matt	Oak	16	11	97.1	81	5	0	0	3	1.000	8	0	1	.00	5.55	0	-1	0	0	-1
Mesoraco, Devin	Cin	13	13	113.0	92	6	1	1	2	.990	11	3	0	.27	4.62	0	1	-2	1	0
Montero, Miguel	ChC	71	64	558.1	550	37	7	2	4	.988	64	5	2	.08	3.19	-3	-6	8	0	-1
Moore, Adam	Cle	9	1	21.1	21	2	1	1	0	.958	4	2	0	.50	9.70	0	0	0	0	0
Murphy, John Ryan	Min	25	23	207.1	187	12	1	0	3	.995	12	4	1	.33	4.12	-2	1	-1	1	-1
Murphy, Tom	Col	12	9	81.2	89	7	2	1	2	.980	10	4	0	.40	5.40	-1	2	0	0	1
Narvaez, Omar	CWS	34	30	269.0	253	11	2	0	1	.992	24	1	1	.04	3.71	-1	-2	0	1	-2
Nicholas, Brett	Tex	15	10	103.0	96	5	0	2	2	1.000	4	1	1	.25	2.88	-2	0	1	0	-1
Pena, Brayan	StL	3	2	19.0	13	1	1	0	1	.933	4	0	0	.00	3.79	-1	-1	0	0	-2
Pena, Francisco	Bal	14	11	96.1	76	5	0	0	1	1.000	8	4	0	.50	6.35	0	0	-1	0	-1
Perez, Roberto	Cle	61	53	451.2	476	29	2	3	3	.996	24	11	2	.46	3.85	2	3	3	0	8
Phegley, Josh	Oak	25	23	199.2	164	13	0	1	3	1.000	9	1	0	.11	5.59	0	-1	-1	-1	-3
Pierzynski, A.J.	Atl	64	59	532.0	457	23	4	5	5	.992	55	12	2	.22	4.06	-7	0	-2	3	-6
Pina, Manny	Mil	17	16	141.0	105	15	1	1	0	.992	18	5	0	.28	4.02	0	0	-1	0	-1
Plawecki, Kevin	NYM	45	38	349.2	321	20	4	2	1	.988	40	9	1	.23	3.47	0	0	2	1	3
Recker, Anthony	Atl	28	26	229.2	179	10	1	4	2	.995	36	7	1	.19	5.33	0	-1	-4	-2	-7
Rivera, Rene	NYM	59	54	481.2	495	37	2	5	3	.996	57	14	4	.25	2.77	-1	2	2	3	6
Romine, Austin	NYY	50	40	355.1	318	22	1	2	2	.997	23	3	1	.13	3.90	1	-3	0	1	-1
Rosario, Alberto	StL	17	8	89.2	82	8	0	1	1	1.000	15	3	1	.20	5.42	0	0	-2	0	-2
Ross, David	ChC	58	50	448.2	433	44	9	3	2	.981	66	17	1	.26	2.39	1	5	5	2	13
Ruiz, Carlos	TOT	56	55	493.0	466	44	4	6	2	.992	36	15	0	.42	4.22	2	4	-3	1	4
Saltalamacchia, J	Det	68	61	548.1	471	19	3	3	1	.994	46	9	3	.20	4.42	-1	-2	-4	0	-7
Sanchez, Gary	NYY	36	36	316.0	304	34	3	1	6	.991	31	12	1	.39	4.41	0	4	-1	0	3
Sanchez, Hector	TOT	14	9	89.2	77	4	2	1	0	.976	5	1	0	.20	6.02	0	0	-3	0	-3
Severino, Pedro	Was	15	8	85.2	84	7	1	0	1	.989	7	3	0	.43	3.99	0	1	-1	0	0
Smith, Kevan	CWS	6	3	28.0	12	1	0	1	0	1.000	3	1	0	.33	4.82	0	0	0	0	0
Soto, Geovany	LAA	23	22	189.0	145	6	1	0	1	.993	28	3	3	.11	4.29	0	-2	-1	0	-3
Stallings, Jacob	Pit	4	3	28.0	28	0	0	0	0	1.000	0	0	0	-	9.32	0	0	0	0	0
Stassi, Max	Hou	8	2	31.0	22	0	0	0	1	1.000	3	0	0	.00	4.65	0	0	0	0	0
Stewart, Chris	Pit	31	26	245.2	193	10	2	1	4	.990	14	3	1	.21	5.28	-2	0	-2	-1	-5
Sucre, Jesus	Sea	9	6	68.0	59	2	0	0	1	1.000	6	0	0	.00	3.44	0	-1	0	0	-1
Susac, Andrew	Mil	6	4	38.0	28	3	1	1	0	.969	3	2	0	.67	3.32	0	0	-1	0	-1
Swihart, Blake	Bos	6	6	52.0	59	3	0	0	3	1.000	4	1	0	.25	5.71	-1	0	0	0	-1
Telis, Tomas	Mia	3	1	12.0	8	2	0	0	0	1.000	2	0	0	.00	7.50	0	0	0	0	0
Thole, Josh	Tor	50	38	343.0	292	18	1	1	17	.997	22	4	2	.18	4.15	-2	0	2	1	1
Vazquez, Christian	Bos	56	49	438.2	423	25	2	3	9	.996	23	8	0	.35	4.27	-1	1	6	-1	5
Wolters, Tony	Col	59	58	501.1	451	29	6	0	3	.988	35	8	4	.23	4.72	-1	2	3	1	5
Zunino, Mike	Sea	52	48	443.2	400	15	0	0	3	1.000	22	3	4	.14	3.43	2	-1	4	3	8

Runs Saved Multi-Year Summary

Lindsay Zeck

Defensive Runs Saved gives an estimate of the number of runs a player saves or costs his team relative to the average player at his position. The Runs Saved Multi-Year Summary shows us how the Runs Saved totals for players have fluctuated over the last six years.

Andrelton Simmons has the highest average number of Runs Saved over his five seasons in the league, fluctuating between his lowest season of 18 Runs Saved in 2016 to his best season of 41 Runs Saved in 2013. Gerardo Parra had positive Runs Saved from 2011 to 2013, averaging 20 Runs Saved per season and with an extremely high 37 Runs Saved in 2013, but has cost his teams an average of 7 runs per year over the last three seasons. Yunel Escobar follows the same trend, saving an average of 8.7 Runs per season between 2011 and 2013 and costing his team 15 runs per year on average between 2014 and 2016.

Mark Reynolds and Lucas Duda showed the biggest improvement in the three most recent seasons compared to the three seasons prior. They cost their teams an average of 13.7 and 12 Runs, respectively, from 2011 and 2013 and saved their teams an average of 2.7 and 3 Runs between 2014 and 2016. The most consistent players that have played in each of the last six seasons are A.J. Ellis and Ryan Zimmerman. Unfortunately, they have been consistently below average defensively, costing their team runs every season.

Adam Eaton has an interesting pattern as he has positive Runs Saved in even-numbered seasons over the last six years and negative Runs Saved in odd seasons. His best performance of 20 Runs Saved was in 2016. Hopefully, for the White Sox's sake, he will repeat his 2016 performance and break his trend by saving his team runs in 2017. It is likely he will if he plays right field where he is much better defensively than he is in center.

A player must have over 2,500 innings played over the past six seasons or 700 innings in the most recent season at his primary position in order to qualify for this list. A secondary position is listed if the player has played at a second position over 1,000 innings over six seasons (or 200 innings in the most recent season).

Defensive Runs Saved by Season

Player	YOB	Position 1	Position 2	DRS 11	12	13	14	15	16
Abreu, Jose	1987	1B					-10	1	-5
Ackley, Dustin	1988	2B		9	11	-4	8	-13	3
Adams, Matt	1988	1B			1	-2	8	5	1
Ahmed, Nick	1990	SS					2	19	13
Alonso, Yonder	1987	1B		-6	2	6	9	9	-5
Altuve, Jose	1990	2B		2	-18	-3	-7	3	-2
Alvarez, Pedro	1987	3B		-9	-5	3	-5	-13	-4
Andrus, Elvis	1988	SS		6	8	11	-14	-1	-3
Aoki, Nori	1982	RF	LF		3	10	-7	-1	-4
Arenado, Nolan	1991	3B			30	16	18	20	
Avila, Alex	1987	C		0	5	-2	3	-7	-1
Aybar, Erick	1984	SS		-1	3	-7	-3	-3	-6
Barney, Darwin	1985	2B		3	29	11	10	-1	9
Barnhart, Tucker	1991	C					2	-3	-3
Bautista, Jose	1980	RF		0	6	6	-2	-3	-8
Beckham, Gordon	1986	2B		5	-6	-3	0	6	-11
Belt, Brandon	1988	1B		3	4	4	3	6	10
Beltran, Carlos	1977	RF		-4	5	-7	-5	-14	-6
Beltre, Adrian	1979	3B		11	13	-5	9	18	15
Betts, Mookie	1992	RF					4	10	32
Blackmon, Charlie	1986	CF		-2	5	-6	2	-7	-2
Bogaerts, Xander	1992	SS			-1	-16	-1	-10	
Bourjos, Peter	1987	CF	RF	10	9	-1	7	-4	1
Bourn, Michael	1982	CF		-5	23	2	-5	6	1
Bradley Jr., Jackie	1990	CF				-3	15	8	11
Brantley, Michael	1987	LF		8	0	4	-1	-2	1
Braun, Ryan	1983	LF		2	6	3	-8	-1	6
Bruce, Jay	1987	RF		0	-1	16	-7	5	-11
Bryant, Kris	1992	3B						4	10
Buxton, Byron	1993	CF						4	3
Byrd, Marlon	1977	RF		0	2	8	9	1	1
Cabrera, Asdrubal	1985	SS		0	-5	-16	-17	-8	-7
Cabrera, Melky	1984	LF			-4	-4	-5	-2	-5
Cabrera, Miguel	1983	1B	3B	-2	-4	-18	-2	4	-6
Cain, Lorenzo	1986	CF		0	5	23	22	18	11
Calhoun, Kole	1987	RF			1	-7	1	6	2
Cano, Robinson	1982	2B		2	15	6	0	-9	11
Carpenter, Matt	1985	3B		-1	-5	0	-2	-10	-5
Carter, Chris	1986	1B		0	-5	-9	0	-6	-5
Castellanos, Nick	1992	3B			-1	-30	-9	-11	
Castillo, Welington	1987	C		0	-4	3	-8	-9	2
Castro, Jason	1987	C			-8	-5	2	11	4
Castro, Starlin	1990	SS	2B	-8	3	-8	-7	-2	-8
Cervelli, Francisco	1986	C		2	0	1	1	8	6
Cespedes, Yoenis	1985	LF			-6	-1	10	11	-3
Chisenhall, Lonnie	1988	3B	RF	5	-4	1	-16	18	3
Choo, Shin-Soo	1982	RF		2	-10	-18	-12	-11	-4
Conger, Hank	1988	C		0	0	8	18	-6	-2
Correa, Carlos	1994	SS						0	-3
Cozart, Zack	1985	SS		4	12	4	19	7	8
Crawford, Brandon	1987	SS		1	12	2	8	20	20
Crawford, Carl	1981	LF		-1	1	0	1	-4	-4
Crisp, Coco	1979	CF		-1	0	3	-18	1	-10
Cron, C.J.	1990	1B					-5	-5	3
Cruz, Nelson	1980	RF		-4	-12	-3	4	-8	-3
Cuthbert, Cheslor	1992	3B						3	-12
Davis, Chris	1986	1B		-5	-4	-7	8	1	6
Davis, Ike	1987	1B		1	-3	1	-4	-1	0
Davis, Khris	1987	LF				-2	4	-6	-1
Davis, Rajai	1980	LF		-8	3	4	-10	3	-8
De Aza, Alejandro	1984	CF		5	-6	-17	0	-4	2
Desmond, Ian	1985	SS	CF	-4	-6	-3	1	1	-4
Dominguez, Matt	1989	3B		-3	0	8	-4		1
Donaldson, Josh	1985	3B			3	12	20	11	2
Dozier, Brian	1987	2B			1	9	0	-5	3
Drew, Stephen	1983	SS		3	-7	-2	4	-3	0
Duda, Lucas	1986	1B		-9	-15	-12	5	4	0
Duvall, Adam	1988	LF					2	-1	16
Dyson, Jarrod	1984	CF		4	4	6	13	11	19
Eaton, Adam	1988	CF	RF		1	-2	11	-14	20
Ellis, A.J.	1981	C		-4	-6	-4	-6	-7	-3

Player	YOB	Position 1	Position 2	DRS 11	12	13	14	15	16
Ellsbury, Jacoby	1983	CF		9	2	13	-3	1	8
Encarnacion, Edwin	1983	1B		-7	-4	-7	-6	0	0
Escobar, Alcides	1986	SS		10	-2	4	-4	-1	-6
Escobar, Yunel	1982	SS	3B	8	14	4	-23	-11	-11
Espinosa, Danny	1987	2B	SS	6	7	3	0	5	8
Ethier, Andre	1982	RF		1	0	0	-7	2	-1
Fielder, Prince	1984	1B		-10	-4	-13	-2	-5	-1
Flowers, Tyler	1986	C		8	9	1	11	14	2
Forsythe, Logan	1987	2B		7	-10	-2	3	6	1
Fowler, Dexter	1986	CF		-5	-12	-4	-20	-12	1
Franco, Maikel	1992	3B					1	-8	-6
Francoeur, Jeff	1984	RF		2	-11	0	0	-11	6
Frazier, Todd	1986	3B		3	-1	5	8	6	-2
Freeman, Freddie	1989	1B		-2	3	7	-7	3	9
Freese, David	1983	3B		0	2	-14	-9	-2	5
Galvis, Freddy	1989	SS			9	-4	-4	-7	5
Garcia, Adonis	1985	3B						-2	-9
Gardner, Brett	1983	LF		23	1	5	4	1	12
Gennett, Scooter	1990	2B				2	-5	3	-4
Giavotella, Johnny	1987	2B		-1	-4	-1	0	-12	-1
Gillaspie, Conor	1987	3B		-1	-3	-5	-12	-10	5
Goldschmidt, Paul	1987	1B		-3	1	13	1	18	4
Gomes, Yan	1987	C			1	21	8	-1	0
Gomez, Carlos	1985	CF		16	2	32	0	-6	-6
Gonzalez, Adrian	1982	1B		12	14	11	11	10	3
Gonzalez, Carlos	1985	RF	LF	8	-13	11	-5	5	4
Gordon, Alex	1984	LF		19	24	17	26	7	4
Gordon, Dee	1988	2B		-3	-14	-3	-5	13	1
Grandal, Yasmani	1988	C			15	4	-5	5	14
Granderson, Curtis	1981	RF	CF	-2	-7	3	-5	11	3
Gregorius, Didi	1990	SS			1	-1	2	5	-9
Grichuk, Randal	1991	CF					4	7	8
Gyorko, Jedd	1988	2B				-4	-9	-6	5
Hamilton, Billy	1990	CF				1	14	8	15
Hanigan, Ryan	1980	C		11	23	2	4	2	-3
Hardy, J.J.	1982	SS		8	18	8	10	4	6
Harper, Bryce	1992	RF				14	4	9	-3
Harrison, Josh	1987	2B		7	-4	0	15	1	8
Headley, Chase	1984	3B		0	-3	5	13	-7	7
Hechavarria, Adeiny	1989	SS			-1	-3	-3	9	9
Hernandez, Cesar	1990	2B			-4	-6	-7	4	
Herrera, Odubel	1991	CF						10	6
Heyward, Jason	1989	RF		10	17	14	26	24	18
Hill, Aaron	1982	2B	3B	0	-2	-9	-10	-3	3
Holliday, Matt	1980	LF		-2	-6	-13	-1	-4	-7
Hosmer, Eric	1989	1B		-10	-6	3	3	0	-6
Howard, Ryan	1979	1B		-13	-6	-1	-10	-9	-4
Hundley, Nick	1983	C		-3	-4	-12	-3	-11	-16
Iannetta, Chris	1983	C		-1	-6	-22	-14	7	-10
Iglesias, Jose	1990	SS		0	7	-1		-3	3
Inciarte, Ender	1990	CF					20	29	15
Infante, Omar	1981	2B		5	7	-5	1	3	-3
Jackson, Austin	1987	CF		26	6	4	-1	-1	-5
Jaso, John	1983	1B		-12	-4	-9	-6	-1	3
Jay, Jon	1985	CF		9	1	-10	6	3	-5
Jennings, Desmond	1986	CF		2	10	-6	4	2	7
Johnson, Chris	1984	3B		-11	-10	-7	-13	-2	1
Johnson, Kelly	1982	2B		1	5	3	2	-7	-2
Jones, Adam	1985	CF		-1	-13	-1	3	4	-10
Joyce, Matt	1984	RF		0	4	-3	1	-3	-2
Kang, Jung Ho	1987	3B						4	-1
Kemp, Matt	1984	CF	RF	-7	-10	-5	-22	-15	-18
Kendrick, Howie	1983	2B		6	2	-3	7	-12	-5
Kepler, Max	1993	RF						0	6
Kiermaier, Kevin	1990	CF			0	14	42	25	
Kinsler, Ian	1982	2B		17	1	11	20	19	12
Kipnis, Jason	1987	2B		-4	3	-1	-11	1	4
Lagares, Juan	1989	CF				28	26	2	8
Lamb, Jake	1990	3B					0	7	-8
Lawrie, Brett	1990	3B	2B	11	20	3	1	-6	-4
LeMahieu, DJ	1988	2B		1	8	11	17	3	3

Player	YOB	Position 1	Position 2	DRS 11	12	13	14	15	16
Lind, Adam	1983	1B		-5	1	-7	-3	5	-2
Lindor, Francisco	1993	SS						10	17
Loney, James	1984	1B		11	6	4	-1	-2	2
Longoria, Evan	1985	3B		20	1	12	-5	-1	-9
Lowrie, Jed	1984	SS	2B	-1	-3	-21	-10	-3	-8
Lucroy, Jonathan	1986	C		19	16	11	24	2	3
Machado, Manny	1992	3B			7	35	6	13	16
Markakis, Nick	1983	RF		5	-7	-7	0	-6	10
Marte, Ketel	1993	SS						2	-2
Marte, Starling	1988	LF			5	20	5	24	17
Martin, Leonys	1988	CF		-1	0	14	16	15	-2
Martin, Russell	1983	C		18	4	21	19	5	6
Martinez, J.D.	1987	RF		2	-2	-9	0	4	-22
Mathis, Jeff	1983	C		11	7	10	8	1	8
Mauer, Joe	1983	1B		4	-6	8	4	0	6
Maybin, Cameron	1987	CF		14	7	-5	2	-16	-11
McCann, Brian	1984	C		9	13	6	6	-4	-5
McCann, James	1990	C				-1	-6	9	
McCutchen, Andrew	1986	CF		2	-6	5	-13	-8	-28
McGehee, Casey	1982	3B		4	-1		-2	1	0
Mercer, Jordy	1986	SS			3	-2	9	0	-9
Middlebrooks, Will	1988	3B			-3	-7	-5	-7	2
Miller, Brad	1989	SS				-3	-5	-20	-17
Molina, Yadier	1982	C		5	29	30	7	9	2
Montero, Miguel	1983	C		19	9	-2	10	7	-2
Moreland, Mitch	1985	1B		-5	0	1	1	2	7
Morrison, Logan	1987	1B		-22	-2	-4	2	-7	-4
Moustakas, Mike	1988	3B		1	14	-3	-2	4	1
Murphy, Daniel	1985	2B		6	-10	-15	-11	-5	-11
Myers, Wil	1990	1B			-1	-8	-6	7	
Napoli, Mike	1981	1B		-7	-12	10	8	1	-4
Navarro, Dioner	1984	C		0	1	1	-15	-1	-14
Norris, Derek	1989	C			6	-1	-3	3	15
Odor, Rougned	1994	2B					-11	-7	-9
Orlando, Paulo	1985	RF						8	10
Ozuna, Marcell	1990	CF				4	9	-3	-5
Pagan, Angel	1981	CF	LF	-9	-5	-9	-5	-20	-6
Panik, Joe	1990	2B					-1	2	3
Parra, Gerardo	1987	RF		14	9	37	0	-10	-11
Pederson, Joc	1992	CF					0	-3	1
Pedroia, Dustin	1983	2B		18	11	15	17	-3	12
Pena, Brayan	1982	C		4	-2	-1	3	-5	-2
Pence, Hunter	1983	RF		2	-6	-8	-1	0	-3
Pennington, Cliff	1984	SS		-12	12	13	4	5	4
Peralta, Jhonny	1982	SS		2	-1	0	17	-7	-8
Perez, Salvador	1990	C		-2	7	11	7	1	3
Phillips, Brandon	1981	2B		7	11	1	6	4	-7
Pierzynski, A.J.	1976	C		-3	-10	-4	-13	-13	-6
Pillar, Kevin	1989	CF				4	3	22	21
Piscotty, Stephen	1991	RF						-5	3
Plouffe, Trevor	1986	3B		-19	-8	0	6	3	-4
Polanco, Gregory	1991	RF					-2	12	2
Pollock, A.J.	1987	CF			1	12	8	14	3
Posey, Buster	1987	C		5	15	16	10	21	24
Prado, Martin	1983	3B		10	18	2	9	10	3
Puig, Yasiel	1990	RF				8	-1	2	7
Pujols, Albert	1980	1B		9	9	1	6	4	-4
Ramirez, Alexei	1981	SS		10	14	1	-4	-6	-20
Ramirez, Hanley	1983	SS	1B	-11	-18	3	-9	-19	-5
Ramirez, Jose	1992	3B				1	6	5	-1
Ramos, Wilson	1987	C		11	-2	10	2	10	-1
Rasmus, Colby	1986	CF		-4	7	12	-6	2	20
Realmuto, J.T.	1991	C					0	1	-13
Reddick, Josh	1987	RF		10	15	13	10	1	6
Rendon, Anthony	1990	3B				-11	16	-1	8
Revere, Ben	1988	CF		-4	10	-3	-16	-1	2
Reyes, Jose	1983	SS		-14	-16	-4	-16	-8	-8
Reynolds, Mark	1983	1B		-21	-9	-11	6	-2	4
Rizzo, Anthony	1989	1B		2	4	16	6	10	11
Rollins, Jimmy	1978	SS		-6	-8	-15	4	-7	-3
Ruiz, Carlos	1979	C		-8	4	0	1	-12	4
Rupp, Cameron	1988	C				0	-1	6	-10
Russell, Addison	1994	SS						19	19

Player	YOB	Position 1	Position 2	DRS 11	12	13	14	15	16
Ryan, Brendan	1982	SS		20	27	6	2	-3	1
Saltalamacchia, J	1985	C		4	5	-5	-21	-5	-9
Sandoval, Pablo	1986	3B		14	-4	-5	4	-11	-1
Santana, Carlos	1986	1B		-17	-14	-19	-10	-5	1
Saunders, Michael	1986	LF		3	-10	-12	5	0	-11
Schoop, Jonathan	1991	2B			-1	11	-3	-1	
Seager, Corey	1994	SS						2	0
Seager, Kyle	1987	3B		0	-4	-8	10	1	15
Segura, Jean	1990	SS	2B	0	3	2	-3	0	
Semien, Marcus	1990	SS			5	-4	5	-6	
Shaw, Travis	1990	3B						-1	14
Simmons, Andrelton	1989	SS			19	41	28	25	18
Smoak, Justin	1986	1B		-1	0	-8	-4	4	-5
Solarte, Yangervis	1987	3B				-7	-1	-2	-3
Soto, Geovany	1983	C		8	0	4	1	2	-3
Souza Jr., Steven	1989	RF					0	-4	2
Span, Denard	1984	CF		9	19	3	-2	-10	-7
Springer, George	1989	RF					-2	6	6
Stanton, Giancarlo	1989	RF		3	9	-6	6	9	4
Stewart, Chris	1982	C		21	11	10	3	4	-5
Stubbs, Drew	1984	CF		-4	1	-7	0	2	-7
Suarez, Eugenio	1991	3B					-4	-12	1
Suzuki, Ichiro	1973	RF		-3	5	10	1	6	6
Suzuki, Kurt	1983	C		-10	-11	-8	-17	-9	-12
Teixeira, Mark	1980	1B		3	17	0	2	5	2
Tejada, Ruben	1989	SS		1	0	-6	3	-18	1
Thole, Josh	1986	C		-6	10	-4	-2	-1	1
Travis, Devon	1991	2B						1	2
Trout, Mike	1991	CF		0	19	-11	-12	5	6
Trumbo, Mark	1986	1B	RF	8	-3	1	-8	-3	-11
Tulowitzki, Troy	1984	SS		12	-6	6	7	5	10
Turner, Justin	1984	3B		-14	-3	0	6	5	7
Upton, Justin	1987	LF	RF	3	1	-8	-3	8	0
Upton Jr., Melvin	1984	CF	LF	-5	-5	0	-8	2	10
Uribe, Juan	1979	3B		4	4	15	17	2	1
Utley, Chase	1978	2B		7	9	-4	3	0	-3
Valbuena, Luis	1985	3B		-1	4	6	-11	1	1
Valencia, Danny	1984	3B		-13	-1	0	-2	-6	-18
Venable, Will	1982	RF		5	-3	1	10	-5	0
Villar, Jonathan	1991	SS			-5	-2	1	0	
Vogt, Stephen	1984	C			0	0	0	-4	-10
Votto, Joey	1983	1B		7	9	6	5	6	-14
Walker, Neil	1985	2B		-3	-4	9	-2	-2	0
Weeks Jr., Rickie	1982	2B		-5	-30	-15	-17	-2	-7
Werth, Jayson	1979	RF	LF	-3	-11	0	-4	-11	-8
Wieters, Matt	1986	C		22	13	-10	-4	-7	-3
Wong, Kolten	1990	2B			0	9	5	4	
Wright, David	1982	3B		-5	16	5	13	-8	-8
Yelich, Christian	1991	LF				1	11	8	6
Young, Chris	1983	CF		17	6	-7	1	-3	-2
Zimmerman, Ryan	1984	3B	1B	-5	-1	-1	-4	-1	-2
Zobrist, Ben	1981	2B		19	5	9	6	-12	-3
Zunino, Mike	1991	C			0	8	8	8	

Baserunning

Lindsay Zeck

Like last season, Billy Hamilton was the best baserunner in baseball this year with +68 bases. He finished second in stolen bases with 58 despite only playing 119 games, and he had a success rate of 88 percent. Interestingly, he was more aggressive in 2016 on his first-to-third opportunities, advancing on 14 of his 18 opportunities—as opposed to 7 of 18 in 2015—and less aggressive on his second-to-home opportunities. He advanced on only 5 of his 11 opportunities in 2016 as opposed to advancing on all 12 of his opportunities in 2015.

Mike Trout has reestablished himself near the top of the leader board in baserunning after finishing tied for 41st overall in 2015. In 2016, he trailed only Hamilton with +58 bases, an improvement of 41 bases over 2015. One of the greatest contributing factors to this increase was his return to stealing more bases. In 2016, he successfully stole 30 of the 37 bases that he attempted (81 percent). He only attempted to steal 18 bases in 2015 and stole 11 of them successfully (61 percent). Another significant difference was in the number of times he was involved in a double play. In 2015, he was doubled up eight percent of his opportunities; he reduced this percentage to only three percent in 2016.

The most improved baserunner was Rajai Davis. While he did have fewer plate appearances in 2015 than in 2016—370 and 495, respectively—he increased his extra bases by 46 in 2016. A difference this significant can not only be explained by having 125 more plate appearances. His biggest change came in the category called Bases Taken, the number of times a player moves up a base on a wild pitch, passed ball, balk, sacrifice fly, or defensive indifference. He went from five Bases Taken in 2015 to 22 in 2016.

The player whose baserunning performance declined the most from 2015 to 2016 was Brandon Phillips, whose extra bases decreased by 36. His Stolen Bases Gained took the biggest hit as it went from +17 to -2. In 2015, he attempted 26 stolen bases and was successful 23 times (88 percent), whereas, in 2016, he attempted 22 stolen bases and was successful only 14 times (64 percent).

Victor Martinez and David Ortiz were the worst baserunners in 2016, finishing with -34 and -32 bases, respectively. Both were hurt by their lack of advancements. Martinez advanced from first to third on only 2 of 31 opportunities (6 percent) and advanced from second to home 2 out of 20 opportunities (10 percent). Ortiz advanced from first to third on only 3 of 28 opportunities (11 percent) and advanced from second to home 4 out of 15 opportunities (27 percent). The overall advancement percentages in these situations are 29 and 60 percent, respectively.

Net Gain is a statistic that measures baserunning production that includes all baserunning advancements on both hits and outs (BR Gain) and stolen bases (SB Gain). It estimates the number of bases a player gained or lost for his team due to his baserunning. BR Gain is the sum of extra baserunning advances a player made over the league average, minus a penalty for the number of BR Outs he made above the league average. SB Gain estimates how many bases each runner gained or lost his team based on his successful and unsuccessful stolen base attempts.

2016 Baserunning

Player	1st to 3rd Moved	Chances	2nd to Home Moved	Chances	1st to Home Moved	Chances	Bases Taken	Out Adv	Doubled Off	BR Outs	GDP	GDP Opps	BR Gain	SB Gain	Net Gain
Abreu,Jose	10	33	6	12	4	13	14	3	1	4	21	139	-11	-4	-15
Adames,Cristhian	2	12	4	9	2	3	8	0	0	0	5	35	+3	-4	-1
Adams,Matt	1	10	4	8	0	6	6	1	0	1	5	72	-1	-2	-3
Ahmed,Nick	9	15	6	8	1	1	10	1	1	2	9	52	+5	+1	+6
Almonte,Abraham	0	5	8	11	0	0	7	2	0	2	5	33	-2	+8	+6
Alonso,Yonder	6	29	10	17	3	6	10	3	0	3	15	102	-9	+1	-8
Altherr,Aaron	1	8	0	4	2	3	7	2	1	3	4	36	-7	+3	-4
Altuve,Jose	18	36	16	26	7	9	21	8	1	9	15	133	-1	+10	+9
Alvarez,Pedro	2	16	4	6	4	5	6	0	0	0	6	69	+5	+1	+6
Amarista,Alexi	1	4	1	2	0	2	6	1	1	2	5	26	-5	+5	0
Anderson,Tim	7	20	9	14	3	5	9	2	1	3	15	81	-6	+6	0
Andrus,Elvis	19	36	16	22	3	8	20	4	2	6	18	99	+1	+8	+9
Aoki,Nori	6	31	12	17	9	12	7	0	1	2	9	80	-1	-11	-12
Arcia,Orlando	1	5	1	1	0	2	7	1	0	1	6	41	0	+8	+8
Arcia,Oswaldo	3	7	2	3	1	3	0	1	1	2	1	36	-3	-1	-4
Arenado,Nolan	16	40	13	19	3	12	16	3	3	6	17	149	-4	-4	-8
Asche,Cody	5	13	5	7	1	3	1	0	0	0	1	37	+4	+1	+5
Avila,Alex	2	15	2	6	0	2	1	1	2	3	3	34	-14	0	-14
Aviles,Mike	3	7	3	5	0	0	9	2	0	2	5	29	+1	-2	-1
Aybar,Erick	4	10	5	7	1	2	20	3	0	3	15	107	+6	-7	-1
Baez,Javier	6	13	8	11	2	4	15	8	1	9	8	102	-8	+6	-2
Bandy,Jett	2	11	2	7	0	3	4	2	2	4	5	39	-15	+1	-14
Barney,Darwin	4	16	6	10	2	5	12	2	0	2	8	50	0	-2	-2
Barnhart,Tucker	1	10	5	11	4	7	6	8	0	8	12	72	-28	+1	-27
Bautista,Jose	4	17	9	14	5	7	14	5	1	6	21	98	-16	-2	-18
Beckham,Gordon	1	7	3	4	0	0	9	0	1	1	12	60	-2	+1	-1
Beckham,Tim	1	7	3	8	1	2	5	1	0	1	3	37	-1	0	-1
Bell,Josh	0	9	2	5	2	2	5	2	0	2	4	33	-5	-2	-7
Belt,Brandon	9	48	13	23	3	8	21	3	2	5	7	144	+4	-8	-4
Beltran,Carlos	3	23	8	15	2	6	17	2	0	3	19	136	-5	+1	-4
Beltre,Adrian	11	28	13	20	3	11	16	3	2	5	10	120	+2	-1	+1
Bethancourt,Christian	3	7	2	3	1	3	5	0	1	1	9	31	-4	-3	-7
Betts,Mookie	22	47	16	19	9	13	27	3	0	3	12	147	+33	+18	+51
Blackmon,Charlie	10	33	14	19	10	12	22	2	2	4	2	77	+20	-1	+19
Blanco,Andres	7	10	2	4	1	3	6	1	0	1	7	35	+2	-4	-2
Blanco,Gregor	4	13	4	6	4	6	10	2	0	2	5	47	+4	0	+4
Bogaerts,Xander	23	39	11	14	13	19	16	3	1	4	14	157	+21	+5	+26
Bour,Justin	3	16	1	5	1	3	3	0	0	0	8	66	-4	0	-4
Bourjos,Peter	10	18	9	13	2	4	12	1	1	2	6	52	+9	-2	+7
Bourn,Michael	12	28	10	13	2	5	8	3	0	3	3	84	+8	+5	+13
Bradley Jr.,Jackie	10	32	16	21	6	9	18	1	1	2	10	134	+18	+5	+23
Braun,Ryan	11	25	9	13	5	10	15	3	1	4	20	109	-4	+6	+2
Bregman,Alex	2	9	4	7	1	5	8	1	1	2	1	44	+3	+2	+5
Brown,Trevor	3	14	3	7	1	1	5	2	0	2	2	29	-3	-2	-5
Broxton,Keon	1	3	2	6	1	1	5	1	1	2	2	41	-1	+15	+14
Bruce,Jay	7	34	5	11	2	9	6	6	0	6	14	134	-21	0	-21
Bryant,Kris	20	39	18	24	5	15	20	2	2	4	3	169	+29	-2	+27
Burns,Billy	2	8	8	11	3	5	10	1	1	2	3	46	+6	+7	+13
Butler,Billy	1	14	4	9	1	4	4	3	0	3	13	54	-19	0	-19
Buxton,Byron	7	11	6	8	5	5	11	0	0	0	2	65	+22	+6	+28
Cabrera,Asdrubal	6	25	8	15	2	7	17	5	0	5	14	113	-7	+3	-4
Cabrera,Melky	2	34	12	20	0	7	21	3	0	3	17	122	-7	+2	-5
Cabrera,Miguel	7	44	6	19	1	7	20	5	0	5	26	140	-24	0	-24
Cabrera,Ramon	1	3	2	3	0	4	3	0	1	1	5	38	-3	-1	-4
Cain,Lorenzo	15	26	10	17	5	5	13	2	1	3	15	84	+5	+4	+9
Calhoun,Kole	8	40	11	19	5	12	30	2	1	3	10	141	+18	-4	+14
Cano,Robinson	6	28	14	22	3	8	17	5	1	6	18	164	-8	-2	-10
Carpenter,Matt	14	34	3	12	4	5	20	8	0	8	4	71	-3	-8	-11
Carrera,Ezequiel	6	19	4	8	2	4	9	1	0	1	8	62	+2	-1	+1
Carter,Chris	3	28	5	16	1	5	13	2	1	3	18	134	-14	+1	-13
Casali,Curt	0	12	4	9	0	2	6	2	0	2	2	31	-6	0	-6
Castellanos,Nick	1	16	9	14	1	7	10	4	2	6	4	92	-10	-1	-11
Castillo,Welington	2	12	2	8	2	10	5	2	0	2	5	84	-7	+2	-5

359

2016 Baserunning

Player	1st to 3rd Moved	Chances	2nd to Home Moved	Chances	1st to Home Moved	Chances	Bases Taken	Out Adv	Doubled Off	BR Outs	GDP	GDP Opps	BR Gain	SB Gain	Net Gain
Castro,Jason	0	10	6	13	2	7	8	2	0	2	9	64	-8	0	-8
Castro,Starlin	7	30	8	14	4	7	13	4	1	5	15	110	-10	+4	-6
Centeno,Juan	0	7	5	8	0	3	3	0	0	0	8	39	-5	0	-5
Cervelli,Francisco	7	22	9	16	1	6	12	0	2	2	14	70	-5	+2	-3
Cespedes,Yoenis	8	27	8	14	1	3	8	1	2	3	14	115	-7	+1	-6
Chisenhall,Lonnie	7	16	6	9	3	5	10	3	1	4	4	83	+4	+6	+10
Choo,Shin-Soo	2	15	8	9	0	1	8	1	0	1	1	33	+6	0	+6
Coghlan,Chris	3	9	8	11	1	5	10	0	1	1	4	50	+7	0	+7
Colon,Christian	1	8	3	5	0	3	3	1	0	1	4	26	-5	-2	-7
Conforto,Michael	5	12	4	6	2	5	6	0	1	1	6	73	+5	0	+5
Contreras,Willson	5	15	6	9	0	2	14	2	0	2	7	41	+4	-2	+2
Correa,Carlos	10	35	16	20	2	5	17	2	1	3	12	125	+8	+7	+15
Cozart,Zack	4	19	7	16	1	8	20	3	0	3	9	52	-2	+2	0
Crawford,Brandon	7	35	13	19	2	4	15	5	0	5	13	150	-2	+7	+5
Crisp,Coco	6	21	10	11	2	3	12	3	0	3	7	62	+4	0	+4
Cron,C.J.	1	24	6	18	1	1	17	3	4	7	9	89	-16	-4	-20
Cruz,Nelson	10	34	9	13	3	11	19	5	0	5	15	135	-1	+2	+1
Cuthbert,Cheslor	4	23	9	13	1	7	2	4	2	6	14	96	-26	+2	-24
d'Arnaud,Chase	3	13	2	4	1	2	8	0	0	0	5	51	+5	+3	+8
d'Arnaud,Travis	2	11	7	9	2	3	1	1	1	2	7	60	-6	0	-6
Dahl,David	8	18	6	7	1	1	11	1	1	2	3	44	+10	+5	+15
Davis,Chris	14	41	16	23	4	11	15	2	0	2	6	116	+15	+1	+16
Davis,Khris	5	28	10	18	5	12	9	1	2	3	19	123	-13	-3	-16
Davis,Rajai	7	18	14	20	5	6	22	1	1	2	9	83	+19	+31	+50
De Aza,Alejandro	6	14	2	6	2	7	10	1	0	1	5	38	+4	-2	+2
De Jesus Jr.,Ivan	1	9	4	8	1	1	7	0	2	2	6	47	-3	+1	-2
Descalso,Daniel	5	16	7	9	1	4	14	0	0	0	2	40	+16	+3	+19
DeShields,Delino	4	10	6	10	3	4	13	2	0	2	1	28	+10	+2	+12
Desmond,Ian	13	34	14	20	6	8	19	4	0	4	11	122	+12	+9	+21
Diaz,Aledmys	14	31	6	8	6	9	12	4	1	5	10	96	+2	-4	-2
Dickerson,Alex	3	11	6	9	1	3	6	2	0	3	5	51	-4	+3	-1
Dickerson,Corey	9	20	8	14	1	3	16	2	1	3	12	102	+6	-4	+2
Dietrich,Derek	4	24	7	10	1	4	10	6	2	8	6	67	-19	+1	-18
Donaldson,Josh	12	35	7	11	5	12	26	5	1	6	16	141	+4	+5	+9
Dozier,Brian	9	25	13	18	2	7	19	2	0	3	12	119	+10	+14	+24
Drew,Stephen	1	5	2	3	0	2	5	1	1	2	3	29	-3	-2	-5
Drury,Brandon	3	27	8	12	1	4	18	1	0	1	14	71	+1	-1	0
Duffy,Matt	4	16	6	10	4	8	11	2	1	3	13	78	-5	-2	-7
Duvall,Adam	9	24	10	21	4	4	13	4	0	5	7	109	+1	-4	-3
Dyson,Jarrod	8	20	12	13	5	6	11	1	0	1	4	59	+16	+16	+32
Eaton,Adam	23	49	20	28	4	7	17	4	5	9	6	104	+3	+4	+7
Eibner,Brett	3	8	3	6	2	4	2	1	0	1	3	43	0	-4	-4
Ellis,A.J.	2	8	5	5	0	1	3	1	1	2	5	33	-4	0	-4
Ellsbury,Jacoby	8	41	8	13	4	6	24	2	1	3	11	100	+8	+4	+12
Encarnacion,Edwin	5	35	11	18	2	7	14	2	0	2	22	164	-7	+2	-5
Escobar,Alcides	11	37	10	20	2	5	23	4	2	6	16	118	-4	+9	+5
Escobar,Eduardo	4	15	1	2	6	6	7	0	1	1	7	64	+5	-5	0
Escobar,Yunel	11	31	17	24	2	10	16	7	1	8	21	83	-22	-6	-28
Espinosa,Danny	9	30	10	17	2	5	12	2	0	2	4	130	+13	+5	+18
Fielder,Prince	3	19	4	12	2	4	6	1	0	1	12	83	-8	0	-8
Flaherty,Ryan	0	8	4	5	0	0	5	2	0	2	1	30	-1	+2	+1
Flores,Ramon	3	10	6	10	0	0	8	0	0	0	11	56	+1	+3	+4
Flores,Wilmer	1	18	2	8	0	1	8	5	1	6	9	77	-20	-1	-21
Flowers,Tyler	2	17	2	16	0	3	6	2	1	3	3	64	-13	0	-13
Forsythe,Logan	6	30	11	16	0	6	27	0	0	0	8	56	+17	-6	+11
Fowler,Dexter	19	32	12	16	4	7	15	1	5	6	3	65	+10	+5	+15
Franco,Maikel	7	28	7	11	2	7	15	2	2	4	13	115	-3	-1	-4
Francoeur,Jeff	2	15	3	8	3	6	16	0	0	1	5	61	+9	-2	+7
Franklin,Nick	2	6	2	2	1	2	6	0	0	0	1	33	+9	+4	+13
Frazier,Adam	3	10	4	4	3	4	2	2	1	3	0	23	-3	+2	-1
Frazier,Todd	5	21	13	24	3	10	17	5	0	5	11	112	-4	+5	+1
Freeman,Freddie	4	36	13	26	3	12	23	1	2	3	12	160	+3	+4	+7
Freese,David	4	30	11	22	0	8	12	4	0	4	15	93	-19	0	-19
Fryer,Eric	2	8	5	5	1	4	5	1	0	1	1	26	+4	-6	-2

2016 Baserunning

Player	1st to 3rd Moved	Chances	2nd to Home Moved	Chances	1st to Home Moved	Chances	Bases Taken	Out Adv	Doubled Off	BR Outs	GDP	GDP Opps	BR Gain	SB Gain	Net Gain
Galvis,Freddy	6	26	5	11	5	9	20	5	0	5	16	131	-2	+5	+3
Garcia,Adonis	11	35	10	20	4	9	16	1	0	1	18	115	+3	-1	+2
Garcia,Avisail	9	26	13	17	4	6	9	3	0	3	9	78	+2	-4	-2
Garcia,Greg	0	12	4	6	7	9	7	0	1	1	3	42	+3	-1	+2
Gardner,Brett	16	36	13	14	8	12	28	1	1	2	6	104	+35	+8	+43
Gattis,Evan	5	20	6	6	1	3	3	1	0	1	12	81	-5	0	-5
Gennett,Scooter	7	27	10	17	0	3	15	7	1	8	11	98	-15	+6	-9
Giavotella,Johnny	6	19	8	11	2	7	8	2	4	6	11	72	-15	-2	-17
Gillaspie,Conor	0	4	3	5	1	4	4	0	0	0	3	46	+3	-3	0
Goeddel,Tyler	1	7	2	2	0	0	4	0	1	1	4	44	0	+3	+3
Goldschmidt,Paul	9	33	15	21	3	7	20	2	1	3	14	133	+7	+22	+29
Gomes,Yan	3	11	4	5	0	1	5	1	1	2	7	46	-4	0	-4
Gomez,Carlos	8	16	4	7	0	2	10	3	4	7	11	74	-15	+8	-7
Gonzalez,Adrian	7	33	5	11	1	9	12	2	0	2	16	124	-8	-4	-12
Gonzalez,Carlos	6	26	13	22	5	10	17	4	1	5	10	137	+1	-2	-1
Gonzalez,Marwin	6	24	5	10	1	4	14	1	0	2	16	105	-2	0	-2
Gordon,Alex	14	33	5	13	4	8	12	1	0	1	9	72	+7	+6	+13
Gordon,Dee	6	17	7	8	2	4	13	0	0	0	4	38	+14	+16	+30
Gosselin,Phil	6	16	1	7	3	3	7	2	0	2	0	26	+2	+3	+5
Grandal,Yasmani	5	17	2	8	2	7	6	4	0	5	11	75	-18	-5	-23
Granderson,Curtis	16	39	7	14	2	5	14	2	0	2	10	88	+7	0	+7
Gregorius,Didi	9	30	12	16	4	8	14	3	1	4	9	116	+5	+5	+10
Grichuk,Randal	5	16	11	14	4	7	24	1	1	2	9	94	+20	-3	+17
Grossman,Robbie	10	25	9	13	1	3	12	2	1	3	3	54	+6	-4	+2
Gutierrez,Franklin	4	12	6	8	0	0	9	0	1	1	6	55	+6	+1	+7
Guyer,Brandon	1	11	5	10	9	13	12	5	0	5	6	49	-6	-1	-7
Gyorko,Jedd	6	21	5	7	1	6	14	2	0	2	11	89	+3	0	+3
Hamilton,Billy	14	18	5	11	4	6	19	0	0	0	5	58	+26	+42	+68
Hardy,J.J.	3	24	10	18	3	6	13	2	0	2	14	80	-6	0	-6
Harper,Bryce	16	30	9	17	9	11	18	4	4	8	11	130	+3	+1	+4
Harrison,Josh	7	24	14	19	2	2	14	4	3	7	10	101	-6	+11	+5
Hazelbaker,Jeremy	2	11	1	6	0	3	5	1	0	1	1	45	-1	+1	0
Headley,Chase	2	24	15	25	4	4	20	2	0	2	7	95	+11	+4	+15
Healy,Ryon	1	8	4	9	1	3	6	1	0	1	7	55	-3	0	-3
Hechavarria,Adeiny	8	23	13	19	1	6	17	1	1	2	10	111	+11	+1	+12
Hernandez,Cesar	13	31	8	13	5	8	9	1	3	4	6	80	0	-9	-9
Hernandez,Kiké	3	17	5	7	2	3	9	3	0	3	3	39	-1	+2	+1
Herrera,Odubel	11	33	11	20	2	5	26	4	1	6	6	108	+9	+11	+20
Herrmann,Chris	3	7	3	4	1	1	1	0	0	0	2	30	+3	+4	+7
Heyward,Jason	6	27	12	18	5	11	16	2	0	2	12	128	+8	+3	+11
Hicks,Aaron	5	12	6	9	2	5	11	0	2	2	7	64	+5	-5	0
Hill,Aaron	7	24	7	11	2	10	13	1	1	2	6	77	+4	0	+4
Holliday,Matt	2	13	5	10	1	5	6	2	0	2	9	89	-6	0	-6
Holt,Brock	10	14	5	8	5	8	14	0	3	3	5	58	+12	-2	+10
Holt,Tyler	6	12	6	9	0	1	11	1	0	1	6	36	+7	-2	+5
Hosmer,Eric	3	23	8	14	3	6	16	2	1	3	18	115	-7	-1	-8
Howard,Ryan	0	8	2	4	1	4	3	1	0	1	7	61	-5	-2	-7
Hundley,Nick	6	18	4	9	2	5	8	0	0	0	12	63	0	0	0
Iannetta,Chris	2	15	1	8	0	2	12	1	1	2	4	60	-1	0	-1
Iglesias,Jose	11	34	13	18	3	5	16	2	2	4	12	87	+2	-1	+1
Inciarte,Ender	21	49	16	21	6	11	25	5	1	6	8	96	+16	+2	+18
Jackson,Austin	1	9	6	9	1	2	6	1	0	1	3	34	+1	0	+1
Jankowski,Travis	6	16	12	14	3	5	19	3	1	4	5	52	+10	+6	+16
Jaso,John	5	21	4	13	2	7	15	5	0	5	8	80	-8	-8	-16
Jay,Jon	8	22	9	10	7	10	12	2	0	2	5	39	+10	+2	+12
Jennings,Desmond	1	5	4	6	3	4	5	1	0	1	4	41	+2	+2	+4
Johnson,Chris	2	17	2	7	1	1	2	1	2	3	13	47	-21	0	-21
Johnson,Kelly	4	18	3	5	2	5	7	1	1	2	6	65	-1	+4	+3
Jones,Adam	14	36	8	18	6	11	17	2	0	2	13	97	+7	+2	+9
Joseph,Tommy	4	17	4	6	0	4	2	1	1	2	11	68	-12	-1	-13
Joyce,Matt	7	19	4	7	1	7	9	0	1	1	9	54	0	-1	-1
Kang,Jung Ho	1	18	6	10	0	2	8	3	1	4	11	69	-15	+1	-14
Kemp,Matt	9	30	12	17	3	6	20	4	0	4	17	147	+6	+1	+7
Kemp,Tony	2	9	2	3	0	1	4	0	0	0	5	25	0	0	0

2016 Baserunning

Player	1st to 3rd Moved	1st to 3rd Chances	2nd to Home Moved	2nd to Home Chances	1st to Home Moved	1st to Home Chances	Bases Taken	Out Adv	Doubled Off	BR Outs	GDP	GDP Opps	BR Gain	SB Gain	Net Gain
Kendrick,Howie	13	23	11	16	2	7	20	1	0	1	20	98	+10	+6	+16
Kepler,Max	5	19	7	9	2	4	17	0	0	1	2	82	+19	+2	+21
Kiermaier,Kevin	9	13	8	10	6	7	13	3	2	5	5	82	+9	+15	+24
Kim,Hyun Soo	8	22	4	8	1	5	7	0	0	0	5	60	+5	-5	0
Kinsler,Ian	12	33	20	24	4	11	21	3	1	4	5	98	+17	+2	+19
Kipnis,Jason	12	41	10	20	4	7	25	1	2	3	21	133	+4	+9	+13
La Stella,Tommy	1	6	3	4	4	4	4	1	0	1	2	33	+3	-2	+1
Lagares,Juan	1	4	3	6	1	1	3	0	1	1	4	30	-2	0	-2
Lamb,Jake	9	30	20	25	5	6	25	1	0	1	13	101	+24	+4	+28
Lawrie,Brett	8	22	8	11	1	3	8	1	0	1	3	76	+11	+1	+12
Lee,Dae-Ho	2	14	2	7	0	5	4	3	0	3	8	67	-14	0	-14
LeMahieu,DJ	10	33	12	19	9	19	24	1	2	3	19	112	+4	-3	+1
Leon,Sandy	4	13	3	7	0	4	9	3	0	3	4	45	-4	0	-4
Lind,Adam	7	18	2	4	0	1	11	3	0	3	14	84	-4	-2	-6
Lindor,Francisco	11	34	17	25	4	6	16	4	0	4	18	141	+1	+9	+10
Loney,James	2	13	6	8	1	2	8	1	1	2	11	76	-3	0	-3
Longoria,Evan	6	18	9	15	2	4	13	1	0	1	13	152	+10	-6	+4
Lowrie,Jed	6	26	7	10	1	6	9	4	0	4	10	57	-11	0	-11
Lucroy,Jonathan	8	22	6	10	3	9	13	2	1	3	20	123	-2	+5	+3
Machado,Manny	7	19	14	19	3	7	18	6	0	6	14	149	+2	-6	-4
Maldonado,Martin	4	10	1	3	2	3	5	1	2	3	6	40	-6	+1	-5
Marisnick,Jake	4	11	9	15	2	2	8	0	3	3	4	41	-1	0	-1
Markakis,Nick	11	39	9	18	2	10	19	1	1	2	16	115	0	-4	-4
Marte,Jefry	4	11	4	8	1	2	4	1	1	2	8	51	-6	-2	-8
Marte,Ketel	8	20	11	15	3	7	15	2	1	3	10	81	+6	+1	+7
Marte,Starling	7	21	11	16	4	5	15	4	0	4	8	95	+5	+23	+28
Martin,Leonys	8	22	9	19	1	4	16	2	1	3	10	112	+4	+12	+16
Martin,Russell	7	25	5	11	2	8	14	2	0	2	12	102	0	0	0
Martinez,J.D.	9	33	7	17	3	5	19	2	2	4	13	99	-2	-3	-5
Martinez,Victor	2	31	2	20	0	9	12	5	0	5	19	122	-34	0	-34
Mauer,Joe	5	23	10	18	3	4	11	2	1	3	11	95	-4	+2	-2
Maybin,Cameron	7	27	13	15	3	4	14	2	2	5	8	80	+1	+3	+4
Mazara,Nomar	6	29	3	9	5	13	16	5	0	5	12	113	-8	-4	-12
McCann,Brian	2	35	3	8	2	6	16	2	2	4	15	87	-15	+1	-14
McCann,James	3	17	2	8	0	2	10	2	0	2	12	68	-8	-2	-10
McCutchen,Andrew	5	29	8	23	4	10	16	1	0	1	15	141	-1	-8	-9
Mercer,Jordy	5	26	18	27	4	7	9	1	0	1	11	116	+4	-1	+3
Merrifield,Whit	5	16	10	15	2	3	6	0	0	0	1	67	+12	+2	+14
Miller,Brad	3	11	5	9	3	9	12	2	1	3	5	101	+4	-2	+2
Molina,Yadier	4	19	10	22	0	9	12	2	2	5	22	106	-27	-1	-28
Montero,Miguel	1	18	5	8	2	2	8	3	0	3	8	61	-7	+1	-6
Morales,Kendrys	3	30	6	11	2	7	5	1	0	1	20	112	-17	0	-17
Moreland,Mitch	2	24	8	16	2	2	8	3	0	3	8	102	-6	+1	-5
Morneau,Justin	1	7	2	5	0	2	7	0	0	0	5	44	+3	0	+3
Morrison,Logan	7	18	3	7	2	7	5	1	3	4	4	63	-7	0	-7
Moss,Brandon	5	18	9	14	2	5	16	2	1	3	8	77	+5	+1	+6
Murphy,Daniel	4	18	10	14	9	14	10	3	1	4	4	115	+5	-1	+4
Myers,Wil	16	33	16	20	10	12	20	3	1	4	12	125	+20	+16	+36
Napoli,Mike	5	30	11	16	2	9	25	10	0	10	15	130	-14	+3	-11
Naquin,Tyler	3	10	12	19	1	3	11	0	0	0	4	47	+10	0	+10
Navarro,Dioner	1	11	2	6	1	6	5	2	0	2	5	56	-7	-3	-10
Nieuwenhuis,Kirk	4	13	5	10	1	3	9	0	1	1	5	80	+6	-10	-4
Norris,Derek	3	17	13	20	1	3	10	0	0	0	9	89	+7	+5	+12
Nunez,Eduardo	5	18	11	20	2	6	21	6	3	9	8	92	-10	+20	+10
O'Malley,Shawn	7	18	2	6	0	0	7	0	0	1	4	38	+2	+2	+4
Odor,Rougned	13	25	8	13	6	7	16	6	3	9	6	131	+3	0	+3
Orlando,Paulo	12	33	14	21	3	4	17	4	1	5	12	75	0	+8	+8
Ortega,Rafael	2	4	6	8	3	5	6	1	0	1	5	38	+4	+2	+6
Ortiz,David	3	28	4	15	1	8	8	5	1	6	22	137	-34	+2	-32
Owings,Chris	7	12	6	11	2	5	14	5	1	6	8	85	-3	+17	+14
Ozuna,Marcell	11	30	11	19	4	8	11	2	1	3	11	106	+1	-6	-5
Pagan,Angel	9	23	15	24	5	7	26	3	0	3	11	91	+17	+7	+24
Panik,Joe	6	28	11	18	4	8	25	2	1	4	14	126	+8	+5	+13
Park,Byungho	5	10	4	5	1	5	6	0	0	0	3	44	+8	+1	+9

2016 Baserunning

Player	1st to 3rd Moved	1st to 3rd Chances	2nd to Home Moved	2nd to Home Chances	1st to Home Moved	1st to Home Chances	Bases Taken	Out Adv	Doubled Off	BR Outs	GDP	GDP Opps	BR Gain	SB Gain	Net Gain
Parker,Jarrett	6	13	4	5	1	3	7	0	2	2	3	35	+4	-2	+2
Parra,Gerardo	4	9	7	10	1	3	8	3	3	6	16	78	-18	-2	-20
Pearce,Steve	4	13	5	6	1	4	12	1	1	2	5	55	+6	-6	0
Pederson,Joc	13	26	6	12	1	3	9	3	1	4	5	89	+3	+2	+5
Pedroia,Dustin	10	46	13	23	6	14	21	5	0	5	24	122	-14	-1	-15
Pence,Hunter	7	24	12	18	7	13	10	3	2	5	10	95	-6	-1	-7
Pennington,Cliff	2	5	5	6	0	2	3	1	0	1	4	26	-1	+1	0
Peralta,David	2	7	4	6	0	2	12	0	0	0	3	34	+11	+2	+13
Peralta,Jhonny	2	8	6	8	0	9	4	1	0	1	5	54	-3	0	-3
Peraza,Jose	2	9	3	7	4	6	2	2	2	4	3	37	-11	+1	-10
Perez,Carlos	1	8	4	10	1	2	4	0	1	1	6	46	-5	+1	-4
Perez,Hernan	6	11	5	9	3	6	15	0	0	1	6	90	+16	+20	+36
Perez,Roberto	1	6	1	1	1	2	5	1	1	2	4	38	-2	0	-2
Perez,Salvador	8	31	12	22	1	4	11	2	0	2	12	95	-2	0	-2
Peterson,Jace	8	24	11	20	4	6	11	3	3	6	9	72	-10	-5	-15
Petit,Gregorio	1	14	4	6	0	3	5	2	1	3	7	37	-12	-1	-13
Pham,Tommy	1	7	6	8	2	4	2	1	0	1	3	30	-2	-2	-4
Phillips,Brandon	9	32	14	21	2	7	17	7	0	7	17	114	-13	-2	-15
Pierzynski,A.J.	3	7	1	4	1	3	3	1	0	1	13	51	-10	+1	-9
Pillar,Kevin	14	30	10	16	2	6	20	1	1	2	12	101	+14	+2	+16
Piscotty,Stephen	7	33	10	19	5	9	16	1	1	2	14	111	+1	-3	-2
Plawecki,Kevin	0	4	1	3	0	1	2	1	0	1	1	31	-2	0	-2
Plouffe,Trevor	3	16	5	10	2	6	8	3	1	4	11	58	-14	+1	-13
Polanco,Gregory	1	30	14	26	2	7	18	2	1	4	13	139	-6	+5	-1
Polanco,Jorge	5	19	3	5	0	1	12	2	1	3	3	41	+2	-2	0
Posey,Buster	11	40	8	22	4	11	20	2	2	4	18	123	-8	+4	-4
Prado,Martin	15	46	15	23	6	14	22	3	2	5	24	160	-2	-2	-4
Profar,Jurickson	2	12	2	5	2	4	10	3	1	4	7	47	-8	0	-8
Puig,Yasiel	5	13	6	7	3	5	9	4	1	5	10	88	-5	+1	-4
Pujols,Albert	6	32	3	11	1	12	19	4	1	6	24	176	-19	+4	-15
Raburn,Ryan	5	10	5	8	0	1	9	0	1	1	6	44	+5	0	+5
Ramirez,Alexei	4	22	7	12	0	2	17	3	0	3	8	74	+1	-10	-9
Ramirez,Hanley	10	34	9	15	4	8	16	6	1	8	17	127	-15	+3	-12
Ramirez,Jose	15	36	18	20	9	14	20	1	1	2	10	113	+25	+8	+33
Ramos,Wilson	1	29	8	17	0	4	14	3	0	3	17	91	-17	0	-17
Rasmus,Colby	4	14	5	8	1	4	7	2	1	3	5	86	-1	+2	+1
Realmuto,J.T.	6	25	15	22	4	8	13	3	3	6	12	93	-10	+4	-6
Reddick,Josh	11	28	13	16	1	3	11	2	1	3	8	69	+4	+2	+6
Refsnyder,Rob	3	14	5	7	0	2	9	2	0	2	5	22	-2	0	-2
Reimold,Nolan	1	11	3	5	0	3	9	1	1	2	8	41	-6	-3	-9
Rendon,Anthony	8	33	17	24	6	12	18	1	2	3	5	97	+12	0	+12
Revere,Ben	7	15	7	11	2	4	14	0	0	0	12	42	+8	+4	+12
Reyes,Jose	5	16	3	6	0	4	21	1	1	2	3	36	+12	+5	+17
Reynolds,Mark	6	20	7	16	3	8	17	1	2	3	6	78	+4	-3	+1
Rickard,Joey	6	13	6	8	6	7	15	2	3	5	3	42	+6	+2	+8
Rivera,Rene	1	3	0	1	0	1	3	1	0	1	4	33	-3	0	-3
Rizzo,Anthony	5	26	11	18	0	10	19	5	1	6	13	172	-5	-7	-12
Robinson,Clint	1	6	1	4	2	5	8	2	0	2	4	48	0	0	0
Rodriguez,Alex	0	10	1	3	0	2	1	1	0	1	4	52	-6	+3	-3
Rodriguez,Sean	4	16	6	12	3	5	10	3	1	4	6	72	-4	0	-4
Rojas,Miguel	2	9	7	9	3	3	4	0	1	1	10	37	-4	0	-4
Rollins,Jimmy	0	6	6	9	0	2	6	2	0	2	2	44	0	+1	+1
Romine,Andrew	3	12	4	4	1	1	4	0	1	1	5	33	-1	+8	+7
Romine,Austin	1	8	3	5	1	1	4	0	0	0	7	37	-1	+1	0
Rosales,Adam	4	12	8	12	0	0	12	0	0	0	2	37	+14	+4	+18
Rosario,Eddie	8	15	7	10	8	9	8	3	1	4	4	66	+6	+1	+7
Ross,David	4	7	3	4	1	1	3	0	0	0	3	40	+6	-2	+4
Rua,Ryan	8	20	8	9	3	4	10	1	0	1	8	55	+9	+9	+18
Ruiz,Carlos	2	16	5	10	1	2	5	1	2	3	4	39	-9	+1	-8
Rupp,Cameron	3	17	5	10	0	1	4	0	1	1	11	62	-9	+1	-8
Russell,Addison	7	37	7	14	4	8	18	2	4	6	11	138	-5	+3	-2
Saladino,Tyler	5	16	8	12	1	2	5	0	1	1	11	61	-3	+1	-2
Saltalamacchia,Jarrod	2	9	1	7	3	6	6	1	1	2	1	56	0	0	0
Sanchez,Gary	5	16	3	7	0	5	6	2	0	2	5	49	-4	+1	-3

2016 Baserunning

Player	1st to 3rd Moved	Chances	2nd to Home Moved	Chances	1st to Home Moved	Chances	Bases Taken	Out Adv	Doubled Off	BR Outs	GDP	GDP Opps	BR Gain	SB Gain	Net Gain
Sano,Miguel	7	18	1	5	1	4	8	4	0	4	8	104	-5	+1	-4
Santana,Carlos	6	23	13	18	4	16	30	3	1	4	18	111	+6	+1	+7
Santana,Danny	8	13	4	8	1	1	5	1	0	1	1	38	+7	-6	+1
Santana,Domingo	3	11	8	10	1	3	9	2	0	2	7	50	+1	-4	-3
Sardinas,Luis	2	8	4	6	1	3	2	1	0	1	3	47	0	0	0
Saunders,Michael	5	21	10	14	4	5	13	2	0	2	14	102	+3	-3	0
Schebler,Scott	2	15	4	4	1	2	9	1	1	2	5	46	+1	-6	-5
Schimpf,Ryan	4	9	7	7	4	6	13	0	0	0	3	53	+19	-1	+18
Schoop,Jonathan	10	25	9	16	2	10	25	1	2	3	16	122	+9	-3	+6
Seager,Corey	10	39	14	18	7	17	25	0	1	1	12	145	+22	-3	+19
Seager,Kyle	11	31	11	18	1	2	15	3	1	4	18	133	-3	+1	-2
Segura,Jean	15	36	19	26	6	9	33	5	4	9	6	70	+12	+13	+25
Semien,Marcus	8	25	13	17	4	6	11	5	0	5	12	119	-2	+6	+4
Shaw,Travis	4	20	7	17	2	8	16	6	0	6	10	108	-10	+3	-7
Shuck,J.B.	2	7	7	11	1	2	3	1	1	2	5	45	-4	-3	-7
Simmons,Andrelton	11	23	7	15	3	7	10	4	2	7	16	95	-18	+8	-10
Smith,Mallex	4	7	5	8	3	3	8	2	0	3	3	34	+2	0	+2
Smith,Seth	9	31	8	20	4	10	12	3	1	4	11	91	-8	0	-8
Smoak,Justin	4	14	5	9	1	3	3	1	1	2	7	50	-7	+1	-6
Smolinski,Jake	0	14	3	6	1	6	8	2	1	4	11	64	-16	-3	-19
Solarte,Yangervis	6	20	6	10	3	5	8	3	2	5	7	77	-8	-1	-9
Soler,Jorge	4	17	6	9	0	2	5	0	1	1	5	53	0	0	0
Souza Jr.,Steven	4	17	7	8	5	7	9	1	1	2	5	78	+7	-5	+2
Span,Denard	12	31	11	15	6	10	26	2	6	9	8	76	+1	-2	-1
Springer,George	17	38	13	25	8	15	38	7	2	9	12	107	+11	-11	0
Stanton,Giancarlo	2	19	6	9	1	7	6	2	0	2	6	94	-4	0	-4
Story,Trevor	6	14	6	7	3	5	9	3	0	3	5	70	+5	-2	+3
Suarez,Eugenio	8	40	10	21	4	9	16	1	0	2	10	101	+1	+1	+2
Suzuki,Ichiro	8	30	11	16	4	7	10	1	1	2	4	57	+5	+6	+11
Suzuki,Kurt	2	14	6	11	1	6	5	3	1	4	9	74	-14	0	-14
Swanson,Dansby	2	8	1	2	2	3	2	0	0	0	2	22	+1	+3	+4
Szczur,Matt	3	9	4	8	1	5	10	1	0	1	2	33	+6	-6	0
Taylor,Michael	4	8	5	7	0	1	8	1	2	3	2	35	+1	+8	+9
Teixeira,Mark	4	21	3	12	3	9	9	1	0	1	7	79	-2	+2	0
Thompson,Trayce	4	12	7	7	2	3	6	0	1	1	3	51	+8	+3	+11
Tomas,Yasmany	4	24	5	12	1	5	12	4	0	4	18	104	-16	-6	-22
Tomlinson,Kelby	6	12	2	5	1	2	4	0	0	0	1	27	+7	+3	+10
Torreyes,Ronald	2	9	4	5	3	3	7	1	1	2	4	26	0	0	0
Travis,Devon	7	18	10	12	1	2	19	2	1	3	6	75	+14	+2	+16
Trout,Mike	25	60	22	33	7	11	32	2	1	3	5	164	+42	+16	+58
Trumbo,Mark	4	25	8	15	4	7	15	4	2	6	14	128	-10	+2	-8
Tulowitzki,Troy	5	23	5	13	1	4	16	3	1	4	14	105	-7	+1	-6
Turner,Justin	17	37	12	18	2	8	14	3	0	3	16	159	+8	+2	+10
Turner,Trea	5	15	7	8	2	2	12	3	1	4	1	36	+4	+21	+25
Upton Jr.,Melvin	6	19	10	15	3	5	13	2	1	3	6	92	+7	+11	+18
Upton,Justin	6	29	10	17	5	6	16	1	0	1	15	141	+9	+1	+10
Uribe,Juan	1	8	2	2	0	3	2	0	1	1	6	41	-6	0	-6
Utley,Chase	11	44	10	15	3	7	21	6	0	6	0	61	+5	-2	+3
Valbuena,Luis	1	11	5	10	1	5	12	2	0	2	5	59	+1	-1	0
Valencia,Danny	5	26	6	13	6	12	20	2	1	3	11	92	+3	-1	+2
Vargas,Kennys	2	9	2	4	1	3	2	0	1	1	2	25	-3	0	-3
Vazquez,Christian	2	11	2	7	0	3	5	0	0	0	3	23	-1	0	-1
Villar,Jonathan	12	25	16	25	1	2	19	7	4	12	7	76	-15	+26	+11
Vogt,Stephen	4	22	8	12	2	6	14	1	1	2	6	94	+7	0	+7
Votto,Joey	3	37	14	29	3	13	15	3	3	6	16	129	-24	+6	-18
Walker,Neil	7	28	8	13	3	8	7	1	1	2	11	90	-4	+1	-3
Wallace,Brett	1	7	5	5	0	3	2	0	0	0	2	26	+1	0	+1
Weeks Jr.,Rickie	1	6	3	5	3	3	1	1	2	3	8	45	-11	+5	-6
Werth,Jayson	12	36	9	18	6	10	20	2	1	3	17	105	+3	+3	+6
White,Tyler	2	7	3	3	0	2	2	0	0	0	6	55	+1	+1	+2
Wieters,Matt	1	21	6	12	2	8	9	1	0	1	10	83	-5	+1	-4
Wilson,Bobby	5	17	1	6	0	0	4	0	0	0	6	53	0	0	0
Wolters,Tony	5	9	3	6	0	0	10	0	0	0	1	41	+14	+2	+16
Wong,Kolten	7	15	4	7	3	6	16	1	1	2	3	68	+15	+7	+22

2016 Baserunning

Player	1st to 3rd Moved	1st to 3rd Chances	2nd to Home Moved	2nd to Home Chances	1st to Home Moved	1st to Home Chances	Bases Taken	Out Adv	Doubled Off	BR Outs	GDP	GDP Opps	BR Gain	SB Gain	Net Gain
Wright,David	2	6	2	2	0	2	2	1	1	2	0	32	-1	-1	-2
Yelich,Christian	7	23	14	22	5	7	20	1	1	2	20	158	+9	+1	+10
Young,Chris	1	7	2	7	2	3	8	0	0	0	4	46	+5	0	+5
Zimmerman,Ryan	11	25	8	12	1	5	17	2	0	2	12	87	+9	+2	+11
Zobrist,Ben	15	38	12	16	5	8	25	1	0	1	17	128	+22	-2	+20
Zunino,Mike	0	11	1	3	0	1	2	0	0	0	0	33	0	0	0

Career Baserunning
Players with 1000 Career Games
(Data goes back to 2002)

Player	1st to 3rd Moved	1st to 3rd Chances	2nd to Home Moved	2nd to Home Chances	1st to Home Moved	1st to Home Chances	Bases Taken	Out Adv	Doubled Off	BR Outs	GDP	GDP Opps	BR Gain	SB Gain	Net Gain
Andrus,Elvis	150	288	120	161	49	73	201	24	20	44	114	890	+127	+75	+202
Aybar,Erick	108	229	126	169	33	55	193	40	19	61	102	976	+59	+28	+87
Bautista,Jose	103	292	105	167	55	103	155	31	20	51	152	1194	-20	+8	-12
Beltran,Carlos	146	449	161	260	64	121	231	23	15	40	156	1703	+122	+158	+280
Beltre,Adrian	144	455	158	264	63	137	233	42	5	47	229	1856	+26	+23	+49
Bourn,Michael	91	277	122	190	52	72	172	18	11	29	34	716	+138	+153	+291
Braun,Ryan	94	286	117	170	54	86	165	28	13	41	136	1201	+45	+81	+126
Bruce,Jay	59	221	76	136	28	58	114	24	6	30	79	1024	+24	-11	+13
Butler,Billy	33	292	57	161	20	106	135	34	8	42	207	1089	-231	-1	-232
Byrd,Marlon	73	315	120	186	49	101	173	28	12	41	115	1144	+16	-6	+10
Cabrera,Asdrubal	85	251	106	162	36	77	167	43	8	55	119	1030	-9	+23	+14
Cabrera,Melky	97	318	108	183	44	95	189	34	14	50	139	1159	-3	+29	+26
Cabrera,Miguel	132	584	173	315	48	141	242	44	14	60	279	1842	-137	-2	-139
Cano,Robinson	109	379	173	273	43	95	218	40	22	62	234	1664	-54	-26	-80
Castro,Starlin	48	201	74	109	27	59	102	21	10	31	121	792	-54	-11	-65
Choo,Shin-Soo	83	295	114	174	39	77	178	23	17	40	66	817	+62	+22	+84
Crawford,Carl	76	308	177	245	60	111	255	36	21	60	79	1303	+124	+262	+386
Crisp,Coco	98	300	158	224	59	98	199	22	11	34	91	1011	+128	+151	+279
Cruz,Nelson	44	227	70	119	13	60	123	26	12	38	95	922	-51	+14	-37
Davis,Chris	45	216	71	126	25	59	87	16	8	26	44	748	+4	-4	0
Davis,Rajai	66	157	82	121	38	47	153	11	7	18	65	668	+129	+179	+308
Desmond,Ian	72	185	73	121	29	43	139	18	8	27	90	819	+60	+57	+117
Drew,Stephen	59	224	76	141	21	69	125	32	11	44	48	820	-11	+3	-8
Ellsbury,Jacoby	75	247	108	186	26	57	176	26	7	34	76	789	+55	+185	+240
Encarnacion,Edwin	78	287	96	153	36	91	128	25	9	34	146	1233	-24	+30	+6
Escobar,Alcides	77	211	104	154	37	56	124	15	12	27	82	755	+58	+92	+150
Escobar,Yunel	107	351	121	173	33	84	142	35	19	55	183	994	-112	-23	-135
Ethier,Andre	67	338	125	181	35	74	111	20	9	30	104	1127	+1	-27	-26
Fielder,Prince	52	414	68	178	36	116	169	30	10	40	159	1329	-124	-4	-128
Fowler,Dexter	137	231	93	144	32	52	162	35	23	59	39	587	+68	+13	+81
Francoeur,Jeff	84	249	92	155	33	89	143	31	15	49	127	1113	-31	-24	-55
Gardner,Brett	82	209	89	137	33	53	162	16	13	29	39	670	+121	+114	+235
Gomez,Carlos	62	164	101	132	25	38	98	32	22	54	64	740	-28	+109	+81
Gonzalez,Adrian	69	400	94	225	43	139	164	35	16	52	195	1558	-163	-6	-169
Gonzalez,Carlos	49	171	98	149	42	71	131	18	6	24	76	842	+70	+58	+128
Gordon,Alex	89	295	119	181	38	73	150	15	9	24	83	904	+84	+17	+101
Granderson,Curtis	113	362	121	213	67	109	184	19	17	36	53	1144	+135	+57	+192
Hamilton,Josh	83	248	83	133	40	62	106	11	14	26	66	878	+64	+18	+82
Hardy,J.J.	69	272	91	165	30	87	133	19	9	29	149	1118	-34	-8	-42
Headley,Chase	58	264	95	172	26	60	150	23	9	34	100	958	-4	+30	+26
Hill,Aaron	81	299	107	169	37	79	157	19	8	28	132	1203	+43	+4	+47
Holliday,Matt	142	427	182	272	64	121	196	43	14	57	206	1594	-1	+33	+32
Howard,Ryan	34	296	79	177	32	119	122	27	10	37	116	1289	-91	+2	-89
Infante,Omar	89	262	109	175	36	68	124	23	18	42	89	1026	+13	+14	+27
Johnson,Kelly	64	243	74	143	39	70	141	13	9	23	70	907	+67	+15	+82
Jones,Adam	86	264	94	141	55	86	149	18	10	29	136	1114	+52	+22	+74
Kemp,Matt	102	281	127	185	41	70	150	39	22	62	138	1226	-25	+61	+36
Kendrick,Howie	119	277	110	179	48	85	161	27	16	45	164	1025	-7	+31	+24
Kinsler,Ian	140	328	176	244	56	102	227	23	20	43	132	1111	+136	+95	+231
Lind,Adam	62	200	59	124	24	71	90	22	6	30	111	907	-55	-4	-59
Loney,James	69	275	82	151	28	65	146	26	11	39	156	1052	-61	-4	-65
Longoria,Evan	64	252	101	160	28	71	137	15	11	26	130	1094	+10	+17	+27
Markakis,Nick	108	457	149	245	44	118	187	24	8	33	164	1289	-8	+7	-1
Martin,Russell	79	312	110	178	40	77	145	27	14	42	169	1099	-63	+7	-56
Martinez,Victor	58	416	100	224	23	132	175	36	8	45	230	1531	-196	-7	-203
Mauer,Joe	121	383	143	217	53	116	216	16	12	30	182	1366	+77	+16	+93
McCann,Brian	46	294	41	135	16	94	101	29	10	40	154	1241	-170	+8	-162
McCutchen,Andrew	78	294	116	168	39	75	121	14	10	24	71	885	+54	+36	+90
Molina,Yadier	58	311	73	170	18	68	127	28	10	40	211	1197	-179	-13	-192
Montero,Miguel	36	218	62	116	26	65	93	26	10	36	100	765	-92	-14	-106
Morales,Kendrys	53	221	49	84	10	59	97	24	3	28	127	741	-83	-20	-103

366

Career Baserunning

Players with 1000 Career Games
(Data goes back to 2002)

Player	1st to 3rd		2nd to Home		1st to Home		Bases Taken	Out Adv	Doubled Off	BR Outs	GDP	GDP Opps	BR Gain	SB Gain	Net Gain
	Moved	Chances	Moved	Chances	Moved	Chances									
Morneau,Justin	55	289	91	174	26	90	152	35	5	40	139	1327	-48	-15	-63
Murphy,Daniel	68	204	74	108	39	66	113	18	8	26	90	809	+35	+14	+49
Napoli,Mike	72	261	87	139	24	70	115	29	7	37	103	976	-24	-6	-30
Navarro,Dioner	25	160	38	98	10	50	72	25	0	25	80	639	-82	-10	-92
Ortiz,David	61	433	100	257	27	136	190	52	16	69	206	1984	-209	-4	-213
Pagan,Angel	86	228	109	170	33	60	164	16	14	33	54	717	+95	+74	+169
Parra,Gerardo	52	176	93	132	22	43	119	33	6	40	84	711	-13	-9	-22
Pedroia,Dustin	89	336	130	205	51	133	179	40	15	57	141	1155	-55	+48	-7
Pence,Hunter	98	309	105	163	65	89	172	20	12	33	138	1122	+64	+7	+71
Peralta,Jhonny	66	354	115	221	35	113	165	38	16	54	198	1480	-142	-37	-179
Phillips,Brandon	132	335	134	197	47	79	231	50	17	69	202	1359	-8	+46	+38
Pierzynski,A.J.	68	345	90	207	23	80	158	48	7	57	233	1486	-202	-19	-221
Prado,Martin	107	292	106	164	35	84	166	29	13	42	152	973	-10	-15	-25
Pujols,Albert	175	532	202	290	57	148	262	69	18	90	315	2257	-99	+30	-69
Ramirez,Alexei	75	246	116	173	41	68	152	21	14	35	139	1080	+22	+17	+39
Ramirez,Hanley	102	311	146	221	48	84	176	50	14	66	111	1102	-14	+98	+84
Rasmus,Colby	69	169	72	101	31	46	94	12	14	26	43	758	+77	0	+77
Reyes,Jose	127	356	176	262	46	80	272	59	20	79	74	972	+81	+250	+331
Reynolds,Mark	53	211	70	127	22	73	124	17	11	28	94	955	-1	0	-1
Rodriguez,Alex	119	382	155	242	50	128	204	36	16	52	181	1724	+19	+104	+123
Rollins,Jimmy	153	462	220	321	50	108	297	38	11	49	131	1324	+161	+227	+388
Ruiz,Carlos	44	167	72	115	13	42	85	15	14	31	102	706	-64	+4	-60
Smith,Seth	57	196	70	117	37	56	96	20	7	29	68	662	+5	+6	+11
Span,Denard	94	252	116	187	35	65	198	22	21	44	65	633	+71	+68	+139
Suzuki,Ichiro	168	635	221	352	72	143	321	34	18	53	87	1441	+171	+248	+419
Suzuki,Kurt	58	221	78	150	25	58	97	15	2	18	113	904	-13	-1	-14
Teixeira,Mark	88	398	121	217	46	131	183	43	8	51	158	1752	-29	+12	-17
Tulowitzki,Troy	98	301	108	173	25	65	160	33	15	49	135	1058	-23	-5	-28
Upton Jr.,Melvin	104	249	107	164	30	59	178	25	13	39	98	1046	+92	+116	+208
Upton,Justin	96	276	111	164	54	89	133	16	15	31	98	1106	+74	+28	+102
Uribe,Juan	86	259	95	151	19	56	133	13	13	28	148	1226	+10	-33	-23
Utley,Chase	164	373	154	211	60	100	207	31	16	47	87	1418	+193	+105	+298
Votto,Joey	91	343	104	179	32	105	150	38	18	57	101	1057	-67	+11	-56
Weeks Jr.,Rickie	85	246	119	167	41	73	148	33	25	58	77	758	-6	+67	+61
Werth,Jayson	105	336	112	177	41	80	167	24	5	30	95	1123	+90	+88	+178
Wright,David	109	348	123	188	53	121	182	33	17	53	152	1425	+7	+66	+73
Young,Chris	46	183	88	133	43	65	115	19	11	30	55	888	+58	+49	+107
Zimmerman,Ryan	88	289	116	179	47	98	162	22	6	28	173	1285	+30	+11	+41
Zobrist,Ben	106	285	100	166	45	91	188	19	10	29	97	1052	+113	+25	+138

2002-2016 MLB Averages

1st to 3rd	2nd to Home	1st to Home
29%	60%	43%

2016 Team Baserunning

Team	1st to 3rd Moved	Chances	2nd to Home Moved	Chances	1st to Home Moved	Chances	Bases Taken	Out Adv	Doubled Off	BR Outs	GDP	GDP Opps	BR Gain	SB Gain	Net Gain
San Diego Padres	79	229	111	157	40	71	155	26	6	33	93	987	+72	+35	+107
Arizona D-Backs	82	275	106	166	32	66	174	27	10	37	117	1052	+31	+75	+106
Cleveland Indians	78	278	129	184	38	81	200	32	11	43	137	1118	+33	+72	+105
Washington Nationals	89	285	101	164	42	81	173	27	14	41	101	1092	+43	+43	+86
New York Yankees	72	317	95	156	40	80	181	22	9	32	120	1108	+33	+28	+61
Minnesota Twins	88	263	92	155	37	75	157	28	10	40	96	1082	+34	+27	+61
Chicago Cubs	98	311	118	178	38	93	194	32	15	47	107	1317	+62	-2	+60
Colorado Rockies	94	284	109	174	43	92	190	20	15	35	113	1100	+69	-12	+57
Boston Red Sox	115	337	105	180	51	109	177	36	9	46	137	1246	+10	+35	+45
Kansas City Royals	93	320	123	200	33	66	142	24	9	33	134	1044	-10	+51	+41
Los Angeles Dodgers	108	320	104	153	32	84	164	31	5	37	120	1167	+43	-7	+36
Milwaukee Brewers	70	233	85	148	23	62	154	29	14	45	131	1128	-34	+69	+35
Atlanta Braves	88	312	96	181	34	79	199	22	10	34	145	1221	+27	+7	+34
San Francisco Giants	90	331	113	199	42	92	201	29	18	49	119	1244	+16	+7	+23
Baltimore Orioles	73	273	98	163	37	84	163	23	8	31	119	1104	+28	-7	+21
Texas Rangers	105	317	105	175	35	76	161	38	13	51	113	1134	-7	+27	+20
Tampa Bay Rays	64	222	74	130	36	81	150	26	12	38	88	1005	+16	-14	+2
Houston Astros	82	250	101	164	31	71	155	30	12	43	134	1100	-17	+14	-3
Toronto Blue Jays	76	285	88	150	33	72	176	31	7	38	153	1165	-13	+6	-7
Seattle Mariners	91	313	94	171	26	67	160	28	8	38	138	1218	-12	0	-12
St Louis Cardinals	75	273	92	163	36	95	171	29	10	40	117	1138	+1	-17	-16
Philadelphia Phillies	76	261	75	132	26	62	128	20	15	36	112	1010	-24	+6	-18
Miami Marlins	79	318	115	188	34	75	148	23	16	39	140	1152	-35	+15	-20
New York Mets	79	293	73	142	21	65	136	26	10	36	122	1179	-30	+6	-24
Chicago White Sox	86	298	123	197	23	72	145	31	12	44	122	1111	-33	+5	-28
Detroit Tigers	75	321	94	176	27	67	178	31	12	44	135	1163	-36	0	-36
Cincinnati Reds	70	267	91	175	32	79	148	37	10	49	129	1048	-78	+37	-41
Pittsburgh Pirates	63	315	117	212	32	85	160	35	10	46	133	1219	-66	+20	-46
Los Angeles Angels	93	324	113	200	31	84	174	34	19	55	147	1201	-62	+5	-57
Oakland Athletics	63	269	98	158	36	84	135	30	7	39	142	1041	-61	+4	-57
MLB Totals	2494	8694	3038	5091	1021	2350	4949	857	336	1219	3714	33894			

Stolen Base Attempt Times

Lindsay Zeck

Stealing bases successfully at the major league level requires a careful blend of independent skills: picking the right pitch on which to run, getting a lead, reading the pitcher, reacting, accelerating, running, and sliding, and avoiding the tag. Some players excel at all of these skills, but Paul Goldschmidt is not one of them. Goldschmidt took an average of 3.76 seconds on his max-effort stolen base attempts of second in 2016, well-below league average. However, a lack of raw speed didn't prevent Goldschmidt from stealing a surprising 32 bases on just 37 attempts for the season. Meanwhile, Wil Myers stole a similar 28 bases on 34 attempts but averaged 3.56 seconds per attempt, a whole two-tenths of a second faster than Goldschmidt, which is enough to put him in the top 15 in baseball. The two sluggers both stole plenty of bases; however, they accomplished the feat in very different ways.

In 2015, Billy Hamilton of the Cincinnati Reds and Jarrod Dyson of the Kansas City Royals finished with the second and third fastest average stolen base times, respectively, to Rico Noel, who did not play in 2016. Both Hamilton and Dyson finished with the same rankings in 2016, even with Hamilton beating his 2015 average stolen base time by 0.03 seconds (3.45 seconds as opposed to 3.48). In 2016, they fell short to Terrance Gore of the Kansas City Royals. Gore, who has played only 37 games in his three seasons in Major League Baseball (17 in 2016), finished with an average time of 3.43 seconds, 0.02 seconds faster on average than Hamilton and 0.06 seconds faster than Dyson. This is the first time Gore has been eligible to appear on the stolen base times leaderboard. Prior to this season, he had only attempted to steal a combined eight bases, five of which were timed with an average of 3.42 seconds. Of all players who have at least 10 timed stolen base attempts between 2014 and 2016, Gore has the fastest average time of 3.43 seconds.

While speed is not the only factor in successful base stealing, it certainly helps. The players with the top five average times had an overall success rate of 84 percent, whereas the bottom five had an overall success rate of only 56 percent. The difference between the fastest and the slowest average stolen base time is about half a second (0.47 seconds) with Avisail Garcia and Alexei Ramirez coming in slowest in 2016 with a 3.90 average stolen base time.

Stolen Base Times 2B Only

Runner	Timed Attempts	Average
Terrance Gore	10	3.43
Billy Hamilton	33	3.45
Jarrod Dyson	19	3.49
Rajai Davis	21	3.50
Jacoby Ellsbury	15	3.51
Keon Broxton	19	3.51
Byron Buxton	8	3.52
Mallex Smith	17	3.54
Jose Altuve	24	3.54
Jonathan Villar	45	3.55
Trea Turner	28	3.55
Tim Anderson	6	3.56
Kevin Kiermaier	13	3.56
Starling Marte	49	3.56
Wil Myers	20	3.56
Charlie Blackmon	19	3.56
Dee Gordon	30	3.56
Cameron Maybin	14	3.56
Carlos Gomez	15	3.56
Ryan Rua	7	3.57
Trevor Story	10	3.57
Travis Jankowski	29	3.57
Billy Burns	13	3.58
Leonys Martin	20	3.58
Ben Revere	14	3.58
Melvin Upton Jr.	23	3.58
Eduardo Nunez	36	3.58
Ian Desmond	12	3.59
Josh Harrison	14	3.59
Mike Trout	19	3.59
Christian Yelich	10	3.59
Michael Taylor	10	3.60
Gregory Polanco	19	3.60
Danny Santana	15	3.60
Chris Owings	10	3.60
Ezequiel Carrera	8	3.61
Kevin Pillar	11	3.61
Jose Ramirez	13	3.62
Jose Peraza	16	3.62
Mookie Betts	21	3.63
Rougned Odor	11	3.63
Cesar Hernandez	20	3.63
Ian Kinsler	9	3.63
Coco Crisp	9	3.63
Ichiro Suzuki	6	3.64
Gregor Blanco	6	3.64
Drew Stubbs	8	3.64
Denard Span	14	3.64
Michael Bourn	11	3.64
Adam Eaton	10	3.64
Xander Bogaerts	8	3.65
Jake Marisnick	10	3.66
Delino DeShields	8	3.66
Anthony Rendon	13	3.66
Brett Gardner	16	3.66
Todd Frazier	8	3.66
Brian Dozier	12	3.67
Jean Segura	23	3.67
George Springer	16	3.67
Aaron Altherr	6	3.67
Whit Merrifield	6	3.68
Odubel Herrera	22	3.68
Javier Baez	11	3.68
Hanley Ramirez	8	3.68
Rafael Ortega	9	3.68
Abraham Almonte	6	3.68
Brett Lawrie	7	3.68
Hernan Perez	21	3.69
Ryan Braun	6	3.69

Runner	Timed Attempts	Average
Francisco Lindor	18	3.69
Jace Peterson	7	3.69
Andrew Romine	6	3.70
Justin Upton	7	3.70
Aaron Hicks	7	3.70
Andrew McCutchen	11	3.70
Jason Kipnis	8	3.71
Jose Iglesias	11	3.71
Angel Pagan	15	3.71
Jackie Bradley Jr.	6	3.71
Peter Bourjos	8	3.72
Dexter Fowler	6	3.72
Ender Inciarte	13	3.72
Jason Heyward	9	3.72
Steven Souza Jr.	8	3.72
Alcides Escobar	11	3.72
Lorenzo Cain	12	3.72
Logan Forsythe	9	3.73
Tyler Saladino	10	3.73
Adam Duvall	7	3.74
Nick Franklin	6	3.74
Freddy Galvis	10	3.74
Ketel Marte	11	3.74
Marcus Semien	6	3.75
Bryce Harper	20	3.75
Alex Gordon	7	3.75
Howie Kendrick	8	3.75
Chase Headley	7	3.76
Paul Goldschmidt	22	3.76
J.T. Realmuto	10	3.76
Nori Aoki	7	3.78
Stephen Piscotty	7	3.78
Elvis Andrus	17	3.78
Kirk Nieuwenhuis	9	3.78
Randal Grichuk	6	3.79
Marwin Gonzalez	6	3.79
Brandon Phillips	9	3.79
Brad Miller	7	3.79
DJ LeMahieu	11	3.83
Dustin Pedroia	6	3.83
Derek Norris	7	3.84
Eugenio Suarez	8	3.84
Kris Bryant	9	3.86
Matt Duffy	8	3.88
Ben Zobrist	7	3.89
Carlos Santana	6	3.89
Avisail Garcia	8	3.90
Alexei Ramirez	7	3.90

Relief Pitching

Joe Rosales

Brad Hand and Zach Duke deserve some appreciation. Neither of them headlined their respective bullpens in 2016, but they did serve prominent roles at the back end of the bullpen, and they both did exemplary work in their roles. In addition to posting strong ERAs of 2.92 and 2.36, respectively, no two pitchers were called on more often than Hand and Duke. Hand led the majors in appearances with 82, while Duke was second with 81. Hand also led the majors in appearances on consecutive days with 29, while Duke tied for fourth with 26.

What is interesting about Duke is that he accumulated those numbers while pitching for two different teams. He began the year with the White Sox and was traded to the Cardinals at the non-waiver trade deadline on July 31. Of his 26 appearances made on consecutive days, 17 came with the White Sox out of 53 total appearances (31 percent) and 9 came with the Cardinals out of 28 total appearances (32 percent). So, neither team was shy about using him on back-to-back days. In fact, the White Sox were not shy about using any of their principle relievers on consecutive days. David Robertson, Nate Jones, and Dan Jennings were all used at least 20 times on back-to-back days, and Matt Albers was used that way on 15 occasions.

In the pages that follow, you will find information related to the performance of the most used relievers from each major league team. To qualify, a reliever must have had at least 10 appearances during the 2016 season. If a guy like Zach Duke pitched for two teams, then you will find him listed with both teams that he pitched for along with the numbers that he accumulated for that team only. In addition to the various performance metrics provided for each pitcher, we also classify each reliever with a specific role: closer (CL), set-up (SU), left-handed specialist (LT), long man (LM), and utility reliever (UR).

The data contained in this section includes:

Usage: Games in Relief (Rel G), the number of times the pitcher entered the game before the seventh inning (Early Entry), pitching on consecutive days (Cons Days), long outings (Long), and Leverage Index (Lev Ind). We use the Leverage Index calculated by Tom Tango and published on FanGraphs.com. An average Leverage Index is 1.0. If a pitcher pitches frequently in late innings with the game on the line, his leverage index will be high. If he generally pitches in the 6th inning of 7-2 ballgames, his leverage index will be very low.

Inherited Runners: The total (#), the number that scored (Scrd), and the percentage that scored (Pct).

Saves: The conversions and opportunities for three different classifications of Saves: "Easy", "Regular", and "Tough". The definitions of each of these save types can be found in the Baseball Glossary at the end of the book.

Relief Results: Clean Outings (Clean), the number of wins the reliever accrued after blowing a save (BS Wins), the total number of Blown Saves (BS), Holds, Save/Hold Percentage (Sv/Hld Pct), Opponent OPS (Opp OPS), and reliever ERA (Rel ERA). The definitions of many of these categories can be found in the Baseball Glossary at the end of the book.

Arizona Diamondbacks

Pitcher	Pos	T	Usage					Inherited Runners			Saves			Relief Results						
			Rel G	Early Entry	Cons Days	Long	Lev Ind	#	Scrd	Pct	Easy	Reg	Tough	Clean	BS Win	BS	Holds	Sv/Hld Pct	Opp OPS	Rel ERA
Ziegler, Brad	CL	R	36	0	11	3	2.2	7	2	.29	12 - 12	5 - 6	1 - 2	26	1	2	0	.90	.724	2.82
Hudson, Daniel	SU	R	70	4	19	8	1.5	22	5	.23	3 - 3	1 - 3	1 - 1	49	0	2	17	.92	.753	5.22
Clippard, Tyler	SU	R	40	0	11	2	1.3	10	4	.40	1 - 1	0 - 2	0 - 0	28	0	2	13	.88	.764	4.30
Chafin, Andrew	LT	L	32	8	8	1	0.8	25	5	.20	0 - 0	0 - 0	0 - 1	21	0	1	6	.86	.703	6.75
Hathaway, Steve	LT	L	24	5	6	1	0.8	12	1	.08	0 - 0	0 - 0	0 - 0	19	0	0	2	1.00	.827	4.91
Escobar, Edwin	LT	L	23	7	8	1	1.2	21	4	.19	0 - 0	0 - 0	0 - 1	14	0	1	4	.80	.874	4.32
Curtis, Zac	LT	L	21	6	2	2	0.8	13	5	.38	0 - 0	0 - 1	0 - 0	14	0	1	1	.50	.864	6.75
Corbin, Patrick	LM	L	12	2	1	9	0.9	4	0	.00	0 - 0	1 - 1	0 - 0	9	0	0	2	1.00	.544	2.70
Delgado, Randall	UR	R	79	29	22	14	0.9	47	17	.36	0 - 0	0 - 0	0 - 3	52	0	3	7	.70	.777	4.44
Barrett, Jake	UR	R	68	16	16	3	1.1	45	18	.40	2 - 3	2 - 4	0 - 2	45	0	5	8	.71	.682	3.49
Burgos, Enrique	UR	R	43	4	7	5	1.1	15	8	.53	0 - 1	1 - 2	0 - 1	25	1	3	7	.73	.779	5.66
Bracho, Silvino	UR	R	26	6	2	6	0.5	19	10	.53	0 - 0	0 - 0	0 - 0	12	0	0	0		.951	7.30
Leone, Dominic	UR	R	25	11	6	4	0.4	11	8	.73	0 - 0	0 - 0	0 - 1	8	0	1	0	.00	1.095	6.33
Godley, Zack	UR	R	18	8	3	6	0.8	10	5	.50	0 - 0	0 - 0	0 - 1	9	0	1	0	.00	.721	4.73
Marshall, Evan	UR	R	15	3	2	2	0.5	13	8	.62	0 - 0	0 - 0	0 - 0	6	0	0	1	1.00	1.083	8.80
Collmenter, Josh	UR	R	15	1	2	9	0.2	6	2	.33	0 - 0	0 - 0	0 - 0	11	0	0	0		.800	4.84

Atlanta Braves

Pitcher	Pos	T	Usage					Inherited Runners			Saves			Relief Results						
			Rel G	Early Entry	Cons Days	Long	Lev Ind	#	Scrd	Pct	Easy	Reg	Tough	Clean	BS Win	BS	Holds	Sv/Hld Pct	Opp OPS	Rel ERA
Johnson, Jim	CL	R	65	1	17	4	1.6	6	2	.33	12 - 13	8 - 9	0 - 1	48	0	3	8	.90	.631	3.06
Withrow, Chris	SU	R	46	6	12	2	1.2	20	7	.35	0 - 0	0 - 2	0 - 1	32	0	3	12	.80	.639	3.58
Cabrera, Mauricio	SU	R	41	2	9	1	1.4	21	4	.19	2 - 3	3 - 3	1 - 1	32	0	1	8	.93	.587	2.82
Krol, Ian	LT	L	63	20	16	6	0.9	47	17	.36	0 - 0	0 - 0	0 - 2	40	0	2	10	.83	.701	3.18
Cervenka, Hunter	LT	L	50	3	16	3	0.9	29	4	.14	0 - 0	0 - 0	0 - 0	40	0	0	9	1.00	.617	3.18
O'Flaherty, Eric	LT	L	39	15	11	3	0.7	24	9	.38	0 - 0	0 - 1	0 - 0	19	0	1	3	.75	.877	6.91
Alvarez, Dario	LT	L	16	4	2	4	1.1	11	2	.18	0 - 0	0 - 0	0 - 0	13	0	0	1	1.00	.642	3.00
Weber, Ryan	LM	R	14	7	0	8	0.4	17	7	.41	0 - 0	0 - 1	0 - 0	4	0	1	0	.00	.802	4.45
De La Cruz, Joel	LM	R	13	11	1	5	0.5	7	1	.14	0 - 0	0 - 0	0 - 0	7	0	0	0		.679	4.32
Vizcaino, Arodys	UR	R	43	0	9	5	1.8	11	3	.27	6 - 7	3 - 6	1 - 1	29	1	4	0	.71	.685	4.42
Ogando, Alexi	UR	R	36	8	11	7	0.8	20	10	.50	0 - 0	0 - 0	0 - 0	20	0	0	3	1.00	.779	3.94
Ramirez, Jose	UR	R	33	5	10	6	1.2	11	4	.36	0 - 0	0 - 0	0 - 0	23	0	0	3	1.00	.700	3.58
Grilli, Jason	UR	R	21	1	4	1	1.5	4	1	.25	1 - 1	1 - 3	0 - 0	13	1	2	2	.67	.779	5.29
Roe, Chaz	UR	R	21	5	5	3	0.7	19	3	.16	0 - 0	0 - 0	0 - 1	15	1	1	3	.75	.604	3.60
Cunniff, Brandon	UR	R	15	6	1	7	0.6	7	2	.29	0 - 0	0 - 0	0 - 0	11	0	0	0		.764	4.24
Gant, John	UR	R	13	5	2	5	0.2	6	3	.50	0 - 0	0 - 0	0 - 0	4	0	0	0		.876	4.95
Norris, Bud	UR	R	12	5	1	4	0.8	6	1	.17	0 - 0	0 - 0	0 - 0	8	0	0	1	1.00	.588	1.96

Baltimore Orioles

Pitcher	Pos	T	Usage					Inherited Runners			Saves			Relief Results						
			Rel G	Early Entry	Cons Days	Long	Lev Ind	#	Scrd	Pct	Easy	Reg	Tough	Clean	BS Win	BS	Holds	Sv/Hld Pct	Opp OPS	Rel ERA
Britton, Zach	CL	L	69	0	19	3	1.8	18	2	.11	28-28	17-17	2-2	62	0	0	0	1.00	.430	0.54
Brach, Brad	SU	R	71	5	13	12	1.2	27	3	.11	0-0	2-5	0-2	54	1	5	24	.84	.578	2.05
O'Day, Darren	SU	R	34	2	5	2	1.5	10	1	.10	2-2	0-2	1-1	27	0	2	10	.87	.717	3.77
Hart, Donnie	LT	L	22	7	4	1	0.5	13	4	.31	0-0	0-0	0-0	17	0	0	4	1.00	.519	0.49
McFarland, T.J.	LT	L	16	7	2	5	0.7	5	3	.60	0-0	0-1	0-2	10	0	3	0	.00	.928	6.93
Duensing, Brian	LT	L	14	4	3	0	0.3	7	0	.00	0-0	0-0	0-0	11	0	0	0		.714	4.05
Worley, Vance	LM	R	31	15	2	16	0.5	24	9	.38	0-0	1-1	0-0	16	0	0	0	1.00	.762	3.20
Bundy, Dylan	LM	R	22	10	1	13	0.7	14	4	.29	0-0	0-0	0-0	12	0	0	3	1.00	.785	3.08
Givens, Mychal	UR	R	66	22	8	15	1.1	39	13	.33	0-0	0-0	0-1	45	1	1	13	.93	.664	3.13
Despaigne, Odrisamer	UR	R	16	8	0	8	0.6	5	2	.40	0-0	0-2	0-0	8	0	2	1	.33	.889	5.60
Drake, Oliver	UR	R	14	4	1	3	0.6	8	4	.50	0-0	0-0	0-1	6	0	1	0	.00	.595	4.00
Hunter, Tommy	UR	R	12	5	3	1	0.9	3	1	.33	0-0	0-0	0-0	10	0	0	1	1.00	.695	2.19
Wilson, Tyler	UR	R	11	6	0	8	0.4	7	4	.57	0-0	0-0	0-0	6	0	0	0		.764	3.86

Boston Red Sox

Pitcher	Pos	T	Usage					Inherited Runners			Saves			Relief Results						
			Rel G	Early Entry	Cons Days	Long	Lev Ind	#	Scrd	Pct	Easy	Reg	Tough	Clean	BS Win	BS	Holds	Sv/Hld Pct	Opp OPS	Rel ERA
Kimbrel, Craig	CL	R	57	0	16	7	1.8	15	4	.27	20-21	9-9	2-3	45	0	2	1	.94	.539	3.40
Tazawa, Junichi	SU	R	53	6	8	4	1.1	22	14	.64	0-0	0-0	0-2	37	1	2	16	.89	.730	4.17
Uehara, Koji	SU	R	50	0	9	3	1.2	1	1	1.00	5-6	2-3	0-0	41	0	2	18	.93	.657	3.45
Ziegler, Brad	SU	R	33	1	9	1	2.0	16	3	.19	1-1	3-5	0-2	26	1	4	8	.75	.597	1.52
Ross Jr., Robbie	LT	L	54	16	6	11	0.8	35	9	.26	0-0	0-0	0-0	39	0	0	8	1.00	.624	3.25
Layne, Tommy	LT	L	34	9	8	2	0.6	15	6	.40	0-0	0-0	0-1	22	0	1	2	.67	.699	3.77
Abad, Fernando	LT	L	18	1	1	1	1.0	11	7	.64	0-0	0-0	0-3	11	0	3	2	.40	.759	6.39
Hembree, Heath	LM	R	38	19	5	15	0.9	26	7	.27	0-0	0-1	0-1	20	1	2	5	.71	.695	2.65
Barnes, Matt	UR	R	62	23	8	14	1.0	50	11	.22	0-0	0-0	1-2	40	0	1	16	.94	.709	4.05
Buchholz, Clay	UR	R	16	4	2	5	0.6	4	0	.00	0-0	0-0	0-0	11	0	0	2	1.00	.571	3.57
Ramirez, Noe	UR	R	14	4	3	1	0.6	12	4	.33	0-0	0-0	0-0	7	0	0	0		1.059	6.23
Kelly, Joe	UR	R	14	3	2	4	1.3	9	4	.44	0-0	0-0	0-1	11	0	1	2	.67	.558	1.02

Chicago Cubs

Pitcher	Pos	T	Usage					Inherited Runners			Saves			Relief Results						
			Rel G	Early Entry	Cons Days	Long	Lev Ind	#	Scrd	Pct	Easy	Reg	Tough	Clean	BS Win	BS	Holds	Sv/Hld Pct	Opp OPS	Rel ERA
Rondon, Hector	CL	R	54	0	11	7	1.6	9	1	.11	11-12	6-8	1-3	40	1	5	7	.83	.641	3.53
Chapman, Aroldis	CL	L	28	0	9	2	1.3	8	4	.50	14-14	1-2	1-2	24	0	2	0	.89	.370	1.01
Strop, Pedro	SU	R	54	1	12	3	1.3	21	6	.29	0-0	0-2	0-2	40	1	4	21	.84	.517	2.85
Wood, Travis	LT	L	77	11	25	5	0.9	37	5	.14	0-0	0-1	0-0	58	0	1	12	.92	.664	2.95
Richard, Clayton	LT	L	25	4	9	0	0.5	15	5	.33	0-0	0-0	1-1	14	0	0	1	1.00	.871	6.43
Montgomery, Mike	LT	L	12	4	1	3	1.0	5	3	.60	0-0	0-0	0-0	8	0	0	2	1.00	.708	1.93
Patton, Spencer	LM	R	16	6	1	6	0.5	5	1	.20	0-0	0-0	0-0	7	0	0	1	1.00	.719	5.48
Grimm, Justin	UR	R	68	8	17	5	0.8	32	6	.19	0-0	0-0	0-0	52	0	0	10	1.00	.679	4.10
Cahill, Trevor	UR	R	49	13	7	14	0.7	17	6	.35	0-0	0-1	0-0	31	0	1	4	.80	.637	2.97
Edwards Jr., Carl	UR	R	36	6	1	4	1.0	24	8	.33	1-1	1-2	0-0	24	0	1	6	.89	.456	3.75
Warren, Adam	UR	R	28	6	2	9	1.1	22	8	.36	0-0	0-0	0-1	15	1	1	6	.86	.802	6.60
Smith, Joe	UR	R	16	0	3	0	0.6	7	3	.43	0-0	0-0	0-0	12	0	0	1	1.00	.769	2.51
Pena, Felix	UR	R	11	1	1	0	1.3	5	0	.00	0-0	0-0	1-1	9	0	0	2	1.00	.479	4.00

Chicago White Sox

Pitcher	Pos	T	Usage Rel G	Early Entry	Cons Days	Long	Lev Ind	Inherited Runners #	Scrd	Pct	Saves Easy	Reg	Tough	Relief Results Clean	BS Win	BS	Holds	Sv/Hld Pct	Opp OPS	Rel ERA
Robertson, David	CL	R	62	0	22	6	2.1	11	2	.18	26 - 28	8 - 12	3 - 4	49	2	7	0	.84	.684	3.47
Jones, Nate	SU	R	71	0	27	4	1.7	36	6	.17	0 - 1	2 - 7	1 - 4	52	2	9	28	.78	.552	2.29
Albers, Matt	SU	R	57	16	15	6	1.2	43	20	.47	0 - 0	0 - 3	0 - 1	31	0	4	13	.76	.964	6.57
Duke, Zach	SU	L	53	4	17	2	1.2	28	10	.36	1 - 1	0 - 0	0 - 3	41	0	3	20	.88	.653	2.63
Jennings, Dan	LT	L	64	15	20	15	0.9	50	21	.42	1 - 1	0 - 0	0 - 2	38	1	2	10	.85	.679	2.08
Purke, Matt	LT	L	12	2	2	5	0.3	7	4	.57	0 - 0	0 - 0	0 - 0	6	0	0	0		.812	5.50
Ynoa, Michael	LM	R	23	6	1	10	0.5	9	3	.33	0 - 0	0 - 0	0 - 0	15	0	0	1	1.00	.573	3.00
Kahnle, Tommy	UR	R	29	7	5	4	0.9	9	3	.33	0 - 0	0 - 0	1 - 2	22	0	1	4	.83	.678	2.63
Beck, Chris	UR	R	25	6	3	4	0.7	9	0	.00	0 - 0	0 - 1	0 - 0	16	0	1	5	.83	.853	6.39
Putnam, Zach	UR	R	25	10	8	5	0.7	17	3	.18	0 - 0	0 - 0	0 - 0	16	0	0	2	1.00	.643	2.30
Turner, Jacob	UR	R	16	3	3	3	0.5	11	7	.64	0 - 0	0 - 0	0 - 0	6	0	0	2	1.00	.919	3.12
Minaya, Juan	UR	R	11	4	2	2	0.7	1	1	1.00	0 - 0	0 - 0	0 - 0	8	0	0	0		.712	4.35

Cincinnati Reds

Pitcher	Pos	T	Usage Rel G	Early Entry	Cons Days	Long	Lev Ind	Inherited Runners #	Scrd	Pct	Saves Easy	Reg	Tough	Relief Results Clean	BS Win	BS	Holds	Sv/Hld Pct	Opp OPS	Rel ERA
Cingrani, Tony	CL	L	65	1	11	10	1.6	29	11	.38	9 - 10	8 - 10	0 - 3	44	1	6	8	.81	.719	4.14
Wood, Blake	SU	R	70	18	12	16	1.3	37	7	.19	1 - 2	0 - 3	0 - 1	45	0	5	15	.76	.752	3.99
Lorenzen, Michael	SU	R	35	7	2	15	1.0	6	0	.00	0 - 0	0 - 2	0 - 0	25	1	2	10	.83	.630	2.88
Iglesias, Raisel	SU	R	32	2	2	18	1.7	3	0	.00	3 - 3	3 - 5	0 - 0	24	1	2	7	.87	.514	1.98
Peralta, Wandy	LT	L	10	3	2	1	0.4	3	0	.00	0 - 0	0 - 0	0 - 0	7	0	0	2	1.00	1.036	8.59
Smith, Josh	LM	R	30	17	1	19	0.8	20	5	.25	0 - 0	0 - 0	0 - 0	14	0	0	1	1.00	.775	4.88
Sampson, Keyvius	LM	R	16	10	2	10	0.2	5	4	.80	0 - 0	0 - 0	0 - 0	3	0	0	0		.908	5.34
Ohlendorf, Ross	UR	R	64	5	9	12	0.9	22	2	.09	0 - 0	1 - 3	1 - 2	39	2	3	3	.63	.792	4.66
Diaz, Jumbo	UR	R	45	12	7	9	0.6	19	6	.32	0 - 0	0 - 0	0 - 1	31	0	1	4	.80	.713	3.14
Ramirez, JC	UR	R	27	9	6	6	0.9	14	5	.36	1 - 1	0 - 1	0 - 2	11	0	3	1	.40	.787	6.40
Cotham, Caleb	UR	R	23	8	7	4	1.0	6	1	.17	0 - 0	0 - 0	0 - 1	14	0	1	3	.75	.880	7.40
Hoover, J.J.	UR	R	18	0	3	6	0.9	5	4	.80	1 - 1	0 - 0	0 - 1	7	0	1	1	.67	1.183	13.50

Cleveland Indians

Pitcher	Pos	T	Usage Rel G	Early Entry	Cons Days	Long	Lev Ind	Inherited Runners #	Scrd	Pct	Saves Easy	Reg	Tough	Relief Results Clean	BS Win	BS	Holds	Sv/Hld Pct	Opp OPS	Rel ERA
Allen, Cody	CL	R	67	0	19	8	1.7	9	1	.11	20 - 21	11 - 13	1 - 1	52	1	3	0	.91	.584	2.51
Shaw, Bryan	SU	R	75	2	22	5	1.4	25	5	.20	1 - 2	0 - 2	0 - 0	58	0	3	25	.90	.686	3.24
Miller, Andrew	SU	L	26	1	8	1	1.4	7	3	.43	1 - 1	2 - 2	0 - 0	20	0	0	9	1.00	.433	1.55
Crockett, Kyle	LM	L	29	14	7	2	0.5	22	4	.18	0 - 0	0 - 0	0 - 0	22	0	0	3	1.00	.716	5.06
Otero, Dan	UR	R	62	27	14	7	0.7	40	12	.30	0 - 0	1 - 1	0 - 1	46	0	1	3	.80	.526	1.53
Manship, Jeff	UR	R	53	21	8	0	0.8	35	8	.23	0 - 0	0 - 0	0 - 1	39	0	1	6	.86	.750	3.12
McAllister, Zach	UR	R	51	13	10	8	0.9	27	6	.22	0 - 0	0 - 0	0 - 1	34	0	1	7	.88	.731	3.10
Hunter, Tommy	UR	R	21	5	3	0	0.8	9	3	.33	0 - 0	0 - 1	0 - 0	13	0	1	0	.00	.668	3.74
Chamberlain, Joba	UR	R	20	6	0	4	0.7	10	4	.40	0 - 0	0 - 0	0 - 0	14	0	0	0		.616	2.25
Adams, Austin	UR	R	19	4	5	1	0.3	9	4	.44	0 - 0	0 - 0	0 - 0	8	0	0	0		1.065	9.82
Colon, Joseph	UR	R	11	5	2	1	1.0	6	0	.00	0 - 0	0 - 0	0 - 0	6	0	0	0		.892	7.20
Anderson, Cody	UR	R	10	5	0	5	0.7	4	0	.00	0 - 0	0 - 0	0 - 0	6	0	0	0		.814	4.34
Armstrong, Shawn	UR	R	10	7	0	3	0.6	9	0	.00	0 - 0	0 - 0	0 - 0	7	0	0	0		.668	2.53

Colorado Rockies

Pitcher	Pos	T	Rel G	Early Entry	Cons Days	Long	Lev Ind	#	Scrd	Pct	Easy	Reg	Tough	Clean	BS Win	BS	Holds	Sv/Hld Pct	Opp OPS	Rel ERA
McGee, Jake	CL	L	57	1	12	3	1.2	11	5	.45	12 - 14	3 - 4	0 - 1	40	0	4	4	.83	.887	4.73
Ottavino, Adam	CL	R	34	0	6	1	1.5	12	3	.25	5 - 6	1 - 2	1 - 4	27	0	5	4	.69	.528	2.67
Logan, Boone	SU	L	66	0	23	2	1.5	45	10	.22	0 - 0	0 - 2	1 - 2	50	0	3	27	.90	.578	3.69
Estevez, Carlos	SU	R	63	1	21	7	1.4	17	4	.24	7 - 10	3 - 6	1 - 2	41	0	7	11	.76	.728	5.24
Castro, Miguel	SU	R	19	2	4	1	1.1	11	5	.45	0 - 0	0 - 0	0 - 1	12	0	1	7	.88	.880	6.14
Rusin, Chris	LM	L	22	16	0	13	0.7	20	5	.25	0 - 0	0 - 1	0 - 0	12	0	1	3	.75	.596	2.58
Bergman, Christian	LM	R	14	8	0	7	0.7	8	6	.75	0 - 0	0 - 1	0 - 0	4	0	1	0	.00	1.060	9.61
Qualls, Chad	UR	R	44	6	9	2	0.5	18	8	.44	0 - 1	0 - 0	0 - 0	31	0	1	4	.80	.848	5.23
Germen, Gonzalez	UR	R	40	12	9	9	0.9	9	4	.44	0 - 0	1 - 1	0 - 1	23	1	1	0	.50	.825	5.31
Miller, Justin	UR	R	40	7	8	7	0.4	20	9	.45	0 - 0	0 - 0	0 - 0	22	0	0	1	1.00	.885	5.70
Lyles, Jordan	UR	R	35	10	7	9	0.8	18	6	.33	0 - 1	1 - 2	0 - 1	16	0	3	3	.57	.740	4.42
Motte, Jason	UR	R	30	0	9	2	0.7	8	4	.50	0 - 0	0 - 0	0 - 0	18	0	0	6	1.00	.940	4.94
Oberg, Scott	UR	R	24	1	7	7	0.7	11	3	.27	1 - 2	0 - 0	0 - 0	16	0	1	1	.67	.713	5.19
Carasiti, Matt	UR	R	19	5	5	2	0.5	9	1	.11	0 - 0	0 - 0	0 - 0	9	0	0	2	1.00	1.052	9.19

Detroit Tigers

Pitcher	Pos	T	Rel G	Early Entry	Cons Days	Long	Lev Ind	#	Scrd	Pct	Easy	Reg	Tough	Clean	BS Win	BS	Holds	Sv/Hld Pct	Opp OPS	Rel ERA
Rodriguez, Francisco	CL	R	61	0	18	6	2.0	16	2	.13	25 - 28	17 - 18	2 - 3	48	1	5	0	.90	.642	3.24
Wilson, Justin	SU	L	66	2	15	5	1.5	21	9	.43	0 - 1	1 - 3	0 - 2	44	0	5	25	.84	.708	4.14
Greene, Shane	SU	R	47	6	13	5	1.4	20	0	.00	0 - 0	1 - 2	1 - 1	31	0	1	16	.95	.687	5.55
Ryan, Kyle	LT	L	56	18	10	6	0.6	38	8	.21	0 - 0	0 - 0	0 - 1	41	0	1	4	.80	.636	3.07
Hardy, Blaine	LT	L	21	5	5	6	0.6	14	6	.43	0 - 0	0 - 0	0 - 0	12	0	0	0		.707	3.51
Wilson, Alex	UR	R	62	28	6	8	1.1	41	16	.39	0 - 0	0 - 2	0 - 2	38	2	4	14	.78	.692	2.96
Lowe, Mark	UR	R	54	0	13	6	0.6	25	10	.40	0 - 0	0 - 0	0 - 1	28	0	1	8	.89	.924	7.11
Rondon, Bruce	UR	R	37	8	7	0	1.0	16	5	.31	0 - 0	0 - 2	0 - 0	27	1	2	6	.75	.583	2.97
VerHagen, Drew	UR	R	19	7	2	5	0.9	9	6	.67	0 - 0	0 - 0	0 - 0	10	0	0	2	1.00	.968	7.11
Farmer, Buck	UR	R	13	5	0	6	0.2	6	3	.50	0 - 0	0 - 0	0 - 0	8	0	0	0		.758	4.07

Houston Astros

Pitcher	Pos	T	Rel G	Early Entry	Cons Days	Long	Lev Ind	#	Scrd	Pct	Easy	Reg	Tough	Clean	BS Win	BS	Holds	Sv/Hld Pct	Opp OPS	Rel ERA
Giles, Ken	SU	R	69	1	15	8	1.8	13	7	.54	10 - 13	5 - 7	0 - 0	46	0	5	18	.87	.709	4.11
Harris, Will	SU	R	66	3	15	4	1.6	9	4	.44	10 - 10	1 - 4	1 - 1	51	0	3	28	.93	.560	2.25
Neshek, Pat	SU	R	60	10	8	2	1.1	31	11	.35	0 - 0	0 - 0	0 - 0	46	0	0	18	1.00	.606	3.06
Gregerson, Luke	SU	R	59	1	13	2	1.8	8	2	.25	10 - 11	5 - 9	0 - 1	40	0	6	15	.83	.589	3.28
Sipp, Tony	LT	L	60	12	12	3	0.7	26	9	.35	1 - 1	0 - 0	0 - 1	39	0	1	12	.93	.953	4.95
Feliz, Michael	LM	R	47	15	4	18	0.8	18	10	.56	0 - 1	0 - 0	0 - 2	30	1	3	5	.63	.659	4.43
Devenski, Chris	LM	R	43	22	5	17	0.7	30	3	.10	0 - 0	1 - 1	0 - 0	32	0	0	5	1.00	.511	1.61
Hoyt, James	LM	R	22	11	7	4	0.5	20	4	.20	0 - 0	0 - 0	0 - 1	12	0	1	1	.50	.707	4.50
Feldman, Scott	LM	R	21	7	0	10	0.9	6	0	.00	0 - 0	0 - 1	0 - 0	15	0	1	0	.00	.686	2.41
Fields, Josh	UR	R	15	4	1	2	0.3	6	0	.00	0 - 0	0 - 0	0 - 0	8	0	0	0		.978	6.89
Gustave, Jandel	UR	R	14	7	2	2	0.3	11	3	.27	0 - 0	0 - 0	0 - 0	10	0	0	0		.676	3.52

Kansas City Royals

Pitcher	Pos	T	Usage					Inherited Runners			Saves			Relief Results						
			Rel G	Early Entry	Cons Days	Long	Lev Ind	#	Scrd	Pct	Easy	Reg	Tough	Clean	BS Win	BS	Holds	Sv/Hld Pct	Opp OPS	Rel ERA
Davis, Wade	CL	R	45	0	12	5	2.0	8	0	.00	19 - 20	8 - 10	0 - 0	39	0	3	0	.90	.537	1.87
Herrera, Kelvin	SU	R	72	0	17	5	1.4	14	3	.21	8 - 8	4 - 5	0 - 2	57	1	3	26	.93	.590	2.75
Soria, Joakim	SU	R	70	4	14	7	1.6	21	8	.38	1 - 2	0 - 5	0 - 1	46	0	7	20	.75	.800	4.05
Hochevar, Luke	SU	R	40	15	6	0	1.2	30	4	.13	0 - 0	0 - 2	0 - 2	29	1	4	14	.78	.703	3.86
Strahm, Matt	LT	L	21	6	2	5	1.4	18	2	.11	0 - 0	0 - 0	0 - 0	15	0	0	6	1.00	.484	1.23
Flynn, Brian	LM	L	35	14	4	13	0.6	25	7	.28	0 - 0	0 - 0	0 - 0	21	0	0	2	1.00	.566	2.21
Young, Chris	LM	R	21	8	1	12	0.7	6	2	.33	0 - 0	1 - 1	0 - 0	14	0	0	1	1.00	.745	4.13
Gee, Dillon	LM	R	19	14	1	16	0.6	11	6	.55	0 - 0	0 - 0	0 - 0	4	0	0	0		.725	3.46
Alexander, Scott	LM	L	17	6	2	5	0.6	7	6	.86	0 - 0	0 - 0	0 - 1	8	0	1	0	.00	.790	3.32
Moylan, Peter	UR	R	50	15	13	7	0.6	38	8	.21	0 - 0	0 - 0	0 - 0	33	0	0	7	1.00	.669	3.43
Wang, Chien-Ming	UR	R	38	10	6	15	0.5	15	8	.53	0 - 0	0 - 0	0 - 0	20	0	0	0		.786	4.22
Duffy, Danny	UR	L	16	7	2	1	0.5	11	5	.45	0 - 0	0 - 0	0 - 0	10	0	0	1	1.00	.665	3.00
Pounders, Brooks	UR	R	13	2	2	4	0.5	6	0	.00	0 - 0	0 - 0	0 - 0	6	0	0	1	1.00	1.083	9.24
McCarthy, Kevin	UR	R	10	4	3	2	0.8	12	2	.17	0 - 1	0 - 0	0 - 0	5	0	1	0	.00	.857	6.48

Los Angeles Angels

Pitcher	Pos	T	Usage					Inherited Runners			Saves			Relief Results						
			Rel G	Early Entry	Cons Days	Long	Lev Ind	#	Scrd	Pct	Easy	Reg	Tough	Clean	BS Win	BS	Holds	Sv/Hld Pct	Opp OPS	Rel ERA
Bailey, Andrew	CL	R	12	0	3	1	1.0	0	0	.00	3 - 3	3 - 3	0 - 0	11	0	0	0	1.00	.594	2.38
Salas, Fernando	SU	R	58	8	11	7	1.3	20	3	.15	2 - 2	4 - 7	0 - 2	39	0	5	13	.79	.750	4.47
Ramirez, JC	SU	R	43	5	12	5	1.0	14	3	.21	1 - 1	0 - 1	0 - 0	28	0	1	12	.93	.659	2.91
Smith, Joe	SU	R	38	2	8	5	1.4	7	2	.29	5 - 5	1 - 3	0 - 1	28	0	3	6	.80	.697	3.82
Alvarez, Jose	LT	L	64	24	12	9	0.7	43	12	.28	0 - 0	0 - 0	0 - 1	42	0	1	11	.92	.745	3.45
Mahle, Greg	LT	L	24	7	7	3	0.7	11	7	.64	0 - 0	0 - 0	0 - 0	15	0	0	6	1.00	.946	5.40
Ege, Cody	LT	L	13	4	4	1	0.5	10	2	.20	0 - 0	0 - 0	0 - 0	10	0	0	3	1.00	.681	1.04
Guerra, Deolis	LM	R	44	19	5	12	0.6	24	11	.46	0 - 0	0 - 1	0 - 3	26	0	4	5	.56	.671	3.21
Morin, Mike	UR	R	60	26	8	4	0.9	42	8	.19	0 - 0	0 - 0	0 - 1	42	0	1	12	.92	.677	4.37
Bedrosian, Cam	UR	R	45	15	10	2	0.8	34	15	.44	0 - 0	1 - 2	0 - 0	29	0	1	7	.89	.532	1.12
Achter, A.J.	UR	R	27	5	3	5	0.3	3	0	.00	0 - 0	0 - 0	0 - 0	19	0	0	3	1.00	.850	3.11
Street, Huston	UR	R	26	0	6	5	1.5	2	1	.50	6 - 8	3 - 4	0 - 0	18	0	3	0	.75	.975	6.45
Valdez, Jose	UR	R	25	6	7	3	1.0	13	3	.23	0 - 0	0 - 0	0 - 1	18	0	1	5	.83	.759	4.24
Rasmus, Cory	UR	R	18	4	3	6	0.4	3	1	.33	0 - 0	0 - 1	0 - 0	9	0	1	0	.00	.703	4.43
Chacin, Jhoulys	UR	R	12	7	0	8	0.7	4	3	.75	0 - 0	0 - 0	0 - 0	5	0	0	0		.590	3.77

Los Angeles Dodgers

Pitcher	Pos	T	Usage					Inherited Runners			Saves			Relief Results						
			Rel G	Early Entry	Cons Days	Long	Lev Ind	#	Scrd	Pct	Easy	Reg	Tough	Clean	BS Win	BS	Holds	Sv/Hld Pct	Opp OPS	Rel ERA
Jansen, Kenley	CL	R	71	0	23	2	1.5	14	1	.07	31 - 31	14 - 18	2 - 4	60	0	6	0	.89	.446	1.83
Blanton, Joe	SU	R	75	7	19	10	1.1	23	10	.43	0 - 0	0 - 0	0 - 1	58	0	1	28	.97	.573	2.48
Howell, J.P.	LT	L	64	24	15	4	0.5	25	10	.40	0 - 0	0 - 0	0 - 0	44	0	0	2	1.00	.730	4.09
Liberatore, Adam	LT	L	58	14	17	3	1.0	32	6	.19	0 - 0	0 - 0	0 - 2	45	1	2	13	.87	.630	3.38
Avilan, Luis	LM	L	27	14	6	2	1.0	26	7	.27	0 - 0	0 - 0	0 - 1	20	0	1	3	.75	.491	3.20
Fien, Casey	LM	R	25	9	4	4	0.7	5	0	.00	0 - 0	0 - 1	0 - 0	17	0	1	5	.83	.846	4.21
Dayton, Grant	LM	L	25	11	4	4	0.9	12	3	.25	0 - 0	0 - 0	0 - 2	19	0	2	6	.75	.495	2.05
Chavez, Jesse	LM	R	23	13	3	6	0.7	13	3	.23	0 - 0	0 - 0	0 - 1	14	0	1	3	.75	.746	4.21
Fields, Josh	LM	R	22	10	3	2	0.6	17	3	.18	0 - 0	0 - 0	0 - 0	15	0	0	2	1.00	.718	2.79
Baez, Pedro	UR	R	73	16	22	9	0.9	27	12	.44	0 - 0	0 - 1	0 - 1	53	0	2	23	.92	.615	3.04
Coleman, Louis	UR	R	61	26	17	5	0.9	37	8	.22	0 - 1	0 - 1	0 - 0	44	0	2	10	.83	.761	4.69
Hatcher, Chris	UR	R	37	8	8	11	0.9	15	3	.20	0 - 0	0 - 1	0 - 0	22	0	1	4	.80	.819	5.53
Ravin, Josh	UR	R	10	4	0	0	0.2	4	2	.50	0 - 0	0 - 0	0 - 0	9	0	0	0		.397	0.93

Miami Marlins

Pitcher	Pos	T	Usage					Inherited Runners			Saves			Relief Results						
			Rel G	Early Entry	Cons Days	Long	Lev Ind	#	Scrd	Pct	Easy	Reg	Tough	Clean	BS Win	BS	Holds	Sv/Hld Pct	Opp OPS	Rel ERA
Ramos, A.J.	CL	R	67	0	20	8	1.9	7	0	.00	25-26	15-17	0-0	53	0	3	2	.93	.600	2.81
Barraclough, Kyle	SU	R	75	3	26	10	1.5	19	4	.21	0-1	0-3	0-0	56	0	4	29	.88	.538	2.85
Phelps, David	SU	R	59	6	16	9	1.6	12	2	.17	3-5	1-4	0-1	49	0	6	25	.83	.590	2.31
Rodney, Fernando	SU	R	39	0	13	7	1.8	0	0	.00	6-8	2-3	0-1	25	0	3	8	.84	.840	5.89
Morris, Bryan	SU	R	24	7	7	1	1.0	22	10	.45	0-0	1-2	0-1	14	0	2	6	.78	.796	3.06
Dunn, Mike	LT	L	51	22	11	5	0.9	31	16	.52	0-0	0-1	0-3	35	0	4	8	.67	.735	3.40
Cervenka, Hunter	LT	L	18	8	6	0	0.7	19	1	.05	0-0	0-0	0-0	14	0	0	2	1.00	.819	4.82
Breslow, Craig	LT	L	15	4	5	1	0.9	7	6	.86	0-0	0-0	0-1	9	0	1	2	.67	.869	4.50
Wittgren, Nick	LM	R	48	19	10	10	1.0	29	5	.17	0-0	0-2	0-0	33	0	2	6	.75	.671	3.14
Urena, Jose	LM	R	16	9	3	6	0.8	9	4	.44	0-0	0-1	1-2	7	0	2	1	.50	.860	7.52
McGowan, Dustin	UR	R	55	19	12	14	0.8	27	14	.52	1-1	0-1	0-0	38	0	1	3	.82	.644	2.82
Ellington, Brian	UR	R	32	12	5	6	0.5	12	3	.25	0-0	0-0	0-0	23	0	0	3	1.00	.652	2.45
Brice, Austin	UR	R	15	9	3	1	0.6	3	1	.33	0-0	0-0	0-0	9	0	0	1	1.00	.598	7.07
Ogando, Nefi	UR	R	14	4	3	2	0.4	7	1	.14	0-0	0-0	0-0	10	0	0	1	1.00	.473	2.30

Milwaukee Brewers

Pitcher	Pos	T	Usage					Inherited Runners			Saves			Relief Results						
			Rel G	Early Entry	Cons Days	Long	Lev Ind	#	Scrd	Pct	Easy	Reg	Tough	Clean	BS Win	BS	Holds	Sv/Hld Pct	Opp OPS	Rel ERA
Jeffress, Jeremy	CL	R	47	0	21	1	1.9	5	2	.40	16-16	10-11	1-1	36	0	1	0	.96	.662	2.22
Torres, Carlos	SU	R	72	22	18	14	1.2	25	7	.28	0-1	2-3	0-1	48	1	3	20	.88	.655	2.73
Thornburg, Tyler	SU	R	67	1	17	12	1.9	16	6	.38	7-7	6-11	0-3	50	5	8	20	.80	.541	2.15
Knebel, Corey	SU	R	35	4	8	3	1.5	0	0	.00	2-3	0-1	0-0	23	0	2	13	.88	.708	4.68
Smith, Will	SU	L	27	3	8	0	1.7	13	4	.31	0-1	0-3	0-0	15	0	4	12	.75	.708	3.68
Suter, Brent	LT	L	12	2	2	1	0.5	5	0	.00	0-0	0-0	0-0	12	0	0	2	1.00	.459	0.00
Marinez, Jhan	LM	R	43	21	8	13	0.5	26	10	.38	0-0	0-0	0-0	25	0	0	5	1.00	.719	3.22
Cravy, Tyler	LM	R	18	11	3	4	0.4	9	4	.44	0-0	0-0	0-0	14	0	0	0		.452	0.81
Capuano, Chris	LM	L	16	10	1	9	0.6	8	1	.13	0-0	0-1	0-0	8	0	1	1	.50	.912	4.13
Boyer, Blaine	UR	R	61	21	9	11	0.8	23	9	.39	1-1	0-1	0-1	36	0	2	5	.75	.767	3.95
Blazek, Michael	UR	R	41	7	11	8	1.2	12	6	.50	0-0	0-1	0-0	25	1	1	9	.90	.932	5.66
Barnes, Jacob	UR	R	27	10	3	2	0.7	5	1	.20	0-0	1-1	0-0	19	0	0	0	1.00	.612	2.70
Scahill, Rob	UR	R	16	5	1	4	0.4	4	4	1.00	0-0	0-0	0-0	12	0	0	1	1.00	.600	2.45
Goforth, David	UR	R	10	0	2	3	0.1	2	0	.00	0-0	0-0	0-0	3	0	0	0		1.047	10.97

Minnesota Twins

Pitcher	Pos	T	Usage					Inherited Runners			Saves			Relief Results						
			Rel G	Early Entry	Cons Days	Long	Lev Ind	#	Scrd	Pct	Easy	Reg	Tough	Clean	BS Win	BS	Holds	Sv/Hld Pct	Opp OPS	Rel ERA
Rogers, Taylor	LT	L	57	14	12	7	0.9	17	10	.59	0-0	0-0	0-0	37	0	0	9	1.00	.719	3.96
Abad, Fernando	LT	L	39	7	9	2	1.5	29	11	.38	0-0	1-1	0-1	26	0	1	6	.88	.614	2.65
Boshers, Buddy	LT	L	37	13	8	4	0.6	18	4	.22	0-0	0-0	0-0	24	0	0	2	1.00	.659	4.25
O'Rourke, Ryan	LT	L	26	10	7	5	0.8	17	2	.12	0-0	0-0	0-0	17	0	0	0		.615	3.96
Dean, Pat	LT	L	10	6	1	7	0.5	5	4	.80	0-0	0-0	0-0	2	0	0	0		.910	5.25
Tonkin, Michael	LM	R	65	26	15	16	0.6	41	14	.34	0-0	0-1	0-1	38	0	2	2	.50	.831	5.02
Pressly, Ryan	UR	R	72	12	18	13	1.3	34	14	.41	0-0	0-3	0-2	45	0	5	13	.74	.725	3.70
Kintzler, Brandon	UR	R	54	1	11	3	1.5	18	2	.11	11-11	6-8	0-1	39	0	3	1	.86	.705	3.15
May, Trevor	UR	R	44	9	10	11	1.0	26	11	.42	0-0	0-1	0-1	29	0	2	6	.75	.757	5.27
Jepsen, Kevin	UR	R	33	1	8	4	1.4	6	3	.50	5-5	2-6	0-0	17	1	4	2	.69	.978	6.16
Chargois, J.T.	UR	R	25	6	9	2	0.6	17	8	.47	0-0	0-0	0-0	17	0	0	2	1.00	.752	4.10
Wimmers, Alex	UR	R	16	6	2	2	1.2	6	1	.17	0-0	0-1	0-0	10	0	1	1	.50	.754	4.15
Light, Pat	UR	R	15	7	3	5	0.7	13	5	.38	0-0	0-0	0-1	9	0	1	0	.00	.790	9.00
Fien, Casey	UR	R	14	4	3	1	0.8	7	0	.00	0-0	0-0	0-0	9	0	0	1	1.00	1.048	7.90

New York Mets

Pitcher	Pos	T	Rel G	Early Entry	Cons Days	Long	Lev Ind	#	Scrd	Pct	Easy	Reg	Tough	Clean	BS Win	BS	Holds	Sv/Hld Pct	Opp OPS	Rel ERA
Familia, Jeurys	CL	R	78	0	26	8	2.0	11	6	.55	36 - 37	15 - 18	0 - 1	59	1	5	0	.91	.574	2.55
Reed, Addison	SU	R	80	1	27	3	1.4	33	12	.36	1 - 1	0 - 2	0 - 2	62	0	4	40	.91	.536	1.97
Henderson, Jim	SU	R	44	7	8	6	1.0	19	3	.16	0 - 0	0 - 1	0 - 1	30	0	2	11	.85	.785	4.11
Salas, Fernando	SU	R	17	1	7	0	1.0	5	0	.00	0 - 0	0 - 0	0 - 0	13	0	0	7	1.00	.516	2.08
Blevins, Jerry	LT	L	73	10	22	1	1.1	55	8	.15	0 - 0	0 - 0	2 - 3	56	0	1	16	.95	.627	2.79
Bastardo, Antonio	LT	L	41	8	8	10	0.6	9	3	.33	0 - 0	0 - 0	0 - 1	25	0	1	7	.88	.765	4.74
Smoker, Josh	LT	L	20	9	7	2	1.0	12	2	.17	0 - 0	0 - 0	0 - 0	13	0	0	2	1.00	.790	4.70
Edgin, Josh	LT	L	16	4	6	2	0.5	20	3	.15	0 - 0	0 - 0	0 - 0	11	0	0	0		.707	5.23
Gilmartin, Sean	LT	L	13	7	2	3	0.5	2	0	.00	0 - 0	0 - 0	0 - 0	10	0	0	1	1.00	.756	4.76
Robles, Hansel	UR	R	68	18	12	20	0.9	48	15	.31	0 - 0	0 - 2	1 - 1	43	0	2	13	.88	.703	3.48
Goeddel, Erik	UR	R	36	14	7	7	0.6	18	2	.11	0 - 0	0 - 1	0 - 0	23	0	1	2	.67	.710	4.54
Verrett, Logan	UR	R	23	6	5	9	0.4	9	4	.44	0 - 0	0 - 0	0 - 0	12	0	0	0		.863	2.84

New York Yankees

Pitcher	Pos	T	Rel G	Early Entry	Cons Days	Long	Lev Ind	#	Scrd	Pct	Easy	Reg	Tough	Clean	BS Win	BS	Holds	Sv/Hld Pct	Opp OPS	Rel ERA
Chapman, Aroldis	CL	L	31	0	10	4	1.9	4	2	.50	13 - 13	7 - 7	0 - 1	24	0	1	0	.95	.519	2.01
Betances, Dellin	SU	R	73	6	24	7	1.8	23	8	.35	5 - 6	7 - 9	0 - 2	50	2	5	28	.89	.577	3.08
Miller, Andrew	SU	L	44	0	11	5	1.9	3	1	.33	5 - 5	3 - 5	1 - 1	35	2	2	16	.93	.521	1.39
Clippard, Tyler	SU	R	29	2	8	4	1.2	8	3	.38	2 - 2	0 - 0	0 - 1	21	0	1	12	.93	.646	2.49
Layne, Tommy	SU	L	29	9	14	0	1.3	25	5	.20	0 - 1	1 - 1	0 - 0	22	0	1	10	.92	.569	3.38
Shreve, Chasen	LT	L	37	8	6	7	0.7	18	2	.11	0 - 0	0 - 0	1 - 1	25	0	0	1	1.00	.823	5.18
Bleier, Richard	LT	L	23	9	4	2	0.3	10	6	.60	0 - 0	0 - 0	0 - 0	18	0	0	2	1.00	.586	1.96
Goody, Nick	LM	R	27	10	3	8	0.3	24	11	.46	0 - 0	0 - 0	0 - 0	13	0	0	0		.878	4.66
Yates, Kirby	UR	R	41	12	6	7	0.6	14	6	.43	0 - 0	0 - 0	0 - 2	22	0	2	2	.50	.746	5.23
Warren, Adam	UR	R	29	6	7	6	1.2	20	7	.35	0 - 1	0 - 0	0 - 1	17	0	2	6	.75	.716	3.26
Swarzak, Anthony	UR	R	26	11	3	4	0.5	17	7	.41	0 - 0	0 - 0	0 - 1	13	0	1	1	.50	.847	5.52
Parker, Blake	UR	R	16	2	1	5	1.2	19	5	.26	0 - 0	0 - 0	1 - 1	11	0	0	0	1.00	.711	4.96
Barbato, Johnny	UR	R	13	3	0	2	0.8	5	0	.00	0 - 0	0 - 0	0 - 0	8	0	0	0		.751	7.62
Severino, Luis	UR	R	11	7	0	7	1.1	5	0	.00	0 - 0	0 - 0	0 - 0	9	0	0	1	1.00	.367	0.39
Heller, Ben	UR	R	10	0	2	2	1.0	5	4	.80	0 - 0	0 - 0	0 - 1	5	0	1	1	.50	1.101	6.43

Oakland Athletics

Pitcher	Pos	T	Rel G	Early Entry	Cons Days	Long	Lev Ind	#	Scrd	Pct	Easy	Reg	Tough	Clean	BS Win	BS	Holds	Sv/Hld Pct	Opp OPS	Rel ERA
Madson, Ryan	CL	R	63	0	15	3	2.0	8	0	.00	17 - 18	13 - 18	0 - 1	46	2	7	3	.83	.701	3.62
Dull, Ryan	SU	R	70	22	14	12	1.1	52	7	.13	2 - 2	1 - 3	0 - 1	48	1	3	15	.86	.577	2.42
Axford, John	SU	R	68	8	17	11	1.2	16	8	.50	1 - 3	2 - 4	0 - 3	49	0	7	15	.72	.711	3.97
Doolittle, Sean	SU	L	44	3	8	1	1.3	18	5	.28	3 - 4	1 - 2	0 - 0	32	0	2	10	.88	.705	3.23
Coulombe, Daniel	LT	L	35	17	6	6	0.4	12	3	.25	0 - 0	0 - 1	0 - 0	23	0	1	2	.67	.634	4.53
Rzepczynski, Marc	LM	L	56	15	13	4	0.8	55	18	.33	0 - 0	0 - 0	0 - 1	37	0	1	6	.86	.721	3.00
Hendriks, Liam	LM	R	53	20	9	15	1.0	34	5	.15	0 - 1	0 - 0	0 - 0	35	0	1	10	.91	.704	3.76
Triggs, Andrew	LM	R	18	9	2	9	0.2	8	4	.50	0 - 0	0 - 0	0 - 0	5	0	0	0		.832	5.58
Rodriguez, Fernando	UR	R	34	12	7	6	0.8	17	3	.18	0 - 0	0 - 0	0 - 0	23	0	0	5	1.00	.625	4.20
Neal, Zach	UR	R	18	6	2	9	0.3	4	3	.75	0 - 0	2 - 2	0 - 1	10	0	1	0	.67	.662	3.03
Smith, Chris	UR	R	13	4	1	7	0.1	8	6	.75	0 - 0	0 - 0	0 - 0	7	0	0	0		.541	2.92

Philadelphia Phillies

Pitcher	Pos	T	Rel G	Early Entry	Cons Days	Long	Lev Ind	#	Scrd	Pct	Easy	Reg	Tough	Clean	BS Win	BS	Holds	Sv/Hld Pct	Opp OPS	Rel ERA
Gomez, Jeanmar	CL	R	70	0	21	5	1.8	11	2	.18	20 - 23	15 - 18	2 - 2	47	0	6	1	.86	.762	4.85
Neris, Hector	SU	R	79	2	24	9	1.3	20	4	.20	2 - 2	0 - 4	0 - 0	59	0	4	28	.88	.620	2.58
Ramos, Edubray	SU	R	42	3	12	2	1.2	17	3	.18	0 - 1	0 - 1	0 - 0	32	0	2	15	.88	.687	3.83
Araujo, Elvis	LT	L	32	8	11	5	0.7	16	3	.19	0 - 0	0 - 0	0 - 1	21	0	1	4	.80	.900	5.60
Rodriguez, Joely	LT	L	12	2	4	1	1.4	8	1	.13	0 - 0	0 - 0	0 - 0	9	0	0	3	1.00	.598	2.79
Bailey, Andrew	LM	R	33	12	6	7	0.8	16	4	.25	0 - 0	0 - 1	0 - 0	19	0	1	4	.80	.812	6.40
Gonzalez, Severino	LM	R	27	8	6	11	0.5	12	8	.67	0 - 0	0 - 0	0 - 0	11	0	0	1	1.00	.804	5.60
Oberholtzer, Brett	LM	L	26	15	2	14	0.5	11	4	.36	0 - 0	1 - 1	0 - 0	12	0	0	0	1.00	.856	4.83
Hernandez, David	UR	R	70	14	16	13	1.2	17	5	.29	1 - 1	0 - 0	0 - 2	47	0	2	15	.89	.785	3.84
Mariot, Michael	UR	R	25	1	6	5	1.0	9	4	.44	1 - 1	0 - 0	1 - 2	17	0	1	4	.86	.781	5.82
Murray, Colton	UR	R	24	8	5	8	0.7	21	10	.48	0 - 0	0 - 0	0 - 0	11	0	0	1	1.00	.848	6.25
Garcia, Luis	UR	R	17	6	4	3	1.0	8	4	.50	0 - 0	0 - 1	0 - 0	10	0	1	1	.50	.895	6.46
Herrmann, Frank	UR	R	14	4	2	4	0.8	9	7	.78	0 - 0	0 - 0	0 - 0	4	0	0	0		1.108	8.40
Hinojosa, Dalier	UR	R	10	2	4	0	1.6	2	0	.00	0 - 0	0 - 1	0 - 0	8	0	1	1	.50	.645	3.27

Pittsburgh Pirates

Pitcher	Pos	T	Rel G	Early Entry	Cons Days	Long	Lev Ind	#	Scrd	Pct	Easy	Reg	Tough	Clean	BS Win	BS	Holds	Sv/Hld Pct	Opp OPS	Rel ERA
Melancon, Mark	CL	R	45	0	12	1	2.0	13	2	.15	20 - 21	10 - 12	0 - 0	36	1	3	0	.91	.516	1.51
Watson, Tony	SU	L	70	0	21	4	1.5	8	1	.13	12 - 12	3 - 7	0 - 1	54	1	5	23	.88	.672	3.06
Feliz, Neftali	SU	R	62	3	17	5	1.5	30	7	.23	2 - 4	0 - 0	0 - 0	45	1	2	29	.94	.696	3.52
Bastardo, Antonio	SU	L	28	12	8	2	1.0	10	4	.40	0 - 0	0 - 1	0 - 0	18	0	1	8	.89	.713	4.13
Rivero, Felipe	SU	L	28	0	8	3	1.4	9	2	.22	0 - 2	0 - 0	0 - 0	22	0	2	10	.83	.666	3.29
Nicasio, Juan	LM	R	40	14	9	16	0.9	11	5	.45	0 - 0	0 - 0	0 - 2	25	0	2	6	.75	.715	3.88
Caminero, Arquimedes	LM	R	39	14	9	7	0.6	23	9	.39	1 - 1	0 - 1	0 - 0	22	0	1	2	.75	.846	3.51
Schugel, A.J.	LM	R	36	17	6	13	0.7	15	3	.20	0 - 1	1 - 1	0 - 0	23	1	1	3	.80	.591	3.63
Lobstein, Kyle	LM	L	14	6	1	9	0.9	3	0	.00	0 - 0	0 - 0	0 - 0	9	0	0	0		.758	3.96
Hughes, Jared	UR	R	67	26	18	6	0.9	46	17	.37	0 - 1	1 - 2	0 - 0	41	0	2	4	.71	.794	3.03
Scahill, Rob	UR	R	15	4	3	3	0.3	9	0	.00	0 - 0	0 - 0	0 - 0	9	0	0	1	1.00	.737	4.41
Locke, Jeff	UR	L	11	6	0	6	1.0	0	0	.00	0 - 0	0 - 0	0 - 0	7	0	0	0		.865	3.38
Vogelsong, Ryan	UR	R	10	6	1	6	0.9	4	1	.25	0 - 0	0 - 0	0 - 0	4	0	0	1	1.00	.906	4.91

San Diego Padres

Pitcher	Pos	T	Rel G	Early Entry	Cons Days	Long	Lev Ind	#	Scrd	Pct	Easy	Reg	Tough	Clean	BS Win	BS	Holds	Sv/Hld Pct	Opp OPS	Rel ERA
Rodney, Fernando	CL	R	28	0	7	0	1.5	4	0	.00	11 - 11	4 - 4	2 - 2	26	0	0	0	1.00	.406	0.31
Hand, Brad	SU	L	82	21	29	14	1.3	55	15	.27	0 - 0	0 - 4	1 - 3	51	0	6	21	.79	.589	2.92
Maurer, Brandon	SU	R	71	2	18	10	1.3	15	10	.67	9 - 10	4 - 7	0 - 2	49	0	6	13	.81	.686	4.52
Buchter, Ryan	SU	L	67	4	20	4	1.1	10	4	.40	1 - 1	0 - 1	0 - 0	56	0	1	20	.95	.559	2.86
Thornton, Matt	LT	L	18	1	2	1	0.2	2	2	1.00	0 - 0	0 - 0	0 - 0	11	0	0	0		.848	5.82
Baumann, Buddy	LT	L	11	6	2	1	0.8	6	0	.00	0 - 0	0 - 0	0 - 0	9	0	0	2	1.00	.529	3.72
Villanueva, Carlos	LM	R	51	22	5	20	0.6	26	10	.38	1 - 2	0 - 0	0 - 0	24	0	1	4	.83	.886	5.96
Hessler, Keith	LM	L	15	5	2	8	0.2	3	0	.00	0 - 0	0 - 0	0 - 0	13	0	0	1	1.00	.799	3.38
Quackenbush, Kevin	UR	R	60	17	15	7	0.9	23	9	.39	1 - 2	1 - 1	0 - 0	38	0	1	9	.92	.743	3.92
Dominguez, Jose	UR	R	34	9	9	7	0.7	21	4	.19	0 - 1	0 - 0	0 - 0	19	0	1	1	.50	.759	5.05
Campos, Leonel	UR	R	18	4	3	5	0.4	1	0	.00	0 - 0	0 - 0	0 - 0	13	0	0	0		.735	5.73
Morrow, Brandon	UR	R	18	7	4	0	0.8	6	1	.17	0 - 0	0 - 1	0 - 0	13	0	1	2	.67	.769	1.69
Perdomo, Luis	UR	R	15	6	2	9	0.8	2	1	.50	0 - 0	0 - 0	0 - 0	4	0	0	0		1.027	9.10

San Francisco Giants

Pitcher	Pos	T	Usage					Inherited Runners			Saves			Relief Results						
			Rel G	Early Entry	Cons Days	Long	Lev Ind	#	Scrd	Pct	Easy	Reg	Tough	Clean	BS Win	BS	Holds	Sv/Hld Pct	Opp OPS	Rel ERA
Casilla, Santiago	CL	R	62	0	21	4	2.3	18	1	.06	15 - 16	13 - 20	3 - 4	46	0	9	3	.79	.710	3.57
Strickland, Hunter	SU	R	72	7	18	3	1.4	35	11	.31	0 - 1	2 - 3	1 - 4	55	1	5	18	.81	.589	3.10
Lopez, Javier	SU	L	68	9	25	1	1.3	53	6	.11	0 - 0	0 - 0	1 - 4	56	0	3	20	.88	.710	4.05
Osich, Josh	SU	L	59	4	21	1	1.2	43	2	.05	0 - 0	0 - 1	0 - 2	42	0	3	18	.86	.769	4.71
Gearrin, Cory	SU	R	56	7	13	2	1.3	40	12	.30	2 - 3	1 - 1	0 - 3	36	0	4	15	.82	.650	4.28
Romo, Sergio	SU	R	40	0	13	0	1.0	11	5	.45	3 - 3	1 - 1	0 - 0	33	0	0	14	1.00	.709	2.64
Smith, Will	SU	L	26	3	7	0	1.2	11	2	.18	0 - 0	0 - 1	0 - 0	22	0	1	11	.92	.551	2.95
Okert, Steven	LT	L	16	7	2	3	0.8	10	2	.20	0 - 0	0 - 0	0 - 1	13	0	1	2	.67	.699	3.21
Law, Derek	UR	R	61	10	13	4	0.9	28	5	.18	0 - 0	1 - 1	0 - 1	46	0	1	14	.94	.570	2.13
Kontos, George	UR	R	57	22	10	7	1.0	29	8	.28	0 - 0	0 - 2	0 - 0	39	0	2	9	.82	.605	2.53
Peavy, Jake	UR	R	10	4	1	1	0.6	2	1	.50	0 - 0	0 - 0	0 - 0	6	0	0	0		.951	6.30
Suarez, Albert	UR	R	10	7	1	7	1.0	0	0	.00	0 - 0	0 - 0	0 - 0	6	0	0	1	1.00	.878	4.30

Seattle Mariners

Pitcher	Pos	T	Usage					Inherited Runners			Saves			Relief Results						
			Rel G	Early Entry	Cons Days	Long	Lev Ind	#	Scrd	Pct	Easy	Reg	Tough	Clean	BS Win	BS	Holds	Sv/Hld Pct	Opp OPS	Rel ERA
Cishek, Steve	CL	R	62	2	19	10	2.0	15	4	.27	12 - 13	12 - 17	1 - 2	45	1	7	9	.83	.600	2.81
Diaz, Edwin	CL	R	49	3	10	8	2.0	19	2	.11	9 - 10	8 - 9	1 - 2	35	0	3	13	.91	.627	2.79
Vincent, Nick	SU	R	60	15	17	3	1.3	27	11	.41	1 - 2	2 - 4	0 - 3	38	1	6	17	.77	.700	3.73
Wilhelmsen, Tom	SU	R	29	5	2	1	1.3	18	1	.06	0 - 1	1 - 1	0 - 0	22	0	1	9	.91	.753	3.60
Benoit, Joaquin	SU	R	26	0	3	4	1.5	3	2	.67	0 - 1	0 - 1	0 - 0	17	0	2	8	.80	.693	5.18
Nuno, Vidal	LT	L	54	15	11	8	0.7	33	14	.42	0 - 0	0 - 1	0 - 1	34	0	2	12	.86	.791	3.09
Rollins, David	LT	L	11	1	2	2	0.2	7	1	.14	0 - 0	0 - 0	0 - 0	6	0	0	0		.904	7.71
Montgomery, Mike	LM	L	30	14	3	12	0.8	15	5	.33	0 - 0	0 - 0	0 - 0	21	0	0	3	1.00	.560	2.15
Storen, Drew	LM	R	19	11	2	2	1.0	13	1	.08	0 - 0	0 - 0	0 - 0	14	0	0	2	1.00	.501	3.44
Peralta, Joel	UR	R	26	1	8	1	0.9	6	4	.67	0 - 0	0 - 2	0 - 0	15	0	2	11	.85	.875	5.40
Caminero, Arquimedes	UR	R	18	2	5	4	0.8	0	0	.00	0 - 0	0 - 1	0 - 0	11	0	1	6	.86	.796	3.66
Johnson, Steve	UR	R	16	2	2	5	0.6	7	0	.00	0 - 0	0 - 0	0 - 0	12	0	0	1	1.00	.685	4.32
Altavilla, Dan	UR	R	15	1	4	1	0.4	6	4	.67	0 - 0	0 - 0	0 - 1	11	0	1	1	.50	.560	0.73
Zych, Tony	UR	R	12	3	2	4	0.4	2	0	.00	0 - 0	0 - 0	0 - 0	7	0	0	1	1.00	.642	3.29
Scribner, Evan	UR	R	12	2	1	1	1.0	3	0	.00	0 - 0	0 - 0	0 - 0	12	0	0	3	1.00	.389	0.00

St Louis Cardinals

Pitcher	Pos	T	Usage					Inherited Runners			Saves			Relief Results						
			Rel G	Early Entry	Cons Days	Long	Lev Ind	#	Scrd	Pct	Easy	Reg	Tough	Clean	BS Win	BS	Holds	Sv/Hld Pct	Opp OPS	Rel ERA
Oh, Seung Hwan	CL	R	76	6	22	9	1.7	19	9	.47	8 - 8	10 - 11	1 - 4	58	1	4	14	.89	.510	1.92
Rosenthal, Trevor	CL	R	45	3	9	10	1.4	8	2	.25	9 - 10	4 - 6	1 - 2	32	1	4	0	.78	.792	4.46
Siegrist, Kevin	SU	L	67	5	15	4	1.5	30	9	.30	2 - 2	0 - 2	1 - 4	49	1	5	17	.80	.650	2.77
Lyons, Tyler	LT	L	30	12	3	7	0.6	13	2	.15	0 - 0	0 - 0	0 - 0	16	0	4	4	1.00	.667	3.38
Duke, Zach	LT	L	28	6	9	1	1.3	25	3	.12	0 - 0	0 - 0	1 - 1	21	0	0	6	1.00	.543	1.93
Kiekhefer, Dean	LT	L	26	6	7	2	0.2	16	11	.69	0 - 0	0 - 0	0 - 0	17	0	0	2	1.00	.746	5.32
Broxton, Jonathan	UR	R	66	6	15	10	0.8	17	5	.29	0 - 1	0 - 1	0 - 1	48	1	3	12	.80	.673	4.30
Bowman, Matt	UR	R	59	19	9	9	0.9	24	7	.29	0 - 0	0 - 1	0 - 0	41	0	1	13	.93	.623	3.46
Maness, Seth	UR	R	29	9	3	6	0.5	12	6	.50	0 - 0	0 - 0	0 - 0	18	0	0	1	1.00	.735	3.41
Socolovich, Miguel	UR	R	15	4	3	3	0.3	11	1	.09	0 - 0	0 - 0	0 - 0	11	0	0	0		.380	2.00
Tuivailala, Samuel	UR	R	12	0	1	2	0.2	0	0	.00	0 - 0	0 - 0	0 - 0	9	0	0	0		.759	6.00
Williams, Jerome	UR	R	11	2	1	4	0.0	4	1	.25	0 - 0	0 - 0	0 - 0	7	0	0	0		.926	5.71

Tampa Bay Rays

Pitcher	Pos	T	Rel G	Early Entry	Cons Days	Long	Lev Ind	#	Scrd	Pct	Easy	Reg	Tough	Clean	BS Win	BS	Holds	Sv/Hld Pct	Opp OPS	Rel ERA
Colome, Alex	CL	R	57	0	12	4	2.1	20	6	.30	25-26	11-13	1-1	47	1	3	1	.93	.572	1.91
Ramirez, Erasmo	SU	R	63	20	13	16	1.4	32	5	.16	1-1	1-4	0-1	38	1	4	15	.81	.787	4.02
Cedeno, Xavier	SU	L	54	5	17	1	1.4	23	7	.30	0-0	0-3	0-2	38	1	5	19	.79	.597	3.70
Boxberger, Brad	SU	R	27	4	6	5	1.5	11	2	.18	0-0	0-3	0-0	19	0	3	7	.70	.734	4.81
Romero, Enny	LT	L	52	9	9	7	0.6	23	7	.30	0-0	1-1	0-1	34	0	1	6	.88	.738	5.91
Eveland, Dana	LT	L	33	7	7	6	0.5	20	1	.05	0-0	0-0	0-0	18	0	0	3	1.00	.964	9.00
Garton, Ryan	UR	R	37	13	8	7	0.6	23	5	.22	1-1	0-0	0-0	23	0	0	2	1.00	.732	4.35
Farquhar, Danny	UR	R	35	6	8	6	0.9	20	11	.55	0-0	0-0	0-1	21	0	1	7	.88	.786	3.06
Geltz, Steve	UR	R	27	7	5	3	0.4	10	4	.40	0-0	0-0	0-1	14	0	1	1	.50	.878	5.74
Jepsen, Kevin	UR	R	25	5	7	0	0.7	10	2	.20	0-0	0-0	0-0	14	0	0	3	1.00	.871	5.68
Webb, Ryan	UR	R	18	4	2	3	0.3	9	5	.56	0-0	0-0	0-0	10	0	0	0		.874	5.19
Sturdevant, Tyler	UR	R	16	5	5	3	0.6	10	2	.20	0-0	0-0	0-0	10	0	0	3	1.00	.706	3.93
Floro, Dylan	UR	R	12	1	0	4	0.8	8	4	.50	0-0	0-0	0-0	6	0	0	0		.813	4.20
Andriese, Matt	UR	R	10	3	0	9	0.8	4	1	.25	0-0	1-1	0-0	5	0	0	4	1.00	.500	2.38

Texas Rangers

Pitcher	Pos	T	Rel G	Early Entry	Cons Days	Long	Lev Ind	#	Scrd	Pct	Easy	Reg	Tough	Clean	BS Win	BS	Holds	Sv/Hld Pct	Opp OPS	Rel ERA
Dyson, Sam	CL	R	73	0	21	3	2.1	18	5	.28	22-23	16-20	0-0	57	0	5	10	.91	.658	2.43
Tolleson, Shawn	CL	R	37	9	6	7	1.4	13	1	.08	7-8	4-7	0-0	23	0	4	1	.75	.904	7.68
Diekman, Jake	SU	L	66	0	13	5	1.3	25	10	.40	1-1	3-3	0-1	49	1	1	26	.97	.594	3.40
Bush, Matt	SU	R	58	0	13	5	1.3	18	5	.28	0-0	1-3	0-1	44	0	3	22	.88	.525	2.48
Barnette, Tony	SU	R	53	14	8	8	1.1	37	10	.27	0-0	0-0	0-1	35	0	1	15	.94	.638	2.09
Kela, Keone	SU	R	35	3	3	5	1.1	11	5	.45	0-1	0-0	0-0	22	0	1	15	.94	.779	6.09
Jeffress, Jeremy	SU	R	12	1	2	0	1.4	1	0	.00	0-0	0-0	0-0	9	0	0	6	1.00	.629	2.70
Alvarez, Dario	LT	L	10	3	0	3	0.2	5	0	.00	0-0	0-0	0-0	5	0	0	0		.978	7.71
Claudio, Alex	LM	L	39	17	5	12	0.6	32	11	.34	0-0	0-0	0-0	20	0	0	2	1.00	.662	2.79
Ramos, Cesar	LM	L	12	8	0	11	0.5	13	3	.23	0-0	0-1	0-0	5	0	0	0	1.00	1.020	6.83
Wilhelmsen, Tom	UR	R	21	8	6	5	0.9	6	4	.67	0-1	0-0	0-1	14	0	2	3	.60	1.161	10.55
Leclerc, Jose	UR	R	12	6	2	3	0.3	6	4	.67	0-0	0-0	0-0	9	0	0	0		.710	1.80
Scheppers, Tanner	UR	R	10	1	4	0	1.3	9	1	.11	0-0	1-1	0-0	8	0	0	2	1.00	.570	4.15

Toronto Blue Jays

Pitcher	Pos	T	Rel G	Early Entry	Cons Days	Long	Lev Ind	#	Scrd	Pct	Easy	Reg	Tough	Clean	BS Win	BS	Holds	Sv/Hld Pct	Opp OPS	Rel ERA
Osuna, Roberto	CL	R	72	0	23	5	1.6	25	6	.24	23-23	10-13	3-6	54	2	6	0	.86	.603	2.68
Grilli, Jason	SU	R	46	0	8	1	1.4	8	2	.25	1-1	1-3	0-0	35	0	2	21	.92	.701	3.64
Storen, Drew	SU	R	38	0	5	3	1.1	3	2	.67	3-3	0-1	0-0	26	0	1	8	.92	.913	6.21
Benoit, Joaquin	SU	R	25	1	8	0	1.4	8	6	.75	0-0	1-1	0-1	21	0	1	10	.92	.545	0.38
Cecil, Brett	LT	L	54	3	12	0	1.2	29	10	.34	0-0	0-2	0-2	41	0	4	9	.69	.742	3.93
Loup, Aaron	LT	L	21	4	6	2	0.4	17	2	.12	0-0	0-1	0-0	14	0	1	1	.50	.855	5.02
Girodo, Chad	LT	L	14	2	2	1	0.3	7	2	.29	0-0	0-0	0-0	7	0	0	0		.855	4.35
Chavez, Jesse	LM	R	39	13	7	7	1.1	31	15	.48	0-0	0-0	0-2	21	0	2	7	.78	.799	4.57
Biagini, Joseph	UR	R	60	20	11	14	1.2	26	5	.19	0-0	1-2	0-1	38	1	2	8	.82	.678	3.06
Floyd, Gavin	UR	R	28	4	3	6	1.2	17	5	.29	0-0	0-0	0-1	16	0	1	6	.86	.640	4.06
Tepera, Ryan	UR	R	20	1	5	1	0.6	14	2	.14	0-0	0-0	0-0	13	0	0	0		.635	2.95
Schultz, Bo	UR	R	16	2	3	3	0.7	7	0	.00	0-0	0-0	0-0	10	0	0	0		.763	5.51
Feldman, Scott	UR	R	14	2	2	5	0.4	4	1	.25	0-0	0-0	0-0	7	0	0	0		.903	8.40
Barnes, Danny	UR	R	12	4	0	4	0.6	3	1	.33	0-0	0-0	0-0	7	0	0	1	1.00	.700	3.95

Washington Nationals

Pitcher	Pos	T	Usage					Inherited Runners			Saves			Relief Results						
			Rel G	Early Entry	Cons Days	Long	Lev Ind	#	Scrd	Pct	Easy	Reg	Tough	Clean	BS Win	BS	Holds	Sv/Hld Pct	Opp OPS	Rel ERA
Papelbon, Jonathan	CL	R	37	0	10	4	1.8	7	3	.43	14 - 16	5 - 6	0 - 0	26	0	3	1	.87	.754	4.37
Melancon, Mark	CL	R	30	0	10	1	1.5	5	4	.80	10 - 10	6 - 7	1 - 1	24	0	1	0	.94	.503	1.82
Treinen, Blake	SU	R	73	12	22	6	1.0	53	13	.25	0 - 0	1 - 1	0 - 2	53	0	2	22	.92	.648	2.28
Kelley, Shawn	SU	R	67	0	16	1	1.1	36	10	.28	2 - 3	3 - 4	2 - 2	50	0	2	13	.91	.635	2.64
Rivero, Felipe	SU	L	47	2	11	7	1.0	20	4	.20	0 - 1	1 - 1	0 - 0	30	0	1	16	.94	.673	4.53
Rzepczynski, Marc	SU	L	14	2	3	0	1.5	7	2	.29	0 - 0	0 - 0	0 - 0	11	0	0	5	1.00	.604	1.54
Perez, Oliver	LT	L	64	13	17	5	1.1	45	6	.13	0 - 0	0 - 0	0 - 1	46	0	1	15	.94	.751	4.95
Solis, Sammy	LT	L	37	6	8	6	0.9	17	4	.24	0 - 0	0 - 0	0 - 1	28	0	1	9	.90	.606	2.41
Burnett, Sean	LT	L	10	5	4	0	0.7	4	1	.25	0 - 0	0 - 0	0 - 0	7	0	0	0		.749	3.18
Belisle, Matt	UR	R	40	17	6	6	0.6	24	9	.38	0 - 0	0 - 0	0 - 0	25	0	0	4	1.00	.611	1.76
Petit, Yusmeiro	UR	R	35	9	3	15	1.2	14	2	.14	1 - 1	0 - 0	0 - 1	18	0	1	1	.67	.787	4.50
Glover, Koda	UR	R	19	4	3	1	0.8	6	2	.33	0 - 1	0 - 1	0 - 0	11	1	2	2	.50	.664	5.03

Pitchers Hitting, Fielding & Holding Runners, and Hitters Pitching

Scott Spratt

The Cy Young Award doesn't consider a pitcher's offensive performance, but if 2016 is any indication, maybe it should. There were four pitchers who hit at least two home runs this season, and three of them—Madison Bumgarner, Noah Syndergaard, and Jake Arrieta—were also in the top 15 in ERA among qualified National League starters. Bumgarner has been particularly impressive. His three home runs this season give him 14 for his career, the most among active pitchers. Bumgarner also had 6 doubles, 16 total hits, and 10 walks in 97 plate appearances this season. The resulting on-base plus slugging (OPS) of .629 doesn't make him the new Babe Ruth, but it is better than 39 non-pitchers with at least 200 plate appearances this season, including Ben Revere, Alexei Ramirez, and Alex Rodriguez. Patrick Corbin's .728 OPS led all pitchers who had at least 40 plate appearances, and that beat Chase Utley, Jacoby Ellsbury, and 131 other non-pitchers with 200 or more plate appearances.

For Bumgarner and every other pitcher who took the mound in 2016, the following table will provide their hitting statistics in both 2016 and for their careers. In addition, the table shows statistics related to pitchers' fielding, holding baserunners, and Defensive Runs Saved—abbreviated RS in the table—which is a comprehensive evaluation of defense that captures things like holding baserunners, fielding range, and avoidance of defensive misplays. Bartolo Colon is a surprising name to see at the top of the Defensive Runs Saved leaderboard for pitchers. Despite his age, Colon remains one of the best in the game at holding baserunners; he allowed just eight stolen bases against seven catcher caught stealings, three pitcher caught stealings, and two pitcher pickoffs this season.

Finally, there is a table that shows the pitching statistics of hitters who took the mound both for this season and for their careers. Five different hitters recorded a strikeout as a pitcher this season. Of the five, Royals backup catcher Drew Butera was perhaps the most impressive on the mound. On Tuesday, July 26, in his second pitching appearance of the season, Butera got out of an inherited bases-loaded jam by inducing a groundball fielder's choice from Johnny Giavotella.

Pitchers Hitting, Fielding and Holding Runners

Pitcher	T	2016 Hitting						Career Hitting										2016 Fielding and Holding Runners											
		Avg	AB	H	HR	RBI	SH	Avg	AB	H	2B	3B	HR	RBI	BB	SO	SH	Inn	PO	A	E	DP	Pct	SBA	CS	PCS	PPO	CS%	RS
Abad, Fernando, Min-Bos	L	.000	1	0	0	0	0	.111	9	1	0	0	0	0	0	5	0	46.2	0	4	0	1	1.000	3	0	0	0	.00	2
Achter, A.J., LAA	R	-	0	0	0	0	0	-	0	0	0	0	0	0	0	0	0	37.2	2	4	0	0	1.000	2	1	0	0	.50	2
Adams, Austin, Cle	R	-	0	0	0	0	0	.000	1	0	0	0	0	0	0	0	0	18.1	0	0	1	0	.000	1	0	0	0	.00	0
Adleman, Tim, Cin	R	.190	21	4	0	3	2	.190	21	4	2	0	0	3	0	11	2	69.2	6	7	0	0	1.000	5	1	0	2	.20	1
Albers, Andrew, Min	L	-	0	0	0	0	0	-	0	0	0	0	0	0	0	0	0	17.0	1	3	0	1	1.000	2	2	0	0	1.00	1
Albers, Matt, CWS	R	1.000	1	1	0	0	0	.086	35	3	1	0	0	0	0	21	3	51.1	2	8	2	2	.833	5	2	0	0	.40	-1
Alburquerque, Al, LAA	R	-	0	0	0	0	0	-	0	0	0	0	0	0	0	0	0	2.0	0	0	0	0	-	0	0	0	0	-	0
Alcantara, Raul, Oak	R	-	0	0	0	0	0	-	0	0	0	0	0	0	0	0	0	22.1	0	2	0	0	1.000	2	0	0	0	.00	-1
Alexander, Scott, KC	L	-	0	0	0	0	0	-	0	0	0	0	0	0	0	0	0	19.0	1	2	1	1	.750	0	0	0	0	-	-2
Allen, Cody, Cle	R	-	0	0	0	0	0	-	0	0	0	0	0	0	0	0	0	68.0	3	6	0	1	1.000	5	3	0	0	.60	1
Altavilla, Dan, Sea	R	-	0	0	0	0	0	-	0	0	0	0	0	0	0	0	0	12.1	0	1	0	0	1.000	2	0	0	0	.00	0
Alvarez, Dario, Atl-Tex	L	-	0	0	0	0	0	-	0	0	0	0	0	0	0	0	0	26.2	0	2	0	0	1.000	2	1	1	0	.50	-1
Alvarez, Jose, LAA	L	.000	1	0	0	0	0	.000	2	0	0	0	0	0	1	0	0	57.1	1	5	1	2	.857	4	2	0	0	.50	0
Anderson, Brett, LAD	L	.000	3	0	0	0	0	.088	68	6	3	0	0	4	5	43	10	11.1	1	3	0	0	1.000	2	1	1	0	.50	-1
Anderson, Chase, Mil	R	.089	45	4	0	1	5	.079	127	10	0	0	0	4	2	64	19	151.2	8	19	1	1	.964	15	8	1	0	.53	5
Anderson, Cody, Cle	R	-	0	0	0	0	0	.000	3	0	0	0	0	0	0	3	0	60.2	4	4	1	2	.889	1	1	0	0	1.00	-1
Anderson, Tyler, Col	L	.114	35	4	1	3	3	.114	35	4	0	0	1	3	4	11	3	114.1	3	29	2	2	.941	9	2	1	2	.22	5
Andriese, Matt, TB	R	.000	1	0	0	0	0	.000	2	0	0	0	0	0	0	0	0	127.2	12	9	1	1	.955	17	1	0	0	.06	-4
Antolin, Dustin, Tor	R	-	0	0	0	0	0	-	0	0	0	0	0	0	0	0	0	2.0	0	0	0	0	-	0	0	0	0	-	-1
Aquino, Jayson, Bal	L	-	0	0	0	0	0	-	0	0	0	0	0	0	0	0	0	2.1	0	0	0	0	-	0	0	0	0	-	-1
Araujo, Elvis, Phi	L	-	0	0	0	0	0	.000	1	0	0	0	0	0	0	1	0	27.1	1	3	0	1	1.000	2	1	0	0	.50	0
Archer, Chris, TB	R	.000	7	0	0	0	0	.000	20	0	0	0	0	0	1	10	0	201.1	14	19	2	0	.943	18	5	1	0	.28	-1
Armstrong, Shawn, Cle	R	-	0	0	0	0	0	-	0	0	0	0	0	0	0	0	0	10.2	1	1	0	0	1.000	1	0	0	0	.00	0
Aro, Jonathan, Sea	R	-	0	0	0	0	0	-	0	0	0	0	0	0	0	0	0	0.2	0	0	0	0	-	0	0	0	0	-	0
Arrieta, Jake, ChC	R	.262	65	17	2	7	1	.188	208	39	5	3	4	15	9	103	15	197.1	12	39	3	6	.944	26	3	0	0	.12	5
Asher, Alec, Phi	R	.091	11	1	0	2	0	.176	17	3	1	0	0	2	0	9	0	27.2	3	4	0	1	1.000	1	1	1	0	1.00	1
Avilan, Luis, LAD	L	-	0	0	0	0	0	.250	4	1	0	0	0	0	0	0	2	19.2	0	4	1	0	.800	3	1	1	0	.33	-1
Axford, John, Oak	R	-	0	0	0	0	0	.000	1	0	0	0	0	0	0	1	0	65.2	2	11	0	0	1.000	4	0	0	0	.00	0
Baez, Pedro, LAD	R	.000	1	0	0	0	0	.000	1	0	0	0	0	0	0	0	0	74.0	0	9	3	2	.750	7	3	0	0	.43	1
Bailey, Andrew, Phi-LAA	R	-	0	0	0	0	0	-	0	0	0	0	0	0	0	0	0	43.2	1	4	0	1	1.000	3	1	0	0	.33	-1
Bailey, Homer, Cin	R	.100	10	1	0	0	0	.156	314	49	6	0	17	10	120	41	23.0	3	1	0	0	1.000	6	1	0	0	.17	-2
Barbato, Johnny, NYY	R	-	0	0	0	0	0	-	0	0	0	0	0	0	0	0	0	13.0	0	0	1	0	.000	2	1	0	0	.50	-1
Barnes, Danny, Tor	R	-	0	0	0	0	0	-	0	0	0	0	0	0	0	0	0	13.2	0	1	0	0	1.000	1	1	0	1	1.00	0
Barnes, Jacob, Mil	R	-	0	0	0	0	0	-	0	0	0	0	0	0	0	0	0	26.2	2	3	1	0	.833	2	1	0	0	.50	0
Barnes, Matt, Bos	R	-	0	0	0	0	0	-	0	0	0	0	0	0	0	0	0	66.2	2	6	0	0	1.000	12	5	0	0	.42	-1
Barnette, Tony, Tex	R	-	0	0	0	0	0	-	0	0	0	0	0	0	0	0	0	60.1	6	2	0	1	1.000	4	1	0	0	.25	0
Barraclough, Kyle, Mia	R	.000	1	0	0	0	0	.000	1	0	0	0	0	0	0	1	0	72.2	1	8	1	1	.900	11	2	0	0	.18	0
Barrett, Jake, Ari	R	-	0	0	0	0	0	-	0	0	0	0	0	0	0	0	0	59.1	4	2	0	1	1.000	4	2	0	0	.50	-1
Bassitt, Chris, Oak	R	-	0	0	0	0	0	.000	2	0	0	0	0	0	0	1	0	28.0	1	0	0	0	1.000	1	0	0	0	.00	-1
Bastardo, Antonio, NYM-Pit	L	-	0	0	0	0	0	.000	8	0	0	0	0	0	1	5	1	67.2	1	4	1	0	.833	13	1	1	0	.08	-2
Bauer, Trevor, Cle	R	.000	5	0	0	0	1	.056	18	1	0	0	0	1	1	10	2	190.0	17	19	0	0	1.000	10	5	1	0	.50	1
Baumann, Buddy, SD	L	-	0	0	0	0	0	-	0	0	0	0	0	0	0	0	0	9.2	0	0	0	0	-	2	1	0	0	.50	0
Beck, Chris, CWS	R	-	0	0	0	0	0	-	0	0	0	0	0	0	0	0	0	25.1	0	0	0	0	1.000	2	0	0	0	.00	-1
Bedrosian, Cam, LAA	R	-	0	0	0	0	0	-	0	0	0	0	0	0	0	0	0	40.1	0	2	1	0	.667	3	2	0	0	.67	-1
Belisle, Matt, Was	R	.000	4	0	0	0	0	.079	89	7	3	0	0	3	3	49	18	46.0	1	3	0	0	1.000	3	2	0	0	.67	-2
Benoit, Joaquin, Sea-Tor	R	-	0	0	0	0	0	.000	9	0	0	0	0	0	0	4	0	48.0	1	4	2	0	.714	4	2	0	0	.50	-1
Bergman, Christian, Col	R	.333	3	1	0	0	0	.118	34	4	0	0	0	1	1	10	3	24.2	0	3	0	0	1.000	0	0	0	0	-	0
Berrios, Jose, Min	R	1.000	1	1	0	0	0	1.000	1	1	0	0	0	0	0	0	0	58.1	1	12	1	0	.929	5	1	0	1	.20	2
Betances, Dellin, NYY	R	-	0	0	0	0	0	-	0	0	0	0	0	0	0	0	0	73.0	4	6	3	1	.769	21	0	0	0	.00	-7
Bettis, Chad, Col	R	.041	49	2	0	2	5	.043	92	4	0	0	0	3	8	39	8	186.0	12	31	2	1	.956	12	4	0	0	.33	0
Biagini, Joseph, Tor	R	-	0	0	0	0	0	-	0	0	0	0	0	0	0	0	0	67.2	3	11	2	0	.875	9	2	2	0	.22	-1
Blach, Ty, SF	L	.500	4	2	0	0	0	.500	4	2	0	0	0	0	0	0	0	17.0	2	0	0	0	1.000	1	0	0	0	.00	0
Blair, Aaron, Atl	R	.048	21	1	0	0	2	.048	21	1	0	0	0	0	0	9	2	70.0	4	9	1	2	.929	7	1	0	0	.14	0
Blanton, Joe, LAD	R	-	0	0	0	0	0	.106	216	23	0	0	0	6	8	92	31	80.0	2	7	0	1	1.000	10	1	0	0	.10	-1
Blazek, Michael, Mil	R	-	0	0	0	0	0	.250	4	1	1	0	0	1	0	2	0	41.1	1	3	1	1	.800	6	4	1	0	.67	0
Bleier, Richard, NYY	L	-	0	0	0	0	0	-	0	0	0	0	0	0	0	0	0	23.0	1	5	0	1	1.000	2	0	0	0	.00	1
Blevins, Jerry, NYM	L	.000	1	0	0	0	0	.000	2	0	0	0	0	0	0	1	0	42.0	1	2	1	0	.750	3	0	0	0	.00	0
Bolsinger, Mike, LAD	R	.000	9	0	0	0	0	.045	66	3	1	0	0	1	0	37	3	27.2	1	4	0	0	1.000	6	1	0	0	.17	-1
Boscan, Wilfredo, Pit	R	.333	3	1	0	1	0	.333	3	1	0	0	0	1	0	1	0	15.1	1	5	0	0	1.000	0	0	0	0	-	0
Boshers, Buddy, Min	L	-	0	0	0	0	0	-	0	0	0	0	0	0	0	0	0	36.0	2	4	1	0	.857	5	0	0	0	.00	-2
Bowman, Matt, StL	R	.000	1	0	0	0	1	.000	1	0	0	0	0	0	0	1	1	67.2	6	17	2	3	.920	3	1	0	0	.33	3
Boxberger, Brad, TB	R	-	0	0	0	0	0	.000	3	0	0	0	0	0	0	1	0	24.1	2	3	0	0	1.000	4	0	0	0	.00	-1
Boyd, Matt, Det	L	-	0	0	0	0	0	-	0	0	0	0	0	0	0	0	0	97.1	7	18	1	1	.857	5	3	1	0	.60	-1
Boyer, Blaine, Mil	R	.000	1	0	0	0	0	.000	9	0	0	0	0	0	6	0	1	66.0	3	7	0	1	1.000	5	2	0	0	.40	-1
Brach, Brad, Bal	R	-	0	0	0	0	0	.000	1	0	0	0	0	0	0	1	0	79.0	5	4	0	0	1.000	4	1	0	0	.25	-3
Bracho, Silvino, Ari	R	.000	1	0	0	0	0	.000	1	0	0	0	0	0	0	1	0	24.2	2	2	0	0	1.000	0	0	0	0	-	0
Bradley, Archie, Ari	R	.070	43	3	0	4	4	.088	57	5	0	0	0	4	0	35	4	141.2	9	9	1	1	.947	17	5	0	0	.29	-2
Bradley, Jed, Atl	L	-	0	0	0	0	0	-	0	0	0	0	0	0	0	0	0	7.0	0	1	0	0	1.000	2	0	0	0	.00	0
Brault, Steven, Pit	L	.250	8	2	0	0	1	.250	8	2	0	0	0	0	0	1	1	33.1	2	2	1	0	.800	5	1	0	0	.20	0

Pitchers Hitting, Fielding and Holding Runners

Pitcher	T	2016 Hitting						Career Hitting										2016 Fielding and Holding Runners											
		Avg	AB	H	HR	RBI	SH	Avg	AB	H	2B	3B	HR	RBI	BB	SO	SH	Inn	PO	A	E	DP	Pct	SBA	CS	PCS	PPO	CS%	RS
Breslow, Craig, Mia	L	-	0	0	0	0	0	.000	4	0	0	0	0	0	0	2	0	14.0	0	2	0	0	1.000	2	2	1	0	1.00	1
Brice, Austin, Mia	R	-	0	0	0	0	0	-	0	0	0	0	0	0	0	0	0	14.0	1	0	2	0	.333	0	0	0	0	-	-1
Bridwell, Parker, Bal	R	-	0	0	0	0	0	-	0	0	0	0	0	0	0	0	0	3.1	0	0	0	0	-	1	1	0	0	1.00	0
Britton, Zach, Bal	L	-	0	0	0	0	0	.625	8	5	1	0	1	2	0	1	0	67.0	1	16	0	0	1.000	1	0	0	0	.00	4
Broadway, Mike, SF	R	-	0	0	0	0	1	-	0	0	0	0	0	0	0	0	1	5.1	0	0	0	0	-	0	0	0	0	-	0
Broxton, Jonathan, StL	R	-	0	0	0	0	0	.000	5	0	0	0	0	0	2	2	1	60.2	3	14	0	1	1.000	7	1	0	0	.14	1
Buchanan, Jake, ChC	R	.000	1	0	0	0	0	.000	2	0	0	0	0	0	0	1	0	6.0	2	0	0	0	1.000	0	0	0	0	-	0
Buchholz, Clay, Bos	R	.000	2	0	0	0	0	.154	13	2	0	0	0	0	1	5	1	139.1	9	61	0	0	.938	7	4	0	0	.57	1
Buchter, Ryan, SD	L	-	0	0	0	0	0	-	0	0	0	0	0	0	0	0	0	63.0	0	5	0	0	1.000	4	2	2	1	.50	1
Bumgarner, Madison, SF	L	.186	86	16	3	9	0	.183	453	83	16	0	14	49	28	184	36	226.2	1	21	0	1	1.000	11	5	4	0	.45	4
Bundy, Dylan, Bal	R	.000	3	0	0	0	0	.000	3	0	0	0	0	0	0	2	0	109.2	4	8	1	0	.923	16	6	0	0	.38	1
Burgos, Enrique, Ari	R	-	0	0	0	0	0	-	0	0	0	0	0	0	0	0	0	41.1	3	5	0	0	1.000	5	0	0	0	.00	-1
Burnett, Sean, Was	L	-	0	0	0	0	0	.069	29	2	1	0	0	4	9	2	5.2	0	3	0	0	1.000	1	1	0	0	1.00	1
Buschmann, Matt, Ari	R	.000	1	0	0	0	0	.000	1	0	0	0	0	0	0	0	0	4.1	0	0	0	0	-	1	0	0	0	.00	0
Bush, Matt, Tex	R	-	0	0	0	0	0	-	0	0	0	0	0	0	0	0	0	61.2	4	14	0	0	1.000	1	0	0	0	.00	3
Butler, Eddie, Col	R	.067	15	1	0	0	4	.045	44	2	0	0	0	0	0	18	5	64.0	3	4	2	0	.778	7	3	1	0	.43	-1
Cabrera, Mauricio, Atl	R	-	0	0	0	0	0	-	0	0	0	0	0	0	0	0	0	38.1	4	6	0	0	1.000	5	1	0	0	.20	0
Cahill, Trevor, ChC	R	.125	8	1	0	1	2	.103	165	17	2	1	0	10	4	58	17	65.2	7	12	2	0	.905	12	1	0	1	.08	-1
Cain, Matt, SF	R	.074	27	2	1	5	1	.119	579	69	11	1	7	32	21	288	71	89.1	5	11	2	3	.889	12	5	0	0	.42	0
Caminero, Arquimedes, Pit-Sea	R	.000	2	0	0	0	0	.000	2	0	0	0	0	0	0	1	0	60.2	1	6	0	0	1.000	6	2	0	0	.33	0
Campos, Leonel, SD	R	-	0	0	0	0	0	-	0	0	0	0	0	0	0	0	0	22.0	1	4	0	0	1.000	1	0	0	0	.00	0
Campos, Vicente, Ari	R	.000	2	0	0	0	0	.000	2	0	0	0	0	0	0	1	0	5.2	1	0	0	0	1.000	0	0	0	0	-	0
Capuano, Chris, Mil	L	-	0	0	0	0	0	.124	371	46	10	0	1	20	10	176	38	24.0	0	1	1	0	.500	1	1	0	0	1.00	0
Carasiti, Matt, Col	R	-	0	0	0	0	0	-	0	0	0	0	0	0	0	0	0	15.2	2	2	0	1	1.000	2	1	0	0	.50	0
Carrasco, Carlos, Cle	R	-	0	0	0	0	0	.125	8	1	0	0	0	0	0	5	4	146.1	6	22	0	0	1.000	8	4	0	1	.50	4
Carroll, Scott, CWS	R	-	0	0	0	0	0	.000	6	0	0	0	0	0	0	0	0	2.1	0	0	0	0	-	0	0	0	0	-	0
Cashner, Andrew, SD-Mia	R	.176	34	6	0	1	3	.161	192	31	2	1	1	7	7	81	17	132.0	6	19	0	0	1.000	17	5	0	0	.29	1
Casilla, Santiago, SF	R	-	0	0	0	0	0	.250	4	1	0	0	0	1	1	1	0	58.0	3	5	0	0	1.000	5	1	0	0	.20	0
Castro, Miguel, Col	R	-	0	0	0	0	0	-	0	0	0	0	0	0	0	0	0	14.2	3	4	1	0	.875	2	0	0	0	.00	0
Cecil, Brett, Tor	L	-	0	0	0	0	0	.000	6	0	0	0	0	0	0	6	0	36.2	2	2	0	0	1.000	6	0	0	0	.00	-2
Cedeno, Xavier, TB	L	-	0	0	0	0	0	.000	1	0	0	0	0	0	0	1	0	41.1	2	7	1	0	.900	1	0	0	0	.00	1
Cervenka, Hunter, Atl-Mia	L	-	0	0	0	0	0	-	0	0	0	0	0	0	0	0	0	43.1	1	7	0	0	1.000	12	3	3	0	.25	-1
Cessa, Luis, NYY	R	-	0	0	0	0	0	-	0	0	0	0	0	0	0	0	0	70.1	1	11	1	0	.923	5	1	0	0	.20	1
Chacin, Jhoulys, Atl-LAA	R	.300	10	3	0	1	0	.186	221	41	5	0	1	16	7	48	11	144.0	21	21	0	1	1.000	6	1	0	1	.17	4
Chafin, Andrew, Ari	L	-	0	0	0	0	0	.200	5	1	0	0	0	1	0	2	0	22.2	1	3	0	0	1.000	1	0	0	0	.00	-1
Chamberlain, Joba, Cle	R	-	0	0	0	0	0	.000	6	0	0	0	0	0	1	2	2	20.0	0	5	0	0	1.000	3	2	0	0	.67	1
Chapman, Aroldis, NYY-ChC	L	-	0	0	0	0	0	.000	2	0	0	0	0	0	0	1	0	58.0	5	5	0	0	1.000	4	1	1	0	.25	1
Chapman, Kevin, Hou	L	-	0	0	0	0	0	-	0	0	0	0	0	0	0	0	0	8.0	3	1	0	0	1.000	1	0	0	0	.00	-1
Chargois, J.T., Min	R	-	0	0	0	0	0	-	0	0	0	0	0	0	0	0	0	23.0	0	1	0	0	1.000	3	0	0	0	.00	-1
Chatwood, Tyler, Col	R	.189	53	10	0	4	3	.238	122	29	2	1	0	12	5	30	14	158.0	13	22	2	2	.946	10	6	0	0	.60	3
Chavez, Jesse, Tor-LAD	R	-	0	0	0	0	0	.091	11	1	0	0	0	0	0	10	3	67.0	1	4	0	0	1.000	5	2	0	0	.40	1
Chen, Wei-Yin, Mia	L	.000	44	0	0	0	5	.000	50	0	0	0	0	0	0	21	6	123.1	4	15	0	1	1.000	2	0	0	0	.00	2
Cingrani, Tony, Cin	L	-	0	0	0	0	0	.192	52	10	1	0	2	1	16	8	63.0	2	14	1	0	.941	5	5	4	2	1.00	5
Cishek, Steve, Sea	R	-	0	0	0	0	0	.000	1	0	0	0	0	0	0	0	0	64.0	0	8	1	0	.889	6	2	0	0	.33	1
Claudio, Alex, Tex	L	-	0	0	0	0	0	-	0	0	0	0	0	0	0	0	0	51.2	1	12	0	1	1.000	0	0	0	0	-	1
Clemens, Paul, Mia-SD	R	.000	21	0	0	0	1	.000	21	0	0	0	0	0	1	11	1	71.1	0	8	1	1	.889	6	1	0	0	.17	0
Clevinger, Mike, Cle	R	.000	2	0	0	0	0	.000	2	0	0	0	0	0	0	0	0	53.0	4	3	0	0	1.000	5	0	0	0	.00	-1
Clippard, Tyler, Ari-NYY	R	-	0	0	0	0	0	.200	15	3	1	0	0	0	6	3	63.0	3	5	1	0	.889	6	4	0	0	.67	0
Cobb, Alex, TB	R	-	0	0	0	0	0	.091	11	1	1	0	0	1	0	2	0	22.0	1	6	1	0	.875	2	1	0	0	.50	1
Coke, Phil, NYY-Pit	L	-	0	0	0	0	0	.000	3	0	0	0	0	0	0	3	0	10.0	0	0	0	0	1.000	0	0	0	0	-	0
Cole, A.J., Was	R	.000	7	0	0	0	1	.000	9	0	0	0	0	0	0	4	1	38.1	0	0	0	0	-	3	1	0	0	.33	-2
Cole, Gerrit, Pit	R	.200	40	8	1	3	2	.178	180	32	1	0	2	12	5	78	16	116.0	11	24	2	1	.946	20	2	0	0	.10	4
Coleman, Louis, LAD	R	-	0	0	0	0	0	.000	1	0	0	0	0	0	0	0	0	48.0	4	7	0	0	1.000	2	1	0	0	.50	0
Collmenter, Josh, Ari-Atl	R	.000	6	0	0	0	1	.123	154	19	2	0	0	6	9	56	14	41.1	3	3	0	0	1.000	3	1	0	0	.33	0
Colome, Alex, TB	R	-	0	0	0	0	0	.000	2	0	0	0	0	0	0	1	0	56.2	3	5	0	0	1.000	1	1	0	0	1.00	1
Colon, Bartolo, NYM	R	.083	60	5	1	2	4	.091	276	25	4	0	1	11	1	153	21	191.2	12	40	3	5	.945	15	7	3	2	.47	8
Colon, Joseph, Cle	R	-	0	0	0	0	0	-	0	0	0	0	0	0	0	0	0	10.0	0	2	0	0	1.000	0	0	0	0	-	1
Concepcion, Gerardo, ChC	L	-	0	0	0	0	0	-	0	0	0	0	0	0	0	0	0	2.1	0	1	0	0	1.000	0	0	0	0	-	0
Conley, Adam, Mia	L	.122	41	5	0	3	4	.153	59	9	0	0	4	1	30	8	133.1	4	15	1	0	.950	9	1	0	1	.11	1
Corbin, Patrick, Ari	L	.306	49	15	0	4	3	.171	175	30	7	2	0	14	7	65	15	155.2	3	17	1	0	.952	6	4	1	1	.67	-1
Cosart, Jarred, Mia-SD	R	.125	16	2	0	0	2	.130	54	7	0	0	0	1	20	6	57.0	3	16	0	2	1.000	1	0	0	0	.00	3
Cotham, Caleb, Cin	R	-	0	0	0	0	0	-	0	0	0	0	0	0	0	0	0	24.1	0	3	1	0	.750	3	0	0	0	.00	-1
Cotton, Jharel, Oak	R	-	0	0	0	0	0	-	0	0	0	0	0	0	0	0	0	29.1	1	1	0	0	1.000	3	0	0	0	.00	0
Coulombe, Daniel, Oak	L	-	0	0	0	0	0	.000	1	0	0	0	0	0	0	1	0	47.2	1	7	0	0	1.000	3	1	1	0	.33	1
Cravy, Tyler, Mil	R	.250	4	1	1	1	1	.083	12	1	0	0	1	1	0	4	3	28.1	3	2	0	0	1.000	2	1	0	0	.50	1
Crockett, Kyle, Cle	L	-	0	0	0	0	0	-	0	0	0	0	0	0	0	0	0	16.0	1	3	0	0	1.000	1	0	0	0	.00	0
Cueto, Johnny, SF	R	.114	70	8	0	5	11	.108	454	49	1	0	0	15	13	148	80	219.2	21	25	2	0	.958	11	7	1	5	.64	3
Cuevas, William, Bos	R	-	0	0	0	0	0	-	0	0	0	0	0	0	0	0	0	5.0	0	1	0	0	1.000	0	0	0	0	-	0
Cunniff, Brandon, Atl	R	-	0	0	0	0	0	-	0	0	0	0	0	0	0	0	0	17.0	0	2	1	0	.667	2	2	0	0	1.00	0
Curtis, Zac, Ari	L	-	0	0	0	0	0	-	0	0	0	0	0	0	0	0	0	13.1	1	4	0	0	1.000	1	0	0	0	.00	0

Pitchers Hitting, Fielding and Holding Runners

Pitcher	T	2016 Hitting						Career Hitting										2016 Fielding and Holding Runners											
		Avg	AB	H	HR	RBI	SH	Avg	AB	H	2B	3B	HR	RBI	BB	SO	SH	Inn	PO	A	E	DP	Pct	SBA	CS	PCS	PPO	CS%	RS
Danish, Tyler, CWS	R	-	0	0	0	0	0	-	0	0	0	0	0	0	0	0	0	1.2	0	0	0	0	-	0	0	0	0	-	0
Danks, John, CWS	L	-	0	0	0	0	0	.083	24	2	0	0	0	0	1	8	3	22.1	1	3	0	1	1.000	1	0	0	0	.00	1
Darvish, Yu, Tex	R	.333	3	1	1	1	0	.214	14	3	1	0	1	1	0	6	0	100.1	3	9	0	2	1.000	13	0	0	0	.00	-2
Davies, Zach, Mil	R	.094	53	5	0	1	7	.091	66	6	0	0	0	1	1	25	8	163.1	8	21	2	0	.935	17	9	0	0	.53	0
Davis, Wade, KC	R	-	0	0	0	0	0	.250	8	2	0	0	0	0	4	3	0	43.1	1	4	0	0	1.000	4	1	0	0	.25	0
Dayton, Grant, LAD	L	.000	1	0	0	0	0	.000	1	0	0	0	0	0	0	1	0	26.1	1	1	0	0	1.000	1	1	1	0	1.00	0
De La Cruz, Joel, Atl	R	.188	16	3	0	1	2	.188	16	3	0	0	0	1	0	8	2	62.2	2	9	1	0	.917	2	1	0	1	.50	1
de la Rosa, Jorge, Col	L	.184	38	7	0	6	1	.127	378	48	4	0	0	27	6	160	29	134.0	3	14	3	0	.850	22	4	1	0	.18	-6
de la Rosa, Rubby, Ari	R	.071	14	1	0	1	3	.106	94	10	0	0	0	3	1	29	8	50.2	5	3	0	1	1.000	2	1	0	0	.50	0
De Leon, Jose, LAD	R	.000	4	0	0	0	0	.000	4	0	0	0	0	0	0	1	0	17.0	2	4	1	0	.857	0	0	0	1	-	-1
De Los Santos, Abel, Cin	R	-	0	0	0	0	0	-	0	0	0	0	0	0	0	1	0	5.2	0	1	0	0	1.000	2	1	1	0	.50	0
Dean, Pat, Min	L	-	0	0	0	0	0	-	0	0	0	0	0	0	0	0	0	67.1	1	8	0	0	1.000	2	1	1	0	.50	0
deGrom, Jacob, NYM	R	.143	42	6	0	2	5	.184	147	27	4	0	0	8	7	41	15	148.0	14	21	2	2	.946	9	4	1	0	.44	1
Delabar, Steve, Cin	R	-	0	0	0	0	0	-	0	0	0	0	0	0	0	0	0	8.0	1	0	0	0	1.000	0	0	0	0	-	0
Delgado, Randall, Ari	R	.000	2	0	0	0	0	.177	79	14	0	0	0	2	1	33	11	75.0	3	8	0	2	1.000	3	1	0	0	.33	-1
Dermody, Matt, Tor	L	-	0	0	0	0	0	-	0	0	0	0	0	0	0	0	0	3.0	0	0	0	0	-	0	0	0	0	-	-1
DeSclafani, Anthony, Cin	R	.122	41	5	0	1	1	.138	109	15	2	0	0	6	5	58	3	123.1	3	17	0	1	1.000	15	6	2	2	.40	-2
Despaigne, Odrisamer, Bal-Mia	R	-	0	0	0	0	0	.037	54	2	1	0	0	0	2	21	6	30.1	0	2	0	0	1.000	1	0	0	0	.00	-1
Detwiler, Ross, Cle-Oak	L	.000	1	0	0	0	1	.060	116	7	0	0	0	3	3	60	10	48.2	2	3	0	0	1.000	1	0	0	0	.00	-1
Devenski, Chris, Hou	R	-	0	0	0	0	0	-	0	0	0	0	0	0	0	0	0	108.1	5	10	0	2	1.000	13	4	0	2	.31	-1
Diamond, Scott, Tor	L	-	0	0	0	0	0	.143	14	2	0	0	0	0	0	7	1	1.0	0	0	0	0	-	0	0	0	0	-	0
Diaz, Dayan, Cin	R	-	0	0	0	0	0	-	0	0	0	0	0	0	0	0	0	6.2	0	0	0	0	-	0	0	0	0	-	0
Diaz, Edwin, Sea	R	.000	1	0	0	0	0	.000	1	0	0	0	0	0	0	0	0	51.2	2	1	0	0	1.000	4	0	0	0	.00	0
Diaz, Jumbo, Cin	R	.000	1	0	0	0	0	.000	1	0	0	0	0	0	0	0	0	43.0	1	3	2	0	.667	6	1	1	0	.17	-2
Dickey, R.A., Tor	R	.000	1	0	0	0	0	.175	206	36	3	0	0	11	4	37	27	169.2	3	31	1	2	.971	3	1	0	4	.33	7
Diekman, Jake, Tex	L	-	0	0	0	0	0	-	0	0	0	0	0	0	0	0	0	53.0	3	5	0	1	1.000	0	0	0	0	-	1
Dominguez, Jose, SD	R	-	0	0	0	0	0	.000	2	0	0	0	0	0	0	2	0	35.2	2	6	0	2	1.000	7	1	0	0	.14	-1
Doolittle, Sean, Oak	L	-	0	0	0	0	0	.000	1	0	0	0	0	0	0	0	0	39.0	0	6	0	0	1.000	1	1	1	0	1.00	1
Drabek, Kyle, Ari	R	-	0	0	0	0	0	.000	2	0	0	0	0	0	0	0	0	2.0	1	0	0	0	1.000	0	0	0	0	-	0
Drake, Oliver, Bal	R	.000	1	0	0	0	0	.000	1	0	0	0	0	0	0	1	0	18.0	2	3	0	0	1.000	0	0	0	0	-	0
Duensing, Brian, Bal	L	-	0	0	0	0	0	.000	7	0	0	0	0	0	0	4	0	13.1	1	2	0	0	1.000	0	0	0	0	-	1
Duffey, Tyler, Min	R	.000	1	0	0	0	1	.000	1	0	0	0	0	0	0	1	1	133.0	9	13	1	1	.957	3	1	0	0	.33	-4
Duffy, Danny, KC	L	.200	5	1	0	1	1	.071	14	1	0	0	0	1	0	6	2	179.2	1	18	3	0	.864	4	3	3	2	.75	0
Duke, Zach, CWS-StL	L	-	0	0	0	0	0	.180	317	57	7	0	2	23	12	117	43	61.0	1	14	1	0	.938	2	0	0	0	.00	1
Dull, Ryan, Oak	R	-	0	0	0	0	0	-	0	0	0	0	0	0	0	0	0	74.1	2	5	2	0	.778	3	1	0	0	.33	0
Dunn, Mike, Mia	L	-	0	0	0	0	0	.200	5	1	0	0	0	0	0	1	0	42.1	3	7	0	1	1.000	5	4	3	0	.80	1
Dyson, Sam, Tex	R	-	0	0	0	0	0	.000	2	0	0	0	0	0	0	0	0	70.1	3	12	0	1	1.000	7	2	0	0	.29	-1
Edgin, Josh, NYM	L	-	0	0	0	0	0	.000	1	0	0	0	0	0	1	0	0	10.1	1	1	0	0	1.000	0	0	0	0	-	0
Edwards Jr., Carl, ChC	R	.000	1	0	0	0	0	.000	2	0	0	0	0	0	2	0	0	36.0	2	4	0	1	1.000	2	1	0	0	.50	1
Eflin, Zach, Phi	R	.261	23	6	0	0	0	.261	23	6	2	0	0	0	0	8	0	63.1	1	8	2	0	.818	9	2	1	0	.22	0
Ege, Cody, Mia-LAA	L	1.000	1	1	0	0	0	1.000	1	1	0	0	0	0	0	0	0	11.2	1	0	0	0	1.000	0	0	0	0	-	0
Eickhoff, Jerad, Phi	R	.131	61	8	0	5	0	.133	75	10	3	0	0	7	1	19	2	197.1	18	26	1	4	.978	14	5	0	1	.36	3
Elias, Roenis, Bos	L	-	0	0	0	0	0	.000	4	0	0	0	0	0	0	1	0	7.2	0	2	0	0	1.000	0	0	0	0	-	1
Ellington, Brian, Mia	R	.000	1	0	0	0	0	.000	1	0	0	0	0	0	0	1	0	33.0	1	2	0	0	1.000	3	1	0	0	.33	0
Eovaldi, Nathan, NYY	R	.000	5	0	0	0	1	.079	140	11	0	0	0	1	5	88	14	124.2	6	14	1	0	.952	5	4	0	2	.80	1
Erlin, Robbie, SD	L	.000	6	0	0	0	0	.067	45	3	0	0	0	2	2	15	3	15.2	0	1	0	0	1.000	1	0	0	0	.00	0
Esch, Jake, Mia	R	.200	5	1	0	0	0	.200	5	1	0	0	0	0	0	2	0	13.0	0	1	0	0	1.000	2	1	0	0	.50	0
Escobar, Edwin, Ari	L	.000	2	0	0	0	0	.000	2	0	0	0	0	0	0	1	0	23.2	3	3	0	0	1.000	0	0	0	0	-	0
Estevez, Carlos, Col	R	-	0	0	0	0	0	-	0	0	0	0	0	0	0	0	0	55.0	2	5	2	0	.778	8	1	0	0	.13	-2
Estrada, Marco, Tor	R	.000	5	0	0	0	0	.146	130	19	4	0	0	7	7	60	20	176.0	8	14	0	1	1.000	13	1	0	0	.08	1
Eveland, Dana, TB	L	-	0	0	0	0	0	.045	22	1	0	0	0	0	2	13	5	23.2	0	3	0	0	1.000	9	0	0	0	.00	-3
Familia, Jeurys, NYM	R	-	0	0	0	0	0	.500	4	2	0	0	0	1	0	1	0	77.2	2	15	0	1	1.000	8	0	0	0	.00	0
Farmer, Buck, Det	R	-	0	0	0	0	0	.250	4	1	0	0	0	0	0	3	0	29.1	6	4	0	0	1.000	2	0	0	0	.00	1
Farquhar, Danny, TB	R	-	0	0	0	0	0	-	0	0	0	0	0	0	0	0	0	35.1	1	9	1	0	.909	2	0	0	0	.00	1
Faulkner, Andrew, Tex	L	-	0	0	0	0	0	-	0	0	0	0	0	0	0	0	0	6.2	0	1	0	0	1.000	0	0	0	0	-	0
Feldman, Scott, Hou-Tor	R	.000	2	0	0	0	0	.164	61	10	3	0	1	9	0	25	5	77.0	6	9	1	0	.938	10	2	0	0	.20	-2
Feliz, Michael, Hou	R	-	0	0	0	0	0	-	0	0	0	0	0	0	0	0	0	65.0	1	4	0	0	1.000	6	1	0	0	.17	-1
Feliz, Neftali, Pit	R	-	0	0	0	0	0	.000	2	0	0	0	0	0	0	1	0	53.2	1	5	0	1	1.000	4	1	0	0	.25	1
Fernandez, Jose, Mia	R	.250	52	13	0	6	8	.213	136	29	4	1	2	14	1	43	21	182.1	7	15	2	0	.917	8	6	1	0	.75	-2
Fields, Josh, Hou-LAD	R	.000	1	0	0	0	0	.000	1	0	0	0	0	0	0	1	0	35.0	5	1	0	2	1.000	2	0	0	0	.00	-1
Fien, Casey, Min-LAD	R	-	0	0	0	0	0	-	0	0	0	0	0	0	0	0	0	39.1	4	4	0	0	1.000	2	1	0	0	.50	0
Fiers, Mike, Hou	R	-	0	0	0	0	0	.082	85	7	0	0	0	2	0	44	18	168.2	13	12	1	0	.962	12	7	1	1	.58	3
Finnegan, Brandon, Cin	L	.113	53	6	0	2	5	.105	57	6	2	0	0	2	3	20	7	172.0	5	12	1	0	.944	21	6	3	0	.29	-1
Fister, Doug, Hou	R	.200	5	1	0	2	2	.155	103	16	3	0	4	3	4	42	10	180.1	11	18	2	1	.935	6	3	0	0	.50	2
Flande, Yohan, Col	L	-	0	0	0	0	1	.121	33	4	0	0	0	2	1	16	6	3.2	0	1	1	0	.500	0	0	0	0	-	-1
Flores, Kendry, Mia	R	.000	1	0	0	0	0	.000	2	0	0	0	0	0	0	2	0	3.0	1	0	0	0	1.000	0	0	0	0	-	0
Floro, Dylan, TB	R	-	0	0	0	0	0	-	0	0	0	0	0	0	0	0	0	15.0	2	3	0	1	1.000	2	0	0	0	.00	0
Floyd, Gavin, Tor	R	.000	1	0	0	0	0	.067	75	5	0	0	0	2	4	43	4	31.0	2	0	2	0	1.000	3	0	0	0	.00	1
Flynn, Brian, KC	L	-	0	0	0	0	0	.286	7	2	0	0	0	0	2	1	1	55.1	2	8	2	3	.833	0	0	0	0	-	1
Foltynewicz, Mike, Atl	R	.139	36	5	0	1	5	.109	64	7	2	0	0	4	1	38	6	123.1	4	18	0	0	1.000	5	3	0	2	.60	3

389

Pitchers Hitting, Fielding and Holding Runners

Pitcher	T	Avg	AB	H	HR	RBI	SH	Avg	AB	H	2B	3B	HR	RBI	BB	SO	SH	Inn	PO	A	E	DP	Pct	SBA	CS	PCS	PPO	CS%	RS
Freeman, Sam, Mil	L	-	0	0	0	0	0	-	0	0	0	0	0	0	0	0	0	7.2	0	1	1	0	.500	0	0	0	0	-	0
Frias, Carlos, LAD	R	.000	1	0	0	0	0	.034	29	1	0	0	0	0	1	17	1	4.0	0	0	0	0	-	0	0	0	0	-	0
Friedrich, Christian, SD	L	.054	37	2	0	2	3	.071	70	5	0	0	0	2	6	40	4	129.1	1	19	1	3	.952	2	1	1	0	.50	4
Fulmer, Carson, CWS	R	-	0	0	0	0	0	-	0	0	0	0	0	0	0	0	0	11.2	1	3	0	0	1.000	2	1	0	0	.50	1
Fulmer, Michael, Det	R	.000	2	0	0	0	0	.000	2	0	0	0	0	0	0	2	0	159.0	16	13	1	2	.967	6	2	0	0	.33	-4
Gallardo, Yovani, Bal	R	.500	4	2	0	0	1	.200	424	85	21	0	12	42	13	149	36	118.0	4	14	0	0	1.000	11	6	2	0	.55	1
Gamboa, Eddie, TB	R	-	0	0	0	0	0	-	0	0	0	0	0	0	0	0	0	13.1	0	6	0	0	1.000	0	0	0	2	-	2
Gant, John, Atl	R	.000	7	0	0	0	3	.000	7	0	0	0	0	0	0	1	3	50.0	3	3	0	1	1.000	5	1	0	0	.20	-1
Garcia, Jaime, StL	L	.171	41	7	0	4	7	.147	272	40	2	1	2	16	11	91	24	171.2	7	28	3	1	.921	20	6	1	0	.30	1
Garcia, Luis, Phi	R	-	0	0	0	0	1	.000	2	0	0	0	0	0	0	1	1	15.1	0	2	0	0	1.000	1	0	0	0	.00	0
Garcia, Yimi, LAD	R	-	0	0	0	0	0	.000	1	0	0	0	0	0	0	0	0	8.1	0	2	0	0	-	0	0	0	0	-	0
Garner, Perci, Cle	R	-	0	0	0	0	0	-	0	0	0	0	0	0	0	0	0	9.1	0	2	0	0	1.000	3	1	0	0	.33	1
Garton, Ryan, TB	R	-	0	0	0	0	0	-	0	0	0	0	0	0	0	0	0	39.1	1	3	1	0	.800	2	1	0	0	.50	-2
Garza, Matt, Mil	R	.036	28	1	0	0	3	.079	239	19	3	0	0	3	6	142	30	101.2	2	6	3	0	.727	4	1	0	0	.25	-1
Gausman, Kevin, Bal	R	.000	2	0	0	0	0	.000	6	0	0	0	0	0	1	5	0	179.2	5	14	2	1	.905	5	2	0	0	.40	-1
Gearrin, Cory, SF	R	1.000	1	1	0	0	0	1.000	1	1	0	0	0	0	0	0	0	48.1	2	5	0	1	1.000	9	0	0	0	.00	-1
Gee, Dillon, KC	R	.000	1	0	0	0	2	.108	194	21	3	1	0	11	9	89	28	125.0	5	12	3	3	.850	7	4	1	1	.57	-2
Geltz, Steve, TB	R	-	0	0	0	0	0	-	0	0	0	0	0	0	0	0	0	26.2	1	1	0	0	1.000	3	1	0	0	.33	0
Germen, Gonzalez, Col	R	.000	3	0	0	0	0	.000	6	0	0	0	0	0	4	0	0	40.2	5	3	0	0	1.000	3	2	0	0	.67	0
Gibson, Kyle, Min	R	.000	7	0	0	0	0	.125	16	2	0	0	0	0	1	9	0	147.1	12	27	0	1	1.000	13	2	1	3	.15	1
Giles, Ken, Hou	R	-	0	0	0	0	0	-	0	0	0	0	0	0	0	0	0	65.2	4	5	0	0	1.000	5	0	0	0	.00	-2
Gilmartin, Sean, NYM	L	-	0	0	0	0	0	.333	6	2	0	0	0	0	0	3	0	17.2	0	5	0	0	1.000	1	0	0	0	.00	0
Giolito, Lucas, Was	R	.250	4	1	0	0	2	.250	4	1	0	0	0	0	0	1	2	21.1	1	3	0	0	1.000	0	0	0	0	.00	0
Girodo, Chad, Tor	L	-	0	0	0	0	0	-	0	0	0	0	0	0	0	0	0	10.1	3	0	1	0	.750	0	0	0	0	-	-1
Givens, Mychal, Bal	R	.000	2	0	0	0	0	.000	2	0	0	0	0	0	0	1	0	74.2	1	13	0	1	1.000	11	4	0	0	.36	2
Glasnow, Tyler, Pit	R	.143	7	1	0	0	0	.143	7	1	0	0	0	0	0	4	0	23.1	0	2	1	0	.667	9	0	0	0	.00	-2
Glover, Koda, Was	R	-	0	0	0	0	0	-	0	0	0	0	0	0	0	0	0	19.2	1	3	1	0	.800	1	1	0	0	1.00	-1
Godley, Zack, Ari	R	.111	18	2	0	0	1	.111	27	3	0	0	0	0	0	15	2	74.2	5	14	2	1	.905	2	0	0	0	.00	-1
Goeddel, Erik, NYM	R	-	0	0	0	0	0	.000	1	0	0	0	0	0	0	0	0	35.2	1	2	1	0	.750	2	1	0	0	.50	-1
Goforth, David, Mil	R	-	0	0	0	0	0	.000	3	0	0	0	0	0	0	3	1	10.2	1	2	0	0	1.000	3	0	0	0	.00	-1
Gomez, Jeanmar, Phi	R	-	0	0	0	0	0	.158	19	3	0	0	0	0	0	11	1	68.2	7	9	1	0	.941	1	0	0	0	.00	-1
Gonzalez, Chi Chi, Tex	R	-	0	0	0	0	0	-	0	0	0	0	0	0	0	0	0	10.1	0	1	0	0	1.000	2	0	0	0	.00	-1
Gonzalez, Gio, Was	L	.135	52	7	0	2	5	.097	268	26	6	0	3	11	3	113	40	177.1	13	26	1	0	.975	15	4	1	0	.27	-2
Gonzalez, Miguel, CWS	R	.000	1	0	0	0	0	.000	10	0	0	0	0	0	0	4	1	135.0	12	13	0	1	1.000	11	1	0	0	.09	1
Gonzalez, Severino, Phi	R	.000	1	0	0	0	0	.091	11	1	0	0	0	1	1	4	1	35.1	2	3	0	0	1.000	1	0	0	0	1.00	-1
Goody, Nick, NYY	R	-	0	0	0	0	0	-	0	0	0	0	0	0	0	0	0	29.0	1	3	0	0	1.000	2	1	0	0	.50	0
Gorzelanny, Tom, Cle	L	-	0	0	0	0	0	.092	217	20	0	0	0	13	9	102	24	3.0	0	0	0	0	-	0	0	0	0	-	0
Gott, Trevor, Was	R	-	0	0	0	0	0	-	0	0	0	0	0	0	0	0	0	6.0	0	0	0	0	-	0	0	0	0	-	0
Grace, Matt, Was	L	-	0	0	0	0	0	-	0	0	0	0	0	0	0	0	0	3.0	0	0	0	0	-	0	0	0	0	-	0
Graham, J.R., Min	R	-	0	0	0	0	0	-	0	0	0	0	0	0	0	0	0	1.2	0	0	0	0	-	0	0	0	0	-	-1
Graveman, Kendall, Oak	R	.000	4	0	0	0	1	.000	4	0	0	0	0	0	0	3	1	186.0	15	27	0	2	1.000	9	2	0	2	.22	2
Gray, Jon, Col	R	.149	47	7	0	4	6	.121	58	7	2	0	0	4	4	36	6	168.0	8	10	1	0	.947	12	2	1	2	.17	-2
Gray, Sonny, Oak	R	.000	2	0	0	0	1	.100	10	1	0	0	0	0	0	6	3	117.0	10	11	1	3	.955	5	1	0	0	.20	-1
Green, Chad, NYY	R	.000	4	0	0	0	0	.000	4	0	0	0	0	0	0	4	0	45.2	4	5	0	2	1.000	4	1	0	0	.25	0
Greene, Shane, Det	R	.000	2	0	0	0	0	.000	7	0	0	0	0	0	0	5	0	60.1	1	6	0	0	1.000	7	3	0	0	.43	0
Gregerson, Luke, Hou	R	-	0	0	0	0	0	.000	2	0	0	0	0	0	0	1	1	57.2	6	14	0	1	1.000	8	1	0	0	.13	3
Greinke, Zack, Ari	R	.212	52	11	0	3	3	.219	343	75	17	0	6	17	19	67	34	158.2	20	28	1	4	.980	7	4	1	0	.57	7
Griffin, A.J., Tex	R	.000	2	0	0	0	0	.000	6	0	0	0	0	0	1	5	0	119.0	1	9	0	1	1.000	9	5	0	0	.56	1
Grilli, Jason, Atl-Tor	R	-	0	0	0	0	0	.200	15	3	0	0	1	3	0	3	3	59.0	2	4	1	0	.857	1	0	0	0	.00	1
Grimm, Justin, ChC	R	-	0	0	0	0	0	.000	4	0	0	0	0	0	0	3	0	52.2	3	5	0	0	1.000	9	5	1	0	.56	0
Gsellman, Robert, NYM	R	.067	15	1	0	0	2	.067	15	1	0	0	0	0	0	9	2	44.2	2	9	0	1	1.000	4	3	1	0	.75	1
Guaipe, Mayckol, Sea	R	-	0	0	0	0	0	-	0	0	0	0	0	0	0	0	0	7.1	0	0	0	0	-	3	1	0	0	.33	0
Guerra, Deolis, LAA	R	-	0	0	0	0	0	.000	1	0	0	0	0	0	0	0	0	53.1	3	2	0	0	1.000	1	0	0	0	.00	0
Guerra, Javy, LAA	R	-	0	0	0	0	0	-	0	0	0	0	0	0	0	1	0	6.1	0	1	0	0	1.000	0	0	0	0	-	0
Guerra, Junior, Mil	R	.229	35	8	0	0	8	.229	35	8	2	0	0	0	0	13	8	121.2	10	11	2	1	.913	8	3	0	0	.38	1
Guerrero, Tayron, SD	R	-	0	0	0	0	0	-	0	0	0	0	0	0	0	0	0	2.0	0	0	0	0	-	0	0	0	0	-	0
Gurka, Jason, Col	L	-	0	0	0	0	0	-	0	0	0	0	0	0	0	0	0	9.2	1	5	1	0	.857	2	1	1	0	.50	1
Gustave, Jandel, Hou	R	-	0	0	0	0	0	-	0	0	0	0	0	0	0	0	0	15.1	1	1	0	0	1.000	3	2	1	0	.67	-1
Hahn, Jesse, Oak	R	.000	1	0	0	0	0	.077	26	2	0	0	0	1	0	15	2	46.1	3	6	0	1	1.000	7	0	0	0	.00	-2
Hale, David, Col	R	-	0	0	0	0	0	.068	44	3	0	0	0	1	0	20	5	2.0	0	0	0	0	-	2	0	0	0	.00	0
Hall, Cody, Mia	R	-	0	0	0	0	0	-	0	0	0	0	0	0	0	0	0	3.0	0	0	0	0	-	0	0	0	0	-	0
Hamels, Cole, Tex	L	.125	8	1	0	0	0	.173	618	107	15	2	1	28	17	258	62	200.2	9	18	3	0	.900	28	5	2	1	.18	-3
Hammel, Jason, ChC	R	.246	65	16	0	7	3	.156	333	52	8	0	1	21	7	130	37	166.2	16	24	1	2	.976	17	2	1	2	.12	1
Hand, Brad, SD	L	.000	4	0	0	0	1	.071	70	5	0	0	0	4	0	22	14	89.1	2	9	1	1	.917	13	2	1	0	.15	-1
Happ, J.A., Tor	L	.286	7	2	0	0	3	.097	186	18	2	0	1	6	9	82	30	195.0	6	26	0	0	1.000	8	1	0	0	.13	5
Hardy, Blaine, Det	L	-	0	0	0	0	0	.000	1	0	0	0	0	0	0	0	0	25.2	2	4	0	0	1.000	1	0	0	0	.00	0
Harrell, Lucas, Atl-Tex	R	.000	8	0	0	0	0	.135	74	10	0	0	0	1	3	39	3	47.0	4	6	1	0	.909	9	2	0	0	.22	1
Harris, Will, Hou	R	-	0	0	0	0	0	.000	1	0	0	0	0	0	0	0	1	64.0	9	7	0	1	1.000	12	1	0	0	.08	-2
Hart, Donnie, Bal	L	.000	1	0	0	0	0	.000	1	0	0	0	0	0	0	0	0	18.1	1	5	0	0	1.000	1	1	0	0	1.00	0
Harvey, Matt, NYM	R	.136	22	3	0	0	3	.129	163	21	7	0	1	12	1	73	12	92.2	5	17	1	2	.957	10	3	0	1	.30	1

Pitchers Hitting, Fielding and Holding Runners

Pitcher	T	2016 Hitting Avg	AB	H	HR	RBI	SH	Career Hitting Avg	AB	H	2B	3B	HR	RBI	BB	SO	SH	2016 Fielding and Holding Runners Inn	PO	A	E	DP	Pct	SBA	CS	PCS	PPO	CS%	RS
Hatcher, Chris, LAD	R	.333	3	1	0	1	0	.083	12	1	0	0	0	1	2	6	0	40.2	3	4	1	0	.875	4	0	0	1	.00	-1
Hathaway, Steve, Ari	L	-	0	0	0	0	0	-	0	0	0	0	0	0	0	0	0	14.2	1	2	0	0	1.000	2	1	1	0	.50	-1
Hayes, Drew, Cin	R	.000	1	0	0	0	1	.000	1	0	0	0	0	0	0	0	1	9.2	0	1	0	0	1.000	0	0	0	0	-	0
Heaney, Andrew, LAA	L	-	0	0	0	0	0	.077	13	1	0	0	0	0	0	5	2	6.0	0	0	0	0	-	0	0	0	0	-	0
Heller, Ben, NYY	R	-	0	0	0	0	0	-	0	0	0	0	0	0	0	0	0	7.0	0	2	1	0	.667	2	0	0	0	.00	1
Hellickson, Jeremy, Phi	R	.167	54	9	0	4	8	.188	101	19	1	0	0	11	6	41	12	189.0	8	28	0	3	1.000	13	3	0	0	.23	3
Hembree, Heath, Bos	R	-	0	0	0	0	0	-	0	0	0	0	0	0	0	0	0	51.0	2	7	1	0	.900	7	1	0	0	.14	-2
Henderson, Jim, NYM	R	-	0	0	0	0	0	-	0	0	0	0	0	0	0	0	0	35.0	2	3	1	0	.833	4	0	0	0	.00	-2
Hendricks, Kyle, ChC	R	.138	58	8	0	2	8	.099	142	14	1	0	0	4	5	64	14	190.0	16	30	0	2	1.000	17	4	0	3	.24	4
Hendriks, Liam, Oak	R	-	0	0	0	0	0	.000	2	0	0	0	0	0	1	1	0	64.2	3	5	0	0	1.000	11	1	0	0	.09	-1
Hernandez, David, Phi	R	-	0	0	0	0	0	.250	4	1	0	0	0	0	0	1	0	72.2	0	6	1	0	1.000	6	1	0	1	.17	-1
Hernandez, Felix, Sea	R	.000	6	0	0	0	2	.093	43	4	1	0	1	7	2	20	7	153.1	6	20	2	1	.929	20	4	3	0	.20	-2
Hernandez, Roberto, Atl	R	.000	4	0	0	0	0	.055	73	4	0	0	0	2	1	40	11	9.0	2	1	0	0	1.000	4	2	0	0	.50	0
Herrera, Kelvin, KC	R	-	0	0	0	0	0	-	0	0	0	0	0	0	0	0	0	72.0	2	7	0	1	1.000	1	1	0	1	1.00	1
Herrmann, Frank, Phi	R	.000	1	0	0	0	0	.000	2	0	0	0	0	0	0	1	0	15.0	0	1	1	0	.500	0	0	0	0	-	1
Hessler, Keith, Ari-SD	L	-	0	0	0	0	0	1.000	1	1	0	0	0	0	0	0	0	21.2	0	4	0	1	1.000	0	0	0	0	-	0
Heston, Chris, SF	R	-	0	0	0	0	0	.192	52	10	2	0	3	0	19	7	5.0	0	0	0	0	-	1	1	0	0	1.00	-1
Hill, Rich, Oak-LAD	L	.000	12	0	0	0	0	.111	126	14	3	0	0	6	2	59	6	110.1	4	17	2	1	.913	10	3	2	0	.30	1
Hinojosa, Dalier, Phi	R	-	0	0	0	0	0	-	0	0	0	0	0	0	0	0	0	11.0	1	3	0	0	1.000	0	0	0	1	-	0
Hochevar, Luke, KC	R	-	0	0	0	0	0	.063	16	1	0	0	0	0	0	10	1	37.1	0	3	0	1	1.000	5	2	0	0	.40	0
Hoffman, Jeff, Col	R	.000	8	0	0	0	1	.000	8	0	0	0	0	0	0	2	1	31.1	3	2	1	0	.833	1	0	0	0	.00	0
Holder, Jonathan, NYY	R	-	0	0	0	0	0	-	0	0	0	0	0	0	0	0	0	8.1	0	0	0	0	-	0	0	0	0	-	-1
Holland, Derek, Tex	L	.500	2	1	0	0	0	.071	14	1	0	0	0	0	2	7	2	107.1	3	8	2	0	.846	6	3	0	0	.50	1
Hoover, J.J., Cin	R	-	0	0	0	0	0	-	0	0	0	0	0	0	1	0	0	18.2	0	1	0	0	1.000	0	0	0	0	-	0
House, T.J., Cle	L	-	0	0	0	0	0	.000	2	0	0	0	0	0	0	0	0	2.2	1	0	0	0	1.000	1	1	1	1	1.00	0
Howell, J.P., LAD	L	.000	2	0	0	0	0	.154	13	2	0	0	0	1	0	7	0	50.2	1	8	0	0	1.000	6	4	1	0	.67	-1
Hoyt, James, Hou	R	-	0	0	0	0	0	-	0	0	0	0	0	0	0	0	0	22.0	3	3	1	0	.857	1	0	0	0	.00	-1
Hudson, Daniel, Ari	R	-	0	0	0	0	0	.226	106	24	5	0	1	21	5	35	14	60.1	5	3	2	1	.800	5	2	0	0	.40	-2
Huff, David, LAA	L	-	0	0	0	0	0	.125	8	1	0	0	0	0	4	2	2	5.1	0	1	1	0	.500	0	0	0	0	-	-1
Hughes, Jared, Pit	R	.000	1	0	0	0	0	.000	6	0	0	0	0	0	0	5	1	59.1	5	8	0	2	1.000	9	2	0	0	.22	-2
Hughes, Phil, Min	R	.000	2	0	0	0	0	.000	17	0	0	0	0	0	0	8	2	59.0	3	6	0	0	1.000	1	0	0	0	.00	0
Hunter, Tommy, Cle-Bal	R	-	0	0	0	0	0	.000	3	0	0	0	0	0	0	2	0	34.0	0	1	0	0	1.000	4	0	0	0	.00	-1
Hursh, Jason, Atl	R	-	0	0	0	0	0	-	0	0	0	0	0	0	0	0	0	1.1	1	0	0	0	1.000	0	0	0	0	-	0
Hutchison, Drew, Tor-Pit	R	.000	1	0	0	0	0	.286	7	2	0	0	0	0	0	3	0	24.0	0	3	0	0	1.000	3	2	0	0	.67	0
Iglesias, Raisel, Cin	R	.091	11	1	0	0	0	.073	41	3	0	1	0	1	0	15	1	78.1	8	8	1	0	.941	1	1	0	0	1.00	1
Iwakuma, Hisashi, Sea	R	.000	2	0	0	0	1	.000	11	0	0	0	0	0	1	8	3	199.0	11	19	1	1	1.000	12	4	1	0	.33	0
Jackson, Edwin, Mia-SD	R	.217	23	5	0	2	1	.173	271	47	4	0	2	13	14	111	23	84.0	5	5	2	0	.833	5	1	0	1	.20	-3
Jackson, Luke, Tex	R	-	0	0	0	0	0	-	0	0	0	0	0	0	0	0	0	11.2	0	1	0	0	1.000	2	1	0	0	.50	0
Jansen, Kenley, LAD	R	-	0	0	0	0	0	.333	3	1	0	0	0	1	1	1	0	68.2	3	1	1	0	.800	5	1	0	0	.20	0
Jeffress, Jeremy, Mil-Tex	R	-	0	0	0	0	0	-	0	0	0	0	0	0	0	0	0	58.0	4	8	0	1	1.000	2	2	0	0	1.00	0
Jenkins, Tyrell, Atl	R	.000	13	0	0	0	4	.000	13	0	0	0	0	0	4	4	4	52.0	1	10	0	0	1.000	4	1	0	1	.25	1
Jennings, Dan, CWS	L	-	0	0	0	0	0	.000	1	0	0	0	0	0	0	0	0	60.2	2	9	1	0	.917	2	1	0	0	.50	1
Jepsen, Kevin, Min-TB	R	-	0	0	0	0	0	-	0	0	0	0	0	0	0	0	0	49.2	0	4	0	1	1.000	3	1	0	0	.33	0
Jimenez, Ubaldo, Bal	R	.000	4	0	0	0	0	.115	286	33	0	0	0	11	17	99	33	142.1	12	12	2	3	.923	30	4	0	0	.13	-4
Johnson, Erik, CWS-SD	R	.000	4	0	0	0	1	.000	7	0	0	0	0	0	0	3	1	31.1	3	2	0	1	1.000	0	0	0	0	-	-2
Johnson, Jim, Atl	R	.000	1	0	0	0	0	.000	2	0	0	0	0	0	0	2	0	64.2	1	10	0	2	1.000	3	0	0	1	.00	1
Johnson, Steve, Sea	R	-	0	0	0	0	0	-	0	0	0	0	0	0	0	0	0	16.2	1	1	0	0	1.000	1	0	0	0	.00	0
Jones, Nate, CWS	R	-	0	0	0	0	0	-	0	0	0	0	0	0	0	0	0	70.2	3	13	1	0	.941	4	2	1	0	.50	1
Jungmann, Taylor, Mil	R	.125	8	1	0	0	0	.244	45	11	2	0	0	1	16	6	26.2	3	4	0	0	1.000	6	3	0	0	.50	0
Kahnle, Tommy, CWS	R	-	0	0	0	0	0	.000	3	0	0	0	0	0	0	1	1	27.1	6	4	0	0	1.000	0	0	0	0	-	1
Karns, Nathan, Sea	R	.000	1	0	0	0	0	.125	8	1	0	0	1	1	0	4	3	94.1	8	5	2	0	.867	14	2	0	0	.14	-3
Kazmir, Scott, LAD	L	.116	43	5	0	2	6	.116	69	8	0	0	0	4	1	34	7	136.1	6	16	0	1	1.000	11	3	1	0	.27	2
Kela, Keone, Tex	R	-	0	0	0	0	0	-	0	0	0	0	0	0	0	0	0	34.0	2	3	0	0	1.000	2	1	0	0	.50	0
Kelley, Shawn, Was	R	.000	1	0	0	0	0	.000	1	0	0	0	0	0	0	1	0	58.0	2	2	0	0	1.000	1	0	0	0	.00	0
Kelly, Casey, Atl	R	.000	2	0	0	0	1	.143	14	2	0	0	0	0	1	5	4	21.2	4	4	0	1	1.000	2	0	0	0	.00	0
Kelly, Joe, Bos	R	-	0	0	0	0	0	.172	87	15	4	0	0	5	0	25	8	40.0	2	3	1	0	.833	0	0	0	0	-	-2
Kennedy, Ian, KC	R	.000	3	0	0	0	0	.127	316	40	11	1	1	18	32	154	42	195.2	9	8	0	2	1.000	16	10	0	1	.63	-1
Kensing, Logan, Det	R	-	0	0	0	0	0	.000	8	0	0	0	0	0	0	3	0	4.2	2	0	0	0	1.000	0	0	0	0	-	0
Kershaw, Clayton, LAD	L	.174	46	8	0	3	3	.154	518	80	7	1	1	27	21	160	83	149.0	2	15	1	0	.944	2	1	0	0	.50	0
Keuchel, Dallas, Hou	L	.000	2	0	0	0	0	.094	32	3	0	0	1	2	18	6	168.0	5	27	0	2	1.000	4	2	0	0	.50	7
Kiekhefer, Dean, StL	L	.000	1	0	0	0	0	.000	1	0	0	0	0	0	0	0	0	22.0	2	3	0	0	1.000	0	0	0	0	-	1
Kimbrel, Craig, Bos	R	-	0	0	0	0	0	.000	1	0	0	0	0	0	0	0	0	53.0	0	2	0	0	1.000	1	0	0	0	.00	0
Kintzler, Brandon, Min	R	-	0	0	0	0	0	.000	2	0	0	0	0	0	0	1	0	54.1	5	15	0	0	1.000	0	0	0	1	-	2
Kirkman, Michael, SD-Mil	L	-	0	0	0	0	0	-	0	0	0	0	0	0	0	0	0	2.1	0	0	0	0	-	0	0	0	0	-	0
Klein, Phil, Tex-Phi	R	.000	2	0	0	0	0	.000	2	0	0	0	0	0	0	2	0	19.1	2	1	0	1	1.000	1	0	0	0	.00	0
Kluber, Corey, Cle	R	.250	4	1	0	0	2	.118	17	2	1	0	0	1	9	3	215.0	19	17	1	1	.973	11	7	1	0	.64	3
Knebel, Corey, Mil	R	-	0	0	0	0	0	-	0	0	0	0	0	0	0	0	0	32.2	1	4	1	0	.833	5	1	0	0	.20	0
Koch, Matt, Ari	R	.000	3	0	0	0	2	.000	3	0	0	0	0	0	1	3	2	18.0	0	0	0	0	-	0	0	0	0	-	0
Koehler, Tom, Mia	R	.098	51	5	0	4	4	.089	191	17	1	0	0	5	4	101	26	176.2	4	12	1	0	.941	17	8	0	1	.47	-3
Kontos, George, SF	R	-	0	0	0	0	0	.000	5	0	0	0	0	0	0	3	3	53.1	6	8	0	1	1.000	7	0	0	0	.00	0

Pitchers Hitting, Fielding and Holding Runners

Pitcher	T	2016 Hitting						Career Hitting										2016 Fielding and Holding Runners											
		Avg	AB	H	HR	RBI	SH	Avg	AB	H	2B	3B	HR	RBI	BB	SO	SH	Inn	PO	A	E	DP	Pct	SBA	CS	PCS	PPO	CS%	RS
Krol, Ian, Atl	L	.000	1	0	0	0	0	.000	2	0	0	0	0	0	0	0	0	51.0	5	10	1	2	.938	8	2	1	0	.25	1
Kuhl, Chad, Pit	R	.087	23	2	0	0	2	.087	23	2	0	0	0	0	1	9	2	70.2	7	12	0	1	1.000	6	2	0	0	.33	2
Lackey, John, ChC	R	.095	63	6	0	2	4	.104	183	19	6	0	0	7	6	74	15	188.1	13	19	0	1	1.000	20	5	0	0	.25	-3
Lamb, John, Cin	L	.050	20	1	0	0	1	.056	36	2	1	0	0	1	1	20	1	70.0	0	10	0	0	1.000	13	3	2	0	.23	-1
Latos, Mat, CWS-Was	R	.200	5	1	1	1	0	.133	324	43	6	0	4	15	6	148	43	70.0	3	10	0	1	1.000	15	3	1	0	.20	1
Law, Derek, SF	R	.000	1	0	0	0	0	.000	1	0	0	0	0	0	0	0	0	55.0	3	9	0	1	1.000	1	1	0	0	1.00	2
Layne, Tommy, Bos-NYY	L	-	0	0	0	0	0	-	0	0	0	0	0	0	0	0	0	44.2	7	8	1	1	.938	6	5	1	0	.83	2
Leake, Mike, StL	R	.143	49	7	0	4	3	.203	413	84	17	1	6	27	12	166	39	176.2	24	37	4	5	.938	20	4	1	2	.20	4
LeBlanc, Wade, Sea-Pit	L	.000	1	0	0	0	0	.250	112	28	1	0	0	2	3	26	15	62.0	2	3	0	0	1.000	2	2	0	0	1.00	0
Leclerc, Jose, Tex	R	-	0	0	0	0	0	-	0	0	0	0	0	0	0	0	0	15.0	0	2	0	0	1.000	0	0	0	0	-	0
Leon, Arnold, Tor	R	-	0	0	0	0	0	-	0	0	0	0	0	0	0	0	0	2.1	0	0	0	0	-	0	0	0	0		0
Leone, Dominic, Ari	R	-	0	0	0	0	0	-	0	0	0	0	0	0	0	0	0	27.0	1	0	1	1	.500	3	1	0	0	.33	-2
Lester, Jon, ChC	L	.102	59	6	0	6	10	.064	157	10	3	0	0	7	10	70	21	202.2	18	17	0	1	1.000	44	13	1	0	.32	1
Lewis, Colby, Tex	R	-	0	0	0	0	0	.259	27	7	1	0	0	5	0	11	1	116.1	1	7	1	0	.889	7	5	0	0	.71	0
Liberatore, Adam, LAD	L	-	0	0	0	0	0	.000	2	0	0	0	0	0	0	2	0	42.2	3	4	0	0	1.000	5	1	1	0	.20	-2
Light, Pat, Bos-Min	R	-	0	0	0	0	0	-	0	0	0	0	0	0	0	0	0	16.2	2	5	0	1	1.000	1	0	0	0	.00	2
Lincecum, Tim, LAA	R	-	0	0	0	0	0	.112	474	53	4	2	0	19	34	244	70	38.1	1	4	0	0	1.000	8	2	1	0	.25	-1
Liriano, Francisco, Pit-Tor	L	.286	42	12	1	5	0	.153	216	33	3	0	2	15	8	85	14	163.0	2	21	4	3	.852	12	1	0	1	.08	-1
Lobstein, Kyle, Pit	L	.000	2	0	0	0	0	.000	2	0	0	0	0	0	0	1	0	25.0	1	4	0	0	1.000	0	0	0	0	-	1
Locke, Jeff, Pit	L	.125	32	4	0	0	6	.097	185	18	1	0	0	2	7	95	21	127.1	2	18	2	1	.909	12	3	1	0	.25	1
Loewen, Adam, Ari	L	-	0	0	0	0	0	.189	37	7	1	0	1	4	3	13	0	6.0	0	0	0	0	-	1	1	0	0	1.00	0
Logan, Boone, Col	L	-	0	0	0	0	0	-	0	0	0	0	0	0	0	0	0	46.1	0	9	1	1	.900	1	0	0	0	.00	0
Lohse, Kyle, Tex	R	-	0	0	0	0	0	.153	509	78	9	0	0	31	9	163	75	9.1	3	0	0	1	1.000	1	0	0	0	.00	0
Lopez, Javier, SF	L	.000	1	0	0	0	0	.083	12	1	0	0	0	1	0	6	2	26.2	1	7	0	2	1.000	0	0	0	0	-	0
Lopez, Reynaldo, Was	R	.083	12	1	0	0	2	.083	12	1	0	0	0	0	0	7	2	44.0	0	6	0	0	1.000	1	0	0	0	.00	1
Lorenzen, Michael, Cin	R	.200	5	1	1	3	0	.244	41	10	0	1	1	7	0	15	4	50.0	10	5	1	0	.938	1	0	0	0	.00	0
Loup, Aaron, Tor	L	-	0	0	0	0	0	.000	1	0	0	0	0	0	0	0	0	14.1	0	5	0	1	1.000	1	1	0	0	1.00	1
Lowe, Mark, Det	R	-	0	0	0	0	0	.000	1	0	0	0	0	0	0	1	0	49.1	2	4	0	0	1.000	3	3	0	0	1.00	1
Luebke, Cory, Pit	L	-	0	0	0	0	0	.143	49	7	0	0	0	2	2	27	2	8.2	0	1	0	0	1.000	0	0	0	0	-	0
Lugo, Seth, NYM	R	.188	16	3	0	1	0	.188	16	3	1	0	0	1	1	2	0	64.0	2	10	0	1	1.000	6	1	0	0	.33	1
Lyles, Jordan, Col	R	.000	8	0	0	0	0	.125	144	18	4	0	2	7	6	68	11	58.2	4	5	1	0	.900	6	0	0	0	.00	-3
Lyons, Tyler, StL	L	.000	4	0	0	0	0	.128	39	5	0	0	0	1	4	15	3	48.0	2	4	0	1	1.000	2	0	0	0	.00	0
Madson, Ryan, Oak	R	.000	1	0	0	0	0	.122	49	6	1	0	0	2	2	21	7	64.2	3	10	0	1	1.000	9	1	0	0	.11	-1
Maeda, Kenta, LAD	R	.123	57	7	1	4	8	.123	57	7	1	0	1	4	1	16	8	175.2	17	24	3	4	.932	13	4	0	0	.31	5
Magill, Matt, Cin	R	-	0	0	0	0	0	.000	7	0	0	0	0	0	0	5	1	4.1	0	2	0	1	1.000	1	1	0	0	1.00	0
Magnifico, Damien, Mil	R	-	0	0	0	0	0	-	0	0	0	0	0	0	0	0	0	3.0	0	0	0	0	-	0	0	0	0	-	0
Mahle, Greg, LAA	L	-	0	0	0	0	0	-	0	0	0	0	0	0	0	0	0	18.1	0	4	0	0	1.000	1	0	0	0	.00	0
Manaea, Sean, Oak	L	.000	2	0	0	0	0	.000	2	0	0	0	0	0	0	1	0	144.2	5	12	1	0	.944	7	4	2	1	.57	-1
Maness, Seth, StL	R	.000	1	0	0	0	0	.214	14	3	0	0	0	0	6	6	0	31.2	4	6	2	0	.833	2	1	0	0	.50	1
Manship, Jeff, Cle	R	-	0	0	0	0	0	.000	10	0	0	0	0	0	0	3	0	43.1	1	2	0	1	1.000	1	1	0	0	1.00	0
Mantiply, Joe, Det	L	-	0	0	0	0	0	-	0	0	0	0	0	0	0	0	0	2.2	0	1	0	0	1.000	1	0	0	0	.00	0
Marinez, Jhan, TB-Mil	R	.000	3	0	0	0	0	.000	3	0	0	0	0	0	0	1	0	62.1	2	12	0	0	1.000	6	2	0	0	.33	1
Mariot, Michael, Phi	R	-	0	0	0	0	0	-	0	0	0	0	0	0	0	0	0	21.2	1	3	0	0	1.000	3	1	0	0	.33	1
Marks, Justin, TB	L	-	0	0	0	0	0	-	0	0	0	0	0	0	0	0	0	9.0	0	2	0	0	1.000	1	0	0	0	.00	0
Marksberry, Matt, Atl	L	-	0	0	0	0	0	-	0	0	0	0	0	0	0	0	0	3.1	0	0	0	0	-	0	0	0	0	-	0
Marquez, German, Col	R	.000	6	0	0	0	2	.000	6	0	0	0	0	0	0	3	2	20.2	1	3	0	0	1.000	2	0	0	0	.00	0
Marshall, Evan, Ari	R	-	0	0	0	0	0	-	0	0	0	0	0	0	0	0	0	15.1	0	3	0	0	1.000	0	0	0	0	-	1
Marte, Kelvin, Pit	L	-	0	0	0	0	0	-	0	0	0	0	0	0	0	0	0	3.1	0	0	0	0	-	0	0	0	0	-	0
Martin, Cody, Sea	R	-	0	0	0	0	0	-	0	0	0	0	0	0	0	0	1	25.2	0	2	0	0	1.000	2	2	0	0	1.00	0
Martin, Rafael, Was	R	-	0	0	0	0	0	-	0	0	0	0	0	0	0	0	0	3.2	0	0	0	0	-	0	0	0	0	-	0
Martinez, Carlos, StL	R	.237	59	14	0	6	4	.194	129	25	3	0	0	8	1	41	10	195.1	25	17	3	3	.933	15	3	0	0	.20	-1
Martinez, Nick, Tex	R	.000	2	0	0	0	0	.000	9	0	0	0	0	0	0	4	0	38.2	1	3	0	1	1.000	6	1	1	0	.17	-1
Matusz, Brian, Bal-ChC	L	-	0	0	0	0	0	.125	8	1	0	0	0	0	0	2	0	9.0	0	1	0	0	1.000	0	0	0	0	-	-1
Matz, Steven, NYM	L	.139	36	5	0	2	4	.180	50	9	2	1	0	7	4	12	4	132.1	4	27	1	3	.969	26	6	2	0	.23	-1
Maurer, Brandon, SD	R	-	0	0	0	0	0	.000	1	0	0	0	0	0	0	0	1	69.2	4	7	1	0	.917	4	1	0	0	.25	0
May, Trevor, Min	R	-	0	0	0	0	0	.000	3	0	0	0	0	0	0	3	0	42.2	1	0	1	0	.500	5	1	0	0	.20	0
Mayers, Mike, StL	R	-	0	0	0	0	0	-	0	0	0	0	0	0	0	0	0	5.1	0	0	0	0	-	1	0	0	0	.00	0
Mazzaro, Vin, SF	R	.000	1	0	0	0	0	.167	18	3	0	0	0	1	0	11	5	1.0	0	0	0	0	-	0	0	0	0	-	0
McAllister, Zach, Cle	R	-	0	0	0	0	0	.167	6	1	0	0	0	0	0	2	0	52.1	5	3	0	0	1.000	8	0	0	0	.00	-2
McCarthy, Brandon, LAD	R	.000	13	0	0	1	0	.053	94	5	0	0	0	5	6	41	8	40.0	2	6	0	0	1.000	8	2	1	1	.25	1
McCarthy, Kevin, KC	R	-	0	0	0	0	0	-	0	0	0	0	0	0	0	0	0	8.1	1	2	0	0	1.000	2	0	0	0	.00	0
McCullers, Lance, Hou	R	.333	3	1	0	0	0	.200	5	1	0	0	0	0	0	1	0	81.0	9	10	0	4	1.000	2	2	0	0	1.00	3
McFarland, T.J., Bal	L	-	0	0	0	0	0	-	0	0	0	0	0	0	0	0	1	24.2	0	3	0	0	1.000	1	1	0	0	1.00	-1
McGee, Jake, Col	L	-	0	0	0	0	0	-	0	0	0	0	0	0	0	0	0	45.2	4	1	0	0	1.000	4	2	0	0	.50	-1
McGowan, Dustin, Mia	R	.000	4	0	0	0	0	.095	21	2	0	0	0	0	0	13	1	67.0	4	5	1	0	.900	8	2	0	0	.25	-2
McHugh, Collin, Hou	R	.000	6	0	0	0	2	.077	26	2	0	0	0	0	0	10	3	184.2	11	19	0	2	1.000	7	3	0	0	.43	1
Medlen, Kris, KC	R	-	0	0	0	0	0	.141	128	18	4	0	1	8	11	59	12	24.1	2	2	0	1	1.000	1	1	0	1	1.00	0
Mejia, Adalberto, Min	L	-	0	0	0	0	0	-	0	0	0	0	0	0	0	0	0	2.1	0	2	0	0	1.000	0	0	0	0	-	1
Melancon, Mark, Pit-Was	R	-	0	0	0	0	0	-	0	0	0	0	0	0	1	0	0	71.1	10	7	0	1	1.000	2	0	0	0	.00	0
Melville, Tim, Cin	R	.000	2	0	0	0	0	.000	2	0	0	0	0	0	0	2	0	9.0	0	3	0	0	1.000	1	0	0	0	.00	0

Pitchers Hitting, Fielding and Holding Runners

Pitcher	T	2016 Hitting						Career Hitting										2016 Fielding and Holding Runners											
		Avg	AB	H	HR	RBI	SH	Avg	AB	H	2B	3B	HR	RBI	BB	SO	SH	Inn	PO	A	E	DP	Pct	SBA	CS	PCS	PPO	CS%	RS
Mendez, Yohander, Tex	L	-	0	0	0	0	0	-	0	0	0	0	0	0	0	0	0	3.0	0	0	0	0	-	1	0	0	0	.00	0
Mengden, Daniel, Oak	R	.000	6	0	0	0	0	.000	6	0	0	0	0	0	0	3	0	72.0	2	7	0	0	1.000	3	2	0	0	.67	1
Merritt, Ryan, Cle	L	-	0	0	0	0	0	-	0	0	0	0	0	0	0	0	0	11.0	0	3	0	1	1.000	0	0	0	0	-	1
Meyer, Alex, Min-LAA	R	-	0	0	0	0	0	-	0	0	0	0	0	0	0	0	0	25.1	1	1	0	0	1.000	3	0	0	0	.00	-1
Miley, Wade, Sea-Bal	L	.182	11	2	0	0	1	.149	208	31	5	0	1	12	8	54	27	166.0	2	21	0	0	1.000	8	5	3	1	.63	3
Miller, Andrew, NYY-Cle	L	-	0	0	0	0	0	.056	72	4	0	0	0	3	0	36	4	74.1	4	2	0	0	1.000	1	0	0	0	.00	-1
Miller, Justin, Col	R	.000	1	0	0	0	0	.000	3	0	0	0	0	0	0	3	1	42.2	3	2	0	0	1.000	5	0	0	0	.00	-2
Miller, Shelby, Ari	R	.125	32	4	0	0	2	.115	192	22	10	1	1	6	7	104	34	101.0	6	5	0	1	1.000	13	5	1	0	.38	-2
Mills, Alec, KC	R	-	0	0	0	0	0	-	0	0	0	0	0	0	0	0	0	3.1	1	1	0	0	1.000	0	0	0	0	-	0
Milone, Tommy, Min	L	1.000	2	2	0	0	0	.222	27	6	0	0	1	6	0	5	4	69.1	3	12	0	0	1.000	9	2	2	0	.22	2
Minaya, Juan, CWS	R	-	0	0	0	0	0	-	0	0	0	0	0	0	0	0	0	10.1	0	0	0	0	-	3	1	0	0	.33	0
Miranda, Ariel, Bal-Sea	L	-	0	0	0	0	0	-	0	0	0	0	0	0	0	0	0	58.0	3	1	1	0	.800	1	1	1	0	1.00	-1
Mitchell, Bryan, NYY	R	-	0	0	0	0	0	.000	1	0	0	0	0	0	0	1	0	25.0	0	1	0	0	1.000	3	2	1	0	.67	1
Molleken, Dustin, Det	R	-	0	0	0	0	0	-	0	0	0	0	0	0	0	0	0	8.1	1	2	0	0	1.000	0	0	0	0	-	0
Montero, Rafael, NYM	R	.000	5	0	0	0	0	.000	18	0	0	0	0	0	0	9	2	19.0	0	2	0	0	1.000	4	1	0	0	.25	0
Montgomery, Mike, Sea-ChC	L	.091	11	1	0	1	0	.071	14	1	0	0	0	1	0	7	0	100.0	6	9	2	0	.882	4	2	0	0	.50	0
Moore, Matt, TB-SF	L	.097	31	3	0	0	4	.079	38	3	0	0	1	0	15	6	198.1	8	18	2	2	.929	8	4	2	1	.50	0
Morales, Franklin, Tor	L	-	0	0	0	0	0	.177	62	11	0	0	0	2	4	27	8	4.0	1	0	0	0	1.000	0	0	0	0	-	0
Morgan, Adam, Phi	L	.094	32	3	0	1	3	.086	58	5	2	0	0	2	1	23	4	113.1	5	17	4	1	.846	12	4	3	0	.33	-1
Morimando, Shawn, Cle	L	-	0	0	0	0	0	-	0	0	0	0	0	0	0	0	0	4.2	1	0	0	0	1.000	0	0	0	0	-	0
Morin, Mike, LAA	R	-	0	0	0	0	0	-	0	0	0	0	0	0	0	0	0	55.2	5	10	0	1	1.000	4	3	0	2	.75	3
Morris, A.J., Cin	R	.000	1	0	0	0	0	.000	1	0	0	0	0	0	0	1	0	10.0	0	3	0	0	1.000	0	0	0	0	-	0
Morris, Bryan, Mia	R	.000	1	0	0	0	0	.143	7	1	0	0	0	0	4	0	17.2	0	2	0	0	1.000	3	1	0	0	.33	0
Morrow, Brandon, SD	R	-	0	0	0	0	0	.000	23	0	0	0	0	0	1	14	0	16.0	0	2	0	0	1.000	1	0	0	0	.00	-1
Morton, Charlie, Phi	R	.167	6	1	0	0	1	.075	255	19	4	0	0	6	3	132	37	17.1	1	2	0	0	1.000	2	1	0	0	.50	0
Moscot, Jon, Cin	R	.000	4	0	0	0	2	.125	8	1	0	0	0	0	0	5	2	21.1	1	1	1	0	.667	4	1	0	0	.25	-2
Motte, Jason, Col	R	-	0	0	0	0	0	.000	4	0	0	0	0	0	0	4	0	23.2	1	5	0	1	1.000	6	1	0	0	.17	0
Moylan, Peter, KC	R	-	0	0	0	0	0	.000	7	0	0	0	0	0	1	6	0	44.2	2	10	3	3	.800	0	0	0	0	-	1
Mullee, Conor, NYY	R	-	0	0	0	0	0	-	0	0	0	0	0	0	0	0	0	3.0	0	0	0	0	-	1	0	0	0	.00	0
Murray, Colton, Phi	R	.000	1	0	0	0	0	.000	1	0	0	0	0	0	0	1	0	31.2	2	2	0	0	1.000	2	0	0	0	.00	-1
Musgrove, Joe, Hou	R	-	0	0	0	0	1	-	0	0	0	0	0	0	0	0	1	62.0	10	8	0	2	1.000	0	0	0	0	-	0
Narveson, Chris, Mia	L	.000	3	0	0	0	0	.210	119	25	3	0	0	13	5	48	16	8.1	0	1	0	0	1.000	0	0	0	0	-	0
Nathan, Joe, ChC-SF	R	-	0	0	0	0	0	.159	63	10	3	0	2	4	3	17	10	6.1	1	0	0	0	1.000	1	0	0	0	.00	0
Neal, Zach, Oak	R	.000	2	0	0	0	0	.000	2	0	0	0	0	0	0	0	0	70.0	3	14	0	1	1.000	4	0	0	0	.00	1
Nelson, Jimmy, Mil	R	.080	50	4	0	3	7	.102	128	13	2	0	0	5	3	75	11	179.1	8	26	5	1	.872	37	7	4	1	.19	-6
Neris, Hector, Phi	R	-	0	0	0	0	0	.000	1	0	0	0	0	0	0	1	0	80.1	7	7	0	0	1.000	6	0	0	0	.00	0
Neshek, Pat, Hou	R	-	0	0	0	0	0	-	0	0	0	0	0	0	0	0	0	47.0	2	6	1	0	.889	2	1	0	0	.50	-1
Nicasio, Juan, Pit	R	.158	19	3	0	1	1	.125	120	15	2	0	0	9	6	69	15	118.0	10	12	1	1	.957	8	4	0	1	.50	0
Nicolino, Justin, Mia	L	.091	22	2	0	0	0	.064	47	3	0	0	0	1	1	19	3	79.1	3	15	1	1	.947	10	2	0	1	.20	1
Niese, Jon, Pit-NYM	L	.100	30	3	0	1	2	.150	347	52	7	1	0	19	35	164	31	121.0	7	16	1	1	.958	4	2	0	1	.50	1
Nola, Aaron, Phi	R	.033	30	1	0	0	1	.057	53	3	1	0	0	1	4	33	3	111.0	7	21	1	0	.966	6	1	0	1	.17	-1
Nolasco, Ricky, Min-LAA	R	.000	3	0	0	0	0	.135	377	51	12	0	1	26	23	177	62	197.2	10	23	2	2	.943	13	5	1	3	.38	0
Norris, Bud, Atl-LAD	R	.222	27	6	0	1	7	.157	204	32	5	1	0	12	7	66	38	113.0	6	10	1	1	.941	13	1	0	1	.08	-1
Norris, Daniel, Det	L	.000	2	0	0	0	0	.250	4	1	0	0	1	2	2	1	0	69.1	4	4	1	0	.889	2	1	0	0	.50	0
Nova, Ivan, NYY-Pit	R	.115	26	3	0	0	2	.100	40	4	0	0	0	0	0	31	5	162.0	10	12	2	2	.917	12	2	0	0	.17	-5
Nuno, Vidal, Sea	L	-	0	0	0	0	0	.080	25	2	0	0	1	0	8	6	58.2	2	4	0	0	1.000	4	2	1	0	.50	-1
Oberg, Scott, Col	R	-	0	0	0	0	0	-	0	0	0	0	0	0	0	0	0	26.0	1	3	0	0	1.000	1	0	0	0	.00	1
Oberholtzer, Brett, Phi-LAA	L	.143	7	1	0	0	0	.143	7	1	0	0	0	0	1	2	2	70.1	1	8	2	1	.818	5	3	0	0	.60	1
O'Day, Darren, Bal	R	-	0	0	0	0	0	.000	1	0	0	0	0	0	0	1	0	31.0	1	1	0	0	1.000	1	0	0	0	.00	0
Odorizzi, Jake, TB	R	.250	4	1	0	1	0	.083	12	1	0	0	0	2	1	6	1	187.2	11	14	2	2	.926	11	6	1	2	.55	1
O'Flaherty, Eric, Atl	L	-	0	0	0	0	0	.000	2	0	0	0	0	0	0	2	0	24.1	0	2	1	0	.667	1	0	0	0	.00	-2
Ogando, Alexi, Atl	R	-	0	0	0	0	0	.500	6	3	0	0	0	0	0	3	0	32.0	1	3	0	0	1.000	7	1	0	0	.14	-2
Ogando, Nefi, Mia	R	-	0	0	0	0	0	-	0	0	0	0	0	0	0	0	0	15.2	3	3	0	0	1.000	3	1	0	0	.33	0
Oh, Seung Hwan, StL	R	.000	2	0	0	0	0	.000	2	0	0	0	0	0	0	2	0	79.2	2	6	1	0	.889	3	1	0	0	.33	-3
Ohlendorf, Ross, Cin	R	-	0	0	0	0	0	.073	137	10	0	0	1	5	4	67	11	65.2	2	3	0	0	1.000	7	2	0	0	.29	-2
Okert, Steven, SF	L	.000	1	0	0	0	0	.000	1	0	0	0	0	0	0	1	0	14.0	0	0	0	0	-	0	0	0	0	-	0
Olson, Tyler, NYY	L	-	0	0	0	0	0	-	0	0	0	0	0	0	0	0	0	2.2	0	1	0	0	1.000	0	0	0	0	-	0
Ondrusek, Logan, Bal	R	-	0	0	0	0	0	.000	7	0	0	0	0	0	0	7	0	6.1	0	2	0	0	1.000	0	0	0	0	-	0
O'Rourke, Ryan, Min	L	.000	1	0	0	0	0	.000	1	0	0	0	0	0	0	0	0	25.0	3	2	0	0	1.000	1	0	0	0	.00	0
Osich, Josh, SF	L	-	0	0	0	0	0	.000	1	0	0	0	0	0	0	1	0	36.1	2	9	1	0	.917	4	0	0	0	.00	0
O'Sullivan, Sean, Bos	R	-	0	0	0	0	0	.121	33	4	2	0	0	1	1	17	2	21.1	0	2	1	0	.667	6	0	0	0	.00	-2
Osuna, Roberto, Tor	R	-	0	0	0	0	0	-	0	0	0	0	0	0	0	0	0	74.0	4	7	0	0	1.000	7	1	0	0	.14	0
Otero, Dan, Cle	R	-	0	0	0	0	0	.000	1	0	0	0	0	0	0	1	0	70.2	7	14	0	3	1.000	1	0	0	0	.00	0
Ottavino, Adam, Col	R	-	0	0	0	0	0	.083	24	2	0	0	0	1	1	17	3	27.0	3	0	0	0	1.000	2	0	0	0	.00	0
Overton, Dillon, Oak	L	-	0	0	0	0	0	-	0	0	0	0	0	0	0	0	0	24.1	1	5	0	0	1.000	2	1	1	0	.50	2
Owens, Henry, Bos	L	-	0	0	0	0	0	.000	2	0	0	0	0	0	0	2	0	22.0	0	0	0	0	-	6	2	0	0	.33	0
Papelbon, Jonathan, Was	R	-	0	0	0	0	0	-	0	0	0	0	0	0	0	0	0	35.0	0	1	0	0	1.000	2	0	0	0	.00	-1
Parker, Blake, Sea-NYY	R	-	0	0	0	0	0	-	0	0	0	0	0	0	0	0	0	17.1	0	2	0	0	1.000	4	2	0	0	.50	0
Parnell, Bobby, Det	R	-	0	0	0	0	0	.111	9	1	0	0	0	0	3	5	5.1	1	1	0	1	1.000	0	0	0	0	-	0
Partch, Curtis, Pit	R	-	0	0	0	0	0	.000	1	0	0	0	0	0	0	0	0	0.2	0	0	0	0	-	1	0	0	0	.00	0

Pitchers Hitting, Fielding and Holding Runners

Pitcher	T	2016 Hitting						Career Hitting										2016 Fielding and Holding Runners											
		Avg	AB	H	HR	RBI	SH	Avg	AB	H	2B	3B	HR	RBI	BB	SO	SH	Inn	PO	A	E	DP	Pct	SBA	CS	PCS	PPO	CS%	RS
Patton, Spencer, ChC	R	.000	2	0	0	0	0	.000	2	0	0	0	0	0	0	1	0	21.1	2	0	0	1.000	3	1	0	0	.33	-1
Paulino, David, Hou	R	-	0	0	0	0	0	-	0	0	0	0	0	0	0	0	0	7.0	1	1	0	1	1.000	1	0	0	0	.00	0
Paxton, James, Sea	L	.000	3	0	0	0	0	.000	7	0	0	0	0	0	2	7	1	121.0	0	12	3	1	.800	4	1	0	0	.25	-1
Pazos, James, NYY	L	-	0	0	0	0	0	-	0	0	0	0	0	0	0	0	0	3.1	0	2	0	1	1.000	0	0	0	0	-	0
Peacock, Brad, Hou	R	-	0	0	0	0	0	.000	9	0	0	0	0	0	0	7	1	31.2	2	2	0	1	1.000	3	1	0	0	.33	1
Peavy, Jake, SF	R	.185	27	5	0	3	2	.168	519	87	17	1	3	33	22	165	52	118.2	4	9	1	0	.929	6	3	0	0	.50	2
Pelfrey, Mike, Det	R	-	0	0	0	0	0	.104	268	28	5	0	0	13	13	72	24	119.0	11	15	0	1	1.000	10	2	0	0	.20	-2
Pena, Ariel, Mil	R	-	0	0	0	0	0	.000	7	0	0	0	0	0	0	6	0	1.2	0	0	0	0	-	0	0	0	0	-	0
Pena, Felix, ChC	R	-	0	0	0	0	0	-	0	0	0	0	0	0	0	0	0	9.0	0	0	0	0	-	0	0	0	0	-	0
Peralta, Joel, Sea-ChC	R	.000	2	0	0	0	0	.143	7	1	1	0	0	2	0	4	0	27.1	1	2	0	1	1.000	3	1	1	0	.33	0
Peralta, Wandy, Cin	L	-	0	0	0	0	0	-	0	0	0	0	0	0	0	0	0	7.1	1	2	0	1	1.000	0	0	0	0	-	0
Peralta, Wily, Mil	R	.128	39	5	1	6	1	.091	187	17	4	0	1	10	6	79	22	127.2	5	19	3	2	.889	21	10	0	1	.48	-2
Perdomo, Luis, SD	R	.132	38	5	0	1	3	.132	38	5	1	0	0	1	1	15	3	146.2	12	18	3	1	.909	12	0	0	1	.00	-5
Perez, Martin, Tex	L	.333	3	1	0	0	1	.091	11	1	0	0	0	0	0	8	2	198.2	9	25	1	3	.971	11	3	0	0	.27	-1
Perez, Oliver, Was	L	.667	3	2	0	0	0	.163	344	56	2	0	0	15	14	116	39	40.0	3	3	0	1	1.000	2	0	0	0	.00	1
Perez, Williams, Atl	R	.000	17	0	0	0	2	.044	45	2	0	0	0	0	2	18	6	53.2	6	7	0	0	1.000	1	0	0	1	.00	-2
Perkins, Glen, Min	L	-	0	0	0	0	0	.000	4	0	0	0	0	0	0	4	3	2.0	0	0	0	0	-	0	0	0	0	-	0
Petit, Yusmeiro, Was	R	.167	6	1	0	0	1	.051	118	6	0	0	0	3	3	49	7	62.0	1	4	1	0	.833	3	0	0	0	.00	-2
Petricka, Jake, CWS	R	-	0	0	0	0	0	-	0	0	0	0	0	0	0	0	0	8.0	1	3	0	1	1.000	1	0	0	0	.00	-1
Phelps, David, Mia	R	.182	11	2	0	1	2	.118	51	6	0	0	0	1	0	22	8	86.2	4	12	3	2	.842	4	0	0	0	.00	-1
Phillips, Zach, Pit	L	-	0	0	0	0	0	-	0	0	0	0	0	0	0	0	0	6.2	0	0	0	0	-	0	0	0	0	-	0
Pinder, Branden, NYY	R	-	0	0	0	0	0	1.000	1	1	1	0	0	1	0	0	0	1.0	0	0	0	0	-	0	0	0	0	-	0
Pineda, Michael, NYY	R	.000	1	0	0	0	0	.125	8	1	0	0	0	0	0	4	0	175.2	9	22	2	1	.939	24	8	1	1	.33	1
Plutko, Adam, Cle	R	-	0	0	0	0	0	-	0	0	0	0	0	0	0	0	0	3.2	0	1	0	0	1.000	0	0	0	0	-	0
Pomeranz, Drew, SD-Bos	L	.143	35	5	1	4	2	.174	69	12	2	0	2	5	1	40	9	170.2	2	17	2	0	.905	14	8	2	0	.57	0
Porcello, Rick, Bos	R	.200	5	1	0	0	0	.179	28	5	0	0	0	2	0	11	3	223.0	6	15	1	0	.955	10	3	0	0	.30	-3
Pounders, Brooks, KC	R	-	0	0	0	0	0	-	0	0	0	0	0	0	0	0	0	12.2	0	1	0	0	1.000	2	2	0	0	1.00	0
Pressly, Ryan, Min	R	-	0	0	0	0	0	-	0	0	0	0	0	0	0	0	0	75.1	3	10	1	1	.929	3	0	0	0	.00	0
Price, David, Bos	L	.000	10	0	0	0	0	.043	47	2	0	0	0	3	24	0	0	230.0	5	22	0	2	1.000	3	2	0	0	.67	2
Purke, Matt, CWS	L	-	0	0	0	0	0	-	0	0	0	0	0	0	0	0	0	18.0	0	3	0	1	1.000	1	0	0	0	.00	1
Putnam, Zach, CWS	R	-	0	0	0	0	0	-	0	0	0	0	0	0	0	0	0	27.1	0	2	0	1	1.000	4	1	0	0	.25	0
Quackenbush, Kevin, SD	R	-	0	0	0	0	0	-	0	0	0	0	0	0	0	0	0	59.2	1	4	0	0	1.000	8	1	0	0	.13	-1
Qualls, Chad, Col	R	-	0	0	0	0	0	.000	6	0	0	0	0	0	0	5	0	32.2	1	1	1	1	.667	3	0	0	0	.00	-3
Quintana, Jose, CWS	L	.000	2	0	0	0	0	.000	24	0	0	0	0	0	1	14	3	208.0	3	18	1	3	.955	9	3	1	1	.33	1
Ramirez, Erasmo, TB	R	-	0	0	0	0	0	.000	8	0	0	0	0	0	0	4	1	90.2	4	13	0	0	1.000	8	1	0	0	.13	1
Ramirez, JC, Cin-LAA	R	-	0	0	0	0	0	.000	1	0	0	0	0	0	0	0	0	78.2	7	9	2	0	.889	10	4	2	0	.40	-3
Ramirez, Jose, Atl	R	-	0	0	0	0	0	-	0	0	0	0	0	0	0	0	0	32.2	0	1	0	0	1.000	10	1	0	0	.10	-1
Ramirez, Neil, ChC-Mil-Min	R	-	0	0	0	0	0	-	0	0	0	0	0	0	0	0	0	24.0	1	2	0	0	1.000	6	3	0	0	.50	0
Ramirez, Noe, Bos	R	-	0	0	0	0	0	-	0	0	0	0	0	0	0	0	0	13.0	0	1	0	0	1.000	2	0	0	0	.00	0
Ramos, A.J., Mia	R	-	0	0	0	0	0	-	0	0	0	0	0	0	0	0	0	64.0	6	5	0	1	1.000	5	1	0	0	.20	1
Ramos, Cesar, Tex	L	-	0	0	0	0	0	.000	6	0	0	0	0	0	0	4	0	47.2	2	7	0	1	1.000	5	1	1	0	.20	0
Ramos, Edubray, Phi	R	-	0	0	0	0	0	-	0	0	0	0	0	0	1	0	0	40.0	2	3	0	0	1.000	5	3	0	0	.60	-2
Ranaudo, Anthony, Tex-CWS	R	.333	3	1	1	1	0	.100	10	1	0	0	1	1	0	6	0	31.1	1	4	0	0	1.000	6	0	0	0	.00	1
Rasmus, Cory, LAA	R	-	0	0	0	0	0	.000	1	0	0	0	0	0	0	0	0	24.2	0	2	0	0	1.000	6	2	1	0	.33	0
Ravin, Josh, LAD	R	-	0	0	0	0	0	-	0	0	0	0	0	0	0	0	0	9.2	0	1	0	0	1.000	0	0	0	0	-	0
Ray, Robbie, Ari	L	.189	53	10	1	2	6	.163	86	14	3	0	1	2	1	40	11	174.1	3	18	2	3	.913	13	3	0	0	.23	0
Rea, Colin, SD-Mia	R	.121	33	4	0	4	4	.143	42	6	1	0	0	1	3	20	6	102.2	5	16	0	2	1.000	15	2	0	0	.13	-2
Reed, Addison, NYM	R	-	0	0	0	0	0	.000	2	0	0	0	0	0	0	0	0	77.2	1	5	0	0	1.000	1	1	0	0	1.00	-1
Reed, Cody, Cin	L	.000	11	0	0	0	2	.000	11	0	0	0	0	0	1	6	2	47.2	3	7	0	0	1.000	8	0	0	0	.00	-1
Reyes, Alex, StL	R	.071	14	1	0	1	1	.071	14	1	0	0	0	1	0	5	1	46.0	0	4	2	0	.667	5	3	0	0	.60	1
Reyes, Jo-Jo, Mia	L	-	0	0	0	0	0	.143	63	9	2	0	0	2	4	24	7	2.0	0	0	0	0	-	0	0	0	0	-	0
Reynolds, Matt, SF	L	-	0	0	0	0	0	.000	5	0	0	0	0	0	1	3	1	6.0	0	0	0	0	-	1	0	0	0	.00	-1
Richard, Clayton, ChC-SD	L	.059	17	1	0	1	3	.115	226	26	8	0	1	21	5	103	26	67.2	2	18	4	0	.833	10	1	1	1	.10	-1
Richards, Garrett, LAA	R	-	0	0	0	0	0	.000	13	0	0	0	0	0	0	5	0	34.2	0	5	2	0	.714	5	1	0	0	.20	-1
Rivero, Felipe, Was-Pit	L	.000	1	0	0	0	0	.000	1	0	0	0	0	0	0	1	0	77.0	1	12	1	2	.929	3	2	0	1	.67	3
Roach, Donn, Sea	R	-	0	0	0	0	0	.400	5	2	1	0	0	1	0	1	0	5.1	0	0	0	0	-	0	0	0	0	-	0
Roark, Tanner, Was	R	.125	64	8	0	3	6	.147	163	24	4	0	0	4	6	60	20	210.0	9	36	1	5	.978	23	7	0	0	.30	-1
Robertson, David, CWS	R	-	0	0	0	0	0	-	0	0	0	0	0	0	0	0	0	62.1	4	6	0	1	1.000	7	0	0	0	.00	0
Robles, Hansel, NYM	R	.000	3	0	0	0	0	.000	3	0	0	0	0	0	0	2	0	77.2	5	3	0	0	1.000	11	3	0	0	.27	-2
Rodgers, Brady, Hou	R	-	0	0	0	0	0	-	0	0	0	0	0	0	0	0	0	8.1	0	0	0	0	-	1	0	0	0	.00	0
Rodney, Fernando, SD-Mia	R	-	0	0	0	0	0	.000	1	0	0	0	0	0	0	0	0	65.1	0	7	1	0	.875	10	4	2	0	.40	0
Rodon, Carlos, CWS	L	.000	3	0	0	0	0	.000	4	0	0	0	0	0	0	3	2	165.0	5	11	1	0	.941	20	3	1	0	.15	-6
Rodriguez, Eduardo, Bos	L	.000	2	0	0	0	0	.000	4	0	0	0	0	0	0	4	1	107.0	4	11	1	1	.938	4	2	0	0	.50	2
Rodriguez, Fernando, Oak	R	-	0	0	0	0	0	.000	4	0	0	0	0	0	0	3	0	40.2	1	2	0	0	1.000	1	1	0	0	1.00	0
Rodriguez, Francisco, Det	R	-	0	0	0	0	0	.500	2	1	0	0	0	0	0	1	0	58.1	6	3	1	0	.900	3	1	0	0	.33	-1
Rodriguez, Joely, Phi	L	-	0	0	0	0	0	-	0	0	0	0	0	0	0	0	0	9.2	0	0	0	0	-	1	0	0	0	.00	-1
Roe, Chaz, Bal-Atl	R	-	0	0	0	0	0	.000	1	0	0	0	0	0	0	0	0	29.2	2	2	0	1	1.000	4	0	0	0	.00	0
Rogers, Taylor, Min	L	-	0	0	0	0	0	-	0	0	0	0	0	0	0	0	0	61.1	4	13	3	1	.850	4	1	0	0	.25	2
Rollins, David, Sea	L	-	0	0	0	0	0	-	0	0	0	0	0	0	0	0	0	9.1	0	2	0	1	1.000	1	1	0	0	1.00	0
Romero, Enny, TB	L	-	0	0	0	0	0	-	0	0	0	0	0	0	0	0	0	45.2	3	5	0	0	1.000	1	0	0	0	.00	1

Pitchers Hitting, Fielding and Holding Runners

Pitcher	T	2016 Hitting						Career Hitting										2016 Fielding and Holding Runners											
		Avg	AB	H	HR	RBI	SH	Avg	AB	H	2B	3B	HR	RBI	BB	SO	SH	Inn	PO	A	E	DP	Pct	SBA	CS	PCS	PPO	CS%	RS
Romo, Sergio, SF	R	-	0	0	0	0	0	.000	6	0	0	0	0	0	0	4	0	30.2	2	0	0	0	1.000	5	3	0	0	.60	0
Rondon, Bruce, Det	R	-	0	0	0	0	0	-	0	0	0	0	0	0	0	0	0	36.1	1	2	0	0	1.000	5	2	0	0	.40	0
Rondon, Hector, ChC	R	.000	1	0	0	0	0	.000	1	0	0	0	0	0	0	1	0	51.0	7	7	0	1	1.000	5	0	0	1	.00	0
Rondon, Jorge, Pit	R	-	0	0	0	0	0	-	0	0	0	0	0	0	0	0	0	3.2	1	0	0	1	1.000	0	0	0	0	-	0
Rosenthal, Trevor, StL	R	.000	1	0	0	0	0	.000	4	0	0	0	0	0	0	4	0	40.1	1	4	0	0	1.000	2	0	0	0	.00	-1
Ross, Joe, Was	R	.244	41	10	0	1	0	.191	68	13	2	0	0	1	3	26	2	105.0	4	13	1	0	.944	4	2	0	0	.50	0
Ross, Tyson, SD	R	.000	1	0	0	0	0	.201	149	30	2	1	1	9	5	62	13	5.1	1	0	0	0	1.000	0	0	0	0	-	0
Ross Jr., Robbie, Bos	L	-	0	0	0	0	0	.000	3	0	0	0	0	0	1	1	0	55.1	4	5	0	0	1.000	1	1	0	0	1.00	1
Roth, Michael, Tex	L	-	0	0	0	0	0	-	0	0	0	0	0	0	0	0	0	3.2	1	0	0	0	1.000	0	0	0	0	-	0
Rowen, Ben, Mil	R	-	0	0	0	0	0	-	0	0	0	0	0	0	0	0	0	3.0	0	0	0	0	-	0	0	0	0	-	0
Rusin, Chris, Col	L	.172	29	5	0	3	1	.174	109	19	0	2	1	9	0	22	7	84.1	6	16	1	1	.957	9	2	2	2	.22	3
Russell, James, Phi	L	-	0	0	0	0	0	.063	16	1	0	0	0	0	0	6	0	4.1	0	0	0	0	-	0	0	0	0	-	0
Ryan, Kyle, Det	L	-	0	0	0	0	0	-	0	0	0	0	0	0	0	0	0	55.2	3	4	1	0	.875	6	2	1	0	.33	0
Ryu, Hyun-Jin, LAD	L	.000	1	0	0	0	0	.179	106	19	5	1	0	7	3	40	14	4.2	0	2	0	0	1.000	0	0	0	0	-	0
Rzepczynski, Marc, Oak-Was	L	-	0	0	0	0	0	.000	1	0	0	0	0	0	0	1	0	47.2	4	3	3	0	.700	4	1	0	0	.25	-2
Sabathia, CC, NYY	L	.000	1	0	0	0	0	.217	115	25	3	0	3	15	1	32	4	179.2	2	18	4	2	.833	3	0	0	0	.00	-3
Salas, Fernando, LAA-NYM	R	-	0	0	0	0	0	.000	4	0	0	0	0	0	0	2	0	73.2	4	7	0	0	1.000	6	2	0	0	.33	0
Salazar, Danny, Cle	R	.000	5	0	0	0	0	.000	14	0	0	0	0	0	0	12	0	137.1	5	9	1	0	.933	9	5	2	0	.56	-4
Sale, Chris, CWS	L	.167	6	1	0	0	0	.100	20	2	0	0	0	0	0	10	1	226.2	12	19	0	1	1.000	7	2	0	0	.29	-1
Samardzija, Jeff, SF	R	.156	64	10	0	9	2	.137	226	31	10	0	2	19	7	93	23	203.1	7	18	1	1	.962	19	6	0	0	.32	-1
Sampson, Adrian, Sea	R	-	0	0	0	0	0	-	0	0	0	0	0	0	0	0	0	4.2	1	1	0	0	1.000	0	0	0	0	-	0
Sampson, Keyvius, Cin	R	.000	7	0	0	0	0	.000	23	0	0	0	0	0	0	17	1	39.1	2	7	0	0	1.000	5	1	0	0	.20	1
Sanchez, Aaron, Tor	R	.000	9	0	0	0	0	.000	9	0	0	0	0	0	1	5	0	192.0	16	32	2	1	.960	14	2	0	0	.14	-1
Sanchez, Anibal, Det	R	.000	6	0	0	0	0	.088	251	22	1	1	0	7	16	119	31	153.1	13	13	2	1	.929	31	9	1	1	.29	-3
Santana, Ervin, Min	R	.000	5	0	0	0	1	.118	93	11	2	0	0	3	2	46	10	181.1	20	8	1	3	.966	6	1	0	0	.17	1
Santiago, Hector, LAA-Min	L	.333	3	1	0	0	0	.188	16	3	0	0	0	0	6	0	0	182.0	9	15	1	1	.960	16	7	4	0	.44	2
Saupold, Warwick, Det	R	-	0	0	0	0	0	-	0	0	0	0	0	0	0	0	0	9.2	0	2	0	0	1.000	0	0	0	0	-	-1
Scahill, Rob, Pit-Mil	R	.000	2	0	0	0	0	.000	4	0	0	0	0	0	1	1	1	34.2	3	7	0	1	1.000	2	0	0	1	.00	0
Scheppers, Tanner, Tex	R	-	0	0	0	0	0	-	0	0	0	0	0	0	0	0	0	8.2	0	1	1	0	.500	0	0	0	0	-	0
Scherzer, Max, Was	R	.186	70	13	0	12	13	.188	218	41	4	0	16	16	8	76	29	228.1	12	19	1	1	.969	11	3	1	0	.27	1
Schugel, A.J., Pit	R	.000	2	0	0	0	1	.000	2	0	0	0	0	0	0	1	1	52.0	1	8	0	0	1.000	3	1	0	0	.33	1
Schultz, Bo, Tor	R	-	0	0	0	0	0	.000	1	0	0	0	0	0	0	0	0	16.1	3	2	0	0	1.000	0	0	0	0	-	0
Schuster, Patrick, Oak-Phi	L	-	0	0	0	0	0	-	0	0	0	0	0	0	0	0	0	8.2	1	1	0	0	1.000	0	0	0	0	-	0
Scott, Robby, Bos	L	-	0	0	0	0	0	-	0	0	0	0	0	0	0	0	0	6.0	0	0	0	0	-	0	0	0	0	-	-1
Scribner, Evan, Sea	R	-	0	0	0	0	0	-	0	0	0	0	0	0	0	0	0	14.0	0	0	0	0	-	1	0	0	0	.00	0
Severino, Luis, NYY	R	-	0	0	0	0	0	.000	2	0	0	0	0	0	0	0	0	71.0	4	13	2	1	.895	2	0	0	0	.00	3
Shaw, Bryan, Cle	R	-	0	0	0	0	0	-	0	0	0	0	0	0	0	0	0	66.2	6	6	0	1	1.000	6	1	0	1	.17	-2
Shields, James, SD-CWS	R	.190	21	4	0	0	2	.169	136	23	3	0	6	6	3	53	8	181.2	8	18	4	0	.867	21	3	0	0	.14	-2
Shipley, Braden, Ari	R	.115	26	3	0	2	1	.115	26	3	1	0	2	0	10	1	0	70.0	6	7	0	1	1.000	4	0	0	0	.00	1
Shoemaker, Matt, LAA	R	.000	2	0	0	0	0	.000	4	0	0	0	0	0	1	2	1	160.0	9	23	2	4	.941	16	4	0	1	.25	0
Shreve, Chasen, NYY	L	-	0	0	0	0	0	-	0	0	0	0	0	0	0	0	0	33.0	2	7	0	0	1.000	2	1	1	0	.50	2
Siegrist, Kevin, StL	L	-	0	0	0	0	0	.000	1	0	0	0	0	0	0	1	0	61.2	0	6	1	0	.857	6	0	0	1	.00	0
Simmons, Shae, Atl	R	-	0	0	0	0	0	-	0	0	0	0	0	0	0	0	0	6.2	1	1	0	0	1.000	0	0	0	0	-	0
Simon, Alfredo, Cin	R	.071	14	1	0	1	3	.101	89	9	3	0	0	3	2	36	10	58.2	4	5	0	0	1.000	6	2	0	0	.33	-2
Sipp, Tony, Hou	L	-	0	0	0	0	0	-	0	0	0	0	0	0	0	0	0	43.2	2	7	1	0	.900	3	1	1	0	.33	0
Skaggs, Tyler, LAA	L	-	0	0	0	0	0	.100	20	2	0	0	0	1	0	11	5	49.2	0	7	0	1	1.000	11	0	0	0	.00	-3
Smith, Blake, CWS	R	-	0	0	0	0	0	-	0	0	0	0	0	0	0	0	0	4.1	1	0	0	0	1.000	1	0	0	0	.00	0
Smith, Carson, Bos	R	-	0	0	0	0	0	-	0	0	0	0	0	0	0	0	0	2.2	0	0	0	0	-	0	0	0	0	-	0
Smith, Chris, Oak	R	-	0	0	0	0	0	.000	2	0	0	0	0	0	1	1	0	24.2	2	2	0	0	1.000	2	1	0	0	.50	0
Smith, Jake, SD	R	-	0	0	0	0	0	-	0	0	0	0	0	0	0	0	0	4.0	0	0	0	0	-	0	0	0	0	-	0
Smith, Joe, Ang-ChC	R	-	0	0	0	0	0	.000	2	0	0	0	0	0	0	2	0	52.0	1	10	0	0	1.000	5	4	3	1	.80	3
Smith, Josh, Cin	R	.182	11	2	0	0	0	.200	20	4	1	1	0	0	8	1	59.2	2	1	0	0	1.000	10	2	0	0	.20	-2
Smith, Will, Mil-SF	L	-	0	0	0	0	0	-	0	0	0	0	0	0	0	0	0	40.1	0	4	1	0	.800	2	0	0	0	.00	-1
Smoker, Josh, NYM	L	.000	1	0	0	0	0	.000	1	0	0	0	0	0	0	1	0	15.1	0	1	0	1	1.000	1	0	0	0	.00	-1
Smyly, Drew, TB	L	.000	2	0	0	0	0	.000	4	0	0	0	0	0	1	1	0	175.1	6	20	1	1	.963	18	4	1	0	.22	0
Snell, Blake, TB	L	.000	2	0	0	0	0	.000	2	0	0	0	0	1	1	0	0	89.0	1	18	0	0	1.000	8	3	1	0	.38	1
Socolovich, Miguel, StL	R	-	0	0	0	0	0	.000	1	0	0	0	0	0	0	0	0	18.0	2	3	0	0	1.000	4	0	0	0	.00	-1
Solis, Sammy, Was	L	.000	3	0	0	0	0	.200	5	1	0	0	0	0	0	1	0	41.0	0	3	0	0	1.000	1	1	0	0	1.00	0
Somsen, Layne, Cin	R	-	0	0	0	0	0	-	0	0	0	0	0	0	0	0	0	2.1	0	1	0	0	1.000	0	0	0	0	-	0
Soria, Joakim, KC	R	-	0	0	0	0	0	-	0	0	0	0	0	0	0	0	0	66.2	5	15	0	1	1.000	4	2	1	0	.50	2
Stephenson, Robert, Cin	R	.000	10	0	0	0	3	.000	10	0	0	0	0	0	0	5	3	37.0	1	2	0	0	1.000	0	0	0	0	-	0
Stewart, Brock, LAD	R	.100	10	1	0	0	0	.100	10	1	0	0	0	0	0	7	0	28.0	0	3	0	0	1.000	4	2	0	0	.50	-1
Storen, Drew, Tor-Sea	R	-	0	0	0	0	0	.500	2	1	0	0	0	1	0	0	0	51.2	2	4	0	0	1.000	6	1	0	0	.17	-1
Strahm, Matt, KC	L	-	0	0	0	0	0	-	0	0	0	0	0	0	0	0	0	22.0	1	0	0	0	1.000	1	1	0	0	1.00	0
Straily, Dan, Cin	R	.019	52	1	0	1	11	.018	55	1	0	0	0	1	4	43	11	191.1	5	12	0	0	1.000	19	7	1	0	.37	0
Strasburg, Stephen, Was	R	.208	48	10	0	2	7	.157	268	42	8	0	1	15	16	100	38	147.2	8	9	1	1	.944	6	3	0	0	.50	-1
Stratton, Chris, SF	R	.000	1	0	0	0	0	.000	1	0	0	0	0	0	0	0	0	10.0	1	0	0	0	1.000	0	0	0	0	-	0
Street, Huston, LAA	R	-	0	0	0	0	0	.000	2	0	0	0	0	0	1	1	0	22.1	2	3	0	0	1.000	2	0	0	1	.00	0
Strickland, Hunter, SF	R	-	0	0	0	0	0	.000	1	0	0	0	0	0	0	1	0	61.0	5	11	0	1	1.000	9	2	0	0	.22	-1
Stripling, Ross, LAD	R	.083	24	2	0	1	1	.083	24	2	0	0	1	2	12	1	100.0	9	26	0	3	1.000	9	0	0	0	.00	2

Pitchers Hitting, Fielding and Holding Runners

Pitcher	T	2016 Hitting						Career Hitting										2016 Fielding and Holding Runners											
		Avg	AB	H	HR	RBI	SH	Avg	AB	H	2B	3B	HR	RBI	BB	SO	SH	Inn	PO	A	E	DP	Pct	SBA	CS	PCS	PPO	CS%	RS
Stroman, Marcus, Tor	R	.000	5	0	0	0	1	.000	5	0	0	0	0	0	0	0	1	204.0	12	29	4	2	.911	18	5	1	0	.28	-1
Strop, Pedro, ChC	R	.000	1	0	0	0	0	.000	1	0	0	0	0	0	0	0	0	47.1	5	5	1	0	.909	0	0	0	0	-	1
Stumpf, Daniel, Phi	L	-	0	0	0	0	0	-	0	0	0	0	0	0	0	0	0	5.0	0	2	0	0	1.000	2	1	1	0	.50	0
Sturdevant, Tyler, TB	R	-	0	0	0	0	0	-	0	0	0	0	0	0	0	0	0	18.1	2	2	0	2	1.000	1	1	0	0	1.00	0
Suarez, Albert, SF	R	.190	21	4	0	2	3	.190	21	4	2	0	0	2	0	11	3	84.0	8	15	1	3	.958	1	1	0	1	1.00	4
Surkamp, Eric, Oak	L	-	0	0	0	0	0	.111	9	1	0	0	0	1	1	5	1	38.2	3	2	1	0	.833	5	2	2	0	.40	-1
Suter, Brent, Mil	L	.000	2	0	0	0	0	.000	2	0	0	0	0	0	0	1	0	21.2	1	5	1	0	.857	1	1	0	3	1.00	2
Swarzak, Anthony, NYY	R	-	0	0	0	0	0	.000	5	0	0	0	0	0	0	4	0	31.0	2	2	0	0	1.000	2	0	0	0	.00	0
Syndergaard, Noah, NYM	R	.190	58	11	3	6	2	.198	101	20	4	0	4	10	8	60	8	183.2	11	21	4	0	.889	57	9	1	1	.16	-6
Taillon, Jameson, Pit	R	.094	32	3	0	2	4	.094	32	3	0	0	0	2	0	17	4	104.0	5	14	2	1	.905	10	2	2	0	.20	0
Tanaka, Masahiro, NYY	R	.000	2	0	0	0	0	.056	18	1	0	0	0	0	1	9	0	199.2	11	30	1	1	.976	10	3	0	0	.30	7
Tazawa, Junichi, Bos	R	-	0	0	0	0	0	-	0	0	0	0	0	0	0	0	0	49.2	3	3	1	1	.857	6	1	0	0	.17	0
Teheran, Julio, Atl	R	.204	49	10	0	2	11	.152	230	35	5	0	0	12	7	63	39	188.0	11	28	1	2	.975	20	3	1	2	.15	0
Tepera, Ryan, Tor	R	-	0	0	0	0	0	-	0	0	0	0	0	0	0	0	0	18.1	2	2	0	0	1.000	0	0	0	0	-	1
Tepesch, Nick, LAD	R	.000	1	0	0	0	0	.167	6	1	0	0	0	0	0	2	0	4.0	0	0	0	0	-	0	0	0	0	-	0
Thompson, Jake, Phi	R	.143	14	2	0	0	3	.143	14	2	1	0	0	0	0	5	3	53.2	4	6	0	2	1.000	2	1	0	0	.50	1
Thornburg, Tyler, Mil	R	-	0	0	0	0	0	.040	25	1	1	0	0	0	0	11	2	67.0	2	4	0	0	1.000	2	1	0	0	.50	1
Thornton, Matt, SD	L	-	0	0	0	0	0	.000	1	0	0	0	0	0	0	1	0	17.0	1	0	0	0	1.000	3	0	0	0	.00	0
Tillman, Chris, Bal	R	.000	2	0	0	0	1	.000	14	0	0	0	0	0	0	7	4	172.0	5	13	2	1	.900	4	4	0	0	1.00	-1
Tolleson, Shawn, Tex	R	.000	1	0	0	0	0	.000	1	0	0	0	0	0	0	1	0	36.1	5	7	0	1	1.000	4	3	0	1	.75	0
Tolliver, Ashur, Bal	L	-	0	0	0	0	0	-	0	0	0	0	0	0	0	0	0	4.2	0	0	1	0	.000	1	1	0	1	1.00	0
Tomlin, Josh, Cle	R	.400	5	2	0	0	1	.500	12	6	1	0	0	1	0	5	1	174.0	16	22	3	1	.927	4	1	0	0	.25	0
Tonkin, Michael, Min	R	.000	2	0	0	0	0	.000	2	0	0	0	0	0	0	1	0	71.2	0	7	0	2	1.000	14	1	1	0	.07	0
Torres, Carlos, Mil	R	-	0	0	0	0	0	.118	34	4	0	0	0	2	2	19	6	82.1	7	11	0	1	1.000	7	2	1	0	.29	2
Torres, Jose, SD	L	-	0	0	0	0	0	-	0	0	0	0	0	0	0	0	0	3.0	0	0	0	0	-	0	0	0	0	-	0
Treinen, Blake, Was	R	-	0	0	0	0	0	.071	14	1	0	0	0	0	1	9	4	67.0	2	13	1	1	.938	2	1	1	0	.50	1
Triggs, Andrew, Oak	R	.000	2	0	0	0	0	.000	2	0	0	0	0	0	0	2	0	56.1	0	5	0	0	1.000	2	1	0	0	.50	0
Tropeano, Nick, LAA	R	.000	2	0	0	0	0	.000	3	0	0	0	0	0	1	1	0	68.1	0	11	1	0	.917	6	3	0	4	.50	1
Tsao, Chin-hui, LAD	R	-	0	0	0	0	0	.214	14	3	2	0	0	0	0	1	2	1.2	0	0	0	0	-	1	0	0	0	.00	0
Tuivailala, Samuel, StL	R	-	0	0	0	0	0	-	0	0	0	0	0	0	0	0	0	9.0	0	0	0	0	-	2	0	0	0	.00	0
Turner, Jacob, CWS	R	-	0	0	0	0	0	.097	72	7	2	1	0	0	1	36	10	24.2	2	1	0	0	1.000	4	0	0	0	.00	-1
Uehara, Koji, Bos	R	-	0	0	0	0	0	.000	2	0	0	0	0	0	1	1	0	47.0	1	4	1	0	.833	1	0	0	0	.00	-1
Urena, Jose, Mia	R	.176	17	3	0	0	4	.133	30	4	0	0	0	1	20	4	83.2	3	13	1	1	.941	1	0	0	0	.00	-1
Urias, Julio, LAD	L	.136	22	3	0	2	4	.136	22	3	0	0	0	2	0	9	4	77.0	1	16	1	0	.944	10	3	3	3	.30	3
Valdez, Jose, LAA	R	-	0	0	0	0	0	-	0	0	0	0	0	0	0	0	0	23.1	2	3	0	1	1.000	0	0	0	0	-	0
Vargas, Cesar, SD	R	.000	8	0	0	0	1	.000	8	0	0	0	0	0	0	5	1	34.0	4	11	0	0	1.000	1	1	0	0	1.00	0
Vargas, Jason, KC	L	-	0	0	0	0	0	.262	61	16	3	0	4	3	16	2	12.0	1	1	0	0	1.000	2	1	1	0	.50	-1
Velasquez, Vince, Phi	R	.200	40	8	0	0	3	.200	40	8	1	0	0	1	16	3	131.0	3	14	2	0	.895	6	4	0	0	.67	-1
Venditte, Pat, Tor-Sea	B	.000	0	0	0	0	0	.000	1	0	0	0	0	0	0	1	0	22.0	0	3	0	1	1.000	1	0	0	0	.00	0
Ventura, Yordano, KC	R	.333	3	1	0	0	0	.154	13	2	0	0	0	0	10	1	186.0	6	27	5	1	.868	8	4	1	1	.50	0
VerHagen, Drew, Det	R	-	0	0	0	0	0	-	0	0	0	0	0	0	0	0	0	19.0	0	4	0	0	1.000	1	1	0	0	1.00	-1
Verlander, Justin, Det	R	.200	5	1	0	0	0	.081	37	3	0	0	0	0	0	17	10	227.2	7	29	1	2	.973	11	6	0	3	.55	5
Verrett, Logan, NYM	R	.053	19	1	0	0	3	.038	26	1	1	0	0	0	0	14	4	91.2	6	12	1	2	.947	8	5	1	0	.63	1
Villanueva, Carlos, SD	R	.000	4	0	0	0	1	.092	120	11	0	0	4	3	61	19	74.0	3	7	0	0	1.000	7	3	0	0	.43	-1
Vincent, Nick, Sea	R	-	0	0	0	0	0	.000	2	0	0	0	0	0	0	2	0	60.1	3	3	0	1	1.000	1	0	0	0	.00	1
Vizcaino, Arodys, Atl	R	-	0	0	0	0	0	-	0	0	0	0	0	0	0	0	0	38.2	3	3	1	0	.857	2	0	0	0	.00	-1
Vogelsong, Ryan, Pit	R	.053	19	1	0	1	2	.138	311	43	9	0	1	12	16	133	41	82.1	8	4	3	1	.800	8	2	0	0	.25	-1
Volquez, Edinson, KC	R	.000	6	0	0	0	0	.082	282	23	2	0	1	8	7	145	43	189.1	13	25	1	0	.974	22	6	0	0	.27	-5
Wacha, Michael, StL	R	.026	39	1	0	0	3	.092	141	13	1	0	0	9	7	70	13	138.0	21	22	1	2	.977	8	2	0	2	.25	4
Wagner, Tyler, Ari	R	.000	2	0	0	0	0	.000	5	0	0	0	0	0	0	3	0	10.0	1	2	0	0	1.000	0	0	0	0	-	0
Wainwright, Adam, StL	R	.210	62	13	2	18	5	.199	582	116	32	2	8	57	21	183	46	198.2	19	22	0	1	1.000	9	4	0	0	.44	1
Walker, Taijuan, Sea	R	-	0	0	0	0	0	.111	9	1	1	0	0	0	5	1	134.1	6	14	1	0	.952	17	1	0	0	.06	-1
Wang, Chien-Ming, KC	R	-	0	0	0	0	0	.051	39	2	1	0	0	1	2	21	1	53.1	1	3	1	0	.800	4	2	0	0	.50	-1
Warren, Adam, ChC-NYY	R	.000	3	0	0	0	1	.000	6	0	0	0	0	0	0	4	1	65.1	5	8	1	1	.929	7	3	0	0	.43	0
Watson, Tony, Pit	L	-	0	0	0	0	1	.167	6	1	0	0	0	0	0	5	3	67.2	5	6	1	0	.917	5	0	0	0	.00	0
Weaver, Jered, LAA	R	.000	6	0	0	0	0	.089	45	4	0	0	0	1	2	19	0	178.0	6	7	1	1	.929	28	8	1	1	.29	-4
Weaver, Luke, StL	R	.385	13	5	0	0	0	.385	13	5	0	0	0	0	0	4	0	36.1	3	7	1	0	.909	0	0	0	0	-	2
Webb, Daniel, CWS	R	-	0	0	0	0	0	-	0	0	0	0	0	0	0	0	0	1.0	0	0	0	0	-	0	0	0	0	-	0
Webb, Ryan, TB	R	-	0	0	0	0	0	.200	5	1	0	0	0	0	4	0	17.1	1	5	0	1	1.000	3	1	1	1	.33	-1
Weber, Ryan, Atl	R	.000	6	0	0	0	0	.000	16	0	0	0	0	0	0	11	0	36.1	3	4	0	0	1.000	3	1	0	0	.33	-1
Wendelken, J.B., Oak	R	-	0	0	0	0	0	-	0	0	0	0	0	0	0	0	0	12.2	0	0	0	0	-	1	0	0	0	.00	0
Whalen, Rob, Atl	R	.200	10	2	0	0	1	.200	10	2	0	0	0	0	3	1	24.2	2	5	1	1	.875	6	0	0	0	.00	-1
Whitley, Chase, TB	R	-	0	0	0	0	0	.200	5	1	0	0	0	0	0	0	0	14.1	1	2	0	0	1.000	3	0	0	0	.00	0
Wieland, Joe, Sea	R	-	0	0	0	0	0	.167	12	2	1	0	0	2	0	5	1	5.0	0	0	0	0	-	0	0	0	0	-	0
Wilhelmsen, Tom, Tex-Sea	R	-	0	0	0	0	0	-	0	0	0	0	0	0	0	0	0	46.1	2	3	0	0	1.000	4	2	0	0	.50	0
Williams, Jerome, StL	R	.000	2	0	0	0	0	.108	167	18	4	0	0	5	2	74	27	17.1	4	1	0	0	1.000	0	0	0	0	-	0
Williams, Trevor, Pit	R	.000	1	0	0	1	0	.000	1	0	0	0	0	1	2	1	0	12.2	2	0	0	0	1.000	1	1	0	0	1.00	0
Wilson, Alex, Det	R	-	0	0	0	0	0	-	0	0	0	0	0	0	0	0	0	73.0	4	7	0	0	1.000	1	0	0	1	.00	-1
Wilson, Justin, Det	L	-	0	0	0	0	0	.000	6	0	0	0	0	0	0	6	1	58.2	1	4	0	0	1.000	6	1	1	0	.17	0
Wilson, Tyler, Bal	R	-	0	0	0	0	0	.000	2	0	0	0	0	0	0	0	1	94.0	5	10	3	1	.833	8	2	0	0	.25	-2

396

Pitchers Hitting, Fielding and Holding Runners

Pitcher	T	2016 Hitting						Career Hitting										2016 Fielding and Holding Runners											
		Avg	AB	H	HR	RBI	SH	Avg	AB	H	2B	3B	HR	RBI	BB	SO	SH	Inn	PO	A	E	DP	Pct	SBA	CS	PCS	PPO	CS%	RS
Wimmers, Alex, Min	R	-	0	0	0	0	0	-	0	0	0	0	0	0	0	0	0	17.1	3	1	1	0	.800	0	0	0	0	-	-1
Winkler, Daniel, Atl	R	-	0	0	0	0	0	-	0	0	0	0	0	0	0	0	0	2.1	0	0	0	0	-	0	0	0	0	-	0
Wisler, Matt, Atl	R	.152	46	7	0	2	5	.147	75	11	0	0	0	3	3	27	10	156.2	7	18	0	0	1.000	17	1	0	0	.06	0
Withrow, Chris, Atl	R	-	0	0	0	0	0	.000	1	0	0	0	0	0	0	1	1	37.2	2	7	1	1	.900	8	0	0	1	.00	-1
Wittgren, Nick, Mia	R	-	0	0	0	0	0	-	0	0	0	0	0	0	0	0	0	51.2	3	6	0	0	1.000	0	0	0	0	-	0
Wood, Alex, LAD	L	.250	16	4	0	2	2	.120	133	16	2	0	0	8	7	86	16	60.1	1	7	0	0	1.000	5	3	0	2	.60	0
Wood, Blake, Cin	R	.000	2	0	0	0	0	.000	3	0	0	0	0	0	0	3	0	76.2	1	6	0	1	1.000	9	1	0	0	.11	-2
Wood, Travis, ChC	L	.182	11	2	0	1	0	.182	280	51	8	1	9	31	7	108	20	61.0	4	11	0	1	1.000	3	1	1	0	.33	0
Worley, Vance, Bal	R	-	0	0	0	0	0	.133	135	18	4	0	0	7	2	53	15	86.2	4	8	0	1	1.000	3	1	0	0	.33	-1
Wright, Daniel, Cin-LAA	R	.000	5	0	0	0	1	.000	5	0	0	0	0	0	0	2	1	39.2	4	5	0	1	1.000	4	2	0	0	.50	-1
Wright, Mike, Bal	R	-	0	0	0	0	0	.500	2	1	0	0	0	0	0	1	1	74.2	1	5	1	1	.857	1	1	0	0	1.00	-1
Wright, Steven, Bos	R	.000	4	0	0	0	0	.000	5	0	0	0	0	0	0	3	1	156.2	8	28	3	5	.923	12	4	0	1	.33	3
Yates, Kirby, NYY	R	-	0	0	0	0	0	-	0	0	0	0	0	0	0	0	0	41.1	2	4	1	0	.857	9	2	0	0	.22	-1
Ynoa, Gabriel, NYM	R	.000	3	0	0	0	0	.000	3	0	0	0	0	0	0	0	0	18.1	3	0	1	0	1.000	3	0	0	0	.00	0
Ynoa, Michael, CWS	R	-	0	0	0	0	0	-	0	0	0	0	0	0	0	0	0	30.0	1	6	1	0	.875	1	0	0	0	.00	1
Young, Chris, KC	R	.000	1	0	0	0	0	.150	207	31	6	1	1	17	10	82	27	88.2	1	9	1	0	.909	14	2	1	2	.14	0
Younginer, Madison, Atl	R	-	0	0	0	0	0	-	0	0	0	0	0	0	0	0	0	7.0	0	2	0	1	1.000	1	0	0	0	.00	0
Zastryzny, Rob, ChC	L	.000	3	0	0	0	0	.000	3	0	0	0	0	0	0	2	0	16.0	1	2	0	0	1.000	0	0	0	0	-	-1
Ziegler, Brad, Ari-Bos	R	-	0	0	0	0	0	.143	7	1	0	0	0	0	0	3	0	68.0	2	11	1	0	.929	1	0	0	0	.00	0
Zimmermann, Jordan, Det	R	.250	4	1	0	0	1	.170	324	55	6	0	1	15	10	99	44	105.1	2	17	2	0	.905	9	3	1	0	.33	2
Zych, Tony, Sea	R	-	0	0	0	0	0	-	0	0	0	0	0	0	0	0	0	13.2	0	0	1	0	.000	1	1	0	0	1.00	-1

Hitters Pitching

Player	2016 Pitching											Career Pitching										
	G	W	L	Sv	IP	H	R	ER	BB	SO	ERA	G	W	L	Sv	IP	H	R	ER	BB	SO	ERA
Amarista, Alexi, SD	1	-	-	-	0.1	-	-	-	-	-	0.00	2	0	0	0	0.2	0	0	0	0	0	0.00
Barney, Darwin, Tor	1	-	1	-	1.0	1	1	1	-	1	9.00	1	0	1	0	1.0	1	1	1	0	1	9.00
Bethancourt, Christian, SD	2	-	-	-	1.2	1	-	-	3	1	0.00	2	0	0	0	1.2	1	0	0	3	1	0.00
Butera, Drew, KC	2	-	-	-	1.1	1	-	-	-	1	0.00	5	0	0	0	4.0	3	2	2	1	4	4.50
Davis, Chris, Bal	-	-	-	-	-	-	-	-	-	-	-	1	1	0	0	2.0	2	0	0	1	2	0.00
Davis, Ike, NYY	-	-	-	-	-	-	-	-	-	-	-	2	0	0	0	2.0	1	0	0	1	1	0.00
Decker, Jaff, TB	-	-	-	-	-	-	-	-	-	-	-	1	0	0	0	1.0	2	0	0	0	0	0.00
Descalso, Daniel, Col	-	-	-	-	-	-	-	-	-	-	-	1	0	0	0	0.1	0	0	0	0	0	0.00
Elmore, Jake, Mil	-	-	-	-	-	-	-	-	-	-	-	2	0	0	0	2.0	3	1	1	0	0	4.50
Escobar, Eduardo, Min	1	-	-	-	1.0	1	-	-	-	-	0.00	1	0	0	0	1.0	1	0	0	0	0	0.00
Flaherty, Ryan, Bal	1	-	-	-	1.0	3	2	2	-	-	18.00	1	0	0	0	1.0	3	2	2	0	0	18.00
Francoeur, Jeff, Atl-Mia	-	-	-	-	-	-	-	-	-	-	-	1	0	0	0	2.0	1	2	2	3	1	9.00
Franklin, Nick, TB	-	-	-	-	-	-	-	-	-	-	-	1	0	0	0	1.0	3	2	2	0	0	18.00
Garcia, Leury, CWS	-	-	-	-	-	-	-	-	-	-	-	2	0	1	0	2.0	2	2	2	2	1	9.00
Gentry, Craig, LAA	-	-	-	-	-	-	-	-	-	-	-	1	0	0	0	1.0	3	2	2	1	0	18.00
Gimenez, Chris, Cle	2	-	-	-	3.0	4	4	4	-	-	12.00	3	0	0	0	4.0	4	4	4	0	1	9.00
Goins, Ryan, Tor	1	-	-	-	1.0	2	-	-	1	-	0.00	1	0	0	0	1.0	2	0	0	1	0	0.00
Harrison, Josh, Pit	-	-	-	-	-	-	-	-	-	-	-	1	0	0	0	0.1	0	0	0	0	0	0.00
Holaday, Bryan, Tex-Bos	1	-	-	-	1.1	-	-	-	-	-	0.00	1	0	0	0	1.1	0	0	0	0	0	0.00
Holt, Tyler, Cin	1	-	-	-	1.0	-	-	-	-	-	0.00	1	0	0	0	1.0	0	0	0	0	0	0.00
Hoying, Jared, Tex	1	-	-	-	1.0	1	1	1	-	-	9.00	1	0	0	0	1.0	1	1	1	0	0	9.00
Janish, Paul, Bal	-	-	-	-	-	-	-	-	-	-	-	2	0	0	0	2.0	9	11	11	2	3	49.50
Kelly, Don, Mia	-	-	-	-	-	-	-	-	-	-	-	1	0	0	0	0.1	0	0	0	0	0	0.00
Kratz, Erik, Hou-Pit	2	-	-	-	2.0	5	2	1	-	1	4.50	2	0	0	0	2.0	5	2	1	0	1	4.50
Ladendorf, Tyler, Oak	1	-	-	-	1.0	1	-	-	1	-	0.00	1	0	0	0	1.0	1	0	0	1	0	0.00
LaMarre, Ryan, Bos	1	-	-	-	1.0	2	-	-	-	-	0.00	1	0	0	0	1.0	2	0	0	0	0	0.00
Maldonado, Martin, Mil	-	-	-	-	-	-	-	-	-	-	-	1	0	0	0	1.0	1	0	0	0	0	0.00
Mathis, Jeff, Mia	-	-	-	-	-	-	-	-	-	-	-	2	0	0	0	2.0	4	2	2	1	0	9.00
Montero, Miguel, ChC	1	-	-	-	1.1	4	1	1	-	-	6.75	1	0	0	0	1.1	4	1	1	0	0	6.75
Moreland, Mitch, Tex	-	-	-	-	-	-	-	-	-	-	-	1	0	0	0	1.0	0	0	0	0	0	0.00
Motter, Taylor, TB	1	-	-	-	0.1	1	-	-	-	-	0.00	1	0	0	0	0.1	1	0	0	0	0	0.00
Phegley, Josh, Oak	1	-	-	-	0.2	-	-	-	-	1	0.00	1	0	0	0	0.2	0	0	0	0	1	0.00
Raburn, Ryan, Col	-	-	-	-	-	-	-	-	-	-	-	2	0	0	0	1.2	1	2	0	1	1	0.00
Ramirez, Alexei, SD-TB	-	-	-	-	-	-	-	-	-	-	-	1	0	0	0	1.0	1	0	0	0	0	0.00
Recker, Anthony, Atl	-	-	-	-	-	-	-	-	-	-	-	1	0	0	0	1.0	1	2	2	1	0	18.00
Robinson, Clint, Was	-	-	-	-	-	-	-	-	-	-	-	1	0	0	0	1.0	1	0	0	0	1	0.00
Robinson, Shane, LAA	-	-	-	-	-	-	-	-	2	-	-	1	0	0	0	1.0	0	0	0	1	1	0.00
Romine, Andrew, Det	1	-	-	-	0.2	-	-	-	2	-	0.00	2	0	0	0	1.2	4	3	3	2	1	16.20
Rosales, Adam, SD	-	-	-	-	-	-	-	-	-	-	-	2	0	0	0	2.0	2	3	2	1	1	9.00
Ross, David, ChC	-	-	-	-	-	-	-	-	-	-	-	2	0	0	0	2.0	0	0	0	0	0	0.00
Ryan, Brendan, LAA	-	-	-	-	-	-	-	-	-	-	-	1	0	0	0	2.0	2	0	0	0	0	0.00
Sardinas, Luis, Sea-SD	1	-	-	-	1.0	-	-	-	-	-	0.00	1	0	0	0	1.0	0	0	0	0	0	0.00
Shuck, J.B., CWS	1	-	-	-	1.0	1	1	1	-	-	9.00	1	0	0	0	1.0	1	1	1	0	0	9.00
Sucre, Jesus, Sea	-	-	-	-	-	-	-	-	-	-	-	2	0	0	0	2.0	6	3	3	0	0	13.50
Suzuki, Ichiro, Mia	-	-	-	-	-	-	-	-	-	-	-	1	0	0	0	1.0	2	1	1	0	0	9.00
Tejada, Ruben, StL-SF	1	-	-	-	1.0	2	2	2	-	-	18.00	1	0	0	0	1.0	2	2	2	0	0	18.00
White, Tyler, Hou	1	-	-	-	1.0	1	1	1	-	-	9.00	1	0	0	0	1.0	1	1	1	0	0	9.00
Worth, Danny, Hou	-	-	-	-	-	-	-	-	-	-	-	2	0	0	0	2.0	4	1	1	0	2	4.50

Hitter Analysis

Ben Jedlovec

The Hitter Analysis section provides a set of detailed information on hitters who had at least 100 plate appearances in 2016. It is information that has not always been widely available because of the logistical challenges in their data collection. The data covers:

PA - Plate Appearances
Pit - Pitches Seen
T - Pitches Taken
Sw - Pitches Swung At
St - Pitches Taken for a Strike
B - Pitches Taken for a Ball
S/M - Swings and Misses
F - Foul Balls Hit
InP - Pitches Hit In Play
P/PA - Pitches Per Plate Appearance
GB - Groundballs Hit
LD - Line Drives Hit
FB - Flyballs Hit

Additionally, we have a pair of categories that combine several of those fields in order to group players into two sets of groupings:

1. Very Patient, Patient, Neutral, Aggressive, or Very Aggressive
2. Groundball Hitters, Medium Hitters, or Flyball (Air) Hitters

Of note:

- In a weird way, Jose Altuve and Jose Abreu aren't very different as hitters. They took a similar number of pitches, hit very similar numbers of ground-balls and flyballs, hit for a high average, and hit virtually the same number of homers. The big difference is that Abreu swung and missed twice as often and fouled off over 100 more pitches. As a result, Abreu saw more pitches overall and put fewer in play. Altuve, instead of wasting his swings, lined the ball all over the field like a machine. The difference was 40 line drives and 40 points of batting average.
- Ben Zobrist and Joe Mauer took 65 percent of the pitches they saw, among the most; Orioles teammates Adam Jones and Jonathan Schoop took just 40 percent, among the least.
- Freddie Freeman took 1,105 balls this year, similar to Jayson Werth's 1,064. However, Freeman took 242 strikes and swung at 1,432, while Werth took nearly three times more strikes (659) and swung at just 1,062. Of course, Freeman used those extras swings to foul off 602 pitches, more than any other player and about 150 more than Werth, and missed completely on 407 swings, third-most in MLB and nearly 200 more than Werth.
- Mike Napoli only put 28 percent of his swings in play this year. By contrast, Mookie Betts put nearly twice as many into play, 54 percent of swings.

Hitter Analysis

Hitter	PA	PS	T	Sw	St	B	S/M	F	In P	P/PA	Group	GB	LD	FB	Hits
Abreu, Jose	695	2695	1318	1377	380	938	313	556	508	3.88	Neutral	231	108	169	Medium
Adames, Cristhian#	256	974	516	458	157	359	93	184	181	3.80	Aggressive	112	32	32	Ground
Adams, Matt*	327	1337	656	681	186	470	168	294	219	4.09	Patient	69	43	105	Air
Ahmed, Nick	308	1045	500	545	163	337	111	203	231	3.39	Very Aggressive	110	49	69	Ground
Almonte, Abraham#	194	725	348	377	98	250	89	145	143	3.74	Aggressive	67	30	43	Ground
Almora, Albert	117	394	190	204	69	121	43	69	92	3.37	Very Aggressive	39	25	26	Ground
Alonso, Yonder*	532	1883	1010	873	281	729	146	315	412	3.54	Very Aggressive	180	92	136	Medium
Altherr, Aaron	227	929	527	402	175	352	112	161	129	4.09	Patient	66	34	29	Ground
Altuve, Jose	717	2474	1272	1202	350	922	169	453	580	3.45	Very Aggressive	238	150	184	Medium
Alvarez, Pedro*	376	1552	840	712	232	608	220	250	242	4.13	Very Patient	114	40	88	Medium
Amarista, Alexi*	150	568	309	259	112	197	42	101	116	3.79	Aggressive	54	29	32	Ground
Anderson, Tim	431	1596	788	808	282	506	241	267	300	3.70	Aggressive	159	61	73	Ground
Andrus, Elvis	568	2083	1180	903	416	764	141	315	447	3.67	Very Aggressive	211	105	126	Ground
Aoki, Nori*	467	1688	879	809	299	580	92	338	378	3.61	Very Aggressive	223	63	81	Ground
Arcia, Orlando	216	793	373	420	109	264	118	148	154	3.67	Very Aggressive	81	26	43	Ground
Arcia, Oswaldo*	222	922	464	458	139	325	161	174	123	4.15	Very Patient	51	30	41	Medium
Arenado, Nolan	696	2743	1424	1319	427	997	237	559	523	3.94	Neutral	184	94	244	Air
Asche, Cody*	218	914	506	408	161	345	77	187	144	4.19	Very Patient	56	31	56	Air
Avila, Alex*	209	948	599	349	179	420	127	130	92	4.54	Very Patient	48	23	21	Ground
Aviles, Mike	181	673	358	315	132	226	51	121	143	3.72	Aggressive	74	27	39	Ground
Aybar, Erick#	459	1641	815	826	271	544	126	348	352	3.58	Very Aggressive	193	66	79	Ground
Baez, Javier	450	1683	790	893	242	548	252	325	316	3.74	Aggressive	133	59	110	Medium
Bandy, Jett	231	847	366	481	101	265	93	210	178	3.67	Very Aggressive	48	36	91	Air
Barnes, Brandon	109	397	173	224	59	114	64	85	75	3.64	Very Aggressive	26	13	27	Air
Barney, Darwin	306	1145	589	556	205	384	95	226	235	3.74	Aggressive	110	52	70	Ground
Barnhart, Tucker#	420	1510	802	708	227	575	136	262	310	3.60	Very Aggressive	145	76	84	Ground
Bautista, Jose	517	2195	1391	804	437	954	167	313	324	4.25	Very Patient	128	61	135	Air
Beckham, Gordon	279	1106	631	475	208	423	96	182	197	3.96	Patient	89	28	79	Air
Beckham, Tim	215	851	428	423	131	297	152	138	133	3.96	Patient	60	23	47	Medium
Bell, Josh#	152	617	342	275	96	246	48	115	112	4.06	Patient	56	24	32	Ground
Belt, Brandon*	655	2721	1432	1289	314	1118	311	580	398	4.15	Very Patient	104	110	182	Air
Beltran, Carlos#	593	2188	1190	998	389	801	185	358	455	3.69	Aggressive	191	95	168	Air
Beltre, Adrian	640	2443	1253	1190	398	855	176	494	520	3.82	Aggressive	209	92	219	Air
Benintendi, Andrew*	118	475	270	205	99	171	36	87	82	4.03	Patient	29	20	31	Air
Bethancourt, Christian	204	751	323	428	89	234	128	162	138	3.68	Very Aggressive	64	22	51	Medium
Betts, Mookie	730	2709	1591	1118	602	989	151	368	599	3.71	Aggressive	247	115	235	Air
Blackmon, Charlie*	641	2614	1382	1232	456	926	201	548	483	4.08	Patient	163	132	179	Air
Blanco, Andres#	209	786	369	417	109	260	110	157	150	3.76	Aggressive	77	29	43	Ground
Blanco, Gregor*	274	1077	609	468	193	416	81	194	192	3.93	Neutral	86	39	61	Ground
Bogaerts, Xander	719	2849	1556	1293	573	983	247	514	532	3.96	Patient	241	104	185	Medium
Bour, Justin*	321	1281	732	549	233	499	129	193	227	3.99	Patient	99	49	78	Medium
Bourjos, Peter	383	1332	610	722	190	420	199	252	271	3.48	Very Aggressive	132	44	83	Ground
Bourn, Michael*	413	1638	951	687	348	603	157	237	293	3.97	Patient	140	61	71	Ground
Bradley Jr., Jackie*	636	2509	1381	1128	453	928	283	425	420	3.94	Neutral	198	77	144	Medium
Braun, Ryan	564	2105	1033	1072	262	771	214	442	416	3.73	Aggressive	231	80	104	Ground
Bregman, Alex	217	834	446	388	139	307	100	138	150	3.84	Neutral	43	42	64	Air
Brown, Trevor	184	686	346	340	106	240	83	123	134	3.73	Aggressive	57	28	49	Air
Broxton, Keon	244	1067	603	464	168	435	163	181	120	4.37	Very Patient	52	29	35	Ground
Bruce, Jay*	589	2302	1118	1184	275	843	294	474	416	3.91	Neutral	154	91	170	Air
Bryant, Kris	699	2699	1390	1309	347	1043	356	501	452	3.86	Neutral	138	107	207	Air
Burns, Billy#	332	1089	523	566	180	343	66	221	279	3.28	Very Aggressive	142	51	74	Ground
Butera, Drew	133	545	277	268	93	184	63	116	89	4.10	Patient	34	19	33	Air
Butler, Billy	274	1057	577	480	194	383	93	176	211	3.86	Neutral	89	61	61	Medium
Buxton, Byron	331	1305	683	622	226	457	201	234	187	3.94	Neutral	60	37	74	Air
Byrd, Marlon	129	496	215	281	52	163	88	113	80	3.84	Neutral	25	20	35	Air
Cabrera, Asdrubal#	568	2082	1027	1055	283	744	225	410	420	3.67	Very Aggressive	155	95	164	Air
Cabrera, Melky#	646	2374	1210	1164	382	828	150	484	530	3.67	Very Aggressive	227	115	184	Medium
Cabrera, Miguel	679	2510	1288	1222	331	957	264	474	484	3.70	Aggressive	202	110	172	Air
Cabrera, Ramon#	185	648	325	323	107	218	69	108	146	3.50	Very Aggressive	59	31	54	Air
Cain, Lorenzo	434	1763	922	841	277	645	183	341	317	4.06	Patient	150	72	95	Ground
Calhoun, Kole*	672	2509	1266	1243	318	948	300	462	481	3.73	Aggressive	182	106	191	Air
Cano, Robinson*	715	2545	1252	1293	344	908	215	518	560	3.56	Very Aggressive	257	101	202	Medium
Carpenter, Matt*	566	2390	1469	921	498	971	170	379	372	4.22	Very Patient	112	96	158	Air
Carrera, Ezequiel*	310	1245	698	547	225	473	120	218	209	4.02	Patient	108	31	48	Ground
Carter, Chris	644	2744	1545	1199	426	1119	439	407	353	4.26	Very Patient	112	69	172	Air
Casali, Curt	256	1066	593	473	181	412	143	183	147	4.16	Very Patient	53	28	63	Air
Castellanos, Nick	447	1729	797	932	229	568	263	364	305	3.87	Neutral	96	78	131	Air
Castillo, Welington	457	1862	1053	809	358	695	213	297	299	4.07	Patient	125	76	98	Medium
Castro, Daniel	139	531	260	271	107	153	47	116	108	3.82	Aggressive	59	21	25	Ground
Castro, Jason*	376	1512	848	664	248	600	200	257	207	4.02	Patient	93	41	69	Medium
Castro, Starlin	610	2251	1088	1163	362	726	259	439	465	3.69	Aggressive	228	96	140	Ground
Centeno, Juan*	192	739	393	346	128	265	69	136	141	3.85	Neutral	68	34	32	Ground

Hitter Analysis

Hitter	PA	PS	T	Sw	St	B	S/M	F	In P	P/PA	Group	GB	LD	FB	Hits
Cervelli, Francisco	393	1597	988	609	294	694	128	222	259	4.06	Patient	144	51	62	Ground
Cespedes, Yoenis	543	2193	1163	1030	351	812	238	415	377	4.04	Patient	140	81	156	Air
Chirinos, Robinson	170	693	384	309	130	254	87	116	106	4.08	Patient	42	15	47	Air
Chisenhall, Lonnie*	418	1590	688	902	185	503	149	431	322	3.80	Aggressive	111	76	131	Air
Choi, Ji-Man*	129	528	315	213	94	221	39	88	86	4.09	Patient	42	14	29	Ground
Choo, Shin-Soo*	210	848	520	328	182	338	69	127	132	4.04	Patient	61	29	40	Ground
Coghlan, Chris*	300	1191	675	516	210	465	125	202	189	3.97	Patient	90	39	59	Ground
Collins, Tyler*	151	589	312	277	96	216	64	114	99	3.90	Neutral	41	19	39	Air
Colon, Christian	161	600	332	268	112	220	54	97	117	3.73	Aggressive	57	23	35	Ground
Conforto, Michael*	348	1410	790	620	239	551	139	263	218	4.05	Patient	79	41	98	Air
Conger, Hank#	137	573	294	279	84	210	93	101	85	4.18	Very Patient	37	15	32	Air
Contreras, Willson	283	1129	591	538	178	413	160	192	186	3.99	Patient	100	33	51	Ground
Correa, Carlos	660	2642	1465	1177	462	1003	282	454	441	4.00	Patient	221	99	121	Ground
Cozart, Zack	508	1898	1010	888	340	670	154	349	385	3.74	Aggressive	151	79	153	Air
Crawford, Brandon*	623	2363	1163	1200	265	898	314	439	447	3.79	Aggressive	188	94	159	Medium
Crisp, Coco#	498	1899	1086	813	367	719	144	295	374	3.81	Aggressive	146	80	139	Air
Cron, C.J.	445	1652	790	862	243	547	190	333	337	3.71	Aggressive	139	66	132	Air
Cruz, Nelson	667	2732	1436	1296	387	1049	368	491	437	4.10	Patient	194	79	164	Medium
Cuthbert, Cheslor	510	2005	1017	988	322	695	218	388	382	3.93	Neutral	181	65	135	Medium
Dahl, David*	237	915	430	485	124	306	140	182	163	3.86	Neutral	74	35	54	Medium
d'Arnaud, Chase	262	977	546	431	192	354	94	151	186	3.73	Aggressive	76	43	64	Medium
d'Arnaud, Travis	276	1058	572	486	194	378	76	206	204	3.83	Neutral	105	34	62	Ground
Davis, Chris*	665	2755	1580	1175	447	1133	410	415	350	4.14	Very Patient	127	69	152	Air
Davis, Khris	610	2331	1119	1212	308	811	398	420	394	3.82	Aggressive	168	67	158	Air
Davis, Rajai	495	1837	880	957	248	632	221	385	351	3.71	Aggressive	156	66	125	Air
De Aza, Alejandro*	267	1087	615	472	206	409	112	191	169	4.07	Patient	56	46	62	Air
De Jesus Jr., Ivan	243	992	545	447	187	358	91	183	173	4.08	Patient	81	46	42	Ground
Descalso, Daniel*	289	1159	692	467	204	488	96	173	198	4.01	Patient	86	47	63	Medium
DeShields, Delino	203	830	472	358	184	288	99	127	132	4.09	Patient	68	21	34	Ground
Desmond, Ian	677	2572	1375	1197	488	887	322	407	468	3.80	Aggressive	249	96	121	Ground
Diaz, Aledmys	460	1744	956	788	294	662	137	299	352	3.79	Aggressive	158	54	135	Medium
Dickerson, Alex*	285	1116	586	530	165	421	96	223	211	3.92	Neutral	78	47	85	Air
Dickerson, Corey*	548	2111	930	1181	270	660	329	473	378	3.85	Neutral	142	66	170	Air
Dietrich, Derek*	412	1609	857	752	268	589	142	338	272	3.91	Neutral	110	59	103	Air
Donaldson, Josh	700	2952	1720	1232	458	1262	291	478	463	4.22	Very Patient	176	98	187	Air
Dozier, Brian	691	2788	1570	1218	537	1033	272	462	484	4.03	Patient	174	76	228	Air
Drew, Stephen*	165	728	419	309	127	292	51	142	116	4.41	Very Patient	37	25	54	Air
Drury, Brandon	499	1947	1076	871	386	690	193	313	365	3.90	Neutral	183	74	108	Ground
Duda, Lucas*	172	688	406	282	133	273	62	101	119	4.00	Patient	44	28	47	Air
Duffy, Matt	366	1411	767	644	238	529	96	262	286	3.86	Neutral	142	61	81	Ground
Duvall, Adam	608	2225	1119	1106	362	757	293	416	396	3.66	Very Aggressive	134	77	185	Air
Dyson, Jarrod*	337	1209	654	555	193	461	71	215	269	3.59	Very Aggressive	139	50	60	Ground
Eaton, Adam*	706	2670	1397	1273	434	963	206	553	514	3.78	Aggressive	264	101	127	Ground
Eibner, Brett	208	823	427	396	126	301	108	149	139	3.96	Neutral	58	25	54	Air
Ellis, A.J.	196	778	479	299	169	310	37	118	144	3.97	Patient	58	31	51	Air
Ellsbury, Jacoby*	626	2334	1248	1086	390	858	172	428	474	3.73	Aggressive	218	107	145	Ground
Encarnacion, Edwin	702	2900	1668	1232	476	1192	280	480	471	4.13	Very Patient	180	96	195	Air
Escobar, Alcides	682	2464	1139	1325	388	751	261	508	556	3.61	Very Aggressive	270	109	162	Ground
Escobar, Eduardo#	377	1407	700	707	245	455	128	296	283	3.73	Aggressive	110	66	105	Air
Escobar, Yunel	567	1956	1004	952	291	713	150	345	457	3.45	Very Aggressive	263	96	94	Ground
Espinosa, Danny#	601	2314	1181	1133	312	869	362	418	353	3.85	Neutral	126	59	140	Air
Fielder, Prince*	370	1375	759	616	221	538	147	202	267	3.72	Aggressive	117	51	99	Medium
Flaherty, Ryan*	176	700	390	310	109	281	70	129	111	3.98	Patient	61	19	29	Ground
Flores, Ramon*	289	1208	693	515	228	465	85	232	198	4.18	Very Patient	106	33	55	Air
Flores, Wilmer	335	1346	687	654	194	493	106	286	262	4.00	Patient	87	57	118	Air
Flowers, Tyler	325	1316	716	600	211	505	160	246	194	4.05	Patient	82	36	76	Air
Forsythe, Logan	567	2352	1421	931	522	899	203	342	386	4.15	Very Patient	162	88	136	Medium
Fowler, Dexter#	551	2429	1476	953	436	1040	201	415	337	4.41	Very Patient	135	79	118	Air
Franco, Maikel	630	2446	1089	1157	294	795	272	406	479	3.57	Very Aggressive	213	96	170	Medium
Francoeur, Jeff	331	1246	543	703	152	391	219	263	221	3.76	Aggressive	107	41	72	Ground
Franklin, Nick#	191	704	356	348	113	243	76	138	134	3.69	Aggressive	50	24	57	Air
Frazier, Adam*	160	625	310	315	119	191	54	140	121	3.91	Neutral	53	40	28	Ground
Frazier, Todd	666	2766	1475	1291	427	1048	350	506	435	4.15	Very Patient	154	68	211	Air
Freeman, Freddie*	693	2779	1347	1432	242	1105	407	602	423	4.01	Patient	128	123	171	Air
Freese, David	492	2062	1147	915	352	795	244	376	295	4.19	Very Patient	179	56	60	Ground
Fryer, Eric	133	547	297	250	86	211	54	101	95	4.11	Patient	47	22	23	Ground
Galvis, Freddy#	624	2365	1115	1250	351	764	251	540	459	3.79	Aggressive	176	103	160	Air
Garcia, Adonis	563	1998	949	1049	299	650	213	396	439	3.55	Very Aggressive	230	92	117	Ground
Garcia, Avisail	453	1722	779	943	201	578	304	339	300	3.80	Aggressive	165	65	70	Ground
Garcia, Greg*	257	1042	638	404	200	438	62	177	165	4.05	Patient	81	41	39	Ground
Gardner, Brett*	634	2591	1625	966	587	1038	144	372	450	4.09	Patient	230	91	119	Ground
Gattis, Evan	499	1901	1040	861	312	728	219	318	324	3.81	Aggressive	133	58	133	Air
Gennett, Scooter*	542	2069	1006	1063	286	720	227	448	387	3.82	Aggressive	172	80	133	Medium
Giavotella, Johnny	367	1221	632	589	234	398	93	182	314	3.33	Very Aggressive	152	69	86	Ground
Gillaspie, Conor*	205	695	321	374	86	235	66	144	164	3.39	Very Aggressive	63	38	63	Air

Hitter Analysis

Hitter	PA	PS	T	Sw	St	B	S/M	F	In P	P/PA	Group	GB	LD	FB	Hits
Gimenez, Chris	155	592	307	285	113	194	68	114	103	3.82	Aggressive	48	21	29	Ground
Goeddel, Tyler	234	904	490	414	164	326	101	150	163	3.86	Neutral	86	27	47	Ground
Goins, Ryan*	196	713	385	328	151	234	76	114	138	3.64	Very Aggressive	71	15	47	Ground
Goldschmidt, Paul	705	3012	1854	1158	585	1269	251	469	437	4.27	Very Patient	203	108	126	Ground
Gomes, Yan	264	913	392	521	116	276	123	214	184	3.46	Very Aggressive	71	30	83	Air
Gomez, Carlos	453	1740	816	924	215	601	293	353	278	3.84	Neutral	116	55	91	Medium
Gonzalez, Adrian*	633	2394	1242	1152	313	929	250	445	457	3.78	Aggressive	210	120	125	Ground
Gonzalez, Carlos*	632	2327	1133	1194	259	874	350	388	456	3.68	Aggressive	210	97	148	Ground
Gonzalez, Marwin#	518	1914	972	942	334	638	234	335	373	3.69	Aggressive	166	72	112	Ground
Gordon, Alex*	506	2126	1201	925	348	853	264	363	298	4.20	Very Patient	113	72	113	Air
Gordon, Dee*	346	1274	637	637	215	422	97	267	273	3.68	Aggressive	152	48	59	Ground
Gose, Anthony*	101	430	248	182	87	161	61	68	53	4.26	Very Patient	30	10	12	Ground
Gosselin, Phil	240	856	488	368	187	301	72	118	178	3.57	Very Aggressive	90	37	46	Ground
Grandal, Yasmani#	457	1971	1199	772	373	826	205	292	275	4.31	Very Patient	122	44	107	Air
Granderson, Curtis*	633	2692	1711	981	597	1114	205	356	420	4.25	Very Patient	152	90	176	Air
Gregorius, Didi*	597	2067	922	1145	277	645	202	453	490	3.46	Very Aggressive	192	94	193	Air
Grichuk, Randal	478	1843	851	992	242	609	284	402	306	3.86	Neutral	124	48	134	Air
Grossman, Robbie#	389	1618	1007	611	332	675	144	231	236	4.16	Very Patient	88	59	86	Air
Gurriel, Yulieski	137	438	195	243	48	147	42	82	119	3.20	Very Aggressive	50	24	45	Air
Gutierrez, Franklin	283	1250	726	524	220	506	167	191	166	4.42	Very Patient	83	30	53	Ground
Guyer, Brandon	345	1210	606	604	182	424	112	252	240	3.51	Very Aggressive	96	51	90	Air
Gyorko, Jedd	438	1700	873	827	235	638	206	316	305	3.88	Neutral	124	58	123	Air
Hamilton, Billy#	460	1773	968	805	336	632	149	326	330	3.85	Neutral	144	66	92	Ground
Hanigan, Ryan	113	468	264	204	105	159	46	80	78	4.14	Very Patient	42	16	20	Ground
Haniger, Mitch	123	497	283	214	90	193	50	81	83	4.04	Patient	32	15	36	Air
Hardy, J.J.	438	1803	1148	655	488	660	94	217	344	4.12	Very Patient	156	63	124	Medium
Harper, Bryce*	627	2547	1484	1063	381	1103	230	434	399	4.06	Patient	160	68	168	Air
Harrison, Josh	522	1896	857	1039	263	594	192	424	423	3.63	Very Aggressive	182	80	149	Medium
Hazelbaker, Jeremy*	224	826	405	421	142	263	96	183	142	3.69	Aggressive	67	20	48	Ground
Headley, Chase#	529	2093	1172	921	355	817	218	349	354	3.96	Neutral	156	84	113	Medium
Healy, Ryon	283	1075	597	478	245	352	104	164	210	3.80	Aggressive	87	41	81	Air
Hechavarria, Adeiny	547	1982	988	994	334	654	154	400	440	3.62	Very Aggressive	207	96	130	Ground
Heisey, Chris	155	636	370	266	133	237	74	96	96	4.10	Patient	29	18	47	Air
Heredia, Guillermo	107	432	260	172	88	172	25	69	78	4.04	Patient	36	15	23	Ground
Hernandez, Cesar#	622	2427	1331	1096	401	930	207	451	438	3.90	Neutral	225	100	85	Ground
Hernandez, Kiké	244	969	538	431	173	365	122	157	152	3.97	Patient	62	26	64	Air
Hernandez, Teoscar	112	469	269	200	79	190	62	65	73	4.19	Very Patient	35	9	29	Medium
Herrera, Odubel*	656	2643	1348	1295	378	970	295	547	453	4.03	Patient	206	96	142	Ground
Herrmann, Chris*	166	678	347	331	100	247	97	128	106	4.08	Patient	46	18	40	Air
Heyward, Jason*	592	2281	1335	946	445	890	152	354	440	3.85	Neutral	203	90	146	Medium
Hicks, Aaron#	361	1381	749	632	200	549	155	214	263	3.83	Neutral	118	44	97	Medium
Hill, Aaron	429	1667	962	705	336	626	110	272	323	3.89	Neutral	120	70	133	Air
Holaday, Bryan	129	503	241	262	76	165	56	114	92	3.90	Neutral	28	12	50	Air
Holliday, Matt	426	1563	809	754	236	573	146	296	312	3.67	Very Aggressive	156	44	112	Ground
Holt, Brock*	324	1406	866	540	357	509	57	247	236	4.34	Very Patient	128	56	51	Ground
Holt, Tyler	208	856	481	375	174	307	87	153	135	4.12	Very Patient	66	29	32	Ground
Hosmer, Eric*	667	2563	1318	1245	351	967	314	454	477	3.84	Neutral	279	78	117	Ground
Howard, Ryan*	362	1372	618	754	139	479	250	284	220	3.79	Aggressive	76	50	94	Air
Hundley, Nick	317	1193	589	604	157	432	142	236	226	3.76	Aggressive	103	40	82	Medium
Iannetta, Chris	338	1403	764	639	205	559	159	265	215	4.15	Very Patient	88	48	78	Air
Iglesias, Jose	513	1987	1096	891	458	638	88	376	427	3.87	Neutral	213	84	117	Ground
Inciarte, Ender*	578	2094	1105	989	362	743	104	424	461	3.62	Very Aggressive	223	107	121	Ground
Infante, Omar	149	526	273	253	96	177	57	79	117	3.53	Very Aggressive	43	23	47	Air
Jackson, Austin	203	862	487	375	163	324	69	160	146	4.25	Very Patient	53	43	46	Air
Jankowski, Travis*	383	1560	917	643	308	609	131	273	238	4.07	Patient	128	57	34	Ground
Jaso, John*	432	1696	1005	691	329	676	115	268	308	3.93	Neutral	160	64	83	Ground
Jay, Jon*	374	1422	679	743	211	468	157	315	271	3.80	Aggressive	146	64	56	Ground
Jennings, Desmond	225	893	509	384	170	339	111	129	144	3.97	Patient	65	23	52	Medium
Johnson, Chris	264	1080	560	520	184	376	146	208	166	4.09	Patient	74	45	46	Ground
Johnson, Kelly*	333	1253	659	594	197	462	127	226	241	3.76	Aggressive	114	50	76	Ground
Jones, Adam	672	2336	924	1412	185	739	358	541	513	3.48	Very Aggressive	218	84	206	Air
Joseph, Caleb	141	575	290	285	95	195	67	112	106	4.08	Patient	43	20	41	Air
Joseph, Tommy	347	1322	652	670	180	472	149	275	246	3.81	Aggressive	91	44	111	Air
Joyce, Matt*	293	1301	811	490	210	601	150	176	164	4.44	Very Patient	75	30	58	Medium
Kang, Jung Ho	370	1523	904	619	316	588	140	238	241	4.12	Very Patient	102	49	90	Air
Kemp, Matt	672	2434	1098	1336	306	792	379	478	479	3.62	Very Aggressive	191	98	190	Air
Kemp, Tony*	136	496	272	224	98	174	32	97	95	3.65	Very Aggressive	41	22	28	Ground
Kendrick, Howie	543	2069	1077	992	329	748	194	404	394	3.81	Aggressive	239	76	77	Ground
Kepler, Max*	447	1732	982	750	338	644	149	292	309	3.87	Neutral	145	50	112	Medium
Kiermaier, Kevin*	414	1611	895	716	261	634	158	265	293	3.89	Neutral	120	59	108	Air
Kim, Hyun Soo*	346	1392	840	552	297	543	79	218	255	4.02	Patient	133	52	68	Ground
Kinsler, Ian	679	2550	1404	1146	490	914	177	463	506	3.76	Aggressive	159	120	224	Air
Kipnis, Jason*	688	2758	1565	1193	550	1015	222	495	476	4.01	Patient	182	111	175	Air
La Stella, Tommy*	169	698	379	319	110	269	66	131	121	4.13	Very Patient	43	34	44	Air
Lagares, Juan	160	644	361	283	130	231	56	107	120	4.03	Patient	49	26	41	Medium

Hitter Analysis

Hitter	PA	PS	T	Sw	St	B	S/M	F	In P	P/PA	Group	GB	LD	FB	Hits
Lamb, Jake*	594	2411	1359	1052	418	941	293	386	373	4.06	Patient	171	65	137	Medium
Lawrie, Brett	384	1460	770	690	269	501	196	251	243	3.80	Aggressive	93	47	103	Air
Lee, Dae-Ho	317	1271	670	601	239	431	138	245	218	4.01	Patient	115	48	55	Ground
LeMahieu, DJ	635	2577	1497	1080	525	972	112	482	486	4.06	Patient	240	126	108	Ground
Leon, Sandy#	283	1196	674	522	225	449	93	237	192	4.23	Very Patient	82	46	58	Medium
Lind, Adam*	430	1612	844	768	318	526	167	287	314	3.75	Aggressive	138	63	113	Medium
Lindor, Francisco#	684	2552	1338	1214	407	931	200	480	534	3.73	Aggressive	262	119	151	Ground
Lobaton, Jose#	114	426	200	226	43	157	48	95	83	3.74	Aggressive	38	17	27	Ground
Loney, James*	366	1248	616	632	177	439	68	256	308	3.41	Very Aggressive	128	73	106	Medium
Longoria, Evan	685	2523	1299	1224	410	889	307	421	496	3.68	Aggressive	158	106	232	Air
Lowrie, Jed#	369	1420	762	658	218	544	108	273	277	3.85	Neutral	117	70	88	Medium
Lucroy, Jonathan	544	2209	1264	945	449	815	178	373	394	4.06	Patient	146	95	152	Air
Machado, Manny	696	2566	1301	1265	355	946	264	476	525	3.69	Aggressive	196	105	224	Air
Mahtook, Mikie	196	779	413	366	151	262	96	151	119	3.97	Patient	45	17	56	Air
Maile, Luke	126	484	250	234	77	173	68	80	86	3.84	Neutral	39	12	32	Medium
Maldonado, Martin	253	999	607	392	192	415	96	140	156	3.95	Neutral	67	27	57	Medium
Marisnick, Jake	311	1129	526	603	157	369	151	243	209	3.63	Very Aggressive	89	38	70	Medium
Markakis, Nick*	684	2626	1566	1060	531	1035	130	423	507	3.84	Neutral	218	111	178	Medium
Marte, Jefry	284	1088	586	502	182	404	128	172	202	3.83	Neutral	93	30	79	Medium
Marte, Ketel#	466	1766	902	864	318	584	151	351	362	3.79	Aggressive	179	75	90	Ground
Marte, Starling	529	1995	914	1081	246	668	263	432	386	3.77	Aggressive	182	88	107	Ground
Martin, Leonys*	576	2232	1080	1152	313	767	330	442	380	3.88	Neutral	156	72	133	Air
Martin, Russell	535	2284	1394	890	444	950	257	320	313	4.27	Very Patient	145	56	111	Medium
Martinez, J.D.	517	2022	964	1058	215	749	293	428	337	3.91	Neutral	143	72	122	Air
Martinez, Michael#	106	350	151	199	59	92	47	73	79	3.30	Very Aggressive	32	14	29	Air
Martinez, Victor#	610	2316	1241	1075	366	875	172	437	466	3.80	Aggressive	174	109	183	Air
Mathis, Jeff	132	447	212	235	72	140	69	75	91	3.39	Very Aggressive	36	14	38	Air
Mauer, Joe*	576	2466	1591	875	608	983	123	349	403	4.28	Very Patient	209	108	86	Ground
Maxwell, Bruce*	101	422	224	198	71	153	45	84	69	4.18	Very Patient	36	14	19	Ground
Maybin, Cameron	391	1510	870	640	302	568	124	233	283	3.86	Neutral	156	60	60	Ground
Mazara, Nomar*	568	2258	1251	1007	436	815	198	398	411	3.98	Patient	201	88	122	Ground
McCann, Brian*	492	2013	1148	865	375	773	163	370	332	4.09	Patient	114	71	146	Air
McCann, James	373	1454	776	678	263	513	179	260	239	3.90	Neutral	96	43	95	Air
McCutchen, Andrew	675	2740	1475	1265	417	1058	300	507	458	4.06	Patient	164	103	191	Air
Mercer, Jordy	584	2292	1296	996	461	835	142	409	445	3.92	Neutral	212	86	139	Ground
Merrifield, Whit	332	1258	650	608	241	409	111	256	241	3.79	Aggressive	105	60	70	Ground
Miller, Brad*	601	2324	1182	1142	352	830	287	453	402	3.87	Neutral	179	74	147	Medium
Molina, Yadier	581	2072	967	1105	262	705	153	479	473	3.57	Very Aggressive	228	103	140	Ground
Mondesi, Raul#	149	515	231	284	73	158	97	94	93	3.46	Very Aggressive	37	9	30	Medium
Montero, Miguel*	284	1134	573	561	129	444	125	251	185	3.99	Patient	92	31	61	Ground
Morales, Kendrys#	618	2468	1284	1184	378	906	273	468	443	3.99	Neutral	196	89	158	Air
Moreland, Mitch*	503	1971	1013	958	279	734	262	354	342	3.92	Neutral	142	72	128	Air
Morneau, Justin*	218	843	378	465	103	275	110	202	153	3.87	Neutral	76	30	47	Ground
Morrison, Logan*	398	1528	817	711	222	595	167	278	266	3.84	Neutral	117	56	92	Medium
Moss, Brandon*	464	1826	899	927	231	668	310	340	277	3.94	Neutral	74	56	144	Air
Moustakas, Mike*	113	467	270	197	82	188	28	78	91	4.13	Very Patient	38	17	36	Air
Moya, Steven*	100	429	180	249	34	146	77	115	57	4.29	Very Patient	22	15	20	Air
Muncy, Max*	133	555	357	198	120	237	40	69	89	4.17	Very Patient	44	16	26	Ground
Murphy, Daniel*	582	2079	1123	956	353	770	107	367	482	3.57	Very Aggressive	175	105	202	Air
Myers, Wil	676	2884	1711	1173	582	1129	241	488	444	4.27	Very Patient	198	95	150	Medium
Napoli, Mike	645	2950	1658	1292	501	1157	370	554	368	4.57	Very Patient	134	68	166	Air
Naquin, Tyler*	365	1515	745	770	211	534	225	332	213	4.15	Very Patient	97	49	63	Ground
Narvaez, Omar*	117	460	242	218	66	176	34	95	89	3.93	Neutral	36	25	28	Medium
Nava, Daniel#	148	580	324	256	115	209	37	116	103	3.92	Neutral	39	29	35	Air
Navarro, Dioner#	334	1350	740	610	253	487	140	232	238	4.04	Patient	81	49	103	Air
Nieuwenhuis, Kirk*	392	1651	966	691	290	676	247	242	202	4.23	Very Patient	92	39	67	Medium
Norris, Derek	458	1901	1054	847	347	707	216	352	279	4.15	Very Patient	98	61	120	Air
Nunez, Eduardo	595	2124	985	1139	317	668	181	485	473	3.57	Very Aggressive	230	77	157	Ground
Odor, Rougned*	632	2177	986	1191	305	681	271	446	474	3.44	Very Aggressive	185	81	194	Air
O`Malley, Shawn#	232	903	484	419	160	324	78	189	152	3.89	Neutral	69	30	36	Ground
Orlando, Paulo	484	1668	727	941	221	506	223	359	358	3.45	Very Aggressive	183	76	90	Ground
Ortega, Rafael*	202	724	379	345	132	247	45	134	165	3.58	Very Aggressive	91	28	40	Ground
Ortiz, David*	626	2478	1399	1079	349	1050	200	421	458	3.96	Patient	150	101	206	Air
Owings, Chris	466	1624	782	842	269	513	172	316	354	3.48	Very Aggressive	172	80	94	Ground
Ozuna, Marcell	608	2224	1180	1044	365	815	267	331	446	3.66	Very Aggressive	196	87	163	Medium
Pagan, Angel#	543	2117	1256	861	462	794	97	329	432	3.90	Neutral	183	108	139	Medium
Panik, Joe*	526	1978	1155	823	375	780	87	311	425	3.76	Aggressive	192	74	156	Medium
Paredes, Jimmy#	167	632	274	358	72	202	121	125	112	3.78	Aggressive	61	19	30	Ground
Park, Byungho	244	1041	563	478	161	402	164	176	138	4.27	Very Patient	57	23	58	Air
Parker, Jarrett*	151	595	318	277	87	231	78	116	83	3.94	Neutral	43	16	23	Ground
Parra, Gerardo*	381	1309	580	729	191	389	147	284	298	3.44	Very Aggressive	159	56	76	Ground
Pearce, Steve	302	1178	649	529	191	458	125	193	211	3.90	Neutral	91	40	80	Air
Pederson, Joc*	476	1999	1165	834	359	806	217	338	279	4.20	Very Patient	108	56	108	Air
Pedroia, Dustin	698	2728	1552	1176	545	1007	136	476	564	3.91	Neutral	276	136	151	Ground
Pence, Hunter	442	1805	981	824	304	677	240	281	303	4.08	Patient	166	51	86	Ground

Hitter Analysis

Hitter	PA	PS	T	Sw	St	B	S/M	F	In P	P/PA	Group	GB	LD	FB	Hits
Pennington, Cliff#	188	760	379	381	126	253	92	169	120	4.04	Patient	46	25	44	Air
Peralta, David*	183	664	319	345	96	223	72	143	130	3.63	Very Aggressive	66	27	37	Ground
Peralta, Jhonny	313	1210	651	559	175	476	107	216	236	3.87	Neutral	96	57	83	Air
Peraza, Jose	256	895	432	463	162	270	60	192	211	3.50	Very Aggressive	90	57	60	Ground
Perez, Carlos	291	1037	544	493	186	358	101	163	229	3.56	Very Aggressive	90	37	92	Air
Perez, Hernan	430	1529	700	829	254	446	203	309	317	3.56	Very Aggressive	136	64	113	Medium
Perez, Roberto	184	767	461	306	136	325	71	118	117	4.17	Very Patient	59	17	34	Ground
Perez, Salvador	546	1875	847	1028	264	583	230	401	397	3.43	Very Aggressive	137	73	187	Air
Peterson, Jace*	408	1607	948	659	322	626	110	263	286	3.94	Neutral	162	52	67	Ground
Petit, Gregorio	223	802	388	414	136	252	105	153	156	3.60	Very Aggressive	77	34	43	Ground
Pham, Tommy	183	766	447	319	142	305	111	119	89	4.19	Very Patient	40	22	26	Ground
Phillips, Brandon	584	2092	887	1205	259	628	218	497	490	3.58	Very Aggressive	225	104	158	Air
Pierzynski, A.J.*	259	825	338	487	96	242	86	180	221	3.19	Very Aggressive	111	44	65	Ground
Pillar, Kevin	584	2124	1071	1053	420	651	193	396	464	3.64	Very Aggressive	207	93	154	Medium
Piscotty, Stephen	649	2481	1181	1300	313	868	317	530	452	3.82	Aggressive	196	91	163	Medium
Plawecki, Kevin	151	568	301	267	89	212	54	114	99	3.76	Aggressive	55	17	27	Ground
Plouffe, Trevor	344	1300	710	590	230	480	111	216	263	3.78	Aggressive	110	52	99	Air
Polanco, Gregory*	587	2401	1294	1107	371	923	222	470	415	4.09	Patient	160	99	153	Air
Polanco, Jorge#	270	1054	601	453	230	371	73	176	204	3.90	Neutral	66	61	74	Air
Posey, Buster	614	2297	1225	1072	355	870	143	450	479	3.74	Neutral	233	103	143	Ground
Prado, Martin	658	2567	1552	1015	646	906	100	379	536	3.90	Neutral	254	133	148	Ground
Presley, Alex*	134	555	300	255	108	192	51	107	97	4.14	Very Patient	45	21	31	Ground
Profar, Jurickson#	307	1307	765	542	261	504	96	233	213	4.26	Very Patient	111	40	60	Ground
Puig, Yasiel	368	1291	620	671	160	460	181	227	263	3.51	Very Aggressive	127	43	92	Medium
Pujols, Albert	650	2516	1363	1153	447	916	169	460	524	3.87	Neutral	230	87	207	Air
Raburn, Ryan	256	1057	572	485	153	419	149	190	146	4.13	Very Patient	67	23	56	Medium
Ramirez, Alexei	506	1840	946	894	346	600	144	332	418	3.64	Very Aggressive	215	84	117	Ground
Ramirez, Hanley	620	2416	1295	1121	389	906	256	432	433	3.90	Neutral	209	81	142	Ground
Ramirez, Jose#	618	2428	1359	1069	476	883	125	436	508	3.93	Neutral	206	115	183	Air
Ramos, Wilson	523	1868	933	935	269	646	171	357	407	3.57	Very Aggressive	221	83	103	Ground
Rasmus, Colby*	417	1680	885	795	235	650	257	285	253	4.03	Patient	88	52	106	Air
Realmuto, J.T.	545	2142	1111	1031	365	746	188	431	412	3.93	Neutral	203	84	125	Ground
Recker, Anthony	112	461	293	168	93	200	42	54	72	4.12	Very Patient	21	15	33	Air
Reddick, Josh*	439	1721	964	757	311	653	114	299	343	3.92	Neutral	140	74	125	Air
Reed, A.J.*	141	556	315	241	94	221	78	88	75	3.94	Neutral	37	9	29	Medium
Refsnyder, Rob	175	673	391	282	139	252	47	109	125	3.85	Neutral	66	33	26	Ground
Reimold, Nolan	227	964	565	399	173	392	106	151	142	4.25	Very Patient	64	28	50	Medium
Rendon, Anthony	647	2604	1492	1112	520	972	177	477	458	4.02	Patient	163	94	200	Air
Revere, Ben*	375	1346	816	530	341	475	50	160	320	3.59	Very Aggressive	171	56	82	Ground
Reyes, Jose#	279	1067	583	484	219	364	94	183	207	3.82	Neutral	72	45	89	Air
Reynolds, Mark	441	1829	987	842	275	712	217	342	283	4.15	Very Patient	118	73	92	Medium
Rickard, Joey	282	1221	716	505	285	431	70	227	208	4.33	Very Patient	84	42	74	Air
Rivera, Rene	207	754	363	391	115	248	107	150	134	3.64	Very Aggressive	63	28	42	Ground
Rivera, T.J.	113	398	180	218	56	124	50	76	92	3.52	Very Aggressive	39	22	31	Medium
Rizzo, Anthony*	676	2656	1463	1193	447	1016	224	491	478	3.93	Neutral	183	97	197	Air
Robinson, Clint*	224	857	491	366	161	330	59	143	164	3.83	Neutral	77	26	60	Medium
Robinson, Shane	111	406	226	180	79	147	35	62	83	3.66	Very Aggressive	37	15	28	Medium
Rodriguez, Alex	243	915	466	449	146	320	125	163	161	3.77	Aggressive	74	30	57	Medium
Rodriguez, Sean	342	1335	700	635	209	491	217	216	202	3.90	Neutral	80	49	72	Air
Rojas, Miguel	214	812	410	402	156	254	64	163	175	3.79	Aggressive	88	33	42	Ground
Rollins, Jimmy#	166	691	385	306	122	263	62	127	117	4.16	Very Patient	56	19	42	Medium
Romine, Andrew#	194	730	319	411	80	239	101	171	139	3.76	Aggressive	70	35	30	Ground
Romine, Austin	176	626	278	348	81	197	65	145	138	3.56	Very Aggressive	64	26	45	Ground
Rosales, Adam	248	1036	594	442	183	411	154	158	130	4.18	Very Patient	48	22	60	Air
Rosario, Eddie*	354	1313	558	755	161	397	210	296	249	3.71	Aggressive	113	47	84	Medium
Ross, David	205	851	456	395	124	332	117	157	121	4.15	Very Patient	38	27	49	Air
Rua, Ryan	269	1022	561	461	184	377	125	170	166	3.80	Aggressive	86	32	47	Ground
Ruiz, Carlos	233	994	630	364	215	415	47	149	168	4.27	Very Patient	77	36	55	Medium
Rupp, Cameron	419	1583	825	758	258	567	219	263	276	3.78	Aggressive	133	48	95	Ground
Russell, Addison	598	2336	1172	1164	318	854	319	449	396	3.91	Neutral	162	83	148	Air
Saladino, Tyler	319	1236	636	600	225	411	100	259	241	3.87	Neutral	121	47	68	Ground
Saltalamacchia, Jarrod#	292	1175	660	515	200	460	176	192	147	4.02	Patient	46	22	79	Air
Sanchez, Carlos#	163	613	308	305	118	190	70	120	115	3.76	Aggressive	42	23	43	Air
Sanchez, Gary	229	941	520	421	170	350	123	152	146	4.11	Patient	72	24	50	Ground
Sano, Miguel	495	2100	1240	860	389	851	299	299	262	4.24	Very Patient	89	53	120	Air
Santana, Carlos#	688	2781	1692	1089	487	1205	205	396	488	4.04	Patient	209	78	201	Air
Santana, Danny#	248	918	417	501	129	288	120	201	180	3.70	Aggressive	89	36	42	Ground
Santana, Domingo	281	1182	697	485	226	471	146	183	156	4.21	Very Patient	69	47	40	Ground
Sardinas, Luis#	197	751	372	379	125	247	89	154	136	3.81	Aggressive	71	23	37	Ground
Saunders, Michael*	558	2383	1318	1065	357	961	295	433	337	4.27	Very Patient	136	75	123	Air
Schebler, Scott*	282	1041	501	540	114	387	148	194	198	3.69	Aggressive	103	36	57	Ground
Schimpf, Ryan*	330	1458	833	625	248	585	170	281	174	4.42	Very Patient	34	27	113	Air
Schoop, Jonathan	647	2231	888	1343	220	661	372	490	481	3.45	Very Aggressive	218	95	168	Medium
Seager, Corey*	687	2512	1192	1320	267	925	291	533	496	3.66	Very Aggressive	229	121	145	Ground
Seager, Kyle*	676	2584	1494	1090	471	1023	194	405	491	3.82	Aggressive	176	107	205	Air

405

Hitter Analysis

Hitter	PA	PS	T	Sw	St	B	S/M	F	In P	P/PA	Group	GB	LD	FB	Hits
Segura, Jean	694	2699	1434	1265	502	932	197	526	542	3.89	Neutral	283	102	148	Ground
Semien, Marcus	621	2586	1403	1183	445	958	269	483	431	4.16	Very Patient	169	76	184	Air
Shaw, Travis*	530	2131	1110	1021	331	779	236	434	351	4.02	Patient	127	67	156	Air
Shuck, J.B.*	241	827	443	384	166	277	38	139	207	3.43	Very Aggressive	107	32	63	Ground
Simmons, Andrelton	483	1584	826	758	265	561	90	253	415	3.28	Very Aggressive	225	80	105	Ground
Smith, Mallex*	215	787	405	382	129	276	97	140	145	3.66	Very Aggressive	75	20	28	Ground
Smith, Seth*	438	1857	1120	737	363	757	159	285	293	4.24	Very Patient	140	63	89	Ground
Smoak, Justin#	341	1374	753	621	217	536	179	255	187	4.03	Patient	57	51	79	Air
Smolinski, Jake	319	1128	592	536	202	390	83	204	249	3.54	Very Aggressive	106	55	87	Medium
Solarte, Yangervis#	443	1589	787	802	235	552	129	328	345	3.59	Very Aggressive	141	75	126	Air
Soler, Jorge	264	1068	586	482	160	426	153	165	164	4.05	Patient	65	28	71	Air
Souza Jr., Steven	468	1836	921	915	276	645	295	347	273	3.92	Neutral	110	67	92	Medium
Span, Denard*	637	2449	1365	1084	460	905	147	436	501	3.84	Neutral	256	110	120	Ground
Springer, George	744	2932	1544	1388	398	1146	373	548	467	3.94	Neutral	225	95	147	Ground
Stanton, Giancarlo	470	1892	1027	865	280	747	296	293	275	4.03	Patient	110	46	119	Air
Stewart, Chris	113	460	303	157	115	188	18	56	83	4.07	Patient	40	14	28	Ground
Story, Trevor	415	1774	960	814	287	673	227	342	245	4.27	Very Patient	71	57	114	Air
Suarez, Eugenio	627	2594	1466	1128	498	968	267	448	413	4.14	Very Patient	167	89	156	Air
Suzuki, Ichiro*	365	1448	813	635	283	530	96	249	290	3.97	Patient	138	79	69	Ground
Suzuki, Kurt	373	1332	690	642	218	472	97	243	302	3.57	Very Aggressive	119	63	114	Air
Swanson, Dansby	145	599	335	264	115	220	60	106	98	4.13	Very Patient	45	22	30	Ground
Szczur, Matt	200	760	349	411	98	251	91	173	147	3.80	Aggressive	61	28	54	Air
Taylor, Michael	237	891	454	437	133	321	137	155	145	3.76	Aggressive	62	38	42	Ground
Teixeira, Mark#	438	1780	1020	760	315	705	168	308	284	4.06	Patient	123	61	100	Medium
Thole, Josh*	136	544	304	240	90	214	41	105	94	4.00	Patient	35	20	36	Air
Thompson, Trayce	262	1128	645	483	216	429	111	202	170	4.31	Very Patient	88	28	54	Ground
Toles, Andrew*	115	388	173	215	36	137	56	78	81	3.37	Very Aggressive	39	18	24	Ground
Tomas, Yasmany	563	1972	837	1135	213	624	335	405	395	3.50	Very Aggressive	188	83	124	Ground
Tomlinson, Kelby	120	420	212	208	71	141	38	81	89	3.50	Very Aggressive	43	24	17	Ground
Torreyes, Ronald	169	563	272	291	87	185	42	111	138	3.33	Very Aggressive	75	27	35	Ground
Travis, Devon	432	1726	871	855	306	565	150	380	325	4.00	Patient	150	62	111	Medium
Trout, Mike	681	3014	1860	1154	567	1293	224	513	417	4.43	Very Patient	172	92	153	Air
Trumbo, Mark	667	2623	1330	1293	408	922	369	481	443	3.93	Neutral	175	77	191	Air
Tucker, Preston*	144	554	296	289	86	210	90	105	94	4.06	Patient	42	15	37	Air
Tulowitzki, Troy	544	2100	1165	935	386	779	183	357	395	3.86	Neutral	160	76	159	Air
Turner, Justin	622	2466	1371	1095	444	927	186	452	457	3.96	Patient	165	109	183	Air
Turner, Trea	324	1232	648	584	216	432	136	198	250	3.80	Aggressive	106	62	78	Medium
Upton, Justin	626	2606	1460	1146	448	1012	337	416	393	4.16	Very Patient	152	72	169	Air
Upton Jr., Melvin	539	2030	1010	1020	310	700	339	336	344	3.77	Aggressive	165	60	115	Ground
Uribe, Juan	259	933	440	493	114	326	99	202	192	3.60	Very Aggressive	88	38	66	Medium
Utley, Chase*	565	2224	1327	897	497	830	168	330	399	3.94	Neutral	174	88	133	Medium
Valbuena, Luis*	342	1488	838	650	226	612	150	284	216	4.35	Very Patient	76	44	88	Air
Valencia, Danny	517	2020	1129	891	368	761	245	288	358	3.91	Neutral	161	83	114	Medium
Van Slyke, Scott	113	401	210	191	68	142	48	64	79	3.55	Very Aggressive	31	19	29	Air
Vargas, Kennys#	177	755	447	308	143	304	91	121	96	4.27	Very Patient	36	14	46	Air
Vazquez, Christian	184	747	395	352	137	258	55	164	133	4.06	Patient	79	33	20	Ground
Villar, Jonathan#	679	2831	1591	1240	490	1101	320	496	424	4.17	Very Patient	224	82	97	Ground
Vogt, Stephen*	532	2124	1159	965	419	740	159	396	410	3.99	Patient	124	95	190	Air
Votto, Joey*	677	2896	1693	1203	460	1233	214	545	444	4.28	Very Patient	191	121	132	Medium
Walker, Neil#	458	1838	980	858	285	695	167	360	331	4.01	Patient	116	70	142	Air
Wallace, Brett*	256	1093	640	453	190	450	146	172	135	4.27	Very Patient	69	28	38	Ground
Weeks Jr., Rickie	205	834	488	346	148	340	103	116	127	4.07	Patient	57	23	47	Medium
Wendle, Joey*	104	353	177	176	58	119	27	67	82	3.39	Very Aggressive	44	17	20	Ground
Werth, Jayson	606	2785	1723	1062	659	1064	214	456	392	4.60	Very Patient	161	68	163	Air
White, Tyler	276	1176	674	502	240	434	116	200	186	4.26	Very Patient	80	33	73	Air
Wieters, Matt#	464	1684	824	860	239	585	188	330	342	3.63	Very Aggressive	123	82	134	Air
Williamson, Mac	127	545	286	259	72	214	93	89	77	4.29	Very Patient	43	13	21	Ground
Wilson, Bobby	251	937	425	512	124	301	150	187	175	3.73	Aggressive	69	40	59	Air
Wolters, Tony*	230	876	470	406	152	318	95	155	156	3.81	Aggressive	69	34	42	Ground
Wong, Kolten*	361	1370	728	642	217	511	109	267	266	3.80	Aggressive	120	52	89	Medium
Wright, David	164	717	443	274	120	323	93	98	82	4.37	Very Patient	19	23	40	Air
Yelich, Christian*	659	2715	1619	1096	504	1115	259	392	445	4.12	Very Patient	251	104	89	Ground
Young, Chris	227	857	497	360	163	334	76	131	153	3.78	Aggressive	39	38	76	Air
Zimmerman, Ryan	467	1829	1029	800	364	665	185	286	329	3.92	Neutral	160	55	114	Ground
Zobrist, Ben#	631	2655	1713	942	597	1116	112	381	449	4.21	Very Patient	211	95	134	Ground
Zunino, Mike	192	810	433	377	120	313	134	143	100	4.22	Very Patient	29	18	52	Air

For some players Swings and Misses, Fouls, and Balls in Play do not add up to overall Swings. This is because of the rare occasions when a swing results in a Catcher Interference.

\#   Switch Hitter

*   Bats Left

Pitcher Analysis

Joe Rosales

Among the many things that went wrong for the Diamondbacks in 2016 was what appeared to be a step back in performance for Robbie Ray. As a 23-year-old in 2015, he finished with a 3.52 ERA in 127.2 innings pitched, and his underlying statistics suggested that that ERA was a true reflection of his talent on the mound. In 2016, his ERA ballooned to 4.90 in 174.1 innings. However, there are reasons to believe that he actually pitched much better than that ERA would suggest. For example, Ray faced 545 batters in 2015 and struck out 119, which is a strikeout rate of 22 percent. In 2016, he struck out 218 out of 776 batters that he faced, an increase to 28 percent. That six-point increase was the fourth largest increase among pitchers who faced at least 500 batters in 2016. The only three pitchers that improved their strikeout rates more were Danny Duffy, Archie Bradley, and Justin Verlander.

Meanwhile, Ray's walk rate and groundball rate remained the same while his flyball rate and line drive rate went down. Given that his home ballpark is one of the more conducive ones to hitting home runs, his reduced flyball rate is especially encouraging. If Ray can maintain the pitching profile that he established in 2016, his results in the future are likely to improve back toward what he was able to achieve in 2015.

The purpose of this section is to give you some insight into the underlying characteristics that make up a pitcher's performance. The data provided includes batters faced and pitches thrown; strikeouts and walks allowed; groundballs, flyballs, and line drives allowed; the percentage of their pitches that were strikes and how many of those were swinging strikes; and how many times they worked their way into certain meaningful ball/strike counts.

Pitcher Analysis
Pitchers with 50+ Batters Faced in 2016

Pitcher	BF	Pitches	K	BB	GB	LD	FB	Str%	S/Str	1-0	0-1	Full	2 Strike	3 Ball
Abad, Fernando	198	784	41	22	57	25	50	61%	13%	77	95	29	98	46
Achter, A.J.	160	568	14	12	60	27	46	63%	16%	69	68	16	66	26
Adams, Austin	88	317	17	7	26	18	20	63%	18%	32	38	9	39	17
Adleman, Tim	287	1107	47	20	76	38	95	65%	16%	100	156	32	147	44
Albers, Andrew	85	326	16	6	30	14	19	64%	11%	33	45	8	44	14
Albers, Matt	237	891	30	19	87	31	61	62%	12%	94	118	31	107	48
Alcantara, Raul	103	380	14	4	32	14	35	63%	10%	40	55	9	42	13
Alexander, Scott	84	324	16	7	41	5	14	64%	20%	31	45	13	42	21
Allen, Cody	264	1133	87	27	67	27	53	64%	22%	118	133	41	170	59
Alvarez, Dario	113	468	41	7	24	13	25	62%	22%	62	43	15	63	26
Alvarez, Jose	256	930	51	15	81	45	60	67%	15%	93	130	23	134	35
Anderson, Brett	62	209	5	4	26	15	11	62%	10%	21	33	6	20	9
Anderson, Chase	647	2639	120	53	165	104	188	61%	14%	276	306	122	359	165
Anderson, Cody	270	996	54	13	80	53	68	66%	18%	114	124	32	133	40
Anderson, Tyler	478	1793	99	28	172	69	97	67%	16%	170	254	62	244	88
Andriese, Matt	527	1983	109	25	167	74	148	67%	16%	179	289	59	267	82
Araujo, Elvis	134	543	29	17	33	17	34	60%	18%	69	58	20	71	32
Archer, Chris	850	3409	233	67	256	95	185	63%	20%	353	419	129	468	184
Arrieta, Jake	795	3124	190	76	272	101	144	63%	17%	328	396	103	427	157
Asher, Alec	111	424	13	4	31	20	37	67%	9%	48	54	14	53	19
Avilan, Luis	82	327	28	10	20	8	11	61%	29%	32	39	6	47	17
Axford, John	289	1194	60	30	104	36	52	60%	18%	141	111	53	152	74
Baez, Pedro	295	1178	83	22	78	36	69	67%	22%	107	156	43	179	51
Bailey, Andrew	190	795	41	17	50	23	52	67%	15%	67	101	29	120	36
Bailey, Homer	111	458	27	7	33	22	18	64%	16%	51	48	15	62	23
Barbato, Johnny	57	235	15	5	16	9	10	65%	22%	20	32	6	35	9
Barnes, Danny	58	234	14	5	15	7	17	61%	20%	23	30	8	37	11
Barnes, Jacob	106	405	26	6	35	15	22	65%	24%	40	55	13	57	19
Barnes, Matt	287	1195	71	31	82	38	60	60%	19%	121	145	43	144	66
Barnette, Tony	246	921	49	16	84	44	50	63%	19%	105	113	36	117	49
Barraclough, Kyle	306	1337	113	44	75	30	39	61%	23%	133	162	57	198	84
Barrett, Jake	250	954	56	28	73	29	61	62%	21%	105	120	29	121	57
Bassitt, Chris	133	503	23	14	44	17	34	63%	14%	56	67	17	70	26
Bastardo, Antonio	297	1223	74	32	56	40	88	63%	23%	118	152	50	177	72
Bauer, Trevor	811	3092	168	70	272	114	172	62%	15%	326	399	109	396	156
Beck, Chris	123	465	20	17	37	21	22	58%	19%	62	45	20	57	32
Bedrosian, Cam	162	655	51	14	47	20	28	63%	18%	62	86	25	95	33
Belisle, Matt	186	671	32	7	68	32	44	71%	13%	59	102	11	87	21
Benoit, Joaquin	204	836	52	24	49	27	49	62%	23%	86	100	33	116	50
Bergman, Christian	119	448	22	6	33	21	35	69%	15%	36	63	10	63	13
Berrios, Jose	281	1144	49	35	71	42	74	58%	15%	127	129	44	133	74
Betances, Dellin	299	1250	126	28	76	27	38	63%	26%	117	165	47	193	76
Bettis, Chad	814	3055	138	59	302	130	158	62%	15%	305	412	113	378	168
Biagini, Joseph	295	1117	62	19	107	44	54	65%	18%	91	165	47	146	58
Blach, Ty	62	241	10	5	26	4	15	64%	9%	22	29	11	31	13
Blair, Aaron	324	1214	46	34	93	52	89	60%	17%	140	144	40	142	75
Blanton, Joe	315	1278	80	26	67	45	94	65%	23%	111	177	45	182	64
Blazek, Michael	201	818	36	27	54	26	53	61%	16%	86	103	28	113	50
Bleier, Richard	92	349	13	4	40	18	16	67%	15%	37	43	6	47	12
Blevins, Jerry	178	728	52	15	49	18	40	65%	17%	70	94	37	111	45
Bolsinger, Mike	122	470	25	9	28	23	32	63%	15%	47	62	20	67	26
Boscan, Wilfredo	67	263	8	7	22	7	22	65%	9%	28	32	7	31	11
Boshers, Buddy	152	542	37	7	49	21	35	66%	19%	66	69	17	73	25
Bowman, Matt	281	1060	52	20	127	39	40	63%	16%	106	147	36	142	51
Boxberger, Brad	114	471	22	19	34	11	26	63%	16%	48	55	21	69	31
Boyd, Matt	412	1683	82	29	112	50	132	66%	15%	153	225	52	231	72
Boyer, Blaine	282	1052	26	17	115	52	68	67%	10%	102	149	23	131	39
Brach, Brad	311	1295	92	25	80	40	73	65%	24%	125	162	45	182	63
Bracho, Silvino	119	463	17	10	25	18	44	64%	17%	45	61	15	61	22
Bradley, Archie	638	2576	143	67	189	105	125	62%	14%	273	304	82	334	145
Brault, Steven	166	662	29	17	51	29	33	59%	17%	85	65	31	85	46
Breslow, Craig	63	210	7	4	15	13	23	65%	13%	24	29	4	23	7
Brice, Austin	59	206	14	5	20	6	12	67%	19%	25	25	5	29	8
Britton, Zach	254	1027	74	18	128	18	14	63%	28%	113	123	34	146	53
Broxton, Jonathan	259	1002	57	24	82	41	48	64%	16%	103	119	39	127	56
Buchholz, Clay	588	2226	93	55	177	68	185	63%	16%	220	296	76	287	123
Buchter, Ryan	247	1127	78	31	28	29	79	60%	17%	113	120	42	157	70
Bumgarner, Madison	912	3571	251	54	232	111	243	66%	18%	319	501	135	515	160

Pitcher Analysis
Pitchers with 50+ Batters Faced in 2016

Pitcher	BF	Pitches	K	BB	GB	LD	FB	Str%	S/Str	1-0	0-1	Full	2 Strike	3 Ball
Bundy, Dylan	474	1951	104	42	115	70	135	65%	17%	184	252	72	275	99
Burgos, Enrique	178	734	43	23	44	22	40	60%	20%	84	84	36	103	54
Bush, Matt	243	941	61	14	70	42	53	68%	20%	82	128	37	145	46
Butler, Eddie	293	1079	47	21	99	53	64	63%	13%	122	133	37	133	54
Cabrera, Mauricio	162	644	32	19	53	19	36	62%	19%	70	82	18	81	37
Cahill, Trevor	284	1162	66	35	99	38	38	58%	20%	129	130	52	140	81
Cain, Matt	397	1568	72	32	103	66	107	63%	15%	148	206	63	193	87
Caminero, Arquimedes	280	1102	50	33	82	36	71	61%	16%	125	128	35	134	57
Campos, Leonel	98	388	24	14	29	7	21	60%	24%	44	46	12	49	24
Capuano, Chris	106	438	27	15	28	8	27	63%	17%	38	58	18	68	25
Carasiti, Matt	83	307	17	11	19	14	19	59%	21%	31	41	11	39	21
Carrasco, Carlos	599	2247	150	34	199	82	129	66%	19%	227	306	68	314	96
Cashner, Andrew	588	2370	112	60	184	81	131	61%	12%	261	267	91	302	147
Casilla, Santiago	241	950	65	19	70	24	53	64%	18%	112	103	25	129	44
Castro, Miguel	67	240	12	5	26	9	13	61%	17%	39	25	9	27	13
Cecil, Brett	157	566	45	8	42	28	30	67%	19%	53	80	16	88	22
Cedeno, Xavier	174	692	43	13	54	27	33	64%	21%	65	96	19	90	31
Cervenka, Hunter	182	759	42	28	50	18	39	59%	19%	100	64	26	97	52
Cessa, Luis	285	1052	46	14	95	43	82	63%	17%	119	136	28	131	48
Chacin, Jhoulys	632	2389	119	55	214	101	127	63%	13%	243	313	92	315	129
Chafin, Andrew	98	351	28	11	28	13	14	62%	24%	39	48	7	46	17
Chamberlain, Joba	82	354	18	11	27	11	13	58%	20%	42	34	18	44	27
Chapman, Aroldis	222	976	90	18	52	28	33	68%	28%	95	108	31	151	44
Chargois, J.T.	100	364	17	12	38	16	15	60%	15%	41	44	17	44	21
Chatwood, Tyler	669	2546	117	70	270	81	121	60%	14%	303	296	83	298	150
Chavez, Jesse	282	1123	63	18	85	35	78	66%	15%	101	150	44	161	57
Chen, Wei-Yin	520	1918	100	24	157	83	148	66%	14%	188	267	55	258	75
Cingrani, Tony	271	1095	49	37	83	28	67	60%	15%	121	125	38	139	66
Cishek, Steve	258	1076	76	21	68	26	61	62%	19%	99	144	54	160	63
Claudio, Alex	217	789	34	10	107	29	35	67%	16%	77	108	22	107	31
Clemens, Paul	314	1196	53	31	88	39	94	61%	11%	127	151	38	141	68
Clevinger, Mike	233	967	50	29	58	33	61	60%	16%	91	119	43	127	61
Clippard, Tyler	262	1059	72	26	49	30	79	63%	21%	112	121	45	149	62
Cobb, Alex	104	386	16	7	42	15	23	65%	12%	37	58	10	46	14
Cole, A.J.	168	674	39	14	36	15	62	64%	17%	69	81	38	93	43
Cole, Gerrit	506	1939	98	36	162	90	103	65%	14%	202	250	63	256	89
Coleman, Louis	211	889	45	24	47	33	55	60%	21%	79	109	41	125	58
Collmenter, Josh	173	687	33	16	53	22	42	61%	13%	68	85	28	87	40
Colome, Alex	226	860	71	15	65	32	41	66%	24%	83	110	22	128	33
Colon, Bartolo	791	2853	128	32	265	139	209	68%	9%	293	397	74	390	97
Colon, Joseph	50	186	10	7	11	7	15	61%	12%	19	25	7	21	11
Conley, Adam	584	2274	124	62	142	77	153	62%	12%	210	310	86	302	127
Corbin, Patrick	701	2539	131	66	263	95	131	61%	16%	304	291	97	300	147
Cosart, Jarred	268	1095	38	39	112	38	34	57%	12%	122	121	55	129	81
Cotham, Caleb	117	431	21	12	35	15	30	60%	17%	55	55	16	48	27
Cotton, Jharel	112	441	23	4	32	12	41	67%	19%	38	62	15	56	19
Coulombe, Daniel	193	731	54	17	74	20	25	64%	22%	76	101	22	104	38
Cravy, Tyler	116	451	22	12	19	20	39	60%	19%	50	61	18	59	27
Crockett, Kyle	70	285	17	7	22	13	11	63%	14%	21	43	7	35	13
Cueto, Johnny	881	3299	198	45	308	128	178	66%	15%	277	483	132	439	155
Cunniff, Brandon	74	304	16	9	10	11	24	61%	18%	30	37	15	43	18
Curtis, Zac	67	271	10	13	16	8	17	56%	17%	29	29	13	30	22
Danks, John	100	387	16	11	22	13	38	59%	15%	46	44	13	44	24
Darvish, Yu	416	1579	132	31	101	49	100	65%	20%	173	202	41	221	72
Davies, Zach	682	2588	135	38	225	109	161	64%	14%	262	350	82	316	121
Davis, Wade	176	719	47	16	53	20	36	63%	21%	81	68	41	98	48
Dayton, Grant	101	468	39	6	14	11	28	68%	24%	42	52	20	72	21
De La Cruz, Joel	276	1008	37	22	90	47	72	63%	15%	119	122	26	122	46
de la Rosa, Jorge	614	2343	108	63	203	90	136	61%	18%	275	277	91	288	141
de la Rosa, Rubby	222	857	54	20	73	26	43	62%	18%	104	97	27	113	45
De Leon, Jose	80	302	15	7	20	9	21	63%	17%	31	38	11	40	20
Dean, Pat	300	1158	50	23	100	43	82	63%	11%	118	141	46	134	68
deGrom, Jacob	604	2353	143	36	187	93	130	66%	17%	218	312	86	334	109
Delgado, Randall	337	1355	68	36	93	48	85	61%	17%	124	177	62	178	84
DeSclafani, Anthony	507	1968	105	30	150	81	127	63%	15%	213	234	53	248	83
Despaigne, Odrisamer	135	534	17	16	40	26	35	59%	14%	64	52	24	63	35
Detwiler, Ross	220	834	26	19	75	38	61	61%	11%	95	101	25	94	39
Devenski, Chris	408	1577	104	20	93	72	113	68%	20%	145	219	48	229	63
Diaz, Edwin	217	831	88	15	52	25	34	67%	29%	90	108	23	134	35

Pitcher Analysis
Pitchers with 50+ Batters Faced in 2016

Pitcher	BF	Pitches	K	BB	GB	LD	FB	Str%	S/Str	1-0	0-1	Full	2 Strike	3 Ball
Diaz, Jumbo	182	767	37	19	57	19	46	62%	18%	77	87	36	105	49
Dickey, R.A.	728	2742	126	63	223	116	191	65%	17%	276	378	85	368	122
Diekman, Jake	221	932	59	26	64	26	43	59%	19%	102	103	43	122	62
Dominguez, Jose	155	597	20	17	54	21	38	61%	13%	64	74	20	75	33
Doolittle, Sean	155	595	45	8	28	15	52	70%	23%	47	88	18	85	23
Drake, Oliver	74	296	21	7	21	6	16	65%	23%	28	40	11	44	15
Duensing, Brian	55	209	10	3	10	14	18	65%	15%	19	29	9	30	11
Duffey, Tyler	596	2278	114	32	209	99	128	65%	14%	216	316	64	307	99
Duffy, Danny	731	2707	188	42	176	101	207	67%	20%	277	372	73	377	110
Duke, Zach	258	1014	68	29	90	27	36	61%	18%	104	126	38	136	59
Dull, Ryan	290	1217	73	15	66	31	102	64%	20%	105	157	46	176	59
Dunn, Mike	176	720	38	11	34	36	52	66%	19%	73	82	28	97	36
Dyson, Sam	285	990	55	23	131	38	32	65%	14%	110	135	25	117	43
Edwards Jr., Carl	138	623	52	14	36	15	21	62%	29%	61	74	23	97	33
Eflin, Zach	272	992	31	17	80	52	89	64%	10%	104	146	29	119	44
Ege, Cody	55	205	11	5	16	10	12	62%	18%	20	30	6	26	11
Eickhoff, Jerad	811	3028	167	42	237	117	229	63%	15%	316	401	88	395	135
Ellington, Brian	142	565	32	16	26	15	48	63%	20%	66	64	13	72	27
Eovaldi, Nathan	525	2064	97	40	190	70	123	65%	15%	187	294	78	287	102
Erlin, Robbie	58	204	13	3	18	10	14	65%	16%	25	25	9	27	11
Esch, Jake	59	214	10	6	21	10	11	63%	16%	28	28	2	25	9
Escobar, Edwin	116	449	17	12	30	20	32	59%	15%	65	43	16	57	25
Estevez, Carlos	246	1025	59	28	67	25	61	62%	19%	106	120	44	141	61
Estrada, Marco	723	2843	165	65	161	88	232	63%	18%	297	342	112	395	165
Eveland, Dana	119	458	21	19	36	17	23	60%	13%	50	50	18	56	31
Familia, Jeurys	321	1262	84	31	126	35	38	65%	24%	139	154	35	175	57
Farmer, Buck	131	505	27	20	43	9	31	60%	18%	51	61	19	69	33
Farquhar, Danny	158	670	46	15	35	26	30	62%	23%	71	71	25	97	37
Feldman, Scott	338	1316	56	19	125	51	75	63%	12%	135	164	43	158	60
Feliz, Michael	270	1148	95	22	64	32	56	63%	23%	134	121	46	162	70
Feliz, Neftali	218	940	61	21	50	30	52	64%	23%	88	113	36	135	51
Fernandez, Jose	737	2940	253	55	165	115	130	65%	22%	286	384	113	459	145
Fields, Josh	158	610	42	11	37	16	50	67%	21%	65	79	16	89	23
Fien, Casey	169	657	35	10	40	25	53	68%	19%	60	85	19	89	24
Fiers, Mike	724	2771	134	42	226	139	171	64%	15%	271	367	100	345	130
Finnegan, Brandon	734	2884	145	84	188	111	194	61%	16%	335	330	103	362	174
Fister, Doug	779	3000	115	62	268	120	203	62%	10%	315	382	110	379	158
Floro, Dylan	72	248	14	5	29	11	13	64%	14%	24	40	6	30	10
Floyd, Gavin	124	475	30	8	35	11	37	63%	25%	46	61	18	65	22
Flynn, Brian	221	815	44	23	80	26	40	60%	19%	99	90	23	91	46
Foltynewicz, Mike	525	2120	111	35	150	78	136	66%	15%	190	293	62	299	89
Friedrich, Christian	567	2139	100	52	182	76	147	64%	14%	224	288	68	268	108
Fulmer, Carson	53	213	10	7	15	9	10	57%	18%	25	21	9	28	16
Fulmer, Michael	647	2473	132	42	223	88	143	64%	17%	252	314	87	314	126
Gallardo, Yovani	526	2107	85	61	161	75	137	59%	11%	242	223	102	248	151
Gamboa, Eddie	54	222	11	8	16	7	11	58%	13%	32	18	13	32	17
Gant, John	222	943	49	21	61	35	49	64%	15%	90	118	34	134	47
Garcia, Jaime	741	2578	150	57	292	94	129	64%	15%	295	345	75	307	130
Garcia, Luis	76	292	14	8	29	8	16	59%	20%	34	35	9	36	15
Garton, Ryan	171	695	33	11	57	26	43	64%	15%	68	86	23	96	32
Garza, Matt	461	1717	70	36	188	59	96	63%	13%	187	220	56	223	78
Gausman, Kevin	757	3113	174	47	231	111	182	64%	18%	326	369	103	427	156
Gearrin, Cory	197	732	45	14	77	21	39	64%	19%	82	93	24	99	35
Gee, Dillon	551	2047	89	37	168	86	156	64%	13%	214	273	64	250	97
Geltz, Steve	112	465	23	9	17	16	46	63%	17%	47	54	18	65	24
Germen, Gonzalez	182	739	32	25	48	30	43	59%	20%	79	80	30	93	47
Gibson, Kyle	653	2468	104	55	236	110	138	61%	16%	266	312	88	300	132
Giles, Ken	286	1117	102	25	61	38	55	67%	30%	102	161	30	182	44
Gilmartin, Sean	79	309	11	7	31	9	14	63%	14%	33	40	9	41	13
Giolito, Lucas	101	398	11	12	30	20	24	62%	10%	45	40	15	48	25
Givens, Mychal	313	1306	96	36	61	44	68	65%	24%	128	160	46	194	64
Glasnow, Tyler	105	439	24	13	30	13	20	59%	20%	40	58	18	61	26
Glover, Koda	83	312	16	7	25	10	24	69%	16%	28	41	12	46	16
Godley, Zack	335	1150	60	25	128	43	67	62%	20%	150	137	30	143	51
Goeddel, Erik	157	630	36	14	30	27	49	65%	18%	60	81	19	92	28
Goforth, David	55	201	9	4	23	4	15	61%	18%	29	19	4	22	8
Gomez, Jeanmar	297	1154	47	22	117	49	59	62%	12%	131	133	44	145	61
Gonzalez, Chi Chi	62	249	7	9	20	11	14	60%	9%	27	30	10	30	15
Gonzalez, Gio	765	3116	171	59	245	118	152	61%	16%	325	359	125	398	175

Pitcher Analysis
Pitchers with 50+ Batters Faced in 2016

Pitcher	BF	Pitches	K	BB	GB	LD	FB	Str%	S/Str	1-0	0-1	Full	2 Strike	3 Ball
Gonzalez, Miguel	566	2100	95	35	171	93	162	65%	13%	223	274	65	274	88
Gonzalez, Severino	151	613	34	7	28	25	56	66%	17%	56	82	17	82	25
Goody, Nick	128	528	34	12	18	17	45	65%	23%	53	67	17	73	25
Graveman, Kendall	786	2832	108	47	323	127	170	63%	12%	278	407	77	326	128
Gray, Jon	712	2793	185	59	192	108	141	65%	19%	268	373	86	381	131
Gray, Sonny	517	1947	94	42	202	70	103	62%	13%	198	257	73	238	107
Green, Chad	198	836	52	15	52	26	48	62%	21%	79	105	36	104	52
Greene, Shane	256	983	59	22	80	35	53	64%	20%	107	127	33	136	50
Gregerson, Luke	230	852	67	18	84	20	36	65%	31%	86	117	31	121	49
Greinke, Zack	667	2503	134	41	221	94	166	65%	17%	215	358	77	330	107
Griffin, A.J.	509	2063	107	46	101	80	166	63%	15%	217	249	81	264	116
Grilli, Jason	251	1072	81	32	40	27	68	61%	22%	109	117	42	152	62
Grimm, Justin	225	906	65	23	56	31	48	61%	21%	98	103	34	132	49
Gsellman, Robert	185	713	42	15	65	27	28	63%	16%	72	95	24	94	33
Guerra, Deolis	220	901	36	7	73	45	55	65%	15%	99	101	37	118	48
Guerra, Junior	492	1866	100	43	153	64	121	62%	19%	203	231	69	239	111
Gustave, Jandel	60	238	16	4	16	9	15	65%	18%	20	32	9	34	13
Hahn, Jesse	203	712	23	19	79	37	44	62%	10%	70	100	20	89	39
Hamels, Cole	848	3253	200	77	277	109	172	63%	20%	361	397	108	429	170
Hammel, Jason	692	2623	144	53	200	94	181	65%	17%	276	346	95	352	132
Hand, Brad	364	1447	111	36	100	37	77	62%	20%	151	177	46	204	76
Happ, J.A.	796	3033	163	60	237	123	198	63%	16%	318	385	95	387	140
Hardy, Blaine	112	444	20	12	38	14	27	64%	15%	40	65	14	63	23
Harrell, Lucas	208	833	36	25	62	32	46	56%	14%	98	92	32	97	58
Harris, Will	255	1045	69	15	98	29	42	65%	22%	93	139	36	152	50
Hart, Donnie	71	271	12	6	30	9	12	62%	14%	35	28	9	36	14
Harvey, Matt	402	1514	76	25	118	73	98	67%	16%	138	218	42	201	62
Hatcher, Chris	181	770	43	21	51	20	44	62%	17%	72	93	24	107	42
Hathaway, Steve	65	253	15	6	22	11	11	63%	11%	30	30	8	37	11
Hellickson, Jeremy	772	2925	154	45	224	137	189	64%	17%	302	373	88	387	125
Hembree, Heath	223	862	47	17	57	37	63	66%	15%	92	105	29	117	39
Henderson, Jim	155	648	40	14	25	20	53	65%	17%	66	67	23	93	28
Hendricks, Kyle	745	2888	170	44	249	104	161	65%	16%	236	437	94	411	127
Hendriks, Liam	275	1081	71	14	75	40	72	68%	17%	94	146	35	155	48
Hernandez, David	322	1276	80	32	76	51	77	64%	19%	135	152	40	184	61
Hernandez, Felix	655	2453	122	65	225	92	131	63%	16%	266	294	90	314	125
Herrera, Kelvin	283	1091	86	12	80	41	60	67%	23%	100	160	25	163	41
Herrmann, Frank	69	280	14	5	13	10	25	68%	16%	24	36	8	42	11
Hessler, Keith	103	418	11	13	29	15	31	60%	12%	44	50	16	56	25
Hill, Rich	439	1819	129	33	120	50	95	66%	17%	174	234	57	277	83
Hochevar, Luke	151	583	40	9	35	15	47	66%	21%	56	79	21	90	24
Hoffman, Jeff	147	556	22	17	53	23	30	62%	11%	62	64	24	68	35
Holland, Derek	461	1828	67	35	136	77	142	64%	12%	176	229	74	223	100
Hoover, J.J.	97	414	15	12	22	16	29	58%	17%	42	47	19	51	29
Howell, J.P.	220	883	44	15	91	29	34	60%	15%	92	111	37	113	46
Hoyt, James	91	375	28	9	28	9	15	63%	24%	34	53	14	55	20
Hudson, Daniel	268	1113	58	22	74	49	58	63%	20%	118	123	51	143	68
Hughes, Jared	257	908	34	22	110	30	50	61%	16%	100	113	23	93	44
Hughes, Phil	259	907	34	13	74	50	85	67%	10%	77	141	31	116	36
Hunter, Tommy	139	483	23	8	52	26	27	67%	15%	48	72	12	62	21
Hutchison, Drew	104	401	22	7	25	16	31	65%	17%	43	53	13	48	21
Iglesias, Raisel	325	1245	83	26	84	44	79	62%	20%	150	141	45	169	65
Iwakuma, Hisashi	836	2981	147	46	255	134	236	67%	12%	299	437	72	370	110
Jackson, Edwin	373	1401	61	41	107	56	103	60%	16%	175	159	44	167	84
Jackson, Luke	62	242	3	8	16	14	21	60%	8%	30	24	14	25	17
Jansen, Kenley	251	1002	104	11	39	20	71	72%	25%	80	150	20	170	25
Jeffress, Jeremy	241	867	42	18	105	41	28	66%	15%	95	119	26	116	41
Jenkins, Tyrell	237	894	26	33	82	31	57	56%	11%	119	85	35	93	69
Jennings, Dan	259	1027	46	28	97	43	40	60%	15%	122	108	32	125	58
Jepsen, Kevin	224	878	35	21	52	44	71	61%	14%	96	100	29	106	46
Jimenez, Ubaldo	638	2492	125	72	212	78	143	61%	14%	270	295	111	311	156
Johnson, Erik	146	572	21	11	48	24	42	62%	12%	62	66	22	71	35
Johnson, Jim	266	1054	68	20	94	38	39	63%	12%	114	132	39	145	58
Johnson, Steve	75	301	17	11	14	7	26	63%	12%	41	27	11	42	18
Jones, Nate	274	1009	80	15	79	36	57	67%	22%	99	138	28	138	40
Jungmann, Taylor	126	513	18	17	38	16	31	57%	11%	51	62	24	61	37
Kahnle, Tommy	119	499	25	20	36	17	21	61%	18%	55	50	21	61	38
Karns, Nathan	417	1679	101	45	106	61	96	62%	18%	177	204	61	221	96
Kazmir, Scott	590	2392	134	52	159	91	140	63%	16%	236	307	97	324	134

Pitcher Analysis
Pitchers with 50+ Batters Faced in 2016

Pitcher	BF	Pitches	K	BB	GB	LD	FB	Str%	S/Str	1-0	0-1	Full	2 Strike	3 Ball
Kela, Keone	150	632	45	17	36	18	28	62%	20%	68	68	25	90	36
Kelley, Shawn	224	907	80	11	48	19	65	70%	24%	76	128	22	149	28
Kelly, Casey	102	376	7	7	38	13	33	62%	12%	51	34	11	43	20
Kelly, Joe	188	739	48	24	53	32	28	58%	19%	90	77	29	93	48
Kennedy, Ian	818	3378	184	66	181	107	258	65%	16%	312	425	139	478	185
Kershaw, Clayton	544	2062	172	11	174	72	106	69%	23%	165	309	56	325	69
Keuchel, Dallas	701	2670	144	48	284	95	122	63%	16%	258	363	98	346	136
Kiekhefer, Dean	98	364	14	7	35	15	24	59%	14%	50	40	13	42	22
Kimbrel, Craig	220	935	83	30	30	23	49	61%	25%	70	127	43	140	62
Kintzler, Brandon	224	828	35	8	109	32	35	67%	11%	78	123	21	110	31
Klein, Phil	86	358	19	9	18	14	23	63%	16%	33	47	15	44	21
Kluber, Corey	860	3189	227	57	249	108	203	66%	20%	320	424	93	449	137
Knebel, Corey	145	612	38	16	38	19	33	60%	14%	56	74	30	83	41
Koch, Matt	69	234	10	4	21	8	22	67%	13%	23	39	3	32	8
Koehler, Tom	774	3089	147	83	223	123	182	61%	17%	314	374	96	392	166
Kontos, George	216	799	35	20	70	37	51	63%	17%	84	101	36	101	49
Krol, Ian	217	890	56	13	79	29	33	65%	17%	86	110	30	125	45
Kuhl, Chad	301	1141	53	20	97	43	79	63%	14%	131	140	36	137	54
Lackey, John	748	2853	180	53	201	111	178	66%	18%	237	385	104	406	139
Lamb, John	318	1264	58	31	91	47	78	63%	13%	137	151	47	163	72
Latos, Mat	309	1184	42	30	99	45	87	62%	12%	134	144	45	147	70
Law, Derek	214	796	50	9	77	33	43	65%	17%	80	105	25	114	32
Layne, Tommy	187	697	38	21	61	21	38	60%	16%	84	87	25	90	40
Leake, Mike	757	2659	125	30	314	123	148	66%	11%	288	355	77	335	102
LeBlanc, Wade	252	945	51	11	64	40	84	66%	14%	93	130	28	130	39
Leclerc, Jose	66	264	15	13	11	10	17	56%	22%	28	31	9	31	22
Leone, Dominic	131	477	23	12	45	16	34	66%	18%	51	58	16	64	26
Lester, Jon	796	3161	197	52	246	106	172	64%	17%	297	404	119	426	152
Lewis, Colby	472	1750	73	28	123	67	171	65%	12%	158	262	55	213	83
Liberatore, Adam	176	716	47	17	42	23	43	62%	16%	71	90	29	94	42
Light, Pat	91	364	16	16	31	11	15	54%	17%	56	27	15	38	31
Lincecum, Tim	200	806	32	23	57	35	48	58%	19%	101	79	26	95	52
Liriano, Francisco	731	2793	168	85	237	81	138	60%	20%	324	322	93	353	160
Lobstein, Kyle	110	412	15	12	40	19	21	57%	13%	58	38	13	43	27
Locke, Jeff	564	2096	73	44	201	87	138	64%	14%	216	267	73	262	109
Logan, Boone	187	748	57	20	52	18	35	62%	27%	64	109	26	106	42
Lopez, Javier	118	443	15	15	52	13	19	61%	11%	46	59	15	52	25
Lopez, Reynaldo	201	806	42	22	55	31	47	63%	16%	88	91	24	109	41
Lorenzen, Michael	202	755	48	13	84	28	22	65%	16%	74	96	26	100	40
Loup, Aaron	62	261	15	4	16	13	11	67%	12%	25	34	6	39	9
Lowe, Mark	224	868	49	21	56	30	67	64%	17%	85	113	37	117	48
Luebke, Cory	53	221	9	11	10	11	10	59%	11%	26	22	9	26	16
Lugo, Seth	260	961	45	21	77	34	69	64%	15%	92	123	33	119	52
Lyles, Jordan	273	957	32	28	105	48	51	61%	12%	109	113	37	113	58
Lyons, Tyler	187	678	46	14	50	30	45	66%	16%	53	108	14	93	30
Madson, Ryan	270	1002	49	20	90	44	60	64%	19%	118	113	40	125	57
Maeda, Kenta	716	2930	179	50	208	97	169	64%	19%	277	376	88	413	127
Mahle, Greg	86	328	14	10	30	11	17	66%	11%	29	47	9	46	14
Manaea, Sean	594	2169	124	37	186	89	146	67%	18%	211	296	67	300	93
Maness, Seth	134	496	16	8	62	22	24	67%	11%	45	73	11	59	20
Manship, Jeff	189	744	36	22	67	17	47	59%	20%	75	97	28	89	48
Marinez, Jhan	269	953	50	21	95	45	49	63%	15%	117	117	27	115	47
Mariot, Michael	95	380	23	14	18	11	29	60%	16%	41	42	16	48	25
Marquez, German	98	351	15	6	39	21	11	64%	15%	35	50	8	44	17
Marshall, Evan	79	284	9	8	35	12	14	59%	15%	31	35	13	29	20
Martin, Cody	107	400	15	9	38	13	29	62%	12%	39	60	10	48	19
Martinez, Carlos	809	3028	174	70	307	96	141	65%	15%	303	408	97	407	149
Martinez, Nick	179	649	16	19	70	22	47	60%	11%	86	75	18	74	35
Matusz, Brian	53	205	3	9	15	9	15	58%	14%	28	20	6	27	13
Matz, Steven	547	2153	129	31	187	77	102	67%	15%	192	309	56	313	77
Maurer, Brandon	300	1229	72	23	76	41	84	63%	19%	121	157	51	172	68
May, Trevor	187	841	60	17	34	28	46	65%	21%	71	105	28	128	42
McAllister, Zach	233	932	54	23	54	33	65	63%	16%	93	106	35	134	49
McCarthy, Brandon	171	701	44	26	33	26	36	62%	13%	67	94	19	95	33
McCullers, Lance	352	1342	106	45	114	43	42	63%	21%	153	165	40	186	74
McFarland, T.J.	112	381	7	10	56	17	20	61%	9%	47	51	9	34	17
McGee, Jake	205	842	38	16	59	32	56	64%	15%	70	117	35	112	45
McGowan, Dustin	279	1080	63	33	98	31	51	60%	24%	114	131	34	139	63
McHugh, Collin	796	3159	177	54	229	114	211	65%	17%	263	454	111	435	148

Pitcher Analysis
Pitchers with 50+ Batters Faced in 2016

Pitcher	BF	Pitches	K	BB	GB	LD	FB	Str%	S/Str	Counts 1-0	0-1	Full	2 Strike	3 Ball
Medlen, Kris	119	475	18	20	38	17	26	56%	16%	69	38	24	56	34
Melancon, Mark	270	1023	65	12	103	39	48	67%	17%	91	144	34	141	43
Melville, Tim	54	203	8	9	12	11	11	58%	14%	21	26	6	23	11
Mengden, Daniel	332	1309	71	33	87	53	80	64%	15%	129	170	41	170	65
Meyer, Alex	117	476	29	17	27	13	31	57%	15%	64	43	16	60	33
Miley, Wade	711	2732	137	49	241	115	154	65%	14%	282	356	89	354	131
Miller, Andrew	275	1118	123	9	76	24	40	70%	24%	105	155	27	199	36
Miller, Justin	194	771	45	20	44	34	48	62%	17%	78	95	28	105	45
Miller, Shelby	460	1740	70	42	143	77	121	63%	12%	186	225	55	205	95
Milone, Tommy	311	1223	49	22	107	57	70	63%	14%	109	164	49	162	70
Miranda, Ariel	232	908	44	18	53	30	87	65%	13%	93	121	29	126	42
Mitchell, Bryan	107	388	11	12	40	16	27	60%	11%	50	44	19	45	25
Montero, Rafael	93	388	20	16	20	18	18	57%	16%	37	50	16	47	28
Montgomery, Mike	414	1513	92	38	157	61	51	61%	19%	180	173	48	196	76
Moore, Matt	838	3285	178	72	219	113	241	64%	17%	322	430	111	453	161
Morgan, Adam	507	1947	95	29	138	93	141	64%	18%	202	243	72	258	98
Morin, Mike	227	848	49	15	62	34	64	67%	19%	74	122	29	124	38
Morris, Bryan	74	282	13	10	25	11	14	56%	17%	34	33	11	28	19
Morrow, Brandon	68	232	8	3	24	14	16	67%	15%	32	26	6	32	10
Morton, Charlie	71	276	19	8	27	9	7	62%	20%	27	38	13	39	20
Moscot, Jon	105	416	10	10	29	23	27	61%	7%	51	46	15	45	23
Motte, Jason	109	462	24	8	32	14	29	66%	14%	35	65	11	61	18
Moylan, Peter	191	668	34	16	83	23	29	65%	15%	80	85	14	83	25
Murray, Colton	142	536	31	13	34	29	30	61%	17%	58	71	17	68	32
Musgrove, Joe	256	980	55	16	79	38	65	66%	15%	98	135	27	140	38
Neal, Zach	281	945	27	6	131	41	75	67%	14%	108	123	22	117	31
Nelson, Jimmy	807	2984	140	86	271	106	172	63%	13%	337	360	84	364	155
Neris, Hector	328	1358	102	30	80	47	64	63%	25%	158	151	46	192	69
Neshek, Pat	185	712	43	11	42	26	58	69%	16%	54	120	9	92	21
Nicasio, Juan	513	2165	138	45	138	69	110	64%	15%	189	263	99	317	120
Nicolino, Justin	346	1209	37	20	130	60	89	64%	8%	129	175	37	134	59
Niese, Jon	546	2011	88	47	203	81	113	64%	12%	204	270	63	257	97
Nola, Aaron	483	1796	121	29	174	63	78	66%	15%	191	250	44	249	75
Nolasco, Ricky	817	3127	144	44	266	116	235	64%	15%	319	405	104	404	151
Norris, Bud	495	2001	102	49	159	72	103	63%	15%	188	250	70	271	112
Norris, Daniel	302	1190	71	22	80	48	81	64%	17%	107	162	48	161	60
Nova, Ivan	684	2310	127	28	271	95	140	66%	15%	259	321	58	282	88
Nuno, Vidal	247	938	51	11	65	43	72	67%	13%	91	125	26	127	32
Oberg, Scott	113	437	20	11	45	9	27	61%	16%	51	49	19	55	30
Oberholtzer, Brett	321	1218	54	29	99	50	85	65%	13%	122	153	41	161	62
O'Day, Darren	131	537	38	13	27	17	35	68%	21%	42	78	18	84	24
Odorizzi, Jake	773	3308	166	54	199	103	241	64%	16%	320	386	118	441	166
O'Flaherty, Eric	136	473	22	11	54	18	28	64%	14%	51	65	12	55	20
Ogando, Alexi	148	618	29	23	36	20	36	59%	16%	71	69	27	79	40
Ogando, Nefi	65	227	8	8	30	12	7	60%	15%	30	29	4	27	12
Oh, Seung Hwan	313	1303	103	18	74	36	75	67%	27%	104	177	37	212	48
Ohlendorf, Ross	290	1138	68	32	58	39	82	60%	18%	127	125	36	142	60
Okert, Steven	58	232	14	4	17	7	16	64%	21%	30	22	6	31	11
O'Rourke, Ryan	101	399	24	10	29	9	26	60%	22%	42	49	11	51	21
Osich, Josh	160	576	25	19	71	13	26	58%	19%	76	57	17	64	36
O'Sullivan, Sean	98	358	13	6	27	20	27	63%	10%	36	52	10	47	14
Osuna, Roberto	288	1134	82	14	62	37	88	70%	23%	86	172	28	173	37
Otero, Dan	269	1001	57	10	124	36	39	68%	12%	90	148	25	134	33
Ottavino, Adam	107	458	35	7	39	11	13	62%	18%	51	52	20	64	25
Overton, Dillon	128	485	17	7	25	15	53	65%	15%	46	64	17	70	23
Owens, Henry	103	419	21	20	18	12	29	55%	18%	49	48	19	50	33
Papelbon, Jonathan	152	570	31	14	37	22	46	63%	17%	65	66	15	75	31
Parker, Blake	79	334	15	9	25	7	20	61%	18%	31	39	15	44	22
Patton, Spencer	101	391	22	14	27	14	23	61%	19%	46	47	15	48	25
Paxton, James	511	1950	117	24	176	80	110	66%	18%	193	263	42	256	71
Peacock, Brad	127	492	28	14	35	8	42	62%	14%	54	62	21	66	32
Peavy, Jake	520	2026	102	36	135	71	165	65%	17%	187	276	70	276	90
Pelfrey, Mike	541	2054	56	46	222	93	110	60%	11%	224	261	75	235	112
Peralta, Joel	119	501	33	8	17	20	40	67%	19%	51	57	20	77	24
Peralta, Wily	554	2132	93	43	202	91	111	61%	15%	247	245	86	254	125
Perdomo, Luis	662	2371	105	46	294	98	106	64%	14%	266	304	67	286	108
Perez, Martin	855	3078	103	76	349	134	173	64%	13%	304	425	109	372	172
Perez, Oliver	182	723	46	20	41	24	40	62%	16%	83	82	19	97	39
Perez, Williams	233	859	27	15	105	28	51	64%	9%	82	119	28	109	41

413

Pitcher Analysis
Pitchers with 50+ Batters Faced in 2016

Pitcher	BF	Pitches	K	BB	GB	LD	FB	Str%	S/Str	1-0	0-1	Full	2 Strike	3 Ball
Petit, Yusmeiro	265	968	49	15	81	34	80	67%	13%	93	135	20	129	36
Phelps, David	352	1497	114	38	90	40	65	62%	17%	156	167	65	223	83
Pineda, Michael	756	3017	207	53	223	105	159	65%	22%	247	434	96	436	135
Pomeranz, Drew	703	2841	186	65	201	72	162	63%	18%	308	330	107	387	150
Porcello, Rick	890	3410	189	32	279	122	246	67%	13%	320	483	99	478	120
Pounders, Brooks	58	249	13	3	14	5	23	68%	15%	21	34	7	37	11
Pressly, Ryan	328	1220	67	23	91	56	84	65%	18%	141	144	37	153	58
Price, David	951	3595	228	50	286	146	222	68%	18%	334	501	104	517	131
Purke, Matt	84	330	15	12	30	15	12	55%	17%	50	26	13	34	24
Putnam, Zach	114	449	30	11	29	24	19	61%	29%	49	56	17	64	23
Quackenbush, Kevin	253	1025	42	22	65	40	79	62%	12%	110	121	42	131	58
Qualls, Chad	152	534	22	9	66	24	30	65%	16%	55	82	12	63	22
Quintana, Jose	837	3282	181	50	241	125	231	63%	13%	293	454	125	416	164
Ramirez, Erasmo	378	1358	63	26	146	43	89	65%	14%	138	185	31	164	61
Ramirez, JC	335	1242	59	22	135	41	70	65%	16%	131	165	36	147	61
Ramirez, Jose	143	571	33	18	29	21	37	60%	21%	60	68	20	77	37
Ramirez, Neil	107	465	24	18	17	9	38	62%	18%	39	63	21	63	29
Ramirez, Noe	61	225	15	8	13	8	15	61%	20%	23	32	7	29	12
Ramos, A.J.	278	1117	73	35	59	42	61	62%	20%	111	141	42	161	67
Ramos, Cesar	212	785	27	20	71	33	60	61%	13%	76	113	34	87	53
Ramos, Edubray	160	612	40	11	40	27	41	66%	17%	66	84	19	87	27
Ranaudo, Anthony	151	624	18	20	45	16	51	62%	9%	57	83	23	78	33
Rasmus, Cory	114	464	17	16	24	14	41	60%	17%	56	50	19	57	29
Ray, Robbie	776	3176	218	71	217	103	155	64%	19%	342	382	102	438	160
Rea, Colin	454	1761	80	44	141	71	101	61%	11%	179	233	65	221	100
Reed, Addison	304	1193	91	13	77	44	73	71%	16%	92	178	29	179	39
Reed, Cody	230	884	43	19	83	34	43	62%	17%	94	104	36	109	51
Reyes, Alex	189	793	52	23	48	17	46	62%	19%	84	88	36	115	53
Richard, Clayton	306	1086	41	31	149	39	41	62%	15%	113	154	27	123	57
Richards, Garrett	148	615	34	15	44	24	28	62%	18%	63	73	26	77	37
Rivero, Felipe	327	1294	92	33	94	42	59	65%	23%	140	163	38	191	67
Roark, Tanner	855	3355	172	73	283	117	181	62%	15%	362	413	115	440	169
Robertson, David	267	1050	75	32	70	22	62	63%	21%	102	136	45	153	60
Robles, Hansel	331	1376	85	36	62	59	85	64%	18%	136	165	54	190	78
Rodney, Fernando	283	1149	74	37	90	36	37	60%	22%	122	143	37	160	65
Rodon, Carlos	715	2795	168	54	211	100	167	63%	17%	326	321	94	352	146
Rodriguez, Eduardo	458	1854	100	40	99	70	144	62%	18%	189	220	75	238	103
Rodriguez, Fernando	163	660	37	17	38	23	45	62%	21%	67	77	28	92	42
Rodriguez, Francisco	235	928	52	21	88	26	47	63%	20%	92	125	31	121	45
Roe, Chaz	124	476	37	14	41	6	24	67%	20%	39	73	11	70	19
Rogers, Taylor	264	1006	64	16	92	36	51	64%	13%	114	124	26	143	44
Romero, Enny	204	811	50	28	47	28	51	62%	21%	90	91	32	112	51
Romo, Sergio	117	469	33	7	29	11	36	65%	20%	41	70	17	74	22
Rondon, Bruce	144	565	45	12	26	14	41	65%	25%	59	72	14	80	23
Rondon, Hector	200	785	58	8	59	26	44	67%	17%	55	120	22	122	27
Rosenthal, Trevor	197	858	56	29	56	27	24	64%	19%	76	103	34	125	52
Ross, Joe	447	1708	93	29	132	84	94	64%	18%	195	200	54	224	85
Ross Jr., Robbie	238	966	56	23	73	37	39	63%	18%	98	125	38	139	50
Rusin, Chris	350	1264	69	23	142	51	50	63%	15%	149	154	46	155	64
Ryan, Kyle	226	837	35	15	96	30	45	64%	14%	86	122	24	96	39
Rzepczynski, Marc	215	840	46	29	89	16	27	55%	21%	106	83	34	93	63
Sabathia, CC	768	2910	152	65	266	90	175	64%	16%	297	367	99	392	156
Salas, Fernando	293	1212	64	19	82	36	91	67%	17%	100	163	38	169	52
Salazar, Danny	584	2404	161	63	170	61	125	63%	18%	271	272	86	322	139
Sale, Chris	907	3431	233	45	247	126	227	67%	18%	344	454	90	484	127
Samardzija, Jeff	829	3190	167	54	278	119	201	66%	15%	304	437	97	441	138
Sampson, Keyvius	188	796	42	27	44	21	50	58%	19%	88	86	33	103	54
Sanchez, Aaron	790	2919	161	63	303	114	140	63%	14%	309	392	94	381	146
Sanchez, Anibal	668	2577	135	53	185	89	193	64%	15%	223	366	95	338	136
Santana, Ervin	748	2931	149	53	229	117	192	62%	17%	308	364	113	374	164
Santiago, Hector	785	3172	144	79	187	87	274	63%	14%	356	376	107	423	166
Scahill, Rob	147	528	27	9	68	19	20	66%	17%	55	72	17	69	23
Scherzer, Max	902	3563	284	56	179	104	260	68%	23%	315	505	104	548	137
Schugel, A.J.	204	817	46	13	61	35	48	66%	14%	72	109	24	116	33
Schultz, Bo	68	260	10	3	30	11	14	66%	13%	25	37	10	31	14
Schuster, Patrick	54	216	8	10	10	10	13	57%	13%	22	25	10	30	16
Severino, Luis	312	1269	66	25	97	51	67	62%	15%	127	156	46	177	64
Shaw, Bryan	275	1158	69	28	94	33	48	62%	19%	128	122	51	157	70
Shields, James	822	3133	135	82	238	126	225	59%	16%	376	354	131	358	207

414

Pitcher Analysis
Pitchers with 50+ Batters Faced in 2016

Pitcher	BF	Pitches	K	BB	GB	LD	FB	Str%	S/Str	1-0	0-1	Full	2 Strike	3 Ball
Shipley, Braden	306	1181	43	28	98	54	77	59%	14%	127	147	43	127	70
Shoemaker, Matt	668	2476	143	30	190	113	174	67%	20%	208	372	74	335	103
Shreve, Chasen	142	569	33	13	40	13	36	63%	23%	55	68	25	83	29
Siegrist, Kevin	248	1050	66	26	52	30	71	62%	17%	101	127	44	153	62
Simon, Alfredo	298	1120	39	31	108	43	67	60%	13%	134	128	33	124	62
Sipp, Tony	195	780	40	18	49	25	62	63%	21%	86	88	35	111	44
Skaggs, Tyler	219	876	50	23	61	33	48	64%	14%	86	113	37	120	52
Smith, Chris	100	439	29	13	26	12	19	59%	25%	37	56	29	64	33
Smith, Joe	217	815	40	18	76	34	41	66%	14%	74	110	27	113	43
Smith, Josh	260	1042	48	26	77	32	75	63%	18%	92	146	39	141	54
Smith, Will	167	650	48	18	34	24	38	63%	19%	50	96	22	92	35
Smoker, Josh	65	258	25	4	10	9	15	68%	23%	16	45	9	40	12
Smyly, Drew	738	2893	167	49	160	99	252	65%	17%	306	363	96	393	133
Snell, Blake	401	1716	98	51	91	68	90	60%	19%	173	194	84	236	116
Socolovich, Miguel	64	236	16	5	23	3	17	64%	20%	33	20	9	33	12
Solis, Sammy	172	663	47	21	42	26	32	64%	20%	61	92	22	98	36
Soria, Joakim	293	1193	68	27	94	37	57	64%	19%	110	161	41	171	60
Stephenson, Robert	170	721	31	19	40	28	48	61%	16%	79	79	28	89	42
Stewart, Brock	126	484	25	12	37	11	40	66%	17%	50	65	16	65	23
Storen, Drew	228	871	48	13	77	31	50	65%	17%	78	131	26	117	37
Strahm, Matt	88	433	30	11	21	11	13	60%	22%	42	44	23	68	29
Straily, Dan	792	3061	162	73	172	107	258	64%	17%	306	406	92	412	150
Strasburg, Stephen	598	2385	183	44	143	77	142	66%	18%	207	319	84	354	113
Street, Huston	105	401	14	12	28	17	33	63%	14%	41	50	17	57	23
Strickland, Hunter	250	1019	57	19	80	38	51	64%	19%	107	123	33	144	46
Stripling, Ross	419	1590	74	30	157	62	90	63%	13%	151	219	59	205	85
Stroman, Marcus	855	3102	166	54	375	122	127	64%	15%	336	419	92	391	129
Strop, Pedro	187	729	60	15	62	17	27	64%	26%	88	83	23	113	33
Sturdevant, Tyler	75	259	14	6	19	15	18	67%	17%	34	29	7	29	12
Suarez, Albert	355	1373	54	26	127	55	83	62%	14%	144	173	56	172	76
Surkamp, Eric	197	735	22	21	48	42	58	60%	12%	87	88	24	85	40
Suter, Brent	91	347	15	5	29	13	25	65%	14%	30	51	14	41	16
Swarzak, Anthony	124	488	31	7	39	9	36	65%	16%	40	76	17	64	23
Syndergaard, Noah	744	2935	218	43	241	102	128	68%	22%	271	407	87	447	112
Taillon, Jameson	418	1550	85	17	161	62	84	66%	13%	161	205	44	200	65
Tanaka, Masahiro	805	2935	165	36	286	123	184	67%	17%	286	402	88	390	120
Tazawa, Junichi	208	838	54	14	55	26	57	64%	21%	78	104	35	113	44
Teheran, Julio	758	2971	167	41	206	100	221	65%	17%	290	389	97	403	136
Tepera, Ryan	85	290	18	8	31	8	14	61%	23%	45	24	11	33	17
Thompson, Jake	237	919	32	28	77	28	61	58%	12%	120	95	38	107	62
Thornburg, Tyler	263	1145	90	25	47	33	65	64%	20%	114	136	42	169	57
Thornton, Matt	77	280	9	6	33	12	16	63%	11%	31	39	5	34	10
Tillman, Chris	715	2936	140	66	205	112	181	62%	15%	309	345	108	376	158
Tolleson, Shawn	168	659	29	10	66	28	33	63%	15%	67	80	19	86	29
Tomlin, Josh	725	2612	118	20	252	121	203	68%	12%	235	398	63	346	87
Tonkin, Michael	315	1287	80	24	70	54	81	64%	18%	125	160	53	177	69
Torres, Carlos	339	1317	78	30	99	46	77	63%	19%	137	166	48	179	66
Treinen, Blake	263	1002	63	31	110	24	33	61%	18%	115	115	28	124	58
Triggs, Andrew	238	929	55	13	84	39	42	63%	17%	108	110	35	121	46
Tropeano, Nick	296	1213	68	31	63	33	93	61%	21%	119	151	50	159	77
Turner, Jacob	122	456	18	16	44	23	19	61%	13%	50	54	19	51	31
Uehara, Koji	184	769	63	11	22	21	60	69%	23%	64	104	24	119	28
Urena, Jose	373	1437	58	29	132	61	84	61%	15%	164	177	52	180	82
Urias, Julio	336	1416	84	31	93	57	63	63%	17%	124	190	59	205	77
Valdez, Jose	100	398	22	16	24	13	25	57%	19%	61	32	17	48	30
Vargas, Cesar	154	607	28	15	57	21	28	59%	15%	62	75	29	70	39
Velasquez, Vince	551	2213	152	45	119	82	141	64%	19%	222	288	73	310	114
Venditte, Pat	102	404	19	11	28	11	31	63%	17%	34	49	14	55	21
Ventura, Yordano	816	3048	144	78	291	110	179	61%	15%	357	358	107	382	173
VerHagen, Drew	90	346	10	7	43	10	19	59%	11%	40	36	17	38	23
Verlander, Justin	903	3668	254	57	194	107	275	67%	19%	324	504	129	541	166
Verrett, Logan	406	1570	66	43	126	65	95	64%	14%	152	211	52	202	82
Villanueva, Carlos	321	1193	61	14	101	58	81	66%	17%	110	170	35	163	46
Vincent, Nick	247	935	65	15	52	33	78	68%	21%	76	149	22	136	36
Vizcaino, Arodys	182	720	50	26	56	17	31	61%	23%	80	89	21	104	41
Vogelsong, Ryan	366	1390	61	40	102	54	96	59%	11%	153	169	58	164	84
Volquez, Edinson	853	3232	139	76	318	123	180	63%	14%	371	406	96	413	160
Wacha, Michael	606	2324	114	45	203	104	129	64%	14%	249	290	74	295	109
Wainwright, Adam	847	3195	161	59	266	155	187	63%	14%	326	411	111	418	163

Pitcher Analysis
Pitchers with 50+ Batters Faced in 2016

Pitcher	BF	Pitches	K	BB	GB	LD	FB	Str%	S/Str	Counts 1-0	0-1	Full	2 Strike	3 Ball
Walker, Taijuan	573	2311	119	37	178	73	153	65%	16%	204	295	81	323	108
Wang, Chien-Ming	231	835	30	18	89	43	48	64%	9%	83	116	28	103	41
Warren, Adam	277	1185	52	29	84	32	76	61%	17%	112	137	43	153	73
Watson, Tony	272	1045	58	20	81	33	71	66%	20%	98	139	33	149	47
Weaver, Jered	767	2835	103	51	174	139	291	65%	13%	277	393	85	365	128
Weaver, Luke	167	682	45	12	31	37	33	63%	16%	73	81	19	87	34
Webb, Ryan	76	292	11	3	30	15	17	65%	14%	26	45	6	39	10
Weber, Ryan	157	539	23	5	64	27	35	67%	9%	57	86	8	70	16
Wendelken, J.B.	64	272	12	9	14	10	19	61%	19%	26	32	11	36	18
Whalen, Rob	110	451	25	12	28	12	27	61%	18%	48	53	20	60	29
Whitley, Chase	61	238	15	3	18	8	17	68%	20%	20	32	9	37	10
Wilhelmsen, Tom	209	808	28	19	80	23	54	61%	14%	92	88	45	101	56
Williams, Jerome	81	291	8	6	24	16	24	62%	16%	31	39	10	32	15
Williams, Trevor	61	224	11	5	20	11	13	64%	15%	27	25	10	29	12
Wilson, Alex	297	1130	49	21	99	42	82	61%	15%	124	135	46	135	66
Wilson, Justin	251	996	65	17	89	24	49	65%	20%	103	122	39	137	53
Wilson, Tyler	414	1470	55	24	148	72	108	64%	11%	178	187	30	171	58
Wimmers, Alex	72	306	14	11	24	4	16	59%	20%	34	34	17	40	22
Wisler, Matt	671	2438	115	49	199	106	190	63%	15%	280	307	65	295	118
Withrow, Chris	158	650	28	17	49	18	41	64%	19%	75	73	25	97	36
Wittgren, Nick	213	842	42	10	61	32	62	67%	10%	80	109	22	117	30
Wood, Alex	255	985	66	20	85	31	43	65%	16%	92	132	35	144	47
Wood, Blake	330	1313	81	38	110	40	57	61%	18%	144	152	51	179	76
Wood, Travis	252	1016	47	24	67	39	73	66%	12%	87	139	32	143	50
Worley, Vance	365	1300	56	35	129	48	91	63%	8%	162	162	37	157	62
Wright, Daniel	179	666	21	8	55	35	52	61%	12%	75	83	27	79	36
Wright, Mike	328	1296	50	26	100	46	93	62%	11%	134	164	49	166	73
Wright, Steven	656	2496	127	57	200	89	169	63%	17%	297	305	91	334	129
Yates, Kirby	184	800	50	19	48	25	37	63%	19%	67	103	35	121	47
Ynoa, Gabriel	88	323	17	7	30	16	15	65%	17%	35	42	15	47	17
Ynoa, Michael	135	546	30	17	31	16	33	57%	15%	62	60	24	61	43
Young, Chris	406	1678	94	43	83	51	131	62%	19%	166	205	65	226	98
Zastryzny, Rob	66	249	17	5	23	5	13	62%	22%	39	24	5	32	9
Ziegler, Brad	289	1035	58	26	126	38	35	63%	19%	127	124	29	133	51
Zimmermann, Jordan	450	1707	66	26	151	63	136	67%	12%	156	242	54	238	72
Zych, Tony	60	252	21	10	14	4	10	61%	18%	32	26	8	35	15

A Repertoire, and a Surgery

Bill James

     Dustin Molleken had Tommy John Surgery in January of 2004. I have not the foggiest idea who Dustin Molleken is, frankly, and I am guessing that none of you do, either, unless you are Detroit Tigers fans or Canadians. He is a 32-year-old right-hander who made his debut with the Tigers in 2016, getting into four games; I just looked him up. He was drafted by the Pittsburgh Pirates in 2003, and has spent all of this time trying to get to the major leagues. He's from the outlands of Alberta, and has competed for the Canadian national team. He finally made it. You have to admire him.

     When you watch a baseball game on your television machine, you will often hear it said that it would now be easier to list the pitchers who have NOT had Tommy John Surgery than to list those who have. After hearing this line eight or ten times I got to wondering, is that actually true?

     It turns out that it isn't true, isn't literally true. Only 26% of major league pitchers have had Tommy John surgery, not that 26% isn't a pretty good percentage. We added this information to this section of the book to create the possibility of learning from it. We are in the business of building understanding about baseball. There are a lot of questions here to which we don't know the answers. How much velocity does a pitcher typically lose after Tommy John Surgery? What is the peak age for Tommy John Surgery? What percentage of effective major league pitchers have had Tommy John Surgery? What percentage of ineffective pitchers? What percentage of starters? What percentage of relievers? What is the normal recovery time frame? What is the normal period of time between Tommy John Surgery and the pitchers' best subsequent season?

You can't build understanding without facts, so somebody has to put the facts on the record. That would be us; that's our job.

The rest of the information here is what has been in this section before, what percentage of each pitcher's pitches are fastballs, sliders, changeups, curves, etc. Do people still use the phrase "changeup", or is it just "change" anymore? Anyway, one thing I always like to figure is the "Pitch Mix Index" for each pitcher. If a pitcher throws three or four different pitches and mixes them up about evenly, that gives a high Pitch Mix Index.

Who mixes up his pitches the most? The major league pitchers who use the deepest pitch mix are, in order, 1. Vidal Nuno, 2. Masahiro Tanaka, 3. Mike Fiers, 4. CC Sabathia, 5. Zack Godley, 6. Clay Buchholz, 7. Tommy Layne, 8. A.J. Ramos, 9. Hisashi Iwakuma, 10. Wade LeBlanc. What you will notice about those pitchers is that none of them really has a good fastball. They're all guys who throw...well, Buchholz and Ramos throw around 92; the other guys throw about 90.

I charted the number of pitchers throwing an average fastball velocity of 97+, 96 to 96.9, etc. That leads to this chart:

Average Fastball Velocity	Number
97 or higher	17
96 to 96.9	29
95 to 95.9	46
94 to 94.9	75
93 to 93.9	96
92 to 92.9	124
91 to 91.9	112
90 to 90.9	91
88 to 89.9	83
Up to 87.9	69

So the center of that chart is 91 to 93; more pitchers throw 91 to 93 than any other group.

As you might expect, the better a pitcher's fastball, the more he will rely on it. Pitchers who throw 96 or higher throw their fastballs 65% of the time; 95 to

95.9, 63%; 94 to 94.9, 61%. Slider usage also peaks for pitchers who throw hard; as fastball usage declines, so does slider usage. And, as slider and fastball usage decline, the Change increases—but what increases most is the curveball. Pitchers who throw 95-95.9 throw only 3% curve balls; pitchers who throw 90-90.9 throw 12% curveballs. Pitchers who throw 90-93 throw the curve as their breaking pitch; hard throwers mostly use the slider. And ALL knuckleball pitchers are in the group of pitchers whose average fastball is less than 88.

Another thing you can study with this data is who is similar to who. If you code pitchers by Left/Right, Fastball A, B, or C, Second Pitch, etc., you can identify which pitchers are most similar to which other pitchers. Sometimes you find two pitchers who are similar, but one of them is successful, the other one isn't. It's a doorway into a question: Why is that? Why is THIS pitcher not succeeding when that pitcher, who has the same fastball and throws the same pitch mix, is successful?

If you can make groups of similar pitchers, you can study whether a hitter who is successful against one pitcher in the group is also successful against similar pitchers. There's a million ways you can study this data. The computer age has buried us all under an avalanche of facts. Eventually, that avalanche of facts will lead to better understanding of many issues, but it will take decades for this to happen. For now, it mostly leads to confusion. We have more data than we can process.

Well...in the spirit of the late, great Henry Gibson, let me conclude with this ten-syllable poem.

Dustin Molleken,

Whaddaya Thenkin?

Player	Tommy John Surgery	Fastball Velocity	Pitch Repertoire						
			Fastball	Slider	Change	Cutter	Curve	Splitter	Other
Abad,Fernando	-	91.4	54%	-	19%	<1%	27%	-	
Achter,A.J.	-	91.1	49%	11%	40%	-	-	-	
Adams,Austin	-	96.1	64%	28%	9%	-	-	-	
Adleman,Tim	-	90.8	63%	-	18%	-	19%	-	
Albers,Andrew	Jan `09	87.3	66%	23%	3%	-	7%	-	
Albers,Matt	-	92.0	74%	14%	9%	-	3%	-	
Alburquerque,Al	Jan `05	91.3	35%	65%	-	-	-	-	
Alcantara,Raul	May `14	93.1	66%	10%	19%	-	4%	-	
Alexander,Scott	-	90.7	72%	23%	5%	-	-	-	
Allen,Cody	Jan `08	94.2	63%	-	-	-	37%	-	
Altavilla,Dan	-	96.5	66%	33%	<1%	-	-	-	
Alvarez,Dario	-	93.1	40%	59%	<1%	-	-	-	
Alvarez,Jose	-	90.6	46%	28%	20%	-	6%	-	
Amarista,Alexi	-	84.0	100%	-	-	-	-	-	
Anderson,Brett	July `11	91.3	59%	17%	8%	-	15%	-	
Anderson,Chase	-	91.1	57%	-	24%	6%	13%	-	
Anderson,Cody	-	94.0	56%	-	27%	6%	11%	-	
Anderson,Tyler	-	90.9	44%	26%	29%	-	1%	-	
Andriese,Matt	-	91.8	46%	-	25%	18%	11%	-	
Antolin,Dustin	June `10	92.2	50%	17%	-	-	-	33%	
Aquino,Jayson	-	89.1	44%	-	31%	-	25%	-	
Araujo,Elvis	Jan `09	92.2	61%	35%	4%	-	-	-	
Archer,Chris	-	94.3	48%	40%	11%	-	-	-	
Armstrong,Shawn	-	92.5	60%	-	-	28%	12%	-	
Aro,Jonathan	-	93.2	60%	-	40%	-	-	-	
Arrieta,Jake	-	93.7	66%	-	5%	18%	12%	-	
Asher,Alec	Jan `06	89.5	59%	14%	18%	-	9%	-	
Avilan,Luis	-	92.0	46%	-	48%	-	6%	-	
Axford,John	Nov `03	95.7	74%	14%	2%	-	10%	-	
Baez,Pedro	-	96.7	75%	12%	13%	-	-	-	
Bailey,Andrew	May `05	92.1	63%	-	-	24%	13%	-	
Bailey,Homer	May `15	92.7	54%	24%	-	-	9%	13%	
Barbato,Johnny	-	94.6	49%	26%	-	-	25%	-	
Barnes,Danny	-	91.7	67%	12%	22%	-	-	-	
Barnes,Jacob	-	94.6	59%	7%	-	33%	-	-	
Barnes,Matt	-	96.8	66%	5%	5%	-	24%	-	
Barnette,Tony	-	92.2	34%	5%	-	40%	12%	10%	
Barney,Darwin	-	85.0	94%	6%	-	-	-	-	
Barraclough,Kyle	-	95.6	54%	42%	4%	-	-	-	
Barrett,Jake	-	94.9	63%	31%	<1%	-	-	6%	
Bassitt,Chris	May `16	92.5	59%	14%	8%	-	19%	-	
Bastardo,Antonio	-	91.5	65%	27%	7%	-	-	-	
Bauer,Trevor	-	93.2	51%	-	12%	17%	19%	-	
Baumann,Buddy	-	88.6	71%	22%	7%	-	-	-	
Beck,Chris	-	94.2	58%	19%	22%	-	-	-	
Bedrosian,Cam	May `11	95.3	68%	32%	-	-	-	-	
Belisle,Matt	-	90.9	56%	33%	1%	-	10%	-	
Benoit,Joaquin	-	94.2	55%	18%	26%	-	1%	-	
Bergman,Christian	-	89.5	48%	33%	16%	-	4%	-	
Berrios,Jose	-	93.3	64%	-	14%	-	22%	-	
Betances,Dellin	-	97.7	43%	57%	-	-	-	-	
Bethancourt,Christian	-	91.9	77%	-	20%	-	2%	-	
Bettis,Chad	-	91.7	56%	-	13%	21%	10%	-	
Biagini,Joseph	-	94.3	59%	18%	6%	-	17%	-	
Blach,Ty	-	91.1	61%	20%	15%	-	4%	-	
Blair,Aaron	-	90.9	58%	-	19%	-	23%	-	
Blanton,Joe	-	91.2	30%	39%	12%	-	20%	-	
Blazek,Michael	-	93.0	51%	28%	-	-	22%	-	

Player	Tommy John Surgery	Fastball Velocity	Fastball	Slider	Change	Cutter	Curve	Splitter	Other
Bleier,Richard	-	89.4	61%	17%	15%	6%	-	-	
Blevins,Jerry	-	89.0	63%	-	6%	-	31%	-	
Bolsinger,Mike	-	87.7	42%	26%	2%	-	30%	-	
Boscan,Wilfredo	-	90.6	69%	-	14%	-	17%	-	
Boshers,Buddy	-	91.7	50%	-	9%	-	42%	-	
Bowman,Matt	-	91.7	63%	22%	15%	-	-	-	
Boxberger,Brad	-	92.0	59%	9%	31%	-	-	-	
Boyd,Matt	-	91.2	61%	11%	16%	-	12%	-	
Boyer,Blaine	-	92.1	58%	32%	<1%	-	10%	-	
Brach,Brad	-	94.5	60%	18%	22%	-	-	-	
Bracho,Silvino	-	92.7	65%	25%	10%	-	-	-	
Bradley,Archie	-	92.4	69%	-	7%	-	24%	-	
Bradley,Jed	-	89.5	63%	22%	15%	-	-	-	
Brault,Steven	-	91.0	67%	24%	8%	-	-	-	
Breslow,Craig	-	89.5	54%	-	17%	25%	4%	-	
Brice,Austin	-	94.1	66%	18%	-	-	16%	-	
Bridwell,Parker	-	91.6	51%	14%	19%	17%	-	-	
Britton,Zach	-	96.3	92%	8%	-	-	-	-	
Broadway,Mike	-	93.3	55%	33%	12%	-	-	-	
Broxton,Jonathan	-	94.4	58%	31%	9%	-	1%	-	
Buchanan,Jake	-	89.4	57%	16%	15%	-	12%	-	
Buchholz,Clay	-	92.1	41%	-	17%	22%	19%	1%	
Buchter,Ryan	-	92.3	84%	8%	-	8%	-	-	
Bumgarner,Madison	-	90.9	48%	33%	3%	-	15%	-	
Bundy,Dylan	June `13	93.8	61%	-	20%	-	18%	-	
Burgos,Enrique	-	95.8	61%	36%	-	-	-	4%	
Burnett,Sean	June `14 Sept `04	88.0	66%	25%	9%	-	-	-	
Buschmann,Matt	-	90.0	66%	20%	15%	-	-	-	
Bush,Matt	Jan `07	97.0	68%	14%	<1%	-	18%		
Butera,Drew	-	88.0	82%	-	18%	-	-	-	
Butler,Eddie	-	92.9	61%	26%	5%	-	8%	-	
Cabrera,Mauricio	-	100.1	71%	-	11%	-	18%	-	
Cahill,Trevor	-	92.0	55%	<1%	26%	-	19%	-	
Cain,Matt	-	90.3	50%	25%	11%	-	14%	-	
Caminero,Arquimedes	Jan `11	97.9	67%	-	-	22%	<1%	10%	
Campos,Leonel	Oct `11	92.8	52%	43%	5%	-	-	-	
Campos,Vicente	Apr `14	88.8	41%	-	43%	-	16%	-	
Capuano,Chris	May `08 May `02	88.5	49%	27%	22%	-	2%	-	
Carasiti,Matt	-	94.2	59%	-	17%	2%	-	22%	
Carrasco,Carlos	Sept `11	93.8	53%	16%	16%	-	15%	-	
Carroll,Scott	Nov `12	88.7	67%	23%	-	-	-	9%	
Cashner,Andrew	-	93.5	65%	21%	6%	-	8%	-	
Casilla,Santiago	-	93.6	53%	18%	2%	-	26%	-	
Castro,Miguel	-	96.1	57%	38%	5%	-	-	-	
Cecil,Brett	-	92.2	40%	-	6%	8%	45%	-	
Cedeno,Xavier	-	-	-	-	-	75%	25%	-	
Cervenka,Hunter	-	92.7	42%	51%	-	-	7%	-	
Cessa,Luis	-	94.6	50%	24%	10%	-	16%	-	
Chacin,Jhoulys	-	90.8	53%	21%	8%	7%	11%	-	
Chafin,Andrew	Jan `10	92.8	72%	28%	<1%	-	-	-	
Chamberlain,Joba	June `11	93.4	53%	35%	-	-	13%	-	
Chapman,Aroldis	-	100.4	81%	16%	3%	-	-	-	
Chapman,Kevin	Jan `08	90.7	49%	30%	14%	-	7%	-	
Chargois,J.T.	Sept `13	96.2	62%	29%	9%	-	-	-	
Chatwood,Tyler	July `14 Jan `06	92.2	71%	-	2%	22%	5%	-	

Player	Tommy John Surgery	Fastball Velocity	Pitch Repertoire						
			Fastball	Slider	Change	Cutter	Curve	Splitter	Other
Chavez,Jesse	-	93.2	34%	8%	10%	41%	8%	-	
Chen,Wei-Yin	Jan `06	90.7	60%	17%	12%	-	11%	-	
Cingrani,Tony	-	94.2	87%	9%	4%	-	-	-	
Cishek,Steve	-	91.4	49%	50%	1%	-	-	-	
Claudio,Alex	-	85.5	56%	15%	27%	3%	-	-	
Clemens,Paul	-	91.7	65%	-	4%	-	31%	-	
Clevinger,Mike	Aug `12	93.4	59%	18%	17%	-	6%	-	
Clippard,Tyler	-	91.1	45%	-	33%	6%	3%	14%	
Cobb,Alex	May `15	90.4	48%	-	30%	-	23%	-	
Coke,Phil	-	92.6	54%	21%	21%	5%	-	-	
Cole,A.J.	-	91.0	57%	27%	7%	-	9%	-	
Cole,Gerrit	-	95.2	67%	18%	5%	-	10%	-	
Coleman,Louis	-	89.0	40%	58%	2%	-	-	-	
Collmenter,Josh	-	84.3	65%	-	26%	-	8%	-	
Colome,Alex	-	94.7	52%	47%	<1%	-	<1%	-	
Colon,Bartolo	-	87.9	89%	6%	5%	-	-	-	
Colon,Joseph	Jan `10	94.5	74%	14%	8%	-	4%	-	
Concepcion,Gerardo	-	91.4	73%	-	2%	-	24%	-	
Conley,Adam	-	91.0	65%	19%	16%	-	<1%	-	
Corbin,Patrick	Mar `14	91.7	63%	27%	10%	-	-	-	
Cosart,Jarred	-	92.3	71%	-	6%	-	24%	-	
Cotham,Caleb	-	92.3	58%	30%	-	-	12%	-	
Cotton,Jharel	-	92.2	47%	-	28%	17%	8%	-	
Coulombe,Daniel	Mar `11	90.0	33%	37%	-	-	30%	-	
Cravy,Tyler	-	91.3	63%	15%	15%	-	7%	-	
Crockett,Kyle	-	88.8	67%	28%	5%	-	-	-	
Cueto,Johnny	-	91.5	50%	8%	17%	22%	3%	-	
Cuevas,William	-	90.1	58%	-	22%	-	19%	-	
Cunniff,Brandon	-	92.6	60%	34%	6%	-	-	-	
Curtis,Zac	-	90.9	60%	35%	5%	-	-	-	
Danish,Tyler	-	91.8	81%	14%	5%	-	-	-	
Danks,John	-	87.1	49%	-	25%	16%	10%	-	
Darvish,Yu	Mar `15	93.3	59%	19%	2%	9%	10%	<1%	
Davies,Zach	-	89.3	56%	-	21%	13%	11%	-	
Davis,Wade	-	94.9	50%	-	<1%	31%	18%	-	
Dayton,Grant	-	92.2	78%	8%	<1%	-	15%	-	
De La Cruz,Joel	-	91.4	52%	23%	24%	-	-	-	
de la Rosa,Jorge	June `11	90.1	36%	-	34%	21%	10%	-	
de la Rosa,Rubby	Aug `11	94.6	62%	29%	8%	-	-	-	
De Leon,Jose	-	91.6	66%	11%	21%	-	1%	-	
De Los Santos,Abel	-	91.9	63%	5%	5%	-	28%	-	
Dean,Pat	-	89.5	56%	25%	11%	-	7%	-	
deGrom,Jacob	Jan `10	93.4	60%	18%	11%	-	11%	-	
Delabar,Steve	Jan `02	92.9	77%	7%	-	-	-	16%	
Delgado,Randall	-	92.0	58%	25%	17%	-	-	-	
Dermody,Matt	-	91.0	57%	42%	2%	-	-	-	
DeSclafani,Anthony	-	92.9	56%	28%	3%	-	13%	-	
Despaigne,Odrisamer	-	92.7	52%	-	7%	25%	16%	-	
Detwiler,Ross	-	91.8	67%	-	14%	-	19%	-	
Devenski,Chris	-	92.4	46%	10%	31%	-	13%	-	
Diamond,Scott	-	88.4	73%	-	12%	-	15%	-	
Diaz,Dayan	Jan `09	93.2	74%	22%	4%	-	-	-	
Diaz,Edwin	-	97.3	68%	32%	<1%	-	-	-	
Diaz,Jumbo	Jan `07	95.9	69%	25%	-	-	-	5%	
Dickey,R.A.	-	82.3	12%	-	4%	<1%	-	-	Knuckleball 84%
Diekman,Jake	-	95.1	74%	26%	<1%	-	-	-	
Dominguez,Jose	-	96.1	70%	20%	9%	-	-	-	
Doolittle,Sean	-	94.8	89%	7%	4%	-	-	-	

Player	Tommy John Surgery	Fastball Velocity	Fastball	Slider	Change	Cutter	Curve	Splitter	Other
Drabek,Kyle	June '12 July '07	88.7	77%	-	4%	15%	4%	-	
Drake,Oliver	-	90.3	54%	-	-	-	-	46%	
Duensing,Brian	Mar '04	91.9	55%	22%	13%	-	10%	-	
Duffey,Tyler	-	90.4	54%	-	7%	-	39%	-	
Duffy,Danny	June '12	94.8	59%	24%	17%	-	-	-	
Duke,Zach	-	89.7	58%	16%	6%	16%	5%	-	
Dull,Ryan	-	90.8	59%	34%	7%	-	-	-	
Dunn,Mike	-	93.6	63%	37%	-	-	<1%	-	
Dyson,Sam	Nov '10	95.3	70%	11%	19%	-	-	-	
Edgin,Josh	Mar '15	90.7	51%	27%	7%	16%	-	-	
Edwards Jr.,Carl	-	95.2	73%	-	<1%	-	26%	-	
Eflin,Zach	-	92.3	63%	25%	7%	-	4%	-	
Ege,Cody	-	86.8	54%	22%	24%	-	-	-	
Eickhoff,Jerad	-	91.0	53%	18%	5%	-	24%	-	
Elias,Roenis	-	92.6	58%	-	17%	-	26%	-	
Ellington,Brian	Sept '07	98.0	76%	-	7%	-	17%	-	
Eovaldi,Nathan	Aug '16 Jan '07	97.1	48%	18%	-	7%	4%	23%	
Erlin,Robbie	May '16	88.0	52%	-	30%	-	18%	-	
Esch,Jake	-	90.0	58%	31%	2%	-	9%	-	
Escobar,Eduardo	-	89.1	81%	-	-	-	19%	-	
Escobar,Edwin	-	91.8	78%	-	2%	-	20%	-	
Estevez,Carlos	-	97.3	71%	20%	9%	-	-	-	
Estrada,Marco	-	88.1	50%	-	29%	12%	10%	-	
Eveland,Dana	-	89.4	50%	47%	4%	-	-	-	
Familia,Jeurys	-	96.2	77%	20%	-	-	-	3%	
Farmer,Buck	-	92.9	60%	-	24%	7%	9%	-	
Farquhar,Danny	-	92.7	43%	-	33%	11%	13%	-	
Faulkner,Andrew	-	92.3	61%	26%	-	-	-	13%	
Feldman,Scott	Jan '03	90.3	33%	-	-	39%	25%	4%	
Feliz,Michael	-	94.9	63%	31%	5%	-	-	-	
Feliz,Neftali	Aug '12	96.1	70%	26%	4%	-	-	-	
Fernandez,Jose	May '14	95.2	54%	27%	13%	-	7%	-	
Fields,Josh	-	94.7	63%	8%	5%	-	24%	-	
Fien,Casey	-	93.2	53%	8%	-	39%	-	-	
Fiers,Mike	-	89.6	42%	7%	19%	14%	19%	-	
Finnegan,Brandon	-	91.7	66%	21%	13%	-	-	-	
Fister,Doug	-	87.0	66%	12%	7%	<1%	15%	-	
Flaherty,Ryan	-	82.1	95%	5%	-	-	-	-	
Flande,Yohan	-	90.1	48%	-	52%	-	-	-	
Flores,Kendry	-	91.2	75%	-	7%	14%	5%	-	
Floro,Dylan	-	92.5	74%	-	4%	21%	2%	-	
Floyd,Gavin	May '13	93.0	51%	-	1%	14%	34%	-	
Flynn,Brian	-	92.6	67%	28%	4%	-	2%	-	
Foltynewicz,Mike	-	95.2	63%	19%	8%	-	10%	-	
Freeman,Sam	Mar '10	94.1	66%	8%	26%	-	-	-	
Frias,Carlos	-	92.2	44%	-	6%	38%	12%	-	
Friedrich,Christian	-	89.2	53%	21%	6%	-	20%	-	
Fulmer,Carson	-	92.8	50%	-	14%	28%	8%	-	
Fulmer,Michael	-	94.8	57%	26%	17%	-	-	-	
Gallardo,Yovani	-	89.5	56%	27%	6%	-	12%	-	
Gamboa,Eddie	May '06	86.6	15%	9%	-	-	-	-	Knuckleball 77%
Gant,John	-	91.8	59%	-	23%	-	19%	-	
Garcia,Jaime	Sept '08	90.5	63%	-	19%	16%	2%	-	
Garcia,Luis	-	96.5	57%	41%	2%	-	-	-	
Garcia,Yimi	-	92.8	70%	23%	7%	-	-	-	
Garner,Perci	-	93.1	90%	10%	-	-	-	-	

Player	Tommy John Surgery	Fastball Velocity	Pitch Repertoire						
			Fastball	Slider	Change	Cutter	Curve	Splitter	Other
Garton,Ryan	-	92.5	49%	-	3%	28%	20%	-	
Garza,Matt	-	92.2	69%	18%	4%	-	9%	-	
Gausman,Kevin	-	94.7	66%	13%	4%	-	-	17%	
Gearrin,Cory	Apr `14	91.6	55%	40%	5%	-	-	-	
Gee,Dillon	-	89.5	46%	21%	17%	-	17%	-	
Geltz,Steve	-	92.4	70%	19%	11%	-	-	-	
Germen,Gonzalez	-	93.6	60%	7%	33%	-	-	-	
Gibson,Kyle	Sept `11	91.0	56%	21%	18%	-	5%	-	
Giles,Ken	-	97.2	52%	48%	-	-	-	-	
Gilmartin,Sean	-	87.8	51%	24%	18%	-	7%	-	
Gimenez,Chris	-	70.1	100%	-	-	-	-	-	
Giolito,Lucas	Aug `12	93.4	71%	-	11%	-	18%	-	
Girodo,Chad	-	86.4	65%	25%	10%	-	-	-	
Givens,Mychal	-	94.3	64%	30%	6%	-	-	-	
Glasnow,Tyler	-	93.5	62%	-	3%	-	35%	-	
Glover,Koda	Jan `11	96.6	45%	46%	<1%	-	8%	-	
Godley,Zack	-	90.8	29%	-	10%	35%	25%	-	
Goeddel,Erik	Jan `07	91.9	52%	1%	-	-	14%	33%	
Goforth,David	-	93.0	49%	49%	-	-	2%	-	
Goins,Ryan	-	85.8	55%	-	36%	-	9%	-	
Gomez,Jeanmar	-	91.5	62%	13%	25%	-	<1%	-	
Gonzalez,Chi Chi	-	91.5	62%	18%	10%	-	10%	-	
Gonzalez,Gio	-	90.8	64%	-	16%	-	20%	-	
Gonzalez,Miguel	Mar `09	91.5	47%	23%	-	-	10%	20%	
Gonzalez,Severino	-	93.4	59%	-	15%	-	26%	-	
Goody,Nick	Apr `13	90.9	52%	48%	-	-	-	-	
Gorzelanny,Tom	-	91.1	59%	28%	13%	-	-	-	
Gott,Trevor	-	94.3	72%	-	-	-	28%	-	
Grace,Matt	-	89.1	77%	23%	-	-	-	-	
Graham,J.R.	-	95.1	48%	43%	9%	-	-	-	
Graveman,Kendall	-	92.7	62%	7%	8%	22%	-	-	
Gray,Jon	-	95.1	55%	27%	7%	-	11%	-	
Gray,Sonny	-	92.7	62%	12%	8%	2%	16%	-	
Green,Chad	-	94.3	53%	29%	2%	15%	-	-	
Greene,Shane	May `08	94.0	41%	21%	<1%	37%	-	-	
Gregerson,Luke	-	89.2	53%	45%	1%	-	-	-	
Greinke,Zack	-	91.3	48%	21%	21%	-	10%	-	
Griffin,A.J.	Apr `14	87.7	54%	18%	9%	-	19%	-	
Grilli,Jason	Jan `02	92.4	62%	36%	2%	-	-	-	
Grimm,Justin	-	94.2	49%	-	-	-	51%	-	
Gsellman,Robert	-	93.7	64%	20%	6%	-	11%	-	
Guaipe,Mayckol	-	92.3	65%	25%	5%	-	5%	-	
Guerra,Deolis	-	90.4	44%	-	45%	3%	8%	-	
Guerra,Javy	Jan `05	92.4	55%	35%	2%	-	8%	-	
Guerra,Junior	-	93.1	62%	15%	-	-	-	23%	
Guerrero,Tayron	-	95.2	86%	14%	-	-	-	-	
Gurka,Jason	-	90.3	60%	-	16%	-	24%	-	
Gustave,Jandel	-	97.1	66%	34%	-	-	-	-	
Hahn,Jesse	Jan `10	93.9	72%	-	8%	-	20%	-	
Hale,David	-	89.6	64%	32%	4%	-	-	-	
Hall,Cody	-	93.0	61%	23%	-	-	-	16%	
Hamels,Cole	-	92.6	44%	-	19%	23%	15%	-	
Hammel,Jason	-	92.1	52%	35%	3%	-	10%	-	
Hand,Brad	-	92.8	61%	30%	1%	-	7%	-	
Happ,J.A.	-	91.6	74%	13%	6%	-	7%	-	
Hardy,Blaine	-	88.4	50%	9%	22%	-	18%	-	
Harrell,Lucas	-	91.5	59%	-	7%	19%	14%	-	
Harris,Will	Jan `09	92.4	66%	-	-	-	34%	-	

Player	Tommy John Surgery	Fastball Velocity	Fastball	Slider	Change	Cutter	Curve	Splitter	Other
Hart,Donnie	-	87.7	46%	40%	14%	-	-	-	
Harvey,Matt	Oct '13	94.5	60%	19%	11%	-	10%	-	
Hatcher,Chris	-	95.7	59%	19%	15%	7%	-	-	
Hathaway,Steve	-	92.6	62%	-	6%	-	32%	-	
Hayes,Drew	-	91.3	70%	20%	9%	-	-	-	
Heaney,Andrew	July '16	90.8	59%	17%	24%	-	-	-	
Heller,Ben	-	95.5	55%	35%	10%	-	-	-	
Hellickson,Jeremy	-	90.1	49%	-	26%	9%	15%	-	
Hembree,Heath	-	93.9	61%	28%	<1%	-	11%	-	
Henderson,Jim	-	93.3	82%	17%	<1%	-	-	-	
Hendricks,Kyle	-	87.8	65%	-	27%	-	8%	-	
Hendriks,Liam	-	94.1	76%	18%	1%	-	5%	-	
Hernandez,David	Apr '14	94.0	64%	-	1%	-	35%	-	
Hernandez,Felix	-	90.5	46%	6%	28%	-	19%	-	
Hernandez,Roberto	-	89.9	54%	18%	28%	-	-	-	
Herrera,Kelvin	-	97.1	60%	16%	19%	-	5%	-	
Herrmann,Frank	Mar '13	93.4	64%	19%	-	-	17%	-	
Hessler,Keith	June '07	91.6	69%	31%	<1%	-	-	-	
Heston,Chris	-	87.3	52%	19%	9%	-	19%	-	
Hill,Rich	June '11	90.2	47%	9%	2%	-	42%	-	
Hinojosa,Dalier	-	92.9	59%	28%	13%	-	-	-	
Hochevar,Luke	Mar '14	94.4	33%	-	-	47%	20%	-	
Hoffman,Jeff	May '14	94.0	59%	10%	15%	-	16%	-	
Holaday,Bryan	-	76.4	67%	-	-	-	-	-	Knuckleball 33%
Holder,Jonathan	-	93.0	43%	-	1%	33%	22%	-	
Holland,Derek	-	91.7	61%	14%	10%	-	14%	-	
Holt,Tyler	-	66.7	60%	-	-	-	-	-	Knuckleball 40%
Hoover,J.J.	-	91.6	65%	17%	4%	-	14%	-	
House,T.J.	-	90.2	74%	23%	4%	-	-	-	
Howell,J.P.	-	85.3	52%	-	1%	-	47%	-	
Hoying,Jared	-	60.9	100%	-	-	-	-	-	
Hoyt,James	-	93.5	38%	54%	-	-	-	8%	
Hudson,Daniel	June '13 July '12	95.7	63%	19%	18%	-	-	-	
Huff,David	-	90.7	56%	-	21%	12%	10%	-	
Hughes,Jared	-	93.0	82%	12%	6%	-	-	-	
Hughes,Phil	-	90.5	49%	-	3%	26%	23%	-	
Hunter,Tommy	-	94.5	63%	-	-	18%	19%	-	
Hursh,Jason	Aug '11	93.6	80%	10%	10%	-	-	-	
Hutchison,Drew	Aug '12	92.0	63%	28%	9%	-	-	-	
Iglesias,Raisel	-	93.0	55%	33%	11%	-	-	-	
Iwakuma,Hisashi	-	87.8	46%	18%	-	9%	9%	18%	
Jackson,Edwin	-	91.9	46%	28%	2%	17%	7%	-	
Jackson,Luke	-	94.1	60%	18%	7%	-	15%	-	
Jansen,Kenley	-	93.6	94%	6%	-	-	-	-	
Jeffress,Jeremy	-	95.1	76%	-	3%	-	20%	-	
Jenkins,Tyrell	-	91.2	65%	-	16%	-	19%	-	
Jennings,Dan	-	90.8	62%	38%	<1%	-	-	-	
Jepsen,Kevin	-	93.6	66%	-	7%	-	27%	-	
Jimenez,Ubaldo	-	89.9	57%	16%	4%	-	7%	16%	
Johnson,Erik	-	89.7	61%	21%	8%	-	10%	-	
Johnson,Jim	-	93.3	69%	-	6%	-	25%	-	
Johnson,Steve	-	89.0	83%	4%	2%	-	11%	-	
Jones,Nate	July '14	96.8	63%	36%	<1%	-	<1%	-	
Jungmann,Taylor	-	89.5	65%	-	4%	-	31%	-	
Kahnle,Tommy	-	96.5	74%	10%	16%	-	-	-	
Karns,Nathan	-	93.0	53%	-	11%	-	36%	-	
Kazmir,Scott	-	91.4	55%	9%	20%	9%	7%	-	

Player	Tommy John Surgery	Fastball Velocity	Fastball	Slider	Change	Cutter	Curve	Splitter	Other
Kela,Keone	-	95.7	62%	-	2%	-	36%	-	
Kelley,Shawn	Sept `10 Jan `03	92.4	56%	44%	-	-	-	-	
Kelly,Casey	Apr `13	90.0	68%	<1%	9%	-	22%	-	
Kelly,Joe	-	96.3	66%	15%	6%	-	13%	-	
Kennedy,Ian	-	92.2	66%	-	12%	8%	14%	-	
Kensing,Logan	Aug `06	90.4	68%	31%	1%	-	-	-	
Kershaw,Clayton	-	93.1	51%	33%	<1%	-	16%	-	
Keuchel,Dallas	-	88.6	50%	26%	9%	14%	-	-	
Kiekhefer,Dean	-	87.3	60%	22%	17%	-	-	-	
Kimbrel,Craig	-	97.3	69%	-	<1%	-	31%	-	
Kintzler,Brandon	-	92.7	88%	7%	5%	-	-	-	
Kirkman,Michael	-	90.8	68%	28%	-	-	-	5%	
Klein,Phil	-	91.8	60%	29%	6%	-	5%	-	
Kluber,Corey	-	92.5	52%	-	5%	24%	20%	-	
Knebel,Corey	-	95.2	72%	-	<1%	-	28%	-	
Koch,Matt	-	92.0	50%	-	5%	39%	6%	-	
Koehler,Tom	-	91.9	47%	24%	7%	-	23%	-	
Kontos,George	July `09	91.0	36%	16%	3%	45%	1%	-	
Kratz,Erik	-	82.9	84%	-	-	-	-	-	Knuckleball 16%
Krol,Ian	-	93.9	65%	-	2%	30%	3%	-	
Kuhl,Chad	-	93.2	61%	29%	9%	-	-	-	
Lackey,John	Nov `11	91.7	58%	24%	5%	-	12%	-	
Ladendorf,Tyler	-	80.5	100%	-	-	-	-	-	
LaMarre,Ryan	-	76.6	100%	-	-	-	-	-	
Lamb,John	June `11	89.4	53%	-	17%	17%	13%	-	
Latos,Mat	-	90.2	58%	20%	4%	<1%	5%	12%	
Law,Derek	June `14	92.9	52%	23%	5%	-	19%	-	
Layne,Tommy	-	90.0	43%	17%	5%	26%	8%	-	
Leake,Mike	-	90.6	48%	9%	8%	29%	6%	-	
LeBlanc,Wade	-	86.9	34%	-	30%	29%	7%		
Leclerc,Jose	-	94.3	61%	-	31%	-	7%	-	
Leon,Arnold	May `10	91.7	59%	22%	7%	-	13%	-	
Leone,Dominic	-	93.1	53%	18%	-	29%	-	-	
Lester,Jon	-	92.1	59%	-	6%	23%	13%	-	
Lewis,Colby	Jan `97	87.3	53%	32%	7%	-	8%	-	
Liberatore,Adam	Jan `09	91.7	67%	17%	16%	-	-	-	
Light,Pat	-	94.6	56%	6%	-	-	-	38%	
Lincecum,Tim	-	87.7	43%	19%	29%	-	9%	-	
Liriano,Francisco	Nov `06	92.8	51%	30%	19%	-	-	-	
Lobstein,Kyle	-	87.5	66%	-	8%	19%	7%	-	
Locke,Jeff	-	91.5	66%	7%	26%	-	1%	-	
Loewen,Adam	-	90.9	71%	25%	5%	-	-	-	
Logan,Boone	-	93.1	47%	53%	<1%	-	-	-	
Lohse,Kyle	-	87.0	62%	21%	12%	-	5%	-	
Lopez,Javier	-	84.2	71%	5%	3%	21%	-	-	
Lopez,Reynaldo	-	95.8	64%	-	10%	-	25%	-	
Lorenzen,Michael	-	96.2	48%	11%	2%	34%	5%	-	
Loup,Aaron	-	91.1	67%	19%	15%	-	-	-	
Lowe,Mark	-	92.4	57%	41%	2%	-	-	-	
Luebke,Cory	Feb `14 May `12	91.8	63%	33%	3%	-	1%	-	
Lugo,Seth	-	92.1	57%	18%	7%	-	17%	-	
Lyles,Jordan	-	92.9	59%	23%	8%	-	9%	-	
Lyons,Tyler	-	90.6	45%	38%	16%	-	<1%	-	
Madson,Ryan	Apr `12	94.2	65%	-	22%	8%	5%	-	
Maeda,Kenta	-	90.0	43%	29%	10%	-	18%	-	
Magill,Matt	May `15	92.8	68%	15%	5%	-	12%	-	

Player	Tommy John Surgery	Fastball Velocity	Pitch Repertoire						
			Fastball	Slider	Change	Cutter	Curve	Splitter	Other
Magnifico,Damien	-	96.7	74%	26%	-	-	-	-	
Mahle,Greg	-	87.1	56%	28%	16%	-	-	-	
Manaea,Sean	-	92.3	58%	14%	28%	-	-	-	
Maness,Seth	-	87.9	70%	5%	25%	-	-	-	
Manship,Jeff	Jan `04	91.0	51%	44%	<1%	-	5%	-	
Mantiply,Joe	-	87.5	68%	18%	13%	-	-	-	
Marinez,Jhan	-	94.7	75%	24%	<1%	-	-	-	
Mariot,Michael	-	92.9	55%	40%	1%	-	5%	-	
Marks,Justin	-	89.6	50%	22%	21%	-	7%	-	
Marksberry,Matt	Jan `09	92.0	57%	-	1%	-	42%	-	
Marquez,German	-	93.3	62%	-	9%	-	28%	-	
Marshall,Evan	-	93.2	69%	-	11%	-	19%	-	
Marte,Kelvin	-	91.6	60%	14%	26%	-	-	-	
Martin,Cody	-	88.3	46%	23%	7%	-	24%	-	
Martin,Rafael	-	87.2	75%	25%	-	-	-	-	
Martinez,Carlos	-	95.6	58%	19%	18%	-	4%	-	
Martinez,Nick	-	91.8	61%	22%	9%	-	8%	-	
Matusz,Brian	-	89.5	51%	25%	15%	-	9%	-	
Matz,Steven	May `10	93.6	61%	10%	12%	-	16%	-	
Maurer,Brandon	-	95.3	55%	32%	13%	-	-	-	
May,Trevor	-	93.9	61%	9%	11%	-	19%	-	
Mayers,Mike	-	93.1	66%	19%	14%	-	-	-	
Mazzaro,Vin	-	92.3	69%	24%	7%	-	-	-	
McAllister,Zach	-	94.2	79%	5%	-	-	15%	<1%	
McCarthy,Brandon	Apr `15	92.2	60%	-	<1%	10%	29%	-	
McCarthy,Kevin	-	93.7	62%	31%	8%	-	-	-	
McCullers,Lance	-	93.8	43%	-	7%	-	49%	-	
McFarland,T.J.	-	91.8	69%	18%	14%	-	-	-	
McGee,Jake	July `08	93.1	84%	7%	-	-	9%	-	
McGowan,Dustin	May `04	94.8	64%	31%	6%	-	-	-	
McHugh,Collin	-	90.2	36%	-	5%	29%	30%	-	
Medlen,Kris	Mar `14 Aug `10	90.7	54%	-	16%	17%	13%	-	
Mejia,Adalberto	-	90.3	45%	21%	24%	-	10%	-	
Melancon,Mark	Oct `06	91.8	11%	-	<1%	63%	26%	-	
Melville,Tim	Oct `12	91.3	57%	23%	3%	-	17%	-	
Mendez,Yohander	-	91.4	48%	12%	30%	-	10%	-	
Mengden,Daniel	-	92.1	56%	-	15%	17%	12%	-	
Merritt,Ryan	-	87.4	51%	-	25%	17%	7%	-	
Meyer,Alex	-	95.2	58%	-	10%	-	31%	-	
Miley,Wade	-	90.3	51%	19%	18%	-	12%	-	
Miller,Andrew	-	94.5	39%	61%	-	-	-	-	
Miller,Justin	-	93.1	67%	33%	<1%	-	-	-	
Miller,Shelby	-	93.0	63%	-	6%	20%	12%	-	
Mills,Alec	July `13	91.9	71%	-	12%	-	17%	-	
Milone,Tommy	-	87.6	39%	<1%	34%	16%	11%	-	
Minaya,Juan	-	94.2	66%	17%	-	-	17%	-	
Miranda,Ariel	-	92.6	58%	4%	22%	-	-	16%	
Mitchell,Bryan	-	94.8	52%	-	3%	23%	21%	-	
Molleken,Dustin	Jan `04	93.7	72%	28%	-	-	-	-	
Montero,Miguel	-	81.1	97%	-	-	-	3%	-	
Montero,Rafael	-	92.6	56%	21%	23%	-	-	-	
Montgomery,Mike	-	93.6	54%	-	10%	12%	24%	-	
Moore,Matt	Apr `14	92.8	60%	-	13%	4%	22%	-	
Morales,Franklin	-	88.3	42%	25%	10%	-	22%	-	
Morgan,Adam	-	90.7	49%	26%	19%	-	6%	-	
Morimando,Shawn	-	90.5	59%	8%	23%	-	10%	-	
Morin,Mike	-	91.3	40%	25%	35%	-	-	-	

Player	Tommy John Surgery	Fastball Velocity	Fastball	Slider	Change	Cutter	Curve	Splitter	Other
Morris,A.J.	Jan `11	88.3	81%	19%	-	-	-	-	
Morris,Bryan	Sept `06	93.1	60%	10%	2%	28%	-	-	
Morrow,Brandon	-	94.2	48%	18%	10%	24%	-	-	
Morton,Charlie	June `12	94.3	51%	-	13%	11%	26%	-	
Moscot,Jon	July `16	90.7	51%	26%	12%	-	11%	-	
Motte,Jason	May `13	93.5	60%	3%	5%	32%	-	-	
Motter,Taylor	-	76.7	100%	-	-	-	-	-	
Moylan,Peter	Apr `14 May `08	90.1	57%	38%	2%	3%	-	-	
Mullee,Conor	June `11	91.8	57%	28%	15%	-	-	-	
Murray,Colton	-	93.5	68%	6%	2%	-	24%	-	
Musgrove,Joe	-	91.7	45%	34%	9%	4%	8%	-	
Narveson,Chris	Oct `01	88.9	35%	28%	29%	-	9%	-	
Nathan,Joe	Apr `15 Mar `10	91.2	58%	31%	2%	-	8%	-	
Neal,Zach	-	89.8	61%	22%	14%	-	2%	-	
Nelson,Jimmy	-	93.1	71%	16%	1%	-	12%	-	
Neris,Hector	-	94.1	45%	3%	-	-	-	52%	
Neshek,Pat	Nov `08	89.2	39%	54%	7%	-	-	-	
Nicasio,Juan	-	93.6	69%	28%	3%	-	-	-	
Nicolino,Justin	-	89.2	52%	-	18%	18%	12%	-	
Niese,Jon	-	89.1	56%	-	10%	25%	9%	-	
Nola,Aaron	-	90.1	58%	-	9%	-	34%	-	
Nolasco,Ricky	-	90.4	48%	33%	-	-	11%	8%	
Norris,Bud	-	93.5	56%	29%	3%	12%	-	-	
Norris,Daniel	-	93.1	62%	16%	14%	-	8%	-	
Nova,Ivan	Apr `14	92.6	65%	-	4%	3%	28%	-	
Nuno,Vidal	-	89.5	32%	33%	19%	7%	9%	-	
O'Day,Darren	-	86.2	55%	45%	-	-	-	-	
O'Flaherty,Eric	May `13	90.6	72%	27%	1%	-	-	-	
O'Rourke,Ryan	-	89.7	46%	32%	19%	-	3%	-	
O'Sullivan,Sean	-	90.1	57%	28%	3%	<1%	11%	-	
Oberg,Scott	Jan `11	94.5	60%	25%	5%	-	10%	-	
Oberholtzer,Brett	-	89.1	58%	-	26%	-	15%	-	
Odorizzi,Jake	-	91.6	60%	11%	20%	6%	4%	-	
Ogando,Alexi	-	94.0	69%	28%	2%	-	-	-	
Ogando,Nefi	-	95.0	70%	29%	1%	-	-	-	
Oh,Seung Hwan	Jan `01	92.8	61%	31%	-	-	<1%	7%	
Ohlendorf,Ross	-	93.9	57%	21%	22%	-	-	-	
Okert,Steven	-	92.2	47%	14%	4%	36%	-	-	
Olson,Tyler	-	87.9	70%	-	2%	-	28%	-	
Ondrusek,Logan	-	92.9	54%	-	-	28%	9%	10%	
Osich,Josh	Jan `10	95.5	66%	-	9%	22%	2%	-	
Osuna,Roberto	July `13	95.8	67%	22%	7%	4%	-	-	
Otero,Dan	Jan `09	90.3	78%	9%	11%	-	2%	-	
Ottavino,Adam	May `15	93.8	55%	45%	-	-	-	-	
Overton,Dillon	July `13	88.3	49%	-	34%	6%	10%	-	
Owens,Henry	-	88.7	55%	3%	31%	-	11%	-	
Papelbon,Jonathan	-	90.9	66%	20%	-	-	-	15%	
Parker,Blake	-	92.2	57%	-	-	-	24%	19%	
Parnell,Bobby	Apr `14	94.0	69%	-	-	-	31%	-	
Partch,Curtis	-	95.3	54%	38%	8%	-	-	-	
Patton,Spencer	-	92.3	64%	27%	9%	-	-	-	
Paulino,David	July `13	92.1	52%	5%	10%	-	34%	-	
Paxton,James	-	96.8	62%	-	8%	16%	14%	-	
Pazos,James	-	95.4	66%	34%	-	-	-	-	
Peacock,Brad	-	91.8	53%	30%	7%	-	10%	-	
Peavy,Jake	-	88.9	45%	10%	9%	31%	5%	-	

428

Player	Tommy John Surgery	Fastball Velocity	Pitch Repertoire						
			Fastball	Slider	Change	Cutter	Curve	Splitter	Other
Pelfrey,Mike	May `12	92.8	70%	10%	-	-	5%	16%	
Pena,Ariel	-	91.7	67%	28%	5%	-	-	-	
Pena,Felix	-	93.5	60%	40%	<1%	-	-	-	
Peralta,Joel	-	89.8	53%	-	-	-	18%	30%	
Peralta,Wandy	-	95.2	62%	6%	32%	-	-	-	
Peralta,Wily	Jan `07	94.8	63%	31%	5%	-	1%	-	
Perdomo,Luis	-	93.6	67%	24%	10%	-	-	-	
Perez,Martin	May `14	92.7	62%	11%	17%	-	11%	-	
Perez,Oliver	-	91.7	57%	43%	-	-	-	-	
Perez,Williams	-	91.2	74%	-	10%	-	16%	-	
Perkins,Glen	-	91.3	58%	42%	-	-	-	-	
Petit,Yusmeiro	-	88.6	50%	21%	14%	-	16%	-	
Petricka,Jake	-	94.2	75%	12%	13%	-	-	-	
Phegley,Josh	-	85.3	80%	20%	-	-	-	-	
Phelps,David	-	93.5	64%	-	2%	22%	11%	-	
Phillips,Zach	-	90.1	47%	29%	24%	-	-	-	
Pinder,Branden	Apr `16	95.1	50%	50%	-	-	-	-	
Pineda,Michael	-	94.1	51%	41%	7%	-	-	-	
Plutko,Adam	-	90.9	63%	18%	6%	-	13%	-	
Pomeranz,Drew	-	90.3	48%	-	<1%	13%	39%	-	
Porcello,Rick	-	90.2	62%	12%	12%	-	14%	-	
Pounders,Brooks	Sept `13	92.6	49%	43%	6%	-	2%	-	
Pressly,Ryan	-	95.1	54%	24%	-	-	21%	-	
Price,David	-	92.9	49%	-	23%	20%	9%	-	
Purke,Matt	May `14	92.4	72%	14%	14%	-	-	-	
Putnam,Zach	-	90.6	31%	-	-	<1%	-	68%	
Quackenbush,Kevin	-	90.5	63%	5%	-	-	32%	<1%	
Qualls,Chad	-	90.2	61%	36%	-	-	-	3%	
Quintana,Jose	-	92.1	67%	-	8%	<1%	25%	-	
Ramirez,Erasmo	-	91.3	64%	15%	20%	-	<1%	-	
Ramirez,JC	-	96.4	73%	26%	-	-	-	1%	
Ramirez,Jose	-	95.3	64%	27%	8%	-	-	-	
Ramirez,Neil	-	92.0	59%	38%	<1%	-	3%	-	
Ramirez,Noe	-	89.7	48%	23%	30%	-	-	-	
Ramos,A.J.	Apr `08	91.9	38%	33%	18%	4%	6%	-	
Ramos,Cesar	-	88.2	43%	21%	21%	-	15%	-	
Ramos,Edubray	-	95.2	54%	45%	1%	-	-	-	
Ranaudo,Anthony	-	91.1	57%	10%	7%	-	27%	-	
Rasmus,Cory	-	91.8	45%	22%	20%	-	13%	-	
Ravin,Josh	-	96.7	71%	29%	-	-	-	-	
Ray,Robbie	-	94.1	71%	18%	6%	-	5%	-	
Rea,Colin	-	91.9	60%	-	-	17%	17%	5%	
Reed,Addison	-	92.4	72%	28%	<1%	-	-	-	
Reed,Cody	-	92.8	53%	36%	12%	-	-	-	
Reyes,Alex	-	96.5	64%	5%	24%	-	8%	-	
Reyes,Jo-Jo	Jan `04	89.1	33%	6%	-	61%	-	-	
Reynolds,Matt	Sept `13	87.6	55%	23%	10%	-	-	11%	
Richard,Clayton	-	90.8	74%	13%	13%	<1%	-	-	
Richards,Garrett	-	95.6	62%	25%	9%	-	4%	-	
Rivero,Felipe	-	95.8	62%	16%	21%	-	1%	-	
Roach,Donn	-	92.6	70%	-	-	-	17%	13%	
Roark,Tanner	-	92.1	62%	15%	10%	-	13%	-	
Robertson,David	-	91.8	68%	-	2%	-	30%	-	
Robles,Hansel	-	95.2	64%	24%	12%	-	-	-	
Rodgers,Brady	-	89.9	47%	28%	8%	7%	10%	-	
Rodney,Fernando	Apr `04	94.4	58%	-	42%	-	-	-	
Rodon,Carlos	-	93.4	64%	26%	10%	-	-	-	
Rodriguez,Eduardo	-	93.5	66%	16%	16%	2%	-	-	

Player	Tommy John Surgery	Fastball Velocity	Pitch Repertoire						
			Fastball	Slider	Change	Cutter	Curve	Splitter	Other
Rodriguez,Fernando	Mar '13	92.9	70%	-	<1%	23%	7%	-	
Rodriguez,Francisco	-	89.2	47%	-	42%	-	11%	-	
Rodriguez,Joely	-	95.0	52%	48%	-	-	-	-	
Roe,Chaz	-	92.6	44%	55%	-	<1%	-	-	
Rogers,Taylor	-	92.6	55%	-	2%	-	43%	-	
Rollins,David	-	91.0	68%	21%	11%	-	-	-	
Romero,Enny	-	96.1	60%	11%	-	28%	-	-	
Romine,Andrew	-	85.2	82%	-	-	-	-	-	Knuckleball 18%
Romo,Sergio	-	85.8	32%	64%	5%	-	-	-	
Rondon,Bruce	Mar '14	97.2	60%	37%	3%	-	-	-	
Rondon,Hector	Aug '10	96.0	64%	34%	3%	-	-	-	
Rondon,Jorge	-	96.7	59%	41%	-	-	-	-	
Rosenthal,Trevor	-	97.1	78%	-	14%	8%	<1%	-	
Ross Jr.,Robbie	-	93.6	52%	28%	-	-	20%	-	
Ross,Joe	-	92.7	52%	39%	9%	-	-	-	
Ross,Tyson	-	92.5	54%	40%	-	5%	-	-	
Roth,Michael	-	90.1	56%	20%	18%	-	6%	-	
Rowen,Ben	-	80.0	68%	32%	-	-	-	-	
Rusin,Chris	-	89.6	44%	4%	18%	28%	7%	-	
Russell,James	-	89.6	47%	32%	10%	2%	9%	-	
Ryan,Kyle	-	89.3	62%	-	9%	21%	9%	-	
Ryu,Hyun-Jin	Jan '04	89.8	56%	12%	19%	-	13%	-	
Rzepczynski,Marc	-	91.3	59%	25%	16%	-	-	-	
Sabathia,CC	-	90.0	34%	25%	11%	29%	-	-	
Salas,Fernando	-	91.1	58%	22%	20%	-	-	-	
Salazar,Danny	Aug '10	94.7	68%	8%	19%	-	5%	-	
Sale,Chris	-	92.8	59%	25%	16%	-	-	-	
Samardzija,Jeff	-	94.3	47%	15%	-	21%	7%	10%	
Sampson,Adrian	July '09	91.1	68%	25%	7%	-	-	-	
Sampson,Keyvius	-	93.1	58%	19%	11%	-	12%	-	
Sanchez,Aaron	-	94.7	74%	-	9%	<1%	16%	-	
Sanchez,Anibal	Jan '03	91.1	57%	14%	17%	3%	9%	-	
Santana,Ervin	-	92.7	53%	37%	10%	-	-	-	
Santiago,Hector	-	91.4	63%	5%	22%	3%	6%	-	
Sardinas,Luis	-	80.2	75%	-	-	-	25%	-	
Saupold,Warwick	-	92.1	56%	-	7%	24%	14%	-	
Scahill,Rob	-	93.2	75%	18%	<1%	-	7%	-	
Scheppers,Tanner	-	94.9	77%	17%	<1%	-	5%	-	
Scherzer,Max	-	94.3	55%	22%	12%	2%	8%	-	
Schugel,A.J.	-	92.3	61%	-	34%	-	5%	-	
Schultz,Bo	-	96.1	70%	10%	2%	18%	-	-	
Schuster,Patrick	-	87.7	45%	43%	12%	-	-	-	
Scott,Robby	-	87.0	44%	-	21%	-	35%	-	
Scribner,Evan	-	90.2	55%	10%	-	-	35%	-	
Severino,Luis	-	96.1	56%	34%	10%	-	-	-	
Shaw,Bryan	-	-	-	18%	-	81%	-	<1%	
Shields,James	-	90.4	44%	1%	20%	19%	16%	-	
Shipley,Braden	-	91.2	56%	-	19%	-	25%	-	
Shoemaker,Matt	-	91.5	49%	13%	-	-	1%	36%	
Shreve,Chasen	-	91.6	50%	19%	-	-	-	31%	
Shuck,J.B.	-	89.3	92%	-	-	-	8%	-	
Siegrist,Kevin	-	93.3	68%	-	22%	-	11%	-	
Simmons,Shae	Feb '15	95.9	62%	-	-	-	31%	7%	
Simon,Alfredo	May '09	92.4	49%	-	-	18%	11%	22%	
Sipp,Tony	July '07	90.8	48%	33%	18%	-	-	-	
Skaggs,Tyler	Aug '14	92.8	59%	-	14%	-	27%	-	
Smith,Blake	-	92.8	71%	-	-	7%	22%	-	
Smith,Carson	May '16	92.0	56%	35%	8%	-	-	-	

430

Player	Tommy John Surgery	Fastball Velocity	Fastball	Slider	Change	Cutter	Curve	Splitter	Other
Smith,Chris	-	87.6	49%	26%	25%	-	-	-	
Smith,Jake	-	91.9	55%	2%	11%	32%	-	-	
Smith,Joe	-	88.3	62%	33%	5%	-	-	-	
Smith,Josh	Jan `07	90.7	39%	37%	2%	-	22%	-	
Smith,Will	-	91.9	50%	37%	-	-	13%	-	
Smoker,Josh	-	95.4	65%	23%	-	-	-	12%	
Smyly,Drew	-	90.2	57%	-	6%	14%	23%	-	
Snell,Blake	-	93.5	57%	12%	18%	-	13%	-	
Socolovich,Miguel	Jan `05	90.0	51%	22%	26%	-	-	-	
Solis,Sammy	Mar `12	93.6	64%	-	8%	-	27%	-	
Somsen,Layne	May `10	88.6	66%	-	2%	-	33%	-	
Soria,Joakim	Apr `12 Jan `03	92.7	62%	8%	19%	-	12%	-	
Stephenson,Robert	-	93.2	64%	-	20%	-	16%	-	
Stewart,Brock	-	93.2	64%	18%	18%	-	-	-	
Storen,Drew	-	91.8	47%	37%	16%	-	-	-	
Strahm,Matt	July `13	93.8	78%	2%	8%	-	11%	-	
Straily,Dan	-	89.3	51%	26%	18%	-	5%	-	
Strasburg,Stephen	Sept `10	94.9	57%	17%	13%	-	13%	-	
Stratton,Chris	-	91.3	62%	18%	9%	-	11%	-	
Street,Huston	-	88.2	47%	34%	19%	-	-	-	
Strickland,Hunter	May `13	96.8	73%	24%	3%	-	-	-	
Stripling,Ross	Apr `14	90.5	46%	22%	10%	-	22%	-	
Stroman,Marcus	-	92.4	58%	15%	5%	12%	10%	-	
Strop,Pedro	-	94.9	42%	52%	-	-	-	6%	
Stumpf,Daniel	-	91.9	38%	32%	30%	-	-	-	
Sturdevant,Tyler	Jan `07	91.4	43%	-	6%	39%	12%	-	
Suarez,Albert	Jan `09	92.0	58%	17%	12%	-	14%	-	
Surkamp,Eric	July `12	88.8	53%	-	8%	20%	19%	-	
Suter,Brent	-	83.8	68%	14%	10%	-	8%	-	
Swarzak,Anthony	-	93.4	48%	52%	-	-	-	-	
Syndergaard,Noah	-	98.0	59%	21%	11%	-	9%	-	
Taillon,Jameson	Apr `14	94.3	63%	-	11%	-	26%	-	
Tanaka,Masahiro	-	90.6	32%	26%	-	8%	5%	29%	
Tazawa,Junichi	Apr `10	92.8	51%	10%	-	-	15%	24%	
Teheran,Julio	-	90.9	56%	26%	8%	-	9%	-	
Tejada,Ruben	-	86.7	79%	-	-	-	21%	-	
Tepera,Ryan	-	95.2	54%	3%	-	42%	-	-	
Tepesch,Nick	-	87.1	50%	-	-	30%	20%	-	
Thompson,Jake	-	91.3	50%	21%	16%	11%	2%	-	
Thornburg,Tyler	-	94.1	66%	-	9%	-	25%	-	
Thornton,Matt	June `02	91.4	74%	5%	21%	-	-	-	
Tillman,Chris	-	91.7	57%	-	15%	16%	12%	-	
Tolleson,Shawn	Mar `06	93.0	61%	22%	11%	5%	-	-	
Tolliver,Ashur	-	92.9	70%	-	30%	-	-	-	
Tomlin,Josh	Aug `12	87.7	38%	-	8%	40%	15%	-	
Tonkin,Michael	-	93.9	71%	29%	<1%	-	-	-	
Torres,Carlos	-	92.1	17%	-	-	70%	14%	-	
Torres,Jose	-	94.6	95%	3%	2%	-	-	-	
Treinen,Blake	-	95.4	69%	30%	<1%	-	-	-	
Triggs,Andrew	Jan `07	90.5	56%	20%	2%	23%	-	-	
Tropeano,Nick	Aug `16	90.9	50%	-	19%	-	26%	6%	
Tsao,Chin-hui	Jan `01	94.0	56%	-	-	42%	3%	-	
Tuivailala,Samuel	-	95.8	65%	26%	-	-	9%	-	
Turner,Jacob	-	94.8	66%	8%	9%	-	18%	-	
Uehara,Koji	-	86.7	50%	-	-	5%	-	45%	
Urena,Jose	-	94.9	66%	16%	17%	-	1%	-	
Urias,Julio	-	92.6	56%	15%	13%	-	16%	-	

Player	Tommy John Surgery	Fastball Velocity	Fastball	Slider	Change	Cutter	Curve	Splitter	Other
Valdez,Jose	-	95.3	60%	40%	-	-	-	-	
Vargas,Cesar	-	89.4	67%	24%	3%	-	6%	-	
Vargas,Jason	Aug `15	86.3	52%	-	33%	-	14%	-	
Velasquez,Vince	Sept `10	93.7	64%	13%	13%	-	10%	-	
Venditte,Pat	-	84.1	52%	46%	2%	-	-	-	
Ventura,Yordano	-	96.1	57%	-	18%	-	25%	-	
VerHagen,Drew	June `08	94.4	63%	-	-	1%	31%	5%	
Verlander,Justin	-	93.5	57%	18%	8%	-	16%	-	
Verrett,Logan	-	90.2	56%	25%	12%	-	8%	-	
Villanueva,Carlos	-	88.1	46%	28%	13%	-	13%	-	
Vincent,Nick	-	89.9	45%	-	5%	50%	<1%	-	
Vizcaino,Arodys	Mar `12	97.4	62%	-	1%	-	37%	-	
Vogelsong,Ryan	Jan `02	90.1	49%	-	13%	23%	16%	-	
Volquez,Edinson	Aug `09	93.2	53%	-	22%	-	25%	-	
Wacha,Michael	-	93.2	53%	-	22%	16%	9%	-	
Wagner,Tyler	-	89.9	30%	14%	20%	36%	-	-	
Wainwright,Adam	Feb `11	90.3	42%	-	2%	29%	27%		
Walker,Taijuan	-	93.9	61%	-	19%	8%	11%	-	
Wang,Chien-Ming	-	91.6	84%	10%	5%	-	1%	-	
Warren,Adam	-	92.8	44%	31%	15%	-	11%	-	
Watson,Tony	-	93.2	67%	9%	25%	-	-	-	
Weaver,Jered	-	83.0	44%	17%	18%	-	22%	-	
Weaver,Luke	-	91.9	60%	-	25%	9%	7%	-	
Webb,Daniel	June `16	92.1	67%	19%	15%	-	-	-	
Webb,Ryan	-	90.9	51%	26%	22%	-	-	-	
Weber,Ryan	-	90.7	50%	-	14%	12%	24%	-	
Wendelken,J.B.	-	92.9	66%	-	25%	-	10%	-	
Whalen,Rob	-	89.1	66%	23%	9%	-	3%	-	
White,Tyler	-	83.8	76%	6%	18%	-	-	-	
Whitley,Chase	May `15	90.2	45%	12%	33%	-	10%	-	
Wieland,Joe	July `12	91.0	55%	-	26%	-	19%	-	
Wilhelmsen,Tom	-	94.8	50%	-	8%	22%	19%	-	
Williams,Jerome	-	89.8	50%	-	18%	29%	3%	-	
Williams,Trevor	-	92.8	67%	24%	9%	-	-	-	
Wilson,Alex	July `07	91.9	56%	7%	<1%	36%	-	-	
Wilson,Justin	-	95.1	65%	-	<1%	29%	5%	-	
Wilson,Tyler	-	89.6	62%	22%	13%	-	4%	-	
Wimmers,Alex	Aug `12	91.6	41%	20%	32%	-	6%	-	
Winkler,Daniel	July `14	92.0	33%	30%	-	36%	-	-	
Wisler,Matt	-	92.8	59%	29%	6%	-	6%	-	
Withrow,Chris	June `14	93.6	55%	39%	-	-	6%	-	
Wittgren,Nick	-	92.2	76%	-	13%	-	11%	-	
Wood,Alex	Jan `09	90.6	53%	-	18%	-	29%	-	
Wood,Blake	May `12	96.0	55%	36%	8%	-	-	-	
Wood,Travis	-	90.5	65%	10%	3%	19%	3%	-	
Worley,Vance	-	89.2	61%	-	3%	28%	7%	-	
Wright,Daniel	-	89.2	52%	14%	18%	-	16%	-	
Wright,Mike	-	93.1	70%	20%	8%	-	2%	-	
Wright,Steven	-	83.2	15%	-	-	-	3%	-	Knuckleball 82%
Yates,Kirby	Jan `06	93.2	60%	32%	3%	-	5%	-	
Ynoa,Gabriel	-	93.5	56%	30%	7%	-	7%	-	
Ynoa,Michael	Aug `10	94.2	67%	18%	4%	-	12%	-	
Young,Chris	-	87.9	46%	53%	<1%	-	<1%	-	
Younginer,Madison	-	94.2	65%	-	7%	-	28%	-	
Zastryzny,Rob	-	89.6	55%	-	2%	18%	26%	-	
Ziegler,Brad	-	83.9	58%	18%	24%	-	-	-	
Zimmermann,Jordan	Aug `09	91.8	53%	31%	3%	-	13%	-	
Zych,Tony	-	95.3	59%	40%	<1%	-	-	-	

432

Average Fastball Velocity

Ben Jedlovec

It feels like Felix Hernandez should be about 37 years old.

Let's flip over to Hernandez's entry of the Register section (page 178) and review his career. If you recall, his debut in 2005 brought much hype and high expectations. After four seasons honing his craft, Felix took a jump forward in 2009, improving his strikeout and walk rates and finishing with a 2.49 ERA and second place in Cy Young Award voting. He repeated the performance the following year, this time winning the Cy Young despite just 13 wins, a record low for a Cy Young starter. Though his ERA rose over a full run the following year, that had more to do with the declining Mariners' defense than his abilities, as his underlying strikeout and walk rates remained constant. That brings us to 2012, when King Felix took his game to yet another level. He improved his strikeout and walk percentages for three straight seasons (2012, 2013 and 2014) and averaged a 2.73 ERA and 224 innings during that span.

Finally, in 2015, Felix took his first step backwards. Though he managed to win 18 games, his underlying stats all went in the wrong direction, resulting in a 3.53 ERA. And, in 2016, Old Man Felix (now 30 years young) proved his mortality. His 3.82 ERA hides a disturbing trend, including career worsts in almost every statistical category and a DL stint due to a calf strain, which kept him from reaching 190 innings for the first time since 2005.

However, the calf strain may be the least of his problems. Felix entered the majors averaging 96 mph on his fastballs and dialing it up from there. He has proven that he doesn't need to throw 96 to be successful; however, his average velocity dropped another 1.4 mph in 2016 to a mere 90, a notch below the rising major league average.

The fact is that Felix's career to date is both common and incredibly unusual for modern pitchers. Pitchers are challenged to exert themselves on every pitch, or the front office will find someone who can throw a 103-mph fastball by the hitter and take their roster spot. It's only natural that pitchers wear down over time and lose some velocity along the way. It's remarkable that it took this long for life to catch up to Felix, and it's unfortunate that he has since declined so quickly.

Unfortunately for Felix, pitchers don't often regain velocity. On the following pages, you will find that 47 of 213 pitchers increased their fastball velocity by at least one mph in 2016, while 91 pitchers lost at least one mph. For the 83 pitchers under 30, the split was much more even: 29 gained velocity and 32 lost velocity.

Three pitchers lost three miles per hour on their fastballs in 2016: John Danks, Edwin Jackson, and Glen Perkins, who had two rough outings in April before succumbing to labrum surgery. So, we could reasonably expect Perkins to rebound in 2017, but it wouldn't be surprising if Danks and Jackson have played their last major league games. Once it's gone, it's gone. As evidenced in this section, many pitchers have no trouble returning to their pre-injury velocity following major surgeries, including Yu Darvish and Matt Harvey who missed entire seasons. Even through the miracle of modern medicine, however, no doctor has a procedure to add speed that wasn't there in the first place.

In the few years we've been producing this table, the exception seems to be the starter-turned-reliever. In fact, this year's biggest velocity gainers were David Phelps, who converted to a full-time reliever for Miami and excelled in the new role, and former starter and current Padres reliever Brandon Maurer, who even closed briefly this season. Last year's biggest gainer was Zach McAllister, who made the same jump in 2015. Before that, there was Zach Britton, Wade Davis, and Tommy Hunter.

Is Felix done as a Cy Young candidate, a staff ace, and even as an above-average pitcher? Our friends at Baseball-Reference—led by Fielding Bible Award tie-breaker Sean Forman—calculate player similarities based on the formula Bill James introduced in *The Politics of Glory*. Through age 29, Felix most resembles Hall of Famer Don Sutton. Sutton, of course, went on the pitch 2,700 more innings over 13 more seasons, retiring (from pitching, at least) at the ripe old age of 43. Granted, at age 30, Sutton was still in the midst of his prime, appearing in the All-Star Game and finishing in the top five in Cy Young voting with a 2.87 ERA. We don't have pitch velocity data for Sutton's career, but there were no signs of diminishing abilities as he turned 31. It's probably safe to say that Sutton is an unrealistic best-case scenario and an unfair expectation for Felix's next decade.

Every pitcher is eventually challenged to learn how to pitch in the majors without the velocity that got them there. Felix has hit that crossroads where he needs to figure it out pretty quickly if he wants to prolong his career. There are a couple more plausible paths for Felix.

He could spend a couple of years trying but failing to regain the form he displayed as recently as 2014. Jered Weaver and CC Sabathia are struggling with this right now, and they may not last much longer. Given how high his peak was, Felix might remain viable but never regain the dominance of his prime. The Mariners might eventually have to move on, but another team or two will give him a shot, enticed by the upside. But, he won't have the velocity or the cozy confines of Safeco Field at his side, and he'll struggle, possibly pitching himself into an injury or two. Four or five years down the road, in his mid-thirties, Felix might have to hang up his spikes following a good career but far short of Cooperstown (check out Felix's career-to-date progress towards the Hall of Fame on page 553).

Alternatively, Felix may be able to transition into a finesse pitcher to significantly extend his career, the way that Greg Maddux, Ferguson Jenkins, and Bartolo Colon were able to do. He may never win a second Cy Young Award, and his lackluster win totals in Seattle will keep him far from 300 wins, but another 5 or 6 above average seasons could put some strong career totals in front of a sabermetric friendly Hall of Fame voting bloc around 2027.

Or, perhaps Felix will be the lucky one to regain velocity, and his previous form will return with it. History tells us this isn't likely, but who could blame us for hoping anyways?

This section contains the average fastball velocity by year, as tracked by Baseball Info Solutions, for each pitcher who has thrown at least 50 innings in at least three of the last four seasons. The listed ages reflect their age as of June 30, 2017.

Average Fastball Velocity by Age

Player	Age	09	10	11	12	13	14	15	16
Fernandez, Jose	24					95	95	96	95
Martinez, Carlos	25					97	97	95	96
Wacha, Michael	25					93	93	93	92
Ventura, Yordano	26					97	97	96	96
Perez, Martin	26				92	93	90	92	93
Teheran, Julio	26			93	92	92	90	91	91
Bauer, Trevor	26				92	93	92	93	92
Wood, Alex	26				92	90	89	91	
Gausman, Kevin	26				96	95	95	95	
Lyles, Jordan	26			89	91	92	91	92	93
Miller, Shelby	26				93	93	93	92	92
Cole, Gerrit	26				96	95	96	95	
Maurer, Brandon	26				93	93	92	95	
Rosenthal, Trevor	27			97	97	97	97	96	
Cosart, Jarred	27				94	94	94	92	
Ramirez, Erasmo	27			93	92	91	91	91	
Odorizzi, Jake	27			90	91	90	90	91	
Hand, Brad	27			90	90	93	92	92	93
Eovaldi, Nathan	27			94	94	96	96	97	97
Delgado, Randall	27			92	92	92	93	93	92
Salazar, Danny	27				96	95	95	95	
Herrera, Kelvin	27			96	99	98	98	98	97
Hendricks, Kyle	27					87	88	88	
Gray, Sonny	27				93	93	93	93	
Familia, Jeurys	27			96	95	96	97	96	
Bumgarner, Madison	27	89	91	92	91	91	92	92	91
Corbin, Patrick	27				91	92		92	92
Cingrani, Tony	27			92	92	91	92	94	
Oberholtzer, Brett	27			90	89	87	89		
Ross Jr., Robbie	28				92	93	91	92	94
Moore, Matt	28			96	94	92	91	92	93
Smyly, Drew	28			91	89	89	88	89	
Nelson, Jimmy	28				94	94	93	93	
Peralta, Wily	28			96	95	96	94	95	
Sale, Chris	28		96	95	92	93	94	94	93
Harvey, Matt	28				95	96		96	94
de la Rosa, Rubby	28			96	94	95	94	94	95
Quintana, Jose	28				89	91	91	91	92
Pineda, Michael	28			95		92	93	94	
Porcello, Rick	28	91	91	90	92	91	90	91	90
Reed, Addison	28			95	95	93	92	93	92
Duffy, Danny	28			93	95	94	93	94	95
Straily, Dan	28			91	90	89	89	89	
Quackenbush, Kevin	28					91	91	91	
Pomeranz, Drew	28			90	91	91	91	89	
Allen, Cody	28				95	95	95	95	94
Greene, Shane	28					91	90	92	
Paxton, James	28				95	94	94	95	
Tanaka, Masahiro	28					91	91	90	
Maness, Seth	28				91	90	89	88	
Archer, Chris	28			94	95	95	95	94	
Grimm, Justin	28			92	92	94	95	94	
Strasburg, Stephen	28		97	96	96	95	95	95	95
Treinen, Blake	29					95	96	95	
deGrom, Jacob	29					93	95	93	
Kelly, Joe	29			94	95	95	95	96	
Kimbrel, Craig	29		95	96	97	97	97	97	97
Richards, Garrett	29			95	95	95	96	95	96
Tillman, Chris	29	92	90	89	91	91	90	91	90
Betances, Dellin	29			93		96	97	97	98
Kershaw, Clayton	29	94	93	93	93	93	93	94	93
Cahill, Trevor	29	90	90	89	89	89	90	92	92
Chapman, Aroldis	29		100	98	98	98	100	99	100
Rondon, Hector	29					93	95	96	96
Gomez, Jeanmar	29		91	90	90	91	91	91	91
Chacin, Jhoulys	29	91	91	91	90	90	88	88	90
Keuchel, Dallas	29				87	89	89	89	88
Britton, Zach	29			92	92	92	95	96	96
Santiago, Hector	29			94	93	91	90	90	91
Latos, Mat	29	94	94	93	93	93	91	91	90
McAllister, Zach	29			91	92	91	93	95	94
Anderson, Chase	29						91	92	91
Locke, Jeff	29			90	91	90	90	91	92
Leake, Mike	29		89	89	89	90	90	91	90
Shaw, Bryan	29			93	93	93	93	92	93
Gibson, Kyle	29				92	91	92	91	
Jansen, Kenley	29		94	93	92	92	94	93	94
Worley, Vance	29		91	90	89	88	88	87	88
Warren, Adam	29			92	93	94	93	93	
Wilson, Justin	29			94	95	94	94	94	
Hoover, J.J.	29			93	93	93	93	92	
Storen, Drew	29		94	95	95	94	93	94	92
Nuno, Vidal	29				88	89	89	89	
McHugh, Collin	30				90	90	92	90	89
Ross, Tyson	30		93	92	92	94	93	93	92
Hellickson, Jeremy	30		91	91	91	90	90	90	89
Morris, Bryan	30				92	92	93	93	91
Carrasco, Carlos	30	92	93	92		95	95	95	94
Farquhar, Danny	30		91		92	90	91	92	
Milone, Tommy	30		87	87	87	86	88	87	
Wood, Travis	30		89	89	88	88	87	89	90
Diekman, Jake	30			95	96	97	96	95	
Nova, Ivan	30		93	93	93	93	92	93	92
Miley, Wade	30			90	91	91	91	91	90
Niese, Jon	30	89	88	90	89	89	88	89	88
Rusin, Chris	30			87	87	87	88	88	
Phelps, David	30			90	89	89	90	93	
Holland, Derek	30	93	92	94	93	94	92	93	92
Roark, Tanner	30				93	91	93	92	
Shoemaker, Matt	30				91	91	90	91	
Ramos, A.J.	30			93	93	91	93	92	
Cashner, Andrew	30		96	95	98	95	94	95	94
Nicasio, Juan	30		94	93	92	93	95	94	
Darvish, Yu	30			92	92	92		93	
Garcia, Jaime	30		89	89	88	87	89	89	89
Hunter, Tommy	30	89	90	90	91	95	96	95	94
Cecil, Brett	30	91	90	88	89	91	92	92	92
Koehler, Tom	31			93	93	93	92	92	
Hughes, Phil	31	93	92	91	92	92	91	90	
Cishek, Steve	31		93	93	92	92	92	91	91
Tazawa, Junichi	31	90		92	94	94	94	94	93
Zimmermann, Jordan	31	93	92	93	94	94	94	93	92
Gee, Dillon	31		89	89	90	89	89	89	90
Brach, Brad	31			93	92	92	93	94	94
Kluber, Corey	31			92	91	92	92	91	91
Hernandez, Felix	31	94	94	93	92	92	92	92	90
Arrieta, Jake	31		93	92	93	94	92	93	93
Detwiler, Ross	31	91	90	92	93	92	93	92	92
Gallardo, Yovani	31	92	93	93	92	91	91	90	90
Cueto, Johnny	31	93	93	93	92	91	92	91	90
Collmenter, Josh	31			87	87	88	86	85	84
Bastardo, Antonio	31	92	94	93	92	92	92	93	92
Gonzalez, Gio	31	92	92	92	93	93	92	92	91
Davis, Wade	31	92	92	91	94	91	95	95	94
Price, David	31	93	95	95	94	92	92	93	92
Chen, Wei-Yin	31			91	91	92	91	91	
Hughes, Jared	31			93	92	92	93	93	
Fiers, Mike	32			88	87	88	89	89	89
Strop, Pedro	32	95	95	94	97	96	95	95	95
Kontos, George	32			91	91	90	90	90	89
Salas, Fernando	32		91	91	92	90	91	91	91
Watson, Tony	32		91	94	94	94	94	94	93
Dunn, Mike	32	93	95	94	94	94	95	95	94
Miller, Andrew	32	91	91	93	95	95	94	94	95
Danks, John	32	89	90	90	89	88	87	89	86
Robertson, David	32	92	92	93	92	92	92	92	92
Melancon, Mark	32	93	93	93	93	92	92	91	91
Norris, Bud	32	94	94	93	92	92	93	94	92
Clippard, Tyler	32	90	92	93	92	91	92	90	90
Samardzija, Jeff	32	94	93	94	95	94	94	94	94
Kennedy, Ian	32	92	89	90	89	90	91	91	91
Petit, Yusmeiro	32	87			88	88	89	88	89

Player	Age				Average FB Velocity				
		09	10	11	12	13	14	15	16
Tomlin, Josh	32		88	87	88	89	88	87	87
Cain, Matt	32	93	92	91	91	91	92	91	90
Harris, Will	32				91	92	92	92	92
Buchholz, Clay	32	94	94	92	91	90	90	91	91
Kintzler, Brandon	32		93	93	93	92	92	91	93
Scherzer, Max	32	94	93	93	94	93	93	94	94
Ramos, Cesar	33	91	92	92	92	91	90	90	88
Broxton, Jonathan	33	98	95	94	95	93	93	94	94
Lincecum, Tim	33	92	91	92	90	90	90	87	88
Gonzalez, Miguel	33				91	91	91	91	91
Gregerson, Luke	33	91	91	90	89	88	88	89	89
Kelley, Shawn	33	93	93	91	92	92	92	92	92
Smith, Joe	33	90	91	90	89	90	89	88	88
Sanchez, Anibal	33	91	91	92	92	93	92	92	91
Fister, Doug	33	88	88	90	89	89	88	86	87
Kazmir, Scott	33	91	91	86		92	90	91	91
Jimenez, Ubaldo	33	96	96	93	92	92	91	91	90
Pelfrey, Mike	33	93	92	92	93	92	91	93	93
Lester, Jon	33	92	92	91	92	92	90	91	91
Hamels, Cole	33	90	91	91	90	91	91	92	91
Wilhelmsen, Tom	33			95	96	96	94	93	92
Villanueva, Carlos	33	89	90	89	89	88	89	88	88
Garza, Matt	33	93	93	94	94	93	93	93	92
Morton, Charlie	33	91	93	91	90	93	91	92	94
Liriano, Francisco	33	92	94	92	93	93	93	92	93
Fien, Casey	33	92	90		91	89	91	91	91
Greinke, Zack	33	94	93	93	92	90	92	92	91
Jackson, Edwin	33	95	94	94	93	93	93	94	91
Chavez, Jesse	33	94	95	93	92	91	90	91	92
Street, Huston	33	92	91	90	89	89	89	89	88
Estrada, Marco	33	90	91	91	90	89	89	89	88
Volquez, Edinson	33	94	94	94	94	92	93	94	93
Johnson, Jim	34	94	94	95	94	94	94	94	93
Duke, Zach	34	89	87	87	89	89	88	88	88
Axford, John	34	94	95	96	96	95	95	96	96
Romo, Sergio	34	90	89	89	88	87	88	87	86
Perkins, Glen	34	90	92	94	95	95	93	94	91
Verlander, Justin	34	96	95	95	94	93	92	93	93
Feldman, Scott	34	91	90	91	91	89	88	89	89
Nolasco, Ricky	34	91	91	91	90	90	90	90	90
Santana, Ervin	34	92	92	93	92	92	92	92	93
O'Day, Darren	34	85	86	84	85	86	87	87	86
Torres, Carlos	34	89	88		90	90	91	91	91
Happ, J.A.	34	88	90	90	90	91	93	92	92
Weaver, Jered	34	89	90	89	88	86	86	83	83
Hammel, Jason	34	92	93	93	94	93	92	92	92
Rodriguez, Francisco	35	93	91	90	92	91	91	90	89
Shields, James	35	89	90	90	91	90	90	89	89
Williams, Jerome	35			90	91	92	90	89	89
Wainwright, Adam	35	91	91		90	90	89	88	88
Peavy, Jake	36	91	90	90	90	90	89	89	87
Simon, Alfredo	36	92	95	94	94	93	93	92	91
Iwakuma, Hisashi	36				90	90	89	88	87
de la Rosa, Jorge	36	93	93	93	90	91	91	90	89
Blanton, Joe	36	90	89	88	90	89		91	91
Papelbon, Jonathan	36	95	95	95	94	92	91	91	91
Hernandez, Roberto	36	93	93	93	91	92	90	89	90
Breslow, Craig	36	90	89	90	89	89	88	89	88
Casilla, Santiago	36	95	97	94	94	93	94	93	94
Sabathia, CC	36	94	93	94	92	91	89	90	89
Ziegler, Brad	37	85	84	85	86	86	85	84	84
Lewis, Colby	37		90	89	88		89	88	87
Young, Chris	38	86	85	85	85		85	87	88
Lackey, John	38	92	91	92		92	92	92	92
Lohse, Kyle	38	90	90	89	90	90	89	89	87
Benoit, Joaquin	39		94	94	94	94	95	94	94
Vogelsong, Ryan	39			91	90	88	90	90	89
Rodney, Fernando	40	96	96	96	96	96	95	95	94
Grilli, Jason	40	92		92	94	93	93	94	92
Dickey, R.A.	42	85	84	84	83	82	82	81	82
Colon, Bartolo	44	89		92	90	90	89	88	88

Pinch Hitting

Lindsay Zeck

Looking at the players with at least 20 pinch-hit at-bats during the 2016 season, only seven players had an on-base plus slugging (OPS) of 1.000 or greater. Amazingly, three of these players—Matt Adams, Brandon Moss, and Kolten Wong—played for the St. Louis Cardinals. Wong led the way with a fantastic line of .400/.538/.750 (Avg/OBP/Slg) in his 20 pinch-hit at-bats. The three Cardinals combined for seven home runs, eight doubles, and 22 RBI in 78 at-bats.

A couple of other standout pinch hitter performers in 2016 were Derek Dietrich of the Miami Marlins and Daniel Descalso of the Colorado Rockies. Dietrich, who had 20 pinch-hit at-bats, had seven hits, two home runs, a walk-off triple, and two doubles with nine RBI. His pinch-hit batting line was an outstanding .350/.500/.850. Descalso had a much improved season as a pinch hitter. In his 26 pinch-hit at-bats, he had nine hits—one of which was a walk-off single—with two home runs and a triple. His performance pinch hitting in 2016 gave him a line of .346/.433/.654. He far surpassed his career pinch-hit performance. Prior to the 2016 season, in his 158 career pinch-hit at-bats, he had only one home run and a batting line of .184/.246/.253.

In order for a player to appear in the following Pinch Hitting table, he needs to have at least 10 plate appearances or 10 total bases as a pinch hitter during the 2016 season. To appear on the Career Pinch Hitting table, he must be an active player who has had at least 100 career plate appearances as a pinch hitter.

Pinch Hitting

Pinch Hitters with 10+ PAs or 10+ Total Bases in 2016

Batter	B	AB	H	2B	3B	HR	RBI	TBB	IBB	SO	GDP	Avg	OBP	Slg	OPS
Cristhian Adames	B	51	14	3	0	0	5	7	0	9	1	.275	.373	.333	.706
Matt Adams	L	37	12	5	0	3	13	0	0	8	2	.324	.316	.703	1.018
Ehire Adrianza	B	18	5	1	0	0	4	1	0	3	0	.278	.316	.333	.649
Abraham Almonte	B	12	1	0	0	0	1	0	0	3	1	.083	.154	.083	.237
Albert Almora	R	10	1	0	0	0	0	0	0	1	1	.100	.100	.100	.200
Yonder Alonso	L	10	2	2	0	0	4	1	0	2	0	.200	.273	.400	.673
Pedro Alvarez	L	11	1	1	0	0	0	2	0	4	0	.091	.231	.182	.413
Alexi Amarista	L	14	0	0	0	0	2	1	0	5	1	.000	.063	.000	.063
Nori Aoki	L	11	5	0	0	0	0	0	0	1	0	.455	.455	.455	.909
Oswaldo Arcia	L	13	0	0	0	0	0	0	0	5	0	.000	.000	.000	.000
Cody Asche	L	14	2	0	0	0	0	0	0	5	0	.143	.143	.143	.286
Erick Aybar	B	9	1	1	0	0	1	0	0	3	0	.111	.200	.222	.422
Javier Baez	R	18	3	0	0	0	0	0	0	3	0	.167	.167	.167	.333
Brandon Barnes	R	10	2	1	0	0	0	1	0	4	0	.200	.273	.300	.573
Gordon Beckham	R	19	4	1	0	1	4	4	0	5	1	.211	.348	.421	.769
Josh Bell	B	9	6	2	0	1	7	3	0	0	0	.667	.750	1.222	1.972
Carlos Beltran	B	9	2	1	0	0	1	2	0	4	0	.222	.364	.333	.697
Christian Bethancourt	R	16	6	0	0	1	3	4	0	4	1	.375	.500	.563	1.063
Andres Blanco	B	31	5	2	0	0	3	0	0	7	0	.161	.212	.226	.438
Gregor Blanco	L	33	7	1	0	1	4	3	0	7	1	.212	.297	.333	.631
Jabari Blash	R	14	2	1	0	0	0	3	0	8	1	.143	.294	.214	.508
Emilio Bonifacio	B	12	4	0	0	0	2	1	0	4	0	.333	.385	.333	.718
Trevor Brown	R	17	3	1	0	0	2	2	0	8	0	.176	.263	.235	.498
Keon Broxton	R	9	2	0	0	2	2	2	0	4	1	.222	.364	.889	1.253
Emmanuel Burriss	B	22	2	0	1	0	0	1	0	7	0	.091	.167	.182	.348
Billy Butler	R	28	8	1	0	1	7	0	0	5	1	.286	.286	.429	.714
Ramon Cabrera	B	14	2	0	0	0	3	0	0	6	0	.143	.133	.143	.276
Eric Campbell	R	11	4	0	0	0	4	4	1	2	0	.364	.533	.364	.897
Stephen Cardullo	R	12	2	0	0	1	1	0	0	2	0	.167	.167	.417	.583
Lonnie Chisenhall	L	12	2	0	0	0	2	1	0	3	1	.167	.267	.167	.433
Ji-Man Choi	L	10	0	0	0	0	0	2	0	5	0	.000	.167	.000	.167
Chris Coghlan	L	17	3	1	0	1	2	1	0	8	0	.176	.300	.412	.712
Tyler Collins	L	10	3	0	1	1	3	1	0	5	0	.300	.333	.800	1.133
Michael Conforto	L	20	4	1	0	0	4	2	0	7	0	.200	.304	.250	.554
Coco Crisp	B	8	0	0	0	0	0	1	0	4	0	.000	.111	.000	.111
Charlie Culberson	R	10	3	0	0	0	1	1	0	3	1	.300	.364	.300	.664
Chase d'Arnaud	R	25	9	1	0	0	0	3	0	7	1	.360	.429	.400	.829
Rajai Davis	R	15	2	0	0	0	0	2	0	3	0	.133	.235	.133	.369
Alejandro De Aza	L	55	14	1	0	2	2	8	0	18	0	.255	.349	.382	.731
Ivan De Jesus Jr.	R	32	9	2	0	0	5	0	0	7	0	.281	.273	.344	.616
Daniel Descalso	L	26	9	0	1	2	5	4	0	7	0	.346	.433	.654	1.087
Alex Dickerson	L	16	5	0	0	2	6	0	0	2	1	.313	.313	.688	1.000
Corey Dickerson	L	15	1	1	0	0	2	0	0	7	0	.067	.067	.133	.200
Derek Dietrich	L	20	7	2	1	2	9	3	0	8	1	.350	.500	.850	1.350
Wilmer Difo	B	10	2	1	0	0	3	4	0	2	0	.200	.429	.300	.729
Stephen Drew	L	26	6	0	1	3	6	1	0	6	0	.231	.286	.654	.940
Brandon Drury	R	14	2	1	0	0	0	1	0	5	0	.143	.200	.214	.414
Jake Elmore	R	30	7	1	0	0	0	7	0	6	1	.233	.378	.267	.645
Eduardo Escobar	B	10	3	1	0	0	1	1	0	3	0	.300	.364	.400	.764
Andre Ethier	L	11	4	1	0	1	2	1	1	3	0	.364	.417	.727	1.144
Taylor Featherston	R	13	1	0	0	0	0	2	0	9	0	.077	.200	.077	.277
Cole Figueroa	L	14	1	0	0	0	0	0	0	1	0	.071	.071	.071	.143
Ramon Flores	L	25	4	0	0	0	0	1	0	10	1	.160	.192	.160	.352
Wilmer Flores	R	14	2	0	0	1	4	1	0	3	0	.143	.200	.357	.557
Jeff Francoeur	R	42	8	0	0	0	4	7	0	15	1	.190	.306	.190	.497
Nick Franklin	B	11	2	2	0	0	4	2	0	1	1	.182	.308	.364	.671
Adam Frazier	L	12	2	0	0	1	1	2	0	2	0	.167	.286	.417	.702
Mike Freeman	L	9	1	1	0	0	0	1	0	2	1	.111	.200	.222	.422
David Freese	R	20	6	2	0	1	3	4	2	7	1	.300	.417	.550	.967
Greg Garcia	L	23	8	1	0	1	3	3	0	5	0	.348	.444	.522	.966
Evan Gattis	R	9	2	0	0	0	0	2	0	4	0	.222	.364	.222	.586
Scooter Gennett	L	12	1	1	0	0	3	1	0	4	1	.083	.154	.167	.321
Conor Gillaspie	L	51	11	3	2	2	9	6	1	10	1	.216	.298	.471	.769
Cole Gillespie	R	29	4	1	1	0	1	1	0	10	0	.138	.161	.241	.403
Tyler Goeddel	R	19	1	0	0	0	1	3	0	7	1	.053	.174	.053	.227
Marwin Gonzalez	B	12	3	0	0	0	0	1	0	3	1	.250	.308	.250	.558
Phil Gosselin	R	77	20	4	0	1	6	4	0	22	0	.260	.289	.351	.640
Yasmani Grandal	B	12	2	0	0	0	4	4	0	7	0	.167	.375	.167	.542

Pinch Hitting
Pinch Hitters with 10+ PAs or 10+ Total Bases in 2016

Batter	B	AB	H	2B	3B	HR	RBI	TBB	IBB	SO	GDP	Avg	OBP	Slg	OPS
Curtis Granderson	L	10	2	0	0	1	1	0	0	3	0	.200	.200	.500	.700
Randal Grichuk	R	14	6	0	0	1	2	3	0	2	0	.429	.529	.643	1.172
Franklin Gutierrez	R	30	6	2	0	0	4	4	0	12	0	.200	.286	.267	.552
Brandon Guyer	R	15	2	1	0	0	3	3	0	2	0	.133	.278	.200	.478
Jedd Gyorko	R	20	5	1	0	0	0	2	0	6	0	.250	.318	.300	.618
Alen Hanson	B	11	2	1	0	0	0	0	0	2	0	.182	.182	.273	.455
Jeremy Hazelbaker	L	41	11	1	0	4	9	1	0	12	0	.268	.286	.585	.871
Chris Heisey	R	41	7	2	0	3	3	2	0	16	0	.171	.227	.439	.666
Kiké Hernandez	R	45	7	0	0	1	1	6	1	14	0	.156	.255	.222	.477
Marco Hernandez	L	10	0	0	0	0	0	2	0	6	0	.000	.167	.000	.167
Chris Herrmann	L	14	0	0	0	0	0	2	0	6	0	.000	.125	.000	.125
Aaron Hill	R	15	6	2	0	1	3	2	1	3	0	.400	.444	.733	1.178
Matt Holliday	R	9	4	0	0	1	2	1	1	2	0	.444	.500	.778	1.278
Brock Holt	L	10	3	1	0	1	1	0	0	0	1	.300	.300	.700	1.000
Tyler Holt	R	34	4	1	0	0	1	5	0	15	1	.118	.225	.147	.372
Ryan Howard	L	19	4	2	0	0	3	2	0	8	1	.211	.286	.316	.602
Jared Hoying	L	9	0	0	0	0	1	1	0	0	0	.000	.100	.000	.100
Hernan Iribarren	L	11	5	0	2	0	0	0	0	3	1	.455	.455	.818	1.273
Travis Jankowski	L	14	2	0	0	0	0	1	0	9	0	.143	.200	.143	.343
John Jaso	L	25	8	1	0	0	2	2	0	7	1	.320	.370	.360	.730
Chris Johnson	R	38	7	1	0	2	5	2	1	9	4	.184	.225	.368	.593
Kelly Johnson	L	45	8	3	0	4	11	4	0	10	2	.178	.255	.511	.766
Tommy Joseph	R	21	3	0	0	1	5	3	0	6	1	.143	.240	.286	.526
Matt Joyce	L	59	13	1	0	4	15	21	0	17	3	.220	.432	.441	.873
Jung Ho Kang	R	12	1	0	0	0	0	1	0	6	0	.083	.154	.083	.237
Ty Kelly	B	14	1	0	0	0	0	3	0	1	0	.071	.235	.071	.307
Tony Kemp	L	17	4	2	0	0	3	1	0	8	0	.235	.263	.353	.616
Howie Kendrick	R	16	3	1	0	0	1	2	0	5	1	.188	.263	.250	.513
Hyun Soo Kim	L	9	6	1	0	1	2	2	0	2	0	.667	.727	1.111	1.838
Tommy La Stella	L	31	5	3	0	0	2	6	0	7	0	.161	.297	.258	.555
Juan Lagares	R	16	5	2	0	1	1	2	0	5	1	.313	.389	.625	1.014
Jake Lamb	L	17	6	1	1	3	4	0	0	6	0	.353	.353	1.059	1.412
Dae-Ho Lee	R	23	7	0	0	2	7	2	1	9	0	.304	.360	.565	.925
Adam Lind	L	21	3	1	0	1	3	2	0	12	2	.143	.217	.333	.551
Jonathan Lucroy	R	9	0	0	0	0	0	2	0	3	3	.000	.182	.000	.182
Jefry Marte	R	11	4	1	0	1	4	1	0	3	1	.364	.417	.727	1.144
Russell Martin	R	7	0	0	0	0	0	3	0	4	0	.000	.300	.000	.300
Victor Martinez	B	8	4	0	0	3	6	3	1	1	0	.500	.636	1.625	2.261
Nomar Mazara	L	8	2	0	0	0	1	2	0	3	0	.250	.455	.250	.705
Brian McCann	L	14	0	0	0	0	0	1	0	5	1	.000	.067	.000	.067
Miguel Montero	L	15	3	0	0	1	3	2	1	4	1	.200	.294	.400	.694
Mitch Moreland	L	11	5	1	0	0	3	2	0	3	0	.455	.538	.545	1.084
Brandon Moss	L	21	6	1	0	3	7	3	1	4	3	.286	.375	.762	1.137
Tom Murphy	R	9	3	1	0	1	2	2	0	3	0	.333	.455	.778	1.232
Tyler Naquin	L	9	1	1	0	0	2	1	1	7	0	.111	.182	.222	.404
Daniel Nava	B	10	0	0	0	0	0	1	0	4	0	.000	.091	.000	.091
Dioner Navarro	B	9	1	0	0	0	1	2	0	4	0	.111	.273	.111	.384
Kirk Nieuwenhuis	L	18	2	0	0	0	0	4	0	9	0	.111	.273	.111	.384
Brandon Nimmo	L	12	6	0	0	0	0	1	0	4	0	.500	.571	.500	1.071
Peter O'Brien	R	12	2	1	0	1	1	0	0	6	0	.167	.167	.500	.667
Rafael Ortega	L	9	5	1	0	0	4	2	0	2	0	.556	.636	.667	1.303
David Ortiz	L	8	2	0	0	0	2	3	0	4	0	.250	.455	.250	.705
Jordan Pacheco	R	20	4	2	0	0	0	0	0	7	0	.200	.200	.300	.500
Jimmy Paredes	B	41	10	1	0	1	6	2	0	16	0	.244	.279	.341	.621
Jarrett Parker	L	18	3	0	0	0	0	1	0	7	1	.167	.318	.167	.485
Joc Pederson	L	13	1	0	0	1	2	4	0	5	0	.077	.294	.308	.602
Hernan Perez	R	20	3	0	1	0	4	0	0	7	0	.150	.150	.250	.400
Jace Peterson	L	18	1	0	0	0	0	1	0	9	0	.056	.105	.056	.161
Tommy Pham	R	14	3	0	0	1	2	2	0	7	0	.214	.313	.429	.741
A.J. Pierzynski	L	15	3	2	0	0	2	1	0	2	1	.200	.278	.333	.611
Manny Pina	R	13	4	0	0	1	5	2	0	5	0	.308	.400	.538	.938
Alex Presley	L	20	4	0	0	1	3	2	0	7	0	.200	.273	.350	.623
Jurickson Profar	B	13	3	0	0	0	4	1	0	3	0	.231	.286	.231	.516
Yasiel Puig	R	16	3	1	0	1	1	1	0	6	0	.188	.235	.438	.673
Ryan Raburn	R	46	11	1	0	4	11	10	0	17	2	.239	.375	.522	.897
Alexei Ramirez	R	13	5	0	0	1	3	0	0	1	0	.385	.429	.615	1.044
J.T. Realmuto	R	9	3	1	0	0	0	1	0	5	0	.333	.400	.444	.844
Nolan Reimold	R	12	4	0	0	1	2	1	0	6	0	.333	.385	.583	.968
Tony Renda	R	14	3	0	0	0	2	1	0	4	0	.214	.267	.214	.481

Pinch Hitting

Pinch Hitters with 10+ PAs or 10+ Total Bases in 2016

Batter	B	AB	H	2B	3B	HR	RBI	TBB	IBB	SO	GDP	Avg	OBP	Slg	OPS
Ben Revere	L	15	2	1	0	0	0	0	0	2	0	.133	.133	.200	.333
Matt Reynolds	R	15	3	1	0	0	2	1	0	6	0	.200	.250	.267	.517
Clint Robinson	L	51	9	2	0	1	4	5	0	11	2	.176	.246	.275	.520
Sean Rodriguez	R	19	4	1	0	1	4	4	0	10	0	.211	.400	.421	.821
Jason Rogers	R	13	1	0	0	0	0	4	0	4	1	.077	.294	.077	.371
Miguel Rojas	R	15	4	1	0	0	0	1	0	2	0	.267	.313	.333	.646
Adam Rosales	R	21	5	3	0	0	2	1	0	12	0	.238	.273	.381	.654
David Ross	R	10	3	1	0	0	0	0	0	3	1	.300	.300	.400	.700
Ryan Rua	R	10	0	0	0	0	0	1	0	2	0	.000	.091	.000	.091
Darin Ruf	R	23	4	0	0	2	4	0	0	11	2	.174	.167	.435	.601
Jarrod Saltalamacchia	B	17	1	0	0	1	1	1	0	12	0	.059	.111	.235	.346
Hector Sanchez	B	12	2	0	0	0	3	1	0	3	0	.167	.231	.167	.397
Domingo Santana	R	9	1	0	0	0	3	4	0	7	0	.111	.357	.111	.468
Scott Schebler	L	15	3	1	0	0	1	1	0	7	0	.200	.250	.267	.517
Rob Segedin	R	14	1	0	0	0	1	3	0	8	1	.071	.278	.071	.349
Mallex Smith	L	12	4	0	0	0	0	4	0	5	0	.333	.500	.333	.833
Seth Smith	L	28	6	1	0	1	2	5	1	11	2	.214	.333	.357	.690
Justin Smoak	B	13	3	0	0	0	1	3	0	4	0	.231	.375	.231	.606
Jake Smolinski	R	11	4	0	0	1	3	0	0	0	0	.364	.364	.636	1.000
Brandon Snyder	R	33	9	4	1	3	8	0	0	12	1	.273	.273	.727	1.000
Jorge Soler	R	15	3	0	0	0	1	6	0	5	0	.200	.429	.200	.629
Giancarlo Stanton	R	9	1	0	0	1	1	1	1	6	0	.111	.182	.111	.293
Ichiro Suzuki	L	57	15	3	0	1	8	7	1	8	1	.263	.353	.368	.721
Matt Szczur	R	46	12	1	1	0	5	3	0	8	0	.261	.306	.326	.632
Raimel Tapia	L	10	2	0	0	0	0	0	0	4	0	.200	.200	.200	.400
Chris Taylor	R	13	2	0	0	0	0	2	0	1	1	.154	.267	.154	.421
Michael Taylor	R	10	0	0	0	0	0	0	0	8	0	.000	.000	.000	.000
Trayce Thompson	R	13	3	0	0	1	1	0	0	6	1	.231	.231	.462	.692
Andrew Toles	L	21	8	3	1	0	2	1	0	4	0	.381	.435	.619	1.054
Kelby Tomlinson	R	17	7	2	0	0	2	3	1	4	1	.412	.500	.529	1.029
Preston Tucker	L	12	1	0	0	0	0	0	0	5	0	.083	.083	.083	.167
Justin Turner	R	8	3	0	0	1	3	1	0	2	0	.375	.400	.750	1.150
Melvin Upton Jr.	R	8	1	0	0	0	1	3	1	1	0	.125	.333	.125	.458
Chase Utley	L	11	1	0	0	0	0	4	0	3	0	.091	.333	.091	.424
Scott Van Slyke	R	15	3	0	0	0	1	3	1	6	1	.200	.316	.200	.516
Stephen Vogt	L	10	1	0	0	0	0	0	0	2	0	.100	.100	.100	.200
Kyle Waldrop	L	9	3	0	0	0	1	1	0	3	0	.333	.400	.333	.733
Brett Wallace	L	52	10	0	0	0	4	4	1	28	0	.192	.263	.192	.455
Colin Walsh	B	17	1	0	0	0	0	10	0	10	0	.059	.407	.059	.466
Rickie Weeks Jr.	R	56	9	5	0	5	8	8	0	24	2	.161	.294	.250	.544
Jayson Werth	R	4	3	1	0	2	6	0	0	0	1	.750	.750	2.500	3.250
Tyler White	R	13	6	4	0	0	4	1	1	3	0	.462	.500	.769	1.269
Andy Wilkins	L	18	1	0	0	1	1	3	0	8	1	.056	.190	.222	.413
Mac Williamson	R	19	5	1	0	1	2	2	0	6	0	.263	.333	.474	.807
Kolten Wong	L	20	8	2	1	1	2	5	0	2	0	.400	.538	.750	1.288
Chris Young	R	13	4	2	0	1	1	2	0	3	0	.308	.438	.692	1.130

Career Pinch Hitting
Active Pinch Hitters with 100+ PAs in their careers

Batter	B	AB	H	2B	3B	HR	RBI	TBB	IBB	SO	GDP	Avg	OBP	Slg	OPS
Matt Adams	L	100	33	6	0	7	28	4	1	29	3	.330	.352	.600	.952
Alexi Amarista	L	100	17	4	0	1	7	5	0	23	1	.170	.208	.240	.448
Brandon Barnes	R	96	25	5	3	3	10	3	0	38	2	.260	.304	.469	.773
Gregor Blanco	L	135	40	8	2	1	22	11	0	34	1	.296	.347	.407	.754
Emilio Bonifacio	B	95	22	2	1	0	4	8	1	34	1	.232	.298	.274	.572
Chris Coghlan	L	101	23	3	1	4	11	5	0	30	6	.228	.278	.396	.674
Rajai Davis	R	91	15	4	1	0	4	12	1	26	2	.165	.267	.231	.497
Alejandro De Aza	L	106	25	4	0	2	6	14	1	32	0	.236	.325	.330	.655
Daniel Descalso	L	184	38	8	1	3	19	15	0	48	1	.207	.274	.310	.583
Andre Ethier	L	129	38	7	1	4	31	22	3	36	7	.295	.405	.457	.863
Jeff Francoeur	R	102	23	4	0	1	17	11	0	33	3	.225	.296	.294	.590
Conor Gillaspie	L	90	20	3	2	5	16	12	2	16	1	.222	.314	.467	.780
Phil Gosselin	R	105	27	6	0	1	7	6	1	31	0	.257	.292	.343	.635
Josh Harrison	R	100	16	2	1	3	14	3	0	17	2	.160	.190	.290	.480
Chris Heisey	R	183	47	10	2	14	40	14	1	55	2	.257	.314	.563	.877
John Jaso	L	118	31	6	0	3	17	23	1	28	3	.263	.380	.390	.770
Jon Jay	L	92	25	3	0	2	10	10	1	24	4	.272	.352	.370	.722
Kelly Johnson	L	154	31	6	1	6	23	26	2	40	4	.201	.319	.370	.689
Matt Joyce	L	162	32	8	1	5	31	39	2	52	5	.198	.355	.352	.707
Adam Lind	L	94	29	6	0	5	22	13	3	31	6	.309	.389	.532	.921
Brian McCann	L	103	19	5	0	3	12	11	4	30	2	.184	.276	.320	.596
Casey McGehee	R	99	25	6	0	3	21	10	2	27	4	.253	.327	.404	.731
Miguel Montero	L	105	20	2	0	4	18	21	3	37	3	.190	.344	.324	.667
Michael Morse	R	99	28	5	2	2	21	13	0	33	2	.283	.363	.434	.797
Brandon Moss	L	132	29	7	1	5	21	15	1	42	5	.220	.316	.402	.717
Daniel Murphy	L	97	25	2	2	4	19	8	2	20	3	.258	.308	.443	.752
Dioner Navarro	B	99	21	3	0	3	18	8	0	29	2	.212	.275	.333	.609
Kirk Nieuwenhuis	L	97	22	8	0	1	6	12	1	47	0	.227	.312	.340	.652
David Ortiz	L	101	19	4	1	5	21	25	3	28	2	.188	.346	.396	.742
Jordan Pacheco	R	106	29	7	0	0	8	6	0	26	2	.274	.313	.340	.652
Gerardo Parra	L	109	24	5	1	1	9	6	1	25	2	.220	.265	.312	.577
Steve Pearce	R	97	19	5	1	1	9	10	1	33	3	.196	.271	.299	.570
Brayan Pena	B	132	33	7	0	2	15	9	0	24	4	.250	.292	.348	.640
A.J. Pierzynski	L	144	37	7	0	5	23	14	5	23	8	.257	.329	.410	.739
Ryan Raburn	R	160	32	8	1	8	34	27	3	49	4	.200	.328	.413	.741
Clint Robinson	L	95	18	4	0	2	10	10	0	23	2	.189	.284	.295	.579
Shane Robinson	R	112	24	4	1	0	7	18	0	21	2	.214	.321	.268	.588
Sean Rodriguez	R	110	16	2	0	2	11	15	0	47	1	.145	.277	.218	.495
Hector Sanchez	B	101	24	5	0	2	18	5	0	32	2	.238	.284	.347	.631
Seth Smith	L	229	68	16	5	9	46	37	3	62	6	.297	.393	.528	.921
Ichiro Suzuki	L	141	36	3	1	1	12	14	2	21	1	.255	.327	.312	.639
Justin Turner	R	152	40	9	0	3	32	11	0	31	7	.263	.310	.382	.691
Juan Uribe	R	94	26	7	0	3	14	11	1	30	2	.277	.355	.447	.802
Will Venable	L	148	27	3	2	2	13	16	1	45	0	.182	.261	.270	.531
Brett Wallace	L	125	28	4	0	4	22	15	2	50	1	.224	.312	.352	.664
Rickie Weeks Jr.	R	157	32	7	1	3	19	23	0	62	6	.204	.326	.318	.645
Eric Young	B	146	31	3	1	1	4	18	0	36	2	.212	.307	.267	.574

Manufactured Runs, Productive Outs, & Unproductive Outs

Ben Jedlovec

You can debate the exact order, but Mike Trout and Mookie Betts were two of the three best players in baseball in 2016. Trout was the better hitter (almost entirely due to the fact that he drew 67 more walks than Mookie), Betts the better fielder (with a league-leading 32 Defensive Runs Saved), and they might have been the two best baserunners in the league. But, if you needed any additional evidence of the impact these two had on their respective teams, look no further. In a section usually dominated by names like Adam Eaton, Billy Hamilton, and Elvis Andrus, Trout and Betts sit in a dead heat atop the manufactured runs leaderboard.

A few other observations:

* For the second straight year, the league set a record for the fewest manufactured runs in a season since 2002, the first season BIS started tracking manufactured runs. Of course, overall run scoring has been on the decline since about 2007, but offense has rebounded in each of the past two years. Manufactured runs have not rebounded in step with the league's offensive level.

- In last year's *Handbook*, Todd Frazier led baseball with 123 Unproductive Outs—30 more than any other player in baseball. Now on the White Sox, Frazier actually performed worse with runners on base (batting .202 in 2016 vs. .247 in 2015), but he dropped way down the Unproductive Outs list, primarily because he had 52 fewer plate appearances with men on base. If the White Sox are to improve offensive production in 2017, Frazier needs to hit better with runners on base, yes, but they also need to put more men on base in front of him.
- Dusty Baker worked his magic in his first season in the nation's capital. After finishing 20th in Manufactured Runs in 2015, the Nationals paced MLB with 173 in 2016. It was a collective effort, with Jayson Werth, Anthony Rendon, Danny Espinosa, Trea Turner, and Ben Revere all manufacturing between 18 and 22 runs.
- Robinson Cano appears in the top 15 in both Productive Outs and Unproductive Outs.

Players with the most Manufactured Runs, Productive Outs, & Unproductive Outs

Manufactured Runs		Productive Outs		Unproductive Outs	
Trout, Mike, LAA	35	Lindor, Francisco, Cle	45	Longoria, Evan, TB	105
Segura, Jean, Ari	34	Escobar, Alcides, KC	40	Upton, Justin, Det	102
Betts, Mookie, Bos	34	Rizzo, Anthony, ChC	39	Bryant, Kris, ChC	100
Hamilton, Billy, Cin	31	Polanco, Gregory, Pit	38	Belt, Brandon, SF	99
Eaton, Adam, CWS	29	Yelich, Christian, Mia	38	Arenado, Nolan, Col	96
Altuve, Jose, Hou	29	Hosmer, Eric, KC	37	McCutchen, Andrew, Pit	94
Inciarte, Ender, Atl	27	Votto, Joey, Cin	37	Trout, Mike, LAA	94
Desmond, Ian, Tex	26	Cano, Robinson, Sea	37	Freeman, Freddie, Atl	93
Herrera, Odubel, Phi	25	Kemp, Matt, SD-Atl	36	Kemp, Matt, SD-Atl	92
Kinsler, Ian, Det	25	Goldschmidt, Paul, Ari	35	Turner, Justin, LAD	92
Davis, Rajai, Cle	24	Gardner, Brett, NYY	34	Russell, Addison, ChC	92
Blackmon, Charlie, Col	24	Zobrist, Ben, ChC	34	Machado, Manny, Bal	92
Nunez, Eduardo, Min-SF	24	Harrison, Josh, Pit	34	Pujols, Albert, LAA	91
Pillar, Kevin, Tor	24	Crawford, Brandon, SF	34	Bradley Jr., Jackie, Bos	90
Springer, George, Hou	23	Gonzalez, Adrian, LAD	34	Cano, Robinson, Sea	89
Jankowski, Travis, SD	23	Encarnacion, Edwin, Tor	34	Betts, Mookie, Bos	87
Bradley Jr., Jackie, Bos	22	Cabrera, Melky, CWS	33	Encarnacion, Edwin, Tor	86
Marte, Starling, Pit	22	Bourn, Michael, Ari-Bal	33	Lucroy, Jonathan, Mil-Tex	86
Harrison, Josh, Pit	22	Mazara, Nomar, Tex	33	Kipnis, Jason, Cle	86
Werth, Jayson, Was	22	Abreu, Jose, CWS	33	Bogaerts, Xander, Bos	86
Frazier, Todd, CWS	21	Bogaerts, Xander, Bos	33	Franco, Maikel, Phi	84
Escobar, Yunel, LAA	21	Pedroia, Dustin, Bos	32	Yelich, Christian, Mia	84
Kendrick, Howie, LAD	21	LeMahieu, DJ, Col	32	Carter, Chris, Mil	84
Pagan, Angel, SF	21	Werth, Jayson, Was	32	Prado, Martin, Mia	84
Marte, Ketel, Sea	21	Altuve, Jose, Hou	32	Heyward, Jason, ChC	84
Rendon, Anthony, Was	21	Markakis, Nick, Atl	32	Trumbo, Mark, Bal	83
Villar, Jonathan, Mil	20	Murphy, Daniel, Was	31	Napoli, Mike, Cle	83
Hernandez, Cesar, Phi	20	Heyward, Jason, ChC	31	Lindor, Francisco, Cle	83
Realmuto, J.T., Mia	19	Franco, Maikel, Phi	31	Miller, Brad, TB	82
Espinosa, Danny, Was	19	Springer, George, Hou	31	Schoop, Jonathan, Bal	82
Escobar, Alcides, KC	19	Betts, Mookie, Bos	31	Goldschmidt, Paul, Ari	82
Phillips, Brandon, Cin	19	Calhoun, Kole, LAA	31	Cabrera, Asdrubal, NYM	82
Suarez, Eugenio, Cin	19	Eaton, Adam, CWS	30	Rizzo, Anthony, ChC	81
Ramirez, Jose, Cle	19	Espinosa, Danny, Was	30	Espinosa, Danny, Was	81
Lindor, Francisco, Cle	19	Longoria, Evan, TB	30	Crawford, Brandon, SF	80
Bryant, Kris, ChC	18	Posey, Buster, SF	30	Odor, Rougned, Tex	79
Turner, Trea, Was	18	Galvis, Freddy, Phi	30	Semien, Marcus, Oak	78
Seager, Corey, LAD	18	Mercer, Jordy, Pit	29	Seager, Kyle, Sea	78
Polanco, Gregory, Pit	18	Ozuna, Marcell, Mia	29	Phillips, Brandon, Cin	78
Utley, Chase, LAD	18	Hechavarria, Adeiny, Mia	28	Abreu, Jose, CWS	78
Revere, Ben, Was	18	Harper, Bryce, Was	28	Shaw, Travis, Bos	77
Headley, Chase, NYY	18	Panik, Joe, SF	28	Donaldson, Josh, Tor	77
Gonzalez, Marwin, Hou	18	Kepler, Max, Min	28	Galvis, Freddy, Phi	77
Perez, Hernan, Mil	18	Gonzalez, Carlos, Col	28	Gonzalez, Carlos, Col	77
Fowler, Dexter, ChC	18	Span, Denard, SF	28	Dickerson, Corey, TB	76
Kipnis, Jason, Cle	18	Marte, Starling, Pit	27	Calhoun, Kole, LAA	76
Andrus, Elvis, Tex	18	Owings, Chris, Ari	27	Piscotty, Stephen, StL	76
Carpenter, Matt, StL	18	Gregorius, Didi, NYY	27	Martin, Leonys, Sea	75
Rosario, Eddie, Min	18	Mauer, Joe, Min	27	Cruz, Nelson, Sea	75
Bogaerts, Xander, Bos	18	Pujols, Albert, LAA	26	Frazier, Todd, CWS	74
Odor, Rougned, Tex	18	Cabrera, Miguel, Det	26	Myers, Wil, SD	74
Hechavarria, Adeiny, Mia	18	Donaldson, Josh, Tor	26	Seager, Corey, LAD	74
		Turner, Justin, LAD	26	Correa, Carlos, Hou	74
		Myers, Wil, SD	26		
		Kipnis, Jason, Cle	26		
		Simmons, Andrelton, LAA	26		
		Bradley Jr., Jackie, Bos	26		

Manufactured Runs, Productive Outs, & Unproductive Outs Produced by Team

Team	Manufactured Runs	Productive Outs	Unproductive Outs
Arizona Diamondbacks	150	267	682
Atlanta Braves	141	297	699
Baltimore Orioles	108	182	715
Boston Red Sox	159	239	741
Chicago White Sox	145	235	690
Chicago Cubs	151	266	795
Cincinnati Reds	152	277	648
Cleveland Indians	170	254	696
Colorado Rockies	161	251	663
Detroit Tigers	131	212	729
Houston Astros	146	230	693
Kansas City Royals	155	237	669
Los Angeles Dodgers	138	224	688
Los Angeles Angels	163	269	660
Miami Marlins	148	262	714
Milwaukee Brewers	134	256	702
Minnesota Twins	139	246	694
New York Yankees	124	232	673
New York Mets	94	210	723
Oakland Athletics	115	186	652
Philadelphia Phillies	127	247	639
Pittsburgh Pirates	155	284	693
San Diego Padres	146	231	663
San Francisco Giants	158	281	769
Seattle Mariners	125	240	726
St Louis Cardinals	130	242	731
Tampa Bay Rays	94	173	716
Texas Rangers	156	234	682
Toronto Blue Jays	123	222	698
Washington Nationals	173	292	629

Manufactured Runs, Productive Outs, & Unproductive Outs Allowed by Team

Team	Manufactured Runs	Productive Outs	Unproductive Outs
Arizona Diamondbacks	148	274	716
Atlanta Braves	186	302	673
Baltimore Orioles	140	218	731
Boston Red Sox	133	207	725
Chicago White Sox	143	232	704
Chicago Cubs	138	233	630
Cincinnati Reds	147	255	775
Cleveland Indians	115	208	629
Colorado Rockies	161	283	734
Detroit Tigers	139	227	637
Houston Astros	123	222	697
Kansas City Royals	130	238	714
Los Angeles Dodgers	132	211	633
Los Angeles Angels	143	230	734
Miami Marlins	139	258	711
Milwaukee Brewers	160	265	726
Minnesota Twins	175	245	721
New York Yankees	123	220	657
New York Mets	129	236	661
Oakland Athletics	149	269	652
Philadelphia Phillies	130	260	687
Pittsburgh Pirates	165	294	722
San Diego Padres	153	258	721
San Francisco Giants	101	240	654
Seattle Mariners	128	195	683
St Louis Cardinals	157	279	717
Tampa Bay Rays	150	219	699
Texas Rangers	125	245	729
Toronto Blue Jays	133	225	704
Washington Nationals	116	230	696

Managers Record

Lindsay Zeck

The Manager's Record is an in-depth look at the managers in Major League Baseball. Rather than providing information about who the best and worst managers are, it gives each manager's strategies for managing his team. It tells us, for example, that Terry Francona of the Cleveland Indians led the league in 2016 in PL%—the percent of players in starting lineups with the platoon advantage at the start of the game—with 73 percent. In contrast, Clint Hurdle of the Pittsburgh Pirates had only 41 percent of his starting players with the platoon advantage.

In his first managerial position in either the minor or the major leagues, Scott Servais of the Seattle Mariners led the American League with his use of 166 pinch hitters, 70 more than the league average and 31 more than second place, Bob Melvin of the Oakland Athletics. The Tampa Bay Rays' Kevin Cash really changed his strategy for using pinch hitters. In 2015, he led the American League with 219, but he used less than half of that total (103) in 2016. Ned Yost of the Kansas City Royals, however, sustained his strategy. For the second year in a row, he used the fewest pinch hitters in the league with 50, 10 more than his 2015 total.

Craig Counsell's Milwaukee Brewers led the league in stolen base attempts with 237. The Brewers' trade acquisition, Jonathan Villar, had over a third of his new team's attempts, leading all of Major League Baseball with 80. Buck Showalter's Orioles had the fewest stolen base attempts with 32 (or 40 percent of Villar's attempts). The greatest number of times any player on the Orioles attempted to steal a base was Joey Rickard with five attempts.

The columns under Pitcher Usage include Quick Hooks and Slow Hooks. For both of these, a score is calculated for each game—the sum of the number of Pitches plus 10 times the number of Runs Allowed. The bottom 25 percent of scores in the league are considered Quick Hooks and the top 25 percent are Slow Hooks. Interestingly, Chip Hale of the Arizona Diamondbacks led the league in Slow Hooks with 66 and had the fewest Quick Hooks (27) in the league. Conversely, Dave Roberts, in his first full season as a manager for the Los Angeles Dodgers, had the fewest Slow Hooks with 26 and led the league in Quick Hooks with 60. Roberts also set the single-season record for the most relievers used with 606.

The table at the end of this section illustrates that the average number of intentional walks in the National League was 40 with 26 of them resulting in a good outcome (65 percent), and 8 of them (20 percent) being bombs where the intentional walk blew up on the manager. Don Mattingly of the Miami Marlins led the league with 62 intentional walks, almost twice the 32 he ordered in 2015 with the Dodgers. In 2016, he had a higher percent of intentional walks with good outcomes than in 2015—68 as opposed to 56—but he also had a higher percentage of his bad outcomes resulting in bombs—70 as opposed to 36.

Brad Ausmus

Year	Team	Lg	G	LINEUPS		SUBSTITUTION			PITCHER USAGE						TACTICS				INTENTIONAL BB				RESULTS		
				LUp	PL%	PH	PR	DS	Quick	Slow	LO	RCD	LS	Rel	SBA	SacA	RM	PO	#	Good	NG	Bomb	W	L	Pct
2014	Tigers	AL	162	103	.51	79	43	44	28	55	43	99	1	473	147	32	144	13	34	17	17	5	90	72	.556
2015	Tigers	AL	161	122	.47	83	38	50	33	59	30	131	4	505	134	37	161	7	32	18	14	7	74	87	.460
2016	Tigers	AL	161	111	.48	89	31	50	41	37	18	93	4	476	87	21	95	3	25	12	13	4	86	75	.534
	162-Game Average			112	.48	84	37	48	34	51	30	108	3	487	123	30	134	8	30	16	15	5	84	78	.519

Dusty Baker

Year	Team	Lg	G	LINEUPS		SUBSTITUTION			PITCHER USAGE						TACTICS				INTENTIONAL BB				RESULTS		
				LUp	PL%	PH	PR	DS	Quick	Slow	LO	RCD	LS	Rel	SBA	SacA	RM	PO	#	Good	NG	Bomb	W	L	Pct
1994	Giants	NL	115	76	.53	177	16	9	29	25	2	86	12	288	154	88		78	40	24	16	8	55	60	.478
1995	Giants	NL	144	97	.41	230	36	13	32	50	8	90	8	381	184	101		77	51	32	19	14	67	77	.465
1996	Giants	NL	162	129	.53	250	17	15	24	58	15	94	8	425	166	103		96	60	37	23	15	68	94	.420
1997	Giants	NL	162	114	.71	212	17	22	46	25	17	132	4	481	170	85		93	57	36	21	12	90	72	.556
1998	Giants	NL	163	130	.62	224	20	12	43	38	8	113	5	433	153	111		41	68	42	26	9	89	74	.546
1999	Giants	NL	162	119	.62	233	16	16	30	51	27	111		450	165	113		40	41	25	16	10	86	76	.531
2000	Giants	NL	162	82	.56	233	26	22	38	50	25	91	3	384	118	86		37	26	17	9	2	97	65	.599
2001	Giants	NL	162	122	.48	261	22	19	40	48	10	114	4	439	99	95		45	49	33	16	6	90	72	.556
2002	Giants	NL	162	118	.43	223	32	38	29	56	53	106	8	417	95	89	42	41	44	28	16	10	95	66	.590
2003	Cubs	NL	162	114	.49	272	25	43	24	58	65	111	3	420	104	93	31	24	36	23	13	4	88	74	.543
2004	Cubs	NL	162	113	.44	254	16	19	37	41	42	129	8	460	94	108	71	62	33	22	11	7	89	73	.549
2005	Cubs	NL	162	121	.59	240	21	29	40	46	36	103	2	457	104	88	107	70	48	27	21	7	79	83	.488
2006	Cubs	NL	162	133	.56	271	9	26	45	39	22	165	2	542	170	108	139	46	44	28	16	11	66	96	.407
2008	Reds	NL	162	119	.58	285	28	27	26	63	39	124	2	507	132	100	101	37	40	28	12	4	74	88	.457
2009	Reds	NL	162	130	.45	252	15	35	30	62	35	115	1	478	136	120	118	23	36	29	7	4	78	84	.481
2010	Reds	NL	162	120	.46	258	19	49	36	41	22	140	0	502	136	91	157	13	32	22	10	9	91	71	.562
2011	Reds	NL	162	142	.42	240	29	42	34	51	20	115	0	501	147	102	226	33	47	26	21	5	79	83	.488
2012	Reds	NL	162	121	.43	201	19	39	33	39	30	78	4	425	114	108	148	19	33	22	11	3	97	65	.599
2013	Reds	NL	162	95	.54	236	20	27	39	40	14	90	3	461	102	110	157	21	28	23	5	3	90	72	.556
2016	Nationals	NL	162	112	.57	220	20	27	35	45	21	119	4	508	160	59	161	3	43	28	15	9	95	67	.586
	162-Game Average			118	.52	243	22	27	35	47	26	114	4	457	138	100	122	46	44	28	16	8	85	77	.525

Jeff Banister

Year	Team	Lg	G	LINEUPS		SUBSTITUTION			PITCHER USAGE						TACTICS				INTENTIONAL BB				RESULTS		
				LUp	PL%	PH	PR	DS	Quick	Slow	LO	RCD	LS	Rel	SBA	SacA	RM	PO	#	Good	NG	Bomb	W	L	Pct
2015	Rangers	AL	162	127	.57	94	51	46	40	47	11	122	0	498	140	66	158	5	29	19	10	5	88	74	.543
2016	Rangers	AL	162	124	.55	84	58	38	47	44	7	85	1	479	135	26	136	3	16	5	11	8	95	67	.586
	162-Game Average			126	.56	89	55	42	44	46	9	104	1	489	138	46	147	4	23	12	11	7	92	71	.564

Bud Black

Year	Team	Lg	G	LINEUPS		SUBSTITUTION			PITCHER USAGE						TACTICS				INTENTIONAL BB				RESULTS		
				LUp	PL%	PH	PR	DS	Quick	Slow	LO	RCD	LS	Rel	SBA	SacA	RM	PO	#	Good	NG	Bomb	W	L	Pct
2007	Padres	NL	163	115	.62	279	18	13	63	28	13	122	0	485	79	85	73	56	48	28	20	11	89	74	.546
2008	Padres	NL	162	113	.63	286	25	20	55	36	17	109	0	491	53	75	78	31	61	30	31	17	63	99	.389
2009	Padres	NL	162	137	.64	264	8	34	50	37	8	118	5	527	111	99	84	55	58	42	16	6	75	87	.463
2010	Padres	NL	162	135	.61	285	16	45	55	33	10	132	7	499	174	99	135	31	51	35	16	8	90	72	.556
2011	Padres	NL	162	140	.58	288	20	43	40	36	10	110	2	490	214	69	184	41	56	31	25	13	71	91	.438
2012	Padres	NL	162	132	.74	280	26	35	45	49	11	126	5	529	201	89	162	21	48	34	14	7	76	86	.469
2013	Padres	NL	162	145	.66	271	24	37	35	46	4	102	1	488	152	78	122	12	31	20	11	8	76	86	.469
2014	Padres	NL	162	157	.74	313	23	29	49	33	13	104	1	481	125	74	116	15	32	24	8	4	77	85	.475
2015	Padres	NL	65	50	.58	113	6	6	8	25	3	40	0	199	54	24	46	2	15	11	4	0	32	33	.492
	162-Game Average			134	.65	283	20	31	48	38	11	115	2	498	138	82	119	31	48	30	17	9	77	85	.475

Bruce Bochy

Year	Team	Lg	G	LINEUPS		SUBSTITUTION			PITCHER USAGE						TACTICS				INTENTIONAL BB				RESULTS		
				LUp	PL%	PH	PR	DS	Quick	Slow	LO	RCD	LS	Rel	SBA	SacA	RM	PO	#	Good	NG	Bomb	W	L	Pct
1995	Padres	NL	144	96	.59	262	30	23	44	41	17	38	3	337	170	68		38	37	19	18	11	70	74	.486
1996	Padres	NL	162	114	.52	289	29	15	51	33	10	67	12	411	164	73		65	47	29	18	12	91	71	.562
1997	Padres	NL	162	111	.60	291	26	9	45	45	3	81	11	426	200	84		58	37	20	17	11	76	86	.469
1998	Padres	NL	162	108	.65	280	62	44	44	45	9	81	12	369	116	84		27	45	31	14	10	98	64	.605
1999	Padres	NL	162	137	.60	298	51	21	44	36	4	68	5	403	241	60		29	48	29	19	13	74	88	.457
2000	Padres	NL	162	134	.52	285	44	14	41	47	14	105	5	443	184	52		27	50	21	29	11	76	86	.469
2001	Padres	NL	162	116	.60	255	54	27	32	47	6	85	10	422	173	43		23	54	31	23	13	79	83	.488
2002	Padres	NL	162	123	.66	259	44	56	39	40	17	106	4	459	115	63	74	14	61	38	23	14	66	96	.407
2003	Padres	NL	162	134	.58	339	20	29	34	43	16	100	3	473	115	63	41	6	52	33	19	12	64	98	.395
2004	Padres	NL	162	96	.54	261	28	47	47	32	15	76	3	437	77	75	96	14	39	24	15	10	87	75	.537
2005	Padres	NL	162	128	.58	285	31	49	46	36	23	87	1	456	143	89	111	16	45	33	12	8	82	80	.506
2006	Padres	NL	162	111	.60	264	64	48	43	42	24	111	2	475	154	77	110	21	63	43	20	10	88	74	.543

Year	Team	Lg	G	LUp	PL%	PH	PR	DS	Quick	Slow	LO	RCD	LS	Rel	SBA	SacA	RM	PO	#	Good	NG	Bomb	W	L	Pct
				LINEUPS		**SUBSTITUTION**			**PITCHER USAGE**						**TACTICS**				**INTENTIONAL BB**				**RESULTS**		
2007	Giants	NL	162	128	.72	264	50	45	26	50	**36**	132	2	496	152	86	119	10	41	29	12	3	71	91	.438
2008	Giants	NL	162	134	.68	276	32	39	24	59	**42**	97	6	478	154	77	**155**	5	59	40	19	8	72	90	.444
2009	Giants	NL	162	134	.65	231	21	52	42	40	32	84	**8**	457	106	93	118	5	49	32	17	10	88	74	.543
2010	Giants	NL	162	126	.55	224	45	**70**	29	37	40	118	**12**	477	87	102	144	12	58	41	17	8	92	70	.568
2011	Giants	NL	162	138	.62	245	**49**	42	38	38	44	108	3	480	136	79	175	11	46	36	10	6	86	76	.531
2012	Giants	NL	162	112	.75	220	32	55	22	50	**31**	136	**9**	526	157	87	**176**	15	42	30	12	5	94	68	.580
2013	Giants	NL	162	109	.70	263	19	45	33	**52**	23	**143**	4	524	93	78	164	7	**64**	**46**	18	6	76	86	.469
2014	Giants	NL	162	131	.66	236	29	**64**	45	41	19	102	1	475	83	53	147	12	35	25	10	9	88	74	.543
2015	Giants	NL	162	124	.63	230	12	21	45	32	11	137	2	557	129	54	173	8	28	20	8	3	84	78	.519
2016	Giants	NL	162	121	.66	268	7	29	31	42	**28**	148	4	575	115	54	**178**	6	30	25	5	4	87	75	.537
	162-Game Average			122	.62	266	36	39	39	42	21	101	6	464	140	73	132	20	47	31	16	9	82	80	.506

Tim Bogar

Year	Team	Lg	G	LUp	PL%	PH	PR	DS	Quick	Slow	LO	RCD	LS	Rel	SBA	SacA	RM	PO	#	Good	NG	Bomb	W	L	Pct
				LINEUPS		**SUBSTITUTION**			**PITCHER USAGE**						**TACTICS**				**INTENTIONAL BB**				**RESULTS**		
2014	Rangers	AL	22	21	.56	1	5	0	10	3	3	11	0	76	29	6	23	1	9	5	4	3	14	8	.636
	162-Game Average			155	.56	7	37	0	74	22	22	81	0	560	214	44	169	7	66	37	29	22	103	59	.636

Kevin Cash

Year	Team	Lg	G	LUp	PL%	PH	PR	DS	Quick	Slow	LO	RCD	LS	Rel	SBA	SacA	RM	PO	#	Good	NG	Bomb	W	L	Pct
				LINEUPS		**SUBSTITUTION**			**PITCHER USAGE**						**TACTICS**				**INTENTIONAL BB**				**RESULTS**		
2015	Rays	AL	162	137	.62	**219**	23	38	**72**	33	10	134	3	**530**	132	27	**173**	2	23	17	6	3	80	82	.494
2016	Rays	AL	162	142	.55	103	11	28	42	52	18	100	8	485	97	24	146	12	25	16	9	4	68	94	.420
	162-Game Average			140	.58	161	17	33	57	43	14	117	6	508	115	26	160	7	24	17	8	4	74	88	.457

Terry Collins

Year	Team	Lg	G	LUp	PL%	PH	PR	DS	Quick	Slow	LO	RCD	LS	Rel	SBA	SacA	RM	PO	#	Good	NG	Bomb	W	L	Pct
				LINEUPS		**SUBSTITUTION**			**PITCHER USAGE**						**TACTICS**				**INTENTIONAL BB**				**RESULTS**		
1994	Astros	NL	115	74	.54	185	20	13	6	6	0	37	4	268	168	90		37	28	17	11	5	66	49	.574
1995	Astros	NL	144	106	.49	302	38	11	15	7	8	100	8	394	236	97		44	39	27	12	8	76	68	.528
1996	Astros	NL	162	111	.41	257	30	28	13	12	9	70	10	371	243	94		35	42	30	12	6	82	80	.506
1997	Angels	AL	162	117	.70	86	34	22	10	16	15	67	8	400	198	55		60	25	13	12	4	84	78	.519
1998	Angels	AL	162	119	.57	100	64	33	15	11	28	86	11	415	138	69		38	16	6	10	4	85	77	.525
1999	Angels	AL	133	113	.56	93	26	16	10	16	10	68	2	315	93	39		7	10	1	9	3	51	82	.383
2011	Mets	NL	162	121	.68	**312**	18	28	32	44	23	126	5	514	165	88	151	9	48	35	13	9	77	85	.475
2012	Mets	NL	162	**141**	.69	**329**	16	38	39	36	19	113	0	505	117	75	149	8	29	18	11	3	74	88	.457
2013	Mets	NL	162	132	.61	266	12	33	33	42	15	131	**4**	**535**	149	67	128	3	38	30	8	3	74	88	.457
2014	Mets	NL	162	135	.55	247	17	26	28	46	23	111	**6**	489	135	73	119	2	38	23	15	4	79	83	.488
2015	Mets	NL	162	138	.52	255	21	40	47	36	6	119	**8**	485	76	49	117	1	43	33	10	6	90	72	.556
2016	Mets	NL	162	129	.68	292	17	50	53	33	6	141	4	538	60	55	80	6	39	26	13	9	87	75	.537
	162-Game Average			126	.59	239	27	30	26	27	14	102	6	458	156	75	124	22	35	23	12	6	81	81	.500

Craig Counsell

Year	Team	Lg	G	LUp	PL%	PH	PR	DS	Quick	Slow	LO	RCD	LS	Rel	SBA	SacA	RM	PO	#	Good	NG	Bomb	W	L	Pct
				LINEUPS		**SUBSTITUTION**			**PITCHER USAGE**						**TACTICS**				**INTENTIONAL BB**				**RESULTS**		
2015	Brewers	NL	137	106	.54	247	14	30	30	47	3	85	1	424	99	56	106	2	30	26	4	3	61	76	.445
2016	Brewers	NL	162	123	.55	284	4	22	40	41	1	115	3	513	**237**	71	160	0	33	16	17	8	73	89	.451
	162-Game Average			124	.55	288	10	28	38	48	2	108	2	508	182	69	144	1	34	23	11	6	73	89	.451

John Farrell

Year	Team	Lg	G	LUp	PL%	PH	PR	DS	Quick	Slow	LO	RCD	LS	Rel	SBA	SacA	RM	PO	#	Good	NG	Bomb	W	L	Pct
				LINEUPS		**SUBSTITUTION**			**PITCHER USAGE**						**TACTICS**				**INTENTIONAL BB**				**RESULTS**		
2011	Blue Jays	AL	162	131	.43	64	**48**	22	40	41	26	62	3	474	183	40	181	22	28	17	11	5	81	81	.500
2012	Blue Jays	AL	162	131	.50	94	30	16	49	44	7	84	3	495	164	46	211	15	20	11	9	7	73	89	.451
2013	Red Sox	AL	162	126	.68	93	41	20	28	46	34	71	4	450	142	32	147	5	10	5	5	3	**97**	65	.599
2014	Red Sox	AL	162	**145**	.55	101	24	17	29	53	28	107	1	493	88	26	124	4	19	11	8	2	71	91	.438
2015	Red Sox	AL	114	96	.56	55	18	20	26	28	6	62	1	326	63	27	105	2	12	6	6	1	50	64	.439
2016	Red Sox	AL	162	118	.53	110	28	11	34	51	26	79	2	463	107	15	169	0	16	8	8	3	93	69	.574
	162-Game Average			131	.54	91	33	19	36	46	22	82	2	474	131	33	164	8	18	10	8	4	82	80	.506

Terry Francona

Year	Team	Lg	G	LUp	PL%	PH	PR	DS	Quick	Slow	LO	RCD	LS	Rel	SBA	SacA	RM	PO	#	Good	NG	Bomb	W	L	Pct
				LINEUPS		SUBSTITUTION			PITCHER USAGE						TACTICS				INTENTIONAL BB				RESULTS		
1997	Phillies	NL	162	98	.66	288	19	28	28	54	22	102	9	409	148	91		30	42	23	19	9	68	94	.420
1998	Phillies	NL	162	84	.53	256	20	19	34	57	20	88	7	385	142	85		16	27	10	17	8	75	87	.463
1999	Phillies	NL	162	85	.51	239	13	31	29	41	16	111	7	441	160	81		27	24	14	10	7	77	85	.475
2000	Phillies	NL	162	108	.53	278	17	14	38	43	25	102	5	414	132	89		16	32	22	10	7	65	97	.401
2004	Red Sox	AL	162	141	.65	116	65	58	41	48	32	105	8	437	98	18	91	28	28	22	6	4	98	64	.605
2005	Red Sox	AL	162	104	.67	110	46	37	25	55	30	99	3	442	57	21	79	11	28	18	10	5	95	67	.586
2006	Red Sox	AL	162	116	.59	93	54	49	36	44	13	94	9	454	74	33	98	16	25	11	14	7	86	76	.531
2007	Red Sox	AL	162	109	.60	84	34	23	41	35	32	89	4	451	120	45	90	14	20	14	6	4	96	66	.593
2008	Red Sox	AL	162	131	.59	62	40	40	50	30	20	90	11	466	155	40	87	8	17	10	7	4	95	67	.586
2009	Red Sox	AL	162	113	.58	85	47	28	36	50	30	68	6	463	165	29	68	6	24	15	9	6	95	67	.586
2010	Red Sox	AL	162	143	.62	125	48	34	32	63	49	84	6	443	85	36	125	26	30	17	13	4	89	73	.549
2011	Red Sox	AL	162	123	.67	89	44	11	52	46	27	89	4	444	144	29	163	34	11	6	5	2	90	72	.556
2013	Indians	AL	162	121	.75	78	45	24	47	34	18	122	2	540	153	41	158	5	26	15	11	6	92	70	.568
2014	Indians	AL	162	133	.78	123	16	24	37	37	18	150	7	573	131	58	128	3	51	29	22	13	85	77	.525
2015	Indians	AL	161	127	.75	138	21	13	40	36	23	85	8	476	114	63	87	4	27	20	7	5	81	80	.503
2016	Indians	AL	161	101	.73	114	27	29	47	39	18	103	3	504	165	44	126	2	34	22	12	7	94	67	.584
	162-Game Average			115	.64	142	35	29	38	45	25	99	6	459	128	50	108	16	28	17	11	6	86	76	.531

Ron Gardenhire

Year	Team	Lg	G	LUp	PL%	PH	PR	DS	Quick	Slow	LO	RCD	LS	Rel	SBA	SacA	RM	PO	#	Good	NG	Bomb	W	L	Pct
				LINEUPS		SUBSTITUTION			PITCHER USAGE						TACTICS				INTENTIONAL BB				RESULTS		
2002	Twins	AL	161	111	.69	141	36	42	54	25	10	84	1	435	141	48	44	11	24	16	8	4	94	67	.584
2003	Twins	AL	162	126	.63	144	50	26	49	33	13	85	2	399	138	59	37	14	35	16	19	6	90	72	.556
2004	Twins	AL	162	131	.59	129	45	29	56	21	20	106	4	435	162	66	121	18	27	15	12	7	92	70	.568
2005	Twins	AL	162	135	.58	104	45	26	50	21	5	87	1	396	146	59	138	16	38	28	10	3	83	79	.512
2006	Twins	AL	162	97	.62	93	36	21	60	31	3	82	5	421	143	48	130	11	25	14	11	4	96	66	.593
2007	Twins	AL	162	139	.63	104	42	25	45	30	8	99	4	438	142	45	148	11	33	14	19	9	79	83	.488
2008	Twins	AL	163	103	.64	109	26	12	47	29	5	115	3	485	144	73	143	17	38	25	13	8	88	75	.540
2009	Twins	AL	163	129	.63	83	54	34	43	25	12	115	3	480	117	62	100	21	20	9	11	6	87	76	.534
2010	Twins	AL	162	112	.62	86	55	30	57	28	5	106	1	465	96	47	140	14	19	12	7	4	94	68	.580
2011	Twins	AL	162	150	.58	93	48	21	34	44	17	82	1	457	131	44	170	5	37	21	16	9	63	99	.389
2012	Twins	AL	162	121	.62	64	45	24	42	31	4	82	1	499	172	49	207	10	43	27	16	6	66	96	.407
2013	Twins	AL	162	139	.66	103	42	28	41	43	6	78	1	511	85	37	137	14	31	13	18	7	66	96	.407
2014	Twins	AL	162	132	.64	97	44	23	40	40	2	82	2	491	135	31	149	5	24	11	13	6	70	92	.432
	162-Game Average			125	.62	104	44	26	48	31	8	92	2	455	135	51	128	13	30	17	13	6	82	80	.506

John Gibbons

Year	Team	Lg	G	LUp	PL%	PH	PR	DS	Quick	Slow	LO	RCD	LS	Rel	SBA	SacA	RM	PO	#	Good	NG	Bomb	W	L	Pct
				LINEUPS		SUBSTITUTION			PITCHER USAGE						TACTICS				INTENTIONAL BB				RESULTS		
2004	Blue Jays	AL	50	36	.68	42	3	2	16	8	7	22	1	130	34	2	47	21	11	5	6	3	20	30	.400
2005	Blue Jays	AL	162	124	.66	148	11	37	55	18	9	77	12	432	107	28	128	45	29	13	16	9	80	82	.494
2006	Blue Jays	AL	162	120	.53	112	32	40	59	33	17	94	16	482	98	20	127	40	56	32	24	12	87	75	.537
2007	Blue Jays	AL	162	131	.46	139	48	33	45	37	31	75	9	420	79	35	99	37	34	17	17	6	83	79	.512
2008	Blue Jays	AL	74	60	.48	53	15	18	12	20	12	43	0	205	70	23	39	10	26	16	10	6	35	39	.473
2013	Blue Jays	AL	162	136	.64	124	31	24	55	44	14	69	2	487	153	41	160	4	33	17	16	6	74	88	.457
2014	Blue Jays	AL	162	128	.72	202	41	49	45	37	20	73	8	449	99	49	161	6	23	17	6	2	83	79	.512
2015	Blue Jays	AL	162	129	.48	97	41	47	46	37	13	85	6	469	111	45	152	2	20	10	10	3	93	69	.574
2016	Blue Jays	AL	162	141	.44	90	37	54	39	30	6	98	6	487	78	33	109	1	10	6	4	3	89	73	.549
	162-Game Average			129	.56	130	33	39	48	34	17	82	8	459	107	36	132	21	31	17	14	6	83	79	.512

Kirk Gibson

Year	Team	Lg	G	LUp	PL%	PH	PR	DS	Quick	Slow	LO	RCD	LS	Rel	SBA	SacA	RM	PO	#	Good	NG	Bomb	W	L	Pct
				LINEUPS		SUBSTITUTION			PITCHER USAGE						TACTICS				INTENTIONAL BB				RESULTS		
2010	Diamondbacks	NL	83	57	.64	154	7	11	25	21	8	43	1	247	69	28	62	19	19	13	6	2	34	49	.410
2011	Diamondbacks	NL	162	118	.57	253	9	13	33	51	15	116	2	463	188	74	143	12	16	10	6	3	94	68	.580
2012	Diamondbacks	NL	162	140	.56	231	11	9	35	50	16	104	4	461	144	77	120	8	18	11	7	1	81	81	.500
2013	Diamondbacks	NL	162	138	.59	285	22	15	31	44	9	121	0	527	103	67	108	3	42	31	11	5	81	81	.500
2014	Diamondbacks	NL	159	135	.55	247	19	18	43	41	5	92	1	479	117	67	140	13	42	28	14	10	63	96	.396
	162-Game Average			131	.57	260	15	15	37	46	12	106	2	484	138	70	128	12	30	21	10	5	79	83	.488

Joe Girardi

Year	Team	Lg	G	LUp	PL%	PH	PR	DS	Quick	Slow	LO	RCD	LS	Rel	SBA	SacA	RM	PO	#	Good	NG	Bomb	W	L	Pct
				LINEUPS		SUBSTITUTION			PITCHER USAGE						TACTICS				INTENTIONAL BB				RESULTS		
2006	Marlins	NL	162	117	.50	250	44	66	46	40	28	76	3	438	168	97	108	42	58	37	21	7	78	84	.481
2008	Yankees	AL	162	114	.63	97	37	42	60	37	12	88	10	475	157	38	173	36	37	22	15	8	89	73	.549
2009	Yankees	AL	162	106	.73	97	61	42	36	45	27	88	13	461	139	44	83	33	28	14	14	9	103	59	.636

Year	Team	Lg	G	LUp	PL%	PH	PR	DS	Quick	Slow	LO	RCD	LS	Rel	SBA	SacA	RM	PO	#	Good	NG	Bomb	W	L	Pct
2010	Yankees	AL	162	114	.72	117	44	31	43	39	33	76	3	430	133	47	152	20	37	26	11	6	95	67	.586
2011	Yankees	AL	162	94	.69	72	41	53	51	36	21	88	2	465	193	50	151	26	43	30	13	4	97	65	.599
2012	Yankees	AL	162	107	.70	149	33	48	37	53	21	115	7	485	120	47	145	10	32	17	15	6	95	67	.586
2013	Yankees	AL	162	141	.59	119	15	29	42	50	23	82	4	428	146	49	131	4	34	20	14	6	85	77	.525
2014	Yankees	AL	162	142	.74	100	27	33	51	28	10	95	7	475	138	44	132	8	23	10	13	9	84	78	.519
2015	Yankees	AL	162	126	.79	118	50	57	48	34	9	80	10	497	88	32	92	6	16	8	8	4	87	75	.537
2016	Yankees	AL	162	143	.72	85	32	48	53	44	8	99	7	483	94	35	89	3	15	9	6	4	84	78	.519
	162-Game Average			120	.68	120	38	45	47	41	19	89	7	464	138	48	126	19	32	19	13	6	90	72	.556

Fredi Gonzalez

Year	Team	Lg	G	LUp	PL%	PH	PR	DS	Quick	Slow	LO	RCD	LS	Rel	SBA	SacA	RM	PO	#	Good	NG	Bomb	W	L	Pct
2007	Marlins	NL	162	96	.50	284	29	34	33	56	20	138	5	560	139	91	79	22	60	36	24	16	71	91	.438
2008	Marlins	NL	161	106	.51	255	38	49	38	39	8	120	3	465	104	61	75	17	66	42	24	14	84	77	.522
2009	Marlins	NL	162	97	.58	281	28	49	48	26	12	116	0	530	110	86	88	20	60	38	22	15	87	75	.537
2010	Marlins	NL	70	31	.41	104	12	16	14	13	11	35	1	193	56	33	64	10	18	11	7	5	34	36	.486
2011	Braves	NL	162	119	.60	260	27	29	53	36	21	144	0	510	121	95	139	19	73	49	24	13	89	73	.549
2012	Braves	NL	162	108	.61	268	18	27	50	34	9	115	4	460	133	67	116	20	40	28	12	11	94	68	.580
2013	Braves	NL	162	115	.50	214	40	51	50	42	8	124	2	466	95	79	94	11	35	26	9	4	96	66	.593
2014	Braves	NL	162	103	.45	206	34	34	27	41	20	122	3	472	128	70	106	23	36	24	12	8	79	83	.488
2015	Braves	NL	162	140	.61	255	21	31	35	55	7	136	0	532	102	80	135	4	45	35	10	5	67	95	.414
2016	Braves	NL	37	34	.73	58	9	11	9	9	3	33	1	131	26	20	36	0	15	11	4	2	9	28	.243
	162-Game Average			110	.54	252	30	38	41	41	14	125	2	504	117	79	108	17	52	35	17	11	82	80	.506

Andy Green

Year	Team	Lg	G	LUp	PL%	PH	PR	DS	Quick	Slow	LO	RCD	LS	Rel	SBA	SacA	RM	PO	#	Good	NG	Bomb	W	L	Pct
2016	Padres	NL	162	130	.56	249	29	25	46	53	6	119	4	510	170	48	138	3	44	26	18	9	68	94	.420
	162-Game Average			130	.56	249	29	25	46	53	6	119	4	510	170	48	138	3	44	26	18	9	68	94	.420

Chip Hale

Year	Team	Lg	G	LUp	PL%	PH	PR	DS	Quick	Slow	LO	RCD	LS	Rel	SBA	SacA	RM	PO	#	Good	NG	Bomb	W	L	Pct
2015	Diamondbacks	NL	162	130	.48	270	14	35	49	35	5	103	8	550	176	67	146	5	45	35	10	6	79	83	.488
2016	Diamondbacks	NL	162	139	.45	266	10	30	27	66	7	130	5	575	168	51	120	0	57	41	16	8	69	93	.426
	162-Game Average			135	.46	268	12	33	38	51	6	117	7	563	172	59	133	3	51	38	13	7	74	88	.457

A.J. Hinch

Year	Team	Lg	G	LUp	PL%	PH	PR	DS	Quick	Slow	LO	RCD	LS	Rel	SBA	SacA	RM	PO	#	Good	NG	Bomb	W	L	Pct
2009	Diamondbacks	NL	133	115	.63	222	10	13	24	50	24	61	5	392	113	64	41	5	24	12	12	6	58	75	.436
2010	Diamondbacks	NL	79	56	.53	120	7	4	12	40	21	39	1	207	58	19	51	7	19	9	10	9	31	48	.392
2015	Astros	AL	162	151	.63	122	40	37	33	41	19	97	0	482	169	31	128	6	17	11	6	2	86	76	.531
2016	Astros	AL	162	143	.55	118	35	27	42	35	9	87	1	500	146	38	137	5	19	11	8	6	84	78	.519
	162-Game Average			141	.59	176	28	24	34	50	22	86	2	478	147	46	108	7	24	13	11	7	78	84	.481

Clint Hurdle

Year	Team	Lg	G	LUp	PL%	PH	PR	DS	Quick	Slow	LO	RCD	LS	Rel	SBA	SacA	RM	PO	#	Good	NG	Bomb	W	L	Pct
2002	Rockies	NL	140	100	.52	274	28	41	33	45	17	104	3	437	139	46	50	13	38	22	16	11	67	73	.479
2003	Rockies	NL	162	108	.47	317	17	32	35	40	5	87	4	500	100	82	26	16	51	31	20	13	74	88	.457
2004	Rockies	NL	162	131	.57	289	18	35	36	63	20	74	1	473	77	128	67	12	84	54	30	12	68	94	.420
2005	Rockies	NL	162	135	.60	273	21	40	42	60	17	89	2	459	97	114	119	22	54	28	26	15	67	95	.414
2006	Rockies	NL	162	111	.49	259	17	22	34	52	17	107	2	499	135	156	114	28	81	45	36	23	76	86	.469
2007	Rockies	NL	163	96	.51	283	32	29	45	37	13	112	1	529	131	112	109	26	61	30	31	14	90	73	.552
2008	Rockies	NL	162	131	.49	253	20	31	40	43	16	85	2	485	178	111	116	43	49	31	18	6	74	88	.457
2009	Rockies	NL	46	42	.60	73	8	10	11	14	3	31	0	135	45	26	34	3	11	8	3	1	18	28	.391
2011	Pirates	NL	162	134	.60	278	26	63	58	27	1	134	3	549	160	101	173	20	65	39	26	13	72	90	.444
2012	Pirates	NL	162	133	.55	270	26	60	50	33	3	74	2	483	125	82	120	17	30	18	12	3	79	83	.488
2013	Pirates	NL	162	127	.51	289	24	61	61	25	7	76	3	465	136	83	172	20	26	22	4	2	94	68	.580
2014	Pirates	NL	162	123	.50	322	28	38	47	40	7	91	0	452	151	85	187	24	43	26	17	7	88	74	.543
2015	Pirates	NL	162	108	.50	269	48	76	39	40	9	124	1	500	143	81	173	9	38	31	7	3	98	64	.605
2016	Pirates	NL	162	125	.41	293	39	73	57	36	1	119	4	525	155	55	154	9	28	15	13	6	78	83	.484
	162-Game Average			122	.52	285	27	46	45	42	10	99	2	494	135	96	123	20	50	30	20	10	79	83	.488

Dan Jennings

Year	Team	Lg	G	LUp	PL%	PH	PR	DS	Quick	Slow	LO	RCD	LS	Rel	SBA	SacA	RM	PO	# Good	NG	Bomb	W	L	Pct
2015	Marlins	NL	124	98	.53	186	14	23	32	30	4	67	3	379	120	63	97	2	22	12	10	5	55	69	.444
	162-Game Average			128	.53	243	18	30	42	39	5	88	4	495	157	82	127	3	29	16	13	7	72	90	.444

Davey Johnson

Year	Team	Lg	G	LUp	PL%	PH	PR	DS	Quick	Slow	LO	RCD	LS	Rel	SBA	SacA	RM	PO	# Good	NG	Bomb	W	L	Pct
1994	Reds	NL	115	79	.54	195	22	12	32	28	2	56	12	261	170	86	0	41	23	15	8	1	66	48	.579
1995	Reds	NL	144	105	.55	257	18	31	56	18	1	60	16	329	258	88	0	10	32	16	16	10	85	59	.590
1996	Orioles	AL	163	99	.68	85	33	38	48	48	13	67	9	378	117	62	0	6	35	13	22	11	88	74	.543
1997	Orioles	AL	162	109	.56	104	36	43	65	23	5	84	11	400	89	75	0	10	31	16	15	9	98	64	.605
1999	Dodgers	NL	162	109	.53	236	22	9	36	40	8	67	4	399	235	126	0	19	26	17	9	7	77	85	.475
2000	Dodgers	NL	162	89	.59	252	26	11	20	15	10		6	371	137	80	51	11	14	8	6	2	86	76	.531
2011	Nationals	NL	83	59	.45	143	20	23	40	13	1	51	1	271	58	51	85	6	19	10	9	6	40	43	.482
2012	Nationals	NL	162	93	.60	252	30	42	57	30	10	105	1	482	140	67	158	2	32	21	11	7	98	64	.605
2013	Nationals	NL	162	108	.54	233	23	33	46	39	27	99	0	440	116	91	148	1	17	8	9	3	86	76	.531
	162-Game Average			99	.35	226	29	18	47	36	18	66	15	354	173	88	176	18	33	18	15	8	92	70	.568

Tom Lawless

Year	Team	Lg	G	LUp	PL%	PH	PR	DS	Quick	Slow	LO	RCD	LS	Rel	SBA	SacA	RM	PO	# Good	NG	Bomb	W	L	Pct
2014	Astros	AL	24	23	.64	18	6	9	8	3	5	7	1	67	39	9	35	3	6	2	4	1	11	13	.458
	162-Game Average			155	.64	122	41	61	54	20	34	47	7	452	263	61	236	20	41	14	27	7	74	88	.457

Jim Leyland

Year	Team	Lg	G	LUp	PL%	PH	PR	DS	Quick	Slow	LO	RCD	LS	Rel	SBA	SacA	RM	PO	# Good	NG	Bomb	W	L	Pct
1994	Pirates	NL	114	94	.56	170	16	13	12	9	1	48	4	285	78	48		38	52	29	23	15	53	61	.465
1995	Pirates	NL	144	124	.56	282	8	4	13	12	11	71	4	391	139	69		51	50	30	20	10	58	86	.403
1996	Pirates	NL	162	117	.53	299	18	14	27	8	11	60	11	422	175	101		46	50	23	27	13	73	89	.451
1997	Marlins	NL	162	105	.59	258	36	31	21	12	18	65	2	404	173	91		38	41	25	16	9	92	70	.568
1998	Marlins	NL	162	96	.56	277	13	15	18	24	31	73	8	420	172	91		31	61	36	25	11	54	108	.333
1999	Rockies	NL	162	124	.56	294	11	12	11	29	21	72	5	421	113	88		11	46	24	22	14	72	90	.444
2006	Tigers	AL	162	120	.53	81	34	38	52	32	16	52	3	390	100	57	128	9	35	23	12	9	95	67	.586
2007	Tigers	AL	162	108	.53	77	31	49	46	43	14	70	5	443	133	35	123	20	41	24	17	13	88	74	.543
2008	Tigers	AL	162	131	.51	66	25	50	29	47	20	72	7	440	94	40	114	10	63	37	26	13	74	88	.457
2009	Tigers	AL	163	126	.55	125	52	50	47	47	38	86	3	439	105	60	132	19	42	26	16	6	86	77	.528
2010	Tigers	AL	162	129	.58	130	11	47	36	54	45	70	6	416	99	54	174	31	29	14	15	9	81	81	.500
2011	Tigers	AL	162	127	.63	86	42	87	43	39	39	84	1	421	69	62	172	7	34	17	17	10	95	67	.586
2012	Tigers	AL	162	121	.58	76	33	62	38	41	37	103	0	420	82	46	151	14	35	21	14	7	88	74	.543
2013	Tigers	AL	162	109	.61	105	40	34	25	48	50	77	6	428	55	42	180	6	29	16	13	8	93	69	.574
	162-Game Average			120	.57	171	27	37	24	33	26	74	5	422	117	65	147	24	45	25	19	11	81	81	.500

Torey Lovullo

Year	Team	Lg	G	LUp	PL%	PH	PR	DS	Quick	Slow	LO	RCD	LS	Rel	SBA	SacA	RM	PO	# Good	NG	Bomb	W	L	Pct
2015	Red Sox	AL	48	40	.58	17	17	4	9	16	10	28	0	149	35	10	32	0	5	3	2	1	28	20	.583
	162-Game Average			135	.58	57	57	14	30	54	34	95	0	503	118	34	108	0	17	10	7	3	95	68	.583

Pete Mackanin

Year	Team	Lg	G	LUp	PL%	PH	PR	DS	Quick	Slow	LO	RCD	LS	Rel	SBA	SacA	RM	PO	# Good	NG	Bomb	W	L	Pct
2005	Pirates	NL	26	24	.52	54	1	5	11	4	1	22	0	94	19	19	20	2	5	2	3	1	12	14	.462
2007	Reds	NL	80	57	.59	130	10	26	20	22	9	58	3	266	62	44	36	12	18	10	8	3	41	39	.513
2015	Phillies	NL	88	82	.76	143	2	16	25	26	5	58	4	278	70	48	93	9	12	7	5	2	37	51	.420
2016	Phillies	NL	162	144	.64	260	14	46	44	44	4	128	2	505	141	61	138	17	30	19	11	10	71	91	.438
	162-Game Average			140	.65	267	12	42	46	44	9	121	4	520	133	78	131	18	30	17	12	7	73	89	.451

Joe Maddon

Year	Team	Lg	G	LUp	PL%	PH	PR	DS	Quick	Slow	LO	RCD	LS	Rel	SBA	SacA	RM	PO	# Good	NG	Bomb	W	L	Pct
1996	Angels	AL		19	.56	21	5	0	7	6	6	10	3	48	11	20		6	4	3	1	1	8	14	.364
1998	Angels	AL	8	4	.57	2	4	0	1	5	3	5	2	13	2	7		0	1	0	1	0	6	2	.750
1999	Angels	AL	29	19	.58	29	4	1	6	0	4	20	0	85	23	12		7	3	1	2	1	19	10	.655

Year	Team	Lg	G	LINEUPS		SUBSTITUTION			PITCHER USAGE						TACTICS				INTENTIONAL BB				RESULTS		
				LUp	PL%	PH	PR	DS	Quick	Slow	LO	RCD	LS	Rel	SBA	SacA	RM	PO	#	Good	NG	Bomb	W	L	Pct
2006	Devil Rays	AL	162	145	.54	81	26	51	41	39	16	79	10	444	186	51	132	48	39	19	20	13	61	101	.377
2007	Devil Rays	AL	162	122	.53	80	19	16	31	56	19	113	1	483	179	40	118	50	31	18	13	4	66	96	.407
2008	Rays	AL	162	115	.69	133	16	39	48	37	14	112	7	448	192	31	113	26	29	15	14	8	97	65	.599
2009	Rays	AL	162	123	.66	140	21	18	28	51	23	139	3	510	255	29	99	15	22	10	12	7	84	78	.519
2010	Rays	AL	162	129	.67	174	31	18	41	34	26	135	2	491	219	45	166	12	34	28	6	3	96	66	.593
2011	Rays	AL	162	130	.67	137	16	31	34	36	47	112	6	438	217	42	187	4	38	23	15	6	91	71	.562
2012	Rays	AL	162	151	.62	156	37	52	43	38	33	123	3	472	178	40	181	7	35	25	10	6	90	72	.556
2013	Rays	AL	163	147	.64	193	27	56	52	38	16	111	6	485	111	26	117	6	38	21	17	11	92	71	.564
2014	Rays	AL	162	130	.58	171	23	15	44	35	26	110	3	494	90	54	143	2	27	20	7	3	77	85	.475
2015	Cubs	NL	162	119	.60	288	22	32	41	31	14	129	2	552	132	48	180	3	38	22	16	10	97	65	.599
2016	Cubs	NL	162	130	.62	236	19	35	56	29	13	100	3	503	100	54	111	6	24	19	5	3	103	58	.640
	162-Game Average			130	.62	162	24	32	42	38	23	114	5	481	167	44	141	17	32	20	12	7	87	75	.537

Charlie Manuel

Year	Team	Lg	G	LINEUPS		SUBSTITUTION			PITCHER USAGE						TACTICS				INTENTIONAL BB				RESULTS		
				LUp	PL%	PH	PR	DS	Quick	Slow	LO	RCD	LS	Rel	SBA	SacA	RM	PO	#	Good	NG	Bomb	W	L	Pct
2000	Indians	AL	162	102	.64	73	40	26	21	12	20	104	7	462	147	59		30	45	28	17	9	90	72	.556
2001	Indians	AL	162	114	.61	105	30	49	28	17	10	120	3	484	120	67		43	44	30	14	11	91	71	.562
2002	Indians	AL	86	67	.61	57	10	19	14	17	25	47	0	222	57	21	34	3	21	12	9	4	39	47	.453
2005	Phillies	NL	162	80	.64	265	36	19	42	28	13	119	6	442	143	86	76	11	51	35	16	9	88	74	.543
2006	Phillies	NL	162	81	.65	301	42	49	28	43	22	126	2	500	117	79	74	16	63	35	28	12	85	77	.525
2007	Phillies	NL	162	87	.64	264	56	75	40	40	19	128	6	498	157	84	90	30	62	41	21	16	89	73	.549
2008	Phillies	NL	162	77	.65	291	62	60	33	42	24	124	1	468	161	88	92	34	64	46	18	11	92	70	.568
2009	Phillies	NL	162	68	.67	283	20	16	32	55	32	107	3	459	147	74	65	3	31	19	12	3	93	69	.574
2010	Phillies	NL	162	94	.64	276	17	19	37	50	39	114	1	451	129	64	120	3	42	27	15	6	97	65	.599
2011	Phillies	NL	162	105	.69	264	26	22	49	39	48	74	1	394	120	80	141	5	41	31	10	5	102	60	.630
2012	Phillies	NL	162	131	.68	281	22	48	35	56	30	93	5	440	139	91	125	6	33	21	12	5	81	81	.500
2013	Phillies	NL	120	90	.61	196	29	29	20	38	16	73	1	331	88	53	90	7	23	13	10	7	53	67	.442
	162-Game Average			97	.65	236	35	38	34	39	26	109	3	457	135	75	98	16	46	30	16	9	89	73	.549

Mike Matheny

Year	Team	Lg	G	LINEUPS		SUBSTITUTION			PITCHER USAGE						TACTICS				INTENTIONAL BB				RESULTS		
				LUp	PL%	PH	PR	DS	Quick	Slow	LO	RCD	LS	Rel	SBA	SacA	RM	PO	#	Good	NG	Bomb	W	L	Pct
2012	Cardinals	NL	162	122	.62	286	37	33	53	37	8	118	5	506	128	95	144	16	28	13	15	7	88	74	.543
2013	Cardinals	NL	162	89	.56	237	30	41	42	49	25	114	4	483	67	73	125	6	26	20	6	6	97	65	.599
2014	Cardinals	NL	162	119	.56	258	21	35	53	32	17	119	5	485	89	81	155	10	35	20	15	10	90	72	.556
2015	Cardinals	NL	162	135	.52	274	46	41	51	29	11	142	8	515	107	60	168	15	37	29	8	3	100	62	.617
2016	Cardinals	NL	162	146	.50	284	39	42	42	39	8	95	2	481	61	56	107	21	35	19	16	8	86	76	.531
	162-Game Average			122	.55	268	35	38	48	37	14	118	5	494	90	73	140	14	32	20	12	6	92	70	.568

Don Mattingly

Year	Team	Lg	G	LINEUPS		SUBSTITUTION			PITCHER USAGE						TACTICS				INTENTIONAL BB				RESULTS		
				LUp	PL%	PH	PR	DS	Quick	Slow	LO	RCD	LS	Rel	SBA	SacA	RM	PO	#	Good	NG	Bomb	W	L	Pct
2011	Dodgers	NL	161	140	.57	233	29	44	45	40	30	86	1	461	166	93	145	13	48	27	21	12	82	79	.509
2012	Dodgers	NL	162	127	.59	247	22	43	51	39	20	118	2	506	148	105	153	8	62	38	24	15	86	76	.531
2013	Dodgers	NL	162	145	.55	210	18	47	40	30	18	118	3	504	106	99	131	10	44	28	16	7	92	70	.568
2014	Dodgers	NL	162	124	.51	237	17	62	49	31	15	107	5	496	188	67	168	2	35	20	15	8	94	68	.580
2015	Dodgers	NL	161	136	.70	276	20	45	50	30	13	119	1	508	93	67	136	2	32	18	14	5	92	70	.565
2016	Marlins	NL	161	111	.48	281	28	69	48	35	10	145	1	559	99	63	101	4	62	42	20	14	79	82	.491
	162-Game Average			131	.57	248	22	52	47	34	18	116	2	507	134	83	145	6	47	29	18	10	88	74	.543

Lloyd McClendon

Year	Team	Lg	G	LINEUPS		SUBSTITUTION			PITCHER USAGE						TACTICS				INTENTIONAL BB				RESULTS		
				LUp	PL%	PH	PR	DS	Quick	Slow	LO	RCD	LS	Rel	SBA	SacA	RM	PO	#	Good	NG	Bomb	W	L	Pct
2001	Pirates	NL	162	131	.51	255	17	32	45	38	2	85	5	410	166	83		52	74	44	30	19	62	100	.383
2002	Pirates	NL	161	121	.45	261	38	65	62	30	3	98	2	458	135	93	73	67	93	61	32	22	72	89	.447
2003	Pirates	NL	161	114	.57	315	27	59	46	35	27	114	10	457	123	99	55	61	58	34	24	13	75	87	.463
2004	Pirates	NL	161	114	.50	278	13	58	50	40	26	133	1	464	103	100	91	61	64	37	27	16	72	89	.447
2005	Pirates	NL	136	123	.53	218	8	19	37	34	15	86	5	357	84	62	83	37	60	32	28	16	55	81	.404
2014	Mariners	AL	162	141	.69	93	48	33	61	21	11	87	3	497	138	48	187	30	36	21	15	9	87	75	.537
2015	Mariners	AL	162	140	.63	133	52	50	53	31	10	114	5	509	114	49	148	30	41	23	18	10	76	86	.469
	162-Game Average			129	.56	227	30	46	52	34	14	105	5	462	126	78	109	51	62	37	25	15	73	89	.451

Bob Melvin

Year	Team	Lg	G	LINEUPS		SUBSTITUTION			PITCHER USAGE						TACTICS				INTENTIONAL BB				RESULTS		
				LUp	PL%	PH	PR	DS	Quick	Slow	LO	RCD	LS	Rel	SBA	SacA	RM	PO	#	Good	NG	Bomb	W	L	Pct
2003	Mariners	AL	162	111	.62	81	62	33	27	46	43	56	6	366	145	44	37	5	24	14	10	4	93	69	.574
2004	Mariners	AL	162	151	.59	109	66	26	26	63	43	82	5	414	152	56	123	24	32	18	14	8	63	99	.389
2005	Diamondbacks	NL	162	120	.68	310	26	38	26	56	36	123	11	458	93	93	101	30	43	27	16	9	77	85	.475
2006	Diamondbacks	NL	162	114	.72	278	11	35	37	42	15	86	0	461	106	83	61	30	44	28	16	8	76	86	.469
2007	Diamondbacks	NL	162	146	.57	243	11	61	35	42	31	96	2	469	133	74	70	25	38	30	8	4	90	72	.556
2008	Diamondbacks	NL	162	134	.57	263	27	30	41	39	16	102	0	444	81	87	79	28	41	27	14	9	82	80	.506
2009	Diamondbacks	NL	29	29	.62	47	6	8	7	4	3	17	0	91	29	17	13	3	3	1	2	2	12	17	.414
2011	Athletics	AL	99	87	.71	33	13	17	24	23	18	59	2	283	103	34	87	23	9	5	4	3	47	52	.475
2012	Athletics	AL	162	132	.71	111	17	18	63	29	5	93	2	462	154	41	116	30	34	21	13	6	94	68	.580
2013	Athletics	AL	162	133	.77	166	14	35	48	28	7	84	7	447	102	32	74	8	23	18	5	3	96	66	.593
2014	Athletics	AL	162	137	.77	187	38	44	45	30	11	101	2	447	103	28	91	16	28	20	8	5	88	74	.543
2015	Athletics	AL	162	137	.65	161	24	35	53	36	10	100	10	487	107	17	130	20	19	8	11	8	68	94	.420
2016	Athletics	AL	162	141	.64	135	28	39	55	36	7	96	3	492	73	19	79	5	28	14	14	8	69	93	.426
	162-Game Average			133	.66	180	29	36	41	40	21	93	4	451	117	53	90	21	31	20	11	7	81	81	.500

Paul Molitor

Year	Team	Lg	G	LINEUPS		SUBSTITUTION			PITCHER USAGE						TACTICS				INTENTIONAL BB				RESULTS		
				LUp	PL%	PH	PR	DS	Quick	Slow	LO	RCD	LS	Rel	SBA	SacA	RM	PO	#	Good	NG	Bomb	W	L	Pct
2015	Twins	AL	162	124	.59	75	34	27	51	27	7	123	4	520	108	44	132	5	34	20	14	8	83	79	.512
2016	Twins	AL	162	148	.61	72	25	18	33	57	4	117	4	533	123	47	157	5	26	13	13	8	59	103	.364
	162-Game Average			136	.60	74	30	23	42	42	6	120	4	527	116	46	145	5	30	17	14	8	71	91	.438

Pat Murphy

Year	Team	Lg	G	LINEUPS		SUBSTITUTION			PITCHER USAGE						TACTICS				INTENTIONAL BB				RESULTS		
				LUp	PL%	PH	PR	DS	Quick	Slow	LO	RCD	LS	Rel	SBA	SacA	RM	PO	#	Good	NG	Bomb	W	L	Pct
2015	Padres	NL	96	84	.56	195	12	10	19	39	11	69	2	314	56	46	60	6	19	10	9	4	42	54	.438
	162-Game Average			142	.56	329	20	17	32	66	19	116	3	530	95	78	101	10	32	17	15	7	71	91	.438

Bo Porter

Year	Team	Lg	G	LINEUPS		SUBSTITUTION			PITCHER USAGE						TACTICS				INTENTIONAL BB				RESULTS		
				LUp	PL%	PH	PR	DS	Quick	Slow	LO	RCD	LS	Rel	SBA	SacA	RM	PO	#	Good	NG	Bomb	W	L	Pct
2013	Astros	AL	162	138	.63	107	40	26	48	43	14	84	6	448	171	51	155	22	32	19	13	8	51	111	.315
2014	Astros	AL	138	120	.66	69	21	15	28	42	16	74	2	371	120	22	127	18	26	13	13	6	59	79	.428
	162-Game Average			139	.63	95	33	22	41	46	16	85	4	442	157	39	152	22	31	17	14	8	59	103	.364

Bryan Price

Year	Team	Lg	G	LINEUPS		SUBSTITUTION			PITCHER USAGE						TACTICS				INTENTIONAL BB				RESULTS		
				LUp	PL%	PH	PR	DS	Quick	Slow	LO	RCD	LS	Rel	SBA	SacA	RM	PO	#	Good	NG	Bomb	W	L	Pct
2014	Reds	NL	162	130	.54	220	21	33	35	37	26	82	3	428	174	87	135	9	33	21	12	5	76	86	.469
2015	Reds	NL	162	118	.57	263	16	26	42	48	15	102	2	521	172	63	144	28	42	29	13	7	64	98	.395
2016	Reds	NL	162	109	.52	230	17	23	37	39	10	67	3	484	190	81	163	26	31	23	8	5	68	94	.420
	162-Game Average			119	.54	238	18	27	38	41	17	84	3	478	179	77	147	21	35	24	11	6	69	93	.426

Mike Redmond

Year	Team	Lg	G	LINEUPS		SUBSTITUTION			PITCHER USAGE						TACTICS				INTENTIONAL BB				RESULTS		
				LUp	PL%	PH	PR	DS	Quick	Slow	LO	RCD	LS	Rel	SBA	SacA	RM	PO	#	Good	NG	Bomb	W	L	Pct
2013	Marlins	NL	162	132	.52	240	8	9	47	30	4	88	1	471	107	81	124	2	58	42	16	7	62	100	.383
2014	Marlins	NL	162	102	.50	279	9	14	51	37	8	107	4	487	79	81	100	8	35	23	12	7	77	85	.475
2015	Marlins	NL	38	22	.39	65	6	2	11	5	0	18	0	107	37	23	21	0	3	2	1	1	16	22	.421
	162-Game Average			115	.50	261	10	11	49	32	5	95	2	477	100	83	110	4	43	30	13	7	69	93	.426

Rick Renteria

Year	Team	Lg	G	LINEUPS		SUBSTITUTION			PITCHER USAGE						TACTICS				INTENTIONAL BB				RESULTS		
				LUp	PL%	PH	PR	DS	Quick	Slow	LO	RCD	LS	Rel	SBA	SacA	RM	PO	#	Good	NG	Bomb	W	L	Pct
2014	Cubs	NL	162	137	.63	275	9	20	50	42	12	103	1	537	105	77	106	5	37	23	14	8	73	89	.451
	162-Game Average			137	.63	275	9	20	50	42	12	103	1	537	105	77	106	5	37	23	14	8	73	89	.451

Dave Roberts

Year	Team	Lg	G	LUp	PL%	PH	PR	DS	Quick	Slow	LO	RCD	LS	Rel	SBA	SacA	RM	PO	#	Good	NG	Bomb	W	L	Pct
2015	Padres	NL	1	1	.63	3	0	0	0	1	0	2	0	3	1	1	0	0	1	1	0	0	0	1	.000
2016	Dodgers	NL	162	120	.69	**325**	11	26	**60**	26	6	143	**5**	606	71	45	120	2	51	36	15	10	91	71	.562
	162-Game Average			120	.69	326	11	26	60	27	6	144	5	605	72	46	119	2	52	37	15	10	90	72	.556

Ron Roenicke

Year	Team	Lg	G	LUp	PL%	PH	PR	DS	Quick	Slow	LO	RCD	LS	Rel	SBA	SacA	RM	PO	#	Good	NG	Bomb	W	L	Pct
2011	Brewers	NL	162	105	.45	260	31	36	36	43	31	92	1	434	125	**104**	141	14	16	9	7	4	96	66	.593
2012	Brewers	NL	162	110	.45	322	20	25	36	50	23	**149**	1	512	197	91	152	8	20	12	8	2	83	79	.512
2013	Brewers	NL	162	125	.47	275	15	34	39	47	7	96	2	501	**192**	86	157	6	29	22	7	6	74	88	.457
2014	Brewers	NL	162	115	.44	253	19	37	33	48	12	114	1	478	145	**92**	127	11	20	16	4	4	82	80	.506
2015	Brewers	NL	25	24	.39	48	4	5	3	9	2	15	0	72	14	18	17	2	6	5	1	1	7	18	.280
	162-Game Average			115	.45	279	21	33	35	47	18	112	1	481	162	94	143	10	22	15	6	4	82	80	.506

Ryne Sandberg

Year	Team	Lg	G	LUp	PL%	PH	PR	DS	Quick	Slow	LO	RCD	LS	Rel	SBA	SacA	RM	PO	#	Good	NG	Bomb	W	L	Pct
2013	Phillies	NL	42	34	.66	66	4	6	6	12	7	18	0	135	14	15	26	0	10	6	4	4	20	22	.476
2014	Phillies	NL	162	105	.70	259	20	31	37	**62**	**30**	111	0	461	135	72	140	1	**43**	**31**	12	6	73	89	.451
2015	Phillies	NL	74	58	.72	114	7	14	16	22	5	63	2	225	50	36	70	2	25	23	2	0	26	48	.351
	162-Game Average			115	.70	256	18	30	34	56	24	112	1	478	116	72	138	2	45	35	10	6	69	93	.426

Mike Scioscia

Year	Team	Lg	G	LUp	PL%	PH	PR	DS	Quick	Slow	LO	RCD	LS	Rel	SBA	SacA	RM	PO	#	Good	NG	Bomb	W	L	Pct
2000	Angels	AL	162	75	.62	110	41	4	56	42	6	95	9	441	145	63		40	44	28	16	7	82	80	.506
2001	Angels	AL	162	130	.62	118	30	8	29	41	5	81	9	384	168	66		50	47	22	25	12	75	87	.463
2002	Angels	AL	162	102	.64	**162**	57	26	36	33	34	88	8	400	168	62	52	30	24	15	9	5	99	63	.611
2003	Angels	AL	162	130	.64	134	54	40	50	48	11	60	4	375	**190**	64	79	25	38	26	12	3	77	85	.475
2004	Angels	AL	162	126	.57	94	32	44	37	40	22	61	11	343	**189**	70	**229**	33	27	18	9	3	92	70	.568
2005	Angels	AL	162	124	.65	92	37	37	47	37	24	88	9	379	**218**	58	**160**	43	24	15	9	4	95	67	.586
2006	Angels	AL	162	114	.63	103	45	38	38	49	21	99	9	380	205	37	**166**	22	27	18	9	6	89	73	.549
2007	Angels	AL	162	127	.66	103	26	19	39	40	14	94	4	396	194	41	**166**	44	22	12	10	5	94	68	.580
2008	Angels	AL	162	125	.63	74	30	36	37	48	**21**	87	1	383	177	39	151	31	32	22	10	6	**100**	62	.617
2009	Angels	AL	162	123	.69	80	26	37	47	47	33	91	1	434	211	55	**137**	**40**	35	22	13	6	97	65	.599
2010	Angels	AL	162	133	.59	96	31	23	41	52	48	76	0	410	156	58	**223**	28	33	17	16	8	80	82	.494
2011	Angels	AL	162	129	.64	88	14	24	31	37	**55**	57	1	386	187	**69**	212	46	34	25	9	5	86	76	.531
2012	Angels	AL	162	121	.55	73	33	47	37	47	31	96	**8**	444	167	**61**	236	33	20	11	9	7	89	73	.549
2013	Angels	AL	162	118	.56	88	26	39	31	44	29	130	**8**	496	116	48	205	41	36	19	17	11	78	84	.481
2014	Angels	AL	162	125	.58	123	46	**59**	49	39	22	141	0	543	120	35	189	14	41	**31**	10	5	**98**	64	.605
2015	Angels	AL	162	125	.53	117	**62**	**73**	38	38	12	**145**	4	518	86	41	168	15	**45**	**34**	11	9	85	77	.525
2016	Angels	AL	162	133	.45	98	54	57	47	32	12	99	2	527	107	38	**211**	14	27	19	8	5	74	88	.457
	162-Game Average			121	.60	103	38	36	41	42	24	93	5	426	165	53	172	32	33	21	12	6	88	74	.543

Scott Servais

Year	Team	Lg	G	LUp	PL%	PH	PR	DS	Quick	Slow	LO	RCD	LS	Rel	SBA	SacA	RM	PO	#	Good	NG	Bomb	W	L	Pct
2016	Mariners	AL	162	114	.72	**166**	33	43	42	38	8	93	7	476	84	36	79	1	30	16	**14**	6	86	76	.531
	162-Game Average			114	.72	166	33	43	42	38	8	93	7	476	84	36	79	1	30	16	14	6	86	76	.531

Buck Showalter

Year	Team	Lg	G	LUp	PL%	PH	PR	DS	Quick	Slow	LO	RCD	LS	Rel	SBA	SacA	RM	PO	#	Good	NG	Bomb	W	L	Pct
1994	Yankees	AL	113	79	.59	95	31	3	24	30	0	38	7	241	95	34		22	24	13	11	4	70	43	.619
1995	Yankees	AL	145	107	.68	124	30	20	29	42	37	57	6	302	80	27		29	21	14	7	1	79	65	.549
1998	Diamondbacks	NL	162	124	.62	252	17	15	34	40	7	43	6	368	111	68		13	32	16	16	9	65	97	.401
1999	Diamondbacks	NL	162	97	.63	220	20	17	37	48	25	74	3	382	176	75		15	48	29	19	8	**100**	62	.617
2000	Diamondbacks	NL	162	99	.60	250	32	11	46	26	18	74	12	390	141	89		10	53	28	25	16	85	77	.525
2003	Rangers	AL	162	133	.61	88	51	41	35	33	12	93	7	**494**	90	35	**80**	12	45	24	21	**14**	71	91	.438
2004	Rangers	AL	162	120	.64	86	15	24	53	30	12	82	10	468	105	30	88	5	29	19	10	3	89	73	.549
2005	Rangers	AL	162	98	.59	57	22	11	42	39	17	79	8	**454**	82	11	103	5	31	10	21	**16**	79	83	.488
2006	Rangers	AL	162	95	.57	39	34	22	41	27	10	85	4	**489**	77	30	72	8	18	11	7	5	80	82	.494
2010	Orioles	AL	57	42	.74	20	11	13	23	9	10	24	1	144	38	13	31	1	10	9	1	1	34	23	.596
2011	Orioles	AL	162	117	.53	60	39	27	43	40	14	61	2	478	106	32	133	6	42	31	11	5	69	93	.426
2012	Orioles	AL	162	120	.62	78	28	31	37	42	10	88	0	492	87	46	145	6	36	25	11	5	93	69	.574

Year	Team	Lg	G	LUp	PL%	PH	PR	DS	Quick	Slow	LO	RCD	LS	Rel	SBA	SacA	RM	PO	#	Good	NG	Bomb	W	L	Pct
				LINEUPS		SUBSTITUTION			PITCHER USAGE						TACTICS				INTENTIONAL BB				RESULTS		
2013	Orioles	AL	162	100	.65	90	23	21	31	39	19	84	4	473	108	37	104	4	32	11	21	**13**	85	77	.525
2014	Orioles	AL	162	120	.49	77	29	51	37	34	17	89	2	479	64	50	101	10	25	16	9	4	96	66	.593
2015	Orioles	AL	162	145	.60	89	21	35	35	41	6	76	8	453	69	26	95	10	27	12	15	8	81	81	.500
2016	Orioles	AL	162	125	.53	74	31	33	36	50	16	68	**9**	443	32	21	55	10	23	13	10	5	89	73	.549
	162-Game Average			115	.60	114	29	25	39	38	15	75	6	438	98	42	97	11	33	19	14	8	85	77	.525

Brian Snitker

Year	Team	Lg	G	LUp	PL%	PH	PR	DS	Quick	Slow	LO	RCD	LS	Rel	SBA	SacA	RM	PO	#	Good	NG	Bomb	W	L	Pct
2016	Braves	NL	124	85	.62	214	8	14	31	36	7	96	1	456	83	64	118	7	40	23	17	10	59	65	.476
	162-Game Average			111	.62	280	10	18	41	47	9	125	1	596	108	84	154	9	52	30	22	13	77	85	.475

Dale Sveum

Year	Team	Lg	G	LUp	PL%	PH	PR	DS	Quick	Slow	LO	RCD	LS	Rel	SBA	SacA	RM	PO	#	Good	NG	Bomb	W	L	Pct
2008	Brewers	NL	12	3	.48	32	2	1	7	2	1	12	0	46	5	13	6	1	2	1	1	0	7	5	.583
2012	Cubs	NL	162	101	.60	277	23	44	46	48	8	117	1	493	139	61	153	13	36	24	12	8	61	**101**	.377
2013	Cubs	NL	162	107	.60	277	12	17	42	47	19	112	1	489	95	58	122	8	43	29	14	**8**	66	96	.407
	162-Game Average			102	.60	283	18	30	46	47	14	116	1	496	115	64	135	11	39	26	13	8	65	97	.401

Alan Trammell

Year	Team	Lg	G	LUp	PL%	PH	PR	DS	Quick	Slow	LO	RCD	LS	Rel	SBA	SacA	RM	PO	#	Good	NG	Bomb	W	L	Pct
2003	Tigers	AL	162	129	.72	138	29	14	48	39	15	73	**14**	451	161	**92**	66	28	35	22	13	7	43	**119**	.265
2004	Tigers	AL	162	131	.65	105	29	19	47	36	26	79	6	432	136	62	99	9	33	16	17	10	72	90	.444
2005	Tigers	AL	162	119	.49	75	26	16	35	39	13	87	2	425	94	56	129	11	33	21	12	7	71	91	.438
2014	Diamondbacks	NL	3	3	.63	6	2	0	1	0	0	1	0	9	2	1	3	0	1	1	0	0	1	2	.333
	162-Game Average			127	.62	107	28	16	43	38	18	80	7	436	130	70	98	16	34	20	14	8	62	100	.383

Robin Ventura

Year	Team	Lg	G	LUp	PL%	PH	PR	DS	Quick	Slow	LO	RCD	LS	Rel	SBA	SacA	RM	PO	#	Good	NG	Bomb	W	L	Pct
2012	White Sox	AL	162	75	.48	72	**64**	23	39	44	34	104	4	466	152	42	174	13	29	17	12	7	85	77	.525
2013	White Sox	AL	162	116	.47	76	47	33	24	**52**	38	**133**	0	470	147	24	132	15	24	12	12	4	63	99	.389
2014	White Sox	AL	162	115	.55	85	49	44	26	**59**	29	96	5	453	121	26	150	28	42	25	17	5	73	89	.451
2015	White Sox	AL	162	114	.47	118	29	35	16	**66**	**43**	94	3	414	110	39	146	18	34	21	13	8	76	86	.469
2016	White Sox	AL	162	116	.56	53	27	13	29	58	29	**128**	4	481	113	37	148	10	30	18	12	2	78	84	.481
	162-Game Average			107	.53	81	43	30	27	56	35	111	3	457	129	34	150	17	32	19	13	5	75	87	.463

Ron Washington

Year	Team	Lg	G	LUp	PL%	PH	PR	DS	Quick	Slow	LO	RCD	LS	Rel	SBA	SacA	RM	PO	#	Good	NG	Bomb	W	L	Pct
2007	Rangers	AL	162	139	.60	89	30	**53**	47	46	4	78	9	467	113	**76**	67	13	38	19	19	11	75	87	.463
2008	Rangers	AL	162	129	.64	118	16	14	31	**53**	11	85	3	458	106	53	74	20	44	19	25	**20**	79	83	.488
2009	Rangers	AL	162	123	.55	48	11	11	39	47	28	80	9	436	185	44	80	5	14	9	5	3	87	75	.537
2010	Rangers	AL	162	112	.52	86	39	31	46	42	35	110	4	481	171	**68**	160	10	24	15	9	0	90	72	.556
2011	Rangers	AL	162	106	.48	66	18	23	43	39	40	76	2	417	188	52	182	3	21	12	9	6	96	66	.593
2012	Rangers	AL	162	79	.47	94	25	37	30	48	33	91	0	428	135	46	155	22	15	10	5	5	93	69	.574
2013	Rangers	AL	163	113	.60	142	23	19	48	41	28	105	3	475	195	**53**	169	11	35	**24**	11	6	91	72	.558
2014	Rangers	AL	140	109	.54	96	16	16	35	51	11	65	0	400	135	43	155	6	34	25	9	4	53	87	.379
	162-Game Average			116	.55	94	23	26	41	47	24	88	4	453	156	55	132	11	29	17	12	7	84	78	.519

Eric Wedge

Year	Team	Lg	G	LUp	PL%	PH	PR	DS	Quick	Slow	LO	RCD	LS	Rel	SBA	SacA	RM	PO	#	Good	NG	Bomb	W	L	Pct
2003	Indians	AL	162	**145**	.67	117	43	27	47	34	18	89	5	428	147	67	54	12	37	22	15	8	68	94	.420
2004	Indians	AL	162	114	.72	91	34	20	44	38	22	121	0	**479**	149	57	129	28	47	26	21	**18**	80	82	.494
2005	Indians	AL	162	111	.66	88	18	16	45	45	15	90	3	409	98	53	79	9	20	11	9	7	93	69	.574
2006	Indians	AL	162	111	.59	98	13	13	31	52	27	48	1	377	78	40	83	15	35	21	14	11	78	84	.481
2007	Indians	AL	162	117	.60	116	41	25	34	38	20	79	2	395	113	40	108	16	42	24	18	9	**96**	66	.593
2008	Indians	AL	162	136	.54	112	31	18	40	35	17	78	4	399	106	56	98	5	28	6	22	11	81	81	.500
2009	Indians	AL	162	**148**	.59	63	28	11	32	41	21	67	3	445	115	52	74	8	31	14	17	9	65	97	.401
2011	Mariners	AL	162	**152**	.68	52	30	22	39	45	30	50	1	351	165	43	161	7	27	20	7	6	67	95	.414

Year	Team	Lg	G	LUp	PL%	PH	PR	DS	Quick	Slow	LO	RCD	LS	Rel	SBA	SacA	RM	PO	#	Good	NG	Bomb	W	L	Pct
				LINEUPS		**SUBSTITUTION**			**PITCHER USAGE**						**TACTICS**				**INTENTIONAL BB**				**RESULTS**		
2012	Mariners	AL	162	141	.69	87	36	21	44	35	14	89	5	451	139	45	116	8	39	20	**19**	7	75	87	.463
2013	Mariners	AL	162	143	.70	78	36	33	50	36	8	82	2	448	72	43	97	3	**48**	19	**29**	12	71	91	.438
	162-Game Average			132	.65	90	31	21	41	40	19	79	3	418	118	50	100	11	35	18	17	10	77	85	.475

Walt Weiss

Year	Team	Lg	G	LUp	PL%	PH	PR	DS	Quick	Slow	LO	RCD	LS	Rel	SBA	SacA	RM	PO	#	Good	NG	Bomb	W	L	Pct
2013	Rockies	NL	162	136	.56	260	18	32	50	42	0	96	2	503	144	80	149	15	52	28	**24**	7	74	88	.457
2014	Rockies	NL	162	134	.51	270	12	26	40	49	2	119	0	**547**	133	69	140	11	32	16	16	7	66	**96**	.407
2015	Rockies	NL	162	122	.56	262	9	36	45	47	2	125	1	538	140	58	138	13	42	26	16	6	68	94	.420
2016	Rockies	NL	162	120	.58	255	7	32	32	57	7	120	2	533	105	69	154	3	38	24	14	7	75	87	.463
	162-Game Average			128	.55	262	12	32	42	49	3	115	1	542	131	69	145	11	41	24	18	7	71	91	.438

Matt Williams

Year	Team	Lg	G	LUp	PL%	PH	PR	DS	Quick	Slow	LO	RCD	LS	Rel	SBA	SacA	RM	PO	#	Good	NG	Bomb	W	L	Pct
2014	Nationals	NL	162	100	.56	248	17	33	**62**	33	11	67	1	458	124	87	91	3	26	15	11	6	**96**	66	.593
2015	Nationals	NL	162	121	.48	225	22	17	45	44	**15**	86	2	468	80	77	79	1	37	17	**20**	10	83	79	.512
	162-Game Average			111	.52	237	20	25	54	39	13	77	2	463	102	82	85	2	32	16	16	8	90	73	.552

Ned Yost

Year	Team	Lg	G	LUp	PL%	PH	PR	DS	Quick	Slow	LO	RCD	LS	Rel	SBA	SacA	RM	PO	#	Good	NG	Bomb	W	L	Pct
2003	Brewers	NL	162	97	.44	304	22	39	23	**59**	18	90	6	460	138	85	40	23	43	28	15	9	68	94	.420
2004	Brewers	NL	161	131	.60	283	25	20	39	41	27	63	2	423	**178**	79	108	8	27	16	11	8	67	94	.416
2005	Brewers	NL	162	99	.46	259	18	35	26	41	**42**	71	2	395	113	89	97	50	52	23	**29**	10	81	81	.500
2006	Brewers	NL	162	106	.48	238	12	14	33	44	18	77	4	427	108	80	82	16	34	14	20	12	75	87	.463
2007	Brewers	NL	162	109	.60	259	11	41	37	42	18	117	**7**	492	128	74	94	19	37	28	9	9	83	79	.512
2008	Brewers	NL	150	74	.48	217	5	16	37	39	23	69	5	399	141	61	105	31	30	17	13	7	83	67	.553
2010	Royals	AL	127	80	.57	56	25	6	22	39	20	65	0	332	127	40	128	18	25	16	9	5	55	72	.433
2011	Royals	AL	162	87	.58	36	28	16	42	42	21	56	7	420	211	65	203	19	42	27	15	5	71	91	.438
2012	Royals	AL	162	118	.57	60	34	15	48	37	10	108	1	**500**	170	37	149	25	**44**	**29**	15	**11**	72	90	.444
2013	Royals	AL	162	127	.60	79	**48**	39	43	44	21	72	2	427	185	48	168	25	21	12	9	5	86	76	.531
2014	Royals	AL	162	101	.52	51	**63**	46	37	51	26	93	1	451	**189**	45	159	3	14	7	7	3	89	73	.549
2015	Royals	AL	162	83	.57	40	40	26	51	42	13	90	3	493	138	45	126	5	10	7	3	1	**95**	67	.586
2016	Royals	AL	162	108	.54	50	38	12	49	44	10	85	2	472	156	**55**	130	0	8	6	2	2	81	81	.500
	162-Game Average			104	.54	152	29	26	38	44	21	83	3	448	156	63	125	19	30	18	12	7	79	83	.488

Categories of this record are Games Managed (G), Number of Different Lineups Used (LUp), the percentage of players who had the platoon advantage at the start of the game (PL%), Pinch Hitters Used (PH), Pinch Runners Used (PR), Defensive Substitutes Used (DS), Quick Hooks (Quick), Slow Hooks (Slow), Long Outings by Starting Pitchers (LO), Relievers Used on Consecutive Days (RCD), Long Saves (LS), Relievers Used (Rel), Stolen Base Attempts (SBA), Sacrifice Bunt Attempts (SacA), Runners Moving with the Pitch (RM), Pitchouts ordered (PO), Intentional Walks issued (#), Intentional Walks resulting in a Good Outcome (Good), Intentional Walks resulting Not in a Good Outcome (NG), Intentional Walks Blowing Up on the Manager (Bomb), Wins (W), Losses (L), and Winning Percentage (Pct).

2016 American League Managers

Manager	G	LINEUPS LUp	PL%	SUBSTITUTION PH	PR	DS	PITCHER USAGE Quick	Slow	LO	RCD	LS	Rel	TACTICS SBA	SacA	RM	PO	INTENTIONAL BB #	Good	NG	Bomb	RESULTS W	L	Pct
Buck Showalter, Bal	162	125	.53	74	31	33	36	50	16	68	9	443	32	21	55	10	23	13	10	5	89	73	.549
John Farrell, Bos	162	118	.53	110	28	11	34	51	26	79	2	463	107	15	169	0	16	8	8	3	93	69	.574
Terry Francona, Cle	161	101	.73	114	27	29	47	39	18	103	3	504	165	44	126	2	34	22	12	7	94	67	.584
Robin Ventura, CWS	162	116	.56	53	27	13	29	58	29	128	4	481	113	37	148	10	30	18	12	2	78	84	.481
Brad Ausmus, Det	161	111	.48	89	31	50	41	37	18	93	4	476	87	21	95	3	25	12	13	4	86	75	.534
A.J. Hinch, Hou	162	143	.55	118	35	27	42	35	9	87	1	500	146	38	137	5	19	11	8	6	84	78	.519
Ned Yost, KC	162	108	.54	50	38	12	49	44	10	85	2	472	156	55	130	0	8	6	2	2	81	81	.500
Mike Scioscia, LAA	162	133	.45	98	54	57	47	32	12	99	2	527	107	38	211	14	27	19	8	5	74	88	.457
Paul Molitor, Min	162	148	.61	72	25	18	33	57	4	117	4	533	123	47	157	5	26	13	13	8	59	103	.364
Joe Girardi, NYY	162	143	.72	85	32	48	53	44	8	99	7	483	94	35	89	3	15	9	6	4	84	78	.519
Bob Melvin, Oak	162	141	.64	135	28	39	55	36	7	96	3	492	73	19	79	5	28	14	14	8	69	93	.426
Scott Servais, Sea	162	114	.72	166	33	43	42	38	8	93	7	476	84	36	79	1	30	16	14	6	86	76	.531
Kevin Cash, TB	162	142	.55	103	11	28	42	52	18	100	8	485	97	24	146	12	25	16	9	4	68	94	.420
Jeff Banister, Tex	162	124	.55	84	58	38	47	44	7	85	1	479	135	26	136	3	16	5	11	8	95	67	.586
John Gibbons, Tor	162	141	.44	90	37	54	39	30	6	98	6	487	78	33	109	1	10	6	4	3	89	73	.549
162-Game Average		127	.57	96	33	33	42	43	13	95	4	487	107	33	124	5	22	13	10	5	82	80	.506

2016 National League Managers

Manager	G	LINEUPS LUp	PL%	SUBSTITUTION PH	PR	DS	PITCHER USAGE Quick	Slow	LO	RCD	LS	Rel	TACTICS SBA	SacA	RM	PO	INTENTIONAL BB #	Good	NG	Bomb	RESULTS W	L	Pct
Chip Hale, Ari	162	139	.45	266	10	30	27	66	7	130	5	575	168	51	120	0	57	41	16	8	69	93	.426
Joe Maddon, ChC	162	130	.62	236	19	35	56	29	13	100	3	503	100	54	111	6	24	19	5	3	103	58	.640
Bryan Price, Cin	162	109	.52	230	17	23	37	39	10	67	3	484	190	81	163	26	31	23	8	5	68	94	.420
Walt Weiss, Col	162	120	.58	255	7	32	32	57	7	120	2	533	105	69	154	3	38	24	14	7	75	87	.463
Dave Roberts, LAD	162	120	.69	325	11	26	60	26	6	143	5	606	71	45	120	2	51	36	15	10	91	71	.562
Don Mattingly, Mia	161	111	.48	281	28	69	48	35	10	145	1	559	99	63	101	2	62	42	20	14	79	82	.491
Craig Counsell, Mil	162	123	.55	284	4	22	40	41	1	115	3	513	237	71	160	0	33	16	17	8	73	89	.451
Terry Collins, NYM	162	129	.68	292	17	50	53	33	6	141	4	538	60	55	80	6	39	26	13	9	87	75	.537
Pete Mackanin, Phi	162	144	.64	260	14	46	44	44	4	128	2	505	141	61	138	17	30	19	11	10	71	91	.438
Clint Hurdle, Pit	162	125	.41	293	39	73	57	36	1	119	4	525	155	55	154	9	28	15	13	6	78	83	.484
Andy Green, SD	162	130	.56	249	29	25	46	53	6	119	4	510	170	48	138	3	44	26	18	9	68	94	.420
Bruce Bochy, SF	162	121	.66	268	7	29	31	42	28	148	4	575	115	54	178	6	30	25	5	4	87	75	.537
Mike Matheny, StL	162	146	.50	284	39	42	42	39	8	95	2	481	61	56	107	21	35	19	16	8	86	76	.531
Dusty Baker, Was	162	112	.57	220	20	27	35	45	21	119	4	508	160	59	161	3	43	28	15	9	95	67	.586
162-Game Average		125	.57	268	18	37	43	42	9	121	3	534	129	60	136	8	40	26	14	8	81	81	.500

Manager	G	LINEUPS LUp	PL%	SUBSTITUTION PH	PR	DS	PITCHER USAGE Quick	Slow	LO	RCD	LS	Rel	TACTICS SBA	SacA	RM	PO	INTENTIONAL BB #	Good	NG	Bomb	RESULTS W	L	Pct
Fredi Gonzalez, Atl	37	34	.73	58	9	11	9	9	3	33	1	131	26	20	36	0	15	11	4	2	9	28	.243
Brian Snitker, Atl	124	85	.62	214	8	14	31	36	7	96	1	456	83	64	118	7	40	23	17	10	59	65	.476

Ballparks and Park Indices

Lindsay Zeck

A park index tells you whether a given park is favorable to hitters or pitchers compared with other MLB parks. If a park has an index of 100, this means it is neutral and should have no effect on any given statistic. If the index is above 100, this means that the ballpark favors that statistic, if the index is below 100, the ballpark is unfavorable towards that statistic.

In 2016, the Yankees and their opponents hit 38 percent more home runs at Yankee Stadium than in Yankees road games. This was the highest HR index. The lowest HR index was at AT&T Park. The Giants and their opponents hit 30 percent fewer home runs in San Francisco than on the road. The Houston Astros and their opponents had a strange season for home runs. In 2016, they combined for only 171 home runs at Minute Maid Park but hit 208 in Astros' road games giving them a HR index of 81 (as opposed to the 116 HR index from 2013-15). This was only 12 home runs fewer than their average between 2013 and 2015 at home but 51 home runs more than their average on the road.

The outfield walls were raised at Coors Field prior to the 2016 season in an attempt to lower the number of home runs. However, the Rockies and their opponents actually hit 25 more home runs at Coors in 2016 than they did on average over the three years prior (215 as opposed to an average of 190). There was not much of a difference in the HR index. From 2013-15, the HR index was 119; in 2016, it was 120.

Not surprisingly, the Colorado Rockies had the highest index for runs at 137, meaning that the Rockies and their opponents scored 37 percent more runs at Coors Field than they did in Rockies road games. The teams with the lowest run index were the Houston Astros and the Los Angeles Dodgers, scoring (along with their opponents) 19 percent fewer runs in home games than in their away games. This was a particularly low index for the Astros, with a three year run index of 91.

Arizona Diamondbacks - Chase Field
LF: 330   CF: 407   RF:334

	2016 Season							2014-2016						
	Home Games			Away Games				Home Games			Away Games			
	D'Backs	Opp	Total	D'Backs	Opp	Total	Index	D'Backs	Opp	Total	D'Backs	Opp	Total	Index
G	81	81	162	81	81	162		241	241	482	245	245	490	
Avg	.270	.287	.279	.252	.260	.256	109	.267	.271	.269	.249	.261	.255	106
AB	2836	2974	5810	2829	2719	5548	105	8277	8634	16911	8589	8209	16798	102
R	411	493	904	341	397	738	122	1115	1238	2353	972	1107	2079	115
H	765	855	1620	714	708	1422	114	2212	2337	4549	2140	2143	4283	108
2B	149	183	332	136	154	290	109	444	502	946	389	449	838	112
3B	35	28	63	21	10	31	194	98	67	165	53	35	88	186
HR	113	108	221	77	94	171	123	243	279	522	219	259	478	108
BB	228	316	544	235	287	522	100	684	760	1444	667	812	1479	97
SO	736	666	1402	691	652	1343	100	1942	1937	3879	1962	1874	3836	100
Foul Outs	42	46	88	62	51	113	74	147	158	305	162	135	297	102
E	42	50	92	59	53	112	82	136	160	296	152	152	304	99
E-Infield	12	22	34	25	23	48	71	50	72	122	63	73	136	91
LHB-Avg	.268	.292	.284	.228	.257	.246	115	.268	.279	.274	.245	.258	.252	109
LHB-HR	28	44	72	19	51	70	98	66	121	187	62	109	171	109
RHB-Avg	.270	.284	.276	.260	.263	.261	106	.267	.265	.266	.251	.264	.257	104
RHB-HR	85	64	149	58	43	101	141	177	158	335	157	150	307	108

Atlanta Braves - Turner Field
LF: 335   CF: 401   RF:330

	2016 Season							2014-2016						
	Home Games			Away Games				Home Games			Away Games			
	Braves	Opp	Total	Braves	Opp	Total	Index	Braves	Opp	Total	Braves	Opp	Total	Index
G	80	80	160	81	81	162		242	242	484	243	243	486	
Avg	.261	.249	.255	.249	.262	.255	100	.250	.248	.249	.247	.269	.258	97
AB	2714	2804	5518	2800	2727	5527	101	7998	8365	16363	8404	8079	16483	100
R	333	399	732	316	380	696	106	899	1045	1944	896	1091	1987	98
H	707	699	1406	697	715	1412	101	2002	2075	4077	2079	2170	4249	96
2B	134	130	264	161	133	294	90	365	382	747	421	410	831	91
3B	15	19	34	12	28	40	85	35	38	73	32	64	96	77
HR	52	78	130	70	99	169	77	162	210	372	183	258	441	85
BB	254	302	556	248	245	493	113	743	825	1568	702	744	1446	109
SO	601	655	1256	639	572	1211	104	1841	2001	3842	1875	1675	3550	109
Foul Outs	46	61	107	46	51	97	110	136	171	307	148	155	303	102
E	60	57	117	41	42	83	143	149	163	312	127	115	242	129
E-Infield	32	30	62	13	18	31	203	75	78	153	51	48	99	155
LHB-Avg	.264	.265	.265	.266	.247	.257	103	.254	.263	.259	.271	.270	.271	96
LHB-HR	27	43	70	38	40	78	89	61	98	159	89	112	201	79
RHB-Avg	.256	.235	.245	.230	.274	.254	97	.248	.236	.241	.227	.267	.247	98
RHB-HR	25	35	60	32	59	91	67	101	112	213	94	146	240	90

Baltimore Orioles - Oriole Park at Camden Yards
LF: 337   CF: 406   RF:320

	2016 Season							2014-2016						
	Home Games			Away Games				Home Games			Away Games			
	Orioles	Opp	Total	Orioles	Opp	Total	Index	Orioles	Opp	Total	Orioles	Opp	Total	Index
G	81	81	162	81	81	162		240	240	480	246	246	492	
Avg	.259	.253	.256	.253	.262	.258	99	.262	.248	.255	.247	.264	.255	102
AB	2657	2766	5423	2867	2701	5568	97	8031	8327	16358	8574	8126	16700	100
R	376	336	712	368	379	747	95	1117	970	2087	1045	1031	2076	103
H	688	699	1387	725	709	1434	97	2103	2075	4178	2114	2081	4195	102
2B	119	142	261	146	167	313	86	362	424	786	413	470	883	91
3B	4	7	11	2	11	13	87	18	25	43	24	36	60	73
HR	131	88	219	122	95	217	104	366	250	616	315	258	573	110
BB	239	261	500	229	284	513	100	650	706	1356	637	794	1431	97
SO	603	642	1245	721	606	1327	96	1813	1835	3648	2127	1820	3947	94
Foul Outs	71	53	124	78	61	139	92	176	172	348	209	194	403	88
E	39	42	81	41	33	74	109	116	123	239	128	111	239	103
E-Infield	18	19	37	15	10	25	148	47	54	101	51	42	93	111
LHB-Avg	.242	.266	.256	.253	.274	.265	97	.251	.251	.251	.243	.256	.250	100
LHB-HR	44	35	79	41	44	85	95	133	105	238	104	106	210	116
RHB-Avg	.267	.243	.256	.253	.254	.253	101	.268	.248	.259	.249	.257	.252	103
RHB-HR	87	53	140	81	51	132	109	233	145	378	211	152	363	106

Boston Red Sox - Fenway Park
LF: 310   CF: 420   RF:302

| | 2016 Season | | | | | | | 2014-2016 | | | | | | |
| | Home Games | | | Away Games | | | | Home Games | | | Away Games | | | |
	Red Sox	Opp	Total	Red Sox	Opp	Total	Index	Red Sox	Opp	Total	Red Sox	Opp	Total	Index
G	81	81	162	81	81	162		243	243	486	243	243	486	
Avg	.300	.260	.280	.264	.231	.248	113	.282	.263	.272	.246	.250	.248	110
AB	2819	2822	5641	2851	2637	5488	103	8321	8562	16883	8540	8138	16678	101
R	477	380	857	401	314	715	120	1234	1137	2371	1026	1025	2051	116
H	845	734	1579	753	608	1361	116	2350	2249	4599	2099	2037	4136	111
2B	209	140	349	134	111	245	139	556	487	1043	363	379	742	139
3B	14	16	30	11	7	18	162	37	50	87	41	37	78	110
HR	102	96	198	106	80	186	104	231	250	481	261	258	519	92
BB	276	242	518	282	248	530	95	810	714	1524	761	736	1497	101
SO	520	676	1196	640	686	1326	88	1688	1946	3634	1957	1847	3804	94
Foul Outs	54	55	109	49	74	123	86	142	170	312	171	199	370	83
E	40	50	90	35	51	86	105	154	168	322	110	133	243	133
E-Infield	16	20	36	16	14	30	120	67	68	135	46	51	97	139
LHB-Avg	.295	.259	.277	.247	.219	.234	118	.281	.265	.273	.242	.239	.241	113
LHB-HR	44	23	67	49	26	75	86	97	84	181	131	110	241	75
RHB-Avg	.303	.261	.282	.276	.237	.257	110	.284	.261	.272	.248	.258	.253	107
RHB-HR	58	73	131	57	54	111	116	134	166	300	130	148	278	106

Chicago Cubs - Wrigley Field
LF: 355   CF: 400   RF:353

| | 2016 Season | | | | | | | 2014-2016 | | | | | | |
| | Home Games | | | Away Games | | | | Home Games | | | Away Games | | | |
	Cubs	Opp	Total	Cubs	Opp	Total	Index	Cubs	Opp	Total	Cubs	Opp	Total	Index
G	81	81	162	81	81	162		243	243	486	243	243	486	
Avg	.254	.203	.228	.258	.221	.240	95	.244	.226	.235	.249	.239	.244	96
AB	2656	2692	5348	2847	2617	5464	98	7967	8322	16289	8535	8020	16555	98
R	389	247	636	419	309	728	87	1023	882	1905	1088	989	2077	92
H	674	546	1220	735	579	1314	93	1944	1879	3823	2121	1920	4041	95
2B	138	102	240	155	103	258	95	396	383	779	439	404	843	94
3B	16	7	23	14	8	22	107	48	38	86	43	38	81	108
HR	90	73	163	109	90	199	84	251	215	466	276	197	473	100
BB	339	255	594	317	240	557	109	859	703	1562	806	703	1509	105
SO	638	755	1393	701	686	1387	103	2095	2197	4292	2239	1986	4225	103
Foul Outs	46	38	84	57	48	105	82	141	118	259	167	158	325	81
E	47	40	87	54	47	101	86	143	116	259	172	133	305	85
E-Infield	17	20	37	15	22	37	100	61	49	110	67	55	122	90
LHB-Avg	.244	.206	.226	.262	.224	.245	92	.240	.234	.237	.252	.232	.243	98
LHB-HR	26	22	48	47	36	83	62	100	71	171	141	76	217	81
RHB-Avg	.262	.201	.230	.255	.219	.237	97	.247	.221	.233	.245	.244	.245	95
RHB-HR	64	51	115	62	54	116	98	151	144	295	135	121	256	116

Chicago White Sox - U.S. Cellular Field
LF: 330   CF: 400   RF:335

| | 2016 Season | | | | | | | 2014-2016 | | | | | | |
| | Home Games | | | Away Games | | | | Home Games | | | Away Games | | | |
	White Sox	Opp	Total	White Sox	Opp	Total	Index	White Sox	Opp	Total	White Sox	Opp	Total	Index
G	81	81	162	81	81	162		243	243	486	243	243	486	
Avg	.261	.251	.256	.254	.264	.259	99	.253	.253	.253	.253	.268	.260	97
AB	2659	2797	5456	2891	2727	5618	97	8128	8501	16629	8498	8125	16623	100
R	345	329	674	341	386	727	93	970	1059	2029	998	1115	2113	96
H	694	702	1396	734	720	1454	96	2060	2152	4212	2149	2181	4330	97
2B	131	136	267	146	154	300	92	383	407	790	433	427	860	92
3B	19	11	30	14	14	28	110	50	43	93	42	52	94	99
HR	83	102	185	85	83	168	113	230	263	493	229	224	453	109
BB	231	240	471	224	281	505	96	673	782	1455	603	770	1373	106
SO	606	661	1267	679	609	1288	101	1919	2034	3953	1959	1747	3706	107
Foul Outs	57	51	108	66	77	143	78	191	162	353	170	176	346	102
E	47	45	92	48	44	92	100	148	151	299	155	141	296	101
E-Infield	21	18	39	21	20	41	95	70	64	134	65	60	125	107
LHB-Avg	.252	.225	.240	.254	.255	.254	94	.244	.240	.242	.260	.266	.263	92
LHB-HR	28	34	62	23	25	48	132	66	102	168	67	77	144	113
RHB-Avg	.268	.264	.265	.254	.268	.261	102	.260	.261	.261	.248	.269	.259	101
RHB-HR	55	68	123	62	58	120	106	164	161	325	162	147	309	107

Cincinnati Reds - Great American Ballpark
LF: 328 CF: 404 RF:325

	2016 Season							2014-2016						
	Home Games			Away Games				Home Games			Away Games			
	Reds	Opp	Total	Reds	Opp	Total	Index	Reds	Opp	Total	Reds	Opp	Total	Index
G	81	81	162	81	81	162		243	243	486	243	243	486	
Avg	.257	.254	.256	.254	.272	.263	97	.251	.247	.249	.243	.259	.251	99
AB	2670	2835	5505	2817	2708	5525	100	8071	8481	16552	8382	8026	16408	101
R	365	416	781	351	438	789	99	1015	1093	2108	936	1127	2063	102
H	687	721	1408	716	736	1452	97	2026	2099	4125	2041	2076	4117	100
2B	132	130	262	145	131	276	95	386	413	799	402	425	827	96
3B	15	5	20	18	13	31	65	37	19	56	43	42	85	65
HR	88	140	228	76	118	194	118	253	323	576	209	275	484	118
BB	247	302	549	205	334	539	102	736	842	1578	627	845	1472	106
SO	651	631	1282	633	610	1243	104	1876	2050	3926	1915	1733	3648	107
Foul Outs	40	57	97	40	41	81	120	156	181	337	158	132	290	115
E	54	48	102	48	61	109	94	125	144	269	139	165	304	88
E-Infield	25	16	41	18	29	47	87	47	53	100	65	75	140	71
LHB-Avg	.278	.260	.268	.272	.271	.271	99	.257	.256	.256	.251	.264	.258	99
LHB-HR	43	51	94	29	45	74	126	100	132	232	72	108	180	129
RHB-Avg	.245	.250	.248	.244	.272	.257	96	.248	.241	.244	.238	.255	.246	99
RHB-HR	45	89	134	47	73	120	113	153	191	344	137	167	304	111

Cleveland Indians - Progressive Field
LF: 325 CF: 405 RF:325

	2016 Season							2014-2016						
	Home Games			Away Games				Home Games			Away Games			
	Indians	Opp	Total	Indians	Opp	Total	Index	Indians	Opp	Total	Indians	Opp	Total	Index
G	81	81	162	80	80	160		242	242	484	242	242	484	
Avg	.288	.246	.266	.236	.240	.238	112	.273	.246	.259	.242	.240	.241	108
AB	2704	2800	5504	2780	2680	5460	100	8112	8431	16543	8386	8020	16406	101
R	452	347	799	325	329	654	121	1142	1027	2169	973	942	1915	113
H	778	688	1466	657	642	1299	111	2211	2077	4288	2030	1925	3955	108
2B	183	155	338	125	132	257	130	501	455	956	394	376	770	123
3B	5	14	19	24	13	37	51	26	38	64	55	52	107	59
HR	99	102	201	86	84	170	117	232	262	494	236	220	456	107
BB	302	225	527	229	236	465	112	832	672	1504	736	678	1414	105
SO	578	704	1282	668	694	1362	93	1714	2168	3882	1878	2087	3965	97
Foul Outs	57	36	93	66	50	116	80	151	105	256	193	166	359	71
E	44	56	100	45	60	105	94	144	139	283	140	152	292	97
E-Infield	20	20	40	22	26	48	82	66	54	120	54	65	119	101
LHB-Avg	.315	.252	.284	.252	.217	.236	121	.283	.247	.267	.250	.227	.240	111
LHB-HR	52	45	97	42	30	72	133	140	119	259	137	95	232	110
RHB-Avg	.260	.240	.250	.220	.258	.240	104	.257	.245	.250	.230	.251	.242	103
RHB-HR	47	57	104	44	54	98	106	92	143	235	99	125	224	105

Colorado Rockies - Coors Field
LF: 347 CF: 415 RF:350

	2016 Season							2014-2016						
	Home Games			Away Games				Home Games			Away Games			
	Rockies	Opp	Total	Rockies	Opp	Total	Index	Rockies	Opp	Total	Rockies	Opp	Total	Index
G	81	81	162	81	81	162		243	243	486	243	243	486	
Avg	.304	.288	.296	.246	.259	.252	117	.309	.291	.300	.234	.263	.248	121
AB	2823	2912	5735	2791	2671	5462	105	8510	8727	17237	8288	7979	16267	106
R	508	477	985	337	383	720	137	1457	1404	2861	880	1118	1998	143
H	857	840	1697	687	692	1379	123	2632	2543	5175	1942	2096	4038	128
2B	189	179	368	129	133	262	134	511	553	1064	388	442	830	121
3B	32	25	57	15	26	41	132	100	72	172	37	63	100	162
HR	116	99	215	88	82	170	120	337	289	626	239	248	487	121
BB	283	257	540	211	290	501	103	702	810	1512	577	847	1424	100
SO	594	636	1230	736	587	1323	89	1712	1721	3433	2182	1688	3870	84
Foul Outs	36	38	74	55	46	101	70	109	119	228	182	143	325	66
E	58	51	109	52	46	98	111	152	149	301	159	132	291	103
E-Infield	20	17	37	25	16	41	90	50	63	113	62	49	111	102
LHB-Avg	.309	.283	.297	.249	.257	.253	117	.313	.286	.300	.239	.257	.247	121
LHB-HR	44	30	74	39	30	69	107	136	96	232	112	83	195	116
RHB-Avg	.299	.292	.295	.244	.260	.252	117	.307	.295	.300	.231	.267	.249	121
RHB-HR	72	69	141	49	52	101	129	201	193	394	127	165	292	125

Detroit Tigers - Comerica Park
LF: 345 CF: 420 RF:330

	2016 Season							2014-2016						
	Home Games			Away Games				Home Games			Away Games			
	Tigers	Opp	Total	Tigers	Opp	Total	Index	Tigers	Opp	Total	Tigers	Opp	Total	Index
G	80	80	160	81	81	162		242	242	484	242	242	484	
Avg	.274	.253	.264	.260	.266	.263	100	.277	.258	.267	.266	.269	.268	100
AB	2660	2749	5409	2866	2708	5574	98	8111	8403	16514	8650	8238	16888	98
R	381	357	738	369	364	733	102	1082	1100	2182	1114	1129	2243	97
H	730	696	1426	746	721	1467	98	2243	2169	4412	2305	2214	4519	98
2B	121	113	234	131	137	268	90	410	391	801	456	455	911	90
3B	20	27	47	10	15	25	194	70	84	154	35	60	95	166
HR	101	107	208	110	75	185	116	246	257	503	271	245	516	100
BB	243	218	461	250	244	494	96	698	692	1390	693	721	1414	101
SO	588	631	1219	715	601	1316	95	1670	1797	3467	2036	1779	3815	93
Foul Outs	69	77	146	57	61	118	128	180	218	398	177	169	346	118
E	32	41	73	43	41	84	88	124	146	270	138	128	266	102
E-Infield	10	15	25	18	9	27	94	47	54	101	60	44	104	97
LHB-Avg	.218	.241	.234	.264	.250	.255	92	.233	.246	.242	.254	.263	.260	93
LHB-HR	21	49	70	23	24	47	147	44	114	158	60	102	162	99
RHB-Avg	.289	.263	.278	.259	.279	.267	104	.289	.268	.280	.270	.274	.272	103
RHB-HR	80	58	138	87	51	138	105	202	143	345	211	143	354	100

Houston Astros - Minute Maid Park
LF: 315 CF: 435 RF:326

	2016 Season							2014-2016						
	Home Games			Away Games				Home Games			Away Games			
	Astros	Opp	Total	Astros	Opp	Total	Index	Astros	Opp	Total	Astros	Opp	Total	Index
G	81	81	162	81	81	162		243	243	486	243	243	486	
Avg	.238	.242	.240	.255	.270	.262	92	.245	.244	.245	.247	.261	.254	96
AB	2722	2897	5619	2823	2740	5563	101	8003	8497	16500	8448	8093	16541	100
R	334	303	637	390	398	788	81	1019	946	1965	1063	1096	2159	91
H	648	702	1350	719	739	1458	93	1961	2074	4035	2086	2112	4198	96
2B	135	152	287	156	168	324	88	386	424	810	423	422	845	96
3B	15	23	38	14	19	33	114	40	65	105	34	44	78	135
HR	98	73	171	100	108	208	81	316	216	532	275	252	527	101
BB	274	208	482	280	245	525	91	773	632	1405	762	728	1490	95
SO	744	786	1530	708	610	1318	115	2169	2054	4223	2117	1759	3876	109
Foul Outs	45	48	93	51	36	87	106	137	147	284	191	141	332	86
E	37	54	91	40	57	97	94	130	149	279	138	153	291	96
E-Infield	19	22	41	19	24	43	95	60	51	111	61	59	120	93
LHB-Avg	.215	.256	.240	.219	.287	.258	93	.223	.244	.235	.229	.267	.249	94
LHB-HR	28	30	58	27	50	77	74	117	91	208	98	101	199	104
RHB-Avg	.248	.232	.240	.271	.256	.264	91	.258	.244	.251	.258	.256	.257	98
RHB-HR	70	43	113	73	58	131	86	199	125	324	177	151	328	99

Kansas City Royals - Kauffman Stadium
LF: 330 CF: 410 RF:330

	2016 Season							2014-2016						
	Home Games			Away Games				Home Games			Away Games			
	Royals	Opp	Total	Royals	Opp	Total	Index	Royals	Opp	Total	Royals	Opp	Total	Index
G	81	81	162	81	81	162		243	243	486	243	243	486	
Avg	.271	.260	.265	.252	.257	.255	104	.268	.257	.263	.260	.248	.255	103
AB	2765	2909	5674	2787	2626	5413	105	8096	8520	16616	8576	8048	16624	100
R	377	371	748	298	341	639	117	1053	1026	2079	997	951	1948	107
H	748	757	1505	702	676	1378	109	2171	2192	4363	2232	1999	4231	103
2B	148	137	285	116	111	227	120	442	427	869	408	337	745	117
3B	23	10	33	10	11	21	150	63	49	112	41	42	83	135
HR	64	91	155	83	115	198	75	169	218	387	212	271	483	80
BB	194	264	458	188	253	441	99	576	693	1269	569	753	1322	96
SO	574	668	1242	650	619	1269	93	1476	1825	3301	1706	1790	3496	94
Foul Outs	60	77	137	59	59	118	111	176	201	377	188	178	366	103
E	44	56	100	50	51	101	99	130	143	273	156	172	328	83
E-Infield	17	18	35	17	21	38	92	47	48	95	57	67	124	77
LHB-Avg	.246	.271	.260	.245	.244	.245	106	.259	.259	.259	.264	.245	.254	102
LHB-HR	30	34	64	41	56	97	67	87	89	176	108	120	228	80
RHB-Avg	.284	.253	.269	.256	.268	.262	103	.274	.256	.265	.258	.251	.255	104
RHB-HR	34	57	91	42	59	101	82	82	129	211	104	151	255	81

Los Angeles Angels - Angel Stadium of Anaheim
LF: 330 CF: 400 RF:330

| | 2016 Season | | | | | | | 2014-2016 | | | | | | |
| | Home Games | | | Away Games | | | | Home Games | | | Away Games | | | |
	Angels	Opp	Total	Angels	Opp	Total	Index	Angels	Opp	Total	Angels	Opp	Total	Index
G	81	81	162	81	81	162		243	243	486	243	243	486	
Avg	.255	.257	.256	.264	.283	.273	94	.252	.241	.247	.257	.261	.259	95
AB	2652	2809	5461	2779	2686	5465	100	8069	8429	16498	8431	8066	16497	100
R	337	351	688	380	376	756	91	1019	959	1978	1132	1073	2205	90
H	676	721	1397	734	759	1493	94	2036	2035	4071	2169	2107	4276	95
2B	123	128	251	156	147	303	83	374	381	755	452	395	847	89
3B	8	7	15	12	13	25	60	30	18	48	42	35	77	62
HR	81	106	187	75	102	177	106	248	231	479	239	269	508	94
BB	231	243	474	240	255	495	96	693	713	1406	705	755	1460	96
SO	476	625	1101	515	511	1026	107	1665	2012	3677	1742	1687	3429	107
Foul Outs	42	62	104	63	72	135	77	157	190	347	159	189	348	100
E	47	51	98	50	44	94	104	134	155	289	139	148	287	101
E-Infield	19	29	48	11	19	30	160	56	80	136	46	64	110	124
LHB-Avg	.222	.255	.243	.247	.270	.262	93	.235	.245	.241	.243	.257	.251	96
LHB-HR	13	42	55	17	34	51	101	57	89	146	62	106	168	87
RHB-Avg	.266	.258	.263	.269	.292	.279	94	.260	.239	.250	.264	.264	.264	95
RHB-HR	68	64	132	58	68	126	108	191	142	333	177	163	340	98

Los Angeles Dodgers - Dodger Stadium
LF: 330 CF: 395 RF:330

| | 2016 Season | | | | | | | 2014-2016 | | | | | | |
| | Home Games | | | Away Games | | | | Home Games | | | Away Games | | | |
	Dodgers	Opp	Total	Dodgers	Opp	Total	Index	Dodgers	Opp	Total	Dodgers	Opp	Total	Index
G	81	81	162	81	81	162		243	243	486	243	243	486	
Avg	.253	.219	.236	.246	.247	.247	95	.253	.227	.240	.257	.252	.255	94
AB	2628	2708	5336	2890	2722	5612	95	7938	8312	16250	8525	8070	16595	98
R	350	261	611	375	377	752	81	1018	832	1850	1092	1018	2110	88
H	664	593	1257	712	673	1385	91	2005	1889	3894	2193	2032	4225	92
2B	128	110	238	144	115	259	97	419	362	781	418	354	772	103
3B	4	9	13	17	17	34	40	31	16	47	54	54	108	44
HR	101	68	169	88	97	185	96	269	218	487	241	234	475	105
BB	251	216	467	274	248	522	94	735	587	1322	872	701	1573	86
SO	633	782	1415	688	728	1416	105	1850	2223	4073	1975	2056	4031	103
Foul Outs	37	48	85	50	58	108	83	117	153	270	169	145	314	88
E	32	61	93	48	42	90	103	125	159	284	137	125	262	108
E-Infield	14	21	35	16	16	32	109	60	50	110	51	45	96	115
LHB-Avg	.263	.215	.243	.257	.246	.253	96	.255	.230	.244	.257	.258	.258	95
LHB-HR	62	21	83	50	25	75	118	145	79	224	117	82	199	117
RHB-Avg	.241	.221	.230	.234	.248	.242	95	.250	.225	.237	.257	.248	.252	94
RHB-HR	39	47	86	38	72	110	81	124	139	263	124	152	276	96

Miami Marlins - Marlins Park
LF: 340 CF: 407 RF:335

| | 2016 Season | | | | | | | 2013-2015 | | | | | | |
| | Home Games | | | Away Games | | | | Home Games | | | Away Games | | | |
	Marlins	Opp	Total	Marlins	Opp	Total	Index	Marlins	Opp	Total	Marlins	Opp	Total	Index
G	80	80	160	81	81	162		243	243	486	243	243	486	
Avg	.250	.238	.244	.275	.264	.270	90	.251	.253	.252	.245	.261	.253	100
AB	2631	2702	5333	2916	2706	5622	96	8000	8447	16447	8450	8026	16476	100
R	302	302	604	353	380	733	83	931	950	1881	840	1048	1888	100
H	658	643	1301	802	715	1517	87	2007	2135	4142	2069	2096	4165	99
2B	132	119	251	127	137	264	100	354	427	781	355	404	759	103
3B	16	13	29	26	18	44	69	68	65	133	39	52	91	146
HR	58	65	123	70	87	157	83	148	151	299	189	225	414	72
BB	215	294	509	232	301	533	101	693	720	1413	615	772	1387	102
SO	567	725	1292	646	654	1300	105	1745	1821	3566	2056	1698	3754	95
Foul Outs	49	54	103	45	46	91	119	143	145	288	164	148	312	92
E	40	48	88	46	58	104	86	121	140	261	141	125	266	98
E-Infield	10	18	28	23	30	53	53	46	48	94	58	50	108	87
LHB-Avg	.268	.259	.263	.278	.273	.275	96	.260	.253	.256	.246	.267	.257	100
LHB-HR	22	28	50	24	34	58	92	42	70	112	71	101	172	64
RHB-Avg	.241	.222	.232	.273	.258	.266	87	.245	.253	.249	.244	.256	.250	100
RHB-HR	36	37	73	46	53	99	77	106	81	187	118	124	242	78

Milwaukee Brewers - Miller Park
LF: 344   CF: 400   RF:345

	2016 Season							2014-2016						
	Home Games			Away Games				Home Games			Away Games			
	Brewers	Opp	Total	Brewers	Opp	Total	Index	Brewers	Opp	Total	Brewers	Opp	Total	Index
G	81	81	162	81	81	162		243	243	486	243	243	486	
Avg	.245	.252	.249	.242	.275	.258	96	.251	.251	.251	.246	.265	.256	98
AB	2599	2812	5411	2731	2697	5428	100	7934	8454	16388	8338	8086	16424	100
R	341	351	692	330	382	712	97	1011	1065	2076	965	1062	2027	102
H	638	709	1347	661	741	1402	96	1989	2124	4113	2054	2144	4198	98
2B	129	142	271	120	151	271	100	414	400	814	406	429	835	98
3B	13	15	28	6	21	27	104	44	37	81	37	54	91	89
HR	102	95	197	92	83	175	113	255	300	555	234	221	455	122
BB	298	261	559	301	271	572	98	750	697	1447	684	783	1467	99
SO	773	629	1402	770	546	1316	107	1956	1962	3918	2083	1719	3802	103
Foul Outs	29	53	82	49	53	102	81	119	148	267	176	160	336	80
E	63	44	107	73	47	120	89	163	146	309	188	147	335	92
E-Infield	29	13	42	22	17	39	108	60	57	117	63	54	117	100
LHB-Avg	.249	.248	.248	.225	.267	.250	99	.267	.258	.261	.242	.256	.251	104
LHB-HR	26	43	69	18	32	50	141	61	142	203	44	90	134	149
RHB-Avg	.244	.256	.249	.250	.282	.264	95	.244	.246	.245	.248	.272	.258	95
RHB-HR	76	52	128	74	51	125	101	194	158	352	190	131	321	111

Minnesota Twins - Target Field
LF: 339   CF: 411   RF:328

	2016 Season							2014-2016						
	Home Games			Away Games				Home Games			Away Games			
	Twins	Opp	Total	Twins	Opp	Total	Index	Twins	Opp	Total	Twins	Opp	Total	Index
G	81	81	162	81	81	162		243	243	486	243	243	486	
Avg	.251	.289	.271	.251	.276	.263	103	.258	.279	.269	.243	.276	.259	104
AB	2773	2990	5763	2845	2732	5577	103	8224	8792	17016	8428	8195	16623	102
R	348	475	823	374	414	788	104	1089	1217	2306	1044	1149	2193	105
H	696	864	1560	713	753	1466	106	2122	2451	4573	2048	2260	4308	106
2B	143	176	319	145	150	295	105	436	495	931	445	445	890	102
3B	21	12	33	14	18	32	100	59	43	102	47	50	97	103
HR	98	114	212	102	107	209	98	250	265	515	234	266	500	101
BB	236	227	463	277	252	529	85	744	629	1373	752	671	1423	94
SO	649	603	1252	777	588	1365	89	1846	1650	3496	2173	1618	3791	90
Foul Outs	67	56	123	51	53	104	114	178	176	354	163	180	343	101
E	82	46	128	44	40	84	152	187	150	337	122	133	255	132
E-Infield	29	17	46	19	15	34	135	68	62	130	48	53	101	129
LHB-Avg	.243	.281	.262	.257	.255	.256	102	.258	.271	.264	.244	.272	.258	102
LHB-HR	24	36	60	39	38	77	75	78	82	160	75	102	177	90
RHB-Avg	.257	.294	.277	.246	.288	.268	103	.258	.285	.272	.242	.278	.260	105
RHB-HR	74	78	152	63	69	132	111	172	183	355	159	164	323	106

New York Mets - Citi Field
LF: 335   CF: 408   RF:330

	2016 Season							2015-2016						
	Home Games			Away Games				Home Games			Away Games			
	Mets	Opp	Total	Mets	Opp	Total	Index	Mets	Opp	Total	Mets	Opp	Total	Index
G	81	81	162	81	81	162		162	162	324	162	162	324	
Avg	.239	.236	.237	.253	.273	.263	90	.236	.236	.236	.254	.262	.258	92
AB	2656	2771	5427	2803	2723	5526	98	5316	5578	10894	5670	5431	11101	98
R	339	301	640	332	316	648	99	652	591	1243	702	639	1341	93
H	634	654	1288	708	743	1451	89	1255	1317	2572	1438	1421	2859	90
2B	110	117	227	130	141	271	85	254	229	483	281	264	545	90
3B	5	10	15	14	19	33	46	12	22	34	24	30	54	64
HR	112	81	193	106	71	177	111	197	160	357	198	144	342	106
BB	277	238	515	240	201	441	119	525	425	950	480	397	877	110
SO	629	784	1413	673	612	1285	112	1249	1482	2731	1343	1251	2594	107
Foul Outs	65	55	120	55	57	112	109	130	113	243	129	113	242	102
E	45	31	76	45	35	80	95	79	68	147	99	85	184	80
E-Infield	17	16	33	17	17	34	97	29	34	63	39	42	81	78
LHB-Avg	.232	.242	.237	.250	.276	.261	91	.236	.247	.242	.252	.267	.259	93
LHB-HR	61	34	95	64	29	93	104	110	76	186	102	63	165	113
RHB-Avg	.247	.231	.238	.256	.271	.264	90	.236	.227	.231	.255	.257	.256	90
RHB-HR	51	47	98	42	42	84	119	87	84	171	96	81	177	100

New York Yankees - Yankee Stadium
LF: 318   CF: 408   RF:314

| | 2016 Season | | | | | | | 2014-2016 | | | | | | |
| | Home Games | | | Away Games | | | | Home Games | | | Away Games | | | |
	Yankees	Opp	Total	Yankees	Opp	Total	Index	Yankees	Opp	Total	Yankees	Opp	Total	Index
G	81	81	162	81	81	162		243	243	486	243	243	486	
Avg	.254	.243	.248	.251	.253	.252	99	.252	.245	.248	.247	.257	.252	99
AB	2647	2813	5460	2811	2665	5476	100	8073	8517	16590	8449	8119	16568	100
R	363	340	703	317	362	679	104	1048	1024	2072	1029	1040	2069	100
H	672	684	1356	706	674	1380	98	2035	2084	4119	2089	2083	4172	99
2B	116	128	244	129	151	280	87	366	364	730	398	433	831	88
3B	9	5	14	11	17	28	50	23	27	50	42	49	91	55
HR	111	119	230	72	95	167	138	313	321	634	229	239	468	135
BB	259	208	467	216	236	452	104	751	647	1398	730	669	1399	100
SO	575	738	1313	613	655	1268	104	1751	2169	3920	1797	1964	3761	104
Foul Outs	50	53	103	50	56	106	97	163	163	326	158	161	319	102
E	42	48	90	44	51	95	95	133	135	268	137	135	272	99
E-Infield	17	22	39	23	23	46	85	55	58	113	66	64	130	87
LHB-Avg	.252	.225	.240	.254	.277	.263	91	.252	.243	.248	.247	.260	.252	99
LHB-HR	64	42	106	37	43	80	132	210	126	336	147	82	229	146
RHB-Avg	.257	.256	.257	.246	.238	.241	106	.252	.246	.248	.248	.254	.252	99
RHB-HR	47	77	124	35	52	87	144	103	195	298	82	157	239	125

Oakland Athletics - O.co Coliseum
LF: 330   CF: 400   RF:330

| | 2016 Season | | | | | | | 2014-2016 | | | | | | |
| | Home Games | | | Away Games | | | | Home Games | | | Away Games | | | |
	Athletics	Opp	Total	Athletics	Opp	Total	Index	Athletics	Opp	Total	Athletics	Opp	Total	Index
G	81	81	162	81	81	162		243	243	486	243	243	486	
Avg	.236	.257	.246	.255	.268	.262	94	.249	.243	.246	.245	.257	.251	98
AB	2658	2812	5470	2842	2746	5588	98	8109	8351	16460	8536	8178	16714	98
R	288	353	641	365	408	773	83	1015	975	1990	1061	1087	2148	93
H	626	722	1348	726	737	1463	92	2022	2030	4052	2089	2100	4189	97
2B	122	145	267	148	132	280	97	393	385	778	407	368	775	102
3B	13	11	24	8	15	23	107	61	19	80	39	31	70	116
HR	67	82	149	102	103	205	74	201	226	427	260	278	538	81
BB	200	222	422	242	242	484	89	739	642	1381	764	702	1466	96
SO	533	600	1133	612	588	1200	96	1545	1792	3337	1823	1819	3642	93
Foul Outs	72	80	152	70	43	113	137	251	260	511	201	152	353	147
E	49	37	86	48	45	93	92	167	145	312	167	150	317	98
E-Infield	21	24	45	28	18	46	98	71	60	131	71	69	140	94
LHB-Avg	.230	.254	.242	.252	.265	.258	94	.248	.242	.245	.240	.257	.247	99
LHB-HR	16	29	45	33	39	72	69	75	89	164	106	108	214	80
RHB-Avg	.239	.259	.249	.258	.271	.265	94	.250	.244	.247	.250	.257	.253	97
RHB-HR	51	53	104	69	64	133	76	126	137	263	154	170	324	81

Philadelphia Phillies - Citizens Bank Park
LF: 329   CF: 401   RF:329

| | 2016 Season | | | | | | | 2014-2016 | | | | | | |
| | Home Games | | | Away Games | | | | Home Games | | | Away Games | | | |
	Phillies	Opp	Total	Phillies	Opp	Total	Index	Phillies	Opp	Total	Phillies	Opp	Total	Index
G	81	81	162	81	81	162		243	243	486	243	243	486	
Avg	.230	.253	.242	.250	.278	.263	92	.239	.256	.248	.248	.276	.262	95
AB	2657	2843	5500	2777	2697	5474	100	8117	8651	16768	8449	8126	16575	101
R	279	363	642	331	433	764	84	920	1082	2002	935	1210	2145	93
H	612	719	1331	693	749	1442	92	1939	2216	4155	2096	2240	4336	96
2B	105	138	243	126	170	296	82	345	431	776	409	461	870	88
3B	18	14	32	17	19	36	88	54	33	87	45	65	110	78
HR	78	122	200	83	91	174	114	214	299	513	202	239	441	115
BB	209	229	438	215	237	452	96	632	737	1369	622	738	1360	100
SO	706	712	1418	670	587	1257	112	1979	2029	4008	1977	1678	3655	108
Foul Outs	65	69	134	43	49	92	145	192	198	390	145	128	273	141
E	53	47	100	44	49	93	108	167	167	334	130	148	278	120
E-Infield	26	23	49	17	22	39	126	85	76	161	49	68	117	138
LHB-Avg	.229	.258	.245	.262	.280	.271	90	.244	.257	.250	.255	.280	.265	94
LHB-HR	39	66	105	37	46	83	128	118	122	240	107	116	223	107
RHB-Avg	.231	.248	.240	.239	.276	.257	93	.233	.255	.246	.239	.273	.258	95
RHB-HR	39	56	95	46	45	91	102	96	177	273	95	123	218	123

Pittsburgh Pirates - PNC Park
LF: 325   CF: 399   RF:320

| | 2016 Season | | | | | | | 2014-2016 | | | | | | |
| | Home Games | | | Away Games | | | | Home Games | | | Away Games | | | |
	Pirates	Opp	Total	Pirates	Opp	Total	Index	Pirates	Opp	Total	Pirates	Opp	Total	Index
G	81	81	162	81	81	162		243	243	486	243	243	486	
Avg	.270	.265	.267	.245	.270	.257	104	.267	.249	.258	.251	.259	.255	101
AB	2681	2811	5492	2861	2768	5629	98	8152	8451	16603	8557	8172	16729	99
R	359	387	746	370	371	741	101	1052	967	2019	1056	1018	2074	97
H	724	744	1468	702	746	1448	101	2180	2104	4284	2144	2119	4263	100
2B	132	173	305	145	149	294	106	404	422	826	440	392	832	100
3B	24	22	46	8	18	26	181	56	38	94	33	52	85	111
HR	70	78	148	83	102	185	82	204	192	396	245	226	471	85
BB	277	272	549	284	261	545	103	772	740	1512	770	745	1515	101
SO	610	607	1217	724	625	1349	92	1781	1901	3682	2119	1897	4016	92
Foul Outs	40	42	82	55	51	106	79	129	130	259	150	157	307	85
E	66	59	125	45	56	101	124	180	161	341	162	148	310	110
E-Infield	23	24	47	26	29	55	85	69	69	138	69	68	137	101
LHB-Avg	.272	.270	.271	.239	.289	.267	102	.251	.252	.252	.237	.262	.250	101
LHB-HR	28	32	60	21	35	56	106	94	68	162	80	80	160	101
RHB-Avg	.269	.261	.265	.248	.258	.253	105	.275	.247	.261	.257	.258	.257	102
RHB-HR	42	46	88	62	67	129	71	110	124	234	165	146	311	76

San Diego Padres - PETCO Park
LF: 336   CF: 396   RF:322

| | 2016 Season | | | | | | | 2015-2016 | | | | | | |
| | Home Games | | | Away Games | | | | Home Games | | | Away Games | | | |
	Padres	Opp	Total	Padres	Opp	Total	Index	Padres	Opp	Total	Padres	Opp	Total	Index
G	81	81	162	81	81	162		162	162	324	162	162	324	
Avg	.242	.253	.247	.229	.263	.246	101	.244	.248	.246	.234	.262	.248	99
AB	2679	2890	5569	2740	2643	5383	103	5330	5650	10980	5546	5323	10869	101
R	350	383	733	336	387	723	101	671	728	1399	665	773	1438	97
H	647	731	1378	628	694	1322	104	1301	1401	2702	1298	1395	2693	100
2B	132	142	274	125	133	258	103	260	272	532	257	271	528	100
3B	13	17	30	13	27	40	72	30	38	68	32	56	88	76
HR	83	93	176	94	90	184	92	157	185	342	168	169	337	100
BB	246	257	503	203	312	515	94	457	515	972	418	570	988	97
SO	721	633	1354	779	589	1368	96	1376	1381	2757	1451	1234	2685	102
Foul Outs	50	62	112	45	50	95	114	102	116	218	100	93	193	112
E	54	47	101	55	42	97	104	102	97	199	99	101	200	100
E-Infield	22	19	41	27	15	42	98	38	39	77	48	38	86	90
LHB-Avg	.254	.238	.245	.238	.250	.244	101	.256	.246	.250	.248	.255	.252	99
LHB-HR	21	35	56	38	35	73	74	36	90	126	59	78	137	90
RHB-Avg	.233	.263	.249	.223	.271	.247	101	.237	.250	.243	.226	.267	.245	99
RHB-HR	62	58	120	56	55	111	105	121	95	216	109	91	200	107

San Francisco Giants - AT&T Park
LF: 339   CF: 399   RF:309

| | 2016 Season | | | | | | | 2014-2016 | | | | | | |
| | Home Games | | | Away Games | | | | Home Games | | | Away Games | | | |
	Giants	Opp	Total	Giants	Opp	Total	Index	Giants	Opp	Total	Giants	Opp	Total	Index
G	81	81	162	81	81	162		243	243	486	243	243	486	
Avg	.273	.250	.261	.244	.236	.240	108	.265	.238	.252	.255	.249	.252	100
AB	2730	2797	5527	2835	2691	5526	100	8084	8284	16368	8569	8079	16648	98
R	371	306	677	344	325	669	101	1026	870	1896	1050	1002	2052	92
H	744	698	1442	693	636	1329	109	2146	1972	4118	2184	2011	4195	98
2B	147	137	284	133	125	258	110	396	382	778	429	392	821	96
3B	39	19	58	15	23	38	153	97	75	172	38	66	104	168
HR	55	64	119	75	94	169	70	161	174	335	237	272	509	67
BB	303	221	524	269	218	487	108	745	625	1370	711	634	1345	104
SO	522	649	1171	585	660	1245	94	1690	1908	3598	1821	1777	3598	102
Foul Outs	54	64	118	65	58	123	96	124	163	287	178	151	329	89
E	24	48	72	48	44	92	78	118	133	251	132	125	257	98
E-Infield	11	23	34	23	23	46	74	48	60	108	56	56	112	96
LHB-Avg	.269	.251	.261	.251	.253	.252	104	.274	.245	.261	.257	.259	.258	101
LHB-HR	27	23	50	42	35	77	63	66	71	137	117	114	231	59
RHB-Avg	.278	.249	.260	.237	.225	.230	113	.257	.233	.244	.253	.242	.247	99
RHB-HR	28	41	69	33	59	92	78	95	103	198	120	158	278	74

Seattle Mariners - Safeco Field
LF: 331   CF: 405   RF:326

	2016 Season							2014-2016						
	Home Games			Away Games				Home Games			Away Games			
	Mariners	Opp	Total	Mariners	Opp	Total	Index	Mariners	Opp	Total	Mariners	Opp	Total	Index
G	81	81	162	81	81	162		243	243	486	243	243	486	
Avg	.256	.245	.250	.262	.261	.262	96	.248	.234	.241	.253	.259	.256	94
AB	2723	2845	5568	2860	2728	5588	100	8039	8350	16389	8538	8202	16740	98
R	370	345	715	398	362	760	94	961	937	1898	1097	1050	2147	88
H	696	698	1394	750	712	1462	95	1991	1956	3947	2162	2124	4286	92
2B	113	144	257	138	129	267	97	341	373	714	419	412	831	88
3B	8	6	14	9	17	26	54	29	22	51	42	45	87	60
HR	116	118	234	107	95	202	116	279	275	554	278	256	534	106
BB	272	218	490	234	242	476	103	701	664	1365	679	750	1429	98
SO	648	706	1354	640	612	1252	109	1950	2047	3997	1906	1871	3777	108
Foul Outs	63	68	131	58	52	110	120	183	200	383	150	155	305	128
E	45	36	81	44	49	93	87	127	130	257	138	140	278	92
E-Infield	24	14	38	22	20	42	90	65	61	126	62	53	115	110
LHB-Avg	.263	.231	.251	.265	.249	.260	97	.257	.235	.248	.261	.258	.260	96
LHB-HR	66	39	105	62	32	94	115	164	100	264	153	92	245	110
RHB-Avg	.244	.254	.250	.257	.268	.264	95	.233	.234	.233	.242	.259	.252	93
RHB-HR	50	79	129	45	63	108	117	115	175	290	125	164	289	102

St Louis Cardinals - Busch Stadium
LF: 336   CF: 400   RF:335

	2016 Season							2014-2016						
	Home Games			Away Games				Home Games			Away Games			
	Cardinals	Opp	Total	Cardinals	Opp	Total	Index	Cardinals	Opp	Total	Cardinals	Opp	Total	Index
G	81	81	162	81	81	162		243	243	486	243	243	486	
Avg	.253	.255	.254	.257	.261	.259	98	.258	.246	.252	.249	.251	.250	101
AB	2695	2832	5527	2853	2721	5574	99	8016	8495	16511	8442	8028	16470	100
R	355	360	715	424	352	776	92	1002	918	1920	1043	922	1965	98
H	681	722	1403	734	710	1444	97	2068	2094	4162	2104	2018	4122	101
2B	144	131	275	155	147	302	92	443	384	827	419	387	806	102
3B	11	8	19	21	14	35	55	42	38	80	50	36	86	93
HR	104	78	182	121	81	202	91	221	193	414	246	212	458	90
BB	256	222	478	270	253	523	92	765	675	1440	738	747	1485	97
SO	599	658	1257	719	632	1351	94	1676	1956	3632	2042	1884	3926	92
Foul Outs	65	48	113	46	43	89	128	171	188	359	156	134	290	123
E	54	46	100	53	56	109	92	142	123	265	149	155	304	87
E-Infield	27	19	46	24	21	45	102	71	45	116	68	65	133	87
LHB-Avg	.242	.257	.250	.250	.250	.250	100	.263	.249	.256	.256	.250	.253	101
LHB-HR	39	39	78	46	25	71	107	89	83	172	102	77	179	98
RHB-Avg	.258	.253	.256	.261	.268	.264	97	.255	.245	.250	.244	.252	.248	101
RHB-HR	65	39	104	75	56	131	82	132	110	242	144	135	279	85

Tampa Bay Rays - Tropicana Field Surface: FieldTurf
LF: 315   CF: 404   RF:322

	2016 Season							2014-2016						
	Home Games			Away Games				Home Games			Away Games			
	Rays	Opp	Total	Rays	Opp	Total	Index	Rays	Opp	Total	Rays	Opp	Total	Index
G	81	81	162	81	81	162		246	246	492	240	240	480	
Avg	.234	.240	.237	.252	.270	.261	91	.243	.235	.239	.252	.252	.252	95
AB	2663	2782	5445	2818	2688	5506	99	8090	8479	16569	8392	7986	16378	99
R	314	338	652	358	375	733	89	946	972	1918	982	1008	1990	94
H	624	669	1293	709	726	1435	90	1966	1992	3958	2111	2009	4120	94
2B	133	108	241	155	125	280	87	393	323	716	436	378	814	87
3B	17	3	20	15	6	21	96	36	23	59	52	23	75	78
HR	103	96	199	113	114	227	89	236	254	490	264	276	540	90
BB	226	255	481	223	236	459	106	725	734	1459	687	716	1403	103
SO	761	727	1488	721	630	1351	111	2004	2208	4212	1912	1941	3853	108
Foul Outs	69	82	151	66	62	128	119	201	242	443	181	198	379	116
E	44	43	87	50	41	91	96	120	120	240	157	127	284	82
E-Infield	17	17	34	20	20	40	85	51	45	96	63	55	118	79
LHB-Avg	.229	.233	.231	.252	.251	.252	92	.251	.227	.238	.254	.238	.246	97
LHB-HR	46	36	82	45	41	86	94	91	101	192	89	99	188	99
RHB-Avg	.238	.245	.242	.251	.281	.266	91	.238	.241	.239	.250	.262	.255	94
RHB-HR	57	60	117	68	73	141	85	145	153	298	175	177	352	85

Texas Rangers - Rangers Ballpark in Arlington
LF: 332   CF: 400   RF:325

| | 2016 Season | | | | | | | 2014-2016 | | | | | | |
| | Home Games | | | Away Games | | | | Home Games | | | Away Games | | | |
	Rangers	Opp	Total	Rangers	Opp	Total	Index	Rangers	Opp	Total	Rangers	Opp	Total	Index
G	81	81	162	81	81	162		243	243	486	243	243	486	
Avg	.279	.266	.272	.245	.255	.250	109	.268	.267	.268	.249	.262	.256	105
AB	2702	2850	5552	2823	2687	5510	101	8109	8572	16681	8387	8087	16474	101
R	425	391	816	340	366	706	116	1127	1203	2330	1026	1060	2086	112
H	755	757	1512	691	684	1375	110	2176	2289	4465	2089	2121	4210	106
2B	126	139	265	131	121	252	104	390	430	820	406	439	845	96
3B	17	12	29	6	10	16	180	52	51	103	31	40	71	143
HR	103	110	213	112	91	203	104	246	277	523	252	255	507	102
BB	242	250	492	194	284	478	102	722	760	1482	634	787	1421	103
SO	578	582	1160	642	572	1214	95	1706	1683	3389	1909	1676	3585	93
Foul Outs	54	44	98	65	48	113	86	139	160	299	185	172	357	83
E	55	49	104	42	44	86	121	172	166	338	150	169	319	106
E-Infield	20	21	41	19	23	42	98	64	70	134	66	74	140	96
LHB-Avg	.259	.251	.256	.239	.257	.246	104	.255	.267	.261	.250	.261	.255	102
LHB-HR	56	35	91	48	36	84	111	126	116	242	125	104	229	105
RHB-Avg	.297	.273	.283	.250	.253	.252	112	.280	.267	.273	.249	.263	.256	107
RHB-HR	47	75	122	64	55	119	99	120	161	281	127	151	278	100

Toronto Blue Jays - Rogers Centre Surface: FieldTurf
LF: 328   CF: 400   RF:328

| | 2016 Season | | | | | | | 2014-2016 | | | | | | |
| | Home Games | | | Away Games | | | | Home Games | | | Away Games | | | |
	Blue Jays	Opp	Total	Blue Jays	Opp	Total	Index	Blue Jays	Opp	Total	Blue Jays	Opp	Total	Index
G	81	81	162	81	81	162		243	243	486	243	243	486	
Avg	.260	.247	.253	.236	.235	.236	107	.268	.242	.254	.249	.254	.252	101
AB	2688	2849	5537	2791	2697	5488	101	8100	8424	16524	8437	8104	16541	100
R	401	363	764	358	303	661	116	1238	987	2225	1135	1035	2170	103
H	698	705	1403	660	635	1295	108	2169	2035	4204	2104	2058	4162	101
2B	159	149	308	117	120	237	129	477	451	928	389	416	805	115
3B	8	14	22	10	10	20	109	30	47	77	29	39	68	113
HR	107	96	203	114	87	201	100	328	264	592	302	243	545	109
BB	319	238	557	313	223	536	103	851	665	1516	853	683	1536	99
SO	644	674	1318	718	640	1358	96	1767	1898	3665	1897	1732	3629	101
Foul Outs	73	59	132	72	62	134	98	231	196	427	218	197	415	103
E	44	45	89	44	43	87	102	128	139	267	135	145	280	95
E-Infield	22	16	38	19	18	37	103	49	52	101	63	54	117	86
LHB-Avg	.235	.257	.249	.218	.224	.222	112	.256	.248	.252	.248	.247	.247	102
LHB-HR	24	51	75	22	34	56	120	79	125	204	71	108	179	109
RHB-Avg	.268	.240	.256	.242	.243	.243	105	.274	.237	.256	.250	.259	.254	101
RHB-HR	83	45	128	92	53	145	92	249	139	388	231	135	366	109

Washington Nationals - Nationals Park
LF: 336   CF: 403   RF:335

| | 2016 Season | | | | | | | 2014-2016 | | | | | | |
| | Home Games | | | Away Games | | | | Home Games | | | Away Games | | | |
	Nationals	Opp	Total	Nationals	Opp	Total	Index	Nationals	Opp	Total	Nationals	Opp	Total	Index
G	81	81	162	81	81	162		243	243	486	243	243	486	
Avg	.252	.231	.241	.259	.238	.249	97	.260	.238	.249	.247	.247	.247	101
AB	2672	2800	5472	2818	2630	5448	100	8061	8434	16495	8399	7994	16393	101
R	365	307	672	398	305	703	96	1087	895	1982	1065	907	1972	101
H	674	646	1320	729	626	1355	97	2092	2014	4106	2077	1975	4052	101
2B	123	122	245	145	130	275	89	406	366	772	392	367	759	101
3B	14	11	25	15	16	31	80	25	29	54	44	55	99	54
HR	102	79	181	101	76	177	102	256	196	452	276	214	490	92
BB	273	222	495	263	246	509	97	819	588	1407	773	596	1369	102
SO	593	774	1367	659	702	1361	100	1862	2134	3996	2038	1972	4010	99
Foul Outs	66	52	118	54	65	119	99	171	178	349	148	172	320	108
E	39	36	75	34	51	85	88	143	141	284	120	149	269	106
E-Infield	22	15	37	8	19	27	137	63	60	123	36	53	89	138
LHB-Avg	.261	.226	.244	.258	.243	.250	97	.269	.240	.253	.252	.256	.254	100
LHB-HR	40	32	72	42	39	81	89	103	81	184	112	104	216	83
RHB-Avg	.245	.234	.239	.259	.234	.248	97	.253	.238	.246	.245	.240	.243	101
RHB-HR	62	47	109	59	37	96	113	153	115	268	164	110	274	99

2016 American League Ballpark Index Rankings

Home Park	Avg	AB	R	H	2B	3B	HR	BB	SO	FO	E	E-Inf	LHB Avg	LHB HR	RHB Avg	RHB HR
Indians (Progressive Field)	112	100	121	111	130	51	117	112	93	80	94	82	121	133	104	106
Red Sox (Fenway Park)	113	103	120	116	139	162	104	95	88	86	105	120	118	86	110	116
Royals (Kauffman Stadium)	104	105	117	109	120	150	75	99	93	111	99	92	106	67	103	82
Blue Jays (Rogers Centre)	107	101	116	108	129	109	100	103	96	98	102	103	112	120	105	92
Rangers (Rangers Ballpark in Arlington)	109	101	116	110	104	180	104	102	95	86	121	98	104	111	112	99
Twins (Target Field)	103	103	104	106	105	100	98	85	89	114	152	135	102	75	103	111
Yankees (Yankee Stadium)	99	100	104	98	87	50	138	104	104	97	95	85	91	132	106	144
Tigers (Comerica Park)	100	98	102	98	90	194	116	96	95	128	88	94	92	147	104	105
Orioles (Oriole Park at Camden Yards)	99	97	95	97	86	87	104	100	96	92	109	148	97	95	101	109
Mariners (Safeco Field)	96	100	94	95	97	54	116	103	109	120	87	90	97	115	95	117
White Sox (U.S. Cellular Field)	99	97	93	96	92	110	113	96	101	78	100	95	94	132	102	106
Angels (Angel Stadium of Anaheim)	94	100	91	94	83	60	106	96	107	77	104	160	93	101	94	108
Rays (Tropicana Field)	91	99	89	90	87	96	89	106	111	119	96	85	92	94	91	85
Athletics (O.co Coliseum)	94	98	83	92	97	107	74	89	96	137	92	98	94	69	94	76
Astros (Minute Maid Park)	92	101	81	93	88	114	81	91	115	106	94	95	93	74	91	86

2016 National League Ballpark Index Rankings

Home Park	Avg	AB	R	H	2B	3B	HR	BB	SO	FO	E	E-Inf	LHB Avg	LHB HR	RHB Avg	RHB HR
Rockies (Coors Field)	117	105	123	123	134	132	120	103	89	70	111	90	117	107	117	129
Diamondbacks (Chase Field)	109	105	122	114	109	194	123	100	100	74	82	71	115	98	106	141
Braves (Turner Field)	100	101	106	101	90	85	77	113	104	110	143	203	103	89	97	67
Padres (PETCO Park)	101	103	101	104	103	72	92	94	96	114	104	98	101	74	101	105
Giants (AT&T Park)	108	100	101	109	110	153	70	108	94	96	78	74	104	63	113	78
Pirates (PNC Park)	104	98	101	101	106	181	82	103	92	79	124	85	102	106	105	71
Reds (Great American Ballpark)	97	100	99	97	95	65	118	102	104	120	94	87	99	126	96	113
Mets (Citi Field)	90	98	99	89	85	46	111	119	112	109	95	97	91	104	90	119
Brewers (Miller Park)	96	100	97	96	100	104	113	98	107	81	89	108	99	141	95	101
Nationals (Nationals Park)	97	100	96	97	89	80	102	97	100	99	88	137	97	89	97	113
Cardinals (Busch Stadium)	98	99	92	97	92	55	91	92	94	128	92	102	100	107	97	82
Cubs (Wrigley Field)	95	98	87	93	95	107	84	109	103	82	86	100	92	62	97	98
Phillies (Citizens Bank Park)	92	100	84	92	82	88	114	96	112	145	108	126	90	128	93	102
Marlins (Marlins Park)	90	96	83	87	100	69	83	101	105	119	86	53	96	92	87	77
Dodgers (Dodger Stadium)	95	95	81	91	97	40	96	94	105	83	103	109	96	118	95	81

2016 AL Home Runs			2016 AL LHB Home Runs			2016 AL RHB Home Runs	
Home Park	Index		Home Park	Index		Home Park	Index
Yankees	138		Tigers	147		Yankees	144
Indians	117		Indians	133		Mariners	117
Mariners	116		Yankees	132		Red Sox	116
Tigers	116		White Sox	132		Twins	111
White Sox	113		Blue Jays	120		Orioles	109
Angels	106		Mariners	115		Angels	108
Rangers	104		Rangers	111		White Sox	106
Orioles	104		Angels	101		Indians	106
Red Sox	104		Orioles	95		Tigers	105
Blue Jays	100		Rays	94		Rangers	99
Twins	98		Red Sox	86		Blue Jays	92
Rays	89		Twins	75		Astros	86
Astros	81		Astros	74		Rays	85
Royals	75		Athletics	69		Royals	82
Athletics	74		Royals	67		Athletics	76

2016 NL Home Runs			2016 NL LHB Home Runs			2016 NL RHB Home Runs	
Home Park	Index		Home Park	Index		Home Park	Index
Diamondbacks	123		Brewers	141		Diamondbacks	141
Rockies	120		Phillies	128		Rockies	129
Reds	118		Reds	126		Mets	119
Phillies	114		Dodgers	118		Reds	113
Brewers	113		Cardinals	107		Nationals	113
Mets	111		Rockies	107		Padres	105
Nationals	102		Pirates	106		Phillies	102
Dodgers	96		Mets	104		Brewers	101
Padres	92		Diamondbacks	98		Cubs	98
Cardinals	91		Marlins	92		Cardinals	82
Cubs	84		Braves	89		Dodgers	81
Marlins	83		Nationals	89		Giants	78
Pirates	82		Padres	74		Marlins	77
Braves	77		Giants	63		Pirates	71
Giants	70		Cubs	62		Braves	67

2016 AL Avg	
Home Park	Index
Red Sox	113
Indians	112
Rangers	109
Blue Jays	107
Royals	104
Twins	103
Tigers	100
Orioles	99
White Sox	99
Yankees	99
Mariners	96
Athletics	94
Angels	94
Astros	92
Rays	91

2016 AL LHB Avg	
Home Park	Index
Indians	121
Red Sox	118
Blue Jays	112
Royals	106
Rangers	104
Twins	102
Orioles	97
Mariners	97
White Sox	94
Athletics	94
Angels	93
Astros	93
Tigers	92
Rays	92
Yankees	91

2016 AL RHB Avg	
Home Park	Index
Rangers	112
Red Sox	110
Yankees	106
Blue Jays	105
Indians	104
Tigers	104
Twins	103
Royals	103
White Sox	102
Orioles	101
Mariners	95
Angels	94
Athletics	94
Astros	91
Rays	91

2016 NL Avg	
Home Park	Index
Rockies	117
Diamondbacks	109
Giants	108
Pirates	104
Padres	101
Braves	100
Cardinals	98
Reds	97
Nationals	97
Brewers	96
Dodgers	95
Cubs	95
Phillies	92
Marlins	90
Mets	90

2016 NL LHB Avg	
Home Park	Index
Rockies	117
Diamondbacks	115
Giants	104
Braves	103
Pirates	102
Padres	101
Cardinals	100
Brewers	99
Reds	99
Nationals	97
Dodgers	96
Marlins	96
Cubs	92
Mets	91
Phillies	90

2016 NL RHB Avg	
Home Park	Index
Rockies	117
Giants	113
Diamondbacks	106
Pirates	105
Padres	101
Cardinals	97
Cubs	97
Nationals	97
Braves	97
Reds	96
Dodgers	95
Brewers	95
Phillies	93
Mets	90
Marlins	87

2016 AL Doubles	
Home Park	Index
Red Sox	139
Indians	130
Blue Jays	129
Royals	120
Twins	105
Rangers	104
Athletics	97
Mariners	97
White Sox	92
Tigers	90
Astros	88
Yankees	87
Rays	87
Orioles	86
Angels	83

2016 AL Triples	
Home Park	Index
Tigers	194
Rangers	180
Red Sox	162
Royals	150
Astros	114
White Sox	110
Blue Jays	109
Athletics	107
Twins	100
Rays	96
Orioles	87
Angels	60
Mariners	54
Indians	51
Yankees	50

2016 AL Errors	
Home Park	Index
Twins	152
Rangers	121
Orioles	109
Red Sox	105
Angels	104
Blue Jays	102
White Sox	100
Royals	99
Rays	96
Yankees	95
Indians	94
Astros	94
Athletics	92
Tigers	88
Mariners	87

2016 NL Doubles	
Home Park	Index
Rockies	134
Giants	110
Diamondbacks	109
Pirates	106
Padres	103
Brewers	100
Marlins	100
Dodgers	97
Reds	95
Cubs	95
Cardinals	92
Braves	90
Nationals	89
Mets	85
Phillies	82

2016 NL Triples	
Home Park	Index
Diamondbacks	194
Pirates	181
Giants	153
Rockies	132
Cubs	107
Brewers	104
Phillies	88
Braves	85
Nationals	80
Padres	72
Marlins	69
Reds	65
Cardinals	55
Mets	46
Dodgers	40

2016 NL Errors	
Home Park	Index
Braves	143
Pirates	124
Rockies	111
Phillies	108
Padres	104
Dodgers	103
Mets	95
Reds	94
Cardinals	92
Brewers	89
Nationals	88
Cubs	86
Marlins	86
Diamondbacks	82
Giants	78

2014-2016 American League Ballpark Index Rankings

Home Park	Avg	AB	R	H	2B	3B	HR	BB	SO	FO	E	E-Inf	LHB Avg	LHB HR	RHB Avg	RHB HR
Red Sox (Fenway Park)	110	101	116	111	139	110	92	101	94	83	133	139	113	75	107	106
Indians (Progressive Field)	108	101	113	108	123	59	107	105	97	71	97	101	111	110	103	105
Rangers (Rangers Ballpark in Arlington)	105	101	112	106	96	143	102	103	93	83	106	96	102	105	107	100
Royals (Kauffman Stadium)	103	100	107	103	117	135	80	96	94	103	83	77	102	80	104	81
Twins (Target Field)	104	102	105	106	102	103	101	94	90	101	132	129	102	90	105	106
Orioles (Oriole Park at Camden Yards)	102	100	103	102	91	73	110	97	94	88	103	111	100	116	103	106
Blue Jays (Rogers Centre)	101	100	103	101	115	113	109	99	101	103	95	86	102	109	101	109
Yankees (Yankee Stadium)	99	100	100	99	88	55	135	100	104	102	99	87	99	146	99	125
Tigers (Comerica Park)	100	98	97	98	90	166	100	101	93	118	102	97	93	99	103	100
White Sox (U.S. Cellular Field)	97	100	96	97	92	99	109	106	107	102	101	107	92	113	101	104
Rays (Tropicana Field)	95	99	94	94	87	78	90	103	108	116	82	79	97	99	94	85
Athletics (O.co Coliseum)	98	98	93	97	102	116	81	96	93	147	98	94	99	80	97	81
Astros (Minute Maid Park)	96	100	91	96	96	135	101	95	109	86	96	93	94	104	98	99
Angels (Angel Stadium of Anaheim)	95	100	90	95	89	62	94	96	107	100	101	124	96	87	95	94
Mariners (Safeco Field)	94	98	88	92	88	60	106	98	108	128	92	110	96	110	93	102

2014-2016 National League Ballpark Index Rankings

Home Park	Avg	AB	R	H	2B	3B	HR	BB	SO	FO	E	E-Inf	LHB Avg	LHB HR	RHB Avg	RHB HR
Rockies (Coors Field)	121	106	143	128	121	162	121	100	84	66	103	102	121	116	121	125
Diamondbacks (Chase Field)	106	102	115	108	112	186	108	97	100	102	99	91	109	109	104	108
Brewers (Miller Park)	98	100	102	98	98	89	122	99	103	80	92	100	104	149	95	111
Reds (Great American Ballpark)	99	101	102	100	96	65	118	106	107	115	88	71	99	129	99	111
Padres (PETCO Park)[1]	101	103	101	104	103	72	92	94	96	114	104	98	101	74	101	105
Nationals (Nationals Park)	101	101	101	101	101	54	92	102	99	108	106	138	100	83	101	99
Mets (Citi Field)[1]	90	98	99	89	85	46	111	119	112	109	95	97	91	104	90	119
Braves (Turner Field)	97	100	98	96	91	77	85	109	109	102	129	155	96	79	98	90
Cardinals (Busch Stadium)	101	100	98	101	102	93	90	97	92	123	87	87	101	98	101	85
Pirates (PNC Park)	101	99	97	100	100	111	85	101	92	85	110	101	101	101	102	76
Phillies (Citizens Bank Park)	95	101	93	96	88	78	115	100	108	141	120	138	94	107	95	123
Giants (AT&T Park)	100	98	92	98	96	168	67	104	102	89	98	96	101	59	99	74
Cubs (Wrigley Field)	96	98	92	95	94	108	100	105	103	81	85	90	98	81	95	116
Dodgers (Dodger Stadium)	94	98	88	92	103	44	105	86	103	88	108	115	95	117	94	96
Marlins (Marlins Park)[2]	90	96	83	87	100	69	83	101	105	119	86	53	96	92	87	77

2014-2016 AL Home Runs

Home Park	Index
Yankees	135
Orioles	110
White Sox	109
Blue Jays	109
Indians	107
Mariners	106
Rangers	102
Astros	101
Twins	101
Tigers	100
Angels	94
Red Sox	92
Rays	90
Athletics	81
Royals	80

2014-2016 AL LHB Home Runs

Home Park	Index
Yankees	146
Orioles	116
White Sox	113
Mariners	110
Indians	110
Blue Jays	109
Rangers	105
Astros	104
Rays	99
Tigers	99
Twins	90
Angels	87
Royals	80
Athletics	80
Red Sox	75

2014-2016 AL RHB Home Runs

Home Park	Index
Yankees	125
Blue Jays	109
White Sox	107
Orioles	106
Twins	106
Red Sox	106
Indians	105
Mariners	102
Tigers	100
Rangers	100
Astros	99
Angels	98
Rays	85
Athletics	81
Royals	81

2014-2016 NL Home Runs

Home Park	Index
Brewers	122
Rockies	121
Reds	118
Phillies	115
Mets[1]	111
Diamondbacks	108
Dodgers	105
Cubs	100
Padres[1]	92
Nationals	92
Cardinals	90
Braves	85
Pirates	85
Marlins[2]	83
Giants	67

2014-2016 NL LHB Home Runs

Home Park	Index
Brewers	149
Reds	129
Dodgers	117
Rockies	116
Diamondbacks	109
Phillies	107
Mets[1]	104
Pirates	101
Cardinals	98
Marlins[2]	92
Nationals	83
Cubs	81
Braves	79
Padres[1]	74
Giants	59

2014-2016 NL RHB Home Runs

Home Park	Index
Rockies	125
Phillies	123
Mets[1]	119
Cubs	116
Reds	111
Brewers	111
Diamondbacks	108
Padres	105
Nationals	99
Dodgers	96
Braves	90
Cardinals	85
Marlins[2]	77
Pirates[1]	76
Giants	74

1. 2015 - 2016 Only
2. 2016 Only

2014-2016 AL Avg	
Home Park	Index
Red Sox	110
Indians	108
Rangers	105
Twins	104
Royals	103
Orioles	102
Blue Jays	101
Tigers	100
Yankees	99
Athletics	98
White Sox	97
Astros	96
Angels	95
Rays	95
Mariners	94

2014-2016 AL LHB Avg	
Home Park	Index
Red Sox	113
Indians	111
Twins	102
Rangers	102
Royals	102
Blue Jays	102
Orioles	100
Athletics	99
Yankees	99
Rays	97
Angels	96
Mariners	96
Astros	94
Tigers	93
White Sox	92

2014-2016 AL RHB Avg	
Home Park	Index
Red Sox	107
Rangers	107
Twins	105
Royals	104
Indians	103
Tigers	103
Orioles	103
Blue Jays	101
White Sox	101
Yankees	99
Astros	98
Athletics	97
Angels	95
Rays	94
Mariners	93

2014-2016 NL Avg	
Home Park	Index
Rockies	121
Diamondbacks	106
Pirates	101
Padres[1]	101
Cardinals	101
Nationals	101
Giants	100
Reds	99
Brewers	98
Braves	97
Cubs	96
Phillies	95
Dodgers	94
Marlins[2]	90
Mets[1]	90

2014-2016 NL LHB Avg	
Home Park	Index
Rockies	121
Diamondbacks	109
Brewers	104
Giants	101
Cardinals	101
Pirates	101
Padres[1]	101
Nationals	100
Reds	99
Cubs	98
Braves	96
Marlins[2]	96
Dodgers	95
Phillies	94
Mets[1]	91

2014-2016 NL RHB Avg	
Home Park	Index
Rockies	121
Diamondbacks	104
Pirates	102
Nationals	101
Padres[1]	101
Cardinals	101
Reds	99
Giants	99
Braves	98
Phillies	95
Cubs	95
Brewers	95
Dodgers	94
Mets[1]	90
Marlins[2]	87

2014-2016 AL Doubles	
Home Park	Index
Red Sox	139
Indians	123
Royals	117
Blue Jays	115
Twins	102
Athletics	102
Astros	96
Rangers	96
White Sox	92
Orioles	91
Tigers	90
Angels	89
Mariners	88
Yankees	88
Rays	87

2014-2016 AL Triples	
Home Park	Index
Tigers	166
Rangers	143
Royals	135
Astros	135
Athletics	116
Blue Jays	113
Red Sox	110
Twins	103
White Sox	99
Rays	78
Orioles	73
Angels	62
Mariners	60
Indians	59
Yankees	55

2014-2016 AL Errors	
Home Park	Index
Red Sox	133
Twins	132
Rangers	106
Orioles	103
Tigers	102
White Sox	101
Angels	101
Yankees	99
Athletics	98
Indians	97
Astros	96
Blue Jays	95
Mariners	92
Royals	83
Rays	82

2014-2016 NL Doubles	
Home Park	Index
Rockies	121
Diamondbacks	112
Dodgers	103
Padres[1]	103
Cardinals	102
Nationals	101
Marlins[2]	100
Pirates	100
Brewers	98
Giants	96
Reds	96
Cubs	94
Braves	91
Phillies	88
Mets[1]	85

2014-2016 NL Triples	
Home Park	Index
Diamondbacks	186
Giants	168
Rockies	162
Pirates	111
Cubs	108
Cardinals	93
Brewers	89
Phillies	78
Braves	77
Padres[1]	72
Marlins[2]	69
Reds	65
Nationals	54
Mets[1]	46
Dodgers	44

2014-2016 NL Errors	
Home Park	Index
Braves	129
Phillies	120
Pirates	110
Dodgers	108
Nationals	106
Padres[1]	104
Rockies	103
Diamondbacks	99
Giants	98
Mets[1]	95
Brewers	92
Reds	88
Cardinals	87
Marlins[2]	86
Cubs	85

1. 2015-2016 Only
2. 2016 Only

2016 Lefty/Righty Statistics

Ben Jedlovec

Right-handed pitchers faced roughly three times as many batters as left-handed pitchers in 2016. They also allowed about three times as many hits, three times as many doubles, and three times as many home runs. Thus, the average hitter had three times as many at-bats against righties.

Franklin Gutierrez was utilized uniquely in Major League Baseball last year. Gutierrez, a right-handed hitter, received 75 percent of his at-bats against lefties. No other hitter with more than 200 total at-bats faced more than 57 percent lefties. Gutierrez made it work, crushing lefties to a higher batting average (.280 vs. .145), OPS (.884 vs. 456), and hit more doubles (7 vs. 2) and homers (12 vs. 2) off of them than righties.

John Jaso represents the opposite end of the platoon spectrum. Jaso, a lefty, had 360 at-bats against righties and just 20 (5 percent) against lefties.

Red Sox righties Mookie Betts, Xander Bogaerts, and Dustin Pedroia had more at-bats against right-handers than any other hitters in baseball. Of the three, only Bogaerts maintained a traditional platoon split by hitting lefties better, but only barely. The three combined to hit .315 and slug .479 against righties. When three key cogs combine for that kind of line without the platoon advantage, it's no wonder Boston outscored the next best team in the American League by over half a run per game!

The following pages include platoon splits for all hitters with at least 20 plate appearances and pitchers with at least 20 batters faced in 2016. It contains batting average, on-base percentage, and slugging percentage along with a count of at-bats, hits, doubles, triples, home runs, RBI, walks, and strikeouts for hitters against both right and left-handed pitchers.

For pitchers, these stats reflect the performance of opposing batters. Most pitchers relatively dominate same-handed hitters but are exposed against opposite-handed batters, while others are equally successful against batters of either hand.

Batters vs. Left-Handed and Right-Handed Pitchers

Batter	vs	Avg	AB	H	2B	3B	HR	RBI	BB	SO	OBP	Slg
Abreu,Jose	L	.262	126	33	6	0	8	22	13	29	.340	.500
Bats Right	R	.301	498	150	26	1	17	78	34	96	.356	.460
Ackley,Dustin	L	.154	13	2	0	0	0	0	2	6	.267	.154
Bats Left	R	.146	48	7	0	0	0	4	6	3	.236	.146
Adames,Cristhian	L	.222	72	16	3	2	0	4	7	18	.291	.319
Bats Both	R	.216	153	33	4	1	2	13	17	29	.310	.294
Adams,Matt	L	.283	46	13	2	0	3	13	2	11	.300	.522
Bats Left	R	.243	251	61	16	0	13	41	23	70	.310	.462
Adrianza,Ehire	L	.353	34	12	2	0	1	4	0	6	.353	.500
Bats Both	R	.138	29	4	0	0	1	3	2	7	.242	.241
Ahmed,Nick	L	.244	82	20	4	0	2	6	3	14	.267	.366
Bats Right	R	.208	202	42	5	1	2	14	12	44	.264	.272
Alberto,Hanser	L	.136	22	3	0	0	0	2	0	9	.136	.136
Bats Right	R	.147	34	5	1	0	0	3	0	8	.147	.176
Almonte,Abraham	L	.279	68	19	9	0	1	11	3	17	.315	.456
Bats Both	R	.254	114	29	11	1	0	11	5	25	.281	.368
Almora,Albert	L	.262	42	11	6	0	2	6	1	5	.279	.548
Bats Right	R	.286	70	20	3	1	1	8	4	15	.324	.400
Alonso,Yonder	L	.227	66	15	4	0	1	8	5	10	.284	.333
Bats Left	R	.257	416	107	30	0	6	48	40	64	.321	.373
Altherr,Aaron	L	.250	40	10	2	0	1	4	5	11	.348	.375
Bats Right	R	.184	158	29	4	0	3	18	18	58	.287	.266
Altuve,Jose	L	.306	160	49	11	2	5	23	19	26	.391	.494
Bats Right	R	.348	480	167	31	3	19	73	41	44	.398	.544
Alvarez,Pedro	L	.237	38	9	2	0	1	6	3	10	.286	.368
Bats Left	R	.251	299	75	18	0	21	43	34	87	.326	.522
Amarista,Alexi	L	.150	20	3	0	0	0	1	0	4	.143	.150
Bats Left	R	.275	120	33	2	0	0	10	8	22	.320	.292
Anderson,Tim	L	.326	92	30	4	1	2	7	2	26	.340	.457
Bats Right	R	.270	318	86	18	5	7	23	11	91	.296	.425
Andino,Robert	L	.273	11	3	0	0	0	0	0	2	.273	.273
Bats Right	R	.308	13	4	0	0	0	1	0	2	.308	.308
Andrus,Elvis	L	.348	115	40	7	2	2	19	11	17	.403	.496
Bats Right	R	.289	391	113	24	5	6	50	36	53	.349	.422
Aoki,Nori	L	.227	97	22	3	0	0	3	9	15	.299	.258
Bats Left	R	.300	320	96	21	4	4	25	25	30	.364	.428
Arcia,Orlando	L	.283	46	13	3	1	1	7	8	10	.389	.457
Bats Right	R	.200	155	31	7	2	3	10	7	37	.235	.329
Arcia,Oswaldo	L	.189	37	7	3	0	0	3	4	16	.268	.270
Bats Left	R	.206	165	34	4	1	8	20	14	64	.271	.388
Arenado,Nolan	L	.267	161	43	9	1	9	23	26	33	.369	.503
Bats Right	R	.304	457	139	26	5	32	110	42	70	.360	.593
Asche,Cody	L	.227	22	5	3	0	0	1	4	8	.370	.364
Bats Left	R	.211	175	37	12	0	4	17	14	46	.272	.349
Asuaje,Carlos	L	.222	9	2	1	0	0	0	0	1	.222	.333
Bats Left	R	.200	15	3	1	0	0	2	1	3	.250	.267
Austin,Tyler	L	.348	23	8	1	0	2	5	4	10	.444	.652
Bats Right	R	.200	60	12	2	0	3	7	3	26	.238	.383
Avila,Alex	L	.250	20	5	0	0	1	1	6	9	.444	.400
Bats Left	R	.208	149	31	6	0	6	10	32	69	.346	.369
Aviles,Mike	L	.203	64	13	1	0	0	1	5	9	.261	.219
Bats Right	R	.214	103	22	4	1	1	5	4	18	.257	.301
Aybar,Erick	L	.234	111	26	6	0	0	7	1	24	.243	.288
Bats Both	R	.247	304	75	13	2	3	27	30	46	.323	.332
Baez,Javier	L	.311	122	38	6	1	4	21	11	25	.375	.475
Bats Right	R	.258	299	77	13	0	10	38	4	83	.288	.401
Bandy,Jett	L	.203	59	12	4	0	3	9	6	13	.273	.424
Bats Right	R	.247	150	37	5	0	5	16	5	25	.284	.380
Barnes,Austin	L	.222	9	2	1	0	0	0	4	2	.462	.333
Bats Right	R	.130	23	3	0	0	0	2	1	7	.167	.130
Barnes,Brandon	L	.222	27	6	2	0	0	1	0	7	.222	.296
Bats Right	R	.219	73	16	4	2	0	7	3	23	.260	.329
Barney,Darwin	L	.306	98	30	5	0	2	7	8	15	.361	.418
Bats Right	R	.249	181	45	8	2	2	12	14	33	.301	.348
Barnhart,Tucker	L	.207	82	17	2	0	2	7	4	24	.241	.305
Bats Both	R	.271	295	80	21	1	5	44	32	48	.344	.400
Bautista,Jose	L	.220	91	20	4	0	5	12	14	16	.324	.429
Bats Right	R	.238	332	79	20	1	17	57	73	87	.376	.458
Beckham,Gordon	L	.221	77	17	3	1	2	5	9	17	.303	.364
Bats Right	R	.208	168	35	13	0	3	26	17	35	.289	.339
Beckham,Tim	L	.276	87	24	5	2	2	7	8	32	.344	.448
Bats Right	R	.225	111	25	7	3	3	9	6	35	.265	.423
Bell,Josh	L	.211	19	4	0	0	0	1	3	3	.304	.211
Bats Both	R	.284	109	31	8	0	3	18	18	16	.380	.440
Belt,Brandon	L	.279	179	50	10	5	6	31	30	48	.392	.492
Bats Left	R	.273	363	99	31	3	11	51	74	100	.395	.466

Batter	vs	Avg	AB	H	2B	3B	HR	RBI	BB	SO	OBP	Slg
Beltran,Carlos	L	.338	151	51	11	0	9	30	10	30	.380	.589
Bats Both	R	.279	401	112	22	0	20	63	25	71	.321	.484
Beltre,Adrian	L	.331	133	44	7	1	9	29	16	14	.403	.602
Bats Right	R	.291	450	131	24	0	23	75	32	52	.344	.498
Benintendi,Andrew	L	.179	28	5	0	0	0	2	3	12	.250	.179
Bats Left	R	.338	77	26	11	1	2	12	7	13	.400	.584
Beresford,James	L	-	0	0	0	0	0	0	1	0	1.000	-
Bats Left	R	.227	22	5	1	0	0	0	0	6	.227	.273
Bethancourt,Christian	L	.244	41	10	2	0	1	3	4	15	.311	.366
Bats Right	R	.224	152	34	7	0	5	22	6	41	.252	.368
Betts,Mookie	L	.264	129	34	8	0	8	21	8	14	.302	.512
Bats Right	R	.331	543	180	34	5	23	92	41	66	.377	.540
Blackmon,Charlie	L	.331	175	58	9	0	4	25	11	27	.392	.451
Bats Left	R	.320	403	129	26	5	25	57	32	75	.376	.596
Blanco,Andres	L	.211	38	8	3	0	0	2	3	10	.262	.289
Bats Both	R	.263	152	40	12	1	4	19	8	31	.329	.434
Blanco,Gregor	L	.242	62	15	2	2	0	4	9	10	.347	.339
Bats Left	R	.218	179	39	8	2	1	14	20	41	.295	.302
Blash,Jabari	L	.118	17	2	1	0	1	1	3	11	.250	.353
Bats Right	R	.185	54	10	1	0	2	4	8	23	.313	.315
Bogaerts,Xander	L	.304	125	38	4	0	6	20	18	25	.393	.480
Bats Right	R	.292	527	154	30	1	15	69	40	98	.347	.438
Bonifacio,Emilio	L	.333	3	1	0	0	0	0	1	2	.500	.333
Bats Both	R	.200	35	7	0	0	0	3	2	10	.243	.200
Bour,Justin	L	.233	30	7	2	0	0	2	0	12	.233	.300
Bats Left	R	.268	250	67	10	1	15	49	38	44	.361	.496
Bourjos,Peter	L	.301	83	25	3	1	0	4	4	18	.333	.361
Bats Right	R	.235	272	64	17	6	5	19	13	73	.279	.397
Bourn,Michael	L	.357	70	25	0	2	1	9	4	19	.387	.457
Bats Left	R	.243	305	74	13	4	4	29	24	73	.297	.351
Bradley Jr.,Jackie	L	.244	164	40	8	1	3	17	14	46	.313	.360
Bats Left	R	.277	394	109	22	6	23	70	49	97	.363	.538
Brantley,Michael	L	.286	7	2	2	0	0	3	0	2	.250	.571
Bats Left	R	.219	32	7	0	0	0	4	3	4	.286	.219
Braun,Ryan	L	.344	122	42	5	1	8	27	15	20	.411	.598
Bats Right	R	.293	389	114	18	2	22	64	31	78	.350	.519
Bregman,Alex	L	.250	56	14	4	0	2	7	5	14	.306	.429
Bats Right	R	.269	145	39	9	3	6	27	10	38	.316	.497
Brentz,Bryce	L	.286	42	12	2	0	1	6	3	12	.333	.405
Bats Right	R	.263	19	5	1	0	0	1	0	5	.263	.316
Brignac,Reid	L	.333	3	1	0	0	0	0	0	1	.333	.333
Bats Left	R	.192	26	5	2	0	0	1	0	7	.192	.269
Brito,Socrates	L	.083	12	1	0	0	0	0	0	5	.083	.083
Bats Left	R	.193	83	16	3	1	4	12	2	18	.212	.398
Brown,Trevor	L	.254	63	16	2	0	2	7	4	12	.299	.381
Bats Right	R	.227	110	25	5	0	3	12	6	27	.274	.355
Broxton,Keon	L	.289	83	24	6	0	4	8	17	37	.410	.506
Bats Right	R	.210	124	26	4	1	5	11	19	51	.315	.379
Bruce,Jay	L	.222	158	35	10	1	6	22	8	39	.266	.411
Bats Left	R	.262	381	100	17	5	27	77	36	87	.326	.546
Bryant,Kris	L	.314	156	49	9	0	14	31	24	36	.419	.641
Bats Right	R	.284	447	127	26	3	25	71	51	118	.372	.523
Burns,Billy	L	.278	79	22	5	1	0	2	1	16	.318	.367
Bats Both	R	.220	232	51	6	3	0	11	9	21	.254	.272
Burriss,Emmanuel	L	.000	8	0	0	0	0	0	0	3	.000	.000
Bats Both	R	.135	37	5	1	1	0	0	2	7	.220	.216
Buss,Nick	L	.000	15	0	0	0	0	0	0	6	.000	.000
Bats Left	R	.242	66	16	7	1	1	8	6	18	.297	.424
Butera,Drew	L	.179	28	5	2	1	0	2	2	9	.233	.321
Bats Right	R	.316	95	30	8	0	4	14	6	27	.356	.526
Butler,Billy	L	.280	125	35	10	0	2	18	11	19	.331	.408
Bats Right	R	.288	125	36	8	0	3	17	10	23	.341	.424
Buxton,Byron	L	.223	94	21	6	4	2	11	11	36	.299	.436
Bats Right	R	.225	204	46	13	2	8	27	12	82	.277	.426
Byrd,Marlon	L	.368	38	14	4	0	1	6	4	11	.409	.553
Bats Right	R	.221	77	17	2	0	4	13	7	27	.282	.403
Cabrera,Asdrubal	L	.321	112	36	7	0	3	11	9	21	.371	.464
Bats Both	R	.269	409	110	23	1	20	51	29	82	.327	.477
Cabrera,Melky	L	.322	121	39	10	1	3	20	6	18	.352	.496
Bats Both	R	.289	470	136	32	4	11	66	41	51	.344	.445
Cabrera,Miguel	L	.302	149	45	5	0	9	21	26	35	.409	.517
Bats Right	R	.321	446	143	26	1	29	87	49	81	.388	.578
Cabrera,Ramon	L	.237	38	9	2	0	0	3	2	8	.268	.289
Bats Both	R	.248	133	33	8	0	3	20	6	22	.282	.376
Cain,Lorenzo	L	.371	89	33	9	1	3	15	9	12	.420	.596
Bats Right	R	.263	308	81	10	0	6	41	22	72	.314	.354

Batters vs. Left-Handed and Right-Handed Pitchers

Batter	vs	Avg	AB	H	2B	3B	HR	RBI	BB	SO	OBP	Slg
Calhoun,Kole	L	.290	155	45	7	1	6	24	17	32	.366	.465
Bats Left	R	.264	439	116	28	4	12	51	50	86	.342	.428
Campbell,Eric	L	.212	33	7	0	0	0	5	5	9	.325	.212
Bats Right	R	.143	42	6	1	0	1	4	5	15	.250	.238
Canha,Mark	L	.158	19	3	0	0	2	3	0	8	.158	.474
Bats Right	R	.091	22	2	0	0	1	3	0	12	.125	.227
Cano,Robinson	L	.275	258	71	9	2	11	34	12	43	.316	.453
Bats Left	R	.312	397	124	24	0	28	69	35	57	.370	.584
Cardullo,Stephen	L	.241	29	7	3	0	0	1	2	9	.290	.345
Bats Right	R	.185	27	5	0	1	2	5	1	3	.214	.481
Carpenter,Matt	L	.270	148	40	9	1	5	20	22	34	.363	.446
Bats Left	R	.271	325	88	27	5	16	48	59	74	.388	.532
Carrera,Ezequiel	L	.329	73	24	4	1	1	6	5	17	.372	.452
Bats Left	R	.218	197	43	5	0	5	17	22	53	.307	.320
Carter,Chris	L	.224	134	30	6	0	12	31	21	43	.338	.537
Bats Right	R	.222	415	92	21	1	29	63	55	163	.316	.487
Casali,Curt	L	.233	73	17	3	0	4	10	8	28	.309	.438
Bats Right	R	.163	153	25	7	0	4	15	17	54	.256	.288
Castellanos,Nick	L	.207	116	24	5	2	5	13	6	35	.242	.414
Bats Right	R	.315	295	93	20	2	13	45	22	76	.365	.529
Castillo,Welington	L	.278	115	32	7	0	7	21	12	29	.346	.522
Bats Right	R	.259	301	78	17	0	7	47	21	92	.312	.385
Castro,Daniel	L	.216	51	11	1	0	0	3	2	9	.245	.235
Bats Right	R	.190	79	15	0	0	0	4	5	15	.238	.190
Castro,Jason	L	.149	87	13	3	1	1	7	9	31	.237	.241
Bats Left	R	.231	242	56	13	2	10	25	36	92	.331	.426
Castro,Starlin	L	.265	162	43	10	1	5	15	9	32	.308	.432
Bats Right	R	.272	415	113	19	0	16	55	15	86	.297	.434
Ceciliani,Darrell	L	.000	7	0	0	0	0	0	1	5	.222	.000
Bats Left	R	.150	20	3	2	0	0	1	0	9	.150	.250
Centeno,Juan	L	.250	44	11	2	0	0	3	0	10	.267	.295
Bats Left	R	.265	132	35	10	1	3	22	12	28	.326	.424
Cervelli,Francisco	L	.385	52	20	1	0	0	3	9	7	.484	.404
Bats Right	R	.241	274	66	13	1	1	30	47	65	.356	.307
Cespedes,Yoenis	L	.341	85	29	6	0	6	16	19	19	.457	.624
Bats Right	R	.266	394	105	19	1	25	70	32	89	.329	.510
Chirinos,Robinson	L	.174	23	4	1	0	2	4	6	7	.345	.478
Bats Right	R	.234	124	29	10	0	7	16	9	37	.307	.484
Chisenhall,Lonnie	L	.217	46	10	4	1	0	4	5	10	.294	.348
Bats Left	R	.295	339	100	21	4	8	53	18	60	.332	.451
Choi,Ji-Man	L	.000	3	0	0	0	0	0	1	0	.250	.000
Bats Left	R	.174	109	19	4	0	5	12	15	27	.272	.349
Choo,Shin-Soo	L	.304	46	14	1	0	4	6	7	10	.429	.587
Bats Left	R	.220	132	29	6	0	3	11	18	36	.331	.333
Clevenger,Steve	L	.000	4	0	0	0	0	0	0	1	.000	.000
Bats Left	R	.234	64	15	3	0	1	7	8	13	.319	.328
Coats,Jason	L	.360	25	9	4	0	1	4	2	5	.407	.640
Bats Right	R	.040	25	1	0	0	0	0	3	7	.200	.040
Coghlan,Chris	L	.120	25	3	1	0	0	1	5	6	.267	.160
Bats Left	R	.195	236	46	11	2	6	29	30	67	.293	.335
Colabello,Chris	L	.000	10	0	0	0	0	0	0	3	.000	.000
Bats Right	R	.105	19	2	0	0	0	1	2	6	.227	.105
Collins,Tyler	L	.111	27	3	0	0	0	3	3	8	.200	.111
Bats Left	R	.266	109	29	2	3	4	12	10	30	.331	.450
Colon,Christian	L	.234	47	11	2	0	1	4	3	13	.308	.340
Bats Right	R	.230	100	23	4	0	0	9	8	18	.287	.270
Conforto,Michael	L	.104	48	5	1	0	0	4	3	15	.170	.125
Bats Left	R	.242	256	62	20	1	12	38	33	74	.336	.469
Conger,Hank	L	.250	8	2	1	0	0	0	1	2	.333	.375
Bats Both	R	.190	116	22	4	0	3	10	11	38	.260	.302
Contreras,Willson	L	.311	74	23	8	0	2	7	4	15	.354	.500
Bats Right	R	.270	178	48	6	1	10	28	22	52	.358	.483
Correa,Carlos	L	.236	148	35	5	1	5	27	25	36	.345	.385
Bats Right	R	.287	429	123	31	2	15	69	50	103	.366	.473
Cowart,Kaleb	L	.294	17	5	2	0	0	0	0	4	.294	.412
Bats Both	R	.147	68	10	2	0	1	8	0	19	.157	.221
Cozart,Zack	L	.226	106	24	6	0	6	15	9	21	.284	.453
Bats Right	R	.260	358	93	22	2	10	35	28	63	.315	.416
Crawford,Brandon	L	.276	181	50	6	2	3	20	14	41	.332	.381
Bats Left	R	.274	372	102	22	9	9	64	43	74	.347	.454
Crawford,Carl	L	.083	12	1	0	0	0	0	0	3	.083	.083
Bats Left	R	.203	69	14	2	1	0	6	4	8	.253	.261
Crisp,Coco	L	.214	98	21	4	0	3	19	9	16	.278	.347
Bats Both	R	.236	348	82	23	4	10	36	37	62	.308	.411
Cron,C.J.	L	.237	93	22	6	1	2	13	6	16	.287	.387
Bats Right	R	.290	314	91	19	1	14	56	18	59	.336	.490

Batter	vs	Avg	AB	H	2B	3B	HR	RBI	BB	SO	OBP	Slg
Cruz,Nelson	L	.293	191	56	8	1	19	35	24	50	.376	.644
Bats Right	R	.284	398	113	19	0	24	70	38	109	.352	.513
Culberson,Charlie	L	.333	48	16	2	0	1	5	1	8	.347	.438
Bats Right	R	.211	19	4	1	0	0	2	0	5	.211	.263
Cunningham,Todd	L	.500	2	1	1	0	0	0	0	0	.500	1.000
Bats Both	R	.120	25	3	2	0	0	1	1	6	.154	.200
Cuthbert,Cheslor	L	.320	122	39	9	0	3	10	6	22	.352	.467
Bats Right	R	.258	353	91	19	1	9	36	26	74	.307	.394
Dahl,David	L	.313	48	15	1	1	0	3	3	13	.353	.375
Bats Left	R	.316	174	55	11	3	7	21	12	46	.360	.534
d'Arnaud,Chase	L	.250	84	21	5	1	1	6	6	16	.312	.369
Bats Right	R	.242	149	36	9	1	0	15	17	34	.320	.315
d'Arnaud,Travis	L	.190	58	11	0	0	0	0	5	15	.266	.190
Bats Right	R	.264	193	51	7	0	4	15	14	35	.319	.363
Davis,Chris	L	.216	176	38	8	0	8	29	23	64	.313	.398
Bats Left	R	.223	390	87	13	0	30	55	65	155	.341	.487
Davis,Khris	L	.267	131	35	7	0	10	27	13	37	.331	.550
Bats Right	R	.241	424	102	17	2	32	75	29	129	.299	.517
Davis,Rajai	L	.235	179	42	8	1	5	17	15	47	.296	.374
Bats Right	R	.258	275	71	15	1	7	31	18	59	.312	.396
De Aza,Alejandro	L	.195	41	8	3	0	0	1	5	13	.313	.268
Bats Left	R	.207	193	40	6	0	6	24	21	54	.294	.332
De Jesus Jr.,Ivan	L	.186	43	8	2	0	0	1	7	14	.300	.233
Bats Right	R	.270	178	48	8	0	1	19	10	37	.314	.331
Decker,Jaff	L	.000	9	0	0	0	0	1	1	3	.091	.000
Bats Left	R	.186	43	8	1	0	0	0	3	11	.239	.209
den Dekker,Matt	L	.000	4	0	0	0	0	0	0	2	.000	.000
Bats Left	R	.200	30	6	1	0	1	4	4	8	.314	.333
Descalso,Daniel	L	.233	43	10	3	1	1	6	5	12	.314	.419
Bats Left	R	.271	207	56	9	1	7	32	29	44	.357	.425
DeShields,Delino	L	.209	67	14	3	0	1	5	3	15	.243	.299
Bats Right	R	.209	115	24	4	0	3	8	12	39	.292	.322
Desmond,Ian	L	.338	142	48	6	0	6	26	8	28	.373	.507
Bats Right	R	.269	483	130	23	3	16	60	36	132	.324	.429
Diaz,Aledmys	L	.256	117	30	8	0	3	11	12	17	.323	.402
Bats Right	R	.317	287	91	20	3	14	54	29	43	.387	.554
Dickerson,Alex	L	.267	60	16	2	1	1	6	4	9	.333	.383
Bats Left	R	.254	193	49	14	1	9	31	22	35	.333	.477
Dickerson,Corey	L	.241	108	26	2	0	2	11	4	35	.274	.315
Bats Left	R	.246	402	99	34	3	22	59	29	99	.297	.510
Dietrich,Derek	L	.200	65	13	4	1	0	6	2	16	.264	.292
Bats Left	R	.297	286	85	16	4	7	36	30	68	.397	.455
Difo,Wilmer	L	.263	19	5	1	0	1	2	1	4	.300	.474
Bats Both	R	.282	39	11	2	0	0	5	7	8	.391	.333
Donaldson,Josh	L	.279	129	36	6	2	7	19	29	23	.413	.519
Bats Right	R	.286	448	128	26	3	30	80	80	96	.401	.558
Dozier,Brian	L	.282	142	40	8	3	11	21	15	34	.352	.613
Bats Right	R	.264	473	125	27	2	31	78	46	104	.336	.526
Drew,Stephen	L	.188	16	3	1	0	0	0	1	1	.235	.250
Bats Left	R	.276	127	35	10	1	8	21	15	30	.351	.559
Drury,Brandon	L	.280	132	37	7	1	6	18	8	24	.319	.485
Bats Right	R	.283	329	93	24	0	10	35	23	76	.332	.447
Duda,Lucas	L	.133	30	4	1	0	1	5	2	8	.188	.267
Bats Left	R	.252	123	31	6	0	6	18	13	28	.329	.447
Duffy,Matt	L	.261	92	24	3	0	2	6	11	13	.343	.359
Bats Right	R	.257	241	62	11	2	3	22	12	40	.297	.357
Duvall,Adam	L	.238	122	29	5	2	7	18	13	38	.311	.484
Bats Right	R	.242	430	104	26	4	26	85	28	126	.292	.502
Dyson,Jarrod	L	.379	29	11	3	1	0	2	1	3	.438	.552
Bats Left	R	.267	270	72	11	7	1	23	25	36	.330	.370
Eaton,Adam	L	.282	156	44	7	1	1	13	18	25	.367	.359
Bats Left	R	.285	463	132	22	8	13	46	45	90	.360	.451
Eibner,Brett	L	.213	80	17	6	0	3	9	12	19	.315	.400
Bats Right	R	.178	107	19	4	1	3	13	7	31	.226	.318
Ellis,A.J.	L	.224	67	15	3	0	0	4	7	13	.297	.269
Bats Right	R	.212	104	22	5	0	2	18	12	18	.303	.317
Ellsbury,Jacoby	L	.247	178	44	7	2	1	14	11	32	.292	.326
Bats Left	R	.271	373	101	17	3	8	42	43	52	.347	.397
Elmore,Jake	L	.255	47	12	2	0	0	3	10	9	.407	.298
Bats Right	R	.161	31	5	0	0	0	1	7	8	.316	.161
Encarnacion,Edwin	L	.242	120	29	6	0	9	26	28	30	.385	.517
Bats Right	R	.268	481	129	28	0	33	101	59	108	.349	.532
Escobar,Alcides	L	.222	153	34	4	1	3	10	8	23	.264	.320
Bats Right	R	.273	484	132	20	5	4	45	19	73	.301	.360
Escobar,Eduardo	L	.207	111	23	3	1	2	10	6	27	.246	.306
Bats Both	R	.249	241	60	11	1	4	27	15	45	.296	.353

Batters vs. Left-Handed and Right-Handed Pitchers

Batter	vs	Avg	AB	H	2B	3B	HR	RBI	BB	SO	OBP	Slg
Escobar,Yunel	L	.314	121	38	12	0	2	10	14	16	.382	.463
Bats Right	R	.301	396	119	16	1	3	29	26	51	.346	.369
Espinosa,Danny	L	.202	119	24	4	0	9	24	6	39	.250	.462
Bats Both	R	.212	397	84	11	0	15	48	48	135	.322	.353
Ethier,Andre	L	.000	1	0	0	0	0	0	0	0	.000	.000
Bats Left	R	.217	23	5	1	0	1	2	2	6	.280	.391
Featherston,Taylor	L	.083	12	1	0	0	0	0	2	6	.214	.083
Bats Right	R	.143	14	2	1	0	0	1	0	5	.143	.214
Federowicz,Tim	L	.455	11	5	1	0	0	1	1	4	.500	.545
Bats Right	R	.050	20	1	1	0	0	2	0	8	.048	.100
Fielder,Prince	L	.181	94	17	3	0	2	14	8	24	.248	.277
Bats Left	R	.224	232	52	13	0	6	30	24	39	.309	.358
Figueroa,Cole	L	.167	6	1	0	0	0	0	0	1	.167	.167
Bats Left	R	.150	20	3	0	0	0	3	1	1	.190	.150
Flaherty,Ryan	L	.300	20	6	0	0	0	3	4	3	.417	.300
Bats Left	R	.204	137	28	7	0	3	12	13	45	.272	.321
Flores,Ramon	L	.226	62	14	0	0	0	3	3	16	.273	.226
Bats Left	R	.198	187	37	8	0	2	16	28	42	.300	.273
Flores,Wilmer	L	.340	100	34	4	0	11	28	7	11	.383	.710
Bats Right	R	.232	207	48	10	0	5	21	16	37	.289	.353
Florimon,Pedro	L	.200	5	1	1	0	0	1	0	1	.200	.400
Bats Both	R	.211	19	4	0	1	0	3	1	11	.250	.316
Flowers,Tyler	L	.258	93	24	7	0	2	13	13	28	.369	.398
Bats Right	R	.277	188	52	11	0	6	28	16	63	.350	.431
Forsythe,Logan	L	.270	115	31	6	2	4	14	8	27	.315	.461
Bats Right	R	.263	396	104	18	2	16	38	38	100	.339	.439
Fowler,Dexter	L	.293	123	36	7	2	4	11	19	22	.396	.480
Bats Both	R	.270	333	90	18	5	9	37	60	102	.392	.435
Franco,Maikel	L	.286	126	36	6	0	8	24	8	23	.336	.524
Bats Right	R	.246	455	112	17	1	17	64	32	83	.298	.400
Francoeur,Jeff	L	.271	133	36	7	0	4	19	9	39	.313	.414
Bats Right	R	.241	174	42	8	1	3	15	11	51	.285	.351
Franklin,Nick	L	.216	37	8	3	0	0	5	2	9	.256	.297
Bats Both	R	.285	137	39	7	1	6	21	10	33	.347	.482
Frazier,Adam	L	.417	24	10	0	0	0	3	1	3	.423	.417
Bats Left	R	.279	122	34	8	1	2	8	11	23	.343	.410
Frazier,Todd	L	.217	115	25	2	0	10	22	14	39	.308	.496
Bats Right	R	.227	475	108	19	0	30	76	50	124	.301	.457
Freeman,Freddie	L	.301	193	58	14	3	7	24	21	64	.389	.513
Bats Left	R	.303	396	120	29	3	27	67	68	107	.405	.596
Freese,David	L	.337	92	31	7	0	4	15	13	29	.419	.543
Bats Right	R	.252	345	87	16	0	9	40	32	113	.333	.377
Fryer,Eric	L	.333	21	7	0	0	0	2	3	2	.385	.333
Bats Right	R	.253	95	24	4	1	0	11	10	23	.324	.316
Fuentes,Rey	L	-	0	0	0	0	0	0	0	0	-	-
Bats Left	R	.317	41	13	1	0	0	5	3	8	.364	.341
Gallo,Joey	L	.000	3	0	0	0	0	0	1	1	.250	.000
Bats Left	R	.045	22	1	0	0	1	1	4	18	.192	.182
Galvis,Freddy	L	.215	144	31	6	0	3	14	2	27	.224	.319
Bats Both	R	.250	440	110	20	3	17	53	23	109	.290	.425
Gamel,Ben	L	.300	10	3	1	0	1	2	3	3	.462	.700
Bats Left	R	.158	38	6	1	0	0	3	3	13	.220	.184
Garcia,Adonis	L	.302	139	42	8	0	2	16	11	22	.362	.403
Bats Right	R	.262	393	103	21	0	12	49	13	71	.293	.407
Garcia,Avisail	L	.222	99	22	6	0	3	13	11	26	.304	.374
Bats Right	R	.252	314	79	12	2	9	38	23	89	.308	.389
Garcia,Greg	L	.233	43	10	2	0	0	4	3	15	.298	.279
Bats Left	R	.287	171	49	9	0	3	13	35	35	.414	.392
Garcia,Leury	L	.176	17	3	0	0	0	0	0	6	.176	.176
Bats Both	R	.258	31	8	1	1	1	5	1	7	.303	.452
Gardner,Brett	L	.247	178	44	5	2	2	12	15	37	.313	.331
Bats Left	R	.268	369	99	17	4	5	29	55	69	.368	.377
Garneau,Dustin	L	.231	26	6	2	0	0	3	3	7	.300	.308
Bats Right	R	.238	42	10	4	0	1	3	3	15	.289	.405
Gattis,Evan	L	.288	156	45	10	0	10	23	12	32	.341	.545
Bats Right	R	.230	291	67	9	0	22	49	31	95	.307	.488
Gennett,Scooter	L	.260	96	25	5	0	2	14	11	30	.333	.375
Bats Left	R	.264	402	106	25	1	12	42	27	84	.313	.420
Gentry,Craig	L	.154	26	4	1	0	0	2	3	3	.267	.192
Bats Right	R	.125	8	1	0	0	0	0	0	3	.125	.125
Giavotella,Johnny	L	.258	97	25	2	0	0	4	3	13	.280	.278
Bats Right	R	.261	249	65	18	1	6	27	10	26	.289	.414
Gillaspie,Conor	L	.227	22	5	1	1	0	0	0	3	.227	.364
Bats Left	R	.266	169	45	7	3	6	25	12	25	.317	.450
Gillespie,Cole	L	.200	15	3	0	0	0	1	2	5	.278	.200
Bats Right	R	.250	36	9	3	2	0	4	1	9	.270	.444

Batter	vs	Avg	AB	H	2B	3B	HR	RBI	BB	SO	OBP	Slg
Gimenez,Chris	L	.229	35	8	1	0	2	2	4	14	.308	.429
Bats Right	R	.212	104	22	3	0	2	9	6	27	.259	.298
Goeddel,Tyler	L	.165	97	16	1	1	1	7	8	23	.229	.227
Bats Right	R	.216	116	25	2	2	3	9	9	29	.281	.345
Goins,Ryan	L	.167	36	6	1	0	0	0	0	9	.189	.194
Bats Left	R	.190	147	28	8	2	3	12	9	39	.237	.333
Goldschmidt,Paul	L	.352	125	44	8	1	6	24	34	33	.494	.576
Bats Right	R	.282	454	128	25	2	18	71	76	117	.386	.465
Gomes,Yan	L	.271	70	19	7	1	1	10	2	20	.297	.443
Bats Right	R	.127	181	23	4	0	8	24	7	49	.163	.282
Gomez,Carlos	L	.241	108	26	6	1	1	8	6	37	.293	.343
Bats Right	R	.228	303	69	16	0	12	45	28	99	.299	.399
Gonzalez,Adrian	L	.244	168	41	5	0	2	16	9	29	.293	.310
Bats Left	R	.303	400	121	26	0	16	74	46	88	.372	.488
Gonzalez,Carlos	L	.273	176	48	7	1	10	40	4	48	.291	.494
Bats Left	R	.309	408	126	35	1	15	60	42	81	.373	.510
Gonzalez,Marwin	L	.253	170	43	15	0	5	17	8	47	.294	.429
Bats Both	R	.255	314	80	11	3	8	34	14	71	.292	.385
Goodwin,Brian	L	.250	4	1	1	0	0	0	0	1	.250	.500
Bats Left	R	.289	38	11	3	1	0	5	2	13	.325	.421
Gordon,Alex	L	.214	140	30	5	0	5	8	16	48	.308	.357
Bats Left	R	.223	305	68	11	2	12	32	36	100	.314	.390
Gordon,Dee	L	.260	73	19	3	0	0	4	3	13	.286	.301
Bats Left	R	.270	252	68	4	6	1	10	15	42	.311	.345
Gose,Anthony	L	.120	25	3	0	0	0	0	4	8	.241	.120
Bats Left	R	.242	66	16	2	2	2	7	5	30	.306	.424
Gosewisch,Tuffy	L	.444	18	8	1	0	3	5	0	2	.444	1.000
Bats Right	R	.083	72	6	0	1	0	2	7	20	.175	.111
Gosselin,Phil	L	.288	52	15	3	0	0	4	4	12	.339	.346
Bats Right	R	.274	168	46	9	1	2	9	11	34	.319	.375
Grandal,Yasmani	L	.224	76	17	1	0	4	12	19	20	.385	.395
Bats Both	R	.229	314	72	13	1	23	60	45	96	.327	.497
Granderson,Curtis	L	.226	146	33	4	2	7	15	12	40	.298	.425
Bats Left	R	.241	399	96	20	3	23	44	62	90	.347	.479
Green,Grant	L	.321	28	9	2	0	1	5	3	5	.375	.500
Bats Right	R	.167	18	3	0	0	0	2	0	3	.167	.167
Gregorius,Didi	L	.324	148	48	10	0	4	24	4	12	.361	.473
Bats Left	R	.258	414	107	22	2	16	46	15	70	.283	.437
Grichuk,Randal	L	.240	121	29	9	0	7	19	13	35	.319	.488
Bats Right	R	.240	325	78	20	3	17	49	15	106	.277	.477
Grossman,Robbie	L	.344	125	43	9	1	6	18	14	29	.418	.576
Bats Both	R	.242	207	50	10	0	5	19	41	67	.367	.362
Gurriel,Yulieski	L	.220	41	9	1	0	1	6	0	2	.220	.317
Bats Right	R	.281	89	25	6	0	2	9	5	10	.323	.416
Gutierrez,Franklin	L	.280	186	52	7	0	12	32	27	60	.373	.511
Bats Right	R	.145	62	9	2	0	2	7	2	25	.182	.274
Guyer,Brandon	L	.336	122	41	9	0	6	17	9	17	.464	.557
Bats Right	R	.216	171	37	8	1	3	15	10	38	.301	.327
Gyorko,Jedd	L	.245	139	34	3	0	7	17	15	28	.318	.417
Bats Right	R	.241	261	63	6	1	23	42	22	68	.299	.536
Hamilton,Billy	L	.221	113	25	4	0	2	6	6	26	.267	.310
Bats Both	R	.275	298	82	15	3	1	11	30	67	.340	.356
Hanigan,Ryan	L	.107	28	3	0	0	0	2	1	7	.138	.107
Bats Right	R	.195	77	15	4	0	1	12	6	20	.262	.286
Haniger,Mitch	L	.172	29	5	1	0	1	3	4	13	.273	.310
Bats Right	R	.250	80	20	1	1	4	14	8	14	.322	.438
Hanson,Alen	L	.143	7	1	0	0	0	0	0	0	.143	.143
Bats Both	R	.250	24	6	1	0	0	1	2	5	.308	.292
Hardy,J.J.	L	.269	104	28	10	0	3	23	11	15	.331	.452
Bats Right	R	.269	301	81	19	0	6	25	15	53	.301	.392
Harper,Bryce	L	.226	146	33	10	0	7	27	23	47	.326	.438
Bats Left	R	.250	360	90	14	2	17	59	85	70	.391	.442
Harrison,Josh	L	.311	90	28	7	2	1	14	2	14	.344	.467
Bats Right	R	.277	397	110	18	5	3	45	16	62	.303	.370
Hazelbaker,Jeremy	L	.195	41	8	2	0	2	4	0	19	.195	.390
Bats Left	R	.245	159	39	5	3	10	24	18	45	.318	.503
Headley,Chase	L	.277	159	44	4	0	3	17	15	24	.339	.358
Bats Both	R	.240	308	74	14	1	11	34	36	94	.327	.399
Healy,Ryon	L	.313	67	21	4	0	4	5	2	12	.333	.552
Bats Right	R	.302	202	61	16	0	9	32	10	48	.338	.515
Hechavarria,Adeiny	L	.207	111	23	3	2	1	10	10	23	.273	.297
Bats Right	R	.244	397	97	14	4	2	28	23	50	.285	.315
Hedges,Austin	L	.400	5	2	1	0	0	0	0	0	.400	.600
Bats Right	R	.053	19	1	0	0	0	1	0	7	.095	.053
Heisey,Chris	L	.239	46	11	1	0	3	5	3	14	.308	.457
Bats Right	R	.204	93	19	2	1	6	12	10	30	.282	.441

Batters vs. Left-Handed and Right-Handed Pitchers

Batter	vs	Avg	AB	H	2B	3B	HR	RBI	BB	SO	OBP	Slg
Heredia,Guillermo	L	.250	68	17	3	0	1	8	7	9	.320	.338
Bats Right	R	.250	24	6	0	0	0	4	5	6	.419	.250
Hernandez,Cesar	L	.341	138	47	4	2	0	8	12	30	.391	.399
Bats Both	R	.279	409	114	10	9	6	31	54	86	.365	.391
Hernandez,Gorkys	L	.273	33	9	3	0	1	1	3	4	.333	.455
Bats Right	R	.238	21	5	2	0	1	3	0	7	.238	.476
Hernandez,Kiké	L	.189	122	23	6	0	5	10	21	35	.308	.361
Bats Right	R	.191	94	18	2	0	2	8	7	29	.248	.277
Hernandez,Marco	L	.500	8	4	0	0	0	2	1	2	.556	.500
Bats Left	R	.256	43	11	1	0	1	3	4	8	.319	.349
Hernandez,Teoscar	L	.278	36	10	2	0	2	5	6	12	.381	.500
Bats Right	R	.203	64	13	5	0	2	6	5	16	.257	.375
Herrera,Odubel	L	.236	144	34	4	1	0	9	17	38	.321	.278
Bats Left	R	.303	439	133	17	5	15	40	46	96	.374	.467
Herrmann,Chris	L	.381	21	8	1	0	1	2	5	5	.500	.571
Bats Left	R	.268	127	34	4	4	5	26	11	39	.324	.480
Heyward,Jason	L	.207	140	29	3	1	2	18	18	30	.300	.286
Bats Left	R	.238	390	93	24	0	5	31	36	63	.309	.338
Hicks,Aaron	L	.161	118	19	4	0	3	11	8	25	.213	.271
Bats Both	R	.249	209	52	9	1	5	20	22	43	.318	.373
Hill,Aaron	L	.273	139	38	4	0	4	13	17	19	.357	.388
Bats Right	R	.255	239	61	10	0	6	25	24	40	.323	.372
Holaday,Bryan	L	.268	41	11	2	0	1	6	2	8	.295	.390
Bats Right	R	.211	76	16	5	1	1	8	5	20	.274	.342
Holliday,Matt	L	.233	116	27	7	0	8	24	9	20	.297	.500
Bats Right	R	.252	266	67	13	1	12	38	26	51	.332	.444
Holt,Brock	L	.103	39	4	0	0	0	1	5	15	.239	.103
Bats Left	R	.279	251	70	16	0	7	33	22	43	.336	.426
Holt,Tyler	L	.204	49	10	1	1	0	1	9	15	.350	.265
Bats Right	R	.246	130	32	4	2	0	12	14	33	.317	.308
Hood,Destin	L	.000	4	0	0	0	0	0	0	3	.000	.000
Bats Right	R	.286	21	6	1	0	1	2	0	8	.286	.476
Hosmer,Eric	L	.233	202	47	4	1	8	40	13	45	.275	.381
Bats Left	R	.283	403	114	20	0	17	64	44	87	.354	.459
Howard,Ryan	L	.121	33	4	0	0	1	2	0	13	.143	.212
Bats Left	R	.205	298	61	10	0	24	57	27	101	.269	.480
Hoying,Jared	L	.167	6	1	0	0	0	1	0	1	.167	.167
Bats Left	R	.225	40	9	2	0	0	4	3	7	.279	.275
Hundley,Nick	L	.333	99	33	10	0	4	17	6	22	.368	.556
Bats Right	R	.221	190	42	10	1	6	31	19	43	.295	.379
Hunter,Cedric	L	.000	1	0	0	0	0	0	0	0	.000	.000
Bats Left	R	.091	33	3	0	0	1	1	2	6	.143	.182
Iannetta,Chris	L	.248	117	29	6	0	3	13	21	33	.364	.376
Bats Right	R	.185	178	33	8	0	4	11	17	50	.259	.298
Iglesias,Jose	L	.254	134	34	10	0	3	10	9	11	.308	.396
Bats Right	R	.255	333	85	16	0	1	22	19	39	.306	.312
Inciarte,Ender	L	.319	138	44	7	1	0	3	9	14	.365	.384
Bats Left	R	.281	384	108	17	6	3	26	36	54	.346	.380
Infante,Omar	L	.241	29	7	2	0	0	2	3	6	.294	.310
Bats Right	R	.238	105	25	7	1	0	9	6	17	.274	.324
Iribarren,Hernan	L	.400	5	2	0	0	0	0	0	1	.400	.400
Bats Right	R	.300	40	12	0	3	0	2	0	10	.300	.450
Jackson,Austin	L	.159	44	7	1	0	0	2	4	13	.229	.182
Bats Right	R	.285	137	39	11	2	0	16	13	26	.346	.394
Janish,Paul	L	.235	17	4	1	0	0	0	2	1	.350	.294
Bats Right	R	.143	14	2	0	0	0	0	1	2	.200	.143
Jankowski,Travis	L	.155	84	13	2	0	0	1	7	25	.220	.179
Bats Left	R	.275	251	69	11	2	2	11	35	75	.368	.359
Jaso,John	L	.050	20	1	0	0	0	0	4	7	.208	.050
Bats Left	R	.281	360	101	25	3	8	42	41	67	.361	.433
Jay,Jon	L	.311	106	33	7	0	0	10	9	24	.381	.377
Bats Left	R	.282	241	68	19	1	2	16	10	54	.319	.394
Jennings,Desmond	L	.194	67	13	4	0	1	8	5	16	.250	.299
Bats Right	R	.203	133	27	3	1	6	12	16	42	.296	.376
Jensen,Kyle	L	.333	15	5	0	1	2	7	0	4	.333	.867
Bats Right	R	.063	16	1	0	0	0	0	2	9	.211	.063
Johnson,Chris	L	.212	99	21	3	0	3	12	10	33	.284	.333
Bats Right	R	.229	144	33	8	0	2	12	9	45	.279	.326
Johnson,Kelly	L	.245	53	13	1	0	3	7	1	10	.273	.434
Bats Left	R	.247	251	62	13	0	7	27	24	55	.313	.382
Jones,Adam	L	.218	147	32	5	0	3	17	10	34	.268	.313
Bats Right	R	.280	472	132	14	0	26	66	29	81	.323	.475
Jones,JaCoby	L	.118	17	2	1	0	0	0	0	11	.118	.176
Bats Right	R	.364	11	4	2	0	0	2	0	1	.364	.545
Joseph,Caleb	L	.083	36	3	0	0	0	0	1	8	.108	.083
Bats Right	R	.208	96	20	3	0	0	6	6	20	.255	.240
Joseph,Tommy	L	.281	89	25	4	0	7	15	10	19	.350	.562
Bats Right	R	.248	226	56	11	0	14	32	12	56	.291	.482
Joyce,Matt	L	.235	34	8	2	0	1	5	8	9	.381	.382
Bats Left	R	.244	197	48	8	1	12	37	51	58	.406	.477
Judge,Aaron	L	.067	15	1	0	0	0	0	3	10	.222	.067
Bats Right	R	.203	69	14	2	0	4	10	6	32	.273	.406
Kang,Jung Ho	L	.209	67	14	4	0	3	11	13	21	.354	.403
Bats Right	R	.267	251	67	15	0	18	51	23	58	.354	.542
Kawasaki,Munenori	L	.000	4	0	0	0	0	0	2	2	.333	.000
Bats Left	R	.412	17	7	2	0	0	1	2	3	.500	.529
Kelly,Don	L	.000	2	0	0	0	0	0	0	1	.000	.000
Bats Left	R	.160	25	4	0	2	0	3	2	4	.214	.320
Kelly,Ty	L	.368	19	7	0	1	0	3	5	1	.500	.474
Bats Both	R	.179	39	7	1	0	1	4	6	8	.277	.282
Kemp,Matt	L	.306	134	41	8	0	11	27	8	29	.342	.612
Bats Right	R	.258	489	126	31	0	24	81	28	127	.293	.468
Kemp,Tony	L	.143	21	3	1	0	0	0	3	5	.250	.190
Bats Left	R	.232	99	23	3	3	1	7	11	22	.306	.354
Kendrick,Howie	L	.234	154	36	9	0	0	5	21	34	.333	.292
Bats Right	R	.264	333	88	17	2	8	35	29	62	.322	.399
Kepler,Max	L	.203	118	24	8	0	2	14	10	34	.273	.322
Bats Left	R	.248	278	69	12	2	15	49	32	59	.325	.468
Kiermaier,Kevin	L	.262	84	22	6	2	2	9	10	22	.364	.452
Bats Left	R	.241	282	68	14	0	10	28	30	52	.321	.397
Kim,Hyun Soo	L	.000	18	0	0	0	0	0	4	4	.217	.000
Bats Left	R	.321	287	92	16	1	6	22	32	47	.393	.446
Kinsler,Ian	L	.309	162	50	10	2	7	18	15	32	.369	.525
Bats Right	R	.281	456	128	19	2	21	65	30	83	.340	.469
Kipnis,Jason	L	.282	209	59	17	0	7	30	14	58	.326	.464
Bats Left	R	.272	401	109	24	4	16	52	46	88	.351	.471
Kratz,Erik	L	.192	26	5	2	0	1	3	1	6	.222	.385
Bats Right	R	.051	59	3	0	0	0	1	0	26	.051	.051
La Stella,Tommy	L	.316	19	6	2	0	0	3	4	2	.435	.421
Bats Left	R	.264	129	34	10	1	2	8	14	25	.345	.403
Ladendorf,Tyler	L	.000	26	0	0	0	0	0	1	7	.037	.000
Bats Right	R	.182	22	4	0	0	0	0	0	6	.182	.182
Lagares,Juan	L	.260	73	19	3	0	1	4	4	12	.308	.342
Bats Right	R	.217	69	15	4	2	2	5	7	15	.295	.420
Lake,Junior	L	.263	19	5	2	0	1	2	1	8	.300	.526
Bats Right	R	.125	16	2	1	0	0	0	3	3	.263	.188
Lamb,Jake	L	.164	110	18	4	2	4	16	10	36	.279	.345
Bats Left	R	.271	413	112	27	7	25	75	47	118	.346	.552
Lawrie,Brett	L	.284	67	19	8	0	2	10	3	24	.310	.493
Bats Right	R	.239	284	68	14	0	10	26	27	85	.310	.394
Lee,Dae-Ho	L	.261	157	41	5	0	8	26	13	38	.329	.446
Bats Right	R	.244	135	33	4	0	6	23	7	36	.292	.407
LeMahieu,DJ	L	.331	151	50	12	2	4	24	23	25	.415	.517
Bats Right	R	.354	401	142	20	6	7	42	43	55	.417	.486
Leon,Sandy	L	.373	67	25	4	0	4	17	10	13	.450	.612
Bats Both	R	.286	185	53	13	2	3	18	13	53	.337	.427
Lind,Adam	L	.240	50	12	3	0	1	5	3	15	.278	.360
Bats Left	R	.239	351	84	14	0	19	53	23	74	.287	.442
Lindor,Francisco	L	.292	202	59	8	1	5	27	14	31	.332	.416
Bats Both	R	.306	402	123	22	2	10	51	43	57	.371	.445
Lobaton,Jose	L	.067	15	1	0	0	0	1	1	2	.176	.267
Bats Both	R	.262	84	22	3	1	2	7	10	17	.344	.393
Loney,James	L	.173	52	9	2	0	1	5	2	10	.218	.269
Bats Left	R	.282	291	82	14	1	8	29	14	27	.323	.419
Longoria,Evan	L	.250	140	35	5	1	6	19	5	24	.303	.450
Bats Right	R	.280	493	138	27	3	32	81	32	112	.323	.542
Lough,David	L	.250	4	1	1	0	0	0	0	2	.250	.500
Bats Left	R	.238	63	15	2	1	0	4	9	6	.347	.302
Lowrie,Jed	L	.298	84	25	3	0	0	7	5	14	.333	.333
Bats Both	R	.252	254	64	9	1	2	20	21	51	.308	.319
Lucroy,Jonathan	L	.233	116	27	2	0	9	18	15	31	.313	.483
Bats Right	R	.310	374	116	22	3	15	63	32	69	.368	.505
Machado,Manny	L	.329	152	50	15	0	5	15	15	25	.393	.526
Bats Right	R	.283	488	138	25	1	32	81	33	95	.328	.535
Mahtook,Mikie	L	.258	66	17	4	0	2	5	1	15	.269	.409
Bats Right	R	.160	119	19	5	0	1	6	6	53	.211	.227
Maile,Luke	L	.242	33	8	1	0	2	5	0	11	.242	.455
Bats Right	R	.221	86	19	6	0	1	10	4	25	.256	.326
Maldonado,Martin	L	.237	59	14	3	0	1	4	9	18	.338	.339
Bats Right	R	.188	149	28	4	0	7	17	27	37	.330	.356
Margot,Manuel	L	.308	13	4	2	0	0	1	0	3	.308	.462
Bats Right	R	.208	24	5	2	1	0	2	0	4	.208	.375

Batters vs. Left-Handed and Right-Handed Pitchers

Batter	vs	Avg	AB	H	2B	3B	HR	RBI	BB	SO	OBP	Slg
Marisnick,Jake	L	.229	109	25	9	1	3	11	8	30	.288	.413
Bats Right	R	.197	178	35	9	0	2	10	8	53	.238	.281
Markakis,Nick	L	.243	181	44	9	0	1	21	14	27	.303	.309
Bats Left	R	.280	418	117	29	0	12	68	57	74	.364	.435
Marte,Jefry	L	.244	78	19	5	0	4	17	7	22	.322	.462
Bats Right	R	.256	180	46	9	0	11	27	11	37	.305	.489
Marte,Ketel	L	.217	143	31	8	1	0	12	4	34	.238	.287
Bats Both	R	.279	294	82	13	1	1	21	14	50	.311	.340
Marte,Starling	L	.292	89	26	3	0	2	5	4	28	.337	.393
Bats Right	R	.315	400	126	31	5	7	41	19	76	.367	.470
Martin,Leonys	L	.261	176	46	5	1	5	15	8	51	.298	.386
Bats Left	R	.240	342	82	12	2	10	32	36	98	.310	.374
Martin,Russell	L	.220	109	24	1	0	5	16	19	38	.333	.367
Bats Right	R	.234	346	81	15	0	15	58	45	110	.336	.408
Martinez,J.D.	L	.306	121	37	10	0	5	21	9	29	.348	.512
Bats Right	R	.307	339	104	25	2	17	47	40	99	.382	.543
Martinez,Michael	L	.250	36	9	1	0	0	1	1	6	.270	.278
Bats Both	R	.231	65	15	3	0	1	3	3	17	.265	.323
Martinez,Victor	L	.295	149	44	3	0	7	20	14	24	.356	.456
Bats Both	R	.287	404	116	19	0	20	66	36	66	.349	.483
Mathis,Jeff	L	.324	37	12	1	1	1	5	2	11	.359	.486
Bats Right	R	.202	89	18	3	0	1	10	2	25	.228	.270
Mauer,Joe	L	.224	116	26	2	0	3	8	11	24	.291	.319
Bats Left	R	.272	378	103	20	4	8	41	68	69	.383	.410
Maxwell,Bruce	L	.200	20	4	1	0	0	0	0	7	.200	.250
Bats Left	R	.306	72	22	5	1	1	14	8	17	.370	.444
Maybin,Cameron	L	.296	98	29	4	1	2	11	14	21	.384	.418
Bats Right	R	.323	251	81	10	4	2	32	22	48	.383	.418
Mazara,Nomar	L	.234	111	26	1	0	1	6	6	29	.277	.270
Bats Left	R	.274	405	111	12	3	19	58	33	83	.332	.459
McBride,Matt	L	.269	26	7	3	0	0	2	0	9	.269	.385
Bats Right	R	.118	17	2	0	0	0	0	1	1	.167	.118
McCann,Brian	L	.218	87	19	2	0	3	9	12	23	.317	.345
Bats Left	R	.249	342	85	11	0	17	49	42	76	.340	.430
McCann,James	L	.258	120	31	3	1	9	26	12	41	.323	.525
Bats Right	R	.201	224	45	6	0	3	22	11	68	.243	.268
McCutchen,Andrew	L	.229	109	25	3	1	5	16	16	25	.328	.413
Bats Right	R	.262	489	128	23	2	19	63	53	118	.338	.434
McGehee,Casey	L	.296	27	8	1	0	0	1	2	4	.367	.333
Bats Right	R	.200	65	13	0	0	0	0	1	10	.212	.200
Mercer,Jordy	L	.275	102	28	6	0	4	12	16	15	.378	.451
Bats Right	R	.252	417	105	16	3	7	47	35	68	.314	.355
Merrifield,Whit	L	.351	77	27	7	2	0	8	6	18	.398	.494
Bats Right	R	.261	234	61	15	1	2	21	13	54	.298	.359
Mesoraco,Devin	L	.154	13	2	0	0	0	0	4	2	.353	.154
Bats Right	R	.135	37	5	1	0	0	1	1	8	.158	.162
Middlebrooks,Will	L	.300	10	3	0	0	0	1	3	2	.462	.300
Bats Right	R	.000	17	0	0	0	0	0	1	11	.056	.000
Miller,Brad	L	.227	110	25	5	1	3	14	12	32	.309	.373
Bats Left	R	.247	438	108	24	5	27	67	35	117	.303	.509
Molina,Yadier	L	.304	138	42	7	0	3	9	11	19	.356	.420
Bats Right	R	.308	396	122	31	1	5	49	28	44	.361	.429
Mondesi,Raul	L	.146	41	6	0	1	0	3	5	15	.239	.195
Bats Both	R	.202	94	19	1	2	2	10	1	33	.227	.319
Montero,Miguel	L	.189	37	7	0	0	0	3	1	8	.250	.189
Bats Left	R	.221	204	45	8	1	8	30	37	50	.340	.387
Morales,Kendrys	L	.330	182	60	9	0	11	37	10	38	.369	.560
Bats Both	R	.231	376	87	15	0	19	56	38	82	.307	.423
Moran,Colin	L	-	0	0	0	0	0	0	0	0	-	-
Bats Left	R	.130	23	3	1	0	0	2	1	8	.200	.174
Moreland,Mitch	L	.277	94	26	4	0	5	18	5	26	.320	.479
Bats Left	R	.221	366	81	17	0	17	42	30	92	.293	.407
Morneau,Justin	L	.278	36	10	1	1	2	6	0	9	.270	.528
Bats Left	R	.257	167	43	13	0	4	19	12	43	.309	.407
Morrison,Logan	L	.258	62	16	5	0	1	7	8	17	.352	.387
Bats Left	R	.234	291	68	13	1	13	36	29	72	.312	.419
Moss,Brandon	L	.232	112	26	5	1	3	15	5	38	.289	.375
Bats Left	R	.223	301	67	14	1	25	52	34	103	.303	.525
Motter,Taylor	L	.348	23	8	2	0	1	3	4	6	.464	.565
Bats Right	R	.123	57	7	1	0	1	6	7	13	.215	.193
Moustakas,Mike	L	.286	21	6	2	0	1	2	1	2	.318	.524
Bats Left	R	.229	83	19	4	0	6	11	8	11	.297	.494
Moya,Steven	L	.600	5	3	1	0	0	4	1	1	.667	.800
Bats Left	R	.236	89	21	3	2	5	7	4	37	.266	.483
Muncy,Max	L	.200	5	1	0	0	0	1	0	1	.200	.200
Bats Left	R	.185	108	20	2	0	2	7	20	23	.313	.259
Murphy,Daniel	L	.329	155	51	12	2	6	30	9	18	.376	.548
Bats Left	R	.354	376	133	35	3	19	74	26	39	.396	.614
Murphy,John Ryan	L	.192	26	5	1	0	0	0	2	8	.250	.231
Bats Right	R	.125	56	7	2	0	1	3	3	11	.167	.214
Murphy,Tom	L	.154	13	2	0	0	1	1	2	7	.267	.385
Bats Right	R	.323	31	10	2	0	4	12	2	12	.382	.774
Myers,Wil	L	.261	142	37	5	0	8	22	18	40	.350	.465
Bats Right	R	.258	457	118	24	4	20	72	50	120	.331	.460
Napoli,Mike	L	.262	164	43	8	1	7	26	28	59	.366	.451
Bats Right	R	.229	393	90	14	0	27	75	50	135	.322	.471
Naquin,Tyler	L	.250	32	8	3	1	0	7	6	7	.368	.406
Bats Left	R	.301	289	87	15	4	14	36	30	105	.372	.526
Narvaez,Omar	L	.333	21	7	1	0	1	4	4	3	.423	.524
Bats Left	R	.250	80	20	3	0	0	6	10	11	.330	.288
Nava,Daniel	L	.500	2	1	0	0	0	0	1	1	.667	.500
Bats Both	R	.219	128	28	6	0	1	13	9	29	.290	.289
Navarro,Dioner	L	.222	90	20	6	0	3	15	6	20	.270	.389
Bats Both	R	.201	214	43	7	2	3	20	17	51	.263	.294
Nicholas,Brett	L	.500	8	4	2	0	0	0	0	2	.500	.750
Bats Left	R	.219	32	7	3	0	2	4	4	7	.324	.500
Nieuwenhuis,Kirk	L	.135	37	5	2	0	1	7	6	17	.256	.270
Bats Left	R	.218	298	65	16	1	12	37	50	116	.332	.399
Nimmo,Brandon	L	.286	7	2	0	0	0	0	1	1	.375	.286
Bats Left	R	.273	66	18	1	0	1	6	5	19	.333	.333
Norris,Derek	L	.203	118	24	4	0	4	13	13	30	.289	.339
Bats Right	R	.178	297	53	13	0	10	29	23	109	.241	.323
Nunez,Eduardo	L	.265	136	36	5	0	7	17	7	19	.295	.456
Bats Right	R	.295	417	123	19	4	9	50	22	69	.336	.424
O'Brien,Peter	L	.136	22	3	0	0	3	7	1	10	.174	.545
Bats Right	R	.143	42	6	1	0	2	2	2	17	.182	.310
Odor,Rougned	L	.269	156	42	8	0	7	20	8	36	.308	.455
Bats Left	R	.272	449	122	25	4	26	68	11	99	.292	.519
Olson,Matt	L	.000	3	0	0	0	0	0	0	1	.000	.000
Bats Left	R	.111	18	2	1	0	0	0	7	3	.360	.167
O'Malley,Shawn	L	.245	98	24	5	1	1	7	4	23	.288	.347
Bats Both	R	.214	112	24	4	1	1	10	14	36	.307	.295
Orlando,Paulo	L	.307	140	43	9	2	4	14	5	32	.331	.486
Bats Right	R	.300	317	95	15	2	1	29	8	73	.328	.369
Ortega,Rafael	L	.200	20	4	0	0	0	0	0	4	.200	.200
Bats Left	R	.236	165	39	8	0	1	16	13	19	.292	.303
Ortiz,David	L	.313	134	42	8	0	5	27	16	20	.382	.485
Bats Left	R	.315	403	127	40	1	33	100	64	66	.407	.665
Owings,Chris	L	.306	108	33	7	3	2	15	7	18	.345	.481
Bats Right	R	.267	329	88	17	8	3	34	13	69	.305	.395
Ozuna,Marcell	L	.289	121	35	5	1	10	18	7	23	.328	.595
Bats Right	R	.259	436	113	18	5	13	58	36	92	.319	.413
Pacheco,Jordan	L	.154	13	2	1	0	0	0	0	3	.154	.231
Bats Right	R	.158	38	6	3	0	0	0	0	11	.158	.237
Pagan,Angel	L	.266	169	45	4	1	7	18	7	22	.291	.426
Bats Both	R	.282	326	92	20	4	5	37	35	44	.352	.414
Panik,Joe	L	.226	133	30	4	3	0	14	11	22	.295	.301
Bats Left	R	.245	331	81	17	4	10	48	39	25	.324	.411
Paredes,Jimmy	L	.175	40	7	0	0	0	2	3	8	.227	.175
Bats Both	R	.237	118	28	8	0	5	17	4	40	.262	.432
Park,Byungho	L	.170	53	9	3	1	2	5	7	18	.279	.377
Bats Right	R	.198	162	32	6	0	10	19	14	62	.273	.420
Parker,Jarrett	L	.108	37	4	1	0	1	2	2	15	.154	.216
Bats Left	R	.289	90	26	2	1	4	12	17	29	.429	.467
Parra,Gerardo	L	.258	97	25	5	1	1	10	2	19	.273	.361
Bats Left	R	.251	271	68	22	2	6	29	7	54	.270	.413
Paulsen,Ben	L	.375	8	3	1	0	0	2	0	2	.375	.500
Bats Left	R	.202	84	17	4	0	1	9	5	25	.247	.286
Pearce,Steve	L	.309	81	25	4	0	7	18	14	20	.411	.617
Bats Right	R	.279	183	51	9	1	6	17	20	34	.357	.437
Pederson,Joc	L	.125	64	8	3	0	1	10	11	22	.250	.219
Bats Left	R	.269	342	92	23	0	24	58	52	108	.371	.547
Pedroia,Dustin	L	.305	118	36	4	0	3	12	18	17	.397	.415
Bats Right	R	.320	515	165	32	1	12	62	43	56	.371	.456
Pena,Francisco	L	.333	15	5	0	0	0	0	1	4	.375	.333
Bats Right	R	.120	25	3	0	0	1	3	1	10	.154	.240
Pena,Ramiro	L	.273	22	6	0	0	0	2	1	4	.304	.273
Bats Both	R	.308	65	20	6	1	1	8	1	12	.338	.477
Pence,Hunter	L	.256	117	30	7	0	7	19	12	28	.326	.496
Bats Right	R	.302	278	84	16	1	6	38	31	67	.371	.432
Pennington,Cliff	L	.095	21	2	0	0	0	0	0	9	.095	.095
Bats Both	R	.225	151	34	4	2	3	10	13	46	.287	.338

Batters vs. Left-Handed and Right-Handed Pitchers

Batter	vs	Avg	AB	H	2B	3B	HR	RBI	BB	SO	OBP	Slg
Peralta,David	L	.211	38	8	1	2	1	3	2	13	.295	.421
Bats Left	R	.263	133	35	8	3	3	12	6	29	.295	.436
Peralta,Jhonny	L	.182	77	14	4	0	2	4	4	17	.229	.312
Bats Right	R	.288	212	61	13	1	6	25	16	39	.335	.443
Peraza,Jose	L	.308	52	16	2	1	1	5	3	6	.351	.442
Bats Right	R	.328	189	62	6	1	2	20	4	27	.352	.402
Perez,Carlos	L	.208	48	10	1	0	1	5	3	8	.255	.292
Bats Right	R	.209	220	46	15	0	4	26	9	41	.241	.332
Perez,Hernan	L	.278	144	40	8	2	6	28	6	34	.301	.486
Bats Right	R	.269	260	70	10	1	7	28	12	60	.303	.396
Perez,Roberto	L	.240	50	12	2	0	2	6	3	14	.283	.400
Bats Right	R	.155	103	16	4	1	1	11	20	30	.286	.243
Perez,Salvador	L	.247	150	37	1	0	11	18	9	34	.289	.473
Bats Right	R	.247	364	90	27	2	11	46	13	85	.287	.423
Peterson,Jace	L	.255	51	13	0	0	0	2	5	12	.316	.255
Bats Left	R	.254	299	76	16	1	7	27	47	57	.355	.385
Petit,Gregorio	L	.222	63	14	3	0	1	7	7	19	.300	.317
Bats Right	R	.255	141	36	10	1	1	10	8	32	.298	.362
Pham,Tommy	L	.206	63	13	2	0	4	9	9	30	.306	.429
Bats Right	R	.240	96	23	5	0	5	8	11	41	.336	.448
Phegley,Josh	L	.250	36	9	3	0	0	2	3	6	.325	.333
Bats Right	R	.262	42	11	3	0	1	8	2	7	.304	.405
Phillips,Brandon	L	.256	129	33	10	1	1	11	4	16	.281	.372
Bats Right	R	.302	421	127	24	0	10	53	14	52	.331	.430
Pierzynski,A.J.	L	.108	37	4	0	0	0	0	0	2	.108	.108
Bats Left	R	.238	210	50	15	0	2	23	6	27	.266	.338
Pillar,Kevin	L	.283	145	41	12	0	2	19	3	23	.302	.407
Bats Right	R	.261	403	105	23	2	5	34	21	67	.303	.365
Pina,Manny	L	.200	25	5	0	0	0	3	6	4	.355	.200
Bats Right	R	.283	46	13	4	0	2	9	4	11	.340	.500
Pinder,Chad	L	.286	28	8	3	0	1	1	1	6	.310	.500
Bats Right	R	.174	23	4	1	0	0	3	2	8	.231	.217
Pirela,Jose	L	.222	9	2	1	0	0	0	0	1	.222	.333
Bats Right	R	.133	30	4	1	0	0	0	1	8	.161	.167
Piscotty,Stephen	L	.297	145	43	11	1	8	19	21	26	.400	.552
Bats Right	R	.265	437	116	24	2	14	66	30	107	.323	.426
Plawecki,Kevin	L	.250	36	9	1	0	1	2	2	9	.289	.361
Bats Right	R	.177	96	17	5	0	0	9	15	24	.301	.229
Plouffe,Trevor	L	.240	75	18	5	0	4	13	8	21	.314	.467
Bats Right	R	.266	244	65	8	1	8	34	11	39	.300	.406
Polanco,Gregory	L	.245	98	24	5	1	5	16	10	32	.312	.469
Bats Left	R	.261	429	112	29	3	17	70	43	87	.325	.462
Polanco,Jorge	L	.309	68	21	4	2	2	13	3	19	.342	.515
Bats Both	R	.271	177	48	11	2	2	14	14	27	.328	.390
Pollock,A.J.	L	.125	8	1	0	0	0	0	2	3	.300	.125
Bats Right	R	.273	33	9	0	0	2	4	3	5	.333	.455
Posey,Buster	L	.312	157	49	10	0	6	20	27	19	.409	.490
Bats Right	R	.277	382	106	23	2	8	60	37	49	.341	.411
Prado,Martin	L	.424	125	53	13	1	1	19	19	13	.500	.568
Bats Right	R	.274	475	130	24	2	7	56	30	56	.318	.377
Presley,Alex	L	.222	27	6	1	0	0	0	4	6	.323	.259
Bats Left	R	.191	94	18	1	0	3	11	7	19	.252	.298
Profar,Jurickson	L	.197	71	14	1	0	0	0	4	16	.250	.211
Bats Both	R	.254	201	51	5	3	5	20	26	45	.345	.383
Puig,Yasiel	L	.261	119	31	7	0	6	19	8	27	.313	.471
Bats Right	R	.265	215	57	7	2	5	26	16	47	.329	.386
Pujols,Albert	L	.279	140	39	4	0	9	30	7	15	.311	.500
Bats Right	R	.265	453	120	15	0	22	89	42	60	.327	.444
Quinn,Roman	L	.333	15	5	2	0	0	0	1	4	.444	.467
Bats Both	R	.238	42	10	2	0	0	6	7	15	.347	.286
Raburn,Ryan	L	.229	96	22	5	2	5	19	18	30	.356	.479
Bats Right	R	.213	127	27	5	0	4	11	10	50	.268	.346
Ramirez,Alexei	L	.313	131	41	6	2	1	18	7	22	.357	.412
Bats Right	R	.213	347	74	16	0	5	30	14	41	.247	.303
Ramirez,Hanley	L	.346	127	44	9	0	11	30	15	26	.420	.677
Bats Right	R	.268	422	113	19	1	19	81	45	94	.344	.453
Ramirez,Jose	L	.311	167	52	13	1	4	22	13	24	.368	.473
Bats Both	R	.312	398	124	33	2	7	54	31	38	.361	.457
Ramos,Wilson	L	.330	103	34	4	0	9	26	9	13	.377	.631
Bats Right	R	.301	379	114	21	0	13	54	26	66	.347	.459
Rasmus,Colby	L	.136	81	11	2	0	2	6	9	28	.220	.235
Bats Left	R	.226	288	65	8	0	13	48	34	93	.305	.389
Realmuto,J.T.	L	.215	93	20	7	0	2	5	4	24	.263	.355
Bats Right	R	.322	416	134	24	0	9	43	24	76	.361	.445
Recker,Anthony	L	.292	24	7	4	0	0	4	5	7	.414	.458
Bats Right	R	.273	66	18	4	0	2	11	11	15	.388	.424

Batter	vs	Avg	AB	H	2B	3B	HR	RBI	BB	SO	OBP	Slg
Reddick,Josh	L	.155	97	15	0	0	0	4	7	19	.212	.155
Bats Left	R	.322	301	97	17	1	10	33	32	37	.386	.485
Reed,A.J.	L	.067	15	1	0	0	0	0	2	9	.176	.067
Bats Left	R	.178	107	19	3	0	3	8	16	39	.282	.290
Reed,Michael	L	.167	6	1	0	0	0	0	1	2	.286	.167
Bats Right	R	.188	16	3	0	0	0	0	1	5	.235	.188
Refsnyder,Rob	L	.274	62	17	5	0	0	7	10	14	.370	.355
Bats Right	R	.233	90	21	4	0	0	5	8	16	.297	.278
Reimold,Nolan	L	.183	104	19	6	0	2	7	11	33	.267	.298
Bats Right	R	.263	99	26	3	1	4	8	11	29	.333	.434
Renda,Tony	L	.143	14	2	1	0	0	0	0	1	.143	.214
Bats Right	R	.196	46	9	1	0	0	3	5	10	.275	.217
Rendon,Anthony	L	.276	105	29	12	0	1	8	22	20	.398	.419
Bats Right	R	.268	462	124	26	2	19	77	43	97	.335	.457
Renfroe,Hunter	L	.333	9	3	1	0	1	1	1	1	.400	.778
Bats Right	R	.385	26	10	2	0	3	13	0	4	.385	.808
Revere,Ben	L	.203	59	12	0	1	1	5	3	7	.262	.288
Bats Left	R	.220	291	64	9	6	1	19	15	27	.260	.302
Reyes,Jose	L	.380	50	19	6	0	4	10	7	7	.456	.740
Bats Both	R	.239	205	49	7	4	4	14	16	42	.293	.371
Reynolds,Mark	L	.250	120	30	5	0	2	11	15	34	.331	.342
Bats Right	R	.297	273	81	19	0	12	42	27	78	.367	.498
Reynolds,Matt	L	.296	27	8	6	0	1	6	1	6	.321	.630
Bats Right	R	.194	62	12	2	0	2	7	3	28	.242	.323
Rickard,Joey	L	.313	83	26	6	0	3	9	7	14	.367	.494
Bats Right	R	.247	174	43	7	0	2	10	11	40	.296	.322
Rivera,Rene	L	.314	35	11	4	0	1	5	7	11	.429	.514
Bats Right	R	.200	150	30	0	0	5	21	9	43	.256	.300
Rivera,T.J.	L	.229	35	8	0	0	0	1	0	10	.229	.229
Bats Right	R	.386	70	27	4	1	3	15	3	7	.397	.600
Rivera,Yadiel	L	.208	24	5	2	0	0	1	2	5	.269	.292
Bats Right	R	.214	42	9	2	0	0	2	0	15	.214	.262
Rizzo,Anthony	L	.261	176	46	12	0	8	33	19	27	.366	.466
Bats Left	R	.305	407	124	31	4	24	76	55	81	.393	.577
Robinson,Clint	L	.300	30	9	0	0	0	4	2	5	.353	.300
Bats Left	R	.223	166	37	4	0	5	22	18	33	.296	.337
Robinson,Shane	L	.185	54	10	2	0	1	7	6	8	.279	.278
Bats Right	R	.159	44	7	1	0	0	3	4	9	.229	.182
Rodriguez,Alex	L	.211	76	16	4	0	3	11	6	22	.265	.382
Bats Right	R	.195	149	29	3	0	6	20	8	45	.238	.336
Rodriguez,Sean	L	.286	77	22	4	1	4	13	16	29	.415	.519
Bats Right	R	.265	223	59	12	0	14	43	17	73	.324	.507
Rogers,Jason	L	.143	14	2	0	1	0	2	3	4	.333	.286
Bats Right	R	.000	11	0	0	0	0	0	4	5	.267	.000
Rojas,Miguel	L	.281	57	16	4	0	1	4	1	6	.293	.404
Bats Right	R	.234	137	32	8	0	0	10	10	21	.287	.292
Rollins,Jimmy	L	.455	22	10	2	1	1	3	4	4	.538	.773
Bats Both	R	.181	127	23	6	0	1	5	12	29	.250	.252
Romine,Andrew	L	.268	41	11	1	0	0	2	3	5	.318	.293
Bats Both	R	.226	133	30	4	2	2	14	10	33	.299	.331
Romine,Austin	L	.274	95	26	6	0	3	15	3	14	.293	.432
Bats Right	R	.200	70	14	5	0	1	11	4	17	.237	.314
Rondon,Jose	L	.000	3	0	0	0	0	0	0	1	.000	.000
Bats Right	R	.136	22	3	0	0	0	1	1	3	.174	.136
Rosales,Adam	L	.237	97	23	5	1	6	19	17	45	.348	.495
Bats Right	R	.222	117	26	7	2	7	16	12	43	.293	.496
Rosario,Alberto	L	.000	7	0	0	0	0	0	2	0	.222	.000
Bats Right	R	.226	31	7	2	0	0	2	0	5	.226	.290
Rosario,Eddie	L	.263	76	20	2	0	0	6	3	22	.305	.289
Bats Left	R	.270	259	70	15	2	10	26	9	69	.293	.459
Ross,David	L	.283	53	15	1	0	4	11	13	17	.418	.528
Bats Right	R	.204	113	23	5	0	6	21	17	37	.299	.407
Rua,Ryan	L	.277	101	28	4	0	3	9	9	26	.348	.406
Bats Right	R	.245	139	34	4	1	5	13	12	50	.318	.396
Ruf,Darin	L	.286	28	8	1	0	1	4	0	9	.267	.429
Bats Right	R	.164	55	9	1	0	2	5	4	16	.220	.291
Ruggiano,Justin	L	.333	18	6	1	0	2	6	2	7	.400	.722
Bats Right	R	.333	6	2	0	0	0	1	0	3	.333	.333
Ruiz,Carlos	L	.271	70	19	2	0	2	5	12	12	.407	.386
Bats Right	R	.260	131	34	6	0	1	10	15	21	.340	.328
Rupp,Cameron	L	.324	68	22	7	1	4	20	4	21	.361	.632
Bats Right	R	.237	321	76	19	0	12	34	20	93	.291	.408
Russell,Addison	L	.223	139	31	7	0	9	28	20	38	.333	.468
Bats Right	R	.244	386	94	18	3	12	67	35	97	.317	.399
Rutledge,Josh	L	.313	16	5	2	0	0	2	3	3	.421	.438
Bats Right	R	.242	33	8	4	0	0	1	3	16	.306	.364

Batters vs. Left-Handed and Right-Handed Pitchers

Batter	vs	Avg	AB	H	2B	3B	HR	RBI	BB	SO	OBP	Slg
Saladino,Tyler	L	.329	79	26	5	0	1	17	5	14	.369	.430
Bats Right	R	.265	219	58	9	0	7	21	8	48	.296	.402
Saltalamacchia,Jarrod	L	.161	62	10	1	0	2	5	8	26	.254	.274
Bats Both	R	.174	184	32	4	1	10	33	33	78	.294	.370
Sanchez,Carlos	L	.167	42	7	0	0	1	4	0	10	.167	.238
Bats Both	R	.223	112	25	9	1	3	17	5	32	.261	.402
Sanchez,Gary	L	.189	53	10	2	0	6	11	9	20	.302	.566
Bats Right	R	.338	148	50	10	0	14	31	15	37	.404	.689
Sanchez,Hector	L	.143	7	1	0	0	0	0	0	2	.143	.143
Bats Both	R	.286	42	12	1	0	3	8	4	8	.362	.524
Sands,Jerry	L	.222	18	4	0	0	0	0	2	8	.300	.222
Bats Right	R	.243	37	9	0	0	1	7	1	16	.263	.324
Sano,Miguel	L	.227	97	22	5	1	6	15	16	39	.333	.485
Bats Right	R	.238	340	81	17	0	19	51	38	139	.315	.456
Santana,Carlos	L	.267	172	46	8	1	4	19	21	20	.347	.395
Bats Both	R	.256	410	105	23	2	30	68	78	79	.374	.541
Santana,Danny	L	.146	48	7	1	1	0	3	2	13	.196	.208
Bats Both	R	.265	185	49	9	1	2	11	10	42	.301	.357
Santana,Domingo	L	.312	77	24	5	0	4	13	12	24	.404	.532
Bats Right	R	.231	169	39	9	0	7	19	20	67	.318	.408
Sardinas,Luis	L	.302	63	19	3	0	3	7	4	16	.343	.492
Bats Both	R	.214	117	25	3	1	1	11	8	32	.270	.282
Saunders,Michael	L	.275	109	30	6	1	8	13	10	36	.358	.569
Bats Left	R	.247	381	94	26	2	16	44	49	121	.332	.451
Schafer,Logan	L	.421	19	8	2	0	0	1	2	5	.500	.526
Bats Left	R	.159	44	7	1	1	0	0	6	11	.275	.227
Schebler,Scott	L	.195	41	8	1	1	1	6	3	7	.267	.341
Bats Left	R	.278	216	60	11	1	8	34	16	52	.342	.449
Schimpf,Ryan	L	.157	51	8	1	2	3	10	5	25	.267	.431
Bats Left	R	.231	225	52	16	3	17	41	37	80	.352	.556
Schoop,Jonathan	L	.243	148	36	8	1	5	17	6	39	.276	.412
Bats Right	R	.274	467	128	30	0	20	65	15	98	.305	.467
Scruggs,Xavier	L	.222	9	2	0	0	0	0	0	2	.222	.222
Bats Right	R	.208	53	11	3	0	1	5	5	18	.300	.321
Seager,Corey	L	.250	196	49	13	2	5	19	15	52	.308	.413
Bats Left	R	.334	431	144	27	3	21	53	39	81	.391	.557
Seager,Kyle	L	.227	216	49	9	1	11	33	17	44	.297	.431
Bats Left	R	.307	381	117	27	2	19	66	52	64	.394	.538
Segedin,Rob	L	.205	39	8	1	1	1	5	3	13	.279	.359
Bats Right	R	.265	34	9	1	0	1	7	3	9	.325	.382
Segura,Jean	L	.275	153	42	6	3	4	12	12	36	.331	.431
Bats Right	R	.333	484	161	35	4	16	52	27	65	.380	.521
Selsky,Steve	L	.500	10	5	1	0	1	2	1	4	.545	.900
Bats Right	R	.268	41	11	1	0	1	5	1	18	.286	.366
Semien,Marcus	L	.257	148	38	5	0	11	19	9	33	.299	.514
Bats Right	R	.231	420	97	22	2	16	56	42	106	.300	.407
Severino,Pedro	L	.200	5	1	0	0	1	2	2	1	.429	.800
Bats Right	R	.348	23	8	2	0	1	2	3	2	.444	.565
Shaffer,Richie	L	.286	14	4	2	0	0	1	2	5	.353	.429
Bats Right	R	.235	34	8	4	0	1	3	3	13	.297	.441
Shaw,Travis	L	.187	107	20	7	0	4	19	5	31	.235	.364
Bats Left	R	.257	373	96	27	2	12	52	38	102	.325	.437
Shuck,J.B.	L	.323	31	10	1	1	0	2	2	2	.382	.419
Bats Left	R	.187	193	36	4	1	4	12	10	19	.225	.280
Simmons,Andrelton	L	.295	105	31	7	1	1	9	8	5	.342	.410
Bats Right	R	.277	343	95	15	1	3	35	20	33	.318	.353
Smith,Mallex	L	.080	50	4	2	0	0	3	5	15	.179	.120
Bats Left	R	.295	139	41	5	4	3	19	15	33	.365	.453
Smith,Seth	L	.167	30	5	2	0	0	5	2	6	.242	.233
Bats Left	R	.256	348	89	13	0	16	58	46	83	.351	.431
Smoak,Justin	L	.209	86	18	2	0	3	9	9	19	.284	.337
Bats Both	R	.221	213	47	8	0	11	25	31	93	.325	.413
Smolinski,Jake	L	.276	105	29	2	1	5	13	9	10	.339	.457
Bats Right	R	.216	185	40	4	1	2	14	10	34	.276	.281
Snyder,Brandon	L	.538	13	7	4	1	2	7	0	3	.538	1.462
Bats Right	R	.121	33	4	1	0	2	2	1	13	.147	.333
Solano,Donovan	L	.250	8	2	1	0	0	0	0	0	.250	.375
Bats Right	R	.214	14	3	1	0	1	2	1	3	.267	.500
Solarte,Yangervis	L	.271	96	26	8	0	3	17	8	17	.324	.448
Bats Both	R	.291	309	90	18	1	12	54	22	46	.346	.472
Soler,Jorge	L	.267	75	20	3	0	4	10	7	21	.345	.467
Bats Right	R	.224	152	34	6	0	8	21	24	45	.328	.421
Soto,Geovany	L	.321	28	9	2	0	2	5	1	7	.345	.607
Bats Right	R	.240	50	12	3	0	2	4	5	14	.309	.420
Souza Jr.,Steven	L	.237	118	28	3	0	5	12	6	47	.274	.390
Bats Right	R	.250	312	78	14	1	12	37	25	112	.314	.417

Batter	vs	Avg	AB	H	2B	3B	HR	RBI	BB	SO	OBP	Slg
Span,Denard	L	.217	184	40	7	1	1	10	16	29	.284	.283
Bats Left	R	.289	388	112	16	4	10	43	37	50	.353	.428
Spangenberg,Cory	L	.333	15	5	1	0	1	5	3	4	.474	.600
Bats Left	R	.182	33	6	0	1	0	3	1	9	.206	.242
Springer,George	L	.274	168	46	8	2	12	29	25	47	.385	.560
Bats Right	R	.256	476	122	21	3	17	53	63	131	.349	.420
Stanton,Giancarlo	L	.273	88	24	5	0	7	17	15	29	.379	.568
Bats Right	R	.231	325	75	15	1	20	57	35	111	.311	.468
Stewart,Chris	L	.316	19	6	1	0	0	0	3	3	.409	.368
Bats Right	R	.190	79	15	3	0	1	7	9	12	.297	.266
Story,Trevor	L	.280	100	28	4	0	9	16	15	40	.385	.590
Bats Right	R	.268	272	73	17	4	18	56	20	90	.324	.559
Stubbs,Drew	L	.216	51	11	0	0	1	2	8	23	.317	.275
Bats Right	R	.241	29	7	0	0	2	5	4	15	.353	.448
Suarez,Eugenio	L	.276	127	35	3	1	9	21	15	37	.354	.528
Bats Right	R	.240	438	105	22	1	12	49	36	118	.306	.377
Sucre,Jesus	L	1.000	5	5	1	0	1	4	1	0	1.000	1.800
Bats Right	R	.350	20	7	1	0	0	1	1	5	.435	.400
Suzuki,Ichiro	L	.339	59	20	1	2	0	5	9	14	.435	.424
Bats Left	R	.280	268	75	14	3	1	17	21	28	.334	.366
Suzuki,Kurt	L	.275	109	30	7	0	4	21	4	19	.296	.450
Bats Right	R	.250	236	59	17	1	4	28	14	29	.304	.381
Swanson,Dansby	L	.294	17	5	1	1	1	3	2	5	.368	.647
Bats Right	R	.304	112	34	6	0	2	14	11	29	.360	.411
Swihart,Blake	L	.800	5	4	0	0	0	0	2	0	.857	.800
Bats Both	R	.211	57	12	0	3	0	5	9	17	.313	.316
Szczur,Matt	L	.225	71	16	4	1	2	8	5	20	.276	.394
Bats Right	R	.281	114	32	5	0	3	16	8	19	.333	.404
Tapia,Raimel	L	.250	8	2	0	0	0	0	0	4	.250	.250
Bats Left	R	.267	30	8	0	0	0	3	2	7	.303	.267
Taylor,Chris	L	.231	26	6	0	2	0	3	1	8	.259	.385
Bats Right	R	.200	35	7	2	0	1	4	3	7	.263	.343
Taylor,Michael	L	.259	81	21	3	0	4	7	6	34	.310	.444
Bats Right	R	.214	140	30	8	0	3	9	8	43	.260	.336
Teixeira,Mark	L	.227	110	25	6	0	2	9	20	23	.348	.336
Bats Both	R	.195	277	54	10	0	13	35	27	82	.268	.372
Tejada,Ruben	L	.267	30	8	4	0	0	4	5	2	.342	.400
Bats Right	R	.083	36	3	1	0	0	1	2	11	.154	.111
Thole,Josh	L	.156	32	5	1	0	1	2	6	6	.282	.281
Bats Left	R	.174	86	15	2	0	0	5	7	22	.242	.198
Thompson,Trayce	L	.219	64	14	4	0	3	8	6	17	.286	.422
Bats Right	R	.227	172	39	7	0	10	24	20	49	.307	.442
Toles,Andrew	L	.231	13	3	0	0	1	2	0	3	.231	.462
Bats Left	R	.326	92	30	9	1	2	14	8	22	.382	.511
Tomas,Yasmany	L	.364	129	47	9	0	11	24	13	33	.423	.690
Bats Right	R	.242	401	97	21	1	20	59	18	103	.276	.449
Tomlinson,Kelby	L	.306	72	22	4	0	0	3	7	12	.367	.361
Bats Right	R	.265	34	9	0	0	0	3	5	6	.375	.265
Torreyes,Ronald	L	.186	43	8	1	0	0	2	6	8	.286	.209
Bats Right	R	.286	112	32	6	4	1	10	4	12	.314	.438
Travis,Devon	L	.260	100	26	4	0	2	10	0	20	.257	.360
Bats Right	R	.313	310	97	24	1	9	40	20	67	.355	.484
Trout,Mike	L	.323	127	41	4	1	7	23	27	27	.436	.535
Bats Right	R	.313	422	132	28	4	22	77	89	110	.442	.555
Trumbo,Mark	L	.173	156	27	3	0	10	24	10	44	.223	.385
Bats Right	R	.284	457	130	24	1	37	84	41	126	.347	.584
Tucker,Preston	L	.105	19	2	1	0	1	1	0	7	.105	.316
Bats Left	R	.174	115	20	7	1	3	7	8	33	.240	.330
Tulowitzki,Troy	L	.266	109	29	3	0	5	18	12	22	.336	.431
Bats Right	R	.251	383	96	18	0	19	61	31	79	.313	.446
Turner,Justin	L	.209	172	36	7	0	5	14	23	34	.303	.337
Bats Right	R	.305	384	117	27	3	22	76	25	73	.356	.563
Turner,Trea	L	.317	63	20	1	1	1	2	2	13	.338	.413
Bats Right	R	.348	244	85	13	7	12	38	12	46	.378	.607
Upton,Justin	L	.236	161	38	7	1	8	28	16	53	.313	.441
Bats Right	R	.249	409	102	21	1	23	59	34	126	.309	.474
Upton Jr.,Melvin	L	.275	120	33	2	1	9	21	13	39	.341	.533
Bats Right	R	.226	372	84	13	2	11	40	24	116	.274	.360
Uribe,Juan	L	.187	75	14	1	0	1	5	5	14	.232	.240
Bats Right	R	.215	163	35	8	0	6	20	10	35	.271	.374
Utley,Chase	L	.154	91	14	4	0	2	9	5	27	.206	.264
Bats Left	R	.273	421	115	22	3	12	43	35	88	.343	.425
Valbuena,Luis	L	.267	75	20	4	0	2	9	8	19	.341	.400
Bats Left	R	.258	217	56	13	1	11	31	36	62	.362	.479
Valencia,Danny	L	.318	129	41	7	0	7	19	14	27	.389	.535
Bats Right	R	.275	342	94	15	1	10	32	27	88	.330	.412

Batters vs. Left-Handed and Right-Handed Pitchers

Batter	vs	Avg	AB	H	2B	3B	HR	RBI	BB	SO	OBP	Slg
Van Slyke,Scott	L	.243	37	9	3	0	1	4	2	7	.333	.405
Bats Right	R	.215	65	14	3	0	0	3	3	17	.268	.262
Vargas,Kennys	L	.378	45	17	4	0	5	10	7	12	.462	.800
Bats Both	R	.168	107	18	7	0	5	10	17	45	.280	.374
Vazquez,Christian	L	.286	35	10	3	1	0	2	5	7	.375	.429
Bats Right	R	.212	137	29	6	0	1	10	5	32	.250	.277
Villar,Jonathan	L	.309	165	51	15	0	8	27	21	51	.385	.545
Bats Both	R	.276	424	117	23	3	11	36	58	123	.363	.422
Vogt,Stephen	L	.196	92	18	5	1	1	13	3	21	.245	.304
Bats Left	R	.264	398	105	25	1	13	43	32	62	.318	.430
Votto,Joey	L	.314	159	50	9	0	5	22	20	41	.396	.465
Bats Left	R	.330	397	131	25	2	24	75	88	79	.448	.584
Waldrop,Kyle	L	.000	4	0	0	0	0	0	0	1	.000	.000
Bats Left	R	.278	18	5	1	0	0	1	1	4	.316	.333
Walker,Neil	L	.330	100	33	4	0	8	16	10	14	.391	.610
Bats Both	R	.266	312	83	5	1	15	39	32	70	.333	.433
Wallace,Brett	L	.278	36	10	1	0	0	2	5	11	.381	.306
Bats Left	R	.171	181	31	9	0	6	18	24	72	.294	.320
Walsh,Colin	L	.000	10	0	0	0	0	0	7	3	.444	.000
Bats Both	R	.108	37	4	1	0	0	2	8	19	.267	.135
Weeks,Jemile	L	.143	14	2	1	0	0	1	0	4	.200	.214
Bats Both	R	.139	36	5	0	1	0	1	3	10	.205	.194
Weeks Jr.,Rickie	L	.284	67	19	4	1	6	12	9	15	.368	.642
Bats Right	R	.212	113	24	5	0	3	15	11	39	.302	.336
Wendle,Joey	L	.333	15	5	0	0	0	2	2	2	.412	.333
Bats Left	R	.247	81	20	1	0	1	9	4	14	.276	.296
Werth,Jayson	L	.322	121	39	9	0	9	22	18	27	.411	.620
Bats Right	R	.220	404	89	19	0	12	47	53	112	.312	.356
White,Tyler	L	.250	88	22	6	0	5	14	7	26	.309	.489
Bats Right	R	.199	161	32	10	0	3	14	16	39	.274	.317
Wieters,Matt	L	.229	105	24	3	0	3	15	11	24	.302	.343
Bats Both	R	.248	318	79	14	1	14	51	21	61	.303	.431
Wilkins,Andy	L	.000	4	0	0	0	0	0	0	3	.000	.000
Bats Left	R	.150	20	3	1	0	1	3	3	7	.261	.350
Williams,Mason	L	.250	8	2	1	0	0	0	0	4	.250	.375
Bats Left	R	.316	19	6	0	0	0	2	1	8	.350	.316
Williamson,Mac	L	.212	66	14	2	0	4	11	6	22	.297	.424
Bats Right	R	.239	46	11	1	0	2	4	7	13	.340	.391
Wilson,Bobby	L	.286	56	16	2	0	2	11	2	13	.310	.429
Bats Right	R	.221	172	38	4	0	5	22	9	51	.258	.331
Wolters,Tony	L	.225	40	9	0	0	1	5	3	10	.279	.300
Bats Left	R	.267	165	44	15	2	2	25	18	43	.339	.418
Wong,Kolten	L	.242	66	16	1	1	1	6	4	12	.320	.333
Bats Left	R	.239	247	59	6	6	4	17	30	40	.329	.360
Worth,Danny	L	.200	25	5	2	0	0	0	1	4	.231	.280
Bats Right	R	.143	14	2	0	0	0	1	0	2	.143	.143
Wright,David	L	.194	36	7	1	0	2	5	7	19	.326	.389
Bats Right	R	.238	101	24	7	0	5	9	19	36	.358	.455
Yelich,Christian	L	.287	150	43	7	1	2	25	9	39	.329	.387
Bats Left	R	.301	428	129	31	2	19	73	63	99	.392	.516
Young,Chris	L	.329	73	24	10	0	3	9	9	17	.410	.589
Bats Right	R	.246	130	32	8	0	6	15	12	33	.319	.446
Zimmerman,Ryan	L	.200	85	17	5	0	4	12	11	15	.283	.400
Bats Right	R	.222	342	76	13	1	11	34	18	89	.269	.363
Zobrist,Ben	L	.301	143	43	10	0	4	11	21	31	.401	.455
Bats Both	R	.261	380	99	21	3	14	65	75	51	.380	.442
Zunino,Mike	L	.200	40	8	1	0	3	6	10	17	.385	.450
Bats Right	R	.210	124	26	6	0	9	25	11	48	.293	.476
AL	L	.258	-	-	-	-	-	-	-	-	.322	.419
	R	.257	-	-	-	-	-	-	-	-	.321	.424
NL	L	.254	-	-	-	-	-	-	-	-	.324	.409
	R	.254	-	-	-	-	-	-	-	-	.321	.413
MLB	L	.256	-	-	-	-	-	-	-	-	.323	.414
	R	.255	-	-	-	-	-	-	-	-	.321	.419

Pitchers vs. Left-Handed and Right-Handed Batters

Pitcher	vs	Avg	AB	H	2B	3B	HR	RBI	BB	SO	OBP	Slg
Abad,Fernando	L	.153	72	11	2	0	2	13	3	17	.195	.264
Throws Left	R	.284	102	29	5	0	2	15	19	24	.397	.392
Achter,A.J.	L	.288	59	17	2	0	4	4	2	4	.311	.525
Throws Right	R	.299	87	26	7	0	3	9	10	10	.374	.483
Adams,Austin	L	.375	40	15	3	2	3	13	3	9	.419	.775
Throws Right	R	.293	41	12	6	0	2	8	4	8	.356	.585
Adleman,Tim	L	.256	117	30	6	0	6	16	10	26	.326	.462
Throws Right	R	.246	138	34	5	2	7	15	10	21	.309	.464
Albers,Andrew	L	.176	17	3	0	0	1	2	0	6	.176	.353
Throws Left	R	.387	62	24	7	1	4	12	6	10	.441	.726
Albers,Matt	L	.308	65	20	4	1	4	16	8	8	.395	.585
Throws Right	R	.326	144	47	12	1	6	35	11	22	.376	.549
Alcantara,Raul	L	.306	49	15	3	0	4	7	3	7	.345	.612
Throws Right	R	.364	44	16	3	0	5	11	1	7	.417	.773
Alexander,Scott	L	.353	34	12	1	0	0	4	2	5	.378	.382
Throws Left	R	.286	42	12	2	1	1	6	5	11	.362	.452
Allen,Cody	L	.218	110	24	4	1	4	12	12	35	.295	.382
Throws Right	R	.139	122	17	4	0	4	12	15	52	.230	.270
Altavilla,Dan	L	.214	14	3	1	0	0	2	0	2	.267	.286
Throws Right	R	.258	31	8	1	0	0	3	1	8	.273	.290
Alvarez,Dario	L	.270	37	10	0	0	1	2	2	18	.341	.351
Throws Left	R	.277	65	18	1	0	5	13	5	23	.333	.523
Alvarez,Jose	L	.283	113	32	2	0	2	11	6	21	.317	.354
Throws Left	R	.312	125	39	7	2	2	23	9	30	.363	.448
Anderson,Brett	L	.611	18	11	1	0	0	3	1	1	.600	.667
Throws Left	R	.368	38	14	3	0	4	10	3	4	.415	.763
Anderson,Chase	L	.203	251	51	9	2	11	28	25	53	.278	.386
Throws Right	R	.313	332	104	29	2	17	48	28	67	.369	.566
Anderson,Cody	L	.326	135	44	9	2	7	23	5	25	.352	.578
Throws Right	R	.342	120	41	6	1	6	16	8	29	.383	.558
Anderson,Tyler	L	.245	102	25	2	2	0	5	9	22	.304	.304
Throws Left	R	.281	335	94	20	2	12	39	19	77	.323	.460
Andriese,Matt	L	.242	227	55	14	0	9	24	13	48	.283	.423
Throws Right	R	.285	267	76	12	0	8	32	12	61	.312	.419
Araujo,Elvis	L	.255	51	13	5	0	0	8	6	11	.356	.353
Throws Left	R	.361	61	22	3	0	4	11	11	18	.452	.607
Archer,Chris	L	.231	368	85	16	1	15	50	34	114	.296	.402
Throws Right	R	.244	401	98	17	1	15	43	33	119	.304	.404
Armstrong,Shawn	L	.238	21	5	1	0	0	1	1	4	.273	.286
Throws Right	R	.235	17	4	0	0	1	1	4	3	.381	.412
Arrieta,Jake	L	.194	319	62	10	2	7	26	51	91	.308	.304
Throws Right	R	.194	391	76	17	0	9	34	25	99	.250	.307
Asher,Alec	L	.241	58	14	4	0	1	7	2	6	.274	.362
Throws Right	R	.182	44	8	1	0	0	2	2	7	.234	.205
Avilan,Luis	L	.200	40	8	0	0	0	7	5	13	.319	.200
Throws Left	R	.143	28	4	1	0	0	2	5	15	.273	.179
Axford,John	L	.256	117	30	5	0	2	17	11	22	.321	.350
Throws Right	R	.259	135	35	5	0	4	16	19	38	.359	.385
Baez,Pedro	L	.160	94	15	2	1	3	9	11	26	.255	.298
Throws Right	R	.214	173	37	6	0	8	27	11	57	.262	.387
Bailey,Andrew	L	.234	64	15	2	0	2	9	4	14	.292	.359
Throws Right	R	.257	101	26	6	1	5	14	13	27	.339	.485
Bailey,Homer	L	.429	42	18	0	0	1	7	3	10	.468	.500
Throws Right	R	.293	58	17	1	0	1	7	4	17	.344	.362
Barbato,Johnny	L	.391	23	9	1	0	2	4	3	6	.462	.696
Throws Right	R	.148	27	4	0	0	0	2	2	9	.258	.148
Barnes,Danny	L	.200	20	4	2	0	0	2	4	5	.333	.300
Throws Right	R	.323	31	10	3	0	0	5	1	9	.324	.419
Barnes,Jacob	L	.318	44	14	2	0	1	3	5	7	.388	.432
Throws Right	R	.185	54	10	3	0	0	5	1	19	.196	.241
Barnes,Matt	L	.234	94	22	2	1	4	14	14	30	.336	.404
Throws Right	R	.256	156	40	9	0	2	18	17	41	.337	.353
Barnette,Tony	L	.287	101	29	2	0	4	12	8	22	.351	.426
Throws Right	R	.205	122	25	5	1	0	10	8	27	.261	.262
Barraclough,Kyle	L	.192	125	24	4	0	1	11	26	45	.336	.248
Throws Right	R	.160	131	21	5	2	0	10	18	68	.263	.229
Barrett,Jake	L	.222	90	20	5	1	4	14	18	22	.357	.433
Throws Right	R	.214	126	27	8	0	2	18	10	34	.275	.325
Bassitt,Chris	L	.210	62	13	4	0	2	4	7	12	.290	.371
Throws Right	R	.386	57	22	4	0	3	14	7	11	.453	.614
Bastardo,Antonio	L	.258	97	25	5	0	6	16	8	19	.321	.495
Throws Left	R	.220	159	35	10	0	5	13	24	55	.328	.377
Bauer,Trevor	L	.239	343	82	22	2	8	40	29	96	.305	.385
Throws Right	R	.257	378	97	14	2	12	49	41	72	.333	.399
Baumann,Buddy	L	.071	14	1	0	0	0	0	1	3	.188	.071
Throws Left	R	.286	21	6	1	0	0	2	3	7	.375	.333

Pitcher	vs	Avg	AB	H	2B	3B	HR	RBI	BB	SO	OBP	Slg
Beck,Chris	L	.385	39	15	3	0	2	6	10	6	.500	.615
Throws Right	R	.250	64	16	3	0	1	7	7	14	.342	.344
Bedrosian,Cam	L	.243	70	17	2	0	0	6	7	34	.312	.271
Throws Right	R	.173	75	13	1	0	1	12	7	17	.259	.227
Belisle,Matt	L	.147	75	11	3	1	1	6	3	19	.190	.253
Throws Right	R	.317	101	32	5	0	1	12	4	13	.340	.396
Benoit,Joaquin	L	.238	80	19	2	0	3	10	10	21	.326	.375
Throws Right	R	.188	96	18	2	0	2	11	14	31	.288	.271
Bergman,Christian	L	.343	35	12	4	0	3	11	4	9	.410	.714
Throws Right	R	.360	75	27	4	1	4	14	2	13	.372	.600
Berrios,Jose	L	.290	124	36	4	0	5	23	20	27	.393	.444
Throws Right	R	.330	115	38	11	0	7	24	15	22	.425	.609
Betances,Dellin	L	.233	120	28	6	0	2	11	10	56	.295	.333
Throws Right	R	.176	148	26	5	0	3	19	18	70	.265	.270
Bettis,Chad	L	.258	361	93	13	6	5	41	36	71	.326	.368
Throws Right	R	.297	374	111	22	3	17	56	23	67	.346	.508
Biagini,Joseph	L	.288	111	32	7	0	1	10	9	32	.347	.378
Throws Right	R	.239	155	37	9	1	2	12	10	30	.296	.348
Blach,Ty	L	.130	23	3	1	0	0	0	2	4	.200	.174
Throws Left	R	.152	33	5	1	0	1	2	3	6	.222	.273
Blair,Aaron	L	.323	130	42	9	3	7	21	22	16	.433	.600
Throws Right	R	.278	144	40	5	2	7	34	12	30	.329	.486
Blanton,Joe	L	.186	97	18	1	0	2	5	14	28	.288	.258
Throws Right	R	.198	187	37	9	1	5	23	12	52	.250	.337
Blazek,Michael	L	.292	65	19	5	0	2	9	15	11	.429	.462
Throws Right	R	.324	102	33	6	2	5	25	12	25	.388	.569
Bleier,Richard	L	.150	40	6	0	1	0	4	2	12	.209	.200
Throws Left	R	.304	46	14	5	0	0	7	2	1	.327	.413
Blevins,Jerry	L	.255	102	26	4	0	1	5	8	35	.313	.324
Throws Left	R	.182	55	10	0	0	3	10	7	17	.266	.345
Bolsinger,Mike	L	.333	39	13	2	0	2	6	5	10	.422	.538
Throws Right	R	.286	70	20	3	0	5	13	4	15	.333	.543
Boscan,Wilfredo	L	.333	30	10	4	0	2	9	3	4	.394	.667
Throws Right	R	.172	29	5	1	0	0	2	4	4	.273	.207
Boshers,Buddy	L	.241	58	14	3	0	0	5	2	17	.267	.293
Throws Left	R	.253	83	21	4	1	3	15	5	20	.293	.434
Bowman,Matt	L	.178	90	16	5	1	1	13	12	20	.282	.289
Throws Right	R	.256	168	43	7	1	3	17	8	32	.288	.363
Boxberger,Brad	L	.244	41	10	0	0	2	8	8	14	.373	.390
Throws Right	R	.255	51	13	0	0	1	7	11	8	.397	.314
Boyd,Matt	L	.172	64	11	2	1	2	5	6	11	.270	.328
Throws Left	R	.276	312	86	13	2	15	41	23	71	.325	.474
Boyer,Blaine	L	.298	124	37	10	0	2	17	10	14	.351	.427
Throws Right	R	.312	138	43	8	0	2	16	7	12	.345	.413
Brach,Brad	L	.288	132	38	7	0	4	11	13	27	.352	.432
Throws Right	R	.126	151	19	4	0	3	11	12	65	.187	.212
Bracho,Silvino	L	.293	41	12	2	1	2	5	5	7	.383	.537
Throws Right	R	.297	64	19	5	0	5	23	5	10	.361	.609
Bradley,Archie	L	.318	277	88	25	1	10	36	44	61	.412	.523
Throws Right	R	.235	281	66	15	3	6	38	23	82	.293	.374
Bradley,Jed	L	.400	15	6	3	0	0	3	2	1	.471	.600
Throws Left	R	.091	11	1	0	0	0	2	4	3	.313	.091
Brault,Steven	L	.318	22	7	1	0	0	4	5	4	.464	.364
Throws Left	R	.311	122	38	11	0	5	19	12	25	.378	.525
Breslow,Craig	L	.400	25	10	1	1	0	6	1	2	.423	.520
Throws Left	R	.333	33	11	0	0	1	6	3	5	.389	.424
Brice,Austin	L	.194	31	6	2	0	1	3	1	7	.265	.355
Throws Right	R	.143	21	3	0	0	1	3	4	7	.280	.286
Britton,Zach	L	.185	54	10	3	0	0	2	5	16	.254	.241
Throws Left	R	.155	181	28	5	0	1	5	13	58	.211	.199
Broadway,Mike	L	.455	11	5	1	0	0	4	0	0	.455	.545
Throws Right	R	.308	13	4	0	0	2	5	1	4	.357	.769
Broxton,Jonathan	L	.230	87	20	1	1	3	6	15	22	.340	.368
Throws Right	R	.229	140	32	7	0	4	23	9	35	.286	.364
Buchanan,Jake	L	.143	7	1	0	0	0	0	0	1	.143	.143
Throws Right	R	.154	13	2	0	0	1	1	1	3	.214	.385
Buchholz,Clay	L	.280	254	71	17	1	6	36	34	44	.363	.425
Throws Right	R	.222	266	59	5	0	15	36	21	49	.286	.410
Buchter,Ryan	L	.147	75	11	6	1	0	5	7	25	.235	.253
Throws Left	R	.168	137	23	7	0	4	13	24	53	.290	.307
Bumgarner,Madison	L	.178	163	29	5	1	4	12	8	58	.218	.294
Throws Left	R	.221	678	150	32	1	22	65	46	193	.276	.369
Bundy,Dylan	L	.256	223	57	12	1	9	28	18	46	.317	.439
Throws Right	R	.259	201	52	7	0	9	24	24	58	.348	.428
Burgos,Enrique	L	.236	72	17	5	0	4	14	14	26	.364	.472
Throws Right	R	.269	78	21	6	0	1	11	9	17	.341	.385

Pitchers vs. Left-Handed and Right-Handed Batters

Pitcher	vs	Avg	AB	H	2B	3B	HR	RBI	BB	SO	OBP	Slg
Burnett,Sean	L	.143	14	2	0	0	1	1	0	2	.143	.357
Throws Left	R	.429	7	3	2	0	0	1	1	1	.500	.714
Bush,Matt	L	.238	84	20	3	0	2	12	7	28	.290	.345
Throws Right	R	.171	140	24	4	0	2	6	7	33	.215	.243
Butler,Eddie	L	.308	107	33	5	1	5	22	11	20	.380	.514
Throws Right	R	.342	158	54	12	2	8	32	10	27	.382	.595
Cabrera,Mauricio	L	.266	64	17	5	0	0	7	8	11	.347	.344
Throws Right	R	.189	74	14	1	0	0	8	11	21	.295	.203
Cahill,Trevor	L	.206	97	20	3	0	3	11	14	21	.330	.330
Throws Right	R	.197	147	29	2	0	4	12	21	45	.302	.293
Cain,Matt	L	.322	149	48	10	2	5	21	12	32	.384	.517
Throws Right	R	.281	196	55	8	0	11	33	20	40	.347	.490
Caminero,Arquimedes	L	.280	107	30	8	2	3	17	13	17	.358	.477
Throws Right	R	.280	132	37	6	1	4	16	20	33	.392	.432
Campos,Leonel	L	.219	32	7	3	0	2	6	8	10	.375	.500
Throws Right	R	.224	49	11	2	0	1	9	6	14	.316	.327
Campos,Vicente	L	.100	10	1	0	0	0	0	0	2	.100	.100
Throws Right	R	.250	12	3	0	0	2	2	2	2	.357	.750
Capuano,Chris	L	.212	33	7	1	0	1	3	4	10	.297	.333
Throws Left	R	.281	57	16	2	1	6	8	11	17	.406	.667
Carasiti,Matt	L	.548	31	17	5	2	0	7	10	5	.667	.839
Throws Right	R	.222	36	8	2	0	1	7	1	12	.268	.361
Carrasco,Carlos	L	.235	247	58	16	1	11	27	21	68	.298	.441
Throws Right	R	.244	311	76	20	1	10	33	13	82	.276	.412
Cashner,Andrew	L	.291	254	74	16	5	11	42	35	58	.380	.524
Throws Right	R	.267	255	68	18	3	8	31	25	54	.339	.455
Casilla,Santiago	L	.265	83	22	5	1	5	9	7	25	.319	.530
Throws Right	R	.215	130	28	4	0	3	11	12	40	.306	.315
Castro,Miguel	L	.389	18	7	1	0	1	5	3	3	.500	.611
Throws Right	R	.262	42	11	1	1	2	7	2	9	.295	.476
Cecil,Brett	L	.258	66	17	1	0	2	8	3	20	.310	.364
Throws Left	R	.278	79	22	4	0	4	16	5	25	.318	.481
Cedeno,Xavier	L	.197	76	15	2	0	0	9	7	21	.259	.224
Throws Left	R	.259	81	21	5	0	2	7	6	22	.310	.395
Cervenka,Hunter	L	.200	85	17	4	0	2	7	12	20	.306	.318
Throws Left	R	.209	67	14	3	2	1	5	16	22	.361	.358
Cessa,Luis	L	.234	111	26	4	0	8	17	7	21	.280	.486
Throws Right	R	.245	155	38	6	0	8	22	7	25	.289	.439
Chacin,Jhoulys	L	.268	280	75	15	1	9	41	28	43	.337	.425
Throws Right	R	.277	282	78	12	2	5	32	27	76	.342	.387
Chafin,Andrew	L	.200	40	8	2	0	0	5	7	15	.319	.250
Throws Left	R	.311	45	14	3	0	1	6	4	13	.380	.444
Chamberlain,Joba	L	.172	29	5	3	0	0	4	7	7	.351	.276
Throws Right	R	.179	39	7	4	0	1	6	4	11	.244	.359
Chapman,Aroldis	L	.135	37	5	2	0	0	2	7	17	.273	.189
Throws Left	R	.163	166	27	4	1	2	10	11	73	.213	.235
Chapman,Kevin	L	.526	19	10	2	0	0	6	1	3	.550	.632
Throws Left	R	.263	19	5	3	0	0	5	3	3	.364	.421
Chargois,J.T.	L	.281	32	9	2	0	0	8	7	5	.415	.344
Throws Right	R	.296	54	16	5	0	0	7	5	12	.356	.389
Chatwood,Tyler	L	.256	308	79	17	3	8	39	37	63	.342	.409
Throws Right	R	.242	281	68	15	0	7	31	33	54	.323	.370
Chavez,Jesse	L	.307	101	31	3	0	4	23	11	24	.381	.455
Throws Right	R	.250	160	40	7	1	8	24	7	39	.284	.456
Chen,Wei-Yin	L	.325	80	26	3	1	1	8	3	17	.353	.425
Throws Left	R	.266	406	108	23	2	21	49	21	83	.303	.488
Cingrani,Tony	L	.207	82	17	3	2	2	16	10	23	.309	.366
Throws Left	R	.252	147	37	7	1	3	19	27	26	.369	.374
Cishek,Steve	L	.216	102	22	5	0	5	5	12	35	.316	.412
Throws Right	R	.169	130	22	4	0	3	17	9	41	.229	.269
Claudio,Alex	L	.177	62	11	2	0	1	6	1	16	.190	.258
Throws Left	R	.310	142	44	8	1	1	19	9	18	.351	.401
Clemens,Paul	L	.188	112	21	5	1	4	9	17	29	.305	.357
Throws Right	R	.313	163	51	10	0	10	28	14	24	.368	.558
Clevinger,Mike	L	.178	90	16	2	0	1	7	12	23	.272	.233
Throws Right	R	.301	113	34	11	0	7	22	17	27	.392	.584
Clippard,Tyler	L	.241	116	28	7	0	6	15	9	34	.296	.457
Throws Right	R	.220	118	26	2	1	4	12	17	38	.324	.356
Cobb,Alex	L	.404	47	19	3	1	4	10	3	6	.440	.766
Throws Right	R	.271	48	13	4	0	1	10	4	10	.321	.417
Coke,Phil	L	.286	14	4	1	0	0	1	3	1	.412	.357
Throws Left	R	.261	23	6	2	1	1	5	4	3	.393	.565
Cole,A.J.	L	.247	81	20	6	1	3	12	9	22	.326	.457
Throws Right	R	.250	68	17	1	1	4	10	5	17	.303	.471
Cole,Gerrit	L	.329	213	70	23	1	3	24	18	55	.381	.488
Throws Right	R	.253	241	61	9	0	4	24	18	43	.312	.340

Pitcher	vs	Avg	AB	H	2B	3B	HR	RBI	BB	SO	OBP	Slg
Coleman,Louis	L	.316	38	12	5	1	0	6	11	7	.480	.500
Throws Right	R	.232	142	33	6	1	5	21	13	38	.302	.394
Collmenter,Josh	L	.246	65	16	3	1	3	11	3	12	.290	.462
Throws Right	R	.233	86	20	2	0	4	8	13	21	.347	.395
Colome,Alex	L	.184	87	16	0	0	1	5	8	31	.260	.218
Throws Right	R	.221	122	27	3	0	5	13	7	40	.269	.369
Colon,Bartolo	L	.270	370	100	18	4	18	44	21	61	.309	.486
Throws Right	R	.267	375	100	18	2	6	33	11	67	.290	.373
Colon,Joseph	L	.200	20	4	2	0	0	2	2	5	.273	.300
Throws Right	R	.348	23	8	2	0	2	6	5	5	.464	.696
Conley,Adam	L	.298	121	36	6	2	0	10	13	18	.379	.380
Throws Left	R	.235	379	89	21	1	13	41	49	106	.333	.398
Corbin,Patrick	L	.241	145	35	3	2	6	16	19	48	.329	.414
Throws Left	R	.300	474	142	28	3	18	73	47	83	.365	.485
Cosart,Jarred	L	.209	110	23	4	0	3	19	25	21	.356	.327
Throws Right	R	.330	115	38	6	0	1	13	14	17	.409	.409
Cotham,Caleb	L	.348	46	16	3	0	1	8	5	10	.426	.478
Throws Right	R	.302	53	16	3	0	2	12	7	11	.387	.472
Cotton,Jharel	L	.146	48	7	1	0	1	4	4	11	.212	.229
Throws Right	R	.217	60	13	2	0	3	6	0	12	.217	.400
Coulombe,Daniel	L	.227	75	17	3	0	1	11	3	24	.250	.307
Throws Left	R	.208	96	20	2	0	5	13	14	30	.306	.385
Cravy,Tyler	L	.250	52	13	3	0	2	7	8	10	.344	.423
Throws Right	R	.163	49	8	3	0	1	6	4	12	.241	.286
Crockett,Kyle	L	.256	39	10	4	0	0	5	3	12	.310	.359
Throws Left	R	.261	23	6	2	1	0	2	4	5	.357	.435
Cueto,Johnny	L	.255	384	98	20	3	6	24	22	96	.300	.370
Throws Right	R	.224	434	97	16	2	9	42	23	102	.269	.332
Cuevas,William	L	.286	7	2	1	0	0	1	2	2	.444	.429
Throws Right	R	.300	10	3	1	0	0	1	4	1	.500	.400
Cunniff,Brandon	L	.240	25	6	1	1	0	2	4	6	.355	.360
Throws Right	R	.229	35	8	2	0	2	5	5	10	.341	.457
Curtis,Zac	L	.310	29	9	2	0	2	7	8	4	.459	.586
Throws Left	R	.182	22	4	1	0	0	2	5	6	.400	.227
Danks,John	L	.308	13	4	0	0	2	5	1	1	.333	.769
Throws Left	R	.324	74	24	5	1	3	12	10	15	.400	.541
Darvish,Yu	L	.207	174	36	6	2	4	18	17	63	.273	.333
Throws Right	R	.221	204	45	7	1	8	21	14	69	.279	.382
Davies,Zach	L	.272	301	82	16	3	10	27	19	59	.323	.445
Throws Right	R	.255	330	84	12	2	10	41	19	76	.297	.394
Davis,Wade	L	.200	80	16	2	0	0	3	6	26	.264	.225
Throws Right	R	.221	77	17	3	0	0	6	10	21	.326	.260
Dayton,Grant	L	.140	43	6	1	0	1	2	2	18	.196	.233
Throws Left	R	.157	51	8	0	0	3	7	4	21	.218	.333
De La Cruz,Joel	L	.260	123	32	7	1	5	23	10	16	.319	.455
Throws Right	R	.266	124	33	11	0	5	15	12	21	.333	.476
de la Rosa,Jorge	L	.297	138	41	7	1	5	21	17	30	.378	.471
Throws Left	R	.291	398	116	24	1	18	59	46	78	.372	.492
de la Rosa,Rubby	L	.198	86	17	3	1	2	7	16	18	.330	.326
Throws Right	R	.236	110	26	5	0	6	14	4	36	.280	.445
De Leon,Jose	L	.212	33	7	1	0	1	5	5	8	.325	.333
Throws Right	R	.364	33	12	2	0	4	11	2	7	.432	.788
De Los Santos,Abel	L	.455	11	5	1	0	1	6	4	2	.600	.818
Throws Right	R	.182	11	2	0	0	0	1	0	0	.231	.182
Dean,Pat	L	.293	58	17	3	1	2	13	5	7	.349	.483
Throws Left	R	.329	216	71	15	1	11	31	18	43	.377	.560
deGrom,Jacob	L	.241	286	69	12	0	5	21	19	70	.288	.336
Throws Right	R	.269	271	73	12	1	10	29	17	73	.317	.432
Delabar,Steve	L	.000	14	0	0	0	0	2	6	4	.300	.000
Throws Right	R	.333	15	5	3	0	1	6	4	6	.500	.733
Delgado,Randall	L	.284	116	33	8	1	4	20	21	25	.393	.474
Throws Right	R	.251	175	44	13	1	4	29	15	43	.309	.406
DeSclafani,Anthony	L	.303	254	77	15	1	11	28	13	60	.337	.500
Throws Right	R	.206	209	43	7	0	5	16	17	45	.274	.311
Despaigne,Odrisamer	L	.327	55	18	2	1	1	4	7	7	.403	.455
Throws Right	R	.295	61	18	8	0	2	14	9	10	.384	.525
Detwiler,Ross	L	.237	38	9	1	0	1	3	3	7	.302	.342
Throws Left	R	.311	161	50	14	0	4	28	16	19	.373	.472
Devenski,Chris	L	.229	188	43	10	3	3	17	12	53	.277	.362
Throws Right	R	.185	195	36	8	0	1	9	8	51	.224	.241
Diaz,Dayan	L	.412	17	7	1	0	1	6	3	1	.476	.647
Throws Right	R	.300	10	3	0	1	1	3	4	2	.500	.800
Diaz,Edwin	L	.195	82	16	5	0	2	7	9	39	.275	.329
Throws Right	R	.248	117	29	2	0	3	10	6	49	.302	.342
Diaz,Jumbo	L	.197	66	13	2	0	4	10	8	14	.284	.409
Throws Right	R	.242	95	23	3	0	4	10	11	23	.327	.400

Pitchers vs. Left-Handed and Right-Handed Batters

Pitcher	vs	Avg	AB	H	2B	3B	HR	RBI	BB	SO	OBP	Slg
Dickey,R.A.	L	.250	276	69	13	1	14	36	32	54	.333	.457
Throws Right	R	.264	379	100	26	4	14	45	31	72	.323	.464
Diekman,Jake	L	.212	66	14	2	1	1	9	7	13	.307	.318
Throws Left	R	.177	124	22	5	0	3	16	19	46	.288	.290
Dominguez,Jose	L	.277	47	13	0	0	1	7	13	8	.426	.340
Throws Right	R	.247	85	21	2	1	4	13	4	12	.312	.435
Doolittle,Sean	L	.206	63	13	4	0	2	5	1	23	.219	.365
Throws Left	R	.250	80	20	5	1	4	13	7	22	.310	.488
Drake,Oliver	L	.154	26	4	1	0	1	4	5	9	.290	.308
Throws Right	R	.175	40	7	5	0	1	7	2	12	.214	.375
Duensing,Brian	L	.190	21	4	2	0	1	1	0	4	.190	.429
Throws Left	R	.290	31	9	1	0	1	5	3	6	.353	.419
Duffey,Tyler	L	.266	278	74	19	1	6	31	13	66	.307	.406
Throws Right	R	.337	276	93	23	4	19	59	19	48	.383	.656
Duffy,Danny	L	.183	109	20	2	0	1	6	4	38	.219	.229
Throws Left	R	.252	567	143	31	3	26	64	38	150	.305	.455
Duke,Zach	L	.233	103	24	7	0	0	9	6	29	.279	.301
Throws Left	R	.203	118	24	4	0	2	11	23	39	.347	.288
Dull,Ryan	L	.244	90	22	5	0	2	8	10	21	.320	.367
Throws Right	R	.156	179	28	7	1	8	19	5	52	.176	.341
Dunn,Mike	L	.278	79	22	3	0	2	18	2	17	.310	.392
Throws Left	R	.263	80	21	2	1	3	12	9	21	.341	.425
Dyson,Sam	L	.274	113	31	4	1	2	13	14	21	.359	.381
Throws Right	R	.221	145	32	5	0	3	7	9	34	.276	.317
Edgin,Josh	L	.235	17	4	0	0	0	2	2	5	.300	.235
Throws Left	R	.300	20	6	0	0	1	4	4	6	.400	.450
Edwards Jr.,Carl	L	.146	48	7	1	0	1	4	3	17	.196	.229
Throws Right	R	.108	74	8	2	0	3	12	11	35	.218	.257
Eflin,Zach	L	.289	121	35	7	2	9	26	9	9	.336	.603
Throws Right	R	.250	128	32	10	2	3	15	8	22	.293	.430
Ege,Cody	L	.208	24	5	0	1	1	2	0	6	.208	.417
Throws Left	R	.500	22	11	2	0	1	8	5	5	.548	.727
Eickhoff,Jerad	L	.278	400	111	24	5	18	49	25	75	.324	.498
Throws Right	R	.220	345	76	19	1	12	32	17	92	.259	.386
Elias,Roenis	L	.500	12	6	2	0	0	4	3	1	.600	.667
Throws Left	R	.375	24	9	3	0	2	7	2	2	.423	.750
Ellington,Brian	L	.288	52	15	4	0	1	8	9	9	.397	.423
Throws Right	R	.174	69	12	3	0	1	4	7	23	.260	.261
Eovaldi,Nathan	L	.268	209	56	14	2	12	26	25	46	.345	.526
Throws Right	R	.245	273	67	14	0	11	36	15	51	.287	.418
Erlin,Robbie	L	.125	16	2	0	1	0	2	1	6	.176	.250
Throws Left	R	.256	39	10	2	1	3	5	2	7	.293	.590
Esch,Jake	L	.269	26	7	1	0	2	5	4	5	.367	.538
Throws Right	R	.385	26	10	0	1	2	3	2	5	.448	.692
Escobar,Edwin	L	.280	50	14	5	0	1	8	2	8	.308	.440
Throws Left	R	.388	49	19	3	1	3	11	10	9	.524	.673
Estevez,Carlos	L	.181	83	15	2	1	0	5	14	21	.310	.229
Throws Right	R	.280	125	35	5	2	6	26	14	38	.359	.496
Estrada,Marco	L	.190	343	65	12	2	11	30	36	86	.270	.332
Throws Right	R	.218	308	67	14	2	12	37	29	79	.287	.393
Eveland,Dana	L	.361	36	13	1	0	2	7	7	9	.467	.556
Throws Left	R	.317	60	19	5	1	1	7	12	12	.446	.483
Familia,Jeurys	L	.239	134	32	10	0	0	15	14	37	.315	.313
Throws Right	R	.204	152	31	3	0	1	10	17	47	.282	.243
Farmer,Buck	L	.233	60	14	2	2	4	13	12	12	.370	.533
Throws Right	R	.229	48	11	2	0	0	5	8	15	.333	.271
Farquhar,Danny	L	.235	51	12	0	0	4	11	4	19	.304	.471
Throws Right	R	.244	86	21	5	0	4	14	11	27	.350	.442
Faulkner,Andrew	L	.250	12	3	0	0	0	0	2	1	.357	.250
Throws Left	R	.313	16	5	0	0	3	6	2	0	.389	.875
Feldman,Scott	L	.325	123	40	8	1	4	12	13	20	.387	.504
Throws Right	R	.254	185	47	9	2	6	26	6	36	.286	.422
Feliz,Michael	L	.237	114	27	4	0	5	22	11	44	.302	.404
Throws Right	R	.212	132	28	3	0	5	16	11	51	.271	.348
Feliz,Neftali	L	.180	89	16	4	0	5	9	8	25	.247	.393
Throws Right	R	.231	104	24	5	0	5	16	13	36	.319	.423
Fernandez,Jose	L	.244	353	86	16	3	8	33	40	111	.319	.374
Throws Right	R	.203	311	63	13	0	5	24	15	142	.250	.293
Fields,Josh	L	.286	56	16	4	2	0	8	6	9	.359	.429
Throws Right	R	.303	89	27	6	1	4	16	5	33	.340	.528
Fien,Casey	L	.279	61	17	2	2	4	6	3	18	.313	.574
Throws Right	R	.289	97	28	4	0	9	16	7	17	.337	.608
Fiers,Mike	L	.272	294	80	18	1	9	31	18	59	.317	.432
Throws Right	R	.287	373	107	29	1	17	45	24	75	.336	.507
Finnegan,Brandon	L	.218	142	31	5	1	2	6	20	28	.323	.310
Throws Left	R	.241	494	119	16	4	27	73	64	117	.327	.453

Pitcher	vs	Avg	AB	H	2B	3B	HR	RBI	BB	SO	OBP	Slg
Fister,Doug	L	.321	377	121	27	3	19	56	37	55	.386	.560
Throws Right	R	.225	329	74	17	0	5	27	25	60	.284	.322
Flande,Yohan	L	.400	5	2	1	0	0	1	0	0	.400	.600
Throws Left	R	.545	11	6	1	1	0	6	3	0	.643	.818
Floro,Dylan	L	.346	26	9	1	0	0	4	2	5	.393	.385
Throws Right	R	.350	40	14	4	0	0	6	3	9	.386	.450
Floyd,Gavin	L	.111	45	5	1	0	2	3	4	11	.184	.267
Throws Right	R	.269	67	18	5	0	2	11	4	19	.333	.433
Flynn,Brian	L	.191	68	13	2	0	2	9	8	15	.276	.309
Throws Left	R	.202	124	25	5	0	3	13	15	29	.291	.315
Foltynewicz,Mike	L	.251	215	54	13	2	9	25	21	52	.320	.456
Throws Right	R	.273	260	71	12	1	9	30	14	59	.319	.431
Freeman,Sam	L	.333	12	4	1	0	0	1	3	4	.467	.417
Throws Left	R	.429	21	9	1	0	2	9	6	4	.517	.762
Friedrich,Christian	L	.239	113	27	5	0	4	15	8	26	.287	.389
Throws Left	R	.265	392	104	21	4	9	44	44	74	.339	.408
Fulmer,Carson	L	.261	23	6	1	0	1	3	5	6	.393	.435
Throws Right	R	.286	21	6	0	1	1	3	2	4	.400	.524
Fulmer,Michael	L	.222	302	67	13	0	6	24	26	60	.297	.325
Throws Right	R	.240	288	69	14	1	10	32	16	72	.284	.399
Gallardo,Yovani	L	.270	196	53	9	1	7	32	35	45	.374	.434
Throws Right	R	.281	260	73	18	2	9	34	26	40	.346	.469
Gamboa,Eddie	L	.238	21	5	1	0	0	0	2	5	.304	.286
Throws Right	R	.160	25	4	0	0	1	1	6	6	.323	.280
Gant,John	L	.248	105	26	8	1	3	14	14	26	.336	.429
Throws Right	R	.315	89	28	4	2	4	18	7	23	.370	.539
Garcia,Jaime	L	.246	134	33	7	1	4	12	7	32	.299	.403
Throws Left	R	.273	534	146	33	0	22	65	50	118	.339	.459
Garcia,Luis	L	.378	37	14	5	0	1	11	2	6	.415	.595
Throws Right	R	.241	29	7	1	0	1	3	6	8	.371	.379
Garcia,Yimi	L	.385	13	5	0	0	0	3	1	1	.429	.385
Throws Right	R	.250	16	4	0	0	0	3	0	3	.263	.250
Garner,Perci	L	.353	17	6	0	0	0	1	1	3	.389	.353
Throws Right	R	.273	22	6	0	1	0	2	4	9	.429	.364
Garton,Ryan	L	.315	54	17	3	0	2	9	6	12	.383	.481
Throws Right	R	.257	105	27	3	0	3	8	5	21	.291	.371
Garza,Matt	L	.292	195	57	10	1	7	31	23	27	.364	.462
Throws Right	R	.274	219	60	17	0	4	32	13	43	.321	.406
Gausman,Kevin	L	.232	323	75	15	1	11	30	17	82	.272	.387
Throws Right	R	.288	375	108	16	0	17	43	30	92	.345	.467
Gearrin,Cory	L	.209	43	9	3	0	1	6	6	9	.306	.349
Throws Right	R	.241	137	33	2	3	3	23	8	36	.284	.365
Gee,Dillon	L	.303	241	73	7	1	10	35	25	40	.370	.465
Throws Right	R	.280	261	73	7	1	14	32	12	49	.320	.475
Geltz,Steve	L	.174	46	8	1	0	3	9	2	9	.220	.391
Throws Right	R	.291	55	16	0	0	8	12	7	14	.371	.727
Germen,Gonzalez	L	.328	67	22	8	1	1	11	17	7	.459	.522
Throws Right	R	.218	87	19	4	0	4	10	8	25	.292	.402
Gibson,Kyle	L	.326	279	91	14	3	9	40	28	45	.392	.495
Throws Right	R	.273	308	84	15	0	11	40	27	59	.331	.429
Giles,Ken	L	.214	126	27	6	0	2	10	12	46	.281	.310
Throws Right	R	.254	130	33	7	3	6	20	13	56	.331	.492
Gilmartin,Sean	L	.226	31	7	0	0	1	4	2	7	.294	.323
Throws Left	R	.359	39	14	2	0	3	10	5	4	.432	.641
Giolito,Lucas	L	.277	47	13	2	0	3	5	7	7	.370	.511
Throws Right	R	.317	41	13	2	1	4	12	5	4	.404	.707
Girodo,Chad	L	.211	19	4	1	0	0	2	1	4	.250	.263
Throws Left	R	.318	22	7	1	0	3	4	1	1	.375	.773
Givens,Mychal	L	.366	82	30	7	0	3	14	15	22	.464	.561
Throws Right	R	.156	186	29	7	0	3	19	21	74	.262	.242
Glasnow,Tyler	L	.308	39	12	1	1	0	3	8	9	.426	.385
Throws Right	R	.204	49	10	3	1	2	5	5	15	.316	.429
Glover,Koda	L	.176	34	6	3	0	1	4	5	9	.282	.353
Throws Right	R	.220	41	9	2	0	2	6	2	7	.273	.415
Godley,Zack	L	.289	135	39	9	2	6	26	17	32	.373	.519
Throws Right	R	.288	163	47	5	2	7	28	8	28	.331	.472
Goeddel,Erik	L	.231	52	12	0	0	2	4	8	14	.344	.346
Throws Right	R	.236	89	21	7	1	3	12	6	22	.281	.438
Goforth,David	L	.381	21	8	2	0	0	4	2	5	.435	.476
Throws Right	R	.333	30	10	4	0	3	8	2	4	.375	.767
Gomez,Jeanmar	L	.287	115	33	6	2	4	18	13	15	.359	.478
Throws Right	R	.290	155	45	7	0	2	19	9	32	.331	.374
Gonzalez,Chi Chi	L	.412	34	14	0	0	0	10	5	4	.475	.412
Throws Right	R	.389	18	7	2	0	1	3	4	3	.500	.667
Gonzalez,Gio	L	.241	145	35	8	1	1	15	10	31	.302	.331
Throws Left	R	.267	539	144	26	2	18	64	49	140	.333	.423

Pitchers vs. Left-Handed and Right-Handed Batters

Pitcher	vs	Avg	AB	H	2B	3B	HR	RBI	BB	SO	OBP	Slg
Gonzalez,Miguel	L	.237	262	62	13	0	7	21	25	50	.308	.366
Throws Right	R	.272	257	70	17	1	4	32	10	45	.304	.393
Gonzalez,Severino	L	.302	63	19	5	0	4	10	4	8	.338	.571
Throws Right	R	.273	77	21	7	2	0	13	3	26	.301	.416
Goody,Nick	L	.375	40	15	4	1	2	12	4	10	.422	.675
Throws Right	R	.205	73	15	4	0	5	12	8	24	.293	.466
Gott,Trevor	L	.333	9	3	1	0	0	1	0	1	.333	.444
Throws Right	R	.200	15	3	1	0	0	2	3	5	.368	.267
Graveman,Kendall	L	.272	390	106	22	2	10	36	35	61	.336	.415
Throws Right	R	.270	333	90	12	0	12	41	12	47	.299	.414
Gray,Jon	L	.239	327	78	9	4	11	47	28	97	.303	.391
Throws Right	R	.248	303	75	19	0	7	35	31	88	.332	.380
Gray,Sonny	L	.286	234	67	15	0	6	34	16	49	.329	.427
Throws Right	R	.286	231	66	15	2	12	38	26	45	.356	.524
Green,Chad	L	.291	86	25	5	0	9	15	7	26	.351	.663
Throws Right	R	.255	94	24	4	0	3	11	8	26	.311	.394
Greene,Shane	L	.283	106	30	9	1	2	14	9	24	.345	.443
Throws Right	R	.233	120	28	1	0	1	17	13	35	.319	.267
Gregerson,Luke	L	.212	99	21	5	2	4	16	16	23	.322	.424
Throws Right	R	.156	109	17	6	1	1	6	2	44	.183	.257
Greinke,Zack	L	.256	344	88	21	2	14	43	20	78	.294	.451
Throws Right	R	.269	271	73	12	3	9	33	21	56	.321	.435
Griffin,A.J.	L	.286	220	63	10	5	18	36	23	52	.355	.623
Throws Right	R	.227	233	53	7	0	10	27	23	55	.311	.386
Grilli,Jason	L	.213	89	19	1	2	7	16	21	36	.372	.506
Throws Right	R	.200	125	25	4	3	3	7	11	45	.261	.352
Grimm,Justin	L	.267	86	23	5	0	2	11	8	36	.337	.395
Throws Right	R	.209	115	24	6	0	3	11	15	29	.300	.339
Gsellman,Robert	L	.230	74	17	4	0	0	3	8	23	.305	.284
Throws Right	R	.281	89	25	3	0	1	7	7	19	.333	.348
Guaipe,Mayckol	L	.250	8	2	0	0	0	1	2	1	.364	.250
Throws Right	R	.286	21	6	1	0	0	4	2	4	.348	.333
Guerra,Deolis	L	.210	105	22	4	0	2	14	2	19	.236	.305
Throws Right	R	.288	104	30	8	0	4	12	5	17	.321	.481
Guerra,Javy	L	.000	3	0	0	0	0	0	4	0	.571	.000
Throws Right	R	.263	19	5	1	0	1	3	3	4	.391	.474
Guerra,Junior	L	.191	194	37	11	1	5	15	24	46	.283	.335
Throws Right	R	.231	247	57	10	3	5	22	19	54	.289	.356
Gurka,Jason	L	.077	13	1	0	0	0	0	0	2	.077	.077
Throws Left	R	.517	29	15	3	1	1	13	2	5	.531	.793
Gustave,Jandel	L	.250	24	6	1	0	0	1	3	7	.333	.292
Throws Right	R	.219	32	7	2	0	2	7	1	9	.242	.469
Hahn,Jesse	L	.361	83	30	2	1	7	19	7	10	.407	.663
Throws Right	R	.273	99	27	3	0	1	7	12	13	.351	.333
Hamels,Cole	L	.208	149	31	4	0	4	12	17	35	.289	.315
Throws Left	R	.252	611	154	26	1	20	67	60	165	.326	.396
Hammel,Jason	L	.239	255	61	16	3	11	32	34	61	.342	.455
Throws Right	R	.238	365	87	15	1	14	40	19	83	.279	.400
Hand,Brad	L	.125	120	15	4	1	1	9	15	46	.221	.200
Throws Left	R	.236	203	48	8	0	7	29	21	65	.310	.379
Happ,J.A.	L	.245	147	36	4	1	3	15	12	29	.304	.347
Throws Left	R	.228	579	132	27	1	19	47	48	134	.292	.377
Hardy,Blaine	L	.200	35	7	3	1	0	4	5	5	.300	.343
Throws Left	R	.281	64	18	1	0	2	11	7	15	.352	.391
Harrell,Lucas	L	.226	84	19	3	1	3	10	11	20	.313	.393
Throws Right	R	.297	91	27	4	1	1	10	14	16	.409	.396
Harris,Will	L	.204	113	23	4	0	1	6	6	38	.248	.265
Throws Right	R	.236	123	29	4	0	2	9	9	31	.286	.317
Hart,Donnie	L	.132	38	5	1	0	0	4	3	11	.190	.158
Throws Left	R	.292	24	7	0	0	1	1	3	1	.370	.417
Harvey,Matt	L	.321	190	61	15	3	4	30	16	39	.370	.495
Throws Right	R	.282	177	50	6	2	4	21	9	37	.317	.407
Hatcher,Chris	L	.150	60	9	0	0	1	2	11	16	.282	.200
Throws Right	R	.316	98	31	7	2	7	21	10	27	.385	.643
Hathaway,Steve	L	.333	36	12	3	0	1	5	4	10	.400	.500
Throws Left	R	.261	23	6	3	0	0	1	2	5	.320	.391
Hayes,Drew	L	.476	21	10	2	0	2	9	3	1	.542	.857
Throws Right	R	.238	21	5	1	0	1	4	3	7	.333	.429
Heaney,Andrew	L	.167	6	1	0	0	1	3	0	1	.167	.667
Throws Left	R	.316	19	6	1	0	1	1	0	6	.316	.526
Heller,Ben	L	.200	15	3	0	0	0	0	3	4	.368	.200
Throws Right	R	.421	19	8	3	0	3	9	1	2	.476	1.053
Hellickson,Jeremy	L	.257	331	85	19	2	11	31	32	65	.325	.426
Throws Right	R	.232	380	88	25	2	13	43	13	89	.261	.411
Hembree,Heath	L	.338	71	24	5	0	2	7	7	12	.397	.493
Throws Right	R	.201	134	27	6	0	4	18	10	35	.255	.336

Pitcher	vs	Avg	AB	H	2B	3B	HR	RBI	BB	SO	OBP	Slg
Henderson,Jim	L	.245	49	12	3	0	2	4	5	15	.327	.429
Throws Right	R	.250	88	22	1	2	5	12	9	25	.323	.477
Hendricks,Kyle	L	.219	292	64	15	1	6	16	17	71	.277	.339
Throws Right	R	.198	394	78	13	1	9	26	27	99	.251	.305
Hendriks,Liam	L	.228	101	23	5	0	2	8	6	33	.271	.337
Throws Right	R	.297	155	46	6	2	4	25	8	38	.327	.439
Hernandez,David	L	.264	129	34	6	0	8	18	18	36	.356	.496
Throws Right	R	.276	156	43	9	0	3	13	14	44	.339	.391
Hernandez,Felix	L	.252	258	65	14	1	8	26	30	50	.332	.407
Throws Right	R	.229	319	73	13	1	11	43	35	72	.322	.379
Hernandez,Roberto	L	.417	12	5	0	0	2	2	1	2	.462	.917
Throws Right	R	.320	25	8	1	0	2	5	0	4	.308	.600
Herrera,Kelvin	L	.206	136	28	7	0	2	14	8	40	.255	.301
Throws Right	R	.223	130	29	7	0	4	11	4	46	.255	.369
Herrmann,Frank	L	.269	26	7	0	0	4	15	5	7	.387	.731
Throws Right	R	.361	36	13	4	0	3	8	0	7	.378	.722
Hessler,Keith	L	.278	36	10	3	1	1	6	7	6	.395	.500
Throws Left	R	.269	52	14	5	0	1	4	6	5	.356	.423
Heston,Chris	L	.300	10	3	1	0	0	3	2	2	.417	.400
Throws Right	R	.500	12	6	2	1	0	6	4	1	.625	.833
Hill,Rich	L	.218	87	19	2	1	0	3	3	17	.258	.264
Throws Left	R	.188	308	58	8	1	4	22	30	112	.272	.260
Hinojosa,Dalier	L	.235	17	4	1	0	0	2	2	3	.316	.294
Throws Right	R	.261	23	6	0	0	1	2	1	5	.280	.391
Hochevar,Luke	L	.164	55	9	0	1	1	3	6	19	.270	.255
Throws Right	R	.268	82	22	4	1	5	16	3	21	.299	.524
Hoffman,Jeff	L	.288	66	19	4	0	3	14	9	6	.373	.485
Throws Right	R	.286	63	18	4	0	4	11	8	16	.366	.540
Holder,Jonathan	L	.143	7	1	1	0	0	2	0	1	.125	.286
Throws Right	R	.292	24	7	1	0	1	2	4	4	.393	.458
Holland,Derek	L	.247	77	19	0	0	1	4	5	17	.293	.286
Throws Left	R	.282	344	97	21	1	14	54	30	50	.341	.471
Hoover,J.J.	L	.368	38	14	4	0	2	10	4	4	.442	.632
Throws Right	R	.326	46	15	3	0	7	22	8	11	.426	.848
Howell,J.P.	L	.299	97	29	3	1	2	13	4	22	.340	.412
Throws Left	R	.265	102	27	3	1	2	11	11	22	.336	.373
Hoyt,James	L	.212	33	7	1	0	2	2	2	10	.278	.424
Throws Right	R	.196	46	9	1	0	3	11	7	18	.296	.413
Hudson,Daniel	L	.283	113	32	6	1	3	17	11	23	.357	.434
Throws Right	R	.256	129	33	7	1	3	18	11	35	.324	.395
Huff,David	L	.200	5	1	0	0	0	0	0	1	.200	.200
Throws Left	R	.522	23	12	2	0	4	10	2	2	.538	1.130
Hughes,Jared	L	.278	97	27	8	3	3	16	8	5	.333	.515
Throws Right	R	.276	127	35	5	0	3	16	14	29	.366	.386
Hughes,Phil	L	.385	78	30	4	0	2	10	9	12	.443	.513
Throws Right	R	.279	165	46	8	1	9	24	4	22	.294	.503
Hunter,Tommy	L	.313	48	15	3	0	0	6	2	8	.340	.375
Throws Right	R	.250	80	20	4	0	1	9	6	15	.318	.338
Hutchison,Drew	L	.343	35	12	1	0	2	5	4	6	.415	.543
Throws Right	R	.281	57	16	3	0	4	9	3	16	.323	.544
Iglesias,Raisel	L	.266	139	37	8	1	5	12	12	28	.331	.446
Throws Right	R	.171	152	26	3	0	2	10	14	55	.253	.230
Iwakuma,Hisashi	L	.290	359	104	20	1	11	42	17	65	.323	.443
Throws Right	R	.276	413	114	23	1	17	46	29	82	.325	.460
Jackson,Edwin	L	.260	146	38	9	1	4	21	25	27	.368	.418
Throws Right	R	.302	179	54	10	3	10	38	16	34	.355	.559
Jackson,Luke	L	.462	26	12	4	0	2	6	4	1	.533	.846
Throws Right	R	.370	27	10	0	0	2	8	4	2	.438	.593
Jansen,Kenley	L	.191	115	22	7	0	2	8	6	52	.238	.304
Throws Right	R	.109	119	13	1	2	2	6	5	52	.151	.202
Jeffress,Jeremy	L	.333	90	30	9	0	2	9	8	18	.406	.500
Throws Right	R	.198	126	25	2	0	0	10	10	24	.261	.214
Jenkins,Tyrell	L	.286	70	20	3	0	3	10	18	10	.427	.457
Throws Right	R	.276	127	35	8	1	8	20	15	16	.352	.543
Jennings,Dan	L	.217	83	18	5	1	1	16	12	20	.316	.337
Throws Left	R	.285	137	39	3	2	0	17	16	26	.358	.336
Jepsen,Kevin	L	.333	72	24	3	0	8	20	7	12	.378	.708
Throws Right	R	.304	125	38	9	1	4	19	14	23	.366	.488
Jimenez,Ubaldo	L	.294	235	69	16	2	10	35	31	59	.378	.506
Throws Right	R	.249	325	81	14	1	6	49	41	66	.336	.354
Johnson,Erik	L	.281	64	18	3	1	6	15	3	12	.300	.641
Throws Right	R	.412	68	28	4	1	8	11	8	9	.474	.853
Johnson,Jim	L	.218	119	26	7	0	1	7	9	37	.288	.303
Throws Right	R	.252	123	31	5	1	2	10	11	31	.313	.358
Johnson,Steve	L	.208	24	5	0	0	1	1	6	5	.367	.333
Throws Right	R	.205	39	8	1	0	2	5	5	12	.289	.385

Pitchers vs. Left-Handed and Right-Handed Batters

Pitcher	vs	Avg	AB	H	2B	3B	HR	RBI	BB	SO	OBP	Slg
Jones,Nate	L	.200	100	20	4	1	5	10	7	38	.257	.410
Throws Right	R	.184	152	28	3	0	2	14	8	42	.233	.243
Jungmann,Taylor	L	.289	45	13	5	2	1	11	10	6	.411	.556
Throws Right	R	.293	58	17	6	1	3	10	7	12	.391	.586
Kahnle,Tommy	L	.143	35	5	1	0	1	3	9	7	.318	.257
Throws Right	R	.250	64	16	5	0	1	7	11	18	.360	.375
Karns,Nathan	L	.206	170	35	8	0	4	17	25	54	.305	.324
Throws Right	R	.305	197	60	13	2	7	30	20	47	.377	.497
Kazmir,Scott	L	.224	143	32	4	1	4	17	12	27	.297	.350
Throws Left	R	.264	383	101	25	1	17	49	40	107	.337	.467
Kela,Keone	L	.175	40	7	2	0	1	8	5	12	.277	.300
Throws Right	R	.264	87	23	4	1	5	15	12	33	.366	.506
Kelley,Shawn	L	.225	80	18	4	2	5	8	6	26	.279	.513
Throws Right	R	.176	131	23	7	1	4	17	5	54	.203	.336
Kelly,Casey	L	.361	36	13	4	1	0	4	2	1	.410	.528
Throws Right	R	.304	56	17	4	1	1	11	5	6	.365	.464
Kelly,Joe	L	.269	52	14	2	0	3	9	13	15	.418	.481
Throws Right	R	.283	106	30	7	2	2	17	11	33	.347	.443
Kennedy,Ian	L	.224	379	85	21	0	16	41	35	89	.303	.406
Throws Right	R	.249	354	88	8	1	17	34	31	95	.315	.421
Kensing,Logan	L	.300	10	3	0	0	0	1	1	0	.364	.300
Throws Right	R	.556	9	5	1	0	0	0	1	1	.600	.667
Kershaw,Clayton	L	.138	138	19	3	0	0	2	2	52	.150	.159
Throws Left	R	.201	388	78	15	1	8	24	9	120	.223	.307
Keuchel,Dallas	L	.237	139	33	5	1	2	11	6	30	.272	.331
Throws Left	R	.265	509	135	30	5	18	71	42	114	.322	.450
Kiekhefer,Dean	L	.209	43	9	2	0	1	5	3	12	.261	.326
Throws Left	R	.333	45	15	2	1	1	17	4	2	.404	.489
Kimbrel,Craig	L	.145	83	12	2	0	2	9	12	36	.273	.241
Throws Right	R	.158	101	16	5	0	2	12	18	47	.292	.267
Kintzler,Brandon	L	.250	92	23	4	0	3	7	4	13	.281	.391
Throws Right	R	.295	122	36	5	1	2	10	4	22	.328	.402
Klein,Phil	L	.342	38	13	3	0	1	4	5	8	.409	.500
Throws Right	R	.286	35	10	2	0	1	9	4	11	.375	.429
Kluber,Corey	L	.226	376	85	19	2	9	28	29	96	.289	.359
Throws Right	R	.206	412	85	20	1	13	42	28	131	.261	.354
Knebel,Corey	L	.172	64	11	0	1	1	6	8	19	.260	.250
Throws Right	R	.333	63	21	2	1	2	8	8	19	.417	.492
Koch,Matt	L	.115	26	3	0	0	0	0	4	5	.233	.115
Throws Right	R	.167	36	6	3	0	1	2	0	5	.211	.333
Koehler,Tom	L	.259	355	92	19	1	12	39	51	87	.353	.420
Throws Right	R	.263	320	84	19	1	10	40	32	60	.333	.422
Kontos,George	L	.243	74	18	2	0	1	7	12	15	.349	.311
Throws Right	R	.203	118	24	4	1	2	13	8	20	.264	.305
Krol,Ian	L	.287	87	25	2	2	1	17	3	24	.330	.391
Throws Left	R	.259	112	29	3	0	3	13	10	32	.320	.366
Kuhl,Chad	L	.301	123	37	10	1	4	15	10	19	.358	.496
Throws Right	R	.240	150	36	12	0	3	15	10	34	.296	.380
Lackey,John	L	.242	277	67	14	2	6	24	30	67	.322	.372
Throws Right	R	.201	393	79	11	0	17	39	23	113	.251	.359
Lamb,John	L	.279	68	19	1	0	2	6	7	14	.355	.382
Throws Left	R	.311	209	65	15	0	12	38	24	44	.380	.555
Latos,Mat	L	.229	140	32	8	1	7	17	19	19	.317	.450
Throws Right	R	.321	131	42	4	1	4	18	11	23	.370	.458
Law,Derek	L	.188	80	15	3	1	2	7	1	20	.198	.325
Throws Right	R	.232	125	29	4	2	1	8	8	30	.278	.320
Layne,Tommy	L	.216	88	19	1	0	1	5	10	21	.310	.261
Throws Left	R	.247	73	18	5	0	2	12	11	17	.353	.397
Leake,Mike	L	.269	323	87	17	1	13	41	18	59	.312	.449
Throws Right	R	.304	382	116	22	2	7	52	12	66	.325	.427
LeBlanc,Wade	L	.224	49	11	5	0	2	6	1	9	.231	.449
Throws Left	R	.253	190	48	11	1	12	26	10	42	.290	.511
Leclerc,Jose	L	.294	17	5	4	0	0	0	9	4	.538	.529
Throws Right	R	.171	35	6	3	0	0	5	4	11	.250	.257
Leone,Dominic	L	.378	45	17	5	0	3	7	9	11	.481	.689
Throws Right	R	.400	70	28	4	0	4	22	3	12	.416	.629
Lester,Jon	L	.200	170	34	8	0	3	8	8	48	.240	.300
Throws Left	R	.214	560	120	17	1	18	43	44	149	.276	.345
Lewis,Colby	L	.229	205	47	6	1	8	24	17	30	.293	.385
Throws Right	R	.241	232	56	10	1	11	27	11	43	.276	.435
Liberatore,Adam	L	.171	82	14	4	1	0	7	7	18	.250	.244
Throws Left	R	.274	73	20	5	0	2	8	10	29	.357	.425
Light,Pat	L	.200	25	5	0	0	1	5	6	5	.355	.320
Throws Right	R	.347	49	17	3	1	3	17	10	11	.467	.633
Lincecum,Tim	L	.367	98	36	4	1	4	14	4	21	.388	.551
Throws Right	R	.432	74	32	6	1	7	26	19	11	.552	.824

Pitcher	vs	Avg	AB	H	2B	3B	HR	RBI	BB	SO	OBP	Slg
Liriano,Francisco	L	.239	142	34	4	2	5	17	15	37	.337	.401
Throws Left	R	.255	482	123	19	2	21	68	70	131	.349	.434
Lobstein,Kyle	L	.083	24	2	0	0	0	1	5	8	.241	.083
Throws Left	R	.324	71	23	7	0	2	7	7	7	.400	.507
Locke,Jeff	L	.282	142	40	8	0	4	24	9	21	.329	.423
Throws Left	R	.305	364	111	27	4	13	52	35	52	.368	.508
Loewen,Adam	L	.222	9	2	0	0	0	1	2	1	.333	.222
Throws Left	R	.385	13	5	0	0	1	6	4	2	.526	.615
Logan,Boone	L	.142	106	15	7	1	1	13	9	40	.222	.255
Throws Left	R	.211	57	12	3	0	3	11	11	17	.338	.421
Lohse,Kyle	L	.381	21	8	2	1	1	4	3	2	.458	.714
Throws Right	R	.333	21	7	1	0	3	9	2	1	.375	.810
Lopez,Javier	L	.211	76	16	2	0	2	8	10	10	.318	.316
Throws Left	R	.333	24	8	1	0	1	4	5	5	.448	.500
Lopez,Reynaldo	L	.193	88	17	4	0	4	16	13	23	.291	.375
Throws Right	R	.353	85	30	10	0	0	9	9	19	.415	.471
Lorenzen,Michael	L	.202	89	18	2	0	1	6	8	16	.290	.258
Throws Right	R	.245	94	23	3	0	4	9	5	32	.304	.404
Loup,Aaron	L	.250	24	6	0	0	2	6	1	7	.321	.500
Throws Left	R	.321	28	9	5	0	0	3	3	8	.382	.500
Lowe,Mark	L	.253	87	22	5	2	5	16	10	25	.320	.529
Throws Right	R	.321	109	35	6	2	7	32	11	24	.379	.606
Luebke,Cory	L	.364	11	4	1	0	1	2	2	3	.462	.727
Throws Left	R	.393	28	11	3	0	1	7	9	6	.538	.607
Lugo,Seth	L	.196	102	20	2	2	4	9	15	18	.299	.373
Throws Right	R	.240	121	29	7	0	3	10	6	27	.289	.372
Lyles,Jordan	L	.316	95	30	8	1	2	17	16	8	.417	.484
Throws Right	R	.275	142	39	8	0	2	20	12	24	.340	.373
Lyons,Tyler	L	.156	64	10	0	0	2	4	5	14	.214	.250
Throws Left	R	.234	107	25	7	0	7	16	9	32	.293	.495
Madson,Ryan	L	.244	119	29	2	1	5	14	8	23	.291	.403
Throws Right	R	.270	126	34	6	0	2	12	12	26	.340	.365
Maeda,Kenta	L	.247	299	74	14	1	10	28	33	65	.328	.401
Throws Right	R	.213	356	76	7	1	10	39	17	114	.257	.323
Magill,Matt	L	.400	5	2	0	0	0	0	4	1	.667	.400
Throws Right	R	.333	9	3	0	0	1	3	1	0	.400	.667
Mahle,Greg	L	.333	39	13	0	0	2	8	5	7	.435	.487
Throws Left	R	.294	34	10	4	0	2	7	5	7	.385	.588
Manaea,Sean	L	.180	100	18	3	0	3	6	4	28	.226	.300
Throws Left	R	.263	445	117	24	2	17	55	33	96	.314	.440
Maness,Seth	L	.244	45	11	1	0	1	3	4	6	.306	.333
Throws Right	R	.291	79	23	11	0	1	13	4	10	.321	.468
Manship,Jeff	L	.241	58	14	3	1	3	9	6	9	.313	.483
Throws Right	R	.241	108	26	4	0	4	12	16	27	.336	.389
Marinez,Jhan	L	.255	102	26	6	1	2	13	10	21	.325	.392
Throws Right	R	.263	137	36	8	0	2	20	11	29	.340	.365
Mariot,Michael	L	.311	45	14	2	0	5	13	7	11	.404	.689
Throws Right	R	.111	36	4	1	0	0	3	7	12	.256	.139
Marks,Justin	L	.313	16	5	0	0	0	0	2	3	.389	.313
Throws Left	R	.118	17	2	1	0	1	1	7	3	.375	.353
Marquez,German	L	.341	44	15	5	2	0	6	4	7	.388	.545
Throws Right	R	.310	42	13	2	1	2	6	2	8	.383	.548
Marshall,Evan	L	.417	24	10	2	0	1	9	3	4	.481	.625
Throws Right	R	.391	46	18	7	0	1	15	5	5	.462	.609
Martin,Cody	L	.314	35	11	2	0	0	3	7	4	.429	.371
Throws Right	R	.288	59	17	1	0	5	8	2	11	.317	.559
Martinez,Carlos	L	.256	390	100	16	1	11	43	48	84	.342	.387
Throws Right	R	.207	334	69	9	0	4	24	22	90	.270	.269
Martinez,Nick	L	.310	71	22	6	0	5	12	12	6	.417	.606
Throws Right	R	.274	84	23	4	1	3	10	7	10	.358	.452
Matusz,Brian	L	.467	15	7	1	0	2	6	5	1	.619	.933
Throws Left	R	.385	26	10	0	0	4	9	4	2	.452	.846
Matz,Steven	L	.269	119	32	7	0	2	13	6	25	.320	.378
Throws Left	R	.253	383	97	12	1	12	38	25	104	.302	.384
Maurer,Brandon	L	.213	136	29	4	2	3	16	18	41	.310	.338
Throws Right	R	.263	137	36	11	0	4	25	5	31	.292	.431
May,Trevor	L	.153	59	9	1	0	2	7	10	22	.275	.271
Throws Right	R	.275	109	30	12	1	5	23	7	38	.331	.541
Mayers,Mike	L	.500	14	7	0	0	1	6	1	1	.533	.714
Throws Right	R	.563	16	9	1	0	2	6	2	1	.600	1.000
McAllister,Zach	L	.242	99	24	4	0	3	9	10	22	.318	.374
Throws Right	R	.269	108	29	9	0	3	16	13	32	.352	.435
McCarthy,Brandon	L	.241	58	14	3	0	1	10	13	20	.375	.345
Throws Right	R	.183	82	15	5	0	1	8	13	24	.306	.280
McCarthy,Kevin	L	.333	18	6	2	0	1	5	3	4	.429	.611
Throws Right	R	.294	17	5	0	0	0	3	2	3	.368	.294

Pitchers vs. Left-Handed and Right-Handed Batters

Pitcher	vs	Avg	AB	H	2B	3B	HR	RBI	BB	SO	OBP	Slg
McCullers,Lance	L	.273	150	41	9	2	2	12	18	62	.351	.400
Throws Right	R	.248	157	39	7	1	3	14	27	44	.359	.363
McFarland,T.J.	L	.367	49	18	6	0	0	6	3	3	.426	.490
Throws Left	R	.313	48	15	3	0	3	13	7	4	.379	.563
McGee,Jake	L	.297	64	19	7	1	0	6	6	16	.384	.438
Throws Left	R	.303	122	37	5	0	9	20	10	22	.356	.566
McGowan,Dustin	L	.290	93	27	5	2	4	13	18	18	.402	.516
Throws Right	R	.148	149	22	2	1	3	12	15	45	.234	.235
McHugh,Collin	L	.291	347	101	18	3	11	38	29	88	.348	.455
Throws Right	R	.274	383	105	22	3	14	44	25	89	.320	.457
Medlen,Kris	L	.288	52	15	5	0	2	11	10	8	.391	.500
Throws Right	R	.333	45	15	4	0	0	5	10	10	.455	.422
Melancon,Mark	L	.221	113	25	4	0	1	8	8	32	.276	.283
Throws Right	R	.190	142	27	4	0	2	11	4	33	.211	.261
Melville,Tim	L	.333	12	4	0	0	1	3	7	2	.579	.583
Throws Right	R	.400	30	12	3	0	4	9	2	6	.455	.900
Mengden,Daniel	L	.283	138	39	11	2	3	17	18	34	.367	.457
Throws Right	R	.286	154	44	6	1	6	29	15	37	.360	.455
Merritt,Ryan	L	.286	7	2	0	0	0	2	0	1	.286	.286
Throws Left	R	.138	29	4	1	0	0	1	0	5	.138	.172
Meyer,Alex	L	.316	38	12	4	1	2	6	6	9	.391	.632
Throws Right	R	.217	60	13	6	0	1	5	11	20	.338	.367
Miley,Wade	L	.234	128	30	8	0	3	12	12	28	.303	.367
Throws Left	R	.301	521	157	31	1	22	78	37	109	.351	.491
Miller,Andrew	L	.181	72	13	2	0	3	5	1	32	.189	.333
Throws Left	R	.153	190	29	7	1	5	11	8	91	.195	.279
Miller,Justin	L	.349	63	22	3	4	4	21	8	17	.411	.714
Throws Right	R	.267	105	28	7	0	2	12	12	28	.350	.390
Miller,Shelby	L	.329	231	76	18	2	9	39	28	36	.402	.541
Throws Right	R	.285	179	51	11	0	5	29	14	34	.337	.430
Milone,Tommy	L	.276	58	16	2	0	4	11	4	10	.333	.517
Throws Left	R	.305	223	68	12	0	11	36	18	39	.352	.507
Minaya,Juan	L	.200	20	4	2	0	0	2	4	3	.360	.300
Throws Right	R	.300	20	6	2	0	0	1	1	3	.364	.400
Miranda,Ariel	L	.310	42	13	4	0	1	5	5	9	.383	.476
Throws Left	R	.200	170	34	8	1	11	21	13	35	.254	.453
Mitchell,Bryan	L	.270	37	10	2	1	0	5	6	9	.372	.378
Throws Right	R	.281	57	16	3	0	1	7	6	2	.349	.386
Molleken,Dustin	L	.267	15	4	2	0	0	3	1	4	.294	.400
Throws Right	R	.381	21	8	1	0	0	2	4	4	.480	.429
Montero,Rafael	L	.424	33	14	2	2	0	3	7	6	.525	.606
Throws Right	R	.205	44	9	1	0	4	13	9	14	.340	.500
Montgomery,Mike	L	.183	115	21	7	0	2	13	13	31	.275	.296
Throws Left	R	.236	246	58	12	1	6	24	25	61	.325	.366
Moore,Matt	L	.240	171	41	3	1	5	22	13	42	.297	.357
Throws Left	R	.246	581	143	22	0	20	64	59	136	.319	.387
Morgan,Adam	L	.259	112	29	7	0	3	9	9	26	.331	.402
Throws Left	R	.316	354	112	26	3	20	64	20	69	.351	.576
Morimando,Shawn	L	.429	7	3	0	1	0	0	1	2	.500	.714
Throws Left	R	.400	15	6	0	0	2	5	4	3	.526	.800
Morin,Mike	L	.257	74	19	3	0	2	13	11	16	.353	.378
Throws Right	R	.246	134	33	5	0	4	19	4	33	.271	.373
Morris,A.J.	L	.200	20	4	1	1	0	2	4	5	.320	.350
Throws Right	R	.278	18	5	0	0	2	5	4	4	.409	.611
Morris,Bryan	L	.222	27	6	0	0	4	8	5	5	.344	.667
Throws Right	R	.250	36	9	1	0	0	6	5	8	.357	.278
Morrow,Brandon	L	.318	22	7	0	0	2	2	2	3	.375	.591
Throws Right	R	.300	40	12	0	1	0	2	1	5	.310	.350
Morton,Charlie	L	.258	31	8	2	0	1	4	3	9	.324	.419
Throws Right	R	.226	31	7	0	0	0	2	5	10	.333	.226
Moscot,Jon	L	.327	49	16	3	0	6	12	7	7	.421	.755
Throws Right	R	.250	40	10	2	0	4	8	3	3	.295	.600
Motte,Jason	L	.295	44	13	4	0	2	6	4	12	.380	.523
Throws Right	R	.278	54	15	6	1	4	12	4	12	.322	.648
Moylan,Peter	L	.333	48	16	1	0	3	10	9	8	.431	.542
Throws Right	R	.218	119	26	4	0	1	11	7	26	.265	.277
Murray,Colton	L	.240	50	12	2	0	2	7	7	17	.333	.400
Throws Right	R	.301	73	22	7	0	4	19	6	14	.366	.562
Musgrove,Joe	L	.270	100	27	5	2	4	14	10	22	.342	.480
Throws Right	R	.235	136	32	12	0	5	12	6	33	.276	.434
Narveson,Chris	L	.333	12	4	1	0	1	5	1	2	.429	.667
Throws Left	R	.261	23	6	0	0	2	3	1	4	.292	.522
Neal,Zach	L	.235	136	32	7	1	5	21	4	6	.255	.412
Throws Right	R	.294	136	40	12	0	4	14	2	21	.307	.471
Nelson,Jimmy	L	.252	318	80	15	3	11	43	49	61	.357	.421
Throws Right	R	.283	375	106	14	1	14	52	37	79	.365	.437
Neris,Hector	L	.210	157	33	4	1	5	17	18	57	.288	.344
Throws Right	R	.193	135	26	7	0	4	12	12	45	.273	.333
Neshek,Pat	L	.250	48	12	3	2	4	15	5	11	.321	.646
Throws Right	R	.172	122	21	4	0	2	10	6	32	.209	.254
Nicasio,Juan	L	.291	206	60	14	2	13	33	24	62	.366	.568
Throws Right	R	.235	243	57	10	4	2	27	21	76	.304	.333
Nicolino,Justin	L	.272	81	22	5	1	1	14	2	11	.292	.395
Throws Left	R	.319	232	74	12	1	7	30	18	26	.368	.470
Niese,Jon	L	.304	125	38	11	1	4	15	13	28	.383	.504
Throws Left	R	.294	364	107	11	6	21	54	34	60	.353	.530
Nola,Aaron	L	.241	203	49	10	1	6	30	20	50	.314	.389
Throws Right	R	.284	236	67	10	3	4	32	9	71	.317	.403
Nolasco,Ricky	L	.254	339	86	21	3	8	32	24	53	.307	.404
Throws Right	R	.278	417	116	20	1	18	58	20	91	.309	.460
Norris,Bud	L	.297	185	55	12	2	8	31	31	43	.402	.514
Throws Right	R	.242	252	61	10	0	6	29	18	59	.293	.353
Norris,Daniel	L	.214	70	15	4	0	2	6	8	27	.291	.357
Throws Left	R	.290	207	60	9	2	8	18	14	44	.332	.469
Nova,Ivan	L	.306	278	85	25	2	10	33	11	40	.339	.518
Throws Right	R	.251	358	90	21	1	13	36	17	87	.292	.425
Nuno,Vidal	L	.293	82	24	4	1	3	15	4	18	.333	.476
Throws Left	R	.287	150	43	7	0	8	22	7	33	.318	.493
Oberg,Scott	L	.361	36	13	0	0	2	8	7	7	.465	.528
Throws Right	R	.200	65	13	3	0	1	8	4	13	.257	.292
Oberholtzer,Brett	L	.277	101	28	3	1	6	17	7	20	.324	.505
Throws Left	R	.303	188	57	13	1	12	31	22	34	.377	.574
O'Day,Darren	L	.243	37	9	4	0	2	4	5	12	.349	.514
Throws Right	R	.200	80	16	2	0	4	8	8	26	.273	.375
Odorizzi,Jake	L	.190	295	56	10	0	10	19	22	86	.252	.325
Throws Right	R	.277	411	114	23	3	19	58	32	80	.327	.487
O'Flaherty,Eric	L	.288	66	19	5	1	1	13	2	12	.329	.439
Throws Left	R	.357	56	20	3	1	2	12	9	10	.446	.554
Ogando,Alexi	L	.314	35	11	3	0	2	12	9	8	.426	.571
Throws Right	R	.256	82	21	5	0	0	12	14	21	.367	.317
Ogando,Nefi	L	.250	28	7	1	0	0	3	5	2	.364	.286
Throws Right	R	.107	28	3	0	0	0	2	3	6	.188	.107
Oh,Seung Hwan	L	.176	131	23	3	0	1	13	8	36	.234	.221
Throws Right	R	.201	159	32	5	0	4	13	10	67	.247	.308
Ohlendorf,Ross	L	.198	111	22	5	0	4	9	13	26	.299	.351
Throws Right	R	.268	138	37	7	0	10	22	19	42	.369	.536
Okert,Steven	L	.259	27	7	0	0	1	3	1	8	.286	.370
Throws Left	R	.259	27	7	1	0	1	4	3	6	.333	.407
Ondrusek,Logan	L	.545	11	6	3	0	1	5	2	1	.615	1.091
Throws Right	R	.200	15	3	1	0	0	0	1	3	.250	.267
O'Rourke,Ryan	L	.077	26	2	0	0	1	3	3	11	.167	.192
Throws Left	R	.262	61	16	1	0	2	4	7	13	.348	.377
Osich,Josh	L	.156	77	12	1	1	2	3	5	18	.235	.273
Throws Left	R	.322	59	19	2	1	5	12	14	7	.452	.644
O'Sullivan,Sean	L	.333	45	15	3	0	1	8	0	7	.326	.467
Throws Right	R	.341	44	15	1	0	2	5	6	6	.442	.500
Osuna,Roberto	L	.237	131	31	6	0	7	18	7	38	.287	.443
Throws Right	R	.176	136	24	6	0	2	9	7	44	.215	.265
Otero,Dan	L	.197	117	23	5	2	0	8	8	29	.248	.274
Throws Right	R	.223	139	31	4	0	2	14	2	28	.234	.295
Ottavino,Adam	L	.256	39	10	0	0	2	6	6	9	.370	.410
Throws Right	R	.136	59	8	0	0	1	5	1	26	.164	.186
Overton,Dillon	L	.375	24	9	3	0	3	8	1	1	.400	.875
Throws Left	R	.415	94	39	8	1	9	21	6	16	.447	.809
Owens,Henry	L	.250	20	5	1	0	0	2	6	5	.444	.300
Throws Left	R	.295	61	18	6	1	5	14	14	16	.421	.672
Papelbon,Jonathan	L	.271	70	19	4	0	2	10	10	12	.363	.414
Throws Right	R	.269	67	18	7	0	1	8	4	19	.310	.418
Parker,Blake	L	.250	28	7	3	0	0	2	4	6	.344	.357
Throws Right	R	.250	40	10	1	0	1	10	5	9	.362	.350
Parnell,Bobby	L	.500	4	2	0	0	0	1	3	1	.714	.500
Throws Right	R	.278	18	5	0	0	1	6	2	3	.350	.444
Patton,Spencer	L	.226	31	7	2	0	0	3	8	11	.400	.290
Throws Right	R	.236	55	13	1	0	3	13	6	11	.311	.418
Paulino,David	L	.278	18	5	2	0	0	2	3	1	.381	.389
Throws Right	R	.143	7	1	0	0	0	0	0	1	.250	.143
Paxton,James	L	.284	74	21	1	2	1	5	7	11	.341	.392
Throws Left	R	.278	406	113	25	2	8	52	17	106	.305	.409
Peacock,Brad	L	.200	50	10	5	0	2	6	7	14	.298	.420
Throws Right	R	.175	63	11	4	0	4	7	7	14	.257	.429
Peavy,Jake	L	.302	205	62	24	4	7	32	18	39	.360	.561
Throws Right	R	.266	271	72	12	4	11	37	18	63	.313	.461

Pitchers vs. Left-Handed and Right-Handed Batters

Pitcher	vs	Avg	AB	H	2B	3B	HR	RBI	BB	SO	OBP	Slg
Pelfrey,Mike	L	.351	245	86	13	2	8	39	24	31	.405	.518
Throws Right	R	.312	237	74	9	1	7	26	22	25	.381	.447
Pena,Felix	L	.000	5	0	0	0	0	0	2	3	.286	.000
Throws Right	R	.185	27	5	0	0	1	2	1	10	.214	.296
Peralta,Joel	L	.245	53	13	2	0	4	8	4	19	.310	.509
Throws Right	R	.304	56	17	6	0	5	13	4	14	.344	.679
Peralta,Wandy	L	.273	11	3	0	0	0	2	4	2	.500	.273
Throws Left	R	.400	20	8	3	0	1	5	3	3	.478	.700
Peralta,Wily	L	.307	241	74	17	3	9	33	21	38	.366	.515
Throws Right	R	.304	257	78	14	0	10	36	22	55	.357	.475
Perdomo,Luis	L	.310	284	88	8	1	15	48	19	43	.357	.504
Throws Right	R	.309	320	99	20	3	8	46	27	62	.368	.466
Perez,Martin	L	.176	136	24	7	0	2	10	17	30	.265	.272
Throws Left	R	.291	622	181	38	1	16	92	59	73	.353	.432
Perez,Oliver	L	.233	86	20	7	0	2	8	8	26	.337	.384
Throws Left	R	.269	67	18	3	0	2	10	12	20	.388	.403
Perez,Williams	L	.295	105	31	3	1	4	12	9	16	.353	.457
Throws Right	R	.248	105	26	5	1	3	21	6	11	.292	.400
Petit,Yusmeiro	L	.275	102	28	9	1	7	10	10	18	.336	.588
Throws Right	R	.271	144	39	2	1	5	19	5	31	.295	.403
Petricka,Jake	L	.250	4	1	0	0	0	0	1	1	.400	.250
Throws Right	R	.269	26	7	0	1	1	8	7	6	.424	.462
Phelps,David	L	.230	135	31	6	0	4	13	27	45	.362	.363
Throws Right	R	.172	174	30	6	0	2	8	11	69	.223	.241
Phillips,Zach	L	.500	8	4	1	1	0	4	0	2	.500	.875
Throws Left	R	.211	19	4	0	0	1	1	1	4	.250	.368
Pineda,Michael	L	.272	302	82	24	3	9	34	29	97	.340	.460
Throws Right	R	.261	391	102	19	3	18	55	24	110	.307	.463
Pomeranz,Drew	L	.240	167	40	9	0	2	10	19	42	.314	.329
Throws Left	R	.209	464	97	20	0	20	51	46	144	.281	.381
Porcello,Rick	L	.225	436	98	22	2	8	34	17	98	.260	.339
Throws Right	R	.235	404	95	14	3	15	45	15	91	.276	.396
Pounders,Brooks	L	.333	27	9	0	0	3	6	2	6	.379	.667
Throws Right	R	.370	27	10	1	0	3	6	1	7	.379	.741
Pressly,Ryan	L	.252	119	30	7	0	0	18	18	30	.348	.311
Throws Right	R	.275	178	49	6	2	8	25	5	37	.301	.466
Price,David	L	.275	218	60	10	3	7	20	7	47	.304	.445
Throws Left	R	.253	661	167	30	3	23	79	43	181	.300	.411
Purke,Matt	L	.167	12	2	0	1	0	3	4	6	.375	.333
Throws Left	R	.300	60	18	5	2	0	9	8	9	.382	.450
Putnam,Zach	L	.229	35	8	0	0	0	3	5	13	.317	.229
Throws Right	R	.258	66	17	2	0	2	5	6	17	.315	.379
Quackenbush,Kevin	L	.295	88	26	5	2	2	13	9	17	.361	.466
Throws Right	R	.209	139	29	9	1	6	16	13	25	.273	.417
Qualls,Chad	L	.300	40	12	2	2	2	8	5	5	.378	.600
Throws Right	R	.307	101	31	7	0	3	18	4	17	.330	.465
Quintana,Jose	L	.246	171	42	10	1	3	14	8	39	.282	.368
Throws Left	R	.247	608	150	36	0	19	57	42	142	.298	.400
Ramirez,Erasmo	L	.290	124	36	10	0	7	17	15	18	.364	.540
Throws Right	R	.251	215	54	8	0	7	20	11	45	.299	.386
Ramirez,JC	L	.247	146	36	6	0	4	18	8	27	.289	.370
Throws Right	R	.266	154	41	2	0	8	25	14	32	.328	.435
Ramirez,Jose	L	.224	49	11	2	0	2	8	8	14	.345	.388
Throws Right	R	.217	69	15	7	1	0	8	10	19	.329	.348
Ramirez,Neil	L	.300	40	12	3	0	5	10	11	7	.442	.750
Throws Right	R	.217	46	10	2	0	3	11	7	17	.309	.457
Ramirez,Noe	L	.300	10	3	1	0	0	2	3	4	.462	.400
Throws Right	R	.333	39	13	2	0	4	10	5	11	.417	.692
Ramos,A.J.	L	.213	127	27	6	0	0	11	19	36	.318	.260
Throws Right	R	.236	106	25	2	0	1	4	16	37	.344	.283
Ramos,Cesar	L	.280	50	14	2	0	3	9	5	7	.351	.500
Throws Left	R	.333	138	46	11	1	9	26	15	20	.394	.623
Ramos,Edubray	L	.260	77	20	2	0	5	9	6	19	.313	.481
Throws Right	R	.225	71	16	5	0	0	10	5	21	.276	.296
Ranaudo,Anthony	L	.232	69	16	4	0	3	9	12	10	.341	.420
Throws Right	R	.339	59	20	3	0	7	17	8	8	.412	.746
Rasmus,Cory	L	.167	42	7	1	0	3	6	9	7	.314	.405
Throws Right	R	.333	54	18	4	0	1	8	7	10	.413	.463
Ravin,Josh	L	.222	9	2	0	1	1	3	1	1	.300	.778
Throws Right	R	.000	22	0	0	0	0	0	3	12	.120	.000
Ray,Robbie	L	.251	171	43	9	2	3	23	11	59	.304	.380
Throws Left	R	.272	523	142	23	3	21	67	60	159	.350	.447
Rea,Colin	L	.259	193	50	7	4	4	25	25	35	.351	.399
Throws Right	R	.257	202	52	11	2	8	31	19	45	.335	.450
Reed,Addison	L	.210	119	25	4	0	1	9	9	36	.264	.269
Throws Right	R	.210	167	35	8	0	3	16	4	55	.227	.311

Pitcher	vs	Avg	AB	H	2B	3B	HR	RBI	BB	SO	OBP	Slg
Reed,Cody	L	.304	46	14	3	0	1	9	2	8	.347	.435
Throws Left	R	.335	158	53	11	0	11	33	17	35	.408	.614
Reyes,Alex	L	.243	70	17	3	2	0	5	9	14	.329	.343
Throws Right	R	.170	94	16	3	0	1	2	14	38	.275	.234
Reynolds,Matt	L	.462	13	6	1	0	0	5	3	2	.529	.538
Throws Left	R	.091	11	1	0	0	0	0	2	1	.231	.091
Richard,Clayton	L	.286	70	20	1	0	0	8	6	15	.354	.300
Throws Left	R	.305	200	61	9	1	4	19	25	26	.379	.420
Richards,Garrett	L	.180	61	11	3	0	0	4	6	15	.254	.230
Throws Right	R	.290	69	20	7	0	2	10	9	19	.380	.478
Rivero,Felipe	L	.289	90	26	5	0	1	9	9	22	.387	.378
Throws Left	R	.204	196	40	8	0	6	19	24	70	.290	.337
Roach,Donn	L	.400	5	2	1	0	1	2	0	1	.333	1.200
Throws Right	R	.263	19	5	2	0	0	4	2	1	.364	.368
Roark,Tanner	L	.214	351	75	11	1	6	22	44	76	.315	.302
Throws Right	R	.241	407	98	9	1	11	45	29	96	.299	.349
Robertson,David	L	.212	118	25	3	0	4	11	10	41	.271	.339
Throws Right	R	.252	111	28	8	0	2	14	22	34	.378	.378
Robles,Hansel	L	.179	117	21	6	1	2	10	18	39	.287	.299
Throws Right	R	.281	171	48	12	0	5	28	18	46	.345	.439
Rodgers,Brady	L	.444	18	8	4	1	0	8	5	0	.583	.778
Throws Right	R	.333	21	7	2	0	0	5	2	3	.375	.429
Rodney,Fernando	L	.241	116	28	2	0	4	12	21	39	.364	.362
Throws Right	R	.215	121	26	6	0	1	10	16	35	.321	.289
Rodon,Carlos	L	.232	125	29	5	1	2	7	5	37	.273	.336
Throws Left	R	.283	519	147	23	1	21	70	49	131	.346	.453
Rodriguez,Eduardo	L	.267	86	23	5	0	1	6	9	25	.351	.360
Throws Left	R	.235	324	76	19	0	15	44	31	75	.300	.432
Rodriguez,Fernando	L	.313	48	15	3	1	2	7	9	8	.421	.542
Throws Right	R	.158	95	15	3	0	1	9	8	29	.229	.221
Rodriguez,Francisco	L	.204	108	22	3	1	5	15	7	19	.259	.389
Throws Right	R	.225	102	23	7	0	1	11	14	33	.311	.324
Rodriguez,Joely	L	.333	18	6	0	0	0	1	3	2	.429	.333
Throws Left	R	.125	16	2	1	0	0	2	1	5	.222	.188
Roe,Chaz	L	.286	49	14	3	4	1	10	9	13	.400	.571
Throws Right	R	.138	58	8	1	0	1	6	5	24	.203	.207
Rogers,Taylor	L	.202	84	17	4	0	1	8	6	27	.261	.286
Throws Left	R	.291	158	46	9	0	6	22	10	37	.349	.462
Rollins,David	L	.200	10	2	0	0	0	0	2	2	.333	.200
Throws Left	R	.333	30	10	2	0	2	6	5	4	.429	.600
Romero,Enny	L	.288	66	19	4	0	2	12	11	19	.385	.439
Throws Left	R	.217	106	23	1	0	5	21	17	31	.317	.368
Romo,Sergio	L	.242	33	8	2	0	2	3	3	9	.306	.485
Throws Right	R	.234	77	18	4	0	3	9	4	24	.272	.403
Rondon,Bruce	L	.159	69	11	0	0	0	4	7	24	.256	.159
Throws Right	R	.207	58	12	2	0	5	13	5	21	.281	.500
Rondon,Hector	L	.260	77	20	2	0	4	8	4	16	.301	.442
Throws Right	R	.200	110	22	3	0	4	13	4	42	.233	.336
Rondon,Jorge	L	.636	11	7	0	1	0	4	1	1	.667	.818
Throws Right	R	.250	8	2	1	0	1	3	0	3	.250	.750
Rosenthal,Trevor	L	.292	65	19	1	0	1	4	17	21	.446	.354
Throws Right	R	.293	99	29	3	1	2	12	12	35	.381	.404
Ross,Joe	L	.317	189	60	7	2	4	18	19	38	.385	.439
Throws Right	R	.225	213	48	6	2	5	22	10	55	.269	.343
Ross,Tyson	L	.412	17	7	3	0	0	4	0	3	.444	.588
Throws Right	R	.286	7	2	1	0	0	2	1	2	.444	.429
Ross Jr.,Robbie	L	.188	80	15	3	0	0	8	13	24	.320	.225
Throws Left	R	.254	126	32	5	0	2	11	10	32	.333	.341
Roth,Michael	L	.375	8	3	1	0	1	3	0	2	.375	.875
Throws Left	R	.538	13	7	2	0	2	4	1	1	.571	1.154
Rusin,Chris	L	.258	97	25	4	2	2	11	5	24	.314	.402
Throws Left	R	.259	220	57	17	1	3	25	18	45	.315	.386
Russell,James	L	.444	9	4	0	0	1	6	2	1	.545	.778
Throws Left	R	.417	12	5	1	0	1	3	3	3	.500	.750
Ryan,Kyle	L	.225	89	20	2	2	2	13	6	22	.271	.360
Throws Left	R	.241	116	28	6	2	0	6	9	13	.313	.328
Ryu,Hyun-Jin	L	.200	5	1	0	1	0	2	0	1	.200	.600
Throws Left	R	.412	17	7	3	0	1	4	2	3	.474	.765
Rzepczynski,Marc	L	.265	102	27	4	1	1	21	6	31	.321	.353
Throws Left	R	.244	78	19	4	0	0	8	23	15	.422	.295
Sabathia,CC	L	.209	134	28	5	1	4	11	15	38	.312	.351
Throws Left	R	.260	553	144	21	1	18	64	50	114	.325	.400
Salas,Fernando	L	.237	131	31	5	0	6	14	6	36	.270	.412
Throws Right	R	.227	141	32	10	0	6	16	13	28	.288	.426
Salazar,Danny	L	.200	235	47	12	1	7	22	25	78	.279	.349
Throws Right	R	.264	280	74	12	0	9	30	38	83	.351	.404

Pitchers vs. Left-Handed and Right-Handed Batters

Pitcher	vs	Avg	AB	H	2B	3B	HR	RBI	BB	SO	OBP	Slg
Sale,Chris	L	.197	127	25	4	0	5	11	3	42	.239	.346
Throws Left	R	.232	710	165	30	3	22	68	42	191	.286	.376
Samardzija,Jeff	L	.272	382	104	26	5	12	49	28	79	.320	.461
Throws Right	R	.225	382	86	11	3	12	35	26	88	.276	.364
Sampson,Adrian	L	.400	5	2	0	0	1	1	1	1	.500	1.000
Throws Right	R	.400	15	6	0	0	1	2	0	1	.400	.600
Sampson,Keyvius	L	.216	51	11	0	0	3	7	12	13	.375	.392
Throws Right	R	.274	106	29	5	0	6	19	15	29	.369	.491
Sanchez,Aaron	L	.217	364	79	12	2	11	35	44	87	.306	.352
Throws Right	R	.231	355	82	19	0	4	28	19	74	.273	.318
Sanchez,Anibal	L	.261	306	80	14	2	11	41	35	75	.343	.428
Throws Right	R	.310	294	91	11	0	19	56	18	60	.347	.541
Santana,Ervin	L	.247	336	83	16	0	7	28	29	63	.310	.357
Throws Right	R	.244	349	85	20	0	12	34	24	86	.293	.404
Santiago,Hector	L	.243	144	35	2	0	7	18	22	31	.347	.403
Throws Left	R	.245	546	134	32	4	26	73	57	113	.318	.462
Saupold,Warwick	L	.294	17	5	1	0	0	1	1	4	.333	.353
Throws Right	R	.462	26	12	4	0	0	6	2	6	.484	.615
Scahill,Rob	L	.321	56	18	5	0	0	7	3	8	.367	.411
Throws Right	R	.208	77	16	1	0	2	10	6	19	.287	.299
Scheppers,Tanner	L	.167	6	1	0	0	0	2	0	2	.167	.167
Throws Right	R	.192	26	5	4	0	0	1	3	3	.276	.346
Scherzer,Max	L	.242	414	100	24	4	17	43	42	118	.315	.442
Throws Right	R	.156	416	65	13	0	14	33	14	166	.189	.288
Schugel,A.J.	L	.161	93	15	2	0	2	8	9	15	.235	.247
Throws Right	R	.268	97	26	4	1	2	12	4	31	.304	.392
Schultz,Bo	L	.320	25	8	0	1	2	5	1	5	.333	.640
Throws Right	R	.231	39	9	2	0	1	2	2	5	.268	.359
Schuster,Patrick	L	.188	16	3	0	1	1	4	5	3	.409	.500
Throws Left	R	.500	24	12	3	1	0	10	5	5	.581	.708
Scott,Robby	L	.250	12	3	0	0	0	0	0	3	.250	.250
Throws Left	R	.300	10	3	0	0	0	1	2	2	.417	.300
Scribner,Evan	L	.200	15	3	2	0	0	0	1	3	.294	.333
Throws Right	R	.067	30	2	1	1	0	0	1	12	.097	.167
Severino,Luis	L	.263	137	36	7	1	4	21	12	32	.331	.416
Throws Right	R	.286	147	42	14	0	7	21	13	34	.348	.524
Shaw,Bryan	L	.255	98	25	6	0	3	8	13	26	.348	.408
Throws Right	R	.214	145	31	3	1	5	16	15	43	.286	.352
Shields,James	L	.287	352	101	19	3	16	41	45	58	.372	.494
Throws Right	R	.288	371	107	22	3	24	69	37	77	.357	.558
Shipley,Braden	L	.270	159	43	10	2	11	25	14	25	.328	.566
Throws Right	R	.325	114	37	10	1	3	14	14	18	.400	.509
Shoemaker,Matt	L	.263	342	90	19	4	8	35	15	72	.293	.412
Throws Right	R	.270	282	76	14	0	10	23	15	71	.319	.426
Shreve,Chasen	L	.275	40	11	2	1	4	6	5	10	.383	.675
Throws Left	R	.212	85	18	4	1	4	9	8	23	.287	.424
Siegrist,Kevin	L	.221	68	15	2	0	3	8	9	18	.308	.382
Throws Left	R	.180	150	27	5	1	7	18	17	48	.265	.367
Simmons,Shae	L	.143	14	2	0	0	0	0	0	2	.143	.143
Throws Right	R	.364	11	4	2	0	0	1	0	1	.364	.545
Simon,Alfredo	L	.369	122	45	9	1	9	34	13	18	.423	.680
Throws Right	R	.331	133	44	6	0	6	25	18	21	.438	.511
Sipp,Tony	L	.284	88	25	5	1	5	18	10	18	.360	.534
Throws Left	R	.310	87	27	6	1	7	13	8	22	.368	.644
Skaggs,Tyler	L	.318	44	14	5	0	0	5	5	9	.373	.432
Throws Left	R	.252	147	37	6	0	5	16	18	41	.339	.395
Smith,Blake	L	.375	8	3	0	0	0	1	0	0	.444	.375
Throws Right	R	.333	12	4	1	0	1	4	0	1	.333	.667
Smith,Chris	L	.188	32	6	0	0	0	5	7	10	.325	.188
Throws Right	R	.151	53	8	3	0	2	6	6	19	.233	.321
Smith,Joe	L	.220	82	18	1	0	5	9	8	20	.312	.415
Throws Right	R	.266	109	29	2	0	3	14	10	20	.341	.367
Smith,Josh	L	.287	94	27	3	0	6	15	13	15	.380	.511
Throws Right	R	.219	137	30	7	0	5	19	13	33	.285	.380
Smith,Will	L	.229	70	16	2	1	1	9	7	23	.299	.329
Throws Left	R	.197	76	15	3	1	2	8	11	25	.303	.342
Smoker,Josh	L	.360	25	9	0	0	2	5	3	7	.448	.600
Throws Left	R	.200	35	7	0	0	2	4	1	18	.222	.371
Smyly,Drew	L	.250	136	34	6	0	7	22	4	39	.276	.449
Throws Left	R	.262	535	140	28	1	25	73	45	128	.315	.458
Snell,Blake	L	.264	72	19	2	0	0	5	12	23	.365	.292
Throws Left	R	.270	274	74	15	1	5	32	39	75	.360	.387
Socolovich,Miguel	L	.125	24	3	0	0	2	4	3	6	.214	.375
Throws Right	R	.059	34	2	0	1	0	0	2	10	.111	.118
Solis,Sammy	L	.200	60	12	5	0	0	4	5	19	.273	.283
Throws Left	R	.218	87	19	4	0	1	6	16	28	.340	.299

Pitcher	vs	Avg	AB	H	2B	3B	HR	RBI	BB	SO	OBP	Slg
Soria,Joakim	L	.246	130	32	5	2	2	17	12	32	.308	.362
Throws Right	R	.297	128	38	7	1	8	18	15	36	.377	.555
Stephenson,Robert	L	.289	76	22	4	0	6	13	9	15	.379	.579
Throws Right	R	.268	71	19	4	0	3	12	10	16	.373	.451
Stewart,Brock	L	.295	44	13	0	0	2	4	1	10	.311	.432
Throws Right	R	.290	69	20	2	0	5	13	11	15	.388	.536
Storen,Drew	L	.319	72	23	8	0	3	6	9	15	.424	.556
Throws Right	R	.244	135	33	7	0	4	17	4	33	.282	.385
Strahm,Matt	L	.292	24	7	1	0	0	1	1	7	.308	.333
Throws Left	R	.118	51	6	1	0	0	2	10	23	.274	.137
Straily,Dan	L	.191	304	58	11	2	10	36	46	69	.306	.339
Throws Right	R	.243	395	96	24	0	21	41	27	93	.300	.463
Strasburg,Stephen	L	.200	265	53	10	1	9	29	25	93	.268	.347
Throws Right	R	.235	281	66	16	2	6	27	19	90	.288	.370
Stratton,Chris	L	.211	19	4	0	0	1	2	3	3	.318	.368
Throws Right	R	.368	19	7	1	0	0	2	2	3	.429	.421
Street,Huston	L	.279	43	12	1	0	0	4	7	7	.373	.302
Throws Right	R	.388	49	19	5	0	5	13	5	7	.444	.796
Strickland,Hunter	L	.270	74	20	3	0	2	8	8	11	.349	.392
Throws Right	R	.197	152	30	4	0	2	16	11	46	.251	.263
Stripling,Ross	L	.222	171	38	9	3	4	15	13	36	.276	.380
Throws Right	R	.272	213	58	14	0	6	27	17	38	.329	.423
Stroman,Marcus	L	.268	399	107	24	1	11	52	32	83	.325	.416
Throws Right	R	.260	393	102	20	2	10	39	22	83	.301	.397
Strop,Pedro	L	.143	56	8	0	1	3	9	9	18	.269	.339
Throws Right	R	.173	110	19	4	0	1	9	6	42	.233	.236
Stumpf,Daniel	L	.429	7	3	0	0	0	1	2	1	.556	.429
Throws Left	R	.400	15	6	0	1	1	7	0	1	.400	.733
Sturdevant,Tyler	L	.250	20	5	2	0	1	3	3	5	.348	.500
Throws Right	R	.283	46	13	1	0	0	3	3	9	.340	.304
Suarez,Albert	L	.253	150	38	12	3	3	15	16	21	.331	.433
Throws Right	R	.274	168	46	17	1	8	23	10	33	.318	.530
Surkamp,Eric	L	.310	42	13	1	0	2	6	5	3	.408	.476
Throws Left	R	.333	126	42	12	0	6	22	16	19	.412	.571
Suter,Brent	L	.394	33	13	1	0	2	4	2	3	.444	.606
Throws Left	R	.235	51	12	1	0	1	4	3	12	.278	.314
Swarzak,Anthony	L	.250	40	10	2	0	3	7	5	15	.333	.525
Throws Right	R	.240	75	18	4	0	7	17	2	16	.266	.573
Syndergaard,Noah	L	.262	298	78	20	0	6	27	28	92	.324	.389
Throws Right	R	.228	394	90	16	3	5	28	15	126	.258	.322
Taillon,Jameson	L	.269	201	54	11	1	6	16	12	37	.308	.423
Throws Right	R	.234	192	45	12	0	7	22	5	48	.265	.406
Tanaka,Masahiro	L	.237	372	88	21	2	11	34	14	79	.263	.392
Throws Right	R	.235	387	91	13	0	11	33	22	86	.281	.354
Tazawa,Junichi	L	.207	82	17	3	0	3	6	8	19	.275	.354
Throws Right	R	.273	110	30	6	0	6	25	6	35	.316	.491
Teheran,Julio	L	.237	312	74	17	4	13	36	29	54	.313	.442
Throws Right	R	.212	391	83	14	1	9	29	12	113	.241	.322
Tepera,Ryan	L	.212	33	7	2	0	1	4	3	10	.316	.364
Throws Right	R	.250	40	10	0	0	0	6	5	8	.348	.250
Thompson,Jake	L	.284	102	29	5	1	5	12	18	15	.402	.500
Throws Right	R	.245	98	24	6	1	5	20	10	17	.319	.480
Thornburg,Tyler	L	.130	100	13	3	0	1	7	11	45	.223	.190
Throws Right	R	.185	135	25	8	1	5	13	14	45	.265	.370
Thornton,Matt	L	.300	20	6	1	0	1	5	3	5	.391	.500
Throws Left	R	.320	50	16	4	0	1	6	3	4	.370	.460
Tillman,Chris	L	.240	292	70	21	2	8	34	34	74	.320	.408
Throws Right	R	.247	344	85	23	1	11	35	32	66	.319	.416
Tolleson,Shawn	L	.318	66	21	2	0	5	14	7	9	.378	.576
Throws Right	R	.352	91	32	4	0	3	14	3	20	.372	.495
Tolliver,Ashur	L	.250	8	2	0	0	1	1	1	3	.333	.625
Throws Left	R	.273	11	3	0	0	0	1	2	2	.385	.273
Tomlin,Josh	L	.229	292	67	15	2	14	31	7	47	.247	.438
Throws Right	R	.299	402	120	22	1	22	60	13	71	.323	.522
Tonkin,Michael	L	.306	98	30	6	3	8	20	12	25	.387	.673
Throws Right	R	.266	188	50	7	1	5	28	12	55	.317	.394
Torres,Carlos	L	.222	135	30	5	1	2	12	14	29	.314	.319
Throws Right	R	.212	165	35	8	2	6	19	16	49	.279	.394
Treinen,Blake	L	.221	77	17	4	0	3	16	15	25	.348	.390
Throws Right	R	.225	151	34	4	1	2	13	16	38	.296	.305
Triggs,Andrew	L	.277	101	28	7	1	2	13	9	27	.333	.426
Throws Right	R	.235	119	28	3	2	3	13	4	28	.278	.370
Tropeano,Nick	L	.277	130	36	7	2	6	12	22	39	.385	.500
Throws Right	R	.264	129	34	5	0	8	14	9	29	.309	.488
Tuivailala,Samuel	L	.300	20	6	1	0	0	1	3	3	.391	.350
Throws Right	R	.316	19	6	0	0	0	2	3	4	.458	.316

Pitchers vs. Left-Handed and Right-Handed Batters

Pitcher	vs	Avg	AB	H	2B	3B	HR	RBI	BB	SO	OBP	Slg
Turner,Jacob	L	.250	40	10	3	0	0	4	8	9	.380	.325
Throws Right	R	.371	62	23	9	0	5	24	8	9	.444	.758
Uehara,Koji	L	.139	79	11	2	0	3	6	6	29	.200	.278
Throws Right	R	.253	91	23	6	1	5	8	5	34	.306	.505
Urena,Jose	L	.303	178	54	7	4	7	34	13	19	.359	.506
Throws Right	R	.242	153	37	13	0	4	23	16	39	.320	.405
Urias,Julio	L	.234	64	15	2	0	3	9	7	24	.333	.406
Throws Left	R	.284	232	66	14	0	2	18	24	60	.354	.371
Valdez,Jose	L	.161	31	5	1	1	1	2	7	8	.316	.355
Throws Right	R	.226	53	12	2	1	3	8	9	14	.339	.472
Vargas,Cesar	L	.271	70	19	4	0	0	7	7	19	.338	.329
Throws Right	R	.333	66	22	4	0	5	12	8	9	.403	.621
Vargas,Jason	L	.333	6	2	1	0	1	1	0	0	.333	1.000
Throws Left	R	.158	38	6	2	0	0	2	3	11	.220	.211
Velasquez,Vince	L	.270	244	66	7	1	11	33	26	75	.337	.443
Throws Right	R	.255	247	63	16	0	10	29	19	77	.308	.441
Venditte,Pat	L	.286	35	10	3	0	2	8	3	10	.333	.543
Throws Both	R	.275	51	14	2	1	3	9	8	9	.381	.529
Ventura,Yordano	L	.249	337	84	16	1	14	46	40	68	.329	.427
Throws Right	R	.275	386	106	19	2	9	39	38	76	.349	.404
VerHagen,Drew	L	.438	32	14	4	1	0	6	3	4	.486	.625
Throws Right	R	.286	49	14	1	1	3	12	4	6	.345	.531
Verlander,Justin	L	.187	406	76	17	2	15	34	34	144	.253	.350
Throws Right	R	.226	421	95	18	2	15	36	23	110	.272	.385
Verrett,Logan	L	.276	174	48	19	3	6	28	15	33	.332	.523
Throws Right	R	.291	179	52	15	0	10	24	28	33	.394	.542
Vincent,Nick	L	.226	84	19	0	1	3	7	8	22	.301	.357
Throws Right	R	.234	145	34	8	0	8	26	7	43	.268	.455
Vizcaino,Arodys	L	.205	73	15	2	0	1	6	14	27	.333	.274
Throws Right	R	.272	81	22	3	0	2	14	12	23	.372	.383
Vogelsong,Ryan	L	.285	137	39	8	3	6	23	25	24	.399	.518
Throws Right	R	.230	178	41	11	3	5	17	15	37	.301	.410
Volquez,Edinson	L	.284	394	112	24	2	11	57	45	72	.360	.439
Throws Right	R	.288	364	105	17	1	12	50	31	67	.348	.440
Wacha,Michael	L	.264	235	62	15	3	5	25	18	47	.316	.417
Throws Right	R	.307	316	97	26	1	10	57	27	67	.358	.491
Wagner,Tyler	L	.190	21	4	2	0	0	2	0	2	.190	.286
Throws Right	R	.294	17	5	1	0	0	2	2	5	.368	.353
Wainwright,Adam	L	.306	343	105	21	2	11	52	31	70	.366	.475
Throws Right	R	.272	423	115	27	2	11	49	28	91	.316	.423
Walker,Taijuan	L	.206	248	51	9	2	16	35	19	59	.269	.452
Throws Right	R	.285	274	78	16	1	11	31	18	60	.338	.471
Wang,Chien-Ming	L	.232	99	23	5	1	4	16	12	18	.327	.424
Throws Right	R	.333	111	37	7	0	2	17	6	12	.368	.450
Warren,Adam	L	.179	84	15	0	0	5	13	11	19	.278	.357
Throws Right	R	.278	158	44	7	1	6	31	18	33	.350	.449
Watson,Tony	L	.211	71	15	2	0	2	4	3	19	.253	.324
Throws Left	R	.216	171	37	9	1	8	18	17	39	.290	.421
Weaver,Jered	L	.298	305	91	15	1	15	43	26	43	.355	.502
Throws Right	R	.296	399	118	23	2	22	52	25	60	.337	.529
Weaver,Luke	L	.377	61	23	4	0	3	12	6	18	.435	.590
Throws Right	R	.264	87	23	4	0	4	17	6	27	.313	.448
Webb,Ryan	L	.389	18	7	1	0	0	4	2	1	.450	.444
Throws Right	R	.364	55	20	1	0	2	11	1	10	.375	.491
Weber,Ryan	L	.333	69	23	4	1	3	11	4	10	.370	.551
Throws Right	R	.288	80	23	5	1	4	15	1	13	.313	.525
Wendelken,J.B.	L	.333	27	9	1	0	2	7	5	7	.438	.593
Throws Right	R	.321	28	9	0	0	1	8	4	5	.406	.429
Whalen,Rob	L	.189	37	7	1	2	2	10	5	10	.279	.486
Throws Right	R	.236	55	13	3	1	2	7	7	15	.354	.436
Whitley,Chase	L	.143	35	5	0	0	0	1	3	9	.211	.143
Throws Right	R	.348	23	8	1	0	2	3	0	6	.348	.652
Wieland,Joe	L	.364	11	4	1	0	0	3	0	2	.364	.455
Throws Right	R	.417	12	5	0	0	1	2	0	1	.417	.667
Wilhelmsen,Tom	L	.292	65	19	2	2	3	7	9	12	.378	.523
Throws Right	R	.336	122	41	9	0	8	28	10	16	.393	.607
Williams,Jerome	L	.120	25	3	2	0	0	3	3	3	.241	.200
Throws Right	R	.404	47	19	4	0	4	13	3	5	.442	.745
Williams,Trevor	L	.350	20	7	3	0	3	8	2	3	.409	.950
Throws Right	R	.333	36	12	3	0	1	4	3	8	.385	.500
Wilson,Alex	L	.239	113	27	10	2	2	11	13	18	.313	.416
Throws Right	R	.261	157	41	8	0	3	25	8	31	.296	.369
Wilson,Justin	L	.308	91	28	3	1	2	17	4	23	.344	.429
Throws Left	R	.234	141	33	3	2	4	14	13	42	.299	.369

Pitcher	vs	Avg	AB	H	2B	3B	HR	RBI	BB	SO	OBP	Slg
Wilson,Tyler	L	.283	191	54	12	2	5	23	13	29	.340	.445
Throws Right	R	.293	191	56	13	1	10	36	11	26	.328	.529
Wimmers,Alex	L	.200	20	4	2	0	0	2	7	5	.407	.300
Throws Right	R	.256	39	10	2	0	2	7	4	9	.311	.462
Wisler,Matt	L	.257	296	76	13	2	11	41	37	49	.343	.426
Throws Right	R	.262	317	83	11	2	15	39	12	66	.290	.451
Withrow,Chris	L	.192	52	10	0	0	1	5	9	12	.323	.250
Throws Right	R	.226	84	19	1	0	4	14	8	16	.298	.381
Wittgren,Nick	L	.242	91	22	2	0	2	3	6	17	.289	.330
Throws Right	R	.264	106	28	5	0	4	18	4	25	.292	.425
Wood,Alex	L	.271	59	16	3	1	1	9	8	16	.368	.407
Throws Left	R	.235	170	40	4	0	4	16	12	50	.290	.329
Wood,Blake	L	.213	127	27	8	1	5	21	18	35	.313	.409
Throws Right	R	.281	160	45	9	0	4	16	20	46	.363	.413
Wood,Travis	L	.128	109	14	4	1	2	5	11	23	.208	.239
Throws Left	R	.265	117	31	12	0	6	15	13	24	.344	.521
Worley,Vance	L	.264	148	39	7	0	5	17	21	29	.351	.412
Throws Right	R	.259	174	45	8	0	6	27	14	27	.323	.408
Wright,Daniel	L	.377	69	26	4	0	3	10	3	9	.405	.565
Throws Right	R	.333	93	31	8	0	4	14	5	12	.388	.548
Wright,Mike	L	.345	119	41	9	1	6	21	10	21	.401	.588
Throws Right	R	.238	168	40	12	1	6	24	16	29	.321	.429
Wright,Steven	L	.209	249	52	8	1	6	26	23	50	.286	.321
Throws Right	R	.254	338	86	9	4	6	37	34	77	.328	.358
Yates,Kirby	L	.204	54	11	1	0	1	4	6	19	.306	.278
Throws Right	R	.286	105	30	6	0	4	18	13	31	.372	.457
Ynoa,Gabriel	L	.359	39	14	0	0	0	3	2	8	.390	.359
Throws Right	R	.308	39	12	0	1	0	8	5	9	.383	.359
Ynoa,Michael	L	.220	50	11	5	0	0	4	10	13	.355	.320
Throws Right	R	.153	59	9	3	0	0	9	7	17	.282	.203
Young,Chris	L	.340	162	55	7	2	17	32	31	44	.441	.722
Throws Right	R	.251	195	49	7	0	11	27	12	50	.295	.456
Younginer,Madison	L	.364	11	4	1	0	0	0	2	0	.462	.455
Throws Right	R	.421	19	8	2	0	0	8	2	4	.478	.526
Zastryzny,Rob	L	.138	29	4	0	0	0	0	1	10	.194	.138
Throws Left	R	.276	29	8	1	0	0	3	4	7	.343	.310
Ziegler,Brad	L	.275	102	28	4	0	1	12	16	15	.380	.343
Throws Right	R	.252	155	39	5	2	1	10	10	43	.301	.303
Zimmermann,Jordan	L	.255	196	50	7	5	7	33	11	32	.289	.449
Throws Right	R	.309	220	68	18	2	7	25	15	34	.357	.505
Zych,Tony	L	.192	26	5	3	0	0	1	5	9	.323	.308
Throws Right	R	.227	22	5	1	0	0	3	5	12	.379	.273
AL	L	.252	-	-	-	-	-	-	-	-	.320	.413
	R	.260	-	-	-	-	-	-	-	-	.320	.428
NL	L	.256	-	-	-	-	-	-	-	-	.333	.417
	R	.253	-	-	-	-	-	-	-	-	.315	.410
MLB	L	.254	-	-	-	-	-	-	-	-	.327	.415
	R	.256	-	-	-	-	-	-	-	-	.318	.419

2016 Leader Boards

Joe Rosales

Leader boards are great for looking up who was the best according to a certain metric or at a particular skill. But any inquisitive individual is going to have questions that range from simple to more complex. For instance, the importance of getting on base is well established, and it is great to know that Mike Trout was better at doing so than anybody else in the league (.441 OBP). However, Mike Trout does so many other things well, including hit for power (fourth in the AL with a .550 slugging percentage), that if you're going to maximize his abilities, you need someone getting on base in front of him. So then you might ask who the best leadoff men are at getting on base, which is another piece of information that we include in this section. In the American League, Jose Altuve had the highest OBP as a leadoff man at .415, which was also higher than his overall OBP of .396. As for Trout, his teammate, Yunel Escobar, was seventh in the AL as a leadoff man with a .357 OBP.

Leader boards are provided on as many things related to offense, pitching, and defense that we could think of. There are batting splits by handedness, position, pitch type, and age. You can look up which players were the most and least likely to swing at the first pitch. You can look up which pitchers threw the most pitches that exceeded 95 mph or which pitchers threw the most pitches below 80 mph. On the defensive side of things, you can find which middle infielders successfully turned the most double plays as the pivot man and who had the best range factors. All of these things are made possible by the extensive game charting and pitch charting data collected by Baseball Info Solutions.

There are also several leader boards consisting of metrics devised by Bill James over the years that evaluate players in unique ways, from Game Scores to Speed Scores to Runs Created and much more. If there are ways that players can distinguish themselves over the course of the season, we have done our utmost to capture that.

Finally, below are definitions to help clarify a few things that you will find in the following tables that not everyone may be familiar with:

BPS stands for "Batting Average Plus Slugging Percentage." BPS makes more sense than OPS for some leaderboards that involve pitches.

OutZ is "Pitches Outside the Strike Zone."

Holds Adjusted Save Percentage is calculated by dividing holds plus saves by holds plus save opportunities.

2016 American League Batting Leaders

Batting Average
(minimum 502 PA)

Altuve, Jose, Hou	.338
Betts, Mookie, Bos	.318
Pedroia, Dustin, Bos	.318
Cabrera, Miguel, Det	.316
Trout, Mike, LAA	.315
Ortiz, David, Bos	.315
Ramirez, Jose, Cle	.312
Martinez, J.D., Det	.307
Escobar, Yunel, LAA	.304
Andrus, Elvis, Tex	.302

On Base Percentage
(minimum 502 PA)

Trout, Mike, LAA	.441
Donaldson, Josh, Tor	.404
Ortiz, David, Bos	.401
Altuve, Jose, Hou	.396
Cabrera, Miguel, Det	.393
Pedroia, Dustin, Bos	.376
Martinez, J.D., Det	.373
Santana, Carlos, Cle	.366
Bautista, Jose, Tor	.366
Ramirez, Jose, Cle	.363

Slugging Average
(minimum 502 PA)

Ortiz, David, Bos	.620
Cabrera, Miguel, Det	.563
Cruz, Nelson, Sea	.555
Trout, Mike, LAA	.550
Donaldson, Josh, Tor	.549
Dozier, Brian, Min	.546
Martinez, J.D., Det	.535
Betts, Mookie, Bos	.534
Trumbo, Mark, Bal	.533
Cano, Robinson, Sea	.533

Home Runs

Trumbo, Mark, Bal	47
Cruz, Nelson, Sea	43
Davis, Khris, Oak	42
Dozier, Brian, Min	42
Encarnacion, Edwin, Tor	42
Frazier, Todd, CWS	40
Cano, Robinson, Sea	39
Cabrera, Miguel, Det	38
Davis, Chris, Bal	38
Ortiz, David, Bos	38

Games

Escobar, Alcides, KC	162
Schoop, Jonathan, Bal	162
Springer, George, Hou	162
Altuve, Jose, Hou	161
Cano, Robinson, Sea	161
Encarnacion, Edwin, Tor	160
Longoria, Evan, TB	160
4 tied with	159

Plate Appearances

Springer, George, Hou	744
Betts, Mookie, Bos	730
Bogaerts, Xander, Bos	719
Altuve, Jose, Hou	717
Cano, Robinson, Sea	715
Eaton, Adam, CWS	706
Encarnacion, Edwin, Tor	702
Donaldson, Josh, Tor	700
Pedroia, Dustin, Bos	698
Machado, Manny, Bal	696

At Bats

Betts, Mookie, Bos	672
Cano, Robinson, Sea	655
Bogaerts, Xander, Bos	652
Springer, George, Hou	644
Altuve, Jose, Hou	640
Machado, Manny, Bal	640
Escobar, Alcides, KC	637
Longoria, Evan, TB	633
Pedroia, Dustin, Bos	633
Desmond, Ian, Tex	625

Hits

Altuve, Jose, Hou	216
Betts, Mookie, Bos	214
Pedroia, Dustin, Bos	201
Cano, Robinson, Sea	195
Bogaerts, Xander, Bos	192
Cabrera, Miguel, Det	188
Machado, Manny, Bal	188
Abreu, Jose, CWS	183
Lindor, Francisco, Cle	182
2 tied with	178

Singles

Pedroia, Dustin, Bos	149
Altuve, Jose, Hou	145
Betts, Mookie, Bos	136
Bogaerts, Xander, Bos	136
Lindor, Francisco, Cle	134
Escobar, Alcides, KC	129
Abreu, Jose, CWS	125
Desmond, Ian, Tex	124
Eaton, Adam, CWS	124
Escobar, Yunel, LAA	123

Doubles

Ortiz, David, Bos	48
Ramirez, Jose, Cle	46
Altuve, Jose, Hou	42
Betts, Mookie, Bos	42
Cabrera, Melky, CWS	42
Kipnis, Jason, Cle	41
Longoria, Evan, TB	41
Machado, Manny, Bal	40
Schoop, Jonathan, Bal	38
4 tied with	36

Triples

Eaton, Adam, CWS	9
Dyson, Jarrod, KC	8
Andrus, Elvis, Tex	7
Bradley Jr., Jackie, Bos	7
Anderson, Tim, CWS	6
Buxton, Byron, Min	6
Escobar, Alcides, KC	6
Gardner, Brett, NYY	6
Miller, Brad, TB	6
13 tied with	5

Total Bases

Betts, Mookie, Bos	359
Cano, Robinson, Sea	349
Machado, Manny, Bal	341
Altuve, Jose, Hou	340
Dozier, Brian, Min	336
Cabrera, Miguel, Det	335
Ortiz, David, Bos	333
Longoria, Evan, TB	330
Cruz, Nelson, Sea	327
Trumbo, Mark, Bal	327

Runs Scored

Trout, Mike, LAA	123
Betts, Mookie, Bos	122
Donaldson, Josh, Tor	122
Kinsler, Ian, Det	117
Springer, George, Hou	116
Bogaerts, Xander, Bos	115
Altuve, Jose, Hou	108
Cano, Robinson, Sea	107
Desmond, Ian, Tex	107
2 tied with	105

RBI

Encarnacion, Edwin, Tor	127
Ortiz, David, Bos	127
Pujols, Albert, LAA	119
Betts, Mookie, Bos	113
Ramirez, Hanley, Bos	111
Cabrera, Miguel, Det	108
Trumbo, Mark, Bal	108
Cruz, Nelson, Sea	105
Beltre, Adrian, Tex	104
Hosmer, Eric, KC	104

Walks

Trout, Mike, LAA	116
Donaldson, Josh, Tor	109
Santana, Carlos, Cle	99
Davis, Chris, Bal	88
Springer, George, Hou	88
Bautista, Jose, Tor	87
Encarnacion, Edwin, Tor	87
Ortiz, David, Bos	80
Mauer, Joe, Min	79
Napoli, Mike, Cle	78

Strikeouts

Davis, Chris, Bal	219
Napoli, Mike, Cle	194
Upton, Justin, Det	179
Sano, Miguel, Min	178
Springer, George, Hou	178
Trumbo, Mark, Bal	170
Davis, Khris, Oak	166
Frazier, Todd, CWS	163
Desmond, Ian, Tex	160
2 tied with	159

2016 American League Batting Leaders

Intentional Walks

Cabrera, Miguel, Det	15
Ortiz, David, Bos	15
Trout, Mike, LAA	12
Altuve, Jose, Hou	11
Mauer, Joe, Min	10
Seager, Kyle, Sea	10
Machado, Manny, Bal	9
Cano, Robinson, Sea	8
Martinez, Victor, Det	8
Abreu, Jose, CWS	7

BA Bases Loaded
(minimum 10 PA)

Alonso, Yonder, Oak	.636
Cron, C.J., LAA	.545
Ellsbury, Jacoby, NYY	.545
Smith, Seth, Sea	.545
Trout, Mike, LAA	.545
Donaldson, Josh, Tor	.500
Gardner, Brett, NYY	.500
Longoria, Evan, TB	.500
Gomez, Carlos, Hou-Tex	.462
3 tied with	.455

Sacrifice Hits

Escobar, Alcides, KC	10
Dyson, Jarrod, KC	8
Perez, Carlos, LAA	8
Carrera, Ezequiel, Tor	7
Eaton, Adam, CWS	7
Iglesias, Jose, Det	7
Wilson, Bobby, Det-Tex-TB	7
Anderson, Tim, CWS	6
Gonzalez, Marwin, Hou	6
Mondesi, Raul, KC	6

Sacrifice Flies

Lindor, Francisco, Cle	15
Abreu, Jose, CWS	9
Encarnacion, Edwin, Tor	8
Jones, Adam, Bal	8
10 tied with	7

BA Close & Late
(minimum 50 PA)

Beltre, Adrian, Tex	.385
Smoak, Justin, Tor	.362
Escobar, Yunel, LAA	.349
Kim, Hyun Soo, Bal	.348
Healy, Ryon, Oak	.347
Cabrera, Miguel, Det	.329
Wieters, Matt, Bal	.329
Forsythe, Logan, TB	.329
Pedroia, Dustin, Bos	.322
Pearce, Steve, TB-Bal	.318

Batting Average w/ RISP
(minimum 100 PA)

Andrus, Elvis, Tex	.378
Altuve, Jose, Hou	.372
Escobar, Yunel, LAA	.362
Garcia, Avisail, CWS	.355
Betts, Mookie, Bos	.355
Ramirez, Jose, Cle	.355
Ortiz, David, Bos	.343
Cron, C.J., LAA	.333
Beltre, Adrian, Tex	.331
Castellanos, Nick, Det	.330

SLG vs. LHP
(minimum 125 PA)

Ramirez, Hanley, Bos	.677
Cruz, Nelson, Sea	.644
Dozier, Brian, Min	.613
Beltre, Adrian, Tex	.602
Beltran, Carlos, NYY-Tex	.589
Grossman, Robbie, Min	.576
Morales, Kendrys, KC	.560
Springer, George, Hou	.560
Guyer, Brandon, TB-Cle	.557
Davis, Khris, Oak	.550

SLG vs. RHP
(minimum 377 PA)

Ortiz, David, Bos	.665
Cano, Robinson, Sea	.584
Trumbo, Mark, Bal	.584
Cabrera, Miguel, Det	.578
Donaldson, Josh, Tor	.558
Trout, Mike, LAA	.555
Altuve, Jose, Hou	.544
Martinez, J.D., Det	.543
Longoria, Evan, TB	.542
Santana, Carlos, Cle	.541

Leadoff Hitters OBP
(minimum 150 PA)

Altuve, Jose, Hou	.415
Pedroia, Dustin, Bos	.394
Santana, Carlos, Cle	.385
Carrera, Ezequiel, Tor	.374
Springer, George, Hou	.362
Eaton, Adam, CWS	.360
Escobar, Yunel, LAA	.356
Betts, Mookie, Bos	.355
Choo, Shin-Soo, Tex	.354
Aoki, Nori, Sea	.348

Cleanup Hitters SLG
(minimum 150 PA)

Ortiz, David, Bos	.635
Abreu, Jose, CWS	.561
Beltre, Adrian, Tex	.555
Cruz, Nelson, Sea	.555
Saunders, Michael, Tor	.551
Davis, Khris, Oak	.536
Sano, Miguel, Min	.534
Encarnacion, Edwin, Tor	.514
Frazier, Todd, CWS	.509
Betts, Mookie, Bos	.500

BA vs. LHP
(minimum 125 PA)

Andrus, Elvis, Tex	.348
Ramirez, Hanley, Bos	.346
Grossman, Robbie, Min	.344
Desmond, Ian, Tex	.338
Beltran, Carlos, NYY-Tex	.338
Guyer, Brandon, TB-Cle	.336
Beltre, Adrian, Tex	.331
Morales, Kendrys, KC	.330
Machado, Manny, Bal	.329
Gregorius, Didi, NYY	.324

BA vs. RHP
(minimum 377 PA)

Altuve, Jose, Hou	.348
Betts, Mookie, Bos	.331
Cabrera, Miguel, Det	.321
Pedroia, Dustin, Bos	.320
Ortiz, David, Bos	.315
Trout, Mike, LAA	.313
Cano, Robinson, Sea	.312
Ramirez, Jose, Cle	.312
Seager, Kyle, Sea	.307
Martinez, J.D., Det	.307

Home BA
(minimum 251 PA)

Ramirez, Jose, Cle	.347
Lindor, Francisco, Cle	.344
Betts, Mookie, Bos	.335
Pedroia, Dustin, Bos	.334
Ortiz, David, Bos	.333
Desmond, Ian, Tex	.330
Trout, Mike, LAA	.330
Bogaerts, Xander, Bos	.323
Cabrera, Miguel, Det	.322
Abreu, Jose, CWS	.315

Away BA
(minimum 251 PA)

Altuve, Jose, Hou	.376
Escobar, Yunel, LAA	.324
Cano, Robinson, Sea	.323
Martinez, Victor, Det	.322
Cabrera, Miguel, Det	.311
Calhoun, Kole, LAA	.307
Andrus, Elvis, Tex	.307
Cruz, Nelson, Sea	.306
Betts, Mookie, Bos	.301
Trout, Mike, LAA	.301

OBP vs. LHP
(minimum 125 PA)

Guyer, Brandon, TB-Cle	.464
Trout, Mike, LAA	.436
Ramirez, Hanley, Bos	.420
Grossman, Robbie, Min	.418
Donaldson, Josh, Tor	.413
Cabrera, Miguel, Det	.409
Andrus, Elvis, Tex	.403
Beltre, Adrian, Tex	.403
Pedroia, Dustin, Bos	.397
Bogaerts, Xander, Bos	.393

OBP vs. RHP
(minimum 377 PA)

Trout, Mike, LAA	.442
Ortiz, David, Bos	.407
Donaldson, Josh, Tor	.401
Altuve, Jose, Hou	.398
Seager, Kyle, Sea	.394
Cabrera, Miguel, Det	.388
Mauer, Joe, Min	.383
Martinez, J.D., Det	.382
Betts, Mookie, Bos	.377
Bautista, Jose, Tor	.376

2016 American League Batting Leaders

Stolen Bases		Caught Stealing		Highest SB Success Pct		Lowest SB Success Pct	
				(minimum 20 SBA)		(minimum 20 SBA)	
Davis, Rajai, Cle	43	Altuve, Jose, Hou	10	Dozier, Brian, Min	90.0	Santana, Danny, Min	57.1
Altuve, Jose, Hou	30	Springer, George, Hou	10	Davis, Rajai, Cle	87.8	Odor, Rougned, Tex	66.7
Dyson, Jarrod, KC	30	Aoki, Nori, Sea	9	Kiermaier, Kevin, TB	87.5	Kinsler, Ian, Det	70.0
Trout, Mike, LAA	30	Santana, Danny, Min	9	Betts, Mookie, Bos	86.7	Pillar, Kevin, Tor	70.0
Nunez, Eduardo, Min	27	Andrus, Elvis, Tex	8	Nunez, Eduardo, Min	81.8	Ellsbury, Jacoby, NYY	71.4
Betts, Mookie, Bos	26	Ellsbury, Jacoby, NYY	8	Dyson, Jarrod, KC	81.1	Maybin, Cameron, Det	71.4
Andrus, Elvis, Tex	24	Dyson, Jarrod, KC	7	Trout, Mike, LAA	81.1	Altuve, Jose, Hou	75.0
Martin, Leonys, Sea	24	Odor, Rougned, Tex	7	Escobar, Alcides, KC	81.0	Andrus, Elvis, Tex	75.0
Ramirez, Jose, Cle	22	Ramirez, Jose, Cle	7	Gardner, Brett, NYY	80.0	Frazier, Todd, CWS	75.0
2 tied with	21	Trout, Mike, LAA	7	Martin, Leonys, Sea	80.0	Ramirez, Jose, Cle	75.9

Steals of Third		Grounded Into DP		Grounded Into DP Pct		Hit By Pitch	
				(minimum 50 GIDP Ops)			
Davis, Rajai, Cle	13	Cabrera, Miguel, Det	26	Merrifield, Whit, KC	1.49	Guyer, Brandon, TB-Cle	31
Trout, Mike, LAA	10	Pedroia, Dustin, Bos	24	Saltalamacchia,J, Det	1.79	Abreu, Jose, CWS	15
Ramirez, Jose, Cle	9	Pujols, Albert, LAA	24	Kepler, Max, Min	2.44	Eaton, Adam, CWS	14
Altuve, Jose, Hou	8	Encarnacion, Edwin, Tor	22	Trout, Mike, LAA	3.05	Kinsler, Ian, Det	13
Dyson, Jarrod, KC	8	Ortiz, David, Bos	22	Buxton, Byron, Min	3.08	Springer, George, Hou	11
Andrus, Elvis, Tex	7	Abreu, Jose, CWS	21	Lawrie, Brett, CWS	3.95	Trout, Mike, LAA	11
Kiermaier, Kevin, TB	6	Bautista, Jose, Tor	21	Castellanos, Nick, Det	4.35	Bradley Jr., Jackie, Bos	10
Burns, Billy, Oak-KC	5	Escobar, Yunel, LAA	21	Odor, Rougned, Tex	4.58	Martin, Russell, Tor	10
Martin, Leonys, Sea	4	Kipnis, Jason, Cle	21	Chisenhall, Lonnie, Cle	4.82	3 tied with	9
3 tied with	3	Morales, Kendrys, KC	20	Miller, Brad, TB	4.95		

Pitches Seen		At Bats Per Home Run		Highest GB/FB Ratio		Lowest GB/FB Ratio	
		(minimum 502 PA)		(minimum 502 PA)		(minimum 502 PA)	
Trout, Mike, LAA	3014	Trumbo, Mark, Bal	13.0	Escobar, Yunel, LAA	2.80	Vogt, Stephen, Oak	0.65
Donaldson, Josh, Tor	2952	Davis, Khris, Oak	13.2	Mauer, Joe, Min	2.43	Longoria, Evan, TB	0.68
Napoli, Mike, Cle	2950	Cruz, Nelson, Sea	13.7	Hosmer, Eric, KC	2.38	Kinsler, Ian, Det	0.71
Springer, George, Hou	2932	Ortiz, David, Bos	14.1	Eaton, Adam, CWS	2.08	Ortiz, David, Bos	0.73
Encarnacion, Edwin, Tor	2900	Encarnacion, Edwin, Tor	14.3	Desmond, Ian, Tex	2.06	Frazier, Todd, CWS	0.73
Bogaerts, Xander, Bos	2849	Dozier, Brian, Min	14.6	Gardner, Brett, NYY	1.93	Perez, Salvador, KC	0.73
Dozier, Brian, Min	2788	Frazier, Todd, CWS	14.8	Pedroia, Dustin, Bos	1.83	Dozier, Brian, Min	0.76
Santana, Carlos, Cle	2781	Davis, Chris, Bal	14.9	Correa, Carlos, Hou	1.83	Napoli, Mike, Cle	0.81
Frazier, Todd, CWS	2766	Donaldson, Josh, Tor	15.6	Iglesias, Jose, Det	1.82	Shaw, Travis, Bos	0.81
Kipnis, Jason, Cle	2758	Cabrera, Miguel, Det	15.7	Lindor, Francisco, Cle	1.74	Dickerson, Corey, TB	0.84

Pitches Per Plate App		Pct Pitches Taken		Best BPS on OutZ		Worst BPS on OutZ	
(minimum 502 PA)		(minimum 1500 Pitches)		(minimum 502 PA)		(minimum 502 PA)	
Napoli, Mike, Cle	4.57	Mauer, Joe, Min	64.5	Ramirez, Jose, Cle	.725	Martin, Russell, Tor	.252
Trout, Mike, LAA	4.43	Hardy, J.J., Bal	63.7	Altuve, Jose, Hou	.679	Davis, Chris, Bal	.271
Mauer, Joe, Min	4.28	Bautista, Jose, Tor	63.4	Ortiz, David, Bos	.672	Gordon, Alex, KC	.285
Saunders, Michael, Tor	4.27	Gardner, Brett, NYY	62.7	Odor, Rougned, Tex	.651	Martin, Leonys, Sea	.304
Martin, Russell, Tor	4.27	Grossman, Robbie, Min	62.2	Pedroia, Dustin, Bos	.641	Napoli, Mike, Cle	.306
Bautista, Jose, Tor	4.25	Trout, Mike, LAA	61.7	Beltran, Carlos, NYY-Tex	.636	Davis, Khris, Oak	.308
Donaldson, Josh, Tor	4.22	Martin, Russell, Tor	61.0	Bogaerts, Xander, Bos	.629	Frazier, Todd, CWS	.328
Gordon, Alex, KC	4.20	Santana, Carlos, Cle	60.8	Andrus, Elvis, Tex	.611	Castro, Starlin, NYY	.333
Semien, Marcus, Oak	4.16	Forsythe, Logan, TB	60.4	Cabrera, Miguel, Det	.594	Donaldson, Josh, Tor	.341
Upton, Justin, Det	4.16	Smith, Seth, Sea	60.3	Ramirez, Hanley, Bos	.579	Semien, Marcus, Oak	.341

2016 American League Batting Leaders

Best OPS vs Fastballs
(minimum 251 PA)

Donaldson, Josh, Tor	1.055
Trumbo, Mark, Bal	1.020
Ortiz, David, Bos	1.014
Machado, Manny, Bal	.995
Cabrera, Miguel, Det	.982
Martinez, J.D., Det	.972
Dozier, Brian, Min	.964
Altuve, Jose, Hou	.961
Odor, Rougned, Tex	.959
Trout, Mike, LAA	.951

Best OPS vs Curveballs
(minimum 50 PA)

Trout, Mike, LAA	1.463
Davis, Khris, Oak	1.118
Napoli, Mike, Cle	1.089
Castellanos, Nick, Det	1.082
Cabrera, Miguel, Det	1.080
Miller, Brad, TB	.985
Ortiz, David, Bos	.961
Altuve, Jose, Hou	.957
Kinsler, Ian, Det	.946
Bogaerts, Xander, Bos	.941

Best OPS vs Changeups
(minimum 50 PA)

Naquin, Tyler, Cle	1.262
Ramirez, Hanley, Bos	1.157
Betts, Mookie, Bos	1.138
Pedroia, Dustin, Bos	1.125
Cuthbert, Cheslor, KC	1.118
Cano, Robinson, Sea	1.048
Correa, Carlos, Hou	1.033
Dozier, Brian, Min	1.029
Calhoun, Kole, LAA	1.021
Martin, Leonys, Sea	1.007

Best OPS vs Sliders
(minimum 32 PA)

Alvarez, Pedro, Bal	1.133
Gregorius, Didi, NYY	1.107
Lee, Dae-Ho, Sea	1.090
Moreland, Mitch, Tex	1.049
Santana, Carlos, Cle	1.032
Cabrera, Miguel, Det	1.019
Sanchez, Gary, NYY	1.019
Beltran, Carlos, NYY-Tex	1.008
Morales, Kendrys, KC	1.007
Bradley Jr., Jackie, Bos	.991

OPS
(minimum 502 PA)

Ortiz, David, Bos	1.021
Trout, Mike, LAA	.991
Cabrera, Miguel, Det	.956
Donaldson, Josh, Tor	.953
Altuve, Jose, Hou	.928
Cruz, Nelson, Sea	.915
Martinez, J.D., Det	.908
Betts, Mookie, Bos	.897
Dozier, Brian, Min	.886
Encarnacion, Edwin, Tor	.886

OPS First Half
(minimum 260 PA)

Ortiz, David, Bos	1.107
Donaldson, Josh, Tor	1.017
Trout, Mike, LAA	.991
Altuve, Jose, Hou	.954
Machado, Manny, Bal	.944
Bradley Jr., Jackie, Bos	.926
Cano, Robinson, Sea	.923
Saunders, Michael, Tor	.923
Trumbo, Mark, Bal	.923
Cruz, Nelson, Sea	.909

OPS Second Half
(minimum 201 PA)

Cabrera, Miguel, Det	1.057
Sanchez, Gary, NYY	1.052
Beltre, Adrian, Tex	1.000
Dozier, Brian, Min	.990
Trout, Mike, LAA	.988
Gattis, Evan, Hou	.951
Ramirez, Hanley, Bos	.947
Martinez, J.D., Det	.945
Betts, Mookie, Bos	.935
Cruz, Nelson, Sea	.923

OPS by Catchers
(minimum 251 PA)

Leon, Sandy, Bos	.840
McCann, Brian, NYY	.751
Martin, Russell, Tor	.736
Wieters, Matt, Bal	.726
Vogt, Stephen, Oak	.724
Suzuki, Kurt, Min	.717
Perez, Salvador, KC	.716
Castro, Jason, Hou	.690
Iannetta, Chris, Sea	.633
Wilson, Bobby, Det-Tex-TB	.626

OPS by First Basemen
(minimum 251 PA)

Cabrera, Miguel, Det	.984
Encarnacion, Edwin, Tor	.933
Santana, Carlos, Cle	.872
Ramirez, Hanley, Bos	.845
Napoli, Mike, Cle	.828
Abreu, Jose, CWS	.828
Davis, Chris, Bal	.787
Cron, C.J., LAA	.765
Hosmer, Eric, KC	.760
Lind, Adam, Sea	.753

OPS by Second Basemen
(minimum 251 PA)

Altuve, Jose, Hou	.922
Cano, Robinson, Sea	.889
Dozier, Brian, Min	.874
Kinsler, Ian, Det	.827
Pedroia, Dustin, Bos	.827
Kipnis, Jason, Cle	.821
Travis, Devon, Tor	.799
Odor, Rougned, Tex	.799
Forsythe, Logan, TB	.781
Schoop, Jonathan, Bal	.752

OPS by Third Basemen
(minimum 251 PA)

Donaldson, Josh, Tor	.957
Beltre, Adrian, Tex	.869
Machado, Manny, Bal	.868
Valencia, Danny, Oak	.868
Longoria, Evan, TB	.863
Healy, Ryon, Oak	.861
Seager, Kyle, Sea	.858
Castellanos, Nick, Det	.833
Valbuena, Luis, Hou	.806
Ramirez, Jose, Cle	.801

OPS by Shortstops
(minimum 251 PA)

Correa, Carlos, Hou	.804
Bogaerts, Xander, Bos	.802
Andrus, Elvis, Tex	.800
Miller, Brad, TB	.800
Lindor, Francisco, Cle	.789
Tulowitzki, Troy, Tor	.754
Gregorius, Didi, NYY	.744
Anderson, Tim, CWS	.738
Semien, Marcus, Oak	.735
Hardy, J.J., Bal	.716

OPS by Left Fielders
(minimum 251 PA)

Grossman, Robbie, Min	.863
Saunders, Michael, Tor	.850
Dickerson, Corey, TB	.818
Davis, Khris, Oak	.814
Cabrera, Melky, CWS	.802
Upton, Justin, Det	.790
Kim, Hyun Soo, Bal	.769
Aoki, Nori, Sea	.752
Gardner, Brett, NYY	.718
Crisp, Coco, Oak-Cle	.701

OPS by Center Fielders
(minimum 251 PA)

Trout, Mike, LAA	1.010
Naquin, Tyler, Cle	.910
Bradley Jr., Jackie, Bos	.835
Maybin, Cameron, Det	.800
Desmond, Ian, Tex	.785
Cain, Lorenzo, KC	.752
Jones, Adam, Bal	.746
Kiermaier, Kevin, TB	.745
Davis, Rajai, Cle	.718
Buxton, Byron, Min	.714

OPS by Right Fielders
(minimum 251 PA)

Betts, Mookie, Bos	.899
Martinez, J.D., Det	.893
Trumbo, Mark, Bal	.888
Bautista, Jose, Tor	.870
Beltran, Carlos, NYY-Tex	.869
Springer, George, Hou	.812
Calhoun, Kole, LAA	.797
Eaton, Adam, CWS	.795
Reddick, Josh, Oak	.794
Chisenhall, Lonnie, Cle	.784

OPS by Designated Hitters
(minimum 125 PA)

Ortiz, David, Bos	1.031
Cruz, Nelson, Sea	.961
Santana, Carlos, Cle	.862
Davis, Khris, Oak	.858
Alvarez, Pedro, Bal	.858
Encarnacion, Edwin, Tor	.843
Beltran, Carlos, NYY-Tex	.838
Park, Byungho, Min	.808
Martinez, Victor, Det	.796
Trumbo, Mark, Bal	.791

2016 American League Batting Leaders

OPS Batting Left vs. LHP (minimum 125 PA)	
Ortiz, David, Bos	.867
Gregorius, Didi, NYY	.834
Calhoun, Kole, LAA	.830
Kipnis, Jason, Cle	.790
Cano, Robinson, Sea	.770
Odor, Rougned, Tex	.763
Seager, Kyle, Sea	.728
Eaton, Adam, CWS	.726
Davis, Chris, Bal	.711
Martin, Leonys, Sea	.684

OPS Batting Left vs. RHP (minimum 377 PA)	
Ortiz, David, Bos	1.072
Cano, Robinson, Sea	.955
Seager, Kyle, Sea	.932
Santana, Carlos, Cle	.915
Bradley Jr., Jackie, Bos	.902
Martinez, Victor, Det	.832
Davis, Chris, Bal	.828
Kipnis, Jason, Cle	.822
Ramirez, Jose, Cle	.818
Lindor, Francisco, Cle	.816

OPS Batting Right vs. LHP (minimum 125 PA)	
Ramirez, Hanley, Bos	1.097
Guyer, Brandon, TB-Cle	1.021
Cruz, Nelson, Sea	1.020
Beltre, Adrian, Tex	1.004
Grossman, Robbie, Min	.994
Trout, Mike, LAA	.971
Beltran, Carlos, NYY-Tex	.970
Dozier, Brian, Min	.965
Springer, George, Hou	.945
Donaldson, Josh, Tor	.932

OPS Batting Right vs. RHP (minimum 377 PA)	
Trout, Mike, LAA	.996
Cabrera, Miguel, Det	.966
Donaldson, Josh, Tor	.960
Altuve, Jose, Hou	.942
Trumbo, Mark, Bal	.932
Martinez, J.D., Det	.925
Betts, Mookie, Bos	.917
Encarnacion, Edwin, Tor	.881
Cruz, Nelson, Sea	.864
Longoria, Evan, TB	.864

OPS vs. LHP (minimum 125 PA)	
Ramirez, Hanley, Bos	1.097
Guyer, Brandon, TB-Cle	1.021
Cruz, Nelson, Sea	1.020
Beltre, Adrian, Tex	1.004
Grossman, Robbie, Min	.994
Trout, Mike, LAA	.971
Beltran, Carlos, NYY-Tex	.970
Dozier, Brian, Min	.965
Springer, George, Hou	.945
Donaldson, Josh, Tor	.932

OPS vs. RHP (minimum 377 PA)	
Ortiz, David, Bos	1.072
Trout, Mike, LAA	.996
Cabrera, Miguel, Det	.966
Donaldson, Josh, Tor	.960
Cano, Robinson, Sea	.955
Altuve, Jose, Hou	.942
Seager, Kyle, Sea	.932
Trumbo, Mark, Bal	.932
Martinez, J.D., Det	.925
Betts, Mookie, Bos	.917

RC Per 27 Outs vs. LHP (minimum 125 PA)	
Beltran, Carlos, NYY-Tex	9.4
Beltre, Adrian, Tex	9.3
Ramirez, Hanley, Bos	9.0
Andrus, Elvis, Tex	8.6
Valencia, Danny, Oak	8.5
Grossman, Robbie, Min	8.2
Guyer, Brandon, TB-Cle	8.2
Trout, Mike, LAA	8.0
Morales, Kendrys, KC	7.9
Donaldson, Josh, Tor	7.4

RC Per 27 Outs vs. RHP (minimum 377 PA)	
Trout, Mike, LAA	9.7
Ortiz, David, Bos	8.7
Seager, Kyle, Sea	7.9
Altuve, Jose, Hou	7.8
Betts, Mookie, Bos	7.7
Donaldson, Josh, Tor	7.4
Trumbo, Mark, Bal	7.1
Cabrera, Miguel, Det	6.9
Santana, Carlos, Cle	6.9
Ramirez, Jose, Cle	6.8

Highest RBI % (minimum 502 PA)	
Betts, Mookie, Bos	44.95
Trout, Mike, LAA	44.52
Ortiz, David, Bos	44.28
Ramirez, Hanley, Bos	41.45
Donaldson, Josh, Tor	41.32
Beltre, Adrian, Tex	41.16
Altuve, Jose, Hou	40.82
Encarnacion, Edwin, Tor	39.53
Trumbo, Mark, Bal	39.17
Morales, Kendrys, KC	39.11

Lowest RBI % (minimum 502 PA)	
Iglesias, Jose, Det	21.68
Gordon, Alex, KC	24.97
Escobar, Yunel, LAA	25.08
Martin, Leonys, Sea	25.12
Gardner, Brett, NYY	25.36
Escobar, Alcides, KC	26.04
Gonzalez, Marwin, Hou	26.86
Cuthbert, Cheslor, KC	26.87
Headley, Chase, NYY	27.10
Saunders, Michael, Tor	28.60

Highest Strikeout per PA (minimum 502 PA)	
Davis, Chris, Bal	.329
Napoli, Mike, Cle	.301
Gordon, Alex, KC	.292
Upton, Justin, Det	.286
Saunders, Michael, Tor	.281
Martin, Russell, Tor	.277
Davis, Khris, Oak	.272
Martin, Leonys, Sea	.259
Trumbo, Mark, Bal	.255
Shaw, Travis, Bos	.251

Lowest Strikeout per PA (minimum 502 PA)	
Iglesias, Jose, Det	.097
Altuve, Jose, Hou	.098
Ramirez, Jose, Cle	.100
Beltre, Adrian, Tex	.103
Pedroia, Dustin, Bos	.105
Cabrera, Melky, CWS	.107
Betts, Mookie, Bos	.110
Pujols, Albert, LAA	.115
Escobar, Yunel, LAA	.118
Andrus, Elvis, Tex	.123

Home Runs At Home	
Trumbo, Mark, Bal	25
Miller, Brad, TB	22
Napoli, Mike, Cle	22
Donaldson, Josh, Tor	21
Dozier, Brian, Min	21
Cabrera, Miguel, Det	20
Encarnacion, Edwin, Tor	20
Ortiz, David, Bos	20
Santana, Carlos, Cle	20
4 tied with	19

Home Runs Away	
Cruz, Nelson, Sea	26
Frazier, Todd, CWS	24
Davis, Khris, Oak	23
Cano, Robinson, Sea	22
Encarnacion, Edwin, Tor	22
Trumbo, Mark, Bal	22
Davis, Chris, Bal	21
Dozier, Brian, Min	21
3 tied with	19

2016 American League Batting Leaders

Under Age 26: AB Per HR
(minimum 502 PA)

Machado, Manny, Bal	17.3
Odor, Rougned, Tex	18.3
Trout, Mike, LAA	18.9
Betts, Mookie, Bos	21.7
Schoop, Jonathan, Bal	24.6
Mazara, Nomar, Tex	25.8
Correa, Carlos, Hou	28.9
Bogaerts, Xander, Bos	31.0
Cuthbert, Cheslor, KC	39.6
Lindor, Francisco, Cle	40.3

Under Age 26: OPS
(minimum 502 PA)

Trout, Mike, LAA	.991
Betts, Mookie, Bos	.897
Machado, Manny, Bal	.876
Ramirez, Jose, Cle	.825
Correa, Carlos, Hou	.811
Bogaerts, Xander, Bos	.802
Odor, Rougned, Tex	.798
Lindor, Francisco, Cle	.794
Schoop, Jonathan, Bal	.752
Mazara, Nomar, Tex	.739

Under Age 26: RC/27 Outs
(minimum 502 PA)

Trout, Mike, LAA	9.3
Betts, Mookie, Bos	7.2
Ramirez, Jose, Cle	6.6
Machado, Manny, Bal	5.8
Correa, Carlos, Hou	5.7
Bogaerts, Xander, Bos	5.4
Lindor, Francisco, Cle	5.0
Odor, Rougned, Tex	4.5
Mazara, Nomar, Tex	4.5
Cuthbert, Cheslor, KC	4.2

Swing and Miss %
(minimum 1500 Pitches Seen)

Davis, Chris, Bal	35.7
Sano, Miguel, Min	35.1
Davis, Khris, Oak	33.2
Rasmus, Colby, Hou	33.1
Souza Jr., Steven, TB	32.9
Gomez, Carlos, Hou-Tex	32.6
Garcia, Avisail, CWS	32.5
Alvarez, Pedro, Bal	31.3
Castro, Jason, Hou	30.6
Anderson, Tim, CWS	30.2

Highest First Swing %
(minimum 502 PA)

Jones, Adam, Bal	44.5
Schoop, Jonathan, Bal	41.3
Springer, George, Hou	39.3
Altuve, Jose, Hou	38.9
Martinez, J.D., Det	37.7
Calhoun, Kole, LAA	37.6
Miller, Brad, TB	37.5
Dickerson, Corey, TB	37.4
Escobar, Yunel, LAA	36.9
Alonso, Yonder, Oak	36.3

Lowest First Swing %
(minimum 502 PA)

Mauer, Joe, Min	7.0
Kipnis, Jason, Cle	11.0
Forsythe, Logan, TB	12.7
Gardner, Brett, NYY	12.8
Pedroia, Dustin, Bos	13.0
Pujols, Albert, LAA	13.0
Betts, Mookie, Bos	16.3
Semien, Marcus, Oak	16.6
Trout, Mike, LAA	16.6
Bogaerts, Xander, Bos	17.4

Home RC Per 27 Outs
(minimum 251 PA)

Trout, Mike, LAA	9.8
Ortiz, David, Bos	9.3
Napoli, Mike, Cle	8.5
Ramirez, Jose, Cle	8.3
Donaldson, Josh, Tor	8.2
Betts, Mookie, Bos	8.2
Beltre, Adrian, Tex	7.4
Ramirez, Hanley, Bos	7.2
Desmond, Ian, Tex	7.2
Kinsler, Ian, Det	7.2

Road RC Per 27 Outs
(minimum 251 PA)

Altuve, Jose, Hou	10.1
Trout, Mike, LAA	8.7
Cano, Robinson, Sea	7.3
Ortiz, David, Bos	7.0
Calhoun, Kole, LAA	6.8
Cruz, Nelson, Sea	6.7
Seager, Kyle, Sea	6.6
Donaldson, Josh, Tor	6.6
Martinez, Victor, Det	6.5
Santana, Carlos, Cle	6.4

Lead Changing RBI

Abreu, Jose, CWS	42
Longoria, Evan, TB	41
Pujols, Albert, LAA	41
Cabrera, Miguel, Det	39
Ortiz, David, Bos	39
Betts, Mookie, Bos	38
Dozier, Brian, Min	38
Altuve, Jose, Hou	36
Encarnacion, Edwin, Tor	36
2 tied with	35

2016 National League Batting Leaders

Batting Average
(minimum 502 PA)

LeMahieu, DJ, Col	.348
Murphy, Daniel, Was	.347
Votto, Joey, Cin	.326
Blackmon, Charlie, Col	.324
Segura, Jean, Ari	.319
Marte, Starling, Pit	.311
Seager, Corey, LAD	.308
Molina, Yadier, StL	.307
Ramos, Wilson, Was	.307
Braun, Ryan, Mil	.305

On Base Percentage
(minimum 502 PA)

Votto, Joey, Cin	.434
LeMahieu, DJ, Col	.416
Goldschmidt, Paul, Ari	.411
Freeman, Freddie, Atl	.400
Belt, Brandon, SF	.394
Fowler, Dexter, ChC	.393
Murphy, Daniel, Was	.390
Zobrist, Ben, ChC	.386
Bryant, Kris, ChC	.385
Rizzo, Anthony, ChC	.385

Slugging Average
(minimum 502 PA)

Murphy, Daniel, Was	.595
Arenado, Nolan, Col	.570
Freeman, Freddie, Atl	.569
Bryant, Kris, ChC	.554
Blackmon, Charlie, Col	.552
Votto, Joey, Cin	.550
Rizzo, Anthony, ChC	.544
Braun, Ryan, Mil	.538
Cespedes, Yoenis, NYM	.530
Seager, Corey, LAD	.512

Home Runs

Arenado, Nolan, Col	41
Carter, Chris, Mil	41
Bryant, Kris, ChC	39
Kemp, Matt, SD-Atl	35
Freeman, Freddie, Atl	34
Bruce, Jay, Cin-NYM	33
Duvall, Adam, Cin	33
Rizzo, Anthony, ChC	32
Cespedes, Yoenis, NYM	31
Tomas, Yasmany, Ari	31

Games

Arenado, Nolan, Col	160
Carter, Chris, Mil	160
Herrera, Odubel, Phi	159
Suarez, Eugenio, Cin	159
Freeman, Freddie, Atl	158
Galvis, Freddy, Phi	158
Goldschmidt, Paul, Ari	158
Markakis, Nick, Atl	158
Votto, Joey, Cin	158
3 tied with	157

Plate Appearances

Goldschmidt, Paul, Ari	705
Bryant, Kris, ChC	699
Arenado, Nolan, Col	696
Segura, Jean, Ari	694
Freeman, Freddie, Atl	693
Seager, Corey, LAD	687
Markakis, Nick, Atl	684
Villar, Jonathan, Mil	679
Votto, Joey, Cin	677
2 tied with	676

At Bats

Segura, Jean, Ari	637
Seager, Corey, LAD	627
Kemp, Matt, SD-Atl	623
Arenado, Nolan, Col	618
Bryant, Kris, ChC	603
Prado, Martin, Mia	600
Markakis, Nick, Atl	599
Myers, Wil, SD	599
McCutchen, Andrew, Pit	598
2 tied with	589

Hits

Segura, Jean, Ari	203
Seager, Corey, LAD	193
LeMahieu, DJ, Col	192
Blackmon, Charlie, Col	187
Murphy, Daniel, Was	184
Prado, Martin, Mia	183
Arenado, Nolan, Col	182
Votto, Joey, Cin	181
Freeman, Freddie, Atl	178
Bryant, Kris, ChC	176

Singles

LeMahieu, DJ, Col	141
Prado, Martin, Mia	135
Segura, Jean, Ari	135
Hernandez, Cesar, Phi	130
Herrera, Odubel, Phi	125
Seager, Corey, LAD	122
Blackmon, Charlie, Col	118
Inciarte, Ender, Atl	118
Molina, Yadier, StL	117
Votto, Joey, Cin	116

Doubles

Murphy, Daniel, Was	47
Freeman, Freddie, Atl	43
Rizzo, Anthony, ChC	43
Gonzalez, Carlos, Col	42
Belt, Brandon, SF	41
Segura, Jean, Ari	41
Seager, Corey, LAD	40
Kemp, Matt, SD-Atl	39
5 tied with	38

Triples

Crawford, Brandon, SF	11
Hernandez, Cesar, Phi	11
Owings, Chris, Ari	11
Lamb, Jake, Ari	9
Belt, Brandon, SF	8
LeMahieu, DJ, Col	8
Turner, Trea, Was	8
8 tied with	7

Total Bases

Arenado, Nolan, Col	352
Freeman, Freddie, Atl	335
Bryant, Kris, ChC	334
Seager, Corey, LAD	321
Blackmon, Charlie, Col	319
Segura, Jean, Ari	318
Rizzo, Anthony, ChC	317
Murphy, Daniel, Was	316
Kemp, Matt, SD-Atl	311
Votto, Joey, Cin	306

Runs Scored

Bryant, Kris, ChC	121
Arenado, Nolan, Col	116
Blackmon, Charlie, Col	111
Goldschmidt, Paul, Ari	106
Seager, Corey, LAD	105
LeMahieu, DJ, Col	104
Freeman, Freddie, Atl	102
Segura, Jean, Ari	102
Votto, Joey, Cin	101
Myers, Wil, SD	99

RBI

Arenado, Nolan, Col	133
Rizzo, Anthony, ChC	109
Kemp, Matt, SD-Atl	108
Murphy, Daniel, Was	104
Duvall, Adam, Cin	103
Bryant, Kris, ChC	102
Gonzalez, Carlos, Col	100
Bruce, Jay, Cin-NYM	99
Yelich, Christian, Mia	98
Votto, Joey, Cin	97

Walks

Goldschmidt, Paul, Ari	110
Harper, Bryce, Was	108
Votto, Joey, Cin	108
Belt, Brandon, SF	104
Zobrist, Ben, ChC	96
Freeman, Freddie, Atl	89
Carpenter, Matt, StL	81
Fowler, Dexter, ChC	79
Villar, Jonathan, Mil	79
Carter, Chris, Mil	76

Strikeouts

Carter, Chris, Mil	206
Espinosa, Danny, Was	174
Villar, Jonathan, Mil	174
Freeman, Freddie, Atl	171
Duvall, Adam, Cin	164
Myers, Wil, SD	160
Kemp, Matt, SD-Atl	156
Suarez, Eugenio, Cin	155
Bryant, Kris, ChC	154
Lamb, Jake, Ari	154

2016 National League Batting Leaders

Intentional Walks			BA Bases Loaded			Sacrifice Hits			Sacrifice Flies	
			(minimum 10 PA)							
Harper, Bryce, Was	20		Kang, Jung Ho, Pit	.571		Scherzer, Max, Was	13		Kemp, Matt, SD-Atl	12
Freeman, Freddie, Atl	18		Barnhart, Tucker, Cin	.500		Cueto, Johnny, SF	11		Carter, Chris, Mil	10
Goldschmidt, Paul, Ari	15		Votto, Joey, Cin	.500		Hamilton, Billy, Cin	11		Harper, Bryce, Was	10
Votto, Joey, Cin	15		Belt, Brandon, SF	.462		Straily, Dan, Cin	11		Crawford, Brandon, SF	9
Espinosa, Danny, Was	12		Gonzalez, Adrian, LAD	.462		Teheran, Julio, Atl	11		Markakis, Nick, Atl	9
Arenado, Nolan, Col	10		Diaz, Aledmys, StL	.455		Lester, Jon, ChC	10		9 tied with	8
Braun, Ryan, Mil	10		Piscotty, Stephen, StL	.455		7 tied with	8			
Crawford, Brandon, SF	10		Robinson, Clint, Was	.455						
Murphy, Daniel, Was	10		Ozuna, Marcell, Mia	.444						
4 tied with	9		3 tied with	.429						

BA Close & Late			Batting Average w/ RISP			SLG vs. LHP			SLG vs. RHP	
(minimum 50 PA)			(minimum 100 PA)			(minimum 125 PA)			(minimum 377 PA)	
Kang, Jung Ho, Pit	.396		Prado, Martin, Mia	.368		Tomas, Yasmany, Ari	.690		Murphy, Daniel, Was	.614
Suzuki, Ichiro, Mia	.380		Piscotty, Stephen, StL	.363		Bryant, Kris, ChC	.641		Freeman, Freddie, Atl	.596
Reynolds, Mark, Col	.375		Votto, Joey, Cin	.356		Werth, Jayson, Was	.620		Blackmon, Charlie, Col	.596
Carpenter, Matt, StL	.362		Arenado, Nolan, Col	.356		Kemp, Matt, SD-Atl	.612		Arenado, Nolan, Col	.593
Molina, Yadier, StL	.358		Barnhart, Tucker, Cin	.355		Braun, Ryan, Mil	.598		Votto, Joey, Cin	.584
LeMahieu, DJ, Col	.339		Murphy, Daniel, Was	.355		Ozuna, Marcell, Mia	.595		Rizzo, Anthony, ChC	.577
Walker, Neil, NYM	.339		Rizzo, Anthony, ChC	.341		Goldschmidt, Paul, Ari	.576		Turner, Justin, LAD	.563
Votto, Joey, Cin	.333		Blackmon, Charlie, Col	.340		Prado, Martin, Mia	.568		Seager, Corey, LAD	.557
Garcia, Adonis, Atl	.325		Diaz, Aledmys, StL	.337		Piscotty, Stephen, StL	.552		Lamb, Jake, Ari	.552
2 tied with	.321		Braun, Ryan, Mil	.336		Murphy, Daniel, Was	.548		Pederson, Joc, LAD	.547

Leadoff Hitters OBP			Cleanup Hitters SLG			BA vs. LHP			BA vs. RHP	
(minimum 150 PA)			(minimum 150 PA)			(minimum 125 PA)			(minimum 377 PA)	
Suzuki, Ichiro, Mia	.427		Cespedes, Yoenis, NYM	.633		Prado, Martin, Mia	.424		LeMahieu, DJ, Col	.354
Hernandez, Cesar, Phi	.405		Arenado, Nolan, Col	.614		Tomas, Yasmany, Ari	.364		Murphy, Daniel, Was	.354
Fowler, Dexter, ChC	.393		Carter, Chris, Mil	.598		Goldschmidt, Paul, Ari	.352		Seager, Corey, LAD	.334
Carpenter, Matt, StL	.386		Rizzo, Anthony, ChC	.573		Braun, Ryan, Mil	.344		Segura, Jean, Ari	.333
Blackmon, Charlie, Col	.380		Bruce, Jay, Cin-NYM	.542		Hernandez, Cesar, Phi	.341		Votto, Joey, Cin	.330
Inciarte, Ender, Atl	.372		Murphy, Daniel, Was	.538		Blackmon, Charlie, Col	.331		Realmuto, J.T., Mia	.322
Villar, Jonathan, Mil	.369		Marte, Starling, Pit	.524		LeMahieu, DJ, Col	.331		Blackmon, Charlie, Col	.320
Segura, Jean, Ari	.368		Kemp, Matt, SD-Atl	.524		Murphy, Daniel, Was	.329		Marte, Starling, Pit	.315
Turner, Trea, Was	.367		Gonzalez, Carlos, Col	.514		Werth, Jayson, Was	.322		Gonzalez, Carlos, Col	.309
Herrera, Odubel, Phi	.359		Joseph, Tommy, Phi	.500		Inciarte, Ender, Atl	.319		Molina, Yadier, StL	.308

Home BA			Away BA			OBP vs. LHP			OBP vs. RHP	
(minimum 251 PA)			(minimum 251 PA)			(minimum 125 PA)			(minimum 377 PA)	
LeMahieu, DJ, Col	.391		Realmuto, J.T., Mia	.352		Prado, Martin, Mia	.500		Votto, Joey, Cin	.448
Murphy, Daniel, Was	.361		Votto, Joey, Cin	.340		Goldschmidt, Paul, Ari	.494		LeMahieu, DJ, Col	.417
Blackmon, Charlie, Col	.335		Prado, Martin, Mia	.340		Tomas, Yasmany, Ari	.423		Freeman, Freddie, Atl	.405
Segura, Jean, Ari	.325		Murphy, Daniel, Was	.333		Bryant, Kris, ChC	.419		Murphy, Daniel, Was	.396
Drury, Brandon, Ari	.322		Hernandez, Cesar, Phi	.327		LeMahieu, DJ, Col	.415		Belt, Brandon, SF	.395
Pagan, Angel, SF	.321		Molina, Yadier, StL	.325		Braun, Ryan, Mil	.411		Rizzo, Anthony, ChC	.393
Seager, Corey, LAD	.321		Freeman, Freddie, Atl	.324		Werth, Jayson, Was	.411		Fowler, Dexter, ChC	.392
Gonzalez, Carlos, Col	.320		Yelich, Christian, Mia	.320		Posey, Buster, SF	.409		Yelich, Christian, Mia	.392
Braun, Ryan, Mil	.317		Marte, Starling, Pit	.319		Zobrist, Ben, ChC	.401		Harper, Bryce, Was	.391
Arenado, Nolan, Col	.312		Blackmon, Charlie, Col	.313		Piscotty, Stephen, StL	.400		Seager, Corey, LAD	.391

2016 National League Batting Leaders

Stolen Bases

Villar, Jonathan, Mil	62
Hamilton, Billy, Cin	58
Marte, Starling, Pit	47
Perez, Hernan, Mil	34
Segura, Jean, Ari	33
Turner, Trea, Was	33
Goldschmidt, Paul, Ari	32
Gordon, Dee, Mia	30
Jankowski, Travis, SD	30
Myers, Wil, SD	28

Caught Stealing

Villar, Jonathan, Mil	18
Hernandez, Cesar, Phi	13
Jankowski, Travis, SD	12
Marte, Starling, Pit	12
Harper, Bryce, Was	10
Peraza, Jose, Cin	10
Segura, Jean, Ari	10
Blackmon, Charlie, Col	9
Nieuwenhuis, Kirk, Mil	9
Ramirez, Alexei, SD	9

Highest SB Success Pct
(minimum 20 SBA)

Owings, Chris, Ari	91.3
Hamilton, Billy, Cin	87.9
Goldschmidt, Paul, Ari	86.5
Broxton, Keon, Mil	85.2
Turner, Trea, Was	84.6
Perez, Hernan, Mil	82.9
Harrison, Josh, Pit	82.6
Myers, Wil, SD	82.4
Gordon, Dee, Mia	81.1
Upton Jr., Melvin, SD	80.0

Lowest SB Success Pct
(minimum 20 SBA)

Hernandez, Cesar, Phi	56.7
Phillips, Brandon, Cin	63.6
Blackmon, Charlie, Col	65.4
Smith, Mallex, Atl	66.7
Harper, Bryce, Was	67.7
Peraza, Jose, Cin	67.7
Inciarte, Ender, Atl	69.6
Jankowski, Travis, SD	71.4
Galvis, Freddy, Phi	73.9
Polanco, Gregory, Pit	73.9

Steals of Third

Hamilton, Billy, Cin	20
Villar, Jonathan, Mil	13
Segura, Jean, Ari	11
Perez, Hernan, Mil	9
Galvis, Freddy, Phi	8
Inciarte, Ender, Atl	7
Goldschmidt, Paul, Ari	6
Phillips, Brandon, Cin	6
Fowler, Dexter, ChC	5
Owings, Chris, Ari	5

Grounded Into DP

Prado, Martin, Mia	24
Molina, Yadier, StL	22
Braun, Ryan, Mil	20
Kendrick, Howie, LAD	20
Yelich, Christian, Mia	20
LeMahieu, DJ, Col	19
Carter, Chris, Mil	18
Garcia, Adonis, Atl	18
Posey, Buster, SF	18
Tomas, Yasmany, Ari	18

Grounded Into DP Pct
(minimum 50 GIDP Ops)

Utley, Chase, LAD	0.00
Bryant, Kris, ChC	1.78
Blackmon, Charlie, Col	2.60
Espinosa, Danny, Was	3.08
Murphy, Daniel, Was	3.48
Bourn, Michael, Ari	4.29
Wong, Kolten, StL	4.41
Fowler, Dexter, ChC	4.62
Flowers, Tyler, Atl	4.69
Belt, Brandon, SF	4.86

Hit By Pitch

Dietrich, Derek, Mia	24
Espinosa, Danny, Was	20
Bryant, Kris, ChC	18
Marte, Starling, Pit	16
Rizzo, Anthony, ChC	16
Kang, Jung Ho, Pit	14
Blackmon, Charlie, Col	13
Piscotty, Stephen, StL	12
Russell, Addison, ChC	12
Segura, Jean, Ari	12

Pitches Seen

Goldschmidt, Paul, Ari	3012
Votto, Joey, Cin	2896
Myers, Wil, SD	2884
Villar, Jonathan, Mil	2831
Werth, Jayson, Was	2785
Freeman, Freddie, Atl	2779
Carter, Chris, Mil	2744
Arenado, Nolan, Col	2743
McCutchen, Andrew, Pit	2740
Belt, Brandon, SF	2721

At Bats Per Home Run
(minimum 502 PA)

Carter, Chris, Mil	13.4
Arenado, Nolan, Col	15.1
Cespedes, Yoenis, NYM	15.5
Bryant, Kris, ChC	15.5
Bruce, Jay, Cin-NYM	16.3
Duvall, Adam, Cin	16.7
Braun, Ryan, Mil	17.0
Tomas, Yasmany, Ari	17.1
Freeman, Freddie, Atl	17.3
Kemp, Matt, SD-Atl	17.8

Highest GB/FB Ratio
(minimum 502 PA)

Kendrick, Howie, LAD	3.10
Yelich, Christian, Mia	2.82
Hernandez, Cesar, Phi	2.65
Villar, Jonathan, Mil	2.31
LeMahieu, DJ, Col	2.22
Braun, Ryan, Mil	2.22
Ramos, Wilson, Was	2.15
Span, Denard, SF	2.13
Garcia, Adonis, Atl	1.97
Segura, Jean, Ari	1.91

Lowest GB/FB Ratio
(minimum 502 PA)

Belt, Brandon, SF	0.57
Carter, Chris, Mil	0.65
Bryant, Kris, ChC	0.67
Carpenter, Matt, StL	0.71
Duvall, Adam, Cin	0.72
Freeman, Freddie, Atl	0.75
Arenado, Nolan, Col	0.75
Rendon, Anthony, Was	0.82
McCutchen, Andrew, Pit	0.86
Granderson, Curtis, NYM	0.86

Pitches Per Plate App
(minimum 502 PA)

Werth, Jayson, Was	4.60
Fowler, Dexter, ChC	4.41
Votto, Joey, Cin	4.28
Goldschmidt, Paul, Ari	4.27
Myers, Wil, SD	4.27
Carter, Chris, Mil	4.26
Granderson, Curtis, NYM	4.25
Carpenter, Matt, StL	4.22
Zobrist, Ben, ChC	4.21
Villar, Jonathan, Mil	4.17

Pct Pitches Taken
(minimum 1500 Pitches)

Zobrist, Ben, ChC	64.5
Granderson, Curtis, NYM	63.6
Werth, Jayson, Was	61.9
Cervelli, Francisco, Pit	61.9
Goldschmidt, Paul, Ari	61.6
Carpenter, Matt, StL	61.5
Grandal, Yasmani, LAD	60.8
Fowler, Dexter, ChC	60.8
Prado, Martin, Mia	60.5
Utley, Chase, LAD	59.7

Best BPS on OutZ
(minimum 502 PA)

Murphy, Daniel, Was	.744
Phillips, Brandon, Cin	.688
Pagan, Angel, SF	.629
Prado, Martin, Mia	.625
Blackmon, Charlie, Col	.604
Marte, Starling, Pit	.593
Span, Denard, SF	.589
Arenado, Nolan, Col	.585
Herrera, Odubel, Phi	.583
Molina, Yadier, StL	.580

Worst BPS on OutZ
(minimum 502 PA)

Duvall, Adam, Cin	.315
Carter, Chris, Mil	.322
Carpenter, Matt, StL	.323
Suarez, Eugenio, Cin	.324
Hechavarria, Adeiny, Mia	.343
Cozart, Zack, Cin	.345
Granderson, Curtis, NYM	.359
Panik, Joe, SF	.359
McCutchen, Andrew, Pit	.361
Werth, Jayson, Was	.364

2016 National League Batting Leaders

Best OPS vs Fastballs
(minimum 251 PA)

Murphy, Daniel, Was	1.044
Bryant, Kris, ChC	1.026
Freeman, Freddie, Atl	1.013
Votto, Joey, Cin	1.008
Blackmon, Charlie, Col	.964
Carpenter, Matt, StL	.946
Pederson, Joc, LAD	.943
Fowler, Dexter, ChC	.937
Ramos, Wilson, Was	.929
LeMahieu, DJ, Col	.908

Best OPS vs Curveballs
(minimum 50 PA)

Bryant, Kris, ChC	1.047
Seager, Corey, LAD	1.038
Harper, Bryce, Was	1.035
Goldschmidt, Paul, Ari	1.029
Duvall, Adam, Cin	1.023
Freeman, Freddie, Atl	1.010
Turner, Justin, LAD	.995
Posey, Buster, SF	.972
Gennett, Scooter, Mil	.956
Yelich, Christian, Mia	.917

Best OPS vs Changeups
(minimum 50 PA)

Braun, Ryan, Mil	1.160
Tomas, Yasmany, Ari	1.097
Gyorko, Jedd, StL	1.070
LeMahieu, DJ, Col	1.063
Freeman, Freddie, Atl	1.052
Arenado, Nolan, Col	1.039
Posey, Buster, SF	1.028
Rizzo, Anthony, ChC	1.015
Polanco, Gregory, Pit	1.003
2 tied with	.993

Best OPS vs Sliders
(minimum 32 PA)

Hernandez, Cesar, Phi	1.238
Rizzo, Anthony, ChC	1.220
Broxton, Keon, Mil	1.131
Joseph, Tommy, Phi	1.103
Diaz, Aledmys, StL	1.052
Arenado, Nolan, Col	1.035
Lucroy, Jonathan, Mil	1.001
Solarte, Yangervis, SD	.982
Puig, Yasiel, LAD	.965
Gonzalez, Carlos, Col	.963

OPS
(minimum 502 PA)

Murphy, Daniel, Was	.985
Votto, Joey, Cin	.985
Freeman, Freddie, Atl	.968
Bryant, Kris, ChC	.939
Blackmon, Charlie, Col	.933
Arenado, Nolan, Col	.932
Rizzo, Anthony, ChC	.928
LeMahieu, DJ, Col	.911
Braun, Ryan, Mil	.903
Goldschmidt, Paul, Ari	.899

OPS First Half
(minimum 260 PA)

Rizzo, Anthony, ChC	1.006
Carpenter, Matt, StL	.988
Murphy, Daniel, Was	.985
Lamb, Jake, Ari	.983
Bryant, Kris, ChC	.962
Cespedes, Yoenis, NYM	.955
Arenado, Nolan, Col	.930
Goldschmidt, Paul, Ari	.930
Belt, Brandon, SF	.928
Gonzalez, Carlos, Col	.924

OPS Second Half
(minimum 201 PA)

Votto, Joey, Cin	1.158
Freeman, Freddie, Atl	1.067
Blackmon, Charlie, Col	1.003
Murphy, Daniel, Was	.985
Segura, Jean, Ari	.954
LeMahieu, DJ, Col	.937
Arenado, Nolan, Col	.934
Turner, Trea, Was	.934
Braun, Ryan, Mil	.931
Molina, Yadier, StL	.926

OPS by Catchers
(minimum 251 PA)

Lucroy, Jonathan, Mil	.898
Ramos, Wilson, Was	.858
Grandal, Yasmani, LAD	.827
Posey, Buster, SF	.788
Molina, Yadier, StL	.786
Flowers, Tyler, Atl	.785
Realmuto, J.T., Mia	.772
Hundley, Nick, Col	.756
Castillo, Welington, Ari	.755
Rupp, Cameron, Phi	.752

OPS by First Basemen
(minimum 251 PA)

Votto, Joey, Cin	.992
Freeman, Freddie, Atl	.968
Rizzo, Anthony, ChC	.929
Goldschmidt, Paul, Ari	.901
Belt, Brandon, SF	.866
Joseph, Tommy, Phi	.834
Carter, Chris, Mil	.824
Bour, Justin, Mia	.818
Myers, Wil, SD	.805
Gonzalez, Adrian, LAD	.795

OPS by Second Basemen
(minimum 251 PA)

Murphy, Daniel, Was	1.002
Schimpf, Ryan, SD	.958
LeMahieu, DJ, Col	.911
Segura, Jean, Ari	.878
Zobrist, Ben, ChC	.832
Walker, Neil, NYM	.827
Hernandez, Cesar, Phi	.765
Peterson, Jace, Atl	.747
Phillips, Brandon, Cin	.743
Gennett, Scooter, Mil	.743

OPS by Third Basemen
(minimum 251 PA)

Arenado, Nolan, Col	.932
Bryant, Kris, ChC	.930
Kang, Jung Ho, Pit	.882
Turner, Justin, LAD	.827
Solarte, Yangervis, SD	.823
Lamb, Jake, Ari	.821
Rendon, Anthony, Was	.795
Prado, Martin, Mia	.779
Suarez, Eugenio, Cin	.743
Garcia, Adonis, Atl	.735

OPS by Shortstops
(minimum 251 PA)

Story, Trevor, Col	.906
Seager, Corey, LAD	.881
Diaz, Aledmys, StL	.865
Cabrera, Asdrubal, NYM	.804
Villar, Jonathan, Mil	.783
Crawford, Brandon, SF	.774
Owings, Chris, Ari	.739
Russell, Addison, ChC	.731
Cozart, Zack, Cin	.730
Mercer, Jordy, Pit	.702

OPS by Left Fielders
(minimum 251 PA)

Braun, Ryan, Mil	.907
Yelich, Christian, Mia	.868
Marte, Starling, Pit	.858
Duvall, Adam, Cin	.796
Dickerson, Alex, SD	.791
Cespedes, Yoenis, NYM	.773
Pagan, Angel, SF	.749
Conforto, Michael, NYM	.728
Upton Jr., Melvin, SD	.720
Werth, Jayson, Was	.719

OPS by Center Fielders
(minimum 251 PA)

Cespedes, Yoenis, NYM	.970
Blackmon, Charlie, Col	.935
Pederson, Joc, LAD	.855
Fowler, Dexter, ChC	.846
Ozuna, Marcell, Mia	.803
Herrera, Odubel, Phi	.780
Grichuk, Randal, StL	.770
Nieuwenhuis, Kirk, Mil	.766
McCutchen, Andrew, Pit	.765
Inciarte, Ender, Atl	.757

OPS by Right Fielders
(minimum 251 PA)

Tomas, Yasmany, Ari	.860
Gonzalez, Carlos, Col	.849
Stanton, Giancarlo, Mia	.825
Bruce, Jay, Cin-NYM	.820
Pence, Hunter, SF	.809
Harper, Bryce, Was	.807
Piscotty, Stephen, StL	.803
Granderson, Curtis, NYM	.780
Kemp, Matt, SD-Atl	.777
Markakis, Nick, Atl	.762

OPS by Pitchers
(minimum 50 PA)

Corbin, Patrick, Ari	.743
Arrieta, Jake, ChC	.720
Syndergaard, Noah, NYM	.673
Wainwright, Adam, StL	.648
Bumgarner, Madison, SF	.608
Hammel, Jason, ChC	.562
Fernandez, Jose, Mia	.505
Martinez, Carlos, StL	.500
Ray, Robbie, Ari	.487
Strasburg, Stephen, Was	.469

2016 National League Batting Leaders

OPS Batting Left vs. LHP (minimum 125 PA)		OPS Batting Left vs. RHP (minimum 377 PA)		OPS Batting Right vs. LHP (minimum 125 PA)		OPS Batting Right vs. RHP (minimum 377 PA)	
Murphy, Daniel, Was	.924	Votto, Joey, Cin	1.033	Tomas, Yasmany, Ari	1.112	Arenado, Nolan, Col	.953
Freeman, Freddie, Atl	.902	Murphy, Daniel, Was	1.010	Goldschmidt, Paul, Ari	1.070	Turner, Justin, LAD	.919
Belt, Brandon, SF	.883	Freeman, Freddie, Atl	1.001	Prado, Martin, Mia	1.068	LeMahieu, DJ, Col	.903
Votto, Joey, Cin	.861	Blackmon, Charlie, Col	.972	Bryant, Kris, ChC	1.060	Segura, Jean, Ari	.900
Blackmon, Charlie, Col	.843	Rizzo, Anthony, ChC	.970	Werth, Jayson, Was	1.031	Bryant, Kris, ChC	.896
Rizzo, Anthony, ChC	.832	Seager, Corey, LAD	.948	Braun, Ryan, Mil	1.010	Braun, Ryan, Mil	.869
Carpenter, Matt, StL	.809	Carpenter, Matt, StL	.920	Kemp, Matt, SD-Atl	.954	Goldschmidt, Paul, Ari	.850
Gonzalez, Carlos, Col	.786	Pederson, Joc, LAD	.918	Piscotty, Stephen, StL	.952	Cespedes, Yoenis, NYM	.839
Harper, Bryce, Was	.764	Yelich, Christian, Mia	.908	LeMahieu, DJ, Col	.931	Marte, Starling, Pit	.837
Inciarte, Ender, Atl	.749	Lamb, Jake, Ari	.898	Villar, Jonathan, Mil	.930	Ramos, Wilson, Was	.806

OPS vs. LHP (minimum 125 PA)		OPS vs. RHP (minimum 377 PA)		RC Per 27 Outs vs. LHP (minimum 125 PA)		RC Per 27 Outs vs. RHP (minimum 377 PA)	
Tomas, Yasmany, Ari	1.112	Votto, Joey, Cin	1.033	Prado, Martin, Mia	12.2	Votto, Joey, Cin	9.6
Goldschmidt, Paul, Ari	1.070	Murphy, Daniel, Was	1.010	Goldschmidt, Paul, Ari	11.1	Murphy, Daniel, Was	8.6
Prado, Martin, Mia	1.068	Freeman, Freddie, Atl	1.001	Werth, Jayson, Was	9.1	Freeman, Freddie, Atl	8.0
Bryant, Kris, ChC	1.060	Blackmon, Charlie, Col	.972	Bryant, Kris, ChC	8.6	Arenado, Nolan, Col	7.7
Werth, Jayson, Was	1.031	Rizzo, Anthony, ChC	.970	Tomas, Yasmany, Ari	8.4	Seager, Corey, LAD	7.5
Braun, Ryan, Mil	1.010	Arenado, Nolan, Col	.953	Murphy, Daniel, Was	8.0	Rizzo, Anthony, ChC	7.5
Kemp, Matt, SD-Atl	.954	Seager, Corey, LAD	.948	Villar, Jonathan, Mil	7.7	Blackmon, Charlie, Col	7.3
Piscotty, Stephen, StL	.952	Carpenter, Matt, StL	.920	Braun, Ryan, Mil	7.6	Turner, Justin, LAD	7.2
LeMahieu, DJ, Col	.931	Turner, Justin, LAD	.919	Piscotty, Stephen, StL	7.4	Carpenter, Matt, StL	7.0
Villar, Jonathan, Mil	.930	Pederson, Joc, LAD	.918	LeMahieu, DJ, Col	7.4	Pederson, Joc, LAD	6.9

Highest RBI % (minimum 502 PA)		Lowest RBI % (minimum 502 PA)		Highest Strikeout per PA (minimum 502 PA)		Lowest Strikeout per PA (minimum 502 PA)	
Murphy, Daniel, Was	46.43	Inciarte, Ender, Atl	18.53	Carter, Chris, Mil	.320	Panik, Joe, SF	.089
Arenado, Nolan, Col	44.24	Hechavarria, Adeiny, Mia	20.83	Espinosa, Danny, Was	.290	Murphy, Daniel, Was	.098
Votto, Joey, Cin	42.23	Heyward, Jason, ChC	23.68	Duvall, Adam, Cin	.270	Prado, Martin, Mia	.105
Blackmon, Charlie, Col	41.58	Kendrick, Howie, LAD	23.78	Lamb, Jake, Ari	.259	Molina, Yadier, StL	.108
Braun, Ryan, Mil	40.92	Hernandez, Cesar, Phi	25.88	Villar, Jonathan, Mil	.256	Posey, Buster, SF	.111
Cespedes, Yoenis, NYM	40.60	Realmuto, J.T., Mia	27.06	Freeman, Freddie, Atl	.247	Phillips, Brandon, Cin	.116
Duvall, Adam, Cin	40.60	Span, Denard, SF	27.40	Suarez, Eugenio, Cin	.247	Inciarte, Ender, Atl	.118
Goldschmidt, Paul, Ari	40.25	Herrera, Odubel, Phi	28.05	Tomas, Yasmany, Ari	.242	Pagan, Angel, SF	.122
Gonzalez, Carlos, Col	39.53	Marte, Starling, Pit	28.12	Myers, Wil, SD	.237	Span, Denard, SF	.124
Myers, Wil, SD	39.17	Mercer, Jordy, Pit	29.41	Kemp, Matt, SD-Atl	.232	LeMahieu, DJ, Col	.126

Home Runs At Home		Home Runs Away	
Arenado, Nolan, Col	25	Bryant, Kris, ChC	22
Carter, Chris, Mil	24	Kemp, Matt, SD-Atl	21
Grandal, Yasmani, LAD	20	Rizzo, Anthony, ChC	20
Lamb, Jake, Ari	19	Freeman, Freddie, Atl	19
Cabrera, Asdrubal, NYM	18	Gyorko, Jedd, StL	18
Gonzalez, Carlos, Col	18	Blackmon, Charlie, Col	17
Myers, Wil, SD	18	Carter, Chris, Mil	17
Seager, Corey, LAD	18	Cespedes, Yoenis, NYM	17
Bruce, Jay, Cin-NYM	17	Duvall, Adam, Cin	17
Bryant, Kris, ChC	17	Granderson, Curtis, NYM	17

2016 National League Batting Leaders

Under Age 26: AB Per HR	
(minimum 502 PA)	
Arenado, Nolan, Col	15.1
Bryant, Kris, ChC	15.5
Tomas, Yasmany, Ari	17.1
Lamb, Jake, Ari	18.0
Harper, Bryce, Was	21.1
Myers, Wil, SD	21.4
Franco, Maikel, Phi	23.2
Polanco, Gregory, Pit	24.0
Seager, Corey, LAD	24.1
Ozuna, Marcell, Mia	24.2

Under Age 26: OPS	
(minimum 502 PA)	
Bryant, Kris, ChC	.939
Arenado, Nolan, Col	.932
Seager, Corey, LAD	.877
Yelich, Christian, Mia	.859
Lamb, Jake, Ari	.840
Villar, Jonathan, Mil	.826
Tomas, Yasmany, Ari	.820
Harper, Bryce, Was	.814
Piscotty, Stephen, StL	.800
Myers, Wil, SD	.797

Under Age 26: RC/27 Outs	
(minimum 502 PA)	
Arenado, Nolan, Col	7.4
Bryant, Kris, ChC	7.3
Seager, Corey, LAD	6.5
Villar, Jonathan, Mil	6.0
Piscotty, Stephen, StL	5.8
Harper, Bryce, Was	5.8
Herrera, Odubel, Phi	5.8
Myers, Wil, SD	5.6
Yelich, Christian, Mia	5.5
Lamb, Jake, Ari	5.5

Swing and Miss %	
(minimum 1500 Pitches Seen)	
Carter, Chris, Mil	37.3
Nieuwenhuis, Kirk, Mil	36.6
Stanton, Giancarlo, Mia	34.7
Moss, Brandon, StL	34.1
Espinosa, Danny, Was	32.9
Tomas, Yasmany, Ari	29.8
Gonzalez, Carlos, Col	29.8
Pence, Hunter, SF	29.8
Rupp, Cameron, Phi	29.4
Grichuk, Randal, StL	29.1

Highest First Swing %	
(minimum 502 PA)	
Tomas, Yasmany, Ari	49.0
Seager, Corey, LAD	42.5
Molina, Yadier, StL	40.5
Freeman, Freddie, Atl	40.2
Crawford, Brandon, SF	38.0
Franco, Maikel, Phi	36.3
Braun, Ryan, Mil	35.8
Belt, Brandon, SF	35.7
Piscotty, Stephen, StL	35.4
Bryant, Kris, ChC	35.3

Lowest First Swing %	
(minimum 502 PA)	
Blackmon, Charlie, Col	7.9
Prado, Martin, Mia	7.9
Granderson, Curtis, NYM	8.3
Werth, Jayson, Was	11.7
Carpenter, Matt, StL	13.6
Zobrist, Ben, ChC	14.7
Pagan, Angel, SF	15.4
LeMahieu, DJ, Col	15.8
Utley, Chase, LAD	16.0
Mercer, Jordy, Pit	16.2

Home RC Per 27 Outs	
(minimum 251 PA)	
Arenado, Nolan, Col	9.1
LeMahieu, DJ, Col	9.0
Murphy, Daniel, Was	8.7
Votto, Joey, Cin	8.4
Myers, Wil, SD	8.0
Blackmon, Charlie, Col	7.8
Gonzalez, Carlos, Col	7.7
Braun, Ryan, Mil	7.4
Belt, Brandon, SF	7.3
Carpenter, Matt, StL	7.3

Road RC Per 27 Outs	
(minimum 251 PA)	
Votto, Joey, Cin	8.9
Bryant, Kris, ChC	8.9
Freeman, Freddie, Atl	8.8
Murphy, Daniel, Was	8.3
Rizzo, Anthony, ChC	7.8
Fowler, Dexter, ChC	7.2
Villar, Jonathan, Mil	6.9
Blackmon, Charlie, Col	6.7
Goldschmidt, Paul, Ari	6.7
Marte, Starling, Pit	6.6

Lead Changing RBI	
Yelich, Christian, Mia	42
Murphy, Daniel, Was	40
Kemp, Matt, SD-Atl	39
Arenado, Nolan, Col	37
Turner, Justin, LAD	37
Rizzo, Anthony, ChC	35
Goldschmidt, Paul, Ari	34
Votto, Joey, Cin	33
3 tied with	32

2016 American League Pitching Leaders

Earned Run Average (minimum 162 IP)		Winning Percentage (minimum 15 Decisions)		Opponent Batting Average (minimum 162 IP)		Baserunners Per 9 IP (minimum 162 IP)	
Sanchez, Aaron, Tor	3.00	Sanchez, Aaron, Tor	.882	Estrada, Marco, Tor	.203	Verlander, Justin, Det	9.33
Verlander, Justin, Det	3.04	Porcello, Rick, Bos	.846	Verlander, Justin, Det	.207	Porcello, Rick, Bos	9.61
Tanaka, Masahiro, NYY	3.07	Happ, J.A., Tor	.833	Kluber, Corey, Cle	.216	Kluber, Corey, Cle	9.80
Kluber, Corey, Cle	3.14	Duffy, Danny, KC	.800	Sanchez, Aaron, Tor	.224	Tanaka, Masahiro, NYY	9.83
Porcello, Rick, Bos	3.15	Tanaka, Masahiro, NYY	.778	Sale, Chris, CWS	.227	Sale, Chris, CWS	10.01
Happ, J.A., Tor	3.18	Hamels, Cole, Tex	.750	Porcello, Rick, Bos	.230	Estrada, Marco, Tor	10.28
Quintana, Jose, CWS	3.20	Tillman, Chris, Bal	.727	Happ, J.A., Tor	.231	Duffy, Danny, KC	10.62
Hamels, Cole, Tex	3.32	Wright, Steven, Bos	.684	Tanaka, Masahiro, NYY	.236	Quintana, Jose, CWS	10.64
Sale, Chris, CWS	3.34	Kluber, Corey, Cle	.667	Kennedy, Ian, KC	.236	Sanchez, Aaron, Tor	10.73
Santana, Ervin, Min	3.38	Price, David, Bos	.654	Archer, Chris, TB	.238	Happ, J.A., Tor	10.80

Games		Games Started		Complete Games		Shutouts	
Shaw, Bryan, Cle	75	Price, David, Bos	35	Sale, Chris, CWS	6	Kluber, Corey, Cle	2
Betances, Dellin, NYY	73	Verlander, Justin, Det	34	Wright, Steven, Bos	4	13 tied with	1
Dyson, Sam, Tex	73	Volquez, Edinson, KC	34	Kluber, Corey, Cle	3		
Herrera, Kelvin, KC	72	8 tied with	33	Porcello, Rick, Bos	3		
Osuna, Roberto, Tor	72			Graveman, Kendall, Oak	2		
Pressly, Ryan, Min	72			Price, David, Bos	2		
Brach, Brad, Bal	71			Santana, Ervin, Min	2		
Jones, Nate, CWS	71			Ventura, Yordano, KC	2		
3 tied with	70			Verlander, Justin, Det	2		
				18 tied with	1		

Wins		Losses		No Decisions		Wild Pitches	
Porcello, Rick, Bos	22	Archer, Chris, TB	19	Odorizzi, Jake, TB	17	Fiers, Mike, Hou	17
Happ, J.A., Tor	20	Dickey, R.A., Tor	15	Pineda, Michael, NYY	14	Gray, Sonny, Oak	15
Kluber, Corey, Cle	18	Nolasco, Ricky, Min-LAA	14	Sanchez, Aaron, Tor	13	Giles, Ken, Hou	14
Price, David, Bos	17	Fister, Doug, Hou	13	Stroman, Marcus, Tor	13	Ventura, Yordano, KC	13
Sale, Chris, CWS	17	Miley, Wade, Sea-Bal	13	Tanaka, Masahiro, NYY	13	Archer, Chris, TB	11
Iwakuma, Hisashi, Sea	16	Sanchez, Anibal, Det	13	Volquez, Edinson, KC	13	Rodon, Carlos, CWS	11
Tillman, Chris, Bal	16	Shoemaker, Matt, LAA	13	Griffin, A.J., Tex	12	Santana, Ervin, Min	11
Verlander, Justin, Det	16	12 tied with	12	Hamels, Cole, Tex	12	6 tied with	10
Hamels, Cole, Tex	15			Perez, Martin, Tex	12		
Sanchez, Aaron, Tor	15			Santana, Ervin, Min	12		

Strikeouts		Walks Allowed		Intentional Walks Allowed		Hit Batters	
Verlander, Justin, Det	254	Santiago, Hector, LAA-Min	79	Neshek, Pat, Hou	7	Sale, Chris, CWS	17
Archer, Chris, TB	233	Ventura, Yordano, KC	78	Rzepczynski, Marc, Oak	6	Kennedy, Ian, KC	13
Sale, Chris, CWS	233	Hamels, Cole, Tex	77	Ramirez, Erasmo, TB	5	Porcello, Rick, Bos	13
Price, David, Bos	228	Perez, Martin, Tex	76	Ryan, Kyle, Det	5	Hernandez, Felix, Sea	10
Kluber, Corey, Cle	227	Volquez, Edinson, KC	76	Vincent, Nick, Sea	5	Bauer, Trevor, Cle	9
Pineda, Michael, NYY	207	Jimenez, Ubaldo, Bal	72	Wilson, Alex, Det	5	Fulmer, Michael, Det	9
Hamels, Cole, Tex	200	Bauer, Trevor, Cle	70	6 tied with	4	Sabathia, CC, NYY	9
Porcello, Rick, Bos	189	Archer, Chris, TB	67			Wright, Mike, Bal	9
Duffy, Danny, KC	188	Kennedy, Ian, KC	66			7 tied with	8
Kennedy, Ian, KC	184	Tillman, Chris, Bal	66				

2016 American League Pitching Leaders

Runs Allowed		Hits Allowed		Doubles Allowed		Home Runs Allowed	
Volquez, Edinson, KC	124	Price, David, Bos	227	Fiers, Mike, Hou	47	Weaver, Jered, LAA	37
Perez, Martin, Tex	110	Iwakuma, Hisashi, Sea	218	Quintana, Jose, CWS	46	Tomlin, Josh, Cle	36
Sanchez, Anibal, Det	108	Volquez, Edinson, KC	217	Perez, Martin, Tex	45	Kennedy, Ian, KC	33
Price, David, Bos	106	Stroman, Marcus, Tor	209	Fister, Doug, Hou	44	Santiago, Hector, LAA-Min	33
Weaver, Jered, LAA	106	Weaver, Jered, LAA	209	Stroman, Marcus, Tor	44	Smyly, Drew, TB	32
Nolasco, Ricky, Min-LAA	104	McHugh, Collin, Hou	206	Tillman, Chris, Bal	44	Shields, James, CWS	31
Stroman, Marcus, Tor	104	Perez, Martin, Tex	205	Iwakuma, Hisashi, Sea	43	Archer, Chris, TB	30
Duffey, Tyler, Min	103	Nolasco, Ricky, Min-LAA	202	Pineda, Michael, NYY	43	Price, David, Bos	30
Smyly, Drew, TB	103	Graveman, Kendall, Oak	196	Duffey, Tyler, Min	42	Sanchez, Anibal, Det	30
3 tied with	100	Fister, Doug, Hou	195	2 tied with	41	Verlander, Justin, Det	30

Run Support Per Nine IP		% Pitches In Strike Zone		Pitches Per Start		Pitches Per Batter	
(minimum 162 IP)		(minimum 162 IP)		(minimum 30 GS)		(minimum 162 IP)	
Porcello, Rick, Bos	7.63	Duffy, Danny, KC	49.1	Verlander, Justin, Det	107.9	Iwakuma, Hisashi, Sea	3.57
Happ, J.A., Tor	6.88	Dickey, R.A., Tor	48.0	Sale, Chris, CWS	107.2	Perez, Martin, Tex	3.60
Price, David, Bos	6.61	Porcello, Rick, Bos	47.7	Gausman, Kevin, Bal	103.8	Tomlin, Josh, Cle	3.60
Santiago, Hector, LAA-Min	6.48	Santiago, Hector, LAA-Min	47.5	Porcello, Rick, Bos	103.3	Graveman, Kendall, Oak	3.60
Fiers, Mike, Hou	6.08	Weaver, Jered, LAA	47.4	Archer, Chris, TB	103.3	Stroman, Marcus, Tor	3.63
Weaver, Jered, LAA	5.81	Sale, Chris, CWS	46.8	Price, David, Bos	102.7	Tanaka, Masahiro, NYY	3.65
Kluber, Corey, Cle	5.78	Iwakuma, Hisashi, Sea	46.4	Quintana, Jose, CWS	102.6	Sanchez, Aaron, Tor	3.69
McHugh, Collin, Hou	5.75	Price, David, Bos	46.3	Kennedy, Ian, KC	102.4	Weaver, Jered, LAA	3.70
Sanchez, Aaron, Tor	5.62	Bauer, Trevor, Cle	46.1	Hamels, Cole, Tex	101.7	Duffy, Danny, KC	3.70
Iwakuma, Hisashi, Sea	5.43	Sanchez, Aaron, Tor	45.8	Odorizzi, Jake, TB	100.2	Kluber, Corey, Cle	3.71

Quality Starts		Batters Faced		Innings Pitched		Most Pitches in a Game	
Verlander, Justin, Det	27	Price, David, Bos	951	Price, David, Bos	230.0	Gonzalez, Chi Chi, Tex	124
Porcello, Rick, Bos	26	Sale, Chris, CWS	907	Verlander, Justin, Det	227.2	Hamels, Cole, Tex	123
Quintana, Jose, CWS	23	Verlander, Justin, Det	903	Sale, Chris, CWS	226.2	Porcello, Rick, Bos	123
Sale, Chris, CWS	23	Porcello, Rick, Bos	890	Porcello, Rick, Bos	223.0	Rodon, Carlos, CWS	122
Sanchez, Aaron, Tor	23	Kluber, Corey, Cle	860	Kluber, Corey, Cle	215.0	Smyly, Drew, TB	122
Hamels, Cole, Tex	22	Perez, Martin, Tex	855	Quintana, Jose, CWS	208.0	Wright, Steven, Bos	122
Kluber, Corey, Cle	22	Stroman, Marcus, Tor	855	Stroman, Marcus, Tor	204.0	Verlander, Justin, Det	121
Price, David, Bos	22	Volquez, Edinson, KC	853	Archer, Chris, TB	201.1	6 tied with	120
Happ, J.A., Tor	21	Archer, Chris, TB	850	Hamels, Cole, Tex	200.2		
4 tied with	19	Hamels, Cole, Tex	848	Tanaka, Masahiro, NYY	199.2		

Stolen Bases Allowed		Caught Stealing Off		Stolen Base Pct Allowed		Pickoffs	
				(minimum 162 IP)			
Jimenez, Ubaldo, Bal	26	Kennedy, Ian, KC	10	Tillman, Chris, Bal	0.0	Duffy, Danny, KC	5
Hamels, Cole, Tex	23	Sanchez, Anibal, Det	9	Duffy, Danny, KC	25.0	Dickey, R.A., Tor	4
Sanchez, Anibal, Det	22	Pineda, Michael, NYY	8	Price, David, Bos	33.3	Gibson, Kyle, Min	4
Betances, Dellin, NYY	21	Weaver, Jered, LAA	8	Kluber, Corey, Cle	36.4	Miley, Wade, Sea-Bal	4
Weaver, Jered, LAA	20	Fiers, Mike, Hou	7	Kennedy, Ian, KC	37.5	Nolasco, Ricky, Min-LAA	4
Rodon, Carlos, CWS	17	Kluber, Corey, Cle	7	Miley, Wade, Sea-Bal	37.5	Santiago, Hector, LAA-Min	4
5 tied with	16	Santiago, Hector, LAA-Min	7	Fiers, Mike, Hou	41.7	Tropeano, Nick, LAA	4
		5 tied with	6	Odorizzi, Jake, TB	45.5	7 tied with	3
				Verlander, Justin, Det	45.5		
				4 tied with	50.0		

2016 American League Pitching Leaders

Strikeouts Per 9 IP
(minimum 162 IP)

Pineda, Michael, NYY	10.61
Archer, Chris, TB	10.42
Verlander, Justin, Det	10.04
Kluber, Corey, Cle	9.50
Duffy, Danny, KC	9.42
Sale, Chris, CWS	9.25
Rodon, Carlos, CWS	9.16
Hamels, Cole, Tex	8.97
Price, David, Bos	8.92
Gausman, Kevin, Bal	8.72

Opp On-Base Percentage
(minimum 162 IP)

Verlander, Justin, Det	.263
Porcello, Rick, Bos	.268
Tanaka, Masahiro, NYY	.272
Kluber, Corey, Cle	.274
Estrada, Marco, Tor	.278
Sale, Chris, CWS	.279
Sanchez, Aaron, Tor	.290
Tomlin, Josh, Cle	.291
Duffy, Danny, KC	.292
Quintana, Jose, CWS	.295

Opp Slugging Average
(minimum 162 IP)

Sanchez, Aaron, Tor	.335
Kluber, Corey, Cle	.357
Estrada, Marco, Tor	.361
Porcello, Rick, Bos	.367
Verlander, Justin, Det	.368
Happ, J.A., Tor	.371
Sale, Chris, CWS	.372
Tanaka, Masahiro, NYY	.373
Hamels, Cole, Tex	.380
Santana, Ervin, Min	.381

Opponent OPS
(minimum 162 IP)

Sanchez, Aaron, Tor	.625
Verlander, Justin, Det	.630
Kluber, Corey, Cle	.631
Porcello, Rick, Bos	.635
Estrada, Marco, Tor	.639
Tanaka, Masahiro, NYY	.645
Sale, Chris, CWS	.651
Happ, J.A., Tor	.665
Santana, Ervin, Min	.682
Quintana, Jose, CWS	.687

Home Runs Per Nine IP
(minimum 162 IP)

Sanchez, Aaron, Tor	0.70
Perez, Martin, Tex	0.82
Kluber, Corey, Cle	0.92
Stroman, Marcus, Tor	0.93
Porcello, Rick, Bos	0.93
Santana, Ervin, Min	0.94
Bauer, Trevor, Cle	0.95
Quintana, Jose, CWS	0.95
Tanaka, Masahiro, NYY	0.99
Tillman, Chris, Bal	0.99

Batting Average vs. LHB
(minimum 125 BF)

Perez, Martin, Tex	.176
Verlander, Justin, Det	.187
Estrada, Marco, Tor	.190
Odorizzi, Jake, TB	.190
Otero, Dan, Cle	.197
Sale, Chris, CWS	.197
Salazar, Danny, Cle	.200
Walker, Taijuan, Sea	.206
Herrera, Kelvin, KC	.206
Karns, Nathan, Sea	.206

Batting Average vs. RHB
(minimum 225 BF)

Hill, Rich, Oak	.202
Kluber, Corey, Cle	.206
Estrada, Marco, Tor	.218
Buchholz, Clay, Bos	.222
Fister, Doug, Hou	.225
Verlander, Justin, Det	.226
Griffin, A.J., Tex	.227
Happ, J.A., Tor	.228
Hernandez, Felix, Sea	.229
Sanchez, Aaron, Tor	.231

Opp BA w/ RISP
(minimum 125 BF)

Salazar, Danny, Cle	.168
Verlander, Justin, Det	.188
Kennedy, Ian, KC	.192
Gausman, Kevin, Bal	.200
Happ, J.A., Tor	.201
Archer, Chris, TB	.206
Estrada, Marco, Tor	.210
Hamels, Cole, Tex	.213
Tanaka, Masahiro, NYY	.215
Santiago, Hector, LAA-Min	.216

OBP vs. Leadoff Hitter
(minimum 150 BF)

Tanaka, Masahiro, NYY	.244
Fulmer, Michael, Det	.258
Santana, Ervin, Min	.259
Carrasco, Carlos, Cle	.260
Verlander, Justin, Det	.266
Kluber, Corey, Cle	.267
Sabathia, CC, NYY	.272
Porcello, Rick, Bos	.275
Happ, J.A., Tor	.275
2 tied with	.276

Strikeouts / Walks Ratio
(minimum 162 IP)

Porcello, Rick, Bos	5.91
Tomlin, Josh, Cle	5.90
Sale, Chris, CWS	5.18
Tanaka, Masahiro, NYY	4.58
Price, David, Bos	4.56
Duffy, Danny, KC	4.48
Verlander, Justin, Det	4.46
Kluber, Corey, Cle	3.98
Pineda, Michael, NYY	3.91
Gausman, Kevin, Bal	3.70

Highest GB/FB Ratio
(minimum 162 IP)

Stroman, Marcus, Tor	2.95
Keuchel, Dallas, Hou	2.33
Sanchez, Aaron, Tor	2.16
Perez, Martin, Tex	2.02
Graveman, Kendall, Oak	1.90
Volquez, Edinson, KC	1.77
Ventura, Yordano, KC	1.63
Hamels, Cole, Tex	1.61
Bauer, Trevor, Cle	1.58
Miley, Wade, Sea-Bal	1.56

Lowest GB/FB Ratio
(minimum 162 IP)

Weaver, Jered, LAA	0.60
Smyly, Drew, TB	0.63
Santiago, Hector, LAA-Min	0.68
Estrada, Marco, Tor	0.69
Kennedy, Ian, KC	0.70
Verlander, Justin, Det	0.71
Odorizzi, Jake, TB	0.83
Duffy, Danny, KC	0.85
Quintana, Jose, CWS	1.04
Iwakuma, Hisashi, Sea	1.08

Sacrifice Flies Allowed

Smyly, Drew, TB	11
Nolasco, Ricky, Min-LAA	9
Perez, Martin, Tex	8
Bauer, Trevor, Cle	7
Gray, Sonny, Oak	7
Iwakuma, Hisashi, Sea	7
Price, David, Bos	7
Verlander, Justin, Det	7
14 tied with	6

Sacrifice Hits Allowed

Perez, Martin, Tex	9
Price, David, Bos	8
Ramirez, Erasmo, TB	7
Archer, Chris, TB	6
Iwakuma, Hisashi, Sea	6
Kluber, Corey, Cle	6
Volquez, Edinson, KC	6
5 tied with	5

GIDP Induced

Perez, Martin, Tex	36
Iwakuma, Hisashi, Sea	25
Pelfrey, Mike, Det	24
Stroman, Marcus, Tor	22
Dickey, R.A., Tor	21
Gibson, Kyle, Min	21
Happ, J.A., Tor	21
Nolasco, Ricky, Min-LAA	21
Sabathia, CC, NYY	21
Ventura, Yordano, KC	21

GIDP Per Nine IP
(minimum 162 IP)

Perez, Martin, Tex	1.63
Iwakuma, Hisashi, Sea	1.13
Dickey, R.A., Tor	1.11
Miley, Wade, Sea-Bal	1.08
Sabathia, CC, NYY	1.05
Tillman, Chris, Bal	1.05
Ventura, Yordano, KC	1.02
Fister, Doug, Hou	1.00
Santana, Ervin, Min	0.99
Stroman, Marcus, Tor	0.97

2016 American League Pitching Leaders

Saves

Britton, Zach, Bal	47
Rodriguez, Francisco, Det	44
Dyson, Sam, Tex	38
Colome, Alex, TB	37
Robertson, David, CWS	37
Osuna, Roberto, Tor	36
Allen, Cody, Cle	32
Kimbrel, Craig, Bos	31
Madson, Ryan, Oak	30
Davis, Wade, KC	27

Blown Saves

Jones, Nate, CWS	9
Axford, John, Oak	7
Cishek, Steve, Sea	7
Madson, Ryan, Oak	7
Robertson, David, CWS	7
Soria, Joakim, KC	7
Gregerson, Luke, Hou	6
Osuna, Roberto, Tor	6
Vincent, Nick, Sea	6
9 tied with	5

Save Pct
(minimum 20 Save Ops)

Britton, Zach, Bal	100.0
Chapman, Aroldis, NYY	95.2
Kimbrel, Craig, Bos	93.9
Colome, Alex, TB	92.5
Allen, Cody, Cle	91.4
Davis, Wade, KC	90.0
Rodriguez, Francisco, Det	89.8
Dyson, Sam, Tex	88.4
Diaz, Edwin, Sea	85.7
Osuna, Roberto, Tor	85.7

Save Opportunities

Rodriguez, Francisco, Det	49
Britton, Zach, Bal	47
Robertson, David, CWS	44
Dyson, Sam, Tex	43
Osuna, Roberto, Tor	42
Colome, Alex, TB	40
Madson, Ryan, Oak	37
Allen, Cody, Cle	35
Kimbrel, Craig, Bos	33
Cishek, Steve, Sea	32

Easy Saves

Britton, Zach, Bal	28
Robertson, David, CWS	26
Colome, Alex, TB	25
Rodriguez, Francisco, Det	25
Osuna, Roberto, Tor	23
Dyson, Sam, Tex	22
Allen, Cody, Cle	20
Kimbrel, Craig, Bos	20
Davis, Wade, KC	19
Madson, Ryan, Oak	17

Regular Saves

Britton, Zach, Bal	17
Rodriguez, Francisco, Det	17
Dyson, Sam, Tex	16
Madson, Ryan, Oak	13
Cishek, Steve, Sea	12
Allen, Cody, Cle	11
Colome, Alex, TB	11
Osuna, Roberto, Tor	10
Kimbrel, Craig, Bos	9
3 tied with	8

Tough Saves

Osuna, Roberto, Tor	3
Robertson, David, CWS	3
Britton, Zach, Bal	2
Kimbrel, Craig, Bos	2
Rodriguez, Francisco, Det	2
13 tied with	1

Holds Adjusted Saves %
(minimum 20 Save Ops + Holds)

Britton, Zach, Bal	100.0
Diekman, Jake, Tex	96.8
Chapman, Aroldis, NYY	95.2
Miller, Andrew, NYY-Cle	94.9
Kimbrel, Craig, Bos	94.1
Harris, Will, Hou	93.0
Colome, Alex, TB	92.7
Herrera, Kelvin, KC	92.7
Uehara, Koji, Bos	92.6
Grilli, Jason, Tor	92.0

Relief Wins

Brach, Brad, Bal	10
Miller, Andrew, NYY-Cle	10
Feliz, Michael, Hou	8
Givens, Mychal, Bal	8
Barnette, Tony, Tex	7
Bush, Matt, Tex	7
7 tied with	6

Relief Losses

Ramirez, Erasmo, TB	11
Soria, Joakim, KC	8
Cecil, Brett, Tor	7
Madson, Ryan, Oak	7
Pressly, Ryan, Min	7
8 tied with	6

Relief Games

Shaw, Bryan, Cle	75
Betances, Dellin, NYY	73
Dyson, Sam, Tex	73
Herrera, Kelvin, KC	72
Osuna, Roberto, Tor	72
Pressly, Ryan, Min	72
Brach, Brad, Bal	71
Jones, Nate, CWS	71
3 tied with	70

Holds

Betances, Dellin, NYY	28
Harris, Will, Hou	28
Jones, Nate, CWS	28
Diekman, Jake, Tex	26
Herrera, Kelvin, KC	26
Miller, Andrew, NYY-Cle	25
Shaw, Bryan, Cle	25
Wilson, Justin, Det	25
Brach, Brad, Bal	24
Bush, Matt, Tex	22

Relief Innings

Ramirez, Erasmo, TB	85.0
Devenski, Chris, Hou	83.2
Brach, Brad, Bal	79.0
Pressly, Ryan, Min	75.1
Givens, Mychal, Bal	74.2
Dull, Ryan, Oak	74.1
Miller, Andrew, NYY-Cle	74.1
Osuna, Roberto, Tor	74.0
Betances, Dellin, NYY	73.0
Wilson, Alex, Det	73.0

Inherited Runners Scrd %
(minimum 30 IR)

Devenski, Chris, Hou	10.0
Hochevar, Luke, KC	13.3
Dull, Ryan, Oak	13.5
Hendriks, Liam, Oak	14.7
Ramirez, Erasmo, TB	15.6
Jones, Nate, CWS	16.7
Morin, Mike, LAA	19.0
Moylan, Peter, KC	21.1
Ryan, Kyle, Det	21.1
Barnes, Matt, Bos	22.0

Relief Opp On Base Pct
(minimum 50 IP)

Miller, Andrew, NYY-Cle	.193
Britton, Zach, Bal	.221
Dull, Ryan, Oak	.228
Devenski, Chris, Hou	.230
Otero, Dan, Cle	.241
Jones, Nate, CWS	.243
Bush, Matt, Tex	.244
Osuna, Roberto, Tor	.251
Gregerson, Luke, Hou	.252
Herrera, Kelvin, KC	.255

Relief Opp Slugging Avg
(minimum 50 IP)

Britton, Zach, Bal	.209
Kimbrel, Craig, Bos	.255
Montgomery, Mike, Sea	.270
Devenski, Chris, Hou	.280
Bush, Matt, Tex	.281
Otero, Dan, Cle	.285
Flynn, Brian, KC	.290
Harris, Will, Hou	.292
Miller, Andrew, NYY-Cle	.294
Ross Jr., Robbie, Bos	.296

2016 American League Pitching Leaders

Relief Opp BA Vs LHB
(minimum 50 AB)

Uehara, Koji, Bos	.139
Montgomery, Mike, Sea	.143
Kimbrel, Craig, Bos	.145
May, Trevor, Min	.153
Abad, Fernando, Min-Bos	.153
Rondon, Bruce, Det	.159
Hochevar, Luke, KC	.164
Grilli, Jason, Tor	.169
Claudio, Alex, Tex	.177
Flynn, Brian, KC	.179

Relief Opp BA Vs RHB
(minimum 50 AB)

Strahm, Matt, KC	.118
Brach, Brad, Bal	.126
Allen, Cody, Cle	.139
Ynoa, Michael, CWS	.150
Smith, Chris, Oak	.151
Miller, Andrew, NYY-Cle	.153
Britton, Zach, Bal	.155
Givens, Mychal, Bal	.156
Gregerson, Luke, Hou	.156
Dull, Ryan, Oak	.156

Relief Opp Batting Average
(minimum 50 IP)

Kimbrel, Craig, Bos	.152
Miller, Andrew, NYY-Cle	.160
Britton, Zach, Bal	.162
Allen, Cody, Cle	.177
Gregerson, Luke, Hou	.183
Flynn, Brian, KC	.186
Dull, Ryan, Oak	.186
Diekman, Jake, Tex	.189
Cishek, Steve, Sea	.190
Jones, Nate, CWS	.190

Relief Earned Run Average
(minimum 50 IP)

Britton, Zach, Bal	0.54
Miller, Andrew, NYY-Cle	1.45
Otero, Dan, Cle	1.53
Devenski, Chris, Hou	1.61
Colome, Alex, TB	1.91
Brach, Brad, Bal	2.05
Jennings, Dan, CWS	2.08
Barnette, Tony, Tex	2.09
Montgomery, Mike, Sea	2.15
Flynn, Brian, KC	2.21

Rel OBP 1st Batter Faced
(minimum 40 BF)

Gregerson, Luke, Hou	.136
Dull, Ryan, Oak	.143
Neshek, Pat, Hou	.172
Harris, Will, Hou	.182
Jones, Nate, CWS	.183
Osuna, Roberto, Tor	.183
Guerra, Deolis, LAA	.186
Bush, Matt, Tex	.193
Herrera, Kelvin, KC	.194
Otero, Dan, Cle	.197

Rel Opp BA w/ Runners On
(minimum 50 IP)

Dull, Ryan, Oak	.132
Miller, Andrew, NYY-Cle	.135
Flynn, Brian, KC	.159
Britton, Zach, Bal	.160
Brach, Brad, Bal	.185
Barnette, Tony, Tex	.188
Colome, Alex, TB	.190
Cishek, Steve, Sea	.198
Shaw, Bryan, Cle	.198
Jones, Nate, CWS	.202

Relief Opp BA w/ RISP
(minimum 50 IP)

Britton, Zach, Bal	.085
Dull, Ryan, Oak	.086
Colome, Alex, TB	.125
Miller, Andrew, NYY-Cle	.136
Shaw, Bryan, Cle	.141
Bush, Matt, Tex	.149
Barnette, Tony, Tex	.149
Diaz, Edwin, Sea	.153
Jones, Nate, CWS	.164
Giles, Ken, Hou	.165

Fastest Avg Fastball-Relief
(minimum 50 IP)

Betances, Dellin, NYY	97.7
Kimbrel, Craig, Bos	97.3
Diaz, Edwin, Sea	97.3
Giles, Ken, Hou	97.2
Herrera, Kelvin, KC	97.1
Bush, Matt, Tex	97.0
Jones, Nate, CWS	96.8
Barnes, Matt, Bos	96.8
Britton, Zach, Bal	96.3
Osuna, Roberto, Tor	95.8

Fastest Average Fastball
(minimum 162 IP)

Ventura, Yordano, KC	96.1
Duffy, Danny, KC	94.8
Sanchez, Aaron, Tor	94.7
Gausman, Kevin, Bal	94.7
Archer, Chris, TB	94.3
Pineda, Michael, NYY	94.1
Verlander, Justin, Det	93.5
Rodon, Carlos, CWS	93.4
Volquez, Edinson, KC	93.2
Bauer, Trevor, Cle	93.2

Slowest Average Fastball
(minimum 162 IP)

Dickey, R.A., Tor	82.3
Weaver, Jered, LAA	83.0
Fister, Doug, Hou	87.0
Tomlin, Josh, Cle	87.7
Iwakuma, Hisashi, Sea	87.8
Estrada, Marco, Tor	88.1
Keuchel, Dallas, Hou	88.6
Fiers, Mike, Hou	89.6
Sabathia, CC, NYY	90.0
Smyly, Drew, TB	90.2

Pitches 100+ Velocity

Chapman, Aroldis, NYY	544
Caminero, Arquimedes, Sea	132
Diaz, Edwin, Sea	59
Betances, Dellin, NYY	51
Eovaldi, Nathan, NYY	37
Paxton, James, Sea	31
Rondon, Bruce, Det	31
Kelly, Joe, Bos	27
Giles, Ken, Hou	18
Ventura, Yordano, KC	12

Pitches 95+ Velocity

Ventura, Yordano, KC	1403
Sanchez, Aaron, Tor	1290
Gausman, Kevin, Bal	1160
Paxton, James, Sea	1130
Eovaldi, Nathan, NYY	971
Duffy, Danny, KC	942
Salazar, Danny, Cle	908
Britton, Zach, Bal	905
Fulmer, Michael, Det	844
Ramirez, JC, LAA	844

Pitches Less Than 80 MPH

Dickey, R.A., Tor	2220
Wright, Steven, Bos	2126
Weaver, Jered, LAA	1569
Nolasco, Ricky, Min-LAA	1254
Estrada, Marco, Tor	1076
McHugh, Collin, Hou	945
Hill, Rich, Oak	920
Quintana, Jose, CWS	746
Keuchel, Dallas, Hou	732
Smyly, Drew, TB	715

Lowest % Fastballs
(minimum 162 IP)

Dickey, R.A., Tor	12.0
Tanaka, Masahiro, NYY	31.6
Sabathia, CC, NYY	34.4
McHugh, Collin, Hou	35.7
Tomlin, Josh, Cle	38.0
Fiers, Mike, Hou	41.6
Weaver, Jered, LAA	43.5
Hamels, Cole, Tex	43.7
Iwakuma, Hisashi, Sea	45.7
Nolasco, Ricky, Min-LAA	48.4

Highest % Fastballs
(minimum 162 IP)

Sanchez, Aaron, Tor	74.3
Happ, J.A., Tor	73.5
Quintana, Jose, CWS	66.5
Gausman, Kevin, Bal	66.3
Kennedy, Ian, KC	66.2
Fister, Doug, Hou	65.8
Rodon, Carlos, CWS	63.7
Santiago, Hector, LAA-Min	63.2
Graveman, Kendall, Oak	61.9
Porcello, Rick, Bos	61.8

Highest % Curveballs
(minimum 162 IP)

McHugh, Collin, Hou	30.0
Ventura, Yordano, KC	25.3
Quintana, Jose, CWS	25.0
Volquez, Edinson, KC	24.8
Smyly, Drew, TB	22.7
Weaver, Jered, LAA	22.2
Kluber, Corey, Cle	19.7
Bauer, Trevor, Cle	19.4
Fiers, Mike, Hou	18.9
Sanchez, Aaron, Tor	16.2

517

2016 American League Pitching Leaders

Highest % Changeups
(minimum 162 IP)

Estrada, Marco, Tor	28.6
Price, David, Bos	22.8
Volquez, Edinson, KC	22.3
Santiago, Hector, LAA-Min	21.8
Odorizzi, Jake, TB	19.6
Fiers, Mike, Hou	19.4
Hamels, Cole, Tex	18.6
Ventura, Yordano, KC	18.0
Weaver, Jered, LAA	17.7
Miley, Wade, Sea-Bal	17.6

Highest % Sliders
(minimum 162 IP)

Pineda, Michael, NYY	41.3
Archer, Chris, TB	40.2
Santana, Ervin, Min	36.8
Nolasco, Ricky, Min-LAA	32.9
Keuchel, Dallas, Hou	26.4
Tanaka, Masahiro, NYY	26.1
Rodon, Carlos, CWS	25.8
Sale, Chris, CWS	25.0
Sabathia, CC, NYY	24.9
Duffy, Danny, KC	23.5

Balks

Andriese, Matt, TB	4
Salazar, Danny, Cle	3
Santana, Ervin, Min	3
Soria, Joakim, KC	3
8 tied with	2

Strikeout/Hit Ratio
(minimum 50 IP)

Kimbrel, Craig, Bos	2.96
Miller, Andrew, NYY-Cle	2.93
Betances, Dellin, NYY	2.33
Allen, Cody, Cle	2.12
Diaz, Edwin, Sea	1.96
Britton, Zach, Bal	1.95
Gregerson, Luke, Hou	1.76
Cishek, Steve, Sea	1.73
Feliz, Michael, Hou	1.73
Giles, Ken, Hou	1.70

Opp OPS vs Fastballs
(minimum 251 BF)

Estrada, Marco, Tor	.618
Sanchez, Aaron, Tor	.621
Happ, J.A., Tor	.633
Quintana, Jose, CWS	.634
Santana, Ervin, Min	.658
Hamels, Cole, Tex	.670
Sale, Chris, CWS	.674
Smyly, Drew, TB	.676
Kennedy, Ian, KC	.682
Porcello, Rick, Bos	.688

Opp OPS vs Curveballs
(minimum 100 BF)

Kluber, Corey, Cle	.419
Verlander, Justin, Det	.467
McCullers, Lance, Hou	.486
Hill, Rich, Oak	.503
Porcello, Rick, Bos	.514
Bauer, Trevor, Cle	.564
Rogers, Taylor, Min	.615
Fiers, Mike, Hou	.628
Ventura, Yordano, KC	.630
Sanchez, Aaron, Tor	.659

Opp OPS vs Changeups
(minimum 100 BF)

Fulmer, Michael, Det	.416
Guerra, Deolis, LAA	.462
Devenski, Chris, Hou	.524
Porcello, Rick, Bos	.533
Manaea, Sean, Oak	.552
Sale, Chris, CWS	.555
Rodriguez, Francisco, Det	.565
Duffy, Danny, KC	.597
Salazar, Danny, Cle	.603
Estrada, Marco, Tor	.605

Opp OPS vs Sliders
(minimum 64 BF)

Jones, Nate, CWS	.389
Cishek, Steve, Sea	.412
Giles, Ken, Hou	.419
Colome, Alex, TB	.433
Neshek, Pat, Hou	.435
Betances, Dellin, NYY	.449
Ross Jr., Robbie, Bos	.458
Diaz, Edwin, Sea	.464
Verlander, Justin, Det	.491
Dull, Ryan, Oak	.497

Earned Runs

Volquez, Edinson, KC	113
Price, David, Bos	102
Sanchez, Anibal, Det	100
Weaver, Jered, LAA	100
Miley, Wade, Sea-Bal	99
Stroman, Marcus, Tor	99
Nolasco, Ricky, Min-LAA	97
Perez, Martin, Tex	97
3 tied with	95

Hits Per Nine Innings
(minimum 162 IP)

Estrada, Marco, Tor	6.75
Verlander, Justin, Det	6.76
Kluber, Corey, Cle	7.12
Sale, Chris, CWS	7.54
Sanchez, Aaron, Tor	7.55
Happ, J.A., Tor	7.75
Porcello, Rick, Bos	7.79
Kennedy, Ian, KC	7.96
Tanaka, Masahiro, NYY	8.07
Tillman, Chris, Bal	8.11

2016 National League Pitching Leaders

Earned Run Average (minimum 162 IP)		Winning Percentage (minimum 15 Decisions)		Opponent Batting Average (minimum 162 IP)		Baserunners Per 9 IP (minimum 162 IP)	
Hendricks, Kyle, ChC	2.13	Lester, Jon, ChC	.792	Arrieta, Jake, ChC	.194	Scherzer, Max, Was	8.95
Lester, Jon, ChC	2.44	Strasburg, Stephen, Was	.789	Scherzer, Max, Was	.199	Hendricks, Kyle, ChC	9.19
Syndergaard, Noah, NYM	2.60	Cueto, Johnny, SF	.783	Hendricks, Kyle, ChC	.207	Lester, Jon, ChC	9.41
Bumgarner, Madison, SF	2.74	Kershaw, Clayton, LAD	.750	Lester, Jon, ChC	.211	Bumgarner, Madison, SF	9.57
Cueto, Johnny, SF	2.79	Scherzer, Max, Was	.741	Bumgarner, Madison, SF	.213	Teheran, Julio, Atl	9.91
Roark, Tanner, Was	2.83	Arrieta, Jake, ChC	.692	Lackey, John, ChC	.218	Lackey, John, ChC	9.94
Fernandez, Jose, Mia	2.86	Fernandez, Jose, Mia	.667	Straily, Dan, Cin	.220	Arrieta, Jake, ChC	10.03
Scherzer, Max, Was	2.96	Hendricks, Kyle, ChC	.667	Teheran, Julio, Atl	.223	Cueto, Johnny, SF	10.16
Martinez, Carlos, StL	3.04	Colon, Bartolo, NYM	.652	Fernandez, Jose, Mia	.224	Fernandez, Jose, Mia	10.37
Arrieta, Jake, ChC	3.10	Greinke, Zack, Ari	.650	Roark, Tanner, Was	.228	Syndergaard, Noah, NYM	10.44

Games		Games Started		Complete Games		Shutouts	
Hand, Brad, SD	82	Bumgarner, Madison, SF	34	Cueto, Johnny, SF	5	Kershaw, Clayton, LAD	3
Reed, Addison, NYM	80	Scherzer, Max, Was	34	Bumgarner, Madison, SF	4	Cueto, Johnny, SF	2
Delgado, Randall, Ari	79	Colon, Bartolo, NYM	33	Kershaw, Clayton, LAD	3	16 tied with	1
Neris, Hector, Phi	79	Eickhoff, Jerad, Phi	33	Nova, Ivan, Pit	3		
Familia, Jeurys, NYM	78	Koehler, Tom, Mia	33	Eflin, Zach, Phi	2		
Wood, Travis, ChC	77	Roark, Tanner, Was	33	Hendricks, Kyle, ChC	2		
Oh, Seung Hwan, StL	76	Wainwright, Adam, StL	33	Lester, Jon, ChC	2		
4 tied with	75	9 tied with	32	18 tied with	1		

Wins		Losses		No Decisions		Wild Pitches	
Scherzer, Max, Was	20	Nelson, Jimmy, Mil	16	Teheran, Julio, Atl	13	Arrieta, Jake, ChC	16
Lester, Jon, ChC	19	Ray, Robbie, Ari	15	Chen, Wei-Yin, Mia	12	Foltynewicz, Mike, Atl	13
Arrieta, Jake, ChC	18	Eickhoff, Jerad, Phi	14	Cashner, Andrew, SD-Mia	11	Niese, Jon, Pit-NYM	11
Cueto, Johnny, SF	18	Corbin, Patrick, Ari	13	Conley, Adam, Mia	11	Perdomo, Luis, SD	10
Fernandez, Jose, Mia	16	Garcia, Jaime, StL	13	Koehler, Tom, Mia	11	Syndergaard, Noah, NYM	10
Hendricks, Kyle, ChC	16	Koehler, Tom, Mia	13	Wainwright, Adam, StL	11	Conley, Adam, Mia	9
Maeda, Kenta, LAD	16	Wisler, Matt, Atl	13	12 tied with	10	Corbin, Patrick, Ari	9
Martinez, Carlos, StL	16	Friedrich, Christian, SD	12			Fernandez, Jose, Mia	9
Roark, Tanner, Was	16	Leake, Mike, StL	12			Hammel, Jason, ChC	9
4 tied with	15	Miller, Shelby, Ari	12			Koehler, Tom, Mia	9

Strikeouts		Walks Allowed		Intentional Walks Allowed		Hit Batters	
Scherzer, Max, Was	284	Nelson, Jimmy, Mil	86	Bradley, Archie, Ari	8	Nelson, Jimmy, Mil	17
Fernandez, Jose, Mia	253	Finnegan, Brandon, Cin	84	Conley, Adam, Mia	7	Roark, Tanner, Was	13
Bumgarner, Madison, SF	251	Koehler, Tom, Mia	83	Koehler, Tom, Mia	7	Gray, Jon, Col	12
Ray, Robbie, Ari	218	Arrieta, Jake, ChC	76	McGowan, Dustin, Mia	7	Conley, Adam, Mia	11
Syndergaard, Noah, NYM	218	Roark, Tanner, Was	73	Perdomo, Luis, SD	7	Martinez, Carlos, StL	11
Cueto, Johnny, SF	198	Straily, Dan, Cin	73	7 tied with	6	Straily, Dan, Cin	11
Lester, Jon, ChC	197	Ray, Robbie, Ari	71			Gonzalez, Gio, Was	9
Arrieta, Jake, ChC	190	Chatwood, Tyler, Col	70			Hammel, Jason, ChC	9
Gray, Jon, Col	185	Martinez, Carlos, StL	70			Lackey, John, ChC	9
Strasburg, Stephen, Was	183	Liriano, Francisco, Pit	69			Teheran, Julio, Atl	9

2016 National League Pitching Leaders

Runs Allowed		Hits Allowed		Doubles Allowed		Home Runs Allowed	
Corbin, Patrick, Ari	109	Wainwright, Adam, StL	220	Wainwright, Adam, StL	48	Scherzer, Max, Was	31
Nelson, Jimmy, Mil	108	Bettis, Chad, Col	204	Hellickson, Jeremy, Phi	44	Straily, Dan, Cin	31
Wainwright, Adam, StL	108	Leake, Mike, StL	203	Eickhoff, Jerad, Phi	43	Eickhoff, Jerad, Phi	30
Bettis, Chad, Col	107	Colon, Bartolo, NYM	200	Wacha, Michael, StL	41	Finnegan, Brandon, Cin	29
Ray, Robbie, Ari	105	Cueto, Johnny, SF	195	Bradley, Archie, Ari	40	Anderson, Chase, Mil	28
Leake, Mike, StL	101	Samardzija, Jeff, SF	190	Garcia, Jaime, StL	40	Bumgarner, Madison, SF	26
Perdomo, Luis, SD	99	Eickhoff, Jerad, Phi	187	Leake, Mike, StL	39	Garcia, Jaime, StL	26
Gonzalez, Gio, Was	98	Perdomo, Luis, SD	187	Anderson, Chase, Mil	38	Wisler, Matt, Atl	26
Garcia, Jaime, StL	94	Nelson, Jimmy, Mil	186	Koehler, Tom, Mia	38	3 tied with	25
2 tied with	93	Ray, Robbie, Ari	185	3 tied with	37		

Run Support Per Nine IP		% Pitches In Strike Zone		Pitches Per Start		Pitches Per Batter	
(minimum 162 IP)		(minimum 162 IP)		(minimum 30 GS)		(minimum 162 IP)	
Arrieta, Jake, ChC	6.84	Colon, Bartolo, NYM	48.4	Bumgarner, Madison, SF	105.0	Garcia, Jaime, StL	3.48
Bettis, Chad, Col	6.39	Nelson, Jimmy, Mil	47.6	Scherzer, Max, Was	104.8	Leake, Mike, StL	3.51
Gray, Jon, Col	5.89	Scherzer, Max, Was	47.2	Cueto, Johnny, SF	103.1	Colon, Bartolo, NYM	3.61
Maeda, Kenta, LAD	5.64	Martinez, Carlos, StL	46.6	Roark, Tanner, Was	100.9	Nelson, Jimmy, Mil	3.70
Martinez, Carlos, StL	5.53	Straily, Dan, Cin	46.3	Arrieta, Jake, ChC	100.8	Eickhoff, Jerad, Phi	3.73
Bumgarner, Madison, SF	5.40	Gray, Jon, Col	46.3	Samardzija, Jeff, SF	99.7	Martinez, Carlos, StL	3.74
Lester, Jon, ChC	5.37	Ray, Robbie, Ari	46.2	Ray, Robbie, Ari	99.3	Cueto, Johnny, SF	3.74
Scherzer, Max, Was	5.36	Garcia, Jaime, StL	45.6	Teheran, Julio, Atl	99.0	Bettis, Chad, Col	3.75
Wainwright, Adam, StL	5.30	Samardzija, Jeff, SF	45.0	Lester, Jon, ChC	98.8	Wainwright, Adam, StL	3.77
Gonzalez, Gio, Was	5.28	Teheran, Julio, Atl	44.9	Martinez, Carlos, StL	97.7	Hellickson, Jeremy, Phi	3.79

Quality Starts		Batters Faced		Innings Pitched		Most Pitches in a Game	
Lester, Jon, ChC	26	Bumgarner, Madison, SF	912	Scherzer, Max, Was	228.1	Moore, Matt, SF	133
Scherzer, Max, Was	26	Scherzer, Max, Was	902	Bumgarner, Madison, SF	226.2	Hendricks, Kyle, ChC	123
Bumgarner, Madison, SF	25	Cueto, Johnny, SF	881	Cueto, Johnny, SF	219.2	Samardzija, Jeff, SF	123
Cueto, Johnny, SF	22	Roark, Tanner, Was	855	Roark, Tanner, Was	210.0	Martinez, Carlos, StL	122
Roark, Tanner, Was	22	Wainwright, Adam, StL	847	Samardzija, Jeff, SF	203.1	Roark, Tanner, Was	121
6 tied with	20	Samardzija, Jeff, SF	829	Lester, Jon, ChC	202.2	Kazmir, Scott, LAD	120
		Bettis, Chad, Col	814	Wainwright, Adam, StL	198.2	Matz, Steven, NYM	120
		Eickhoff, Jerad, Phi	811	Arrieta, Jake, ChC	197.1	Teheran, Julio, Atl	120
		Martinez, Carlos, StL	809	Eickhoff, Jerad, Phi	197.1	Wainwright, Adam, StL	120
		Nelson, Jimmy, Mil	807	Martinez, Carlos, StL	195.1	4 tied with	119

Stolen Bases Allowed		Caught Stealing Off		Stolen Base Pct Allowed		Pickoffs	
Syndergaard, Noah, NYM	48	Lester, Jon, ChC	13	(minimum 162 IP)		Cingrani, Tony, Cin	6
Nelson, Jimmy, Mil	30	Peralta, Wily, Mil	10	Fernandez, Jose, Mia	25.0	Cueto, Johnny, SF	6
Lester, Jon, ChC	28	Davies, Zach, Mil	9	Cueto, Johnny, SF	36.4	Urias, Julio, LAD	6
Arrieta, Jake, ChC	23	Syndergaard, Noah, NYM	9	Davies, Zach, Mil	47.1	Colon, Bartolo, NYM	5
Matz, Steven, NYM	20	Anderson, Chase, Mil	8	Koehler, Tom, Mia	52.9	Nelson, Jimmy, Mil	5
Cole, Gerrit, Pit	18	Koehler, Tom, Mia	8	Colon, Bartolo, NYM	53.3	Bumgarner, Madison, SF	4
de la Rosa, Jorge, Col	18	5 tied with	7	Bumgarner, Madison, SF	54.5	DeSclafani, Anthony, Cin	4
Teheran, Julio, Atl	17			Wainwright, Adam, StL	55.6	Rusin, Chris, Col	4
3 tied with	16			Straily, Dan, Cin	63.2	12 tied with	3
				Eickhoff, Jerad, Phi	64.3		
				Bettis, Chad, Col	66.7		

2016 National League Pitching Leaders

Strikeouts Per 9 IP (minimum 162 IP)		Opp On-Base Percentage (minimum 162 IP)		Opp Slugging Average (minimum 162 IP)		Opponent OPS (minimum 162 IP)	
Fernandez, Jose, Mia	12.49	Scherzer, Max, Was	.254	Arrieta, Jake, ChC	.306	Hendricks, Kyle, ChC	.581
Ray, Robbie, Ari	11.25	Hendricks, Kyle, ChC	.262	Hendricks, Kyle, ChC	.319	Arrieta, Jake, ChC	.583
Scherzer, Max, Was	11.19	Bumgarner, Madison, SF	.265	Roark, Tanner, Was	.327	Lester, Jon, ChC	.602
Syndergaard, Noah, NYM	10.68	Lester, Jon, ChC	.268	Martinez, Carlos, StL	.333	Bumgarner, Madison, SF	.619
Bumgarner, Madison, SF	9.97	Teheran, Julio, Atl	.275	Lester, Jon, ChC	.334	Scherzer, Max, Was	.619
Gray, Jon, Col	9.91	Arrieta, Jake, ChC	.277	Fernandez, Jose, Mia	.336	Fernandez, Jose, Mia	.624
Maeda, Kenta, LAD	9.17	Lackey, John, ChC	.281	Cueto, Johnny, SF	.350	Cueto, Johnny, SF	.633
Lester, Jon, ChC	8.75	Cueto, Johnny, SF	.284	Syndergaard, Noah, NYM	.351	Roark, Tanner, Was	.634
Gonzalez, Gio, Was	8.68	Syndergaard, Noah, NYM	.287	Bumgarner, Madison, SF	.354	Syndergaard, Noah, NYM	.639
Arrieta, Jake, ChC	8.67	Fernandez, Jose, Mia	.288	Maeda, Kenta, LAD	.359	Martinez, Carlos, StL	.643

Home Runs Per Nine IP (minimum 162 IP)		Batting Average vs. LHB (minimum 125 BF)		Batting Average vs. RHB (minimum 225 BF)		Opp BA w/ RISP (minimum 125 BF)	
Syndergaard, Noah, NYM	0.54	Hand, Brad, SD	.125	Scherzer, Max, Was	.156	Hand, Brad, SD	.171
Cueto, Johnny, SF	0.61	Kershaw, Clayton, LAD	.138	Pomeranz, Drew, SD	.173	Lester, Jon, ChC	.173
Fernandez, Jose, Mia	0.64	Oh, Seung Hwan, StL	.176	Arrieta, Jake, ChC	.194	Hendricks, Kyle, ChC	.184
Martinez, Carlos, StL	0.69	Bumgarner, Madison, SF	.178	Hendricks, Kyle, ChC	.198	Lackey, John, ChC	.189
Hendricks, Kyle, ChC	0.71	Robles, Hansel, NYM	.179	Lackey, John, ChC	.201	Scherzer, Max, Was	.199
Roark, Tanner, Was	0.73	Clemens, Paul, Mia-SD	.188	Kershaw, Clayton, LAD	.201	Straily, Dan, Cin	.200
Arrieta, Jake, ChC	0.73	Guerra, Junior, Mil	.191	Fernandez, Jose, Mia	.203	Bumgarner, Madison, SF	.206
Lester, Jon, ChC	0.93	Straily, Dan, Cin	.191	DeSclafani, Anthony, Cin	.206	Conley, Adam, Mia	.206
Gonzalez, Gio, Was	0.96	Barraclough, Kyle, Mia	.192	Martinez, Carlos, StL	.207	Eickhoff, Jerad, Phi	.217
Gray, Jon, Col	0.96	Arrieta, Jake, ChC	.194	Teheran, Julio, Atl	.212	Bradley, Archie, Ari	.225

OBP vs. Leadoff Hitter (minimum 150 BF)		Strikeouts / Walks Ratio (minimum 162 IP)		Highest GB/FB Ratio (minimum 162 IP)		Lowest GB/FB Ratio (minimum 162 IP)	
Kershaw, Clayton, LAD	.193	Scherzer, Max, Was	5.07	Garcia, Jaime, StL	2.26	Straily, Dan, Cin	0.67
Maeda, Kenta, LAD	.222	Syndergaard, Noah, NYM	5.07	Martinez, Carlos, StL	2.18	Scherzer, Max, Was	0.69
Scherzer, Max, Was	.229	Bumgarner, Madison, SF	4.65	Leake, Mike, StL	2.12	Teheran, Julio, Atl	0.93
Teheran, Julio, Atl	.240	Fernandez, Jose, Mia	4.60	Bettis, Chad, Col	1.91	Bumgarner, Madison, SF	0.95
Hendricks, Kyle, ChC	.242	Cueto, Johnny, SF	4.40	Arrieta, Jake, ChC	1.89	Finnegan, Brandon, Cin	0.97
Greinke, Zack, Ari	.247	Leake, Mike, StL	4.17	Syndergaard, Noah, NYM	1.88	Eickhoff, Jerad, Phi	1.03
Cueto, Johnny, SF	.253	Teheran, Julio, Atl	4.07	Cueto, Johnny, SF	1.73	Hammel, Jason, ChC	1.10
Hellickson, Jeremy, Phi	.258	Colon, Bartolo, NYM	4.00	Gonzalez, Gio, Was	1.61	Lackey, John, ChC	1.13
Lester, Jon, ChC	.263	Eickhoff, Jerad, Phi	3.98	Nelson, Jimmy, Mil	1.58	Hellickson, Jeremy, Phi	1.19
Gray, Jon, Col	.266	Hendricks, Kyle, ChC	3.86	Roark, Tanner, Was	1.56	Koehler, Tom, Mia	1.23

Sacrifice Flies Allowed		Sacrifice Hits Allowed		GIDP Induced		GIDP Per Nine IP (minimum 162 IP)	
Eickhoff, Jerad, Phi	10	Bettis, Chad, Col	10	Martinez, Carlos, StL	33	Martinez, Carlos, StL	1.52
Leake, Mike, StL	10	Roark, Tanner, Was	10	Roark, Tanner, Was	28	Wainwright, Adam, StL	1.22
Wainwright, Adam, StL	9	Velasquez, Vince, Phi	9	Wainwright, Adam, StL	27	Roark, Tanner, Was	1.20
Lackey, John, ChC	8	8 tied with	8	Chatwood, Tyler, Col	22	Garcia, Jaime, StL	1.10
Blair, Aaron, Atl	7			Garcia, Jaime, StL	21	Hellickson, Jeremy, Phi	1.00
Bradley, Archie, Ari	7			Hellickson, Jeremy, Phi	21	Nelson, Jimmy, Mil	0.90
Nicasio, Juan, Pit	7			Perdomo, Luis, SD	20	Colon, Bartolo, NYM	0.89
5 tied with	6			Cashner, Andrew, SD-Mia	19	Finnegan, Brandon, Cin	0.89
				Colon, Bartolo, NYM	19	Gonzalez, Gio, Was	0.86
				Samardzija, Jeff, SF	19	Samardzija, Jeff, SF	0.84

2016 National League Pitching Leaders

Saves			Blown Saves			Save Pct			Save Opportunities	
						(minimum 20 Save Ops)				
Familia, Jeurys, NYM	51		Casilla, Santiago, SF	9		Jeffress, Jeremy, Mil	96.4		Familia, Jeurys, NYM	56
Jansen, Kenley, LAD	47		Thornburg, Tyler, Mil	8		Ramos, A.J., Mia	93.0		Jansen, Kenley, LAD	53
Melancon, Mark, Pit-Was	47		Estevez, Carlos, Col	7		Melancon, Mark, Pit-Was	92.2		Melancon, Mark, Pit-Was	51
Ramos, A.J., Mia	40		Cingrani, Tony, Cin	6		Familia, Jeurys, NYM	91.1		Gomez, Jeanmar, Phi	43
Gomez, Jeanmar, Phi	37		Gomez, Jeanmar, Phi	6		Ziegler, Brad, Ari	90.0		Ramos, A.J., Mia	43
Casilla, Santiago, SF	31		Hand, Brad, SD	6		Rodney, Fernando, SD-Mia	89.3		Casilla, Santiago, SF	40
Jeffress, Jeremy, Mil	27		Jansen, Kenley, LAD	6		Jansen, Kenley, LAD	88.7		Jeffress, Jeremy, Mil	28
Rodney, Fernando, SD-Mia	25		Maurer, Brandon, SD	6		Johnson, Jim, Atl	87.0		Rodney, Fernando, SD-Mia	28
Johnson, Jim, Atl	20		Phelps, David, Mia	6		Papelbon, Jonathan, Was	86.4		4 tied with	23
2 tied with	19		9 tied with	5		Gomez, Jeanmar, Phi	86.0			

Easy Saves			Regular Saves			Tough Saves			Holds Adjusted Saves %	
									(minimum 20 Save Ops + Holds)	
Familia, Jeurys, NYM	36		Melancon, Mark, Pit-Was	16		Casilla, Santiago, SF	3		Blanton, Joe, LAD	96.6
Jansen, Kenley, LAD	31		Familia, Jeurys, NYM	15		Blevins, Jerry, NYM	2		Jeffress, Jeremy, Mil	96.4
Melancon, Mark, Pit-Was	30		Gomez, Jeanmar, Phi	15		Gomez, Jeanmar, Phi	2		Buchter, Ryan, SD	95.5
Ramos, A.J., Mia	25		Ramos, A.J., Mia	15		Jansen, Kenley, LAD	2		Feliz, Neftali, Pit	93.9
Gomez, Jeanmar, Phi	20		Jansen, Kenley, LAD	14		Kelley, Shawn, Was	2		Ramos, A.J., Mia	93.3
Rodney, Fernando, SD-Mia	17		Casilla, Santiago, SF	13		Rodney, Fernando, SD-Mia	2		Melancon, Mark, Pit-Was	92.2
Jeffress, Jeremy, Mil	16		Jeffress, Jeremy, Mil	10		24 tied with	1		Baez, Pedro, LAD	92.0
Casilla, Santiago, SF	15		Oh, Seung Hwan, StL	10					Treinen, Blake, Was	92.0
Chapman, Aroldis, ChC	14		Cingrani, Tony, Cin	8					Hudson, Daniel, Ari	91.7
Papelbon, Jonathan, Was	14		Johnson, Jim, Atl	8					Rodney, Fernando, SD-Mia	91.7

Relief Wins			Relief Losses			Relief Games			Holds	
Thornburg, Tyler, Mil	8		Estevez, Carlos, Col	7		Hand, Brad, SD	82		Reed, Addison, NYM	40
Blanton, Joe, LAD	7		Ohlendorf, Ross, Cin	7		Reed, Addison, NYM	80		Barraclough, Kyle, Mia	29
Quackenbush, Kevin, SD	7		Quackenbush, Kevin, SD	7		Delgado, Randall, Ari	79		Feliz, Neftali, Pit	29
Barraclough, Kyle, Mia	6		Johnson, Jim, Atl	6		Neris, Hector, Phi	79		Blanton, Joe, LAD	28
Dunn, Mike, Mia	6		Rivero, Felipe, Was-Pit	6		Familia, Jeurys, NYM	78		Neris, Hector, Phi	28
Oh, Seung Hwan, StL	6		10 tied with	5		Wood, Travis, ChC	77		Logan, Boone, Col	27
Robles, Hansel, NYM	6					Oh, Seung Hwan, StL	76		Rivero, Felipe, Was-Pit	26
Siegrist, Kevin, StL	6					4 tied with	75		Phelps, David, Mia	25
Wood, Blake, Cin	6								3 tied with	23
6 tied with	5									

Relief Innings			Inherited Runners Scrd %			Relief Opp On Base Pct			Relief Opp Slugging Avg	
			(minimum 30 IR)			(minimum 50 IP)			(minimum 50 IP)	
Hand, Brad, SD	89.1		Osich, Josh, SF	4.7		Jansen, Kenley, LAD	.194		Barraclough, Kyle, Mia	.238
Torres, Carlos, Mil	82.1		Cervenka, Hunter, Atl-Mia	10.4		Kelley, Shawn, Was	.232		Iglesias, Raisel, Cin	.250
Neris, Hector, Phi	80.1		Lopez, Javier, SF	11.3		Melancon, Mark, Pit-Was	.241		Jansen, Kenley, LAD	.252
Blanton, Joe, LAD	80.0		Perez, Oliver, Was	13.3		Oh, Seung Hwan, StL	.241		Oh, Seung Hwan, StL	.269
Oh, Seung Hwan, StL	79.2		Wood, Travis, ChC	13.5		Reed, Addison, NYM	.243		Ramos, A.J., Mia	.270
Familia, Jeurys, NYM	77.2		Blevins, Jerry, NYM	14.5		Thornburg, Tyler, Mil	.247		Melancon, Mark, Pit-Was	.271
Reed, Addison, NYM	77.2		Grimm, Justin, ChC	18.8		Law, Derek, SF	.248		Familia, Jeurys, NYM	.276
Robles, Hansel, NYM	77.2		Liberatore, Adam, LAD	18.8		Baez, Pedro, LAD	.259		Buchter, Ryan, SD	.288
Rivero, Felipe, Was-Pit	77.0		Wood, Blake, Cin	18.9		Rondon, Hector, ChC	.261		Thornburg, Tyler, Mil	.294
Wood, Blake, Cin	76.2		Coleman, Louis, LAD	21.6		Blanton, Joe, LAD	.263		Reed, Addison, NYM	.294

2016 National League Pitching Leaders

Relief Opp BA Vs LHB
(minimum 50 AB)

Hand, Brad, SD	.125
Wood, Travis, ChC	.128
Thornburg, Tyler, Mil	.130
Logan, Boone, Col	.142
Strop, Pedro, ChC	.143
Belisle, Matt, Was	.147
Buchter, Ryan, SD	.147
Hatcher, Chris, LAD	.150
Osich, Josh, SF	.154
Lyons, Tyler, StL	.156

Relief Opp BA Vs RHB
(minimum 50 AB)

Edwards Jr., Carl, ChC	.108
Jansen, Kenley, LAD	.109
Iglesias, Raisel, Cin	.115
Ottavino, Adam, Col	.136
Chapman, Aroldis, ChC	.139
McGowan, Dustin, Mia	.148
Dayton, Grant, LAD	.157
Barraclough, Kyle, Mia	.160
Stripling, Ross, LAD	.167
Buchter, Ryan, SD	.168

Relief Opp Batting Average
(minimum 50 IP)

Jansen, Kenley, LAD	.150
Buchter, Ryan, SD	.160
Thornburg, Tyler, Mil	.162
Iglesias, Raisel, Cin	.165
Barraclough, Kyle, Mia	.176
Oh, Seung Hwan, StL	.190
Siegrist, Kevin, StL	.193
Blanton, Joe, LAD	.194
Kelley, Shawn, Was	.194
Baez, Pedro, LAD	.195

Relief Earned Run Average
(minimum 50 IP)

Melancon, Mark, Pit-Was	1.64
Jansen, Kenley, LAD	1.83
Oh, Seung Hwan, StL	1.92
Reed, Addison, NYM	1.97
Iglesias, Raisel, Cin	1.98
Law, Derek, SF	2.13
Thornburg, Tyler, Mil	2.15
Treinen, Blake, Was	2.28
Phelps, David, Mia	2.31
Blanton, Joe, LAD	2.48

Rel OBP 1st Batter Faced
(minimum 40 BF)

Kelley, Shawn, Was	.149
Jansen, Kenley, LAD	.169
Law, Derek, SF	.180
Logan, Boone, Col	.185
Strickland, Hunter, SF	.208
Maurer, Brandon, SD	.211
Reed, Addison, NYM	.213
Neris, Hector, Phi	.215
Buchter, Ryan, SD	.224
Gearrin, Cory, SF	.232

Rel Opp BA w/ Runners On
(minimum 50 IP)

Thornburg, Tyler, Mil	.140
Jansen, Kenley, LAD	.149
Iglesias, Raisel, Cin	.162
Wood, Travis, ChC	.165
Siegrist, Kevin, StL	.174
Hand, Brad, SD	.176
Casilla, Santiago, SF	.182
Buchter, Ryan, SD	.183
Lorenzen, Michael, Cin	.186
Ramos, A.J., Mia	.186

Relief Opp BA w/ RISP
(minimum 50 IP)

Iglesias, Raisel, Cin	.087
Ramos, A.J., Mia	.118
Watson, Tony, Pit	.119
Wood, Travis, ChC	.137
Phelps, David, Mia	.146
Jansen, Kenley, LAD	.149
Barraclough, Kyle, Mia	.151
Kelley, Shawn, Was	.152
Grimm, Justin, ChC	.154
Thornburg, Tyler, Mil	.157

Fastest Avg Fastball-Relief
(minimum 50 IP)

Estevez, Carlos, Col	97.3
Strickland, Hunter, SF	96.8
Baez, Pedro, LAD	96.7
Familia, Jeurys, NYM	96.2
Lorenzen, Michael, Cin	96.2
Feliz, Neftali, Pit	96.1
Wood, Blake, Cin	96.0
Rondon, Hector, ChC	96.0
Rivero, Felipe, Was-Pit	95.8
Hudson, Daniel, Ari	95.7

Fastest Average Fastball
(minimum 162 IP)

Syndergaard, Noah, NYM	98.0
Martinez, Carlos, StL	95.6
Fernandez, Jose, Mia	95.2
Gray, Jon, Col	95.1
Scherzer, Max, Was	94.3
Samardzija, Jeff, SF	94.3
Ray, Robbie, Ari	94.1
Arrieta, Jake, ChC	93.7
Nelson, Jimmy, Mil	93.1
Lester, Jon, ChC	92.1

Slowest Average Fastball
(minimum 162 IP)

Hendricks, Kyle, ChC	87.8
Colon, Bartolo, NYM	87.9
Straily, Dan, Cin	89.3
Davies, Zach, Mil	89.3
Maeda, Kenta, LAD	90.0
Hellickson, Jeremy, Phi	90.1
Wainwright, Adam, StL	90.3
Garcia, Jaime, StL	90.5
Leake, Mike, StL	90.6
Gonzalez, Gio, Was	90.8

Pitches 100+ Velocity

Chapman, Aroldis, ChC	544
Cabrera, Mauricio, Atl	328
Syndergaard, Noah, NYM	157
Caminero, Arquimedes, Pit	132
Ellington, Brian, Mia	29
Estevez, Carlos, Col	24
Martinez, Carlos, StL	24
Reyes, Alex, StL	18
Rivero, Felipe, Was-Pit	12
2 tied with	10

Pitches 95+ Velocity

Syndergaard, Noah, NYM	1722
Rivero, Felipe, Was-Pit	1278
Martinez, Carlos, StL	1226
Gray, Jon, Col	1078
Fernandez, Jose, Mia	1043
Ray, Robbie, Ari	968
Cashner, Andrew, SD-Mia	966
Foltynewicz, Mike, Atl	928
Strasburg, Stephen, Was	903
Familia, Jeurys, NYM	888

Pitches Less Than 80 MPH

Hill, Rich, LAD	920
Wainwright, Adam, StL	854
Clemens, Paul, Mia-SD	742
Eickhoff, Jerad, Phi	742
Davies, Zach, Mil	731
Kazmir, Scott, LAD	627
Nola, Aaron, Phi	614
Pomeranz, Drew, SD	611
Maeda, Kenta, LAD	603
Gonzalez, Gio, Was	601

Lowest % Fastballs
(minimum 162 IP)

Wainwright, Adam, StL	41.6
Maeda, Kenta, LAD	42.9
Koehler, Tom, Mia	46.7
Samardzija, Jeff, SF	47.4
Bumgarner, Madison, SF	48.3
Leake, Mike, StL	48.4
Hellickson, Jeremy, Phi	49.4
Cueto, Johnny, SF	49.9
Straily, Dan, Cin	51.0
Hammel, Jason, ChC	51.9

Highest % Fastballs
(minimum 162 IP)

Colon, Bartolo, NYM	89.5
Ray, Robbie, Ari	71.1
Nelson, Jimmy, Mil	71.0
Finnegan, Brandon, Cin	65.6
Arrieta, Jake, ChC	65.5
Hendricks, Kyle, ChC	65.2
Gonzalez, Gio, Was	64.4
Garcia, Jaime, StL	62.9
Roark, Tanner, Was	62.3
Syndergaard, Noah, NYM	59.1

Highest % Curveballs
(minimum 162 IP)

Wainwright, Adam, StL	26.7
Eickhoff, Jerad, Phi	24.2
Koehler, Tom, Mia	22.5
Gonzalez, Gio, Was	19.8
Maeda, Kenta, LAD	17.9
Hellickson, Jeremy, Phi	15.2
Bumgarner, Madison, SF	15.1
Roark, Tanner, Was	12.7
Lester, Jon, ChC	12.6
Nelson, Jimmy, Mil	12.4

2016 National League Pitching Leaders

Highest % Changeups
(minimum 162 IP)

Hendricks, Kyle, ChC	27.1
Hellickson, Jeremy, Phi	26.1
Davies, Zach, Mil	20.6
Garcia, Jaime, StL	18.7
Straily, Dan, Cin	18.4
Martinez, Carlos, StL	18.3
Cueto, Johnny, SF	16.9
Gonzalez, Gio, Was	15.7
Finnegan, Brandon, Cin	13.3
Bettis, Chad, Col	12.9

Highest % Sliders
(minimum 162 IP)

Hammel, Jason, ChC	35.1
Bumgarner, Madison, SF	33.3
Maeda, Kenta, LAD	28.8
Gray, Jon, Col	26.9
Fernandez, Jose, Mia	26.7
Teheran, Julio, Atl	26.3
Straily, Dan, Cin	25.9
Lackey, John, ChC	24.3
Koehler, Tom, Mia	23.7
Scherzer, Max, Was	22.2

Balks

Bastardo, Antonio, NYM-Pit	4
Anderson, Tyler, Col	3
Clippard, Tyler, Ari	3
Kershaw, Clayton, LAD	3
8 tied with	2

Strikeout/Hit Ratio
(minimum 50 IP)

Jansen, Kenley, LAD	2.97
Barraclough, Kyle, Mia	2.51
Thornburg, Tyler, Mil	2.37
Buchter, Ryan, SD	2.29
Kelley, Shawn, Was	1.95
Oh, Seung Hwan, StL	1.87
Phelps, David, Mia	1.87
Kershaw, Clayton, LAD	1.77
Hand, Brad, SD	1.76
Neris, Hector, Phi	1.73

Opp OPS vs Fastballs
(minimum 251 BF)

Familia, Jeurys, NYM	.519
Arrieta, Jake, ChC	.542
Kershaw, Clayton, LAD	.549
Martinez, Carlos, StL	.601
Hendricks, Kyle, ChC	.621
Scherzer, Max, Was	.621
Lester, Jon, ChC	.623
Cueto, Johnny, SF	.628
Strasburg, Stephen, Was	.646
Guerra, Junior, Mil	.654

Opp OPS vs Curveballs
(minimum 100 BF)

Grimm, Justin, ChC	.439
Bumgarner, Madison, SF	.491
Hellickson, Jeremy, Phi	.568
Pomeranz, Drew, SD	.574
Nola, Aaron, Phi	.584
Eickhoff, Jerad, Phi	.672
Wainwright, Adam, StL	.700
Bradley, Archie, Ari	.702
Hernandez, David, Phi	.706
Roark, Tanner, Was	.711

Opp OPS vs Changeups
(minimum 100 BF)

Hendricks, Kyle, ChC	.478
Fernandez, Jose, Mia	.581
Rodney, Fernando, SD-Mia	.592
Hellickson, Jeremy, Phi	.618
Greinke, Zack, Ari	.621
Garcia, Jaime, StL	.647
Cueto, Johnny, SF	.659
Bettis, Chad, Col	.666
Kazmir, Scott, LAD	.700
Davies, Zach, Mil	.715

Opp OPS vs Sliders
(minimum 64 BF)

Logan, Boone, Col	.319
McGowan, Dustin, Mia	.350
Kershaw, Clayton, LAD	.371
Lackey, John, ChC	.381
Barraclough, Kyle, Mia	.446
Strop, Pedro, ChC	.454
deGrom, Jacob, NYM	.460
Withrow, Chris, Atl	.473
Cervenka, Hunter, Atl-Mia	.489
Fernandez, Jose, Mia	.489

Earned Runs

Wainwright, Adam, StL	102
Bettis, Chad, Col	99
Ray, Robbie, Ari	95
Perdomo, Luis, SD	93
Leake, Mike, StL	92
Nelson, Jimmy, Mil	92
Gonzalez, Gio, Was	90
Corbin, Patrick, Ari	89
Garcia, Jaime, StL	89
Wisler, Matt, Atl	87

Hits Per Nine Innings
(minimum 162 IP)

Arrieta, Jake, ChC	6.29
Scherzer, Max, Was	6.50
Hendricks, Kyle, ChC	6.73
Lester, Jon, ChC	6.84
Lackey, John, ChC	6.98
Bumgarner, Madison, SF	7.11
Straily, Dan, Cin	7.24
Fernandez, Jose, Mia	7.35
Roark, Tanner, Was	7.41
Teheran, Julio, Atl	7.52

2016 American League Fielding Leaders

2B Pivot % (minimum 98 G)	
Odor, Rougned, Tex	0.760
Pedroia, Dustin, Bos	0.739
Cano, Robinson, Sea	0.731
Travis, Devon, Tor	0.679
Schoop, Jonathan, Bal	0.661
Kinsler, Ian, Det	0.660
Forsythe, Logan, TB	0.636
Dozier, Brian, Min	0.636
Castro, Starlin, NYY	0.613
Altuve, Jose, Hou	0.565

SS Pivot % (minimum 98 G)	
Hardy, J.J., Bal	0.764
Simmons, Andrelton, LAA	0.710
Correa, Carlos, Hou	0.685
Semien, Marcus, Oak	0.656
Iglesias, Jose, Det	0.643
Lindor, Francisco, Cle	0.620
Tulowitzki, Troy, Tor	0.600
Marte, Ketel, Sea	0.571
Escobar, Alcides, KC	0.563
Bogaerts, Xander, Bos	0.517

Highest Pct CS by Catchers (minimum 600 INN or 50 SBA)	
McCann, James, Det	43.1
Perez, Salvador, KC	42.9
Leon, Sandy, Bos	39.4
Wieters, Matt, Bal	31.7
Perez, Carlos, LAA	30.0
Iannetta, Chris, Sea	26.2
Castro, Jason, Hou	22.4
McCann, Brian, NYY	20.3
Vogt, Stephen, Oak	20.3
Navarro, Dioner, CWS-Tor	18.5

Lowest Pct CS by Catchers (minimum 600 INN or 50 SBA)	
Suzuki, Kurt, Min	11.9
Martin, Russell, Tor	12.9
Wilson, Bobby, Det-Tex-TB	14.9
Navarro, Dioner, CWS-Tor	18.5
Vogt, Stephen, Oak	20.3
McCann, Brian, NYY	20.3
Castro, Jason, Hou	22.4
Iannetta, Chris, Sea	26.2
Perez, Carlos, LAA	30.0
Wieters, Matt, Bal	31.7

2B Double Play % (minimum 98 G)	
Schoop, Jonathan, Bal	0.628
Cano, Robinson, Sea	0.619
Dozier, Brian, Min	0.617
Odor, Rougned, Tex	0.615
Kinsler, Ian, Det	0.600
Pedroia, Dustin, Bos	0.595
Forsythe, Logan, TB	0.568
Travis, Devon, Tor	0.567
Altuve, Jose, Hou	0.508
Kipnis, Jason, Cle	0.504

3B Double Play % (minimum 98 G)	
Seager, Kyle, Sea	0.627
Escobar, Yunel, LAA	0.500
Beltre, Adrian, Tex	0.482
Shaw, Travis, Bos	0.475
Longoria, Evan, TB	0.475
Frazier, Todd, CWS	0.438
Ramirez, Jose, Cle	0.438
Machado, Manny, Bal	0.434
Donaldson, Josh, Tor	0.431
Castellanos, Nick, Det	0.364

SS Double Play % (minimum 98 G)	
Hardy, J.J., Bal	0.676
Simmons, Andrelton, LAA	0.652
Iglesias, Jose, Det	0.649
Tulowitzki, Troy, Tor	0.611
Marte, Ketel, Sea	0.609
Semien, Marcus, Oak	0.602
Correa, Carlos, Hou	0.595
Lindor, Francisco, Cle	0.588
Andrus, Elvis, Tex	0.583
Bogaerts, Xander, Bos	0.580

Errors	
Odor, Rougned, Tex	22
Seager, Kyle, Sea	22
Marte, Ketel, Sea	21
Semien, Marcus, Oak	21
Escobar, Yunel, LAA	19
Miller, Brad, TB	19
Sano, Miguel, Min	18
Andrus, Elvis, Tex	17
Cuthbert, Cheslor, KC	16
Shaw, Travis, Bos	16

Fielding Errors	
Seager, Kyle, Sea	18
Odor, Rougned, Tex	17
Miller, Brad, TB	14
Semien, Marcus, Oak	13
Marte, Ketel, Sea	12
Sano, Miguel, Min	12
Polanco, Jorge, Min	11
Castro, Starlin, NYY	10
Desmond, Ian, Tex	10
Napoli, Mike, Cle	10

Throwing Errors	
Escobar, Yunel, LAA	14
Cuthbert, Cheslor, KC	9
Marte, Ketel, Sea	9
Andrus, Elvis, Tex	8
Semien, Marcus, Oak	8
Shaw, Travis, Bos	8
7 tied with	7

Range Factor for 2B (minimum 98 games)	
Kinsler, Ian, Det	5.09
Odor, Rougned, Tex	5.03
Cano, Robinson, Sea	4.84
Dozier, Brian, Min	4.77
Schoop, Jonathan, Bal	4.57
Travis, Devon, Tor	4.46
Castro, Starlin, NYY	4.25
Kipnis, Jason, Cle	4.25
Pedroia, Dustin, Bos	4.23
Forsythe, Logan, TB	4.11

Range Factor for 3B (minimum 98 games)	
Seager, Kyle, Sea	3.11
Beltre, Adrian, Tex	2.99
Machado, Manny, Bal	2.90
Shaw, Travis, Bos	2.89
Headley, Chase, NYY	2.83
Donaldson, Josh, Tor	2.63
Frazier, Todd, CWS	2.62
Castellanos, Nick, Det	2.51
Longoria, Evan, TB	2.44
Cuthbert, Cheslor, KC	2.41

Range Factor for SS (minimum 98 games)	
Semien, Marcus, Oak	4.63
Simmons, Andrelton, LAA	4.61
Andrus, Elvis, Tex	4.47
Iglesias, Jose, Det	4.40
Lindor, Francisco, Cle	4.37
Hardy, J.J., Bal	4.24
Tulowitzki, Troy, Tor	4.18
Correa, Carlos, Hou	4.17
Escobar, Alcides, KC	4.12
Anderson, Tim, CWS	4.04

2016 National League Fielding Leaders

2B Pivot % (minimum 98 G)	
Segura, Jean, Ari	0.708
Harrison, Josh, Pit	0.677
Hernandez, Cesar, Phi	0.674
Panik, Joe, SF	0.659
Phillips, Brandon, Cin	0.658
Walker, Neil, NYM	0.649
Murphy, Daniel, Was	0.618
LeMahieu, DJ, Col	0.526
Zobrist, Ben, ChC	0.518
Utley, Chase, LAD	0.460

SS Pivot % (minimum 98 G)	
Espinosa, Danny, Was	0.714
Diaz, Aledmys, StL	0.673
Galvis, Freddy, Phi	0.671
Villar, Jonathan, Mil	0.656
Cabrera, Asdrubal, NYM	0.640
Mercer, Jordy, Pit	0.588
Crawford, Brandon, SF	0.579
Cozart, Zack, Cin	0.571
Ramirez, Alexei, SD	0.568
Seager, Corey, LAD	0.567

Highest Pct CS by Catchers (minimum 600 INN or 50 SBA)	
Lucroy, Jonathan, Mil	37.7
Castillo, Welington, Ari	34.4
Ramos, Wilson, Was	33.3
Posey, Buster, SF	32.9
Realmuto, J.T., Mia	30.1
Barnhart, Tucker, Cin	26.1
Ross, David, ChC	25.8
Rivera, Rene, NYM	24.6
Rupp, Cameron, Phi	22.4
Pierzynski, A.J., Atl	21.8

Lowest Pct CS by Catchers (minimum 600 INN or 50 SBA)	
Flowers, Tyler, Atl	3.2
Montero, Miguel, ChC	7.8
Hundley, Nick, Col	10.9
Norris, Derek, SD	14.6
d'Arnaud, Travis, NYM	16.4
Cervelli, Francisco, Pit	18.3
Molina, Yadier, StL	20.2
Grandal, Yasmani, LAD	21.3
Pierzynski, A.J., Atl	21.8
Rupp, Cameron, Phi	22.4

2B Double Play % (minimum 98 G)	
Panik, Joe, SF	0.578
Hernandez, Cesar, Phi	0.547
Segura, Jean, Ari	0.543
Murphy, Daniel, Was	0.514
Phillips, Brandon, Cin	0.512
Harrison, Josh, Pit	0.512
Walker, Neil, NYM	0.484
Zobrist, Ben, ChC	0.465
Gennett, Scooter, Mil	0.445
LeMahieu, DJ, Col	0.444

3B Double Play % (minimum 98 G)	
Prado, Martin, Mia	0.443
Rendon, Anthony, Was	0.436
Arenado, Nolan, Col	0.407
Suarez, Eugenio, Cin	0.400
Bryant, Kris, ChC	0.350
Turner, Justin, LAD	0.333
Garcia, Adonis, Atl	0.326
Franco, Maikel, Phi	0.308
Lamb, Jake, Ari	0.212

SS Double Play % (minimum 98 G)	
Galvis, Freddy, Phi	0.657
Diaz, Aledmys, StL	0.649
Cabrera, Asdrubal, NYM	0.636
Crawford, Brandon, SF	0.622
Espinosa, Danny, Was	0.621
Mercer, Jordy, Pit	0.608
Ramirez, Alexei, SD	0.602
Cozart, Zack, Cin	0.546
Russell, Addison, ChC	0.538
Hechavarria, Adeiny, Mia	0.536

Errors	
Villar, Jonathan, Mil	29
Suarez, Eugenio, Cin	23
Lamb, Jake, Ari	20
Espinosa, Danny, Was	18
Garcia, Adonis, Atl	18
Seager, Corey, LAD	18
Kang, Jung Ho, Pit	17
Diaz, Aledmys, StL	16
Baez, Javier, ChC	15
4 tied with	14

Fielding Errors	
Villar, Jonathan, Mil	16
Suarez, Eugenio, Cin	15
Kang, Jung Ho, Pit	14
Lamb, Jake, Ari	12
Peterson, Jace, Atl	12
Carter, Chris, Mil	11
Espinosa, Danny, Was	11
Phillips, Brandon, Cin	11
3 tied with	10

Throwing Errors	
Villar, Jonathan, Mil	13
Garcia, Adonis, Atl	10
Hechavarria, Adeiny, Mia	10
Seager, Corey, LAD	10
Flores, Wilmer, NYM	9
Realmuto, J.T., Mia	9
Russell, Addison, ChC	9
4 tied with	8

Range Factor for 2B (minimum 98 games)	
Harrison, Josh, Pit	5.24
LeMahieu, DJ, Col	5.06
Panik, Joe, SF	4.96
Gennett, Scooter, Mil	4.66
Segura, Jean, Ari	4.61
Hernandez, Cesar, Phi	4.55
Phillips, Brandon, Cin	4.54
Walker, Neil, NYM	4.47
Murphy, Daniel, Was	4.06
Zobrist, Ben, ChC	3.94

Range Factor for 3B (minimum 98 games)	
Arenado, Nolan, Col	3.12
Lamb, Jake, Ari	2.59
Bryant, Kris, ChC	2.57
Suarez, Eugenio, Cin	2.57
Rendon, Anthony, Was	2.50
Garcia, Adonis, Atl	2.31
Turner, Justin, LAD	2.26
Prado, Martin, Mia	2.23
Franco, Maikel, Phi	2.20

Range Factor for SS (minimum 98 games)	
Villar, Jonathan, Mil	4.65
Cozart, Zack, Cin	4.58
Mercer, Jordy, Pit	4.32
Crawford, Brandon, SF	4.28
Ramirez, Alexei, SD	4.21
Hechavarria, Adeiny, Mia	4.14
Galvis, Freddy, Phi	4.11
Cabrera, Asdrubal, NYM	3.93
Diaz, Aledmys, StL	3.93
Espinosa, Danny, Was	3.88

2016 Active Career Batting Leaders

Batting Average (minimum 1000 PA)		On Base Percentage (minimum 1000 PA)		Slugging Average (minimum 1000 PA)		Home Runs	
Cabrera, Miguel	.321	Votto, Joey	.425	Pujols, Albert	.573	Rodriguez, Alex	696
Suzuki, Ichiro	.313	Trout, Mike	.405	Cabrera, Miguel	.562	Pujols, Albert	591
Votto, Joey	.313	Cabrera, Miguel	.399	Trout, Mike	.557	Ortiz, David	541
Altuve, Jose	.311	Goldschmidt, Paul	.398	Ortiz, David	.552	Cabrera, Miguel	446
Pujols, Albert	.309	Pujols, Albert	.392	Rodriguez, Alex	.550	Beltre, Adrian	445
Mauer, Joe	.308	Mauer, Joe	.391	Braun, Ryan	.544	Beltran, Carlos	421
Posey, Buster	.307	Holliday, Matt	.382	Stanton, Giancarlo	.539	Teixeira, Mark	409
Cano, Robinson	.307	Harper, Bryce	.382	Votto, Joey	.536	Howard, Ryan	382
Trout, Mike	.306	Fielder, Prince	.382	Goldschmidt, Paul	.525	Fielder, Prince	319
Lindor, Francisco	.306	McCutchen, Andrew	.381	Bryant, Kris	.522	Encarnacion, Edwin	310

Games		At Bats		Hits		Total Bases	
Rodriguez, Alex	2784	Rodriguez, Alex	10566	Rodriguez, Alex	3115	Rodriguez, Alex	5813
Beltre, Adrian	2720	Beltre, Adrian	10295	Suzuki, Ichiro	3030	Pujols, Albert	5232
Suzuki, Ichiro	2500	Suzuki, Ichiro	9689	Beltre, Adrian	2942	Beltre, Adrian	4940
Beltran, Carlos	2457	Beltran, Carlos	9301	Pujols, Albert	2825	Ortiz, David	4765
Pujols, Albert	2426	Rollins, Jimmy	9294	Beltran, Carlos	2617	Beltran, Carlos	4572
Ortiz, David	2408	Pujols, Albert	9138	Cabrera, Miguel	2519	Cabrera, Miguel	4414
Rollins, Jimmy	2275	Ortiz, David	8640	Ortiz, David	2472	Suzuki, Ichiro	3920
Cabrera, Miguel	2096	Cabrera, Miguel	7853	Rollins, Jimmy	2455	Rollins, Jimmy	3889
Pierzynski, A.J.	2059	Pierzynski, A.J.	7290	Cano, Robinson	2210	Cano, Robinson	3589
Teixeira, Mark	1862	Cano, Robinson	7210	Pierzynski, A.J.	2043	Teixeira, Mark	3533

Doubles		Triples		Runs Scored		RBI	
Ortiz, David	632	Crawford, Carl	123	Rodriguez, Alex	2021	Rodriguez, Alex	2086
Pujols, Albert	602	Reyes, Jose	121	Pujols, Albert	1670	Pujols, Albert	1817
Beltre, Adrian	591	Rollins, Jimmy	115	Beltran, Carlos	1522	Ortiz, David	1768
Rodriguez, Alex	548	Suzuki, Ichiro	96	Beltre, Adrian	1428	Beltre, Adrian	1571
Beltran, Carlos	536	Granderson, Curtis	89	Rollins, Jimmy	1421	Cabrera, Miguel	1553
Cabrera, Miguel	523	Beltran, Carlos	78	Ortiz, David	1419	Beltran, Carlos	1536
Rollins, Jimmy	511	Fowler, Dexter	72	Suzuki, Ichiro	1396	Teixeira, Mark	1298
Cano, Robinson	479	Bourn, Michael	69	Cabrera, Miguel	1321	Howard, Ryan	1194
Holliday, Matt	448	Drew, Stephen	63	Holliday, Matt	1104	Holliday, Matt	1153
Gonzalez, Adrian	415	Span, Denard	60	Teixeira, Mark	1099	Gonzalez, Adrian	1146

Walks		Intentional Walks		Hit By Pitch		Strikeouts	
Rodriguez, Alex	1338	Pujols, Albert	302	Utley, Chase	190	Rodriguez, Alex	2287
Ortiz, David	1319	Cabrera, Miguel	220	Rodriguez, Alex	176	Howard, Ryan	1843
Pujols, Albert	1214	Ortiz, David	209	Weeks Jr., Rickie	131	Ortiz, David	1750
Beltran, Carlos	1051	Suzuki, Ichiro	180	Pierzynski, A.J.	129	Beltran, Carlos	1693
Cabrera, Miguel	1011	Fielder, Prince	164	Fielder, Prince	124	Reynolds, Mark	1631
Teixeira, Mark	918	Gonzalez, Adrian	154	Holliday, Matt	121	Granderson, Curtis	1589
Bautista, Jose	881	Howard, Ryan	154	Choo, Shin-Soo	115	Beltre, Adrian	1584
Votto, Joey	862	Mauer, Joe	137	Teixeira, Mark	111	Upton Jr., Melvin	1561
Fielder, Prince	847	Martinez, Victor	112	Pujols, Albert	100	Cabrera, Miguel	1516
Mauer, Joe	822	Votto, Joey	112	Byrd, Marlon	93	Teixeira, Mark	1441

2016 Active Career Batting Leaders

Sacrifice Hits			Sacrifice Flies			Stolen Bases			Seasons Played	
Andrus, Elvis	99		Rodriguez, Alex	111		Suzuki, Ichiro	508		Rodriguez, Alex	22
Kershaw, Clayton	83		Beltran, Carlos	104		Reyes, Jose	488		Ortiz, David	20
Crisp, Coco	80		Pujols, Albert	99		Crawford, Carl	480		Beltran, Carlos	19
Cueto, Johnny	80		Ortiz, David	92		Rollins, Jimmy	470		Beltre, Adrian	19
Lohse, Kyle	75		Beltre, Adrian	89		Davis, Rajai	365		Colon, Bartolo	19
Aybar, Erick	72		Martinez, Victor	77		Bourn, Michael	341		Pierzynski, A.J.	19
Cain, Matt	71		Cabrera, Miguel	75		Rodriguez, Alex	329		Rollins, Jimmy	17
Escobar, Alcides	70		Morneau, Justin	74		Ellsbury, Jacoby	321		6 tied with	16
Lincecum, Tim	70		Utley, Chase	69		Beltran, Carlos	312			
Infante, Omar	64		Gonzalez, Adrian	67		Crisp, Coco	309			

At Bats Per Home Run (minimum 1000 AB)			Grounded Into DP			Highest SB Success Pct (minimum 100 SBA)			Lowest SB Success Pct (minimum 100 SBA)	
Stanton, Giancarlo	14.3		Pujols, Albert	336		Utley, Chase	87.9		Castro, Starlin	63.7
Howard, Ryan	14.9		Cabrera, Miguel	279		Werth, Jayson	86.5		Parra, Gerardo	64.1
Rodriguez, Alex	15.2		Rodriguez, Alex	261		Beltran, Carlos	86.4		De Aza, Alejandro	67.2
Carter, Chris	15.2		Beltre, Adrian	259		Dyson, Jarrod	85.4		Aoki, Nori	67.7
Davis, Chris	15.3		Pierzynski, A.J.	241		Trout, Mike	83.6		Hill, Aaron	67.9
Pujols, Albert	15.5		Ortiz, David	236		Stubbs, Drew	82.6		Pence, Hunter	68.2
Davis, Khris	15.5		Cano, Robinson	234		Ellsbury, Jacoby	82.5		Martin, Russell	68.3
Ortiz, David	16.0		Martinez, Victor	230		Escobar, Alcides	82.2		Fowler, Dexter	69.0
Cruz, Nelson	16.5		Molina, Yadier	211		Hamilton, Billy	82.1		Ramirez, Alexei	69.4
Bautista, Jose	16.7		Butler, Billy	207		Rollins, Jimmy	81.7		Johnson, Kelly	70.7

Strikeouts / Walks Ratio (minimum 1000 AB)			At Bats Per GIDP (minimum 1000 AB)			OPS (minimum 1000 PA)			Secondary Average (minimum 1000 PA)	
Pujols, Albert	.867		Bourn, Michael	140.7		Pujols, Albert	.965		Trout, Mike	.458
Aoki, Nori	1.044		Stubbs, Drew	140.6		Trout, Mike	.963		Votto, Joey	.430
Mauer, Joe	1.052		Blackmon, Charlie	140.1		Cabrera, Miguel	.961		Goldschmidt, Paul	.428
Pedroia, Dustin	1.054		Hamilton, Billy	127.7		Votto, Joey	.961		Bautista, Jose	.421
Hanigan, Ryan	1.069		Bonifacio, Emilio	116.9		Ortiz, David	.931		Ortiz, David	.420
Santana, Carlos	1.125		Bryant, Kris	116.2		Rodriguez, Alex	.930		Stanton, Giancarlo	.419
Votto, Joey	1.165		Granderson, Curtis	115.6		Goldschmidt, Paul	.924		Rodriguez, Alex	.413
Panik, Joe	1.173		Gordon, Dee	114.2		Braun, Ryan	.910		Harper, Bryce	.413
Martinez, Victor	1.177		Eaton, Adam	107.9		Bryant, Kris	.900		Pederson, Joc	.409
Ruiz, Carlos	1.185		Suzuki, Ichiro	107.7		Holliday, Matt	.897		Pujols, Albert	.408

Highest Strikeout per PA (minimum 1000 PA)			Lowest Strikeout per PA (minimum 1000 PA)			Plate Appearances			At Bats Per RBI (minimum 1000 AB)	
Carter, Chris	.331		Aoki, Nori	.080		Rodriguez, Alex	12207		Howard, Ryan	4.8
Nieuwenhuis, Kirk	.324		Simmons, Andrelton	.089		Beltre, Adrian	11260		Ortiz, David	4.9
Zunino, Mike	.324		Revere, Ben	.093		Pujols, Albert	10552		Pujols, Albert	5.0
Flowers, Tyler	.323		Molina, Yadier	.095		Beltran, Carlos	10522		Cabrera, Miguel	5.1
Arcia, Oswaldo	.315		Pedroia, Dustin	.096		Suzuki, Ichiro	10466		Rodriguez, Alex	5.1
Davis, Chris	.313		Panik, Joe	.098		Rollins, Jimmy	10240		Teixeira, Mark	5.3
Reynolds, Mark	.310		Suzuki, Ichiro	.099		Ortiz, David	10091		Stanton, Giancarlo	5.5
Stubbs, Drew	.306		Pujols, Albert	.100		Cabrera, Miguel	9001		Goldschmidt, Paul	5.6
Saltalamacchia,J	.305		Shuck, J.B.	.101		Teixeira, Mark	8029		Hamilton, Josh	5.6
Wallace, Brett	.300		Altuve, Jose	.104		Cano, Robinson	7845		Braun, Ryan	5.6

2016 Active Career Pitching Leaders

Earned Run Average
(minimum 750 IP)

Kershaw, Clayton	2.37
Rodriguez, Francisco	2.73
Nathan, Joe	2.87
Bumgarner, Madison	2.99
Sale, Chris	3.00
Hernandez, Felix	3.16
Wainwright, Adam	3.17
Strasburg, Stephen	3.17
Price, David	3.21
Cueto, Johnny	3.23

Winning Percentage
(minimum 100 Decisions)

Kershaw, Clayton	.677
Wang, Chien-Ming	.667
Price, David	.651
Scherzer, Max	.644
Wainwright, Adam	.638
Lester, Jon	.635
Iwakuma, Hisashi	.630
Strasburg, Stephen	.627
Verlander, Justin	.620
Weaver, Jered	.617

Opponent Batting Average
(minimum 750 IP)

Rodriguez, Francisco	.205
Kershaw, Clayton	.205
Nathan, Joe	.206
Arrieta, Jake	.220
Benoit, Joaquin	.223
Sale, Chris	.224
Strasburg, Stephen	.226
Estrada, Marco	.227
Young, Chris	.229
Archer, Chris	.231

Baserunners Per 9 IP
(minimum 750 IP)

Kershaw, Clayton	9.21
Sale, Chris	10.09
Strasburg, Stephen	10.10
Bumgarner, Madison	10.16
Nathan, Joe	10.30
Iwakuma, Hisashi	10.39
Rodriguez, Francisco	10.42
Estrada, Marco	10.48
Price, David	10.50
Kluber, Corey	10.58

Games

Rodriguez, Francisco	920
Lopez, Javier	839
Qualls, Chad	825
Nathan, Joe	787
Rodney, Fernando	767
Thornton, Matt	748
Benoit, Joaquin	712
Papelbon, Jonathan	689
Frasor, Jason	679
Broxton, Jonathan	674

Games Started

Colon, Bartolo	500
Sabathia, CC	482
Lohse, Kyle	418
Lackey, John	416
Peavy, Jake	377
Hernandez, Felix	359
Verlander, Justin	352
Shields, James	351
Greinke, Zack	349
Santana, Ervin	343

Complete Games

Sabathia, CC	38
Colon, Bartolo	36
Hernandez, Felix	25
Kershaw, Clayton	24
Shields, James	23
Verlander, Justin	23
Wainwright, Adam	22
Lackey, John	18
Cueto, Johnny	17
2 tied with	16

Shutouts

Kershaw, Clayton	15
Colon, Bartolo	13
Sabathia, CC	12
Hernandez, Felix	11
Wainwright, Adam	10
Lohse, Kyle	9
Shields, James	9
5 tied with	8

Wins

Colon, Bartolo	233
Sabathia, CC	223
Lackey, John	176
Verlander, Justin	173
Greinke, Zack	155
Hernandez, Felix	154
Peavy, Jake	152
Weaver, Jered	150
Lohse, Kyle	147
Lester, Jon	146

Losses

Colon, Bartolo	162
Lohse, Kyle	143
Sabathia, CC	141
Lackey, John	135
Peavy, Jake	126
Santana, Ervin	116
Shields, James	116
Jackson, Edwin	114
Hernandez, Felix	109
Dickey, R.A.	108

Innings Pitched

Colon, Bartolo	3172.1
Sabathia, CC	3168.1
Lackey, John	2669.2
Lohse, Kyle	2531.2
Hernandez, Felix	2415.2
Peavy, Jake	2377.0
Verlander, Justin	2339.0
Shields, James	2294.1
Greinke, Zack	2253.1
Hamels, Cole	2214.1

Batters Faced

Colon, Bartolo	13379
Sabathia, CC	13233
Lackey, John	11299
Lohse, Kyle	10839
Hernandez, Felix	9906
Peavy, Jake	9838
Verlander, Justin	9664
Shields, James	9606
Greinke, Zack	9279
Santana, Ervin	9163

Strikeouts

Sabathia, CC	2726
Colon, Bartolo	2365
Hernandez, Felix	2264
Peavy, Jake	2207
Verlander, Justin	2197
Lackey, John	2145
Hamels, Cole	2122
Greinke, Zack	2021
Shields, James	1977
Kershaw, Clayton	1918

Walks Allowed

Sabathia, CC	959
Colon, Bartolo	888
Jimenez, Ubaldo	790
Lackey, John	762
Perez, Oliver	723
Peavy, Jake	708
Verlander, Justin	699
Hernandez, Felix	695
Lohse, Kyle	694
2 tied with	681

Hit Batters

Lackey, John	121
Sabathia, CC	104
Santana, Ervin	92
Cueto, Johnny	91
Lohse, Kyle	87
Shields, James	85
Hernandez, Roberto	82
Hernandez, Felix	81
Dickey, R.A.	80
Verlander, Justin	80

Wild Pitches

Hernandez, Felix	132
Lackey, John	114
Lincecum, Tim	107
Jackson, Edwin	94
Shields, James	91
Jimenez, Ubaldo	90
de la Rosa, Jorge	89
Liriano, Francisco	85
Santana, Ervin	84
Dickey, R.A.	78

2016 Active Career Pitching Leaders

Saves		Save Pct (minimum 50 Save Ops)		Home Runs Allowed		Strikeouts Per 9 IP (minimum 750 IP)	
Rodriguez, Francisco	430	Britton, Zach	93.8	Colon, Bartolo	379	Rodriguez, Francisco	10.59
Nathan, Joe	377	Kimbrel, Craig	91.1	Lohse, Kyle	316	Strasburg, Stephen	10.55
Papelbon, Jonathan	368	Holland, Greg	90.1	Sabathia, CC	315	Sale, Chris	10.09
Street, Huston	324	Chapman, Aroldis	89.7	Shields, James	300	Scherzer, Max	9.98
Rodney, Fernando	261	Nathan, Joe	89.1	Lackey, John	283	Kershaw, Clayton	9.81
Kimbrel, Craig	256	Miller, Andrew	89.1	Santana, Ervin	276	Nathan, Joe	9.51
Soria, Joakim	203	Tolleson, Shawn	88.5	Peavy, Jake	259	Kluber, Corey	9.49
Jansen, Kenley	189	Jansen, Kenley	88.3	Hamels, Cole	246	Perez, Oliver	9.43
Chapman, Aroldis	182	Papelbon, Jonathan	88.2	Weaver, Jered	246	Archer, Chris	9.34
Melancon, Mark	168	Melancon, Mark	88.0	Dickey, R.A.	238	Lincecum, Tim	9.29

Opp On-Base Percentage (minimum 750 IP)		Opp Slugging Average (minimum 750 IP)		Hits Per Nine Innings (minimum 750 IP)		Home Runs Per Nine IP (minimum 750 IP)	
Kershaw, Clayton	.263	Kershaw, Clayton	.301	Kershaw, Clayton	6.62	Kershaw, Clayton	0.54
Sale, Chris	.280	Nathan, Joe	.331	Rodriguez, Francisco	6.69	Wainwright, Adam	0.64
Strasburg, Stephen	.280	Rodriguez, Francisco	.332	Nathan, Joe	6.73	Lynn, Lance	0.67
Bumgarner, Madison	.281	Arrieta, Jake	.345	Arrieta, Jake	7.29	Rodney, Fernando	0.68
Nathan, Joe	.282	Rodney, Fernando	.346	Benoit, Joaquin	7.42	Wang, Chien-Ming	0.69
Rodriguez, Francisco	.285	Strasburg, Stephen	.351	Sale, Chris	7.48	Morton, Charlie	0.72
Estrada, Marco	.286	Sale, Chris	.352	Strasburg, Stephen	7.55	Wilson, C.J.	0.74
Iwakuma, Hisashi	.287	Hernandez, Felix	.355	Estrada, Marco	7.63	Gonzalez, Gio	0.74
Price, David	.287	Archer, Chris	.357	Young, Chris	7.69	Hernandez, Felix	0.76
Scherzer, Max	.290	Wilson, C.J.	.358	2 tied with	7.76	Pelfrey, Mike	0.76

Strikeouts / Walks Ratio (minimum 750 IP)		Stolen Base Pct Allowed (minimum 750 IP)		GIDP Induced		GIDP Per Nine IP (minimum 750 IP)	
Sale, Chris	4.78	Cueto, Johnny	39.2	Colon, Bartolo	296	Wang, Chien-Ming	1.20
Strasburg, Stephen	4.59	Miley, Wade	41.3	Sabathia, CC	289	Keuchel, Dallas	1.12
Kluber, Corey	4.52	Tillman, Chris	41.3	Lackey, John	246	Morton, Charlie	1.11
Bumgarner, Madison	4.29	Fister, Doug	47.6	Hernandez, Felix	236	Pelfrey, Mike	1.11
Iwakuma, Hisashi	4.03	Iwakuma, Hisashi	51.1	Shields, James	196	Garcia, Jaime	1.09
Kershaw, Clayton	4.02	Kershaw, Clayton	51.3	Lohse, Kyle	192	Qualls, Chad	1.08
Scherzer, Max	3.93	Lynn, Lance	52.3	Lester, Jon	187	Duke, Zach	1.07
Zimmermann, Jordan	3.92	Greinke, Zack	53.7	Wainwright, Adam	179	Richard, Clayton	1.07
Price, David	3.80	Duke, Zach	55.2	Porcello, Rick	174	Porcello, Rick	1.07
Greinke, Zack	3.68	Colon, Bartolo	55.6	Santana, Ervin	174	Hernandez, Roberto	1.02

Complete Game % (minimum 100 GS)		Quality Start Pct (minimum 100 GS)		Walks Per 9 IP (minimum 750 IP)		Games Finished	
Sale, Chris	0.09	Sale, Chris	73.6	Iwakuma, Hisashi	1.83	Rodriguez, Francisco	657
Kershaw, Clayton	0.09	Kershaw, Clayton	73.0	Zimmermann, Jordan	1.85	Nathan, Joe	587
Wainwright, Adam	0.09	Price, David	68.1	Fister, Doug	1.95	Papelbon, Jonathan	585
Keuchel, Dallas	0.08	Wainwright, Adam	68.1	Porcello, Rick	2.04	Street, Huston	523
Sabathia, CC	0.08	Hamels, Cole	66.9	Bumgarner, Madison	2.07	Rodney, Fernando	481
Kluber, Corey	0.07	Hernandez, Felix	66.9	Kluber, Corey	2.10	Soria, Joakim	343
Colon, Bartolo	0.07	Bumgarner, Madison	66.8	Sale, Chris	2.11	Kimbrel, Craig	341
Hernandez, Felix	0.07	Verlander, Justin	65.3	Nolasco, Ricky	2.12	Broxton, Jonathan	285
Harrison, Matt	0.07	Lester, Jon	64.2	Chen, Wei-Yin	2.13	Jansen, Kenley	276
Cueto, Johnny	0.07	Darvish, Yu	64.0	Hughes, Phil	2.17	Melancon, Mark	274

2016 American League Bill James Leaders

Top Game Scores

Pitcher	Date	Opp	IP	H	R	ER	BB	SO	GS
Duffy, Danny, KC	8/1	TB	8.0	1	0	0	1	16	95
Sale, Chris, CWS	4/15	TB	9.0	2	0	0	0	9	92
Walker, Taijuan, Sea	9/13	LAA	9.0	3	0	0	0	11	92
Santana, Ervin, Min	7/6	Oak	9.0	2	0	0	0	8	91
Smyly, Drew, TB	4/19	Bos	8.0	1	0	0	2	11	89
Wright, Steven, Bos	8/5	LAD	9.0	3	0	0	1	9	89
Andriese, Matt, TB	5/14	Oak	9.0	2	0	0	0	5	88
Fulmer, Michael, Det	8/14	Tex	9.0	4	0	0	0	9	88
Graveman, Kendall, Oak	8/19	CWS	9.0	2	0	0	0	5	88
Kluber, Corey, Cle	6/21	TB	9.0	3	0	0	2	9	88
Shoemaker, Matt, LAA	7/16	CWS	9.0	6	0	0	0	13	88

Worst Game Scores

Pitcher	Date	Opp	IP	H	R	ER	BB	SO	GS
Volquez, Edinson, KC	6/24	Hou	1.0	8	12	11	3	0	-12
Holland, Derek, Tex	5/5	Tor	2.2	11	11	11	3	0	-11
Rodriguez, Eduardo, Bos	6/27	TB	2.2	11	9	9	1	2	1
McHugh, Collin, Hou	7/29	Det	1.2	10	8	8	0	1	4
Miley, Wade, Sea	6/2	SD	4.2	12	9	9	2	2	4
Lincecum, Tim, LAA	7/24	Hou	1.1	7	8	8	2	0	6
Manaea, Sean, Oak	5/10	Bos	2.2	10	8	8	0	1	7
Perez, Martin, Tex	7/6	Bos	4.0	9	11	7	2	1	7
Bauer, Trevor, Cle	8/3	Min	2.2	8	8	7	5	1	8
Ranaudo, Anthony, CWS	9/4	Min	4.2	11	9	9	1	3	8
Shields, James, CWS	6/18	Cle	1.2	7	8	8	3	2	8
Smyly, Drew, TB	5/31	KC	4.0	12	8	8	1	3	8

Runs Created

Trout, Mike, LAA	137
Altuve, Jose, Hou	132
Betts, Mookie, Bos	130
Ortiz, David, Bos	123
Donaldson, Josh, Tor	121
Seager, Kyle, Sea	110
Beltre, Adrian, Tex	108
Cabrera, Miguel, Det	106
Kinsler, Ian, Det	105
2 tied with	104

Runs Created Per 27 Outs

Trout, Mike, LAA	9.3
Ortiz, David, Bos	8.3
Altuve, Jose, Hou	7.7
Donaldson, Josh, Tor	7.4
Betts, Mookie, Bos	7.2
Beltre, Adrian, Tex	6.8
Ramirez, Jose, Cle	6.6
Seager, Kyle, Sea	6.5
Cabrera, Miguel, Det	6.5
Kinsler, Ian, Det	6.2

Offensive Winning %

Trout, Mike, LAA	.825
Altuve, Jose, Hou	.782
Ortiz, David, Bos	.753
Betts, Mookie, Bos	.698
Donaldson, Josh, Tor	.697
Seager, Kyle, Sea	.689
Beltre, Adrian, Tex	.678
Cabrera, Miguel, Det	.668
Correa, Carlos, Hou	.662
Cruz, Nelson, Sea	.661

Secondary Average
(minimum 502 PA)

Trout, Mike, LAA	.501
Donaldson, Josh, Tor	.466
Ortiz, David, Bos	.458
Bautista, Jose, Tor	.428
Santana, Carlos, Cle	.418
Encarnacion, Edwin, Tor	.414
Dozier, Brian, Min	.407
Davis, Chris, Bal	.396
Cruz, Nelson, Sea	.377
Napoli, Mike, Cle	.375

Isolated Power
(minimum 502 PA)

Ortiz, David, Bos	.305
Dozier, Brian, Min	.278
Davis, Khris, Oak	.277
Trumbo, Mark, Bal	.277
Cruz, Nelson, Sea	.268
Encarnacion, Edwin, Tor	.266
Donaldson, Josh, Tor	.265
Longoria, Evan, TB	.248
Cabrera, Miguel, Det	.247
Machado, Manny, Bal	.239

Power / Speed Number
(minimum 502 PA)

Trout, Mike, LAA	29.5
Betts, Mookie, Bos	28.3
Altuve, Jose, Hou	26.7
Dozier, Brian, Min	25.2
Frazier, Todd, CWS	21.8
Desmond, Ian, Tex	21.5
Odor, Rougned, Tex	19.7
Kinsler, Ian, Det	18.7
Martin, Leonys, Sea	18.5
Kipnis, Jason, Cle	18.2

Speed Scores

Kiermaier, Kevin, TB	8.50
Burns, Billy, Oak-KC	8.07
Betts, Mookie, Bos	7.70
Eaton, Adam, CWS	7.52
Cain, Lorenzo, KC	7.29
Martin, Leonys, Sea	7.22
Pillar, Kevin, Tor	7.12
Trout, Mike, LAA	7.08
Odor, Rougned, Tex	7.03
Gardner, Brett, NYY	6.87

Cheap Wins

Fiers, Mike, Hou	4
Fister, Doug, Hou	4
Andriese, Matt, TB	3
Dickey, R.A., Tor	3
Duffey, Tyler, Min	3
Iwakuma, Hisashi, Sea	3
Perez, Martin, Tex	3
Ventura, Yordano, KC	3
18 tied with	2

Tough Losses

Archer, Chris, TB	9
Quintana, Jose, CWS	8
Shoemaker, Matt, LAA	6
Dickey, R.A., Tor	5
Gausman, Kevin, Bal	5
Nolasco, Ricky, Min-LAA	5
Sabathia, CC, NYY	5
Santana, Ervin, Min	5
Verlander, Justin, Det	5
9 tied with	4

2016 National League Bill James Leaders

Top Game Scores

Pitcher	Date	Opp	IP	H	R	ER	BB	SO	GS
Bumgarner, Madison, SF	7/10	Ari	9.0	1	0	0	1	14	98
Garcia, Jaime, StL	4/14	Mil	9.0	1	0	0	1	13	97
Velasquez, Vince, Phi	4/14	SD	9.0	3	0	0	0	16	97
Gray, Jon, Col	9/17	SD	9.0	4	0	0	0	16	95
Kershaw, Clayton, LAD	5/1	SD	9.0	3	0	0	0	14	95
Kershaw, Clayton, LAD	5/12	NYM	9.0	3	0	0	1	13	93
Teheran, Julio, Atl	6/19	NYM	9.0	1	0	0	0	7	92
deGrom, Jacob, NYM	7/17	Phi	9.0	1	0	0	1	7	91
Bettis, Chad, Col	9/5	SF	9.0	2	0	0	0	7	90
Arrieta, Jake, ChC	4/21	Cin	9.0	0	0	0	4	6	89
Cueto, Johnny, SF	5/23	SD	9.0	2	0	0	0	6	89
Kershaw, Clayton, LAD	5/23	Cin	9.0	2	0	0	1	7	89

Worst Game Scores

Pitcher	Date	Opp	IP	H	R	ER	BB	SO	GS
Simon, Alfredo, Cin	5/17	Cle	4.1	14	10	10	1	2	-4
Locke, Jeff, Pit	6/9	Col	4.2	11	11	11	3	2	-3
Shields, James, SD	5/31	Sea	2.2	8	10	10	4	1	-1
Blair, Aaron, Atl	5/17	Pit	1.1	9	9	9	1	1	0
Mayers, Mike, StL	7/24	LAD	1.1	8	9	9	2	1	1
Strasburg, Stephen, Was	8/17	Col	1.2	9	9	9	3	3	1
Greinke, Zack, Ari	8/14	Bos	1.2	10	9	9	0	3	2
Godley, Zack, Ari	8/27	Cin	2.0	9	9	9	0	1	3
Lamb, John, Cin	7/16	Mil	2.0	9	9	9	2	3	3
Locke, Jeff, Pit	4/20	SD	3.0	11	8	8	4	2	3

Runs Created

Votto, Joey, Cin	130
Arenado, Nolan, Col	128
Bryant, Kris, ChC	120
Freeman, Freddie, Atl	119
Rizzo, Anthony, ChC	119
Murphy, Daniel, Was	115
Goldschmidt, Paul, Ari	113
Blackmon, Charlie, Col	110
Seager, Corey, LAD	110
Segura, Jean, Ari	107

Runs Created Per 27 Outs

Votto, Joey, Cin	8.7
Murphy, Daniel, Was	8.5
Freeman, Freddie, Atl	7.4
Arenado, Nolan, Col	7.4
Rizzo, Anthony, ChC	7.3
Bryant, Kris, ChC	7.3
Blackmon, Charlie, Col	7.2
Goldschmidt, Paul, Ari	7.0
LeMahieu, DJ, Col	7.0
Belt, Brandon, SF	6.9

Offensive Winning %

Votto, Joey, Cin	.791
Murphy, Daniel, Was	.790
Rizzo, Anthony, ChC	.755
Bryant, Kris, ChC	.755
Freeman, Freddie, Atl	.725
Seager, Corey, LAD	.715
Fowler, Dexter, ChC	.707
Belt, Brandon, SF	.706
Braun, Ryan, Mil	.685
Carpenter, Matt, StL	.682

Secondary Average
(minimum 502 PA)

Harper, Bryce, Was	.453
Goldschmidt, Paul, Ari	.437
Votto, Joey, Cin	.433
Freeman, Freddie, Atl	.428
Carter, Chris, Mil	.421
Villar, Jonathan, Mil	.411
Carpenter, Matt, StL	.406
Bryant, Kris, ChC	.400
Lamb, Jake, Ari	.394
Belt, Brandon, SF	.391

Isolated Power
(minimum 502 PA)

Carter, Chris, Mil	.277
Arenado, Nolan, Col	.275
Freeman, Freddie, Atl	.267
Bryant, Kris, ChC	.262
Lamb, Jake, Ari	.260
Duvall, Adam, Cin	.257
Bruce, Jay, Cin-NYM	.256
Rizzo, Anthony, ChC	.252
Cespedes, Yoenis, NYM	.251
Murphy, Daniel, Was	.249

Power / Speed Number
(minimum 502 PA)

Villar, Jonathan, Mil	29.1
Myers, Wil, SD	28.0
Goldschmidt, Paul, Ari	27.4
Segura, Jean, Ari	24.9
Harper, Bryce, Was	22.4
Blackmon, Charlie, Col	21.4
Braun, Ryan, Mil	20.9
Polanco, Gregory, Pit	19.2
Herrera, Odubel, Phi	18.8
Galvis, Freddy, Phi	18.4

Speed Scores

Hamilton, Billy, Cin	8.95
Gordon, Dee, Mia	8.37
Blackmon, Charlie, Col	7.85
Owings, Chris, Ari	7.76
Fowler, Dexter, ChC	7.71
Inciarte, Ender, Atl	7.28
Herrera, Odubel, Phi	7.28
Segura, Jean, Ari	7.14
Hernandez, Cesar, Phi	7.10
Marte, Starling, Pit	6.97

Cheap Wins

Wainwright, Adam, StL	5
Arrieta, Jake, ChC	4
Kazmir, Scott, LAD	4
Peralta, Wily, Mil	4
7 tied with	3

Tough Losses

Bumgarner, Madison, SF	6
Eickhoff, Jerad, Phi	5
11 tied with	4

Additional Bill James Leaders

AL Batters Win Shares

Altuve, Jose, Hou	36
Trout, Mike, LAA	35
Seager, Kyle, Sea	30
Beltre, Adrian, Tex	29
Betts, Mookie, Bos	29
Kinsler, Ian, Det	29
Cano, Robinson, Sea	28
Donaldson, Josh, Tor	28
Machado, Manny, Bal	28
2 tied with	26

NL Batters Win Shares

Votto, Joey, Cin	33
Bryant, Kris, ChC	32
Murphy, Daniel, Was	31
Rizzo, Anthony, ChC	29
Seager, Corey, LAD	29
Freeman, Freddie, Atl	28
Arenado, Nolan, Col	26
Goldschmidt, Paul, Ari	25
Herrera, Odubel, Phi	25
Turner, Justin, LAD	25

AL Pitchers Win Shares

Kluber, Corey, Cle	20
Verlander, Justin, Det	20
Britton, Zach, Bal	19
Miller, Andrew, NYY-Cle	19
Porcello, Rick, Bos	19
Happ, J.A., Tor	18
Tanaka, Masahiro, NYY	18
Sale, Chris, CWS	17
Sanchez, Aaron, Tor	17
Hamels, Cole, Tex	16

NL Pitchers Win Shares

Scherzer, Max, Was	20
Bumgarner, Madison, SF	19
Cueto, Johnny, SF	19
Lester, Jon, ChC	18
Syndergaard, Noah, NYM	18
Fernandez, Jose, Mia	17
Hendricks, Kyle, ChC	17
Jansen, Kenley, LAD	17
Roark, Tanner, Was	17
6 tied with	16

Batters Win Shares

Rodriguez, Alex	491
Pujols, Albert	463
Cabrera, Miguel	381
Beltran, Carlos	365
Beltre, Adrian	349
Suzuki, Ichiro	319
Ortiz, David	316
Rollins, Jimmy	303
Cano, Robinson	296
Utley, Chase	280

Pitchers Win Shares

Sabathia, CC	218
Colon, Bartolo	198
Hernandez, Felix	183
Verlander, Justin	177
Greinke, Zack	168
Rodriguez, Francisco	168
Nathan, Joe	165
Lackey, John	163
Hamels, Cole	158
Kershaw, Clayton	157

AL Component ERA
(minimum 162 IP)

Verlander, Justin, Det	2.54
Kluber, Corey, Cle	2.62
Porcello, Rick, Bos	2.64
Tanaka, Masahiro, NYY	2.80
Estrada, Marco, Tor	2.88
Sale, Chris, CWS	2.88
Sanchez, Aaron, Tor	2.90
Happ, J.A., Tor	3.22
Quintana, Jose, CWS	3.23
Santana, Ervin, Min	3.39

NL Component ERA
(minimum 162 IP)

Hendricks, Kyle, ChC	2.19
Scherzer, Max, Was	2.35
Arrieta, Jake, ChC	2.45
Lester, Jon, ChC	2.47
Bumgarner, Madison, SF	2.57
Fernandez, Jose, Mia	2.66
Cueto, Johnny, SF	2.71
Teheran, Julio, Atl	2.79
Syndergaard, Noah, NYM	2.79
Lackey, John, ChC	2.81

Highest Avg Game Score
(minimum 30 GS)

Verlander, Justin, Det	61.65
Sale, Chris, CWS	60.63
Kluber, Corey, Cle	60.41
Porcello, Rick, Bos	58.67
Sanchez, Aaron, Tor	57.53
Tanaka, Masahiro, NYY	57.29
Quintana, Jose, CWS	56.84
Happ, J.A., Tor	56.31
Hamels, Cole, Tex	55.66
Price, David, Bos	54.97

AL Lowest Avg Game Score
(minimum 30 GS)

Volquez, Edinson, KC	44.97
Weaver, Jered, LAA	45.29
Miley, Wade, Sea-Bal	47.00
Fister, Doug, Hou	47.56
Perez, Martin, Tex	47.73
Fiers, Mike, Hou	49.07
Ventura, Yordano, KC	49.38
Santiago, Hector, LAA-Min	49.42
Graveman, Kendall, Oak	49.84
Smyly, Drew, TB	50.13

AL Lowest Offensive Win %

Iglesias, Jose, Det	.351
Escobar, Alcides, KC	.355
Gordon, Alex, KC	.368
Gonzalez, Marwin, Hou	.386
Pillar, Kevin, Tor	.416
Perez, Salvador, KC	.429
Vogt, Stephen, Oak	.433
Moreland, Mitch, Tex	.436
Castro, Starlin, NYY	.442
Cuthbert, Cheslor, KC	.446

Highest Avg Game Score
(minimum 30 GS)

Scherzer, Max, Was	63.50
Bumgarner, Madison, SF	61.62
Lester, Jon, ChC	61.59
Hendricks, Kyle, ChC	61.20
Cueto, Johnny, SF	60.00
Arrieta, Jake, ChC	59.42
Syndergaard, Noah, NYM	59.37
Teheran, Julio, Atl	57.73
Roark, Tanner, Was	57.45
Martinez, Carlos, StL	57.29

NL Lowest Avg Game Score
(minimum 30 GS)

Nelson, Jimmy, Mil	47.38
Bettis, Chad, Col	47.66
Leake, Mike, StL	48.23
Anderson, Chase, Mil	48.83
Wainwright, Adam, StL	48.97
Garcia, Jaime, StL	49.00
Koehler, Tom, Mia	49.45
Ray, Robbie, Ari	49.50
Gonzalez, Gio, Was	50.19
Finnegan, Brandon, Cin	51.58

NL Lowest Offensive Win %

Hechavarria, Adeiny, Mia	.288
Heyward, Jason, ChC	.387
Galvis, Freddy, Phi	.395
Mercer, Jordy, Pit	.422
Garcia, Adonis, Atl	.427
Inciarte, Ender, Atl	.429
Cozart, Zack, Cin	.434
Panik, Joe, SF	.447
Phillips, Brandon, Cin	.458
Espinosa, Danny, Was	.458

Home Run Robberies

Lindsay Zeck

The Upton brothers, Justin and Melvin Jr., led the league in home run robberies in 2016. In first place was Justin with an incredible four home runs robbed. Melvin Jr. came in second place overall with three. Together, they comprised 15 percent of all of the home runs robbed last season. Amazingly, prior to this season, Justin Upton had only one home run robbery in his entire career, and Melvin had zero.

The most times any player was robbed this season was two. There were eight players robbed twice: Anthony Rizzo, Leonys Martin, Jose Abreu, Manny Machado, Freddie Freeman, J.J. Hardy, Albert Pujols, and Hyun Soo Kim. Chris Carter of the Milwaukee Brewers was robbed by Jay Bruce back in July, causing him to have to share his first place finish on the National League home run race with Nolan Arenado of the Colorado Rockies.

The only teams that were not involved in a game with a home run robbery were the Cleveland Indians and the San Francisco Giants. The Baltimore Orioles had 11 of their batters' home runs stolen away but still topped the leader board for the most home runs of any team in 2016 with 253.

Just like at the end of the 2015 season, Carlos Gomez and Torii Hunter are tied for the most home runs robbed since 2004 when we began tracking them as part of Bill James' Good Plays/Misplays data. Gomez did not add to his career total of 12 this season. Mike Trout only robbed one home run in 2016, as opposed to his three in 2015. However, he did it in style by robbing a grand slam from Leonys Martin. This put his career total to nine home runs robbed, now trailing Gomez and Hunter by only three.

Home Run Robberies

Date	Matchup	Fielder	Pos	Pitcher	Batter	Inn.	Outs	Men On	Score
08/22/2016	Red Sox@Rays	Andrew Benintendi	7	David Price	Steven Souza Jr.	8	0	1__	3-0
08/12/2016	Diamondbacks@Red Sox	Mookie Betts	9	David Price	Jake Lamb	8	2	_2_	3-9
08/13/2016	Rockies@Phillies	Charlie Blackmon	8	Carlos Estevez	Tommy Joseph	7	1	1_3	3-5
09/07/2016	Cubs@Brewers	Keon Broxton	8	Tyler Thornburg	Anthony Rizzo	9	1	___	1-2
07/15/2016	Brewers@Reds	Jay Bruce	9	Anthony DeSclafani	Chris Carter	4	1	___	1-0
09/16/2016	Blue Jays@Angels	Nick Buss	7	Cody Ege	Devon Travis	7	1	___	2-0
04/07/2016	Twins@Orioles	Byron Buxton	8	Phil Hughes	Jonathan Schoop	5	1	___	2-0
07/25/2016	Cubs@White Sox	Melky Cabrera	7	Miguel Gonzalez	Kris Bryant	1	1	___	0-0
09/05/2016	Tigers@White Sox	Melky Cabrera	7	Chris Sale	Cameron Maybin	1	0	___	0-0
06/07/2016	Royals@Orioles	Lorenzo Cain	8	Yordano Ventura	Pedro Alvarez	1	1	1__	0-4
08/15/2016	Mariners@Angels	Kole Calhoun	9	Mike Morin	Kyle Seager	7	2	1__	3-2
08/23/2016	Mets@Cardinals	Yoenis Cespedes	7	Josh Smoker	Stephen Piscotty	6	2	___	6-4
08/04/2016	Athletics@Angels	Coco Crisp	7	Zach Neal	Ji-Man Choi	5	2	___	5-5
08/25/2016	Royals@Marlins	Jarrod Dyson	8	Edinson Volquez	Christian Yelich	1	2	___	0-0
08/07/2016	Orioles@White Sox	Adam Eaton	9	Matt Albers	Matt Wieters	2	1	1__	8-0
08/21/2016	Yankees@Angels	Jacoby Ellsbury	8	Chad Green	Albert Pujols	5	2	1__	0-1
08/20/2016	Yankees@Angels	Brett Gardner	7	Tyler Clippard	C.J. Cron	7	1	1__	5-0
04/20/2016	Cubs@Cardinals	Randal Grichuk	8	Carlos Martinez	Anthony Rizzo	1	2	1__	0-0
05/13/2016	Cardinals@Dodgers	Randal Grichuk	8	Michael Wacha	Howie Kendrick	1	0	___	1-0
04/15/2016	Reds@Cardinals	Billy Hamilton	8	Dan Straily	Matt Carpenter	6	0	___	3-7
05/15/2016	Reds@Phillies	Tyler Holt	8	Dan Straily	Ryan Howard	5	0	1__	7-0
09/21/2016	Braves@Mets	Ender Inciarte	8	Jim Johnson	Yoenis Cespedes	9	2	12_	4-3
09/16/2016	Rays@Orioles	Kevin Kiermaier	8	Danny Farquhar	Hyun Soo Kim	7	1	123	4-2
09/20/2016	Red Sox@Orioles	Hyun Soo Kim	7	Darren ODay'	Mookie Betts	9	0	___	5-2
04/19/2016	Mets@Phillies	Juan Lagares	8	Rafael Montero	Maikel Franco	8	2	_23	11-1
08/19/2016	Nationals@Braves	Nick Markakis	9	Julio Teheran	Clint Robinson	5	0	___	1-0
05/26/2016	Diamondbacks@Pirates	Starling Marte	7	Neftali Feliz	Rickie Weeks Jr.	8	0	___	3-5
08/29/2016	Mariners@Rangers	Leonys Martin	8	Arquimedes Caminero	Ian Desmond	7	0	___	3-6
04/23/2016	Rangers@White Sox	Nomar Mazara	9	Tom Wilhelmsen	Todd Frazier	9	2	___	3-3
06/24/2016	Rays@Orioles	Taylor Motter	7	Matt Moore	Adam Jones	4	0	___	3-0
07/08/2016	Angels@Orioles	Daniel Nava	7	Matt Shoemaker	Manny Machado	1	1	___	2-1
08/12/2016	Pirates@Dodgers	Josh Reddick	9	Ross Stripling	Josh Harrison	5	1	___	4-1
08/19/2016	Nationals@Braves	Ben Revere	8	Tanner Roark	Freddie Freeman	4	2	___	1-0
06/19/2016	Blue Jays@Orioles	Michael Saunders	7	Jesse Chavez	J.J. Hardy	7	1	___	6-11
08/03/2016	Cardinals@Reds	Scott Schebler	9	Cody Reed	Jedd Gyorko	5	0	___	4-2
05/08/2016	Mariners@Astros	George Springer	9	Collin McHugh	Leonys Martin	3	0	___	0-1
05/19/2016	Astros@White Sox	George Springer	9	Collin McHugh	Jose Abreu	1	2	___	0-0
09/23/2016	Diamondbacks@Orioles	Yasmany Tomas	9	Shelby Miller	Chris Davis	1	1	12_	1-0
08/07/2016	Angels@Mariners	Mike Trout	8	Matt Shoemaker	Leonys Martin	4	0	123	1-1
04/26/2016	Athletics@Tigers	Justin Upton	7	Mike Pelfrey	Chris Coghlan	3	2	___	0-0
07/24/2016	Tigers@White Sox	Justin Upton	7	Anibal Sanchez	Jose Abreu	3	0	___	0-4
08/27/2016	Angels@Tigers	Justin Upton	7	Michael Fulmer	Albert Pujols	3	0	12_	2-1
09/09/2016	Orioles@Tigers	Justin Upton	7	Michael Fulmer	Hyun Soo Kim	3	2	___	0-1
04/20/2016	Pirates@Padres	Melvin Upton Jr.	7	Luis Perdomo	Matt Joyce	9	0	1__	2-8
06/08/2016	Braves@Padres	Melvin Upton Jr.	7	Drew Pomeranz	Freddie Freeman	5	0	___	3-1
06/28/2016	Orioles@Padres	Melvin Upton Jr.	8	Erik Johnson	J.J. Hardy	2	1	1__	1-1
04/22/2016	Twins@Nationals	Jayson Werth	7	Gio Gonzalez	Byron Buxton	3	1	___	0-4
05/31/2016	Red Sox@Orioles	Chris Young	8	Eduardo Rodriguez	Manny Machado	3	2	_2_	5-1

Win Shares

Bill James

What we call a Win Share is intended to represent about one-third of a Win, which is, in most cases, about three runs. It is *about* three runs, but it is *precisely* one-third of a win. If a team wins 100 games, they have 300 Win Shares. If a team wins 80 games, they have 240 Win Shares. One win; three shares of a win. It's a fixed ratio.

Win Shares are then assigned from team to player based on the good things that each player does, the things that each player has done to help the team win games. If a player hits a single, that represents a small portion of a Win. If he steals a base, strikes out an opposing hitter, or turns a double play, that's a small part of a Win. At the end of the year all of the little things that a player has done that are parts of a Win are added together, and each one-third of a win is a Win Share.

The first objection that we always hear from the peanut gallery is that this favors a player who plays on a good team, but actually it does not. Take two players with the same stats, same defensive performance, one on a good team, one on a bad team, their Win Shares will be the same. Good teams win not because the ratio changes, but simply because winning teams have more good players. Win Shares will vary with the run context of the team; that is to say, there is (of course) a difference between hitting .300 in Colorado and hitting .300 in Dodger Stadium. It takes more runs to win a game in Colorado than it does in Dodger Stadium, so of course it takes more runs created to earn a Win Share. But good or bad team isn't a variable, unless a team is inefficient at turning runs into wins.

The second issue that people often raise is that they don't understand why there are three Win Shares for each win, rather than 10 to 1 or 1 to 1. There is an extremely good reason for that, but it's harder to explain. Some things simply have a natural size. You wouldn't use a grocery sack that was six feet deep and four feet across; it's too big for the task. You wouldn't use a grocery sack that was six inches deep and four inches across; it's too small for the task. You wouldn't sit on a dining room chair that was seven feet deep; you wouldn't sit on a dining room chair that was a foot across. There is a natural size for a chair.

I know that there are other systems which measure a player's contribution to victory in tenths of a win, but here's what people don't get about that. It's a fraud. OK, harsh word, fraud; my point is that we can't actually measure accurately exactly how many tenths of a win a player has contributed to his team. A tenth of a win is a little bit less than a run; it's basically a run, but a little bit less. None of our systems of analysis, none of our weights and measures, are actually accurate enough to measure reliably how much a player has contributed to the success of his team with an accuracy of less than a run. People like to *pretend* that they can do that, but they can't. They're pulling your leg. Yes, you can take any form of measurement and state it as a decimal, but it's a meaningless decimal. A player with 2.4 WAR is not actually better than a player with 2.3 WAR, most of the time. It's a pretend difference.

Suppose, on the other hand, that we measured win contributions only in whole wins, undivided into shares, undivided into decimal points. If you do that, you're basically operating on a one-to-ten scale, with the MVP usually coming in around 10 wins, maybe 7 or 8 in some seasons.

But if you do that, you're losing distinctions that you actually CAN perceive. If you state win contributions only in whole wins, you'll have two players listed at "6", but one of them is clearly and pretty obviously better than the other one. You've lost a distinction that you didn't need to lose. The system has failed to distinguish between players who are clearly different.

A third of a win is the smallest unit of measurement that one can reliably see-a third, or a fourth, but a third works better than a fourth.

OK, so we measure how many Win Shares each player has contributed to his team. The highest number in the majors in 2016 was 36, by Jose Altuve. The scale is this:

29 or above, MVP candidate

25 to 28, obvious All Star

21 to 24, marginal All Star, high quality regular

17 to 20, a regular player of more than ordinary value

13 to 16, a regular player having a modest season, or a quality player who missed part of the season.

9 to 12, good bench player or a one-year regular who will lose his job next year

5 to 8, bench player, middle reliever

1 to 4, player with limited playing time, small role on the team

This outline describes position players more than it does pitchers. It used to be that pitcher's Win Shares were on the same scale as position players, and the highest total in baseball would not infrequently be for a pitcher. But in the modern world, with the five-man starting rotations and eight-man bullpens, Win Shares for pitchers are dispersed so widely that individual pitchers rarely break 20 anymore; they're on a little different scale. Pitchers rarely have MVP seasons anymore.

Players who were 29 and above in 2016 include Altuve, Trout, Mookie Betts, Kris Bryant, Adrian Beltre, Ian Kinsler, Daniel Murphy, Anthony Rizzo, Joey Votto, and both of the Seager brothers. That's it; I think that's the complete list. The MVP candidates.

Players who were 25 to 28 in 2016 include (but are not limited to) Elvis Andrus, Nolan Arenado, Manny Machado, Carlos Correa, Josh Donaldson, Paul Goldschmidt, Freddie Freeman...guys who might be MVP candidates next year or were last year, but who just don't quite make the serious MVP candidates list for this season.

Players who were in the 21 to 24 range in 2016 include Wilson Ramos, Ian Desmond, Nelson Cruz, Brian Dozier, Dexter Fowler, Francisco Lindor. Mark Trumbo...guys who are among the best players on the playoff teams, generally, and a few really good players who somehow got stranded on bad teams.

Players in the 17 to 20 range in 2016 include Chris Davis, Adam Jones, Rougned Odor, Eric Hosmer, Wil Myers, Addison Russell, Chase Utley. These are good players, quality regulars, All Stars who just aren't quite having All Star seasons.

Players in the 13 to 16 range in 2016 include Danny Valencia, Starlin Castro, C. J. Cron, Josh Harrison, Matt Kemp, Brad Miller, Jordy Mercer, Angel Pagan, Devon Travis...players who were regulars and who did enough to remain regulars, generally, but who aren't going to sign big, big contracts based on their current level of play.

Players in the 9 to 12 range of value in 2016 include Josh Reddick, Nori Aoki, Corey Dickerson, Adeiny Hechavarria, Jon Jay, Matt Joyce, Logan Morrison...guys whose hold on a regular position is tenuous or who have slipped into a bench role, plus some guys who are blasting through this range on the way up, like Alex Bregman and Yasmany Tomas.

Players in the 5 to 8 range of value in 2016 include Nick Hundley, Chris Coghlan, A.J. Ellis, Chris Iannetta, Jed Lowrie, Jarrod Saltalamacchia...guys who used to be regulars but aren't now and probably never will be again.

Players in the 1 to 4 range of value are mostly 4-A players who move up and down between the majors and the minors, or who were injured and not able to perform most of the season.

The chart below contain the 2016 and career Win Shares for almost every player. You don't have to agree with all of the values; we do the best we can but we're not always right. There are lots and lots of players who have 1 or 2 Win Shares, and space prevents us from listing them all. There is some sort of rule that if you don't have either 8 Win Shares or 10 in your career, then you're not listed. Thanks.

WIN SHARES BY YEAR

Player	<07	07	08	09	10	11	12	13	14	15	16	Career
Abreu, Jose									29	27	20	76
Ackley, Dustin						14	16	11	12	3	0	56
Adams, Matt								1	12	15	13	41
Albers, Matt	0	0	4	2	5	3	6	5	1	6	0	32
Allen, Cody							1	8	14	12	14	49
Alonso, Yonder					0	4	17	12	6	8	12	59
Altuve, Jose						2	17	11	30	27	36	123
Alvarez, Pedro					14	3	22	18	11	10	8	86
Amarista, Alexi						1	6	10	13	6	2	38
Anderson, Brett				8	9	4	3	0	3	8	0	35
Anderson, Tim											10	10
Anderson, Tyler											8	8
Andrus, Elvis				17	20	18	23	15	13	21	26	153
Aoki, Nori							15	17	17	12	9	70
Archer, Chris							0	10	11	14	8	43
Arenado, Nolan								9	12	26	26	73
Arrieta, Jake					5	5	0	3	12	27	16	68
Asche, Cody								4	10	10	2	26
Avila, Alex				3	7	27	15	6	14	6	2	80
Aviles, Mike			17	2	10	5	10	8	5	3	1	61
Axford, John				1	11	15	7	3	3	7	5	52
Aybar, Erick	1	2	15	20	9	20	16	14	20	13	6	136
Baez, Javier									2	1	14	17
Bailey, Andrew				17	11	6	0	3		0	2	39
Bailey, Homer			2	0	5	5	5	12	11	8	0	48
Barnette, Tony											8	8
Barney, Darwin					1	14	15	5	6	1	6	48
Barnhart, Tucker									1	4	12	17
Barraclough, Kyle										3	9	12
Bastardo, Antonio				0	1	10	3	6	3	6	3	32
Bauer, Trevor							0	0	5	8	11	24
Bautista, Jose	9	12	8	6	34	36	13	18	28	25	15	204
Beckham, Gordon				12	11	14	13	7	5	3	3	68
Belisle, Matt	7	5	0	1	11	7	8	5	3	3	5	55
Belt, Brandon						5	17	24	5	20	24	95
Beltran, Carlos	184	25	29	14	8	26	18	22	7	14	18	365
Beltre, Adrian	145	16	13	10	26	16	25	22	27	20	29	349
Benoit, Joaquin	22	10	2		9	8	7	14	12	9	6	99
Betances, Dellin							0	0	14	14	12	40
Bettis, Chad								0	0	7	10	17
Betts, Mookie									8	23	29	60
Blackmon, Charlie						1	1	7	16	20	22	67
Blanco, Andres	6			2	4	1			2	9	7	31
Blanco, Gregor				11	0	6	12	13	15	10	3	70
Blanton, Joe	23	13	7	11	4	1	5	0		8	10	82
Blevins, Jerry		0	3	1	3	2	7	5	2	2	6	31
Bogaerts, Xander								1	7	22	19	49
Bonifacio, Emilio		1	2	7	5	20	6	7	11	1	0	60
Bour, Justin									3	12	11	26
Bourjos, Peter					3	16	5	4	7	2	5	42
Bourn, Michael	0	4	7	23	18	22	28	14	11	7	7	141
Brach, Brad						0	3	1	5	9	12	30
Bradley Jr., Jackie								1	5	10	19	35
Brantley, Michael				3	5	11	18	21	31	21	1	111
Braun, Ryan		22	23	36	25	37	28	9	17	20	20	237
Bregman, Alex											10	10
Breslow, Craig		2	6	6	8	3	6	7	0	3	0	41
Britton, Zach						6	3	1	17	15	19	61
Broxton, Jonathan	9	10	10	16	6	0	11	1	9	4	3	79
Bruce, Jay			7	9	16	22	18	21	10	10	18	131
Bryant, Kris										30	32	62
Buchholz, Clay		3	0	6	18	6	9	12	2	8	5	69
Bumgarner, Madison				1	8	12	11	12	16	17	19	96
Burnett, Sean	2		2	5	7	5	7	1	0		0	29
Bush, Matt											9	9
Butler, Billy		7	8	18	20	17	21	16	12	9	6	134
Byrd, Marlon	29	13	12	20	19	8	1	23	16	12	4	157
Cabrera, Asdrubal		7	12	18	9	25	19	12	15	11	21	149
Cabrera, Melky		13	12	5	14	28	19	25	12	20	10	158
Cabrera, Miguel	91	29	20	25	30	38	32	37	28	26	25	381
Cahill, Trevor				7	16	9	11	6	0	2	5	56
Cain, Lorenzo					6	0	7	12	19	27	13	84
Cain, Matt	16	12	14	20	15	15	16	5	1	0	0	114

WIN SHARES BY YEAR

Player	<07	07	08	09	10	11	12	13	14	15	16	Career
Calhoun, Kole							0	8	20	21	19	68
Cano, Robinson	29	21	12	18	34	30	34	35	34	21	28	296
Carpenter, Matt						0	9	35	27	30	21	122
Carrasco, Carlos				0	3	5		0	12	14	12	46
Carter, Chris					0	0	8	13	15	10	11	57
Cashner, Andrew					2	1	2	10	9	3	2	29
Casilla, Santiago	0	4	3	0	8	8	9	6	12	9	8	67
Castellanos, Nick								0	13	13	15	41
Castillo, Welington					1	0	4	10	12	10	14	51
Castro, Jason					4		8	18	10	7	9	56
Castro, Starlin					12	25	23	7	20	13	15	115
Cecil, Brett				3	10	4	1	6	6	6	2	38
Cervelli, Francisco			0	3	7	4	0	3	7	17	9	50
Cespedes, Yoenis							24	14	18	27	19	102
Chacin, Jhoulys				0	10	12	4	15	2	2	5	50
Chapman, Aroldis					2	4	21	12	13	15	13	80
Chatwood, Tyler						3	3	11	1		11	29
Chen, Wei-Yin							12	7	12	14	2	47
Chisenhall, Lonnie						6	4	7	18	9	14	58
Choo, Shin-Soo	4	1	16	23	27	8	25	31	9	25	5	174
Cishek, Steve					1	6	10	14	10	3	11	55
Clippard, Tyler		1	1	5	9	13	11	10	10	9	7	76
Cobb, Alex						3	6	13	13		0	35
Coghlan, Chris				21	8	4	1	5	15	16	6	76
Cole, Gerrit								8	7	18	6	39
Collmenter, Josh						10	5	7	12	6	3	43
Colome, Alex								1	2	6	12	21
Colon, Bartolo	131	1	2	3		8	9	17	7	7	13	198
Contreras, Willson											9	9
Corbin, Patrick							4	13		5	5	27
Correa, Carlos										18	26	44
Cozart, Zack						1	11	12	8	4	12	48
Crawford, Brandon						5	13	11	22	20	20	91
Crawford, Carl	82	20	11	19	32	8	3	13	12	4	0	204
Crisp, Coco	54	16	11	4	14	15	18	21	15	0	14	182
Cron, C.J.									8	9	14	31
Cruz, Nelson	3	4	7	16	19	16	17	16	22	26	21	167
Cueto, Johnny			6	7	12	12	21	5	22	12	19	116
Cuthbert, Cheslor										2	10	12
Danks, John		4	17	16	16	8	1	3	7	5	0	77
Darvish, Yu							14	18	10		8	50
Davies, Zach										2	8	10
Davis, Chris			8	7	1	4	19	33	12	27	17	128
Davis, Ike					16	6	15	7	10	3	0	57
Davis, Khris								6	12	11	15	44
Davis, Rajai	0	5	5	13	14	6	11	6	14	6	13	93
Davis, Wade				2	8	6	7	2	15	19	11	70
De Aza, Alejandro		1		1	1	9	18	16	11	8	3	68
de la Rosa, Jorge	4	3	5	12	8	4	0	12	11	9	5	73
deGrom, Jacob									11	15	11	37
Descalso, Daniel					1	10	5	11	3	1	8	39
Desmond, Ian				2	11	16	18	25	19	12	22	125
Devenski, Christopher											11	11
Diaz, Aledmys											18	18
Diaz, Edwin											8	8
Dickerson, Alex										0	8	8
Dickerson, Corey								4	15	8	9	36
Dickey, R.A.	11		3	3	15	11	19	11	11	10	7	101
Dietrich, Derek								5	6	6	15	32
Donaldson, Josh					0		8	32	27	32	28	127
Doolittle, Sean							5	8	11	2	4	30
Dozier, Brian							4	19	19	24	24	90
Drew, Stephen	6	16	21	16	20	10	6	17	4	7	5	128
Drury, Brandon										0	9	9
Duda, Lucas					0	11	13	8	25	17	3	77
Duensing, Brian				6	13	4	2	5	4	3	1	38
Duffy, Danny						1	2	3	12	7	15	40
Duffy, Matt									2	22	5	29
Duke, Zach	20	2	3	12	1	4	2	2	7	5	8	66
Dull, Ryan										1	8	9
Dunn, Mike				0	2	5	0	7	6	3	4	27
Duvall, Adam									0	2	16	18
Dyson, Jarrod					2	2	8	7	9	6	12	46

WIN SHARES BY YEAR

Player	<07	07	08	09	10	11	12	13	14	15	16	Career
Dyson, Sam							0	0	4	9	14	27
Eaton, Adam							2	5	20	24	24	75
Eickhoff, Jerad										4	12	16
Ellis, A.J.			0	0	4	3	20	16	7	10	6	66
Ellsbury, Jacoby		6	16	21	1	34	6	22	22	9	17	154
Encarnacion, Edwin	18	16	14	6	8	11	31	22	19	24	19	188
Eovaldi, Nathan						2	3	5	4	9	6	29
Escobar, Alcides			0	4	12	8	14	10	20	15	13	96
Escobar, Eduardo						0	2	2	13	14	7	38
Escobar, Yunel		12	13	24	14	20	9	18	10	16	15	151
Espinosa, Danny					4	22	18	2	6	10	18	80
Estrada, Marco			0	0	0	4	8	7	5	12	12	48
Ethier, Andre	11	13	23	21	22	18	22	16	10	15	0	171
Familia, Jeurys							0	0	9	15	16	40
Feldman, Scott	4	1	4	14	2	2	4	10	9	5	4	59
Feliz, Neftali				6	15	12	4	1	6	1	6	51
Fernandez, Jose								16	4	6	17	43
Fielder, Prince	18	27	23	36	23	33	27	18	3	24	2	234
Fiers, Mike						0	8	0	7	9	7	31
Fister, Doug				4	7	18	11	14	14	4	6	78
Flaherty, Ryan							2	7	9	4	4	26
Flores, Wilmer								2	7	16	9	34
Flowers, Tyler				0	0	3	3	3	10	7	10	36
Floyd, Gavin	2	2	15	13	12	11	10	0	3	1	2	71
Forsythe, Logan						3	8	3	4	16	16	50
Fowler, Dexter			0	15	13	16	15	13	16	22	22	132
Franco, Maikel									1	13	17	31
Francoeur, Jeff	27	20	5	9	8	17	6	1	0	5	4	102
Frazier, Todd						3	13	15	20	13	15	79
Freeman, Freddie					0	19	18	35	28	22	28	150
Freese, David				1	8	13	19	9	12	15	13	90
Fulmer, Michael											14	14
Gallardo, Yovani		9	2	10	11	13	16	8	9	14	3	95
Galvis, Freddy							3	4	2	15	16	40
Garcia, Adonis										3	11	14
Garcia, Avisail							1	5	4	10	11	31
Garcia, Jaime			1		12	7	6	2	2	12	6	48
Gardner, Brett			3	9	17	16	2	22	19	19	17	124
Garza, Matt	1	4	12	12	10	10	5	10	8	0	2	74
Gattis, Evan								11	12	11	15	49
Gausman, Kevin								1	6	5	12	24
Gee, Dillon					3	5	4	10	5	0	6	33
Gennett, Scooter								9	14	7	11	41
Gentry, Craig				0	0	5	9	11	8	0	0	33
Gillaspie, Conor			0			1	0	9	16	3	4	33
Goldschmidt, Paul						6	17	36	20	35	25	139
Gomes, Yan							2	14	18	5	4	43
Gomez, Carlos		2	13	6	4	7	12	21	27	14	11	117
Gomez, Jeanmar					2	3	0	4	4	5	7	25
Gonzalez, Adrian	18	25	24	34	35	27	24	24	26	22	20	279
Gonzalez, Carlos			6	9	25	20	15	15	5	18	18	131
Gonzalez, Gio			0	2	15	15	17	11	8	9	6	83
Gonzalez, Marwin							2	2	6	8	7	25
Gonzalez, Miguel							10	10	10	5	7	42
Gordon, Alex		12	15	2	3	24	20	21	26	16	9	148
Gordon, Dee						6	3	2	22	26	7	66
Gorzelanny, Tom	3	11	0	2	7	4	6	4	3	0	0	40
Grandal, Yasmani							11	4	12	15	19	61
Granderson, Curtis		26	25	20	20	16	26	4	17	29	13	217
Graveman, Kendall									0	5	9	14
Gray, Jon										1	9	10
Gray, Sonny								5	13	16	0	34
Gregerson, Luke				5	9	4	9	7	8	11	10	63
Gregorius, Didi							0	10	9	17	16	52
Greinke, Zack	13	9	15	26	11	10	16	17	15	26	10	168
Grichuk, Randal									1	12	13	26
Grilli, Jason	6	4	7	2			4	6	9	2	6	52
Grossman, Robbie								7	10	0	10	27
Guerra, Junior										0	10	10
Gutierrez, Franklin	1	6	5	21	14	4	5	3		7	7	73
Guyer, Brandon							0	0	8	11	10	29
Gyorko, Jedd								12	11	11	12	46
Hamels, Cole	8	15	18	10	16	17	18	13	15	12	16	158

WIN SHARES BY YEAR

Player	<07	07	08	09	10	11	12	13	14	15	16	Career
Hamilton, Billy								2	15	5	9	31
Hammel, Jason	0	2	3	10	8	5	10	4	9	9	9	69
Hand, Brad						1	0	1	3	1	8	14
Hanigan, Ryan		1	4	8	13	11	18	5	8	4	2	74
Happ, J.A.		0	2	15	6	1	5	3	7	10	18	67
Hardy, J.J.	14	19	20	6	10	22	20	16	17	5	14	163
Harper, Bryce							21	19	9	38	20	107
Harris, Will							0	5	1	9	11	26
Harrison, Josh						5	4	3	25	12	15	64
Harvey, Matt							5	14		14	2	35
Headley, Chase		0	8	16	15	16	32	17	15	16	17	152
Healy, Ryon											11	11
Hechavarria, Adeiny							3	5	13	13	9	43
Heisey, Chris					4	8	8	5	3	3	2	33
Hellickson, Jeremy					3	15	11	4	1	5	12	51
Hendricks, Kyle									7	8	17	32
Hernandez, Cesar								3	1	12	24	40
Hernandez, David				3	6	10	9	3		1	5	37
Hernandez, Felix	16	14	13	26	23	16	15	16	22	14	8	183
Herrera, Kelvin						0	10	5	10	8	13	46
Herrera, Odubel										16	24	40
Herrmann, Chris							0	3	0	1	8	12
Heyward, Jason					23	11	22	14	23	21	12	126
Hill, Aaron	23	20	5	25	12	13	25	12	10	5	9	159
Hill, Rich	5	13	1	0	1		3	0	1	4	12	41
Hochevar, Luke		1	3	1	4	7	1	10		3	3	33
Holland, Derek				2	3	14	8	13	4	2	4	50
Holliday, Matt	45	27	21	25	25	21	21	25	26	12	10	258
Holt, Brock							3	1	12	14	6	36
Hosmer, Eric						13	10	18	14	22	17	94
Howard, Ryan	40	26	24	26	20	21	7	9	15	11	5	204
Howell, J.P.	3	0	11	11		0	3	6	5	6	2	47
Hudson, Daniel					1	9	16	0	0	4	4	34
Hughes, Phil		4	0	10	11	1	9	2	14	8	0	59
Hundley, Nick			3	10	10	12	2	10	6	7	6	66
Hunter, Tommy			0	8	10	3	4	10	8	4	3	50
Iannetta, Chris	1	5	17	10	3	16	8	10	17	8	5	100
Iglesias, Jose						0	1	13		12	13	39
Inciarte, Ender									10	15	14	39
Infante, Omar	30	4	9	7	19	18	14	16	9	3	2	131
Iwakuma, Hisashi							8	20	11	8	10	57
Jackson, Austin					18	14	22	15	11	14	5	99
Jackson, Edwin	3	2	10	17	9	12	9	1	0	4	1	68
Jansen, Kenley					6	6	15	16	11	12	17	83
Jaso, John				0	16	5	21	9	9	6	11	77
Jay, Jon					8	13	15	17	16	3	12	84
Jeffress, Jeremy					1	1	0	1	3	7	10	23
Jennings, Desmond					0	11	13	20	13	2	2	61
Jepsen, Kevin			0	4	5	0	4	1	6	12	0	32
Jimenez, Ubaldo	0	4	11	19	22	6	3	13	3	11	2	94
Johnson, Chris				0	15	8	17	20	11	3	1	75
Johnson, Jim	0	0	8	7	3	11	17	11	0	7	10	74
Johnson, Kelly	9	19	19	6	21	16	14	12	7	10	8	141
Jones, Adam	1	0	9	13	15	16	26	23	25	15	18	161
Jones, Nate							9	4	0	2	10	25
Joyce, Matt			6	1	10	19	13	11	10	1	11	82
Kang, Jung Ho										17	11	28
Kazmir, Scott	24	13	12	6	0	0		8	10	11	4	88
Kelley, Shawn				3	2	2	2	4	3	4	8	28
Kelly, Joe							5	9	5	6	2	27
Kemp, Matt	3	10	19	26	15	37	21	6	20	18	16	191
Kendrick, Howie	6	9	15	15	19	18	16	13	27	18	11	167
Kennedy, Ian		2	0	0	11	20	11	2	9	4	14	73
Kepler, Max										0	8	8
Kershaw, Clayton			5	12	15	23	19	22	22	21	16	155
Keuchel, Dallas							0	3	16	22	6	47
Kiermaier, Kevin								0	9	19	13	41
Kim, Hyun Soo											12	12
Kimbrel, Craig					4	17	18	17	16	11	9	92
Kinsler, Ian	12	17	24	24	13	22	15	20	24	21	29	221
Kipnis, Jason						6	24	27	10	22	19	108
Kluber, Corey						0	1	9	21	14	20	65
Lackey, John	56	21	13	12	11	1		10	11	17	11	163

WIN SHARES BY YEAR

Player	<07	07	08	09	10	11	12	13	14	15	16	Career
Lagares, Juan								7	15	13	2	37
Lamb, Jake									1	9	16	26
Latos, Mat				1	13	8	16	13	5	3		62
Lawrie, Brett						10	14	9	10	13	11	67
Leake, Mike					7	9	8	12	10	10	5	61
Lee, Dae-Ho											8	8
LeMahieu, DJ						0	6	8	9	14	22	59
Leon, Sandy							0	0	1	3	12	16
Lester, Jon	5	4	18	17	17	14	8	12	18	13	18	144
Lewis, Colby	2	0			13	11	8		3	10	8	55
Lincecum, Tim		8	25	22	14	16	0	4	3	3	0	95
Lind, Adam	3	7	7	21	9	11	9	15	13	20	7	122
Lindor, Francisco										14	21	35
Liriano, Francisco	16		4	2	14	4	4	12	7	12	6	81
Lobaton, Jose			0			1	5	9	5	3	3	26
Logan, Boone	0	3	1	0	4	3	5	5	0	2	6	29
Lohse, Kyle	45	9	12	3	0	9	16	12	11	0	0	117
Loney, James	3	16	14	18	18	16	5	19	13	6	5	133
Longoria, Evan			19	24	28	25	14	24	21	18	20	193
Lopez, Javier	8	4	6	0	6	6	4	5	3	5	2	49
Lowrie, Jed			7	1	8	5	11	23	11	6	8	80
Lucroy, Jonathan					4	15	15	19	26	10	22	111
Machado, Manny							7	20	12	27	28	94
Madson, Ryan	19	5	8	10	8	12				9	8	79
Maeda, Kenta											11	11
Maldonado, Martin						0	7	3	4	5	7	26
Markakis, Nick	12	20	23	16	22	19	16	11	20	20	17	196
Marte, Starling							5	20	17	20	17	79
Martin, Leonys						0	1	14	14	5	13	47
Martin, Russell	14	22	20	16	9	14	12	16	22	17	15	177
Martinez, Carlos								1	4	14	16	35
Martinez, J.D.						6	7	3	19	25	17	77
Martinez, Victor	64	29	7	21	17	24		11	30	4	15	222
Mathis, Jeff	0	2	7	4	3	4	5	4	1	1	3	34
Matusz, Brian				3	10	0	4	5	3	4	0	29
Matz, Steven										4	9	13
Mauer, Joe	58	21	30	32	27	10	25	23	14	18	14	272
Maybin, Cameron		0	3	2	8	17	13	0	5	16	14	78
Mazara, Nomar											16	16
McCann, Brian	28	15	18	20	19	23	12	16	19	21	12	203
McCann, James									0	10	9	19
McCarthy, Brandon	10	3	1	5		11	7	3	8	0	0	48
McCutchen, Andrew				18	22	28	40	34	33	35	17	227
McGee, Jake					0	2	8	5	15	7	4	41
McGehee, Casey			0	17	23	9	5		17	1	0	72
McHugh, Collin							0	0	13	13	8	34
Medlen, Kris				3	7	0	18	13		3	0	44
Melancon, Mark				1	2	10	0	15	15	17	16	76
Mercer, Jordy							2	13	10	8	13	46
Merrifield, Whit											8	8
Mesoraco, Devin						1	3	8	26	0	0	38
Miley, Wade						2	14	10	7	9	3	45
Miller, Andrew	0	2	0	2	0	2	4	2	9	13	19	53
Miller, Brad								10	11	15	15	51
Miller, Shelby							2	10	10	11	1	34
Milone, Tommy						2	10	6	5	8	1	32
Molina, Yadier	28	12	15	20	17	18	29	29	19	16	21	224
Montero, Miguel	0	3	4	13	9	29	26	10	15	12	6	127
Moore, Matt						1	8	13	1	1	10	34
Morales, Kendrys	2	2	0	23	8		14	17	2	21	15	104
Moreland, Mitch					6	8	9	10	3	16	10	62
Morneau, Justin	43	18	28	18	17	4	10	14	16	5	3	176
Morrison, Logan					9	11	4	7	11	9	9	60
Morrow, Brandon		5	7	4	7	7	10	0	0	2	2	44
Morse, Michael	7	2	0	2	9	25	13	3	13	3	0	77
Morton, Charlie			0	4	0	8	0	6	4	2	1	25
Moss, Brandon		1	5	5	0	0	13	20	17	7	11	79
Motte, Jason			2	2	6	9	14		1	6	1	41
Moustakas, Mike						4	14	5	9	21	1	54
Murphy, Daniel			6	10		14	20	22	21	19	31	143
Myers, Wil								14	6	9	19	48
Napoli, Mike	10	8	12	10	12	23	12	16	10	8	14	135
Naquin, Tyler											13	13

WIN SHARES BY YEAR

Player	<07	07	08	09	10	11	12	13	14	15	16	Career
Nathan, Joe	75	16	16	16		5	12	17	6	0	2	165
Nava, Daniel						5	5	18	11	2	1	42
Navarro, Dioner	9	6	17	5	2	3	4	11	17	5	3	82
Neris, Hector									0	2	11	13
Neshek, Pat	6	8	1		0	1	3	2	13	4	5	43
Niese, Jon			0	1	6	4	13	6	8	5	3	46
Nolasco, Ricky	5	0	14	6	7	5	8	9	3	0	8	65
Norris, Bud				3	3	7	4	8	11	0	4	40
Norris, Derek							7	11	16	19	3	56
Nova, Ivan					2	11	5	13	0	2	8	41
Nunez, Eduardo					2	8	4	6	3	6	15	44
O'Day, Darren			2	9	9	0	10	8	10	12	3	63
Odor, Rougned									11	16	18	45
Odorizzi, Jake							0	1	7	11	11	30
O'Flaherty, Eric	0	4	0	4	5	12	8	3	2	0	0	38
Ogando, Alexi					6	13	7	8	0	4	2	40
Oh, Seung Hwan											16	16
Orlando, Paulo										7	13	20
Ortiz, David	132	27	15	11	18	18	15	22	19	15	24	316
Osuna, Roberto										11	15	26
Otero, Dan							0	5	9	0	10	24
Ottavino, Adam						0	5	7	6	4	5	27
Owings, Chris								2	8	6	11	27
Ozuna, Marcell								8	19	10	15	52
Pagan, Angel	3	5	3	12	23	15	27	11	14	9	15	137
Panik, Joe									10	17	13	40
Papelbon, Jonathan	23	15	15	15	10	12	14	11	14	10	4	143
Parnell, Bobby				0	2	2	4	8	9	0	0	25
Parra, Gerardo				9	6	19	9	15	6	14	2	80
Pearce, Steve		2	2	2	1	0	6	4	19	5	9	50
Peavy, Jake	53	21	13	6	6	5	17	7	9	6	1	144
Pederson, Joc									0	15	19	34
Pedroia, Dustin	2	18	26	24	12	27	17	25	17	12	21	201
Pelfrey, Mike	0	1	12	4	12	3	2	3	0	7	2	46
Pena, Brayan	1	0	0		2	4	5	3	2	8	0	33
Pence, Hunter		18	19	17	21	24	18	25	26	7	16	191
Pennington, Cliff			3	7	19	18	10	5	4	3	2	71
Peralta, David									7	20	2	29
Peralta, Jhonny	45	21	19	10	16	22	12	19	22	20	6	212
Peralta, Joel	7	6	0	0	5	8	6	7	3	2	0	44
Peralta, Wily							3	5	12	3	4	27
Perez, Hernan							0	1	0	4	11	16
Perez, Martin							1	8	2	3	9	23
Perez, Salvador						7	10	23	17	18	18	93
Perkins, Glen	1	2	7	2	0	8	10	13	9	9	0	61
Peterson, Jace									1	14	9	24
Phelps, David							7	3	4	3	12	29
Phillips, Brandon	19	17	19	19	18	22	19	22	13	17	12	197
Pierzynski, A.J.	96	8	8	10	12	11	19	17	6	14	2	203
Pillar, Kevin								1	1	15	15	32
Pineda, Michael						10			8	7	6	31
Piscotty, Stephen										11	22	33
Plouffe, Trevor					0	6	8	8	17	18	7	64
Polanco, Gregory									8	17	14	39
Polanco, Jorge									1	1	8	10
Pollock, A.J.							2	14	10	27	1	54
Pomeranz, Drew						1	4	0	5	5	12	27
Porcello, Rick				13	5	8	7	9	13	5	19	79
Posey, Buster				0	20	9	38	24	30	29	24	174
Prado, Martin	2	1	9	12	22	12	23	15	15	17	22	150
Price, David			1	6	17	13	19	12	16	19	14	117
Puig, Yasiel								17	27	9	10	63
Pujols, Albert	210	32	34	39	32	26	25	10	19	18	17	462
Qualls, Chad	20	9	11	8	0	5	1	6	7	3	2	72
Quintana, Jose							9	13	12	15	15	64
Raburn, Ryan	0	4	3	9	11	10	1	13	0	6	2	59
Ramirez, Alexei			18	15	20	20	14	15	21	16	9	148
Ramirez, Hanley	25	27	32	34	22	10	17	23	18	7	17	232
Ramirez, Jose								1	7	4	22	34
Ramos, A.J.							0	5	8	14	11	38
Ramos, Wilson					3	13	3	8	10	11	24	72
Rasmus, Colby				13	17	11	15	20	8	15	9	108
Realmuto, J.T.									1	10	19	30

						WIN SHARES BY YEAR						
Player	<07	07	08	09	10	11	12	13	14	15	16	Career
Reddick, Josh				0	1	7	16	13	13	17	12	79
Reed, Addison						0	7	12	7	4	13	43
Reimold, Nolan				10	0	11	4	0	2	6	3	36
Rendon, Anthony							12	26	9	22		69
Revere, Ben					0	9	11	10	16	17	4	67
Reyes, Jose	60	24	28	5	19	26	23	15	19	13	8	240
Reynolds, Mark		14	17	20	16	16	12	11	7	7	9	129
Richard, Clayton			0	8	10	2	7	0		3	4	34
Richards, Garrett					0	1	6	13	14	2		36
Rivera, Rene	4				2		2	14	5	6		33
Rizzo, Anthony				0	12	14	28	32	29			115
Roark, Tanner							7	15	4	17		43
Robertson, David			2	3	4	11	7	12	12	13	10	74
Rodney, Fernando	15	3	4	10	6	1	19	11	10	4	7	90
Rodon, Carlos										9	8	17
Rodriguez, Alex	339	37	23	23	21	14	14	4		15	1	491
Rodriguez, Francisco	58	15	16	10	11	10	5	7	13	12	11	168
Rodriguez, Sean			3	0	9	10	8	4	6	2	13	55
Rollins, Jimmy	126	28	24	19	14	25	21	20	19	5	2	303
Romo, Sergio			4	4	8	9	11	9	8	5	4	62
Rondon, Hector							2	11	16	7		36
Rosales, Adam			0	3	8	0	1	2	5	1	7	27
Rosenthal, Trevor					2	7	11	14	1			35
Ross, David	23	7	5	6	6	7	6	2	2	1	6	71
Ross, Joe									4	8		12
Ross, Tyson				0	3	0	5	13	12	0		33
Ruggiano, Justin	0	1			4	11	8	8	5	1		38
Ruiz, Carlos	2	13	6	13	19	18	24	9	15	3	8	130
Rupp, Cameron							1	1	7	16		25
Russell, Addison									13	18		31
Ryan, Brendan		5	2	14	8	13	11	4	1	2	0	60
Sabathia, CC	76	24	23	18	20	19	14	8	0	5	11	218
Saladino, Tyler										3	10	13
Salas, Fernando					1	12	2	0	4	4	6	29
Salazar, Danny							4	4	14	10		32
Sale, Chris				5	11	19	15	17	15	17		99
Saltalamacchia, J		5	6	6	0	7	8	15	5	5	6	63
Samardzija, Jeff			3	0	0	7	8	7	11	6	11	53
Sanchez, Aaron									6	6	17	29
Sanchez, Anibal	10	1	0	5	11	10	10	17	8	5	1	78
Sanchez, Gary										0	11	11
Sandoval, Pablo			6	27	9	23	18	22	21	6	0	132
Sano, Miguel										16	11	27
Santana, Carlos					7	22	21	26	22	13	19	130
Santana, Ervin	18	3	19	6	14	14	2	14	9	7	11	117
Santiago, Hector					1	7	8	5	11	7		39
Saunders, Michael			1	6	2	17	10	10	0	12		58
Scherzer, Max			4	9	13	10	14	20	18	18	20	126
Schimpf, Ryan											15	15
Schoop, Jonathan							0	6	9	18		33
Seager, Corey										6	29	35
Seager, Kyle					3	24	23	28	17	30		125
Segura, Jean						4	21	13	12	23		73
Semien, Marcus							2	7	10	21		40
Shaw, Bryan					3	4	7	8	7	7		36
Shaw, Travis										7	12	19
Shields, James	6	12	15	11	3	20	12	18	15	9	2	123
Shoemaker, Matt							1	11	5	9		26
Siegrist, Kevin							6	0	12	7		25
Simmons, Andrelton					8	19	13	14	14			68
Simon, Alfredo			0	0	4	3	6	7	11	5	0	36
Sipp, Tony				3	4	7	2	1	6	6	0	29
Smith, Joe		3	6	2	3	8	6	9	14	8	4	63
Smith, Seth	1	3	14	9	13	11	10	20	11	13		105
Smoak, Justin			7	10	9	12	4	10	4			56
Smyly, Drew					6	10	10	5	4			35
Solano, Donovan					8	9	10	1	1			29
Solarte, Yangervis							16	18	16			50
Soria, Joakim		13	17	12	15	7		2	6	10	5	87
Soto, Geovany	0	3	21	8	15	10	5	8	2	3	3	78
Souza Jr., Steven								0	7	10		17
Span, Denard			16	21	20	6	15	19	26	12	15	150
Springer, George									10	13	23	46

						WIN SHARES BY YEAR						
Player	<07	07	08	09	10	11	12	13	14	15	16	Career
Stanton, Giancarlo					13	19	19	15	31	14	12	123
Storen, Drew					5	15	5	3	12	9	2	51
Story, Trevor											13	13
Straily, Dan							2	7	1	0	9	19
Strasburg, Stephen					5	2	14	11	13	8	11	64
Street, Huston	30	10	10	15	9	7	9	8	14	12	0	124
Stroman, Marcus								9	3	10		22
Strop, Pedro			0	0	3	10	5	6	8	5		37
Stubbs, Drew			5	18	13	6	10	11	2	2		67
Suarez, Eugenio								9	10	16		35
Suzuki, Ichiro	158	33	19	28	23	15	11	10	8	4	10	319
Suzuki, Kurt		7	17	17	10	8	10	6	14	8	7	104
Syndergaard, Noah										9	18	27
Tanaka, Masahiro								12	10	18		40
Tazawa, Junichi			0		0	6	6	6	4	4		26
Teheran, Julio					0	0	12	15	8	13		48
Teixeira, Mark	90	25	28	26	24	22	16	1	10	17	7	266
Tejada, Ruben			3	11	14	4	15	11	0			58
Thole, Josh			2	8	9	4	1	2	0	1		27
Thornburg, Tyler						1	6	2	1	13		23
Thornton, Matt	10	4	10	12	12	5	7	3	4	5	0	72
Tillman, Chris			2	1	1	8	14	13	6	13		58
Tomas, Yasmany										4	11	15
Tomlin, Josh				4	9	0	0	2	6	10		31
Torres, Carlos				0	0		3	4	7	2	9	25
Travis, Devon										11	14	25
Treinen, Blake									4	3	8	15
Trout, Mike					3	38	40	40	42	35		198
Trumbo, Mark					0	14	19	14	8	10	22	87
Tulowitzki, Troy	1	24	9	24	25	25	5	21	16	14	18	182
Turner, Justin			0	0	15	4	3	18	18	25		83
Turner, Trea									0	17		17
Uehara, Koji			4	9	8	5	18	13	9	6		72
Upton, Justin		1	8	19	14	26	16	21	21	21	14	161
Upton Jr., Melvin	6	22	23	13	18	20	17	3	9	9	11	151
Uribe, Juan	72	13	11	13	16	2	2	15	14	10	2	170
Utley, Chase	65	28	30	32	25	18	13	22	24	5	18	280
Valbuena, Luis			1	6	4	0	5	9	17	9	12	63
Valencia, Danny				12	10	1	5	4	12	16		60
Vargas, Jason	5	0		3	10	8	11	7	10	3	1	58
Venable, Will			3	8	15	12	17	14	10	10	0	89
Ventura, Yordano							1	13	10	10		34
Verlander, Justin	15	16	8	21	17	27	23	14	8	8	20	177
Villanueva, Carlos	4	8	6	2	2	7	6	6	2	5	1	49
Villar, Jonathan							3	5	4	24		36
Vogelsong, Ryan	4				14	10	0	5	2	2		37
Vogt, Stephen					0	4	8	18	9			39
Volquez, Edinson	0	2	16	2	3	0	6	0	11	13	5	58
Votto, Joey		3	19	24	33	33	27	30	8	33	32	242
Wacha, Michael							4	7	14	2		27
Wainwright, Adam	9	13	11	21	20		9	16	23	3	10	135
Walker, Neil			0	16	20	21	20	21	22	19		139
Warren, Adam					0	6	8	9	3			26
Watson, Tony				3	5	8	11	12	9			48
Weaver, Jered	14	12	11	17	19	24	16	10	12	5	5	145
Webb, Ryan			1	4	4	4	5	3	4	0		25
Weeks, Jemile				15	8	0	1	0	1			25
Weeks Jr., Rickie	19	14	16	7	29	18	14	4	9	0	4	134
Werth, Jayson	22	13	17	26	22	17	13	26	27	6	13	202
Wieters, Matt			9	12	23	23	19	5	7	16		114
Wilhelmsen, Tom				3	13	8	8	7	2			41
Wong, Kolten							1	10	18	9		38
Wood, Alex						4	13	8	2			27
Wood, Travis			6	3	5	15	3	6	5			43
Worley, Vance			2	11	5	0	7	3	6			34
Wright, David	65	34	27	20	25	14	30	26	15	7	4	267
Wright, Steven					1	1	4	11				17
Yelich, Christian						8	22	15	21			66
Young, Chris (P)	24	12	5	1	3	3		9	11	0		71
Young, Chris (OF)	2	14	17	8	19	21	9	7	8	9	5	119
Young, Eric			0	2	4	5	11	6	1	0		29
Ziegler, Brad		12	7	5	6	8	13	7	13	12		83
Zimmerman, Ryan	26	20	9	21	23	15	22	23	8	10	3	180

WIN SHARES BY YEAR												
Player	<07	07	08	09	10	11	12	13	14	15	16	Career
Zimmermann, Jordan				3	1	11	15	15	16	11	4	76
Zobrist, Ben	2	1	8	27	21	28	27	26	18	17	19	194
Zunino, Mike								2	11	5	8	26

Instant Replay

Ben Jedlovec

Managers are starting to get the hang of this whole instant replay thing. Managers challenged about 12 percent more calls in 2016 than in 2015 (1,305 vs. 1,161), even while getting a higher percentage of calls overturned (54 percent vs. 52 percent).

And it's making a difference in major league games. There were 49 replay reviews in extra innings, 62 in the bottom of the ninth, and 107 in the top of the ninth. Of these 218 replay reviews, 78 were overturned, potentially making the difference at a crucial point in the game. Some of the first and second-year hurdles and rule clarifications seem to be behind us.

Managers no longer look overmatched by the replay rules. Well, ok, they don't look AS overmatched as they have in previous years. The notable exception was in the last week of the regular season, when the Cardinals were fighting to stay alive in the playoff race. Reds manager Bryan Price challenged the Cardinals' walk-off hit, but it was "too late", in the umpire's mind, to go back and resume the game if the call had been overturned.

New Marlins manager, Don Mattingly, led the way with 35 overturned calls, a new record. New Padres manager Andy Green challenged more calls than any other manager (57), more than double the number of calls challenged by Twins skipper Paul Molitor (28).

Molitor and the Twins, in fact, carry the dubious honor of having been 2015's biggest beneficiaries of instant replay but finishing dead last in 2016. Twins' opponents got 27 calls overturned, while the Twins themselves had just 17 overturned in their favor.

2016 Instant Replay Summary

Replay Type	Total Replays	Overturned	Percent
Tag Play	648	311	48.0
Force Play	558	342	61.3
Boundary Call (Over Fence)	94	30	31.9
Hit By Pitch	79	38	48.1
Fair or Foul	55	16	29.1
Trap or Catch	24	15	62.5
Record Keeping	9	2	22.2
Missed Base	8	2	25.0
Passed Runner	2	1	50.0

2016 Challenges

Team	Challenges	Overturned	Pct	Opponent Challenges	Overturned	Pct	Net
Indians	49	28	57.1	29	14	48.3	14
Marlins	54	35	64.8	52	26	50.0	9
Giants	50	32	64.0	48	25	52.1	7
Rays	49	29	59.2	39	22	56.4	7
Royals	39	27	69.2	41	22	53.7	5
Rockies	54	32	59.3	41	27	65.9	5
Cardinals	56	29	51.8	40	25	62.5	4
Rangers	51	23	45.1	42	19	45.2	4
Athletics	35	22	62.9	28	18	64.3	4
Braves	42	18	42.9	38	17	44.7	1
Angels	38	21	55.3	45	20	44.4	1
Orioles	39	22	56.4	43	21	48.8	1
Padres	57	30	52.6	50	29	58.0	1
Mets	30	20	66.7	41	19	46.3	1
Reds	51	25	49.0	41	24	58.5	1
Phillies	46	26	56.5	50	26	52.0	0
Red Sox	46	20	43.5	43	21	48.8	-1
Tigers	35	20	57.1	32	21	65.6	-1
Mariners	37	22	59.5	42	24	57.1	-2
Yankees	28	19	67.9	34	21	61.8	-2
Brewers	48	23	47.9	53	26	49.1	-3
Dodgers	34	18	52.9	46	22	47.8	-4
Pirates	56	27	48.2	55	31	56.4	-4
Nationals	47	20	42.6	48	25	52.1	-5
Astros	37	17	45.9	37	22	59.5	-5
Blue Jays	50	20	40.0	41	26	63.4	-6
Diamondbacks	38	23	60.5	49	29	59.2	-6
Cubs	42	21	50.0	57	28	49.1	-7
White Sox	39	20	51.3	58	29	50.0	-9
Twins	28	17	60.7	42	27	64.3	-10

Hall of Fame Monitor

Bill James

There are certain advantages inherent in organized thought or organized understanding, and there are certain advantages inherent in intuitive understanding. Organized thought is precise, limited. It can be tested against external realities and refined, and thus improved over time, but it is also limited in that it excludes any input which cannot be quantified. Intuitive understanding is vague, imprecise, and impossible to explain to someone who lacks a background in the field, but it has the great advantage of being open to a much wider array of inputs. 99% of what we do is driven by intuitive understanding; only a tiny portion of it is driven by organized thought. You don't use a flow chart to decide who to ask out on a date, when to ask the boss for a raise or what book to read next. It's a feel; it's intuition. A detective doesn't use an Excel sheet to figure out who to question in a murder investigation, or what questions to ask. You don't use a formula to decide when the grocery store is charging too much for a gallon of milk and you're going to have to go to some other grocery store. It's a feeling, a sense. But if you're buying a car or a house, then you use organized information, and you draw on sources which are driven by formulas that you don't understand, but which you know are there somewhere.

The Hall of Fame monitor—like many things that we do—operates in the gray area between organized and intuitive understanding. Intuitively, we all know that Adrian Beltre, with his great season in 2016, has about closed the deal for getting into the Hall of Fame. He has 2,942 hits, 445 homers, four Gold Gloves at third base. One knows intuitively that it is enough.

What we're trying to do with the Hall of Fame monitor is to take this intuitive understanding, and build an organized understanding based on the same information and the same process. Many times people who are not in my business, not in sabermetrics, assume that we believe that organized understanding is superior to intuitive understanding. That is not actually what we believe, at all, or at least it is not what I believe. What I believe is that there are advantages to organized information, like stats, and advantages to less organized information and understanding. What we are trying to do here is to create a hybrid system which has advantages of both types.

So...Jose Altuve has now had 200 hits for three seasons in a row, and has now led his league in hits for three seasons in a row, and also won the batting title in 2016, but let's focus just on the 200 hits. We know intuitively, and can confirm easily, that players who get 200 hits in a season are much more likely to go into the Hall of Fame than players who do not get 200 hits in a season. The question is, how much more likely? Is getting 200 hits more or less helpful to a Hall of Fame campaign than getting 100 RBI? Obviously it is less helpful to a Hall of Fame career than an MVP Award, but how does it compare to a Gold Glove?

Those questions have objective answers. For example, among players who had 17-year careers...there are 119 players in history who had 17-year major league careers and are now eligible for the Hall of Fame. Of those 119 players, 95 never had 200 hits in a season, and 12 of the 95 who never had 200 hits in a season are in the Hall of Fame anyway. Among those with one 200-hit season, 1 out of 12 is in the Hall of Fame, so we can see that having one 200-hit season is not an accomplishment impressive to Hall of Fame voters. But among those with two or three 200-hit seasons, two of five are in the Hall of Fame, and among those with four or more 200-hit seasons in a 17-year career, all are in the Hall of Fame, five out of five.

We can contrast that data with the similar data for 100-RBI seasons. First of all, 100-RBI seasons are much more common than 200-hit seasons, so we assume that they are of less impact based on the fact that they are more common. But research shows that they are, in fact, of less impact. Of 13 players with one 100-RBI season, none are in the Hall of Fame, and of 13 players with two or three 100-RBI seasons, only three are in the Hall of Fame. Of four players with seven 100-RBI seasons, only one is in the Hall of Fame.

Doing studies of this nature enables us to estimate where a player is along the pathway that begins with his first major league game, and ends in Cooperstown. Is he 20% of the way there? Is he 30% of the way there? Where is he? We are not trying to say whether a player SHOULD be a Hall of Famer; that is for the wise men of the BBWAA. We are mere accountants, trying to calculate the odds.

In our system, if a player retires with less than 70 points, he has little chance of being selected to the Hall of Fame, although you never know. Stranger things have happened, and not merely in politics. If a player retires with 100 or more points, he will be selected to the Hall of Fame unless his career is tainted by scandal. We thus believe that Ichiro, Derek Jeter, Albert Pujols and Miguel Cabrera are certain Hall of Famers, and that A-Rod will join them unless he is considered too damaged by scandal. We believe that Robinson Cano, Francisco Rodriguez and Carlos Beltran are in good shape but not certain Hall of Famers, and we believe that Evan Longoria, Buster Posey and Clayton Kershaw, while they are having outstanding careers and are collecting Hall of Fame markers, still have a long way to go before they can be regarded as qualified Hall of Famers.

This system is based on a melding of two entirely separate systems, one developed in the 1970s and one in the 1990s, put together about ten years ago. I have taken some criticism about some of the results published in previous years, and I am inclined to believe that the criticism is justified. I think in some respects we could do better, and that it is time to re-visit the research and re-construct the system.

Regarding David Ortiz, for example, it would have seemed to me intuitively that Ortiz was a likely Hall of Famer by about 2011, and that the last question about his qualifications would have been answered when he carpet-bombed the St. Louis pitching staff in the 2013 World Series. The Hall of Fame monitor, for some reason, has never liked Ortiz; it still shows him in the gray area. I don't buy it; I don't think there is any question about his qualifications. The system shows David Ortiz and Robinson Cano as about even, which I don't really buy; Cano is a strong candidate, but I don't think he is on the same level at this time as David Ortiz.

Another issue is the relievers. Whereas there is a wide array of career standards which are meaningful to a hitter (3000 hits, 300 homers, 400 homers, 500 homers, 500 stolen bases, a .300 average, etc.)...whereas there is a wide array of career numbers which are meaningful to a hitter, there isn't really any career number which is meaningful for a relief pitcher, and, when I designed part of this system in the 1970s, there REALLY wasn't any career number which was meaningful for a relief pitcher. Because their career totals are not meaningful, I had to base a reliever's position on the numbers from each season. The result of that is that relievers pile up points early in their careers much more rapidly than position players. The position players get even, late in their careers, because they get big bonuses for things like getting their 3000th hit or even their 2500th hit and hitting their 500th home run, so it works out alright by the end of the career, but it gets weird results when you compare a 27-year-old reliever to a 27-year-old outfielder or a 33-year-old reliever to a 33-year-old infielder. That's a problem. I probably should have addressed that problem years ago.

The advantage of organized systems of thought is that they can be improved over time—but that is a bogus argument unless you actually improve them over time. I haven't done as much as I should have done to refine and fine-tune these systems. The advantage of the intuitive approach is that it is open to a wider range of information—but I'm not really taking advantage of this being a hybrid method unless I open it up to a wider range of information. So I'll try to work on it, and I'll try to have a better system for you next year. Thanks.

Leading Hall of Fame Candidates Born in 1992

Player	Points
Bryce Harper	17
Manny Machado	9
Kris Bryant	5

Leading Hall of Fame Candidates Born in 1991

Player	Points
Mike Trout	41
Nolan Arenado	11

Leading Hall of Fame Candidates Born in 1990

Player	Points
Jose Altuve	27
Starlin Castro	20
Salvador Perez	13
Trevor Rosenthal	13

Leading Hall of Fame Candidates Born in 1989

Player	Points
Freddie Freeman	19
Giancarlo Stanton	16
Madison Bumgarner	15
Chris Sale	15
Anthony Rizzo	14
Jason Heyward	12

Leading Hall of Fame Candidates Born in 1988

Player	Points
Clayton Kershaw	45
Craig Kimbrel	40
Aroldis Chapman	29
Elvis Andrus	20
Dee Gordon	16
Neftali Feliz	15
Dallas Keuchel	10

Leading Hall of Fame Candidates Born in 1987

Player	Points
Buster Posey	41
Paul Goldschmidt	27
Justin Upton	20
Kenley Jansen	19
Michael Brantley	18
Zach Britton	15
Jason Kipnis	14
Kyle Seager	12
Jay Bruce	12
Austin Jackson	11
Pedro Alvarez	10
Alex Avila	10
Brian Dozier	10

Leading Hall of Fame Candidates Born in 1986

Player	Points
Felix Hernandez	38
Andrew McCutchen	38
Chris Davis	26
Pablo Sandoval	18
Matt Wieters	17
Billy Butler	16
Jonathan Lucroy	16
Johnny Cueto	14
Carlos Santana	12
Dexter Fowler	12
Jake Arrieta	11
Jordan Zimmermann	11

Leading Hall of Fame Candidates Born in 1985

Player	Points
Evan Longoria	29
David Price	26
Matt Carpenter	23
Josh Donaldson	22
Adam Jones	20
Greg Holland	20
Carlos Gonzalez	20
Mark Melancon	16
Asdrubal Cabrera	16
Neil Walker	13
Daniel Murphy	12
Ian Desmond	12

Leading Hall of Fame Candidates Born in 1984

Player	Points
Prince Fielder	53
Brian McCann	40
Troy Tulowitzki	36
Matt Kemp	33
Tim Lincecum	31
Joakim Soria	28
Ryan Zimmerman	24
Jon Lester	24
Max Scherzer	23
Melky Cabrera	23
Alex Gordon	19
Chase Headley	17

Leading Hall of Fame Candidates Born in 1983	
Player	**Points**
Miguel Cabrera	127
Joe Mauer	79
Ryan Braun	60
Hanley Ramirez	50
Justin Verlander	50
Dustin Pedroia	49
Joey Votto	48
Jose Reyes	47
Huston Street	42
Zack Greinke	34
Nick Markakis	26
Russell Martin	25

Leading Hall of Fame Candidates Born in 1981	
Player	**Points**
Curtis Granderson	38
Josh Hamilton	36
Justin Morneau	33
Carl Crawford	31
Adam Wainwright	29
Ben Zobrist	29
Brandon Phillips	28
Jake Peavy	21
Alex Rios	17
James Shields	17
Alexei Ramirez	15
Omar Infante	13

Leading Hall of Fame Candidates Born in 1979	
Player	**Points**
Adrian Beltre	68
Ryan Howard	54
Adam Dunn	50
Mark Buehrle	31
Rafael Soriano	26
Jayson Werth	24
Carlos Ruiz	20
Michael Cuddyer	17
Coco Crisp	17
Adam LaRoche	17
Juan Uribe	16
David DeJesus	13

Leading Hall of Fame Candidates Born in 1982	
Player	**Points**
Robinson Cano	79
Francisco Rodriguez	76
Adrian Gonzalez	59
David Wright	55
Yadier Molina	53
Ian Kinsler	38
Jhonny Peralta	28
Jered Weaver	26
Shin-Soo Choo	24
Grady Sizemore	23
Andre Ethier	21
Aaron Hill	19

Leading Hall of Fame Candidates Born in 1980	
Player	**Points**
Albert Pujols	163
Mark Teixeira	65
Jonathan Papelbon	63
Matt Holliday	61
CC Sabathia	45
Jose Bautista	41
Dan Uggla	30
Shane Victorino	22
Nelson Cruz	22
Nick Swisher	19
Dan Haren	18
C.J. Wilson	14

Leading Hall of Fame Candidates Born in 1978	
Player	**Points**
Jimmy Rollins	68
Chase Utley	63
Victor Martinez	56
Aramis Ramirez	56
Cliff Lee	37
Jose Valverde	35
Vernon Wells	33
Jason Bay	31
Barry Zito	23
John Lackey	19
Kevin Gregg	14
Chad Qualls	10

Leading Hall of Fame Candidates Born in
1977

Player	Points
Carlos Beltran	71
Roy Halladay	61
Juan Pierre	36
Rafael Furcal	34
Fernando Rodney	32
Roy Oswalt	31
Marlon Byrd	16
A.J. Burnett	13
Bronson Arroyo	12
Grant Balfour	10
Javier Lopez	6

Leading Hall of Fame Candidates Born in
1976

Player	Points
Lance Berkman	72
Michael Young	69
Alfonso Soriano	63
Paul Konerko	50
A.J. Pierzynski	39
Matt Thornton	8
Jason Grilli	7
Randy Wolf	7

Leading Hall of Fame Candidates Born in
1975

Player	Points
Alex Rodriguez	200
David Ortiz	74
Torii Hunter	40
Tim Hudson	36
Placido Polanco	34
Koji Uehara	11
Rafael Betancourt	6

Leading Hall of Fame Candidates Born in
1974

Player	Points
Derek Jeter	164
Miguel Tejada	83
Bobby Abreu	79
Joe Nathan	79
R.A. Dickey	11

Leading Hall of Fame Candidates Born in
1973

Player	Points
Ichiro Suzuki	106
Todd Helton	98
Bartolo Colon	32

Leading Hall of Fame Candidates Born in
1972

Player	Points
Andy Pettitte	56
Raul Ibanez	30
LaTroy Hawkins	27

Hitter Projections

Bill James

So, who do you think will hit more homers in 2017, Chris Davis or Rajai Davis? Who do you think will drive in more runs, Miguel Cabrera, or Melky? Who do you think will score more runs, Carlos Gonzalez or Marwin Gonzalez? Who do you think will steal more bases, Leonys Martin or Russell Martin?

My point is that certain things about the future are, in fact, known. The future is not *entirely* a blank canvas; that's just what we tell ourselves when we do self-destructive things. Most of us will continue to do the things we have done before. This, at least, is the theory on which we operate. If a player hits 20, 30 homers a year, we predict that he will hit 25 next year. Sometimes it works out.

We predicted that Albert Pujols would hit 31 homers, and he did:

Hitter	Label	G	AB	R	H	D	T	HR	RBI	BB	SO	SB	Avg	Slg
Pujols,Albert	Actual	152	593	71	159	19	0	31	119	49	75	4	.268	.457
Pujols,Albert	Projected	141	547	80	147	31	0	31	93	55	68	5	.269	.495

We predicted that Adam Jones would hit 29 homers, and he did:

Hitter	Label	G	AB	R	H	D	T	HR	RBI	BB	SO	SB	Avg	Slg
Jones,Adam	Actual	152	619	86	164	19	0	29	83	39	115	2	.265	.436
Jones,Adam	Projected	154	618	88	173	32	2	29	91	27	123	6	.280	.479

We predicted that Randal Grichuk would hit 24 homers, and he did:

Hitter	Label	G	AB	R	H	D	T	HR	RBI	BB	SO	SB	Avg	Slg
Grichuk,Randal	Actual	132	446	66	107	29	3	24	68	28	141	5	.240	.480
Grichuk,Randal	Projected	155	486	76	124	30	6	24	67	29	128	7	.255	.490

We predicted that Chase Headley would hit 14 homers, and he did:

Hitter	Label	G	AB	R	H	D	T	HR	RBI	BB	SO	SB	Avg	Slg
Headley,Chase	Actual	140	467	58	117	18	1	14	51	51	118	8	.251	.383
Headley,Chase	Projected	152	554	68	143	31	1	14	64	61	139	4	.258	.394

We predicted that David Freese would hit 13 homers, and he did:

Hitter	Label	G	AB	R	H	D	T	HR	RBI	BB	SO	SB	Avg	Slg
Freese,David	Actual	141	437	63	118	23	0	13	55	45	142	0	.270	.412
Freese,David	Projected	135	453	54	120	25	1	13	63	40	116	1	.265	.411

We predicted that another guy with the same initials would hit the same number of homers, and he did:

Hitter	Label	G	AB	R	H	D	T	HR	RBI	BB	SO	SB	Avg	Slg
Fowler,Dexter	Actual	125	456	84	126	25	7	13	48	79	124	13	.276	.447
Fowler,Dexter	Projected	147	553	91	146	30	7	13	49	81	143	17	.264	.414

We predicted that Kelly Johnson would hit 10 homers, and he did:

Hitter	Label	G	AB	R	H	D	T	HR	RBI	BB	SO	SB	Avg	Slg
Johnson,Kelly	Actual	131	304	25	75	14	0	10	34	25	65	4	.247	.391
Johnson,Kelly	Projected	104	272	34	64	13	1	10	33	28	75	3	.235	.401

Also Nick Hundley; we had predicted 10 homers for Hundley:

Hitter	Label	G	AB	R	H	D	T	HR	RBI	BB	SO	SB	Avg	Slg
Hundley,Nick	Actual	83	289	30	75	20	1	10	48	25	65	0	.260	.439
Hundley,Nick	Projected	110	349	35	88	18	2	10	41	24	85	3	.252	.401

We predicted that Conor Gillaspie would hit 6 homers, and he did:

Hitter	Label	G	AB	R	H	D	T	HR	RBI	BB	SO	SB	Avg	Slg
Gillaspie,Conor	Actual	101	191	24	50	8	4	6	25	12	28	1	.262	.440
Gillaspie,Conor	Projected	100	289	29	75	15	2	6	32	23	48	0	.260	.388

We had also predicted that Conor Gillaspie would suddenly become Lou Gehrig in the playoffs against the Cubs, but unfortunately we forgot to publish that one before it happened. We predicted that Nolan Reimold would hit 9 doubles and 6 homers and would draw 22 walks, and he did:

Hitter	Label	G	AB	R	H	D	T	HR	RBI	BB	SO	SB	Avg	Slg
Reimold,Nolan	Actual	104	203	25	45	9	1	6	15	22	62	1	.222	.365
Reimold,Nolan	Projected	70	179	23	46	9	0	6	22	22	43	2	.257	.408

We predicted that Gordon Beckham would hit 5 homers, and he did:

Hitter	Label	G	AB	R	H	D	T	HR	RBI	BB	SO	SB	Avg	Slg
Beckham,Gordon	Actual	88	245	25	52	16	1	5	31	26	52	1	.212	.347
Beckham,Gordon	Projected	86	210	26	49	12	0	5	22	16	39	1	.233	.362

We predicted that Peter Bourjos would hit five homers, and he did:

Hitter	Label	G	AB	R	H	D	T	HR	RBI	BB	SO	SB	Avg	Slg
Bourjos,Peter	Actual	123	355	40	89	20	7	5	23	17	91	6	.251	.389
Bourjos,Peter	Projected	118	241	35	57	10	4	5	20	19	67	7	.237	.373

We predicted that Chris Stewart would hit only 1 homer, and he did:

Hitter	Label	G	AB	R	H	D	T	HR	RBI	BB	SO	SB	Avg	Slg
Stewart,Chris	Actual	34	98	10	21	4	0	1	7	12	15	0	.214	.286
Stewart,Chris	Projected	56	147	12	37	6	0	1	13	12	23	1	.252	.313

On the other hand, we also predicted that Joey Gallo might hit 35 homers, which was substantially off the mark:

Hitter	Label	G	AB	R	H	D	T	HR	RBI	BB	SO	SB	Avg	Slg
Gallo,Joey	Actual	17	25	2	1	0	0	1	1	5	19	1	.040	.160
Gallo,Joey	Projected	132	487	71	114	24	2	35	93	66	217	6	.234	.507

My philosophy is that if we think a young player MIGHT play regularly, we project that he WILL play regularly. This causes some embarrassing projections, like the one above, but we'll live with those because we take pride in our ability to project hitting stats for major league players based on minor league performance. Before sabermetrics, it was universally believed among baseball men that you couldn't predict what a player would hit in the majors based on what he had hit in the minors. This is completely untrue; we do it all the time, and these projections are as accurate as the projections based on major league stats. Corey Seager had played only 27 games before last season, but we had a pretty good projection for what he would do:

Hitter	Label	G	AB	R	H	D	T	HR	RBI	BB	SO	SB	Avg	Slg
Seager,Corey	Actual	157	627	105	193	40	5	26	72	54	133	3	.308	.512
Seager,Corey	Projected	155	589	93	170	43	4	21	88	46	97	6	.289	.482

We had Trea Turner projected as a .295 hitter with 38 stolen bases, and OK, we were a little light in our projections for him, but we had a handle on who he was:

Hitter	Label	G	AB	R	H	D	T	HR	RBI	BB	SO	SB	Avg	Slg
Turner,Trea	Actual	73	307	53	105	14	8	13	40	14	59	33	.342	.567
Turner,Trea	Projected	146	562	83	166	30	6	12	62	46	119	38	.295	.434

But at this point I have to confess.

It has always been our policy to project playing time for young players, and this is one of the prime reasons that many people buy our book, that we are willing to put ourselves on the line to say whether a young player can play or not. But somehow, last year, we screwed up. I shouldn't say "somehow"; it was my fault. Last year's book failed to include projections for Trevor Story, Aledmys Diaz, Nomar Mazara, Tim Anderson, Cheslor Cuthbert, Alex Bregman, Jeremy Hazelbaker, Ryan Healy, Tommy Joseph, Max Kepler, Tyler Naquin, Gary Sanchez, Ryan Schimpf, Alex Dickerson, Whit Merrifield, Jeff Bandy, Jose Peraza, Travis Jankowski, Wilson Contreras and other rookies who got significant 2016 playing time.

There is no excuse for this; it was a screw-up, plain and simple. I wasn't paying attention. We'll try to avoid this in the future. Part of our job in this section is to make projections for young players so that, when that young player comes to the major leagues, you can pull out our book to see what kind of a hitter he is.

Well, anyway, I was getting ready to confess to a lesser sin, which is just being wrong about some players. Prince Fielder, we had projected to hit .292 with 26 homers, which didn't turn out to be real close:

Hitter	Label	G	AB	R	H	D	T	HR	RBI	BB	SO	SB	Avg	Slg
Fielder,Prince	Actual	89	326	29	69	16	0	8	44	32	63	0	.212	.334
Fielder,Prince	Projected	160	575	79	168	31	0	26	99	80	96	0	.292	.482

That was our worst projection from last year; Joey Gallo was the second-worst. We had a substantially off-target projection for Jonathan Villar of Milwaukee:

Hitter	Label	G	AB	R	H	D	T	HR	RBI	BB	SO	SB	Avg	Slg
Villar,Jonathan	Actual	156	589	92	168	38	3	19	63	79	174	62	.285	.457
Villar,Jonathan	Projected	61	148	21	37	6	1	3	14	13	41	16	.250	.365

DJ LeMahieu, we missed his batting average by 64 points; we had his at bats exactly right, oddly enough, but we were just way off on everything else:

Hitter	Label	G	AB	R	H	D	T	HR	RBI	BB	SO	SB	Avg	Slg
LeMahieu,DJ	Actual	146	552	104	192	32	8	11	66	66	80	11	.348	.495
LeMahieu,DJ	Projected	147	552	70	157	25	4	5	52	41	101	18	.284	.371

We didn't have any idea that Cameron Maybin was going to hit .300:

Hitter	Label	G	AB	R	H	D	T	HR	RBI	BB	SO	SB	Avg	Slg
Maybin,Cameron	Actual	94	.349	65	110	14	5	4	43	36	69	15	.315	.418
Maybin,Cameron	Projected	134	480	64	124	20	4	9	47	45	103	19	.258	.373

Oddly enough we got his runs scored and RBI about right, but the ratios are all wrong. Daniel Murphy has been around a few years, but we still didn't have a good line on what kind of player he was:

Hitter	Label	G	AB	R	H	D	T	HR	RBI	BB	SO	SB	Avg	Slg
Murphy,Daniel	Actual	142	531	88	184	47	5	25	104	35	57	5	.347	.595
Murphy,Daniel	Projected	148	596	76	174	42	2	13	76	38	67	7	.292	.435

You might be surprised to learn...actually, the hardest players to project are not young players, but old players. Young players, they are what they are; sometimes they take a step forward and sometimes they don't. But older players fall off a cliff, and you never know when it is going to happen. Like the always popular A.J. Pierzynski:

Hitter	Label	G	AB	R	H	D	T	HR	RBI	BB	SO	SB	Avg	Slg
Pierzynski,A.J.	Actual	81	247	15	54	15	0	2	23	6	29	1	.219	.304
Pierzynski,A.J.	Projected	120	416	39	113	20	1	10	48	17	50	0	.272	.397

Or Andre Ethier:

Hitter	Label	G	AB	R	H	D	T	HR	RBI	BB	SO	SB	Avg	Slg
Ethier,Andre	Actual	16	24	2	5	1	0	1	2	2	6	0	.208	.375
Ethier,Andre	Projected	139	412	51	113	25	2	12	55	46	85	2	.274	.432

Or Mark Teixeira, or Jose Bautista, or Alejandro De Aza:

Hitter	Label	G	AB	R	H	D	T	HR	RBI	BB	SO	SB	Avg	Slg
Teixeira,Mark	Actual	116	387	43	79	16	0	15	44	47	105	2	.204	.362
Teixeira,Mark	Projected	120	431	62	103	22	0	26	77	60	99	2	.239	.471

Hitter	Label	G	AB	R	H	D	T	HR	RBI	BB	SO	SB	Avg	Slg
Bautista,Jose	Actual	116	423	68	99	24	1	22	69	87	103	2	.234	.452
Bautista,Jose	Projected	154	571	103	147	28	1	39	106	108	116	7	.257	.515

Hitter	Label	G	AB	R	H	D	T	HR	RBI	BB	SO	SB	Avg	Slg
De Aza,Alejandro	Actual	130	234	31	48	9	0	6	25	26	67	4	.205	.321
De Aza,Alejandro	Projected	123	390	54	102	22	3	8	38	35	97	11	.262	.395

So sometimes we're mostly right about what a player will do, and sometimes we're completely wrong. Take it for what you think it is worth.

2017 Hitter Projections

Hitter	Team	Age	G	AB	H	2B	3B	HR	R	RBI	RC	RC27	BB	SO	SB	CS	SB%	Avg	OBP	Slg	OPS
Abreu,Jose	CWS	30	158	619	190	36	1	30	80	108	113	6.85	47	120	0	0	.00	.307	.369	.514	.883
Ackley,Dustin	NYY	29	55	130	32	6	1	3	16	13	15	3.94	13	24	1	1	.50	.246	.319	.377	.696
Adames,Cristhian	Col	25	92	206	53	8	1	2	23	18	21	3.5	17	34	4	3	.57	.257	.320	.335	.655
Adams,Matt	StL	28	122	312	85	20	1	15	39	52	49	5.61	22	70	1	0	1.00	.272	.322	.487	.810
Adrianza,Ehire	SF	27	45	114	28	5	1	2	12	10	12	3.55	10	21	3	2	.60	.246	.317	.360	.677
Ahmed,Nick	Ari	27	100	285	67	13	2	4	31	24	27	3.18	18	49	6	3	.67	.235	.285	.337	.622
Albies,Ozzie	Atl	20	90	240	69	14	2	2	35	22	33	4.85	23	41	14	6	.70	.288	.350	.388	.737
Alfaro,Jorge	Phi	24	84	257	65	14	1	8	32	32	30	4.04	12	71	2	1	.67	.253	.286	.409	.695
Almonte,Abraham	Cle	28	89	246	64	15	2	4	33	25	31	4.33	22	52	11	4	.73	.260	.323	.386	.710
Almora,Albert	ChC	23	150	566	148	35	4	9	75	60	63	3.86	23	77	13	6	.68	.261	.290	.385	.675
Alonso,Yonder	Oak	30	152	471	126	31	1	8	51	54	61	4.57	47	73	4	2	.67	.268	.335	.389	.724
Altherr,Aaron	Phi	26	137	477	116	28	3	14	63	62	60	4.24	45	122	18	7	.72	.243	.315	.403	.718
Altuve,Jose	Hou	27	160	648	207	43	4	17	95	73	114	6.56	47	69	32	11	.74	.319	.371	.477	.848
Alvarez,Dariel	Bal	28	145	523	143	33	1	9	54	58	62	4.21	23	72	6	3	.67	.273	.304	.392	.696
Alvarez,Pedro	Bal	30	122	356	87	17	1	21	45	58	54	5.2	39	108	2	1	.67	.244	.321	.475	.795
Amarista,Alexi	SD	28	84	190	46	7	1	2	19	19	18	3.21	12	31	6	2	.75	.242	.291	.321	.612
Anderson,Tim	CWS	24	154	601	166	28	7	11	85	47	73	4.27	20	146	28	9	.76	.276	.301	.401	.702
Andrus,Elvis	Tex	28	156	586	162	29	4	6	81	60	74	4.43	53	83	26	10	.72	.276	.341	.370	.711
Aoki,Nori	Sea	35	116	387	108	18	2	4	51	27	47	4.3	32	41	9	5	.64	.279	.347	.367	.714
Arcia,Orlando	Mil	22	148	533	138	30	5	10	67	59	64	4.13	33	97	24	8	.75	.259	.302	.390	.692
Arcia,Oswaldo	SD	26	112	389	97	19	2	22	52	65	57	5.06	32	119	2	1	.67	.249	.310	.478	.788
Arenado,Nolan	Col	26	155	607	176	43	4	36	99	115	115	6.91	51	97	2	2	.50	.290	.347	.552	.899
Arroyo,Christian	SF	22	130	510	136	35	2	4	56	49	57	3.95	29	75	1	1	.50	.267	.306	.367	.673
Asche,Cody	Phi	27	86	224	57	15	1	8	27	27	30	4.64	18	53	2	1	.67	.254	.316	.438	.753
Austin,Tyler	NYY	25	144	549	142	33	2	20	72	78	81	5.12	67	155	9	4	.69	.259	.339	.435	.775
Avila,Alex	CWS	30	93	283	62	15	0	9	32	33	35	4.12	50	108	0	0	.00	.219	.338	.367	.706
Aviles,Mike	Det	36	56	107	25	4	0	2	12	10	9	2.82	5	16	2	1	.67	.234	.281	.327	.608
Aybar,Erick	Det	33	146	533	139	27	2	5	60	46	56	3.65	31	75	9	5	.64	.261	.308	.347	.655
Baez,Javier	ChC	24	142	428	120	22	1	20	59	71	65	5.38	24	115	15	6	.71	.280	.326	.477	.803
Bandy,Jett	LAA	27	69	202	49	11	0	6	23	28	22	3.71	11	37	1	1	.50	.243	.288	.386	.675
Barney,Darwin	Tor	31	94	248	61	12	1	3	29	19	24	3.32	16	37	2	1	.67	.246	.297	.339	.636
Barnhart,Tucker	Cin	26	97	319	80	17	1	5	28	38	37	4.03	33	54	1	0	1.00	.251	.323	.357	.680
Bautista,Jose	Tor	36	146	537	130	26	1	33	90	91	94	5.98	103	121	4	2	.67	.242	.369	.479	.848
Beckham,Gordon	SF	30	86	205	48	12	0	5	25	22	22	3.62	17	40	1	1	.50	.234	.308	.366	.674
Beckham,Tim	TB	27	95	288	71	15	3	7	38	31	34	4.02	22	82	5	3	.62	.247	.302	.392	.695
Bell,Josh	Pit	24	146	539	158	30	4	14	74	78	89	6.01	72	83	5	4	.56	.293	.376	.442	.818
Belt,Brandon	SF	29	154	532	147	38	5	19	76	76	94	6.32	82	148	3	2	.60	.276	.377	.474	.851
Beltran,Carlos	Tex	40	138	477	129	27	1	21	59	69	72	5.36	41	92	2	1	.67	.270	.331	.463	.794
Beltre,Adrian	Tex	38	144	556	164	31	1	24	78	86	92	6.09	42	70	1	1	.50	.295	.350	.484	.834
Benintendi,Andrew	Bos	22	147	551	160	38	5	12	87	73	85	5.5	51	72	21	11	.66	.290	.352	.443	.794
Bethancourt,Christian	SD	25	67	180	47	9	0	4	20	23	20	3.85	8	37	3	2	.60	.261	.293	.378	.670
Betts,Mookie	Bos	24	155	646	205	45	6	27	121	103	130	7.54	57	75	27	7	.79	.317	.374	.531	.905
Bird,Gregory	NYY	24	146	549	146	39	1	29	80	89	94	6.05	65	124	1	1	.50	.266	.344	.499	.843
Blackmon,Charlie	Col	30	154	608	178	35	4	21	97	73	95	5.61	42	107	21	10	.68	.293	.347	.467	.815
Blanco,Andres	Phi	33	85	172	44	11	1	4	21	17	21	4.23	13	31	2	1	.67	.256	.323	.401	.724
Blanco,Gregor	SF	33	92	202	50	9	2	2	27	16	23	3.86	25	44	6	3	.67	.248	.333	.342	.675
Bogaerts,Xander	Bos	24	157	617	186	35	2	17	99	84	98	5.84	51	109	11	5	.69	.301	.360	.447	.807
Bour,Justin	Mia	29	136	433	115	24	0	21	53	79	69	5.64	49	80	1	0	1.00	.266	.340	.467	.807
Bourjos,Peter	Phi	30	96	189	46	8	3	3	25	15	20	3.59	12	50	4	2	.67	.243	.306	.365	.671
Bourn,Michael	Bal	34	88	235	59	9	2	2	29	18	25	3.61	21	61	9	4	.69	.251	.315	.332	.647
Bradley Jr.,Jackie	Bos	27	153	547	142	34	5	21	89	76	83	5.28	61	128	9	4	.69	.260	.340	.455	.796
Brantley,Michael	Cle	30	152	586	172	38	2	12	78	76	89	5.51	55	63	17	6	.74	.294	.356	.427	.783
Braun,Ryan	Mil	33	137	514	149	29	2	26	81	87	92	6.45	50	108	14	6	.70	.290	.359	.506	.864
Bregman,Alex	Hou	23	152	585	165	40	5	23	108	103	106	6.47	66	99	11	6	.65	.282	.355	.516	.871
Brinson,Lewis	Mil	23	153	580	153	33	6	23	80	82	79	4.7	28	126	25	10	.71	.264	.298	.460	.758
Brito,Socrates	Ari	24	89	277	73	9	5	6	35	30	32	4	11	53	8	4	.67	.264	.292	.397	.689
Brown,Trevor	SF	25	65	160	39	8	0	3	15	17	16	3.44	10	32	0	0	.00	.244	.292	.350	.642
Broxton,Keon	Mil	27	132	430	109	22	6	15	65	51	65	5.06	54	146	39	13	.75	.253	.337	.437	.774
Bruce,Jay	NYM	30	152	561	138	32	3	30	79	93	83	5.07	55	143	6	3	.67	.246	.317	.474	.791
Bryant,Kris	ChC	25	157	597	185	37	3	42	124	95	139	8.67	83	159	11	5	.69	.310	.405	.593	.998
Burns,Billy	KC	27	85	234	62	9	2	1	33	14	25	3.69	14	34	16	4	.80	.265	.317	.333	.651
Butera,Drew	KC	33	69	154	32	7	0	3	14	13	12	2.56	10	36	0	0	.00	.208	.261	.312	.572
Butler,Billy	NYY	31	107	311	88	20	0	8	35	43	46	5.36	31	55	0	0	.00	.283	.354	.424	.778
Buxton,Byron	Min	23	150	588	153	34	11	23	104	75	89	5.25	46	182	25	6	.81	.260	.316	.473	.789
Cabrera,Asdrubal	NYM	31	150	563	148	34	2	18	74	68	76	4.73	44	115	7	3	.70	.263	.323	.426	.749
Cabrera,Melky	CWS	32	151	588	170	36	3	13	74	74	85	5.26	44	76	4	2	.67	.289	.340	.427	.767
Cabrera,Miguel	Det	34	158	599	189	38	1	34	96	114	132	8.35	83	117	1	1	.50	.316	.401	.553	.954
Cabrera,Ramon	Cin	27	64	173	45	9	0	2	15	19	19	3.86	13	23	1	0	1.00	.260	.312	.347	.659
Cain,Lorenzo	KC	31	137	524	151	29	3	11	76	65	74	5.06	38	110	19	7	.73	.288	.341	.418	.759
Calhoun,Kole	LAA	29	156	587	158	33	3	20	87	76	85	5.13	55	128	4	2	.67	.269	.336	.438	.774
Canha,Mark	Oak	28	145	520	134	31	2	20	74	80	73	4.88	47	124	6	3	.67	.258	.322	.440	.762
Cano,Robinson	Sea	34	160	632	187	39	1	28	92	96	108	6.3	50	99	2	1	.67	.296	.353	.494	.847
Carpenter,Matt	StL	31	150	568	155	42	3	19	96	75	96	6.01	87	130	2	2	.50	.273	.374	.458	.832
Carrera,Ezequiel	Tor	30	92	189	49	7	1	3	29	16	22	3.97	17	38	9	4	.69	.259	.327	.354	.681
Carter,Chris	Mil	30	147	510	113	26	1	33	73	86	75	4.89	69	191	5	2	.60	.222	.320	.471	.791

564

2017 Hitter Projections

Hitter	Team	Age	G	AB	H	2B	3B	HR	R	RBI	RC	RC27	BB	SO	SB	CS	SB%	Avg	OBP	Slg	OPS
Casali,Curt	TB	28	83	229	52	12	0	9	25	32	30	4.41	33	67	0	0	.00	.227	.330	.397	.727
Castellanos,Nick	Det	25	150	540	146	33	4	19	60	73	78	5.13	39	130	2	1	.67	.270	.322	.452	.774
Castillo,Rusney	Bos	29	76	203	54	10	1	2	26	19	22	3.79	12	35	5	2	.71	.266	.310	.355	.665
Castillo,Welington	Ari	30	111	376	93	21	0	14	37	53	47	4.3	30	106	1	1	.50	.247	.311	.415	.726
Castro,Daniel	Atl	24	62	153	39	5	0	1	15	13	13	2.94	7	19	1	1	.50	.255	.288	.307	.595
Castro,Jason	Hou	30	114	362	80	21	1	11	42	38	41	3.77	41	124	1	1	.50	.221	.304	.376	.679
Castro,Starlin	NYY	27	150	558	152	31	3	15	62	64	72	4.58	28	103	6	3	.67	.272	.312	.419	.731
Cecchini,Gavin	NYM	23	129	473	137	27	2	7	57	45	65	5	38	62	4	2	.67	.290	.344	.400	.743
Centeno,Juan	Min	27	59	155	39	7	1	1	12	17	15	3.33	10	24	1	1	.50	.252	.297	.329	.626
Cervelli,Francisco	Pit	31	119	422	118	19	2	4	53	45	56	4.74	55	84	5	3	.62	.280	.369	.363	.732
Cespedes,Yoenis	NYM	31	149	565	153	31	3	30	85	95	90	5.64	45	129	5	3	.62	.271	.331	.496	.827
Chirinos,Robinson	Tex	33	100	340	79	19	0	14	41	44	42	4.18	33	83	0	0	.00	.232	.308	.412	.719
Chisenhall,Lonnie	Cle	28	124	382	102	25	2	10	46	53	51	4.7	27	76	4	2	.67	.267	.320	.421	.742
Choi,Ji-Man	LAA	26	89	204	52	12	1	6	25	28	29	4.86	28	39	4	3	.57	.255	.345	.412	.757
Choo,Shin-Soo	Tex	34	142	526	138	29	1	17	76	61	78	5.15	74	143	11	6	.65	.262	.366	.418	.784
Coghlan,Chris	ChC	32	112	303	73	19	2	7	40	29	38	4.26	37	70	5	2	.71	.241	.329	.386	.716
Collins,Tyler	Det	27	62	130	31	5	1	4	14	16	15	3.9	11	31	2	1	.67	.238	.303	.385	.687
Colon,Christian	KC	28	70	169	43	7	0	2	18	15	17	3.45	14	22	4	2	.67	.254	.315	.331	.647
Conforto,Michael	NYM	24	149	570	158	41	3	25	83	86	98	6.14	64	129	5	3	.62	.277	.354	.491	.845
Conger,Hank	TB	29	69	163	37	8	0	5	16	19	18	3.71	15	39	0	0	.00	.227	.296	.368	.664
Contreras,Willson	ChC	25	118	415	127	29	3	15	61	65	77	6.86	45	76	5	4	.56	.306	.378	.499	.877
Correa,Carlos	Hou	22	153	569	163	39	3	25	82	82	105	6.66	72	119	17	4	.81	.286	.371	.497	.868
Cowart,Kaleb	LAA	25	137	495	118	29	3	9	56	58	53	3.59	37	122	20	7	.74	.238	.291	.364	.655
Cozart,Zack	Cin	31	149	512	125	28	2	14	68	50	58	3.88	35	92	5	2	.71	.244	.295	.389	.684
Crawford,Brandon	SF	30	155	555	142	29	5	13	64	72	71	4.44	54	124	6	3	.67	.256	.326	.396	.723
Crawford,J.P.	Phi	22	137	542	130	24	3	8	66	45	61	3.79	72	85	14	7	.67	.240	.329	.339	.668
Crisp,Coco	Cle	37	78	207	48	10	1	5	27	21	23	3.71	23	35	6	2	.75	.232	.309	.362	.671
Cron,C.J.	LAA	27	138	482	131	30	2	19	56	78	68	5.01	26	87	3	2	.60	.272	.316	.461	.776
Cruz,Nelson	Sea	36	158	610	164	30	1	38	86	101	103	5.98	58	168	3	2	.60	.269	.337	.508	.845
Cuthbert,Cheslor	KC	24	148	557	148	32	2	17	61	69	75	4.74	44	97	4	2	.67	.266	.319	.422	.741
Dahl,David	Col	23	156	582	165	34	7	20	107	75	94	5.74	50	151	26	9	.74	.284	.340	.469	.809
d'Arnaud,Chase	Atl	30	74	214	52	10	2	2	28	15	22	3.45	15	38	12	4	.75	.243	.296	.336	.632
d'Arnaud,Travis	NYM	28	100	344	92	21	1	11	42	42	49	5.06	32	62	1	0	1.00	.267	.333	.430	.764
Davidson,Matt	CWS	26	88	234	52	12	0	9	25	30	27	3.86	23	76	0	0	.00	.222	.292	.389	.681
Davis,Chris	Bal	31	158	560	138	29	0	39	92	100	94	5.66	75	213	1	1	.50	.243	.338	.499	.837
Davis,Khris	Oak	29	150	530	136	30	1	36	80	93	87	5.71	47	140	3	2	.60	.257	.323	.521	.844
Davis,Rajai	Cle	36	134	439	109	23	2	8	63	41	48	3.67	28	99	33	10	.77	.248	.299	.364	.664
De Aza,Alejandro	NYM	33	92	198	50	10	1	4	27	19	23	3.96	19	52	5	3	.62	.253	.333	.374	.707
Descalso,Daniel	Col	30	117	275	66	15	2	5	36	31	31	3.82	30	58	3	2	.60	.240	.319	.364	.683
DeShields,Delino	Tex	24	139	463	113	21	3	7	85	42	55	3.94	57	120	38	13	.75	.244	.330	.348	.677
Desmond,Ian	Tex	31	156	590	154	31	2	20	79	74	78	4.58	43	163	17	7	.71	.261	.316	.422	.738
Diaz,Aledmys	StL	26	146	535	150	38	3	20	82	76	86	5.75	48	76	6	4	.60	.280	.344	.475	.819
Diaz,Elias	Pit	26	45	135	37	7	0	2	13	18	16	4.2	10	21	1	1	.50	.274	.324	.370	.695
Dickerson,Alex	SD	27	136	414	121	30	3	15	64	64	69	6.08	30	70	4	2	.67	.292	.343	.488	.831
Dickerson,Corey	TB	28	149	507	142	36	5	24	69	72	84	5.95	35	115	2	2	.50	.280	.328	.513	.841
Dietrich,Derek	Mia	27	130	305	81	17	3	10	42	37	43	4.97	27	70	1	1	.50	.266	.354	.439	.794
Difo,Wilmer	Was	25	131	455	119	21	3	6	68	47	52	3.91	31	74	31	10	.76	.262	.309	.360	.669
Donaldson,Josh	Tor	31	159	613	167	36	2	33	108	104	111	6.43	87	132	6	3	.67	.272	.368	.499	.867
Dozier,Brian	Min	30	158	623	154	37	3	30	100	82	91	4.98	64	140	16	6	.73	.247	.324	.461	.785
Dozier,Hunter	KC	25	142	535	129	38	1	18	72	62	68	4.32	50	149	7	3	.70	.241	.306	.417	.723
Drew,Stephen	Was	34	88	213	48	12	2	7	26	25	25	3.92	23	48	1	1	.50	.225	.304	.399	.703
Drury,Brandon	Ari	24	154	542	151	38	1	15	63	62	76	5.04	34	96	2	1	.67	.279	.324	.435	.759
Duda,Lucas	NYM	31	142	490	122	29	0	24	65	74	75	5.28	65	131	1	1	.50	.249	.344	.455	.799
Duffy,Matt	TB	26	148	567	168	30	4	10	76	72	81	5.2	40	87	15	6	.71	.296	.347	.416	.763
Duvall,Adam	Cin	28	149	547	133	30	3	31	76	92	76	4.74	39	141	5	3	.62	.243	.297	.479	.776
Dyson,Jarrod	KC	32	119	313	81	11	4	1	47	22	36	3.9	28	52	32	8	.80	.259	.324	.329	.653
Eaton,Adam	CWS	28	155	613	176	32	7	12	97	54	91	5.33	61	116	16	7	.70	.287	.361	.421	.782
Eibner,Brett	Oak	28	139	512	127	24	3	21	74	67	71	4.75	56	129	8	4	.67	.248	.322	.430	.752
Ellis,A.J.	Phi	36	81	216	50	9	0	4	20	25	23	3.58	32	45	1	1	.50	.231	.336	.329	.665
Ellsbury,Jacoby	NYY	33	149	560	150	27	3	11	76	55	72	4.48	49	93	23	8	.74	.268	.331	.386	.717
Encarnacion,Edwin	Tor	34	155	583	149	32	0	38	91	110	103	6.16	83	123	3	1	.75	.256	.353	.506	.859
Escobar,Alcides	KC	30	159	589	154	25	4	5	65	49	60	3.54	26	85	18	6	.75	.261	.298	.343	.641
Escobar,Eduardo	Min	28	54	169	44	10	1	3	19	18	20	4.13	11	32	1	1	.50	.260	.309	.385	.694
Escobar,Yunel	LAA	34	141	517	144	24	1	7	60	47	64	4.45	45	70	1	1	.50	.279	.342	.369	.712
Espinosa,Danny	Was	30	151	501	110	23	1	18	65	56	53	3.49	44	165	9	4	.69	.220	.299	.377	.677
Ethier,Andre	LAD	35	140	422	113	25	2	12	51	56	60	5.03	44	91	2	1	.67	.268	.343	.422	.764
Fisher,Derek	Hou	23	141	513	125	22	3	20	68	73	76	4.96	80	166	33	10	.77	.244	.346	.415	.761
Flaherty,Ryan	Bal	30	77	169	39	8	1	5	20	20	19	3.77	16	43	1	1	.50	.231	.305	.379	.684
Flores,Ramon	Mil	25	61	116	28	5	1	2	14	11	13	3.8	14	22	1	1	.50	.241	.328	.353	.682
Flores,Wilmer	NYM	25	115	345	94	19	1	14	44	51	49	5.06	20	47	1	1	.50	.272	.316	.455	.771
Flowers,Tyler	Atl	31	114	371	90	19	0	12	36	46	45	4.16	35	127	0	0	.00	.243	.320	.391	.710
Forsythe,Logan	TB	30	152	532	137	26	3	17	72	57	72	4.69	54	126	8	4	.67	.258	.334	.414	.747
Fowler,Dexter	ChC	31	145	529	140	29	6	13	90	48	80	5.25	83	141	14	7	.67	.265	.371	.416	.786
Franco,Maikel	Phi	24	151	576	156	31	2	25	74	91	84	5.19	38	93	2	1	.67	.271	.319	.462	.781
Francoeur,Jeff	Mia	33	75	138	33	7	0	4	14	15	14	3.43	7	36	1	1	.50	.239	.286	.377	.663
Franklin,Nick	TB	26	60	127	32	7	1	4	15	15	17	4.6	13	31	4	1	.80	.252	.326	.417	.744
Frazier,Adam	Pit	25	147	561	172	34	5	3	78	44	80	5.1	53	67	26	19	.58	.307	.367	.401	.769

2017 Hitter Projections

Hitter	Team	Age	G	AB	H	2B	3B	HR	R	RBI	RC	RC27	BB	SO	SB	CS	SB%	Avg	OBP	Slg	OPS
Frazier,Clint	NYY	22	151	578	148	34	4	19	80	58	80	4.76	55	156	18	7	.72	.256	.321	.427	.748
Frazier,Todd	CWS	31	158	600	146	32	1	33	84	90	85	4.79	56	154	13	7	.65	.243	.313	.465	.778
Freeman,Freddie	Atl	27	158	587	168	41	3	27	93	95	111	6.86	83	155	4	2	.67	.286	.382	.504	.886
Freese,David	Pit	34	136	451	114	24	0	12	55	59	55	4.24	43	134	0	0	.00	.253	.329	.386	.714
Gallo,Joey	Tex	23	150	527	121	24	4	36	84	94	86	5.48	79	229	5	2	.71	.230	.330	.495	.825
Galvis,Freddy	Phi	27	156	572	141	26	4	15	64	59	62	3.69	29	112	14	6	.70	.247	.285	.385	.670
Gamel,Ben	Sea	25	141	546	152	30	4	8	74	55	72	4.66	45	111	18	8	.69	.278	.333	.392	.725
Garcia,Adonis	Atl	32	144	573	158	33	1	15	70	71	73	4.54	25	88	6	3	.67	.276	.308	.415	.724
Garcia,Avisail	CWS	26	104	365	99	14	2	11	51	47	48	4.64	26	88	5	3	.62	.271	.327	.411	.738
Garcia,Greg	StL	27	88	196	52	10	1	2	27	17	25	4.45	26	39	4	2	.67	.265	.357	.357	.714
Gardner,Brett	NYY	33	147	540	139	24	4	10	84	48	69	4.41	66	119	17	6	.74	.257	.345	.372	.717
Gattis,Evan	Hou	30	129	428	110	21	2	27	54	71	66	5.38	32	97	1	1	.50	.257	.315	.505	.819
Gennett,Scooter	Mil	27	140	484	132	29	3	11	60	49	63	4.61	29	89	7	3	.70	.273	.317	.413	.730
Giavotella,Johnny	LAA	29	114	383	105	24	1	6	47	42	48	4.44	27	43	6	3	.67	.274	.324	.389	.713
Gillaspie,Conor	SF	29	81	190	50	10	1	5	20	21	24	4.43	14	28	1	1	.50	.263	.317	.405	.722
Gimenez,Chris	Cle	34	73	180	41	8	0	4	21	19	18	3.37	18	44	1	0	1.00	.228	.298	.339	.637
Goins,Ryan	Tor	29	90	219	54	12	1	3	22	21	23	3.6	16	46	1	1	.50	.247	.301	.352	.652
Goldschmidt,Paul	Ari	29	155	577	173	41	2	28	102	105	125	7.89	106	153	23	8	.74	.300	.412	.523	.935
Gomes,Yan	Cle	29	99	372	92	23	1	14	43	54	45	4.18	19	92	0	0	.00	.247	.291	.427	.719
Gomez,Carlos	Tex	31	140	516	127	28	3	17	71	61	63	4.12	38	150	23	9	.72	.246	.308	.411	.719
Gonzalez,Adrian	LAD	35	157	583	161	35	0	22	72	95	90	5.55	60	119	0	0	.00	.276	.348	.449	.797
Gonzalez,Carlos	Col	31	150	559	160	34	3	29	89	95	99	6.42	49	132	6	2	.75	.286	.346	.513	.859
Gonzalez,Marwin	Hou	28	123	376	95	21	1	9	41	36	41	3.73	19	83	8	5	.62	.253	.294	.386	.680
Gordon,Alex	KC	33	139	492	123	27	2	17	68	57	68	4.75	60	142	7	3	.70	.250	.342	.417	.759
Gordon,Dee	Mia	29	147	612	176	21	8	2	87	37	75	4.3	35	101	56	17	.77	.288	.327	.358	.685
Gosselin,Phil	Ari	28	89	191	53	10	1	2	24	15	23	4.3	13	34	3	1	.75	.277	.327	.372	.699
Grandal,Yasmani	LAD	28	127	382	94	19	1	21	52	63	63	5.67	66	99	1	1	.50	.246	.360	.466	.826
Granderson,Curtis	NYM	36	153	552	131	24	3	27	85	69	79	4.84	75	147	6	3	.67	.237	.335	.438	.773
Gregorius,Didi	NYY	27	150	544	146	28	4	15	70	62	70	4.54	33	76	6	3	.67	.268	.317	.417	.735
Grichuk,Randal	StL	25	148	526	134	33	5	29	82	80	77	5.06	31	140	6	4	.60	.255	.299	.502	.801
Grossman,Robbie	Min	27	95	367	95	19	1	9	50	35	50	4.69	54	92	8	5	.62	.259	.355	.390	.745
Gurriel,Yulieski	Hou	33	50	120	30	6	0	3	11	14	13	3.76	5	16	1	0	1.00	.250	.286	.375	.661
Gutierrez,Franklin	Sea	34	95	268	63	13	0	11	33	35	32	4.04	24	84	2	1	.67	.235	.303	.407	.709
Guyer,Brandon	Cle	31	118	314	86	21	2	8	49	34	43	4.84	22	54	7	3	.70	.274	.352	.430	.782
Gyorko,Jedd	StL	28	133	434	109	18	0	24	54	65	62	4.96	37	95	1	0	1.00	.251	.313	.459	.771
Hamilton,Billy	Cin	26	145	501	127	20	4	5	77	34	59	3.93	43	97	67	16	.81	.253	.314	.339	.653
Hanigan,Ryan	Bos	36	56	129	28	5	0	1	12	13	11	2.83	16	27	0	0	.00	.217	.318	.279	.597
Haniger,Mitch	Ari	26	34	120	33	7	1	5	17	19	20	5.91	14	26	2	1	.67	.275	.356	.475	.831
Hardy,J.J.	Bal	34	141	491	120	24	0	12	53	52	52	3.64	30	91	0	0	.00	.244	.289	.367	.656
Harper,Bryce	Was	24	150	537	153	30	3	32	101	87	114	7.54	104	124	17	9	.65	.285	.404	.531	.934
Harrison,Josh	Pit	29	141	528	150	34	4	6	68	53	66	4.45	23	83	17	8	.68	.284	.320	.398	.718
Hazelbaker,Jeremy	StL	29	83	191	49	8	2	7	28	24	26	4.63	16	53	10	4	.71	.257	.314	.429	.743
Headley,Chase	NYY	33	136	449	114	23	1	12	55	52	58	4.46	51	115	6	3	.67	.254	.338	.390	.728
Healy,Ryon	Oak	25	147	540	159	39	2	20	73	76	88	5.99	33	107	1	1	.50	.294	.336	.485	.821
Hechavarria,Adeiny	Mia	28	141	473	122	18	5	4	49	41	49	3.61	28	75	4	2	.67	.258	.301	.342	.643
Hedges,Austin	SD	24	112	404	100	20	1	14	45	60	45	3.84	17	74	2	1	.67	.248	.280	.406	.686
Heisey,Chris	Was	32	88	179	40	8	1	8	24	21	21	3.9	17	51	2	1	.67	.223	.302	.413	.715
Hernandez,Cesar	Phi	27	153	532	153	20	7	5	70	43	72	4.81	56	102	18	10	.64	.288	.357	.380	.736
Hernandez,Kiké	LAD	25	77	220	53	11	1	7	26	21	26	4	20	47	3	2	.60	.241	.307	.395	.703
Hernandez,Marco	Bos	24	94	245	73	12	2	5	30	27	34	5.08	12	49	4	2	.67	.298	.331	.424	.755
Hernandez,Teoscar	Hou	24	150	548	139	28	2	15	85	56	67	4.1	45	123	35	16	.69	.254	.310	.394	.704
Herrera,Dilson	Cin	23	138	534	142	30	3	18	76	68	73	4.72	43	112	13	10	.57	.266	.322	.434	.756
Herrera,Odubel	Phi	25	159	584	172	26	5	12	83	54	86	5.31	51	123	23	9	.72	.295	.356	.418	.774
Herrmann,Chris	Ari	29	75	196	46	9	1	4	26	22	21	3.59	20	48	3	2	.60	.235	.306	.352	.658
Heyward,Jason	ChC	27	151	553	146	31	3	13	76	62	77	4.86	65	101	14	5	.74	.264	.347	.401	.748
Hicks,Aaron	NYY	27	97	285	72	14	2	7	39	30	37	4.45	34	57	6	3	.67	.253	.334	.389	.724
Hill,Aaron	Bos	35	115	335	84	17	1	9	40	40	40	4.11	29	56	3	2	.60	.251	.318	.388	.706
Holaday,Bryan	Bos	29	65	167	40	9	1	3	17	18	17	3.48	10	35	0	0	.00	.240	.287	.359	.646
Holliday,Matt	StL	37	125	438	118	27	1	18	62	69	70	5.67	52	86	2	1	.67	.269	.359	.459	.818
Holt,Brock	Bos	29	109	351	98	19	2	4	49	32	46	4.67	34	63	7	3	.70	.279	.346	.379	.725
Hosmer,Eric	KC	27	156	574	158	31	2	20	79	85	86	5.34	55	114	6	3	.67	.275	.341	.441	.781
Howard,Ryan	Phi	37	93	254	56	11	0	14	29	44	31	4.07	23	87	0	0	.00	.220	.295	.429	.725
Hundley,Nick	Col	33	92	317	79	17	1	9	32	40	38	4.13	24	79	1	1	.50	.249	.306	.394	.700
Iannetta,Chris	Sea	34	98	275	58	13	0	8	29	33	30	3.59	44	82	0	0	.00	.211	.326	.345	.672
Iglesias,Jose	Det	27	132	453	123	20	1	4	54	33	49	3.8	27	48	8	5	.62	.272	.321	.347	.668
Inciarte,Ender	Atl	26	149	594	174	28	5	7	89	40	80	4.86	44	68	22	8	.73	.293	.345	.387	.732
Jackson,Austin	CWS	30	105	347	93	18	3	5	49	31	43	4.33	30	87	8	4	.67	.268	.330	.380	.710
Jankowski,Travis	SD	26	146	524	142	21	5	3	84	31	65	4.22	60	118	45	18	.71	.271	.347	.347	.694
Jaso,John	Pit	33	120	356	92	12	1	8	44	42	48	4.71	48	71	1	1	.50	.258	.353	.393	.746
Jay,Jon	SD	32	105	314	88	17	1	3	43	29	38	4.33	23	63	4	2	.67	.280	.349	.369	.718
Jennings,Desmond	TB	30	135	515	123	27	3	13	75	47	62	4.05	55	123	17	6	.74	.239	.316	.379	.695
Johnson,Chris	Mia	30	90	240	62	13	0	5	21	27	27	3.94	13	71	1	0	1.00	.258	.302	.375	.677
Johnson,Kelly	NYM	35	92	190	45	8	1	7	21	22	23	4.1	18	49	2	1	.67	.237	.310	.400	.710
Jones,Adam	Bal	31	159	620	169	28	1	29	87	88	88	5.05	32	121	4	2	.67	.273	.317	.461	.778
Joseph,Caleb	Bal	31	69	170	40	8	0	4	16	20	17	3.4	12	34	0	0	.00	.235	.290	.353	.643
Joseph,Tommy	Phi	25	138	459	118	25	0	26	56	71	66	5.02	28	91	1	1	.50	.257	.303	.481	.784
Joyce,Matt	Pit	32	112	258	59	14	1	10	35	35	36	4.68	43	71	2	1	.67	.229	.345	.407	.752

2017 Hitter Projections

Hitter	Team	Age	G	AB	H	2B	3B	HR	R	RBI	RC	RC27	BB	SO	SB	CS	SB%	Avg	OBP	Slg	OPS
Judge,Aaron	NYY	25	142	537	135	26	2	27	77	84	81	5.2	63	167	7	3	.70	.251	.331	.458	.789
Kang,Jung Ho	Pit	30	140	465	125	26	1	26	68	82	77	5.84	46	103	4	3	.57	.269	.354	.497	.850
Kelly,Carson	StL	22	35	112	29	6	0	2	13	10	12	3.76	7	21	0	0	.00	.259	.308	.366	.674
Kemp,Matt	Atl	32	153	570	155	33	2	28	82	95	89	5.54	44	149	6	3	.67	.272	.326	.484	.811
Kemp,Tony	Hou	25	140	462	125	18	5	3	61	35	55	4.1	50	69	21	12	.64	.271	.342	.351	.692
Kendrick,Howie	LAD	33	147	490	134	26	2	9	62	54	62	4.48	36	97	8	4	.67	.273	.328	.390	.718
Kepler,Max	Min	24	152	534	142	31	9	18	80	88	85	5.58	66	98	11	4	.73	.266	.349	.459	.808
Kiermaier,Kevin	TB	27	150	502	134	26	8	14	74	47	72	4.98	43	90	23	8	.74	.267	.330	.434	.764
Kim,Hyun Soo	Bal	29	121	427	131	23	1	10	52	33	71	6.22	52	66	1	1	.50	.307	.387	.436	.823
Kinsler,Ian	Det	35	158	642	171	34	3	20	101	79	87	4.74	51	104	13	6	.68	.266	.328	.422	.750
Kipnis,Jason	Cle	30	149	567	155	35	3	16	84	69	84	5.22	60	127	16	6	.73	.273	.348	.430	.778
La Stella,Tommy	ChC	28	69	155	43	10	1	2	15	16	22	5.11	18	20	1	0	1.00	.277	.356	.394	.750
Lagares,Juan	NYM	28	133	360	97	19	3	5	40	34	42	4.09	19	67	9	4	.69	.269	.312	.381	.692
Lamb,Jake	Ari	26	151	533	145	35	7	26	81	90	96	6.4	65	140	5	2	.71	.272	.353	.510	.864
Lawrie,Brett	CWS	27	129	492	124	28	3	16	59	55	62	4.33	36	127	8	4	.67	.252	.308	.419	.727
Lee,Dae-Ho	Sea	35	102	280	77	10	0	14	30	49	41	5.25	19	61	0	0	.00	.275	.332	.461	.793
LeMahieu,DJ	Col	28	152	552	170	27	5	8	82	57	85	5.7	51	90	12	6	.67	.308	.369	.418	.787
Leon,Sandy	Bos	28	106	360	89	19	1	7	42	39	42	4.03	37	80	0	0	.00	.247	.319	.364	.683
Lind,Adam	Sea	33	123	387	103	21	0	19	49	60	58	5.31	36	85	0	0	.00	.266	.330	.452	.782
Lindor,Francisco	Cle	23	158	616	185	30	5	16	93	79	99	5.85	59	91	22	9	.71	.300	.364	.443	.807
Lobaton,Jose	Was	32	55	187	45	8	0	4	19	19	21	3.85	21	43	1	0	1.00	.241	.321	.348	.668
Loney,James	NYM	33	94	279	77	14	0	5	26	33	34	4.38	19	32	1	0	1.00	.276	.329	.380	.709
Longoria,Evan	TB	31	159	612	162	37	1	29	83	96	94	5.42	58	140	2	1	.67	.265	.333	.471	.804
Lowrie,Jed	Oak	33	104	345	87	20	1	7	39	37	41	4.13	33	64	0	0	.00	.252	.321	.377	.698
Lucroy,Jonathan	Tex	31	136	508	142	30	2	17	65	74	78	5.51	50	92	4	2	.67	.280	.346	.447	.793
Machado,Dixon	Det	25	141	526	132	29	1	4	57	45	56	3.64	50	80	17	6	.74	.251	.316	.333	.649
Machado,Manny	Bal	24	158	672	194	42	2	35	106	95	118	6.38	55	119	5	3	.62	.289	.345	.513	.859
Mahtook,Mikie	TB	27	104	309	77	19	2	6	33	33	35	3.87	22	83	8	3	.73	.249	.301	.382	.683
Maile,Luke	TB	26	107	344	78	18	1	5	33	31	32	3.13	27	71	0	0	.00	.227	.283	.328	.612
Maldonado,Martin	Mil	30	88	233	52	10	0	7	23	28	25	3.59	27	58	0	0	.00	.223	.312	.356	.668
Mancini,Trey	Bal	25	136	517	150	28	3	20	76	70	85	6.01	46	123	2	1	.67	.290	.349	.472	.821
Margot,Manuel	SD	22	149	603	160	29	8	5	84	53	67	3.81	31	79	39	14	.74	.265	.301	.365	.666
Marisnick,Jake	Hou	26	92	205	49	11	1	5	27	20	22	3.58	11	53	11	4	.73	.239	.288	.376	.663
Markakis,Nick	Atl	33	155	590	160	33	1	11	70	64	78	4.71	64	92	1	1	.50	.271	.347	.386	.733
Marte,Jefry	LAA	26	61	127	31	7	0	5	16	18	16	4.29	11	25	2	1	.67	.244	.314	.417	.732
Marte,Ketel	Sea	23	135	496	137	28	3	3	64	41	58	4.12	28	79	20	7	.74	.276	.316	.363	.679
Marte,Starling	Pit	28	148	562	166	34	6	14	83	61	84	5.31	30	127	40	15	.73	.295	.349	.452	.801
Martin,Leonys	Sea	29	145	522	131	22	3	12	70	50	60	3.9	41	134	24	9	.73	.251	.309	.374	.683
Martin,Russell	Tor	34	136	451	101	19	0	18	59	64	55	4.06	62	128	3	2	.60	.224	.330	.386	.715
Martinez,J.D.	Det	29	145	549	156	36	2	26	73	87	93	6.12	48	155	3	2	.60	.284	.345	.499	.844
Martinez,Michael	Cle	34	72	160	39	7	1	2	19	14	16	3.38	11	29	3	2	.60	.244	.292	.338	.630
Martinez,Victor	Det	38	150	541	151	27	0	20	62	83	81	5.4	50	76	0	0	.00	.279	.345	.440	.784
Mathis,Jeff	Mia	34	42	129	25	5	0	2	11	14	9	2.25	8	41	0	0	.00	.194	.246	.279	.525
Mauer,Joe	Min	34	126	468	129	27	1	9	62	55	68	5.2	67	90	2	1	.67	.276	.368	.395	.763
Maxwell,Bruce	Oak	26	54	170	42	9	0	4	17	24	20	4.06	17	34	0	0	.00	.247	.316	.371	.686
Maybin,Cameron	Det	30	122	449	119	21	4	7	64	45	56	4.32	44	95	17	7	.71	.265	.333	.376	.710
Mazara,Nomar	Tex	22	152	544	152	21	3	21	69	74	81	5.37	46	109	0	0	.00	.279	.339	.445	.784
McCann,Brian	NYY	33	104	367	87	13	0	18	45	58	48	4.46	41	78	1	0	1.00	.237	.325	.420	.745
McCann,James	Det	27	106	350	85	18	1	9	33	42	38	3.71	21	86	1	1	.50	.243	.288	.377	.665
McCutchen,Andrew	Pit	30	157	596	170	35	4	24	93	85	106	6.38	82	136	11	6	.65	.285	.379	.478	.857
Meadows,Austin	Pit	22	50	174	47	9	2	7	28	26	27	5.53	17	38	1	0	1.00	.270	.335	.466	.801
Mercer,Jordy	Pit	30	149	508	131	28	1	10	59	56	60	4.12	42	88	2	2	.50	.258	.318	.376	.694
Merrifield,Whit	KC	28	145	558	145	37	3	7	71	47	65	4	36	101	26	9	.74	.260	.305	.375	.679
Mesoraco,Devin	Cin	29	115	379	93	21	1	15	44	55	51	4.62	39	78	1	1	.50	.245	.319	.425	.744
Miller,Brad	TB	27	150	541	138	27	5	23	72	71	78	4.98	54	126	8	4	.67	.255	.325	.451	.776
Molina,Yadier	StL	34	139	508	146	31	0	8	69	61	66	4.79	37	63	3	2	.60	.287	.341	.396	.736
Moncada,Yoan	Bos	22	84	291	71	16	3	9	49	38	44	5.08	43	93	27	5	.84	.244	.341	.412	.754
Mondesi,Raul	KC	21	150	516	121	16	9	12	66	57	57	3.68	31	153	49	8	.86	.234	.279	.370	.649
Montero,Miguel	ChC	33	91	278	67	13	0	9	30	40	35	4.31	36	71	0	0	.00	.241	.339	.385	.723
Morales,Kendrys	KC	34	156	562	147	31	0	25	65	89	81	5.07	49	119	0	0	.00	.262	.327	.450	.778
Moreland,Mitch	Tex	31	139	452	111	24	0	20	52	65	59	4.49	37	112	1	1	.50	.246	.310	.431	.741
Morneau,Justin	CWS	36	74	267	72	16	1	8	29	37	37	4.93	22	54	0	0	.00	.270	.332	.427	.759
Morrison,Logan	TB	29	115	389	92	20	2	14	46	48	50	4.35	44	82	4	2	.67	.237	.320	.406	.727
Moss,Brandon	StL	33	145	466	105	24	1	25	62	71	62	4.45	50	154	1	1	.50	.225	.308	.442	.750
Moustakas,Mike	KC	28	137	480	123	29	1	19	57	66	65	4.72	37	76	1	1	.50	.256	.315	.440	.754
Moya,Steven	Det	25	141	529	136	30	3	24	64	78	69	4.53	22	146	5	3	.62	.257	.287	.461	.748
Muncy,Max	Oak	26	72	178	42	9	1	4	22	21	22	4.18	26	41	2	1	.67	.236	.333	.365	.699
Murphy,Daniel	Was	32	148	580	175	43	2	17	79	83	94	5.99	37	66	7	3	.70	.302	.348	.471	.819
Murphy,John Ryan	Min	26	73	225	54	13	0	4	24	26	23	3.5	19	46	0	0	.00	.240	.296	.351	.647
Murphy,Tom	Col	26	86	303	82	21	2	15	44	52	48	5.62	19	87	2	1	.67	.271	.314	.502	.815
Myers,Wil	SD	26	157	566	155	31	2	27	97	95	96	5.91	65	138	21	7	.75	.274	.351	.479	.830
Napoli,Mike	Cle	35	142	485	112	24	1	25	66	74	69	4.78	69	168	3	2	.60	.231	.333	.439	.772
Naquin,Tyler	Cle	26	152	554	152	28	6	16	87	62	83	5.28	60	151	14	7	.67	.274	.347	.433	.781
Narvaez,Omar	CWS	25	62	212	52	9	0	2	22	18	21	3.41	19	27	0	0	.00	.245	.307	.316	.623
Navarro,Dioner	Tor	33	91	271	64	12	0	7	24	32	28	3.5	22	55	1	1	.50	.236	.296	.358	.654
Nicholas,Brett	Tex	28	56	121	32	7	0	3	13	16	15	4.38	9	26	1	0	1.00	.264	.315	.397	.712
Nieuwenhuis,Kirk	Mil	29	114	287	66	18	1	10	39	35	36	4.16	35	94	6	4	.60	.230	.316	.404	.720

2017 Hitter Projections

Hitter	Team	Age	G	AB	H	2B	3B	HR	R	RBI	RC	RC27	BB	SO	SB	CS	SB%	Avg	OBP	Slg	OPS
Nimmo,Brandon	NYM	24	131	512	142	24	5	9	65	46	68	4.69	50	106	9	7	.56	.277	.343	.396	.739
Norris,Derek	SD	28	120	369	85	20	1	12	50	48	44	3.99	39	109	7	3	.70	.230	.309	.388	.697
Nunez,Eduardo	SF	30	142	540	149	27	3	12	69	60	69	4.46	30	86	32	11	.74	.276	.316	.404	.720
O'Brien,Peter	Ari	26	132	510	117	26	4	28	63	81	62	4.09	24	168	2	1	.67	.229	.264	.461	.725
Odor,Rougned	Tex	23	145	577	159	31	7	29	86	87	88	5.37	26	108	13	8	.62	.276	.314	.504	.818
O'Malley,Shawn	Sea	29	95	286	71	10	3	3	38	24	30	3.55	26	60	13	5	.72	.248	.313	.336	.649
O'Neill,Tyler	Sea	22	132	496	138	23	3	24	67	80	85	6.1	58	148	13	4	.76	.278	.354	.482	.836
Orlando,Paulo	KC	31	138	498	135	23	3	7	56	50	56	3.94	21	97	17	7	.71	.271	.305	.371	.676
Owings,Chris	Ari	25	130	443	121	24	6	6	56	46	55	4.37	21	90	18	5	.78	.273	.310	.395	.706
Ozuna,Marcell	Mia	26	149	565	157	31	5	22	76	79	87	5.53	43	116	1	1	.50	.278	.332	.467	.799
Pagan,Angel	SF	35	115	388	105	20	3	6	51	36	48	4.35	29	61	11	4	.73	.271	.321	.384	.705
Panik,Joe	SF	26	143	521	141	27	4	10	73	59	69	4.7	51	51	5	2	.71	.271	.339	.395	.735
Paredes,Jimmy	Phi	28	62	115	30	6	1	3	14	12	14	4.23	6	30	3	1	.75	.261	.298	.409	.706
Park,Byung-ho	Min	30	125	415	86	18	1	28	59	45	50	3.94	33	130	1	1	.50	.207	.274	.458	.732
Parker,Jarrett	SF	28	73	184	48	7	1	10	29	26	29	5.46	22	63	3	2	.60	.261	.346	.473	.819
Parra,Gerardo	Col	30	156	556	150	34	4	11	71	53	69	4.34	32	106	10	7	.59	.270	.313	.405	.718
Pearce,Steve	Bal	34	104	317	82	19	1	14	42	43	49	5.4	37	70	1	1	.50	.259	.342	.457	.799
Pederson,Joc	LAD	25	154	485	124	25	1	30	83	72	88	6.23	86	147	12	6	.67	.256	.372	.497	.869
Pedroia,Dustin	Bos	33	153	626	183	38	1	14	90	73	95	5.53	65	78	7	4	.64	.292	.361	.423	.784
Pence,Hunter	SF	34	155	612	166	31	3	22	87	87	89	5.15	56	139	6	3	.67	.271	.334	.440	.774
Pennington,Cliff	LAA	33	82	169	38	7	1	2	18	13	16	3.15	16	43	3	1	.75	.225	.296	.314	.609
Peralta,David	Ari	29	148	498	145	29	8	14	67	70	78	5.68	36	97	7	4	.64	.291	.343	.466	.809
Peralta,Jhonny	StL	35	150	550	143	32	1	15	60	70	70	4.46	47	112	1	1	.50	.260	.322	.404	.725
Peraza,Jose	Cin	23	152	505	147	20	5	5	65	43	62	4.33	23	61	34	14	.71	.291	.326	.380	.706
Perez,Carlos	LAA	26	120	357	87	22	0	7	34	39	38	3.65	23	59	2	1	.67	.244	.289	.364	.654
Perez,Hernan	Mil	26	142	488	131	27	4	10	55	53	60	4.26	21	90	31	9	.77	.268	.299	.402	.700
Perez,Roberto	Cle	28	79	209	47	11	1	5	26	27	25	4.01	34	58	0	0	.00	.225	.333	.359	.692
Perez,Salvador	KC	27	143	526	136	29	2	20	57	72	66	4.4	21	98	0	0	.00	.259	.293	.435	.729
Peterson,Jace	Atl	27	148	512	126	25	4	7	61	47	59	3.9	65	96	10	7	.59	.246	.333	.352	.685
Petit,Gregorio	LAA	32	72	157	38	8	0	2	16	14	15	3.25	10	32	1	1	.50	.242	.292	.331	.623
Pham,Tommy	StL	29	143	509	135	25	5	18	77	64	77	5.25	59	146	18	7	.72	.265	.343	.440	.783
Phegley,Josh	Oak	29	60	195	49	12	0	6	22	26	23	4.1	11	36	0	0	.00	.251	.295	.405	.700
Phillips,Brandon	Cin	36	147	568	157	28	1	12	69	70	69	4.3	28	77	12	6	.67	.276	.318	.393	.711
Pillar,Kevin	Tor	28	153	560	158	40	2	10	69	59	73	4.64	27	80	17	7	.71	.282	.320	.414	.734
Pina,Manny	Mil	30	45	115	29	7	0	2	11	14	13	3.93	9	18	0	0	.00	.252	.306	.365	.672
Piscotty,Stephen	StL	26	153	568	156	38	3	19	81	81	86	5.36	52	110	8	5	.62	.275	.342	.452	.794
Plawecki,Kevin	NYM	26	64	163	39	8	0	3	15	19	16	3.35	12	27	0	0	.00	.239	.299	.344	.643
Plouffe,Trevor	Min	31	130	475	119	27	1	17	58	65	61	4.44	38	100	2	1	.67	.251	.310	.419	.729
Polanco,Gregory	Pit	25	154	492	131	30	3	16	80	71	72	5.07	51	96	20	8	.71	.266	.335	.437	.772
Polanco,Jorge	Min	23	146	512	140	27	6	10	56	60	68	4.66	40	83	12	7	.63	.273	.329	.408	.737
Pollock,A.J.	Ari	29	149	578	172	37	4	15	94	67	93	5.8	47	80	30	11	.73	.298	.351	.453	.805
Pompey,Dalton	Tor	24	140	503	141	22	4	8	87	46	70	4.85	57	98	31	13	.70	.280	.355	.388	.742
Posey,Buster	SF	30	146	553	169	34	1	18	76	89	97	6.53	61	69	4	2	.67	.306	.378	.468	.846
Prado,Martin	Mia	33	151	583	166	34	2	10	67	67	78	4.84	45	74	2	2	.50	.285	.340	.401	.742
Presley,Alex	Det	31	66	161	43	6	1	3	19	15	19	4.08	13	26	4	3	.57	.267	.326	.373	.698
Profar,Jurickson	Tex	24	132	427	108	18	3	10	58	45	52	4.19	45	78	7	4	.64	.253	.327	.379	.706
Puig,Yasiel	LAD	26	146	481	141	27	5	20	74	69	83	6.24	46	96	9	6	.60	.293	.363	.495	.858
Pujols,Albert	LAA	37	153	594	155	29	0	31	80	101	90	5.31	56	76	4	2	.67	.261	.329	.466	.795
Quinn,Roman	Phi	24	145	566	153	25	8	6	91	39	76	4.64	50	132	52	13	.80	.270	.331	.385	.716
Raburn,Ryan	Col	36	88	175	40	10	0	6	21	24	20	3.85	17	56	0	0	.00	.229	.308	.389	.696
Ramirez,Alexei	TB	35	143	500	127	24	1	8	50	52	51	3.5	24	67	11	6	.65	.254	.292	.354	.646
Ramirez,Hanley	Bos	33	145	541	147	30	1	25	80	89	86	5.6	55	114	10	5	.67	.272	.344	.470	.814
Ramirez,Jose	Cle	24	147	538	151	34	4	9	81	57	74	4.85	45	54	24	10	.71	.281	.338	.409	.747
Ramos,Wilson	Was	29	85	313	85	14	0	12	33	47	43	4.9	20	56	0	0	.00	.272	.317	.431	.749
Rasmus,Colby	Hou	30	120	379	87	18	1	17	51	51	49	4.24	40	125	3	2	.60	.230	.306	.417	.723
Realmuto,J.T.	Mia	26	125	466	132	28	3	10	60	54	64	4.92	30	78	11	4	.73	.283	.331	.421	.751
Reddick,Josh	LAD	30	135	463	121	23	3	16	62	59	64	4.81	43	74	7	4	.64	.261	.325	.428	.753
Reed,A.J.	Hou	24	142	508	132	32	2	22	69	77	79	5.46	61	144	0	0	.00	.260	.339	.461	.800
Refsnyder,Rob	NYY	26	55	117	33	7	0	2	16	12	16	4.89	12	20	3	1	.75	.282	.354	.393	.747
Reimold,Nolan	Bal	33	80	166	41	8	0	5	20	18	21	4.33	20	42	2	1	.67	.247	.332	.386	.717
Rendon,Anthony	Was	27	153	577	159	40	3	20	95	78	93	5.72	68	106	10	5	.67	.276	.357	.459	.816
Renfroe,Hunter	SD	25	144	574	155	32	3	26	75	89	82	5.05	27	142	6	3	.67	.270	.303	.472	.775
Revere,Ben	Was	29	151	597	168	16	6	2	75	38	66	3.91	30	58	33	10	.77	.281	.318	.338	.656
Reyes,Jose	NYM	34	134	525	143	27	4	10	76	46	69	4.61	42	76	21	7	.75	.272	.326	.396	.722
Reynolds,Mark	Col	33	125	387	90	18	0	17	49	53	51	4.45	49	127	2	1	.67	.233	.327	.411	.737
Rickard,Joey	Bal	26	68	177	50	10	1	3	25	16	25	5.04	18	34	5	2	.71	.282	.352	.401	.753
Rivera,Rene	NYM	33	81	195	44	9	0	5	15	23	19	3.27	13	47	0	0	.00	.226	.281	.349	.630
Rivera,T.J.	NYM	28	75	285	88	17	1	5	33	37	41	5.38	11	39	1	1	.50	.309	.337	.428	.765
Rizzo,Anthony	ChC	27	157	595	165	41	2	32	91	103	109	6.53	76	117	6	4	.60	.277	.373	.514	.887
Robinson,Clint	Was	32	114	240	63	14	0	7	29	31	33	4.85	27	42	0	0	.00	.263	.342	.408	.750
Rodriguez,Sean	Pit	32	116	235	55	12	1	9	32	33	28	4.02	20	74	2	1	.67	.234	.310	.409	.719
Rojas,Miguel	Mia	28	99	199	49	8	1	2	22	16	19	3.25	14	24	3	2	.60	.246	.299	.327	.626
Romine,Andrew	Det	31	106	198	48	6	1	2	24	15	19	3.21	15	40	9	4	.69	.242	.302	.313	.615
Romine,Austin	NYY	28	60	150	37	8	0	3	16	19	16	3.68	10	26	1	0	1.00	.247	.294	.360	.654
Rosales,Adam	SD	34	96	233	51	11	1	8	30	28	25	3.53	23	77	3	2	.60	.219	.295	.378	.672
Rosario,Eddie	Min	25	125	466	127	27	5	15	68	56	62	4.69	19	102	10	5	.67	.273	.302	.448	.751
Rua,Ryan	Tex	27	76	185	48	9	1	7	26	22	25	4.68	16	49	4	2	.67	.259	.328	.432	.761

2017 Hitter Projections

Hitter	Team	Age	G	AB	H	2B	3B	HR	R	RBI	RC	RC27	BB	SO	SB	CS	SB%	Avg	OBP	Slg	OPS
Ruiz,Carlos	LAD	38	94	298	74	17	0	5	30	30	34	3.93	33	47	2	1	.67	.248	.337	.356	.693
Rupp,Cameron	Phi	28	110	355	86	20	1	14	33	45	44	4.25	26	96	1	0	1.00	.242	.299	.423	.722
Russell,Addison	ChC	23	151	524	135	30	2	22	74	89	76	5.04	52	127	6	3	.67	.258	.332	.448	.780
Saladino,Tyler	CWS	27	95	298	74	12	1	6	36	33	33	3.75	24	57	15	5	.75	.248	.309	.356	.664
Saltalamacchia,Jarrod	Det	32	84	218	45	12	0	9	28	30	25	3.76	27	85	0	0	.00	.206	.297	.385	.682
Sanchez,Carlos	CWS	25	79	209	51	11	1	4	22	20	21	3.39	11	45	6	3	.67	.244	.288	.364	.652
Sanchez,Gary	NYY	24	122	461	127	28	0	25	62	78	77	5.94	42	94	7	3	.70	.275	.337	.499	.836
Sandoval,Pablo	Bos	30	112	411	112	24	1	12	45	53	56	4.87	31	64	0	0	.00	.273	.328	.423	.751
Sano,Miguel	Min	24	149	561	143	33	2	38	90	81	103	6.39	82	201	3	1	.75	.255	.351	.524	.875
Santana,Carlos	Cle	31	155	552	139	33	1	26	80	87	93	5.81	103	109	5	3	.62	.252	.371	.457	.828
Santana,Danny	Min	26	86	244	66	13	3	3	34	20	28	3.96	10	51	12	6	.67	.270	.305	.385	.690
Santana,Domingo	Mil	24	152	555	146	28	1	24	84	88	86	5.4	72	185	8	5	.62	.263	.350	.447	.797
Sardinas,Luis	SD	24	141	512	130	21	2	4	61	45	48	3.2	25	88	18	8	.69	.254	.290	.326	.616
Saunders,Michael	Tor	30	137	489	117	28	3	19	68	55	66	4.58	58	152	4	3	.57	.239	.322	.425	.748
Schebler,Scott	Cin	26	136	441	116	22	6	18	59	58	64	5.07	33	93	6	3	.67	.263	.319	.463	.781
Schimpf,Ryan	SD	29	148	475	109	26	2	30	76	81	74	5.24	65	131	2	1	.67	.229	.327	.482	.809
Schoop,Jonathan	Bal	25	156	588	153	32	1	25	76	76	76	4.53	24	125	2	1	.67	.260	.296	.446	.742
Schwarber,Kyle	ChC	24	148	538	144	20	2	32	107	100	98	6.42	91	157	5	3	.62	.268	.376	.491	.866
Seager,Corey	LAD	23	157	619	190	45	5	26	105	83	117	7.06	53	115	4	2	.67	.307	.364	.522	.885
Seager,Kyle	Sea	29	160	614	166	37	2	26	89	89	96	5.53	62	111	5	3	.62	.270	.344	.464	.808
Segura,Jean	Ari	27	146	584	166	26	7	13	80	54	79	4.81	29	74	28	10	.74	.284	.328	.420	.747
Semien,Marcus	Oak	26	156	559	141	29	4	24	78	69	81	4.99	58	123	11	4	.73	.252	.323	.447	.770
Severino,Pedro	Was	23	62	205	53	10	0	3	20	18	22	3.74	14	29	2	1	.67	.259	.309	.351	.660
Shaffer,Richie	TB	26	65	172	40	12	0	7	22	22	23	4.5	23	53	1	1	.50	.233	.327	.424	.751
Shaw,Travis	Bos	27	140	458	113	28	2	17	59	63	62	4.65	48	107	4	2	.67	.247	.321	.428	.749
Shuck,J.B.	CWS	30	74	154	40	6	1	1	19	13	16	3.59	12	14	4	2	.67	.260	.317	.331	.649
Simmons,Andrelton	LAA	27	149	551	146	26	3	7	59	52	62	3.94	38	51	9	4	.69	.265	.316	.361	.677
Sisco,Chance	Bal	22	97	355	100	22	1	4	39	36	49	4.98	44	74	2	1	.67	.282	.361	.383	.744
Smith,Mallex	Atl	24	144	580	164	22	11	6	99	54	84	5	64	120	64	21	.75	.283	.355	.390	.745
Smith,Seth	Sea	34	136	388	96	23	2	13	54	50	54	4.81	48	94	0	0	.00	.247	.338	.418	.755
Smoak,Justin	Tor	30	129	295	65	14	0	12	33	37	35	3.96	37	91	0	0	.00	.220	.311	.390	.701
Smolinski,Jake	Oak	28	96	261	66	15	1	7	33	29	33	4.36	26	42	4	2	.67	.253	.330	.398	.728
Sogard,Eric	Oak	31	126	360	91	16	1	3	43	33	37	3.51	31	45	9	5	.64	.253	.314	.328	.642
Solarte,Yangervis	SD	29	141	517	146	31	1	15	64	68	74	5.17	38	62	1	1	.50	.282	.335	.433	.768
Soler,Jorge	ChC	25	91	258	69	15	1	12	38	43	43	5.92	33	74	1	0	1.00	.267	.355	.473	.828
Soto,Geovany	LAA	34	72	179	40	10	0	7	19	23	21	3.93	19	52	0	0	.00	.223	.302	.397	.698
Souza Jr.,Steven	TB	28	136	462	122	25	1	21	72	63	70	5.24	49	148	13	7	.65	.264	.339	.459	.797
Span,Denard	SF	33	149	606	167	30	5	8	82	50	78	4.56	56	79	15	6	.71	.276	.340	.381	.721
Spangenberg,Cory	SD	26	137	452	128	20	7	8	61	42	61	4.73	33	99	20	11	.65	.283	.333	.412	.745
Springer,George	Hou	27	158	630	175	30	3	33	112	90	113	6.36	88	168	15	7	.68	.278	.373	.492	.865
Stanton,Giancarlo	Mia	27	142	526	137	31	1	39	81	100	101	6.73	75	175	3	1	.75	.260	.357	.546	.903
Stassi,Max	Hou	26	58	201	44	9	1	6	20	24	19	3.15	12	56	1	0	1.00	.219	.263	.363	.626
Stewart,Chris	Pit	35	56	152	37	6	0	1	14	13	14	3.17	15	21	0	0	.00	.243	.324	.303	.626
Story,Trevor	Col	24	147	564	149	36	6	34	96	94	98	6.04	55	175	15	7	.68	.264	.333	.530	.863
Suarez,Eugenio	Cin	25	154	552	143	28	3	20	75	70	75	4.7	49	132	10	6	.62	.259	.325	.429	.754
Sucre,Jesus	Sea	29	40	117	28	4	0	1	9	9	9	2.63	5	18	0	0	.00	.239	.276	.299	.576
Susac,Andrew	Mil	27	46	103	25	6	0	4	12	14	14	4.67	11	26	0	0	.00	.243	.316	.417	.733
Suzuki,Ichiro	Mia	43	108	229	59	8	1	1	24	14	22	3.33	15	31	6	2	.75	.258	.309	.314	.623
Suzuki,Kurt	Min	33	122	399	98	22	0	7	37	49	41	3.54	26	55	1	0	1.00	.246	.302	.353	.655
Swanson,Dansby	Atl	23	155	577	163	33	6	13	93	78	90	5.58	68	121	19	5	.79	.282	.358	.428	.786
Swihart,Blake	Bos	25	110	380	107	20	3	6	53	45	52	4.9	38	79	5	3	.62	.282	.347	.397	.744
Szczur,Matt	ChC	27	72	116	29	6	1	2	15	10	13	3.8	9	22	4	2	.67	.250	.304	.371	.675
Tapia,Raimel	Col	23	141	538	166	23	7	8	82	45	75	5.03	25	69	26	16	.62	.309	.339	.422	.761
Taylor,Michael	Was	26	88	237	60	11	1	8	33	29	31	4.45	21	73	15	4	.79	.253	.317	.409	.726
Telis,Tomas	Mia	26	62	189	53	9	1	3	22	21	23	4.36	10	22	2	1	.67	.280	.320	.386	.706
Thole,Josh	Tor	30	52	144	34	6	0	1	11	13	13	3.07	15	24	0	0	.00	.236	.313	.299	.611
Thompson,Trayce	LAD	26	80	250	60	14	2	10	35	30	33	4.45	25	62	3	2	.70	.240	.309	.432	.741
Tilson,Charlie	CWS	24	144	569	149	22	7	5	74	40	63	3.78	39	80	32	13	.71	.262	.309	.351	.661
Toles,Andrew	LAD	25	149	606	170	39	6	15	94	72	84	4.81	37	105	35	18	.66	.281	.323	.439	.762
Tomas,Yasmany	Ari	26	145	551	154	31	2	29	73	86	87	5.67	31	130	3	2	.60	.279	.319	.501	.820
Tomlinson,Kelby	SF	27	58	166	48	6	1	1	23	14	21	4.48	16	27	10	4	.71	.289	.355	.355	.711
Torreyes,Ronald	NYY	24	56	104	27	5	1	1	13	8	11	3.67	6	9	2	1	.67	.260	.300	.356	.656
Travis,Devon	Tor	26	144	586	173	40	3	16	85	77	90	5.63	38	105	8	3	.73	.295	.339	.456	.795
Trout,Mike	LAA	25	160	594	186	37	7	36	128	104	146	9.13	106	152	27	8	.77	.313	.425	.581	1.006
Trumbo,Mark	Bal	31	155	601	152	29	1	36	81	102	89	5.14	47	164	2	1	.67	.253	.309	.484	.793
Tulowitzki,Troy	Tor	32	139	524	147	28	1	26	78	86	89	6.12	54	110	2	1	.67	.281	.353	.487	.840
Turner,Justin	LAD	32	150	539	123	31	1	17	73	75	60	3.73	46	102	4	2	.67	.228	.297	.384	.681
Turner,Trea	Was	24	152	633	190	36	12	19	111	75	115	6.6	52	125	57	10	.85	.300	.354	.485	.839
Upton Jr.,Melvin	Tor	32	146	489	110	22	2	16	62	52	55	3.7	47	158	22	8	.73	.225	.296	.376	.672
Upton,Justin	Det	29	150	535	138	29	2	26	81	79	82	5.3	59	160	10	5	.67	.258	.337	.465	.803
Uribe,Juan	Cle	38	91	258	62	12	0	8	25	31	29	3.85	18	56	1	0	1.00	.240	.295	.380	.675
Utley,Chase	LAD	38	135	475	114	24	2	12	62	54	54	3.87	41	95	4	2	.67	.240	.320	.375	.695
Valbuena,Luis	Hou	31	130	439	103	25	1	17	57	53	58	4.47	58	112	1	1	.50	.235	.327	.412	.739
Valencia,Danny	Oak	32	129	440	116	26	1	15	56	58	59	4.72	32	103	1	1	.50	.264	.315	.430	.745
Van Slyke,Scott	LAD	30	97	248	68	17	1	9	32	35	39	5.54	27	58	4	3	.57	.274	.353	.460	.812
Vargas,Kennys	Min	26	112	338	85	17	1	17	48	57	54	5.55	51	91	0	0	.00	.251	.351	.459	.810
Vazquez,Christian	Bos	26	76	239	59	14	0	2	28	23	25	3.59	22	46	2	1	.67	.247	.313	.331	.644

2017 Hitter Projections

PLAYER			BATTING												BASERUNNING			AVERAGES			
Hitter	Team	Age	G	AB	H	2B	3B	HR	R	RBI	RC	RC27	BB	SO	SB	CS	SB%	Avg	OBP	Slg	OPS
Villar,Jonathan	Mil	26	152	570	152	29	4	15	89	60	83	4.95	64	155	57	18	.76	.267	.342	.411	.752
Vogelbach,Dan	Sea	24	146	516	136	27	1	20	74	68	84	5.75	91	118	0	0	.00	.264	.374	.436	.810
Vogt,Stephen	Oak	32	135	479	126	26	2	15	56	65	65	4.79	41	77	0	0	.00	.263	.324	.420	.743
Votto,Joey	Cin	33	158	549	168	37	1	26	92	86	123	8.33	119	129	7	3	.70	.306	.434	.519	.953
Walker,Neil	NYM	31	143	534	143	27	2	21	70	74	79	5.23	51	108	4	2	.67	.268	.337	.444	.781
Weeks Jr.,Rickie	Ari	34	83	153	35	8	1	6	21	17	19	4.15	17	47	3	1	.75	.229	.333	.412	.745
Wendle,Joey	Oak	27	141	566	148	34	6	11	75	62	67	4.12	27	114	14	5	.74	.261	.295	.401	.696
Werth,Jayson	Was	38	136	492	123	27	1	18	73	64	70	4.91	67	130	5	2	.71	.250	.346	.419	.764
White,Tyler	Hou	26	74	213	53	11	0	9	27	33	29	4.68	24	43	1	1	.50	.249	.328	.427	.755
Wieters,Matt	Bal	31	130	442	112	23	1	17	50	64	59	4.63	39	93	1	1	.50	.253	.317	.425	.742
Williams,Nick	Phi	23	148	575	152	35	6	16	81	66	72	4.36	26	143	10	6	.62	.264	.296	.430	.726
Williamson,Mac	SF	26	137	522	133	28	2	22	77	82	72	4.79	44	133	4	2	.67	.255	.315	.443	.758
Wilson,Bobby	TB	34	60	125	27	5	0	2	11	15	10	2.65	9	28	0	0	.00	.216	.274	.304	.578
Winker,Jesse	Cin	23	147	526	148	31	1	8	64	59	77	5.28	80	88	2	1	.67	.281	.376	.390	.766
Wolters,Tony	Col	25	103	357	86	19	2	4	40	40	37	3.51	34	83	6	3	.67	.241	.307	.339	.646
Wong,Kolten	StL	26	142	497	131	21	6	12	70	52	65	4.56	41	76	15	5	.75	.264	.330	.402	.732
Wright,David	NYM	34	100	380	99	22	1	12	50	49	55	5.02	49	106	8	4	.67	.261	.348	.418	.766
Yelich,Christian	Mia	25	150	580	176	37	4	17	90	79	104	6.6	72	124	13	6	.68	.303	.383	.469	.852
Young,Chris	Bos	33	72	201	44	12	0	7	28	25	23	3.76	22	51	4	2	.67	.219	.305	.383	.688
Zimmer,Bradley	Cle	24	147	536	126	28	4	16	78	66	71	4.32	75	187	44	17	.72	.235	.329	.392	.721
Zimmerman,Ryan	Was	32	125	464	118	26	1	19	64	68	64	4.78	43	109	3	2	.60	.254	.322	.438	.759
Zobrist,Ben	ChC	36	149	563	149	35	3	16	87	72	86	5.35	86	92	7	4	.64	.265	.365	.423	.788
Zunino,Mike	Sea	26	133	411	92	19	1	23	52	63	52	4.24	35	124	0	0	.00	.224	.296	.443	.739

Pitcher Projections

Bill James

Formulas, formulas, formulas; it is all a mass of formulas. That's not strictly true; we DO look at the data and ask ourselves whether it is reasonable, and, if it isn't reasonable, we make adjustments.

I created most of the formulas which create charts and stuff in this book, or, if I didn't create them, I created the formula that was used BEFORE this formula, so I sort of understand what is happening there. When my formula says that Bartolo Colon has a 20% chance to win 300 games, I just laugh that off because I created that formula, so I understand why it doesn't work sometimes, and I have some idea what would have to be done to fix it.

I never had the courage to try to create a set of formulas which would project pitching stats; I always thought that was too complicated. John Dewan and some of his men created those formulas, so I don't really understand them, so when they do something that doesn't seem reasonable I just scratch my head and complain about the damned computers like anybody else. Their formula says that Kenley Jansen will have a 1.46 ERA in 2017, and I don't know why it says that but it seems reasonable enough, since that's about what he usually does. Their formula says that the six pitchers who will have ERAs lower than Clayton Kershaw will all be relievers, which seems reasonable enough, and that Clayton Kershaw will have the best ERA of any starting pitcher, and you don't know whether that is right or not, but it seems reasonable. Their formula says that within the next year, people will finally stop giving starts to Mike Pelfrey, which, you know, it has to happen sometime.

Their formulas say that Chris Sale will lead the majors in strikeouts with 259, which I am certainly willing to accept, although I think perhaps we should add 10% because strikeouts seem to go up 10% every year. Their formulas say that Josh Tomlin might lead the majors in home runs allowed, and that certainly seems reasonable. Their formulas say that Tyler Glasnow will lead the majors in walks, which, since he is 6-foot-8 and 23 years old and throws 35% curveballs, certainly seems like something that might happen.

Some things happen that you could never have predicted, and this is true of hitting and it is true of pitching, but it is a lot MORE true of pitching. No one could have predicted Sam Dyson of Texas getting 38 Saves in 2016, I don't think; we had actually predicted that he would get zero. I don't think anyone would fault us for failing to predict that J. A. Happ would win 20 games, or that Aaron Sanchez would go 15-2.

I remember when Stephen Strasburg was an amateur, he was supposed to be the greatest pitching prospect ever—and he's been pretty good, you know? He's 28 games over .500 in his career; that's really good. But everything rests on the pitcher's health. A pitcher can't make progress unless he gets regular work, and he can't get regular work if he's not 100% healthy. We don't always know who the injury buffalo will trample upon.

2017 Pitcher Projections

PLAYER			HOW MUCH			WHAT HE WILL GIVE UP					THE RESULTS				
Pitcher	Team	Age	G	GS	IP	H	HR	BB	SO	HB	W	L	Pct	Sv	BR/9	ERA
Abad,Fernando	Bos	31	60	0	52	49	6	22	45	2	3	3	.500	0	12.6	3.98
Achter,A.J.	LAA	28	35	0	45	39	7	14	35	1	3	2	.600	0	10.8	3.40
Adleman,Tim	Cin	29	19	19	110	112	12	33	81	4	6	7	.462	0	12.2	3.93
Albers,Andrew	Min	31	12	4	34	45	4	11	24	1	1	3	.250	0	15.1	5.82
Albers,Matt	CWS	34	60	0	57	58	7	18	40	2	3	4	.429	0	12.3	4.11
Allen,Cody	Cle	28	66	0	68	51	6	26	86	1	4	4	.500	33	10.3	2.65
Alvarez,Dario	Tex	28	68	0	68	56	10	30	98	8	3	4	.429	0	12.4	3.97
Alvarez,Henderson	Oak	27	29	29	177	180	15	43	99	7	9	10	.474	0	11.7	3.71
Alvarez,Jose	LAA	28	60	0	54	58	6	18	41	2	2	4	.333	0	13.0	4.33
Anderson,Brett	LAD	29	25	25	146	161	13	37	104	3	8	8	.500	0	12.4	4.01
Anderson,Chase	Mil	29	29	29	157	158	21	50	128	5	8	10	.444	0	12.2	4.07
Anderson,Cody	Cle	26	32	6	79	87	11	21	57	2	4	5	.444	0	12.5	4.33
Anderson,Tyler	Col	27	30	30	181	174	12	54	159	5	12	8	.600	0	11.6	3.48
Andriese,Matt	TB	27	32	14	95	100	10	21	81	3	5	6	.455	0	11.7	3.79
Archer,Chris	TB	28	33	33	207	186	21	68	213	7	12	11	.522	0	11.3	3.48
Arrieta,Jake	ChC	31	32	32	208	162	15	66	195	7	17	6	.739	0	10.2	2.90
Asher,Alec	Phi	25	27	27	152	154	23	36	107	3	7	10	.412	0	11.4	3.91
Axford,John	Oak	34	66	0	69	64	7	35	76	2	3	4	.429	0	13.2	4.04
Baez,Pedro	LAD	29	70	0	72	61	8	20	74	2	5	3	.625	0	10.4	3.00
Bailey,Andrew	LAA	33	58	0	55	49	6	21	58	1	3	3	.500	0	11.6	3.60
Bailey,Homer	Cin	31	27	27	171	175	21	61	144	8	8	11	.421	0	12.8	4.32
Barbato,Johnny	NYY	24	64	0	61	57	6	30	62	3	3	4	.429	0	13.3	4.13
Barnes,Jacob	Mil	27	56	0	59	58	4	21	55	3	3	3	.500	5	12.5	3.66
Barnes,Matt	Bos	27	63	0	60	61	7	28	59	2	3	4	.429	0	13.6	4.50
Barnette,Tony	Tex	33	62	0	64	62	5	17	49	4	4	3	.571	0	11.7	3.52
Barraclough,Kyle	Mia	27	75	0	78	51	1	48	112	2	6	3	.667	8	11.7	2.42
Barrett,Jake	Ari	25	68	0	61	60	5	29	56	1	3	4	.429	0	13.3	4.13
Bassitt,Chris	Oak	28	11	11	65	63	4	25	54	5	3	4	.429	0	12.9	3.74
Bastardo,Antonio	Pit	31	67	0	65	50	6	31	77	3	4	3	.571	0	11.6	3.18
Bauer,Trevor	Cle	26	31	31	184	171	21	72	174	9	10	11	.476	0	12.3	3.91
Beachy,Brandon	LAD	30	18	18	102	87	10	54	97	3	6	6	.500	0	12.7	3.79
Beck,Chris	CWS	26	40	0	41	46	3	18	27	2	2	3	.400	0	14.5	4.83
Bedrosian,Cam	LAA	25	65	0	61	51	3	26	78	3	4	3	.571	2	11.8	2.95
Belisle,Matt	Was	37	43	0	51	53	3	11	40	2	3	3	.500	0	11.6	3.53
Benoit,Joaquin	Tor	39	57	0	55	38	6	23	60	1	4	2	.667	0	10.1	2.62
Berrios,Jose	Min	23	28	28	148	140	16	59	151	8	8	9	.471	0	12.6	3.95
Betances,Dellin	NYY	29	69	0	70	53	5	28	95	4	4	3	.571	43	10.9	2.70
Bettis,Chad	Col	28	31	31	186	202	21	61	149	7	9	11	.450	0	13.1	4.40
Biagini,Joseph	Tor	27	62	0	74	74	4	22	53	3	4	4	.500	0	12.0	3.41
Blach,Ty	SF	26	28	10	75	80	6	19	46	1	4	4	.500	0	12.0	3.72
Blair,Aaron	Atl	25	29	29	156	157	18	68	124	7	7	10	.412	0	13.4	4.44
Blanton,Joe	LAD	36	72	0	79	81	11	23	69	2	4	5	.444	0	12.1	4.10
Blazek,Michael	Mil	28	48	0	48	47	5	24	43	2	2	3	.400	0	13.7	4.50
Blevins,Jerry	NYM	33	71	0	42	36	4	15	42	2	3	2	.600	1	11.4	3.00
Boshers,Buddy	Min	29	61	0	63	58	3	23	68	1	4	3	.571	0	11.7	3.14
Bowman,Matt	StL	26	62	0	68	75	6	22	49	1	3	4	.429	0	13.0	4.24
Boxberger,Brad	TB	29	60	0	60	47	7	34	80	2	3	4	.429	2	12.4	3.75
Boyd,Matt	Det	26	28	28	163	159	25	50	142	5	8	10	.444	0	11.8	4.03
Boyer,Blaine	Mil	35	63	0	66	71	5	17	38	1	3	4	.429	0	12.1	3.82
Brach,Brad	Bal	31	69	0	74	61	7	27	82	1	5	3	.625	0	10.8	2.92
Bracho,Silvino	Ari	24	61	0	60	58	8	17	68	3	3	3	.500	0	11.7	3.75
Bradley,Archie	Ari	24	30	30	160	158	12	78	153	8	8	10	.444	0	13.7	4.16
Britton,Zach	Bal	29	67	0	67	60	4	17	56	1	5	3	.625	44	10.5	2.82
Broxton,Jonathan	StL	33	62	0	59	53	5	22	57	2	4	3	.571	0	11.7	3.36
Buchholz,Clay	Bos	32	26	26	143	138	15	48	109	6	8	8	.500	0	12.1	3.78
Buchter,Ryan	SD	30	69	0	68	52	4	36	81	3	4	3	.571	3	12.0	3.04
Bumgarner,Madison	SF	27	33	33	219	187	21	47	218	7	16	9	.640	0	9.9	3.00
Burgos,Enrique	Ari	26	57	0	55	51	5	33	65	2	3	3	.500	0	14.1	4.42
Bush,Matt	Tex	31	64	0	73	58	7	18	80	2	6	2	.750	0	9.6	2.47
Butler,Eddie	Col	26	42	9	96	112	12	35	53	3	* 4	7	.364	0	14.1	5.16
Cahill,Trevor	ChC	29	56	0	60	58	6	31	46	2	3	3	.500	0	13.6	4.50
Cain,Matt	SF	32	25	25	149	141	19	54	119	6	8	9	.471	0	12.1	3.93
Caminero,Arquimedes	Sea	30	55	0	61	58	7	31	62	5	3	4	.429	0	13.9	4.43
Campos,Leonel	SD	29	51	0	63	57	4	37	79	1	3	4	.429	0	13.6	3.86
Capps,Carter	SD	26	52	0	51	42	4	20	71	3	3	2	.600	0	11.5	3.00
Capuano,Chris	Mil	38	35	10	79	82	10	37	68	2	3	6	.333	0	13.8	4.67
Carrasco,Carlos	Cle	30	31	31	195	181	21	45	193	6	12	9	.571	0	10.7	3.37
Cashner,Andrew	Mia	30	30	30	180	177	17	71	151	6	9	11	.450	0	12.7	3.95
Casilla,Santiago	SF	36	59	0	56	46	5	19	52	3	4	2	.667	12	10.9	2.89
Cecil,Brett	Tor	30	62	0	44	43	5	11	41	2	3	2	.600	0	11.5	3.48
Cedeno,Xavier	TB	30	64	0	43	39	3	13	43	1	3	2	.600	0	11.1	2.93
Cervenka,Hunter	Mia	27	63	0	39	33	2	25	42	2	2	2	.500	0	13.8	3.69
Cessa,Luis	NYY	25	27	27	144	157	19	41	115	3	7	9	.438	0	12.6	4.44
Chacin,Jhoulys	LAA	29	35	21	146	142	13	55	108	5	8	8	.500	0	12.5	3.82
Chapman,Aroldis	ChC	29	63	0	64	38	3	25	104	3	5	2	.714	37	9.3	1.83
Chargois,J.T.	Min	26	56	0	56	54	2	24	56	2	3	3	.500	0	12.9	3.54
Chatwood,Tyler	Col	27	29	29	163	169	15	71	112	6	8	10	.444	0	13.6	4.36
Chavez,Jesse	LAD	33	63	0	72	74	9	21	64	2	4	4	.500	0	12.1	4.00
Chen,Wei-Yin	Mia	31	31	31	190	196	27	38	147	4	10	11	.476	0	11.3	3.84

573

2017 Pitcher Projections

Pitcher	Team	Age	G	GS	IP	H	HR	BB	SO	HB	W	L	Pct	Sv	BR/9	ERA
Cingrani,Tony	Cin	27	62	0	62	52	7	37	66	2	3	4	.429	1	13.2	4.06
Cishek,Steve	Sea	31	65	0	64	54	4	23	68	3	4	3	.571	2	11.2	2.95
Claudio,Alex	Tex	25	46	0	63	62	3	14	47	1	4	3	.571	0	11.0	3.00
Clemens,Paul	SD	29	28	28	160	174	24	72	119	6	6	12	.333	0	14.2	5.17
Clevinger,Mike	Cle	26	27	15	82	77	8	34	77	3	4	5	.444	0	12.5	3.84
Clippard,Tyler	NYY	32	75	0	70	51	8	29	76	2	5	3	.625	2	10.5	2.83
Cobb,Alex	TB	29	25	25	150	149	13	51	131	7	8	9	.471	0	12.4	3.84
Cole,A.J.	Was	25	28	28	159	167	19	53	133	4	8	10	.444	0	12.7	4.30
Cole,Gerrit	Pit	26	31	31	201	191	12	52	184	10	13	9	.591	0	11.3	3.36
Coleman,Louis	LAD	31	47	0	36	31	4	16	37	1	2	2	.500	0	12.0	3.50
Collmenter,Josh	Atl	31	45	12	108	104	13	35	75	2	6	6	.500	0	11.8	3.67
Colome,Alex	TB	28	62	0	62	60	4	18	55	3	3	3	.500	36	11.8	3.48
Colon,Bartolo	NYM	44	30	30	179	192	21	27	121	3	10	10	.500	0	11.2	3.72
Conley,Adam	Mia	27	29	29	159	153	12	69	137	10	8	9	.471	0	13.1	3.96
Cook,Ryan	Sea	30	60	0	60	49	5	31	67	3	4	3	.571	0	12.4	3.00
Corbin,Patrick	Ari	27	26	26	158	167	18	59	136	6	8	10	.444	0	13.2	4.44
Cosart,Jarred	SD	27	14	14	78	79	7	44	54	2	3	5	.375	0	14.4	4.62
Cotton,Jharel	Oak	25	26	26	157	139	21	47	167	0	9	8	.529	0	10.7	3.44
Coulombe,Daniel	Oak	27	43	0	59	51	4	25	66	1	4	3	.571	0	11.7	3.20
Cravy,Tyler	Mil	27	30	2	42	39	4	18	37	2	2	2	.500	0	12.6	3.86
Crockett,Kyle	Cle	25	45	0	31	31	2	12	28	1	2	2	.500	0	12.8	4.06
Cueto,Johnny	SF	31	32	32	218	189	18	47	184	10	15	9	.625	0	10.2	3.06
Cunniff,Brandon	Atl	28	51	0	64	57	6	36	59	2	3	4	.429	0	13.4	4.08
Darvish,Yu	Tex	30	27	27	161	130	16	53	200	5	11	7	.611	0	10.5	3.13
Davies,Zach	Mil	24	28	28	169	171	15	49	143	5	9	10	.474	0	12.0	3.73
Davis,Wade	KC	31	69	0	66	58	5	22	62	2	4	3	.571	33	11.2	3.00
Dayton,Grant	LAD	29	62	0	64	52	6	17	84	2	5	2	.714	0	10.0	2.53
De La Cruz,Joel	Atl	28	28	0	90	103	10	35	54	5	3	7	.300	0	14.3	5.10
de la Rosa,Jorge	Col	36	28	28	161	160	20	73	130	7	8	10	.444	0	13.4	4.47
de la Rosa,Rubby	Ari	28	14	14	81	81	10	29	70	3	4	5	.444	0	12.6	4.11
Dean,Pat	Min	28	25	9	76	98	10	21	43	2	3	6	.333	0	14.3	5.45
deGrom,Jacob	NYM	29	28	28	181	165	14	42	174	3	13	8	.619	0	10.4	3.13
Delgado,Randall	Ari	27	70	0	69	68	8	32	62	2	3	4	.429	0	13.3	4.43
DeSclafani,Anthony	Cin	27	31	31	187	192	22	47	159	6	10	11	.476	0	11.8	3.90
Despaigne,Odrisamer	Mia	30	41	0	62	68	6	22	42	4	3	4	.429	0	13.6	4.65
Detwiler,Ross	Oak	31	21	14	90	103	10	36	59	5	3	7	.300	0	14.4	5.00
Devenski,Christopher	Hou	26	55	0	54	49	5	13	48	1	4	2	.667	0	10.5	2.83
Diaz,Edwin	Sea	23	60	0	66	60	5	20	83	4	4	3	.571	36	11.5	3.27
Diaz,Jumbo	Cin	33	57	0	58	51	6	21	57	2	3	3	.500	0	11.5	3.41
Dickey,R.A.	Tor	42	33	33	209	194	26	71	152	10	12	12	.500	0	11.8	3.79
Diekman,Jake	Tex	30	62	0	49	42	3	24	59	2	3	2	.600	0	12.5	3.31
Dominguez,Jose	SD	26	48	0	53	50	5	33	50	5	2	4	.333	0	14.9	4.75
Doolittle,Sean	Oak	30	56	0	55	42	5	11	67	0	5	2	.714	2	8.7	2.13
Doubront,Felix	Oak	29	40	12	97	101	10	38	82	3	4	6	.400	0	13.2	4.27
Duffey,Tyler	Min	26	40	10	95	101	11	26	80	3	5	6	.455	0	12.3	4.07
Duffy,Danny	KC	28	30	30	186	171	22	52	169	9	11	9	.550	0	11.2	3.58
Duke,Zach	StL	34	80	0	66	68	6	31	51	2	3	4	.429	0	13.8	4.50
Dull,Ryan	Oak	27	66	0	68	55	8	16	71	1	5	3	.625	8	9.5	2.65
Dunn,Mike	Mia	32	67	0	53	47	5	19	60	2	3	3	.500	0	11.5	3.23
Dyson,Sam	Tex	29	67	0	68	65	3	22	49	5	4	3	.571	37	12.2	3.31
Edwards Jr.,Carl	ChC	25	62	0	62	37	3	37	77	1	5	1	.833	2	10.9	2.18
Eflin,Zach	Phi	23	27	27	156	165	17	34	90	5	7	10	.412	0	11.8	3.87
Eickhoff,Jerad	Phi	26	32	32	197	186	27	49	171	7	10	12	.455	0	11.1	3.65
Elias,Roenis	Bos	28	22	22	135	139	16	64	115	8	6	9	.400	0	14.1	4.73
Ellington,Brian	Mia	26	55	0	57	44	3	33	63	3	4	3	.571	0	12.6	3.16
Escobar,Edwin	Ari	25	61	0	60	70	8	26	43	3	2	4	.333	0	14.8	5.55
Estevez,Carlos	Col	24	62	0	52	51	5	24	56	3	3	3	.500	0	13.5	4.33
Estrada,Marco	Tor	33	30	30	178	148	25	61	153	4	11	9	.550	0	10.8	3.44
Familia,Jeurys	NYM	27	77	0	81	71	4	29	81	2	5	4	.556	50	11.3	3.00
Farmer,Buck	Det	26	39	5	66	72	9	26	57	2	3	5	.375	0	13.8	5.05
Farquhar,Danny	TB	30	61	0	63	59	6	21	66	3	3	4	.429	0	11.9	3.57
Feldman,Scott	Tor	34	40	2	61	64	7	16	39	2	3	4	.429	0	12.1	3.84
Feliz,Neftali	Pit	29	60	0	55	47	7	21	52	2	3	3	.500	2	11.5	3.44
Fields,Josh	LAD	31	50	0	46	40	3	15	53	1	3	2	.600	0	11.0	2.93
Fiers,Mike	Hou	32	31	30	172	160	22	48	165	6	10	9	.526	0	11.2	3.61
Finnegan,Brandon	Cin	24	32	32	186	173	29	94	170	5	8	12	.400	0	13.2	4.45
Fister,Doug	Hou	33	33	33	176	184	18	52	118	9	9	10	.474	0	12.5	4.09
Floyd,Gavin	Tor	34	60	0	64	62	8	18	52	4	4	4	.500	0	11.8	3.66
Flynn,Brian	KC	27	43	0	60	63	5	26	50	2	2	4	.333	0	13.6	4.50
Foltynewicz,Mike	Atl	25	30	30	167	169	22	63	155	9	8	11	.421	0	13.0	4.37
Friedrich,Christian	SD	29	28	28	157	178	20	61	125	4	6	11	.353	0	13.9	4.93
Fulmer,Michael	Det	24	30	30	179	165	18	50	163	7	11	9	.550	0	11.2	3.47
Gallardo,Yovani	Bal	31	27	27	143	142	16	62	119	2	7	9	.438	0	13.0	4.15
Garcia,Jaime	StL	30	27	27	155	154	16	46	128	4	9	8	.529	0	11.8	3.77
Garcia,Yimi	LAD	26	59	0	58	47	8	11	66	4	4	2	.667	0	9.6	2.64
Garton,Ryan	TB	27	50	0	55	52	3	21	56	1	3	3	.500	0	12.1	3.44
Garza,Matt	Mil	33	29	29	181	182	21	65	144	5	9	11	.450	0	12.5	4.03
Gausman,Kevin	Bal	26	32	32	204	203	27	58	193	4	11	12	.478	0	11.7	3.88
Gearrin,Cory	SF	31	63	0	55	48	3	17	54	3	4	2	.667	0	11.1	2.95
Gee,Dillon	KC	31	33	17	140	149	18	39	102	6	6	10	.375	0	12.5	4.24
Germen,Gonzalez	Col	29	38	0	39	39	4	22	34	1	2	3	.400	0	14.3	4.85

574

2017 Pitcher Projections

Pitcher	Team	Age	G	GS	IP	H	HR	BB	SO	HB	W	L	Pct	Sv	BR/9	ERA
Gibson,Kyle	Min	29	29	29	179	192	17	63	128	5	8	12	.400	0	13.1	4.27
Giles,Ken	Hou	26	67	0	69	54	4	25	96	1	4	3	.571	35	10.4	2.48
Givens,Mychal	Bal	27	68	0	78	60	4	33	99	6	6	3	.667	0	11.4	2.77
Glasnow,Tyler	Pit	23	28	28	169	133	9	105	202	4	10	8	.556	0	12.8	3.51
Godley,Zack	Ari	27	35	7	58	64	7	21	47	4	3	4	.429	0	13.8	4.81
Goeddel,Erik	NYM	28	66	0	66	65	6	27	64	2	3	4	.429	0	12.8	3.95
Gomez,Jeanmar	Phi	29	69	0	64	69	6	19	43	2	3	4	.429	21	12.7	4.08
Gonzalez,Gio	Was	31	31	31	172	158	13	61	167	5	11	8	.579	0	11.7	3.51
Gonzalez,Miguel	CWS	33	30	30	175	173	24	50	130	8	9	11	.450	0	11.9	3.91
Gonzalez,Severino	Phi	24	53	0	60	70	8	13	43	3	2	4	.333	0	12.9	4.65
Goody,Nick	NYY	25	41	0	42	36	6	15	51	1	3	2	.600	0	11.1	3.43
Graveman,Kendall	Oak	26	31	31	196	210	21	54	120	6	9	12	.429	0	12.4	4.09
Gray,Jon	Col	25	30	30	172	172	16	61	172	3	10	10	.500	0	12.7	3.98
Gray,Sonny	Oak	27	31	31	206	192	17	67	172	4	12	11	.522	0	11.5	3.50
Green,Chad	NYY	26	13	11	56	58	5	16	54	2	3	3	.500	0	12.2	3.86
Greene,Shane	Det	28	62	1	60	67	5	20	50	4	3	4	.429	0	13.6	4.65
Gregerson,Luke	Hou	33	63	0	62	49	5	16	61	2	5	2	.714	5	9.7	2.47
Greinke,Zack	Ari	33	32	32	214	192	20	49	198	3	15	8	.652	0	10.3	3.15
Griffin,A.J.	Tex	29	26	26	136	129	26	52	116	6	6	9	.400	0	12.4	4.37
Grilli,Jason	Tor	40	63	0	57	46	6	27	74	2	3	3	.500	0	11.8	3.47
Grimm,Justin	ChC	28	66	0	54	50	4	24	53	2	3	3	.500	0	12.7	3.67
Gsellman,Robert	NYM	23	28	28	152	158	10	46	107	5	8	8	.500	0	12.4	3.79
Guerra,Deolis	LAA	28	53	0	58	61	7	11	50	2	3	3	.500	0	11.5	3.72
Guerra,Junior	Mil	32	28	28	172	144	16	67	162	4	11	8	.579	0	11.2	3.35
Gustave,Jandel	Hou	24	55	0	61	57	2	26	54	5	4	3	.571	0	13.0	3.54
Hahn,Jesse	Oak	27	24	24	135	136	10	57	96	7	6	9	.400	0	13.3	4.13
Hamels,Cole	Tex	33	31	31	201	181	20	69	193	7	12	10	.545	0	11.5	3.54
Hammel,Jason	ChC	34	29	29	162	154	21	46	135	7	10	8	.556	0	11.5	3.78
Hand,Brad	SD	27	35	20	130	126	15	49	111	2	7	8	.467	2	12.3	3.88
Happ,J.A.	Tor	34	31	31	194	187	23	58	165	4	11	11	.500	0	11.6	3.71
Hardy,Blaine	Det	30	57	0	51	47	4	18	42	1	3	3	.500	0	11.6	3.35
Harrell,Lucas	Tex	32	18	18	96	103	8	61	64	4	3	7	.300	0	15.8	5.34
Harris,Will	Hou	32	65	0	64	52	5	18	68	2	5	2	.714	0	10.1	2.53
Harrison,Matt	Phi	31	6	6	35	36	3	16	22	0	2	2	.500	0	13.4	4.37
Harvey,Matt	NYM	28	28	28	172	156	14	40	169	5	12	7	.632	0	10.5	3.19
Hellickson,Jeremy	Phi	30	30	30	181	181	23	46	145	6	9	11	.450	0	11.6	3.83
Hembree,Heath	Bos	28	45	0	59	54	6	20	58	2	4	3	.571	0	11.6	3.36
Henderson,Jim	NYM	34	58	0	57	52	8	29	64	2	3	4	.429	0	13.1	4.26
Hendricks,Kyle	ChC	27	31	31	194	168	14	45	166	8	15	6	.714	0	10.3	3.02
Hendriks,Liam	Oak	28	63	0	73	77	6	14	59	2	4	4	.500	0	11.5	3.58
Hernandez,David	Phi	32	66	0	73	66	10	31	78	3	3	5	.375	0	12.3	3.95
Hernandez,Felix	Sea	31	31	31	201	175	18	69	190	8	13	9	.591	0	11.3	3.36
Herrera,Kelvin	KC	27	72	0	76	61	5	19	79	3	6	3	.667	5	9.8	2.37
Herrmann,Frank	Phi	33	58	0	61	68	9	16	51	1	2	4	.333	0	12.5	4.43
Hessler,Keith	SD	28	60	0	65	64	6	27	61	2	3	4	.429	0	12.9	4.22
Heston,Chris	SF	29	30	30	175	174	16	72	131	10	8	11	.421	0	13.2	4.11
Hill,Rich	LAD	37	22	22	122	96	7	43	140	10	9	4	.692	0	11.0	3.02
Hochevar,Luke	KC	33	56	0	52	52	7	17	43	2	2	4	.333	0	12.3	4.15
Holland,Derek	Tex	30	28	28	156	159	21	51	124	4	8	10	.444	0	12.3	4.15
Holland,Greg	KC	31	55	0	55	42	3	27	70	0	4	2	.667	0	11.3	2.62
Hoover,J.J.	Cin	29	52	0	52	45	7	24	55	1	3	3	.500	0	12.1	3.81
Howell,J.P.	LAD	34	61	0	48	43	3	16	43	2	3	2	.600	0	11.4	3.19
Hoyt,James	Hou	30	52	0	52	41	4	18	67	2	4	2	.667	0	10.6	2.60
Hudson,Daniel	Ari	30	71	0	64	65	6	23	58	2	3	4	.429	20	12.7	4.08
Hughes,Jared	Pit	31	73	0	66	67	5	23	44	6	3	4	.429	0	13.1	3.95
Hughes,Phil	Min	31	29	29	182	202	26	25	141	4	9	11	.450	0	11.4	4.01
Hunter,Tommy	Bal	30	60	0	60	63	8	13	39	2	3	3	.500	0	11.7	3.90
Iglesias,Raisel	Cin	27	65	0	62	54	7	19	63	4	4	3	.571	23	11.2	3.34
Iwakuma,Hisashi	Sea	36	33	33	202	197	25	41	163	3	12	10	.545	0	10.7	3.56
Jackson,Edwin	SD	33	34	11	86	95	11	39	68	2	3	6	.333	0	14.2	4.92
Jansen,Kenley	LAD	29	69	0	68	43	5	12	104	2	6	2	.750	46	7.5	1.46
Jeffress,Jeremy	Tex	29	63	0	63	60	3	21	58	2	4	3	.571	2	11.9	3.29
Jenkins,Tyrell	Atl	24	55	0	62	68	6	33	38	1	2	4	.333	0	14.8	5.08
Jennings,Dan	CWS	30	66	0	61	60	2	27	52	1	3	4	.429	0	13.0	3.69
Jepsen,Kevin	TB	32	68	0	67	63	7	27	61	1	3	4	.429	0	12.2	3.76
Jimenez,Ubaldo	Bal	33	25	25	161	156	17	75	147	6	8	10	.444	0	13.2	4.19
Johnson,Jim	Atl	34	69	0	72	74	5	24	56	5	4	4	.500	29	12.9	3.88
Jones,Nate	CWS	31	66	0	69	57	7	16	74	2	5	3	.625	0	9.8	2.61
Jungmann,Taylor	Mil	27	26	26	147	144	13	88	126	13	6	10	.375	0	15.0	4.78
Kahnle,Tommy	CWS	27	40	0	41	33	3	25	44	1	2	2	.500	0	13.0	3.51
Karns,Nate	Sea	29	32	17	110	107	15	48	113	4	5	7	.417	0	13.0	4.34
Kazmir,Scott	LAD	33	28	28	157	150	18	54	138	7	9	9	.500	0	12.1	3.84
Kela,Keone	Tex	24	46	0	46	36	4	18	58	1	3	2	.600	0	11.0	2.93
Kelley,Shawn	Was	33	66	0	58	47	7	14	70	0	4	2	.667	2	9.5	2.48
Kelly,Joe	Bos	29	62	0	61	63	6	24	49	3	3	4	.429	0	13.3	4.28
Kennedy,Ian	KC	32	33	33	209	198	29	69	197	10	10	14	.417	0	11.9	3.92
Kershaw,Clayton	LAD	29	33	33	230	166	13	29	257	4	20	4	.833	0	7.8	2.15
Keuchel,Dallas	Hou	29	32	32	219	214	20	56	167	4	14	11	.560	0	11.3	3.49
Kimbrel,Craig	Bos	29	61	0	56	32	4	27	87	2	4	2	.667	37	9.8	2.09
Kintzler,Brandon	Min	32	60	0	61	66	4	12	43	1	3	3	.500	24	11.7	3.54
Kluber,Corey	Cle	31	32	32	219	201	20	53	225	9	14	10	.583	0	10.8	3.33

575

2017 Pitcher Projections

Pitcher	Team	Age	G	GS	IP	H	HR	BB	SO	HB	W	L	Pct	Sv	BR/9	ERA
Knebel,Corey	Mil	25	63	0	65	52	6	26	80	2	4	3	.571	2	11.1	3.05
Koch,Matt	Ari	26	33	8	71	85	6	14	43	3	4	4	.500	0	12.9	4.31
Koehler,Tom	Mia	31	33	33	182	178	20	80	142	6	9	11	.450	0	13.1	4.20
Kontos,George	SF	32	65	0	65	56	6	18	53	1	4	3	.571	0	10.4	2.77
Krol,Ian	Atl	26	70	0	56	55	5	21	58	2	3	3	.500	0	12.5	3.86
Kuhl,Chad	Pit	24	26	26	146	152	16	40	104	6	8	8	.500	0	12.2	3.95
Lackey,John	ChC	38	30	30	194	185	22	51	160	6	13	9	.591	0	11.2	3.62
Lamb,John	Cin	26	25	25	131	138	16	53	120	6	5	9	.357	0	13.5	4.67
Latos,Mat	Was	29	24	24	143	134	14	53	119	3	8	8	.500	0	12.0	3.71
Law,Derek	SF	26	65	0	61	55	3	14	60	0	5	2	.714	0	10.2	2.51
Layne,Tommy	NYY	32	65	0	48	46	3	23	38	3	3	3	.500	0	13.5	3.94
Leake,Mike	StL	29	30	30	180	187	21	37	121	6	10	10	.500	0	11.5	3.80
LeBlanc,Wade	Pit	32	29	10	86	91	9	21	70	2	5	5	.500	9	11.9	3.87
Leone,Dominic	Ari	25	63	0	60	60	7	25	56	2	3	4	.429	0	13.0	4.35
Lester,Jon	ChC	33	31	31	213	187	19	52	203	7	16	7	.696	0	10.4	3.13
Lewis,Colby	Tex	37	32	32	200	207	29	47	151	8	10	12	.455	0	11.8	4.05
Liberatore,Adam	LAD	30	59	0	53	46	3	20	54	2	4	2	.667	0	11.5	2.89
Liriano,Francisco	Tor	33	30	30	170	151	17	80	175	6	9	10	.474	0	12.5	3.81
Locke,Jeff	Pit	29	29	11	96	100	10	34	70	4	5	6	.455	0	12.9	4.22
Logan,Boone	Col	32	62	0	46	42	5	20	54	3	3	3	.500	0	12.7	3.91
Lopez,Javier	SF	39	68	0	38	32	2	19	26	1	2	2	.500	0	12.3	3.08
Lorenzen,Michael	Cin	25	50	0	71	73	8	25	53	4	3	5	.375	0	12.9	4.31
Lowe,Mark	Det	34	59	0	58	59	8	20	58	1	3	4	.429	0	12.4	4.19
Lugo,Seth	NYM	27	26	15	112	118	12	32	91	5	6	7	.462	0	12.5	4.10
Lyles,Jordan	Col	26	56	2	55	63	5	24	37	3	2	4	.333	0	14.7	5.07
Lynn,Lance	StL	30	31	31	180	173	13	65	167	7	11	9	.550	0	12.2	3.70
Madson,Ryan	Oak	36	64	0	64	57	5	18	58	2	4	3	.571	34	10.8	2.95
Maeda,Kenta	LAD	29	31	31	171	148	19	49	173	8	11	8	.579	0	10.8	3.37
Manaea,Sean	Oak	25	27	27	163	152	20	46	156	5	9	9	.500	0	11.2	3.59
Maness,Seth	StL	28	68	0	64	69	6	14	40	2	4	4	.500	0	12.0	3.80
Manship,Jeff	Cle	32	49	0	43	44	4	19	31	0	2	3	.400	0	13.2	4.40
Marinez,Jhan	Mil	28	58	0	78	72	8	31	76	5	4	5	.444	0	12.5	3.81
Mariot,Michael	Phi	28	64	0	63	62	8	29	57	2	3	4	.429	0	13.3	4.43
Martin,Cody	Sea	27	34	8	71	72	8	27	65	3	3	4	.429	0	12.9	4.31
Martinez,Carlos	StL	25	31	31	201	185	14	72	186	11	13	10	.565	0	12.0	3.54
Martinez,Nick	Tex	26	30	14	89	96	10	28	54	6	4	6	.400	0	13.1	4.45
Matz,Steven	NYM	26	29	29	174	158	14	45	170	5	12	8	.600	0	10.8	3.26
Maurer,Brandon	SD	26	65	0	64	67	6	20	56	2	3	4	.429	14	12.5	4.08
May,Trevor	Min	27	31	25	144	146	16	47	147	6	7	9	.438	0	12.4	4.06
McAllister,Zach	Cle	29	62	0	64	67	6	23	55	2	3	4	.429	0	12.9	4.22
McCarthy,Brandon	LAD	33	26	26	159	170	20	58	124	4	7	10	.412	0	13.1	4.53
McCullers,Lance	Hou	23	30	30	180	152	12	81	215	5	12	8	.600	0	11.9	3.40
McGee,Jake	Col	30	57	0	46	45	5	14	52	2	3	2	.600	2	11.9	3.33
McGowan,Dustin	Mia	35	58	0	72	68	9	42	61	2	3	5	.375	0	14.0	4.63
McHugh,Collin	Hou	30	33	33	196	195	20	55	175	8	11	10	.524	0	11.8	3.77
Medlen,Kris	KC	31	18	18	103	103	14	46	83	4	4	8	.333	0	13.4	4.54
Melancon,Mark	Was	32	75	0	75	61	4	13	69	2	5	3	.625	45	9.1	2.04
Meyer,Alex	LAA	27	22	22	127	128	10	69	143	6	6	9	.400	0	14.4	4.54
Miley,Wade	Bal	30	30	30	164	171	18	52	129	4	8	10	.444	0	12.5	4.06
Miller,Andrew	Cle	32	71	0	75	56	6	14	99	4	6	2	.750	10	8.9	2.16
Miller,Justin	Col	30	52	0	53	49	4	20	52	3	3	3	.500	0	12.2	3.57
Miller,Shelby	Ari	26	31	31	177	171	18	61	156	5	8	11	.421	0	12.1	3.81
Milone,Tommy	Min	30	18	18	102	108	13	25	81	2	5	6	.455	0	11.9	4.06
Mitchell,Bryan	NYY	26	37	8	77	82	5	38	63	2	4	5	.444	0	14.3	4.56
Montero,Rafael	NYM	26	14	6	34	34	3	17	31	0	2	2	.500	0	13.5	4.24
Montgomery,Mike	ChC	27	43	11	102	101	10	39	79	6	6	5	.545	0	12.9	4.06
Moore,Matt	SF	28	33	33	202	184	24	73	197	7	11	11	.500	0	11.8	3.70
Morgan,Adam	Phi	27	24	23	127	146	20	34	92	5	4	10	.286	0	13.1	4.89
Morin,Mike	LAA	26	65	0	59	57	6	15	59	3	3	3	.500	0	11.4	3.51
Morrow,Brandon	SD	32	45	0	45	47	5	15	40	1	2	3	.400	0	12.6	4.20
Morton,Charlie	Phi	33	26	26	160	163	11	56	118	14	7	11	.389	0	13.1	3.99
Motte,Jason	Col	35	55	0	45	42	6	14	41	2	3	2	.600	0	11.6	3.60
Moylan,Peter	KC	38	66	0	52	50	3	18	42	3	3	3	.500	0	12.3	3.46
Neal,Zach	Oak	28	32	10	108	124	12	17	62	4	5	7	.417	0	12.1	4.17
Nelson,Jimmy	Mil	28	31	31	173	163	16	74	149	14	9	11	.450	0	13.1	4.01
Neris,Hector	Phi	28	76	0	80	72	10	33	81	4	4	5	.444	14	12.3	3.71
Neshek,Pat	Hou	36	59	0	47	41	5	10	42	1	3	2	.600	0	10.0	2.87
Nicasio,Juan	Pit	30	61	0	65	68	8	26	60	2	3	4	.429	0	13.3	4.57
Nicolino,Justin	Mia	25	45	6	77	89	8	18	38	2	4	5	.444	0	12.7	4.32
Niese,Jon	NYM	30	36	5	50	54	6	17	37	2	2	3	.400	0	13.1	4.50
Nola,Aaron	Phi	24	28	28	168	168	17	40	158	6	9	10	.474	0	11.5	3.64
Nolasco,Ricky	LAA	34	31	31	192	212	22	45	148	6	9	12	.429	0	12.3	4.17
Norris,Bud	LAD	32	26	14	77	79	10	30	69	4	4	5	.444	0	13.2	4.44
Norris,Daniel	Det	24	28	28	154	162	16	63	154	3	7	10	.412	0	13.3	4.38
Nova,Ivan	Pit	30	31	31	179	194	23	39	134	11	9	11	.450	0	12.3	4.17
Nuno,Vidal	Sea	29	54	0	59	59	9	13	49	2	3	3	.500	0	11.3	3.81
Oberholtzer,Brett	LAA	27	55	0	67	73	9	21	50	1	3	5	.375	0	12.8	4.57
O'Day,Darren	Bal	34	58	0	56	43	6	17	60	4	4	2	.667	0	10.3	2.73
Odorizzi,Jake	TB	27	32	32	187	172	24	54	171	4	10	10	.500	0	11.1	3.56
Ohlendorf,Ross	Cin	34	60	0	62	64	8	28	52	4	2	4	.333	0	13.9	4.79
O'Rourke,Ryan	Min	29	60	0	60	56	6	24	68	1	3	3	.500	0	12.2	3.75

2017 Pitcher Projections

PLAYER			HOW MUCH			WHAT HE WILL GIVE UP					THE RESULTS					
Pitcher	Team	Age	G	GS	IP	H	HR	BB	SO	HB	W	L	Pct	Sv	BR/9	ERA
Osuna,Roberto	Tor	22	71	0	77	58	9	16	86	2	5	3	.625	42	8.9	2.22
Otero,Dan	Cle	32	65	0	79	78	4	11	55	2	5	3	.625	0	10.4	2.73
Ottavino,Adam	Col	31	66	0	62	61	6	19	61	3	4	3	.571	28	12.0	3.63
Owens,Henry	Bos	24	12	12	69	61	8	44	66	4	3	4	.429	0	14.2	4.57
Papelbon,Jonathan	Was	36	64	0	64	53	5	19	66	4	5	3	.625	18	10.7	2.81
Parker,Blake	NYY	32	58	0	59	49	6	22	67	2	4	3	.571	0	11.1	3.20
Parker,Jarrod	Oak	28	25	25	151	144	14	30	113	6	9	7	.563	0	10.7	3.34
Paxton,James	Sea	28	26	26	160	163	14	46	147	1	9	9	.500	0	11.8	3.71
Peacock,Brad	Hou	29	32	16	106	104	14	45	100	4	5	7	.417	0	13.0	4.33
Peavy,Jake	SF	36	28	28	164	160	20	47	135	5	9	9	.500	0	11.6	3.79
Pelfrey,Mike	Det	33	12	12	73	89	7	25	39	4	3	5	.375	0	14.5	5.18
Peralta,Wily	Mil	28	30	30	175	191	20	61	134	6	8	12	.400	0	13.3	4.53
Perez,Martin	Tex	26	32	32	188	202	16	67	121	4	9	12	.429	0	13.1	4.21
Perez,Oliver	Was	35	65	0	44	42	5	20	49	4	2	3	.400	0	13.5	4.30
Perez,Williams	Atl	26	22	22	112	114	9	39	76	7	6	7	.462	0	12.9	4.02
Perkins,Glen	Min	34	45	0	45	46	5	9	43	1	3	2	.600	2	11.2	3.60
Petit,Yusmeiro	Was	32	35	1	64	63	9	14	58	0	4	3	.571	0	10.8	3.52
Petricka,Jake	CWS	29	55	0	53	54	3	26	38	1	2	3	.400	0	13.8	4.25
Phelps,David	Mia	30	51	0	92	88	9	35	85	4	5	5	.500	8	12.4	3.82
Pineda,Michael	NYY	28	31	31	182	178	22	43	186	5	11	9	.550	0	11.2	3.66
Pomeranz,Drew	Bos	28	31	31	177	163	21	67	170	3	11	9	.550	0	11.8	3.92
Porcello,Rick	Bos	28	33	33	220	231	24	37	158	9	13	12	.520	0	11.3	3.72
Pressly,Ryan	Min	28	65	0	70	72	5	24	57	1	4	4	.500	0	12.5	3.73
Price,David	Bos	31	33	33	229	211	23	48	222	5	16	10	.615	0	10.4	3.22
Putnam,Zach	CWS	29	47	0	46	43	4	20	46	1	2	3	.400	0	12.5	3.72
Quackenbush,Kevin	SD	28	62	0	62	55	4	20	60	1	4	3	.571	4	11.0	2.90
Qualls,Chad	Col	38	60	0	52	57	6	12	39	1	3	3	.500	0	12.1	4.15
Quintana,Jose	CWS	28	32	32	210	208	18	49	173	5	12	11	.522	0	11.2	3.51
Ramirez,Erasmo	TB	27	63	0	89	90	11	24	67	5	4	6	.400	5	12.0	3.94
Ramirez,JC	LAA	28	71	0	83	83	10	28	61	3	4	5	.444	4	12.4	4.01
Ramirez,Jose	Atl	27	57	0	58	55	6	33	60	5	3	4	.429	0	14.4	4.50
Ramirez,Noe	Bos	27	48	0	43	41	4	17	43	2	2	2	.500	0	12.6	3.98
Ramos,A.J.	Mia	30	64	0	64	46	3	32	74	3	4	3	.571	38	11.4	2.67
Ramos,Edubray	Phi	24	68	0	67	60	4	16	66	3	4	3	.571	0	10.6	2.82
Ranaudo,Anthony	CWS	27	40	11	97	98	14	32	71	3	4	6	.400	0	12.3	4.27
Ray,Robbie	Ari	25	31	31	176	186	17	74	185	7	8	11	.421	0	13.7	4.50
Rea,Colin	Mia	26	20	20	110	104	8	41	87	6	6	6	.500	0	12.4	3.68
Reed,Addison	NYM	28	75	0	73	65	7	17	79	1	5	3	.625	0	10.2	2.71
Richard,Clayton	SD	33	33	17	114	128	12	38	65	3	5	8	.385	0	13.3	4.50
Richards,Garrett	LAA	29	28	28	177	163	13	67	146	6	10	9	.526	0	12.0	3.56
Rivero,Felipe	Pit	25	75	0	78	70	6	31	80	4	5	4	.556	3	12.1	3.46
Roark,Tanner	Was	30	33	33	205	193	19	63	155	9	12	10	.545	0	11.6	3.60
Robertson,David	CWS	32	63	0	63	49	6	25	83	1	4	3	.571	36	10.7	2.86
Robles,Hansel	NYM	26	65	0	72	64	8	30	75	3	4	4	.500	3	12.1	3.63
Rodney,Fernando	Mia	40	69	0	67	58	5	35	69	5	4	4	.500	0	13.2	3.76
Rodon,Carlos	CWS	24	31	31	184	180	20	72	191	9	9	12	.429	0	12.8	4.06
Rodriguez,Eduardo	Bos	24	31	31	172	171	20	53	148	4	10	9	.526	0	11.9	3.87
Rodriguez,Fernando	Oak	33	61	0	62	53	5	25	63	2	4	3	.571	0	11.6	3.19
Rodriguez,Francisco	Det	35	60	0	60	48	7	18	62	1	4	3	.571	43	10.0	2.85
Rodriguez,Joely	Phi	25	46	0	48	56	4	19	31	0	2	4	.333	0	14.1	4.69
Rodriguez,Paco	LAD	26	56	0	48	36	3	19	55	1	4	2	.667	0	10.5	2.63
Roe,Chaz	Atl	30	45	0	45	44	4	18	42	2	2	3	.400	0	12.8	4.00
Rogers,Taylor	Min	26	64	0	68	80	4	20	55	3	3	5	.375	0	13.6	4.50
Romero,Enny	TB	26	50	0	45	46	5	23	40	1	2	3	.400	0	14.0	4.60
Romo,Sergio	SF	34	63	0	57	46	6	11	65	2	4	2	.667	26	9.3	2.37
Rondon,Bruce	Det	26	50	0	50	43	4	27	60	3	3	3	.500	0	13.1	3.96
Rondon,Hector	ChC	29	66	0	64	55	6	12	62	2	4	3	.571	37	9.7	2.67
Rosenthal,Trevor	StL	27	65	0	65	57	3	36	79	3	4	3	.571	2	13.3	3.74
Ross Jr.,Robbie	Bos	28	58	0	54	52	5	21	55	4	3	3	.500	0	12.8	3.67
Ross,Joe	Was	24	24	24	135	129	12	36	122	5	8	7	.533	0	11.3	3.47
Ross,Tyson	SD	30	30	30	185	176	12	77	174	9	10	11	.476	0	12.7	3.79
Rosscup,Zac	ChC	29	51	0	48	34	4	25	66	1	4	2	.667	0	11.2	2.81
Rusin,Chris	Col	30	39	3	87	100	10	25	57	3	4	6	.400	0	13.2	4.66
Ryan,Kyle	Det	25	62	0	61	65	5	21	37	1	3	4	.429	0	12.8	3.98
Ryu,Hyun-Jin	LAD	30	26	26	155	156	12	21	130	2	11	6	.647	0	10.4	3.25
Rzepczynski,Marc	Was	31	67	0	46	45	3	25	43	3	2	3	.400	0	14.3	4.30
Sabathia,CC	NYY	36	29	29	171	174	22	58	149	7	9	10	.474	0	12.6	4.21
Salas,Fernando	NYM	32	72	0	68	60	8	16	66	2	5	3	.625	0	10.3	3.04
Salazar,Danny	Cle	27	30	30	186	166	21	71	211	4	10	10	.500	0	11.7	3.68
Sale,Chris	CWS	28	33	33	231	195	24	47	259	14	16	10	.615	0	10.0	3.04
Samardzija,Jeff	SF	32	32	32	208	197	24	51	181	7	12	11	.522	0	11.0	3.55
Sampson,Keyvius	Cin	26	32	12	89	85	10	49	84	3	4	6	.400	0	13.9	4.45
Sanchez,Aaron	Tor	24	31	31	196	169	15	75	158	8	13	9	.591	0	11.6	3.40
Sanchez,Anibal	Det	33	28	28	177	173	21	58	159	4	9	10	.474	0	11.9	3.86
Santana,Ervin	Min	34	29	29	182	176	21	55	143	6	10	10	.500	0	11.7	3.76
Santiago,Hector	Min	29	32	32	183	171	26	77	157	9	9	12	.429	0	12.6	4.18
Scahill,Rob	Mil	30	61	0	64	68	5	26	51	4	3	4	.429	0	13.8	4.36
Scheppers,Tanner	Tex	30	45	0	39	38	4	20	34	3	2	3	.400	5	14.1	4.62
Scherzer,Max	Was	32	33	33	220	182	25	48	249	6	16	8	.667	0	9.7	2.99
Schugel,A.J.	Pit	28	40	0	51	56	4	15	40	2	3	3	.500	0	12.9	4.06
Scribner,Evan	Sea	31	60	0	62	53	8	9	68	2	5	2	.714	0	9.3	2.61

2017 Pitcher Projections

PLAYER			HOW MUCH			WHAT HE WILL GIVE UP					THE RESULTS					
Pitcher	Team	Age	G	GS	IP	H	HR	BB	SO	HB	W	L	Pct	Sv	BR/9	ERA
Severino,Luis	NYY	23	29	29	165	159	14	52	155	6	10	8	.556	0	11.8	3.65
Shaw,Bryan	Cle	29	72	0	66	59	6	24	57	2	4	3	.571	0	11.6	3.41
Shields,James	CWS	35	30	30	172	171	24	70	150	7	7	12	.368	0	13.0	4.40
Shipley,Braden	Ari	25	29	29	174	193	16	54	118	3	9	11	.450	0	12.9	4.29
Shoemaker,Matt	LAA	30	29	29	182	191	24	38	154	7	9	11	.450	0	11.7	3.91
Shreve,Chasen	NYY	26	48	0	44	39	5	19	46	1	3	2	.600	0	12.1	3.68
Siegrist,Kevin	StL	27	67	0	63	47	6	28	74	3	4	3	.571	2	11.1	2.86
Simon,Alfredo	Cin	36	21	15	82	87	11	33	55	5	3	6	.333	0	13.7	4.83
Sipp,Tony	Hou	33	57	0	44	37	7	15	47	1	3	2	.600	0	10.8	3.48
Skaggs,Tyler	LAA	25	27	27	157	148	14	54	150	5	9	8	.529	0	11.9	3.61
Smith,Carson	Bos	27	40	0	38	29	1	12	47	3	3	1	.750	0	10.4	2.37
Smith,Chris	Oak	36	55	0	63	59	6	24	60	1	3	4	.429	0	12.0	3.57
Smith,Joe	ChC	33	49	0	48	39	4	14	40	3	4	2	.667	0	10.5	2.81
Smith,Josh	Cin	29	65	0	63	68	7	24	51	3	3	4	.429	0	13.6	4.57
Smith,Will	SF	27	63	0	48	48	5	19	48	1	2	3	.400	0	12.8	4.13
Smoker,Josh	NYM	28	69	0	63	57	6	21	84	1	4	3	.571	0	11.3	3.29
Smyly,Drew	TB	28	29	29	175	164	25	51	171	2	9	10	.474	0	11.2	3.70
Snell,Blake	TB	24	30	30	185	165	13	94	224	3	10	11	.476	0	12.7	3.75
Socolovich,Miguel	StL	30	58	0	62	51	4	20	63	1	5	2	.714	0	10.5	2.61
Solis,Sammy	Was	28	57	0	62	57	2	27	63	3	4	3	.571	0	12.6	3.34
Soria,Joakim	KC	33	71	0	67	61	7	23	69	2	4	4	.500	0	11.6	3.49
Stephenson,Robert	Cin	24	27	27	156	146	24	92	147	6	6	11	.353	0	14.1	4.90
Storen,Drew	Sea	29	66	0	60	55	5	15	58	4	4	3	.571	0	11.1	3.15
Straily,Dan	Cin	28	32	32	190	176	25	67	176	9	10	11	.476	0	11.9	3.84
Strasburg,Stephen	Was	28	28	28	172	146	17	44	200	5	12	7	.632	0	10.2	3.03
Street,Huston	LAA	33	62	0	62	54	8	24	57	0	4	3	.571	29	11.3	3.48
Strickland,Hunter	SF	28	68	0	61	51	5	15	61	2	5	2	.714	13	10.0	2.51
Stripling,Ross	LAD	27	37	14	93	94	9	27	74	0	5	5	.500	0	11.7	3.68
Stroman,Marcus	Tor	26	31	31	205	200	18	55	182	5	12	10	.545	0	11.4	3.56
Strop,Pedro	ChC	32	65	0	60	42	4	22	67	4	5	2	.714	0	10.2	2.40
Suarez,Albert	SF	27	32	12	85	89	9	26	59	2	4	5	.444	0	12.4	4.13
Suter,Brent	Mil	27	27	4	43	47	3	11	31	2	2	3	.400	0	12.6	3.98
Swarzak,Anthony	NYY	31	55	0	62	70	7	14	42	1	3	4	.429	0	12.3	4.21
Syndergaard,Noah	NYM	24	32	32	204	184	18	48	235	4	14	9	.609	0	10.4	3.18
Taillon,Jameson	Pit	25	28	28	174	166	15	25	154	6	12	7	.632	0	10.2	3.16
Tanaka,Masahiro	NYY	28	31	31	200	180	25	36	178	3	14	8	.636	0	9.9	3.19
Tazawa,Junichi	Bos	31	58	0	56	55	6	15	57	1	3	3	.500	0	11.4	3.54
Teheran,Julio	Atl	26	32	32	203	186	23	53	173	9	13	10	.565	0	11.0	3.46
Tepera,Ryan	Tor	29	61	0	56	52	5	22	50	4	3	3	.500	0	12.5	3.86
Thompson,Jake	Phi	23	23	23	135	135	15	52	102	7	6	9	.400	0	12.9	4.20
Thornburg,Tyler	Mil	28	66	0	70	58	8	28	79	2	4	4	.500	37	11.3	3.34
Tillman,Chris	Bal	29	32	32	198	190	24	74	152	5	11	11	.500	0	12.2	3.95
Tomlin,Josh	Cle	32	30	30	178	183	32	21	126	4	10	10	.500	0	10.5	3.79
Tonkin,Michael	Min	27	60	0	66	65	7	20	68	3	3	4	.429	0	12.0	3.82
Torres,Carlos	Mil	34	70	0	80	74	8	28	72	2	5	4	.556	0	11.7	3.49
Treinen,Blake	Was	29	73	0	72	70	4	30	59	2	4	4	.500	0	12.8	3.63
Triggs,Andrew	Oak	28	35	10	78	72	4	18	72	7	5	4	.556	0	11.2	3.00
Tuivailala,Samuel	StL	24	62	0	61	54	4	34	77	4	3	3	.500	0	13.6	3.84
Uehara,Koji	Bos	42	54	0	51	36	6	11	62	1	4	1	.800	4	8.5	2.12
Urena,Jose	Mia	25	27	19	113	121	12	42	78	6	5	7	.417	0	13.5	4.46
Valdez,Jose	LAA	27	48	0	47	44	5	29	44	1	2	3	.400	0	14.2	4.40
Vargas,Jason	KC	34	30	30	185	192	24	40	125	4	9	12	.429	0	11.5	3.84
Velasquez,Vince	Phi	25	30	30	173	156	23	61	197	3	9	10	.474	0	11.4	3.69
Venditte,Pat	Sea	32	47	0	53	50	5	23	54	2	3	3	.500	0	12.7	3.91
Ventura,Yordano	KC	26	33	33	200	193	19	81	179	9	9	13	.409	0	12.7	3.96
Verlander,Justin	Det	34	33	33	220	192	22	56	214	6	15	10	.600	0	10.4	3.15
Verrett,Logan	NYM	27	45	8	86	88	11	34	66	3	4	6	.400	0	13.1	4.40
Villanueva,Carlos	SD	33	41	0	64	66	9	15	55	2	3	4	.429	0	11.7	3.94
Vincent,Nick	Sea	30	65	0	66	58	7	18	72	2	4	3	.571	0	10.6	3.00
Vizcaino,Arodys	Atl	26	62	0	61	55	4	34	68	2	3	4	.429	2	13.4	3.84
Vogelsong,Ryan	Pit	39	38	14	103	103	12	42	80	4	5	6	.455	0	13.0	4.28
Volquez,Edinson	KC	33	30	30	184	182	18	71	148	8	8	12	.400	0	12.8	4.01
Wacha,Michael	StL	25	28	28	170	162	16	55	148	4	10	9	.526	0	11.7	3.65
Wainwright,Adam	StL	35	33	33	199	189	14	55	168	5	13	9	.591	0	11.3	3.39
Walden,Jordan	StL	29	55	0	51	43	3	25	58	1	3	2	.600	0	12.2	3.18
Walker,Taijuan	Sea	24	29	29	178	168	26	52	167	12	10	10	.500	0	11.7	3.89
Warren,Adam	NYY	29	67	0	75	73	7	28	59	3	4	4	.500	0	12.5	3.84
Watson,Tony	Pit	32	70	0	69	56	6	18	61	4	5	3	.625	32	10.2	2.61
Weaver,Jered	LAA	34	31	31	180	173	25	48	131	6	10	10	.500	0	11.4	3.80
Weber,Ryan	Atl	26	32	5	44	50	4	8	27	2	2	3	.400	0	12.3	4.09
Wheeler,Zack	NYM	27	11	11	62	55	5	28	60	4	4	3	.571	0	12.6	3.63
Whitley,Chase	TB	28	39	12	84	83	8	23	73	4	4	5	.444	0	11.8	3.64
Wilhelmsen,Tom	Sea	33	55	0	57	52	6	23	48	2	3	3	.500	0	12.2	3.63
Williams,Trevor	Pit	25	30	12	84	97	7	29	61	2	4	6	.400	0	13.7	4.61
Wilson,Alex	Det	30	62	0	71	70	6	18	55	2	4	4	.500	0	11.4	3.42
Wilson,C.J.	LAA	36	29	29	172	158	15	65	149	9	10	9	.526	0	12.1	3.66
Wilson,Justin	Det	29	65	0	59	52	5	19	56	2	4	3	.571	0	11.1	3.05
Wilson,Tyler	Bal	27	40	5	64	71	8	16	46	2	3	4	.429	0	12.5	4.36
Wimmers,Alex	Min	28	59	0	60	63	5	29	55	1	3	4	.429	0	14.0	4.50
Wisler,Matt	Atl	24	30	30	172	177	23	52	136	5	8	11	.421	0	12.2	4.19
Withrow,Chris	Atl	28	65	0	59	51	5	31	58	2	3	3	.500	0	12.8	3.66

2017 Pitcher Projections

PLAYER			HOW MUCH			WHAT HE WILL GIVE UP					THE RESULTS					
Pitcher	Team	Age	G	GS	IP	H	HR	BB	SO	HB	W	L	Pct	Sv	BR/9	ERA
Wittgren, Nick	Mia	26	64	0	63	62	7	12	56	1	4	3	.571	0	10.7	3.29
Wood, Alex	LAD	26	36	11	87	82	7	27	79	3	6	4	.600	0	11.6	3.31
Wood, Blake	Cin	31	69	0	74	74	6	39	74	2	3	5	.375	0	14.0	4.38
Wood, Travis	ChC	30	73	0	57	53	6	23	48	2	3	3	.500	0	12.3	3.79
Workman, Brandon	Bos	28	51	0	48	49	8	24	44	1	2	3	.400	0	13.9	5.06
Worley, Vance	Bal	29	34	6	67	72	7	21	48	2	3	4	.429	0	12.8	4.16
Wright, Daniel	LAA	26	12	11	60	72	6	19	46	3	2	4	.333	0	14.1	4.95
Wright, Mike	Bal	27	33	0	88	96	10	28	63	5	4	6	.400	0	13.2	4.50
Wright, Steven	Bos	32	30	30	198	195	20	70	152	7	11	11	.500	0	12.4	3.91
Yates, Kirby	NYY	30	62	0	62	53	8	27	77	4	4	3	.571	0	12.2	3.77
Ynoa, Gabriel	NYM	24	65	0	64	73	7	16	35	3	3	4	.429	0	12.9	4.50
Young, Chris	KC	38	37	6	75	71	14	31	55	1	3	5	.375	0	12.4	4.44
Ziegler, Brad	Bos	37	68	0	66	59	3	22	46	2	5	3	.625	4	11.3	3.00
Zimmermann, Jordan	Det	31	29	29	175	173	18	37	137	6	10	9	.526	0	11.1	3.55
Zych, Tony	Sea	26	58	0	61	62	3	21	59	4	3	3	.500	0	12.8	3.69

The Favorite Toy

Lindsay Zeck

The Favorite Toy is a method invented by Bill James to estimate a player's chance to both meet career milestones and to break records. It uses the additional number of seasons a player is likely to play, the performance he needs in each of those seasons to meet said goal, and the rate at which the player has been moving toward the goal.

This season, Ichiro Suzuki recorded his 3,000th hit against the Colorado Rockies to become the 30th ever player to do so. Adrian Beltre has a 95 percent chance of reaching this milestone, and with only 58 hits to go, he will likely do so in the 2017 season. Albert Pujols increased his chance to meet the milestone to 83 percent with his addition of 159 hits in 2016; he is now only 175 hits below the 3,000-hit mark.

After the 2015 season, Alex Rodriguez had a 92 percent chance to reach the amazing 700 career home runs milestone. However, with only 65 games played and nine home runs in 2016, and having now retired, he fell short of this achievement by four home runs. Only three players have ever reached 700 home runs in their careers: Barry Bonds (762), Hank Aaron (755), and Babe Ruth (714). Pujols is now the most likely player to reach this milestone with a 42 percent chance of hitting the 109 additional home runs that he needs before he retires. There is a 96 percent chance that Pujols will become the ninth member of the 600 home run club. Needing only nine home runs, we will likely see him do it during the 2017 season.

Pujols still has a small (nine percent) chance of breaking Bonds' 762 home run record. He has an even better (18 percent) chance of breaking Hank Aaron's record of 2,297 RBI. The 36-year-old still needs 481 RBI to break this record. His RBI total of 119 in 2016 was the greatest number of runs he has batted in since 2009. He now only needs 183 RBI (and has a 76 percent chance) to become the fifth player to achieve 2,000 RBI in his career.

It is definitely worth mentioning that Jose Fernandez would have been at the top of the leader board for having the greatest percent chance of pitching a no-hitter over the rest of his career at 47 percent. This was 20 percentage points higher than Max Scherzer, who currently tops the list. It is not surprising that the extremely talented 24-year-old, Fernandez, had the best chance by a wide margin. He led the league in 2016 with 12.5 strikeouts per 9 innings, and his 2.30 FIP (Fielding Independent Pitching) was second to only Noah Syndergaard. At such a young age, he should have still had many more seasons to play, and with the dominance with which he pitched, many more outings that would likely have been opportunities to pitch a no-hitter.

3,000 Hits	
% chance to reach milestone	
Rodriguez, Alex	done
Suzuki, Ichiro	done
Beltre, Adrian	95%
Pujols, Albert	83%
Cabrera, Miguel	64%
Cano, Robinson	51%
Markakis, Nick	27%
Altuve, Jose	22%
Cabrera, Melky	19%
Andrus, Elvis	16%
Trout, Mike	14%
Castro, Starlin	14%
Jones, Adam	14%
Hosmer, Eric	13%
Pedroia, Dustin	12%
McCutchen, Andrew	11%
Gonzalez, Adrian	11%
Bogaerts, Xander	11%
Freeman, Freddie	11%
Machado, Manny	11%
Arenado, Nolan	10%
Kemp, Matt	10%
Longoria, Evan	9%
Betts, Mookie	9%
Segura, Jean	9%
Upton, Justin	9%
Yelich, Christian	8%
Rizzo, Anthony	8%
LeMahieu, DJ	7%
Escobar, Alcides	6%
Kinsler, Ian	6%
Beltran, Carlos	5%
Harper, Bryce	5%
Goldschmidt, Paul	4%
Heyward, Jason	4%
Seager, Kyle	4%
Braun, Ryan	3%
Eaton, Adam	3%
Mauer, Joe	3%
Seager, Corey	2%
Odor, Rougned	2%
Prado, Martin	2%
Lindor, Francisco	< 1%
Blackmon, Charlie	< 1%
Desmond, Ian	< 1%

Career Targets

762 Home Runs
% chance to break record

Pujols, Albert	9%
Trout, Mike	2%

2,298 RBI
% chance to break record

Pujols, Albert	18%
Cabrera, Miguel	9%
Arenado, Nolan	3%

2,296 Runs Scored
% chance to break record

Trout, Mike	9%

4,257 Hits
% chance to break record

Altuve, Jose	3%

900 Home Runs
% chance to reach milestone

2,000 RBI
% chance to reach milestone

Rodriguez, Alex	done
Pujols, Albert	76%
Cabrera, Miguel	47%
Arenado, Nolan	11%
Trout, Mike	8%
Beltre, Adrian	4%
Rizzo, Anthony	1%

6,857 Total Bases
% chance to break record

Trout, Mike	6%
Cabrera, Miguel	5%
Pujols, Albert	2%
Machado, Manny	< 1%

4,000 Hits
% chance to reach milestone

Altuve, Jose	7%
Cabrera, Miguel	3%
Trout, Mike	< 1%
Bogaerts, Xander	< 1%

800 Home Runs
% chance to reach milestone

600 Home Runs
% chance to reach milestone

Rodriguez, Alex	done
Pujols, Albert	96%
Cabrera, Miguel	35%
Davis, Chris	15%
Trout, Mike	13%
Arenado, Nolan	12%
Encarnacion, Edwin	12%
Stanton, Giancarlo	9%
Machado, Manny	8%

793 Doubles
% chance to break record

Altuve, Jose	7%
Cabrera, Miguel	6%
Freeman, Freddie	1%
Betts, Mookie	< 1%
Rizzo, Anthony	< 1%

Most Likely No-Hitter
% chance to reach milestone

Scherzer, Max	27%
Ray, Robbie	24%
Syndergaard, Noah	23%
Strasburg, Stephen	20%
Bumgarner, Madison	20%
Archer, Chris	20%
Pineda, Michael	18%
Velasquez, Vince	18%
Salazar, Danny	18%

700 Home Runs
% chance to reach milestone

Pujols, Albert	42%
Trout, Mike	8%
Arenado, Nolan	4%
Cabrera, Miguel	2%
Machado, Manny	1%
Davis, Chris	< 1%

500 Home Runs
% chance to reach milestone

Rodriguez, Alex	done
Pujols, Albert	done
Ortiz, David	done
Cabrera, Miguel	74%
Beltre, Adrian	64%
Encarnacion, Edwin	44%
Davis, Chris	34%
Upton, Justin	21%
Teixeira, Mark	21%
Bruce, Jay	21%

1,000 Stolen Bases
% chance to reach milestone

The 300-Win Candidates

Bill James

Max Scherzer is emerging as the best candidate among the current crop to get 300 wins; Max Scherzer or Clayton Kershaw. Kershaw is excluded from the list below because we have a rule in the system that says you're not a candidate if your innings pitched in the season plus your career wins are less than 300. Since Kershaw pitched only 149 innings this year, he didn't make the list, and there's actually a really good reason for that; history shows that if a pitcher gets hurt one year he will tend to get hurt the next, and many of the most dominant pitchers in history did not get to 300 wins.

But let's add Kershaw to our mental list, anyway; he'll be back near the top of the list if he stays healthy in 2017. CC Sabathia and Roy Halladay were the last really good candidates for 300 wins, but after they both collapsed three or four years ago it looked like we might not see another 300-game winner for a good many years. That still might be true, but what happens over time is that the pool of potential 300-game winners collapses and then starts slowly to re-form. Scherzer, Kershaw, Bumgarner, David Price, Verlander, Jon Lester, Cole Hamels, Johnny Cueto, Felix Hernandez, Zack Greinke; the odds are against each one of these pitchers, but not necessarily against ALL of them. One of them might make that death-defying march across the last 100 wins.

Bartolo Colon is on our list. You know, sometimes the formulas work beautifully, and sometimes they don't really work, but what Bartolo has already done defies belief, so you have to give him that. The closest historical parallel to Colon is Robin Roberts. Roberts didn't have a slightly comical body, and his last good season was when he was 38, which is quite different than 43, but Roberts was a pitcher (like Colon) who had a tremendous fastball when he was young; he wasn't ONE OF the best pitchers in baseball in the early 1950s, he was the best. He passed through a serious career crisis in his early thirties, as Colon did, and after he re-emerged from that crisis he stopped throwing anything except the fastball. He never threw a lot of other stuff anyway, but as he got old he just threw 100% fastballs or nearly 100%, like Colon; the fastball wasn't that good, but what he could do with it was amazing. He could clip corners with his fastball like Edward Scissorhands. He never walked anybody, and, like Colon and Koji Uehara, who is also in his forties, he just had an inexplicable ability to throw an 88-MPH fastball through the heart of the strike zone and have people swing and miss. The odds are that one pitcher now active will get to 300 career wins. I guess my money would be on Verlander.

Pitchers on Course For 300 Wins

Name	2016 Age	R/L	W	L	EWL	Momentum	Chance
Scherzer, Max	31	R	125	69	18.4	.881	30%
Bumgarner, Madison	26	L	100	67	15.7	.890	23%
Colon, Bartolo	43	R	233	162	12.7	.733	20%
Price, David	30	L	121	65	15.8	.862	19%
Verlander, Justin	33	R	173	106	14.3	.818	17%
Lester, Jon	32	L	146	84	15.4	.820	14%
Lackey, John	37	R	176	135	11.4	.799	9%
Hamels, Cole	32	L	136	96	13.3	.810	7%
Cueto, Johnny	30	R	114	75	14.7	.810	7%
Porcello, Rick	27	R	107	82	16.2	.743	3%
Sale, Chris	27	L	74	50	15.2	.788	3%
Sabathia, CC	35	L	223	141	8.7	.662	3%
Hernandez, Felix	30	R	154	109	11.1	.755	2%
Greinke, Zack	32	R	155	100	12.6	.719	2%
Wainwright, Adam	34	R	134	76	11.1	.770	2%
Shields, James	34	R	133	116	8.4	.746	<1%
Santana, Ervin	33	R	133	116	8.1	.700	<1%
Weaver, Jered	33	R	150	93	9.7	.622	<1%
Nolasco, Ricky	33	R	108	103	8.0	.676	<1%

EWL: Established Win Level

Baseball Glossary

% Inherited Scored
The percentage of inherited baserunners a relief pitcher allows to score.

% Pitches Taken
The percentage of pitches that a batter does not swing at out of the total number of pitches thrown to him.

1st Batter Average
The Batting Average that a relief pitcher allows to the first batter he faces when he enters a game.

1st Batter OBP
The On-Base Percentage that a relief pitcher allows to the first batter he faces when he enters a game.

1st to 3rd (Baserunning)
"Moved" is the number of times a runner goes from 1st base to 3rd base on a SINGLE. "Chances" are the number of times a runner is on 1st base and a batter is credited with a SINGLE.

1st to Home (Baserunning)
"Moved" is the number of times a runner goes from 1st base to home on a DOUBLE. "Chances" are the number of times a runner is on 1st base and a batter is credited with a DOUBLE.

2nd to Home (Baserunning)
"Moved" is the number of times a runner goes from 2nd base to home on a SINGLE. "Chances" are the number of times a runner is on 2nd base and a batter is credited with a SINGLE.

Active Career Batting Leaders
A list of batting leaders among active (appearing in the most recent season) players. An active player is eligible when he meets the minimum requirements for the following categories:

> 1,000 At Bats—Batting Average, On-Base Percentage, Slugging Average, At
>   Bats Per HR, At Bats Per GDP, At Bats Per RBI, Strikeout to Walk Ratio
> 100 Stolen Base Attempts—Stolen Base Success Percentage

Active Career Pitching Leaders
A list of pitching leaders among active (appearing in the most recent season) players. An active player is eligible when he meets the minimum requirements for the following categories:

> 750 Innings Pitched—Earned Run Average, Opponent Batting Average, all "Per
>   9 Innings" categories, Strikeout to Walk Ratio
> 250 Games Started—Complete Game Frequency
> 100 Decisions—Win-Loss Percentage

AVG Allowed ScPos
The Batting Average allowed by a pitcher while pitching with runners in scoring position.

AVG Bases Loaded
The Batting Average of a hitter while batting with the bases loaded.

Base Taken
A player is credited with a Base Taken whenever he moves up a base on a Wild Pitch, Passed Ball, Balk, Sacrifice Fly, or Defensive Indifference.

Batting Average
Hits divided by at bats.

Blown Save
When a relief pitcher enters a game in a Save Situation (see definition for Save Situation) and allows the other team to score the tying or go-ahead run.

Bomb (Intentional Walk)
An Intentional Walk is counted as a "Bomb" if
1. The next batter, after the IBB, does not ground into a double play, and
2. Multiple runs are scored in the inning, after the intentional walk.

BR Gain (Baserunning)
BR Gain (or Loss if a negative number) is the total of all the types of extra baserunning advances minus the (triple) penalty for all the BR Outs compared with what would be expected based on the MLB averages.

BR Outs (Baserunning)
BR Outs include the sum of Outs Advancing, Doubled Offs, and when a runner is tagged out on the bases when another runner moves up on a Wild Pitch, Passed Ball, or scores on a Sacrifice Fly.

BS Win
A Blown Save Win is a "win" credited to a reliever who has blown a save opportunity.

Career Targets
This method, also called the Favorite Toy, is a way to estimate the probability that a player will achieve a specific career goal. In this example, 3,000 hits will be used. The four components of the formula are:

1. Needed Hits. This is the number of Hits (or any statistic) that a player needs to reach a desired goal.

2. Years Remaining. This is the estimated number of years remaining in the player's career. It is determined using the player's age (on June 30th of the previous year; use 2016 when making the calculation after the 2016 season is complete). The formula is (42 - age) divided by two. This means a player who is 20 years old will have 11 remaining seasons, a player who is 25 years old will have 8.5 remaining seasons and a player who is 35 years old will have 3.5 remaining seasons. If the player is a catcher, then multiply his remaining seasons by .7. The only stipulation is that years remaining must always be greater than or equal to 1.5.

3. Established Hit Level. The Established Hit Level is a weighted average of the player's hits over the past three seasons. To calculate the Established Hit Level after the 2016 season is complete, add 2014 Hits, (2015 Hits multiplied by two) and (2016 Hits multiplied by three), then divide by six. If the Established Hit

Level is less than 75% of the most recent performance (2016 Hits in this case), then the Established Hit Level is equal to .75 times the most recent performance.

4. Projected Remaining Hits. This is calculated by multiplying Years Remaining by the Established Hit Level.

The probability of achieving the specified goal is found by dividing Projected Remaining Hits by Needed Hits, then subtracting .5. The maximum that any player has of achieving a goal is .85 raised to the power of (Need Hits / Established Hit Level). This prevents the possibility of a player reaching a goal from being higher than 100 percent, which is impossible.

Catcher's ERA
The ERA for a catcher is equal to the ERA of pitchers pitching while the catcher is playing behind the plate. It is calculated exactly like ERA for pitchers. Take the number of earned runs allowed while the catcher is playing, multiply it by 9 and then divide it by the total number of defensive innings that the catcher was behind the plate.

Cheap Win
A starting pitcher who wins the game with a game score under 50 gets credit for a cheap win. See Game Score.

Clean Outing
A Clean Outing is a game in which the reliever is not charged with a run (earned or otherwise) AND does not allow an inherited runner to score.

Cleanup Slugging Average
The Slugging Average of a batter when he bats in the cleanup spot, or fourth, in the batting order.

Close and Late
A situation in a game that is very similar to a Save Situation. The following requirements are necessary for a Close and Late game:
1. The game is in the seventh inning or later AND
2. The batting team is either leading by one run or tied OR
3. The tying run is on base, at bat, or on deck.

Component ERA (ERC)
A statistic that estimates what a pitcher's ERA should have been, based on his pitching performance. The ERC formula is calculated as follows:

1. Subtract the pitcher's Home Runs Allowed from his Hits Allowed.
2. Multiply Step 1 by 1.255.
3. Multiply his Home Runs Allowed by four.
4. Add Steps 2 and 3 together.
5. Multiply Step 4 by .89.
6. Add his Walks and Hit Batsmen.
7. Multiply Step 6 by .475.
8. Add Steps 5 and 7 together.

This yields the pitcher's total base estimate (PTB), which is:

$$PTB = 0.89 \times (1.255 \times (H - HR) + 4 \times HR) + 0.475 \times (BB + HB)$$

For those pitchers for whom there is intentional walk data, use this formula instead:

$$PTB = 0.89 \times (1.255 \times (H - HR) + 4 \times HR) + 0.56 \times (BB + HB - IBB)$$

9. Add Hits and Walks and Hit Batsmen.
10. Multiply Step 9 by PTB.
11. Divide Step 10 by Batters Facing Pitcher. If BFP data is unavailable, approximate it by multiplying Innings Pitched by 2.9, then adding Step 9.
12. Multiply Step 11 by 9.
13. Divide Step 12 by Innings Pitched.
14. Subtract .56 from Step 13.

This is the pitcher's ERC, which is:

$$\frac{(H + BB + HB) \times PTB}{BFP \times IP} \times 9 - 0.56$$

If the result after Step 13 is less than 2.24, adjust the formula as follows:

$$\frac{(H + BB + HB) \times PTB}{BFP \times IP} \times 9 \times 0.75$$

Consecutive Days
A count of how many times the pitcher was used after having pitched on the previous day or (in a few cases) in an earlier game on the same day.

Defensive Runs Saved
Defensive Runs Saved (Runs Saved, for short) is the innovative metric introduced by John Dewan in *The Fielding Bible—Volume II* and modified in *The Fielding Bible—Volume III* and *The Fielding Bible—Volume IV*. The Runs Saved value indicates how many runs a player saved or cost his team in the field compared to the average player at his position. A player of zero Runs Saved is about average; a positive number of runs saved indicates above-average defense, below-average fielders post negative Runs Saved totals. There are eight components of Runs Saved:

Range and Positioning Runs Saved (all positions except Catcher)
Adjusted Earned Runs Saved (Catchers)
Strike Zone Runs Saved (Catchers)
Stolen Base Runs Saved (Catchers, Pitchers)
Bunt Runs Saved (Corner Infielders, Pitchers, Catchers)
Double Play Runs Saved (Infielders)
Outfield Arm Runs Saved (Outfielders)
Good Play/Misplay Runs Saved (All Positions)

Double Play %
Successful Double Plays divided by the number of Double Play opportunities. This statistic includes both the fielder who started the play and the pivot man.

Double Play Opportunity
A fielder is considered to have a double play opportunity when a ground ball is hit with a runner on first base and less than 2 outs and that fielder is involved in the play. This is used to calculate Double Play % and Pivot %.

Doubled Off
A runner is Doubled Off when he is out for failing to get back to his base before he, or the base, is tagged after a ball hit in the air is caught.

Early Entry
A count of the number of times the reliever entered the game in the sixth inning or earlier.

Earned Run Average
The number of earned runs that a pitcher surrenders per nine innings that he pitches. It is calculated by multiplying the total earned runs allowed by nine and dividing by the total number of innings pitched.

Easy Save
This label is used to separate Saves by difficulty level (Easy or Tough). A Save is considered Easy if the relief pitcher enters the game, pitches one inning or less, and the first batter he faces does not at least represent the tying run.

Fielding Percentage
The percentage of plays a player makes in the field without making an error out of the total number of opportunities. It is calculated by adding (Putouts plus Assists) and dividing by (Putouts plus Assists plus Errors).

Games Finished
The relief pitcher who is in the game for each team when the game ends is credited with a Game Finished.

Game Score
To determine the starting pitcher's Game Score:
Start with 50.
Add 1 point for each out recorded by the starting pitcher.
Add 2 points for each inning the pitcher completes after the fourth inning.
Add 1 point for each strikeout.
Subtract 2 points for each hit allowed.
Subtract 4 points for each earned run allowed.
Subtract 2 points for an unearned run.
Subtract 1 point for each walk.

GDP
Grounded into Double Play.

GDP Opportunity
This is a situation where the batter has a chance to ground into a double play. It occurs with at least a runner on first base and less than two outs.

Ground / Fly Ratio (Grd/Fly, GB/FB)
Calculated for both batters and pitchers. For batters, it is the number of groundballs hit divided by the number of flyballs hit. For pitchers, it is exactly the same but uses the number of groundballs and flyballs allowed. Every fair batted ball is included except for bunts and line drives.

Hold
A relief pitcher is given a Hold anytime he enters the game in a Save Situation (see definition for Save Situation), records one out or more, and exits the game without giving up the lead. If the pitcher finishes the game, then he will only earn credit for a Save. He cannot receive credit for both a Hold and a Save.

Holds Adjusted Save Percentage (same as Save/Hold Percentage)
Holds plus Saves divided by Holds plus Saves Opportunities.

Inherited Runner
When a relief pitcher enters the game, any runner who was on base at the time is considered an Inherited Runner.

Isolated Power
Slugging Average minus Batting Average.

K/BB Ratio
Strikeouts divided by Walks.

Leadoff On-Base Percentage
The On-Base Percentage of a batter when he bats leadoff, or first, in the batting order.

Leverage Index
Leverage is the amount of swing in the possible change in win probability, compared to the average swing in all situations. The average swing value, by definition, is indexed to 1.00.

If the score of the game is 12-0 or 14-1 the possible changes in win probability will be very close to negligible. Whether the pitcher gives up a home run or gets a double play ball doesn't really change the outcome of the game. There won't be much swing in either direction for the probability of the win. But in the late innings of a close game, the change in win probability among the various events will have rather wild swings. With a runner on first, two outs, down by one, and in the bottom of the ninth, the game can hinge on one swing of the bat. A home run and an out will both end the game, but with different outcomes for the teams involved. The Leverage Index we use (LI) was developed at the website Tangotiger.net, and compiled at the website FanGraphs.com.

Long Outing
A Long Outing is one in which the starting pitcher throws more than 110 pitches. Prior to 2002, we used 120 pitches as the cutoff in the Manager's Record section.

Long Save
A Long Save is when the pitcher credited with a save pitches more than one inning.

Manufactured Runs
1. A run that scores without a hit, or a run on which the only hit(s) is/are infield hits, is always scored as a Manufactured Run.
2. A run which is driven in by a home run is never scored a Manufactured Run, under any circumstance.
3. A run which is driven in by a double or a triple is scored as a Manufactured Run only if *two* of the four bases result from advancing on one of these four acts: a sacrifice bunt, a stolen base, a hit and run, or a bunt single.
4. Otherwise, a run is considered to be a Manufactured Run if two of the four bases do not result from the runner being forced along by a walk, a hit batsman, or a safe hit reaching the outfield.
5. A forceout or fielder's choice which does not improve the position of the base runners should not be counted as contributing toward a Manufactured Run. Advancing on a forceout or a fielder's choice DOES count toward a manufactured run, if the play is one which improves the position of the baserunners.
6. A base "gained" on a double play does not count as a contribution to a Manufactured Run. A run scored on a double play is a Manufactured Run only if two of the OTHER bases are not attributable to forced advancement.

Not Good Outcome (Intentional Walk)
A Not Good Outcome (NG) for an Intentional Walk occurs when one run scored in the inning after the intentional walk (and the next batter after the intentional walk did not ground into a double play).

Offensive Winning Percentage (OWP)
A player's Offensive Winning Percentage is the winning percentage of a hypothetical team which has an offense consisting of nine of that player, and pitching and defense which is average for the player's league. It is calculated by taking the square of RC/27 (see the definition for Runs Created per 27 Outs), dividing it by the sum of the square of RC/27 and the square of the average runs scored per game in the league.

On-Base Percentage
(Hits plus Walks plus Hit by Pitcher) divided by (At Bats plus Walks plus Hit by Pitcher plus Sacrifice Flies).

$$\frac{H + BB + HBP}{AB + BB + HBP + SF}$$

Opponent Batting Average
Hits Allowed divided by (Batters Faced minus Walks minus Hit Batsmen minus Sacrifice Hits minus Sacrifice Flies minus Catcher's Interference).

$$\frac{H}{BFP - BB - HBP - SH - SF - CI}$$

Opposition OPS
The OPS of the hitters facing the pitcher.

Out Advancing
A runner is out advancing when he is tagged out attempting to score from 2nd base on a single or from 1st base on a double, or attempting to go from 1st base to 3rd base on a single.

PA*
Used in the denominator for the calculation of On-Base Percentage. It is calculated by subtracting (Sacrifice Hits plus Times Reached Base on Defensive Interference) from Plate Appearances (see definition for Plate Appearances).

Park Index
To calculate the park index for home runs in a given ballpark, we take the total home runs of both the home team and its opponents at the ballpark and compare it to the total home runs of the home team and its opponents in other games. We then divide each of those totals by the at-bats in the equivalent situations, so that if there are more at-bats in either situation the index is not skewed. The result is then multiplied by 100 to yield the familiar form.

The park indices for doubles, triples, walks, strikeouts and home runs by lefties and righties are determined like home runs above—relative to at-bats. Indices of at-bats, runs, hits, errors and infield fielding errors (E-Infield) are calculated relative to games. The three batting average indices are calculated as is, since these are already relative to at-bats.

PCS (Pitchers' Caught Stealing)
The number of runners officially scored as Caught Stealing where the pitcher initiated the play. The normal Caught Stealing is when a runner is out attempting to steal a base but the play was initiated by the catcher. PCS plays are often referred to as pickoffs, but differ when the runner breaks towards the next base as opposed to returning to the base he was currently on. Pickoffs occur when the pitcher throws to a base that a runner is leading from, and the runner is out attempting to return to that base. Pickoffs are not an official statistic.

Pitches per PA
The total number of pitches a hitter sees divided by his total Plate Appearances.

Pivot %
Successful Double Plays turned by pivot man divided by the number of Double Play opportunities with that pivot man involved.

Plate Appearances
At Bats plus Total Walks plus Hit By Pitches plus Sacrifice Hits plus Sacrifice Flies plus Times Reached on Defensive Interference.

Platoon Advantage %
Platoon Advantage % is the percentage of players in the starting lineup who have the platoon advantage (i.e. bats right against a left-handed pitcher or bats left against a right-hander) against the starting pitcher; e.g. if the opposing starting pitcher is right handed and the batting team has six left-handed batters in its lineup, the platoon advantage for that game would be 67%.

Power/Speed Number

A single number that reflects a combination of power and speed. To calculate the Power/Speed Number, multiply Home Runs by Stolen Bases by two, and divide by the sum of Home Runs and Stolen Bases.

$$\frac{2 \times HR \times SB}{HR + SB}$$

PPO (Pitcher Pickoff)

The number of baserunners thrown out when a pitcher throws to a base with a leading baserunner, and the runner is tagged out attempting to return to the base. PPO is not an official statistic and does not count toward Caught Stealing totals.

Productive Out

An out made by the batter which moves at least one baserunner up at least one base. See also Unproductive Out.

Quality Start

A game where the starting pitcher pitches for at least six innings and allows no more than three earned runs.

Quality Start Percentage

Quality Starts divided by Games Started (see the definition for Quality Start).

Quick Hooks

Used in the Manager's Record. For Quick Hooks and Slow Hooks, a score is calculated for each game that is the sum of the number of Pitches plus 10 times the number of Runs Allowed. The bottom 25% of scores in the league are considered to be Quick Hooks.

Range and Positioning System

Formerly called the Plus/Minus System, the Range and Positioning System is a method for evaluating defensive play on batted balls. It is made possible by a game scoring system in which each batted ball is rated for type (line drive, grounder, etc.), velocity within its type (based on hang time for flyballs and time to the infielder or through the infield on groundballs), and location on the field. A player gets credit (a "plus" number) if he makes a play that at least one other player at his position missed during the season and he loses credit (a "minus" number") if he misses a play that at least one player made. The size of the credits are proportional to the percentage of times all players make the play. All plays for each player at his position are summed to get his total Plays Saved for the season. A total of zero would be average and any other number would approximate how many plays more or less the player made than the average player at the position for the number of chances the player had to field batted balls.

Range Factor

The number of Successful Chances (Putouts plus Assists) times nine divided by the number of Defensive Innings Played.

RBI %

The percentage of all potential runs driven in by a certain hitter. Simply put, it's RBIs divided by RBI Opportunities. RBI Opportunities are a weighted total for baserunners available to be driven in by the batter. They are defined like so:

1.00 for each runner on third base with less than 2 outs, plus

.70 for each runner on third base with 2 outs, plus

.70 for each runner on second base, plus

.40 for each runner on first base, plus

.10 for each bases-empty plate appearance.

Regular Saves

Any save which does not meet the definition either of an Easy Save or a Tough Save is a "Regular" Save.

Run Support Per 9 IP

The total number of runs scored by a pitcher's team while he is in the game multiplied by nine and divided by total Innings Pitched.

Runs Created

"Runs Created" is an estimate of the number of a team's runs which are created by each individual hitter. Let's assume the Cubs scored 820 runs last year. How many of those were created by Kris Bryant? How many by Anthony Rizzo? How many by Addison Russell?

There are many different formulas for estimating runs created. . .did you want the one that involves swinging a dead cat in the cemetery under a full moon? Yeah, I don't blame you. . .worm-eaten persimmons are so hard to find in the modern world.

This is the one we use now; it is complicated enough. First, there is an "A" Factor in the formula, a "B" Factor, and a "C" factor. The "A" Factor, which represents the number of times the hitter is on base, is Hits, Plus Walks, Plus Hit Batsmen, Minus Caught Stealing, Minus Grounded Into Double Play. The "B" Factor, which represents the hitter's ability to advance other runners, is 1.125 times the player's Singles, plus 1.69 times his Doubles, plus 3.02 times his Triples, plus 3.73 times his Home Runs, plus .29 times his Walks and Hit Batsmen, not counting intentional walks, plus .492 times Sacrifice Hits, Sacrifice Flies and Stolen Bases, minus .04 times Strikeouts. The "C" Factor, which represents opportunities, is At Bats, Plus Walks, Plus Hit By Pitch, Plus Sacrifice Hits, Plus Sacrifice Flies.

Having made these initial calculations of the A, B and C factors, we then change the "A" factor to "A plus 2.4 times C".

We change the "B" factor to "B plus 3 times C".

We change the "C" factor to "9 times C".

Multiply A times B, divide by the new C ("9 times C"), and subtract .90 times by the original C.

This is our first, temporary estimate of the player's runs created. What we have done here is to ask these questions:

1. How many runs would a team probably score that consisted of eight "ordinary" type of hitters, plus this particular hitter?
2. How many of those runs would be created by the eight ordinary type of hitters?
3. What is the difference and thus, how many runs did our player create?

To estimate this, we have placed our player in the context of eight hitters with a .300 on base percentage (2.4 divided by 8) and a .375 advancement percentage (3 divided by 8). For each trip through the batting order, the eight ordinary-type hitters would produce 9/10 of a run (2.4 times 3, divided by 8). The "9" in the denominator is eight ordinary hitters plus our man. The "-.9" being subtracted at the end is the runs created by the "ordinary" hitters. In essence, we have placed the hitter in a neutral solution, measured the neutral solution without our hitter, measured it with our hitter, and then estimated the contribution of this hitter as being the difference between the two.

We're not quite done. After that, we adjust the player's runs created estimate for his performance in two "run-sensitive" situations. Suppose that a player whose overall batting average is .250, has batted 100 times with runners in scoring position, and has gone 30-for-100. That's five hits better than expected, 30 hits where we would have expected 25. His team will score an extra five runs because he has done that, and so we increase the player's runs created estimate by five runs. If the player has hit poorly with runners in scoring position, we decrease it by the shortfall in the same way.

Suppose that a player has batted 250 times with runners on base, 250 times with the bases empty, and that he has hit 20 home runs overall. We would expect him to have hit 10 with men on base, 10 with the bases empty, right?

Suppose that he didn't. Suppose that he hit 12 with the bases empty, 8 with men on base. His team would score two runs less than expected because he did this, and we would thus penalize him two runs for the shortfall.

This is our second runs created estimate the player's runs created, adjusted for his batting performance in run sensitive situations.

Suppose, however, that we figure the runs created for all of the individuals on a team, and we add them up, and it doesn't match the runs actually scored by the team? What if the formulas say that the team should have scored 800 runs, but they actually scored 820?

Then obviously, the formulas missed. We're trying to measure the runs ACTUALLY created by each hitter as best we can, in the real world, not the theoretical impact of some combination of singles, doubles, triples and walks. If the actual number is different than the estimates, we have to adjust the estimates to fit the facts. In this case—820 runs scored with only 800 runs created— we would multiply each runs created estimate by 820/800, or 1.025. Then we round it off to an integer, and that's the player's estimated runs created.

Let go of that cat, Arthur. Heck, the moon isn't full for three weeks, anyway.

Runs Created per 27 Outs (RC/27)

This statistic estimates the number of runs per game that a team made up of nine of the same player would score. To calculate RC/27, multiply Runs Created by league outs per team game, divide the result by outs made by the player (the sum of at bats plus sacrifice hits plus sacrifice flies plus caught stealing plus grounded into double plays, minus hits). The formula written out is:

$$\frac{\dfrac{RC \times 3 \times LgIP}{2 \times LgG}}{AB - H + SH + SF + CS + GDP}$$

Runs Saved

See Defensive Runs Saved.

Save Opportunities

The sum of Saves and Blown Saves (see Save Situation).

Save/Hold Percentage (same as Holds Adjusted Saves Percentage)

The sum of Saves and Holds, divided by the sum of Saves, Holds, and Blown Saves.

For several years we figured "Save Percentage", which is simply Saves divided by Save Opportunities, and this stat had some currency in the game. But the Save Percentage severely discriminates against middle relievers, who have no real chance to be credited with the Save, since they will be taken out of the game and replaced by the Closer even if they throw 110 miles an hour and strike out everybody they see. Middle relievers typically have Save Percentages of zero, even if they pitch well. The Save/Hold Percentage is a much more realistic evaluation of a pitcher's success in Save situations.

Save Percentage

A pitcher's Saves divided by the total number of Save Situations he faces (see definition for Save Situation).

Save Situation

A relief pitcher is in a Save Situation when he enters the game with his team in the lead, has the opportunity to finish the game, is not the winning pitcher of record at the time, and meets any one of the three following conditions:

1. The pitcher's team is leading by no more than three runs and the pitcher has the chance to pitch for at least one inning,

OR

2. The pitcher enters the game with the potential tying run on base, at bat, or on deck,

OR

3. The pitcher pitches three or more effective innings regardless of the lead. The determination of a save in this situation is made by the official scorer.

It is not possible to have more than one save credited to a single team in a game.

SB Gain (Baserunning)

Stolen Base attempts must be successful greater than about two thirds of the time to have a positive result on the number of runs scored. SB gain is therefore the number of bases stolen minus two times the number of caught stealing (SB Gain = SB - 2CS). For example, a runner steals 30 bases and is caught stealing 7 times. His SB Gain would be 30 - 2 * 7 = +16. Another runner steals 10 bases and is caught stealing 6 times. His SB Gain (actually a loss) would be 10 - 2 * 6 = -2.

SB Success Percentage

Stolen Bases divided by the number of Stolen Base attempts (Stolen Bases plus Caught Stealing).

$$\frac{SB}{SB + CS}$$

Secondary Average

A number meant to reflect everything else except for batting average. A player will have a high Secondary Average if he hits for power, takes walks and steals bases. It is calculated with the following formula:

$$\frac{TB - H + BB + SB}{AB}$$

Similarity Score

A number which reflects the similarity between two different statistical lines, either for a player or for a team. A score of 1,000 means that the statistical lines are identical.

Slow Hooks

Used in the Manager's Record. For Quick Hooks and Slow Hooks, a score is calculated for each game that is the sum of the number of Pitches plus 10 times the number of Runs Allowed. The top 25% of scores in the league are considered to be Slow Hooks.

Slugging Average

Total Bases divided by At Bats.

$$\frac{TB}{AB}$$

Speed Score

Speed score is an estimate of a player's running speed, based on six indicators of running speed found in his batting and fielding records. Those six indicators are stolen base success rate, the frequency of stolen base attempts, triples, grounding into double plays, runs scored as a percentage of times on base, and defensive position and range.

The full process of estimating Speed Scores is long and complex, and can be found on Bill James Online or by contacting Baseball Info Solutions.

Total Bases

Hits plus Doubles plus (2 times Triples) plus (3 times Home Runs).

$$H + 2B + (2 \times 3B) + (3 \times HR)$$

Tough Loss

A starting pitcher who loses the game with a game score (see definition for Game Score) over 50 gets credit for a tough loss.

Tough Save

This label is used to separate Saves by difficulty level (Easy or Tough). A Save is considered Tough if the relief pitcher enters the game with the tying run on base.

Unproductive Out

An out made by the batter which is not the third out of an inning, but comes with runners on base which fails to advance any baserunner, or results in a weaker baserunner configuration than before the out. See also Productive Out.

Win Probability

The probability of a team winning the game determined at any time during the game based on the score, inning, outs and base situation.

Winning Percentage

Wins divided by (Wins plus Losses).

Minor League Abbreviation Key

Abbreviation	Team	Level	League	MLB Affiliate	First Year	Last Year
Abrdn	Aberdeen IronBirds	A-	New York-Penn League	Baltimore Orioles	2012	2016
Akron	Akron Aeros	AA	Eastern League	Cleveland Indians	2012	2013
Akron	Akron RubberDucks	AA	Eastern League	Cleveland Indians	2014	2016
Albq	Albuquerque Isotopes	AAA	Pacific Coast League	Los Angeles Dodgers	2012	2014
Albq	Albuquerque Isotopes	AAA	Pacific Coast League	Colorado Rockies	2015	2016
Altna	Altoona Curve	AA	Eastern League	Pittsburgh Pirates	2012	2016
Amarill	Amarillo Sox	IND	Independent League	Independent	2013	2013
Angels	AZL Angels	R	Arizona League	Los Angeles Angels	2012	2016
Ark	Arkansas Travelers	AA	Texas League	Los Angeles Angels	2012	2016
As	AZL Athletics	R	Arizona League	Oakland Athletics	2012	2016
Ashvll	Asheville Tourists	A	South Atlantic League	Colorado Rockies	2012	2016
Astros	GCL Astros	R	Gulf Coast League	Houston Astros	2012	2016
Auburn	Auburn Doubledays	A-	New York-Penn League	Washington Nationals	2012	2016
Augsta	Augusta GreenJackets	A	South Atlantic League	San Francisco Giants	2012	2016
B Jays	GCL Blue Jays	R	Gulf Coast League	Toronto Blue Jays	2012	2016
Batvia	Batavia Muckdogs	A-	New York-Penn League	St Louis Cardinals	2012	2012
Batvia	Batavia Muckdogs	A-	New York-Penn League	Miami Marlins	2013	2016
Beloit	Beloit Snappers	A	Midwest League	Minnesota Twins	2012	2012
Beloit	Beloit Snappers	A	Midwest League	Oakland Athletics	2013	2016
BG	Bowling Green Hot Rods	A	Midwest League	Tampa Bay Rays	2012	2016
Billings	Billings Mustangs	R+	Pioneer League	Cincinnati Reds	2012	2016
Biloxi	Biloxi Shuckers	AA	Southern League	Milwaukee Brewers	2015	2016
Bklyn	Brooklyn Cyclones	A-	New York-Penn League	New York Mets	2012	2016
Bkrsfld	Bakersfield Blaze	A+	California League	Cincinnati Reds	2012	2014
Bkrsfld	Bakersfield Blaze	A+	California League	Seattle Mariners	2015	2016
Bluefld	Bluefield Blue Jays	R+	Appalachian League	Toronto Blue Jays	2012	2016
Bnghtn	Binghamton Mets	AA	Eastern League	New York Mets	2012	2016
Boise	Boise Hawks	A-	Northwest League	Chicago Cubs	2012	2014
Boise	Boise Hawks	A-	Northwest League	Colorado Rockies	2015	2016
Bowie	Bowie Baysox	AA	Eastern League	Baltimore Orioles	2012	2016
Bradtn	Bradenton Marauders	A+	Florida State League	Pittsburgh Pirates	2012	2016
Braves	GCL Braves	R	Gulf Coast League	Atlanta Braves	2012	2016
Brewrs	AZL Brewers	R	Arizona League	Milwaukee Brewers	2012	2016
Brham	Birmingham Barons	AA	Southern League	Chicago White Sox	2012	2016
Brstol	Bristol White Sox	R+	Appalachian League	Chicago White Sox	2012	2013
Brstol	Bristol Pirates	R+	Appalachian League	Pittsburgh Pirates	2014	2016
BrvdCt	Brevard Co. Manatees	A+	Florida State League	Milwaukee Brewers	2012	2016
Buffalo	Buffalo Bisons	AAA	International League	New York Mets	2012	2012
Buffalo	Buffalo Bisons	AAA	International League	Toronto Blue Jays	2013	2016
Burlgtn	Burlington IA Bees	A	Midwest League	Oakland Athletics	2012	2012
Burlgtn	Burlington IA Bees	A	Midwest League	Los Angeles Angels	2013	2016
Burlgtn	Burlington NC Royals	R+	Appalachian League	Kansas City Royals	2012	2016
Cards	GCL Cardinals	R	Gulf Coast League	St Louis Cardinals	2012	2016
Carlina	Carolina Mudcats	A+	Carolina League	Cleveland Indians	2012	2014
Carlina	Carolina Mudcats	A+	Carolina League	Atlanta Braves	2015	2016
Charllt	Charlotte NC Knights	AAA	International League	Chicago White Sox	2012	2016
Charltt	Charlotte FL Stone Crabs	A+	Florida State League	Tampa Bay Rays	2012	2016
Chatt	Chattanooga Lookouts	AA	Southern League	Los Angeles Dodgers	2012	2014
Chatt	Chattanooga Lookouts	AA	Southern League	Minnesota Twins	2015	2016
Clinton	Clinton LumberKings	A	Midwest League	Seattle Mariners	2012	2016
Clmbs	Columbus Clippers	AAA	International League	Cleveland Indians	2012	2016
Clrwtr	Clearwater Threshers	A+	Florida State League	Philadelphia Phillies	2012	2016
ColSpr	Colorado Spr. Sky Sox	AAA	Pacific Coast League	Colorado Rockies	2012	2014
ColSpr	Colorado Spr. Sky Sox	AAA	Pacific Coast League	Milwaukee Brewers	2015	2016
Conn	Connecticut Tigers	A-	New York-Penn League	Detroit Tigers	2012	2016
CpChr	Corpus Christi Hooks	AA	Texas League	Houston Astros	2012	2016
Crpds	Cedar Rapids Kernels	A	Midwest League	Los Angeles Angels	2012	2012
Crpds	Cedar Rapids Kernels	A	Midwest League	Minnesota Twins	2013	2016
CtnSC	Charleston RiverDogs	A	South Atlantic League	New York Yankees	2012	2016
Cubs	AZL Cubs	R	Arizona League	Chicago Cubs	2012	2016
Danvle	Danville Braves	R+	Appalachian League	Atlanta Braves	2012	2016
Dayton	Dayton Dragons	A	Midwest League	Cincinnati Reds	2012	2016

Minor League Abbreviation Key

Abbreviation	Team	Level	League	MLB Affiliate	First Year	Last Year
Dbcks	AZL D-backs	R	Arizona League	Arizona Diamondbacks	2012	2016
Ddgrs	AZL Dodgers	R	Arizona League	Los Angeles Dodgers	2012	2016
Dlmrva	Delmarva Shorebirds	A	South Atlantic League	Baltimore Orioles	2012	2016
Dnedin	Dunedin Blue Jays	A+	Florida State League	Toronto Blue Jays	2012	2016
Drham	Durham Bulls	AAA	International League	Tampa Bay Rays	2012	2016
Dytona	Daytona Cubs	A+	Florida State League	Chicago Cubs	2012	2014
Dytona	Daytona Tortugas	A+	Florida State League	Cincinnati Reds	2015	2016
Elizab	Elizabethton Twins	R+	Appalachian League	Minnesota Twins	2012	2016
ElPaso	El Paso Chihuahuas	AAA	Pacific Coast League	San Diego Padres	2014	2016
Erie	Erie SeaWolves	AA	Eastern League	Detroit Tigers	2012	2016
Eugene	Eugene Emeralds	A-	Northwest League	San Diego Padres	2012	2014
Eugene	Eugene Emeralds	A-	Northwest League	Chicago Cubs	2015	2016
Everett	Everett AquaSox	A-	Northwest League	Seattle Mariners	2012	2016
Frdrck	Frederick Keys	A+	Carolina League	Baltimore Orioles	2012	2016
Fresno	Fresno Grizzlies	AAA	Pacific Coast League	San Francisco Giants	2012	2014
Fresno	Fresno Grizzlies	AAA	Pacific Coast League	Houston Astros	2015	2016
Frisco	Frisco RoughRiders	AA	Texas League	Texas Rangers	2012	2016
FtMyrs	Fort Myers Miracle	A+	Florida State League	Minnesota Twins	2012	2016
FtWyn	Fort Wayne TinCaps	A	Midwest League	San Diego Padres	2012	2016
GdJunc	Grand Junction Rockies	R+	Pioneer League	Colorado Rockies	2012	2016
Giants	AZL Giants	R	Arizona League	San Francisco Giants	2012	2016
Gr Falls	Great Falls Voyagers	R+	Pioneer League	Chicago White Sox	2012	2016
Grnsbr	Greensboro Grasshoppers	A	South Atlantic League	Miami Marlins	2012	2016
Grnvlle	Greeneville Astros	R+	Appalachian League	Houston Astros	2012	2016
Grnvlle	Greenville Drive	A	South Atlantic League	Boston Red Sox	2012	2016
Gt Lks	Great Lakes Loons	A	Midwest League	Los Angeles Dodgers	2012	2016
Gwnntt	Gwinnett Braves	AAA	International League	Atlanta Braves	2012	2016
Helena	Helena Brewers	R+	Pioneer League	Milwaukee Brewers	2012	2016
Hgrstn	Hagerstown Suns	A	South Atlantic League	Washington Nationals	2012	2016
Hi Dsrt	High Desert Mavericks	A+	California League	Seattle Mariners	2012	2014
Hi Dsrt	High Desert Mavericks	A+	California League	Texas Rangers	2015	2016
HiroCrp	Hiroshima Carp	IND	Independent League	Independent	2008	2016
Hkry	Hickory Crawdads	A	South Atlantic League	Texas Rangers	2012	2016
Hlsbro	Hillsboro Hops	A-	Northwest League	Arizona Diamondbacks	2013	2016
Hntsvl	Huntsville Stars	AA	Southern League	Milwaukee Brewers	2012	2014
Hrsbrg	Harrisburg Senators	AA	Eastern League	Washington Nationals	2012	2016
HudVal	Hudson Valley Renegades	A-	New York-Penn League	Tampa Bay Rays	2012	2016
Idaho	Idaho Falls Chukars	R+	Pioneer League	Kansas City Royals	2012	2016
Indns	AZL Indians	R	Arizona League	Cleveland Indians	2012	2016
Indy	Indianapolis Indians	AAA	International League	Pittsburgh Pirates	2012	2016
InldEm	Inland Empire 66ers	A+	California League	Los Angeles Angels	2012	2016
Iowa	Iowa Cubs	AAA	Pacific Coast League	Chicago Cubs	2012	2016
Jacksn	Jackson Generals	AA	Southern League	Seattle Mariners	2012	2016
Jaxnvl	Jacksonville Suns	AA	Southern League	Miami Marlins	2012	2016
Jhscty	Johnson City Cardinals	R+	Appalachian League	St Louis Cardinals	2012	2016
Jmstwn	Jamestown Jammers	A-	New York-Penn League	Miami Marlins	2012	2012
Jmstwn	Jamestown Jammers	A-	New York-Penn League	Pittsburgh Pirates	2013	2014
Jupiter	Jupiter Hammerheads	A+	Florida State League	Miami Marlins	2012	2016
Kane	Kane County Cougars	A	Midwest League	Kansas City Royals	2012	2012
Kane	Kane County Cougars	A	Midwest League	Chicago Cubs	2013	2014
Kane	Kane County Cougars	A	Midwest League	Arizona Diamondbacks	2015	2016
Knapol	Kannapolis Intimidators	A	South Atlantic League	Chicago White Sox	2012	2016
Kngspt	Kingsport Mets	R+	Appalachian League	New York Mets	2012	2016
Lakwd	Lakewood BlueClaws	A	South Atlantic League	Philadelphia Phillies	2012	2016
Lancst	Lancaster JetHawks	A+	California League	Houston Astros	2012	2016
Lk Cty	Lake County Captains	A	Midwest League	Cleveland Indians	2012	2016
Lk Els	Lake Elsinore Storm	A+	California League	San Diego Padres	2012	2016
Lkland	Lakeland Flying Tigers	A+	Florida State League	Detroit Tigers	2012	2016
Lnsng	Lansing Lugnuts	A	Midwest League	Toronto Blue Jays	2012	2016
Lowell	Lowell Spinners	A-	New York-Penn League	Boston Red Sox	2012	2016
LsVgs	Las Vegas 51s	AAA	Pacific Coast League	Toronto Blue Jays	2012	2012
LsVgs	Las Vegas 51s	AAA	Pacific Coast League	New York Mets	2013	2016
Lsvlle	Louisville Bats	AAA	International League	Cincinnati Reds	2012	2016
LV	Lehigh Valley IronPigs	AAA	International League	Philadelphia Phillies	2012	2016

Minor League Abbreviation Key

Abbreviation	Team	Level	League	MLB Affiliate	First Year	Last Year
Lxngtn	Lexington Legends	A	South Atlantic League	Houston Astros	2012	2012
Lxngtn	Lexington Legends	A	South Atlantic League	Kansas City Royals	2013	2016
Lynbrg	Lynchburg Hillcats	A+	Carolina League	Atlanta Braves	2012	2014
Lynbrg	Lynchburg Hillcats	A+	Carolina League	Cleveland Indians	2015	2016
Mdest	Modesto Nuts	A+	California League	Colorado Rockies	2012	2016
Mdlnd	Midland RockHounds	AA	Texas League	Oakland Athletics	2012	2016
Memp	Memphis Redbirds	AAA	Pacific Coast League	St Louis Cardinals	2012	2016
Mets	GCL Mets	R	Gulf Coast League	New York Mets	2012	2016
MhVlly	Mahoning Valley Scrappers	A-	New York-Penn League	Cleveland Indians	2012	2016
Missi	Mississippi Braves	AA	Southern League	Atlanta Braves	2012	2016
Mobile	Mobile BayBears	AA	Southern League	Arizona Diamondbacks	2012	2016
Mont	Montgomery Biscuits	AA	Southern League	Tampa Bay Rays	2012	2016
Mrlns	GCL Marlins	R	Gulf Coast League	Miami Marlins	2012	2016
MrtlBh	Myrtle Beach Pelicans	A+	Carolina League	Texas Rangers	2012	2014
MrtlBh	Myrtle Beach Pelicans	A+	Carolina League	Chicago Cubs	2015	2016
Ms	AZL Mariners	R	Arizona League	Seattle Mariners	2012	2016
Msoula	Missoula Osprey	R+	Pioneer League	Arizona Diamondbacks	2012	2016
Nashv	Nashville Sounds	AAA	Pacific Coast League	Milwaukee Brewers	2012	2014
Nashv	Nashville Sounds	AAA	Pacific Coast League	Oakland Athletics	2015	2016
Nats	GCL Nationals	R	Gulf Coast League	Washington Nationals	2012	2016
NewOr	New Orleans Zephyrs	AAA	Pacific Coast League	Miami Marlins	2012	2016
Nexen	Nexen Heroes	IND	Independent League	Independent	2012	2016
Nham	New Hampshire Fisher Cats	AA	Eastern League	Toronto Blue Jays	2012	2016
Nippon	Hokkaido Nippon Ham Fighters	IND	Independent League	Independent	2013	2016
Norfolk	Norfolk Tides	AAA	International League	Baltimore Orioles	2012	2016
NWArk	NW Arkansas Naturals	AA	Texas League	Kansas City Royals	2012	2016
NwBrit	New Britain Rock Cats	AA	Eastern League	Minnesota Twins	2012	2014
NwBrit	New Britain Rock Cats	AA	Eastern League	Colorado Rockies	2015	2015
Ogden	Ogden Raptors	R+	Pioneer League	Los Angeles Dodgers	2012	2016
OkCity	Oklahoma City RedHawks	AAA	Pacific Coast League	Houston Astros	2012	2014
OkCity	Oklahoma City Dodgers	AAA	Pacific Coast League	Los Angeles Dodgers	2015	2016
Omha	Omaha Storm Chasers	AAA	Pacific Coast League	Kansas City Royals	2012	2016
Orem	Orem Owlz	R+	Pioneer League	Los Angeles Angels	2012	2016
Orioles	GCL Orioles	R	Gulf Coast League	Baltimore Orioles	2012	2016
Padres	AZL Padres	R	Arizona League	San Diego Padres	2012	2016
Peoria	Peoria Chiefs	A	Midwest League	Chicago Cubs	2012	2012
Peoria	Peoria Chiefs	A	Midwest League	St Louis Cardinals	2013	2016
Phillies	GCL Phillies	R	Gulf Coast League	Philadelphia Phillies	2012	2016
Pirates	GCL Pirates	R	Gulf Coast League	Pittsburgh Pirates	2012	2016
PlmBh	Palm Beach Cardinals	A+	Florida State League	St Louis Cardinals	2012	2016
Pnscla	Pensacola Blue Wahoos	AA	Southern League	Cincinnati Reds	2012	2016
Portlnd	Portland ME Sea Dogs	AA	Eastern League	Boston Red Sox	2012	2016
Prnctn	Princeton Rays	R+	Appalachian League	Tampa Bay Rays	2012	2016
Ptomc	Potomac Nationals	A+	Carolina League	Washington Nationals	2012	2016
Pulski	Pulaski Mariners	R+	Appalachian League	Seattle Mariners	2012	2014
Pulski	Pulaski Yankees	R+	Appalachian League	New York Yankees	2015	2016
Pwtckt	Pawtucket Red Sox	AAA	International League	Boston Red Sox	2012	2016
QuadC	Quad Cities River Bandits	A	Midwest League	St Louis Cardinals	2012	2012
QuadC	Quad Cities River Bandits	A	Midwest League	Houston Astros	2013	2016
Rays	GCL Rays	R	Gulf Coast League	Tampa Bay Rays	2012	2016
Rchmd	Richmond Flying Squirrels	AA	Eastern League	San Francisco Giants	2012	2016
Rcuca	Rancho Cucamonga Quakes	A+	California League	Los Angeles Dodgers	2012	2016
Rdng	Reading Phillies	AA	Eastern League	Philadelphia Phillies	2012	2012
Rdng	Reading Fightin Phils	AA	Eastern League	Philadelphia Phillies	2013	2016
RdRck	Round Rock Express	AAA	Pacific Coast League	Texas Rangers	2012	2016
Reds	AZL Reds	R	Arizona League	Cincinnati Reds	2012	2016
RedSx	GCL Red Sox	R	Gulf Coast League	Boston Red Sox	2012	2016
Reno	Reno Aces	AAA	Pacific Coast League	Arizona Diamondbacks	2012	2016
Rngrs	AZL Rangers	R	Arizona League	Texas Rangers	2012	2016
Roch	Rochester Red Wings	AAA	International League	Minnesota Twins	2012	2016
Rome	Rome Braves	A	South Atlantic League	Atlanta Braves	2012	2016
Royals	AZL Royals	R	Arizona League	Kansas City Royals	2012	2016
Salem	Salem Red Sox	A+	Carolina League	Boston Red Sox	2012	2016
Salt Lk	Salt Lake City Bees	AAA	Pacific Coast League	Los Angeles Angels	2012	2016

Minor League Abbreviation Key

Abbreviation	Team	Level	League	MLB Affiliate	First Year	Last Year
Savann	Savannah Sand Gnats	A	South Atlantic League	New York Mets	2012	2015
Sbend	South Bend Silver Hawks	A	Midwest League	Arizona Diamondbacks	2012	2014
Sbend	South Bend Cubs	A	Midwest League	Chicago Cubs	2015	2016
Scrmto	Sacramento River Cats	AAA	Pacific Coast League	Oakland Athletics	2012	2014
Scrmto	Sacramento River Cats	AAA	Pacific Coast League	San Francisco Giants	2015	2016
SlKzr	Salem-Keizer Volcanoes	A-	Northwest League	San Francisco Giants	2012	2016
SnAnt	San Antonio Missions	AA	Texas League	San Diego Padres	2012	2016
SnJos	San Jose Giants	A+	California League	San Francisco Giants	2012	2016
Spkane	Spokane Indians	A-	Northwest League	Texas Rangers	2012	2016
Sprgfld	Springfield Cardinals	AA	Texas League	St Louis Cardinals	2012	2016
Stcktn	Stockton Ports	A+	California League	Oakland Athletics	2012	2016
StCol	State College Spikes	A-	New York-Penn League	Pittsburgh Pirates	2012	2012
StCol	State College Spikes	A-	New York-Penn League	St Louis Cardinals	2013	2016
Stluci	St. Lucie Mets	A+	Florida State League	New York Mets	2012	2016
Stnlld	Staten Island Yankees	A-	New York-Penn League	New York Yankees	2012	2016
S-WB	Scranton WB Yankees	AAA	International League	New York Yankees	2012	2012
S-WB	Scranton WB RailRiders	AAA	International League	New York Yankees	2013	2016
Syrcse	Syracuse Chiefs	AAA	International League	Washington Nationals	2012	2016
Tacom	Tacoma Rainiers	AAA	Pacific Coast League	Seattle Mariners	2012	2016
Tampa	Tampa Yankees	A+	Florida State League	New York Yankees	2012	2016
Tenn	Tennessee Smokies	AA	Southern League	Chicago Cubs	2012	2016
Tigers	GCL Tigers	R	Gulf Coast League	Detroit Tigers	2012	2015
Toledo	Toledo Mud Hens	AAA	International League	Detroit Tigers	2012	2016
TriCity	Tri-City WA Dust Devils	A-	Northwest League	Colorado Rockies	2012	2014
TriCity	Tri-City NY ValleyCats	A-	New York-Penn League	Houston Astros	2012	2016
TriCity	Tri-City WA Dust Devils	A-	Northwest League	San Diego Padres	2015	2016
Trntn	Trenton Thunder	AA	Eastern League	New York Yankees	2012	2016
Tucsn	Tucson Padres	AAA	Pacific Coast League	San Diego Padres	2012	2013
Tulsa	Tulsa Drillers	AA	Texas League	Colorado Rockies	2012	2014
Tulsa	Tulsa Drillers	AA	Texas League	Los Angeles Dodgers	2015	2016
Twins	GCL Twins	R	Gulf Coast League	Minnesota Twins	2012	2016
Vancvr	Vancouver Canadians	A-	Northwest League	Toronto Blue Jays	2012	2016
Visalia	Visalia Rawhide	A+	California League	Arizona Diamondbacks	2012	2016
Vrmnt	Vermont Lake Monsters	A-	New York-Penn League	Oakland Athletics	2012	2016
Wichita	Wichita Wingnuts	IND	Independent League	Independent	2012	2012
Wilmg	Wilmington Blue Rocks	A+	Carolina League	Kansas City Royals	2012	2016
WinSa	Winston-Salem Dash	A+	Carolina League	Chicago White Sox	2012	2016
Wisc	Wisconson Timber Rattlers	A	Midwest League	Milwaukee Brewers	2012	2016
Wmich	West Michigan Whitecaps	A	Midwest League	Detroit Tigers	2012	2016
Wmspt	Williamsport Crosscutters	A-	New York-Penn League	Philadelphia Phillies	2012	2016
Wsox	AZL White Sox	R	Arizona League	Chicago White Sox	2013	2016
WV	West Virginia Black Bears	A-	New York-Penn League	Pittsburgh Pirates	2015	2016
WV	West Virginia Power	A	South Atlantic League	Pittsburgh Pirates	2012	2016
Yakima	Yakima Bears	A-	Northwest League	Arizona Diamondbacks	2012	2012
Yanks1	GCL Yankees	R	Gulf Coast League	New York Yankees	2012	2015
Yanks2	GCL Yankees2	R	Gulf Coast League	New York Yankees	2013	2015

Baseball Info Solutions

It's hard to believe, but Baseball Info Solutions has been around long enough now to be a teenager. Since the beginning, analytics' place in the sport has changed a lot, but BIS remained true to its objective. The mission is to provide the most accurate, in-depth, timely professional baseball data, including cutting-edge research and analysis, striving to educate major league teams and the public about baseball analytics. BIS is thrilled to work with 25 of the 30 teams in Major League Baseball as a part of that goal.

It all begins with the data collection operation. BIS's staff of operations analysts does excellent work in organizing the ever-expanding crew of highly trained video scouts, and together they record data from every Major League Baseball game and many minor league ones. That data covers everything from basic box score data to pitch locations, types, and velocities to batted ball hang times, defensive shifts, and much more. BIS collects a lot of data that cannot be found any place else, and each game is reviewed multiple times to ensure that the data is as accurate as possible.

The data itself is valuable to many clients, but BIS's research and development department creates analytics and undertakes research projects with the data to help it reach its full potential utility. Their most well-known endeavor is the Defensive Runs Saved statistic, which estimates how many runs fielders save their teams because of a variety of skills such as range, throwing, prevention of stolen bases, pitch framing, and many other factors. Most recently, they worked to synthesize new data available in StatCast with BIS's own data and research projects.

John Dewan founded Baseball Info Solutions in 2002 after already spending a couple of decades in the industry at the forefront of the sabermetric movement. He got his start in the field as the Executive Director of Project Scoresheet, which was a Bill James-led effort to comprehensively collect baseball data. This led to the incorporation and development of STATS Inc. from a bedroom office to its sale to News Corp in 2000. Without those efforts, many of the statistics and analytics that we all take for granted may not even be available at all.

If you would like to contact Baseball Info Solutions for data inquiries, potential job openings, or additional information, you can reach us at:

Baseball Info Solutions
41 S. 2nd Street
Coplay, PA 18037
610-261-2370
www.baseballinfosolutions.com

Acknowledgments

The Bill James Handbook is a massive undertaking that requires a lot of late nights from everyone involved in its production. From the moment the regular season ended on October 3 to the publisher's deadline on October 14, we all worked tirelessly to ensure that every stat was double-checked and every word was proofread so that the *Handbook* would live up to its high standard. Because of that extraordinary effort, we want to thank everyone who helped make the book possible.

The first thank you is reserved for Bill James, whose original Baseball Abstract in 1977 became the foundation of the current *Handbook*, which is still going strong 40 years later. Bill continues to be a major part of the book's production. He helped design and wrote introductions for two new sections—Long Outs & Home Run Distances and Run Impact of Events. He also wrote the intros for the Pitchers' Repertoires, Win Shares, Hall of Fame Monitor, 300 Wins, and Hitter and Pitcher Projections sections. In addition, he provided valuable input on the hitter and pitcher projections.

John Dewan and his wife Sue Dewan are the owners of Baseball Info Solutions. John is the final editor for every printed word in this book in addition to several other leadership roles. Sue provides direction for BIS in Human Resources among other things over the course of the year.

This is the eighth *Handbook* Ben Jedlovec has been a part of, from his early days in Research and Development to his current role as President. He manages the entire *Handbook* process and also contributes to a variety of sections and introductions.

Director of IT Rob Dougherty has more than 15 years of industry experience and now has made it through two *Handbooks* as part of BIS. In addition to his contributions to the book, Rob makes sure that all of our clients' needs are met in this critical time of the baseball season.

Joe Rosales was promoted to Director of Business Operations earlier this year. In addition to maintaining much of his workload in the Research and Development department—including organizing the Fielding Bible Award voting process and writing many of the introductions in the *Handbook*—he liaises with the different BIS departments to make sure everyone is working in concert.

Patrick Coyle is now 4-and-0 in his four years as the producer of the *Handbook*. It's a massive job that Pat makes look easy, not to mention all of the other great work he does as a Senior IT Analyst throughout the year. The rest of the IT department features Greg Thomas, Ben Stanczak, Will Creager, Craig Saboe, and IT interns Joe Gownley, Alex Szilagyi, and Jake Balderama. They are also instrumental during the *Handbook* process, both in producing the book and in keeping up with their many other IT demands. Pete Zundel and Craig Scurlock have also contributed to the department from afar this year.

With our expansion into football data collection, our Operations Department has grown to include Jon Vrecsics, Jim Swavely, Dan Casey, Todd Radcliffe, Kevin Morrissey, Tim Kwilos, Dan Foehrenbach, James Mehall, Nathan Phares, Jason Paff, Michael Churchward, and Josh Hofer. Despite now being in charge of multiple levels of multiple sports, the Operations staff has gracefully maintained its excellent standards of timeliness and accuracy of data collection. With 11-year *Handbook* veteran Jon as the organizer, their efforts ensure that every statistic we publish in the *Handbook* has been checked and rechecked such that we are confident that, in cases where there are discrepancies between our numbers and those of other published sources, we have the correct numbers.

The Research and Development Department of Scott Spratt and Lindsay Zeck is responsible for many different *Handbook* tasks including the hitter and pitcher projections process, section intros and data discrepancies. They with interns Josh Lipman, Sierra Doherty, Liam Bressler, and James Ridgeway undertake research projects and create analytics that demonstrate the value of the data BIS collects.

Director of Business Development Jim Capuano and Business Development Associate Corey March together lead the effort to bring our data, research, and analysis to our clients and the public. Ryan Allor also helped out with these efforts earlier in the year. Former NFL scout Matt Manocherian also joined us this season and has been a big help with multiple facets of our football operation.

Office Administrator Carol Olsen is the glue that holds the office together. She wears a number of hats in the running of the business, from Human Resources to Accounting to Office Management.

As our collection efforts continue to expand, so too does our collection of video scouts. Their dedication and attention to detail provide the foundation of our business. They include Ted Baarda, Kit Banko, Mitchell Bley, Alex Boyer, Alex Botts, Wil Broadwell, Sean Burke, Mark Carlozzi, Sam Cassell, Jack Cecil, Mike Chernow, Nathan Cooper, Forrest Djavaherian, Alec Dopp, Matt Ducondi, Andrew Dunklee, Michael El-Far II, Anthony Flora, Sean Gallagher, Noah Gatsik, Chris Goudoras, Zack Greenfield, Brandon Haney, Aidan Hanlon, Adam Hayes, Kyle Hutson, Erik Knutsen, Tyler Kuhns, Yen Lai, Hank LaRue, Thomas Lear, Stefan Lechmanik, Derek Lescarbeau, Tyler Lloyd, Kevin Lyman, Brent Minta, Matt Mistretta, Patrick O'Donnell, Jack Olszewski, Chris Ouellette, Jordan Perrine, Nick Rabasco, Cole Ratliff, Brian Reiff, Matt Risko, Marc Roche, Ryne Rogers, Dan Romano, Connor Salter, Brooks Sandler, Nick Shnider, Ben Sniezek, Kyle Stephany, Bryce Stevens, Justin Stine, Aaron Thorn, Sam Trecaso, Matt Unangst, Dan Wallie, Tanner Watkins, and Ryan Wormeli.

Our partners at ACTA Publications include President Greg Pierce, Tom Wright, Mary Eggert, Abby Pierce, Brian Tobin, Patricia Lynch, Mary Doyle, Hugh Spector, Richard (Isz) and Mary Struben.

Thank you to our friends in the baseball industry who have helped us over the years. They include Andy Andres, David Appelman, Dave Cameron, Sean Forman, Peter Gammons, Vince Genarro, Marshall Greenhut, Eric Karabell, Brian Kenny, Peter Kreutzer, Michael Lehrer, Bob Meyerhoff, Mike Murphy, Noel Nash, Rob Neyer, Alex Patton, Mike Phillips, David Pinto, Joe Posnanski, Adam Richman, Hal Richman, Peter Schoenke, Ron Shandler, Joe Sheehan, Mark Simon, Dave Studenmund, Tom Tango, Mark Watson, and Don Zminda.

Thank you to Steve Ruskowski for your assistance in stat-checking.

In just a few pages, it is impossible for us to thank everyone who made this book possible, and so thank you to everyone who we could not mention by name but who helped make it happen. And finally, thank you to our readers. The reason we make this extreme effort to produce the *Handbook* so quickly and to such a high standard is because we know that you share our passion for baseball. We hope you have enjoyed all of our hard work.